WORLD AUTHORS
2000 – 2005

EDITORS
Jennifer Curry
David Ramm
Mari Rich
Albert Rolls

CONSULTING EDITORS
Andrew I. Cavin
Clifford Thompson

STAFF WRITERS
Jeremy K. Brown
Dimitri Cavalli
Forrest Cole
Kathleen D'Angelo
Karen E. Duda
Ronald Eniclerico
Seth Hartig
Peter G. Herman
Christopher Mari
Paul B. McCaffrey
Bertha Muteba
Geoff Orens
David H. Pickering
Liliana Segura
Kate Stern
Hope Tarullo
Selma Yampolsky

EDITORIAL ASSISTANT
Carolyn Ellis

THE H. W. WILSON COMPANY
NEW YORK   DUBLIN
2007

PRINTED IN THE UNITED STATES OF AMERICA

International Standard Book No. – 978-0-8242-1077-9

Table of Contents

PREFACE

Not taking into account the four-volume *World Authors 1900–1950*, published in 1997, *World Authors 2000–2005* is the 16th installment of the Wilson Authors series, begun in 1942. This volume comprises biographical articles on some 300 novelists, poets, dramatists, essayists, social scientists, biographers, and other authors who have published significant work within the period indicated.

Each article in *World Authors 2000–2005* provides a starting point for understanding the subject's contributions to the world of books, and, taken together, they reveal the wide variety of influences, experiences, opinions, and approaches to the creative process that shape contemporary literature.

Many of the authors profiled here have contributed autobiographical essays, crafted solely for use in this book. A number of these essays detail a lifelong love of literature. Sandra Benítez, for example, writes, "Being a writer was something magical I never dreamed I could attain. But while growing up, I frequently had a book in my lap, and so I was linked, early on, to writing and to the spell that stories cast." Emmanuel Dongala echoes that theme, writing that in his native French colonial Africa, "Books were magical and seemed to us to contain all the knowledge in the world. I became an avid reader and being an avid reader gave me an irresistible desire to . . . become a writer."

These profiles make plain that writing is never simply a job. Joan Didion writes that putting pen to paper is a way of asserting herself to the world: "In many ways writing is the act of saying *I*, of imposing oneself upon other people, of saying *listen to me, see it my way, change your mind*," she once wrote. For Augusten Burroughs, producing the 1,800-page first draft of *Dry*, a memoir about his recovery from alcoholism, was a form of salvation: "I would stay inside on a beautiful day to write. I wasn't thinking about publishing, or that someone would read this someday; I just had to write. That's what *Dry* came from." For Bernardo Atxaga, writing can be likened to a "battle between giraffes": "When you see two lions fighting, you know what's going on: they roar, claw at each other, roll on the ground. But when you watch a pair of giraffes fighting, it looks as if they're caressing each other. They're not though, they're trying to break each other's necks: and that's the kind of struggle the writer is engaged in with language, with tradition, with sense."

Editing this volume has been a pleasure and an honor. I am grateful to the following people for their assistance in doing so: Mark Gauthier, H. W. Wilson's vice president for Editorial Services; the staff writers listed on the title page, without whom this book could not have been published; my fellow editors Jennifer Curry, David Ramm, and Albert Rolls, whose hard work and dedication is beyond compare; Andrew Cavin, whose move to the University of Michigan is academia's gain, but our loss; and Clifford Thompson, who has overseen this volume and has, as always, provided immeasurable guidance and support.

Mari Rich
March 2007

List of Biographical Sketches

WORLD AUTHORS
2000 – 2005

Courtesy of Christopher Abani

Abani, Christopher

1967– Poet; novelist; playwright

A political dissident in his native Nigeria, Christopher Abani has endured imprisonment, torture, and exile. "However much [he] deserves respect for his political courage," Dan Cryer wrote for the *Chicago Tribune* (February 29, 2004), "that's no rationale for praising his fiction. . . . His writing can stand on its own." Since his first novel, *Masters of the Board*, debuted in 1985, when he was still a teenager, Abani has published several other works, among them the poetry collections *Kalakuta Republic* (2000), *Daphne's Lot* (2003), and *Dog Woman* (2004), as well as the critically acclaimed novel *GraceLand* (2004). "*GraceLand*," Merle Rubin wrote for the *Los Angeles Times* (April 5, 2004), "amply demonstrates that Abani has the energy, ambition and compassion to create a novel that delineates and illuminates a complicated, dynamic, deeply fractured society."

Christopher Abani was born in 1967 in Afikpo, Nigeria, a nation in West Africa that won its independence from Great Britain in 1960. The postcolonial years found Nigeria in the grip of a civil war, a series of oppressive military regimes, increasing tensions between the Christian population and fundamentalist Muslims, and mob violence. In a brief reminiscence for the *New York Times Magazine* (February 1, 2004), Abani recalled that as a 10-year-old boy he watched a man accused of stealing be burned alive by an angry mob: "As the man burned, people began to file past him in an orderly manner like the offertory line in the Catholic Church I attended," Abani wrote. "As they walked past, they spat on the incandescent figure. My aunt spat. I looked away, hand held over my nose at the smell of burning flesh, horrified that it reminded me of kebabs. 'Spit,' she snapped, rapping me on the head with her knuckles. I spat."

Abani started writing as a teenager and completed his first novel, *Masters of the Board*, when he was 16. Speaking with Andie Miller for the South Africa *Mail & Guardian* (March 11, 2005, on-line), Abani described his first novel as "a very bad crime thriller about neo-Nazis taking over Nigeria to reinstate the Fourth Reich." He explained, "Thrillers were fascinating to me because you can indulge all your adolescent fantasies about guns and women in them. I thought it would bring me fame and wealth." The manuscript won Nigeria's Delta Fiction Award, in 1983, and was published two years later. Abani was then arrested for treason by the Nigerian government, then under General Ibrahim Babangida. The head of the Association of Nigerian Authors, General Mamman Vatsa—who also happened to be Abani's mentor at the time—was accused of plotting a coup and using Abani's novel as a blueprint. "In the novel certain strategic targets had to be blown up, and when he [Vatsa] was arrested he was carrying a copy [of] my novel," Abani told Miller. Abani was imprisoned for six months, and though, as he told Miller, he had not been political before his internment, he emerged from prison with "a mix of idealism and a saviour complex."

In 1987, while a university student, Abani ran afoul of the authorities once again, this time for belonging to an allegedly subversive theater group that conducted impromptu performances outside of government buildings. The manuscript for his second novel, *Sirocco*—a tale of Palestinian terrorists planting a biological agent in Europe's water supply—was seized by the government, and Abani was sent to Kiri-Kiri, an infamous prison located in the Nigerian capital of Lagos, where he was subjected to torture, before being released one year later. "I'm not sure what they were thinking when they released me," he told Michael Datcher for *Black Issues Book Review* (May–June 2005). "That I would stop making art?"

In 1991 Abani graduated magna cum laude from Imo State University in Imo, Owerri, Nigeria, with a bachelor's degree in English and literary studies. For his university's convocation ceremony, he wrote *Song of a Broken Flute*, a controversial play that criticized the rampant corruption in Nigeria's government; the government responded by arresting him a third time. Sentenced to death Abani endured almost two years of imprisonment—six months of which he spent in solitary confinement—before friends bribed prison officials to arrange for his escape.

Settling in Great Britain Abani completed a master's degree in gender, society, and culture at Birkbeck College, at the University of London, in 1995. He then wrote a collection of poems, *Kalakuta Republic,* that served as a sort of prison memoir in verse. In an interview posted on the Voices in Wartime Web site, Abani explained that he began writing poetry in an attempt to capture his experiences as a political prisoner: "What really drew me to poetry, I suppose you could say, is the brevity in it. . . . It's a form that resists sentimentality. And when you are dealing with a difficult subject, sentimentality is a problem because you're sign-posting how people should feel." Described by Robert Winder for the *New Statesman* (May 21, 2001) as "a sequence of poems scraped from the harsh walls of a prison cell in Nigeria," *Kalakuta Republic* is composed of "short, bloodstained notes from a place where few of us have any wish to go." One poem from the collection, "Ode to Joy," as quoted on the Web site of the New Zealand Electronic Poetry Centre, details the brutal death of a young inmate: "John James, 14 / Refused to serve his conscience up / to indict an innocent man / handcuffed to chair; they tacked his penis / to the table / with a six inch nail / and left him there / to drip / to death / 3 days later." The British playwright Harold Pinter avowed, as quoted on Abani's official Web site, "Abani's poems are the most naked, harrowing expression of prison life and political torture imaginable. Reading them is like being singed by a red hot iron."

While Abani was living in Great Britain, the Nigerian government accused him of treason and sought to have him extradited. When Abani's neighbor, the only other Nigerian in the apartment building, was mysteriously murdered, the writer began to suspect that he was being targeted for assassination by agents from his homeland. He subsequently left Great Britain and moved to Los Angeles, California. In 2002 Abani earned a master's degree in English from the University of Southern California (USC).

The poems contained in Abani's 2003 compilation, *Daphne's Lot*, address war and violence, as well as the universal themes of compassion and coming-of-age. In a representative review Ronald Gottesman, a professor emeritus at USC, wrote, as quoted on Abani's Web site, "Chris Abani's poems remind us of what happens when moral boundaries are obliterated and the sacredness of life becomes a kind of cynical joke. But these poems also remind us of the human capacity for compassion and love in the face of unspeakable cruelty and fiendish conditions."

Abani's novel *GraceLand* is set in the late 1970s and early 1980s in Maroko, a slum on the outskirts of Lagos. The protagonist of this dark bildungsroman is Elvis Oke, a bookish Nigerian teenager who earns his living by impersonating his namesake, Elvis Presley, for tourists. Elvis's widowed father, Sunday, is unemployed, alcoholic, and bereft of hope for himself and his country. Elvis, in his struggle to escape his surroundings, enters Nigeria's criminal under-world, trafficking in drugs and human organs for a mysterious and sinister figure, dubbed the Colonel. Scattered throughout are excerpts from Elvis's deceased mother's journal, which recall the family's earlier life in the countryside, with its singular folklore and recipes. Though some critics felt the passages from Elvis's mother did not always mesh seamlessly with the rest of the story, *GraceLand* by and large earned high praise, particularly for its evocation of the squalid streets of Lagos; in a passage quoted by Chris Lehmann for the *Washington Post* (February 3, 2004), Abani described the Maroko slum: "Half of the town was built of a confused mix of clapboard, wood, cement and zinc sheets, raised above a swamp by means of stilts and wooden walkways. The other half, built on solid ground reclaimed from the sea, seemed to be clawing its way out of the primordial swamp, attempting to become something else." Writing for the *Boston Globe* (April 11, 2004), Melvin Jules Bukiet opined, "Abani's *GraceLand* is both a poetic meditation on urban decay and a coming-of-age picaresque. . . . Abani creates an intensely vivid portrait of an artificial nation whose people have as much emotional vigor as natural resources and, scarily, some have as much likelihood of throwing away their potential as making the most of it." Sophie Harrison wrote for the *New York Times Book Review* (February 22, 2004) that the notion of a Nigerian teen doing Elvis Presley impressions was "almost too weird to swallow." She admitted, however, "The book works brilliantly in two ways. As a convincing and unpatronizing record of life in a poor Nigerian slum, and as a frighteningly honest insight into a world skewed by casual violence, it's wonderful."

In 2006 Abani published the novella *Becoming Abigail*, another coming-of-age tale about a Nigerian youth, but with a female protagonist this time. Left to fend off the sexual advances of her male relatives after her mother's untimely death, young Abigail acts out, practicing self-mutilation. Her situation only worsens when she is sent to live with relatives in London. "This portrait of a brutalized girl given no control over her life or body . . . features Abani's lyrical prose (Abigail's father's armchair 'smelled of the dreams of everyone who had sat in it') and deft moves between short chapters titled 'Then' and 'Now'— with the latter offering little promise," a reviewer wrote for *Publishers Weekly* (January 9, 2006). In a review for *Library Journal* (February 1, 2006), Kevin Greczek wrote, "Abani's abundant talent is clearly evident throughout, as is his willingness to be brutally honest without being grotesque. Perhaps because of the book's brevity, Abani also refrains from polemics and focuses solely on the artistic presentation of a young, tragic life, leaving interpretation to the reader."

In 2006 Abani also published the poetry collection *Hands Washing Water*. His most recent novel, *The Virgin of Flames*, was published in 2007.

In addition to the works already noted, Abani has published a bilingual, Dutch/English poetry collection, issued in the Netherlands in 2003, entitled *Maar mijn hart is onvergankelijk* (*My Heart Is Unending*). His poetry collection *Dog Woman* was described by the poet Maurya Simon as "a mesmerizing, haunting, and sometimes subversive exploration of the personal and cultural politics of disempowerment and power," according to Abani's Web site. Abani has also written several plays, including one aimed at young adults, entitled *The Poet, the Soldier, the Lover and the Paper-Kite Maker* (2003). Abani has received a number of honors and awards, including a Prince Claus Award, the PEN USA Freedom to Write Award, a Hellman/Hammett Grant from Human Rights Watch, a Lannan Foundation Literary Fellowship, and the PEN/Hemingway Prize.

Abani, who received a doctoral degree in literature and creative writing from USC in 2004, has taught writing as an associate professor at Antioch University, in Los Angeles, since 2001; he has also been a visiting assistant professor at the University of California, at Riverside.

In addition to writing Abani enjoys playing the saxophone.

—P.B.M.

Suggested Reading: *Boston Globe* D p7 Apr. 11, 2004; *Chicago Tribune* C p3 Feb. 29, 2004; Christopher Abani's Web site; *Los Angeles Times* E p10 Apr. 5, 2004; *New Statesman* May 21, 2001; *New York Times Book Review* p8 Feb. 22, 2004; *New York Times Magazine* p74 Feb. 1, 2004; *Washington Post* C p4 Feb. 3, 2004

Selected Books: fiction—*Masters of the Board*, 1985; *GraceLand*, 2004; *Becoming Abigail*, 2006; The Virgin of Flames, 2007; poetry—*Kalakuta Republic*, 2000; *Daphne's Lot*, 2003; *Dog Woman*, 2004; *Hands Washing Water*, 2006

Aczel, Amir D.

Nov. 6, 1950– Nonfiction writer

Although Amir Aczel had written books on business statistics and on taxes (including a provocative 1995 volume entitled *How to Beat the I.R.S. at Its Own Game*), it was when he started publishing engaging accounts of the history of scientific and mathematical concepts that he became better known to the general reading public. Such titles include *Fermat's Last Theorem: Unlocking the Secret of an Ancient Mathematical Problem* (1996); *Probability 1: Why There Must Be Intelligent Life in the Universe* (1998); *God's Equation: Einstein, Relativity, and the Expanding Universe* (1999); *The Mystery of the Aleph: Mathematics, the Kabbalah, and the Search for Infinity* (2000); *The Riddle of the Compass: The Invention that Changed the World* (2001); *Entanglement: The Greatest Mystery in Physics* (2002); *Pendulum: Leon Foucault and the Triumph of Science* (2003); *Chance: A Guide to Gambling, Love, the Stock Market, and Just about Everything Else* (2004); *Descartes's Secret Notebook: A True Tale of Mathematics, Mysticism, and the Quest to Understand the Universe* (2005); and *The Artist and the Mathematician: The Story of Nicolas Bourbaki, the Genius Mathematician Who Never Existed* (2006). Bryce Christensen, in a review for *Booklist* (October 1, 2000), wrote of Aczel's "gift for interpreting complex concepts" and ability to penetrate "to the human drama behind the formulas."

Amir D. Aczel was born in Carmel, Israel, on November 6, 1950. He earned bachelor's and master's degrees in mathematics from the University of California, at Berkeley, in 1975 and 1976 respectively. He the went on to earn a Ph.D. in statistics from the University of Oregon, in Eugene.

Pierre de Fermat, a French jurist living in the 17th century, had a passionate interest in mathematical theory, and in about 1637 he scribbled a note in the margin of one of his books stating that he had solved a well-known mathematical problem—but neglected to show his solution. For more than three centuries, mathematicians tried, fruitlessly, to piece together

Debra Gross Aczel/Courtesy of Harcourt

Amir D. Aczel

the puzzle Fermat had left. Finally, in 1995, a mathematician named Andrew Wiles discovered the answer. *Fermat's Last Theorem: Unlocking the Secret of an Ancient Mathematical Problem* is Aczel's account of the mathematics, people, and sometimes highly dramatic events involved. "The author has taken a recent and newsworthy mathematical topic and made it into a fascinating story," Gary Klinger wrote in a review for *Mathematics Teacher* (September 1997). "Presented in a conversational tone that is both readable and attractive, the story downplays the technical jargon and mathematical details while still presenting a logical and adequately complete picture of the solution. The middle of the book discusses the various mathematical contributions even remotely related to Fermat's conjecture, from ancient times to the present." [Aczel] "has written a tale of buried treasure, the treasure here being immaterial, intellectual, of no practical benefit, but rooted in the pleasure of pure knowledge," Richard Bernstein wrote for the *New York Times* (December 16, 1996, on-line). "His book is modestly but lucidly presented, most (though not all) of the technical material understandable to people with only a smattering of mathematical skill. This is a captivating volume even when it comes to those few passages that you might not entirely understand." While praising Aczel's lucidity, Bernstein concluded, "Equally important is the sense of awe that Mr. Aczel imparts for the hidden, mystical harmonies of numbers, and for that sense of awe alone, his slender volume is well worth the effort."

Aczel used his skills as a statistician to support the thesis of his next book, *Probability 1: Why There Must Be Intelligent Life in the Universe.* Chris Aylott, writing for Space.com (January 24, 2000), noted that "Aczel bases his argument on Frank Drake's method for calculating how many civilizations might currently exist in our galaxy. By estimating all the factors likely to influence the answer, this method—famous as 'Drake's Equation'—cuts the problem down to size." Aylott continued, "Drake suggested figuring out how many habitable planets there are in the galaxy, how many are likely to develop life, how likely that life is to develop civilization, and so on. . . . Aczel spends most of *Probability 1* going through each of the factors in Drake's Equation, presenting what astronomers now know about how common planets are and how likely life is to develop. His writing is clear and engaging, and Drake's Equation is so broad in scope that *Probability 1* becomes an excellent general survey of current astronomy. Fans of Asimov, Sagan and other science writers will find much of the material familiar, but Aczel also presents a lot of exciting new developments in the field." Atlott, finding the book ultimately disappointing, concluded, "Unfortunately, the final 'proof' that appears in the book's final chapter wastes this survey of astronomy and math, using almost none of it. Instead, Aczel simply makes the point that even using arbitrarily tiny values for the factors in Drake's Equation, the number of stars in both our galaxy and the greater universe is so vast that it's impossible for the equation not to return the practical certainty of alien life. Therefore, he announces triumphantly, it's certain there's at least one other civilization somewhere in our galaxy."

In *God's Equation: Einstein, Relativity, and the Expanding Universe*, Aczel examines the "cosmological constant," a component of Einstein's field equation for general relativity that the famed physicist later disavowed. In a review for *Booklist* (October 15, 1999), Bryce Christensen wrote, "Even readers without exceptional mathematical sophistication will grasp why Einstein first conceived of a cosmological constant and then later repudiated it as [a] bad mistake. But Aczel's greatest accomplishment lies in his deft weaving together of the seemingly disparate research projects in cosmology and quantum physics that have unexpectedly provided fresh evidence for the validity of Einstein's cosmological constant as the key to understanding the 'strange energy' filling quantum space and driving our universe ever outward. A marvelous distillation of epoch-making science." Writing for *Discover* (November 1999), Jeffrey Winter concurred: "It is . . . a wonderful time to glance back over Einstein's path in developing the field equation. [But] it's not an easy road to follow. . . . Fortunately, we have a fabulous guide in Amir D. Aczel."

The Mystery of the Aleph: Mathematics, the Kabbalah, and the Search for Infinity is Aczel's look at the concept of infinity and includes the story of Georg Cantor, a 19th-century German mathematician who formulated an equation using the aleph, the first letter of the Hebrew alphabet, to describe infinity. "A single formula that purports to hold within itself the deepest mysteries of existence: the idea rings with all sorts of spiritual and scientific implications. The drama deepens because at least two of the mathematicians who explored the mystery most avidly—Cantor and Kurt Godel—went mad," Richard Bernstein wrote for the New York Times (November 15, 2000, on-line). Bernstein, while complaining—as did many reviewers—that The Mystery of the Aleph was less accessible to the layperson than some of Aczel's previous efforts, concluded, "Mr. Aczel's book remains highly enjoyable and frustrating at the same time. It deals, after all, with great minds venturing into the farthest reaches of speculation, with the nature of endlessness itself, both mathematical and religious, subjects that were not meant to be easy."

In the first chapter of The Riddle of the Compass: The Invention That Changed the World, Aczel wrote about growing up on a passenger ship that his father captained around the Mediterranean. (He spent a few months ashore each year, to attend school.) When Aczel was not yet in his teens, his father taught him to steer the massive vessel. "Steering by compass is both an art and a science, as I learned at the age of ten," he wrote. "Many years later I can still hear in my mind the ticking of the compass, degree by degree, as the ship turned." Inspired by his childhood experiences, Aczel wrote The Riddle of the Compass, a richly detailed history of the instrument. The book received largely mixed reviews, with most critics praising its accessibility but wishing for more detail. In a representative assessment, Robert C. Cowen wrote for the Christian Science Monitor (September 13, 2001), "This [is an] interesting little book. . . . One wishes that the author had given his story greater depth and set it in [a] broader context. Instead, we have a sketchy account fleshed out with potted histories of such relevant developments as Marco Polo's travels and the rise of Venice as a mini-superpower. If you take this essay on the level of an after-dinner conversation, it's an entertaining read. Meanwhile, we await a more incisive history."

Entanglement: The Greatest Mystery in Physics discusses a phenomenon that occurs in quantum physics in which two subatomic particles remain bafflingly connected, even when separated physically. (If a change is made to one of the particles, then instantaneously the same change is manifested in its entangled partner.) In Pendulum: Leon Foucault and the Triumph of Science, Aczel examines another area of physics, visiting the life of the 19th-century French physicist Leon Foucault, whose pendulum experiments resulted in the first real proof of the Earth's rotation. With Chance: A Guide to Gambling, Love, the Stock Market, and Just About Everything Else, Aczel returned to statistics and probability. A reviewer for Publishers Weekly (September 13, 2004, on-line) wrote, "[Aczel] untangles a number of urgent conundrums, including why buses always seem to run late, why any group of 31 people will include two with the same birthday and why random walks can model the stock market. The book abounds in counterintuitive life lessons. You shouldn't gamble, he says, but if you do then you are better off, probability-wise, if you blow your whole wad on a single spin of the roulette wheel than if you parcel it out in smaller bets. And the lovelorn can take comfort in knowing that, if you just keep dating, the odds are surprisingly good that your soul mate will turn up. . . . Aczel's treatments of some topics, like game theory, are so perfunctory as to barely register, but his light touch generally makes probability come alive." In an assessment for Booklist (November 1, 2004), a critic wrote, "People, as a rule, perform poorly when it comes to estimating risk and chance. Casinos profit from this ignorance about probability, and statistics in the news tend not to be well understood by the public. Aczel takes on the noble mission of enlightening readers with the theory behind everyday probability. . . . Extending his winning track record of popularizing science, Aczel entertains readers with ways to tame the guesswork."

In Descartes's Secret Notebook: A True Tale of Mathematics, Mysticism, and the Quest to Understand the Universe and The Artist and the Mathematician: The Story of Nicolas Bourbaki, the Genius Mathematician Who Never Existed, Aczel delivers the type of human drama that has proven exceedingly popular with his readers. Of the first volume, a Publishers Weekly (August 29, 2005, on-line) reviewer wrote, "What Aczel did for mathematician Fermat (Fermat's Last Theorem) he now does for Descartes in this splendid study about the French philosopher and mathematician (1596-1650) most famous for his paradigm-smashing declaration, 'I think; therefore, I am.' Part historical sketch, part biography and part detective story, Aczel's chronicle of Descartes's hidden work hinges on his lost secret notebook. . . . As Aczel so deftly demonstrates, Descartes's mathematical theories were paths to an understanding [of] the order and mystery of the cosmos, and he kept the notebook hidden because it contained a formula that—because it supported Copernicus's model of the solar system—Descartes feared would lead to his persecution by the Inquisition. Aczel lucidly explains the science, mystery and mathematics of Descartes, who has never been so lively as he is in the pages of this first-rate [book]." The other volume tells the story of a group of French mathematicians who published their collective work under an imaginary name in the 1930s.

(Although it started as simply a prank, the group published several highly influential works.) *The Artist and the Mathematician* stirred some excitement when the *Washington Post Book World* (October 15, 2006) published a particularly vicious review by Charles Siefe, who accused Aczel of plagiarism: "A reader without a PhD in mathematics will be baffled by Aczel's prose. In all probability, so would an intellectual property lawyer. Even in passages dealing with mathematicians, Aczel seems more than a little inspired by other writers." Aczel responded in a letter to the publication on October 22, 2006: "Unlike Seife, I am doubtful that an intellectual property lawyer would ever be 'baffled' by my book—but perhaps a libel lawyer might be baffled by his review."

Aczel has taught at various institutions, including Bentley College, in Waltham, Massachusetts. He is currently a visiting researcher in the Department of the History of Science at Harvard University, in Cambridge, Massachusetts. The departmental Web site states, "Our faculty and students employ historical, textual, ethnographic, and social scientific methods to ask larger questions about how the various sciences work in practice, the basis of their authority, how ethical and political decisions are made about their regulation and applications, how they relate to larger intellectual, cultural, social, and political trends and changes, and much more."

Aczel lives with his wife and daughter in Brookline, Massachusetts. On his Amazon.com profile page, he described his next book: "I began work on this book in China in the summer of 2005, when I visited the Peking Man site—the place 25 miles southwest of Beijing at which fossils of 'the missing link' were found in 1929. Several skulls and bones dated to 500,000 years ago were discovered here and recognized as belonging to the human ancestor named *Homo erectus*. This was a hominid found in Africa and in Asia that predates the Neanderthals and modern humans. My book describes this amazing discovery by an international team of scientists, which included the enigmatic figure of Pierre Teilhard de Chardin—a Jesuit priest who was also a mystic and a renowned paleontologist. Teilhard remained a devout Jesuit all his life, but he also believed in evolution. The Jesuits exiled him to China for his views on evolution, which he often expressed publicly. As fate would have it, he arrived in China just in time to take part in one of the most important discoveries in support of evolution. The title of the book is 'The Jesuit and the Skull,' and it [is scheduled to] appear in September of 2007."
—S.Y.

Suggested Reading: *American Libraries* p68 Dec. 2000; *Booklist* p206 Oct. 15, 1999, p296 Oct. 1, 2000, p450 Nov. 1, 2004; *Choice* p1,375 Apr. 1997; *Christian Science Monitor* p21 Sep. 13, 2001; *Economist* p9 July 17, 1999; *Mathematics Teacher* p498 Sep. 1997; *New Scientist* p49 Oct. 19, 1996; *New York Times* E p8 Nov. 15, 2000; *New York Times Book Review* Nov. 15, 1998; *Publishers Weekly* (on-line) Sep. 13, 2004, Aug. 29, 2005; *Science News* p50 Jan. 27, 2001; *Scientific American* (on-line) Feb. 1999; Space.com Jan. 24, 2000; *Washington Post Book World* p5 Nov. 19, 2000, p2 Aug. 23, 2001, p10 Oct. 15, 2006

Selected Books: *How to Beat the I.R.S. at Its Own Game: Strategies to Avoid—and Survive—an Audit,* 1995; *Fermat's Last Theorem: Unlocking the Secret of an Ancient Mathematical Problem,* 1996; *Probability 1: Why There Must Be Intelligent Life in the Universe,* 1998; *God's Equation: Einstein, Relativity, and the Expanding Universe,* 1999; The *Mystery of the Aleph: Mathematics, the Kabbalah, and the Search for Infinity,* 2000; *The Riddle of the Compass: The Invention that Changed the World,* 2001; *Entanglement: The Greatest Mystery in Physics,* 2002; *Pendulum: Leon Foucault and the Triumph of Science,* 2003; *Chance: A Guide to Gambling, Love, the Stock Market, and Just about Everything Else,* 2004; *Descartes's Secret Notebook: A True Tale of Mathematics, Mysticism, and the Quest to Understand the Universe,* 2005; *The Artist and the Mathematician: The Story of Nicolas Bourbaki, the Genius Mathematician Who Never Existed,* 2006

Alexander, Caroline

Mar. 13, 1956– Travel writer

Though Caroline Alexander, the author of six nonfiction titles, began her career as a travel writer, she is perhaps best known for her extremely popular revisionist works about Sir Ernest Shackleton's doomed expedition to the South Pole and the famous mutiny on the British armed vessel *Bounty.* In the former of these books, *The Endurance: Shackleton's Legendary Antarctic Expedition* (1998), Alexander's text frames 170 previously unpublished photograph's that had been taken by the expedition's photographer, Frank Hurley, bringing to life the struggle for survival endured by the Shackleton expedition during its many months trapped on the Antarctic ice. In the later book, *The Bounty: The True Story of the Mutiny on the* Bounty (2003), Alexander uses historical records, diaries, and eyewitness accounts to reassess popular thinking about why the master's mate, Fletcher Christian, led a mutiny against the *Bounty's* commander, William Bligh, in 1789.

The eldest daughter of a British-born, Jewish mother, Caroline Alexander was born on March 13, 1956, in Gainesville, Florida. Her parents divorced while she was still a child, and her mother, Elizabeth Ann Kirby, who later earned a doctorate in art history, struggled to raise Alexander and her younger sister, Joanna, without any child support. Still, the girls were fortunate enough to spend their summers at a camp in Tennessee, where their mother taught swimming lessons, and Kirby arranged for the family to live overseas for two years, first in Florence, Italy, and then the Netherlands, where Alexander learned to speak French, German, and Italian. In 1976, at the age of 20, Alexander earned her bachelor's degree in classics from Florida State University, in Tallahassee, and then became one of the first women to be named a Rhodes Scholar, studying at the University of Oxford's Somerville College for three years. While pursuing her education, Alexander also competed as a world-class athlete in five sports—swimming, running, fencing, pistol shooting, and horseback riding. She served as an alternate for the American women's pentathlon team in the 1978 World Games.

After graduating from Oxford with degrees in philosophy and theology, in 1980, Alexander convinced the university's virology department to send her and two others to the Southeast Asian island of Borneo on an insect-collecting expedition, though she knew little about entomology. In 1982 she returned to the U.S. to train for the World Games, but her plans were interrupted by an invitation, offered at the behest of the president of the small, land-locked African nation of Malawi, to create a classics program at the University of Malawi, in the city of Zomba. After completing this project in 1985, Alexander once again returned to the U.S., this time to attend the graduate program in classics at Columbia University, in New York City, as the recipient of a prestigious Mellon Fellowship. When she showed one of her favorite professors, Laura Slatkin, an article she had written about her travels in Borneo, Slatkin put her in touch with a literary agent, who quickly sold the piece to the *New Yorker*. "It was a turning point," Alexander told Catharine Reeve for the *Chicago Tribune* (April 8, 1990), "because it showed me that people had faith in my ability to convey my experiences."

Alexander's agent then parlayed that success into a book contract for the travelogue *One Dry Season: In the Footsteps of Mary Kingsley*, which was published in 1990. The book describes Alexander's travels in Gabon, a former French colony in West Africa, where she traced the path of Mary Kingsley, a Victorian woman who, defying the social customs of the time, traveled to Africa, in 1895, to conduct research for a book that her father had failed to complete before his death. Alexander first learned of this intrepid adventurer in December 1986. Browsing through her local library, she discovered a copy of *Travels in West*

Africa, in which Kingsley had chronicled her explorations. Leafing through the 700-page tome, which was a best-seller when first published in 1897, Alexander noticed that the preface ended with the rather bold declaration, according to Catharine Reeve, that if the reader should travel to West Africa, "you will find things as I have said." Alexander told Reeve, "Even before I checked her book out of the library, let alone read it, I had made up my mind to take Miss Kingsley up on her offer."

A few months later Alexander put her graduate studies on hold and set off for Gabon. Though much had changed there in the last century, her book reveals that many aspects of life there had remained unaltered. "Weaving a narrative pattern of 'then and now,' Alexander evokes images of chugging river steamers packed with passengers, roads of red dust, pirogues paddled against the current, and more," Janet L. Stanley wrote for *Library Journal* (November 15, 1989). "As she travels in the footsteps of others, she reflects on the different faces of interpretive writing, selective recollection, and the disparity between fact and fiction. But ultimately this is Alexander's own story of discovery and can be read and enjoyed as such. She avoids the patronizing, exaggerated tone of much contemporary travel writing about Africa; she is sympathetic and gently self-effacing." Though Caroline Moorehead, writing for the *Times Literary Supplement* (January 26, 1990), felt that Mary Kingsley's "presence adds virtually nothing" to the book, she was fascinated with "the incidental characters, early travellers turned up during Alexander's diligent research, and whose stories—and the brief passages she quotes—are charming and lively." Moorehead concluded: "But Alexander is not only good on history. Her own travels are well told, with considerable powers of description and a true sense of adventure. If [the book] is at times a little humourless, it makes up for it in sympathy and perceptiveness. As a companion to an armchair traveller, she is resourceful, without prejudice and full of insights."

In 1991 Alexander was awarded her doctorate from Columbia University and began writing full-time. In her second book, *The Way to Xanadu* (1994), Alexander sought to find the real-life locations that correspond to the mythical landscape in Samuel Taylor Coleridge's 1816 poem "Kubla Khan," which immortalized—in the Western world, at least—Kublai Khan, the founder of the 13th-century Mongol Dynasty of China. In her travels the author explored the ruins of Shangdu, Kublai Khan's summer palace, and visited Ethiopia, Kashmir, and Florida—places where mystical ice caves and fountains were supposed to be found. "The literary sleuthing that lies behind [the author's] travel gives *The Way to Xanadu* an aura of madcap scholarship," Rand Richards Cooper wrote for the *New York Times Book Review* (June 5, 1994). "Extensive chains of citation, deduction and inference are required to deliver Ms. Alexander's destinations to her. Her identification of Florida as a source, for example, arises from a reference to 'fragrant groves' and 'perfumed' trees in the American naturalist William Bartram's 1791 account of his travels through the American Southeast. . . . If such moves seem a little dodgy, and if the travel narrative they produce . . . sometimes seems to bear little direct relation to Coleridge or his poem, it doesn't really matter. . . . It is this elevation of the imagination, and not any far-flung destination, that makes her slight and graceful book the truly romantic text it is." On the other hand, Robert Carver, in his review for the *New Statesman and Society* (December 17, 1993), was more critical: "[This is] a good idea, perhaps for a travel book, but it doesn't come off. . . . Alexander travels with supportive, old-fashioned boyfriend George, and in considerable luxury. She falls ill and doesn't really care for the rigours of a not very rigorous trip. The poverty in Africa refuses stubbornly to turn into poetry for her, and she wonders in print, rather plaintively, that perhaps she should be tampering with the material to make it sound hardier and more romantic. Hers is a tourist jaunt out of litcrit-land and it doesn't make for either an original or a stimulating read."

With her third book, *Battle's End: A Seminole Football Team Revisited* (1995), Alexander looked at the impact of high-school sports and athletic scholarships on the quality of the education that athletes receive. The book's genesis lay in Alexander's experience as a writing tutor for college freshmen football players, a position she took shortly after returning to Tallahassee, Florida, in 1981. The relationship that she had forged with her students was strong enough that, over a decade later, she sought them out to see how their lives were progressing. Much of the book's text consists of interviews with the players, who recount their lives since their college days. "This is the book for all those outsiders—be they intellectuals, social reformers, liberals, or conservatives—who have ever deluded themselves into believing they understand what it can be like to be young, black, and male in the U.S. today," Wes Lukowsky wrote for *Booklist* (December 15, 1995). "Most of Alexander's young men defined themselves athletically; the classroom was where they were mocked and failed, and reading was something they learned to distrust and dismiss as uncool. . . . Alexander lets them present their stories without interference, and the result is an intimate look at the hopes, dreams, regrets, and plans of seven young men who were once college football players. There are no types here, no statistical standards—just individuals who've had to come such a long way to get to where so many people start." In the *New York Times Book Review* (January 14, 1996), Carolyn T. Hughes called the book "an interesting but flawed study," noting that Alexander "is a talented interviewer, but what she does not do—and what the book desperately

needs—is to draw some conclusions about the effects of big-time college athletics on the men's lives, and on society generally." Hughes concluded: "Every Saturday during the season, millions of Americans eagerly await the entrance of the players onto the gridiron. What becomes apparent after reading *Battle's End* is just how few care what happens to the athletes once the game is over."

While researching her next book, an investigation into the 1914–15 expedition by Sir Ernest Shackleton to the South Pole, Alexander discovered that the beloved cat aboard the ship *Endurance*, Mrs. Chippy, had to be left behind to die after the crew found themselves stuck in the ice for many months. A cat lover herself, the author decided to fashion a diary of the trip for Mrs. Chippy. *Mrs. Chippy's Last Expedition: The Remarkable Journal of Shackleton's Polar-Bound Cat* was published in 1997 to generally positive reviews. Claire Hutchings, writing for *Geographical* (January 1998), found that the book "offers a rather unique perspective of this much written about expedition. For example, Alexander includes comic details about the scarcity of mice aboard the ship and the dubious nature of Darwin's theories, in the cat's view, when despite months stuck in ice no-one seems to show signs of evolving into penguins! This tongue-in-cheek account of the expedition is accompanied by some wonderful black and white photographs taken by the official expedition photographer James Francis Hurley. A unique and beautifully presented book particularly for all cat-lovers and Shackleton admirers."

Alexander followed this book's publication with *The Endurance*, her immensely popular study of the Shackleton expedition, which is illustrated with some 170 previously unpublished photos. In it, she describes the famous story of how, in his effort to become the first man to traverse Antarctica, Shackleton and the crew of the *Endurance* found themselves trapped by ice floes that eventually destroyed their ship. Despite these disastrous events, the Shackleton story is now seen as a heroic tale of survival, one in which every member of the *Endurance*'s crew was saved. "The expedition has been described more than once. Ms. Alexander has sensibly, and ably, concentrated on the characters and interactions of the men . . . and used her text as a frame for previously unpublished pictures by the expedition's Australian photographer, Frank Hurley," Phoebe-Lou Adams wrote for the *Atlantic Monthly* (February 1999). "The pictures are dazzling. There is no other word for the patterns of black rigging against snow, or for the angles and shadows Hurley recorded as he climbed to improbable places and clung to unlikely surfaces." In a review for the *New York Review of Books* (June 10, 1999), Jonathan Raban criticized the work: "Given the splendors of Hurley's photographs, it may seem niggardly to carp at the shortcomings of Caroline Alexander's text, which is a workmanlike retelling of a story told many times before. The best-known version is Alfred Lansing's *Endurance* (1959); much the best-documented is to be found in Roland Huntford's splendid 1985 biography, *Shackleton*. In a somewhat condescending note of acknowledgement at the end of her book, Alexander belittles Lansing's as 'a rip-roaring narration,' which does it a calculated injustice. Alexander has taken pains to distance herself from Lansing; . . . and [she] has added a mass of new details, many of them from Huntford. Yet in its essential shape and tone, *The Endurance* seems more than faintly derivative of *Endurance*. What she has not done—and it is a huge missed opportunity—is to bring Frank Hurley fully into the foreground of the story." Hurley's photographs were also prominently displayed in the documentary *The Endurance: Shackleton's Legendary Antarctic Expedition* (2000), which was based on Alexander's book.

Alexander's most recent book is *The Bounty*, a revisionist look at the events that led up to the famous mutiny aboard the British transport ship. The book recounts how Fletcher Christian led a mutiny against the commander of the ship, William Bligh, and set Bligh and his loyalists adrift on a longboat in the South Pacific, before sailing away. Eventually, after two grueling months at sea, Bligh's party reached Timor. Christian and his cohorts established a colony on Pitcairn Island, where their descendants can still be found today; some mutineers later returned to Tahiti, where the *Bounty*'s voyage had begun, and three of those crew members were court-martialed and hanged. Alexander reevaluates the traditional accounts of Bligh's villainy and alleged abuse of his crew to deliver a more balanced judgment on the incident. As to the cause of the mutiny, Alexander had few qualms about placing blame. As she told Jessica Jernigan, in an interview posted on the Borders Web site: "If the Bounty's mission was doomed from the start it was because Fletcher Christian was on board. . . . There are many reasons why Christian did break—family circumstances, his pride, Bligh's undoubted nagging, the memory of an easy life in Tahiti, his probable drinking on the night before the mutiny; but it is my belief that if he had not broken down there would have been no mutiny."

Verlyn Klinkenborg proclaimed in the *New York Times Book Review* (September 14, 2003): "Alexander's vigorous retelling . . . leads to lots of vigorous rethinking . . . . [This] is a story of enormous complexity, one with ramifications that seem to spin off in every direction. . . . Alexander is more than equal to the task. With this and her previous book, *The Endurance*, she has made the wondrous genre of open-boat-voyage narratives still more wondrous. . . . A sea mist hangs over this age-old tale. Alexander dispels it, to the reader's fascination. But when all the facts are told and the fates of the cast are duly chronicled, the sea mist settles in again, as impenetrable and yet more interesting than it has ever been." Frank McLynn, writing for the *New Statesman* (November 3, 2003), was far more critical in his assessment, proposing that "Alexander's work is poorly structured, with a Godardian problem about beginnings, middle and ends that dissipates narrative tension. To borrow a term from the movies (appropriately, in this case), one might say that it suffers from a very poor second act, when Alexander reproduces the courtmartial proceedings of those mutineers who had been recaptured . . . at unconscionable length. It seems her main thesis is that Bligh was guilty of no more than flashes of temper, that Fletcher Christian was the mentally unbalanced one. . . . Although she writes well and has done a lot of archival sleuthing, Alexander tells me nothing new. Let us hope that this talented author will find a subject that has not already been written into the ground and will produce something truly original in her next book."

Caroline Alexander has been a contributor to such noted periodicals as the *New Yorker*, *Granta*, *Condé Nast Traveler*, *Smithsonian*, *Outside*, and *National Geographic*. She is a fellow of the Royal Geographic Society and a member of the American Philological Association, the Society for the Promotion of Hellenic Studies, and a number of environmental organizations. She lives in England.

—C.M.

Suggested Reading: *Atlantic Monthly* p106 Feb. 1999; *Boston Globe* (on-line) Nov. 13, 2003; *Chicago Tribune* N p1 Apr. 8, 1990; *Christian Science Monitor* p12 Mar. 23, 1990; *Geographical* p84 Jan. 1998; *New Statesman and Society* p71 Dec. 17, 1993; *New York Review of Books* p14 June 10, 1999; *New York Times Book Review* p3 June 5, 1994, p18 Jan. 14, 1996, p9 Sep. 14, 2003; *Times Literary Supplement* p97 Jan. 26, 1990

Selected Books: *One Dry Season: In the Footsteps of Mary Kingsley*, 1990; *The Way to Xanadu*, 1994; *Battle's End: A Seminole Football Team Revisited*, 1995; *Mrs. Chippy's Last Expedition: The Remarkable Journal of Shackleton's Polar-Bound Cat*, 1997; *The Endurance: Shackleton's Legendary Antarctic Expedition*, 1998; *The Bounty: The True Story of the Mutiny on the* Bounty, 2003

John Foley/Opale/Courtesy of Simon & Schuster

Ali, Monica

Oct. 20, 1967– Novelist; short-story writer

Hailed as one of Britain's most promising young novelists, even before her first book reached bookstores, Monica Ali found both critical and popular success with the 2003 publication of *Brick Lane,* a novel that takes its title from the area of London's East End where many impoverished Bangladeshi immigrants reside. She also earned the ire of some members the Bangladeshi community in Great Britain, who organized strong protests against her characterization of their lives. One organization, the Greater Sylhet Welfare and Development Council, which represents many Bangladeshis living in England, went so far as to demand, in an 18-page letter to the London *Guardian* and the panel that was to decide the winner of the Booker Prize, that passages be cut. As Amit Roy reported for the London *Daily Telegraph* (December 04, 2003), "A spokesman for the council said, 'We have serious objections to most of the content of this book, which is a despicable insult to Bangladeshis at home and abroad. It says we got here by jumping ship, that we have lice in our hair and live like rats. These comments are hurtful and untrue.' Kalam Mahmud Abu Taher Choudhury, the leader of the protesters, said that a 'team of intellectuals' had gone through the novel twice and drawn up a list of offending lines they wanted excised. 'We want to correct the idea that Bangladeshis are uneducated and cannot read,' he said." In 2006, during the filming of a movie based on the novel—which will be released in 2007— protests continued to be staged, forcing producers to conceal the set's location. In the meantime, Ali

had moved on, writing her second novel, *Alentejo Blue* (2006), which is about British expatriates in Portugal.

Monica Ali was born on October 20, 1967 in Dhaka, a city in former East Pakistan (now Bangladesh), to an English mother and a Bangladeshi father. The family moved to England after the outbreak of the civil war that led Bangladesh to gain independence from Pakistan, in 1971. The family settled in Bolton, where Ali attended the Bolton Girls' School. She continued her education at Wadham College, Oxford, from which she graduated with honors, in 1989. She later took jobs in the advertising and public-relations industries, married, and had two children. Meanwhile, she toyed with the idea of being a writer, having grown up with a love of literature and having, she told Harriet Lane in an interview for the London *Observer* (June 1, 2003): "an idea that it would be a nice thing to be a writer, which is quite a different thing to having the urge to write. That came quite late. And so did the confidence." Ali began writing short stories and anonymously sharing them with other aspiring writers through a Web site. "I'd joined these on-line writing groups—critique groups," she explained to Shahnaz Yousuf in an interview for the Adhunika Web site. "Other people would submit their short stories, you would send in yours. You would swap criticisms. That was very good just to get me into the habit and discipline of writing on a regular basis. I couldn't get out of the house very easily with a baby. . . . I don't think it's how I learnt to write, but I learnt quite a lot about how not to write. Because if something didn't work, you'd have to really think why. That was useful. That got me started."

In July 2001 Ali began writing a novel, the opening chapters of which earned her an attention-grabbing two-book contract with Doubleday at the beginning of the following year. Shortly thereafter, *Granta,* a literary journal, included her on its list of Britain's best young authors—based on reading a manuscript version of the chapters that won her the contract. As a result, Ali's name was well known before she had even published her first book. The finished product, *Brick Lane,* received enthusiastic reviews, justifying the early confidence in Ali's ability. The novel examined the lives of two Bangladeshi girls: Nazneen, who immigrates to England on her 18th birthday to marry Chanu, a middle-aged man whom she has never met, and Hasina, who stays in Bangladesh and marries for love but is forced, after her husband dies, to turn to prostitution to survive. Harriet Lane described the work as "warm, shrewd, startling and hugely readable: the sort of book you race through greedily, dreading the last page." Diana Abu-Jaber observed for the *Nation* (October 20, 2003), "*Brick Lane* fulfills [Ali's] early promise and establishes Ali as a writer of real literary depth and dimension. There is an elegance and a steadfast, patient, careful construction of observed detail to this prose, a meticulous layering of character and social observation that endows *Brick Lane* with a sophistication and maturity that might surprise readers who've come to expect flash and dash in modern fiction."

Some critics were less enthusiastic, however. Chris Lehmann, in a review for the *Washington Post* (October 12, 2003), acknowledged Ali's achievement but also called attention to her faults, writing: "In a feverishly fragmenting and often character-resistant fictional landscape, *Brick Lane* manages to do many of the things that fiction does best: to create a fully rounded, satisfyingly complicated world of its own that opens onto our own lives, provoking us to measure ourselves by its terms rather than vice versa. Ali's novel also has some notable shortcomings: Like many books that revolve around a central character struggling to make up her mind, it can grow frustratingly longsome, and for all the inventive care that Ali shows with language, she also tosses off some unwieldy and/or cliched metaphors. But in all the ways that fiction matters most, *Brick Lane* is no ordinary achievement."

Ali's next novel, *Alentejo Blue*, appeared in 2006 but received decidedly less favorable reviews. Set in Portugal and lacking a clear storyline, the novel contains nine loosely linked chapters, each narrated by a single character. Sean O'Brien complained for the London *Independent* (June 2, 2006): "The book should be a chamber piece, rich in design and moral understanding, but it reads as 'late' work undertaken too soon. It rubs up against serious themes—love, endurance, time, making do—only to move quickly on. As yet Ali lacks the dramatic economy which her form requires. The novel seems strangely modular, relying on the reader's consent to a kind of shorthand which recalls the empty 'issues' and mechanical *gravitas* of soap opera. Predictably, the political and historical dimensions—Salazar's version of Fascism, the failure of revolution to keep the land from slipping back into the hands of the rich—are no sooner introduced than they are tidied away." Lionel Shriver wrote for the London *Daily Telegraph* (June 3, 2006), "*Alentejo Blue* is a frustrating novel, for page by page it is well written and often entertaining. But the book is structurally more akin to the linked short-story collections recently in vogue than a fully fledged novel. Each set piece on different denizens of Mamarrosa has its merits, and many of these chapters could stand on their own as stories; strung together, they fail to form the arc that makes the form of the novel so rewarding. The fact that none of these characters is going anywhere is, of course, part of Ali's point. Yet if her charges are staying put, kidding themselves about getting away, or passing through on the way to nowhere, her readers should still have a reasonable expectation of taking a journey of some sort from the first to last page."

Not all reviewers found fault with the novel's structure, however. In a review for the *Chicago Tribune* (August 6, 2006), Julia Livshin observed that *Alentejo Blue* "features characters who don't do much other than pine—for professional success, for sustaining companionship, for a fresh start, for what could have been. The plot of one chapter revolves around a portly cafe owner sadly contemplating his last remaining almond tart. Spoon poised, he agonizes over whether to eat it as he cycles through the highlights and disappointments in his life. It's not that [the novel], which unfolds as a series of linked vignettes set in a village in a poor agricultural region of Portugal, is wholly devoid of event. It opens with a suicide and moves on to adultery, an illegal abortion, a murder charge and the much-anticipated (but ultimately anticlimactic) return of a native son who has struck it rich. These bits of plot, however, feel decidedly peripheral; they function mainly as pegs on which the characters' interior lives are hung. Like all books that ask the reader to dwell in a character's mind, the challenge facing *Alentejo Blue* is that its motley assemblage of voices be distinct and arresting enough to offset the lack of momentum. And for the most part they are."

Ali lives with her husband, Simon, who works as a management consultant, and their children in south London. The couple also spend a few months of each year in Portugal, in the same region in which Ali set her second novel.

—P.B.M./A.R.

Suggested Reading: Adhunika Web site; *Chicago Tribune* C p9 Aug. 6, 2006; (London) *Daily Telegraph* p3 Dec. 04, 2003, June 3, 2006; (London) *Independent* June 2, 2006; (London) *Observer* Review Pages p5 June 1, 2003; *Nation* p25 Oct. 20, 2003

Selected Books: *Brick Lane*, 2003; *Alentejo Blue*, 2006

Ammaniti, Niccolò

Sep. 25, 1966– Novelist; short-story writer; screenwriter

Niccolò Ammaniti is widely considered one of Italy's brightest literary talents. His novel *Io non ho paura* (2001) remained on best-seller lists in Italy for nearly a year. The book won the prestigious Viareggio-Repaci Prize for fiction, making Ammaniti the youngest author ever to receive the award. *Io non ho paura* has since been translated into 20 languages and became the first of Ammaniti's books to be published in English.

Born on September 25, 1966, Niccolò Ammaniti was raised in the Italian capital of Rome. Unlike many of his contemporaries, he did not devote his

Courtesy of Canongate Books

Niccolò Ammaniti

education to studying the tradition of Italian literature. Instead, Ammaniti studied biology at La Sapienza, a university in Rome; he left before completing his degree. In an interview with James Eve for the London *Times* (January 8, 2003), he described the differences between his approach to writing and that of other authors. "Among young Italian writers there's a kind of deep traditionalism," he said. "Many young Italian writers have an academic training—they've read and learnt a lot about Italian literature. I don't have that same grounding, so I've never read in such a prescriptive way, or had someone say to me: 'read this, read that.' I keep up with English writing a lot more than I do with Italian."

Ammaniti has listed among his favorite writers such American masters of horror and crime fiction as James Ellroy and Stephen King. Ammaniti's sharp, spare sentences often exhibit the clipped, tense pace of these writers rather than the more elaborate, academic style of such contemporary Italian authors as Umberto Eco. Thematically, Ammaniti's works often explore life in modern Italy, demonstrating the influence of comic books, kung fu videos and other pop-culture references.

"L'Ultimo capodanno dell'umanità" (which translates as "humanity's last New Year's Eve"), one of the longer stories from Ammaniti's 1996 short-fiction collection, *Fango* (which translates as "mud"), became the basis for a 1998 film, *L'Ultimo Capodanno*. Ammaniti co-wrote the screenplay for the film, which is about a diverse group of people (including an aging countess, a prostitute, and a soccer team) heading for tragedy one New Year's Eve. His first novel, *Branchie* (1994), which translates as "gills," was also adapted into a film, in 1999.

Ammaniti's novel *Io non ho paura*, which was published in the U.S. as *I'm Not Scared*, in 2003, is different from the author's earlier pulp works. "It has a more universal appeal than the others," he explained to Eve. "Those spoke about Italy here and now, and they had a narrower range of reference, whereas this is a very simple story that can be read easily anywhere." Set in the small Southern village of Acqua Traverse, during the summer of 1978, the novel is narrated by nine-year-old Michele Amitrano. A mischievous youngster, he is playing near an abandoned farmhouse one day when he discovers another child who has been kidnapped, blindfolded, and chained to a wall. Michele befriends the boy and begins bringing him food and water. As he becomes increasingly involved in the situation, he learns the grim truth behind the crime—and the number of his own townspeople who are involved. Ammaniti's novel employs a series of surprising plot twists, while tackling such larger themes as Michele's coming-of-age, his complex relationship with his father, and the economic troubles of southern Italy. The story, which came to Ammaniti as he was driving between the regions of Campania and Puglia in southern Italy, took only six months to complete. "It was during a hot spell and the landscape was much as I describe it: just corn fields," he told Eve. "There are no trees, few houses, nothing. I was really struck by it. I'd never expected the area to make such a strong visual impression on me. Seeing these things I said to myself: what would kids do in a place like this?" Because Ammaniti originally set out to write the story as a film, the work initially took on a very visual style. Once he began, he said, "the other part came together: the child's-eye viewpoint, Michele's fears—all the things I hadn't considered when I was writing a screenplay."

I'm Not Scared resonated with readers and became an instant best-seller in Italy. The book was hailed by critics and earned Ammaniti the 2001 Viareggio-Repaci Prize for fiction. When it was published in its English-language version, American and British critics offered even more praise for the work. Calling it "a spellbinding novel," Jan Winburn, writing for the *Baltimore Sun* (February 2, 2003), found the book to be "surprising, to the last word." In his *New York Times* (February 16, 2003) review, Lawrence Venuti opined, "In prose that is by turns poetic and hard boiled, [Ammaniti] unfolds the story of a violent crime while simultaneously evoking a child's vivid imaginative life. Although a page turner, his novel avoids cheap thrills and forces its readers to reflect on intractable social problems, most notably the impact of regional and class divisions on the Italian family."

Many critics noted similarities between this work and Stephen King's novella *The Body*, which was the basis for the 1986 film *Stand By Me*. "Like King," Tawny Sinasac observed for the *Hamilton Spectator* (April 19, 2003), "Ammaniti has the ability to create a breathless atmosphere, one that grows more oppressive not only because of the summer's unrelenting heat but because Michele begins to piece together the boy's story and finds himself more and more enmeshed in it. He also has the gift of writing cleanly. Sentences are usually short, descriptions are dead on . . . and the story moves smoothly and quickly toward a dramatic ending." Writing for the London *Observer* (March 9, 2003), Ian Thomson affirmed, "Ammaniti's sparse prose creates a truly evil tension, and his caustic intelligence would be impressive in a writer twice his age." *I'm Not Scared* was adapted for film—with Ammaniti again co-writing the screenplay—and premiered at the Berlin Film Festival in February 2003.

After the success of *I'm Not Scared*, Canongate books published *I'll Steal You Away* (2006), an English translation of *Ti Prendo e Ti Porto Via* (1999). As with *I'm Not Scared*, this novel focuses on the travails of a young boy living in a small Italian village. Pietro Moroni is a skinny, introspective child who is ignored at home and tormented at school. His story is juxtaposed with

that of Graziano Biglia, a washed-up flamenco guitarist and the town's ladies' man. "Ammaniti weaves almost seamlessly between his characters as they spiral slowly toward their inevitable sad conclusions," according to Tina Jordan for *Entertainment Weekly* (September 22, 2006). A reviewer for *Publishers Weekly* (May 29, 2006) wrote that the novel, which features a "quasi call-and-response" narration, "feels awkward at first, but once the reader settles in, Hunt's translation adds welcome depth to seemingly simple folk. . . . Chilling and intimate, Ammaniti's work brings life to a deceptively quiet town and its wealth of eclectic and unsettling residents."

—K.D.

Suggested Reading: *Baltimore Sun* F p11 Feb. 2, 2003; *Los Angeles Times* V p11 Feb. 19, 2003; *New York Times* VII p14 Feb. 16, 2003; *Washington Post* T p15 Mar. 9, 2003

Selected Books in English Translation: *I'm Not Scared*, 2003; *I'll Steal You Away*, 2006

Ashbery, John

July 28, 1927– Poet

"To create a work of art that the critic cannot even talk about ought to be the artist's chief concern," John Ashbery—the most renowned poet of the so-called New York School—wrote for *Art News* (May 1972), and though he was discussing the visual artist Brice Marden's work, his statement is equally relevant to his own. (The poetry associated with the New York School emerged in the late 1950s in response to the confessional verse then enjoying popularity. In addition to Ashbery the New York School included such writers as James Schuyler, Frank O'Hara, Barbara Guest, and Kenneth Koch, many of whom were deeply influenced by such abstract painters as Jackson Pollock and Willem de Kooning.) Critics, attempting to discuss Ashbery's poems, have often found themselves confounded by their obscurity and complexity. The difficulty is in part a consequence of Ashbery's juxtaposition of disparate elements. A typical Ashbery poem might, for example, mix snippets of phone conversations that he has had while writing or citations of cartoons with highbrow references. "It seems that throughout my poetry," Ashbery explained to Sarah Rothenberg for an interview posted on the Ashbery Resource Center Web site, "I'm constantly talking about assembling as broad a spectrum as possible of whatever it is I'm talking about at that particular moment. There's a passage from *Three Poems* in which I state this: 'Thus everything and everybody were included after all, and any thought that might ever be entertained

Mikki Ansin/Getty Images

about them. The irritating drawbacks each possessed along with certain good qualities were dissolved in the enthusiasm of the whole, yet individuality was not lost for all that, but persisted in the definition of the urge to proceed higher and further, as well as the counter-urge to amalgamate into the broadest, widest kind of uniform continuum.' Then I go on to say: 'The effect was as magnificent as it was unexpected, not even beyond his wildest dreams since he had never had any, content as he had been to let the process reason itself out.'" The jumps from one element to the next, however, sometimes seem incoherent, something that has led some critics to discount the value of Ashbery's poetry altogether. Over time, however, his talent and the inherent musicality of his verse have led other critics, including some of the most respected, to laud his contribution to the tradition of American poetry. The world-renowned critic Harold Bloom, for example, wrote, as Vernon Scannell reported for the London *Sunday Telegraph* (December 17, 2000), "No one writing poems in the English language is likelier than Ashbery to survive the severe judgments of time."

John Lawrence Ashbery was born in Rochester, New York, on July 28, 1927 to Chester Frederick Ashbery, a farmer, and Helen (Lawrence) Ashbery, a biology teacher. For the first seven years of his life, Ashbery lived with his grandparents in the city of Rochester but then moved to his parent's farm outside the city's limits, nearer to Lake Ontario. When he was nine or ten, he decided he wanted to be a painter. "I saw all these paintings from the 'Fantastic, Dada, and Surrealism' show at the Museum of Modern Art in *Life* magazine," he told John Freeman for the *Pittsburgh Post-Gazette* (May 29, 2005). "I decided then and there I wanted to be a surrealist when I grew up." Between the ages of 11 and 15, he attended weekly classes at the art museum in Rochester. When he was 13, his brother, Richard, died of leukemia, something Ashbery was unprepared for because no one had discussed the possibility with him, and the following years were among the unhappiest of his life. "I was extremely lonely. I had very few friends. In school I was considered weird, which I was I guess," he told Jim Schley for the *New Yorker* (November 7, 2005). "I always felt that I was a disappointment to my parents, especially my father. My brother loved sports and was very extroverted. He would I'm sure have been straight, have gotten married and had children, probably would have taken over the farm, which my father obviously wanted." When Ashbery was 16 a neighbor paid for him to become a boarder at the Deerfield Academy, in Massachusetts, where he was introduced to such poets as Wallace Stevens, Dylan Thomas, and W. H. Auden and consequently developed a serious interest in poetry. He started to write it himself and was soon published. (*Poetry Magazine* published his first piece, but under the name of a fellow student, who had stolen and submitted the poem himself.)

Ashbery's interest in poetry grew, and when he entered Harvard University in Cambridge, Massachusetts, in 1945, he majored in English. During his sophomore year he began to submit poems to the recently revived *Harvard Advocate*, which was then being edited by Robert Bly, Donald Hall, and Kenneth Koch, all of whom earned fame as poets later in life. They not only accepted his poems but also offered him a position on the editorial board. Harvard proved to be filled with aspiring poets, and besides the editors at the *Harvard Advocate*, Ashbery met the now-renowned writers Barbara Epstein, Frank O'Hara, Robert Creeley, and Peter Davison, as well as the cartoonist Edward Gorey. Ashbery, who wrote his senior thesis on Auden, graduated from Harvard, in 1949, and completed an M.A. at Columbia University, in New York City, in 1951. He then entered publishing, working as a copyeditor, first for Oxford University Press and then for McGraw Hill. All the while, he continued publishing in small literary journals, and, in 1953, the Tibor de Nagy Gallery put out a chapbook of his poems entitled *Turandot, and Other Poems*. Two years later Ashbery was awarded a Fulbright fellowship to study in Paris, where he lived for the next 10 years, with the exception of brief stays back in the U.S., for example, during the 1957–58 academic year, when he took graduate courses at New York University and wrote for *Art News*. In France Ashbery lived with the French poet Pierre Martory, worked as an editor for the European edition of the New York *Herald Tribune*, and wrote art criticism for *Art International*.

While Ashbery was in France, his reputation as a poet began to grow. In 1956 Auden selected Ashbery's first full-length collection of poems, *Some Trees*, for the acclaimed Yale University Press's Younger Poets Series. Auden had turned down all of the manuscripts that he had received and declared that there would be no winner. Auden then learned that Ashbery and O'Hara had submitted manuscripts that had not been given to him and asked to see them. In the end he chose Ashbery's. *Some Trees* was, for the most part, ignored, but it did attract the attention of the critic Harold Bloom, who has, as his own reputation has grown, remained among Ashbery's greatest supporters. Ashbery wrote two more collections of poetry in France. The first of these books, *The Tennis Court Oath* (1962), was received hostilely because of its experimental nature. "The trouble with Ashbery's work is that he is influenced by modern painting to the point where he tries to apply words to the page as if they were abstract, emotional colors and shapes," James Schevill complained for the *Saturday Review*, as quoted on the Interviews with Poets Web site. "Consequently, his work loses coherence . . . There is little substance to the poems in this book." Even Harold Bloom "angrily criticized" the collection "as mostly 'calculated incoherence' that resisted the Stevensian genealogy [that is, the influence of the poet Wallace Stevens] Bloom had established for Ashbery," David Sweet wrote for an essay published in *Comparative Literature* (Fall 1998). Ashbery, however, recalls that he had not been considering publishing the poems as a book when he wrote them, telling John Tranter for *Jacket* (May 1988, on-line) that he never thought he would get the opportunity again and "was also rather interested in trying something new, [and] having difficulty in doing this, living in a country were the language spoken was not my own. . . . These were . . . experiments which I thought would perhaps lead to something, but I didn't really intend them to be finished poems. I didn't at that point know how to write a finished poem in the way that I felt I had done so before, at least in the new way that I wanted to write. And quite unexpectedly I had an opportunity to publish another volume. So I used what I had. My intention was to be after . . . kind of . . . taking language apart so I could look at the pieces that made it up. I would eventually get around to putting them back together again, and would then have more of a knowledge of how they worked, together."

The second of the books that Ashbery wrote while in France, *Rivers and Mountains*, was published, in 1966, a year after Ashbery had returned to the U.S., in part to take up the position of executive editor at *Art News*—a position he held until the magazine was sold, in 1972. Ashbery had by this time gained some notoriety, having been designated a member of the New York School, and his experiments with language were greeted positively. Indeed, the publication of *Rivers and Mountains* "marked what several of his critics regard as his real arrival as a poet, with poems such as 'These Lacustrine Cities,' 'Clepsydra' and 'The Skaters' all demonstrating for the first time what one of them has called the 'astonishing range and flexibility of Ashbery's voice,'" according to the Interviews With Poets Web site observed. Ashbery attributed the change in readers' interest in his work to a change in attitudes about poetry, telling Nicholas de Jongh for the London *Guardian* (May 9, 1987), "While I'd been away the beat poets had become prominent and suddenly everyone was reading their poems. . . . They opened things up for others."

Ashbery's next books include *Selected Poems* (1967); *The Double Dream of Spring* (1970), which includes the critically acclaimed long poem "The Fragment"; *Three Poems* (1972), for which he was awarded the Modern Poetry Association's Frank O'Hara Prize; and, in 1975, *Self-Portrait in a Convex Mirror*. This last book—which John Malcolm Brinnin called for the *New York Times Book Review* (August 10, 1975) a "collection of poems of breathtaking freshness and adventure in which dazzling orchestrations of language open up whole areas of consciousness no other American poet has even begun to explore"—secured Ashbery a reputation for being among the most important living poets. Writing for the *Times Literary Supplement* (July 25 1975), David Kalstone observed: "[Ashbery] is at that enviable and arresting stage of a poet's career when he knows how to say what he wants to say—things no one else would. . . . The long and brilliant title poem . . . is sparked by a Renaissance painting, Parmigianino's self-portrait, against which Mr. Ashbery matches what proves to be his own; a

mirror of the state of mind in which the poem was written, open to wave after wave of discovery, and aware of the unframed and unframeable nature of experience." Michael Madigan, by contrast, wrote for *Library Journal* (May 15, 1975), "Though Ashbery's voice is sometimes musical, it is estranged from silence, and lacks the resonance of passion, wit, piety, vision, or character. Rarely do his associational notations have imaginative form. The poems in this latest book are not even verbally playful. Curiously enough, the individual images or ideas that a reader might focus on in one of Ashbery's poems have much in common with the platitudes found in genteel verse." Despite such criticism *Self-Portrait* achieved the rare feat of winning three major literary awards, the Pulitzer Prize, the National Book Award, and the National Book Critics Circle Award.

Ashbery next published *Houseboat Days* (1977), *As We Know* (1979), and *Shadow Train* (1981), but it was his 1984 collection, *A Wave*, that earned him the most critical success. The 44 pieces that comprise the book, including the long title poem, have been described as disconcerting and melancholy but sprinkled with bits of hilarity. Ashbery recollected that it was written during a time of joy in the midst of a great love affair. "I was mainly very happy because it seemed it would not end, unlike most of them have," he told de Jongh. Controversy over Ashbery's poems still reigned. "Reading John Ashbery's poems is a bit like playing hide-and-seek in a sprawling mansion designed by M.C. Escher. . . . Strictly speaking, hardly any of the titles of the 44 pieces in [this book] are thematic, so [the author's] themes and concerns have to be snatched more or less out of the air," Christopher Middleton wrote for the *New York Times Book Review* (June 17, 1984). *A Wave*, nonetheless, received much critical praise. David St. John remarked, in a review for the *Washington Post* (May 20, 1984) that the book "characteristically throws caution to the winds in pursuit of things unattempted yet in prose and rhyme. The results are exhilarating. To top it off, the 21-page title poem is easily Ashbery's finest single achievement since *Self-Portrait in a Convex Mirror*."

In 1985 Viking Press released *Selected Poems*. The 300-page book begins with *Some Trees* and represents each of his collections with a relatively equal number of pages, providing readers with an overview of his career, one that certain critics felt not worth having. "There were times during my reading of this *Selected Poems* . . . when I actually thought I was going to burst into tears of boredom," James Fenton wrote for the *New York Times* (December 29, 1985). "What I see now, where once I saw a relaxed and exquisite mockery, is an esthetic loneliness, like the loneliness of secret work . . . I don't believe in this ontology—or lack of it. I don't believe in this esthetic. I still respect the talent, but not the resort to the sad shadows." Other critics found the selection more compelling.

"At least a few of these poems, the really good ones, will grow on you because they repay rereading," Tom D'Evelyn observed for the *Christian Science Monitor* (December 31, 1985). "They connect with what the greatest lyric poet, Charles Baudelaire, called 'the profound.' Despite the accidents of time and place and mood of reading, their substance doesn't change. Perhaps they are a part, though an unwilling part, of our eternal present. Ashbery pads along the beach, collecting shells and arranging them according to color and shape, not according to their original or inherent nature."

In 1987 Ashbery published *April Galleons* and the long prose poem *The Ice Storm*, and then in 1989, he put out a collection of his art criticism, *Reported Sightings: Art Chronicles, 1957–1987*, which he followed, in 1991, with *Flow Chart*, a book-length stream-of-consciousness meditation broken into six parts, which, again, inspired debate. "Ashbery is considered a major poet. I cannot share that view," Robert Nye wrote for the London *Times* (November 7, 1991). "I reckon him the Salvador Dali of modern verse by which I mean that he is a clever draughtsman who has designs on his audience to convince them that he is something more. Like Dali, he has no one recognizable or characteristic manner." "John Ashbery's standing at 64 is unmistakably that of the leading American poet; but his new book-length poem, his longest poem to date . . . is very nearly unreadable," Paul Driver wrote for the *Financial Times* (October 5, 1991) and went on to observe that "the common reader, certainly in this country [England], will be inclined to throw down his Ashbery volume exclaiming 'Pfiffle!'" Thomas M. Disch, writing for the *Washington Post* (July 14, 1991), found the complexity of *Flow Chart* exhilarating: "The most remarkable thing about the book, for me, was simply how enjoyable it was to read. Ashbery is generally regarded, and even dreaded, as one of those poets who can't be read without making a major intellectual effort, on the principle: No pain, no gain. One can dip into *Flow Chart* anywhere with a good likelihood of being either amused or beguiled or simply astonished at the way the poet zips down the page, like a skier negotiating moguls, with a major swerve from the oracular to the demotic to some other antithetical tone in almost every line."

Ashbery went on to publish *Hotel Lautréamont* (1992), *And the Stars Were Shining* (1994), *Can You Hear the Birds* (1995), *Wakefulness* (1998), and *Girls on the Run* (1999). This last book was inspired by the artist Henry Darger's more than 15,000-page self-illustrated novel, *The Story of the Vivian Girls, in what Is Known as the Realms of the Unreal, of the Glandeco-Angelinnian War Storm, Caused by the Child Slave Rebellion*. The novel tells the story of seven princesses (the Vivian Girls) from an imaginary kingdom on a planet that resembles Earth but, like the moon, orbits another large planet. The sisters, upset with living under an evil tyrant who promotes child slavery, take part in a rebellion. "I was fascinated by the color and the sort of helter-skelter composition and the fact that these girls were of the same vintage as my own childhood, when I was fascinated by little girls." Reviews of the book dwelled on Ashbery's insularity and lack of narrative, but their respectful tone also showed Ashbery's importance.

"Learning to enjoy Ashbery on his own terms means learning to live without plot, learning to enjoy and sympathize with his playful 'seething ambiguity' and to appreciate his category mistakes, pseudocausality ('This / pen is for you because you're about twenty-four'), mock argument ('Count the dogs as furniture / as otherwise there will be no chairs'), and deictics that could point anywhere," Steve Burt wrote for the *Village Voice* (March 30, 1999). Burt went on to claim: "*Girls* proves Ashbery's genius by compelling our attention even as the props of plot go AWOL; his creative fecundity and supple syntax set scenes up as fast as he knocks them down." John Palattella observed for New York *Newsday* (April 4, 1999), in a less laudatory review, "Yes, *Girls on the Run* is a difficult book, but not because Ashbery has created an obstacle course that promises a prize—the sneer of cultural elitism, the badge of political commitment—to any reader who successfully plumbs its paradoxes or negotiates its sand traps. The book is simply a maze, and it promises no prize other than the experience of reading it. At its best, *Girls on the Run*, like much of Ashbery's work, but with more gusto and less finesse, confronts the reader again and again with a mystery whose explanation merely creates another mystery. Ashbery's is an art so intellectually precise that its ideas cannot be pried loose from its words."

Age has not diminished Ashbery's productivity. In 2000 he published *Your Name Here*, a series of lyrical prose poems. As with any book of Ashbery's, it received mixed reviews, but this collection led critics to discuss Ashbery's confrontation with his own mortality. "*Your Name Here*, like all of Ashbery's best work, finds its emotions in the deepest reaches of the self, but finds its expressive idiom almost exclusively in this vast territory of what might be called 'legal tender' American language," Dan Chiasson observed for *Raritan* (Fall 2001), but later, he takes issue with a specific poem, "The History of My Life," complaining that it is made up of "the fussy and fatuous idiom of someone who has held the floor for too long, who takes his listener's silence for spell-boundedness. Of course it is the way a poem about subjectivity and its relation to language would talk; but it is also how a poet afraid of his own death would talk." In 2000 Ashbery also published *Other Traditions*, a group of essays based on lectures that he delivered at Harvard that discuss John Clare, Thomas Lovell Beddoes, Raymond Roussel, John Wheelwright, Laura Riding, and David Schubert, six so-called minor poets who have provided him with inspiration. "*Other Traditions* is an entertaining and shrewd little book. To begin with, the life stories of the six poets he discusses are all amazing. Ashbery is an accomplished raconteur and the lectures are full of delightful anecdotes. . . . [and] provide abundant hints about Ashbery's own method," Charles Simic wrote for the *New York Review of Books*, as quoted on Complete-review.com.

Over the following two years, Ashbery published *As Umbrellas Follow Rain* (2001) and *Chinese Whispers* (2002), and released, in 2004, *Selected Prose*, a collection of essays about artists, poets, and the consequences of their creations. Many critics praised the book, arguing that reading Ashbery's opinions about the works of others enabled them to finally see into the complex workings of his poetry. "Because Ashbery's own poetry is at least as daunting as any he dissects, watching him prod the insides of other people's work reveals a lot about the gimmicks at the core of his own," Diane Middlebrook observed for the *Los Angeles Times* (March 20, 2005). "By the end of the book, Ashbery has laid out not only a course in contemporary poetics but a portrait of the artist teaching himself to become a thoroughly Modernist poet—in small bites, easy to savor, easy to digest."

The following year Ashbery's *Where Shall I Wander* (2005) was published. It contained 51 short free-verse and prose poems that touch upon images of a lost American culture and show Ashbery meditating on his own impending mortality. Critics continued to comment on Ashbery's obscurity, but they rarely did so without also acknowledging his achievement. "Ashbery blends highbrow with lowbrow, pop culture and classical culture, clichéd or banal language with original turns of phrases. The effect of such mixing up can make the poetry seem obscure and difficult—and indeed it is," Jacob Stockinger wrote for the Wisconsin *Capital Times* (November 18, 2005). "But if instead of seeking the meaning of a whole poem you search for the music and meaning of a single line or even phrase, the world of Ashbery opens up more easily and becomes accessible and even memorable." More recently Ashbery released *A Worldly Country* (2007), a collection, Bryan Appleyard wrote for the *Philadelphia Inquirer* (February 11, 2007), that "will, for regular readers, appear much of the time very familiar. Ashbery even seems to be quoting himself. 'Opposition to a Memorial' sounds, to my ear, like 'The Ecclesiast,' and 'The Handshake, the Cough, the Kiss'—the longest poem here—evokes 'A Last World' and 'The Skaters,' all three written decades ago. But the effects seem intensified. With old age—he is 80 this year—Ashbery's fondness for autumnal regret has become more pronounced. Time, as ever, passes too quickly—'Spring came and went so fast this year'—and the sense of the ungraspable seems more urgent—'What if we are all ignorant of all that has happened to us...?' Most poignant of all, there is the constant, nagging suspicion that there is, in fact, something to say."

Besides the works mentioned above Ashbery, who was named a MacArthur Fellow in 1985, has also written three plays—*The Compromise* (1960), *The Heroes* (1960), and *The Philosopher* (1964)—and collaborated with James Schuyler on a novel called *A Nest of Ninnies* (1969). He divides his time between an apartment in the New York City neighborhood of Chelsea, and a home in Hudson, New York. He has been with his partner, David Kermani, since 1970.

—F.C.

Suggested Readings: *Chicago Tribune* C p8 Sep. 8, 1991; *Christian Science Monitor* p19 Dec. 31, 1985; *Financial Times* p19 Oct. 5, 1991; *Jacket* (on-line) May 1998; (London) *Guardian* May 9, 1987; (London) *Independent* p31 Nov. 16, 1991; (London) *Times* Nov. 7, 1991; *Los Angeles Times* R p4 Mar. 20, 2005; (New York) *Newsday* B p12 Apr. 4, 1999; *New York Times* VII p10 Dec. 29, 1985; *New Yorker* p87 Nov. 7, 2005; *Newsweek* p78 July 16, 1984; *Philadelphia Inquirer* H p2 Apr. 18, 1999; *Pittsburgh Post-Gazette* J p4 May 29, 2005; *Raritan* p139+ Fall 2001; *Village Voice* p135 Mar. 30, 1999; *Washington Post* p6 May 20, 1984; (Wisconsin) *Capital Times* A p9 Nov. 18, 2005

Selected Books: poetry—*Some Trees*, 1956; *The Tennis Court Oath*, 1962; *Rivers and Mountains*, 1966; *Selected Poems*, 1967; *The Double Dream of Spring*, 1970; *Three Poems*, 1972; *Self-Portrait in a Convex Mirror*, 1975, *Houseboat Days*, 1977; *As We Know*, 1979; *Shadow Train*, 1981; *A Wave*, 1984; *Selected Poems*, 1985; *April Galleons*, 1987; *The Ice Storm*, 1987; *Flow Chart*, 1991; *Hotel Lautréamont*, 1992; *And the Stars Were Shining*, 1994; *Can You Hear the Birds*, 1995; *Wakefulness*, 1998; *Girls on the Run*, 1999; *Your Name Here*, 2000; *As Umbrellas Follow Rain*, 2001; *Chinese Whispers*, 2002; *Where Shall I Wander*, 2005; *A Worldly Country* (2007); fiction—*A Nest of Ninnies* (with James Schuyler), 1969; nonfiction—*Reported Sightings: Art Chronicles 1957–1987*, 1989; *Other Traditions*, 2000; *Selected Prose*, 2005

Atkinson, Kate

Dec. 20, 1951– Novelist; playwright

The English-born, Scottish-based writer Kate Atkinson was 44 when her first novel, *Behind the Scenes at the Museum* (1995), captured Britain's prestigious Whitbread Award, winning out over the works of more established writers. With that book and her two follow-up novels, *Human Croquet* (1997) and *Emotionally Weird* (2000),

Peter Ross/Courtesy of Random House

Kate Atkinson

Atkinson, a onetime Ph.D. candidate in literature, established a reputation for works whose sometimes deliriously comic tone belies the seriousness of their themes: bleak family histories, parents' betrayals of children, and irreparable loss. Following the publication of her 2002 story collection, *Not the End of the World*, Atkinson turned to the mystery/thriller genre, to write the well-reviewed novels *Case Histories* (2004) and her most recent work, *One Good Turn* (2006). In the London *Telegraph* (August 29, 2004, on-line), Helen Brown expressed the view that the writing of mysteries is well-suited to Atkinson's talents. Referring to Jackson Brodie, the detective-protagonist of *Case Histories*, Brown wrote, "Considering the intimate details of other people's lives for a living is something Jackson and Atkinson have in common."

An only child, Kate Atkinson was born in York, England, on December 20, 1951. Her parents ran a surgical-supplies store, and the family lived in an apartment above the store until Atkinson was two years old. Atkinson read voraciously as a child; among her favorite books were Richmal Compton's 1922 comic novel *Just William* and the works of Lewis Carroll, including *Alice's Adventures in Wonderland*, which she has recalled reading once a week between the ages of five and 10. She attended a private elementary school and the Queen Anne Grammar School for Girls before enrolling at Dundee University, in Scotland; she matriculated thereafter failing the entrance examinations for the University of Oxford, the University of Cambridge, and the University of Edinburgh. (Between secondary school and college she worked briefly as a maid in a hotel, a fact that

the press would later publicize widely. She has also, by her own account, worked as a legal secretary, headed a welfare-benefits office, run a youth program for visiting the elderly, and served as a home aide, among other jobs. "The more experience you get the better," she wrote for the Web site Write Words, with reference to becoming a writer.) Atkinson graduated from Dundee with an M.A. degree in English literature, in 1974, and thereafter she made Scotland her home. In 1973 she married another Dundee student, and two years later her first daughter, Eve, was born. Atkinson was divorced soon afterward but remained at Dundee, where, having become fascinated by the work of such American writers as Donald Barthelme and Kurt Vonnegut, she studied for a Ph.D. degree in American literature and completed a dissertation, "The Post-Modern American Short Story in Its Historical Context." She failed her oral examination, however, and fell short of obtaining her degree. Having done so, she "suddenly had no creative outlet" and was "very unhappy," as she stated for Write Words. She added, "Unhappiness is a great kick start to writing."

Atkinson married for the second time in 1982, giving birth to her second child, Helen, the same year. After five years that marriage, too, ended. Meanwhile, she had begun working part-time and writing fiction. One of her short stories won the *Woman's Own* magazine prize in 1988, and two years later she was runner-up for the Bridport Short Story Prize. She told Wendy Smith for an interview in New York *Newsday* (June 22, 1997), however, that she did not make a conscious commitment to a writing career until she was 40. Her career took off in earnest when she won the prestigious Ian St. James Award for her story "Karmic Mothers—Fact or Fiction?"

Atkinson's first novel, *Behind the Scenes at the Museum*, appeared in 1995. She has recalled that the inspiration for the book came in part from a dream she had; in it, she was visiting the Castle Museum of Yorkshire Life, in York, when the displays came to life. The novel brought its author the Whitbread Book of the Year Award, winning over the celebrated novelist Salman Rushdie's *The Moor's Last Sigh*, among other books by better-known writers. (In response, one British newspaper ran a headline reading, "44 Year Old Chambermaid Wins Whitbread.") Ruby Lennox, the narrator and protagonist of *Behind the Scenes at the Museum*, mainly presented as a teenager, describes a century of events in her family prior to—and including—her own birth. She also tells of her life in York, spent above the family pet shop with her two older sisters and her bickering parents—a philandering father and a mother who admits to not liking children. While the novel is in some respects reminiscent of the York author Laurence Sterne's 18th-century comic tour de force *Tristram Shandy*, Ben Macintyre noted for the *New York Times Book Review* (March 31, 1996) that even "by traditional standards of Yorkshire gloom, what happens to the intervening generations of Ruby's family is pretty dire. Most end up married to people they cordially detest or with children they did not expect or much want; many die violent, early deaths and almost all are miserable, some quite happily so. . . . Like Yorkshire itself, *Behind the Scenes at the Museum* is all sharp edges; it is a caustic and affectionate portrayal of a world in which bleak but nourishing wit is the only safety net." Georgia Jones-Davis, writing for the *Los Angeles Times* (December 27, 1995), called the novel "a powerhouse of storytelling, a treasure chest bursting with the painful, pitiful, sad, always fascinating details of the most ordinary of lives." In addition to the Whitbread, *Behind the Scenes at the Museum* earned Atkinson the Lire Book of the Year prize, from France, and the Yorkshire Post Book Award for best first work. Atkinson was presented with the E. M. Forster Award from the American Academy of Arts and Letters in 1997.

Stung by assumptions that *Behind the Scenes at the Museum*, set in her native York, was the story of her own life, Atkinson deliberately made *Human Croquet*, her 1997 novel and the second in what she termed a trilogy, "purely a product of the imagination," as she told Wendy Smith. Isobel Fairfax, the main character in *Human Croquet*, slips "in and out of linear time" and "experiences Christmas Eve and Day, 1960, over and over again, with increasingly and hilariously disastrous results," in Smith's words. Isobel and her older brother, Charles, grow up without their mother, who "ran off with a fancy man," according to the children's aunt; the novel's humor aside, its "central motif," as Rosemary Goring noted in a review for *Scotland on Sunday* (March 9, 1997), is "a profound sense of loss." Claire Harman, writing for the London *Independent* (March 9, 1997), called *Human Croquet* "interestingly confusing" and noted that "the device of time-warping . . . is taken very much further than the reader anticipates, beyond the point at which it appears fanciful and into a region where all sorts of possibilities open up. . . . Once you've given up trying to follow the real plot—if there is one—the problem of the book having no message becomes irrelevant; the author makes you attend to her contradictory stories for their own sake." Rosemary Goring observed, "Atkinson stirs together her cast like a witch flavouring her cauldron, the result [is] a faintly gothic and beguiling concoction that is inimitable. One of her talents is to invest mundane detail with surreal significance, while at the same time deflating horrors, such as violence or abuse, by the clarity of her observation, unloaded with comment, but seen as through a youngster's camera eye. . . . The joists of life, where farce and dullness and cruel despair lie beneath a placid surface, are Atkinson's terrain."

In her novel *Emotionally Weird*, set in the early 1970s, Atkinson again explored the themes of family history and mother-daughter relationships. Effie, while studying at Dundee University and maintaining her relationship with her drug-addled boyfriend, shares a house—and trades dubious autobiographical stories—with Nora, the woman she believes at first to be her mother. Meanwhile, Effie realizes that she is being followed. Rosemary Goring noted for *Scotland on Sunday* (February 20, 2000) that *Emotionally Weird* forms a continuum with *Behind the Scenes at the Museum* and *Human Croquet*. Each of the first two novels, she wrote, "took the form of family archaeology, the narrator prying into secrets, digging up the past and piecing together the fragments until a whole, if cracked, picture emerges. In both books we were drawn into the past as well as watching the unfolding present, Atkinson slipstreaming into history with the ease of a greased diver cutting through the waves." Goring found that with *Emotionally Weird*, Atkinson had used the same approach, and taken on similar themes, less successfully. "The design and central issues of *Emotionally Weird* are identical, but where the earlier books held their plot tightly controlled, and with it your interest, this time the structure is stretched so thin it's transparent. . . . Atkinson's cast of hundreds and attention to specifics is a good idea that runs out of control." Stephanie Zacharek, writing for the *New York Times Book Review* (June 25, 2000), arrived at much the same conclusion. Noting that *Emotionally Weird* starts with "lively, crackling prose" and "deft character descriptions," Zacharek ultimately found that "a problem with too much clever wordplay and so many enticingly detailed descriptions" is that "they can build you up just to let you down. . . . Atkinson is so good at describing her characters that she introduces altogether too many of them, and many of the better ones don't have much to do. . . . *Emotionally Weird* is clearly supposed to be a rumination on the bond between mothers and daughters, and Effie's shaggy-dog story is most likely intended as a metaphorical reflection of her emotional state. Too bad it untwirls itself halfway through."

Atkinson explained to Kim Bunce for the London *Observer* (March 12, 2000) her realization that her first three books were "based on *Alice in Wonderland* in one way or another but the young girl has now reached 21 and is grown up." She added, "I've had enough of that kind of writing." Accordingly, she next wrote *Not the End of the World* (2002), a short-story collection. The 12 stories each stand alone, but there are recurring characters among them; the first and last stories, both of which are set in a drastically decayed London and feature the characters Charlene and Trudi, fully reveal the thread running through the book. "These jazzy, offbeat stories studded with pop cultural references will appeal to Atkinson's fans and all readers of smart, trendy fiction,"

Barbara Love wrote for *Library Journal* (September 1, 2003).

Case Histories, Atkinson's 2004 novel, marked another departure. Her first entry into crime fiction, the book centers on the policeman-turned-private-detective Jackson Brodie, who attempts to solve the mysteries surrounding three events of years past: the disappearance of a three-year-old girl; the killing of a young woman; and the ax-murder of a young husband and father, apparently by his wife. In describing her choice of a protagonist, Atkinson told Helen Brown, "I wanted to write about a man man, who's interested in cars . . . you know? A man man. It's been said that the men in my books have been absent, or weak, or creepy. Jackson is 'the last good man standing.'" Carrie O'Grady wrote for the London *Guardian* (October 2, 2004), "*Case Histories* is essentially a balancing act, with evil and ignorance stacked opposite truth and healing. In this aspect the book is more satisfying than many detective novels—not just because it is so well written, but in its defiant refusal to let the dark side win the day merely for the sake of looking gritty and 'real.' Of course, *Case Histories* is not all sunshine and trite happy endings, but this is a book that rests on a strong and well-constructed moral framework, and is all the more powerful for it." Katie Owen, writing for the London *Daily Telegraph* (August 29, 2004, on-line), pronounced *Case Histories* to be Atkinson's "best book yet."

In *One Good Turn* (2006), her most recent book, Atkinson again turned to the crime/mystery genre—this time to tell the story of Martin Canning, a 50-year-old, sedentary mystery writer who performs an uncharacteristic act of physical bravery that makes him the target of a killer. Assessing the murder-filled novel for the *New York Times Book Review* (October 29, 2006, on-line), Liesl Schillinger observed that prior to Atkinson's forays into crime fiction, "her novels and stories were puzzles of interpersonal connection: sometimes homey and nostalgic, like a jigsaw, sometimes experimental, like a Rubik's Cube, but always recognizable once assembled. Paradoxically, murder has given her a framework that helps liberate her insights on the living, as the lurking presence of corpses reminds readers that there are worse offenses than bad parenting and worse fates than unhappy marriages." Once, Schillinger concluded, "domestic dynamics were Atkinson's whole subject. Now they're her fuel tank."

Atkinson lives in Edinburgh. Catherine Lockerbie reported for the *Scotsman* (February 3, 1996) that contrary to an article in the London *Daily Mail* describing Atkinson as being "pale" and "rather pimply" with "unwashed" hair, and as looking "like any tired London tourist," the novelist is "a strikingly beautiful and vivacious woman—with very well-washed hair." In addition to publishing fiction, Atkinson has written dramatic works. Her short 1996 play, *Nice*, was written for the Traverse Theatre, in Edinburgh. Her play *Abandonment* was published in 2000 and opened at the Edinburgh Festival in the same year.

—S.Y.

Suggested Reading: (Glasgow) *Herald* p12 Nov. 2, 2002; *Kirkus Reviews* p755 Aug. 15, 2004; (London) *Daily Telegraph* p12 Aug. 28, 2004, (on-line) Aug. 29, 2004; (London) *Independent* p29 Mar. 9, 1997, (on-line) Sep. 10, 2004; (London) *Observer* p13 Mar. 12, 2000; *Los Angeles Times* E p5 Dec. 27, 1995; (New York) *Newsday* G p11 June 22, 1997; *New York Times Book Review* p13 Mar. 31, 1996, p5 June 25, 2000, (on-line) October 29, 2006; *People* (on-line) Jan. 12, 2004; *Scotland on Sunday* Spectrum p13 Mar. 9, 1997, p12 Feb. 20, 2000; *Scotsman* p16 Feb. 3, 1996

Selected Books: fiction—*Behind the Scenes at the Museum*, 1995; *Human Croquet*, 1997; *Emotionally Weird*, 2000; *Not the End of the World*, 2002; *Case Histories*, 2004; *One Good Turn*, 2006; plays—*Abandonment*, 2000

Atwood, Margaret

Nov. 18, 1939– Poet; novelist; short-story writer; essayist

Margaret Atwood, the Canadian poet, novelist, short-story writer, and critic, has been described as "the most discussed and widely read writer in Canada and the Canadian national heroine of the arts," according to the Web site for the Oregon Public Electronic Network. Since 1966, when she won Canada's highest literary honor for *The Circle Game*, a poetry collection, Atwood has enjoyed an international reputation for being among the most important writers working today. Her books, which include everything from adult and children's books to literary criticism, are not only critically acclaimed best-sellers but have also been translated into more than 30 languages. Though she was initially recognized as a poet, she is now more widely known as a highly inventive novelist whose thematically diverse works include *The Handmaid's Tale* (1985), a speculative look at a future U.S. run by religious fundamentalists; *Alias Grace* (1996), a historical novel set in 19th-century Canada; *The Blind Assassin* (2000), a postmodern family saga; and *Oryx and Crake* (2003), a frightening look at the future of genetic engineering.

Margaret Eleanor Atwood was born on November 18, 1939 to Carl Edmund, a forest entomologist, and Margaret Dorothy (Killam) Atwood, a dietician. She has a brother, Harold Leslie, who is two years older and a professor of physiology and zoology, and a younger sister,

Scott Barbour/Getty Images

Margaret Atwood

Ruth, born in 1951. Six months after she was born—Atwood wrote for an earlier edition of *World Authors*: "I was taken by my family to a lake in northern Quebec (remote then, accessible now), and for the next eleven years I alternated this way between the bush (first in Quebec, then on the northern shore of Lake Superior, then Quebec again) and various cities—Ottawa, Sault Sainte Marie, Toronto. I did not spend a full year in school until I was in Grade Eight. I began to write at the age of five—poems, 'novels,' comic books and plays—but I had no thought of being a professional writer until I was sixteen. I entered Victoria College, University of Toronto, when I was seventeen and graduated in 1961. I won a Woodrow Wilson Fellowship to Harvard, where I studied Victorian literature, and spent the next ten years in one place after another: Boston, Montreal, Edmonton, Toronto, Vancouver, England, and Italy, alternately teaching and writing.

"I had my first poem accepted for professional publication when I was nineteen. It took me a while to discover modern Canadian poetry because the literary culture at that time in Canada was largely underground: authors were published in small editions and not generally known. This changed during the next decade, when I was becoming active as a poet and prose fiction writer. At the beginning of the sixties there was only a handful of magazines and indigenous publishing houses; at its end there were many, and writers had become public figures.

"I and many other members of my generation were part of this expansion. Because of our beliefs and the extraordinary amount of blood and energy that sustaining a Canadian literary culture in the face of U.S. domination required, many of us also did time as publishers, and I served a three-year sentence with the House of Anansi in Toronto. It was during this period that I wrote *Survival*, which was originally intended as the first beginner's guide to Canadian literature but which turned into a treatise of sorts on the case for nationalism. It caused a certain amount of uproar, which has always puzzled me, as it seems to me merely to state the obvious. Largely because of it, I became a combination target and cult figure, and began to feel a rather pressing need for privacy. I now live on a farm in southern Ontario, where I'm still not finding as much time to write as I'd like. When I'm not writing or thinking about it, I play with my young daughter (born in May 1976), work in the garden or go canoeing, when I can. Writing is still my main occupation or obsession, but should I find myself with nothing new to try or say I will stop without regret and do something else."

While she had taken up writing at five, Atwood abandoned that interest after a couple of years in favor of plans for a career in home economics. In high school she once again began to write poetry, which was influenced by that of Edgar Allan Poe, and began considering pursuing writing as a career. Indeed, she recalls the exact moment when she decided to dedicate her life to literature: she was 16 and walking home across a football field composing a poem in her head. "It was suddenly the only thing I wanted to do," she explained to Joyce Carol Oates for the *New York Review of Books* (May 21, 1978). Atwood went on to study English literature in the honors program at Victoria College of the University of Toronto. As an undergraduate she reviewed books and wrote articles for *Acta Victoriana*, the college literary magazine, and in 1961, the year she received her B.A. degree, *Double Persephone*, her first volume of poetry, was published. In the following year she obtained a Master of Arts degree from Radcliffe College, the women's college connected to Harvard University, in Cambridge, Massachusetts. During her year at Radcliffe, Atwood concentrated on Victorian literature, and after winning a Woodrow Wilson fellowship, she continued her study of Victorian literature and of Gothic romances at Harvard in the 1962-63 academic year. For the next two years she worked at such jobs as market researcher, cashier, and waitress, using whatever free time she had at her disposal to write. She returned to Harvard in 1965 to continue her doctoral work but left two years later without completing her dissertation, "The English Metaphysical Romance," a thesis topic that reflected her unabated interest in "the Gothic, the supernatural fantasy, and related forms," as she told Oates.

During the 1960s Atwood contributed book reviews and articles to *Alphabet*, *Poetry*, and *Canadian Literature*, among other periodicals. In the early 60s her poems began to appear in such magazines as *Kayak*, *Quarry*, and the *Tamarack*

Review and in the mid-1960s a number of pamphlet-sized collections of her poetry—*The Circle Game* (1964), *Kaleidoscopes: Baroque* (1965), *Talismans for Children* (1965), *Expeditions* (1966) and *Speeches for Doctor Frankenstein* (1966)—were published in limited editions by the Cranbrook Academy of Art in Bloomfield Hills, Michigan. In 1966 Atwood published her second full-length, also called *The Circle Game*, which went on to win the Governor General's Award that for the best book of poetry, giving her a national reputation in Canada. Discussing her work during this period, Gary Ross, in an essay for *Canadian Literature* (Spring 1974), saw her use of the wilderness and of the external world in general as symbols of human isolation and congratulated her for resolving the conflict between inner and outer worlds, between individuality and community. The 40 spare, free-verse poems in *The Animals in That Country* (1968), her next book of poems, are also rooted in Canadian soil, so that it seemed a singularly appropriate gesture when a group of poems from that collection received first prize in Canada's 1967 Centennial Commission poetry competition.

Among the themes that Atwood was exploring at this time were the individual's quest for identity, human isolation, love as a power struggle, technology as dehumanizing, and the inefficacy of language. In *Procedures for Underground* (1970), she employed images of drowning, journeys, and dreams, creating a sense of imminent danger and a lack of personal control over one's fate in the process. The poems, nevertheless, are informed with an element of hope, however tentative. Writing for *Canadian Literature* (Autumn 1971), Peter Stevens detected a movement in the book "towards a fundamental belief in the prerogatives of poetry in a threatening, tense world," a view that Melvin Maddocks echoed in his review for *Time* (October 26, 1970). "The Atwood message is beyond formulated pessimism," Maddocks wrote. "It has the rhythmic cycling of hope and despair natural to life itself. A lyricism as honest as a blade of grass in a boulder's crack keeps thrusting through."

For her 1970 collection of poems, *The Journals of Susanna Moodie*, Atwood adopted the persona of a historical figure—the 19th-century emigrant from England who wrote novels based on her experiences in the Canadian bush. In Atwood's text Moodie perceives the land as both the source of her sustenance and as the force that destroys her. Canadians, Atwood had begun to contend around this time, for too long shared the pioneers' attitude that literature was created by dead Englishmen, or occasionally by an American, and thus native art was largely ignored until the 1960s, when Canadian nationalism and a strong resentment against literary tastes that were being dictated by the U.S. began to emerge. Native authors started several literary magazines as vehicles for Canadian writing, and in support of the movement many

writers, including Atwood, worked in the publishing industry. During her period in publishing, Atwood released *Power Politics* (1971), which many critics then ranked among her best poetry collections. In that series of poems, which are about a failed love affair, she exposed the mutual manipulation inherent in any human relationship and the use of language as a weapon. Writing for *Parnassus: Poetry in Review* (Spring/Summer 1974), Rosellen Brown marveled that Atwood was able to employ images that those familiar with her poetry had seen her use before and "which must by now be comfortable to her, nearly domesticated by familiarity, and make them live so fiercely."

Having realized during her years at Harvard that no critical study of the body of Canadian literature had ever been published, Atwood set out to compile one and also prepared an introductory survey, *Survival: A Thematic Guide to Canadian Literature*, which triggered a controversy when it was published, in 1972. Canadian literature, she contended in *Survival*, reflects the tendency of Canadians to be willing victims—to the influences of their powerful neighbor to the south, to the land itself, to the still-prevalent colonial mentality, among other things—but also mirrors their tendency to be survivalists. Although nationalists liked the attention that the study brought to Canadian literature, some scholars and critics were incensed by the study's conclusions and asserted that Atwood had chosen to examine only those works that fit her pre-established theories, ignoring, for example, the novels, plays, and criticism of Robertson Davies. The debate made *Survival* "an instant phenomenon," and by 1982 more than 85,000 copies had been sold, an amazing number for a critical study.

Survival's overwhelming success also had drawbacks: The attention that she received threatened her privacy, and she gave up her editorial job and moved to the country. About the time *Survival* was published, Atwood also ended her five-year marriage to the American novelist Jim Polk—whom she had met at Harvard and married in January 1967—and began living with the Canadian novelist Graeme Gibson. Gibson and Atwood later married and had a daughter, Eleanor, known as Jess, who was born in May 1976. Her brightening circumstances may account for the marked change in outlook of the poems in *You Are Happy* (1974). The poems in that collection explored many of Atwood's recurring concerns, but the affirmative, freely given, joyful commitment of the lovers in the book's fourth and final section led several critics to remark that she had radically altered her vision.

Atwood's increasing involvement during the mid-1970s in human-rights issues, her membership in Amnesty International, and her extensive travels in the southern Caribbean resulted in a considerable expansion of her horizons. She began to explore political as well as personal and sexual violence and the relationships among countries and cultures as well as those among individuals—concerns that became particularly evident in *Two-Headed Poems* (1978) and *True Stories* (1981). In her introduction to *Second Words* (1982), a selection of her critical prose, she explained her need to widen her vision: "When you begin to write you're in love with the language, with the act of creation, with yourself partly; but as you go on, the writing—if you follow it—will take you places you never intended to go and show you things you would never otherwise have seen. I began as a profoundly apolitical writer, but then I began to do what all novelists and some poets do: I began to describe the world around me."

The poems in *Interlunar* (1984) are darker in tone and more muted in imagery than some of Atwood's earlier work, but they once again deal with struggles between the sexes and within each individual. Writing in the Toronto *Globe and Mail* (July 7, 1984), John Bemrose detected "a new humanity and depth" in the collection and considered it "an omen that her best may be yet to come." Her most recent poetry collections include *Morning in the Burned House* (1996), *Eating Fire: Selected Poems, 1965–1995* (1998), and "The Door," which is scheduled to be released in the fall of 2007.

Despite being a well-respected poet, Atwood is more popularly known for writing novels, a literary form that she had been interested in since the beginning of her career. Even before *The Circle Game* was released, she had written a still-unpublished novel. Her first published novel, *The Edible Woman*, appeared in 1969. Its protagonist, Marian MacAlpin, tries to make a place for herself in society, either by resigning herself to her dead-end career or by escaping through marriage to a lawyer. She feels that the men in her life are conspiring to smother her identity, and she becomes so obsessed with the ideas of consuming and consumption that she stops eating. When her fiancé refuses to eat a cake in the shape of a woman that she baked for him—symbolic of his attempt to "assimilate" her—she is freed from her anorectic obsession. Critics found her attempt at black humor unsuccessful, her characters bland, and her plot thin, but feminists seized upon it as a "product of the movement," as Atwood pointed out in her introduction to a 1981 edition.

Atwood won both critical and popular acclaim for *Surfacing* (1972). Using a stream-of-consciousness technique, the unnamed heroine narrates her return to the Canadian bush to search for her missing father, a scientist working in the far north. That search quickly becomes a quest for her identity. When she discovers her father's drowned and bloated corpse, she retreats to an island where she depends on nature for sustenance and embarks on a psychic exploration of her suppressed past. She emerges from her experience whole, having come to terms with her barbarous and "civilized"

natures, and ready to re-enter society. Writing for the *Saturday Review* (April 1973), Benjamin DeMott argued that "what is most striking about *Surfacing* is the integrity of the writer's imagination. . . . Everywhere in the language of this story there are dependencies, associative prefigurings, linkages extending and refining meaning. Moments of dramatic crisis evolve from metaphor itself."

Lady Oracle, Atwood's 1976 novel, was a humorous account of a woman's attempt to escape. The heroine, however, is not fleeing the role that others wish to impose on her but the many different roles she herself has assumed—and kept hidden—over the years: fat teenager, author of Gothic romances, mistress of a would-be artist, a poet whose work is, as Peter S. Prescott explained for *Newsweek* (October 4, 1976), "a cross between Kahlil Gibran and Rod McKuen," among others. Afraid that her multiple identities are about to be exposed and convinced that the woman who underlies them all is essentially unlovable, Joan Foster fakes her own drowning in Lake Ontario and hides out in Italy. Critical response to *Lady Oracle* was mixed. Although several reviewers agreed with Linda Sandler's opinion in *Saturday Night* (September 1976) that it was a well-made novel and an "exquisite parody of an obsolete generation," Katha Pollitt maintained in a critique for the *New York Times Book Review* (September 26, 1976) that it was a "familiar tale of feminist woe," slow-moving, and full of "clumsy contrivances."

In *Life before Man* (1979) Atwood molds intermeshing love triangles into a disturbing social-psychological study. The three main characters—Elizabeth, who works at a natural-history museum; Lesje, a female paleontologist also employed there; and Nate, Elizabeth's husband and Lesje's lover—are constantly contemplating the extinction of the dinosaurs (which Lesje fantasizes living among), of lovers and love affairs, of themselves, and of all homo sapiens. Paradoxically, the theme of *Life before Man* is survival, continuing even if life is pointless or even threatening, whether love is realizable or not. "Organisms adapt to their environments," reflects Lesje. "Of necessity, most of the time . . . often with a certain whimsy, you could almost say perversity." Marilyn French wrote for the *New York Times Book Review* (February 3, 1980) that Atwood combined "several talents—powerful introspection, honesty, satire and a taut, limpid style—to create a splendid, fully integrated work."

In *Bodily Harm*, Atwood's 1981 novel, a young lifestyles reporter retreats to a politically unstable Caribbean island on the pretext of writing a travel article. Her shaky mental and physical states, brought on by the trauma of a mastectomy, are clearly mirrored by the world around her. Unwittingly drawn into a revolution and imprisoned, she emerges a politically aware woman with a sense of her own identity. *Bodily*

Harm rivaled *Life before Man* in the warmth of its critical reception, and the Periodical Distributors of Canada honored it as their 1983 book of the year.

The novel most often credited with cementing Atwood's international reputation is *The Handmaid's Tale*, a work of speculative fiction set in the Republic of Gilead, a near-future version of the U.S., in which religious fundamentalism holds sway. The narrator of the story, a woman named Offred, serves as the handmaid to one of the Commanders of the Faithful, a leader of the government. Her job is to produce an heir for the commander, with the help of his wife, who like many women in the story, is unable to conceive. Though now widely hailed as one of her best novels and nominated for the Booker Prize, *The Handmaid's Tale* divided critics upon its release. Writing for the *New York Times* (February 9, 1986), Mary McCarthy complained: "If *The Handmaid's Tale* doesn't scare one, doesn't wake one up, it must be because it has no satiric bite. . . . The most conspicuous lack, in comparison with the classics of the fearsome-future genre, is the inability to imagine a language to match the changed face of common life," such as the Newspeak that George Orwell imagined for his *Nineteen Eighty-Four* (1949). McCarthy concluded, "It seems harsh to say again of a poet's novel—so hard to put down, in part so striking—that it lacks imagination, but that, I fear, is the problem." I. M. Owen, by contrast, disagreed, writing for *Books in Canada* (October 1985): "The great glory of the book is its technique of gradual revelation, sustained with dazzling skill from beginning to end. It was this that kept me reading with delight. But it must be said that the second reading was much less pleasurable; without the constant puzzles, constantly resolved in new surprises, it became a chore. . . . So here is a novel that should be read, and that can be read with pleasure and excitement, at least the first time. After that, it remains a valuable tract for the times; its details . . . have been brilliantly worked out and are well worth examining carefully."

In *Cat's Eye*, Atwood's 1988 novel, Elaine Risley, a famous 50-year-old Canadian painter, has journeyed back to her native city, Toronto, to view a retrospective of her career. As she moves through the city, now so different from the one she had lived in as a child, she finds herself recalling her youthful companion, Cordelia, a girl with whom she had a love/hate relationship. Carole Angier, reviewing the novel for *New Statesman and Society* (January 27, 1989), wrote: "This is a very personal, very intellectual, very complex novel. Despite that Booker nomination I thought *The Handmaid's Tale* a bore. *Cat's Eye* is Margaret Atwood's return to form, her best book since *Surfacing*. . . . But a lot of people are going to hate this book. Torontonians, for example ('Toronto is nowhere, and nothing happens in it'); especially feminists. . . . *Cat's Eye* is going to get [Atwood] into trouble. If so, I'm on her side. No good writer

can belong to any group, almost by definition. But I have my own reservations. The novel is extremely bleak about humanity. . . . It's written with a glassy detachment. . . . Through most of this novel you feel distance, dissection: a cat's eye. It ends on a note of gaiety, forgiveness and hope: but I don't quite believe it." Alice McDermott remarked in the *New York Times Book Review* (February 5, 1989): "Given the artist narrator and the retrospective that frames the novel, . . . it is tempting to use the book as a guide to Ms. Atwood's own work, to hear the author's voice in Elaine's. . . . But while reading the novel as Ms. Atwood's own midlife assessment of her life and her work adds a certain significance to its conclusion and may lead us to speculate further on some elements of the story that the character does not confront, . . . it in no way adds to the pleasure the book provides. For finally *Cat's Eye* is not only about memory, nor is it the chronicle of a particular life. It is a novel of images, nightmarish, evocative, heartbreaking and mundane, that taken together offer us not a retrospective but an addition: a new work entirely and Margaret Atwood's most emotionally engaging fiction thus far."

In *The Robber Bride* (1993), Atwood explored the relationships among three middle-aged women who have been friends since college. The novel begins on Tuesday, October 23, 1990, when the three women meet for lunch at a trendy restaurant called The Toxique. Though the trio seem vastly different on the surface—Charis is a flower child; Roz, an entrepreneur; and Tony, a military historian—they are united not only by their history but also by their loathing of a fourth classmate, Zenia. In the past Zenia had stolen their lovers but now the friends worry she might also have the ability to return from the grave. In the *Atlantic Monthly* (December 1993), Phoebe-Lou Adams proclaimed: "Atwood makes her characters believable, as she does the men whom they inexplicably value—for not one of those fellows could be trusted even to put out the garbage. The settings, from bohemian Toronto to a rundown farm to a college building mustily devoted to 'worthy but impoverished departments,' are as clearly evoked as the characters. The amoral, spiteful, ruthlessly self-interested Zenia is almost too bad to be true, but she represents all the impulses that Tony, Roz and Charis have repudiated or suppressed. Good women, in Ms. Atwood's view, are their own enemies, and whether one agrees with her opinion or not, she has written a brilliantly intelligent novel to support it." Writing for the *Christian Science Monitor* (November 19, 1993), Merle Rubin remarked : "Although Atwood, addressing the American Booksellers Association earlier this year, spoke of achieving a wiser, more balanced and realistic brand of feminism, one that takes account of the fact that women as well as men have the capacity for evil, men—and women who believe that men are people, not just sex objects—might well complain that the three men in this novel are portrayed as ciphers. . . . Nor is Zenia a very compelling or enlightening portrait of evil: She is merely a stereotypical vamp. . . . Readers may well enjoy Atwood's crisp writing, neatly interwoven plotting, sharp-eyed descriptions; and wry sense of humor. But those who imagine *The Robber Bride* to be a work of large significance with anything profound or new to say about gender, power, love, hate, or the nature of good and evil, are simply kidding themselves."

Alias Grace was based on the story of Grace Marks, an Irish immigrant who was imprisoned for murdering her employer, Thomas Kinnear, in 1843. In the book Dr. Simon Jordan, who studies mental problems, journeys to western Canada in 1859 at the request of a minister who believes that Grace is innocent of the murder; the book presents the the reader with Grace's version of events as told to the doctor. Claiming to have no memory of the killing, Grace also says that she has forgotten two key figures: one, the woman who had been Kinnear's housekeeper and lover, and the other, James McDermott, supposedly her own lover and the man who was hanged for his part in the murder. Donna Seaman noted for *Booklist* (September 15, 1996) that this was "perhaps [Atwood's] strongest work to date. . . . Grace's enduringly enigmatic tale embodies Atwood's signature theme—and, as she portrays a fictionalized Grace in prose as elegant as [George] Eliot's or [Edith] Wharton's, she also gleefully exposes all the hypocrisy, sexism, ignorance, and fear embedded in Victorian culture. . . . Atwood uses conversations [between Grace Marks and Simon Jordan], which are electric with suppressed desire and suspense, as a forum for considering everything from the class system to treatment of the insane, prostitution, spiritualism, and sensationalized journalism. Atwood's humor has never been slier, her command of complex material more adept, her eroticism franker, or her descriptive passages more lyrical. This is a stupendous performance." Francine Prose, for the *New York Times Book Review* (December 29, 1996), observed: "Alias Grace has the physical heft and weighty authority of a 19th-century novel. In its scope, its moral seriousness, its paradoxically ponderous and engrossing narrative, the book evokes the high Victorian mode, spiced with the spooky plot twists and playfully devious teases of the equally high Gothic. . . . Some readers may feel that the novel only intermittently succeeds in transcending the burden of history, research and abstraction. . . . Others will admire the liveliness with which Ms. Atwood toys with both our expectations and the conventions of the Victorian thriller. Such fans will be delighted by the plot's many riddles, its edifying Victoriana, the enigmas that continue to perplex us even after we've finished this latest installment in the mystery of a pretty young woman who was either the loathsome perpetrator or another innocent victim of an infamous crime."

Atwood finally won the Booker Prize for *The Blind Assassin*, which describes the lives of the Chase sisters, Iris and Laura, who came of age in the small textile town of Port Ticonderoga. Atwood slowly reveals the Chase family saga over the course of the first half of the 20th century through a memoir Iris is writing, newspaper clippings about the family, and finally as chapters of a novel written by Laura before her death. (Laura's novel depicts an affair between a young woman and a bohemian writer who scrapes by selling science-fiction stories to pulp magazines.) Margaret Anne Doody, reviewing the novel for the *London Review of Books* (October 5, 2000), observed: "Atwood illuminates the placid obscurities of life in Canada's 20th century, from the plush ambitions and dubious traditions of the late Victorians through the false glow of the Edwardian era to the troubled aftermath of World War One, the fear of Bolshevism, the Depression. As a history of an era, the novel is compassionate and satiric, the satire heightened by quotations from local and regional newspapers." A reviewer for *Time* (September 4, 2000) also approved of the work, observing: "English professors will relish [Atwood's] postmodern trick—a novel within a novel. . . . The less theoretically inclined can simply kick back and marvel at Atwood's gripping tale. . . . There is enough suspense in *The Blind Assassin* . . . to stock a shelfful of ordinary mysteries, with the added benefit that Atwood's plot comes with fully rounded characters and reams of beautiful prose."

Oryx and Crake postulates a future in which animals are altered to create viable vaccines for human beings and to serve as incubators for growing transplantable organs. When the novel opens most of the population has already been killed by a virus, but among the few survivors is Snowman, whose narration tells the reader of what happened decades earlier, leading up to the point in which he finds himself alone in a barren world, except for the Children of Crake, who look upon him as a monster. Though popular, the book received mixed reviews. Michiko Kakutani wrote for the *New York Times* (May 13, 2003): "The book is not as dreary as Doris Lessing's recent post-apocalyptic novel *Mara and Dann* or Tatyana Tolstaya's futuristic satire *The Slynx*, which is due entirely to the sympathetic charm of Ms. Atwood's hero, Jimmy a k a Snowman. She lavishes on him all the emotional detail that the other characters in this novel lack, delineating his adolescent angst, his hero worship of Crake and his later guilt over his failure to stop Crake's nefarious plans with ardor and panache. By the time we've plowed through *Oryx and Crake*, we can only wish that Ms. Atwood had inserted Jimmy Snowman into a different novel, not this lame piece of sci-fi humbug." Lorrie Moore proclaimed for the *New Yorker* (May 19, 2003): "In her towering and intrepid new novel, *Oryx and Crake*, Atwood, who is the daughter of a biologist, vividly imagines a late-twenty-first-century world ravaged by innovations in biological science."

Atwood's most recent novel is *The Penelopiad* (2005), a re-imagining of Homer's epic poem *The Odyssey*. Instead of focusing on Odysseus, the poem's hero, who has spent years away from his wife and homeland fighting the Trojan War, Atwood looks at the life of Penelope, Odysseus's long-suffering wife, who has spent those years awaiting his return. As with *Oryx and Crake* the book divided critics. Caroline Alexander, for the *New York Times Book Review* (December 11, 2005), complained that the "marvelous material [upon which Atwood drew] seems not to have been metabolized by Atwood's imagination, and the result is merely a riff on a better story that comes dangerously close to being a spoof. Most fatally, the maids, whose tragic end in the *Odyssey* is what in part inspired Atwood to choose this story, also remain mere outlines of characters." Thomas Jones wrote for the *London Review of Books* (November 17, 2005): "'Now that I'm dead I know everything,' Penelope's narrative begins. 'This is what I wished would happen'—when she was alive, presumably—'but like so many of my wishes it failed to come true.' The voice that Atwood gives Penelope's ghost is modern, matter-of-fact, smart, funny, unillusioned: 'Every once in a while the fogs part and we get a glimpse of the world of the living. It's like rubbing the glass on a dirty window, making a space to look through. Sometimes the barrier dissolves and we can go on an outing. Then we get very excited, and there is a great deal of squeaking.' This novel is one such outing, if without the squeaking. The narrator exists neither in the world she lived in nor in ours, but in limbo somewhere in between—the ideal place from which to tell her story."

Among Margaret Atwood's other works are several short-story collections: *Dancing Girls* (1977), *Bluebeard's Egg* (1983), *Murder in the Dark* (1983), *Through the One-Way Mirror* (1986), *Wilderness Tips* (1991), *Good Bones* (1992), *Good Bones and Simple Murders* (1994), *The Tent* (2006), and *Moral Disorder* (2006). She has written four children's books—*Up in the Trees* (1978); *Anna's Pet* (1980), with Joyce C. Barkhouse; *For the Birds* (1990), with Shelly Tanaka; and *Princess Prunella and the Purple Peanut* (1995), and in addition to *Survival*, her nonfiction titles include *Days of the Rebels 1815–1840* (1977), *Strange Things: The Malevolent North in Canadian Literature* (1995), *Negotiating with the Dead: A Writer on Writing* (2002), and *Writing with Intent: Essays, Reviews, Personal Prose, 1983–2005* (2005). She is also the editor of several literature anthologies.

Atwood has received numerous awards for her writing. Besides those mentioned above she has won the 1977 Canadian Booksellers Association Award, the 1977 Toronto Book Award, the 1978 St. Lawrence Award for fiction, the 1982 Arts Council of Wales International Writers Prize, the 1986 Governor General's Literary Award for fiction, the 1987 Arthur C. Clarke Award, the 1987 Los Angeles Times Book Prize, the 1994 Sunday Times Award for literary excellence, the National Arts Club Medal of Honor for literature in the U.S., and many more.

—C.M.

Suggested Reading: *Atlantic Monthly* p142 Dec. 1993; *Booklist* p180 Sep. 15, 1996; *Books inCanada* p13 Oct. 1985; *Christian Science Monitor* p19 Nov. 19, 1993; *Kirkus Reviews* p687 July 15, 2006; (London) *Guardian* p9 Oct. 14, 1970, p9 Oct. 23, 1982; *London Review of Books* p27+ Oct. 5, 2000, p23 Nov. 17, 2005; *Mother Jones* p24+ July/Aug. 1997; *New Statesman and Society* p37 Jan. 27, 1989; *New York Times* C p9 Dec. 30, 1996, E p9 May 13, 2003; *New York Times Book Review* p15+ May 21, 1978, p1 Feb. 9, 1986, p6 Dec. 29, 1996, p16 Dec. 11, 2005; *New Yorker* p88+ May 19, 2003; *People* p69+ May 19, 1980; *Time* p70 Sep. 4, 2000

Selected Books: poetry—*Double Persephone*, 1961; *The Circle Game*, 1966; *The Animals in That Country*, 1968; *The Journals of Susanna Moodie*, 1970; *Procedures for Underground*, 1970; *Power Politics*, 1971; *You Are Happy*, 1974; *Selected Poems*, 1976; *Two-Headed Poems*, 1978; *True Stories*, 1981; *Interlunar*, 1984; *Morning in the Burned House*, 1996; *Eating Fire: Selected Poems, 1965–1995*, 1998: novels—*The Edible Woman*, 1969; *Surfacing*, 1972; *Lady Oracle*, 1976; *Life Before Man*, 1979; *Bodily Harm*, 1981; *The Handmaid's Tale*, 1985; *Cat's Eye*, 1988; *The Robber Bride*, 1993; *Alias Grace*, 1996; *The Blind Assassin*, 2000; *Oryx and Crake*, 2003; *The Penelopiad*, 2005; short stories—*Dancing Girls*, 1977; *Bluebeard's Egg*, 1983; *Murder in the Dark*, 1983; *Through the One-Way Mirror*,1986; *Wilderness Tips*, 1991; *Good Bones*, 1992; *Good Bones and Simple Murders*, 1994; *The Tent*, 2006; *Moral Disorder*, 2006; nonfiction—*Survival: A Thematic Guide to Canadian Literature*, 1972; *Days of the Rebels 1815–1840*, 1977; *Second Words*, 1982; *Strange Things: The Malevolent North in Canadian Literature*, 1995; *Negotiating with the Dead: A Writer on Writing*, 2002; *Writing with Intent: Essays, Reviews, Personal Prose, 1983–2005*, 2005; children's books—*Up in the Trees*, 1978; *Anna's Pet* (with Joyce C. Barkhouse), 1980; *For the Birds* (with Shelly Tanaka), 1990; *Princess Prunella and the Purple Peanut*, 1995

Ander Gillenea/Getty Images

Atxaga, Bernardo

(ah-CHA-ga)

July 27, 1951– Novelist; poet; children's book author; playwright

The Basque novelist, poet, children's book author, and playwright Bernardo Atxaga—the pen name of Joseba (or, in Spanish, José) Irazu Garmendia—has been compared with such South American writers as Jorge Luis Borges and Julio Cortázar and with such French modernists as Raymond Queneau and Georges Perec. A recipient, in 1989, of the Spanish National Literary Prize (Premio Nacional de Literatura) for fiction, Atxaga writes in Euskera, more commonly referred to in English as Basque, but also contributes to the Spanish translations of his works, which have appeared in more than 20 languages. His novels *Obabakoak* (1992), *The Lone Man* (1996), *The Lone Woman* (1998), and *Two Brothers* (2001), all translated from Spanish into English by Margaret Jull Costa, evoke an imaginative version of Basque life and culture, as well as presenting a moral universe in which real politics play a part. Nick Caistor, writing for the London *Independent* (September 12, 1992), observed that while Atxaga uses the "paraphernalia of the naturalistic novel, he comes down firmly on the side of literature as sleight of mind." In his conversation with Caistor, Atxaga compared the author's attempt to wrest literature out of mundane material ("memories, the events of one's own life and of the community you find yourself in") to "a battle between giraffes." Atxaga elaborated: "When you see two lions fighting, you know what's going on: they roar, claw at each other, roll on the ground. But when you watch a pair of giraffes fighting, it looks as if they're caressing each other. They're not though, they're trying to break each other's necks: and that's the kind of struggle the writer is engaged in with language, with tradition, with sense." Reviewing *An Anthology of Basque Short Stories: Basque Literature Series*, edited by Mari Jose Olaziregi, Mark Kurlansky wrote for the *Los Angeles Times* (April 15, 2005) that Atxaga, a contributor to the volume, was "a natural storyteller whose work is marked by curious detail and rich characters" and "one of those rare writers who can instantly seduce his readers."

Bernardo Atxaga was born Joseba Irazu Garmendia on July 27, 1951 in Asteasu, a village near San Sebastián in a rural area of the Basque province of Guipúzcoa, in Spain; he has at least two brothers. His mother taught school and his father, grandfather, and great-grandfather worked as carpenters; all of them spoke Basque. "Historically, Basque existed only in private," Atxaga told Richard Gott for the London *Guardian* (July 29, 1996). "It had no social existence. There were no books, no literature. It was invisible. That's why there have been books in Basque only in the 20th century. After the civil war, the first book permitted to be printed [in Basque] was in 1959." Yet in Atxaga's youth, Basque was under a particularly sharp threat from the dictator Francisco Franco, who first established his hold over the entire country in 1939, at the end of the Civil War, and retained it until 1975. As part of his extremist nationalist policies, Franco had banned the use of any of the country's native languages other than Castilian Spanish, with the result that Basque became even more marginalized than it had already been. "Political repression was fierce when I was a child," Atxaga told Lucia Iglesias Kuntz for the *UNESCO Courier* (April 2000). "My brothers and I were beaten at school if we were caught speaking Euskera, the language we spoke at home. We knew we risked punishment if we spoke Basque in public." (Though Basque itself is carved up into a number of distinct dialects—and in its standardized form is to some degree an artificial creation—the language as a whole is one of the few in the world to have no close relationship to any other known tongue. Not only is it not related to Spanish, Basque is not even a part of the massive language grouping known as Indo-European—a category that subsumes languages as distinct as classical Greek and modern Urdu.)

Thanks in part to Franco's attempted suppression of Basque language and culture, opposition to Franco in the Basque region crystallized into Basque nationalism, which came to be represented by ETA (Euskadi ta Askatasuna, generally translated as "Basque homeland and freedom"). In his youth Atxaga was a part of the nationalist movement, working with the cultural front—as distinct from the military, political, and labor fronts—of the ETA movement. In the era after

Franco's death, Atxaga gradually detached himself from active involvement in ETA, coming to believe that although socialism should be instituted and Basque culture preserved, there was no need for a Basque nation separate from Spain.

After finishing his primary education close to home, Atxaga attended the Colegio La Salle, in the much larger town of San Sebastián, and received his *bachillerato*, a level of certification roughly between a high school diploma and an associate's degree. He studied economics at the University of Bilbao (now the University of the Basque Country) and worked briefly in a bank in Bilbao. Between 1981 and 1984 he studied philosophy at the University of Barcelona.

Atxaga's work first saw print in 1972 in an anthology of Basque writing called *Euskal literatura 72*. Four years later he released his first book of poems, *Ziutateaz*, and in 1978, his second, *Etiopia* (Ethiopia), earned him the Premio de la Crítica ("critic's prize") for poetry in Basque in 1978. (Some sources state that he received the Premio de la Crítica again in 1985, 1988, 1993, and 2003.)

Obabakoak, initially published in Euskera, in 1988, was Atxaga's first book to be translated into English and remains his best-known novel. The word at the root of the book's title is Obaba, the name of an imaginary mountain village, and the title as a whole has been variously translated as "everything about Obaba," "people and things from Obaba," and "stories from Obaba." Laden with tales from Basque folk tradition, the book offers a series of linked stories that call on such varying literary techniques as magical realism, intertextuality, and didactic narrative. The first part of the book, called "Childhoods," is composed of five stories, all of them set in Obaba and all suggesting the type of stories Basque children might have heard from their grandparents. Brief stories related to another imaginary small town comprise the second part, "Nine Words in Honor of the Village of Villamediana," which is told by a dwarf poet. The third part, "In Search of the Last Word," drifts furthest afield from narrative, with chapters about such subjects as "How to Write a Story in Five Minutes" and "How to Plagiarize," with examples provided. "However contrived this may seem," Caistor observed, "Atxaga holds the attention by his sheer craft" and "shows that, however recent Basque literature may be, it is not coming cap in hand asking to be admitted as a humble part of our 'great tradition.'"

Obabakoak established Atxaga as an impressive new voice in European literature. "Obaba is a micro-Europe," Chris Dolan wrote for *Scotland on Sunday* (July 27, 1997). "It feels the tremors of small events in Germany and London, and the ripples caused by its own people wash up in the Far East and the Amazonian rainforest. Atxaga writes about what it means to be Basque; we read about what it means to be human." Abigail Lee Six, writing for the *Times Literary Supplement* (August

21, 1992), argued: "Above all, it is the tone of the novel which is one of its most attractive features, for it maintains a lightness of touch without ever becoming flippant; there is humour shot through with pathos and irony that is wry rather than biting, a novel that is entertaining without ever becoming lightweight." Javier Cillero, reviewing the book for *World Literature Today* (Summer 1993), wrote: "There are so many narrative levels in *Obabakoak* that eventually the reader can choose his or her own position. Whether one is an old-fashioned reader who loves the art of storytelling, or a modern reader who enjoys discovering references and linking stories to one another, *Obabakoak* is sure to delight." In a review for the *New York Times Book Review* (June 20, 1993), Eugenio Suarez-Galban observed: "It is precisely the unexpected marriage of styles traditionally considered as incompatible in any one story that gives *Obabakoak* its peculiar originality and strength." Margaret Jull Costa's translation found favor in Suarez-Galban's eyes for retaining "Atxaga's magically flowing and seemingly simple style." In 2005 a film version of *Obabakoak* was released to wide acclaim, becoming Spain's official nomination for best foreign language film for the Oscars.

Having made his mark with *Obabakoak*, which was quickly disseminated in translation across Europe, Asia, and North America, Atxaga followed a somewhat more conventional narrative path with his next book, *The Lone Man*. Originally published in 1993 as *Gizona bere bakardadean*, the book takes on perhaps the most troubling issue about Basque nationalism: the violent tactics employed by ETA. Set in Barcelona at the time of the 1982 soccer World Cup, the novel follows Carlos, an ex-ETA activist who now runs and co-owns, with a group of former comrades, a hotel paid for with booty from their years as outlaws. Over the five days in which the novel takes place, Carlos attempts to help two current ETA members, Jon and Jone, both acknowledged killers, who are hiding in Carlos's secret den. Carlos is, in a sense, held prisoner by his past, while the other old activists are more interested in their new lives. According to Julian May, who reviewed *The Lone Man* for *New Statesman* (August 9, 1996), Atxaga's "greatest achievement is the clarity with which he delineates the 'territory of Fear' that Carlos inhabits" while trying to balance "his immediate need—to get the bombers away—with his loyalty to his friends and the vestiges of an idealism that once gave him identity. Beyond this lies a struggle to construct a meaningful life in the aftermath of the violence he has committed." Comparing the novel with the writings of the French existentialists Jean-Paul Sartre and Albert Camus, Colm Tóibín noted for the *Observer* (August 4, 1996) that "Carlos is plagued by a literary device whereby two dead characters whisper comments and warnings into his ear, and most of the time this is irritating and disconcerting. But his character is so carefully imagined and rendered with such precision and authenticity that the narrative becomes compelling." In a review for the *Irish Times* (August 29, 1997), Paddy Woodworth wrote that "the profuse, intricate imagery" of *Obabakoak* had been "stripped back to the bare branches here" but judged that "as a psychological portrait of a reformed revolutionary at the end of his tether, this book flashes with steely insights. It is also endowed with a page-turning power that speeds up impressively in the closing chapters."

Atxaga continued his dissection of the political, psychological, and philosophical implications of Basque nationalism with the brief novel *The Lone Woman*, originally published in 1996 as *Zeru horiek*. The eponymous woman, Irene, a former nurse, having just been released from prison on the promise that she will denounce the unnamed organization for which she acted, takes a bus from Barcelona to Bilbao. Her memories and dreams make up the substance of the book. Dogged by undercover police and annoyed by her fellow passengers, she eventually is comforted by a fat woman and two nuns. "Irene's journey is from prison to freedom, from exile to home," Julian May wrote for the London *Independent* (April 24, 1999), adding: "The fictional journey is almost always mythic, but in Atxaga's hands this ride becomes a psychological thriller reminiscent of [Graham] Greene." In a review for the *Irish Times* (April 10, 1999), Eileen Battersby wrote: "Brilliantly observed, the narrative juxtaposes ordinary life, as represented by the other passengers, with Irene's private hell of memories, doubt and regret. Stark and cinematic, it is an unusually convincing study of a state of mind." James Hopkin, for *New Statesman* (June 28, 1999), felt that Atxaga's minimalist approach in *The Lone Woman* established "a disturbing, transitory world in which all proportion and compassion have been lost. . . . Such a strategy delicately reinforces Irene's isolation; she has, after all, just been released from the gloomy uniformity of prison into a world of difference and light." *The Lone Woman* was adapted for Spanish television in 2005.

Translated from a revised Spanish version of its 1985 Basque original, *Bi anai*, *Two Brothers* is set in the village of Obaba and tells how the 16-year-old Paulo inherits his father's sawmill as well as the care of his mentally retarded brother, Daniel. Older than Paulo by four years, Daniel has recently begun to show an overpowering interest in women. "Daniel's late sexual awakening, the depression suffered by Paulo, and the conspiracies of two girls who vie for Paulo's affection, make for a tragic story," Lucia Graves wrote for the London *Daily Telegraph* (January 5, 2002). "Atxaga universalizes the problem of the social outcast and the cruelty of ignorance." In *Two Brothers* Atxaga employed the unusual narrative techniques of telling the story through the voices of a series of nonhuman narrators, including a bird, some squirrels, a star, a snake, and a wild goose, each of which is linked by what the book refers to as an "inner voice." Julian May, writing for the London *Independent* (November 24, 2001), found Atxaga's use of animals in *Two Brothers* "a disconcerting narrative device. . . . Chillingly, these animals take up the story when, at the insistence of the inner voice, they kill the previous narrator. The snake eats the bird, splitting open its head, and then has its own crushed in the bill of the goose."

In 2003 Atxaga published the novel *Soinujolearen Semea* (which can be translated as "the accordion player's son"). Translations of the book have already been published in Spanish, Catalan, and Dutch, and an English translation is reportedly forthcoming.

In addition to writing fiction and poetry, Atxaga is a well-regarded author of children's books in Basque; among his works in this genre are *Nikolasaren abenturak eta kalenturak* (1979), *Ramuntxo detective* (1979), *Chuck Aranberri dentista baten etxean* (1982), and *Xolak badu lehoien berri* (1995).

English-language reviewers have consistently praised Atxaga's writing, often following a line of thought expressed by Jan Fairley, writing for the London *Independent* (November 28, 1990) about *Obabakoak*: "By managing to be specifically Basque but rooted in the retelling of world stories, Atxaga's novel offers a possible paradigm for a European literature." Atxaga's position has not been an easy one, as he told Jon Lee Anderson for an article in the *New Yorker* (February 12, 2001) on the escalation of the Basque war for independence.: "I don't mind living within Spain," Atxaga said. "It has a more appropriate scale for a country than Euzkadi does. But it's difficult to stomach so many attacks on our culture. We have a minority group of *integristas*, fundamentalists, on the inside, and then on the outside we have a state that wants to destroy everything the minority stands for. Most of us are stuck in the middle, and we no longer know which way to turn."

Anderson described Atxaga in 2001 as "a rumpled, impish man of fifty with wild curly hair." Atxaga has lectured at Dartmouth University, in New Hampshire, and lived briefly in Scotland while his wife, Asun, taught the Basque language at the University of St. Andrews. Atxaga is featured prominently in Julio Medem's controversial and widely admired documentary about the Basque separatist conflict *La pelota vasca: la piel contra la piedra* (2003). (Also known by its Euskera title, *Euskal pilota: larrua harriaren kontra*, and the English translation of its main title, *Basque Ball*, the film takes its title from the unique game *pelota*, a variety of which is known abroad as jai alai. The film's subtitle can be translated as "skin against stone.") The last words in Medem's documentary are spoken by Atxaga, who says, according to a paraphrase by Giles Tremlett in a review of the film for the London *Guardian* (October 23, 2003, online): "The Basque country should be like a city,

. . . embracing all, ending violence and thereby producing a form of communal levitation." Tremlett commented: "It would be a perfect ending, if only poetry really could stop violence."

In late March 2006 ETA announced what it claimed would be a permanent cease-fire. Atxaga recognized the occasion with an essay, translated into English for the *New York Times* (March 29, 2006), in which he acknowledged the many responses the announcement had brought but suggested that relief and a sense of optimism were utmost: "But still and all, through the clamor of opinion, the feeling of happiness, of lightness, doesn't go away." On December 30, 2006 a bomb exploded in an airport car park in Madrid, killing two people; ETA claimed responsibility for the bombing but also insisted that the cease-fire was still in effect. According to a report by the BBC (January 9, 2007, on-line), Spanish Interior Minister Alfredo Perez Rubalcaba responded by saying that after the bombing, negotiations with ETA were "finished."

—S.Y.

Suggested Reading: *Irish Times* p14 Aug. 29, 1997, p67 Apr. 10, 1999; (London) *Daily Telegraph* p5 Jan. 5, 2002; (London) *Guardian* p27 Jan. 24, 1992, p9 Aug. 5, 2000, p16 Oct. 23, 2003; (London) *Independent* p19 Nov. 28, 1990, p26 Sep. 12, 1992, p12 Apr. 24, 1999, p12 Nov. 24, 2001; *Los Angeles Times* E p15 Apr. 15, 2005; *New Statesman* p47 Aug. 9, 1996, p49 June 28, 1999; *New Yorker* p40+ Feb. 12, 2001; *Scotland on Sunday* July 27, 1997; *Times Literary Supplement* p18 Aug. 21, 1992; *UNESCO Courier* Apr. 2000; *World Literature Today* p649 Summer 1993

Selected Books in English Translation: *Obabakoak*, 1992; *The Lone Man*, 1996; *The Lone Woman*, 1998; *Two Brothers*, 2001

Courtesy of Jimmy Santiago Baca

Baca, Jimmy Santiago

Jan. 2, 1952– Poet; memoirist; short-story writer; screenwriter

When Jimmy Santiago Baca entered prison, at 21, he was illiterate. When he was released five years later, he was not only literate but was also a poet, with a self-titled chapbook already in print and a book from a major academic publisher on the way. Since the publication of his first full-length collection of poetry, *Immigrants in Our Own Land* (1979; reissued in 1990 as *Immigrants in Our Own Land and Selected Early Poems*), Baca has published a number of poetry collections, the most important of which was *Martín and Meditations on the South Valley* (1987). He has also turned his hand to writing short stories and screenplays, and in 2001 he published a memoir, *A Place to Stand: The Making of a Poet.* Born into a Mexican American and Native American family, Baca most often refers to himself as Chicano, a term that, in academic U.S. circles, is denotatively identical with Mexican American but suggestive of a stronger degree of political identification, a quality clearly discernable in Baca's work. "His aim," Frederick Luis Aldama explained in an introduction to a recent interview with Baca for *Melus* (Fall 2005), "was from the start to give literary expression to his uniquely located and time-bound experiences, not to craft 'poetry for poetry's sake.' . . . Words, for Baca, were the seeds he would plant to grow roots in a land that had constantly discriminated against, excluded, displaced, and discarded not only him but also his Chicano/a compatriots, the Mexican and other Latino immigrants, the African Americans, the Asian Americans, as well as numerous other groups of fellow citizens." Baca's political ideas come through in his work and in interviews, and he also demonstrates them by his commitment to teaching writing to people whose backgrounds resemble his own. Baca frequently lectures or offers writing workshops in prisons and community centers, where he tries to encourage a love of language that he has often said saved his life. In his interview with Aldama, Baca acknowledged that teaching in academia "can be rich and fulfilling and meaningful, and important to the society we live in," yet, he added, "I couldn't see myself using what God had given me when I've heard with my own ears and seen with my own eyes kids in the *barrio*, [or] little white kids up in the mountains who know in their soul the power of language: its rhythms, sounds, images. I was one of those kids. So instead of teaching in a classroom at Harvard, I reach out to these kids and use the gift that God gave me to give them that tool and see where they go with it."

Born in Santa Fe, New Mexico, on January 2, 1952, Jimmy Santiago Baca was the youngest of three children, two of them boys; some authoritative sources give his birth name as José. (Accounts of Baca's life often differ in important details, in part because Baca himself has given varying information about his past, especially his early years. The general outlines of Baca's story, as he tells it, are nonetheless clear.) Of mixed Native American and Mexican heritage, Baca's father, Damacio Baca, was raised in the small town of Estancia, southeast of Albuquerque and just north of another small town, Willard, the home of Baca's mother, Cecilia Padilla. The youngest of seven children, Padilla was unusual among her Mexican American family for her light skin color, a quality that later allowed her to pretend to be Anglo American. Damacio Baca, by contrast, worked primarily among other Hispanics and strongly preferred speaking Spanish to English. Baca told Adam Fuss in an interview for *Bomb* (Summer 2003) that his father "was voted the person in the village most likely to make it, and good lord, he tried so hard to make it." Though he aspired to political office, Damacio Baca undercut his own ambitions with his tendencies toward violence and alcoholism, making him a fleeting and frightening presence in the household he and Padilla formed when, according to *A Place to Stand*, they were both 16. Baca's father later died of an alcoholism-related illness, presumably sometime during or after the 1967–71 administration of New Mexico governor David F. Cargo, in which Baca has said Damachio held some position.

Baca's first years were passed in Estancia and Santa Fe, in a home environment marked by neglect, poverty, and brutality. In *A Place to Stand*, he described watching his father rape his mother one afternoon when his father was drunk, and he has elsewhere claimed that his mother at times used him as a shield against his father's rage. When Baca was still young, his mother ran off to California with an Anglo American named Richard, leaving her children behind with Damacio Baca's parents. Baca enjoyed his grandparents' ranch, but when his grandfather died, his grandmother could no longer take care of the three children. Baca and his brother, Mieyo, were then sent to St. Anthony's Orphanage in Albuquerque, while his sister, Martina, stayed with their grandmother to help take care of her. Mieyo eventually died a violent death, as did Baca's mother, who was shot in the head by her second husband.

Indifferent to school and oppressed by the conditions at St. Anthony's, Baca often fled the orphanage during his years there and in his mid-teens abandoned it altogether. By the time he dropped out of school in about the ninth grade, Baca had only limited literacy skills. He was not, as profiles often suggest, fully illiterate but "functionally illiterate," as he explained to Robert Stuart in a 1991 interview for the radio program *New Letters on the Air*, according to a transcript available on the Modern American Poetry Web site. "Anybody can read 'it,' or 'you,' or 'a,' 'and,' 'but.' . . . It's not so much the fact that you can read or not read. I couldn't read, but it's what happens to an individual who is not able to read. What condition does that person fall into?"

Living anywhere he could, Baca worked odd jobs and began abusing alcohol and drugs. He eventually began selling drugs as well, and in about 1973, in Arizona, an acquaintance of Baca's sold drugs to an undercover law-enforcement official and, to avoid arrest, shot him; Baca has always insisted that he was not involved with the crime. Still, to avoid capture, he crossed back into New Mexico but in Albuquerque soon gave himself up to the police. After three months in jail, awaiting extradition, Baca was sent to Arizona for trial. He attempted to plead innocent but his lawyer, whom Baca portrayed in *A Place to Stand* as indifferent to his fate and clubby with the prosecution, insisted he enter a guilty plea, which he did, on November 16, 1973. He was later sentenced to five to 10 years in a maximum-security state prison in Florence for possession with intent to distribute. In interviews Baca has maintained that during his time in prison he spent four years in solitary confinement, was sometimes slipped debilitating drugs, and was subjected to electroshock therapy.

Over the years Baca has also given many explanations for what prompted him to develop his reading and writing skills while in prison. Among the most basic reasons was his desire to avoid punishment. Often put into solitary confinement for breaking rules, Baca decided he should learn to read English so that he could know the rules on his own. Another incentive was the arrival of "the only letter ever sent to me until that time," Baca told Peter Stack for the *San Francisco Chronicle* (July 15, 2001). Written by a stranger named Harry, a veteran of World War II, the letter was sent as part of a church program to write letters to prisoners who otherwise received no mail.

In *A Place to Stand*, Baca portrayed his first encounter with poetry in prison as an act of politically motivated revenge against a cruelly insensitive college student. Before his transfer to Florence, Baca was helping out at the local jail when the student, a white woman working the late shift, joined a couple of detectives in mocking a Chicano who resisted giving up what Baca called a "talisman pouch." When the woman looked away, Baca stole her English literature textbook.

Later he slowly pieced together the words from what he knew of the sounds of letters. The book included poems by such Romantic-era poets as William Wordsworth and Samuel Taylor Coleridge, and their work, particularly Wordsworth's *The Prelude*, brought back pleasant childhood memories.

As he grew more comfortable reading and writing, Baca began trading his skills for cigarettes or other difficult-to-obtain materials. He wrote letters for other inmates and even composed poems that they passed off as their own. He also began setting down poems for himself. In 1977, at the urging of a fellow inmate, he sent a selection of his work to *Mother Jones*. The magazine's poetry editor at that time, the renowned poet Denise Levertov, accepted three of the poems and, by Baca's account, paid him $100 per poem. Thrilled by his sudden success, Baca bought ice cream for the other men in his cellblock. "Since everybody had been supporting me for a few years," Baca told Robert Stuart, "I decided it was my turn [to] give them something."

By the time Baca left prison in 1978, his first chapbook, *Jimmy Santiago Baca*, had appeared and he had signed the contract for his first full-length book, *Immigrants in Our Own Land*. The book received generally positive reviews, including strong praise in the *Northwest Review* and the *American Book Review* and from Levertov in *Commonweal*. On the Web site of the New Mexico Culturenet, R. W. French commented on what he saw as Baca's "terse, concrete and direct" writing in this first book. "Typically, Baca confronts his situation with an unflinching eye. Beauty has nothing to do with it; understanding is everything, and understanding demands total commitment to honesty. Despite the lyric impulse central to the poems of *Immigrants in Our Own Land*, Baca's work avoids the merely 'pretty' or 'poetic.' It is apparent throughout that efforts toward formal aesthetic pleasures would be evasive, a betrayal of the forces that have brought these poems into being."

Though Levertov and other established poets, particularly Virginia Love Long and Gary Soto, supported Baca in his early work, he had trouble accepting his vocation as aa poet. Over the seven or eight years after he was first released from prison, he abused alcohol and drugs and drifted back and forth across the country, taking odd jobs. Though Baca has sometimes suggested that he did not write poetry during this time, he produced three chapbooks between 1981 and 1986, *Swords of Darkness* (1981), *What's Happening* (1982), and *Poems Taken from My Yard* (1986), none of which received much critical notice. Official biographies list Baca as having received a bachelor's degree in English from the University of New Mexico, in 1984.

Baca's second major book, *Martín and Meditations on the South Valley*, appeared in 1987. Published by New Directions and carrying an introduction by Levertov, the book followed the semiautobiographical figure of Martín as he moved across the U.S. searching for a comfort he eventually found in the barrio. The book enjoyed almost unanimous, if sometimes condescending, praise from critics. J. N. Igo, writing for *Choice* (June 1988), called Baca "a dynamic member of the growing tribe of Chicano poets who take the Chicano as their subject matter" and the book "a powerful sociological, semipoetic document" that was "extremely articulate." "Baca," Igo added, "seizes upon and explores details that haunt the imagination of the poet and the reader. Not for standard poetry collections, but certainly for all collections intended to offer insights into a rich but painful alternate tradition." In a critique for *Library Journal* (October 15, 1987), Ivan Arguelles wrote that there were moments when the book "really works in a strong, haunting way, evoking an almost twilight and gritty sense of growing up as a 'de-tribalized apache' in the Southwest. The sometimes prosaic reminiscences often leap to the vividly super-real, achieving a powerful, nightmarish quality. . . . Personification, as of La Muerte (Death), reminds us how close to the 'primitive' and to other cultures this poetry is."

Baca's career changed significantly after *Martín and Meditations on the South Valley* was awarded the American Book Award, in 1988. Having already received a grant from the National Endowment for the Arts, in 1986, Baca went on to win the 1989 Hispanic Heritage Award from the Hispanic Heritage Foundation. That same year he was selected for a visiting teaching position at Yale University, in New Haven, Connecticut, and the following year at the University of California, at Berkeley, where he was a regents' lecturer. Baca's *Black Mesa Poems* also appeared in 1989, to little critical notice.

Baca's next collection of poetry was not published until 2001. In the interim, he worked on a number of projects, including an as-yet unpublished novel, and a play, *Los tres hijos de Julia* (which can be translated as "the three sons of Julia"), which premiered, in 1991, in Los Angeles and reappeared in short-story form in Baca's 2004 fiction collection *The Importance of a Piece of Paper*. Baca's first collection of nonfiction, *Working in the Dark: Reflections of a Poet of the Barrio*, was published to mixed but generally negative reviews, in 1991. Considering the book "less an autobiography than a romantic paean, taking form as a series of essays, to the redemptive, ecstatic possibilities of poetry," a reviewer for *Publishers Weekly* (February 3, 1992) judged that Baca was "at his best when evoking barrio culture: his stately grandmother, the village cantinas and the quiet solidarity of Mexican workers. The book finally disappoints, however; too many reflections are self-indulgent, gratuitously profane, incoherent, or simply lost in torturous metaphors." John Wilson, for *Magill Book Reviews* (January 1, 1993), found similar fault and added: "From essay to essay there's a good deal of repetition, and as hyperbole is piled upon hyperbole the law of diminishing returns begins to take effect. Still, Baca's voice, once heard, won't be forgotten." In 1993 the Border Regional Library Association gave the book one of its Southwest Book Awards.

During this period Baca also served as a screenwriter and executive producer for the film *Bound by Honor* (also known as *Blood In/Blood Out*), a three-hour-long gangster film directed by Taylor Hackford. Released in 1993 the film was a critical and box-office disappointment and prompted protests by some Hispanics. Baca appeared in the PBS series, hosted by Bill Moyers, entitled *Language of Life*, which was first broadcast in 1995. In 1996 and 1997 Baca was awarded the title World Heavyweight Champion Poet by the Taos Poetry Circus, a now-defunct poetry-slam festival held in New Mexico.

In 2001 Baca released three books, two of them collections of poetry (*Healing Earthquakes* and *Set This Book on Fire!*) and the third, his autobiography. The books of poetry received generally positive reviews. A *Publishers Weekly* reviewer characterized *Healing Earthquakes* as "a sprawling journal of epic proportions. . . . Heavy with metaphor throughout, the 'Healing' in the title no doubt resonates with the poem's epi-center: the falling in and falling out of love with his wife, a process steeped in contradictions as much as self-indulgence. The poems, correspondingly, are intensely personal, contradictory and completely forthcoming." Writing for the *Nation* (March 4, 2002), Ilan Stavans acknowledged that "the style of *Healing Earthquakes* is at times flat, even repetitive, and the book's plot insinuates itself with the accumulation of insights. But overall the work is stunning, the product of a poet in control of his craft, one worth paying attention to."

Reviews of *A Place to Stand* tended to be more emphatic, with many critics moved by Baca's story while also criticizing the quality of his prose; a small number of reviewers questioned the book's truthfulness or pointed to inaccuracies or inconsistencies. Stavans's review in the *Nation* was among the most unstinting in its praise. "I was often overwhelmed by the sorrow and commiseration conveyed in Baca's memoir," Stavans wrote. "It is a luminous book, honest to a fault." Donna Seaman, a writer for *Booklist* (July 2001), also commended what she termed the "riveting exactitude and remarkable evenhandedness" of Baca's approach to the material. "Baca's harrowing story," Seaman predicted, "will stand among the world's most moving testimonies to the profound value of literature." A number of reviewers noted moments where the prose drifted into cliché or sentimentalism, but David Romo, in Austin's *Texas Observer* (August 3, 2001), directed his criticisms toward what he considered to be the unlikely elements in the story. "I feel guilty,"

Romo wrote, about expressing his incredulity, "in part because it's a good book, but at least 20 percent must be bulls**t." After describing some parts of the book that struck him as unlikely, particularly Baca's adventures in prison, Romo concluded: "I don't think it's a 'journalistically accurate' account of Baca's life, but so what? His memoir reaches for a deeper truth. It's a search for personal and collective myths, a first-hand account that goes to the heart of an American reality that's often ignored. . . . In fact, unlike the cinematic bravado of some of the plot inside the prison walls, the emotional vulnerability of much of his prose—especially that dealing with his childhood—made me uncomfortable. Its honesty made it difficult to read."

In 2002 Baca brought together two long poems—the first, "C-Train," subtitled "Dream Boy's Story"—to form his sixth book of poetry, *C-Train and Thirteen Mexicans*. In 2004, Baca published his first book of short stories, *The Importance of a Piece of Paper*. Keeping for the most part to the rough-and-tumble world portrayed in his memoir and some of his poems, Baca's stories received generally strong praise, though most reviewers criticized the story "Mother's Ashes" for being far-fetched. A writer of a starred notice in *Kirkus Reviews* (December 15, 2003) called the pieces "vivid, horrific, visionary, [and] disarmingly sentimental," while *Publishers Weekly* (December 22, 2003) commented that "in the best of these eight stories, gritty realism is deftly leavened by flights of lyricism." Sandra Márquez, writing for *Hispanic Magazine* (March 2004), argued that "at their best, the stories do not try to impose a world view, rather they transport the reader to a vividly drawn world where nature and animals come to life and marginal yet tender characters make their way in the world, searching for family." At the same time, Márquez noted, "the notion of Hispanic identity that many of Baca's characters are struggling against at times feels rooted in a nativist and even racist mold that seems out of step from the much more fluid, cross-cultural identity embraced by Latinos in this country today."

In 2004 Baca published *Winter Poems along the Rio Grande*. Widely reviewed, the book was considered a success by most critics, who often noted the poet's softer turn, both in terms of the tone of the work and in the looser lines, which many compared to Whitman's. Writing for the *Oklahoman* (June 20, 2004), Nathan Brown suggested that the collection "reveals a quiet, deeply rooted joy that has overtaken and consumed the author after all his difficulties. Nothing of his past (which, honestly, it doesn't appear he should have survived) has succeeded in conquering his soul." Characterizing the poems in the book as "long-lined, casual and determinedly optimistic," a reviewer for *Publishers Weekly* (April 26, 2004) concluded: "many of the images and themes here are predictable, but readers who have followed Baca this far will certainly want to come along for his heartfelt exploration of the American Southwest and of 'the contradictions/ that come with being human.'" His next book, *Spring Poems Along the Rio Grande*, is scheduled for release in April 2007. He is presently working on his as-yet-untitled novel and another book of poems that will be called, according to his official Web site, "Bi-lingual."

In addition to his many other awards, Baca was given an honorary doctorate by the University of New Mexico, in 2003.

Baca lives in Albuquerque. His marriage to his first wife, Beatrice Narcisco, ended in about 2002; they had two sons, Antonio and Gabriel, now both adults. A third son, Isai, was born in about 2003 to Baca's partner, Stacey.

—D.R.

Suggested Reading: *Bomb* p59 Summer 2003; *Choice* p1,552 June 1988; Jimmy Santiago Baca's Web site; *Los Angeles Times* V p1 Feb. 15, 1989; *Melus* p113+ Fall 2006; Modern American Poetry Web site

Selected Works: poetry—*Immigrants in Our Own Land*, 1979; *Poems Taken from My Yard*, 1986; *Martín and Meditations on the South Valley*, 1987; *Black Mesa Poems*, 1989; *Set This Book on Fire!*, 2001; *Healing Earthquakes*, 2001; *C-Train and Thirteen Mexicans*, 2002; *Winter Poems along the Rio Grande*, 2004; nonfiction—*Working in the Dark: Reflections of a Poet of the Barrio*, 1992; *A Place to Stand: The Making of a Poet*, 2001; fiction—*The Importance of a Piece of Paper*, 2004

Backer, Sara

1957– Novelist; poet; playwright

The poet, playwright, and fiction writer Sara Backer is primarily known for her 2001 debut novel *American Fuji*, a book that was inspired by her impressions of living in Japan, where she was the first American and the first woman to serve as visiting professor of English at Shizuoka University. But the experience of living in Japan did more than merely provide her a setting for her book; it gave shape to the ideas that provide the narrative with significance. Living in Shizuoka taught her, perhaps more than living in Tokyo, where many Westerners reside, what it was like to live as an Other. Indeed, Wanda A. Adams wrote for the *Honolulu Advertiser* (June 2, 2002), she was unprepared for "what she calls 'the Japanality of it all.' Things like sidewalk scrubbing. No one told her—because they didn't know that she needed to be told—that in Japan, apartment dwellers take turns cleaning up the trash area and pathways around the building. It was only after a certain amount of smoldering resentment had built up that she discovered her social solecism. At which point, she said, 'the only thing to do was apologize and get down on my knees with a scrub brush. Which I did, singing Italian arias the whole time,' she said. The incident—one of many humorous clashings of culture that later would provide the comic relief in *American Fuji*—illustrates a theme of the book: the assumptions people make, and how wrong we often are about each other."

Sara Backer was born in 1957 and lived in Holdon, Massachusetts, until she was 14, when she moved with her family to Oregon. She began writing as a young child and quickly found success, publishing, at the age of 6, a poem in the Worcester, Massachusetts, *Sunday Telegram*'s Happy Times pages. "They gave me a dollar, and I was rich!" she told Pamela H. Sacks for the Worcester *Telegram & Gazette* (March 14, 2002). Little else has been written about her childhood, but as an adult she studied at the University of California, at Davis, with the poet Gary Snynder and is often referred to as his protégé. After completing her M.A. in creative writing, she heard that Snyder had gotten another graduate a job; Backer, Adams reported, "chided him: 'Hey, where's my job?' The next week Snyder came back to her and said, 'Sara, be careful what you wish for . . . I've got a job for you but it's in mainland Japan and it's a three-year commitment.' Snyder assured her that her total ignorance of the Japanese language was no problem. 'You'll pick it up,' he said, blithely."

She used her experience in Japan as the background for *American Fuji*, which has been described by critics as being simultaneously a mystery, a love story, and a literary novel. The protagonist, Gaby Stanton, has been fired from her job teaching English and now sells elaborate funeral parties for a living. In her new line of work, she meets Alex Thorn, an American psychologist and author of self-help books, who has come to Japan to learn more about the death of his son, an exchange student who had attended the university where Gaby taught. As the duo team up to solve the mystery of the young man's demise, they are confronted with Japanese people who look upon them as outsiders and treat them accordingly; a romance soon blossoms between the two Americans, and they gain a better understanding of themselves and their foreign surroundings.

In her review for the Book Reporter Web site, Jana Siciliano cheered: "*American Fuji* is a wondrously complex and compelling first novel with a strong, fully fleshed-out female protagonist. I kept imagining the movie in my head as I read, it was so perfectly orchestrated. . . . *American Fuji* is a powerful book and a stunning debut." Susan Chira, writing for the *New York Times Book*

Review (March 25, 2001), was more reserved in her praise: "The leading characters in *American Fuji* are complex and the plot twists clever, but Backer's novel occasionally lapses into pedantry because of the weight placed on Gaby, who must explain Japan both to Alex and to the reader. There is plenty of contempt for foreigners, and a villain who is cartoonish in his callousness and superiority, yet there is also considerable knowledge and appreciation of the ways Japan forces the foreigner toward self-reflection, a heightened sensitivity to gesture and an earnestness unencumbered by irony." Beverley Curran, writing for the Tokyo *Daily Yomiuri* (November 18, 2001), while not quite as dismissive, did fault the novel for being a little obvious: "'Expect the unexpected' is a mantra repeated throughout *American Fuji*, but for anyone who has been living in Japan for a while, the characters in Sara Backer's first novel are very familiar: the British Berlitz English teacher who spends most of his time drinking and attempting to seduce his young students; the American university instructor who has not had sex since she came to Japan; the humorless Japanese university professor . . . You get the picture. Still, there are enough twists in this story to make it a fairly entertaining read for those wishing to confirm their generally critical view of Japan."

An early draft of *American Fuji* was named as a finalist in the competition for the James Jones First Novel Fellowship, and it has since been translated into French, Italian, Spanish, Dutch, and Polish. Backer's short stories and poems have been published in such literary journals as *Poetry, Southern Poetry Review, Poetry Northwest, Slant, Bakunin, Oxford Magazine*, and the *Seattle Review*. In June 2000 one of her plays was chosen for performance at the Edward Albee Theatre Conference, which is held in Valdez, Alaska. While Backer continues to be interested in poetry—telling Sacks, "A poem is a metaphor for the human condition that makes sense on an inexplicable level"—she has found that writing a novel has turned her off the short-story form. "The short story illuminates a single life moment," Backer told Sacks. "That was interesting when I was in my 20s. As I get older, I find I'm interested in larger themes and truly understanding people."

Backer lives in San Luis Obispo, California, and while she has written some novels in manuscript she does not know when her next book will appear, noting on her official Web site, "Publishers don't buy authors; they buy books. None of my other novels are set in Japan and they are quite different from *American Fuji*. I suspect *American Fuji* was a fluke, a lucky break. But I just keep writing."

—C.M./A.R.

Suggested Reading: Book Reporter Web site; *Honolulu Advertiser* D p1 June 2, 2002; *New York Times Book Review* p20 Mar. 25, 2001; Sara Backer's Official Web site; (Worcester, Massachusetts) *Telegram & Gazette* C p3 Mar.14, 2002;

Selected Books: *American Fuji*, 2001

Badami, Anita Rau

(bah-DAH-mee, ah-NEE-tah RAUW)

1961– Novelist

Anita Rau Badami was born in India and has lived in Canada since the early 1990s. Both countries figure largely in her novels: *Tamarind Mem* (1996), *The Hero's Walk* (2000), and *Can You Hear the Nightbird Call?* (2006). "I was twenty-nine years in India and ten years here [in Canada], so I have a foot in India and a couple of toes here," she once told an interviewer, as quoted on the Random House of Canada Web site. "I am both doomed and blessed, to be suspended between two worlds, always looking back, but with two gorgeous places to inhabit, in my imagination or my heart."

Anita Rau Badami was born in 1961 in Rourkela, a village in Orisson, a state in the eastern region of India. Her father was a mechanical engineer who worked for the Indian Railways Company, and as a result of his job, the family relocated to a different city every few years. Badami also lived occasionally in "saloons," which were, as she explained to an interviewer for the BookBrowse Web site, "a sort of house on tracks designed for the railway engineer who was obliged to tour remote landscapes for extended periods of time. These 'homes' usually had three bedrooms, living and dining rooms, and an office. In some saloons the rear wall would be a large sheet of glass. I would sit in front of this window pane for hours, mesmerized by miles of track slipping away into the distance as the train sped forward."

Badami grew up speaking three languages: Kannada (her mother tongue), English, and Hindi. The members of her extended family often regaled her with stories drawn from mythology and folklore, and her fascination with these traditional tales developed into a passion for reading, particularly the works of such British writers as Enid Blyton, Agatha Christie, and P. G. Wodehouse. She generally attended Catholic schools—"the only schools which taught really good English . . . and gave you a [well-rounded] education about the world, not just about India," as she explained to Angela Kozminuk for the *Peak*, the student-run newspaper of Simon Fraser

Richard-Max Tremblay/Courtesy of Random House
Anita Rau Badami

University, a mid-sized Canadian institution in Vancouver, British Columbia (July 10, 1996). She continued: "The religion was left out completely. . . . I know the Bible very thoroughly, but not because they forced it down our throats. It was just taught as literature."

Badami attended the University of Madras, earning a bachelor's degree in English. She began writing as a way to earn pocket money for books, selling her first piece to a women's lifestyle publication, *Femina Magazine*, at age 18; she was paid the equivalent of about $2. Badami went on to Sophia College, in Bombay, where she studied communications, and after graduation she worked as an advertising copywriter and freelance journalist, writing articles for three local English-language newspapers: the *Hindu, Deccan Herald,* and *Indian Express.* The steady income afforded Badami the opportunity to indulge in writing fiction for children's magazines, which paid little but which she enjoyed greatly. She told Mary Soderstrom for *Quill & Quire* (September 2006, on-line), "The point of view of a child is an extremely interesting way to tell a story. Children are sensitive to things, they half-know, half-understand, and if the point-of-view character realizes after the fact what things meant, the hints advance the [plot]."

Badami married her husband, Madhav, in 1984, and traveled to northern Indian for their honeymoon. Their return home coincided with the assassination of Prime Minister Indira Gandhi by two of her Sikh bodyguards. Her description of the violence that broke out in the wake of the assassination is quoted on the Random House of Canada Web site: "In Modinagar, a town close to

Delhi, we saw a Sikh man standing on a bridge over a dry stream, his turban removed, his long hair unbound, his arms pinned to his sides by a car tire, surrounded by a group of hoodlums. Somebody tossed something at him and the next moment the man was on fire. His body arched over the low wall of the bridge and one of the thugs who had set him alight leaned forward and shoved him with a crowbar so that he dropped over the edge. I can still feel the shock that ran through me at that casual brutality." The incident haunted her, as did the bombing by Sikh separatists, less than a year later, of Air India Flight 182 (departing from the Montréal-Mirabel International Airport, in Quebec). The bombing claimed the lives of 329 people, including one of Badami's neighbors; most of the victims were Canadian citizens, and almost a third of them were children.

In 1987 Badami gave birth to a son, Aditya. In March 1991 she and Aditya joined Madhav in Calgary, Canada, where he was pursuing a master's degree in environmental studies at the University of Calgary. The family lived in a modest apartment, and Badami soon found work at a shopping mall, selling dinnerware and porcelain figurines. Soon after her arrival she enrolled in a master's program in creative writing at the University of Calgary. "Adjusting to new situations came easily to me," she told the BookBrowse interviewer. "In India, my geographies were in a permanent state of flux; I was always moving away somewhere, perennially settling in. Change was my only constant, and my perspective was that of a nomad. The only difference was that now, . . . instead of toys and a change of clothes, I carried words and stories. . . . These would travel with me wherever life took me." Several of her early short stories appeared in the *Malahat Review* and other Canadian literary journals. At the suggestion of one of her university instructors, Aritha Van Herk, Badami developed one of the pieces—her master's thesis project—into a full-length novel and sent it to a publishing house.

In 1995 Badami graduated from the University of Calgary, and the following year Penguin Canada published her debut novel. *Tamarind Mem* examines the combative relationship between Saroja, a woman born into a traditional Indian household, who is forced by her parents to abandon her plans for a medical career in favor of an arranged marriage to a railway engineer, and her daughter Kamini, who has moved to Canada to pursue a graduate education and to escape both the caste system and her strong-willed mother. (The title refers to the nickname given to Saroja by her servants, who find her tongue as sharp as the acidic tamarind fruit; mem is short for memsahib—a form of address similar to madame.)

The story, set against the backdrop of the railway colonies in northern India, is told from the widely differing perspectives of mother and daughter. In the first portion of the novel, a grown Kamini reflects on the past in order to find clues to her mother's unhappiness and bitterness; in the second half Saroja, now widowed and on a train tour of India, tells the story of her life to fellow passengers. *Tamarind Mem* was well received by critics. Valerie Compton, in a review for the *Edmonton Journal* (August 1996), wrote, "It is rare these days to come across a book so unselfconscious it begs to be read aloud. *Tamarind Mem . . .* is such a book. Badami allows her characters to float their stories on the air in a first-person narrative as jewel-bright and weightless as a silk sari shaken out of its folds. . . . As with a fine piece of furniture, the plain lines of the story emphasize the texture of the beautiful material used: Badami's gorgeous language is as rich and sharp and surprising as are her insights." Donna Nurse, writing for *MacLean's* (September 9, 1996), was similarly impressed, calling *Tamarind Mem* a "vivid, almost cinematic tale." Nurse continued, "The novel is a solid accomplishment—an exciting addition to the burgeoning tradition of Indo-Canadian writing that includes Rohinton Mistry, M. G. Vassanji, and Shyam Selvadurai." (The novel was published in the U.S. in 2002, under the title *Tamarind Woman*.)

In the late 1990s Badami and her family moved from Calgary to Vancouver, so her husband could study for a doctoral degree at the University of British Columbia. In Vancouver she wrote her second book, *The Hero's Walk*, which tells the story of a young girl who is rendered mute after the death of her parents in a car accident. She is sent to live in India with her mother's family, headed by Sripathi Rau, the hero of the title. Rau agrees to take in his orphaned granddaughter despite his estrangement from the girl's mother, who years before had shunned the traditional marriage he had arranged for her. Badami explores what ultimately constitutes a hero. "The book actually started with this fascination I had for mythological heroes or people of mythic proportion, those grand heroes of yore that you find in every mythology, in every culture," she explained to Penelope Dening for the *Irish Times* (June 16, 2001). "But for most people, life itself is a challenge, from the beginning to the end. And I started thinking that each one of us is heroic simply to be able to survive with hope intact and with reasonable amount of dignity."

Much like her debut novel, *The Hero's Walk* drew critical praise for its vivid language and engrossing story. Jaswinder Gundara wrote for the *Multicultural Review* (September 2001), "Badami's novel is peopled with engaging characters capable of great pathos and strength. It is replete with local customs, colors, and smells, as well as the interminable frustrations, quirks, and humor of life in a small Indian town." James Gerein, in a critique for *World Literature Today* (Winter 2002), similarly opined, "This is a novel of extraordinarily strong characters living simple, believable lives. . . . Badami's writing is lucid, clear, and at times pleasantly poetic." *The Hero's Walk* earned Badami the distinction of being the youngest woman in history to receive the Marian Engel Award (2000), presented annually by the Writers' Trust of Canada. She also received a Regional Commonwealth Writers Prize, Italy's Premio Città di Gaeta and Giuseppe Berto Literary Prize. The book was also nominated for an International IMPAC Dublin Literary Award, the prestigious Orange Prize for Fiction, the Kiriyama Prize (for books about the Pacific Rim and South Asia), and the Ethel Wilson Fiction Prize (one of the British Columbia Book Prizes).

In 2001, when her husband accepted a teaching position at McGill University, Badami and her family moved again, from Vancouver to Montreal. She began work on her third novel, largely inspired by two historic events that continued to have a deep impact on her—the anti-Sikh riots of 1984 and the 1985 terrorist bombing of Air India Flight 182. In the process of researching the book, *Can You Hear the Nightbird Call?*, Badami studied Sikh religious practices, examined testimony from survivors of the riots, and read interviews with young terrorists. The novel traces the interwoven lives of three women from Sikh and Hindu backgrounds and examines how India's frequent periods of tumult and violence affect them. "It is difficult not to be a little wary of books that are timely, political, and tug at the heartstrings," Ingrid Ruthig wrote for *Books in Canada* (October 2006). Ruthig was nonetheless won over: "This book is ambitious in its intellectual and emotional scope and in its historical breadth. . . . Badami's strength lies in portraying individuals and their interactions. The tensions and emotional intensity she manages to build draw the reader into each of her characters' lives, so that we're better able to understand and empathize with all sides. This subtle balancing act is no small achievement." Chris Kurata, in a review for the Toronto *Globe and Mail* (September 16, 2006), was also taken with the novel's historical backdrop, writing, "The book's manipulation of suspense as the plot expands [from the 1947 partition of India and Pakistan] toward the Air-India bombing in 1985 is a timely draw for those who regard terrorism as something new in history, especially if they wish to view the perspectives of characters inured to these seemingly sudden eruptions of violence. If the pathology of terrorism is simplified here, it is to give deference to the larger enterprise, the telling of stories too often lost in the slippage of countries and generations, of old identities and new." (Badami dedicated the novel to the Sikh man whose death she had witnessed right after her honeymoon and to the victims of Air India Flight 182.)

Badami currently lives with her husband and son in Montreal. In an essay titled "My Canada" for the *Imperial Oil Review* (Summer 2000, on-line), she described returning to her adopted land after a visit to her native country: "While I still cherished the brilliant colours of India, I was also beginning to recognize and appreciate the subtle tints and textures of the Canadian fabric. And I knew that even though a part of me would always look with love towards the land of my birth, and deep inside I would [forever] straddle two continents, two realities (the East and the West), my home was now here, in Canada."

—B.M.

Suggested Reading: BookBrowse Web site; *Books in Canada* p9 Oct. 2006; *Imperial Oil Review* (on-line) Summer 2000; *Irish Times* p65 June 16, 2001; *January Magazine* (on-line) Aug. 2000; *Maclean's* p53 Sep. 9, 1996; (Montreal) *Gazette* J p7 Sep. 9, 2006; *Ottawa Citizen* C p9 Aug. 18, 1996, C p1 Sep. 3, 2006; *Quill & Quire* (on-line) June 1996, Sep. 2006; Random House of Canada Web site; (Toronto) *Globe and Mail* D p16 Sep. 16, 2006

Selected Books: *Tamarind Mem*, 1996; *The Hero's Walk*, 2000; *Can You Hear the Nightbird Call?*, 2006

Bahal, Aniruddha

1967– Novelist

Aniruddha Bahal, who garnered international attention for his second novel, *Bunker 13*, when it appeared in 2003, is better known in India, the country of his birth, as a journalist, which he initially became to pay his bills as he worked on establishing himself as a novelist. He became more serious about pursuing journalism after his first novel, *A Crack in the Mirror*, failed to find a readership after its appearance in 1991. Over the next decade he wrote for newspapers, eventually earning a reputation as an innovative investigative journalist, employing computer technology to expose corruption in professional cricket. He then switched over to Web-based publications and began focusing on governmental corruption. *Bunker 13*, however, fully established Bahal as an important voice for the new India, presenting the country, Alexander Zaitchik observed for the *Sunday Review* (November 19, 2006), "at terminal literary velocity. . . . [The novel] exists on a yet higher post-pity plane, one that eradicates most of the new India books that have piled up in the last decade. As India's 'creamy class'—the preferred local term—grows and accelerates, so does the rate of obsolescence of certain so-deemed culturally representative books. Yet *Bunker 13* . . . remains the closest thing to a Declaration of Independence for Indian fiction, signed with a Ralph Steadman exclamation-point splat."

Born in 1967 in the northern Indian city of Allahabad, where he attended St. Joseph's College, Aniruddha Bahal moved to Calcutta after graduating from university and found work as a journalist while he was writing *A Crack in the Mirror*. The book sold only about 500 copies and failed to interest reviewers. Bahal then moved to Delhi and began taking his journalism career more seriously, apparently giving up on the idea of being a novelist altogether and taking positions with such Indian newspapers as *Outlook* and *India Today*. (Today he virtually denies the existence of *A Crack in the Mirror* and refers to *Bunker 13* as his first novel.)

Bahal made a name for himself as an investigative reporter when, writing for an Indian sports weekly, he used new-media technologies, in 1997, to expose the existence of match fixing among international cricket players, whom bookmakers, in order to guarantee their winnings, paid to perform badly. "When bookmakers approach players," he revealed, as Peter Popham reported for the London *Independent* (December 10, 1998), "there are three stages. First they ask for information about who's playing and who's not playing, the state of the pitch and so on, for which they pay well. Next they say, 'would you like to take a free bet with us?' If the player wins, he wins; but if he loses, the loss is overlooked. Then finally they say, 'could you arrange to get out for under 15? Or to bowl outside off stump for a couple of overs?' Once the player gets sucked in, what's to stop the bookies from blackmailing them?"

Three years later Bahal founded, with Tarun Jit Tejpal, Buffalo Networks, a media company, which launched *Tehelka*, an investigative-news Web site. The company was also said to have a television division, a design division, a music division, and a book division, which apparently was going to release, in 2000, "Fallen Heroes" by Bahal, the publicity blurb for which read, Namita Bhandare reported for *India Today* (on-line, March 26, 2001), "the 'sensational undercover investigation' into the 'world of match-fixing and cricketing icons who have betrayed our trust.'" This book, however, never seems to have been published, though a 90-minute documentary film about the breaking of the story apparently was. Bahal's next coup, uncovered in what *Tehelka* called Operation West-End, was his and Samuel Mathew's four-month sting operation involving India's defense ministry, which uncovered widespread corruption in the form of government employees demanding kickbacks for buying equipment for the Indian military. Their investigation led to the resignations of several senior government officials, including the defense minister. To uncover the corruption Bahal and Mathew posed as promoters of a fictitious London arms-manufacturing company called West End International, filming all their meetings with government officials using cheap electronic cameras; eventually one of the officials, Bangaru Laxman, demanded a $30,000 bribe. "There were moments of intense anxiety," Bahal said, as Chetan Krishnaswamy reported for the *Times of India* (March 15, 2001). "Everytime we met a person, we were nervous about being detected and beaten. But now the satisfaction is tremendous."

The government, however, fought back, launching an investigation into *Tehelka,* and Bahal and another *Tehelka* reporter were arrested, in 2002, apparently for what Operation West-End had uncovered. Bahal told Adam Dunn for *Publishers Weekly* (April 28, 2003): "I wasn't jailed for Operation Westend. It was more a case of the system trying to find an excuse to teach me a lesson. An officer from the Central Bureau of Investigation, which has been trying to frame us in an Official Secrets Act case for a story that we did in October 2000, came to my office to interrogate me and some staffers. I asked him to serve us with some written notice first as that was the way our lawyers had advised us. But he failed to do so and instead lodged a complaint that I had manhandled and threatened him. They arrested me the next day, but the judge saw through the case and granted me bail within a few hours. Fortunately, the entire Indian media expressed their solidarity with me around the incident and labeled it a witch-hunt."

In the meantime Bahal worked on his second novel, *Bunker 13,* which tells the story of Minty Mehta (MM for short), a cynical, debauched ex-soldier who takes a job as an investigative reporter and becomes embroiled in arms smuggling and drug running while on assignment with Indian special forces near the Kashmiri border. Upon its release critics compared it to such acclaimed literary works as Norman Mailer's *The Naked and the Dead* (1948) and Joseph Heller's *Catch-22* (1961). "Bahal's style," Burhan Wazir wrote for the London *Observer* (May 18, 2003), "is full of pace and character. He appears to relish the new lease of life fiction offers and his prose is influenced by the hard-bitten, women and alcohol-fuelled language of the modern thriller genre: 'Man, you have enough alcohol in here to launch a polar satellite vehicle. Johnnie Walker Blue Label! The only time I have seen the bottle is in a Star TV ad, the one with that slinky blonde in it that blows her skirt in the ventilator.'" Amitava Kumar, writing for the *Nation* (August 18, 2003), called attention to some of the novel's flaws but concluded, "the book's gift is greater than its conclusion, or the plotting that stretches plausibility almost to the breaking point. *Bunker 13* gives flesh and blood to the ingenuity and rapacity of India's new entrepreneurial class. Writers and journalists aren't exempt either. The novel shows that the desire to find and tell the truth is only a move in a high-risk gamble. It follows that there is also a sinister side to MM. At his most chilling, he reminds you of his more modest cousins who have been in the news—those affluent Hindus who took directions on their cell phones and arrived in their SUVs, during the riots in Gujarat last year, to loot the shops owned by Muslims."

Bahal currently runs his own investigative-news Web site, Cobrapost, which he founded in 2003. He lives in Doida, near New Delhi.

—P.B.M./A.R.

Suggested Reading: (London) *Observer* p17 May 18, 2003; *Nation* p46 Aug. 18, 2003; *Publishers Weekly* p44 Apr. 28, 2003; *Spectrum* (on-line) Aug. 3, 2003; *South Asian* (on-line) Aug. 2003; *Sunday Review* p18 Nov. 19, 2006; *Time Asia* (on-line) July 7, 2003; *Times of India* Mar. 15, 2001

Selected Books: *A Crack in the Mirror,* 1991; *Bunker 13,* 2003

Paul Hawthorne/Getty Images

Baitz, Jon Robin

Nov. 4, 1961– Playwright; television writer

"It's so hard to write," Jon Robin Baitz observed to Terry Byrne for the *Boston Herald* (June 12, 1996). "If you're going to do it, you might as well hit the big themes." Baitz has expressed disapproval of such labels as "modern-day moralist," as a headline in the *New York Times* (May 7, 1992) described him. Nonetheless, he has steadfastly addressed serious moral and ethical questions in his plays—but without moralizing—largely because of what he saw, heard, and experienced firsthand in the 1970s as an American adolescent living in South Africa, where the black majority had long suffered the brutal oppression and racial segregation institutionalized by the white minority through the nation's apartheid laws; indeed, most of his plays are semiautobiographical. "I think something kicked in for me in South Africa, something about feeling impotent to change things that I found repugnant," he recalled to Misha Berson for the *Seattle Times* (October 23, 1995). "And with that came rage and a modified, complex liberal guilt." In the *New York Times* (March 3, 1996), the cultural critic Margo Jefferson wrote that Baitz has focused on such questions as these: "How does the home prepare one for the evils of the world? How does the family and country we belong to shape us for good or ill? And what do we do with all the treacherous ambiguities in between; with the choices that must be made and the catastrophes that must be acknowledged?"

The first of Baitz's plays to be mounted, in 1985, was the original version of his one-act comedy *Mizlansky/Zilinsky*. The second, *The Film Society*, opened in New York in 1988 and earned Baitz the 1989 George Oppenheimer Award (called the Oppy), which honors the most impressive New York debut of an American playwright; the play was published in 1987. His later works for the stage include *The Substance of Fire*, *The End of the Day*, *Three Hotels*, *A Fair Country*, *Ten Unknowns*, *Chinese Friends*, and *The Paris Letter*. Known for his love of and sensitive ear for language, Baitz has written screenplays and a contemporary version of Henrik Ibsen's *Hedda Gabler* and has appeared in three films: *Last Summer in the Hamptons* (1995), *One Fine Day* (1996), and *Sam the Man* (2000). In recent years he has also written for television. "I'll keep writing about the decreasing power of the individual and the increasing responsibility of the individual," he once said, as quoted on Virginia Commonwealth University's Arts Web site. "I'm in pursuit of something, and it's a long-term notion."

Jon Robin Baitz, called Robbie by friends and relatives, was born on November 4, 1961 in Los Angeles, California. His brother, Richard K. "Rick" Baitz, born in 1954, is a composer and arranger who has written scores for HBO and PBS presentations as well as for productions of works by his brother. His father, Edward Baitz, now deceased, was an executive with the international division of the Carnation evaporated-milk company; his job transfers dictated the family's subsequent moves. For two years beginning when Robbie was eight, the Baitzes lived in Brazil. In 1972 they set up house in Durban, in the Republic of South Africa. Explaining to Michael Lassell for *Interview* (April 1992) why, in his words, he "has always felt old," Baitz said, "You're so much on your own when you live overseas as a kid of parents who are kind of doing their own thing. Being sad as a child makes people grow up faster." He told a reporter for *New York Newsday* (August 3, 1989), "Growing up as a traveler, you learn to listen and observe in order to determine what the rules of the game are going to be in any given place." By the early 1970s in South Africa, the black majority's plight under apartheid had led to increasingly open and frequent rebellion. Some of the strikes, marches, and other protests ended in violence, with the police killing dozens of the participants. Baitz's first memory of South Africa is of a sign reading "This door for whites only" at the airport arrivals building. On his first day at his all-white, Anglican boys' school, he told William Grimes for the *New York Times* (May 7, 1992), after seeing all the students stand whenever a white adult entered the classroom, he alone rose from his seat when a black janitor came in. He also remembers seeing blacks stopped on the streets of Johannesburg by white policemen armed with machine guns in 1976, after residents of the nearby black township of Soweto protested the national edict that instruction in black schools must be in Afrikaans, the language spoken by the descendants of South Africa's Dutch settlers. Once, when a heated argument between his mother and one of her black employees led her to summon a police officer, he heard the policeman advise her to buy a gun.

During the six years Baitz spent as an outsider in South Africa—in particular at his school, where he was the only Jew as well as the only American—he grew "increasingly comfortable, increasingly integrated, increasingly anguished, because as a teenager you get anguished. So the more comfortable I became, the less comfortable I was," as he recalled to Grimes. Baitz told Misha Berson that he was "always struck by the kind of moral ambiguity that living in South Africa required." He told Grimes, "When one is confronted with such day-to-day evil, it should be very clear how to respond. And yet I found myself lacking—found myself, my peers, my parents, my parents' friends, the world lacking." He told Stephen Gaghan for *Bomb Magazine* (2004, on-line), "South Africa made me who I am. Being party to, not mere witness to, pure and simple state-run racism, the subjugation of entire peoples, [led to] my interest in how systems operate and how we lull ourselves into letting them operate with impunity. I write about that as much as I do parents and children; they're exactly the same thing." Baitz also told Gaghan that his mother "has contributed vastly to my personality; both of us struggling to understand, struggling to fit in . . . . She's not so much a muse as she is a half-me."

Baitz's family returned to Los Angeles in time for Baitz to spend his last year before college at Beverly Hills High School, where the students' disengagement from nearly all societal problems astonished him. He decided against continuing his education after his high-school graduation. "Because of the moving around, I'd never really focused on my schoolwork," he explained to Mervyn Rothstein for the *New York Times* (August 2, 1988). "Being a student seemed unreal, and going to college seemed evasive—a kind of side-stepping maneuver." Instead, he embarked on a series of "the usual drifter's jobs," as he put it to Rothstein, mostly in Israel and Europe.

At age 20 Baitz returned to Los Angeles. He got a job as a gofer with a producer of substandard films who was struggling to survive on Hollywood's margins. During this time he also worked as a salesclerk in a bookstore and started to attend plays. A turning point in his life came when he saw a production of Anton Chekhov's *The Cherry Orchard*, in which, because of debts and inattention, an old landowning family loses their property to Lopakhin, a former serf who has become a rich merchant. "The scene where Lopakhin says 'I told you this was going to happen,' I understood that moment of revenge," Baitz told Bruce Weber for the *New York Times* (October 30, 1994). "And I wanted revenge." He came to view the stage as "a forum to jumpstart something" and fight the "ever-present impulse to disengage," as he put it to Grimes.

For a while Baitz studied playwriting at the now-defunct Padua Hills Playwrights' Workshop and Festival, in Northridge, California. At 22 he wrote his first play and got his first rejection, from the Actors Theater of Louisville, in Kentucky, whose letter offered suggestions and encouragement. He next penned *Mizlansky/Zilinsky* (1985), inspired by his Hollywood employer's "byzantine, elusive business dealings," as Naomi Pfefferman wrote for the *Jewish Journal of Greater Los Angeles* (April 7, 2000, on-line). Referring to a writer of comedies and a tragedy by Arthur Miller, Baitz told Pfefferman that *Mizlansky/Zilinsky* was "like a Neil Simon version of *Death of a Salesman*, with all the little dramas of trying to get to the next good deal." Mounted in a storefront theater in Los Angeles, the play brought Baitz an *L.A. Weekly* Award. At the time, he told Pfefferman, "I had such an entitlement complex that my response was, 'This is right. What's next?'"

Baitz's next play, *The Film Society*, takes place in 1970 at a fictitious boys' school in Durban that resembles the one Baitz attended. Through his six characters, Baitz portrayed the school as a "fascinating microcosm of South Africa," as Mimi Kramer wrote for the *New Yorker* (August 8, 1988). The protagonist is a teacher who precipitates a crisis by inviting a black priest to speak at the school's centennial celebration. The possibility that the school will mistakenly be thought to be fomenting antiapartheid activity pushes some of the otherwise goodhearted characters "out of their amiable bumbling into fear-induced beastliness," as John Simon wrote for *New York* (August 1, 1988). In one of many complimentary reviews, Sylviane Gold wrote for the *Wall Street Journal* (August 2, 1988), "Baitz's South Africa is awash in moral ironies" and "full of betrayals, large and small. Mr. Baitz's understated writing . . . lets the point of the play slip out around the edges of the story: In a society based upon a lie, good faith is not possible. . . . In the end, we see that self-interest is the only creed that can survive in white South Africa." In Mimi Kramer's view *The Film Society*

"reverberates like the best work of [the renowned South African playwright] Athol Fugard." The play was published as a book in 1987.

Dutch Landscape, Baitz's next play, centers on an American family living in 1970s South Africa; the parents and their two sons have "lost touch with [their] roots in 1960s idealism . . . [and] are isolated and far away, not only from their home in America, but from each other," according to a blurb posted on the Web site of the Kennedy Center for Performing Arts in Washington, D.C. The play, which opened in late 1988 at the Mark Taper Forum, in Los Angeles, failed resoundingly. The harsh words of critics devastated its author, who grew angry, depressed, and confused. Afraid that the negative response to *Dutch Landscape* might paralyze Baitz professionally, Gordon Davidson, the artistic director of the forum's Center Theatre Group, persuaded him to start writing again immediately. Baitz described the negative reception to *Dutch Landscape* to Richard Stayton for the *Los Angeles Times* (January 17, 1993) as "the most seminal experience of my life." "Right after it I wrote *Substance [of Fire]*, *Three Hotels*, and *End of the Day* in rapid succession," he said. "And I attribute all of that to *Dutch Landscape*, to learning from the extraordinary battle of that play. It fueled a great growth for me."

Baitz wrote *The Substance of Fire* with the actor Ron Rifkin, a friend of his, in mind for the leading role. At its premiere, at Playwrights Horizons, in New York City, in March 1991, Rifkin portrayed Isaac Geldhart, a refugee from Nazi Germany whose family perished during the Holocaust; he now owns a publishing company along with his adult children. In Act I his children urge Isaac to bring out a trashy novel to bolster the firm's shaky finances. Instead, against their vehement objections and warnings of disaster, he insists on publishing a six-volume account of the medical experiments conducted by the Nazis on Jews and others deemed undesirable by the German dictator Adolf Hitler and his cohorts during the 1930s and World War II. Victimized by evildoers as a child, Isaac habitually attacks his own children verbally. In Act II, set three years later, his business is in the hands of a Japanese corporation; a now-retired, mentally unstable Isaac confronts his past from a different perspective when visited by a troubled psychiatric social worker sent by one son in hopes of having his father deemed incompetent. "For all his nastiness, it is hard to dislike Isaac," Frank Rich wrote for the *New York Times* (March 18, 1991). "Once Mr. Baitz ruthlessly challenges the premises by which Isaac has lived—examining the real meaning of his survival, the substance of his 'fire'—the audience is caught up in the sad reckoning facing him in late middle age. Is Isaac's proud insistence on holding onto his past the choice that allowed him to survive, or is it a burden that robbed him of any hope for happiness?" Rich also wrote, "It is the searing achievement of *The Substance of Fire* that it keeps chipping and chipping away at its well-worn, well-defended protagonist until finally he and the century that shaped him and then reshaped him are exposed to the tragic quick." Ron Rifkin starred in the film version of *The Substance of Fire* (1996), for which Baitz wrote the screenplay; the text of the play was published in 1993.

"On the heels of his daunting patriarch in *The Substance of Fire*, Baitz stacks up as a true American virtuoso" with *Three Hotels*, Jan Stuart declared in *New York Newsday* (April 7, 1993), expressing an opinion shared by many other reviewers. Baitz wrote *Three Hotels* for a presentation on the PBS television series *American Playhouse* in 1991 that he directed as well. Two years later the play was published as a book and the stage version opened at the Circle Repertory Theater, in New York City. *Three Hotels* has only two characters, Ken Hoyle and his wife, Barbara, and three acts, each set in a different hotel room overseas; in the first and third acts, only Ken is on stage (except for a moment at the very end, when a silent Barbara is seen); in the second act, only Barbara. Ken (the child of an American communist of Russian and Jewish heritage) is a hard-nosed executive with a company that markets baby formula to underdeveloped nations, fully aware that the food is a poor and even dangerous substitute for breast milk, because in many areas the water necessary to prepare the formula is contaminated, and many users will not understand the proper way to mix it. (Baitz's father did not think that Hoyle's business tactics mirrored his. "I don't think I'm that venal a character," he told Bruce Weber. "I never thought [my son] was portraying me in that sense.") Ken is unaware that his wife, after two decades of seeming compliancy in her marriage, has become embittered and desperate. Barbara, who like Ken is a former Peace Corps volunteer, disapproves of his company's misleading sales tactics. In Act II she discloses that in a talk to company wives, she has not-so-subtly warned the women of the harm in store for them as appendages to their husbands in Third World environments. In Act III Ken reveals that his wife's subversive speech has cost him his job and that she has left him. The confident, combative corporate climber whom Ken presented to the world in Act I is barely discernible. "Kenneth and Barbara's alternating spiels reveal classic case histories of good liberal intentions gone awry," according to Jan Stuart. In the *New York Times* (April 18, 1993), David Richards wrote, "The playwright has not only painted a vivid picture of a marriage in collapse and a freewheeling career on the rocks, he's also indicted a whole society for which ethics is just a bothersome form of nit-picking."

Baitz took the title of *A Fair Country* from the poem "Refugee Blues," by W. H. Auden. A reworking of *Dutch Landscape*, the play opened at a Lincoln Center theater on February 19, 1996 and was published as a book in 1996. It features Harry Burgess, an idealistic U.S. Foreign Service officer

stationed in Durban; his wife, Patrice, a "walking nervous breakdown," as Vincent Canby described her in the *New York Times* (February 20, 1996), whose emotional turmoil is linked to her keen understanding of the horrors of apartheid and its damaging effects on her family; their adult son, Alec, a fiery, countercultural journalist who is visiting from New York; and their agonized, homosexual 17-year-old son, Gil, "the play's conscience," in Canby's words. Eager to remove Patrice and Gil from South Africa, Burgess succeeds in getting a job with the Voice of America in Europe—but with a string attached: he must divulge to the U.S. Central Intelligence Agency (CIA) the names of South African antiapartheid organizers who are Alec's friends. His acquiescence leads to the destruction of his family. *A Fair Country* left the *New York Times*'s Margo Jefferson with questions about the characters' inner lives and actions; nevertheless, she described what she called "Baitz's angry, intelligent new play" as "the best contemporary American play I have seen at Lincoln Center for some time."

In 1996 Baitz developed a life-threatening infection in one of his heart valves and underwent open-heart surgery. His illness left him "more fragile than I realized, with perhaps a diminished capacity for laughter, boldness and bravery," as he wrote for the *New York Times* (February 1, 1998). The Los Angeles Theater Works' request, in 1997, that he adapt *Mizlansky/Zilinsky* for broadcast on the radio helped him emerge from his gloom; "administering a kind of literary CPR on myself," as he put it in the *New York Times*, he made major changes in the play, which was published as a book, in 1998, as *Mizlansky/Zilinsky, or Schmucks*.

Meanwhile, for about two years after his recuperation, Baitz worked on scripts for the silver screen—a lucrative but, for him, highly unsatisfying activity. "It left me feeling practically worthless as a writer," he told Bernard Weinraub for the *New York Times* (March 14, 1999). "The variables that I could not control just stymied me. I was left feeling impotent." A new project for the stage—adapting *Hedda Gabler* for contemporary audiences—enabled him to become "reacquainted with the exhilaration of writing," as he put it to Weinraub. Baitz's version of *Hedda Gabler* was mounted in Los Angeles in 1999 and at the Williamstown Theater Festival, in Massachusetts, in 2000. The text of Baitz's revision was published in 2000.

Baitz's more recent plays include *Ten Unknowns*; premiering in 2001 and published three years later, the play is about the mysteries of artistic creation and corruption in the world of fine art. First produced in 2004, *Chinese Friends* is set in 2030 in a dystopian U.S. The play amounts to a "jeremiad," as the playwright put it to Jason Zinoman for the *New York Times* (May 30, 2004), that grew out of his anger over the policies and actions of the administration of President George W. Bush. *The Paris Letter*, which was first produced and published in 2005, deals with "the survivors, the benefactors and the victims of a sexual revolution," as Baitz, who is gay, described it to Stephen Gaghan. "I had been somewhat elliptical or cautious about sexuality in my work," he explained. "And it had started to bother me."

For more than a decade, Baitz lived in New York City with the actor and director Joe Mantello, who directed some of his plays. He then moved to Venice, California. His honors include the Playwrights USA Award from the Theatre Communications Group; the Humanitas Prize, from the Human Family Educational and Cultural Institute; and fellowships from the Rockefeller and Revson foundations, the American Academy of Arts and Letters, and the National Endowment for the Arts (NEA), which gave him a $15,000 grant in 1992. Later that year, to protest the refusal of the NEA's acting director to give grants to an arts center and a gallery despite the recommendations of the NEA's advisory panel, on the grounds that the funds would be used for exhibiting sexually explicit material, Baitz gave $7,500 each to the center and the gallery. He is a founding member of Naked Angels, a nonprofit New York City theater company of actors, writers, directors, designers, and producers. Baitz lamented to Gloria Goodale for the *Christian Science Monitor* (April 21, 2000) that theater is largely peripheral to contemporary American society. "The sense of futility, the feeling that the culture has passed you by is the most difficult part of being a playwright, that you're doing work that nobody knows about; most of the time I can't bear it," he told her. "I can't pretend I'm happy about it or reconciled or at peace with it, but I'm addicted [to writing]."

Baitz recently began trying his hand at a new medium, writing for the ABC television drama *Brothers and Sisters*, which premiered in 2006 and for which Baitz also works as an executive producer. The show centers around the Walkers, a wealthy California family that includes both liberals and conservatives; much of the dialogue is comprised of passionate political banter. (Baitz, an avowed Democrat, contributes frequently to the Huffington Post, a political blog.) The show features an openly gay character who is accepted and loved by the entire family: When he shows up alone at a family dinner, his mother, played by the veteran actress Sally Field, bemoans his single state and expresses hope that he will find a boyfriend soon. Baitz has also written individual episodes of the TV shows *Alias* and *The West Wing* and finds television an interesting challenge. "[TV] moves a little differently," he told Drew Mackie for AfterElton.com (September 25, 2006). "[It] requires an almost brutal brevity."

—H.T.

Suggested Reading: *Chicago Tribune* C p14 June 19, 1994; *Jewish Journal of Greater Los Angeles* (on-line) Apr. 7, 2000; *New York Times* C p15 Aug. 2, 1988, C p11 Mar. 28, 1991, C p1+ May 7, 1992, II p1+ Oct. 30, 1994; *Seattle Times* Tempo p12 Oct. 23, 1992

Selected Books: *The Film Society*, 1987; *The End of the Day*, 1993; *Three Hotels*, 1993; *The Substance of Fire, and Other Plays*, 1993; *A Fair Country*, 1996; *Mizlansky/Zilinsky, or Schmucks*, 1998; *Ten Unknowns*, 2004; *The Paris Letter*, 2005

Selected Films: as screenwriter—*The Substance of Fire*, 1996; as actor—*Last Summer in the Hamptons*, 1995; *One Fine Day*, 1996; *Sam the Man*, 2000

Selected Television Series: *Brothers and Sisters*, 2006–

Barker, Nicola

Mar. 30, 1966– Novelist; short-story writer

"Nicola Barker has published novels and short story collections, and they form one of the strangest oeuvres in contemporary English fiction," James Ley wrote for the Melbourne *Age* (February 15, 2003). "Her characters, who are usually emotionally damaged misfits, inhabit a world that is comic and unsettling. . . . It would be easy to mistake much of her bizarre inventiveness for frivolity, but there is real angst in her stories." Since emerging on the British literary scene with her short-fiction collection *Love Your Enemies* (1993), Barker has distinguished herself as one of the most original British writers of her generation. Of her penchant for dwelling on the eccentric, Barker told Maggie O'Farrell for the London *Independent* (February 6, 2000), "There's this huge stereotype in fiction about what a normal person is, and I often feel as if writers are trying to write about normal people, or a concept of normality, so that everyone will be comforted. Well, I'm not interested in comforting people. . . . I think the effect I want is to make things that aren't entirely conventional more accessible, to make people more accepting of peculiar things."

Nicola Barker was born on March 30, 1966, in Ely, a town in the county of Cambridgeshire, England, where her father was stationed in the Royal Air Force. Barker's father, Derek, took up a career as a sales executive when he left military service, and her mother, Rayne, worked as a teacher. When Nicola was nine years old, her father moved the family to South Africa, where they resided in a whites-only area of Johannesburg. As Barker recalled to Penelope Dening for the *Irish*

Times (May 27, 2000), her experiences in South Africa proved quite traumatic. "It was a very scary place," she explained. "Murder capital of the world. When we were there it was the heart of apartheid. You're in a sort of white bubble and the newspapers don't tell you about what's going on, so you don't really know. There was a whole series of moral dilemmas that become part of your daily life." In response to the rampant racism that afflicted the region, Barker's mother was actively involved in efforts to aid black South Africans. She worked at an educational newspaper, and when that publication folded she began teaching black children in Soweto.

When Barker was 15 years old, her parents separated, and she and her mother returned to England to live with her grandparents in Manchester. Her older sister, however, remained in South Africa with her father. Although she had been eager to return to England, Barker found the readjustment process difficult. Barker faced discrimination in her native land due to the heavy South African accent she had acquired in her years there. She nonetheless never took steps to regain her British accent, telling Jasper Rees for the London *Evening Standard* (May 12, 2000), "I hate people adopting accents. You should never deny what you are. . . . People just find out."

Barker and her mother eventually moved from Manchester to London, but she soon returned north, to Cambridge, after she was admitted to King's College (part of the University of Cambridge). There she began studying for a degree in philosophy and law but changed her focus to English, completing an undergraduate thesis on teen fiction. At one point in her research, she interviewed the British novelist Martin Amis. "He made such a positive impression," she told Dening. "So it's people like him and [English writer] Angela Carter—they gave me a taste of writing a more modern kind of fiction which hadn't been around really." Around this time Barker began writing seriously and started work on the book that would eventually become her first novel.

After earning her bachelor's degree, with honors, from King's College, in 1988, Barker returned to London, where she held a series of odd jobs to support her writing career. She worked in a betting shop and as a cashier in a Soho bakery; the latter position led to a job at the Queen Elizabeth Hospital for Children, where she spent four years as a cook. Throughout this period, Barker remained committed to her writing, rising two hours early each morning to work on her fiction. In 1996 she began pursuing writing full time.

With the publication of her first book, the short-story collection *Love Your Enemies*, Barker began building her reputation as one of Britain's most promising young writers. The stories in that volume feature a cast of unusual characters, each of whom is in the midst of a personal crisis. In "Layla's Nose Job," for example, a young girl confronts her obsession with her large nose, as well as the disappointing results of plastic surgery; in "John's Box" an AIDS victim builds his own casket as a means of coming to terms with his death; and in "Symbiosis: Class Cestoda" a young woman on the heels of a breakup ingests a tape worm to lose weight and develops a relationship with the insect that far exceeds the one she shared with her ex-lover. *Love Your Enemies* became a critical success. Many reviewers praised her ability to tackle both the humorous and painful aspects of a situation or relationship. As Julian Evans described for the London *Guardian Weekly* (March 7, 1993), "[Barker] has an exact and lawless imagination and a voice to transmit it sweetly, without too much interference. These stories are about Here-and-Now, but the opposite of commonplace. They are about small bits of the world. They're only stories. Yet to use a word reeling with recent fatigue, they are a showcase for a talent." For *Love Your Enemies*, Barker received both the 1993 David Higham Prize for Fiction and the 1994 PEN\Macmillan Silver Pen Award.

Her next work, *Reversed Forecast* (1994), is a full-length novel about a group of urban misfits. The story revolves around Ruby, a brash girl who works in a betting shop, and Vincent, an oddball known for his fits of violence and other strange habits. Additional characters include Sylvia, who is adored by birds despite her allergy to them; her half-sister, Samantha, a hopeful cabaret singer; and the girls' mother, Brera. While several critics praised Barker's funny prose and "idiosyncratic creations," as one reviewer wrote for the London *Sunday Times* (September 18, 1994), others found the characters and the plot somewhat underdeveloped. Nevertheless, Robin Blake, writing for the London *Independent* (August 6, 1995), opined, "Barker is a superbly physical writer, and the rough material of her characters' lives is vividly realised. There is a fair quotient of quiet desperation, but also plenty of wit and spiritual toughness and it is all completely believable. A first novel which has you ready to queue for the second."

Barker's second novel, *Small Holdings* (1995), is the story of Phil, a man who works at a public park in northern London. In the opening pages of the book, Phil, who is participating in an assertiveness-training course, walks into a pharmacy to request a pack of extra-small condoms. The plot largely explores Phil's interaction with his unusual coworkers: Doug, a man disillusioned with his marriage, and a one-legged vixen named Saleem. The book received mixed reviews. In her critique for the London *Guardian* (August 18, 1995), Jenny Turner noted, "At her best, Barker tents a delicate web of poetry about the privet hedging of the unremarkable little park into which her characters dig their raging resentments and dreams." Nevertheless, Turner found the book fraught with contrivances and ultimately concluded: "*Small Holdings* is an artistically timid book. And at the moment, it is this timidity which is holding a talented writer back."

Barker returned to short stories in her fourth work, *Heading Inland* (1996). The collection again features a bizarre set of characters, each caught in unusual circumstances. In "Inside Information" a pregnant petty criminal begins using her belly's zipper—a secret feature that her fetus shares with her so she may avoid labor—to shoplift goods by hiding them inside her womb. In "G-String" Gillian uses her underwear and a Swiss army knife to finally free herself from her boyfriend's obsession with the actress Katherine Hepburn. Three of the stories—"Blisters," "Braces," and "Mr. Lippy"—center around Wesley, a young man attempting and failing to find emotional freedom. Like Barker's first short-fiction collection, *Heading Inland* received significant critical praise. As Rachel Cusk suggested in her laudatory review for the London *Times* (July 18, 1996), the short story may be a better showcase for Barker's talent than the novel. "Barker's characters here no more belong in a novel than they do in life," she noted. "Their interest lies in their imperviousness to narrative. They're not misfits, Barker half-humorously, half-maliciously implies: they're special." *Heading Inland* garnered the Mail on Sunday/John Llewellyn Rhys Prize in 1996. Many of Barker's stories from both *Love Your Enemies* and *Heading Inland* were collected in *The Three Button Trick, and Other Stories* (1999), which Judith Ann Akalaitis, writing for *Library Journal* (July 1999), described as "a stunning assortment." A reviewer for *Publishers Weekly* (May 31, 1999) hailed the collection as "wildy imaginative and thoroughly entertaining" and praised Barker's "penchant for writing about the freakish twists life holds for average or extraordinary misfits, neurotics and the walking wounded."

Barker next began working on a novel that would explore much darker themes than those in her earlier works. The result, *Wide Open* (1998), is set on the Isle of Sheppey, on a bleak section of the Thames River estuary. Here, Barker places a number of complex and peculiar characters, including Sara, a wild-boar farmer; her deranged daughter, Lily (who worships a miscarried fetal boar that she calls The Head); Ronny, a pesticide sprayer; Nathan, his estranged brother; and Luke, a pornographer. The novel contains several strange and surprising plot twists, although the main focus is the redemption of Ronny and Nathan, who both suffered at the hands of their violent, pedophiliac father.

With its complex and often confusing plot, *Wide Open* received mixed reviews from critics, although most praised Barker's skill at evoking the bleak landscape of Sheppey and the vivid inner lives of her characters. As Jennifer Berman wrote for New York *Newsday* (November 1, 1998), "[Barker's] style is fast, funny, profound and sharp.

She is a remarkable writer who comes up with some of the rarest, most unexpected images I've read. . . . Barker is not shy, nor is she squeamish, and she is capable of handling the most violent scenes as adeptly as she does the most wrenching and tragic." However, many reviews acknowledged problems with the "deeply perplexing novel that constantly hints at greater meanings and profound symbols but doesn't always deliver," as Rachel Hartigan wrote for the *Washington Post* (November 29, 1998). In her review for the London *Independent* (April 4, 1998), Louise Doughty suggested that Barker's linguistic quirkiness ultimately diminishes the story's clarity. "Her alliteration sometimes feels self-indulgent," she noted. "Broken sentences abound. And the halting prose is mirrored in the short chapters and the fractured nature of each character's life. . . . Barker's story collections routinely win awards but her novels suffer from the qualities that make the stories so good. In a novel, we need more than evocative glimpses of character; we need a complete picture." Berman acknowledged that the characters and scenarios were so bizarre that they threatened to alienate the reader but concluded, "In the end, however, *Wide Open* is so beautifully written, so imaginatively drawn, that whether you completely believe it is somehow not the point. The fact that Barker has come up with such crazy characters is reason enough for resounding applause." Despite such mixed criticism, *Wide Open* received the 2000 International IMPAC Dublin Literary Award, which carried a cash prize of £75,000 ($115,000). In announcing the prize, the international panel noted that Barker's work possessed a "manic energy and taut eloquence worthy of a large, serious and global readership," as quoted by a reporter for the London *Evening Standard* (May 10, 2000). "*Wide Open* is word perfect, witty and ironic. Its dialogue sparkles and its chiselled sentences display both a razor-sharp comic sensibility and flawless structure."

Barker did not write any fiction for nearly a year after completing *Wide Open*. "It was an incredibly traumatic book to write," she told Rees. "I didn't think it would be published. It just seemed such a huge, negative, angry, complicated thing. I think of it as a slightly maladjusted child that looks strange but is very beautiful inside." Despite the personal toll, however, she remained committed to presenting unusual characters in an honest way. "I think everybody is weird," she explained. "But the whole point of my work is to express weirdness in a normal way that doesn't seem frightening to people. I want people to be more accepting. That's my mission, I suppose." Nevertheless, in approaching her next novel, *Five Miles from Outer Hope* (2000), Barker wanted to shift tone and deliver a work that was lighthearted and romantic. "It was cocking a snook [British slang meaning to make a gesture of derision] at everyone who took me too seriously," she explained to Dominic

Bradbury for the London *Times* (February 5, 2000). "And *Wide Open* was also a hard and boring book to write—it was very complex structurally. So I wanted to move away from that and for the next book to be fun. It was a release. My favourite genre is actually romantic comedy—films like *Bringing Up Baby*—so this was my attempt at saying, 'I can do this as well.'" Barker completed the novel in just three months.

Set on a small island off Britain's Devon coast, *Five Miles from Outer Hope* is the coming-of-age story of 16-year-old Medve, a six-foot three-inch giantess, during the summer of 1981. Medve's unpredictable family members, who run a dilapidated art-deco hotel on the island, contribute to many of the novel's comic elements. The discontented teenage narrator, however, is less than tolerant towards her eccentric family—a father who crochets, an older sister with recently enlarged breasts, bothersome younger siblings, and a mother who is traveling the U.S. selling an anal probe she designed for prisons. When a 19-year-old South African boy arrives on the island, Medve develops something of a love/hate relationship with the outsider. As Bradbury wrote for the London *Times* (February 12, 2000), the novel "gradually becomes the oddest of love stories, a coming-of-age drama that outdoes *Catcher in the Rye* for hormonal angst and teenage confusion." *Five Miles from Outer Hope* received generally favorable reviews, although most critics had some quibbles. Bradbury called the book "occasionally grating," but concluded that it "is always fresh, original and tightly written. It is certainly Barker's lightest and perhaps her most accessible novel to date." In her review for the *Edmonton Journal* (June 4, 2000), Margaret Macpherson opined, "Barker is a very clever writer and following her serpentine train of thought and savouring her language is an adventure in itself. But the work never goes beyond mere cleverness. . . . If Barker weren't so wordy, the novel would make a great short story."

In *Behindlings* (2003) Barker explores the character of Wesley, who had previously appeared in several of her short stories. (In those stories, readers learned that Wesley was traumatized as a child when he accidently killed his brother by locking him in an abandoned freezer; a radical environmentalist, he has in the past liberated live eels from a fish-and-chip shop and once fed his own hand to an owl.) Here Wesley has been inflated to the status of a cult figure; he is followed by a group of "behindlings" who trail his every move. As the novel begins Wesley has agreed to take part in a promotional treasure hunt for a confectionary company, in which followers can track clues to his whereabouts to earn a grand prize. When one of the contestants accidently drowns, Wesley abandons his involvement in the hunt, leaving the candy company in a frenzy. Wesley's regular followers—who include a tattooed hippie, a nurse, and a blind ex-policeman,

to name a few—track him to Canvey Island—a dreary place in the Thames estuary—where the novel follows a number of ambitious plot lines. "As you would expect," Michael Pye noted in his review for the *New York Times* (December 29, 2002), "there will be revelations; there will be conflict among the behindlings. Crimes and tragedies will emerge. Certainties will be spoiled, lives wrecked and salvaged. An elaborate puzzle will be solved and a jigsaw of memories put together—all this with the exuberant, violent energy of a Saturday morning cartoon show, laced with the easy bits of [Austrian philosopher Ludwig] Wittgenstein."

Behindlings received mixed reviews from critics, who found the novel both technically ambitious and overly convoluted. As Keith Gessen wrote for the *Washington Post* (April 6, 2003), "It's an intriguing premise for a novel, though Barker, who is a very hot literary property in England, does not pull it off. One problem is the peculiar style: a thesaurusized, caffeinated, abusively italicized narration that deploys interior monologue with utter abandon, constantly interrupting speech with the characters' supposedly truer thoughts." Writing for *New Statesman* (September 2, 2002), Hephzibah Anderson opined, "In the space of just a couple of pages, Barker is capable of hauling in everything from the Spanish Armada to bathrobes and brass doorknobs. Sometimes it works well, but more often it doesn't." Nevertheless, other critics celebrated Barker's energetic language and excessive attention to detail. "There are times when this kind of bombast can seem indulgent," James Ley noted, "but at its best, the writing has an almost Joycean sense of liberation." He added, "It is the often astounding collision of the serious and the absurd that is perhaps the most distinctive feature of *Behindlings* and Barker's work in general. There is a reckless glee behind many of her ideas."

Shortly after celebrating the release of *Behindlings*, Barker was inspired to write a picaresque, *Clear: A Transparent Novel* (2005), after witnessing a stunt by famed American magician David Blaine. In 2003 Blaine encased himself in a plexiglass box suspended over the Thames River, a short distance from Barker's London apartment. Eating nothing during the 44 days that he lived in the box, Blaine was repeatedly taunted by a crowd of onlookers who tempted him with hamburger dangling from a radio-controlled helicopter.

That stunt serves as the centerpiece for Barker's novel: the main character, Adie, works in an office building next to Blaine's box, and the enterprising young man uses the spectacle as an opportunity to pick up women in the crowd. Meanwhile, the suffering of Adie's friend Aphra—who lies dying in a hospital bed, unable to swallow food—stands in stark contrast to Blaine's performance. "Despite her postmodern metafictional high jinks," Jean Nathan wrote for the *New York Times* (September

25, 2005), "Barker leaves us with an old-fashioned message: we're all trapped in boxes, and we can't be freed by the contents of our boxlike televisions, computers, iPods and cellphones, which only encourage us to 'hold life cheap.'"

Nicola Barker lives in Hackney, a borough of East London, with her long-term boyfriend (the music journalist Ben Thompson) and her two dogs. In January 2003 she was named one of Britain's best writers under the age of 40 by *Granta* magazine.

—K.D.

Suggested Reading: (London) *Evening Standard* p17 May 10, 2000, p30 May 12, 2000; (London) *Independent* p10 Feb. 6, 2000; (London) *Times* July 18, 1996, Feb. 12, 2000; (New York) *Newsday* B p14 Nov. 1, 1998; *New York Times* VII p7 Dec. 29, 2002; *Washington Post* T p6 Apr. 6, 2003

Selected Books: short stories—*Love Your Enemies*, 1993; *Heading Inland*, 1996; *The Three Button Trick, and Other Stories*, 1999; novels— *Reversed Forecast*, 1994; *Small Holdings*, 1995; *Wide Open*, 1998; *Five Miles from Outer Hope*, 2000; *Behindlings*, 2003; *Clear: A Transparent Novel*, 2005

© Giovanni Photography 2001/Courtesy of Houghton Mifflin

Barth, John

May 27, 1930– Novelist; short-story writer; essayist

John Barth is considered a leading practitioner, along with such writers as William Gass and Robert Coover, of the postmodern literary style known as metafiction, which places as much emphasis on exposing the artifice of story-writing as on the telling of the story itself. "Good art in any medium," Barth told Patrick T. Reardon for the *Chicago Tribune* (January 2, 2006), "is seldom simply but nearly always also about itself. My stories are seldom simply but nearly always also about Storytelling, for better or for worse. But love, pain, mortality, & such have more than walk-on

roles as well, I hope. The Teller who's aware that he's storytelling is as old as storytelling itself." Barth's many works of fiction—including *Giles Goat-Boy* (1966), *Lost in the Funhouse* (1968), *Letters* (1979), *Sabbatical: A Romance* (1982), and *Coming Soon!!!* (2001)—are noted for their complex, involuted style, a concern with mythic personalities and themes, and a flair for humor and linguistic hijinks—as well as for their ability to divide critics. To his adamant admirers he combines daring originality with a deft sense of parody; to his detractors his predilication for self-reflexive narratives results in novels lacking genuine characters and psychological insight. Barth's stature has waned slightly since the 1960s and 1970s, when postmodernism was making waves, but his early books continue to be read by college literature students, and most critics concede that, as his influence on such well-known authors as David Foster Wallace and Dave Eggers suggests, he has had a significant impact on modern American letters.

John Simmons Barth was born in Cambridge, Maryland, on May 27, 1930 to John Jacob Barth, a candy-store owner, and Georgia (Simmons) Barth. He has a twin sister, Jill, and an older brother, William. In an interview with Mopsy Strange Kennedy for the *Washington Post* (September 2, 1967), Barth's father commented on his son's literary bent: "This talent must have come later. I didn't notice it when he was younger. He always liked stories, though—I like to tell stories myself. Funny stories." Barth's twin sister, Jill, recalled to Kennedy: "He's always been more serious than outgoing. . . . He got a lot of things without trying very hard at school." Of their father's influence she said: "If there is a thread it comes from him—no particular talent, but just creative ability passed along in some form." Barth's brother told the interviewer: "Looking back I'd never have expected him to be a writer. . . . I will say he always had a vivid, overactive imagination. . . . What amazes me is how he imagines so much when he's experienced so little. . . . He's a dreamer, and an iconoclast. In a way I don't understand him; he's a mystery to me."

Barth's first aspiration was to make music. In high school he played drums in the school band, and after graduation he enrolled at the Juilliard School of Music, in New York City, to study orchestration. Partly for financial reasons he left Juilliard after one term and transferred to Johns Hopkins University, in Baltimore, Maryland, as a journalism major. At Johns Hopkins he experienced what he has called his "love affair" with Scheherazade—the heroine storyteller of *The Book of One Thousand and One Nights* (also known as *The Thousand Nights and a Night* and *Arabian Nights*). "As an illiterate undergraduate," he recalled in an article for the *New York Herald Tribune* (September 26, 1965), "I worked off part of my tuition filing books in the Classics Library at Johns Hopkins, which included the stacks of the Oriental Seminary. One was permitted to get lost for hours in that splendiferous labyrinth and intoxicate, engorge oneself with story. Especially I became enamoured of the great talecycles and collections: Somadeva's *Ocean of Story* in ten huge volumes, [Sir Richard] Burton's *Thousand Nights and a Night* in twelve, the *Panchatantra*, the *Gesta Romanorum*, the *Novellini*, and the *Pent-Hept-* and *Decameron*. . . . Most of those spellbinding liars I have forgotten, but never Scheherazade."

In *The Book of One Thousand and One Nights*, Scheherazade, to prevent her jealous husband from executing her, tells him every night a new story that leaves him in suspense until the following day. "Though the tales [Scheherazade] tells are not my favorites, she remains my favorite teller," Barth explained in his *New York Herald Tribune* article. "Like a parable of [Franz] Kafka's or a great myth, the story of deflowered Scheherazade, yarning tirelessly through the dark hours to save her neck, corresponds to a number of things at once and flashes meaning from all its facets. For me its rich dark circumstances, mixing the subtle and the coarse, the comic and the grim, the realistic and the fantastic, the apocalyptic and the hopeful, figure, among other things, both the estate of the fictioner in general and the particular endeavors and aspirations of this one, at least, who can wish nothing better than to spin like that vizier's excellent daughter, through what nights remain to him, tales within tales, full-stored with 'description and discourse and rare traits and anecdotes and moral instances and reminiscences . . . proverbs and parables, chronicles and pleasantries, quips and jests, stories and . . . dialogues and histories and elegies and other verses . . .' until he and his scribblings are fetched low by the Destroyer of Delights." Other major formative influences on Barth were Kafka, James Joyce, and Thomas Mann. Barth received a bachelor's degree from Johns Hopkins, in 1951, and a master's degree, from the same institution, in 1952.

Barth began writing short stories while he was still a student. The idea for Barth's first novel, *The Floating Opera* (1956), was inspired by a showboat—a river steamer with a theater and actors on board—that used to ply the tidewater Maryland area when he was a child. "When I came across a photograph of that old show boat in 1954," he told John Enck for *Wisconsin Studies in Contemporary Literature* (Winter–Spring 1965), "I thought it would be a good idea to write a philosophical minstrel show. . . . I started to do it and it ended up being a novel instead." The narrator of *The Floating Opera* is Todd Andrews, a rakish tidewater lawyer with an absurdist philosophy of life. He plans to commit suicide out of existentialist boredom but changes his mind when he realizes that killing himself would be just as meaningless as any other action in his life. The novel ends with Andrews coming to terms with an existence bereft of absolutes: "A value is no less authentic . . . for its being relative. . . . These [relative values] at least we have, and if they are all we have, then in no way whatsoever are they inferior." Melvyn Bragg, writing for the London *Observer* (September 2, 1968), noted that the philosophizing was carried out with Barth's characteristic "intellectual agility, gossipy tone, [and] comic brio."

Barth's second novel, *The End of the Road*, was published in 1958. In it Jacob Horner, paralyzed by indecision about everything, is advised by his psychotherapist to seek a cure in role-playing. Accordingly, he becomes a teacher of prescriptive grammar at a Maryland teachers college, where he clashes with an opposite personality type, Joe Morgan, and seduces Morgan's wife, Rennie. The comedy of manners—in which psychiatric and academic jargon are parodied—ends tragically, with Rennie choking to death on her own vomit during an illegal abortion. Some critics found the book tasteless, but Talliaferro Boatwright asserted in the *New York Herald Tribune* (July 20, 1958): "Given his premise that we live in a world without standards, taste becomes a side issue, not to be considered. Whether or not his diagnosis of the plight of modern man, and his prognosis of his fate, are correct, he has stated them persuasively."

Barth moved away from realistic fiction with his third novel, *The Sot-Weed Factor* (1960). The story of a tobacco peddler named Ebenezer Cooke, his twin sister, and their tutor, it is set in the Restoration era and is written in the spirit and language of that period. "It is a huge sprawling book, filled with dry, rarefied quips," Douglas M. Davis wrote for the *National Observer* (February 15, 1965). "It parodies at once the grand costume novel, Elizabethan literature, Ph.D. theses, and mankind at large." Richard McLaughlin observed for the *Springfield Republican* (September 25, 1960) that "in spite of the wild vagaries . . . his book does have . . . a genuine seriousness at the bottom of its racy, comic adventures. . . . The fact that . . . Ebenezer has a none too easy time of it maintaining his virtue in an unvirtuous world rather points up the serious moral of this boisterously diverting farce."

For his fourth novel, *Giles Goat-Boy*, Barth reimagined the political poles of the Cold War world as two campuses: one ostensibly symbolizing the capitalist West and the other the communist East. Each campus is under the control of a monster computer. For the Informationalist New Tammany College, the computer is named WESCAC, and for the Student-Unionist Nikolay College, EASCAC. The computers are programmed to destroy one another on provocation. Upon that scene arrives Giles Goat-Boy, conceived by accident by the computer WESCAC and born mysteriously of a virgin. Rescued from automatic destruction in the computer's tape-lift by Max Spielman (apparently representing the Jewish side of the Judeo-Christian heritage), Giles is raised on the university goat farm. There, during mating season, he makes the painful discovery that he is not really a goat. That discovery, coupled with his mysterious origin, leads him to believe that he is a savior of mankind. Wearing a foul goatskin, the sexually aroused Giles goes to the West Campus to preach his Revised New Syllabus and prove his right to be Grand Tutor. At once guileless and lustful, he wanders through countless weird adventures and extraordinary trials, rejecting various philosophies and temptations on the way to his ultimate goal, which is to enter the computer WESCAC, change its programming, and thus bring the student body (mankind) to Redemption.

The publication of *Giles Goat-Boy* was a major literary event. The novel received long front-page reviews, was distributed by two book clubs, and became a best-seller. Its critical reception was nevertheless rather mixed. A few complained that the book, although inventive, lacked depth. Alfred Alvarez remarked for the London *Observer* (April 2, 1967): "The allegory is worked out down to the smallest expletive. . . . The figures are so rigorously symbolic that they can never be more than puppets, and the whole development is governed by the simple principle of exploring obsessively every logical possibility of every situation. . . . The result is . . . an intricate, academic game of logic-chopping. Even the wrought, archaic style has a pedantic ring." Webster Schott, writing for *Life* (August 12, 1966), opined: "*Giles Goat-Boy* is the novel with something to offend everyone. Barth distributes his hostility and nihilism with cold impartiality. His psychiatrists encourage sodomy. His moralists preach immorality. His pacifists want blood. Humanity is totally perverted. . . . The novel deteriorates into a game of matching Barth's inventions to their corresponding realities." Phyllis Grosskurth, writing for the Toronto *Globe and Mail* (September 3, 1966), praised the work: "Here is a novel of dazzling synthesis, embodying religion, myth, science, and politics, and narrated in the most literate, controlled prose since Joyce.

Any cavil on the part of a mere critic seems tawdry, if not downright impertinent."

As Barth's reputation grew so did the demand for him to give readings at universities and other intellectual centers. He became interested in the voice as a narrative instrument, and that interest reinforced his intention—based on his premise that the realistic novel had run its course—to affirm the artificial element in his art and "make the artifice part of [the] point." He began composing pieces specifically for voice and tape recorder and rendering them before his audiences. His short pieces for tape and live voice were included among the 14 stories, meditations, and parodies published in *Lost in the Funhouse*. "Many things can happen in John Barth's funhouse, but getting lost is not likely to be one of them," a reviewer for *Time* (September 27, 1968) commented. "Whenever the rubber spiders and indiscreetly aimed jets of air become too threatening, the lights suddenly flash on and Proprietor Barth himself ambles in and starts explaining the machinery. Those who take their funhouses seriously may grow confused and exasperated. But readers of *The Sot-Weed Factor* and *Giles Goat-Boy* are familiar with Barth's impulses toward farce, his intellectual mobility, shaggy doggerel, and merry nihilism. These people are apt to accept the clever gimmickry as one would a party favor. . . . Taken together, as Barth urges they should be, these fictions interreact to produce a series of constantly changing and enticing illusive forms. . . . Another bit of Barth cunning is to turn daily life into mythology while turning mythology into domestic comedy."

In 1972 Barth published *Chimera*, a volume of three interconnected novellas that offered retellings of the classical stories of Perseus, who slew Medusa; Bellerophon, who tamed the winged horse Pegasus; and Scheherazade. The book was the joint winner (with John Williams's *Augustus*) of the 1973 National Book Award for fiction. Barth did not publish another book of fiction until 1979, when his novel *Letters* appeared. That work is composed of seven letters, each representing a letter in the word "letters." Three of the seven fictional letters are authored by characters from Barth's earlier works, two are by descendants of characters, and one is by a character named John Barth. The novel received mixed reviews. Benjamin DeMott, for the *Atlantic Monthly* (November 1979), suggested: "While Barth's fascination with the technology of narrative is often wearing, it does stimulate brooding on the meaning, for contemporary life, of the decline of the storytelling craft. . . . [More important than] this is the scrupulousness with which the book's basic theme—call it the fiction of fiction—is explored. . . . Whether the novel as hitherto constituted is the proper setting for such instruction can be debated. So too can the wisdom of promoting complex epistemological fiction in a manner suggesting that a swell evening's reading lies ahead. . . . Yet despite all this, *Letters* remains worth wrestling with. It is by turns a brain-buster, a marathon, an exasperation, a frustration, a provocation, to earnest thought." Paul Gray, writing for *Time* (October 8, 1979), offered a negative assessment: "Barth seems to have taken pains to make his letter writers as unattractive as possible. . . . The chief virtue of the old epistolary novel was suspense; the tense was present, and the letter writers did not know what would happen once they put down their quills. Barth strips the form of any forward thrust. His interest is not in progress or advancement but in recapitulation. . . . It takes a major writer to commit a major blunder. What Barth publishes matters, in capital Letters. . . . As he talks on and on, piling analysis upon explanation, the audience slowly files out. If Joyce's *Ulysses* was the milestone of modernism, Barth's *Letters* may well be its tombstone."

In *Sabbatical: A Romance* Susan Seckler has decided she needs to come to a decision about her life; either she should return to teaching or have a child with her husband, Fenwick Turner, a former CIA operative who has recently written a scathing book about the intelligence agency. Married for seven years the couple decide to take the winter off to sail the Caribbean in their boat and reflect on their lives. Along the way they must also confront other issues they've been unwilling to deal with, including the disappearance of Fenwick's brother, who has vanished along with his partner in the CIA, and the brutal gang rape of Susan's sister by SAVAK, the internal-security agency for the Shah of Iran. In a review for the *Washington Post* (May 23, 1982), Charles Trueheart cheered: "Although the novel is no retrogression, stylistically or thematically, for Barth, it does represent those rudiments of storytelling Barth has been willing to sacrifice of late. He attends to characters and the illumination of their drama more scrupulously and straightforwardly than in anything he has written since his first pair of novels, *The Floating Opera* and *The End of the Road*. As a consequence, *Sabbatical* lodges itself firmly in our imaginations and memories—and it is a pleasure to read besides." For the *New York Times Book Review* (June 20, 1982), Michael Wood suggested that the novel "reads easily enough and persuasively makes the story seem to belong to its inhabitants. . . . But there is a flatness in the book that these likable characters cannot redeem. Partly this is the result of heavy-handedness that is felt everywhere." Wood added, "The problem is not that Barth fails to deliver grander meanings but that he looks so hard for them, so restlessly tries to convert a modest and engaging trip into a wind-filled portent."

Barth published his first nonfiction work of nonfiction, *The Friday Book*, in 1985. The title refers to the author's habit of writing fiction four days a week and devoting every Friday to such nonfiction work as essays, lectures, or addresses.

The Friday Book is a collection of those works and reveals a side of the author not previously seen in print. Walter Kendrick, for the *New York Times Book Review* (November 18, 1984), observed: "Mr. Barth's still-debatable standing in the literary tradition will be determined by his fiction, not the slight and sometimes scrappy pieces that make up [this work]. They portray him in a wide variety of moods, from the rather inflated rhapsody brought on by his beloved Chesapeake Bay to the painstakingly analytical approach he takes to his favorite book of all time, *The Arabian Nights*. They reveal little about his private life, but they have a consistent tone of warm personal enthusiasm that is often beguiling. They are not . . . the products of his closest attention or deepest engagement. Their value—not great, but not negligible—resides in the light they cast on the work to which Mr. Barth devotes the other four-fifths of his week." John R. Dunlap remarked in *America* (April 13, 1985): "If it is true that children are the toughest critics (because they stop reading whatever bores them), John Barth tends to make me, well, childlike. And since I did not expect much, I cannot say his first collection of nonfiction is a disappointment—although the duty of reading *The Friday Book* cover-to-cover was a tad painful. In most of his work, Barth seems to address an audience of flummoxed English professors like himself, of the hapless students of these English professors, and of with-it critics prone to the turgid ('Very likely, John Barth is the most brilliant American novelist now at work') and fascinated by the infantile."

Barth returned to two of his favorite themes—storytelling and the sea—with his next novel, *The Tidewater Tales* (1987). In it, the minimalist novelist Peter Sagamore and his wife, Katherine, have decided to take a two-week boat trip around Chesapeake Bay. In their boat, named Story, they tell each other stories and try to come to terms with some of their problems. Peter has been self-editing his writing so mercilessly that his pieces end up no more than a few words in length; Katherine, who has a master's degree in library science, is a "maximalist" whose epic oral histories are the center of her universe. Their two conflicting ideologies, however, don't pose nearly as much of a challenge as their debates on life. Though Katherine is in the late terms of her pregnancy, they question the purpose of having children, while at the same time being comically pursued by Katherine's father and her obstetrician. Along the way the couple encounter a variety of modern-day versions of literary characters, including Ulysses, Don Quixote, and Scheherazade. For *Library Journal* (June 15, 1987), Edward B. St. John proclaimed: "A strong addition to the Barth canon, *Tidewater Tales* is probably the only piece of experimental fiction that can double as summer beach reading." On the other hand, Jonathan Raban, for the *Times Literary Supplement* (August 19–25, 1988), was far more critical: "For a book which promises to be bottomless . . . The *Tidewater Tales,* in parts at least, is disconcertingly shallow and banal. . . . It is an exasperating book. It is hugely self-indulgent (with Barth working the titles of his own earlier novels, like the sot-weed factor and the floating opera, into the text in hide-and-seek lower case). . . . [But] *The Tidewater Tales* seems mysteriously to improve after one's finished reading it. In retrospect, you can wander around the text, taking in its bizarre juxtapositions and narrative tricks at a glance."

Maintaining the sailing theme Barth published *The Last Voyage of Somebody the Sailor* (1991). While taking a cruise that traced the voyages of Sinbad the Sailor, the popular journalist Simon Behler finds himself washed overboard and rescued by contemporaries of the real Sinbad. Tossed back in time, Simon struggles to come to terms with his new situation by regaling his fellow sailors with tales of his adventures living as a boy in Maryland, falling in love, and gaining early success as a writer. Critics offered slight praise for the novel. "Though I have been interested in, or entertained by, many passages in [Barth's] work, have marveled at others, and have been bored or exasperated by still more, I have never been moved by his fiction, or been captured by it for a moment," Robert Towers wrote for the *New York Review of Books* (April 25, 1991). "He seems unable to give his characters a deeply grounded or significant inner life." Jonathan Raban, for the *New York Times Book Review* (February 3, 1991), noted: "On any page, you can find at least one act of verbal contortionism to applaud. Yet the overall effect after several hundred pages is jocose, long-winded and arbitrary. . . . Behler's wartime boyhood is the one true novelty in the book, and it makes his adventures in the world and style of [Sir Richard] Burton seem pallid by comparison."

With *Once upon a Time* (1994), Barth again mined the theme of sailing as a representation of his characters' journeys through life, though this time the protagonist was based on Barth himself. Presented as a novel in the form of a memoir, *Once upon a Time* describes a middle-aged writer and his wife sailing into a time warp, known as the "Chesapeake Triangle," where they recall his development as a writer, with a particular emphasis on his early novels. The book received mostly favorable reviews. R. H. W. Dillard, for the *New York Times Book Review* (July 3, 1994), noted: "[This work] is an appropriately complicated texture of riffs and motifs, reflexive images and echoes from [the author's] other books. But while it tinkers with time and flouts the very possibility of order with the inventive comic skills of one of Mr. Barth's favorite authors, Laurence Sterne, it manages at the same time to impose a symmetrical order every bit as contrived and pleasing as any of those of another of his 18th-century favorites, Henry Fielding. *Once Upon a Time* is, then, its own complex complete self, but it is also the satisfying last chapter and tying up of a much larger 12-volume work, the remarkable and altogether noteworthy opera and virtual voyages of John Barth." Wilfrid Mellers wrote for the *Times Literary Supplement* (November 25, 1994): "The story of *Once Upon a Time* enacts the basic myth of the eternal return, involving a quest and a perilous journey: from a mysterious birth, initiation, exile, confrontation with demons of sundry sorts, to a return by way of death and transfiguration. Such patterns of behaviour were outlined by key writers of the 1960s, such as Joseph Campbell, Northrop Frye and Marshall McLuhan, all of whom play vicarious roles in this book. But it is not an anthropological, let alone a theological, tract, and what matters is the identity it achieves between the present reality of narration and its putative, sometimes contradictory meanings. . . . Barth started the book in the year devoted to the (sometimes denunciatory) celebration of Columbus's discovery of the New World; and he has produced a 'memoir' which recreates not only himself, but also a world."

The plot of *Coming Soon!!!* centers around a competition between an aging novelist, known as Novelist Emeritus (N. E.), and his protégé, Johns Hopkins Johnson, known as Aspiring Novelist (A. N.). Believing the print novel to be dead, A. N. argues that cyberspace can create a better storytelling medium through hypertext. A wager is made: the older author begins to write a new print novel while the student begins work on a hypertext version, each racing the other to see who finishes first. Their combined work is presented in *Coming Soon!!!,* which contains representations of a Web site, clickable icons, and underlined hypertext links. For the London *Guardian* (March 20, 2002, on-line), Sarah Churchwell called Barth's latest "a meditation on the fear of endings and the simultaneous drive towards them, confronting and mocking Barth's fears about the death of the novel; the end of his 'potency', both artistic and sexual; the end of his career; and the end of his life. . . . At his finest Barth balances his sportive self-consciousness with a lyrical recognition of our unconscious desires and fears. His virtuosic brilliance remains, but the barrages of jokes about laughing in the face of death in *Coming Soon!!!* ultimately seem as frantic—and unconvincing—as all those exclamation marks." Steven More for the *Washington Post Book World* (November 25, 2001) proclaimed: "Barth is back in full metafictional finery, sporting all the bells and whistles of postmodernism like boutonnieres, the three exclamation points in the title announcing that he intends to go out with a bang. For he implies this might be his last novel, and while that is grievous news to those of us who consider him one of the greatest novelists of our time, it is bracing to have this final display of his matchless power."

With *Where Three Roads Meet* (2005), Barth returned to the intersecting novella form used for *Chimera.* The title (sometimes rendered as *Where*

3 Roads Meet) is both a reference to the place where Oedipus unknowingly killed his father in Sophocles' tragedy *Oedipus Rex* and a future novella collection of a character in the first of the book's three novellas, "Tell Me"—only one example of the book's seemingly countless metafictional twists. Brent Bowles, for the *Virginian-Pilot* (December 18, 2005), wrote that the book's "delighting puzzle . . . is how Barth manages to celebrate and parody the beauty and variability of language. He merrily lampoons writers who have retold the same story in guises both pedantic and esoteric." Barth's interest in language, Bowles argued, means that the book "will demand a greater focus and determination than do most contemporary novels. Barth does not stop for stragglers. But the trip to this narrative confluence, however taxing, is a trek worth its weight in words." On the other hand, Deborah Friedell, writing for the *New York Times* (December 25, 2005), found the book stale: "Indeed, those who have read even a small amount of Barth's previous outpourings will recognize little that is innovative in these three novellas (which one character defines as stories that are 'too long to sell to a magazine and too short to sell to a book publisher'). The settings and themes are familiar Barth territory: Greek myth, the university, the central metaphor of sperm bravely heading toward ovum." Though she found "much here to admire" in Barth's intelligent language and humor, Friedell remarked that "his self-indulgence becomes overweening, with sentences glutted with bad puns, French bons mots and self-references. The prose often seems in love with its own sophistication, a bit of a bully."

In addition to the works cited above, Barth is the author of another collection of nonfiction, *Further Fridays: Essays, Lectures, and Other Nonfiction, 1984–1994* (1997), and two additional collections of short fiction, *On with the Story* (1996) and *The Book of Ten Nights and a Night* (2004). Barth has also been an influential teacher, beginning his career at Pennsylvania State University, in State College, from 1953 to 1965, before becoming a professor of English at the State University of New York, in Buffalo, from 1965 to 1973. In 1973 he returned to his alma mater, Johns Hopkins University, to teach creative writing, and 19 years later the university made him an emeritus professor; he only retired completely from teaching in 1995. In 1998 he received a lifetime achievement award from the Lannan Foundation.

John Barth and Harriette Anne Strickland were married on January 11, 1950. They had three children—Christine, John, and Daniel—before divorcing, in 1969. Barth married Shelly I. Rosenberg on December 27, 1970. After years of living in Baltimore, he and Shelly now split their time between Chestertown, Maryland, and Bonita Springs, Florida.

—C.M.

Suggested Reading: *America* p309 Apr. 13, 1985; *Atlantic Monthly* p89 Nov. 1979; *Chicago Tribune* Tempo p1 Jan. 2, 2006; *Horizon* p36+ Jan. 1963; *Library Journal* p82 June 15, 1987; *Life* p8 Oct. 18, 1968; (London) *Guardian* (online) Mar. 10, 2002; *New York Review of Books* p46 Apr. 25, 1991; *New York Times Book Review* p22 Aug. 7, 1966, p1 June 20, 1982, p16 Nov. 18, 1984, p3 Feb. 3, 1991, p13 July 3, 1994, p15 Dec. 25, 2005; *Time* p109 Mar. 17, 1967, Oct. 8, 1979; *Times Literary Supplement* p901 Aug. 19–25, 1988, p21 Nov. 25, 1994; *Virginian-Pilot* E p3 Dec. 18, 2005; *Washington Post Book World* p1 May 23, 1982, p6 Nov. 25, 2001; *Wisconsin Studies in Contemporary Literature* p3+ Winter–Spring 1965

Selected Books: fiction—*The Floating Opera*, 1956; *The End of the Road*, 1958; *The Sot-Weed Factor*, 1960; *Giles Goat-Boy*, 1966; *Lost in the Funhouse*, 1968; *Chimera*, 1972; *Letters;* 1979, *Sabbatical: A Romance*, 1982; *The Tidewater Tales*, 1987; *Floating Opera and the End of the Road*, 1988; *The Last Voyage of Somebody the Sailor*, 1991; *Once upon a Time*, 1994; *On with the Story*, 1996; *Coming Soon!!!*, 2001; *The Book of Ten Nights and a Night*, 2004; *Where Three Roads Meet*, 2005; nonfiction—*The Friday Book*, 1985; *Further Fridays: Essays, Lectures, and Other Nonfiction, 1984–1994*, 1997

Baruth, Philip E.

1962 (?)– Novelist; radio commentator

Philip E. Baruth is best known for his novel *The X President* (2003), a mixture of political satire and science-fiction audacity; in the year 2055, a time when the U.S. is reeling from home-grown terrorism and facing an imminent invasion from hostile foreign nations, a government plot is hatched to send a few select operatives back in time to prevent a former president, who served in the 1990s and is identified only as BC, from making certain decisions that set America on its current ill-fated course. (In interviews Baruth has conceded that BC is modeled on President Bill Clinton.) Baruth, a professor of English at the University of Vermont, in Burlington, is also a regular contributor to Vermont Public Radio.

Philip Edward Baruth was born in about 1962. He graduated from Brown University, in Providence, Rhode Island, with a bachelor's degree, in 1984, and continued his studies at the University of California, at Irvine, receiving his Ph.D. in English, in 1993. Baruth was subsequently appointed to the faculty of the University of Vermont, where he remains. His academic research deals primarily with Restoration and 18th-century drama as well as autobiography;

Philip E. Baruth

Baruth also teaches courses in critical theory and creative writing. In addition to his academic work, Baruth is a longtime contributor to Vermont Public Radio (VPR); he authors and presents two three-minute commentaries a month, mostly about urban life in Vermont. He spends a considerable amount of time on the pieces, as he explained to Sally Pollak for the *Burlington Free Press* (May 27, 2002): "I've never in my life had this kind of audience." He added, "There are a huge number of people all around who give you feedback immediately. It's not something that's just going to find a knothole and drop in. It's an active part of people's lives. With that kind of attention, comes more responsibility." Baruth also worked on a series for VPR entitled *Camel's Hump Radio*, which featured local notables reading from their favorite children's books.

Baruth's little-noted debut novel, *The Millennium Shows* (1994), grew out of a short story he published in the *Denver Quarterly* in the early 1990s called "I Am These Dead," which was nominated for a Pushcart Prize. The book chronicles the adventures of a protagonist named Story, a self-professed deadhead—the name for devoted fans of the psychedelic-rock band the Grateful Dead. Story makes his way through the counterculture world of tie-dye, drugs, and parking-lot bazaars, from the 1960s through the 1990s on his way to a show on New Year's Eve of 1999. The book's publication was a proud moment for Baruth, as he explained in an on-line chat for the SCI FI Web site: "I remember . . . the first time I saw my book stacked in a bookstore window. I bought a camera. I have the photo."

In 1998 Baruth published *The Dream of the White Village*, a collection of 13 stories set in Burlington, Vermont. Featuring such characters as a Taiwanese lesbian waitress, an arsonist who burned down an AIDS outreach center, the racist son of a corrupt police officer, and a Native American drifter furious at the government's treatment of his people, the book seeks to show that Burlington, which is a largely Caucasian, wealthy, and liberal community—the "White Village" of the novel's title—conceals beneath it's idyllic appearance a seething tempest of ethnic, racial, class, and generational tensions. A critic for *Publishers Weekly* (June 1, 1998) observed, "Baruth's gritty collection is a dogged, if rather obvious, unmasking of white middle-class hypocrisy and of the racism planted deep in America's soul." The critic concluded: "Although [Baruth's] Burlington lacks the compelling immediacy of, say, William Kennedy's Albany, N.Y., his disquieting, timely novel transcends regional appeal."

For *Introducing Charlotte Charke: Actress, Author, Enigma* (1998), Baruth compiled and edited a selection of scholarly articles examining the life of the controversial 18th-century actress. Charke, the daughter of the renowned English playwright Colley Cibber, shocked British society with her unconventional ways, which included cohabiting with another woman and subverting established gender roles by, for example, cross-dressing both onstage and off. Charke—who was commonly known as Mr. Charles Brown—was also a novelist and writer; she published a scandalous autobiography, which Baruth discusses in his introductory chapter. Other contributors to the volume include Jean Marsden, Sidonie Smith, Kristina Straub, and Felicity A. Nussbaum.

In 2002 Baruth teamed up with fellow VPR contributor Joe Citro to edit *Vermont Air: The Best of the Vermont Public Radio Commentaries*. "It's a kind of all-encompassing free-for-all," Citro explained to Pollak. "It looks at a whole spectrum of topics that are rooted in Vermont." The editors asked the regular VPR commentators to compile a list of their five favorite commentaries and then chose three from each contributor. They focused on pieces that would translate well to print, as Baruth told Pollak: "One of the things that makes the series [of VPR on-air commentaries] so great is the intimacy of somebody speaking to you in your car or kitchen, and that gets lost." But, Baruth added, with a print publication "we gained something: People are always saying, 'I caught the last 40 seconds of your piece.' Now they can get it all."

The X President begins with several pages of explanatory background material. In 2055, BC, now 109 years old, is withered in body but passionate in spirit; he feels guilty, moreover, about the damaging effects of two key decisions he made more than half a century earlier, when he was president: first, he expanded the North

Atlantic Treaty Organization (NATO), which prompted the military alliance of Russia, China, and India; second, he launched a major anti-tobacco campaign that forced Big Tobacco to exploit foreign markets. The combination of the these moves has produced an interminable, brutal conflict known as the Cigarette Wars. With the U.S. about to be invaded, the government has concocted a plan to fix the present by revising the past: two agents, code-named George Stephanopoulous and James Carville, will travel back in time to both the 1960s and the 1990s in an attempt to persuade BC, first as a teenager and later as the president, about the error of his ways. The agents enlist the expertise of Sal Hayden, a female historian writing BC's authorized biography; it is through Sal's eyes that the story unfolds.

"Cheerfully embracing the paradoxes inherent in time travel," Gerald Jonas observed for the *New York Times Book Review* (November 9, 2003), "*The X President* provides as good an explanation as any for the uncanny political instincts and against-all-odds success of one of the century's most engaging and enraging political figures." Jonas added, "Baruth's portraits of young BC and very old BC are touching, even loving caricatures, warts, wens and all." For the *Washington Post Book World* (December 8, 2003), Patrick Anderson described *The X President* as an "ingenious, often hilarious novel," noting, "If you can handle a fanciful plot and an onslaught of irreverence, you'll devour it the way the young BC did his first Big Mac." A critic for *Publishers Weekly* (September 29, 2003) offered measured praise: "Baruth's facility for leaking and withholding information helps sustain interest, although the story is almost too neat at times. A disappointing ending mars this interesting blend of satire and sci-fi."

In an interview posted on the Random House Web site, Baruth cited two books in particular as major influences on the writing of *The X President*: *First in His Class*, a Clinton biography by David Maraniss, and Neal Stephenson's cyberpunk novel *Snow Crash*. The former, Baruth explained, "keeps the focus on the young Clinton, the formative events, the weird combinations of talent and upbringing and social change that lands him in the White House." The latter "rolls like a freight train, short cliffhanger chapters, never letting up, even as it flashes by enticing little bits of future history and an impressive amount of information about computers, language, viruses and ancient Sumerian culture. . . . I wanted the narrative [in *The X President*] to pump along, never letting up, even as fairly detailed political scenarios rolled past." When asked what prompted him to focus on Clinton, Baruth explained: "The first three presidential elections I voted in, I was on the losing side. And life on the losing side during the Reagan/Bush years was not fun. Then, in 1992, I voted for a winner. I remember being at a party on election night with a bunch of other people who'd never voted for a winner, and we didn't even know

what to do when Clinton went over the top. We had had no practice with champagne bottles, for instance. A cork? What the heck is that? But one thing I did do was to begin reading voraciously about Clinton, trying to figure out what made him different, what made him tick. I think I've read probably a hundred books on the guy, at this point. At a certain point, you have to do something with all of that information."

Despite his success as an author, Baruth explained in his chat for the SCI FI Web site that his students' achievements give him more satisfaction than his own: "I teach writers here at [the] University of Vermont all the time. The biggest rush was when one of *them* published."

—P.B.M.

Suggested Reading: *Burlington Free Press* D p1 May 27, 2002; *New York Times Book Review* p26 Nov. 9, 2003; *Publishers Weekly* p42 Sep. 29, 2003; Random House Web site; SCI FI Web site; University of Illinois Press Web site; University of Vermont Web site; *Washington Post Book World* C p2 Dec. 8, 2003

Selected Books: *The Millennium Shows*, 1994; *The Dream of the White Village*, 1998; *The X President*, 2003; as editor—*Introducing Charlottte Charke: Actress, Author, Enigma*, 1998; *Fresh Air: The Best of the Vermont Public Radio Commentaries* (with Joe Citro), 2002

Bauman, Beth Ann

1964– Short-story writer

"If you're compelled to write something, and you feel it's something you have to do, I think you have to honor it. Because truthfully, the world really doesn't care if you write your book or not," Beth Ann Bauman, the author of *Beautiful Girls* (2003), told Leslie Koren for the North Jersey Web site (March 30, 2003). Bauman, it might be said, owes her life to this compulsion to write: for more than a year, up until late August 2001, she did temporary work for Cantor-Fitzgerald in the World Trade Center, refusing several of the firm's offers of full-time employment in order to concentrate more fully on her writing. Consequently, she narrowly avoided losing her life during the terrorist attacks of September 11, 2001. Bauman's brush with tragedy inspired her to complete *Beautiful Girls*, her well-received short-story collection.

Born in 1964, Beth Ann Bauman grew up in Metuchen, New Jersey. Her father was a police officer and her mother, a secretary. Baumann began to consider becoming a professional writer when she took part in a writers' workshop at Richard Stockton College, located in southern New

Courtesy of MacAdam/Cage

Beth Ann Bauman

Jersey, and a year after she graduated, she entered the M.F.A. program at Brooklyn College. Unhappy with this program, she transferred to the University of Arizona, from which she received an M.F.A., in 1992. Bauman then returned to the east coast, settling in New York, where she hoped to write a novel, and financed her writing by taking various temporary jobs. Recalling this period, which lasted much longer than she—or her professors in Arizona, for that matter—thought would last, she told Joanna Smith Rakoff for the *New York Times* (February 16, 2003), "I'm so consumed by this, by writing stories, by trying to arrive somewhere as a writer. Sometimes, when I look back on everything, on how long it took me to get where I am, I'm just overwhelmed."

While she had published stories in several literary journals and made some contacts in the literary world, Bauman didn't feel that she had the material for a book until 2000; that year she sent a collection of short stories to the agent Tina Bennett, whom she had met in the mid-1990s. Not expecting Bennett to be interested in the book but hoping she might know someone who would be, Bauman was surprised by Bennett's response to the collection. Bennett would represent her, if she agreed to replace two of the stories with new ones. For the next year Bauman fussed over the new stories but only managed to get around to finishing them late in 2001, in the aftermath of the terrorist attacks on New York City. With the collection complete in December, Bennett began trying to sell the book, and while editors at publishing houses were impressed by the stories, they were unwilling to take a risk on a collection by an unknown writer. Most short-story collections sell a few thousand copies at most, after all.

Finally, in August 2002, MacAdam/Cage, an independent publisher known for championing new writers, accepted the manuscript; *Beautiful Girls* appeared the following year and was well received by critics. The stories, which have a strong New Jersey flavor, are "mainly about adolescent and young women who are struggling with their identities and trying to cope in dysfunctional relationships with parents and lovers," as Koren wrote. Kevin Sampsell praised the work in a review for the Powell's Books Web site (August 16, 2003), remarking, "[Bauman's] voice is cool, her tone is smart, and her storytelling vibrates on the page like the real thing." Heller McAlpin, writing for New York *Newsday* (March 23, 2003), observed, "There is nothing flip or charming about the sad, spare tales in this debut collection. Bauman depicts an inverted world in which children often are more responsible than their dysfunctional parents. . . . *Beautiful Girls* features oddly touching moments, although Bauman skirts the sentimental with her sharply distinctive characters. A tendency toward willful weirdness creates some situations that strain credulity, as when the mild divorcee in [the story] 'Safeway' pelts a stranger with yams. But Bauman's stories remind us that girls can be beautiful not just for their physical attributes, but for their fighting spirits." Dan Kaufman, writing for the *New York Times* (May 4, 2003), found less to praise. Noting that the stories focus "on middle-class girls and women struggling with loneliness, resentment, sexual frustration and grief," he went on to complain: "To compensate for the dullness of the milieu, Bauman frequently tries to shock us: in one story, a father's mistress calls his 8-year-old daughter and tells the girl she's sleeping with her dad; in another, an impotent married police officer seduces a baby sitter. But mostly these episodes make you feel Bauman is trying too hard."

Beth Ann Baumann lives in New York City. She currently has no writing projects in the works, having decided to take a break following the completion of her short-story collection. She continues to take temporary jobs but hopes that paperback sales of *Beautiful Girls* will provide the financial security necessary for her to concentrate on writing full time.

—P.B.M./A.R.

Suggested Reading: MacAdam/Cage Publishing Web site; *New York Times* XIV p1 Feb. 16, 2003, p24 May 4, 2003; North Jersey Web site Mar. 30, 2003

Selected Books: *Beautiful Girls*, 2003

Beaton, Roderick

*Sep. 29, 1951– Literary critic; novelist;
biographer*

Ever since childhood and throughout his
prestigious career, the British scholar Roderick
Beaton has been captivated by the language and
literature of Greece: as a literary critic, he has
occupied a prominent position in the academic
explication of Modern Greek literature, publishing
Folk Poetry of Modern Greece (1980) and *An
Introduction to Modern Greek Literature* (1994). In
addition, his first novel, *Ariadne's Children*
(1995), draws on ancient Greek heritage, as well as
on the juxtaposition of sunlight and shadow that
characterizes Greek literature. Most recently, he
wrote *George Seferis: Waiting for the Angel* (2003),
the first full-length biography of the Nobel Prize–
winning Greek poet.

Roderick Beaton wrote the following for *World
Authors 2000–2005*:

"I was born and brought up in Edinburgh,
Scotland. I think what had the greatest effect on me
during my schooldays was the month each
summer when my parents, on a modest income,
used to take their three young sons camping round
Europe. I quickly acquired the taste for the
opposite end of Europe from my own;
temperamentally I feel I belong at least as much to
the Mediterranean as to Britain.

"The defining moment came in 1965, when I
was just 13. The destination that year was Greece;
and as it happened, I was about to start learning
ancient Greek at school. After that, I never looked
back. It was a close-run thing whether I would
study Classics or English at university; when the
time came to go to Cambridge, English literature
was the eventual choice. But I took classes in
modern Greek while I was there, and was lucky
enough to be accepted to study for a PhD in modern
Greek—and to spend three of the next four years in
Greece, based in Athens.

"I was there during the last year of the infamous
rule of the 'Colonels' (1967–74); some of the
brutality of that regime I saw at first hand. The
experience of living under a military dictatorship,
even as a privileged outsider, is something that
never leaves you. The transition to civilian rule in
1974 was a heady, exciting time; I've never before
or since been so wholly involved in public events.

"But it wasn't only politics in those years: my
thesis was on Greek folk poetry, an art form with
a long tradition and highly esteemed by Greeks. In
the course of my work I travelled all over Greece,
and to Cyprus, with a tape recorder. I learned at
first hand how traditional singer-poets in remote
villages still performed. I have always loved music,
played violin and viola in orchestras at school and
university; now I began to learn a completely
different musical language. Greek music belongs
more to the Middle East than to the west; it's a
music of improvisation and of haunting melodies

that take some getting used to. I immersed myself
in this music, as well as in the language and the
poetry, and even learned to play several stringed
instruments. For many years after I came back to
Britain, a group of university friends kept up a
band, and played traditional Greek music at the
most unlikely of venues: academic conferences!

"Greece, Greek history, the Greek language and
its heritage have always been at the heart of my
writing. My first published book was an academic
one, *Folk Poetry of Modern Greece*, based on my
doctoral thesis. Since 1977 I have worked in
universities, first at Birmingham, then at King's
College, part of the federal University of London.
For nine years from 1988, when I was appointed to
the Koraes Chair of Modern Greek and Byzantine
History, Language and Literature, I was head of the
Department of Byzantine and Modern Greek
Studies. This is a specialist department; its
students are relatively few. But during that time it
was possible to build it up considerably, both in
student numbers and staff, and it remains a
privilege to work among a small group of dedicated
people who share my passion for the Hellenic
world.

"As well as academic books and articles, I have
published fiction, a biography, translations, and in
my younger days a small amount of poetry. My first
novel, *Ariadne's Children*, was published in
Britain in 1995 (1996 in the US) and was translated
into Greek and Danish. It tells the story of three
generations of English archaeologists in Crete, in a
way turning the real story of the discovery of
Minoan civilisation into a parable of the 20th
century (the story starts with assassination of the
archduke Ferdinand in Sarajevo in 1914, and ends
with the start of the Bosnian civil war in the same
city in 1992). I believe very much in place and
atmosphere in fiction.

"My biography of the Greek poet and diplomat
George Seferis was published in autumn 2003 in
Britain and the U.S. (by Yale University Press);
when it came out in Greek translation just before
Christmas 2003 it became a surprise bestseller.
Seferis was the first Greek to win a Nobel Prize (for
Literature in 1963); the story of his life makes an
eventful narrative which draws in much of Greek
history during the first 70 years of the last century.

"As an academic I try to make sense of the
world, to make connections and find patterns. But
I've always believed that the best way in which our
species has always tried to do these things is by
telling stories. (I'm greatly struck by the fact, for
instance, that one of the most successful attempts
to explain modern cosmology to the lay reader, by
Stephen Hawking, is entitled *A Brief History of
Time*). History (good history), tells a story; so does
biography, and so, of course, does fiction. It may
not always, and certainly not only, be about the
Greek world, but I like to think I have a good many
stories left to tell."

Courtesy of Roderick Beaton

Roderick Beaton

Roderick Beaton was born in Edinburgh, Scotland, on September 29, 1951. There he received his secondary education at George Watson's College. After earning his bachelor's degree in English from Peterhouse College at the University of Cambridge, in England, he earned a doctorate in Modern Greek studies from the same institution, in 1976. He then served as the Ouranis Foundation fellow in Modern Greek language and literature at the University of Birmingham. In 1981 he became a lecturer at King's College London at the University of London, and in 1988 he was promoted to his current post, Koraes Professor of Modern Greek and Byzantine History, Language and Literature.

While Beaton's first two books, F*olk Poetry of Modern Greece* and T*he Medieval Greek Romance* (1989), were intended for an academic audience, his next book, A*n Introduction to Modern Greek Literature* (1994), was intended for general audiences as well as academic specialists. Vassilis Lambropoulos argued, however, in an article for W*orld Literature in Review* (Winter 1995), that the book would be of little interest to scholars due to Beaton's refusal to address pressing epistemological issues, such as those raised by feminists. "All the established figures in each genre remain on their pedestals unchallenged," Lambropoulos wrote. "The book has no fresh appraisals of its own to make—it simply reiterates and organizes the dominant ones. Expect to find no contestations or revisions here, only a confirmation of what has been already deemed canonical." Nonetheless, M. Kotzamanidou, writing for C*hoice* (April 1995), did not feel that Beaton's adherence to the canon detracted from the

book: "Though the author follows the established canon of modern Greek letters, the contents of the entire work are interesting because he also reviews the changes in critical attitudes toward specific writers and/or works, as well as changes within the canon itself. Beaton does not avoid expressing a personal opinion in regard to the material he discusses, a refreshing change from the pseudo-objective stance of most literary histories." A*n Introduction to Modern Greek Literature* won the Anglo-Hellenic League's 1995 Runciman Award.

In 1995 Beaton tried his hand at fiction with *Ariadne's Children*, a family saga centered around the excavation of an ancient Greek palace. Dan Robertson, a dissatisfied employee at the Institute of Chronometry, must dig through family records in order to prove that his father and grandfather did not commit any improprieties while digging at a site known as Ariadne's Summer Palace and, in the process, struggles to come to terms with his emotional legacy as well. "The destructive impulse that laps the edges of civilization haunts Roderick Beaton's first novel," Linda Barrett Osborne wrote for the N*ew York Times Book Review* (June 23 1996). "[It] is the engaging story of the Robertsons, but it is also a subtle inspection of the differing ambitions and values of succeeding generations. Lionel, Daniel and Dan each find in Minoan culture—supposedly dedicated to beauty and peace, but conveying hints of death and debasement—a mirror of their own sensibilities and the world around them."

Next Beaton turned to biography, with *George Seferis: Waiting for an Angel*. Alongside Constantine Cavafy, Seferis (1900–1971) is regarded as one of the greatest Greek poets of the 20th century. Beaton's biography, which was the first on Seferis to be published in any language, was described by Philip McDonagh, writing for the I*rish Times* (November 22, 2003), as "a comprehensive and ground-breaking study, scholarly yet accessible, well-written, and enlivened by juicy anecdotes." Characterizing Beaton's "summaries of the political and ideological developments in 20th-century Greece" as "models of concision, illuminating even to those who know the facts," a reviewer for the E*conomist* (November 20, 2003, on-line) noted that "at heart this book is the portrait of a man, and throughout the reader is conscious of the sensitivity and restraint with which Mr. Beaton treats his subject," who was known as a deeply private person. "Like Seferis," the reviewer concluded, Beaton "is aware that a mystery is not better revealed under a fierce light." Alan Marshall reached a similar conclusion in his review for the London D*aily Telegraph* (December 6, 2003): "Beaton consistently sheds light on the circumstances from which the poetry emerges, without encroaching on the mystery of it, and unlike some biographers, especially when presenting a poet who writes in another language, he never tries to foreground his role as mediator. He has built an invaluable bridge, and one best crossed with the *Complete Poems* to hand, which is how it should be."

In addition to writing fiction and nonfiction, Beaton has served as the editor or co-editor for the scholarly texts T*he Greek Novel, AD 1–1985* (1988), T*he Making of Byzantine History: Studies Dedicated to Donald M. Nicol* (1993), and D*igenes Akrites: New Approaches to Byzantine Heroic Poetry* (1993), and he has translated novels and poetry from Modern Greek to English. Beaton, married and the father of two grown children, lives in London.

—S.Y.

Suggested Reading: *Choice* p1,293 Apr. 1995; *Economist* (on-line) Nov. 20, 2003; *Irish Times* p60 Nov. 22, 2003; (London) *Daily Telegraph* p4 Dec. 6, 2003; *World Literature Today* p197+ Winter 1995

Selected Books: fiction—*Ariadne's Children*, 1995; nonfiction—*Folk Poetry of Modern Greece*, 1980; *The Medieval Greek Romance*, 1989; *An Introduction to Modern Greek Literature*, 1994; *George Seferis: Waiting for the Angel*, 2003; as editor—*The Greek Novel, A.D. 1–1985*, 1988; *Digenes Akrites: New Approaches to Byzantine Heroic Poetry* (with David Ricks), 1993; *The Making of Byzantine History: Studies Dedicated to Donald M. Nicol* (with Charlotte Roueche), 1993

Francois Durand/Getty Images

Beigbeder, Frédéric

(baig-beh-DEH, freh-
deh-REEK)

Sep. 21, 1965– Novelist

The French nightclub habitué and ubiquitous television presence Frédéric Beigbeder has received acclaim at home and in the Anglophone press for his dark, satirical fiction. Though his diatribe about the advertising industry, *£9.99* (2002), was not his first novel, it attracted more attention and better sales than his previous efforts—a result of the publicity he received when his employer, a reputable international advertising firm, fired him after the book's publication. Beigbeder then published the critically praised *Windows on the World* (2005), a recounting of the terrorist attacks of September 11, 2001 through the eyes of a fictional character trapped in the eponymous restaurant.

Frédéric Beigbeder was born in Neuilly-sur-Seine, one of the ritzier neighborhoods just outside Paris, France, on September 21, 1965. His father, Jean-Michel Beigbeder, was a corporate headhunter, and his mother, Christine de Chasteigner, was a literary translator. He attended the Collège Lycée Montaigne Paris, a well-regarded public school that also boasts such noteworthy alumni as the filmmaker René Clair and Michel Debré, the principal author of France's current constitution. Beigbeder also reportedly attended the Lycée Louis le Grand, which features an even more impressive list of alumni, including Jean-Paul Sartre, the Marquis de Sade, and Voltaire, among others. After completing his secondary education, he enrolled in L'Institut d'études politique de Paris, from which he earned a diploma in 1989. Beigbeder then accepted a position with the Paris branch of Young & Rubicam, one of the world's largest consumer advertising agencies.

Beigbeder published his first novel, *Mémoires d'un jeune homme dérange* (which translates as "memoirs of a deranged young man"), in 1990. Though this first novel has yet to be translated into English, the British branch of HarperCollins is slated to publish a compilation of his second and third novels—*Vacances dans le coma* (1994) and *L'amour dure trois ans* (1997)—under the title "Holiday in a Coma; and Love Lasts Three Years," in June 2007. His 1999 short-story collection, *Nouvelles sous ecstasy* (which translates as "tales on ecstasy"), has not been translated into English.

While working on these books and moonlighting as a literary critic on a prime-time television show, Beigbeder continued working at Young & Rubicam—that is, until the company fired him, shortly after the publication of *99 francs*, in 2000. The novel, which two years later was translated into English as *£9.99*, mercilessly satirizes the advertising industry and features a slew of thinly disguised agencies and clients from the real world. Though the cocaine-addicted, prostitute-loving protagonist, Octave Parango, claims at the opening of the book that he is writing his account in an attempt to get fired, Beigbeder was displeased when he lost his job and sued his employer for wrongful termination. The publicity from the incident, however, propelled *£9.99* to the top of the best-seller lists in France.

Though some critics in the U.K. thought the book was a brilliant satire, Jonathan Patrick, writing for *Scotland on Sunday* (June 23, 2002), felt that "Beigbeder obviously wants Octave to take his place alongside [Louis-Ferdinand] Celine's Bardamu in *Journey to the End of Night* and [Michel] Houellebecq's Bruno in *Atomised*, as a cynical, embittered, unsympathetic narrator who vomits his rage at consumer capitalism and shows how the pleasures it brings—sex, drugs, travel— are synthetic and illusory. But this is Celine Lite, Decaff Houellebecq." On the other hand, Georgia de Chamberet, writing for the London *Independent* (June 15, 2002), described *£9.99* as a "relentlessly funny diatribe against the advertising industry."

Beigbeder's next novel, *Windows on the World*, drew its name from the famed restaurant situated at the top of the north tower of the World Trade Center, which was destroyed in the September 11, 2001 terrorist attacks on New York City. The novel begins at 8:30 that fateful morning, shortly before Al Qaeda hijackers crash American Airlines Flight 11 into the tower, and ends at 10:29, when the towers collapse. The events of that morning are told through the eyes of Carthew Yorston, a fictional real estate agent from Texas who has finally brought his two young sons to the restaurant for a long-promised breakfast.

When it was first published in France, in 2003, *Windows on the World* debuted in second place on the best-seller list. It also won the prestigious Prix Interallié, despite having "two handicaps," Beigbeder told a reporter for the *National Post* (November 13, 2003)—"its success and its English title." The English translation—which was published in England in September 2004 and in the U.S. in March 2005—was slightly different from the original version. Beigbeder told the press, "There were, I felt, moments when it was starker and perhaps more likely to wound than I intended," according to a staff writer for *Publishers Weekly Reviews* (January 24, 2005). That same staff writer took little offense at the dark humor that remained in the English version: "Abundant doses of gallows humor at once add levity and underscore the drama. Yorston's overheard snatches of fatuous cell-phone conversations, for example, would be funny in another context, while the enforced exit of a cigar-smoking guest at Windows on the World 'thereby proves that a cigar

can save your life.' Though some readers may be put off by this novel's subject matter, Beigbeder invests his narrators with such profound humanity that the book is far more than a litany of catastrophe: it is, on all levels, a stunning read."

Josh Lacey, writing for the London *Guardian* (September 11, 2004), was not bothered by the liberties that Beigbeder took in re-creating real-life events but complained that the author did not take the story to its natural fruition: "Beigbeder is a smart, sarcastic writer who likes to shock; confronted by 9/11, he is not only cowed, but cowardly. When he comes to the climax of his novel—the deaths of his characters, the collapse of the north tower—he refuses to write about it." Lacey did enjoy, however, the even-numbered chapters, which featured Beigbeder's own ruminations on the terrorist attacks, "mingling polemic, confession and autobiography." The English edition of *Windows on the World* was awarded the 2005 Independent Foreign Fiction Prize, which Beigbeder shared with the book's translator, Frank Wynne.

In addition to writing novels, Beigbeder has contributed reviews and essays to numerous French periodicals, including *Lire*, *Paris Match*, *Elle*, and *Le Figaro*. During the 1990s he founded three magazines: *Genereux* in 1992, *Deluxe* in 1993 (some sources state 1994), and *NRV* in 1996. He has authored a nonfiction book on the world's most celebrated fashion doll, which was published in English as *Barbie* (1998). He is a regular contributor to the radio program *Masque et la Plume*.

Beigbeder lives in France. He is divorced and has one daughter, Chlöe.

—S.Y.

Suggested Reading: (London) *Guardian* p27 Sep. 11, 2004; (London) *Independent* F p32 June 15, 2002, F p24 Mar. 22, 2003; *New York Times* Sep. 3, 2003; *Scotland on Sunday* p5 June 23, 2002

Selected Books in English Translation: fiction— *£9.99*, 2002; *Windows on the World*, 2005; nonfiction—*Barbie*, 1998

Bender, Aimee

1969(?)– Short-story writer; novelist

Aimee Bender has made a name for herself as the author of quirky modern fairy tales, many of which feature young women in extremely unusual situations. She first received notice with her acclaimed short-story collection *The Girl in the Flammable Skirt* (1998), drawing praise for her imaginative characters and story lines. The collection was a New York Times Notable Book of the Year for 1998. In 2000 she published her first

Aimee Bender

novel, *An Invisible Sign of My Own*, which told the story of a girl willing to sacrifice all her joys in life in order to keep her father healthy. Her second collection of short stories, *Willful Creatures*, was released in 2005.

Aimee Bender was born in about 1969 and grew up in Santa Monica, California. As a child she enjoyed reading fairy tales, especially Hans Christian Andersen and the Brothers Grimm. "I liked Hans Christian Andersen because the tales were so dark and tragic," Bender told Larry Weissman in an interview for the on-line journal *Bold Type*. "My favorites were 'The Tinderbox' and 'The Steadfast Tin Soldier.'" By age seven Bender was writing her own stories. Two years later she tried writing a novel. "I had a big red folder with unicorn stickers on it—you know, very girlie—and a lengthy start of a novel about a unicorn and a fox," she told Dennis McLellan in an interview for the *Los Angeles Times* (September 9, 1998). "I wrote a lot. I really loved it." Her mother encouraged her writing, as well as her interest in music and dance. Bender's literary interests, however, temporarily dissipated during her years at Palisades High School. She didn't fit in—it was an "incredible surfer high school," she recalled to McLellan—but found an outlet for her creative energies by taking choir and drama classes.

Bender received her bachelor's degree in English from the University of California, at San Diego, in 1991. As an undergraduate she began to feel the need to write stories again. "I remember writing really weird stories—mothers wearing tutus on their heads—and getting a lot of encouragement for that," she told McLellan. But she began to feel that she should take writing more

seriously. When she attempted to write more traditional pieces, however, she didn't enjoy it as much.

After graduation she spent three years teaching elementary school in San Francisco, in a neighborhood populated predominantly by Russian immigrants. In fall of 1995 she entered the graduate program for creative writing at the University of California, at Irvine. There she was the only one out of 11 students writing short stories instead of a novel. For class she wrote both realistic and fanciful tales, but she found that her classmates had stronger responses to her more magical stories. A workshop teacher, Judith Grossman, described one of her stories—about a librarian coping with the death of her father by seducing men in a back room of the library—as moving towards surrealism and becoming more mythic.

"I hadn't thought of the word 'mythic,'" Bender told McLellan. "It was just like opening a door and gently giving me a little push, and then I sort of ran through the door! I felt so excited by that idea of myth." She followed her surrealist tendencies, writing stories that hovered just above the surface of reality. She sent one of them to the *Santa Monica Review*, the Santa Monica College literary journal, which later published the story in an anthology, *Absolute Disaster: Fiction from Los Angeles* (1997). An editor from Doubleday picked up a copy of the anthology at a book festival and read it on his return flight to New York. Impressed, he called Bender and offered her a contract.

Bender's first collection of stories, *The Girl in the Flammable Skirt*, was published by Doubleday in 1998. The stories in it explore many facets of the extraordinary. In "The Rememberer" a woman is confronted with a boyfriend who is regressing daily down the evolutionary scale; in "Drunken Mimi" a teenage mermaid hides her tail under long skirts and falls for the school imp; in "What You Left in the Ditch," a soldier's wife, distraught when her husband returns from the war without lips, resorts to making love with a young grocery clerk. In Bender's interview with Weissman, she acknowledged that physical deformities and sex were recurring themes in her writing, although not necessarily intentionally so: "My ideas just hit me, I've got to admit. For the stories, I would just think of a first line, and if it has some kind of pull to it, it will write me through the story. Often the first line does have something to do with either sex or deformity, it's about the body, really. Everything a human experiences happens on the body. . . . That's the place where pain happens, and love happens, all the good and bad things. It's just a resonant setting."

The Girl in the Flammable Skirt generally met with favorable reviews, though some critics expressed reservations about it. Lorin Stein, in a review for New York *Newsday* (July 26, 1998), cheered: "[The book] is an endearing, promising first collection of grotesquely romantic fairy tales. . . . [Bender] will beguile readers. Few first story collections are as accessible or inventive, or seriously funny, as hers." In *Entertainment Weekly* (July 10, 1998), Margot Mifflin remarked: "Some of Bender's forays into magical realism feel like collegiate exercises, while others, like her account of a woman whose lover evolves backward, are superbly imagined. And even though the fairy-tale format she too often employs is—one hopes—just a youthful affectation, Bender has hit the ground running with this debut." Stephanie Zacharek, in *Salon* magazine (July 24, 1998, on-line), had similar doubts: "Many of the stories in Aimee Bender's debut collection are wonderful in theory, and some of them are beautifully executed. . . . Bender's ear is undeniably musical. But she also has a weakness for spelling out too much of the obvious."

In 2000 Bender published her first novel, *An Invisible Sign of My Own*, which focused on the life of Mona Gray. On her 10th birthday, Mona's father tells her a story about a magical kingdom where everyone lives forever, but the king must ask one volunteer from each family to die to prevent overcrowding. When Mona's father becomes ill, she attempts to make sacrifices the way the inhabitants of that magical kingdom did, to the point that she removes herself from everything she enjoys, with the exception of math. Reviews of the novel were largely favorable. Verity Ludgate-Fraser wrote in the *Christian Science Monitor* (August 17, 2000): "Displaying the considerable gifts of a natural writer, Bender constantly draws us into Mona's distressed world with surprising humor and dazzling, original description. . . . I wish Bender could deliver herself in less depressing ways of both her clear writing ability and keen understanding of human nature. We expend too much energy dreading the horror that comes with so much unrelenting dysfunction." Bliss Broyard offered a similar opinion in a critique for the *New York Times Book Review* (August 20, 2000): "Bender's affection for numbers . . . suffuses [the book] with the authority of a novelist who has found her turf. Less convincing is the feeling between Mona and her father that led her to alter her life so dramatically. . . . Nevertheless, [the novel] has much to recommend it." Beth E. Anderson's review in *Library Journal* (May 15, 2000) was more complimentary: "Filled with terrific wit and lovely helpings of life's tougher truths, Bender's fairy tale fulfills the promise of her highly regarded collection of short stories, *The Girl in the Flammable Skirt*."

Rebecca Meyers, writing for *Time* (September 19, 2005), described Bender's second collection of modern fairy tales, *Willful Creatures*, as "whimsical and yet elegantly stark." The stories in this book, according to Joy Press of the *New York Times* (August 21, 2005), "alternate between absurd scenarios imbued with recognizable human pathos, and apparently ordinary tales pitched at an oblique angle that reveals their true strangeness."

Though Press goes on to complain that "too often, overbearing symbolism throws Bender's fragile concoctions out of whack, or she twists her plots too far," she lauded the author for her "chatty prose style" that "carries the reader effortlessly over the road bumps of implausibility." Christina Schwarz, writing for the *Atlantic Monthly* (October 2005), singled out the story "The Meeting" for particular praise but commented that in all the pieces in *Willful Creatures*, Bender "arranges words in unconventional combinations, uses rhyme, chops some sentences off at a single word—'Oven.' 'But.' 'Wet'—and lets others run on, all of which have the effect of giving her writing a life of its own, seemingly unfettered by a controlling author. But these techniques also call attention to the words, emphasizing the distance between language and the ideas it's meant to convey. Bender never pretends that stories capture the real world on the page; instead she creates her own world somewhere between the familiar and the absurd."

Aimee Bender's work has been published in *Harper's*, *GQ*, *LA Weekly*, the *Missouri Review*, *Granta*, *Faultline*, the *Colorado Review*, *Story*, the *North American Review*, and the *Paris Review*. She has also contributed stories to such fiction anthologies as *McSweeney's Mammoth Treasury of Thrilling Tales* (2003), *Lit Riffs* (2004), and *The Secret Society of Demolition Writers* (2005). In keeping with the conceit of *The Secret Society*, however, her contribution there is anonymous, forcing readers to guess which of the book's 12 stories she wrote.

Aimee Bender teaches creative writing and contemporary literature at the University of Southern California, in Los Angeles, and lives in West Hollywood. Discussing her affection for her neighborhood, Bender wrote for the *Los Angeles Times* (September 14, 2006): "Here, the houses and apartments are most charming to me because of how they all interact with one another. . . . The houses person-sized, the apartments person-sized: appealing but not big—two-bedroom houses, or duplexes with small backyards. Something feels in proportion on these blocks. Up above, in the Hollywood Hills, everything goes on steroids. Voluminous space. Enormous windows. Ceilings made for giants. A million rooms. Down here, most of the houses feel connected to the neighborhood at large. The prices are immodest, yes, but the houses themselves have a modesty to their shape and size."

—K.D.

Suggested Reading: *Atlantic Monthly* p124 Oct. 2005; *Bold Type* (on-line); *Christian Science Monitor* p16 Aug. 17, 2000; *Entertainment Weekly* p68 July 10, 1998; *Library Journal* p123 May 15, 2000; *Los Angeles Times* E p1 Sep. 9, 1998, F p3 Sep. 14, 2006; (New York) *Newsday* B p12 July 26, 1998; *New York Times Book Review* p19 Aug. 20, 2000, p20 Mar. 23, 2003; *Salon* (on-line) July 24, 1988

Selected Books: *The Girl in the Flammable Skirt*,
1998; *An Invisible Sign of My Own*, 2000; *Willful
Creatures*, 2005

Courtesy of Sandra Benítez

Benítez, Sandra

Mar. 26, 1941– Novelist

Sandra Benítez began writing at the age of 39 and
first found success with *A Place Where the Sea
Remembers* (1993), a novel set in a Mexican
village. Her next novels, *Bitter Grounds* (1997) and
The Weight of All Things (2001), trace a bloody 50-
year period in the history of El Salvador, starting
in 1932; in them, Benítez weaves the personal
stories of men and women into larger events,
making her characters, in the estimation of
reviewers, come vividly to life. She has since
published the novel *Night of the Radishes* (2004)
and the memoir *Bag Lady* (2006).

In 2004 Benítez submitted the following
statement, in both third person and first person, to
World Authors 2000–2005:

"Sandra Benítez has spent her life moving
between the Latin American culture of her Puerto
Rican mother and the Anglo-American culture of
her father. Benítez was born on March 26, 1941 in
Washington, D.C. She was one of a pair of identical
twins. Her sister, Susana, died only a month after
their birth. A year later, Benítez and her parents
moved to Mexico where Anita, another sister, was
born. Benítez's childhood was spent in Mexico and
El Salvador. When she thinks of those years, the
images that come to her are awash in the color
saffron—the Spanish language, the pervasive scent

of cedar and leather, the shimmering beat, the color
of the women in the household, the stories they
told, the lives they shared.

"In Latin America, Benítez learned that life is
frail and most always capricious, that people find
joy in the midst of unsurmountable obstacles, that
in the end, it is hope that saves us.

"When Benítez became a teenager, she was sent
to live for three years on her paternal grandparents'
farm in Northeastern Missouri. She went to high
school there. Back then, she was the first Latina the
town people had ever known. She pictures those
years in a pale blue light—the thin sheen the
setting sun cast on the snow banks, the color of her
father's eyes, the doleful bawl a cow makes when
it's lost its calf, the backbreaking work that is the
farmer's lot, the reticent way he conducts his life.

"In Missouri, Benítez learned that life is what
you make it, that satisfaction comes with a job well
done, that in the end, it is steadfastness that saves
us.

"Benítez received both an undergraduate degree
and a master's degree from Truman State
University, Kirksville, Missouri. Over the years she
has been an English, Spanish and literature teacher
at both the high school and university levels. She
has been a translator, and worked in the
international division of a major training
corporation. While there, she traveled extensively
throughout Latin America. Since 1980, she has
been a fiction writer and creative writing teacher.

"Benítez has two sons, Christopher and
Jonathon Title. She lives with her husband, Jim
Kondrick, in Edina, Minnesota.

"How I Came to Write:

"I came to writing late. I was 39 before I gathered
enough courage to begin. When I hear other writers
talk about writing, I'm amazed by those who say
they always knew they had to write. When I was
a girl, I never wished to do it. Being a writer was
something magical I never dreamed I could attain.
But while growing up, I frequently had a book in
my lap, and so I was linked, early on, to writing
and to the spell that stories cast.

"Over the years I didn't know a writing life was
lying in store for me. I had to live and grow before
I caught the faint call. Since heeding the call, I've
worked hard at being faithful to it.

"I've been a writer for 18 years, though it took
13 years to first get published. In that time, I had
to suppress the knowledge that mainstream
America often ignores the stories of 'the other
America,' 'la otra America.' In my heart were
stored the stories of my Latin American and
Midwestern heritage, of a childhood lived in
Mexico, El Salvador and Missouri. It was from that
core I chose to write and not from what seemed
marketable. For 13 years, until I was finally
published, I persevered, despite the setback of a
host of rejections.

"In the end, I've learned these things about
writing: it's never too late to begin; we know all we
need to know in order to do it; persistence and

tenacity will take us all the way; there are angels on our shoulders. Be still to catch their whisperings."

———————————

Discovering that she did not need to conform to mainstream America did not immediately occur to Benítez. Indeed, she had finished the manuscript of a murder mystery before she did so. In 1984 she took this manuscript to the Bread Loaf Writers' Conference in Vermont and was told that it was terrible. "It was like someone threw me to the sharks," Benítez told George Monaghan for the Minneapolis, Minnesota *Star Tribune* (September 28, 1993). "They gobbled me up. They told me it was awful and it was a soap opera. I felt bad, like I couldn't write anymore and that I was doing the wrong thing and that maybe I should quit and go back to work." Instead, Benítez abandoned her attempts to write to Anglo America and took up Hispanic subjects, beginning, after a trip to Mexico in 1985, what would become *A Place Where the Sea Remembers*, a novel no one is on record as having decried as awful. Cristina Garcia, writing for the *Washington Post* (September 5, 1993), called it a "delicately wrought first novel" and went on to observe, "Benitez chronicles the hopes and disappointments of a handful of distinctive characters in the Mexican seaside village of Santiago. There are no 'types' here, no generic situations, only a poignancy rendered through language as steady and sure-footed as a mountain burro. Profound in its simplicity and rhythm, *A Place Where the Sea Remember*s is a quietly stunning work that leaves soft tracks in the heart." The book won the first Barnes & Noble Discover Great New Writers Award for literary merit.

Four years later Benítez published her second novel, *Bitter Grounds*, which is set in El Salvador during years that culminated in a 1980 civil war and focuses on three generations of women who are connected to La Abundancia, a plantation—including the wives and daughters of the owners and the servants as well as their friends and rivals. The book, critics found, did not quite succeed. Complaining that Benítez had oversimplified the socio-political nature of the El Salvadorin environment, Pamela Constable complained, in a review for the *Washington Post* (August 25, 1997), that "after a short and powerful first section in which a peasant village is destroyed in the infamous matanza—the mass slaughter of rebellious Salvadoran coffee-pickers in 1932—the book moves to the plantation manor, where the plot becomes melodramatic and incestuous. For nearly 200 pages spanning 30 years, we gallop from one doomed romance to the next, from one family feud to another." Constable continued: "The author often weaves social commentary and political foreshadowing into these entertaining developments, but sometimes the result is clumsy

or misplaced. The topic of land reform—a central factor in the Salvadoran conflict—is dismissed in one brief conversation, in which two landowners guffaw over the notion of having a 'social conscience.' In contrast, the book lingers ad nauseam over the details of the opulent oligarchic lifestyle. . . . Yet we almost never learn what the poor think of all this, rarely glean a hint of their rage or despair." Others were not quite so harsh. Susan C. Hegger, for example, wrote for the *St. Louis Post-Dispatch*, "Befitting a melodrama, the plot is chock full of familiar devices: adultery, violence, unrequited love, betrayal, passion and extraordinary coincidences. In conjunction with the basically sympathetic characters, these are the elements of a lightweight but entertaining page turner. On that more limited level, *Bitter Grounds* succeeds quite well." She concluded: "despite its shortcomings, it's hard not to get hooked. Or to admire Benitez, who approaches her subject in such an admirably earnest way. . . . *Bitter Grounds* ends up providing the same kind of guilty pleasure as a cup of cappuccino and a sinfully rich dessert." The novel, despite such qualified praise, won the American Book Award.

As undeterred by the reviewers as the American Book Award judges, Benítez continued to write about El Salvadoran history in her fiction, and her next novel, *The Weight of All Things*, turns to the civil war. Exploring its significance through the eyes of a nine-year-old boy, the novel "blends fact with imagination, evoking the trauma of war more vividly than any newspaper account," a reviewer for *Publishers Weekly* (December 11, 2000) explained, adding: "Benitez's novel is both political and spiritual, beautifully illuminating the effects of war on the innocent. . . . [Her] style is both quiet and intense. Her achievement here is considerable; in this brief narrative, she gives voice to the silenced. Those who seek a deeper understanding of Latin American conflict and who appreciate Benitez's moral stance will find the novel especially gratifying." Some critics did, however, make note that the book's politics lacked subtlety, but as Michael Porter pointed out for the *New York Times* (March 25, 2001): "In this graceful and unabashedly tenderhearted novel, the politics behind the fighting is almost beside the point."

In her next novel—the title of which, *Night of the Radishes*, is the name of a traditional Mexican festival held on December 23 during which participants, take part in a sculpting competition using radishes—Benítez tells the story of the semi-autobiographical character Annie Hart Rush, a woman of Puerto Rican and Anglo American heritage who grew up on a farm, in Minnesota rather than Missouri, and whose twin sister died, at the age of nine rather than as an infant. Taking care of her mother, who is dying of emphysema, Annie revisits her childhood traumas—her sister's death, her father's suicide, and the disappearance of her older brother—and sets off to find her long-lost brother, a quest that leads to Mexico, where she reconnects with her Hispanic heritage. Jane Ciabattari wrote for the *Washington Post* (February 22, 2004): "Benítez has a firm grasp of the quotidian on both sides of the border. She precisely describes the farm vehicles of Annie's childhood . . . and persuasively details the comforts of a secure marriage. Similarly, she is masterful at evoking the special fragrance of Oaxaca [Mexico]." Ciabattari added: "Despite the traumatic events that underlie the storyline, *Night of the Radishes* is written in a lighter vein than Benítez's earlier novels, which may be why, at times, her emotional lushness veers into sentimentality. But the appealing characters and settings, the lyrical language and steadily moving plot, give this novel satisfactions of its own." In a more positive vein, Rigoberto Gonzalez wrote for the *El Paso Times* (March 28, 2004), "After witnessing Annie's burdens grow page after page, the reader will be pleased to know that Annie's blues finally take a breather. *Night of the Radishes* is a life-affirming tale and a lush sensory experience, which makes the narrative, despite its bleak beginning, seductive and enjoyable. Benitez has given her readers yet another book that's difficult to put down."

Benítez's latest book, *Bag Lady* (2006), is a memoir about her grief at losing her twin sister, her struggle with alcoholism, her shame over leaving her two young sons, and her battle with ulcerative colitis, a bowel disease that forced her to get a colostomy—the bag of the title is the colostomy bag that she must wear. "I never would have thought to write a memoir. It was so painful for me; the hardest thing I've ever done. I needed to be honest about all the things that affected my gut," Benítez told Mary Ann Grossmann for the *Saint Paul Pioneer Press* (May 7, 2006). Grossmann went on to observe that Benítez "discusses with frankness and humor topics such as what food looks like when it comes out her stomach, how she decorated her bag during intimate moments with her husband, the way her sewn-up bottom is 'smooth as a Barbie's' and how she accomplished a couple of emergency bathroom clean-ups when she was adjusting to wearing her bag."

In 2006 Benítez was recognized with the National Great American Comebacks Award, given to a person who has made notable achievements after recovering from bowel disease. That year she was also named a United States Artists (USA) Gund Fellow, one of the first to be honored in the pilot fellowship program.

Benítez and her husband continue to reside in Edina, Minnesota.

—S.Y./A.R.

Suggested Reading: *Booklist* p207 Sep. 15, 1997; *Boston Globe* p31 Dec. 29, 1993; *Christian Science Monitor* (on-line) Jan. 21, 1998; *Denver Post* (on-line) Sep.14, 1997; *Hispanic* p12 Aug. 1995; *Library Journal* p218 Sep. 1, 1993, p214 Sep. 1, 1997, p184 Dec. 2000; *Los Angeles Times* E p3 Oct. 28, 1997; *Minnesota Daily* (on-line) Mar. 13, 1997; *Ms.* p87+ Dec. 1997; *New York Times Book Review* (on-line) p25 Oct. 31, 1993, Mar. 25, 2001; *Publishers Weekly* p64 Dec. 11, 2000; *Washington Post Book World* p4 Sep. 5, 1993

Selected Books: *A Place Where the Sea Remembers*, 1993; *Bitter Grounds*, 1997; *The Weight of All Things*, 2001; *Night of the Radishes*, 2004; *Bag Lady*, 2006

Joe Pacheco/Courtesy of Random House

Bissell, Tom

1974– Journalist; short-story writer

As a young man serving in the Peace Corps, the journalist and fiction writer Tom Bissell was stationed in Uzbekistan, in Soviet Central Asia. Though he left after only a few months, unable to bear the burdens of disease and depression, he has returned many times since and has published two books set in and around the vicinity—the travelogue *Chasing the Sea: Lost among the Ghosts of Empire in Central Asia* (2003) and a collection of short fiction, *God Lives in St. Petersburg, and Other Stories* (2005). "Bissell . . . is one of a group of hot young writers who have been evolving a new prose style," Keith Taylor wrote for the Arbor Web (on-line). "On the surface this style evinces an ironic detachment that is often very funny. It also abounds in pop references—to everything from music to brand names—that can easily confuse readers even just a little older who haven't kept up. This popular referentiality is often combined with the grammar and diction of high culture. But beneath all these flourishes—and the real explanation for this new style's success—is a genuine moral sensibility that usually lies outside any of the familiar political categories."

Tom Bissell wrote the following autobiographical statement for *World Authors 2000–2005*:

"I was born in Escanaba, Michigan, in 1974. I had a sensationally undistinguished academic career prior to college, and all I ever really cared about was reading. (I remember one jarring instance of being caught reading "Portrait of the Artist as a Young Man" during a droolingly boring remedial high-school math class.) My father's friendship with the writers Philip Caputo (with whom he served in Vietnam) and Jim Harrison (with whom he occasionally hunted) went some way toward interesting me in first-class contemporary literature a bit earlier than my rural, small-town surroundings might have otherwise occasioned. My literary interests during college were mostly concerned with American novels. I was an unreconstructed fiction chauvinist and believed nonfiction to be a waste of time. Which makes my subsequent career as a travel writer and journalist somewhat unexpected.

"The Peace Corps began me on this path. I joined out of desperation: every MFA writing program I applied to rejected me. I had done almost no traveling prior to the Peace Corps, and going from Michigan to the former Soviet Union shattered my consciousness and many of my cozy understandings of the world. I now believe consciousness-shattering is of absolute importance to a young writer. Out of the shards of one's old certainties and the wreckage of one's new understandings one often finds entirely new things to write about. In this way I have often felt that I am a writer who is living a completely different literary existence than the one I had long imagined for myself—not a bad thing, surely.

"Following my Peace Corps experience (aborted after a mild nervous breakdown [see above: Consciousness, Shattering of]) I moved to New York to work as an intern for *Harper's Magazine*. Here I began to make my peace with the unavoidable but curiously faith-strengthening contingencies of the business side of literature. I learned, too, for the first time, how editing gets done and more importantly how to edit myself. After a few weeks at *Harper's* I was taking 60-page drafts of stories and turning them into 25-page drafts and seeing them much improved for it. From *Harper's* I went on to W.W. Norton, as an assistant editor, and finally to Henry Holt, as an editor. A week before September 11, 2001, I quit to become a full-time writer.

"My personal interests as a writer are, for better or worse, largely international. I am most interested in writing about people far afield of their native habitats, and of the inevitable disconnects and terrors that result. Conflict of all kinds interest me, whether cultural or political or religious. Fanaticism interests me. Futility interests me. Optimism in the face of all these forces interests me above all. I find very little value in writing that is not humorous, or life-affirming, in some way. I do not say that writing must be funny—only that I have a hard time getting interested in writing that is not. I have also created within myself a truce between fiction and nonfiction. Until fairly recently, I agonized about which sort of writer I *really* was: a fiction writer or a nonfiction writer? I now believe that a piece of writing is, or should be, an emotional human experience. Writing, to me, is joy, even when the material at hand is intolerable."

Thomas Carlisle Bissell was born in 1974, in Escanaba, a town on the upper peninsula of Michigan. While attending public high school, Bissell was a disinterested student, and as a result he attended a local community college, Bay de Noc Community College, for a year before he was able to transfer to Michigan State University (MSU), in East Lansing. "Small-town kids in the rural Midwest have access to maybe one-tenth of the resources that kids in suburban high schools have access to," he explained to Robert Birnbaum in an interview for the *Morning News* (March 31, 2005, on-line). "For a kid that was as serious about reading as I was and basically as smart as I was, even when I was a f—-up, the fact that nobody pulled me aside and tried to right my ship, that no one saw that and identified this in me except for one man, one teacher, and just one, that in retrospect seems to me to be a damning thing."

After graduating MSU with a bachelor's degree in English, in 1996, he volunteered for the Peace Corps and was sent to Uzbekistan, a former Soviet republic, to teach English. Seven months into his 27-month assignment, he dropped out of the program, after losing 50 pounds of his body weight due to a bout of dysentery and suffering a nervous breakdown. He then returned to the U.S., moving to New York City, where he worked for several years in book publishing at W.W. Norton & Company and Henry Holt and Company. In 2000 he got his first big break as a magazine journalist, when an editor at *Harper's Magazine*—for which Bissell had interned briefly after leaving the Peace Corps—asked him to write an article about a film that was being shot in his hometown, Escanaba. Since then Bissell has written for numerous periodicals, including *Esquire*, *Salon*, the *New York Observer*, the *New York Times Book Review*, and the *New York Times Magazine*.

Bissell also continued to contribute to *Harper's*, and in 2001 he proposed that the magazine return him to Uzbekistan to write about the shrinking Aral Sea, a salt lake in southwestern Kazakhstan and northwestern Uzbekistan. In previous generations the lake had supported local fishing industries, but in the 1950s the Soviet Union, which dominated central Asia at the time, diverted much of the water from the Syr Darya and Amu Darya rivers for large scale irrigation projects, which resulted in an ecological disaster. Since 1960 the surface area of the lake has shrunk by half, wreaking devastating consequences for the local ecology and industry, as well as significant health problems for local residents. *Harper's* agreed to Bissell's story proposal, and he returned to Uzbekistan later that year.

Bissell's article "Eternal Winter: Lessons of the Aral Sea Disaster," appeared in the April 2002 issue of *Harper's*, and in 2003 he published his first book, *Chasing the Sea: Lost among the Ghosts of Empire in Central Asia*, a travelogue of the writer's journeys in the vicinity of the disappearing Aral Sea. Describing the book as a "hilarious and insightful misadventure in the post-Soviet bureaucratic badlands," Steve Hendrix wrote for the *Washington Post Book World* (October 12, 2003): "Bissell is a born raconteur, but he is also a prodigious scholar, uncoiling the tangled history, ancient and modern, of this crossroads society in bright, taut cords. . . . And he is such an ambidextrous writer that his mini-treatise on Anglo-Russian statecraft is as readable as the dish on his college sweetheart. Bissell may have been a flop as a Peace Corps volunteer. (The toughest job he ever flubbed?) But his failure has still provided some benefit to humanity—at least to the part of humanity that enjoys a great read." Bill Beuttler, writing for the *Boston Globe* (January 25, 2004), noted that "Bissell doesn't reach the Aral Sea until his final chapter, but he makes vivid the full extent of this underreported disaster and the Soviet obsession with cotton growing that caused it. He gives us just enough history on the despots who have brutalized the region over the ages and of the political tensions that the collapse of the Soviet Union has unleashed in Central Asia today. Bissell's translator, a slang-happy 24-year-old he calls Rustam, is a funny and worthy sidekick. The narrative is propelled by a strong literary sensibility and Bissell's droll, self-deprecating humor."

Around the same time *Chasing the Sea* was issued in its paperback edition, in 2005, Bissell published a collection of short fiction, *God Lives in St. Petersburg, and Other Stories*. Comparing these two books for the *Chicago Tribune* (January 23, 2005), Michael Upchurch wrote that while Bissell "goes a little berserk with his metaphors" in *Chasing the Sea*, "no such prose wackiness mars the six astonishing stories in *God Lives in St. Petersburg*." Most of the short stories in this collection are also set in central Asia but were written before the terrorist attacks of September 11, and in his review Upchurch noted that the world had changed a great deal since then: "But the authority with which Bissell pins down his particular historical moments in fiction is easily as convincing as the observations he makes in *Chasing the Sea*. And the writing is better. . . . Here's hoping that he brings the cruel, honed edge of *God Lives in St. Petersburg* to his next book, whatever genre he chooses to write in."

Bissell lives in New York City. He travels frequently and has mentioned a desire to write a book about the arctic.

—S.Y.

Suggested Reading: *Boston Globe* H p9 Jan. 25, 2004; *Chicago Tribune* C p5 Jan. 23, 2005; *Entertainment Weekly* p86 Jan. 28, 2005; *Los Angeles Times Book Review* p10 Feb. 6, 2005; *Morning News* (on-line) Mar. 31, 2005; *Washington Post Book World* T p13 Oct. 12, 2003

Selected Books: nonfiction—*Chasing the Sea: Lost among the Ghosts of Empire in Central Asia*, 2003; fiction—*God Lives in St. Petersburg, and Other Stories*, 2005

Mark Mainz/Getty Images

Bloom, Harold

July 11, 1930– Literary critic; editor

Harold Bloom, according to David Lehman, writing for *Newsweek* (August 18, 1986), is "arguably the best-known literary critic in America, probably the most controversial and undoubtedly as idiosyncratic as they come." Michael Dirda, writing for the *Washington Post*, once designated Bloom, the author of nearly 30 books of criticism, as one of the top-three most-important critics of the 20th century, along with the Cambridge don F. R. Leavis and the American writer Edmund Wilson, as cited by Joseph Epstein for the *Hudson Review* (Summer 2002). Writing for the *Australian* (January 10, 2001), Joanna Coles called Bloom "America's best-read man" and added that "it seems as if he has the entire Western canon committed to memory." With a career spanning nearly 50 years, Bloom has distinguished himself as an authority on literary figures from Shakespeare to the Romantic poets, as well as on religious topics ranging from Biblical texts to the Gnostic tradition. Along the way he has achieved something uncommon among literary critics: the status of being a best-selling author. Several of Bloom's recent books, including his comprehensive volumes *The Western Canon: The Books and School of the Ages* (1994), *Shakespeare: The Invention of the Human* (1998), and *How to Read and Why* (2000), have all made national bestseller lists, earning him an unusual place as a celebrity academic. While his influence on contemporary criticism is well established, Bloom's provocative ideas are not always universally accepted. As he once said of himself, "I am the pariah of my profession." Indeed, Bloom's name has been associated with controversy since the publication of his early book *The Anxiety of Influence: A Theory of Poetry* (1973), in which he set forth a bold new doctrine on poetic influence. His concept—that poetry was not the result of a benign and enriching literary tradition, but was in fact the product of a poet's usurpation and revisionism, or "misreading," of the work of predecessor poets—was received by fellow critics with a flurry of skepticism and debate. Nevertheless, the theory continues be discussed in graduate-school literature programs, inspiring both admiration and antagonism. In addition to his books of criticism, Bloom has edited several anthologies on Romantic poetry, as well as hundreds of critical anthologies, including such series as Bloom's Major Poets and Major Literary Characters, through a venture with the publishing firm Chelsea House. Since 1955 he has taught at Yale University, in New Haven, Connecticut, where he is currently the Sterling Professor of the Humanities; he has also been the Berg Visiting Professor of English at New York University, in New York City, since 1988.

Harold Bloom was born in New York City on July 11, 1930, the youngest by many years of the five children of William and Paula (Lev) Bloom, both of whom had immigrated to the U.S. from Eastern Europe following World War I. Bloom was raised in the Bronx, in an Orthodox Jewish home where only Yiddish was spoken. From an early age he expressed a strong love for reading, a practice that was largely self- taught. He taught himself to read Yiddish at age three, Hebrew at age four, and, finally, English at age five. (Bloom did not actually hear English spoken until he was six.) To learn the English language he did not read children's books, but rather volumes of poetry by William Blake and Hart Crane; since this introduction poetry has remained his first love. As he later recalled in an essay collected in *Agon: Toward a Theory of Revisionism* (1982), "I became cathected upon poems very early, when I was about ten years old, and I have spent forty years trying to understand that initial cathexis." Due to his Orthodox upbringing, Bloom also became a close reader of Jewish religious texts. At one point he balked at becoming a Bar Mitzvah (a Jewish boy who, upon his 13th birthday, reaches the age of religious duty and responsibility) because he had serious doubts about certain aspects of the Biblical texts.

Although he remained an avid reader throughout his youth, demonstrating uncanny abilities in both speed reading and memorization, Bloom was not a strong student. In fact, when he attended the academically well-regarded Bronx High School of Science—which he described to David Remnick for the *Washington Post* (August 20, 1985) as "that ghastly place"—he generally performed poorly. Nevertheless, Bloom scored first on the statewide New York regents examination and was thus awarded a full scholarship to Cornell University, in Ithaca, New York. There his most important teacher was likely M. H. Abrams, an influential author of books on Romanticism and literary criticism. Bloom dedicated one of his early books to Abrams, but he soon departed from many of his former teacher's views.

In his interview with Remnick, Bloom spoke of his "astonishing memory" for the poetry he has read: "When I was a student I would get a bit drunk and recite Hart Crane's 'The Bridge' frontwards, then backwards, quite like a tape recorder running wild." Another recollection of himself as a student appears in an *Agon* essay, in which Bloom describes himself as "a young man, deeply in love with the whole range of Romantic poetry, British and American." When Bloom entered Yale University, after receiving his B.A. degree at Cornell, in 1951, the English department was widely considered the citadel of New Criticism—a mode of literary criticism that emphasized rigorous study of the text and eschewed consideration of social, historical, or other external elements to explain a work. Many members of Yale's English faculty, which included Cleanth Brooks, Robert Penn Warren, and W. K. Wimsatt, heeled to T. S. Eliot's conservative attachment to 17th-century metaphysical and religious poets to the neglect of the Romantics.

Displaying the rebellious spirit that has characterized all of his literary studies, Bloom chose to write his doctoral dissertation on the Romantic poet Percy Bysshe Shelley, whom he saw as an impassioned intellectual skeptic. In 1955 Bloom was awarded his Ph.D. degree and appointed an instructor of English at Yale. Four years later he published *Shelley's Mythmaking* (1959), which he had developed from his dissertation. In examining the mythmaking aspect of many of Shelley's principal poems—his effort to replace received myths with his own experience of reality—Bloom turned to the distinction that Martin Buber made between "I-It" and "I-Thou" attitudes. Mythmaking in Shelley's "Hymn to Intellectual Beauty," for example, is an encounter not between subject and object, but between subject and subject: a relationship, or communion, of existences.

With his defense of Shelley against a host of detractors, Bloom began his attack on anti-Romanticism. In *The Visionary Company: A Reading of English Romantic Poetry* (1961), he sought to establish Romanticism as the central tradition of English poetry and as a continuing force in literature. He defined the tradition through interpretative readings, or prose paraphrases, of the important poems of the six major Romantic poets of the late 18th and early 19th centuries—William Blake, William Wordsworth, Samuel Taylor Coleridge, Lord Byron, Shelley, and John Keats. The book also includes a chapter on some of the lesser poets of the period. While maintaining that the Romantics were not poets of nature, Bloom showed in *The Visionary Company* that one of their common themes was the relationship, or dialectic, between nature and the imagination in the process of creating poetry. As if in defiance of the New Critics' treatment of a poem as a self-contained, nonreferential "well-wrought urn," he sought out other shared themes, patterns of crisis and quest, analogues, borrowings, recurring images. In his epilogue, moreover, he countered the structuralist assertion that "myths have no authors and come into existence only when incarnated in a tradition" by arguing that "the myths of Romanticism have authors and then are embodied by tradition." He traced the transmission, for example, of John Milton's "Il Penseroso" to the character of Crispin in the poem "The Comedian as the Letter C" by the American modernist Wallace Stevens, following the development of the character through kindred figures in the poems of intervening English Romantic poets. Bloom edited an anthology, *English Romantic Poetry* (1961), to accompany his book.

Two books other than the one on Shelley that Bloom devoted to a single English poet are *Blake's Apocalypse: A Study in Poetic Argument* (1963) and *Yeats* (1970). The latter is an exhaustive, systematic study of Yeats's work, especially as it relates to the Romantic tradition extending from Milton to Robert Browning. Various aspects of that tradition were also Bloom's concern in *The Ringers in the Tower: Studies in Romantic Tradition* (1971), a collection of 21 essays that had first appeared, mainly during the 1960s, in periodicals and in introductions to anthologies and other books. Milton had clearly emerged in *The Visionary Company* as the precursor of the Romantic poets: "It is one of the great

characteristics of the Romantic period that each major poet in turn sought to rival and surpass Milton, while also renewing his vision." That rivalry became more intense in *The Ringers in the Tower*: "Somewhere in the heart of each new poet there is hidden the dark wish that the libraries be burned in some new Alexandrian conflagration, that the imagination might be liberated from the greatness and oppressive power of its own dead champions. Something of this must be involved in the Romantics' loving struggle with their ghostly father, Milton." As Bloom noted in his preface, the unifying theme of *The Ringers in the Tower* "is poetic influence (perhaps rather poetic misprision) conceived as an anxiety principle or variety of melancholy, particularly in regard to the relation between poets in the Romantic tradition."

"Having hit a kind of universal nerve with a little book, *The Anxiety of Influence*, published in January 1973," Bloom said in a 1981 lecture at the University of California, at Irvine, "I have had a number of years in which to reflect upon the joys and sorrows of giving offense." In his interview with David Remnick, he explained that he began to develop his theories about literary influence in 1965, "in the midst of a personal crisis," during which he started reading Sigmund Freud and Ralph Waldo Emerson almost continuously. When his book on influence was eventually published, he told Remnick, "the nastiness with which it was received was unprecedented." Basic to the theory set forth in *The Anxiety of Influence*—which remains perhaps Bloom's most talked-about work—is his contention that a poem's substance is an intra-poetic relation, that a poem is both a response to and a defense against another poem, or antecedent. The relationship is ambivalent, but necessarily adversarial because the "ephebe" or "belated" poet must clear a space in which to achieve personal fulfillment. Bloom offers as an analogue the Satan of Milton's *Paradise Lost*, who struggles against God, and as a Freudian paradigm, the parricidal Oedipus. Satan goes so far as to consider himself "self-begot, self-rais'd." Just as every man, according to Freud, has the unconscious wish to be his own father, the poet would like to be his own literary precursor, the possessor, as Satan boasts of being, of his "own quick'ning power."

Bloom described poetic influence in the book as a process in which the poet copes with his precursor by an act of misreading, or misprision, that is, in fact, a misrepresentation, or falsification, a "wilful revisionism." To the six "revisionary ratios," by which such a poet creatively corrects a prior text, Bloom applied the terms *clinamen* (swerving), *tessera* (completing), *kenosis* (emptying), *daemonization* (displacing), *askesis* (diminishing), and *apophrades* (the return of the dead). They are kinds of strategies, he says, that have "the same function in intrapoetic relations that defense mechanisms have in our psychic life."

The controversy over *The Anxiety of Influence* came as much from the language that Bloom used to explain his new theory as from the ideas proposed. Perry Meisel, a former student of Bloom's who is now a professor at New York University, recalled to Larissa MacFarquhar for the *New Yorker* (September 30, 2002), "We all remember that great night at Ezra Stiles College when Harold was going to unveil his new theory of poetry. It was a very big event. We didn't understand a word of it, but we all remembered one line: 'There are no poems, only relations between poems.'" Despite the general view that Bloom's language and style were often hard to penetrate, critics immediately recognized the innovation of the author's concepts. "Unconvinced as I am by this book as argument," Edward Duffy noted for *America* (April 14, 1973), "I must confess to its pragmatic effectiveness. It talks about literature in such a way that it has illuminated, for me at least, some poems which I thought I had already known. If, as he says, Bloom intends his book as a goad toward a new kind of particular criticism, then he has much of great value to say even (or perhaps especially) to the Apollonians among us." Meanwhile, John Hollander, writing for the *New York Times* (March 4, 1973), observed, "[This book] may outrage and perplex many literary scholars, poets and psychologists; in any event, its first effect will be to astound, and only later may it become quite influential. . . . After being debated and mulled over, it may turn out to embody what is after all a theory of American poetry."

In his next work, *A Map of Misreading* (1975), Bloom presented an example of how to read a poem in accordance with the theory set forth in *The Anxiety of Influence*. The map the book describes has not only six revisionary ratios and six psychic defenses but also six sets of images, six rhetorical tropes, and three stages of creation. Bloom demonstrated how the interplay of his map's images and tropes produces meaning by testing his map on Browning's baffling "Childe Roland to the Dark Tower Came," of which he had given a detailed and illuminating reading in *The Ringers in the Tower*. With his map as a guide, he also examined the way Milton influenced the English Romantics, some of whom in turn influenced each other, and how Emerson influenced Walt Whitman, Stevens, John Ashbery, and other American poets. In *A Map of Misreading* and elsewhere Bloom made clear that he was not involved in a search for sources, similarities in style, and verbal echoes: "I continue *not* to mean the passing-on of images and ideas from earlier to later poets. Influence, as I conceive it, means that there are *no* texts, but only relationships *between* texts." It is a relationship, moreover, in which "poets need not *look* like their fathers."

Remarkably erudite, Bloom has ready access to a vast store of religious, philosophical, historical, and literary information, much of it esoteric, that supplies him with paradigms and underpinnings in the explication of his theory of poetic influence. In the work on the Kabbalah of the 16th-century Jewish mystic Isaac Luria, along with that of the modern Jewish scholar Gershom Scholem, he discovered "a dialectic of creation astonishingly close to revisionist poetics," as he maintained in his next critical work, *Kabbalah and Criticism* (1975). He later stated, moreover, in *Agon* that the "sole concern" of *Kabbalah and Criticism* was "to use Kabbalah, or Jewish Gnosticism, and Scholem's analyses as paradigms for a theory of reading poetry." But in a critique for the *New York Review of Books* (February 19, 1976), Leon Wieseltier argued that if Bloom had demanded from the Kabbalah "no more than models, paradigms, and maps, *Kabbalah and Criticism* would have been a *tour de force* which, like all his other books, would stand or fall on the validity of his theory of influence. Unfortunately, however, . . . he advances the further and unfelicitous claim that Kabbalah itself is a theory of influence because it is likewise 'a theory of writing.'"

Bloom's use of arcane Lurianic Kabbalah terminology, which he had also found useful in earlier books, aroused some protest from reviewers of both *Kabbalah and Criticism* and his next work, *Poetry and Repression: Revisionism from Blake to Stevens* (1976). Arguing in the latter that the "true subject" of a poem is its "repression of the precursor poem," Bloom furthered the study of intrapoetic relations begun in *The Anxiety of Influence*. One reviewer recommended the last chapter, on Wallace, as "a stunner, a celebration of the Sublime." Most of the essays in *Figures of Capable Imagination* (1976) illustrate Bloom's theory of influence by detailing Emerson's role as the poetic father of modern American Romantic poets, notably Stevens, A. R. Ammons, and Ashbery. In *Wallace Stevens: The Poems of Our Climate* (1977), Emerson again, along with Whitman, emerges as the progenitor as the book traces the "revisionary swerves" between poet and precursor in his interpretative reading of Stevens's poetry.

One year after—and apparently as a result of—the publication of *The Anxiety of Influence*, Bloom removed himself from Yale's English department (where he had obtained his full professorship, in 1965, but was becoming increasingly isolated from his colleagues because of his views) to become the university's DeVane Professor of the Humanities. (Since 1983 he has had the title of Sterling Professor of the Humanities.) The theory of reading that Bloom developed, beginning with *The Anxiety of Influence*, was antithetical to the rising school of literary analysis known as deconstructionism, which has had several distinguished proponents at Yale. Although deconstructionism, in Bloom's opinion, exerted a despiritualizing effect on criticism, he nevertheless joined some of them, including Paul de Man and Jacques Derrida, in writing

Deconstruction and Criticism (1979), which attempts to clarify the deconstructionist approach to literature and its philosophical method of analyzing meaning.

Bloom returned to the familiar subjects of Emerson, Whitman, Stevens, and other poets in the essays that make up *Agon: Toward a Theory of Revisionism*. The book provided Bloom an opportunity to indulge his longstanding interest in Kabbalist commentary as well as the theology of Valentinus, the second-century founder of a Gnostic sect. While Freud's mythmaking and methods of interpretation greatly appealed to him, he specified in *Agon*, "My mode of interpreting literary texts can be described more accurately as a Valentinian and Lurianic approach than as being Freudian, Nietzschean or Viconian." (A reincarnated Valentinus is one of the characters in Bloom's only attempt at fiction, *The Flight to Lucifer; A Gnostic Fantasy* [1979]. This novel, depicting the schematic of Gnosticism, received mixed reviews from critics, who often found it underdeveloped as a piece of fiction; Bloom later expressed regret that it had been published.) In addition to his theological bent, Bloom confirmed his undiminished regard for Freud in some of the essays in *Agon*, as well as in one of the lectures he gave as the first Wellek Library Lecturer, at the University of California, at Irvine, in spring 1981. These lectures were published in *The Breaking of the Vessels* (1982), which owes its title to the second, or catastrophic, stage of the Kabbalistic myth of the world's creation, degeneration, and restoration. In 1987 Bloom published *The Strong Light of the Canonical: Kafka, Freud, and Scholem as Revisionists of Jewish Culture and Thought*.

Bloom's next two works returned to some of the themes of his earlier critical theory: *The Poetics of Influence* (1989) features selections from his previously published books of criticism, while *Ruin the Sacred Truths: Poetry and Belief from the Bible to the Present* (1989) is composed of a series of Norton lectures he delivered at Harvard University from 1987 to 1988. The book explores the tradition of mythmaking from the Bible, through the classics, and in the English canon.

Bloom undertook more original—and controversial—criticism in 1990 with the publication of *The Book of J*, in which he reinterpreted the Torah (the first five books of the Hebrew Bible, known in the Christian tradition as the Pentateuch) with the assistance of the translator David Rosenberg. In modern religious scholarship, the term "J" is used to refer to the sections of the Torah that refer to God as Jahwe (modern Jehovah), or Yahweh; it is believed that an editor known as the Redactor (or "R") later combined this document with other texts to create the Torah. Despite some scholarly claims that "J" is not the work of one person, Bloom theorized that the author was in fact a woman living in the early 10th century, who likely was a member of the royal court of Rehoboam of Judah, the son of Solomon.

Although evidence supporting the idea is scant, Bloom arrived at his contention that the author was female largely because all the complex and sympathetic characters throughout the text are women. The book also advances an intricate theory about the purpose of these original texts. As David Stern wrote for the *New Republic* (February 4, 1991), "The real J, whom Bloom seeks to rescue from oblivion, was neither a historian nor a theologian, nor even a religiously inclined writer. She was, he insists, a teller of tales, surpassingly ironic and sophisticated, essentially 'a comic writer . . . in the difficult mode of Kafka' who brought her imaginative vision to bear upon telling, or retelling, the early history of her nation, the people of Israel, and their God, Yahweh." In this way, Bloom argued, Yahweh was "the central character in a book of fiction before he became the object of religious belief and worship," according to K. L. Woodward and L. Wilson for *Newsweek* (October 1, 1990). Bloom's innovative theory incited a fair amount of critical umbrage, with many religious scholars questioning the accuracy of his assertions. In addition, linguists called into question aspects of Rosenberg's new translation, which Bloom included as a separate text. While Stern found the idea of printing "J" in this manner "brilliant," he nonetheless considered Bloom and Rosenberg's efforts unsuccessful. "Some have suggested that Bloom, whose control of Hebrew seems from several indications to be less than perfect, was misled by Rosenberg's translations. . . . My impression is the opposite: that Rosenberg's translation was produced with Bloom's reading in mind." Despite the mixed reception, Bloom's critical work was widely viewed as provocative, attracting significant attention from both literary and religious scholars.

Bloom continued his emphasis on religious studies in *The American Religion: The Emergence of the Post-Christian Nation* (1992), in which he proposed that the true American religion is more Gnostic than Christian. Generally, Gnostic belief involves the idea that the universe was at one time completely separated from God, and that the world as it exists was created by an evil figure as a sort of prison. The only remnant of God on earth is a "pneuma," or a small fragment that resides within people, but is not accessible without a Gnostic unveiling. In this way, Gnostics seek to gain "knowledge" of spiritual truths through ritualistic practices but also through an exploration of the self. Examining the sacred texts of such denominations as Mormons, Christian Scientists, Pentecostalists, Jehovah's Witnesses, and Seventh Day Adventists, Bloom argued that the tendency among American religions to focus on gaining a knowledge of the inner self and a personal, intimate relationship with God is evidence of an emerging Gnostic tradition. Again, Bloom's ideas generated significant debate among religious scholars, with one reviewer for *Publishers Weekly* (March 23, 1992) calling the work the author's "most controversial to date." While critics generally appreciated his thorough evaluation of several prominent religions, they often questioned his larger conclusions. Writing for the *New York Times* (May 10, 1992), Jay P. Dolan found that Bloom "is correct in emphasizing the importance of the individual in the American religious pantheon, but he is off the mark when he elevates that to a national religion." Meanwhile, Alfred Kazin opined in the *New Republic* (June 8, 1992), "What is most remarkable about Bloom is his increasing sense of himself as one of the sacred company that he writes about. . . . My chief image of the book is Bloom interrogating American religions to find just where he, in his exceptionality as a 'Gnostic Jew,' fits in."

Bloom's next major work, *The Western Canon: The Books and School of the Ages* (1994), presents a summary of the major authors who, in his view, define the core of Western literature. Among the 26 authors Bloom discussed, he singled out William Shakespeare as perhaps the single most important figure in the Western canon, in the sense that his works have served to establish the standards by which all literature is judged. Other authors touched upon in the book are Dante, Chaucer, Cervantes, Montaigne, Milton, Samuel Johnson, Goethe, Wordsworth, Jane Austen, Whitman, Emily Dickinson, Charles Dickens, George Eliot, Leo Tolstoy, Henrik Ibsen, Freud, Marcel Proust, James Joyce, Virginia Woolf, Kafka, Jorge Luis Borges, Pablo Neruda, Fernando Pessoa, and Samuel Beckett. Throughout, Bloom eschewed what he called the "School of Resentment" in contemporary literary criticism—a group in which he includes feminist critics, Marxists, queer theorists, multiculturalists, New Historicists, deconstructionists, and semioticians; the practitioners of such criticism, Bloom asserted, are guilty of various sins, including their dismissal of the creative power of the author, their neglect of the importance of fictional character, their attempts at historicizing or politicizing works of fiction, and, more generally, their attempts to overturn the traditional canon of "dead white male" authors in favor of a greater variety of texts.

Overall, *The Western Canon* was considered a significant literary achievement for its thorough analysis of many important writers. Nevertheless, some critics questioned Bloom's criteria for determining which authors comprise the canon; others took issue with his disdain for the present course of literary scholarship. As Daniel J. Silver noted for *Commentary* (December 1994), "With an exception here or there, few are likely to quarrel with Bloom's principal choices. . . . But there are larger problems with *The Western Canon*, and they have to do precisely with Bloom's notion of aesthetic merit, his criterion of canonical status. . . . In the end, Bloom's approach to literature, even when it 'works,' is a peculiarly airless and smothering one." Writing for the *New Republic* (October 10, 1994), Robert Alter asked,

"How does a writer get into the canon? In Bloom's plausible view, he barges his way in through sheer imaginative energy and wholly unanticipated resourcefulness with words, ideas, and the formal dimensions of his medium." He continued: "Bloom's understanding of the power of literature is invigorating, in our moment of ideological self-righteousness, but it exhibits serious deficiencies. . . . The canonicity of all the writers discussed by Bloom is defined almost exclusively in terms of their original solution to expressing the problematics of selfhood." *The Western Canon* became a national best-seller and earned Bloom the Boston Book Review Rea Nonfiction Prize in 1995.

Bloom returned to a discussion of Gnosticism in *Omens of Millennium: The Gnosis of Angels, Dreams, and Resurrection* (1996), in which he again explored Gnosticism as America's new national religion. While examining the present-day focus on angel worship, dream interpretation, and near-death experiences, he also considered the growth of such mystical traditions as Christian Gnosticism, Muslim Sufism, and Jewish Kabbalism. The book draws a distinction between Gnosticism, which is the religion of secret knowledge, and the concept of "gnosis," which is the spiritual knowledge itself. Mark C. Taylor noted for the *New York Times* (September 8, 1996, on-line): "Analyzing the relationship between millenarianism and Gnosticism, Mr. Bloom has written three books in one: a history of ideas, a religious-cultural critique and a spiritual autobiography." Other critics also observed that the work occasionally assumed the tone of a memoir, with Bloom revealing himself fully as a Gnostic and discussing the experiences that helped shape his thesis; some reviewers drew comparisons to St. Augustine's personal revelations in his *Confessions*. Nevertheless, Bloom's theories on religion were again met with some skepticism. Writing for the *New York Times* (September 27, 1996, on-line), Michiko Kakutani opined: "Provocative as many of these ideas are, they are not laid out in a persuasive—or even systematic—fashion, leaving the reader feeling frustrated, toyed with and often downright perplexed. . . . To make matters worse, Mr. Bloom's prose has a way of becoming as muddled and muddy as the New Age writings he so vehemently condemns." In contrast, one reviewer for the *Economist* (December 7, 1996) called the book a "brilliant, idiosyncratic study of millennial omens," adding, "Though often hard to follow, Mr. Bloom's latest book is full of dazzling insights and unexpected connections."

Elaborating on an idea approached in *The Western Canon, Shakespeare: The Invention of the Human* proposes that Shakespeare's plays and poems provide a type of "secular Scripture" from which modern-day notions of personality, psychology, and mythology were derived. Writing for the *New York Times* (November 1, 1998, on-line), James Shapiro explained Bloom's "bold argument" as the notion "that Shakespeare remains so popular and his most memorable characters feel so real because through them Shakespeare invented something that hadn't existed before. Bloom defines this as 'personality,' inwardness, what it means to be human. In so doing, Bloom adds, Shakespeare invented us as well." The book includes a thorough critical analysis of Shakespeare's work, grouping plays by genre and often focusing most heavily on the playwright's characters. In fact, as Larissa MacFarquhar described, "[Bloom's] focus is astonishingly narrow: he cares only about character. He doesn't care about structure—what the play shows and what it leaves out, how the action unfolds. . . . Bloom doesn't care about circumstance or luck or disaster or choice or other people or any of these forces that make up plot. He emphatically rejects the Aristotelian claim that plot generates character, rather than the other way around. He barely even discusses the plays' language." The work represented such a divergence from the concerns of contemporary academic criticism that John Hollander, a friend and colleague of Bloom's at Yale, remarked (aware that it would please his friend) that the book had set Shakespeare criticism back 100 years. In publications outside the academy, Bloom's work was often hailed for offering significant insights into Shakespeare's body of work. Writing for the *Yale Review* (April 1999), Richard Howard called the book "the best comprehensive interpretation of all Shakespeare's plays, addressed to common readers and theatergoers, to have appeared in my lifetime." "Moreover," he added, "its particular concern—which Bloom calls, quite deliberately, Bardolatry—with characters, with the creation of individuals who exist for and against others, undivided, is of a particular utility to the tribe of teachers nowadays. . . . It is a pretty common experience in our classes to hear someone . . . ask with all the gleeful certainty of a child discovering the emperor's nakedness, 'What's so good about Shakespeare? Why should we read this stuff?' Harold Bloom tells why." *Shakespeare: The Invention of the Human* was named a National Book Award finalist for nonfiction, a National Book Critics Circle Award finalist for criticism, a New York Times Notable Book of the Year, one of *Publishers Weekly*'s Best Books of the Year, and the ALA/Booklist Editor's Choice for 1998.

Bloom's next work, *How to Read and Why* (2000), serves as a compelling introduction to literary study. Divided into individual sections on such topics as short stories, poetry, novels, plays, and American fiction, the book provides five guiding principles to help readers approach each of these genres; it also offers several arguments about the benefits of reading. For example, Bloom suggested that through reading people can learn more about themselves, experience new realities, find companionship from characters in literature,

and attain knowledge that would otherwise be inaccessible. Despite earning a place on best-seller lists, *How to Read and Why* received mixed reviews from critics. Michael Gorra, writing for the *New York Times* (June 18, 2000), called the work "a book that resembles nothing so much as an instructor's manual for one of those anthologies through which students are introduced to literary study." He added: "It would be a good anthology, though one whose selections seem terribly safe, and would provide the basis of a good course for beginning students. But *How to Read and Why* is not a good book. . . . Bloom has said almost everything that is here before—and better—at greater length and with a more nuanced sense of detail." In a review for the *Wilson Quarterly* (Summer 2000), James Morris observed, "The surprising thing about Bloom's answers, his how and why of reading, is how unsurprising they are—not that they're in the least wrong or objectionable, but that they're entirely traditional." Nevertheless, Morris concluded, "[Bloom's] devotion sets an example that will survive the lapses in this book."

In 2002 Bloom edited a collection of classic works entitled *Stories and Poems for Extremely Intelligent Children of All Ages*. Featuring nearly 100 selections, mostly from the 19th century, the volume is designed to train children for more elevated reading. "If readers are to come to Shakespeare and Chekhov, to Henry James and to Jane Austen," Bloom explained to a reporter for the *Australian* (November 21, 2001), "then they are best prepared if they have read Lewis Carroll and Edward Lear, Robert Louis Stevenson and Rudyard Kipling." In addition to poems by John Keats and Christina Rosetti, the book includes often dark and ironic stories such as Hans Christian Andersen's "The Red Shoes," O. Henry's "Witches' Loaves," and Mark Twain's "Journalism in Tennessee."

In *Genius: A Mosaic of One Hundred Exemplary Creative Minds* (2002), Bloom stressed that literary appreciation, as an approach to reading, is more valuable and rewarding than the gamut of contemporary methods of literary analysis. The book is thus devoted to celebrating the top 100 literary "geniuses," with discussions on Shakespeare, Dante, Cervantes, Homer, and Virgil, as well as more modern writers (though all are deceased) such as Stevens, Robert Frost, Whitman, and Hart Crane. Some critics responded to the volume with laments of the sort commonly hurled at Bloom. For example, Judith Shulevitz, in a review for the *New York Times* (October 27, 2002, on-line), found Bloom's language at times rambling and verbose ("it defies every rule of elegance and economy"), his arguments repetitive, and his observations often "grandiose and indefensible." Nevertheless, Shulevitz did not altogether dismiss Bloom's ideas on the essence of genius, which she described as authentic. Other reviews were more favorable. Peter Ackroyd, writing for the London *Times* (October 23, 2002), called the book "engaging, refreshing and impassioned," while

Shana C. Fair for *Library Journal* (September 15, 2002) noted, "Although the book is a delight to read, its real value lies in the author's ability to provoke the reader into thinking about literature, genius, and related topics. No similar work discusses literary genius in this way or covers this many writers."

Bloom's *Hamlet: Poem Unlimited* (2003) takes a detailed look at Shakespeare's tragic play. He noted in the preface that this critical piece is largely an elaboration of his previous discussion of *Hamlet* in *Shakespeare: The Invention of the Human*. Bloom classifies *Hamlet* as a "poem unlimited"—a quote from the play—because he felt that it properly belongs to no genre, but rather offers a form of greatness that "competes only with the world's scriptures," as quoted in *Kirkus Reviews* (February 1, 2003).

In *Where Shall Wisdom Be Found?* (2004), Bloom outlined the wisdom he has gleaned from the such wide-ranging works as the Talmud and *King Lear*. The book emphasizes that "wisdom literature teaches us to accept natural limits," according to Andrew Delbanco for the *New York Times* (October 10, 2004). While noting that "Bloom can be an annoyingly extravagant writer, given the sweeping pronouncements . . . that he contradicts without revising his initial certitude," Delbanco argued that "a critic who writes this well has a right to instruct us, even imperiously—but the best thing about Harold Bloom is that he would be disappointed if we did not resist."

With his next book, *Jesus and Yaweh: The Names Divine* (2005), Bloom made, in the words of Merle Rubin, writing for the *New York Times* (October 3, 2005), a "foray into the shadowy realm between literature and religion." While examining the characters of the Christian and Jewish gods as given in scripture, the book also reveals a great deal about Bloom's own feelings toward religion. "To talk of this book's central thesis would be misleading; Bloom is not so much proposing a thesis as offering up his personal impressions based on a lifetime of thoughtful reading," Rubin wrote.

In addition to his critical writings, since 1983 Bloom has been associated with one of the most ambitious publishing ventures of its kind, editing and writing the introductions for a formidable number of critical anthologies published by Chelsea House. Bloom, an insomniac who once told Lehman that he has "been doing nothing but read for 50 years now," seemed born for the job. To date he has published more than 600 volumes in conjunction with Chelsea House, including such series as Bloom's Guides, Bloom's Period Studies, and Bloom's Major Novelists, with books on such varied subjects as Holden Caulfield, the angst-ridden protagonist of J. D. Salinger's *Catcher in the Rye* (1951); the Harlem Renaissance; and the writer Edgar Allen Poe. Typically, each book includes a collection of critical essays and an introduction by Bloom. As MacFarquhar noted, Bloom has not shied away from writing introductions about authors whose work he has professed to dislike. For example, in what she called his "delicately worded introduction" to *Bloom's BioCritiques: Alice Walker*, Bloom wrote, "There is a tenacity in her quest that compensates the reader for at least part of what is sacrificed in storytelling and in the representation of character." In addition to these books, he served as editor (with David Lehman) for *The Best of the Best American Poetry 1988–1997* (1998).

Bloom has earned numerous honors and awards, including a Fulbright Fellowship (1955), the John Addison Porter Prize from Yale University (1956), a Guggenheim Fellowship (1962), the Newton Arvin Award (1967), the Melville Cane Award from the Poetry Society of America (1971) for *Yeats*, the Zabel Prize from the American Institute of Arts and Letters (1982), a MacArthur Fellowship (1985), the Christian Gauss Award for *Ruin the Sacred Truths* (1988), the Gold Medal for criticism from the American Academy of Arts and Letters (1999), and the 14th Catalonia International Prize (2002). He holds honorary degrees from Boston College, Yeshiva University, the University of Bologna, St. Michael's College, and the University of Rome.

Harold Bloom married Jeanne Gould on May 8, 1958; they have two sons, Daniel Jacob and David Moses. Outside of reading Bloom has few hobbies or diversions, although he is a devoted fan of baseball, with a passionate love for the New York Yankees. Bloom and his wife reside in New Haven, Connecticut.

In his article "The Tyranny of the Yale Critics," in the *New York Times Magazine* (February 9, 1986), Colin Campbell described Bloom as "large, shaggy-haired and courteous" and reported that "as a teacher, he's known as a sage, genius, and comic rolled into one—Zarathustra cum Zero Mostel." Remnick, in his *Washington Post* article, similarly profiled Bloom as a teacher who is free of the antagonistic tone of his books: "Nowhere is Bloom's personality more evident and powerful than in the classroom. He is an affectionate and generous teacher, an easy grader, ... Some students say they adore Bloom, some admit they cannot make head or tail of his lectures." As one former student remembered, he emits "a kind of personal power as a figure that's hard to escape."

—K.D.

Suggested Reading: *Australian* Jan. 10, 2001, Nov. 21, 2001; *Harvard Business Review* p63 May 2001; *Hudson Review* p213+ Summer 2002; *New Republic* p34+ Feb. 4, 1991; *New York Times* (on-line) Sep. 8, 1996, Sep. 27, 1996, Oct. 27, 1998, Nov. 1, 1998, June 2, 2000, June 18, 2000, Oct. 27, 2002; *New York Times Book Review* p20+ Feb. 9, 1986; *New Yorker* p86+ Sep. 30. 2002; *Newsweek* p56+ Aug. 18, 1986, p62 Oct. 1, 1990; *Washington Post* C p1+ Aug. 20, 1985

Selected Books: literary criticism—*Shelley's Mythmaking*, 1959; *The Visionary Company: A Reading of English Romantic Poetry*, 1961; *Blake's Apocalypse: A Study in Romantic Argument*, 1963; *Yeats*, 1970; *The Ringers in the Tower: Studies in Romantic Tradition*, 1971; *The Anxiety of Influence: A Theory of Poetry*, 1973; *A Map of Misreading*, 1975; *Kabbalah and Criticism*, 1975; *Poetry and Repression: Revisionism from Blake to Stevens*, 1976; *Figures of Capable Imagination*, 1976; *Wallace Stevens: The Poems of Our Climate*, 1977; *Agon: Toward a Theory of Revisionism*, 1982; *The Breaking of the Vessels*, 1982; *The Strong Light of the Canonical: Kafka, Freud, and Scholem as Revisionists of Jewish Culture and Thought*, 1987; *Poetics of Influence*, 1989; *Ruin the Sacred Truths: Poetry and Belief from the Bible to the Present*, 1989; *The Book of J*, 1990; *The American Religion: The Emergence of the Post-Christian Nation*, 1992; *The Western Canon: The Books and School of the Ages*, 1994; *Omens of Millennium: The Gnosis of Angels, Dreams, and Resurrection*, 1996; *Shakespeare: The Invention of the Human*, 1998; *How to Read and Why*, 2000; *Genius: A Mosaic of One Hundred Exemplary Creative Minds*, 2002; *Hamlet: Poem Unlimited*, 2003; *Where Shall Wisdom Be Found?*, 2004; *Jesus and Yaweh: The Names Divine*, 2005; fiction—*The Flight of Lucifer: A Gnostic Fantasy*, 1979; as co-author—*Deconstruction and Criticism* (with Jacques Derrida, Geoffrey H. Hartman, J. Hillis Miller, and Paul de Man), 1979; as editor—*English Romantic Poetry*, 1961; *The Romantic Tradition in American Literature*, 1973; *Romantic Prose and Poetry* (with Lionel Trilling), 1973; *Victorian Prose and Poetry* (with Trilling), 1973; *Oxford Anthology of English Literature*, two volumes (with Frank Kermode and John Hollander), 1973; *Robert Browning: A Collection of Critical Essays* (with Adrienne Munich), 1979; *The Best of the Best American Poetry 1988–1997* (with David Lehman), 1998; *Stories and Poems for Extremely Intelligent Children of All Ages*, 2002

Bobrick, Benson

1947– Nonfiction writer

The nonfiction writer Benson Bobrick is perhaps best known for his informative historical studies. His works have gained attention for both their accessibility and their thoroughness and have run the gamut in their subject matter. His first book, *Labyrinths of Iron* (1981), looked at the historical and contemporary uses of underground transportation. Two later books, *Fearful Majesty* (1987) and *East of the Sun* (1992), focused on Russian history and two others, *Angel in the Whirlwind* (1997) and *The Fight for Freedom* (2004) on the American Revolution; one other, *Testament* (2003), looks at the Civil War. His other books include a history of stuttering, *Knotted Tongues* (1995); an account of the Bible's translation into English, *Wide as the Waters* (2001); and a history of one of the oldest engineering firms in the United States, *Parsons Brinckerhoff* (1985). His most recent book, *The Fated Sky* (2005), offers a history of the belief in astrology.

Benson Bobrick was born in 1947. He received a doctorate from Columbia University and worked for some time as a freelance journalist and poet. He first received notice as a historian with the publication of *Labyrinths of Iron: A History of the World's Subways*. Over the course of about 350 pages, Bobrick chronicles the advent and subsequent development of underground transportation, from the gold mines of ancient Egypt and the tunnels of the Romans to the innovations of the Industrial Revolution, particularly the creation of subways in London,

Lois Wadler/Courtesy of Simon & Schuster

England; Paris, France; and New York City. The book received many positive reviews. B. C. Hacker observed in *Library Journal* (September 1, 1981): "Without neglecting nostalgia or the technological underpinnings of subway construction and operation, [Bobrick] finds much to say about the social, political, and economic factors that shaped subways. The book's chief distinction, however, may be Bobrick's attention to the aesthetic and psychological dimensions of subway history. A thoughtful book, written with style, it is an excellent piece of popular history." However, a reviewer for *Choice* (January 1982) felt that the author's "notion of history is so naive that he never grasps either the social or technical reality of modern subway systems. . . . The illustrations are diverting, but the author's evident commitment to keeping the narrative light, fast, and easy ensures that nothing of intellectual substance will be attempted."

Parsons Brinckerhoff: The First Hundred Years, a study of one of the oldest continuously operating American engineering firms, with a long history of innovations in tunneling, was published to little notice in 1985. Bobrick's next book was *Fearful Majesty: The Life and Reign of Ivan the Terrible* (1987), which explores the life of the Russian czar best known for his cruelty but also attempts to show the reasoning behind some of the monarch's actions, including how his relationships with his fellow European rulers affected his decision making. The book received generally favorable reviews. In the *New York Times Book Review* (November 8, 1987), Alfred J. Rieber proclaimed: "In probing this Czar's complex character, Benson Bobrick . . . wisely avoids amateur psychologizing. Instead he finds clues to Ivan's aberrant behavior in biology and politics. He traces the flawed genetic legacy of the Byzantine line of Ivan's paternal grandmother, as shown in the extreme nervousness and irritability of his ancestors. And he explores the frightening effect on Ivan of the intrigue-filled, faction-ridden court milieu of his youth. . . . In the end [Ivan] left Russia a shambles. Despite this sobering conclusion, it is the chief merit of Mr. Bobrick's biography that it gives us a portrait of Ivan the Terrible as a figure of high tragedy rather than a madman or a villain."

Bobrick continued his examination of Russian history with his next book, *East of the Sun: The Epic Conquest and Tragic History of Siberia*, which details how generations of Russians have explored, settled, and developed the large swath of land known as Siberia. The book begins with 16th-century explorers and continues through the collapse of the Soviet Union, in 1991. Bobrick sought to counter the popular image of Siberia as nothing more than a barren wasteland or a penal colony, pointing out that the region harbors sizable resources of oil, coal, natural gas, diamonds, and gold and contains considerable amounts of fertile land. Like its predecessors *East of the Sun* was well received. "Bobrick again demonstrates his ability to produce interesting popular history," Mark R. Yerburgh wrote for *Library Journal* (September 15, 1992). "Especially effective are the descriptions of [Joseph] Stalin's nightmarish Gulag and the ways in which an enormous ever-shrinking frontier affected Russia's historical development." In a review for *New Statesman and Society* (March 26, 1993), Robert Shannan Peckham attested: "One of Benson Bobrick's achievements in *East of the Sun*

is to show how deeply rooted notions of a frontier territory are in Russian culture. An account of Russia's settlement in Siberia involves more than a description of consecutive mapping expeditions. With a firm grasp of his material, Bobrick balances summaries of Russian political and social history with Russia's diplomatic relations and descriptions of Siberia's geography and indigenous populations."

In 1995 Bobrick published *Knotted Tongues: Stuttering in History and a Quest for a Cure*. Inspired by his own difficulties with the ailment—which caused a nervous breakdown and forced him to give up on his dreams of teaching—the author detailed the history of the disease, including the various treatments attempted over the centuries, the beliefs that scholars have held about its origins, and profiles of famous stutterers throughout history, from Moses to Marilyn Monroe. Ray Olson, writing for *Booklist* (April 1, 1995), called the book "compelling" and "fascinating." In the *New York Times Book Review* (May 7, 1995), Derek Bickerton wrote: "[Bobrick] was himself a stutterer, and his final chapter includes an account of his own struggles with this mysterious difficulty. But most of the book tries, not quite successfully, to interweave two general themes: medical treatments for stuttering and the problems faced by its more famous victims. . . . In general, the book would have benefitted from a more focused presentation."

Angel in the Whirlwind: The Triumph of the American Revolution (1997) presents a narrative history of the American Revolution, beginning with the French and Indian War of 1754–63 and ending with the inauguration, in 1789, of George Washington as the new country's first president. The author was particularly interested in the subject, having had ancestors who fought on both sides of the conflict. "[Bobrick] has produced a splendidly lively retelling of 'a remarkable story,'" Phoebe-Lou Adams remarked in the *Atlantic Monthly* (August 1997). "[He] does not hurry his narrative," Adams added. "He quotes lavishly and effectively from letters by men who were not haunted by nitpicking journalists and had no need to mask themselves with bland governmentese. . . . One encounters, directly, [Thomas] Jefferson's liking for formally polished rhetoric, [John] Adams's lawyerly addiction to accumulated evidence, and Washington's awe-inspiring ability to combine—with no hint of effort—lucidity, courtesy, and enormous practical intelligence." Frederick Allen, for the *New York Times Book Review* (July 6, 1997), was equally generous in his summation, noting that the book "entertainingly but authoritatively lays out the texture of life at the time, with all the necessary sense of how people lived and thought—what the average person was doing through the whole period, soldier or civilian, as well as the great man. And it covers a war half again as long as the Civil War in satisfying detail without ever losing momentum."

Turning his attention to England, Bobrick published *Wide as the Waters: The Story of the English Bible and the Revolution It Inspired* (2001). The book begins with the first attempt, sponsored by John Wycliffe in 1382, to translate the various texts of the Bible into English, an activity that culminated in the edition, initially published in 1611, of the text known as the King James Version. Those efforts made the scriptures directly accessible to the English-speaking public but may have provoked both religious and civil strife, such as the Civil War of 1642–49. Bobrick also argued that the translation helped to standardize the English language, bring about widespread literacy, and may have been a contributing factor in the creation of modern democracy, which questioned the divine right of kings and other beliefs regarding societal inequality. In the *New York Times Book Review* (April 8, 2001), Simon Winchester wrote: "Bobrick is an exceptionally able writer of popular histories. . . . This new book is by far his most ambitious, and if at times his tone is a little dense and solemn, he succeeds entirely in the challenge he sets himself." Guy Davenport, in *Harper's* (May 2001), called the work an "admirably clear and abundantly informative history." "[Bobrick] knows how to engage readers with a rollicking narrative," Susan M. Felch wrote for the *Christian Century* (November 7, 2001). "[He] is a consummate teacher who summarizes complex historical and linguistic movements without reducing them to caricature."

Bobrick's *Testament: A Soldier's Story of the Civil War* (2003) is a unique work in that the subject of the book, Benjamin "Webb" Baker, was the author's great-grandfather. Between August 1861, when Webb was 19 years old, and September 1864, he saw combat as a member of the 25th Illinois Volunteer Infantry Regiment; he participated in such major battles as Pea Ridge, Perryville, and Chickamauga, and was wounded three times. The narrative weaves together excerpts from Webb's detailed letters, most of which were addressed to his mother; the letters are included in their entirety in an appendix. In a review for the *Seattle Times* (October 19, 2003), Steve Raymond noted: "Bobrick's commentary places the letters in historical context, and while some of this will certainly be 'old news' to Civil War buffs, it will definitely aid the understanding of readers who have spent less time studying the war. . . . Baker was a far more literate writer than most Civil War correspondents (he earned a doctorate in history after the war). Despite their relative lack of emotional impact, his letters present an unusually detailed and articulate portrait of the hard life of a Civil War solider." A reviewer for *Publishers Weekly*, as quoted on Amazon.com, remarked, "This is a compelling story, rendered in vivid, graceful prose."

In 2004 he published *Fight for Freedom: The American Revolutionary War*, which was intended for preteen through adult readers. "Bobrick offers readers a huge amount of information about the Revolutionary War, but smartly organizes it into brief chapters that each focus on a battle or aspect of the war," Karen MacPherson wrote for the Scripps Howard News Service (June 30, 2004). "Bobrick obviously knows and loves his subject, and does a great job at making history both interesting and accessible. From time to time, his writing is a bit awkward, but this is a mere quibble. A more serious flaw, however, is the almost total lack of information about African-Americans' role during the conflict, although Bobrick does offer a look at the role of women and American Indians."

Bobrick's most recent book, *The Fated Sky: Astrology in History*, traces the influence that astrology has had on Western society from its nascency in ancient Babylonia to modern times. Though astrology is scorned by most contemporary scientists, Nicolaus Copernicus and Isaac Newton consulted astrology charts, and interest in the field has reappeared in academe. Nonetheless, Dick Teresi wrote for the *New York Times Book Review* (February 5, 2006) that Bobrick sought to entertain, not to stir up controversy, with his latest book. "He simply reports astrology's 'impact on history and on the history of ideas.' He likens it to 'an underground river through human affairs.' He is convincing." In a review for the *Washington Post* (November 20, 2005), Anthony Grafton wrote, "This synthetic, anecdote-rich book explains the basics of astrology in a non-technical way. It also uses the art as a thread on which to string a potted history of ancient and medieval civilizations and brief studies of individual astrologers. It is a cosmopolitan and amusing first look at a big subject."

In 2002 Benson Bobrick received the Literature Award of the American Academy of Arts and Letters. He and his wife, Hilary, live in New York City and Brattleboro, Vermont.

—C. M.

Suggested Reading: *Atlantic Monthly* p96 Aug. 1997; *Choice* p646 Jan. 1982; *Harper's* p66+ May 2001; *Library Journal* p1,641 Sep. 1, 1981, p74 Sep. 15, 1992, p175 Feb. 15, 1995; *New Statesman and Society* p40 Mar. 26, 1993; *New York Times Book Review* p60 Nov. 8, 1987, p14 May 7, 1995, p8 July 6, 1997, p8 Apr. 8, 2001; *Seattle Times* K p12 Oct. 19, 2003; *Wall Street Journal* A p 18 Oct. 13, 1992

Selected Books: *Labyrinths of Iron: A History of the World's Subways*, 1981; *Parsons Brinckerhoff: The First Hundred Years*, 1985; *Fearful Majesty: The Life and Reign of Ivan the Terrible*, 1987; *East of the Sun: The Epic Conquest and Tragic History of Siberia*, 1992; *Knotted Tongues: Stuttering in History and the Quest for a Cure*, 1995; *Angel in the Whirlwind: The Triumph of the American Revolution*, 1997; *Wide as the Waters: The Story of the English Bible and the Revolution It Inspired*, 2001;

Testament: A Soldier's Story of the Civil War, 2003; *Fight for Freedom: The American Revolutionary War*, 2004; *The Fated Sky: Astrology in History*, 2005

Bertrand Parres/AFP/Getty Images

Bolaño, Roberto

Apr. 18, 1953–July 15, 2003 Poet; novelist; short-story writer; nonfiction writer

Although the Chilean writer Roberto Bolaño lived only 50 years and did not produce his first novel until he was 43, he has become known internationally as one of Chile's most influential writers. "Bolaño, it seemed to me, hovers over many young Latin American writers, even those in their 40's, the way Garcia Marquez must have over his generation and the following one," Francisco Goldman wrote for the *New York Times Magazine* (November 2, 2003). "Bolaño wrote somewhat in the manner that Martin Amis calls the 'higher autobiography'—with the high-voltage first-person braininess of a Saul Bellow and an extreme and subversive personal vision of his own." In the London *Financial Times* (November 27, 2004), Angel Gurria-Quintana wrote, "From his earliest writings to his last, hefty volume, Bolaño seemed to be developing, and expanding on, a specific type of book—part novel of ideas, part deranged road novel, part literary essay. He became increasingly preoccupied with an image of the deserted wasteland—whether Antarctica or Santa Teresa— towards which civilisation is hurtling. "

"Bolaño's genius is not just the extraordinary quality of his writing, but also that he does not conform to the paradigm of the Latin American writer," Ignacio Echeverria, a former literary editor of the Spanish daily *El Pais*, told Larry Rohter for the *New York Times* (August 9, 2005). "His writing is neither magical realism, nor baroque nor localist, but an imaginary, extraterritorial mirror of Latin America, more as a kind of state of mind than a specific place." Indeed, though Bolaño is identified as a Chilean writer, he was more of a postnationalist; Bolaño lived in several different countries during his life, returning to Chile only once after Augusto Pinochet's successful coup, in 1973—a situation reflected in his many vagabond characters. "Roberto was one of a kind, a writer who worked without a net, who went all out, with no brakes, " Jorge Herralde, his Spanish editor, told Rohter, "and in doing so, created a new way to be a great Latin American writer."

Roberto Bolaño was born on April 18, 1953 in Santiago, Chile, to Victoria Ávalos and León Bolaño. A skinny, bookish (though dyslexic) child, he spent his early years in Santiago, before moving with his parents to Mexico City, in 1968. At 17 he dropped out of school to work as a journalist and became involved in left-wing politics. In late 1970 the socialist Salvador Allende was elected the president of Chile, prompting Bolaño to return to his native country, in 1973, just a month before the army, under the command of General Augusto Pinochet, seized power. Bolaño was arrested and held prisoner for a week in the city of Concepción. He was fortunate enough to be recognized by two former classmates who were serving in the national police, and they authorized his release. Bolaño then spent a brief period in El Salvador, associating with the poet Roque Dalton and the guerrillas of the Farabundo Marti National Liberation Front, before returning to Mexico to live the life of a Bohemian poet, supporting himself by writing book reviews. Shortly after his return, in 1974, he co-founded, along with the poets Mario Santiago and Bruno Montané an avant-garde literary movement known as "infrarealism." The following year he published his first collection of poetry, *Gorriones cogiendo altura*, and in 1976 his second, *Reinventar el amor*. He departed for Europe in 1977, settling for a while in Paris, then moving to Barcelona, Spain.

In Spain Bolaño worked as a dishwasher, campground custodian, bellhop, garbage collector, and at other temporary jobs while he wrote. In 1984 he collaborated with Antoni García Porta to write the novel *Consejos de un discípulo de Morrison a un fanático de Joyce*, which won the Premio Ámbito Literario de Narrativa award. Two of his early novels, *La senda de los elefantes* (which translates as "the elephant path," 1982) and *La pista de hielo* (which translates as "the ice track," 1993), were published by local government authorities and won prizes in provincial literary contests. In the mid-1980s he married Carolina

López, with whom he later had a son and a daughter, and settled in the village of Blanes, on the Costa Brava. Jorge Herralde told Rohter that though Bolaño had thought of himself as a poet, he "abandoned his parsimonious beatnik existence" and began to focus on narrative fiction, after the birth of his son, in 1990, when he "decide[d] that he was responsible for his family's future and that it would be easier to earn a living by writing fiction." In 1993 Bolaño published a compilation of the poetry that he had written between 1977 and 1990, *Los perros románticos* (which translates as "the romantic dogs"), and three years later he established himself as a novelist with the publication of *La literatura Nazi en America* (which translates as "Nazi literature in America"), a miniencyclopedia of fictitious Nazi literature from Latin America. In a review for the London *Independent* (July 24, 2003), Chris Andrews, who translated three of Bolaño's other books into English for New Directions Publishing, called it a "tour de force of black humour and imaginary erudition [that] has a lineage that runs back through [Jorge Luis] Borges' *Universal History of Infamy* to the *Imaginary Lives* of Marcel Schwob." Ilan Stavans, writing for the *Los Angeles Times* (January 31, 2005), described *La literatura Nazi en America* as "one of the most courageous and imaginative books produced in the region since Gabriel Garcia Marquez's *One Hundred Years of Solitude* appeared in 1967."

Bolaño published the short-story collection *Llamadas telefónicas* (which translates as "telephone calls") in 1997, and followed that with his breakthrough novel *Los detectives salvajes* (1998), which is scheduled for publication in 2007 as *The Savage Detectives*. Described by Nick Caistor, writing for the London *Guardian* (July 17, 2003), as "a challenging mixture of thriller, philosophical and literary reflections, pastiche and autobiography," the novel follows the characters Arturo Belano and Ulises Lima, founders of the fictional "visceral realist" movement, as they attempt to discover what became of a fellow writer who supposedly disappeared after the Mexican revolution. Not only did the novel draw critical acclaim and garner both the Premio Herralde de Novela and the Premio Rómulo Gallegos, it also led many critics to compare Bolaño's work to such Latin American literary giants as Carlos Fuentes and Borges—the latter being one of Bolaño's most revered influences. Chris Andrews noted that critics had compared *Los Detectives salvajes* to Julio Cortázar's *Hopscotch*, which he considered well-justified, given the book's "energy and humour, its formal ingenuity and the intercontinental sweep of its action." Bolaño revived a minor character from *Los detectives salvajes* to narrate his 1999 novel *Amuleto* (which translates as "amulet"). Another novel, *Monsieur Pain*, was released that same year, and the following year he published a collection of poetry, *Tres*. In 2001 he published another collection of stories, *Putas asesinas*, and in 2002 two novellas, *Amberes* and *Una novelita lumpen*.

Bolaño's 2000 novel *Nocturno de Chile* (*By Night in Chile*), was translated into English in 2003. A bitter satire of Chilean politics and religion, *By Night in Chile* is written as a night-long confessional rant by a dying priest and member of Opus Dei, Sebastian Urrutia Lacroix (whose character was loosely based on José Miguel Ibañez Langlois, the leading literary critic of a right-wing newspaper under Pinochet). Through Urrutia's memories Bolaño illustrates the problems of Chile, and, by extension, the modern world. *By Night in Chile* was universally admired by anglophone critics, and Chris Andrews won plaudits for his translation as well. "This is a wonderful and beautifully written book by a writer who has an enviable control over every beat, every change of tempo, every image," Ben Richards wrote for the London *Guardian* (February 22, 2003). "The prose is constantly exciting and challenging—at times lyrical and allusive, at others filled with a biting wit (Bolaño has dissected the Chilean literary tradition with such gleeful eloquence that the novel may not win him many dinner invitations back in the country of his birth)." The London *Times* (February 1, 2003) critic James Hopkin described *By Night in Chile* as "deadly earnest, foreboding, and yet joyfully whimsical" and "a wonderful introduction to Bolaño's work." For the *New York Times Book Review* (January 11, 2004), Mark Kamine wrote, "In Chris Andrews's lucid translation, Bolaño's febrile narrative tack and occasional surreal touches bring to mind the classics of Latin American magic realism; his cerebral protagonist and nonfiction borrowings are reminiscent of Thomas Bernhard and W. G. Sebald."

Bolaño died in a Barcelona hospital while awaiting a liver transplant, on July 15, 2003. Shortly after his death, the novel *El gaucho insufrible* (2003) was published, which was followed by a collection of essays, *Entre paréntesis* (2004). In the years that followed, interest in his work continued to grow in the U.S., with Farrar, Straus and Giroux acquiring the rights to publish the U.S. editions of *Los detectives salvajes* and a novel that was published posthumously under Bolaño's working title, *2666*. Though Bolaño had intended to publish his final work as five separate novels, released one per year, it was printed as one large tome that was divided into five sections when it was launched in Barcelona, in 2004. The novel won nearly every Spanish-language literary award for which it was eligible—yet reviewers were divided. "Critics are already arguing over whether *2666* is a work of genius or a self-indulgent, sprawling behemoth. Surely the answer lies somewhere between the two. Bolaño's death has certainly left everyone wondering whether, given more time, he would have made it leaner and tighter," Angel Gurria-Quintana wrote, noting that "the final irony is that for all his [Bolaño's] vitriolic depiction of critics as enthusiastic cannibals, interested less in literature than in literary criticism, he has left behind a body of work so dense in veiled references and sly allusions that it will keep them employed for generations to come."

New Directions, which published *By Night in Chile*, planned to release translations of the rest of Bolaño's works (excepting those acquired by Farrar, Straus and Giroux). In 2004 it published the novel *Distant Star*, which was originally published in 1996, under the title *Estrella distante*. The novel, set in Chile during Pinochet's rule, was described by Ian Thomson, writing for the London *Sunday Telegraph* (November 28, 2004), as "a haunting addition to that well-worn genre, the Latin-American 'dictator novel'." When compiling *La literatura nazi en America*, Bolaño had become obsessed with one character, Carlos Wieder (aka Alberto Ruiz-Tagle), a fascist poet who unsettled the Chilean literary establishment during the Pinochet era, and though the author dedicated more than twenty pages of that book to the character, he was unsatisfied and used Wieder as the main character in *Distant Star*. A pilot as well as a poet, Wieder offers his support for the Pinochet regime by infiltrating intellectual circles in Concepción and disseminating his "New Chilean Poetry"—that is, sky-writing pro-junta slogans over the skies of numerous Chilean cities. "This absurd, oddly egalitarian poetic technique is contrasted in the novel by a very disturbing account of Wieder murdering two girls and their aunt," Chad W. Post wrote for the *Review of Contemporary Fiction* (March 22, 2005). "And these aren't the only people he 'disappears' following the coup. In fact he creates a poetic display of pictures of those tortured and murdered for the 'amusement' of other members of the military. . . . There's definitely some black humor in this novel, but its core is horrifying, as the tales of poets killed or exiled following the coup are placed in juxtaposition to Wieder's story." Ilan Stavans argued that this complicated portrait of a disturbed artist sets Bolaño's work apart from his contemporaries: "Far too often in Latin American letters, authority figures, especially dictators, are turned into cartoons. Authors minimize their lives by turning them into senseless marionettes. What makes Bolaño so fascinating is his refusal to simplify those who pushed him out of Chile. . . . Bolaño's literature is about silences and absences, about reevaluating national memory. As today's Chile moves to distance itself from the atrocities of the military period, it is forced to confront the ghosts of its past. In Bolaño's able hands, those treacherous ghosts have universal value."

The third English translation that New Directions released, *Last Evenings on Earth*, is a collection of short stories set in Chile, Spain, Mexico, and Germany. In these tales, as in much of Bolaño's work, he examined the relationship of the artist to society. "Most of Bolaño's stories are about writers, and this concern sometimes grows to an obsession with petty literary politics," Benjamin Lytal wrote for the *New York Sun* (May 3, 2006). "But his obsession actually works as an anti-obsession, exorcising Latin American literary circles of their self-seriousness. . . . Bolaño is not a satirist, however. He reserves an important respect for serious, sensitive literary affairs. 'We never stop reading, although every book comes to an end,' he writes, 'just as we never stop living, although death is certain.' Literature is a way of breathing in Bolaño's world—in a world, to borrow one character's phrase, 'where vast geographical spaces could suddenly shrink to the dimensions of a coffin.'" Lytal concluded: "If this collection is any indication, Bolaño's late work will ensnare more and more American readers. Our own tradition of noir is rendered not magical, but refreshingly alien—and politically relevant, after Bolaño's fashion."

—S.Y.

Suggested Reading: (London) *Guardian* Saturday Pages p28 Feb. 22, 2003; (London) *Independent* p16 July 24, 2003; (London) *Times* Features p14 Feb. 1, 2003; *Los Angeles Times Book Review* p4 Dec. 14, 2003; *New York Times* E p3 Aug. 9, 2005; *World Literature Today* p217 Winter 2002

Selected Works in English Translation: *By Night in Chile*, 2003; *Distant Star*, 2004; *Last Evenings on Earth*, 2006

Bolger, Dermot

(BUL-jer)

Feb. 6, 1959– Novelist; poet; playwright; editor; publisher

Dermot Bolger has become internationally known for presenting Ireland not as it has been viewed traditionally—centered around rural life, poverty, alcoholism, and the church—but as a place that has embraced modernity and postmodernity with such haste that tradition has become lost. Bolger began his writing career while still in his teens and, over his nearly three-decade-long career, has produced at least seven full-length volumes of poetry, nine novels, and about half a dozen plays, as well as editing and publishing more than 100 other books, many of them prescient selections of work by unknown, little-known, or nearly forgotten Irish writers. Both as a publisher and a writer, Bolger is credited with helping usher in a Renaissance in Irish writing, thanks in part to his interest in the seedy side of contemporary Irish life, particularly in Dublin and more particularly in Finglas, the part of Dublin in which he was raised. "I hate the idea of a straitjacket, of being labelled as one kind of writer," Bolger told Mary Holland for the London *Observer* (June 2, 1991). Bolger added: "Where I grew up it was unthinkable that people might want to read or write poetry. They were supposed to speak in four letter words and drink cans of [the beer] Harp. But people in Finglas experience birth and death, sudden joy and growing old. I hate the assumptions of high art, and the literary novel." Bolger has admitted that he treats tradition like a rummage sale, telling Sarah Hemming for the London *Independent* (September 26, 1990), "We often feel in Ireland we should serve tradition. For me it's more a question of scavenging through it to take something that suits me."

Dermot Bolger was born February 6, 1959 in Finglas, on the northern side of Dublin, Ireland, to Roger and Bridie (Flanagan) Bolger. His mother died in 1969, and his father, a ship's steward, spent long periods of time away from home; both circumstances strongly influenced his later work. (Although largely deprived of parental oversight after his mother's death, he has said his brothers and sisters took good care of him.) Bolger was educated entirely in Finglas, first at Saint Canice's Boys' National School, then at Beneavin College, a Catholic secondary school. Bolger told Olivia Kelly for an article under his byline in the *Irish Times* (May 8, 2001) that at Beneavin, "They knew I was different and they gave me the space to be different." Part of what set him apart was his desire to become a poet. "I remember saying to a fella in primary school who wanted to be a soldier that I wanted to be a poet, and he said you couldn't be a poet unless you went to university," Bolger recalled in the same *Irish Times* article. "We couldn't think of anyone where we were from who'd been to university. Free second-level education was only just coming in, so I didn't imagine university would be an option for me." Bolger had an early mentor, however, who encouraged him to keep writing and assured him that all he needed to do so was a piece of paper and a pen. At 15 or 16 Bolger, having already begun to publish pastoral poems in the local press, met the celebrated Irish poet Anthony Cronin, and he and Bolger's influential teacher at Beneavin helped change the young writer's direction. "At that time I thought poetry had to be about things like [lilies] and clouds," Bolger told Caoimhe Young for the London *Sunday Mirror* (January 17, 1999). "I didn't know I could write poetry about events which occurred in the life around me." The landscape in which Bolger lived was also inspiring, albeit in its plainness rather than its splendor. John Waters, writing about the pop-star Bono, Bolger's childhood neighbor, for the *Irish Times* (September 30, 1994), paraphrased Bolger as saying that the landscape of Finglas was "unsuitable for visual depiction, there was nothing to paint or draw, only flat surfaces and slow curves. To say who you were you would have to write or sing."

Bolger began his working life as a teenager, taking part-time jobs while still in school and becoming a full-time factory worker soon after graduating from Beneavin, in 1977. After about a year and a half of factory work, Bolger became what he described in the Dublin *Sunday Independent* (November 21, 2004) as "undoubtedly the worst library assistant in the history of the now defunct Dublin County Council." By then Bolger was already beginning to make inroads in the Irish publishing world with Raven Arts Press, the company he founded in 1977. The press's first release was a mimeographed pamphlet of Bolger's own poems, *Finglas Watching the Night* (1977), which carried an introduction by Cronin. Over the next 15 years, Raven Arts published more than 120 books, including early work by such writers as Patrick McCabe, Roddy Doyle, and Colm Tóibín; the press also published writers from other countries in the European Union and proved instrumental in reviving the flagging reputations of some older Irish writers, including Cronin and the controversial novelist, poet, and playwright Francis Stuart. (Much like the American poet Ezra Pound, Stuart was an anti-Semite and a staunch believer in fascism, going so far as to live in Berlin, Germany, during World War II and work as a radio propagandist on behalf of the Nazis.) Raven Arts also published four of Bolger's full-length collections of poetry: *The Habit of Flesh* (1980), *Finglas Lilies* (1981), *No Waiting America* (1982), and *Leinster Street Ghosts* (1989). In 1992 Bolger closed the press to give himself more time to write. The successful publishing house New Island Books, which Bolger cofounded as the successor to Raven Arts and for which he continues to serve as executive editor, published two other collections of Bolger's verse, *Taking My Letters Back: New and Selected Poems* (1998) and *The Chosen Moment* (2004). (Bolger's 1986 collection, *Internal Exiles,* was published by Dolmen Press.) As with his prose Bolger's poetry registers his furor at Ireland's transformation into a politically corrupt and drug-laden society. Surveying Bolger's career as a poet in a review of *Taking My Letters Back*, Caitriona O'Reilly praised Bolger for the *Irish Times* (January 16, 1999) as "a witness to Dublin working-class life and a keen and sympathetic observer of the difficulties of estate and high-rise existence: poverty, boredom, addiction. The sheer spitting anger of this work is admirable. However, strong feeling is no guarantee of good poetry, and too often these poems descend into adjective-laden histrionics where a calmer eye might better have served Bolger's intentions." Yet O'Reilly also criticized Bolger for his "unvarying line lengths and metre, the over-use of full rhyme, and verbal bagginess" and concluded: "Ultimately, this is a poetry that lives in its detail. Poems such as 'Bluebells for Grainne,' 'Ireland: 1967' and 'Botanic Gardens Triptych' are enjoyable pieces of observation, and reveal an engaging troubled affection for city and country. In its more controlled moments *Taking My Letters Back* makes a success of its defiantly humanist arguments."

Bolger's first novel, *Night Shift*, appeared in 1985, the year after he quit his job at the library. The story of a young couple, Donal and Elizabeth Flynn, coming to maturity and struggling to make ends meet in Dublin, the novel grew out of his time at the welding parts manufacturing company Oerlikon Welding, in Finglas, leading Bolger to call the book, in an article for the *Irish Times* (December 27, 2004), "the welding rod's sole contribution to world literature." Reviewing one of the novel's many reissues, a critic for the London *Observer* (August 1, 1993) termed *Night Shift* a "vivid, sharp and condensed tale" and a "tour de force," with a "sense of hope and poetry [achieved by] only the best Irish prose."

The Woman's Daughter, Bolger's second novel, was published in 1987, with a revised and enlarged edition coming out in 1991. Separated into three parts the novel begins in the 20th century with Sandra, a Finglas woman whose internal monologue tells about her life and attempts to justify the vicious abuse to which she subjects her daughter, a child of incest whose own thoughts—as well as the daughter's imaginary trip back in time, to the 19th century—also figure into the narrative. "It is a narrative that brings together numerous voices and perspectives from different times," Derek Hand noted for the *Irish Times* (September 13, 2003), "and Bolger's novel succeeds in knitting together these different strands powerfully and poetically. . . . Bolger brilliantly allows the past and the present to exist side by side in his descriptions of an ever-changing and utterly fluid landscape. A palpable sense of longing for a simpler time pervades the sections set in the present, which of course is undercut by the shifting narrative that suggests no time—in the past or the present—is ever simple or straightforward."

The Journey Home (1990), Bolger's next novel, was characterized by Desmond Christy for the London *Guardian* (June 21, 1990) as "a violent book with a violent purpose." Christy quoted Bolger as saying that when writing the book, he "wanted to take the Irish literary novel and kill it. Hold its head under water until it stopped shaking." The central characters in the novel are Francis (Hano) Hanrahan, Shay, and Katie, three Dubliners who fall into the hands of the villainous Plunkett brothers, part of the cabal of grafters and drug lords that rule the city economically and politically. Shay, the eldest, winds up dead, and Hano, the new kid on the block, flees with young Katie. Tom Adair observed for the London *Independent* (June 16, 1990): "Bolger's sharpness in portraying [the] inexorable subjugation of ordinary lives is unforgettable. Here, meticulous prose whooshes with life. It imbues the passionate restraint of Bolger's indictment of dirty politics, of the leeching profiteering ethic, with a filleting edge." Patricia Craig, also writing for the London *Independent* (June 24, 1990), noted that exposure of "the shocking state of Ireland" was Bolger's goal

in writing *The Journey Home*. Craig, however, felt that as "an exercise in social criticism *The Journey Home* goes right over the top. Even Hano, on an ordinary visit to his parents, succumbs to hyperbole: 'I was like a wound inside their house, festering without air.' Dermot Bolger is a forceful commentator with an instinct for the strong theme, but he would do much better to tone down the portentous element in his approach."

At the center of Bolger's fourth novel, *Emily's Shoes* (1992), is Michael McMahon's conflicted feelings about his fetishism over women's shoes and the difficult childhood, including the deaths of his parents, that brought him to where he is. Shena Mackay, for the London *Independent* (June 14, 1992), found that in the novel a "sensuous melancholy pervades; a child's impacted grief at his mother's death and unacknowledged mourning for the father he never knew are rendered with painful accuracy. . . . Bolger has turned aside from the poetic and violent depictions of Dublin nightlife and political corruption which made his name, and has written a quiet, occasionally funny memoir of an almost wasted life." Alison Roberts, writing for the London *Times* (July 30, 1992), concluded that "McMahon does not like himself, Bolger does not like McMahon, and neither does the reader very much. Somehow, McMahon's childhood and the death of 'mammy' are not sufficiently traumatic to explain an adulthood of such self-hatred."

A Second Life (1994) is another novel about a man striving to come to terms with his past. Sean Blake, a 36-year-old Dublin photographer, has an out-of-body experience after an automobile crash. He is sent back to his body, however, and spends his time recovering from the accident in a search for his lost mother, who was forced by the cruel custom of her time to give him up for adoption because he was illegitimate. He and his birth mother search for each other telepathically, but she dies before they make contact in person. Bolger's "sub-text is history, personal and national and how one can impact upon the other," Carl MacDougall observed for the Glasgow *Herald* (May 14, 1994). "He is especially concerned," MacDougall added, "with the way the past continues, how it leaks into the present; that events and decisions we thought were of little consequence continue to affect our lives and often the lives of others. He is particular about decisions made on our behalf or those we cannot remember making, using the past to inform the present, exploring both recent history and buried memories." Mark Ford, for the London *Guardian* (May 17, 1994), judged the writing toward the end of the book to be "horribly sentimental" and the novel's climax "mawkish" in the extreme. "Bolger is an energetic writer," Ford concluded, "but also a monotonous one. Certainly *A Second Life* has more than its fair share of longueurs, during which it becomes hard not to wish its hero had died for more than just a few seconds in the crash described in the book's opening pages."

A critic for the *Economist* (April 19, 1997) termed Bolger's next novel, *Father's Music* (1997), a continuation of "Bolger's profound chronicling of Irish life." The novel begins in London, where Tracey Evans, a young drug user and club-hopper meets Luke Duggan, a middle-aged man from a family of criminals. Though Luke thought that by leaving Ireland he had his criminal past as well, he returns to his home country after his brother is killed, taking Tracey along under the guise of being his illegitimate daughter. Tracey eventually realizes that her father, whom she had assumed was English, is actually an Irish fiddler. "Bolger's exploration of an Irishness which arouses in him mingled feelings of love and resentment, pride and a sense of inferiority, provides the sub-text of the novel," Allan Massie wrote for the *Scotsman* (April 19, 1997). "Irish music, sentimental, deceiving, yet speaking to the heart, throbs through the narrative. Ireland's pride and Ireland's old poverty, now set against the glossy New Ireland, determinedly European, are questions that obsess and disturb him." Though Massie considered the novel too long by roughly 50 pages, he nonetheless considered *Father's Music* "a novel which will give far more enjoyment and satisfaction than many more exact works. It has a verve that is all but irresistible, and a knowledge of where it is coming from that is powerfully persuasive." Calling *Father's Music* "a haunting and often moving tale," Joanna Hunter argued, in a review for the London *Times* (February 21, 1998), that "where Bolger really shines is his canny depiction of the Anglo-Irish love-hate obsession, which elevates his novel when the plot fails."

In an article for the *Irish Times* (June 17, 2000), Bolger explained that he started work on his next novel, *Temptation* (2000), a week after turning 40. "In my previous novels," Bolger wrote, "characters' lives were transformed by major, often brutal, political or social events. But in *Temptation* I wanted to explore the life of a seemingly happily married woman enjoying what seems on the surface to be a normal family holiday." Many reviewers judged Bolger successful in conveying the thoughts of a middle-aged woman, Alison Gill, facing the temptation of re-encountering her first love. Rupert Shortt, however, writing for the *Financial Times* (July 29, 2000), observed that Bolger was promoted by the book's publishers for "his gift for getting inside [Alison's] head, but since Alison is short-tempered and childish, many readers will find this a tedious place to be." Alex Benzie, the reviewer for the *Scotsman* (July 29, 2000), praised "Bolger's fine, strong-willed prose" as a means of evoking "thoughts of mortality, the illusion of redemption of the past and the wisdom of keeping the past exactly where it is, without making an unholy upheaval of the present."

With *The Valparaiso Voyage* (2001), Bolger returned to the wider ranging political and social sphere that characterized many of his earlier novels. The title comes from "Thánaig Long ó Valparaiso," an Irish language poem by Pádraig de Brún that evokes the nostalgic feelings of someone rooted in Ireland but longing for a voyage to a sunny and exotic place such as the Chilean city Valparaiso. Brendan, the main character in *Voyage*, is treated brutally as a boy by his stepmother and forced to sleep in a shed used for his father's filing cabinets. He picks the locks to the cabinets and discovers evidence of corruption on the part of his father, a local planning officer. When Brendan grows up he marries and has a son but is unable to care for them. A convenient railroad accident allows him to fake his own death and disappear. He returns, ghostlike, when he hears of his father's death. "This is a tempestuous, loose-knit political thriller, a fictional expose of modern times, a tub-thumping rant against the recent past and current attempts to cover up," Helen Falconer observed for the London *Guardian* (November 10, 2001). "It is also a sad, distressing story of refugees from evil, piled upon ships destined never to dock at Valparaiso. Maybe it always was a mythical city? Unless, of course, as Brendan dare not fantasise, Valparaiso is what we find on coming home—the solid shore beneath the dreamer's feet." Tom Adair, for the *Scotsman* (November 24, 2001), noted that "with Bolger there is always the lonely childhood to negotiate." Adair concluded: "The tale rattles forward, interrupted by Brendan's maudlin introspection, becoming almost a state-of-the-nation audit of Ireland's present-day struggle to come to terms with itself. . . . Always best as a gripping expression of family warfare, and of rural, small-town Irishness, sometimes *The Valparaiso Voyage* loses its way— washed up in Dublin, in love with the past. Sometimes it soars. And Valparaiso, what of it? It never figures. It too is a ghost."

For the novel *The Family on Paradise Pier* (2005), Bolger drew on interviews he had conducted with Sheila Goold Verschoyle Fitzgerald, a woman born in the first years of the 20th century who had spent her youth in a manor house and her old age in a trailer. Two of her brothers became virulent communists and suffered deeply for their convictions, often at the hands of the Russian government, which ostensibly represented the embodiment of their beliefs. Sheila had once aspired to becoming an artist or a writer, but little of her work was ever seen by the public. "Sheila's quest was spiritual, to strip away the veneer of complexity and strive—despite tragedies and setbacks—to grasp the joy at the core of life," Bolger wrote in the *Irish Times* (March 22, 2005). "She was still a bohemian alternative thinker at the age of 73, when I met her first in 1977. . . . She taught me to believe in my dreams, and my life was never the same again." Bolger spent two years trying to turn her story into a nonfiction book but discovered that her recollections were not always in accord with history, so he recast the work as fiction. Katie Wink for the Dublin *Sunday Independent* (April 17, 2005) argued that "Sheila's story deserves to be told, and Bolger is the man to tell it. His sympathy for the Goold Verschoyle children is full of fatherly patience; in whatever ways they may go astray, he understands their good intentions and portrays them with compassion." Fintan O'Toole, writing for the London *Guardian* (May 7, 2005), went even further in praise of *The Family on Paradise Pier*, calling it Bolger's "best novel since *The Journey Home*" and a "remarkably vivid account of the way those who don't count may nevertheless matter."

Bolger's plays have taken up many of the same themes that have preoccupied him in his fiction. His first work for the stage, *The Lament for Arthur Cleary*, which premiered in 1989, is based on "The Lament for Art O'Leary," an Irish-language poem about an actual Irish Catholic nobleman who, in the 18th century, had returned home after English protestants seized control of the country and who refused to accept his nearly serf-like status under the English; O'Leary's wife is said to have composed the lament over his murdered body, though it was not written down until the 19th century. Bolger's play is set in contemporary Ireland, when Arthur Cleary, who has been a guest worker all over northern Europe, finds himself forced to return to a country held in thrall not by the English but by drug lords and the bureaucrats in the European Community. Joyce Macmillan, discussing a revival of the play for the London *Guardian* (October 20, 1992), commented that the play is "not only an exquisite post-modern tragedy, with a deep sureness of emotional and narrative structure underlying its fragmented episodes and imagery; it's also, possibly, the first play written in English in which the 'European Community' figures as a felt reality, rather than a form of words."

Bolger followed *The Lament for Arthur Cleary* with two one-act plays, *In High Germany* and *The Holy Ground*, both first produced at the Gate Theatre, in Dublin, in 1990. *In High Germany*, perhaps the more frequently revived of the two, depicts a deracinated Irishman named Eoin—now living in Hamburg, Germany—who is waiting for a train after attending the 1988 European Football Championships with two childhood friends. Eoin muses on the game and its implications, and it soon becomes apparent that the sport gives him his only sense of identity. "It's not a train he waits for: It's a reconciliation," Patti Hartigan wrote for the *Boston Globe* (May 25, 1994). "The play," Hartigan added, "touches a raw nerve for anyone forced to live a life of exile, straddled in cultural limbo. It is serious, yet the end result is somewhat slight. Bolger tries so hard to reconcile his own issues that the play creaks in its most obvious moments." John McKeown noted, for the *Irish Times* (August 17, 2001), that the road to the character's epiphany "involves a feast of drinking, lunatic incidents and vividly recaptured memories that encapsulate the common experience of a generation."

In 1997 Bolger served as playwright in association at Dublin's famed Abbey Theatre, the first home of many of his plays, including *One Last White Horse* (1991) *April Bright* (1995), and *The Passion of Jerome* (1999). In *April Bright* a couple expecting a child moves into a house in Dublin only to have an unknown woman come to their door and conjure up the spirits of the previous inhabitants, a family named Bright. Fintan O'Toole, writing for the *Irish Times* (August 29, 1995), observed that "this co-existence of generations is a source, not of conflict but of sympathy. As the play unfolds we soon realise that past and present are there, not to wage war, but to fulfill each other." Bolger, David Nowlan wrote for the *Irish Times* (August 24, 1995), "has contrived an intricate interplay of both attitudinal change between generations and emotional continuance within successive generations. The snag is that, as the two generations co-exist in the space of this terrace house, and as one admires the literary skill with which the author intermingles their separate but related familial concerns, the theatrical contrivance of the piece becomes increasingly apparent."

The Passion of Jerome is, as the title implies, a foray into the realm of the spiritual and is considered his most metaphysical piece. "This isn't a Catholic play," Bolger told Mic Moroney for the *Irish Times* (February 11, 1999), explaining that the play partly represented an argument with the prevailing idea that religious ideas should be left out of the theater or at least treated less than seriously. "It seems that if you deal with Catholicism in this day and age, you have to be sneering and post-modern. There is this notion that people are afraid to explore religion because there's a sense that it's a cliched part of the past." In the play Jerome is not a father of the Catholic Church but a married architect who sleeps with his mistress in an apartment once occupied by a boy who committed suicide. The boy now haunts his former home and scores Jerome's hands with the stigmata. Lara Marlowe, writing for the *Irish Times* (June 4, 2002) about a production of the play in Paris, France, quoted the French critic Jean-Luc Jeener, who called Bolger "a great playwright" and the play "a story of redemption. Simple, powerful, without hackneyed words, superfluous explanations or moralising." David Nowlan, writing for the *Irish Times* (February 18, 1999), argued that *The Passion of Jerome* "might be taken as a metaphor for the rescue of a Catholic soul from some kind of living purgatory. Or maybe it is a kind of allegory about a dysfunctional materialistic society, larded with social comment (some of it [straightforwardly] didactic and some glancingly satirical) about scandal and inequality."

The apartment in which Jerome's affair takes place is part of the public housing projects of Ballymun, a group of seven apartment towers built in the 1960s amid much ballyhoo and demolished at the end of the century as urban blight. Bolger returned to that setting for *From These Green Heights* (2004), the story of a middle-aged couple who attempt to come to terms with their memories of the Ballymun and its roller-coaster history. "What makes Bolger's play important is the compassion and clarity with which he depicts Ballymun's development as a vibrant community," Karen Fricker noted for the *Guardian* (May 17, 2005). Fricker commented, however, that during the latter half of the play "Bolger the novelist grapples with Bolger the dramatist, and the play is overwhelmed by its complicated plot and themes." In February 2005 *From These Green Heights* was declared the best new play at the 2004 Irish Times ESB Irish Theatre Awards.

The *Passion of Jerome* and *From These Green Heights*, as well as Bolger's play *A Dublin Bloom: An Original Free Adaptation of James Joyce's* Ulysses (1995), were published as books during the same year that they first appeared on stage, while *April Bright* was first published, in 1997, in an edition with another short play, *Blinded by the Light*. Bolger's 1992 collection *A Dublin Quartet* brought together *The Lament for Arthur Cleary*, *In High Germany*, *The Holy Ground*, and *One Last White Horse*. *Plays: I* (2000) included all the works from *A Dublin Quartet* with the exception of *One Last White Horse*, which was replaced by *Blinded by the Light*.

In addition to his work as a poet, fiction writer, playwright, and publisher, Bolger has had notable success as an editor. In 1993 he edited *The Picador Book of Contemporary Irish Fiction*, which also includes a sample of his own work, and in 1997 he published *Finbar's Hotel*, a serial novel about a seedy Dublin hotel. He conceived and edited the book and contributed one chapter and small bits of connecting material; the remainder was written, in unsigned chapters, by Roddy Doyle, Anne Enright, Hugo Hamilton, Jennifer Johnston, Joseph O'Connor, and Colm Tóibín. Reviewers have said that readers could have fun either by trying to guess which author wrote which chapter or by not worrying about the authorship and just enjoying the book. Katherine Weber, for the *New York Times Book Review* (May 2, 1999), judged that Bolger did "a superb job of allowing his colleagues their freedom, while at the same time imposing enough structure to make the whole greater than the sum of the parts." The result is a book that "brings together a good deal of distinctive writing with energy and charm—and surprising harmony. American readers will probably be far less intent than their Irish counterparts on guessing the identity of the author of each unsigned chapter. Instead, readers here . . . will be drawn in by the novel itself, an appealing series of intersecting vignettes." A surprise best-seller, *Finbar's Hotel* was followed, in 1999, by *Ladies' Night at Finbar's Hotel*, in which Bolger was joined by Maeve Binchy, Clare Boylan, Emma Donoghue, Anne Haverty, Éilís Ní Dhuibhne, Kate O'Riordan, and Deirdre Purcell. In the second version the old hotel

has been renovated under the new ownership of an Irish rock star and his Dutch wife. "Finbar's cosmopolitan refurbishment reflects the new Ireland's Celtic Tiger boosterism, but the chic atmosphere doesn't lend itself to the cohesion of a novel as well as did the nostalgic air of the old hotel," a reviewer commented for *Publishers Weekly* (February 14, 2000). "However, the amusing crossovers of recurrent characters, such as the unnamed musical celebrity who appears in the charming nun-on-the-run tale and who throws a fit in another story, capture some of the hotel's charm and add wit and style to Bolger's creative concept."

The word *home* carries a strong weight for Bolger. He continues to live in Dublin, in the section known as Drumcondra, not far from Finglas, with his wife Bernadette, a nurse. They have two sons: Donnacha, born in 1990, and Diarmuid, born in 1992. He is a member of Aosdána, the Irish writers' association. "It's the job of art to point out things that are wrong with society," Bolger told Sarah Hemming. "But there are many parts of Dublin that are very beautiful. I certainly wouldn't want to live anywhere else."

—S.Y.

Suggested Reading: (Dublin) *Sunday Independent* on-line Nov. 21, 2004; *Irish Times* Arts p14 Feb. 11, 1999, p70 June 17, 2000, p61 May 8, 2001; (London) *Independent* p35 Sep. 26, 1990; (London) *Observer* p54 June 2, 1991; (London) *Sunday Mirror* Features p2+ Jan. 17, 1999

Selected Books: poetry—*The Habit of Flesh*, 1980; *Finglas Lilies*, 1981; *No Waiting America*, 1982; *Internal Exiles*, 1986; *Leinster Street Ghosts*, 1989; *Taking My Letters Back: New and Selected Poems*, 1998; *The Chosen Moment*, 2004; fiction—*Night Shift*, 1985; *The Woman's Daughter*, 1987 (revised edition, 1991); *The Journey Home*, 1990; *Emily's Shoes*, 1992; *A Second Life*, 1994; *Father's Music*, 1997; *Temptation*, 2000; *The Valparaiso Voyage*, 2001; *The Family on Paradise Pier*, 2005; plays—*A Dublin Quartet*, 1992; *A Dublin Bloom: An Original Free Adaptation of James Joyce's* Ulysses, 1995; *April Bright; and, Blinded by the Light*, 1997; *The Passion of Jerome*, 1999; *Plays: I*, 2000; *From These Green Heights*, 2004; as editor and contributor—*The Picador Book of Contemporary Irish Fiction*, 1993; *Finbar's Hotel*, 1997; *Ladies Night at Finbar's Hotel*, 1999

Booker, Stephen Todd

1953– Poet

An accomplished poet whose language ranges from the formal to the vernacular, Steven Todd Booker is a unique voice in modern American verse. Booker has spent, however, the last quarter-century on death row for murder. He did not begin seriously writing poetry until after he was incarcerated. His writing, he claims, allows him to travel to places he might never be allowed to see again. "Writing is like a magic carpet or a time machine," he told Bruce Weber for the *New York Times* (March 9, 2004). Booker added, "I remember thinking one time—I'd already been [in prison] a while—and I hadn't seen a star in 12 years. And I started to wonder about them, thinking they'd changed or something, and I wrote this poem imagining stars but from the perspective of a bat." The resulting poem is called "I, When a Bumblebee Bat." As quoted by Weber, it reads in part, "Only twice in twelve long years / Has the self in me transformed / To weighing less than a cent, / And blended with the evening, / Or heard ringing in my ears, / Or seen a star do its thing, / Umbrellaed aloft on air." Though he is imprisoned, Booker's confinement has allowed his imagination to take flight.

Steven Todd Booker was born in Brooklyn, New York, in 1953. After his father deserted the family, Booker and his older brother were raised by his mother and two aunts. While his mother worked as a civil servant to provide for her sons, Booker became involved with petty crime, drugs, and alcohol at an early age. In a poem titled "Wisdom," as quoted by Weber, Booker wrote of this period: "We kids did chase and stone a goofy square. / None of us knew the dude. A lapsed rabbi? . . . / Maybe . . . none of us cared. Shoeless, he ran / Through Crown Heights, and on into East New York."

Booker's rough street persona, however, masked an inquisitive and scholarly nature, which manifested itself while he was home reading. He read the works of Virgil, Homer, Edgar Allan Poe, and Robert Louis Stevenson, among others. "I lived two lives," Booker remarked to Weber. "Outside I was a thief and a hustler. I used drugs. But I was a bookworm in the house. Both my aunts belonged to the Book-of-the-Month Club, and as they got older, they worked as domestics for white families, and the families would throw away books. So they brought books home. I was never at a loss for anything to read."

Leaving school at age 14, Booker drifted for a few years. After watching his mother die of a stroke, Booker enlisted in the U. S. Army. He was shipped overseas, to Okinawa, Japan, where he began a love affair with a Japanese woman, later memorialized in the poem "Sandii." He was discharged from the army after being involved in a fight with a fellow soldier, and he soon became hooked on heroin, among other drugs. His drug and alcohol abuse eventually led him to robbery; after serving most of a five-year prison sentence for robbery, he was released and shortly thereafter committed the crime that sent him to death row.

Booker was living in Florida at the time, not far from Lorine Demoss Harmon, a 94-year-old widow who lived by herself in a small apartment in Gainsville. On November 9, 1977 Harmon was coming home from a bridge game and found Booker, high on drugs and alcohol, robbing her apartment. Booker raped the elderly woman, brutally beat her, and stabbed her eight times with knives from her own kitchen. Less than a year later, Booker was sentenced to death for Harmon's murder.

About a year after his conviction, Booker received a letter from Page Zyromski, the grand-niece of the woman he had murdered. She told him that she forgave him. He wrote back asking if she was "some kind of goody-two-shoes," as quoted by Weber. Zyromski, a teacher, contributor to *Catechist* magazine, and author of several books on Catholicism has written to him often since that first exchange and has even visited him on several occasions. Booker and Zyromski have developed a relationship, and she has petitioned the courts repeatedly to stay his execution.

Booker has spent nearly 30 years on death row. He remains alive because of a maze of court motions and appeals that have prevented his execution from going forth. In 1988 a U.S. District Court judge ruled that the case be remanded for re-sentencing, but it took until 1998 for that re-sentencing to occur. When his trial finally reached the courts, a new jury also imposed the death penalty.

Zyromski opposes the death penalty because of her Roman Catholic faith, which opposes capital punishment. She acknowledges, however, that forgiving her great-aunt's murderer was initially difficult. But, as she remarked in an interview with Grant Segall for the Cleveland *Plain Dealer* (March 10, 2004): "I knew that I needed to forgive this guy. That's sort of bottom-line for a Christian." Aiding her in her efforts to reduce Booker's sentence are a number of literary figures, among them the poets Denise Levertov (before her death) and Hayden Carruth, who have argued that Booker's contributions to such journals as *Field*, the *Kenyon Review*, and *Seneca Review* prove that he is an important poet whose voice should continue to be heard.

In addition to his publication in various journals, Booker has written two books of poetry, *Waves & License* (1983) and *Tug* (1994). Fielding Dawson, reviewing *Tug* for the *American Book Review* (March–May 1995), noted: "I read every poem in this book until I understood it or, better, until I understood it as best I could. It has a mobius feel: twenty-seven poems in interweaves we're not used to. . . . Acrostics where you would, nor could, not believe it possible. They aren't related to entertainment, nor is he. They are serious, of the highest wit, artistry, irony, and fury. Booker is a very serious man, make no mistake about it: he is very angry, but, you see he has gone where we have not. . . . Booker is inside himself inside a cell inside a prison in a special section called Death Row, far beyond our clocks, and calendars, our nine to five, he's inside the inside." E. J. Zimmermann, for *Choice* (December 1994), remarked: "[This] is a captivating book—and a disturbing one. Almost all of its poems, in varied formats, address, in varied ways and with a certain chill, the small world of the author's past-cum-present. . . . The poems are generally precise and carefully constructed with an occasional and unusual use of rhyme and, more frequently, the surprising but appropriate word. The result, collectively, makes it difficult to believe that

Booker only began to write while in prison. He limns well. As the title poem says, 'Guests, we are, in one riff, one chest, one drum.'"

Booker has reportedly contributed some of the proceeds from his books to the education of Page Zyromski's children. "[His] is very much a story of redemption," she told Grant Segall.

—C.M.

Suggested Reading: *African American Review* p506 Fall 1996; *American Book Review* p25 Mar.–May 1995; (Cleveland) *Plain Dealer* B p4 Mar. 10, 2004; *Choice* p597 Dec. 1994; *New York Times* E p1+ Mar. 9, 2004

Selected Poetry Collections: *Waves & License,* 1983; *Tug,* 1994

Star Black/Courtesy of Laure-Anne Bosselaar

Bosselaar, Laure-Anne

Nov. 17, 1943– Poet

"Poetry for me is passion, solace, joy," Laure-Anne Bosselaar told Suzanne Frischkorn for the *Samsara Quarterly* (Vol. 2, Issue 2, 2000–01, on-line). "The poet's job is to reach out, grab, and give back the truth." Bosselaar, in the opinion of Barbara Hoffert, as expressed in *Library Journal* (April 1, 1998), "writes wonderfully evocative poems, pinpointing with exquisite accuracy 'the worlds in this world' even as she airs personal and spiritual concerns." Strongly autobiographical, Bosselaar's work "embodies the concept that poetry springs from

moments of intense emotion recalled at leisure," as Lynn Flewelling wrote for the *Bangor (Maine) Daily News* (May 10, 1997). Within the past 20 years, Bosselaar has published *Artemis,* which came out in Belgium, her native land; *The Hour between Dog and Wolf* (1997); *Small Gods of Grief* (2001), and *A New Hunger* (2007). Some of her poems have appeared in *Ploughshares,* the *Harvard Review,* the *Georgia Review,* the *Washington Post,* and *Agni,* among other periodicals, and her poetry has been included in many anthologies. She has edited three collections of poems by others—*Outsiders: Poems about Rebels, Exiles and Renegades* (1999), *Urban Nature: Poems about Wildlife in the City* (2000), and *Never Before: Poems about First Experiences* (2005)—and with her husband, Kurt Brown, she co-edited the anthology *Night Out: Poems about Hotels, Motels, Restaurants, and Bars* (1997). Also with Brown, she translated from Dutch into English the poems in *The Plural of Happiness: Selected Poems by Herman de Coninck* (2006). Bosselaar teaches graduate courses in poetry at Sarah Lawrence College, in Bronxville, New York, and has led many poetry workshops. She has also given many public readings of her poems. At one of them, Flewelling reported, Bosselaar "read a few well-chosen poems that rocked a roomful of experienced poets and poetry-phobic prose artists such as myself back on our emotional heels."

An only child, Laure-Anne Bosselaar was born on November 17, 1943 in Belgium. Her parents maintained a home in the Belgian port of Antwerp. In her poem "The Worlds in This World," she wrote that while one of her grandfathers was imprisoned by the Germans during World War I, he "sewed perfect, eighteen-buttoned / booties for his wife with the skin of a dead / dog found in a trench." During World War II her father sympathized with the Nazis. Bosselaar's "deepest shame," she told Suzanne Frischkorn, was "being the daughter of anti-Semites"; her knowledge of her father's wartime activities "haunted" her, as Lynn Flewelling wrote. Her father in effect benefited from the war, becoming wealthy as a merchant of steel and iron after its conclusion, during the massive rebuilding effort in Europe. Her father's manner and behavior at home further alienated her from him. In her poem "The Cellar" (*Massachusetts Review*, Spring 1995), she recalled being sent to her family's basement on an errand: "From up there, comes father's call, weary / irked, the same every time, with the same pitch and / threat after the last consonant in my name. / Deaf with terror, I grab the potatoes or his gin, / run out, slam the door, slap the hasp, / holding my offering to father as far as I can / from my body, throw it on the kitchen formica / in the escape to my room." In her poem "Seven Fragments on Hearing a Hammer Pounding," from *Small Gods of Grief*, she described her parents' laughter when remarks they had made about Jews led her, at age five, to ask out of ignorance what sort of animals Jews were. In the same poem she wrote about a visit to her father's office as a seven-year-old girl; when her father discovered that she had used his pen, he slapped her face and struck her chest with his knee.

For much of her childhood, Bosselaar lived in misery in a Roman Catholic convent in Bruges, Belgium. She was "more often punished than praised," as she wrote in her poem "English Flavors," and had "no access to radio, television, or movies," as she recalled to Frischkorn. "We were only allowed to read books given to us, most of which were telling religious stories. I had to make up the outside world because I didn't see it. So I would tell myself stories. I would see the Atlantic Ocean in a mud puddle for example. . . . I would make up people's lives just by looking at them, to the point of imagining the color of their towels, how they ate and where, in the kitchen or in the living room?" In her poem "The Rat Trinity," published in *Ploughshares* (Fall 2001), Bosselaar wrote of seeing a rat waiting "with the same tenacity I had / as a child, hungry to grow strong / enough to escape the nunnery / without being caught. . . . There were times, when / beatings seared my skin with hues / of oil on the river Scheldt, and I / squeezed my thumbs / in my fists through dormitory / nights, there were times I prayed / to the Rat Trinity. To show me the way / out of the convent." In another poem, "The Pallor of Survival," she wrote of the experience of a childhood friend: "I'd seen / what the nuns did to her when she confessed / she masturbated: bending her over, pulling down / her panties to ram the longest part of an ivory crucifix / into her, hissing: HE is the Only One Who Can Come / Inside You—No One Else—You Hear?" In her conversation with Flewelling, Bosselaar alluded to being the victim of a rape as a young adult.

Bosselaar attended the Conservatoire Royal de Bruxelles, in Belgium, a school that specializes in music, theater, and "the art of the word," according to its Web site. She earned a first prize in elocution and a B.A. degree in French literature, in 1962. She remained in Brussels to enroll at what is now called the Institut National Superieur des Arts et Spectacles et des Techniques de Diffusion, which offers courses in many aspects of the entertainment industry; there, in 1964, she earned another B.A., in theater arts. During the next decade she devoted herself to homemaking and motherhood. She entered the workforce in 1974, taking voice-over and other jobs in theater, television, and radio in Belgium and neighboring Luxembourg. She next taught literature and poetry courses at the International School of Brussels, a day school for students up to age 18. She left that job in 1986, the year that her first volume of poetry, *Artemis*, was published. The poems in *Artemis* are in French, one of the four languages in which she is fluent. Bosselaar told Frischkorn that her knowledge of French, Dutch, and Flemish idioms that don't exist in English is helpful to her as a poet writing in English: since "a cliche in one language isn't a cliche in another," knowing them helps her to meet "the challenge of finding an exact way of describing an image, emotion, or sensory detail," which is of prime importance to her.

In 1987 the now-divorced Bosselaar settled in the U.S. From 1989 until 1991 she co-directed the Aspen Writers' Conference, in Colorado. When it was founded, by the poet Kurt Brown, in the mid-1970s, it served as a retreat for poets. By the time Bosselaar had joined the staff, it was catering to a range of prose writers as well. (Currently called Aspen Summer Words, it now welcomes readers as well as writers.) In 1992 Bosselaar and Brown married. At around that time Bosselaar entered the graduate writing program at Warren Wilson College, in Asheville, North Carolina. A so-called low-residency program, it requires a master's-degree candidate to complete four half-year semesters, during each of which the student spends 10 days on campus. Before graduation, according to the school's Web site, each student "must complete an analytical paper on some topic of literature, contemporary letters or craft; read 50–80 books; teach a class to fellow students; give a public reading of his or her work; and prepare a manuscript of fiction or poetry." in 1994 Bosselaar earned an M.F.A. degree from the college.

Bosselaar's first collection of poems in English, *The Hour between Dog and Wolf*, contains an introduction by the Pulitzer Prize–winning, Yugoslavian-born poet Charles Simic and poems whose subjects include both Bosselaar's childhood experiences and aspects of her adult life. Its first poem, "The Worlds in This World," is introduced with lines by the poet Stephen Dobyns—"This is the world to love. There is no other"—and begins, "Doors were left open in heaven again: / drafts wheeze, clouds wrap their ripped pages / around roofs and trees. . . . / all this in one American street. / Elsewhere, somewhere, a tide / recedes, incense is lit, an infant / sucks from a nipple, a grenade / shrieks, a man buys his first cane. / Think of it: the worlds in this world." In the year 1916, the poem continues, "thousands and thousands of Jews / from the Holocaust were already—were / still—busy living their lives; / while gnawed by self-doubt, [the German poet Rainer Maria] Rilke couldn't / write a line for weeks in Vienna's Victorgasse, / and fishermen drowned off Finnish coasts, / and lovers kissed for the very first time, / while in Kashmir an old woman fell asleep, / her cheek on her good husband's belly." The poem's last stanza, after mentioning a speck of dust that has landed on the poet's desk, reads, "Say now, at this instant: / one thornless rose opens in a blue jar above / that speck, but you—reading this—know / nothing of how it came to flower here, and I / nothing of who bred it, or where, nothing / of my son and daughter's fate, of what grows / in your garden or behind the walls of your chest: / is it longing? Fear? Will it matter?" The poem ends with the words, "Listen to that wind, listen to it ranting / The doors of heaven never close, / that's the Curse, that's the Miracle." In a review of the book for *Ploughshares* (Fall 1997, on-line), the poet Wyn Cooper wrote that the poems set in Belgium "do more than address life there—they evoke it in every color, smell, texture, and taste." Another poet, Andrea Hollander Budy, writing for the *Arkansas Democrat-Gazette* (April 26, 1998), found "the foreignness of Bosselaar's perspective [to be] especially enlightening, whether she is describing her Flemish neighbors in postwar Belgium, or when she turns her focus onto things American." A third poet, Marilyn Krysl, in an assessment for the *Iowa Review* (Summer/Fall 1998), remarked on the coexistence of Bosselaar's attention to "the smallest detail" and capacity to "encompass the whole" and noted her ability to articulate in her poems "a child's rich chiaroscuro of emotion," her "gift for humor, whimsy, [and] irony," her "preoccupation with the sensuous and sensual," and the "ardor with which Bosselaar embraces her material." *The Hour between Dog and Wolf* was a finalist for the Nicholas Roerich Prize and the Walt Whitman Award, among other honors.

In her conversation with Frischkorn, Bosselaar described in detail her creative process: "I work exclusively when an image strikes me; that, for me, is the beginning of a poem. An image is like opening the door to a poem. Often I'll start by describing things around me to get into the imaginative space of a poem, and later I'll discard those descriptions because I don't need them anymore. . . . Once an image has triggered my imagination and/or a memory I will then introduce characters, dialogue or lyric based on the image. What I also do is listen to the sounds of the first line, and use that as guide for the rest of the poem. The sound of the first line, for me, sonorously tells me the emotion of the poem." She also said, "Nine times out of ten I will start a poem in answer to a poem I have just read. When I was writing *The*

Hour Between Dog and Wolf, it was as if I was in constant dialogue with a novelist I have never met: Ron Hanson who wrote the extraordinary novel *Mariette In Ecstasy.*" (That novel is set in a convent). An extremely slow writer, by her own account, Bosselaar typically rewrites every poem 20 to 30 times and discards 85 percent of her work. She has named Brigitte Pegeen Kelly, Louis Aragon, and the Flemish poet Herman de Coninck as "masters" whose poems she has studied in depth.

Bosselaar told Frischkorn that many of the poems in *Small Gods of Grief* were inspired by writings of the poet Jane Kenyon. That collection earned Bosselaar the 2001 Isabella Gardner Prize for Poetry, which BOA Editions (the book's publisher) gives every other year to a poet in mid-career for work of "exceptional merit." The title of the book comes from one section of the seven-part poem "Seven Fragments on Hearing a Hammer Pounding," in which news accounts about the increasing influence of right-wing politicians in some countries spark the speaker's fears that her father's "tongue" is still alive. "O Gods of Grief, grant me this," she wrote: "some tongues will die, some tongues must." In an evaluation of the book for the *Crab Orchard Review* (on-line), Debra Kang Dean wrote, "Small Gods of Grief is marked by [Bosselaar's] irrepressible spirit and essentially redemptive imagination." A reviewer for *Poetry* (July 2003) wrote, "As good poems ought, Bosselaar's best suggest more than they say, but they do so with refreshing clarity. . . . With admirable economy, Bosselaar makes a near-epigram out of material lesser poets would belabor." In an assessment for the *Harvard Review* (Spring 2002), Andrea Hollander Budy wrote, "Bosselaar's concision is equaled by her ability to choose exactly the right details—a vital attribute in a genre so dependent upon the relative power of an image." Noting that she did not want to "neglect the book's pulse and heart," Budy added, "Good lyric poems allow us to empathize with their author; the best rouse our own emotional centers. Bosselaar's poems do both."

Bosselaar's poem "English Flavors" won first prize in the 1996 National Poetry Contest. Bosselaar has taught at the University of Southern Maine as well as at Sarah Lawrence College and has been a writer in residence at Hamilton College and the Vermont Studio Center. Her latest collection of poems, *A New Hunger*, was published in 2007.

A "small, serene woman with a wonderfully gentle accent," according to Flewelling, Bosselaar has what she described to Frischkorn as "a maniacal curiosity—I'm so curious that I could stay in a hotel lobby all day and never be bored." She lives in New York City with her husband, Kurt Brown. She told Frischkorn that she and Brown are "each other's first readers. When I show a poem to Kurt 90 percent of the time he'll read it and say, 'So?' 'And?' and 75 percent of the time he's right.

When he shows me work I will often say, 'This is great but . . .' and he will energetically defend the part that I doubt, then hours later come back and say, 'You were right again, damn it!'" She continued, "We're very, very supportive of each other. The only time we literally had a fight was one day in the car. The radio commented on something so fascinating that I said 'I'm going to write a poem about that,' and he had the guts to say 'I thought about it first!'" She told Frischkorn that she adopted the habit of writing from 4:30 to 10:30 a.m. when she was raising her son and daughter and, for a number of years, the child of a friend. Her son is a physician; her daughter works as a food stylist in Hollywood. Bosselaar is a passionate cook and gardener.

—R.E.

Suggested Reading: *Bangor (Maine) Daily News* May 10, 1997; Laure-Anne Bosselaar's Web site; *New York Times Book Review* p14 July 6, 1997, p32 Nov. 4, 2001; *Samsara Quarterly* (on-line) Vol. 2, Issue 2, 2000–01

Selected Books: *The Hour between Dog and Wolf*, 1997; *Small Gods of Grief*, 2001, *A New Hunger*, 2007; as editor—*Night Out: Poems about Hotels, Motels, Restaurants, and Bars* (with Kurt Brown), 1997; *Outsiders: Poems about Rebels, Exiles, and Renegades*, 1999; *Urban Nature: Poems about Wildlife in the City*, 2000; *Never Before: Poems about First Experiences*, 2005

Alex Wong/Getty Images

Branch, Taylor

Jan. 14, 1947– Biographer; journalist; historian; novelist

Though Taylor Branch has been a journalist, novelist, and ghostwriter at various points during his long career, he is best known as the author of one of the definitive histories of the civil rights movement, which he chronicled in three massive volumes written over a nearly 25-year period. These three books—*Parting the Waters* (1988), *Pillar of Fire* (1998), and *At Cannan's Edge* (2006), all subtitled *America in the King Years*—chronicle not only the metamorphosis of the civil rights movement through the 1950s and 1960s but also

the evolving ideology of its central figure, the Reverend Dr. Martin Luther King Jr., whose assassination, in 1968, marked the end of an era. Branch's books examine King as a person and as a central leader of a movement that successfully brought an end to legalized segregation in the U.S. The trilogy also offers detailed portraits of the many other people involved, from such figures as Rosa Parks, whose refusal to give up her seat on a bus prompted a successful boycott of Montgomery, Alabama's segregated public-transportation system, to presidents John F. Kennedy and Lyndon B. Johnson, whose administrations were strongly marked by their involvement in the movement. Moreover, Branch's monumental series, which runs to almost 3,000 pages, puts the civil rights movement in the context of the post–World War II era as a whole, making it at times a condensed national history of the years between 1954 and 1968. "People think of the movement as taking place in an era of simplicity," Branch told Mark Harris for *Publishers Weekly* (December 16, 1988). "If you believe that, then civil rights history is in danger of collapsing into platitude. But certainly, it's not true that the civil rights movement is over and the good guys won. In fact, there's been a strong tendency to repudiate the '60s as a time of excess and non-patriotism. But that'll go down the tubes as well."

Taylor Branch was born on January 14, 1947 in Atlanta, Georgia, the eldest of six children by the former Jane Worthington and Franklin T. Branch, the owner of an extensive dry-cleaning chain, consisting at one time of as many as 17 stores, and a smaller chain of bowling alleys. Growing up in Atlanta, Branch had the opportunity to experience history firsthand, with the fledgling civil rights movement taking shape before his eyes. Yet being young and white and with seemingly apolitical parents—Branch's father had a law degree but called politics a "deadbeat's game," Branch recalled to Kim Hubbard and Linda Kramer for *People* (December 19, 1988)—Branch for many years knew almost nothing about the movement. That changed after he saw newspaper and television images of civil rights protests in Birmingham, Alabama, in 1963, including one of the most famous images of the era: a photo of a police dog, teeth bared, leaping on a passively resisting African-American teenager. "Until those dogs in Birmingham, which penetrated my little world of high school sports and chasing girls, I thought that everything in America was wonderful," he told Harris. "I had the rosy view that all of the authority figures were doing the right thing." Branch's interest in King in particular was fired by hearing King's voice. "I knew that I wanted to investigate the life that could produce that voice," he told Harris, "and I had never even heard a whole King speech."

After graduating, in 1964, from the private Westminster Schools in Atlanta, Branch attended the University of North Carolina, at Chapel Hill, with a full, four-year scholarship from the John Motley Morehead Foundation. While at Chapel Hill he became directly involved in the civil rights movement and in protests against the Vietnam War. During that time his family also made contributions to ending segregation. When activists organized protests in Georgia's Forsyth County to draw attention to the violence faced there by African-Americans—who were threatened if they stayed after sundown anywhere in the county, even as servants in white households—Branch's father drove a group of protestors to Forsyth and lent a laundry truck to take another group there as well. "I was unbelievably proud of him," Branch told Hubbard and Kramer. "I considered myself a campus activist, but I had never done anything like that then. But my daddy did it, and he never wanted to talk about it. It was a very isolated thing." Branch's father and his partner in the bowling alley venture also helped the cause by becoming the first bowling alley in the area to allow blacks and whites to bowl alongside each other.

Branch earned his undergraduate degree in political science and history, in 1968, and followed that, in 1970, with a master's degree in public affairs from the Woodrow Wilson School of Public and International Affairs at Princeton University, in New Jersey. Having worked on Eugene McCarthy's failed 1968 bid for the Democratic presidential nomination, Branch kept up his political activism during this time by devoting part of one summer to outreach among African-American voters in rural Georgia. Arrested that summer for the only time in his life, Branch was officially charged, he told an audience of inmates at a New York City prison, with "'being in Niggertown' illegally," according to Herbert Mitgang, for the New York Times (January 7, 1989). "I got out of jail after the Mayor looked at my I.D. from Princeton and said they didn't want anyone from that university in their jail and that I better not show up in that county ever again, and I

haven't." When Branch wrote about his work that summer for a school report, he gave the professor the journal he had kept during that time, and the professor, in turn, sent selections of the journal to the Washington Monthly, then in its infancy. The magazine's founder and editor, Charles Peters, published the selections and offered Branch a position on the staff.

Branch worked for the Washington Monthly until 1972, when he left to work for Senator George McGovern's presidential campaign. That same year a collection of essays from the Washington Monthly, edited and written by Branch and Peters, appeared under the title Blowing the Whistle: Dissent in the Public Interest. The collection detailed a number of then-current issues of corruption and mismanagement facing corporations and the government, while at the same time looking at the lives of those willing to risk their livelihoods to reveal these offenses. In Library Journal (May 15, 1972), Renate Hayum argued that Peters and Branch "do their whistle blowing in a refined way. They speak the truth as they see it and do not editorialize. . . . A well-balanced, sane account of frightening things happening in government and to those who try to speak out." In the New York Times (April 30, 1972), V. S. Navasky called the book a "unique collection of essays" and praised Branch's contributions to the volume. Navasky continued: "I don't wish to be the one to blow the whistle on the editors, who are frank and modest in their claims, but it should be noted that [some of the] essays . . . really have more to do with protest [and analysis] than whistle-blowing."

After Richard M. Nixon trounced McGovern in the 1972 presidential election, Branch returned to journalism, taking a staff position at Harper's, in New York City, in 1973. He remained at Harper's until 1975, when he began a short stint at Esquire that ended the following year. During this period Branch also began working as a ghostwriter and co-author of autobiographies. After ghostwriting Blind Ambition (1976), the memoirs of the Nixon White House lawyer John Dean, he co-authored Second Wind: The Memoirs of an Opinionated Man (1979), the autobiography of the basketball star Bill Russell. Branch's contribution to Dean's book went unacknowledged for a time, but reviewers noted his assistance to Russell. For the New Republic (October 20, 1979), Larry McMurtry wrote that Russell's "analyses of the psychology, tactics, and geometry of basketball make fascinating reading. They will hold the attention of any fan, but they are not Bill Russell's central concern. . . . What he has in mind is serious autobiography—an attempt to understand and describe his own experience—and with a certain amount of unobtrusive help from Taylor Branch, he achieves it."

Having worked in a collaborative capacity for some time, Branch wanted to tackle a book of his own for his next project, especially since he was starting to feel pigeonholed as a ghostwriter. "I do think that it's good exercise for someone like myself who wants to write fiction," Branch told Judy Klemesrud for the *New York Times Book Review* (December 9, 1979), "because basically it's putting yourself in the skin of another character. But if I thought I was going to be a ghostwriter for the rest of my life, I don't think I'd like that." Branch then finished his first (and, to date, only) novel, *The Empire Blues*, which met with little fanfare when it was published, in 1981.

Branch's next book, *Labyrinth* (1982), co-authored with Eugene M. Propper, a former federal prosecutor, is about the assassination of the Chilean ambassador Orlando Letelier. In *Library Journal* (May 1, 1982), M. S. Stohl described the main narrative of the book as "well told and highly readable" but added that "many of the more difficult questions regarding American foreign policy and respect for the law and human rights are not well addressed." Philip Taubman, for the *New York Times Book Review* (March 21, 1982), wrote: "Like a good thriller, *Labyrinth* begins with the crime itself and then skillfully weaves back and forth between the killers and the investigators until they finally meet. In places, particularly early in the book, the narrative line becomes opaque as the authors pause to give us lengthy sections of background about individuals whose importance to the story does not become clear until much later. The story is kept moving with crisp dialogue, dozens of pages of it. The only problem is that most of the exchanges were manufactured by the authors. . . . These are minor irritants, however, because the book, at a deeper level, delivers an honest, uncompromising description of Government investigators and prosecutors at work. This insider's account spares no one, including Mr. Propper, whose mistakes are fully chronicled along with those of officials in the F.B.I., the State Department and the C.I.A."

Though Branch had decided as early as the mid-1970s to write a one-volume biography of Martin Luther King, he was told that, at that time, his reputation was not strong enough for a publisher to give him an advance that would pay for the time needed to research and write what he already knew would be a complex book. In 1980, however, with several successful books already under his belt, he was able to get the contract he needed, and the following year he went to work. "I spent six months reading books," he told Mark Harris, "and the more I got into it, the harder the books were to find. Civil rights books do not have a long shelf life. I established relationships with specialty bookstores and search services, read all the footnotes in every book, and went on from there. After six months, I started doing interviews, but I didn't start writing until 1984." After realizing that three years had been consumed by research alone, Branch asked his agent to renegotiate the contract. "[My agent] said, 'You have zero leverage,'" Branch told Robert Marquand for the *Christian Science Monitor* (February 3, 1989). "I said I needed another year. The publisher said that doesn't mean we'll sell more books."

When he submitted his first draft to his editor, Alice Mayhew, the manuscript ran to 1,900 pages and the story of King's life was still incomplete. After Branch decided to end the first volume with the assassination of President John F. Kennedy in November 1963, he and Mayhew pruned some 600 additional pages from the manuscript. When *Parting the Waters: America in the King Years, 1954–63* finally appeared, it totaled a massive 1,064 pages, including scores of notes and an extensive index—yet few critics commented negatively on its length. Instead, most reviewers praised Branch for offering a compelling but refreshingly human portrait of King and the world around him. A chronicle of the first decade of the civil rights era filtered through King's evolving participation in it, *Parting the Waters* suggests that King, at 26, was initially reluctant to become a spokesman for other black Americans during the boycott of the Montgomery bus system. The book portrays King as having been inspired by his beliefs in basic Christian ethics and in the idea of human equality before God; it also casts him as a leader willing to make tough decisions while fighting for civil rights through nonviolent means, frequently risking imprisonment. King's battles with local and national officials also figure prominently in the account, particularly the persecution of King by the FBI, then under the direction of J. Edgar Hoover, who sought to paint King as a communist sympathizer and to tarnish his image with suggestions of infidelity. The book concludes in 1963, after chronicling King's famous "I Have a Dream" speech and the far more bitter event that followed a few weeks later in Birmingham, Alabama: a church bombing that killed four African-American girls and injured 23 other people.

In *Newsweek* (November 28, 1988), Jim Miller, like many other critics, compared Branch's first volume with another King biography, David J. Garrow's *Bearing the Cross: Martin Luther King Jr. and the Southern Christian Leadership Conference* (1986), which won the 1987 Pulitzer Prize for biography. Miller saw Branch's rendering of King's life and times as the stronger account, particularly for the emphasis in *Parting the Waters* on "the black church—a largely invisible world to most white Americans that Branch evokes as few writers before." Calling the book "a landmark achievement and a paradigm of the new American history at its best," Miller commented: "As few writers can, Branch creates the illusion of reality. Deeply skeptical of those with power and suspicious of the anodyne gloss they put on events as they happen, Branch—in this regard, a model new historian—has searched out the hidden reality and often tragic human drama of the King years. On his best pages, the past, miraculously, seems to spring back to life. King himself appears human, all too human. Yet when the reader is done, his remarkable virtues and ordinary vices seem of a piece, the component parts of a coherent, towering personality." Eleanor Holmes Norton, for the *New York Times Book Review* (November 27, 1988), also praised Branch's ability to breathe life into the past, arguing that "he has penetrated unusually difficult territory, where records are not kept and the story must be elaborately pieced together. He has done so with great skill and often with language literary in its quality. Much of the ambiance of the period would have been lost without a writer of his talent." Still, Holmes acknowledged that "there is much more in this bulky volume than some will want to know" and suggested that the work "is least successful when it attempts to be more than a history of the movement. Its references to major unrelated events of the period, such as the Hungarian revolt or the Suez crisis, are necessarily disconnected from the stories of the struggle for civil rights and become mere intermissions to the main attraction. Mr. Branch's burden—to cover, and bring together the scattered impressions that convey a movement—is awesome enough." Short-listed for many prizes, including the National Book Award for nonfiction, the book went on to receive the Los Angeles Times Book Award for current interest (1989), the National Book Critics Circle Award for nonfiction (1988), the English-Speaking Union Book Award (1989), and, shared with James M. McPherson's *Battle Cry of Freedom: The Civil War Era* (1988), the Pulitzer Prize for history (1989). In 1991 Branch was awarded a $275,000 fellowship, often called the genius grant, from the John D. and Catherine T. MacArthur Foundation.

Though planned for publication in 1990, Branch's second volume, *Pillar of Fire: America in the King Years, 1963–65*, was not published until eight years later. The delay was occasioned in part by the author's continuing research, but the blossoming demands made on his schedule by groups eager for him to speak, coupled with an unsuccessful attempt to turn a version of his King biography into a film, also took their toll. *Pillar of Fire* chronicles the civil rights during one of its most intense periods, as the movement secured fundamental rights for all Americans with the Civil Rights Act of 1964, which Lyndon Johnson signed into law following Kennedy's assassination. Much of the book looks at King's relationship with Kennedy and Johnson, as well as the challenge to the strategy of nonviolence posed by Elijah Muhammad and Malcolm X—at one time both important leaders in the separatist religious group the Nation of Islam who often criticized King's approach to social change. The volume ends, however, shortly after Malcolm X, having split completely from Muhammad, had traveled to Selma, Alabama, to offer King his support; within weeks, Malcolm X was assassinated by members of the Nation of Islam. The book also gives a detailed account of Hoover's continuing obsession with King.

Branch's second volume in the series met with a somewhat cooler reception than his first, though critics were still generally favorable. For *Booklist* (January 1-15, 1998), Brad Hooper noted: "Branch's research is impeccable and his knowledge of his material solid as he focuses on the civil rights movement's 'peak years.' . . . But the prose is so airless, the reader will gasp for breath. . . . The book is significant for marshaling so much information, particularly the profiles of all the many individuals involved in the race issues of that time, but it lacks fluidity." John Meacham, for *Newsweek* (January 19, 1998), found similar faults but still saw the work important as a whole: "Branch's scholarship is strong, his storytelling colorful. The only quibble is that the detail can be overwhelming, but even in that vice there is a virtue: the trilogy will stand as a definitive history of the movement's politics, personalities and theology." Like its predecessor, *Pillar of Fire* earned several awards, including the American Bar Association Silver Gavel Award (1999) and the Sidney Hillman Book Award (1999).

Branch brought his series to a close with *At Canaan's Edge: America in the King Years, 1965–68*. During this period in his life, King not only challenged the Black Power movement, which often took issue with King's nonviolent approach and his emphasis on integration, but also condemned U.S. involvement in the Vietnam War, which put him directly at odds with Johnson, who had lent his support to the civil rights movement at key moments. The book begins with the pivotal march from Selma to Montgomery in 1965 and ends with King's assassination in Memphis, Tennessee, in 1968.

John McWhorter, for the *National Review* (February 27, 2006), followed many critics in using the occasion of the final volume of the trilogy as an opportunity to assess all three. Calling the series "magisterial" McWhorter argued: "thinking people's culture has so thoroughly internalized the concept that 'race matters' that the sheer existence of Branch's trilogy figures larger in most critics' estimation than its quality of composition. *At Canaan's Edge*, while usefully getting a massive volume of facts between two covers, is not precisely history written with lightning, and few will be inclined to read it all the way through. Branch reports more than he interprets, and his narrative crackles only occasionally. In the first two books this was less of a problem, because civil-rights history until 1965 was dominated by clean triumphs with beginnings, middles, and ends. But after this came fragmentation and questions; as a result, *At Canaan's Edge* is exhaustingly episodic." Richard Nicholls, for the *American Scholar* (Spring 2006), also gave his overall impression of Branch's trilogy: "Branch's remarkable talent for amassing details and incorporating them into a swiftly paced narrative makes these books seem fresh, startling, and compelling." Nicholls concluded: "What emerges most powerfully is Branch's conviction that King is the defining figure of America in the 1960s and one of the great prophetic figures in the American tradition. King's goals were breathtakingly audacious—he was attempting to bring about an end to the Vietnam War, to extend his campaigns to confront racism in the North, and to tackle head-on the vexing question of poverty and class in American society. Martin Luther King Jr. had a willingness no longer in evidence in these less altruistic times to believe that economic and political justice and equality are attainable and necessary, that they are the most essential elements of an American vision."

Shortly after *At Canaan's Edge* was published, Branch discussed his feelings on completing a work that had taken up almost half his life, telling Sarah F. Gold for *Publishers Weekly* (January 9, 2006):"I feel a loss, but it's a real jumble because I'm thrilled that it's done, in part because I've been doing it for so long." Branch added: "I think this book reflects my conviction that it's not just dusty history, that it's contemporary, that these are the same issues that still define our politics about how you create freedom."

In November 2006 Branch received a 2006 Common Ground Award from the international conflict-resolution group Search for Common Ground. That same month he was given the *Chicago Tribune*'s Heartland Prize for nonfiction for *At Canaan's Edge*. Among the projects Branch has said that he might take up next is a book about Bill Clinton, with whom Branch had lived, in 1972, in Texas, where they were working on George McGovern's presidential campaign. During Clinton's presidency, Branch occasionally acted as a speechwriter and adviser to Clinton on racial issues.

Taylor Branch lives in Baltimore, Maryland, with his second wife, Christina Macy, the senior speechwriter for Hilary Rodham Clinton during the last few years of the Clinton administration. Branch and his wife have two children, Macy and Franklin. In addition to his books, Branch had also written articles and essays for such publications as the *New York Times*, the *New York Times Magazine*, *Sport*, the *New Republic*, and *Texas Monthly*.

—C.M.

Suggested Reading: *American Scholar* p133+ Spring 2006; *Booklist* p741 Jan. 1–15, 1998; *Christian Science Monitor* p12 Feb. 3, 1989; *Library Journal* p1,796 May 15, 1972, p876 May 1, 1982; *National Review* p43+ Feb. 27, 2006; *New Republic* p32 Oct. 20, 1979; *Newsweek* p84+ Nov. 28, 1988, p62 Jan. 19, 1998; *New York Times* B p4 Mar. 31, 1989; *New York Times Book Review* p4 Apr. 30, 1972, p38 Dec. 9, 1979, p8 Mar. 21, 1982, p1 Nov. 27, 1988; *People* p75+ Dec. 19, 1988; *Publishers Weekly* p62+ Dec. 16, 1988, p42 Jan. 9, 2006; Taylor Branch's Web site

Selected Books: nonfiction—*Blowing the Whistle: Dissent in the Public Interest* (with Charles Peters), 1972; *Blind Ambition* (ghostwritten for John Dean), 1976; *Second Wind* (with Bill Russell), 1979; *Labyrinth* (with Eugene M. Propper), 1982; *Parting the Waters: America in the King Years, 1954–63*, 1988; *Pillar of Fire: America in the King Years, 1963–65*, 1998; *At Canaan's Edge: America in the King Years, 1965–68*, 2006; fiction—*The Empire Blues*, 1981

Marc Alcarez/Courtesy of Random House

Brock-Broido, Lucie

May 22, 1956– Poet

Lucie Brock-Broido is the author of three poetry collections, *A Hunger* (1988), *The Master Letters* (1995), and *Trouble in Mind* (2004). She is a "poet who cultivates elegant nervousness and a riveting clairvoyance, daring the soul to push deeper and deeper into unwrit dimensions," as William Matthews wrote for the *Los Angeles Times* (January 25, 2004). Brock-Broido is currently the director of poetry in the writing division of Columbia University's School of the Arts, in New York City. As an instructor of poetry composition, she has been ranked among the best in the field.

A native of Pittsburgh, Pennsylvania, Lucie Brock-Broido was born on May 22, 1956. (Brock-Broido is a synthesis of her mother's maiden name and her father's last name.) She attended Johns Hopkins University, in Baltimore, Maryland, earning a B.A., in 1979, and an M.A. soon thereafter. She subsequently moved to New York City to study poetry at Columbia University under the noted poet Stanley Kunitz. In 1982 she received her M.F.A. Brock-Broido then received several poetry fellowships and began to teach composition to undergraduates at Wheaton College, in Illinois, and Tufts University, in Massachusetts. In 1988 she became the Briggs Copeland Assistant Professor in Poetry at Harvard University, in Cambridge, Massachusetts, and served from 1992 to 1993 as the director of Harvard's creative-writing program. Brock-Broido then returned to Columbia, accepting a position as an associate professor and the director of poetry at the university's School of the Arts. She has since become a full professor. According to some sources, while interviewing for the job at Columbia, Brock-Broido was asked what she could offer the program that her predecessor and mentor, Stanley Kunitz, could not; she is said to have replied, "more hair." Brock-Broido has also taught at Bennington College, in Vermont, from 1993 to 1995, and at Princeton University, in New Jersey, as a visiting professor in 1995.

The poems in Brock-Broido's debut collection, *A Hunger*, "are original, strange, often unsettling, and mostly beautiful," Stanley Kunitz said, as quoted in the *Boston Globe* (October 2, 1988). In *A Hunger* Brock-Broido "creates a world based on varied reading in classic and contemporary myth and popular literature. Her tastes are eclectic, and the poems spring from many different starting points. Yet each poem achieves a startling leap into the self—that composite of metaphor and memory and color that defines our lives," M. Gillan commented for *Choice* (May 1989). However, some critics found fault with Brock-Broido's emphasis on popular culture and sensational news stories; William Logan, writing for the *Washington Post* (December 28, 1988), dubbed her "the poet laureate of *People* magazine and the evening news. . . . A poem that begins with an exhumation of Josef Mengele may move through the imagined death of Marlene Dietrich, a fire in an English football stadium, and the biological death of half of the Rhine before settling into the narrator's self-regarding address to a past lover." Helen Vendler offered a particularly harsh characterization for the *New Yorker* (August 7, 1989), criticizing the collection's "preciousness" and Brock-Broido's overuse of the words "'small,' 'little,' 'tiny,' 'frail,' 'fragile,'" and others, on the grounds that the "unconscious repetition of the self-deprecating adjectives suggest an as yet incomplete control over psychic material." These reviews aside, *A Hunger* received high praise from other quarters: Gillan, for example, described Brock-Broido's voice as "definite, haunting, fey, and uniquely her own."

Three unsent letters penned by the poet Emily Dickinson—two addressed "Dear Master"—provide the thematic framework for Brock-Broido's second poetry compilation, *The Master Letters*. Stylistically many of the poems in the collection recall Dickinson. As a glimpse into the

history of poetry, however, the selections in *The Master Letters* do not focus exclusively on Dickinson (though she remains central) but also examine the works of William Shakespeare, John Donne, the Romantic poets, and others. Wyn Cooper observed for *Ploughshares* (Winter 1995–96), "This is not an easy book, though it does not require a thorough knowledge of Dickinson in order to satisfy. It is an elaborate homage that is by turns hypnotic, frightening, and hilarious, and at all times brilliant." Cooper quoted a poem titled "When the Gods Go, Half-Gods Arrive": "Once you knew the powers / Of conversion, white powder cut / With nothing on the scales, / Delicate, pythagorean, bold as a compass / Needle pointing—North, a commerce / Of tiny clean white envelopes, / Your letters to me long since / Lost, I've been loving you so long." Cooper pointed out that the title of the poem derives from Ralph Waldo Emerson, the final line from the singer Otis Redding, the punctuation from Dickinson, and the closing couplet from Gerard Manley Hopkins. The voice, however, he claimed, "is pure Brock-Broido, lilting and staccato by turns, made all the more powerful by the echoes." Steven R. Ellis, writing for *Library Journal* (October 1, 1995), remarked that "these poems are hard to pin down, and perhaps that is the point: Brock-Broido gives the impression of writing within her subject—a solitary voice trapped in simultaneous history where truth and cliche lie only in the ruins of revelation." More effusive in his compliments, Willard Spiegelman raved for the *Yale Review* (April 1996), "The urgent jaggedness of every poem bespeaks an explosive disposition as sure of itself and its power as of its nervous relation to everything and everyone outside it. Like her tutelary Dickinson, Brock-Broido has got a loaded gun ready to use against the world."

Trouble in Mind, Brock-Broido's last collection, "displays, with near Jacobean relish, 50 poems about death and dissolution that clothe themselves in garments of gorgeous language," Peter Davison wrote for the *Boston Globe* (February 29, 2004). *Trouble in Mind* addresses Brock-Broido's feelings about death—"First, my father died. Then my mother / Died. My father died again," a reviewer for *Publishers Weekly* (December 22, 2003) quoted—and about growing old. In a selection entitled "Domestic Mysticism," Brock-Broido wrote, "In the next millennium, I will be middle aged. I do not do well / In the marrow of things," as quoted by Maureen N. McLane for the *New York Times Book Review* (February 29, 2004). *Trouble in Mind* brought Brock-Broido her most laudatory reviews to date.: "These poems confirm Brock-Broido as a poet who finds renewed languages for the recurrent dilemmas such hearts contain," the *Publishers Weekly* reviewer wrote. Davison concluded on a similar note: "Brock-Broido's poems, with their richly caparisoned death wish, seem to discover a more vivid presence in language than in life."

Lucie Brock-Broido has received numerous awards, including the Harvard Phi Beta Kappa Teaching Award, the Harvard-Danforth Award for distinction in teaching, the Witter-Bynner Prize in Poetry, and the Jerome J. Shestack Poetry Prize from the journal *American Poetry Review*. She has also been honored with a Guggenheim fellowship and two National Endowment for the Arts fellowships. She currently divides her time between New York City and Cambridge, Massachusetts.

—P.B.M.

Suggested Reading: Borzoi Reader Web site; *Boston Globe* D p9 Feb. 29, 2004; *Choice* p1512 May 1989; Columbia University Web site; *Library Journal* p86 Oct. 1, 1995; *Los Angeles Times* R p14 Jan. 25, 2004; *New York Times Book Review* (on-line) Feb. 29, 2004; *New Yorker* p93 Aug. 7, 1989, p107 May 3, 2004; *Publishers Weekly* p54 Dec. 22, 2003; *Washington Post* X p6 Dec. 25, 1988; *Women's Review of Books* p24 Nov. 1996; *Yale Review* p160 Apr. 1996

Selected Books: *A Hunger*, 1988; *The Master Letters*, 1995; *Trouble in Mind*, 2004

Brodrick, William

1960– Novelist

The character of Father Anselm Duffy in William Brodrick's two novels, *The Sixth Lamentation* (2003) and *The Gardens of the Dead* (2006), became a friar after a stint as a lawyer. For the author himself, however, the course was reversed: Brodrick went from being an Augustinian friar to following a career as a lawyer and then became a writer.

William Brodrick was born in Bolton, Lancashire, England, in 1960. His father was a miner, but seeing the mines closed in the mid-1960s, he decided to emigrate and took Brodrick and the rest of his family to Australia, where Brodrick's mother had family. "It didn't work out for all sorts of reasons but my father then got work in Canada through someone he had known in Bolton," Brodrick recalled to David Whetstone during an interview for the Newcastle, England, *Journal* (March 28, 2006). Meanwhile Brodrick was sent back to England. He became a student at the Austin Friars School, in Carlisle, which was run by Augustinian friars. After finishing there he traveled to Canada, where he worked for a year in a British Colombia logging camp. Then, at 19, he returned to England and joined the Augustinian Friars. He stayed with the friars for six years, serving part of his novitiate in Dublin and London, earning a degree in theology and philosophy at Heythrop College during that period. Then Cardinal Basil Hume asked him to go to London and set up a charity for homeless people, The Depaul Trust. In London Brodrick—just before he was to take his vows—left his order and began to consider pursuing another field. He subsequently took up the law and found a place working as a barrister in Newcastle, a city in North East England. He still wanted to do something else. "I had always wanted to write. My father used to write and I grew up in an atmosphere of appreciation and respect for the written word. I was approaching 40 and I thought if I didn't start writing now, I would never get around to it,"

Brodrick told Louise Redvers for the Newcastle *Evening Chronicle* (February 1, 2003).

Three years after he turned 40, Brodrick's first novel, *The Sixth Lamentation*, appeared. Inspired by his mother—who during the Nazi occupation of Holland in World War II smuggled Jewish children to safety, until she was caught and imprisoned for a year—the book follows two stories. The first concerns Agnes, who was a member of a group called the Round Table, which helped smuggle Jewish children out of France until someone betrayed its members and they were sent to a concentration camp; now near death Agnes reveals a long-held secret to her granddaughter, Lucy. The second story involves Father Anselm's investigation into the life of Eduard Schwermann, a man who has sought sanctuary in Anselm's monastery but who is suspected of Nazi war crimes. Anselm's pursuit of the truth leads to startling and disturbing discoveries. These stories eventually become entwined, leading to the emergence of a number of mysteries, foremost among them who betrayed the Round Table and why the French branch of Father Anselm's order aided Schwermann and another suspected collaborator after World War II. The work received high praise from critics. "Brodrick shows all the skill of a detective-story writer in repeatedly proffering what seems to be the key to one or other of these mysteries, only for the reader to discover that, no, it won't open the door. He has crammed so many people into his narrative that one keeps fearing the life will be crushed out of them. But, miraculously, they survive in all their remarkable depth. As a result, this supremely confident first novel never ceases to drive home its message that, in the right circumstances, even the most ordinary people are capable of both extraordinary evil and extraordinary heroism. Such a combination of narrative mastery, psychological insight and moral vision suggests a John le Carre in the making," Francis King wrote for the London *Daily Telegraph* (March 29, 2003). Kate Ayers, writing for Bookreporter.com, stated, "While this is his first book, [Brodrick] writes with the polish of a veteran author and brings his readers a story filled with tragedy, love, redemption and forgiveness. . . . This is a dazzling debut." Edward Smith, commenting on Brodrick's handling of the Holocaust, observed for the London *Sunday Telegraph* (April 13, 2003), "*The Sixth Lamentation*, thankfully, is not another Holocaust book that was conceived in anger, coloured by horror, and wrapped up with redemption. Instead, William Brodrick's highly intelligent first novel is an original exploration of law, theology and the past."

Brodrick's next book, *The Gardens of the Dead*, revived Father Anselm, who here investigates a mystery that stems from a case he had worked on when he was a lawyer. Elizabeth Glendinning, a former colleague, dies of a rare heart disease while plotting to bring to justice Graham Riley, a client she and Anselm had successfully defended years earlier, even though they knew he was guilty. The book received decidedly mixed reviews. "Sharply etched characters who owe a lot to the darker side of Dickens lift Brodrick's sequel to his well-received debut. . . . Unfortunately, many of the descriptive scenes—a homeless man endlessly sharing toast and hot chocolate with a shrewd London female barrister for whom he acts as an informant, for example—start off with poignant power, but eventually become just padding. Brodrick has all the right moves, but fewer slices of toast would have made for a tighter plot," a reviewer for *Publishers Weekly* (July 31, 2006) wrote. "*The Gardens of the Dead* has gravity and grace, as well as a powerful atmosphere of creeping dread. But there are problems, too. Characters' actions tend to telegraph moral status rather than drive the plot, the writing is sometimes portentous, and for some reason nobody ever makes a phone call or sends an email if they can convey the information in person or by letter. Yet Brodrick uses flashback skilfully, and can, when he relaxes, write with stark beauty," John O'Connell observed for *Time Out* (April 5, 2006). By contrast, Christina Hardyment, writing for the London *Times* (April 1, 2006), had the opposite experience. "I did not make much headway with William Brodrick's *The Sixth Lamentation*, for all its acclaim," she wrote, adding: "But his second novel, *Gardens of the Dead*, held me spellbound and fascinated. It is something of a tour de force to set up such a thoroughly unprepossessing villain (he even secretly slays his wife's much needed love-substitute hamsters), keep us rooting for his downfall for four hours and then turn the tables to such an extent that our hearts bleed for him as the last of the many tangled knots are teased apart."

Brodrick lives in France with his wife, Ann, and their children.

—P.B.M./A.R.

Suggested Readings: (London) *Times* p17 Apr. 1, 2006; (Newcastle, England) *Evening Chronicle* p10 Feb. 1, 2003; (Newcastle) *Journal* p20 Mar. 28, 2006; *Publishers Weekly* p50 July 31, 2006

Selected Books: *The Sixth Lamentation*, 2003; *The Gardens of the Dead*, 2006

Bromwich, David

Dec. 15, 1951– Literary critic; poet

The literary critic David Bromwich is a respected authority on Romantic and modern poetry, whose work, according to Daniel T. O'Hara for the *Journal of Modern Literature* (Summer 2003), is "elegantly written and measured even in its most pointed judgements, [and] has been a tonic and sometimes an antidote to the prevailing fashion in elite critical circles." An adherent of the great man theory—the idea that history is best told through the biographies of extraordinary individuals—Bromwich has received critical praise for his examination of the poet William Wordsworth's early work and for reviving interest in William Hazlitt, a major 19th-century essayist.

David Bromwich was born on December 15, 1951 in New Haven, Connecticut, to Leo Bromwich and Rose (Meyer) Bromwich. His father worked as a lawyer, and his mother was a professor. Bromwich attended Yale University, also in New Haven, and graduated summa cum laude, in 1973, with a bachelor's degree. After receiving a poetry fellowship from the Ingram Merrill Foundation, he continued his studies at Yale, becoming a student of the noted literary critic Harold Bloom. Bromwich began by focusing on 18th-century poets from the Romantic movement—which, in reaction against neoclassism, emphasized the use of imagination and emotion in literature and art—and this led him to discover the works of Hazlitt, who captivated his interest and would later serve as the subject of his dissertation. In addition to his literary studies, Bromwich wrote poetry, and in 1976 the magazine *Poetry* awarded him the Oscar Blumenthal Prize for his poem entitled "From the Virtuous Man Even the Wild Beasts Run Away." After Bromwich earned his doctorate, in 1977, he accepted a position as an assistant professor at Princeton University, in New Jersey. While in that post he, along with the literary critics Irving Howe and John Hollander, co-edited *Literature as Experience: An Anthology* (1979), a textbook designed for incoming college students. In 1979 he was awarded a year-long fellowship by the National Endowment for the Humanities and selected by the faculty at Princeton for a three-year preceptorship.

Courtesy of Yale University Press

David Bromwich

In 1983 Bromwich was promoted to associate professor. That same year he published *Hazlitt: The Mind of a Critic*, a full-length book that expanded upon his doctoral thesis. In the book Bromwich examined the critical and political philosophies underpinning Hazlitt's work, which covers a broad range of topics, including art, theater, literature, philosophy, economics, and politics. Bromwich, most critics agreed, successfully established that the Hazlitt's work was far more revolutionary than that of his peers; indeed, he was highly critical of such upper-class radicals as Percy Bysshe Shelley and Lord Byron. Describing the book as a "work of advocacy as well as appreciation," in a review for *Studies in English Literature* (Autumn 1984), Nina Auerbach wrote, "Hazlitt exemplifies the virtues Bromwich wants us all to have: he chooses historicism over apocalypse, a public and broadly communicative idiom over oracular symbolism, a literature inseparable from the world of power and politics. . . . Bromwich's book is not technically a biography, but . . . the biography of a mind in its culture." Though Claude Rawson, writting for the *New York Times* (January 15, 1984), thought that *Hazlitt* "betrays doctoral thesis origins," he praised the book as "rich in detail, alert in perception and strong in feeling—academic in the best sense and not merely academic." *Hazlitt* earned Bromwich his first nomination for a National Book Critics Circle Award for criticism.

In 1987 Bromwich edited the anthology *Romantic Critical Essays*, which included literary criticism from Hazlitt, Wordsworth, Thomas De Quincey, Leigh Hunt, Charles Lamb, Thomas Love Peacock, and others. The following year he left

Princeton, returning to his alma mater, Yale, as a full professor. The spectre of Hazlitt continued to loom large in the next book Bromwich authored, *A Choice of Inheritance: Self and Community from Edmund Burke to Robert Frost* (1989), a book of essays that contest some of the literary theories that dominated the field in the 1970s and 1980s. "For Bromwich, the schools of [Jacques] Derrida, [Michel] Foucault, Marxism, and feminism together express 'a general distrust of literature,'" according to Robert Weisbuch for *Modern Philology* (February 1992). "The practitioners of this 'sonorous nonsense' are accused of an egomaniacal provincialism, 'as if genuine dissent were largely a matter of the successful displacement of some books by others.'" In the opinion of a reviewer for the *Journal of Modern Literature* (Fall/Winter 1990), "Few contemporary critics combine Bromwich's grasp of moral philosophy, intellectual history, and literary aesthetics, and fewer still can write with such authority and grace. Best of all, one feels that important issues are at stake when he sets about showing why the public-minded spirit usually associated with eighteenth-century thought is as limited a model for contemporary readers as is the equally conventional view that nineteenth-century writing wholeheartedly embraced individualism. For Bromwich, the writers who matter most— Burke, Hazlitt, Emerson—tend to reflect the view that human nature is, in Burke's words, 'at once given and chosen.'" *A Choice of Inheritance* was nominated for the 1989 National Book Critics Circle Award for criticism.

In *Politics by Other Means: Higher Education and Group Thinking* (1992), Bromwich scrutinized, as he explained in the introduction, two environments in contemporary America: "a conservative political culture outside the academy and a radical political culture inside." He argued that both, having isolated themselves from criticism, are on their way to ruin. "Both cultures have grown provincial rather than cosmopolitan: their members talk to the same people, receive the same narrow and defensive advice, from one occasion of judgement to the next," Bromwich wrote. "But they are provincial in another sense as well. They make such sparing use of our traditions that they are wrecking the chances of continuity with the moral ideals of liberalism—the very ideals of free expression and personal autonomy which have long been what the world rightly admires about America." Reviewing the book for the *Washington Post* (Oct. 18, 1992), William A. Galston wrote, "Bromwich writes as a staunch partisan of 'political liberalism' and the 'Enlightenment ideals of rational discussion and individual choice.' His core commitment is to independence of mind and spirit—the capacity and opportunity of every individual to reflect on experience, work toward self-knowledge, and construct a way of life free from coercive interference and fear of social disapproval. At one time this independence could be cultivated and displayed by free-floating intellectuals and 'intellectual journalists.' Today, Bromwich notes, this class has all but disappeared. For better or worse, prospects for freedom of the mind are linked to the performance of a single institution—the university. . . . Bromwich sees individual freedom . . . locked in a two-front war: against political conservatives (George Will and William Bennett are prominent examples) who want to use the humanities as weapons for inculcating virtue and defending Western civilization; and against radicals (deconstructionists, followers of Michel Foucault, and Stanley Fish–style nihilists, among others) who want to subvert all standards of taste and judgement in the name of politicized approaches to literature that focus on power relations, oppression and group consciousness."

For his next book, *Disowned by Memory: Wordsworth's Poetry of the 1790s* (1998), Bromwich analyzed the early works of Wordsworth, whom he described in the book's introduction as "a disagreeable man and an interesting poet." "Bromwich is that rare thing among literary critics—an independent thinker," Willard Spiegelman wrote for *Raritan* (Fall 1999). "He belongs to no single school except that of his own intellect. Consequently, he is an ideal guide to the poetry of a man who stood alone, at least partly visible even when in hiding. For Bromwich, the poetry is 'a portrait of the conditions for thinking,' not thinking per se but that which precedes and accompanies it. . . . Bromwich takes Wordsworth seriously as a poetic moralist. . . . As a defender of the whole human being, Wordsworth was—as Bromwich paints him—'an antagonist of the very idea of the rational person,' a proponent, instead, of a way of seeing human identity as 'coherent and irreducible by analysis.'"

Bromwich went on to edit *On Empire, Liberty and Reform: Speeches and Letters* (2000), a collection of Edmund Burke's most important speeches, letters, and pamphlets. In 2001 he published *Skeptical Music: Essays on Modern Poetry,* which offers an in-depth examination of such 20th-century poets as T. S. Eliot, Hart Crane, Elizabeth Bishop, Adrienne Rich, and John Ashbery. *Skeptical Music* won the Spielvogel-Diamonstein Award for the Art of the Essay by the PEN American Center in 2002. The following year he co-edited, with George Kateb, a new edition of John Stuart Mill's *On Liberty* (2003).

Bromwich's works, including his poetry, essays, and reviews of books and films, have appeared in the *Washington Post, London Review of Books, New Republic, New York Times Book Review, Parnassus,* and *Poetry,* among other publications. From 1993 to 1994 he was the film critic for the *New Leader,* and he has served on the editorial boards of *Dissent* and *Raritan.* In addition, he has served as a consultant for National Public Radio's *Poets in Person* series. Bromwich is the recipient

of an Academy Award from the American Academy of Arts and Letters and a Guggenheim Fellowship, among other honors.

—B.M.

Suggested Reading: *New York Times Book Review* p30 Jan. 15, 1984; *Raritan* p114+ Fall 1999; *Washington Post* X p5 Oct. 18, 1992

Selected Books: *Hazlitt: The Mind of a Critic,* 1983; *A Choice of Inheritance: Self and Community from Edmund Burke to Robert Frost,* 1989; *Politics by Other Means: Higher Education and Group Thinking,* 1992; *Disowned by Memory: Wordsworth's Poetry of the 1790s,* 1998; *Skeptical Music: Essays on Modern Poetry,* 2001; as editor—*Literature as Experience* (with Irving Howe and John Hollander), 1979; *Romantic Critical Essays,* 1987; *On Empire, Liberty, and Reform: Speeches and Letters, 2000; On Liberty* (with George Kateb), 2003

Chris Jackson/Getty Images

Brown, Dan

June 22, 1964– Novelist

What if Jesus Christ, the central figure of Christianity, had been married to the repentant prostitute Mary Magdalene, fathered a child, and spirited his family away to France in order keep them safe from his persecutors in the Middle East? That provocative question forms the basis of Dan Brown's blockbuster novel *The Da Vinci Code.* The book, the action of which takes place over the course of 24 hours, traces the exploits of Robert

Langdon, a Harvard professor and symbologist (an expert in symbols and their meanings), as he uncovers the mystery surrounding the secret lineage of Jesus and finds himself at odds with those who would die to keep it unsolved. Since its publication, in the spring of 2003, *The Da Vinci Code* has become an unqualified success, selling more than 60 million copies and making Brown a household name. Translated into more than 40 languages, the book has proven wildly popular outside the U.S., and it has attracted renewed interest in Brown's previous three books, all of which became best-sellers as well. In addition, it has sparked numerous debates among religious scholars and academics over its core theory. A number of books, including *Breaking the Da Vinci Code* (2004), have been written in response to Brown's book or inspired by the discussion it triggered, and it has spawned so many imitators that Brown has been said to have created a new genre of thrillers.

Brown's books offer labyrinthine plots and focus on shadowy conspiracies and, most famously, secret societies. Each of his four novels—the others are *Digital Fortress* (1998), *Angels & Demons* (2000), and *Deception Point* (2001)—sheds light on a real-life group largely hidden from the public, be it the Priory of Sion, supposedly charged with concealing the bloodline of Jesus; the National Security Agency (NSA), a U.S. government organization that has the power to intercept personal E-mail messages and wiretap the phones of private citizens; or the Illuminati, a group of scientists (including Galileo Galilei) who swore vengeance on the Catholic Church for the persecution and execution of those who championed science over religion. "My interest [in secret societies] sparks from growing up in New England," Brown told an interviewer for his official Web site, "surrounded by the clandestine clubs of Ivy League universities, the Masonic lodges of our Founding Fathers, and the hidden hallways of early government power." A former teacher of English at Phillips Exeter Academy, Brown also weaves many other historical elements into his stories. "One of the aspects that I try very hard to incorporate in my books is that of learning," he told Edward Morris for *BookPage* (April 2003, on-line). "When you finish the book—like it or not—you've learned a ton."

Dan Brown was born on June 22, 1964 in Exeter, New Hampshire, and grew up on the campus of Phillips Exeter Academy, one of the nation's most prestigious boarding schools, at which his father was a Presidential Award–winning mathematics teacher. His mother performed sacred music—music rooted in spirituality and religion. The Brown house was filled with books; in addition, the family enjoyed working on puzzles and exchanging coded messages. Every Christmas, for example, Brown and his sister were given poems that provided clues to the locations of their gifts. At Phillips Exeter Brown was exposed daily to

people of other races and cultures. His first baby-sitter was a student from Nigeria. "I grew up on a campus with kids from 37 countries," Brown told Julie Flaherty for the *New York Times* (June 25, 2003). "Racism just didn't occur to me." In addition, he would often spend time with some of the older students. "A lot of these guys missed their younger siblings, and plus it's a very high-pressure environment," he told Flaherty. "It's probably therapeutic on some level to stop and talk to some 9-year-old kid about Hot Wheels."

After graduating from Phillips Exeter, in 1982, Brown attended Amherst College, in Amherst, Massachusetts. While enrolled there he spent a semester in Seville, Spain, studying art history at the city's university. Brown graduated from Amherst with a B.A. degree in 1986; at that time, as he told Claire E. White for the Web site Writers Write (May 1998), he "had two loves—writing fiction and writing music." He moved to Hollywood, California, where he focused on writing songs and playing the piano. While in Hollywood he released four CDs of original material. (Though Brown has often claimed that a song of his called "Peace in Our Time" was performed at the 1996 Olympic Games in Atlanta, Georgia, no records exist of a song with that title having been performed during those Games, according to an article by Seth Mnookin, writing for *Vanity Fair* [July 2006]. The 1988 Olympics, however, featured a song called "Peace in Our Time," but the copyright holders for that work are veteran songwriters Andy Hill and Pete Sinfield.) In 1990, inspired by encounters with people in Los Angeles who struck him as strange, Brown penned a joke book entitled *187 Men to Avoid*; the book was published, with the subtitle *A Survival Guide for the Romantically Frustrated Woman*, in 1995, under the name Danielle Brown.

Earlier, in 1993, Brown had returned to Phillips Exeter to teach English and creative writing. Brown has often said that in 1995 one of his students was briefly detained by the Secret Service, which was concerned that the boy posed a threat to national security. "As it turned out," Brown explained to Claire E. White, "the kid had been on the Internet the night before having a light-hearted political debate via E-mail with one of his friends and had made the comment that he was so mad at the current political situation he was ready to kill President [Bill] Clinton. The Secret Service came up to make sure he wasn't serious." The incident made an impression on Brown, particularly the notion that the Secret Service keeps such close tabs on private citizens. "I began wondering how the Secret Service knew what these kids were saying in their e-mail," he told D. Quincy Whitney for the *Boston Globe* (July 19, 1998), "and discovered the National Security Agency, an intelligence agency as large as the CIA that is home to the country's eavesdroppers. I realized it was a great backdrop for a novel." Brown began conducting extensive research, communicating with two NSA cryptographers via anonymous remailers—Internet sites that forward E-mail messages to specified destinations without revealing the original sources of the messages. "At first, I was surprised with the information they were sharing," he noted during an interview for his Web site, "and I suspected, despite their obvious knowledge, that they were probably not who they said they were. But the more we spoke, the more I was convinced they were authentic. Neither one knew about the other, and yet they told almost identical stories." (Mnookin and others have cast doubt on the truthfulness of Brown's story about the Secret Service, pointing out that while newspaper reports indicate that, in 1996 and 1997, high school students at other New Hampshire schools had been approached by the Secret Service for writing E-mails deemed to be threatening to President Clinton, those reports did not mention Phillips Exeter. On his personal Web site, in a post dated September 28, 2006, Mnookin noted that the Secret Service had assured him that no such search had taken place.)

The product of Brown's work, the novel *Digital Fortress*, received positive notices. "In this fast-paced, plausible tale," Sybil Steinberg wrote for *Publishers Weekly* (December 22, 1997), "Brown blurs the line between good and evil enough to delight patriots and paranoids alike." The story centers on a computer program that generates impenetrable codes, which could cripple U.S. intelligence, and on the efforts of a brilliant cryptographer, Susan Fletcher, to prevent such a disaster. The novel also provides the reader with a look inside the walls of the NSA and raises long-debated questions about the extent to which the federal government has invaded citizens' privacy. "The World Wide Web is anything but private," he noted on his Web site, as quoted by Whitney. "Many computer users still don't realize that the Web sites they visit will, in many cases, track their progress through the site, how long a user stays, what he lingers over, what files he downloads. If you're visiting sites on the Web that you don't want anyone to know you're visiting, you better think again."

Brown's second novel, *Angels & Demons*, introduced readers to Robert Langdon, the Harvard symbologist who would become the hero of *The Da Vinci Code*. The idea for *Angels & Demons*, which places its protagonist at the center of a wide-ranging conspiracy involving the Vatican and the Illuminati, came to Brown while he was vacationing in Rome, Italy. "I was beneath Vatican City touring a tunnel called il passetto—a concealed passageway used by the early Popes to escape in event of enemy attack," he recalled on his Web site. "According to the scholar giving the tour, one of the Vatican's most feared ancient enemies was a secret brotherhood known as the Illuminati—the 'enlightened ones'—a cult of early scientists who had vowed revenge against the Vatican for crimes against scientists like Galileo

and Copernicus. I was fascinated by images of this cloaked, anti-religious brotherhood lurking in the catacombs of Rome. Then, when the scholar added that many modern historians believe the Illuminati is still active today and is one of most powerful unseen forces in global politics, I knew I was hooked. . . . I had to write an Illuminati thriller."

As was the case with *Digital Fortress*, Brown thoroughly researched the topics covered in *Angels & Demons*, which include the Vatican, the Illuminati, and the Conseil Européen pour la Recherche Nucléaire (CERN), a Swiss research facility that is credited with the invention of (among other things) the World Wide Web. *Angels & Demons* received solid reviews. "One of the best international thrillers of recent years, Dan Brown's *Angels & Demons* is both literate and extremely well researched, mixing physics with religion," Nancy Pearl wrote for *Library Journal* (November 15, 2000). Such praise notwithstanding, at the time of its initial publication, the book sold only 10,000 copies.

In his third novel, *Deception Point*, Brown again built his story around the inner workings of a clandestine organization, in this case the National Reconnaissance Office (NRO), an intelligence agency that employs cutting-edge spy technology. The plot involves an asteroid, found beneath the arctic ice, that may contain evidence of extraterrestrial life, and the events that ensue when a female intelligence analyst attempts to uncover the conspiracy to keep the asteroid hidden. *Deception Point* received mixed notices from critics. Writing for *Publishers Weekly* (September 10, 2001), Jeff Zaleski called the book "an excellent thriller—a big yet believable story unfolding at breakneck pace, with convincing settings and just the right blend of likable and hateful characters. [Brown has] also done his research, folding in sophisticated scientific and military details that make his plot far more fulfilling than the norm." Offering a different take, in a review for *Booklist* (September 15, 2001), David Pitt wrote, "In the end, what does Brown's mixed bag add up to? Those who require only that thrillers deliver the requisite number of chills will have a good time here, but those looking for a little artistry, a little panache, are likely to be disappointed."

The idea for *The Da Vinci Code* came to Brown as he was researching *Angels & Demons*. Its seeds had been planted, however, during his college years. "I first learned of [the Italian artist, engineer, and architect Leonardo] Da Vinci's affiliation with the Priory of Sion when I was studying art history at the University of Seville," he told Edward Morris. "One day, the professor showed us a slide of *The Last Supper* and began to outline all the strange anomalies in [Da Vinci's] painting"; those oddities, such as the disembodied hand holding a knife and the feminine appearance of the figure who should have been John the Apostle, according to the teacher, suggested that Da Vinci had hidden messages in the painting. Knowing that a novel based on this idea would have to be complexly plotted, Brown began working out the details of the story during his morning exercise sessions. "I would go running with a Dictaphone and discuss the plot aloud with myself. I felt like a juggler who was trying to keep 13 balls in the air simultaneously," he told Aurelia C. Scott for *Audiofile* (June/July 2003, on-line). "Imagine if someone had found the Dictaphone. They would have heard a panting guy talking about Rome and Mary Magdalene's child and assassinations—and would have turned it in to the police!"

To write the story Brown drew on a number of sources, including histories of the Knights Templar (a monastic military order founded in 1118, in the aftermath of the First Crusade, to help the new Kingdom of Jerusalem protect itself from its Muslim neighbors and ensure the safety of the large numbers of European pilgrims to Jerusalem); the Dead Sea Scrolls (hundreds of leather or papyrus scrolls and fragments, in Hebrew, Greek, or Aramaic, believed to have been written largely by a Jewish sect known as the Essenes between the third century BCE and 68 A.D., which were discovered between 1947 and 1956 in caves near Qumran, near the Dead Sea); and the Holy Grail. Many passages in *The Da Vinci Code* suggest that history as many of us know it is false. According to the book the Holy Grail is not, as Christian legend has it, the cup that Christ used at the Last Supper or the vessel that caught Christ's blood at the Crucifixion; instead, it is a series of documents that offer proof of Jesus's marriage to Mary Magdalene and of his royal bloodline, the so-called Merovingian Kings. While some may dismiss these notions as the ravings of a conspiracy theorist, Brown has insisted that there is historical evidence to support them. "Since the beginning of recorded time," he noted on his Web site, "history has been written by the 'winners' (those societies and belief systems that conquered and survived). Despite an obvious bias in this accounting method, we still measure the 'historical accuracy' of a given concept by examining how well it concurs with our existing historical record. Many historians now believe (as do I) that in gauging the historical accuracy of a given concept, we should first ask ourselves a far deeper question: How historically accurate is history itself?"

The Da Vinci Code arrived in bookstores in March 2003 and immediately shot to number one on the *New York Times* best-seller list, a rare feat for an author with no previous successes to his credit. The enthusiastic public reception was expected, as there had been talk about the book in the publishing community since the summer of 2002. When 100 pages of the manuscript were circulated to the sales force at Doubleday, the reaction was uniformly positive. "There was a unanimous 'Oh my God' response," Stephen Rubin, the president of the Doubleday Broadway publishing group, which published the book, told Bill Goldstein for the *New York Times* (April 21,

2003). "If people [within the publishing house] are responding unanimously and rhapsodically, there's no reason to think that [other people] won't react the same way." For the most part, critical response was positive as well. "In this gleefully erudite suspense novel, Mr. Brown takes the format he has been developing through three earlier novels and fine-tunes it to blockbuster perfection," Janet Maslin wrote for the *New York Times* (March 17, 2003). "Not since the advent of Harry Potter has an author so flagrantly delighted in leading readers on a breathless chase and coaxing them through hoops." In *Entertainment Weekly* (March 28, 2003), in a somewhat less enthusiastic review, Scott Brown wrote that "the story is a straightforward, code-cracking mystery quest for the Sunday Jumble set. . . . The cliches click pleasantly into place, like the tumblers of an old, easy-to-pick lock." Writing for *Publishers Weekly* (February 3, 2003), Jeff Zaleski observed, "Brown sometimes ladles out too much religious history at the expense of pacing, and Langdon is a hero in desperate need of more chutzpah. Still, Brown has assembled a whopper of a plot that will please both conspiracy buffs and thriller addicts."

The success of *The Da Vinci Code* sparked a flurry of debate, with religious leaders challenging the veracity of Brown's claims and historians calling into question some of Brown's knowledge of Leonardo da Vinci. "How much does this murder mystery have to do with the real Leonardo?" Bruce Boucher asked in a *New York Times* (August 3, 2003) article titled "Does *The Da Vinci Code* Crack Leonardo?" "The short answer is not much, and the author's grasp of the historical Leonardo is shaky." In an article for *Crisis* (September 2003) entitled "Dismantling *The Da Vinci Code*," Sandra Miesel systematically picked the novel apart, concluding that Brown's knowledge of history as reflected in the book is at best questionable and at worst completely based on misperceptions. "So error-laden is *The Da Vinci Code*," she wrote, "that the educated reader actually applauds those rare occasions where Brown stumbles (despite himself) into the truth."

In addition, much of the Christian community has expressed displeasure over the book. In an article in *Catholic New World,* as quoted by Mark O'Keefe in the *Houston Chronicle* (February 28, 2004, on-line), Francis Cardinal George called *The Da Vinci Code* "a work of bizarre religious imaginings" based on "a facade of scholarship" that takes advantage of readers' "gullibility for conspiracy." However, some have defended the book's assertions, arguing that, accurate or not, they might lead people to learn more about the life of Jesus. "It's only a threat if people read this fictional book naively, don't think critically about it and don't pursue truth," the Reverend Mark Roberts told O'Keefe. "Now that we have people thinking and talking, we can look at the real evidence of Jesus." Stephen Prothero, the chairman of the religion department at Boston

University, told Ron Charles for the *Christian Science Monitor* (March 19, 2004) that the book "taps into a lot of longstanding stories about Jesus in America. Americans have been ruminating since the Colonial period about finding documents that would settle all the mysteries about Jesus."

The Da Vinci Code spent nearly three years on the *New York Times* hardcover best-seller list—about a third of that period at the top spot—before a paperback edition of the book was finally released, in 2006, with a reported advanced printing of 6 million copies. The novel's success spurred sales of Brown's earlier books, which have gone on to sell a total of more than 7 million copies; in fact, during one week in early 2004, all four of his novels appeared on the *New York Times* best-seller list. In 2006 the film adaptation of *The Da Vinci Code*, directed by Ron Howard, was released to largely negative reviews but solid popular success. Costing approximately $175 million ($125 million for production and approximately $50 million for publicity), the film earned more than $224 million worldwide during its opening weekend and went on to gross approximately $758 million internationally.

In 2005 Brown succeeded in preempting a legal battle with a fellow novelist, Lewis Perdue, who in a letter to Random House had argued that *The Da Vinci Code* borrowed a wealth of specific material from Perdue's novels *Daughter of God* (2000) and *The Da Vinci Legacy* (1983). Random House responded to the letter by suing Perdue in federal court, demanding a declaratory judgment that his claims were false. The suit was successful, and Perdue's attempts at appeal, including a petition to the Supreme Court, have failed.

In 2006 Brown again quashed charges of plagiarism that had been lodged against him by Michael Baigent and Richard Leigh, two of the three authors of the book *The Holy Blood and the Holy Grail* (1982). (The third author, Henry Lincoln, refused to participate in the suit.) Baigent and Leigh had sued Random House for what they alleged to be copyright violations, though Brown had acknowledged their influence directly in the text. Brown's trial became an international media event, and the two days he spent giving testimony, in March 2006, offered fans an unusually detailed sense of his work routine. The case was dismissed the following month, and Baigent and Leigh were ordered to pay approximately £1.8 million to Random House to cover legal fees. In January 2007 Baigent and Leigh succeeded in convincing an appeals court to hear their case again, though few observers believe that their appeal will be successful.

Dan Brown makes his home in New Hampshire with his wife, Blythe, a painter and art historian who, Brown explained during his testimony in London, prepares voluminous research materials to help him write his books.

Due to the controversy surrounding *The Da Vinci Code*, Brown no longer grants interviews. He is currently at work on his next Robert Langdon novel, which will be set in Washington, D.C. "I was skeptical when I first started thinking of setting a book here that it could have the same sort of grandeur and punch as a place like Paris or Rome," he told Linda Wertheimer during an interview for the National Public Radio program *Weekend Edition* (April 26, 2003). "In fact, the more I researched about Washington's architecture and its history, the more I'm starting to think . . . it may surpass Rome in its secret history. What a fascinating place." As of early 2007 no firm date of publication had been announced for the novel, which is tentatively titled "The Solomon Key."

—J.K.B.

Suggested Reading: *Boston Globe* (on-line) July 19, 1998; Dan Brown's Web site; *Houston Chronicle* (on-line) Feb. 28, 2004; National Public Radio Web site; *New York Times* C p11 Apr. 21, 2003, E p8 Mar. 17, 2003; *Vanity Fair* p100+ July 2006; Writers Write Web site

Selected Books: *Digital Fortress*, 1998; *Angels & Demons*, 2000; *Deception Point*, 2001; *The Da Vinci Code*, 2003

Brown, Laura Catherine

Novelist

Laura Catherine Brown, the author of the novel *Quickening* (2000), is a graduate of the School of Visual Arts, in New York City. Brown had not originally planned to pursue a career as a novelist. "When I graduated from the School of Visual Arts, I was a major in graphic design, and I really thought that's what I would do—I would love it and it would be creatively fulfilling," she told Ron Hogan in an interview posted on the Beatrice Web site. "It didn't take me long, working in an ad agency, to realize that while graphic design was a craft, my heart couldn't be in it because it was work for someone else. Then writing became where I put my creative energy."

Brown quit her full-time job and began writing. She supported herself with freelance graphic-design work. "And for a while that was harder because I became paranoid about money and couldn't write at all. There was no time. I took on every freelance job offered me. I never refused a job," she explained to Dani Shapiro, a fellow novelist, in an interview posted on the Random House Web site. "But eventually I learned to turn down those jobs. I learned to have faith in what I was doing, and I gave myself permission to write the book." The book took a total of seven years to finish, with much of the work done at artist-residency programs to which Brown had been admitted. (These included the Norcroft Writing Retreat, in Lutsen, Minnesota; the Ucross Foundation, in Ucross, Wyoming; and the Hambidge Center, in Dillard, Georgia.) The residency programs were a great help, Brown recalled to Hogan: "Being away in an environment where everyone else is also away, working in the creative moment, is just wonderful."

The novel went through several drafts before Brown was satisfied with it. She told Shapiro, "It was a long and convoluted process. The book was initially written in a third-person voice. I never used to like first-person novels when I was young. If it was an 'I' book—that's how I thought of first-person narration—I didn't want to read it. I always wanted to read about he, she, and they. So the first draft of *Quickening* was in the third-person past tense, and that wasn't working. There was no real voice or point of view. It felt distant and generic to me." She continued, "So then I took it to the first-person present, believing that made it really immediate—which is something I think a lot of beginning writers believe. But the present tense wasn't working, either, because [the protagonist] could only know what was right there in front of her. She could only comment on what was going on in her mind. There was no sense of distance or perspective—there really couldn't be. So it wasn't reading as I hoped it would; instead, it was reading as immovable. Finally, I tried first-person past tense—a very close past tense. She wasn't far from the events, yet she had gotten through them, so she had a slight sense of perspective. And suddenly it seemed to work. The idiosyncrasies of her speech and ways of thinking suddenly had room to exist. And once I had that, there was a momentum to the writing. I think I learned how to write while writing this book."

As the novel opens the 19-year-old protagonist, Mandy Boyle, is heading off to college, thereby escaping from her demanding, sickly mother. Her relief is short-lived, however; she soon faces a series of challenges, including the death of her beloved father and an unwanted pregnancy. (Brown's own father died about a year before she finished the book, making the scenes involving Mandy's father particularly difficult for her to write.)

The title *Quickening* is derived from the stage of pregnancy at which an expectant mother first feels her baby moving; the baby can thus be said to be developing an independent life of its own. Promotional materials for the book note that Mandy undergoes something of an "adult quickening," in getting ready to strike out on her own. Brown elaborated to Shapiro: "I see [*Quickening*] more as a coming-of-adulthood novel [than a traditional coming-of-age novel]. Coming-of-age usually is more about a younger protagonist and a loss of innocence. . . . The book isn't about discovering an ugly truth about life—it's about leaving home to enter the world at large. In the

beginning, she leaves home believing herself to be free, finally away from the limits and confinements of her background. But, in fact, although she physically leaves, she has not left, and she is pulled back. The whole novel is, in a sense, a struggle to leave." She concluded, "By the end of *Quickening*, Mandy has truly left home, and that leaving is something that happens internally."

A reviewer for *People* (May 15, 2000) praised the work, writing, "In this impressive debut novel, Brown explores a young woman's emotional upheavals with sincerity and grace. . . . Brown is a talent to watch." A critic for *Publishers Weekly* (May 15, 2000) concurred, writing, "Mandy is a heroine worth rooting for. When she recognizes the power of choice in determining her own course in life, most readers will cheer."

Laura Catherine Brown currently lives in New York City and is reported to be at work on another novel.

—P.B.M.

Suggested Reading: Beatrice Web site; *People* May 15, 2000; *Publishers Weekly* May 15, 2000; Random House Web site

Selected Books: *Quickening,* 2000

Broyard, Bliss

1966– Short-story writer

With the success of her critically acclaimed short-fiction collection, *My Father, Dancing* (1999), Bliss Broyard, the daughter of the famed literary critic and author Anatole Broyard, has earned a reputation as a literary talent in her own right. The volume has been praised for revealing the most intimate and tender moments of her characters, who are often young women. Broyard told Daniel Zwerdling for National Public Radio's *Weekend All Things Considered* (August 28, 1999), "What I enjoy in writing is trying to get down the texture of an experience, and to bring people who perhaps had no idea what was running through that young girl's mind as she sat on a bench in a courtyard or she was walking down the street. And so I do search for a kind of honesty in experience in my writing, and that's the same thing that I look for in other people's writing as well."

Bliss Broyard was born in 1966 to Anatole and Alexandra "Sandy" (Nelson) Broyard. Along with her older brother, Todd, she grew up in Fairfield County, Connecticut. She attended the University of Vermont and later the University of Virginia's creative-writing program, for which she was named a Henry Hoyns Fellow.

In late 1989 Anatole was diagnosed with terminal prostate cancer. Sandy, a white woman of Norwegian descent, decided to share a long-

Scott Gries/Getty Images

Bliss Broyard

standing family secret with her children a few days before their father's death, in October 1990: Anatole, born in New Orleans, was black. The son of two light-skinned African-Americans, he had spent his life hiding his black heritage and was, in fact, what the Creoles called *passe-blanc*, a black man "passing" for white. Anatole, in addition to being a critic and essayist, had harbored ambitions of becoming a novelist and had denied his ancestry so as to avoid being pigeonholed as a black writer. (Despite high expectations from the literary community, he never completed a novel. The writer John Updike once told Henry Louis Gates Jr. for the *New Yorker* [June 17, 1996], "The most famous non-book around was the one that Anatole Broyard was not writing." Many literary critics have since surmised that Anatole's well-known writer's block stemmed from his own inhibitions about his racial identity.)

After learning the truth about her father, Bliss Broyard told Chris Gray for the New Orleans *Times–Picayune* (February 5, 2001), that she could see there had been earlier clues, including Anatole's strong love of Afro-Cuban music. More notably, the family had never returned to New Orleans, and Anatole had largely terminated his relations with his darker-skinned sister, as well as other relatives. Once, a visitor to the family's summer home on Martha's Vineyard told Broyard that she had overheard an older woman calling Anatole a "black Haitian." "I remember questioning my father, 'Are you sure we're just French?'" Broyard recalled.

While the news of her heritage initially surprised Broyard, she soon became eager to learn more about the family's past. She regretted that she

was never able to discuss the information with her father, who fell in and out of lucidity towards the end of his life. Eventually, Broyard began spending time in New Orleans, searching for family connections and clues to better understand her father's—and her own—identity. In her travels there, she met Broyards with widely varying skin pigmentation. "People of my father's generation are still invested in the term Creole," she told Gray. "They don't think of themselves as black. They know themselves as something different, in the way they were raised. For the younger relatives, Creole doesn't mean as much."

Over time Broyard has come to terms with her father's decision to distance himself from his past. "This is a journey he couldn't take because of the times," she said of her research and her desire to one day tell her father's story. "We couldn't have lived where we lived if my father was openly black. He presented the version of himself he wanted people to know. He didn't want us to go through what he went through—being betwixt and between. He thought: Why voluntarily subject yourself to limited opportunity if you have the chance?"

Around the time of her father's death, Broyard began working on a series of short stories focusing on the theme of fathers and daughters. "Losing him got me to thinking about what his influence had been in my life and the person I'd become, the person I was becoming," she told Zwerdling. She continued, "I think my father, in particular, and the fathers of the daughters in these stories, are not only fathers to their daughters; they're also men in the world. And they tend to bring their interests home, their experiences in the world home. I think a lot of the daughters in my stories tend to see their fathers as human beings, you know, warts and all."

Broyard's collection, *My Father, Dancing*, includes eight stories, five of which feature fathers and daughters; many of the stories also contain autobiographical elements. In the title story, for example, Kate sits beside her father's hospital bed as he lies dying of cancer and lovingly recalls her memories of dancing with him throughout her childhood. "As my body grew and pushed out in new places, I wriggled these parts and tried on different movements, the way I would try on new clothes," Broyard wrote, as quoted by Christopher Lehmann-Haupt for the *New York Times* (July 29, 1999). "He was my first male audience, and I used him as a mirror to understand what I looked like to the world." "The Trouble with Mr. Leopold" presents Celia, who attends the prestigious Woodbridge Country Day School. When Celia's teacher, Mr. Leopold, assigns her to write a film review, she elicits the help of her father, a film critic, who in turn writes the paper himself. After the review earns only a mediocre grade, Celia's father sets out to have Mr. Leopold fired. In another emotionally charged story, "Mr. Sweetly Indecent," which was included in *The Best American Short Stories 1998*, a young woman confronts her father in a restaurant after she has caught him kissing his mistress. Other stories explore themes of female growth, such as "Snowed In," in which a group of teens stranded together in a storm self-consciously engage in sex games, and "Ugliest Faces," in which a college student who is dating an older, intellectual type suddenly finds herself attracted to a young man she has hit with her car.

My Father, Dancing was generally well received by critics, who often praised Broyard's skill at exploring the delicate and complex relationships among her characters. Mary A. McCay wrote for the New Orleans *Times–Picayune* (November 14, 1999), "All of the stories turn on a moment, and Broyard successfully navigates most of them." While some critics found Broyard's dialogue to be stiff and a few of the stories to be forced, most others applauded the depth of her writing. "It is between the lines that Ms. Broyard's writing is most effective," Lehmann-Haupt observed.

"Between the lines, her personae confront the sexuality with which their fathers overwhelm them. . . . In these eight arresting stories, Ms. Broyard proves herself a powerful writer who never looks away."

Broyard is reportedly working on a nonfiction book about her father, as well as a novel. She frequently contributes book reviews and other articles to such publications as the *New York Times* and the *Washington Post*.

Bliss Broyard lives in the New York City borough of Brooklyn.

—K.D.

Suggested Reading: *Houston Chronicle* p14 Oct. 24, 1999; *New York Times* E p9 July 29, 1999; VII p8 Aug. 15, 1999; (New Orleans) *Times–Picayune* Metro p1 Feb. 5, 2001; *Weekend All Things Considered* Aug. 28, 1999

Selected Books: *My Father, Dancing*, 1999

Budbill, David

June 13, 1940– Poet; playwright; fiction writer; essayist

The poet, playwright, fiction writer, and performance artist David Budbill has steeped himself in the life of a village in northern Vermont, where he and his wife, the artist Lois Eby, live and work. Originally a writer of verse drama, Budbill later turned to poetry. Several of his dramatic and poetic works featuring the voices and stories of the inhabitants of "Judevine"—the name of the mountain near Budbill's home, a source of inspiration for the poet—were combined in *Judevine: The Complete Poems, 1970–1990* (1991). Budbill has joined with musicians, notably William Parker, Hamid Drake, and Erik Nielson, to create collaborative musical pieces.

David Budbill composed the following autobiographical statement for *World Authors 2000–2005*:

"I was born in Cleveland, Ohio, in 1940, to a street car driver and a minister's daughter. Neither one of my parents graduated from high school.

"My grandfather, on my father's side, was an occasional woodworker and an abusive alcoholic who beat my grandmother, stole money from my father and abandoned his family to go on long drunken benders. When my grandmother was a young woman she was John D. Rockefeller's washerwoman. Even when she was in her 90s I can remember her face flushing with rage when she told how Rockefeller would pass out nickels to the poor on the streets of Cleveland.

"My grandfather, on my mother's side, worked his way through Northwestern University and then received a graduate degree in theology and became a Methodist minister. My grandmother graduated from medical school in 1896 with a degree in homeopathic medicine. A few years later, my grandparents married and went to Portuguese South East Africa, now Mozambique, where they were missionaries for three years.

"My father, who organized and managed Credit Unions most of his working life, said to me again and again, "Stick up for the Little Guy, Bud."

"My mother was a semi-professional church choir singer when I was a baby. She sang a lullaby to me which went: "Baby's boat's a silver moon / sailing in the sky / and I see it sailing there / as the stars go by. / Sail baby's boat / out across the sea / only don't forget to come / home again to me." Many years later, after I had developed my life long interest in music, I realized that "Baby's Boat," the way my mother sang it, was in a minor key.

"My mother was a housewife and homemaker, but the day I left for college she got a job managing a Teamsters' Union Credit Union and worked out of the house every day after that until she died. After I graduated from college—and, as my mother put it, there was no more danger of my college scholarship being taken away by the government—my mother joined The Women's International League for Peace and Freedom.

"I spent most of my time as a child day dreaming and fishing. I did not read. I wasn't good at anything. In elementary school I did only moderately well, but almost every year I won the good citizenship award. I never really read a book cover to cover until I was in high school. Throughout my childhood and adolescence both my parents and I were deeply involved in the Methodist church.

"In high school I ran track and played jazz trumpet, both of which I did quite well; I was also the school clown. Track, trumpet and buffoonery gave me an identity. During high school I had acne so bad that it often took all the courage I had just to go to school.

"My average grade coming out of high school was about a C-. In my senior year, however, I had an English teacher who inspired me greatly and who was very enthusiastic about some little things I was beginning to write and I got seriously interested in writing religious verse.

"Colleges were interested in me only because I was a very good hurdler. One college offered to get me a tutor to help me through my courses. When I got to college I had to go to the reading lab where they told me I was reading at an 8th grade level. The dean at the college I attended told me in my freshman year that if I worked hard I could be a good solid C+ or maybe even a B- student. This condescension pissed me off so much that after my first semester on academic probation I got on the Dean's List and stayed there for the next seven semesters.

"I, like my father before me, have waged a lifelong struggle with depression.

"I majored in philosophy and art history in college.

"I write poems and plays, occasionally a novel, and on a regular basis essays also. I'm interested in the invisible people, the downtrodden, the put upon and the forgotten.

"I am deeply involved in the Peace Movement and write many essays on the subject. In recent years on my website—www.davidbudbill.com—I have been publishing a cyberzine called THE JUDEVINE MOUNTAIN EMAILITE, an unabashedly left-wing publication for my own essays and others', devoted primarily to the issues of the Right Wing take-over in the United States and to issues of race in America.

"I am devoted to reading the ancient Chinese and Japanese poets and my recent writing is heavily influenced by them as it is by Taoism and Buddhism. I am a beginning student—and I will always be a beginning student—of the shakuhachi, a vertical, bamboo Japanese flute.

"I have always been somewhat embarrassed about being a writer, an artist. I don't like the elite and elitist air that so often casts itself over artists and the arts. It is obvious that many people involve themselves with the arts in order to distinguish themselves from the common people out of which I come and with whom I still fiercely identify. I hate pretense. I want to make art that the common people can understand, use, find meaningful and enjoy."

David Budbill was born on June 13, 1940. He was educated at Muskingum College in New Concord, Ohio, and in New York City at Columbia University and Union Theological Seminary, where he earned a master of divinity degree. He has worked as a short-order cook, carpenter's helper, forester, and gardener, among other jobs. In addition, he has taught English at the high-school and college levels and served as a church minister.

Budbill began his writing career as a crafter of poetic drama. His first play, *Mannequins' Demise,* was published in 1965. (Some sources say 1966.) Another dramatic work, *Knucklehead Rides Again,* followed in 1967, after which more than a decade passed before the publication of *The Pulp Cutters' Nativity: A Christmas Poem in Two Acts, Being a Contemporary Adaptation of the Medieval English Miracle Play,* The Second Shepherds' Play (1981). Meanwhile, in 1969, Budbill and his wife moved to a remote area in Vermont and built their own house. They have remained there, often working together, as they did on Budbill's books of poems *The Chain Saw Dance* (1977) and *From Down to the Village* (1981), both illustrated by Lois Eby. Those volumes, along with the collection *Barking Dog* (1968), helped secure Budbill a Guggenheim Fellowship in poetry. In 1976 he published a short-story collection for young readers, *Snowshoe Trek to Otter River,* which was a Kirkus Choice Book and was nominated for the Dorothy Canfield Fisher Award. *Bones on Black Spruce Mountain,* a novel Budbill called a sequel to the story collection, appeared in 1978.

Budbill's first book with "Judevine" in the title was *Why I Came to Judevine,* published in 1987, with illustrations by Eby. In 1991 Budbill published *Judevine: The Complete Poems.* The culmination of 20 years' work, that volume contains "a distillation," as Janice Arkatov remarked in the *Los Angeles Times* (March 8, 1992), of *The Chain Saw Dance, From Down in the Village,* and *Why I Came to Judevine,* as well as *The Pulp Cutters' Nativity.* An ongoing project, *Judevine* interweaves stories of the ordinary people of the region in which Budbill lives.

Staged productions of *Judevine* have been accompanied by music and feature actors' imitations of bird calls and other sounds. Budbill has created a performance piece, *A Love Supreme: A Found Poem for Black Music,* made up of quotations from jazz musicians interwoven with improvised music. He has performed as part of a group with William Parker, a multi-instrumentalist and composer, and other musicians. *Zen Mountains/ Zen Streets: A Duet for Poet and Improvised Bass,* by Budbill and Parker, was released as a CD in 1999. In 2000 Budbill wrote the libretto for *A Fleeting Animal: An Opera from Judevine,* with music by Erik Nielsen. The recording *Songs for a Suffering World: Incantation and Improvisation; A Prayer for Peace; A Protest against War,* featuring William Parker and the percussionist Hamid Drake along with Budbill, appeared in 2003.

Moment to Moment, a book of poems largely composed by "Judevine Mountain," a recluse and alter-ego of Budbill, appeared in 1999. As Budbill explained to Lisa Simeone for the National Public Radio program *Weekend All Things Considered* (March 31, 2001), he needed a "persona to hide behind." In a review of Budbill's most recent collection of poetry, *While We've Still Got Feet: New Poems* (2004), for the *New York Times* (July 17, 2005), Joel Brouwer wrote, "Budbill belongs to the tradition in American letters inaugurated by Thoreau and continuing today in manifestations both benign (Wendell Berry) and malignant (Ted Kaczynski), wherein the writer abandons the cacophony of human society for a little paradise in the woods, but instead of quietly living out his days in smog-free solitude insists on coming to town (or writing an essay, or mailing a bomb) every few months to remind us of what a benighted existence we're living."

Budbill is currently working on a play called "Papa."

—S.Y.

Suggested Reading: *American Libraries* p76 Nov. 1999; *American Theatre* p13 Mar. 1994; *Antioch Review* p135+ Spring 2002; *Booklist* p59 Sep. 1, 1999; David Budbill's Web site; *Judevine Mountain Emailite* (on-line) Aug. 13, 2002, Oct. 28, 2002, Dec. 30, 2002; *Library Journal* p86 Sep. 15, 1999; *Los Angeles Times* C p92 Mar. 8, 1992; *New York Times* G p10 May 19, 1999; *New York Times Book Review* p32 Apr. 30, 1978; *Parnassus: Poetry in Review* (on-line) 1993; *Weekend All Things Considered* (on-line) Mar. 31, 2001

Selected Books: juvenile—*Christmas Tree Farm* (illustrated by Donald Carrick), 1974; *Snowshoe Trek to Otter River* (illustrated by Lorence Bjorklund), 1976; *Bones on Black Spruce Mountain*, 1978; poetry—*Judevine: The Complete Poems, 1970-1990*, 1991; *Moment to Moment*, 1999; *While We've Still Got Feet*, 2004; drama—*Mannequins' Demise*, 1965; *The Pulp Cutters' Nativity: A Christmas Poem in Two Acts, Being a Contemporary Adaptation of the Medieval English Miracle Play,* The Second Shepherds' Play, 1981; *Judevine*, 1999; as editor—*Danvis Tales: Selected Stories by Rowland E. Robinson*, 1995

Budnitz, Judy

Apr. 24, 1973– Novelist; short-story writer

Judy Budnitz writes fiction that highlights the grotesqueries and indignities of modern life. In her collections of short stories, *Flying Leap* (1998) and *Nice Big American Baby* (2005), and her novel, *If I Told You Once* (1999), she "reveals both the pleasures and pitfalls of high-concept fiction that has untethered itself from the pesky obligations of verisimilitude," Tom Perrotta wrote for the *New York Times Book Review* (February 20, 2005). "Budnitz takes great pains to avoid the specificity essential to the illusion of realism, as if she's warning the reader not to get too invested in her characters, to look elsewhere for the meaning of her stories." He concluded with the hope that Budnitz would "turn her attention more directly to the world we actually live in. She's a gifted writer; there's a lot she could tell us." In a review for *Newsweek* (March 28, 2005), Jeff Giles commented, "Budnitz has misgivings about America's place in the world. But she avoids even the names of countries, burning away anything that will distract from the primal questions of who we are and what we owe each other." One reviewer, in what seems to be a reference to Perrotta, "recently advised Budnitz to write realistic fiction—a patronizing suggestion, as well as a naive one. She already does."

Jeff Linnell/Courtesy Random House

Judy Budnitz was born on April 24, 1973 in Newton, Massachusetts. Her mother, Paula, was a social worker, and her father, Mark, was a law professor. She was raised in Atlanta, Georgia, and attended Harvard University, in Cambridge, Massachusetts, earning a bachelor's degree, in

1995. She was then awarded a fellowship at the Provincetown Fine Arts Work Center, in Massachusetts. Upon completing the fellowship Budnitz entered New York University, and in 1998 she earned an M.F.A. By the time she had received her master's degree, Budnitz had embarked on a career as a cartoonist for the *Village Voice* and had published stories in such prestigious venues as the *New Yorker*, *Harper's*, and the *Paris Review*.

In 1998 Budnitz collected some two dozen stories in *Flying Leap*. The tales start out conventionally, but at some point almost all of them change course—"the moment when she leaves the comfort zone for the Twilight Zone," as J. D. Biersdorfer wrote for the *New York Times Book Review* (January 25, 1998). One of the stories in the collection often singled out by reviewers is "Guilt," in which the protagonist is so worn down by the carping of his aunts, who insist that he donate his heart to his dying mother, that he decides that "one quick operation will be so much easier than struggling for the rest of my life to do back to her all the things she thinks she's done for me," as quoted by Biersdorfer. In another, "Got Spirit," school spirit carries away a group of high-school cheerleaders to the point that they immolate themselves in a bonfire. "Like so many stories in this collection," Biersdorfer wrote, "'Got Spirit' is a skewed, bitter little performance that's also morbidly hysterical. In a consistently impressive debut, Budnitz takes her *Flying Leap* and hits the ground running." Jeff Giles, writing for *Newsweek* (February 23, 1998), compared Budnitz to the acclaimed writer Shirley Jackson and concluded, "Her jacket copy praises her 'sense of humanity and hope.' Me, I like her mean streak."

In 1999 Budnitz's first novel, *If I Told You Once*, the story of four generations of women, was published. Budnitz told Lisa Gee in an interview for the Orange Prize Web site that the novel grew out of an accumulation of ideas, some of them related to the Holocaust. "Most eyewitnesses of the [Holocaust] will be dead in twenty years, and it made me wonder where we could turn to then for proof, for indisputable evidence that it happened," she explained to Gee. "And that made me think more generally about the subjectivity of memory, and the paradox that the most reliable source of information about an event ought to be an eyewitness, yet at the same time one person's version is inherently subjective, shaped by his personal angle. And that made me want to try to write a novel which was narrated by several different characters with very different points of view, a novel which would force the reader to have to decide which narrator to trust to find the truth." The initial point of view in the novel is that of Ilana, a young woman living in a gray, desolate forest in what seems to be the middle of Europe but is really the fairy-tale forest of legend. Through magic and sheer will, she gets to a city in the New World, a metaphorical simulacrum for the immigrant experience. She eventually marries and has a daughter, Sashie; a granddaughter, Mara; and a great-granddaughter, Nomie. In an interview for the *Jerusalem Post* (February 4, 2000), Budnitz told Nan Goldberg, "Ilana is self-reliant and stubborn. But with each generation that strength gets turned in on itself and gets warped. I wanted to say that strength can become a bad thing instead of a good thing." The men in the novel die, are killed, or magically disappear. "I had to eliminate the men," Budnitz told Goldberg, "because I wanted to focus on the relationships between the women. . . . The oppression of women by men is written about so much, and I wanted to show that women also oppress each other, put themselves in bad positions. It's not only the men's fault."

Lelia Ruckenstein, writing for the *Washington Post Book World* (January 30, 2000), described *If I Told You Once* as a series of "stories within stories, like a series of Russian wooden dolls that fit one inside the other." Ruckenstein opined, "Combining folk tale, haunting evocations, hallucinations and dreams, this wildly imaginative epic explodes the boundaries between reality and fantasy. . . . But even when this twisted folk tale threatens to overwhelm and float away into magic realism, it resonates with historical and psychological meaning. Budnitz's apocalyptic visions evoke the devastation of the pogroms and World War I. . . . But there are humor and tenderness in this dark, eerie tale." For the *Publishers Weekly* (September 6, 1999, on-line) reviewer, "Budnitz's hypnotic prose, as tight as coiled spring, dream imagery (both poetic and fierce) and instinct for the grotesque cast a weird light on familiar subject matter, and owe as much to Isaac Bashevis Singer's . . . demon-haunted fables as to contemporary multigenerational sagas." *If I Told You Once* won the Edgar Lewis Wallant Award for fiction and was short-listed for the Orange Prize, a literary award for women writing in English.

For *Nice Big American Baby*, her critically celebrated 2005 book, Budnitz returned to the short-story form. Many of the stories in the collection concern the relationships among children and parents, as with "Where We Come From," in which a woman trying desperately to get over the border into the U.S. manages to keep her child in the womb for years so that she can have "a nice big American baby," and "Flush," in which a mother and her daughters deal with the results of a series of mammograms. Others concern issues of race and class politics. In "Immersion," for example, a group of black children playing in a public pool are purposely exposed to polio by a disgruntled white person, and in "Nadia" an eastern European mail-order bride must face the resentment of her husband's female American friends. "Miracle," a parable in which an ink-black child is born to a Caucasian couple, touches on both the political and the parental. "This is a collection that offers much in the way of both emotion and imagination, which dares to be magical without bothering about realism," Lydia Millet wrote for the *Washington Post Book World* (February 27, 2005). "Budnitz manages to be both funny and serious, whimsical and substantive: With a wry rap across the knuckles she draws our attention to small and vital things." Gillian Flynn, in a review for *Entertainment Weekly* (February 11, 2005), wrote, "Budnitz's collection is jarring, humane, funny, and so lively it practically buzzes."

Budnitz—who has taught writing at Brown University, in Providence, Rhode Island, and Columbia University, in New York City, among other institutions—told Lisa Gee, "I like creating a story that conveys some strong emotion or idea,

that makes readers pause and look around and see the world in a new way. I think that's the objective of most writers."

—S.Y.

Suggested Reading: *Jerusalem Post* B p12 Feb. 4, 2000; *Los Angeles Times Book Review* p12 Feb. 20, 2005; *New York Times Book Review* p12 Jan. 25, 1998, p8 Feb. 20, 2005; *Newsweek* p68 Feb. 23, 1998; Orange Prize Web site; *Publishers Weekly* (on-line) Sep. 6, 1999; *Washington Post Book World* p7 Jan. 30, 2000, p6 Feb. 27, 2005

Selected Books: *Flying Leap*, 1998; *If I Told You Once*, 1999; *Nice Big American Baby*, 2005

Kevin Winter/Getty Images

Burroughs, Augusten

Oct. 23, 1965– Memoirist; essayist; novelist

"When I was 13, my crazy mother gave me away to her lunatic psychiatrist, who adopted me. I then lived a life of squalor, pedophiles, no schools and free pills." With those words, spoken to Claude Peck for the Minneapolis-St. Paul *Star Tribune* (November 16, 2003, on-line), the writer Augusten Burroughs summarized the contents of *Running with Scissors* (2002), a memoir of his turbulent teenage years. A critically acclaimed best-seller, *Running with Scissors* was made into a feature film in 2006. "There have been a lot of authors writing about their screwed-up life—Tobias Wolff is a perfect example, with *This Boy's Life*," Dan Peres, the editor of *Details* magazine, told Peck. "The

difference with Augusten is that he took an extremely intense and upsetting and traumatizing childhood and wrote about it in a way that doesn't necessarily make you feel sorry for him. He didn't write a tearjerker. He wrote a very honest book that makes you laugh." Similarly, Peter Neil Nason wrote for the *Tampa Tribune* (June 8, 2003), "Burroughs has the uncanny ability to do what so many authors strive for but few can accomplish with equal aplomb: He makes you laugh and then he tears out your heart." Burroughs, whose formal education ended with primary school, is also the author of *Sellevision* (2000), a well-received satirical novel based on his years as an advertising copywriter; *Dry*, a memoir describing his addictions to drugs and alcohol, his treatment at a rehabilitation center that catered to homosexuals, and his struggles to remain sober after the death of his lover from AIDS; and two collections of personal essays, *Magical Thinking: True Stories* and *Possible Side Effects*. Regarding Burroughs's success, Claude Peck commented, "It's the kind of career in writing that might make Burroughs the envy of classmates at his high-school reunion, if only he had gone to high school."

Burroughs was born Christopher Robison on October 23, 1965 in Pittsburgh, Pennsylvania. He has claimed to be a direct descendant of King James II of Scotland (1430–60). At age 18 he legally changed his name to Augusten X. Burroughs. His father, John Robison, taught math and philosophy at the college level (he retired as head of the philosophy department at the University of Massachusetts, at Amherst); he also suffered from alcoholism. His mother, Margaret Robison (called Deirdre in *Running with Scissors*), an aspiring poet, had bouts of manic depression and psychosis. As a child, in attempts to escape his parents' unending quarreling, Burroughs would fantasize about becoming an airline steward, a soap-opera star, or a hair-care-products tycoon. He yearned in vain for the sort of idealized happy life depicted on the 1950s sitcom *Leave It to Beaver*. "My parents had this relationship that was really terrifying," he recalled to Litsa Dremousis for Bookslut.com (October 6, 2003). "I mean, the level of hatred that they had, and the level of physical abuse—my mother would beat up my father, basically—and I think I was drawn to images on television that were bright and reflective. And shallow, very superficial." When he was young, his parents gave him a tape recorder as a gift. "Before I could write, I would talk into it," he told LoAnn Halden for the *Weekly News* (January 8, 2004, on-line), a Florida publication. "I would make up plays sometimes, but mostly what I would do is talk about my day."

During his adolescence Burroughs's parents divorced, and his father disappeared from his life for many years. When he was 13 his mother relinquished guardianship of him to her psychiatrist, Rodolph Harvey Turcotte (called Dr. Finch in *Running with Scissors*), who lived in Northhampton, Massachusetts, with his wife and children. (Burroughs's older brother, John, nine years his senior, had already left home. He now owns a car dealership in Springfield, Massachusetts.) An assortment of the psychiatrist's patients and former clients also lived in the Turcottes' home for varying periods. All the while Burroughs maintained contact with his mother, who was repeatedly institutionalized for psychiatric treatment.

As Burroughs has described events, Rodolph Turcotte physically resembled Santa Claus, but he was far from benign. Viewing himself as a "full-time theologist," he believed that God communicated to him through the shape of his feces, which he examined at the dining room table. Turcotte and his wife raised their daughters with few rules: They did not object to the children's playing with an obsolete electroshock-therapy machine, for example; according to Burroughs the girls strapped him into it during his first visit to the house. Further contributing to the strangeness of the household, Mrs. Turcotte ate dog food, and her husband had given legal guardianship of one daughter, who was then 13, to a tennis pro nearly 30 years her senior, who abused her during their ensuing three-year relationship. Turcotte also enabled the 13-year-old Burroughs to quit school, by helping him to fake a suicide attempt (by administering whiskey and Valium to the boy until he passed out); at the mental hospital at which Burroughs was briefly held afterward, he was labeled psychologically unfit to attend school.

That year a man whom Burroughs has called Neil Bookman, who was then in his 30s, began having sex with him. The relationship, which Turcotte and other adults in the house knew about, continued for several years, until Bookman vanished. Explaining why he submitted to Bookman, Burroughs told Colin Waters for the Scottish newspaper *Sunday Herald* (February 16, 2003), "I didn't have any adults in my life that were paying attention to me. My mother was crazy and my father wasn't around. Neil was an adult who

was giving me a tonne of attention and time. It became sexual. I think what happened to me could happen to any kid, regardless of whether they're gay or straight. You get sucked into something like that because in order to get the attention and affection you crave, you have to pay the price, and that's sex. It's only years later you realise how horrible and wrong it was."

Burroughs received his GED (general equivalency diploma) at 17 and then enrolled at a community college; he soon flunked out. At about that time his mother accused Dr. Turcotte of raping her, and Burroughs moved out of the Turcottes' home. Although, in light of his mother's mental problems, he was unsure whether to believe her charge of rape, "knowing Dr. Finch, I would say that he probably did rape my mother," as he told Waters. Finch, he said, had much in common with the American mass murderer Charles Manson, in that he "had charisma and was to some degree a leader. He was able to get vulnerable people to follow him. Finch had moments of clarity, possibly even brilliance, but these were heavily diluted with real madness." The doctor lost his medical license in 1986, when he was found guilty of insurance fraud; he died in 2000.

Burroughs lived in Boston, Massachusetts, and Chicago, Illinois, before moving to San Francisco, California, where he remained for five years. After working at a series of relatively unskilled jobs (waiter, dog trainer, candy-store clerk, and store detective), he attended a trade school with the intention of becoming a computer programmer. Then, by his own account, while watching TV one day, he saw a badly made commercial for the school; thinking he could do better, he rewrote every ad in a copy of *Fortune* magazine that happened to be at hand. (As a child he had loved the TV sitcom *Bewitched*, in which the main character's husband, Darren Stevens, was an advertising executive.) Soon afterward he landed a job with the advertising agency Ogilvy & Mather in San Francisco. "The only thing I could do was write ads, because it's manipulating people, telling them to look on the bright side—and I was good at that. I'd had a lot of practice," he told Jackie McGlone for the *Scotsman* (February 15, 2003). "I knew all about taking a situation that was [expletive] and finding the positive. Advertising is taking a wart and transforming it into a beauty mark."

Working in advertising is "pretty cushy in a lot of ways, but I hated it," Burroughs told Litsa Dremousis. Nevertheless, in the early 1990s he took another job in the field, this time with an ad agency in New York City. During that period he began smoking crack cocaine and drinking to excess. Every night he would consume a bottle of whiskey; to disguise the smell of alcohol on his breath when he was at his office, he would spray his tongue with cologne. "I had been very successful as an advertising copy writer, but I always felt like I had this horrible, dirty secret," he told James MacGowan for the *Ottawa Citizen* (July 28, 2002). "I really felt like my childhood, my past and my lack of any education was this extra, deformed leg I was dragging around behind me, trying to keep under my jacket. I was really ashamed of it and I felt like a prisoner of it. And try explaining it to someone on a third date who says, 'So, tell me about your parents.'"

Burroughs's drug and alcohol problems intensified until his co-workers persuaded him to enter a 30-day rehabilitation program specifically designed for homosexuals, at the Pride Institute, in Eden Prairie, Minnesota, outside Minneapolis (dubbed the Proud Institute in *Running with Scissors*). In 2000 he quit drinking and within weeks wrote a novel, *Sellevision*. Published the same year, *Sellevision* focuses on a fictitious home-shopping network and several of the people associated with it. Burroughs described *Sellevision* to LoAnn Halden as a "total cheese popcorn of a book"—"which is exactly what he wanted it to be," as Halden reported. "Light and funny, with a bitter aftertaste," according to an assessment by Regina Marler for Amazon.com, *Sellevision* earned mixed reviews in *Publishers Weekly* and *Kirkus Reviews*, among other periodicals. As quoted on Amazon.com, more enthusiastic notices appeared in *People*, in which a critic called it "one of the hoots of this fall"; the New York *Daily News*, which labeled it "an absolute howl . . . wicked fun"; and *Booklist*, for which James Klise wrote, "As a bubbly soap opera, *Sellevision* is good company for the beach or the plane. Its literary value may be low, but the material sparkles."

At the suggestion of his agent, Christopher Schelling, Burroughs next began writing a memoir about his teen years. "I thought my childhood was a disgusting mess so I never thought anyone would be interested in reading about it, even with a gallows humour," he told Phillip McCarthy for the *Sydney Morning Herald* (April 5, 2003). "And so I never really thought about holding back. Should I tell about my pedophile relationship? Sure. Should I tell about eating dog food watching television? Why not." As reference, Burroughs used his extensive journals, which he began keeping at 14. "These journals were hilarious," he told Waters. "There I was, with a mother who was talking to the lampshades and eating peanut butter and cigarette sandwiches, and all I could think about was how I'd give myself an ulcer unless I started up my own line of hair-care products." Burroughs mined terrain already covered in countless childhood memoirs; what set his book apart from most of them was its combination of ghastliness and humor. "Hopefully the book isn't about self-pity and being a victim and whining and sniveling about how horrible my life was," Burroughs said to Waters. "Even at the time I saw how my life was so appalling it was funny." "*Running with Scissors* is—in every sense I can think of—a blast," Lynne Truss wrote for the London *Sunday Times* (February 2, 2003).

"Burroughs is a likeable and wry narrator, and a born writer. . . . In the world of horrific and self-amazed childhood memoirs, *Running with Scissors* sets a new standard for, basically, getting over it and getting out more." Sara O'Leary, in a review for the *Vancouver Sun* (August 17, 2002), wrote that *Running with Scissors* "appears to do more than reinvent the genre [of personal memoir]—it completely obliterates it, or at least handily dispatches one of its many subgenres: the tell-all account of the dysfunctional family. After reading this memoir I don't see any point in anyone ever writing about an unhappy childhood again." According to O'Leary, Burroughs's "mix of cynicism, resilience, and self-deprecating humour . . . makes a highly readable book out of an often sickening story. . . . It's hard to believe that all his claims are literally true, but perhaps they are. At a certain point, if the story is good enough you just don't care." While several other reviewers also challenged the book's veracity, Burroughs told McCarthy that all of it was true. "I don't think you could really make up stuff like this," he asserted. "It would be too unbelievable. But I was writing it down in my journals my whole life . . . writing for four hours every day."

As the film version of the memoir was being prepared, members of the Turcotte family sued Burroughs for $2 million, alleging that despite changing their last name to Finch in the book, he had included details that made them easily identifiable, defaming them and causing emotional distress. They also alleged that Burroughs had grossly exaggerated some incidents described in the book and completely fabricated others. The lawsuit remains unsettled as of early 2007, although Sony Pictures reached a separate settlement with the family in late 2006, preventing a threatened lawsuit over the film. (Like members of the Turcotte family, Burroughs's mother has also taken issue with his depiction of some events, such as the scene in which he discovers her having sex with a minister's wife.)

In his next book, *Dry* (2003), which was written before both *Sellevision* and *Running with Scissors*, Burroughs described his struggles with alcohol and drug addiction, his recovery, and his relationship with his best friend and lover George Stathakis (called Pighead in *Dry*), whom he helped care for when Stathakis was ill with AIDS. Burroughs had started writing *Dry* after his friend's death, in 1998, in an effort to stay sober. "I was like, 'What do I do all day?'" he told Jeff Baker for the *Oregonian* (June 6, 2003). "Everything was vibrating with intensity and I had all this energy. When I drank, I didn't keep a journal—I did some in rehab, but it didn't help at all—but when I got out I just wrote all day, every day." Burroughs explained to Claude Peck that after he completed rehab, "I was so exuberant, and so manic . . . I would stay inside on a beautiful day to write. I wasn't thinking about publishing, or that someone would read this someday; I just had to write. That's what *Dry* came from." The completed manuscript filled about 1,800 pages; with the help of Schelling and Jennifer Enderlin, an editor at St. Martin's Press, the author reworked it; the published book ends on page 293. Burroughs has said that in writing *Dry*, he took liberties with the truth, by combining characters, for example, and changing some details and time periods.

While critiques of *Dry* were favorable, they were not as positive as those for *Running with Scissors*. Among the most enthusiastic reviewers was Connie Ogle, who wrote for the *Miami Herald* (June 29, 2003), "What made *Scissors* so overwhelmingly enjoyable also makes *Dry* compelling: Burroughs can see himself at his lowest . . . and turn his pain into an unforgettable comic portrait. . . . The trick is that Burroughs can laugh at himself, and when he writes he reminds us that maybe we ought not to take ourselves and our problems so seriously. And he's more than just a garden variety wise guy: *Dry* takes a heart-breaking turn at the end, and the shift is perfect, moving and redemptive, an excellent counterpoint to the outrageous humor." By contrast, Kim Hughes wrote for the *Toronto Star* (July 27, 2003), "While the slyly funny *Dry* might be as easy to knock back as Burroughs' preferred Ketel One martinis, it's relatively light on alcohol-fuelled disasters. Moreover, its rarefied setting . . . keeps us at an emotional distance. . . . Burroughs is to be commended for having the courage to examine his shortcomings publicly. And there's absolutely no doubt our man can sucker-punch the senses with a supple turn of phrase and many alert observations. But transparency is only as interesting as what lies beneath. In the case of *Dry*, the declarations of a privileged, well-heeled recovered alcoholic are only slightly more illuminating than avowals of a regular one."

In Burroughs's next effort, *Magical Thinking: True Stories* (2004), he continued to mine his life for literary material, which he set down this time in essay form. Although there were numerous favorable comparisons made between him and other essayists with a taste for the grotesque and amusing (among them David Sedaris, Jonathan Ames, and David Rakoff), Burroughs's collection struck some critics as flat, especially in light of the outsized carnival-sideshow attraction of *Scissors* and *Dry*. "Now comes the revenge of the quotidian," John Leland wrote about *Magical Thinking* for the *New York Times Book Review* (October 12, 2004). "After a few tales from his past, he muses here on the tamer oddities of life after rehab: his relative fame, his flirtation with steroids, telemarketers, moisturizer, tacky tourists in Key West, the stresses of buying a country house and, centrally, his happy Upper West Side domesticity with an art director named Dennis."

Burroughs's latest book, *Possible Side Effects* (2006), is another collection of personal essays. The book received largely mixed reviews. "*Possible Side Effects* is slight in subject matter

and shaky in chronology. (The essays jump back and forth through time; certain facts are repeated arbitrarily.) It's less spiky than *Magical Thinking*," Janet Maslin wrote for the *New York Times* (May 1, 2006, on-line). "But it's also more inviting and less forced, perhaps because there is less at stake here. While Mr. Burroughs treads water until he either returns to outright fiction (his first book, *Sellevision*, was a novel about advertising) or has adult experiences to rival the indelibly crazy ones of his childhood, he makes good, snarky company even with nothing serious in mind."

Burroughs has written frequently for the on-line magazine *Salon* and recently became a contributing editor at *Details* magazine. "He's one of the most prolific writers I know, and unbelievably fast," Dan Peres, the editor of *Details*, told Claude Peck. "We can agree on a column idea at noon, say, and by 2 o'clock he's filed it to me." Burroughs has said that he learned much about writing during his career in advertising, including the importance of entertaining readers, cutting material that doesn't work, and writing even when one does not feel up to it. "You can't sit around waiting for inspiration or you'll never get anything done," he told Baker. "I write every day, whether I'm in the mood or not, and I got that from advertising."

Burroughs has included his E-mail address on his Web site, and he spends about five hours a day answering mail from readers. He has named *A Confederacy of Dunces*, by John Kennedy Toole, and Todd Haynes's *Safe*, starring Julianne Moore, as his favorite book and film, respectively, and Elizabeth Berg as one of the writers he most admires. The relationship between Burroughs and his mother, who has been confined to a wheelchair since she suffered a stroke in 1989, is strained; he has made peace with his father, who has remarried. Burroughs and his partner, Dennis Pilsits, a former graphic designer who now manages Burroughs's business affairs, live with their two French bulldogs. Burroughs writes frequently about the dogs, who are named Bentley and the Cow.

—K.E.D.

Suggested Reading: Bookslut.com Oct. 6, 2003; (Minneapolis-St. Paul) *Star Tribune* (on-line) Nov. 16, 2003; *Oregonian* Arts and Living p10 June 6, 2003; *Ottawa Citizen* C p8 July 20, 2003; *People* p229 Sep. 23, 2002; *Sydney Morning Herald* Books p13 Apr. 5, 2003; *Weekly News* (on-line) Jan. 8, 2004

Selected Books: *Sellevision*, 2000; *Running with Scissors*, 2002; *Dry*, 2003; *Magical Thinking: True Stories*, 2004; *Possible Side Effects*, 2006

Byler, Stephen Raleigh

1971(?)– Short-story writer

Stephen Raleigh Byler's novel *Searching for Intruders* (2002) established Byler's place among a tradition of writers that includes Raymond Carver, Andre Dubus, and Ernest Hemingway in large part because they share an overarching theme: the conflicts men face as they navigate through the demands placed upon them by conventional notions of masculinity and the realities of the modern world. Byler's exploration of this theme, however, is as much personal as it is literary. "I come from a family of boys on my father's side, and they were all hunters and fishermen. My father left us, and my mother raised me, and she came from a farm family. I grew up with a lot of feminine energy, so I had to deal with how to keep from becoming a completely emasculated mama's boy," Byler has said to explain the obsessions of his fiction, as reported by Lynn Cline for the *Santa Fe New Mexican* (February 08, 2002). Byler's combining of the personal and the literary enabled him to produce a group of "stories, of lives wasted and lives saved, [that] are acute, accurate and painful. They do not surprise, but instead they examine what might be called a tragedy that even at this late date, sensitivity still fits so poorly on modern American men," Ben Schrank observed for the *Hartford (Connecticut) Courant* (December 23, 2001).

Stephen Raleigh Byler, who was born in about 1971, didn't grow up wanting to be a writer. As a boy in Lancaster, Pennsylvania, where he attended Lancaster Mennonite High School, and later as an undergraduate at Eastern Mennonite University, in Virginia, he enjoyed writing but never felt he would be able to succeed at it professionally. After receiving a bachelor's degree in sociology, in 1992, he had what he described to Jo Kadlecek, in an interview for the *Columbia News* (January 30, 2002, on-line), as a "meaning crisis," which led him to study philosophy and religion at Princeton University, in New Jersey. His intellectual forays eventually triggered a creative awakening, in which he came to believe that literature offered the best means of engaging his questions. "I realized that there are certain intense experiences you can't really describe with critical language," he told Kadlecek. "You need to evoke, to make the reader or listener feel what you're trying to communicate in the context of a narrative." Byler, then, set a goal for himself of writing his first novel by the time he was 30; he dropped out of Princeton after his second year and spent the following six months traveling around the U.S. and writing. He later enrolled at Yale University, in New Haven, Connecticut, where he earned a master's degree in religion and literature; there he studied under the novelist Robert Stone and the literary critic Harold Bloom. He subsequently received an M.F.A. from Columbia University, in New York City.

At Columbia Byler began to construct his novel as a collection of stories, each of which could be read either individually or as part of a whole. The result was *Searching for Intruders*, which is composed of 11 interlocking stories—each of which is preceded by a short vignette—that depict the development of Wilson Hues, a troubled man in his 30s who works at low-paying jobs, drifts aimlessly from place to place, and occasionally experiences moments of stunning clarity and illumination. Brad Hooper greeted the book enthusiastically, remarking for *Booklist* (November 15, 2001), "Newcomer Byler's 11 stories are like tightly fitting mosaic pieces, contributing individual luster to a vibrant collective pattern, each story illuminating a crucial milestone in the history of the narrator Wilson's tough relationships with his wife, family, and lovers." In a similarly positive review Harold Bloom wrote, as quoted on the Associated Colleges of the Midwest Web site, "*Searching for Intruders* returns us to the Hemingway of *The Nick Adams Stories*. At their best, Byler's stories are tersely eloquent and marked by a vivid exuberance."

Other reviewers were less enthusiastic. Byler's stories, Dwight Garner wrote for the *New York Times Book Review* (December 30, 2001) "sound terrific right from the start" but went on to note that the book "loses a great deal of its force in its second half. . . . The book's final story, 'Perrito,' sends the collection out on a ridiculous note when a stranger in Chile, where Wilson has traveled on a kind of emotional sabbatical, puts him on the receiving end of a bogus lecture." Brian Miller, writing for *Seattle Weekly* (March 7, 2002), was harsher, asserting that "Stephen Raleigh Byler's unrelentingly flat, affectless prose has hardly a memorable sentence in its 200-plus pages. Again, this seems intentional—but calculated to what end? His hero's vacuous, whiny tone recalls nothing so much as Jack Handy's old 'Deep Thoughts' on *Saturday Night Live*. (Handy's rewrite of Byler would be: 'My father used to drown puppies, which was sad. But later in high school, I used the story to get girls. . . .'"

Byler, who was included in the national Barnes & Noble Discover Great New Writers promotion, divides his time between Lancaster, Pennsylvania and Montana. He has toured the country promoting his book and is at work on a novel, which is to be set in Cuba. He has also participated in the Lancaster Literary Guild lecture series, visiting schools throughout Lancaster County.

—C.M./A.R.

Suggested Reading: *Booklist* p550 Nov. 15, 2001; *Columbia News* (on-line) Jan. 30, 2002; *Library Journal* p148 Jan. 2002; *New York Times Book Review* p6 Dec. 30, 2001

Selected Books: *Searching for Intruders*, 2002

Arizona State University

Carlson, Ron

Sep. 15, 1947– Novelist; short-story writer

Ron Carlson is perhaps best known for his highly praised short-story collections, including *The News of the World* (1987), *Plan B for the Middle Class* (1992), *The Hotel Eden* (1997), *At the Jim Bridger* (2002), and *A Kind of Flying* (2003). Carlson writes largely about the everyday struggles of ordinary men and women in a style that, according to critics, incorporates both a poignant realism and a zany, offbeat sense of humor. His short stories have appeared in such notable publications as *Harper's*, *GQ*, *Esquire*, *Story*, *Playboy*, and the *New Yorker*, as well as in numerous anthologies, including *A Literary Christmas* (1992), *The Norton Anthology of Contemporary Fiction* (1998), and *The Best American Short Stories* (1987 and 2000). He has written such well-received novels as *Betrayed by F. Scott Fitzgerald* (1977) and *Truants* (1981) and is also the author of a novel for young adults, *The Speed of Light* (2003). As Kyrie O'Connor noted in a review of *At the Jim Bridger* in the *Hartford Courant* (May 26, 2002): "For clarity and sure-footedness in pursuit of the American short story, Ron Carlson knows no equal. Now, mind you, that's not 'few' equals, and there's no 'probably' involved."

The eldest of three brothers, Ronald Frank Carlson was born in Logan, Utah, on September 15, 1947, the son of Edwin Carlson and the former Verna Mertz. In 1950 the family relocated to Poplar Grove, a working-class neighborhood on the west side of Salt Lake City, Utah, where Carlson's father worked as a welder and his mother as a homemaker. "I grew up in a golden era, in a very blue collar part of town," Carlson explained to Dennis Lythgoe for the Salt Lake City *Deseret News* (August 11, 2002). "My neighbors worked for the railroad or the copper mine. It was like growing up in a village. Everyone knew who swore and who smoked. We had the river and the railroad tracks— and every kind of baseball there ever was. I loved it. It was like a Garden of Eden." Carlson has suggested that he might have inherited his storytelling gifts from his mother, who, in 1959, entered a 25-words-or-less contest for the computer giant Remington Rand and won $15,000. She had won a number of similar contests throughout that decade, so many in fact that she was photographed for the local newspaper with all of the prizes she won, including stereos, records, books, and basketballs.

Carlson began writing while he was at Edison Elementary School, in Salt Lake City; among his earliest efforts was a story that his teacher selected to read aloud at a parents' meeting. By fifth grade he was writing skits that he and his friends would perform for the class. The characters were taken primarily from films he had seen or books he had read—the Wolfman, Tarzan, Dracula, and so forth—but the stories were entertaining enough that he was allowed to perform them. At West High School he began writing pieces for the school literary magazine, *West Winds*, beginning with a haiku and culminating in a senior-year skit, "Caesar Disgustus," a Roman-gladiator extravaganza.

Shortly after Carlson finished high school, his father received a promotion and the family moved to Houston, Texas. Carlson spent a year studying at the University of Houston before transferring to the University of Utah, in Salt Lake City, in 1966, so he could be closer to his girlfriend, Georgia Elaine Craig, whom he later married. At the University of Utah, he met a number of professors who made an impression on him, among them David Kranes, who became Carlson's mentor. During this period Carlson began doing his first serious writing, turning out term papers, poetry, stories, and plays. After graduating he and his new wife taught for a summer in Connecticut, and when they returned to Utah in the fall, Carlson sold art supplies while his wife worked as a waitress.

After being classified 4-F (physically unfit for military service) for the draft, in 1970, Carlson decided to go to graduate school and later that year returned to the University of Utah. In 1972 he completed his master's degree; his thesis was a collection of short fiction, "Cutting Teeth: The Larry Stories." Though never published as a whole, some of the stories in his thesis were later published in a number of small literary journals. In the fall of 1971, he moved to Lakeville, Connecticut, where he taught English at the Hotchkiss School until 1981. In Connecticut he began to write his first novel—a coming-of-age tale about a young poet named Larry Boosinger who leaves graduate school to write, tours Mexico, returns to America, winds up in jail, escapes with his baseball team, and tries to prove his innocence. Published under the title *Betrayed by F. Scott Fitzgerald*, the book was placed by Richard R. Lingeman, for the *New York Times* (July 14, 1977), "most directly in the coming-of-age tradition, with the contemporary attributes of humor and cool." Lingeman concluded: "*Betrayed* is written in a seriocomic vein, flecked with apt observations, often very funny, though more successful on the comic than it is on the serio side. . . . Larry is more happened to than happening; a humorous counterpuncher to the heavyweight, life. Still I liked him for his unpretentiousness, his wry, caring angle on experience."

Written primarily during a sabbatical year away from teaching, Carlson's second novel, *Truants*, chronicles the misadventures of Collin Elder, a 16-year-old boy who runs away from a home for troubled juveniles in Arizona to seek his uncaring father in California. Along the way, while shoveling cow dung at a summer job at the Arizona State Fair, he meets Louisa Holz, a girl of about his age who has had similar problems with her father, a motorcycle stuntman performing at the fair. The duo soon find jobs at an old-age home, where they meet Will Clare, an octogenarian who wants to run away to find the son who institutionalized him. For the *New York Times Book Review* (February 15, 1981), Barry Yourgrau observed, "The situations in *Truants* (including highly detailed family histories of its main characters) develop the theme of how . . . most families, and their surrogates, wretchedly mishandle the business of nurturing and succoring. Mr. Carlson . . . presents all of this in an affecting manner, with a very decent heart and a tart tongue. He practices a kind of wit that is at once tender, canny and vivid, capable of burnishing a passing moment with a quick touch." Yourgrau added, "Mr. Carlson is not, however, above the too improbable (the degree of Will's spryness, for example) and a much-heavier-than-air sentimentalism. Also, I'm really not comfortable with the sudden ending he's given *Truants*; but there are numerous small pleasures that appeal about this book."

For his next book Carlson had intended to write another novel, tentatively titled "A Thousand People Later." However, he had difficulty completing it and took a number of part-time jobs as he labored through it, including teaching at the division of continuing education at the University of Utah and serving as a writer for schools in the Utah Arts Council, the Idaho Commission on the Arts, and the Alaska Arts Council. He held these positions between 1981 and 1986 and found that he was spending more time writing short stories than working on the novel. Though he had not planned on writing a short-story collection, he found story writing easy and enjoyable. Many of the stories that would make up *The News of the World*, including "The H Street Sledding Record"

and "The Status Quo," were originally published in *Network*, a Salt Lake City monthly magazine.

In a review for *Los Angeles Times Book Review* (February 1, 1987), Richard Eder had many good things to say about *The News of the World*: "Ron Carlson sees patterns in lives. He sees love, struggle that is sometimes rewarded and bravery. He also sees love turned cannibal, defeat, poltroonery and the doping effects of contemporary life. But the outcome of his stories, whether upbeat or the opposite, tends to be an outpouring instead of an evaporation of spirit. So he is a warm writer, and this makes the collection in *The News of the World* relatively unusual. This should not be exaggerated, but our better-known short-story writers tend to write cool, with more irony than assertion. They end with cadences that are not full but interrupted and that suggest drawing away more than coming together." Eder concluded, "*The News of the World* is an uneven collection. Carlson does not have impeccable taste. We can feel shoved. But quite a few of his discoveries are more than worth the shoving." A reviewer for *Playboy* (April 1987) noted that Carlson "knows how regular guys feel and writes about it thoughtfully, wittily, expertly. The 16 stories in this collection, which cover everything from wives who are friendly to dogs that are not, have more dynamism than you'll find in ten other story collections put together." One of the stories, "Milk," appeared in *The Best American Short Stories 1987*, edited by Ann Beattie and Shannon Ravenel.

Many of the pieces in Carlson's next collection of stories, *Plan B for the Middle Class*, also found their way into magazine publication, including "The Chromium Book," which began the author's long association with *Harper's*. The collection was received very favorably. "Carlson specializes in the astute observations of daily life, and yet he is sarcastic about what one takes to be both his subject and the object of his affection: namely, modern marriage, families and suburbia," Debra Spark wrote for the *Washington Post* (September 4, 1992). "Carlson's device for combining his contradictory feelings about the everyday is the bizarre. He uses strange behaviors, moderately mad voices and odd details to allow himself to look at the mundane without quite appearing to do so. In the past, the effect has been entertaining and intelligent but, until this collection, only occasionally magical or profound." Writing for the *New York Times Book Review* (July 26, 1992), Maxine Chernoff described the book as "a gathering of tender and often humorous tales of people coping with conflicts and disasters at work, at home, even in the marriage bed." She further noted that "Ron Carlson is a brilliant comedic writer; in his best stories, he captures the ability of people to adapt to the worst situations and still see the results as triumphant. With its wildy humorous but truthful look at how much we can bend without breaking, *Plan B for the Middle Class* is a revealing—and sometimes unsettling—look at what we may really mean when we talk about 'family values.'"

In 1997 Carlson published *The Hotel Eden*, his third collection of stories. Like its predecessors, the collection was almost universally praised. Writing for the *Los Angeles Times Book Review* (June 8, 1997), Judith Freeman opined: "*The Hotel Eden* is a strange eclectic mixture of some of the funniest and saddest stories ever to cozy up together in one volume. Some stories are brilliant and deeply moving; others are wild and surreal. Taken together, they represent the idiosyncratic vision of an original writer who does what only good writers can do: make us see and feel what his characters see and feel and draw us into their world as if we had been born there." In a critique for the *New York Times Book Review* (July 6, 1997), Margot Livesey was only slightly more reserved in her praise, noting, "I must confess . . . that I was not absolutely swept along by the opening story, 'The Hotel Eden.' . . . But from then on, I was entirely and happily in Carlson's thrall. The word 'happily' seems especially apt for this writer, who is a master of that rarity in contemporary fiction, the happy ending. Throughout the stories, disaster hovers, with despair in the wings, but sometimes the characters do win through, and when that happens we are glad." The *New York Times* named the collection a notable book of the year and the *Los Angeles Times* placed it among the best 100 books of the year. A number of the stories were optioned to be made into films.

The primary focus of Carlson's fourth collection, *At the Jim Bridger* (2002), is American men at various crossroads in their lives. While some of the men are suffering through midlife crises, others are adolescents who are confused about themselves and their futures. "The nine fully developed stories, as varied and uneven a lot as are the contents of [Carlson's three previous collections], uniformly employ a witty, knowing (usually first-person) narrative voice and a tangy colloquial style that often bursts into authentic comic aphorism," a critic for *Kirkus Reviews* (March 1, 2002) observed. "A few stories fall flat. . . . But when Carlson creates a protagonist with an original relationship to his milieu and circumstances, he can dazzle." The critic concluded, "At his (frequent, though inconsistent) best, this is one of our better storytellers. It's about time for a Ron Carlson Selected Stories."

For many years Carlson had been writing stories about his youth in Salt Lake City, the majority of them set during the summer of 1959 and describing a friendship he had with another boy during that period. Carlson had planned on collecting the stories into a single volume but then thought better of it, instead reworking the tales into a novel, *The Speed of Light*, which was published in 2003 and marketed to a young-adult audience. It received generally favorable reviews, though some critics, such as one writing for *Publishers Weekly* (July 7,

2003), expressed reservations about it: "Carlson . . . divides the book into three sections, one for each month of the boys' summer exploits, and this structure is both the novel's strength and weakness. The framework emphasizes accurately the malaise of being 12 years old and not knowing what you want from life, but while individual episodes stand out here and there, the overall effect is akin to a high-minded *Beavis and Butthead* [a popular animated comedy show that aired on MTV during the 1990s], minus the laughs."

In 2007 Carlson is scheduled to publish *Five Skies*, a novel about three men who convene in the Rocky Mountains to help with a summer-long construction project. An early review of the novel, written for *Publishers' Weekly* (March 5, 2007), called the novel "stunning."

Carlson taught at Arizona State University, in Tempe, for nearly 20 years, beginning, in 1986, as a writer in residence, before becoming, in 1994, a full professor of English. In 2006 he took over as the head of the fiction section within the creative-writing program at the University of California, at Irvine.

Carlson has received numerous awards for his writing, including a grant from the Connecticut Commission on the Arts (1978), a Bread Loaf Fellowship (1983), a Cohen Award (1993) from the literary journal *Ploughshares*, the Pushcart Prize (1998 and 2000), and the O. Henry Award from the Texas Institute of Letters (2001). His essays, articles, and book reviews have appeared in such publications as the *New York Times Book Review*, the *Los Angeles Times Book Review*, *Slate*, *Esquire*, and *Writer's Journal*.

Carlson has been married to his high-school sweetheart, the former Georgia Elaine Craig, since June 14, 1969. The couple have two sons, Nicholas and Colin, whom they adopted in 1984.

—C.M.

Suggested Reading: *Hartford Courant* G p3 May 26, 2002; *Kirkus Reviews* Mar. 1, 2002; *Los Angeles Times Book Review* p3 Feb. 1, 1987, p13 June 8, 1997; *New York Times Book Review* p12 Feb. 15, 1981, p8 July 26, 1992, p22 July 6, 1997, p 10 Dec. 28, 2003; *Playboy* p25 Apr. 1987; *Ploughshares* p202+ Fall 2006; *Publishers Weekly* p37 Oct. 20, 2003, p73 July 7, 2003, p36 Mar. 5, 2007; (Salt Lake City) *Deseret News* E p1 Aug. 11, 2002, E p2 Dec. 28, 2003; *Washington Post* B p3 Sep. 4, 1992

Selected Books: short fiction—*The News of the World*, 1987; *Plan B for the Middle Class*, 1992; *The Hotel Eden*, 1997; *At the Jim Bridger*, 2002; *A Kind of Flying*, 2003; novels—*Betrayed by F. Scott Fitzgerald*, 1977; *Truants*, 1981; *The Speed of Light*, 2003

Courtesy of Peter Smith

Carson, Anne

June 21, 1950– Poet; essayist; translator

Over the past decade Anne Carson has taken her place at the forefront of American poetry. In the *Village Voice* (May 19, 1998), Karen Volkman referred to Carson as "unclassifiable," due in part to the blurring of genres that takes place in many of her works, some of them blending poetry and prose, others story and essay. While Carson has been reluctant to discuss with interviewers more than the bare facts of her life, the sadder elements of that life—her father's dementia, the disappearance of her brother, the painful dissolution of her marriage—have often found their way into her work, which did not stop Gail Wronsky from writing for the *Antioch Review* (Spring 1997), echoing others, "Carson's poems are also sometimes wickedly funny." Carson, a university professor and scholar of classical literature, has often infused her poetry with references to mythology and the great works of antiquity, along with images from modern life; perhaps the most celebrated aspects of her work, in fact, are its eclectic nature and the connections made between things that are, on the surface, wildly unrelated. In her profile of Carson for the *New York Times Magazine* (March 26, 2000), Melanie Rehak reported, "When I try to get her to nail down her main themes as a writer, she's baffled: 'I have no idea. Whatever I bump into, I do. It's an act of impulse.'"

Carson's works include the essay volumes *Eros the Bittersweet* (1986) and *Economy of the Unlost: Reading Simonides of Keos with Paul Celan* (1999), the poetry volumes *Plainwater* (1995), *Glass, Irony*

and God (1995), *Autobiography of Red: A Novel in Verse* (1998), and *Decreation* (2005), and translations of ancient works by the Greek masters Sophocles and Sappho. The winner of a number of prestigious awards, Carson was the recipient of a $500,000 MacArthur Fellowship, commonly referred to as the "genius" grant, in 2000.

Anne Carson was born June 21, 1950 in Canada and grew up in various towns in northern Ontario. Her father was a bank manager; her mother was a homemaker. Carson's early life was made difficult by her father's long struggle with Alzheimer's disease. Her older brother, Michael, who was addicted to drugs, dropped out of contact with the family in about 1970 and was in touch with Carson again only after their mother's death, in 1997. He died in 2000. Writing for the *New York Times* (March 27, 2004, on-line), Dinitia Smith reported that Carson's childhood was "redeemed" when, in her last year of high school, her Latin teacher introduced her to classical literature, giving her informal lessons in Greek and reading the works of Sappho with her. "She really changed my life," Carson told Smith about the teacher.

Carson pursued her interest in classical literature at the University of Toronto, in Ontario, where she earned a B.A. degree in 1974, an M.A. in 1975, and a Ph.D. in 1981. She was also awarded a diploma in classics by the University of St. Andrews, in Scotland, in 1976. Carson began her academic career at the University of Calgary, in Alberta, Canada, in 1979 and then taught at Princeton University, in New Jersey, from 1980 to 1987. She then went on to McGill University, in Montreal, teaching classics in the history department and directing graduate studies while devoting alternate semesters to visiting professorships at various universities in the U.S. She has taught at the University of Michigan, in Ann Arbor; the University of California, at Berkeley; Emory University, in Atlanta, Georgia; and the California College of Arts and Crafts, in Oakland.

In 1986 Princeton University Press published Carson's *Eros the Bittersweet: An Essay*, which grew out of her doctoral dissertation. (Dalkey Archive Press reissued the book as a trade paperback in 1998.) The volume consists of 34 essays about the human expression of love and desire, with emphasis on how "the Greeks displayed eros in poetic discourse," according to John Peter Anton, writing for *Choice* (December 1986). Carson, he wrote, "combines critical insight, poetic sensibility, and intimate knowledge of classical literature" to "illustrate the multifaceted nature of eros and also provide a point of departure for expansive explorations into the depths of erotic myth and motive." Stephen Burt, in his article on Carson for *Publishers Weekly* (April 3, 2000), called *Eros the Bittersweet* "a startling, lucid argument about love, lust and jealousy in Greek poetry."

What Carson has described as a "changeful" occurrence in her career took place when she was living at the 92nd Street Y, in New York City, known as a venue for authors' readings, for a year in 1986 and 1987. As she told Stephen Burt, a friend of hers suggested that she contact Ben Sonnenberg, the founding publisher of the literary journal *Grand Street*, "since he was a man of letters and I was a person of letters." Carson took her friend's advice, with the result that Sonnenberg published her series of prose pieces, "Kinds of Water," which Carson described to Burt as "something in between a story and an essay" that traces the route of the Catholic pilgrimage to Santiago de Compostela, in Spain. Carson described Sonnenberg's response to her work as playing a crucial part in her development as a writer: "It's very important to have someone you trust tell you your writing is good," she told Burt, adding that Sonnenberg's acceptance of her writing "made me validate that way of writing, because up until that time . . . I thought I had to make things be either an academic thesis or else fiction, and I couldn't write fiction." A *New York Times Book Review* (November 20, 1988) critic called "Kinds of Water" an example of "a kind of inspired lunacy." Annie Dillard included an essay from "Kinds of Water" in *The Best American Essays 1988*.

In Carson's volume *Short Talks* (1992), prose works are intermingled with poems, each piece titled a "Short Talk" on a different subject, examples being "Short Talk on Hopes" and "Short Talk on Ovid." The pieces concern transformations, sometimes subtle, sometimes surreal, as in the transformation of the actress Brigitte Bardot into the mythological figure Circe in "Short Talk on Brigitte Bardot." Alexander M. Forbes wrote for *Canadian Literature* (Spring 1995), "If *Short Talks* transforms its subjects, it also transforms the prose paragraphs which comprise it. In Carson's hands the prose paragraph sometimes becomes a prose poem ('Short Talk on Autism') and sometimes an essay ('Short Talk on the Rules of Perspective'). . . . The stories that are told usually prove . . . to be 'parables and paradoxes'. . . . At every level, the *Short Talks* record unexpected transformations."

Carson's 1995 volume *Plainwater* includes "Kinds of Water" and *Short Talks* as well as "The Life of Towns" and "Canicula di Anna," a long poem based on the work of the 16th-century Italian painter Perugino. The book's overriding image is, as the title suggests, water. "The theme of water that floods each part lends credence to one's notion of seldom having a metaphysical floor to stand on, the aberrations of grammar, syntax, punctuation, and linear movement floating one weightless," Richard Holinger wrote for the *Midwest Quarterly* (Winter 1997). Holinger found the most successful part of the book to be "The Anthropology of Water," which consists of three essays. "At the outset of the third essay," he wrote, "Carson

explains that her brother ran into 'bad luck' in high school, and then disappeared while trying to reach Asia. What follows is an anthology of lovely dreamlike prose poems about a man's daily swim in a beautiful lily lake. He is perfectly at home, as are we, thanks to Carson's sure, exquisite language." Brian Evenson, writing for the *Review of Contemporary Fiction* (Fall 1995), found Carson's "short essays on father's madness" to be "superb" and wrote that "at her best, Carson's imagination is so vivid and the links she makes so unexpected that her images are revelatory, skirting the very edge of madness. At her worst, which is seldom, a pretentiousness can creep into her style." He concluded that, like the poet Ezra Pound, Carson uses "erudition without obscurity, and knows how far her readers are willing to go with her."

Carson's *Glass, Irony and God*, also published in 1995, consists of five long poems and an essay, "The Gender of Sound." In *Publishers Weekly* (September 25, 1995), a reviewer wrote, "Fusing confession, narrative and classicism, Carson's poetry witnesses the collision of heart and mind with breathtaking vitality." Writing for the *New York Times Book Review* (May 14, 2000), Calvin Bedient judged the poem "The Glass Essay" from *Glass, Irony and God* to be (along with "The Anthropology of Water") one of Carson's strongest works, calling it "stunningly unsparing."

Autobiography of Red: A Novel in Verse, Carson's 1998 volume, is a modern retelling of the Greek myth of Geryon, a red monster with wings who, along with his red cattle, is killed by Herakles as one of the hero's 12 labors. Carson's Red is first a schoolboy, then an adolescent, and finally a mature artist with a passion for photography and volcanos. Years after he falls in love with—and is abandoned by—Herakles, the two meet again, when Herakles has a new lover. "The resulting love triangle erupts like a volcano," Anne Szumigalski wrote for *Quill & Quire* (July 1998). "*Autobiography of Red* is a strange bildungsroman, a portrait of the artist as red winged creature," Karen Volkman wrote. "With her unnerving gift for portraying inner turmoil and terror, Carson records the tremors of this fugitive sensibility, tracing Geryon's life through his childhood molestation, tortured romance with Herakles, obsession with photography, and impulsive pilgrimage to the extreme reaches of the Andes and the volcano Icchantikas, culminating in a delirious act of self-assertion as his dormant wings test themselves at last." *Autobiography of Red* was nominated for the National Book Critics Circle Award for poetry in 1998.

In 1999 Carson and her students created the libretto for an opera, *The Mirror of Simple Souls*, based on the life of Marguerite Porete, a medieval French mystic who was burned at the stake for heresy. The original production, at the University of Michigan, required seven rooms—or installations—that corresponded to the seven parts of the opera. In the same year Carson published *Economy of the Unlost: Reading Simonides of Keos with Paul Celan*, comprising her Martin Classical Lectures, given at Oberlin College, in Ohio. The volume is a critical comparison of the writings of Simonides, who lived in the fifth century B.C.E. in Greece, with those of Paul Celan (1920–70), a Romanian Jew who lived in Paris and wrote in German.

Men in the Off Hours, Carson's 2000 offering, is another volume of poems and poetic essays. "Most verse collections are a miscellany of pieces written over a number of years, without much connection, and of uneven consistency," Phoebe Pettingell wrote for the *New Leader* (March/April 2000). "Carson's latest compilation should be read as a whole, for images and concepts accumulate meaning throughout the work, like a rolling snowball. A peruser might wonder why such diverse forms belong together, yet upon closer reading the work's coherence becomes luminous." In "Father's Old Blue Cardigan," from *Men in the Off Hours*, Carson addressed her father's decline into Alzheimer's disease: "His laws were a secret. / But I remember the moment at which I knew / he was going mad inside his laws. / He was standing at the turn of the driveway when I arrived. / He had on the blue cardigan with the buttons done up all the way to the top. / Not only because it was a hot July afternoon / but the look on his face—as a small child who has been dressed by some aunt early in the morning / for a long trip / on cold trains and windy platforms / will sit very straight at the edge of his seat / while the shadows like long fingers / over the haystacks that sweep past / keep shocking him / because he is riding backwards." *Men in the Off Hours* also contains an elegy for Carson's mother, "Appendix to Ordinary Time." Another section of the volume, entitled "TV Men," had its origins in the work Carson did for a 1995 public-television documentary on Nobel Prize winners. Since most of the laureates were scientists, "I was supposed to attack science from the view of a humanist in these little 30-second sound bites. It was just ridiculous," Carson told Melanie Rehak. "They referred to my function as 'putting the poetry in.'" She told Burt for the *Publishers Weekly* profile that her work on the documentary was "one of the worst experiences of my life." Calvin Bedient wrote in his assessment of *Men in the Off Hours* for the *New York Times Book Review*, "There's a good reason that Carson's reputation has soared to a level equal to that of the half-dozen most admired contemporary American poets. She's tremendously gifted and, without lowering standards, often writes in a middle range between philosophy and lyricism, where many can find her. At the same time, she has great intellectual and emotional knowledge, a vast habitat, to every bit of which she brings powerful perception and a freshness as startling as a loud knock at the door."

In her 2001 volume, *The Beauty of the Husband: A Fictional Essay in 29 Tangos*, Carson returned to the autobiographical mode that had informed *Plainwater* and *Glass, Irony and God*. *The Beauty of the Husband* tells the story of a couple's courtship, marriage, and painful parting. "The plot emerges through Carson's meditative, elusive fragments, mysteriously isolated couplets, excerpts from versified conversations and letters, interior monologues and (as Carson's readers have come to expect) digressions on matters of classical scholarship," the *Publishers Weekly* (December 18, 2000) reviewer wrote. Over the next couple of years, Carson brought out her translations of work by Greek masters. Her edition of *Electra*, by the dramatist Sophocles, appeared in 2001, followed by *If Not, Winter: Fragments of Sappho*, her translation of the poet's work, in 2002. Her translation of Euripides's *Hecuba* had a staged reading in 2004 at the 92nd Street Y.

Decreation appeared in 2005. The volume is representative of the eclectic nature of Carson's work. The *Publishers Weekly* (August 15, 2005) reviewer wrote that in "13 intricately related, supple and confident works in verse and prose," Carson "takes on the meaning and function of sleep; the art and attitudes of Samuel Beckett; the last days of an elderly mother; guns; a solar eclipse; 'Longing, a Documentary'; the films of Michelangelo Antonioni; and the vexing, paradoxical projects of women mystics, among them Simone Weil and the medieval heretic Marguerite Porete." The *Publishers Weekly* reviewer concluded that for "all its variety . . . the strongest work in this strong collection may be the short, spiky, individual poems."

Carson received the prestigious Lannan Literary Award for poetry in 1996. In the following year she was awarded the Pushcart Prize for her work, and she was the recipient of a Guggenheim Fellowship in 1998. In 2000 the John D. and Catherine T. MacArthur Foundation presented Carson with one of its coveted "genius" fellowships—a no-strings-attached cash award of $500,000, given both to recognize past accomplishments and to assist with future creative endeavors. One measure of the popularity of the poet's work is that it was mentioned on the television series *The L Word*; one character said that Carson's books "practically changed my life."

Dinitia Smith described Carson as "tall, lanky and shy"; Melanie Rehak noted, "She can seem reserved to the point of diffidence, but she's also prone to extravagant gestures like wearing green, purple and blue iridescent nail polish on alternating fingers." Carson's eight-year marriage to a man she described to Smith as "an entrepreneur" ended in 1980. Smith wrote in 2004 that Carson "lives by herself most of the time" and quoted the poet as saying, "Loneliness is not an important form of suffering. It's undeniable, but it's just not significant."

—S.Y.

Suggested Reading: *Antioch Review* p247 Spring 1997; *Choice* p637 Dec. 1986; *New York Times* E p13 Feb. 14, 2001; *New York Times Magazine* p36+ Mar. 26, 2000; *Ploughshares* p229+ Winter 1997; *Publishers Weekly* p77 May 29, 1995, p70 Feb. 7, 2000, p56+ Apr. 3, 2000, p73 Dec. 18, 2000; *Village Voice* p152+ May 19, 1998

Selected Books: *Eros the Bittersweet*, 1986; *Plainwater: Essays and Poetry*, 1995; *Glass, Irony and God*, 1995; *Autobiography of Red: A Novel in Verse*, 1998; *Economy of the Unlost: Reading Simonides of Keos with Paul Celan*, 1999; *Men in the Off Hours*, 2000; *The Beauty of the Husband: A Fictional Essay in 29 Tangos*, 2001; *Decreation*, 2005

Carter, Vincent O.

1924–1983 Novelist; memoirist

Vincent O. Carter "wrote on the side," Urs Frauchiger, the eminent Swiss cellist, recalled in a memorial, as Steve Paul reported for the *Kansas City Star* (May 30, 2002), "working for days on one page, for years on one book, without ever worrying for a moment about whether anything he wrote would ever be published." During his lifetime Carter had very little success with publishers, selling only one book, a memoir called *The Bern Book,* which failed to find an audience. The book for which he will be remembered, *Such Sweet Thunder,* was even less successful, garnering little more than rejection letters. It has since found a publisher and a readership among those who are interested in good literature, for as Renee Graham observed for the *Boston Globe* (May 5, 2003), the work is "ambitious and resonant . . . [and] often achieves brilliance; at its best, it has the kinetic energy of an August Wilson play. . . . Though its publication comes 20 years too late for him to enjoy the public embrace the book deserves, this is a rich addition to our literary understanding of the 20th-century African-American experience."

Vincent O. Carter, the only child of Joseph and Eola Carter, was born in Kansas City, Missouri, in 1924, and grew up in a poor section of that city. His father was a hotel porter who worked in a manufacturing plant during World War II, and his mother worked in a laundromat. "I came from a noisy, jostling town," Carter once wrote, as Steve Paul reported, "where the people sing in the streets, where friend shouts to friend from one side to the other and stranger speaks to stranger with or without a formal introduction. They fight when they are angry, work and sweat naked to the waist, and complain because the boss is mean. They crush each other to death under the skidding wheels of careening autos and catch the streetcars on the run." As a student at Lincoln High School,

from which he graduated in 1941, Carter distanced himself from the other students. Those who recall him have described him as haughty, a nerd, and someone who, when others were having fun, "probably would be off somewhere reading a book," according to Paul. After high school Carter was drafted into the U.S. Army and was among the American forces that landed at Normandy and took part in the allies' "drive toward Paris," as Herbert R. Lottman described it in his foreword to *Such Sweet Thunder.* When Carter returned to the U.S., he worked as a railroad cook for the Union Pacific Railroad, attended Lincoln University in Pennsylvania, and did a year of graduate work at Wayne State University in Detroit, Michigan, where he also worked in an automobile factory.

Aspiring to be a writer, Carter returned to Europe. He spent time in Paris, Munich, and Amsterdam: in 1953 he settled in Bern, Switzerland. Carter once explained, according to Steve Paul, "I was the only American Negro in a city of over one hundred thousand." Paul continued: "As such, he was a curiosity. But he settled in and lived a humble, creative and introspective life. He wrote. He frequented cafes and taverns. He hung out with musicians and made long-lasting friendships. He listened to Chopin, Bach and King Oliver. He couldn't get his writing published. To make money, he gave English lessons."

Carter completed his first book, a memoir about his life as an African-American expatriate in Switzerland, in 1957; it was published under the title *The Bern Book,* in 1973, after Carter reportedly had quit writing and began drawing and painting. He "was happy [when the book appeared] . . . but he didn't do anything to promote it. It was reviewed somewhat favorably. 'It is impossible for a reader not to like this black Don Quixote,' *The Kansas City Star*'s reviewer wrote at the time, but *The Bern Book* and its author were soon forgotten," Paul noted. In a review for *Library Journal* (April 15, 1973), A. R. Shucard proclaimed: "Carter has written one of the most striking autobiographies to appear in print in a long while. Or perhaps it is inaccurate to label it 'autobiography' since it is also a travel book, a political commentary, a sociological tract, and more. . . . The book is fascinating because Carter writes brilliantly, with the eye of a [Norman] Mailer mapping a political convention or a [Truman] Capote exploring a murder." Lottman recalled that when he first saw the manuscript: "I was charmed. I thought of his daybook as a new *Anatomy of Melancholy* [by Robert Burton, a meditation on life disguised as a medical tract, which was published in the early 17th century]. His digressions also reminded me of that earlier continental visitor, [the 18th-century novelist]Lawrence Sterne. Indeed *The Bern Book*, which its author considered to be a record of the voyage of the mind, so defied current conventions . . . that it couldn't be published, however letter-perfect it may have been."

Six years after finishing his memoir, Carter completed a novel, which he called "The Primary Colors" but which was published posthumously under the title *Such Sweet Thunder*. (Eleven publishers had rejected the manuscript, in the 1960s, before Carter gave up on the idea of trying to sell it.) A Depression-era coming-of-age story, the novel tells the story of Amerigo Jones, an African-American youth growing up in the Kansas City of the 1920s and 1930s, and has been described as a masterpiece of mid-century fiction. "Most unpublished manuscripts stay that way for a reason," Whitney Terrell wrote for the *New York Times Book Review* (April 20, 2003). "*Such Sweet Thunder* . . . is an exception. The novel has its share of technical hurdles, but patient readers will be rewarded with a dense and vibrant portrait of African-American life at the nation's crossroads." The narrative, John Mark Eberhart wrote for the *Kansas City Star* (April 6, 2003), "feels more like vision than exposition, it's not an easy read. There aren't even any chapters—just breaks in the texts now and then, like breath pauses. Sprawling and searching, it is Dickensian or even Joycean in scope. It wears its feelings on its sleeve, even as its prodigious young hero seeks to fill his mind with knowledge in a world hostile to his presumptions, to his very skin." Eberhart went on to note: "Carter's greatest triumph, though, is his dreamlike depiction of Amerigo's childhood mind and soul. Few writers have captured that strange, off-kilter, almost mystical feeling of what it is like to exist on this planet as a preadolescent."

Carter died of cancer in 1983, in Bern, where he had lived with his partner, Liselotte Haas, who has surmised, Paul reported, that Carter failed to get the attention he deserved when he was alive because, during the period in which he was seeking to get his books into print, he refused to become involved with the political battles that African-Americans were fighting in the U.S. "He always said, 'No, that's not my duty. I have something else I need to do,'" Haas recalled. "And I think, funny enough, you know the years he spent here, he touched so many people, perhaps many more than if he had been back and fighting and doing political things." Chip Fleischer, who was instrumental in getting Carter's novel into print, took a similar position, blaming, George Elliott Clarke reported for the Toronto *National Post* (May 17, 2003), "casual racism" for Carter's failure to find a publisher for his novel. Fleischer argued that *Such Sweet Thunder* did not fall in line with "what publishers were looking for in the way of 'Negro literature.' Carter was not writing manifestos of integration, a la James Baldwin, nor hurling lyrics like Molotov cocktails at the white 'Establishment,' a la Amiri Baraka."

—C.M./A.R.

Suggested Reading: *Boston Globe* B p8 May 5, 2003; *Kansas City Star* J p1 Apr. 6, 2003, May 30, 2002; *Library Journal* p1,273 Apr. 15, 1973; *New York Times Book Review* p30 Apr. 20, 2003;

Selected Books: *The Bern Book*, 1973; *Such Sweet Thunder*, 2003

Chace, James

Oct. 16, 1931–Oct. 8, 2004 Nonfiction writer; novelist; memoirist

James Chace, who lived from 1931 to 2004, spent his life trying to marry politics with aesthetics, developing a worldview and a masterful writing style that impressed and inspired politicians and intellectuals. Chace overcame a harsh childhood, contending with an alcoholic mother, an abusive older brother, and his once-wealthy family's decline, as well as his own nervous tics. Starting as an aesthete he became a keen observer of statecraft, which he explained in his books on foreign policy, *A World Elsewhere: The New American Foreign Policy* (1973), *Solvency: The Price of Survival* (1981), *Endless War: How We Got Involved in Central America and What Can Be Done* (1984), *America Invulnerable: The Quest for Absolute Security from 1812 to Star Wars* (with Caleb Carr, 1988), and *The Consequences of the Peace: The New Internationalism and American Foreign Policy* (1992). He turned to memoir and biography in his later writings, *What We Had*

(1990) and *Acheson: The Secretary of State Who Created the American World* (1998). In *1912: Wilson, Roosevelt, Taft, and Debs; The Election That Changed the Country* (2004), he examined some of the origins of the current liberal-conservative split in American politics. He was also the author of *The Rules of the Game* (1960), a coming-of-age novel set in Paris that failed to attract much attention.

"If there is any kind of theme in my work, it's the degree to which your own formation, your own past, the past itself, can haunt one, can affect one," Chace told Joshua A. Brook for *Publishers Weekly* (August 3, 1998). One of Chace's core convictions, according to Mark Danner, as quoted by Tim Weiner in the *New York Times* (October 11, 2004), was that "the true statesman, even one leading a superpower, understands that resources—blood, treasure and above all political will—are by definition limited, and must devise ways of protecting those interests that do not bankrupt his country. Vietnam, to James, was a classic example of the failure prudently to balance interests and resources. The current Iraq war is another." Ronald Steel remembered him in an article for the *New*

Enrico Ferorelli/Courtesy of Simon & Schuster

James Chace

York Review of Books (December 2, 2004), to which Chace was a frequent contributor, as someone who "offered uncommonly sensible insights into the way the world worked, and why the United States so often managed to confound its own interests." Steel found that some of the power and grace of Chace's writing had their origins in his determination to overcome his unhappy childhood. "His tragic sense of life's vagaries, and of how a family, like a nation, can through a series of bad judgments and illusions lose its way, helped to form his political sensibilities. . . . He was a skeptic but never a cynic. Although he decried the abuse of American power, he also recognized its uses."

James Clarke Chace was born October 16, 1931 in Fall River, Massachusetts, the second son of Harriet Mildred Clarke Chace and Hollister (called Holly) Remington Chace. Chace's family had formerly been both rich and prominent in the town's important textile business, his grandfather having been president of the Massachusetts senate, but in the decade before Chace was born, the textile mills had moved South, sending the town into decay. At the time of Chace's birth, his family retained the aura of the upper class but was poor. His father ran for mayor but was unsuccessful, forever unable to recapture the high position the family had once held. One reason for his grandfather's political success and his own father's failure was the fact that Chace's grandfather had spent extravagantly on elections. Deprived of income from the textile mills, Chace's family essentially went broke. His mother lapsed into a stuporous alcoholism, and only at the end of her life, when she was forced to stop drinking, was

Chace able to establish a loving relationship with her.

Chace was able to be educated at Harvard University in Cambridge, Massachusetts, because friends of the family took up a collection to pay his fees. At Harvard he studied literature and languages and worked on a literary magazine, the *Harvard Advocate*. After graduating, in 1953, he traveled to Paris on a fellowship from Rotary International to do graduate work at the University of Paris (also called the Sorbonne). Some of his time in Paris was spent collecting information on French politics for the CIA, by using such straightforward means as reading newspapers and chatting with friends.

In 1954, after finishing his fellowship and refusing a higher position with the CIA in Florence, Italy, Chace was drafted for a two-year stint in the U.S. Army and was by chance sent back to Paris. The three years he spent there came during a critical period in French history, when the colonial empire was crumbling amid great violence, and Chace became engrossed by the political ferment around him, particularly the French wars in Vietnam and Algeria. "The opposition between art and politics that had seemed inherent at Harvard was being resolved in Paris," Chace once said, as quoted by Steel.

Chace returned to the U.S., in 1956, and took up residence in New York City. He worked for a time at *Esquire* and wrote captions for what was then *Gentlemen's Quarterly* before becoming, in 1959, an editor at *East Europe*, a magazine published by Radio Free Europe that dealt with the political, economic, and cultural affairs of Soviet-bloc nations. He also served as managing editor of *Interplay*, a foreign policy journal, beginning in about 1965.

In 1969 he edited, for the H. W. Wilson Company, a volume titled *Conflict in the Middle East*, and the following year he became the managing editor of *Foreign Affairs*, a position he held until 1983, when he began a four-year stint as a member of the editorial board of the *New York Times Book Review*. After a year-long position as a senior associate with the Carnegie Endowment for International Peace, Chace began teaching in universities: first in New York City at Columbia University, between 1988 and 1990, as a visiting professor; and then at Bard College, in Annandale-on-Hudson, New York. Between 1990 and 1998 he was the Henry Luce professor in freedom of inquiry and expression at Bard, and from 1998 until his death, Chace was the college's Paul W. Williams professor of government and public law and administration.

Written during the presidency of Richard M. Nixon, *A World Elsewhere: The New American Foreign Policy*, analyzed a shift in the balance of power that Chace imagined would take place as a Cold War–world with two superpowers, the U.S. and the Soviet Union, gave way to a global power structure distributed among a greater number of nations. Charles DeBenedetti, for *Library Journal* (December 15, 1972), felt that Chace's ideas in the book "alternate between the banal and the perceptive, but they are always cogent and pleasantly presented." Henry Brandon, in the *New York Times Book Review* (April 8, 1973), criticized Chace's emphasis on national security issues in the book, arguing that "the seventies will be a period of not military but economic wars, and it is these that are likely to be the real threat to the balance of power policy." Brandon nonetheless considered the book "thoughtful and enlightened and worth reading."

Chace's *Solvency: The Price of Survival* considered the potentially devastating ramifications of America's seeming inability to judiciously balance its economic, political, and military priorities. Calling on America's leaders to make economic renewal their greatest concern, Chace also asked ordinary Americans to accept a diminished standard of living and recognize the limitations on American power. Perhaps because the book was published in the aftermath of a particularly contentious presidential election that saw Democratic President Jimmy Carter replaced with Republican Ronald Reagan, critical response to *Solvency* tended to break down along partisan lines, with more liberal commentators finding Chace's claims and arguments worth considering and more conservative ones attacking it roundly. Writing for the *New Republic* (June 6, 1981), David Fromkin called the book "illuminating and eloquent," while Peter W. Rodman, for *Commentary* (June 1981), wrote: "All the moralizing myopia of the Carter administration is here . . . even if clothed in more sophisticated 'analysis': the notion that all leftist revolutions in Central America are indigenous and autonomous, that the Soviet Union is never involved, that they raise no threat to the United States, that we must be on the side of progressive change—in short, that the main enemy is our own overweening power."

Chace's next book, *Endless War: How We Got Involved in Central America and What Can Be Done*, grew out of his experiences in Central America, covering the region's many complex military conflicts for a series of articles that originally appeared in the *New York Review of Books*. One evening in Nicaragua, as Chace was reviewing his notes in his hotel, a group of Contras (the U.S.–supported fighters battling the ruling Sandinistas) started shooting into his room. Only when another journalist warned him that he was being singled out because his light was on did Chace realize he needed to hide in the dark, under his bed. "Chace has never been content to be an armchair intellectual, coolly surveying the chaos of world politics from his comfortable perch," Brook wrote, and quoted Chace: "You can't make foreign policy simply by going to conferences and seeing the same people all the time. You have to go and find out what the hell is happening." In the book Chace analyzed the previous century of U.S.

policy toward Central America and argued against American military involvement in the region, particularly when that involvement undermined democracy and fostered military repression; he also emphasized the important role Mexico plays in U.S. security. Roderic A. Camp, writing for *Library Journal* (October 15, 1984), called the book "well-written" and "concise," and E. M. Dew, in *Choice* (February 1985), labeled it "a first-rate primer on US involvement in Central America."

Caleb Carr, the child of a friend of Chace's and later famous for his novels, had helped Chace with his research in Central America, and Chace mentored him to the extent of making Carr the co-author of *America Invulnerable: The Quest for Absolute Security from 1812 to Star Wars*. The book takes the somewhat contrarian position that it has not been a desire for an empire nor for commercial or financial gain that has motivated many U.S. military and foreign policy initiatives. Rather, it has been an unattainable quest for absolute security, starting with the British invasion of 1812 and continuing onward to Ronald Reagan's initiation of the so-called Star Wars program, which was supposed to render the U.S. invulnerable to foreign missle attacks. (Still in development, the program is now under the U.S. military's Missile Defense Agency.) The *Economist* (September 10, 1988) reviewer found in the book "many thoughtful profiles of the men who directed American policy, mostly the presidents, and their subordinates," but added: "At times, however, the search for security seems more an excuse than a reason. It is hard, for example, to see the annexation of the Philippines and America's expansion of the defensive perimeter throughout East Asia in the same light as the incorporation of Florida, Texas, and California into the union." Jefferson Morley, in a critique for the *Los Angeles Times Book Review* (March 13, 1988), called *America Invulnerable* "a series of witty and illuminating historical essays" that "provide an enlightening history of U.S. imperial ambitions." Morley concluded, however, that Chace and Carr might be "less likely to succeed in their secondary goal of prodding a current generation of U.S. policy-makers to rethink the American empire before it is too late." Writing for the *New York Times Book Review* (April 10, 1988), Gaddis Smith found deeper flaws in Chace and Carr's arguments. "The authors seldom clarify the difference between necessary responses to real threats to national security and violent, irrational reactions to imaginary enemies," he wrote. "Leaders in the history of American foreign policy are depicted, with few exceptions, as obsessed devotees of unilateralism, violence and absolute security. . . . Sometimes the authors criticize the use of military power; at other times they complain that it was given second place to moralistic, legalistic norms. In general they favor those who made deals with other nations, but they also deplore the vagueness that is often an essential element in compromise."

Smith also argued that the book was sometimes inaccurate, citing occasional factual errors in Chace and Carr's account and taking issue with their interpretations of some events.

Chace turned to writing about his own history in *What We Had*, which narrated his family's decline and his own nerve-wracked childhood and youth, ending the story around the time he turned 25. Susan Kenney, writing for the *New York Times Book Review* (June 17, 1990), called *What We Had* "a sad and desperate tale." The book, she added, also contains "moments of lunatic humor —$30,000 in cash, proceeds from the sale of Aunt Sue's house to be shared among the impoverished siblings, gets stashed in an oven for safekeeping on Thanksgiving Day; though most of it is recovered, a good chunk still literally goes up in smoke." Patrick T. Reardon, for the *Chicago Tribune* (July 23, 1990), judged such scenes to contain "too much bare pain . . . for humor." Reardon concluded: "There is a sense of expiation to this book, of demons exorcised. Yet, in recounting the pain, Chace . . . writes with great beauty and restraint. It is easy to read, and hard to read."

In *The Consequences of the Peace: The New Internationalism and American Foreign Policy,* Chace again took up the argument that the U.S. should remain involved in the world and refrain from acting unilaterally, this time in the context of the fall, beginning in 1989, of the Soviet-bloc and the dissolution of the Soviet Union itself. Joanna Spear, for *Political Studies* (December 1993), observed that Chace "presents an elegant case for a new American internationalism based on a recognition of shared needs and interests." Chace's thesis, she added, "is that America needs to seize the opportunity of the end of the Cold War to scale down and re-orient its military forces and place a new emphasis on geoeconomics" in order to prevent the world from becoming divided into "hostile trading blocks," in which Europe, Asia, and the Americas compete excessively instead of harnessing their collective powers for their collective benefit. While noting that Chace offers few concrete solutions for turning his ideas into American policy, Walter LaFeber, for the *Washington Post Book World* (May 10, 1992), commended *The Consequences of the Peace* as a whole, calling it "an important book that can advance one of the most important debates in 20th-century foreign policy, if anyone out there outside of the Pentagon and some think-tanks is listening."

The book for which Chace became best known was *Acheson: The Secretary of State Who Created the American World*, a biography of Dean Acheson, Harry S. Truman's secretary of state. Acheson, whose father was an Episcopalian bishop, had an elite education and was considered to have betrayed his class by becoming a New Dealer under President Franklin Roosevelt and by bonding strongly with Truman, who had been a failed haberdasher. Acheson was one of the architects of the Marshall Plan, NATO (the North Atlantic Treaty Association), the Bretton Woods agreement that established the World Bank and International Monetary Fund, and other American commitments that, in the opinion of many, prevented communism from sweeping over Europe. "Chace has produced an enjoyable and masterfully written biography of Acheson," Francis J. Gavin declared in *Orbis* (Spring 1999). Gavin added, however, that the "book is not perfect," especially in "its attempt to present Acheson not as a hardened 'Cold Warrior,' but as a level-headed realist throughout his career." On the other hand, Robert D. Ubriaco Jr., writing for the *Historian* (Spring 2000), contended that Chace "presents a balanced account of Acheson's career. He exonerates Acheson's China policy and implies that Acheson adopted a realist stance towards Mao." Ubriaco concluded that the "book is extremely valuable for anyone interested in twentieth-century America," but the idea that Acheson is "the most important figure in American foreign policy since John Quincy Adams," as Ubriaco quoted Chace as claiming, "remains questionable."

In *1912: Wilson, Roosevelt, Taft and Debs; The Election That Changed the Country*, Chace examined the election of 1912, in which Theodore Roosevelt ran as a Progressive against the Republican candidate William Howard Taft, his former friend and chosen successor to lead the Republican Party. Eugene V. Debs entered the race as the candidate of the Socialist Party, and Woodrow Wilson won the election for the Democrats. Chace explained in an article for the *Smithsonian* (October 2004) that a clash of values arose when "Roosevelt called for a 'New Nationalism,' in which government would regulate big business. Under Wilson's 'New Freedom,' government's task was to break up the trusts and restore competition to a world dominated by technology and mass markets. For Debs, America needed federal control of basic industries and a broad-based trade unionism. Taft called for better enforcement of existing laws to restrain industry's excesses." To Chace the election of 1912 ushered in the modern era by introducing "'a conflict between progressive idealism . . . and conservative values' that raged through the rest of the 20th century and continues today," Michael Kazin wrote for the *Washington Post Book World* (May 23, 2004), partially quoting Chace. "The most affecting passages in the book," Kazin added, "describe the troubled relationship between Taft and [Roosevelt]." Kazin argued, though, that "a good story does not make up for the lack of sound historical judgment. . . . As stirring as it was, the 1912 campaign neither signified nor resulted in . . . momentous change." A reviewer for *Publishers Weekly* (March 1, 2004) felt, however, that "Chace brings sharply alive the distinctive characters in his fast-paced story. There won't soon be a better-told tale of one of the last century's major elections."

Chace, as he died suddenly in Paris on October 8, 2004, while doing research for a planned book on the French statesman the Marquis de Lafayette, who, along with Acheson, was one of his heroes. Chace was married and divorced from Jean Valentine, the poet, and Susan Chace. He was survived by both wives; his companion in his last years, Joan Bingham; and his three daughters from his two marriages. His death occurred at the peak of his powers, according to many who remembered him.

—S. Y.

Suggested Reading: *Chicago Tribune* C p3 July 23, 1990; *Commentary* p72 June 1981; *Economist* p105 Sep. 10, 1988; *Historian* p651 Spring 2000; *Los Angeles Times Book Review* p1 Mar. 13, 1988; *New York Review of Books* p44 Dec. 2, 2004; *New York Times* B p7 Oct. 11, 2004; *New York Times Book Review* p12 Apr. 10, 1988, p6

June 17, 1990; *Orbis* p336+ Spring 1999; *Political Studies* p713 Dec. 1993; *Publishers Weekly* p58 Aug. 3, 1998; *Smithsonian* p57+ Oct. 2004; *Washington Post Book World* p13 June 7, 1981, p4 May 23, 2004

Selected Books: nonfiction—*A World Elsewhere: The New American Foreign Policy*, 1973; *Solvency: The Price of Survival*, 1981; *Endless War: How We Got Involved in Central America and What Can Be Done*, 1984; *America Invulnerable: The Quest for Absolute Security from 1812 to Star Wars* (with Caleb Carr), 1988; *What We Had*, 1990; *The Consequences of the Peace: The New Internationalism and American Foreign Policy*, 1992; *Acheson: The Secretary of State Who Created the American World*, 1998; *1912: Wilson, Roosevelt, Taft, and Debs; The Election That Changed the Country*, 2004; fiction—*The Rules of the Game*, 1960

Chessman, Harriet Scott

Jan. 16, 1951– Novelist; literary critic

Harriet Scott Chessman provided the following third-person biographical statement for *World Authors 2000–2005*:

"Harriet Scott Chessman is the author of the acclaimed novels *Someone Not Really Her Mother*, *Ohio Angels*, and *Lydia Cassatt Reading the Morning Paper*, as well as *The Public Is Invited to Dance*, a book of literary interpretation about the experimental writings of Gertrude Stein. She was born in Newark, Ohio, on January 16, 1951. Her father, G. W. Chessman, is a Professor Emeritus of History at Denison University in Granville, Ohio, and her mother, Eleanor Osgood Chessman, who died in May 2002, was a psychiatric social worker. Harriet Chessman lived in Granville, Ohio for most of her childhood, apart from a year spent in Hampshire, England when she was seven and her father was on sabbatical at the University of Southampton. She received her B.A. from Wellesley College in 1972, and her PhD in English from Yale University in 1979. After teaching English at Yale for 11 years, she began to write children's stories and fiction while teaching courses in creative writing, autobiography, and the novel at Wesleyan University's Graduate Liberal Studies Program and Middlebury College's Bread Loaf School of English. Chessman has three children, Marissa, Micah, and Gabriel Wolf. Her husband Bryan Wolf, formerly Professor of American Studies at Yale University, is now a Professor of Art History at Stanford University. Chessman moved to the Bay Area of San Francisco, California, with her family in 2002, where she is at work on her fourth novel."

During the first phase of Chessman's career, she taught about American women novelists, modern British fiction, and the works of the early 20th-century avant-garde writer Gertrude Stein, at Yale University, in New Haven, Connecticut. Her first book, *The Public Is Invited to Dance: Representation, the Body, and Dialogue in Gertrude Stein* (1989), was an academic analysis of the writer's work in the context of feminism and modernism. Chessman co-edited, along with Catherine R. Stimpson, the collections *Gertrude Stein: Writings, 1903–1932* and *Gertrude Stein: Writings, 1932–1946*, both of which were published by the Library of America in 1998. She has also edited *Literary Angels* (1994), which includes works by John Donne, Eudora Welty, Virginia Woolf, and Anne Sexton, among others. A reviewer for *Publishers Weekly* (October 10, 1994) described that volume as "a richly satisfying anthology of prose and poetry."

After Chessman was rejected for tenure at Yale (though she continued to teach), she began to focus less on academic work, publishing her first novel, *Ohio Angels*, in 1999. It is the tale of Hallie, an artist living with her architect husband in Brooklyn, who returns to her hometown in Ohio to succor her depressed mother. While there she is forced to revise her own memories of what she had once thought was a rather idyllic childhood. "The pitfalls of kitchen-sink melodrama lie in wait," Amanda Heller wrote for the *Boston Globe* (December 23, 2003), "but Chessman's luminous narrative style—Hallie is one artist-narrator who plausibly thinks like an artist—prevents any precipitous tumble into banality." Ellie Barta-Moran, writing for *Booklist* (April 1, 1999), complained that "at times, the passages leap from narrator, accompanied by abrupt flashbacks to childhood, which can be a little confusing," but "on the whole," she concluded, "it is a poetic and moving first novel." Despite such mixed reviews, *Ohio Angels* proved popular with readers, selling out its first hardcover printing, as well as two trade paperback printings. It was re-released in hardcover, in 2002, following the critical and popular success of Chessman's second novel.

Initially setting out to write a scholarly text on the American Impressionist painter Mary Cassatt, Chessman instead produced the historical novel *Lydia Cassatt Reading the Morning Paper* (2001). Illustrating each of the five chapters with reproductions of the paintings that Mary Cassatt made of her sister Lydia, Chessman limned a portrait of the Cassatt family, a pair of wealthy Americans who settle with their two daughters in Paris, in the latter part of the 19th century. Mary Cassatt often used her sister as a model because of her availability, because she loved her dearly, and because her sister was soon to die of kidney failure. While researching Lydia's life, with the aid of her research assistant at Yale, Chessman was unable to find any writings by the lesser-known Cassatt sister. "I was almost glad. I stopped looking," she told Amy Boaz for *Publishers Weekly* (November 12, 2001). Instead the author pieced together Lydia's personality by examining her image in Mary's paintings; as she explained to Boaz, "I have thought, imagined and dreamt my way into her world."

Reviewers were generally impressed with *Lydia Cassatt Reading the Morning Paper*, and it topped the Book Sense 76 list, a ranking of the books most highly recommended by independent bookstore owners, in November and December of 2001. "A browser blessed with good taste and good luck might discover this book by accident, simply charmed to find something so well made," a reviewer wrote for the *Canberra Times* (June 22, 2002). "The text is elegantly presented, the photographs of paintings are clear and sharp, even the end-papers are a most gracious, opulent shade of eggshell blue. Style fits subject. Grace notes on and in the cover open the way into a quiet, sad, clever story. Physical pleasure in encountering the book gives way to sustained intellectual and emotional delight in reading it." Susan Salter Reynolds, writing for the *Los Angeles Times Book Review* (November 11, 2001), felt that Chessman had enhanced Cassatt's paintings with her "sweet, pretty little novel," making the reader want to climb inside them, "carry a parasol, read a book in the afternoon, embroider." On the other hand, in a critique for the *New York Times Book Review* (March 31, 2002), Mary Elizabeth Williams described Lydia Cassatt's character as too much "in the style of a woman who's read too many floridly romantic fictional diaries" and concluded that it was a "dainty, forgettable novel." The more scholarly Diana Postlethwaite, writing for the *Women's Review of Books* (April 2002), concluded that it was "clear why Harriet Chessman didn't need to write her academic study of Mary Cassatt.

Using Lydia's voice, she can satisfyingly merge her critical sensibilities with the 'exquisite pleasure' she takes in Cassatt. . . . Chessman burnishes the simple moments of ordinary life with an elegant meditation on art and flesh."

In Chessman's third novel, *Someone Not Really Her Mother* (2004), she created a portrait of a French-born Jewish woman who is moved to a nursing home in Connecticut, after having lost her family to the Holocaust, her husband in the war, and her own sense of herself to Alzheimer's. "The author uses Hannah's condition as the starting place for a series of finely crafted meditations that blur the lines between past and present, English and French," a critic for *Publishers Weekly* (June 28, 2004) wrote. "Chessman creates a lovely if precious world filled with snapshots, letters and internal dialogue, but the gradual fading away of the protagonist leaves a hole at the book's center." Other reviewers agreed that the pictures drawn by Chessman of Hannah's daughter and two granddaughters remain "shadowy," as Jill Wolfson phrased it in a review for the *San Jose Mercury News* (August 29, 2004). Wolfson expressed a desire for Chessman to have probed more fully "the triangle created when a mother loses her own mother and granddaughters strive to make sense of their legacy." A reviewer for the *San Francisco Chronicle* (December 12, 2004) argued, however, that "in this narrow setting, Chessman explores some major themes: memory, family history, personal identity and the redemptive power of art" and named *Someone Not Really Her Mother* one of the best books of 2004.

—S.Y.

Suggested Reading: *Canberra Times* A p22 June 22, 2002; *New York Times* E p1 Mar. 4, 2002; *Publishers Weekly* Nov. 12, 2001

Selected Books: nonfiction—*The Public Is Invited to Dance: Representation, the Body, and Dialogue in Gertrude Stein*, 1989; fiction—*Ohio Angels*, 1999; *Lydia Cassatt Reading the Morning Paper*, 2001; *Someone Not Really Her Mother*, 2004; as editor—*Literary Angels*, 1994; *Gertrude Stein: Writings, 1903–1932* (with Catherine R. Stimpson), 1998; *Gertrude Stein: Writings, 1932–1946* (with Stimpson), 1998

San Diego State University

Chin, Marilyn

Jan. 14, 1955– Poet

Sometimes referred to as an activist poet, Marilyn Chin—whose books include *Dwarf Bamboo* (1987), *The Phoenix Gone, The Terrace Empty* (1994), and *Rhapsody in Plain Yellow* (2002)—has established a reputation for writing poems, both political and personal in nature, that are reflections of her experience as an immigrant, that is, of someone who simultaneously feels the need to assimilate to her adopted country and fears losing touch with her native culture. "I am afraid of losing my Chinese, losing my language, which would be like losing a part of myself, losing part of my soul," she told Bill Moyers, as quoted on the Web site for the Department of English at the University of Illinois, at Urbana-Champaign (UIUC). "Poetry seems a way to recapture that, but of course the truth is we can't recapture the past. The vector only goes one direction and that is toward the future." For this reason, Chin acknowledged, in the same interview, that "assimilation is a particularly important issue for me." Her poetry has helped her to weave her Chinese identity into her American identity, and vice-versa, something she suggested when she said in an interview for *Meridians* (Spring 2002) that her poetry is "a medium for the cross-fertilization of East and West, ancient and contemporary, the traditional and the experimental, the personal and the political." Adrienne McCormick argued in an essay also posted on UIUC's Web site, "[Chin's] treatment of Asian American identity in particular addresses national identification and the contradictions involved in being asked, on the one hand, to assimilate to mainstream American culture, while on the other, being made to feel irrevocably foreign. Thus, Chin theorizes identity as something that is constantly being re/produced; it shifts upon entry into 'the new country' as much as it shifts with the dying and birthing of old and new customs. Identity, for Chin, is something to kill and regenerate."

Marilyn Chin, the daughter of the restaurateur George Chin and his wife, Rose, was born Mei Ling Chin on January 14, 1955 in Hong Kong. Her first years were spent in a tiny apartment occupied by 10 people in Wanchai—a district of Hong Kong once known for being among the bawdier parts of town and for being frequented by sailors. While she was still a young girl, Chin's family immigrated to Portland, Oregon. During the move from Hong Kong to the U.S., she was given her American name "somewhere between Angel Island and the sea, / when my father the paperson / in the late 1950s / obsessed with a bombshell blonde / transliterated 'Mei Ling' to 'Marilyn,'" she wrote in "How I Got That Name: An Essay on Assimilation," a poem included in her second book, *The Phoenix Gone, The Terrace Empty*. Her father would later abandon his family for a blonde woman, obliging Chin's mother to raise the children on her own. Chin began writing poetry in the sixth grade, but only when she was a student at the University of Massachusetts, at Amherst—which she entered because she mistakenly believed James Baldwin was teaching there—did she decide to devote her life to the poetic arts. She had, in fact, entered college with the intention of going into social work or the legal field, areas of study that would allow her to help Asian American immigrants. Then, as she told the interviewer for *Meridians*, "One day as I was walking near the UMass library and the harsh wind was entangling my long hair, it dawned on me that this was my *dao*, my 'way'—I would become a poet!"

Chin learned her art translating Asian poetry, which she studied under Ching-Mao Cheng and Alvin P. Cohen at Amherst. In 1977, the same year she graduated with a bachelor's degree in Chinese literature, she applied to the Writer's Workshop at the University of Iowa, in Iowa City, and also to its translation workshop. She secured a job as a translator in the university's International Writing Program, and three years later she published a translation of the Japanese poet Gozo Yoshimasu's *Devil's Wind: A Thousand Steps or More* (1980). In 1982, a year after she received her master of fine arts degree, she published a translation, with Peng Wenlan and Eugene Chen Eoyang, of the *Selected Poems of Ai Qing*, a popular Chinese poet who was living and working in Iowa in the late 1970s. Over the next five years, Chin lived in San Francisco (which she has called her spiritual home), working in a psychiatric hospital tutoring patients. She also worked on an anthology of world literature, *Writing from the World* (1985), and her own poetry, publishing her first collection of original poetry, *Dwarf Bamboo*, in 1987. In *Critical Survey of*

Poetry (2003), C. L. Chua and Teresa Ishigaki praised the collection for being "much more than a capable first book": "The whole is the product of a subtle, gifted intelligence, a redoubtable maker of images; it forms an intensely persuasive portrayal of a woman's sensibility grappling with the perplexity and the experience of being American, and Asian, and female." The collection is divided into four sections that seem to reenact Chin's personal development: the first containing poems set in Asia, particularly China and Japan; the second, seemingly written from a young person's perspective, set in the U.S. and critiquing the notion that America is a land of promise for immigrants; the third offering more positive poems, spoken by a more mature speaker, that move between Asia and North America; and the fourth bringing together poems that are pessimistic about unifying the speaker's Asian and American identities.

The year after publishing *Dwarf Bamboo*, Chin secured a teaching position at the San Diego State University in the master of fine arts program, and in 1991 she published another literary anthology, *Dissident Song: A Contemporary Asian American Anthology*, which she edited with David Wong Louie. She also worked on her second book of poems, *The Phoenix Gone, The Terrace Empty*. Upon its release, in 1994, Matthew Rothschild, writing for the *Progressive* (May 1994), declared that "Marilyn Chin has a voice all her own—witty, epigraphic, idiomatic, elegiac, earthy," noting that in her latest collection "she covers the canvas of cultural assimilation with an intensely personal brush." Imbued with an elegiac tone, the book seemed to Richard Oyama, who reviewed it for *AsianWeek* (July 14, 1995), to be "the song of an exile in 'the new diaspora,' of an exile's 'fierce and tender' heart strung between contraries and countries." He continued: "Amid the voices of berating Chinese ancestors and the predatory menace of barbarians, she recounts the indignities suffered and exhortations required to shape a hybrid Asian American 'womanist' identity in America. Hers is a strange, fugitive music, a poetry of paradox and juxtaposition." Critics were impressed by Chin's mastery of poetic form, her ability to interweave, as Linda Wertheimer noted on NPR's *All Things Considered* (May 26, 1999), "such traditional forms as the sonnet and the haiku with modern day migrant worker ballads and the rhythms of funk," as much as they were interested by her approach to the themes that she addressed.

Eight years passed before Chin published her third book, *Rhapsody in Plain Yellow*, and during that time both her mother and her grandmother died within a couple of years of each other and her boyfriend died in an airplane crash. "Therefore," Chin told Nhien Nguyen for the *International Examiner* (February 19, 2002), "the center of the book is made up of elegies. . . . What saves the book from drowning in a deep dark sadness is that—as in all my books—there is a wide range of themes and concerns both personal and political." The combination helped Chin produce, according to Donna Seaman for *Booklist* (January 1 and 15, 2002), an "electrifying collection of protests and laments." Although she revisited themes she had written about in her earlier books—cross-cultural identity, family, love, and the suffering women face in patriarchal cultures—and again drew upon traditional Chinese stories and thought as well as American life, Chin was also attempting to experiment more with poetic form, producing "compressed self-contained quatrains that I borrowed from the Chinese chueh-chu . . . and ballads that reference the *Book of Songs* as well as English and American frontier ballads," as she told Nguyen. Cynthia Quimpo Ignacio, writing for the on-line journal *Yolk: Generasian Next* (2002), called the collection "a triumph of past-present experimentation" and went on to observe that it "is an eclectic mixture of ancient poetic forms and jazzy contemporary rhythms, thrumming with the vital energy of the modern world, while honoring traditional Chinese myths." Nonetheless, all were not entirely impressed by her formal experiments. Michael Scharf and Jeff Zaleski, in their review for *Publishers Weekly* (September 22, 2001), acknowledged the power of the collection but noted, "Chin's ambitions can outrun her technique: some poems, especially those in short lines, lack aural or emotional power. Overall, though, this collection's speaker has a strong sense of herself and of her times—a sense to which readers of many concerns could respond."

Chin has received, among other honors, two writing fellowships from the National Endowment for the Arts, the Mary Roberts Rinehart Award, the PEN/Josephine Miles Award, four Pushcart Prizes and a Stegner Fellowship. She still teaches at San Diego State University, but throughout the years she has taught at institutions all over the world, including schools in Singapore, Hong Kong, Sydney, and Berlin.

—A.R.

Suggested Reading: *AsianWeek* p15 July 14, 1995; *International Examiner* p26 Feb. 19, 2002; *Meridians* p67+ Spring 2002; *Progressive* p49 May 1994

Selected Books: *Dwarf Bamboo*, 1987; *The Phoenix Gone, The Terrace Empty*, 1994; *Rhapsody in Plain Yellow*, 2002

Cohen, Elizabeth

June 13, 1959– Journalist; memoirist

Elizabeth Cohen is the author of the evocative memoir *The House on Beartown Road: A Memoir of Learning and Forgetting* (2003), which was reissued, in 2004, as *The Family on Beartown Road: A Memoir of Love and Courage*; the book is about the struggles she faced raising her daughter and taking care of her father. "I came to see that while it was very painful, it was also very beautiful taking care of the two of them," she wrote for the Binghamton, New York, *Press & Sun-Bulletin* (April 5, 2003). "Daily, I could see the struggles of people at the two far edges of the life arc. It seemed an extraordinary thing to watch, sort of like watching the sun rise and set at the same time. . . . When I hold [my book] in my hand I cannot really believe it. That all I wrote and much of what I felt has become distilled into this thing, this object I can hold in my hand. I know that there is so much that didn't fit in there, so much I forgot. But there is so much in there that I remembered, too. . . . I hope that this book can provide to other people taking care of their parents and children what that long-ago essay on my miscarriage provided to other women who had undergone the experience: The knowledge that these are universal experiences."

Elizabeth Cohen was born on June 13, 1959 in Indianapolis, Indiana. She received a BA degree from the University of New Mexico, in Albuquerque, and went on to obtain a master's degree at Temple University, in Philadelphia, Pennsylvania, in 1983, and an M.F.A. from Columbia University, in New York City, in 1987. She was briefly an editorial assistant to the writer Anna Quindlen, but she has made her living primarily as a journalist, writing—often first-person essays—for publications such as *Newsweek*, *Rolling Stone*, and the *New York Post*. She has also written a column, Close to Home—which formed the basis of her memoir—for the *Press & Sun-Bulletin* in Binghamton, New York, since 1999. That was the year that she and her husband, a painter, left Manhattan—moving to upstate New York to raise their daughter, Ava—and her father, Sanford, moved into her home. "They were living a charmed life in a secluded farmhouse when her father, a retired economics professor, came to live with them. Within weeks her husband [who was fifteen years her junior] had taken off to live with an 18-year-old in Mexico and Cohen was left to get the family through the winter alone," Geeta Sharma-Jensen reported for the *Milwaukee Journal Sentinel* (March 23, 2003).

The House on Beartown Road recounts Cohen's experiences as a single mother trying to raise her newborn daughter, Ava, while simultaneously caring for her ailing, Alzheimer's-stricken father, during the first winter after her husband left. Rather than being a bitter complaint against her husband, however, the memoir is half a commemoration of the beauty of life and somber observance of her father's decline. "I celebrated all my daughter's firsts," Cohen wrote in her prologue, as quoted by Sharma-Jensen. "Likewise, I had to mourn all my father's losses. There were numerous coincidences. She said 'Mama' on the same day he first asked me who I was." A reviewer for *Publisher's Weekly* (February 17, 2003) remarked, "Cohen's fluid prose lifts her forceful story to a higher level, making it a tribute to her father and her family." Other reviews were less admiring. "Not all parts of *The House on Beartown Road* . . . work equally well," Maggie Jones wrote for the *New York Times* (April 6, 2003). "Most of the narrative takes place over one long winter with too much snow and too little heating oil. And just as Cohen seems to lose track of time, in her repetitive, diarylike descriptions of the weather and her domestic life, so do we. The details of her schedule, her father's forgetfulness and her lonely nights watching infomercials occasionally read like filler substituting for deeper analysis. And yet," Jones concludes, "it's hard not to be charmed by her simple, straightforward style and her self-deprecation."

Cohen, under the name Elizabeth Cohen Van Pelt, also co-authored, with Lori Alvord, *The Scalpel and the Silver Bear,* Alvord's memoir about her becoming "a white man's doctor," as she calls it in the book. Cohen, whose column Close to Home still appears every Sunday in the *Press & Sun-Bulletin,* currently lives in Port Crane, New York. She enjoys hiking and skiing but spends most of her time with her daughter. Her favorite books include *To Kill a Mockingbird* by Harper Lee and *Things Fall Apart* by Chinua Achebe. Her father died in 2004: he was suffering from double pneumonia, and Cohen and her sister decided to allow him "to die without extraordinary medical intervention," as Barbara Bedway described it for *Editor & Publisher* (June 1, 2005).

—P.B.M./A.R.

Suggested Reading: (Binghamton, New York) *Press & Sun-Bulletin* D p1 Apr. 5, 2003; *Milwaukee Journal Sentinel* E p6 Mar. 23, 2003; *Publisher's Weekly* p63 Feb. 17, 2003

Selected Books: *The House on Beartown Road,* 2003

Cole, Henri

May 9, 1956– Poet

Identified by the noted literary critic Harold Bloom as one of the most crucial poets of his generation, Henri Cole has transformed himself as a writer: while many of the poems in his early collections—

The Marble Queen (1986), *The Zoo Wheel of Knowledge* (1989), and *The Look of Things* (1995)—adhere to a formalist, detached style, he has eased into a more confessional, freer mode with *The Visible Man* (1998) and *Middle Earth* (2003). "His recent metamorphoses have been, like Ovid's, violent and sexual," Maureen N. McLane wrote for the *New York Times Book Review* (April 27, 2003), noting that the "sexual frankness and emotional harrowing" in *The Visible Man* "marked a turn away from the elegance and restrained, observational stance that had characterized his earlier work." Cole's poetry is pervaded by animal imagery, and his tone is poetic even in his everyday speech. For example, in an interview with Christopher Hennessy for the *American Poetry Review* (June 2004), Cole stated: "The two biggest influences on my work are sleeping and reading. I wish I could do them simultaneously. They make the little hamster of the unconscious run wild on its wheel."

Roger Henri Cole was born on May 9, 1956 in Fukuoka, Japan, to Marianne Derderian and Crawford Lee Cole, who was serving in the American military at the time. Cole's father was an engineer, and his mother was a civil servant. Not long after Cole's birth the family returned to the U.S., settling in Virginia. "When I was eight I received a typewriter for Christmas," Cole wrote in the essay "How I Grew," which is posted on the Borzoi Reader Web site. "It was not intended as a gift to the poet I would one day become; rather, in our lower middle-class household, it was a reminder that business skills would be necessary to improve my circumstances in the world. Inexplicably, I understood a higher purpose of my machine-a-ecrire to be the instrument of an artist. It was something like the human mind, to my Roman Catholic self, and was to remain uncorrupted, tenacious, and true. I knew better than to share this belief with my parents, who were unsentimental about life." He continued in his essay to describe a childhood marked by domestic violence and relative solitude: "For several years, I lived alone in a tree house in the woods behind our suburban Virginia home. It was there that I learned the true meaning of the state of being necessary to become a writer, the state of exile and aparthood."

While attending the College of William and Mary in Williamsburg, Virginia, Cole was finally able to develop friendships with others who were interested in the arts, and in his junior year he began writing poetry. "Everything I wrote was autobiographical," he explained in his essay. "These were the poems of a closeted homosexual. [They] were about the men I knew and were filled with yearning and anger." In 1978 he graduated with a bachelor's degree in English, and in 1980 he earned a master's degree from the University of Wisconsin, at Milwaukee, where he had also worked as an English instructor. Next he moved to New York City, earning a master of fine arts degree

from Columbia University, in 1982. During this time he also worked as an instructor and served as an editorial intern at the Paris Review and the managing editor and, later, the editor of *Columbia: A Magazine of Poetry and Prose*. In 1982 he was named executive director of the Academy of American Poets, a post he held until 1988. After that Cole devoted his career to writing poetry and teaching. He has taught at Columbia University; Reed College, in Portland, Oregon; Yale University, in New Haven, Connecticut; the University of Maryland, in College Park; Harvard University, in Cambridge, Massachusetts; Smith College, in Northampton, Massachusetts; and Brandeis University, in Waltham, Massachusetts.

Cole's first collection, *The Marble Queen*, contains poems on a variety of subjects, including nature and art, but particularly focuses on the relationships of the child to the parent and of the adult to his child self. Phoebe Pettingell, writing for the *New Leader* (July 14, 1986), found *The Marble Queen* "so polished, we might easily take it to be the latest collection by an established writer." She noted, "For all his urbanity, Cole's touch is light and even inclines to playfulness. 'Diana and the Adder,' for example, presents the eye with an excellent pun as it snakes its way down the page in graceful curves. . . . In another bit of whimsy, Cole describes driving 'in a Lilliputian car across a mammoth landscape / towards the south, the sea looming like Gulliver in our hearts.' A vague feeling of adult insecurity makes him 'wish to be small / as every child's fantasy of Swift's island, / small enough to be in a soup spoon, / just a speck in an ignorant world.' Cole experiments with perspective as if he were someone alternately looking through the two ends of a telescope, and his delightful shifts from tiny to gigantic are accomplished with a dexterity that reminds us of Lewis Carroll." In the *New York Times Book Review* (April 19, 1987), Lynne McMahon wrote that the best poems in the collection demonstrate "a confluence of the mythic and ordinary that is magical." Cole, she added, had fashioned something new from the elements of the poems: "Eve and the lamia are recast; the queen mother and sailor father are broken from archetype, then unexpectedly returned; a struggling plant becomes the vehicle for ardent make-believe." While acknowledging that "Cole manages a graceful omniscience that allows him to see things beyond the usual temporal and spatial limitations of first-person poetry," B. Weigl, writing for *Choice* (October 1986), complained that the poet "sometimes sacrifices what is otherwise an elegantly natural diction for one that feels forced into its formality, straining too hard to be 'poetic.'"

In Cole's next collection, *The Zoo Wheel of Knowledge*, many of the poems deal with homoerotic sensuality. "Cole's subjects—family, boyhood, death, nature—would be conventional were it not for the willingness to convey within them some ugly or grisly detail," Helen Vendler wrote for *Parnassus: Poetry in Review* (1991), citing the title poem as an example: "Above us the ape's lips are cracked and bleeding, / his pink tits pumped up from swinging / in the canopy." She felt, however, that his poetry needed more satirical bite. "Sweetness needs astringency to be aesthetically believable," Vendler argued, concluding that Cole seems "to be a poet of 'sensibility' but also—if he would value it more—a potential poet of satire." According to Phoebe Pettingell, writing for the *New Leader* (March 13, 1995), *The Zoo Wheel of Knowledge* exhibits "a fresh, childlike eye for the wonder in familiar sights and a probing intelligence alert to irony as well as ambivalence."

The Look of Things confirmed, in most critics' opinion, Cole's stature as a major poet. "His previous guarded language yields to a new openness that overcomes the impulse to cling to privacy," Phoebe Pettingell wrote, pointing to "The House Guest Looks at Love and Life," a poem she deemed "a gently self-mocking portrait of a 'perfect guest'":

Even standing bare, whichever
way he turns he leaves no traces: the bed
that looks unslept-in; the bathroom mirror
rubbed of fog; the bright shower stall rinsed
of wiry gray hairs weeded from his chest.
And most of the time he is happy since
no one guesses what was so cleverly repressed.

Pettingell added, "Cole has abandoned this invisible man to pursue the risky enterprise of 'the heart excavating itself,' as one poem puts it. His lyrics here resonate with regret and sexual longing; the desire to be loved conflicts with a yearning for solitude and autonomy; anger in the face of loss alternates with moments of blinding, transcendent joy." Wayne Koestenbaum, writing for the *New Yorker* (May 1, 1995), also noted a shift in Cole's poetry: "In his first two volumes . . . virtuosity seemed pushed to its extremes; here he has relaxed, and, as a consequence, he produces lines of natural and nonchalant brio. . . . Commanding a full range of idioms, he assembles poems of a sculptural fineness. Most often, they achieve beauty by sounding a note of severe, unsentimental forlornness."

The Visible Man was published in 1989, and a decade later William Logan, writing for the *Washington Post Book World* (January 10, 1999), referred to it as "Cole's most brutal and despairing book—what earlier was a dapper young man's mild self-absorption has become self-hatred fit for the burning rain of the Inferno." The poem sequence "Apollo" won particular acclaim from Logan: "The break with the proprieties of Cole's earlier style, the invention of a self so harrowing in character, will remind readers of the confessions in Robert Lowell's *Life Studies*, published 40 years ago. If Cole's poems are not quite formed, if they are still raw with half-born shouts, most other books would be reduced to ashes by the

comparison." In a review for *Lambda Book Report* (November 1998), Timothy Liu wrote: "Resisting the constraints that accompany a formalist poetics, Cole breaks through to dark confessional truths in his fourth book with all of his Catholic guilt and self-loathing in tact. Like marks that score the backs of self-flagellant monks, these poems are 'nourished on violent adult fare' and sting—with love's cruel lash. . . . Ironically, Cole's book is haunted by the ghost of formalism in poem after poem, with more than two dozen pseudo-sonnets strung throughout his penitent opus like rosary beads. Remarkably, his insistence on such a poetics becomes metaphor to the very Catholic laws he cannot free himself from, Cole himself a 'soul-animal [who] prefers the choke-chain.'"

As the recipient of a writing fellowship from the American Academy of Arts and Letters, Cole once lived in Italy, serving a year-long residency at the at the American Academy in Rome, and as he told Hennessy, "It Romanized my poems . . . making them more naked. This was partially a result of viewing Italian art and seeing thousands of images of a man nailed to a cross, of a man dead in his mother's arms, and of a man rising out of a tomb. It made me want to foreground emotion rather than the brain." Cole also spent a long period in Japan, this time through a fellowship offered by the Japan–U.S. Friendship Commission. "In Japan, the country of my birth, I tried to write in a neutral style, without either elegance or inelegance," he told Hennessy. "Many of the poems in *Middle Earth* were written in Japan, where poetry often emphasizes a quiet life, free from worldly concerns. It praises simple, austere beauty. Ornate beauty is vulgar. In my two tatami mat rooms, in the foothills north of Kyoto where I was living, I wanted to write poems that conveyed both the intensity and the simplicity of my life."

Maureen N. McLane noted the Japanese influence in *Middle Earth*: "In several 'self-portrait' poems the lyric 'I' emerges as if translated into a common yet foreign language. 'Self-Portrait in a Gold Kimono' typifies this strategically naive self-presentation: 'Born, I was born. / Tears represent how much my mother loves me, / shivering and steaming like a horse in rain.' This new voice transfixes us by its incantatory clarity. The strangeness of its lyric spell arises in part from the japonaiserie of such poems—an aspect that registers as neither coy nor exoticizing but delicately estranging. Daring to traffic in Orientalism (one thinks of Pound's 'Cathay'), Cole here takes a risk that pays off." In a critique for the *Los Angeles Times Book Review* (May 4, 2003), Dana Goodyear wrote, "*Middle Earth*, Cole's transcendent fifth collection, is a gift to pagan literature. A questioning Catholic, Cole finds another religion in seeing. These are the poems of a conjurer, ceremonial and hypnotic. He sets the mood in the title poem, turning down the lights and beginning an ars poetica mantra: 'I repeat things in order to feel them, / craving what is no longer there. / The past dims like a great, tiered chandelier. / The present grows fragmentary / and rough.'"

Cole is the recipient of numerous awards, including a Berlin Prize fellowship from the American Academy in Berlin, in Berlin-Wannsee, Germany. His poems have appeared in the *Atlantic*, the *Nation*, the *New Republic*, the *New Yorker*, and the *Paris Review*, among other publications.

—S.Y.

Suggested Reading: *American Poetry Review* p43+ May/June 2004; Borzoi Reader Web site; *Choice* p303 Oct. 1986; *Lambda Book Report* Nov. 1998; *Los Angeles Times Book Review* p11 May 4, 2003; *Midwest Quarterly* p341+ Spring 1996; *New Leader* p17+ July 14, 1986, p14+ Mar. 13, 1995; *New York Times Book Review* p20 Apr. 19, 1987, p8 Apr. 27, 2003; *Washington Post Book World* p11 Jan. 10, 1999

Selected Books: *The Marble Queen*, 1986; *The Zoo Wheel of Knowledge*, 1989; *The Look of Things*, 1995; *The Visible Man*, 1998; *Middle Earth*, 2003

Ellen M. Augarten/Courtesy of Simon & Schuster

Colt, George Howe

1954– Memoirist; journalist

In *The Big House: A Century in the Life of an American Summer Home* (2003), the author and journalist George Howe Colt offers his recollections of more than four decades of summer vacations spent in his family's ancestral dwelling—a four-story, 11-bedroom architectural relic on the Cape Cod peninsula, in Massachusetts. The home serves as the focal point for Colt to detail the changing fortunes and vanishing lifestyle of his family, which belongs to the elite social group the Boston Brahmins, known for its distinction and wealth. Prior to the publication of *The Big House*, Colt worked for many years as a staff writer at *Life* magazine and penned a highly praised work of nonfiction, *The Enigma of Suicide* (1991). His

articles have also appeared in the *New York Times*, *Mother Jones*, *Civilization*, and various other publications.

Colt was born in 1954 into a family of Boston Brahmins whose financial clout, although once considerable, had long since evaporated. "It is not so much wealth as former wealth that defines Old Money families," Colt explained in *The Big House*, as quoted by a reviewer for *Publishers Weekly* (May 12, 2003). Colt was raised in Dedham, Massachusetts, but moved frequently, living in four different houses by the time he turned 12. Colt's parents both pursued careers in education: his father, Henry, worked for a time as the director of development at the Perkins School for the Blind, in Watertown, Massachusetts; his mother, Elizabeth, taught English and art at the Noble and Greenough School, in Dedham. Every summer during Colt's youth the family would vacation at the Big House, their ramshackle and sprawling abode overlooking Buzzard's Bay, on Wings Neck, a section of Cape Cod that had been in the family for generations and was the last remnant of their former fortune. After high school Colt attended Harvard University, in Cambridge, Massachusetts, graduating with honors. He then went to Johns Hopkins University, in Baltimore, Maryland, where he obtained his master's degree in creative writing. Not long afterward Colt took a position at *Life* magazine; he continued working there until the magazine ceased publication (temporarily) in 1998. As a staff writer at *Life*, Colt composed stories on a diverse array of topics, including the former Israeli Prime Minister Yitzhak Shamir, the artist Andrew Wyeth, angels, earthquakes, roller coasters, and migrant farm workers.

In 1983 Colt was assigned to write an article about the "Westchester Cluster" for *Life*. The Westchester Cluster referred to a spate of adolescent suicides—eight in number—that occurred over a four-month period in the suburbs outside of New York City. Out of that piece grew *The Enigma of Suicide*, an encyclopedic analysis of suicide, charting its history from the earliest recorded reference—in a 4,000-year-old Egyptian papyrus—up to its present-day incarnations. Colt discusses case histories, cultural and religious perspectives on suicide, the moral and legal issues involved, the right-to-die movement, prevention programs, and the effects on survivors. Critical response to the book was positive. Steve Oney, writing for the *Los Angeles Times Book Review* (June 2, 1991), called it "a work that in almost every way is a great and moving triumph." Colt, he added, "always remains aware of historical context, traversing the ages to reveal how primitive cultures, the Greeks and Romans, early Christians, European rationalists like Voltaire and [Jean Jacques] Rousseau, and such relative contemporaries as [Sigmund] Freud, regarded suicide. . . . Not only is this a masterly piece of journalism, it is also, strangely enough, a profoundly life-affirming study." Dave Sobel, writing for the *New York Times Book Review* (April 14, 1991), characterized the work as "an utterly fascinating, admirably well-written and sad book. . . . [Colt] examines suicide from every imaginable angle: historical, moral, sociological, psychological." Anthony Storr opined for the *Washington Post* (May 19, 1991), "[Colt] has written one of the most comprehensive studies of the phenomenon of suicide that I know of." (In 2006 *The Enigma of Suicide* was republished under the title *November of the Soul: The Enigma of Suicide*.)

Colt's subsequent book, *The Big House: A Century in the Life of an American Summer Home*, charts the history of Colt's family dwelling on Cape Cod. The house was built in 1903 by his great-grandfather Edward W. Atknison, an eminent Bostonian importer; every year, for the next century, the family returned to its summer retreat. "Behind its imposing shingled walls, the Big House exemplifies that peculiar combination of wealth and masochism which conclusively identifies it as the summer retreat of Boston Brahmins," Colt wrote, as quoted by Jonathan Yardley for the *Washington Post* (June 29, 2003). "It is furnished with that culture's traditional mix of Victorian mahogany dressers, cast-iron bedsteads, caned chairs (with most of the caning intact), plastic porch furniture, and 1950s Sears Roebuck appliances. The house has no indoor shower, no television, no VCR, and no stereo, though there is a battered portable radio, used primarily during hurricanes and Red Sox games." *The Big House*, Colt noted, has been witness to five weddings, four divorces, three deaths, and countless parties, anniversaries, and love affairs. Colt had been going there since his childhood—42 summers in all; it was where he learned to swim and play tennis, and where he had his first kiss. Not all of Colt's memories were idyllic: the family has also seen perhaps more than its share of mental breakdowns and alcoholism. Nevertheless, with its pre-modern furnishings, mismatched décor, and artifacts accumulated over the past century, the retreat was, Colt wrote, a receptacle and museum of the family's eccentric history. By the 1990s, the cost of taxes and upkeep, however, had retaining the house unfeasible. In the book, as the sale of the house becomes imminent, Colt returns for what may be one last summer, intent on coming to an understanding of his family history and the house's place in it.

Carol Haggas, writing for *Booklist* (May 15, 2003), opined, "In [this] touching, deeply felt memoir, reminiscent of Willie Morris' *North Toward Home* (1967), Colt goes beyond his own wistful longing, rendering keen observations of a lifestyle borne of privilege, perpetuated by tradition, and celebrated through elegance." Yardley offered similar praise, stating, "*The Big House* is a pensive, reflective, leisurely book, and a frankly nostalgic one as well. Colt has a keen eye for details, and uses them to create pointillist pictures." A reviewer for *Publishers Weekly* (May 12, 2003) observed, "Colt, like playwright A. J. Gurney, is adept at exposing the dark underbelly of WASP restraint, recording the mental illness, alcoholism and despair that have plagued his family. . . . This love letter to the past is a quiet delight." *The Big House* was a nominee for the National Book Award in 2003.

In 1989 Colt married the poet Anne Fadiman, a fellow Harvard graduate whom he met while the two were working at *Life* magazine. Colt has described her as having "always been my best editor," as quoted by Daniel Okrent in *Life* (December 1995). The couple live in Whately, a small town in a rural region of western Massachusetts, with their two children, Henry and Susannah. Colt is an ardent fan of the Boston Red Sox baseball team. When Colt first told his son that he had been nominated for the NBA (National Book Award), the boy, misunderstanding, responded, "Daddy, you don't even play basketball," Carol Beggy and Mark Shanahan recounted for the *Boston Globe* (October 17, 2003). After explaining to his son that a second career in basketball was unlikely, Colt celebrated his nomination by taking his children out for candy.

—P.B.M.

Suggested Reading: *Booklist* p1,635 May 15, 2003; *Boston Globe* D p7 June 10, 2003, J p1 Sep. 7, 2003, D p2 Oct. 17, 2003; *Los Angeles Times* M p1 June 2, 1991, *Los Angeles Times Book Review* p1 June 2, 1991; National Book Award Web site; *New York Times* F p1 Aug. 29, 2003; *New York Times Book Review* p67 Mar. 5, 1989, p7 Apr. 14, 1991, p8 July 6, 2003; *Washington Post* X p6 May 19, 1991, T p2 June 29, 2003

Selected Books: *The Enigma of Suicide*, 1991; *The Big House: A Century in the Life of an American Summer Home*, 2003

Cook, Claire

Feb. 14, 1955– Novelist

Claire Cook, who transformed her own life by becoming a novelist, writes about women who have broken away from conventional domesticity to find either romance, professional fulfillment, or simply a renewed appreciation of what they already have. *Ready to Fall* (2000), *Must Love Dogs* (2002), *Multiple Choice* (2004), and the upcoming *Life's a Beach* (2007) all feature spunky heroines well past the first blush of youth and have thus been called "hen-lit" to differentiate them from books in the "chick-lit" genre, which typically feature young, unmarried protagonists.

Claire Cook submitted the following autobiographical statement to *World Authors 2000–2005*:

"I was born in Alexandria, Virginia, on Valentine's Day, 1955. I'm one of eight children, and by the time my next youngest sister was born, two years later, we'd already moved on to Providence, Rhode Island, and from there to Indiana, a couple of places in Pennsylvania, and finally to Massachusetts.

"My mother was five years older than my father. She was his teacher in a business-writing class he took when he went back to college on the GI bill. The family joke was that marrying her was the only way he passed. She was brilliant and a voracious reader, and he was charming and an outrageous storyteller. Her death at the age of 44, just short of my 11th birthday, was the defining family tragedy.

"I first knew I was a writer when I was three. My mother entered me in a contest to name the Fizzies whale, and I won in my age group. It's quite possible that mine was the only entry in my age group since "Cutie Fizz" was enough to win my family a six-month supply of Fizzies tablets (root beer was the best flavor) and a half dozen turquoise plastic mugs with removable handles. My father's contribution to my growth as a writer was that he was always embellishing. Growing up we were never quite sure which stories to believe. Were we really direct descendents of Captain Cook? (No.) Or P.T. Barnum? (Yes, though on our mother's side.) Even as something was happening, I began to tweak it in my head to make it more interesting. At six I had my first story on the Little People's Page in the Sunday paper (about Hot Dog, the family Dachshund, though I'm pretty sure we actually had a fox terrier at the time), and at 16 I had my first front-page feature in the local weekly.

"I majored in film and creative writing in college and fully expected that the day after graduation a brilliant novel would emerge, fully formed, like giving birth. When that didn't happen, I felt like an imposter. I wrote shoe ads for an inhouse agency for five weeks, became continuity director of a local radio station for a couple of years, wrote a few freelance magazine pieces, took some more detours. Eventually, I had two children and followed them to school as a teacher.

"Years later, when I was in my forties and sitting in my minivan outside my daughter's swim practice at 5 AM, it hit me that I might live my whole life without ever writing a novel. So, for the next sixth months I wrote a rough draft in the pool parking lot, and in May 2000, *Ready to Fall* was published. Two years later, *Must Love Dogs* was published, and *Multiple Choice* was published two years after that.

"So many women have written to say that my story has been an inspiration to them, and I hope that's true. I've received, and answered, thousands of emails from readers, and what I love about my website, www.clairecook.com, is that it makes it so easy for readers and book groups to communicate with me.

"Looking back, I can see how all those years I wasn't writing informed my books. *Ready to Fall* was about a woman drowning in a sea of swim moms. I wouldn't have been able to write the classroom scenes in *Must Love Dogs* as convincingly if I hadn't been a teacher. My stint at a quirky little radio station gave me parts of *Multiple Choice*.

"Still, my fiction never feels particularly autobiographical to me. It's as if I take all the things that are real, all the stories I've heard, plus everything I imagine, and put them into a paper bag, shake them up, and then take them out in a completely new configuration.

"I relate to all the characters, both two- and four-legged, in my novels. I think you have to, at least to some degree, in order to write the characters. It's all about being a good eavesdropper and it's all grist for the mill. I've always been that person at the restaurant listening to the conversation at the next table. It's nice to finally have found a career where that becomes non-deviant behavior.

"I often say that I'm 'having a blast' as a novelist, though this does not necessarily mean that on any given day I'm having a blast with the actual writing. The people part—meeting readers and booksellers and librarians and the media—is very social and I'm having lots of fun with that. The writing part is great, too, once you get past the procrastination, the self-doubt, the feelings of utter despair. It's all of the stuff surrounding the writing that's hard; once you find your zone, your place of flow, or whatever it is we're currently calling it, and lose yourself in the writing, it really is quite wonderful. I've heard writers say it's better than sex, though I'm not sure I'd go that far.

"As for a typical working day, I've found that every day of my life presents me with dozens of perfectly valid reasons not to write. My kids, my house, my hair. And occasionally even more glamorous things like interviews and movie deals. So, for me, the only way to actually write a novel is to get really disciplined with myself. I write two pages a day, every day, or I'm not allowed to go to sleep. It gets ugly sometimes, but it works.

Claire Cook

"I love books that don't wrap everything up too neatly at the end, and I think it's a big compliment to hear that a reader is left wanting more. After each novel, I hear from readers asking for a sequel—they say they just *have* to find out what will happen to these people next. I think it's wonderful that the characters have come to life for them. But, for now, I think I'll grow more as a writer by trying to create another group of quirky characters. Maybe a few books down the road, I'll feel ready to return to some of them—who knows?

"I'm always surprised when I'm introduced at a book event, and I hear, 'Claire Cook writes about relationships.' Or transitions or suburbia or family. I thought I was writing about the Hurlihys or the Monroes! But I suppose I am fascinated by people and by relationships, and I'm particularly drawn to characters in transition. That's where you find the fireworks—people trying to let go of something and move on to something else are often messy and always interesting.

"My favorite comments from readers are, 'I can't remember when I laughed out loud like that,' 'I couldn't put it down' and 'Ohmigod, you're writing my life!' Also, a woman came to one of my book events to tell me that, the week before, she'd missed her subway stop because she was reading one of my books. That might well be the litmus test for a good read, don't you think?"

After graduating, in 1977, from Syracuse University, in New York, Claire Cook lived a life similar in some respects to those portrayed in chick-lit novels—working at an ad agency and a radio station, among other places. Like the heroines of many of those books, she eventually met the right man and settled down to marriage, children, and a teaching career. While this attainment of domestic bliss is generally depicted in the final chapter of frothy chick-lit offerings, Cook then opened a whole new chapter in her life—much like one of her own heroines—by pursuing a career as a writer. She told Amy Boaz, in an interview for *Publishers Weekly* (July 26, 2004), "I've met a lot of women who have these lifelong unrealized dreams and put everything into their families, you know, schlepping kids around and doing all this stuff, and even if you carve out the time, you're not getting to that big thing—when I think of it now, I think, how messed up was this?"

After finally finishing her first novel, which she wrote in longhand on legal pads, Cook had a difficult time finding a literary agency to represent her. She sent numerous letters to agents whose names she found in a copy of the reference book *Writer's Market*, but most were loath to work with a totally unknown author. "[They'd write back], 'If your novel is half as funny as your query letter, you will definitely find someone. However, it won't be me,'" she told Boaz. Eventually, Cook discovered Bridge Works, a small publisher who agreed to buy the manuscript without an intermediary. (She soon gained representation, however, thanks to a budding friendship with the novelist Elizabeth Berg, who invited Cook to join a writing workshop and introduced the fledgling author to her own agent. At the workshop Cook made revisions on her first book and began her second.)

Beth, the protagonist of Cook's first novel, *Ready to Fall*, is a frustrated housewife whose husband and children seem to acknowledge her only when they run out of toilet paper or some other household staple. Feeling lonely and unappreciated, she enters into an E-mail flirtation with a neighbor undergoing his own marital problems. "The tension of whether or not their budding relationship will be consummated keeps the plot going at a decent clip," a *Publishers Weekly* (April 3, 2000) reviewer commented. "Despite its cliched elements, the narrative has some witty scenes of domestic miscommunication, and Cook's perky take on midlife angst will undoubtedly appeal to women who fantasize about changing their lives." Genre fiction aimed at women often garners such mixed critical notices, but *Ready to Fall* was a hit with readers, and when Cook's new agent sent out the manuscript for her next book, *Must Love Dogs*, to 10 large publishers, four of them responded within days with offers. (Viking ultimately won the rights to publish the book.)

In *Must Love Dogs* Sarah Hurlihy, a divorced teacher, is prodded by her large Irish family to begin dating again. They place a personal ad on her behalf, calling for a man who loves dogs (despite the fact that Sarah owns no dog and must borrow one to bring on her first dates). Stacy Alesi, in a review for *Library Journal* (June 15, 2002), called the book "utterly charming," an opinion echoed by many critics, although some expressed predictable quibbles about the book's breezy tone and lack of seriousness. Ann Prichard, for example, writing for *USA Today* (July 18, 2002), faulted it for being "self-consciously wacky." In 2005 *Must Love Dogs* was made into a movie starring Diane Lane and John Cusack. Cook wrote on her official Web site, "Even if I hadn't written the book it's based on, I'd be standing in line to see this movie! . . . [It] captures the spirit of the novel and yet sparkles with its own wit and originality. . . . I don't think an author whose book has been adapted for the screen has ever been luckier!"

In *Multiple Choice* March Monroe, a middle-aged mother, goes back to college and lands an internship position at a local radio station. In a comic coincidence her fractious daughter, Olivia, has also won an internship at the station. Their fights fascinate the station manager, and they wind up hosting their own show about mother-daughter relations. Kaite Mediatore, writing for *Booklist* (July 2004) called the novel a "sweet and humorous suburban domestic comedy with likable characters." A reviewer for *Publishers Weekly* (May 31, 2004) was less charmed, opining, "The story meanders, detouring into asides about family pets, the generation gap, the stresses of being overscheduled and other typical suburban family disasters. Despite (or because of) the stabs at domestic insight, the cluttered result reads like warmed-over Erma Bombeck."

Cook's fourth novel, *Life's a Beach*, is scheduled for publication in June 2007. It examines the relationship of Ginger Walsh—41 years old, single, and living in a FROG (finished room over garage)—and her married sister, as the pair discuss fertility issues, their trash-picking father, films, and a host of other topics over the course of a summer. (Inspired by Cook's experiences on the set of the big-screen version of *Must Love Dogs*, a segment in the book deals with a movie crew that visits the sisters' hometown.) Cook helped promote *Life's a Beach* by mailing out scores of personalized letters to booksellers, decorating the missives with glued-on sand, miniature beach shoes, and seashells. She has told interviewers that she anticipates greatly enjoying the book tour for her latest novel, because she plans to wear flip-flops, instead of high heels.

Claire Cook still lives in Scituate, Massachusetts, where she has spent most of her life. She and her husband, a land surveyor, have two grown children. As a longtime teacher at the local Montessori school, she was a familiar figure in the small town, even before her success as a novelist. Now, however, she has achieved celebrity status. "I'm the only novelist around," she explained to Boaz, "except for maybe a few mimeographing their own books."

—S.Y.

Suggested Reading: *Booklist* p1,816 July 2004; *Library Journal* p93 June 15, 2002; *Publishers Weekly* p63 Apr. 3, 2000, p49 May 31, 2004, p33 July 26, 2004; *USA Today* D p4 July 18, 2002

Selected Books: *Ready to Fall*, 2000; *Must Love Dogs*, 2002; *Multiple Choice*, 2004

Courtemanche, Gilles

(CORT-a-MONCH, ZH-EEL)

1943– Journalist; novelist

After nearly 40 years covering Canadian politics and serving as a foreign correspondent, the French-Canadian journalist Gilles "Gil" Courtemanche penned his first novel in 2000. A best-seller among French-language texts in Canada, the work was translated into English, in 2003, under the title *A Sunday at the Pool in Kigali*, which likewise achieved best-seller status in Canada. The novel follows a French-Canadian journalist as he becomes caught up in the genocide that swept the central African nation of Rwanda in 1994. Having visited Rwanda several times prior to 1994, Courtemanche was personally affected by the violence, since many of the friends and contacts he had made there were among the victims. *A Sunday at the Pool in Kigali* is an effort to bear witness to the

horror that claimed so many lives. "What I tried to do is write a contemporary historical novel, a type of literature that was once important in France," Courtemanche explained to Judy Stoffman for the *Toronto Star* (April 14, 2003). "In French literature, writers have turned their eyes inward. I'm not a writer's writer. I write to change the world."

One of seven children, Gilles Courtemanche was born in 1943 in Montreal, Quebec, Canada. His father sold insurance. As a child Courtemanche developed an interest in political activism and protest. When he was 12 years old, he organized a strike at his school. "I was first in my class but a bad influence," he recalled to Jane Sullivan for the Melbourne *Age* (August 9, 2003). In 1960, at age 17, Courtemanche was expelled from his high school, the College des Eudistes. That same year he campaigned for René Lévesque, a Liberal Party candidate running for a seat in the Quebec provincial legislature. (Lévesque would later leave the Liberal Party and form the Parti Québécois, which unsuccessfully sought to establish national sovereignty for the province of Quebec; Lévesque served as the province's premier from 1976 to 1985).

At age 19, in 1962, Courtemanche began his career as a journalist, getting his start with the newspaper *La Presse* in Montreal. In 1974 he helped found *Le Jour*, a Quebec newspaper organized by Lévesque and his allies to communicate their vision of an independent province; Courtemanche eventually became one of its editorial writers. From 1975 to 1985, he worked as a foreign correspondent, covering the civil war in Lebanon and unrest in Haiti, among other stories. "I was kind of ignorant," he explained to Sullivan. "I began to cover war because nobody wanted to go." He also served as a political commentator for the Canadian Broadcasting Company (CBC) television network but was fired for insubordination in 1985.

During the late 1980s Courtemanche focused his attention on Canadian politics and Third World issues. In 1989 he published his first book in French, *Douces colères: Journal*, which was about the Canadian national election of 1988. Courtemanche's second book, *Chroniques internationales*, a collection of his newspaper columns, was published in 1991. Two years later Courtemanche produced a documentary for Canadian television, *The Gospel of AIDS*, which chronicled the battle against the disease in Africa. As part of his research for the film, in 1989 Courtemanche traveled to Rwanda, where he would return several times over the next five years, making many friends and developing a profound connection to the country.

In April 1994 Rwanda exploded into genocidal violence after Rwandan President Juvenal Habyarimana and Burundian President Cyprien Ntaryamira were killed when their plane was shot down shortly before its scheduled landing at the airport in Kigali, Rwanda. Tensions and strife between Rwanda's majority Hutus and minority Tutsis had long plagued the nation, and the deaths of the two presidents catalyzed a wave of terror as government troops and Hutu militia groups began slaughtering Tutsis and their Hutu sympathizers. By the time the violence ended, in July, as many as 800,000 Tutsis had been killed. Courtemanche was in Paris when the hostilities initially broke out. "I realised that most of my friends and colleagues would be dead," he told Sullivan. In 1995 Courtemanche returned to Rwanda. Profoundly affected by the genocide and the murders of his friends and associates, he felt compelled to do something to preserve their memory and the memory of all those affected by the tragedy. At first he considered making another documentary or writing a work of nonfiction, but nothing came of these efforts. Finally, Courtemanche found notes he had taken during his first visit to Rwanda. Sitting by the pool in the Hotel des Mille-Collines in Kigali, which, as was dramatized in the motion picture *Hotel Rwanda* (2004), served as a safe-haven during the 1994 turmoil, Courtemanche had recorded his impressions of the eclectic mix of people he observed. Inspired, he began to expand on the scene. "Five or six days later, I discovered I was writing a novel," he told Stoffman. Courtemanche's editor encouraged this approach, explaining that a novel would likely sell better than his earlier nonfiction books.

The French edition of Courtemanche's novel, *Un dimanche à la piscine à Kigali*, debuted in Quebec in 2000. It spent more than a year on the best-seller lists and captured the Prix des Libraires award for outstanding book of the year. The English translation, by Patricia Claxton, was a finalist for the Rogers Writers' Trust Fiction Prize. The novel's protagonist is Bernard Valcourt, a weary French-Canadian journalist who is in Kigali to film a documentary about AIDS. Valcourt spends his free time by the pool at the Hotel des Mille-Collines in the company of visiting foreigners from Western countries, Rwandan government officials, the hotel's staff, and prostitutes. Valcourt falls in love with Gentille, a waitress of mixed heritage who works at the hotel. The characters in *A Sunday at the Pool in Kigali* are based on—and named after—people Courtemanche met and befriended during his trips to Rwanda; Gentille was a waitress at the hotel for whom he had developed a secret passion. He later learned that she was among the victims of the massacres. In the novel, when the genocide begins, many of the hotel's residents are indifferent or oblivious to the carnage. However, Valcourt finds that he cannot isolate himself since Gentille, who looks like a Tutsi, is in danger.

A Sunday at the Pool in Kigali earned substantial critical acclaim. "Courtemanche narrates coolly, at one remove, emboldened by the facts of history and the objectivity distance provides," Noah Richler wrote for the Toronto *National Post* (April 12, 2003). "His novel is, on the one hand, a portrait of, and tribute to, the dear friends he lost in Rwanda; on the other, it is a relentless indictment of the Rwandan catastrophe." Richler was especially impressed by Courtemanche's touching portrayal of a farewell party for Methode, a Rwandan dying of AIDS, who warns his friends from his deathbed that an even graver illness—hatred—will soon traumatize the country. "There are many unsettling qualities to Gil Courtemanche's extraordinary novel," the reviewer concluded. "But, above all, it is his insistence on love, and the right to live one's life passionately and well, even in the face of AIDS and the genocide, this double helix of devastating African tragedies, that makes the book great." Writing for the *New York Times* (October 26, 2003), Christopher Dickey lauded the work: "The appeal of *A Sunday at the Pool in Kigali* is not in Valcourt's story, or the ill-fated romance, but in the novel's chillingly evocative sense of people and place," he observed. "When Courtemanche describes the decadence by the pool at the Mille-

Collines, or the fear at the roadblocks manned by drunken soldiers, or one friend who comes to die of AIDS in Valcourt's hotel room, or another murdered and hacked to bits with his wife, the effect is devastating. When the author writes so simply that 'Valcourt got up very early, with the mists and the ravens, before the dogs and the children,' this land of the dying comes alive." *A Sunday at the Pool in Kigali* has adapted into a French-language feature film, *Un dimanche à Kigali*, starring Luc Picard and directed by Robert Favreau, which is slated to premiere in May 2006.

Courtemanche has published three other nonfiction books in French: *Québec* (1998), which features the photography of Philippe Renault; *Nouvelles douces colères* (1999), and *La Seconde Révolution tranquille: Démocratiser la démocratie* (2003). His latest novel, *Une belle morte* (2005), explores the emotional turmoil experienced by a man forced to watch as his father slowly dies from Parkinson's disease over a six-month period. Yet to be translated into English, the book is "inspired by what's happening around me and in my family,"

Courtemanche explained, as quoted by Pat Donnelly for the Montreal *Gazette* (September 24, 2005). "Not by the individual character but by the situation." Courtemanche is a columnist for the newspaper *Le Devoir* in Montreal and has written for *Moi et l'Autre*, one of Quebec's most popular television comedies. Courtemanche's first marriage ended in divorce; he married his second wife, France-Isobel Langlois, in 2003. He is known for his sometimes acerbic personality and his predilection for cigarettes, coffee, and alcohol.

—D.C.

Suggested Reading: (Melbourne) *Age* Review p3 Aug. 9, 2003; (Montreal) *Gazette* J p4 May 29, 1999, J p3 Apr. 14, 2001; *New York Times* E p10 Oct. 13, 2003; Random House Canada Web site; (Toronto) *National Post* Books p11 Apr. 12, 2003; *Toronto Star* E p1 Apr. 14, 2003

Selected Books in English Translation: *A Sunday at the Pool in Kigali*, 2003

Couto, Mia

(COO-too)

July 5, 1955– Novelist; short-story writer; journalist; poet

In 2002 a panel of 16 African scholars and critics named Mia Couto's first novel, *Terra sonâmbula* (1992), one of the 12 best works of 20th-century African literature. Published in English as *Sleepwalking Land* (2006), the novel tells two intertwining stories about the civil war that tore apart Mozambique, Couto's home country, between the time it gained independence from Portugal, in 1975, and 1990, when a new constitution opened up the country to democratic reforms. (Some sources date the end of the war to the 1992 cease-fire between the two main warring parties and others to 1994, when the country held its first open, multiparty elections.) By the time *Sleepwalking Land* appeared, Couto had already developed a commanding reputation as a columnist, poet, and short-story writer. In 1990 he became the first person to win his country's national literary award, the Grande Prémio da Ficção Narrativa de Moçambique, for *Vozes anoitecidas* (1986), a book of short fiction translated as *Voices Made Night* (1990). This was followed by the translation of Couto's second story collection, *Every Man Is a Race* (1994), and later by the novels *Under the Frangipani* (2001) and *The Last Flight of the Flamingo* (2004). In June 2001 this last novel, about the disappearance of a group of U.N. peacekeepers, won Couto the first-ever Mário António Prize from the Calouste Gulbenkian

Courtesy of Serpent's Tail

Foundation in Lisbon, Portugal. At the awards ceremony Couto, a political activist since his youth and since 1989 a university lecturer on environmental issues, told the audience, according to a translation posted on the African Review of Books Web site: "*The Last Flight of the Flamingo* speaks of a perverse manufacturing of absence—a lack of a completely whole land, an extreme theft of hope committed by the ruthlessness of the powerful. The advance of these consumers of nations forces us, ourselves, writers, to a growing moral obligation. Against the indecency of those who enrich themselves at the expense of everything and everyone, against those who have their hands dripping with blood, against the lies and crime and fear, against all of this the words of writers should be constructed." Couto added that this conviction had shaped all his novels, and in them, "I have been confronted with the same demons and have felt the need to invent the same treasured territory, where it should be possible to recreate beliefs and repair the [calluses] of suffering in our lives."

António Emilio Leite Couto was born on July 5, 1955 in Beira, Mozambique, to Fernando and Maria de Jesus Couto; he was given the nickname Mia while still quite young. (Some sources give Couto's day of birth as July 7.) His father was a poet, newspaper editor, and railroad administrator who, like Couto's mother, had come to Mozambique from northern Portugal. Couto published his first poems in the paper his father edited, *Notícias da Beira*, when he was 14 and stayed in his hometown until 1971, when he matriculated to Lourenço Marques University (now known as Eduardo Mondlane University) in the nation's capital, Maputo (then known as LourenSo Marques), to study medicine. Like many students around the world at that time, Couto was a dedicated political reformer, and he and others like him "lived in a heady atmosphere of struggle and protest," he wrote in an article for *Le Monde Diplomatique* (April 2004, on-line).

Part of Couto's struggle was against the Portuguese government itself, which was then under the control of the political heirs of the dictator António Salazar, but for Couto the more pressing struggle was against colonialism. To speed independence Couto joined with the Liberation Front of Mozambique (Frente de Libertação de Moçambique, or Frelimo), which directed him, he explained in *Le Monde Diplomatique*, "to abandon my studies and get a job with a newspaper, to infiltrate the Portuguese-controlled media with educated Mozambicans." In April 1974 a bloodless coup brought democracy to Portugal, and in 1975 Frelimo's 10-year-long campaign for independence bore fruit. Hopes for a democratic and stable Mozambique soon faded, however. Frelimo declared a one-party communist state aligned with the Soviet Union, and two of Mozambique's most powerful neighbors, Zimbabwe (then called Rhodesia) and South Africa, responded to the events in Mozambique by funding the counterrevolutionary Resistência Nacional Moçambicana (Renamo). The subsequent civil war killed an estimated one million Mozambicans, pushed roughly 1.7 million out of the country altogether, and left the country littered with millions of landmines.

Couto's work toward independence was rewarded, beginning in 1977, with a roughly two-year appointment as the head of the Mozambique Information Agency. From there he moved to the magazine *Tempo*, for which he served as general editor for three years. In 1981 he began to edit the daily newspaper *Notícias de Maputo* and the weekly *Domingo*. While continuing an active career as a writer and editor, Couto eventually returned to Eduardo Mondlane University, receiving a degree in biology, in 1989, and beginning a secondary career as an environmental activist and, at his alma mater, a lecturer and researcher in ecology. Couto also continued to write for *Notícias de Maputo*, and in subsequent years his columns there and in the weekly paper *Savana* have made him a highly visible commentator on his country's political scene; his books *Cronicando* (1988) and *O país do queixa andar* (2003) collect some of these "chronicles," as they are called.

Couto published his first book, the poetry collection *Raiz de orvalho* (which translates as "root of dew"), in 1983. He became famous, however, on the publication of his first collection of short stories, *Vozes anoitecidas*. The stories in that collection, *Voices Made Night,* and in much of Couto's subsequent work, mingle the mundane and the spiritual in a manner that has been compared to the magical realism associated with such South American writers as Gabriel García Márquez.

In *African Writers* (1997), David Brookshaw, the translator of all Couto's work published thus far in English, traced some of the fantastical elements in Couto's stories to the Mozambican oral storytelling tradition, which Brookshaw also detected in Couto's use of gnomes at the openings of his stories. The fantastical quality of Couto's fiction also has a political dimension, Brookshaw noted: "the stories [in *Voices Made Night*] derive from a preoccupation with the power of fantasy and its ability to rule the lives of those who are all but destitute. Fantasy becomes a compensatory mechanism, but it is equally a destructive force, as Couto explained in the forward: 'There exists in nothingness that illusion of plenitude which causes life to stop and voices to become night.'" Karima Effendi argued for the value of this type of storytelling for the South African publication *Inter Action: Proceedings of the Fourth Postgraduate Conference* (1996): "By injecting into his stories an element of the fantastic, Couto is . . . able to talk about the atrocities of poverty in a way which leaves the reader, not motionless with pity or sympathy for the poor, but inspired to the point of wanting to correct what has gone wrong. In this sense we are no longer passive voyeurs."

Couto took a similar approach in *Cada homem é uma raça*, his 1992 story collection, translated as *Every Man Is a Race*. The stories in Couto's second collection find somewhat more concrete historical moorings, with several of the stories set during the Mozambican war for independence and the civil war that followed it, but *Every Man Is a Race* is also a thematic relative of *Voices Made Night*. Couto's work in the former is, Brookshaw wrote, "full of fragmented characters, social outcasts who are either orphans or widows, deprived in some way of the 'other' with which their personalities might be completed." Commenting that Couto "is on his way to becoming Mozambique's foremost author of extraordinary tales," Gerald Moser for *World Literature Today* (Autumn 1994) compared Couto to another Lusophone writer, the Brazilian novelist João Guimarães Rosa, in that Couto also "invents a Portuguese sui generis that cannot easily be transferred to any other language. It seems to me that Couto is creating a literary idiom that looks and feels like the Portuguese which untutored black Mozambicans may be speaking, not just due to ignorance of standard Lisbonese usage, but attuned to African modes of thought, including an animistic view of the world." While this led Moser to conclude that Couto's work can only be fully appreciated in Portuguese, he judged Brookshaw's translation somewhat successful, especially in re-creating the Mozambican atmosphere of Couto's stories. In *Every Man Is a Race*, Moser added, "a hallucinatory world rises before the mind's eye, peopled by real human beings tragically surviving for a while in an all-too-real country being devastated by a civil war between 'bandits' and 'soldiers' and simultaneously rendered crazy through the demands of party hacks and bureaucrats on plain folk."

Bandits, soldiers, and plain folk also figure prominently in Couto's next book, *Sleepwalking Land*. The novel tells two stories that come together only at the end. The first is about an older man named Tuahir, who is traveling during the Mozambican civil war with Muidinga, a boy he helped nurse back to health while they were in a refugee camp together. Walking down a road the two discover an abandoned bus full of dead bodies and, in a suitcase, a set of notebooks that tell about the life of Kindzu, a man who left his own village to join an elusive, proud, and highly principled warring group, the Naparamas. Providing the second narrative strand in the novel, Kindzu's story takes an almost mythic turn when he meets Farida, a beautiful woman who draws him into a quest to locate her son, Gaspar. A reviewer for *Publishers Weekly* (February 6, 2006) called the book "a brutally absorbing tale of those who suffered a devastated country's vicissitudes," and Uzodinma Iweala, writing for the *New York Times Book Review* (July 30, 2006), essentially concurred. Though Iweala criticized some of the passages depicting Tuahir and Muidinga reading Kindzu's notebooks as resembling "static stage directions," he praised "Couto's attention to detail [that] makes the unreality of his novel tangible. When a Portuguese settler rises from the dead, Couto describes him 'balancing on the tightrope of his dizziness, having lost his vertical habits.' Kindzu's brother, Twenty-Fifth of June, named after Mozambique's independence day, vividly masquerades as a chicken with 'flea-bitten plumage.' In a similar fashion, Couto takes the actors in Mozambique's violent political drama and turns them into demons and ghosts that terrorize the common people. If magic realism traditionally offers understanding through escape from the heaviness of reality, Couto's novel is an anomaly in the genre. It creates a dream that weighs more heavily than reality itself."

After another book of stories—titled, with an untranslatable neologism, *Estórias abensonhadas* (1994)—Couto published his second novel, *A varanda do frangipani* (1996), a mystery translated as *Under the Frangipani*. What lies under the scented, flowering tree mentioned in the title is the grave of a carpenter, whose wandering ghost inhabits the body of the humble policeman assigned to find out who murdered the brutal director of the old-age home and former fort that occupies the grounds where the frangipani grows. With only six days to conduct his work, the policeman turns up six witnesses: four who confess to the crime and two who admit they wanted the director dead. A reviewer for South Africa *Business Day*, as carried by Africa News (October 24, 2001), found that Couto had "drawn inspiration in his style and plotting from a legacy of Brazilian authors as well as from Mozambican aural narrative. Where he succeeds is in . . . plunging the reader into the recent tormented history of his native Mozambique. The reader is left with no sentimental view of the aftermath of Mozambique's civil war. He deals crisply and unemotionally with the grim reality of events that have damaged irrevocably old attitudes and responsibilities." Couto's novel, Carl MacDougall wrote for the Glasgow *Herald* (July 7, 2001), "occupies a territory which is familiar through folk tales, fusing the living and the dead and amalgamating people with other living creatures, while continuingly questioning the nature of reality and language with mordant wit, [verve] and endless invention."

Couto described how he came to write *O último vôo do flamingo* (1996), published in English as *The Last Flight of the Flamingo*, in his July 2001 speech acknowledging the receipt of the Mário António Prize. Finding a single flamingo feather on a beach that, in years past, had been a nesting site for flocks of flamingos, Couto said that he felt an "inexplicable anguish" and asked himself: "what if those birds never returned again? And what if the flamingos from all the beaches had been swallowed by distant shadows? . . . . My chest tightened in anxious premonition. It was not a simple longing for those creatures. It was a definitive absence of those messengers of the skies, those discrete, divine couriers." Couto took the feather home and set it on his computer, and during the novel's two-year gestation, "that feather confronted me as if it were a narrow window in the sky through which the birds . . . filed."

The Last Flight of the Flamingo begins with the discovery that around Tizangara, a Mozambican town still recovering from the ravages of civil war, a group of U.N. peacekeepers has disappeared, leaving nothing behind but their helmets and penises. An Italian U.N. official, Massimo Risi, arrives to investigate, and his translator serves as the narrator—"our guide through the hazy borderlands between the living and the dead," Rob Nixon wrote for the New York Times Book Review (July 17, 2005). Nixon characterized The Last Flight of the Flamingo as "a wry poignant fable about any society lost in translation, any society sent through the ideological wringer by colonists, Marxist-Leninists, counterrevolutionaries, NGO's [nongovernmental organizations], globalizing capitalists and authoritarian kleptocrats. As the novel's narrator observes of his people's mangled identity, 'We hadn't understood the war, and now we didn't understand the peace.'" Calling the novel "a protest novel of sorts, a cry against the debasements of politics and language inflicted upon ordinary inhabitants of the 'developing' world," Nixon emphasized Couto's light touch, writing: "The Last Flight is a serious novel that doesn't take itself too seriously. On almost every page of this witty magic realist whodunit, we sense Couto's delight in those places where language slips officialdom's asphyxiating grasp."

Among Couto's works yet to be translated into English are the short-story collections Contos do nascer da terra (1997) and Na berma de nenhuma

estrada (2001), the novel Um rio chamado tempo, uma casa chamada terra (2002), and the novellas Vinte e zinco (1999), Mar me quer (2000), and Chuva pasmada (2004). His work has been published in more than a dozen languages, with Terra sonâmbula alone appearing in print in at least 16 countries, from Brazil to Norway.

Couto lives in Maputo. He has been married several times and is the father of three children, Dawany, Luciana, and Rita. He continues his outcries against such injustices as the murder of Carlos Cardoso, a crusading journalist, said to have been assassinated by hired thugs at the government's request. Couto is the head of the environmental organization Impacto.

—S.Y.

Suggested Reading: African Review of Books Web site; Africa News Oct. 24, 2001; African Writers (on-line) 1997; (Glasgow) Herald p12 July 7, 2001; Inter Action p96+ 1996; New York Times Book Review p25 July 17, 2005; World Literature Today p866+ Autumn 1994, p81 July–Sep. 2003

Selected Books in English Translation: Voices Made Night, 1990; Every Man Is a Race, 1994; Under the Frangipani, 2001; The Last Flight of the Flamingo, 2004; Sleepwalking Land, 2006

Cummins, Ann

1960– Short-story writer; novelist

"My stories are very much character-driven stories," Ann Cummins, the author of the short-story collection Red Ant House (2003) and the novel Yellowcake (2007), stated in an interview posted on the Readers Read Web site (March 2003). "I'm attracted to the wild in human beings—not the psychotic, but the dark, hidden places in all of us." When her book of short stories appeared, Cummins found herself being compared to the likes of Flannery O'Connor and Denis Johnson, and while, "she does take a few cues from [those writers] in [her] stories, many of which are set on Indian reservations and uranium mills," Kera Bolonik wrote for the Westchester County, New York, Journal News (June 15, 2003), "more often than not, she takes risks all her own and you can't help but admire her daring."

Ann Cummins, the daughter of Cyril P. and Barbara R. Cummins, was born in the Rocky Mountain town of Durango, Colorado, where her father—the descendant of Irish immigrants who made their living as miners—worked as a uranium miner. When Cummins was nine, her father was

transferred to a uranium mine in Shiprock, New Mexico, and the family moved to a Navajo Indian reservation, where Cummins spent the rest of her youth. After high school she entered the University of Oregon but transferred to Johns Hopkins University, in Baltimore, Maryland, earning her B.A. there, in 1987, her B.A. She then entered the University of Arizona's writing program, earning her M.F.A., in 1989. Thereafter, Cummins saw her short stories published in such magazines as McSweeney's, the New Yorker, and the Sonora Review, as well as in the anthology The Best American Short Stories 2002.

Red Ant House is a collection of 12 short stories that focus on "those moments when the civilized, driven by desire, passion, fear, begin to misbehave," as Cummins told the Readers Read interviewer. The stories are set in the rural American Southwest, on Indian reservations and in desolate towns. Stephen Deusner, reviewing the work for Bookreporter.com, noted the author's "rough-hewn prose that bursts with short, targeted sentences and blunt declarations of brutal insights," and opined, "these solid, sturdy stories . . . reveal Cummins as a genuinely talented and immensely sensitive writer." Donna Stokes was equally impressed, writing for the Albuquerque

Steve Willis/Courtesy of Houghton Mifflin

Ann Cummins

Journal (September 7, 2003) that "Cummins rips the veils of normalcy off her intense characters, revealing the itchy, light-sensitive underside of people as they drag their loved ones along on life's dirty road." She concluded, "Cummins' writing is from the gut. Her dark characters are sad, intriguing and painfully human in a way most of us try to forget." The reviewer for *Publishers Weekly* (April 7, 2003) offered a more tempered view, observing "Cummins doesn't always create convincing alternate universes—her deliberately off-kilter prose sometimes falters and her attempts at interior logic aren't always consistent—but these are mostly clever and entertaining experiments"

Yellowcake, Cummins's debut novel—which takes its title from the slang term for uranium oxide, the material that remains after uranium is separated from its ore—was released in 2007. Set, like her stories, in the American Southwest, *Yellowcake* is about a Navajo family, the Atcittys, and an Anglo family, the Mahoneys, who about 30 years prior to the events of the novel lived near a uranium mill. Now, Becky Atcitty, who is involved in a lawsuit that seeks damages for the people harmed by the mill's radioactive dust, arrives at the Mahoney's door, and Ryland Mahoney, the family patriarch, is unable to prevent the past from being dredged up. "By fusing suspenseful love entanglements with family angst, Native American concerns, grief over the poisoning of the land, penetrating compassion, and ironic humor, Cummins brilliantly conflates the insidious damage wrought by radiation sickness with the maladies of the soul caused by prejudice, poverty, nature's abuse, and love's betrayal," Donna Seaman wrote for *Booklist*, as quoted on Amazon.com.

Cummins lives in Oakland, California, with her husband, the musician Steven Evans Willis,; she also maintains a residence in Flagstaff, Arizona, where she teaches creative writing at Northern Arizona University. She was the recipient of a Lannan Literary Fellowship in 2002.

—P.B.M./A.R.

Suggested Reading: *Albuquerque Journal* F p8 Sep. 7, 2003; Bookreporter.com; *Publishers Weekly* p46 Apr. 7, 2003; Readers Read Web site, Mar. 2003

Selected Books: *Red Ant House*, 2003; *Yellowcake*, 2007

Cusk, Rachel

Feb. 8, 1967– Novelist; memoirist

The word critics have most often applied to Rachel Cusk's writing is "mordant." On the surface, her novels *Saving Agnes* (1993), *The Temporary* (1995), and *The Country Life* (1997)—each set in either the professional, fast-paced world of London society or the surrounding countryside—are comic works, but there is an undercurrent of malignity and despair that cuts through the humor, giving her stories an unmistakable bite. Her first venture into the world of nonfiction, *A Life's Work: On Becoming a Mother* (2001), was written in a similar vein. Composed while she was expecting her second child in order to capture and record the sensations of pregnancy, childbirth, and child rearing, the book was called by Craig Seligman, for the *New York Times Book Review* (March 14, 2004), a "rumination on motherhood, which is variously unsentimental, self-pitying, passionate, naked and, when you least expect it, hilarious." Her continuing attempts to transform her raw emotions and experiences into literature next resulted in *The Lucky Ones* (2003), which although not "funny," according to Seligman, "touches greatness in its psychological incisiveness." Her latest offering, *Arlington Park* (2006), examines the many frustrations of life in suburbia.

Rachel Cusk was born February 8, 1967 in Canada to English parents, Carolyn and Peter, an independent business woman and a financial controller, respectively. The family moved to Los Angeles, California, where Cusk spent her early childhood. When she was eight, the family relocated to Bury St. Edmunds in East Anglia, England. Cusk attended a convent school, which, she told Hester Lacey for the London *Independent* (September 1, 1996), she "detested. . . . I spent five years there, living for the day I could leave." She studied English at New College, part of the University of Oxford, graduating in 1989. Cusk then traveled to Spain, spending a year there after

Rachel Cusk

Adrian Clark/Courtesy of HarperCollins

leaving Oxford. "I went to Spain, determined to become this successful person in secret, returning in triumph to England," she told Annie Taylor in an interview for the London *Guardian* (August 3, 1995). "It didn't work out like that: I couldn't get a job, or a flat, didn't even have enough money to come home. After a couple of months, I ended up sleeping on a friend's floor." She succeeded in landing an editorial job in England, but she found that she had to return to Bury St. Edmunds and her parents' home, where she lived while she wrote her first published novel, *Saving Agnes*. That time was "weird. Kind of like the Betty Ford [drug rehabilitation] clinic," she told Claire Messud in an interview for the London *Guardian* (December 6, 1993).

The book's protagonist, Agnes Day, a somewhat altered version of the author, lives in London with two roommates, Nina and Merlin, and works as an assistant editor at a magazine called *Diplomat's Week*. She is unsatisfied with both her life and her boyfriend. Reviewers almost universally reveled in Cusk's writing, comparing her to a latter-day Jane Austen. *Saving Agnes* went on to receive the Whitbread Prize for first novel and prompted one of the judges, Philip Hobsbawm, to remark in the London *Guardian* (November 9, 1993), "This is a sceptical, ironic, beautifully resonant prose, articulate throughout, with never a lapse." By the time of the book's publication in the U.S., in 1999, many American reviewers were comparing it to *Bridget Jones's Diary* (a popular 1998 novel by Helen Fielding) and were as impressed as their British counterparts with *Saving Agnes*. "Cusk's use of telling detail is exquisite and sometimes diabolical. The dialogue is often hilarious,

illuminating even minor characters with pithy elan," a *Publishers Weekly* (November 15, 1999) critic declared. "Readers will find themselves . . . savoring Cusk's rich explorations into the life of a young woman whose view of the world is never rosy, but who, in the book's closing scenes, comes to understand that future happiness can lurk in an event as ordinary as a bus ride."

Although, as Cusk admitted to Messud, she found the experience of reading even the most glowing reviews of her work to be "singularly disturbing," the success of *Saving Agnes* opened up other literary doors for Cusk, who was asked to become a fiction reviewer for the London *Times*. She was also able to move up the date of her first marriage, to her boyfriend, Josh, a banker, to 1995. That year her novel *The Temporary* was published. *The Temporary* tells the story of a mismatched couple—Francine and Ralph. In her less-than-enthusiastic review for the London *Independent* (August 13, 1995), Christina Patterson wrote that she felt Ralph was a well-realized character whose "loneliness and insecurity is sympathetically conveyed, as is his growing fear, bewilderment and irritation," but she found Cusk's portrayal of Francine "less than convincing, almost a parody of a brainless tart," suggesting to Patterson the low regard in which Cusk held the character. The critic John Bayley, however, expressed in the London *Times* (July 20, 1995) almost the opposite viewpoint. He judged *The Temporary* to be a "step forward" for Cusk because "the inner feel of a social world is triumphantly but unobtrusively realised." He added that Cusk tells this "everyday story" and portrays her characters with great sympathy. Although she "is certainly lacking in the modern 'caring and compassionate' version of sentimentality . . . that does not mean that she has no feeling for her characters. With a concealed ingenuity which shows a strong sense of the culture and history of the novel form, she takes a well-worn situation and characters from fiction's past, and brings them sparklingly up to the moment." For Kate Kellaway, writing for the London *Observer* (July 16, 1995), Cusk's language is both a handicap and a strength, filled with "intense affectation" and "mannered dislocations. . . . But gradually you get the hang of it: nothing can be performed unreflectingly. Life is all performance and potential snares. And gradually 'against the odds' the novel takes hold."

Stella Benson, the protagonist of Cusk's next novel, *The Country Life*, is named for the British author of *Tobit Transplanted* (1931), called *Faraway Bride* in its American publication. The latter title is an appropriate description of Cusk's Stella, who has fled her husband, along with the city and her career as a lawyer, to take a position as caregiver and companion to Martin, a crippled teenager, in the country. Unfortunately, she is woefully ill equipped for life in her new surroundings. Sunburn, rashes, and hayfever play havoc with her body, and she is unable to drive, a necessary qualification for her position. Martin's parents, an odd couple, make her life very difficult, as does Martin himself. Nevertheless, a strange alliance develops between Martin, aged 17, and Stella, aged 29. "Cusk follows the subtle dynamics of their growing interdependence beautifully, and the result is a refreshingly unusual love story," Heller McAlpin noted for New York *Newsday* (January 31, 1999). "*The Country Life* is about rejecting 'an acknowledged life, stamped and certified,' and striking out 'at whatever risk to set things right' when dissatisfied with one's lot. Cusk's enchanting story makes a pitch for adventure and fulfillment but also, as Martin sagely lectures Stella, the importance of facing difficulties and loving people despite imperfections." Alex Clark, writing for the London *Guardian* (July 10, 1997), called *The Country Life* "a fine entertainment" that is "both witty and humorous" and "succeeds as comedy precisely because of the discord between Stella's impeccable narrative voice and the chaos of her experiences. In thrall not to her circumstances but to her obsessional ratiocination, Stella is the perfect vehicle for Cusk's verbosity and archness."

In 2001 Cusk temporarily abandoned fiction to write *A Life's Work: On Becoming a Mother*. The book was begun during her second pregnancy, which had started only six months after the birth of her first child. Cusk told Maureen Freely for the London *Independent* (September 6, 2001), "It was my impression, when I became a mother, that nothing had been written about it at all; this may merely be a good example of that tone-deafness . . . with which a non-parent is afflicted whenever a parent speaks, a condition we acquire as children and which leads us as adults to wonder with bemusement why [we] were never told—by our friends, BY OUR MOTHERS!—what parenthood was like." Cusk proceeded to write a frank and, for many readers, disturbing account of her experience with motherhood. As much as she happened to like the book, for instance, even Freely admitted, "If I were a mother-to-be, I think I would find it rather frightening." Cusk described for Freely the kinds of reactions she was receiving from the nay-sayers: "They've said, 'You're a bad mother, we disown you, busy mothers won't have time to read this.' It's as if the organism of good mothers has produced an antibody to reject me."

Nevertheless, there were many critics who enjoyed *A Life's Work*. Suzanne Moore, in the *New Statesman* (September 3, 2001), called it "a very funny book about very serious things." Quoting from Cusk, Moore added, "in this wonderful book, 'The experience of motherhood loses nearly everything in its translation to the outside world. In motherhood a woman exchanges her public significance for a range of private meanings, and, like sounds outside a certain range, they can be difficult for other people to identify.'" Moore then described the book as "full of enormous insight and sly wit" and "a work of profundity and depth."

Tracey Macleod, writing for the London *Sunday Times* (September 2, 2001), however, failed to see the humor in *A Life's Work*: "Cusk's writerly instincts outpace her human ones at every stage. Each mood of alienation and moment of despair is exhaustively scrutinised, but joy and tenderness seem to be missing from the mix. Repeatedly drawing on the imagery of imprisonment, of death, of power and powerlessness, she creates an atmosphere of tragedy that reads like survivor literature, or the account of a terminal illness."

Cusk's grimmer side was also displayed in *The Lucky Ones*. Billed as a novel, the book is actually five "loosely, though deftly, linked stories," as Craig Seligman observed. The stories deal largely with motherhood and marriage, often from the point of view of despairing young mothers. In the first story, "Confinement," Kirsty, a young pregnant woman unjustly jailed (or, in Cusk's play on words, "confined"), starts her labor in a prison cell and gives birth in the back of a police car. In the final story, a couple with seemingly happy lives and healthy children have to face the husband's imminent death. Craig Seligman, in pointing to the social consciousness displayed in "Confinement," declared that, with that story, "Cusk is exploring new ground," and that in *The Lucky Ones* in general, "Cusk has brought her writing to a new level." He concluded that if Cusk were to regain her sense of humor, "she'll do more than touch greatness." Lisa Allardice, for *New Statesman* (April 7, 2003), concurred that Cusk was one of the more important novelists in the U.K. She wrote of *The Lucky Ones*, "In contrast to Cusk's earlier books, the intricate storylines are more torturous than her prose. A distinctive stylist, she treats language with the greedy indulgence her fictional mothers lavish on their babies. While family resentments, infidelities and discord are hardly original themes, the clarity of her observations makes this mundane world seem freshly new."

Arlington Park, Cusk's most recent novel, is a tale of suburban angst. As Lucy Ellmann wrote for the *New York Times Book Review* (January 28, 2007), "*Arlington Park* isn't the end of the world; it's just suburbia. But, with a little exaggeration, the two become interchangeable." Calling the novel—which follows a group of wealthy housewives as they shop, argue with their children, and meet for coffee—"the kind of book that makes you burn things on the stove and berate your husband," Ellmann complained, "There are some great moments, but she tends to over-egg the pudding with metaphor, simile and melodramatic hyperbole when all she's describing is a set of materially advantaged women getting through the day." Christina Schwartz, in a review posted on Powell's Books Web site, was more impressed, calling Cusk's writing "so diamond sharp and so lushly metaphorical that even had this substantial book no substance, one would read it happily."

Brought up Roman Catholic, Cusk told Lacey, "I would describe myself as a Christian rather than a Catholic." She lives with her second husband and two children "at the edge of Exmoor," as Maureen Freely noted for the London *Independent* (September 6, 2001). She has continued to write essays for the London newspapers, in addition to her endeavors as a novelist. For the London *Guardian* (September 14, 2001), Cusk authored a response to the tragedy of September 11, 2001, writing of individuals connected by cell phone to their loved ones who were about to die. Cusk compared their situation to that of a woman who was on the phone with her husband as he was hopelessly stranded on Mount Everest, his phone's battery fading along with his life. In describing the event, she set forth her own philosophy of writing: "She was with him and not with him; she could hear him suffer but couldn't help him or even comfort him, except with words. . . . That's a big

'except.' The love that survives us is inextricably bound up with words. . . . I'm not sure I could have found the words. But perhaps we just haven't known how to talk to each other. Perhaps we're learning."

—S. Y.

Suggested Reading: (London) *Guardian* p11 Nov. 9, 1993, p11 Dec. 6, 1993, T p14 Aug. 3, 1995, T p14 July 10, 1997, p12 Sep. 14, 2001; (London) *Independent* p31 Aug. 13, 1995; p2 Sep. 1, 1996, p7 Sep. 6, 2001; (London) *Observer* p16 July 16, 1995; *New Statesman* p37 Sep. 3, 2001; *New York Times Book Review* p15 Jan. 28, 2007; *Publishers Weekly* p54 Nov. 15, 1999

Selected Books: *Saving Agnes,* 1993; *The Temporary,* 1995; *The Country Life,* 1997; *A Life's Work: On Becoming a Mother,* 2001; *The Lucky Ones,* 2003, *Arlington Park,* 2006

Davis, Kenneth C.

Nonfiction writer

The playful titles of the books in the *Don't Know Much About* series are derived from the lyrics of "Wonderful World," a song co-written and recorded in the late 1950s by the soul artist Sam Cooke. Cooke famously sang, "Don't know much about history / Don't know much biology / Don't know much about a science book / Don't know much about the French I took / But I do know that I love you / And I know that if you love me too / What a wonderful world this would be." The series, which covers most of the topics mentioned in Cooke's enduring hit, plus many more, has been credited with bringing various academic topics to life with offbeat humor and contemporary references.

Kenneth C. Davis, the author of the series, was born in Mount Vernon, New York. According to the *Don't Know Much About* Web site, he "coasted through high school and never finished college." (He did attend Concordia College, in Bronxville, New York, and Fordham University at Lincoln Center, in New York City. In 1998 he was awarded an honorary doctorate from Concordia.) In a message posted on the Web site, Davis wrote, "When I was a teenager, I used to pose questions like this: 'Mom, can I borrow five bucks for a movie?' Or, 'May I get an extension on that term paper?' When Albert Einstein was a teenager, he asked, 'What would the world look like if I rode on a beam of light?' That's why Einstein rewrote the laws of physics and, thirty years after my school days, his question still leaves me scratching my head. The point is we all have questions— admittedly some are more interesting than others." In Davis's Web site message he explained that this

was the genesis of the pithy question-and-answer format that has made his books so popular. "The *Don't Know Much About* series is built around quirky, offbeat and occasionally irreverent questions—whether it means asking, What did Washington say when he crossed the Delaware? Why did Thomas Jefferson keep slaves? Where was the Garden of Eden? Or Was Jesus really born on Christmas? These questions are meant to spark the imagination and get people thinking in new ways, examining the easy assumptions we all hold. Underlying the [entire] series is the notion that learning should be a lot more interesting than it was for most of us back in school."

Davis began publishing the *Don't Know Much About* series in 1990, with *Don't Know Much About History.* That book spent more than 35 weeks on the *New York Times* best-seller list and sold more than a million copies. It was followed, in 1992, by *Don't Know Much About Geography,* another successful volume, with more than 400,000 copies sold. Since that time, the series has focused on the Bible, the Civil War, the Earth, and other such significant topics. Each volume has sold briskly.

While some reviewers found the tone of the books too flippant, others appreciated Davis's lighthearted but informative approach. In a review of *Don't Know Much About Mythology* (2005), for example, a critic wrote for *Publishers Weekly* (September 5, 2005, on-line), "What is a myth? How does it differ from legend, fairy tale and allegory? Do myths cross cultures? Davis answers these and many other questions with his characteristic humor and charming storytelling. He examines the myths created by societies ranging from Egypt, Greece and Rome to Africa, India and the Americas, proceeding, as in his other books, by way of question and answer as he surveys each mythmaking culture. . . . Because Davis ranges widely and with such sparkling wit through a broad sweep of myths, his survey provides a superb starting point for entering the world of mythology."

In 2001 Davis expanded his franchise to include picture books for elementary-school children and more sophisticated volumes for middle-schoolers. The first volumes in the elementary series covered the solar system and the 50 states in the union; the middle-school series covered outer space and the planet Earth. Subsequent volumes have dealt with the American presidents, pilgrims, English royalty, dinosaurs, and mummies. Davis has also written a series of biographies aimed at schoolchildren, covering such notable figures as George Washington, Sitting Bull, Abraham Lincoln, Rosa Parks, Thomas Jefferson, and Martin Luther King Jr. Recommending *Don't Know Much About the Presidents* (2002) as a good book to read on President's Day, Jane Clifford wrote for the *San Diego Union-Tribune* (February 18, 2007), "The facts that fill this slim volume will amaze as many adults as children."

Davis is a frequent guest at school assemblies across the country. During his presentations he hosts mock quiz shows that have proven highly popular with students. He serves as a contributing editor for *USA Weekend*, for which he provides weekly quizzes. His writing has appeared in the *New York Times*, the *San Francisco Chronicle*, and the *Washington Post*, among other publications. He is married to the book editor Joann Davis, with whom he has two children, Jenny and Colin. They have homes in New York City and Vermont.

—C.M.

Suggested Reading: *Don't Know Much About* Web site; *Publishers Weekly* (on-line) May 10, 1991, Aug. 24, 1992, Oct. 11, 1993, Sep. 14, 1998, July 30, 2001, Oct. 22, 2001, Jan. 7, 2002, Dec. 9, 2002, Mar. 15, 2003, Apr. 5, 2004, Sep. 5, 2005; *San Diego Union-Tribune* Books p5 Feb. 18, 2007; *Washington Post* C p14 Feb. 16, 2007

Selected Books: *Don't Know Much About History*, 1990; *Don't Know Much About Geography*, 1992: *Don't Know Much About the Civil War*, 1996; *Don't Know Much About the Bible*, 1998; *Don't Know Much About the Solar System*, 2001; *Don't Know Much About the Fifty States*, 2001; *Don't Know Much About Planet Earth*, 2001; *Don't Know Much About the Universe*, 2001; *Don't Know Much About Space*, 2001; *Don't Know Much About the Presidents*, 2002; *Don't Know Much About the Pilgrims*, 2002; *Don't Know Much About the Dinosaurs*, 2002; *Don't Know Much About Sitting Bull*, 2003; *Don't Know Much About George Washington*, 2003; *Don't Know Much About the Pioneers*, 2003; *Don't Know Much About Abraham Lincoln*, 2004; *Don't Know Much About Mythology*, 2005

Davis-Goff, Annabel

Feb. 19, 1942– Novelist; memoirist

"With the eye of an anthropologist," Alice Truax wrote for the *New York Times Book Review* (October 12, 2003), the author Annabel Davis-Goff "scrutinizes the world of the Anglo-Irish gentry in which she grew up, teasing apart its social fabric and holding up its various conventions for inspection." Truax's observation is borne out in the four successful books Davis-Goff has published over the last 15 years—the memoir *Walled Gardens: Scenes from an Anglo-Irish Childhood* and the novels *The Dower House*, *This Cold Country*, and *The Fox's Walk*—all of which expertly probe the customs, traditions, and social mores of 20th-century Ireland's so-called Anglo-Irish Ascendancy. Though she left Ireland as a teenager, living first in England then eventually emigrating to the U.S., Davis-Goff can never be said to have truly left her homeland, as she returns constantly to it in her work; she told Daphne Uviller for New York *Newsday* (September 7, 2003), "Of course I miss [Ireland], think about it, write about it. I can't write about America. I can't get that dispassionate, affectionate view I have of Ireland."

Annabel Davis-Goff was born on February 19, 1942 in County Waterford, in the Republic of Ireland, the first of four children of a "fox-hunting baronet and a wife 15 years his junior," as Michael Packenham wrote for the *New York Times Book Review* (September 24, 1989). With Irish independence, the Anglo-Irish Ascendancy, of which the Davis-Goffs were members, lost the last of their waning power. Thomas Mallon, writing for the *Washington Post* (April 19, 1998), quoted heavily from *The Dower House* in describing the Anglo-Irish of Davis-Goff's time "as 'not exactly English,' a small progeny of transplants and hybrids 'living on leftovers' and probably 'headed for extinction' in the new independent Irish republic. Success in their tight-knit world still requires 'a good seat on a horse, wit, nerves of steel about unpaid bills, the ability to hold large quantities of alcohol, a way with words, good enough circulation to live in large, cold houses, and the ability to eat awful food.'" The declining fortunes of the Davis-Goffs—and the Anglo-Irish in general—were reflected in the faded elegance of the author's upbringing. "Financially troubled," Pakenham wrote, "the family moved through a series of mildly decaying houses, all with gardens and most with grooms." Davis-Goff's first home, Glenville, was on the outskirts of Waterford; the family moved to Ballinaparka when Davis-Goff was 13.

An assortment of eccentric relatives provided the children with amusement, offering "strong opinions and curious histories," as Isabel Colegate wrote for the *Washington Post* (September 3, 1989). The children, for the most part, however, busied themselves. Davis-Goff told Uviller, "The entertainment of children was not a priority. . . . We didn't listen to the wireless or have television, and nobody was very interested in amusing us. . . . We read, [or] we played outside." The children spent much of their time riding horses and walking in the surrounding countryside. The cultural influence of the rest of the world was limited because Anglo-Irish children rarely even went to the movies, as their parents feared contact with typhoid or polio sufferers. (There were frequent outbreaks of those diseases in Ireland at the time.) In some ways that state of affairs helped Davis-Goff develop the depth of perception that has served her so well as a writer. "The author," Uviller explained, "attributes her own unwavering recall abilities to an absence of the hyperstimulation that riddles modern society. 'I remember, because I was paying attention [Davis-Goff stated]. We had no distractions.'" It was not an entirely idyllic childhood; her parents' marriage disintegrated gradually, and Davis-Goff has recalled meals eaten in "agonized silence."

Life in Ireland at that time did not present the opportunities or choices for girls that it now does, and higher education for female students was not as common as at present. Additionally, Davis-Goff lacked the proficiency in the Irish language necessary for either entrance to an Irish university or for some jobs. The education she had received, as she recalled to Uviller, "wouldn't have got me into even a third-rate university." Marriage or emigration seemed to be the choices available to her, but as she told Uviller, "there were about four Protestants geographically convenient, and none of them was terribly tempting." Moreover, the rituals designed to encourage pairing off between marriageable Anglo-Irish men and women were ineffective: "Three or four times a year," Davis-Goff recalled in *Walled Gardens*, as John Wyse Jackson quoted for the London *Sunday Times* (March 18, 1990), "we would change into not particularly becoming dresses, and, with home-curled hair, pale goose-pimpled arms and shoulders, we would have three or four hours to attract a lifetime mate. And, what's more, we were meant to do it while pretending we weren't." With no realistic marriage or university prospects, Davis-Goff opted instead for secretarial school and traveled, at the age of 17, across the Irish Sea to Oxford, England, to begin her training.

Upon completing her secretarial course, Davis-Goff moved to London, where she obtained a position "providing live audiences for bad television shows," as she told Uviller. She then found work in the booming British motion-picture industry, as a script supervisor. In the early 1970s, Davis-Goff relocated to the U.S. She then began writing and soon published two novels, *Night Tennis* (1978) and *Tailspin* (1980).

Published in 1989 by Alfred A. Knopf, *Walled Gardens: Scenes from an Anglo-Irish Childhood* first brought Davis-Goff to widespread attention.

The memoir describes not only Davis-Goff's childhood but provides an evocative portrait of a time and place. The work, Davis-Goff told Uviller, "started without a plan. When my son was little and he had difficulty going to sleep, I used to sit up on the landing outside his room and write down everything I remembered. I don't know why I did it. I would start with a great-aunt and write about her. Then summers at the seaside with my grandmother." The story begins as Davis-Goff returns to Ireland for her father's funeral; the situation provides the impetus for a prolonged reminiscence on her childhood. Going further back in family history, she described the life of an ancestor, William Goffe, a member of Cromwell's parliament and signatory of Charles I's death warrant who, following the Restoration of the Stuarts in 1660, fled to America. The book recounts the life of the regicide who, with a price on his head, spent the rest of his life in hiding. The end of the memoir describes a visit with her children to a cave in Connecticut where Goffe hid. He died without ever seeing his family again. (The book includes an extract from a touching letter from Goffe to his wife.) Colegate wrote, "The author conveys brilliantly the inexplicable clarity of certain childhood recollections, and her descriptions of places and people are evocative, sometimes moving and sometimes very funny." "*Walled Gardens*," Michael Pakenham wrote, "is a book that does not make you laugh aloud, or cry. It is a book that, in fact, resolutely, explicitly denies you either of those purgations or privileges. In that denial is the soul of the work. . . . The book's joys, lean and simple, are the wordless chant of survival."

In 1996 Davis-Goff edited *The Literary Companion to Gambling*, a compilation of poetry and prose examining the use of gambling as a metaphor in literature. She published her next book, the novel *The Dower House*, in 1998. The work was chosen as a New York Times Notable Book of the Year—as were her two subsequent novels—and was named one of the ten best novels of the year by the *New York Post*. The book's main characters are Molly Hassard and her cousin Sophie, Anglo-Irish girls who come of age during the 1950s. Sophie marries into a rich English bourgeois family and proceeds to spend her husband's money with fierce abandon; Jacqueline Carey wrote for the *New York Times Book Review* (March 15, 1998) that Sophie provides "a sympathetic, convincing portrait of a conflicted woman whose choice brings no one any real happiness." Molly, orphaned early in the novel, is undemanding and self-effacing. While still an adolescent, she falls secretly and painfully in love with a neighbor who is struggling to keep his family land intact. Despairing of gaining his love, or even attention, she joins Sophie in London, where she is bewildered by the changing world of the 1960s. "If Davis-Goff insists a bit too often on the particularity of this milieu [the Anglo-Irish in general]," Thomas Mallon wrote for the *Washington Post* (April 19, 1998), "one cannot deny its vividness, any more than one can miss the full development and sympathy of the characters she has created." Mallon termed Davis-Goff "a find," and added, "*The Dower House* may depict a damp and worn-out world, but the novel itself stays crisp and invigorating."

In *This Cold Country* (2002), Daisy Creed, a young English woman, falls in love with an Anglo-Irish soldier named Patrick Nugent who is serving in the British armed forces during World War II. "After prolonged exposure to Patrick's friends and family," however, as Alida Becker observed for the *New York Times Book Review* (June 16, 2002), "[Daisy] has become painfully aware 'that people lived with secrets, small guilts, with shame.' The problem is, 'she hadn't thought she would be one of them.'" Becker offered considerable praise for the book and for Davis-Goff, stating, "Crisply and gracefully, and with her habitual wry empathy, she [Davis-Goff] shows us how Daisy comes to a singular discovery: that while loneliness can contort or destroy her ties to other people, it can have the opposite effect on her feelings about her surroundings."

Much of the inspiration for Davis-Goff's next novel, *The Fox's Walk* (2003), arose from her mother's memories of growing up during World War I. In the book the 1965 reburial of the Irish republican hero Roger Casement, executed and interred by the British during that war, serves as the catalyst for a long recollection by the protagonist, Alice Moore. Just after the war's outbreak, nine-year-old Alice is left by her parents to live with her grandmother and great-aunt in a declining house in the Irish countryside. Alice, as Daphne Uviller wrote, "lurks around the crumbling estate of Ballydavid, making endearingly methodical attempts to decode adult conversation, trying earnestly to make sense of family and national politics." A reviewer for *Publishers Weekly* (August 25, 2003) observed, "With deft assurance, Davis-Goff conveys the complex social order of the Anglo-Irish hierarchy, in which class, religion and political thought, heretofore stratified, are undergoing vital challenges."

Davis-Goff has two children, a daughter named Jenny and a son named Max, by her former husband, the acclaimed movie director Mike Nichols. She currently teaches at Bennington College, in Vermont.

—P.B.M.

Suggested Reading: Annabel Davis-Goff's Web site; *New York Times* VII p20 Sep. 24, 1989; (New York) *Newsday* D p47 Sep. 7, 2003; *Washington Post* X p1 Sep. 3, 1989

Selected Books: nonfiction—*Walled Gardens: Scenes from an Anglo-Irish Childhood*, 1989; fiction—*The Dower House*, 1998; *This Cold Country*, 2002; *The Fox's Walk*, 2003

Courtesy of Bloomsbury

Dawson, Jill

Apr. 8, 1962– Novelist; poet; editor

Jill Dawson's protagonists are often women trying to transform their lives—sometimes successfully, sometimes not. Her novels include: *Trick of the Light* (1996), in which a young woman living on public assistance in England moves to a remote area of the American West with her abusive lover and their child; *Magpie* (1998), in which a single mother from Yorkshire acquires a Jamaican lover and learns to live prudently but exuberantly; and *Fred & Edie* (2000), the tale, based on a real-life court case, of a woman who is tried and hanged for a murder in which she might not have been involved. Dawson's next novel, *Wild Boy* (2003), is also based on a true story—that of a 12-year-old boy who was discovered living alone in the woods near Aveyron, France, in the 19th century. With her latest book, *Watch Me Disappear* (2006), Dawson once again employs a female main character—Tina Humber, who returns to her childhood home in the fens of Great Britain for her brother's wedding, only to be visited by disturbing memories. Dawson has also conducted interviews with young British women, published in *How Do I Look?* (1990), and compiled such anthologies as *School Tales* (1990), *The Virago Book of Wicked Verse* (1992), *The Virago Book of Love Letters* (1994), and, with Margo Daly, *Wild Ways: New Stories about Women on the Road* (1998). Her poetry chapbook *White Fish with Painted Nails* was published in 1994.

Jill Dawson was born on April 8, 1962. She attended the Boston Spa School, in West Yorkshire, and received a degree in American studies from Nottingham University, in 1983. In 1996 she was awarded an M.A. degree in writing (with distinction) from Sheffield Hallam University. She is the recipient of an honorary doctorate from Anglia Ruskin University, in England.

Dawson provided the following account of her life and work to *World Authors 2000–2005:*

"I was born in County Durham in the North of England to bright parents who had come from a mining background. That part of the UK has a very strong mining tradition and a strong regional dialect too but I didn't pick this up as we'd moved away before I was two. I always have trouble telling British people where I'm 'from' as we moved around quite a lot—from a new town in Staffordshire (the Midlands) to a Southern suburb to a Yorkshire village, because of my father's job. He was an engineer, educating himself in the evenings, bettering himself. All of these places signify a certain class, a certain background of course to other British people and mine was always subtly shifting. People, I imagined, found it hard to place me. Even my accent kept changing. I mention this because class feels like an undercurrent in all my writing and my decision to be a writer—if decision isn't too strong a word for the slow journey I took—was something to do with daring.

"In an early poem I wrote about feeling 'like a girl too big for my boots' and that was definitely a message I picked up from somewhere. Women writers I pictured as blue-stockinged Oxbridge types. Virginia Woolf and Jane Austen. But by some stroke of luck I chose to study American literature at Nottingham University rather than English and had my eyes opened to other possibilities by Faulkner, Twain, Kate Chopin, Zora Neale Hurston, Alice Walker, Toni Morrison. . . . At 18 I studied for a term (semester) at Carroll College, Wisconsin, and began a lifelong love affair with America and American literature. I've since had several extended trips to the States, including a term teaching at Amherst College, Massachusetts, in 1997.

"My first novel (published in 1996), *Trick of the Light,* tells the story of a young English girl who goes to live in Washington state in a log cabin in the middle of nowhere (as I did in 1992, having won a poetry prize which funded me for six months). Although the landscape is dazzlingly beautiful, Rita, the protagonist, hasn't really faced up to the violence in her relationship with Mick and the risk that she and her small daughter are exposed to. This novel has been optioned for a film. At times it was painful to write as I really wanted to look at what keeps women in violent relationships. Rita is quite a tough character who thinks she can 'take on' Mick and finds it hard to admit defeat. I did feel as if I turned myself inside out to find Rita. But Margaret Atwood said once in an interview that 'to assume everything a woman writes is autobiographical denies her imagination' and I like that quote. I do find it limiting to always talk of fiction as if it were disguised autobiography. The thing I like to research, to feel is realistic in my fiction, is the landscape, the place. I did a lot of research for *Fred & Edie,* set in Ilford, a commuter suburb just outside of London in 1922. The previous novel (my second), *Magpie,* was set in East London—Hackney—an area I lived in for 11 years.

"My favourite quote about writing is Katherine Mansfield. When asked why write? she answered: why breathe? That sums it up for me. I don't know. I can't help it. Because I have to. And also, most of all, in order to live."

Trick of the Light was nominated for a Betty Trask Award, given to a book of a romantic or traditional nature written by an author under 35. Graham Lord, one of the Trask judges, wrote for the London *Times* (July 13, 1996): "[This] is a moving, beautifully written tale, taut with narrative tension and memorable for its superb descriptions of landscape and a multitude of deft touches that always seem just right. Above all, this is a genuinely romantic novel." Lord warned that *Trick of the Light* was sexually explicit and contained a liberal sprinkling of four-letter words, but noted, "What makes the book memorable is that all this foulness seems absolutely right in the context of the story and that, far from diminishing the romantic nature of the novel, it actually enhances it. For the book is about love as well as lust, and love can be [startlingly] physical and violent."

Magpie received even more effusive praise and won for Dawson the London Arts Board New Writer Award. Christina Koning wrote for the London *Times* (November 7, 1998), "A novel about a single mother coping with poverty and lonliness on an east London council estate sounds like a depressing read; in fact, Jill Dawson's latest is anything but. . . . Dawson takes this unpromising material and turns it into compelling drama, full of subtle observation and wry humour, which engages the reader's sympathies. One of the reasons for the book's success is its likeable central character; another is the truthfulness and sensitivity with which it depicts ordinary life." A reviewer for the London *Mail on Sunday* (November 15, 1998) agreed, writing that the book was "a crackling page-turner of a novel, written with consummate skill and feeling."

While *Trick of the Light* and *Magpie* had bought Dawson some critical attention, that attention increased exponentially with the publication of *Fred & Edie,* which was short-listed for two prestigious literary prizes: the Orange Prize and the Whitbread Novel of the Year title. (It was also on the long list for a Dublin IMPAC award.) *Fred & Edie* was based on the case of Freddy Bywaters and his lover, Edith Thompson, who were hanged in 1923 for the killing of Edith's husband, Percy. Freddy had stabbed his rival but insisted he had planned the murder with no help from Edith. The jurors, who were shown love letters written by Edith to Freddy, were scandalized by her adultery and ordered her to be executed along with him— despite uncertainty as to the extent of her involvement. The case has since spawned several books, movies, and television shows. Of Dawson's book, John McCrystal wrote for the *New Zealand Herald* (September 30, 2001), "This is a dazzling novel, gripping and moving. It reminds the reader of how far we have come as a society, at the same time as it raises awareness of unsettling resonances." Similarly, in a review for the *Hartford Courant* (December 2, 2001), M. A. Turner wrote, "*Fred & Edie* is a well-written and engrossing novel that embraces the voyeuristic appeal of its subject and then takes it to a higher, smarter level."

The real-life case of Victor, a feral child found wandering about in the woods near Saint Sernin sur Rance, in southern France, at the turn of the 19th century, provided the inspiration for Dawson's next book, *Wild Boy*. About 12 years old at the time of his discovery, Victor couldn't speak and was covered in scars, prompting authorities to theorize that he had been abandoned by his parents years before. Amanda Craig wrote for *New Statesman* (October 13, 2003), "Dawson is faithful to what can be imagined from the facts. Her novel, suffused with wisdom and a compassion for each of her main characters, only just misses being of the very first rank. . . . She will only get the readership she deserves [however] when she delivers the consolations of fairy tales as well as their real-life shadows." A reviewer for the London *Independent* (July 16, 2004) called the book "persuasive and thought provoking" and described certain scenes as " heartbreaking." *Wild Boy* was the first novel ever to be long-listed for the British Academy Book Prize, awarded to a work that makes scholarly ideas accessible to laypeople. (Dawson had originally read about Victor when she was researching Aspberger's Syndrome, a mild form of autism. Her older son, Lewis, whom she was then raising as a single mother, had been diagnosed with the condition.)

In Dawson's latest novel, *Watch Me Disappear*, a woman returns to her hometown to attend her brother's wedding and while there is haunted by the long-ago disappearance of her best childhood friend. The book was placed on the long list for the Orange Prize, and although it did not make it onto the short list, critics found it undeniably praiseworthy. Christina Koning, in an assessment for the London *Times* (January 27, 2007), called it "powerfully absorbing and impossible to put down," and a review for the London *Mail on Sunday* (January 7, 2007), lauded the novel's combination of "seat-edge psychological drama with vivid reflections on the mysteries of memory and childhood."

In addition to Lewis, Dawson has another son, Felix. She is married to Meredith Bowles, an architect, who designed the family's home near Ely, a cathedral city in east England.

—S.Y.

Suggested Reading: *Booklist* p2,112 Aug. 1991; *Hartford Courant* G p3 Dec. 2, 2001; (London) *Guardian* p2 June 8, 1999, T p8 July 14, 1999; (London) *Independent* p27 July 16, 2004; (London) *Mail on Sunday* p70 Jan. 7, 2007; (London) *Observer* p16 Nov. 4, 2001; (London) *Times* p1 July 13, 1996, p19 Nov. 7, 1998, p17 Aug. 26, 2000, p14 Jan. 27, 2007; *Marie Claire* (on-line) May 2000; *Publishers Weekly* p53 Aug. 20, 2001

Selected Books: poetry—*White Fish with Painted Nails*, 1994; fiction—*Trick of the Light*, 1996; *Magpie*, 1998; *Fred & Edie*, 2000; *Wild Boy*, 2003; *Watch Me Disappear*, 2006; as editor— *How Do I Look?*, 1990; *School Tales*, 1990; *The Virago Book of Wicked Verse*, 1992; *The Virago Book of Love Letters*, 1994; *Wild Ways: New Stories about Women on the Road* (with Margo Daly), 1998; *Gas and Air: Stories about Childbirth*, 2002

Dé, Shobhaa

(DAY, SHO-ba)

1948– Novelist; nonfiction writer

Shobhaa Dé has established herself as India's most commercially successful English-language author with a series of steamy novels that have often drawn comparisons to the work of the American writer Jackie Collins. She has also been widely denounced in her traditionally conservative country, where the graphic depictions of sex in her work have earned her the nicknames "the Maharani of Muck," "the Princess of Porn," and "the Queen of Quickies." Much of the criticism has been aimed at the way women in her novels are portrayed. "Her women characters come out on top through sex or manipulation. It's just soft porn," Rita Dewan, a professor of gender economics at a university in Mumbai, told Miranda Kennedy for the *Nation* (May 27, 2004). Dé defends her female characters, describing them as strong and not just sexual. "The women in my books are definitely not doormats. They're not willing to be kicked around," she told Ajay Singh in an on-line interview for *Asiaweek* (February 28, 1997). However, even her harshest critics cannot disregard the impact she has had on India's female population. "Writing about somebody dropping a sari and having an orgasm doesn't mean you're striking big notes for women," the film critic Shubra Gupta told Kennedy, "But she is India's

Sebastian D'Souza/AFP/Getty Images

Shobhaa Dé

first and only glamorous female brand name, and that means something." Ultimately, Dé is less concerned by reviewers' remarks than she is about her audience. "I think I know my readers better than the critics know them," she told Samita Bhatia for the Calcutta *Telegraph* (February 26, 2005, on-line). Dé's books consistently appear at the top of India's best-seller lists, and in 2003 she was named by Penguin India as part of its 10,000 Club, for authors whose books have sold more than 10,000 copies each. Ten of Dé's books have sold 10,000 copies or more and are still in print. Her fellow club members include such esteemed writers as Vikram Seth, Yann Martel, and Arundhati Roy.

Shobhaa Dé was born Shobha Rajadhyaksha in 1948 in Maharashtra, India. The youngest of four children in a middle-class family, she was raised in Bombay from the age of eight. Her father was a bureaucrat who was based in Delhi for many years. Dé attended Queen Mary School and St. Xavier's College, a Jesuit school in Bombay, from which she graduated with a degree in psychology. Upon graduation, Dé decided to begin modeling. Although her conservative parents opposed her career choice, Dé's promise that she would not dress in revealing outfits, pose with male models, or do anything to embarrass the family changed their minds. By the time she was 21, Dé had risen to the top ranks of the modeling world. After a few years of modeling, however, she began working briefly as a copywriter for Hira's Creative Unit, an advertising agency founded by the publishing tycoon Nari Hira. In 1970 Hira offered Dé the position of editor of *Stardust* magazine, despite her lack of editorial experience. Patterned after

Hollywood gossip publications, *Stardust* reported on the rich and famous in Bollywood, as India's best-known film sector is known. As editor Dé popularized the use of Hinglish, a combination of English and Bombay Hindi. Following her 10-year stint at *Stardust*, Dé moved to another gossip magazine, *Society*, in the same capacity. In 1982 she launched *Celebrity*, an Indian version of the British magazine *Hello!*, which was itself an offshoot of the famous Spanish publication *Hola!*.

Dé, who had been married once before, married the widower Dilip Dé, a Mumbai-based shipping mogul of Bengali origin, shortly after meeting him at a 1984 party. "Dilip proposed to me in just 10 minutes," she told Singh. "I made up my mind in four days." A year after her marriage, she sold *Celebrity*. She continued to write for prominent Indian periodicals while raising her six children (four boys and two girls—two from her first marriage, two from Dilip Dé's previous marriage, and the remaining two from her marriage with Dé).

In 1988 Dé's life changed dramatically with a knock at the door at her $3 million penthouse overlooking the Arabian Sea. As she recounted to Singh, "There was this hunk of a man standing there. He asked me to write a nonfiction book about Bombay." The man turned out to be David Davidar, the former editor and publisher of the Penguin Group's Indian division and current publisher of Penguin Group Canada. Dé reluctantly agreed to the project, and within three and a half months, she had completed not a nonfiction work but a novel, written in longhand at her kitchen table. "I was like a woman possessed. I just wrote and wrote until it was done," she told Singh. The work, her first novel, was called *Socialite Evenings* (1989), the tale of a middle-class girl's rise into Bombay's high society based on Dé's own social circle. The book became an instant best-seller among the urban middle-class in her native country, selling 40,000 copies, a considerable triumph by Indian standards. (In India, publishers of English-language novels break even financially when they sell 2,000 copies.) However, Dé drew criticism for writing about sex and adultery, which literary reviewers charged bordered on the pornographic. As quoted in a piece by Edward A. Gargan for the *New York Times* (January 17, 1993), the freelance journalist Geeta Doctor, writing for the *Indian Review of Books*, opined, "Penguin India, who have published Ms. Dé's books, should feel proud of themselves. Instead of merely aiming to produce good literature as we have been led to expect, they have decided to put themselves in the service of the country, masturbating the nation." The article also included comments by Dilip Roate for the *Economic Times*, who described Dé's writing as "coarse, without class." He complained, "The two or three scenes of the kind that are described by mental juveniles as 'torrid' are narrated with the elegance of a bullying lout bragging about his conquests." Dé countered, telling Gargan, "It wasn't that explicit. It explored adultery, women walking out of marriages because they were bored. People found that shocking."

Some critics, including male members of Bombay's high society, were also less than enthusiastic about Dé's second novel, *Starry Nights* (1991). The reviewer S. Nihal Singh was quoted in the *Chicago Tribune* (February 7, 1993) as saying of the novel's protagonist, "We have a heroine, of the films and of the novel, who lives on a diet of men for breakfast, lunch and dinner, and sometimes in between. Four-letter words come thick and fast from those sharing her bed, among others." The book was groundbreaking for its unflinching look at India's film industry and its portrayal of a strong, sexual female protagonist. Miranda Kennedy wrote, "*Starry Nights* provided the first long-form, unflattering portrait of Bollywood. . . . The Hindi film industry, far more than Hollywood, has been reluctant to expose its dirty underbelly, because it relies heavily on family-oriented films and the pristine image of virgin stars. Dé has made it one of her life's missions to blow a hole in those perceptions."

Sisters (1992), her follow-up to *Starry Nights*, focused on the battle between two half-sisters for control of their father's industrial empire and continued to explore strong, sexually liberated female characters, this time set against the backdrop of big business. She pushed the envelope even further with *Strange Obsession* (1994), broaching the subject of a love relationship between two female characters, a topic rarely covered in South Asian literature and considered taboo in Indian society. (Though it is rarely enforced, part of the Indian penal code makes any homosexual act illegal and punishable with life imprisonment.) Simran Bhargava wrote for the New Delhi *Pioneer* on January 9, 1993, as reprinted in the *New York Times* (January 17, 1993), "I couldn't put down Shobha Dé's new book, *Strange Obsession*. And I didn't even like it." Dé's next two books prompted similarly mixed responses. In her fifth novel, *Sultry Days* (1995), Dé tackled the romance between a teenager and a man named God amid the world of journalism; *Second Thoughts* (1996) focused on a middle-class housewife trapped in an arranged marriage who enters into an adulterous relationship.

Although many have characterized her books as second rate or non-literary, Dé told Alexandre M. Barbosa for *Goa Today* (January 1988), "I really don't care about labels and definitions. These are the books I have within me; they are the books I want to write and anybody is free to call it whatever they wish to. I don't like to categorise them. It is contemporary writing." However, the impact of her writing cannot be overlooked. Today, four of her books (*Socialite Evenings*, *Starry Nights*, *Sisters*, and *Strange Obsession*) are part of a prestigious post-graduate, popular-culture course at the University of London's School of Oriental and African Studies and part of the curriculum at universities in Chicago, Illinois, and

Sydney, Australia. The University of Mumbai has also selected *Starry Nights* as a required text. In addition, college students have submitted dissertations on her books.

Dé ventured into the world of nonfiction with the release of her book *Surviving Men: The Smart Woman's Guide to Staying on Top* (1997), a radical departure from the sexual exploits depicted in her previous works. The book, which explored the difficulties faced by women balancing careers and marriage in a male-dominated society, struck a chord with a large number of Indian women who were starting to work outside the home. On a *Voice of America* program aired on January 23, 1997, Dé argued that the book was not an attempt to bash the opposite sex. "I believe Indian women have changed qualitatively, and are part of the modern world, and ready for the new millennium. But the Indian male is still in the 15th or 16th century, very medieval and refusing to be shaken out of this torpor." Dé next published *Speedpost: Letters to My Children about Living, Loving, Caring and Coping with the World* (1999), which touched on family values and adolescent anxieties, written in the form of a series of letters to her six children. "The letters were a literary device to raise certain issues. It was my way of marking [the new millennium]. And my kids loved it too," she told Subha J. Rao for the national Indian newspaper the *Hindu* (February 10, 2003). The book has found a large audience and has been translated into Hindi (the official language of India) and Marathi (spoken mainly in the Indian state of Maharashtra and in the central part of the country), with upcoming versions in Malayalam (spoken by about 35 million people, mainly in southwest India) and Gujarati (the official language of the Indian state of Gujarat on the country's west coast, spoken by about 40 million people). She continued to distance herself from her pop-fiction work with her next effort, the autobiographical *Selective Memory: Stories from My Life* (1999), which openly discusses how she abandoned her first husband, a member of the wealthy Kilachand family, and two eldest children, with whom she has since reconciled.

In 2001 Dé chose to take a break from writing books. "At that time I felt the pressing need to slow down and to do different things," she told Samita Bhatia. She turned her attention to television and became a writer for the serials *Swahbhimaan*, *Sukanya*, and *Lipstick*. She also conceptualized and wrote for the defunct serial *Kittie Party*, which aired on Zee TV. Dé explained to Seema Pherwani in an on-line interview for *Indian Television* (October 20, 2004), "Television writing is an extremely stimulating experience for me. But it's all about being disciplined, as you have to write about eight to nine scenes for each episode." She also embraced her spiritual side in 2003, adding an extra "a" to the end of her first name on the advice of a numerologist.

Dé's debut in front of the television cameras came in 2004 with the prime-time program *Power Trip*, which gave viewers an inside look into the lives of leading men and women in the corporate world. Besides her anchor duties, Dé was also responsible for the research, content, and look of the show, which was canceled after 28 episodes.

Dé returned from her self-imposed sabbatical from writing books with the release of the nonfiction work *Spouse: The Truth about Marriage* (2005), written in longhand on 11 lined notepads over the course of eight months. "Other people watch birds, I watch marriages," she told Dilip Bobb for *India Today* (February 28, 2005). The book asserts that despite the racy content of her earlier novels, Dé considers herself a staunch traditionalist. "I am glad that I have cleared the confusion between real life and fiction. In real life, I have never been anything else but consistent," she said to Madhumita Bhattacharyya for the Calcutta *Telegraph* (March 19, 2005). The book sold more than 10,000 copies in just three days and a record-breaking 22,000 copies in one month. Its success has been attributed to the sharp increase in the number of divorces among young urban Indians—which was ultimately what spurred her to write the book. Unlike her earlier works, *Spouse: The Truth about Marriage* received favorable reviews from the literary set. As Bobb wrote, "There is the all-important issue of sex but again, she dissects this clinically, with intelligence and understanding. As someone who has performed a delicate balancing act between her career, husband, children, and friends, Dé is uniquely qualified to write on what makes a marriage work and what doesn't. She is quick to admit that this is not a how-to book and that there is no magic formula. Yet there is enough insight, examples and analyses, including self-analysis, that *Spouse* should be an essential wedding gift for all Indian couples."

Although Dé is not the first female novelist in India to write about sex, she is credited with taking sex out of the closet and making it an open topic of discussion among the women in her country. Despite the strong women's voices in her novels, Dé refuses to categorize them as feminist works. "My books try to find ways that women can survive and cope in a world that's cruel to them," she told Kennedy. "But I tell stories in an entertaining format. I am not doing a Germaine Greer or Betty Friedan [noted North American feminists]. It's not just get up and fight for your rights; it is more sly and subversive."

In her current position as consulting editor for fiction at Penguin India, Dé works primarily with first-time authors and women's fiction. She is also a freelance writer and columnist for several newspapers and magazines, including the *Times of India*, the *Statesman*, and the *Sunday Observer*. (Her advice columns in the *Bombay Times*, the *Sunday Times*, and the *Week* have a readership of 25 million each month.) Her latest television serial, *Sarrkkar*, debuted on April 25, 2005. The show is about a woman caught between family obligations and the power games thrust upon her by high-level politics. Although Dé has generally enjoyed her celebrity status in India, one disturbing consequence has been the inordinate amount of attention paid to her by one specific fan—a woman who had been stalking her for 25 years before being arrested in May 2005.

In 2006 Dé renewed her interest in the fashion industry, launching her own label, Serendipity. The clothing line features rich brocades and other traditional handiwork from India. "In Italy recently I was being bombarded with statements about the brilliance of garments from Versace and others and I told them that nothing can better the elegance of the saree—it is the most perfect piece of garment and the West still does not have an answer to that," she told a reporter for Business Line (September 26, 2006). "Indian fashion does not need to look to the West for inspiration. We have to look inwards at our old traditions of weaving and embroidery and colours and establish ourselves just as the Japanese or Chinese have taken pride in their textile traditions. There is no point trying to be the poor man's [Roberto] Cavalli."

Dé still prefers to write her columns and books in longhand form, from her home. "I love the feel of pen on paper. I have to see the work in my own writing to believe it is mine," she explained to Subha J. Rao. "Writing is a passion that I can never give up. The day things cease to excite, life is over. I don't want that to happen to me."

—B.M.

Suggested Reading: *Asiaweek* (on-line) Feb. 28, 1997; (Calcutta) *Telegraph* Feb. 26, 2005; *Hindu* Feb. 10, 2003; *India Today* p85 Feb. 28, 2005; *Nation* June 14, 2004; *New York Times* IX p3 Jan. 17, 1993; Penguin Books India Web site

Selected Books: fiction—*Socialite Evenings*, 1989; *Starry Nights*, 1991; *Sisters*, 1992; *Strange Obsession*, 1994; *Sultry Days*, 1995; *Second Thoughts*, 1996; nonfiction—*Surviving Men: The Smart Woman's Guide to Staying on Top*, 1997; *Speedpost: Letters to My Children about Living, Loving, Caring and Coping with the World*, 1999; *Selective Memory: Stories from My Life*, 1999; *Spouse: The Truth about Marriage*, 2005

de Botton, Alain

Dec. 20, 1969– Novelist; nonfiction writer

In his three novels, *On Love* (1993, published in Great Britain as *Essays in Love*), *The Romantic Movement: Sex, Shopping, and the Novel* (1994), and *Kiss & Tell* (1996), the Swiss-born English writer Alain de Botton delved so deeply into philosophy and abstract sociology for his tales about the course of modern love that it became clear that philosophy was his true metier. His next books—*How Proust Can Change Your Life: Not a Novel* (1997), *The Consolations of Philosophy* (2000), *The Art of Travel* (2002), *Status Anxiety* (2004), and *The Architecture of Happiness* (2005) provide a way for readers to insert their own concerns into the theories, philosophies, and even great novelistic renderings of life propounded by such minds as Marcel Proust, Friedrich Nietzsche, Gustave Flaubert, and Socrates, among others.

Alain de Botton contributed, in 2003, the following self-interview to *World Authors 2000–2005*:

"Q. How do you describe yourself? A writer or philosopher?

"A. I don't feel comfortable with the standard categories that writers are slotted into; novelist or poet or historian etc. I like writing what could best be called essays—with a personal voice, but concerned with the great topics of life. The people who have inspired me are: La Rochefoucauld, his *Maxims*; Milan Kundera, *The Book of Laughter and Forgetting*; Cyril Connolly, *The Unquiet Grave*; Stendhal, *On Love*; Roland Barthes, *S/Z*; Nicholson Baker, *U and I*. All of these books are genre-breaking. That's what I'm drawn to.

"Q. Tell us about your first real success, or your first real failure, and how they affected you.

"A. My first real success was publishing my book *On Love* at the age of 23. It was a huge bestseller around Europe. I bought a car as a result, and then an apartment. I thought I'd be happy—I was for a while, but then reality set in again.

"Q. What was the best or worst job you've ever had, and how did it affect your writing career?

"A. I was motoring correspondent for a magazine in London called the *Tatler*. I got to drive lots of big new cars. It came to an unfortunate end when I crashed one into a lamppost. There were no injuries, apart from my job prospects in that field.

"Q. Why do you write?

"A. A few years ago, I was browsing in a bookshop in Paris when my eye was caught by a quote on the cover of a paperback: 'To be psychologically alive means either being in love, or in psychoanalysis, or in the spell of literature.' The book was called *Tales of Love*, it was written by the psychoanalyst Julia Kristeva and because I had always liked her first name (I'd been in love with a little one with glasses at nine), I bought the book. Unfortunately, Julia let me down badly, for in over 300 pages, she did nothing to elaborate on the fascinating sentence that her publisher had so cunningly placed on the back cover. Still, the thought seemed valuable and stayed with me: of an important connection between love and reading, of a comparable pleasure offered by both. A feeling of connection may be at the root of it. There are books which speak to us, no less eloquently—but more reliably—than our lovers. It explains why literature is such a consolation when love has failed.

"The idea that we are not alone in the world is a cosy one. Nevertheless, there is a darker side: we still like to feel special, to feel unique, and this is not something literature suggests we in fact are. Take the following: 'Some people would never have fallen in love if they had not heard there was such a thing.' I recall reading this gem from La Rochefoucauld on a flight between London and Edinburgh. 'For God's sake, that's my idea!' was my immediate response, and I stared crossly out at the window at the cottony Midlands. 'He's stolen my thought.' But it seemed unlikely, given that he was born in the spring of 1613 and I in 1969, so more generously, I reflected, 'Maybe I've stolen it from him'—equally impossible, given that I had until then never laid eyes on the maxims. It suggested an answer at once humbling and ennobling: that both La Rochefoucauld and I have lived in the same world, and could hence at times be expected to think roughly the same thoughts, even though he's a genius and I am not (La Rochefoucauld would immediately have picked up on the self-pity in this last comment, and could well have squashed it with a withering: 'There are few people more convinced of their own genius than those who complain of how stupid they are.')

"Q. Is writing clearly very important to you?

"A. For centuries now, serious objections have been levelled at the way that academics write books and express themselves. Of course, attacking academic obscurity has something of the ease of firing that proverbial rifle at barrelled fish. One might more generously ask why human beings have such an appetite for obscurity in the first place, as readers and writers. Perhaps because so many important subjects present challenges to the intellect and do not reveal their secrets when skip-read in the bath, it is natural that an association should be formed between what is difficult and what is serious. Science presents the most impressive example of ideas that are both hard to understand and still correct—and it is in part due to our awe of the powers of science that we may form a general belief that the more obscure a book, the more profound it must be—its impassibility seems to guarantee its value, its intelligibility its shallowness. How easy then to exploit the ambiguity, playing on the prestige of difficulty without having earned the right to it.

"Q. Why did you decide to write about philosophy?

Courtesy of Charlotte de Botton

Alain de Botton

"A. In a secular age, philosophy looks like the ultimate authority on life's great questions, the natural place to seek answers to the riddles of human unhappiness. Philosophers, like rocket scientists, look as if they have access to some very complex and important truths. But despite an enticing exterior, philosophy often disappoints those who study it more closely. Issues that seem so urgent to many philosophers (is this a table? what is a sentence?) don't often echo our own priorities (why am I so shy? am I in the right job?). Were it not for politeness and an ingrained respect for learning, novices might be tempted to declare the subject bunk and throw their books out of the window. Which would be a pity, because philosophy is like a lobster—with an impenetrable outer shell, certain dark sections that should be left untouched, but also more nourishing flesh which can be hardest to reach. *The Consolations of Philosophy* aims to do for philosophy what a claw-cracker and a long cleft probe can do for lobster-consumption.

"Q. What's the point of your latest book, *The Art of Travel*?

"A. For most of us, when we think of how to be happy, we think of one (or all) of three things: falling in love, finding satisfaction at work and going travelling. But the reality of travel seldom matches our daydreams. The tragi-comic disappointments are well-known: the disorientation, the mid-afternoon despair, the lethargy before ancient ruins. And yet the reasons behind such disappointments are rarely explored. *The Art of Travel* is an attempt to tackle the curious business of travelling—why do we do it? What are we trying to get out of it? In a series of essays, I write about airports, landscapes, museums, holiday romances, photographs, exotic carpets and the contents of hotel mini-bars. I mix my own thoughts about travel with those of some great figures of the past: Edward Hopper, Baudelaire, Wordsworth, Van Gogh and Ruskin among them. The result is a work which, unlike existing guidebooks on travel, actually asks what the point of travel might be—and modestly suggests how we could learn to be happier on our journeys.

"Q. What then are some of the reasons why our travels go awry?

"A. Well, we won't just be in India/South Africa/Australia/Prague/Peru in a direct, unmediated way, we'll be there with ourselves, still imprisoned in our own bodies and minds—with all the problems this entails. I remember a trip to Barbados a few years ago. I looked forward to it for months, I anticipated a beautiful hotel on the shores of a sandy beach (as pictured in a glossy brochure called 'Winter Sun'). But on my first morning on the island, I realised something at once obvious and surprising: that I had brought my body with me and that, because of a fateful arrangement in the human constitution, my interaction with the island was critically to depend on its co-operation. The body proved a temperamental partner. Asked to sit on a deckchair so that the mind could savour the beach, the trees, and the sun, it collapsed into difficulties; the ears complained of an enervating wind, the skin of stickiness, and the toes of sand lodged between them. After 10 minutes, the entire machine threatened to faint. Unfortunately, I had brought something else that risked clouding my appreciation of my surroundings: my entire mind—not only the aesthetic lobe (that had planned the journey and agreed to pay for it), but also the part committed to anxiety, boredom, melancholy, self-disgust and financial alarm.

"Q. What else goes wrong when we travel?

"A. Another great problem of vacations is that they rob us of one of the important comforts of daily life: the expectation that things won't be perfect. We are therefore prone to be not only miserable on our travels—but miserable about the fact that we are miserable. I remember a trip to a hotel in France with my girlfriend. The setting was sublime, the room flawless—and yet we managed to have a row which, for all the good the room and setting did us, meant that we might as well have stayed at home. Our row (it started with who had forgotten the key in the room and extended to cover the whole of our relationship) was a reminder of the rigid, unforgiving logic to which human moods seem subject—and which we ignore at our peril when we encounter a picture of a beautiful country or hotel and imagine that happiness must naturally accompany such magnificence. Our capacity to draw happiness from aesthetic or material goods seems critically dependent on first satisfying a more important range of emotional or psychological needs, among them the need for understanding, for love, expression, and respect. We will not enjoy—we are not able to enjoy—sumptuous gardens and attractive bedrooms with en suite bathrooms when a relationship to which we are committed abruptly reveals itself to be suffused with incompatibility and resentments."

Alain de Botton was born in Zurich, Switzerland, on December 20, 1969, the son of Jacqueline Burgauer and Gilbert de Botton, a financier and patron of the arts who came from Alexandria, Egypt. De Botton was educated in Switzerland and, from the age of eight, in England, attending Harrow, the exclusive English public school, and later the University of Cambridge, where he studied history. Despite their background of great wealth and privilege, de Botton's family believed he should make his own way in life, and he has supported himself since the age of 23. He first considered a career in academia and took graduate courses in history and philosophy at Harvard University and at Kings College of London University. He dropped out without obtaining a Ph.D. but became an associate research fellow in the philosophy program at the School of Advanced Study of the University of London, a position he held in 2000.

His first two books, On Love and The Romantic Movement: Sex, Shopping, and the Novel, were published before de Botton had turned 25. The first sold well throughout Europe, affording de Botton independence from his family but failing to impress some critics. "Essays In Love is one of those books which feels obliged to advertise itself as 'A Novel' on the dustjacket because the casual reader might otherwise have mistaken it for a mathematical tract," Jonathan Coe wrote for the London Sunday Times (January 2, 1994). Coe concluded: "As an evocation, then, of the bliss and heartache shared by two people when they love and lose one another, this novel must be considered a failure. But if de Botton intended to write a book about self-love, about a young man's deep and lasting infatuation with his own voice and pseudo-erudition, he could hardly have produced a more passionate or convincing one."

Others were hesitantly fascinated. For example, Kate Kellaway, writing for the London Observer (August 14, 1994), described her experience of the first two novels in these terms: "If you were to eat a surprising, excellent cake, commend the chef to your friends and before you had regained your appetite had a second cake thrust your way, then that would approximate the experience of reading Alain de Botton's first novel, Essays in Love, and following it immediately with his second, The Romantic Movement." She concluded on a more ambiguous note, observing: "De Botton's own books are self-helpless, except that they show us how thought will always prove a defence against

feeling." "De Botton's idea of a philosophical analysis of an ordinary relationship smacks of precious writing. Any such exercise which insists on using diagrams and endless quotations from philosophers would become tiresomely pretentious in the hands of a second-rate writer. There are, indeed, places where his relentless analysis does become precious. Yet de Botton's wit, curiosity and originality make him more than equal to the task," Simon Sebag Montefiore wrote for the London Times (August 25, 1994), concluding that the novel's faults "do not subtract from the success of a novel that places its author in the first rank of young British novelists. The book is difficult to penetrate; but once penetrated, it is enormously enjoyable."

De Botton's third novel, Kiss & Tell, is a fictional biography of Isabel Rogers, who works for a stationery manufacturer, written by a man who decides, while moping about his unsatisfactory love life, to write a biography of the next person he meets. "Mr. de Botton plays around on every level, mixing erudite meditations on biography, love and other grand subjects with pedantic analyses of the quirks of Isabel's undistinguished existence. The purported biography is largely just an excuse for telling the story of the couple's romance, and occasionally it gets in the way of the real business at hand. Mr. de Botton has tried to do too many things," Elizabeth Gaffney observed for the New York Times (August 4, 1996). She concluded: "Kiss & Tell is neither fish nor fowl—not fully satisfying as a novel or as a mock biography." Ren Fenwick, writing for the Auckland Sunday Star-Times (July 14, 1996), found "de Botton's Kiss and Tell . . . superb [because] although the whole thing could be made up, you never once, while you're reading, feel as if it is."

For his next book, How Proust Can Change Your Life, de Botton experimented with the self-help genre, analyzing Marcel Proust's great novel In Search of Lost Time as if it were a tract for self-improvement. For example, the book claims, as Derwent May wrote for the London Times (April 10, 1997), "we can learn from Proust's long sentences how to take our time. The longest sentence in Proust, in standard-sized text, would be four metres long and would stretch round the base of a wine bottle 17 times. . . . De Botton suggests that Proust's sentences can teach us how to go slow, look properly at things, enlarge our sympathies." The experiment, Edmund White wrote for the London Observer (April 13, 1997), was "good-humoured, whimsical and convincing, especially since the lessons are far from bromidic and often are refreshingly perverse. In fact, How Proust Can Change Your Life, can even be read as a parody of an American self-help book: Q: How long can the average human expect to be appreciated? A: Fully appreciated? Often, as little as a quarter of an hour . . . Q: Did Proust have any relevant thoughts on dating? What should one talk about on a first date? And is it good to wear black?

A: Advice is scant. A more fundamental doubt is whether one should accept dinner in the first place."

Three years later, de Botton released *The Consolations of Philosophy,* which was accompanied by a television series. Revisiting the idea behind his Proust book but taking his words of advice from the Greek philosophers Socrates and Epicurus, the Roman philosopher and dramatist Lucius Annaeus Seneca, the French essayist Michel de Montaigne, and the German philosophers Arthur Schopenhauer and Friedrich Nietzsche, de Botton again drew on great works from the past to offer readers advice for improving their present selves. Calling the book "a commentary rather than a work of original thought," Humphrey Carpenter observed for the London *Sunday Times* (March 26, 2000), "few discussions on the great philosophers can have been so entertaining. De Botton takes us on a brisk, playful tour of the lives and ideas of half-a-dozen of the big names in the history of philosophy." He concluded, "this is an ingenious, imaginative book which will not disappoint fans of *How Proust Can Change Your Life,* and might even win over a few readers to study philosophy at a more demanding level." Others, however, pointed out that the advice from the different philosophers often proved contradictory, and Tom Cubbock, writing for the Edinburgh, Scotland *Sunday Herald* (March 26, 2000) argued that the insights de Botton culled from them weren't all that profound, observing "that this advice is not always off the point. It's just that we don't need to go to the philosophers for it. We can get it anywhere. And the whole de Botton production is pure bluff and reader-trifling—a trick to make familiar reflections seem challenging, and their playful handling look brilliant."

De Botton's next book, *The Art of Travel,* was, Jan Morris wrote for the *New Statesman* (May 6, 2002), "an elegant and entertaining evocation of all the sensations of travel, and a manual of how to get the best out of it. Half of it concerns de Botton's own reflections; half of it is about the attitudes of great writers, painters and, yes, philosophers towards the whole business of going away from home." Some critics found de Botton unsuited for the project. "He may have travelled the highways of the mind, but there's a certain insouciance in his writing a book about travel that seems so little acquainted with the byways of the world," Henry Hitchings observed for the *Financial Times* (May 11, 2002). Others argued that advice about actual trips was not what readers should be seeking from the book. "There is not much that is original in *The Art of Travel* but that is not its point. It is a book that invites you to enjoy its gentle formalism, its sweet flow and the writerly-ness of its reflections. If it is a little precious sometimes ('craft' for car seems excessive, unless de Botton owns a Batmobile), then that is a small price to pay for its playful erudition," Melanie McGrath wrote for the London *Evening Standard* (May 13, 2002).

Again drawing on famous philosophers, de Botton next wrote *Status Anxiety.* "Status anxiety is a fascinating topic. It is disappointing, therefore, that this study of it ultimately fails to deliver," Selina Hastings complained for the London *Sunday Telegraph* (February 29, 2004). "De Botton begins promisingly enough by introducing the subject of how we assess ourselves and how much our self-conception depends on others' regard. . . . The reader is then treated to a brief course in the history of western history and philosophy as retailed in the writings of such famous figures as Herodotus, Socrates, Saint Augustine, [Niccolo] Machiavelli, La Rochefoucauld, [Jean-Jacques] Rousseau, [Friedrich] Engels, [Henry David] Thoreau, William James and Karl Marx. As each writer is wheeled on, he is set neatly in context before a patronising *precis* is given of the relevant extract." She concluded: "[de Botton's] book is the work of a schoolboy swot who has read widely, always got his homework in on time, but who has nothing new to give us." Laurie Taylor was equally disappointed, noting for the London *Independent* (March 5, 2004): "Until now, no one would have suggested that Alain de Botton was a player in this vacuous self-help either/or advice market. . . . But this new offering is desperately disappointing. De Botton has nothing much to say about status anxiety that hasn't already been said a thousand times by knowing journalists or populist sociologists."

De Botton followed his 2004 book with *The Architecture of Happiness*—which argues that good architecture can contribute to one's sense of well-being—and seemed to return to form, as critics found the book appealing despite its faults. "The book's argument suffers from its beautiful descriptive surface—big contradictions open up underneath," Kester Rattenbury wrote for *Building Design* (April 21, 2006), adding: "De Botton clearly loves the symbolic surface, and surface is his architectural focus. He describes a man (we assume de Botton) weeping over an Adam ceiling, but you won't catch him talking about circulation, or massing, or materiality and he is also surprisingly slight on proportion. It makes you long for iconoclastic but pragmatic books such as [Jane Jacobs's] *The Death And Life of the Great American Cities* or *Learning from Las Vegas* [by Robert Venturi, Denise Scott Brown, and Steven Izenour]. . . . This is a great, stimulating read, even if its yearning quality suggests more about de Botton's quest for self-knowledge than architecture's." Even his detractors acknowledged the book's power. Calling it "an elegant, stimulating read, " a reviewer for the *Irish Times* (April 29, 2006) noted that it was primarily "about the issues that affect people who are rich enough to be able to influence the designs of the spaces that surround them."

De Botton lives with his wife, Charlotte, and child in a multistory Victorian row house in West London.

—S.Y./A.R.

Suggested Reading: *Irish Times* (on-line) Apr. 1, 2000, p73 Apr. 14, 2001; (London) *Independent* p27 Sep. 3, 1994, p35+ July 2, 2000; (London) *Observer* p3 Mar. 19, 2000; (London) *Sunday Times* (on-line) Jan. 2, 1994, Feb. 25, 2001; (London) *Times Literary Supplement* p20 Sep. 15, 1995; (New York) *Newsday* B p10 June 8, 2000; *New York Review of Books* p35 Jan. 13, 1994; *New York Times* B p7 June 3, 2000; *New York Times Book Review* p18 Aug. 4, 1996, p22 Aug. 18, 2002; *New Yorker* p106 Aug. 28, 1995, Sep. 9, 2002; *Scotsman* p11 Mar. 25, 2000; *Time* p71 June 12, 1995; *Washington Post Book World* p8 May 4, 1997, p7 July 21, 2002

Selected Books: fiction—*On Love*, 1993; *The Romantic Movement: Sex, Shopping, and the Novel*, 1994, *Kiss & Tell*, 1996; nonfiction—*How Proust Can Change Your Life: Not a Novel*, 1997; *The Consolations of Philosophy*, 2000; *The Art of Travel*, 2002; *Status Anxiety*, 2004; *The Architecture of Happiness*, 2005

Veronica Solari/Courtesy of Susanna Zevi Agencia

De Luca, Erri

(day LOO-ka, EHR-ray)

1950– Novelist

Erri De Luca is the author of more than a dozen books, many of them imaginative embroideries of his unusually varied life. Raised by middle-class parents to become a diplomat, De Luca instead became a radical leftist, dedicating himself to a revolutionary communism that, unlike other prominent members of his generation, he has never repudiated. Refusing a university education he worked as a manual laborer for more than 20 years, even after publishing his first book, *Non ora, non qui* (which translates as "not now, not here"), when he was 39. Since then he has become one of Italy's most celebrated authors, writing three additional works of extended prose fiction, all of them straddling the line between novel and novella and all available in English: *Tu, mio* (1998), titled *Sea of Memory* in its 1999 English version; *Tre cavalli*, published in Italian in 1999 and in English as *Three Horses* in 2005; and *Montedidio* (2001), appearing as *God's Mountain* in English in 2002. De Luca has also published collections of his short stories, plays, and a book of poetry, as well as a wealth of commentary for left-wing Italian newspapers and a number of difficult-to-categorize works, including a novel in verse, *Solo andata* (2005; which translates as "one way"). In the 1980s De Luca, raised Catholic but now a nonbeliever, taught himself ancient Hebrew in order to read the Hebrew Bible and has since published at least six short books of translations of some of the most famous episodes or chapters; in the 1990s he taught himself Yiddish as a way of acknowledging the horrors of the Holocaust. His novels have been translated into at least five languages and have been praised by critics inside and outside of his home country, particularly in the U.S., Israel, and France, where in 2002 his book *Montedidio* received one of the country's two most prestigious literary awards for foreign authors, the Prix Femina. In the afterword to his translation of *Three Horses*, Michael F. Moore quotes De Luca as having told Silvio Perrella, in an interview posted on the Web site of the author's Italian publisher: "Writing is an attempt to create a definitive version—shorter, more brusque and abusive—of the life you've lived: Arrested, detained for a spell, fixed inside a container that prevents it from aging."

Erri De Luca was born in 1950 in the southern Italian city of Naples (or Napoli, as it is known in Italian)—"a very hard, exuberant, exaggerated, and crowded city" that did not suit his temperament, De Luca told Paolo Di Paolo for an April 13, 2004 interview posted on the Italia Libri Web site, as translated by *World Authors*. From an early age De Luca enjoyed writing and reading, often taking up books from his father, an infantryman during World War II whom he described to Di Paolo as "a huge, voracious reader who bought books by the kilo and read them all." The desire to tell stories, De Luca continued, came from "the books I read and the stories I was told, the ones adults told each other back then—stories of . . . war, earthquakes, ghosts (because Naples was full of ghosts, then; they were part of the first-aid kit)." One likely distinction between many of the stories De Luca heard and the ones he read in his father's books was the language in which they were told. For the young De Luca, Italian was his "father tongue, quite literally," because it was the language of his father and his father's books, as Moore pointed out in his afterword to *Three Horses*. But De Luca's mother tongue—his first language, as well as the means by which he communicated with his mother—was Neapolitan. Closely related to Italian but linguistically distinct, Neapolitan was his birth city's lingua franca. "Italian was a language . . . that came from outside," De Luca told Di Paolo. "It was the language of the State, of the police . . . of the lawyers, the language that I used with my father, who demanded [that I speak] unaccented Italian. This has helped me keep the two languages separate. I have screamed in Neapolitan, I have been moved in Neapolitan, I have argued in Neapolitan, but I have always written in Italian. That is the language that was inside books, mute and beautiful to follow." Despite the distance separating him from Italian, De Luca feels close enough to claim the language itself, and not Italy, as his home country and for that reason prefers not to be regarded as an Italian writer but, as he told Di Paolo, "a writer in Italian."

Though middle-class, De Luca's parents lived under straitened circumstances after allied bombing destroyed their home during the war; Shiri Lev-Ari, in a June 30, 2003 article for the Tel Aviv newspaper *Ha'aretz* (on-line), paraphrased De Luca as saying that "his parents' life story after World War II [was] a tragedy." In 1968, after finishing the first step on the path to a diplomatic career by graduating from a French secondary school in Rome, De Luca chose not to go on to a university but instead joined the widespread social protests raging among students throughout the U.S. and Europe, eventually becoming a leader in the revolutionary communist group Lotta Continua (which can be translated as "ongoing struggle"). In the late 1960s and early 1970s, an era in Italy dubbed "the years of lead," when political violence was rife in every quarter of the country, Lotta Continua took a hard communist line but did not join in the calls for violent revolution made by other groups. Instead, De Luca and his comrades preferred to keep a steady pressure on politicians and industrialists by advocating immediate and forceful public protests and workplace revolts. (According to a January 30, 1997 article by Julian Coman in the *European*, Lotta Continua was associated with such slogans as "Let's kidnap the bosses" and "Let's take over the city.")

During this period, De Luca, like other members of Lotta Continua, worked in a factory for the automaker Fiat. He continued working there after the dissolution of Lotta Continua in 1976 but stopped in the fall of 1980, when Fiat threatened to lay off more than 20,000 workers, prompting a massive strike that made headlines around the world. In his afterword to *Three Horses*, Moore quoted a short story by De Luca called "Conversazione di fianco," from the collection *In alto a sinistra* (1994; which translates as "up above, to the left"), in which De Luca touched on this event: "In a single night the great factory had gotten rid of twenty-four thousand meals in the cafeteria, and forty-eight thousand hands, perhaps fewer, since people injured on the job were also among the expelled. 'Go outside to eat,' they said. And outside we would stay for forty days and forty nights, by fires to keep us warm. No one exited, no one entered the factory we were blockading. In the end we would all remain outside: friends, strangers, defeated." (Contemporaneous American press accounts put the figure of the potential layoffs at 23,000 and the duration of the strike at a less biblical 38 days. Reports also suggest that the strike was largely effective, though a November 11, 1980 Associated Press report on Fiat's operating losses noted that even before the strike the company employed 10,000 fewer workers in 1980 than it had the year before.)

With Lotta Continua having faded away and the wider revolutionary communist movement dramatically losing steam, many of De Luca's contemporaries began rethinking their views and moving into more traditional places in the country's political and cultural hierarchy. De Luca, however, has remained singularly attached to his early ideals, telling Di Paolo in 2004 that he had a "loyal relationship" with the revolutionary actions he took part in when he was younger. "We were a commune of young people who struggled for democratic values in factories, in prisons," De Luca told Lev-Ari. "We did the right thing at the time. It wasn't communism in the style of communist governments and parties, but rather active communism. Nowadays communism no longer exists, because it's not an idea but a way of life, a daily experience, which doesn't say 'Maybe tomorrow will be good,' but operates within the present."

In 1983 De Luca began preparing to leave Italy for Tanzania, where he would drive a truck on a humanitarian relief mission. Coming across an Italian translation of a Christian Bible, he took it up and found that the book spoke to him, particularly the section referred to as the Hebrew Bible, which closely corresponds to the Old Testament of recent Christian tradition and Judaism's Tanakh. For De Luca the appeal was not spiritual; he has made it clear in interviews that he does not believe in the religion of his childhood, nor seemingly any other, though he speaks respectfully of a number of faiths, including Judaism and Catholicism.

Instead, the stories struck him as aesthetically singular. "It's not ordinary literature in my eyes," he told Lev-Ari, "because ordinary literature tries to come close to the reader, and maybe to flatter him. Here the reader has to go toward it." The Hebrew Bible also fulfilled a psychological need for De Luca during a time that he described to Di Paolo as finding himself in a desert. "I needed to go deeper into this desert, not take myself out of it," De Luca continued, and the "remote stories" of the Hebrew Bible thrust him deeper into that desert. "The Bible has words that a person needs in the desert—not in the centers of his life or the center of the city," he told Lev-Ari. "In the desert a person encounters the boundary, 'the boundary of his sanctity,' as it says in Psalms, a boundary for God and a boundary for man." Over the years De Luca has cemented his attachment to Hebrew by reading it every day immediately after waking. He is "grateful" for the habit, he told Lev-Ari, "because it has helped me physically. I'm not a believer, but it has helped me get through the day. The simplicity, the sentence structure. Even today I wake up in the morning in Hebrew."

De Luca's work as a truck driver was not limited to his single stint in Tanzania but was one of the many blue-collar jobs De Luca has held over the years, including construction worker, mason, and airport porter. (In the mid-1990s De Luca again drove a truck for a humanitarian mission, this time bringing aid to refugees displaced by the war in the former Yugoslavia.) In 1989 he published his first novel, *Non ora, non qui*. Clearly autobiographical, this brief novel or novella, running only 91 pages, uses a first-person, present-tense narration to tell the story of a boy's Neapolitan childhood and his feelings of being "torn between the exuberance and noise of the streets and the orderly stillness of his home life," according to Moore's afterword to *Three Horses*. "When his family's fortunes improve, the narrator experiences it not as a welcome improvement but as an irremediable loss."

In the early 1990s De Luca traveled to Poland at the time of an anniversary commemoration of the Warsaw Ghetto Uprising, an insurrection by Polish Jews against the Nazi occupiers; the German forces, which had created the ghetto in 1940, were on the verge of finishing their extermination of the area's hundreds of thousands of residents when fighting broke out in January 1943 and became a sustained battle between April 19 and May 16 of that year. Virtually all of the roughly 60,000 Jews living in the ghetto at the time the battle began were eventually killed, either during the battle itself or shortly afterwards, in concentration camps. Reflecting on the event and on the Holocaust as a whole, De Luca decided to teach himself Yiddish (a language spoken by the Jews of Central and Eastern Europe) just as he had taught himself Hebrew before, though with a somewhat different motivation. "It's one of the only things that can be done after what happened to the Jewish

people—to preserve this language," De Luca told Lev-Ari. "I owed it to historical truth."

De Luca's next major book was the 1992 short-story collection *Aceto, arcobaleno* (which translates as "vinegar, rainbow"). In 1998 De Luca published *Tu, Mio*, which was translated into English by Beth Archer Brombert and put out as *Sea of Memory* (1999). The novel takes a setting and subject similar to *Non ora, non qui*, with a first-person narrator telling the story of a boy growing up in Naples in the 1950s. In this case, the boy is a 16-year-old whose name is never given, and the action takes place at some remove from the city itself, on an island where the boy is spending the summer with his uncle, learning to fish and getting to know the other people on the island. Particularly drawn to older people, the boy befriends an experienced fisherman named Nicola and keeps company with his cousin Daniele. The boy also develops a strangely paternal affection for a visiting woman named Caia, whom he learns is Jewish and a Holocaust survivor. Near the novel's end, Caia suggests that the boy might be the reincarnation of her father.

The first of De Luca's work to see print in English, the novel was generally praised, though several reviewers questioned some of the novel's departures from realism. For the *Denver Post* (August 8, 1999), Tom Walker wrote that De Luca "uses a deft touch with the passions of youth to give the reader a haunting tale." The author, Walker added, "also uses the novel to peer inside how Italians felt about themselves after the cataclysmic days of the early '40s. Guilt was everywhere. The young man has a burning desire to talk about the war days, but the adults in his life refuse to discuss that time, as if by ignoring it they can forget about it." For the *New York Times* (August 29, 1999), Lucy Ferriss described *Sea of Memory* as a "lyrical but strangely ominous novella" and "a poetic novel charged with anger and desire. For that reason, one wishes its poetry had been more evenly matched to its narrative of adolescent epiphany. The two main characters' last words to each other are closer to operatic monologue than to the clumsy poetry of young lovers." In a review of the 2003 Hebrew version of the novel—called *Ata, Sheli* and translated by Ioram Melcer and Menachem Perry—that was published in *Ha'aretz* (July 25, 2003, on-line), Gaby Levin acknowledged that some events in the novel "might sound far-fetched and even ridiculous" but that these "become believable in De Luca's hands." In this novel, Levin added, "as in all De Luca's books, there are mystic, fantastical elements in his protagonists' search for self—a blend of fact, hearsay and fiction. Past and present live alongside one another, and every character is a cluster of questions for which there is no answer." For a reviewer for *Publishers Weekly* (July 5, 1999), Caia's intuitions that the boy might be the reincarnation of her father "hinder what is otherwise an alluring and poignant story about an adolescent in love, in search of himself and of history." The translation, the reviewer added, "ranges from clear to shimmeringly lyrical." For Ferriss, however, Brombert's work "occasionally lapses into either glaring literalisms ('I couldn't make him resume his previous manner') or cliche ('going full sail'). But De Luca's symbolic writing about the island and its fishing culture more than makes up for these faults."

In 1999 De Luca's *Tre cavalli* was published in Italian. Another first-person, present-tense narrative, *Tre cavalli* is unique among De Luca's novels for being the story of an older man and for its somewhat vague setting. The main character is a gardener who returns to Italy after living abroad, in Argentina, where he suffered under the so-called Dirty War, which the Argentine government waged on its citizens between 1976 and 1983, slaughtering somewhere between 10,000 and 30,000 Argentineans. In Italy the gardener works in a small town near the coast and develops a relationship with two other people who feel sharply out of place in the area, a Russian immigrant named Laila and an African man named Selim.

Reviewing the Italian edition for *World Literature Today* (Autumn 2000), Giovanni d'Angelo described the book as a "long short story that is in no sense a novel" told in "dry, simple, very spare" prose. "Sometimes articles are missing, some verbs are merely implied, the present tense changes place with the past tense and vice-versa. The idea is to indicate the speech and the thoughts of an uneducated ex-emigrant who has difficulty finding his roots in Italy. However, the style is softened by intermittent waves of a dry lyricism that echoes ancient popular wisdom." Reviews of the American edition, titled *Three Horses* and published in 2005, were mixed, particularly regarding the style of the prose, translated here by Moore. Noting that the novel has "an intricate, engaging story," Richard Wakefield, in the *Seattle Times* (November 6, 2005), compared moments of confusion he felt while reading the book to watching "a grainy black-and-white foreign film with subtitles that seem to be from another movie: elusive, allusive, obscure." Unsure whether the translation or the original was at fault, Wakefield nonetheless noted that "at times the obscurity falls away, replaced by lyricism." Benjamin Lytal submitted the book to a light mocking in the *New York Sun* (March 15, 2006). Commenting that the narrator "lives a Hemingwayesque life of sensuality," Lytal argued that De Luca "feasts" on detailed descriptions of his narrator's tasks; at the same time, the prose "also recalls epic speech, or the Song of Solomon." The book, Lytal concludes, "will deeply satisfy the romantic, Spartan reader, though it may also embarrass him."

In 2002 De Luca published his most recent long-form work of fiction. Titled *Montedidio* in Italian and published in English the next year as *God's Mountain* (also translated by Moore), the book

returns to Naples and the subject of youth. This time the narrator is a 13-year-old boy who has recently left school to begin an apprenticeship with a carpenter named Master Errico. Sharing part of his master's shop is a Yiddish-speaking Holocaust survivor called Rafaniello, who spends his days repairing shoes for the poor and whose humped back slowly sprouts the wings that will take him, he hopes, to Jerusalem, where he had been heading when he accidentally ended up in Naples. At home the boy's father spends most of his time attending to his sick wife, while the boy slowly falls in love with a neighbor girl who, though his own age, is more experienced in the darker side of the world. The boy records his first-person, present-tense impressions in diary form on a scroll, much of it given over to imagining how he will throw the boomerang his father gave him when he grows strong enough and there is enough room in his family's confining Neapolitan neighborhood, Montedidio.

The Italian and French editions of the book were strong successes, and the novel received generally positive reviews in the U.S and Canada. Charles Klopp, discussing the Italian edition for *World Literature Today* (Summer–Autumn 2002), wrote that it "might be called a 'pious' novel for its conviction that there are still connections between heaven and earth and its insistence on the need for compassion in human relations. In it the folk wisdom of the people of Naples and that of the Jews of Central Europe are reconciled and mutually enriched through the author's perception of the analogous suffering of the two peoples. Thanks to the unique cultural perspective he brings to his writing, De Luca . . . has once again demonstrated that his is not only an original but also a strikingly valuable voice in the panorama of contemporary Italian fiction." Describing the book as an "international best-seller," a reviewer for *Booklist* (December 15, 2002) also noted the book's thematic importance: "More impressionistic than linear, this is a haunting, atmospheric novel that muses on religion, language, community, and what it means to be an adult, all against the backdrop of a rough, often violent city where 'you grow up quickly.'" In a generally appreciative review for the *Toronto Star* (March 9, 2003), Len Gasparini called *God's Mountain* "a poignant and honest slice of life" but noted: "Although the author takes care to avoid sentimentality—especially the kind that tends to present all human instincts as naturally good—perhaps a willing suspension of cynicism is required of the intellectually jaded reader who finds happy endings suspect."

Never married, De Luca lives in the countryside near Rome in a house he renovated himself. In addition to his prominent political commitments, he is a dedicated mountain climber. In 2003 he served as one of the nine members of the jury that awards the Palme d'Or at the Cannes Film Festival in France and that same year had a small part in the film *L'Isola* (*The Island*), which was directed and written by Constanza Quatriglio. De Luca played a mechanic.

—D.R.

Suggested Reading: *Ha'aretz* (on-line) June 30, 2003, July 7, 2003; *Italian Culture* p123+ Dec. 22, 2002

Selected Books in English Translation: *Sea of Memory*, 1999; *God's Mountain*, 2002; *Three Horses*, 2005

Charles Harris/Corbis/Courtesy of Simon & Schuster

Deaver, Jeffery

1950– Novelist

Jeffery Deaver's well-researched suspense novels include forays into the minds of the mentally ill, as well as the the the spheres of television-news production, computer technology, magic tricks and illusions, immigrant smuggling, and major New York law firms. Among the most popular of his more than 20 books are those featuring Lincoln Rhyme, a quadriplegic detective who solves crimes using only mental agility—and a few high-tech devices. These include *The Bone Collector* (1997), *The Coffin Dancer* (1998), *The Empty Chair* (2000), *The Stone Monkey* (2002), *The Vanished Man* (2003), *The Twelfth Card* (2005), and *The Cold Moon* (2006). Deaver told John Connolly for the *Irish Times* (June 16, 2003), "I wanted to write a very cerebral, Holmesian character who combats crime with his thought processes more than fast car chases and shooting."

Jeffery Wilds Deaver was born in 1950 in the Chicago area and raised in the suburb of Glen Ellyn, Illinois. His father was an advertising copywriter, and his mother was a homemaker and an artist. His younger sister, Julie Reece Deaver, became a writer of young-adult novels. (Some sources, however, have described Deaver as an only child.) Deaver's parents allowed him to read any book he liked. "I discovered Ian Fleming [the creator of James Bond] when I was eight," he told Ray Chesterton for the Melbourne *Herald Sun.* " There were some sex scenes in the James Bond books, but they were written with such nuance and innuendo, I skimmed through to the shoot-em-ups and car chases." Deaver was inspired, at age 11, to write his own book—which ended up being two pages long, including illustrations by the author. "I've forgotten . . . but my hero was probably named Fred Bond or something like that," he told Chesterton.

Deaver was educated at the University of Missouri, earning a B.A. in journalism. Wanting to write about legal matters, he attended Fordham University, in New York City. He graduated with a law degree and actually began a brief career at a firm in New York, although he has told several interviewers that he was a terrible lawyer. Deaver's first book, published in 1984, was *The Complete Law School Companion*, a nonfiction manual for students.

During the long commute to his law office, Deaver also began to write fiction. His first widely available novel, *Manhattan Is My Beat*, was published in 1988. (He published two books before that, with a little-known publisher who provided no editorial input, but those are out of print— "mercifully," as Deaver has told interviewers.) The protagonist of *Manhattan Is My Beat* is a female video-store clerk named Rune, who stumbles upon a murder while retrieving a rented film from a customer. Rune also appeared in Deaver's next two books, *Death of a Blue Movie Star* (1990) and *Hard News* (1991). Deaver, who was by then earning enough from his books to give up his law practice, next wrote a series of books featuring a male protagonist, John Pellam, a film location scout. (The Pellam books were originally written under the pen name William Jeffries but have since been issued with Deaver's name on the cover.) The series includes *Shallow Graves* (1992), *Bloody River Blues* (1993), and *Hell's Kitchen* (written in 1994 but not published until 2001).

Deaver generally maintained a schedule of writing a book a year, and during the mid-1990s he published several stand-alone mysteries (non-series books not featuring a recurring protagonist.) *The Lesson of Her Death* (1993), in which a detective investigates the deaths of several Midwestern college students; *Praying for Sleep* (1994), about a convicted murderer who escapes from a mental hospital; and *A Maiden's Grave* (1995), a hostage drama in which a group of deaf girls is kidnapped, were all tautly plotted thrillers that garnered Deaver a large group of fans. With the appearance of Lincoln Rhyme in *The Bone Collector* (1997), however, Deaver reached a new level of fame. The novel followed what the author came to call the "Deaver framework"—a book "taking place over a short time frame, involving multiple plots, frequent deadlines, surprising plot twists and turns, endings that bring together all the plot strands in a whammy twist or two," as Deaver explained to Jeff Glorfeld in an interview for the Melbourne *Age* (May 6, 2002, on-line).

While there is plenty of murder and mayhem in the Lincoln Rhyme books, none of it is created by Rhyme himself, who is confined to a wheelchair, able to move only a finger and his head slightly. The real hero of *The Bone Collector*, according to Marilyn Stasio for the *New York Times Book Review* (March 16, 1997), is the technology. Although Lincoln Rhyme, "known in the trade as 'the world's foremost criminalist,'" cannot function physically, he uses "a scanning electron microscope, an energy-dispersive X-ray unit, a vacuum metal fingerprint unit and a computerized gas chromatograph and mass spectrometer to analyze the tantalizing clues (rat hairs, bone dust, pocket lint, ladies' underwear) harvested from a serial killer's gruesome crime scenes." A *Publishers Weekly* (December 16, 1996) reviewer wrote that the novel was aimed at an audience that was "uncritical and doting on violence." If so, that description fit a large slice of the reading public; the book sold exceptionally well and was optioned for the big screen. Rhyme was played by Denzel Washington in a 1999 film, *The Bone Collector*, directed by Phillip Noyce. (Harrison Ford was also considered for the role.) Angelina Jolie played Amelia Sachs, Rhyme's fellow detective and love interest.

In *The Coffin Dancer* Rhyme and Sachs track down an assassin who targets grand jury members investigating stolen weapons. The duo appear together again in *The Devil's Teardrop*, searching for a crazed killer called the Digger, and *The Empty Chair*, pitted against a suspect called the Insect Boy, for his creepy obsession with bugs. *The Stone Monkey*, their next outing, is set against a Chinatown backdrop; its plot concerns a people-smuggling operation with horrific consequences. Marilyn Stasio, writing for the *New York Times Book Review* (March 17, 2002), opined, "Whether it's a high-speed chase through Manhattan's Chinatown district, a breathless dive to the underwater grave of a corpse-laden ship or a battle of wits in an impulsive match of wei-chi [a popular Asian game of strategy], Deaver knows how to play this game for all it's worth." In *The Vanished Man*, Rhyme is helped by Sachs and a young illusionist to catch a nefarious quick-change artist who escapes the police by employing ingenious disguises and sleight-of-hand tricks. "*The Vanished Man* has so many tricks that readers may have to unscrew it from the shelf," Connolly wrote.

Although Lincoln Rhyme and Amelia Sachs became two of his most popular characters, Deaver interspersed those books with stand-alone thrillers. In *The Blue Nowhere* (2001), for example, Deaver turned to cyberspace—the "Blue Nowhere" of the title. The book's villain tracks his victims through their computer use so that his hunter has to be extremely cyber-savvy as well. Mary Jane Boland, reviewing the book for the Wellington *Evening Post* (June 22, 2001), called it "a startling trip through the world of crackers, hackers and phreaks." Jon Dugdale, writing in the London *Sunday Times* (July 8, 2001), found, on the other hand, that "Deaver's customary brilliant plotting is impeded by the continual need to translate jargon or explain technicalities."

Set in Berlin, Germany, in 1936, *Garden of Beasts: A Novel of Berlin 1936*, satisfies Deaver's requirement for interesting bad guys by featuring a cameo appearance by Adolf Hitler, along with his chief lieutenants, but "it's the smart shaded-gray characterizations of the principals that anchor the exciting plot," a *Publishers Weekly* (May 3, 2004) reviewer noted. A *Library Journal* (May 15, 2004) reviewer thought that Deaver had done well in portraying "the blanket of evil that is snuffing out dissent and freedom" in Nazi Germany. In 2005 Rhyme and Sachs, their romantic relationship deepening, returned in *The Twelfth Card*, in which they protect a Harlem schoolgirl who is being targeted for murder because of information contained in a research paper she has written.

Deaver, who is divorced, maintains homes in Virginia and California. He researches and writes from 10 to 14 hours a day. "Cops have to work the streets. Books have to be written," Phil McCombs reported Deaver as saying in the *Washington Post* (April 19, 1997). Deaver is also famed, however, for the elaborate theme parties he hosts for his many friends. Besides being devoted to his human friends, Deaver considers his dogs an important part of his life. He breeds Briards (muscular herding dogs with wavy coats) and has been known to auction off character-naming rights for his novels to benefit animal-related causes. Of his many fans he told Glen Coleman for the Sydney *Daily Telegraph* (May 4, 2002), "I want to make them feel edgy; to stay up late reading. I want them to be scared . . . but happy."

—S.Y.

Suggested Reading: *Entertainment Weekly* p52 Nov. 12, 1999; *Irish Times* p12 June 16, 2003; Jeffery Deaver's Web site; *Library Journal* p105 Feb. 1, 1997, p113 May 15, 2004; *Los Angeles Times* E p1 Oct. 19, 1998; *New York Times Book Review* p28 Mar. 16, 1997; *Publishers Weekly* p166 May 3, 2004; *Washington Post* CO p1 Apr. 19, 1997; (Wellington) *Evening Post* p6 June 22, 2001

Selected Books: Lincoln Rhyme series—*The Bone Collector*, 1997; *The Coffin Dancer*, 1998; *The Empty Chair*, 2000; *The Stone Monkey*, 2002; *The Vanished Man*, 2003; *The Twelfth Card*, 2005; *The Cold Moon*, 2006; other novels—*Manhattan Is My Beat*, 1988; *Death of a Blue Movie Star*, 1990; *Hard News*, 1991; *Shallow Graves*, 1992; *Bloody River Blues*, 1993; *The Lesson of Her Death*, 1993; *Praying for Sleep*, 1994; *A Maiden's Grave*, 1995; *The Devil's Teardrop*, 1999; *The Blue Nowhere*, 2001; *Hell's Kitchen*, 2001; *Twisted*, 2003; *Garden of Beasts*, 2004

Jerry Bauer/Courtesy of Random House

Delaney, Frank

Oct. 24, 1942– Nonfiction writer; novelist

Frank Delaney always considered himself a writer, even though he took a few detours before he began writing professionally in the early 1980s, working variously as a bank clerk and a broadcaster. When he was asked why he became a writer in an undated interview posted on the Bibliofemme Irish Book Club Web site, he observed, "I didn't have any choice. It's been an impulse for as long as I can remember. I think about writing all the time." At first, he wrote nonfiction books, such as *James Joyce's Odyssey: A Guide to the Dublin of* Ulysses (1981) and *The Celts* (1986), in a mode that he hoped would impress upon the minds of ordinary readers the importance of both literature and history. He turned to literature himself in the late 1980s, when he began to write fiction; he has since published 10 novels, many of which deal with the

ways history affects ordinary lives. Praised for his command of the language and for his ability to spin a tale, he has earned a reputation for turning out popular novels, all of which have a serious undertone. What Sherie Posesorski, writing for the *Philadelphia Inquirer* (March 13, 2005), wrote about the stories that make up Delaney's most recent novel, *Ireland* (2004), could well stand as a description of Delaney's entire oeuvre: "These lively tales narrated by the storyteller in colorful, idiomatic prose," she wrote, "have a vivid, dramatic immediacy. The storyteller, a figure both archetypal and touchingly human in his passions and frailties, is in his own way a preserver and protector of Ireland, just like the heroes whose stories he relates."

The youngest of eight children, Frank Delaney was born on October 24, 1942 in a small town in Tipperary, Ireland. His parents, Elizabeth Josephine and Edward Delaney, were both teachers, and he grew up surrounded by books, believing he would become a writer. When he was 11 Delaney was sent to the Abbey School, run by the Christian Brothers. Amanda Doherty, in an article for the *Sunday Mirror* (September 6, 1998), a British tabloid, quotes Delaney as saying that his teachers "wore long black cassocks and some of the Brothers kept a leather strap up their sleeves to beat us. But I received a fabulous education. There was violence but I learned quickly how to dodge and evade it. . . . I did not work at subjects taught by teachers who would let me get away with it and worked like a slave at those subjects taught by teachers who were strict. In Latin exam I got 398 marks out of 400 because I was terrified of the teacher." Despite his desire to become a writer, Delaney did not do well enough on his exit exams for Irish secondary school to get into a university. He thus took an exam for a job at the Bank of Ireland, where one of his older brothers already worked, and having done well on this exam, he headed to Dublin at the age of 17 for training. He was then placed in a country branch of the bank and stayed for 11 years. Throughout these years, he dabbled with being a writer, publishing short stories in the *Irish Times* and book reviews in papers at home and abroad. He also set his sights on a broadcasting career. He applied to RTE, Ireland's national broadcasting company, 30 times before getting a response from the company and then endured 15 auditions and five training courses before finally being given a job as a newsreader at the age of 28. A few years later, he moved to BBC Northern Ireland to become a reporter, and in 1978 he went to London to become the host of the radio program *Bookshelf*, a show he had pitched to the BBC and on which he interviewed more than 1,000 authors, including John Updike and Margaret Atwood. In the early 1980s, Delaney became the host of a self-titled Saturday-night television talk show, and according to Chris Dunkley, writing for the *Financial Times* (December 22, 1982), the show was "a great improvement on previous chat shows."

In 1981 Delaney published *James Joyce's Odyssey: A Guide to the Dublin of* Ulysses. "Part Dublin guidebook, part Joyce biography, part *Ulysses* crib," Kathleen Leverich wrote for the *Christian Science Monitor* (June 11, 1982), "this compendium of *Ulysses* lore and background information is marked by Delaney's ardent pleasure in the great work. He leads us, pointing and gesticulating exuberantly, through the paces of the novel." Delaney, in fact, wanted his book to make *Ulysses* accessible to the masses, so "instead of illuminating what is esoteric in *Ulysses* and what has kept so many readers from finishing the book," Christopher Lehmann-Haupt wrote for the *New York Times* (February 2, 1982), "Mr. Delaney emphasizes what is most accessible. With all due respect for 'the huge body of academic work Joyce has inspired,' he announces, 'This is a plain man's guide to a novel, perhaps the novel, of the plain man.'" Delaney next published *Betjeman Country* (1983), a book that shared with the Joyce book a travel theme. In it he introduced places associated with the poems of Sir John Betjeman, a poet laureate of England and one of the top 20 writers living in England in 1981, according to the National Book League, of which Delaney was the chairman.

Delaney continued working for the BBC, and in 1986 he combined the roles of broadcaster and writer, hosting a six-part BBC series about the Celts and writing an accompanying book, *The Celts*, "in which literature ranging from the Book of Kells to Seamus Heaney takes its place among a mass of archeological evidence and beautifully carved artifacts," as Anthony Curtis reported for the *Financial Times* (November 22, 1986). *The Celts* was followed by two other books with a historical theme, *A Walk through the Dark Ages* (1988) and *The Legends of the Celts* (1988), a retelling of 20 ancient Irish myths.

In 1989 Delaney published his first full-length piece of fiction, *My Dark Rosaleen*, a novella about an innocent Irish bank clerk who has grown up learning to sing patriotic songs and has thus come to idealize his country. In the course of the story, he meets Rosaleen, both a woman and the personification of Ireland, and a crew of young men who abuse and eventually rape her. "It's all a great shame," Desmond Christy wrote for the London *Guardian* (May 19, 1989), "because the theme of Delaney's book [the gap between the ideal and the corrupt reality] is important and he is brave to tackle it. You just wish he had not used a pedestrian thriller to say it but had written a novel in the Ireland he actually knows so well and peopled it with flesh and blood, not the gang of goths we get here. This book is so much less intelligent than the man we've heard on the radio."

The Sins of the Mother (1992), his next novel and the first in a series of books about Ireland of the 20th century, is set in Deanstown, a village in Tipperary, between 1925 and 1927. It tells the story of Ellen Morris, a young schoolmaster who arrives in Deanstown to take a position at a two-teacher national school (public primary school) and marries the other school teacher, Thomas Kane, who had been in a command unit of Michael Collins, a legendary Irish fighter and nationalist. The book garnered widespread praise for its writing and was short-listed for the Sunday Express Book of the Year award. Penelope Fitzgerald, for example, wrote for the *Evening Standard* (June 25, 1992), "Delaney has taken affectionate care in his detailed reconstruction of two slow passing years. He uses songs, newspaper cuttings and recipes as well as his knowledge, which is hardly likely to let him down, of the way people talk in the south of Ireland." Some critics, however, thought the book was too long. Sandra Barwick, writing for the London *Daily Mail* (June 18, 1992), noted that it had a "slow start," but went on to claim that this was only a minor problem and that the "book takes hold on the imagination, until it is clear that the fabric of Ireland is being described." Alannah Hopkin, for the *Financial Times* (August 8, 1992), by contrast, complained that the subject matter "could have made an interesting short novel but the gold-embossed jacket and its 509 pages suggest that the publishers were aiming at a . . . blockbuster leading to a TV mini-series, and, sure enough, the proceedings are enlivened by a shooting, a hero in [a] coma for months, and a near-miraculous recovery."

Delaney followed *The Sins of the Mother* with *Telling the Pictures* (1993). Set in Belfast in 1942, the novel relates the story of Belle MacKnight, a Protestant mill worker who has a talent for retelling and reenacting Hollywood movies. Her co-workers, too poor to attend the movies individually, combine their resources and send Belle so that they can collectively participate in the movie when she reenacts it. "In her apron and turban-tied headscarf she climbed on the table of the spinning-room in Rufus Street and dramatised, in her own sharp accent, the passions of Hollywood. With her wide eyes, and her wit, and her hands weaving gestures like a magician casting spells, she pierced the overcast of their long, dirty days," Carl Macdougall quoted from the novel in the Glasgow *Herald* (November 20, 1993). Belle soon falls in love with Eugene Crawford, a Catholic from Southern Ireland who works in the mill beginning a love story that suggests the divisions that continue to dominate the lives of those in Northern Ireland. As they had done when they had reviewed Delaney's previous novel, some critics found fault with the length of *Telling the Pictures*. "The narrative has a succession of false starts, and twists, eventually culminating in Gene's arrest and trial, which in itself is anything but straightforward," Macdougall wrote before going on to complain, "As with his early accounts of the film sequences, Delaney tells too much." Other critics, however, found the length of the book helpful because it allowed Delaney to provide a detailed account of the novel's themes. Sian

Phillips wrote for the London *Daily Mail* (November 20, 1993), for example, "Delaney dodges none of the issues as they appeared in 1942 and it is one of the great virtues of the book that the account of the trial of an innocent young man and the ruin of two young lives is so deeply felt that it provokes feelings of outrage and pity that are acute and fresh as though one were hearing of such a tragedy for the first time." Similarly, Rachel Billington wrote for the *Financial Times* (December 4, 1993), "Delaney is revealed to have a serious purpose, to be intent on revealing corruption in high places, showing the cruelty of sectarian loyalties, the bitter unfairness of Ulsterman towards Catholic. It is a black picture, turning a book that seems set to be a romance into a thriller."

Delaney's next novel, *A Stranger in Their Midst* (1995), revisited the Deanstown of *The Sins of the Mother*. Set in the 1950s the novel takes up the story of Ellen and her husband, Thomas, who now have two daughters, Grace and Helena. The stranger of the title is Dennis Sykes, an ambitious womanizer who works his way through women and to the top of the engineering business, a career path that brings him to Deanstown to build a hydroelectric dam and furnish the village with electricity. The ensuing conflict between progress and tradition, decency and immorality produces the drama of the novel. Unfortunately, as Albert Read objected for the London *Evening Standard* (June 19, 1995), "we are over halfway through the novel before the stranger finally does arrive. . . . The over-long build-up to the beginning of the main plot unbalances the novel." Delaney's presentation of detail could impress as well as dismay critics. Peter Cunningham, for example, praised Delaney in the *Irish Times* (July 14, 1995) for using "his racy, raunchy skills in presenting this period piece" and noted that "the closed way of life in a rural parish comes across well," but he also joined other critics in doubting the book needed to be so long. David O'Donoghue of the *Sunday Business Post* (September 5, 2004), by contrast, was "won over by the author's intricate portraits of county people's lives in post–civil war Ireland."

In his next novel, *The Amethysts* (1996), Delaney took his readers beyond the shores of Ireland to tell the story of Nicholas Newman, a British architect whose lover, Madeleine, a child during the Holocaust, was brutally murdered three years before the novel opens. While on a short holiday in Switzerland, Newman encounters an elderly Hungarian couple and observes in the photographs they are showing him an amethyst Eiffel Tower, an object that was stolen from Madeleine at the time of her murder. Attempts to destroy Newman's life follow. His shampoo is replaced with acid the night he sees the photograph, and the next day he finds that his credit cards are invalid and his bank accounts have been emptied. Back in London he is attacked by joggers, and while he is recovering in the hospital, he is visited by an elderly man who gives him a file that reveals why Madeleine has been murdered and why he is being pursued. During World War II Madeleine had been the victim of a Nazi experiment that sought to find ways to undermine Jewish culture by destroying the family unit. This part of the story "defies logic," Phillip Knightley observed for the *Mail on Sunday* (July 20, 1997), but he went on to say, "It could be argued that it doesn't matter because this is a compelling novel. It's written with pace, verve and imagination, and the reader is so carried along with the plot as to be convinced that everything the author says happened could have happened." Delaney's writing also impressed Chris Petite for the London *Guardian* (August 7, 1997). "Writing quality, gift-of-the-gab prose," he observed, "broadcaster Delaney effortlessly hooks the reader." Vincent Banville, writing for the *Irish Times* (July 1, 1997) found fault with the details of the story but went on to note, "one continues reading, for in this case the whole is greater than the parts, and the book, when viewed with the correct amount of incredulity, becomes an enjoyable read."

Delaney's next novel, *Desire and Pursuit* (1998), is again set in Ireland and again deals with the problems that have plagued Northern Ireland. Beginning in 1972 and following its protagonists over the next two decades, *Desire and Pursuit* tells the story of Ann Martin, an upper-class Irish woman, and Christopher Hunter, an English journalist covering the Irish troubles who observes Ann on her wedding day and unbeknownst to her falls madly in love. Calling the story "mad," Janet Chimonyo, writing for the *Australian* (November 30, 1998), nonetheless argued, "Delaney more or less carries it off, along with several companion improbabilities concerning stolen toddlers and women who get locked up in the nuthouse by disaffected husbands." While also admitting the events of the novel "might have gone a bit over the top," Betty Kirkpatrick, writing for the Glasgow *Herald* (September 30, 1998), concluded, "This is a moving and highly successful novel and at least part of its success lies in the author's skilful use of language."

Delaney followed *Desire and Pursuit* with two more thrillers, *Pearl* (1999) and *At Ruby's* (2001). Both novels resurrect Nicholas Newman from *The Amethysts* and again explore the influence Nazism continues to have on Europe. Frances O'Rourke observed for the *Irish Times* (November 6, 1999), "Our collective fascination with the legacy of Nazi evil, with the power of events close to 60 years ago to haunt the present, has provided many a thriller writer with the basis of a good plot. Frank Delaney proves that it's a source that can still be mined with success." The plot of *At Ruby's* deals with the theft of property from Jews during the war. "Sometimes poetic, sometimes melodramatic, Frank Delaney has combined passion and suspense with a serious underlying theme. This is a very superior thriller,"

David Shukman wrote for the London *Daily Mail* (June 29, 2001). "The storytelling is pacy and the descriptions meticulous. My only doubt is about the characters. Far from the usual literary pattern of normal people being thrust into abnormal situations, Delaney's people start off odd and become odder—which wouldn't matter if their behaviour was a little more convincing." In 2001 Delaney also published *Jim Hawkins and the Curse of Treasure Island*, using the pseudonym Francis Bryan. The book is a sequel to Robert Louis Stevenson's *Treasure Island* (1883) in which the narrator of Stevenson's novel, Jim Hawkins, is obliged to return to the island. "Aficionados of Stevenson's classic," John Harper wrote for the *Orlando Sentinel* (July 7, 2002), "will not be disappointed by *Curse* because it captures every bit of the swashbuckling spirit of the earlier work. Written in a high style, it is masterfully crafted with much care given to logistical accuracy."

In 2004 Delaney released his first novel in the U.S. Simply called *Ireland*, the novel integrates a history of Ireland as told by an itinerant storyteller or *seanchai* and Ronan O'Mara, who at the age of nine welcomes the seanchai into his home and later sets out to find him. In the process Ronan becomes, in effect, a seanchai himself. The fictionalized account of Irish history that emerges led some reviewers to fault the book for being overly ideal. Dermot Bolger, for example, wrote for the *Irish Times* (October 3, 2004) that the novel is "decidedly old-fashioned" and complained that it "falls into the trap of viewing Irish history as one grand narrative or a morality tale." In a similar vein David O'Donoghue, for the Dublin *Sunday Business Post* (September 5, 2004), observed, "we get a potted history. . . . And just like the Folen's history books of old, everything ends in the shining light of liberation from English rule. There is no mention of the civil war, which would only spoil Delaney's rose-tinted vision of the glorious new state." Other critics, however, found the novel compelling. Greg Langley, in a review for the Baton Rouge *Advocate* (February 27, 2005), lauded it for "exalting the art of storytelling as well as demonstrating the author's love of all things Irish" and went on to note that Delaney's "characters are very vivid, and their speech is so accurate, you almost hear their brogue as they read." Bill Sheehan, writing for the *Washington Post* (March 16, 2005), observed, "The stories of Irish history are familiar but still stirring, and Delaney brings a fresh perspective and a depth of understanding to the telling. His detailed grasp of Irish history lends weight and authority to this long, discursive tale."

Following the success of *Ireland* Delaney returned to nonfiction, writing *Simple Courage: A True Story of Peril on the Sea* (2006), a book that tells the story of the 1951 shipwreck of the freighter *The Flying Enterprise*, the rescue of its crew and passengers, and the captain, Henrik Kurt Carlsen. Many critics were unimpressed by both the story and Delaney's retelling of it. The rescue of the passengers and crew, a reviewer wrote for *Publishers Weekly* (May 15, 2006), "was indeed harrowing—and it's over by page 92 of this overblown maritime-distress yarn. The rest of the book is about the *Enterprise*'s captain, Kurt Carlsen, who insisted on staying aboard to await a tugboat to tow the floundering ship to harbor. . . . Carlsen's story generated a lot of breathless press hoopla at the time, and it still has the feel of a trumped-up media sensation." Others were more impressed by the story. Delaney, Larry Cox wrote for the *Tucson Citizen* (July 6, 2006), "has written a gripping, absorbing narrative that highlights one man's outstanding fortitude and heroic sense of duty."

Delaney had almost died in 1995, after sustaining a small cut while changing at the gym. He had contracted septicaemia, a blood-poisoning disease, and spent three weeks in the hospital. "I am working to achieve a certain balance in my daily routine. I changed my diet and my lifestyle very fast after the illness," he told Yvonne Swann for the London *Daily Mail* (August 5, 1997). "I had been doing the usual things—overworking, eating steak and chips and giving in to my sweet tooth. I automatically gave up red meat and ate loads of fish and fresh vegetables." After almost 20 years of living in England, where he has three grown sons, Frank, Bryan, and Owen, from his first marriage, Delaney moved to the U.S. He now divides his time between Connecticut and New York. In 2002 he married Diane Meier, the owner of Meier Inc., an advertising and marketing company in New York City. When he is not working, Delaney retreats from his professional life as much as possible, avoiding both his books and the radio shows he has recorded. Discussing the books he has written, he told Amanda Doherty, "I just can't pick them up. If I did I would continually find faults in them that would haunt me. I also can't bear to listen to myself on radio because I always hear faults in my presentation."

—A.R.

Suggested Reading: (Glasgow) *Herald* p11 Sep. 4, 1993; (London) *Daily Mail* p37 Nov. 20, 1993; (London) *Mail on Sunday* p38 July 20, 1997; *Publishers Weekly* p44 Dec. 13, 2004; *New York Times* C p9 Feb. 2, 1982

Selected Books: nonfiction—*James Joyce's Odyssey: A Guide to the Dublin of* Ulysses, 1981; *Betjeman Country*, 1983; *The Celts*, 1986; *A Walk through the Dark Ages*, 1988; *A Walk to the Western Isles: After Boswell and Johnson*, 1993; *Simple Courage: A True Story of Peril on the Sea*, 2006; fiction—*My Dark Rosaleen*, 1989; *The Sins of the Mother*, 1992; *Telling the Pictures*, 1993; *A Stranger in Their Midst*, 1995; *The Amethysts*, 1998; *Desire and Pursuit*, 1998; *Pearl*, 1999; *At Ruby's*, 2001; *Ireland*, 2004; as Francis Bryan—*Jim Hawkins and the Curse of Treasure Island*, 2001

Courtesy of Greg Delanty

Delanty, Greg

July 19, 1958– Poet

Greg Delanty composed the following for *World Authors 2000–2005*:

"I was born in Cork city in 1958. My mother, Eileen O'Sullivan, came from a working class background and began full-time work in the local textile mill at the age of 14. My father, a compositor, was from a middle-class background of teachers and nurses on his mother's side and compositor printers on his father's. I have one brother, Norman, who is now a doctor. I was educated in Scoil and Coláiste Chríost Rí, a very Catholic and Gaelic orientated school system, and received my B.A. degree from University College Cork in English and History. We lived in a housing estate right in the outskirts of the city and within view of farmed hills, the city dump, the city airport, and a dilapidated English army garrison. I've lived in this type of zone for the most part of my 45 years. My home now is on the outskirts of Burlington, Vermont, looking out over Lake Champlain and the Adirondacks, with planes continually flying over from and to Burlington airport. Perhaps, I can only feel at home on the periphery, the outside, the Cimmerian land between city and country. Or, is it here that I've made or found a center where I can keep tabs on the rural and the urban world and the connection between both?

"My emigration and immigration poems from *Southward* (1992) to *The Blind Stitch* (2001) open up from my specific experience as an Irish emigrant/immigrant in America to the metaphorical search for home, and all that means, for everyone:

> Perhaps now I understand the meaning of home
> For I'm in a place, but it is not in me . . .
> –'Home from Home'

"As Joel Brouwer has said in a review of *Southward* in the *Harvard Review* (Fall 1993): '. . . deracination, more than anything else, is what defines twentieth century culture. If this is so, Greg Delanty's keen remembrances and deep longing for his native land should speak to all of us.' The theme of the emigrant/immigrant continues from *Southward* into *American Wake (1995)*—an 'American Wake' was the get-together people had in Ireland for those emigrating to America, which was both festive and mournful:

> . . . In them uncover the destiny
> of everyone,
> For all are exiled and in search
> of a home,
> As you settle the eroding
> island of each poem . . . .
> –'The Splinters'

"*The Hellbox* (1998) refers to the box or bin in which broken or worn type was thrown to be recast in the printer's composing room. This is a metaphor for breaking down language into a renewed type, for the melting pot of America, for remaking oneself in general:

> I trekked to the Eagle and the unassuming redbrick
>   where you first set *Leaves*, forecasting how you
> and all you composed in your time would be
>   dismantled and distributed in the composing room
> of America before being finally cast aside,
>   melted down and recast in the likes of us,
> each life set in its unique and sometimes fitting
>   fonts and distributed or flung in
> the hellbox, turning up again diffused in others.
>   But it's our time to set our lives down,
> to select and fix them with our own measure
>   in a ligature affixing characters who've gone
> before to those close by now and way off in the future
>   –'Ligature' (this poem is addressed to Walt Whit-
>   man and should be set in ligature type)

"*The Blind Stitch* is less directly involved with deracination, and more taken up with intimating connections with the human past and present, and with the natural world. The book is sewn with two main conceits and arranged thematically in the form of a palindrome. In the poem 'The Malayalam Box' the palindrome gives the 'kibosh' to the notion that an artist must choose either perfection of the work or of the life, stating, 'poetry and life/ [are] a kind of palindrome of one another like the word *Malayalam*.' One of the metaphorical conceits is that of a leper, which concerns personal and public suffering and complicity; the other conceit is that of needlework, the threads that run through our public and private lives, seen and unseen, 'stitching us all together.' Metaphor in all my books is the portal through which layers of revitalizing surprise connections and shared experience are revealed. Like many poets I have tried to make, out of the experience of my own life, a shape-changing metaphor for other people's lives no matter how distant they are in place and time— indeed, the more foreign and distant the better.

"*The Ship of Birth* (2004) logs the days before and after a child is born and is written from the vantages of a father, his hopes, fears, wonder, and perplexity:

I'm back again scrutinizing the Milky Way
    of your ultrasound, scanning the dark
        matter, the nothingness, that now the heads say
is chockablock with quarks & squarks,
gravitons & gavitini, photons & photinos. Our sprout
who art there inside the spacecraft
    of your ma, the time capsule of this printout,
        hurling & whirling towards us, it's all daft
on this earth. Our alien who art in the heavens,
our Martian, our little green man, we're anxious
to make contact, to ask divers questions
        about the heavendom you hail from, to discuss
            the whole shebang of the beginning&end,
        the pre-big bang untime before you forget the why
and lie of thy first place. And, our friend,
to say Welcome, that we mean you no harm, we'd die
    for you even that we pray you're not here
        to subdue us, that we'd put away
        our ray guns, missiles, attitude and share
our world with you, little big head, if only you stay.
    –'The Alien'

"The poems in *The Ship of Birth*, in a different way than in previous books, register the seen and unseen interconnections of place, people and the natural world, and the continuity of the past with the present and the future. This is achieved not alone in content, but in the style and form of the poems, recalling the line and open voice of the 17th-century religious poets such as Herbert and Vaughan, the immediacy of Gaelic poetry, the interplay of traditional forms such as the sonnet and the more open forms of the 20th and 21st centuries.

"I've sought to keep form and content in sync, utilizing traditional and open form. For instance, with regard to traditional form, an early practitioner of the sonnet was Spenser who played [an] important role in the colonization of Cork and Munster. I have used this form throughout my poems as a symbol of complicity, both overtly and also covertly in poems that are not political. Spenser, returning from the dead, speaking in sonnet form within the longish poem 'The Splinters' admonishes:

Had shed blood been ink, I could still be
quilling The Faerie Queene, but I did not
allow a drop to blot a mere sonnet
    that you, trapped in complicity, can never
quite break free of. Admit it, hypocrite.
    In your time few are not guilty of slaughter.
Even the page you'll pen this upon is of pine
that Amazonians were shot for. I could go on.

"All my books since *American Wake* are intended to be read from start to finish. Almost all the poems stand on their own, but they also work together as a loose, larger poem. I have, for the most part, wanted my poetry be accessible while concealing complexity and interconnectedness below the surface. I do not want cleverness to overwhelm the poetry's impetus.

"Apart from my own poems I have translated mainly from Greek and Gaelic. I've done versions of Aristophanes' *The Knights*, which I retitled *The Suits*, and also Euripides's *Orestes*—which I would retitle now *The Family*. I was helped in these translations by my now deceased friend Katharine Washburn. I also translated the Gaelic poems of Liam Ó Muirthile, and I am presently translating the first modernist Gaelic poet, Sean O'Riordain, who also came from Cork. Along with these I have edited with Nuala Ni Dhomhnaill, *Jumping Off Shadows: Selected Contemporary Irish Poets* and edited and selected with Robert Welch *The New and Selected Poems of Patrick Galvin*. The latter two books are centered in Cork and the southwest of Ireland. This region's writing—with its mixture of Gaelic and English traditions and its Latin sensibility—I've tried to bring attention to.

"I live in Burlington, Vermont with my wife, Patricia Ferreira, and my son Daniel Delanty, named after my father. I teach in the English department of St. Michael's College. I became an American citizen in 1994 and have always been publically active, demonstrating against political policy I disagree with, and particularly against military actions and the destruction of the environment, taking part in protests, vigils and committing civil disobedience. This public commitment emanates as much from my writer self as from my civic self. I believe in poetry not as a career, but as a way of life."

———————

The poet Greg Delanty was born on July 19, 1958 in Cork, Ireland. From an early age he was determined to pursue his literary aspirations, despite his mother's wish that he enter a more profitable line of business. "She always wanted me to get a job in a bank," Delanty told Brian Lavery for the London *Sunday Times* (March 12, 2006), "They wouldn't have given me a job in a bank, anyway. From 17, I knew what I wanted to do. I wanted to write poems and that was it, and I put my head down and I've stayed true to that. I said I was going to be a great poet, because you're arrogant as a young fella. But you have to be a bit arrogant to take it on." At the National University of Ireland's University College Cork (UCC), he studied under the noted professors Sean Lucy and John Montague, and for that reason he is often lumped in with what later became known as the Cork school of poets, which includes such figures as Gregory O'Donoghue, Sean Dunne, and Nuala Ní Dhomhnaill. Delanty received bachelor's degrees in English and history, in 1980, and earned a diploma in education from UCC, in 1982. He then taught English for four years at an educational and vocational college, which was also in Cork. In 1983 he won the first of many literary prizes yet to come, the prestigious Patrick Kavanagh Award, and three years later the Dolmen Press, which had published the works of the Irish literary luminary William Butler Yeats, issued Delanty's first collection of verse, *Cast in the Fire* (1986). That same year he left his native country for the U.S., where served as a visiting poet at the University of Vermont, in Burlington, from 1986 to 1987. Since then Delanty has taught English at Saint Michael's College, in Colchester, Vermont.

In 1992, with Delanty's first publication in the U.S., *Southward*, the poet established himself as a "a particularly distinctive voice in the generation of Irish poets emerging in the 1990s," according to Thomas O'Grady, writing for the *Irish Literary Supplement* (Fall 1994). While most of the poems in the collection are primarily set in the poet's homeland—particularly Cork and the nearby County Kerry—Delanty included pieces that both detail his struggles as an emigrant and his impressions of his new home in America. "There are, in the textures of Delanty's speech and thought, a directness, an honesty, and a verve that are always engaging," David R. Slavitt wrote for the Louisiana State University Press Web site. "The achievements of *Southward* promise a long and vibrant career for this prizewinning young poet."

In Delanty's next collection of poetry, *American Wake* (1995), exile is the predominant theme around which the "poems whirl and veer," according to a reviewer for *Publishers Weekly* (January 22, 1996). "In Delanty's hands, the issue is quite humbly (and refreshingly) domesticated," the reviewer continued, "brought not only down to earth but to the Bronx, to his adopted Vermont, cherished for its snow, which 'covers / any resemblance / to that other one / & its perpetual row.' Still, one feels the longing in the voice, and at times the seducer seems set upon an Irish prey, not an American one. The collection is none the worse for that, however, for Delanty's voice indeed is Irish—making music of earthenware, a poetry 'hewn out of bones' and displaying a deceptively casual mastery of form and softly muffled rhyme." In the London *Independent* (November 12, 1995), William Scammell pointed out that Delanty "allows that he may be 'a parody of the Irish / with my hangover & rebellious inferiority, or was it superiority? / Both, perhaps'." Nevertheless, Scammell concluded, "The stronger poems, such as 'On the Renovation of Ellis Island' and 'Backfire', get down past the stereotypes into an unvarnished and convincing present." In 2004 the poetry from *American Wake* was featured in a movie of the same title, which was directed by the Irish American filmmaker Maureen Foley.

Delanty's 1998 collection, *The Hellbox*, takes its title from the bin which typesetters once used—before the current computer-based design programs made such work unnecessary—to discard broken type so that it could be melted down for recycling. The volume not only contains poems about typesetting but also has several poems printed as they would be typeset—backwards. "In choosing the conceit of typography," a reviewer wrote for *Publishers Weekly* (September 28, 1998), "Delanty is able to spell out the life of his father, a printer in Cork; convey his fascination with the English language in all its materiality; and in the end, somehow break type, shattering the increasingly heavy burden of being an Irish writer in exile without becoming just another American poet. . . . The discarded fonts of memory, more obliquely reflected in earlier books like *Southward* and *American Wake*, are here recast and set into a strong book of verse, solid in its frame."

In 1999 Delanty won second prize in the Poetry Society's National Poetry Competition—Britain's longest-running poetry competition—with his "Behold the Brahminy Kite," a poem inspired by his travels in India. Imagery from his trip to the subcontinent was also woven into Delanty's 2001 collection, *The Blind Stitch*. The title uses the technique of blindstitching, which is employed by quilters to hide all but a tiny bit of thread from view, as a metaphor for the unseen connections that exist among people in daily life. "Delanty's stitching can seem all too visible, with wobbly syntax and uncertain diction slowing the pace of the weaker poems here," Patrick Crotty wrote for the *Irish Times* (June 23, 2001). "His book exploits an elaborate figurative machinery, linking the Cork of his childhood to the India of a recent sojourn through the figure of the leper priest Father Damien, to whom he was devoted as a boy. The poet's mother's remembered needlework connects to the sewing of children in Third World sweatshops and to the relentless poetic stitching of her son." Carol Muske-Dukes, writing for the *Los Angeles Times Book Review* (November 3, 2002), characterized *The Blind Stitch* as "engaging" and pointed to the "heavily inflected, heady music of his mother tongue" as one of the book's "many beauties."

In *The Ship of Birth* (2004), which written in anticipation of the arrival of Delanty's son, Daniel, the poet expresses his desire to be a seahorse so that "I, / being the male, would be the one in the family way," according to Colin Graham, writing for the *Irish Times* (April 3, 2004). Graham praised the poems in this volume, in which "new parental experiences mix with vivid childhood memories," as "fascinatingly intimate, open and unashamedly domestic." Brian Lavery noted that the "bright and often light-hearted tone" of *The Ship of Birth*, stood in "sharp contrast to the darkness" of the collection of 15 previously unpublished poems—titled "Aceldama," meaning "field of blood"—that were included in Delanty's *Collected Poems 1986–2006* (2006). Though these new pieces reflected the poet's anger over the 2003 U.S.-led invasion of Iraq, Lavery argued that "there are no Bush-bashing screeds, anti-war manifestos or impassioned pleas about common humanity." The poet explained to the reporter: "If you get too explicitly political, you close down the space for the reader to make up their own mind, and that's lecturing or standing on a soapbox. It's anti-art, really. If you're too upfront you'll shut people out. It's about leaving space for people to enter. When people try to figure it out they become part of it."

Delanty, who has remained politically active since he started advocating for the homeless and supporting nuclear disarmament campaigns in the 1980s, unsuccessfully ran for office of high baliff in Vermont on the Green Party ticket in 2004. "It was a joke, like," he told Brian Lavery. "We were putting ourselves on the ballot just so people knew that we existed." Nonetheless, he nearly won, drawing 38 percent of the vote.

Delanty was recently named a Guggenheim Foundation fellow for 2007–08.

—S.Y.

Suggested Reading: *Irish Times* Weekend p9 Nov. 18, 1995, Weekend p10 Apr. 1, 2006; (London) *Independent* Features p12 Mar. 21, 1999; (London) *Sunday Times* Features p18 Mar. 12, 2006; *Los Angeles Times Book Review* p14 Nov. 3, 2002

Selected Works: *Cast in the Fire*, 1986; *Southward*, 1992; *American Wake*, 1995; *The Hellbox*, 1998; *The Blind Stitch*, 2001; *The Ship of Birth*, 2004; *Collected Poems, 1986–2006*, 2006; as editor—*Jumping Off Shadows: Selected Contemporary Irish Poets* (with Nuala Ní Dhomhnaill), 1995; *New and Selected Poems of Patrick Galvin* (with Robert Welch), 1996; as translator—*Selected Poems of Kyriakos Charalambides*, 2005

D'Emilio, John

1948– Essayist; biographer; historian

Lost Prophet: The Life and Times of Bayard Rustin (2003), a biography of a noted civil rights activist, earned John D'Emilio, its author, a National Book Award nomination in the nonfiction category. For D'Emilio, a Distinguished Professor of history, gender studies, and women's studies at the University of Illinois, at Chicago, as well as a longtime political activist, the success of the Rustin book is representative of the two principles that he has successfully fused throughout his career—the academic's search for truth and the idealist's quest for social justice.

Born in 1948, D'Emilio grew up in the New York City borough of the Bronx, where at an early age he developed a strong idealistic bent; in an editorial article for *New York Newsday* (October 25, 1992), D'Emilio recalled a description of the U.S. that he had memorized as a child: "The land of the free and the home of the brave, conceived in liberty and dedicated to the proposition that all men are created equal." Such sentiments left a lasting impression on him, and this belief in equality became one of the chief principles of his later work. After completing high school in the mid-1960s, D'Emilio entered Columbia University, in New York City. It proved a tough transition as he began to wrestle with his sexuality: "The only thing I remember about [freshmen] orientation was that a campus minister told me that God was dead. It did little to comfort my Roman Catholic soul. No one spoke to me about being gay. If someone had, I might not have tried to commit suicide in my dorm room; I might not have remained isolated from most of my peers on campus, and I might not have had to struggle for several more years with my

sexual identity before coming to peace with myself," he wrote in a letter to the *New York Times* (September 20, 1992).

Despite his difficulties, in 1970 D'Emilio graduated cum laude and Phi Beta Kappa from Columbia. He remained there and in 1972 earned a master's degree. He received a New York State Lehman Fellowship for the years 1972 to 1976, during which he worked as a contributing editor for the *New Columbia Encyclopedia*, became a founding member (and board member) of the Gay Academic Union, and developed into a fervent gay-rights activist. In 1975 D'Emilio was named a Kent fellow by the Danforth Foundation and held the fellowship through 1977. Around this time he began doctoral studies in history at Columbia. In 1979 he edited *The Civil Rights Struggle: Leaders in Profile*, which gave brief accounts of the movement's luminaries. In addition to his academic duties and writing, he worked as a program developer for the Bank Street College Day Care Consultation Services from 1977 to 1978, as assistant director of Voters Against the Prison Construction Bond in 1981, and as a policy analyst for the Day Care Forum from 1981 to 1983.

D'Emilio completed his doctoral coursework in 1982; his dissertation on gay history in the U.S. was nominated for Columbia University's prestigious Bancroft Prize. After obtaining his doctorate D'Emilio accepted a position as an assistant professor of history at the University of North Carolina, at Greensboro (UNCG), a post he held from 1983 through 1988. In his first year at UNCG, D'Emilio released his revamped dissertation as *Sexual Politics, Sexual Communities: The Making of the Homosexual Minority in the United States, 1940–1970* (1983). The book was dubbed "a milestone in the history of the American gay movement," by Rudy Kikel, writing for the *Boston Globe*, as quoted on

Amazon.com. The book catalogs the various forms of oppression homosexuals were subjected to, pointing out, for example, that during the McCarthy era alleged homosexuality resulted in more lost jobs than supposed communist sympathies. D'Emilio also examined the movement's early trailblazers, men and women who struggled to gain acceptance for homosexuals at a time when the cultural atmosphere was decidedly more hostile to such endeavors than it is today. A critic for the *New York Times Book Review* wrote, "John D'Emilio provides homosexual political struggles with something that every movement requires—a sympathetic history rendered in a dispassionate voice," as quoted on Amazon.com. The work established D'Emilio as one of the foremost chroniclers of the homosexual experience in the U.S.; it has become a classic in the field and a required text for many college courses.

In 1988 D'Emilio became an associate professor at UNCG and that year published *Intimate Matters: A History of Sexuality in America*, a book he co-wrote with Estelle B. Freedman. The volume surveyed American sexual practices and attitudes over the course of four centuries. The work was exhaustive in its scope: "The authors," a critic for *Publishers Weekly* wrote, as quoted on Amazon.com, "cram into 400 pages balanced discussions of racial sex-stereotyping, Chinese slave rings, abortion, same-sex relationships, women's rights and AIDS-engendered conservatism." One of the central propositions put forward in the work, as Barbara Ehrenreich noted for the *New York Times Book Review* (April 24, 1988), was that "the most persistent and inexorable force pushing America toward sexual liberalization was capitalism itself." Ehrenreich continued, "John D'Emilio and Estelle Freedman are not the first to say this, but they say it so convincingly and with such a wealth of suggestive evidence that they might as well take the credit. . . . John D'Emilio and Estelle B. Freedman deserve our gratitude for putting sex in its proper place—which is in the long, uneven movement toward a more diverse and democratic society." Johnathan Yardley offered similar praise, opining for the *Washington Post* (May 8, 1988), "*Intimate Matters* is comprehensive, meticulous and intelligent; it also resists, at every turn, titillation and prurience."

From 1988 through 1993 D'Emilio served as UNCG's director of graduate studies. During that time he published an essay collection, *Making Trouble: Essays on Gay History, Politics, and the University*. Fusing academic scholarship with his personal experience, he focused on the reality of American gay history in the post–World War II era, the university's response to the emergence of homosexual awareness, and the political aspect of the gay-rights movement. In *Making Trouble*, a *Library Journal* critic noted, "D'Emilio advocates nothing less than a total reevaluation of our society's sexual paradigm," as quoted on Amazon.com.

In 1993 D'Emilio received a full professorship at UNCG; he left in 1998 to serve as a visiting scholar in Washington, D.C., at George Washington University's graduate program in public policy. The next year he accepted a professorship in the gender and women's studies program and the department of history at the University of Illinois, at Chicago. In 2000 D'Emilio edited, with William B. Turner and Urvashi Vaid, the essay collection *Creating Change: Sexuality, Public Policy, and Civil Rights*. The collection "chronicles the history, successes, and failures of the gay agenda, from the passionate immediacy of public protest marches to the plodding maneuverings of political and public policy initiatives," according to a reviewer for *Library Journal* (August 2000). Contributors included the activist Frank Kameny and Congressman Barney Frank of Massachusetts. Like D'Emilio's previously published works, *Creating Change* received a positive reception: A critic for *Publishers Weekly* (July 31, 2000) wrote, "Vaid, D'Emilio, and Turner know their material well. . . . This collection of 26 articulate, scholarly essays [is] both necessary and commendable."

D'Emilio next published *The World Turned: Essays on Gay History, Politics, and Culture* (2002). The work consisted of previously published personal essays, reviews, and biographical sketches; the covered topics included D'Emilio's sex life, Pat Buchanan's homophobia, and the possible genetic root of homosexuality. A *Library Journal* critic (July 2002) offered ringing praise for the volume, writing, "The 16 pieces collected here, which cover historical topics, contemporary issues, and personal essays, blend together into a vivid portrait of gay thought in the past 15 years, showing how the gay community became a vital part of American life during the 1990s." as quoted on Amazon.com.

Lost Prophet: The Life and Times of Bayard Rustin is D'Emilio's latest book. In it he examined the life of the influential and complex civil rights leader who provided the organizational mettle behind the legendary 1963 march on Washington. Born into an African-American Quaker family in Pennsylvania, Rustin began working for civil rights—and leftist causes more generally—early in life. He espoused Gandhian nonviolence (serving time in prison for refusing to fight in World War II) and was instrumental in converting Dr. Martin Luther King Jr. to the doctrine; for this, D'Emilio wrote, "Rustin was as responsible as anyone else for the insinuation of nonviolence into the very heart of what became the most powerful social movement in 20th-century America." Early in his career, Rustin flirted with communism before resigning from the party following the announcement of Stalin's non-aggression pact with Hitler. What proved even more damaging to Rustin's career than his communist past was his open homosexuality, for which he was periodically arrested and persecuted. Rustin never lost faith in his mission, however, observing, "God does not require us to achieve any of the good tasks that humanity must pursue. What God requires of us is that we not stop trying," as quoted by D'Emilio.

The critical response to the biography was overwhelmingly positive: Brian Palmer wrote for New York Newsday (August 3, 2003), "D'Emilio's prose is clear and unadorned, scholarly in a straightforward way without being academic"; a critic for Kirkus Reviews (June 1, 2003) characterized the work as an "eye-opening look at the personal ordeal underlying a revolutionary quest."

D'Emilio has been the recipient of many awards and commendations over the years. In 1995 he received a fellowship from the National Humanities Center, which he declined; he later accepted fellowships from the National Endowment for the Humanities and the Guggenheim Memorial Foundation. D'Emilio is currently the gender and women's studies program director at the University of Illinois, a position he will relinquish when his five-year term expires in 2007.

Summing up his philosophy in his New York Newsday editorial, D'Emilio wrote, "The essence of the American social contract is that we keep reaching for a better order of things, for a vision of justice and human dignity that has always been a bit beyond our grasp. This is what gays, lesbians and all good Americans are fighting for today."

—P.B.M.

Suggested Reading: Boston Globe F p8 Nov. 11, 2003; Los Angeles Times R p3 Aug. 24, 2003; National Book Award Web site; New York Newsday p7 Oct. 25, 1992; New York Times A p16 Sep. 20, 1992, B p7 Aug. 23, 2003; New York Times Book Review p1 Apr. 24, 1988, p13 Nov. 9, 2003; Washington Post Z p3 May 8, 1988, T p2 Sep. 7, 2003

Selected Books: Sexual Politics, Sexual Communities: The Making of a Homosexual Minority in the United States, 1940–1970, 1983; Intimate Matters: A History of Sexuality in America (with Estelle B. Freedman), 1988; Making Trouble: Essays on Gay History, Politics, and the University, 1992; The World Turned: Essays on Gay History, Politics, and Culture, 2002; Lost Prophet: The Life and Times of Bayard Rustin, 2003; as editor—The Civil Rights Struggle: Leaders in Profile, 1979; Creating Change: Sexuality, Public Policy, and Civil Rights (with William B. Turner and Urvashi Vaid), 2000

D'Erasmo, Stacey

1961– Novelist

Praised for her luminous prose, the novelist Stacey D'Erasmo has emerged as a leading light of the post-Stonewall generation of writers to whom being gay is simply a natural part of life, not something to be fought for or against. This attitude is evident in her two novels, *Tea* (2000) and *A Seahorse Year* (2004), in which the alternative lifestyles of the characters serve as background to dramatic tensions that emanate from more conventional family troubles. D'Erasmo's ethos is probably best articulated in a review she wrote for the *New York Times* (January 11, 2004), in which she praised the television series *The L Word* for presenting lesbians as "ambitious, modern women living their complicated lives with one another." She noted, "The fight for liberation is as grand as opera, but the dailiness of living a liberated life can come closer to soap opera; the police might not arrest you anymore, but it doesn't mean the girl you just slept with will call you back. . . . Being an L myself, a member of a group that has had a spotty presence on the small screen, I can testify with authority to the despair of bouncing along a life of risk, mystery and heartbreak only to turn on the TV and see two women in bad pantsuits

© Matt Carr/Courtesy of Houghton Mifflin

gingerly touching one another on the forearm. *The L Word* tosses those pantsuits to the wind, and good riddance to them."

Stacey D'Erasmo was born in New York City in 1961 and grew up near Washington, D.C. She has been writing fiction since the age of 10 and described her juvenilia as "a weird combination of bad TV, movies, the backs of cereal boxes, Louisa May Alcott, and Nancy Drew," according to Paula Martinac, writing for the *Lambda Book Report* (January 2000). As an undergraduate at Barnard College, in New York City, D'Erasmo wrote fiction that included blatantly homoerotic elements. "It was a very natural thing to me to be queer and to write about it," she told Martinac. After receiving her bachelor's degree, in 1983, she went on to obtain a master's degree in English and American literature, at New York University, in 1988. By the time she finished her master's degree, Erasmo decided she had had enough of academic life; instead she chose to work as a journalist, writing for such periodicals as New York *Newsday* and the *New York Times Book Review*. She also worked at the *Village Voice*, serving as a senior editor for the weekly's literary supplement. Later she was appointed the first editor of *Bookforum*. Though D'Erasmo enjoyed her work, she longed to write fiction again. She was finally afforded the opportunity to focus on creative writing after receiving a Stegner Fellowship from Stanford University, in California, in 1995. "To be given a gift like a Stegner fellowship when you're old enough to really understand what it means is fantastic," she told Martinac. "If I'd gotten something like that at 22, I would never have understood how precious it was. I was the happiest little Stegner in the world."

During her fellowship D'Erasmo finished her first novel, *Tea*, but it took her some time to find a publisher. "It's hard to know if it's because of the queer content," she told Martinac. "There's also the fact that not a lot happens in *Tea*. I'm not sure if the publishing industry is really as wildly homophobic as it is wildly profit-conscious. If Isabel had stuck up a bank or been mutilating herself at night, it probably would have sold faster." Finally, in 2000, the small, independent trade publisher Algonquin Books issued D'Erasmo's tale of a young lesbian coming of age in 1970s Philadelphia. D'Erasmo admitted to Liza Featherstone in an interview for New York *Newsday* (January 16, 2000) that Isabel, the principal character, shared certain traits with her creator: "To sit here and say, well, I wrote a book about a woman who's a lesbian who's about my age, but I didn't steal anything from myself, would be so obviously and patently a lie. I couldn't really pull that off. . . . The thing that I gave that was most like me is that she spends all this time thinking that she knows what's going on, and, in fact, she never does. . . . Probably the other thing I share with her is that her lesbianism is kind of natural to her. She comes out; it isn't some trauma, she just sort of proceeds. It's not the core of her; it's not her drama." The dramatic elements in the story arise from the suicide of Isabel's mother, who is an alcoholic. *Tea* is narrated in three sections: "Morning," when Isabel is 8; "Afternoon," when she is 16; and "Evening," when she is 22. "I wanted to write a novel in three parts, a kind of triptych about loss," she explained to Martinac. "I knew there would be a suicide and three different parts in the character's life about how she understood that loss at different times."

Reviewers generally found her successful, not only in presenting her plot, but in the beauty of her writing. Calling the book "lushly written," Donna Seaman noted for *Booklist* (November 1, 1999) that "D'Erasmo's prose possesses both the elan of a child playing make-believe and the insights gleaned from a truly literary writer's openness to subtle gradations of emotion and change." Victoria Segal, writing for the London *Times* (January 5, 2002), called *Tea* "a beautiful book, every bit as complex and inscrutable as its heroine, but equally engaging." While the reviewer also described the novel as "written with such quiet intensity that every detail seems to carry a symbolic weight," she noted that it "never seems overwrought," because "D'Erasmo has created a forceful, intuitive poetry out of everyday life, unafraid to use details of popular culture in her measured, multilayered narrative." *Tea* was selected as a New York Times Notable Book of the Year for 2000.

In 2004 D'Erasmo published her second novel, *A Seahorse Year*, in which she "explores how a supposedly unconventional family is no different from a traditional one when confronted with difficult choices," according to Misha Stone, writing for *Library Journal* (June 15, 2004). The unconventional San Francisco family in *A Seahorse Year* consists of Nan and Marina, lovers, who live with Christopher, the biological son of Nan and Hal, a gay man who works as an accountant. Crisis descends on the family when Christopher is diagnosed with schizophrenia and runs away. "Despite the unconventional setup, his parents sometimes act with the confused stiffness of the most traditional of families," a reviewer wrote for *Publishers Weekly* (May 17, 2004). In the *New York Times Book Review* (August 15, 2004), Margot Livesey agreed, noting that "a significant part of D'Erasmo's accomplishment is the absolute normalizing of Christopher's less-than-conventional family." She continued: "In the tradition of writers like Carol Shields and A. S. Byatt, [D'Erasmo] gives us a novel whose tension is almost entirely domestic. . . . Like Byatt and Shields, D'Erasmo is too interested in conveying the texture of lived experience to reach a neat conclusion. Certain aspects of her characters remain properly mysterious, and the novel's ending leaves them, as it should, in the midst of their lives. But what is abundantly clear throughout is D'Erasmo's talent and intelligence. *A Seahorse Year* succeeds in being both deeply satisfying and quietly subversive."

D'Erasmo has continued to write book reviews for such publications as New York *Newsday*, the *Nation*, and the *New York Times Book Review*. She is an assistant professor in the English department at Barnard College and lives in New York City, with Robyn Selman, a poet.

—S.Y.

Suggested Reading: *Lambda Book Report* p6 Jan. 2000; (New York) *Newsday* B p11 Jan. 16, 2000; *New York Times Book Review* p18 Aug. 15, 2004;

Selected Books: *Tea*, 2000; *A Seahorse Year*, 2004

Peter Waldvogel/Courtesy of CUNY Graduate Center

Dickstein, Morris

Feb. 23, 1940– Critic; essayist

The author of several prominent works of literary criticism, Morris Dickstein has focused much of his work on the cultural and literary history of the 1950s and 1960s. His well-known book *Gates of Eden: American Culture in the Sixties* (1977)—which established his place in contemporary criticism and was nominated for a National Book Critics Circle Award—explored the intellectual community of the 1960s, with a particular focus on the novel. With his work *Leopards in the Temple: The Transformation of American Fiction, 1945–1970* (2002), Dickstein expanded his exploration into the relation between literature and American society, examining how the post-World War II environment of the 1950s shaped numerous

American writers and gave way to the counterculture revolution of the 1960s. Dickstein's other major work, *Double Agent: The Critic and Society* (1992), sought to determine the role of the critic in contemporary literature. In 2004 he published *The Mirror in the Roadway: Literature and the Real World*, which was written for both students of literature and general audiences alike.

Morris Dickstein wrote the following for *World Authors 2000–2005*:

"No one ever grew up with the dream of becoming a literary critic. Certainly not a boy born, as I was, in 1940, to immigrant parents on the Lower East Side of New York, who went on to twelve years of schooling at an Orthodox Jewish yeshiva. In retrospect, a Talmudical education might orient one to textual commentary, but literary exegesis wasn't really what I wanted to do. I merely enjoyed reading and writing, and had a knack for talking about books.

"Early on I had a simple ambition: to know everything. With undiscriminating appetite, I devoured whatever I could lay my hands on: history, biography, fiction. Week by week, I read through whole sections of the local public library starting with art and anthropology. I looked for titillating details: I can still recall Margaret Mead's accounts of puberty rites in Samoa and New Guinea.

"Always in a hurry, I plowed through Somerset Maugham's egregious abridgements of the world's top ten novels: *Wuthering Heights*, *Old Man Goriot*, etc.—the classics with all the fat removed. I also had two exacting high school English teachers, careful speakers, close readers, unsparing critics of my own hapless prose and poetry. Still, when I went off to Columbia in 1957 I thought I would become a lawyer or journalist, since I was a facile writer and had a big mouth—I edited the school paper and traveled with the debating team.

"All this changed during my first two years in college. My religious friends gave way to tough-minded intellectuals from the Bronx High School of Science who had already taken college-level courses and had read even more than I did. My freshman English teacher, Jim Zito, who would later become a legend at Sarah Lawrence, had the most dazzling mind and acid style I ever encountered. Writing had always come easily to me but he made me work at it, boil it down to essentials, make every adjective, every metaphor count. At the same time the famous Humanities course exposed me to world literature from Homer to Dostoevsky with an exhilarating intensity. I began to devour books, not simply to read them; they became part of me.

"At the end of my sophomore year I read Lionel Trilling's *Liberal Imagination* and got a glimpse of what critical writing could really be. I was hooked. For the first time I thought of staying on in a university so I could keep reading, keep writing, keep talking about the books I desperately loved. Good teachers reinforced this passion: Andrew

Chiappe and Jim Zito on Shakespeare, F. W. Dupee on the classics, Trilling on modernism, Steven Marcus on the Romantic poets. They talked less like strenuous citizens of a community of letters rather than professional critics. They preferred personal or historical insight to technical analysis. Their love of ideas was infectious. They were not so much scholars as intellectuals, and the air was filled with politics, culture, and big ideas, not the safe prospect of graduate school.

"When I arrived at Yale as a graduate student in 1961 something else was in the air: an established critical formalism, demanding the kind of close reading I had never encountered outside Cleanth Brooks's *The Well Wrought Urn*. It was a conservative department, best known for its medievalists and 18th-century scholars. But there were also vague stirrings from a junior faculty stocked with beleaguered young romanticists like Harold Bloom, Geoffrey Hartman, and E.D. Hirsch, none of whom as yet taught graduate students. After two years I got a fellowship to Cambridge, where I worked informally with F. R. Leavis and Raymond Williams, then returned to Yale to tackle Keats under the newly tenured Bloom, just admitted grudgingly to graduate teaching.

"Seeing Keats as a tragic realist, a poet of self-making, I could not have been further from Bloom's view of the Romantics as a "visionary company." But I got a delicious pleasure out of our working friendship and his always provocative mind. My book *Keats and His Poetry* appeared in 1971 when I was back teaching at Columbia. But by then the big carnival of the 1960s, especially the antiwar movement, the counterculture, the student uprisings, and new writers like Pynchon and Heller, had already drawn me to contemporary issues.

"For years I had been reviewing new books for *Partisan Review*, *Commentary*, and the *New Republic*, more the pattern of a New York intellectual than the academic critic plowing his field. Finally, in an essay on Allen Ginsberg, I saw a way of synthesizing the serious culture of the sixties, bringing the work of novelists, poets, journalists, and rock singers together with my own personal and political experiences, including the 1968 student uprising at Columbia. While teaching at Queens College after 1971, I wrote a series of review-essays for the *Times Book Review* on contemporary writers like Barthelme, Mailer, Malamud, Roth, then published my book on the sixties, *Gates of Eden*, in 1977. It began with Ginsberg and concluded with a chapter of autobiography, very much in the spirit of personal witness I identified with the sixties.

"Much of my later work followed from this book. One turn took me towards film and popular culture, another passion of the sixties that had been a blind spot for older intellectuals. I began writing film criticism for *American Film*, the *Bennington Review*, and *Partisan Review*. Another turn took me back toward the 1930s, yet another

decade of social crisis, political tension, and cultural ferment. I was especially fascinated by the films of the thirties—gangster films, dance musicals, screwball comedies, protest movies, creature features—with their mixture of escapism and social consciousness. I began writing essays on film genres: horror movies, spy thrillers, films noirs, historical dramas, war movies. I grew fascinated by the tensions between an intransigent modernism and a highly accessible mass culture.

"Finally, as the work of my academic colleagues shifted towards theory and criticism, I found myself exploring the tradition behind my own blend of critical journalism, literary commentary, personal writing, and cultural history. Essays on practical criticism and book reviewing, polemics against post-structuralist theory, and reassessments of critics like Arnold, Trilling, and Kazin eventually led me to *Double Agent: The Critic and Society* (1992). The book emphasized the critic's need to balance art and social concern, personal response and public discourse, both neglected by theorists caught up in academic jargon and professionalism. I wrote essays that were salvos in the culture wars: on the literary canon, political correctness, identity politics, and new forms of ideological and historical criticism.

"In 1993 I created a Center for the Humanities at CUNY's graduate school and over the next seven years developed many public programs: tributes to leading writers and scholars like Ralph Ellison, Irving Howe, Alfred Kazin, Arthur Schlesinger Jr., Michael Harrington; panels and symposia on African-American art, law and literature, the work of Edward Hopper and Berenice Abbott. In 1995 I organized a two-day conference on pragmatism and expanded the results into a large book, *The Revival of Pragmatism* (1998). The impersonality of literary theory stimulated my autobiographical impulse, and I began publishing fragments of a future memoir. At the same time I completed a survey of American fiction after World War II for the *Cambridge History of American Literature* (vol. 7, 1999) and expanded it into a book, *Leopards in the Temple* (2002). Whichever way I turned, literature remained the center of gravity—to be served, not dominated, by critical writing.

"My favorite writers were displaced preachers, moral ironists as different as Wordsworth and Kafka, Blake and Benjamin, Hawthorne and Malamud, Henry James and Joseph Heller. To a remarkable extent, my values could be traced to those I had formed when young: the moral and textual exigency of my Jewish education, the urban cacophony and ethnic buzz of growing up in New York, my undergraduate faith in criticism as a form of *writing*, a branch of the intellectual life. I saw criticism, finally, as a visceral response to art in its moral and social complexity, at once personal and public, deeply attuned to how the imagination reshapes our common experience."

Morris Dickstein was born on February 23, 1940 in New York City. He received a B.A. degree from Columbia University, in 1961, and conducted postgraduate work at Yale University, in New Haven, Connecticut, where he earned his master's degree, in 1963, and his Ph.D., in 1967. In an essay for *Partisan Review* (No. 4, 1984–85), he acknowledged the shaping influence of his religious heritage on his later work: "My immersion in The Book became a passion for books. The stress on right conduct, which Matthew Arnold called the essence of Hebraism, was gradually directed into a new framework—secular, moral, and political rather than religious." By his own account Dickstein found himself becoming a "double agent," the critic who combines "a deep feeling for art with a powerful sense of its changing place in human society."

After publishing *Keats and His Poetry: A Study in Development* (1971), an analysis of the poet John Keats, Dickstein shifted his critical focus to American cultural studies. *Gates of Eden: American Culture in the Sixties*, nominated for a National Book Critics Circle Award in 1977, is a cultural history of the 1960s—through an analysis of the decade's prominent literature—written from the eyewitness point of view of a young graduate student and then college teacher. Observing the campus in his double role, Dickstein shared both the idealism of a generation inspired by the civil rights and other liberating movements and the bitter disillusion over the war in Vietnam. For him, as for many others, the 1960s was a period when the "search for personal authenticity" became identified with the "quest of social justice." In the 1968 student uprising on the campus of Columbia University, he served on a faculty committee attempting to conciliate and mediate—an experience that, he said, "finally showed me that I *was* a liberal rather than a radical." Overall, Dickstein judged the decade as having "a liberating effect on many of our lives." Rethinking the decade in an introduction he wrote for the paperback edition of *Gates of Eden* in 1989, Dickstein reiterated his judgment that the sensibility of the American people had been profoundly changed: "Many of the fundamental rights we now accord to women, gay people, and blacks belong to the legacy of the sixties."

Although throughout the book Dickstein predominantly focused on the genre of the novel, he also took a wider approach, exploring novels and novelists from earlier decades (particularly the 1950s) to determine the evolutionary process that influenced modern fiction. Issues such as civil rights, rock music lyricism, U.S. imperialism, the hippie movement, and education factor into his analysis. In *Gates of Eden* Dickstein maintained that he was different from many critics who "are still unable to acknowledge . . . that the line between popular culture and high culture gave way in the sixties," as quoted by Jerome L. Rodnitzky for the *American Historical Review*

(December 1977). Rather, he considers such material relevant for a thorough critical reading of the decade's literature. While many critics praised his analysis of what Rodnitzky called the "intellectual life in the 1960s," others found the overall work to be lacking in its coverage of nonliterary arts. Writing for the *National Review* (July 8, 1977), Allen G. Weakland opined, "Certainly the panorama which his title indicates should have included, to be complete, some analysis of the serious music, art, drama, architecture, and sculpture of America in the Sixties." Rodnitzky, however, concluded: "[Dickstein's] challenging generalizations and skill in tying ideas to broad cultural transition makes what could have been a mere compendium of critiques of cult writers a creative approach to the last decade. . . . The book is a triumph of literary and cultural criticism rather than a basic contribution to literary or intellectual scholarship."

During the 1970s and 1980s, Dickstein pursued his studies in literary and popular culture, lecturing and writing on contemporary fiction, Romantic and contemporary poetry, film, and such controversial questions of contemporary education as multiculturalism and revision of the literary canon. The course that Dickstein defined for himself in *Gates of Eden*, that "criticism, which is often tempted to be hermetic, can tell us something of the real world," led to his survey of criticism *Double Agent: The Critic and Society*, in which he set out to establish whether contemporary critics can contribute meaningful literary analysis in a way that may actually influence people's lives. Moreover, he examined whether criticism had evolved into a purely academic field, relevant only to other professional critics. The book also presents a thorough history of 20th-century public criticism.

The critic to whom Dickstein gives closest attention in *Double Agent* is Matthew Arnold, a Victorian, whose goal, Dickstein wrote, "was not to create a timeless canon, a perfect society, or an absolute set of values, but to find whatever was needful for a given age." To that end "Arnold emphasized the reflection that should precede action: he insisted on the many-sidedness of the traditional humanist ideal." Dickstein's book argues that 20th-century critics who have worked in the Arnoldian tradition are double agents—both intellectuals and public critics, academics and journalists. Much of the book is spent discussing what Dickstein termed the "heroic period" of modern British and American criticism, from 1920 to 1960, when public critics served as double agents and thus provided a larger cultural service to readers. Among those critics Dickstein singled out for praise were Lionel Trilling, Alfred Kazin, Edmund Wilson, and George Orwell. "Dickstein has a knack for getting at the heart of a critic's sensibility, even if on occasion he seems fair-minded to a fault," Arthur Krystal wrote for the

Times Literary Supplement (February 26, 1993). "All too polite," John Sutherland wrote in the *New York Times Book Review* (February 7, 1993). "Diatribe rather than dialogue seems to be called for, assault rather than genteel subversion." In the *New York Review of Books* (March 25, 1993), Denis Donoghue judged the book "a little dispirited. . . . *Double Agent* has the features of an epitaph. Dickstein does well to inform students that criticism was once a public art, reaching beyond the academy. . . . But he doesn't explain what precisely has changed and why." hristopher Lehmann-Haupt concluded his review of *Double Agent* for the *New York Times* (October 15, 1992) with an "Amen" to Dickstein's description of literary journalism as "criticism by fits and starts, bound to the moment, happily unable to systematize or break free from either its cultural setting or its very specific relation to readers and the marketplace." Lehmann-Haupt added, "[He] strives to be the exemplar of his ideal, the balanced observer who bestrides multiple worlds and can discriminate between writers, their works and the implications of their utterances."

In 1999 Dickstein served as editor for a collection of essays entitled *The Revival of Pragmatism: New Essays on Social Thought, Law, and Culture*, which deals largely with the revival of pragmatism—a philosophical doctrine emphasizing the practical impact of beliefs—in many intellectual communities. In his introduction he argued that pragmatism is "once again recognized not only as a distinctive American contribution to philosophy but as a new way of approaching old problems in a number of fields," according to Thomas R. Degregori for the *Journal of Economic Issues* (December 1999).

Dickstein's critical work *Leopards in the Temple: The Transformation of American Fiction, 1945–1970* explores the 25-year period following World War II in which he contends that numerous writers began expressing transgressive ideas that questioned the popular image of the prosperous and carefree 1950s. In fact, Dickstein argues that many seeds of the revolutionary 1960s were actually planted in the 1950s by novelists and poets such as Norman Mailer, Jack Kerouac, Thomas Pynchon, James Baldwin, Donald Barthelme, Tom Wolfe, Hunter S. Thompson, Allen Ginsberg, Gore Vidal, Tennessee Williams, Truman Capote, Saul Bellow, Joseph Heller, Philip Roth, and Ralph Ellison. According to Mark Shechner in a review for *Tikkun* (November 2002), the book argues that "the disenchantment and rebellion that flourished in the 1960s had already been beta-tested in literature, music, and film a decade earlier and had uncovered a vast popular audience. When it hit the streets in the mid-Sixties, fueled by anti-war and racial passions, the ground had already, in a way, been laid. The popular arts not only paved the way for the revolution, but the novel in particular opened a window to it. More amply and more precisely than any sociology

could be, the novel was in touch with its spiritual core." Dickstein's title refers to a parable from the author Franz Kafka in which "leopards break into the temple and drink to the dregs what is in the sacrificial pitchers; this is repeated over and over again; finally it can be calculated in advance, and it becomes part of the ceremony itself," as quoted by Shechner. Dickstein's leopards are the writers under analysis, many of whom emerged from marginalized parts of society—writers who were Jewish, African-American, homosexual, or first-generation children of immigrants—to put their mark on American popular culture. In addition to presenting what Steven G. Kellman for the *Virginia Quarterly Review* (Winter 2003) called "an exercise in literary historiography," Dickstein offered significant critical analysis, providing close readings of many of the period's most prominent literary works.

Leopards in the Temple was deemed a critical success. Although some reviewers noted a lack of attention to female authors of the period, most critics applauded what Kellman termed Dickstein's mastery of "a vast library of fiction and criticism." Perhaps the most acclaimed aspect of the work was what many reviewers described as its straightforward readability, particularly as a piece of literary criticism. As Shechner opined, "I can give no stronger endorsement to any literary study than to say that it makes sense. By that I mean two things that are distinctly different but obviously connected: one, that I understand it . . . and two, that its arguments have the ring of truth about them. In brief, that the writing is both lucid and sensible. *[Leopards in the Temple]* makes sense; it is lucid and sensible and then some. It manages also to be engaging, comprehensive, measured, penetrating, voracious, provocative, worldly, and even courageous."

In 2004 Dickstein published *A Mirror in the Roadway: Literature and the Real World*, a collection of 20 essays that examine how literature has interpreted America's ever-changing society. The title for the volume is drawn from a metaphor in Stendhal's *The Red and the Black* (1830): the novel is like a mirror being carried down a dirt road—sometimes it reflects the sky, sometimes the muck of the puddles. Dickstein thus argued that the novel serves a social function when in the hands of such writers as Upton Sinclair, whose book on the meat-packing industry, *The Jungle* (1906), had a significant impact on American history. A reviewer for *Library Journal Reviews* (April 1, 2005) wrote that by "blending cultural history and literary biography with the barest traces of memoir," Dickstein "has produced in his newest essay collection that rarest species of literary criticism: one as genial to the general reader as to the academic."

Dickstein began his teaching career at Columbia University (1966–71). Since 1994 he has been Distinguished Professor of English at the City University of New York Graduate Center. He lectured in France and in England (1980–81) as a Fulbright fellow and in 1980 was also visiting professor of English and American Studies at the University of Paris. He received a Guggenheim Fellowship (1973–74), a Rockefeller Humanities Fellowship (1981–1982), a Mellon Research Fellowship (1989–90), as well as grants and fellowships from the Danforth Foundation, the American Council of Learned Societies (ACLS), and the National Endowment for the Humanities (NEH). He married Lore Willner, a writer, in 1965. They have two children and live on the Upper West Side of New York City.

—K.D.

Suggested Reading: *Chicago Tribune* Jan. 10, 1993; *New York Review of Books* Aug. 4, 1977; Mar. 25, 1993; *New York Times* Mar. 9, 1977;

Oct. 15, 1992; *New York Times Book Review* Mar. 13, 1977; Feb. 7, 1993; *Newsweek* Mar. 28, 1977; *Partisan Review* No. 4, 1984–85; *Times Literary Supplement* Feb. 26, 1993.

Selected Books: *Keats and His Poetry: A Study in Development*, 1971; *Gates of Eden: American Culture in the Sixties*, 1977; *Double Agent: The Critic and Society*, 1992; *Leopards in the Temple: The Transformation of American Fiction, 1945–1970*, 2002; *A Mirror in the Roadway: Literature and the Real World*, 2004; as editor—*Great Film Directors: A Critical Anthology* (with L. Braudy), 1978; *The Revival of Pragmatism: New Essays on Social Thought, Law, and Culture*, 1999

Peter Kramer/Getty Images

Didion, Joan

Dec. 5, 1934– Essayist; novelist; journalist; memoirist; screenwriter

The technical virtuosity of Joan Didion's intensely personal journalism and of her understated, elliptical novels has led a number of critics to second the opinion of James Dickey, who considered her one of contemporary Anglophone literature's finest prose stylists. During a career spanning five decades, Didion has communicated her often somber view of post–World War II America, especially of her native California, with fierce eloquence. Intensely individualistic, Didion

has shunned psychoanalysis and written critically of feminism, and though she has written extensively about politics, her own political ideas have never settled into straightforward categories. Raised in a family of staunch Republicans, Didion was a supporter of the conservative Arizona senator Barry Goldwater, who made an unsuccessful bid for the presidency in 1964. After Ronald Reagan's election as governor of California in 1966, she began slowly moving into the Democratic Party's camp, believing that religious conservatives had hijacked the Republicans' principles. Despite the switch she is not a big booster for any party. "Sometimes I vote, sometimes I don't," she admitted to Natasha Wimmer for *Publishers Weekly* (October 15, 2001). She seems to view the U.S. as a place of disintegration, where, as she quotes from William Butler Yeats: "Things fall apart; the center cannot hold." The quotation comes from the preface to her celebrated collection of magazine essays, *Slouching towards Bethlehem* (1968), but it could just as well serve as an introduction to her other books of nonfiction or her novels, including *Play It as It Lays* (1970) and *A Book of Common Prayer* (1977). Didion and her husband of just under 40 years, the author John Gregory Dunne, formed one of the most famous literary couples of the 20th century, and in 2005 she published *The Year of Magical Thinking*, a memoir about her life following Dunne's death from a massive heart attack, while the couple's only daughter, Quintana Roo Dunne Michael, lay hospitalized in a coma.

Joan Didion was born into a family that had lived for five generations in the Sacramento Valley—which she described in *Slouching towards Bethlehem* as the real California, "a place in which a boom mentality and a sense of Chekhovian loss meet in uneasy suspension." She was born on December 5, 1934, the daughter of Frank Reese and Eduene (Jerrett) Didion. Her father's family originally came from Alsace-Lorraine. Her mother is descended from English settlers who came to America during the War of Independence and kept pushing westward along the frontier. Didion has one younger brother, James J. Didion, born December 1939, who worked for the real estate company Coldwell Banker; her father also worked in real estate.

During World War II Joan Didion left Sacramento with her family to follow her father, then an Army Air Corps finance officer, from base to base. After the war ended she returned to Sacramento, where during the week she attended public schools and on Sundays, religious classes at the Trinity Episcopal Cathedral. Although she has insisted that her childhood was happy, Didion has admitted to being "one of those children who always thought the bridge would fall in if you walked across it." "I was just one of those fearful children," she told Sally Quinn for the *Washington Post* (April 4, 1977), "always working out how the funicular at Royal Gorge would crash. Yes, I did have a happy childhood . . . except for these terrible fears. I thought about the atomic bomb a lot . . . after there was one."

By the age of 13 Joan Didion was typing pages from the fiction of Ernest Hemingway and Joseph Conrad just to see "how sentences worked," as she has told reporters. After graduating from high school, she attended the University of California, at Berkeley, where she majored in English literature and edited the school paper. Shortly before her graduation in 1956, she submitted a long article she had written on William Wilson Wurster, the father of the San Francisco style of architecture, to *Vogue*'s Prix de Paris contest for young writers and won first prize. Entitled either to a free trip to Paris or a cash award and a job at *Vogue*, Didion prudently chose the job, arriving in New York City in the summer of 1956. At *Vogue* she worked her way up from writing merchandising and promotional copy to a position as associate features editor. By the early 1960s she was also freelancing for *Mademoiselle* and the *National Review*. In 1963 she began writing *Vogue*'s movie reviews and went on leave from her staff position to finish her first novel.

Set in the Sacramento Valley that Joan Didion knows so well, *Run River* (1963) centers on the gradual self-destruction of an old Sacramento family during the years after World War II. "I started . . . *Run River* in New York because I was homesick," the author explained to Elizabeth Fishel for New York *Newsday* (October 2, 1971). "That's why there's too much landscape in it, too much social detail." Although it lacked the spare, sinewy quality of her later fiction, the novel encountered an admiring critical reception. "She is, above all, cool, and an impressively skilled writer," Robert Maurer wrote for *New York Herald Tribune Books* (May 12, 1963). "Even in this first novel there seems to be nothing technically that she cannot do."

A few months after the publication of *Run River*, on January 30, 1964, Joan Didion married John Gregory Dunne, who was then working on the staff of *Time*. In an interview with Beth Austin for the *Chicago Tribune* (March 13, 1988), Didion recalled: "I had known John for years. We were great friends. Then we kind of right out of the blue began seeing each other in a different way, and we got married. We got married with the idea that we were both going to be doing the same thing, essentially. We had thought that we might try doing a screenplay sometime." In April 1964 they left New York for Southern California, where they began freelance writing careers. Over the next few years, Didion continued writing film reviews for *Vogue* as well as contributing to the *Saturday Evening Post*, *Holiday*, the *New York Times Magazine*, and the *American Scholar*. She became a contributing editor to the *National Review*, and in 1967 she and her husband began alternately writing a column for the *Saturday Evening Post* called Points West, which continued until the *Post* stopped publication, in February 1969. They took up the column again, in 1976 and 1977, for *Esquire*. In an interview with Chris Chase for the *Chicago Tribune* (April 3, 1977), Didion admitted that she hated doing magazine columns. "I do it to force myself to go out and report," she said. "It's a way of forcing yourself into other people's worlds. . . . An awful lot of stuff in my novels came out of stuff I encountered reporting."

A selection of Didion's brooding essays from the *Saturday Evening Post* and other journals is included in *Slouching towards Bethlehem*. Those articles, including her celebrated title piece on the hippies of San Francisco's Haight-Ashbury district during the summer of 1967, deal mainly with contemporary life in California and her reactions to it. "A substantial element of spiritual biography is present in these pieces of wary skepticism," Melvin Maddocks wrote for the *Christian Science Monitor* (May 16, 1968). "Though she has a journalist's weakness for converting her themes into 'myths,' 'dreams,' and 'folk' symbols—she is an original observer and even better, an original thinker."

Didion has characterized her second novel, *Play It as It Lays*, as "a book in which anything that happened would happen off the page, a 'white' book to which the reader would have to bring his or her own bad dreams." Written in tough, jagged prose, the novel consists of 84 terse chapters, some only a few lines long. Chapter 52, for example, reads: "Maria made a list of things she would never do. She would never: walk through the Sands or Caesar's alone after midnight. She would never: ball at a party, do S-M unless she wanted to, borrow furs from Abe Lipsey, deal. She would never: carry a Yorkshire in Beverly Hills." The book's deliberately disjointed narrative relates the story of Maria Wyeth, a second-rate Hollywood actress who aimlessly drives the freeways of Southern California and keeps a precarious grasp on life despite adultery, divorce, abortion, the institutionalization of her brain-damaged daughter, and the suicide of her best friend.

"Miss Didion is shocking in the way that Jane Austen is shocking," Robert Nye wrote for the London *Guardian* (March 17, 1971) in an admiring review typical of the others. "She calculates her effects with imperturbable iciness. . . . *Play It As It Lays* deserves the attention of anyone still interested in the possibilities of narrative prose." A commercial as well as a critical success, the book became a best-seller and was nominated for a National Book Award.

In December 1969 Didion began a biweekly column for *Life*, introducing herself to her readers with characteristically dramatic directness as a woman sitting in a hotel room in Honolulu "in lieu of filing for a divorce." The column lasted for only a few months, but her marriage to Dunne endured, and the husband-and-wife team went on to write several screenplays together. The first to be produced was *The Panic in Needle Park* (1971), a modestly budgeted Cannes Film Festival prize-winner, starring a young Al Pacino, about youthful heroin addicts on the Upper West Side of New York. The pair then adapted *Play It as It Lays* into a 1972 screen version that was directed by Frank Perry and starred Tuesday Weld and Anthony Perkins. Having come up with the idea of turning *A Star Is Born*—already filmed in 1937 and 1954—into a rock musical, they wrote three screenplays for the film that, after many tribulations, eventually became the 1976 Barbra Streisand and Kris Kristofferson vehicle. Didion and Dunne's other collaborations include the screenplays for the films *True Confessions* (1981), based on Dunne's best-selling 1977 novel of the same name, and *Up Close and Personal* (1996); they also wrote television scripts for an adaptation of the Hemingway story "Hills Like White Elephants," included in an HBO series titled *Women and Men: Stories of Seduction* (1990), and *Broken Trust* (1995). Didion has told interviewers that she finds screenwriting a lucrative activity and a welcome break from writing fiction. "It's not like writing," she explained to Evelyn Renold for New York *Newsday* (April 24, 1977). "You're really making notes for a director. . . . It's like working a puzzle; there's no real involvement in it."

At the center of Didion's third novel, *A Book of Common Prayer*, is Charlotte Douglas, a wanderer who drifts through the American South and the countries of Central America, refusing to come to terms with her 18-year-old daughter's career as a hijacker and political terrorist. Charlotte's final stop is a steamy, decadent banana republic called Boca Grande, where she is killed during one of the country's periodic "colorful" revolutions. As in *Play It as It Lays*, Didion tempers the melodrama of *A Book of Common Prayer* with a spare, ironic narrative that mixes first and third person points of view. Although a few critics found this narrative technique obtrusive, the reviewer for *Library*

Journal (February 15, 1977) praised the book as "an almost Faulknerian reconstruction in which the drama of the action is matched by a second drama of narration." Equally admiring was Peter S. Prescott, who wrote for *Newsweek* (March 21, 1977): "Her laconic prose, compressed into short chapters and staccato paragraphs, allows for occasional repetitions that lend a liturgical echo to her tale. Her exposition of situations and details adroitly conceals their significance—until much later their meaning flares before our eyes. This is a remarkably good novel."

Didion's next collection of essays, *The White Album*, was published in 1979. Largely a meditation on life on the West Coast, the essays vary widely in their particular subjects, from a sound studio to a Black Panther Party press conference. Like many other reviewers, Lance Morrow, for *Time* (August 20, 1979), compared *The White Album* to Didion's first collection, describing it as "mellower than *Slouching Towards Bethlehem*" and noting that in the later book "Didion ranges more widely." Calling Didion "an alert and subtle observer, with a mordant intelligence and a sense of humor with touches of Evelyn Waugh in it," Morrow argued that "Didion is best when the literary transaction is personal and direct, when she is a live character reporting her own wanderings through the splendidly strange California of the late '60s and the '70s." Ann Hulbert's review for the *New Republic* (June 23, 1979) was more critical, suggesting that Didion's "'temperamentally unobtrusive' reporter of a decade ago is now a literary figure who is taking her own pulse in her pages, not just observing American styles and states of mind. And that pulse is racing with anxiety. . . . Didion writes in an intense and agitated style—the style of the haunted characters of her novels. Instead of the often insightful, ironic, deft stories of her first collection, her new essays tend to lose their shape and sharpness in her angst." In the majority of the pieces, Hulbert added, "Didion is still writing about the 1960s and the golden land. But the revealing stories, the little ironies she once found in the 1960s aren't there anymore."

In June 1982 Didion and her husband spent two weeks in El Salvador, then in the throes of a protracted civil war between leftist revolutionaries and the El Salvadoran military that began in 1980 and ended in 1992. Didion's observations on El Salvador were first published in November and December 1982 in three extensive essays for the *New York Review of Books* and were collected the following year as *Salvador*. In a vitriolic review of the book for *Commentary* (May 1983), Mark Falcoff argued: "Since Miss Didion is a writer of exceptional talent, the impact is precisely what is intended: to convince us that El Salvador is the quintessential Heart of Darkness—a black hole into which even the best of deeds and intentions are bound to disappear. . . . With [this book], however, there are two big problems. One has to do with the facts, the other with Joan Didion. There are some serious inaccuracies in the text, and many, many more half-truths. . . . What is even more disturbing about *Salvador* than Miss Didion's disingenuous use of facts and fugitive quotations is the way in which she makes the tiny republic of El Salvador into a mirror reflecting her own basic contempt for liberal democracy and—why not say it?—the American way of life." By contrast, Warren Hoge, the *New York Times Book Review* (March 13, 1983), praised Didion's work: "No one in El Salvador has interpreted the place better. *Salvador* shines with enlightening observation, and its language is lean and precise, in short what we have come to expect from Miss Didion. . . . I doubt whether any reporter who has worked in El Salvador can come away from a reading of this book without envy of her gift. I don't know if policy makers will have the same reaction, though to her credit, she resists the facile maneuver of simply depicting American officials as errant boobs and in particular treats United States Ambassador Deane R. Hinton with sensitivity. Her novelist's eye examines policy on a plane seldom reached in Congressional hearings or State Department briefings."

Though featuring a reporter character named Joan Didion, the writer's next book, *Democracy* (1984), marked her return to fiction. The main character is Inez Christian Victor, a Hawaiian married to U.S. senator and failed presidential candidate Harry Victor. Much of the action in the book takes place in 1975, when Jessie, one of the Victors' two children, runs away. He finds a job in Saigon, Vietnam, around the time of the collapse of the South Vietnamese government; almost simultaneously, Inez's sister is accidentally killed by their father. The stress of her sister's death, compounded by the disappearance of her own child, causes Inez to leave her husband and her other son in search of Jessie. During her quest Inez encounters Jack Lovett, with whom she had been romantically involved 23 years earlier. Walter Clemons, for *Newsweek* (April 16, 1984), called the book "very chic, knowing and romantic" and "by far the wittiest of Didion's orchidaceous, highly specialized fictions." Didion, Clemons added, "is as good as Somerset Maugham on the Pacific exotica of steamy weather and repressed passion. She is attracted more by celebrity and sensation than by the deepest potential of her rich subject, the Hawaiian colonial mentality. But she has a perfect ear for her characters' edgy, brittle repartee and a gift for bringing her scenes to a crisp curtain line. Watch for a brilliant four-page press interview in which Inez is asked about the 'major cost' of public life. *Democracy* is an ideal entertainment for readers too fastidious to go for Judith Krantz." Paul Stuewe offered more measured praise in *Quill & Quire* (June 1984): "Didion's upper-crust American characters haven't been adequately differentiated in appearance and voice; consequently, one can't always track them though

the book's frequent shifts of time-frame and point of view. Considered as a social canvas, however, *Democracy* is a fascinating portrait of contemporary American mores, and several of its component vignettes are masterpieces of trenchant observation. More glittering mosaic than coherent novel, it is nonetheless an engrossing read."

In *Miami* (1987) Didion examined the lives and changing political fortunes of that portion of the Cuban American community in Miami, Florida, who have tenaciously clung to the hope that the American government will ultimately help them overthrow the Cuban dictator Fidel Castro. The book considers the influence of these Cuban refugees on American politics since the early 1960s, when President John F. Kennedy's administration supported an invasion of the island by Cuban exiles that was mercilessly suppressed by the Castro government at the Bay of Pigs. As Didion herself noted to James Atlas, writing for *Vanity Fair* (October 1987), "There's been an awful lot going on [in Miami] since the Kennedy assassination that would seem to lend itself to conspiratorial interpretations." Reviewing *Miami* for *Choice* (March 1988), J. Raftery wrote that Didion "focuses on her subjects with the sharpness of a photographer." In a review for the *Christian Science Monitor* (November 12, 1987), Ruth Walker noted that Didion "has an excellent eye for detail, a sense of the phrase or image that tells the whole story. Indeed, her style is so distinctive that she sometimes teeters on the edge of self-parody. Occasional sentences go on and on, like a high note held after it has become uncomfortable for the listener, if not the singer. She clearly does her homework. This relatively slender volume is obviously based on reams of research, distilled like fragrance from whole fields of blossoms. *Miami* is an insightful book illustrating the dangers both of overzealous ideological engagement and of moral disengagement. To one who reads it, the discussion of United States policy in Latin America will never be quite the same again."

In 1992 Didion published *After Henry*, a collection of essays named for and dedicated to her longtime editor Henry Robbins, who first worked with her at the publishing house Farrar, Straus and Giroux before moving on to Simon & Schuster; Robbins died in 1979. "I never had the relationship with anybody that I had with Henry," Didion told Natasha Wimmer. Previously published in such periodicals as the *New Yorker* and the *New York Review of Books*, the 11 essays in the book are grouped into three geographic categories— "California," "Washington," and "New York"— and discuss a variety of topics, including the presidency of Ronald Reagan, the 1988 presidential campaign, and the brutal rape of a jogger in New York's Central Park, in 1989. In the *National Review* (June 22, 1992), David Klinghoffer remarked: "Instead of one of the most devastating reporters in America, Miss Didion has turned into a media critic. She can still be devastating, as she is in the best essays in this new collection. . . . [However], readers of her earlier, and more exhilarating, work will . . . miss the greater comedy and sadness of real lives observed at first hand." In a more favorable review, R. Z. Sheppard wrote for *Time* (June 29, 1992): "About half this collection deals with such Didion standbys as California's earthquakes, airheads and the mayhem found on what she likes to call the 'freak-death pages' of the newspapers. Readers should welcome the chance to savor the vintage sotto voce style that more than 20 years ago distinguished this careful writer from New Journalism's noisier competition."

Twelve years after her previous novel, Didion published *The Last Thing He Wanted* (1996). Atypically for Didion, the book was an espionage thriller. "I did not have a good time writing *Democracy*, so I wasn't eager to get started again [on another novel]," she told Mark Marvel for *Interview* (September 1996). "And when I finally did start this one, it was very easy to set it aside and do other things, like go report on something more current or work on a movie. Plus, I've never written novels very fast. So I just let time go by and then a couple of years ago I started feeling the impulse again pretty strongly." Set in 1984 *The Last Thing He Wanted* focuses on the journalist Elena McMahon, who has recently survived cancer and suffered the loss of her mother. Throughout her life Elena has needed to reinvent herself and finds that she must do so once again, this time by taking on a false identity in order to help her father, an illegal arms dealer who has recently become incapacitated. In the *New Yorker* (September 16, 1996), John Weir declared that Didion's "fiction is no less indispensable than her five books of essays and reportage are." Weir described "an animating tension in Didion's fiction between her achingly sure control as storyteller and stylist and the numbing vagueness of the people she depicts" that made her novels "simultaneously lucid and surreal." Paul Gray, however, in his review for *Time* (September 9, 1996), was more critical: "Although at 227 pages [this] is a short book, it seems an interminable accretion of mannerisms around a small, straightforward series of mishaps. . . . Much of the narrator's time is spent striking different attitudes toward the story. Sometimes these display Didion's characteristic cleverness and bite . . . . But for every one of these palpable hits there are many examples of flatfooted prose."

For *Political Fictions* (2001) Didion brought together essays first published in the *New York Review of Books* that reflected her thoughts on the workings of the American political process between the 1988 and 2000 elections. Often critical of the two major political parties, Didion appeared to see them as two sides of the same coin, virtually indistinguishable. David Klinghoffer, for the *National Review* (December 17, 2001), took issue with precisely this point, arguing that the idea "that somehow both liberals and conservatives have an interest in narrowing the field of crucial voters . . . is of course a fiction—a 'political fiction,' if you will—but it's expressed with such a distinct style, and creates such a delicately terrorized atmosphere, that a reader in the correct mood won't begrudge [Didion] the fantasy of her right-wing takeover plot." Klinghoffer added: "Once the charm of the Didion schtick has worn off, however, the plain facts begin to appear: first, that her big observations aren't always very original. . . . [Second], cynicism really does wear thin after 300-plus pages. There is almost nothing about which Didion is not cynical." Scott McLemee, for New York *Newsday* (October 28, 2001), saw Didion making a less partisan argument: "What bothers Didion about U.S. politics is that 'the center' is now all there is. The media and its minders have seen to that. Gone, or much weakened, is the notion (essential to any democratic life worthy of the name) that politics is a conflict among groups with divergent interests; that the electoral process itself is aggression, with rules; that campaigns are contests between fundamentally incompatible accounts of the country's past, present and future." Calling Didion's ideation in the book "plausible" if "at times, almost too familiar," McLemee concluded by touching on his ideas about Didion's cynicism: "Didion presents, with some elegance, the suspicions that have already crossed your mind in moments of darkest cynicism. Then she doubles back, revealing that your cynicism is merely another element of 'the [political] process.' Indeed, its cheapest necessary resource."

Didion and her family had moved from California, where they had been living for more than 20 years, to New York City, in 1988. The move prompted considerable reflection on Didion's part about what California meant to her and how it had changed. These thoughts ultimately culminated in *Where I Was From* (2003), a book that looked back on her West Coast upbringing. In the *New York Times* (September 24, 2003), Michiko Kakutani expressed her disappointment with the book. Commenting on what she considered to be its "decidedly elliptical feel," Kakutani wrote: "Part memoir, part Californian scrap book, part jittery postmodernist collage, [the book] trades the high-definition dichotomies of the author's earlier work for a more shaded, shadowed meditation on the golden land and American Dream." David Thomson, for the *London Review of Books* (March 18, 2004), argued that "what [Didion] means by California is America as a whole, or the westward tendency, the restless, vague assertion that it is all going to turn out for the best." Didion's analysis of this, Thomson continued, did not produce "a cosy book about an idyllic upbringing or a flawless America" or a book "without irony (though it can take a reader some time to catch up with Didion's mirthless amusement). And it isn't remotely comfortable or reassuring—beyond the evidence

DIDION

that sentences can still open up such clamped souls."

On December 30, 2003 Didion's husband, Dunne, died of a massive heart attack at their New York City apartment. They had just returned from visiting their only daughter, Quintana Roo, who had been in a coma following a bout with pneumonia and septic shock. (Named for a Mexican state on the Yucatán Peninsula, Quintana Roo had been adopted by Didion and Dunne shortly after she was born on March 3, 1966.) Quintana regained consciousness about a month later but then suffered a massive hematoma. She underwent brain surgery, followed by months of rehabilitation, and during this time Didion attempted to piece back together her fragmented life, in part by writing *The Year of Magical Thinking* (2005). Bill Gunlocke, for *America* (February 13, 2006), noted the "beauty in Didion's recollections of [the couple's] life together: the California homes, the meals with literary friends and movie people, the dinners with just the two of them together, the swimming-pools, the travels, the clothes—recollections that evoke a mood, an atmosphere. She gives the reader what the reader appreciates most. That is what makes even Joan Didion's sad tale somehow stimulating to read. Wherever she finds herself, be it in sunlight or loneliness, her experience is palpable to the reader, who is transported to where she is—and wants to be there with her." Cathleen McGuigan, for *Newsweek* (October 10, 2005), called the book a "slender, stunning memoir," adding: "Didion's intricate narrative moves forward, circles back, pauses to describe a memory with Dunne—a long-ago swim in a coastal cave, a rain-soaked walk in Paris—or to recall a fragment of a poem or a clue in a crossword puzzle. Then it dives down again to grasp a deeper meaning. There's something especially moving about her famously spare style here, how her elegant prose never threatens to spill over into the realm of the tell-all, even though she's telling us quite a lot. For us, her words, never squandered, are more than enough. For her, of course, they must be nowhere near."

After months of being in intensive care, Qiuntana Roo Dunne Michael died, at 39, on August 26, 2005 from acute pancreatitis, shortly before *The Year of Magical Thinking* was published. When asked by her editors if she wanted to revise the manuscript to include her daughter's death, Didion reportedly replied: "It's finished." The book won the 2005 National Book Award for nonfiction and was a finalist for the 2005 National Book Critics Circle Award. Didion is currently collaborating with the playwright David Hare in adapting the book for the Broadway stage; it will be a one-person show and is scheduled to open in April 2007.

In October 2006 Didion collected all of her previous books of nonfiction, with the exception of *The Year of Magical Thinking*, into one volume, *We Tell Ourselves Stories in Order to Live*. The book provided critics with an opportunity to reassess Didion's work as a whole, and the resulting evaluations were often strongly divided. While praising *The Year of Magical Thinking* as "wrenching," Adam Kirsch, for the *New York Sun* (October 6, 2006), argued that the version of Didion's persona that comes across in her collected nonfiction "is clearly a literary descendant of Hemingway, who created the genre in which she excels: what might be called modernist melodrama. Just as a Method actor was ostentatiously inarticulate where a [19th-century] ham would rant and rave, so Ms. Didion employs tranced repetition, ironic understatement, and blank space to create an atmosphere of psychic prostration. She always seems to be writing on the brink of a catastrophe so awful that her only available response is to withdraw into a kind of autism." Calling Didion "one of America's truly original writers," Gaylord Dold, for the *Wichita Eagle* (October 15, 2006), wrote that Didion's "sentences sing and her radiant intellect shines through the pain. She's writing against all our best interests. This new . . . edition of her collected nonfiction is must reading for every thinking person interested in the fate of our political, social and moral ideals."

Didion has described herself as shy and reticent and has often said that she never feels articulate unless she is writing. "In many ways writing is the act of saying *I*, of imposing oneself upon other people, of saying *listen to me, see it my way, change your mind*," she wrote in the essay "Why I Write," first published in the *New York Times Book Review* (December 5, 1976). "It's an aggressive, even a hostile act. You can disguise its aggressiveness all you want with veils of subordinate clauses and qualifiers and tentative subjunctives, with ellipses and evasions—with the whole manner of intimating rather than claiming, of alluding rather than stating—but there's no getting around the fact that setting words on paper is the tactic of a secret bully, an invasion, an imposition of the writer's sensibility on the reader's most private space."

—C.M.

Suggested Reading: *America* p24+ Feb. 13, 2006; *Chicago Tribune* Apr. 3, 1977; *Choice* p1,160 Mar. 1988; *Christian Science Monitor* p24 Nov. 12, 1987; *Commentary* p66 May 1983; *Harper's* p112+ Dec. 1971; *Interview* p84+ Sep. 1996; *London Review of Books* p3+ Mar. 18, 2004; *Ms.* p65+ Feb. 1977; *National Review* p53 June 22, 1992, p54+ Dec. 17, 2001; *New Republic*, p35 June 23, 1979; (New York) *Newsday* B p12 Oct. 28, 2001, C p31 Oct. 15, 2006; *New York Post* p17 July 25, 1970; *New York Times* E p8 Sep. 24, 2003; *New York Times Book Review* p1+ Apr. 3, 1977, p3 Mar. 13, 1983; *Newsweek* p86 Apr. 16, 1984, p63 Oct. 10, 2005; *New Yorker* p95 Sep. 16, 1996; *People* p50+ July 26, 1976; *Publishers Weekly* p41+ Oct. 15, 2001; *Time* p69 Aug. 20,

1979, p81 June 29, 1992, p69 Sep. 9, 1996; *Washington Post* D p1+ Apr. 4, 1977; *Vanity Fair* p48+ Oct. 1987

Selected Books: fiction—*Run River*, 1963; *Play It as It Lays*, 1970; *A Book of Common Prayer*, 1977; *Democracy*, 1984; *The Last Thing He Wanted*, 1996; nonfiction—*Slouching towards Bethlehem*, 1968; *The White Album*, 1979; *Salvador*, 1983; *Miami*, 1987; *After Henry*, 1992; *Political Fictions*, 2001; *Where I Was From*, 2003; *The Year of Magical Thinking*, 2005; *We Tell Ourselves Stories in Order to Live*, 2006

Courtesy of Canongate Books

Dierbeck, Lisa

1963– Novelist

"Dierbeck is brilliant at capturing what it feels like to be a young girl looked at by an older man: a sense that one is powerful and in control; sort of disgusted by how predictable even an adult male can be; but also a bit intrigued by how far can she take things," Emily Lloyd wrote for the *School Library Journal* (January 2004), announcing Lisa Dierbeck's literary debut, *One Pill Makes You Smaller* (2003), a novel that placed Dierbeck in the company not only of Lewis Carroll and J. D. Salinger, the two authors whose works she makes the most use of to construct her story, but also Vladimir Nabokov, whose novel *Lolita* (1955) also explores the relationship between a young girl and an older man.

Lisa Dierbeck was born in 1963 and raised in New York City, where she came of age in the 1970s, growing up on Manhattan's Upper East Side during what she has described, *Publishers Weekly* (August 11, 2003) reported, as a "'self-consciously amoral' era . . . when 'adults behaved like children and children behaved like adults.'" By the age of 11 Dierbeck was already being described as tall, leggy, and buxom, and she recalled experiencing, she told *Publishers Weekly*, "this strange and intriguing phenomenon where cool, 17-year-old guys would want to hang out with me, and I thought, 'Wow! They don't even care that I'm 11.'" Her experiences as an early bloomer as well as the summers she spent in the 1970s attending an arts camp on a 100-acre farm figure largely in *One Pill Makes You Smaller*. After high school she attended Wesleyan University, in Middletown, Connecticut, earning her bachelor's degree in philosophy before moving to Italy for several years. She later returned to New York, and in about 1997, began writing a novel about an adult Alice Duncan and her encounter with a man who may have raped her when she was a child. However, in the course of constructing the background to the adult story, Dierbeck found that she had the material for a novel about Alice's childhood and put off writing the one about Alice's adulthood until later.

One Pill Makes You Smaller is essentially a revisionist telling of Carroll's *Alice's Adventures in Wonderland*, updated and seen through the filter of the countercultural movement of the 1970s. "It's a story of a very young girl at some ways in war with her own body," Dierbeck told *Publishers Weekly*. "It is a real phenomenon from a statistical perspective; young girls enter puberty at younger and younger ages, so she's wrestling with a divided self which feels like it's half sexualized, half innocent." Alice Duncan is 11 years old and lives in Manhattan with her 16-year-old half-sister, whom she refers to as Aunt Esme. Her mother has left for Italy with a boyfriend; her father, an artist, is in a mental asylum. More immediately problematic is that Alice's body is developing rapidly, attracting unwanted attention not only from boys her own age but also her classmates' fathers and her sister's boyfriends. Esme, wanting to be unencumbered so that she can pursue an affair with a punk musician, sends Alice to an arts camp in North Carolina, where she becomes involved with an odd assortment of drug dealers, would-be artists, and a man in his mid-30s named J. D.

Critical response to the novel and Dierbeck's use of *Alice's Adventures in Wonderland* was decidedly mixed. In a review for New York *Newsday* (September 28, 2003), Claire Dederer called the novel "an up-all-night page-turner, an artful Polaroid of a painful girlhood, and something more besides. In telling Alice's story, Dierbeck gives us a small landscape of the 1970s. The novel reads like a dark report of the counterculture's effect on children; at the same time, it never underestimates the allure and the transformative power of breaking the rules. You get the feeling that if Dierbeck were somehow to meet Charles Dodgson [Lewis Carroll's real name], she'd thank him for the source material and promptly kick his butt." Chris Lehmann, however, wrote for the *Washington Post Book World* (September 2, 2003), "Beware the too-clever premise. . . . [Though] Dierbeck is an undeniably talented writer . . . her frequent and elaborate nods to the Carroll original are both needlessly distracting and more important, invite comparisons to Carroll's own achievements that are never flattering." Others were even less kind. Kate Tylor, writing for the *New Leader* (September–October 2003), observed, "Though she doesn't think much of her father's work, Alice has artistic aspirations of her own. She pastes together collages from cut-outs of magazines and rock album covers" Tylor added: "Dierbeck performs this sort of borrowing—her main sources are Carroll and J. D. Salinger—too

often and with inadequate care. Alice's identification here with Holden Caufield adds little to his fantasy by draping it in pop culture, and after several of these pilferings *One Pill* starts to read like a teen novel that has broken out in a pox of literary allusions."

Lisa Dierbeck's work has been published in a number of literary journals and anthologies, as well as in the *New York Times Book Review* and *Barron's*. She lives in New York City, where she works in an art gallery.

—C.M./A.R.

Suggested Reading: *New Leader* p34 Sep.–Oct. 2003; (New York) *Newsday* D p35 Sep. 28, 2003; *New York Times* p8 Sep. 7, 2003; *School Library Journal* p163 Jan. 2004; *Washington Post Book World*, C p3 Sep. 2, 2003

Selected Books: *One Pill Makes You Smaller*, 2003

Scott Gries/Getty Images

Doctorow, E. L.

Jan. 6, 1931– Novelist; short-story writer; screenwriter

E. L. Doctorow is considered one of the leading lights of contemporary American literature. Best known for putting historical figures into fictionalized settings, Doctorow has sometimes been pigeonholed as a writer of historical fiction, though he has always written in a variety of modes. While some of his most famous novels—including

Ragtime (1975), *Billy Bathgate* (1989), and *The March* (2005)—do use historical figures as characters, other books, particularly *Loon Lake* (1980) and *City of God* (2000), have both ventured further afield, both in terms of subject matter and form. His two earliest novels, *Welcome to Hard Times* (1960) and *Big As Life* (1966), attempted to reinterpret what Doctorow has called "disreputable" genres—respectively, the Western and science fiction. Doctorow has also frequently centered his fiction in the greater New York City area, as exemplified by his autobiographical novel *World's Fair* (1985), which explored his childhood during the Great Depression. Before becoming a full-time writer, Doctorow was a highly regarded editor for a variety of publishing houses. Now, having won the PEN/Faulkner Award for fiction two times and the National Book Critics Circle Award three times, Doctorow holds the Lewis and Loretta Glucksman Chair in English and American Letters at New York University.

Edgar Laurence Doctorow was born in the New York City borough of the Bronx on January 6, 1931 to David Richard Doctorow and the former Rose Levine, whom he has described as "old-fashioned social democrats." His grandparents, on both sides, were Jewish immigrants from Russia. Doctorow grew up on Eastburn Avenue, in the same area of the Bronx that he later chose for the youth of Daniel Isaacson, the hero of his 1971 novel, *The Book of Daniel*. His mother was a pianist, and his father, who died in 1955, owned a store that sold musical instruments, radios, and records. Although Doctorow told Al Ellenberg for the *New York Post* (August 31, 1971) that there was "never any money" and that his father would have to be considered "a failed man," he nevertheless had pleasant boyhood memories of his bar mitzvah, visits to the theater, summers at camp, and playing stoop ball in the neighborhood streets.

By the time he was in the third grade, Doctorow knew that he wanted to be a writer. Part of his motivation came from his older brother, who, after serving at the front in World War II, wrote a book about his experiences at the family's kitchen table. "He never published it, but he made writing—which for me had always been a dream—a reality," Doctorow told Marie Arana-Ward for the *Washington Post Book World* (April 17, 1994). At the Bronx High School of Science, one of New York City's elite public schools, he worked on the literary magazine *Dynamo*, wrote poetry and music, and took up an interest in painting After graduating he went on to Kenyon College in Gambier, Ohio, to study under the poet John Crowe Ransom. At Kenyon he majored in philosophy and acted in school plays. He did not belong to a fraternity because, he told Ellenberg, "If you were Jewish, black, or had acne, you just didn't get invited."

After receiving his B.A. from Kenyon, in 1952, Doctorow returned to New York City for a year of graduate study in English at Columbia University; he wrote several plays during this time but never finished his M.A. thesis. Drafted in 1953 he served for two years in the United States Army Signal Corps. After his discharge, in 1955, he returned to New York and wrote in his spare time while working at a variety of odd jobs, including a stint as an airline reservations clerk. For three years he worked for Columbia Pictures reading, according to Alex Hamilton for the London *Guardian* (January 19, 1976), "indescribably awful screenplays." In 1959 Doctorow took a position as an associate editor at the New American Library, and by the time he left, five years later, he was a senior editor, having worked on a wide array of books, from works by Shakespeare to others by Ian Fleming. In 1964 Doctorow moved to Dial Press, where he was editor in chief until 1969, as well as being, during his last year, vice president and publisher.

The Wild West was an unlikely locale for Doctorow's first novel, since he had never related to that time and place and did not like Western movies as a child. Doctorow told Martha MacGregor for the *New York Post* (July 9, 1966) that he was hoping, with *Welcome to Hard Times*, "to take a disreputable genre, cheap materials of a nonliterary kind and try to fuse them in some way that was valid. I was interested in the counterpoint of what I was doing and what the reader might expect me to do." The plot, as summarized by the reviewer S. E. B. for the Massachusetts *Springfield Republican* (September 18, 1960), "revolves around a badman who destroys the town of Hard Times in one day, casually and cruelly; a mayor who is too weak to kill the badman but is hopeful enough to rebuild the town; and a woman of easy virtue who waits, in terror and hatred for the return of the badman." To that reviewer *Welcome to Hard*

Times presented "the timeless tragedy of the strength of destructiveness and the weakness of good will." Michael McNay, who interviewed Doctorow for the London *Guardian* (March 10, 1972), saw the book's theme as "the idea of the West having developed as a series of failures." When the book was reissued in 1975, it evoked fresh praise from Kevin Starr, who called it, in the *New Republic* (September 6, 1975), "a superb piece of fiction: lean and mean, and thematically significant." The reviewer was especially struck by Doctorow's "profound sense of American myth and his marvelous sensitivity to American materials." A film version of *Welcome to Hard Times* was released by MGM in 1967. Though the film was critically panned, it nevertheless earned some money for Doctorow, enabling him to make a down payment on the 1906 house in New Rochelle, New York, that helped to inspire him a few years later to write *Ragtime*.

What Doctorow calls "the myth of the monstrous visitation" was borrowed from science fiction to serve as the basis of his next novel, *Big as Life*, which tells of what happens to a group of New Yorkers when two enormous naked human figures appear in the harbor, towering over the buildings. The book troubled some readers and reviewers when it was first released. "The general reader dismisses it as science fiction," Doctorow told Martha MacGregor, "and the science fiction buffs are furious because it isn't science fiction enough—I have departed from the formula." Asked by MacGregor about the meaning of the book and whether it might be about the atom bomb, he said that he preferred to "keep whatever ambiguity it has" but thought the book "related much more to contemporary conflict and anxiety." In recent years Doctorow has made plain his distaste for *Big as Life*. "It was quite a bad book," Doctorow told Eleanor Randolph for the *Los Angeles Times* (March 30, 1997). "It was the worst thing I have ever done. It had some good things in it, but I didn't really make it work. It had—fortunately—a very small first printing. And I never let it get back in print."

As editor in chief at Dial Press, Doctorow worked with such notable writers as James Baldwin, Norman Mailer, Howard Fast, and Richard Condon, but in May 1969 he left his job to complete *The Book of Daniel*, which he had begun the year before. "I couldn't write and still handle a 60-hour-a-week executive position," Doctorow admitted in an interview with John F. Baker for *Publishers Weekly* (September 12, 2005). He received an offer to serve as a writer in residence at the University of California, at Irvine, but before accepting, he consulted the ancient Chinese text known as the I Ching, which, according to a number of reports, told him that he would cross "a great water." His wife, believing that "great water" to be the Mississippi River, encouraged him to take the position.

While living and teaching in California, Doctorow finished *The Book of Daniel*, which he has said was inspired by what he has called "a major political crime in the 1950's"—the execution of Ethel and Julius Rosenberg for passing on U.S. atomic secrets to the Soviet Union. Although the repressions of the McCarthy era made a profound impression on him, Doctorow was not personally involved in the 1953 protests against the executions, nor did he research the Rosenbergs' personal lives in preparation for the book. He has denied that *The Book of Daniel* is a roman à clef, explaining that it is not about the Rosenbergs but about the "idea" of the Rosenbergs. As Al Ellenberg observed in the *New York Post*: "For Doctorow, the Rosenbergs are the occasion illustrative of this judgment: all children are witnesses to their parents' destruction by the institutions of society."

The Book of Daniel ended up being a succès d'estime. Critic Stanley Kauffmann's judgment of it, in the *Saturday Review* (July 26, 1975), as "the best American political novel in a generation" was echoed in Great Britain by David Caute, who wrote for the London *Guardian* (February 17, 1972): "I would place Mr. Doctorow's achievement as a political novelist above that of any contemporary except Solzhenitsyn. . . . Line by line he wrenches from the reader the tribute of absolute assent and recognition: yes, it is, it was exactly like that. . . . This novel represents a marvelous marriage of the intellect and the imagination." *The Book of Daniel* was nominated for a National Book Award in 1971.

Soon after completing his third book, Doctorow began a daily stint at his desk in search of an idea for a new novel, but he found himself more emotionally drained from his work on *The Book of Daniel* than he realized. For months nothing came to him; then, suddenly inspired by the atmosphere of his 1906 house, he imagined escape artist Harry Houdini visiting the people who lived in the house shortly after it was built. He was unable to explain the reason for that particular image, which was soon joined by other images of the U.S. in the years before World War I. Doctorow turned to history books, biographies, and collections of photographs of the period to nudge his imagination, but he purposely kept that process haphazard. In an interview with John F. Baker for *Publishers Weekly* (June 30, 1975), Doctorow said that *Ragtime*, completed in two years, was a "happy, easy book to write—it didn't fight me."

In addition to introducing Houdini, Doctorow brought into the book such historical figures as Emma Goldman, Evelyn Nesbit, Harry K. Thaw, J. P. Morgan, Henry Ford, Admiral Robert E. Peary, Booker T. Washington, Sigmund Freud, and Carl Jung. These figures interact with a wealth of fictional characters, including members of a New Rochelle WASP family and a family of Lower East Side Jewish immigrants. A pivotal character in *Ragtime* is the fictitious African-American ragtime pianist Coalhouse Walker, a character apparently inspired by the tragic life of the ragtime composer Scott Joplin, as well as by Heinrich von Kleist's historical novel *Michael Kohlhaas*, about a 16th-century German horse trader who becomes a revolutionary bandit. *Ragtime* also seems to have been influenced in style and content by Doctorow's familiarity with such radically oriented literature of the 1930's as John Dos Passos's trilogy, *U.S.A.* Unconcerned about the historical accuracy of *Ragtime*, Doctorow told John F. Baker, in 1975: "Let's just say that *Ragtime* is a mingling of fact and invention—a novelist's revenge on an age that celebrates nonfiction."

Ragtime met with a wave of ecstatic reviews. Stanley Kauffmann, for the *Saturday Review* (July 26, 1975), praised the author's skill in re-creating the pre–World War I atmosphere and noted that "the 'ragtime' effect of the book's prose captures a change in the rhythm of American life, a change to the accelerated, impelling beat of a new century." In the *New Republic* (July 5, 1975), Doris Grumbach called *Ragtime* "a model of a novel"—"compact," "spare," and "completely absorbing," because once in, there is no possible way out except through the last page." However, John Seelye noted, in a later article for the *New Republic* (April 10, 1976), that the initially enthusiastic reception accorded to *Ragtime* was eventually tempered by negative criticism, in part because the book's success had endowed it with "an aura of trashiness"; Seelye also pointed out that *Ragtime* was conspicuously absent from the list of National Book Award nominees. In England, where the book was published in 1976, reviewers were generally more critical than their American counterparts. Jeremy Brooks, writing for the London *Sunday Times* (January 18, 1976), found *Ragtime* "often funny and always entertaining," but complained of the book's "inability to grasp at and hold on to the reader's emotions." In addition to being a best-seller and a Book-of-the-Month Club selection, *Ragtime* was among the four winners of the first-ever National Book Critics Circle Awards.

Loon Lake, Doctorow's follow-up to *Ragtime*, is considered one of Doctorow's less successful novels. Set in the era of the Great Depression, it tells the story of Joe, the son of a poor mill worker in Paterson, New Jersey. After running away from home, Joe travels around the country, first as a hobo and later with a carnival, before stumbling across an immense estate known as Loon Lake and owned by steel tycoon F. W. Bennett. After an affair with a gun moll, Joe is taken in by the elderly Bennett. Reviewing the novel for the *New Republic* (September 20, 1980), Mark Harris called the book "a failed work of a serious man" and added: "This book tells again things Doctorow has told before, but nothing more mature." While not as overtly critical, Anthony Burgess put forward a similar opinion of the book's merits in the *Saturday Review* (September 1980), arguing that it "is a difficult book and I don't think it is a successful one. But it is a very honorable attempt at expanding the resources of the genre. . . . That *Loon Lake* breaks new technical ground and yet possesses so many of the traditional virtues of fiction must be accounted its peculiar distinction."

Doctorow's next novel, *World's Fair*, is considered by many critics to be something of a sequel to *Ragtime*. Conceived as an autobiographical novel, *World's Fair* tells the story of Edgar, a nine-year-old boy who wins a free visit to the 1939–40 World's Fair in New York City. While Edgar narrates much of the novel, some chapters are given from the point of view of his mother and older brother. Each of the characters recounts the family's troubles—the failure of Edgar's father's business, his grandmother's death, his brother's departure from home—against the backdrop of hopefulness that the World's Fair inspires in Edgar. Robert Towers, for the *New York Review of Books* (December 19, 1985), wrote: "The characters, while convincingly reproduced and analyzed, are not really memorable, and the book as a whole lacks the movement and suspense of good fiction. . . . The mislabeling of *World's Fair* [as a novel] by no means spoils one's enjoyment of many passages in the book, but it does result in a degree of aesthetic smudging and the raising of expectations that remain unfulfilled." On the other hand, Edmund White, writing for the *Nation* (November 30, 1985) considered *World's Fair* "a novel in which the brick buildings and the summer light are as intense, as substantial and as present as in a Hopper painting. . . . The characters themselves are as clear as if they had been etched out of wood with fire. . . . [Doctorow] finds feelings that are deep in the settings of a more innocent past. His past purrs and hisses and is capable of scratching deep enough to draw blood." The novel was a best-seller and won the 1986 National Book Award for fiction.

Doctorow continued to mix fictional characters with historical figures in his next novel, *Billy Bathgate*, which depicts the Depression-era life of the teenage Billy, who, after growing up on Bathgate Avenue in the Bronx, becomes a low-level hoodlum for the real-life gangster Dutch Schultz. Billy then falls in love with Drew Preston, a beautiful girl who happens to be Schultz's latest romantic conquest and who eventually falls for Billy as well. As their relationship develops Billy begins to question his mob's actions and attempts to protect Drew from it. Barbara Hoffert wrote for *Library Journal* (February 15, 1989) that although "at times 15-year-old Billy seems far too precocious, even for a streetwise punk, ultimately we are made to feel his apprehension of the world." The result, Hoffert continued, is a work that "successfully re-creates worlds gone by in loving and meticulous detail." In the *New York Times Book Review* (February 26, 1989), Anne Tyler argued that *Billy Bathgate* "is Mr. Doctorow's shapeliest piece of work: a richly detailed report of a 15-year-old boy's journey from childhood to adulthood, with plenty of cliff-hanging adventure along the way." Billy, Tyler concluded, is "Huck Finn and Tom Sawyer with more poetry, Holden Caulfield with more zest and spirit—a wonderful new addition to the ranks of American boy heroes." *Billy Bathgate* won a number of awards, including the 1989 National Book Critics Circle Award, the 1990 PEN/Faulkner Award, and the 1990 William Dean Howells Medal from the American Academy of Arts and Letters. In 1991 the novel was made into a film, directed by Robert Benton and starring Dustin Hoffman and Nicole Kidman.

Published in 1994, *The Waterworks* is Doctorow's only novel from the 1990s. It takes place in New York City, during the 1870s, a period of widespread corruption in the city. The plot centers around freelance reporter Martin Pemberton, who disappears after claiming to have seen his dead father, the rich and amoral Augustus Pemberton, on a horse-drawn omnibus. After the younger Pemberton vanishes, his editor, McIlvane, contacts perhaps the only police officer in the city untouched by graft, Inspector Edmund Donne. Working together the two men discover that Augustus is among a small number of very wealthy men who have paid a scientist, Dr. Sartorius, to lengthen their lives. Merle Rubin, for the *Christian Science Monitor* (June 13, 1994), considered the book "an instantly arresting, vivid re-animation of the American past that does not quite succeed in satisfying the expectations it arouses. . . . Why exactly one comes away from this spellbinding novel with a sense of mild disappointment is hard to explain. After so much is said and done, one has learned little more about avarice, corruption, and the amorality of science and technology than one was already led to suspect at the outset." Calling Doctorow "a remarkable writer," Ted Solotaroff wrote for the *Nation* (June 6, 1994) that *The Waterworks* "settles in the mind like a kind of missing link in our literary evolution. Hints and glints of Poe are embedded in its twinned interests in mystery and science, its detective-story format, its necrological overlay, its protagonist—a brilliant, noir, disinherited literary journalist—its man-about-New York ambiance, even a mansion named Ravenwood." Each of Doctorow's books, Solotaroff concluded, "is a kind of relay network between its time and ours, keeping our awareness in touch with American experience."

Doctorow's next novel, *City of God*, was a nonlinear work in which the author attempted to summarize the spiritual trials of the 20th century through the mysterious disappearance of a brass crucifix from an Episcopal church on Manhattan's Lower East Side. Narrated by a writer named Everett, the novel's main character is the Reverend Thomas Pemberton, who goes in search of the crucifix only to find it on the roof of a decrepit building that houses a fledgling religious group called the Synagogue of Evolutionary Judaism, begun by Joshua and Sarah Gruen. While trying to understand what happened, Pemberton finds himself confronting his own ideas about faith and eventually converts to Judaism. Everett, meanwhile, hopes to turn the mystery into a novel. Calling the book "dazzling" and "polyphonic," Paul Gray, writing for *Time* (February 14, 2000), acknowledged that "it takes a while for the narrative strategies of *City of God* to start meshing" but added: "The true miracle of *City of God* is the way its disparate parts fuse into a consistently enthralling and suspenseful whole." Bruce Bawer, in the *Hudson Review* (Winter 2000), sharply criticized the book for what he termed its "seriously off-base" portrayal of the Episcopal Church. Adducing a series of what he considered to be errors in Doctorow's rendering of Episcopalianism, Bawer went on to describe *City of God* as the work "of a writer who, apparently incapable of shaking his decades-long preoccupation with politics and political categories, plainly feels that in an America suffering from the absence of a vigorous Marxist faith of the sort that animated the likes of the Rosenbergs, Reform congregations like the Synagogue for Evolutionary Judaism and 'Beacons of Faith' like Joshua and Sarah Gruen are the best substitute we have. That Doctorow fails to understand that such substitution is not the proper function of religion—Christian, Jewish, or otherwise—will probably not surprise any of his longtime readers, though it is responsible for the fact that *City of God*, perhaps the most ambitious of his novels, is at the same time his most abhorrent work and his most conspicuous failure."

Set during the American Civil War, Doctorow's most recent novel, *The March* (2005), examines Union general William T. Sherman's famous and destructive march through Georgia and wide swaths of the Carolinas—an event that left much of the South's infrastructure in tatters. Though still a controversial action, Sherman's march is credited by many historians with successfully breaking the back of the Southern Confederacy and speeding the end to the bloodiest war in American history. Against this background, Doctorow places Pearl, a mixed-race girl who passes for white; Walsh, a lieutenant in Sherman's army who falls in love with Pearl; Emily Thompson, a Southern belle who attracts the attention of the army field doctor Wrede Sartorius—the same character Doctorow used in *The Waterworks*. Sherman himself also appears, though as Michiko Kakutani remarked in the *New York Times* (September 20, 2005), "the central character of this novel is not Sherman, but the Army he commands—and its inexorable march through Dixie." Though Kakutani found *The March* "less inventive, less innovative than [Doctorow's] 1975 classic *Ragtime*," she argued that, "in recounting Sherman's march, [Doctorow] manages to weld the personal and the mythic into a thrilling and poignant story. He not only conveys the consequences of that campaign for soldiers and civilians in harrowingly intimate detail, but also

creates an Iliad-like portrait of war as a primeval human affliction—'not war as adventure, nor war for a solemn cause,' but 'war at its purest, a mindless mass rage severed from any cause, ideal, or moral principle,' a 'characterless entanglement of brainless forces' as God's answer 'to the human presumption.'" To Harry L. Carrigan Jr., however, writing for *Library Journal* (August 2005), "Doctorow's fictional re-creation of the event lacks compelling characters, forceful structure, and dominant themes and so fails to make it much more than a romp in the park." The book won the PEN/Faulkner and National Book Critics Circle Awards for fiction.

In 2006 Doctorow released *Creationists: Selected Essays, 1993–2006*, a collection of 16 nonfiction meditations on the creative act, whether carried out by F. Scott Fitzgerald, the Marx Brothers, or the makers of the first atomic bomb. Many of the pieces were originally written as stand-alone essays for periodicals, while others were prepared as lectures or introductions. In the *New York Times Book Review* (September 24, 2006), Ron Powers called the collection "luminous" and added that the book "sustains a pitch of fascination, borne on a cascade of glittering aphorism, rarely encountered in the unforgiving genre of literary criticism." John Freeman, writing for the *Hartford Courant* (September 24, 2006), chose a similar adjective to describe the book, calling it "illuminating," but he also noted: "In contrast to his novels and stories, which often are highly worked and rhythmically beautiful, these essays feel somewhat unadorned."

In addition to the 1969–70 academic year that Doctorow spent at the University of California, at Irvine, he has also been on the faculty or served as a visiting writer at, among other schools, Sarah Lawrence College (1971–78), in Bronxville, New York; and the School of Drama at Yale University (1974–1975), in New Haven, Connecticut. He has been on the faculty of New York University since 1982.

Doctorow lives in New York City but spends summers in Sag Harbor, Long Island. He married Helen Esther Setzer, whom he met at Columbia University, on August 20, 1954. They have two daughters, Jenny and Caroline, and a son, Richard. In addition to his novels, Doctorow has also written a play, *Drinks Before Dinner* (1979); a collection of essays, *Jack London, Hemingway, and the Constitution: Selected Essays, 1977–1992* (1993); two collections of short fiction, *Lives of the Poets* (1984) and *Sweet Land Stories* (2004); and several screenplays, including three published as a book, in 2003. All of the scripts given in *Three Screenplays* are adaptations of Doctorow's own novels: *The Book of Daniel* (called simply *Daniel*), *Ragtime*, and *Loon Lake*. The 1981 screen adaptation of *Ragtime*, directed by Milos Forman from a different script, earned eight Academy Award nominations. A musical stage adaption of the book opened on Broadway in January 1998; nominated for 12 Tony Awards, it won four.

Doctorow is cautiously optimistic about the future of American literature and culture. In an interview with Gregory Kirschling for *Entertainment Weekly* (September 16, 2005), Doctorow opined: "there's a lot of junk in the culture today—cheap, tawdry nonsense being pumped out everywhere, and it's like people who eat too much candy. After a while, they get sick of it, and they want a decent meal, so I think novels will last. It would be nice if some of my books lasted, but they've lasted so far. It's nice to think that when you're gone, the work will still be there."

—C.M.

Suggested Reading: *Entertainment Weekly* p42+ Sep. 16, 2005; *Hartford Courant* G p4 Sep. 24, 2006; *Library Journal* p175 Feb. 15, 1989; (London) *Guardian* p10 Mar. 10, 1972; p8 Jan. 19, 1976; *Los Angeles Times* R p6 Sep. 24, 2006; *Nation* p594 Nov. 30, 1985, p784 June 6, 1994; *New Republic* p31 Sep. 20, 1980; *New York Post* p33 Aug. 31, 1971; p25 July 12, 1975; *New York Review of Books* p23 Dec. 19, 1985; *New York Times* E p1+ Sep. 20, 2005; *New York Times Book Review* p1 Feb. 26, 1989; *Newsweek* p58 Feb. 21, 2000; *Publishers Weekly* p6+ June 30, 1975, p25+ Sep. 12, 2005; *Saturday Review* p66 Sep. 1980; *Washington Post Book World* p6 Apr. 17, 1994

Selected Books: fiction—*Welcome to Hard Times*, 1960; *Big as Life*, 1966; *The Book of Daniel*, 1971; *Ragtime*, 1975; *Loon Lake*, 1980; *Lives of the Poets*, 1984; *World's Fair*, 1985; *Billy Bathgate*, 1989; *The Waterworks*, 1994; *City of God*, 2000; *Sweet Land Stories*, 2004; *The March*, 2005; drama—*Drinks Before Dinner*, 1979; nonfiction—*Jack London, Hemingway, and the Constitution: Selected Essays, 1977–1992*, 1993; *Creationists: Selected Essays, 1993–2006*, 2006

Courtesy of Simon's Rock College

Dongala, Emmanuel

July 16, 1941– Novelist; short-story writer

Raised in the Republic of the Congo—not to be confused with the Democratic Republic of the Congo, formerly known as Zaire—Emmanuel Dongala has been compared to Chinua Achebe, the Nigerian novelist, for his zeal for opening readers to the many-sided realities of African life, as well as for his need to flee his home country for the sake of his and his family's safety. A political idealist when he was young, eager for the brutality of colonization to end, Dongala watched ruefully as the end of French rule over his home country brought a series of coups d'etat by a succession of dictators rather than a stable democracy. What has most concerned Dongala—a scientist and educator as well as a writer of poetry, plays, and fiction—is how children develop under such circumstances. The three of his five works of fiction to have been translated into English—*The Fire of Origins* (2001), *Little Boys Come from the Stars* (2001), and *Johnny Mad Dog* (2005)—all belong to the tradition of the *Bildungsroman* (a German word meaning "novel of formation"). *The Fire of Origins* traces the life of one man, but in doing so it also takes the reader from the traditional past in the Congo, through the coming of the French, to independence, when the spiritual values of both the Africans and the French are lost to corruption, greed, and violence. Despite the grim subject matter, Dongala's fiction is laced with humor—as is, by his interviewers' accounts, Dongala's own conversation. In *Johnny Mad Dog* the humor can be quite bitter, as it comes from the mouth of a 16-year-old member of a militia—a killer and a rapist whose nickname gives the book its title. In *Little Boys Come from the Stars*, however, Dongala "created a whimsical, indeed hilarious satire out of Africa's decidedly unfunny post-independence woes," Susie Linfield wrote for the *Los Angeles Times Book Review* (March 18, 2001), adding: "The barbarities that have been visited on the Congo, and that it has visited on itself, have not crushed Dongala; he has emerged with the robust capacity to see through lies, to root himself in history rather than myth and even, miraculously, to laugh at tyranny."

Emmanuel Dongala submitted the following statement for *World Authors 2000–2005*:

"Even though I know precisely on which day and what year I was born, July 16, 1941, I do not know the season. The reason for this is simple. My father is from the Republic of Congo and my mother from the Central African Republic. It happens that the first country lies below the equator while the second one lies above it and one of the consequences of this is that seasons are reversed. So, on my mother's side they say that I was born during the rainy season, while my father's family pretend that I was born during the dry season. To make matter worse, my paternal family is matrilinear, therefore, for them, I belong to my mother's clan, while to my mother's family, which is patrilinear, I belong to my father's clan. This position of belonging to a netherland, or rather of belonging nowhere, had made me long for certainty at a very early age, and one of the places I always thought I could find this certainty was in books.

"In these territories of French colonial Africa, books were magical and seemed to us to contain all the knowledge in the world. I became an avid reader and being an avid reader gave me an irresistible desire to 'write books myself,' in other words to become a writer.

"I studied at the Lycée Savorgnan de Brazza in Brazzaville, the capital of the Republic of Congo. Then with a grant from the Ford Foundation, I went to the United States to study. I earned a B.A. from Oberlin College, a M.S. from Rutgers University. I left the U.S. for France where I earned a doctorate in chemistry from the University of Montpellier in France. I taught in France before joining the faculty of the University of Brazzaville, first as chairman of the chemistry department and then as the dean of academic affairs of the university.

"I started first by writing juvenile poetry which was heavily influenced by the French writers we learned in school—Victor Hugo, Baudelaire, Rimbaud. African literature did not really exist then. Later, I read the great authors of the world and started writing seriously. I have published four novels, a collection of short stories and a play. The collection of short stories, *Jazz et vin de palme* (Jazz and Palm Wine), published while the Congo was a one-party Marxist-Leninist state was banned because it satirized those in power. The ban was lifted only in 1990, after the collapse of the Soviet Union followed by the collapse of the Congolese one-party state.

"I am the founder and former president of both the National Association of Congolese Writers and the Congolese chapter of PEN. I am also the founder and director of a theater company called Le Théâtre de l'Eclair.

"I write in French but my books have been translated into a dozen languages.

"I have won, among other awards, the Grand Prix de Littérature d'Afrique Noire, the Prix de la Fondation de France, Prix Radio France Internationale. I was a finalist for the Caine Prize (usually referred to as the 'African Booker Prize') in 2003. I won the Fonlon-Nichols prize for 'excellence in creative writing and for human rights and freedom of expression' in 2003 and a Guggenheim Fellowship in 1999.

"I left the Congo in 1998 to escape from a bitter civil war and I am now on the faculty of both Simon's Rock College of Bard, where I teach chemistry, and at Bard College, where I teach the literature of Francophone Africa."

In 1961, the year after the Republic of the Congo achieved independence, Emmanuel Boundzéki Dongala came to the U.S. to study chemistry. He told an interviewer for Qmag.org (August 2001) that during his youth he "was a romantic revolutionary," and it was partially this quality that fueled his desire to study chemistry. Dongala told Terry Gross, host of the syndicated radio show *Fresh Air* (April 12, 2001), that he shared "this dream, that we're going to change Africa. We need scientists, engineers, doctors, and all that. So that's why I went into science." His time in America allowed Dongala to meet a number of important civil rights leaders, including Martin Luther King Jr. and Malcolm X, and it exposed him to jazz, transforming him into a devotee of such musicians as John Coltrane, Miles Davis, and Thelonious Monk.

Dongala published his first novel, *Un fusil dans la main, un poeme dans la poche* (which can be translated as "a gun in the hand, a poem in the pocket"), in 1973. The story of the development of a political revolutionary, Mayela dia Mayela, who eventually becomes the leader of an imaginary central African country, the book won the Ladislas Dormandi prize for the best novel in French written by a nonnative of France. Koffi Anyinefa, in *Research in African Literatures* (Spring 1993), called the book, which has been translated into Dutch, German, Portuguese, and Hungarian, "one of the most important *Bildungsromane* to have emerged from francophone Africa." (Dongala has distanced himself from the book a bit in recent years, describing it to the Qmag.org interviewer "as more of an action novel" and "a little bit dated.") In 1982 Dongala published *Jazz et vin de palme*. Set partially in the U.S., with John Coltrane's music figuring importantly in the title story, the book satirized African politics.

Le feu des origines, Dongala's next work of fiction, was originally published in 1987. Translated by Lillian Corti as *The Fire of Origins*, the novel follows the life of Mandala Mankunku, who is born in a village in the Congo before the arrival of the French and lives to see Congolese independence. He is a questioner and a seeker of truth, not fully accepting the traditions of his village and later trying to understand the ways of those who colonize it. A larger-than-life figure, he learns to be a sculptor, a blacksmith, and a healer and then is conscripted to work on the railroads when the French assume control. He escapes to the city and struggles there until he is again conscripted, this time to fight in World War II. Reviewing the book for *World Literature Today* (Spring 2002), Adele King remarked that when, after World War II, Mankunku is regarded as a revolutionary hero, it becomes an empty honor since "this revolution is subverted by a dictatorial president with a gang of party thugs." In the book, King added, "Dongala mocks Congolese tribalism, blind obedience to traditional rules, even his compatriots' amazement at voices coming from a phonograph record. More forcefully, however, he attacks the colonial rulers who can only use overpowering brutality against peasant riots. Worse still are the new African rulers, with their torture of any opponents." For King, however, the novel's meditative turns often overwhelmed its characters and its story: "While the style is frequently witty and ironic, the plot becomes overlong and excessively complicated at times." A critic for *Kirkus Reviews* (January 1, 2001), on the other hand, wrote: "A remarkable amount of felt life, as well as representative historical fact, is subtly woven into Dongala's narrative, which is further enlivened by a descriptive lushness that has the thematic amplitude, verbal dignity, and suggestive force of creation myth. . . . A great African novel. Not to be missed."

The Republic of the Congo's volatile political situation reached a head in 1997, when civil war pushed Dongala and his family out of their home in Brazzaville. With food scarce, and packed into a house outside the capital with 30 other people, Dongala and the other men in the group sometimes ate only every other day, alternating with the women. "We lost everything," Dongala told Marcela Valdes for *Publishers Weekly* (May 13, 2005). "I saw somebody killed because she didn't have a hundred francs"—the equivalent in Congelese currency, he explained, of 25 U.S. cents. His youngest daughter was mistakenly evacuated by the French to Chad, and the family lost track of her for several weeks; far from being traumatized by the experience, his daughter returned as though from a vacation. Still, the family was eager to escape the constant threats to their safety. Thanks to the intervention of Philip Roth and others in the American literary community, whom Dongala had gotten to know as the head of the Republic of the Congo branch of the writing and human-rights organization International PEN, he was able, in early 1998, to come to the U.S., where a teaching position had been secured for him by Leon Botstein, the president of Bard College, in Annandale-on-Hudson, New York. He was offered a post in the French department at Bard and made a professor of chemistry at Simon's Rock College, a division of Bard geared toward high-school-aged students, in Great Barrington, Massachusetts. "Let me stress that I am not a political exile," Dongala told Michael T. Kaufman, for the *New York Times* (May 7, 1998). "I did not suffer because I was a writer or an intellectual. I suffered like everybody else did because the mortars and the rockets we call Stalin's organs kept firing on our house, because anarchy spread and children with machine guns took what they wanted. It was not ideological." The use of child soldiers in the war seemed to disturb Dongala particularly. "One day you wake up and you see all these kids with guns," he told Valdes. "Sometimes the guns are taller than they are. And you say, where do they come from? I mean, they have no parents? What kind of society brings up children like that?"

Little Boys Come from the Stars was translated by Joel Rejouis and Val Vinokurov from *Les petits garçons naissent aussi des étoiles*, originally published in 1998. It is another look into the history of Africa through a young person's eyes. The central character in the novel is Michel, a little boy whose nickname, Matapari, means "trouble" or "problem child" but who is, in a sense, a miraculous child, a triplet born two days after his other two brothers. His uncle, Boula Boula, becomes a star politician in the communist dictatorship that succeeds colonial rule. His scholarly, somewhat absent-minded father later overthrows that regime, while his grandfather serves as the family's repository of traditional African thought. "Matapari's growth from childhood to adolescence parallels Africa's growth from animism to an embrace of modernization and democracy, but the journey is never smooth," Koom Kankesan noted for the Montreal *Gazette* (May 26, 2001), adding: "In the end, like his father, Matapari chooses a more noble and bookish path. The character of the father, obsessed with Fermat's last theorem while Matapari's uncle is coming up with a plan to convert the forest pygmies to Marxism-Leninism, balances the book's playful cynicism with a celebration of life and learning." Writing that the book was replete with "clamorous slapstick, razor sharp characterization and vivid detail of central African village life, " Philip Herter, for the *St. Petersburg (Florida) Times* (May 27, 2001), argued that "Dongala's sly narrative uses the coming-of-age form to tweak colonialism and socialism, among other political forces, that have plagued and destabilized his country. Missionary priests, pompous bureaucrats and local sorcerers all take their lumps in wide-eyed Michel's tale. . . . By novel's end, violence erupts as demonstrations for political pluralism sweep the country. While Matapari keeps a vigil for his dying grandfather, the old man teaches him that true heroism doesn't come from an earthly agenda." A *Publishers Weekly* (January 22, 2001) reviewer described Matapari's "keen and comic voice" as "refreshing" but felt that "Dongala sometimes wedges historical information and family asides into improbable spots."

Johnny Mad Dog is Maria Louise Ascher's translation of *Johnny chien mechant*, first published in 2002 and told by two narrators who have nothing in common but their age, 16. The title character is one of the child soldiers spawned from the chronic disorder in the Congo. He belongs to a militia that is really just a gang of looters who have joined one side in the conflict in order to gain as much as they can. They do not hesitate to kill and rape for pleasure. His opposite is Laokolé, a girl with educational aspirations whose murdered father was an architect. Laokolé attempts to save her maimed and disabled mother and her younger brother from the onslaught but loses them both, becoming a lone refugee. In an iconic scene she is pushed away from a rescue helicopter by a team of Westerners because their mission is to rescue gorillas, not people. "Dongala has written an unrelentingly bleak story, occasionally lightened by Mad Dog's laughable pronouncements," wrote Luisita López Torregrosa, for the *New York Times Book Review* (July 10, 2005), "and he grabs us from the start with a language that is rude and raw (Mad Dog's) and lyrical (Laokolé's)." *Johnny Mad Dog*, Chris Abani wrote for the *Los Angeles Times Book Review* (June 5, 2005), "is a novel about war like few others. [Dongala] has lived through it to bring us these pages of awe and illumination." The critic for *Kirkus Reviews* (March 15, 2005), however, contrasted the book unfavorably with Dongala's previous two novels, arguing that *Johnny Mad Dog* "offers a simplistic contrast of innocence with rampant amorality." The writer concluded: "One respects this earnest tale's passion and indignation, but little else. Johnny is a posturing monster, Laokolé a stoical saint, and every action and thought of each is reduced to melodramatic cliche. The result is an all-too-credible horror story, but not a good novel."

In 1989 Dongala was named a Chevalier des Arts et des Lettres by the French ministry of culture.

Now the Richard B. Fisher Chair in natural sciences at Simon's Rock, Dongala and his wife, Pauline Milondo, a librarian, live in Great Barrington, Massachusetts. They have four daughters: Assita, Nefertiti, Nora, and Myriam.

—S.Y.

Suggested Reading: *Africa Today* p101+ Winter 2003; *Los Angeles Times Book Review* p3 Mar. 18, 2001, p6 June 5, 2005; (Montreal) *Gazette* J p4 May 26, 2001; *New York Times Book Review* p16 July 10, 2005; *Publishers Weekly* p301 Jan. 22, 2001, p26+ June 13, 2005; *St. Petersburg (Florida) Times* D p4 May 27, 2001; *World Literature Today* p127+ Spring 2002

Selected Books in English Translation: *The Fire of Origins*, 2001; *Little Boys Come from the Stars*, 2001; *Johnny Mad Dog*, 2005

Donoghue, Emma

Oct. 24, 1969– Novelist; short-story writer; playwright; literary historian

Emma Donoghue, in 2004, wrote the following autobiographical statement for *World Authors 2000-2005*:

"Born in Dublin in 1969, I grew up in the prosperous Southside suburb of Mount Merrion beside University College Dublin, where my father, Denis Donoghue, was Professor of English. I was the youngest of eight—three boys, five girls—and so had a very cushy life.

"The walls of our house were lined with books, and my mother, Frances Donoghue (a former English teacher) taught me to read at the age of three. Though I had a particular passion for fairy-tales from all round the world, and then later for science fiction, I always read a real mixture: Enid Blyton one day, Jane Austen (after whose novel, *Emma*, I'd been named) the next. At about seven, I started writing poetry: ghastly stuff about fairies or the Holy Spirit, but still, good practice with words.

"The most stimulating event in my childhood was a year that I spent in New York (with my parents and two of my sisters) in 1979. For a rather cautious Irish nine-year-old, being offered a joint by a classmate on my first day was a shock to the system, as were the revelations that not everyone in the world was white, and that most of my new friends' parents were divorced.

"The schools I went to, back in Dublin, were traditional Catholic convents: Mount Anville National School in Kilmacud and Muckross Park in Donnybrook. I resented the bossy nuns—who spent a disproportionate amount of time ranting about abortion—but I do have to credit them with encouraging us to become ambitious 'career girls.'

"Being a teenaged lesbian in the closet in 1980s Ireland was rather grueling. Even more so when I found a girlfriend; for the last three years of school, we had to keep our relationship a secret, and we lived in constant (and justifiable) fear of being expelled, separated, and sent to psychiatrists. I think what helped me survive relatively unscathed was that I was very confident, and thought of myself as a poet, who didn't have to be 'normal.'

"For years I went to weekly drama classes at the Betty Ann Norton school, where I learned how to improvise short plays and act everything from a king to a piece of inter-galactic debris. Later at UCD (studying English and French) I joined Dramsoc, which gave me a chance to direct several adaptations, including a play I based on Shakespeare's sonnets. I set up a Creative Writing Group and an American male friend and I won

Claire McNamee

Emma Donoghue

much mockery, I'm sure, for running Anti-sexism workshops together. Actually, most of my close friends at college were men; having lived in an all-girl environment through my schooldays, I now relished the different ways mens' minds seemed to work. The GaySoc gave me the nerve to start coming out: most of my friends reacted fine, but I used to find rather startling graffiti about me in the toilets, such as 'Emma Donoghue is an AIDS-spreading bitch.'

"In my second year I saw an ad on an accommodation noticeboard in UCD which gave me the idea for a novel, *Stir-fry*. Overnight I switched from poetry to prose, and over the course of eight drafts, gradually taught myself how to write fiction.

"In 1990 I decided to go to England to do my PhD, partly because I wanted a break from Ireland. In my teens I would have described myself as an introvert, but moving to Cambridge—being 'out' from the start, and leaving the Catholic church—gave me the chance to remake myself. I discovered that I was highly sociable, and that being a lesbian was not just about sleeping with a woman, but about community (I lived in a women's co-op), a lively sub-culture, a shared sense of humour.

"My PhD thesis was on the mid-18th-century English novel and the concept of friendship between men and women. But I have never liked to work on one thing at a time, so I wangled my first contract from a small, newly formed women's press to write a book about 18th-century lesbian representations, *Passions Between Women*. I was lucky enough to find an agent in London, Caroline Davidson, who kept encouraging me, while gathering rejection letters for *Stir-fry* for several

years, before getting me a two-novel deal with Penguin. Without Caroline, I remind myself sometimes, I could very easily be one of the many restless academics who've got an unfinished novel in the bottom drawer.

"Instead, 1994 saw me launched as a novelist, mildly notorious as 'Ireland's only lesbian,' and presenting the first (if short-lived) prime-time literary programme on RTE, Book 94. For the rest of my 20s I continued to experiment in a variety of genres: contemporary novels and short stories, fairy-tales, stage plays for a Dublin theatre company, radio plays for RTE and for BBC Radio 4, as well as lesbian literary history. I also wrote reviews, gave lectures, taught creative writing, sat on judging panels, and slowly finished my PhD.

"At a Cambridge seminar in that same busy year of 1994 I met a Canadian professor of French, Chris Roulston, and I divided the next few years between Cambridge and London, Ontario—a city of 330,000 people, about two hours west of Toronto. In 1998 I moved there permanently, and I gave birth to our son Finn Roulston in 2003.

"In my 30s so far I have concentrated on fiction; my bestselling novel about an 18th-century murder, *Slammerkin*, won me a wider audience and I followed it up with two more fact-based fictions, *The Woman Who Gave Birth to Rabbits* and *Life Mask*. I relish giving readings, and tour about every two years, particularly in the United States, which is my biggest market. Books in the pipeline include several collections of short stories, a contemporary novel about immigration and another about a Victorian divorce trial."

Now best known for her fiction, Emma Donoghue, who was born on October 24, 1969, made her literary debut with a play, *I Know My Own Heart*, which was produced in 1993 and later published in an anthology, *Seen and Heard: Six New Plays by Irish Women* (2001). *I Know My Own Heart* is based on the diaries of an Englishwoman of the first part of the 19th century who lived as a lesbian and recorded three love affairs. Fintan O'Toole, writing for the *Irish Times* (November 13, 1993), termed the play "an effort, not to awake from the nightmare of history, but to invent an alternative history in which a young Irishwoman can place herself." O'Toole noted that gender and sexuality replace nationality for the play's audience and concluded that the play is "the work of a real writer with a gift for dialogue, a hard-edged wit and an admirable determination to make her own world." The same year that *I Know My Own Heart* appeared on the stage, Donoghue's first book, *Passions between Women: British Lesbian Culture, 1668–1801*, appeared in print. Calling it a "challenging and often exciting book," Elaine Hobby noted for the *Journal of Gender Studies* (March 1995) that cumulatively "Donoghue establishes beyond doubt that dictionary-makers and the theorists who have trusted them are wrong: Lesbianism as an identity, the possibility of the (female) homosexual being seen 'as a species,' in [Michel] Foucault's terms, is not a modern invention."

In 1994 *Stir-fry*, Donoghue's first novel, was published. Set in a college campus in Dublin, the novel is the coming-of-age story of Maria, a 17-year-old student from rural Ireland who arrives in Dublin for her first year at the university and rents a room in the home of a lesbian couple, Ruth and Jael. Reviewers were generally impressed by Donoghue's fictional debut. Eileen Battersby wrote for the *Irish Times* (January 22, 1994), "Confidence, intuition and a sharp, clinical intelligence sustain *Stir-fry*. . . . In Maria's fluctuating sensations, the concept of love as an affirmation of worth is intelligently understood and dissected. A novel which impresses more for its psychological insights than for its set piece exchanges between characters, *Stir-fry* testifies to its heroine's helpful loss of her youthful emotional resilience and to the formidable Emma Donoghue's firm, if kindly, reading of complex, indefinable human needs." Other reviewers saw in Donoghue's work an evocation of the new Irish culture that was beginning to emerge in the early 1990s. "The language, wit and iconography make this a very Irish piece of work," Aisling Foster observed for the London *Times* (January 27, 1994). She went on to note: "where else would you get a humorous, liberal and anti-apartheid view of lesbianism which is sympathetic to men, condemns power politics in relationships between either sex, and sends up its paranoid and bandwagon sisterhood? With this clever, interesting and very assured first novel Donoghue has put down a marker for the so-called New Ireland and its fictions."

Donoghue followed *Stir-fry* with *Hood*, in 1995, a novel that explores how the main character, Pen O'Grady, deals with her grief in the week that follows the loss of her lover of 13 years in an automobile accident. Calling Donoghue a "born writer," Catherine Lockerbie argued, in an article for the *New York Times Book Review* (March 24, 1996): "The charm of the book—and it is utterly charming—lies in its lack of political aggression, in its insouciant avoidance of the bandwagon." Lockerbie went on to observe: "The achievement of *Hood* may lie in its very ordinariness. It states indirectly that love, homosexual or heterosexual, is simply love. The sex of the partner cannot alter its effects." Sylvia Brownrigg wrote for the London *Guardian* (March 14, 1995) that Donoghue's style was "passionate without taking itself too seriously." She concluded: "Donoghue is honest enough to give Pen an awareness of the flaws and excesses in the women's relationship, but she crucially fails to make Pen's grief seem deep or moving."

Donoghue drew on fairy tales for her 1997 short-story collection, *Kissing the Witch*, adapting such classic stories as "Cinderella," "Rumpelstiltskin," "Rapunzel," and "Beauty and the Beast" and retelling them from the perspective of their principal female characters. The experiment was an overwhelming success. "Donoghue keeps us in the Jungian fairy-tale world of castles, witches, princes and goose-girls, but her perceptions and wryness are of today," Fay Weldon wrote for the London *Mail on Sunday* (August 3, 1997). "Lyrically focused," Weldon added, "you can find all the hurt and joy of being alive and female—the casual cruelty of mothers, the reluctance of daughters, the desires of fathers, the passion of kings—and the hidden and inner life made abundantly clear. The writing is as impressionistic as a Van Gogh cornfield, and as masterly." Lucy Atkins, writing for the London *Guardian* (May 8, 1997), called the collection "an original and playful endeavour" and noted that these "bold rewritings of fairy tales . . . are salvaged from the political soap-box by Donoghue's sense of humour and delight in the rhythmic mythologies of the genre." Reviewers for the *Journal of Adolescent & Adult Literacy* (September 1997) called *Kissing the Witch* "a provocative look at the stories that were, for many of us, our initiation into the wonder of imaginative literature." (Donoghue later adapted the title story for the stage.)

As she was writing her novels and stories, Donoghue was also working on her Ph.D., which she completed in 1996, submitting her dissertation, "Male-Female Friendship and English Fiction in the Mid-eighteenth Century." She continued her scholarly research after receiving her degree, publishing, in 1998, *We Are Michael Field*, a biography of two late 19th-century women, Katherine Bradley and Edith Cooper. Together, these women, who were lovers, made up the writer Michael Field, a prolific author of poetry, plays, and novels. Kimberly Clarke, the reviewer for *Library Journal* (April 1, 1999), observed that "Donoghue sheds light on the obscure careers of these women, who collaborated to write 30 plays and 11 volumes of poetry. . . . Donoghue provides an engaging, informal overview of their history, including family origins, their decision to use a male pseudonym, their rise to fame, their intimate relationship, and their colorful circle of friends."

Slammerkin (2000), Donoghue's third novel, was based to some extent on her research into the manners and mores of the long 18th century, which is generally said to run from 1660 to 1790 or 1798. The book's title refers to a loose dress, and, by extension, a loose woman. Using an actual murder case as her starting point, Donoghue narrates the short, brutal life of Mary Saunders, a maid who was executed, in 1764, for hacking her employer to death with a cleaver. "*Slammerkin* sees the historical circumstances of its heroine as a trap, impossible to escape from alive," Roz

Kaveney observed for the London *Independent* (September 9, 2000). He went on to observe: "Mary's adventures as whore, as penitent, as runaway and as servant are sensuously vivid, and for once we get a sense of religious life as something more than hypocrisy. Yet our pre-knowledge of Mary's end means that all this lived experience comes to seem no more than a theorem that will end by confirming what it began by announcing." Margot Livesey, writing for New York *Newsday* (July 22, 2001), by contrast, maintained: "Mary Saunders is *Slammerkin*'s central jewel, a robust, vivid unpredictable character, by turns sympathetic and exasperating, touching and infuriating, capable of odd tenderness and sudden violence, whose adventures we follow with a suspense that amounts almost to anguish as we watch her, repeatedly, act in her own worst interests. This suspense comes not entirely from wondering about Mary's ultimate fate—the prologue shows her already in jail—but from those more complex emotions that we bring to a story whose outcome we already know and dread."

Donoghue's short-story collection *The Woman Who Gave Birth to Rabbits*, which came out in 2002, also grew out of historical research, "the flotsam and jetsam of the last seven hundred years of British and Irish life: surgical case notes, trial records, a plague ballad, theological pamphlets, a painting of two girls in a garden, an articulated skeleton," Carrie Brown explained for the *Washington Post Book World* (May 19, 2002). Brown went on to note, "Donoghue dedicates *The Woman Who Gave Birth to Rabbits* to her father, the literary critic Denis Donoghue, who taught her 'that books are for letting us imagine lives other than our own,' and the generous scope of her curiosity is apparent in the sheer variety of these 17 tales." Populated with women who are victims of terrible circumstances or of their struggle to be strong, these stories revive history in an almost conversational style. Yvonne Nolan thus argued for the *Irish Times* (July 27, 2002), "Donoghue is eruditely familiar with the 18th century in particular, and her informed imaginings combined with her sheer cleverness and elegance as a writer breathe vivid life into real characters who heretofore resided in the footnotes of history (if even that). For this alone she should be saluted, but for this reader at least, it is in the quiet stories of this volume that Donoghue is at her descriptive, empathetic best."

For her 2004 novel *Life Mask*, Donoghue once again delved into 18th-century history, depicting a decade in the lives of Eliza Farren, one of the leading actresses at London's Drury Lane Theatre; Lord Derby; and Anne Damer, a English sculptor who had a reputation for pursuing the love of women. "From these real-life personages—and a host of other period figures like [Richard Brinsely] Sheridan, William Pitt and George III—Donoghue has sculpted a fabulously dense portrait of the social and political landscape of England," Dermot Bolger observed for the Dublin, Ireland *Sunday Independent* (September 5, 2004). The *Publishers Weekly* (July 26, 2004) reviewer noted that Donoghue "has an extraordinary talent for turning exhaustive research into plausible characters and narratives; she presents a vibrant world seething with repressed feeling and class tensions." For Walter Olson, writing for the *New York Times Book Review* (September 26, 2004), the book was "a sprawling, leisurely and enjoyable novel that draws on Donoghue's own varied accomplishments as a skillful investigator of literary and lesbian history. . . . Donoghue's method is tightly controlled: all her major characters are historical people, and their doings are amply enough documented in surviving papers . . . to reconstruct a dinner party or a set of amateur theatricals with an accurate guest list. The dialogue, naturally is invented, but often arises from the news or known table talk of the day. . . . By sticking so close to verifiable events, [Donoghue] gives up any hope of a driving plot. . . . But these characters do provide a chance to explore in satisfying detail the interlocking worlds of London at the time."

For her next book, *Touchy Subjects* (2006), a collection of short stories, Donoghue returned to the present. Divided into five thematic sections—babies, domesticity, strangers, desire, and death—each of the stories deals with an issue that people are normally uncomfortable discussing. "Despite the title, Emma Donoghue isn't out to shock—rather, to prove that shocking situations still happen to ordinary, everyday people," Danielle O'Donohue wrote for the Adelaide, Australia *Advertiser* (January 20, 2007). He went on to observe: "Donoghue has a great deal of affection for her subjects no matter how dysfunctional they are—guy or girl, gay or straight—and she has the gift of the gab. Her stories sparkle with humour and vitality." Others were equally impressed. Stevie Davies, for instance, wrote for the London *Guardian* (December 16, 2006), "Donoghue displays and anatomises the diseased cells of her characters. Her touch is so light and exuberantly inventive, her insight at once so forensic and intimate, her people so ordinary even in their oddities, that she is able to exhibit the small shames, shortcomings, prevarications and betrayals that we hope to keep in the dark. The tales at their best hit a nerve in the reader which corresponds to that in the character. They bring out, often through isolating a minor freakish activity or an apparently trivial object, the hidden rash that marks an inner blemish, anatomising these tender places in an unnervingly exact way."

Donoghue's next novel, *Landing*, is set for release in May 2007. "That's a post-closet novel, about a flight attendant for Aer Lingus. My mother was a flight attendant for Aer Lingus before she married. The Irish woman in the book falls in love with a woman living in a small town in Canada, so it has a half Canadian setting," Donoghue told Judy Stoffman for the *Toronto Star* (January 13, 2007). "The Sealed Letter," a historical novel about the sensational divorce of the Codringtons, a Victorian couple, is scheduled for release in 2008, and Donoghue is reportedly working on a study of hidden lesbian plots in literary works throughout the ages.

Besides the works discussed above, Donoghue has written a number of radio plays, including *Trespasses* (1996); *Don't Die Wondering* (2000), which was adapted for the stage, in 2005; *Exes* (2001), a series of five short plays about getting along with one's ex; and *Humans and Other Animals* (2003), a five-play series about pets; and *Mix* (2003). She has also produced stage plays, including *Ladies and Gentlemen* (1996); contributed to *Ladies' Night at Finbar's Hotel*, a novel for which a number of established Irish women authors contributed chapters; and edited *What Sappho Would Have Said* (entitled *Poems between Women* in the U.S., 1997) and *The Mammoth Book of Lesbian Short Stories* (1999), among other collections.

Donoghue, as well as writing prolifically, reads three books a week, giving each away after she has finished it.

—S.Y.

Suggested Reading: *Irish Studies Review* p73+ No. 1, 2000; *Irish Times* Supplement p5 Nov.13, 1993; *Journal of Adolescent & Adult Literacy* p80 Sep. 1997; *Journal of Gender Studies* Mar. 1995; *Library Journal* Apr. 1, 1999; (London) *Guardian* T p8 Mar. 22, 1995, T p10 May 8, 1997; (London) *Independent* p10 Sep. 9, 2000; (London) *Times* Jan. 27, 1994; (New York) *Newsday* B p9 July 22, 2001; *New York Times Book Review* p12 Mar. 24, 1996, Sep. 26, 2004; *Publishers Weekly* p38 July 26, 2004; *Washington Post* T p11 May 19, 2002

Selected Books: novels—*Stir-fry*, 1994; *Hood*, 1995; *Slammerkin*, 2000; *Life Mask*, 2004; short stories—*Kissing the Witch*, 1997; *The Woman Who Gave Birth to Rabbits*, 2002; *Touchy Subjects* (2006); nonfiction—*Passions between Women: British Lesbian Culture, 1668–1801*, 1993; *We Are Michael Field*, 1998; drama—*I Know My Own Heart*, 1993; *Ladies and Gentlemen*, 1996

Doughty, Louise

1963– Novelist; playwright

Louise Doughty "writes about people who don't usually get written about," Emma Hagestadt observed for the London *Independent* (March 23, 1996), referring to Doughty's first two novels, *Crazy Paving* (1995) and *Dance with Me* (1996), in which the author portrays the experiences of single women in their 20s, living in London, leading turbulent lives, and struggling with sex, relationships, and loneliness. In an article for the on-line magazine O*penDemocracy* (April 4, 2003), Doughty welcomed Hagestadt's praise: "[That] is one comment that pleases me above all others. . . . By that she meant that although my [early] heroines were young and female, they were not the glamorous city girls of 'chick-lit'. They were ordinary women leading ostensibly ordinary lives beneath which a variety of torrents raged." Doughty has shifted focus in her subsequent novels but preserved her interest in the marginal. In *Honey-Dew* (1998), which was published in the U.S. as *An English Murder* (2000), she added a new twist to the mystery genre by writing a novel about a young reporter covering a small-town murder in the English countryside that emphasized the ambitiousness of provincial journalism and the soullessness of rural life over the investigation of the murder itself. With *Fires in the Dark* (2003), Doughty offered a fictionalized account of the persecution of the Roma by the Nazis during World War II, a topic of particular importance to the author, who is one-sixteenth Roma. (Better known as Gypsies, the Roma are now more often called— and generally call themselves—Roma or, as Doughty prefers, Romany, though usually the latter word is used to indicate the Roma's language.) In *Stone Cradle* (2006) Doughty drew on her family history to shed light, once again, on the culture and history of the Roma. Both of these novels express what she termed in her article for *OpenDemocracy* "a new and highly politicised evangelism": they attempt to correct public misperceptions about the Roma, who are generally depicted "as exotic symbols of freedom or sexual licence" or "thieves, beggars or any of the other tiresome litany of racist stereotypes which are used to characterise Romany people in newspapers and magazines on a daily basis."

Louise Doughty was born in 1963 in Rutland, England, the second of three children. "As a child," Doughty wrote in a statement archived on the British Council Web site, "I was shy and bookish, constantly making up stories and inventing imaginary friends." With her dark complexion, Doughty was often teased by her classmates. When she was 17 her father informed her that there was Gypsy blood in the family: her great-great-grandmother, whose parents had emigrated to England in the mid-19th century, was Roma. A traditionally nomadic people, the came to be known as Gypsies because, when the population spread throughout Europe between the 15th and 16th centuries, they were erroneously believed to have come from Egypt. (They are now thought to have originated in India.) Due to their unique customs and closed society, the Roma have long faced discrimination and harassment in Europe. "When my father first told me these stories, he said that it would be a good idea not to mention our Romany blood to friends or neighbours," Doughty explained to David Altheer for the London *Times* (July 10, 2003). "But when I went to school the next day, I told everyone who would listen. I thought it was wonderful, and it explained something: my brother, sister and I all have black hair and brown eyes, and I am olive-skinned."

At 22 Doughty was "unpublished and living on the dole [a British expression for 'unemployed'] in Leeds," as she wrote in an article for the London *Guardian* (November 9, 1992). She moved to Norwich to attend the one-year master's course in creative writing at the University of East Anglia, a program that has produced such respected authors as Ian McEwan and Kazuo Ishiguro. "By the time I had finished," Doughty recollected, "I was 23, still spotty, still unpublished and living on the dole in Norwich. But I had learned to structure my narrative and trim down my metaphors. More importantly someone had taken me seriously."

Relocating to London Doughty worked at "a series of dire jobs," as she recalled to Altheer. From 1989 to 1991, she worked as a part-time secretary in London Transport's property division, an endeavor she found "so consummately awful," she had to write about it, she told Justina Hart for the London *Guardian* (March 23, 1998). "The work," Doughty explained, "was mind-numbing: doing dictation tapes, typing letters and specs. There's nothing so confidence-sapping as boredom." Doughty added, "All my writing has come out of things I feel passionate about. And since this job got up my nose, I knew there was a book in it."

In 1990 Doughty's commitment to writing began to pay off: a short story she wrote won the Ian St. James Award, and her play *Maybe* won a Radio Times Drama Award and was aired on BBC Radio 3. Doughty soon began getting freelance work, writing pieces for such publications as the London *Guardian* and the London *Sunday Express*. She also served for a time as the theater critic for the London *Mail on Sunday*. In 1994 her play *The Koala Bear Joke* was aired on BBC Radio 4. Her first two attempts at novels, meanwhile, were rejected by publishers.

In her first published novel, the black comedy *Crazy Paving*, Doughty drew on her clerical experience in London and detailed the lives of three secretaries in the employ of a nebulous transit bureaucracy called Capital Transport. Annette, Joan, and Helly have little control, whether over the policies of the organization for which they work or the random occurrences that determine their fates. The work was short-listed for

the John Llewellyn Rhys Prize and received generally encouraging reviews. Jonathan Coe, writing for the London *Sunday Times* (February 12, 1995), stated, "Somewhere inside the book lurks the seed of something more adventurous and intriguing, but, for the time being, the author's ambitions in that direction have been submerged beneath a general desire to please and to tell a simple story. . . . What lets the book down is not its plot, then, but the failure of its dialogue and characterisation to spark into consistent life." A critic for the London *Evening Standard* (January 23, 1995), although unsatisfied with the novel's ending, remarked, "Here is a first novel bubbling with talent. When one reads that one character was 'married to a man who always bought her garden tokens for her birthday'. . . one knows at once that here is a writer with constantly alert powers of observation and a happy gift for a phrase." The critic concluded, "For all its miscalculations, here is a debut of outstanding promise."

In her novel *Dance with Me*, Doughty again wrote about 20-something women with London office jobs. The book examines the dysfunctional romantic lives of two women, Iris and Bet: the former pines away in a dilapidated office for a lover who has spurned her; the latter goes on drinking bouts at local wine bars and has flings in the bedrooms of men with whom she is only marginally acquainted. The supernatural also becomes a factor: "The fates of [Iris and Bet] enmesh and twist eerily together," Penny Perrick wrote for the London *Times* (February 17, 1996). "Surroundings become increasingly scary: ghosts are seen, or imagined; people are raised from the dead." Perrick added, "Sometimes, the gruesome pranks that Doughty delights in can seem a bit too heady but her observations on women's lives are breathtakingly original." "*Dance with Me* is a painfully accurate record of mating rituals and dating nightmares," Emma Hagestadt wrote for the London *Independent* (March 23, 1996). "It is a novel about delusions—particularly the kind women have about men."

In 1996 Doughty's third play, *Nightworkers*, was aired on BBC Radio 4. Her third novel, *Honey-Dew*, was published in 1998. Set in a small and picturesque English village, the novel offers a satire of the conventional murder mystery. "I had never written a murder story before," Doughty explained in an interview for *BookEnds*, the magazine of the British on-line bookstore The Book Place, "but I knew before I began *Honey-Dew*, that I wanted to send the whole thing up." *Honey-Dew* follows the intrepid, if slow-witted, small-town reporter Alison Akenside as she examines the stabbing of a local couple whose missing 17-year-old daughter is the prime suspect in the crime. However, as Akenside's investigation proceeds, she soon uncovers more than she bargained for. Excerpts from the missing daughter's diary and from Akenside's articles propel the plot forward, and the observations of some of the locals contribute to a growing sense of unease.

DOUGHTY

"Each word of this book seems as carefully chosen as the blooms in a bridal bouquet," Kate Munger wrote for the *Washington Post* (June 25, 2000). "Even the black humor, used to chilling effect, is perfectly keyed to character and never obtrusive." Munger added, "In exploring events building up to the killing as well as its aftereffects, Doughty challenges the traditional givens of murder mysteries, suggesting, for example, that murder may well be one of the most ordinary events of human existence rather than an extraordinary occurrence. Because of this, readers are forced to examine many of their preconceptions about life, death and human nature." Gill Hornby, in a review for the London *Times* (April 18, 1998), offered tempered praise: "The portrayal of country life out of kilter is the most successful aspect of this slight novel. . . . Alison's bovine stupidity combined with her irritating cockiness mean that the narrative has to somehow drive along despite her. And at the end, when we know the truth but our hapless detective is none the wiser, you can't help but regret the absence of that obvious ingredient of the traditional murder mystery, the satisfying conclusion."

In an interview with Emily Bromfield for *Southbank* magazine (November 2003, on-line), Doughty explained that after her first three novels, "I felt ready to tackle some big historical themes. I reached a point as a writer when I had to make a choice. You can keep writing the same novels over and over again or you can make an imaginative leap and do something completely different." Accordingly, Doughty's novel *Fires in the Dark* ventured into uncharted and ambitious territory for the author, tackling the persecution of the Roma during World War II, when between 250,000 and 500,000 Romanies lost their lives in Nazi concentration camps. In 1999, as a writer-in-residence in the Czech town of Brno, Doughty began research into the Romany genocide; she also familiarized herself with Gypsy customs, a difficult endeavor considering the private nature of Gypsy society and the small amount of scholarly work on the subject. The novel begins in 1927, when a son is born in rural Bohemia to Josef Maximoff, the leader of a family of the Coppersmith sect of the Roma, and his wife, Anna. The boy, named Emil, grows up during the Great Depression of the 1930s, a time when Gypsies in Europe were subjected to strict registration and documentation requirements in an attempt to limit the movements of the nomads. The discrimination comes to a head when Nazi forces invade Czechoslovakia; Emil is sent to an internment camp but manages to escape. He reaches occupied Prague, while the rest of his family is transported to Auschwitz, the largest of the Nazi death camps.

Critical response to the novel was generally favorable. "The characters are absorbing individuals, and the reconstruction of Roma life has a loving and compelling vitality," Jane Jakeman wrote for the London *Independent* (May 10, 2003). "This journey into hell is scarcely bearable, yet made compelling reading by the humanity which it reveals. . . . History can give us the facts; a novel such as this has the emotive power to restore dignity to those who were so appallingly robbed of it." Tom Deveson, writing for the London *Sunday Times* (June 8, 2003), was less complimentary, describing the work as "well intentioned but rather cumbersome. . . . [Doughty's] uneasy blend of hereditary custom and modern psychology isn't convincing. The appalling history behind the story is more memorable than the way it is told." Steve Davis, however, opined for the London *Guardian* (June 7, 2003), "If the novel falters with its romantic and unlikely conclusion, this does not detract from the magnanimity and power of Doughty's achievement in recreating a generation that lived according to its own laws and died by lawless butchery."

Doughty gave a fictionalized account of her own ancestry for her fifth novel, *Stone Cradle*. Following her family history to the town of Peterborough, England, she recounts "a very human story," she remarked to the *Peterborough Evening Telegraph* (May 10, 2006). "It tells of the lives of Clementina and Rose, two women who adored my great-grandfather and gave up everything for him. It's about the mistakes we can all make in our lives and how misunderstandings in families can go on for 30-odd years." Clementina is the mother of Elijah, who was born on a rainy afternoon atop a gravestone in Wellington. This young family of two endure ostracism and other tribulations but none as horrifying for Clementina as when her teenage son falls in love with Rose, a *gorjer* (a non-Gypsy). When Elijah enlists in the service to fight in World War I, the women are forced to live together along with Elijah and Rose's children. "In the end, this warm, wry, wonderfully engaging novel is as much about the familiar fictional territory of motherhood as it is about the challenges of living with another race," Amanda Craig opined for the *New Statesmen* (May 29, 2006). In a review for the Glasgow *Herald* (June 24, 2006), Vicky Collins wrote, "Doughty's most admirable skills are portraying people realistically and balancing a plot on their relationships. Her understanding of Romanies and their culture is used in exactly the way it should be: to create a unique and dramatic backdrop to the lives of ordinary but fascinating characters."

BBC Radio 4 broadcast Doughty's play *Geronimo!* in 2004 and two years later her adaptation of the Thomas Hardy story "The Withered Arm."

Doughty makes her home in London. She has two daughters. According to her personal Web site, she "is currently working on several screen projects, including an adaptation of her novel *Honey-Dew* and an original screenplay."

—P.B.M.

Suggested Reading: British Council Web site; (Glasgow) *Herald* Guide p9 June 24, 2006; (London) *Evening Standard* p24 Jan. 23, 1995; (London) *Guardian* p28 June 7, 2003; (London) *Independent* p27 Jan. 28, 1995, p12 Mar. 23, 1996, p16 Mar. 28, 1998, p25 May 10, 2003; (London) *Times* Mar. 6, 1995, Feb. 17, 1996, Feb. 25, 1996, Apr. 18, 1998, p48 June 8, 2003, p11 July 10, 2003; Louise Doughty's Web site; *New Statesman* May 29, 2006; *OpenDemocracy* (on-line) Apr. 4, 2003; *Washington Post* X p13 June 25, 2000

Selected Books: *Crazy Paving*, 1995; *Dance with Me*, 1996; *Honey-Dew*, 1998 (published in the U.S. as *An English Murder*, 2000); *Fires in the Dark*, 2003; *Stone Cradle*, 2006

Dudman, Martha Tod

Jan. 4, 1952– Memoirist

Martha Tod Dudman is known in business circles as both a radio-station executive and a professional fundraiser; she is recognized in the literary world, however, for her brutally honest and revealing memoirs: *Augusta, Gone* (2001), which recounts her relationship with her troubled teenage daughter, and *Expecting to Fly: A Sixties Reckoning* (2004), in which she recalls her own youthful rebelliousness. In an interview with Patricia Corrigan for the *St. Louis Post-Dispatch* (March 10, 2004), Dudman explained her reasons for writing her kind of memoirs: "There are two benefits to writing this kind of book. One is for myself. You write a memoir to figure things out, to come to terms, to understand yourself better. The only way to do this is to be completely honest. [The other reason is that] all of us have secrets that are shameful, private and painful. We guard them. Yet if someone else tells their story, it frees everybody else in the room to do the same. You can't do that without talking about things that are uncomfortable or unflattering."

Martha Tod Dudman was born on January 4, 1952 in St. Louis, Missouri, the daughter of Richard Dudman, the former Washington bureau chief of the *St. Louis Post-Dispatch*, and Helen Dudman, the owner of Dudman Communications, a network of radio stations. (In 1970 Richard was captured by North Vietnamese forces and held prisoner for 40 days while on assignment covering the Vietnam War.) Dudman attended an exclusive girl's institution, the Madeira School, located in McLean, Virginia. Her summers were spent at the family home on an island off the coast of Maine. She kept a daily journal from the age of seven and hoped to one day become a writer.

Dudman attended Antioch College, in Ohio. During her college years she taught English in Portugal and Brazil. In 1974 she earned a degree in English literature, and after graduation, she spent a year in Yellow Springs, Ohio, working as a waitress. In 1975 she moved back to Maine, to live on the island where she had summered as a child and write.

For the next three years Dudman worked doggedly at her writing, while supporting herself with a number of odd jobs, including a stint as a maid. During this time she wrote two books of fiction—neither of which was ever published. Eventually she sold a single essay to the *New York Times*. Discouraged, she moved off the island to Maine's mainland to work as a special-education teacher. Dudman continued to write during this period of her life, but it was something she did for her own pleasure—not publication.

After marrying and having two children, she found it hard to find time for any writing at all. Then, deciding that she again wanted to pursue her desire to become a writer, she contacted Constance Hunting, a professor at the University of Maine who ran a small publishing house called the Puckerbrush Press. Dudman arranged to take private lessons in writing with Hunting, who met with her once a week to discuss her progress. With Hunting's encouragement Dudman began to write more earnestly and soon saw several pieces of her short fiction published in the *Puckerbrush Review*. Her first collection of stories, *Dawn*, was published by Puckerbrush Press in 1989.

As Dudman's writing blossomed, other aspects of her life began to deteriorate; she and her husband divorced while their two children were still toddlers. No longer able to support herself and her children, Dudman accepted a part-time position at one of her mother's radio stations to help make ends meet. In 1990 her mother decided to leave the radio business entirely, and Dudman was made president and general manager of Dudman Communications, a position she held until 1999, when she sold the radio stations. (Dudman also works in the field of fundraising and economic development. She was instrumental, for example, in the effort to build a children's museum in Bangor, Maine.)

While she was managing Dudman Communications, Dudman quit her writing classes. She continued to write regularly, however, and began work on a novel. "I started writing this romance about a middle-aged woman living in Maine," she explained to Daniel Paul Simmons III for *Publishers Weekly* (February 26, 2001). "But no matter what I tried to do with her, she kept relentlessly going back into her daughter's room. I realized after a while that I was writing the story of what happened with my daughter."

Dudman was referring to her own daughter's case of extreme teenage rebellion, which included bouts of truancy, promiscuity, bulimia, and drug and alcohol abuse. Augusta (a pseudonym) was sent to a wilderness program in Idaho, where she attempted suicide, and to a school for troubled teens in Oregon, from which she ran away repeatedly. Convinced that she was meant to be writing a memoir rather than a novel, Dudman wrote the first draft of *Augusta, Gone* in eight weeks and found an agent, Betsy Lerner. Lerner made extensive suggestions on revising the book and Dudman spent three months making the changes. Right before the book was sold to Simon & Schuster, Dudman informed her daughter, then on the road to recovery, that she had written about their experiences. Without seeing the manuscript, her daughter agreed to the book's publication.

In an interview with Cheryl Dellasega for *Writers Write* (May 2001, on-line), Dudman explained that "as a mother, I was sensitive to how my children might feel about the book, and didn't tell anyone I was working on it for a long time. Then, when I'd done the editing, I sat down with my daughter and went over it with her. Betsy had it, but I wouldn't have published it if my daughter didn't want me to."

Augusta, Gone was met with critical acclaim. In a review for *Readings* (September 2001), Elinor B. Rosenberg wrote: "With unsentimental honesty, Dudman reveals the fear, guilt, and blame she feels during her struggle to save the girl. As the story unfolds, we are able to see the convergences of family structure, dynamics, development, and circumstances that contribute to the way that each member functions. . . . It is a simply told story of a parent's pain, but also of love transcending despair." Writing for the *New York Times Book Review* (March 18 2001), Martha Beck opined: "Dudman's blunt, honest writing searingly articulates the agony of a mother whose child has disappeared emotionally and sometimes physically (Augusta's frequent runaway periods often lasted weeks). Interacting with her daughter, Dudman writes, was 'like sticking my hand into the garbage disposal.' Trying to identify the cause of Augusta's behavior was an exercise in bewilderment. . . . Though Dudman blames herself for her daughter's behavior as mercilessly as anyone could, her descriptions of Augusta's wild resistance to every offer of help makes it impossible to level simplistic accusations. The frankness of *Augusta, Gone* will help other parents in similar circumstances, if only by facilitating open discussion of problems they may be ashamed to admit." (*Augusta, Gone* aired as a made-for-TV movie on Lifetime in 2006.)

In her second memoir, *Expecting to Fly: A Sixties Reckoning*, Dudman chose to focus on her own rebelliousness as a child of privilege in the tumultuous 1960s and early 1970s. In this book she describes being kicked out of the Madeira School for smoking marijuana and experimenting with drugs and sex throughout her formative years. In a review for the *New York Times* (February 23, 2004), Janet Maslin noted that Dudman "has a gift for making small details sound scarily,

embarrassingly true. . . . Here is Grandma, remembering Woodstock, wondering how she turned into a 50-year-old professional fund-raiser who goes for a walk wearing a pedometer every day. How did she get here? And is it possible to turn back the clock, at least in memory? This recollection of her first experiences with sex, drugs and rebellion in the 1960s manages to accomplish just that." Reviewing the book for the *Calgary Herald* (March 13, 2004), Elsa Dixler wrote, "This memoir is both ruthlessly honest—in its depiction of teenage Martha's discomfort in her own skin and her clueless fumbling with boys, in its description of stomach troubles on her travels in Spain—and evasive. . . . This book is a reckoning of the '60s, as the subtitle has it, only in the sense of a recollection; it isn't an attempt to understand the hippie culture in which Dudman participated, or what it meant then or now. Paying attention to the details and forgetting the big arguments can get you only so far."

Dudman resides in Northeast Harbor, Maine, where she continues to work as a professional fundraiser.

—C.M.

Suggested Reading: *Calgary Herald* E p3 Mar. 13, 2004; *New York Times Book Review* p23 Mar. 18, 2001; *Publishers Weekly* p26+ Feb. 26, 2001; *Readings* p26 Sep. 2001; *St. Louis Post-Dispatch* E p1 Mar. 10, 2004; *Writers Write* (on-line) May 2001

Selected Books: fiction—*Dawn*, 1989; nonfiction—*Augusta, Gone*, 2001; *Expecting to Fly: A Sixties Reckoning*, 2004

Dunant, Sarah

Aug. 8, 1950– Novelist; broadcaster

Sarah Dunant earned her literary reputation as a mystery writer but has successfully expanded her purview to include historical fiction. Dunant's suspense novels include *Snow Storms in a Hot Climate* (1987); the Hannah Wolfe mysteries *Birth Marks* (1990), *Fatlands* (1993), and *Under My Skin* (1995); and the taut thrillers *Transgressions* (1997) and *Mapping the Edge* (1999). At the beginning of her career as a fiction writer, while also producing or hosting radio and television programs for the BBC and authoring articles for a variety of publications, including the London *Times* and the London *Observer*, Dunant co-wrote two mysteries with Peter Busby, *Exterminating Angels* (1983) and *Intensive Care* (1986), under the combined name Peter Dunant. The lessons she learned from her years as a suspense novelist proved instrumental to her achieving international success with such historical novels as *The Birth of Venus* (2003) and

Courtesy of Random House

Sarah Dunant

In the Company of the Courtesan (2006). As the author told Sybil Steinberg for *Publishers Weekly* (March 8, 2004), writing mysteries "made me realize how important the structure of the story is. Your style must be eloquent and muscular, and you must force your reader to read fast. Writing *Venus* allowed me to touch the fabric, as it were. It allowed me to slow down so the reader can luxuriate."

Sarah Dunant was born on August 8, 1950 in London, England. Her father, David, worked for the British Overseas Airline Corporation (BOAC), which would later become part of British Airways. Her mother, the former Estelle Joseph, was a teacher. Dunant completed her primary education at the Godolphin and Latymer School in Hammersmith, London; she studied history at Newnham College, Cambridge, graduating in 1973. Because of her father's career in the airline industry, Dunant was able to fly inexpensively throughout the world in her youth; she consequently traveled to a variety of exotic locales both before and after completing her college education. "By the time I was 30, I'd been to Japan, Asia and the United States for the price of a British Rail ticket to Edinburgh," Dunant informed Ann McFerran for the London *Times* (November 5, 1995). "I didn't have a career in those days, just stints of work to finance stints of travel; it was the mid-1970s and early 1980s, when traveling was a version of discovering who you were, before the grip of Thatcherism took hold." (Thatcherism refers to the system of political thought attributed to Prime Minister Margaret Thatcher; it stressed a free-market economy, privatization of business, and opposition to unions.)

Dunant initially looked for work as an actress but found little success; in 1974 she began a long relationship with BBC Radio when she was hired as a producer. She eventually became a host of BBC Radio 4's *Woman's Hour*, as well as BBC Radio 3's *Night Waves*. Dunant moved to BBC Television in the late 1980s, and in 1988 she began hosting art and culture discussions on various programs.

While working for BBC Radio, Dunant collaborated with Peter Busby on her first two novels. *Exterminating Angels* details the exploits of an ironic group of terrorists. They kidnap a racist politician and give him injections that dye his skin black. In another episode the terrorists fill a polluter's swimming pool with oil. The authorities, however, quickly close in on the gang. A reviewer for *Time Out* described the work as "a smoothly written and provocative book" and "quite simply, one of the best novels about terrorism I've read," as quoted on the now-defunct British Web site TrashFiction. (The editors of the site explained that it was so named because the books reviewed were notable for their entertainment value but that this criterion does not preclude works of literary merit.) Dunant and Busby's second joint effort, *Intensive Care*, was not widely reviewed.

Snowstorms in a Hot Climate, Dunant's first solo literary effort, was published in the U.K., in 1987, and in the U.S. the following year. The novel's narrator, Marla, a bored English academic, visits America to help an old friend, Elly, disentangle herself from a romantic relationship with a charismatic and possibly murderous drug dealer named Lenny. Writing for the *New York Times Book Review* (January 1, 1989), Michael Freitag called the book "intelligent and rarely predictable" and observed: "As Marla tries to rescue Elly from an inevitable downfall, she finds that she too has become caught in a complex web of emotions: friendship, romance, curiosity, jealousy and revenge." The work, which displayed a decidedly feminist perspective, contained "refreshingly economical and astute" prose, Freitag averred, though he also noted that Dunant "relies too heavily on secondhand storytelling to advance her plot."

In *Birth Marks* Dunant introduced the private detective Hannah Wolfe, a "coolly pragmatic London operative, [who] uses brains over charm, relies on psychology rather than intuition and does not confuse compassion with sentimentality," Marilyn Stasio wrote for the *New York Times Book Review* (October 25, 1992). In the novel Wolfe is hired to locate a missing ballerina, who is soon found drowned in London's Thames River. The horror is compounded when it is discovered that the dancer was eight months pregnant and that she appears to have killed herself. Wolfe investigates and learns that the young woman was leading a startling double life in France. Marcel Berlins, writing for the London *Times* (April 4, 1991), offered high praise for *Birth Marks* and for Hannah

Wolfe, declaring "Hannah is a real person, wise and sensitive, lacking in confidence but making up for it in stubborn effort and conscience. Dunant's barbed observations of life and men and things that go wrong are a delight." Overall, Berlins concluded, *Birthmarks* is "intelligent, extremely well written and compassionate."

Dunant's second Hannah Wolfe mystery, *Fatlands*, was published in the U.K. in 1993 and in the U.S. the following year. Hired to watch over Mattie, the adolescent daughter of a research scientist, Wolfe cannot save her charge from a car bomb set by animal-rights activists targeting Mattie's father. As Wolfe investigates the scheme, she uncovers disturbing revelations about both Mattie's private life and her father's scientific endeavors. The animal-rights movement provides the backdrop to the novel as Wolfe unwittingly discovers how corporate greed promotes animal exploitation. "What Dunant does brilliantly is to use the thriller as a vehicle for the novel of ideas, without ever letting ideas get the better of pace or plot," Lisa Appignanesi wrote for the London *Times* (July 18, 1993). "What she does even better is create a fictional voice that is as barbed and wise-cracking and lucid and laid-back as [Raymond] Chandler's." Paul Skenazy, writing for the *Washington Post* (November 20, 1994), criticized Dunant's encyclopedic digressions on the impact of chemicals on animals but generally found much to praise: "The topic of animal rights could lead to a lot of polemics, but Dunant keeps the issues clear without hammering her points home. . . . most of the writing has a lively intelligence and convincing humanity to it. There's solid craft here, in everything from the landscape to the problems of buying underwear at Harrod's." Dunant received the Crime Writers Association Silver Dagger Award for *Fatlands*.

Hannah Wolfe surfaces once again in *Under My Skin*. Called upon to investigate a series of costly pranks at an elite health spa, Wolfe manages to catch the saboteur and is in turn hired by the spa's owner to find out who is behind a series of death threats being sent to her husband, a plastic surgeon. The plastic surgeon is soon murdered, and Wolfe, in order to solve the mystery, is forced to delve into the seamy underworld of the artificial-beauty business. "Like many feminists," Maureen Corrigan observed for the *Washington Post* (December 24, 1995), "Hannah is both repelled and mesmerized by the beauty industry, and her contradictory feelings give *Under My Skin* emotional depth." Marcel Berlins remarked for the London *Times* (June 10, 1995), "It is [Dunant's] ability to integrate a stimulating intellectual argument with her thoroughly structured plot, spot-on atmosphere and convincing characters that places Dunant very near the top of modern British crime writing."

Dunant's next novel, *Transgressions,* aroused a firestorm of criticism. The novel's protagonist, Elizabeth Skvorecky, lives by herself in a London mansion; she is working on translating a violent and lurid Czech mystery novel. When accosted by a rapist who has been stalking her, Elizabeth responds by seducing the rapist—and experiences in the act a moment of real, if hardly unalloyed, pleasure. Long identified as a feminist, Dunant was vociferously faulted by critics who found the work degrading to women. Jane Gordon excoriated *Transgressions* for the London *Mail on Sunday*, calling it "little more than polished pornography," as quoted by Harvey Porlock for the London *Times* (June 15, 1997). Discussing the reaction to the book with Angela Neustatter, in an article for the London *Guardian* (May 27, 1997), Dunant said that she wrote the book after reading "a whole series of thrillers, and I had been disturbed by how much careless misogyny there is in them. It seems a good killer thriller has to have a lot of dead and mutilated women's bodies and I am convinced the impact of this constant onslaught is that most of us have a sort of vibrating fear of sexual threat and mutilation—the feeling that if we are in a rape situation, for instance, we would not be strong enough physically or emotionally to cope." Instead, she hoped writing *Transgressions* would enable her "to breathe life into the victims because in popular thriller fiction, they are usually silenced—literally, in most cases, because they are dead." While critics on both sides of the Atlantic took issue with the book on aesthetic and ethical grounds—a reviewer for *Publishers Weekly* (February 16, 1998) called the book an "ill-conceived, poorly disguised appeal to prurience"—others responded positively to Dunant's main idea, even if the book as a whole proved disappointing to some. In a review for the London *Daily Mail* (June 6, 1997), Carla McKay noted that the idea of a rape victim feeling aroused was "a dangerous and contentious notion that feminists have been trying to slough off for decades" but found that the moment in the book that depicts this experience "carries conviction, distasteful though it is." McKay added: "My problem with this book is that although it's an interesting, unsettling read, Dunant's preoccupation with getting a message across to her readers—don't let yourself become a victim—tends to get in the way of the story. In particular, it affects our heroine/narrator Eliza, who at best remains a shadowy figure and at worst fails to elicit much sympathy despite her plight."

In *Mapping the Edge* Dunant follows the story of Anna Franklin, a single mother who turns up missing during a trip to Florence. Left behind is Anna's daughter, Lily, as well as her surrogate family of friends who wonder if the disappearance was the result of malfeasance or if Anna had willfully vanished. Michael Upchurch had tempered praise for the work in the *New York Times Book Review* (February 18, 2001), writing that it "succeeds admirably in concept and structure—even if, line by line, it's less of a sure thing." Christina Schwartz wrote for the

Washington Post (March 11, 2001), "*Mapping the Edge* may not be quite frightening enough for those who enjoy a thriller, and neither the writing nor the characters will particularly impress those whose tastes run to literary novels, but it's a good read for those who crave some of each."

The idea for *The Birth of Venus* came to Dunant soon after she purchased a small apartment in Florence, Italy. "The book took two years to write," Dunant wrote for the London *Times* (March 22, 2003). "Laptop in hand, I commuted [from England] every month for a long weekend, and snatched holiday weeks alone. I slept some nights, wrote my way through others." Set in 15th-century Florence, *The Birth of Venus* begins with the death of a nun, Sister Lucrezia, and the discovery, on her stomach, of a shocking tattoo of a curled serpent. The deceased sister's life story forms the basis of the novel. Born Alessandra Cecchi, she had come of age at a turbulent time in Florentine history; following the death of Lorenzo de Medici in 1492, Florence is held in thrall by a reactionary Dominican, Girolamo Savonarola, and his cohorts, who strive to return the city to its pre-Renaissance religiosity, banning women from the streets and bemoaning the moral corruption of the age. A gifted artist, Alessandra pursues painting surreptitiously and develops a passion for the artisan hired to refurbish the family chapel. While still in her teens, Alessandra is wed to a much older man; her new husband, however, is in love with Alessandra's brother and feels compelled to marry to avoid Savonarola's campaign against homosexuality. Given her passionless marriage, Alessandra begins a sensual relationship with the chapel painter as the political situation in Florence deteriorates. "However strong the scent of commercial calculation in Dunant's book—there's nothing like the Renaissance to give tone to sex and bloodshed—[*The Birth of Venus*] turns out to be a beguiling story," Richard Lacayo observed for *Time* (February 23, 2004). A reviewer for *Publishers Weekly* (December 15, 2003) wrote, "Dunant's vivid, gripping novel gives fresh life to a captivating age of glorious art and political turmoil." Despite minor complaints about the work's ending and some of its subplots, Sarah A. Smith wrote for the London *Guardian* (March 22, 2003) that "Dunant's passionate knowledge of her subject, the fluidity of her prose and her commitment to storytelling . . . make [the book] an accomplished delight."

Dunant's second historical novel, *In the Company of the Courtesan*, is also set in Renaissance Italy. At the center of the tale is a courtesan, Fiammetta Bianchini, whose beauty is marred when she and her servant, Bucino Teodoldo, who is also the book's narrator, flee from Rome to Venice in 1527. Once Fiammetta has healed enough to return to work, their fortunes begin to rise but not without trouble brought by a mix of players including a passionate lover looking for more than his allotted nights. Writing for the

Washington Post (February 12, 2006), Philippa Stockley praised Dunant's handling of setting and characterization and concluded: "The novel's plot is not particularly tight, but there are some great set-pieces. . . . Otherwise, this amiable, intelligent story ambles along pretty much of its own accord, toward a good surprise at the end." Mary Ellen Quinn, in a review for *Booklist* (October 15, 2005), called Dunant "the kind of writer a reader will follow anywhere, trusting completely in her ability both to bring a time and place to life and to tell an enthralling story."

Besides writing novels, Dunant edited the anthology *The War of Words: The Political Correctness Debate*, which was published in 1994 in the U.K. and in 1995 in the U.S. The essay collection addresses various facets of the effort to create a more inclusive lexicon for political discourse, one that avoids excluding or marginalizing traditionally disadvantaged groups. Laurie Taylor lauded the work for the London *Times* (October 8, 1994), writing, "What brings the book to life is the evidence it provides of what Dunant calls the 'remarkable double whammy [of political correctness], its capacity to offend both the Right and a good deal of the Left at the same time.'" Dunant also edited, with Roy Porter, the essay collection *The Age of Anxiety* (1996), which considered widespread unease about the future of the world through the lens of the impending change of the millennium.

Sarah Dunant lives primarily in London, England, but also spends part of the year at her home in Florence, Italy. She has had two daughters, Zoe and Georgia, with television producer Ian Willox. *Transgressions*, *Mapping the Edge*, and *Birth of Venus* are all reportedly being adapted for the silver screen.

Wanting to spend more time with her daughters, Dunant no longer works for the BBC. In an interview posted on the Barnes & Noble Web site, Dunant stated, "The most important things in my life are my work, my children, my friends, and the possibility of a plane ticket to somewhere I have not yet been."

—P.B.M.

Suggested Reading: *Booklist* p5 Oct. 15, 2005; (London) *Daily Mail* p52 June 6, 1997; (London) *Guardian* p86 Dec. 10, 1993, T p8 May 27, 1997; (London) *Times* July 18, 1993, Nov. 5, 1995, June 15, 1997, Mar. 22, 2003; *New York Times Book Review* p14 Jan. 1, 1989, p29 Oct. 25, 1992, p39 Nov. 19, 1995, p34 Feb. 18, 2001, p9 Mar. 7, 2004; *Publishers Weekly* p203 Feb. 16, 1998, p43 Mar. 8, 2004; *Time* p62 Feb. 23, 2004; *Washington Post* T p4 Mar. 11, 2001, T p9 Feb. 22, 2004, Feb. 12, 2006

Selected Books: *Snow Storms in a Hot Climate*, 1987; *Birth Marks*, 1990; *Fatlands*, 1993; *Under My Skin*, 1995; *Transgressions*, 1997; *Mapping the Edge*, 1999; *The Birth of Venus*, 2003; *In the

Company of the Courtesan, 2006; co-written as Peter Dunant—*Exterminating Angels,* 1983; *Intensive Care,* 1986; as editor—*The War of Words: The Political Correctness Debate,* 1994; *The Age of Anxiety* (with Roy Porter), 1996

Duncker, Patricia

June 29, 1951– Novelist; short-story writer

Patricia Duncker has chosen to set her fiction in the realm of the paranormal. Her books *Hallucinating Foucault* (1996), a look into the world of postmodern intellectuals; *The Doctor* (1999), a biographical novel about a 19th-century female military surgeon masquerading as a man; *The Deadly Space Between* (2002), a gothic tale of forbidden love and the dark places in the psyche that lead to murder, and a short-story collection, *Monsieur Shoushana's Lemon Trees* (1997), deal with many varieties of border crossing, from sanity to madness, from female to male, and from the possible to the impossible. Her works contain "a characteristically rich blend of unsettling psychology and literary playfulness," Nicola Upson wrote in the *New Statesman* (March 11, 2002).

In the playful spirit for which she is noted, in 2002 Patricia Duncker contributed the following statement to *World Authors 2000–2005,* stating that it is "not conventional" but "does give the right idea about who I am as a writer. I am not conventional either":

"Patricia Duncker—Curriculum Vitae

"Born: 51 years ago in Kingston, Jamaica, then a British colony.

"Educated: At the local High School, then at a classy British boarding school, seriously classy universities, Cambridge and Oxford.

"Further education: In Germany as stable maid, butcher's assistant and supermarket cheese girl.

"Attended: Various rock concerts

"Married: Several times

"Religion: Savage Christianity

"Languages: Numerous, foreign and dead

"Jobs: Teaching young people in universities to think rather than obey

"Interests: Food, reading, driving South to warmer climates

"Ambitions: To be very rich

"Regrets: None"

Duncker next explained what has influenced her most strongly:

"Seasons: All European writers and some American ones have very powerful relationships with the seasons. I think it was Robert Graves who said that love, death, and the changing of the seasons; that's what you write about if you're a poet. I never saw seasons until I was in my teens. In the tropics we have different seasons. We have the dry season, the rainy season, and the hurricane season. We have the season when we are at risk from the bush fires. And it's not the same. If you live without seasons, it changes how you are, how you breathe, how you think. You can't believe in European Christianity, not in the same way that the people of the North do, if you haven't lived with seasons, because Christianity is predicated on death and resurrection. We never see the earth die and rise again. If you don't see it then it cannot be true. What you can believe in is eternity—unchangingness. The tropics do not die and do not change. We rot, and then grow even taller. But you can't believe in the death change or in the earth that rises again, and so that is the reason that I do not believe in immortality. But I do believe in eternity.

"What made me decide to be a writer? My aunt told me that I was going to be one, because she was. But the other person who told me that I should write was my creative writing tutor. We didn't call it creative writing. We were not encouraged to be creative. Creativity was subversive and intellectually suspect. People who were creative were either sodomites or had affairs with other men's wives. So we weren't creative. We called it English Composition and we were told that we had to be properly punctuated and grammatically correct. If we wrote poetry we would be wise to rhyme. When I was at school in Jamaica I had a wonderful creative writing tutor called Mrs. Davies. And she was one of those teachers from hell. If she didn't like what you had written, or what you were reciting, after about the first line, she pulled no punches whatsoever. We had to write out our poems, or learn one by a Great English Author, and then stand up in class, one after another, bolt upright beside our desks, and speak the lines aloud. Stand up straight. Breathe. Louder, girl! Don't mutter. None of us can hear you. Next! I remember one girl describing 'The moon like a yellow banana on a blue enamel plate. . . .' 'NEXT!' shouted Mrs. Davies. I can still hear her shouting 'NEXT!'

"Mrs. Davies used to teach English Literature by making us learn massive chunks of poetry by heart and then recite them. She made us learn and recite Wordsworth. 'I wandered lonely as a cloud.' But of course, none of us had ever seen a daffodil. Ever, because we were children of the tropics. And Great English Authors didn't write poems about sea-grapes, bougainvillaea, or hibiscus. So when she described daffodils we just looked blank. She went home and came back with a calendar called Flowers of Britain. She turned to March and held it up for us and said 'This is a daffodil.' We all looked at it, and I remember one of my classmates whispering to me, 'Oh, it's yellow.'

"The thing that now strikes me about the daffodil incident is this. If you have never seen the earth die, if you have never seen it go grey, brown, blue and die, if you have never smelt frost on dead leaves, then you have no idea what daffodils mean. For they are the first real sign of spring. They are the first sign of colour that comes back. They are the yellow of the sun. So the resonance of the seasons had no meaning. We saw a single yellow daffodil.

"I can remember everything Mrs. Davies taught me. She was a very effective teacher. I can still see her straight back and flowered dresses. Studying Great English Authors in the tropics had a very peculiar effect on my brain. When I came to England I was under the impression that English people all talked as they did in Shakespeare's Julius Caesar, and went around saying, 'Oh, I do love thee, Brutus.'

"But I came to England and I discovered that it wasn't like that at all. I didn't like England. Not because it was different from everything I had ever known. I didn't like it here because it was cold. I still don't like it because it's cold. I don't like coldness. I shall never get used to this climate, and to the sense of The North. To people who live in England, obviously it doesn't feel like The North, because they're aware of Scotland, the Orkneys, the Shetlands, Iceland, Scandinavia, and all these white desert spaces in Northern Europe and beyond. But to me, England feels very North.

"I long to go South in the winter."

Patricia Duncker is the daughter of Noel Aston and Sheila Johna (Beer) Duncker. One of her early mentors was her aunt, the poet Patricia Beer. Duncker earned a Ph.D. degree in English and German Romanticism at St. High's College, Oxford University. She was an academic of standing—a professor of writing, literature, and feminist theory at the University of Wales—when she wrote her first novel. *Hallucinating Foucault* is the story of a transgressive love affair between a reader and the writer with whom he falls in love. The *Publishers Weekly* (October 21, 1996) reviewer praised *Hallucinating Foucault* as a "moving, mysterious answer" to the question of what happens when the reader attempts to consummate his or her love for the author. *Hallucinating Foucault* garnered for Duncker the Dillon's First Fiction Award in 1997. In addition, she won a McKitterick Prize that year.

Also in 1997, Duncker's book *Monsieur Shoushana's Lemon Trees*, a collection of stories, appeared. Described as "fabulist tales" by Barbara Hoffert for *Library Journal* (March 15, 1998), the stories take place in the interstices between reality and the shadow world in which the unexpected and the near-impossible occur. In one of the longest stories, "The Arrival Matters," a young woman is drawn into what might be described as a coven, consisting of powerful women who maintain a male musician and practitioner of magic to do their bidding. "Many of these stories are meditations on love—primarily between women—and the emotional and sexual struggles for control and emancipation between lovers," Graham Fraser noted in the *Review of Contemporary Fiction* (Fall 1998). Hoffert termed the stories "utterly original in conception and told in a clear, dry voice that glints like metal left out in the sun."

Duncker's next work of fiction was a historical novel. *The Doctor*, published in 1999 (and titled *James Miranda Barry* in Great Britain), is the fictionalized story of James Miranda Barry, a 19th-century girl disguised as a boy by her mother so that she could enjoy the benefits of an education then denied to women. Barry became a British military surgeon, wearing the clothing and living the life of a man until she died. Some reviewers have called the book a fictionalized biography. (Barry's love interest in the novel, Alice Jones, a young maid who becomes a famous actress, is an entirely fictional creation of Duncker.) Joan Smith, writing in the London *Independent on Sunday* (June 6, 1999) termed *The Doctor* "an interrogation of the very idea of gender."

In the *New Statesman* (May 13, 2002), Duncker reviewed *Tomb Raider; Scanty Particulars: The Life of Dr. James Barry* by Rachel Holmes. She contrasted Holmes's factual book with her own, observing, "Biography has a duty to the facts. Fiction has a duty to the reader. Real lives are random and chaotic, governed by chance and accident. Fiction arranges accidents into patterns." Duncker praised Holmes's work, admitting that "Barry's sexual secret has overshadowed and determined all our speculation concerning his origins and sexuality. But should it? His genius as a surgeon, his creation of a leper colony in Africa, his achievement as the first doctor to perform a successful Caesarean operation, his innovative hygiene reforms, his fame as a conversationalist and elegant dandy all gave him a tremendous reputation in his lifetime." She thus made it abundantly clear why she had chosen Barry as her hero and concluded that if Barry, "who was almost certainly born and raised as Margaret Bulkley, could have studied medicine, joined the army, risen to a senior rank and travelled the world while remaining female, he probably wouldn't have bothered to change sex. He had a choice: a life of unmarried boredom, genteel poverty and embroidery, or independence and adventure. Which would you choose?"

The choice 18-year-old Tobias must make in Duncker's 2002 novel, *The Deadly Space Between*, is how to relate to a man, Roehm, who seduces both his very young mother, Iso, and—in a way—himself. After Tobias tries unsuccessfully to kill Roehm, he and his mother flee to the Swiss Alps. Roehm follows them but is soon found dead in a crevice. When Iso confesses to the murder, the police inform her that the corpse is 200 years old. "I love the horror genre," Duncker told Nicholas Wroe for an interview in the London *Guardian* (August 12, 2000). "I think the reason crime fiction has become so respectable is that the French literary establishment has thrown its weight behind it, but this hasn't happened yet with horror. There are so many possibilities and resonances."

Speaking of her aunt Patricia Beer, Duncker told Wroe that Beer has "shaped my mind. I hugely admire her ruthless imagination. There is a real ice-queen chill in her writing." She committed herself to her aunt's standards of excellence as well: "never be sloppy, go to the sixth, seventh, eighth revision. Leave your best scenes on the cutting room floor. Work work work."

—S.Y.

Suggested Reading: *Advocate* p82 Apr. 25, 2000; (London) *Independent on Sunday* (on-line) June 6, 1999; (London) *Guardian* p11 Aug. 12, 2000; *Library Journal* p98 Mar. 15, 1998; *New Statesman* (on-line) Mar. 11, 2002, May 13, 2002; *New Statesman and Society* p37 Mar. 1, 1996; *Publishers Weekly* p68 Oct. 21, 1996; p32 May 6, 2002; *Review of Contemporary Fiction* p244+ Fall 1997, p255 Fall 1998; *Times Literary Supplement* p24 Aug. 29, 1997

Selected Books: novels—*Hallucinating Foucault*, 1996; *The Doctor* (published in the U.K. as *James Miranda Barry*), 1999; *The Deadly Space Between*, 2002; short fiction—*Monsieur Shoushana's Lemon Trees*, 1997; as editor—*Sisters and Strangers: An Introduction to Contemporary Feminist Fiction*, 1992; *Cancer: Through the Eyes of Ten Women* (with V. Wilson), 1996; *The Woman Who Loved Cucumbers* (with J. Thomas), 2002

Eberstadt, Fernanda

Nov. 10, 1960– Novelist; nonfiction writer

Fernanda Eberstadt, the granddaughter of the legendary poet and humorist Ogden Nash, is the author of four novels that provide keen insight into the society and culture of modern New York and, within that, the world of the rich and the artistically inclined—a milieu that Eberstadt knows firsthand as a result of her unusual upbringing. In 2006 she published her first nonfiction book, *Little Money Street*, about a community of Roma people—better known as Gypsies—in southern France.

Fernanda Eberstadt was born in New York City on November 10, 1960, the daughter of a wealthy photographer, Frederick Eberstadt, and a writer, the former Isabel Nash. Her parents, frequently described in the press as "socialites," threw lavish parties attended by such figures as Andy Warhol, Diana Vreeland, and Truman Capote, among others. As a child Eberstadt was an avid reader and delighted in making up her own stories, which her mother would transcribe for her. At age 11 she took a sabbatical from grade school to pen a novel about the Bolshevik Revolution. Five years later, at age 16, she was writing regularly for *Interview*, a magazine founded by Warhol in the 1970s, and spending her nights at New York's infamous Studio 54 dance club.

At age 18 Eberstadt moved to England to study at the University of Oxford's Magdalen College. In 1982 she received her bachelor's degree and in 1986 her master's degree, both from Oxford. At Magdalen, she discovered "how to work and make friends who read, thought and argued hard," as she explained to Cynthia Joyce for *Salon* (May 5, 1997, on-line). Eberstadt began her first novel, *Low Tide* (1985), as a student at Magdalen, writing the first draft in six weeks. She then spent the next five years revising it.

The story of two wealthy misfits, *Low Tide* chronicles the relationship between Jezebel, an adolescent who lives in New York with her mother, and Jem, the son of an Oxford don and a Mexican heiress. Eberstadt's debut received generally favorable notices. In a review for the *Washington Post* (May 10, 1985), Edmund Morris observed: "'Youth,' sighed [George Bernard] Shaw, 'is wasted on the young.' Any writer *d'un certain age* must have similar emotions when he sees youthful talent squandered as recklessly—and enchantingly—as here by Fernanda Eberstadt, in her first novel. *Low Tide* is a slender sapling of a book, but it has enough sap rising to foliate an orchard. . . . Her only problem now is to control this force, and channel it upward, rather than outward in all directions." In a review for the London *Times* (August 18, 1985), Jane Thynne remarked: "Eberstadt uses language as her extravagant wastrels use their fortunes—inventively, indulgently at times, with a surfeit of purple imagery. Mostly, however, her [sumptuous] and lyrical style more than compensates for the hollow centre of her story."

Isaac and His Devils, Eberstadt's second novel, was published in 1991. The coming-of-age novel centers around Isaac Hooker, an adolescent genius from an impoverished New England family who is encouraged by his spinster math teacher to attend Harvard University. Zachary Leader, writing for the *Times Literary Supplement* (July 5 1991), was critical of the novel, noting that it "is much more assured and ambitious than *Low Tide*, but still suffers from overwriting at the level of the sentence or phrase and in large units as well. Too often the narrative is interrupted by passages of 'fine writing' and unremarkable speechifying—a special shame given the author's obvious narrative gifts, her ability in particular to modulate time's passage, and to gather together and interrelate the fortunes of a varied cast of characters. It is the depiction of Isaac himself, though, on which the novel's claims depend, and in the end Isaac's greatness—his genius—remains shadowy, unrealized. His 'devils,' on the other hand, bode well for the future." Barbara Quick, writing for the *New York Times Book Review* (June 30 1991), liked the book, but she had some reservations: "[The

Courtesy of Random House

Fernanda Eberstadt

characters] are all quirky, as were the folks who populated Ms. Eberstadt's first novel, *Low Tide*. But while the members of the cast of *Low Tide* could be annoyingly opaque, those in *Isaac and His Devils* fully engage the reader's interest and sympathy. Ms. Eberstadt seems to understand perfectly the pain and passion of the gifted child. Like Isaac's mind, her pen roams with 'a commanding clarity' over a startling range of subjects. At times she displays a tendency toward overdescription, but she is so adept a storyteller that the reader forgives and forgets—and races to the end."

Eberstadt's third novel, *When the Sons of Heaven Meet the Daughters of the Earth* (1997), is a sequel to *Isaac and His Devils*. Isaac, now 25 years old, has moved to New York to become a painter of religious imagery. He is quickly snatched up by the Aurora Foundation, which sponsors budding young artists. Before long Isaac finds himself embroiled in the lives of the wealthy Gebler family, whose patronage supports the foundation. Like its predecessor, the novel received widely varying reviews. Ken Johnson, writing for *Art in America* (July 1997), complained: "There are moments when Eberstadt gives a vivid, you-are-there feeling for high-culture scenery. . . . [But] mostly her characters lie flat on the page and refuse to come to life. She can write passages of lyrical description (she might do better as a short story writer), but her dialogue feels forced and mechanical. . . . The book's problems are most evident in the character of Isaac. Though supposedly the moral and spiritual pivot of Eberstadt's novel, he hardly ever dramatically demonstrates the admirable qualities attributed to

him. . . . As it stands, one can't help feeling annoyed by the novel's underlying neoconservative polemic, even if one agrees with Eberstadt that the art world in all its venality sorely warrants some kind of comeuppance. Perhaps what's needed is the spiritual heroism that Isaac is supposed to represent, but without his cranky, censorious attitude. Unfortunately, that attitude cramps the spirit of what one wishes were a more generously comical and imaginative novel." On the other hand, Donna Seaman found much to praise in a review for *Booklist* (March 1 1997): "Eberstadt's new novel flows like a sun-spangled brook on a bright spring day. It continues the saga of New Hampshireman Isaac Hooker that began in *Isaac and His Devils* (1991), but no prior knowledge of Isaac is required for total immersion in this astute, animated, and funny tale about the sublime and the ridiculous in love and art. . . . Each page is an adventure as Eberstadt animates her marvelous characters, struts her fine psychological stuff, and offers provocative musings on the meaning of art and the nature of love."

Eberstadt's fourth novel, *The Furies* (2003), describes the unusual relationship between Gwen Lewis, the wealthy director of an institute that is working to establish a free-market economy in the former Soviet Union, and Gideon Wolkowitz, a puppeteer and Jewish mystic whose ideology harkens back to the radical politics of the 1960s. This unlikely pair first meets in New York City's Central Park, in September 1995, when Gwen takes him for a homeless man; they meet again, only days later, in Russia and begin a passionate affair that culminates in an unexpected pregnancy and a rocky marriage. In the *New York Times Book Review* (September 14, 2003), Bruce Bawer observed: "The facts are indisputable: Gwen's a spoiled princess who's gone slumming; Gideon's just plain obnoxious. If these lovebirds are less than lovable, however, the novel's prose—taut, fresh and vividly descriptive—can be a positive delight. Like Tom Wolfe, Eberstadt is a precise and witty observer of life in Manhattan, where 'murderously ambitious 26-year-olds' sip cocktails at midtown hotel bars while pianists play 'Miss Otis Regrets,' where uptown 'power nannies' mind their 'power babies.'" Bawer continued, "Like Wolfe, too, Eberstadt is no neutral party in the culture wars: she manifestly esteems the more conservative side of each of her protagonists, sharing Gwen's disdain for Gideon's stale leftism while preferring his zeal for parenthood and religion to Gwen's arid, takeout-menu lifestyle, which is more or less equated with the zeitgeist." Writing this time for the *Chicago Tribune* (October 26, 2003), Donna Seaman was again enthusiastic: "The true test of the significance of a novel is its ability to precisely capture the texture and spirit of the age it depicts, and to link that particular milieu to the entirety of the human experience. This Eberstadt masterfully accomplishes with a heady blend of drama and levity, intellect and emotion. And if, as Gideon sees it, 'We are all living in an age of antilove,' we recognize that we've been there before, and we have survived. As has love and our faith in redemptive power."

In 2006 Eberstadt published *Little Money Street*, a nonfiction account of her time spent among members of the Gypsy community in Perpignan, a small city in the south of France. Initially intending to write about the Gypsy musical group Tekameli, Eberstadt eventually became friends with Diane, the common-law wife of the band's lead singer, Moïse Espinas, and with Diane's help began a wider exploration of Gypsy culture. Noting that the book's title is both a reference to one of the streets in Perpignan's Gypsy neighborhood and a statement about the people who live there, Molly Lori, in a review for *Seattle Weekly* (June 28, 2006, on-line) called the book "ultimately dispiriting," adding: "With a nomadic caravan life long past, Gypsies have become poorer and poorer, living off government handouts. *Little Money Street* is a place they'll likely never leave, no matter how far their music travels." In a critique for the *Washington Times* (March 19, 2006, on-line), Bart McDowell, who also lived with Gypsies for a time, lauded Eberstadt's portrait of that culture. "At last—a book worthy of its subject. . . . The author writes with the warmth and wit of a novelist . . . the eye and ear of a detective and the vocabulary of a multilingual sailor. She knows her Gypsies." In a review for the *New Yorker* (April 10, 2006), John Updike called the book "piquant" and observed: "As writing, *Little Money Street* is lively and varied, moving proficiently between statistics and anecdote, warm sympathy and cold condemnation. As narrative, *Little Money Street* has a distracting double focus; trying to see the Gypsies, we keep seeing the hip, assertive, irresistible journalist."

Fernanda Eberstadt lives with her husband, Alistair Bruton, a British journalist, and their two children, Maud and Theodore, in France. In addition to writing books, Eberstadt has contributed essays to the *New Yorker, the New York Times Magazine, Vogue, Vanity Fair,* and *Commentary.*

—C.M.

Suggested Reading: *Art in America* p29 July 1997; *Booklist* p1,109 Mar. 1, 1997; *Boston Globe* C p9 Jan. 4, 2004; *Chicago Tribune* C p4 Oct. 26, 2003; *New York Times Book Review* p13 May 26, 1985, p20 June 30, 1991, p30 Sep. 14, 2003; *Salon* (on-line) May 5, 1997; *Seattle Weekly* (on-line) June 28, 2006; *Times Literary Supplement* p20 July 5, 1991; *Washington Post* p9 May 10, 1985; *Washington Times* (on-line) Mar. 19, 2006

Selected Books: fiction—*Low Tide*, 1985; *Isaac and His Devils*, 1991; *When the Sons of Heaven Meet the Daughters of the Earth*, 1997; *The Furies*, 2003; nonfiction—*Little Money Street*, 2006

Edgerton, Clyde

May 20, 1944– Novelist; memoirist

The confluence of two propitious events—discovering an abandoned well beneath the floorboards of his house and seeing Eudora Welty read a short story on PBS—worked to propel Clyde Edgerton, then a professor of education, towards a career as a fiction writer. Known for his unique characters and superb dialogue, Edgerton has won wide acclaim for his humorous and heartwarming accounts of rural family life in the American South. Since his debut novel, *Raney*, appeared in 1985, Edgerton has published seven more works of fiction—*Walking across Egypt* (1987), *The Floatplane Notebooks* (1988), *Killer Diller* (1991), *In Memory of Junior* (1992), *Redeye* (1995), *Where Trouble Sleeps* (1997), and *Lunch at the Piccadilly* (2003)—and these have earned him a "reputation as one of this country's funniest and most accomplished novelists," Howard Frank Mosher wrote for the *Washington Post* (November 22, 1992). In 2005 he published his first book of nonfiction, *Solo: My Adventures in the Air.*

Clyde Carlyle Edgerton was born on May 20, 1944 in Durham, North Carolina, the only child of Ernest Carlyle Edgerton, an insurance salesman, and the former Susan Truma Warren, a homemaker. Raised in the rural enclave of Bethesda, NC, Edgerton was surrounded by a network of 23 aunts and uncles as well as dozens of cousins. "My mother was [almost] 40 when I was born," Edgerton told Teresa K. Weaver for the *Atlanta Journal-Constitution* (September 7, 2003). "She had an older sister and a slightly younger sister. Both of the sisters were childless, and I was an only child, so I spent a lot of time with those three women. . . . I didn't know I was sopping up good stories and nuances and perspectives of the world. But I think that's why it's been easy for me to write about older people—especially older women." The extended family regularly socialized with one another, visiting each other's homes and helping out with the yearly clean-up of the family burial plot, all the while telling the stories and anecdotes that were to form the basis of Edgerton's later novels. This country setting provided the young Edgerton with a wealth of activities to pass the time: "Drama during this period . . . came from baseball, hunting, and playing Robin Hood with my friends in the woods," Edgerton recalled, as quoted by R. Sterling Hennis in *Contemporary Fiction Writers of the South* (1993), an excerpt of which is posted on Edgerton's Web site. At his mother's behest, Edgerton began taking piano lessons at the age of seven; his interest in music continues to this day.

After graduating from Southern High School in Durham, Edgerton matriculated at the University of North Carolina, at Chapel Hill (UNC Chapel Hill), where he participated in a U.S. Air Force ROTC program and graduated, in 1966, with a degree in English. The decision to major in English came about during his sophomore year, when he read Ernest Hemingway's *A Farewell to Arms* and decided he wanted to become an English teacher. While attending UNC Chapel Hill, Edgerton wrote a few short stories and a handful of poems criticizing those who opposed the Vietnam War, but beyond these halfhearted forays, he showed little interest in pursuing writing as a career. Having learned to fly in the ROTC program, Edgerton received his U.S. Air Force commission following graduation and served as a pilot in the armed forces until 1972, when he was discharged with the Distinguished Flying Cross medal. Edgerton's five-year tenure in the service was traumatic; his experience in Southeast Asia, in the Vietnam conflict, had a particularly scarring affect and drastically altered his political consciousness: formerly an adherent of the Republican senator and presidential aspirant Barry Goldwater and an opponent of the anti-war movement, Edgerton, upon returning home to North Carolina, campaigned for Goldwater's polar opposite on the political spectrum, the anti-war Democratic Senator George McGovern, in his bid for the presidency. Edgerton also returned to UNC Chapel Hill to study for his master's in education. Upon receiving his degree, Edgerton accepted a position as an English teacher at his alma mater, Southern High School, where he taught until 1973. In part because of his achievements and facility in the classroom, Edgerton was urged to pursue a doctorate in education. Returning to UNC Chapel Hill, Edgerton took up his doctoral studies while working as a teaching assistant. Edgerton received his Ph.D., in 1976, whereupon he accepted an associate professorship at Campbell University, a Baptist-affiliated school located in Buies Creek, North Carolina.

While teaching at Campbell University, Edgerton had two pivotal experiences that led to his becoming a writer. During Christmas vacation, 1977, Edgerton became curious about a soft area on the floor of his kitchen; he climbed into the crawlspace underneath his home and discovered an abandoned well. The experience compelled him to compose a short story in which a boy falls through his kitchen floor and into an underlying well. While revising the story six months later, on May 14, 1978, Edgerton watched Eudora Welty read from her short story "Why I Live at the P.O." on public television. Welty's story, which featured characters very much like those Edgerton himself had encountered while growing up in the rural South, inspired the novelist-to-be to scribble in his journal, "Tomorrow, May 15, 1978, I would like to start being a writer," Edgerton recalled, as quoted by Weaver. With a strengthened sense of purpose he began writing a number of short stories. Although his early attempts to get his writing published resulted in more than 200 rejection letters, he refused to give up hope. After the intercession of friends, several of Edgerton's short

stories were finally published. Inspired by some of the characters in his early short stories, Edgerton began crafting his first novel, *Raney*. That work was rejected by several major publishers before Louis Rubin, a professor at UNC Chapel Hill whose reputation and scholarship on Southern literature Edgerton knew well, offered to publish the book for his new publishing house, Algonquin Books, and introduced the aspiring novelist to the editor Shannon Ravenel.

Raney Bell Shepherd, the title character of *Raney*, is a down-home country girl, a Free Will Baptist from Bethel, North Carolina. Raney has recently married Charles Shepherd; a Methodist who would rather be an Episcopalian, Charles is more liberal and sophisticated than his bride. A love of music brought the couple together, but on nearly every other point they differ. The book follows them through the first two years of their marriage, as Raney's well-meaning but meddling country kin clash with Charles and his more modern conceptions of wedded bliss. Edgerton is "in perfect command of Raney's voice [and] provides wonderful small surprises throughout," Gene Lyons remarked for *Newsweek* (February 25, 1985). "[He makes] us care for his characters and wish them well." A critic for *Publishers Weekly* (January 4, 1985) opined, "Edgerton's ear for idiom is exact, the two central characters perceptibly develop and other members of the small cast are given dimension and personality. Few readers will fail to respond with sympathy and understanding to a young couple whose problems are neither epic nor earth-shaking but very much like our own." Carol Verderese, writing for the *New York Times Book Review* (June 23, 1985), was particularly impressed with the nuances of Raney's character: "Like Charles, we are both appalled by Raney's provincial attitudes and awed by her simple wisdom. She is ingenuous but not naive, and her exploration of life's limitations and possibilities is as poignant as it is funny. Utterly beguiling, Raney lives beyond the pages of this short novel."

Despite the many glowing reviews for *Raney*, the book provoked considerable controversy at Campbell University. Administrators there expressed concern that the parochialism, racism, and religious fervor of Raney's Baptist family gave readers an unfair impression of Baptists and the novel did not generally further the purpose of the university. Edgerton subsequently had several meetings and exchanges with administrators, who delayed renewing his teaching contract despite Edgerton's strong popularity among both the faculty and the student body. Eventually his contract was renewed, but Edgerton did not receive a raise or tenure, although his chairperson had previously recommended he receive both. Edgerton accused the university of violating his academic freedom, and controversy swirled around the campus in the months that followed. The dispute was widely publicized in regional papers, and soon the American Association of

University Professors and other Baptist colleges had become involved. The university finally offered the expected salary increase, but Edgerton, feeling that the administrators had not properly addressed the issue of academic freedom, decided to leave Campbell and take a teaching position at St. Andrews Presbyterian College, in Laurinburg, North Carolina.

Edgerton remained at St. Andrews until 1989, during which time he published two more books, *Walking across Egypt* and *The Floatplane Notebooks*. The protagonist of *Walking across Egypt*, Mattie Rigsbee, is elderly and widowed. Still plucky at 78 years old, she acknowledges that she may be slowing down a bit but keeps herself busy by supporting the local Baptist church, planning for her own funeral and playing hymns at the parlor piano. ("Walking across Egypt" is one of her favorites.) She longs for grandchildren, but her own children have not married. Her life takes a new dimension when a young delinquent named Wesley comes to her attention. Concerned that Wesley, an orphan, is not being well fed at at his juvenile detention center, Mattie begins taking him home-cooked meals, against the objections of her family and neighbors. Her affections—and skill in the kitchen—win over the wayward youth, who returns the favor by breaking out of the facility and paying Mattie a surprise visit. Writing for the *New York Times Book Review* (March 29, 1987), Karthryn Morton opined that *Walking across Egypt* "lacks the coherent form of [*Raney*] and struggles at the start against the author's penchant for picturesque farce." Morton continued, however, "Eventually we are treated to the round-robin activities of the hungry, habitual young thief, his uncle Lamar, the gun-toting neighbors, indignant church folk, Mattie's sullen grown children, the law, and gutsy old Mattie herself—a past master with skillet and stove and purposeful non sequitur. The novel redeems itself after some delays." Donald McClaig praised the book for the *Washington Post Book World* (June 2, 1987), remarking, "I can't think of anything I've read quite like [it]. . . . Not many writers have dealt, fondly, with the life of an ordinary Christian believer." McClaig added, "Some will call *Walking Across Egypt* a regional novel, and in a sense it is. It is deeply rooted in a particular people, a place you could get in your car and find. In this precise sense, much of American fiction is regional. Clyde Edgerton's book is brilliant, brief and kind."

Much of the narrative in Edgerton's innovative 1988 work *The Floatplane Notebooks* is delivered by an unconventional narrator: a wisteria vine. The novel, which was 10 years in the making, examines the trials of the Copeland family, a small-town North Carolina clan, from the 1950s through the Vietnam War. The wisteria vine, located in the family's burial plot—where everyone comes together once a year to clean up the graves and tell old stories—sheds light back in time as it recounts the memorable incidents in the lives of the family's ancestors. Vietnam is a focal point of the work, and in his portrayal of the effects of the war on those who served in it, Edgerton relied heavily upon his own experiences. A central character of the narrative is the family's oddball patriarch, Albert, and his 15-year mission to launch his ill-fated floatplane. Frank Levering hailed the work for the *Los Angeles Times* (November 6, 1988): "Edgerton's comedy is as deft as his narrative is inventive." Levering voiced particular admiration for the material dealing with Vietnam: "A reader senses here a depth of feeling and a hard edge that mark a new departure in Edgerton's work. . . . The last third of the book, in which [two of the characters] go off to war . . . is among the wisest, most heartfelt writing to emerge from the South in our generation."

Killer Diller (1991) picks up with the characters Wesley and Mattie eight years after the events of *Walking across Egypt* and returns to the more straightforward, linear narrative techniques used in that earlier work. However, Lisa Koger remarked in the *New York Times Book Review* (February 10, 1991), *Killer Diller* is "too independent, really, to be called a sequel." Wesley has now found God and music as he instructs mentally challenged youths as part of his residency in the BOTA (Back on Track Again) halfway house. He falls for Phoebe, an obese client of Project Promise, a weight-loss program sponsored by the nearby Ballard University's School of Nutrition, and strives to seduce her. He reconciles his shady plan with his newfound faith by perusing the Bible for passages containing a similarly flawed sexual morality. Meanwhile, the pompous Sears twins, the brothers who head Ballard University, work avidly to raise their school's profile and endowment while espousing a discrete 1950s sensibility regarding racial matters. "*Killer Diller* is a romp," Michael Upchurch declared for the *Washington Post* (February 24, 1991), "but it's a subtly nuanced and pointed romp. . . . Edgerton packs a lot into his smallscale entertainment. His mix of love for his characters with dry pinches of skepticism about them works beautifully." Koger noticed a marked evolution in Edgerton's talent as a writer: "A slew of unforgettable characters . . . give this book a broader, more accomplished feel than either *Walking Across Egypt* or *Raney*." Koger added, "Rare are writers who can create characters so lifelike, so entertaining, that we can finish their books and be genuinely sorry to see their characters consigned to the literary attic or cellar." A film version of *Killer Diller*, directed by Tricia Brock, was released in 2006.

Edgerton's highly regarded fifth novel, *In Memory of Junior*, is colored by the theme of looming death: three characters are each succumbing to disease as the story unfolds, with an expensive piece of real estate hanging in the balance. A dead stepson causes trouble from beyond the grave as survivors argue over the inscription on his tombstone, and the curmudgeonly comedic Uncle Grove tries unsuccessfully to shoot himself in his own coffin. (The bullet misses, and he climbs out of the coffin to go fishing.) "Edgerton's method is simple," Frank Levering observed for the *Los Angeles Times* (November 12, 1992). "Virtually every character, from the gravedigger to those soon to be in the grave, takes one or more short turns as narrator, as if the novel were a relay race with each character/runner passing the baton. Often the same events are narrated twice, even three times. As characters filter those events through their own biases, or as they retell a story that they heard another character tell first, we learn not only who they are and how they feel about each other but also how stories themselves create a family's and a community's mythology." Levering added, "With all his characters, Edgerton's ear is so good it can make your hair stand on end. But the real splendor is in the storytelling—and in the characters who do the telling. Edgerton lets them do the talking, and they can say things you won't forget." Howard Frank Mosher noted, "[The novel] abounds with anecdotes as tasty as a freshly caught Carolina bluefish . . . and, as is the case in most of the best comic fiction, there's always an intimation of the sadnesses of human existence, as well, lurking just around the corner."

Foregoing the usual rural North Carolina setting of his previous novels, Edgerton located his sixth effort, *Redeye*, in the American West of the 1890s, crafting what Thomas Kilpatrick characterized in *Library Journal* (April 15, 1995) as "a rollicking tale of cowboys and Indians, Englishmen and maidens." Set in southwestern Colorado, "The outrageous plot of this tall tale is almost impossible to summarize," Joanne Wilkinson explained for *Booklist* (March 15, 1995), "but revolves around an infamous Mormon attack on pioneers and the excavation of newly discovered cliff dwellings." *Redeye* drew high praise from critics. Tim Sandlin, writing for the *New York Times Book Review* (April 30, 1995), stated, "A Hollywood pitchman might call *Redeye* 'Eudora Welty meets Mark Twain.' An admirer of good fiction might say that Clyde Edgerton has combined structure, character and style to create a small gem of a novel." Kilpatrick likewise averred, "A master storyteller, Edgerton proves that he is in full command of his craft no matter what the setting."

With the novel *Where Trouble Sleeps* Edgerton returned to writing about his familiar locale. In 1950 the con-man Jack Umstead wheels into the small North Carolina town of Listre in a purloined car and sets about relieving the townsfolk of their money and the town's daughters of their virtue. "What action there is in the novel—and the con man generates most of it—occurs largely as a result of [Edgerton's narrative technique of] shifting points of view," Roy Hoffman observed for the *Washington Post* (November 20, 1997). However, "since each of their stories is tied into Umstead's adventure, the novel's conclusion provides the

satisfaction of an intricate puzzle, completed with no pieces missing," Mark Childress remarked for the *New York Times Book Review* (September 28, 1997), adding that the novel is "as much the story of a man who brings random badness into a good place as it is the story of a boy's search for his own salvation. And the seriousness of this underlying quest is what makes the novel ever so much more than just charming." Michael Harris wrote for the *Los Angeles Times* (September 15, 1997): "What makes *Where Trouble Sleeps* different from other novels is Edgerton's gentle touch with potentially explosive material. He shows us a society whose blind spots are obvious—this is, after all, the South in the Jim Crow era—but whose Christianity is vital and sincere. Separating the faith's 'good' and 'bad' parts, he demonstrates, is no easier than imagining a character whose vices aren't, in some sense, a function of his virtues."

Growing old is the central theme of Edgerton's eighth novel, *Lunch at the Piccadilly*. Lil Olive, a spunky and eccentric elderly woman, is confined to the Rosehaven Convalescent Center after a fall in the bathtub. She longs to return home but makes the most of her time in the facility, meeting new friends and engaging them in various misadventures, such as when she inadvertently steals a car to take the ladies out for a spin. Meanwhile, her bachelor nephew, Carl, visits her often, striking up a friendship with an acquaintance from the facility and eventually playing bass in his band. A reviewer for *Publishers Weekly* (August 25, 2003) wrote, "Edgerton hits the mark with his quirky characterizations, and his sympathy for his subjects is evident as they struggle to retain their dignity through their twilight years." The reviewer faulted some of the novel's humor, calling it "stuffy and outdated," adding, "This underplotted novel isn't one of Edgerton's best efforts, but it remains a solid, touching treatment of a neglected subject." Andrew Ervin, however, writing for the *Washington Post* (September 7, 2003), called *Lunch at the Piccadilly* "one of the most graceful and humane studies of old age we could hope to find." Sherie Posesorski likewise described the work for the *New York Times Book Review* (September 28, 2003, on-line) as "graceful and often painfully funny. . . . Among the delights here are the smart dialogue, the pointed satire of the nursing home industry and, most of all, the chorus of idiosyncratic, opinionated characters who've got more life left in them than anyone quite expects."

Edgerton's first nonfiction book, *Solo: My Adventures in the Air*, chronicles his longstanding love for airplanes and his years as a civilian and military pilot. The book received mixed reviews, with many critics commenting on the difference between Edgerton's frantic fiction and his comparatively subdued memoir. "Fans and readers of the author may have a difficult time accepting Edgerton as a real person in this autobiographical account of his love affair with airplanes," Rodney Barfield opined for the *Roanoke Times* (November 13, 2005). "He is so mild and balanced, so unlike the personalities in his novels." Writing for the *Atlanta Journal-Constitution* (September 18, 2005), Diane Roberts voiced a similar feeling: "Edgerton's novels are full of delightfully sneaky, often dark, humor, moving stories, and engaging characters, nearly all of which are AWOL here. . . *Solo* may be a faithful account of Edgerton's airborne life, but it's as flat as Kansas from 20,000 feet." Charmed by Edgerton's story of returning to flying after a hiatus of more than 15 years, William Grimes wrote for the *New York Times* (September 7, 2005): "One of the great pleasures of this modest, winning memoir is [Edgerton's] rediscovery of his youthful passion. In *Annabelle*, a funny-looking, high-nosed three-person plane, Mr. Edgerton finds true love a second time around. It's a match made in sky-blue heaven, with just enough room, in the back seat, to accommodate a happy reader." In 2006 the book earned Edgerton the Ragan Old North State Award for nonfiction from the North Carolina Literary and Historical Association, which in 1998 had given him its Sir Walter Raleigh Award for fiction.

Edgerton has served as a visiting professor at Agnes Scott College, in Decatur, Georgia; Millsaps College, in Jackson, Mississippi; and Duke University, in Durham, North Carolina. As he came into his own as a novelist, he shifted his academic focus to teaching creative writing. After four years as a visiting professor in creative writing at the University of North Carolina, at Wilmington, Edgerton accepted tenure at the institution in late 2002. In addition to his novels, Edgerton has contributed short fiction to the *Southern Review*, the *Old Hickory Review*, *Just Pulp*, *Pembroke Magazine*, and *The Best American Short Stories*, among other publications. Edgerton has received many distinctions over the years, including the North Carolina Award for Literature, a Guggenheim Fellowship, and a Lyndhurst Fellowship; five of his novels have been named a Notable Book of the Year by the *New York Times*. Edgerton married his first wife, Susan Ketchin, in the early 1970s and his second wife, Kristina, several years ago. His first marriage produced a daughter, Catherine, and his second a son, Nathaniel. In his spare time Edgerton enjoys playing bluegrass music; he is adept at both the piano and the banjo. He wrote or co-wrote many of the songs performed in the 2006 musical adaption of his novel *Lunch at the Piccadilly*.

—P.B.M.

Suggested Reading: *Atlanta Journal-Constitution* F p2 Sep. 7, 2003; *Charlotte Observer* A p16 Feb. 8, 1998, F p1 Feb. 8, 1998; Clyde Edgerton's Web site; *Los Angeles Times* E p8 Nov. 12, 1992; *New York Times Book Review* p11 Feb. 10, 1991; *Southern Cultures* Summer 2001; *Washington Post* X p15 Feb. 24, 1991, C p14 Sep. 27, 2005

Selected Books: fiction—*Raney*, 1985; *Walking across Egypt*, 1987; *The Floatplane Notebooks*, 1988; *Killer Diller*, 1991; *In Memory of Junior*, 1992; *Redeye*, 1995; *Where Trouble Sleeps*, 1997; *Lunch at the Piccadilly*, 2003; nonfiction—*Solo: My Adventures in the Air*, 2005

Ellmann, Lucy

Oct. 18, 1956– Novelist

In Lucy Ellmann's latest novel, *Doctors and Nurses* (2006), the author wastes no time, according to Patrick Ness for the London *Guardian* (February 11, 2006), diving into her signature style— curmudgeonly rants underscored by the idiosyncratic use of capital letters: "I refute, deplore, abhor and CONDEMN acknowledgments in novels," she wrote in lieu of any acknowledgements. Transforming the details of her own somewhat-discombobulated life into an outcry against the middle-class world, Ellmann has endeared herself to critics as a caricaturist of "a febrile modern time of clangorous material connections and very faint social and personal ones," as Richard Eder wrote for New York *Newsday* (June 7, 1998). Her novels, *Sweet Desserts* (1989), *Varying Degrees of Hopelessness* (1991), *Man or Mango?: A Lament* (1998), and *Dot in the Universe* (2003), have found a wide audience among those who love satire.

The youngest of three children, Lucy Ellmann was born into a highly intellectual family on October 18, 1956 in Evanston, Illinois, a suburb of Chicago. Her father, Richard Ellmann, was described by Rosemary Goring for the Glasgow *Herald* (May 10, 2003) as "arguably the greatest biographer of his generation, whose works on [James] Joyce, [William Butler] Yeats and [Oscar] Wilde are unmatched." Her mother, Mary Ellmann (née Donahue), authored *Thinking About Women*, which, since its publication in 1968, has been considered a classic feminist text. Lucy Ellmann's siblings also went on to prestigious careers in academia—her sister, Maud, is a professor of English at the University of Notre Dame, in Indiana, and her brother, Stephen, is an associate dean at the New York Law School, in New York City—so she was always (and still feels like) "the flop of the family," as she explained to Goring. "I was bullied into reading sooner than I wanted to be. I was behind in my class and my father taught me at weekends until I wept." She continued, "I hated it. But I did begin to enjoy books, I guess." When she was 13, her father, who had been

Lucy Ellmann

teaching at Yale University, in New Haven, Connecticut, was appointed to a professorship at the University of Oxford, and the family moved to England.

After completing her secondary education at the Falmouth School of Art, in 1978, Ellmann attended the University of Essex, graduating with a bachelor's degree in art and literature in 1980. She earned a master's degree in 1981 from the Courtauld Institute of Art, in London. After working various odd jobs, she settled down to write professionally, producing columns and reviews for such British publications as the London *Guardian*, the *New Statesman*, and the London *Independent*. She had a daughter, Emily Firefly Gasquoine, with a man to whom she was briefly married, and then lived the hermit-like life, alone in a little house with her child. She has described her life as marred by serious depression, but her columns tended more toward the curmudgeonly hilarious. For example, she wrote in "Millennium Baby Blues," which was published by the London *Guardian* (April 1, 1999), "People are full of justifications for having children but they never ring true because there is not, never was and can never be any moral purpose in depositing somebody into the world. The only explanation is that people are either at the mercy (despite birth control) of their genitals or hormones, they mistakenly believe their children might be willing to take them on in old age, or they want heirs. But this inheritance stuff is just habit. You'd get as much satisfaction out of leaving your pennies to a pet, a charity, or someone you just met on the street. What's so poignant about leaving it to someone who LOOKS vaguely like you? . . . How

many of these Millennium Babies will end up ORTHODONTISTS, bent coppers, rapists, spies, landlords? How many will hunt a species into extinction, drink the last bottle of some rare wine, fail to pay their TV licence? How many will crash their cars or play darts or annoy their neighbours? It's just so WASTEFUL and DESTRUCTIVE being alive, so unecological, so selfish!"

Ellmann's first novel, *Sweet Desserts*, was published in 1989. It is highly autobiographical, describing the life of Suzy Schwarz, an American writer, the daughter of a famous professor, who lives with her daughter in London. In his review for the *Sydney Morning Herald* (January 21, 1989), Tom Gilling wrote that this "passionate and paradoxical" novel "grapples with disjointed lives and broken hopes and it is written in prose that manages to be both sardonic and tender." He went on to note, although "the narrative leaps in and out of recipe books, Shakespeare and assorted bizarre diets, playing fast and loose with its chronology," Ellmann threads a "coherent path through all these disparate borrowings, running up against quotations that serve both to emphasise and undercut her own text." Gilling saw "Ellmann's deft use of conflicting texts" as an act of literary subversion, but Michiko Kakutani, the reviewer for the *New York Times* (June 6, 1989), deemed the author's many asides "empty post-modern gestures." Kakutani nonetheless praised the final chapters of *Sweet Desserts,* in which Ellmann exchanged "the flippant tone that has informed so much of the novel for a darker, more lyric mode," proving that the author "is not merely a clever collage maker, but a gifted writer capable of exploring the tragedies as well as the absurdities of family life." Ellmann won the 1988 Guardian Fiction Prize for *Sweet Desserts*, and it was later adapted for the stage. Sara Villiers, writing for the Glasgow *Herald* (August 14, 1995), called the play "frothy, frenetic fun," but John Peter, the reviewer for the London *Sunday Times* (January 12, 1992), wrote that he could not "remember offhand a more boring 90 minutes in the theatre or indeed anywhere else."

Isabel, the heroine of Ellmann's second novel, *Varying Degrees of Hopelessness* (1991), is a 31-year-old art student whose obsession with romance novels has left her virginal and clinging to unrealistic expectations of love. She devours the works of "Babs Cartwheel"—an obvious parody of one of the most prolific authors in the genre, Barbara Cartland. In a review for the London *Sunday Times* (July 28, 1991), the novelist Nick Hornby complained that mocking Cartland was much like shooting fish in a barrel: "Pastiche is an art particularly unsuited to full-length fiction; one joke, however uproarious, begins to look a little threadbare after 100 pages or so, and in any case, a send-up of Barbara Cartland's admittedly limited prose style is hardly the acme of comedic invention." Other reviewers, such as Jonathan Coe, writing for the London *Guardian* (July 18, 1991), disagreed. "*Varying Degrees* is no solemn treatise on the corrupting effects of romantic fiction but a liberating and richly inventive farce," Coe wrote. "Ellmann has not set out to draw a realistic portrait. . . . Isabel is an accurate caricature, and as such carries a truth and immediacy greater than anything which realism alone could convey."

Ellmann's third novel, *Man or Mango?: A Lament* (1998), features another sexually frustrated woman. Eloise has had little luck with men—she remains obsessed with the American writer with whom she had an affair six years earlier—and after finally resigning herself to celibacy, she seeks comfort in her cats and begins obsessively compiling lists on such topics as "HOW EVERYTHING WRONG WITH THE WORLD IS MEN'S FAULT" to vent her growing misanthropy. In a review for the *New Statesman* (March 27, 1998), Jason Cowley wrote that *Man or Mango?* "isn't really a novel at all; merely an assemblage of fragments, lists, half-remembered allusions, quotations, fractured observations and autobiographical sketches." But, he continued, "There is little doubt that . . . Lucy Ellmann is the real thing. Unlike most contemporary novelists, she is not hamstrung by convention and seems utterly oblivious to failure. There is no risk she will not take. Yet, for this reason, her work can be showy, exhibitionistic. She is a bit like a magician who is constantly being arrested by the swagger of his own invention: look at me, she cries. But this, I think, is merely opening-night nerves, the jitters of a writer finding her voice." Writing for the *New York Times* (June 19, 1998), Michiko Kakutani noted that not only did Eloise share many personality traits with the heroine of *Sweet Desserts*, but the collage-like narrative technique in both novels was strikingly similar: "Ellmann's use of this technique not only feels a little tired the second time around, but in this case it has also become a formulaic—and loaded—means of putting her heroine's self-pitying life into perspective. After all, what individual's petty romantic and familial concerns don't pale in comparison with the great tragedies of history? . . . What keeps *Man or Mango* from devolving into a predictable portrait of an unhappy woman are Ms. Ellmann's raucous, bawdy sense of humor and her highly tuned radar for the absurdities of modern life."

The eponymous heroine of *Dot in the Universe* (2003) "is just that, a dot, a speck in an unremittingly vicious universe," according to Stuart Kelly for *Scotland on Sunday* (February 2, 2003). Dot, a pretty but shallow housewife, leads a typically dull middle-class life until she accidentally runs over a little boy with her car and develops a taste for blood. Having lost any sense of the value of life, she begins murdering old ladies and—when her troubled marriage eventually falls apart—commits suicide. After briefly visiting hell, Dot returns to earth in myriad reincarnations. The novel contains all of Ellmann's trademarks: jokes, rants, lists, exclamations, and the frequent use of capital letters. "Probably everyone has received, at some time or another, one of those crazy, fulminating letters that have lots of capitalizations and passionately scratched-out phrases and unwarranted exclamation points," Claire Dederer wrote for the *New York Times* (February 29, 2004). "Such letters, sent by a tormented friend or a lonely cousin or a complete stranger, suggest ignorance at first, then insanity. But sometimes, if read to the end, they have an internal clockwork of idiosyncratic logic. *Dot in the Universe* is a literary version of that kind of letter, a deliciously subversive message. . . . Ellmann, though a novelist, has been compared by one British critic to [the French essayist Michel de] Montaigne. And, ultimately, the pleasures of this book are the pleasures of an essay: the strong point of view, the surprising tug of moralism. Dot waxes and wanes as a character, but Ellmann emerges as a voice of clarity and reason." Kelly correctly predicted that the book would divide critics: "Its tirade raised to the level of literature may be something of an acquired taste: nonetheless it's not one you need to struggle to acquire. The sheer anarchic energy of the novel thrills as much as it spills out into digressions on middle-age, the arrogance of scientists and the peculiar reproductory organs of the opossum. It is daring, dangerous and supremely funny."

Ellmann's most recent novel, *Doctors and Nurses* (2006), follows an affair between Jen, an incompetent and obese nurse, and Roger, a depraved doctor. "Cross Tom Robbins with James Joyce and throw in a George Carlin rant (only don't make it funny), and you might have this novel; if its incessant Riot Of Capital Letters isn't off-putting enough, perhaps its constant vulgarity will be," Christine Perkins wrote for *Library Journal* (February 1, 2006). Describing the novel as "tiresome and self-indulgent," Perkins noted that by the conclusion of the tale many of the characters "have been overdosed, sodomized, or hacked with knives" and suggested that the author might have the misplaced sense that she was being "incredibly clever and liberated by all these expressions of rage." On the other hand, Jennifer Rees, writing for *Entertainment Weekly* (February 24, 2006), declared the novel "filthy, hilarious, and absolutely furious," noting, "You may be puzzled by Ellmann's penchant for capital letters, but you'll find they keep you paying ATTENTION to this strange and fascinating book."

In 1997 Ellmann married Todd McEwen, an American novelist, and moved to Edinburgh, Scotland.

—S.Y.

Suggested Reading: (Glasgow) *Herald* p14 May 10, 2003; (London) *Guardian* July 18, 1991; (London) *Guardian* (on-line) Feb. 1, 2003; *New Statesman* p54 Mar. 27, 1998, p53 Feb. 3, 2003; (New York) *Newsday* B p10 June 7, 1998; *New*

York Times C p19 June 6, 1989, E p49 June 19, 1998; *New York Times Book Review* (on-line) Feb. 29, 2004; *Sydney Morning Herald* p81 Jan. 21, 1989

Selected Books: *Sweet Desserts,* 1989; *Varying Degrees of Hopelessness,* 1991; *Man or Mango?: A Lament,* 1998; *Dot in the Universe,* 2003; *Doctors and Nurses,* 2006

Espada, Martín

Aug. 7, 1957– Poet; essayist

The verse of the acclaimed Puerto Rican poet, lawyer, and academic Martín Espada resides at "the cross roads of poetry and politics," as he explained in an interview for the PBS program *Conversations with Ilan Stavans* (September 24, 2002), as quoted by Espada's Web site, "a place where craft encounters commitment, where the spirit of dissent encounters the imagination, where we labor to create a culture of conscience." For Espada, this idealism is not merely an element of his poetry; it goes to the core of his identity. Raised by a Puerto Rican political activist, Espada grew up with the struggle for social justice permeating every aspect of his life. After graduating college, he became a public-interest lawyer, working on behalf of tenants in low-income housing and for bilingual education, and wrote his poetry on his own time. Espada published his first collection, *The Immigrant Iceboy's Bolero,* in 1982, and followed that up with *Trumpets from the Islands of Their Eviction* (1987); *Rebellion Is the Circle of a Lover's Hands* (1990); *City of Coughing and Dead Radiators* (1993); *Imagine the Angels of Bread* (1996), which earned him an American Book Award; *A Mayan Astronomer in Hell's Kitchen* (2000); *Alabanza: New and Selected Poems, 1982–2002* (2003); and his latest work, *The Republic of Poetry* (2006). He has also edited two poetry anthologies—*Poetry Like Bread: Poets of the Political Imagination* (1994) and *Coro: A Chorus of Latino and Latina Poetry* (1997)—and authored an essay collection entitled *Zapata's Disciple* (1998). Dubbed "the true poet laureate of this nation" by the editors of the *Bloomsbury Review,* Espada is one of the preeminent figures in modern American poetry, earning comparisons to the late Chilean Nobel Prize–winner Pablo Neruda.

Born in the New York City borough of Brooklyn, on August 7, 1957 to a Puerto Rican father (then working as a draftsman for an electrical contractor) and a Jewish mother, Martín Espada was raised first in housing projects within the borough and later in Valley Stream, a blue-collar area of Long Island. Formerly a member of the U.S. Air Force, Espada's father, Frank, underwent a political awakening in 1949, when he was arrested in Biloxi, Mississippi, while on leave, after refusing to move to the back of a bus. (Jim Crow laws were sometimes enforced against Latinos in the South.) He spent the next week in jail, during which time he vowed to dedicate his life to fighting such discrimination. Frank first got involved in the civil rights movement and later became a leader in New York's Puerto Rican community. At the New York World's Fair in 1964, Frank was arrested once again as he demonstrated against the discriminatory hiring policies of the Schaeffer Brewing Company. During his father's subsequent weeklong imprisonment, nobody told Espada, then seven years old, what was going on. "I simply assumed that my father was dead," Espada recalled to Stavans. "I would sit holding a picture of him and crying, and that's the way it was until the moment he walked through the door."

Espada often accompanied Frank to demonstrations and to his headquarters, East New York Action, in the East New York neighborhood of Brooklyn. "I was raised with an ethos of resistance all around me," Espada told Stavans. In 1967, when he was 10 years old, Espada traveled to Puerto Rico for the first time. He found himself overwhelmed by the island: "It was absolutely remarkable to see the trees," he explained to Stavans. "For the first time in my life, to actually hold a real coconut in my hand, not the hairy shriveled up husk we see in the supermarket, but a big green shell, and to watch someone cut the top of that shell off so I could drink right out of the damn thing—it was a revelation. It was miraculous. I was surrounded by miracles. The island revealed itself to me in that way as an explosion of the senses."

In school Espada endured ethnic slurs and occasional violence. He enjoyed drawing as a youth, but was not a particularly good student; in high school he experimented with drugs and ignored his studies. At 15, however, he discovered poetry. A teacher assigned Espada and several of his classmates the task of assembling their own magazine based on an issue of the *New Yorker*. Espada was charged with writing a poem; he took to the medium immediately and thereafter continued writing in his spare time. "I used to write instead of sleeping," Espada told Tracy Rysavy for the journal *Yes!* (Fall 1999). "I learned to become a time bandit, to steal minutes. I learned how to walk down the street and compose a poem in my head."

The first person in his family to attend college, Espada graduated from the University of Wisconsin, at Madison, in 1981 with a B.A. in history. The following year his first collection, *The Immigrant Iceboy's Bolero,* was published. The volume interspersed Espada's verse with his father's photography. Though the book was not widely reviewed, the poems contained therein expressed a profound identification with the poor and underprivileged as well as a commitment to social justice, attributes which would become hallmarks of Espada's style. One entry describes an apartment building inhabited by Latinos that is set ablaze by its landlord; another details police misconduct and discrimination against Puerto Ricans in Harlem. Espada next entered the Northeastern University School of Law, in Boston, Massachusetts, and in 1985 completed his degree. Reflecting on his decision to pursue a legal career, Espada told Robert Elder Jr. for *Texas Lawyer* (November 24, 1997), "I think I saw law and to some degree still see law as [an] opportunity to use the power of the word to create a more just society. I'm fully aware of [the] limitations of that. . . . What motivated me to move into law school was a way of achieving justice every now and then in some small ways." Espada remained in Boston after finishing law school, working first with Multicultural Education, Training and Advocacy (META), a nonprofit, public-interest law firm specializing in the rights of linguistic and cultural minorities, before joining Su Clinica Legal as a supervisor. Su Clinica Legal offered legal assistance to low-income, non-English-speaking tenants in the city of Chelsea, outside Boston. "We did the things that tenant lawyers do: eviction defense, no-heat cases, rats and roaches, crazy landlords," Espada explained to Stavans. In addition to his legal work, Espada found time to author three more poetry collections: *Trumpets From the Islands of Their Eviction*, *Rebellion Is the Circle of a Lover's Hands*, and *City of Coughing and Dead Radiators*. When the administrators of Su Clinica Legal decided to merge two attorney positions into one, in 1994, Espada resigned so that his associate, Nelson Azócar, a political dissident from Chile, could keep his job. Espada now embarked on his academic career: "There was an opening at UMass-Amherst [the University of Massachusetts, at Amherst]," Espada recalled to Elder, "and I said, let's just try this and see what happens."

Espada has taught creative writing and Latino poetry at UMass for more than a decade now, while continuing to publish his own writing. Though ensconced in academia, he has remained very much committed to progressive causes. In 1997 he was invited to write an original poem for broadcast on National Public Radio (NPR). He wrote "Another Nameless Prostitute Says the Man is Innocent," about Mumia Abu-Jamal, an African-American journalist on Pennsylvania's death row for the murder of a Philadelphia police officer in 1981. There was a great deal of controversy surrounding Abu-Jamal's conviction, and NPR refused to broadcast the work; in turn, Espada contacted the journal the *Progressive*, which subsequently published the poem as well as an account of Espada's NPR silencing. (In similar fashion, upon receiving an offer from the ad agency of the Nike sneaker company to contribute a poem for a commercial to be broadcast during the 1998 Winter Olympics, Espada delivered a scathing reply, taking the company to task for its labor practices.)

Espada's *Trumpets from the Island of Their Eviction*, earned significant critical plaudits. Published by Bilingual Press, the work included Espada's poetry in both English and Spanish. In the collection's title poem, a woman is evicted from her rodent-infested apartment after sending the dead mice she trapped to the landlord. Other topics addressed include police brutality and the complicated (Espada has termed it colonial) relationship between the U.S. and Puerto Rico. Linda Frost wrote for the *Minnesota Review* (Fall 1991) that "Espada takes us by the hand and leads us straight into the core of boredom, poverty, hostility and violence. He indeed gives a voice to the silenced, gathering together the tales of the ignored and forcing us to see the faces in the crowd."

In honoring Espada with a PEN/Revson Foundation Fellowship for *Rebellion Is the Circle of a Lover's Hand*, his next collection, the judges declared, "The greatness of Espada's art, like all great art, is that it gives dignity to the insulted and the injured of the earth." Among the many themes addressed in the 34 "energetic and dynamic" poems of the collection are those "endemic to [Espada's] Latino background and his struggle for ethnic identy," R. Ocasio noted for *Choice* (May 1991). "On one hand, his dear Puerto Rico, green and peaceful, is contrasted against the violent history of American intervention." The title poem describes the movements of a woman's hands as she tries to finish sewing her wedding dress even though she has just been told her fiancé is dead. Another entry, "The Savior is Abducted in Puerto Rico," details what happens after a statue of Jesus is stolen from a church. Espada also delves into the personal; in "Cusin and Tata" Espada tells the traumatic stories of his aunt and grandmother, who stayed in Puerto Rico, undergoing profound hardship after his father left for New York. Writing for the *Boston Review* (October 1991), Alan Gilbert declared, "The individuality of Espada's voice is one to which any attentive reader can respond. These poems deserve an audience."

In *City of Coughing and Dead Radiators*, Espada "moves across the page with bold strokes and aggression," Elizabeth Lund observed for the *Christian Science Monitor* (March 3, 1994). "Like a skater who begins his program with the most challenging jumps, Espada writes about difficult, often ugly situations." One poem describes a man stuck between the doors of a crowded subway, while another details the massacre of peasants at the hands of the Salvadoran military in 1992. A poem entitled "The Other Alamo" offers an unidealized version of the U.S.—one in which "the vigilantes hooded like blind angels / hunting with torches for men the color of night / gathering at church, the capital, or the porch / for a century all said this: Alamo," as quoted by John R. Keene for *MELUS* (Spring 1996). Though Keene expressed a minor caveat, stating that some of the poems lacked the depth of Espada's earlier efforts, he otherwise lauded the work, declaring, "Almost always, Espada's anger, his pain, his empathy, and by extension the conjoined anger, pain and empathy of all Puerto Ricans, peoples of color, scions of the 'fateful encounter,' are clearly visible, palpable. . . . Among contemporary poets, Martin Espada stands among the finest at pointing to, painting and passing through those crossroads where the essential human concerns, the imperatives of art, history, politics and humanity, intersect."

Espada's first editorial effort, *Poetry Like Bread: Poets of the Political Imagination*, contains work by several activist poets, with a particularly strong emphasis on Central Americans. Among the authors included are Leonel Rugama, Otto René Castillo, and Roque Dalton—all of whom were martyred for their politics. Writing for the *Nation* (December 19, 1994), Ray Gonzalez described the collection as "impressive," adding, "Espada's eye for memorable and necessary poems . . . results in a worthwhile contribution to a field whose political content makes most poetry editors nervous." The second collection edited by Espada, *El Coro: A Chorus of Latino and Latina Poets*, contained work by 43 artists and, as with *Poetry Like Bread*, received glowing reviews.

Espada's American Book Award–winning collection *Imagine the Angels of Bread* "demonstrates mastery of many levels of emotional experience: wry humor, gentle sadness, lofty tribute, righteous anger," Frank Allen wrote for the *American Book Review* (May/June 1997). In one poem, "The Sign of My Father's Hand," Espada examines his father imprisonment during the World's Fair for protesting the hiring practices of a large brewery and his own emotional reaction to it. The collection concludes with a piece celebrating the Puerto Rican nationalist poet Clement Soto Vélez. "Implicit in Espada's work is the conviction that the only thing worse than a rebel without a cause is a rebel without a community," Demetria Martínez wrote for the *Progressive* (September 1996). "This achievement demands respect," Allen concluded, "but what is most striking is [Espada's] delicacy of compassion."

Zapata's Disciple "is a supremely literary book; it's about how poetry is made," Barbara Hoffert wrote for the *American Book Review* (September/October 1999). The essays contained in the collection offer a context for many of Espada's poems and his life as a whole, explaining his ideals and the real-life stories that inspired his verse. Espada details both his father's arrest at the World's Fair and his imprisonment in Biloxi, including an account of how he went on a journey to Biloxi himself to view the site of his father's political conversion. In another selection, Espada's wife's injury at the hands of her abusive father is juxtaposed with the strength she displayed during the delivery of Espada's son. "Espada's book reminds us with every indelible page why poetry must matter," Rafael Campo wrote for the *Progressive* (April 1999). "He demonstrates that poetry, like birth itself, may be one of the last ways to sustain hope in our damaged world." Hoffert wrote, "it would be a mistake to sideline [Espada] as a Latino or activist poet. He is, simply, one of the better poets at work in America today."

In *A Mayan Astronomer in Hell's Kitchen*, "Martin Espada, like some postmodern yet pre-Columbian Orpheus, takes us on an unforgettable journey to the underworld of our inner-city tenements, death row prisons, and poisoned rivers," Rafael Campo observed for *American Book Review* (March/April 2001). Espada's foremost talent "is his uncanny eye for the countless lapidary details amidst the deceptively bleak wasteland of the barrio." In one memorable poem in the collection, a doctor implores the poet's father, who suffers from heart disease, to stop working, but the elder Espada refuses because his landlord will not permit him: "The heart pills are dice / in my father's hand / gambler who needs cash / by the first of the month," as quoted in a *Boston Globe* (December 16, 2000) editorial.

Compiled from Espada's previously published work and featuring some new poems as well, *Alabanza* (which means praise in Spanish) serves as a sort of paean to the world's downtrodden. Replete with stories of immigrants struggling to enter the U.S., as well as fruit pickers, activists, and military deserters, *Alabanza* maintains a sense of humor that mitigates its otherwise sorrowful subject matter. John Freeman wrote for the *San Francisco Chronicle* (May 4, 2003), "Neruda is dead, but if *Alabanza* is any clue, his ghost lives through a poet named Martín Espada." The volume was selected as an American Library Association Notable Book and won the Paterson award for Sustained Literary Achievement.

The poems in *The Republic of Poetry* (2006), Espada's most recent collection, discuss the politics of both Chile and the U.S., with emphasis on one particularly important day, September 11, in the history of each. On September 11, 1973, General Augusto Pinochet, with the covert backing of the U.S. government, toppled the democratically elected government of President Salvador Allende in a bloody coup d'état. In recounting the September 11, 2001 terrorist attacks on New York City and Washington, D.C., Espada captures not only the horror of the events but also his anger at the response of President George W. Bush's administration. "Espada's work is lyrical," Doris Lynch wrote for *Library Journal* (November 15, 2006), "and its power comes from strong images; two lines from 'Not Here' illustrate these features: 'The fountain speaks in the water's tongue' and 'I am the one navigating the night without stars.' But as powerful as Espada's images are, sometimes they seem off-target: '[T]he blond officer / who smiled at his work as if churches sang in his head.' Overall, however, this is a powerful collection, as evidenced by the last poem, 'The Caves of Camuy,' which combines the political and personal in a moving tribute to his wife."

Espada makes his home in Amherst, Massachusetts, where he lives with his wife, Joan, and son. He has been the recipient of a Massachusetts Artists Foundation fellowship, and two National Endowment for the Arts fellowships. He has been named the first poet laureate of Northhampton, Massachusetts, among other honors.

Reflecting on the future of modern poetry, Espada told Stavans, "I want to see poems pinned on the refrigerator, carried in wallets until they crumble, read aloud on the phone at 3 AM. I want to see poems that are political in the broad sense of urgent engagement with the human condition, poems that defend human dignity."

—P.B.M.

Suggested Reading: Academy of American Poets Web site; *American Book Review* p20 May/June 1997, p25 Sep./Oct. 1999, p23 Mar./Apr. 2001; *Boston Globe* D p1 July 30, 1997, A p18 Dec. 16, 2000; *Choice* p1,478 May 1991; *Christian Science Monitor* Mar. 6, 1991, p16 Mar. 3, 1994; Martín Espada's Web site; *MELUS* p133 Spring 1996; *Multicultural Review* p74 Mar. 1994; *New York Times Book Review* p24 Apr. 20, 2003; *Progressive* p43 Sep. 1996, p4 July 1997, p4 Jan. 1998, p43 Apr. 1999; *Texas Lawyer* Nov. 24, 1997; *YES!* Fall 1999

Selected Books: *The Immigrant Iceboy's Bolero*, 1982; *Trumpets from the Islands of Their Eviction*, 1987; *Rebellion Is the Circle of a Lover's Hands*, 1990; *City of Coughing and Dead Radiators*, 1993; *Imagine the Angels of Bread*, 1996; *Zapata's Disciple*, 1998; *A Mayan Astronomer in Hell's Kitchen*, 2000; *Alabanza: New and Selected Poems, 1982–2002*, 2003; *The Republic of Poetry*, 2006; as editor—*Poetry Like Bread: Poets of the the the Political Imagination*, 1994; *Coro: A Chorus of Latino and Latina Poetry*, 1997

Everett, Percival

Dec. 22, 1956– Novelist; short-story writer; poet

Like the protagonist of his satirical 2001 work *Erasure*, Percival Everett is an African-American writer of books that are difficult to categorize but have at least one thing in common: they contrast sharply with the many stereotype-filled contemporary novels by and about blacks. "Of course my experience as a black man in America influences my art; it influences the way I drive down the street," Everett told an interviewer for the University Press of New England Web site. "But certainly John Updike's [writing] is influenced by his being white in America, but we never really discuss that. I think readers, black and white, are sophisticated enough to be engaged by a range of black experience . . . just as one accepts a range of so-called white experience." In his novels and short-story collections, Everett, a former graduate student in philosophy, has turned a ruthlessly analytical eye and acid humor on subjects ranging from race to families to Greek myth to government to the publishing industry, featuring characters who include a baseball player, a retired doctor, a hydrologist, a racist cowboy, and the god Dionysus. Jabari Asim noted for the *Washington Post Book World* (October 2, 2001) that in Everett's works, "'conventional' narrative passages abruptly give way to philosophical speculations." "I've never had a bestseller, and I'm not going to have one," Everett told Ed Newton for the University of Southern California's *Trojan Family Magazine* (Spring 1999, on-line). "I watch our culture, and I see what sells. That's not what I write. I do make demands on the reader."

Courtesy of Blue Flower Arts

Percival L. Everett was born on December 22, 1956 in Fort Gordon, Georgia, near Augusta, to Dorothy Stinson Everett and Percival Leonard Everett, a sergeant in the U.S. Army who later became a dentist. He has a sister, Vivian. Shortly after his birth the family moved to Columbia, South Carolina, where Everett grew up, and where his childhood was "filled with books," as he told Ed Newton. After graduating from A.C. Flora High School, he attended the University of Miami, in Florida, where he received a B.A. degree in philosophy, with a minor in biochemistry, in 1977. He went on to study the philosophy of language from 1978 to 1980 at the University of Oregon, in Portland. Everett intended to become a professor of philosophy, having been "seduced completely by [Ludwig] Wittgenstein," as he told Ed Newton, and agreeing with Wittgenstein's "theory that most philosophical problems were semantic—misunderstandings caused by imprecise language," as Newton put it. He ultimately grew disillusioned with philosophy, however, having lost the belief that it "could be a genuine intellectual pursuit instead of an academic game," as he told an interviewer for the *Houston Chronicle* (June 30, 1985). Instead of completing his dissertation, Everett sent some of his fiction to the creative-writing department at Brown University, in Providence, Rhode Island. He was accepted to the well-regarded graduate program there and received an M.A. degree in 1982. At the same time he maintained his interest in Wittgenstein. "He still informs my way of thinking," he told Newton. "The root for me is matters of language."

While journalists have written of Everett's varied career as a jazz musician, sheep-ranch hand, and high-school teacher, he devoted only a few years to those pursuits before joining the creative-writing faculty at the University of Kentucky, in 1985. He went on to teach at Notre Dame University and at the University of California, at Riverside. In 1999 he became a professor of English at the University of Southern California, in Los Angeles.

Meanwhile, Everett's master's thesis at Brown University was published as *Suder*, his first novel, in 1983. *Suder* portrays the flight of the title character, a third baseman for the Seattle Mariners, from marriage, parenthood, and his botched career. As Suder becomes involved with cocaine smugglers and a small runaway girl, among others, flashbacks return him to his childhood in the rural South, where he was mentored by a jazz pianist who helped relieve the stress brought on by his dysfunctional family. Carolyn See, assessing *Suder* for the *Los Angeles Times Book Review* (July 31, 1983), called it "a mad work of comic genius, combining symbols and myths from ancients and moderns, white culture and black, juxtaposing heartbreak with farce." Jabari Asim commented in the *Washington Post Book World* (November 7, 1999) that "although *Suder* is about a black character, rarely does race influence the outcome of his adventures." Asim noted the "lack of heavy-handedness and the absence of an overt sociological approach" in *Suder*. With "sly matter-of-factness, in language and dialogue impressively devoid of the deadly earnestness that frequently burdens" such explorations, Asim commented, Everett examined "stereotypical images of black men—jock, musician, sexual threat—while putting his hero through a series of comic misadventures, leavening his subtle social commentary with dry irony." *Suder* won Everett a D.H. Lawrence fellowship from the University of New Mexico.

In the years that followed, Everett proved himself to be a prolific novelist and short-story writer. His second novel, *Walk Me to the Distance* (1985), tells of a Vietnam War veteran who, unsettled by his experiences in combat, flees his family in Georgia and winds up in the fictional Slut's Hole, Wyoming, where he gets a surer grip on his life. In his 1986 book, *Cutting Lisa,* which Richard Eder—in the *Los Angeles Times Book Review* (November 26, 1986)—termed "a bleakly survivalist story," a widowed, semi-retired physician, John Livesey, "embittered . . . by what he sees as the failure of honor and loyalty in the world around him," becomes "the judge of this world and, in a manner of speaking, its executioner," in Eder's words. Everett, he wrote, "has the uncommon skill to work his story up into an ending of genuine though troublesome shock, even while broadcasting it all along." After the publication of *The Weather and Women Treat Me Fair* (1987), a short-story collection, Everett turned to futurist fantasy for the novel *Zulus*, published in 1990. Set in a time after nuclear holocaust, *Zulus* is the story of an obese woman who has eluded mandatory sterilization, thus becoming the only fertile woman on Earth. Impregnated by a rapist, she attracts the interest of rebels who oppose the nihilist regime and want to restart the human race. *Zulus* was followed later in the year by *For Her Dark Skin* (1990), a reworking of Greek myth.

The One That Got Away (1992), illustrated by Dirk Zimmer, represented Everett's entry into the world of children's literature. In it, cowboys rope number ones—represented as figures with faces and limbs—corralling nine of them. While the captors are asleep, however, the biggest number one escapes, and the cowhands go looking for it. "This offbeat but endearing little book exhibits a congenial marriage between text and illustration, at once whimsical and humorous," the *School Library Journal* (May 1992) reviewer, Ann Welton, wrote.

God's Country, Everett's 1994 novel, is his foray into the "unspoiled" and untamed American West of the 1870s. Curt Marder, the central character, is a Union Army deserter homesteading land in "God's country." When marauders dressed as Indians kidnap his wife, loot and pillage his farm, and kill his dog, he hires a "tracker," a black man named Bubba, and sets off looking for vengeance. Noting that at one point, Marder complains to Bubba, "Man, it's 1871, ain't you people ever gonna forget about that slavery stuff?," David Bowman, writing for the *New York Times Book Review* (June 5, 1994), called *God's Country* "Everett's extended answer to that question." The novel, Bowman wrote, "starts sour, then abruptly turns into Cowpoke Absurdism, ending with an acute hallucination of blood, hate and magic. It's worth the wait. The novel sears." Eric Miles Williamson, writing for *American Book Review* (February 1995), disagreed strongly: "Rather than illuminating an aspect of America's grisly past, and rather than presenting an allegory from the past in order to enrich the present, and rather than aspiring to the condition of Art or Literature or even entertainment, Mr. Everett has given us an angry essay. Mr. Everett is a fine writer of prose. Perhaps his next book will be a novel. We hope so."

The stories in *Big Picture,* Everett's 1996 collection, "chart the inexplicable moments when life takes unexpected turns," according to Maggie Garb in the *New York Times Book Review* (September 15, 1996). "There are no shattering epiphanies here, just the casual comment or quirky object that can set off a rumble of change through a habitually dreary life." The characters in the book include "an unlikely assemblage of cowboys and painters, veterans and veterinarians," Garb wrote.

Further expanding his range, Everett made the central character of his 1996 novel, *Watershed,* a hydrologist. As Everett told the interviewer for University Press of New England, "I love research and it never stops. Reading, as with many writers, is what usually leads me to my characters and stories. My characters force research. . . . I knew nothing of hydrology, but I needed [the main character] to have a job that put him in touch with his landscape and water being so important in the west. I wanted to think like a hydrologist, so I had to attempt to internalize some of the knowledge he would possess." He told the interviewer that he had read books on hydrology and then "created a fictitious landscape for the character to know. I drew topographical maps of this place and wrote hydrologic reports about the watershed, of which one appears in the novel." Everett's hydrologist, Robert Hawks, a black man from Virginia, although not particularly involved in politics, is caught up in a dispute between the FBI and a fictional Native American tribe in Colorado. After beginning a romantic relationship with the mysterious Louise Yellow Calf, Hawks uncovers a toxic dumping ground, together with a dam built to divert water from that area into the reservation where Louise's people live. Recalling his grandfather and father, who became activists in the civil rights movement despite themselves, he joins the struggle against the government.

Watershed received a mixed response. The *Publishers Weekly* (March 4, 1996) review referred to the "bumpy ride" the novel offered readers, with its "leaden excerpts from secondary sources (ranging from topographical reports to a 1916 treaty granting water rights to the Plata Indians). . . . It's an ambitious novel, but Everett's dolorous subplots about broken families and failed relationships lack the nuance of the cultural background he gives them, one of black and Native American communities waging turf battles against rogue cops and racist whites." In the *New York Times Book Review* (December 1, 1996) James Polk presented the opposite viewpoint: "Illuminating his novel with excerpts from broken Indian treaties, F.B.I. memos and hydrologists' reports hinting at the scope of what Hawks has stumbled

into, . . . Everett builds a taut story." The *Small Press* (February 1997) reviewer, Joseph Ferguson, agreed: "Everett syncopates his text between events, past and present, and direct quotations from Indian treaties, hydrology reports, and other documents. Small details and matter-of-fact dialogue lend credibility to the plot while serving to define even minor characters. The result is not only a high-quality, fast-paced mystery, but an empathetic portrait of a man and how he came to be what he is."

Frenzy, Everett's 1997 novel, is the story of Dionysus, the ancient Greek god of wine and pleasure, as related by his mortal assistant Vlepo. The central character in *Glyph* (1999) is the unnaturally intelligent Ralph, age four, who narrates the story of the first years of his life—during which he has not spoken but has written poetry and read adult-level books, including complex philosophical works, insatiably. Ralph is kidnapped on separate occasions, and for varying reasons, by a mad child psychologist, a Pentagon officer, and a married couple desperately seeking a child, among others. The *Washington Post Book World* (November 28, 1999) critic, Steven Moore, deemed *Glyph* to be "a strange novel, but not strange enough. The premise of an infant with full linguistic capacities but little life experience should yield a defamiliarized language, yet too often Ralph sounds like . . . well, like Professor Percival Everett of the University of Southern California." Nevertheless, he concluded that since "*Glyph* is a farce, it's probably a mistake to get too literal-minded. . . . Everett is a clever writer with a gift for parody and a formidable library in his head. *Glyph* is obviously written for a small, select audience." David Galef, writing for the *New York Times Book Review* (November 28, 1999), praised Everett's "sendups of everything from semiotics to military intelligence, deconstruction and cognitive psychology. . . . Here his omnivorous intelligence and wordplay match Ralph's imperiled intellect perfectly." In *Grand Canyon Inc.*, a short novel published in 2001, "Rhino" Tanner, a greedy and violent man not terribly concerned with truth, sets out to turn the Grand Canyon into a theme park. Jabari Asim in the *Washington Post Book World* (October 2, 2001) found the book to be "slight, absurd and consistently funny" and filled with "semiotics, signifying and fun with names."

Ironically, it was his next novel, a scathing satire about the book-publishing business, that brought Everett more than his previous share of recognition in the literary world. In *Erasure* (2001) Everett parodied literary accounts of black ghetto life that are written by people with little or no knowledge of their subject and embraced by the mostly white-controlled book industry, which has often ignored other kinds of writing by African-American authors. The main character, Thelonious "Monk" Ellison, is a Harvard University graduate and the author of a number of ill-selling highbrow novels, which some critics have pronounced "not black enough." Monk leaves his California university teaching job to go home to Washington, D.C., where he tries to help the members of his family: his mother, who has been stricken by Alzheimer's disease; his brother, who has abandoned his wife and children for a gay lifestyle; and his sister, a doctor who performs abortions and is later murdered for her work. Among his sister's possessions Monk finds a copy of *We's Lives in Da Ghetto*, a best-seller supposedly detailing life in Harlem, which both appalls him and gives him an idea for how to support his family. Taking the pseudonym Stagg. R. Leigh, Ellison pens his own "ghetto" tale, *My Pafology* (included in its entirety in *Erasure*), which becomes a runaway best-seller and is nominated for the country's top literary award. "Monk's experience is very much my own, though he of course is not me at all," Everett told the University Press of New England interviewer. "Yes, I have been hit with the 'not black enough' complaint, but always from white editors and critics. I find that curious."

Everett's "stinging satire enables him to take deadly aim at . . . the narrow categories and bookstore shelves to which black novelists are often confined; some blacks' obsession with 'ghetto fabulous'-ness and 'keeping it real'; and the still-stupefying ignorance of publishers who can't or won't conceive of black authors who may be more interested in ideas than in 'gritty' urban drama," Jabari Asim wrote in his review of *Erasure* for the *Washington Post Book World* (October 2, 2001). David McGoy noted in Bookreporter.com (2001), "With multiple layers of satire, *Erasure* takes no prisoners in its assault on the publishing industry and its notions of 'African American literature.' Percival Everett thumbs his nose at the literary snobs and the commercial hounds alike. Television is also a target for his wrath, as he dedicates several unforgettable scenes to exposing the adverse role it can play in literature and the stereotyping of Black people."

Everett published two novels in 2004: *American Desert* and *A History of the African-American People (Proposed) by Strom Thurmond,* the second written with James Kincaid. These books, according to Sven Birkerts, writing for the *New York Times Book Review* (May 9, 2004), confirm Everett's "standing as one of the wilder of our wild-card satirists." In *American Desert*, Theodore Street is on his way to end his unhappy life by drowning himself when he is decapitated in a traffic accident. Street's head is crudely sewn back on his body for his funeral, at the close of which he sits up in his coffin. Seemingly alive, he returns home to his wife and children, only to be abducted by members of a religious cult, who believe that he is Satan. (He is later sheltered by another cult, whose members consider him a messianic figure.) The full title of *A History* refers to the real-life U.S. senator and onetime segregationist (who after his death, in 2003, was revealed to have fathered a

child with a black woman); the novel takes the form of letters between Thurmond's assistant and members of a publishing firm. The result, a *Publishers Weekly* (April 26, 2004) reviewer wrote, "is a truly funny sendup of the corrupt politics of academe, the publishing industry and politics, as well as a subtle but biting critique of racial ideology."

The short-story collection *Damned If I Do* was published in late 2004. Many of the tales in the book deal with racial issues; one of these, "Appropriation of Culture," was singled out for particular praise by critics, who enjoyed the irony in this story of a college-educated black man who buys a used vehicle with a Confederate flag sticker affixed to it; he refuses to remove the decal, adopting the symbol as his own and offending the perplexed white citizens of his town. The following year Everett published another novel, *Wounded*. The book's protagonist is John Hunt, a black rancher who unwillingly becomes embroiled in the mystery surrounding the murder of a gay man in his insular Wyoming town. *Wounded* won a PEN USA Literary Award for fiction.

Everett has also been the recipient of the New American Writing Award, in 1990, the PEN/Oakland-Josephine Miles Award, in 1996, and the Hillsdale Prize for Fiction, presented by the Fellowship of Southern Writers, in 2001. He served as a fiction judge for the 1991 PEN/Faulkner Award and the 1997 National Book Award.

Everett's other recent projects have included a 2006 collection of poetry titled *re: f (gesture)* and an introduction to a 2004 edition of the Jefferson Bible, a volume also known as *The Life and Morals of Jesus of Nazareth*. (The book, published numerous times since Thomas Jefferson's death, was the statesman's attempt to purge the Bible of supernatural aspects and present its teachings in a rational, chronological manner.) Everett is married to Francesca Rochberg, a professor of ancient history at the University of California, at Riverside. The couple live on a farm and raise horses in a bucolic setting not far from Los Angeles. They reportedly also have a home in British Columbia.

Everett's latest novel, called "Water Cure," is scheduled for publication in late 2007.

—S.Y.

Suggested Reading: *Bomb* (on-line) Summer 2004; *Boston.com* Dec. 9, 2001; *Callaloo* p62+ Winter 2001; *Houston Chronicle* p4 June 30, 1985; *Poets & Writers* p32+ May/June 2004; University Press of New England Web site; *USC Trojan Family Magazine* (on-line) Spring 1999; *Washington Post Book World* p8 Oct. 2, 2001

Selected Books: *Suder*, 1983; *Walk Me to the Distance*, 1985; *Cutting Lisa*, 1986; *The Weather and Women Treat Me Fair*, 1987; *For Her Dark Skin*, 1990; *God's Country*, 1994; *The Big Picture*, 1996; *Watershed*, 1996; *Frenzy*, 1997; *Glyph*,

1999; *Erasure*, 2001; *American Desert*, 2004; *A History of the African-American People (Proposed) by Strom Thurmond* (with James Kincaid), 2004; *Damned If I Do*, 2004; *Wounded*, 2005

Sigrid Estrada/Courtesy of Linda Fairstein

Fairstein, Linda

May 5, 1947– Novelist; former district attorney

In her decades-long career with the Manhattan District Attorney's Office, Linda Fairstein gained a reputation as one of the country's foremost authorities on crimes of sexual assault and domestic violence. She spent 25 years as the chief prosecutor in the D.A.'s sex-crimes unit and has tried several high-profile cases, including those known in the tabloid press as the "Preppie Murder" and the "Rape of the Central Park Jogger." An indefatigable champion of victims' rights, Fairstein helped campaign for the dismissal of an archaic requirement that rape victims have corroborating witnesses and worked to place a ban on cross-examining rape victims about their sexual histories and institute other procedural changes. Additionally, she is widely considered a pioneer in the use of DNA evidence to identify sex offenders in the U.S. Fairstein's real-life experiences have provided the basis of a second career; she is also the author of a popular series of novels featuring a savvy prosecutor named Alexandra Cooper, who has—as readers have noted—much in common with her creator. (Fairstein frequently tells interviewers, however, that her fictional protagonist is younger, thinner, wealthier, and "blonder" than herself.)

Linda Fairstein was born, according to most sources, on May 5, 1947 in Mount Vernon, New York. (Other sources indicate her year of birth as 1948.) Her father, Samuel, was an anesthesiologist, and her mother, Alice, was a nurse. Fairstein has recalled her childhood in a leafy middle-class suburb as peaceful. "Growing up, I never knew anyone who was the victim of a crime; I don't think I even knew what rape was until I was in high school," she told Anna Sobkowski for *Executive Female* (May 1989, on-line). Her father introduced her to classic mysteries by Edgar Allan Poe and Arthur Conan Doyle. "I always loved Poe. For me, he was the point in adolescence where I went from Hardy Boys and Nancy Drew to my first adult mystery. His short stories were always pointedly chilling," she told Fran Wood for the Newhouse News Service (January 3, 2005). After graduating from high school, Fairstein attended Vassar, an elite single-sex college in Poughkeepsie, New York, where she majored in English literature and dreamed of being "the next Mary McCarthy [a renowned 20th-century writer]," as she told Jackie McGlone for the Glasgow *Herald* (February 7, 2004). In 1969 Fairstein graduated, as part of one of the last all-women's classes at the school, which began admitting men in 1970.

Confounding her parents' expectations that she would go into a traditionally female-dominated field like teaching, she then enrolled at the University of Virginia School of Law. (Coincidently, Poe had attended the University of Virginia but had been expelled for failing to pay his debts.) According to some sources Fairstein's brother, Guy, then a law student himself, influenced her decision to pursue this line of work. Fairstein first became interested in specializing in criminal law after taking a class in the subject during her first year of law school. "To me, it was the most immediate and alive subject matter, the only class that I didn't do the crossword puzzle in," she told Sobkowski. Although there were not many women working in criminal law at the time, Monrad Paulsen, Fairstein's professor, who also served as the dean of the law school, encouraged her.

In 1972 Fairstein earned her law degree and on the advice of Paulsen, she interviewed with Frank Hogan, then the Manhattan D.A., hoping to become one of the few female prosecutor in his largely male-dominated office. Hogan, who held traditional views on the role of women in law enforcement, questioned her reason for pursuing such a career. "When he interviewed me he said, 'This work is too tawdry for a woman. . . . Why [does] a nice girl like you, an English lit major from a nice home, want to spend a career trawling through a moral cesspit?'" she told Stuart Jeffries for the London *Guardian* (February 27, 2004). Fairstein was passionate about using her law degree to perform public service, however, and, thanks to her tenacity and Paulsen's glowing recommendation, in November 1972 Hogan hired her as one of only seven female assistant district attorneys (in a pool of about 170 men) at the Manhattan D.A.'s office. At that time no female lawyer had ever prosecuted a murder case. "When I started out, women [lawyers] did not do trial work. Blood and guts and the courtroom were no place for a woman, according to Mr. Hogan. This was a world in which women were always the victims, never the prosecutors," she told McGlone.

Fairstein prosecuted a wide range of criminal cases before being asked to join the sex-crimes prosecution unit, in 1974. "At the time, I was one of the few women who had tried a rape case," she explained to Christine Jackman for the Sydney *Sunday Telegraph* (March 19, 2000). The sex-crimes unit, devoted to the investigation and prosecution of sexual-assault and domestic-violence cases, was the first of its kind in the entire country. Headed initially by a staunch feminist lawyer named Leslie Crocker Snyder, the unit was a division of the D.A.'s office, which was then being managed by Robert Morgenthau, who had taken over following Hogan's death, in 1974. In the mid-1970s testimony from the victim of a sexual assault was not sufficient to obtain a rape conviction; a traumatized woman was not seen as a reliable witness in court. New York law required corroboration from an additional witness of three elements of the crime: identification of the attacker, proof of force, and proof of penetration. The new sex-crimes unit pushed through several legal changes that influenced the prosecution of rape cases, including the elimination of the corroboration requirements.

Snyder resigned, in 1976, to pursue a criminal-court judgeship, and Morgenthau offered Fairstein the top spot in the unit. Continuing her predecessor's commitment to victims' rights, Fairstein was instrumental in helping pass, in 1977, New York's rape-shield law, prohibiting the common practice by defense attorneys of questioning rape victims about their sexual history. (If a victim had previously been sexually active, the defense would intimate that she had invited her attack in some way.) In 1978 Fairstein prosecuted her first high-profile case, that of Marvin Teicher, a dentist accused of sexually assaulting sedated female patients. She has jokingly told reporters that the hardest part of the case was finding an undercover female police officer with a severe enough dental problem to require sedation; she is serious, however, when discussing the importance of the case. "It was an opportunity for me to explain to a disbelieving public that sex offenders don't always look like the bum hiding behind a tree in the park," she told Danielle Cantor for *Jewish Woman* (Spring 2004, on-line), "and that victims can be young professional women." The next year she prosecuted a landmark case, charging a 15-year-old boy, who had a previous record of 16 arrests and six major convictions in family court, with the rape and sodomy of a 15-year-old girl. He became the first youth to be tried as an adult under a recently enacted juvenile-justice law in New York State.

Date-rape cases, in which the victims had previously been friendly with their attackers, were particularly hard to prosecute, because juries often found it difficult to believe consent had actually been withheld. In 1981, however, Fairstein obtained a widely publicized date-rape conviction against four clerks at the New York Public Library's central branch who were charged with the sexual assault of two of their co-workers, whom they had lured to an apartment with the promise of concert tickets. That year Fairstein became deputy chief of the D.A.'s trial division. She was beginning to attract the attention of Hollywood, serving as the inspiration for the female attorney characters in the television movie *Farrell for the People* (1982) and the Oscar-winning film *The Accused* (1985), a rape-case drama that starred Jodie Foster. (The actress Greta Scacchi shadowed Fairstein while conducting research for her role as an assistant district attorney in the 1990 movie adaptation of the Scott Turow novel *Presumed Innocent*.)

Fairstein solidified her reputation as a tough prosecutor with her first murder trial, serving in 1986 as the lead attorney prosecuting Robert Chambers, then a 19-year-old drop-out from the affluent Upper East Side of Manhattan. In what became known as the "Preppie Murder" case, Chambers was charged in the strangulation death of 18-year-old Jennifer Levin, whose partially clad body was discovered in New York City's Central Park in August of that year. According to witnesses, Levin was last seen leaving a now-defunct Upper East Side bar, Dorrian's Red Hand, with Chambers, whom she had dated briefly when they were in high school. Chambers immediately became the prime suspect after police detectives noticed fresh scratches on his face and arms. After initially explaining that his cat had scratched him, Chambers confessed to the police that he and Levin had engaged in a sexual encounter that morning and that he had accidentally killed her when she became aggressive during the act.

Following the testimony portion of the trial, which lasted almost three months, the jury deliberated for nine days but failed to reach a verdict. Fairstein, fearing that the trial might end in a hung jury, reluctantly negotiated an agreement with Chambers, who was allowed to plead guilty to a lesser charge of manslaughter, rather than murder, and received a prison sentence of five to 15 years. (Chambers was released from prison in February 2003, after serving the maximum sentence.) "I would have considered it a greater triumph if he had been convicted of murder. Unfortunately, jurors are still influenced by class and race," Fairstein told Alix Kirsta for the London *Times* (October 30, 1999).

In April 1989, in one of the most infamous incidents of her career, Fairstein supervised the prosecution of five African-American and Hispanic boys, between the ages of 14 and 16, who had been accused with the rape and savage beating of a 28-year-old female investment banker, left for dead after jogging in Central Park. The teens were arrested as part of a group of 30 people committing a series of physical assaults against joggers and bicyclists in Central Park. (Press coverage introduced the evocative term "wilding," as the group mayhem was termed, to the general public.) The victim, whose identity was protected under the rape-shield law, suffered a severe skull fracture and lost almost 80 percent of her blood; she was so viciously attacked that the only parts of her body not misshapen or bruised were the soles of her feet. She survived only because her head was left resting in a puddle of cool mud, which kept her brain from fatally swelling. After emerging from a 12-day coma, the woman, whom the press had dubbed the "Central Park Jogger," had no memory of the incident. Despite the lack of physical evidence connecting the five teenagers to the attack, four of the five boys were charged based on their videotaped police statements, in which they confessed—in graphic detail—their involvement in the rape and the acts of violence committed preceding the sexual assault. A detective testified at trial that the fifth had made incriminating admissions to him but never on videotape. Although supporters argued that the confessions had been coerced, the five were found guilty of assault and rape and sentenced to five to 10 years in prison. In September 2002, Matias Reyes, a convicted murderer and rapist, claimed sole responsibility for the rape and assault. His participation was corroborated with DNA testing, which had not been available in the late 1980s. Reyes was not convicted because he confessed after the statute of limitations had expired. The five young men, who had already served 13 years, were acquitted and released in December 2002, when their convictions were overturned. A New York City government panel later ruled, as posted on the New York Police Department Web site, "Some have analyzed the case as if there were only two possible scenarios: either Reyes acted alone or the defendants did. Our examination of the facts leads us to suggest an alternate theory of the attack on the jogger: that both the defendants and Reyes assaulted her, perhaps successively." The report explained, "The most likely scenario for the events of April 19, 1989 was that the defendants came upon the jogger and subjected her to the same kind of attack, albeit with sexual overtones, that they inflicted upon other victims in the park that night. Reyes either joined in the attack as it was ending or waited until the defendants had moved on to their next victims before descending upon her himself, raping her and inflicting upon her the brutal injuries that almost caused her death. On this theory of the facts, there is no reason to believe that the defendants were prompted into making erroneous statements." Fairstein, incredulous at the turn of events, told Linley Boniface for the Wellington, New Zealand, *Dominion Post* (April 3,

2004), "My view is that this was about racial politics: overturning the convictions was a politically expedient thing to do. The boys were all in the park that night and they admitted beating her up. We never claimed that they all sexually assaulted her."

In 1996 Fairstein prosecuted the first computer-related sex case in history, in which Oliver Jovanovic, a Columbia University student, was charged with kidnapping and committing sadomasochistic torture and sexual assault against a Barnard College sophomore he had encountered in an Internet chat room. Although Jovanovic received a sentence of five years to life imprisonment, the ruling was successfully appealed in 1999, after it was discovered that the judge had not allowed part of an e-mail written by the accuser to be introduced as evidence because of a possibly overzealous application of the rape-shield law; the e-mail included references she had made to sadomasochistic practices she enjoyed. (In October 2004 Jovanovic filed a $10 million federal lawsuit against Fairstein, claiming false arrest and malicious prosecution.)

In February 2002 Fairstein made the decision to step down from her position as chief of the sex-crimes unit. "My 30 years were up, and [the terrorist attacks of] 9/11 made it seem the right time to put it all behind me," she told Jeffries. Fairstein, who had been considered a promising candidate for the post of attorney general of the United States—the nation's top law-enforcement position—under President Bill Clinton, continued to serve as a consultant on sex crimes to police and prosecutors around the country. (Clinton ultimately appointed Janet Reno instead, but remained a big fan of Fairstein, whose novels he frequently read during vacations.)

Fairstein began writing while still at the D.A.'s office. She documented her years as a sex-crimes prosecutor in the nonfiction book *Sexual Violence: Our War against Rape* (1993). In a review of the volume, Mary Ellen Sullivan wrote for *Booklist* (September 15, 1993), "By blending reports of real cases she has worked on with explanations of the machinations of the U.S. legal system, [Fairstein's] book serves as a true eye-opener about how rape is treated, how far that treatment has come in 20 years, and how much it still needs to change. If any one person can change things, it will be Fairstein, whose book reflects her intelligence, compassion and brilliance. . . . Anyone who wants to understand the impact of rape really should read it." In 1994 the book was named a *New York Times* Notable Book of the Year.

Fairstein's first foray into fiction was *Final Jeopardy* (1996), which introduced readers to the character of Alexandra Cooper. The plot follows two cases: the murder of an actress friend, whose body is discovered at Cooper's weekend home on Martha's Vineyard—initial press reports mistakenly indicate that the corpse is, in fact, Cooper—and the ongoing investigation of a serial rapist by the New York City police. The book was welcomed by fans of the genre. In a representative review, Marilyn Stasio wrote for the *New York Times* (July 28, 1996), "Whenever Ms. Fairstein's brainy, principled heroine is on the job—interviewing a victim of date rape, dragging a confession from a serial rapist, advising a young lawyer on his first case—the writing is crisp and decisive." (*Final Jeopardy* was made into a television movie of the same name; it aired in April 2001.)

In her follow-up novel, *Likely to Die* (1997), Alexandra Cooper investigates the fatal stabbing of a female neurosurgeon, who has been sexually assaulted and is found, at the opening of the story, barely breathing in her office at a New York hospital. In reviewing the book, Madeline Blais wrote for the *New York Times Book Review* (August 24, 1997): "As in her previous novel, *Final Jeopardy*, the author . . . places a smart and driven Manhattan prosecutor . . . at the center of the action. Since Dr. Gemma Dogen was a single, professional woman, no children, no pets, no one to depend on her for contact, Alex is left to discover the victim through her work—which makes a suspect out of everyone at the hospital. . . . . Such a wide net might daunt some investigators, but not Fairstein's fearless heroine, whose portraits of her boss and fellow prosecutors are as engaging as her asides about history and neurology. Throw in a little romance, a hurried trip to England and a valentine to Martha's Vineyard, and the result is a stylish and oddly antic book, despite the gruesome nature of its subject." For her first two fiction books, both published by Scribner, Fairstein reportedly received an advance of $500,000.

Fairstein's third novel, *Cold Hit* (1999) is set in New York City's art world, as Alexandra Cooper investigates the murder of a wealthy gallery owner whose body is found in the river. During an interview with Katie Couric for the *Today Show* (August 18, 1999), Fairstein said, "When I began to research . . . I was fascinated by this world that seems so refined and elegant in auction houses and galleries. . . . But there have been so many stories in the last few years, just right out of the *New York Times* and shows like yours, about crimes that have occurred, major thefts from art museums, provenances that have been faked on great paintings. . . . It seems such a world layered with deceit and fraud beneath. So that was the setting I chose." This novel, like Fairstein's first two, met with favorable reviews. "Fairstein has first-hand experience of every aspect of a murder investigation, and it shows. In fact, it puts her in a class of her own," Nicola Upson wrote for the *New Statesman* (February 7, 2000). "It's not simply the accuracy of forensic detail or legal procedure that makes these books so real. The emotional accuracy is also quite superb; when Fairstein writes about the fears of women who have experienced sexual assault . . . you believe her."

Molly Gorman wrote for *Library Journal* (August 1999), "Fairstein, a D.A. in Manhattan's sex crimes unit, is dazzling in her third Alexandra Cooper mystery. . . . Smart, sexy, and indefatigable, bluestockingish Alex is relentlessly likeable." Although she found the frequent descriptions of police procedure unsettling, Gorman ultimately found the book "fascinating and fast-paced."

Fairstein continued to draw on her own professional experiences and her love of New York City history for her next releases, which included *The Deadhouse* (2001), about the murder of a Columbia University professor, which takes Cooper to Manhattan's Roosevelt Island, where victims of such diseases as tuberculosis and smallpox were sent in the 19th century; *The Bone Vault* (2003), which provides readers with a detailed, behind-the-scenes look at New York City's famed Museum of Natural History; and *The Kills* (2004), about a murder in Harlem of an elderly woman who was a former mistress of the Egyptian king Farouk. (The book takes its title not just from the homicides involved, but also from the old Dutch name for the system of waterways in lower Manhattan.)

The influence of Edgar Allan Poe is apparent in Fairstein's next book, *Entombed* (2005), in which Cooper investigates a murder that takes place in Poe's townhouse in lower Manhattan. Fairstein drew the inspiration for the novel from an article in the *New York Times* stating that the Poe House, a downtown building in which the writer had lived and worked, was being demolished and replaced with a high-rise law school.

In 2006 Fairstein published *Death Dance*, the story of the murder of a world-renowned ballerina at the Metropolitan Opera. (The tale had been inspired by a real-life case in which a musician had been killed during a break in the performance.) Connie Fletcher wrote for *Booklist* (October 15, 2005), "Cooper delivers what has made this series so good: solid legal, procedural, and forensic detail surrounding an intriguing case. The book's added punch comes from Fairstein's *Phantom of the Opera*-like re-creations of the labyrinthine environs of the Met, beneath and behind the stage. A great read." Rebecca House Stankowski wrote for *Library Journal* (November 2005), "This thriller is chock-full of authentic detail, showcasing Fairstein's extensive knowledge of legal and forensic issues and the New York arts and theater scene. Her measured prose has enough plot twists to engage any reader, and her well-rounded characters add depth and believability. Fun, smart, and creepy . . . Fairstein's latest is a real winner." In early 2007 Fairstein published *Bad Blood*, which follows the investigation of a real-estate mogul who may have murdered his wife.

Fairstein continues to perform *pro bono* work on behalf of victims of sex crimes and domestic abuse. Her efforts have earned her Columbia University's School of Medicine and School of Nursing Award for Excellence, the Anti-Violence Project Courage

Award, the American Heart Association Women of Courage Award, and the *Glamour* Woman of the Year title, among many others. Fairstein is a member of the Choice Cares DNA Advisory Board and the board of the New York City Task Force on Sexual Assault, among other groups. She is married to Justin Feldman, a lawyer who helped manage the U.S. Senate campaign for Robert F. Kennedy in 1964. (Fairstein inserts a minor character named after her husband in each of her novels.) The two divide their time between New York City and Martha's Vineyard.

During book tours Fairstein sometimes attracts more than literary fans. Once, the families of the teens convicted in the Central Park Jogger case showed up to picket her appearance at a New York City bookstore. Often, she is visited by victims of sexual assault whom she has helped. "I've had so many healthy, vibrant women show up years later—especially at book signings and readings," Fairstein told McGlone. "And they'll say to me, 'Those were my darkest days, but I survived.' That's what I loved about my job—the knowledge that despite all the atrocities, I could make a tremendous difference. I could turn to a woman who had been to hell and back and say that her rapist was behind bars. Justice had been done." It has been estimated that, thanks in large part to Fairstein, the conviction rate in New York City rape cases rose from 10 percent in the mid-1970s to almost 75 percent a decade later.

—B.M.

Suggested Reading: *Executive Female* (on-line) May 1989; (Glasgow) *Herald* p14 Feb. 7, 2004; *Legal Times* p70 July 22, 1996; (London) *Guardian* T p6 July 2, 1996; (New York) *Daily News* p8 June 2, 1996; *New York Post* p23 Aug. 31, 1999; *New York Times* VI p21 Feb. 25, 1990, B p2 Aug. 27, 1999; *People* p77 Sep. 27, 1993; *Pittsburgh Post-Gazette* C p6 Mar. 19, 2005; *Village Voice* p39 Nov. 26, 2002

Selected Books: nonfiction—*Sexual Violence: Our War against Rape*, 1993; fiction—*Final Jeopardy*, 1996; *Likely to Die*, 1997; *Cold Hit*, 1999; *The Deadhouse*, 2001; *The Bone Vault*, 2003; *The Kills*, 2004; *Entombed*, 2005; *Death Dance*, 2006; *Bad Blood*, 2007

Fesperman, Dan

Sept. 15, 1955– Journalist; novelist

As a foreign correspondent for the *Baltimore Sun*, Dan Fesperman has traveled to 30 countries and three war zones. He has used his experiences covering the wars in the Balkans and Afghanistan as fodder for his critically acclaimed thrillers *Lie in the Dark* (1999) and *The Small Boat of Great Sorrows* (2003)—which are set against the backdrop of Yugoslavia's troubled and bloody history—and *The Warlord's Son* (2004), which takes place in Afghanistan in the aftermath of the terrorist attacks of September 11, 2001. His descriptions of war and its consequences have been termed masterly; "Fesperman is that rare journalist who is also a gifted novelist," Patrick Anderson wrote for the *Washington Post* (September 20, 2004). The Crime Writers' Association awarded Fesperman the John Creasey Memorial Award for his debut novel in 1999 and the Ian Fleming Steel Dagger for best thriller in 2003 for *The Small Boat of Great Sorrows*.

Dan Fesperman sent the following statement to *World Authors 2000-2005*:

"I was not one of those children who naturally took to writing—no plotting of novels at age 6, or scribbling plays for the gathered cousins at 10. Writing was a classroom chore, an assignment to be embraced reluctantly, and only as the due date approached. Not that I didn't have a certain vanity about my earliest attempts. I was pleased and prideful whenever a teacher or parent praised a

Amy Deputy/Courtesy of Alfred A. Knopf

composition, and inwardly thrilled whenever a rhythmic turn of phrase seemed to leap to the page of its own accord.

"But those were aberrations. Creation was a joy to be encountered in the imagination, not within the lines of a notebook. My friends and I marshalled our powers of invention in the woods and playing fields of whitebread suburbia in

Charlotte, N.C., where I was born September 15, 1955.

"We felt safe there. A glare from the principal or a scolding from the manager of the A&P was about as frightening as life got. The wanderlust which would eventually supply the raw materials of my novels was every bit as late in blooming as my desire to write.

"Yet, something of the uncertainty of those times must have marked me, because my first living memory, from age 2, is that of our neighbors gathered on a starlit lawn during a cookout, scanning the skies for a gliding white dot. They pointed to it in awe until some waggish fellow broke the tension by holding aloft a hotdog poked with toothpicks, shouting gleefully, 'Look, it's Sputnik!'

But for the most part, even war and death were subjects for play. You fired a cap pistol at your victims, counted to 50 when you were dead, and rose to fight again from the red mud of the newest lot being graded for construction.

"All my early creations were ephemeral. The greatest of these was the baseball league I organized in my head, a collection of fictitious teams stocked with made-up stars and journeymen, heroes and villains whose names and personalities I still vividly recall but never put to paper. They played out their seasons to the tempo of a rubber ball thrown against a brick wall, pitch by pitch, for hours of every summer day. I supplied the soundtrack of a roaring crowd and a play-by-play commentary, foolishly certain that no one but me was ever listening. The games were morality plays, and the seasons were the great levelers of the undeserving.

"We were not rebels in our neighborhood. On the day of the Vietnam War Moratorium, most of us in the eighth grade sneered at those who wore black armbands to class. Skepticism was for the kids who smoked cigarettes, or whose brothers were off at war. Nowadays, whenever I have trouble grasping the political dynamic of Blue States, I need only think back to the way I saw the world then—through a narrow lens of naïve hopefulness, believing pretty much everything the authorities told me about outsiders and people of other faiths, colors and cultures.

"The first departure from this pattern came in high school, shortly after the Supreme Court ordered the Charlotte-Mecklenburg schools to integrate. While most of us continued to be preoccupied with proms, ballgames and algebra tests, we also began dealing with riots, fights, name-calling and tense classroom discussions over just whose school this was, and would become. The halls and classrooms of the main building were laid out around a central mall, and most kids of both races tended to watch any fighting from the bannister around the second level. We gaped and cheered in the manner of Roman spectators, trying to swallow our anxieties in misplaced laughter, while frantic teachers urged us to our classrooms to await the arrival of police.

"The most instructive encounters were more subdued, and took place among cooler heads in locker rooms and at cafeteria tables. The two sides never mixed in the way that idealists had hoped, but we did learn from each other, speak to each other, share rides home from after-school events, and compete together. I suppose that this is the age when, no matter what, everyone begins to question the assumptions they've grown up with. But this kind of atmosphere makes it a mandate, not a choice.

"From there, my university years in Chapel Hill brought me the joys of helping to write, edit, and publish a daily newspaper, which in turn pushed me ever so slightly into the surrounding world to ask about why things happen the way that they do. With each year after graduation I pushed those horizons a little further—to Florida and into the West, then abroad to Amman and Kuwait City, Sarajevo and Berlin, Gaza and Kiev, Kabul and Peshawar. Setting novels in these places allows you, in a sense, to bookmark what you've observed. You set aside your experiences and look them over for a while, evaluating the worth of various causes and passions, and trying to fathom where they came from. The frustration, of course, is in discovering—as so many others before you have already done—that the more you learn, the more there is that you still don't know."

———

After graduating from Olympic High School in 1973, Fesperman attended the University of North Carolina, at Chapel Hill, studying journalism under the renowned North Carolina newspaperman Jim Shumaker. Upon graduating with a bachelor's degree in journalism, in 1977, he became a reporter, working at various newspapers—the *Fayetteville Times*, *Durham Morning Herald*, *Charlotte News*, and *Miami Herald*—before finally joining the *Baltimore Sun*, in Maryland. He was first dispatched overseas, in 1991, to cover the Persian Gulf War from Jordan, Saudi Arabia, and Kuwait. He was later sent to Berlin, Germany, to run the newspaper's European bureau, and in the wake of the terrorist attacks of September 11, 2001, he was assigned to cover Afghanistan and Pakistan, during which time he survived a fatal ambush on a convoy of journalists riding from Jalalabad to Kabul.

While serving as head of the European bureau, Fesperman covered the civil war that pulled apart Yugoslavia in the 1990s, making about a dozen trips to Bosnia between 1993 and 1996. He spent most of that time in Sarajevo, but whether he was in a remote village or in the cosmopolitan city, he experienced "the same surreal mix—bullets and shells flying around at times and people trying to act as if they could still lead a normal life," as he noted in an interview posted on the Vintage Web site. "I was always fascinated by the little things people did to get by, not just their survival techniques for getting food and water but also the small rituals and routines that they adopted to try and convince themselves that life could still have a certain rhythm, a semblance of normalcy." Fesperman's first novel, *Lie in the Dark*, published in 1999, attempted to recapture that same benumbed atmosphere; the book's protagonist, Vlado Petric, is a police inspector with the almost ludicrous task of investigating routine murders in the middle of a decimating war. When an old acquaintance, the head of the the Interior Ministry's special police, is found dead, Petric discovers a conspiracy and begins to unravel an international smuggling ring. "Our hero is, of course, estranged from his wife, half-kempt and sour in spirit and body odour and in the course of his investigation puts his life on the line not once but half a dozen times. All par for the thriller course, though with the added frisson of a wartime Sarajevo setting." a reviewer wrote for the London *Guardian* (January 8, 2000). "It's hard not to feel uneasy about Fesperman hanging his narrative on the Yugoslav conflict, but *Lie in the Dark* makes the terror of living in the midst of a civil war come horribly and numbingly to life." Fesperman "catalogues in unmitigated detail the innumerable daily humiliations and dangers associated with nothing more ambitious than trying to stay alive," according to Dominique Baldy, writing for the *Scotsman* (October 2, 1999). "The mystery itself," Baldy writes, "centred on a plan to smuggle Bosnia's expensive art collection from the country, is nothing out of the ordinary, and the only quibble with *Lie in the Dark* is that it does go off the boil on the fortunately rare occasions when the criminal plot and not the characterisation becomes the central device in driving the story forward. But that is a minor drawback, because Fesperman for the most part concentrates his energies on creating a depressingly complete picture of the realities of life for those unlucky enough to be called upon to carry on their daily lives amid the devastation wreaked by the war."

Vlado Petric reappears in Fesperman's 2003 book, *The Small Boat of Great Sorrows*. As the novel begins, the hero has fled Sarajevo and rejoined his wife and child, in Berlin, Germany, where he has found a job as a construction worker. He gets back into the investigation trade, however, when an American who works for the war-crimes tribunal at the Hague recruits him to track down a former member of the Ustache fascists, a ferocious pro-Nazi group that took over Croatia during World War II. The old man, still in hiding, is believed to have been a friend of Petric's father, and the former investigator is curious about his father's role in the war. The truth about the war, as with much of Yugoslavia's history, has been deliberately obfuscated, and Petric, like others of his generation, knows little of the real history of his country. Writing for the London *Guardian* (October 4, 2003), Chris Petit described *The Small*

Boat of Great Sorrows as an "engrossing exercise in what author Robert Littell calls 'walking back the cat', or working a case backwards to see what dank truths are revealed—in this case a sequence of shunts that connects recent Balkan atrocities with previous genocides and a history of ethnic violence unresolved for centuries." Jonathan Mahler noted, writing for the *New York Times Book Review* (September 28, 2003), that Fesperman had strayed from the formula of literary espionage novels: Petric is not an ambivalent and flawed hero but a good man, who is devoted to his wife and child, and Fesperman's portrait of the villain, Nazi collaborator Pero Matek, also lacks any shades of gray. Nevertheless, Mahler wrote, "*The Small Boat of Great Sorrows* manages to survive its Hollywood finish, much as it transcends its black-and-white moral landscape. There's even something reassuring, if unfashionable, in being able to distinguish the good guys from the bad. But Fesperman's greatest contribution to his genre may be his discovery of the narrative potential of the Balkans. Cold war Europe, with its shadowy deceptions and murky defections, has a worthy successor in this land of divided loyalties and uncomfortably overlapping layers of violent history."

Next Fesperman relied on his experiences in post-Taliban Afghanistan to supply the background for *The Warlord's Son*. The novel's protagonist, Skelly, is a burned-out reporter, who has been relegated to covering town meetings for a local paper in the Midwest. He jumps when offered the opportunity to report the U.S. military's response to the September 11 terrorist attacks, seeing this as his last chance to return to the big time. In Peshawar, Pakistan, Skelly hires Najeeb, the eponymous warlord's son, to serve as his "fixer" (translator and go-between), and the pair, after being tested by the dangerous journey into Afghanistan, develop an enduring friendship. "Almost alone in depicting the main theatre of the war on terror, Fesperman proves equal to the challenge, producing impressively vivid portraits of Peshawar and the mountainous borderlands," John Dugdale wrote for the London *Sunday Times* (December 12, 2004). Sue Arnold noted in the London *Guardian* (December 11, 2004, on-line) that this "exciting story, of an ageing American foreign correspondent hoping that his last ever war assignment in Afghanistan will give him the scoop he's been chasing all his life, offers a subtle take on the different viewpoints of west and east, religious, social and moral." A reviewer for *Publishers Weekly* (August 16, 2004) described *The Warlord's Son* as a "gripping portrayal of shameless media frenzy and hopeless geopolitical gamesmanship."

Fesperman's most recent novel, *The Prisoner of Guantanamo*, was published in July 2006. He is currently on an extended leave from the *Sun*, while he finishes his next novel. He has been married to journalist Liz Bowie since 1988. They and their two children, Emma and Will, live in Baltimore.
—S.Y.

Suggested Reading: Dan Fesperman's Web site; (London) *Sunday Times* p53 Dec. 12, 2004; *New York Times Book Review* p17 Sep. 28, 2003; *Scotsman* p10 Oct. 2, 1999

Selected Books: *Lie in the Dark*, 1999; *The Small Boat of Great Sorrows*, 2003; *The Warlord's Son*, 2004

Christopher Jackson/Getty Images

Fforde, Jasper

1961– Novelist

Jasper Fforde's satirical novels starring the detective Thursday Next abound in puns—characters include agents named Phodder and Kannon—and literary references—Next is called on at one point to defend herself in an abdurdist courtroom based on Franz Kafka's novel *The Trial*. Next is featured in *The Eyre Affair* (2001), *Lost in a Good Book* (2002), *The Well of Lost Plots* (2003), and *Something Rotten* (2004), all set largely in a fantasy world in which the Crimean War has lasted more than a century, Russia continues to be ruled by the Romanoffs, and the massive Goliath Corporation controls everything from the military industrial complex to the price of cheese. Next travels back and forth in time and actually leaps into such works as *Jane Eyre*, *Hamlet*, and *Great Expectations*, whose characters help her in her detective work.

Fforde is also the author of a series of books starring the detective Jack Spratt of the Nursery Crimes Division. Helped by an ambitious, but contrary young colleague named Mary Mary, he solves the mystery of Humpty Dumpty's demise in *The Big Over Easy* (2005) and of Goldilocks's disappearance in *The Fourth Bear* (2006). Fforde observed in an interview with Murray Waldren for the *Weekend Australian* (September 21, 2002), "I've always enjoyed making bizarre connections between ideas, and I have a boy's factoid head—I collect curious facts in every field from nature to vintage cars to philosophy, which means I can then scatter in-jokes through the text."

Jasper Fforde was born in London, England, in 1961, the third of four children of Marya and John Fforde. His father was an economist who had been a Royal Air Force pilot during World War II and later became a director of the Bank of England. Fforde's siblings all earned doctoral degrees. One of his older brothers became a member of Parliament, another a college professor. His younger sister, too, became a professor. Fforde, in contrast, was a poor student and was sent to a progressive school with less rigorous academic requirements; he decided not to go on to a university. After he left school at the age of 18, Fforde worked as a handyman and then went into the film business. He worked his way up from gofer to assistant cameraman (also known as focus puller) on such films as *GoldenEye*, *The Mark of Zorro*, and *The Saint*.

By the late 1980s, Fforde had discovered that he wanted to write and scrambled to find periods of time between film shoots to do so. He told several interviewers that he received 76 rejection notices before a publisher saw the merit of *The Eyre Affair*, his first published novel. The book, which he had initially envisioned as a film script, became an almost instant cult favorite, and Fforde left the movie business to devote himself to writing full-time. *The Eyre Affair* is a genre-bending spoof of detective and science-fiction novels. Set in Great Britain in 1985, it introduces the literary sleuth Thursday Next. Fforde's is an alternative universe in which people travel in dirigibles, and the science of cloning is so advanced that the dodo, now brought out of extinction, is a favorite pet. Literature is the main passion of everyday people, replacing pop music, movies, and sports. Like proselytizers for the Jehovah's Witnesses, missionaries go door to door to convert people to the idea that Francis Bacon is the real author of Shakespeare's plays. There are no football hooligans, but gangs of surrealists and abstract expressionists challenge those who question their philosophies. Thursday's first quest is to bring the villain Acheron Hades to justice for the ghastly kidnapping of the fictional Jane Eyre from Charlotte Brontë's gothic novel, thus leaving blank pages in every copy of the book in existence. "There's much, much more," James Sallis wrote in *Fantasy & Science Fiction* (September 2002). "Thesaurus Maggots; Thursday speeding backtime in a roadster to put an earlier self on alert; great names; a myriad allusions, jokes, pickle barrels of puns, shaggy dogs. The whole thing's as silly as can be, but always great fun. . . . Satire and pastiche? Of itself as much as anything (or should I say everything?) else."

Michiko Kakutani wrote for the *New York Times* (February 12, 2002), "Although Hades and the rest of the supporting cast of *The Eyre Affair* are all cartoonish folk—a sort of cross between the goodies and baddies in a James Bond film and the stock characters from a Victorian melodrama—they gradually emerge as useful foils to the driven Thursday, who acts more and more like a conflicted yuppie when she isn't in her gun-packing Clint Eastwood mode." Kakutani continued, "The gratuitous whimsy that was so cloying in the early chapters gradually gives way to genuinely clever invention, just as the literary jokes—which run the gamut from bad puns (one character is named Millon de Floss) to postmodern capers—slowly evolve from knee-jerk spasms of humor into a larger, comedic point of view. . . . By the end of the novel, Mr. Fforde has, however belatedly, found his own exuberant voice."

Fforde's publishers demanded a quick sequel, and the subsequent Thursday Next outing, *Lost in a Good Book*, was released the following year. (Fforde has announced his intention of writing a book a year, a schedule he has maintained thus far.) In this new adventure, Next is still chasing crooks so nefarious they stoop to counterfeiting Shakespearean plays and tacking different endings on such famous works as Lord Byron's *Don Juan*. She is joined in her work for the "JurisFiction" division by Miss Havisham, a character from Charles Dickens's *Great Expectations*. In the *Washington Post Book World* (April 6, 2003), Lloyd Rose praised Fforde's "head-spinning narrative agility," and his incorporation of "satire, fantasy, literary criticism, thriller, whodunit, game, puzzle, joke, postmodern prank and tilt-a-whirl." Rose noted, however, that those without "a working acquaintance of [Charles] Dickens, [the] Brontë [sisters], Lewis Carroll, and [Edgar Allan] Poe are as likely to be irritated as entertained, as if they'd been asked to work a crossword with unnecessarily esoteric clues."

In *The Well of Lost Plots*, Next leaves her hometown of Swindon to rest up in the eponymous well, which Jay MacDonald described for the BookPage Web site as "part Moroccan thieves' market [and] part B-movie back lot." MacDonald continued, "The Well is also where A-list heroes and villains take a break from their classic novels to vacation in unpublished works via the Character Exchange Program." Here Next meets Miss Havisham once more and is projected into the world of another Brontë—Emily—in a trip to *Wuthering Heights*. She encounters a rampaging Minotaur, a group of bat-like creatures called grammasites who delete text, and the Cheshire Cat, of *Alice in Wonderland* fame. Again battling a colorful cast of strange villains, Thursday remains unflappable. "If Thursday Next existed, I would be in love with her," Fforde told an interviewer for

BookBrowse (July 14, 2003). MacDonald pointed out that Fforde had been denied permission from Disney to use the character of Eeyore, and the estate of H.G. Wells had forbidden mention of the mutant Morlocks from *The Time Machine*. MacDonald asked, "How in the world, then, did he manage the neat trick of bringing in Godot from Samuel Beckett's classic existential play, *Waiting for Godot*, much less as a head-in-a-bag plot device?" Fforde replied, "The good thing about Godot is, he doesn't actually appear in the play; they're waiting for him but he never appears! He's not actually a copyrighted character because he doesn't exist, he's not there. And now you know why: his head is in a bag in *The Well of Lost Plots*."

Something Rotten finds Next back in Swindon with her two-year-old son, Friday, and the character of Hamlet, who masquerades as her Cousin Eddie. Threatened by a horde of Napoleon Bonaparte clones, the evil Emperor Zhark, and a madman named Yorrick Kaine, Next must prevent Shakespeare's Merry Wives of Windsor from staging a coup and save the world from Armageddon by winning a croquet match, among other tasks. "The pileup of all these ingredients, not to mention the hedgehog Mrs. Tiggy-Winkle from the Beatrix Potter books and cameo appearances by certain *Alice in Wonderland* characters, make *Something Rotten* more than clever," Janet Maslin wrote for the *New York Times* (August 5, 2004). "Fforde's penchant for plotting knows no bounds, nor does his taste for awful puns." Lev Grossman wrote for *Time* (August 2, 2004) that Fforde is "always charming company, and if he sometimes strays too far into fantasy, well, what's so great about reality? 'If the real world were a book,' Hamlet remarks, 'it would never find a publisher.'"

Fforde's next two books star the detective Jack Spratt, who had been seen previously as a minor character in the Thursday Next novels. *The Big Over Easy*, one of Fforde's early writing attempts that had originally been rejected by publishers, and *The Fourth Bear* feature the same abundant use of literary allusion and punning that marked his first published books, and most reviewers agreed that Thursday Next's fans would find much to enjoy in this other series. In a representative review Anita Sama wrote for *USA Today* (July 27, 2005, on-line), "*Over Easy* is an interesting reminder of the violent nature of the building blocks of children's literature. Greek myths and fairy tales are turned inside out, familiar names surface in peculiar circumstances. It's as if the Marx brothers were let loose in the children's section of a strange bookstore—a duck soup of loony lit. How else to describe a plot that turns on the discovery of a giant wart and turns again on a stale sandwich used as a detonator?" Sama continued, "In whatever form he delivers his writing, Fforde is above all funny. His self-styled 'daft novels' are not for the lazy brained but for the actively engaged reader, one who knows the secret pleasures of a word puzzle and can draw on a lifetime of literature."

Fforde, who has four children, lives with his companion, Mari Roberts, in Wales. He is an avid pilot and often flies his 1937 DeHavilland biplane over the Welsh countryside. When asked by Ron Hogan for the Beatrice Web site what book he himself would most like to step into, Fforde replied, "I guess I could go into one of my books and meet the characters, tell them, 'Hi, I'm Jasper! I wrote you!' Then they'd ask, 'Well, couldn't you have written me a little more handsome?' Then I'd try to apologize, and everybody would start complaining about the mole on their face, or how old they are."

—S.Y.

Suggested Reading: *BookBrowse* (on-line) July 14, 2003; *Fantasy & Science Fiction* p30+ Sep. 2002; *New York Times* E p8 Feb. 12, 2002, Aug. 5, 2004; *New York Times Book Review* p12 June 22, 2003; *School Library Journal* p175 June 2003; *Time* Aug. 2, 2004; *Washington Post Book World* p7 Apr. 6, 2003; *Weekend Australian* B p10 Sep. 21, 2002

Selected Books: *The Eyre Affair*, 2001; *Lost in a Good Book*, 2002; *The Well of Lost Plots*, 2003; *Something Rotten*, 2004; *The Big Over Easy*, 2005; *The Fourth Bear*, 2006

Fischer, David Hackett

Dec. 2, 1935– Historian

Throughout his career as an author and academic, the Pulitzer Prize–winning historian and Brandeis University professor David Hackett Fischer has offered a vivid counterpoint to those in his field who, like a sequestered jury, espouse a distinctly impersonal approach to their studies: "The phrase some historians use is, 'The past is a foreign country,'" Fischer told David Mehegan for the *Boston Globe* (February 16, 2004). "They write about it as if it were very distant from themselves. I never thought about the past that way. The past is our country, and the people who lived there were our forebears. For me, there's always a connection between these people in the past and us." Fischer, who has written more than a dozen books—most notably *Albion's Seed: Four British Folkways in America* (1989), *Paul Revere's Ride* (1994), *The Great Wave: Price Revolutions and the Rhythm of History* (1996), *Liberty and Freedom: A Visual History of America's Founding Ideas* (2004), and *Washington's Crossing* (2004)—has developed a "braided" writing method that effectively draws together aspects of classical history, with its heavy emphasis on the actions of individuals (generals, kings, etc.), and the more modern social and economic histories, which have a more sweeping, if less intimate, framework. As Stephen Saunders Webb observed for the *Washington Post* (February 11, 1990), "This design is a laudable effort to make the impersonal and barren structures of 'the new social history' more appealing and accessible to readers who still treasure the human dimensions and appealing decorations of more traditional constructions."

David Hackett Fischer was born on December 2, 1935 to Norma and John Fischer in Baltimore, Maryland. The Fischer family is part "Old Maryland"—that is, descendants of the state's early settlers—and part Baltimore German. Fischer developed an abiding passion for history while still a child: "I grew up in the midst of history," he recalled to David Mehegan. "It had happened in my own family, which had been in most American wars. The Civil War was very much a presence in my youth. My Aunt Eliza was in her 90s in the late 1930s and '40s, and had been a young teenager during the Civil War. She described once hearing a sound like the wind outside the farm, and when she went out, she saw it was the cries of wounded Union soldiers in wagons as far as the eye could see, being carried to hospitals. There were many stories like that. So history had a kind of reality to me." Raised as he was in the midst of World War II, Fischer intuitively grasped that history was not simply a product of the past but could be witnessed and experienced in the present. Later, while a teenager, Fischer watched as his father, the superintendent of Baltimore's public schools, helped integrate the city's classrooms after the Supreme Court's ruling in *Brown v. Board of Education* (1954), which outlawed racial segregation in public schooling. "I had a sense of seeing things sort of worked out, or developing, around the table at my house, and then I'd read about them in *The Baltimore Sun* the next day," he told John Koch for the *Boston Globe Magazine* (March 23, 1997). "It gave me a sense of how history happened. It gave me a feeling of the importance of contingency in the world, that is, of people making choices and choices making a difference. I was a witness to those choices; a lot of historians don't have that experience."

Upon completing high school, Fischer entered Princeton University, in Princeton, New Jersey, completing a bachelor's degree in 1958. He then began his doctoral studies in American history at Johns Hopkins University, in Baltimore, where he developed the wide-ranging interests that would characterize his later work: "I started as a specialist in the year 1804," he told Bob Thompson for the *Washington Post* (April 3, 2004), "[but soon] started showing interest in 1805 and even 1807 and they started calling me a generalist." Upon completing his doctorate, in 1962, Fischer headed north to Waltham, Massachusetts, where he had accepted a professorship at Brandeis University; he has remained there since, except for the occasional visiting appointment at the University of Washington, in Seattle; Harvard University, in Cambridge, Massachusetts; and the University of Otago, in Dunedin, New Zealand; among other educational institutions. His research interests have included early American history, the American Revolution, the early republic, the Civil War era, and World War II. In addition to the works listed above, Fischer has authored *The Revolution of American Conservatism: The Federalist Party in the Era of Jeffersonian Democracy* (1965); *Historians' Fallacies: Toward a Logic of Historical Thought* (1970); *Growing Old in America* (1977); and *Bound Away: Virginia and the Westward Movement* (2000), with James C. Kelly. He has also edited *Concord: The Social History of a New England Town, 1750-1850* (1983) and co-edited, with James M. McPherson, the Oxford University Press series Pivotal Moments in American History.

Albion's Seed, the first volume in a series that examined regional cultures in the U.S., offered a radical theory to explain the cultural development of the nation. As Alvin P. Sanoff and Sharon F. Golden noted in *U.S. News & World Report* (December 4, 1989), "Fischer argues that settlers from different sections of England—called Albion by the ancient Greeks—brought divergent values to the new world, where they established distinctive regional cultures that remain central to the nation's fabric even today." The four cultural groups identified by Fischer are the Puritans, who came from eastern England and settled in the New England states; the Cavaliers, who originated in the south and west of England and settled in the American South; the Quakers, from the northern midlands and Wales, who came to reside in the mid-Atlantic states; and the North British borderers, or Scotch-Irish, who came mostly from Scotland and the province of Ulster, in northern Ireland, and settled in Appalachia. Fischer argues that the individual peculiarities of these cultures continue to exert their influence: for example, he claims, that New England, Southern, and Appalachian accents originated in the region of England from which the settlers hailed. Likewise, the educational, political, and domestic practices of the individual folkways are still palpable today: for example, that the Puritans valued education to a greater degree than their early American counterparts is reflected in the higher college attendance rates—not to mention the multitude of universities—found in New England; by the same token, according to Fischer, the South's historic political conservatism is a natural outgrowth of the Cavalier culture that was transferred from England. Describing the response to *Albion's Seed*, Sanoff and Golden observed that Fischer has been "accused of underplaying differences within a regional culture and of presenting a framework

that, all in all, is a little too tidy." "But whatever the shortcomings of his encyclopedic, 946-page work," Sanoff and Golden continued, "historians who have read it generally agree that the book is a masterpiece of scholarship. . . . What Fischer has done is to shatter the myth that America has evolved into one homogeneous mass culture."

In *Paul Revere's Ride* "Fischer manages to evoke Paul Revere as a striking heroic figure while, at the same time, giving us the particulars of the world in which he lived and the cause he served," Jonathan Kirsch wrote for the *Los Angeles Times* (May 4, 1994). "And so [the book] turns out to be both a well-executed biography of Revere and a refresher course on the American Revolution." Though the story of Paul Revere's ride has long been a staple in American elementary schools, when Fischer set to work on his book, no serious history text had ever been written about it; indeed, in the American consciousness, the ride had come to resemble folklore more than history. After examining the archives of the Massachusetts Historical Society, Fischer discovered an abundance of material relating to the ride, including Revere's personal documents. Far from the solitary rider of American legend, Revere, Fischer discovered, was very much a man of his community; he enthusiastically joined and formed civic organizations, taking a lead role in the social life of the region. When he made his ride, he was one among 60 such men sent to inform the countryside that British soldiers were on the march, intent on confiscating the colonists' weapons caches. In Revere's character, Fischer perceived a synthesis of individualism and a communal ethos: "We misunderstand Paul Revere's revolutionary thinking if we identify it with modern ideas of individual freedom and tolerance," he wrote, as quoted by Kirsch. "We remember individual rights and forget the collective responsibilities."

Fischer later sold the film rights to *Paul Revere's Ride* to Paramount Pictures; however, the prospects for the film's eventual production are considered unlikely. After signing the deal, Fischer remarked, "I tend to live in the 18th century; all of this (Hollywood deal-making) has a certain remoteness from a scholar's world," as quoted by Laurence Chollet for the *Bergen Record*, in an article reprinted by the Denver, Colorado, *Rocky Mountain News* (November 24, 1994). "All I can say is, dealing with people in California has been an experience I've found very interesting."

In *The Great Wave* Fischer shifted his gaze from American history to global economics, theorizing that over the past 800 years the world has experienced four great waves of inflation—when the price of goods and services rise while wages stagnate. These inflation waves, which occurred between 1200 and 1320, 1520 and 1620, 1720 and 1820, and 1896 and 1997, were accompanied by increased poverty, violence, and social turmoil, but were followed by periods of price stability and prosperity. Commended for its readability and ambition, *The Great Wave* was well received in the business community but did not fare as well among traditional economists. For *Foreign Affairs* (July/August 1997), the economist Paul Krugman wrote, "I plan to keep *The Great Wave* on my shelf both as a useful source of facts and figures and as a guide to data sources; the author did do a lot of homework. It is therefore a shame that the book turns out to be quite wrong-headed. But let that not be too harsh a judgment: it is wrong-headed in interesting ways, and much can be learned by examining how and where Fischer went astray." Krugman felt Fischer failed to account for the impact of the Industrial Revolution on economic models and lacked a clear understanding of certain fundamental concepts in the discipline. Nonetheless, a reviewer for the *Economist* (July 19, 1997) declared *The Great Wave* "a provocative and thoughtful journey through history."

Liberty and Freedom, the second volume in the series that began with *Albion's Seed*, is composed "of several dozen profusely illustrated brief essays, each devoted to a particular artifact or clutch of items from which Fischer extracts larger historical meanings," Sean Wilentz wrote for the *Los Angeles Times* (November 28, 2004). Through his chronological analysis of various flags, statues, and other paraphernalia, Fischer shows that while liberty and freedom have always been central to the American identity, what these terms actually mean has been debated since the nation's inception. Thus this "shared vocabulary has given Americans the appearance of cohesion," Wilentz wrote. "But the conflicts have been as enduring as the commonalities." Though he felt the work faltered in the later stages and that "when pressed too far . . . [Fischer's] retrospective anthropology can become a doggedly schematic form of cultural history that effaces ideas and material interests," Wilentz nevertheless characterized *Liberty and Freedom* as a "powerful book" that "affirms that without these basic values, and our conflicts over them, we are lost." For the *Seattle Times* (January 16, 2005), Steve Raymond declared, "Every American should read this book. . . . Fischer has fashioned an elaborate history of American liberty and freedom—where those ideas have come from and where they may be going."

As with *Paul Revere's Ride*, *Washington's Crossing* illuminated one of the seminal events in American history, removing the aura of myth that had long surrounded it to reveal the underlying facts. After a string of military disasters, on a cold Christmas night in 1776, General George Washington, at the head of the Continental army, crossed an icy Delaware River to attack Hessian mercenaries in New Jersey. His subsequent victories at Trenton and Princeton rejuvenated American morale and changed the character of the war. Fischer began his book by discussing events prior to the crossing: how the Americans were driven out of Manhattan and Long Island by superior British forces and Washington's

incredible efforts to hold together his tattered army. In examining the battles in New Jersey, Fischer corrects certain popular misconceptions: far from a drunken, undisciplined rabble, the Hessian mercenaries ambushed by Washington were actually a highly disciplined and professional force who fought valiantly in defeat. Moreover, far from merely symbolic, morale-boosting victories, Washington's triumphs in New Jersey actually had great strategic value: they significantly sapped British troop strength and forestalled the capitulation of the New Jersey countryside. *Washington's Crossing* earned considerable plaudits from critics: Joseph J. Ellis, writing for the *New York Times* (February 15, 2004), singled out Fischer's descriptions of combat for particular praise, remarking that his narrative provides "an overarching picture of the way armies move, with a genuine sense of what it looks and feels like to face a bayonet charge or to witness the man abreast of you disemboweled by a cannonball." The book, Michael Kenney observed for the *Boston Globe* (February 16, 2004), "is history at its best, fascinating in its details, magisterial in its sweep." Fischer was awarded the 2005 Pulitzer Prize in history for *Washington's Crossing*.

Fischer and his wife, Judith, a biology professor at Lesley University, in Cambridge, Massachusetts, divide their time between Wayland, outside of Boston, and Mount Desert Island, Maine. Together the couple have a daughter, Susie, who is a barrister in London, England. Fischer is currently working on a biography of the renowned 19th-century painter and adventurer Samuel Emery Chamberlain. In addition to the Pulitzer, Fischer has received, among other awards, the Ingersoll Prize, the Irving Kristol Award, the Louis Dembitz Brandeis Prize for Excellence in Teaching, and the 1991 Massachusetts Teacher of the Year award. Despite his remarkable success as an author, Fischer shows no sign of resting on his laurels and remains firmly committed to both his writing and to his teaching. Fischer's eminent standing in his field was aptly characterized by fellow historian Alice Kelikian, who described him as "the most imaginative historian of early America working today," as quoted by Catherine Sheffield for the Waltham, Massachusetts, *Daily News Tribune* (April 7, 2005, on-line). "Unlike so many historians of the late 20th century, he links the new social history to the great theme of American political history, and all this with rich archival research and grand narrative sweep."

—P.B.M.

Suggested Reading: *Booknotes* (on-line) July 17, 1994; *Boston Globe* C p1 Feb. 16, 2004; *Boston Globe Magazine* p10 Mar. 23, 1997; (Waltham, Massachusetts) *Daily News Tribune* (on-line) Apr. 7, 2005; *Washington Post* C p1 Apr. 3, 2004

Selected Books: *The Revolution of American Conservatism: The Federalist Party in the Era of Jeffersonian Democracy*, 1965; *Historians' Fallacies: Toward a Logic of Historical Thought*, 1970; *Growing Old in America*, 1977; *Albion's Seed: Four British Folkways in America*, 1989; *America: A Cultural History*, 1989; *Paul Revere's Ride*, 1994; *The Great Wave: Price Revolutions and the Rhythm of History*, 1996; *Bound Away: Virginia and the Westward Movement* (with James C. Kelly), 2000; *Liberty and Freedom: A Visual History of America's Founding Ideas*, 2004; *Washington's Crossing*, 2004; as editor— *Concord: The Social History of a New England Town, 1750–1850*, 1983

Fisher, Antwone Quenton

Aug. 3, 1959– Memoirist; screenwriter

Antwone Quenton Fisher is the acclaimed author of *Finding Fish* (2001), a memoir of growing up as an abused foster child during the 1960s and 1970s. Fisher's life story caught the attention of producers while he was working as a security guard at a Hollywood movie studio, and in 2002 the Oscar-winning actor Denzel Washington co-starred in and directed a feature film, *Antwone Fisher*, based on a screenplay written by Fisher himself. Recalling his remarkable rise to an interviewer for *Jet* (January 13, 2003), Fisher said, "Having my story told gives me faith and encouragement and reminds me that there are good and unselfish people in the world; people who would help an absolute stranger by giving him the tools to pull himself up, giving him the chance to benefit society. Despite the unfortunate circumstances of my life, there is hope. How peculiar and blue that the words 'You ain't nothing. You ain't never gonna be nothing 'cause you come from nothing' made for fervent fuel that gave me strength and the courage to persevere."

Fisher was born in an Ohio prison on August 3, 1959 to a 17-year-old inmate named Eva Mae Fisher. His father, Edward Elkins, had been killed two months before Fisher's birth by an enraged 19-year-old ex-girlfriend, who was also the mother of two of his daughters. When Eva Mae failed to pick him up after she was released from prison, Antwone was placed in a succession of foster homes.

At the age of two, Fisher was placed in the care of the Reverend Ulysses and Isabella Pickett in Cleveland, Ohio, where over the next 14 years, he and the other foster children who lived in the Picketts' home were subjected to a wide variety of torment. The Picketts never explained to him why he had a different last name from them or the fact that he was a foster child. Thus, he didn't realize for years that the Picketts, who had adult children

and grandchildren of their own, were not his biological parents. The Picketts made it clear, however, that he was unwanted and unloved. In addition to their physical and emotional abuse, a babysitter began sexually abusing him when he was just three years old.

When he was about 16, with little warning, Isabella Pickett gave him bus fare and told him to leave the house. He returned to the social-services agency responsible for his placement with the Picketts, and workers there concluded that at his age it would be unlikely that he would get another foster family; he was sent instead to a reform school, despite the fact that he hadn't committed a crime. The school turned out to be a positive influence, providing his life with the structure that it had been lacking. Knowing that funding for his care would cease when he turned 18, he applied himself to earning his high-school diploma. After leaving the reform school, he moved to Cleveland, Ohio, where he lived briefly at a local YMCA. Desperate to earn enough money to go to art school, he found himself working briefly for a drug dealer and pimp. When he discovered that the man was trafficking children, Fisher ran away and began living on the streets.

Recalling that a social worker had once suggested that he join the military, Fisher enlisted in the Navy. Thriving in the regimented atmosphere, he excelled in his duties as a barber, orderly, and service manager. Despite being an excellent recruit, however, Fisher soon gained a reputation for having a quick temper. He was ordered by his superior officers to receive counseling. From a series of psychiatrists (who were condensed into one character, played by Denzel Washington, in the film version of his life), he learned how to manage his anger, and he emerged from his 11 years in the Navy a changed man. (While in the service Fisher was also diagnosed with dyslexia, and with the proper guidance he began to read all he could about African-American history, as well as great works by William Shakespeare and Fyodor Dostoevsky.)

When Fisher ended his Naval career, he joined the Federal Bureau of Prisons as a guard, working mainly at Terminal Island Federal Prison, near Los Angeles. After a few years he became a security guard at Sony Pictures Entertainment. He then decided to contact his biological family, something that had been suggested to him previously by a Navy psychiatrist. When he made contact with his father's family, the Elkins were surprised to discover that Edward had fathered a son, but despite their shock, they invited him to visit them in Cleveland. He also met his biological mother, who had borne four more children and then given them up because of her drug addiction. Fisher returned to Los Angeles after the visits, determined to move on with his life.

Fisher's immediate supervisor at Sony felt the tale of his upbringing would make an interesting movie and approached executives at the company.

Stephen Shugerman/Getty Images
Antwone Quenton Fisher

They agreed and purchased the rights to Fisher's life story. When Fisher expressed interest in writing the screenplay himself, however, they were hesitant. He persevered, and after taking a series of free screenwriting classes, Fisher wrote the script and presented it to the producer Todd Black. Black turned down the early effort but offered to pay Fisher to keep working on it. "He wrote with such clarity and command of character," Black recalled, as quoted by Christina Cheakalos for *People* (January 27, 2003). "I knew the rest would get there." After Fisher had completed more than 40 drafts, Black agreed to buy the 120-page screenplay.

Fisher wrote *Finding Fish*, his memoir, only after the screenplay was finished. Co-authored with Mim Eichler Rivas and published in 2001, the book allowed him to expand on the screenplay by including a wider array of characters and a greater number of events. Landing on the *New York Times* best-sellers' list, the book met with mostly positive reviews upon its publication. Lise Funderburg wrote for *Time* (February 26, 2001): "The facts of [Fisher's] life have a movie-of-the-week ring: relentlessly abusive foster care; redemption through military service; and irrepressible intellect. But detailed accounting distinguishes the tale, and Fisher's searing, luminous portrait of his childhood transcends the familiar, as does his retroactive (and likely hard-won) tenderness toward the boy no one else loved." Reviewing the memoir for *Library Journal* (January 2001), Antoinette Brinkman wrote: "Like Cinderella, Fisher rose above the abuse of a dismal foster care childhood in Cleveland to success as a screenwriter and producer in Hollywood. . . .

This is a story of resilience based on personal character as well as the kindness and inspiration of mentors; it is also a gripping exposé of a foster care system that undersupervises caretakers and provides little transitional assistance for its 'graduates.'" On the other hand, Michael Harris, in the *Los Angeles Times* (February 13, 2001), was more critical: "[*Finding Fish*] isn't bad, but—compared to such memoirs as Tobias Wolff's *This Boy's Life*—it's ordinary. Fisher's prose veers from stiff formality to street crudities to a gushy lyricism. Only rarely does it seem to find the precise words, the exact tone, to render the life it cost him so much to live."

The film version of Fisher's life, *Antwone Fisher*, was released in 2002 and marked Denzel Washington's directorial debut. Washington had been intrigued by Fisher's story for years and invested a reported $2 million of his own money into the project. "I promised Antwone I would take good care of him," Washington told Cheakalos. "I said, 'I know you've been through a lot and I promise I won't screw you up.'" Washington arranged for an office at the 20th Century Fox studios to be made available to Fisher so that he could work on revisions. In addition to his screenwriting credit, Fisher is listed as one of the film's co-producers.

Since the movie's release, Fisher has written numerous screenplays and served as a script doctor for many others; his most recent writing credit is *ATL* (2006)—a drama about Rashad, Esquire, New-New, Teddy, and Anton, a group of inner-city youths from Atlanta. "It's a film about growing up and working, about falling in love, about planning for your future, and about the importance of friends," Roger Ebert wrote for the *Chicago Sun-Times* (March 31, 2006, on-line). "I doubt *ATL* is as autobiographical as [Fisher's] 2002 film, but it reflects lives of focus and determination; Rashad and his friends are young and sometimes foolish and like to party, but they're also smart and determined to survive and prevail." Ebert continued, "I sense that somewhere in the film, if we know where to look, maybe in the support of [an adult character] Uncle George, [and] the friendships involving Rashad, Esquire and New-New, we can find clues about how Antwone Fisher evolved from a kid with a shaky future into a screenwriter with a big one."

In 2003 Fisher published a collection of his poetry under the title *Who Will Cry for the Little Boy?* He and his wife, LaNette, whom he married in 1996, have two daughters, Indigo and Azure.

—C.M.

Suggested Reading: *Black Issues Book Review* p24+ July–Aug. 2002; *Los Angeles Times* E p3 Feb. 13, 2001; *Newsweek* p67 Dec. 23, 2002; *People* p127+ Jan. 27, 2003; *Salon* (on-line) Dec. 20, 2002; *Time* p72 Feb. 26, 2001

Selected Books: nonfiction—*Finding Fish*, 2001; poetry—*Who Will Cry for the Little Boy?*, 2003

Grant Delin/Courtesy of Miami Book Fair

Foer, Jonathan Safran

1977– Novelist

Even before Jonathan Safran Foer's first novel was published, he was designated a "genius" and a "wunderkind": his book, *Everything Is Illuminated* (2002), elicited almost universal advance praise and counted the novelists Joyce Carol Oates and Russell Banks, both former writing professors of Foer's, among its boosters. "*Everything Is Illuminated* pretends to be about a young man's search for the Ukranian woman who saved his grandfather from the Nazis but is really about pretty much everything else: love, history, memory, narrative, and death—and that's just for starters," Daniel Mendelsohn wrote for *New York* (April 22, 2002). By turns funny, bawdy, and puzzling, the book was inspired by Foer's real-life, unsuccessful search for the woman who rescued his grandfather during World War II. The author has credited his own book with giving his life direction. "I realized rather late in the game that writing presents itself as a kind of answer to that question, 'What should I be doing?'" he told Joyce Wadler for the *New York Times* (April 24, 2002). "What I realized is that the question is the final answer. That what I wanted to do with my life is figure out what I wanted to do with my life." Critical response to Foer's second novel was more equivocal; *Extremely Loud and Incredibly Close* (2005) was alternately hyped and reviled, according to Boris Kachka for *New York* (May 16, 2005, on-line).

The second of three sons, Jonathan Safran Foer was born in 1977 in Washington, D.C. His mother, Esther Foer, is the executive vice president of the

Hawthorn Group, an international public-relations firm; his father, Albert A. "Bert" Foer, an attorney, entrepreneur, and educator, currently heads the American Antitrust Institute, a think tank he founded in 1998. "My parents are creative in the way I most admire," Jonathan Safran Foer told Sarah Bernard for *New York* (April 15, 2002), "which has nothing to do with the outside world. It has everything to do with what they think is fun." Foer's older brother, Franklin, is the editor of the *New Republic* and the author of *How Soccer Explains the World: An Unlikely Theory of Globalization* (2004); his younger brother, Joshua, is a freelance science writer whose first book, "Moonwalking with Einstein: A Journey into Memory and Mind," is slated for publication in 2009. Foer attended the private Georgetown Day School, where he was a good student but, by his own account, not especially creative. "I wasn't somebody who was writing or making things, and I wasn't even reading really," he explained to Peter Terzian for New York *Newsday* (May 30, 2002). "I was just sort of doing kid stuff . . . playing Atari and eating sugar cereals and watching a lot of TV." His Jewish upbringing was "a formality," he told Susan Josephs for the *Jewish Week* (December 20, 2001). "I had no interest in Hebrew school. They were like weekly doctor's appointments and everyone I knew felt the exact same way."

In the fall of 1995, Foer enrolled at Princeton University, in Princeton, New Jersey, where he majored in philosophy. During his freshman year he had a revelation in a sculpture class, after he was introduced to the work of the assemblage artist Joseph Cornell. Cornell, well known for his intricate dioramas, "is the most important person ever to enter my life," Foer told Peter Terzian. "His work just opened up a world to me, a world of having physical examples of things that you believe in." In an interview with Louis Jacobson for the *Princeton Alumni Weekly* (May 15, 2002, on-line), Foer elaborated on Cornell's impact on his life. "What captured my attention," he said, "was the way my attention was captured. I was in love with the way that I loved his art. I loved the way that it inspired me to go to the art library and look at all the images of his works, or to read his biography when it came out. It was something no one had done for me before." Combining his interest in Cornell's art with a newly uncovered passion for creative writing—nurtured by Joyce Carol Oates and others among his professors—he solicited fiction and poetry from other writers inspired by Cornell's work and collected the pieces in a single volume, *A Convergence of Birds*, which was printed in 2001 by Distributed Art Publishers. (The title refers to a frequent subject in Cornell's work.)

The summer after his sophomore year at Princeton, Foer took a brief trip to the Ukraine in pursuit of knowledge about his family's history. Although he had heard that his maternal grandfather, who had died when Foer was very young, had been saved from the Nazis by a woman in the town of Trachimbrod, discussion of the Holocaust was generally taboo in the family. Foer went to Trachimbrod in search of information and of anyone who might have known his grandfather. But he found that the town is "no longer extant," as he told Louis Jacobson. "It's just a field with a stone marker in the middle of it." He described his experience to Julia Llewellyn Smith for the London *Daily Telegraph* (May 31, 2002): "I went for three days and I did have this photograph of my grandfather—all we knew of him was that he had survived the destruction of this village in what used to be in Poland. But I was completely unprepared. I did no research, so I more or less jeopardised the trip before I had even started." Nonetheless, in an interview with Soledad O'Brien for NBC's *Saturday Today* (May 11, 2002), Foer described the trip as a turning point for him: "There was nothing in it in the sense that I didn't find the person I was looking for and I didn't find anything resembling what I thought I was looking for, which is to say, an explicit connection to somebody I had never met, my grandfather. But, what I did find was this great hole to replace."

From the Ukraine, Foer retreated to Prague, Czech Republic, where he spent 10 weeks furiously writing what would become *Everything Is Illuminated*. The novel's characters include a young American Jew named Jonathan Safran Foer who goes on a trip to find the woman who saved his grandfather. "But then the book quickly moves into fiction, and becomes very imaginative," Foer told Soledad O'Brien. "I tried to use other names [for the protagonist]," he explained to Susannah Meadows for *Newsweek* (June 17, 2002). "Even at the end I did one of those search-and-replaces, [but] it didn't feel genuine. This is how I am honest, by beginning with the life of my circumstances. You learn all these things you never could have known. My God, I was interested in Jewish things? I had no idea! Here's a piece of evidence of what I actually was. It's like looking at a picture of yourself and realizing you were pudgier than you thought." Among the novel's other characters are a Ukranian university student, Alex, who acts as a guide and translator for the Foer character, mangling one English idiom after another; Alex's melancholy and possibly blind grandfather, who is Foer's driver; and the grandfather's flatulent Seeing Eye dog, Sammy Davis Junior Junior.

The narrative of *Everything Is Illuminated* has three sections. One tells the story of Foer's visit to Trachimbrod; one comprises Alex's correspondence with him, after Foer's departure; and a third section—written in the magical-realist style—traces the fictional history of Trachimbrod, from the late 18th century through the beginnings of World War II. Foer did no research on the real town of Trachimbrod, as he told Peter Terzian: "I sort of went out of my way to be ignorant about a lot of stuff I was writing about just so I'd have more imaginative latitude."

Although Foer wrote his opus in a single summer, he spent more than two years editing and refining it. "It was excruciating," he admitted to Edward Guthmann for the *San Francisco Chronicle* (June 8, 2002). "It was like the greatest act of will I've ever committed in the sense that I didn't really want to do it." The editing of the book "changed it completely," he told Louis Jacobson—in spite of his having tried to remain true to the original spirit of the work. "What I was trying with the book was to create this sort of document of my 20-year-old self. Which is why, when I look back at it and I see things that are embarrassing, that I would change, I don't want to change them because then I would be making the book that I should make now," he explained to Guthmann.

After graduating from Princeton, in 1999, Foer held a variety of low-paying jobs, including tutoring, ghostwriting, and working as a receptionist at a public-relations firm. He spent his free time editing his book, writing other pieces, and cultivating relationships with a wide range of artists and writers. He also collected and framed blank sheets of paper from well-known writers, whom he had asked to give him the sheets they would have written on next. Foer explained the origins of his offbeat project to Joyce Wadler: "When [Isaac Bashevis] Singer's archivists entered what was his apartment, they found this incredibly old typewriter and next to it a stack of paper—paper with carbon between each sheet. . . . It had no obvious archival use, so my friend sent it to me. I loved this. I became obsessed with it. I found it moving in so many ways. . . . It hadn't been realized yet. Because it was an artifact of his life. Because it was waiting for him. It felt to me heavy with potential."

As for his novel, Foer did not have specific plans for it until a friend persuaded him to find an agent. After signing with Nicole Aragi, he found his manuscript the object of a bidding war; more than a dozen publishing houses competed for the rights to *Everything Is Illuminated*. Houghton Mifflin won out and proffered an advance reported to be between $400,000 and $500,000. (HarperCollins purchased the paperback rights for more than $900,000.) "Surprised is not even the right kind of word," Foer told Clark Collis for the London *Observer* (June 2, 2002) about those developments. "I was a receptionist at a PR firm when I sold the book. I was just the guy who picked up the phone, making $11,000 a year. I always had this number of $20,000 floating in my head. I thought that if I made that then I could go away to Spain for a couple of months. . . . But then . . . it became a different story." In the midst of all the excitement over his book, Foer appeared to remain calm, staying at his receptionist job for another two months and opting not to move from his shared apartment in the New York City borough of Queens. "It's frustrating that a lot of people are so concerned with [the amount of the advance]," he said in an interview with CNN.com (June 17, 2002, on-line). "I'm extremely grateful . . . but other than that, it's no big deal." He did admit, however, to one new indulgence. "I have dessert all the time," he told Peter Terzian, "ice cream, cookies and brownies and all of that. I never bought it before because I filed it into 'luxury items that we're not going to do.' But now, I'll go to the big grocery store, and half of my cart will be ice cream."

The reviews of *Everything Is Illuminated*, which was published in April 2002, were mostly positive. (A brief portion of the book appeared in the *New Yorker* before its publication.) "Under it all there's a funny, moving, unsteady, deeply felt novel about the dangers of confronting the past and the redemption that comes with laughing at it, even when that seems all but impossible," Lev Grossman wrote for *Time* (April 29, 2002). "This is a brilliant but occasionally exasperating book . . . ," Janet Maslin wrote for the *New York Times* (April 22, 2002). "*Everything Is Illuminated* is a complex, ambitious undertaking, especially as its characters and events begin to run together in keeping with the author's ultimate plan. Mr. Foer works hard on these effects, and sometimes you will, too. But the payoff is extraordinary: a fearless, acrobatic, ultimately haunting effort to combine inspired mischief with a grasp of the unthinkable." The novel won the *Guardian* First Book Award, the National Jewish Book Award, the New York Public Library's Young Lions Fiction Award, and the inaugural Saroyan Writing Prize, which is co-sponsored by the William Saroyan Foundation and Stanford University Libraries.

Foer went on a brief tour to promote the book, which led to another curatorial project: at each stop on the tour, he handed out index cards and envelopes, asking fans to create self-portraits and send them to him. "I couldn't help feeling that I—I owed them something," he explained to Soledad O'Brien. "And also I wanted the experience, this exchange of a book, to continue. Not to continue past the covers, to continue past this hour we get to spend with each other in a bookstore and to have a chance to communicate further. Which is what it's been. It's been more wonderful than I could have ever imagined."

The actor Liev Schreiber wrote the screenplay for and directed a film version of *Everything is Illuminated*, which was released in 2005. Critics were divided as to whether the film, which starred Elijah Wood as Foer, was as good as the book. In the *New York Times* (September 16, 2005), A.O. Scott described the story as "a gentle comedy of understanding and forgiveness played in the shadow of the Holocaust. This is a difficult feat to attempt in the best of circumstances, as well as, perhaps, an unseemly one. Mr. Foer's verbal and imaginative energies brought him close to succeeding. Mr. Schreiber, plucking a single thread of the novel's interwoven narratives, shows himself to be a sincere and serious reader, but his effort at translation does not quite work. Taken on

its own, without comparison with its literary source, the movie, Mr. Schreiber's first as writer and director, is thin and soft, whimsical when it should be darkly funny and poignant when it should be devastating."

Oskar Schell, the precocious nine-year-old protagonist of Foer's second novel *Extremely Loud and Incredibly Close*, is an amateur inventor, jewelry designer, astrophysicist, tambourine player, and pacifist. The young hero sets off on a quest to find the lock that fits the key that his father left him shortly before perishing in the terrorist attacks that toppled the World Trade Center on September 11, 2001. "Foer embellishes the narrative with evocative graphics, including photographs, colored highlights and passages of illegibly overwritten text, and takes his unique flair for the poetry of miscommunication to occasionally gimmicky lengths, like a two-page soliloquy written entirely in numerical code," a reviewer wrote for *Publishers Weekly* (January 31, 2005). "Although not quite the comic tour de force that *Illuminated* was, the novel is replete with hilarious and appalling passages, as when, during show-and-tell, Oskar plays a harrowing recording by a Hiroshima survivor and then launches into a Poindexterish disquisition on the bomb's 'charring effect.' It's more of a challenge to play in the same way with the very recent collapse of the towers, but Foer gambles on the power of his protagonist's voice to transform the cataclysm from raw current event to a tragedy at once visceral and mythical."

Other reviewers were more critical of such textual embellishments, particularly of the inclusion of a flip book created from video stills—arranged in reverse order—of a person jumping from one of the World Trade Center towers. Though acknowledging that in *Extremely Loud and Incredibly Close* Foer demonstrated "the same high-flown ambition" as in his first novel, Michiko Kakutani, the *New York Times* (March 22, 2005, on-line) reviewer, felt that the results were "decidedly more cloying" this time around. "While it contains moments of shattering emotion and stunning virtuosity that attest to Mr. Foer's myriad gifts as a writer, the novel as a whole feels simultaneously contrived and improvisatory, schematic and haphazard. . . . *Extremely Loud and Incredibly Close* tends to be at its most powerful when Mr. Foer abandons his willful use of experimental techniques and simply writes in an earnest, straightforward manner, using his copious gifts of language to limn his characters' state of mind. . . . Sadly, these passages are all too few and far between in what is an admirably purposeful but ultimately mannered and irritating novel." Such reviews notwithstanding, *Extremely Loud and Incredibly Close* was a commercial success, peaking in the 12th slot on the *New York Times* best-seller list.

Foer lives in the Park Slope neighborhood in Brooklyn, New York, with his wife, the novelist Nicole Krauss, and their son, Sasha.

—K.S.

Suggested Reading: *Book* p31+ Jan./Feb. 2002; *Entertainment Weekly* p108+ Apr. 26, 2002; (London) *Times* Features June 5, 2002; *New York* p34+ Apr. 15, 2002; (New York) *Newsday* B p8 May 30, 2002; *New York Times* B p2 Apr. 24, 2002, (on-line) Mar. 22, 2005

Selected Books: *Everything Is Illuminated*, 2002; *Extremely Loud and Incredibly Close*, 2005; as editor—*A Convergence of Birds*, 2001

Jon Rou/Emory Creative Group

Fox-Genovese, Elizabeth

May 28, 1941–Jan. 2, 2007 Historian

When Elizabeth Fox-Genovese died, in 2007, she was a pariah among feminists; although she had been a pioneer in the field of women's studies and continued to define herself as a feminist, she drew ire from women's groups for her criticisms of the movement, which she said had become largely irrelevant to the majority of women today. While she conceded that women have made important strides in recent decades, she argued that contemporary feminism, with its prevailing emphasis on single, career-oriented women, neglects the importance of family life and motherhood. "Conservatives," she wrote, as quoted by Jennifer C. Braceras for the Independent Women's Forum Web site (March 1, 2003), "talk as if they want to imprison women in motherhood; feminists talk as if they want to liberate women from it." In her books *Feminism without Illusions: A Critique of Individualism* (1991) and *Feminism Is Not the Story of My Life: How Today's Feminist*

Elite Has Lost Touch with the Real Concerns of Women (1996), she made a case for a more family- and community-oriented feminism.

One of two children, Elizabeth Fox-Genovese was born on May 28, 1941 in Boston, Massachusetts. Her father, Edward Whiting Fox, whose ancestors date back to the Plymouth Bay Colony, taught history at Cornell University, in Ithaca, New York. Fox-Genovese recalled to Cynthia Grenier in an interview for the *Washington Times* (January 31, 1995) that her mother, Elizabeth (Simon) Fox, "loved reading and read beautifully to us from the time we were very young." Fox-Genovese and her brother grew up on their parents' farm and enjoyed a comfortable upbringing in a cultured environment. "About the time I was to go into the seventh grade, my parents decided the public school in [Ithaca] wasn't making the grade, and they took me and my brother and put us in a boarding school," Fox-Genovese told Grenier. "It was rather small, and in the country. In addition to our studies, we all had to work—milking cows, mucking out horses' stables, doing farm work, planting, harvesting—all the while getting a first-rate education. It was a wonderful experience." During her teenage years Fox-Genovese lived in France for about a year, attending a Huguenot school and eventually becoming fluent in French.

Fox-Genovese attended Bryn Mawr College, a private school for women, in Pennsylvania. "What I got was a very demanding education with professors for whom the best student in every class had to be a woman," she told an interviewer for the *Atlanta Journal and Constitution* (October 8, 1994). "They were smart people who were taking us seriously. What I also gained was respect for other women my age. Not just friendship, but respect. I dated a lot at Bryn Mawr, but it was a lovely feeling that if you had a lot of work to do or if you were not seeing someone, studying in the dorm on a Saturday night was perfectly all right." She also spent a year studying at Cornell University and a year at the Institut d'Etudes Politiques, better known as Sciences Po, in Paris. In 1963 Fox-Genovese graduated cum laude from Bryn Mawr College, with her A.B. degree in history and French literature.

Fox-Genovese continued her education at Harvard University, in Cambridge, Massachusetts, receiving a master's degree in history, in 1966. That same year, she joined the faculty of Harvard as a teaching fellow. In 1967 she met Eugene Genovese, a history professor and a well-known Marxist. "My family wasn't too enthusiastic, as Gene was 11 years older, came from a working-class family in Brooklyn, [and] had been married and divorced twice," she recalled to Grenier. "I knew—absolutely knew—he was the man I wanted. It wasn't romantic; it was a sense that this was someone I could trust utterly. And that's the way it's been ever since." In June 1968 the couple married.

In 1969 Fox-Genovese moved to upstate New York when her husband was appointed chairman of the history department at the University of Rochester. "For academic couples at that time, the husbands were the professors and the wives were hired, at a pittance, to teach part time, even though they were sometimes the better-known scholar," she told Ron Grossman for the *Chicago Tribune* (November 24, 1993). After playing "the role of the chairman's wife" for two years, as Fox-Genovese told Grenier, she was encouraged by her husband to continue her studies. She returned to Harvard University, receiving a doctorate in 1974. "[Gene] financed my research, advised and counseled me through the writing of my dissertation," she told Grenier. "He supported me utterly, unselfishly, throughout."

In 1973 Fox-Genovese began teaching history and liberal arts at the University of Rochester as an assistant professor. Three years later she was promoted to associate professor. In 1977 she and her husband founded the scholarly journal *Marxist Perspectives*. In 1980 she joined the faculty of the State University of New York, at Binghamton, as a professor of history. In 1986 Fox-Genovese accepted an offer to establish a women's studies department at Emory University, in Atlanta, Georgia. "Women's studies can unearth a good deal of information about women that would not emerge from a general course," she explained to Maggie Riechers for *Humanities* (January/February 2004). "My goal was to develop a program that was intellectually rigorous and ideologically open." In 1988 Fox-Genovese was named the Eleonore Raoul Professor of the Humanities at Emory University. She served as the director of the women's studies department at Emory until she resigned— reportedly under pressure from university officials—in 1991.

The problems that led to her resignation became public in 1993, when Virginia Meacham Gould, the associate director of the women's studies department under Fox-Genovese and a former student of hers as well, filed a sexual discrimination suit against Fox-Genovese and Emory University. In her suit Gould alleged that Fox-Genovese had made demands of her and policed her activities to a degree that she would not have done had Gould been a man; Emory was named in the suit on the grounds that it had allegedly allowed Fox-Genovese's behavior to go unchecked, despite a persistent pattern of complaints. Fox-Genovese vehemently denied the charges and a small rally in support of her was staged a few days after Gould's claims were made public. In March 1996, having already exhausted both private and court-ordered mediators' attempts to resolve the dispute and with a jury already impaneled and television crews gathered to film what was expected to be a six-week-long affair, the case was settled out of court for an undisclosed sum. (Interest in the case was revived in 2005, when the historian Jon Wiener included a chapter on Fox-Genovese in his book *Historians in Trouble*, which detailed a dozen scandals to strike the history profession in recent years.)

Fox-Genovese's first book, *The Origins of Physiocracy: Economic Revolution and Social Order in Eighteenth-Century France* (1976), grew out of her dissertation at Harvard, "The Forging of a Bourgeois Ideology: A Study in the Origins of Physiocracy." (The physiocrats were a group of French Enlightenment thinkers in the 18th century who advocated an economic system that called for the strengthening of agriculture, which would lead to an increase in the overall wealth of a society, through *laissez-faire* methods. The leading thinker of the group was François Quesnay, a physician at the court of King Louis XV.) In the book Fox-Genovese argues that the physiocrats' economic theories played a key role in the development of capitalism in France. The book impressed most reviewers. "Economic, intellectual, and political historians will find much of interest in Fox-Genovese's clear exposition of the origins and development of physiocracy," a critic for *Choice* (December 1976) asserted. "Her carefully documented work chooses to emphasize only Quesnay and the Marquis de Mirabeau, but it opens up new areas by probing the revolutionary implications of the movement, and by exposing its interconnections with the broader philosophical trends of the Enlightenment." Reviewing the book for *Library Journal* (August 1976), Jacques Fomerand called it well written, well researched, and an "outstanding work of intellectual history."

In 1983 Fox-Genovese and her husband published the essay collection *Fruits of Merchant Capital: Slavery and Bourgeois Property in the Rise and Expansion of Capitalism*. "The authors focus on economic and legal aspects of slavery in the United States (the expertise of Genovese) and 18th-century French history (the expertise of Fox-Genovese) but are not entirely successful in making the connections between the two apparent," William J. Hausman observed for *Library Journal* (November 15, 1982). "Taking a frankly polemical (but never shrill) Marxist viewpoint, the essays are interpretative, innovative, and critical, but provide little new information." For the *Journal of American History* (March 1984), Peter Kolchin lauded *Fruits of Merchant Capital*. "This is an exciting book, staggering in breadth and erudition," Kolchin asserted. "The authors seem equally at ease discussing a huge range of topics, from slavery to physiocracy, from the French Revolution to the women's question, from law and psychology to 'new' social history. It is brilliant, witty, difficult, polemical, cantankerous, and important."

In her next book, *Within the Plantation Household: Black and White Women of the Old South* (1988), Fox-Genovese discusses the relationship between white women and black female slaves in the pre–Civil War South. "Fox-Genovese finds little evidence of 'sisterhood' across the deep chasm of race and class and rejects the notion that many planters' wives and daughters were secret abolitionists because they saw an analogy between the oppression of blacks and the oppression of women," George M. Fredrickson remarked for the *Times Literary Supplement* (May 5, 1989). "Somehow, the black women themselves recede behind the shifting grid of class, race and gender that Fox-Genovese creates to interpret them," Christine Stansell observed for the *Nation* (March 27, 1989). "In contrast, readers come to know the [white] mistressess well. Fox-Genovese has a psychological grasp on the ladies from the start; the abstractions class/race/gender illuminate but never subordinate her white historical subjects." The book was honored with the C. Hugh Holman Prize of the Society for the Study of Southern Literature and the Julia Cherry Spruill Prize of the Southern Association of Women Historians; it was also named outstanding book of the year by the Augustus Meyer Foundation for the Study of Human Rights.

Fox-Genovese sparked controversy among many of her feminist colleagues with her book *Feminism without Illusions: A Critique of Individualism*, which argues that contemporary feminism's emphasis on individual rights in seeking the equality of women neglected women who still experience discrimination based on their class or race, instead of only their gender. As a remedy Fox-Genovese proposes that feminist theory should be reconstructed in communitarian terms, which would take race and class factors into account in formulating a wider critique of society and its treatment of women. Fox-Genovese illustrates her thesis with chapters on such issues as abortion, affirmative action, pornography, and the impact of feminism on academic curricula. *Feminism without Illusions* divided critics. "Fox-Genovese writes convincingly that the triumph of individualism as a political philosophy has, in fact, subverted its intent, and that all of us, no matter what our political preferences, are in danger of being overtaken by a radical individualism that makes collective identity or action as a people impossible," Rosemary L. Bray wrote for the *New York Times Book Review* (May 5, 1991). "There are few chapters of *Feminism Without Illusions* that will not disturb someone, but that is the inevitable effect of a book this ambitious. Elizabeth Fox-Genovese has been fearless in her attempts to mitigate the competing claims of women and men as hungry for acknowledgment as they are for a national identity. It will be tough work to gain both, but Ms. Fox-Genovese has given us an intriguing place to begin." Writing for the *Washington Post* (April 21, 1991), Phyllis Palmer faulted the book. "Fox-Genovese's nuanced analysis is marred by two defects," Palmer observed. "Despite her criticism that feminists have pursued personal gratification at the expense of community-building, Fox-Genovese concludes her treatise as one more 'women can have it all'

book. . . . Moreover, though Fox-Genovese has made some attempt to integrate what is essentially a set of articles and [aperçus], the book is often repetitious and offers no coherent answers to the hard and valuable questions it poses."

In *Feminism Is Not the Story of My Life: How Today's Feminist Elite Has Lost Touch with the Real Concerns of Women*, Fox-Genovese contends that most women no longer identify with feminism and that the cause of this alienation is the hostility toward childbearing and the family that is felt, Fox-Genovese claims, by many of the movement's most prominent leaders. She also argues that the movement has championed affluent, single, career-oriented women while neglecting the needs of the majority of women, who, while seeking gender equality, also seek to fulfill themselves as mothers and wives. To support these claims the author cites informal conversations and interviews with women of various backgrounds, including African-Americans, Latinas, Southerners, college students, career women, single mothers, and blue-collar workers. To ease the burden on working mothers, Fox-Genovese called for such changes in public policy as the revision of tax laws, federally guaranteed maternity leave, and the creation of more part-time jobs with benefits. In a review for the *Christian Science Monitor* (January 25, 1996), Marilyn Gardner dismissed the book's arguments and methodology. "Some of the charges Fox-Genovese levels against feminism have an oddly dated quality," Gardner opined. "They give the impression that she is shadow-boxing, punching away at stereotypes left over from the 1960s and '70s. Among them: 'Feminists have not had much patience with femininity . . .'; 'Feminists tend to disapprove of love stories . . .'; 'Most feminists minimize the importance of marriage.' So sweeping and vague are the charges that readers may wonder: Just who are these nameless, faceless feminists, anyway?" The reviewer added that Fox-Genovese "writes more like a sociologist than an academic. That serves her readers well by making her prose accessible and engaging. But it becomes a liability in the anecdotal evidence she offers to support her thesis. Real-life women appear briefly and pseudonymously, floating in and out so quickly that most remain as faceless as those unidentified feminists." In *Commonweal* (March 22, 1996), Margaret O'Brien Steinfels found that Fox-Genovese's "research does not carry the weight of representative samples and in-depth interviews," but added, "It has something better— the ring of reality. . . . This is a book that will please neither feminists nor proponents of 'family values.' But it is a brave book that raises all the right questions."

In 1998 Fox-Genovese and her husband joined other scholars in forming the Historical Society, an organization whose members contend that the issues of race, class, and gender have overwhelmed the study of history, and that diplomatic, intellectual, political, and economic questions, along with an emphasis on objective truth, should be returned to the foreground. Fox-Genovese serves as the editor of the *Journal of the Historical Society*. In 1999 she and Elisabeth Lasch-Quinn co-edited the book *Reconstructing History: The Emergence of a New Historical Society*, a collection of essays written by scholars affiliated with the organization. In 2000 a lecture that Fox-Genovese delivered at the Center for Public Justice, in Annapolis, Maryland, was published that same year in the book *Women and the Future of the Family*, which includes responses from such scholars as Stanley J. Grenz, Mardi Keyes, and Mary Stewart Van Leeuwen.

In 2005 Fox-Genovese and her husband published *The Mind of the Master Class: History and Faith in the Southern Slaveholders' Worldview*. In an extensively footnoted text running to more than 800 pages and integrating previously published articles and book chapters, the authors analyze the writings of antebellum intellectuals in the South and suggest how their ideas reflected and shaped the attitudes of the society around them. "The book retains the scholarly texture and intensity of the journal articles that largely compose it," George McKenna wrote for *First Things* (March 2006). "As such, it is sometimes fatiguingly over-documented, piling up example after example; some of those examples would have been better consigned to endnotes. But chief among the book's many virtues is the authors' sympathetic but not uncritical ear to the dominant voices of the South as it drifted toward catastrophe." In a review for the *Atlantic Monthly* (October 2005), Benjamin Schwarz called *The Mind of the Master Class* "brilliant but at times exasperating, always tough-minded, often mischievous, and occasionally disappointing" but, like McKenna, felt that the importance of the text outweighed its flaws: "Among its many contributions it provides significant and powerful support to the now academically unfashionable argument that the antebellum North and South were separate cultures with divergent political, economic, moral, and religious values; a work of searching historical anthropology, it reveals a profoundly alien society and culture. The Genoveses have accomplished the most difficult and intellectually imaginative feat of the historian: they have allowed us to understand the past on its own terms."

In 2003 Fox was appointed to the prestigious National Council on the Humanities, which oversees the federal government's National Endowment for the Humanities. In November of that year Fox-Genovese was given the National Humanities Medal by President George W. Bush.

Elizabeth Fox-Genovese converted to Roman Catholicism in 1995, while the sexual discrimination suit against her was still moving forward. The following year Eugene Genovese also returned to the Church. They were later remarried by a Catholic priest.

On January 2, 2007, Fox-Genovese died of complications from surgery; she had reportedly been suffering from a long illness.

—D.C.

Suggested Reading: *Atlantic Monthly* p111 Oct. 2005; *Chicago Tribune* V p1+ Nov. 24, 1993; *Choice* p1,334 Dec. 1976; *Christian Science Monitor* B p4 Jan. 25, 1996; *Commonweal* p24 Mar. 22, 1996; *First Things* p55+ Mar. 2006; *Humanities* p15+ Jan./Feb. 2004; *Journal of American History* p863 Mar. 1984; *Library Journal* p1,631 Aug. 1976, p2,172 Nov. 15, 1982; *New York Times Book Review* p12 May 5, 1991; *Times Literary Supplement* p477 May 5, 1989; *Washington Post Book World* p4 Apr. 21, 1991; *Washington Times* C p11 Jan. 31, 1995

Selected Books: *The Origins of Physiocracy: Economic Revolution and Social Order in Eighteenth-Century France*, 1976; *Within the Plantation Household: Black and White Women of the Old South*, 1988; *Feminism without Illusions: A Critique of Individualism*, 1991; *Feminism Is Not the Story of My Life: How Today's Feminist Elite Has Lost Touch with the Real Concerns of Women*, 1996; with Eugene D. Genovese—*Fruits of Merchant Capital: Slavery and Bourgeois Property in the Rise and Expansion of Capitalism*, 1983; *The Mind of the Master Class: History and Faith in the Southern Slaveholders' Worldview*, 2005

Frank, Thomas

1965– Writer; essayist; cultural critic; publisher

The author and cultural critic Thomas Frank is often compared to his hero, the essayist H. L. Mencken. Though both Frank and Mencken's works are characterized by stinging political analysis and a satirical approach, their politics are often widely divergent. "Frank is a radical leftist, but not of the French Theory strain," Gerald Marzorati wrote in the *New York Times* (November 30, 1997). "Both his thinking and his prose hark back to a time when the radical left was something more in America than conferences and seminars attended by Foucault-steeped professors. Frank has thrown off the mandarin jargon; for him it's about wealth and power, haves and have-nots, loud and simple. . . . He's just about the last thing you'd expect to come along in these relatively sanguine times (or then, maybe not): a lonely, seething avatar of a new New Left."

Raised in one of the wealthiest and most staunchly conservative neighborhoods in Kansas, as a youth Frank admired President Ronald Reagan and was a Republican until his freshman year at college. As he became more aware of the benefits

Photo by Wendy Edelberg

Thomas Frank

that are doled out to the privileged elite—and the fact that he was not one of them—his politics took a hard turn to the left. He founded *The Baffler*, a magazine that skewered both postmodern academia and American business culture. He went on to publish two highly contentious polemics, *One Market Under God: Extreme Capitalism, Market Populism, and the End of Economic Democracy* (2000) and *What's the Matter With Kansas?: How Conservatives Won the Heart of America* (2004)—both of which reflected his concern for the ever-widening gap between the poorest and wealthiest Americans. Though left-leaning, Frank does not refrain from criticizing Democrats as well as Republicans; his politics are better described as contrarian. In *LA Weekly* (November 24, 2000), Brendan Bernhard wrote, "One can quibble with Frank's vision of the world, as people often do, for its sometimes overly black-and-white view of things. . . . But no one else has examined our country's corporate mind-set with such indefatigable zeal and wit in order to show us how the people who drive our economy actually think."

Frank was born in 1965 and raised in Mission Hills, an affluent suburb of Kansas City, Missouri, located just across the state line in Kansas. Frank describes the neighborhood, in his book *What's the Matter With Kansas?*, as a "solid redoubt of conservativism" populated by corporate executives, lawyers, and doctors. As an adolescent and Reagan supporter, his right-wing politics were solidified when he saw *Free to Choose*, a documentary featuring the Nobel Prize–winning economist Milton Friedman, on PBS. "A lot of people became conservative watching that show,"

Frank told Fred McKissack for the *Wisconsin State Journal* (October 3, 2003). "And as an ideology, it fit together really well. But it did the classic thing that ideologies are supposed to do: it justified your position in life. My family was not really well-to-do, but we had a nice perch in life." Frank's father was an engineer, and his family lived in a modest home nestled among the more palatial houses of Mission Hills. "Growing up in the Edenic preserves the local elite had fashioned for themselves had anesthetized me to the system that made them an elite in the first place," Frank wrote in *What's the Matter With Kansas?* "I honestly thought that Mission Hills, with its castellated palazzi, was normal and that other places were the aberration. I played with the tots of millionaires and convinced myself that America was a classless society, where all that mattered was ability and one's willingness to work."

This illusion of a classless society began to fracture in the summer 1983, after Frank graduated from Shawnee Mission East High School in Prairie Village, Kansas; while his better-connected friends were offered jobs at law firms and banks, he worked monotonous temporary jobs in various offices around Kansas City. "To make matters worse, I did not win a spot at some highly selective eastern college, as many of the other kids from Mission Hills did," Frank wrote in *What's the Matter With Kansas?*. "I did not understand what had caused me to be sifted one way and them the other; I just took myself dutifully off to KU [the University of Kansas], which had open admissions for all." There his frustrations with the class system were reinforced; his friends who had been accepted into the more exclusive fraternities on campus stopped talking to him, and he became disgusted with the College Republicans after attending only a few of their meetings. "The leadership had all been chosen, it seemed, by some mysterious process to which the rank and file was not privy," Frank wrote in *What's the Matter With Kansas?* "Maybe I just missed the election; I don't remember. At any rate, the leaders all knew one another, they were all such great friends, and they made no effort to disguise their oozing insincerity." He recognized that these young Republicans were angling for positions in "Kansas's Republican machine" and saw them as utterly lacking in idealism. Frank acknowledges in *What's the Matter With Kansas?*, "These complaints are of course small beer by the usual standards of oppression and unfairness. . . . But these developments were nonetheless sufficient to awaken me to the existence of class, of the elite. Also to the startling fact that I was not part of it. . . . So I did a very un-Kansan thing: I started voting Democratic. And then I did something that, I have since found, was utterly typical of my generation of college-educated Kansans: I left."

After his freshman year at the University of Kansas, Frank transferred to the University of Virginia, in Charlottesville. He graduated with his bachelor's degree in 1987, and the following year he founded *The Baffler*, a magazine of cultural criticism, with some of his college friends. A writer for *The Baffler* (on-line) described the magazine's genesis: "Thanks to the forces of academic professionalization, it seemed to us, cultural criticism had become specialized and intentionally obscure. The authority of high culture may have collapsed, but the high-culture critics had no intention of allowing their authority to collapse with it. Instead they abandoned the mundane project of enlightenment and aimed for bafflement, for a style that made much of its own radicalism but had astonishingly little to say about the conditions of life in late twentieth-century America. We set out to puncture their pretensions and to beat them at their own game."

Later that year Frank moved to the South Side of Chicago, Illinois, to attend graduate school at the University of Chicago, and *The Baffler* went with him. Frank served as editor and contributed essays to the magazine, which continued to take a literary approach to cultural criticism. "The precedent for that was things like the *American Mercury*, H. L. Mencken stuff," Frank told Brendan Bernhard. "For several issues the magazine focused on the role of hip in our culture, the commodification of dissent, and the way the imagery and language of dissent had become part of the official culture. . . . When you say I don't think the counterculture was very revolutionary at all, people think that's a curious statement. So for a while that was definitely the guiding theme, and that sort of mutated into being a more general criticism of business culture." Reviewers praised the publication for its wit, but *The Baffler* did not catch the national media's attention until 1993, when it exposed a hoax perpetrated in a *New York Times* article about youth culture. The article, "Grunge: A Success Story," was accompanied by a glossary of grunge slang, which *The Baffler* revealed to be completely fabricated by one of the article's sources.

Frank completed his Ph.D. in history in 1994, and the University of Chicago Press published an expanded version of his doctoral thesis, *The Conquest of Cool: Business Culture, Counterculture, and the Rise of Hip Consumerism*, in 1997. It was only the second dissertation that the press had agreed to publish in 20 years. "For a renovated dissertation, *The Conquest of Cool* is blessedly free of academic throat-clearing and professional jargon," Alan Wolfe wrote in *Slate* (December 10, 1997, on-line). "There isn't a dull page in the book."

The Conquest of Cool examines the close ties between the counterculture that emerged in the 1960s and business culture, particularly advertising. "Regardless of the tastes of Republican leaders, rebel youth culture remains the cultural mode of the corporate moment, used to promote not only specific products but the general idea of life in the cyber-revolution," Frank wrote in the introduction to the book. "Commercial fantasies of rebellion, liberation, and outright 'revolution' against the stultifying demands of mass society are commonplace almost to the point of invisibility in advertising, movies, and television programming."

While examining how advertisers co-opted the counterculture, Frank also challenges the notion of the counterculture as wholly authentic and business culture as wholly conformist. Long before the counterculture emerged, he argues, admen were looking to jettison the restrictive conformity and hierarchy of the old business model. "The story of the counterculture—and of insurgent youth culture generally—now resides somewhere near the center of our national self-understanding, both as the focus of endless new generations of collective youth-liberation fantasies and as the sort of cultural treason imagined by various reactionaries," Frank wrote in *The Conquest of Cool*. "And even though countercultural sympathizers are willing to recognize that co-optation is an essential aspect of youth culture, they remain reluctant to systematically evaluate business thinking on the subject, to ask how this most anticommercial youth movement of them all became the symbol for the accelerated capitalism of the sixties and the nineties, or to hold the beloved counterculture to the harsh light of historical and economic scrutiny."

In her review of the book for the *New York Times* (December 5, 1997), Michiko Kakutani wrote that Frank makes a compelling case that "the ad industry recognized the roots of the Me Generation's consumerism in the counterculture's insistence on self-expression," but Kakutani argued that "he tends to mistake defiant gestures on the part of admen, like wearing flamboyant clothes or making ironic ads, for real rebellion." She continues: "When Mr. Frank turns from theorizing—which he does clumsily, repeating the same points over and over—to simple reporting, the results are considerably better. He provides the reader with a succinct if somewhat familiar account of Doyle Dane Bernbach's innovative campaign for Volkswagen and the explosive effect that its introduction of irreverence and skepticism had on the heretofore staid world of Madison Avenue in the early 60's. He also provides the reader with a wide-ranging, and often hilarious, overview of ads that attempted to adopt the language, pose or style of the youth and counterculture movements."

Also in 1997 Frank edited, along with Matt Weiland, a compilation of essays from *The Baffler* titled *Commodify Your Dissent: Salvos from the Baffler*. In the introduction Frank suggests that business culture and counterculture are the same. The youth have become so convinced that they can express rebellion by purchasing certain products, he claims, that they take no real action against the "Culture Trust"—the companies in the telecommunication and entertainment industry that control the public discourse. "Denunciation is becoming impossible," Frank wrote in his essay "Closing Slavo: The Dark Age." "We will be able to achieve no distance from business culture since we will no longer have a life, a history, a consciousness apart from it. . . . It is putting itself beyond our power of imagining because it has become our imagination, it has *become* our power to envision, and describe, and theorize, and resist."

In her review of *Commodify Your Dissent* for the *Los Angeles Times* (November 30, 1997), Deborah Goldman wrote, "As would be expected, the collection features a lot of howling at target-marketed youth culture deviance, designed to exhaust itself in the purchase of the right beer or jeans or CD. And the boomers, of course, get theirs. . . . Frank himself, whose name appears on six pieces in the collection, is, as his own book would suggest, fairly obsessed with his fate as prisoner of boomer history. But obsession often makes for good prose. In these essays, Frank pours outrage and disgust with a rhetorical inventiveness at which the scholarly sobriety of *The Conquest of Cool* only hints."

Frank's next book, *One Market Under God* (2000), was an all-out assault on what Frank terms "market populism"—the notion that the market is a democratic entity whereby people vote with their dollars, and that this form of democracy is more accurate and in tune with the needs of the people than the democratically elected government. In Frank's view, America is an economic oligarchy, where the gap between the rich and poor continues to widen and consumers are enslaved under the guise of market choice. The majority of American workers saw their wages fall or barely keep pace with inflation in the nineties, he noted; CEO compensation, however, rose from 85 times the average wage of a blue-collar worker in 1990 to 475 times the average blue-collar wage in 1999. Frank also argued that the much touted "new economy"—the idea that the new technologies fueling unprecedented market growth in the nineties would make the economy impervious to business cycles and inflation—was not so new; it was essentially what wealthy elites had wanted all along: free trade, cheap labor, and deregulation. "In a sweeping, savage and witty indictment of American business, Mr. Frank, 35, slams the notion that the 1990's lived up to the promise of the new economy," John Schwartz wrote in the *New York Times* (December 21, 2000).

When *One Market Under God* was published, *The Baffler* ran a full-page ad with the heading "Great Minds of the New Economy Deplore Cynical Account of Bountiful New Era," under which were quoted only negative reviews. While Frank's book was applauded by some critics, he certainly had his share of vociferous detractors, in both the moderate and right-wing presses. Steven Pearlstein wrote in the *Washington Post* (November 2, 2000), "Frank's *One Market Under God* is but another in a series of superficial, ill-informed, poorly thought-out screeds on the

shortcomings of modern capitalism." Frank gives readers, he said, "a long and self-indulgent sneer from a writer who seems more intent on rallying his band of true believers than on marshaling facts and analysis that might enlighten a wider audience." Jacob Heilbrunn, writing in the *National Review* (November 6, 2000), describes Frank as "hip and cool and authentic—a culture critic who mixes academic theories with smartass prose," but he goes on to say, "Unfortunately, Frank's punches fly so furiously that he ends up completely missing his target. He ignores fundamental truths about today's economy—like, umm, the fact that it's been good for just about everybody."

In late 2000, shortly after the publication of *One Market Under God*, the stock-market bubble burst. Many dot-com companies had been greatly overvalued, and stock prices plummeted, putting companies out of business. These events prompted Adam Bresnik, writing for the *Los Angles Times* (January 14, 2001), to observe, "Given the stock market free-fall of 2000, Frank's book could not have arrived at a more apposite time, and his piercing skepticism about the inflated and myopic claims of the market analysts appears very prescient indeed." Frank was not pleased to be proven correct, as he and many people he knew lost money in the failing market. The fact that Frank had invested in the market came as a surprise to some; but as he has often explained, he is not against capitalism per se, just what he terms "extreme capitalism."

In 2002 Prickly Paradigm Press published a series of pamphlets on wide-ranging political topics, among them Frank's *New Consensus for Old: Cultural Studies from Left to Right*. As he again takes aim at postmodern academia, Frank analyzes the cultural studies movement in this 53-page pamphlet. "By the 1990's, Mr. Frank contends, facile 'cult stud' arguments about the 'subversive potential' of a television sitcom or the 'counter-hegemonic' impact of shopping malls had come to look uncomfortably like the market populism promoted by the pro-business right: both groups appear to equate consumerism with democratic self-expression," Emily Eakin wrote in the *New York Times* (August 10, 2002).

Frank and a co-editor, David Mulcahey, released *Boob Jubilee: The Mad Cultural Politics of the New Economy: Salvos from the Baffler* in 2003. The previously published essays in this collection focus on debunking myths about the new economy, and the volume features an introduction by the essayist Studs Terkel. A reporter for *Kirkus Reviews* (June 15, 2003) wrote, "The Chicago-based *Baffler* brought, and brings, skepticism, dissent, and critical intelligence. There's not a rotten apple in these 32 articles, but all have range, depth, and purpose. . . . Fine muckery, with fingers pointed and blame apportioned. Like being lifted up high, where the air is clear."

Frank drew the title of his latest book, *What's the Matter With Kansas?*, from an 1896 essay written by the renowned Kansan and Pulitzer-prize winning journalist William Allen White. White's essay was a discourse against Populism, the radical, leftist movement that swept Republicans out of almost every minor and major public office in 1890. Frank's book turned the meaning of White's question on its head: He wonders how a state that had once ignited "the first of the great American Leftist movements" had become so steadfastly Republican. Frank examines how free-market capitalism has hurt various communities throughout the state and argues that culture wars—debates about values (i.e., abortion, gay marriage, etc.)—have been used by Republicans to distract Kansans from the damage that right-wing economic policies have inflicted on farmers and blue-collar workers.

The release of *What's the Matter With Kansas?* was well timed. On the *New York Times* best-seller list for nine weeks, it came out a month before the Democratic National Convention during a highly contentious election year, and the book became a talking point with many pundits. Frank made the rounds on the political talk-show circuit, appearing on PBS, NPR, and even the conservative icon Bill O'Reilly's show, *The O'Reilly Factor*, among others. In his review for the *Chicago Tribune* (June 27, 2004), Jefferson Cowie accurately predicted that Frank's book would serve as "a revelation to many and a source of outrage for others"; it was received warmly by reviewers from the left and denounced in the right-wing press. George Scialabba, writing for the leftist periodical the *Nation* (June 14, 2004), praised Frank's book as "one of the best so far this decade on American politics." George Will, a staunch conservative, assailed the book in his nationally syndicated column, which ran in the *Washington Post* (July 8, 2004) and numerous other newspapers. "If you believe, as Frank does, that opposing abortion is inexplicably silly," Will wrote, "and if you make no more attempt than Frank does to empathize with people who care deeply about it, then of course you, like Frank will consider scores of millions of your fellow citizens lunatics." Josh Chafetz, in his review for the *New York Times* (June 13, 2004), accused Frank of characterizing his fellow Kansans as knaves and fools. "Frank's book is remarkable as an anthropological artifact," Chaftez wrote. "Although not terribly successful at explaining the cultural divide, it manages to exemplify it perfectly in its condescension toward people who don't vote as Frank thinks they should."

Andrew O'Hehir responded to such criticism in an article for *Salon* (June 28, 2004, on-line): "Frank's freewheeling examination of how and why the left-wing economic populism of the 1890s was transformed into the right-wing cultural populism of today is hilarious, angry and often riveting. It ranges from history to sociology to memoir to old-fashioned street journalism, and despite what you may have read in a thoroughly disgraceful *New York Times* review, Frank does not mock his fellow Kansans for their political beliefs. If anything, he is awed and amazed by the right-wing activists he meets on his visits home, highly principled and selfless people who have sacrificed much to fight for causes and policies that (he believes) will prove immensely destructive to their own way of life."

Frank noted that when his book came out there were dozens of books written by liberals denouncing conservatives, and vice versa, but he felt that his book stood apart because he had made a genuine effort to understand the people he wrote about. He traveled across Kansas, talking to people along the way, hanging out in their towns, visiting their churches, and reading their periodicals. "Instead of really lambasting these people, who I obviously disagree with, I'm, you know, attracted to them. I think that's really obvious," he told O'Hehir. "People with pretty extreme-right politics—they're fighting to close abortion clinics, to ban the teaching of evolution or, you know, basically shut down the school system. And they're remarkable people. They renounce prosperity and personal gain in favor of their idea of righteousness. They choose principle over their own personal interest." Frank also told O'Hehir that while the local papers in Kansas were "hopping mad" about the book, he had been welcomed warmly at public readings in the state and had received numerous e-mails from Kansans who said that he had told their life story.

In the closing chapter of *What's the Matter With Kansas?*, Frank offended many potential allies in the Democratic party by accusing Democrats of spending too much time pursuing white-collar voters and corporate contributions, thereby giving too much headway to Republicans on economic issues. Republicans were then free to pursue blue-collar voters on the basis of cultural issues. "Mr. Frank's willingness to scold his own side; his irreverence and his facility with language; his ability to make the connections that other writers fail to make—all of this puts *What's the Matter with Kansas?* in a different league from most political books that have come out in recent years," Kevin Canfield wrote in the *New York Observer* (June 14, 2004).

Frank also writes for numerous periodicals; his essays and articles have appeared in the *Village Voice*, the *Chicago Reader, Artforum*, the London *Guardian*, the *Financial Times*, and the French weekly *Le Monde Diplomatique*, among others. He is a contributing editor to *Harper's*. In 2004 Frank was selected for a fellowship from the Lannan Foundation, an organization dedicated to cultural freedom, diversity, and creativity. In 1997 *Newsweek* named Frank one of the "100 people to watch as America prepares to pass through the gate to the next millennium." He is also a recipient of the Eugene V. Debs Award.

Frank recently moved from Chicago to Tenleytown, a neighborhood in Washington, D.C. His wife is an economist, and together they have two young children.

—J.C.

Suggested Reading: *Chicago Tribune* p1 Apr. 13, 2002; *LA Weekly* p37 Nov. 24, 2000; *New York Times* C p1 Dec. 21, 2001; *Salon* (on-line) June 28, 2004; *Washington Post* C p1+ Oct. 29, 2004

Selected Books: *The Conquest of Cool*, 1997; *One Market Under God: Extreme Capitalism, Market Populism, and the End of Economic Democracy*, 2000; *What's the Matter With Kansas?: How Conservatives Won the Heart of America*, 2004

Courtesy of Princeton University Press

Frankfurt, Harry G.

May 29, 1929– Philosopher

"I got interested in philosophy because of two things," Harry G. Frankfurt, a moral philosopher and the author of five books on the topic, told Peter Edidin in an interview for the *New York Times* (February 14, 2005). "One is that I was never satisfied with the answers that were given to questions, and it seemed to me that philosophy was an attempt to get down to the bottom of things. The other thing was that I could never make up my mind what I was interested in, and philosophy enabled you to be interested in anything." As a result of these two factors, Frankfurt became the author of what Edidin described as "a small and scrupulous body of work that tries to make sense

of free will, desire and love," establishing over the years a reputation as a writer with a clear, layman-accessible prose style, who illustrates his points with examples that readers will readily recognize. Such examples have come to be called the "Frankfurt example" by philosophers. Fellow philosopher Sarah Buss explained to Edidin, "He's dealing with very abstract matters, but trying not to lose touch with the human condition. His work keeps faith with that condition."

Harry G. Frankfurt was born on May 29, 1929 in Langhorne, Pennsylvania, to Bertha (Gordon) Frankfurt and Nathan Frankfurt, a bookkeeper. He grew up mostly in the New York City borough of Brooklyn, New York, and was educated at Johns Hopkins University, in Baltimore, Maryland, where he majored in philosophy and received his B.A. in 1949, his M.A. in 1953, and his Ph.D. in 1954. After completing his graduate studies, he served for two years in the United States Army, and then returned to civilian life to pursue an academic career, teaching at Ohio State University, in Columbus, (1956–62); the State University of New York, at Binghamton (1962–63); Rockefeller University, in New York City, (1963–76); and Yale University, in New Haven, Connecticut, (1978–90). In 1990 he was appointed professor of philosophy at Princeton University, in New Jersey, and remained there until his retirement.

Frankfurt published his first book, *Demons, Dreamers, and Madmen: The Defense of Reason in Descartes's Meditations*, in 1970. Though René Descartes, a 17th-century mathematician and scientist, is regarded as the father of modern philosophy, his work has been heavily criticized by postmodern scholars. In his book, Frankfurt defends the validity of Descartes's arguments for the use of reason and clarity as criteria for belief and truth. Charles Parsons, writing in the *Journal of Philosophy* (January 27, 1972), called the author's presentation "thorough, clear, and philosophically interesting." He concluded that the "book is an important contribution to the discussion of skepticism, independently of whether [Frankfurt's] interpretation of Descartes is correct."

Over the next 18 years, Frankfurt published numerous essays in philosophical journals, and in 1988 he collected a selection of his pieces—those that had drawn the most attention in his field—into the book *The Importance of What We Care About: Philosophical Essays*. The 13 articles gathered here address such perennial philosophical concerns as the nature of free will, moral responsibility, how equality can be misjudged as a goal, and the nature of the self and its relation to the outside world. In the essay "The Importance of What We Care About," Frankfurt attempts to disprove the theory that we care about something because it is good or beautiful or valuable in some objective way, arguing instead that the investment we make in caring about something is really what gives the object its value.

Frankfurt's next collection of essays, *Necessity, Volition, and Love*, was published in 1999. All of the chapters were drawn from previously published articles, with the exception of "On Caring," the final piece in the book. "One concern with a collection such as this is that one will fail to be interested in all of the essays," James Stacey Taylor wrote for *Philosophical Quarterly* (January 2001). "Fortunately, in this case this concern is unfounded, for Frankfurt manages to intrigue with every issue that he addresses in this collection. . . . Although all of the papers in this collection are absorbing, the most important are undoubtedly those in which Frankfurt develops his influential views on what it is for one to identify with one's desires, and what it is for a person to be autonomous." Paul H. Benson, reviewing the volume for *Ethics* (October 2000), praised "the depth and integrity of Frankfurt's thought, as well as the sheer delight of his prose," but noted that many will "disagree sharply with Frankfurt's insistence that autonomy arises from volitional necessities that define the essential natures of persons."

In 2001, as part of the University of Kansas's Lindley Lecture Series, Frankfurt delivered the speech "Some Mysteries of Love," which was also published in pamphlet form. His 2004 book, *The Reasons of Love* (2004), was a revised version of another speech that he presented at a Romanell–Phi Beta Kappa lecture at Princeton University and a Shearman lecture at the University College London, in England. Reviewing the book for *Ethics* (October 2005), Gabriel Richardson Lear wrote, "Frankfurt addresses a question that is 'both ultimate and preliminary: how should a person live?' . . . The result is a book that is ambitious, plainspoken, funny, and often extraordinarily provocative. Anyone familiar with his earlier work will be interested to see how he brings together ideas about freedom, caring, selfhood, identification, and practical reasoning that he has developed and defended in greater detail elsewhere." *The Reasons of Love* won the 2004 Association of American Publishers's Professional and Scholarly Publishing Award for best book in philosophy.

Although well known among academic philosophers, Frankfurt became a cynosure to the general public after the publication of his best-selling book *On Bullshit*, in 2005. Originally written for a weekly, interdisciplinary seminar that he attended while teaching at Yale, the lengthy essay was first published in the fall 1986 issue of *Raritan*, a quarterly review published by Rutgers University, in New Jersey, and later reprinted in *The Importance of What We Care About*. The essay had staying power among the select readership of scholarly journals, and for years after its initial publication, xeroxed copies were passed around academic circles; a man from Wales even set the text to music. "In the 20 years since it was published," Frankfurt told Peter Edidin, "I don't think a year has passed in which I haven't gotten one or two letters or e-mails from people about it."

Still, the philosopher was surprised by the commercial success of the 67-page book version, which attempts to tease out the difference between lying, which is roundly condemned as a moral transgression, and bull——, which is tolerated even when recognized—as when it comes from the mouths of politicians. "One of the most salient features of our culture is that there is so much bull[——]," Frankfurt's book begins. "Everyone knows this. Each of us contributes his share. But we tend to take the situation for granted. Most people are rather confident of their ability to recognize bull[——] and to avoid being taken in by it. So the phenomenon has not aroused much deliberate concern, nor attached much sustained inquiry." Bull—— may not necessarily be false, Frankfurt concludes, but it is marked by a deliberate disregard for truth, which makes the practice far more insidious than the act of lying, because a liar at least acknowledges and is responding to the truth. "Frankfurt's account of bull[——] is doubly remarkable," Jim Holt wrote for the *New Yorker* (August 22, 2005). "Not only does he define it in a novel way that distinguishes it from lying; he also uses this definition to establish a powerful claim: 'Bull[——] is a greater enemy of truth than lies are.'" Holt worries, however, that the author's account is "a little too flattering to the liar," who, regardless of his motivations, strikes a momentary alliance with untruth, "to be abandoned the moment it ceases to serve [his] goal." Reviewing *On Bullshit* for *Books in Canada* (December 2005), Gordon Phinn praised it as a "calm, clear-headed deconstruction of everyday deceit [that] is without parallel," and the "perfect antidote to our culture's daily dose of garish scandal and scatterbrained ideology."

Frankfurt was married to Marilyn Rothman, with whom he had two daughters, Katherine and Jennifer. He lives in Princeton, New Jersey, with his second wife Joan Gilbert. He is described by Peter Edidin as "a courtly man, with a broad smile and a philosophic beard."

—S.Y.

Suggested Reading: *Ethics* p202 Oct. 2000; *Journal of Philosophy* p38 Jan. 27, 1972; *New York Times* E p1 Feb. 14, 2005; *Philosophical Quarterly* Jan. 2001

Selected Books: *Demons, Dreamers, and Madmen: The Defense of Reason in Descartes's Meditations*, 1970; *The Importance of What We Care About: Philosophical Essays*, 1988; *Necessity, Volition, and Love*, 1999; *The Reasons of Love*, 2004; *On Bullshit*, 2005; as editor— *Leibniz: A Collection of Critical Essays*, 1972

Freeman, Charles

1947– Nonfiction writer

Charles Freeman is an expert on the impact the ancient world has had on the modern one. His popular and sometimes lavishly illustrated histories distill complex situations and events into highly accessible prose. Frequently tapped by the editors of historical series and encyclopedias, Freeman has also written many well-regarded stand-alone volumes, including *The Greek Achievement: The Founding of the Western World* (1999), *The Closing of the Western Mind* (2002), and *The Horses of St. Marks* (2004).

Born in 1947, Freeman has been on archaeological digs in Europe, Asia, and Africa and has directed academic programs on Renaissance Italy. Freeman's book *The World of the Romans* (1993) was an entry in the Illustrated Encyclopedia of World History series, published by Oxford University Press. The volume's glossy paper and lavish color photographs moved it, as a reviewer for *Book News, Inc.* (on-line) noted, "into the category of lovely-book-on-nonfiction-topic-for-the-general-reader, a category which is not usually the domain of university press publishers." *Egypt, Greece, and Rome: Civilizations of the Ancient Mediterranean* (1996) was also heavily illustrated and targeted to the general reader. Writing for *Booklist* (December 15, 1996), Gilbert Taylor observed: "Covering an immense variety of material with competence and sensitivity to nuance, Freeman relates the familiar parts of the classical story, but his is no mere rehash of the Persian War or the fall of the Roman Republic. He analytically recounts political events, religious movements, and society, with steady awareness of the fragmented character of the surviving evidence. Still, Freeman hasn't forgotten that popularity presupposes pace, and his narrative moves steadily, intriguingly, and informatively." Christopher Kelly, in the *Times Literary Supplement* (March 14, 1997) wrote: "If nothing else, this is a triumph of tenacity; a skillful exercise in the compression of the past. . . . Freeman recognized that writing a survey volume is a matter of often difficult compromise. With some regret, he elected to elide unseemly scholarly wrangling and 'to impose an order and coherence on past societies which the evidence does not justify.' Both aims have been amply fulfilled. In welding together Egypt, Greece and Rome into one manageable whole, unity has been bought at the price of dull uniformity. . . . But whatever the overall result, no one can deny Freeman's enthusiasm and his concern that a survey volume, whatever its faults, should—like any properly run prep school—'provide the springboard into further study of these fascinating societies.'"

Freeman followed this work with an illustrated volume that focused specifically on the Egyptians, comparing and contrasting the Egypt of legend with the Egypt of history. *The Legacy of Ancient Egypt* (1997), a volume in the Facts on File Legacies of the Ancient World series, was a coffee-table book with more than 350 illustrations and timelines. A critic for the *Midwest Book Review* (on-line) called it "a completely new, stunningly illustrated presentation of the facts and legends behind one of the world's most fascinating civilizations of antiquity."

Freeman's next survey of the ancient world was *The Greek Achievement: The Foundation of the Western World* (1999). This book, unlike many earlier volumes, looked at Greek society not only as the glorious civilization that brought about great advances in the arts and sciences but as a brutal entity capable of savage warfare, misogyny, and slavery. As Jean Dubail wrote for the Cleveland *Plain Dealer* (December 12, 1999): "As Charles Freeman reminds us, our quite justified admiration of the Greek's virtues sometimes blinds us to their vices, including a pervasive misogyny, a casual contempt for non-Greek 'barbarians,' an indefensible reliance on slavery and a near-suicidal weakness for settling disputes through war. . . . Freeman is not, however, a mere debunker. His appreciation for Greek culture is genuine and deep, and he has an uncommon ability to make it understandable to a modern audience. Nor does his enthusiasm give out, as does that of many historians, when the subject turns from political and military history to art, science and philosophy." Bob Trimble, writing for the *Dallas Morning News* (December 5, 1999), expressed a similar appreciation: "Charles Freeman offers a new look at those people, with all their warts, to whom Western civilization owes the most. . . . Mr. Freeman has written much more than a compendium of Greek accomplishments; he offers a compelling overview of Greek history from the Bronze Age to the Byzantine Empire. Abstract mathematics, philosophy, drama, history, scientific inquiry, all are gifts from the Greeks. Despite such gifts, Mr. Freeman is firm in his belief that their flaws cannot be ignored."

The Closing of the Western Mind (2002) is a scholarly study of the impact of the Catholic Church on Western civilization. According to Freeman, the Church stifled intellectual reasoning and replaced it with unbending faith (in both the teachings of Jesus and those of the Church). The controversial book received widely varying reviews. In a critique for the *New York Times Book Review* (February 15, 2004), Anthony Gottlieb argued: "Each part of [the book's] argument is highly questionable, but Freeman tells an entertaining story, and on the way produces an excellent and readable account of the development of Christian doctrine. It is not easy to make an interesting or even comprehensible subject out of the angry controversies about the Trinity that preoccupied early Christians. But he manages it. . . . The book is particularly good on the development of the biblical canon: it is always a useful reminder, and not just for fundamentalists, to see how happenstance and politics determined the shape of what many now take as immutable holy writ. Freeman is judicious, too, on the origins of early Christian asceticism and abhorrence of sex. . . . Although the most important Christian thinkers, from St. Paul to Augustine, did everything they could to stifle the rationalist tradition they sought to displace, as Freeman effectively demonstrates, it is impossible to lay the aptly named Dark Ages entirely at their door. Just why the lights went out when they did remains something of a mystery." A reviewer for *Publishers Weekly* (August 4, 2003), on the other hand, was highly critical of the work: "Freeman repeats an oft-told tale of the rise of Christianity and the supposed demise of philosophy in a book that is fascinating, frustrating and flawed. He contends that as the Christian faith developed in the first four centuries it gradually triumphed over the reigning Hellenistic and Roman philosophies. . . . Yet Freeman . . . fails to show that faith became totally dominant over reason. First, he asserts that Paul of Tarsus, whom many think of as the founder of Christianity, condemned the Hellenistic philosophy of his time. Freeman is wrong about this, for the rhetorical style and the social context of Paul's letters show just how dependent he was on the philosophy around him. Second, Freeman glosses over the tremendous influence of Clement of Alexandria's open embrace of philosophy as a way of understanding the Christian faith. Third, the creeds that the church developed in the fourth century depended deeply on philosophical language and categories in an effort to make the faith understandable to its followers. Finally, Augustine's notions of original sin and the two cities depended directly on Plato's philosophy; Augustine even admits in the *Confessions* that Cicero was his model. While Freeman tells a good story, his arguments fail to be convincing."

In 2004 Freeman published *The Horses of St. Mark's*, a look at the famous statuary from St. Mark's Basilica, in Venice, and the societies in which they have been displayed. The four gilded horses were in Constantinople at its founding; in Venice, both at the height of its glory and its fall to Napoleon Bonaparte in 1797; and in Paris, as the spoils of war. Freeman examines the horses' artistic merits and symbolic value as witnesses to some of the most turbulent events in European history.

Freeman has written extensively for children, as well. *The Ancient Greeks* (1996) was part of a series of histories aimed at young audiences. (Other entries in this series include *The Romans* by John Haywood, *The Egyptians* by Neil Grant, and *Prehistoric Life* by Dougal Dixon.) The book serves as a primer on the subject for students between the ages of nine and 12. Freeman also wrote *The Rise of the Nazis* (1998), a children's book detailing Adolf Hitler's ascent to power and the Holocaust.

Crisis in Rwanda (1998), an overview for grade-school students, details the genocide that swept across the nation in the mid-1990s and the response of the international community in handling the crisis. In *Booklist* (December 15, 1998), reviewer Hazel Rochman wrote: "For all those shocked by the images of genocide in Rwanda and bewildered by the names and the politics, this is a stirring, nonexploitative, accessible account of what happened, written with clarity and fairness and a strong commitment to human rights. Part of the excellent *New Perspectives* series, the design is like a magazine article, with photos on every page and with boxed quotes from survivors, journalists, and aid workers who were there. They take us beyond snapshots of piled bodies and wandering orphans to stories of individual anguish."

Charles Freeman lives in Suffolk, England. In addition to writing he leads organized tours of Venice.

—C.M.

Suggested Reading: *Booklist* p706 Dec. 15, 1996, p741 Dec. 15, 1998; *Dallas Morning News* J p9 Dec. 5, 1999; *New York Times* (on-line) Feb. 15, 2004; *Publishers Weekly* p73 Aug. 4, 2003; *Student Library Journal* p116 Feb. 1999

Selected Books: *The World of the Romans*, 1993; *Egypt, Greece, and Rome: Civilizations of the Ancient Mediterranean*, 1996; *The Ancient Greeks*, 1996; *The Legacy of Ancient Egypt*, 1997; *The Rise of the Nazis*, 1998; *Crisis in Rwanda*, 1998; *The Greek Achievement: The Founding of the Western World*, 1999; *The Closing of the Western Mind*, 2002; *The Horses of St. Mark's*, 2004

French, Howard W.

Oct. 14, 1957– Journalist

Howard W. French has spent more than 20 years as a foreign correspondent in various parts of the world, but no other place has fascinated him more than Africa. French moved to the continent shortly after graduating from college and spent many years reporting on it for the *New York Times* and other periodicals. What he experienced there as the newspaper's West Africa bureau chief—the rampant diseases and poverty, the civil wars, the government corruption—made him want to write a book about the subject, to go beyond simply reporting on Africa's problems and instead write about what he saw as the root causes of modern Africa's woes. In 2004 he published *A Continent for the Taking: The Tragedy and Hope of Africa*, a memoir about his time in Africa, in which he takes to task both the corrupt dictatorships that plague

Stuart Isett/Courtesy of Random House

Howard W. French

the continent as well as the Western governments that have supported them. The book received widespread praise and was nominated for a Lettre Ulysses Award for the art of reportage in 2004.

Howard W. French, the son of David Marshall French and the former Carolyn Alverda Howard, was born on October 14, 1957 in Washington, D.C. His father, a prestigious surgeon, once served on a government fact-finding mission in southeast Asia at the request of Senator Edward M. Kennedy. The family relocated to a Boston suburb just before French entered junior high school, and later, when his father—who had been actively involved in the civil rights movement—shifted his practice from surgery to public health, with a focus on Africa, the family contemplated moving to Cameroon.

Around the time that French entered the University of Massachusetts, at Amherst, as an undergraduate, in 1975, his parents moved to Africa, specifically Abidjan, the capital city of Côte d'Ivoire (the Ivory Coast), where his father served as the project director of a 20-country health delivery system in central and West Africa for the the World Health Organization. Upon completing his bachelor's degree, in 1979, French followed his family to Abidjan, where he had spent his summer vacations during college. In an interview posted on the Random House Web site, French explained that as an African-American he had long felt a "fraternal identification with Africa, and especially a political sympathy for what were seen then as the continent's more 'progressive' governments, and especially for the anti-apartheid movement." Describing the excitement he felt before his first trip to the continent, he said: "I also remember the feeling of dismay and almost insult

when a liberal white friend of my father told me not to expect that if we moved to Africa, we would be treated like 'brothers.' In a very simplistic way his comment turned out to be true. Africans are generally not waiting at the shores to embrace black Americans seeking to 'return.' At the same time, I eventually learned, there tends to be a refreshing degree of relaxation about matters of race that contrasted dramatically with the America I knew at that time, and indeed even with the America of today."

After settling in Africa, French first worked as a French-English translator from 1979 to 1980. He then became an assistant professor of English, a position that he held until 1982, at a university in Abidjan. Though he was initially more interested in writing fiction than working as a journalist, French began working as a stringer for the *Washington Post,* while still teaching. He also wrote freelance articles for such prestigious periodicals as the *Economist* and the *Chronicle of Higher Education.*

In 1986 French returned to the U.S., after accepting an offer from the *New York Times* to serve as a metropolitan reporter in New York City. French covered a broad range of topics for the newspaper, including health care, law enforcement, and the federal courts. After four years on the metro desk, French longed for a foreign posting; the newspaper wanted him to return to Africa, but he was hesitant, fearing that his reportage from the continent would receive little play at the *Times.* "It was not that I thought poorly of Africa—but I knew that they did," he said, according to Shelley Neumeier, writing for the Overseas Press Club of America's Web site. In 1990 he moved to Miami, Florida, began covering the Caribbean, Central America, and northern South America for the newspaper. During his first year in that post, Haitian president Jean-Bertrand Aristide was overthrown, providing French with the opportunity to cover what quickly became one of the most important stories of the year. In 1994 he was once again offered a post in Africa, this time as the *Times*'s West Africa bureau chief. In 1997 he reported on the fall of Zaire's dictator, Mobutu Sese Seko, for which he earned a Pulitzer Prize nomination and the Bob Considine Award for the best newspaper or wire service interpretation of international affairs from the Overseas Press Club of America. In addition to working for the *Times,* French contributed articles on African affairs to a number of other periodicals, including the *Economist,* the *International Herald Tribune,* and the *Washington Post.*

French's experience as he traveled across the region made him want to go beyond mere reportage and write about the state of African affairs as he saw them. In his book, *A Continent for the Taking,* he not only addressed many of Africa's problems—including the AIDS epidemic, civil strife, and genocide—but also examined the historical and systemic roots of the continent's political disarray.

He criticized Europe for its previous colonial policies, which resulted in a hodgepodge of African states that had been created by arbitrarily drawn borders and contained citizenries divided along tribal lines; he also chided European nations for their unwillingness to adequately address postcolonial issues in Africa. French was no more forgiving to the U.S. government for its willingness to support African dictators who served American political or business interests, while showing little regard as to how these policies affected the local populace. French was especially reproachful of President Bill Clinton's administration for its refusal to confront the genocide in Rwanda, where, in 1994, political upheaval and ethnic tension led to the genocide of roughly 800,000 Tutsis and moderate Hutus. However, he also pointed out the positive aspects of modern Africa, citing former Malian president and current chairman of the Commission of the African Union, Alpha Oumar Konare, as a role model for African leaders.

A Continent for the Taking received mostly positive notices. "[French's] strength as a reporter is evident as he takes the reader across the continent, recounting in vivid detail the genocide in Rwanda and the AIDS and Ebola outbreaks," a reviewer wrote for *Publishers Weekly* (February 16, 2004). "His prose is evocative without being melodramatic in describing the suffering he saw. The 'powerful and eerily rhythmic' wailing of those who had lost loved ones to the Ebola virus 'was painful to hear, and clearly bespoke of the recent or imminent deaths of loved ones.' French is just as eloquent discussing his ambivalence about covering African crises after criticizing other journalists for their pack mentality in focusing on such crises rather than on giving a more rounded picture of life on the continent." In the *American Prospect* (July 2004), Daphne Eviatar praised the book for providing "the context necessary to understand Africa's current problems and the deeper reasons for the indifference—and complicity—of European governments and the United States."

For the *New York Times Book Review* (April 25, 2004), Jeremy Harding wrote, "*A Continent for the Taking* fingers many villains on the ground—among them [Charles] Taylor, Mobutu [Sese Seko] and Mobutu's successor, the rebel Laurent Kabila—but the real enemy for French, a native son of Washington, is the United States. Above all, he cannot forgive the Clinton administration, which he believes allowed the Rwandan Tutsi to take their revenge on the Hutu in the years that followed the 1994 genocide. This is an honest position, backed up by French's firsthand reports from eastern Zaire in 1996 and '97, when the tables had turned and the Rwandan Army, under a new Tutsi-led government installed with Washington's approval, pursued the fleeing Hutu into eastern Zaire, killing as they went." Though Joshua Hammer, writing for the *Washington Monthly* (April 2004), also found much to praise in the

book, he disagreed with other critics, arguing that French "is too willing to let Africans themselves off the hook." Hammer explained: "The ruinous depredations of Zimbabwe's Robert Mugabe, for example, the horrors perpetrated by Charles Taylor in Liberia and Foday Sankoh in Sierra Leone can't all be laid at the doorstep of European slave merchants and colonizers. Africa's ruinous civil wars and ethnic strife also reflect a total failure of the political class, of elites who view government office as an opportunity for personal gain, of rulers who owe their primary allegiance to clan or tribe."

In 1997, while reporting from the Congo, French contracted malaria, which precipitated his departure from the continent. "I began to conclude that Africa was starting to kill me," he wrote in *A Continent for the Taking*, as quoted by Deborah Scroggins for the *Nation* (June 14, 2004, on-line). "So many loves had kept me going here: the beauty and the unfussy grace of the people, the amazing food—yes, the food—music rich beyond comparison, the sheer immediacy of human contact, the pleasure of living by my wits. But the grim truth was that a single mosquito bite had contained enough deadly force to lay me very low indeed." French, according to Scroggins, also felt as though, despite his best intentions, he had become a "fireman" who chased after disaster stories in order to feed "the world media's insatiable market in images of horror." After leaving Africa in 1998, French spent a year as a visiting scholar at the University of Hawaii, where he studied East Asian affairs and the Japanese language. The following spring he was a Jefferson Fellow at the East West Center in Honolulu, Hawaii. From 1999 to 2003 he served as the Tokyo bureau chief for the *New York Times*, reporting on affairs in North and South Korea, Japan, and the Russian Far East.

Howard W. French has been married to Agnes Koffi since October 5, 1987; they have two sons, William Howard and Henry Nelson. He is a member of the National Association of Black Journalists, the Institute of the Americas, and the African Studies Association. French has earned the *New York Times*'s highest award, the Publisher's Award, six times for work that included his reporting from Pakistan in 2002. He and his family now live in Shanghai, China, where he has served as the *Times*'s Shanghai bureau chief since August 2003.

—C.M.

Suggested Reading: *American Prospect* p38+ July 2004; Borzoi Reader Web site; Lettre Ulysses Award Web site; *Publishers Weekly* p161 Feb. 16, 2004; *New York Times* E p6 June 7, 2004; *New York Times Book Review* p25 Apr. 25, 2004; *Washington Monthly* p49+ Apr. 2004

Selected Books: *A Continent for the Taking*, 2004

Bruno Vincent/Getty Images

Freudenberger, Nell

1975– Short-story writer; novelist

While working as an editorial assistant at the *New Yorker*, in the spring of 2001, Nell Freudenberger, then only 26 years old, published a short story in that magazine's Summer Fiction issue, which featured debut pieces by several previously unpublished authors. The story, "Lucky Girls," attracted considerable attention from some very important people in publishing, most notably, the powerful literary agent Amanda "Binky" Urban. With Urban as her representative, Freudenberger found herself at the center of a bidding war between publishing houses for a collection of short stories she had yet to write. She ultimately signed with Ecco, an imprint of HarperCollins, for $100,000—reportedly turning down an offer of $500,000—because she wanted to work with the poet and editor Daniel Halpern. "Signing up to write a book based on one short story is ridiculous," she told Tim Cribb for the *South China Morning Post* (March 5, 2006). "And signing up to write two books based on one story is just crazy. I wasn't sure I could do it. I thought I could take the chance with one book, but not two." Despite her reservations, Freudenberger has since published two books—a collection of short stories, *Lucky Girls* (2003), and her first novel, *The Dissident* (2006)—both of which received plaudits from reviewers.

The older of two daughters, Nell Freudenberger was born in New York City in 1975. Her father, Daniel, a television writer and playwright, moved the family to Los Angeles when she was seven. (He divorced Freudenberger's mother, Carol Hofmann, when their daughter was in college.) Freudenberger was interested in literature from an early age. "Sometimes I think that the books you fall in love with as a child are the ones that make the greatest impression," Freudenberger wrote for an interview posted on the Barnes & Noble Web site. "I'm thinking of two in particular: *D'Aulaires' Book of Greek Myths*, and a poetry anthology called *Reflections on a Gift of Watermelon Pickle*. The stories of the Greek gods as they're presented in *D'Aulaires*, with its evocative (sometimes violent) illustrations, were the most stimulating stories I'd read until that point: they made me want to write my own. I remember showing my parents an 'ode' (at least, that was what I called it) that I'd written about Helen of Troy. They were nice enough not to point out that the subject of the Trojan War had been taken by another poet, quite some time ago." While attending Harvard University, in Cambridge Massachusetts, she worked on the school's literary magazine with her friend Benjamin Kunkel, who would later become a best-selling author as well. She graduated magna cum laude in 1997 and went on to receive an M.F.A. in fiction from New York University. She taught English in Bangkok, Thailand, and New Delhi, India, before accepting a job as an editorial assistant at the *New Yorker*.

When Freudenberger's much-anticipated collection of stories, *Lucky Girls*, was finally published, it was widely reviewed; most critics praised the work, although some found that it did not live up to expectations. Four of the collection's five stories are drawn from Freudenberger's experiences living among Americans in Asia. In the title story, "Lucky Girls," a young American woman living in India recalls her five-year relationship with Arun, a married man from New Delhi who recently died. While dealing with her own grief, the woman comes face-to-face with the scorn and contempt of Arun's family.

A critic for the *New York Times Book Review* (October 5, 2003) called *Lucky Girls* "a poised but sharp-toothed first collection of stories about Americans abroad, mostly privileged young women; though they have, or used to have, parents and lovers, their primary loyalties are to their own memories." "It seems impossible that a writer of Freudenberger's youth could know so much about the world, but she does," Don Lee wrote for *Ploughshares* (Winter 2003–04). "[The stories] crackle with acuity and authenticity." Writing for the *Los Angeles Times* (September 24, 2003), Carmela Ciuraru offered more reserved praise, noting that if the book was "a collection of, say, 12 stories, it might have been fine for a few to seem more mediocre than the rest. Yet there are just five long stories in this debut, so each one ought to be outstanding and, unfortunately, that isn't the case. Throughout the book, however, are moments of sharp humor and wise insight, especially into the dysfunctional layers of family dynamics. Unfortunately those moments are not sustained."

Freudenberger was inspired to write her first novel, *The Dissident*, after seeing a Chinese scroll painting by the 13th century artist Zhao Cangyun at the Metropolitan Museum of Art. Titled "Liu Chen and Ruan Zhao in the Tiantai Mountains," the scroll relates the tale of two men who discover a passage through time. The main character in Freudenberger's novel, a Chinese artist and political activist named Yuan Zhao, spends a year living with a Beverly Hills family. During that time he makes a detailed copy of Zhao's scroll.

Reviewing *The Dissident* for the on-line magazine *Salon* (August 29, 2006), Andrew O'Hehir wrote that Freudenberger had lept "into the upper quartile of American novelists with this impressive debut." Though many reviewers expressed similar sentiments, others agreed with Maureen Corrigan who expressed her disappoint with the Freudenberger's sophomore effort in her review for the NPR program *Fresh Air* (September 20, 2006): "*The Dissident* isn't funny enough to be a comedy. Nor is it profound enough to be a commentary on cross-cultural blindness. Nor, I'm sorry to say, is it as compelling as Freudenberger's amazing short story collection *Lucky Girls*, which deservedly made her the literary wunderkind of 2003. Freudenberger tackles the same themes in this novel as she did in *Lucky Girls*, namely people from disparate cultures trying and failing to only connect. And to give *The Dissident* its due, the sudden cruel plot twists and offbeat but precise way with words that distinguished *Lucky Girls* are also present intermittently throughout this novel. . . . But proportional to its 400-plus page length, there just aren't enough of these shimmering moments to really lift *The Dissident* into the exalted literary league of its predecessor. . . . It's a commonplace piece of wisdom among writing teachers that the hardest student papers to improve upon are not the C-range disasters, but rather those pesky B-plus essays that are good, just not good enough. That's what *The Dissident* feels like to me. Good, but especially in light of *Lucky Girls*, just not good enough."

Freudenberger has won several awards for her writing, including the Sue Kaufman Prize from the American Academy of Arts and Letters, the PEN/Malamud Award for Short Fiction, and the Whiting Writers' Award. In September 2006 Freudenberger married Paul Logan, an architect whom she met at a party in East Hampton, New York. The film and stage actor John Lithgow, who is also her godfather, officiated.

—C.M.

Suggested Reading: *Los Angeles Times* V p9 Sep. 24, 2003, E p5 Aug. 13, 2006; *New York Times Book Review* p26 Oct. 5, 2003; (Toronto) *National Post* Oct. 11, 2003;

Selected Books: *Lucky Girls*, 2003; *The Dissident*, 2006

Paulina Lavista/Courtesy of Harcourt

Fuentes, Carlos

Nov. 11, 1928– Novelist; short-story writer; essayist

"Without risk, there is no art, no literature," Carlos Fuentes observed in the documentary *The Journey of Carlos Fuentes: Crossing Borders* (1989), as quoted by Jeremy Gerard in the *New York Times* (October 5, 1989). "You should always be on the edge of a cliff, about to fall down and break your neck." For Fuentes, considered to be one of Mexico's most important authors, art, politics, and history are closely related. His novels, short stories, and essays cover a diverse variety of genres and topics, from historical fiction and gothic horror to thrillers and political essays. His most famous works, such as *The Death of Artemio Cruz* (1964), *Terra Nostra* (1976), *The Old Gringo* (1985), and more recently, *The Years with Laura Diaz* (2000), are fictions of epic sweep and portent that have earned him a position, according to many observers, among the handful of great living writers and have made him a likely contender for the Nobel Prize in Literature for many years.

Descended from coffee planters, merchants, and bankers, Carlos Fuentes was born in Mexico City on November 11, 1928, one of the two children of Rafael Fuentes Boettiger, a career diplomat, and the former Berta Macías Rivas. His ancestors on his mother's side had lived in the Mexican states of Sonora and Sinaloa. Among his paternal ancestors, who settled in Veracruz, were natives of the Canary Islands and a Lassallean Socialist who emigrated to Mexico from Darmstadt, Germany, in the 1870s. Carlos and his sister, Berta, grew up in Western Hemisphere capitals, where their father—who later became chief of protocol in the Mexican Foreign Affairs Ministry and Ambassador to the Netherlands, Portugal, and Italy—was serving in diplomatic posts. At the age of four, Fuentes learned English while living in Washington, D.C. Later the family resided in such cities as Santiago, Chile; Rio de Janeiro and Buenos Aires, Brazil; Montevideo, Uruguay; and Quito, Ecuador.

Fuentes's early interest in becoming a writer was encouraged by his father. By the time he was 13 he had his first stories published in Chilean magazines. As a secondary-school student at the exclusive Grange School, in Santiago, and at the Colegio México, in Mexico City, he edited school magazines and acted in student dramatic productions. After completing his secondary education, in 1946, Fuentes studied law at the Colegio Francés Morelos, in Mexico City, where he took part in debate and public speaking and won first prize in a literary competition. He graduated in 1948 and entered the National University of Mexico, from which he received a degree in international law. Having taught himself French by reading Honoré de Balzac with the help of a dictionary, he went to Geneva, Switzerland, to study for a year at the Institut des Hautes Études Internationales. His dissertation, entitled "The *Rebus Sic Stantibus* Clause in International Law," was privately published in 1951.

Between 1950 and 1952 Fuentes lived in Geneva, where he was a member (and later secretary) of the Mexican delegation to the International Labor Organization. At the same time he was secretary of the Mexican delegation to the International Law Commission of the United Nations and cultural attaché to the Mexican Embassy. When he returned to Mexico City, Fuentes was appointed assistant chief of the press section of the Foreign Affairs Ministry in 1954 and also became press secretary of the United Nations information center. In the 1955–56 academic year he was secretary and assistant director of the cultural department of the National University of Mexico, and from 1957 to 1959 he was back at the Foreign Affairs Ministry as head of the department of cultural relations.

In 1955 Fuentes and Emmanuel Carballo founded the prestigious bimonthly literary revue *Revista Mexicana de Literatura,* dedicated to the national culture while preserving a universal perspective. Fuentes served as editor until 1958. He also edited or co-edited *El Espectador* from 1959 to 1961 and the periodicals *Siempre* and *Política* in 1960. His first book of short stories, *Los dias enmascarados* (which can be translated as "masked days"), was published in 1954 by Los Presentes, founded by Juan José Arreola to provide an outlet for young writers. In the stories, Fuentes depicts Mexico's moral and spiritual decay by blending fantasy with reality and elaborates on his countrymen's obsession with the mythology of their Indian heritage.

A fellowship from the Centro Mexicano de Escritores in 1956 enabled Fuentes to write his first novel, a kaleidoscopic panorama of Mexico City entitled *La región más transparente* (which can be translated as "the most transparent region"), which was published in 1958. An English version, by Sam Hileman—who was later responsible for many English translations of Fuentes's books—was published in 1960 as *Where the Air Is Clear.* Fuentes intended this novel to be both a biography of the city and an encapsulation of contemporary Mexico. The main action of the novel takes place in 1951, but Fuentes delves into Mexico's revolutionary past with flashbacks and cinematic techniques. Among the dozens of characters, representing all social strata of Mexican society, the most clearly defined personality is that of Federico Robles, a former revolutionist of humble origin, who rises to the top of the financial world by shady means. His nemesis is Ixca Cienfuegos, a kind of mythical prophet who acts as a universal conscience and principal witness. Ixca sees Mexico as a land of spiritual decadence that had severed its ties with its primitive past but failed to establish a meaningful society through its revolution.

Although some critics pointed out that *Where the Air Is Clear* lacked technical perfection, many felt that Fuentes had created a work of lasting significance. A critic for *Kirkus Reviews* (September 15, 1960) remarked: "Written with a fervor that is both fierce and compassionate, this is a complex, powerful novel of huge scope." In the *New York Times Book Review* (November 13, 1960), Selden Rodman proclaimed: "This is the most ambitious and skillful novel to come out of Mexico in a long time, and by all odds the most 'modern.' It's the most readable, too, if the reader is not thrown off by the confusing switches and martini-maelstroms of the opening pages."

Fuentes's second novel, *Las buenas conciencias* (1959), published in English as *The Good Conscience* (1961), is a more conventional work, originally intended as the first part of a tetralogy that was later abandoned. Written in the narrative style of the Spanish novelist Benito Pérez Galdós, the novel traces the intellectual development of the adolescent Jaime Ceballos, scion of a rich and powerful family in the provincial capital of Guanajuato. Torn between the liberal Christian humanism of his convictions and the sanctimonious conservatism of his family, Jaime ultimately capitulates to the latter. Although *The Good Conscience* attracted less attention than Fuentes's first novel, critics complimented his charting of Jaime's moral conflicts. In the *Chicago Sunday Tribune* (December 10, 1961), R. A. Jelliffe praised how "the richness of the narrative lies rather in the tone and spirit of the story, in the honesty and fidelity and understanding of the boy's life, a boy struggling towards manhood in a hostile environment." Thomas Curley, writing for *Commonweal* (January 19, 1962), remarked:

"Fuentes has grasped something important in allowing Jaime to appear so thoroughly naive. Since he is young, he can take Christ seriously and, though it is obvious that his failure to accept Father Obregon's advice lies primarily within himself, surely the occasion of his failure is the contradiction between the professions and actions of his elders."

Fuentes followed *The Good Conscience* with the book that established his international reputation, *La muerte de Artemio Cruz* (1962), which was published as *The Death of Artemio Cruz* in 1964. As *Where the Air Is Clear* did, the novel traces the disintegration of revolutionary ideals in modern Mexico. In *The Death of Artemio Cruz* the nation is symbolized by a wealthy tycoon and media baron who, on his deathbed, looks back upon those episodes of his life that led to a sacrifice of principle and deterioration of character. Hovering in the background is the voice of Artemio's conscience, which always speaks in the second person and in the future tense. Far from depicting his protagonist as the personification of absolute evil, Fuentes shows him to be, as Luis Harss and Barbara Dohmann observed in *Into the Mainstream* (1966), a man who is "humorous, shrewd, hardheaded, cruel, endearing, taciturn, admirable, pitiable." Jean Franco pointed out in *The Modern Culture of Latin America* (1967) that Cruz embodies a basic flaw in the Mexican's character, the "need to impose himself violently on other people in order to assert his machismo, or masculinity."

To evoke the past, Fuentes relies on flashbacks, temporal jumps, interior monologues, and stream of consciousness. Although some reviewers found the novel too fragmented, critical comment was highly favorable. In the *New Statesman* (August 4, 1964), Stephen Hugh-Jones wrote: "*The Death of Artemio Cruz* is a novel of great power and great imagination. It sweeps through the history of modern Mexico in one man's life—which is no novelty. What is unusual . . . is the understanding of people and of history that fuses these elements into a continuously revealing whole." He concluded, "I was dazzled by the richness of this book, in texture, construction, psychology and description. I won't swear it is a masterpiece; but it may well be."

The gothic style of Fuentes's novella *Aura* (1962), translated into English by Lysander Kemp under the same title in 1965, reminded some critics of such writers as Edgar Allen Poe, Oscar Wilde, and William Faulkner. Mingling fantasy and reality in a second-person narrative, the story is set in an old mansion and revolves around a young scholar, engaged to work on some documents by an elderly matron who shares a mysterious connection with her beautiful young niece. With the publication of *Cantar de ciegos* (Song of the Blind, 1964), a collection of seven short stories, Fuentes earned praise as an outstanding *cuentista,* or storyteller. Set in contemporary Mexico, the stories, some of which tend toward the bizarre, satirize the pretentious banality that Fuentes deplores in some of his compatriots. His next novel, *Zona sagrada* (Sacred Zone, 1967), about a famous film actress who completely dominates her effeminate son, evoked little enthusiasm from critics.

Cambio de piel (1967), published as *A Change of Skin* in 1968, is one of Fuentes's most complex and controversial novels. It concerns an ill-fated Holy Week pilgrimage from Mexico City to Veracruz, undertaken by four people: Javier, an unsuccessful middle-aged Mexican poet and scholar; Elizabeth, his love-starved American-born Jewish wife; Franz, a Sudetenland German with a Nazi background; and Isabel, his pleasure-seeking young Mexican mistress. Although the action takes place on a single day in 1965 between Mexico City and the historic town of Cholula, flashbacks evoke scenes of earlier events, in such locations as New York, Argentina, Italy, Czechoslovakia, and Greece, as well as Germany during World War II. Unlike Fuentes's other major novels, *A Change of Skin* had to do mainly with the inner conflicts and search for self-fulfillment or redemption of the four central characters, whose fates are intertwined. Some critics frowned on the book because of what they considered to be its sexual excesses and its inordinate use of symbolism; others were generous in their praise. R. J. Coleman, writing in the *Saturday Review* (January 27, 1968), admitted that his "initial reactions were hostile" but that in the end he was aware that he had "experienced a great book," a novel that is "bursting in energy, capacious in content, gripping in evocation, and humanitarian in its universal tolerances." In Francoist Spain, where the book was officially banned as "pornographic, communistic, anti-Christian, anti-German, and pro-Jewish," it earned Fuentes his first major literary award, the 1967 Premio Biblioteca Breve of the Barcelona publishing house Seix Barral.

Returning to Mexico in 1969 after four years of self-imposed European exile, Fuentes published *Cumpleaõnos* (which can be translated as "birthday"), a short novel in which he deals with eternity, reincarnation, immortality, life, and death. He also authored *Paris: La revolución de Mayo* (which can be translated as "the May revolution," 1968), a report on the student and worker uprising in Paris in 1968; and the essay collections *La nueva novela hispanoamericana* (which can be translated as "the new Spanish-American novel," 1968), *Casa con dos puertas* (which can be translated as "house with two doors," 1970), and *Tiempo Mexicano* (which can be translated as "Mexican time," 1971). His plays, *Todos los gatos son pardos* (which can be translated as "all cats are gray," 1970) and *El tuerto es rey* (which can be translated as "the one-eyed man is king," 1970), were staged in such cities as Paris, Avignon, Vienna, Brussels, and Barcelona during this period. Fuentes also wrote the text of the book *El mundo de José Luis Cuevas* (which can be translated as "the world of José Luis Cuevas" 1969), featuring the work of the noted Mexican artist.

Fuentes's next major work was the novel *Terra Nostra* (1975), published under the same title in an English translation in 1976. In it, the author incorporates a series of Spanish kings and queens into a figure named Felipe, also known as El Señor. After returning from the Crusades, Felipe builds a monumental cathedral and castle in Spain. Shortly after construction begins, a man called the Pilgrim arrives at the royal court and recounts his journey to the New World. The novel ends with the Spanish colonization of the Americas. The ambitious work, which was mildly praised when it was first published, has since become considered one of the author's masterworks. In the *Saturday Review* (October 30, 1976), Robert Maurer remarked: "What one senses in *Terra Nostra* most is [Fuentes's] reaching out for a direction and a voice of his own. . . . When he is successful in his reach, his speech rhythms and tones (extremely well translated by Margaret Sayers Peden) are like cathedral music, organ and chorus combined, stately and moving, with amazing powers to sustain intensity."

The high-action thriller *La cabeza de la Hidra* (1978), translated into English as *The Hydra Head* (1978), displayed the author's great versatility. In it, a Mexican secret agent named Felix Maldonado must attempt to foil the plans of Israeli and Arab agents who are trying to gain access to Mexico's oil reserves. The book met with high praise. In *Library Journal* (December 15, 1978), Ruth Dougherty cheered: "Espionage and international intrigue are skillfully and vividly portrayed in this fast-paced latest novel by one of Mexico's major writers. . . . Sophisticated narrative techniques including sudden changes of perspective advance a plot with topical philosophical and political ideas as well as just plain action. Many types of readers will find this well-written and well-translated book attractive." Alan Cheuse, in the *New Republic* (December 23 & 30, 1978), observed: "Carlos Fuentes . . . has looked the spy novel in the eye and produced a controversial world-class thriller. *The Hydra Head* reads as though it has been freshly minted out of the turmoil and subterranean intrigue of current world affairs. . . . [*The Hydra Head* is] a tour de force." Fuentes strengthened his reputation in the English-speaking world with the publication of *Burnt Water* (1980), a collection of Gothic tales, which was his first volume of short stories to be published in English; and the play *Orchids in the Moonlight* (1982), about two aging film stars, which was his first play to be produced in the United States. In 1982 he also published the novel *Distant Relations.*

In 1985 *The Old Gringo,* one of Fuentes's most famous novels, was published. It tells the story of the American writer Ambrose Bierce, who fought with Pancho Villa's revolutionaries during the 1910 Mexican Revolution. Bierce disappeared in Mexico, never to be heard from again. Much of the conflict of the novel concerns Bierce's relationship with Tomas Arroyo, a Villa general, and an American governess in Mexico named Harriet Winslow. In the *Atlantic Monthly* (December 1985), Phoebe-Lou Adams proclaimed: "Mr. Fuentes has erected a narrative of brilliant complexity and sophistication, describing brisk military action and philosophically contrasting national character, or social tradition, or styles of revolt, or regional strengths, weaknesses, and prejudices." L. M. Lewis, writing for *Library Journal* (November 1, 1985), agreed: "Fuentes has made clever fictional use of an actual literary mystery, but his more remarkable achievement here is the portrait of the writer as a father figure to an American governess and to a general in Pancho Villa's army, each of whom has been betrayed by a real father. . . . This is a novel to be savored; it deserves more than a single reading."

In 1988 Fuentes published a collection of essays entitled *Myself with Others,* seven selections written in English for an American audience. In addition to two autobiographical essays about growing up as a diplomat's son and essays on other artists, he writes about 20th-century politics, including U.S. relations with Latin America. Throughout the 1980s Fuentes was harshly critical of American foreign policy in the region.

With *Cristóbal Nonato* (1987), published in the United States as *Christopher Unborn* (1989), Fuentes returned to his ambitious style of storytelling. The narrator of the novel is an unborn fetus, Christopher, conceived in the hopes that his birthday will come closest to the 500th anniversary of Columbus's arrival in the Americas, and thereby win a contest to become the new ruler of Mexico. In utero, Christopher recalls Mexico's history as well as observes the troubled country he would be inheriting. The novel's nine chapters parallel the nine months of his mother's pregnancy and allude to Columbus's journey to the New World. The book received mixed reviews. "For a novel purporting to be the vision of Mexico City, *Christopher Unborn* carries remarkably little sense of the place," Dan Bellm observed for the *Voice Literary Supplement* (September 1989). "Still, the novel's second half somewhat rewards a reader's patience, finally hitting upon a great satiric theme to channel this aimless energy. Fuentes probably can write the book of Mexico City someday, but this is the book of a man looking at himself." "There is throughout a display of endless verbal pyrotechnics, a relentless desire to amuse, to be clever which becomes fatiguing and ultimately tedious," Robert Carver opined in the *New Statesman & Society* (October 27, 1989). "Through this, though, glint some sharper apercus. . . . The comic invention is sharp, too." Carver concluded, "Beneath all the jokiness and flip multicultural references one can discern the torments of a cultured, intelligent man who is agonised by the moral and physical squalor of contemporary Mexico."

In the early 1990s English translations of Fuentes's books were published in rapid succession, including *Constancia, and Other Stories for Virgins* (1991), originally published in Spain in 1989; *The Campaign* (1991), a novel about revolution; and *Geography of the Novel* (1993), a collection of essays. *The Buried Mirror: Reflections on Spain and the New World* (1992), a volume of essays written in tandem with a television documentary on the influence of Spain on Latin America, was a highly ambitious nonfiction work. David Keymer, writing for *Library Journal* (March 1, 1992) observed, "[Fuentes argues that] Spanish America's predicament is that it inherited from Spain neither institutions nor attitudes necessary for full partnership in the modern capitalist world. Latin America remains derivative in culture and economy. Every page in this lapidary essay offers profound insight into the Spanish American psyche."

Fuentes's book *El Naranjo* (1994), translated and published in English as *The Orange Tree* (1995), was unique in that it collected five of his novellas for the first time. The novellas are all first-person narratives and are linked by the presence of an orange tree—a symbol of renewal that connects different cultures as its seeds are spread from the Orient to Arabia to Rome and finally to Spain and the New World. The collection received generally favorable reviews. Harold Augenbraum, writing for *Library Journal* (March 14, 1994), noted, "Although the irony is sometimes a bit too thick, Fuentes's imagination creates vivid worlds, and his writing is powerful." Merle Rubin, in the *Christian Science Monitor* (April 20, 1994), noted that the novellas are "artfully arranged to serve as distant mirrors of one another." In the *Chicago Tribune* (April 17, 1994), Alan Cheuse called it a "fascinating new addition to Fuentes's fictional history of Latin America."

In his novel *Diana: The Goddess Who Hunts Alone* (1995), Fuentes fictionalizes a love affair he had with the actress Jean Seberg, who is portrayed here as Diana Soren. Reviews of the novel were varied. In the *New York Times Book Review* (October 22, 1995), Paul Theroux wrote: "One of the odd lessons of this book by a novelist of world-class stature is the way it demonstrates the artlessness and banality of machismo. The character of Diana Soren has a weak ego and so she takes revenge on men, because they represent the authority of the United States. The novelist-narrator sees Americans as 'without exception' problematical and lacking in substance, and so he rants. He is Mexico. You are a gringo. She is your victim. It makes for an entirely humorless and strangely sclerotic novel." Adam Mazmanian's review for *Library Journal* (September 1, 1995) was more positive: "The narrative is marked by digressions into Sixties revolutionary politics, the meaning of literary creation, and the Puritan origins of the United States. But these never distract from the central themes of the novel—the hunger with which Diana and Carlos consume each other, the tragic link between the eternity of desire and the finitude of love; the wish to create and the inexorable will to destroy."

Fuentes followed this novel with a collection of essays, *A New Time for Mexico* (1996), and *The Crystal Frontier: A Novel in Nine Stories* (1997), both of which received mixed reviews at best. However, with his novel *Los Años con Laura Diaz* (1999), translated into English as *The Years with Laura Diaz* (2000), Fuentes received some of his best reviews in years. The story of a Mexican woman descended from German grandparents who settled in Mexico in the late 1800s, it tells of her life during the Mexican Revolution and her subsequent experiences with such notable Mexican figures as the revolutionary painter Diego Rivera. In *Library Journal* (October 1, 2000), Jack Shreve proclaimed: "This fictionalized memoir brilliantly recaptures the turbulent and exciting history of 20th-century Mexico. . . . A mural-mosaic of recent Mexican history by an author who has witnessed, scrutinized, and interpreted that history like no other, this roman fleuve of a novel can hardly fail to entertain and enlighten." Veronica Scrol, in a review for *Booklist* (September 1, 2000), agreed: "In many ways, Laura Diaz is the female counterpart to Artemio Cruz, the hero of Fuentes's 1962 novel, *The Death of Artemio Cruz*. If Cruz, the former revolutionary turned capitalist, symbolized for Fuentes Mexico's quest for wealth at the expense of moral values, then Diaz, the politically committed artist, stands as the pillar of integrity and hope for twentieth-century Mexico. In Laura Diaz, Fuentes has created a remarkable heroine."

In 2002 Fuentes published *The Eagle's Throne*, the translation of which was released in 2006, a futuristic tale in which the Mexican president engages in a trade war with the U.S., while the American president Condoleezza Rice uses her country's technology to cripple Mexico's communications system. Calling it "a satiric novel whose real target is the way politics and presidential succession work in Mexico now," Francisco Goldman observed for the *Washington Post* (June 18, 2006), "the somewhat cumbersome futuristic framework merely provides Fuentes with a rationale for launching an epistolary novel in the exuberantly cynical manner of *Les Liaisons Dangereuses*." He concluded: "Other sources of this book's considerable pleasures are Fuentes's characteristic dazzling, razor-sharp, intellectual flights. In his vast and multi-faceted oeuvre, this may be a minor work, but it provides a feast of political insight, aphorisms and maxims, in the spirit of Machiavelli and Sun Tzu's *The Art of War*. . . . For anyone aspiring to be a Mexican politician, this should be an indispensable manual. For those seeking to apply such knowledge—if only as a vicarious pleasure—to their own circumstances, well, it can only make you wiser."

In the last few years, Fuentes has focused on producing mostly nonfiction, authoring the Spanish-language book *Contra Bush* (2004)—which translates as "against Bush"—and an unconventional memoir, *This I Believe: An A to Z of a Life* (2004), which consists of such alphabetized topical entries as "Globalization," "Sex," and "Zurich." "Most writers, certainly most writers in English," Ian Jack wrote for the *New York Times* (June 12, 2005), "would have tackled their life and thoughts in a different way, not encyclopedic but narrative, not telling but showing, their story informed with wisdom but not necessarily proclaiming it. Wisdom is what he [Fuentes] wishes to impart, and while it may be unfair to describe his voice as sermonic, the whiff of the pulpit, the lectern and the platform hangs around many of his pages." Though noting that Fuentes is at times "affecting and illuminating" when describing his personal relationships, Jack wrote that the "political-pulpit style tarnishes too much" of the book.

Carlos Fuentes married the film star Rita Macedo, in 1959. The marriage ended in divorce in 1969. In 1973 he married Sylvia Lemus. He has a daughter, Cecilia, from his first marriage, as well as a son, Carlos, and a daughter, Natasha, from his second.

—K.D.

Suggested Reading: *Atlantic Monthly* p118 Dec. 1985; *Booklist* p6 Sep. 1, 2000; *Christian Science Monitor* p13 June 30, 1992, p17 Apr. 20, 1994; *Chicago Sunday Tribune* p3 Dec. 10, 1961; *Commonweal* p439 Jan. 19, 1962; *Kirkus Reviews* p825 Sep. 15, 1960; *Library Journal* p2,536 Dec. 15, 1978, p109 Nov. 1, 1985, p103 Mar. 15, 1994, p206 Sep. 1, 1995, p147 Oct. 1, 2000; *New Republic* p39 Dec. 23 and 30, 1978; *New Statesman* p189 Aug. 7, 1964; *New Statesman and Society* p36 Oct. 28, 1989; *New York Times* II p1+ June 8, 1982; *New York Times Book Review* p44 Nov. 13, 1960, p3 Nov. 7, 1976, p12 Oct. 22, 1995; *People* p93+ Mar. 3, 1986; *Saturday Review* p38 Oct. 30, 1976; *Times Literary Supplement* p672 June 17–23, 1988; *Voice Literary Supplement* p27 Sep. 1989; Harss, Luis and Barbara Dohmann. *Into the Mainstream,* 1966; Langford, Walter M. *The Mexican Novel Comes of Age,* 1971; Schwartz, Kessel. *A New History of Spanish American Fiction,* 1971

Selected Books in English Translation: fiction—*Where the Air Is Clear,* 1960; *The Good Conscience,* 1961; *The Death of Artemio Cruz,* 1964; *Aura,* 1965; *A Change of Skin,* 1968; *Terra Nostra,* 1976; *The Hydra Head,* 1978; *Burnt Water,* 1980; *Distant Relations,* 1982; *The Old Gringo,* 1985; *Christopher Unborn,* 1989; *Constancia, and Other Stories for Virgins,* 1991; *The Campaign,* 1991; *The Orange Tree,* 1995; *Diana: The Goddess Who Hunts Alone,* 1995; *The Crystal Frontier: A Novel in Nine Stories,* 1997; *The Years with Laura Diaz,* 2000; nonfiction—*Myself with Others,* 1988; *The Buried Mirror: Reflections on Spain and the New World,* 1992; *A New Time for Mexico,* 1996; *This I Believe: An A to Z of a Life,* 2004; *The Eagle's Throne*

Fuguet, Alberto

(foo-GET, ahl-BEAR-
tow)

1964– Novelist; short-story writer

The Chilean writer and filmmaker Alberto Fuguet is one of the most prominent figures in the McOndo movement, a literary rebellion of sorts that draws its name from the title of a 1996 anthology of fiction that Fuguet co-edited with Sergio Gómez. The name is a pun on Macondo, the rural village at the center of Gabriel García Márquez's *One Hundred Years of Solitude,* a seminal book in the magic realism genre, which dominated Latin American literature for the last half of the 20th century. The young, urbanite contributors to *McOndo* did not recognize their own experiences in the typically pastoral scenes described by their predecessors. For them, the South American experience is focused on the continent's metropolises, with their imported McDonald's chain restaurants and condos. In a *Newsweek* (May 6, 2002) article entitled "Is Magical Realism Dead?," Mac Margolis described the stories in *McOndo* as "irreverent, often aggressive, scatological riffs on contemporary urban life, told to a backbeat of sex, drugs and pop music." The Hispanic literary establishment was appalled, dismissing the *McOndo* authors, whose characters are steeped in American pop culture, as "shallow and flippant," but Fuguet and his collaborators have, in the decade since, established their reputations as the new faces of Latin American literature.

Alberto Fuguet was born in 1964 in Santiago, Chile, but he was taken to the U.S. as a baby and spent most of his childhood in Encino, California, in the San Fernando Valley near Los Angeles. English was his first language, and he was in a program for gifted children at the Rhoda Street Elementary School. His father worked at Los Angeles International Airport and a Wonder Bread factory, and the family's lifestyle was decidedly middle class and suburban. In 1973 General Augusto Pinochet overthrew Chile's democratically elected socialist president,

Salvador Allende. Shortly afterward, Fuguet's conservative mother decided to move the family back to her homeland. "Coming to Chile as an immigrant was going down in every sense of the word for me," Fuguet told Marcela Valdes for *Críticas* (September 1, 2003, on-line). "From democracy to dictatorship, from first world to third world, from English to Spanish. Spanish wasn't so cool then as it is now. It wasn't the second language of the world." Although he was also a right-winger, Fuguet's father preferred life in America and returned to California, splitting the family.

Though he saw Spanish as possessing less cultural cachet than English, Fuguet decided to adopt the former as his primary language. As a child he had dreamed of a career as a reporter, so when he had completed secondary school, he enrolled in the journalism program at the Universidad de Chile, in Santiago. There Fuguet bristled at the restrictions placed on him by the conventions of traditional newswriting. "A teacher basically told me if you want to write weird, write your own things," he told Valdes. He began experimenting with fiction and was accepted into workshops run by the novelists José Donoso and Antonio Skármeta. Donoso initially rejected Fuguet's irreverence and appreciation of American culture, but later they reconciled, and in 1994 Donoso secured a spot for Fuguet in the International Writing Program at the University of Iowa, in Iowa City. He was not a successful student in Iowa, however, because the program administrators had expected a typical Latin American author—in other words, a magic realist. By that point, he had already published his distinctly styled prose in various Spanish-language anthologies and had authored three books: *La azarosa y sobreexpuesta vida de Enrique Alekán* (1990), a collection of columns that he had written for the newspaper *El Mercurio*; the short-story collection *Sobredosis* (1990), and *Mala Onda* (1991), a novel. *Sobredosis*, which can be translated as "overdose," won Santiago's Municipal Prize of Literature.

In 1997 *Mala Onda* became the first of Fuguet's novels to be published in English. Translated as *Bad Vibes*, the novel features a 17-year-old narrator named Matias, who after spending a holiday in Rio de Janeiro, Brazil, returns home to Santiago just in time for the 1980 referendum on Pinochet's power. While free expression is threatened under the oppressive regime, a hedonistic atmosphere prevails among the upper-class teenagers, who indulge in drugs, sex, and rock and roll. Many reviewers in the U.S. compared Matias with Holden Caulfield, the protagonist of J. D. Salinger's *The Catcher in the Rye*. "Already popular in his native Chile, Fuguet will be a welcome new voice to American readers," a reviewer wrote for *Publishers Weekly* (February 24, 1997). "*Bad Vibes* . . . artfully captures a tense moment in a country's political history, the lifestyle of a society and the personal development of its jaded young narrator. . . . For Matias, Fuguet crafts a memorable narrative voice—candid, prone to overheated insight and exhibiting mastery of telling detail."

Though Fuguet continued to publish in South America, he did not put out another English translation until 2003, when his novel *Las películas de mi vida* was simultaneously published with its translation, *The Movies of My Life*. The novel is semiautobiographical: Beltran Soler, the protagonist, lived in Encino, California, as a child and later returned to Chile. Unlike Fuguet, however, Beltran is a seismologist. "I was looking for a profession that consumes Chile and yet also represents California," Fuguet explained in an interview for the HarperCollins Web site. "One day we had a quake (3 or 4, the typical Santiago jolt) and I saw this seismologist on TV and bingo! I became obsessed with this strange profession." Beltran, on his way to a conference in Japan, decides to hole up in a Los Angeles hotel and begin writing his memoirs, tracing his life through the movies that influenced him. A reviewer for *Publishers Weekly* (July 14, 2003) found the setup for the novel somewhat stiff, but, the reviewer noted, "once Fuguet begins piecing together Beltran's lopsided, bicultural life, the novel speeds along, overflowing with ironic insight. . . . The movie titles heading each chapter serve as subtle triggers for reminiscence, but never become a structural straitjacket, and Fuguet's pop archness is tempered with honest feeling. Despite the rocky start, this is a fresh, notable effort." In the *Washington Post Book World* (October 19, 2003), Michael Dirda wrote, "Fuguet writes well—his translator, Ezra Fitz, appears to have done a terrific job—in what seems a largely autobiographical book, and though often melodramatic he can also make you laugh. . . . Despite a certain O. Henry–like neatness, the double-whammy of the novel's final pages—as Beltran assumes adulthood in both the most natural and the most unexpected way—is quite touching. But Fuguet's greatest strength lies in evoking the joys, traumas, fears and hopes of childhood and adolescence, and these, it would seem, transcend any nationality."

In *Shorts* (2005), translated from *Cortos* (2004), Fuguet again used movies as symbols and touchstones in many of the stories. In one, two Chilean documentary makers sit in a Denny's restaurant and bemoan their failure to win an Academy Award. Passing teenage girls, however, are impressed because they think the documentary makers are chauffeurs for real celebrities. In a critique for the *New York Times Book Review* (November 6, 2005), Lenora Todaro found much to praise in *Shorts* but unfavorably compared Fuguet's work to that of the magic realists: "Fuguet comes across as a clever writer—an old-fashioned cafe realist—who portrays a certain stratum of Latin American society on its bruised knees: the haves who have little in the way of personal happiness and less in the way of love, and egoistic 30-somethings who prolong adolescence beyond its expiration date. . . . While his observations about cultural dislocation seem spot on, intrusive bits of conventional wisdom flicker through the stories like news crawl. . . . To set Fuguet against the outsized talents of García Márquez & Company is unfair, but by fronting McOndo, he raised the gloves. This round goes to the elders."

In addition to writing fiction, Fuguet has occasionally worked as a screenwriter, producer, and director. He wrote and directed the feature films *Las hormigas asesinas* (2004) and *Se arrienda* (*For Rent*, 2005). He also teaches a program on contemporary audio and visual culture at Universidad Alberto Hurtado, in Santiago.

Fuguet lives in Santiago, but he travels a great deal and frequently visits the U.S.

—S.Y.

Suggested Reading: *Críticas* (on-line) Sep. 1, 2003; *Los Angeles Times* A p1 Feb. 23, 2000, V p1 July 26, 2002; *Newsweek* p52 May 6, 2002; *Time* p23 Mar. 16, 1998, p51 Apr. 3, 2000

Selected Books in English Translation: *Bad Vibes*, 1997; *The Movies of My Life*, 2003; *Shorts*, 2005

© Margaret Bonner/Courtesy of Penguin

Fuller, Alexandra

Mar. 29, 1969– Memoirist

Discussing her family's reaction to her memoir *Don't Let's Go to the Dogs Tonight* (2002), which is about growing up as a white girl in Africa—as Africans fought for their independence—and the person that she has become, Alexandra Fuller told John Mark Eberhart for the *Kansas City Star* (November 8, 2003), "I am purely an African. And my mum struggles with that. She's the one still living in Africa; I'm the one living over here [in America]. But I'm the one who's really sort of celebrated the new Africa, and Mum sees what's going on in Zimbabwe, and, yes, it feels hopeless at times. But for me it feels inevitable—part of our growth as a nation. But for Mum it feels like, 'Well, you know, we gave them independence, and look

what they did with it.' So her take on the book, I think, was very much that I had been a traitor—that I'd written from the inside." Since publishing *Don't Let's Go to the Dogs Tonight*, Fuller has continued to explore the nature of the white community in Africa from the inside, writing *Scribbling the Cat: Travels with an African Soldier* (2004), a study of the psyche of a soldier who fought to protect Rhodesia's colonial rulers and the people who benefited from the colonial system.

Alexandra Fuller, nicknamed Bobo by her family, was born in Glossop, Derbyshire, England, on March 29, 1969. In 1972 her family moved to Africa, where her parents, supporters of colonial rule in Africa, had lived before her birth, and thereafter she grew up on a succession of African farms, primarily in what was then Rhodesia but has since become Zimbabwe. Fuller had four siblings, of whom only one, a sister, lived into adulthood. The backdrop of her childhood was the Rhodesian civil war, in which blacks and whites fought for dominance in the postcolonial country. Fuller's mother suffered from alcoholism and depression; her father disappeared for days into the bush to fight rebels—only to return home to scold her because she, at seven, had not learned to strip down a machine gun fast enough. Nonetheless, she loved, and still loves, Africa, and as an adult she set out to write her story, first in fictionalized form, but after completing eight or nine unsatisfactory novels, she decided to write a memoir.

Fuller's childhood memoir, *Don't Let's Go to the Dogs Tonight*, was highly praised upon its release. Calling it "gripping," Michiko Kakutani wrote for the *New York Times* (December 21, 2001), "Fuller does not judge, rationalize or explain her parents' commitment to white rule. Instead she simply describes what it was like to grow up in Rhodesia in the 70's, knowing that she had the power to fire her nanny if she wanted to, knowing that she attended a Class A school while black children attended a Class C school. The resulting narrative, much like the early fiction of Nadine Gordimer [an acclaimed South African writer], gives the reader an intimate sense of what daily life was like in a segregated and racist society and its insidious emotional fallout on children and grown-ups alike." Similarly, Gail Caldwell wrote for the *Boston Globe* (December 23, 2001), "Fuller's loving but skeptical narrative distance is established from the outset, when she watches her mother—rendered here as an astonishing character—take a kind Englishman hostage, ply him with alcohol, and force him to listen to the all-night tragedy of *Being Nicola Fuller*. Fuller the younger, having heard it a hundred times before, goes to sleep. The dog next to her is already snoring, accompanied by the lamentations of her mother. 'We were prepared to die, you see,' she tells the Englishman, 'to keep one country white-run.' The rare story that subsequently unfolds is so grippingly real and matter-of-fact that one has an intimate regard for Fuller's interior experience—what it must have felt like to have this childhood—even without her elaborating on that psychic dimension." Not everyone, however, found Fuller's account compelling. Danna Bell-Russel noted for *Library Journal* (August 15, 2003), "Though it is interesting to hear about her life in Africa and the hardships she and her family faced, Fuller seems to complain constantly about arguments with her sister, sob when she can't get water during a cattle roundup, and cry when she doesn't get her way. The book does better with its descriptions of the history of Zimbabwe, the family's travels into South Africa and Malawi, and depictions of the people they encounter."

Fuller followed *Don't Let's Go to the Dogs Tonight* with *Scribbling the Cat: Travels with an African Soldier*, a memoir detailing her return to Africa and her journey with a white soldier, whom she calls K. and who fought against native Africans during the war of independence in which she was raised. (The title alludes to the aphorism "curiosity killed the cat.") The two travel from K.'s farm in Zambia, where he, as well as Fuller's parents, now lives in exile, through Zimbabwe and into Mozambique, revisiting the battlefields on which K. fought. Along the way, Fuller becomes his confessor and recounts his stories, exploring, she writes, as cited by David Herndon for New York *Newsday* (May 2, 2004), "why that particular African war had created a man like K.," who can play the stereotypical tough guy but also breaks into tears often, as he remembers the death of his five-year-old son and his wife's cheating on him with his best friend. The book found a more tempered reception than its predecessor upon its release: "Fuller evokes place and character with the vivid prose that distinguished her unflinching memoir of growing up in Africa," a critic wrote for *Publishers Weekly Reviews* (March 8, 2004), "but here she handles subject matter that warrants more than artful word painting and soul-searching. Writing about war—its scarred participants, victims and territory—Fuller skimps on the history and politics that have shaped her and her

subjects." Others, however, were more impressed. "Fuller is at her prosaic best here. Her rich and distinct dialect resonates from the first page of this book, as does the hardship of the African people," Karen Algeo Krizman wrote for the *Rocky Mountain News* (May 7, 2004), and the book won the Lettre Ulysses Award for the Art of Reportage in 2005.

Alexandra Fuller received a bachelor's degree from Acadia University, in Nova Scotia, Canada, in 1993. She lives in Wyoming with her husband and two children, but she is always, she says, considering moving back to Africa.

—C.M./A.R.

Suggested Reading: *Boston Globe* D p3 Dec. 23, 2001; *Kansas City Star* Nov. 8, 2003; *Library Journal* p151 Aug. 15, 2003; *New York Times* E p21 Dec. 21, 2001; *Rocky Mountain News* D p25 May 7, 2004

Selected Books: *Don't Let's Go to the Dogs Tonight*, 2002; *Scribbling the Cat: Travels with an African Soldier*, 2004

Furman, Laura

Nov. 19, 1945– Novelist; short-story writer

Laura Furman has unflinchingly turned her own early sorrows—the loss of her mother and a subsequent bout of emotional disturbance and self-destructiveness—into the stuff of fiction that, without sensationalism or melodrama, delineates, especially for women, the enormous gap between childhood security and the uncertainties of later life. Her story collections, *The Glass House: A Novella and Stories* (1980), *Watch Time Fly* (1983), and *Drinking with the Cook* (2001), have been widely praised. Her novels, *The Shadow Line* (1982), a literary mystery, and *Tuxedo Park* (1986), often described as a "sleeping beauty" story, provide insights into the social complexities of life in upper-class New York. In her memoir, *Ordinary Paradise* (1998), she detailed her early life—from a pleasant existence in New York City, with happy summers spent in New Jersey, to the death of her supportive mother, which left her family barely able to speak of their loss. Robin Bradford, writing for the *Austin Chronicle* (April 20, 2001), observed that Furman "applies her even sense of grace to each sentence so that if there is drama in her stories, it is not usually the life and death kind. It is the daily, wearing, ineffable drama of living as a human island among others who invariably seem more attractive, more connected, or simply more 'normal.'"

Furman submitted the following autobiographical statement to *World Authors 2000–2005*:

Laura Pickett Calfee/Courtesy of Random House

Laura Furman

"For much of my life, I have been one place thinking of another, in the present thinking of the past or the future, and my writing reflects these pulls and anxieties.

"I grew up in New York City, first in Brooklyn Heights and then in Manhattan, but, until I was 12, my best times were spent in New Jersey dairy country, in a house my parents bought in 1944, a year before I was born.

"My mother died when I was 12. Until then I had been writing sketches and stories, and I read all the time. The life my mother gave me in the country was full of chances to read, during rainy afternoons by a window, on the hammock. I had wanted to become an actress or a dancer, both odd ambitions because I had no talent in either. After her death, both reading and writing helped me bear the fact of an utterly changed family, and I began to think of myself as a writer, or rather that I wrote. Writing was then and remains the way I try to understand living.

"In my mid-20s, in an attempt to write with full concentration, I moved to Washington County, New York, and lived there alone in a farmhouse I renovated as I could. The first summer I lived on a screened-in porch, and in October moved inside. I stayed for five years, often lonely, often ecstatic with the beauty of the countryside and the instinctual knowledge that never again would I be able to focus so exclusively on writing. When I'd lived there a few years, my short story, 'Last Winter,' was published in the *New Yorker*, and other publications followed.

"After five years there, I moved to Houston, Texas, to work on a city magazine. I had been supporting myself with a freelance editing job that originated in Houston for the Menil Foundation. When that work ended, I stayed on in the country, earning a precarious living. By October 1978 I was ready for a change, and living in Texas gave me a chance to make my way in an unknown place, away from familiar Northeastern cities and countryside. I've since lived in Houston, Galveston, Dallas, Lockhart, and Austin. For six months, I lived with my dog on a ranch outside of Austin and learned about the beauties and troubles of the Central Texas countryside: limestone cliffs, creeks, floods, snakes, lightning storms, heat and cold in one day. In a way, my time on the Paisano Ranch was a return to the freedom and happiness of my childhood summers.

"For almost 20 years, I've lived and worked in Central Texas. In 1981, I married Joel Warren Barna, with whom I worked at *Houston City Magazine* when he was a writer and I his editor. When we'd been married eight years, we adopted our son, and now we live in a house on the edge of a cliff in Austin.

"In my mid-50s, I feel a greater contentment, and, concomitantly, a feeling of greater power as a writer. After three collections of stories, a memoir, two novels, co-authoring a play, journalism—and my unpublished novels—I feel surer of what I take on in my writing. My work needs time so that I can develop it fully, and this is as true with stories as with longer works of fiction. I have always felt my way with a novel for years and then plunged into certainty out of a desire to see it whole; this habit of mind and work will probably never change, no matter how I wish for certainty from the start. The difference is that at my best I greet the process with some pleasure as well as with recognition of my ways."

Laura Furman was born on November 19, 1945 in the New York City borough of Brooklyn. She was educated at Bennington College, in Vermont, from which she graduated in 1963. Furman's first collection of short fiction, *The Glass House: A Novella and Stories*, included "Last Winter" and other somber tales. Reviewing the book for *Library Journal* (August 1, 1980), Mary Soete wrote, "These are moody, stylish *New Yorker* set pieces full of cool observations and even chillier ironies, secrets, unspoken words and unacted gestures, and women who come to quietly nihilistic conculusions about their perfectly organized lives. . . . Furman's is the sure, unsettling voice of a gifted newcomer."

Two years after her story collection appeared, Furman debut novel, *The Shadow Line*, was published. The book's protagonist, Liz Gold, has just moved from New York to Houston in the hopes of starting anew. Her first assignment as a new reporter for a local magazine, however, is to uncover the truth about the mysterious death of the mistress of a powerful businessman—which proves a dangerous task. Describing *The Shadow Line* as "a memorable, remarkably finished first novel," Michele M. Leber suggested in her review for *Library Journal* (July 1, 1982) that "this finely crafted, understated novel may establish Furman as the fictive voice of southeast Texas; here Houston and Galveston are as well realized as most characters, and the plot seems rooted in the region."

Furman's next book was her second collection of short stories, *Watch Time Fly*. "The success of these quiet, plotless stories rests largely on Furman's unusually strong sense of place, whether they are set in cities (New York, London) or in the rural Northeast (Vermont, upstate New York)," Lynette Friesen wrote for *Library Journal* (July 1, 1983). "The environment is evoked so vividly that it functions in the reader's imagination almost as a second protagonist: houses, furniture, streets, gardens, all enrich the stories with their presence and their importance. . . . Written in a cadenced prose that is a pleasure to read, this collection never falters."

Sadie Ash, the heroine of Furman's next novel, *Tuxedo Park*, is orphaned at age 12 and spends the rest of her life in pursuit of meaningful human connections. While still a teenager she becomes pregnant by Willard Weaver, a failed painter from a wealthy family. They marry, but several years later, after the birth of a second daughter, Willard demands a divorce, which Sadie, who clings to traditional notions of romance and marriage, is unwilling to grant without a fight—even if her idealism is maintained at the expense of her daughters' best interests.

Reviewing the novel for the *Christian Science Monitor* (October 21 1986), Sara Terry wrote that Furman "has a keen eye for mannerisms and detail. That talent serves her well in crafting this very human tale which underscores the dangers of living in the past or the future at the expense of commitment to the present—and to those who live in the present." Describing *Tuxedo Park* as "rewarding, if melancholy, reading," Laura E. Obolensky pointed out in the *New Republic* (January 5–12 1987) that Furman "decries the twin bedrocks of wifely virtue, fidelity and domesticity, and recycles one of fiction's most overworked motifs: our disconnectedness from one another and from our own inner selves. . . . [The author] proves once again that she is a writer of enormous grace and sensitivity who possesses a keen if unsettling genius for stripping the psyche of its deceptions—self and otherwise—in order to reveal the subliminal conceits that at their most insidious make human compatibility such a formidable challenge."

Ordinary Paradise, Furman's memoir, focuses on the impact that her mother's untimely death from ovarian cancer had on her family. Unable to discuss her grief with her emotionally reserved father, Furman took to self-mutilation and was eventually hospitalized for her depression.

According to GraceAnne A. DeCandido, writing for *Booklist* (September 1, 1998), "Furman takes us through her adolescence and writing career hiding from and seeking her mother's life and memory. . . . Some of the vignettes along the way—corn on the cob, spilled milk, a silver ring that had to be cut from her finger—are a bit too small, or recounted too narrowly, to resonate widely. Still, the larger aspect of Furman's need for a way to cope with her mother's illness and death is spun out with steely clarity." While Andrea Cooper, a critic for the *New York Times Book Review* (January 24 1999), praised Furman's prose as "dreamy" and "imagistic," she felt that the author left too many questions unanswered: "By turns emotionally muted and fiercely angry, she is forthright about the possible distortions of memory. However, for all its honesty and heroic appeal, the memoir feels muffled, as if a layer of story lies hidden. How did she lead herself from loneliness to a happy marriage, from numbing depression to stories that would earn a Guggenheim fellowship and publication in *The New Yorker*?"

Furman's most recent short-story collection is *Drinking with the Cook*. Most of the heroines in these 13 melancholy tales are suburban women whose lives are lonely and isolated. "Though a few of the narratives are stretched thin by their heroine's caution or inertia, in the main Furman's quiet observations of lonely lives ring true, and she establishes a small universe of people looking for connection but unable to escape the bonds of self-doubt," a reviewer wrote for *Publishers Weekly* (March 19, 2001). In the *New York Times Book Review* (June 3, 2001), Deborah Mason wrote: "This stinging collection . . . shows that she is still adept at conjuring up scenes of domestic bliss gone south, constructing houses that are unnerving blueprints of their owner's emotional capaciousness, or lack of it. . . . There is an abiding melancholy in most of the lives [Furman] depicts here, a sadness that is seldom relieved by irony or humor. But Furman's portraits of her characters are rich in telling detail, showing them utterly and convincingly rooted in their worlds. Her luxuriant histories of grief are sure and exact, drawing the reader in and rarely loosening their grip."

—S.Y.

Suggested Reading: *Austin Chronicle* (on-line) Apr. 4, 2001; *Boston Globe* B p2 Sep. 13, 1998; *Houston Chronicle* Z p16 May 20, 2001; *Los Angeles Times* E p3 Apr. 2, 2001; *New Republic* p41+ Jan. 5, 1987; *New York Times Book Review* p18 Jan. 24, 1999, p53 June 3, 2001; *San Francisco Chronicle* p4 Sep. 7, 1986; *Washington Post Book World* p5 Sep. 19, 1982

Selected Books: fiction—*The Glass House: A Novella and Stories*, 1980; *The Shadow Line*, 1982; *Watch Time Fly*, 1983; *Tuxedo Park*, 1986;

Drinking with the Cook, 2001; nonfiction—
Ordinary Paradise, 1998; as editor—*Bookworms: Great Writers and Readers Celebrate Reading* (with E. Standard), 1997

Ralph Orlowski/AFP/Getty Images

Gaarder, Jostein

(GOUHRD-er, YOH-styn)

Aug. 8, 1952– Novelist

The best-selling novel in the world in 1995 was a lightly reworked philosophy textbook. Called *Sofies verden: roman om filosofiens* and written by the Norwegian author Jostein Gaarder, the book was initially intended to be a history of philosophy for people in their mid- to late teens—about the same age as the students in the philosophy classes Gaarder had been teaching when he wrote it. Gaarder, however, quickly grew tired of writing a pure history of ideas and introduced a narrative thread, creating a kind of didactic mystery story. The resulting book, Gaarder's fifth, was published in 1991, in Norway, where it became a surprise best seller. Editions in nearby Sweden and Denmark followed, and thereafter, interest in the book snowballed, leading, in 1995, to the book's appearance in English as *Sophie's World: A Novel about the History of Philosophy* and its ultimate recasting as, among other things, a 1997 video game and a 1999 film that was reported to be the most expensive Norwegian movie made up to that time. According to the Web site of Gaarder's Norwegian publisher, Aschehoug & Co., *Sophie's*

World has been translated into 53 languages—including Albanian and Tigrinya, one of the most widely spoken languages in the West African nation of Eritrea—and some 25 million copies of the book have been sold. Many of Gaarder's other books have also been translated into English, and though none of them has come close to reproducing the success of *Sophie's World*, many of them have been well received.

Jostein Gaarder was born on August 8, 1952 in the Norwegian capital of Oslo. His father, Knut Gaarder, was the director of a school and his mother, Inger Margrethe Gaarder, an author of children's books. After attending the Ingieråsen Secondary School outside his hometown, Gaarder went to Oslo University, where he studied Scandinavian languages and the history of philosophy and religion. He is reported to have pursued a Ph.D. in philosophy at Oslo but quit before finishing due to lack of money. Almost always referred to as a former high-school philosophy teacher, Gaarder seems instead to have taught philosophy primarily at a type of postsecondary boarding school called a folk school (Folkehøgskole) in the small town of Fana, just south of the city of Bergen and far to the west of Oslo. Gaarder began teaching at the Fana folk school, in 1981, and taught there until about 1992, when the success of *Sophie's World* allowed him to become a full-time writer.

Gaarder's first book, a collection of short fiction called *Diagnosen og andre noveller* (which can be translated as "the diagnosis and other stories"), appeared, in 1986, and was followed by *Barna fra Sikhavati* (which can be translated as "the children from Sukhavati"), in 1987. Both books remain unavailable in English translations, but Gaarder's 1988 children's story *Froskeslottet* was translated into English and released as *The Frog Castle*, in 1999. Praised by a number of reviewers for its simplicity and sometimes compared to Lewis Carroll's *Alice's Adventures in Wonderland*, the book tells the story of a boy named Gregory Peggory, who one night finds himself in the bewildering place called Frog Castle. (The hero's name is presumably a reference to the 1978 Frank Zappa song "The Adventures of Greggery Peccary," itself a reference to the actor Gregory Peck.) A reviewer in the *Scotsman* (December 4, 1999) wrote, "Gaarder's airy prose style is ideal for this story which snatches memories from reality and threads them through an extraordinary dream sequence in which Gregory is the hero. The depiction of that unquestioning acceptance which allows us all to dream our best dreams is excellent." The reviewer went on to note that the "occasional observation about the meanings of life" that Gaarder makes sometimes intrude upon the the story, but he urged readers to overlook them. Those moments might have contributed to what Eileen Batersby, in a review for the *Irish Times* (May 19, 2001), identified as the "heavy-handedly moral and drawn out" qualities of the story.

In 1990 Gaarder's fourth book, *Kabaalmysteriet*, appeared in Norway to great acclaim, winning an award from the Norwegian ministry of cultural affairs and a prize for books for children and young adults from the country's literary critics association. (Awards from organizations in other countries appeared in the following years, as the book reached a wider audience in the wake of the fame Gaarder achieved after the appearance of *Sophie's World*.) Published in English as *The Solitaire Mystery*, in 1996, the book is divided into 53 chapters in imitation of a deck of cards, with the joker as its "hero," Gaarder told Jeffrey Staggs for the *Washington Times* (October 7, 1994), "because he is the outsider." At the center of the story is a boy named Hans Thomas, who joins his alcoholic father on a trip to Greece, where they think Hans's mother went when she left them to find herself years ago. Reviews of the book were often negative, but sales, particularly in the U.S., were fairly strong. (It should be noted that because the book appeared in English after *Sophie's World*, many reviewers often assumed it had been written later and commented that Gaarder appeared not to have improved as a storyteller since his success.) Offering one of the few unqualified expressions of praise, Beth Crome wrote for the *San Antonio Express-News* (July 21, 1996) that *The Solitaire Mystery* was "the kind of good book that makes you feel like a kid again" and that it "beautifully expresses a wonder at the world we live in." Other writers pointed to what they considered to be Gaarder's weaknesses as a storyteller and compared the book unfavorably to Carroll's *Alice* or to the Italian author Italo Calvino's *If on a Winter's Night a Traveler*, which Gaarder's book echoes formally. A writer for *Kirkus Reviews* (May 1, 1996) described the book as "fascinating and frustrating in equal measure" and pointed particularly to sections "that are ingenious and startling, reminiscent of the philosophical fantasies of the Victorian writer George MacDonald. But too often Gaarder's musings seem repetitious, the imagery hazy, the conclusions unsurprising."

In 1990 Gaarder began working on *Sophie's World* while on leave from the Fana folk school. His chief motivation, he has often told interviewers, was to write a history of philosophy that could be read by people of all educational backgrounds and ages but particularly by people in their teens. "My motto, when I wrote the book, was 'philosophy for all,'" Gaarder told Nicholas A. Basbanes for the Allentown, Pennsylvania *Morning Call* (January 8, 1995). Gaarder was also hoping to counter the proliferation of philosophical and religious writings loosely grouped under the term New Age. "I call the New Age material philosophical pornography," Gaarder told Basbanes, using words similar to those he put into the mouth of the book's philosopher character, Alberto Knox, at the end of the book. "Pornography gives people instant access to the erotic. Nobody really needs pornography, of course. What we really want is love, but love takes time. There are no shortcuts to real love, nor to philosophical insight. I think people are getting tired of this instant philosophy; what they want is the real stuff." After trying to write a purely discursive book, Gaarder gave up because he felt "like a professor sitting behind a desk," he told Jeffrey Staggs. The story Gaarder used to liven up the book focuses on Sophie Admundsen, an almost-15-year-old girl who one day begins receiving letters with lessons on philosophy sent to her by a mysterious older man, Alberto Knox. The lessons begin, Basbanes reported, with such questions as "Who are you?" and "Where does the world come from?" After that, they become a simplified, textbook-like series of essays on the history of philosophy, beginning with the early Greek philosophers known as the Pre-Socratics and moving up through the 20th century to discuss such figures as Jean-Paul Sartre and Simone de Beauvoir, both 20th-century philosophers, alongside references to the more recent philosophy of the environment as well. Over the course of the book, Sophie meets such philosophers as Socrates and Plato and learns, at a point, that she is in fact only a character in a novel, written by a man named Albert Knag for his daughter Hilde.

Early reviews of the Norwegian edition were apparently positive. In an essay for *Bookbird* (2006), Anne-Kari Skardhamar translated a Norwegian newspaper reviewer's description of the book as "audacious, moving—and clean." The book landed on the country's best-seller list and stayed there for at least the next three and a half years. Versions for other Scandinavian countries soon followed, with the Danish buyers alone snapping up a reported 110,000 copies by July 1994. By that time, about 350,000 copies were in print in Germany, and the English-language translation was set to appear. When the latter appeared, in the fall of 1994, German sales had reached more than half a million, and the book, already available in about 30 countries, had become one of the most popular in recent memory across all of Europe—a shock to perhaps no one as much as it was to Gaarder himself. After first chalking up his success to a particularly Scandinavian, then Germanic interest in philosophy, Gaarder eventually had to accept that in virtually every country in which it appeared it sold surprisingly, if not extraordinarily, well. "It's incredible, it's crazy, it's insane," Gaarder said in an interview with Mark Phillips for *CBS This Morning* (March 9, 1995). "This book, this odd book became a best-seller. It's—it's stupid."

Reviews of *Sophie's World* in the Anglophone press were almost uniformly mixed. Perhaps the most enthusiastic review, and one of the few to praise Gaarder's writing per se, came from the *Economist* (January 14, 1995). Calling the book "a marvellous piece of narrative fiction," the reviewer wrote, "The writing has clarity, an ease of style, and a way of presenting difficult ideas simply. Just occasionally an 'international bestseller' is not a tasteless confection of tripe and hype. *Sophie's World* is such a book. It leaves you wondering a little at the world—rather in the way that children do." Offering a more qualified but still positive assessment, Nicholas Tucker, writing for the *New Statesman & Society* (January 13, 1995), called attention to Sophie's relatively static character and a "sometimes po-faced" translation and argued that the book's narrative "is not sufficiently compelling to drag too many reluctant young philosophers along in its wake." Tucker nevertheless felt that the book was "an achievement. It proposes interestingly eclectic philosophical dilemmas and describes them with skill. [Charles] Darwin and [Karl] Marx get a look-in as well as [René] Descartes and [John Stuart] Mill, and the passages about [Sigmund] Freud are extremely fair. Philosophy is treated primarily as a quest for meaning and not as endless quibbling about the meaning of meaning. And we ignore at our peril its stress on today's 'ecophilosophy' movement."

Sometimes, reviewers called attention to the book's shortcomings as a narrative and occasionally faulted its handling of the philosophical material. "In this long, self-referential novel (to use the word loosely)," a writer for *Kirkus Reviews* (August 15, 1994) argued, "Gaarder presents philosophy in a clear, cogent way, using Sophie's and Hilde's experiences to illustrate his points. The reader who is expecting something other than a creative textbook, however, will be disappointed." Like many subsequent reviewers, this writer also expressed doubt that teenagers outside northern Europe would have much interest in the history of ideas, asserting: "Maybe Gaarder can fool Norwegian youths into learning philosophy, but savvy American kids won't be so easily hoodwinked." In the *New York Times Book Review* (September 25, 1994), John Vernon called Gaarder's writing "plain as a box" and the characters "tissue thin." Vernon continued: "Moreover, there is enough about the wonder and magic of philosophy in *Sophie's World* to make some readers reach for their guns. The meat of the book—its account of Western philosophical thought—ranges in quality from philoso-Disney to a series of accurate and intelligent précis. Alberto the philosopher is a kind of latter-day Mr. Wizard; whether we swallow his generously sweetened bait and become hooked on philosophy depends on the philosophy being expounded. On [Baruch] Spinoza and [David] Hume he is superb, but when he gets to Romanticism we see the supermarket encyclopedias lying open before his hidden God, Mr. Gaarder." Despite such reviews the book went on to win at least nine awards from various organizations or publications and turned Gaarder into one of his country's most visible citizens, and foreign publishers began actively releasing more of Gaarder's books, with two appearing in the U.S. in 1996 alone.

In addition to *The Solitaire Mystery*, Gaarder's work came to English readers through the translation of the 1992 children's book *Julemysteriet*, which was translated as *The Christmas Mystery,* in 1996. As with other books by Gaarder, *The Christmas Mystery* begins as a story about one young person, a boy named Joachim in this case, before moving on to tell the story of another young person, a girl named Elisabet, who is magically able to witness the birth of Jesus Christ. Reviews of the book were generally positive. The story, Sarah Johnson wrote in the London *Times* (November 16, 1996), "is outrageously old-fashioned, Christocentric and pedagogic—which is to say that many children, especially eight-to-twelves, will adore it." While joining other reviewers in suggesting that some of the references—from Scandinavian history to the present-day conflict between Israelis and Palestinians—might throw some readers off, Johnson nonetheless felt the book was "a skilful and lasting achievement, with all the elements of a perfect Christmas tale."

Gaarder's next book, *Bibbi Bokkens magiske bibliotek* (which can be translated as "Bibbi Booken's magic library") was published in Norway, in 1993, but has not been translated into English. *I et speil, I en gate*, which appeared in English, in 1998, as *Through a Glass, Darkly*, was also released in 1993. Reviews of the English translation were generally negative, with many critics finding the story of a conversation between an angel named Ariel and a dying girl named Cecilia to be superficial. Karen Armstrong, writing for the London *Times* (July 16, 1998) complained, "the novel represents an almost perverse flight from the tragic to the trivial. The reader longs to know what Ariel's God thinks about the death of children, mortality and the state of the world, but these great questions are kept firmly at bay. Occasionally Gaarder tries to introduce a more profound note. . . . But because Gaarder's narrative sticks so firmly to the literal, these remarks sound banal, statements of the self-evident." By contrast, Robert Dunbar, writing for the *Irish Times* (August 8, 1998), called the book "stunning," "beautiful," and "sad," noting that Gaarder demonstrates "the ease with which [he] has always presented complex ideas in accessible terms."

Gaarder's 1996 book *Hallo? Er det noen her?* was also published in English, in 1998. Translated as *Hello? Is Anybody There?*, the story is told in a letter to a young girl soon to be joined by a sibling. In the letter the girl's uncle explains what happened when his younger brother was born many years before. The fantastic events that follow led many critics to compare the book to Antoine de Saint-Exupéry's *The Little Prince*, in part because the illustrations for Gaarder's text, done by Sally Gardner, clearly refer to those Saint-Exupéry drew to accompany his story; most of these comparisons were made, however, in Saint-Exupéry's favor. A reviewer for *Publishers Weekly* (August 10, 1998) called Gaarder's work a "limp imitation" of *The Little Prince* and dismissed the book as "a tepid exercise." GraceAnne A. DeCandido, writing for *Booklist* (December 15, 1998), also called attention to the connections between the two books but concluded, "Odd but engaging, [Gaarder's tale] will surely sing to some children."

In 1996 Gaarder also published *Vita Brevis: Floria Aemilias brev til Aurel Augustin*, a novella about the relationship between a presumably real historical person whom Gaarder calls Floria Aemilia and her canonized former lover, St. Augustine, who was also the father of her son, Adeodatus. Written in the form of a letter and purporting to be a translation of a text Gaarder stumbled across in a Buenos Aires bookstore, the novella records Floria's response to reading Augustine's *Confessions*, which describes their relationship and discusses his decision to abandon her and their son as a prelude to his conversion to Christianity. The book was published in Great Britain and Australia as *Vita Brevis: A Letter to St. Augustine*, in 1997, with a translation by Sarah Perkins; its American edition, translated by Anne Born, appeared the following year under the title *That Same Flower: Floria Aemilia's Letter to Saint Augustine*. Reviewers found Gaarder's premise evocative but were divided over the question of how well he had imagined Floria's feelings and thoughts. Tony Baker, writing for the South Australian *Advertiser* (December 13, 1997), praised the book for being "large in themes and lightly worn erudition" and concluded that "Floria Aemilia emerges not as a bimbo of ancient history but as an educated sceptical peer . . . who questions Augustine's beliefs and who finds him timid, self-centered and terrified of pleasure." Lanae Hjortsvang Isaacson argued for *World Literature Today* (Spring 1998) that "Gaarder frames two opposing views of life brilliantly" but that "the text becomes somewhat repetitive, as Floria reiterates her argument at every turn, using Augustine's own words to chide and rebuke him." For some readers the result was that Augustine remained the more sympathetic and commanding figure. Calling Augustine "one of history's subtlest, most thoroughly ironic writers," a reviewer for *Publisher's Weekly* (November 17, 1997) chided Gaarder for attempting to make the saint "a straw man" and added: "Would that [Augustine] could reply to this patchwork of anodyne feminism, coy pseudo-scholarly footnotes and hack psychoanalysis. . . . Although Floria's arguments are occasionally poignant and witty, it is hard to imagine her as the lover of the fourth-century genius—easier to envision her in the faded clippings of a 1970s *Ms.* magazine."

Gaarder continued using the epistolary form in his next book, though this time the correspondence at the heart of the novel is conducted by E-mail.

Entitled *Maya* and originally published in 1999, the book appeared in English the following year. The narrator in this case is John Spooke, an English writer, and the story he tells relates an experience he had on the eve of the millennium on the South Pacific island of Taveuni. *Maya*'s unusually large adult cast, its fascination with natural history, and its characteristic emphasis on ideas seemed to intrigue reviewers, but many came away dissatisfied. "For all its weird cast, odd mixture of topics and deliberate weaving of mystery," Chris Arthur wrote for the *Scotsman* (October 21, 2000), "*Maya* offers a rather pedestrian, often ponderous, reflection on the nature of the universe and the meaning of life." Still, Arthur conceded, "this odd mongrel of a book poses some intriguing questions—about beginnings, chance, kinship, loss, and meaning. It also keeps readers guessing and often displays a nice, if sometimes overblown, turn of phrase."

Reviewers generally greeted Gaarder's next novel more warmly; indeed, perhaps no other work by Gaarder up to that time had been as resistant to charges of ponderousness and poor characterization. Called *Sirkusdirektørens datter* and appearing first in 2001, the book was issued in English translation the following year as *The Ringmaster's Daughter*. Its main character is a ghost writer named Petter, also called "The Spider," whose fertile imagination gives rise to story after story—making him a much in-demand figure in the literary world—but also thrusts him into a confusing world of lies. In the Alberta, Canada, *Edmonton Journal* (December 8, 2002), Tim McNamara echoed the book's relatively few other reviewers by calling the novel "engrossing." The stories Petter tells, McNamara added, "are often so good that the reader hopes they will keep going. I felt the same about the novel as a whole. The reader would like it to go on and on. It is hard to think of a higher compliment than that."

Critics found Gaarder's most recent novel similarly appealing. Titled *Appelsinpiken* (2003) and published in English under the title *The Orange Girl* (2004), the book weaves together the recollections of a son named Georg with a letter from his father, Jan—a letter written more than a decade before the novel opens, when Jan was about to die of cancer, but received by Georg only recently. John Moore, writing for the British newspaper *Morning Star* (November 1, 2004), found the book "well measured" and argued that Gaarder's "instructive style" was "only slightly intrusive." John Peters, writing for *School Library Journal* (January 2005), noted that over the course of the book, Gaarder "pops a Big Question" but argued that "the leisurely way he prepares readers for it may lose most of them."

In 2006, Gaarder published an anthology of selections from his works, entitled *Sjakk matt* (which can be translated as "checkmate"). Besides being a writer, Gaarder runs a foundation, which he and his wife created in 1997. The foundation offers an annual $100,000 award, called the Sophie Prize, to a person or group making a creative effort to provide for the world's long-term well-being, principally in environmental terms. (Human-rights and peace activists as well as journalists, however, have also received the award.) To Gaarder, the type of work that they carry out is closely related to the work of a writer. At a meeting of the Norwegian branch of the organization International PEN, Gaarder said, according to a report for the *Warsaw Voice* (October 3, 2004): "The question for writers and artists at the start of the third millennium must be: what shift in consciousness do we need? What is a sustainable wisdom? Which qualities of life are the most important? Which values are the true values? What is the good life? And importantly: what kind of mobilization is possible in the global village?" Defining literature as "nothing less than a celebration of mankind's consciousness," Gaarder asked: "So shouldn't an author be the first to defend human consciousness against annihilation?"

Gaarder lives in Oslo. He married Siri Dannevig, a drama teacher, in 1974, and they have two sons. The younger, Kristoffer, was born around 1983. The elder, Nikolas, was born around 1976 and is listed as a jury member for the Sophie Prize.

—D.R.

Suggested Reading: Aschehoug Agency Web site; *Bookbird* p30 2006; *Economist* p77 Jan. 14, 1995; *Irish Times* p75 May 19, 2001, p14 Dec. 21, 2005; *Kirkus Reviews* Aug. 15, 1994; *Los Angeles Times* E p1 Sep. 8, 1994; *Morning Call* F p3 Jan. 8, 1995; *New York Times* p42 Sep. 25, 1994

Selected Books in English Translation: *Sophie's World*, 1994; *The Christmas Mystery*, 1996; *The Solitaire Mystery*, 1996; *Hello? Is Anybody There?*, 1998; *That Same Flower: A Letter to St. Augustine*, 1998; *Through A Glass, Darkly*, 1998; *The Frog Castle*, 1999; *Maya*, 2000; *The Ringmaster's Daughter*, 2002; *The Orange Girl*, 2004

Galgut, Damon

1963– Novelist; short-story writer; playwright

Though the South African novelist Damon Galgut published his first book, *A Sinless Season*, in 1982, while still a teenager, he did not receive much international attention until 2003, when he published *The Good Doctor*—an allegorical tale about racial strife in his homeland that earned him a spot on the short list for both the Booker Prize for Fiction, the Commonwealth Writers' Prize, and the International IMPAC Dublin Literary Award. The recognition "made a huge difference to my life and career already," he told Ginanne Brownell for *Newsweek* (October 6, 2003). "My first book got a fair amount of attention primarily because I was so young when I wrote it. Since then my career has been steadily shrinking till this turnaround. It is nice to know that the spotlight can still fall so far south."

Damon Galgut sent the following autobiographical statement to *World Authors 2000–2005*:

"I was born in 1963 in Pretoria into a family well known in South African legal circles—my grandfather, Oscar, was a prominent judge in the Appeal Court in Bloemfontein, the country's highest court. Later my father, then an advocate, would also become a judge, as would an uncle, while three of my cousins also went into law. It was hoped, if not expected, that I would follow suit, but I knew from an early age that writing was the only activity that felt meaningful to me.

Scott Barbour/Getty Images

"At the age of six I fell seriously ill with a cancer that almost killed me. During several months in hospital and through the five years of chemotherapy that followed, I learned to associate love and attention with being read to by various relatives—which set off in me a deep desire to make stories of my own. My mother was a journalist at one time, and encouraged this vaguely subversive love of words in her eldest son. I wrote my first attempt at a novel when I was 14 years old, at a time when 'normal' South African white boys were launching themselves into sports and other 'healthy' activities. *A Sinless Season*, my first published book appeared when I was 18 and drew enough attention to keep me quiet for another seven years. It's not a book I'm especially proud of today, but it did confirm me in a path I might otherwise have been forced to abandon.

"I wrote some plays too in those early years, and went on to study and teach drama at the University of Cape Town, but prose was always my first passion. I have published five books in all. My second book, *Small Circle of Beings*, appeared when I was 24 and dealt with my childhood illness and the subsequent breakup of my family. *The Beautiful Screaming of Pigs* came out in 1991 and was my first tentative venture into South Africa's political terrain. *The Quarry* (1995) tried to make myth out of obdurate reality, and *The Good Doctor* (2003) is an expression of how it feels to be a disempowered white man in the new South Africa.

"I belong, I suppose, to a strange in-between generation—not old enough to have made or dismantled apartheid, but also not young enough not to know what it meant. I benefitted from its material privileges while I was growing up, and participated in its power structures (like military service), while never feeling part of its values or ideology. So to some extent I stand outside both the society I was born into as well as the one which has replaced it. It's an odd fate being a white observer in Africa at this point in history. But I also don't believe that being human is entirely circumscribed by politics. I have experienced enough personal tragedy to know how much the interior world of psychology and personality propels a life along. As a writer, I would like to be true to both the inner and outer worlds—most specifically, to the place where they meet, which is where most of us live."

Galgut first earned media attention with *A Sinless Season*, which was considered an excellent showing for such a young author. The novel opens as three 15-year-old friends are sent off to Bleda Reformatory for committing a crime. Shortly after their arrival one of the boys is murdered and another raped. These events precipitate a downward spiral that ends with the reformatory students chasing the principal, who fears for his life, from the school grounds. According to Kem Nunn, writing for the *New York Times* (March 31, 1985), the novel "asks to be taken seriously on at least one level, as an inquiry into the nature of sin, while on another it seeks to entertain as a kind of Gothic murder mystery. . . . It is as a study of sin that the novel is least satisfying, particularly in light of the revelation with which the book ends. . . . The ending cheats by saving the author from moving into the near-Dostoyevskian depths the crime in question seems to call for if we are to

make sense of motivation and character. On the other hand, the novel does succeed on some levels. There is a richly drawn physical environment—a wild, dark land—and much of the best writing is given over to its description. It is a landscape we eventually come to see as reflecting the even darker emotional and sexual undercurrents of Bleda itself. And in making these undercurrents palpable, Mr. Galgut best demonstrates his talents." In a review for *Library Journal* (May 1, 1985), Grove Koger wrote that the young author had failed to "communicate sufficient insight into the nature of the relationships uniting the three friends, relationships that precipitate a shocking but never-quite-believable sequence of events." But, he noted, the novel "possesses a unique and poetic vision."

It took Galgut several years to publish his next work of prose fiction, *Small Circle of Beings* (1988), a novella accompanied by four short stories, all of which are set in South Africa in the 1980s. Though the eponymous novella is semiautobiographical—it is the story of a six-year old cancer patient—Galgut made the daring move of narrating the novel from the mother's perspective. "Throughout the book Galgut's characters find themselves stuck in emotional prisons and pacts," Austin MacCurtain wrote for the London *Sunday Times* (December 2, 1990), "and he is a writer of considerable subtlety and insight, although his emotional dramas are no holiday for the reader."

Galgut's next full-fledged novel, *The Beautiful Screaming of Pigs*, is the story of Patrick Winter, a young odd man out, who does not share his father's macho sensibilities nor the values of his privileged peers. Nonetheless, he dutifully shows up for his compulsary service in South Africa's military and is sent to the Namibian border. There, Patrick is traumatized by the death of another soldier, sending him into an emotional breakdown. He later revisits Namibia with his mother, and while there is finally forced to come to terms with his own part in the region's politics. "Galgut's sensitive and economic prose both encapsulates the young man's anguish and isolation and conveys a strong attachment to the battle-torn continent," a reviewer wrote for the London *Sunday Times* (October 11, 1992). J. D. F. Jones, writting for the *Financial Times* (June 15, 1991), described *The Beautiful Screaming of Pigs* as "a striking near-debut promising great things in the future" and "the sort of brusque, subbed-back novel that reminds you of what good, taut prose can achieve." *The Beautiful Screaming of Pigs* was selected for the Central News Agency Literary Award in 1992.

Considered by most to be Galgut's finest novel to date, *The Good Doctor* is set in a rural hospital in postapartheid South Africa. Dr. Frank Eloff, who formerly served as a soldier, forms an unlikely friendship with a young, idealistic colleague, Laurence Waters. Through their relationship Galgut explores the influence of the generational divide on South African society. "The changeover in South Africa happened overnight," he explained to Brownell. "I taught at the University of Cape Town, and the kind of young people rising up through the university have no idea of what apartheid was about, what it entailed and what its values meant. To young people, black and white, it is a vague demi-event at the edge of things; it is not central in the way that it was to us when we were growing up. Maybe it should give us hope for the future and the remaking of the country that people do not carry that memory around with them."

The Good Doctor reinvigorated Galgut's career and many reviewers compared it with the works of such noted authors as Graham Greene and, unsurprisingly, J. M. Coetzee, the South African–born Nobel laureate. "Both Coetzee and Galgut write ruthlessly regimented prose, spring-load their books with sudden acts of violence, and do not reach too hard for pat resolution," John Freeman wrote for the Boston Globe (March 7, 2004). "But the similarities end there. What is unspoken in Coetzee's work is spelled out in Galgut's, making The Good Doctor an easier book to read, but somehow less satisfying." Though he described the book as "avowedly South African," Phil Whitaker wrote for the Lancet (December 20, 2003) that it "transcends its setting to become an exploration of clashes between perspectives, and the wreckage of upheaval. One might wish for a more invisible marriage between rounded character and novelistic theme, but that should not detract unduly from this complex, thought-provoking, and absorbing book."

Though Galgut's novel The Quarry was first published in South Africa in 1995 and made into an award-winning feature film in 1998, it was not issued in the U.S. until 2005, following the critical success of The Good Doctor. The unnamed protagonist of The Quarry is a penniless fugitive from justice. After a minister provides him with some aid, the fugitive repays his kindness by killing him and assuming his identity. "With increasingly stomach-tightening intensity, Galgut chronicles his troubled protagonist's struggles to evade capture under the ever-watchful eye of the authorities in his new town," a reviewer wrote for Publishers Weekly (November 29, 2004). "The suspenseful narrative never strays from the dreary force of its understated character development ('He reached out with his filthy, his bloody hands and began to eat without looking at them'). As the story builds to a climax, Galgut heightens the book's emotional power with tense one-page chapters until justice—cosmic justice, in this case—comes to call." Hazel Rochman, writing for Booklist (Nov 15, 2004), declared that Galgut's "clear, elemental prose is never generic," but Greg Bottoms unfavorably compared The Quarry to The Good Doctor in his review for Artforum International (April 2005). "The Quarry . . . is of a different, lesser order altogether," Bottoms wrote. "It is not

a bad book compared with what sometimes passes for literary fiction, but it comes across as fairly atrocious if you have just put down, as I had, Galgut's prizeworthy newer work. . . . Perhaps there's a lesson in this. It is a common mystification to think brilliant writers spring onto the scene fully formed, when in fact they almost always labor and improve over long years. Given Galgut's gargantuan subject—a nation in violent flux, a culture grappling with a new identity in the face of an oppressive past—it's understandable that he has struggled to find a suitable narrative form. His recent fiction, though, which deftly unearths South Africa's troubled history, has indeed been years in the making. Let's look forward to his next novel and, like one of his protagonists, avoid the past."

Galgut's dramatic works include Echoes of Anger, Party for Mother, Alive and Kicking, and The Greens Keeper. He lives in Cape Town and travels frequently. According to some press reports, he owns neither a television nor a car.

—S.Y.

Suggested Reading: Boston Globe H p7 Mar. 7, 2004; Economist p81 Sep. 20, 2003; (London) Sunday Times Features p53 Sep. 14, 2003; New York Times E p27 Jan. 21, 2000; New York Times Book Review p7 Mar. 31, 1985; Newsweek p66 Oct. 6, 2003

Selected Books: A Sinless Season, 1982; Small Circle of Beings, 1988; The Beautiful Screaming of Pigs, 1991; The Quarry, 1995; The Good Doctor, 2003

Gerritsen, Tess

June 12, 1953– Novelist

Tess Gerritsen, a popular writer of medical thrillers, often finds inspiration in the daily newspaper. Her novels—which include Harvest (1996), Life Support (1997), Bloodstream (1998), Gravity (1999), The Surgeon (2001), The Apprentice (2002), The Sinner (2003), Body Double (2004), and Vanish (2005)—deal with such contemporary problems as the illegitimate use of organs for transplant, the quest for longer life at any price, and the ramifications of sexual abuse. While Gerritsen is sometimes derided by critics—one, quoted on her official Web site, admitted a desire to slap her and suggested that readers accost her on the street—her fans disagree, and her books have landed on the best-seller list numerous times.

Tess Gerritsen was born on June 12, 1953 in San Diego California. Her parents, Ruby Tao and Ernest Tom, were of Chinese descent, and her father owned a Chinese seafood restaurant. Gerritsen's great-grandfather had been a poet, and she told an interviewer for Bookreporter.com that she had a "childhood of great books and great food." Gerritsen's novels are sometimes accused of being too horrific, and she has attributed her affinity for such topics to her mother. "When [my mother] came to the U.S., her command of English was a bit spotty. The one thing she understood, and enjoyed, was American horror films. No need to understand English in a horror film. You see Frankenstein or the Mummy coming after you, and you don't need English to understand that this is a bad thing," Gerritsen wrote on her Web site. "My mother dragged me and my younger brother to every horror film that came to San Diego. I grew up cowering in fright in movie theaters. My girlhood was fraught with nightmares of *Body Snatchers* and *Them* and those alien ships from *Robinson Crusoe on Mars*. If you want to understand where my books come from, all you need to do is watch a few horror films from the 60's. . . . [My mother] awakened my imagination. She (and Hollywood) made me think: 'What's the worst that can happen?' And that's exactly what goes on in my books. I'm always thinking: 'What's the worst that can happen?' And then I try to make it happen."

As a child Gerritsen had an avid interest in science and sometimes collected snakes and lizards in order to study them. She majored in physical anthropology at Stanford University, graduating in 1975, and went on to study medicine at San Francisco State University. After earning her medical degree, in 1979, she moved to Honolulu, Hawaii, to complete a residency in internal medicine, along with her husband, Jacob, also a physician, whom she had married in 1977.

Gerritsen and her husband practiced medicine in Honolulu, and she soon had two sons, Joshua and Adam. While on maternity leave in the early 1980s, Gerritsen began to write romance fiction. Her interest in the genre had been sparked during her residency by a grateful patient who had passed on a bagful of romance novels she had read during her hospital stay. Although Gerritsen originally intended to donate the books to Goodwill, she became hooked. "A week [after I got them], I'd read every book in that sack," she wrote on her official Web site. "Soon I found myself slipping romance novels into my grocery cart, along with the milk and eggs. Exhausted though I was by the demands of medical training, I became a voracious romance reader . . . all the time feeling slightly sheepish about my secret addiction. Wait, I was a medical doctor! A Stanford graduate! Why wasn't I reading, oh . . . Proust instead? Then one night, while on Intensive Care rotation, I happened to glance around at the ICU nurses who were taking their coffee breaks, and I realized that they were all reading romance novels. They were doing it happily and unashamedly. If you've ever worked in a hospital, then you know that the smartest people in the building are probably the ICU nurses. I thought: if these women aren't embarrassed by their reading material, why should I be?"

Gerritsen found that she had a talent for writing and began publishing a chain of Harlequin romances, some with medical settings or elements, including *Call After Midnight* (1987), *Under the Knife* (1990), *Never Say Die* (1992), *Whistleblower* (1992), *Presumed Guilty* (1993), *Peggy Sue Got Murdered* (1993), *In Their Footsteps* (1994), *Thief of Hearts* (1995), and *Keeper of the Bride* (1996). Although the books, like most in their genre, were not critically successful, they can still be found on shelves, and fans of her later thrillers are sometimes surprised to find that Gerritsen was once a prolific Harlequin author. Gerritsen continued to practice medicine until 1989, when she stopped to write for Harlequin full-time. In 1990 she and her family moved to the small town of Camden, Maine.

At the encouragement of her agent, Gerritsen, who had also written the screenplay for *Adrift*, a 1993 CBS Movie of the Week, tried her hand at a new genre: the medical thriller. It was, she has told interviewers, a chance to reach a wider audience, earn more money, and tackle various issues that interested her. *Harvest*, published in 1996, was inspired by a conversation in which a security specialist told her that he had heard that children were being kidnapped in Moscow by the Russian mafia for use as organ donors for wealthy patients. Although she was not able to verify the story, she used the idea behind it for *Harvest*, in which an idealistic young surgical resident gives a heart to a deserving boy instead of to the rich woman whose husband is willing to pay for it. She angers the senior staff at the hospital and gets into real trouble when her boyfriend, a transplant surgeon, tries to harvest her own liver. The novel marked Gerritsen's first appearance on the *New York Times* best-seller list, but many critics panned it. J. D. Reed wrote for *People* (October 8, 1996) that despite "frantic action and flashing scalpels, *Harvest* remains a terminally bad read." On her Web site Gerritsen quotes a *Publishers Weekly* reviewer who stated that the book would appeal to "only readers who move their lips." Gerritsen compares receiving reviews as vicious as that one to being a mother whose infant is attacked with an ice pick; she writes, "I doubt there's an author alive with skin thick enough to be able to just brush these off. After all these years as a novelist, truly cruel reviews still make me double over in pain and make me want to crawl into bed and pull the sheets over my head."

The quest for eternal youth provided the background for *Life Support*, published the following year to mixed reviews. Dr. Toby Harper, the book's protagonist, becomes suspicious when an old man disappears after coming into the hospital through the emergency room. The patient, seemingly senile, may have been part of a secret experiment to rejuvenate the wealthy. A *Publishers Weekly* (June 23, 1997) critic found that Gerritsen "adeptly integrates medical details into a taut and troubling thriller." Cynthia Sanz, the reviewer for *People* (August 18, 1997), agreed that the "chilling science (footnoted to real journal articles) and breathless, ER-style pacing make it a quick delightfully scary read," but she found the characters "paper-thin."

Bloodstream, Gerritsen's 1998 novel, is set in a small town ironically named Tranquillity, where the widowed main character, Dr. Claire Elliot, hopes to establish her new medical practice and keep her son away from bad influences. When violence erupts among the town's teenagers, Elliot must try to track down the cause, which might lie in an organism in the polluted town lake—or might be supernatural. Some reviewers thought *Bloodstream* demonstrated that Gerritsen was honing her writing skills, and with her next book, *Gravity* (1999), which she has described as one of her favorites, she chanced a move into the realm of science fiction. Her fans were disappointed. "I've puzzled over just why this book sold so poorly," she wrote on her Web site. "I've heard criticism from some readers that it was simply too technical, or that the topic of space travel didn't appeal to them. I guess not everyone's an old [*Star Trek* fan] like me. But every time I look up at the sky, I feel both a great sense of wonder and a deep sense of dread about what's up there—and whether it wants to exterminate us. I just had to explore that issue of doom falling upon us from space, because it's a recurrent nightmare of mine, and one that I still haven't shaken. Readers who happen to be big fans of *Gravity* often write to ask me why I don't write more books like it. The truth is, I want to! I wish there was a market for it."

Gerritsen returned to the genre of medical thriller with her next book, the first in a series featuring Jane Rizzoli, a homicide detective. In *The Surgeon* Rizzoli pursues a case in which a female doctor is stalked by a serial killer whose moniker is "The Surgeon," because of his habit of cutting out the wombs of his victims before he slits their throats. (Despite garnering the review in which the critic confessed to wanting to slap Gerritsen, *The Surgeon* won an award from the Romance Writers of America as best romantic suspense novel of the year.) Both the Surgeon and Rizzoli returned in 2002 in *The Apprentice*. A *Publishers Weekly* (July 22, 2002) reviewer called Rizzoli "a terrific lead character . . . who rivals Patricia Cornwell's Kay Scarpetta for intensity and complexity." In *The Sinner* (2003) Rizzoli makes another appearance, joined this time by Dr. Maura Isles, a Boston medical examiner. "While Rizzoli handles the crimes, " a *Kirkus Reviews* (June 15, 2003) critic wrote, "Dr. Isles delivers arias on death and the sweet hell of human existence. . . . 'A place of death has a power all its own. Long after the body is removed and the blood scrubbed away, such a place still retains the memory of what has happened there. It holds echoes of screams, the lingering scent of fear. And like a black hole, it sucks into its vortex the rapt attention of the living who cannot turn away, cannot resist a glimpse into hell.'"

Rizzoli and Isles appear together again in *Body Double* (2004), considered by many reviewers to be Gerritsen's best novel to date. In it, Rizzoli, hunting a serial killer who stalks pregnant women, is about to become a mother for the first time. In a representative critique, a writer for *Kirkus Reviews* opined, "Doc Gerritsen rises to her best yet, skirting neatly around the cliche plotting usually tied to serial killers. . . . Gerritsen always does well on the [sales] charts, but this masterful outing should rocket her into the top bracket of suspense writers."

Gerritsen, who maintains a strict schedule of publishing a book a year, featured Rizzoli and Isles in her 2005 effort, *Vanish*. This time Rizzoli, still pregnant, is taken hostage by a desperate young woman. The book, which explores the themes of sexual slavery and human trafficking, was nominated in the category of best novel for a prestigious Edgar Award from the Mystery Writers of America. In 2006 Rizzoli and Isles returned in *The Mephisto Club*, in which they struggle to find the killer of a young woman who has been found with mysterious symbols and Latin phrases scrawled on her corpse with blood.

Tess Gerritsen, whose Web site includes an extensive section labeled "Creepy Biological Facts," is an amateur violinist and enjoys growing roses; her gardens have been admiringly written up in several local magazines.

—S.Y.

Suggested Reading: *Kirkus Reviews* p823 June 15, 2003, p509 June 1, 2004; *Library Journal* p135 July 1, 1996; *People* p35 Aug. 18, 1997; *Publishers Weekly* p66 Mar. 16, 1990, p67 June 23, 1997, p159 July 22, 2002; Tess Gerritsen's Web site

Selected Books: *Harvest*, 1996; *Life Support*, 1997; *Bloodstream*, 1998; *Gravity*, 1999; *The Surgeon*, 2001; *The Apprentice*, 2002; *The Sinner*, 2003; *Body Double*, 2004; *Vanish*, 2005; *The Mephisto Club*, 2006

Gibson, Miles

Feb. 10, 1947– Novelist

Miles Gibson is known for his unique brand of fiction, which places intense, passionate characters in imaginative, often surreal, circumstances. Because Gibson regularly experiments with setting and style—his works range from crime fiction to romantic comedy—his novels are difficult to categorize. One characteristic distinguishing them all, however, is the author's witty, satirical sense of humor. Nevertheless, as Gibson told James Keating for an interview posted on the Unofficial Miles Gibson

Fan Page (on-line), he does not consider himself a comic writer. "In fact, I've always felt I was writing tragedy. The human condition is farcical—that's the tragedy. It helps to explain our endless struggle for dignity. We're absurd creatures. We want to be heroic but we're merely buffoons. I suppose we laugh when we spot the difference."

Born on February 10, 1947 in New Forest, England, Miles Gibson spent much of his childhood in what he described in an essay on his unofficial fan site as "the draughty little seaside town of Christchurch, Dorset," on the southern coast. He studied at the Somerset Junior School and later at Somerset Secondary Modern (now called the Grange), but he failed to make a strong academic impression at either institution. (A biographical statement posted on the Do-Not Press Web site satirically mentions crafting a toast rack in woodworking class as one of his significant accomplishments.) Gibson did enjoyed reading as a hobby, however, and has since observed, as posted on his fan page, "I think I became a writer because I was bad at school games. When you're never picked for the football team you're left with time to read the wrong books and take long flights of imagination."

Because of his poor grades, upon the completion of his secondary education Gibson had few prospects for attending college. Instead, he turned to the field of advertising—which he described as "the artist's equivalent of joining the army." While training to become an art director, Gibson was largely relegated to making tea and running errands. Nevertheless, he entered a writing competition organized by a large London advertising agency, and his submission made a strong impression. Within a few months, he had been offered a job as a junior copywriter at J. Walter Thompson, where he remained from 1968 to 1972. As Gibson recalled on his fan page, "I wrote for several years in praise of dog biscuits, cough drops and women's underwear." However, during this time, he also began writing his own fiction. In 1969 Gibson won a Young Writer of the Year award from the London *Daily Telegraph*. After leaving advertising in 1972, he supported himself doing freelance writing, often for the *Telegraph*'s Sunday magazine section. During this period, he published two books of poetry, *The Guilty Bystander* (1970) and *Permanent Damage* (1973).

In approaching his first novel, *The Sandman* (1984), Gibson decided that he wanted to break the pattern of many first-time novelists, who often present thinly veiled autobiographies. As he wrote on his fan page, "*The Sandman*, the journal of a serial killer written as a black comedy, seemed the perfect challenge. No-one would accuse me of writing myself into the story." Nevertheless, *The Sandman* did contain some biographical elements. For example, the main character, Mackerel Burton, like Gibson, grew up in a small seaside town, where he often amused himself with tricks and dark magic. As an adult, he finds himself stalking the streets of London looking for random victims. The novel received many positive reviews, although one critic, Isabel Quigly, writing for the London *Financial Times* (January 21, 1984), described it as "compelling and talented, readable and promising, but not powerful enough to shock."

Gibson's next novel, *Dancing with Mermaids* (1985), was also set in an English seaside town, this one known as Rams Horn. The story explores the odd and often surreal lives of the town's residents, many of whom are motivated by lust and sexual fantasy. A group of schoolboys, for example, plot to give a friend's mother sleeping pills so that they can take off her clothes and indulge their imaginations; a doctor takes steps to seduce a clairvoyant widow with an herbal aphrodisiac, and an African sailor beds both his landlady and her daughter. The novel drew many comparisons to *Under Milk Wood*, a play by the Welsh poet Dylan Thomas that explores the love lives of inhabitants of a small coastal village in Wales. Yet, as Richard Eder noted for the *Los Angeles Times* (November 12, 1986), "*Dancing with Mermaids* is an *Under Milk Wood* with the volume turned up and everybody trying much harder." He added, "Its characters get up to more hare-brained schemes than the Milk Wooders, and are consumed by even more extravagant longings. What is missed is Dylan Thomas' tender balance. The delicate path between waking and sleeping, between reality and magic, becomes a floodlit pedestrian mall." Gibson was praised, however, for his "vibrant, electric prose that occasionally alternates with a beautiful, dreamlike passage or poetic description," by Thomas Lavoie, writing for *Library Journal* (November 15, 1986).

For his third novel, *Vinegar Soup* (1987), which was released in the United States under the title *Hotel Plenti*, Gibson drew inspiration from his travels in West Africa and his love of English cooking in shaping the main character, Gilbert Firestone, whom he described on his fan site as "a romantic, a dreamer, a man who wants to eat the world and suck on the bones." After the death of his wife, who drowns in a pan of soup, Firestone travels to Africa to work at the Hotel Plenti, known for such delicacies as crocodile stew and ape's foot. The book received widely varying reviews. In his critique for the *Guardian* (August 28, 1987), Normal Shrapnel opined, "Gibson writes with a nervous versatility that is often very funny and never lacks a life of its own, speaking the language of our time as convincingly as the aerosol graffiti on the steamy café window." A reviewer for the *New Yorker* (October 19, 1988) countered, "But where first you are won by language you are balked by stitch after dropped stitch. Objects are animated at the expense of character. . . . The disappointment is in proportion to the promise."

In *Kingdom Swann* (1990) Gibson presents a comical exploration of the pornography industry that existed in Victorian and Edwardian England. The novel's main character, the Kingdom Swann of the title, is a portrait painter known for his beautiful nudes and his skillful depictions of the human form; in the midst of the photography craze that gripped England after the Great Exhibition of 1851, he picks up a camera and soon finds himself one of the most popular pornographers in London. In her review for the London *Times* (March 15, 1990), Sabine Durrant praised the book's unique exploration of Victorian England. "The humour of Miles Gibson's writing rests in its combination of crudity and coyness, in the fine line it draws between mock 19th-century titillation and serious historic biography. Intricate, heavy-breathing details of the various imaginative states of dress and undress adopted by Swann's clients knock shoulders with explicit references to royal deaths and coronations, aeronautical inventions, and suffragette demonstrations." *Kingdom Swann* was adapted for BBC Television as *Gentleman's Relish* (2001), starring Billy Connolly and Sarah Lancashire.

Gibson's next novel, *Fascinated* (1993), revolves around Frank Fisher, a timid junior manager for the Fancy Wholesale Fruits Corporation, whose wife is having an affair with his boss. Through a series of strange accidents, he becomes involved with the beautiful daughter of a mob boss and must learn how to kill to win her heart. Max Rodenbeck, in his review for the London *Financial Times* (July 31, 1993), found much to both admire and criticize. "Gibson's writing is rich and randy, the plot as slick as it is predictable. But the characters are celluloid, the scenes a cartoon pastiche mixing Raymond Chandler with Arnold Schwarzenegger. A good read for sure, but *Fascinated* is little more than a clever kid's screenplay." Jo-Ann Goodwin for the London *Independent* (September 5, 1993) affirmed, "Miles Gibson clearly had a marvellous time writing this. Sad to say, [it] is a difficult pleasure to share."

In his next work, *The Prisoner of Meadow Bank* (1995), Gibson aims his satirical eye at Holly Walker, a thirty-something housewife who has become bored with her mundane life, which involves little more than gossiping with her friends and gorging on junk food in front of the television. Although her dull husband, Jack, a marketing manager who specializes in household items, is content with their situation, Holly feels trapped. She puts herself on a crash diet, takes a lover, and eventually leaves Jack, who is horrified at his wife's metamorphosis. Critics generally commended Gibson's exploration of everyday life. While Jason Cowley, writing for the London *Independent* (July 22, 1995), found fault with the fact that all the characters speak in "the unmistakably quirky voice of the author," he nonetheless praised Gibson's handling of the material. "What stops this normality from becoming a drag is that Gibson, unlike many writers, clearly cares for his characters and is moved by their difficulties. He may be sentimental but he is never mocking. Their small, diminished

lives interest him, and he will not condemn them. He delights in their eccentricities, in the waywardness and deficiencies of their speech, its fractured rhythms, repetitions and exaggerations. . . . It's hard not to be swayed by this authorial generosity, this largeness of heart."

After taking a long break from fiction, Gibson returned with *Mr. Romance* (2002), a comic novel narrated by 18-year-old Skipper Wandsworth, who shares his parent's boarding house. His mother enjoys nothing more than watching wrestlers on TV, while his father spends most of his time working on inventions, such as the Life Expectancy Wristwatch, in the basement. Their unusual lodgers include Senior Franklin, an unpublished novelist who spends hours disparaging other authors, and Janet, a shy department-store clerk with a fondness for romance novels. The action begins when the mysterious Mr. Marvel appears at the boarding house with a cardboard suitcase and a small wooden box. In the course of the novel Skipper develops a romantic interest in a returning boarder, Dorothy, an ex-dancer whom he last saw when he was just eight years old. *Mr. Romance*, a quirky comedy, ultimately explores many of the conventions of romance novels. In his laudatory review for the *New York Times* (January 19, 2003), David Finkle wrote, "True to form, at the end two pairs of lovers are united—but only after one of them has been reduced to spouting nonsense syllables. And here the story gently floats away, like a bubble that hasn't yet burst." David Peters, a reviewer for *Time Out* (August 14, 2002), found the novel "beautifully written" and concluded: "*Mr. Romance* is a novel brimming over with observations and quirks, wit and erudition. It is, however, devoid of murder, war, gratuitous sex and all the other apparent essentials of a bestseller. Still, there won't be many better novels from any better authors this year."

The title character of Gibson's most recent novel, *Einstein* (2004), is a clever mutt, who is rescued from the streets by Charlie Nelson, a dissatisfied man who is retracing his life in the hopes of proving that he has committed at least one meaningful act. "Used to employing the outrageous and the atrocious as the material of farce, Gibson now presses home the theme which has underpinned his other work: that modern life is rubbish," Richard Cabut wrote for *Time Out* (August 4, 2004). "Despite some excessive zaniness and an unhealthy measure of didacticism," Cabut continued, "*Einstein* celebrates escape from the deadening effects of routine and resistance to the destructive power of the mindless consumer. Beneath the surface wackiness, the book is an emphatic shout for those of us caught small and scared in the teeth of forces that sometimes we can neither control nor avoid."

Gibson, who prefers to remain outside of the literary circuit, currently resides with his wife in London. As he explained to James Keating, "I'm something of a recluse. I'm not a performance artist." Gibson described his writing habits on his fan site: "These days I like to write as I've always written, slowly and in pencil, draft after draft, half a page at a time, until I'm ready to transfer the work to computer. Language is everything. And whenever I lose my sense of purpose I turn to the perfect, polished prose of writers like [John] Updike and Bruno Schultz. I'll stop when I've mastered it."

—K.D.

Suggested Reading: (London) *Independent* p8 July 22, 1995; *Los Angeles Times* V p10 Nov. 12, 1986; *New York Times* VII p19 Jan. 19, 2003; *Time Out* p59 Aug. 14, 2002

Selected Books: *The Sandman*, 1984; *Dancing with Mermaids*, 1985; *Vinegar Soup*, 1987; *Kingdom Swann*, 1990; *Fascinated*, 1994; *The Prisoner of Meadow Bank*, 1995; *Mr. Romance*, 2002; *Einstein*, 2004

Lee Rothchild

Giddins, Gary

Mar. 21, 1948– Music critic

Gary Giddins has written book reviews and biographies, but his life has mainly been dedicated to the appreciation of jazz and its practitioners. He has been a concert and record producer, a writer of liner notes, a jazz columnist for the *Village Voice* and other media outlets, and the author of the essay collections *Riding on a Blue Note: Jazz and American Pop* (1981), *Rhythm-a-ning: Jazz*

Tradition and Innovation in the '80s (1985), *Faces in the Crowd: Players and Writers* (1992), *Visions of Jazz: The First Century* (1998), *Weather Bird: Jazz at the Dawn of its Second Century* (2004), and *Natural Selection: Gary Giddins on Comedy, Film, Music, and Books* (2006). His biographies— *Celebrating Bird: The Triumph of Charlie Parker* (1986), *Satchmo* (1988), and *Bing Crosby: A Pocketful of Dreams, the Early Years, 1903–1940* (2001)—have been widely praised. In the *New York Times Book Review* (July 4, 1993), Giddins wrote that folk-music collector Alan Lomax's "discerning reconstructions . . . miraculously evade the blurring of time. They give life to a domain most of us can never know, and yet one that summons us with an oddly familiar sensation of reverence and dread." The same could be said of Giddins's writings in the domain of jazz.

Gary Giddins sent the following autobiographical sketch, entitled "The Writing Life," to *World Authors 2000–2005*:

"I was born, the first of two children, to Leo and Alice Giddins in Brooklyn, New York, in 1948. Four years later, we relocated to East Rockaway in Nassau County, where I attended school until I entered Grinnell College in Iowa. The '50s and '60s were a splendid time to discover the arts, as modernism was about to carom into a skepticism that undermined all but the most rigorous assumptions; one enjoyed the benefits of a classical education, before classicism itself was under siege, and the challenge of indiscriminate anxiety. After leaving Grinnell in 1970, I wrote unsuccessfully for two years, before landing a position reviewing movies for the *Hollywood Reporter*, while placing music reviews in *Down Beat*. In 1973, having made a decision to focus my energies on jazz, I sold my first piece to the *Village Voice*, which led to a column in 1974, called Weather Bird.

"Jazz was in the doldrums in the late 1960s and early 1970s, but it was young enough to offer up its entire history on a platter. I was able to see several iconic figures of the 1920s—Louis Armstrong, Duke Ellington, Coleman Hawkins, Benny Carter, Earl Hines—even as I could hear, first-hand, major figures from subsequent eras: swing, modern jazz, the avant-garde, and so forth. Jazz revved up with a new energy in the mid-1970s, and though the public spurned it, it was an exhilarating experience to cover the remaking of an idiom. Still, the question critics are asked most frequently is, How did you become one? The answer is, through indirection. You set out to become a writer; then at some point you realize that your writerly strengths are in criticism. Writers are admonished to write about what they know and critics know the arts. If you attend art with scrupulous love, it will yield the whole world—every star, every grain of sand.

"For me, the process began early, but the moment of revelation remains vivid. My dad kept stacks of *Esquire* behind the hat boxes in his closet, and I was now at an age when it was necessary to know why they had been relegated to that shadowy second shelf. So on a night when he was out, I investigated, and in the first issue I opened, I was detoured from the abiding Varga girl by a letter to the editor. The correspondent was annoyed that film critic Dwight Macdonald had complained of Anglophobic casting and conflicting accents in *Ben Hur*, when all she, the letter writer, could see was ancient Rome and ancient Romans going about their business. This struck me as hilarious. I had seen *Ben Hur* a couple of years earlier, in 1959, and even I knew it was a movie. On the other hand, unable to articulate my own complaints about the film, I had cravenly surrendered them before the approbatory consensus in and out of my elementary school classroom. Rifling through the stack, I located and read Macdonald's review. Then I read his columns in the other issues. The veil fell from my eyes.

"Macdonald's irreverence, wit, and independence made for a tonic so intoxicating I never recovered. The critical voice was entirely new to me, a razor to cut your way through the suffocating world of received opinion. Having confessed my transgression, I was given the magazines and began to read other *Esquire* critics (the M brigade: Malcolm Muggeridge, Norman Mailer, Martin Mayer). I discovered the *New York Times Book Review*. Upon learning of a certain Edmund Wilson who remarked that every time he saw an issue of *Life* he felt like an alien from another planet, I went in pursuit of his books and found a second home in *The Shores of Light* and *Classics and Commercials*. Among the numerous critics I devoured were two, Martin Williams and Dan Morgenstern, who spoke to me most compellingly about my other obsession, jazz.

"Jazz came into my life with corresponding immediacy one summer in New Orleans, when I was touring the country's perimeters with a dozen or so other 15-year-old New Yorkers. All any of us knew about the deep South were riots, hoses, attack dogs, and politicians who spoke—as Louis Armstrong said of Orval Faubus—like 'uneducated ploughboys.' Half asleep as our bus pulled into the motel court, we peered out the window and stared in disbelief at a wall with three doors: Men, Women, and Colored Men. Later in our room, we decided that Colored Women must have been around the corner, though for a while we wondered if segregation was different for women. We also determined to hear jazz, chiefly out of curiosity. A newspaper ad promoted an afternoon concert at a hotel: Emanuel Sayles and His Silverleaf Ragtimers, featuring George Lewis.

"Pushing through swinging doors into a small red ballroom, we saw a world far removed from the one represented by the shops we had passed on the way, their display shelves festooned with Confederate flags and pickaninny dolls. Here before us were white and black men and women, cigarettes and cocktail glasses in hand, chatting as though they all belonged to the same country club.

The enlightened promise of the gathering was more than matched by the music, a charging, thumping, polyphonic gallimaufry that made my head and heart soar. At intermission, I stood gawking near the bandstand and the pianist, Joseph Robichaux, beckoned me over and asked me about school and how I liked the music, and then called the others over to say hello. We left after two sets and my feet didn't touch the ground for half a mile. Weeks later I heard Armstrong's 1928 recordings and knew there was no human emotion that jazz could not express and flatter.

"Over the years, I've worked both sides of the critical divide, producing records and concerts, writing and directing documentary films and, from 1986 through 1992, serving as artistic director for the American Jazz Orchestra, a repertory ensemble I co-founded. But first and last I'm a writer and whatever I've contributed to an appreciation of American music may be found in my biographies of Louis Armstrong, Charlie Parker, my critical history, *Visions of Jazz*, and a life of Bing Crosby, in progress."

Gary Giddins was born on March 21, 1948 to a decorator and a businessman. He was educated at Grinnell College, in Iowa, but he describes himself as having left it rather than having graduated, because there was no commencement ceremony in 1970, when Giddins graduated. Student protests against the Vietnam War caused the college to close down early that year. Nevertheless, Giddins was mentioned by the president of the college in 1991, when the class dedicated a peace grove, as one of the successful graduates from that era, along with Thomas Cech, a Nobel Prize winner in chemistry.

Giddins began his career as a critic in 1972, writing movie reviews for the *Hollywood Reporter*, a California-based trade magazine. From 1972 to 1973 he served as a contributing editor to the jazz magazine *Down Beat*. In 1973 he joined the staff of New York City's famous left-wing weekly, the *Village Voice*, and the following year he was given his own jazz column. While he continued to write for that paper, he also authored music columns for *New York* and *Modern Maturity*. He not only wrote criticism of jazz; he produced records and concerts; served as an announcer and producer for WBAI, a listener-sponsored radio station in New York; and taught and lectured at various colleges and universities, including New York University and Columbia University, both in New York City.

By the time his first book, *Riding on a Blue Note*, came out, Giddins was hailed as a seasoned jazz critic. Robert Palmer compared the collection of essays for the *New York Times Book Review* (July 19, 1981) with two contemporaneous jazz memoirs, by veteran critics Whitney Balliett and Leonard Feather. "Because it is the first book by an important new jazz critic, *Riding on a Blue Note* is the most significant," Palmer concluded. He found Giddins's appreciation of Ethel Waters superior to that of the other critics and praised "his account of the Chicago avant-garde's move to New York City in the mid-'70's" as "a valuable historical document." Palmer's favorite piece was Giddins's narration of "the musical and criminal career of Red Rodney," a trumpeter and con artist, which demonstrated to Palmer that Giddins "has the makings of a first-rate storyteller."

Giddins collaborated with the photographer Carol Friedman on *A Moment's Notice: Portraits of American Jazz Musicians* (1983). The volume combines Friedman's photographs of 74 musicians with Giddins's comments, which the *Library Journal* (March 1, 1984) reviewer Gordon Lutz found "always to the point."

Giddins founded and served as artistic director of the American Jazz Orchestra, an ensemble that played from 1985 to 1992, at which point he told Peter Watrous of the *New York Times* (December 10, 1992), they stopped "partly because there's no more funding." The last major concert they were able to perform, at Cooper Union in New York City, featured saxophonist David Murray. "We hoped that we would have been taken up by another hall, but we haven't been," Giddins remarked, adding that the orchestra was "willing to reconvene."

When Giddins's second collection of essays, *Rhythm-a-ning*, came out, he had already cemented his reputation as an important jazz critic, one able "to recognize and convey the historical and esthetic subtleties surrounding any given jazz performance," as Francis Davis put it in the *New York Times Book Review* (April 7, 1985). *Rhythm-a-ning* examines the impact of Cecil Taylor, Frank Sinatra, Ornette Coleman, Illinois Jacquet, and David Murray, among many others. The *Newsweek* (June 24, 1985) reviewer Walter Clemons characterized Giddins as "the best jazz critic now at work" and cited his "loving, encyclopedic knowledge of the past." "He's an elegant enthusiast," Clemons concluded.

Giddins's next two books were biographies of jazz greats: *Celebrating Bird* and *Satchmo*, his 1988 biography of Louis Armstrong. In both biographies, Giddins dealt with his subjects compassionately. Although Parker was a heroin addict for most of his short life, Giddins wrote in *Celebrating Bird*, the drug "never entirely subverted his personality. He remained dignified, open, generous, curious, concerned." Jason Berry, writing for the *New York Times Book Review* (January 11, 1987), termed the book "as penetrating a character study of Bird as any yet written." In Louis Armstrong's case, most critics regard the 1920s and 1930s as the high point of his career. Afterward, critics contend, Armstrong—affectionately known as Satchmo—became a mere entertainer, a self-parodist, and a clown. In the opinion of Charles Fox, the *Times Literary Supplement* (April 7, 1989) reviewer of *Satchmo*, Giddins wrote his book partly to mount

"an impassioned attack" on that attitude toward Armstrong. Fox felt that Giddins's judgments "spring from a generosity that is part of an attempt to view one of this century's greatest musicians on his own terms." Documentary films, shown on PBS, were adapted from both books; Giddins directed the film *Satchmo* (1989).

Faces in the Crowd: Players and Writers, another compendium of Giddins's essays, was republished in 1996 as *Faces in the Crowd: Musicians, Writers, Actors & Filmmakers*. Most reviewers agreed with Robin Lippincott, whose opinion appeared in the *New York Times Book Review* (August 23, 1992): "Praising a virtuosic performance by the saxophonist Sonny Rollins, Mr. Giddins writes: 'Imagine writing one perfect sentence on top of another without hesitation.' Mr. Giddins not only imagines it, he does it; these essays are marked by elegance and informed intelligence." A critic for *Kirkus Reviews* (May 15, 1992), however, called Giddins's piece on the comedian Jack Benny "surprisingly bland." Gay Talese and Robert Atwan, the editors of *The Best American Essays 1987*, expressed their disagreement by including Giddins's overview of Benny's career in their volume. Lippincott deemed the chapter on Jack Benny "a wonderful piece."

Visions of Jazz was termed by its publisher "an evocative journey" through the first 100 years of jazz. In 78 chapters it covers the major innovators of the quintessential American music, going back to what Giddins considered its roots in 19th-century minstrel shows. Giddins also explained that jazz differs from classical music in that jazz "musicians are superior to the songs they perform . . . In jazz, performance is the text." Alfred Appel Jr. wrote in the *New York Times Book Review* (October 18, 1998) that in describing Dexter Gordon's playing, Giddins presented "the pan-racial, multicultural, and even utopian essence of so-called modern jazz." He called Giddins "our best jazz critic." Dexter Morrill, who reviewed *Visions of Jazz* for *America* (March 27, 1999), observed that Giddins's "expansive style" embodied "solid content: 'Through much of its history, jazz made avid converts with the simple promise of undying excitement, whether maximized by throbbing rhythms, bloodcurdling high notes, violent polyphony, layered riffs, hyperbolic virtuosity, fevered exchanges, or carnal funk. . . .' Such linguistic technique could only be exercised by a mature jazz writer with a special way of solving the age-old problem of choosing appropriate words for the often abstract world of sound."

Bing Crosby, Giddins's third book-length biography, focused on the early years in the singer's career. "Those who remember Bing Crosby only for 'White Christmas' may be surprised to find jazz-critic Giddins singing Der Bingle's praises as 'one of the handful of artists who remade American music in the 1920s,'" a reviewer wrote for *Booklist* (January 1, 2002). "Artie Shaw called Crosby the 'first hip white person born in the United States,' and Giddins shows us why he was right." Though James Marcus, writing for the *Atlantic Monthly* (February 2001), felt that Giddins "makes a strong case for Crosby as the prime mover of American pop culture, who shaped it in his own affable image for more than three decades," Charles Winecoff, who reviewed the book for *Entertainment Weekly* (January 26, 2001), was considerably less impressed. "This obsessively panegyric account gently glosses over Crosby's well-known alcoholism, gambling, philandering, and parenting deficiencies to focus on his pioneering use of the microphone and his numerous studio recordings," Winecoff wrote. "Unfortunately, except for the occasional human touch . . . , the book is so academic and reverential that it borders on the bu-bu-bu-boring."

Most of the more than 140 essays, articles, and reviews that comprise *Weather Bird* were originally published in Giddins's *Village Voice* column of the same name, which ran for 30 years. "The breadth and depth of his knowledge is extremely impressive, his ear is astounding, and his masterly style routinely achieves the near impossible in writing engagingly about something that inherently eludes description," Mark Woodhouse wrote for *Library Journal* (October 15, 2004). "For instance, in reading the delightful and seemingly nonsensical 'If Ornette Coleman Were Jim Hall, He Would Be Joe Morris,' a fan immediately begins to approximate in the mind's ear what Joe Morris might sound like. . . . Jazz fans will head back to their collections for another listen to classic albums and to the record bins to seek out music they've overlooked."

Weather Bird was published by Oxford University Press, which put out another collection of Giddins's work, *Natural Selection: Gary Giddins on Comedy, Film, Music, and Books*, in 2006. The latter anthology featured previously uncollected essays on music, film, and comedy, as well as a few new pieces written expressly for this volume. "Giddins is that rare creature, the deadline-driven journalist with a distinctive voice," Jack Helbig wrote, reviewing *Natural Selection* for *Booklist* (August 1, 2006). "This collection also reveals that, while best known for his award-winning writing on jazz, his range is really quite remarkable. Besides jazz, he writes authoritatively about film noir, silent comedy, and contemporary fiction; about Jack Benny and Friedrich Durrenmatt; and, in intelligent, heartfelt reflections on a youth spent reading it, that late but seldom lamented comic-book series, *Classics Illustrated*. . . . Giddins has chosen to corral the best of his elegantly written, exquisitely argued pieces, most of them written in the last 15 years or so, for this eclectic collection, which should please film buffs, jazz fans, and anyone, really, who loves the fine art of literary journalism."

In addition to writing books, Giddins has contributed to such publications as *Vanity Fair*, the *New York Times*, the *Boston Globe*, and *Esquire*. He has received numerous honors for his writing, including an American Book Award for *Celebrating Bird*, the 1998 National Book Critics Circle Award for criticism for *Visions of Jazz*, a Peabody Award for his screenplay of the PBS documentary *John Hammond: From Bessie Smith to Bruce Springsteen* (1990), and several awards from the American Society of Composers, Authors and Publishers. He has also written the album notes for more than 60 records, and in 1986 he won a Grammy Award for the album notes that he co-wrote for *The Voice: The Columbia Years (1943–1952)* by Frank Sinatra.

Giddins has been married twice, has two children, and lives in New York City.

—J.C.

Suggested Reading: *America* p24+ Mar. 27, 1999; *New York Times* C p15 Dec. 10, 1992; *New York Times Book Review* p10 July 19, 1981, p9 Apr. 7, 1985, p19 Jan. 11, 1987, p16 Aug. 23, 1992, p9 July 4, 1993, p18+ Oct. 18, 1998; *Times Literary Supplement* p376 Apr. 7, 1989

Selected Books: *Riding on a Blue Note: Jazz and American Pop*, 1981; *A Moment's Notice: Portraits of American Jazz Musicians* (with C. Friedman), 1983; *Rhythm-a-ning: Jazz Tradition and Innovation in the '80s*, 1985; *Celebrating Bird: The Triumph of Charlie Parker*, 1986; *Satchmo*, 1988; *Faces in the Crowd: Players and Writers*, 1992; *Visions of Jazz: The First Century*, 1998; *Bing Crosby: A Pocketful of Dreams, the Early Years, 1903–1940*, 2001; *Weather Bird: Jazz at the Dawn of its Second Century*, 2004; *Natural Selection: Gary Giddins on Comedy, Film, Music, and Books*, 2006

Gilbert, Jack

Feb. 17, 1925– Poet

Jack Gilbert has earned a reputation as one of America's most talented living poets almost in spite of himself. In a career spanning more than 40 years, he has published only four full-length books of poetry—*Views of Jeopardy* (1962), *Monolithos* (1982), *The Great Fires* (1994), and *Refusing Heaven* (2005)—and two chapbooks, *Kochan* (1984) and *Tough Heaven: Poems of Pittsburgh* (2006). For much of his career his work has been, as Fredric Koeppel observed for the Memphis *Commercial Appeal* (April 17, 1994), "unconnected with and unaffected by literary and cultural concerns or fashions." Furthermore, Gilbert has generally failed to participate in some of the events—from literary festivals to writing

Julio Granda/Courtesy of Random House

Jack Gilbert

took his bachelor's degree in about 1947. At 23 he traveled to Italy and France, where he eked out an existence, some sources claim, by illegally selling gasoline, which was being rationed in the aftermath of the Second World War.

When Gilbert returned to the U.S., he settled in San Francisco and became involved in that city's vibrant literary scene, attending the poet Kenneth Rexroth's weekly poetry meetings, associating with such Beat writers as Allen Ginsberg and Lawrence Ferlinghetti, and, in the late 1950s, participating in a series of workshops, called Poetry as Magic, led by the poet Jack Spicer. Gilbert also took graduate courses at the University of California, at Berkeley, during the 1958–59 academic year and, in 1962, received a master's degree from what is now San Francisco State University. In between, he returned for a time to Italy, where he met Pound in the northern Italian city of Merano.

In 1962 Yale University Press published Gilbert's first book, *Views of Jeopardy*, as part of the Yale Series of Younger Poets, a distinction often described as winning the Yale Younger Poets prize. While looking back in recent years, some critics have noted the ways in which this first collection seems aligned with the larger Beat poetry movement, but in the *New Hampshire Review* (Summer 2005, on-line), Elizabeth Kennedy argued that the emphasis in *Views of Jeopardy* on "classical mythology, romantic love, [and] 'the spaces between the notes' . . . was very much the exception in an era of clever Beat articulations." Indeed, one poem, "Malvolio in San Francisco," has been read as Gilbert's rejection of the Beat aesthetic. Referring to the arguably frivolous nature of some of the Beats' projects, Gilbert wrote, according to Meghan O'Rourke: "Two days ago they were playing the piano / With a hammer and a blowtorch. / Next week they will read poetry / To saxophones They laugh so much. / So much more than I do. / It doesn't wear them out / As it wears me out. . . ."

Nominated for the Pulitzer Prize for poetry, the book quickly made Gilbert a literary and popular culture star, and it reportedly became, in the early 1960s, one of the books most often stolen from libraries. He was featured in such magazines as *Esquire, Glamour,* and *Teen Magazine,* and in 1962 the literary journal *Genesis West* devoted a special section to celebrating his work. Uncomfortable with his celebrity status, and using money from a 1964 Guggenheim fellowship, Gilbert left the country in about 1965 and returned to Europe, living in Greece and elsewhere before moving to Japan. "The idea of being a professional poet bored me," he said, according to Kennedy. While outside the country, he occasionally took jobs, including positions teaching English as a second language, but quit them soon after saving enough money to support himself, often not in comfort, so that he could work on his poetry in peace. He returned periodically to the U.S. during this time,

workshops—that poets can attend to call attention to themselves, gain an audience, and earn an income. "As [Gilbert] implies in the poem 'Going Wrong,' his solitude is not a result of stubbornness or vanity but of an elemental creative necessity immensely greedy for the time and space required for consummation," Koeppel noted. "Gilbert is not playing games, nor do his poems." Assessing Gilbert's contribution to contemporary poetry, Meghan O'Rourke commented for *Slate* (May 9, 2005, on-line): "No other poet I know captures so well a mind torn between the pleasures of austerity and the fecund, intoxicating powers of abundance. What Gilbert is searching for, poem after poem, are the ideal circumstances where the two intersect, and privation becomes a form of richness, a sharpening of the attention."

The son of James Plummer and Della Florence (Ingram) Gilbert, Jack Gilbert was born February 17, 1925 in Pittsburgh, Pennsylvania, the city in which he was raised. Gilbert's father, who at one time had been a member of a circus, fell from a window and died when Gilbert was only 10. At that same age, Gilbert began helping his uncle fumigate houses. "The cyanide could knock you out with just one breath," he latter recalled, according to Sarah Manguso for the Poetry Foundation's Web site. He later held a variety of other jobs while in Pittsburgh, including time spent as a door-to-door salesman and a steel worker. After attending Peabody High School, Gilbert matriculated to the University of Pittsburgh. There, inspired in part by such modernists as Ezra Pound and T. S. Eliot, Gilbert made his first attempts at composing poetry, alongside friend and fellow poet Gerald Stern, and maintaining a relationship with the Poetry Center at San Francisco State University until 1971, and in 1975 he toured 15 countries on behalf of the U.S. Department of State, lecturing on American literature.

Two decades after the publication of his first book, Gilbert brought out his second, *Monolithos*, reportedly at the urging of writer and editor Gordon Lish, one of the relatively small circle of admirers who had helped keep Gilbert's name alive. Titled after a small village on the Greek island of Rhodes, *Monolithos* is divided into two sections: one, dated 1962, contains revised selections from *Views of Jeopardy*, while the other, dated 1982, presents poems previously unpublished in book form. Many of the later poems concern Gilbert's long-term relationship with Linda Gregg, with whom he had lived during part of his time abroad, although they never married, as is sometimes reported. David Kirby wrote for *Library Journal* (February 15, 1982) that the poems in *Monolithos* "offer fresh insights into the bittersweet relations between the sexes." Gilbert's primary subject in the volume is love, as Richard Tillinghast observed in the *New York Times Book Review* (October 12, 1982). "The poems present [Gilbert] as a traveler, a loner, a pilgrim in the quest for Eros," Tillinghast wrote. He added, however, that Gilbert's "poems too often simply report, stopping short of the work of transformation that turns an experience into a poem." Others found the poems more compelling, including a *Washington Post* (September 2, 1984) reviewer, who called them "intelligent, striking, pleasing poems, with many classical allusions, about the futility of love, the fragility of friendship, and the precariousness of art, as in 'Poetry Is a Kind of Lying': 'Poetry is a kind of lying, / necessarily. To profit the poet / or beauty. But also in / that truth may be told only so.'" The book earned nominations for the 1982 Pulitzer Prize for poetry and that year's National Book Critics Circle Award for poetry.

After the publication of *Monolithos*, Gilbert took a teaching position at Syracuse University, in New York, during the 1982–83 academic year, participating in readings and publishing, in 1984, a chapbook called *Kochan*, which contains elegies for his wife of 11 years, Michiko Nogami, who had succumbed to cancer in 1982, at 36. (The chapbook includes four poems by Nogami as well.) Published in a limited edition, the chapbook was not widely reviewed or read, and Gilbert waited until 1994 to put out another full-length collection with a major press. Titled *The Great Fires*, the book contained Gilbert's poems in *Kochan* and other work written through 1992. Fredric Koeppel was among the critics who greeted the book warmly, writing: "One reads *The Great Fires* . . . with gratitude and envy. One plunges into [the poems] as into an acid bath, emerging purified and chastened." Others found the collection compelling for different reasons. In the *New York Times* (May 15, 1994), Patricia Hampl described

The Great Fires as "a book of farewells and leave-takings, yet it conveys a rare serenity, or a stoicism so fully achieved it passes for serenity. Mr. Gilbert's enormous relish for the physical world and his immaculate diction are about nothing less than 'searching for a base line of the Lord.'" The book also proved popular, going into seven printings, an unusually high number for a book of poems, and later that year Gilbert received a $50,000 fellowship for poetry from the New Mexico–based Lannan Foundation.

Gilbert waited another 11 years before publishing his fourth book, *Refusing Heaven*, which is dedicated to Nogami and Gregg. Elizabeth Hoover, in the *Los Angeles Times* (March 8, 2005), argued that the book suggested Gilbert's indifference to contemporary trends: "As poetry increasingly falls into two categories (confessional-style and experimental language poetry), Gilbert refuses the modes of either; rather he forges his own path with writing that is at once intellectually dense and profoundly human. His work radiates with humility and awe, and he brings an intellectual heft that is often lacking in contemporary poetry." In the *New Criterion* (December 1, 2005), William Logan offered a more severe assessment: "Gilbert's prosy, cheerless sentences pile up in patient suffering, suffering that prides itself on being without pity or delusion (which means it's riven with self-pity and self-delusion)." Gilbert's poems, Logan added, "indulge in the consoling passions of memory, and the consoling negations of grief. Yet the memories too often seem thumbed over, his love a kind of knight-errant narcissism: 'We are allowed / women so we can get into bed with the Lord, / however partial and momentary that is.'" *Refusing Heaven* went on to win the 2005 National Book Critics Circle Award for poetry.

In January 2006 Gilbert began a two-year term as poet laureate of Northampton, Massachusetts, and later that year he released another chapbook, *Tough Heaven: Poems of Pittsburgh*. In the *Pittsburgh City Paper* (August 31, 2006, on-line), Bill O'Driscoll described the book as "a collective portrait" of the city during the mid-twentieth century. "Gilbert's Pittsburgh, it's true, is limited by his mere generation of long-ago experience here," O'Driscoll noted, and the city might have "grown bigger in his imagination. But his tone is searching, and he is keen to avoid sentimentality."

Gilbert lives by himself in western Massachusetts. He does not have any children. As he told Sarah Fay for the *Paris Review* (Fall/Winter 2005): "I could never have lived my life the way I have if I had children. There used to be a saying that every baby is a failed novel. I couldn't have roamed or taken so many chances or lived a life of deprivation. I couldn't have wasted great chunks of my life."

—A.R.

Suggested Reading: *Hartford Courant* G p2 Apr. 24, 2005; *Los Angeles Times* E p12 Mar. 8, 2005; (Memphis) *Commercial Appeal* G p3 Apr. 17, 1994; *New Hampshire Review* (on-line) Summer 2005; *New York Times* VII p26 May 15, 1994; *New York Times Book Review* p42 Oct. 12, 1982; *Paris Review* (on-line) Fall/Winter 2005; *Slate* (on-line) May 9, 2005

Selected Books: *Views of Jeopardy,* 1962; *Monolithos,* 1982; *The Great Fires,* 1994; *Refusing Heaven,* 2005

V. Tony Hauser/Courtesy of Random House

Gildiner, Catherine

Mar. 31, 1948– Nonfiction writer; novelist

In 1999 Catherine Gildiner's first book, *Too Close to the Falls*, met with wide critical acclaim and went on to enjoy impressive sales in Canada, where it was first released and where Gildiner, born and raised in New York State, has lived since 1970. A memoir of her unusual childhood during the 1950s, *Too Close to the Falls* won many readers with its sharply drawn portraits of Gildiner's parents, particularly her spirited and independent mother, and of the other people in their small town. In 2005 Gildiner made her first venture into fiction with her next book, *Seduction*, a murder mystery that drew on her professional training in clinical psychology, particularly her interest in the work of pioneering psychoanalyst Sigmund Freud. In an interview for a reading guide for *Too Close to the Falls* posted on the Penguin Group Web site and available in some editions of the book,

Gildiner was asked about the relationship between her writing and her practice as a psychologist. "Hearing all of my patients' histories," she answered, "gave me the courage to tell my story. All of our stories are just variations on the same theme. I think being a psychologist gave me an inside track on that."

Catherine Ann McClure Gildiner was born on March 31, 1948 in Lewiston, a small town north of Niagara Falls and across the Niagara River from Canada. She was the only child of James McClure, a pharmacist, and Janet McClure, a math teacher. Though in many ways the family reflected the middle-class norms typical of the 1950s, Gildiner was born relatively late in her parents' lives, and her mother steadfastly preferred pursuing intellectual interests in history and anthropology to housework, particularly cooking, leading the family to eat virtually all their meals, even breakfast, in restaurants. Janet also urged her daughter "never to learn to cook or type," Gildiner, in her memoir, recalled her mother saying, "or you'd be requested to do both against your will forever."

A rambunctious child, Gildiner had to be rescued by the town fire department after making her way to the top of a cherry tree when she was three. At that same age she flew off a playground swing while trying to make a complete loop and was knocked unconscious; she did the same thing the next day. Gildiner told Kim Covert for the Canadian Press (December 15, 1999) that her mother thought she "was really over the top" when, at age four, Gildiner received money for performing her imitations of television entertainers Ed Sullivan and Jack Benny in a local store. "That was the profound and deep humiliation when she decided that I was seriously ill," she told Covert. Brought to her family doctor, Gildiner was first judged to have worms. Once this diagnosis proved incorrect, the doctor, Gildiner wrote in *Too Close to the Falls*, "explained that we all had metronomes inside our bodies and mine was simply ticking faster than most: I had to do more work than others to burn it off."

Gildiner thus became a full-time employee at her father's drugstore. "I had to tell people whether makeup looked good or bad," she wrote in her memoir, "point out what cough medicines had sedatives, count and bottle pills. I also had to sound as though I knew what I was talking about in order to pull it off. I was surrounded by adults, and my peer group became my coworkers at the store." Having already learned to read, Gildiner was also tasked with giving the store's African-American delivery driver, Roy, who was illiterate, directions from maps as he made his rounds in the area. Seeing people from all walks of life, and seeing them partially through the eyes of such an even-tempered adult as Roy, widened Gildiner's sense of the world. She became familiar with everyone from the very poor residents of a nearby Native American reservation to movie star Marilyn

Monroe, who was in the area while working on the movie *Niagara* (1953).

Gildiner continued working full-time until she turned six and began attending a local Catholic school, after which point she worked before and after classes. Her family sold the pharmacy when she was 13 and relocated to Buffalo, New York. At some point after the move, while her parents were still relatively young, they both became ill and died. These changes ended what Gildiner, in the interview on the Penguin Group Web site, called "the carefree mood of what I felt was my childhood." She added: "My life in the 1950s in Lewiston was light years away from my life in public school in Buffalo. Just as the '50s were politically innocent and carefree in the Eisenhower years, so was my life. The 1960s and '70s were full of political tumult, as was my life."

In 1966 Gildiner graduated with a bachelor's degree in English literature. Relocating four years later to Canada, Gildiner pursued graduate study in English literature, earning her first master's degree in 1971. Her second master's degree, this time in psychology, came, in 1976, from York University, in Toronto, Ontario; her thesis was titled "An Empirical Investigation of Dream Characteristics as Postulated by Psychoanalytic Theory." Her doctoral studies also concerned psychoanlytic theory, though this time with an additional interest in the work of Charles Darwin. York granted her a doctoral degree in clinical psychology, in 1983, upon her completion of her dissertation, which is called "The Evolutionary Foundations of Freud's Theory of Female Psychology." She worked for a period at Lakeshore Psychiatric Hospital, which closed in 1979, and at the Clarke Research Institute (now the Centre for Addiction and Mental Health), both in Toronto, before eventually going into private practice. She has also served as a teacher at York University and the University of Toronto.

Gildiner's professional writing career began as early 1991, when she began publishing occasional essays in the Toronto *Globe and Mail.* In 1995 she started writing for the Canadian women's magazine *Chatelaine,* putting her training and experience as a psychologist to use in a monthly advice column. The idea of writing a memoir, however, did not come to her until she reached an impasse while working on the manuscript of what later became *Seduction.* "I thought I'd had a totally average childhood," she told Kim Covert. "My parents didn't argue, I wasn't an incest survivor, I wasn't poor . . . Middle-class girl grows up, big deal." Her ideas changed after telling a story about her childhood at a party. "Someone at the party told me to write the story and send it to a publisher," she told an interviewer for York University's *Alumni Matters* (February/March 2005, on-line). "So I quickly wrote up the tale and then mailed it in on a Friday. On the following Monday I received an advance cheque in the mail with a yellow post-it attached which said 'finish it'. Not wanting to give back the cheque, I finished the book."

Most critics of *Too Close to the Falls* found the details of Gildiner's childhood appealing, particularly her portraits of her mother and Roy. In the *Toronto Star* (January 2, 2000), Jamie Zeppa emphasized the many unusual qualities of Gildiner's early life, calling her "an extraordinary child," but added: "A fascinating childhood is no guarantee of a fascinating memoir. It still takes a gifted writer to translate the past into a work of art, and Gildiner is a gifted writer. Her prose is intensely colourful, like a concentrate, but never overwhelming or labourious in its details. Against a vivid backdrop, she brings into focus those moments when the child's world and the adult world intersect, when illusions are shattered and understanding begins." While Zeppa wrote, "I cannot recommend this book enough," a critic for *Kirkus Reviews* (December 15, 2000) called the book "uneven," praising Gildiner's "considerable narrative gifts" but pointing out several factual errors and noting that her extensive use of dialogue "[requires] of the reader an eager suspension of disbelief." The reviewer concludes: "A messy portrait of a messy childhood, but rather moving in spite of itself." A hit in Canada, where it spent well over a year on best-seller lists, the book was also short-listed, in 2000, for the Trillium Award, the Ontario government's annual literary prize.

Gildiner's inspiration for her second book, *Seduction,* came from an idea she had when she was working on her doctoral degree. While studying the psychoanalytic theories of Sigmund Freud, Gildiner came to wonder why, in 1897, the year Freud began advancing the idea of the Oedipus complex, he suddenly seemed to be pulling back from an earlier idea, called the seduction theory, which held that a primary cause of hysteria in adults was one or more negative sexual experiences in youth, with a close relative typically acting as the instigator. "I went to my adviser and said, 'Look, we've got to write about this!'" Gildiner told Rebecca Wigod for the *Vancouver Sun* (February 19, 2005). "And he said, 'Cathy, we're scientists. We're writing about hermaphroditic eels right now. These are things for a novel." Part detective story and part history of psychoanalysis, *Seduction* tells the story of Kate Fitzgerald, a murderer with a doctoral degree in the philosophy of science who has spent her years in prison immersed in Freud's writings. When Anders Konzak, a major figure among Freud scholars, boasts that his new research will expose Freud and probably crush the field Freud created, the psychiatrist in Fitzgerald's prison offers her parole if she will investigate what Konzak has discovered before he publishes his alleged findings. To keep tabs on Fitzgerald, the psychiatrist pairs her with Jackie Lawton, a private detective with a long criminal record. Wayne Grady, for the Montreal *Gazette* (February 12, 2005), characterized the book as "a fast-paced modern novel filled with snappy dialogue, exotic settings and juicy intellectual plums, somewhat in the manner of *The Da Vinci Code*." Many other critics, however, found fault with the book's premise—that a murderer would be set free to investigate a dispute among Freud scholars—and commented negatively on Gildiner's extensive explanations of psychoanalytic theory. In the Canadian *National Post* (March 5, 2005), Marnie Woodrow argued that "the characters and story are at their best when no one is expounding in an effort to validate their (a) intelligence (b) legendary anger issues or (c) repressed sexual chemistry." The novel, Woodrow concluded, "is certainly a romp, and the author's pleasure in writing it comes across, a rare enough literary event. Her devotion to the subject matter is apparent, yet it snarls up when she plugs in characters she doesn't seem to understand. Another weapon required in the art of full seduction: genuine empathy."

Gildiner lives in Toronto with her husband, Michael Gildiner, a radiologist, whom she married in April 1975. In addition to her writing, Gildiner trains five days a week as a member of a competitive rowing team. She is also the mother of three sons: Jamey, born in about 1979, and Sam and Dave, both born in 1981. According to an article by Gildiner in the Toronto *Globe and Mail* (April 29, 2006), Sam and Dave were "the largest identical twins ever born at Toronto's Women's College Hospital." She does not cook.

—B.M.

Suggested Reading: (Canada) *Vancouver Sun* D p16 Feb. 19, 2005; Catherine Gildiner's Web site; (Montreal) *Gazette* E p1 May 14, 2001; Penguin Group Web site

Selected Books: nonfiction—*Too Close to the Falls*, 1999; fiction—*Seduction*, 2005

Courtesy of Yale University

Glück, Louise

(GLICK)

Apr. 22, 1943– Poet; critic

Louise Glück has established herself as one of the most important poets of her generation, a reputation that was cemented in October 2003, when she was named the U.S. poet laureate. While she often writes about being a wife and mother, the trauma of divorce and death, and other autobiographical experiences, Glück tends to defy

the conventions of confessional poetry, frequently narrating her work from the perspective of biblical figures or characters in classical mythology and shaping her poems around fiercely controlled lines that grip readers as much with what she leaves out as with what she includes. Glück explained some of her aesthetic convictions in her essay "Disruption, Hesitation, Silence," collected in her 1994 volume *Proofs and Theories: Essays on Poetry*, as quoted on the Modern American Poetry Web site, "I do not think that more information always makes richer poem. I am attracted to ellipsis, to the unsaid, to suggestion, to eloquent, deliberate silence. The unsaid, for me, exerts great power: often I wish an entire poem could be made in this vocabulary. It is analogous to the unseen for example, to the power of ruins, to works of art either damaged or incomplete. Such works inevitably allude to larger contexts; they haunt because they are not whole, though wholeness is implied: another time, a world in which they were whole, or were to have been whole, is implied." Glück, who has been compared to such important poets as Sylvia Plath and Stanley Kunitz, received the Pulitzer Prize for poetry in 1993.

Louise Elisabeth Glück was born on April 22, 1943 in New York City, the daughter of Daniel Glück, a businessman who is said to have developed the X-Acto knife (a popular tool with craftspeople), and the former Beatrice Grosby. She has a sister, Tereze, who is now a banker. Glück, who suffered from severe anorexia as a teen, grew up in Long Island and graduated from Hewlett High School, in Hewlett, New York, in 1961. She attended Sarah Lawrence College, in Bronxville, New York, for one year before transferring to Columbia University, in New York City, where she studied poetry with Kunitz and in 1966 received the Academy of American Poets prize. During this period she taught poetry to dropouts in New York City. She has since taught at such institutions as the Fine Arts Work Center in Providence, Rhode Island; Goddard College in Plainfield, Vermont; the University of North Carolina, in Greensboro; the University of Virginia, in Charlottesville; the University of Iowa, in Iowa City; the University of California (at Berkeley, Davis, Irvine, and Los Angeles); Harvard University and Brandeis University, both in Massachusetts; and Columbia University. She began teaching at Williams College, in Williamstown, Massachusetts, in 1984, eventually becoming a senior lecturer, but in 2004 she moved to Yale University, in New Haven, Connecticut, where she is currently an adjunct professor and a writer in residence.

Firstborn, published in 1968 when Glück was just 25 years old, attracted significant critical attention. The poems move among various narrators, each with an angry and disaffected voice. As R. D. Spector wrote for the *Saturday Review* (March 15, 1969), "No softness enters the work of Miss Glück. None of the personæ she adopts in *Firstborn* speaks gently or regards the world kindly. Her vision is harsh, her verse forms terse and stripped to essentials." Many reviewers offered favorable comparisons to the work of such poets as Kunitz, Robert Lowell, Plath, and Randall Jarrell. While some critics lamented Glück's dark outlook, others praised her controlled use of language, rhythm, and meter. Spector concluded, "Miss Glück demands a reader's attention and commands his respect." Duane Schneider, writing for *Library Journal* (March 1, 1968), declared, "Louise Glück's first collection of poems confirms her status as a respectable and promising young poet."

The poet's vision remained grim in *The House on Marshland*, the collection of 35 brief poems that followed in 1975, after a long silence. In this volume Glück continued her exploration of pain, death, and darkness, although her tone tends to be more mild, reflective, and even lyrical than in her first book. *The House on Marshland* presents a number of poems dissecting landscapes, home life, and personal relationships, most of which feature her characteristic short, broken lines. For example, in the verse titled "Poem," Glück observes a couple's marriage from the viewpoint of an unborn child. She writes: "In the early evening, as now, a man is bending / over his writing table. / Slowly he lifts his head; a woman / appears, carrying roses. / Her face floats to the surface of the mirror, / marked with the green spokes of rose stems." In her review for the *New York Times* (April 6, 1975), Helen Vendler found that the new poems represented a "phenomenal" advance over the old ones, writing, "[They] are almost dreamy; they drift in a reflection like the moon in a pool (the moon and the pool recur as powerful counters in her private language). . . . A very peculiar power, and a new style, commanding in its indifference to current modes." J. D. McClatchy, writing for the

Yale Review (Autumn 1975), affirmed the work as "one of the year's enduring books." He noted that Glück had "scoured both her experience and her style, and while one regrets so slim a sheaf, one is grateful for its achieved balance."

In her next volume, *Descending Figure* (1980), Glück used both autobiographical experiences and larger mythical elements to explore the themes of frustration, helplessness, absence, and despair. For example, in the four-poem sequence entitled "Lamentations," she presents a revision of the creation story of *Genesis*, tracing the separation of the sexes and the evolution of humanity. In "The Gift," she offers a poem composed in the form of a prayer for her young son, while in another poem, "The Sick Child," she takes on the voice of a mother in a museum painting. William Logan wrote for *Library Journal* (October 15, 1980) that the book represents "a frightening mixture of sensuous pain and anxiety." He added, "[Glück's] flat, almost affectless voice records an extraordinary violence against the self as she describes the 'thrust and ache' of love, the 'formless / grief of the body,' and the 'terrible charity of marriage.' These notations of wounded spirit are joined to a world alien and hostile, from the 'cold, receptive earth' to the 'blue waste of the sea.'" Overall, *Descending Figure* received praise from critics. Although Vendler, writing for the *New York Review of Books* (October 12, 1980), found that "Glück is not at her best in expository verse, where her hieratic rhythms can begin to sound portentous," she nonetheless noted, "Her wonderfully suggestive poems about art (whether about its governing dreams or its formal expression in a medium) bring her embattled oppositions into their finest confrontation."

Glück addressed a variety of archetypal themes in her fourth collection, *The Triumph of Achilles* (1985), in which she presents subjects from classic myths, fairy tales, and Biblical lore. In his review for *The Nation* (January 18, 1986), Don Bogen wrote, "Larger and more varied than her earlier books, *The Triumph of Achilles* shows her experimenting with new types of poems, from Orientalist attempts to capture the moment to songs, narratives and long mixed sequences. Language is looser, embracing the casual as well as the concise, and Glück's sense of the line has broadened too." Critics widely praised Glück's attention to her craft, as well as her control of subject. Writing for the *New York Times* (December 22, 1985), Liz Rosenberg opined, "Miss Glück's language is clearer, purer and sharper than ever before, and sometimes ravishing and sexy." Rhoda Yerburgh wrote for *Library Journal* (September 15, 1985), "Her genius lies in her passionate restraint, a mingling of plain and elevated diction, a reliance on indirection and understatement. . . . Glück is foremost among her generation of poets." For *The Triumph of Achilles*, Glück was awarded the National Book Critics Circle Award, the *Boston Globe* Literary Press

Award, and the Poetry Society of America's Melville Kane Award.

For her fifth volume, *Ararat* (1990), Glück fashioned a book-length sequence of 32 short poems, which many critics described as functioning almost as a single poem. The title refers to a mountain in present-day Turkey on which the biblical figure of Noah allegedly landed his ark. The volume includes an epigraph from the Greek philosopher Plato: "Human nature was originally one and we were a whole, and the desire and pursuit of the whole is called love," as quoted by Stephen Dobyns for the *New York Times* (September 2, 1990). Accordingly, the book deals with issues of family, exploring the poet's reaction to her father's death from cancer and its effect on her mother and sister, as well as the relationships coloring her personal history. Many of the poems evoke larger subjects of grief and tragedy, often alluding to biblical symbols and elements of Greek tragedy. As H. Cole wrote for *The Nation* (April 15, 1991), "The poems are testimony from a survivor. And thankfully, the human story that unfolds has a kind of mythic cast to it, sparing the reader the everyday banalities that ensnare so much contemporary American poetry." Overall, the book was well received. While Steven Cramer, in a review for *Poetry* (November 1990), found the work "comfortless, at times exasperating," on the whole he called it an "uncompromisingly honest book." Similarly, Dobyns wrote, "*Ararat* has relentlessness more common in fiction than poetry. Coupled with precision and clarity, it makes some of the poems difficult to read. They feel too bright. The lives they reveal too often contain much we had hoped to forget. The world they describe is a world from which we too often try to escape. No American poet writes better than Louise Glück; perhaps none can lead us so deeply into our own natures." For *Ararat* Glück was awarded the 1992 Rebekah Johnson Bobbitt National Prize from the Library of Congress.

After using autobiographical experiences as fodder in *Ararat*, Glück returned to a more symbolic, mythical strain in *The Wild Iris* (1992). The book's 52 pieces are presented by varying narrators, most frequently the voices of flowers talking to a gardener-poet; the poet, yearning for youth and passion, occasionally prays to a nameless god, who in turn addresses her. The dialogue that ensues between the poet, the natural world, and the divine concerns a number of weighty issues, including mortality, loss, despair, desire, and emotion. As one critic wrote for the New York State Writers Institute's on-line magazine (Summer 1997), as quoted on the Modern American Poetry Web site, "In the absence of a loving God, the poet's task is to celebrate the splendor of the natural world with language and to locate the door at the end of suffering where, 'from the center of my life came a great fountain, deep blue / shadows on azure sea water.'" Although many critics found the structure and theatrical style of the book to be somewhat risky, most nonetheless agreed that Glück's lyrical efforts proved successful. "[The author's] language is of the simplest and highest, gaining unusual beauty and authority," Constance Hunting noted for *Small Press* (Summer 1992). "With the exception of one or two poems which do not fit seamlessly in, the book becomes not a mere collection but a fully unified work. Its combination of simplicity, daring, and thematic quality ensure *The Wild Iris* a place unique in current American poetry." Fred Muratori, writing for *Library Journal* (May 15, 1992), observed that "repeated readings unveil subtle reversals and shadings, evoking the ghostly consciousness that has always invested Glück's best work." *The Wild Iris* earned Glück the 1993 Pulitzer Prize for poetry and the William Carlos Williams Award from the Poetry Society of America.

In *Meadowlands* (1996) Glück explores the domestic sphere through a revisionist interpretation of events from *The Odyssey*. Glück's Penelope is not the patient and resourceful heroine of Homer but rather an angry and long-suffering figure; her Odysseus is often cruel and violent. While the parallel stories do not line up exactly, Glück's intersection provides a larger context for the subject of marital woe. In a review of *Meadowlands*, as posted on the Modern American Poetry Web site, Briggs Seekins wrote, "By presenting the mythic alongside the everyday and contemporary, Glück is successful in reminding us that her themes, love, grief and loss, are ones which have been with us since before there was even a written literature. And the pain and difficulty which they present us with in our own lives is the same pain and difficulty which they have always presented." Critics found much to praise in Glück's experimental material, most notably her unique characterization of the epic figures. Maureen McLane wrote for the *Chicago Review* (Winter 1997), "One of Glück's most striking inventions is her Telemachus [the son of Odysseus and Penelope], who more than any other speaker in the book attains a kind of judicious and wry balance: it is the thoughtful, matured child who can assemble the shards of his parents' experience. That Telemachus exists in this book suggest that there is, if not a God's-eye view of suffering, at least the possibility of a loving and just assessment." Praising the overall collection, James Longenbach wrote for the *Yale Review* (October 1996), "[This volume] is remarkable precisely because it is not Glück's most exquisite effort: it is something more than that—her most ambitious and compelling book. *Meadowlands* suggests that its much-honored author is not willing to take her own achievement for granted, and the result is a poetry more stringently dissatisfied and beautiful than ever."

Thematically, Glück's next volume of poems, *Vita Nova* (1999), begins where her previous work ended—during the period after her marriage failed.

This book chronicles the poet's resilience in the aftermath of divorce, her metaphorical rebirth into a new life and a new locale. Opening with a poem narrated by Persephone, the wife of Hades and goddess of the underworld, Glück again juxtaposes classic mythology and fable with images of contemporary life. Writing for *Booklist* (February 1, 1999), Donna Seaman described the poems as "meditation[s] on spring, that is on renewal, return, and reincarnation, and this endlessly poignant theme is perfectly expressed in Glück's confident resurrection of the timeless tales of ancient Greece and Rome." A reviewer for *Publishers Weekly* (December 21, 1998) observed, "The poems rely on negative space—on what's left out—and on psychological acuity; their stripped-down self-analyses cast their cold illumination far past her own life. Glück's psychic wounds will impress new readers, but it is Glück's austere, demanding craft that makes much of this . . . collection equal the best of her previous work—bitter, stark, careful, guiltily inward, alert to myth." A widespread critical success, *Vita Nova* was named winner of the *Boston Book Review*'s Bingham Poetry Prize.

In 2001 Gück received the Bollingen Prize for poetry, in recognition of her lifetime contributions to the form. That same year she published *The Seven Ages*, which deals with, among other subjects, Glück's relationship with her sister, her childhood, and a recent love affair. Glück again employed her characteristically spare lyrical style, eschewing lush metaphors and longer lines in favor of highly disciplined language, and throughout the book, the pomes pose such questions as "Why should my poems not imitate my life?" and "Why do I suffer? Why am I ignorant?" as quoted by William Logan for *New Criterion* (June 2001). Yet, as Logan suggested, "Such raw questions, written after the end of love, the end of eros, don't want answers—they revel in their long-suffering suffering." Melanie Rehak, reviewing the volume for the *New York Times* (May 13, 2001), found it "a weighty, incandescent marvel," while other critics noted some reservations. For example, in the *Christian Science Monitor* (April 26, 2001), Elizabeth Lund wrote, "The journey is not always smooth, and there are several poems in *The Seven Ages* that fall flat. Readers who are expecting a flawless golden girl will be a bit disappointed, but there is some consolation in her efforts to consistently overcome her limitations. It reminds one how difficult it can be to be human, and how valuable and rare truly great poems are."

In 2004 Sarabande Books published Glück's chapbook *October*, which is composed of a single long poem originally published in the *New Yorker*. That poem is reprinted in Glück's next full-length book of poetry, *Averno* (2006), which takes up the Greek myth of Persephone, the goddess of the underworld and the daughter of Zeus and Demeter. In a critique for the *New York Review of Books* (June 22, 2006), Charles Simic commented that Glück's "poems, one comes to realize with her tenth collection, are part of a continuous narrative, an attempt to give voice to certain decisive moments in her life. What impresses me about her work is the moral passion, her stubborn conviction that poetry can lead to truth, not just the truth of one's own life, but also that other one, which mystics and philosophers have been after." William Logan, writing for the *New Criterion* (June 2006), criticized what he called "the tense, overwrought poems in *Averno*, nervous in their very syllables" and concluded: "Not all Glück's previous encounters with myth have evaded blind comedy, but the success of *Averno* is that the reader isn't tempted to laugh too often. Limited in range and tone and figure, limited to a degree you're surprised they work at all, these eighteen poems repeat themselves until her repetitions have a mythic squalor. . . . If you want to avert your eyes from the pain recorded, the fretful worrying, the bloodless anxiety, you must remember that the torment Glück suffers is to be stuck eternally writing Louise Glück poems."

In addition to her poetry collections, Glück has published *Proofs and Theories: Essays on Poetry*. Although she states in the work that she is "uneasy with commentary," she presents essays on such varied topics as Stanley Kunitz, Hugh Seidman, T. S. Eliot, poetic craft, education, and the nature of courage. The work won the PEN/Albrand Award for nonfiction.

Throughout her career Glück has received numerous honors and awards, including the Rockefeller Foundation Fellowship (1967), grants from the National Endowment for the Arts (1969 and 1979), the Eunice Tietjens Memorial Prize from *Poetry* magazine (1971), two Guggenheim Fellowships (1975 and 1987), the American Academy Award (1981), the Sara Teasdale Memorial Prize (1986), and a National Endowment for the Arts Fellowship (1988). In 1990 she was named the Phi Beta Kappa poet at Harvard University, and in 1994 she was named the poet laureate of Vermont. Glück was elected a fellow of the American Academy of Arts and Sciences in 1993 and a chancellor of the Academy of American Poets in 1999. She holds honorary doctoral degrees from Williams College (1993), Skidmore College (1995), and Middlebury College (1996). She served as editor, with David Lehman, for the volume *The Best American Poetry 1993*.

On October 21, 2003 Glück assumed the role of poet laureate of the United States, succeeding Billy Collins. Observers lauded the choice but expressed concerns that Glück, known for being reclusive and camera shy, would find it difficult to follow in Collins's footsteps. (Collins frequently traveled the country, enthusiastically championing poetry to the public.) Glück announced that she would fill the laureate's role as she saw fit and that she looked forward to interacting with promising young poets. "I have no concern with widening audiences [for poetry]," she told Justin Pope for the Associated Press (October 26, 2003), adding that she preferred her audiences to be "small, intense, [and] passionate."

Louise Glück's first marriage, to Charles Hertz, ended in divorce. She has a son, Noah (currently a sommelier in California), by her 1977 marriage to John Dranow, which also ended in divorce.

—K.D.

Suggested Reading: *American Poetry Review* p52+ Jan.–Feb. 1993; *Chicago Review* p120+ Winter 1997, p180 Summer–Fall 1999; *Contemporary Literature* p58+ Spring 1990;

Kenyon Review p166+ Winter 2001; *New Criterion* p68 June 2001; *New Republic* p35+ May 24, 1993; *New York Times* VII p16 Oct. 12, 1980, VII p22 Dec. 22, 1985, VII p5 Sep. 2, 1990, VII p24 May 13, 2001; *Poetry Chronicle* p119+ Winter 1991

Selected Books: poetry—*Firstborn*, 1968; *House on the Marshland*, 1975; *Descending Figure*, 1980; *The Triumph of Achilles*, 1985; *Ararat*, 1990; *The Wild Iris*, 1992; *Meadowlands*, 1996; *Vita Nova*, 1999; *The Seven Ages*, 2001; *October*, 2004; *Averno*, 2006; essays—*Proofs and Theories: Essays on Poetry*, 1994

Courtesy of Pan Macmillan

Gourevitch, Philip

1961– Journalist; editor

"I'm very wary of the journalistic urge to explain by simplification, by reducing everything to its most basic elements, because there are some stories you can only understand by respecting their complexity," Philip Gourevitch told Alex French in an interview for the *Small Spiral Notebook* (September 4, 2001, on-line). "That means getting inside of the stories, prowling around and pushing against the places that most invite one to ignore them. Being ignored is precisely what the people who inflict great suffering hope for, and I don't like to see such people getting what they want." Gourevitch's detailed, compelling, and intellectually unflinching accounts of seemingly inexplicable events, whether the impulsive

murder of two men or the systematic slaughter of about 800,000, have made him one of the most respected nonfiction writers in the U.S. The author of two books, *We Wish to Inform You That Tomorrow We Will Be Killed with Our Families: Stories from Rwanda* (1998) and *A Cold Case* (2001), Gourevitch has also written for the *New Yorker*, for which he served as a staff writer between 1997 and 2005, and a host of other prestigious publications, including *Commentary*, the *Forward*, *Harper's*, the *New York Review of Books*, the *New York Times Magazine*, the *Village Voice*, and the *Washington Post*. Explaining his approach to nonfiction, Gourevitch explained to Mark Brennock for the *Irish Times* (April 22, 1999) that "rather than say 'here's the way it made me feel', I prefer to say, 'feel it, experience it, go through it, think it'."

Philip Gourevitch was born in 1961 in Philadelphia, Pennsylvania, to Jewish parents who independently of each other immigrated to the U.S. in 1940 to escape the Holocaust. As Gourevitch explained in an article for *Harper's* (July 1993), "Both my parents, in their separate youths, escaped the Nazi effort to murder all Jews; many in my family were not so lucky. I knew this fact, in some form, from as early in my life as I remember knowing anything significant." Gourevitch's Parisian-born mother, Jacqueline Hermann Gourevitch, is a painter; Gourevitch's father, Victor Gourevitch, at one time a student of the famous University of Chicago philosopher Leo Strauss, taught political philosophy at Temple University, in Philadelphia, before moving on to Wesleyan University, in Middletown, Connecticut, where Gourevitch and his brother Marc, now a physician, grew up. Gourevitch decided early on that he wanted to be a writer, telling Mark Brennock, "I never really considered being anything else." Entering Cornell University, in Ithaca, New York, in about 1979, Gourevitch took liberal-arts classes for at least two years before deciding to take time off to write fiction. Gourevitch told Alex French: "I figured I ought to determine if I would write on my own. I did. I was only writing fiction at that point. It had never occurred to me to write nonfiction, probably because I hadn't read much of it that sparked my imagination the way short stories and novels did." Gourevitch returned to Cornell and graduated with his bachelor's degree in English in 1986. He then moved to New York City, which has been his home ever since.

By the beginning of the 1990s, Gourevitch was writing book reviews for such newspapers as the *Village Voice* and the *Washington Post*, while continuing to work on his own short fiction, some of which was published in such prominent literary magazines as *Zoetrope: All-Story*, *Southwest Quarterly*, and *Story*. Around that time he entered the graduate program in creative writing at Columbia University, where he studied fiction writing but also served as the nonfiction editor for *Columbia: A Journal of Literature and Art*. He worked on nonfiction, he explained to Alex French, because "it struck me that for writers who are still developing their chops and finding their voices nonfiction can offer a much more concrete foundation than unfettered imagination, and I enjoyed working with writers whose work was firmly grounded in an external, objective reality." In 1992, the same year he received his M.F.A. degree from Columbia, Gourevitch made the transition from aspiring literary figure to journalist by becoming the New York bureau chief for the *Forward*, a Jewish newspaper with a storied history as a socialist-leaning Yiddish-language daily, which had recast itself as a weekly and launched an English-language supplement in 1983. While turning out roughly three news stories for each English edition of the *Forward*, Gourevitch also found time to develop freelance work for magazines.

Gourevitch contributed numerous articles to *Commentary*, including two pieces that probed the tensions between members of African-American and Jewish communities in New York City. The first article, published in March 1992, discussed the career of the controversial Afrocentric political scientist Leonard Jeffries, while the second, published in January 1993, dealt with the deadly 1991 riots in the Crown Heights section of the borough of Brooklyn. Gourevitch's first article for a high-circulation national glossy—a profile of documentary filmmaker Errol Morris—was published in the August 9, 1992 issue of the *New York Times Magazine*. In July 1993 Gourevitch, by then the *Forward*'s cultural editor, published a long essay on the United States Holocaust Memorial Museum in Washington, D.C., which had opened in April of that year, in *Harper's*. While Gourevitch's articles for *Commentary* had provoked strong responses, his *Harper's* essay became the subject of intense debate, in no small part because it questioned not only the value of dedicating an American museum to "a European event," as Gourevitch referred to it, but also because he seemed to doubt that any museum

could accomplish the ethical mission that the museum's founders had set for themselves, which was, according to the museum's Web site, "to advance and disseminate knowledge about this unprecedented tragedy; to preserve the memory of those who suffered; and to encourage its visitors to reflect upon the moral and spiritual questions raised by the events of the Holocaust as well as their own responsibilities as citizens of a democracy." Gourevitch wrote: "There is something dangerously facile about opposing evil fifty years after the fact. Yet that is the price one pays for Americanizing the Holocaust; as soon as the Holocaust is set up as a metaphor for national ideology, it comes back to haunt us, making its utterance a constant potential embarrassment and tainting the otherwise irreproachable impulse to commemorate the dead. As an American, and as a Jew, I am deeply discomforted to have to point out these things. I do not, for a moment, want to suggest that the Holocaust should be forgotten, remembered in silence, or ignored. I want only to serve a reminder, as this museum becomes a major new touchstone in America's narrative of national identity, that denouncing evil is a far cry from doing good." In the February 1994 issue of *Commentary* Gourevitch took on another popular and widely praised effort to depict the Holocaust, the director Steven Spielberg's 1993 film adaptation of Thomas Keneally's fact-based novel *Schindler's List*. In a version of the same article published in the *Washington Post* (January 16, 1994), Gourevitch argued that Spielberg's film falsifies the actual life of the German industrialist Oscar Schindler, who helped save more than 1,000 Jews during World War II, in order to create a character "who can only be described by the self-contradictory label 'good Nazi.'" Gourevitch concludes by observing, "It is commonly asserted that anything that increases public awareness of the most extreme moment of 20th-century history can only be a good thing. But awareness is a vague concept, not always synonymous with knowledge. To present as historical fact a morally and historically fictitious creation—the good Nazi—corrupts the past in the name of preserving it."

In May 1994 Gourevitch returned to the Holocaust museum for another visit. "Waiting amid the crowd," he wrote in his first book, "I tried to read a local newspaper. But I couldn't get past a photograph on the front page: bodies swirling in water, dead bodies, bloated and colorless, bodies so numerous that they jammed against each other and clogged the stream." The bodies were from Rusumo Falls in the small central African nation of Rwanda, where, over a roughly 100-day period beginning on April 6, 1994, about 800,000 members of the country's Tutsi minority ethnic group were murdered by members of the Hutu majority, who typically used machetes to hack to death their victims—who were often friends, neighbors, or even close relatives. As a systematic attempt to annihilate an entire ethnicity, it was an act of genocide. Thinking about this as he stood in front of the Holocaust museum, Gourevitch noticed that museum staffers were wearing buttons that read "Remember" and "Never again" and became aware, thanks in part to his family background, of "the juxtaposition of the very safe rhetoric of 'never again' with what was happening," as he told Mark Brennock.

Gourevitch first visited Rwanda in May 1995, returning several times after that to gather information for a series of articles for the *New Yorker* and then his first book, *We Wish to Inform You That Tomorrow We Will Be Killed with Our Families: Stories from Rwanda*, which was published in September 1998. Critically acclaimed, the book went on to win the 1998 National Book Critics Circle Award for general nonfiction, the 1998 *Los Angeles Times* Book Prize for best current interest book, the 1998 George Polk Book Award for foreign reporting, the 1998 Overseas Press Club's Cornelius Ryan Award for best nonfiction book on international affairs, the 1999 PEN/Martha Albrand Award for first nonfiction, the 1999 New York Public Library Helen Bernstein Book Award, and the 1999 Guardian First Book Award.

Writing for *Time* (August 6, 2001), Belinda Luscombe called *We Wish to Inform You* "the best-titled book of the '90s." The name is taken, slightly elided, from a letter written by a group of Tutsi Seventh-day Adventist parishioners to the pastor of their church. "We wish to inform you that we have heard that tomorrow we will be killed with our families," the letter read, as Gourevitch records it in *We Wish to Inform You.* "We therefore request you to intervene on our behalf and talk with the mayor." The pastor's response, according to Gourevitch's conversation with a survivor of the massacre that the letter had hoped to prevent, was, "Your problem has already found a solution. You must die." Stories such as this one, with its back and forth between the methodical mass slaughter and the memories of survivors, form the core of Gourevitch's book. To Americans, the best known of the stories Gourevitch uncovered is that of a Hutu hotel manager named Paul Rusesabagina, who in his modest way tells how he protected at least 1,200 people from being killed during the genocide. Rusesabagina's story served as the basis for the award-winning movie *Hotel Rwanda* (2004), a film that is in many ways analogous to *Schindler's List.* Woven into these individual stories are Gourevitch's reflections on the experience of reporting the events as well as a brief overview of Rwandan political history, centered around the separation of Rwandans into these two arguably fictional ethnicities and the political events leading up to April 1994. Roughly the second half of the book details the aftermath of the genocide: the Hutu forces that brought it about had been chased from power but continued to remain a potent element in the country's political and cultural dynamic. In the final chapters, Gourevitch

offers a sustained attack on the members of international community who had turned a blind eye, including the United Nations, humanitarian aid organizations, and such significant Western powers as the U.S. and France. "The West might later wring its hands over the criminal irresponsibility of its policies," Gourevitch wrote, "but the nebulosity known as the international community is ultimately accountable to nobody. Time and again in central Africa, false promises of international protection were followed by the swift abandonment of hundreds of thousands of civilians in the face of extreme violence."

Most reviews of *We Wish to Inform You* praised Gourevitch's skill and dedication as a writer, reporter, and storyteller, though more specialized reviewers often took issue with aspects of Gourevitch's analysis. In the *Contemporary Review* (December 1999), Tom Phillips wrote that the book's "crisply-written history" of the African nation "gives the book a degree of scholarship which few similar works of reportage can match and means that the largely depressing conclusions about the violent legacies of colonialism and the weakness of the response to the genocide from the 'international community' carry considerable weight." As with many other critics, though, Phillips considered that "it is those voices, voices of ordinary Rwandans, which give the book its authority and make it essential reading at a time when much of Central Africa remains at war with itself." Colette Braeckman, writing for *World Policy Journal* (Winter 1998/1999), described this approach to the subject as "conjugating Rwanda in the singular." Similarly, in a review for *Booklist* (September 15, 1998), Mary Carroll wrote, "In a world where too many groups seek their enemies' extermination, his conversations with central Africans shed light on the worst and best of which humans are capable."

Gourevitch's analysis in *We Wish to Inform You*—his reflections on his own position as a reporter, his way of explaining the events leading up to and following the genocide, as well as his sketches of individual political leaders or the groups they represented—proved more divisive for critics. "Like the best storytellers, Gourevitch is self-conscious," Mark Gevisser wrote in a generally positive review for New York *Newsday* (September 20, 1998). "He listens carefully to the cadences of his informants and analyzes their elisions and hiata. And he submits his own storytelling to similar rigor." Gevisser also noted approvingly that "Gourevitch is avowedly partisan; indeed, the book draws much of its energy from the question, 'How is it possible not to be?' He is passionate enough to be readable, but not so passionate as to swamp the evidence with his own emotions." Still, Gevisser differed with Gourevitch over some details: "Sometimes, one is frustrated by Gourevitch's imprecision about who—or what—the indicted 'international community' is. Perhaps this is because [Gourevitch] wishes to make the point that the very reason the 'international community' was so ineffective in the Rwandan conflict is because it is so nebulous and inchoate. But the imprecision also sets into play a subtle dynamic whereby we, the readers, and he, the writer, become part of that vague planetary polity that sat by and did nothing." Other reviewers took issue with Gourevitch's apparent support of the Tutsi military leader Paul Kagame who directed the rebel forces, called the Rwandan Patriotic Front (RPF), that overtook the country when the genocide was underway and subsequently became the country's vice-president and, later, president; others took issue with what was considered a flattering portrait of the Zairian leader Laurent Kabila. A small number of critics found fault with Gourevitch's treatment of history. One of the historians whose work Gourevitch cites in his acknowledgements, the political scientist René Lemarchand, contended, in an article for the magazine *Transition* (2000), "In essence, Gourevitch's story reduces the butchery to a tale of bad guys and good guys, innocent victims and avatars of hate. His frame of reference is the Holocaust." In a February 1999 review for *Commentary* Gary Rosen also took issue with Gourevitch's very infrequent references to the Holocaust, albeit in this case for not being "sufficiently aware of how high a standard" Gourevitch and another writer under discussion had "set for themselves when they prompt comparisons to the Holocaust."

Gourevitch spent nearly three years working on *We Wish to Inform You*, while also writing articles for the *New York Times Magazine*, the *New Republic*, and the *New York Review of Books*. In April 1997 he became a staff writer for the *New Yorker*. In 1999 he began working on an article for the magazine about Andy Rosenzweig, a New York City police officer who was retiring from the force after decades of service and at that time was serving as the chief of investigations at the Manhattan district attorney's office. As Gourevitch told Matt Lauer, the host of NBC's *Today* (August 1, 2001), the "reporter's god smiled on me" that day, because what Rosenzweig told him was not "a little human interest story" but the story of a double murder that had gone unsolved for 27 years before the investigator reopened the case and eventually found the killer, a career criminal named Frankie Koehler. First published as a more than 13,000-word-long article in the February 14, 2000 issue of the *New Yorker* and sold, almost simultaneously, as a film to the production company of the Hollywood star Tom Hanks, the story of Rosenzweig's hunt for Koehler was expanded to book length, at the suggestion of the publisher John Straus of the literary house of Farrar, Straus, and Giroux. After a month's work at the Saratoga Springs, New York, artists' colony Yaddo, Gourevitch had finished his second book, *A Cold Case*, which was published in July 2001.

After the acclaim given to *We Wish to Inform You*, critics found less to praise and less to debate with *A Cold Case*, and reviews overall were mixed, with many writers commenting on the book's brevity. (In its first hardback American edition, the book runs fewer than 200 pages, 12 of which are taken up with photos.) In *Library Journal* (May 15, 2001), Deirdre Bray Root wrote that Gourevitch "covers not only the way investigators attack a 'cold case' but the lives of both Koehler and Rosenzweig and how a similar milieu could birth both a dedicated lawman and a cold-blooded killer." Calling *A Cold Case* "an elegant and extraordinary little book," John Palattella, writing for *New York Newsday* (July 29, 2001), noted that during the nearly 30 years that had passed between the time of the crime and Koehler's arrest, "Rosenzweig and Koehler have been immersed in their own lives, and time's churn has polished them without abrading their quirks and imperfections. Through his deft use of interviews and letters, Gourevitch has carefully placed those men in the clearest possible light, one that catches the pocks and striations, the puzzles of character and conduct, just beneath their dusky surfaces." Other reviewers found *A Cold Case* insufficiently searching and even slight. "Fascinating through and through," Eric Wargo wrote for *Book* (July 2001), "this book feels too brief, our acquaintance with Koehler and Rosenzweig too passing. The reader is left wanting to know more about both men." In *Washington Monthly* (July 2001), Peter Slevin wrote: "This is not an ambitious book. Gourevitch . . . teases an engaging yarn from a simple set of details and a choice group of characters who never stray far from stereotype. The grizzled, two-bit tough; the dogged, old-school detective and his energetic young protégés; the long-suffering wife and the speak-no-evil girlfriend; the theatrical mob lawyer. . . . It is a smooth, sparingly written story, but if Gourevitch had only dug deeper, everyone—including the accomplished author—might have had more to say."

Gourevitch was named the editor of perhaps the nation's most famous literary magazine, the *Paris Review*, in March 2005. Renowned for the quality of its fiction and poetry and long-identified with its detailed interviews with writers, the magazine had never emphasized nonfiction, but Gourevitch began introducing more of it with his first issue, number 174.

Gourevitch lives in New York City with his wife, the *New Yorker* staff writer Larissa MacFarquhar. They have a daughter, Clio.

—D.R.

Suggested Reading: *Irish Times* p15 Apr. 22, 1999; *Ottawa Citizen* B p7 July 4, 1993; *Small Spiral Notebook* (on-line) Sep. 4, 2001

Selected Books: *We Wish to Inform You That Tomorrow We Will Be Killed with Our Families: Stories from Rwanda*, 1998; *A Cold Case*, 2001

Gregory, Philippa

Jan. 9, 1954– Novelist; children's author

The British novelist Philippa Gregory is one of her country's most renowned writers of historical fiction. In an interview related to the publication of her novel *The Other Boleyn Girl* (2001) on the Web site for the Reading Group Guides, Gregory explained the allure of historical novels: "I think people want to know where they came from and where they are going, and stories about the past satisfy that. I think this is such a fundamental desire that it is not surprising that people choose to read historical fiction. The other great ingredient is that historical fiction has become a lot better written, better researched, and more interesting in the last few years. Very fine writers like Antonia Byatt, Rose Tremaine, and Margaret Atwood have written novels which have raised the standard of writing. Other writers, me among them, have raised the standards of research." In the 20 years since her career began, in 1987, with her best-selling novel *Wideacre*, Gregory has written more than 15 additional novels, six children's books, and a collection of short stories.

The second of two daughters, Philippa Gregory was born on January 9, 1954 in Nairobi, Kenya to Arthur Percy and Elaine (Wedd) Gregory. In 1955 her father, a radio operator and navigator for East African Airways, died in an airplane crash, and about a year later the family left Kenya for England, moving to her mother's home county, Somerset, before going to Bristol when she was four. She and her sister attended the Duncan House School for Girls, in Bristol's Clifton neighborhood, until the school closed; they then transferred to the Colston's Girls' School, also in Bristol. A self-described rebel, Gregory became interested in social issues while in her mid-teens, taking up such causes as disarmament, poverty, and debt relief in the developing world. She also organized a student union and coordinated a protest against the school's policy of requiring its pupils to wear uniforms. "It was a time when society was very politicised, and it seemed that every Saturday you went out and carried a banner for one thing or another," she told Harvey McGavin for the *Times Education Supplement* (November 19, 2004). Schoolwork, by contrast, felt tedious; even history, she told Alice Wignall for the London *Guardian*'s *Education Weekly* (February 3, 2004, on-line), "seemed designed for the purpose of turning people off" the subject. As a result Gregory earned low scores in several subjects, including history, on the qualifying exams, called A-levels, that largely determine where British secondary school students can continue their education.

In 1971 Gregory began studying journalism at Cardiff University, in Wales; she also worked during this time as an apprentice reporter at the *Portsmouth News*. In 1974, after three years at the paper, Gregory started school again, this time in England, at Sussex University, where her poor A-levels mattered less. Intending to major in English literature, she switched to history during her first term after taking a course under the European history professor Maurice Hutt. "What he cared about was making you think," Gregory told McGavin, adding: "We went to a conference once and he made this speech about how women in the French revolution were there to take the sans-culottes their lunch. He knew that it would kick off a passionate debate about the role of women in revolution. He absolutely switched me on to history." In 1978 she graduated from Sussex with honors and took a position as a reporter and producer for BBC Radio Solent, the station broadcasting to two of England's southern coastal counties, Hampshire and Dorset, as well as the Isle of Wight.

In 1980 Gregory left England for Scotland and began pursuing a Ph.D. in 18th-century literature at the University of Edinburgh, supporting herself by working as a freelancer for BBC Radio Four and Radio Scotland. "I fell in love with history," she told Elisabeth Winkler for the *Bristol Evening Post* (January 23, 1999), "and the 18th century is my favourite period because it's when everything changes: people moved from villages to towns, started working in factories and formed nuclear families. The society we live in now is based on decisions taken then." For her dissertation, supervised by Geoffrey D. Carnall and entitled "The Popular Fiction of the Eighteenth-Century Commercial Circulating Libraries," Gregory attempted to read 100 of the 18 century's best-selling novels, but to do so she first had to discover what novels those were. She scoured all available records of the commercial libraries of the time, and in the process nearly tripled the number of known records for those institutions. This research taught her lessons about storytelling and writing, while also giving her insights into how 18th-century popular fiction responded to and helped shape the culture around it. She told Suzie Mackenzie for the London *Guardian* (April 17, 1991) that before about 1760 heroines were portrayed as active and openly libidinous; after about that point they were cast as delicate and virginal. Accompanying this literary change was a shift in cultural attitudes toward marriage. "Post 1760, instead of arranged marriages, people were choosing their partners for love," Gregory told Mackenzie. Yet, Gregory added, "Romantic love subordinated women. It meant they measured their success in terms of whether their marriage was happy, and this quickly came to mean whether the man was happy."

While finishing her doctorate, which she received in 1984, Gregory moved to the small northern city of Hartlepool with her first husband, Peter Chislett, and their infant daughter, Victoria. She taught part-time at various institutions in England, including the Workers' Educational Association, the University of Durham, and the former Teesside Polytechnic (now the University of Teesside), and the Open University. At the same time, with Chislett rarely at home and their relationship falling apart, she wrote columns about country life for the London *Guardian*—using her aunt's name, Kate Wedd—and began *Wideacre*. While working on the manuscript, Gregory sent three finished chapters, along with a summary, to several publishers. One of the publishers encouraged her to keep writing, and when she was finished, the rights to publish the manuscript were auctioned for £121,000 in the U.K. and $500,000 in the U.S.

The novel centers around a young woman, Beatrice Lacey, who is not legally permitted to purchase her ancestral country estate and the extraordinary lengths—including murder and incest—to which she is willing to go in order to control it by other means. Peter Ackroyd, for the London *Times* (April 16, 1987), called *Wideacre* "a very engaging book" and went on to note: "The 18th-century woman is a neglected creature (or at least she was until recently) but, in the figure of her heroine, Philippa Gregory has defined a certain kind of wildness, a female assertiveness, which may have a great deal to do with the 20th century, but which is here buttressed by the novelist's close understanding of the 18th. Murder and incest are two of the less egregious elements in the book; but the danger of [*Wideacre*] turning into a historical farrago is notably diminished by Philippa Gregory's powerful involvement in the story. This is a novel written from instinct, not out of calculation, and it shows." The book was an immediate success, spending nine weeks, in 1987, on the best-seller lists in the U.K; with paperback sales of over 200,000, the novel went on to be among the 40 best-selling books in Britain in 1988. Gregory credited the success of *Wideacre* to the timing of its release, which was "at a time when people wanted a new sort of historical fiction: more realistic, more radical, more sexy, and harder edged," she said in an interview on the Barnes & Noble Web site. "That's how I see the world, so I never wrote for a market, I always wrote to reflect my own view of the period, and it has been phenomenally successful."

Setting teaching aside, Gregory became a full-time novelist, and her next two novels, *The Favoured Child* (1989) and *Meridon* (1990), were sequels to *Wideacre*. (Collectively, the books are called the Lacey trilogy or the Wideacre trilogy, since the family and their titular property are common to all three.) The battle between two siblings over the inheritance of the country estate is at the heart of *The Favoured Child*, while Gregory's third novel, *Meridon*, centered on a young woman, Sarah Lacey, who was raised by gypsies and later sold to a traveling circus; upon returning to Wideacre, Sarah faces a fierce battle for control of the estate. Dora Sowden for the *Jerusalem Post* (March 16, 1990) praised *The Favoured Child* for "its fluent modern style [that]

is faithful to place and period. In fact, it never strays out of its century. Set in the England of the era of the French Revolution, it mirrors the gulf between the 'quality' and the working classes, and the beginnings of trouble in relations between landed gentry and tenants, landowners and farm hands. . . . Gregory knows the countryside and makes it vivid but never distinct from the characters—some living in poverty, others in wealth." On the other hand, Philippa Toomey, in the London *Times* (June 10, 1989), dismissed the book as "extremely well written, high class tosh." Reviewing *Meridon* for the London *Sunday Times* (May 13, 1990), Miranda Seymour judged Gregory "a very good story-teller indeed" and noted that Gregory's training in literary history "hasn't made her into the kind of writer who crams her pages with gratuitous snippets of information; it has, on the contrary, helped to give her a confident and easy approach to the period." Seymour went on to record, however, that by the time she put the novel down, she "had the strong impression of having read two quite separate" novels. One was the story of Sarah's time at Wideacre, which Seymour described as "clearly emblazoned with the stamp of commerce" and "an average, romantic frolic, light, readable and wholly unmemorable. The second, the gypsy-circus book, is original, enthralling and bursting with vitality. Now that the Wideacre trilogy is complete, I hope Gregory will give us more in her second and better style."

In 1992 Gregory published her fourth novel, *The Wise Woman*, a historical thriller set in England during the 16th century. The story follows Alys, a young woman who develops magical healing powers under the direction of a wise woman named Morach. Jan Maxwell Avent for the *Knoxville News-Sentinel* (January 2, 1994) called Alys "Gregory's most developed character" but added: "it becomes more difficult for the reader to care what happens to her as the book progresses. It is only Gregory's skill as a storyteller . . . that keeps the reader turning the pages." Also in 1992 Gregory published her first novel with a contemporary setting, *Mrs. Hartley and the Growth Centre* (1992; later issued as *Midlife Mischief*). A satire of contemporary sexual mores, the novel traces Alice Hartley's drift from a lifeless marriage with a sagging academic husband into a romance with a younger man and the adventure of opening a multi-purpose New Age counseling business (the titular "growth centre"). Gregory also wrote the screenplay for the book, which appeared, in 1995, on BBC television, with Pam Ferris as Alice. Alongside these works for adults, Gregory also produced a series of feminist fairy tales for younger readers: *Princess Florizella* (1988), *Florizella and the Wolves* (1991) and *Florizella and the Giant* (1992).

Gregory's next novel, *Fallen Skies* (1993), takes place in the aftermath of the First World War. Recounting the story of Lily Valance, a young cabaret singer enduring a troubled marriage to a former captain tormented by memories of war, the book was judged by Frank Delaney, for the London *Sunday Times* (August 8, 1993), as having been "written in better prose than [its] seemingly romantic themes might be presumed to warrant."

Following the publication of the children's book *The Little Pet Dragon* (1994), Gregory produced a novel about a weightier and more controversial subject—the history of the African slave trade in England at the end of the 18th century. *A Respectable Trade* (1995) told the story of a poor but well-educated governess, Frances Scott, who becomes Mrs. Josiah Cole after entering into a marriage of convenience with a shipping merchant and eventual slave trader. Directed by her husband to teach English social graces to the slaves in hopes of being able to charge more for their sale, Frances ultimately falls in love with one of them, a Yoruban priest named Mehuru. Gregory's frank and carefully researched treatment of Bristol's involvement in the slave trade drew criticism from some of the city's residents, but Gregory insisted that her point was to raise awareness about the past. "People think of slavery as being an American trade, an African tragedy," Gregory told Taylor for the London *Guardian* (April 6, 1998). "But they were British-owned ships, British plantations and British profits. *A Respectable Trade* . . . is my way of bringing the story of slavery back home." Penny Perrick for the London *Times* (March 25, 1995) argued that "the great roar and sweep of history is successfully braided into the intimate daily detail of provincial life in this compelling and intelligent book." Perrick also saw Gregory making a statement with the novel that transcended its historical setting: "In rich, melodious and supple prose, Gregory puts not only the horrors of the slave trade in the dock but capitalism itself." Barry Unsworth, however, contended in the London *Sunday Times* (April 9, 1995) that the novel failed precisely because its historical setting lacked metaphorical resonance: "There is a good deal of information about the [slave] trade [in the novel], at least as it is viewed by Bristol merchants. But there is nothing in the organisation of the novel which would allow us to see connections with other forms of buying and selling, for example, or with the burgeoning commercial vitality of the city. Bristol stinks but all this means is that Mrs Cole is frequently obliged to press a square of cambric to her nose." Gregory wrote the screenplay for BBC's 1998 adaptation, which won widespread praise from television critics in both England and the U.S.

Gregory followed up *A Respectable Trade* with another contemporary social satire, *Perfectly Correct* (1996); the children's book *Diggory and the Boa Conductor* (1996); and the psychological thriller *Little House* (1996), set in contemporary England. She then returned to historical fiction with the novels *Earthly Joys* (1998) and *Virgin Earth* (1999), both 17th-century sagas told through the eyes of royal gardeners, the senior John

Tradescant for the first book and the junior for the second. Her 1998 effort earned praise from Betsy Groban, who wrote for the *New York Times Book Review* (November 1, 1998): "This tale of forbidden love set against the turmoil of a country in chaos makes for both intelligent and satisfying reading." Lisa Jardine for the London *Times* (April 3, 1999) called the second novel in the series "a brilliant continuation of Gregory's meticulously researched story of the Tradescant gardening family." Noting that Gregory was forced, in telling the story of the younger Tradescant, to invent more because less is known about his actual life, Jardine commented that "this time [Gregory] is able to give her imagination freer rein," concluding: "Gregory manages to provide the reader with an utterly gripping, believable account of the everyday lives and loves of a loyal London family caught up in the seismic political changes surrounding the execution of Charles I, the English Commonwealth and, finally, Charles II's Restoration."

Following *Zelda's Cut* (2000), another contemporary thriller, and *Bread and Chocolate* (2000), a collection of contemporary short stories, Gregory published perhaps her most commercially successful novel since *Wideacre*, *The Other Boleyn Girl* (2001), which follows the journey of Mary Boleyn, a 16th-century English aristocrat who entered royal circles in her early teens and later became mistress to King Henry VIII; two of Mary's children are alleged to have been by Henry before his subsequent (doomed) marriage to her sister, Anne. Gregory conducted three years of research, providing readers with little-known facts on a figure she considered overlooked. "Gregory captures not only the dalliances of court but the panorama of political and religious clashes throughout Europe," Kathy Piehl wrote for *Library Journal* (April 15, 2002). "She controls a complicated narrative and dozens of characters without faltering, in a novel sure to please public library fans of historical fiction." The novel received the Romantic Novelists' Association award for romantic novel of the year (2002), and in 2003 British actresses Jodhi May and Natascha McElhone played the lead roles in the BBC television adaptation of the book, which was filmed using improvisation and hand-held cameras. A Hollywood adaptation of the book, starring Scarlett Johansson as Mary, is slated for release in 2007.

Gregory gave another fictional account of sibling rivalry in England's Tudor dynasty with her next novel, *The Queen's Fool* (2003). This time the rivalry splits two half-sisters—Queens Mary I and Elizabeth I—and the narrator is a young woman who served under each of them. In October 2004 she published *The Virgin's Lover*, also set in Tudor England. The novel recounts the first two years of the reign of Queen Elizabeth I, the daughter of Henry VIII and Anne Boleyn, and Elizabeth's purported affair with Sir Robert Dudley. Narrated by Dudley's wife, Amy, the book was described by

Kristi Gray for the Christchurch, New Zealand *Press* (November 13, 2004) as "a fascinating look at the intrigue, the politics, and the back-stabbing plotting of court life, as well as a well-researched portrait of the times." Gray added: "The book rattles along at a dazzling pace, and although a little repetitive in its details of Amy's despair at the pair's relationship, is certainly hard to put down." Susannah Goddard for the Melbourne *Herald Sun* (December 17, 2005) criticized Gregory's characterization of the book's central female characters, calling Amy and Elizabeth "frequently weak-minded and indecisive."

The subject of *The Constant Princess* (2005) is Catalina, the daughter of Queen Isabella and King Ferdinand of Spain and better known as Catherine of Aragon. Briefly married to England's teenage Prince Arthur shortly before his death, Catalina subsequently marries his younger brother, King Henry VIII. Elizabeth Buchan for the London *Sunday Times* (December 11, 2005) praised Gregory's decision to tell the story using two points of view: "The story switches between first- and third-person narrative, a device that permits Catherine to confide the secrets of her first marriage to Arthur (by which her second marriage stood or fell) and to construct the emotional scaffolding around the historical facts. Whether or not you are convinced by Gregory's answer to the question of whether Catherine's marriage to Arthur was consummated . . . the novel is a reminder of the lonely, difficult and frequently perilous condition of a Tudor royal." Jessica Feder for *Entertainment Weekly* (December 9, 2005) judged the novel only slightly better than average and singled out Gregory's shifting points of view for particular criticism, calling them "disconcerting." Ultimately, Feder decided, "the book's messy framework fails to do justice to the majestic subject."

Gregory's next novel, *The Boleyn Inheritance* (2006), also examined the the reign of Henry VIII. This time the story is told by three first person narrators: Lady Jane Rochford and the two queens, Anne of Cleves and Katherine Howard, for whom Rochford acted as lady in waiting. "It's the story of the queens that we think we know, but we don't know anything about them really," Gregory told Jamie Stengle for the Associated Press (October 14, 2006). "They have an extraordinary history that hasn't really been told." The reviewer for *Publishers Weekly* (August 7, 2006) joined other critics of some of Gregory's earlier books by finding Gregory's male characters less compelling than her female ones but concluded: "Gregory's accounts of events are accurate enough to be persuasive, her characterizations modern enough to be convincing. Rich in intrigue and irony, this is a tale where readers will already know who was divorced, beheaded or survived, but will savor Gregory's sharp staging of how and why."

In addition to her writing, Gregory still works as a broadcaster, appearing on the *Round Britain Quiz* show on BBC Radio 4 and as the featured expert on the Tudor period for the Channel 4 television show *Time Team*. Gregory has been a guest book reviewer for the London *Sunday Times* since 1989.

In 1993 Gregory founded Gardens for the Gambia, a small charity in Gambia that builds wells in school gardens and provides water to irrigate gardens, which in turn provide food for the schools' students. To date 56 wells have been built with funds donated by Gregory and others, and in 2005 the BBC series *Inside Out* documented Gregory's visit to a number of these sites.

Gregory lives in the north of England, near Stokesley, in Yorkshire, with her third husband, Anthony Mason, a personal transformation trainer; she has two children by her previous marriages—Victoria, born in 1982 and Adam, born in 1993—and four stepchildren. In February 2006 she suffered serious spinal injuries after being thrown from her horse, Cracker.

—B.M.

Suggested Reading: Philippa Gregory Web site; *Boston Globe* D p12 Dec. 14, 2004; (London) *Mail on Sunday* p6+ Oct. 17, 2004; (London) *Sunday Times* Features p8 Nov. 28, 2004; (Newcastle) *Journal* p11 Nov. 13, 2001

Selected Books: *Wideacre*, 1987; *The Favoured Child*, 1989; *Princess Florizella*, 1988; *Meridon*, 1990; *Florizella and the Wolves*, 1991; *The Wise Woman*, 1992; *Mrs. Hartley and the Growth Centre*, 1992; *Florizella and the Giant*, 1992; *Fallen Skies*, 1993; *The Little Pet Dragon*, 1994; *A Respectable Trade*, 1995; *Diggory and the Boa Conductor*, 1996; *Perfectly Correct*, 1996; *The Little House*, 1996; *Earthly Joys*, 1998; *Virgin Earth*, 1999; *Zelda's Cut*, 2000; *Bread and Chocolate*, 2000; *The Other Boleyn Girl*, 2001; *The Queen's Fool*, 2004; *The Virgin's Lover*, 2004; *The Constant Princess*, 2005; *The Boleyn Inheritance*, 2006

Grooms, Anthony

Jan. 15, 1955– Novelist; short-story writer; poet

The writer Anthony Grooms grew up during the civil rights struggles of the 1950s and 1960s. He drew on his background for the *Ice Poems* (1988) and for the short-story collection *Trouble No More* (1995), fictional representations of the mobilization—by Martin Luther King Jr. and other leaders—of ordinary people whose values and courage were tested as they fought for equal rights. In his novel *Bombingham* (2001), the protagonist becomes a killer in Vietnam at the age of 19, after a youth that was shaped by the civil rights movement.

Anthony Grooms sent, in 2004, the following third-person account of himself for *World Authors 2000–2005*:

"Tony Grooms was born on January 15, 1955, and was raised and educated in rural Louisa County, Virginia, 120 miles south of Washington, D.C. The eldest of six siblings, he grew up among a large extended African American family that also claimed Native and European heritage.

"His father, a refrigeration mechanic, and his mother, a textile worker and housewife, encouraged his education. In 1967, as a preface to the forced racial integration of Virginia's public school system, his parents enrolled Grooms in the Freedom of Choice plan that brought about limited integration of white public schools. Though he notes that many of his attitudes about race and class in the United States were formed before 1967, the school integration experience was, nonetheless, a landmark event in his life, contributing to a perspective that is evident in many of his writings.

"Later, he studied at The College of William and Mary earning a Bachelor of Arts in Theater and Speech in 1978. His focus was playwriting, and student theater groups produced several of his plays. Next, he studied at George Mason University, where he developed a professional interest in creative writing and graduated in 1984 with a Master of Fine Arts, the terminal degree for that field. It was not until after graduate school, when he moved to Georgia to teach, that he found a subject in the American Civil Rights Movement of the 1960s.

"Grooms is the author of a collection of poems, *Ice Poems*, and of a collection of stories, *Trouble No More*. His stories and poems have been published in *Callaloo*, *African American Review*, *Crab Orchard Review*, *George Washington Review*, and other literary journals. He is the recipient of the Lillian Smith Prize for Fiction, the Sokolov Scholarship from the Breadloaf Writing Conference, the Lamar lectureship from Wesleyan College, and an Arts Administration Fellowship from the National Endowment for the Arts.

"Writing in *MELUS*, a critical journal of multi-ethnic literature, Professor Diptiranjan Pattanaik says that Grooms demonstrates 'the insider's profound knowledge of the history and struggles of African Americans, while consistently managing to circumscribe his breadth of understanding with a tender story-telling art.'

"Though the subject matter of his work varies, his most notable work has focused on characters struggling with the uncertainty of the American Civil Rights Movement. His novel, *Bombingham*, set against the activism for and resistance against civil rights in Birmingham, Alabama in 1963, was published by The Free Press imprint of Simon & Schuster in October 2001. Reviewing the novel for the *Washington Post*, critic Jabari Asim wrote, 'In its insistence that "the world is a tumultuous place and every soul in it suffers," this powerful, resonant novel offers no consolations. Grooms offers consolation, however, in allowing us to be present at the emergence of a brave and promising talent, fully equipped to take on the writer's task of confronting chaos and wrestling it into form.'

"Grooms's teaching career has taken him to positions at a variety of universities in Georgia, U.S.A., including the University of Georgia, Clark Atlanta University, Emory University, and Morehouse College; and to the University of Cape Coast, in Ghana, West Africa. For the past seven years, he has been a Professor of Creative Writing at Kennesaw State University near Atlanta, Georgia. He teaches a range of writing and literature courses, but specializes in creative writing and American literature.

"He lives in Atlanta with his wife, Pamela B. Jackson, a federal administrative judge."

Ice Poems, a chapbook in which Grooms plays with death imagery, received, like many such books, little attention. *Trouble No More,* a collection of 12 short stories, many of which are set in the South during the civil rights movement, brought him a larger audience, impressing a number of critics. Ronda Racha Penrice, for example, wrote for the *Black Book Review* (February 28, 1996), "Grooms explores the different shades of courage it took in bringing down Jim Crow, but the strongest stories in the collection show the paradoxes everyday Southern black people live with now." Alida Becker noted for the *New York Times* (September 24, 1995) that many of the stories are set in "a time when the 'colored' sign at a fast-food restaurant may have been removed, but 'still people knew which line was which.'" She went on to observe, "What his upwardly mobile black characters don't know, just yet, is where to draw their own personal lines. And the talk that animates these vignettes—from lunch counters to juke joints to family dinner tables—is an affecting reminder of the quiet courage, ingrained wariness and rueful humor with which such individual decisions reshaped an uncertain community."

Bombingham concerns Walter Burke, an African-American soldier serving in Vietnam, who recounts his and his family's experiences in Birmingham, Alabama, during 1963, the year that the 16th Street Baptist Church, in Birmingham, was firebombed, an event that left four little girls dead and galvanized the country. Walter, who was 11 at the time, and his sister, Josie, ignored their parents and participated in local protests organized by such activists as Martin Luther King Jr., Fred Shuttlesworth, and James Bevel. Explaining his motivation for choosing this moment in history as the setting for his novel, Grooms told Clarence Reynolds for *Black Issues Book Review* (April 30, 2002), "Whereas much nonfiction—particularly memoir—has been written about the Civil Rights Movement, I find that little fiction is set in that period. My interest in writing the novel was first to tell a good story, and, second, to contribute—through storytelling—to what is known about individual lives during this struggle."

Ishmael Reed, writing for the *Village Voice* (December 4, 2001), noted that the novel takes its title from the name African-Americans gave to Birmingham during the 1960s, because "bombings were so common" there. Reed goes on to write, "*Bombingham* is constructed so well that it could be used as a textbook in writing classes. It's a perfect traditional novel. There are characters whom you feel for. The scenes are so vivid that they could be staged without any adaptation. The characters' speeches tell you as much about the characters as the excellent descriptions. Well-crafted novels are common, however. Grooms brings more to his book. . . . He has the rare ability to transport the reader to those times about which he writes." Tayari Jones observed for the *Progressive* (March 1, 2002), "With lyric intensity and quiet authority, Grooms writes the story not included in news headlines or historical retrospectives. He reminds us that the civil rights movement, like all cultural movements, is about the people who make up the families, which make up the neighborhoods, which make up the cities, which make up our nation. In Grooms's world, the grief of an eleven-year-old boy matters, just as the bus boycotts and freedom marches that change his community forever."

A consummate craftsman, Grooms understands that discipline is one of the writer's greatest assets, a notion he tries to instill in his students. Discussing his approach to teaching writing, the year in which he was asked to direct Emory University's Summer Writer's Institute, Grooms told the *Atlanta Journal and Constitution* (July 2, 1992) that he attempts to get his students to understand: "To write every day, not only when inspired, just as one would practice a musical instrument to attain proficiency in that performing art, is a necessary habit."

—S.Y./A.R.

Suggested Reading: *Choice* p278 Oct. 1996; *MELUS* p193+ Fall 1999; *MultiCultural Review* p62 June 1996; *Publishers Weekly* p66 Sep. 24, 2001; *Washington Post* C p11 Oct. 9, 2001; *Village Voice* p74 Dec. 4, 2001

Selected Books: poetry—*Ice Poems*, 1988; fiction—*Trouble No More*, 1995; *Bombingham*, 2001

Guest, Barbara

Sep. 6, 1920–Feb. 15, 2006 Poet; novelist; biographer

Barbara Guest was the only female member of the so-called New York School of poetry, a movement that emerged in the late 1950s in response to the confessional verse then enjoying popularity. The New York School poets, who included John Ashbery, James Schuyler, Frank O'Hara, and Kenneth Koch, were deeply influenced by such abstract painters as Jackson Pollock and Willem de Kooning. Margalit Fox explained for the *New York Times* (March 4, 2006, on-line): "The New York Poets shared a concern with language as pure form, using words much as a painter uses paint." Fox continued, "Ms. Guest's poetry is intended for both the eye and the ear, straddling the border between the painterly and the musical. . . . Ms. Guest wielded English as Picasso wielded a brush."

Before her death, in 2006, Guest sent the following third-person statement to *World Authors 2000–2005*:

"Barbara Guest was born in Wilmington, North Carolina, in 1920. She spent her childhood in West Virginia, Florida, and, after her father died, with her aunt and uncle in Los Angeles, California. She attended the University of California, at Los Angeles, and graduated from the University of California, at Berkeley. The Metaphysical Poets of the 17th century, whom she studied in college,

Judy Dater/Courtesy of Wesleyan University Press

became an influence on her poetry. Following graduation, she arrived in New York City in the 1950s, where she became part of a group of poets, influenced by the French modernist poets, who became later well-known as the New York School along with John Ashbery, Frank O'Hara, and James

Schuyler. In the '50s New York was filled with scholars and artists who had arrived earlier from Europe to escape World War II. This lent true sophistication to New York City, particularly through the influx of the painters from France, Germany and Italy. Now York was altered by a European profile. The poets and painters responded.

"Guest was influenced by the group of artists living in New York devoted to Abstract Expressionism; art has been a continued influence on her poetry. She wrote art reviews for such journals as *Art News* and *Art in America*; in 1962, with B. H Friedman, she published *Robert Goodnough, Painter*. In the 1960s she published several books of poetry, including *The Location of Things* (published with the art Gallery Tibor De Nagy, 1960, Longview Award, 1968); *Poems* (1962); and *The Blue Stairs* (1968). During the 1970s, with such books of poetry as *Moscow Mansions* (1973), which continued in a more abstract mode; *The Countess from Minneapolis* (1976); *The Turler Losses* (1979); and her novel, *Seeking Air* (1979) Guest continued in an experimental direction.

"In the 1980s Guest published *Biography* (1980); and *Quilts* (1981); along with a vivid biography of the poet H.D., *Herself Defined: The Poet H.D. and Her World* (1984), which has had a major influence on the writing of biography in the United States, and a British edition (Collins, 1985). Her next book of poems, *Fair Realism* (1989), won the Lawrence Lipton Award for Literature (1990); it continued her move toward the abstract, although Guest has always experimented with the idea of language as a way to go within and beyond the surface of the poem. *Fair Realism* and the books which followed, *Defensive Rapture* (1993); *Quill, Solitary APPARITION* (1996); and *Rocks on a Platter* (1999) especially won her recognition from readers in their 20s and 30s, and her work continues to have a major influence on a new generation of poets and critics.

"In 1994 Guest returned to California, settling in Berkeley in the San Francisco Bay area. Since then she has published several books of poetry, such as her *Selected Poems* (1995), with a British edition (Carcanet Press, 1996); *Quill, Solitary APPARITION* (1996); *The Confetti Trees* (1999), with fictional stories based on her girlhood in Los Angeles and the European refugee film-makers of that time; *Rocks on a Platter* (1999), a poetic treatise on the art of the poem; and her most recent work, *Symbiosis* (2000), a long poem which muses on the collaboration of poet and artist, with art by Laurie Reid. In every new book, as she has done throughout her career, she continues her forays into new territory of language, image, thought, and the spiritual dimension of poetry.

"Throughout her career, Guest never falters in pushing back the borders of literature. She has collaborated with artists, including poem-paintings with artists Mary Abbott and Fay Lansner and the French artist Anne Slacik, with a poem, 'The Nude,' (1986), with artist Warren Brandt; *The Altos* (1992), with artist Richard Tuttle; *Stripped Tales* (1995) with artist Ann Dunn, She has written plays, several of which have been produced; recently, *The Office* (1960) and *Port* (1964), and *Often* (in collaboration with Kevin Killian, 2000) at the California College of Arts and Crafts, San Francisco, December 8, 2000."

Barbara Guest was born Barbara Ann Pinson on September 6, 1920 to Ann Hetzel and James Harvey Pinson, a probation officer. The family moved often, depending on where James could find work, and Guest has told interviewers that it was purely by chance that she was born in North Carolina: her family had no roots there, and Guest spent most of her first decade in a series of small Florida towns. She moved to California at age 11. In *The Confetti Trees: Motion Picture Stories* (1998), a volume of prose pieces, excerpts of which appeared in *Jacket* (no. 10, October 1999), Guest wrote, "When I was a girl in Los Angeles, the city became a haven for emigres of World War II. People of the arts and film, experts in languages, arrived. The brothers Mann, the composers Mahler and Schoenberg. In the studios were Lang, Milestone, Lubitsch. Cameramen, story writers. They were people of experience and imagination. They were sad with a different kind of sadness. They did not know about our maturing under their guidance, abstract as it might be. It was an emigre climate we never lost." Her peripatetic childhood had a lasting effect: in an oft-quoted line, she once said, "When I say the word 'home' I almost whisper it."

After graduating from the University of California, at Berkeley, in 1943, Guest moved to New York City, working for a time as a reviewer for *Art News*. (She continued, throughout her life, to write articles and reviews for art magazines. She collaborated with artists on several illustrated volumes, and in some instances she herself created the artwork that appeared on her book covers.) In 1960, when she was 40 years old, Guest published her first collection of poems, *The Location of Things*. The volume was followed by *Poems* and *Blue Stairs*. Although her verse received favorable notice, "by the end of the decade," Fox wrote, "the spotlight had shifted to poets like Denise Levertov and Adrienne Rich, whose work was overtly political."

Still, Guest continued to write poetry throughout the next decades. Reviews, although infrequent, were generally favorable. Commenting on *Fair Realism*, for example, a critic wrote for *Publishers Weekly* (May 5, 1989, on-line), "In these lush, free-form poems, her ninth collection, Guest grasps at reality through shifting perspectives as she aims for a truth beyond abstractions or idealizations. Kandinsky's view from his window,

Alexander the Great's ancient world of conquest and Flaubert's quest for literary perfection are some of the props in this shadow-play of the mind. The effects of a nude on the viewer, the underlying structure of the cosmos unveiled by a piano piece, the alteration of memories in the crucible of time give rise to Guest's exploratory meditations. Now and again, the reader is nudged into a sense of recognition at 'encountering the marble exactitude of things.'" A reviewer for the same publication (August 19, 2002), wrote of *Miniatures and Other Poems*, "*Miniatures* divides into three parts; [the last] two are single, extended open field poems proffered with extraordinary economy and elegance, and a wry take on reflexive poetic reference to language: 'mirror moving backward, / impromptu surface of the alphabet when she fell sideways.'" The reviewer continued, "The first section of 24 brief poems, 'Miniatures,' gives quick takes on everything from the Aeneid to Chekhov to Coleridge. (On Schönberg: 'This is not "dinner music." This is a power structure, / heavy as eyelids.') These three short works go together beautifully, held together by a will-to-inquiry that is as funny and skeptical as it is open and determined."

Of the more recent *The Red Gaze*, Ann Vickery wrote for the journal *How2* (on-line): "To enter Guest's poetry is an experience of intense sensuousness (dealing with affective and aesthetic dimensions) as well as being a philosophical (cognitive) pursuit; do not expect to be led through some linear narrative with confined walls and rooms with clearly marked entry and exit points. For Guest the act of reading is all about letting go: an intuitive rather than rational passage toward the discovery of meaning. The focus is on the process, whether it be the act of looking or the act of reading. As she declares in 'The Beautiful Voyage,' '[G]o inside the poem itself and *be in the dark* at the beginning of the journey.'"

Theories abound as to why Guest did not get the recognition she deserved throughout much of her life. The male members of the New York School inarguably received the lion's share of attention in the literary world. "Critics intent on securing the reputations of Ashbery and O'Hara in particular," Geoff Ward wrote for the London *Independent* (February 22, 2006), "neglected Guest under the imperative to establish those poets as being as important to American poetry after 1945 as [T. S.] Eliot and [Ezra] Pound had been to an earlier generation." Additionally, the male poets—especially O'Hara, Ashbery, and Koch—could be cliquish, prompting Schuyler to famously write to Guest complaining that the trio thought of themselves as points on a trefoil, when Schuyler and Guest should rightfully make the configuration a five-pointed star. In an article posted on the Poetry Foundation Web site, Guest's daughter, Hadley, told Cynthia Haven, "There was a certain jealousy because she was so experimental. I've always considered her,

personally, the most experimental of the whole group. . . . She was very independent in her thinking; she could be outspoken. . . . She wouldn't go along to get along—she paid a price for that. No doubt about that."

Haven put forth yet another reason for Guest's relative obscurity: "[She] refused the academic path that kept many of her peers in print. 'She didn't approve of workshops—she thought it was kind of fraudulent, with many people claiming to be poets who weren't. She looked warily at academics, said Hadley Guest. Her daughter recalled her saying, 'I can't be a teacher and a poet at the same time. First, I don't approve of academia, and second, I don't have the energy to do both.'"

Towards the end of her life, Guest began to attract attention that most agreed was long overdue. When she was presented with the prestigious Robert Frost Medal for Distinguished lifetime achievement from the Poetry Society of America, on April 23, 1999, Charles Bernstein, a fellow poet, introduced her, saying, "[Her] works have become an integral part of the fabric of contemporary American poetry, touchstones crucial for understanding not just the poetry of the generation of poets born in the 1920s—but also for the understanding of the activity—I want to say the possibilities—of poetry in the postwar period." He continued, "Yet I read Guest, and I think I share this with many of my contemporaries and also with a large number of younger poets, not as an historical figure whose achievement has been assimilated, but rather as a contemporary, a poet for whom each new poem seems to exist in that very difficult to define now. That is, Guest is not only an important influence on contemporary American poetry but also someone who is actively creating its present terms and tense." He concluded, "At [a] Barnard [college] poetry conference, just two weeks ago. . . . Barbara Guest was an incandescent center, illuminating the entire proceedings. At a panel discussion at this milestone conference, Guest told a packed crowd that she had come to us unprepared. I want to thank Barbara Guest for a lifetime of poetry for which we have been unprepared, for continually testing the limits of form and stretching the bounds of beauty, for expanding the imagination and revisioning—both revisiting and recasting—the aesthetic. As readers we have been unprepared for Guest: she has never quite fitted in to our pre-made categories, our expectations, our explanations. She has written her work as the world inscribes itself, processurally, without undue obligation to expectation, and with a constant, even serene, enfolding in which we find ourselves folded. We are unprepared for Barbara Guest and for that we thank her, for this lifetime of work that is still unravelling before our eyes and ears, unraveling so that we may revel in it. It has taken so long to recognize Barbara Guest's work, to acknowledge it, perhaps because this work seeks neither recognition nor acknowledgement but that a fair realism may awake in us as we read, inspired not by the author but by the whirls and words and worlds that she enacts."

Aside from her poetry, the work for which Guest is perhaps best known is her still widely read biography of the poet H.D. The book continues to polarize critics: some dislike Guest's somewhat unflattering views of Hilda Doolittle as opportunistic and eccentric; others have welcomed the wealth of biographical detail Guest unearthed. In a mixed review for the *New York Times* (January 4, 1984, on-line), Michiko Kakutani wrote, "Because H. D.'s work is incompletely understood by the general public, the lack of critical analysis in *Herself Defined* seems particularly unfortunate. In this volume, there is little assessment of her maturation as a poet and barely any examination of the momentous effect that analysis—with Freud himself—had on her later work," but Kakutani concluded, "Still, few poets' work is as rooted in autobiographical details as H. D.'s, and for readers curious about her life, *Herself Defined* is essential reading. Instead of dwelling on the poet's celebrated liaisons with Ezra Pound, Richard Aldington and D. H. Lawrence, Barbara Guest weaves these relationships and others into a shimmering, delicately patterned narrative that is never less than absorbing."

Guest is the recipient of, among other honors, the Longwood Award, the Lawrence Lipton Award, the Columbia Book Award, and a grant from the National Endowment for the Arts.

Guest was first married to the painter and writer John Dudley; the pair ultimately divorced. In 1948 she married Stephen Guest, who was later given a peerage; that marriage lasted six years. When it ended, in 1954, she married the military historian Trumball Higgins; they remained married until Higgins's death, in 1970. In addition to her daughter, Hadley Guest, the poet has one son, Jonathan Higgins.

On February 15, 2006 Barbara Guest died in Berkeley, California. She had suffered a series of strokes and had been in ill health since the end of 2004.

Guest was described by a *Publishers Weekly* (June 28, 1999) reviewer as "a major force in innovative poetics" whose "near-flawless ear and synaesthetic sense of word values" produce "carved jewel-like word-clusters." A major writing on her work, "Implacable Poet, Purple Birds: The Work of Barbara Guest" by the critic Sara Lundquist, includes this quote from Guest herself: "How empty is all the dazzle of style, without the imagination."

—S.Y.

Suggested Reading: *American Poetry Review* p23+ Aug. 1992, p7+ Feb. 1996, p11+ July 2000; *Booklist* p712 June 15, 1962; *Kirkus Reviews* p312 Mar. 15, 1962; *Library Journal* p96 Aug.

1999; *London Review of Books* p25+ Aug. 22, 1996; *New York Times* (on-line) Mar. 4, 2006; *New York Times Book Review* p7 Mar. 11, 1984; Poetry Foundation Web site; *Publishers Weekly* p65 Apr. 24, 1995, p81+ Aug. 19, 2002; *San Francisco Chronicle* p4 July 16, 1995, R p12 Jan. 9, 2000

Selected Books: *The Location of Things*, 1960; *Blue Stairs*, 1968; *Moscow Mansions*, 1973; *The Countess from Minneapolis*, 1976; *Seeking Air*, 1979; *Herself Defined: The Poet H. D. and Her World*, 1984; *Fair Realism*, 1989; *Defensive Rapture*, 1993; *Selected Poems*, 1995; *Quill, Solitary APPARITION*, 1996; *The Confetti Trees*, 1999; *If So, Tell Me*, 1999; *Rocks on a Platter: Notes on Literature*, 1999; *Miniatures and Other Poems*, 2002; *Forces of the Imagination: Writing on Writing*, 2003; *The Red Gaze*, 2005

Gullar, Ferreira

(GOO-yar, feh-HER-RA)

Sep. 10, 1930– Poet; art critic

When Ferreira Gullar published a collection of poetry, *A luta corporal* (which can be translated as "the bodily struggle"), in 1954, it opened many literary and artistic doors for him in his native Brazil, and he became known for experimenting with avant-garde styles. Although he enjoyed critical acclaim and established his reputation as a poet and writer, Gullar found himself disillusioned with his work. He concluded that avant-garde art and poetry were ineffective in addressing many of the social problems that plagued Brazil, including poverty, illiteracy, and racism. As a result, Gullar's work became more political, and he ran afoul of Brazil's military dictatorship, which had seized power in April 1964. Denounced as a communist, Gullar fled Brazil in 1971. He settled in Santiago, Chile, but found little respite there, as Chile was in the throes of its own political turmoil. Gullar witnessed the violent overthrow of the democratically elected government of Salvador Allende, a socialist, by Augusto Pinochet, who established a ruthless dictatorship.

Considered an enemy of the regime because of his support for Allende and his status as a Brazilian expatriate, Gullar found refuge in Buenos Aires, Argentina. Depressed by the traumatic events of the preceding years and his separation from his family, he wrote a book-length poem entitled *Poema Sujo* (*Dirty Poem*), which drew on his adult experiences and childhood memories. In 1975 *Poema Sujo* was published in Brazil and earned substantial acclaim, and two years later Gullar returned to his native land and resumed his career as a journalist and poet. He has since written numerous poetry collections, volumes of literary and artistic criticism, and an autobiography.

One of 11 children, Ferreira Gullar was born on September 10, 1930 in São Luis, the capital city of the Maranhão state in northeastern Brazil. Gullar's father, Newton, was a merchant. Gullar began reading and writing poetry during his teenage years. One of Gullar's teachers was impressed with a poem, "Dia do Trabalho," that he wrote for a classroom assignment. The teacher's favorable reaction encouraged the young Gullar to pursue a career as a writer, and a revised version of that assignment became the first poem Gullar published in a journal.

In 1948 Gullar began writing for the *Diário de São Luis,* a local literary supplement. A year later, he published his first book, *Un pouco acima do chão,* a collection of poetry, with the financial assistance of the Gonçalves Dias Cultural Center.

Gullar then went to work as a broadcaster for the state-owned Rádio Timbira. In 1950 he witnessed the police killing of a worker at a political rally. He was fired after refusing to read an official government statement over the radio that blamed communists for the killing. That year Gullar's poem, "O galo," won a competition held by the *Jornal de Letras.* The competition's judges included such established Brazilian poets and writers as Manuel Bandeira, Odylo Costa, and Willy Lewin.

In 1951 Gullar moved to Rio de Janeiro, Brazil's largest city and the nation's capital until 1960. After becoming acquainted with several young artists and the acclaimed writer and art critic Mário Pedrosa, Gullar began writing about art. Gullar edited articles for *O Cruzeiro,* one of Brazil's most popular and influential magazines.

In 1954 Gullar became an editor for *Manchete,* a popular magazine. (He also served as an editor for *Diário Carioca,* a newspaper.) His second collection of poetry, *A luta corporal* (1954), brought him wide literary success. (His first had met with little fanfare.) In his book *Seven Faces: Brazilian Poetry since Modernism* (1996), Charles A. Perrone described *A luta corporal* as "a benchmark in modern Brazilian lyric, a point of departure for the contemporary. This markedly diverse collection moves from metrified verse and more conventional lyric to brief epiphanies, dense prose poems, automatic writing, and other audacious linguistic trials." Many other artists and writers praised *A luta corporal,* which established Gullar as a promising new poet.

Impressed with his book, the poets Augusto de Campos, Haroldo de Campos, and Décio Pignatari, who were the leaders of postwar Brazil's experimental Concretist movement, reached out to Gullar and encouraged him to try writing poetry in the new style. (Unlike conventional poetry, Concretist poetry adds a visual effect because of the ways in which words and sentences are arranged in the poem.)

In December 1956 Gullar participated in the first National Exposition of Concrete Art, at the Museum of Modern Art, in the city of São Paulo. He later participated in the second National Exposition of Concrete Art, at the Palácio Gustavo Capanema, in Rio de Janeiro. In 1957, however, Gullar publicly broke with the Concretist movement. In the introduction to his 1990 translation of Gullar's *Poema Sujo,* Leland Guyer wrote that Gullar concluded that Concretist art, while intellectually ingenious, negated the essence of poetry. Gullar has attributed the split to his disagreement with the views of an article calling for a mathematical composition for concrete poetry, published by the Concretist group in São Paulo.

In 1959 Gullar drafted the Neoconcrete Manifesto, which was published on March 23, 1959 in the *Suplemento Dominical do Jornal do Brasil.* Many artists and writers signed the manifesto. "We do not conceive of a work of art as a 'machine' or 'object' but as a 'quasi-corpus'; that is, a being whose reality is not exhausted by the external relationships of its elements," the manifesto read, as quoted by Regina Célia Pinto in her article, "The Neoconcrete Movement: 1959– 1961." "We believe that a work of art surpasses the material mechanism on which it rests, but not because it has an extraterrestrial quality: it surpasses it by transcending such mechanical relationships . . . and [creating], in and of itself, a tacit meaning . . . that emerges for the first time." In 1959 Gullar participated in the first National Exposition of Neoconcrete Art. That same year, he published his first book of art criticism, *Teoria do não-objeto* (which can be translated as "the theory of the non-object").

Guyer described one of Gullar's experiments with Neoconcretism in the introduction to the translation of *Poema Sujo.* "[Gullar] joined forces with painters and sculptors to create what he has called, 'spatial poems,' culminating in a work which he entitled *Poema Enterrado* [Buried Poem]," Guyer wrote. "The work, a joint creation of Ferreira Gullar and the painter Hélio Oiticica, went beyond his initial experiments. This unusual and historically important work was installed in a basement room, behind a door. Beyond this door one 'entered the poem' and in the middle of the room found a red cube, half a meter square. Lifting the red cube revealed a green cube beneath it. Lifting the green cube revealed a white one. On the face of this white cube was written 'Rejuvenate' [*Rejuvensça*]. This experimental poem, created in 1959, had a brief but well-remembered existence and came to a luckless end when the basement unexpectedly flooded with water."

In 1961 Gullar was appointed the director of the Fundação Cultural de Brasilia, a cultural foundation in the newly built capital city of Brasilia. Gullar, however, resigned from the foundation shortly thereafter. According to Guyer, Gullar became disillusioned with the avant-garde and experimental poetry that he had been writing, concluding that it would not help him find solutions to such chronic social problems as poverty and racism. "Recognizing that, in certain ways, he had become part of the problem and that he had become untrue to his own reality," Guyer observed, "Gullar decided that he must 'return to his roots,' identify and reveal those qualities he deemed most Brazilian, and create a truer, more responsible art."

In 1962 Gullar joined a local Centro Popular de Cultura (CPC or the Popular Culture Center), a left-wing organization and branch of the União Nacional dos Estundantes (UNE or the National Union of Students). He began writing folk ballads with the aim of reaching a wider audience. (He did not abandon his other work, however; he published two books of poetry that year, *Quem matou Aparecida?* and *João Boa-Morte, cabra marcado pra morrer.*) A year later, Gullar was elected president of his CPC.

In April 1964 a military dictatorship seized power in Brazil and shut down the CPCs. The police broke into Gullar's home and confiscated several of his books and other belongings. One of Gullar's poems, "August 1964," as translated in 1983 by William Jay Smith in the book *Brazilian Poetry (1950–1980)*, recalled Gullar's feelings of the time: "I must pay cash / to buy life from the world's proprietors. / Verse is suffocating under the weight of taxes, / and poetry is subjected to a secret-police inquiry."

Gullar and a group of other artists responded to the new censorship by forming *Grupo Opiniãdo* (Group Opinion), a theater troupe that performed plays critical of the regime. While continuing to write poetry and art criticism, Gullar wrote pieces for performance. In 1966 he co-wrote the production *Se correr o bicho pega, se ficar o bicho come* (which can be translated as "if you run the beast will get you, if you stay the beast will eat you"). Staged in Rio de Janeiro, the show won the Molière Award (the French equivalent of the American Tony Award), among other honors. Over the next two years Gullar wrote several additional pieces for the group.

In December 1968 Gullar was arrested by the government and imprisoned for a brief time. After his release, he resumed his political and literary activities and was denounced as a communist. Fearing for his safety, he went into hiding for almost a year and then fled Brazil. Over the next few years, he lived in Moscow, Russia; Santiago, Chile; Lima, Peru; and Buenos Aires, Argentina. Under the pseudonym of Frederico Marques, Gullar continued to write.

In September 1973 Gullar was living in Santiago when Augusto Pinochet, a general, overthrew Salvador Allende and established a ruthless military dictatorship that suppressed dissent and eventually killed thousands of people. According to Guyer, the Chilean government suspected that Gullar was a terrorist because he was among the many Brazilian exiles living in the country who had backed Allende. Gullar's apartment was searched twice. One time, the military threatened to arrest him and send him to the National Stadium in Santiago, where executions of political dissidents and other civilians were carried out. Gullar won his release by persuading the soldiers that, as a journalist, he was exempt from arrest. He then fled to Buenos Aires. Gullar kept writing. In 1975 more of his poetry was published in the book *Dentro da Noite Veloz.* A year later, he wrote *Augusto do Anjos ou morte e vida nordestina,* a tribute to the Brazilian poet Augusto do Anjos.

During his exile in Buenos Aires, Gullar greatly missed his family, which included a wife, Thereza, and three children. Guyer wrote that these feelings led Gullar, in 1975, to write what he considered his last will and testament, a book-length poem entitled *Poema Sujo (Dirty Poem).* In it, Gullar recalled his childhood memories of growing up in São Luis do Maranhão by creating vivid images of the decaying city and the social injustice he observed. Recordings of Gullar reciting *Poema Sujo* were smuggled into Brazil and played privately for audiences. A year later, *Poema Sujo* was published in book form in Brazil. The work earned substantial praise. In *World Literature Today* (Autumn 1991), Richard A. Preto-Rodas opined (referring to Guyer's translation), "Writing during a period of severe depression as a middle-aged political exile in Buenos Aires, Gullar interweaves reverie, regret, and nostalgia into a rich lyric tapestry—in effect, the background of a social revolutionary." Preto-Rodas continued, "However, he transcends ideology to create a hauntingly sincere remembrance of things past, warts and all. . . . The work begins as a kaleidoscope of impressions from a poor but not destitute childhood with snatches of color, glimpses of long-dead pets, furtive sexual experiences, modest family dinners, and a barrage of smells, from open sewers and cooking oil to ground ginger grass and mint leaves. The reader is enveloped in a sensuous world where bright sunlight gives way to velvety darkness, where the sounds of songbirds rustling in overarching trees meld with the taste of friend cracklings."

In the wake of the poem's publication, numerous artists and intellectuals called on the government to allow Gullar to return to the country. (In 1974 a Brazilian court had acquitted him of the charge of being a member of the Cultural Committee of the Brazilian Communist Party.) On March 10, 1977, Gullar returned to Rio de Janeiro. The day after his arrival, he was arrested by the police and interrogated for more than 72 hours. Gullar was then released, however, and not charged with a crime.

Back home, Gullar resumed his literary and artistic endeavors. In 1979 he released a recording, *Antologia poética de Ferreira Gullar,* which earned him the title Personalidade Literária do Ano (Literary Person of the Year) from the Câmara

Brasileira do Livro, an independent organization devoted to the promotion of reading. In the following decades, he published more of his poetry in such books as *Na vertigem do dia* (1980), *Crime na flora ou Orden e progresso* (1986), *O formigueiro* (1991), *Muitas vozes* (1999), *Um gato chamado Gatinho* (2000), *O rei que more no mar* (2001), and *Dr. Urubu e Outras Fábulas* (2005). Gullar's books on art and literature include *Uma luz do chão* (1978), *Sobre arte* (1982), *Etapas da arte contemporanea: do cubismo à arte neoconcreta* (1985), *Indagações de hoje* (1989), *Argumentação contra a morte da arte* (1993)—an attack on avant-garde art that sparked considerable controversy in Brazilian literary and artistic circles—and *Relampagos* (2003).

Gullar has translated many classical texts into Portuguese. His 1985 translation of Edmond Rostand's play *Cyrano de Bergerac* earned him a Molière Award. From 1992 to 1995, Gullar served as the director of the Instituto Brasileiro de Arte e Cultura (IBAC or the Brazilian Institute for Art and Culture). In 1998 Gullar published his autobiography, *Rabo de foguete.* (The title roughly translates to the "tail end of a rocket.") In 2000 the Museum of Art in Rio de Janeiro celebrated Gullar's 70th birthday with an exhibit devoted to his work.

In 2002 Gullar was nominated for the Nobel Prize in Literature. (The honor ultimately went to Imre Kertész, a Hungarian novelist.) That year he was also given the Prince Claus Prize, an award from the Netherlands Academy of Arts and Sciences that recognizes artists and writers whose work contributes to the improvement of society and culture.

—D.C.

Suggested Reading: *World Literature Today* p685+ Autumn 1990; Perrone, Charles A. *Seven Faces: Brazilian Poetry Since Modernism*, 1996

Selected Works in English Translation: *Brazilian Poetry, 1950–1980*, 1983; *Dirty Poem: Poema Sujo*, 1990

Gunesekera, Romesh

(goo-neh-SAY-keh-reh)

Feb. 26, 1954– Novelist; short-story writer

When Romesh Gunesekera's *Reef* (1994) was short-listed for the Booker Prize, it was the odds-on favorite to walk away with one of the most prestigious prizes in English literature—quite an accomplishment for a first novel. His first book, *Monkfish Moon* (1992), a collection of short stories that are mostly set in his homeland, Sri Lanka, had been published the same year that his compatriot Michael Ondaatje won the Booker Prize for *The English Patient*, leading many critics to compare the two. Unlike those of Ondaatje, however, Gunesekera's writings almost inevitably return to Sri Lanka and the brutal strife between the majority Sinhalese (from whom Gunesekera is descended) and the Tamil separatists—or, more specifically, the plight of the postcolonial exile, who mourns the memory of his homeland and struggles to make sense of conflicting identities. "The world being what it is I write to redress the balance, at least in my own mind," Gunesekera wrote for an author's statement posted on the British Council Web site. "I want to keep an inner life alive and, with luck, somebody else's too. Imaginative writing, to me, is a way of discovering who we are, and what we have to contend with; discovering what is out there, and also what is not there. It enables me to think and explore and make something new with language, while trying to make sense of our lives."

Courtesy of Bloomsbury

Romesh Gunesekera was born in Colombo, Sri Lanka, on February 26, 1954. The country was still called Ceylon at that time, though it had won independence from Great Britain in 1948. He was brought up bilingually; his first language was Sinhalese, one of the two official languages of the country, with English a close second. "My biggest childhood memory is of my father's friends, who all seemed to be journalists," Gunesekera told James Wood for the London *Guardian* (July 30,

1994). "When they got drunk, they would recite lines and lines of poetry. It was a very literary culture: in Jaffra, now devastated, where my mother grew up, she was given a box of chocolates and a book of Keats's poems on one of her birthdays." His father, a government bank executive, moved the family to the Philippines when Gunesekera was 12. As a teenager he moved to England and completed his secondary education at a small boarding school in Liverpool. "I was terribly homesick," Gunesekera told Wood. "But you know, I have felt nostalgic all my life, if that doesn't sound too precious. I think I was probably nostalgic for Sri Lanka even when I lived there, because there is something imaginary about the place. It can't be grasped."

Gunesekera then attended the University of Liverpool, where he studied English and philosophy. He won awards for his scholarship in philosophy and his poetry, though, according to his own account, he spent most of his time reading books from the public library. "One of the advantages of my strange exile in Liverpool was that I was left alone; this focused my attention," he told Wood. "I was able to drink in lots of Milton and Shakespeare." Before dedicating himself to writing, Gunesekera worked as a development-aid officer in several countries. He then accepted a position in London as an assistant regional director of the British Council, a cultural organization. He continued to write during this time, winning first prize in the Peterloo Poets Annual Open Poetry Competition, in 1988.

Gunesekera's first book, *Monkfish Moon*, included nine tales primarily focused on the suffering and loss that Sri Lankans have endured during the current rein of political turmoil. "The unusual power of Gunesekera's writing stems from his graceful manipulation of contrasts: set mostly in Sri Lanka, the stories oppose the almost Baudelairean voluptuousness of the geography with seemingly uncontrollable political violence, the innocence of the observed characters with the omniscience of the narrators . . . ," a reviewer wrote for *Publishers Weekly* (March 22, 1993). "The natural surroundings are sharply scrutinized and sturdily evoked in unassuming, surprisingly potent descriptive passages. Plotting remains deliberately uncomplicated, and while the protagonists themselves measure the dramas of their own destinies against vaster social upheavals, Gunesekera never loses sight of his characters' worth and dignity." In the *New York Times Book Review* (August 1, 1993), Suzanne Berne wrote, "Everyone may feel guilty and scared in Mr. Gunesekera's stories, yet the most startling aspect of this slender, evocative book is how distinct one tale proves from another. Certain ironic details are repeated—several characters, for instance, refurbish dilapidated buildings as Sri Lanka falls apart—and the question 'What's happened?' becomes a plaintive refrain, but despair bred by civil unrest has endless variations, as Mr. Gunesekera eloquently demonstrates."

In *Monkfish Moon* Gunesekera used a "simple story-telling style against a backdrop of a lush and verdant Sri Lanka with the suggestion of the distant thunder of rot, political unrest and death under the surface," Julie Chatterjee wrote for the Singapore *Straits Times* (October 21, 1995), and in the author's sophomore effort, *Reef*, "it is the same sense of loss of a pristine paradise that echoes through the nuances and images of a highly-charged novel." The novel's protagonist, Triton, is sent at the age of 11 to live with and serve as the houseboy to Mister Salgado, a marine biologist who is obsessed with studying the environmental devastation of the coral reefs surrounding Sri Lanka. Triton learns to become an excellent cook from working for Salgado and eventually becomes a successful restaurateur in London. The personal tale at the heart of the novel is contrasted with the political turmoil. "This was my greatest struggle, to make a place that seemed like paradise while also admitting the real," Gunesekera told Wood. "Because as a writer, when things happen in the world, I have to deal with them, I have to incorporate them. And what happened in 1983, when the war really began, was that Sri Lanka went from being a paradise to a hellhole. There was a real sense of the Fall, of the desecration of Eden. So what I wanted to do with this book was to write about this paradisal landscape, to create a kind of tropical Asian island of the imagination; while at the same time, I wanted to give readers a premonition of what was ahead."

Reef, in addition to making the short lists for the Booker Prize and *Guardian* Fiction Prize, won the Yorkshire Post Book Award for best first work and the plaudits of critics. Gunesekera "brings a moving combination of innocence and wisdom to Triton's first-person narration," a reviewer wrote for *Publishers Weekly* (December 19, 1994). "His spare, lyrical prose evokes the sensuous heat of the tropical island and conveys mouthwatering descriptions of Triton's many culinary triumphs. And his take on the synergies of politics, nature and personal striving is subtle and intriguing." Julian Evans, writing for the London *Guardian* (July 5, 1994), compared Gunesekera's skills at characterization to those of R. K. Narayan and Graham Greene. "*Reef* is a delightful novel," Evans wrote. "With no resolution (an escape from Sri Lanka to Earls Court hardly counts as a fictional resolution), *Reef* is a long story more than a novel, a long episode of childhood that ends with the characters fading out into real life on the last page, a comedy with a vein of sadness."

The Sandglass (1998), Gunesekera's third book, begins with the funeral of Pearl Ducal, an exiled Sri Lankan who is living in London. She is the widow of Jason Ducal, whose death remains shrouded in mystery. In Colombo the Ducal family had lived next door to a clan of robber barons, the Vatunas family. While the Ducals are plagued by tragedy and death, the Vatunases prosper, benefiting financially from Jason's mysterious death. The story is narrated by Chip, a former tenant of Pearl's in London, who gets together with her son to investigate the family's downfall. According to Pico Iyer, writing for *Time* (September 7, 1998), in *The Sandglass*, the "meticulous evocation of the marketing of paradise" that made *Reef* such an artistic success, is swept up "into an even ampler examination of how independent Sri Lanka devolved into bloody anarchy and its people got scattered around the globe." In the London *Mail on Sunday* (February 15, 1998), Philip Hensher noted that many fans of the rather slender *Reef* had eagerly awaited *The Sandglass*, expecting a deeper exploration of the same themes, and were somewhat disappointed. "It has many of the same qualities as *Reef*, with its beautifully written prose, its deft way with characterisation and description, dialogue which is full of life, and buckets of charm," Hensher wrote. "Yet, in trying to tell a grand family saga, Gunesekera seems to extend the delicate and tender qualities of the earlier book on to a dangerously large scale; the allusive, short-breathed manner of his writing is made to carry more weight than it can bear." Such reviews notwithstanding, *The Sandglass* won the BBC Asia Award for achievement in writing and literature.

Heaven's Edge (2002) is set on a fictional island that resembles Sri Lanka, a few decades into the future. The protagonist, Marc, is the son of Sri Lankan parents, though he was born and raised in England. Nonetheless, his grandfather, who died when Marc was still a boy, used to paint such an idyllic picture of his homeland that Marc is inspired to return as an adult. He finds, however, that the island is far from his grandfather's paradise: it is a land ravaged by violence, political oppression, and ecological disaster. "We never learn the precise nature of the disaster that has taken place on Marc's island," Akash Kapur wrote for the *New York Times Book Review* (February 23, 2003). "This indeterminacy can be troubling: the narrative sometimes unfolds in a state of delirium, and there are moments when it veers dangerously away from storytelling toward vague metaphysical ponderings. . . . But Gunesekera's prose is spare and muscular, and ultimately it is the writing that rescues his novel from its 'ethereal' digressions. For every moment of vagueness, there is a precise—and often beautiful—description of nature, a vivid action sequence or an all-too-real encounter with violence. Gunesekera's story may be dreamlike, but his prose is resolutely grounded, and the result—as in the best science fiction writing—is a story that uses realism to transcend reality, to hint at deeper mysteries and more profound truths." A writer for *Publishers Weekly* (January 27, 2003) acknowledged that *Heaven's Edge* explored many of the same theme's as Gunesekera's early works but felt that the "compelling romance" between Marc and a Sri Lankan eco-terrorist "makes this one of his best efforts."

The Match, which was published in Britain in 2006, is Gunesekera's most recent novel. After moving to Manila, following his mother's untimely death, 16-year-old Sunny misses the cricket games he enjoyed back in Colombo, so he and his father introduce the sport to their new neighborhood. Cricket fever not only sweeps up the local boys but also Tina, the attractive girl next door, whom he continues to think about even as an adult living in London. The grown-up Sunny finds himself increasingly alienated—that is, until the Sri Lankan cricket team plays an exhibition game in England, stirring something deep in Sunny and jolting him into self-awareness. "This is a most intimately and precisely imagined novel," Paul Binding wrote for the London *Independent* (March 19, 2006). "Those who have followed Gunesekera from the debut stories of *Monkfish Moon* and his subtle first novel, *Reef*, won't be surprised. Yet so complete a match (to use the novel's central image) between empathy and artistry, between lively observation and intellectual grasp of cultural tensions, always surprises. Henry James said about Balzac's relation to his characters: 'It was by loving them that he knew them.' Loving, while remaining in sharp moral control, is a hard business, but it leads to the profoundest kind of knowledge, as *The Match* so movingly demonstrates."

Gunesekera, who was awarded the distinction Sri Lanka Ranjana in 2005, lives in London and has spent time as a writer in residence in Copenhagen, Singapore, and Hong Kong, among other places. He has two daughters.

—S.Y.

Suggested Reading: (Glasgow) *Herald* p16 July 25, 2002; (London) *Guardian* Features p29 July 30, 1994; (London) *Mail on Sunday* p35 Feb. 15 1998; (London) *Sunday Times* Features Mar. 8, 1992; *New York Times Book Review* p10 Aug. 1, 1993; *Time* p80 Sep. 7, 1998

Selected Books: *Monkfish Moon*, 1992; *Reef*, 1994; *The Sandglass*, 1998; *Heaven's Edge*, 2002; *The Match*, 2006

Halberstam, David

Apr. 10, 1934– Journalist; historian

The Pulitzer Prize–winning journalist and historian David Halberstam has written a wealth of critically acclaimed books on history, politics, and culture. He first made a name for himself as a journalist in the 1960s, when he observed and reported in candid detail on the tragedies of the Vietnam War. *The Best and The Brightest* (1972), his book about the political and military men steering U.S. foreign policy during the war, is now hailed as a classic study of power in America. The

Robert Mora/Getty Images

David Halberstam

then to Winsted, Connecticut, where in grammar school Halberstam competed for high grades with Ralph Nader (the future consumer-protection advocate and 2000 presidential candidate).

After World War II Halberstam's father returned from service in Europe, and the family moved to Westchester County in New York. As a student at Roosevelt High School in Yonkers, Halberstam was a member of the track team and worked on the school newspaper. He graduated in 1951 and then entered Harvard University, in Cambridge, Massachusetts. There he became the managing editor of the *Harvard Crimson* and did freelance reporting for the *Boston Globe*. He graduated in 1955 with a B.A. Deciding to pursue a career in journalism and discerning that the subject of race relations was developing into a central issue in American life, he went south to Mississippi and found work as a reporter for the West Point *Daily Times Leader*. He also wrote several articles on politics and race for the now-defunct magazine the *Reporter*. He was fired after 10 months at the *Daily Times Leader*, but in April 1956 he took a job on the Nashville *Tennessean*, where he remained for more than four years, covering mostly politics, while continuing to contribute to the *Reporter* and other publications.

During his time in Tennessee, Halberstam also began working on his first novel, *The Noblest Roman* (1961). A story of bootlegging and political chicanery in a Southern community, it earned critical approval for its well-drawn characters, absorbing action, and closely observed details of small-town life.

In fall 1960 Halberstam joined the Washington bureau of the *New York Times*, where he reported on the early days of President John F. Kennedy's time in office. In 1961 the newspaper assigned Halberstam to the Congo (now the Democratic Republic of the Congo, or DRC) to cover the attempt by U.N. forces to end the secession of Katanga Province. To dispatch his cables he regularly had to travel through hazardous regions; once he was nicked by shrapnel, and on another occasion he and a colleague were fired on by soldiers at a roadblock. "It was a remarkable story: exciting and dangerous," he wrote of the event in *The Making of a Quagmire: America and Vietnam during the Kennedy Era* (1965), labeling it "a small but very nasty street war." His coverage of the conflict won him a 1962 Page One Award from the Newspaper Guild of New York.

In September 1962 Halberstam was assigned to South Vietnam, where the National Liberation Front, a Communist-front organization of Vietnamese nationalists, was attempting to overthrow the repressive anti-Communist government of U.S.–backed Ngo Dinh Diem. Halberstam accompanied South Vietnamese troops and their U.S. advisors on military operations in the Mekong Delta. The optimism of the official reports was sharply contradicted by what Halberstam saw in the field—the growing

recipient of a score of honorary degrees, Halberstam, whose narrative style has been described as anecdotal, energetic, and dramatic, has since written such books as *The Powers That Be* (1979), about the rise of modern media; *The Fifties* (1993), about the people and events of that pivotal decade in American history; and *The Children* (1998), about the growth of the civil rights movement in Nashville, Tennessee, in the 1960s. Halberstam is also the author of several highly regarded sports books, which combine historical detail with social commentary; these include *The Breaks of the Game* (1981), *Summer of '49* (1989), *October 1964* (1994), and *Playing for Keeps: Michael Jordan and the World He Made* (1999). Nearly all of Halberstam's books have been national best-sellers, and he has won numerous journalism and book awards. His most recent books are *War in a Time of Peace: Bush, Clinton, and the Generals* (2001), *Firehouse* (2002), *The Teammates: A Portrait of a Friendship* (2003), and *The Education of a Coach* (2005).

David Halberstam was born in New York City on April 10, 1934, the son of an army surgeon, Dr. Charles A. Halberstam, and a schoolteacher, Blanche (Levy) Halberstam. He has one brother, Dr. Michael Halberstam, a physician and writer. As their father was transferred from one army post to another, the family lived in numerous places throughout the country. "It was a marvelous boyhood of auto trips," Halberstam recalled in *Harper's Bazaar* (August 1972). "Best of all was our home in El Paso, [Texas,] where there were . . . horses to be ridden . . . and polo to be watched at Fort Bliss—the last days of that particular empire." The family moved on to Rochester, Minnesota, and strength of the Viet Minh (the Vietnamese Communist movement, also known by the derogatory name Viet Cong), the reluctance of the South Vietnamese Army to engage the enemy, and disasters in battle publicized as victories. Halberstam decided that it was necessary to write honestly about the deteriorating situation in Vietnam. He was joined by a handful of other American journalists in reporting on the growing resistance to the Diem government, including anti-government street demonstrations; the 1963 Buddhist protests, in which a number of monks set themselves on fire to protest repression; and the government's brutal attempts to stifle dissent.

Halberstam's reports were attacked as inaccurate and irresponsible by the Pentagon, the White House, and the Vietnamese authorities. According to Gay Talese in *The Kingdom and the Power* (1969), Halberstam became "the most conspicuous *bête noire* of the American State Department and the White House," and President Kennedy personally suggested that the *New York Times* transfer him to a less sensitive post. After the overthrow of the Diem regime, the widow of Diem's brother Ngo Dinh Nhu said: "Halberstam should be barbecued, and I would be glad to supply the fluid and the match." The *New York Times* supported Halberstam, however, and his reports from Vietnam brought him the 1964 Pulitzer Prize for international reporting (shared with another Vietnam reporter, Malcolm W. Browne) and the George Polk Memorial Award. Halberstam also received, with two of his colleagues, the first Louis M. Lyons Award for conscience and integrity in journalism.

Halberstam left Vietnam at the end of 1963 and spent the next year in New York. In 1965 he published *The Making of a Quagmire: America and Vietnam during the Kennedy Era*, an account of his experiences in the Congo and more particularly in Vietnam, including his struggles with officialdom and his views on American policy. George Eagle, writing in the *New Republic* (May 15, 1965), praised Halberstam's previous reporting but found the book "choppily constructed and written in the nondescript style of a journeyman journalist." Charles Mohr, however, writing in the *Nation* (May 17, 1965), called it "a sensitive and brilliant book." Coinciding as it did with the beginning of the teach-ins against the war, it had, according to Bert Cochran in the *Nation* (January 8, 1973), "an electrifying effect on a new generation of dissenters. It opened the eyes of a wider public to the sordid activities concealed by official fustian."

At the beginning of 1965 Halberstam was assigned to the *New York Times* bureau in Warsaw, Poland, where his insistence on writing what he saw rather than what the Polish government wanted him to see once more earned him official disapproval. In December 1965 he wrote a piece in which he said that the Warsaw government was weak and the Polish people "restless and alienated"; a week later he was ordered out of the country. During his stay in Poland he had met Elzbieta Czyzewska, one of the country's most-popular actresses, to whom he was married in June 1965. In 1966 he was posted to Paris, where his wife subsequently joined him. Having grown increasingly disenchanted with newspaper journalism in general and particularly the *New York Times*, where his rapid ascent had soured relations with some of his colleagues, Halberstam spent most of his time in Paris working on a novel. After being recalled to New York, he put in another year on the *New York Times* metropolitan staff but in April 1967 resigned to become a contributing editor at *Harper's*.

Among the articles Halberstam wrote for *Harper's* were several on Vietnam, which he revisited in 1967, and others on American politics and politicians, including the 1968 presidential campaign. He published his second novel, *One Very Hot Day* (1968), which describes a crucial day in the life of a company of Vietnamese troops and their American advisers. Critics praised the novel for bringing out a range of attitudes and relationships. "Mr. Halberstam's reporter's ear has caught with uncanny accuracy the inflections and nuances of relevant conversations," Elizabeth Pond wrote for the *Christian Science Monitor* (January 25, 1968). "The characters are authentic," she added. "What Mr. Halberstam knew intimately . . . back in the days when very few Americans thought much about Vietnam, he has now committed to fiction that is bitter and warm—and true." Halberstam also published *The Unfinished Odyssey of Robert Kennedy* (1969), a detailed account of Senator Kennedy's political career, his campaign for the presidency in 1968, and the circumstances of his assassination; and *Ho* (1971), a brief biography of the North Vietnamese leader Ho Chi Minh.

Halberstam has written that he regarded the Vietnam War as "the worst tragedy to befall this country since the Civil War." In the late 1960s he became preoccupied with the origins of American involvement in Vietnam and the subsequent escalation of the war. He began a study of the "architects" of the war—certain high officials in the administrations of Kennedy and Lyndon B. Johnson—and the social forces that shaped their attitudes and assumptions. Halberstam's portraits of McGeorge Bundy (a presidential assistant on national security) and Robert S. McNamara (the former defense secretary) had already appeared in *Harper's* when, in March 1971, the magazine's editor, Willie Morris, unexpectedly resigned in an unrelated dispute with the magazine's publisher. Three other senior editors, as well as several contributing editors, resigned as well, including Halberstam.

After departing *Harper's* Halberstam freelanced for *Esquire*, the *Atlantic Monthly*, *McCall's*, and other publications while completing his study of the nature of power in America. The result of his research, *The Best and the Brightest*, offered biographical portraits of several important figures behind the Vietnam War, including Bundy, McNamara, Dean Rusk, Walt W. Rostow, General Maxwell Taylor, General William Westmoreland, and presidents Kennedy and Johnson. Halberstam sought to convey in the book why these able and dedicated men—America's "best and brightest"— dragged the country into the quagmire of Vietnam. Halberstam concluded, as W. W. MacDonald wrote for *Library Journal* (November 1, 1972), "that they became victims of their own brilliance, of hubris, and of the cold war mentality."

Today *The Best and the Brightest* is widely considered a classic work on Vietnam and American policy makers, though recent historians have begun to question some of Halberstam's fundamental claims, particularly regarding the competence of South Vietnamese President Ngo Dinh Diem. At the time of its release, the book garnered mostly favorable reviews, although several critics found fault with various aspects of the work. Bert Cochran, writing for the *Nation* (January 8, 1973), wrote that the book "has a rich texture woven of inside stuff that connects individuals and decisions, anecdotal detail that blows the breath of life into the musty bureaucratese of memo writers, gossip that adds flash and dazzle. But because he is unclear in his own mind about his concepts, the book is a failure in terms of offering the answer that he set out to provide." Since Halberstam based his work largely on about 500 interviews that he had personally conducted, he was consequently unable to corroborate many of his revelations, a fact that was harshly criticized by Mary McCarthy in a famously vicious article written for the *New York Review of Books* (January 25, 1973). Nevertheless, most critics evinced admiration; P. S. Prescott, for example, writing for *Newsweek* (November 20, 1972), opined, "[This] is a staggeringly ambitious undertaking that is fully matched by Halberstam's performance; it is also a staggeringly long book which, thanks to Halberstam's technical virtuosity and narrative skill, is seductively readable." *The Best and the Brightest* became a national best-seller and in 1973 brought Halberstam the National Book Award for nonfiction, as well as the Overseas Press Club's award.

Halberstam turned his investigative powers towards the media industry with *The Powers That Be*. He covers the rise of modern media in the 20th century, using four major news outlets—the *Washington Post*, CBS News, *Time*, and the *Los Angeles Times*—as examples to show how media venues gained the power to bring down President Richard Nixon (through their coverage of the Watergate scandal) and at the same time grow into highly profitable corporate entities. In a review of the book for *Library Journal* (April 15, 1979), Daniel Levinson proclaimed: "This massively detailed, fascinatingly anecdotal study . . . is destined to have as much influence on American

thought as Halberstam's *The Best and The Brightest*." Richard Rovere, writing for the *New York Times Book Review* (April 22, 1979), noted that the book "is a prodigy of research and of tendentious but sharply focused narrative and analysis, not only of American journalism in the last 30 years or so but also American life, values and politics. . . . *The Powers That Be* will remain stirring history."

The Breaks of the Game was Halberstam's first book about professional sports. During the 1979–80 basketball season, the author traveled with the struggling Portland Trail Blazers, who, just three seasons earlier, had been the champions of the National Basketball Association (NBA). He profiles players, coaches, and owners and places them in the context of their era, depicting the influence of television on basketball's popularity, the sport's rapid growth, new management strategies, and the creation of the players' union. Taylor Branch, in a review for the *New Republic* (February 10, 1982), found the book to be "better than [Halberstam's] others precisely because it is different: he shows more heart, and his talent stands out in sharp relief." In the *Student Library Journal* (April 1982), John Offen remarked, "Halberstam covers not only the professional level of the game but, through his analysis of the lives of the players and coaches, presents a total picture of the game today—from big-city ghetto playground pick-up games to high-pressure college level and the grind of the professional seasons. . . . [This account] also provides an awareness and understanding of the American character."

Halberstam's next book on sports, *The Amateurs* (1985), depicted the quest of four young unknowns who compete for a chance to represent the U.S. in single-scull racing (a type of rowing event) at the 1984 Olympics, in Los Angeles. In *The Reckoning* (1986), a prodigious book that was the result of five years of research, Halberstam compared the auto industries of the U.S. and Japan. That book was widely reviewed and drew much praise for its astute analysis.

One of Halberstam's best-known books, *Summer of '49*, recalled one of the last great seasons of the famous baseball player Joe DiMaggio, the centerfielder for the New York Yankees, and his team's rivalry with the Boston Red Sox. In the 1949 season the Yankees and the Red Sox had one of the most memorable pennant races in baseball history, distinguished as much by the vacillating fates of the teams—the Yankees finally beat Boston to capture the American League championship—as by the personalities of such players as DiMaggio, Ted Williams, Tommy Henrich, and Bobby Doerr. In a review for *Newsweek* (April 17, 1989), Jack Kroll wrote: "*Summer of '49* is a gorgeous story with personalities and anecdotes jampacking every page. . . . Baseball does wonders for Halberstam's style, turning his slow stuff into fast balls." In *BusinessWeek* (May 22, 1989), John Friedman was more tempered in his assessment, noting that Halberstam's "nostalgia sometimes verges on corniness. And he occasionally waxes as enthusiastic about journalists as he does about ballplayers, forgetting that his readers may not share his professional bias. But chiding Halberstam for these errors is like criticizing [Ted] Williams, arguably the greatest hitter of all time, for less-than-brilliant fielding."

Halberstam had planned for his subsequent book, *The Next Century* (1991), to be part of a publishing experiment—books with advertisements, a concept promoted and developed by Whittle Communications. When that project fell through, Halberstam took his manuscript to William Morrow & Company for publication; it subsequently spent numerous weeks on the best-seller lists. The slim volume was as much a memoir as it was the speculative tract its title might suggest; the author coupled his more than 30 years of reporting experience with his thoughts about America's future in the next century. In 1991 the country was experiencing fiscal woes, domestic discord, and a minor identity crisis brought on by the collapse of the Soviet Union and heightened competition in the international economy. Halberstam's view of America's future is a pessimistic one, although he does leave room for hope. Senator Bill Bradley of New Jersey wrote for the *New York Times Book Review* (February 17, 1991): "Mr. Halberstam's is one of the few books to recognize that the challenge facing the United States is not finding a scapegoat for our economic blunders but making the most of our physical and mental capacities, improving our productivity in an open, democratic structure."

With *The Fifties* Halberstam revisited the middle decade of the 20th century, a period in which the U.S. underwent dramatic transformations in politics, morals, media, and the arts. He chronicles the defining events of the decade, including the communist witch-hunts, the Korean War, economic expansion, racial integration, the emergence of television, and the growth of suburbia, as well as describing the many colorful personalities of the day, including President Dwight D. Eisenhower, the writer Jack Kerouac, the singer Elvis Presley, and the civil rights activist Rosa Parks. Some critics, like Douglas T. Miller for *New York Newsday* (May 30, 1993), found much to praise about the book, which was more than 800 pages long. Miller called it a "monumental re-examination of the decade," and noted: "With a deft style and a flair for dramatic narration, Halberstam portrays a host of major and minor figures. . . . Though a frustrating book for serious students of mid-century America due to the absence of any overall analytic framework, *The Fifties* will prove a fun read for those interested in the fascinating personalities of the period." A reviewer for *Publishers Weekly* (February 26, 1993) commended Halberstam for "a brilliant job of putting together a treasure trove" of information,

adding, "If not a great prose stylist, Halberstam is a clear, thoughtful reporter and a thorough researcher." In a review for the *Wall Street Journal* (June 23, 1993), John Podhoretz was more critical of the book, noting sarcastically that "it is as inspired and as clever as its title. There is nothing about this immensely long book that explains why Mr. Halberstam would spend so much time and effort to produce it. It has no passion, no narrative drive and no real theme except for the startlingly obvious observations that the social upheavals of the '60s were the result of the social trends of the '50s."

In *October 1964* Halberstam recounted the spectacular 1964 baseball season leading up to the World Series in which the St. Louis Cardinals defeated the New York Yankees. The author argues that the two teams represented the past (the Yankees) and the future (the Cardinals) of baseball; he also ties the story into the larger social context, with discussions on race relations and the Vietnam War. In the *Christian Science Monitor* (September 16, 1994), Larry Eldrigdge wrote: "*Summer of '49* is a tough act to follow—but it quickly becomes apparent that Halberstam has pulled it off. . . . These books are companion pieces, going far beyond the misleading specific years of their titles to give us a two-volume chronicle of the evolution of baseball within the American social fabric from pre–World War II days into the 1970s." A reviewer for the *Economist* (October 29, 1994) expressed similar feelings: "Those who know baseball will appreciate this richly textured narrative of one of the best seasons on record. Those who are less knowledgeable will at times find the book confusing because it assumes a basic understanding of baseball. Even so, they ought to persevere. They will gain a true insight into America's love of its national pastime and all that it embodies."

Halberstam's next book, *The Children*, offers a telling reexamination of the civil rights movement of the 1960s by focusing on the lives of eight young black college students he had met in Nashville when he was covering the lunch-counter sit-ins as a young reporter. The book was widely praised. Mary Carroll, writing for *Booklist* (January 1–15, 1998), cheered: "As in books from *The Best and the Brightest* (1972) to *October 1964* (1994), Halberstam makes vivid the interaction between unique individuals and the groups whose support enables them to exercise their individuality. [This is] a powerful story of young people justly seen as heroes because they risked their lives to challenge Jim Crow apartheid." Thomas J. Davis, in a review for *Library Journal* (February 15, 1998), wrote: "Detailing the speeding cycle of racial protest that divided the 1950s and 1960s and created a new age and a new America, Halberstam renders the private and public struggles of a generation of young impassioned black students. With impressive sweep he reports on both what happened in the movement and what happened to it."

In 1999 Halberstam published *Playing for Keeps: Michael Jordan and the World He Made*, a popular biography of the basketball superstar. Halberstam is "fascinated by character, with a psychologist's eye for telling tics, nuances, and turning points, and he's especially intent on character in a moral sense," L. S. Klepp wrote for *Entertainment Weekly* (February 5, 1999). "The underlying theme," Klepp added, "is that Jordan, the greatest player in the history of the game, drew unprecedented crowds, publicity, and money to it, which didn't corrupt him but did corrupt the sport."

Returning once again to the realm of politics, Halberstam wrote *War in a Time of Peace: Bush, Clinton, and the Generals*, a study of U.S. foreign and military policy in the 1990s. "[This is] a book that most journalists would give their right arm to have written, a tour de force of reportorial narration very much in the *Best and the Brightest* genre," Richard Bernstein wrote for the *New York Times* (October 10, 2001). An anonymous critic for the *Economist* (September 8, 2001) remarked, "The book is not quite what its subtitle promises—an analysis of civil-military relations in the United States during the 1990s—but rather a finely crafted and enjoyable account of the shared culture and personal chemistry of America's political and military power-brokers." The critic went on to complain that Halberstam possessed a "relatively uncritical attitude towards the powerful and sophisticated Americans who form his subject matter."

Halberstam's next book, *Firehouse*, tells of the tragedy that befell a group of 13 New York City firefighters who were called to the World Trade Center following the terrorist attacks of September 11, 2001. Only one of the 13 survived. Frederick R. Lynch, writing in the *Washington Times* (September 8, 2002), called the book "a remarkable study of a tightly knit workplace world and the impact of September 11 upon it. Anyone who doubts the sociological maxim that the group is more than the sum of its parts must read this brief but excellent book. . . . Mr. Halberstam reveals the strong interplay of tradition, history, family and honor pulsing through the firehouse and the entire FDNY [New York City Fire Department] as if it were a living organism."

In *The Teammates: A Portrait of a Friendship*, Halberstam chronicles a road trip taken in October 2001 by the former Boston Red Sox players Dominic DiMaggio (a brother of Joe DiMaggio), then 84 years old, and Johnny Pesky, then 82, on their way from Massachusetts to Florida to visit their dying teammate Ted Williams. Another teammate and close friend, Bobby Doerr, remained in Oregon to care for his sick wife. Halberstam's narrative uses the road trip to reflect back on the lifelong friendship of these four ballplayers and explore the changing nature of the game; in particular, Halberstam suggests that modern baseball could no longer cultivate such a relationship. "As in his other sports books," a critic noted in *Publishers Weekly* (April 14, 2003), "Halberstam has a great eye for the telling detail behind an athlete's facade." In a review for the *New York Times* (May 25, 2003), Charles McGrath noted: "As authors go, David Halberstam has never been known as a singles hitter. He's not so much a Williams as a Mo Vaughn [a famous home-run hitter]. When he is not writing about sports, he writes big books about big subjects, and his sentences sometimes lurch mightily for the fence. But in style and spirit *The Teammates* is pure Pesky: not a home run but a line drive stroked smartly and with delicate bat control. If anything, you wish it were longer—and not quite so sad at the end."

Halberstam's *The Education of a Coach* is a profile of Bill Belichick, the coach of the New England Patriots football team. In a review for the *New York Times* (November 27, 2005), Richard Sandomir wrote that the book "feels like something conceived on a dare," as the subject matter "poses a narrative problem" unlike any that Halberstam had previously faced; though Belichick cooperated with the author in his research, the coach "disdains celebrity, resists introspection, dresses to be ignored, [and] reluctantly deals with an invasive news media," according to Sandomir. "While Halberstam makes Belichick interesting and occasionally compelling," Bill Plaschke wrote for the *Los Angeles Times* (November 25, 2005), "he does not make him human. . . . We rarely see Belichick at home, or in the office, or anywhere but in the playbooks that have defined his legacy team. This is, one supposes, a book that Bill Belichick would have loved to have written. Not surprisingly, that makes it ultimately unsatisfying to read."

David Halberstam has been married twice. His first marriage, to Elzbieta Czyzewska, ended in divorce in 1977. He married Jean Sandness Butler on June 29, 1979; with her he has a daughter, Julia Sandness. In addition to his work as an author and journalist, Halberstam has been the editor of a number of books, including *Kansas Century: 100 Years of Championship Jayhawk Basketball* (1997) and *The Best American Sports Writing of the Century* (1999). He also wrote the introduction for *New York September 11: By Magnum Photographers* (2001). Halberstam lives in New York City.

—K.D.

Suggested Reading: *BusinessWeek* p16 May 22, 1989; *Christian Science Monitor* p15 Dec. 30, 1981, p11 Sep. 16, 1994; *Commentary* p30+ Jan. 1965; *Economist* p104 Oct. 29, 1994; *Esquire* p57+ Jan. 1964; *Harper's Bazaar* p27+ Aug. 1972; *Houston Chronicle* p18 July 21, 2002; *Library Journal* p937 Apr. 15, 1979, p156 Feb. 15, 1998; *National Review* p62+ Nov. 5, 2001; *New York* p42+ May 8, 1989; *New York Times* C p21 Oct. 20, 1986; *New York Times Book Review* p1 Apr.

22, 1979, p9 Feb. 17, 1991, p8 Sep. 30, 2001, p9 May 25, 2003; *Newsweek* p68 Apr. 17, 1989; *Publishers Weekly* p44+ Oct. 17, 1986, p42 Dec. 21, 1990; *Wall Street Journal* p17 Aug. 16, 1985, A p12 June 23, 1993; Talese, Gay. *The Kingdom and the Power*, 1969

Selected Books: nonfiction—*The Making of a Quagmire: America and Vietnam during the Kennedy Era*, 1965; *The Unfinished Odyssey of Robert Kennedy*, 1969; *Ho*, 1971; *The Best and the Brightest*, 1972; *The Powers That Be*, 1979; *The Breaks of the Game*, 1981; *The Amateurs*, 1985; *The Reckoning*, 1986; *Summer of '49*, 1989; *The Next Century*, 1991; *The Fifties*, 1993; *October 1964*, 1994; *The Children*, 1998; *Playing for Keeps: Michael Jordan and the World He Made*, 1999; *War in a Time of Peace: Bush, Clinton, and the Generals*, 2001; *Firehouse*, 2002; *The Teammates: A Portrait of a Friendship*, 2003; *The Education of a Coach*, 2005; fiction— *The Noblest Roman*, 1961; *One Very Hot Day*, 1968

Courtesy of Ohio University

Hamby, Alonzo L.

Jan. 13, 1940– Historian

The historian Alonzo L. Hamby has devoted his career to studying the rise and fall of American liberalism in the 20th century, primarily through the examples of two of its greatest exponents: Franklin Delano Roosevelt (often referred to as FDR) and Harry S. Truman. During the 1930s and 1940s, Hamby has argued, FDR served as a beacon of democratic liberalism; although the president's New Deal programs failed to bring about total recovery for the American economy, his inspirational leadership helped preserve democratic values during the dark days of the Great Depression and World War II. Later, under the presidential administrations of Truman and others, liberalism's message of equality and freedom lent strength to containment—the policy to prevent the spread of communism—as well as to the early civil rights movement. Hamby's major works—*Beyond the New Deal* (1973), *The Imperial Years* (1976), *Liberalism and Its Challengers* (1985), *Man of the People* (1995), and *For the Survival of Democracy* (2004)—have earned him praise from both conservative and liberal critics alike for their well-balanced approach, in which he gives credit to liberalism's major advocates while also examining their flaws.

In an autobiographical sketch prepared for *World Authors 2000–2005*, Hamby writes:

"My first memory of a specific historical event is of hearing the announcement of the death of Franklin D. Roosevelt on the radio. I was five years old. I knew the president, a revered figure in my home, was an important person. I ran to tell my mother.

"I grew up in Humansville, Missouri, a small town on the fringes of the Ozarks. My parents owned a mom and pop grocery store, worked very hard at it, and barely managed to get by. Just as Roosevelt had been a presence in my home, so was his successor, our fellow Missourian Harry S. Truman. As if to make life more interesting, the town and surrounding area was heavily Republican. From a very young age, I realized I was a member of an embattled minority. From an early age, I developed quite an interest in politics, history, and maps, from which I have frequently been diverted by a fifty-five year obsession with the fortune of the St. Louis Cardinals baseball team.

"Excessive work and low pay was a common experience in my home town. It was part of the life of the primary and secondary school teachers who attempted to educate me and seldom got the effort from me they deserved. I had the good fortune to attend two small state colleges (Southwest Missouri and Southeast Missouri) in a time when 'student retention' was not the imperative it has now become. Deans told students at orientation, 'Look at the person on your left, then the one on your right. One of them probably won't be here next year.' They meant it. Faced with serious demands, I found I could do pretty well.

"During my freshman year, I often browsed through magazines in the library. One day I ran across a piece in *Esquire* on the early political career of Franklin D. Roosevelt. It was excerpted from Arthur Schlesinger, Jr.'s forthcoming first volume on FDR, *The Crisis of the Old Order*. It opened my eyes to the possibilities of serious, vividly written history and established a standard to which I still aspire.

"Four years later, much to my amazement, I had received a Woodrow Wilson fellowship and was a master's student in history at Columbia University—at least as fascinated as Thomas Wolfe had been by the big city, if less inclined to roam all over it at odd hours of the early morning. My two most important mentors there were John A. Garraty, my thesis adviser, and William E. Leuchtenburg, with whom I took a superb and difficult two-semester course in twentieth-century American history. The political scientists David B. Truman and Richard Neustadt offered memorable courses which I took against the earnest advice of the history department's M.A. adviser. In all, Columbia and New York were a wonderful experience, the richness of which was matched only by the uncertainty of continued financial support.

"Thus I wound up in the doctoral program at the University of Missouri in the fall of 1962, lured there by a National Defense Education Act fellowship that assured I could live in the relative poverty to which I had become accustomed and by the opportunity to become a member of the first generation of scholars to investigate the presidency of my old childhood presence, Harry Truman. My dissertation mentor, Richard S. Kirkendall, channeled my enthusiasm with skill and patience.

"My dissertation was the first half of a big work published in 1973: *Beyond the New Deal: Harry S. Truman and American Liberalism*. It was at least as much about liberalism as about Truman and perhaps was a passable survey of his presidency. It was not, however, a biography, which I resolved to write someday when the sources were available. That work finally appeared twenty-two years later. In the meantime, I did other things that in one way or another probed the changing nature of American liberalism in the course of the twentieth century.

"I had landed my first teaching appointment at Ohio University in 1965 with no inkling that it would be my only permanent job. Forty years later (and now semi-retired) I am still there with no regrets. It has been a source of satisfaction to participate in the building of a history program that has achieved national visibility.

"I have remained influenced by the important historians of my own student days—scholars such as Schlesinger, James MacGregor Burns, Henry Steel Commager, Allan Nevins, C. Vann Woodward, Eric F. Goldman, and Richard Hofstadter. All wrote with enviable literary skill. All understood that historians have a duty to write for a nonprofessional audience that tends to place politics at the center of any historical narrative. All understood that politics could be broadly construed and sophisticated scholarship explained in language intelligible to ordinary educated individuals. The current academic trend toward either ignoring political history or subsuming it within ideologically driven social/cultural studies has taken our profession to the margins of popular discussion. A counter tendency to make political history a field of study that is essentially a subset of political science has produced interesting work of little popular appeal.

"The great early-twentieth century historian Carl Becker in his presidential address to the American Historical Association, 'Everyman His Own Historian,' wrote: 'The history that lies inert in unread books does no work in the world.' I have done my best to heed Becker's admonition."

Alonzo L. Hamby was born on January 13, 1940 in Humansville, Missouri, the son of David A. Hamby, a merchant, and the former Lila Summers. Hamby received his education at Southeast Missouri State College (now University), in Cape Girardeau, earning a bachelor's degree in 1960. He then moved to New York City to study at Columbia University; there he received his master's degree, in 1961. He earned his doctoral degree in history at the University of Missouri, in 1965, and subsequently joined the faculty at Ohio University as an assistant professor. In 1969 he was made an associate professor, and in 1975 he became a full professor. He chaired the history department for a time and is now a Distinguished Professor. In addition to his teaching duties, he serves as a manuscript adviser for several scholarly journals, reviews, and university presses.

Hamby's first book, *Beyond the New Deal*, focuses on the course of American liberalism following the death of President Franklin D. Roosevelt in April 1945. When the presidency passed into the hands of Harry S. Truman, the little-known vice president, many intellectuals in the United States believed that Truman was ill-equipped to provide both the wartime leadership and the visionary ideals Roosevelt had demonstrated so masterfully during his 12 years as president. Following the end of World War II, Hamby argues, Truman was able to give consistent and effective leadership to the liberal movement. *Beyond the New Deal* (which was published not long after Truman's death, in 1972) received impressive reviews. In the *New Republic* (February 9, 1974), Chilton Williamson declared the book to be "an example of academic letters at their best. It is well organized, well argued and very well written, a welcome volume at a time when history is written increasingly by self-important 'social scientists' of mediocre talents rather than by the kind of polished and civilized men who formerly dominated the profession." Ronald Radosh, in the *New York Times Book Review* (September 1, 1974), asserted: "Hamby's book is the most important of the new Truman books. Unlike the others, Hamby's well written account is based on extensive use of manuscript material, archival research and personal interviews. In his study of the shifting relationship of American liberals and liberal intellectuals to the Truman Administration,

Hamby allows readers to live through and fight again the tumultuous political battles of the 1950's. One may disagree with the author's interpretation yet come away with new insights and fresh information about the Truman era."

In 1976 Hamby published *The Imperial Years*, which charts the development of American power from 1939 through the 1970s. The author argues that America's dominance in global affairs came about as a result of World War II, from which the country emerged as virtually the only industrialized nation not devastated by years of warfare. Since American infrastructure remained untouched by bombings and battles, it was able to recover quickly and convert its significant war industries into peacetime reconstruction efforts, resulting in a booming U.S. economy and an extension of American influence abroad. The book also covers the social changes of the 1960s, when the civil rights movement was reshaping American politics and the Vietnam War was changing perceptions of the United States around the world. The book received mostly positive reviews. "Hamby's focus is political, though he takes some side trips into cultural history as well," David Isaacson wrote for *Library Journal* (June 15, 1976). "His narrative is more informative than argumentative, a discussion of important personalities as much as events; in fact, the book is too often more a record than an interpretation of recent history. It is, however, useful as a concise and objective account written in a refreshingly unpedantic style." Frank Freidel, writing in the *New York Times Book Review* (July 11, 1976), called it "a clear and thoughtful synthesis of American political history [that] . . . delineates the course from Franklin D. Roosevelt to Lyndon B. Johnson's Great Society and since. [Hamby] is particularly effective in summing up some of the major controversies among historians. And . . . he succeeds in being both liberal and at least mildly optimistic."

Liberalism and Its Challengers, Hamby's third book, focuses on the developments of democratic liberalism between the 1930s and the 1980s. The author provides biographical sketches of the presidents who served during the period, including Roosevelt, Truman, Dwight Eisenhower, John F. Kennedy, Lyndon Johnson, and Richard Nixon, as well as other notable political figures, including Senator Joe McCarthy, Senator Robert F. Kennedy, and Reverend Martin Luther King Jr., while attempting to demonstrate, through an analysis of their backgrounds and upbringing, how these figures shaped liberal ideals in the 20th century. *Liberalism and Its Challengers* received mixed reviews. Roger Kaplan, in *Commentary* (January 1986), found the biographical essays "numbing in their superficiality combining conventional pieties about the accomplishments of presidents and other political figures since FDR with psychological speculations that are embarrassing when they are not distracting."

Forrest McDonald, writing for the conservative-minded *National Review* (July 26 1985), argued: "The work is largely derivative, a synthesis of secondary accounts organized around a succession of presidential administrations, with a chapter on Martin Luther King Jr. thrown in for color. Such a format is as inherently soporific as a textbook." Brian Champion, however, in a review for *Library Journal* (March 1, 1985), observed: "The early chapters on Roosevelt and Truman explain the New Deal/Fair Deal heritage of public policy. The best chapter is Nixon's; it provides a refreshingly balanced view of his first term." Champion noted that "Hamby dabbles in psychohistory when dealing with Johnson's crudity and Nixon's pathological fear of failure and/or the press," but concluded, "This is a very useful book for understanding what Hamby calls the 'exhaustion of liberalism.'" A second edition of this book was published in 1992; it covered liberal developments up through the presidency of the conservative George Herbert Walker Bush.

Man of the People: A Life of Harry S. Truman, published in 1995, was the author's first full-length biography of the 33d president. Hamby revisits some of the more controversial aspects of Truman's administration, including his early support for civil rights (in particular the desegregation of the armed forces), his tough stance against the expansion of communism, and his decision to use the atomic bomb on Japan at the end of World War II. Though many modern critics have argued that Japan was already defeated and that the use of the bomb was unnecessary, Hamby contends that Truman sanctioned its deployment in order to prevent the massive American casualties that would likely have occurred if the Allied forces had opted to invade Japan.

Man of the People was widely praised. Marc Landy, in a review for *America* (May 18, 1996), cheered: "Alonzo Hamby's biography of Truman is a masterpiece—arguably the best biography of any modern President. Its greatest strength is the steadfast willingness to confront the complexity of its subject. For those who want a simple Truman, a salty cracker-barrel philosopher who always knew where the buck stopped, or a venal graft-dispensing, A-bomb-tosser, there are plenty of other places to look. Because Hamby, a historian at Ohio University and the author of a seminal study of Truman's relationship to postwar liberalism, loves Truman, he does not need to like him all that much. He makes Truman's greatness into a fascinating puzzle." David Oshinsky, in the *New York Times Book Review* (October 29, 1995), remarked: "The need to be recognized and respected dominated Harry Truman's life. That is the main theme of Alonzo L. Hamby's superb new biography. . . . The Truman we meet in these pages is more troubled, complicated and genuine than the man we have read about before. While Mr. Hamby's account lacks the narrative drive of David McCullough's Pulitzer Prize–winning *Truman*, published in 1992, it is superior, I think, in providing a clear interpretive framework for understanding the relationship between Truman's personal traits and his momentous presidential decisions. . . . What Mr. Hamby has done, with great skill, is to remind us of the real Harry Truman, to demythologize him without slighting his accomplishments or his rough road to success."

For the Survival of Democracy evokes the dismal world of the 1930s, when the Great Depression had rocked economies worldwide. Hamby compares and contrasts the world's three biggest capitalist economies—Germany, Britain, and the United States—and argues that, whereas Germany saw its democratic government toppled, America was able to survive the tumultuous period intact due to the leadership of Roosevelt, whose New Deal programs, although they may not have been responsible for pulling the country out of the Depression, added greatly to the confidence of Americans in their system of government. As a *Publishers Weekly* (October 27, 2003) critic noted: "Hamby credits FDR with saving American democracy if not its economy, which was saved by the war. The president thus made possible the survival of free governments elsewhere. The author's clarity and balance of judgement are marred somewhat with a cascade of facts. But his characterizations of people are always deft and occasionally surprising. He revives the reputation of Britain's Prime Minister Stanley Baldwin and even has good things to say of the often reviled Neville Chamberlain. But at the center of this somewhat old-fashioned political and economic history is FDR's leadership. And that's what will draw readers to this solid, authoritative history."

Hamby has edited several books, including *The New Deal: Analysis and Interpretation (1969)*, *Harry S. Truman and the Fair Deal (1974)*, and *Access to the Papers of Recent Public Figures: The New Harmony Conference* (1978). He is a contributor to the *Encyclopedia Britannica* and has published articles in such periodicals as the *Review of Politics*, *Historian*, the *Journal of American History*, the *American Historical Review*, and the *American Spectator*.

Hamby married Joyce Ann Litton on June 6, 1967. They live in Athens, Ohio.

—C.M.

Suggested Reading: *America* p27 May 18, 1996; *Chicago Tribune* XIV p5 Jan. 14, 1996; *Choice* p1,202 Nov. 1976; *Commentary* p75 Jan. 1986; *National Review* p42 July 26, 1985; *New Republic* p23 Feb. 9, 1974; *New York Times Book Review* Sep. 1, 1974, p2 July 11, 1976, p10 Oct. 29, 1995; *Publishers Weekly* p51 Oct. 27, 2003

Selected Books: *Beyond the New Deal*, 1973; *The Imperial Years*, 1976; *Liberalism and Its Challengers*, 1985; *Man of the People*, 1995; *For the Survival of Democracy*, 2004

Pierre Andrieu/AFP/Getty Images

Hamilton, Hugo

Jan. 28, 1953– Novelist; memoirist

In the novels *Surrogate City* (1990), *The Last Shot* (1992), *The Love Test* (1995), *Headbanger* (1996), and *Sad Bastard* (1998), as well as the short-story collection, *Dublin Where the Palm Trees Grow* (1996), Hugo Hamilton has both portrayed postwar Germany—with its atmosphere of fear in the face of inevitable change—and epitomized the new Ireland, contrasting it with received ideas, some of them mythical, of the Ireland of the past. The tone of his novels might be described as comedy *noir*. Hamilton's background, as the son of a German woman who grew up in an anti-Nazi household and a father who was an ardent Irish nationalist, is the subject of his memoir *The Speckled People* (2003); its was followed by a second memoir, in 2006, *Sailor in the Wardrobe*, which was reissued in the U.S. as *The Harbor Boys* later that year. Hamilton told Liam Fay in an interview for the London *Sunday Times* (August 30, 1998), "All you can do as a writer is watch how things unfold. A writer is a critic of the country he lives in. We're losing the Irishness of things. All the features that made us Irish 20 years ago have disappeared. Good and bad."

Hamilton has been hailed as a master of poetic English prose in the Irish tradition of J. M. Synge and Brendan Behan. After his first two novels were published, Michael Hofmann wrote of him in the London *Times Literary Supplement* (August 9, 1991), "Hamilton is a natural storyteller, with poise, daring and control, and, after two books, he is already quite unmistakable." For Joseph O'Connor, writing in the London *Daily Mail*

(February 21, 2003), Hamilton's "prose becomes poetry, it is so beautiful and intensely charged. English may not be Hugo Hamilton's mother tongue, but he writes it with ethereal grace."

Hugo Hamilton was born in Dublin on January 28, 1953 and named Johannes O h'Urmoltaigh. His mother, Irmgard Kaiser, a German, was in Ireland when she met Jack Hamilton, an engineer, who called himself Sean O'hUrmoltaigh.

In 2004 Hugo Hamilton wrote the following autobiographical statement for *World Authors 2000–2005*:

"I was born in 1953 and grew up in a speckled, German-Irish household in Dublin. Speckled was my father's word for describing our family, coming from the Irish or Gaelic word *breac,* meaning mixed or coloured or spotted like a trout. But that idea of cultural mixture became an ordeal for us, a confused childhood full of painful and comical cultural entanglements out of which we have been trying to find some sense of identity and belonging ever since.

"My mother spoke to us in German while my father, a revolutionary Irish nationalist who wanted to get rid of all things British, spoke to us in Irish and would not allow us to speak a word of English. Beyond our hall door was a different country where everybody spoke English, an alien tongue for which we were punished if were caught speaking it. So much so that I recall how my older brother Franz once had his nose broken by my father for uttering some words that he had heard on the street.

"After World War II, my parents had great ambitions to create a good, decent family that would put behind it all the awful memories of the past. My mother wanted to retain some of her German heritage and dressed us up in 'Lederhosen' while my father, not to be outdone, made us wear Aran Sweaters from the west of Ireland. We were truly speckled, Irish on top, German below, except that in reality, we were anything but speckled. My father's rigid idealism in pursuit of Irish Ireland, created a place where we became isolated from the world outside.

"On the streets of Dublin we were mocked for being Irish speakers and mocked for being German. At a time when Ireland itself was very remote and isolated from the rest of the world, we were called Nazis. The Nuremberg Trials and the Eichmann trial which were prominent in the news at the time were re-enacted in a mock seaside court where I became Eichmann facing justice. The great irony in all this is that we could never deny anything or explain that my mother's family actually stood against the Nazis in the Third Reich. Her uncle, a lord mayor, refused to join the party and was ousted from his post in 1933. They had a phrase for passive resistance. 'The Silent Negative' my mother called it, but this silence was eventually turned into action when her eldest sister began to harbour Jewish people in Salzburg.

"It must have been doubly painful for her and her children to be called Nazis on the streets of Dublin. It was painful, too, to discover that after she escaped from the ruins of Germany in 1949 and came to Ireland on a pilgrimage, she married an Irishman from Cork whose initial courage and idealism increasingly resembled the ruthless principles she had experienced under Nazism. Before they met, my father founded a political party in Ireland and made speeches on O'Connell Street. To us, he was always making a speech. He seemed like a man who had failed to convince the nation but who then tried to create a republic of his own inside the home, a country that would be fully Irish and fully German.

"As I recall in *The Speckled People*, he conscripted us into his army. We became his weapons, his foot soldiers in a language war. I describe him and his generation as people who tried to hold back the waves, at a time in Ireland when rock and roll and TV serials were beginning to march into every household and the very idea of the Irish language was like a step back into the past, into poverty, famine and emigration. My recollection is that my mother was always homesick for Germany, while my father was always homesick for Irish Ireland, so much so that we became the homesick children with no real sense of belonging, either at home or on the streets of Dublin.

"It was my mother who rescued us at every turn with her stories and her humour. In contrast to his stern attitudes, and counter to all the stereotypes, it was my German mother who had the humour which softened his hard regime. She made us aware of the ironies that we had to live with. She also began the resistance with which I eventually questioned my father's laws. She also began to uncover the secrets which they both kept from each other and from us in the wardrobe. It was my mother who brought out the truth.

"As a child it was impossible to explain these ironies and contradictions to myself. It is only as a writer that I could go back into that confused childhood mind in order to extract some meaning from this alienated experience. All I can remember doing as a child was hiding. I developed ways in which I could conceal myself from the world, ways in which I could be invisible, the most effective of which was remaining silent, in my own imagination. We became very isolated and reticent. I remember in my twenties, as a trainee journalist, being advised that the most important characteristic of the trade was an enquiring mind. But I was afraid to ask questions at that time in case people would then also ask me awkward questions and I would also have to reveal myself.

"Becoming a writer of fiction was the only way of liberating myself from this silence. As a writer of novels and short stories, it was the only way that I could come out from my hiding place and finally tell the story of my childhood, a story that was so full of shame and embarrassment that my only impulse was always to run away from it."

———————————

Set in Germany in the 1970s, *Surrogate City* tells the tale of an Irish woman who is searching for the man whose child she is carrying. "Hamilton is a fastidious writer with a fascination for life's minutiae. *Surrogate City* reverberates with echoes of [Christopher] Isherwood, not just because of the shared setting, but because of [the narrator's] detachment from the drama he describes. It's a clever book, and a promising debut," John Nicholson wrote for the London *Times* (November 8, 1990). Not every critic was so positive. C. J. Fox, for example, wrote for the London *Independent* (November 10, 1990), "The destinies of Hamilton's lacklustre characters seem inconsequential, and his indulgence in obtrusive narrative devices hardly helps the cause of the reader's interest. However, for those who thrived in that weird enclave west of the Wall, the limbo-like world he deals with may well become the subject of considerable nostalgia in the years ahead."

The Last Shot, set in the immediate aftermath of World War II, confidently portrays German military personnel in a positive light and liberated Polish prisoners as villains. Hamilton's development of this unorthodox perspective is matched, a reviewer for the London *Times* (August 22, 1991) opined, "by an adroit interweaving of two separate stories. At the heart is an adventure: how a young German escapes at the end of the war from the Czechoslovakian town of Laun before the arrival of the Russian Army. At points of tension this is interrupted by the first person narration of a contemporary German Canadian who is searching for information about wartime activities in Laun (who, he asks, fired the last shot?). . . . Hamilton has a cool dispassionate tone, as adept with the cinematic sweep as the salient detail." Jeff Black, taking a similar stance, wrote for the *Jerusalem Post* (November 27, 1992), "Thanks to Hamilton's great skill as a storyteller, *The Last Shot* works on many levels and presents a sympathetic yet convincing portrait of Germans under the Third Reich, as well as an indictment of a modern materialistic society which, in its pride at its recent accomplishments, ignores the evil from which it sprang."

Hamilton followed *The Last Shot* with *The Love Test*, which is set in a post–Berlin Wall Germany and concerns Mathias and Claudia, an affluent, liberal, and young Berlin couple. Their happy life unravels when Mathias, a journalist, is contacted by and decides to help Christa, a woman who was imprisoned by East Germany's communist authorities for attempting to defect to the West with Ralf, her lover, when she got pregnant. She claims that a prison officer named Erwin Puckler stole her newborn baby. The book was positively received. Tibor Fischer wrote for the *Financial Times* (January 21, 1995), "Hamilton's writing is

clear and enticing and (helped no doubt by his half German parentage) he presents a convincing picture of life in the unified Germany, with telling observations and humour." Fischer concluded by remarking that there was "not a comma too much, not a word out of place." Stephen Amidon opined for the London *Sunday Times* (February 5, 1995), "Where the novel succeeds best is in the graceful way the author interweaves the personal with the political. The novel's two central couples are ironically counterpoised to show how people can be made trivial by freedom. . . . This ironic deftness pervades the book. . . . Hamilton has created characters we care for deeply. There are moments that are singularly harrowing." Sylvia Brownrigg, however, faulted Hamilton's over logical view, complaining for the London *Guardian* (February 14, 1995) that the novel was "altogether rational. . . . The maddest thing anyone does in [it] is to go on a shopping binge. One reads this ordered and moving tale waiting for abandon, or poetry, or the passion missing from the lives of its characters."

With his next book Hamilton changed course, leaving Germany behind and writing stories of modern Ireland. *Headbanger* tells the tale of Pat Coyne, a policeman who describes himself as "the Dublin Dirty Harry" and who is working to rid the city of a criminal gang led by Drummer Cunningham. "Hamilton took a tremendous risk in moving so dramatically from the territory he staked out in his previous three novels, but his gamble has added an extra dimension to his writing. Hamilton has discovered a real comic genius, and it is this, combined with the intelligence of his vision, which makes *Headbanger* such an impressive departure," Antonia Logue wrote for the London *Times* (April 3, 1997). The year *Headbanger* appeared, Hamilton also published a collection of short stories, *Dublin Where the Palm Trees Grow* (1996), that are set in Ireland. "His brood of stories has a wonderful booze-swilling, chimney corner charm. The raconteur spits into the fire. Silence follows in the wake of hissing phlegm. And yet they are anything but folksy, these biting tales. Their Ireland is modern. Its manifestations of menace lie not in vague externals—the supernatural, the arcane— but in the deep darkness where people have lost the power to connect—with themselves, with others," Tom Adair observed for *Scotland on Sunday* (January 28, 1996). "These stories of fragmented identities do not come with neat endings or smugly ironic outlines, and some leave the reader feeling short-changed, but their effect is as lingering as that of finding a strange object lying in the grass," David Buckley noted for the London *Observer* (January 7, 1996).

Following on the success of *Headbanger*, Hamilton revived Pat Coyne for *Sad Bastard*. Coyne, who is on leave from his job on the police force and receiving psychoanalysis, finds himself trying to protect his son, who has stolen money from a small-time criminal after witnessing him murder someone. "*Headbanger* was funny and frantic, brimming with bile. Hamilton found its creation so satisfying that he quickly produced a sequel, *Sad Bastard*. Written with the punchy urgency of a ransom note, its plot and set pieces have been ripped straight from today's headlines. The cast includes Romanian immigrants smuggled ashore in fishing boats, bar-stool republicans desperately clinging to the last vestiges of local clout and, inevitably, *Riverdance* fanatics," Liam Fay wrote for the London *Sunday Times* (August 30, 1998) "The writing is very fine throughout the book, but there is something unsatisfying about its construction," Tim Haigh remarked for the London *Independent* (September 20, 1998). "The relation of Coyne's psychology of stalled momentum to the almost thriller-like plot motor is too diffuse. Coyne's main desire is to get back together with his estranged wife, Carmel, but my main desire was to get back to the crook and the policeman. While Hamilton has thoughtful ambitions, the style of the book is what is now called black comedy, which is to say that it employs the rhythms and cadences of humour without going so far as to be funny."

Hamilton followed the fictional books discussed above with two memoirs about his childhood, *The Speckled People* and *Sailor in the Wardrobe* (2006). The first dealt with Hamilton's entire youth, ending with his father's heart attack, while the second primarily focused on one summer, perhaps in 1970. Discussing the move from fiction to memoir, Hamilton told Arminta Wallace for the *Irish Times* (January 11, 2003), "I needed to make a story out of a childhood that was extremely awkward and didn't lend itself to a story. To do that, I had to distance myself to a certain extent. Even though the characters in a memoir are people you lived with and the events are real, you do need to turn them into characters like they are in a novel. That was very important for me to do—particularly in terms of my father." He went on to explain: "I don't see the memoir as being very different to a novel. I think the novel is a great way of mining the truth. That's really what interests me most."

The Speckled People was widely acclaimed as among Hamilton's best books. "Hamilton has always been an excellent storyteller. His sense of pace and necessary detail were evident in his earlier books, like *The Last Shot* and *Sad Bastard*, but here he moves onto another plane altogether. To recall and articulate the child's understanding and sensibility without sounding coy, sentimental or simply false is a very difficult task. To use this sensibility in a language that consistently reveals more than an ordinary adult's account is an extraordinary achievement," George Szirtes wrote for the *Irish Times* (January 18, 2003). "The domestic world created by this dictator [Hamilton's father] is wonderfully evoked, an atmosphere of terror trembling on the edge of hysterical laughter. Hamilton conveys the sense of a world marooned in space, in a windy seaside

suburb of Dublin,'" Roy Foster observed for the London *Times* (January 22, 2003). The second memoir was deemed less successful by some critics. As Foster, for example, noted for the London *Times* (January 21, 2006), "Hamilton was clearly a writer who would repay watching, but it was not clear where he was going. Several books intervened in different genres: with *The Speckled People* style and subject at last converged to produce a classic. This new book reads like a gloss on that story, a less supercharged companion-piece, and its impact is lessened. Still, in a world where 'identity' has become a worn-out concept indeed, Hamilton's Irish-German-English voice remains unique. The question is where he will project it next."

Hamilton, according to some sources, has published or, according to other sources, is working on a novel called "Sucking Diesel," apparently a third Coyne novel, which, in the late 1990s, he had told journalists he was writing. He lives in Dun Laoghaire (pronounced DUN LEER-ee)—a seaside town that lies on Ireland's east coast, south of Dublin—with his wife, the author Mary Rose Doorley, and their three children.

—S.Y./A.R.

Suggested Reading: *Financial Times* W p4 Feb. 1, 2003; *Irish Times* S p15 Dec. 24, 1994, S p9 Jan. 6, 1996, S p8 Mar. 22, 1997; (London) *Daily Mail* (on-line) Feb. 21, 2003; (London) *Independent* (on-line) Nov. 10, 1990, F p12 Sep. 20, 1998; (London) *Observer* p61 Sep. 29, 1991; (London) *Sunday Times* (on-line) Aug. 30, 1998; *New York Times Book Review* p32 Nov. 4, 2001; *Publishers Weekly* p222 May 7, 2001; *Times Literary Supplement* p36 Aug. 9, 1991

Selected Books: fiction—*Surrogate City*, 1990; *The Last Shot*, 1992; *The Love Test*, 1995; *Dublin Where the Palm Trees Grow*, 1996; *Headbanger*, 1996; *Sad Bastard*, 1998; memoir—*The Speckled People*, 2003; *Sailor in the Wardrobe*, 2006 (reissued in the U.S. as *The Harbor Boys*, 2006)

Han Shaogong

Jan. 1, 1953– Novelist; short-story writer

Han Shaogong, whose work is only beginning to be appreciated in the West, is one of the foremost fiction writers in China today. During the 1980s he became a strong proponent of the root-seeking literary movement, which set out to produce works that would be grounded in China's cultural heritage as opposed to the West's traditions and the social realism that Chinese communist ideologues favored. Theorizing a rigid opposition between the Chinese and Western traditions in his famous 1985 essay "Wenxue de gen" (which can be translated as

Courtesy of Han Shaogong

Han Shaogong

"roots of literature"), Han, nonetheless, "developed a more nuanced view of Chinese tradition over the years. The exaggerated dichotomy between Chinese national literature and the West in his essays in the mid-1980s gave way to a more softened attitude that stressed creativity in opposition to a superficial imitation of the West," Rong Cia explained in a review of Mark Leenhouts's *Leaving the World to Enter the World: Han Shaogong and Chinese Root-Seeking Literature* (2005) for *China Review International* (September 22, 2005). "Moreover," Rong continued, citing Leenhout, "'there is a relationship of opposition, struggle, and distrust' between what Han propagates in his essays on root-seeking and what he portrays in his fiction. In the essays Han may still be 'China-obsessed' as a public intellectual, but as an individual writer he is more concerned with literary creativity." Han, who, in 1990, translated Milan Kundera's *Unbearable Lightness of Being* into Chinese, has thus developed a reputation for blending traditional Chinese culture, mythology, and folklore with Western literary technique, creating a unique voice that often leads critics to compare him to Franz Kafka or Gabriel García Márquez.

Han Shaogong was born to Han Ke Xian and Zhang Jing Xin on January 1, 1953 in Chang Sha, Hunan Province, China. During the Cultural Revolution he was sent, at the age of 16, to the countryside, along with hundreds of thousands of other young people, and for six years he was forced to perform manual labor and spread the philosophy of Mao Zedong. He nonetheless developed an interest in writing, and his first book, which can be transliterated as *Shi niu yang* but has

never appeared in English, was published in 1973. Six years later he published, with Zhengwen Gan, a biography of Ren Bishi, an important 20th-century Chinese politician. In 1980 and 1981 he won the Best Chinese Short Story award. The book of short stories, *You huo* (which can be translated as 'lure'), appeared in 1983. Han then returned to the Hunan Province, and he, Judith Shapiro reported for the *New York Times* (January 11, 1987), "visited local ethnic minorities in the hill areas, where he wrote down legends and superstitions." Han used the material that he gathered to develop, Carole Murray noted for the *Financial Times* (December 18, 1987), stories that were set in "enigmatic rural worlds" in which "the entrenched feudalism and superstition which Mao sought to destroy are described with an earthy realism." Han published two other short-story collections in the 1980s, but the work he is primarily known for in the West was all released in the 1990s. This work includes *Homecoming?, and Other Stories,* which was published in China in 1992 and in English translation in 1995; *Pa Pa Pa,* a book published in 1993, which remains unavailable in English but can be found in a 1996 French-language edition; and *A Dictionary of Maqiao,* which was published in China in 1996 and appeared in English translation in 2003.

Han's *The Homecoming?, And Other Stories,* the Astral Ed Web site noted contained "stories incorporating the magical, the psychological, stories which suggest many things without finally resolving in any definite form—perhaps a cunning way to avoid official censorship." Another reviewer noted, as cited on the Renditions Web site: "An atmosphere of doubt and mystery, a lack of ready answers, pervades Han's work—a major departure from the moralist, didactic and propaganda modes which marked Chinese literature in the recent past." *Pa Pa Pa* concerns a mentally disabled man whose verbal abilities are limited to his pronunciation of the syllables "pa pa pa," which give the book its title. Years before his father had abandoned him and he is now cared for by his mother. Through his story Han explores, Rong Cia pointed out, the opposition of "modernity and tradition and rationality and superstition" in contemporary Chinese life.

The book that has brought Han the most attention in the English-speaking world is *A Dictionary of Maqiao,* which was inspired by his relocation to a rural village when he was a young man. The book contains no central character or narrative. Rather, it explores the life of the imaginary village of Maqiao through lengthy definitions of about 100 Maqiao words. The innovative novel was widely praised. In a review for the *Village Voice* (September 17–23, 2003, online), Ben Ehrenreich called it "a magnificent book, epic in its ambitions and sweep without any of the sentimental obfuscation." Roger Gathman wrote for the *San Francisco Chronicle* (August 10, 2003, on-line), "Under the guise of an excursion in ethnographic linguistics, Han Shaogong creates a compendium of stories, observations and reflections that, stroke by stroke, give the place more textual density, more history and, finally, more reality than all of the county seats of Utah and Montana combined." Rachel Hartigan Shea observed for the *Washington Post* (October 9, 2005) that telling the story through definitions of words was "a counterweight to Mao Zedong's penchant for issuing language manuals in an effort to standardize discourse in a country with many dialects. But Han's aim is hardly didactic," she continued. "Take the definition of 'low,' for instance, which means any sort of sexual or deviant behavior. Maqiao, he writes, used to be particularly 'low'—until the arrival of Mr. He, the commune head. At one meeting, Mr. He brandishes a strange object: 'What are these, you ask? X-ray glasses! With these, I can see every single low-down thing you get up to! If I catch someone, I'll punish 'em! Catch ten, punish ten! No mercy!' The X-ray glasses were really binoculars, but 'many people said they didn't even dare touch their wives during that time.' In the

entry 'The Qoqo Man,' Wanyu, the local foul-mouthed singer, objects to wielding his own hoe in a peasant opera: 'It makes me sweat,' he complains. 'Nine Pockets' recounts the difficulty that the authorities had defining the class status of a beggar in the nearby city of Changle who lived better than they did. Local and individual idiosyncrasies survive, Han seems to be saying, even under a vast, oppressive regime."

Han, who is married to Liang Yu Li, with whom he has a daughter, is a member of the Hainan Writer's Association, and he was made, in 2002, a Chevalier of the Order of Arts and Letters by the government of France.

—C.M./A.R.

Suggested Reading: *China Review International* p469 Sep. 22, 2005; *San Francisco Chronicle* (on-line) Aug. 10, 2003; *Washington Post* T p11 Oct. 9, 2005; *Village Voice* (on-line) Sep. 17–23, 2003

Selected Books in English Translation: *Homecoming?, And Other Stories*, 1995; *A Dictionary of Maqiao*, 2003

Hansen, Eric

1947(?)– Travel writer

The best-selling author Eric Hansen spent most of his life wandering across the globe, working as everything from a prawn fisherman to a volunteer at Mother Teresa's mission in Calcutta. "I travelled through Afghanistan, along the Russian-Afghan border, got thrown in jail there. I got in so much trouble travelling, usually for travelling in areas without permission," he told Marina Skinner for the Wellington, New Zealand, *Dominion Post* (May 24, 2005). "I always like going a little bit further than I'm supposed to go." This reckless wanderlust has placed the author in danger on more than one occasion, providing him with the material for travelogues and adventure essays that transcend the genre: he traversed corners of the world that no Westerner had ever seen to write *Stranger in the Forest: On Foot across Borneo* (1988); returned to an island where he had once been shipwrecked for *Motoring with Mohammed: Journeys to Yemen and the Red Sea* (1991); spent years investigating an international smuggling racket for *Orchid Fever: A Horticultural Tale of Love, Lust, and Lunacy* (2000); and revisited some of his most unusual adventures for a collection of essays, *The Bird Man and the Lap Dancer: Close Encounters with Strangers* (2004).

Eric Hansen was born in 1947 (some sources state 1948) in San Francisco, California. His first exposure to foreign cultures came in 1968 (some sources state 1967), when his grandmother sent him to the Soviet Union to study for the summer.

Dick Sonnen/Courtesy of Random House

"She sent me to St. Petersburg, which was Leningrad in those days, and I studied city planning and art history," Hansen, who knew no Russian before the trip, explained to Skinner. "It was the height of the Cold War and I really had my reservations about going there, but the students, the teachers, the people couldn't have been nicer. It really made me wonder about the US media and about perceptions of us and them and the good guys and the bad guys. The Russian people were so wonderful. I came back from two months in the Soviet Union with a completely different mindset about who I was in the world." He studied architecture at the University of California, at Berkeley, and shortly after graduating, in 1971, he was drafted for the Vietnam War. Hansen did not support the military action and fled to Vancouver, British Columbia, Canada. After spending some time there, he went to live in Sydney, Australia, for two years. He then began a peripatetic life, visiting such places as North Africa, Afghanistan, Southeast Asia, and the Indian subcontinent and living for almost a year in villages along the border of Nepal and Tibet. Hansen began writing in 1982, after encounters with noted travel writers Bruce Chatwin and Robyn Davidson.

Stranger in the Forest: On Foot across Borneo recounts the five months in 1982 that Hansen spent crossing the island's deep jungles, traveling roughly 2,500 miles through largely unmapped terrain. During his arduous journey he carried only a camera, mosquito net, bed sheet, backpack, jungle knife, one change of clothes, tennis shoes, and such goods as colored beads, chewing tobacco, fabric, and shotgun shells to trade with the people he met. "Everything I needed came from the jungle—food, water, medicine from plants, huge leaves for rain cover, flint for starting fires, bamboo for cooking containers and leaves for dinner plates," Hansen told Tim Elledge for United Press International (September 17, 1983). With the aid of his native traveling companion, Hansen told Elledge, he learned to live off a variety of foodstuffs available in the forest, including "bee larva and rice soup, roasted vines, boa constrictors, lizards, monkeys, bats, fish heads and stomachs, sago flour and blood fried in pig fat."

In his book, Hansen "admits at the outset that his vision of the trip was colored by childhood fantasies and a certain romantic naivete," according to Tim Cahill for the *New York Times Book Review* (March 6, 1988). "The mind envisions noble savages; the traveler encounters shrewd traders. By the time we become comfortable with this formulation—ah, so they're folks, just like us—*Stranger in the Forest* goes careening off into realms of curious danger. Descending into the Kayan River valley, for instance, Mr. Hansen was distressed to see that women and children fled at his approach. . . . . For all the leeches, the hard walking, the close calls, Mr. Hansen's trek across Borneo is an experience to envy, if not emulate. It is beguiling to encounter a man who is more interested in the people he meets than in discussing his own considerable courage and endurance. And there is a charm beyond simple romance in Mr. Hansen's insights." Though Cahill concluded his review by describing *Stranger in the Forest* as "a gracefully written and passionate book that is full of such unexpected delights," Jack Mathews, writing for the *Los Angeles Times Book Review* (March 20, 1988), complained that reading

the book "takes almost as much determination as the trip itself." Hansen, Mathews continued, "is a game adventurer, but he is no storyteller. The events are laid out in dull, dispassionate chronological detail, with missed dramatic opportunities buried in almost every paragraph." Reviews were generally positive, however, and *Stranger in the Forest* is regarded by many as a classic piece of travel writing.

Motoring with Mohammed: Journeys to Yemen and the Red Sea is not only a travel story but also a tale of self discovery. In 1978 a yacht on which Hansen was sailing from the Maldives to Athens, Greece, was shipwrecked on Uqban, a desert island in the Red Sea. He and four other survivors were eventually rescued by goat smugglers, who had no room to transport anything but people, so Hansen left seven years' worth of travel journals buried in the sand of that desert island. Ten years later he returned to the island to look for the journals. "*Motoring With Mohammed* is not a psychological or a very stylish book," Diane Ackerman wrote for the *New York Times Book Review* (February 24, 1991). "Its charm lies in its wild hairpin turns of event and its superbly detailed descriptions of seafaring and of daily life in Yemen. Mr. Hansen's observations, at once plangent and revelatory, give so much texture to the story that before the reader can say, *Look, I'm not really interested in another rambling car ride,* he pauses to describe a market toilet in such vigorous detail that it nabs your attention. . . . . I wish the book were more contemplative, but it's saturated with the piquant sensations of Yemeni culture and Eric Hansen's life, both of which come across as beguiling, slightly farouche and great fun." Describing Hansen's book as "a model of concision, curiosity and sheer good writing," Paul William Roberts declared, in a review for the *Toronto Star* (April 20, 1991), that "*Motoring With Mohammed* firmly establishes Hansen as one of the best offbeat tour guides since Bruce Chatwin."

Hansen then provided the text for *The Traveler: An American Odyssey in the Himalayas* (1993), a coffee-table book that paid tribute to and featured the photographs of the great Himalayan trekker Hugh Swift, who died in 1991. "Hansen looks at Swift as part of the generation of Americans who came of age during the Sixties, a generation that traveled to Asia and elsewhere to experience other cultures without the preconceived notion that remote and different meant backward," Lisa J. Cochenet wrote for *Library Journal* (October 1, 1993). Reviewing *The Traveler* for the *Los Angeles Times Book Review* (December 5, 1993), Kevin Coyne lauded the "understated beauty" of Swift's photographs and praised Hansen's text, which "captures the gentle, questing spirit of Swift, including his ambivalence at leading trekkers through these once-unreachable places."

In 1993 Hansen returned to the Borneo rain forest intent on repaying the indigenous Penan people for the hospitality they had shown him back in 1982. Because their hunting grounds were shrinking as the logging industry encroached upon their lands, the Penans' livelihood was in danger, and Hansen had hoped to help the group start a nursery that specialized in the region's rare orchids. "I soon discovered that the project and the orchids were doomed because of conservation laws that prevent the rescue and sale of rare orchids from endangered habitats," he explained in an interview posted on the Random House Web site. "I became fascinated with these laws and this is what led to my interest in orchids and the orchid trade." After spending seven years studying the topic, Hansen published *Orchid Fever: A Horticultural Tale of Love, Lust, and Lunacy.* As Hansen explained in the Random House interview, he had originally intended to write a book about how smugglers were furthering the demise of rare orchids, but after about 18 months of intense research, he discovered "that the 'smugglers' were beginning to look more like conservationists, and less like criminals." Meanwhile, "certain powerful botanical institutions and botanists started to come across as ignorant thugs intent on maintaining exclusive use of rare plant material at all costs." The orchid world, Hansen explained to Michelle Hurley for the Sydney *Daily Telegraph* (September 8, 2001), is "tightly controlled by a powerful group of botanists and bureaucrats who were passing ridiculous laws and making the resolutions and all of them were benefiting financially from them."

Orchid Fever caused quite a stir: Hansen received thousands of supportive E-mails from concerned orchid lovers and was threatened with a libel suit by the Royal Botanic Gardens, Kew, in England. In a review for the *Seattle Times* (March 26, 2000), Michael Upchurch noted that Hansen clearly came down on the side of the smugglers and argued that the author would have made a more persuasive case if he had spent more time talking to those responsible for upholding the current regulations. "While Hansen falls short in his investigative-journalist duties," Upchurch continued, "he's never less than a treat to read. His sexy flower descriptions, his quick sketches of orchid rogues and visionaries, and his ready sense of humor—'We also called on Kemal Kucukonderuzunkoluk (pronounced Kucukonderuzunkoluk)'—make *Orchid Fever* a riotous, blossomy tonic for the brain." Most critics were particularly impressed with Hansen's descriptions of some of the eccentric figures who are obsessed with collecting orchids. "The international cast of characters Hansen unearths are every bit as captivating as the plants themselves," Donna Marchetti wrote for the Cleveland *Plain Dealer* (April 2, 2000). "Both bloom in his highly entertaining story of fanatics and their flowers."

In 2004 Hansen published *The Bird Man and the Lap Dancer: Close Encounters with Strangers,* a collection of short essays about his travels over the past four decades. "This extraordinary collection of short essays may leave readers disoriented as it leaps from the French Riviera to the South Pacific, India, Manhattan, California, Borneo, and back to California," Mark Knoblauch wrote for *Booklist* (September 15, 2004). "But the characters Hansen meets along the way anchor themselves indelibly in the reader's imagination. . . . Delightful, affecting surprises await in these narratives of uncommon and daring lives." In a review for the London *Daily Telegraph* (May 28, 2005), Paul Mansfield wrote that "several things set Hansen head and shoulders above other 'adventure' writers. The first is his prose, which has a limpid, deceptively simple quality. Then there's his ability to form sympathetic relationships with odd characters while still remaining clear-headed."

In addition to his books, Hansen has written about his travels for various periodicals, including the *New York Times, National Geographic, Travel and Leisure, Condé Nast Traveler,* and *Outside.*

When he is not traveling, Hansen lives with his wife in the San Francisco Bay area, within a five-mile range of where he was born.

—S.Y.

Suggested Reading: (London) *Daily Mail* p57 Mar. 24, 2000; (London) *Daily Telegraph* Travel p13 May 28, 2005; *Los Angeles Times Book Review* p11 Mar. 20, 1988; *New York Times Book Review* p8 Mar. 6, 1988, p29 Feb. 24, 1991; (Sydney) *Daily Telegraph* G p13 Sep. 8, 2001; *Washington Post Book World* p4 Mar. 3, 1991; *Weekend Australian* B p11 Aug. 25, 2001

Selected Books: *Stranger in the Forest: On Foot across Borneo,* 1988; *Motoring with Mohammed: Journeys to Yemen and the Red Sea,* 1991; *The Traveler: An American Odyssey in the Himalayas,* 1993; *Orchid Fever: A Horticultural Tale of Love, Lust, and Lunacy,* 2000; *The Bird Man and the Lap Dancer: Close Encounters with Strangers,* 2004

Harington, Donald

Dec. 22, 1935– Novelist

At his best, Donald Harington is "one of the most powerful, subtle and inventive novelists in America," according to Peter Straub for the *Washington Post* (June 6, 1993). "Everywhere, his work is full of mystery and heartbreak kept afloat by high spirits, sensual pleasure and intellectual joy." Over the course of his 40-year career as an author, Harington, a professor of art history at the University of Arkansas, at Fayetteville, has written more than a dozen books and earned comparisons to such literary giants as Vladimir Nabokov, Gabriel García Márquez, William Faulkner, and Mark Twain. Despite such high praise, Harington has remained relatively obscure to the general reading public; indeed, he is often referred to as "America's greatest unknown novelist."

In his 12 novels, most of which are set in the fictional community of Stay More, a tiny hamlet in the Ozark Mountains of his native Arkansas, Harington "has not only invented [a] dense, deeply loved fictional world," Straub wrote, "but created an inclusive fictional manner, a voice and style at once playful, thoughtful and lyrical, utterly his own." Harington is a distinctively postmodern author; his work is often described as metafictional, possessing what a University of Arkansas press release (February 26, 2003) described as a "penchant for narrative trickery, fantastical plot twists and the blending of fiction with reality." However, Harington explained, as quoted in the press release, "My work is not metafictional in the sense of escaping the boundaries of ordinary storytelling. I have always considered the storytelling the most important thing. I've played with tense shifts and metaphysical devices simply to give the story greater impact and to make the reader an important participant in the story."

Donald Harington was born on December 22, 1935 in Little Rock, Arkansas, to Conrad Fred Harington and the former Jimmie Walker. In his youth Harington lived in Little Rock during the school year but spent his summers with his grandparents in the small, secluded town of Drakes Creek, which is situated in Arkansas's Ozark Mountains, 20 miles east of Fayetteville. These summers at Drakes Creek, more than the months spent in Little Rock, came to shape Harington's artistic sensibilities: "Well, I don't want to wax poetic . . . but for me the mountains rising up were like a constant visual embrace, like someone hugging you. And if you leave the hills and mountains and go down in the flatlands, it's like their arms open up and just let go of you. And you feel bereft of that hug . . . ," he explained in an interview with Gene Hyde for *Southern Quarterly* (Winter 2002). "My grandmother used to talk about how lonesome it was here in these mountains, and it used to make me feel as if there was something about being in the mountains that made you lonesome. . . . I was aware of that sense of alienation that comes from the isolation of the mountains."

Though Harington tried his hand as a novelist at a six year old and remained committed to becoming an author throughout his youth, he read mostly comic books up until the age of 12, when he was stricken with meningococcal meningitis, which caused permanent hearing loss. "That was the time, in the late 1940s . . . when radio and television were first coming in and were about to wipe out the old time mountain speech . . . ," Harington told Gene Hyde, "I was fortunate that I could still hear the way people talked before they started trying so hard to sound like the radio." Harington told Cyd King, writing for the *Arkansas*

Democrat-Gazette (July 30, 2000), that his malady ultimately proved a blessing to his writing: "If I had kept perfect hearing I probably would not have remembered as well the accents and the expressions they [the inhabitants of the Ozarks] used." During Harington's recovery, his older brother, Conrad, compiled a lengthy syllabus— which included William Faulkner, Fyodor Dostoevsky, Leo Tolstoy, and Joseph Conrad—for his younger sibling to read.

After high school Harington attended the University of Arkansas, at Fayetteville, graduating in 1956, with a bachelor's degree in art. He remained in Fayetteville after graduation to pursue a master of fine arts degree in printmaking, which he completed in 1958. Harington then studied art history at Boston University, in Massachusetts, receiving his master's degree in 1959. Though still intent on becoming a novelist, he then entered a doctoral program in art history at Harvard University, in Cambridge, Massachusetts. Harington left the program in 1960, without completing his degree, and began teaching art history at Bennett College, a two-year women's finishing school, in Millbrook, New York.

Prior to leaving Harvard, Harington had begun a correspondence with the author William Styron, whose book *Set This House on Fire* (1960) had profoundly influenced the would-be novelist. After moving to Millbrook, a town not too far from Styron's home in Roxbury, Connecticut, Harington struck up an enduring friendship with the author. For the first two years of their friendship, Harington, who had started writing but never finished almost a dozen novels by that time, did not tell Styron about his literary ambitions. Then, in 1962, Harington left his post at Bennett, retiring to a shack in Vermont to finish a novel called "Land's Ramble." Styron introduced him to Robert Loomis, his editor at Random House. While Loomis passed on "Land's Ramble," he expressed interest in one of Harington's unfinished manuscripts. Styron then offered Harington the use of his guest cottage, which had been used by the authors Philip Roth and James Baldwin, to help complete the novel. Published in 1965, *The Cherry Pit* chronicles the return of Clifford Stone to his hometown of Little Rock after a disappointing stint in Boston, Massachusetts. Nominated by the William Faulkner Foundation for an award for best first novel, a prize that ultimately went to Cormac McCarthy for his debut, *The Orchard Keeper*, *The Cherry Pit* received a robust critical reception but did not fare as well commercially, setting the precedent for Harington's subsequent novels.

In 1964, after completing *The Cherry Pit*, Harington reentered academia, heading to Windham College, in Putney, Vermont, where he taught for the next 14 years. During that time he authored three more novels and developed a friendship with a young, unpublished author named John Irving. Irving had been hired to replace Harington as an English teacher at

Windham, while he was on sabbatical in Europe. Upon his return to Windham, Harington began teaching art history again so that his protégé could continue on in the English department. Irving later emerged as one of the more celebrated writers in contemporary American literature, authoring such acclaimed works as *The World According to Garp* (1978), *The Cider House Rules* (1985), and *A Prayer for Owen Meany* (1989), among others.

Harington's second novel, *Lightning Bug* (1970), was the first to be set in the mythical town of Stay More, which was based on Drakes Creek. The novel, which is narrated by a young boy named Dawny, depicts the struggle of Latha Bourne, Stay More's postmistress, to come to terms with the return of Every Dill, who ten years earlier had raped her and robbed the local bank before disappearing. Martha Duffy, writing for *Time* (August 17, 1970), described *Lightning Bug* as a "modest but totally satisfying novel," noting that the author "reveres the most ordinary aspects of the lives of unexceptional people, and with lyrical comedy and irony, he makes his joy infectious."

Harington initially intended *Lightning Bug* as a swan song to Drakes Creek, but in his next novel, *Some Other Place. The Right Place.*, he returned to the outskirts of his mythical Stay More. "I was hooked," he told Mark Harris for *Publishers Weekly* (March 31, 1989). "I would just have to devote the rest of my life to what Faulkner referred to as his 'little postage stamp [of] earth.' I realized that my experience would enable me to write about more sophisticated locales and characters. But if I stick with Stay More, I've got everything I need and can work with, right in that little village." In *Some Other Place. The Right Place.*, Diana Stoving, a recent graduate of Sarah Lawrence College, meets Day Whittacker, a young Eagle Scout, who, his English teacher believes, is the reincarnation of Stoving's deceased grandfather, Daniel Lyam Montross. Together Stoving and Whitaker embark on a riveting cross-country investigation into Montross's life and death. A writer for the *New York Times Book Review* (November 12, 1972) observed, "There is much to admire here— structure, characterization, tonal and thematic complexity, evidence of hard and fruitful labor— all tempered with healthy dollops of self-mockery." *Some Other Place. The Right Place.* was adapted into an independent motion picture by Andrew Silver; entitled *Return* (1986), the film opened to mixed reviews and did not fare well commercially.

In *The Architecture of the Arkansas Ozarks* (1975), Harington told the history of Stay More, detailing the town's 150 years through the prism of six generations of the Ingledew clan. *The Architecture of the Arkansas Ozarks* received praise from certain quarters: R.H. Donahugh, writing for *Library Journal* (January 15, 1976), declared that the hamlet depicted in this "fine novel" is populated with a "magnificent cast of characters." Nevertheless, Harington was

disappointed with the work's overall reception: "I thought I'd done something important," he told Mark Harris. "Reviewers did not share that sentiment, unfortunately. Either it was totally ignored or got very bad reviews."

Following *The Architecture of the Arkansas Ozarks*, Harington did not publish another novel for more than a decade; he later described this period to Cyd King as his "Dark Ages." His difficulties began not long after the publication of *The Architecture of the Arkansas Ozarks*, when his editor at Little, Brown left the publishing industry, and soon after, Harington's father died. Then, in 1978, Windham College closed, forcing Harington to find another teaching position; subsequently, while a visiting professor at the University of Missouri, at Rolla, in 1979, Harington separated from his first wife, Nita Harrison. In 1980 he left Rolla for the University of Pittsburgh, in Pennsylvania, where he taught writing. Later that year he left Pittsburgh and went to South Dakota State University, in Brookings, where he resumed teaching art history for a year before returning to Arkansas. During these tribulations, Harington started to lose control of his drinking. "I went into a skid," he told Mark Harris. "I wrote another novel that I was unable to find a publisher for. I was strictly a mid-list writer with a very bad track record."

Prior to leaving Vermont, Harington had begun a correspondence with Kim Gunn McClish, a fan from Arkansas, who, inspired by his novels, later decided to explore Arkansas's ghost cities—small, rural, and declining towns—and interview their inhabitants. Once back in Arkansas, Harington traveled throughout the state with McClish, compiling material for a book. They fell in love during their travels and married in 1983. Looking back, Harington credits Kim with saving his life, telling Cyd King, "I had sort of bottomed-out personally and she rescued me. It's very true that I probably would not be alive today if she had not come along exactly when she did." With McClish's assistance, Harington swore off alcohol and tobacco, and in 1986, returned to teaching, taking up a post as an instructor of art history at the University of Arkansas, where he has remained ever since.

In *Let Us Build Us a City: Eleven Lost Towns* (1986), Harington described the histories of the Arkansas ghost towns he had visited, as well as his burgeoning romance with McClish. Wendy Kaminer, writing for the *New York Times Book Review* (December 21, 1986), classified *Let Us Build Us a City* as "an earnest and affectionate book, which, like country towns, is intermittently lively." *Let Us Build Us a City* went on to receive the Porter Fund Literary Prize. Reflecting on the book's impact on his writing in general, Harington told Mark Harris, "[It] probably affected my fiction [by] giving me a stronger sense of actual places and people who confirm or corroborate what I already believe about loss, about hope thwarted and unfulfilled ambition."

Let Us Build Us a City likewise allowed Harington to break the writer's block that had plagued him since the mid-1970s; while in the midst of writing *Let Us Build Us a City*, Harington began *The Cockroaches of Stay More* (1989), in which he shifted his gaze from the fictional town's human citizens to its cockroaches. These insects, who take their names from the humans in whose homes they reside, have developed a distinct society, complete with fiery preachers and religious factions who worship humans as gods. "Harington is a daring and confident writer," Donald McCaig wrote for the *Washington Post* (February 19, 1989), "and *The Cockroaches of Stay More* is surprising and funny and frequently brilliant. The reader will find himself in a world where perspectives are different, a small world where a single raindrop can knock you off your gitalongs and blood is no thicker than ichor." Harry Middleton for the *New York Times Book Review* (April 23, 1989) likewise described the work as "a truly captivating and appealing book, one as honest as it is imaginative and fanciful, one that probes the transitory and fragile worlds of man and cockroach alike."

In 1991 Harington followed up *The Cockroaches of Stay More* with *The Choiring of the Trees*, a novel inspired by the real-life story of an innocent Arkansas man, who, in the early part of the century, had been condemned to die for supposedly raping a young girl. In Harington's retelling, the wrongly convicted man, Nail Chism, is a Stay More native, or Stay Moron, whose innocence is championed by Viridis Monday, an artist hired to sketch the execution for a newspaper. The novel charts the romance that develops between Monday and Chism, as well as Chism's three harrowing reprieves from the electric chair and his subsequent escape from jail. In its searing portrayal of "The Walls," the Little Rock penitentiary, where Chism is confined, and the deeply flawed individuals who seek to engineer the convict's demise, *The Choiring of the Trees* offers a powerful indictment of capital punishment. Though he found Harington's evocation of the romance between Chism and Monday somewhat disappointing, Frank Levering, for the *Washington Post* (April 21, 1991), favorably compared the novel to the work of Charles Dickens: "Not only in its scope, but also in its transparent reformer's zeal and in its unambiguous distinctions between good and evil, this resembles a Dickens novel." Levering concluded, "If, as it should, 'regional writing' has meaning as a non-reductive term, *The Choiring of the Trees* is regional in the best sense: It is rooted in the particulars of time and place, yet reaches out, like a spreading oak, to suggest issues and themes of universal interest."

In his 1993 novel, *Ekaterina*, Harington paid homage to Vladimir Nabokov. *Ekaterina* both parallels and inverts the Russian author's classic novel *Lolita* (1955): "Just as that earlier novel was a man's fantasy about a woman, a very young woman," Susan Larson observed for the New Orleans, Louisiana, *Times-Picayune* (May 30, 1993), "so *Ekaterina* is another male fantasy about a woman, an older woman who lusts after prepubescent boys." The title character is a former Russian princess and mushroom expert who escapes to the U.S. from a prison camp, where she was tortured by Bolshakov, a dastardly psychiatrist. She stays for a time in Pittsburgh, where she takes a writing course and seduces her landlord's young son. After settling in Stay More, here called "Stick Around," *Ekaterina* pens an erotic novel entitled *Georgie Boy*, which details the allure of young males and becomes a major success. "Ekaterina's metamorphosis from comic-pathetic refugee to best-selling author and connoisseur of 12-year-old boys forms the main narratives of this playful and many-voiced story," Edward Allen wrote for the *New York Times Book Review* (June 13, 1993). *Ekaterina* earned widespread plaudits from critics, with Peter Straub declaring, "Harington's seductive, artful novel is another reminder of the splendor [he] can offer us as long as we are willing to entertain the notion that the word 'reality' should always have quotation marks around it."

In the fall of 1994, Harington underwent successful treatment for throat cancer, a malady he attributed to many years of smoking, which he had given up 12 years earlier. While recovering, Harington questioned his doctors about their profession and subsequently used the information to write his next novel, *Butterfly Weed* (1996), which chronicles the life of Doc Colvin Swain, Stay More's resident physician. The story is told from the vantage point of one of Swain's former patients, the folklorist Vance Randolph. Trained by an unconventional hillbilly physician, Swain develops his "dream cure," which allows him to heal his patients by visiting them in their dreams. Unable to make ends meet as a doctor, Swain must moonlight as a teacher at a local academy, where he falls tragically in love with a student and is ensnared by a fellow teacher, who uses witchcraft to turn him into her love slave. Like *Ekaterina*, *Butterfly Weed* earned a mostly positive reception from reviewers. "Harington, an ingenious, wise storyteller and a sly stylist, able to catch the tang and vigor of the spoken word, makes Doc and the other inhabitants of Stay More as real as the mountains they inhabit—and also as mysteriously timeless," a critic for *Kirkus Reviews* (March 15, 1996) observed. Though he felt Harington's narrative technique was unwieldy at times, Peter Givler, writing for the *Washington Post* (May 23, 1996), declared the story a success, adding "I think we need every book we can get where invention and energy reign, where marvelous and fantastic things happen just because we have the glorious power to imagine them."

When Angels Rest (1998) is set in Stay More during World War II. Isolated from the outside world, the young residents of Stay More conduct their own war, dividing into Axis and Allies and battling one another as the older male residents leave town for the conflict overseas. Dawny, inspired by the famous war correspondent Ernie Pyle, takes up the task of reporting on the local war, as well as local events more generally, producing his own weekly newspaper. "Seen through Dawny, this is a poignant coming-of-age tale, not only for him and the town's young people but also for a nation whose innocence is sorely tested . . . ," a writer for *Publishers Weekly* remarked, according to Amazon.com. "Harington maintains the breezy originality that makes his 10th book a welcome addition to this talented writer's work."

In Harington's eleventh novel, *Thirteen Albatrosses (or, Falling Off the Mountain)* (2002), Vernon Ingledew, a Stay Moron first introduced in *The Architecture of the Arkansas Ozarks*, having grown rich off a thriving ham business, embarks on a quixotic run for the Arkansas governor's mansion. Vernon's bid for high office is complicated by 13 albatrosses that may make him unpalatable to the state's voters; among these potential deal breakers are Vernon's avowed atheism, his lack of education, his common-law marriage to his cousin, and his stated desire to ban pistols and hospitals. Undeterred—and with plenty of cash on hand—Vernon assembles a crack team of political consultants, some of whom helped engineer Bill Clinton's successful presidential campaign. "This is a wonderful entertainment in all senses," Thomas Gaughan declared for *Booklist* (February 15, 2002). "Its characters are interesting, engaging, funny, and memorable. . . . The political milieu is knowing, and the storytelling is as fine as a tall glass of sweet tea on a sultry afternoon."

But like so many of Harington's earlier novels, *Thirteen Albatrosses* failed to capture the public's attention, and Harington's publisher rejected his next novel, *With* (2004), on the grounds that it was "prurient," forcing the author into a long search for a new publisher. After virtually every American publishers had turned it down, *With* eventually found a home with a small but ambitious publisher, Toby Press. "*With* begins like a sleazy story out of an old Police Gazette but ends like a feminist revision of Genesis," Steven Moore wrote for the *Washington Post* (April 11, 2004). Harington himself has compared *With* to the W.H. Hudson novel *Green Mansions* (1985) and the motion picture *Nell* (1994), which feature young girls growing up alone in the wilderness. The plot of his novel revolves around the kidnapping of a young girl named Robin Kerr by a state trooper named Sog Allen, who spirits her off to a secluded Ozark Mountain retreat north of Stay More. Robin survives her captor, whose physical maladies have kept him from abusing her, but for more than 10 years she is unable to escape from the inaccessible mountain homestead. "*With* is a joy to read," Moore wrote, "partly due to the variety of audacious techniques Harington uses. First, each chapter is narrated from the point of view of a specific character, which may not sound all that innovative until you learn that many of these characters are not human. . . . [It] is as whimsical as a paper-doll show while being deeply rooted in the earth; it gives the Garden of Eden myth a happy ending, and should find the wide readership that Harington so richly deserves."

Not only was *With* a critical success, but it also sold better than any of Harington's previous books, after which Toby Press reprinted all of Harington's novels. Such attention inspired Harington to write his latest novel, *The Pitcher Shower* (2005), which is about a Stay More man who earns his living as an itinerant motion-picture projectionist in the backwoods of the Ozarks. According to a reviewer for *Publishers Weekly*, "A lighthearted Ozark take on Shakespeare drives the latest whimsical installment of the Stay More series. . . . Harington has tackled heavier themes in previous volumes, but sly narrative commentary and winning humor make this a welcome addition to the series."

In addition to his novels and *Let Us Build Us a City*, Harington also wrote the text for the art history book *On a Clear Day: The Paintings of George Dombek, 1975–1994* (1995). Harington is a regular contributor to the *Arkansas Democrat-Gazette,* and his short fiction has appeared in *Esquire*, among other publications. He is a recipient of the Robert Penn Warren Award for Fiction, which was bestowed upon him by the Fellowship of Southern Writers.

Currently Harington makes his home in Fayetteville, where he lives with his wife, Kim, and continues to teach art history at the University of Arkansas, with the title of distinguished professor. He has three daughters, Jennifer, Calico, and Katy, from his first marriage. In his leisure time he enjoys gardening.

—P.B.M.

Suggested Reading: *Arkansas Democrat-Gazette* D p1 July 30, 2000; Donald Harington Web site; *Publishers Weekly* p39+ Mar. 31, 1989; *Southern Quarterly* p69+ Winter 2002; *Washington Post* X p9 June 6, 1993

Selected Books: *The Cherry Pit*, 1965; *Lightning Bug*, 1970; *Some Other Place. The Right Place.*, 1972; *The Architecture of the Arkansas Ozarks*, 1975; *Let Us Build Us a City: Eleven Lost Towns*, 1986; *The Cockroaches of Stay More*, 1989; *The Choiring of the Trees*, 1991; *Ekaterina*, 1993; *On a Clear Day: The Painting of George Dombek, 1975–1994*, 1995; *Butterfly Weed*, 1996; *When Angels Rest*, 1998; *Thirteen Albatrosses (or, Falling off the Mountain)*, 2002; *With*, 2004; *The Pitcher Shower*, 2005

© Joyce Ravid/Courtesy of Bloomsbury

Harrison, Colin

Nov. 27, 1960– Novelist; editor

Though fans and critics of Colin Harrison have cited his well-drawn characters as a central component of the success of his novels, his work has often been lumped into the thriller category—a situation that might annoy some literary-minded authors. Not so with Harrison, who seeks to redefine readers' perception of thrillers. "The question is, what is a thriller?" Colin Harrison remarked in an interview with Adam Dunn for *Publishers Weekly* (December 6, 1999). "The term is often used pejoratively to mean a poorly written, fast-moving story that sells a lot of copies and yet which is utterly forgettable. And that's correct. On the other hand, a lot of books are protected by the term 'thriller.' . . . They're allowed to travel the world with 'thriller' on the suitcase and, therefore, they live. I am not intimidated by the word 'thriller,' because I think that the word 'thriller' means 'thrilling.'"

Colin Harrison was born in New York City on November 27, 1960 and raised in Westtown, Pennsylvania, near Philadelphia. He is the son of Earl Grant Harrison Jr., the headmaster of a Quaker boarding school, and the former Jean Spencer, an actress and teacher. He described his childhood home to Lucinda Dyer for *Publishers Weekly* (November 3, 2003) as "a very safe place," adding: "that's probably why I'm fascinated by the convulsive danger of the city. New York City scares me, motivates me, beckons me and turns my head around. As a kid from the country, it's still magical to me."

Harrison studied at Haverford College, located about 15 miles from Westtown. While there, he decided to become a writer and began work on a novel. After graduating with a bachelor's degree, in 1982, he went to the University of Iowa, from which he received his M.F.A. degree, in 1986. There he met his future wife, Kathryn, who is also a novelist. After another year of postgraduate study, Harrison took an editorial position in New York City at *Harper's*; as he moved up through the ranks to become the deputy editor, he commissioned and edited works by such noted authors as David Guterson, Bob Shacochis, and David Foster Wallace. As he explained in his interview with Dunn, his dual existence as writer and editor has been beneficial for him. "The two worlds definitely feed each other," Harrison noted. "There's no doubt about that. At the magazine, I'm standing in a river of information and perceptions about what's going on in culture, and that benefits me. I always try to get the language better and sharper. Magazine work benefits my discipline and creativity. I've thought about how to look at the world as a writer, and that helps me as an editor. On another level, I work with a lot of writers. I understand, watching what other writers go through, how difficult it is, how lonely it is, how you have to be psychologically tough. As much as possible, I've tried to apply some of those observations to my own practice."

Harrison published his first novel, *Break and Enter*, in 1990, while still working at *Harper's*. In it, he relates the story of Peter Scattergood, an up-and-coming assistant district attorney with a wife, a nice townhouse in an expensive area of Philadelphia, and a seemingly bright future. That all changes when he is assigned to a high-profile homicide case—the murder of the mayor's nephew. While trying to unravel the murder, his wife leaves him. Now he must not only solve this difficult murder case, but the complexities of his own life as well. In a review for the *Chicago Tribune* (July 8, 1990), Alice Cromie called Harrison's debut novel "both suspenseful and unpredictable to the very last page." Michele Slung, writing for the *Washington Post Book World* (June 24, 1990), noted that "*Break and Enter* succeeds . . . on a level that touches us more deeply than the ordinary thriller, even as we can admire the orderly working-out of its plot mechanisms. . . . [It] is dense with detail and memorable scenes. . . . Behind the sharp surface details, however, it is Peter's imperfect relationships that are the book's texture."

Bodies Electric, Harrison's second novel, was published in 1993. As the book opens, Jack Whitman, a distant relative of the poet Walt Whitman, has had his life forever altered by a random act of violence: his pregnant wife was gunned down in a drive-by shooting. Since her death he has lived alone in a half-renovated Brooklyn brownstone and buried himself in his job as an executive at a large multimedia corporation.

Just as he's about to help cement a deal between his company and a German counterpart, he becomes involved with a beautiful homeless woman and her child, both of whom eventually move in with him. Like its predecessor, the novel was well received. Randall L. Schroeder, for *Library Journal* (March 15, 1993), wrote: "This is a hard-boiled detective novel without the detective. Harrison has a feel for the rhythm of New York, just as Dashiell Hammett had for San Francisco. The plot, told from the perspective of corporate businessman Jack Whitman, oozes sex, blood and greed. At first, the reader feels sorry for Whitman when he is pulled into a corporate coup d'etat and is caught up in a dangerous love affair after the brutal murder of his pregnant wife. Later, however, it becomes apparent that Whitman is a metaphor for the greed of our era with his amoral ability to use money and people interchangeably. . . . The beauty of this book is in the characters' depth." In a review for the *New York Times Book Review* (June 6, 1993), Robert Nathan was effusive: "Along with his narrative skill and the extraordinary sureness of his voice, Mr. Harrison has abundant gifts for phrasemaking and the music of words. . . . From his heartless yet febrile corporation, from his hollow, broken men and women, he has wrought a work of fiction as relentlessly bleak as any in recent memory, making no peace with cheap hopes of redemption. A daring, haunting book, *Bodies Electric* demonstrates that in storytelling as in life it's not how far out you go or what you see out there, it's what you bring back. Mr. Harrison has brought back a novel that serves one of the essential purposes of fiction: to remind us of what we have always known but forgotten, sometimes what we most want to forget."

In *Manhattan Nocturne* (1996) Harrison explored the life of a tabloid newspaper columnist, Peter Wren, who begins an affair with a beautiful woman distraught over the death of her famous filmmaker husband. Wren agrees to help the woman solve her husband's murder, though by doing so he ultimately endangers his own family's safety. The novel received more mixed reviews than its predecessors. Mark Annichiarico, for *Library Journal* (August 1996), expressed doubts: "*Manhattan Nocturne* rehashes the same theme of Harrison's earlier novels: A relatively wealthy man must come to terms with his small evils while working to right a larger, societal evil. Incessant name-dropping and an anticlimactic ending shave some points from what is otherwise a well-written, very entertaining story peopled by intriguing and fully fleshed characters. Ultimately, this will do well in popular fiction collections, but one can't help but expect better from this author." However, Jim Shepard, reviewing *Manhattan Nocturne* for the *New York Times Book Review* (October 13, 1996), found much to praise: "[There is] a nice dovetailing between the world view of a novel like *The Bonfire of the Vanities* and the premises of

noir: that vision of society as wilderness, a world of deceptive surfaces where guilt, because it's all-pervasive, can be assigned to sacrificial victims. These corollary aspirations generate some of the greatest pleasures in Mr. Harrison's novel, so that the same narrative that impresses us with its top-to-bottom knowledge of New York City fauna is also illuminating about the quiet acts of omission that irrevocably damage a marriage. *Manhattan Nocturne* is also filled with tips for the street-smart. . . . The novel's protagonist is most memorable when that small-town boy, for all his bluster, articulates with real sadness his understanding of his own wrongdoing, and of the damage he's done to those he loves."

Harrison's fourth novel, *Afterburn* (2000), focuses on the multimillionaire Charlie Ravich, who, having lost his son years earlier to leukemia, learns that his daughter is unable to have children and hires a woman to have his third child, who would inherit his fortune. Christina Wells, the intelligent, angry woman he picks for the job, has just been released from prison for "conspiracy to possess stolen property." Pursued through New York City by her ex-boyfriend and the police detective who arrested her, she attempts to throw off the vestiges of her old life; she sees an opportunity in Ravich's offer—an offer that comes with consequences for everyone involved. The book was widely praised. In a review for *Booklist* (September 1, 1999), Vanessa Bush wrote simply: "This is a compelling, thrilling, and intelligent novel with sharply drawn characters." Tom De Haven, in a review for *Entertainment Weekly* (January 7, 2000), observed, "Unlike so many other recent American crime novels . . . *Afterburn* never splinters into cheap nihilism. Heroism and loyalty are still virtues here; they're just awfully hard to practice. Hard, not impossible. Harrison has created a world that's dangerous cruel, overbright, too fast, and unreliable—but a world that's worth staying alive in. This is a serious, stylish, generously humane work of fiction."

In 2004 Harrison released *The Havana Room*. The protagonist, a Manhattan-based corporate lawyer named Bill Wyeth, is leading a comfortable life. His marriage is deteriorating, but he has a son that he loves and takes pride in his work. However, when his son's friend dies while in Wyeth's care, he finds himself losing everything, including his job and his family. After months of depression and guilt, Wyeth begins hanging around at a Midtown steakhouse, where he becomes enchanted by the beautiful manager, Allison Sparks. Wyeth soon notices that select patrons are allowed into a private lounge, known as the Havana Room, where, it is rumored, illicit transactions take place. One night Allison invites him in, asking him to help out a friend by acting as his lawyer in a last-minute real-estate deal. The deal looks suspicious, but Wyeth agrees, partly to please Allison—but the consequences are far worse than he imagines. In the *New York Times* (January 6, 2004), Michiko

Kakutani commented: "Though at least two of the novel's last-act revelations can be seen coming a mile off, Mr. Harrison's emotionally detailed portrait of his narrator and his penchant for seeding his narrative with intriguing digressions—about everything from Manhattan real estate to the perils of eating the deadly fugu fish—combine to create a consistently entertaining story." A reviewer for the *Economist* (January 10, 2004) concurred, noting that the author "keeps the pages turning at a spanking clip. The book is nicely put together for maximum suspense, and is strong on characterization. Mr. Harrison is much more interested in the subtler shadings of goodness and weakness than he is in the gaudy displays of bang-pow-splat that typify so many other thrillers."

In 2000 Harrison left *Harper's* to join the publishing imprint Scribner, part of Simon & Schuster, as a senior editor. He and his wife, Kathryn, were married in 1988. They live in the New York City borough of Brooklyn with their three children.

—C.M.

Suggested Reading: *Booklist* p8 Sep. 1, 1999; *Chicago Tribune* C p7 July 8, 1990, XIV p3 May 30, 1993; *Entertainment Weekly* p105 Oct. 25, 1996; *Library Journal* p106 Mar. 15, 1993, p112 Aug. 1996, p134 Oct. 1, 1999; *Los Angeles Times* p11 Jan. 11, 2004; *New York Times* IX p4 May 23, 1993, E p1 Jan. 6, 2004; *New York Times Book Review* p16 June 16, 1993, p13 Oct. 13, 1996; *People* p32 June 28, 1993; *Philadelphia Inquirer* (on-line) Jan. 11, 2004; *Publishers Weekly* p48+ Dec. 6, 1999, p31+ Nov. 3, 2003; *Washington Post* B p1 June 16, 1993, p4 June 24, 1990

Selected Books: *Break and Enter*, 1990; *Bodies Electric*, 1993; *Manhattan Nocturne*, 1996; *Afterburn*, 2000; *The Havana Room*, 2004

Hartley, Aidan

1965– Journalist; memoirist

The former war correspondent Aidan Hartley's *The Zanzibar Chest: A Story of Life, Love, and Death in Foreign Lands* (2003) was hailed by James Astill, writing for the London *Guardian* (August 23, 2003), as "the most startling memoir of Africa for a generation." In the book, Hartley recounts his experiences covering Africa's bloodiest conflicts, while weaving in the story of a close personal friend of his father, an Englishman named Peter Davey, who was killed in a shoot-out outside of Dhala, Yemen, in 1947. He had served as a colonial administrator and after falling in loved with an Arabian princess, he converted to Islam. Setting off to uncover more information about Davey's mysterious death, Hartley gained insight into his father's life and his own.

Aidan Hartley, who was born in 1965 to a family of British colonialists, grew up in Kenya following the sale of the family's ranch in Tanzania. He attended boarding school in Great Britain and later studied English at Balliol College at the University of Oxford and politics at the University of London. "I am what the Afrikaners called a 'salt dick': one foot in Africa, one foot in Europe, tackle hanging down in the sea between," he explained to Chris Martin in an interview for the on-line magazine *BookEnds*. "This split identity is at the core of every white African, but obviously it's important to lots of different people in this hybridised world. I'm glad I feel this way. It hurts sometimes, but I've also derived great enjoyment and intellectual stimulation from it too."

While still in his 20s, Hartley began working as a correspondent for Reuters News Service, at various times covering events in Russia, the Balkans, and the Middle East. He also witnessed firsthand the brutal military conflicts and genocidal madness that plagued Africa during his 12-year tenure with the news agency, reporting on the tragic events in Somalia, Ethiopia, and Burundi. During most of that time, he felt as if he was making a valuable contribution through his journalism, but he was left shaken after witnessing the wave of mass genocide that spread across Rwanda in 1994, leaving almost 500,000 people dead. He told Martin, "Rwanda was different. . . . Of course Rwanda left bad memories. I would have had cause to really worry if Rwanda didn't haunt me."

When Hartley sat down to write *The Zanzibar Chest*, in 1996, he initially intended to write a memoir of his experiences as a foreign correspondent, but he quickly realized that was a "big mistake," as he told Martin: "I drafted some of the opening riff after Rwanda, when I was fried, and once I did that the floodgates opened," he explained to Martin. "Then my Dad died, which forced me to take stock even more. Then I found the diaries of his friend Peter Davey, so I went to Yemen, hoping to bin the war material and confine myself to an exotic colonial story. But I discovered I couldn't write one without the other."

Reviews of *The Zanzibar Chest*, while largely positive, offered occasional criticism. "Hartley has seen, and survived, the worst of which man is capable. What he has lived through makes a sedentary reviewer feel utterly inadequate," Allan Massie wrote in the London *Daily Telegraph* (August 16, 2003). Calling it "a profoundly serious and disturbing book," Massie added, "It is written with an intensity of feeling that is rare, and deserves to sell hugely. That said, it is also in some respects intensely irritating. . . . For an experienced reporter, Hartley too often tells a story clumsily, with too many digressions, too many unidentified characters." "Hartley's greatest literary strength comes from the living he has done; many M.F.A.–programmed writers would trade a limb for just a month's worth of his stories," Rob Nixon wrote for the *New York Times* (August 24, 2003). "But *The Zanzibar Chest* suffers, especially early on, from story overload. Family forebears, African strongmen, aid workers, transitory lovers, ground-down foreign correspondents, doped-up border guards and plane-crash survivors pass before us in a high-speed cavalcade, as if Hartley had no idea how long to stay with a character or scene." Nixon continued, "There is rich material here for self-inquiry, but by instinct and conditioning Hartley is not an introspective writer.

When he stands back from his plunges into danger, his writing feels less secure. He struggles to integrate reports from countries torn by violence and famine with the very different tonal demands of the family memoir and the historical quest."

Hartley lives on the Laikipia plateau, a Kenyan highland district between Mount Kenya and the Rift Valley, with his wife, Claire, and their two children. He frequently contributes articles on wildlife to the *Spectator*. His second book, "Wild Life: Adventures on an African Farm," is slated for publication in 2008.

—P.B.M.

Suggested Reading: (London) *Daily Telegraph* p5 Aug. 16, 2003; (London) *Guardian* Aug. 23, 2003; *New York Times* VII p22 Aug. 24, 2003

Selected Books: *The Zanzibar Chest: A Story of Life, Love, and Death in Foreign Lands*, 2003

Courtesy of the University of Iowa Press

Harty, Ryan

1965– Short-story writer

In his starkly evocative short-story collection *Bring Me Your Saddest Arizona* (2003), Ryan Harty "displays an incredibly assured sense of storytelling . . . grounding his stories in telling details, noble gestures and a palpable sense of place," Joanne Wilkinson wrote in a review for *Booklist* (October 2003, on-line). "His stories will break your heart."

Born in 1965 Harty was raised in Arizona and Northern California. He graduated from the University of California, at Berkeley, and then earned an M.F.A. from the Iowa Writers' Workshop at the University of Iowa, in Iowa City. Prior to the publication of *Bring Me Your Saddest Arizona*, Harty's work appeared in the *Missouri Review* and *Tin House*, among other literary journals. He is married to the writer Julie Orringer, with whom he lives in San Francisco, California. The two were dubbed "one of San Francisco's hottest young literary couples" by Aidin Vaziri in an On the Town feature for the *San Francisco Chronicle* (March 13, 2005, on-line). (In the piece the couple listed "the places in San Francisco that inspire and feed their creative lives." Included were an art showroom called the Luggage Store Gallery, a bar called Sadie's Flying Elephant, a theater called the Red Victorian Movie House, and a cafe called the Bashful Bull that served cheap and plentiful breakfast specials.)

Bring Me Your Saddest Arizona consists of eight short stories that delve into the darkness and gloom that pervade otherwise ordinary lives in the sun-drenched American Southwest. These include "What Can I Tell You about My Brother," in which a marine, home on leave, kills a romantic rival's dog; "Crossroads," which features two brothers— one on his way to fight in Vietnam—who attend a rock concert together; "Between Tubac and Tumacacori," which finds a heroin addict trying to tempt a friend to join him; "Don't Call It Christmas," about the relationship between a homeless girl and a lonely creative-writing teacher; "Why the Sky Turns Red When the Sun Goes Down," a futuristic tale in which a couple debate what to do with their ailing robot son; "Ongchoma," which features a protagonist who is losing her ambition to work in academia;

"September," in which Tom, the narrator of "What Can I Tell You about My Brother," looks back on his life; and "Sarah at the Palace," in which a divorced middle-aged man cleans out his dead sister's Las Vegas apartment. ("Why the Sky Turns Red When the Sun Goes Down" also appeared in *The Best American Short Stories 2003*.)

Many critics singled out for particular praise the collection's first story, "What Can I Tell You about My Brother." The story opens: "On his first night home from marine boot camp, my brother killed Rob Dawson's German shepherd with a Phillips screwdriver. Rob was the captain of my football team at Arcadia High School. He was an all-league quarterback and a popular guy, and since the end of the summer he'd been seeing a girl named Jessica Lynn Armstrong, who'd gone out with my brother before he joined the marines. She and Victor had been together for a year and a half, and they'd been serious enough to talk about getting married after he finished boot camp. But during his tenth week of training, she called to say she was seeing Rob, and it must have made my brother crazy. He killed the dog in the backyard of the Dawsons' house, a three-story Spanish villa overlooking the whole sleeping valley. He left the body floating on the lighted blue pool, disappeared over a row of yuccas, and didn't come home until the next afternoon."

Wilkinson called the stories "unbearably sad," and a reviewer for *Publishers Weekly* (August 4, 2003, on-line) concurred: "No one would call these stories uplifting or optimistic but they are fully realized and elegantly told—and quite often quietly surprising. Harty excels at creating a three-dimensional desert suburbia populated by seeking, reaching characters, for whom happiness is always just a bit out of reach." Similarly, Ann Cummins wrote for the *San Francisco Chronicle* (October 19, 2003, online), "With face-lifted mothers and war-burned sons, Harty's world is as Orwellian as, well, the daily news. . . . In the tradition of American writers such as John Cheever and Philip K. Dick, who unflinchingly engaged the troubles of their time, Harty fearlessly and beautifully digs into the cracks of ours. His collection could as well be called *Bring Me Your Saddest America*."

Harty, a former Stegner Fellow and Jones Lecturer at Stanford University, has also been a recipient of the Henfield/Transatlantic Review Award.

In an interview for the Powell's Books Web site, Harty's wife, Julie Orringer, commented on the fact that her first book, *How to Breathe Underwater*, came out shortly before his: "In many ways it's an incredible coincidence, and yet somehow it doesn't seem strange at all. We never planned or expected to have first books coming out at the same time, though I suppose we always knew it was a possibility; we met at the Iowa Writers' Workshop in 1996 and have been together ever since. Later we were both at Stanford. Our writing lives have followed amazingly similar tracks. In addition to

being an incredibly talented writer, Ryan has always been a fantastic reader for me—honest and demanding and sensitive. Writing fiction is a lonely and scary endeavor, and it's an unspeakable relief to be able to share the good and bad times with my best friend."

—P.B.M.

Suggested Reading: *Booklist* (on-line) Oct. 2003; *Publishers Weekly* (on-line) Aug. 4, 2003; *San Francisco Chronicle* (on-line) Oct. 19, 2003, Mar. 13, 2005

Selected Books: *Bring Me Your Saddest Arizona*, 2003

Haruf, Kent

(HER-if)

Feb. 24, 1943– Novelist

The acclaimed writer William Faulkner set many of his books in Yoknapatawpha County, a fictional locale based on his actual home in Lafayette County, Mississippi. Yoknapatawpha, as Faulkner famously wrote, was meant to serve as a "cosmos in miniature." Similarly, Kent Haruf has created the town of Holt, on the plains of eastern Colorado, as the setting for his novels: *The Tie That Binds* (1984), *Where You Once Belonged* (1990), *Plainsong* (1999), and *Eventide* (2004). The inhabitants of Holt "know how to survive a landscape that in equal measure nurtures and negates them, and thereby makes them heroic," Laura Hendrie wrote for the *Boston Review* (on-line). "Set apart out in the middle of the prairies of Colorado, [the people of Holt] are outlined and magnified by the enormous, windswept emptiness around them, so that who they are, what they believe in and how they survive becomes suddenly not just another . . . story about a small town in the American West, but a story of universal concern."

One of four children, Kent Haruf was born on February 24, 1943 in Pueblo, Colorado, to the former Eleanor Shaver, a teacher and homemaker, and Louis Haruf, a Methodist minister. As Louis was assigned to various parishes, the family moved from one small rural town to another. Haruf attended Nebraska Wesleyan University, in Lincoln, earning a B.A., in 1965. For the next two years, he served in the Peace Corps, as an English teacher in the Turkish village of Anatolia. Upon his return he took a series of odd jobs, working on construction sites, railroads, farms, and in libraries in Colorado, Montana, Wyoming, and Kansas.

Haruf was a conscientious objector during the Vietnam War, and instead of being sent to combat, he fulfilled his service by working at hospitals and orphanages. Denied entrance once to the prestigious Iowa Writers' Workshop at the

University of Iowa, he took a job as a janitor until he was finally granted admission. He received his M.F.A. in 1973. Needing a steady source of income to support the three daughters that he had by his first wife, Virginia Koon, he taught high school English in Wisconsin and Colorado from 1976 to 1986. He then joined the faculty of Nebraska Wesleyan, where he remained until 1991. He was a professor at Southern Illinois University, in Carbondale, from 1991 to 2000, when the success of *Plainsong* made it possible for him to retire from academia.

In an essay for the *New York Times* (December 24, 2004), Haruf remembered his father with deep affection and pride as "his own best witness for the virtues of compassion, generosity and faith." Because of a raging blizzard, his father's simple funeral was attended by only five people. It "seems appropriate now, thinking about it, remembering where my father came from and how he was. He was well acquainted with bad weather, and he would not have wanted any fanfare," Haruf wrote. Many of Haruf's characters display a similar humility and strength.

In *The Tie That Binds* Haruf introduced the fictional geography of Holt County, in northeastern Colorado, which was to become his sole literary turf. As the novel opens, Edith Goodnough lies in the hospital at the age of 80 with a sheriff on guard outside her door; her neighbor narrates her story to an unknown interlocutor. Edith has grown up on a farm, where she has been forced to do her mother's work as well as her own after the older woman's early death. When her father, an angry, demanding man, loses most of his fingers in an accident, he becomes dependent on Edith and her brother, Lyman. Lyman escapes for a while but ultimately returns to the farm. Instead of enjoying a well-earned peaceful old age together, Lyman descends into senility. Edith, in an act of desperation, sets fire to the house, resulting in Lyman's death and a charge of attempted murder against her. The novel, although not a great commercial success, was critically acclaimed and won Haruf a Whiting Foundation Writer's Award and a citation from the PEN/Hemingway Foundation.

Haruf's second novel, *Where You Once Belonged*, another tale of Holt, is the story of Jack Burdette, a man who had a wild youth, was expelled from college, joined the army, returned to the town, and worked for the cooperative that ran the grain elevator. Over the course of the book, Burdette embezzles the cooperative's money and flees, abandoning his wife, Jessie. The editor of the local newspaper, Pat Arbuckle, who has taken up with Burdette's deserted wife, narrates the story. Richard Eder, writing for the *Los Angeles Times Book Review* (February 11, 1990), described the narrator as "both a dispassionate recounter and a chief victim of the devils that are in Burdette." Eder concluded that in the end, "like all evil, Burdette is a mystery. And what is most

mysterious is not what separates his evil from the town's virtue but what joins them. Haruf does not spell out the link for us; it is part of what resonates in the bitten-off silences of this stirring and remarkable book." Dan Cryer, writing for *New York Newsday* (January 8, 1990), called Jack's voice "unmistakable" and observed that "Jack looms over this story like some smiling, malicious death's head."

The next installment in the Holt saga, *Plainsong*, established Haruf's reputation as a major force in American letters. This time Haruf places at the center of his stage two saintly bachelor brothers, Harold and Raymond McPheron, who, despite their tendency to remain isolated, take in Victoria, a pregnant teenager thrown out by her mother. This situation is orchestrated by Maggie, a teacher, whose love interest is raising his young sons after their mother has deserted the family. The novel covers one day in the life of the town, alternating chapters about the various characters. Maria Russo remarked for the on-line publication *Salon* (October 18, 1999), "Haruf tells each of their stories with the same steady, unstrained rhythm and generous unflinching tone, so that the unexpected intersections of his character's lives come to seem not just interesting but deeply, reassuringly right." Elizabeth Gleick, writing for *Time* (October 25, 1999), opined, "There are some echoes here—of [Ernest] Hemingway, Cormac McCarthy, even Harper Lee." She added, "Haruf's gentle novel gives off a familiar backwoods, cold-mountain whiff. . . . The cliches are plentiful, but this is a lovely read, illuminated by sparks of spare beauty."

Plainsong, a critical and commercial hit, was nominated for a National Book Award, and Haruf was able to give up teaching and move with his second wife, the former Cathy Dempsey, a high-school classmate whom he married in 1995, to Salida, Colorado, where they settled into a picturesque log home. When *Plainsong* was filmed for television, in 2004, Haruf's financial situation improved even more dramatically, although he told Christy Karras for the *Salt Lake Tribune* (May 16, 2004) that he didn't much care for the result, because "they took the sting out of [the book]."

In an interview posted on the Random House Web site, Haruf explained why he had named his novel after the unisonous, unadorned vocal music sometimes used in Christian church services: "There's an obvious pun that this is kind of a song or an emblem for the Plains or an anthem for the Plains. Sung in a plain style. These are regular, ordinary sort of elemental characters and I think they're presented sort of directly and I wanted the prose to be kind of simple and direct."

In *Eventide*, his next Holt novel, Haruf revisits Victoria and the McPheron brothers. "If *Eventide* offers its readers one steadfast component, it's Haruf's unornamented prose," John Mark Eberhart noted for the Monterey County, California, *Herald* (May 23, 2004). While he found Haruf overly fond of describing the open landscape of Holt and the town's iron-haired men, the reviewer concluded, "Even Hemingway had his devices—his aperitifs; his clean, well-lighted places, his Parisian cafes." When one of the McPheron brothers is killed by a bull, the surviving brother is drawn out of his loneliness and isolation by a social worker—who has designs on him. "In the hands of another writer these events might read like a hick town soap opera," Michiko Kakutani observed for the *New York Times* (May 25, 2004), "but Mr. Haruf's understated prose, combined with his emotional wisdom and his easy affection for his characters turns these events into affecting drama. . . . His story, while lacking the fierce originality of *Plainsong*, possesses the haunting appeal of music, the folksy rhythms of an American ballad and the lovely, measured grace of an old hymn."

Interviewers often comment on Haruf's gentle nature and kindness. "Readers make a critical mistake when they assume that the virtues—or vices—of a novel's characters are the same as those

of it's creator," Alden Mudge wrote for *BookPage* (May 2004, on-line). "But . . . it is more than tempting to find in Haruf's direct, thoughtful, and self-effacing conversation everything that is most uplifting in the characters who populate his fictional town of Holt, Colorado."

—S.Y.

Suggested Reading: *BookPage* (on-line) May 2004; *Boston Review* (on-line); *Los Angeles Times Book Review* p3 Feb. 11, 1990; (Monterey County, California) *Herald* May 23, 2004; *New York Newsday* II p6 Jan. 8, 1990; *New York Times* E p7 May 25, 2004, A p23 Dec. 24, 2004; *New York Times Book Review* p13 May 23, 2004; *Salon* (on-line) Oct. 18, 1999; *Salt Lake Tribune* D p2 May 16, 2004; *Time* p130 Oct. 25, 1999

Selected Books: *The Tie That Binds*, 1984; *Where You Once Belonged*, 1990; *Plainsong*, 1999; *Eventide*, 2004

Haruka, Yoko

(ha-ROO-ka, YO-koh)

Nonfiction writer; essayist

In the beginning of her book *Kekkon Shimasen* (which can be translated as "I won't get married," 2001), the Japanese writer and television personality Yoko Haruka recalls her father's funeral, at which her supposed inferiority to her male siblings was made painfully clear. As recounted by Ayako Doi, writing for *Foreign Policy* (November–December 2003, on-line) "[Haruka] was told to sit and walk behind her five brothers— younger as well as older—and made to understand that she wasn't wanted on the receiving line to greet relatives and family friends." This was only one of many radicalizing experiences that inspired Haruka to become one of her country's best-known feminist figures. The author of several books and essays that examine the institutionalized sexism of Japanese society, Haruka exhorts young women to first consider their own needs before bowing to the expectations of a rigid patriarchy. "Men, company, marriage, these are the things you can use to achieve your goals," she writes, as quoted by Brendan Pearson in the *Australian Financial Review* (December 1, 2003). "But if they are no use, discard them." Noting Haruka's position at "the vanguard of a social revolution," Pearson wrote, "[She] has become the poster girl for a fast-growing breed of more independent Japanese women."

Many women are taking Haruka's advice. In recent years Japan has seen its fertility rate plunge dramatically, coinciding with trends that find younger women rejecting traditional roles in order

to live on their own, pursue a career, and eschew marriage. If these trends continue some experts note with alarm, the next century will see Japan's population sliced in half. Haruka's words are thus seen by many as subversive, or even dangerous, in their influence.

Yoko Haruka was born in Osaka, Japan, in the late 1960s, an era in which unmarried women were often referred to as "leftover Christmas cake," implying that they were undesirable or had outlived their usefulness. As Haruka does not disclose her exact age in interviews, reporters generally refer to her as "thirtysomething." During her childhood and adolescence, her needs were routinely ignored in favor of those of her five brothers. When she got her first bra, for example, she kept it on around the clock, sleeping in it, because no family member had explained that she didn't have to. Only when she went on an overnight school trip did she discover her error. "It was a great relief to me," she said, as quoted by Ginko Kobayashi for the Tokyo *Daily Yomiuri* (June 24, 2000). As Haruka grew older, she chafed at her brothers' sense of entitlement. Her oldest brother, she noted in *Kekkon Shimasen*, is verbally abusive to his wife, who, in addition to bearing sole responsibility for all domestic chores, must accommodate both her husband and his mother, who, as dictated by Japanese tradition, lives with them. Haruka's sister-in-law, according to Ayako Doi, "manages to smile self-effacingly even as she scurries to provide for their material needs, right down to putting a cold beer in her husband's hand as he steps out of his nightly bath." Haruka also recalls in the book her annoyance at an aunt's wish to find an "ordinary girl" to marry her son—by which she meant a complacent woman with no personal ambition besides keeping her husband fed and happy. Such family experiences were at the root of Haruka's early stirrings of feminist consciousness.

While in her early 20s, Haruka began a career in television, working as a kind of hostess or sidekick on a variety show—a common role for pretty young women on Japanese TV. Describing these shows, which are quite popular in Japan, Stephen Lunn, writing for the *Australian* (July 27, 2000), explained that typically "a charismatic host [is] accompanied by an attractive 'flower.' No prizes for guessing the gender of the respective participants." The programs are a "microcosm of Japanese society," Lunn wrote, in that they "reduce the women to little more than a sounding board for the male host's ideas. If [the women] try to increase their profile or offer an unwanted opinion, trouble quickly follows." Male hosts, when feeling affronted by some instance of female audacity, frequently make disparaging comments about their female counterparts' age or marital status. Haruka often found the work demoralizing, but at first, she did not fight back against the overt sexism. "Earlier in my career," she told Lunn, "I tried to hide the fact that I believed in feminism for fear I would lose my job."

Haruka worked on several such programs, acting as an emcee or a panelist; one of her more notable stints was on a popular quiz show called *Seikatsu Shohyakka*. By the mid-1990s, she was an established presence on the Japanese television circuit. Despite her professional success, Haruka felt dissatisfied. "I had worked many years in television, but the longer I worked, the more hurdles were put in my path," she told Lunn. She had grown tired of the patronizing way in which she was treated by the men with whom she shared the camera. Her discontent extended to her personal life. Recently engaged, she feared that her fiancé would expect her to be a traditionally submissive wife, a role she was unprepared to adopt; she broke off the engagement. "I think we loved each other very much," she told Pearson. "But the best partner for him was someone who does not have a job, and stays home for him."

Haruka decided to attend classes taught by the feminist scholar Chizuko Ueno, at Tokyo University. Coming from a profession in which a heavy premium is placed on women's looks, Haruka found academia, with its focus on brains rather than beauty, to be liberating. Although she was initially intimidated by Ueno, soon Haruka was learning effective debate skills and reading seminal feminist essays. (She continued television hosting during her three years as a student.) At the end of her studies, Haruka wrote *Todai de Ueno Chizuko ni Kenka o Manabu* (which can be translated as "learning how to argue from Chizuko Ueno at Tokyo University"). It was published in early 2000; by summer it had sold 160,000 copies. The book summarized much of what Haruka learned under Ueno, including a list of 10 tips for winning arguments; the first tip was "Be defiant when necessary." After the book's publication, Haruka took her own advice and started confronting men who made sexist comments on the air.

The success of her first book prompted Haruka, in 2001, to write two more: *Hataraku Onna Wa teki bakari* (which can be translated as "all a working woman gets is enemies"), which sold over 100,000 copies, and *Kekkon Shimasen*. Haruka's books were indicative of a major generational shift regarding marriage and family. Official statistics, as of 2004, report that half of all Japanese women in their late 20s are single. The number of unmarried women in their 30s, meanwhile, has tripled since the 1970s. Women who do marry are doing so later and having their children later as a consequence. "These trends have important economic implications for Japan, and are exacerbating an already ageing society," Pearson wrote. "Official figures [show] that the number of babies born [in 2002] was the lowest number since records began in 1899. In 2002, the national fertility rate stood at an all-time low of 1.32 children per women." There is even a name in Japan for this crisis: *shoshika*, which means "decline in childbearing." The answer to why Japan is seeing such dramatic shifts can, in part, be found in the pages of *Kekkon Shimasen*. In the book Haruka compares being a working mother in Japan to playing "a cleverly designed computer game that one can never win," as Doi explains. "[A woman] can spend an eight-hour day at work and arrive home exhausted, but if she leaves the laundry to the weekend, or serves up a TV dinner, her husband is likely to say, 'What kind of woman are you?'—and mean it. On top of that he will expect her to peel his apples, go out for [his] cigarettes, make his coffee and still have enough energy for sex."

Haruka's most recent book is *Hybrid Woman* (2003). For this volume, Haruka moderates her position, advising women that they can achieve their goals without totally challenging patriarchal norms. The book recommends employing feminine wiles to influence men, rather than using more strident techniques. Though Haruka's softer stance in *Hybrid Woman* is a disappointment to some hard-line feminists, she is not concerned with the criticism. Many of her opinions simultaneously straddle feminist ideals and the realities of daily life in male-dominated Japan. On the rising trend of plastic surgery among women in television, for example, she told Lunn, "I've heard a lot of women do that. But I don't think it's a bad thing if they can assure their job by making their breasts bigger or padding their bra." Indeed, Lunn writes, "Haruka has no desire to martyr herself to the cause of feminism on Japanese TV. She plans to work within the system, knowing that in Japan, unlike Australia, the U.S., or Europe, if she spoke out against a male colleague and was sacked, laws covering unfair dismissal are virtually non-existent."

Haruka lives in Osaka, where she is currently working on various TV programs and continuing to write. After little romantic luck and the dissolution of her engagement, she concluded that a man was not a necessary part of her life. "I need someone who understands me and who supports me, but I have come to the realization that someone does not have to be male," she told Pearson. "When I ticked off my must-have list in my ideal partner, there was only one thing that required [the] male sex."

—L.S.

Suggested Reading: *Australian* M p8, July 27, 2000; *Australian Finanical Review* p10 Dec. 1, 2003; (Tokyo) *Daily Yomiuri* p8 June 24, 2000; *Foreign Policy* (on-line) Nov.–Dec. 2003

Selected Books: *Todai de Ueno Chizuko ni Kenka o Manabu*, 2000; *Kekkon Shimasen*, 2001; *Hataraku Onna Wa teki bakari*, 2001; *Hybrid Woman*, 2003

Courtesy of Canongate Books

Haskell, John

1958– Short-story writer; novelist; playwright

John Haskell, the author of the innovative collection of short fiction entitled *I Am Not Jackson Pollock* and the novel *American Purgatorio* (2005), has found success writing "about how it is precisely in pretence and myth that we can explore and convey truths. . . . Haskell sets his plough deep, exploring moments of profound psychological strain in his characters," Vicky Allan wrote for the Edinburgh

Sunday Herald (May 14, 2006). Lee Henderson, writing for the Toronto *Globe and Mail* (April 16, 2005), has called attention to other elements of Haskell's writing, observing "If it's not for his poignant and unmatched blend of pop culture and literary intelligence, then the reason Haskell is the United States' most significant new voice is because of sentences like this one: 'As I watched her walk I told myself, This is what I have to do, meaning, This is what I feel, meaning, This is who I think I have to be.'"

Born in California in 1958, John Haskell attended the University of California, at Los Angeles, and earned an M.F.A. from Columbia University, in New York City. He began his career working as an actor, performance artist, and playwright, co-founding, in 1982, the Huron Theatre in Chicago, Illinois, for which he was, for a time, the only dramatist, writing works such as *Gallop*, a play that was performed at the Eugene O'Neill Theater Center in Waterford, Connecticut, in 1984, and *Scenes from Hell* (1988), which David McCracken described for the *Chicago Tribune* (October 21, 1988) as a "typically funny, quirky, semi-autobiographical performance about—what else—a narrator who returns to Chicago after an extended stay in New York City." Meanwhile, Haskell described it, according to McCracken, as "a tongue-in-cheek, post–Thomas Wolfe thing, with all the requisite sex and death." During that period, Haskell supported himself with various odd jobs. "Chicago was cheap back then," Haskell told Dylan Foley for the *Denver Post* (March 15, 2005). "Most of the time I was a house painter. I was once a vending machine repairman. I worked as a proofreader and at an envelope factory."

In *I Am Not Jackson Pollock*, a reviewer for *Publishers Weekly* (March 24, 2003) wrote, "Haskell evades definition . . . creating an innovative blend of fact and fiction and deliberately eliding the difference between them. Most of the nine stories are imaginative extrapolations of the lives of real people (or, in some cases, real animals)" The reviewer continued "Haskell mixes anecdotes from the lives of these artists and celebrities with fictitious events to compose deceptively simple vignettes in which he distills and clarifies moments of intense psychological struggle." The stories "aim to create a genre all their own, describing bits of famous movies and artists' lives, then layering these depictions on top of one another in a kind of montage," as John Freeman wrote for the *Portland Phoenix* (June 13–29, 2003). Haskell tackles, among other topics, the relationship between the actors Janet Leigh and Anthony Perkins in the movie *Psycho*; the plight of Laika, the Sputnik satellite's canine passenger; and the dynamic between Jackson Pollock and his long-suffering wife. Michael Spinell opined for *Booklist* (April 1, 2003), "the wonderful, quirky, even extraordinary tales [contained in the book] intersperse Hollywood gossip with plumbing the depths of the human spirit." Nevertheless, Freeman concluded, "That readers are supposed to treat this goulash of criticism and film appreciation as fiction says a lot about the bankrupt state of fiction writing today."

Haskell's debut novel, *American Purgatorio*, which is loaded with references to Dante's *Divine Comedy*, follows Jack, an empty husk of a man, as he frantically searches the country for his wife, Anne, after she mysteriously disappears from a gas station in New Jersey. "I like to think the book is funny," Haskell told Robert Dahlin for *Publishers Weekly* (August 9, 2004), "but it also concerns itself with death, which is not funny. I think it's fast-paced, but it's intricate as well. It took some mental preparation in the beginning, and it was different from a short story because everything became a little fuller, a little deeper, a little rounder and thus longer. Other than that, the process of writing a novel or a short story is basically the same." Haskell added, "It's not a page-turner like a mystery story or a spy novel, but it does bare that element of emotional intensity." "This is a hypnotic and sometimes maddening novel, heady yet grounded in straightforward prose," Joy Press wrote for the *Village Voice* (January 18, 2005). "And it's nearly impossible to summarize in a review without detracting from the impact of the gradually unraveling structure. *American Purgatorio* teases us with its genre possibilities: Is this a thriller? Amnesia fiction? A metaphysical road novel? A puzzle? The answer is all of the above, of course."

Haskell lives in the New York City borough of Brooklyn. He has contributed to such journals as the *Paris Review, Granta, Conjunctions*, and *Ploughshares* and to the radio show *The Next Big Thing*.

—P.B.M./A.R.

Suggested Reading: *Portland Phoenix* (on-line) June 13–19, 2003; *Publishers Weekly* p129 Aug. 9, 2004, p58 Mar. 24, 2003; (Toronto) *Globe and Mail* D p26 Apr. 16, 2005; *Village Voice* Aug. 11, 2003

Selected Books: *I Am Not Jackson Pollock*, 2003; *American Purgatorio*, 2005

Hensher, Philip

Feb. 20, 1965– Novelist; short-story writer

In June 1998, when he was only 33, Philip Hensher was made a fellow of the British Royal Society of Literature, an honor that cemented him in the minds of some of his countrymen as one of the most significant authors of his generation. Hensher's writing—intricate and graceful in style—is often filled with alienated characters, people whose interpersonal relationships crumble when faced with the strife that comes with sexual betrayal, abuse of power, or familial rivalry. History is an important backdrop to his novels, often serving to emphasize the hypocrisy behind a public face. On his personal page on the Web site of the University of Exeter, in England, Hensher writes: "My interests are rooted in the realist traditions, but extend to explorations of intertextuality, self-aware narrations, pastiche and disruptive techniques deriving from other art forms, particularly music. In addition, I've tried to import literary forms from other cultures." Tentatively titled "The Northern Clemency" and forthcoming in 2007, Hensher's sixth novel is, he writes on the Exeter Web site, "a straightforward narrative of two families, told through the history of the energy industry."

Philip Michael Hensher was born on February 20, 1965 in the Kingston borough of London, England. His father, R. J. Hensher, managed a bank, while his mother, M. Foster Hensher, was a librarian for a university. Both parents had family ties to the evangelical Christian denomination the Salvation Army, better known in the U.S. as a charity group; his father played the French horn in a Salvation Army band and his mother sang for one of its choruses. When Hensher was nine, his father moved the family to Sheffield so that Hensher and his sister might get away from the strikes then plaguing southeastern England. Hensher and his sister began taking piano lessons around that time, and he later took up the double bass, which he played on tours with the Sheffield Youth Orchestra. In an article for *Granta* (number 76, 2002, on-line), Hensher recalled his teenage fascination with music: "Between the ages of twelve and eighteen, I did nothing, it seems to me now, but write music. That must be an illusion; I must have gone to school and learned about the ordinary things; I had friends and learned about sex and boys, I had a religious phase lasting six months, I rode my bike and daringly got drunk on Guinness on my sixteenth birthday. I made desultory attempts to have sex with girls. . . . I sat in the kitchen of a sympathetic girl called Miriam and told her that I was homosexual, and faked an anguish I didn't really feel. Several times, too, I hopefully said, late at night to a handsome boy, when we were alone, what everyone like me says and never really believes, that of course, everyone is basically bisexual, until one of them crossed the room and kissed me, and after that I never said anything so foolish ever again. All that faded, all that life, afterwards; it seemed, even at the time, like the sort of things that everyone does. What mattered was what I did, ceaselessly, in solitude; wrote music."

Always a good student, Hensher particularly excelled in English, French, German, and music. During this same period he also became infatuated with such authors as George Orwell, Lawrence Durrell, and Marcel Proust. His greatest admiration, however, was reserved for 18th-century literature, particularly the poet Alexander Pope. In an interview with the London *Observer* (August 16, 1998), he described "spending a whole term at university reading nothing but Alexander Pope" and argued: "If you read Pope for eight weeks, inch by inch and really understand it, my God, he teaches you how to begin to write. Pope's just the greatest writer in English." By the time Hensher entered the University of Oxford's Lady Margaret Hall College as an undergraduate, he had come to realize that he had no real talent as a composer. At 17, a professional orchestra performed one of his original works, the recollection of which caused the author, as recently as 2004, to squirm with embarrassment when discussing it during an interview.

He received his undergraduate degree in English literature from Oxford in 1986 and later began work on a doctoral degree in English at Cambridge University. In about 1990, two years before he completed his Ph.D. with a thesis titled "The Diffusion of Satire in Art and Literature, 1750–1800," Hensher took a position as a clerk at the British House of Commons, working first with the Energy Select Committee before moving to the Journal Office and ending at the Treasury Committee. "What's fascinating about the job," he remarked in an interview with John Walsh for the London *Independent* (April 19, 1996), "is that you're physically very close to these people, to ministers and the PM, but you still know nothing about them. The work itself is not without influence. . . . Clerks get the witnesses to come and give evidence, and write the questions the ministers are supposed to ask. In my experience, most of what ends up in print—the actual form of words—is the work of the clerk."

In addition to this work, Hensher began writing for several newspapers, serving as an art critic for the *Mail on Sunday*, a book reviewer for the *Spectator*, and columnist for the London *Independent*. He also began writing his first novel, *Other Lulus* (1994), which drew extensively on his background in music, particularly the work of Viennese composer Alban Berg, who died in 1935 before completing the final act of his second opera, *Lulu*. In the novel Hensher writes from the perspective of a German woman, Friederike, who travels to Austria in the early 1970s to study voice at the Vienna Conservatory. She marries one of her teachers, an Englishman named Archy, who claims to have something that no one else in the world possesses—notebooks containing the finishing touches for Berg's *Lulu*. The two characters are set apart by their temperaments. While Friederike never desires attention and does not fully realize how gifted a singer she is, Archy believes that his

obsession with Berg will lead to fame. In a review for the London *Sunday Times* (March 20, 1994), John Melmoth described *Other Lulus* as an "intelligent, complex, [and] rebarbative" book that "takes precious few prisoners. Hensher writes equally well about marriage and music, and can be very funny." On the other hand, Jason Cowley, writing for the London *Independent* (April 2, 1994), remarked: "What strikes one most about the book . . . is Hensher's stylistic daring. Not only does he succeed throughout in maintaining a consistent tone of voice, he actually sounds like a woman. . . . His prose is fresh and bold and often memorable. What he doesn't do, however, is write with any real conviction about Berg's music."

Hensher began his second novel, *Kitchen Venom* (1996), while still employed at the House of Commons. A damning account of the British parliamentary system during the end of Margaret Thatcher's administration, the novel centers around John, a clerk who has an affair with a young Italian male prostitute named Giacomo. When Giacomo winds up murdered, John suspects his fellow clerk Louis of being the murderer. In a review for the London *Guardian* (April 26, 1996), Jeremy Maule called the book "a tightly cross-cut London melodrama of hateful sisters and restaurant embarrassments, clerkly ennuis and afternoon sex. Add a probable suicide, the murder of a beautiful and charming Italian rentboy and a stylish, angled account of the Last Days of Thatcher, and it all sounds a gloopy mix, impossibly bustling. Nothing could be further from the effect and tone. Airy, felicitous, superintendent, Hensher releases his staggered secrets and recognitions in a smart but unpredictable procession of bad behaviours. If Royal divorces were staged, and not just casually exhibited at tedious length, Hensher would be their perfect commentator: sharp to field-pattern, not a little sententious, acidly voluptuous on dress-sense and dress-nonsense." Jason Cowley, in the London *Observer* (April 28, 1996), criticized some of Hensher's stylistic excesses but noted how "in the end, what one remembers most about the book is not the grand political intrigue, the strange back-to-front sentences or the intricate obliquity of the prose, but the tenderness with which Hensher describes his fragile rent boy, and the sense of sadness and suffering he brings to writing about lust and unfulfilled desire."

Hensher was fired from his position in the House of Commons in April 1996, around the time *Kitchen Venom* was published and shortly after he gave an interview to the London magazine *Attitude*, which describes itself on its Web site as "the leading gay men's lifestyle magazine in the UK." In his interview Hensher claimed that at least 60 members of Parliament were closeted homosexuals and called most members of Parliament ugly. At the time he portrayed his firing as an unintentional, if welcome, consequence of a thoughtless interview; years later, however,

Hensher suggested to Sally Vincent, in an article in the London *Guardian* (July 3, 2004), that the interview was a deliberate ploy to get fired without having to compromise his otherwise exemplary work history.

Hensher's third novel, *Pleasured* (1998), begins in Germany at the very end of 1988 and goes into 1989, the year the Berlin Wall fell and Communist-controlled East Germany was reunited with the West. The lead character, Friedrich Kaiser, is sharing a car with two others: an English businessman, Peter Picker, who hates East Germany and is plotting to bring about the end of Communism there, and Daphne, a student whose leftist ideology often prompts her to rail against the bourgeois attitudes of West Berlin. Phil Whitaker, writing for the *New Statesman* (August 14, 1998), observed: "There is much to admire in *Pleasured*, even though the pace is uneven and the narrative too often static. Hensher, who occasionally overwrites, is, I think, a little unsure of his voice. . . . [Yet] Hensher has shown himself willing to engage with contemporary Europe, a refreshing contrast to the cozy Anglo-European writing of Julian Barnes and others. The challenge for him now is to marry this large ambition with the taut narrative control we glimpsed in *Kitchen Venom*. When he does so, *Pleasured* will be seen as a stepping stone in the development of an important new voice in British fiction." In the London *Independent* (July 24, 1999), reviewers Emma Hagestadt and Christopher Hirst called *Pleasured* "an engrossing novel as memorable for its cinematic set pieces—a couple tangoing on a strip of deserted Autobahn, a cyclist's bid for freedom during the Tour de France—as for its reflections on East and West."

Hensher published his first collection of short stories, *The Bedroom of the Mister's Wife*, in 1999. Many of the stories originally appeared in such notable literary periodicals as *Granta,* and one piece in the collection, "Dead Languages," was the only story by a writer of Hensher's generation to be anthologized in the 1998 edition of *The Oxford Book of English Stories*, edited by novelist A. S. Byatt. In the *New Statesman* (September 20, 1999), Tamsin Todd argued: "There's often a cold cleverness to much of Hensher's writing, and some of the stories can read like the work of a callous teenager—Hensher as the smart kid who twists the teacher's words and throws them back at her. In 'Work' and 'A Chartist', unnecessarily complicated and sometimes nasty plotting disguises the thinness of the storylines. But for the most part Hensher is acute, and his prose is gorgeous. He reminds us that even the briefest glimpse of the possibility of desire is worth celebrating." James Urquhart, writing for the London *Independent* (August 14, 1999), offered a similarly mixed, but generally positive, assessment: "Though not entirely coherent as a collection, this volume combines 13 refreshingly tart slices of short fiction. Hensher's hallmark is literary sleight of hand, and

most stories, in their own way, conceal as much as they reveal. His tales, though often edged with a gleeful darkness, are neither adult fables nor vignettes burdened with a heavy yoke of morality. But they do invite closer reading, and the carapace of his brightly gleaming prose often encloses an unexpected heart."

In the afterward to his fourth novel, *The Mulberry Empire, or the Two Virtuous Journeys of the Amir Dost Mohammed Khan* (2002), Hensher notes that the book grew in part out of a suggestion from A. S. Byatt, who thought Hensher should try his hand at a long novel. The result was a historical epic set in Afghanistan in the 1830s, when the British Empire was suffering one of the worst defeats in its history. Hensher's main character is a British explorer named Alexander Burnes, a friend of the Afghan emir, Dost Mohammed Khan, who comes to Burnes seeking British support against an invasion by the Persians. Instead of helping the emir, the British send troops to push him out of power—only to have those troops decimated by the resistance. Writing for the *Christian Science Monitor* (August 29, 2002), Ron Charles described the book as "a stunningly accurate analysis of depravity, stupidity, and hubris across cultures. Readers who persist through its thick style will find *The Mulberry Empire* flatters them with its erudition and wit. . . . What's particularly brilliant is the way the novel returns, after all the planning and scheming and mayhem and destruction, to find both societies essentially unchanged." Jason Goodwin, in the *New York Times Book Review* (September 1, 2002), praised Hensher's ability to imitate a range of 19th-century authors, but worried that Hensher "may be too preoccupied with intellectual risk to bring off quite the emotional relationship an author must forge with his readers . . . . Hensher is taking us with dexterity and invention toward a kind of tragedy, but *The Mulberry Empire* is sensationally long, and while the art of high camp is to be always, remorselessly, even savagely pushing the envelope of other people's expectations, it often betrays, somewhere along the line, the weakness that is also its greatest fear: that on any performance, however brilliant, the spectators retain the option of simply turning away."

After spending years researching and writing *The Mulberry Empire*, Hensher bet his boyfriend that he could write his next novel in only a month. Walking his dog later that same evening, Hensher came across a man strolling the streets in his underwear, and Hensher's fifth novel, *The Fit* (2004), came to life. He completed a draft in the month, winning his bet, but subsequently rewrote the book substantially. The novel is narrated by John, an indexer who develops the hiccups shortly after being left by his wife. Apparently indifferent to the end of his marriage, John demonstrates throughout the book a narcissistic and pessimistic attitude that masks a great tragedy: the murder and rape of his sister Frankie when she was a teen. In *New Statesman* (July 12, 2004), Hugo Barnacle described *The Fit* as "a curiosity, a compendium of the things that Hensher happened to think about at the time of composition," but concluded that was still "a highly readable curiosity." In the *Spectator* (July 10, 2004), Sebastian Smee criticized the book's first half, with its "jerry-built plot" and "inconsistent tone," but found the second half "genuinely wonderful." Smee added: "The dialogue throughout is terrific, full of snappy non-sequiturs and sense-shifting lapses in logic. Overall, however, I felt that the book might have benefited from a longer—or at least a more careful—gestation. On the other hand, Hensher is such a marvellous writer that one wants to read almost anything he writes."

In addition to his books and journalism, Hensher has also written a libretto for the chamber opera *Powder Her Face*, with music by Thomas Adès. First produced in 1995, the opera has been revived frequently in the ensuing years. In addition to receiving a Somerset Maugham Award in 1997, Hensher was the only writer of his generation to be included in the eighth edition of *The Oxford Companion to English Literature* (1995). He is attached to the School of English at the University of Exeter.

—C.M.

Suggested Reading: *Christian Science Monitor* p15+ Aug. 29, 2002; *Granta* (on-line) number 76, 2002; (London) *Guardian* p29 Apr. 20, 1996, T p20 Apr. 26, 1996, p28 July 3, 2004; (London) *Independent* p29 Apr. 2, 1994, p2 Apr. 19, 1996, p15 Aug. 15, 1998, p11 July 24, 1999, p11 Aug. 14, 1999; (London) *Observer* p15 Apr. 28, 1996, p15 Aug. 16, 1998; (London) *Sunday Times* (on-line) Mar. 20, 1994; *New Statesman* p45+ Aug. 14, 1998, p58 Sep. 20, 1999, p55 July 12, 2004; *New York Times Book Review* p7 Sep. 1, 2002; *Spectator* p33+ July 10, 2004; University of Exeter Web site

Selected Books: *Other Lulus*, 1994; *Kitchen Venom*, 1996; *Pleasured*, 1998; *The Bedroom of the Mister's Wife*, 1999; *The Mulberry Empire*, 2002; *The Fit*, 2004

Herrick, William

Jan. 10, 1915–Jan. 31, 2004 Novelist; memoirist

The great battles of the 20th century—the fights against fascism and communism, the struggles for unionization and civil rights—provided the focus for William Herrick's life, as well as his fiction. His work typically explores the lives of individuals caught up in momentous events, as he, himself, was so often during his lifetime. As Stephen Schwartz wrote for the *Weekly Standard* (March 15, 2004) shortly after Herrick's death, on January 31, 2004: "Bill Herrick was one of those whose lives, and whose writings, must not be neglected if we are to understand the century from which we have just emerged, as well as the century before us."

William Herrick was born William Horvitz on January 10, 1915 in Trenton, New Jersey. His parents, Nathan Horvitz and the former Mary Saperstein, were Jewish immigrants from a former Soviet republic now known as Belarus. They were avowed Communists, and Herrick reportedly slept in a crib surrounded by embossed tin portraits of Lenin, Trotsky, and Stalin. When Herrick was four, his father died. His mother remained a Communist Party loyalist, and, as Paul Grondahl wrote for the Albany *Times Union* (February 4, 2004), "drifted through a series of party-approved free-love assignations." Herrick was educated in the public schools of Newark, New Jersey and New York City. After graduating from high school, in June 1932, he took a number of odd jobs, including stints as a busboy in cabarets on New York's East Side. He later took to the road.

During the Great Depression, Herrick was just one of a score of migrant workers throughout the country, men and women trying to survive the economic upheaval that began with the market crash of October 1929. He traveled by freight trains to various parts of the country and lived for a time in an anarchist commune. Later he worked in a hotel in Miami Beach and was a union organizer for black sharecroppers in Georgia—an experience that helped him to find work in the New York fur trade, which was run by a strong Communist-influenced union.

When the Spanish Civil War broke out, in July 1936, Herrick volunteered for one of the international units traveling to Spain, the Abraham Lincoln Battalion, which was more commonly known as the Lincoln Brigade. (The alternate name was intentional; at the time Spanish brigades consisted of three to four battalions, and the Communists wanted to exaggerate the number of their volunteers.) The majority of the Lincoln Brigade was comprised of young American men, eager to fight for the communist beliefs espoused by the Spanish Republic.

Spain of the 1930s was at a crossroads; its Second Republic was a left-leaning democratic government with strong ties to both communism and anarchism. The Republic's cause was supported by Stalin, who sought greater influence in Western Europe. Allied against the Republic were General Francisco Franco and his right-wing Falangist Party, which was in turn supported by Nazi Germany and Fascist Italy. In November 1936 it seemed likely that the capital of Madrid would fall to Franco's forces, but Republican and international forces kept them at bay.

Herrick was wounded in Madrid, on February 23, 1937. He had been shot in the neck, and the bullet lodged close to his spinal column. Unable to remove the bullet (which remained in his neck for the rest of his life) and return him to active duty, physicians sent him back to the United States. His experience in the war reshaped his feelings about the Communist Party. After witnessing the savage manner in which party members dealt with dissidents, he began to question the righteousness of his political leanings. After Hitler and Stalin signed a non-aggression pact, in August 1939, Herrick protested the action to the Fur and Leather Worker's Union and he was summarily fired. (In 1953 he denounced his former comrades before the House Committee on Un-American Activities.)

Back in America Herrick continued to wander. He eventually landed in California, where he met such actors as Rita Hayworth and Orson Wells. In 1943 he began working as a court reporter, a position he held until 1969. Sometime during the mid-1950s he began writing fiction at night. For a decade he worked steadily, honing his craft, but didn't publish anything until 1966 when *The Itinerant*, his first novel, appeared. He was 51 years old at the time.

The Itinerant was a semiautobiographical novel. It follows the adventures of Zeke Gurevich, a young man who grew up during the Great Depression, traveled around the country, associated with Communists, and eventually fought in the Spanish Civil War. The novel details Zeke's return home from the war, his adjustment to married life, and his participation in the civil rights movement. It received mixed notices. In the *Saturday Review* (August 19, 1967), Granville Hicks called it "a strange novel, full of energy, written in a rough-and-ready style, wandering as restlessly as the itinerant himself. A late starter— he was born in 1915—Herrick has written a first novel that is full of flaws but does bring to life the Thirties and Forties." On the other hand, Harry Roskolenko, in the *New York Times Book Review* (April 23, 1967), harshly declared: "How did this completely mechanical novel about the depression days, with all its leftist political paraphernalia . . . get written? Is it the experimental product of a proletarian prose computer? . . . Nothing has been left out of the radical drollery that Herrick deals with except art, writing and character development."

Herrick quickly followed his first novel with another, *Strayhorn* (1968), but it was his third novel, *Hermanos!* (1969), which drew the attention of critics. In this novel Jake Starr, a union organizer, travels to Spain to join the Spanish Civil War and fight on behalf of the Republic. His conscience soon gets the better of him as he realizes that the Communist Party might not be all he hoped, and he becomes involved in an illicit affair. In a review for *Library Journal* (September 1, 1969), R. D. Harlan declared: "When it is good, this novel . . . is very good. The battle scenes are

particularly well done; they are terrifying! Equally terrifying are the cynicism and brutality with which the idealism of the rank and file and very survival of the Republic are exploited and subverted by the novel's protagonists—party-line Communists—to the party's own ends. At the conclusion of this story, one has qualified sympathy for the defeated brigade, no sympathy at all for the chief protagonist . . . and a great deal of sympathy for the people of Spain. Like most good war novels, this work is profoundly antiwar." In the *New York Times Book Review* (October 26, 1969), Martin Levin cheered: "This compelling novel's . . . greatest distinction is its author's ability to articulate the Byzantine conflicts among the Loyalists with the flesh-and-blood participants who illustrate the name of the game. . . . Mr. Herrick, a veteran of the International Brigade, enlarges his hero's personal tragedy into the tragedy of Spain and the betrayal of political idealism everywhere."

Following the commercial and critical success of *Hermanos!*, Herrick stopped working as a court reporter to devote himself to writing full-time. He produced a number of novels over the next few years, among them *Last to Die* (1971), *Golcz* (1976), and a political trilogy of terrorism and espionage: *Shadows and Wolves* (1980), *Love and Terror* (1981), and *Kill Memory* (1983). In a critique of *Love and Terror* for the *New York Times Book Review* (June 14, 1981), Michael Malone wrote: "William Herrick's anatomy of a young German terrorist, written with dispassionate intelligence and documentary density, offers not a flutter of the pulse but a chill in the bone."

In 1985 Herrick published *That's Life*. The book was not traditionally written as a novel or collection of interconnecting stories, but rather as a compendium of letters, telephone conversations, and other recollections stemming from three generations of a Jewish American family. The tale begins during the Great Depression with the accidental death of the family patriarch, Eli Miller. His 15-year-old son, Max, then leaves for parts unknown and becomes a part of the union movement. He enters a tumultuous marriage to Rebecca, the daughter of a Ukrainian revolutionary. In the *New York Times Book Review* (June 16, 1985), Howard Frank Mosher observed: "As experimental fiction about family ties, *That's Life* is only partly successful. Even its sympathetic examination of Max and Rebecca's midlife marital crisis seems oddly flat compared with Max's rough-and-tumble days on the road or the dramatic battle scenes in *Hermanos!*, the author's acclaimed novel about the Spanish Civil War. Even so, Mr. Herrick's hobos, anarchists, squabbling immigrant families and striking factory workers are fine creations, and his depiction of the devastated America of the early 1930's is superb."

Herrick's next novel, *Bradovich*, was published in 1990. The title character is a former football player turned internationally celebrated sculptor who is placed under constant surveillance by a group called the Authority. The Authority's operatives appear throughout his daily life; they surprise him in the shower, interrupt the shows he's watching on television, and prevent him from leaving the city by keeping him from buying tickets from the local travel agency. No matter where he turns, Bradovich is confronted by the fact that his individual rights have become virtually nonexistent. James Kaufman, in the *Washington Post* (December 14, 1990), observed: "William Herrick's *Bradovich* is a vigorous and unrelenting parable, politically charged, that appears to have high on its agenda the reintroduction of Franz Kafka to today's literary audience. Given the various recent incursions on individual rights in our world, the ideological burden of this novel—the state can arbitrarily invade one's life at any moment—is quite timely."

Herrick's final book was a memoir. *Jumping the Line: The Adventures and Misadventures of an American Radical* (1998) recalls his life as a Communist, a volunteer in the Spanish Civil War, and a union organizer. More than any of his novels, the memoir reveals the extent of his misdeeds as a member of the Lincoln Brigade, including his involvement in the assassinations of political dissidents by the Communist Party. It reveals his later disavowal of his past attitudes, including his confessions before the House Committee on Un-American Activities. Dorothy Gallagher, in the *New York Times Book Review* (May 3, 1998), noted: "[In this] direct and unadorned memoir (Herrick is a plain speaker if no great stylist), he sets out to tell the full truth about his life as a Communist in Spain. At the center of his book he bravely places his shame, and shows us a deep sense of unease. . . . A terrible test of loyalty was set him [in Spain]. He was forced to witness the execution of three young Spanish revolutionaries. . . . 'I am standing there shaking with fear, with shame—oh, the shame of it,' Herrick writes. 'These are my comrades who are murdering my comrades.'" A. Hirsh wrote for *Choice* (October 1998), "Offered as part of the 'Wisconsin Studies in American Autobiography' series, this work by the novelist and longtime American radical (b. 1915) reads like an oral memory in which the memories are clearer the closer the writer nears the present. Memory, sometimes sketchy in details, serves the author, as opposed to research, in order to re-create his boyhood milieu. . . . After all, Herrick is a primary source. Readers will find fascinating these recollections of his ethnic heritage. . . . Born with the name Horvitz, the author grew up among socialists and communists, a distinction that is an overriding theme of this book. The bulk of the narrative discusses his experiences as a member of the Lincoln Brigade in the Spanish Civil War, and here, particularly, he emphasizes his ideological growth from dogma to reason."

William Herrick died on January 31, 2004 following a long illness. He is survived by his wife, Jeanette Esther Wellin, a sculptor and former psychologist whom he married on August 31, 1948, and their three children: Jonathan, Michael, and Lisa. (The Herricks also have four grandchildren.) His wife donated his body to the Albany Medical College, with the stipulation that the bullet lodged in his neck be returned to her. "He was a fighter to the very end, true to his own character, a curmudgeon," she told Paul Grondahl.

—C.M.

Suggested Reading: (Albany) *Times Union* B p4 Feb. 4, 2004; *Choice* p315 Oct. 1988; *Library Journal* p2,955 Sep. 1, 1969; *New York Times* (on-line) Feb. 9, 2004; *New York Times Book Review* p40 Apr. 23, 1967, p64 Oct. 26, 1969, p14 June 14, 1981, p7 June 16, 1985, p31 May 3, 1998; *Saturday Review* p23 Aug. 19, 1967; *Washington Post* B p3 Dec. 14, 1990; *Weekly Standard* (on-line) Mar. 15, 2004

Selected Books: *The Itinerant*, 1967; *Strayhorn*, 1968; *Hermanos!*, 1969; *Last to Die*, 1971; *Golcz*, 1976; *Shadows and Wolves*, 1980; *Love and Terror*, 1981; *Kill Memory*, 1983; *That's Life*, 1985; *Bradovich*, 1990; *Jumping the Line*, 1998

Hettche, Thomas

Nov. 30, 1964– Novelist

As a leading member of the second generation of postwar German writers, Thomas Hettche first became famous for his postmodernist storytelling techniques, but in his true-crime novel *Der Fall Arbogast* (2001), translated into English by Elizabeth Gaffney as *The Arbogast Case* (2003), Hettche eschewed flashy literary devices and offered readers a more straightforward story of a miscarriage of justice. The characters, according to Roger K. Miller, writing for the *Denver Post* (January 26, 2004), are fascinating rather than charming and serve "as expressions of a changing society under pressure" in "an excellent depiction of postwar Germany."

Thomas Hettche was born November 30, 1964 in Treis, a small town in the German region of Hesse (also called Hessen). He studied German and philosophy, earning the equivalent of a master's degree, in 1991, before going on to complete his doctorate in philosophy, in 1999. While completing his degree, he moved around within Germany, spending time in such cities as Stuttgart and Berlin, and also lived for periods in Italy, Poland, and the U.S.

Hettche made an impressive literary debut with his novel *Ludwig muß sterben* (which can be translated as "Ludwig must die," 1989). That novel and his succeeding books, *Inkubation* ("incubation," 1992), *Nox* (which takes its title from the Latin word for "night," 1995), and *Animationen* ("animations," 2000) gave Hettche a reputation as a postmodernist writer able to deploy a wealth of "literary fireworks," as Ulf Zimmermann wrote in a review of *Nox* for *World Literature Today* (Summer 1996).

Neil H. Donahue, reviewing *Inkubation* for *World Literature Today* (Autumn 1993), emphasized the stylistic uniformity of the book and noted that Hettche had described his philosophy of composition in *Inkubation* in one of the short burst of prose that make up the novel. Donahue argued, however, that "such cogitations only suggest the author's familiarity with some rudiments of literary theory. The derivative formalism, theoretical self-justifications, existentialist posturing, awkward metaphors, and the would-be-bold but in fact sophomoric treatment of sexuality . . . are all, to my mind, egregious pretensions that make the book seem half-baked, as if not long enough 'brooded' upon, as if the incubation of the title might have ended too soon."

Nox narrates some of the events of November 9, 1989, the night the Berlin Wall fell, signaling the reunification of Germany after more than four decades of being separated into East and West, communist and capitalist. The story the novel tells, built around a violent woman and the man who dies under her sexual ministrations, is clearly intended to be seen as a parable of Berlin and its reunification. According to a Greek myth Hettche invokes in the book, the sexes were once united as one being, only to be later split in two by the gods. The gods spared the newly formed creatures from extinction by creating reproductive organs. Humans were thus condemned to a constant effort to return to their unified state—much as Berlin, Hettche seems to warn, could be consumed by an attempt to heal. Zimmermann contended that Hettche's approach to the story "makes [the novel] seem too much an effort to construct a model text for apprentice deconstructionists."

The images of decaying and morbid flesh and Hettche's insistence on the links between sex and death continue in *Animationen*, a mingling of essays and illustrations—some of them frankly erotic, even pornographic—all associated to some degree with a narrative, possibly autobiographical, about a man's visit to Venice and the attentions he receives from a countess who is also his landlady. In a review for *World Literature Today* (Summer 2000), Theodore Ziolkowski called *Animationen* "accessibly and sometimes even wittily written" but somewhat disconnected. "Indeed," Ziolkowski concluded, "any unity that these free associations may have is provided in the last analysis solely by the consciousness of the author himself, who, for those curious enough to unfold the unusually thick dust jacket and examine its other side, gazes out somberly from a 16″ x 19″ photograph."

Following a more conventional narrative line than Hettche's previous books, *The Arbogast Case* is based on an actual event that occurred nearly 50 years before the book was published. Set in 1953 the novel tells the story of the traveling salesman Hans Arbogast, who one night has quick and violent sex with a hitchhiker—at the end of which the hitchhiker dies. Panicked, the married Arbogast hides her body and flees, only to later confess. Expecting, at worst, a charge of manslaughter, Arbogast is instead given a life sentence for murder, largely on the basis of the testimony of a prominent pathologist. Chris Lehmann, writing for the *Washington Post* (December 16, 2003), called the book a "legal procedural" that turns into "a bleak and existential meditation on the psychic toll that confinement in prison takes on a person, and a somewhat Kafkaesque tour through the detailed and harrowing business of getting a legal bureaucracy to admit a terrible mistake." For Charles Wilson, writing for the *New York Times Book Review* (December 21, 2003), *The Arbogast Case* is "a subtle psychological and historical drama dressed up in the garb of a legal thriller. . . . Hettche forces us to abandon rigid ideas of justice, morality and even redemption." Josh Cohen, writing for *Library Journal* (August 2003), felt that the "weighty issues" Hettche explores, such as "the fairness of the justice system, and the issue of whether Arbogast—like postwar Germany itself—is innocent or guilty" do not prevent the novel from being entertaining. For Lehmann, however, Hettche's emphasis on the system that draws Arbogast into despair means that "Hans Arbogast steadily ceases . . . to be not just a sympathetic character but really any sort of character; and the intransigent judicial system becomes, in yet another irony, the main source of the novel's dramatic interest."

Hettche's next novel, *Woraus wir gemacht sind* (which can be translated as "from which we are made," 2006), concerns a German couple who travel to the U.S. a year after the terrorist attacks of September 11, 2001.

In 1999, in preparation for the coming millennium, Hettche began an on-line literary forum called *Null*. After a year of writers posting their work or responding to the work of others, the site stopped collecting material, and in 2000 a book of the same title was published in Germany.

Since 2005 Hettche has lived in Berlin, Germany. He has a daughter, Antea, born in 1993.

—S.Y.

Suggested Reading: *Denver Post* F p13 Dec. 7, 2003; *Library Journal* p130+ Aug. 2003; *New York Times Book Review* Dec. 21, 2003; *Washington Post* C p4 Dec. 16, 2003; *World Literature Today* p812 Autumn 1993, p683 Summer 1996, p641 Summer 2000

Selected Books in English Translation: *The Arbogast Case* (2003)

Hicok, Bob

1960– Poet

Critics have frequently praised Bob Hicok for the truth embodied in his poetry. "While I was in school, I found myself upset by the recent literary theory that we can't really decide anything, that the ability to make decisions is a tenuous thing," Hicok noted in an interview with Kevin Lynch for the Madison, Wisconsin *Capital Times* (November 10, 1995). "I accept the consideration that we might be deluding ourselves. But if you can't be sure about anything, what harm is there to proceed with your best judgment to truth, till you know otherwise?"

Hicok's poetry covers a broad range of topics, including class, violence, racism, and family life. While assuming the guise of ordinary people—an old man contemplating his mortality, a young girl struggling with her self-image—Hicok presents the material of everyday life and confronts the moral dilemmas that go along with simply being alive. His work——direct and occasionally political— has received numerous awards, including the Felix Pollack Prize for his collection *The Legend of Light* (1995).

Hicok was born in 1960 and raised in a working-class family of seven. He has been publishing his poetry in such journals as the *American Poetry Review* and the *Kenyon Review* for the past decade. *The Legend of Light*, Hicok's first collection, received solid reviews. W.V. Davis, in *Choice* (May 1996), suggested: "Taken individually, some of the poems seem slight; too often they disappoint by failing to realize themselves fully. But this book sneaks up on the reader. In poems like 'AIDS' and 'Visiting the Wall,' . . . Hicok movingly documents some of the ceremonies of individual lives and deaths in ways that seem to make people mean differently—and better—than they did before he made his case with these words. As he says at the end of 'AIDS,' 'you love as you have to / and die the best you can.' Several of these poems will long burn in memory." Elizabeth Gaffney wrote for the *New York Times Book Review* (January 21 1996), "With both grace and apparent ease, Bob Hicok assumes a diverse array of personæ in this collection of poems: an old man gazing toward death and a young girl examining a painting, a blood-spattered doctor and a foundry worker gossiping with his crew. Each of Mr. Hicok's poems is marked by the exalted moderation of his voice—erudition without pretension, wisdom without pontification, honesty devoid of confessional melodrama. . . . His judicious eye imbues even the dreadful with beauty and meaning."

In his second collection, *Plus Shipping* (1998), Hicok focused on the eccentric: urban legends, weird characters, odd objects and historical figures. A reviewer for *Publishers Weekly* (September 28, 1998) wrote of the collection:

"Readers can follow Hicok's offhand and personable speaking voices and alter egos as they re-imagine *Citizen Kane*, meet a saddened UPS clerk, remember the Belgian bourgeois who purchased Magritte's house, or describe 'pyromancers fireworking / end-time,' 'a klatch of hardware gurus,' and a ghetto child who offers the author a piece of his rib."

Hicok's third collection, *Animal Soul* appeared in 2001. Shortly after it appeared, Hicok gave an interview to Dannye Romine for the *Charlotte Observer* (August 22, 2002). Romine had initially been attracted to Hicok's work by a poem titled "Sudden Movements," published in an issue of the *Georgia Review*. As quoted by Romine, the semi-autobiographical poem about an illness suffered by Hicok's father, contains the lines, "When he moves his head his eyes / get big as roses filled / with the commotion of Spring." Hicok explained to Romine that he had long wanted to write about his father's medical condition—"something with a long name I can never remember"—and "one day this poem came out." He continued, "One of the most interesting things about writing is how tied to a particular moment each poem is. Another day, I'd have written a different poem." He elaborated on his approach to poetry: "Typically, I sit down and go with the first things that comes to mind, that interests me when I read it. If I can get down three or four lines, I'll usually finish the poem. By then there's a rhythm to the poem. I have a sense of the subject, and most importantly, I'm curious [and] want to see how it comes out. Only rarely do I know what I want to write about, so most of what comes out surprises me." *Animal Soul* was a finalist for the National Book Critics Circle Award.

When Hicok published *Insomnia Diary* (2004), critics noted a new assurance in his writing. A reviewer for *Publishers Weekly* (February 23, 2004) remarked: "In his fourth collection, Hicok writes with a newfound maturity and an appealing lack of obsession with the self, examining the joys and pains (mostly pains) of ordinary others. As in earlier books, he chronicles a blue-collar life, a life in which 'no matter what happens you have to punch in.'" Writing for the *New York Times Book Review* (April 4, 2004), David Kirby noted that "ultimately the most potent ingredient in virtually every one of Bob Hicok's compact, well-turned poems is a laughter as old as humanity itself, a sweet waggery that suggests there's almost no problem that can't be solved by this poet's gentle humor."

In 2007 Hicok published *This Clumsy Living*, solidifying his reputation, Ilya Kaminsky wrote for *Library Journal* (December 1, 2006), for using "muscular, witty, and charming language." Kaminsky went on to write, "if poetry is a surrealist mechanism made of words, then this is a perfect poet. But is poetry such a mechanism? Though Hicok never misses a chance to make fun and to have fun, his poems offer a great deal more than ready playfulness. What elevates Hicok above many talented—but limited—pyrotechnists is his brave openness toward his (and our) feelings. . . . Ultimately, this collection works because it dwells on human experience and because at its best the language is charged with unforgettably lyrical wisdom."

Bob Hicok lives in Ann Arbor, Michigan. He has worked as an automotive-die designer, creating the molds that are used to produce car parts, and during the 2002–03 academic year, he was a visiting poet at Western Michigan University, in Kalamazoo.

—C.M.

Suggested Reading: *American Poetry Review* p36 Nov./ Dec. 2001; (Madison, Wisconsin) *Capital Times* Nov. 10, 1995; *Charlotte Observer* Aug. 22, 2002; *Choice* p1,478 May 1996; *Kenyon Review* p3+ Spring 2003; *New York Times Book Review* p21 Jan. 21, 1996, p20 Apr. 4, 2004; *Publishers Weekly* p98 Sep. 28, 1998, p67 Feb. 23, 2004

Selected Poetry Collections: *The Legend of Light*, 1995; *Plus Shipping*, 1998; *Animal Soul*, 2001; *Insomnia Diary*, 2004; *This Clumsy Living*, 2007

Chip Somodevilla/Getty Images

Hillenbrand, Laura

1967– Journalist; nonfiction writer

Laura Hillenbrand had been writing about thoroughbred racing for some of the nation's most popular magazines for more than a decade before she published her best-selling book *Seabiscuit* (2001). Much like the titular character of that nonfiction work, Hillenbrand overcame adversity to achieve critical and popular success: plagued with chronic fatigue syndrome (CFS), a disease that makes it almost impossible for her to leave her home, she spent most of the four years it took to write *Seabiscuit* working from her sickbed. "The subjects that I've written about—the men and the horse—were radically different individuals, but the one thread that pulls through all of their lives and through the events that they lived through together is this struggle between overwhelming

hardship and the will to overcome it," she told Jennifer Frey for the *Washington Post* (March 9, 2001). "It's a central theme in this book, and it is the central struggle of my life as well."

Born in 1967 in Fairfax, Virginia, and raised in Maryland, Hillenbrand enjoyed writing as a child. "For me, being a writer was never a choice. I was born one," she told Anne A. Simpkinson in an interview for the Beliefnet Web site (May 21, 2001). "All through my childhood I wrote short stories and stuffed them in drawers. I wrote on everything. I didn't do my homework so I could write." She also loved horses and had dreams of becoming a jockey. In 1987, however, while she was attending Kenyon College, in Ohio, Hillenbrand developed CFS, which forced her to drop out of school. "I had difficulties with just about everyone taking it seriously at first," she told Frey. "I definitely had a lot of problems with people thinking that this is some sort of hypochondria or some sort of willful attempt to get attention." The effects of her condition were crippling: plagued by exhaustion, vertigo, and other incapacitating symptoms, Hillenbrand became physically unable to leave her bed. She told Simpkinson, "I've spent about 6 of the last 14 years completely bedridden."

In 1988, after her health had improved a little, she was watching the Kentucky Derby when she became inspired to try writing again. In the years that followed, Hillenbrand, when not incapacitated by her illness, produced articles, primarily on history and thoroughbred racing. Her work appeared in such media outlets as *Equus, Talk,* and *Thoroughbred Times.* Recalling a favorite book from her childhood entitled *Come On Seabiscuit,* Hillenbrand researched the story of the real-life horse, uncovering a wealth of intriguing information. In 1998 she published a story about Seabiscuit in *American Heritage.* The piece won Hillenbrand the Eclipse Award for magazine writing, the highest honor among journalists covering thoroughbred racing; she also received numerous offers from publishing houses to lengthen the piece into a book, and Hollywood movie producers sought to purchase the rights to adapt the story to film. Hillenbrand soon signed with Random House and sold the movie rights to Universal and Larger Than Life Productions.

Seabiscuit, which takes place during the Great Depression, chronicles the horse's unlikely rise from obscurity to superstardom, a journey that culminates in Seabiscuit's famous match against his archrival, War Admiral, in 1938. The event, which pitted racing fans from the West Coast against fans from the East Coast, was one of the decade's biggest sporting events. The main characters in the book are Seabiscuit's caretakers: his jockey, Red Pollard, who was an unlucky former boxer with a shock of red hair, a drinking problem, and an affinity for Shakespeare; his owner, Charles Howard, who was a self-made millionaire who built his fortune selling Buicks in California at the dawn of the automobile age; and his trainer, Tom Smith, who was a reticent, rugged westerner who spent decades developing his horse sense on ranches and at hardscrabble rodeos and race tracks.

The famously fastidious critic Michiko Kakutani, writing for the *New York Times* (March 6, 2001), described *Seabiscuit* as "an absorbing book that stands as the model of sportswriting at its best. . . . Hillenbrand gives us a visceral appreciation of [thoroughbred racing] as refracted through the tumultuous lives of Seabiscuit and his

human companions, while at the same time creating a keenly observed portrait of a Depression-era America bent on escapism and the burgeoning phenomenon of mass-media-marketed celebrity." Jesse Birnbaum wrote for *Time* (April 2, 2001), "Hillenbrand's prose is often breathless and overwrought, but readers should ride this one to the wire." *Seabiscuit* sold more than 2.5 million copies and was on the *New York Times* best-seller list for almost two years. The movie adaptation of *Seabiscuit* was released to popular acclaim in the summer of 2003.

Hillenbrand currently lives in Washington, D.C., with her longtime companion, Borden Flanagan. Since the publication of *Seabiscuit*, Hillenbrand has, most notably, written a personal account of her struggle with CFS for the *New Yorker* and served as a consultant on the motion picture *Seabiscuit*.

—P.B.M.

Suggested Reading: Beliefnet Web site; *New York Times* E p7 Mar. 6, 2001, E p1 July 25, 2003; *New Yorker* p56 July 7, 2003; *Newsweek* p54 July 28, 2003; *Washington Post* C p1 March 9, 2001

Selected Books: *Seabiscuit*, 2001

Him, Chanrithy

June 4, 1965– Memoirist

Chanrithy Him is the author of the noted memoir *When Broken Glass Floats: Growing Up Under the Khmer Rouge* (2000). When Him was nine years old, in April 1975, the Khmer Rouge, an organization of communist guerilMas, seized power in Cambodia in the aftermath of the war in Southeast Asia. The leader of the Khmer Rouge, Pol Pot, established a dictatorship and ruthlessly implemented his schemes to establish a utopian society in Cambodia that would be classless, agrarian, and free of Western influences. He evacuated cities, closed schools, banks, and factories, and forced large numbers of people onto collective farms that were essentially labor camps. Many civilians were executed or died of starvation. By the time Pol Pot's rule was overthrown, in early 1979, by invading Vietnamese troops, an estimated 1.5 million Cambodians had died—out of a population that had previously numbered about seven million. Him lost both of her parents and five brothers and sisters. In 1981 Him and the surviving members of her family came to live in the United States with one of her uncles, who had escaped Cambodia before the Khmer Rouge took power. Still haunted by nightmares and painful memories that she preferred to forget, Him was encouraged to write as a form of therapy by a university

Courtesy of Ohio University

counselor. Him's memoir, *When Broken Glass Floats*, recalls her childhood memories in a land swept by evil, where she and her family struggled to carry on amid hunger, disease, terror, and death. "Throughout a childhood dominated by war, I learned to survive," she wrote in the preface. "In a country faced with drastic changes, the core of my soul was determined to never let the horrific situations take away the better part of me. I mentally resisted forces I could only recognize as evil by being a human recorder, quietly observing my surroundings, making mental notes of the things around me. There would come a day to share them, giving my voice to children who can't speak for themselves. Giving voice, as well, to my deceased parents, sisters, brothers, and extended family members, and to those whose remains are in unmarked mass graves scattered throughout Cambodia, the once-gentle land."

Chanrithy Him submitted the following statement to *World Authors 2000–2005*:

"Born on June 4, 1965, in the Takeo province that borders South Vietnam, my life is forever affected by the Vietnam War that had already begun near Cambodia's doorstep. On a night in 1968 my mother, whom I called *Mak*, excitedly hurried my older siblings and me out of our living room to see a comet. On the balcony, our excitement rose like the mercury in a hot sun as *Mak* lifted me up to see the heavenly star with a long, luminous tail. A moment later her joy seemed to fade—even a child could feel it.

"She told us of an old folk superstition: When the tail of the comet pointed to a particular place, Cambodia would be drawn into war with that country. The word 'war' about which I wondered came crushing down on us in 1969, when the already raging war spilled over into Cambodia.

"We fled to Phnom Penh. When we returned to Takeo, our two-story stucco home was bombed. I remember tugging at my father's hand asking him to take me away from this dead home as he surveyed it. While *Pa* and *Mak* considered rebuilding, *Mak*'s uncle let us stay with his family in their home overlooking the Bassac River.

"In 1969, it was over this river that I witnessed the silhouettes of planes my father called *B-cinquante-deux*. [American B-52 jets flew on numerous bombing raids over Cambodia during the Vietnam War.] Before we could see them, the explosions they caused shook our home, our beds. We crowded against the front window, helplessly watching them charging from the dark skies, dropping sequins of light with each one spitting out a loud explosion, forming a huge mushroom of smoke mixed with fire.

"*Pa* said some civilians died from direct hits and others died from the intense heat created by the bombs. Adults talked about villagers fleeing their homes, staggering up the river bank. Deprived of our sheltered home, my playground was now on the street, along the river. As *Mak* was overwhelmed with her pregnancy, I, four years old at the time, let my curiosity take me to the river bank. There, standing by the railing, I watched the distressed families dock their boats.

"My older brother, Chantharitheavy, and prematurely born brother, Bosaba, died from lacking access to proper medical care.

"In 1972 we moved into a house in Phnom Penh. Here, we found some comfort in the safety of the distance that separated us from the fighting in the outlying provinces. My older siblings and I re-enrolled in public schools.

"On April 17, 1975, the growing Khmer Rouge, which thrived in part on the tumultuous political instabilities brought on by the Vietnam War, took over Cambodia. They emptied the cities. Two million people in Phnom Penh, including my family, were forced out. On foot, my family headed to *Pa*'s birthplace, called Year Piar, a village on the outskirts of Takeo, carrying a few belongings and food supplies. At nine, I thought that when the Khmer Rouge won, there would be no more killings as I would hear reported on the radio or TV. But little did I know or understand about the other kind of war that would later be waged against my father and uncles, who had worked for the former government of Lon Nol.

"An idealist, *Pa* revealed his and my uncles' professions to the Khmer Rouge. He believed that the Khmer Rouge wouldn't just take the country, but would also save the people. Khmer officials brought ox carts to take him and my uncles for an orientation. It started with an excavation, what would become their grave. *Pa* denounced the Khmer Rouge as a *traitor*. They killed him instantly. Unbeknownst to him, I tearfully made a calendar marking the remaining days of when he would return.

"*Pa*'s death was just the beginning. The Khmer Rouge ordered us to leave Year Piar. On a humid, sunny day, hundreds of people and my family were loaded onto a train as rifles were pointed at us. They separated family members, brushing off our miserable cries. They didn't kill us that day, but dumped us in the woods. We built our own hut and shared it with another family, separated in the middle by a wall of thatch. Our food rations continued to diminish. With little food, a lack of sanitation surrounding this makeshift village, and with no proper medical care, my baby brother, Vin, and young sister, Avy, died. *Mak* was next, then my oldest sister Chea, whom I idolized.

"Before her death, I asked her questions, one of which was in the hope of understanding our pain and the loss of those I loved. "Chea, how come good doesn't win over evil? Why did the Khmer Rouge win if they are bad people?"

"Chea's answer became the seed of my survival. She said, "Loss will be God's, victory will be the devil's." When good appears to lose, it is an opportunity for one to be patient, and become like God. "But not very long, *p'yoon srey* [young sister]," she explained, referring to a Cambodian proverb about what happens when good and evil are thrown together into the river of life. Good is symbolized by *klok*, a type of squash, and evil by *armbaeg*, shards of broken glass. "The good will win over evil. Now *klok* sinks, and broken glass floats. But *armbaeg* will not float long. Soon *klok* will float instead, and then the good will prevail."

"As I was growing up in the Khmer Rouge labor camps, the death of each of my family members compounded my own powerlessness, my pain. To cope with the loss of Chea, who died of a prolonged fever and deprivation, I promised her in my own mind that I would become a doctor if I survived, to help people medically because I couldn't help her.

"On January 7, 1979, the Vietnamese invaded Cambodia and installed a new government. I reunited with my remaining siblings—Chantara, Channary, Chanthan, and Phalkundarith.

"Due to drought and food shortage, we migrated to a makeshift camp near Thailand. Later we were brought inside a refugee camp after a Khmer Rouge attack. Fortunately, we learned of a relative, Uncle Seng, who lived in Portland, Oregon. He sponsored us, along with our adopted sister, Savorng, and Chantara's husband, Vantha, and their baby, Syla, to come to Portland. On November 14, 1981, we touched down at the Portland International Airport.

"In 1982, at age 16, I resumed my education as a freshman at Cleveland High School. Despite lacking formal schooling for seven years, I managed to graduate with honors and a GPA of 3.7. Before my graduation on June 2, 1985, my confidence grew even more. I was awarded a summer internship in biochemistry, working as a research assistant for the Portland School of Dentistry.

"I was ready for college and chose Brigham Young University, Hawaii Campus, after a friend told me about it. There, I imagined it would be warm like Cambodia. I would not get sick with flu or cold as I would in Oregon. I figured I couldn't afford to miss school since I would be in a pre-med program.

"But there were unwelcome surprises, triggered by the tropical climate, the young mango leaves swaying in the sun. . . . I was homesick; however, I excelled in my classes until I had to read George Orwell's *1984* and *Animal Farm*.

"The former began to trigger nightmares related to the Khmer Rouge regime and then the latter compounded everything. I told my teacher that I would stop reading the books. I was sadly shocked to learn of the similarities in these books with my own traumatic experiences. My teacher mentioned my history to my seemingly bored classmates and students from other classes who were also reading these novels. Everyone was curious as to who I was, making these novels more interesting to them than ever before.

"Later a BYU school counselor encouraged me to write a book to let the painful memories out of my system. In the spring of 1986, after I applied for a transfer to the University of Oregon, I returned to Portland. I began taking notes of whatever memories easily came to me. At UO, I transferred these memories onto papers for writing assignments. Joan Mariner, my English composition instructor, told me that I was a natural storyteller—but I wanted to be a doctor!

"In 1999, after my literary agent sold my book proposal to Norton, Amy Cherry, my editor at Norton, said that my memories added so much color to my story. "Would you like to work together? . . ."

"On April 17, 2000, marking the 25th anniversary of the Khmer Rouge takeover of Cambodia, *When Broken Glass Floats: Growing Up Under the Khmer Rouge* was released internationally to wide acclaim. It won the Oregon Book Award for literary nonfiction and was a finalist for the Kiriyama Pacific Rim Book Prize.

"Since its publication, through personal appearances internationally, I have brought the gift of storytelling with a touch of spunk, good-natured teasing, humor, and love. "Unbroken Spirit" was what I was told I have. Now it's the title of the sequel. Joan Mariner was right!"

Chanrithy Him was one of many Cambodian immigrants at Cleveland High School, in Portland. "Most of our scars were well hidden, set aside in our battle for academic success," Him recalled in *When Broken Glass Floats.* "Out of forty students at Cleveland High School who lived under Pol Pot, half were diagnosed with PTSS [Post Traumatic Stress Syndrome], and half suffered from some form of depression." Dan Dickason, a teacher of English as a second language (ESL), was initially skeptical of many of the stories that the students told him about the things that had gone on in their home country a decade earlier. Dickason became convinced, however, after he watched a news broadcast display a mountain of human skulls in Cambodia, the remains of some of those who had perished under the Khmer Rouge. Dickason brought psychiatrists to the school to interview the students and provide them with counseling. Him was unwilling to participate, preferring to leave her past behind. In 1989 Dr. William Sack, one of the psychiatrists and a professor with the Department of Child Psychiatry at Oregon Health and Science University (OHSU), in Portland, recruited Him to assist in a project that was sponsored by the National Institute of Mental Health, studying PTSS in Cambodian refugees. Him acted as interpreter and interviewed many of the participants. As part of her training, Him had to watch films about the genocide in Cambodia. One such film was *The Killing Fields* (1984); "After a few minutes, I stormed out," Him recalled in her book. "I remember taking refuge in the women's restroom, leaning against the wall and weeping. For the first time in years, I had allowed myself to feel the pain of the past that was buried in my soul." Him found that interviewing survivors triggered her own painful memories. "As a researcher, my job was to be a cultural voyeur," she wrote. "I was to use my knowledge of Cambodian customs, culture, and my own wartime experiences to establish a common ground with other refugees. In theory, they would be more comfortable talking to someone who knew what they had endured. It was a strange role for me. In conducting psychiatric interviews, I was both the insider, who knew their trauma, and the outsider, the dispassionate, clinical researcher." Him added that the process of "efficiently recording details . . . jogged so many of my own harsh memories. Unlike during my training experience, I couldn't run away and take sanctuary in a restroom. I couldn't stop listening when subjects' and their parents' or guardians' distressing stories awakened my emotions. My job was to listen, to record answers, and continue to ask questions, pressing until some of these people broke down as they confronted things that had been successfully repressed." (Him eventually earned a B.S. degree in biochemistry from the University of Oregon, in Eugene.)

Him's book, *When Broken Glass Floats: Growing Up Under the Khmer Rouge*, was published in 2000. In the memoir, Him relates her family background and early childhood memories before moving on to recount the horrific experiences she and her family suffered during the years of Pol Pot's rule. In a review of the book for Amazon.com, Chloe Byrne called it "remarkable for both its unflinching honesty and its refusal to despair. In wrenchingly immediate prose, [Him] describes atrocities the rest of the world might prefer to ignore. . . . And yet what emerges most strongly from this memoir is the triumph of life." Reviewing both *When Broken Glass Floats* and Loung Ung's book, *First They Killed My Father: A Daughter of Cambodia Remembers* (2000), for the *New York Times* (April 19, 2000), Richard Bernstein noted, "Neither of these writers speculate on why the French-educated Khmer Rouge leaders, who seized power after a long guerilla war, forged a regime in which cruelty and murder become revolutionary values. But they do tell, graphically enough so that it is sometimes difficult to keep on reading, what it meant to be in the way of those values in the years that they prevailed in Cambodia." Bernstein added that "these two books by two intelligent and morally aware young women tell us what it was like to struggle while others played out utopian dreams above them." In the journal *War, Literature, and the Arts* (2002, Volume 14, Numbers 1 and 2), David M. Kirkham hailed Him's book. "Perhaps not since Anne Frank's diary has there been as stirring an account of a young girl's efforts to survive and thrive in a world torn apart by terror as Chanrithy Him's *When Broken Glass Floats*," Kirkham wrote. "Him's style is to state facts directly and to understate emotions, in such a way that resonates truth without recourse to hyperbole and rhetorical flourishes." The reviewer concluded that the book "is simply and hauntingly powerful. Born in a country where literacy was once a death warrant, her writing reminds us what reading can do to

preserve those institutions most likely to protect the human spirit, mind and body."

Chanrithy Him works as a medical interpreter with Oregon Health and Services University, serving as a translator for Cambodian patients. She frequently lectures around the country and performs classical Cambodian dance. "Some people hear only about war [in Cambodia]," Him explained to Chris Higashi, a contributor to the *International Examiner* (September 3, 1997). "We have many beautiful things in our culture. I want to show people that all Cambodians are not warlike people. People look at Cambodia differently when they see my dances because it is so different from what they see in the news."

Him, who is single, lives in Eugene, Oregon. She is working on a sequel to *When Broken Glass Floats*, tentatively titled "Unbroken Spirit." She is currently shopping around a screenplay adaptation of her first book.

—D.C.

Suggested Reading: *Buffalo News* H p1+ Oct. 15, 2000; *International Examiner* p8+ Sep. 3, 1997; *New York Times* E p1 Apr. 19, 2000; *War, Literature, and the Arts*, 2002

Selected Books: *When Broken Glass Floats: Growing Up Under the Khmer Rouge*, 2000

Hollander, Paul

Oct. 3, 1932– Nonfiction writer; sociologist

Paul Hollander survived the Holocaust during World War II and then a repressive Communist regime in his native Hungary to build a successful career as a sociologist and writer in the United States. Among the topics Hollander has addressed in his numerous scholarly essays and books are communism in Eastern Europe and the former Soviet Union, anti-Americanism, and Western intellectuals' alienation from their own societies. Jay Nordlinger, writing for the *National Review Online* (July 22, 2004), placed Hollander among "the scholars and writers in the West who told the truth about Communism, often at tremendous cost to themselves," and identified him as "a nearly all-purpose sociologist and intellectual, ranging far and wide. Few subjects in politics and social affairs seem to have escaped his attention. Hollander is as trenchant a commentator on O. J. Simpson as he is on [the former North Korean leader] Kim Il Sung. He dissects feminism, affirmative action, and various follies of the intellectuals, as well as Communism and its aftermath (in those places that are lucky enough to have an aftermath, rather than Communism itself). He would be called a conservative—not inaccurately—but he is not a pigeon-holable conservative."

Paul Hollander submitted the following statement to *World Authors 2000–2005*:

"My choice of sociology as a field of study and subsequent profession was not the culmination of carefully nurtured aspirations, of the desire to serve humanity by becoming a virtuous critic of social injustice, or becoming a hard-nosed scientist tracking social facts and rules of life. There was nonetheless a lurking hope that in this occupation I could eventually shed some light on the many puzzling and disturbing aspects of social existence and especially the horrific results of political conflict and the associated dehumanization I was privileged to experience first hand in my native country, Hungary, between 1944 and 1956.

"My original, early interests were literary and had I been able to attend university in Hungary I would have studied English and Hungarian or Russian and Hungarian literature leading to the position of high school teacher. The elite high school, or *gymnasium* I attended in Budapest was a major influence on my intellectual development and aspirations. By the standards of comparable American institutions it was an extremely demanding institution; there were virtually no electives; requirements included years of Latin, Russian (as well as one other foreign language before this requirement was abolished), mathematics, geometry, algebra, chemistry, biology, zoology/botany, Hungarian literature, world literature, history, art history and physical education. Homework was abundant as were in-class tests. A much feared comprehensive written and oral examination covering several years of learning and lasting for several days concluded the attendance of the *gymnasium*. Most graduates went on to university. While not everybody in my classes was bookish there were enough of us who took pride in reading books not required in school constituting a small subculture not held in contempt by the 'jocks.' The pursuit of popularity characteristic of American high schools was absent from our sex-segregated institution.

"Although initially admitted to the University of Budapest (to study Russian and Hungarian literature) I had no chance to attend since in 1951 (just after finishing the *gymnasium*) I was deported with my family to a small village designated as a 'forced place of residence' for groups defined by the authorities as politically suspect. In our case this was due to the social status of my maternal grandfather, who used to be a businessman before the communist government confiscated his properties. Upon reaching draft age I was placed into a so-called 'building battalion' for the politically unreliable who were not given military training. I escaped in late November 1956 after the defeat of the Revolution by the invading Soviet forces.

"I was one of 300 Hungarian refugee students British universities admitted and supported in the wake of the 1956 Revolution. I had a wide range of choices and I could just as easily have picked political science, social psychology, cultural anthropology or contemporary history and probably would have ended up writing the kind of books I wrote as a certified sociologist. Becoming a sociologist has not been a major source of my professional-intellectual identity.

"The major political-historical events and experiences influencing my professional-sociological leanings were World War II, the Jewish persecution in 1944, the imposition of communist rule between 1948 and 1953, and the Hungarian Revolution of 1956. Each impressed on me the large part played by intolerance, aggression, violence, and irrationality in human affairs. These experiences also implanted seeds of skepticism toward theoretical schemes in sociology that emphasized consensus and rational conflict resolution. By the same token I also became dubious about visions of utopia, of sweeping revolutionary transformation and the possibility of dramatically improving human nature entertained by the social protest movements during the 1960s in the United States.

"While surviving the persecution of Jews in Hungary and experiencing (and later escaping) Soviet style communism were truly formative experiences, the former did not show up in my work. Rather than incorporating and reflecting the truly traumatic experiences of the Jewish persecution much of my work came to focus on Soviet totalitarianism, communist systems and ideologies and the attraction the latter held for Western intellectuals. The reasons for this preoccupation were far from self-evident since the communist regime in Hungary was not life threatening. The explanation lies in the fact that I came to the realization (especially after escaping from Hungary) that the moral and historical issue of Nazism has been settled. No decent, respectable, or moderately intelligent person would defend Nazism or try to minimize its misdeeds. Nobody writing about Nazism was ever cautioned about the danger of making value-judgments, unlike those writing about communist systems; refugees from Nazi Germany or former inmates of Nazi concentration camps were not considered unreliable witnesses by leading Western intellectuals (as were for example the Cambodian refugees under Pol Pot by Noam Chomsky). The condemnation of Nazism was (or seemed) universal, at any rate in the West. (I did not know about the popularity of the *Protocols of Zion* in Arab countries.) By contrast there was a lively debate about the nature of communist systems and their supporting ideas—a debate that has persisted even after the collapse of Soviet communism in 1991. Many distinguished Western intellectuals have remained impressed by the apparent good intentions of these systems and believed that their unfortunate deformations had nothing to do with their sublime theoretical-ideological foundations. Consequently and correspondingly I became 'energized' (as my friend, the late Stanley Milgram put it) by what struck me as the ignorance, wishful thinking and self-deception I discerned among many Western intellectuals. The major product of these sentiments was *Political Pilgrims*, the best known and most widely reviewed of all my publications.

"To this day these issues remain intellectually and morally unsettled and many idealistic Western intellectuals remain impressively uninformed about communist systems (extinct and surviving). They are also inclined to detect a moral equivalence between the failings of Western democratic-capitalist countries and far more detestable systems and movements around the world. Seeking to contribute to public enlightenment about such matters I put together a rather large volume about repression in communist states utilizing excerpts from the personal recollections of those who experienced such mistreatment. This book remained for many years unpublished for want of interested publishers. [The book appeared in 2006 as *From the Gulag to the Killing Fields: Personal Accounts of Political Violence and Repression in Communist States*.]

"My professional and personal interests were not limited to political and sociological matters. My longstanding interest in literature found expression in my doctoral dissertation, which (unusually for a sociologist) was based on the analysis of novels (Soviet and Hungarian socialist realist types) which I used as sources of information about the prevailing official political values and ideals of human nature in these societies. My literary interest found further expression in the sociology of literature course I taught from the beginning to the end of my teaching career. While for the most part it consisted of an examination of how literary works (novels) reflect and deal with major human preoccupations, problems and social realities, it also provided opportunities for discussing many of my favorite authors, classics as well as contemporary ones. I intend to write a book rooted in this course.

"Not surprisingly, given my background and comparative perspectives on matters social and political, I have been a critic of the attitudes and beliefs designated as 'political correctness' and the cognate entity labeled as the 'adversary culture.' I also wrote and edited books about anti-Americanism, probing its irrational aspects while fully recognizing the social, historical, and cultural roots and explanations of the phenomenon. At the same time I have also been critical of many aspects of American culture and society, especially of popular culture (including the celebrity cult), the fluctuations between moral relativism and absolutism, the excesses of individualism and the excesses of egalitarianism as well as of anti-intellectual tendencies and certain naive American beliefs about the solubility of all human and social problems.

"This sketch of my background and beliefs explains my perceived status as an outsider. Thus I cannot say without hesitation that I am 'American.' My Hungarian accent, if nothing else reminds me that I am not. It doesn't however follow, that I have a strong Hungarian (or Jewish) identity although I speak Hungarian fluently and without an accent. When I visit Hungary (something I do almost every year since the 1980s) I do not feel that it is the place where I 'belong.'

"Likewise I had no such feelings on my visit to Israel in 1968. All of which suggests that I qualify for the designation 'rootless cosmopolitan' devised by the Soviet ideological commissar, Andrei Zhadanov. But being an outsider in this tolerant society has not been uncomfortable or stressful, quite to the contrary. I am particularly satisfied with living in New England (western Massachusetts) and feel strongly attached to it.

"Although, as noted above, I drifted into sociology in a casual, unpremeditated way, I found it to provide opportunities for what I enjoy to do— reading, writing and reflecting. My writings express beliefs I never sought to hide but I also believe that a degree of impartiality is attainable and there is a social and human reality that is independent of our perceptions and preferences. I think poorly of postmodernism and the numerous similar academic fads and fashions of the past few decades conveyed usually in impenetrable jargon.

"In retirement, writing, reading and outdoors activities (hiking, kayaking and cross country skiing) remain my major activities. I am an ardent environmentalist with a strong aversion to SUVs. I consider their popularity a discouraging reflection of many things wrong with American society and the tastes, needs and judgments of its members."

Paul Hollander was born on October 3, 1932 in Budapest, Hungary. In 1944 Nazi Germany invaded his country. The Nazis and their fascist collaborators in Hungary began arresting Jews and deporting them to the Nazi death camps. Hollander and his family hid in Budapest until the Soviet troops liberated Hungary, in January 1945. "In the beginning during 1945–47, I was attracted to the Communist Party because it was closely identified with the Soviet Union," Hollander recalled in an essay published in his book *Discontents: Postmodern and Postcommunist* (2002). "I had warm feelings toward the Soviet Union because it was the Soviet Army which liberated Hungary from the Nazi troops and a pro-Nazi political system which engaged in rounding up and killing the Jews." As a student Hollander participated in the communist youth movement at his high school. One time Hollander and his fellow students were called to testify against one of their teachers who had made disparaging comments about the Soviet troops who occupied Hungary. The teacher was found guilty and sentenced to 18 months in prison for slander. Discussing his participation in that incident, Hollander wrote in *Discontents* that it "was not an episode I can look back on with pride and satisfaction." Hollander's enthusiasm for communism and the Soviet Union evaporated after a repressive, pro-Soviet communist government took power in 1948. In *Discontents* Hollander recalled how the new government changed the country: "The school curriculum changed, Western movies were no longer shown and few Western books were published. The compulsory public veneration of [the Soviet dictator Joseph] Stalin and his Hungarian disciple Mathias Rákosi reached new heights. Even more ominous were the political trials in which the accused were coerced into making fantastic self-incriminating confessions."

After escaping Hungary during the unsuccessful revolt against Soviet rule in 1956, Hollander was admitted to the U.K. as a refugee and received financial support that allowed him to pursue his higher education. In 1959 he graduated with honors from the prestigious London School of Economics and Political Science, receiving his bachelor's degree in sociology. Hollander then went to the U.S. to continue his education. In 1960 he earned his master's degree in sociology from the University of Illinois, in Urbana-Champaign. Hollander then enrolled at Princeton University, in New Jersey, receiving a second master's degree in sociology, in 1962, and his doctorate in sociology, in 1963.

In 1963 Hollander joined the faculty of Harvard University, in Cambridge, Massachusetts, as an assistant professor of sociology. After five years at Harvard, Hollander moved to the University of Massachusetts, in Amherst, in 1968, beginning there as an associate professor of sociology before being promoted to full professor six years later. Hollander's association with Harvard's Davis Center for Russian and Eurasian Studies (originally the Russian Research Center) dates to 1963, when he started as a research fellow; he later became an associate, a position he still holds.

In 1969 Hollander edited *American and Soviet Society: A Reader in Comparative Sociology and Perception*, a collection of articles by Russian and American sociologists on such topics as the family, alcoholism, and juvenile delinquency. A critic for *Choice* (December 1969) described the book as a "unique collection of Soviet and American sociological writings by an impressive array of authorities." The reviewer observed that the "selections are well chosen, highly readable, and well translated (some of the Russian ones appear in English here for the first time). A lengthy general introduction and shorter introductions to each section provide the needed integrative device."

Hollander's next book, *Soviet and American Society: A Comparison* (1973), compared social conditions in the U.S. and the Soviet Union by analyzing a wide range of factors and trends, including religion, education, the treatment of the elderly and ethnic minorities, and crime. "The principle conclusion of this massive comparative study of the institutions, values and practices of the American and Soviet societies of the 1960s and 1970s is depressing," a writer for the *Economist* asserted. "[Neither] Russia nor America can look forward to an especially bright future. According to Professor Hollander . . . things are going to get worse rather than better in both countries. . . . Even those who may disagree with the gloomy predictions offered in this book will find much that is both instructive and fascinating in the huge amount of evidence that its author has collected in support of his thesis."

In *Political Pilgrims: Travels of Western Intellectuals to the Soviet Union, China, and Cuba* (1981), Hollander examined the motivations of prominent journalists, artists, and political activists, including the French existentialist philosopher Jean-Paul Sartre and the British playwright George Bernard Shaw, who have visited communist countries over the decades and praised conditions and life there—contrary to the realities of state persecution and economic misery. Hollander found that, for the most part, many of these intellectuals were alienated from their own societies and perceived communist countries as providing serious utopian alternatives. For the *American Scholar* (Autumn 1982), James Hitchcock wrote: "There are few surprises in the book, but it is nonetheless extremely thorough, well argued, and well written. Hollander shows that the reaction of these people has not been the result of an occasional personal aberration but has been consistent and according to pattern—almost predictable in its forms. What he also shows, although he does not belabor the point, is that it cannot be excused as mere naivete. Most people who sent back glowing reports of the Red experiments were deceived because they wanted to be deceived." In the *American Historical Review* (June 1982), Robert Booth Fowler was also impressed with the book. "*Political Pilgrims* has three strengths that taken together make it a good book," Fowler observed. "Hollander writes well and his tale often makes intriguing, if sad, reading. Although some readers will not find his analysis plausible, the presentation is undoubtedly stimulating. Second, it effectively weaves together disparate periods and thinkers to fashion a remarkably coherent and clear result. Third, it is a bold essay. Writing this book took guts, since it attacks so many intellectual and political parties." Fowler concluded that *Political Pilgrims* "is an interesting book, bold in its critiques and fascinating in its documentation of the romance between (some) intellectuals and Marxist authoritarian regimes."

In 1983 Hollander published *The Many Faces of Socialism: Essays in Comparative Sociology and Politics*, a collection of articles discussing life in various communist countries. The book includes Hollander's account of a visit to his native Hungary, as well as essays on such subjects as communist governments' use of border controls and the "problem," as authorities in China viewed it, of love in a centrally planned state where everyone's primary loyalty is supposed to be to the state. Ivan Szelenyi for *Contemporary Sociology* (May 1984) wrote: "This is a bitter book. Hollander is skeptical about the future of the world; he feels that most kremlinologists do not understand the danger the Soviet Union represents, and he despises the intelligentsia for its prosocialism and anti-Americanism. . . . This is also a conservative book. Hollander was a neoconservative before the label was invented, and there is an astonishing consistency in his political views. Finally, this is a powerful book. It presents the neoconservative view as credibly as it can be presented. Though I dislike his politics I admire the consistency of his reasoning, and I read with great pleasure his fine, ironic analyses of the intelligentsia and the paradoxes of East European life."

Another collection of Hollander's essays, *The Survival of the Adversary Culture: Social Criticism and Political Escapism in American Society*, appeared in 1988. In these essays Hollander discusses the open hostility that many academics, artists, religious figures, and intellectuals appear to have for American culture and politics. In his review for *Academic Questions* (Winter 1989/1990), Theodore S. Hamerow was impressed with most of the pieces in the book. "The author contends that the disillusionment of the educated classes of America with the political and social system of their country does not derive from disagreement with any particular policy its government may be pursuing," Hamerow asserts. "It reflects, rather, a deep-rooted alienation of an emotional or psychological nature that finds expression in a persuasive attitude of civic disagreement. Thus a perceptive article, 'The Antiwar Movement and the Critiques of American Society' maintains that it was not the conflict in Vietnam that turned a large part of the intelligentsia against established values, but rather the rejection of established values that fed opposition to the war."

In 1992 Hollander published two books, *Decline and Discontent: Communism and the West Today* and *Anti-Americanism: Critiques at Home and Abroad: 1965–1990*. In the first book, a collection of previously published articles and original essays, Hollander examined why many left-wing intellectuals in the West remained devoted to socialist ideas despite the collapse of communism. R.J. Mitchell, writing for *Choice* (October 1992), called Hollander's argument "penetrating and convincing," but felt that the book "as a whole lacks the cohesiveness and incisiveness of the introduction and epilogue, which are stirring defenses of Western democratic culture." In *Anti-Americanism* Hollander documented what he

believed to be the irrational hostility to the United States on the part of many left-wing authors, journalists, churches, and the entertainment industry. In the *New York Times* (January 2, 1992), Herbert Mitgang dismissed *Anti-Americanism*, writing, "The author's main failure is that he confuses 200 years of devoted, and often idealistic, American self-criticism in politics, the arts, and other forums with Anti-Americanism." (In 1995 Hollander published an updated edition of the second book as *Anti-Americanism: Irrational and Rational*.)

Political Will and Personal Belief: The Decline and Fall of Soviet Communism was published in 1999. Drawing on information obtained from newly opened Russian archives and books written by former Soviet officials, Hollander argued that the Soviet Union collapsed in December 1991 because Soviet government officials had lost their faith in communism. In his review for the *New Leader* (December 13, 1999), David E. Powell hailed the book:. "Hollander's two central findings are what make his volume so intriguing," Powell wrote. "(1) The leaders in Communist Europe suffered a crisis of conscience, especially after Nikita S. Khrushchev's 'Secret Speech' [denouncing the crimes of his predecessor Joseph Stalin] at the 20th Soviet Party Congress in 1956, then again after the invasions of Hungary (1956) and Czechoslovakia (1968). (2) Most of those who became disillusioned with the official ideology, or the contrast between official rhetoric and everyday reality (especially the privileges for the elite), had experienced or witnessed utterly unnecessary cruelties during the Stalin era. As a result, they lacked the conviction of their 'true-believer' predecessors—and wavered in the face of challenges." The reviewer praised Hollander for "bringing together a rich array of quotations that reveal the doubts and concerns of the men against whom the Cold War was fought. He is, of course, right: Economic, political and ethnic difficulties were becoming increasingly grave, but it was the decline of faith, the reluctance to use coercion—the end, for a while, of ideology—that caused a decaying empire to crumble. This is an important book precisely because it demonstrates how the absence of political will and personal belief ultimately brought down the Soviet Union and its Eastern European satellites."

The essays that make up *Discontents: Postmodern and Postcommunist* are grouped in two sections, the first about social and cultural problems in American society and the second exploring the aftermath of the fall of communism. Reviewing *Discontents* for the *New Criterion* (September 2002), Digby Anderson wrote, "Paul Hollander is very funny and very cheerful, the very opposite of discontent. His book is a collection of previously published essays on intellectuals and Communism. Both are deeply depressing subjects, but Hollander, while being analytically incisive and damning about them, still retains his good humor. That's a rare and very powerful combination." The reviewer concluded that "*Discontents* is a fascinating, erudite, and good-natured book, a book for our time."

In 2004 Hollander edited *Understanding Anti-Americanism: Its Origins and Impact at Home and Abroad*. Strongly embraced by reviewers for conservative magazines in the U.S., the book brought together essays by scholars who, for the most part, analyze anti-Americanism in the U.S. and elsewhere as an enduring and essentially baseless hatred. "With varying levels of persuasiveness, each essay isolates a different strand of anti-Americanism in its cultural context of origin," a critic for *Publishers Weekly* (May 3, 2004) wrote. "Because the collection emphasizes anti-Americanism as a vitriolic intellectual construction," the critic concluded, "some readers may find its tone overly defensive, particularly in relation to American foreign policy. Nevertheless, the sense of cultural contradictions and differing philosophical legacies that the collection conveys is enriching and allows anti-Americanism to be viewed less as a bundle of generalizations and more in terms of the cultural particularity of each country and region."

In 2006, the same year as the appearance of *From the Gulag to the Killing Fields*, Hollander published *The End of Commitment: Intellectuals, Revolutionaries, and Political Morality in the Twentieth Century*, an analysis of how some notable intellectuals and functionaries in communist states, as well as some distinguished Western intellectuals, abandoned or modified their ideological commitments in response to manifest moral, political, and economic failures of communist states; the book also includes a chapter about well-known Western intellectuals whose left-wing views have, for the most part, been maintained despite these problems in the communist world. "*The End of Commitment* is about a loss of faith; in some [respects], it is also about faith's beginnings," Maximilian Pakaluk of *National Review Online* (June 29, 2006) opined. "It was partly a denial of the persisting and unavoidable reality of human imperfection that ensured Communism would be so misguided; yet it is this same reality that ensures people will continue to look to place their faith in something."

Hollander is married to the former Mina Harrison and has a daughter, Sarah, from a previous marriage. He lives in Northampton, Massachusetts.

—D.C.

Suggested Reading: *Academic Questions* p85+ Winter 1989/1990; *American Historical Review* p751+ June 1982; *American Scholar* p582+ Autumn 1982; *Choice* p1,492 Dec. 1969, p377 Oct. 1992; *Economist* p135 Oct. 22, 1973; *Library Journal* p2,630 July 1969; *Modern Age* p244+ Spring 2002; *National Review Online* July 22, 2004, June 29, 2006; *New Criterion* p76+ Sep.

2002, p71+ Oct. 2006; *New Leader* p15 Dec. 13, 1999; *New York Times* C p19 Jan. 2, 1992; *Publishers Weekly* p185 May 3, 2004

Selected Books: *Soviet and American Society: A Comparison*, 1973; *Political Pilgrims: Travels of Western Intellectuals to the Soviet Union, China, and Cuba*, 1981; *The Survival of the Adversary Culture: Social Criticism and Political Escapism in American Society*, 1988; *Decline and Discontent: Communism and the West Today*, 1992; *Anti-Americanism: Critiques at Home and Abroad, 1965–1990*, 1992; *Political Will and Personal Belief: The Decline and Fall of Soviet Communism*, 1999; *Discontents: Postmodern and Postcommunist*, 2002; *The End of Commitment: Intellectuals, Revolutionaries, and Political Morality*, 2006; as editor—*American and Soviet Society: A Reader in Comparative Sociology and Perception*, 1969; *Understanding Anti-Americanism: Its Origins and Impact at Home and Abroad*, 2004; *From the Gulag to the Killing Fields: Personal Accounts of Political Violence and Repression in Communist States*, 2006

Hollingshead, Greg

Feb. 25, 1947– Novelist; short-story writer

Greg Hollingshead produced the following autobiographical statement for *World Authors 2000–2005*:

"I was born in Toronto in 1947 and grew up in Woodbridge, then a village on the north edge of the city, now consumed by it. My father worked in the cotton mills across the street, my mother did clerical work. He had left school in Grade 8, she in Grade 10. For most of his life, my father served in local politics. Shortly before his death at 66, he ran for mayor. I was an only child until 1959, when my brother Paul was born. That same year my mother's desire to see her children well educated had me starting Grade 9 at an academically advanced day school for boys in the city, the University of Toronto Schools, where I was miserable for five years but had good teachers. My primary school teachers had taught me grammar; at UTS I was introduced to modern literature by a scathing but compassionate Irishman named R.G. Harrison. I can still remember the excerpt from *Portrait of the Artist as a Young Man*. That was Grade 12. In 1968 I completed a B.A. in Honours English at the University of Toronto. The same year, the poet and editor Dennis Lee included some of my poems in a collection called *T.O. Now: The Young Toronto Poets*. After a year in Europe (where, in a cave in Crete, at age 20, I began my first unpublishable novel, 'Monster Weather,' about a climate change), I returned to Toronto to complete an M.A. in English.

Courtesy of the Banff Centre

Greg Hollingshead

"From 1970 to 1975, I lived in England, first in Ladbroke Grove, London, then Oxted, Surrey, while writing a PhD at the University of London on the philosopher George Berkeley and his influence on 18th-century poetry. In 1975 I took a job as Assistant Professor in 18th-century literature at the University of Alberta, in Edmonton. Soon after arriving, I met the novelist and short story writer Matt Cohen, the university's first writer in residence, and we became friends. In the British Library, I had read and liked his first story collection, *Columbus and the Fat Lady*. At the end of the school year, we drove back to Ontario together in his truck. Matt Cohen was a mentor, model, and editor in my early days as a writer and a good friend until his early death in 1999. Before the five-day conversation we had on that drive back to Ontario, it had never occurred to me to write short stories. I began my first as soon as I got out of the truck. Matt Cohen edited (and named) my first book, *Famous Players* (1982), a collection of stories published in Toronto by Coach House Press. Over the next ten years I published approximately 50 stories while trying to write a publishable novel. During that time, I bought a cluster of isolated cabins on a lake in Algonquin Park in Ontario, where I still spend the summers. In 1983, I married Rosa Spricer, a psychologist. Our son David was born in 1984.

"In 1992 my second story collection, *White Buick*, and my first novel, *Spin Dry*, were published. When sorting through 30 or so stories written over 18 years, in order to create *White Buick*, I set aside the more comic for another book. This became *The Roaring Girl* (1995), edited by Patrick Crean at Somerville House. My other books

had garnered various provincial awards, but *The Roaring Girl* won what was then the most visible Canadian fiction prize, the Governor General's Award. *The Roaring Girl* sold well and was published in the U.K., Germany, and China. In 1998, working with Phyllis Bruce at HarperCollins Canada, I published my second novel, *The Healer*, which was also published in the U.K. and U.S. *The Healer* was shortlisted for the Giller Prize and won another national award, the Rogers Writers' Trust Fiction Prize. In 1999 I became Director of Writing Programs at the Banff Centre in Banff, Alberta. In 2004 I published my third novel, in which I was able to combine my fiction and 18th-century interests. *Bedlam* was longlisted for the IMPAC Dublin Literary Award and shortlisted for the Commonwealth Prize for Best Book in the Caribbean and Canada region as well as for various provincial awards. It has also been published in the U.S. In 2005 I became Professor Emeritus at the University of Alberta. In addition to my work at the Banff Centre, I now devote myself mainly to writing.

"Literature is now mostly taught in Canadian and U.S. universities as a category of cultural studies. My interest has always been in literature as art. For the ten years from 1995 I taught mainly creative writing workshops, currently the places in the university where the teaching of literature as art has persisted, as it has at institutions such as the Banff Centre, where the approach is one-on-one editorial mentoring. I write because when I don't, I am more or less miserable. My brain has trouble knowing what to do with information if not turn it over for possible use in a work in progress. My inspirations have been cosmic comedians such as Swift, [Laurence] Sterne, [Mikhail] Bulgakov, Flannery O'Connor, [Samuel] Beckett, William Burroughs, [Thomas] Pynchon, as well as virtuoso masters of the story-telling craft: Emily Brontë, [Anton] Chekhov, [Gustave] Flaubert, Raymond Carver, Cormac McCarthy, Alice Munro. It seems to me that the world is a mad place, and that all a writer needs to do is tell the truth, but in a voice and with details that penetrate the veils of cliché, and habit, and normalcy, for a while. As a writer, I am sometimes mistaken for despairing, but I do believe in the saving, universal power of human intelligence, which for me finds its most available expression as comedy."

Born on February 25, 1947 to Joyce (McGlashan) and Albert Hollingshead, Greg Hollingshead sees himself as a quintessentially Canadian writer. "I got to know how Canadian I am by living in England for five years in the early '70s. I might have stayed, except that I wanted to write and I knew that for me it would have to be in the Canadian way," he told Mark Young for an interview in *Blood and Aphorisms* (Spring 1996).

"More personally, I have strong emotional connections to my father's voice and sensibility. . . . The sensibility that informed me growing up I think of as a national one, with some regional variation. It's the sense of humour, a loser's really, chipping away at pretension. It's the space left for mystery. The assumption of darkness." Hollingshead's debut, a collection of short stories called *Famous Players*, began to establish him as a postmodernist because of its "elaborate, sophisticated verbal games," as Dennis Duffy wrote for the Toronto *Globe and Mail* (September 25, 1982). Duffy went on to call the stories "outrageous" and "brilliant" but caviled at the excessive verbal pyrotechnics that might "dehydrate and exhaust a reader." He concluded, "Wit, imagination, intensity abound in the collection, yet the total effect is austere, determinedly distanced. This, no doubt, is a desired effect, the hallmark of an elegant sensibility that has outgrown earlier conventions of storytelling."

Over the next 10 years Hollingshead published stories in journals and magazines. Then, in 1992, he released a collection of short stories, *White Buick*, and his first novel, *Spin Dry*. The story collection met with mixed reviews. Laurel Wellman, writing for the *Vancouver Sun* (October 24, 1992), called it "a depressing little book about depressing little people. It contains one standout piece, 'The Comfort of Things as They Are,' a work reminiscent of Raymond Carver's short masterpiece, 'A Small, Good Thing'. . . . The rest of the collection suffers by comparison. One story reads like a writing exercise on the lines of 'Imagine you are a paranoid psychotic,' while another seems more than slightly derivative of *The Silence of the Lambs*." Similarly, Claire Rothman, writing for the Montreal *Gazette* (January 16, 1993), took note of Hollingshead's "message of despair and violence." He "can't seem to find comfort anywhere. . . . At his best, Hollingshead is a true-north version of Raymond Carver" and "a writer of some talent. Unfortunately, the dark-tinted glasses through which he looks at the world tend to obscure rather than illuminate human truths."

Spin Dry, the action of which takes place in a suburb built over a toxic dump, met with a more positive reception. T.L. Craig characterized it for *Letters in Canada* (Fall 1993) as a "comic updated version of [Robertson] Davies' *The Manticore*, but far more readable. . . . It is the comic characters, flailing at stereotypes, that make the novel work and ultimately render it no more comic than *The Manticore*. A light satire of contemporary suburban social and psychological agoraphobia, *Spin Dry* is a successful . . . first novel." Mark Anthony Jarman, in a review for the *Calgary Herald* (May 16, 1993), called attention to the novel's "impressive writing: funny, mean, impressive prose, a session with a crazed shrink, a spin doctor tunneling hellishly under the developers' guilt and greed and the innocence and angst-ridden desire of the postwar suburban dream of flight, refuge, home sweet home. As the narrator says, as Rachel takes a last look at the townhouses and condos done in 'Contractor modern,' it's all 'pretty ordinary and pretty strange. Like most life anywhere.'"

The publication, in 1995, of the prize-winning *The Roaring Girl* fully established Hollingshead as an important figure in Canadian literary circles and helped to build him an international reputation. Charles Foran noted for *Maclean's* (November 27, 1995) that for readers, it is encountering "a fictional sensibility at once contemplative and spontaneous, whimsical and harsh that makes *The Roaring Girl* so exhilarating." The success of the book was perhaps better illustrated by the fact that Hollingshead's dark vision no longer seemed to be represented as a problem by critics. Philip Marchand, writing for the *Toronto Star* (October 28, 1995), observed, "The difficulties of the helpless human characters in making sense of the world . . . are agonizing. The problem, this collection suggests, is that they never quite overcome their difficulties. . . . In one story, 'The Death of Brule,' a small boy and his girlfriend play out their drama of love and friendship in 'caves and forts and tents made out of blankets.' At the same time, they are fascinated by the houses adults make—mysterious domains of grownup emotion and sexuality. But these stories demonstrate that adult houses, seemingly the product of reason and maturity, are, in fact, as vulnerable to the chaos of the world as childish tents made of blankets. No human structure, however solidly built, can keep out nightmare. Hollingshead's vision, then, is a daunting one. Reading the stories is not a depressing experience, however." On the book's publication, in 1997, in the U.S., the *Publishers Weekly* (January 27, 1997) reviewer remarked, "these characters offer a wealth of unexpected reactions and impulses and, in so doing, reveal rich interior lives. Like the characters themselves, Hollingshead's crisp, energetic prose offers surprising pleasures—expressions unique enough to press the narrative forward, but not so odd that they are halting. These lean narratives never feel forced and are frequently funny. Perhaps most impressively, the humor seems completely natural, as human and necessary as grief or ecstasy."

Hollingshead next novel, *The Healer*, tells the story of a young widower, Tim Wakelin, a journalist who goes to a small mining town to interview a young woman who is supposed to be a faith healer. Caroline, the purported healer, is only 20 and lives with an abusive father and an alcoholic mother. When she eventually flees from her father, Tim pursues her into the wilderness. "Circumstances put Caroline and Wakelin together in the wilderness—he rescues her, then she rescues him—for the better part of the novel," Joel Yanofsky noted for the Montreal *Gazette* (October

3, 1998). "Caroline's father chases after them too, adding suspense to the story and providing Hollingshead with what he's been manoeuvring toward all along—an excuse to strand his characters in the woods and strip them of any shred of civilization. . . . There's nothing majestic or reassuring about his wilderness. Instead, it's a reflection of our own flaws. . . . Wakelin says: 'If deprivation and suffering and failure make character, then the real question is why pretend the character of this country is not as bitter and wretched and unforgiving as the experiences that formed it?'" For James Urquhart, writing for the London *Guardian* (February 6, 1999), "Hollingshead does not burden *The Healer* with solutions but allows the unfathomable impulses of love and hurt to enmesh these fractured and dislocated lives. . . . Hollingshead's unhysterical comprehension of the human capacity for harm is convincing and unsettling; such raw exposure of emotion lends an edge of agoraphobia to his isolated, northern community." Neil Besner observed in *Letters in Canada* (Winter 2000) that "the precision and economy of Hollingshead's descriptions of milieus such as the small-town Ontario coffee shop are . . . very fine. His language is often honed and distinctive. And the novel's plot is engaging. . . . However the novel sometimes suffers from lurid overwriting when Hollingshead turns his eye to the details of landscape."

Hollingshead followed *The Healer* with *Bedlam*, a historical novel that is set in the 18th century and written in the language of the period. The project gave him the opportunity to return to his scholarly fascination with the 18th century. He had, he told Michael Bryson for the *Danforth Review* (January 2005), wanted to "do something gritty and eighteenth- or nineteenth-century for some time, . . . using eighteenth-century language." The novel takes its name from the popular name for St. Mary's of Bethlehem, a lunatic asylum in London in which mentally ill people were incarcerated under horrendous conditions, and is narrated by three main characters, all of whom are historical figures: James Tilly Matthews, a man committed to Bedlam because he attempted a peace mission to France during the French Revolution, not because of his mental state; his wife, Margaret, who spent her life trying to secure his release; and John Haslam, who is a member of the Bedlam staff and, historically, chronicled Matthews's progress, which is often counted as the first scientific account of a mental illness.

"As with all copiously researched fiction, Hollingshead's novel is best served when he shows not merely a dungeon of pitiables and grotesques but also inmates whose infirmity reflects the novel's wider themes—men like Richard Pocock, 'whose conviction it is that as soon as he thinks of something, it's destroyed' and who stands in his cell with his eyes closed, trying to undo the damage repeating, 'I never thought of America, nor

Jersey, nor Spain, nor Portugal, nor Plymouth Dock' and so on," Andrew Sean Greer noted in the *New York Times Book Review* (October 16, 2006). He went on to observe, "Bedlam has no end of gorgeous writing. Ostentatious language is always a danger when using narrators from the distant past, but Hollingshead's descriptions stand tastefully back from such overexuberance." Greer, however, did not find the novel without fault, concluding "Hollingshead's elegant, heartfelt writing and smart research almost make up for the novel's oddly static feeling. The author seems too in love with the past to be willing to take liberties with it. . . . Haslam, Matthews and his wife, true to the real people who inspired them, remain glued in history, unable to change." Anna Mundow wrote for the *Boston Globe* (October 15, 2006), "*Bedlam* is a decidedly intellectual yet profoundly moving examination of both mental and political lunacy." A reviewer for *Kirkus Reviews* (July 1, 2006), by contrast, complained, the novel "suffers from too much history and not enough story."

—S.Y.

Suggested Reading: *Blood and Aphorisms* p39+ Spring 1996; *Boston Globe* E p5 Oct. 15, 2006; (London) *Guardian* p10 Feb. 6, 1999; *Kirkus Reviews* p649 July 1, 2006; *Letters in Canada* (on-line) Fall 1993; (Montreal) *Gazette* J p2 Jan. 16, 1993, J p1 Oct. 3, 1998; *New York Times Book Review* p30 Oct. 15, 2006; *Publishers Weekly* p76 Jan. 27, 1997, p50 July 10, 2006; (Toronto) *Globe and Mail* C p3 Sep. 25, 1982; *Toronto Star* H p17 Oct. 28, 1995

Selected Books: *Famous Players*, 1982; *White Buick*, 1992; *Spin Dry*, 1992; *The Roaring Girl*, 1995; *The Healer*, 1998; *Bedlam*, 2004

Hosseini, Khaled

(KHAH-lehd hoh-SAY-nee)

Mar. 4, 1965– Novelist

Khaled Hosseini's childhood experiences in Kabul, the capital of Afghanistan, served as the basis for his first novel, *The Kite Runner* (2003), a coming-of-age tale about two boys from different ethnic backgrounds whose shared pleasure in flying kites brings them together despite the economic and ethnic barriers that separate them. Set in the years before the country was invaded by the Soviet Union, the story is told in first person from the perspective of one of the boys, offering Western readers an unusually direct sense of life in Hosseini's home country. "Too often, stories about Afghanistan center around the various wars, the opium trade, the war on terrorism," he told Farhad Azad for the *Afghan Magazine* Web site (June

John Dolan/Courtesy of Penguin

Khaled Hosseini

2004). "Preciously little is said about the Afghan people themselves, their culture, their traditions, how they lived in their country and how they manage abroad as exiles." From the start the novel, buoyed by positive reviews, sold well, but beginning in 2004, once it was released in paperback and began being adopted by reading clubs around the country, *The Kite Runner* turned from a solid success to a startling best-seller, becoming, in 2005, the third highest-selling book in the U.S. By late 2006 Hosseini's novel, generally described as the first English-language novel by a person of Afghan origin, had sold more than three million copies and been translated into more than 25 languages. Remarking on his success Hosseini told one of the many audiences he has addressed since the book's publication, as quoted by Jan Sjostrom for the Cox News Service (March 22, 2006): "If the book has in some way given a face and voice to a people who have been faceless and voiceless for a long time, I am honored."

The oldest of five children, Khaled Hosseini was born on March 4, 1965 in the northern section of Kabul, where, he told Liane Hansen for National Public Radio's *Weekend Edition* (July 27, 2003), "we lived a comfortable—not privileged, but probably a comfortable life." His father worked for the Afghan foreign ministry as a diplomat, and his mother taught history and Farsi (the language also called Persian) at a secondary school for girls. In 1970 Hosseini's family moved to Iran, where his father held a post in the Afghan embassy in Tehran for three years before returning to Kabul. At that time the city was relatively open and cosmopolitan, and Hosseini grew up surrounded by the intellectuals, artists, and upper-middle-

class professionals who made up his family's circle of friends. As a child he was an avid reader of Persian poetry, but for prose narratives he had to turn to the literary traditions of other cultures. "I came into contact with prose fiction by reading Farsi translations of American or Western novels—I used to read Ian Fleming and Mike Hammer novels in Farsi," he told Philip Marchand for the *Toronto Star* (August 5, 2003). "I read *The Exorcist* in Farsi—it was serialized in a magazine." Hosseini began writing short stories while in grade school, inspired partially by his reading of Western fiction but also strongly influenced by Afghan popular culture and the oral tradition. "I grew up with my grandmother telling us stories, my father telling us stories and on the radio there was a series called *Tales Of The Night*," Hosseini told Marchand. "I grew up with that tradition of old-fashioned and sort of straightforward story-telling." During the winter months, when school was out, he also indulged in a national pastime, kite flying.

In October 1976 the family again left Afghanistan, after Hosseini's father was assigned as a second secretary to the Afghan embassy in Paris, France. In April 1978 a Marxist-led coup toppled the administration led by Afghan president Daoud Khan, creating an atmosphere of intense anxiety throughout the country but also in Paris, among Hosseini's family. In an interview available on the Web site of the Bloomsbury Publishing company, Hosseini said that during that time "it felt a little like I was living in a spy novel. Whenever we'd travel anywhere my father would insist we all wait by the elevator in the garage while he went clear across the parking lot to get the car and bring it to us. People were getting killed and he was afraid that someone may have planted a bomb in the car. And you had to be careful about what you said, and to whom, because the new regime sent its own diplomats to Paris." When Soviet military forces began occupying Afghanistan in the last days of 1979, igniting a more than nine-year-long war, Hosseini's father applied for political asylum in the U.S., and, in September 1980, the family moved to San Jose, California.

Hosseini spoke only Farsi and French at the time of his arrival, but by the end of his freshman year at San Jose's Independence High School, he had become fluent in English as well. Still, he found the initial adjustment to life in America trying. "For my siblings and me," Hosseini said in the Bloomsbury interview, "in addition to the anxiety of learning a new language, there were the usual fears of adolescence and pre-adolescence: Will I fit in? Will I make friends? Am I ever going to learn English? And will the other kids make fun of me?" The relocation proved to be equally difficult on Hosseini's parents, who for a time were forced to rely on government support programs to feed themselves and the rest of the family. "Probably the single most difficult thing was not having money," Hosseini told Marchand. "It was really losing your identity. My parents had established careers in their own country and established identities. For them to give that up in one fell swoop in a new country with a new culture was very hard. But I think the notion of being on welfare was the hardest thing for them to accept." When Hosseini's father accepted a position as a driving instructor, he immediately cut the family off from welfare. His mother also continued to work to support the family, taking jobs as a waitress at the chain restaurant Denny's and as a beautician.

In 1984 Hosseini graduated from high school and began his undergraduate studies at Santa Clara University, in California. He made the decision to abandon his dream of being a writer, pursuing a career in medicine—a choice that was influenced by his ready grasp of science as well as his sense of responsibility. "I had this notion that, when you're an immigrant, you come here with a sense of purpose," Hosseini told Adair Lara for the *San Francisco Chronicle* (June 8, 2003). "When you don't speak English and you're just starting out, being a writer is not exactly something you think about. I wanted to work with people. Something honorable. I never wanted to get up in the morning and feel what I'm doing doesn't serve a purpose." In 1989, the year after he received his bachelor's degree in biology from Santa Clara, Hosseini entered medical school at the University of California, at San Diego; he took his M.D. four years later.

Hosseini found work as an internist in 1996, at the conclusion of a three-year residency in internal medicine at the Cedars-Sinai Medical Center, in Los Angeles. In 1999 he returned to northern California after taking a position in the internal medicine department at a branch of the Kaiser Permanente Medical Group, in Mountain View. Around that same time, he began writing short stories again, beginning with a horror story and progressing, over the next two years, until he had accumulated about a dozen, some of which were published in literary magazines. One of the early and unpublished stories he wrote during this time concerned two boys in Kabul during the 1970s and their shared love of flying kites. The story was inspired by a news report about the Taliban—a fundamentalist Sunni Muslim group that controlled most of Afghanistan from 1996 to 2001—having banned kite flying. (Announced without explanation in January 1997, the ban also extended to such activities as dogfighting, quailfighting, and cockfighting, which were typically occasions for gambling, something expressly forbidden in the Koran. The rationale for criminalizing the flying of kites, however, was less clear. Some considered the ban a way of keeping children from wasting money on such relatively expensive items as string; others assumed it was frowned upon for being a distraction from more important religious duties. As Hosseini remarked

to Marchand, the Taliban "banned anything that was halfway fun and took away from Qu'ran studies.")

Within 12 hours of hearing about the ban, Hosseini had completed a draft of the short story, also titled "The Kite Runner," which he later mailed to the *New Yorker, Esquire,* and the *Atlantic Monthly.* All three magazines rejected it, and the story remained largely untouched until March 2001, when his wife and father-in-law read it. At his father-in-law's urging, Hosseini began expanding the short story. "That was really my first crack at writing a novel," he told Vik Jolly for the *Orange County Register* (February 22, 2006). In order to have time to write, Hosseini woke at around 5 a.m. and worked for about three hours before heading to his full-time job.

Following the September 11, 2001, attacks on the World Trade Center in New York City and the Pentagon in Washington, D.C., Hosseini, who had completed two-thirds of his novel at the time, put the manuscript aside. "I was embarrassed that my country had been involved in this attack on the States," he told Adair Lara. "The first time I heard the word 'Taliban' on TV that day, I cringed. And I thought Afghans would be persecuted." He soon picked up the manuscript again, and by midsummer 2002, after altering the ending to suit his wife and other early readers, he was ready to find an agent and, after that, a publisher. In September 2002 he sold the manuscript to the publishing house Riverhead Books.

In March 2003, two weeks before the novel was officially published, Hosseini visited Kabul for the first time in 27 years. "I returned to Afghanistan because I had a deep longing to see for myself how people lived, what they thought of their government, how optimistic they were about the future of their homeland," he explained to Razeshta Sethna for the Pakistani on-line magazine *Newsline* (November 2003). "I was overwhelmed with the kindness of people and found that they had managed to retain their dignity, their pride, and their hospitality under unspeakably bleak conditions." During the trip, he visited his childhood home, which was then being occupied by seven soldiers from the anti-Taliban group the Northern Alliance.

The two motherless boys at the heart of *The Kite Runner* come from different ethnic groups: Amir, the educated son of an upper-class businessman called Baba and a Pashtun, traditionally the country's dominant ethnic group; and Hassan, the son of one of Baba's servants and a Hazara, an ethnic minority generally excluded from the country's corridors of power. The turning point in their friendship occurs following Amir's failure to intercede during a brutal attack against Hassan, who also serves as Amir's "kite runner"—the person designated, in Afghan kite flying competitions, to find a kite after it has been cut by the ground glass–coated string of an opponent. The book documents the boys' lives over four decades, as Amir, who immigrated to the U.S. as a child, returns to Afghanistan after learning that the Taliban killed Hassan and his wife and left their son, Sohrab, an orphan.

Stella Algoo-Baksh, for *Canadian Literature* (Spring 2005), wrote that the book was full of "surprising twists and turns" and "as tightly and intricately woven as a rich tapestry." The book Algoo-Baksh added, "transcends time, place, and the immediate locale, for it may be read as an ethical parable for all peoples who are confronted daily with personal struggles pertaining to family, love, betrayal, guilt, fear, and redemption." Calling the book "shattering," Amelia Hill, for the London *Guardian* (September 7, 2003, on-line), wrote: "Amir's story is simultaneously devastating and inspiring. His world is a patchwork of the beautiful and horrific, and the book a sharp, unforgettable taste of the trauma and tumult experienced by Afghanis as their country buckled. *The Kite Runner* is about the price of peace, both personal and political, and what we knowingly destroy in our hope of achieving that, be it friends, democracy or ourselves." Some critics, however, considered the book uneven—albeit still strong for a first novel—and a few found fault with the ending. In the Dublin *Sunday Business Post* (September 21, 2003), Elizabeth McGuane described the novel as having "a curiously opaque feeling," and suggested that "the places and events [the author] describes feel unreal, as if they have been researched rather than remembered. . . . Yet when, later in the book, the setting shifts to the United States, the tone becomes more personal and authentic. It is a shame that Hosseini's attempt to re-imagine the Afghanistan of his childhood, and thus to show its alternative history, is itself oppressed by the weight of recent history. Had the novel been written in a more immediate manner, with less reliance on dates and more on characters, the effect of this commendable but less than powerful novel could have been far greater."

According to interviews with Hosseini, less formal responses to the book from other people from Afghanistan have also generally been positive. "Some Afghans may think the book airs dirty laundry during a sensitive time, but I think they are in the minority," he told Chauncey Mabe for the Fort Lauderdale *Sun-Sentinel* (March 14, 2004). "Most of the Afghans I've heard from are proud one of their own has written a book that captures a slice of their history and is getting national attention."

In December 2004 Hosseini began an extended leave of absence from his full-time position at Kaiser Permanente to work on his second book. Scheduled for publication in May 2007, the novel, tentatively titled "A Thousand Splendid Suns," is reported to be about a friendship between two Afghan women.

Hosseini met his wife, Roya, at a weekend gathering at his parents' house in San Jose. Before a week passed he proposed, and the two were married six weeks later. For years a practicing attorney, Roya served as the initial editor for *The Kite Runner*; she is also now working at home, assisting Hosseini with his second novel. They live in the foothills of South San Jose with their son, Haris, and daughter, Farah.

—B.M.

Suggested Reading: Khaled Hosseini's Web site; *Florida Times-Union* L p1 Mar. 11, 2006; *Contra Costa Times* p1 May 6, 2005; *Modesto Bee* H p1 Feb. 1, 2004

Selected Books: *The Kite Runner*, 2003

Michael Latz/AFP/Getty Images

Houellebecq, Michel

(WELL-beck)

Feb. 25, 1958– Novelist; poet

"Michel's not depressed," the wife of the French writer Michel Houellebecq told Emily Eakin for the *New York Times* (September 10, 2000). "It's the world that's depressing." Houellebecq, a tortured literary giant and provocateur whose novels have attracted hundreds of thousands of readers in his native France and around the world, has caused an unprecedented upheaval in the world of French letters. He is considered by many to be a breath of fresh air in a national literary milieu in which using experimental forms such as the *nouveau roman*—that is, the new novel, a novelistic form that was developed by writers such as Alain Robbe-Grillet, who sought to avoid metaphor in his prose in favor of exact descriptions—had become the norm. Houellebecq's novels, by contrast, are lurid and contemporary; they address such topical issues as cloning, terrorism, and sex tourism. Nonetheless, his critics allege that, innovator or no, Houellebecq is an unrepentant racist, misogynist, and homophobe whose novels reveal his universal disgust for the world.

Michel Houellebecq was born on February 25, 1958 in La Reunion, a French island off the coast of Madagascar. His parents, as he tells it, joined the hippie generation, which, in France as in America, was characterized by political idealism and a belief in the virtues of sexual liberation. Houellebecq's father was a trail guide and his mother was an anesthesiologist; according to their son, neither were competent parents. "What I felt was fear of my father and disgust with my mother," Houellebecq recalled to Alan Riding for the *New York Times* (March 2, 1999). "It's funny, but she never realized that I hated her." Houellebecq's mother left him in the care of his paternal grandmother when he was only six years old so that she could pursue a hedonistic lifestyle, he has said; he now knows nothing of her whereabouts—nor, for that matter, those of his father and half-sister.

Houellebecq was raised by his grandmother in Yonne, a southwestern suburb of Paris and then in Crecy-la-Chapelle. He eventually left home for a boarding school in Meaux, near Paris. There, he encountered "a panoply of incomprehensible political movements, leftists, environmentalists, who awakened in me profound repulsions," as he explained to Riding. In the six years he weathered at Meaux, Michel was a social outcast and a sexual pariah who spent much of his time reading. He had already developed a much stronger affinity with the dystopian works of Aldous Huxley and George Orwell than with the literary canon of his own country.

At age 18 Houellebecq was exempted from France's obligatory military conscription because of an addiction to morphine. Instead he enrolled in a preparatory school—a requisite step for students who plan to sit the entrance exams for France's elite universities. In 1978 his grandmother and caretaker died. With no family to speak of, he found a refuge among writers and began to frequent Parisian literary circles. In school he pursued the sciences, especially biology and physics, and in 1980 he took a degree in agronomy, a branch of agriculture dealing with field-crop management. His interest in the subject, however, was fleeting: "I was good at science," he told Eileen Battersby for the *Irish Times* (June 15, 2002), "but suddenly at 23 when I had completed my course, I decided 'I don't want to do this.' It took me a very long time to decide what I wanted to do in life." Also in 1980 he married the sister of a former classmate, with whom he had a child, Etienne, in 1981.

After Etienne turned four, Houellebecq divorced his wife and fell into a deep depression, a condition exacerbated by his inability to find a job. He spent much of the next few years in and out of psychiatric hospitals, drinking heavily and watching television. But he also found time to write, and in 1985 he met Michel Bulteau, the editor of a small Parisian literary review who agreed to publish some of his poems. Bulteau pushed Houellebecq to write his first book, an essay on the American science–fiction and fantasy writer H. P. Lovecraft. Houellebecq chose his subject because he felt an emotional connection with Lovecraft's misanthropy. "When you love the world, you don't read about it," he wrote in the first lines of the book, as quoted by *Le Figaro* (February 10, 2000) and translated by *World Authors*. "Whatever else may be said, the artistic universe is more or less reserved for those who are fed up." The book, *H. P. Lovecraft, contre le monde, contre la vie* (1991), which was translated as *H. P. Lovecraft: Against the World, Against Life*, in 2005, was billed as a biography but likened by some to a novel because of its freewheeling style. Also in 1991 Houellebecq published *Rester vivant, methode* (which can be translated as "staying alive: a method"). The following year he published a collection of poems, *La poursuite du bonheur* (which can be translated as "the pursuit of happiness"), which went on to win the Prix Tristan Tzara, an annual prize for French-language poetry.

Houellebecq's literary productions did not suffice to make ends meet, and in 1991 he was forced to take a job as a software technician for the French Parliament. Although he found working with computers lonely and alienating, the job inspired him to write his first novel—about a software technician named Michel. Published in France in 1994, *L'extension de la domaine de la lutte* (published in English as *Whatever*) contains the first articulation of an idea that is central to Houellebecq's oeuvre: natural selection favors the sexually virile. "In a perfectly liberal economic system," Houellebecq wrote, as quoted by Eakin, "some will accumulate considerable fortunes; others will wallow in unemployment and misery. In a perfectly liberal sexual system, some will enjoy a varied and exciting erotic life; others will be reduced to masturbation and solitude." Though largely overlooked by the press, *Whatever* sold over 20,000 copies in France. Some compared the novel to Albert Camus's *The Stranger* because of its sparse style and because one scene, in which a character contemplates committing a murder on a beach, was seen as an allusion to Camus's 1942 classic.

But it wasn't until 1998, with the publication of *Les Particules Elementaires* (published in the U.S. as *Elementary Particles* and as *Atomised* in Britain), that Houellebecq stepped into France's literary spotlight. "Houellebecq's book is an original work of art—ironic, intelligent, and as airtight and elegant as a geometry proof," Eakin wrote. The novel, the title of which refers to the idea that individuals, like particles, are disconnected from one another, tells the story of Bruno and Michel, two brothers who are abandoned as children by their hippie parents and go on to develop parallel but opposite sexual perversions. Bruno is a pathetic wretch with an insatiable sexual appetite that dominates his personality; Michel is an asexual molecular biologist who escapes from women into science. Both brothers inhabit a world of fierce and dehumanizing sexual competition that is the unwanted bequest of their parents' hippie generation. "In a sense," muses Bruno, as quoted by Eakin, "the serial killers of the 1990s were the spiritual children of the hippies of the '60s."

Houellebecq's indictment of the 1960s, an era that many in France hold sacrosanct, brought him notoriety. Many members of the literary and political establishment had come of age in the '60s and felt personally attacked by *Elementary Particles*: they responded with accusations that Houellebecq was a misogynist, a racist, and a reactionary. The recriminations culminated with Houellebecq's banishment from the pages of the literary review *Perpendiculaire*, which he had helped found in 1996. "We are distancing ourselves from Houellebecq," Christophe Duchatelet, a co-founder of *Perpendiculaire*, told Jean Luc Douin for *Le Monde* (September 11, 1998), as translated by *World Authors*, "because we have realized, in the process of interviewing him, that the author subscribes to the ideas developed by his character. . . . As a result, his book leaves the domain of allegory, of metaphor, to become something else." With hundreds of thousands of copies of *Elementary Particles* sold in the first months of publication alone, Houellebecq was not apologetic. A bitterly divided jury decided not to give Houellebecq the Prix Goncourt, the "French Pulitzer," in 1998, though he did win that year's Grand Prix National des Lettres for young talent—a much less prestigious accolade—for his collected literary works and won, in 2002, the Dublin IMPAC award, after the book appeared in English translation.

In the wake of the furor over *Elementary Particles*, Houellebecq beat a retreat from France with his second wife, Marie-Pierre Gauthier, a publishing agent he has known since 1992. The couple first moved to Dublin, Ireland, and then to a secluded island off Ireland's southeast coast. In 1999 Houellebecq collaborated with Phillippe Harel on a screen adaptation of *Whatever*, and in the spring of 2000 he released an album, *Presence humaine*, for which he recited his poetry to the music of French composer Bertrand Burgalat. Houellebecq also published *Lanzarote*, which appeared in English, in 2003, under the same title. Taking its name from a European holiday island, the novel critiques the hedonistic, and in Houellebecq's view, destructive, nature of Europe's holiday culture. Much shorter than its predecessor, the book found disfavor even among Houellebecq's fans. "The most charitable thing to say about this new book . . . is that it might be a spoof. Michel Houellebecq's usual obsessions with the sexual convenience of global tourism and the cruel absurdities of the Islamic faith are on display once again, but in a curiously truncated form. The book reads like a lackadaisical afterthought or a story that the author feels too lazy to tell. The narrative is abandoned, rather than brought to a natural end. It can be read in 40 minutes, and it won't be time well spent," Paul Bailey wrote for the London *Sunday Times* (June 29, 2003). Similarly, David Sexton wrote for the London *Evening Standard* (June 30, 2003), "*Lanzarote* is little more than a minor variation on the themes of *Platform*, most worth reading for a few characteristically sardonic asides."

In August 2001 Houellebecq published *Plateforme*, which appeared as *Platform* in English, a novel that celebrates Third World prostitution and, at the same time, condemns the free-market economy that, in Houellebecq's view, fuels sex tourism. The novel, which contains a passage that calls Islam "a stupid religion," was widely decried as racist. Several Muslim groups brought criminal charges against Houellebecq in France, where law prohibits the dissemination of materials that could incite racism. In October 2002 a Paris court found the author not guilty, concluding that his remarks were simply part of a "system of thought" that could be refuted, but not declared illegal. Though the court acknowledged that Houellebecq's views lacked "subtlety in their expression," it judged that they did not imply that Muslims were stupid. In his own defense, Houellebecq told the court, "I have never shown the slightest contempt for Muslims, but I have always held Islam in contempt," as quoted by Philip Delves Broughton for the *Chicago Sun-Times* (October 23, 2002).

In 2005 Houellebecq released *La possibilité d'une île*, which was released in an English translation as *The Possibility of an Island*. The book presents a dialogue across the centuries between Daniel1, an early 21st century comedian who joins the Elohimites, a cult that saves cells for creating clones in the future, and Daniel24, the other Daniel's future replica, who is writing a commentary on Daniel1's diaries. A reviewer for the *Economist* (September 17, 2005), observed, "Houellebecq does not disappoint. His deftly constructed novel is a bleak comment on contemporary society, at times funny, brutal and revolting, which pushes notions of hope and hopelessness to a dismal logical conclusion. If there are weaknesses, it is the familiarity of themes from his previous work: the commodification of sex, the interaction between modern science and spirituality, the link between happiness and suffering. Moreover, the effort to shock with semi-pornographic scenes is increasingly tiresome; his female characters are flat; and, at times, the storytelling is slow." Other critics were more harsh. Houellebecq's "crude directness makes him like the Quentin Tarantino of the contemporary novel," Michael Savage wrote for the Culture Wars Web site. "But just as Tarantino seems less and less brilliant with the passage of time, we should avoid over-praising Houellebecq. *The Possibility of an Island*, his latest book, is a variation on a familiar Houellebecq theme (sun, sea and sex, plus cults and cloning). . . . His critique is relentlessly literal and forcefully unsubtle. Political culture is insistently multicultural, so Houellebecq says Islam is a stupid religion. Society is feminised, so Houellebecq is crudely pornographic. Fear of scientific progress is rampant, so Houellebecq's anti-heroes are clones. Houellebecq's outrageous naughtiness, nihilistic misery and crude sexiness appeal to the inner teenager."

Besides the works discussed above, Houellebecq has published a number of other books including the poetry collection *Renaissance* (1999) and the essay collection *Interventions: recueil d'essais* (1998). He has been married to Marie-Pierre Gauthier, with whom he maintains an open relationship, since 1998.

—D.H.P.

Suggested Reading: (London) *Independent* p9 Jan. 2, 1999, p37 Apr. 30, 2000; *New York Times* E p1 Mar. 2, 1999; *New York Times Magazine* p36 Sep. 10, 2000

Selected Books in English Translation: *Whatever*, 1994; *Elementary Particles*, 1998; *Platform*, 2001; *Lanzarote*, 2001; *The Possibility of an Island*, 2005

Jana Marcus/Courtesy of Random House

Houston, James D.

Nov. 10, 1933– Novelist; nonfiction writer

James D. Houston is considered primarily a California writer. His novels, *Between Battles* (1968), *Gig* (1969), *A Native Son of the Golden West* (1971), *Continental Drift* (1978), *Love Life* (1985), *The Last Paradise* (1998), and *Snow Mountain Passage* (2001), chronicle life in California (and elsewhere on the Pacific Rim) from the mid-19th-century Gold Rush through the present time. In his nonfiction volumes, *Californians: Searching for the Golden State* (1982) and *In the Ring of Fire: A Pacific Basin Journey*

(1997), Houston has assessed California from personal, geographical, and sociological points of view. He has also authored books of reminiscences: *Three Songs for My Father* (1974) and *Men in My Life and Other More or Less True Recollections of Kinship* (1987). With his wife, Jeanne Wakatsuki Houston, he co-wrote *Farewell to Manzanar: A True Story of Japanese American Experience During and After the World War II Internment* (1973). His most recent books are *Hawaiian Son: The Life and Music of Eddie Kamae* (2004), which he co-wrote with Kamae, a ukulele virtuoso, singer, and composer, and the novel *Bird of Another Heaven*, published in 2007.

Houston wrote the following autobiographical statement for *World Authors 2000–2005*:

"My grandparents on both sides came from farming families in the southern United States. My mother was born in Alabama, my father in Oklahoma, the son of a cotton sharecropper and itinerant blacksmith. They met in the Texas panhandle, where she had grown up. In the early days of the Great Depression, they joined the multitudes heading west in search of better times.

"I was born in San Francisco on November 10, 1933, into a transplanted subculture of country music, country food, compulsive story-telling, and Bible Belt fundamentalism. But I saw myself as a city kid, and I worked overtime distancing myself from my parents' downhome ways. It took me quite a while to recognize the many gifts hidden right alongside what I was so earnestly rejecting. It took many years, for example, to see how the very desire to be a writer was seeded in those long ago Sunday morning services where language itself was the primary means for connection with a higher power.

"We were so fundamental that almost everything had been stripped away from the place of worship, and all that remained were words—the sermons, the prayers, the exhortations, the Bible readings. The opening verse in the Gospel of St. John summed it up: 'In the beginning was the Word, and the Word was with God, and the Word was God.'

"Quote a verse like that, of course, and you run the risk of sounding self-congratulatory, as if you have hit upon some true path to salvation via the sacred calling of prose or poetry. I don't want to suggest that writing became another form of religion. But as I grew up in the presence of scripture, a lasting belief was internalized. Long after I left the family church behind, at the age of 17, the role and the appeal of words stayed with me, the idea that words themselves might somehow save you.

"Another gift, another feature of the family legacy, was the nature of their pilgrimage from the Dust Bowl out to the coast. It spurred what has become a lifelong fascination with the many journeys, the multiplicity of travelers who have shaped this part of the world and continue to shape it. Eventually I would learn that their trip had its counterpart in the migratory journey of my wife's parents, who reached these shores from the opposite direction. Her background is Japanese. A hundred years ago her parents had traveled east across the Pacific to a California that was not 'the end of the line,' or 'the farthest edge,' but the point of arrival, the starting place.

"My wife, Jeanne Wakatsuki Houston, was born in Inglewood, California. We were married in Honolulu in 1957. Fifteen years later we co-wrote *Farewell to Manzanar* (now in a 56th printing from Bantam Books, and a standard work in schools and colleges across the country), the story of her family's experience during and after the World War II internment of Japanese Americans.

"Over the years these two stories, her family's and my family's, have had quite a bit to do with what I have chosen to write about. It has been a prolonged exploration, in both fiction and nonfiction, of the cultures and histories of the western U.S. and the Asia/Pacific region—from my early novel, *A Native Son of the Golden West* (Dial Press, 1971), set mostly in Hawaii, to *Snow Mountain Passage* (Alfred Knopf, 2001), based on the experiences of a family who came into California with the infamous Donner Party. What led me to take up that material, by the way, is the strange coincidence that we live in an old Victorian house once inhabited by Patty Reed, younger daughter of James Frazier Reed, who co-organized the Donner Party out of Springfield, Illinois, in 1846.

"My wife and I met at San Jose State University, where I received a B.A. in drama in 1956. After three years in the U.S. Air Force as an Information officer with a NATO tactical fighter bomber wing in England, I came back to Stanford for an M.A. in American literature (1962). I had the good fortune there to study with Malcolm Cowley; Yvor Winters; Irving Howe; Frank O'Connor, the Irish short story master; and Wallace Stegner, who was

an important mentor and became a longtime friend and colleague.

"In 1966 I returned to Stanford as a Stegner Writing Fellow, and while there finished my second novel, *Gig* (Dial Press, 1966), which won the 1967 Joseph Henry Jackson Award. These two honors, one right after the other, not only bought some precious writing time but provided the jump-start and validation I needed just then to continue along this path made of words and not turn back.

"It is a path that has allowed me to travel both inward and outward. Stints as visiting writer have taken me to the University of Hawaii, the University of Oregon at Eugene, the University of Michigan at Ann Arbor, and George Mason University, Fairfax, Virginia. There were two trips to Asia as a lecturer with the U.S.I.S. 'Arts America' program, a south Pacific cruise as a Smithsonian Lecturer on Cunard's Royal Viking Sun, a Rockefeller Foundation Residency at Bellagio, Italy. But most of my time has been spent here in Santa Cruz, where we have lived now for nearly 40 years, where the stories have been composed, in this old house at the edge of Monterey Bay."

James D. Houston began writing while still serving in the military. One early short story was published in *GEMINI,* a London-based literary journal, in 1959, and another story won the U.S. Air Force Short Story Contest later that year. Upon leaving the Air Force, he visited Belgium, France, Germany, Spain, Scotland, Scandinavia, and the Soviet Union, before returning to the U.S. to earn his master's degree in American literature from Stanford University.

The most heralded of his early works is arguably *Farewell to Manzanar,* which details the three years his wife spent living in the Manzanar Relocation Camp with her family during World War II. Covering both her assimilation into American life during her childhood, in the 1930s, and her life after internment, the book was praised for its insight. A writer for the *New York Times Book Review* (January 13, 1974) observed, "Although there are brief recreations of some of the internal ferment at the camp . . . the deeper political and social implications of Manzanar are largely ignored. The co-author, Jeanne's husband, is a novelist, and their book provides an often vivid, impressionistic picture of how the forced isolation affected the internees. All in all, a dramatic, telling account of one of the most reprehensible events in the history of America's treatment of its minorities." A reviewer for the *New Yorker* (November 5, 1973) wrote, "In this book a particularly ignominious chapter in our history is recounted with chilling simplicity by an internee." (By the time he and Jeanne met in college, American fear and suspicion of the Japanese had dissipated, and although they were the only interracial couple on campus, their relationship caused little comment.)

Despite the book's scope and importance, Houston, as the *New York Times* reviewer of *Farewell to Manzanar* mentioned, remained known mainly as a novelist; he had already written several fictional works, including, among others, *Gig,* which takes place over one night in a piano bar, and *A Native Son of the Golden West,* about a pair of surfers living in Hawaii. After *Farewell to Manzanar* he returned to fiction with *Continental Drift,* which focuses on the family of Montrose Doyle, who lives with his wife, Leona, on a small California ranch and works as a newspaper columnist. When one of Monty's sons, Travis, returns home from his service during the Vietnam War, the happy family reunion is disrupted by the investigation of a series of murders. (Evidence seems to suggest that Travis might be the one who committed the crimes.) Alan Cheuse wrote for the *New Republic* (September 30, 1978), "[Houston] acutely renders the lore of the region—the redwood enclaves, abandoned mountain towns, the coast, rightists, faddists, Buddhists, the dress, the music, the codes, the endless free way caravan of mutated autos and pickups, the look and smell, the very cell and bone-structure of northern California. It is all here, and it works. His fusion of moral suspense and physical adventure, however, stands as his greatest triumph. In the evocative depiction of Montrose Doyle's struggle to keep his family intact in the midst of great psychological and physical danger, Houston has created a fictional state we recognize because we live there." N. J. Loprete wrote for *Best Sellers* (January 1979), "[The book] is superb fiction, and James Houston is a faultless novelist who has captured the way we are now, for we are all Californians at heart. . . . It is a literate, suspenseful, amusing, and provocative record of a world no one intended to make."

Houston did write more nonfiction: in *Californians: Searching for the Golden State* he examines a host of issues ranging from the state's film, oil, and computer industries to environmental causes to freeway travel. Roger W. Fromm remarked for *Library Journal* (October 15, 1982), "As the prologue indicates, the author is searching as much for California as for Californians. . . . However, despite his insistence that California is so different, much of what he relates could be about other states. This is a personal search, and one might question the author's choices, e.g., a lengthy account of a talk show hostess, yet only two paragraphs on the defense industry (military and the contractors), though Houston admits that perhaps 40 percent of the federal defense budget is spent in California and that it is the state's biggest business." Lee Hopkins, however, wrote for the *National Review* (September 30, 1983), "A seasoned local writer, Houston examines every facet of his native state,

traveling all over its vast, variegated surface in grids producing the literary equivalent of a geodetic survey map. What he accomplishes is a remarkable blend of travel writing, interpretive profiles, and reflective essay. . . . Houston addresses the very difficult problem of defining California in all its diversity. Most people living in the state do not understand its totality any better than the tourists who usually see only its long, spectacular coastline. The state is the sum of many parts and perceptions, kept separate by an intense regionalism. . . . A genial, lyrical, and rational man, James Houston avoids extremes, and in his fair-minded, very equitable way is the ideal observer and chronicler."

Love Life, the novel Houston penned after *Californians,* looks at the life of a wife and mother of two named Holly, who discovers that her husband has become seriously involved with another woman. Houston's use of a female narrator divided critics. Elizabeth Chamish wrote for the *Christian Science Monitor* (December 9, 1985), "[This] is a curiously virtuous book affirming in the midst of betrayal and infidelity the solid values of persistence, courage, and self-reliance. . . . Although the story flows through vaguely poetic chapter titles and believable dialogue, there are, nevertheless, some major irritations. Holly's macho husband, for one. His feeble attempts to become a more sensitive man of the '80s will make readers wonder why she wants him at all. Generously speaking, he is simply not a likable enough character. The author's female voice is another flaw. While Henry James made successful forays into the female psyche and D.H. Lawrence did not, James D. Houston makes a decent effort. But as often as it is accurate, fair and likable, Houston's female perspective is also weak, detached, and essentially untrue." Jamie Baylis, on the other hand, wrote for the *New Republic* (November 11, 1985), "The plot, to be sure, has its share of cliches, the characters their occasional platitudes. . . . The pat story line is salvaged, however, by Holly's first-person narrative. . . . James Houston's foray into the female psyche is entirely convincing to this reviewer (a woman)."

Houston's novel *Snow Mountain Passage* is a piece of historical fiction—his take on the famed Donner Party, who in 1846 found themselves trapped in the mountains during a snowstorm on their way to California. (The Donner Party is best known in popular culture for having resorted to cannibalism in order to survive their ordeal.) Unlike much of Houston's previous fiction, this novel received several negative reviews. Benjamin Schwarz wrote for the *Atlantic Monthly* (April 2001), "Houston has given himself an opportunity to explore complex motives and characters, and his writerly skills are a match for the task. . . . Yet this work of fiction can't match George Stewart's 1936 history, *Ordeal by Hunger*—the most terrifying book I've read." Bruce Barcott had similar complaints in the *New York Times Book*

Review (April 8, 2001), opining, "The details of the Donner Party still retain their power to shock and horrify. The classic tale of disaster in the American wilderness has all the makings of Shakespearean drama: ambition, greed, jealousy, revenge, murder, cannibalism and bad directions. . . . Houston takes these grand elements and turns them into an undistinguished work of historical fiction."

Houston's most recent novel, *Bird of Another Heaven,* was published in 2007. In it, a radio talk-show host in the San Francisco Bay Area named Sheridan "Dan" Brody is surprised when a woman calls into his show claiming to be his grandmother. In order to discover the truth about her, he embarks on a quest to better understand his origins and finds that his great-grandmother, a half-Indian, half-Hawaiian women from California, was once the consort of the last king of Hawaii. A *Publishers Weekly* (December 18, 2006) reviewer remarked, "Houston interweaves Dan's life in mid-1980s San Francisco with the Hawaiian tribal legacy of his great-grandmother, Nani Keala ('Nancy Callahan'), a pioneer who learned the Hawaiian ways of life and took her place at the side of Hawaii's last king, David Kalakaua. The two story lines converge as Dan learns of and begins to hunt for a secret audio recording made at San Francisco's Palace Hotel during King Kalakaua's final days. Though it gets off to a slow start, Houston builds momentum as the novel's scope widens, and the historical detail is mesmerizing." In *Kirkus Reviews* (January 15, 2007), a critic called the book "compelling evidence that he's one of the best historical novelists working today."

Houston has served as the Villa Montalvo writer in residence in Saratoga, California (Fall 1980 and Spring 1992); the Distinguished Visiting Writer at the University of Hawaii (1983); a member of the California Council of the Humanities (1983–87); the Allen T. Gilliland Chair in Telecommunications at San Jose State University (1985); a visiting writer at the University of Michigan, at Ann Arbor (Fall 1985); a writer in residence at the Centrum Foundation, in Port Townsend, Washington (Winter 1992); a writer in residence at George Mason University, in Fairfax, Virginia (Fall 1999); a writer in residence at the German Federal Reserve Bank, in Frankfurt (May 2002); and most recently, the Lurie Chair and Distinguished Visiting Professor of Creative Writing at San Jose State University (Spring 2006).

Houston has received numerous awards for his work, including the Joseph Henry Jackson Award for *Gig*; his teleplay for *Farewell to Manzanar* won the 1976 Humanitas Prize and earned an Emmy Award nomination the same year for outstanding writing in a drama. He is the recipient of an NEA Individual Writing Grant (1976–77), two travel grants to Asia from the Arts America Program (1981 and 1984), the 1983 American Book Award (for *Californians*) from the Before Columbus Foundation, the 1999 Distinguished Achievement Award from the Western Literature Association,

the 1999 American Book Award (for *The Last Paradise*) from the Before Columbus Foundation, the 2000 Carey McWilliams Award from the California Studies Association, a 2001 commendation from the California State Assembly, and the 2005 Award of Excellence in General Hawaiian Culture and Award of Excellence in Nonfiction from the Hawaii Book Publishers Association.

The Houstons have three grown children: Corinne, Joshua, and Gabrielle.

—S.Y./C.M.

Suggested Reading: *Atlantic Monthly* p107 Apr. 2001; *Best Seller* p299 Jan. 1979; *Kirkus Reviews* Jan. 15, 2007; *Library Journal* p107 Oct. 15, 1982, p110 Sep. 15, 1985; *National Review* p35 Sep. 30, 1983; *New Republic* p39 Sep. 30, 1978, p193 Nov. 11, 1985; *New York Times Book Review* p31 Jan. 13, 1974, p29 Apr. 8, 2001; *New Yorker* p186 Nov. 5, 1973; *Publishers Weekly* p39+ Dec. 18, 2006

Selected Books: fiction—*Between Battles,* 1968; *Gig,* 1969; *A Native Son of the Golden West,* 1971; *Adventures of Charlie Bates,* 1973; *Continental Drift,* 1978; *Love Life,* 1985; *The Last Paradise,* 1998; *Snow Mountain Passage,* 2001; *Bird of Another Heaven,* 2007; nonfiction— *Farewell to Manzanar: A True Story of Japanese American Experience During and After the World War II Internment* (with Jeanne Wakatsuki Houston), 1973; *Californians: Searching for the Golden State,* 1982; *In the Ring of Fire: A Pacific Basin Journey,* 1997; *Hawaiian Son: The Life and Music of Eddie Kamae* (with Eddie Kamae), 2004; memoirs—*Three Songs for My Father,* 1974; *Men in My Life and Other More or Less True Recollections of Kinship,* 1987

Hoy, Claire

July 21, 1940– Nonfiction writer

"Every country's journalism requires at least one Claire Hoy," Kirk Lapointe remarked for the *Hamilton Spectator* (November 27, 1999), referring to the renowned Canadian author, conservative political columnist, and television commentator. "He can be counted upon to be the guy who will ask the politically incorrect question at the most vulnerable time. He's the guy who will take down an ideologue as his fellow reporters simply take down dictation at a news conference. He's the guy who will call a cabinet minister's doublespeak what is in the straight street vernacular." Combining an acerbic wit with a profound skepticism about government and politicians, Hoy has described himself as belonging to the same school of journalism as the late American social

Claire Hoy

critic H. L. Mencken. As he explained to Joe O'Donnell for the *Toronto Star* (November 1, 1987), "Reporters should have the same relationship to politicians as dogs have to telephone poles."

Hoy is the author of nine books, three of which profile prominent Canadian politicians, while three others attack corruption and dishonesty in Canadian politics. Hoy also collaborated with Victor Ostrovsky, a former Israeli intelligence agent, on the book *By Way of Deception* (1990), which leveled sensational allegations against the Mossad, Israel's intelligence service, and garnered considerable international media attention. In *The Truth about Breast Cancer* (1995), Hoy shifted his focus to the deadly medical condition, examining efforts to understand its causes and find its cure. In his latest book, *Canadians in the Civil War* (2004), Hoy explored how his compatriots influenced the American Civil War. Hoy has worked for a number of Canadian newspapers during his career, frequently running afoul of his editors; he has served as a columnist for Southam Newspapers, a division of CanWest Global Communications, since 1988. From 1994 to 1999, Hoy co-hosted the political talk show *Face Off* with Judy Rebick on the Canadian Broadcasting Company (CBC) Newsworld channel. Though his conservative ideals stand in marked contrast to Canada's traditional political culture, with its strong emphasis on moderation and social democracy, Hoy has steadfastly refused to temper his beliefs or tone down his often scathing rhetoric; as he remarked to Greg Enright for the *Toronto Star* (January 19, 1997), "I tend to say what I think."

Claire Hoy was born on July 21, 1940 in Brockville, Ontario, Canada, to James David Hoy and the former Jennie May Richmire. He grew up in the small town of Prescott on the St. Lawrence River across from Ogdensburg, New York. Raised as a Presbyterian, Hoy has described his upbringing as a conservative one. In 1964 he graduated from the Ryerson Polytechnic Institute (today Ryerson University), in Toronto, with a degree in journalism. After completing his education, Hoy wrote for a number of different newspapers in his native Ontario, including the *Belleville Intelligencer*, from 1965 to 1966; the *Kitchener-Waterloo Record*, from 1967 to 1968; the *Toronto Telegram*, from 1968 to 1970; and the *Toronto Star*, from 1970 to 1974. He subsequently moved to the *Toronto Sun*, where he remained for the next 13 years, serving as a reporter and political columnist. In 1980 he made a brief foray into television, serving as a political commentator for Global TV. Hoy's outspoken conservative views and frequent attacks on politicians, regardless of their political affiliation, made him a controversial and polarizing figure. In 1984 Hoy emerged as a fierce critic of Prime Minister M. Brian Mulroney, whose Progressive Conservative (PC) party won the national election in a landslide that year. Writing about Mulroney on a regular basis, Hoy asserted that the prime minister was untrustworthy, vain, and shallow.

In 1985 Hoy published his first book, a biography entitled *Bill Davis*. A member of the PC party, Davis served as the premier of the province of Ontario from 1971 to 1985. During his time in office, Davis substantially increased government spending on education and health care and played an important role in the passage of Canada's new constitution in 1982. Hoy interviewed members of the premier's Cabinet, his close associates, and advisors, whom he described as a "Palace Guard" that protected Davis throughout his career. In 1983 Davis made a bid to lead the PC, which would have made him a candidate for prime minister, but his candidacy generated little enthusiasm outside of Ontario. A few months after Davis stepped down as premier in 1985, Ontario voters ousted the PC from power for the first time in 42 years. "Hoy paints a good picture of the small-town, teetotaling, United Church background that shaped Davis's character and his career," Paul Marshman observed in his review for the Toronto *Financial Post* (July 6, 1985). "It's on Davis as a political animal, however, that Hoy treads firmer ground, and the book's best moments come in his descriptions of how Queen's Park [the seat of Ontario's provincial government] operated under Davis's rule: the Big Blue Machine [the powerful Ontario Progressive Conservative Party], the 'palace guard' that kept MPPs [members of the provincial parliament] at bay, the patronage lists that kept the party oiled and functioning, the major decisions made without the knowledge of caucus. The picture that emerges is that of a decent, yet opportunistic man who built a huge supporting structure around himself to avoid what he feared most—personal confrontation, especially when it involved telling someone no." Marshman, however, criticized Hoy's conservative bias and his "relentless parade of facts and characters," which he thought detracted from the overall quality of the book.

In his second book, *Friends in High Places: Politics and Patronage in the Mulroney Government* (1987), Hoy examined Prime Minister Mulroney's political career and the many difficulties Mulroney encountered during his first three years in power as various scandals forced the resignations of several cabinet members, embarrassed the prime minister personally, and eroded the public's confidence in his government. Expanding on what he wrote about Mulroney in his column, Hoy traced the prime minister's problems to what he alleged were character flaws. Joe O'Donnell offered high praise for *Friends in High Places*, which was a best-seller in Canada. "In page after damning page, Hoy documents the legacy of broken promises, inconsistencies, character flaws and outright political blunders that have brought Prime Minister Brian Mulroney's 3-year-old government from historic highs in public support to record lows," O'Donnell wrote. "Hoy's tales of infighting, indecisiveness, confusion and conflicting statements resurrect in graphic detail Mulroney's difficulties. He also did dozens of interviews and re-read hundreds of speeches and news clippings to single out times and places when Mulroney appears to have said one thing and later said or did exactly the opposite." In a review for the Toronto *Financial Post* (November 2, 1987), Andrew Cohen expressed mixed feelings about the book. "After a while, this kind of relentless character assassination becomes a bit trying," Cohen noted. "The tone is shrill and the language excessive. The attack is unhoneyed by humor. The book is larded with too many quotations from political enemies, who are unlikely to say anything nice about Mulroney. While there is much new material, most of this we have seen before." Despite these criticisms, Cohen concluded that the book "offers a useful and creditable antidote to other studies written by admirers of Mulroney. In its attempt to separate truth from fiction, the book is a public service. If Hoy ever had friends in high places, he will have fewer now."

A year after the publication of *Friends in High Places*, Hoy left the *Toronto Sun*. He alleged that Mulroney, who was reelected by a wide margin in 1988, had pressured Paul Godfrey, the *Sun*'s publisher, to dismiss him. Godfrey countered Hoy's accusation, however, claiming that the columnist voluntarily left the newspaper when he failed to report for a new position in Toronto, after he was transferred there from Ottawa. Hoy filed a lawsuit against his former employer, alleging wrongful dismissal and damage to his reputation; however, nothing came of this litigation. After

leaving the *Toronto Sun*, Hoy became a freelance columnist for Southam Newspapers, where he has remained ever since.

In *Margin of Error: Pollsters and the Manipulation of Canadian Politics* (1989), Hoy criticized the growing dependence of politicians on information supplied by their pollsters. The author wrote that far from being a precise gauge of voter preferences, polls can be inaccurate because different factors, such as unrepresentative samples and poorly worded questions, can produce skewed results. According to Hoy, Mulroney tailored his political platform in 1988 to whatever his pollsters told him, and erroneous polling data led both John Turner, the leader of the Liberal Party, and Edward Broadbent, the leader of the New Democratic Party, to make embarrassing political mistakes. "Hoy portrays the pollsters as self-important publicity-seekers who pose as social scientists, but are disturbingly prone to conflict of interest, ethical lapses, statistical oversights, and partisan overstatement," Martin Cohn wrote for the *Toronto Star* (December 9, 1989). "Yet they are still held in awe as political gurus imbued with mystical clairvoyance. Polling is a growth industry in Canada, fed by the truism that information is power—and that a statistical printout of voters' views confers an extra edge to politicians, bureaucrats, and journalists." Cohn described *Margin of Error* as "a powerful indictment of how we conduct and consume polls," but added that it "is also tedious at times. Statistical sampling is not sexy stuff, particularly when Hoy indulges in lengthy comparisons of questionnaire wording in order to prove bias or skewed results. While the errors and abuses are instructive, few readers are likely to pay close attention to his analysis."

Hoy next assisted Victor Ostrovsky, a former Mossad operative, in writing the controversial *By Way of Deception*, which chronicled Ostrovsky's tenure with the elite intelligence agency. Claiming that the book threatened Israel's security and endangered the lives of Mossad agents, the Israeli government sought to block its publication. Many critics faulted these efforts, arguing that such actions brought *By Way of Deception* valuable publicity and lent credibility to Ostrovsky's allegations. In the book Ostrovsky, who was born in Canada and moved to Israel with his family when he was two years old, described how he was recruited by the Mossad while in the Israeli military and trained as a *katsa*, a case officer. At first, Ostrovsky took pride in serving in the Mossad, believing that he was helping to protect Israel. However, after speaking with senior agents and accessing the agency's computers, he learned of numerous abuses and widespread corruption within the Mossad and became increasingly disillusioned. Among the book's most sensational allegations, Ostrovsky claimed that the Mossad had uncovered intelligence regarding an imminent terrorist attack against an American target in Beirut, Lebanon, in 1983, but refused to share the information with the U.S. because the agency wanted U.S.–Arab relations to deteriorate. Subsequently, on October 23, 1983, 241 American marines, who were stationed in Lebanon as part of an international peacekeeping force, were killed when a terrorist drove a truck filled with explosives into the compound where they were housed. Ostrovsky also wrote that the Mossad conducted clandestine operations in the U.S. and other countries friendly toward Israel. The Israeli government strongly denied the book's claims, dismissing them as lies. *By Way of Deception* became an immediate best-seller and was eventually translated into numerous languages. Most reviewers were unsure how much of the book was true since there was no way to independently verify Ostrovsky's charges. "Given the veil of secrecy that cloaks the nether world of espionage, no lay reader could hope to pass judgment on whether *By Way of Deception* is a work of fact or fiction," George D. Moffett observed for the *Christian Science Monitor* (November 7, 1990). "It should be taken rather as something suggestive, as a highly readable, vastly entertaining account of the way nations operate in a realm where democratic values often take a back seat to national security concerns."

In 1992 Hoy shifted his focus back to Canadian politics with the publication of another biography, *Clyde Wells*. From 1989 to 1996, Wells, a member of the Liberal Party, served as the premier of the province of Newfoundland. As Hoy explained to a writer for *Maclean's* (July 29, 1991), he found Wells an intriguing subject: "Some of the other premiers hate his guts, and they have said so. I have always been interested in people who attract strong emotional responses, positive or negative." As premier Wells played a key role in the defeat of the controversial Meech Lake Accord, a set of amendments to Canada's constitution that would have officially recognized the French-speaking province of Quebec as a "distinct society." The biography received mixed reviews. "Hoy has done a workman-like job assembling what is generally known about Clyde Kirby Wells," Ray Guy wrote for the Montreal *Gazette* (December 12, 1992). "He seems inclined to be positive toward Wells as a politician—or at least sets him a little above the Hoyeseque Ottawa dunghill. Most of it is already known on Wells's home ground, Newfoundland; elsewhere in Canada the need to know has dropped well below fever pitch. It is dry stuff—but so is the subject." For the *Ottawa Citizen* (November 21, 1992), A. Brian Peckford faulted the book, arguing that it was riddled with mistakes and exaggerated Wells's humble upbringing. "Most of the 'information' contained in the book is not new," Peckford wrote. "Perhaps other Canadians may find some interest in knowing about Wells and Newfoundland. This, no doubt, is of some value. However, one hopes that if Hoy wishes to explain a Newfoundlander and Newfoundland to other Canadians in the future, he will spend more

time on fact, less on exaggeration, and place an emphasis on substance and style."

In September 1994, Hoy and the left-wing political activist Judy Rebick began a five-year run as hosts of the debate program *Face Off*, which aired on CBC Newsworld. "Each night this pair of combatants along with two guests, go at each other on some of the touchiest issues of the day, from Quebec separatism to abortion to gun control," Greg Enright observed. Though the show was considered groundbreaking for its time, it went off the air in 1999.

Hoy had a personal interest in the subject of his next book, *The Truth about Breast Cancer* (1995), as his first wife, Beverley, died of the disease in 1976, when she was only 33 years old. Hoy found that despite all of the money spent annually on research in recent decades, doctors have made little progress in determining either what causes breast cancer or how to cure it. "For those who want to know 'the truth' about breast cancer—what it is, who gets it, how it is treated—this is not the right book," a reviewer for *Quill & Quire* (April 1995) wrote. "But for those interested in increasing awareness, activism, and funding for breast cancer research, it provides valuable ammunition, giving a wide-ranging critique of the current medical establishment, its clinical trials, and its crude methods of treating breast cancer." The reviewer criticized the book for making several exaggerated claims and leaving many questions unanswered, concluding, "All in all, *The Truth About Breast Cancer* is useful and very thought-provoking, but it doesn't tell the whole story."

Hoy's subsequent book, *Nice Work: The Continuing Scandal of Canada's Senate* (1999), was highly critical of the Canadian Senate. Canada's parliament has two houses, the House of Commons, whose members are elected, and the Senate, whose members are appointed by the prime minister. Hoy wrote that the Senate consumes millions of dollars every year in salaries and perks for its members—many of whom, he claims, do little work—and is rife with corruption. The author observed that the reputation of the Senate has declined to such an extent with the Canadian public that many prominent politicians have refused appointments to the body. In order to reform the Senate, Hoy called for its members to be elected, instead of appointed, thus making them accountable to the voters. In his review for the *Hamilton Spectator* (November 27, 1999), Kirk Lapointe described *Nice Work* as a disorganized book and criticized Hoy for devoting little attention to how the Senate could be reformed into an effective legislative body. "Still, [*Nice Work*] is a serious book in most respects," Lapointe observed. "The writing is direct, the use of adjectives is surprisingly restrained. The data can numb the senses after a few dozen pages, but it remains a swift read. What could have been an opinionated rant—and I could imagine Claire telling it that way—proves to be more withering by playing it straight."

In 2000 Hoy completed his third political biography, *Stockwell Day: His Life and Politics*. Starting in 1999, the articulate and telegenic Stockwell Day, a legislator and treasury minister in the province of Alberta, was seen by many Canadian conservatives as the one candidate capable of uniting the fractured parties of the political right in time for the general election of November 2000. However, Day became a polarizing rather than a unifying figure in Canadian politics. His call for lower taxes and tougher anti-crime measures resonated with voters in western Canada, but many citizens in eastern Canada were alarmed by Day's fundamentalist Christian beliefs—which included opposition to abortion and homosexuality and support for government funding of religious schools—and feared that if he took power, he would impose his religious views on the country. At the time Hoy's book was published, Day was seeking the leadership of the Canadian Alliance, a new conservative party that had supplanted the PC as the primary Canadian opposition party. (In 1993 voters swept the PC out of power, and the party fared poorly in subsequent elections; in 2000 the PC merged with the Canadian Alliance to form the Conservative Party of Canada.) In his book, Hoy discussed Day's background, religious conversion, family life, and political views. A college dropout, Day worked at different jobs before entering politics. Hoy, who interviewed Day and his wife, argued that the candidate had been unfairly portrayed as a religious extremist and concluded that fears that he would impose his views on the country were greatly exaggerated by his political enemies. Critiquing the work for *Maclean's* (July 17, 2000), Brian Bethune and Barbara Wickens described it as "a sympathetic but reasonably thorough treatment by a prominent right-wing journalist." The reviewers observed that the most interesting parts of the book "consist of Day's frank explanation of his religious conversion and his views on the intersection of religion and politics." Day won the leadership of the Canadian Alliance, and subsequently embarked on his campaign for prime minister, taking on the Liberal candidate, Prime Minister Jean Chretien. In the general election, Day was unable to broaden his appeal or alleviate the concerns of many voters, who returned Chretien's government to power.

"In turning to the writing of a history of Canadian-American relations during the U.S. Civil War, [Hoy] has suppressed his polemic ferocity," Neil Cameron observed, in a review of Hoy's *Canadians in the Civil War*, for the Montreal *Gazette* (December 31, 2004). "[The book] is a well-written, well-researched and well-balanced study of a topic that, as Hoy correctly observes, has received far less attention than it deserves." More than 30,000 Canadians participated in the conflict, Hoy notes, and of these, 5,000 died. Interspersed within the narrative are colorful accounts of Confederate conspirators hatching plots in Montreal hotels and draft-dodgers finding refuge in Canada more than a century before Vietnam. Hoy also explores how the Canadian Confederation of 1867, which began the process of uniting a group of distinct colonies under one government, was influenced by the not entirely unfounded fear that the victorious Union army might turn north to invade Canada. *Canadians in the Civil War* earned a robust critical reception: a writer for *Maclean's* (January 10, 2005) termed it "a fine historical survey." Reviewing the work for the *Edmonton Journal* (February 6, 2005), Brian Hodgson had several caveats, complaining that "[Hoy's] selection of many of the more interesting and intriguing personalities is at times rendered less effective by his lengthy digressions. This and the somewhat episodic nature of the book make it a bit choppy in places." Hodgson also felt that "Hoy never really confronts the question of whether those from north of the U.S. border actually thought of themselves as Canadian or something else." Nevertheless, Hodgson concluded, "The mythic assertion that Canadian history is dull certainly would not be sustained after reading this book. It's all there: tales of cross-border raids, attempts to burn New York City, planning a Confederate mass prisoner of war escape and, indeed, the assassination of President Lincoln, all with Canadian connections."

Hoy has two children, Paul and Kathy, by his first wife, Beverley Sykes, who died in 1976. His second marriage, to the writer Lydia Huber, produced three children, Zachary, Clayton, and Scarlet; Huber and Hoy divorced in 2000, after 18 years of marriage. Hoy makes his home in Toronto. In his leisure time, he enjoys hockey and golf. Though belonging to a profession that produces few teetotalers, Hoy eschews both alcohol and cigarettes and remains a committed Presbyterian.

—D.C.

Suggested Reading: (Canada) *Vancouver Sun* A p13 Nov. 3, 1992; *Hamilton Spectator* W p7 Nov. 27, 1999; *Toronto Star* E p1 Jan. 19, 1997

Selected Books: *Bill Davis*, 1985; *Friends in High Places: Politics and Patronage in the Mulroney Government*, 1987; *Margin of Error: Pollsters and the Manipulation of Canadian Politics*, 1989; *By Way of Deception* (with Victor Ostrovsky), 1990; *Clyde Wells*, 1992; *The Truth about Breast Cancer*, 1995; *Nice Work: The Continuing Scandal of Canada's Senate*, 1999; *Stockwell Day: His Life and Politics*, 2000; *Canadians in the Civil War*, 2004

Courtesy of the University of the South

Hudgins, Andrew

Apr. 22, 1951– Poet; essayist

"The power of [Andrew] Hudgins's poems to describe the world," Peter Stitt wrote for the *New York Times Book Review* (May 4, 1986), "is as profound as their power to affect it is negligible. He lives in a realm that is lost and fallen, but also lush and tragically grand. Perhaps the greatest compliment one could pay a writer like him is to say that his poems are equal to their landscape." Hudgins's debut poetry collection, *Saints and Strangers* (1985), was a runner-up for the Pulitzer Prize, and his collection *The Never-Ending* (1991) was a finalist for the National Book Award. His work betrays a profoundly Southern sensibility, reminding many reviewers of Flannery O'Connor and William Faulkner. Eschewing the free verse so common among modern poets, Hudgins, a professor of English at Ohio State University, favors blank verse, which places greater emphasis on meter and rhythm, and consequently, he has been dubbed a New Formalist. His other poetry collections are: *After the Lost War: A Narrative* (1988), *The Glass Hammer: A Southern Childhood* (1994), *Babylon in a Jar* (1998), and *Ecstatic in the Poison* (2003). His verse, essays, and short stories have appeared in a number of publications, including the *New Yorker*, *Poetry*, the *Southern Review*, the *Missouri Review*, and *American Poetry Review*.

Andrew Hudgins was born on April 22, 1951 in Killeen, Texas. His father, Andrew L. Hudgins, was an officer in the U.S. Air Force but had served in all three major branches of the service: "My father joined the Navy," Hudgins explained in a November 17, 1997 interview posted on the Southern Voices Web site. "He went to naval flight school, was getting ready to be shipped overseas, and then took an [army] appointment to West Point. He had liked flying when he was in the Navy, so he opted to switch to the Air Force." Hudgins moved often as a child, relocating from one military town to another, depending on his father's postings; during his youth the family lived variously in New Mexico, California, North Carolina, and Ohio, as well as overseas in England and France, before finally settling in Montgomery, Alabama. Despite their transient lifestyle, the Hudginses considered themselves Georgians, and that sense of a distinctly Southern identity was deeply absorbed by the young Hudgins: "Wherever we were, our family was a Southern family," he explained in the Southern Voices interview. The Hudginses were Southern Baptists, and Hudgins's upbringing had a strong Christian component, as he told Mark Jarman in an interview for the journal *Image,* as posted on the Poetry Daily Web site: "Since my father read the Bible to my brothers and me every night before prayers, it was the living word, not something detached from life as I lived it. It really is in my bones." As a boy Hudgins, whose poetry has been praised for its rich descriptions of the physical world, developed an odd sensual proclivity for strong smells: "I reacted viscerally to odors more than, say, sounds—and I was often both fascinated and repulsed at the same time." One time Hudgins brought home a few starfish from a school trip; "I threw them on the garage roof to dry," he told Jarman. "Instead they rotted. But I kept crawling up on the garage roof to smell them, study them as they decayed, and think about them, even though the smell was overwhelmingly nasty. . . . It was both evidence that I had killed them for no purpose, and punishment for doing it."

Hudgins did not stand out in school and was a poor athlete. "I was encouraged to do these things I was lousy at," he explained for the Southern Voices interview, "and I felt kind of badgered and bullied, and so mostly, I just wanted to be left alone by adults." Reading and writing became solitary refuges for Hudgins; "A few people were vaguely encouraging, but my parents didn't really know what to make out of it, so they left me alone. I liked that part," he recalled for the Southern Voices interview. He enjoyed children's books, such as the Hardy Boys series and a book by Ellis Credle, *Tall Tales from the High Hills,* and in junior high he began reading the works of Shakespeare and Sophocles. During his sophomore year of high school, in Montgomery, Alabama, he discovered the writing of T. S. Eliot, which proved to have a lasting influence on his artistic sensibility, though Hudgins's own style is much different: "He's the first poet that really excited me," Hudgins recalled in the Southern Voices interview, "and he's the poet that I keep teaching and thinking about and reading regularly."

Upon graduating from high school, Hudgins continued his studies at Huntingdon College, a Methodist school in Montgomery, while living at home and working part-time. Hudgins majored in English and earned a teacher's certificate before graduating in 1974. Huntingdon was a small school with limited course offerings; consequently, Hudgins explained for the Southern Voices interview, "What was offered was what I took, and there was no contemporary fiction class or modern poetry class." After completing his bachelor's degree, Hudgins remained in Montgomery and found work as a sixth-grade teacher at Carver Elementary School, a rough school in an impoverished neighborhood. He reflected at length to Jarman on his short tenure in the classroom, describing it as "what must have been the worst year of my life. I've done a lot of crappy jobs over the years, including one that involved digging up a septic tank and spending a couple of afternoons standing in what is euphemistically called 'gray water.' But nothing was as bad as knowing that I would have to go back to my out-of-control job that, in a rotation of ninety students in three classes, had twelve kids who had to report to their probation officer regularly. I couldn't even have art class because boys snapped the crayons into pellets and threw them at the girls so hard that they left welts on their skin. I didn't have a clue how to teach them, and on Sunday nights, about ten o'clock, I often started crying, knowing I had to go back to work the next morning and be incompetent for another week." In his spare time Hudgins concentrated on his writing.

After resigning from his teaching position at Carver, Hudgins worked various odd jobs while studying for his master's degree in English at the University of Alabama, where he was honored as a dean's scholar. Upon completing his master's thesis, "Tom Jones and the Monomyth," in 1976, Hudgins moved north to attend Syracuse University, in New York. There Hudgins continued his studies in English, working towards a Ph.D. while his wife pursued a law degree. Though he did not complete his doctoral studies, Hudgins was recognized for his talent as a writer, receiving the Delmore Schwartz Award. In 1978 Hudgins returned to Alabama and began teaching creative writing as an adjunct instructor in composition at Auburn University, a junior college in Montgomery, where he remained until 1981, when he gained acceptance to the Iowa Writer's Workshop. At Iowa Hudgins studied with Don Justice, Marcia Southwick, Henri Coulett, Marvin Bell, and Lynn Sharon Schwartz; he also began to accept his vocation as a writer. Before that time, Hudgins recalled in the Southern Voices interview, "I felt self-conscious about it: when people would say, 'What are you doing?' I didn't want to say, 'I'm a writer.' I'd say, 'Well, I'm writing books, mumble, mumble,' and 'Well, I'm teaching part-time, mumble, mumble,' and it wasn't until I was thirty and at the Iowa Writers

Workshop that . . . the answer was either 'I'm a poet' or 'I'm a fiction writer,' and that was the un-self-conscious answer that people gave at Iowa, and that was when it happened for me." In 1983 Hudgins was awarded his M.F.A.

From 1984 to 1985 Hudgins taught creative writing at Baylor University, in Waco, Texas, as a lecturer in composition. In 1985 he accepted a position at the University of Cincinnati, where he remained for the next 17 years, publishing a number of works before moving, in 2001, to a post at Ohio State University, in Columbus. The Ohio State Web site lists modern poetry, contemporary poetry, and 19th-century American poetry as his primary areas of expertise. Hudgins considers himself "a dedicated, teacher, a better than average classroom technician, a very good practical critic of what poems do and what they can do, and someone who will go the extra mile for his students. I push them hard to be better while still being encouraging," he told Jarman. Thematically, the fundamental questions that Hudgins addresses in his poetry, he explained in the interview for Southern Voices, are "What do you do with the drive for perfection in a fallen world?" and the related question, "What do you do in a world where you're going to be in for a limited amount of time and then die? . . . Those are the issues that I keep circling back to and picking at, though the subject I'm writing about changes."

With *Saints and Strangers*, Hudgins unveiled his signature poetic style. Describing his rationale for using blank verse as opposed to the more protean free verse, Hudgins explained for the Southern Voices interview, "With free verse, I never could figure out why the lines stopped where they stopped. . . . Some people say that in free verse, because you're not locked into that beat count in the lines, the lines are more sensual, but they did not work that way for me. What happened with me was because the line could stop anywhere, it became over-intellectualized. . . . Once I started writing in meter, I knew that the line had to have these five beats in it, and I wanted to have this kind of a weight on the last foot, then everything became not an intellectual decision, but a sensual decision."

Saints and Strangers received complimentary notices. "Hudgins's well-nigh perfect first book considers the plight of a frail humanity in a universe that permits, or at any rate seems to permit, the existence of evil," a reviewer wrote for *Publishers Weekly*, as quoted on Amazon.com. "The poems themselves are as plain, graceful and compulsively readable as they are resonant and profound. Both Hudgins's vision and his mechanics are impeccable." *Saints and Strangers* is marked by its "richness of style, preoccupation with guilt and sacrifice and a sense of ill-spent blood dripping from the honeysuckle and verbena, soaking into the tragic Confederate soil," Stitt observed. "The title poem, in eight sections, reads like Mr. Hudgins's rewriting of [Flannery]

O'Connor's *Wise Blood*—this time with a female rather than a male protagonist." In the section entitled "Something Wakes Me Up," the narrator describes conflicted feelings while overhearing the gutting of a deer by two poachers. In "Mary Magdalene's Left Foot," Hudgins reveals his earthy Christian sensibility: "But gold is meretricious flattery / for the whore who washed Christ's feet with tears, / who rubbed sweet oil into his sores, then kissed / each suppurating wound that swelled his flesh, / knowing that it was God's clear flesh beneath / its human dying. And that is more than you or I / will ever know of where we place our lips," he writes, as quoted by Clay Reynolds in the *Dictionary of Literary Biography, Volume 120: American Poets Since World War II* (1992).

Despite the strong Christian current running through *Saints and Strangers* and his later works, Hudgins does not consider himself a Christian in any strict, dogmatic sense: "I continue to see the world from a Christian ethical perspective, though now I add to it my own doubts about that perspective," he explained to Jarman. "The spiritual issue, the issue of faith, is much more difficult for me, fluid, and painful. I am, I think, an instinctive believer, but I balk at the intellectual level. No matter how much I want to make the leap I can't do it."

In *After the Lost War: A Narrative* (1988), Hudgins offered a poetic homage to the poet and Civil War veteran Sidney Lanier. In this narrative poem, "Hudgins turns from a collection of tortured individuals, dark scenes, and religious themes to focus on . . . Lanier; Hudgins follows Lanier's life through one of the most horrible series of events any man could face: war and the knowledge of his own, impending death," Reynolds wrote. "Once more, Hudgins penetrates history and biography to reveal a deeper meaning, a truer self." Although the book was not as well received as *Saints and Strangers*—some critics expressed dismay at its violent tone, which they felt clashed with Lanier's actual life and work—*After the Lost War* further established Hudgins's standing as a poet of depth and importance. As Reynolds noted, "Other critics tend to agree that, regardless of the wisdom of Hudgins's choice of Lanier as a character of focus, the contemporary poet's work far outstrips his subject's importance and, possibly, Lanier's talent as well."

Hudgins's next work, *The Never-Ending*, contains poems on such subjects as nature, religion, family, and love. Reviews of the book were enthusiastic. His chief tools "include linear narrative and anecdotal drama, a static speaker, traditional lineation with formalized line breaks, a fondness for blank verse, clarity, public expression, and shared experience," David Baker observed for *Poetry* (February 1992). "He writes what in most hands is tidy, safe, party-line poetry favored by many literary magazines. But Hudgins can be brilliant. Sometimes the most valuable and difficult articulations are those originating from deep within the confines of traditional method, those which reinvigorate otherwise conventional gestures." Doris Lynch wrote for *Library Journal* (May 15, 1991) , "The poems are blessed with startling imagery: deer are 'enormous rats on stilts;' sirens are 'lullabies / they sound like making love.' In one 'prayer' poem, Hudgins speaks in slang to God; he tells God he hears from an old girlfriend, then asks, 'Do you?' It's surprisingly effective."

The 65 entries in Hudgins's collection *The Glass Hammer: A Southern Childhood* (1994) offer a vision of childhood and adolescence in the South during a great period of change, in the 1950s and 1960s. In this loosely autobiographical work, Hudgins explores such difficult issues as racism, poverty, and class conflict. Jay Rogoff wrote for the *Kenyon Review* (Spring 1995) that the book "stands as an idiosyncratic social document, revealing as much about a time and place as about a self and family. Our hero, Andrew Hudgins, springs from a mixture of memory and desire, in a series of reconstructed selves growing up before our eyes." The work was not immune from criticism; David Wojahn wrote for *Poetry* (January 1995) that "in many cases his humor devolves into cheap shots, easy ridicule and a kind of adolescent guffawing. . . . *The Glass Hammer* is an exasperating combination of Hudgins at his best as well as at his worst." Most critics praised the volume, however, as did Christine Stenstrom in a review for *Library Journal* (June 1, 1994): "The powerfully direct, anecdotal quality of these poems," she wrote, "invites the reader to experience a deeply flawed world the poet has transformed into a more palatable place by his humor and compassion."

The Glass Anvil (1997), an anthology of Hudgins's literary essays, includes tales from his childhood; reflections on language, religion, racism, and Southern literature; homages to the 19th-century poet Frederick Goddard Tuckerman and to the contemporary poet Galway Kinnell; and revelations about which parts of *The Glass Hammer* are factual and which are fiction.

A bizarre array of characters populate Hudgins's fifth collection, *Babylon in a Jar*, among them "a man who artfully hangs dead and dying animals from a tree, a young patricide who likes to show his night-school classmates the newspaper accounts of the slaying, . . . and a drunken bleacher bum whose beaming face suggests to the poet the loving visage of God," David Yezzi observed for *Poetry* (June 1999). John Taylor wrote for the *Antioch Review* (Fall 1999), "Often black-humored, Hudgins can also tenderly ruminate on the ephemeral beauty of flowers. . . . A strikingly earnest poet, Hudgins searches for whatever meanings or values—despite the 'cold capricious / laughter' of the 'goat god'—can genuinely be attributed to our lives." Though Yezzi characterizes the poems as "memorable tales to be sure, full of pathos and quirky humor," he found fault in Hudgins's spare diction, commenting that "certain passages lack the intensity of language necessary to make the works as engaging as the stories they tell."

In his 2003 work, *Ecstatic in the Poison*, Hudgins "mixes taut anecdotes and autobiography with more lyrical work," a reviewer noted for *Publishers Weekly* (July 21, 2003). The title poem evokes an image of children playing in a cloud of DDT spray used to cut down the mosquito population: "The white clouds tumbled down our streets / pursued by spellbound children / who chased the most distorting clouds, / ecstatic in the poison," Hudgins writes, as quoted by Matthew Flamm for the *New York Times Book Review* (December 28, 2003). Flamm observed, "There is a subversive streak to Andrew Hudgins's orderly, accessible poetry that sets him apart from his more transcendent peers: he consistently undercuts himself. Metaphysically and otherwise, he is forever seeing his life clearly and spilling a Coke on his lap at the same time." *Ecstatic in the Poison* features Hudgins's usual formal poetic structure and includes comic interludes, such as the entry "A Joke Walks into a Bar," as well as biblical parables. "Part of what makes Hudgins such a pleasure—and carries the reader over the occasionally repetitive arrangements—is his great storytelling gift and his role as an acidly self-deprecating central character," Flamm commented. "It might seem wrong to praise a collection of poems this way, but *Ecstatic in the Poison* reads like a novel." "'In the midst of life, we are in death' often seems to be Hudgins' motto, yet no contemporary poet of his distinction writes more of joy and wonder," Ray Olson noted in *Booklist*, as quoted on Amazon.com.

Though Hudgins has written fiction, penning a number of short stories, poetry remains his metier: "I trained my brain to be a poet's brain, so it's very difficult to move into other structure sometimes, and sometimes I think that writers who go back and forth bring the limitations of the one to the other," he explained in the interview for Southern Voices. In regards to his essay writing, Hudgins prefers pieces that combine the personal with the literary. As for his advice for aspiring authors, Hudgins demurs, remarking in the Southern Voices interview, "There's several pat answers; the first one is, read; the second one is, don't. . . . I don't really have any advice for anybody. If you truly want to do it, then you have to take it very seriously and hold yourself to a high standard, and that means reading and writing as hard as you can, and taking hard criticism, and go about it as honestly and at as deep a level as you possibly can."

Hudgins has received numerous awards in recognition of his artistic achievements over the years, including two fellowships from the National Endowment for the Arts, the Hanes Prize for Poetry from the Fellowship of Southern Writers (1995), the Ohioana Krout Poetry Award (1997), and the Witter Bynner Foundation Prize for poetry from the American Academy and Institute of Arts and Letters. Hudgins lists his primary influences as Shakespeare, Robert Lowell, Walt Whitman, T. S. Eliot, and Emily Dickinson. Noted for his sense of humor, Hudgins was described by Rita Dove, the former poet laureate of the United States, as "one of the funniest people I know," as quoted by Bill Eichenberger for the *Columbus Dispatch* (August 6, 2003). "I'm talking seriously comedic: He can keep a dinner pary in stitches from salad to cappuccino, and not with one liners—no, Andrew Hudgins is a natural storyteller, a spinner of shaggy-dog tales that suddenly turn to make a point." Despite his well-regarded body of work and many accolades, Hudgins is modest regarding his output thus far: "As to what all this work has actually accomplished," Hudgins remarked to Jarman, "what can I say? I'm dissatisfied. I want it to be better than it is."

Hudgins married his first wife, Olivia Hardy, in 1974; the couple divorced several years later. In 1992 Hudgins married the novelist Erin McGraw. They currently live in Columbus, Ohio.

—P.B.M.

Suggested Reading: *Library Journal* May 15, 1991, p110 June 1, 1994; Ohio State University Web site; *New York Times Book Review* p22 May 4, 1986, p13 Dec. 28, 2003; *Poetry* Feb. 1992, p219 Jan. 1995; Poetry Daily Web site; *Publishers Weekly* p189 July 21, 2003; Southern Voices Web site; *Dictionary of Literary Biography, Volume 120: American Poets Since World War II*, 1992

Selected Books: *Saints and Strangers*, 1985; *After the Lost War: A Narrative*, 1988; *The Never-Ending*, 1991; *The Glass Hammer*, 1997; *Babylon in a Jar*, 1998; *Ecstatic in the Poison*, 2003

Huneven, Michelle

Aug. 14, 1953– Novelist; journalist

The critically acclaimed journalist and novelist Michelle Huneven has earned a reputation for successfully depicting life-weary characters in a fully realized Southern California setting. Elizabeth Judd, writing for the *Atlantic Monthly* (October 2003), likened Huneven to the Pulitzer Prize–winning author Richard Russo: "Both have an old-fashioned authorial munificence, a leisurely way of developing their threadbare characters, and an exasperated affection for unlovable places." Huneven's first novel, *Round Rock* (1997), offers a look into the turbulent lives of a group of recovering alcoholics; her second, *Jamesland* (2003), focuses on a colorful cast of characters who all seem to share some connection to, or interest in, the life and thought of the American philosopher and psychologist William

Marion Ettlinger/Courtesy of Random House

Michelle Huneven

James. In 2006 Huneven co-authored, with Bernadette Murphy, the nonfiction book *The Tao Gal's Guide to Real Estate: Six Modern Women Discover the Ancient Art of Finding, Owning, and Making a Home*, which details the Eastern philosophy–tinged house-hunting adventures of members of a longstanding women's group who share an interest in Eastern philosophy, particularly the Tao Te Ching.

Michelle Huneven was born in Altadena, California, on August 14, 1953. Her father, Arthur Huneven, was a carpenter and teacher; her mother, the former Shirley Blechman, was a pianist. She received her bachelor of arts degree from Scripps College, in Claremont, California, in 1970. She attended Grinnell College, in Iowa, from 1970 to 1972, and Eastern Washington University, in Cheney, Washington, from 1973 to 1974; in both cases she left before receiving a degree. She ultimately received her M.F.A. degree from the Iowa Writers' Workshop, in 1978.

Since 1984 Huneven has been working as a journalist and freelance writer. In 1984 she received the General Electric Younger Writers Award for her short story "The Foot." In an interview with David L. Ulin for the *Los Angeles Times* (November 13, 1997), she explained that when she started writing fiction, it was for the wrong reasons. "I wanted to be famous," she told Ulin. "I was writing to be published, to build a career, but where I ended up was on a route of self-deprivation leading nowhere." Her work as a journalist, however, helped her "to desacralize writing," she added. "Always in the holy hall of fiction, everything had to be so perfect, so precious, so self-conscious, but with journalism, I wasn't so impossibly hard on myself."

Huneven suffered from a drinking problem for a time in her life, but recovered from it sufficiently in the early 1990s to study to become a Unitarian Universalist minister. Between 1990 and 1992 she attended the Claremont School of Theology, in California, and while there was urged by a psychologist to stop flitting lightly from one interest to another and devote herself fully to one thing. "No one had ever said that to me before," Huneven recalled to Ulin. "And it made me decide to do a novel after all." Instead of focusing on "publication, money, [and] fame," she began writing simply for the sake of writing itself.

The result was her first novel, *Round Rock*. The story takes place in the small town of Rito, in California's Santa Bernita Valley. There, at a rehabilitation retreat for recovering alcoholics known as Round Rock Ranch, a romantic triangle develops among Red Ray, a recovering alcoholic who founded Round Rock; Lewis Fletcher, a graduate-student cocaine addict who has been sleeping in his professor's garage; and Libby Daw, a barroom fiddle player, for whom both men feel some affection.

Round Rock was highly praised. In the *New York Times Book Review* (August 3, 1997), Valerie Sayers noted: "Deftly shifting the narrative's focus from one character to another, Huneven lays bare these three searching souls." Philip Lopate, in *Esquire* (July 1997), wrote: "Huneven has fashioned a sexy, moving, and (mostly) unsentimental novel about romantic folly that takes place in the most improbable of settings: a drunk farm. . . . The real brilliance of the novel lies in how it balances cynicism and hope. Huneven gives both doubters of and believers in twelve-stepism equal time." In the *Los Angeles Times* (August 3, 1997), Valerie Miner observed: "Huneven follows people into disaster, toward recovery, through estrangements of venerable vintage to marriage and reproduction, all against a shifting backdrop of concealed desire and hidden memory. Essentially, *Round Rock* chronicles an odyssey toward forgiveness, toward absolution of self and others." Miner added, "Huneven is an audacious novelist, casting the narrative light evenly on various idiosyncratic characters while summoning the generationally and culturally distinct voices of a diverse population. She forfeits fashionable audience-protagonist cathexis for a more complex portrayal of multiple situations and relationships, thereby introducing readers to this tight, fractious community as if they were newcomers, free to form their own fresh allegiances." *Round Rock* was named a *New York Times* Notable Book of the Year and a *Los Angeles Times* Best Book of the Year.

In Huneven's second novel, *Jamesland* (2003), Alice Black, the fictional great-great-granddaughter of the philosopher William James, is in need of some emotional and spiritual aid. Alice is in her 30s and seriously depressed; she is involved with a married man, tends bar for a living, and resides alone in a house once inhabited by her great-aunt Kate Gordon. Kate, now fairly senile, is in a nursing home, working on an obsessive project that has occupied the last 40 years of her life: writing a biography of James and his family. Alice, on the other hand, has tried to distance herself from the influence of her illustrious ancestor. While waiting for her lover, Nick Lawton, to divorce his wife, the aging movie star Jocelyn Nearing, Alice meets and befriends some of the other residents of the Los Feliz district of Los Angeles, notably Pete Ross, a former chef who lost his family and his middle-class life after his restaurant failed, and Helen Harland, the down-to-earth minister of a nearby Unitarian Universalist church. The trio make a habit of dining together, with gourmet dinners prepared by Pete, and engage in avid discussions about—among other things—the writings of William James.

In *L.A. Weekly* (October 17, 2003), Mona Simpson declared: "One of the goals of the novel since the beginning of the form has been to realistically capture love, that ever-flitting butterfly, in its contemporary incarnation. Huneven is one of our few writers who can deliver an authentic love story, with characters as unlikely for redemption as possible, as failed and weird and hopeless as ourselves." Jennifer Egan, writing for the *New York Times Book Review* (October 12, 2003), observed, "Offbeat and vigorously written, [*Jamesland*] is engrossing in part because it wears its preoccupation with the paranormal so lightly." A critic for *Kirkus Reviews* (August 1, 2003) described the novel as inhabiting "Anne Tyler/Gail Godwin/Jon Hassler territory, and Huneven works it efficiently, scattering expository details throughout her characters' successive communications, meetings, and quarrels. The only problem: her warm and fuzzy empathy with eccentrics and misfits, initially gratifying, is hard to sustain over the course of a long novel. Still, *Jamesland* meanders agreeably, and gets better as it goes along. Another charmer from a gifted and very likable writer."

In an interview posted on the Knopf Web site, Huneven commented on the presence of religion in her two novels: "Both are concerned with how people who don't consider themselves religious—like almost all of my friends—still have these crises, these emergencies, that are essentially spiritual or religious in nature and therefore require a spiritual or religious solution. In *Round Rock*, such crises came in the form of alcoholism, and the solution was found in AA [Alcoholics Anonymous] and personal recovery. But even AA spirituality is somewhat institutionalized, and certainly has its own vocbulary. After finishing *Round Rock*, I wanted to write about people who didn't qualify for any such program, who had to forge their own spiritual paths, invent their own religious vocabularies, find their own like-minded communities simply in order to survive."

In 2006 Huneven co-wrote, with Bernadette Murphy, *The Tao Gal's Guide to Real Estate: Six Modern Women Discover the Ancient Art of Finding, Owning, and Making a Home.* The Tao Gals, a group of Los Angeles–area women, have for years been holding weekly meetings, and according to Susan Carpenter for the *Los Angeles Times* (February 9, 2006), they use the Tao Te Ching, a Chinese spiritual text written more than 25 centuries ago, "to reflect on spiritual principles and their real-life application." Under the influence of this ancient Chinese text, two of the Tao Gals, Huneven and Murphy, have presented "a book that addresses not only the practical aspects of home-buying, but also the emotional ones," Sandy Dunham wrote for the *Seattle Times* (February 8, 2006). "The market will tell you where you belong," Murphy told Penelope Green for the *New York Times* (January 26, 2006), "but you can't take that as a reflection of who you are. At least you're not supposed to. Of course we all did. The market will also tell you to 'get in, get in, before it's too late.' The point of the book, what we learned after years, is not to let our lives be defined by externals." Carpenter found that the book's strengths lay in two areas: "the comfort women feel in hearing other women's stories and getting solid nuts-and-bolts information."

Huneven has contributed essays and short fiction to a number of publications, including the *Los Angeles Times*, *Redbook*, *Harper's*, and *Buzz*. For many years she has been a restaurant critic for *LA Weekly*. She has received the James Beard Journalism Award for newspaper feature reporting (1995) and the Whiting Writers' Award (2002). She lives in Altadena, California, next door to her husband, Jim Potter, an attorney. They married in September 2005. The ceremony took place in his yard, the reception in hers.

—C.M.

Suggested Reading: *Atlantic Monthly* (on-line) Oct. 2003; *Esquire* p28 July 1997; *LA Weekly* p120 Oct. 17, 2003; *Los Angeles Times* p 2 Aug. 3, 1997, E p1 Nov. 13, 1997, R p6 Nov. 23, 2003, F p6 Feb. 9, 2006; *New York Times* (on-line) Oct. 12, 2003, F p1 Jan. 26, 2006; *New York Times Book Review* p9 Aug. 3, 1997; *Times Literary Supplement* p25 Oct. 31, 1997

Selected Books: *Round Rock*, 1997; *Jamesland*, 2003; *The Tao Gal's Guide to Real Estate: Six Modern Women Discover the Ancient Art of Finding, Owning, and Making a Home* (with Bernadette Murphy), 2006

Jack Guez/AFP/Getty Images

Huston, Nancy

Sep. 16, 1953– Novelist; essayist; literary theorist

Nancy Huston was born in Canada but moved to France more than three decades ago. Her work, like her life, has been marked by experimentation and change. First a feminist theorist, she later became a novelist and writes most often in French—not her native language. "Huston's own changes and developments make her hard to place as Calgarian, Parisian, or anything else," Harry Vandervlist wrote for the Calgary arts magazine *FFWD* (on-line). Huston told Vandervlist, "If I'm like anyone, I'm like [Samuel] Beckett [who also moved to France and adopted French for his writings], because he wanted to get away from childhood tensions." She explained that for both herself and Beckett, the use of French "was a totally personal and psychologically-determined choice, not a politically-determined choice. We are both refugees from mental disaster." Vandervlist concluded, "If [Huston] has a place, perhaps it is the 'between' in the relations between men and women, her birthplace and her adopted home, or her mother tongue and the language of art. Between may be the best place to be for the kind of vital empathy and imagination Huston brings to a life and work spent puncturing preconceptions." Although she writes in French, Huston often translates her own novels for publication in English.

Nancy Huston wrote the following autobiographical statement for *World Authors 2000–2005*:

"I was born in 1953 to a couple of beautiful, brilliant and extremely young intellectuals who happened to be living in Calgary at the time. Their other two children, my older brother and younger sister, were both born in Edmonton and my mother claims that *in toto* the family moved house 18 times in the nine years their marriage lasted.

"I've been on the move ever since. . . .

"Both my parents came from families with a typically Canadian mixture of backgrounds—descendants of Irish, Scots, English and German immigrants, their own folks were hardworking Puritans with humble beginnings who'd managed to acquire a modicum of education, culture and financial ease. My father taught math and physics; my mother was impassioned by everything from literature and music to political science. I see my parents as a 1950's couple akin in many ways to Sartre and de Beauvoir—striving to be free and strong and egalitarian despite the dictates of the feminine mystique. Unfortunately, things didn't pan out in their case because, unlike the famous French couple, they also had a slough of kids and financial difficulties. The marriage fell apart in 1959; my mother left the country and my father at once became engaged to a young German woman. In the fall of 1959, my future stepmother took me and my younger sister to Germany with her for four months; this experience—learning a new language at an extremely critical moment in my life and feeling that it somehow turned me into a new and better person—probably prepared my brain and soul for my later conversion to French.

"In 1968, my father decided to leave the University of Alberta in Calgary for a teaching job in a tiny Waldorf school in the backwoods of New Hampshire. I was 15, and fairly incensed at being uprooted yet again. But it was at this school that I first tasted the true joy of learning—Shakespeare, Dante, art history, pottery, creative writing, French—suddenly the whole world opened up to me and I felt I could exist.

"A number of fairly rocky years ensued—working as a medical secretary at the Harvard Psychiatric Clinic in Cambridge, taking night classes in philosophy, doing lots of dabbling with love and sex, then living in a roach-infested ground-floor apartment in the Bronx, studying at Sarah Lawrence in Bronxville while supporting myself with typing on the side. Two courses at Sadie Lou were to have a lasting effect on me—writing with E.L. Doctorow and harpsichord with Joel Spiegelman. In 1973 I came to Paris on my Junior Year Abroad. Having fallen in love with a Frenchman, I wangled permission to also spend my senior year abroad, and now, several decades down the line, I've come up with the perfect inscription for my tombstone, *Once a broad, always a broad.*

"Shortly after my arrival in Paris I got involved with the women's movement and was asked to write book reviews for a new women's literary journal called *Sorcières* (Witches). I found the experience of writing in French exhilarating—the writer's block I'd been struggling with magically evaporated and I could hear the music of the language, perhaps because in French I wasn't hampered with the norms of academic discourse or intimidating role models. Moreover, I had no childhood memories in French and thus no unconscious, no bad dreams, no dark demons. I got a cushy job teaching English at the Ministry of Finance and found I could support myself working by ten or fifteen hours a week; this left luscious amounts of time for pursuing my studies, my relationships, and my love affair with the French language. In 1977, having attended Roland Barthes's seminar for two years and written a thesis on linguistic taboo, I received the equivalent of a Master's degree from the Ecole des Hautes Etudes en Sciences Sociales. Two years later, also indirectly through Barthes, I met Bulgarian-born critic and philosopher Tzvetan Todorov, and from then on my exile was irreversible. We married in 1981; our children were born in 1982 (Lea) and 1988 (Sacha); and we're still very much together.

"[The year] 1979 also marked the publication of my first book, a nonfiction work on men and little girls; my swearwords thesis was published the following year and my first novel, *The Goldberg Variations*, in 1981; ever since then I've continued to alternate between fiction and nonfiction, with occasional forays into screenwriting, playwriting, children's books and even some feeble attempts at poetry. Essentially, over all these years and in all these genres, I've explored various ways of interweaving the same themes: death and aging, transgression and madness, love and music, fatherhood and motherhood, prostitution and war, exile and identity, the importance of childhood. . . .

"Another major turning-point in my life occurred in 1989–90 when I finally decided to revive my mother tongue and write a novel set in my home province of Alberta. *Plainsong* caused rather an upset in my career, partly because my French publisher dumped me (I'd started working with an agent and French publishers tend to hate agents) and it was two years before I found another one, and partly because Quebec publishers and journalists were infuriated when the novel's French translation *Cantique des plaines* won the Governor General's prize. Things eventually calmed down, however, and—the *Plainsong* experience having taught me that translating my books helped me to improve them—I decided to accept my linguistic duplicity once and for all. The complex, multilingual, multicultural identity of Romain Gary (to whom I devoted a short book in 1995) was inspiring and encouraging to me in this matter. Though I continue to write nonfiction only in French, occasionally translating bits and pieces for journals in North America, my novels are written in French or English depending on the language my characters speak, and I now never show a manuscript to a publisher until I've completed both versions.

"I'm an insatiable traveler and an insatiable listener. I drink in other people's stories and love to slip into their skins. I work with voices and have preserved a deep, constant involvement with music (piano, harpsichord, flute, numerous stage performances with musicians accompanying my readings); my books tend to be polyphonous. I have an unending fascination for the theme of identity— not, as people often hastily surmise, because I'm looking for mine, but because the checkered story of my life has given me precious distance on the matter, and I'm acutely aware of the extent to which all our identities are arbitrary—and thus in a sense, despite the devastating effects they produce in reality, illusory.

"I believe in the virtue, not of identity but of identification, which is the overriding virtue of the novel.

Nancy Huston was born to Mary Louise Engels and James Huston in Calgary, Alberta, Canada, on September 16, 1953. Her mother left the family when Huston was six. She grew up in Calgary and Edmonton. Her father then got a teaching job in Wilton, New Hampshire, where Huston attended high school and began learning French. "It was not my Canadian upbringing but actually my American high school that made me a francophone," she told Pat Donelly for the Montreal *Gazette* (October 18, 2003). Charles Foran wrote for the Canadian *National Post* (February 15, 2003) that Huston's childhood, by her own accounts, was one of "Protestantism, wheat fields, country and western music, oil derricks, freight trains, piano lessons, picnics, mountain lakes." She does not remember it as idyllic. "I began to see my childhood as a spiritually very superficial existence," she explained to Don Gillmor for the journal *Saturday Night* (June 1995). "The New World Protestantism is the most imagination-throttling thing."

In France Huston studied under Roland Barthes, the prominent literary and social theorist, and acquainted herself with the work of such French intellectuals as Jacques Derrida, Claude Levi-Strauss, Jacques Lacan, Michel Foucault, and Julia Kristeva. Huston soon grew disillusioned with literary theory. She told Joel Yanofsky for the Montreal *Gazette* (September 11, 1993), "You know how when you go to tropical countries you get vaccinated against certain maladies, well, when I went to France, no one vaccinated me against theory. I got ill with theory. . . . It's made to be very intimidating, but it is really bodiless, hollow. It is discourse about discourse about discourse." She continued, "I like writers whose work has flesh, who believe in the virtue of telling stories. . . . With all my reading of Lacan, with all my note-taking, all my seminars, has any of it helped me to live one second? No. Has [the fiction writer] Flannery O'Connor? Yes."

Huston published her first novel, *Les Variations Goldberg*, in 1981, and translated it in 1996 as *The Goldberg Variations*. The book is dedicated to Roland Barthes, who "had longings to write a novel but was never able to. He was crippled by his own intelligence," Huston told Gillmor. "I think that his death [in 1980] gave me the green light to write novels." *The Goldberg Variations* consists of the musings of 30 guests as they wait to hear Liliane, a musician, play Bach's *Goldberg Variations* on the harpsichord. (One of the main characters is an intellectual apparently based on Barthes.) Calling it "a jewel of a book," Marianne Ackerman wrote for the Montreal *Gazette* (November 23, 1996), "This is an intellectual exercise that throbs with the smell of life. We learn a lot about music, criticism, literary circles, but most of all, we learn a lot about Liliane—her love affairs, her appetites, her lust for mystery, her husband, her eccentricities, her hubris. And yet, Liliane remains, as she must, a mystery. As people sit on the hard chairs and wait for the concert to begin, they think all the bitchy little thoughts people think in public situations. Jealousies abound. Insecurities flourish. . . . The result is an utterly delightful cacophony of brainy people wallowing in art, a wonderful explanation, by way of character, of why it is so great to share culture. Bach, Liliane and her mysterious need to perform are what draws these lives together, and the mix is simply more intoxicating that anything else they could be doing with their evening." *The Goldberg Variations* was short-listed for the Prix Femina and won the Prix Contrepoint.

Huston continued to publish fiction, nonfiction, children's books, drama, and screenplays, becoming well known in the French-speaking world. She wrote the novel *Plainsong* (1993) in English, because of its subject matter. "*Plainsong* dealt with the things I grew up with—hymns and prayers, cowboys, country and western music, Christianity. It had to be in English," Huston told Yanofsky. The novel tells of a man named Paddon Sterling, from the point of view of his granddaughter Paula, who has inherited his diaries. Yanofsky called *Plainsong* "a touching lyrical family saga about time and history. . . . . It's also the story of a man who believes he's a failure but whose daily life has a grandeur he is never quite able to see. It's up to the narrator to see it, to redeem her grandfather through love and memory." Gregory F. McGillis opined in a review for the *Ottawa Citizen* (January 29, 1994), "*Plainsong* is part letter and part prayer, part song of faith and part work of art. It is, in every part, a brilliant achievement of language and imagination." A controversy arose when Huston's translation of the novel, *Cantique des Plaines* won the Governor-General's Literary Award for French-language fiction. Objections were raised that the book had been originally written in English and that, furthermore, the author was not French-Canadian. According to Claire Rothman, writing

for the Montreal *Gazette* (January 29, 1994), Huston "lobbed a question that summed up matters with the clarity of a Zen koan: 'If I didn't write *Cantique des Plaines*,' she said, 'I'd like to know who did.'"

Slow Emergencies, Huston's translation of *La Virevolte*, her 1994 novel, was published in Canada in 1996. (Some sources say 1997.) The novel relates the story of Lin, a passionate dancer who abandons her husband and children for an international career on the stage. In a review for the *Washington Post Book World* (March 18, 2001), Lisa Russ Spaar called the novel a "story of domestic quicksand and exigency, of artistic force and its price" and wrote, "*Slow Emergencies* may strike some readers as self-indulgent and gestural at times, perhaps owing to the novel's mimetic, stylistic choreography. . . . This novel's 'slow emergencies,' its motions of emergence and submersion, resemble the temporal arc of human experience. It mirrors our transformation—however briefly and impossibly, however fairy tale—into 'musical instruments, vibrant angels, streaming luminous clouds. This is . . . the preserved miracle of being alive.'"

Instruments of Darkness (1997) is Huston's translated version of *Instruments des tenebres*, which had been published the previous year. Like *Slow Emergencies*, it is the story of a creative woman, this time a writer, who has rejected domesticity. Nadia, the divorced protagonist, is researching a book about an 18th-century French servant who has been raped by her employer and is forced to hide the resulting pregnancy. The narrative alternates between the tale of the hapless maid and Nadia's own life story, which includes an alcoholic father and a mentally ill mother. Barbara Carey wrote for the *Toronto Star* (April 5, 1997) that despite its somber themes, "[*Instruments of Darkness*] is a captivating novel with both intellect and heart. As for that question of motherhood vs. creative achievement, it doesn't make the two seem any easier to reconcile. But it does imply there are rewards in trying to pull off a balancing act between them."

The Mark of the Angel, which was published in 1999, is Huston's translation of *L'Empreinte de l'ange* (1998); it has become one of her best-known works. The book examines a love triangle between Saffie, a German woman who has come to post–World War II Paris to work as a maid; Raphael, a flutist who employs her and later becomes her husband; and Andras, a Hungarian-Jew who repairs musical instruments. Huston has turned "an ostensibly melodramatic romance into a story of fierce, doomed lovers about whom the reader cares a great deal," S. T. Meravi wrote for the *Jerusalem Post* (November 12, 1999). "Despite the trappings of soap opera, this novel is an intelligent and deeply felt meditation on the havoc that modern history wreaks in the lives of innocents in search of wholeness, integrity, and a little bit of love." Eugenia Zukerman, reviewing *The Mark of* the Angel for the Washington Post Book World (December 12, 1999), was somewhat less enthusiastic, writing that "[the book] has the makings of a sensual and emotionally blistering tale. Instead it reads like a mix of Greek tragedy, French farce, history lesson and soft porn. . . . Not only is the tone unfocused; the narrative is often interrupted by omniscient statements that are needlessly portentous." Despite the occasional poor review, The Mark of the Angel was short-listed for the Giller Prize, a Canadian literary award. (It was also nominated for a Governor-General's Literary Award in the category of translated works.) She found attending the Giller awards ceremony an onerous chore, telling Pat Donnelly, "I found it humiliating to be bought all the way over from Paris and put through that gala evening. I hate gala evenings. I hate shmoozing. I hate cocktail parties." Thereafter, Huston requested that her publishers stop submitting her work for Canadian literary awards, on the grounds that she had not lived there since leaving for the U.S. as a teen.

Prodigy was translated in 2001 by Huston; the French version, Prodige: polyphonie, had been published two years earlier. The story of a pianist of questionable talent and her daughter, the eponymous prodigy, the book received largely mixed reviews. Nancy Schiefer, for example, writing for the Toronto Sun (December 24, 2000), declared it no competition for its predecessor, The Mark of the Angel, which she deemed "an incomparable work that combined elegance and precision of style with the quiet astonishments of a tale well told." Huston, she concluded, "is a superb writer, and Prodigy is touched, here and there, with traces of her talent. At times, the story is exquisitely told, but far too often it succumbs to the banal, to strained metaphors, tired symbols and unlikely happenings."

Huston translated Dolce agonia: Roman in 2001, the same year it was published in France. The title means "sweet agony" in Italian, and Huston did not initially change it for the English-language version. (A later edition was published as Sweet Agony.) The novel takes place during a Thanksgiving dinner in New England. The host is a university professor and poet. The narrator of the story is God, who explains the choice of setting: his favorite episodes in the history of mankind include, as Merilyn Simonds quoted in the Ottawa Citizen (October 14, 2001), "'The Hundred Years' War, The Death of Cleopatra, Thanksgiving dinner at Sean Farrell's, circa 2000. There's no point in looking for reasons. All I can say is that a multitude of minor coincidences and unexpected undercurrents in the conversation made this dinner party into a poem. Sudden beauty. Sudden drama. Flames of fury, gales of laughter.'" As the party progresses, God interrupts the narrative to reveal each character's eventual fate. Simonds wrote, "These advance obituaries have an extraordinary effect. One minute, you're deeply

involved in the repartee around the table, the flirting, the bridling, and the next, you're whisked to the heavens to watch God play out the end of a person's life, then whoosh! You're back watching dessert being served. It's like an out-of-body experience, one that shifts your perspective again and again—the intimacy of the table, the broad sweep of a life—until we come to know these people not the way we know our own dinner-table companions, by their pasts and present circumstance, but by their futures, too. It is this that lends each living moment its dolce agonia, its sweet agony."

Une adoration (An Adoration) was published in 2003, in both English and French. The book takes the form of an inquest into the death of Cosmo, an actor (patterned on the still-living French actor Phillippe Caubère, with whom Huston traveled for research purposes); the reader is addressed as the judge and jury, as testimony is given by other characters, including Cosmo's mistress, Elke. "To her, stories are as elemental as carbon and oxygen. . . . The more Elke talks about her lover, the more she interrupts and dominates the testimony of others, the more she creates a Cosmo who befits the sensual creature she now sees herself as. One of the themes of the novel is how stories can be used to engage or disengage with life," Elizabeth Johnston wrote for the Toronto Star (December 7, 2003). "Far from being an inaccessible, bloodless experiment in postmodern literature, in Huston's hands it seems child's play, a romp through the mind of a sprightly character who has known the darker aspects of life but never strays far from the intoxicating realms of sensuality and pleasure." An Adoration, which was later adapted as a stage play, was nominated for a Dublin IMPAC prize.

Lignes de faille ("Fault Lines"), was published in 2006 and won the Prix Femina, considered one of France's most prestigious literary prizes, but it has not yet been issued in an English version because her publisher felt that American readers would object to its references to President George W. Bush, the war in Iraq, and the Abu Ghraib prison scandal. A multigenerational saga that examines how one generation's political decisions affect the next, the novel follows a family from World War II–era Germany to the present day. James Adams, in an article for the Toronto Globe and Mail (November 2, 2006), quoted Huston as saying in an earlier French-language interview, "Contemporary America is reproducing the worst traits of Nazi Germany. I believe we are in a pretotalitarian state."

Huston's popular nonfiction work includes Losing North: Musings on Land, Tongue and Self, her 2002 translation of Nord perdu (1999). The book contains Huston's musings on her expatriate state. As Dawne McCance wrote for Letters in Canada (Winter 2004), "In English . . . the title of this collection of essays . . . suggests the country, Canada—'the North, the Great North, the True

North Strong and Free'—that Huston lost, and feels she betrayed. . . . In French, however, 'losing north' means 'forgetting what you were going to say. Losing track of what's going on. Losing your marbles. It is something that you should avoid at all costs.' Paradoxically, when Huston loses her marbles—for instance by 'letting off steam, freaking out, swearing, singing, yelling, surfing on the pure pleasure of verbal delirium'—she does so in her lost tongue, her first tongue, English, which, like the piano of her childhood, she regards as a motherly instrument, 'emotional, romantic, manipulative, sentimental and crude.'" McCance continued, "If, in 1973, Huston was running away from the 'carmine lipstick and heavy Mexican silver-and-turquoise earrings' Alberta of her youth in favour of the sophistications of French literary theory . . . what she has discovered by 1998, when these essays were written, is that expatriation is loss." In 2005 Huston published another collection of essays, *Longings and Belongings*. The pieces in the collection, as described on the Northwest Passages Canadian Literature Web site, concern "motherhood, eroticism, war, madness, exile, the search for identity, the transgression of taboo, [and] the moral implications of creation."

In addition to *Losing North: Musings on Land, Tongue and Self* and *Longings and Belongings*, Huston has written several other nonfiction books, many relating to feminism and motherhood. She has taught at such institutions as Harvard University, in Cambridge, Massachusetts, and the University of Paris.

In 1994 Huston attracted some notoriety when she published an essay on the ramifications of being born beautiful and intelligent. (The essay's first words, which have been widely quoted, are "I'm beautiful.") The essay appeared initially in the journal *Salmagundi* and was then reprinted in *Brick* and *Harper's*, among other periodicals. It has since been translated into several languages. "You can never tell what's going to draw people's attention," she told P. Scott Lawrence for the Montreal *Gazette* (December 15, 1996), explaining that she had written the piece mainly as a reaction to the rigid atmosphere of political correctness at Harvard, where she was then teaching. Lawrence defended Huston against the charges of conceit and immodesty that had been levied against her: "The underlying subject of her article—which many commentators chose to ignore—is how the 'shimmering, shifting mix of public and private, physical and spiritual, proximity and distance, conformity and spontaneity' is being annulled by what she terms 'maniacal moralism and ludicrous legalism.'" Lawrence did, in the course of his article, confirm Huston's beauty; many other journalists have also been moved to make observations about her physical appearance; Gillmor described, for example, her "sensual face and reddish hair"; Yanofsky called her "strikingly attractive"; and Donnelly wrote, "She has the cheekbones, the [French actress Bridget] Bardot

lips, the feline grace. . . . At 50, she could pass for 35."

—S.Y.

Suggested reading: *Irish Times* p57 Mar. 2, 2002; *Jerusalem Post* B p13 Nov. 12, 1999; *Letters in Canada* p350 Winter 2004; (Montreal) *Gazette* Books p14 Sep. 11, 1993, H p1 Jan. 29, 1994, H p11 Nov. 23, 1996, Books p11 Oct. 18, 2003, D p6 Apr. 1, 2005; *Ottawa Citizen* B p7 Jan. 29, 1994, C p9 Oct. 14, 2001; *Time* p107 Nov. 8, 1999; *Toronto Star* M p15 Apr. 5, 1997, D p14 Dec. 7, 2003; *Toronto Sun* C p13 Dec. 24, 2000; *Washington Post Book World* p5 Dec. 12, 1999, p9 Mar. 18, 2001

Selected Books in English: fiction—*Plainsong*, 1993; *The Goldberg Variations*, 1996; *Slow Emergencies*, 1996; *Instruments of Darkness*, 1997; *The Mark of the Angel*, 1999; *Prodigy*, 2001; *Dolce Agonia*, 2001; *An Adoration*, 2003; nonfiction—*Losing North: Musings on Land, Tongue, and Self*, 2002; *Longings and Belongings*, 2005

Isegawa, Moses

1963– Novelist

Following the American publication, in 2000, of his debut novel, the poignant and disturbing coming-of-age story *Abyssinian Chronicles*, the Ugandan-born Dutch novelist Moses Isegawa earned comparisons to such august literary figures as Gabriel García Márquez, Salman Rushdie, and Günter Grass. In the months preceding the 1998 publication of the Dutch edition of *Abyssinian Chronicles*, Isegawa piqued public interest in the upcoming book through a series of captivating interviews. Isegawa has since written another work, *Snakepit*, which hit Dutch and American bookstores in 1999 and 2004 respectively. In his adopted country he has evolved into a controversial media figure, known for opinionated pronouncements on world affairs.

Moses Isegawa was born in 1963 in rural Uganda, a small, land-locked African nation south of the Sudan, on the north shore of Lake Victoria. When he was still young, his family relocated to the city of Kampala, Uganda's capital. A prolific reader as a child, Isegawa decided at 14 to pursue writing as a vocation: "I thought it must be magical to be a writer," the author once remarked, as quoted by Mel Gussow for the *New York Times* (August 5, 2000). "To tell a story and somebody deep in a village in Uganda reads it and can identify with the place and the characters—I never lost that idea of the magic and the excitement of literature." Isegawa's grandfather, a lawyer, regaled the young Moses with stories about the

Jerry Bauer/Courtesy of Random House
Moses Isegawa

family's ancestors and relatives, tales that Isegawa would later expand upon and embellish once he began writing in earnest. Isegawa's upbringing, during a turbulent time in Ugandan history, also provided plenty of material for an aspiring writer. After seizing power in a 1971 coup, the bellicose Ugandan dictator Idi Amin began instituting popular economic and political reforms; however, despite the promising signs at its outset, Amin's reign quickly descended into a brutal totalitarian nightmare. Amin's rule lasted nine years—long enough to leave a sad and indelible legacy that continues to haunt the impoverished nation 25 years later. (Amin's reign and its tumultuous aftermath provided the backdrop for *Abyssinian Chronicles*.)

Isegawa received his education at a Roman Catholic seminary, where he began composing his first short stories. Through the aid of a Dutch friend, Isegawa managed to have some of his work published in a Dutch religious periodical that eventually offered him a regular column. After completing his education Isegawa became a history teacher but remained intent on writing. In order to pursue this dream, at the age of 26, he left Uganda for the Netherlands. His departure was relatively quiet: "It was like stealing away," he explained to Gussow. The aunt and cousin who accompanied him to the airport "didn't even know that I was going to be a writer. They thought I was going to do what other young people do"—that is, find a job overseas and send money to family members in Uganda.

Upon arriving in the Netherlands, Isegawa had to adjust to a new and wholly alien culture: "I had burned all my bridges," he explained to Gussow.

"I think writers need a shock. In Amsterdam, I had to begin at zero level. I had to learn the language, and find my own feet. When people would ask what are you doing, I would say I was a bookkeeper." Soon after his exodus to the Netherlands, Isegawa began writing his novel, a task that would occupy him on and off for the next several years. In 1997, when he was finally finished, Isegawa sent the manuscript off to four Dutch publishers, one of whom, De Bezige Big, agreed to purchase the work. Isegawa's manuscript initially had to be translated from English into Dutch for its Netherlands edition; during this process, Isegawa began conducting radio interviews. He proved a captivating guest and soon developed into a recognizable media figure before his book was even published.

Upon its publication in Dutch, *Abyssinian Chronicles* won wide acclaim for its author and was hailed as a Ugandan relative of Günter Grass's *Tin Drum* (1959). Subsequently, Isegawa's Dutch editor canvassed publishing houses abroad in order to have the work issued overseas. The English version of the *Abyssinian Chronicles* also received an impressive critical response. From its startling first sentence—"Three final images flashed across Serenity's mind as he disappeared into the jaws of the colossal crocodile: a rotting buffalo with rivers of maggots and armies of flies emanating from its cavities; the aunt of his missing wife, who was also his longtime lover; and the mysterious woman who had cured his childhood obsession with tall women"—*Abyssinian Chronicles* displayed haunting and evocative imagery, as well as a cast of singular characters. The work was described by Isegawa as 10 percent memoir and 90 percent invention, but, as Gussow noted, "it resonates with the knowledge of first-hand experience."

The story follows Mugezi, a rural Ugandan boy, as he grows up amid the brutality of the Amin regime. Mugezi is an omniscient narrator, able to inhabit the minds of his parents; this unusual perspective "takes some getting used to," Paul Gray wrote for *Time* (July 10, 2000), "but the effort is worth making. Isegawa's method of portraying a broad swath of national history through the wise eyes of a young observer has precedents in such reality-bending epics as Günter Grass's *The Tin Drum* and Salman Rushdie's *Midnight Children*." Mugezi is not the traditional sympathetic protagonist found in most coming-of-age novels: though he suffers at the hands of his abusive parents and the priests at the seminary where he studies, Mugezi responds viciously in kind; after completing his schooling he finds employment as an anti-corruption official under Amin, but becomes thoroughly corrupt himself. "I tried to get away from the love-me kind of book," Isegawa explained to Gussow. "I wanted to treat everybody the same way. I was not going to be soft on myself and then go out punching people below the belt. I wanted to write a challenging book, challenging to myself and to others." Finally, with the country in ruins and AIDS running rampant, Mugezi leaves for Amsterdam, where he casts his withering gaze on the decadence of the West.

Several critics complained that Isegawa had a tendency to ramble at certain points in the 500-page work and used overblown language at times; Bruce Allen, for example, wrote for the *Boston Globe* (June 18, 2000) that "Isegawa's cavalier attitude toward structure," was a serious shortcoming. Despite its flaws *Abyssinian Chronicles* was widely praised. Sophie Radcliffe, writing for the London *Times* (October 28, 2000), observed that Isegawa's "achievement is to give, through fiction, a real sense of the 'abyss' around which his people and country have skirted—a void that swallows feelings, people and unspeakable acts with equal ease."

"Having won himself an audience [with *Abyssinian Chronicles*]," Matt Steinglass wrote for *The Nation* (April 5, 2004), "Isegawa proceeded to scandalize it. . . . In interviews, he attacked the media and his public for expecting him to represent the African viewpoint; denounced Western development as a scheme to sink African countries further into debt; and characterized the Dutch welfare state as a way of bribing the population into political quiescence." In a 2001 essay entitled "Two Chimpanzees," Isegawa suggested that Western-backed African inoculation programs, far from improving the health of those vaccinated, had served to weaken their immune systems, crippling their ability to fight off illness. Furthermore, he held the United States responsible for Africa's AIDS epidemic, stating that the American government had been complicit in spreading the disease throughout the continent. "Isegawa's enormous literary talent began to be overshadowed by his politics," Steinglass remarked. Isegawa's critiques were not all so incendiary, however; he argued persuasively against Western stereotypes concerning Africa, stating in an interview with *Transition* magazine, as quoted by Steinglass, "Every time you see something about Africa, it has to be negative. But 90 percent of our African experience is not about war or violence; it is about people getting on with their lives."

Isegawa's second novel, *Snakepit*, was described by a reviewer for *Publishers Weekly* (March 18, 2004) as "another ambitious narrative of trouble and turmoil near the end of Idi Amin's dictatorship in Uganda, a country 'like a madwoman of untold beauty.'" The protagonist is Bat Katanga, a Cambridge-educated Ugandan who joins Amin's Ministry of Power and Communication and is put in charge of the nation's energy sector. He soon becomes embroiled in the institutional crime, corruption, and brutality that typified the Amin regime. Offering a mixed review, Steinglass described *Snakepit* as rushed, disorganized, and brutal—a "magical-realist Tom Clancy thriller, with far more violence and no good guys. The book's cruelty and amorality are positively Jacobean." The *Publishers Weekly* reviewer had a more positive take on *Snakepit*, characterizing it as "a headlong and blurry novel filled with violence and sex, deceit and revenge—a messy, captivating portrait of a desperate time and place."

Isegawa currently lives in the Netherlands. He has stated that he would like to do for African literature what Márquez did for Latin American fiction. Questioned by Gussow as to whether his work might offend his parents and relatives in Uganda, who may see themselves in certain unsympathetic characters, Isegawa replied philosophically, "I think Philip Roth said, if a family gets a writer in its midst, there's going to be trouble."

—P.B.M.

Suggested Reading: *Boston Globe* Books p1 June 18, 2000; (London) *Guardian* p10 Nov. 18, 2000; *New York Times* E p42 June 23, 2000, B p9 Aug. 5, 2000; *New York Times Book Review* p8 July 2, 2000; *Publishers Weekly* p55 Feb. 9, 2004; *Time* p104 July 10, 2000

Selected Books in English: *Abyssinian Chronicles*, 2000; *Snakepit*, 2004

Istarú, Ana

1960– Poet; playwright; actress

"Erotic poetry written by women represents a different viewpoint," the playwright, poet, and actress Ana Istarú told Sasha Campbell Barr for the Calle 22 Web site, as translated by *World Authors*, "a woman is no longer an object of desire, but an active subject." Since her earliest stirrings of feminist consciousness when she was a teenager, Istarú has been creating work that seeks to challenge and dispel the sexist conventions about women and femininity that permeate her native Costa Rica. A published poet at age 15, she first won national recognition for her work a year later; in 1982 her fourth book of poems, *La Estación de Fiebre* (which can be translated as "fever season"), won Costa Rica's National Poetry Prize. In addition to her poetry, Istarú has been recognized for her playwriting and acting—she frequently performs in her stage pieces. Istarú's work is provocative and fiercely feminist, the themes often evident in the titles she gives her pieces, which can be translated as "our mother, who art on earth," "baby boom in paradise," and "men in marinade." These works are bold, cutting, and often funny. "Among her tools is comedy," Jorge Boccanera noted for *Rio Negro* (January 13, 2004, on-line), as translated by *World Authors*. Boccanera quoted Istarú on her use of humor as a conduit for social commentary:

Courtesy of Editorial Costa Rica

Ana Istarú

"Through hilarity, the barriers behind which a conservative public might shield itself are broken, and laughter ensures that the play's ideas are absorbed." Istarú's work has been translated into English, Italian, and Dutch and has been performed throughout Europe and North America. Her early and continued successes have made her one of the most recognized members of Costa Rica's literary elite; her compatriot, the acclaimed actor and writer Daniel Gallegos, told Camilo Rodriguez Chaverri for *Art Studio* magazine (February/March 2004) that Istarú is, as translated by *World Authors*, "one of the most important figures in theatre today."

Istarú characterizes her work as constantly pushing cultural and societal boundaries. "Women's literature is transgressive," she explained to Ana Maria Echecerria for the Associated Press (November 8, 2002), as translated by *World Authors*, "perhaps because it has obstacles to overcome. . . . [It is] more rebellious, more subversive, and more critical." As a Central American artist, Istarú creates work that continues the legacies of Latin American women writers who have struggled against formidable obstacles to produce and show their work in a traditionally male-dominated field. In a speech at the Inter American Development Bank in 1998, as reprinted in the IDB newsletter, *Encuentros* (September 1998), the Colombian writer Gloria Guardia noted the difficulties faced in the past and present by women writers in South and Central America. "Today, as yesterday, women who want to write in Central America run many risks. Together with the desire for recognition is the terror not just of censorship but also self-censorship, fostered by a

cultural conditioning in which 'artistic temperament' is understood to mean 'inferiority.' There is no doubt that the feminine culture in our region symbolizes all that is repressed, especially within the canons of a society where traditionally the habits of daily and family life, religion, and the law are still inescapably machista. . . . In Central America, the woman who thinks, reads, reflects, and writes is considered a threat to the established order." Istarú thrives on tackling subjects in her work that have been traditionally taboo. "As a writer coming from a Latin, patriarchal society," she told audience members at a reading in New York in 2002, as quoted by Ana Maria Echeverria, "I have written about the body, sexuality, and pleasure. Maybe if I hadn't been born in Costa Rica I would have written about something different."

Ana Istarú was born in 1960 in Costa Rica's capital city, San José. As a young girl she was first exposed to theater by her mother, and her father introduced her to literature. Istarú cultivated the interests she inherited from her parents, and her early and acute observation of gender roles and social mores, coupled with her creative inclinations, led her to begin writing poetry. At age 15 she published her first collection of poems, *Palabra nueva* (which can be translated as "new word"). The following year she published her second volume, *Poemas para un dia cualquiera* (which can be translated as "poems for any given day"), which won the Premio Joven Creación de la Editorial Costa Rica, a national poetry prize. Though she continued to write poetry, Istarú decided to study acting at the University of Costa Rica, where she enrolled in the late 1970s. In 1980, while still a student, she won the National Prize for best debut actress for her role in *La Celestina*, a famous play by Francisco de Rojas. That same year she published a third poetry collection, *Poemas Abiertos y otros Amaneceres* (which can be translated as "open poems and other awakenings"). Of her early work and her increasing exploration of erotic, feminist themes, Istarú told Jorge Boccanera, "I always wrote from my body; it is the spine of my work. Since I was very young, I faced up to the fact that as a woman I was meant to subjugate myself to my anatomy. Patriarchal society sees a woman's body as a beauty object and generator of desire, and for that very reason, deserving of martyrdom."

She graduated college in 1981 with a degree in theater and two years later, her fourth and most popular poetry collection, *La Estación de Fiebre*, was published to national acclaim. The title poem in *La Estación de Fiebre* (which literally means "season of fever" but is closer to "season of lust") is an erotic ode to sexual awakening that mixes the vivid imagery of the body with religious themes, weaving in the organic textures of the natural world, such as flowers, milk, and velvet. The writer and poet Carmen Naranjo called it, as quoted on the Web site of the Spanish publishing house Terramozas and translated by *World*

Authors, "a long love poem and shout for liberation." The book received the Central American EDUCA prize, bestowed by the Confederación Universitaria Centroamericana (Confederation of Central American Universities), and when *La Estación de Fiebre* was released in Spain by Torremozas in 1986, critics praised both Istarú's bold approach to erotic subject matter and her cunning use of language and metaphor. Juan Cameron, writing for the Web site of the Liberation press, observed, "Ana Istarú's poetry is highly erotic, but it isn't this that surprises and gratifies the reader. Rather, it is her development of language as shown by the text." Istarú's most recent volume of poems, *Verbo Madre* (which can be translated as "mother verb"), was published in 1995.

After graduating from college Istarú continued to develop as a playwright and actress. In 1984 she wrote her first play, *El Vuelo de la Grulla* (which can be translated as "the flight of the crane"), and four years later finished her second, *Madre Nuesta que Estás en la Tierra*, (which can be translated as "our mother, who art on earth"), a work whose very title (a play on the Lord's Prayer, which begins "Our father, who art in heaven") inverted the patriarchal trifecta of Christianity in a pointedly feminist way.

The debut of Istarú's most famous theatrical piece, *Baby Boom en el Paraíso* (which can be translated as "baby boom in paradise"), was in 1996. According to Istarú, as quoted on her page on the Editorial Costa Rica Web site and translated by *World Authors*, the play attempted to "unveil, for those who don't know, the physical odyssey, the emotional ordeal that is found within us women who are privileged by nature to give birth." She wrote the play in just over two weeks and has called it the most autobiographical of her works—according to Istarú, the role and dialogue of the nurse in the play was lifted almost exactly from the woman who coached her through childbirth. *Baby Boom en el Paraíso* was not only about giving birth; it also questioned the subservient roles females have been historically allotted in society and pointed out the ways in which they continue to affect modern women. The play also took to task the sexist societal double standards that render women either virgins or whores, and it ridiculed the historically accepted notion that women's sexuality is a potentially rabid and monstrous force that must be contained and controlled. (She singled out Catholicism over the course of the play.) "What Moses never told us," a character in *Baby Boom en el Paraíso* notes, as quoted on Istarú's page on Editorial Costa Rica, "and what they never taught us in Catechism is that there are two types of women . . . the one you take home to meet your mother—and 'the other,' the one who could eat her boyfriend whole, without cutlery and with mustard." The play also lampooned the absurdity of a culture that demanded that women be virginal and pure, but which allowed men to enjoy casual sexual encounters. "Moses," the character in the play points out, "did not say: 'Attention, ladies, it is prohibited to abandon your hymen in the lost and found. Please sit with your legs crossed.' No, the 'no fornicating' command was to apply directly, expeditiously, and immediately to whatever human creature walked the earth." On the impossible standards women are expected to fulfill in order to make suitable partners for men, Istarú asked through her protagonist: "What is it that men want? A virgin with history? [The overtly sexual pop music icon] Madonna doing her first communion?" While it was quite confrontational in its humor, the play was not relentlessly anti-male; much of the humor had to do with the illogical societal constructs relating to religion and family. ("It's so strange, the term 'political family.' Political, why? As far as I know, one cannot vote for one's mother-in-law. Though it would be very practical.") *Baby Boom en el Paraíso* was well received and performed throughout Costa Rica, as well as in Spain and the United States. A radio version, translated into German, was aired in Germany by the Westdeutscher Rundfunk (WDR) station. It won the Maria Teresa Leon prize for dramatists, an award given by the Spanish Directors Association.

In 1999 Istarú mounted *Hombres en Escabeche* (which can be translated as "men in marinade"), which she wrote in two months and which she characterized as "an acid portrait of Latin sexual mores," in a comment she wrote for her page at the Editorial Costa Rica Web site. The play was inspired by a scene Istarú had witnessed in a restaurant, in which an argument between a man and a woman at a nearby table culminated in the woman's dropping her date's cell phone into a cup of coffee. From that seed came what Istarú called "the romantic odyssey of a woman who, with irony and finesse, presents a gallery of men spanning her first boyfriend to her last lover." Istarú hoped to communicate the way in which women's notions of sex and gender is formed from their first relationship with a man—their fathers—to future partners. "There is an emotional void generated by the traditional paternal figure, indifferent or absent—if not, frankly, negative—in the life of a girl," Istarú told Jorge Boccanera. "I always compare sadly the abundant and excessive attention and affection that a son receives from his mother with that which a girl receives from her father, which is almost always negligible. And he is her first love, who will determine her relationship with men." While *Hombres en Escabeche* criticized this cultural failing, it did not seek to indict any particular villain or even men in general for the larger machinations of a sexist society. The play, Istarú explained to Norma Niurka for the Spanish-language edition of the *Miami Herald*, *El Nuevo Heraldo* (June 2, 2000), as translated by *World Authors*, "deals with the romantic failures in one woman's life, beginning with the initial failure of her relationship with her father. Without condemnation and treating the subject with humor, I take the opportunity to say something about the double standards in our society and the perception of sex women have since they are little." (Moreover, while Istarú's plays often paint a wretched portrait of the lot women have been made to endure in a sexist society, she acknowledges that the narrowness of traditional gender roles affects men as well. "The privilege enjoyed by men in a patriarchal society is up for debate," she told Boccanera. "Men are also victims, obligated to follow a stereotype that inflicts violence on an individual. It isn't easy to be macho in Latin America: men cannot cry, express one's sensitivity, emotions, feelings, weaknesses, kiss and hug their friends like women do.") There were other reasons for Istarú to write *Hombres en Escabeche*. "I knew I had to write a play in order to provide myself with work as an actress," she said, as quoted on the Editorial Costa Rica Web site, "given that I didn't want to be part of a banal, low-quality play like those that comprise the majority of works performed at theaters." *Hombres en Escabeche* won the Hermanos Machado Theatre Award in 1999, a prize given by the City Hall of Seville, in Spain. Alberto Cañas, writing for *La Republica* and quoted on the Editorial Costa Rica Web site, described the play as "farcical at times, sharp and penetrating all the time. *Hombres en Escabeche* functions admirably as a humorous spectacle and as a ruthless social critique." *Hombres en Escabeche* and *Baby Boom en el Paraíso* were published together in book form by Editorial Costa Rica in 2001. The following year *Poesia Escogida* (which can be translated as "selected poems") was also issued by Editorial Costa Rica.

Istarú's next play, *Sexus Benedictus*, debuted in 2002. Another humorous portrayal of sex and gender, it played at the Lucha Barahona Theatre in San José into 2003. The play became very popular, and both lead actors—Marcela Ugalde and Marco Martín—won top prizes at Costa Rica's Premios Nacionales, sponsored by the Costa Rican Ministry of Culture, Youth, and Sports. Istarú began exploring a new medium—film—with the 2003 movie *Caribe*, for which she wrote the screenplay. *Caribe* is the story of a woman who discovers, upon the death of her mother, that she has a sister. The film includes explorations of romantic and familial relationships, as well as a story about Costa Rican townspeople protesting an oil company's destructive presence in nearby waters. *Caribe* was inspired by a short story by the Costa Rican writer Carlos Salazar Herrera, and while it featured popular actors from across Latin America and Spain, the film was unique in its strong sense of locality—to Istarú, who was skeptical about her ability to write a screenplay, one of the most rewarding parts of the project was that it marked the emergence of a Costa Rican film industry. "When [director Esteban Ramírez] proposed the project . . . I thought he was crazy, I had never

written a script before, not even a public service announcement, so I didn't feel capable of doing it," she told Lizeth Castro for the television program *7 Dias* (May 26, 2003), as translated by *World Authors*. "But eventually he called me again, I considered his proposal and I realized that we are a country in which this cinematographic phenomenon is incipient." Moreover, the story, which was based in part on the American-based Harken Oil Company's petroleum explorations along the Caribbean coast—a presence that was fervently protested by Costa Ricans in the coastal town of Puerto Viejo—makes *Caribe*, according to Castro, "a film with a Costa Rican soul."

Istarú has won many awards for acting in addition to her writing, including the National Prize for best lead actress in 1997 and the Premio Ancora de Teatro in 1999 and 2000. She was named a Guggenheim Fellow in 1990, an honor bestowed by the John Simon Guggenheim Memorial Foundation to individuals "who have demonstrated exceptional capacity for productive scholarship or exceptional creative ability in the arts," as noted on the foundation's Web site. English translations of her poetry have appeared in several North American literary journals, including the *Massachusetts Review*, the *Crab Creek Review*, the *Colorado Review*, the *Five Fingers Review*, and *The Raddle Moon*. She lives in Paris, France.

—L.S.

Suggested Reading: Agence France-Presse (on-line) Nov. 8, 2002; Editorial Costa Rica Web site; *El Nuevo Heraldo* C p2, June 2, 2000; *Rio Negro* (on-line) Jan. 13, 2004

Selected Books: poetry—*Palabra Nueva*, 1975; *Palabras Para un dia Cualquiera*, 1976; *Poemas Abiertos y otros Amaneceres*, 1980; *La Estacion de Fiebre*, 1982; *Verbo Madre*, 1995; plays—*El Vuelo de la Grulla*, 1984; *Madre Nuestra que estas en la Tierra*, 1988; *Baby Boom en el Paraiso*, 1996; *Hombres en Escabeche*, 2000; *Sexus Benedictus*, 2002

Jaffa, Harry V.

Oct. 7, 1918– Political scientist

The political scientist and author Harry V. Jaffa, a disciple of the late political philosopher Leo Strauss (1899–1973), has devoted his academic career to studying the philosophical origins of the U.S.'s founding, the importance of the Declaration of Independence, the interpretation of the U.S. Constitution, and the philosophy of President Abraham Lincoln. For Jaffa, the Declaration of Independence, which was adopted on July 4, 1776, established equality—which he argued is rooted in natural law, a system of justice that is derived from nature and common to all humankind—as a key principle in the nation's founding. Jaffa examined the views of Lincoln and those of his opponent, Stephen Douglas, in the Illinois Senate race in 1858 in his book *Crisis of the House Divided: An Interpretation of the Issues in the Lincoln-Douglas Debates* (1959), which scholars regard as a classic in the field. Over the decades, Jaffa has clashed with many of his fellow conservatives over such issues as equality, the interpretation of Strauss's ideas, the meaning of the Declaration, and various interpretations of the Constitution. Jaffa has collected many of his scholarly articles in several books including *Equality and Liberty: Theory and Practice in American Politics* (1965), *The Conditions of Freedom: Essays in Political Philosophy* (1975), and *American Conservatism and the American Founding* (1984). In two books, *Original Intent and the Framers of the Constitution: A Disputed Question* (1994) and *Storm over the Constitution* (1999), Jaffa took prominent conservatives to task for ignoring the concept of natural law in their interpretations of the Constitution. In 2000 he published his long-awaited sequel to *Crisis of a House Divided*, the book *A New Birth of Freedom: Abraham Lincoln and the Coming of the Civil War*, an examination of Lincoln's views on Southern secession.

The son of Arthur S. and Frances (Landau) Jaffa, Harry Victor Jaffa was born on October 7, 1918 in New York City. In 1939 he graduated from Yale University, in New Haven, Connecticut, with a bachelor's degree in English. Jaffa then enrolled in the New School for Social Research, in New York City to pursue a doctorate in political science, which he completed in 1951. At the New School, he studied under Leo Strauss, a Jewish refugee from Nazi Germany and a political philosopher. Strauss articulated a basis for ethics and moral judgments in politics that ran against the prevailing trends of moral relativism and scientific materialism by drawing on classical texts and traditions. Strauss's ideas influenced many political philosophers and contributed to the development of the present-day neoconservative movement.

From 1945 to 1948 Jaffa taught at Queens College, in New York City. After teaching at the College of the City of New York (now called City College, part of the City University of New York system) from 1948 to 1949 and then at the University of Chicago, in Illinois, from 1949 to 1951, Jaffa joined the faculty of Ohio State University, in Columbus. In 1964 Jaffa became a professor of political philosophy at both the Claremont Men's College (today Claremont McKenna College) and the Claremont Graduate School (today Claremont Graduate University), in Claremont, California, and in 1971 he was appointed a Henry Salvatori research professor at these institutions.

In 1952 Jaffa published his first book, *Thomism and Aristotelianism: A Study on the Commentary by Thomas Aquinas on the Nicomachean Ethics.* "This rather technical volume is a most important contribution to the literature on natural law theory," a reviewer for the *United States Quarterly Book Review* (September 1952) wrote. "By careful comparison of the text of Aristotle's *Ethics* and St. Thomas Aquinas' *Commentary*, the author seeks to determine whether the Neo-Thomist doctrine of natural law does have its claimed philosophical foundation in Aristotle."

In 1959 Jaffa published two books—*In the Name of the People: Speeches and Writings of Lincoln and Douglas in the Ohio Campaign of 1859*, which he co-edited with Robert W. Johannsen, and *Crisis of the House Divided,* in which he contrasted the political views and visions of Abraham Lincoln and Stephen Douglas. In 1858 Lincoln, the candidate of the newly formed Republican Party, ran for a U.S. Senate seat for Illinois against the Democratic incumbent, Douglas. During the campaign, Lincoln and Douglas met in seven debates, presenting their views on some of the most important issues of the time, including the expansion of slavery into the territories, the morality of slavery itself, the equality of the black and white races, and popular sovereignty. The debates drew thousands of spectators and received extensive attention in the national press. (Douglas narrowly defeated Lincoln in the Senate race, but in 1860 Lincoln beat Douglas in the presidential election.) Examining the content of these debates, Jaffa argued that both men had radically different visions of democracy and equality. "Mr. Jaffa . . . demonstrates with considerable skill that the debates were an intellectual and moral contest of the highest order," E.C. Rozwenc wrote in his review for *Political Science Quarterly* (December 1960) and went on to observe, "Despite the tedious character of Mr. Jaffa's close analysis of key words and paragraphs in the utterances of Lincoln and Douglas, this book deserves to be read carefully by all historical scholars who seek to explain America's greatest political crisis." In the *New York Times Book Review* (September 13, 1959), P.M. Angle described Jaffa's reasoning as "rigorous, exhaustive and sometimes hard to follow." Angle suggested that Jaffa had overreached in his analysis, explaining, "One wonders whether the author may not have discovered more shades of meaning, implications and reservations in these speeches than either principal was aware of. One wonders also whether even the first-rate minds of Lincoln and Douglas were as complex and sophisticated as Mr. Jaffa has found them." Nonetheless, Angle writes, Jaffa has produced "a convincing demonstration of the soundness of the conventional verdict of history." In 1960 *The Crisis of the House Divided* won the Ohioana Book Award for nonfiction.

When Senator Barry Goldwater, a Republican from Arizona, made a bid for the presidency, in 1964, Jaffa worked for his campaign as a speechwriter. Throughout the primaries Goldwater was often labeled a political extremist by his opponents. Nevertheless, he won his party's nomination, and in his acceptance speech, which was drafted by Jaffa and delivered at the Republican National Convention in San Francisco, Goldwater used the opportunity to respond to these accusations: "I would remind you that extremism in the defense of liberty is no vice. I would also remind you that moderation in the pursuit of justice is no virtue." Goldwater told delegates at the convention, as quoted by Jaffa in an article for *National Review* (August 1984). Although most of the delegates enthusiastically applauded Goldwater's speech, it nonetheless confirmed the suspicion of many voters that he was a reactionary; in the general election, Goldwater was defeated by incumbent Lyndon B. Johnson, a Democrat from Texas, by a landslide.

In 1965 Jaffa collected 10 of his previously published essays in the book *Equality and Liberty*. Among other topics, the essays discuss the origins of the party system in the U.S., draw a connection between morality and patriotism, and devote more attention to Abraham Lincoln. "These pieces are of good quality, though better for the striking sentence or passage than for a thoroughly achieved argument," George Kateb wrote in his review for *Commentary* (August 1965). "There is, however, not the slightest change in Jaffa's moral temper: his devotion to Lincoln's devotion to equality remains constant. Reading Jaffa on the Emancipation Proclamation, or on the Ohio campaign of 1859 in which Lincoln and Douglas took part, one would have to infer that the writer [despite his involvement in the Goldwater campaign] is a dedicated liberal, that his politics [are] humane and generous." Reviewing the book for *America* (May 29, 1965), Francis Canavan recommended the collection: "While this reviewer thinks that Prof. Jaffa would have written a better book if he had reworked his essays into a more coherent whole, it must be said that he has made a penetrating analysis of our political history. Jaffa regards the Civil War as 'an epitome of all the great conflicts in American history,' and so gives most of his attention to the issues in that struggle. Though he writes with scholarly calm, his sympathies are never in doubt. . . . Students will find his exegesis of Lincoln illuminating and, for all its realism, inspiring."

Another collection of Jaffa's previously published articles, *The Conditions of Freedom*, was published in 1975. "These essays (mostly reprinted articles and reviews written between 1957 and 1974) set Jaffa's *Crisis of the House Divided* within a wider context and range in subject from American constitutional history to Aristotle, *King Lear, Tom Sawyer*, and Thoreau," Evan Simpson wrote for *Library Journal* (July

1975). "Leo Strauss's views provide the book's philosophical inspiration. Following Strauss, Jaffa compiles compelling evidence against the thesis of subjectivity of values, but his evidence for the existence of 'laws of Nature and of Nature's God' is less impressive. The book's main argument—good government must be enlightened by classical political thought—is stated with clarity and passionate intensity."

In Jaffa's next book, *How to Think about the American Revolution: A Bicentennial Celebration* (1978), he critiqued different views on the Declaration of Independence that were held by such scholars as Willmoore Kendall, Irving Kristol, Martin Diamond, Richard Hofstadter, and M.E. Bradford. Discussing the book for *National Review* (December 22, 1978), M. J. Sobran wrote that "Jaffa is concerned to redeem equality, generally a bad word among conservatives, as a central value of the American regime." Sobran continued: "Far from agreeing (with, e.g., Tocqueville) that it coexists tensely with liberty, Jaffa argues that equality is merely another *aspect* of liberty. He means, of course, equality 'rightly understood'—which is to say: as Locke understood it, as Jefferson and Madison understood it, as Lincoln understood it." Sobran added that although *How to Think about the American Revolution* is a brief book, it manages to cover "a remarkable number of disputed questions with a comprehensive trenchancy" and "brilliantly tears away conceptual distractions, and reveals our own first principles to us."

In 1984 Jaffa published a third collection of his essays, *American Conservatism and the American Founding*. The author devoted further attention to the Declaration of Independence and discussed, among other topics, James Madison, the 1980 presidential election, human rights, and the Supreme Court's notorious decision in *(Dred) Scott v. Sandford* (1857), which declared that African-Americans were not citizens. Jaffa asserted that such conservative authors as Walter Berns and George F. Will, along with the liberal author Garry Wills, a former conservative himself, have distorted the meaning of the American founding. (In the last few decades, Jaffa has frequently clashed with Berns, who also studied under Leo Strauss, over the interpretation and meaning of Strauss's ideas. Jaffa is acknowledged as the leader of an unofficial group of Strauss's followers who are known as the West Coast Straussians. By contrast, Berns, who is affiliated with the American Enterprise Institute for Public Policy Research, a conservative think tank based in Washington, D.C., leads the East Coast Straussians.) In the *National Review* (November 1, 1985), Joseph Sobran expressed a mostly favorable opinion of the book: "As always, Jaffa's great project is the vindication of Lincoln. He holds that Lincoln, at a critical moment, kept the American political tradition in harmony with the great principles of the Declaration and the Constitution, which in turn derive from [John] Locke, Aquinas, and Aristotle. And he contends that American conservatism has been corrupted by hostility to the Declaration, a hostility that unites such disparate men as [the pro-slavery Senator John C.] Calhoun, Kendall, Wills, and various Marxists, along with the pro-slavery polemicist George Fitzhugh." Sobran added, "The great virtue of Jaffa's work is simply that he is a philosopher in the classical tradition, discussing politics with full moral seriousness, in contrast to the terrible triviality we have come to expect on all sides in current discussion."

In 1994 Jaffa published *Original Intent and the Framers of the Constitution*. The book includes the reprint of an essay Jaffa originally published in the *University of Puget Sound Law Review* in 1987, in which he agreed with most conservatives that judges should interpret the Constitution along the lines intended by its framers. Jaffa, however, argued that natural law is crucial to understanding what the framers specifically intended when they drafted the Constitution and asserted that many conservatives have ignored natural law in interpreting it. The book contains critiques of Jaffa's essay by such legal scholars as Bruce Ledewitz, Robert L. Stone, and George Anastaplo, as well as Jaffa's responses to them. In the *Review of Politics* (Spring 1996), Matthew J. Franck found the exchanges between Jaffa and his critics entertaining: "In many passages of this book, Jaffa is at the top of his form in expounding the meaning of the Declaration, and the sense in which it sets the standard of the justice that the Constitution seeks to establish." Franck, however, noted that Jaffa contradicts himself in his rejoinders to his critics and provides a shallow analysis of the Dred Scott decision. "The failure of this book to make out a coherent doctrine for judicial interpretation of the Constitution is truly a shame," Franck concluded. "Few scholars are Jaffa's equals when it comes to expounding the true principles of legitimate political power, and the proper sensitivity of statesmen to the self-evident truths on which our constitutional structure rests. But he would have left well enough alone had he never taken up the question of the judicial function as it relates to those principles and that structure. For the reader wishing to know what role 'the Laws of Nature and of Nature's God' have in courts of law, there remain more questions than answers after reading Harry Jaffa's *Original Intent*—and even the questions are rendered murkier." By contrast, in his review for *Choice* (September 1994), M.A. Foley was impressed with the book: "This is an extremely well-written and well-argued set of essays on original intent and constitutional interpretation. Jaffa's interpretation of 'original intent' is challenging and thought provoking. The responses to Jaffa, and Jaffa's replies to his critics, are, from the perspective of academic scholarship, noteworthy contributions to the ongoing debate over the boundaries of Supreme Court decision making."

In *Storm over the Constitution*, Jaffa disputed the notion held by many conservatives—including Supreme Court Justice Antonin Scalia—that judges should apply no theory to their interpretation of the Constitution. Instead, Jaffa argues, jurists should use the Declaration of Independence as a guide. "Jaffa makes a strong case, but it would be even stronger if not for the book's conspicuous fault—the author's tendency to engage in too many personal animadversions against his critics," Michael Potemra wrote for *National Review* (November 22, 1999). "Many readers will find these comments entertaining, but others will find them distracting."

In 2000 Jaffa published *A New Birth of Freedom*, the long-awaited sequel to *Crisis of the House Divided*. In the new book, Jaffa examined President Lincoln's arguments, which he articulated in his inaugural address on March 4, 1861 and in an address to a special session of Congress on July 4, 1861, on why the Southern states had no right to secede from the Union. Lincoln believed that no state, even if a majority of its citizens supported secession, had the constitutional right to leave the Union without the consent of the other states. In his addresses Lincoln warned that secession would destroy democratic government and result in anarchy. "The new volume will not prove a disappointment," Glenn Tinder wrote in his review for the *Weekly Standard* (November 27, 2000). "It is a product of rigorous reasoning, reflects a profound knowledge of Lincoln and his era, and is cast in vigorous prose. And like the earlier volume, it expresses a deep moral seriousness." Although Tinder criticized Jaffa for failing to devote sufficient attention to several vital areas of Lincoln's thought, the reviewer wrote that "most readers will find *A New Birth of Freedom* to be a powerful work."

Harry Jaffa serves as a distinguished fellow with the Claremont Institute—a conservative think tank in Claremont, California—which has also published monographs of his work, including *The American Founding as the Best Regime: The Bonding of Civil and Religious Liberty* (1990) and *Homosexuality and the Natural Law* (1990). Jaffa is currently working on a third book about Abraham Lincoln.

He and his wife, Marjorie E. (Butler) Jaffa, live in in Claremont. Together they have three grown children.

—D.C.

Suggested Reading: *America* p807 May 29, 1965; *Choice* p209 Sep. 1994; Claremont Institute Web site; *Commentary* p71+ Aug. 1965; *Harper's Magazine* p114 May 1964; *National Review* p1,601+ Dec. 22, 1978, p36 Aug. 10, 1984, p62+ Nov. 1, 1985, Nov. 22, 1999; *New York Times Book Review* p59 Sep. 13, 1959; *Political Science Quarterly* p604 Dec. 1960; *Review of Politics* p390+ Spring 1996; *Weekly Standard* p31+ Nov. 27, 2000

Selected Books: *Thomism and Aristotelianism: A Study of the Commentary by Thomas Aquinas on the Nicomachean Ethics*, 1952; *Crisis of the House Divided: An Interpretation of the Issues in the Lincoln-Douglas Debates*, 1959; *Equality and Liberty: Theory and Practice in American Politics*, 1965; *The Conditions of Freedom: Essays in Political Philosophy*, 1975; *How to Think about the American Revolution: A Bicentennial Celebration*, 1978; *American Conservatism and the American Founding*, 1984; *The American Founding as the Best Regime: The Bonding of Civil and Religious Liberty*, 1990;

Homosexuality and the Natural Law, 1990; *Original Intent and the Framers of the Constitution: A Disputed Question*, 1994; *Storm over the Constitution*, 1999; *A New Birth of Freedom: Abraham Lincoln and the Coming of the Civil War*, 2000; as editor—*In the Name of the People: Speeches and Writings of Lincoln and Douglas in the Ohio Campaign of 1859* (with Robert W. Johannsen), 1959; *Statesmanship: Essays in Honor of Sir Winston Spencer Churchill*, 1981; *Emancipating School Prayer*, 1996

Jelinek, Elfriede

(YEL-i-nek, el-FREED)

Oct. 20, 1946– Novelist

When the Austrian novelist, poet, and playwright Elfriede Jelinek was selected for the Nobel Prize in Literature, in 2004, many observers expressed surprise; outside of Germany and France, her work was rather obscure. Those who were familiar with it, knew her to be a particularly divisive figure—a feminist who counts human cruelty and the latent fascism in her native culture among her most-constant themes. Stephen Schwartz, writing for the right-wing *Weekly Standard* (October 8, 2004), accused the Swedish Academy of trying to destroy literary standards by awarding top honors to an "unknown, undistinguished, leftist fanatic," whose "writings mainly verge on gross pornography." In a rare interview, the normally reclusive Jelinek told Ben Naparstek for the *Financial Times* (October 28, 2006), "I don't understand why so much hate is brought against me. I don't mean negative reviews, which are of course acceptable, but contemptuous and hate-filled writings, which have destroyed me personally. . . . A man can increase his erotic value through success, regardless of whether he is 30 or 80. A woman is erotically devalued by achievement, because she becomes intimidating. She is forever chained to her biological being."

Though equally controversial at home, Jelinek was praised by Austria's Socialist president Heinz Fischer, who hailed her victory as a "tribute to all Austrian literature." Jelinek, however, stated that she did not want her award to be viewed as a "feather in Austria's cap," a writer reported for the Agence France-Presse (October 7, 2004). She also confessed that she felt no sense of patriotism regarding her country. Indeed, the greatest affinity between Jelinek and Thomas Bernhard—the noted Austrian writer and composer to whom reviewers often compare her—lies in their grim sensibility and scathing view of humanity in general and their countrymen in particular. Describing her artistic

vision in an interview with a reporter for the Agence France-Presse (October 7, 2004), she stated, "My writings are limited to depicting analytically, but also polemically, the horrors of reality. Redemption is the specialty of other authors."

The writer Elfriede Jelinek was born on October 20, 1946 in the town of Mürzzuschlag, in the Austrian province of Styria. Her father was of Czech-Jewish origin and a chemist by profession, and her mother hailed from a prosperous Viennese-Catholic family. During the occupation of Austria by Nazi Germany during World War II, Jelinek's father experienced the Nazis' virulent anti-Semitism but was spared the concentration camps because his job in industrial production was considered valuable to the German war effort. The persecution suffered by her father during the war and afterward would become a prime motivator for Jelinek: "My whole life I wanted to avenge my father," she told a writer for Agence France-Presse (October 9, 2004).

While growing up Jelinek found herself torn between her parents' conflicting values: her father's Jewish cultural heritage and left-wing political views clashed with her mother's conservative Catholicism and bourgeois sensibilities. "On May Day [a holiday honoring organized labor] I would walk with my father wearing red ribbons in my hair," Jelinek recalled to Desmond Christy for the London *Guardian* (October 15, 1992). "On the feast of Corpus Christi I'd wear my white Catholic dress. And between these two poles is Austria. On the one side this social-democratic tradition and on the other a Catholic reactionary tradition." Pressured by her overbearing and socially ambitious mother, Jelinek took ballet lessons from the age of three and began studying music several years later, learning to play the piano, organ, and recorder. For 11 years, beginning in 1960, she attended the prestigious Vienna Conservatory, receiving an organist's diploma in 1971. Concurrent with her studies at the conservatory, Jelinek attended the Albertsgymnasium high school. She graduated in 1964 and matriculated at the University of Vienna,

Courtesy of Serpent's Tail

Elfriede Jelinek

where she took classes in theater and art history. In 1967 Jelinek's first collection of poetry, *Lisas Schatten* (which translates as "Lisa's shadow"), was published; at about that time she also started to write fiction.

During these years Jelinek's father suffered from severe mental illness and was eventually institutionalized in a psychiatric clinic before his death, in 1969. Jelinek herself has struggled with a similar malady: after several semesters at the University of Vienna, she experienced a nervous breakdown and spent the whole of 1968 secluded in her parents' home. "When I was a young woman I couldn't leave the house," Jelinek told Christy, "and even now I have problems." After emerging, Jelinek never returned to the University of Vienna to complete her studies. She did, however, become involved in the student movement of the late 1960s, and her writing started to take on darker, more political overtones. Published in 1970, Jelinek's second work, the satirical novel *wir sind lockvögel baby!* (which translates as "we are bait, baby!"), "revealed linguistic rebellion against popular culture's deceptive description of the good life," a writer for Agence France-Presse (October 7, 2004) observed. "Like with many of her later works, Jelinek shocked readers with her unemotional descriptions of brutality and power play in human relations." Jelinek's next novel, *Michael: Ein Jugendbuch für die Infantilgesellschaft* (1972), focused on similar themes. Contemporaneous with the publication of these novels, Jelinek also wrote radio plays, one of which was among the most successful productions of 1974. That same year Jelinek married Gottfried Hüngsberg and joined the Austrian Communist

Party, of which she remained a member until 1991. Dividing her time between Vienna and Munich, Germany, Jelinek continued to write. She garnered her best sales and critical reception to date with her novel *Die Liebhaberinnen* (1975), which was originally printed in Germany and later translated into English by Martin Chalmers under the title *Women As Lovers* (1994).

In *Women As Lovers*, "the lives of two young women desperate to improve their lots are contrasted in a short, sharp, shockingly frank assessment of sexual politics and modern life," a writer for *Kirkus Reviews* (on-line) observed. Brigitte, a factory seamstress, hopes to be the wife of Heinz, an electrician, while Paula, a dressmaker, pines after Erich, a woodcutter. The women see their desired mates as the means of rescuing them from their otherwise unsatisfying lives. Brigitte tries to ensnare Heinz through sex, whereas Paula stuffs Erich with food and drink. Despite the antipathy of the parents of Erich and Heinz and of the men themselves, the women succeed in their machinations after they both become pregnant. However, once they are married, Paula and Brigitte come to despise their husbands as their lives take drastically different directions. "The banal horrors of everyday life, and the layers of love and dreams are dissected with savage indifference," the *Kirkus Reviews* critic declared. "[*Women As Lovers* is] a chilling but truthful vision of women's precarious position in a society still dominated by money and men."

Jelinek next published the novels *Bukolit* (1979) and *Die Ausgesperrten* (1980). *Die Ausgesperrten* was translated into English by Michael Hulse under the title *Wonderful, Wonderful Times* (1990). Set in 1950s Vienna, the novel "concerns four teenage rebels and their efforts to assault citizens and relieve them of their wallets, not for money but for existentialist kicks," Charlotte Innes remarked for the *Nation* (March 18, 1991). The group is composed of Rainer Witkowski, the gang's nominal leader; his twin sister, Anna, a young pianist; Sophie, a girl from a wealthy family; and Hans, a working-class boy with whom Anna falls in love. The Witkowski children are the offspring of an unrepentant former officer of the S.S. (the Nazi paramilitary organization notorious for committing crimes against humanity) and his compliant schoolteacher wife, whom he beats and subjects to extreme sexual abuse. "Jelinek's characters, and the voice she uses to tell of them, are fashioned with black irony and jarring distortion," Richard Eder wrote for the *Los Angeles Times* (December 16, 1990). "Yet the ultimate effect is grace, a dark image delivered in terms appropriate to it, but in a draftsmanship that conveys a hint of delicacy and lyricism, as if these had been ejected from the room but continued to haunt it." Innes observed, "[Jelinek's] goal is to examine society with a cool, analytical eye. Youth, love, art, political systems, memory, religion, intellectualism and even nature are placed on the

Jelinek operating table and stripped of all our most treasured notions."

Published in 1983, Jelinek's semiautobiographical novel, *Die Klavierspielerin*, was translated into English under the title *The Piano Teacher* (1988). In the English-speaking world, *The Piano Teacher* is Jelinek's most acclaimed work. Set in Vienna, the novel details the exploits of Erika Kobut, an unmarried piano teacher whose dream of becoming a concert pianist has never materialized. She lives with her aging and overly possessive mother who keeps track of her every move, going so far as to share a bed with her in order to keep her from acquiring even a small measure of independence. Deeply troubled, Erika mutilates herself with razors and sometimes sneaks off to seedy pornography shops where she watches strippers disrobe. Her life changes when one of her students becomes sexually fixated on her. "Confronted by an actual male presence, Erika's precarious mental balance tips into psychosis, and her covert sexual practices finally become uncontrollable, driving the novel to a violent and scarifying climax," Elaine Kendall noted for the *Los Angeles Times* (January 16, 1989). The Vienna detailed in *The Piano Teacher* is not the romantic cultural center of the popular imagination but rather a profoundly decadent "netherworld of masochism, oppression, and violence in which no romantic illusions can survive the first chapter," Kendall observed. While applauding "Jelinek's uncompromising vision: her reluctance to make even one of the characters in this novel remotely sympathetic, her unwillingness to give any of them a way of transcending their predicament," the *New York Times* (December 7, 1988) critic Michiko Kakutani wrote and went on to say that "too often her descriptions of Erika's violent fantasies seem willfully perverse—as though they'd been concocted for the purpose of shocking the reader— and her relentless focus on the dark underbelly of Viennese life can seem equally artificial and contrived. In the end it makes for a novel that depresses rather than genuinely disturbs." Kendall offered a much more positive critique: "Though not for the faint-hearted or squeamish, *The Piano Teacher* is compelling fiction, ensnaring the reader with the intensity of the author's vision and the bitter irony she uses to present her view of the city." Jelinek, while acknowledging that the novel possesses autobiographical elements, has not elaborated on how much of the work is derived from her own experience. The novel was later adapted into an award-winning motion picture, *La Pianiste* (*The Piano Teacher*, 2001). The film was directed by Michael Haneke and starred Isabelle Huppert; it earned the top prize at the 2001 Cannes International Film Festival and a best-actress award for Huppert for her portrayal of Erika.

In her next novel, *Lust*, published in Germany in 1989 and translated into English in 1992, "Jelinek lets her social analysis swell to fundamental criticism of civilization by describing sexual violence against women as the actual template of our culture," the Nobel Prize Committee observed in a statement on the Nobel e-Museum Web site. The novel centers around Hermann, the manager of a provincial paper mill, and his wife, Gerti. When the AIDS epidemic persuades Hermann to give up his extramarital exploits, he forces Gerti to do his bidding, raping and beating her mercilessly. Gerti in turn embarks on an equally abusive relationship with a student. Although the book became a best-seller in Europe, the critical response was largely one of moral outrage: Lucasta Miller, writing for the London *Times* (December 26, 1992), declared that Gerti and Hermann's "function in the book is both allegorical and political, and their marriage is presented as a paradigm for all male-female relations in capitalist society. Peddling an unimaginative, bastardized version of Marxist-feminist thought, Jelinek takes for her premise the crass, simplistic line that all men are rapists and all women victims." Jelinek defended the book to Desmond Christy, explaining, "Every sexual relationship between a man and a woman is a relationship of violence. In all of these relationships a master gives and a slave receives. . . . These are such old, deep things in people's nature. The class society and private property can't allow any other kind of love-relationship."

Though never translated into English, Jelinek's 1995 novel *Die Kinder der Toten* (which translates as "the children of the dead"), was described by Elisabeth Juliane Vogel, a professor of German literature at the University of Vienna, as "the most important Austrian book of the '90s," as Sonya Yee reported for the *Los Angeles Times* (October 8, 2004). The novel portrays Austria as a nation of zombies who have failed to acknowledge their Nazi past. "This book shows what happens when you displace guilt and mass murder for such a long time," Vogel commented.

In addition to her novels, Jelinek has written a variety of other works over the years, including more than a dozen plays and an opera libretto. English versions of these works have yet to be published. Since Jelinek writes in a peculiar German dialect, her works are difficult to translate; her plays are particularly troublesome in this regard. "They cannot be translated," Jelinek told Sonya Yee. "I am sort of a provincial writer, because my works cannot be read by many people." Jelinek's plays have frequently created controversy in Austria. Her 1984 play *Burgtheater* referenced Paula Wessely, an acclaimed Austrian stage actress and a supporter of the Nazi regime. Wessely was quickly forgiven after World War II, an incident that Jelinek used to draw attention to Austria's failure to acknowledge the unsavory aspects of its past. In a similar vein, Jelinek's 1998 play *Ein Sportstück* depicted athletics as rife with violence and latent fascism. One of her most recent plays, *Bambiland* (2003), is an indictment of the

U.S.–led occupation of Iraq. Making use of her musical training, Jelinek collaborated with Olga Neuwirth on an opera, *Lost Highway*, based on the 1997 film of the same name by the director David Lynch. The opera debuted in Graz, Austria, in the fall of 2003.

Given the controversial nature of her work and her willingness to criticize Austrian culture and history, Jelinek has often earned the open enmity of certain politicians in her homeland. In particular, Jörg Haider and his right-wing Freedom Party launched the first in a series of attacks on Jelinek, in 1995, accusing her of fostering "degenerate art," a loaded term in Austria that recalled the language used by the Nazis to attack the Jews. Such tactics were not new for Haider and the Freedom Party, who often employed such language in their attacks against the European Union and immigrants. Initially Jelinek refused to respond to these assaults. In January 2000, however, Haider and the Freedom Party became part of a right-wing coalition government. Jelinek subsequently announced that as long as Haider and the Freedom Party were part of the ruling coalition, she would not allow her works to be performed in Austria. In the ensuing months, as the international community voiced dismay at his newfound prominence, Haider resigned from his post. In the November 2002 elections, the Freedom Party was roundly beaten in the polls.

On October 7, 2004 the Swedish Academy awarded Jelinek the Nobel Prize in Literature "for her musical flow of voices and counter-voices in novels and plays that with extraordinary linguistic zeal reveal the absurdity of society's clichés and their subjugating power." Speaking on behalf of the academy, Horace Engdahl, according to the transcript of his presentation speech that is posted on the Nobel Prize Web site, praised Jelinek for the singularity and strength of her work. "What first perplexes when reading Elfriede Jelinek," he noted, "is the strange, mixed voice that speaks from her writing. The author is everywhere and nowhere, never quite standing behind her words, nor ever ceding to her literary figures in order to allow the illusion that they should exist outside her language. There is nothing but a stream of saturated sentences, seemingly welded together under high pressure and leaving no room for moments of relaxation."

In addition to the Nobel Prize, Jelinek has received the 1969 Young Austrian Culture Week Poetry and Prose Prize; the 1969 Austrian University Students Poetry Prize; the 1972 Austrian State Literature Stipendium; the 1979 West German Interior Ministry Prize for Film Writing; the 1983 West German Ministry of Education and Art Appreciation Prize; the 1989 City of Vienna Literature Appreciation Prize; the 1996 Bremer Literature Prize; the 1998 Georg Buchner Prize, Germany's highest literary award; the 2002 Berlin Theatre Prize; the 2003 Else Lasker Schuler Prize; and the 2003 Mainz Prize, among others.

Greed, the first English translation of a novel that was published in German in 2000, is slated for publication in spring 2007. Besides penning her own original work, Jelinek has earned a living by translating into German the works of Christopher Marlowe and Thomas Pynchon, among other writers. With the $1.3 million that comes with the Nobel Prize, Jelinek hopes she will now be able to fully concentrate on her own writing. "The biggest luxury," she explained to Susanna Loof for the Associated Press (October 7, 2004), "is simply to write what one wants to write." Jelinek currently divides her time between Vienna, where she shares a house with her mother, and Munich. Jelinek is a renowned recluse; her social anxiety is so acute that she delivered her Nobel Prize acceptance speech via telecast instead of in person. "Of course, I'm very happy and proud to have received it," Jelinek told Ben Naparstek, explaining her anxiety over becoming a Nobel laureate. "My problem is that, because of my anxiety disorder, publicity is close to torture."

—P.B.M.

Suggested Reading: Agence France-Presse Oct. 7, 2004; Associated Press Oct. 7, 2004; (London) *Guardian* p11 Oct. 15, 1992, p7 Oct. 8, 2004; *Los Angeles Times* A p3 Oct. 8, 2004; *New York Times* II p10 May 13, 2001, A p3 Oct. 8, 2004; *Washington Post* C p1 Oct. 8, 2004; *World Literature Today* p61 Jan.–Apr. 2005

Selected Works in English Translation: *The Piano Teacher*, 1988; *Wonderful, Wonderful Times*, 1990; *Lust*, 1992; *Women As Lovers*, 1994; *Greed*, 2007

Jennings, Kate

1948(?)– Novelist; poet; essayist; short-story writer

The Australian-born poet, essayist, and novelist Kate Jennings began her writing career as a dedicated feminist and has never wavered from that position, though her views may have grown more nuanced over time. Her collections of poetry, *Come to Me My Melancholy Baby* (1975) and *Cats, Dogs and Pitchforks* (1993), and her volumes of essays, *Save Me, Joe Louis* (1988) and *Bad Manners* (1993), have a feminist tilt. The short stories in *Women Falling Down in the Street* were reportedly influenced by the works of two prominent early 20th-century women writers, Djuna Barnes and Jean Rhys. Jennings has since published two critically praised novels: *Snake* (1996) is set against the harsh background of life on a farm in the remote Australian outback, while the action in *Moral Hazard* (2002) takes place in the luxurious but ethically treacherous climate of Wall Street.

Courtesy of Harper Perennial

Kate Jennings

Kate Jennings submitted the following third-person biographical statement for *World Authors 2000–2005*:

"Kate Jennings is gaining an international readership for her subversive, honed-to-the-bone fiction. Her first novel, *Snake*, which was a *New York Times* Notable Book of the Year and came into contention for the Booker shortlist, was described variously as 'lethal and fast-moving' (*Publishers Weekly*), 'a narrative of pure anguish' (*Times Literary Supplement*), and 'possessing a holographic shimmer' (*New York Times Book Review*). Her second novel, *Moral Hazard*, explores the connections between our public and private selves and has been called 'humane and unsparing; witty, unsettling, and wildly intelligent' by Shirley Hazzard, author of *The Transit of Venus*.

"Jennings grew up on a farm in outback Australia in the fifties. 'Kids from the Australian bush know about the long haul, about surviving,' she says. 'We're also proud, stubborn, independent little sods. Make up our own minds about things. Put ourselves on the line.' She attended the University of Sydney in the 1960s, where she began her career as a poet, essayist, and fiction writer. A passionate feminist, she gained notoriety in her native country for an exceptionally confrontational speech that launched the modern feminist movement in Australia. 'I spent the first half of my life getting on a high horse, the second half trying to get off it,' she says, happy to laugh at herself. She adds, 'They were wild years. We went at everything full tilt. I lived by Jane Austen's motto: 'Run mad as often as you choose but do not faint.'

"In the early 1970s, Jennings edited an anthology of poetry by Australian women that made the front pages of newspapers. 'That anthology sold an astonishing—for poetry and for a small country—10,000 copies,' she remembers. Her own poetry has been described by fellow poet Les Murray as 'full of the graces of accuracy and resource.' Critic Judy Cotton, writing in Vogue, has said that 'Kate Jennings' words cut to the heart of the matter, a scrutiny that is a sustained act of courage.' Her book of short stories, *Women Falling Down in the Street*, won the Steele Rudd Award. Subsequently, her work was honored by the Philip Hodgins Memorial Prize for Literary Excellence.

"Jennings moved to New York in 1979. For a time, she was preoccupied with the subject of expatriation and the fate of '60s radicalism, writing essays that were collected in two volumes, *Save Me, Joe Louis* and *Bad Manners*. She then turned to her childhood for *Snake*. The story of a desperate postwar rural marriage, the surprise of the book is the even-handedness in Jennings's portrayal of her protagonists. As English critic Cherry Smyth expressed it, 'Rather than pit feminism against patriarchy, both husband and wife are horribly trapped by the expectations of their era. The sad emotional restraint is born in the language itself which gnaws at conjugal conventions brilliantly.'

"At the beginning of the 1990s, Jennings's husband, Bob Cato, an art director known for his work at CBS-Columbia Records, Revlon, and United Artists, was diagnosed with Alzheimer's. To pay for his care, she took a job as an executive speechwriter on Wall Street, and this became the milieu for her new novel, *Moral Hazard*. '[She] was the last person you would ever think to find on the Street. Truly a stranger in a strange land. But who knew that men in suits with thinning hair could be so mesmerizing, so chock full of juicy hypocrisy and fabulous vainglory. Ripe for the picking!' When asked if *Moral Hazard* is a roman à clef, she says, 'Well, it might make it onto reading lists at a couple of the big investment banks. And I most certainly will never eat lunch downtown again.'

"Andrew Field, a prominent Nabokov scholar, describes Jennings as a 'ferocious truth-teller' and predicts that she will soon be as well regarded in literary circles as Christina Stead, another Australian writer who lived for many years in New York. It will happen, writes Field, 'because of her humor, her obdurate individuality, and her willingness to say what other people won't.'"

A farmer's daughter, Kate Jennings was born in 1948 (some sources state 1949) and raised in a small town in the prosperous agricultural region known as the Riverina, in New South Wales, Australia. She has said in interviews that her experiences as a country girl helped to toughen her up. "A word of praise has never passed my father's lips," she told W. Fraser for the Melbourne *Herald* (September 7, 1988). (The Melbourne *Herald* has since merged with another newspaper and is now known as the Melbourne *Herald Sun*.) She later moved to Sydney, Australia, to attend college. There she established a reputation not only as a feminist and poet but also as the young woman who rode her motorcycle around town while wearing a helmet that read, "Better dead than wed."

According to Andrew Field, writing for the Queensland *Courier Mail* (May 3, 1997), though Jennings has received more press coverage for her fiction, there are many who still consider her first and foremost a poet. *Come to Me My Melancholy Baby*, her first collection of poetry, "is now partially dismissed by her as being both too confessional and too obscure," according to Field. Her second collection, *Cats, Dogs and Pitchforks*, was nominated for the C. J. Dennis Prize for Poetry, in 1993. Though she lost the award to the prolific poet and critic Les Murray for his *Translations from the Natural World* (1993), Murray praised Jennings's work, declaring that she "has become a truly fine poet, full of the graces of accuracy and resource," as quoted by Field.

Jennings's first collection of essays, *Save Me, Joe Louis*, includes 15 short pieces. Praising the collection as "witty and thoughtful," J. Power wrote for the Australia *Courier Mail* (January 21, 1989) that Jennings's "narrative style invites harmony: reader and writer move along in concert, sorting and tidying up a vast grab-bag of ideas, opinions, stories and memories—ranging from schooling, family, travel, love, war, eccentrics, the Japanese, the Americans, life, death—and Dusty Springfield."

Next Jennings published a collection of short fiction, *Women Falling Down in the Street*, which featured tales about women running headlong into relationships. Reviewing the collection for the Melbourne *Sunday Herald* (August 26, 1990), Alison Croggon wrote that the "stories seem more like the raw clay of prose than its sculpted art. It feels impossible to read them as anything except directly autobiographical notes, whether they are or not." One of Jennings's old boyfriends, an Australian journalist, seemed to agree; his lawyer contacted her shortly after the book's publication, claiming that his client was easily recognizable as one of the characters and threatening legal action. Jennings dismissed the claim, explaining to Margaretta Pos for the *Hobart Mercury* (August 25, 1990) that the story in question, "Mistakes, Too Many to Mention," was a satire, a send-up of another author's short story. (There are no press accounts indicating whether the ex-boyfriend ever took legal action.) Despite such complaints, however, the book's reception was generally positive. Giles Hugo, writing for the *Hobart Mercury* (October 13, 1990), described Jennings's style as "iconoclastic and cocky—but

compassionate. Her characters are truly weird and wonderful."

Jennings's 1993 book of essays, *Bad Manners*, "appeared to almost total silence in Australia," according to Field. "Of course, the snub had a lot to do with the many plainspoken comments about Australia in the very fairly labelled collection, but it doubtless had deeper causes as well. I have been told that there are many old friends from the days of the old Sydney Push [arts movement], in which she was one of the leading feminist figures, who are deeply disappointed that she didn't self-destruct as so many in that movement did." Nonetheless, Fields continued, "*Bad Manners* shows that Kate Jennings has remained a radical in the best sense of the word, and her essays should be read by anyone with any interest in Australian literature, Australia, or America, not to mention votive painting, nude beaches, the sex lives of Madonna and Eleanor Roosevelt and folly gardens. Her voice is unique. It's not necessary to agree with everything she says, or even half of it, to enjoy her style and method of argumentation."

Snake, Jennings's first novel, is set on a remote Australian farm in the 1950s. Irene is the wife of Rex, an upstanding farmer, and the mother of his two children. Their lives would be ideal, if it were not for the inexplicable hatred that Irene harbors for her husband. "Domestic dystopia has rarely been distilled into such concentrated literary form," a reviewer wrote for *Publishers Weekly* (March 10, 1997). "In her American debut, Jennings . . . paints a devastating portrait of a rotten marriage in post–WWII rural Australia. . . . The opening section (written in the second person and addressed to Rex) and the concluding one (addressed to Irene) pale next to Jennings's deliciously ironic, parable-like third-person narrative, which enriches the story of a doomed marriage with intimations of the spouses' thwarted desires and better selves. Almost whimsical chapter headings stand in contrast to the lean, startling prose. This snake of a novel is lethal and fast-moving—and so spare it will leave readers wishing for more."

Though many elements of *Moral Hazard* parallel the events in Jennings's life, she has insisted in press interviews that it is a work of fiction. Like the author, the protagonist of *Moral Hazard*, Cath, is an Australian-born former radical who must take a job on Wall Street to pay for the treatment of her husband's Alzheimer's disease. As the story unfolds, the deterioration of Cath's husband is mirrored by the collapse of her firm. "Jennings's title is the term used on Wall Street to describe dubious transactions (often high-risk ones that rely upon government bailouts)," a reviewer wrote for the *New Yorker* (July 15, 2002), "and in her spare, unsettling novel the human transactions are far more harrowing than the financial ones. . . . She is disgusted by the greed that surrounds her, but her unsentimental chronicle of the progress of a disease is what makes this fine, short novel almost unbearably sad."

Jennings's husband, Bob Cato, died in 1999 from complications due to Alzheimer's disease. She continues to reside in New York City. "Expatriates are held in contempt in Australia," she told Field, "but they have their uses, the main one being an ability to size up their native country with faculties that haven't been dulled by familiarity."

—S.Y.

Suggested Reading: Bookmunch Web site; *Canberra Times* A p19 June 1, 2002; (Queensland) *Courier-Mail* Weekend p8 May 3, 1997; *Library Journal* p127 Apr. 1, 1997; *New Statesman* p53 Apr. 15, 2002; *New York Times Book Review* p11 May 11, 1997, p5 June 30, 2002; *New Yorker* p87 July 15, 2002

Selected Books: poetry—*Come to Me My Melancholy Baby*, 1975; *Cats, Dogs and Pitchforks*, 1993; nonfiction—*Save Me, Joe Louis*, 1988; *Bad Manners*, 1993; fiction—*Women Falling Down in the Street*, 1990; *Snake*, 1996; *Moral Hazard*, 2002

Jha, Raj Kamal

1966– Novelist

Among the most exciting authors to have written in English over the last 50 years are a group of Indian writers that includes Salman Rushdie, Rohinton Mistry, Arundhati Roy, and Jhumpa Lahiri. Raj Kamal Jha joined that group when he published *The Blue Bedspread* (1999), shocking the staid Indian establishment with its tale of illicit family relations. Jha garnered praise as a writer of "breathtaking and precise" prose more like that of Raymond Carver and Don DeLillo than that of Rushdie and Roy, according to a reporter for the Southeast Asia Journalists Association (SAJA). Rushdie, nonetheless, is the author who helped Jha see the value of English: Jha's reading of Rushdie's *Midnight's Children* allowed him to regard English, which he still does not speak at home, as "an aesthetic instrument," he told Baret Magarian for the London *Guardian* (June 22, 1999). "Until then, I had always associated English with homework, nothing more. Rushdie's book showed me that English could be taken out of the school satchel and played with creatively." Jha followed *The Blue Bedspread* with *If You Are Afraid of Heights* (2003) and *Fireproof* (2007), solidifying his reputation for exploring taboo subjects and employing an impressionistic prose style.

Raj Kamal Jha was born in Bhagalpur, India, in 1966 and grew up in Calcutta, now known as Kolkata, where his father worked as a college professor. After finishing secondary school, Jha entered the prestigious Indian Institute of Technology (IIT), in Kharagpur, at which he studied mechanical engineering. He found that his zeal did not match that of his fellow students and vaguely began to consider the idea of becoming a writer, though, lacking the confidence to pursue the idea wholeheartedly, he completed his studies at IIT and obtained his mechanical-engineering degree, in 1988. At this point, he applied and was accepted to the journalism program at the University of Southern California, in Los Angeles, from which he earned his M.A., in 1990. Jha then became a working journalist, taking internships at the *Los Angeles Times* and the *Washington Post* and finding a staff position on a local Salinas Valley newspaper. He returned to India as a journalist, in 1994, taking a position at the Kolkata *Statesman*. He later worked briefly at *India Today* and, in 1996, accepted the position of deputy editor of the *Indian Express*, where he continues to work, now as an executive editor.

While working as a journalist, Jha wrote fiction by night, profiting from the insomnia that had always plagued him. Sometime in about 1996 he wrote a couple of pieces that he thought might be part of a larger whole, and a friend put him in touch with Pankaj Mishra, an Indian writer and publisher who encouraged him to expand the pieces into a novel. After completing four more chapters, Jha—with the help of Mishra—found a publisher in England who gave him a deadline, something that forced him to complete the project. The novel *The Blue Bedspread*, which was both a critical and financial success, relates the tale of a family from the point of view of a man whose sister has died in childbirth. He has been given charge of the child, who sleeps on the eponymous bedspread, until the family who will adopt her arrives the next morning. Over the course of a night, the man, trying to give shape to his life and somehow arrange a future for the child, relates in an elliptical and often obfuscated fashion, how he and his sister hid under that same bedspread, trying to escape from the reality of their alcoholic, violent father and oppressed mother. His recollections may not be entirely true, but they hint at the illicit sexual relationships that the siblings endured as children.

Magarian called *The Blue Bedspread* "an incantatory, audacious book, notable for moments of great poignancy," adding that "the fleeting quality of the book, its preoccupation with moments that plug straight into an emotional terrain, is primarily what Jha wishes readers to connect with." Richard Bernstein wrote for the *New York Times* (April 7, 2000), "Jha's world is a cruel one in which all normal yearnings for happiness are thwarted by poverty, or the dead hand of custom, or the untrustworthiness of others. But what is really a dismal horror story is told with a . . . loveliness that transforms it into an elegant, melancholy meditation on love and courage. Mr. Jha exhibits a remarkable honesty as a writer, and he is in impressive command of a technique that creates a powerful psychological realism out of a near phantasmagoric collage. . . . In short, *The Blue Bedspread* is a brilliant beginning for a writer whose voice already shows a maturity well beyond his years." Others, however, were unimpressed by Jha's method of storytelling. A reviewer complained for the *Hindu* (May 2, 1999), for example, "This is a story of love and hate and incest, and Jha has a narrative that conveys them, but somewhere they do not all link up. There are the memories, sometimes graphic, but they do not connect. This too could be one of the results of the effects of the distracted generation. Love and hate get their poignancy only if they are connected to a great memory. If they are disjointed, even if graphic, they do not have a cumulative impact. This is why the book makes for engrossing reading but in the end leaves you with little residue."

The Blue Bedspread was followed by *If You Are Afraid of Heights*, a novel whose fragmentations and ellipses are similar to those of its predecessor. In three sections, "Of Heights," "You Are Afraid," and "If," children and mysterious adults go about their shrouded business. A man hawks rides on a crow that he keeps in a cage, promising onlookers that they can peer into the windows of tall buildings and see the life of the city that is ordinarily barred to them. The crow, with a tiny human on his back, does indeed survey the entire scene. One of the characters, Amir, a postal worker whose job is to write letters for the illiterate and the blind, has an accident and is tended by a strange woman in her luxury apartment. The woman disappears when the cry of a child is heard. A little girl has been raped and murdered, and a little girl in a red dress, who may or may not be that same child, looks longingly into a shop window while her mother listens to the crow owner's spiel.

Alfred Hickling noted for the London *Guardian* (August 16, 2003) that it "takes a special kind of imagination to fuse such extreme ideas together, particularly as there is no such binding element as a conventional plot. . . . Readers are left to formulate their own theories and connections. But Jha's writing functions more through the power of association than sequential narrative. His prose has the febrile, cold-sweat quality of the most vivid waking nightmares. He suspends his work in a realm of improbability where it is possible to think the unthinkable. . . . Jha's prose ascends to some incredible heights. But it is the depths that are truly frightening." A reviewer for *Publishers Weekly* (August 2, 2004) called the novel "a dark, impressionistic collage about the collective history and the unseen connections between people and events," concluding that, like *The Blue Bedspread*, it "contemplates incest and domestic violence through the screen of repressed memory, but it is more self-consciously allegorical, and while rich in poetry, it lacks some of the emotional weight of its predecessor." Tiffany Lee-Youngren wrote for the *San Diego Union-Tribune* (August 1, 2004, on-line), "With fragments and hints strewn about this story like marigolds at a Hindu puja, one suspects

Jha's poetic and fulfilling work would be even better the second time around. 'See, that's what I mean, you look at facts, you draw the first pattern the facts make and then you stick to that pattern even if it's wrong. That's the problem. The truth, I have often found, lies somewhere else, it's linked to the facts but outside the pattern. . . . You may not get any answers . . . but no harm in looking, I say. Look, look wherever you can look.'"

Jha's third novel, *Fireproof*, was released in 2007. Opening in the Indian city of Ahmedabad, which is beleaguered by a wave of religious violence in which 100 Muslims die, the novel is narrated by a man, Jay, who possesses an unspeakable secret.

Jha, who lives in New Delhi, has done his best to keep his personal life private, telling Nilanjana S. Roy for the *Hindu* (November 2, 2003), "I want my books to do all the talking, even if in whispers. . . . The only thing I want people to see of me are my books. The books are my public space. I would like my readers to walk into the page."

—S.Y.

Suggested reading: *Hindu* (on-line) Nov. 2, 2003; (London) *Guardian* (on-line) June 22, 1999, Aug. 16, 2003; *New York Times* E p48 Apr. 7, 2000; *Publishers Weekly* p50 Aug. 2, 2004; *San Diego Union-Tribune* (on-line) Aug. 1, 2004

Selected books: *The Blue Bedspread*, 1999; *If You Are Afraid of Heights*, 2003; *Fireproof*, 2007

Johnson, Chalmers A.

Aug. 6, 1931– Nonfiction writer

Chalmers A. Johnson, a renowned scholar, political scientist, and author, has, in the last five years, emerged from the cocoon of academia to become "a distinguished doomsayer," as George Scialabba observed for the *Boston Globe* (April 25, 2004). Johnson's analysis of Japan's economic and political structure was essential to the development of a revisionist school of thought that argued that the key to Japan's economic success was "its unique variant of capitalism, which included a heavy dose of government direction over the economy and tight links among corporate families of manufacturers, suppliers, distributors, and banks," as Paul Blustein explained in the *Washington Post* (August 16, 1998). In recent years, however, Chalmers has broadened his gaze, writing the prescient work *Blowback: The Costs and Consequences of American Empire* (2000), in which he predicted that U.S. foreign policy would make the nation and its citizens the prime targets of terrorists. The book marked the transformation of Johnson—initially a Central Intelligence Agency

(CIA) analyst and Korean War veteran who had supported the use of American force on both the Korean peninsula in the 1950s and in Indochina during the 1960s and 1970s—to a passionate skeptic of what he has dubbed the "American Empire." Johnson continued this critique of American power in his follow-up work, *The Sorrows of Empire: Militarism, Secrecy, and the End of the Republic* (2004), a book that "conveys a sense of impending doom rooted in a belief that the United States has entered a perpetual state of war that will drain our economy and destroy our constitutional freedoms," as Ronald D. Asmus wrote for the *New York Times* (March 3, 2004). In 2007 Johnson published *Nemesis: The Last Days of the American Republic*, which is described as the final volume in the trilogy that began with *Blowback*.

The son of David F. Johnson Jr. and the former Katherine Ashby, Chalmers Ashby Johnson was born on August 6, 1931 in Phoenix, Arizona, and grew up in Buckeye, a town 30 miles away, at the confluence of the Gila and Hassayampa Rivers. During World War II, Johnson's father served in the Pacific theater for the U.S. Navy. After he returned from the war, the family relocated to Alameda, California.

Johnson attended the University of California, at Berkeley, receiving his bachelor's degree in economics, in 1953. Johnson then joined the Navy and subsequently traveled to Japan and Korea as part of the Korean War effort. He served until 1955 and finished his naval career with the rank of lieutenant. Upon his return to California, Johnson studied political science at Berkeley, obtaining his master's degree in the discipline in 1957 and his doctorate in 1961. While studying for his doctorate, Johnson authored his first book, *Freedom of Thought and Expression in China: Communist Policies toward the Intellectual Class* (1959). From 1961 to 1962 Johnson studied in Japan courtesy of a Ford Foundation fellowship.

Back in the U.S., Johnson taught at Berkeley from 1962 to 1988, serving as chair of the Center for Chinese Studies from 1967 to 1972. During his time at Berkeley, Johnson wrote prolifically on Asia; his titles include *Peasant Nationalism and Communist Power: The Emergence of Revolutionary China, 1937–1945* (1962); *An Instance of Treason: Ozaki Hotsumi and the Sorge Spy Ring* (1964); *Revolution and the Social System* (1964); *Revolutionary Change* (1966); *Conspiracy at Matsukawa* (1972); *Autopsy on People's War* (1973); *Japan's Public Policy Companies* (1978); and *MITI and the Japanese Miracle: The Growth of Industrial Policy, 1925–1975* (1982). Johnson also edited several scholarly works, including *Change in Communist Systems* (1970), *Ideology and Politics in Contemporary China* (1978), and *The Industrial Policy Debate* (1984). In 1988 Johnson left Berkeley for the University of California, at San Diego, where he served as a professor at the Graduate School of International Relations and

Pacific Studies until his retirement in 1992. During his tenure at San Diego, Johnson wrote *History Restarted: Japanese-American Relations at the End of the Century* (1992) and edited (with Laura D'Andrea Tyson and John Zysman) *Politics and Productivity: The Real Story of Why Japan Works* (1989). Two years after his retirement, Johnson founded, along with Steven C. Clemons, the Japan Policy Research Institute (JPRI); the Institute's purpose is "to promote greater public awareness and understanding of Japan's role in world affairs and Asian area studies," according to its Web site. In looking over Johnson's illustrious academic career, Patrick Smith wrote for the *Nation* (August 7, 2000) that many of Johnson's books "turned out to subvert the orthodoxy." In particular, *Peasant Nationalism and Communist Power* "forced late-McCarthyist America to acknowledge the treasonous truth that the Chinese Communists enjoyed immense popularity in the years leading up to the revolution." Similarly, Johnson's *MITI and the Japanese Miracle* was a seminal tome for the revisionist view of Japan that has now become prevalent. In the book, Johnson traces the activities of Japan's Ministry of International Trade and Industry (MITI), which was an integral part of Japan's economic growth. "As Johnson sees it," Don Oberdorfer wrote for the *Washington Post* (January 9, 1983), "the underlying element of 'the miracle' has been unrelenting determination to develop economically, which is an outgrowth of Japan's large population, lack of natural resources, late development and other factors. This determination has been channeled through institutions and practices that are uniquely Japanese." Oberdorfer anticipated the book's transformative impact, commenting, "For those who write, speak and argue about Japanese performance and especially about Japan's experience with a government-guided market economy, this is a book which cannot be circumvented or ignored. Its evidence will have to be taken into account."

The revisionist analysis of Japan, as illustrated in *MITI and the Japanese Miracle*, argues that the nation does not possess a typical capitalist, free-market economy; rather, as Johnson commented in the *New York Times* (September 6, 1990), Japan "is what we term a 'capitalist developmental state.'" In other words, Japan has an established, nationalistic industrial policy that includes "governmental affirmative action on behalf of domestic industry to foster orderly retreat of declining industries and to build the high-value-added industries of the future. It works on the supply side and takes as its criterion the number of truly valuable jobs held by a nation's workers. It favors computer chips over potato chips." Revisionists received that designation because, in recognizing Japan's economic singularity, they argued that orthodox American policy needed to be revised with specific trade measures tailored specifically for Japan. In his book *Japan, Who*

Governs?, published in 1995, Johnson concluded, as quoted by Paul Blustein for the *Washington Post* (August 16, 1998), "Japan's combination of a strong state, industrial policy producer economics and managerial autonomy seems destined to lie at the center, rather than the periphery, of what economists will teach their students in the next century."

Throughout most of the 1980s and 1990s, the revisionist school was ascendant. However, with the decline of Japan's economic fortunes during the late 1990s, some considered the Japanese paradigm and revisionism obsolete, arguing that market-driven models had proven more productive in the long run. Johnson, however, remained defiant, calling such criticism "Ideological piffle. The worst kind of American triumphalism," according to Blustein. "It misleads Americans into believing that they are truly triumphant, when they are in fact merely enjoying one phase of a global economic crisis that, for the time being, happens to be working out in their favor." Furthermore, he added, "Japan is still the main source of long-term capital in the world today, and the United States is still the largest debtor nation."

Blowback, a term used by the CIA to describe the unintended side effects of clandestine operations, "is shorthand for saying that a nation reaps what it sows, even if it does not fully know or understand what it has sown," Johnson wrote in his book of the same name, according to Tariq Ali for the London *Guardian* (March 16, 2002). Johnson explains early in *Blowback* that he had long been a proponent of American power. However, through his research on Japan's industrial policy, he wrote, as quoted by Richard Bernstein for the *New York Times* (March 29, 2000), he began "to see clearly for the first time the shape of the empire I had so long uncritically supported." One of the central foundations of the argument set forth in *Blowback* is that the U.S. is indeed an empire, propagated through America's control of global financial institutions and through its network of military bases located around the globe. With these military and financial assets, Johnson argued, the American empire is able to bully its client states into line. However, in analyzing the impact of U.S. policy in Korea, Okinawa, Afghanistan, and elsewhere, Johnson predicted that the nation was setting itself up for a violent comeuppance; specifically, he cited al Qaeda's 1993 attack on the World Trade Center and its bombing of U.S. embassies in Africa as blowback from America's Cold War policy in Afghanistan and the Islamic world. The book forecasts a hopeless, violent 21st century, in which terrorism will become a regular feature of American life, and the U.S. will not emerge victorious. "I believe our very hubris ensures our undoing," Johnson stated, according to Patrick Smith. The only way this outcome can be avoided, he argued, is if America dismantles its empire and constructs a new international order based on true democratic and humanitarian ideals.

Bernstein dismissed the book as "a take-no-prisoners tirade against what [Johnson] portrays as a classic imperial overextension worthy of Rome or the Ottoman Empire." Moreover, Bernstein found especially troubling Johnson's contention that South Korea and Japan—both democracies—were comparable, in their relationship with the U.S., to the Eastern European nations under Soviet domination during the Cold War. Still, Bernstein singled out Johnson's analysis of U.S. excesses in Okinawa and of the nuclear crisis in North Korea in the mid-1990s as relatively illuminating. Overall, however, Bernstein stated, the book is "marred by an overriding, sweeping and cranky one-sidedness."

Bruce W. Nelan, writing for *Time* (May 29, 2000), shared some of Bernstein's misgivings, describing *Blowback* as "more a scattershot polemic than an academic analysis. It suffers from its contradictions and its overstatements, as well as its lack of evidence for some accusations." However, he concluded that though "Johnson's denunciations are debatable and not all of his predictions are probabilities . . . if self-absorbed America goes on ignoring the world, some of them might come true." Karen M. Paget offered a similar critique for the *American Prospect* (December 4, 2000), making note of Johnson's excesses while observing that "Johnson has thrown down enough red flags on the triumphalist field to give us pause. And the issues he raises are ignored at our own peril."

With the attacks of September 11, 2001, Johnson's dire predictions about terrorists targeting the U.S. were borne out. Soon after, in a piece for the *Los Angeles Times*, he argued that the terrorists were not targeting America, but American foreign policy, and that, in response, the U.S. should seek to be more evenhanded with the Islamic world and avoid a retributive military overreaction that would embolden terrorists and otherwise isolate the nation. His remarks digressed markedly from the zeitgeist and earned him comparisons to the likes of Noam Chomsky, an influential linguist and a fervent critic of U.S. power.

In his second critique of America's global might, *The Sorrows of Empire*, Johnson details the spread of American militarism. In it Johnson argues that the U.S. military, with its hundreds of far-flung bases (imperial outposts in his analysis) and enormous yearly budgets, has become more and more removed from democratic oversight. The military-industrial complex has evolved into a state unto itself, according to Johnson. Moreover, far from serving to protect the U.S., the powerful armed forces actually incite violence, creating more anti-American sentiment, particularly in and around foreign military bases; this increased insecurity in turn spurs more military spending and further perpetuates the problem. The outcome of all this, Johnson predicts, are four "sorrows": perpetual war; the decline of democracy and individual rights as the executive branch supplants the Congress; a burgeoning propaganda apparatus that glorifies militarism and disseminates disinformation; and, finally, the nation's insolvency. Andrew J. Bacevich, reviewing the volume for the *Washington Post* (February 29, 2004), noticed some inconsistencies in the overall argument, stating that Johnson seemed torn between blaming the rise of militarism and empire on President George W. Bush and his advisers and acknowledging that the seeds of empire were planted in previous administrations. Nevertheless, the book is not simply an anti-Bush polemic; in fact, Johnson claims President Bill Clinton was the more effective imperialist of the two, "because he understood the need to impose the national will on the world indirectly via globalization," as Ronald D. Asmus explained in the *New York Times* (March 3, 2004). Asmus was scathing in his critique of the book, remarking, "No doubt Mr. Johnson's motives in drawing public attention to these concerns are well intended. But there is no doubt in my mind that his analysis is deeply flawed and his judgments at times grotesque." Despite some misgivings, Bacevich ultimately offered high praise for the work, writing, "The role of the prophet is an honorable one. When a nation falls into sinful ways, angry words and dire prognostications may be necessary to awaken people to the truth. In Chalmers Johnson the American empire has found its Jeremiah. He deserves to be heard; but the proper response to his gloomy message is not despair, but thought followed by action."

Chalmers Johnson married the former Sheila Knipscheer in 1957. She is a Berkeley-educated anthropologist specializing in cross-cultural gerontology, according to the Japan Policy Research Institute's Web site. In 1976 Johnson became a fellow of the American Academy of Arts and Sciences. He served as an adviser on the PBS television series *The Pacific Century* and was an integral contributor to *Losing the War with Japan*, an edition of PBS's *Frontline* documentary series; both of these programs earned Emmy Awards for the network.

—P.B.M.

Suggested Reading: American Empire Project Web site; *American Prospect* p43 Dec. 4, 2000; *Boston Globe* D p8 Apr. 25, 2004; *Bulletin of Atomic Scientists* p71 Nov./Dec. 2000; *Humanist* p43 May/June 2001; Japan Policy Research Institute Web site; *New York Times* E p8 Mar. 29, 2000, A p13 Oct. 6, 2001, E p1 Mar. 3, 2004; *Publishers Weekly* p58 Dec. 8, 2003; *Time* p73 May 29, 2000; *Washington Post* H p1 Aug. 16, 1998, T p4 Feb. 29, 2004

Selected Books: *Freedom of Thought and Expression in China: Communist Policies toward the Intellectual Class*, 1959; *Peasant Nationalism and Communist Power: The Emergence of Revolutionary China, 1937–1945*, 1962; *An Instance of Treason: Ozaki Hotsumi and the Sorge Spy Ring*, 1964; *Revolution and the Social System*, 1964; *Revolutionary Change*, 1966; *Conspiracy at Matsukawa*, 1972; *Autopsy on People's War*, 1973; *Japan's Public Policy Companies*, 1978; *MITI and the Japanese Miracle: The Growth of Industrial Policy, 1925–1975*, 1982; *History Restarted: Japanese-American Relations at the End of the Century*, 1992; *Blowback: The Costs and Consequences of American Empire*, 2000; *The Sorrows of Empire: Militarism, Secrecy, and the End of the Republic*, 2004; *Nemesis: The Last Days of the American Republic*, 2007

Courtesy of HarperCollins

Jones, Edward P.

Oct. 5, 1950– Novelist; short-story writer

Having grown up in a series of predominantly African-American neighborhoods in Washington, D.C., Edward P. Jones has crafted tales of that world: his well-regarded story collections, *Lost in the City* (1992) and *All Aunt Hagar's Children* (2006), describe the lives of ordinary residents of Washington, capturing their struggles, foibles, and occasional heroism. Jones's Pulitzer Prize–winning novel, *The Known World* (2003), about slave society in the years preceding the Civil War, also brought him a measure of attention and acclaim. Gene Seymour wrote for New York *Newsday* (August 24, 2003), "Jones' novel is a significant contribution to the growing body of work by such African-American novelists as Toni Morrison (*Beloved*) and John Edgar Wideman (*The Cattle Killing*) who are seizing imaginative autonomy over their shared history."

The oldest of three children, Edward Paul Jones was born on October 5, 1950 in Arlington, Virginia, to Aloysius and Jeanette Majors Jones. He was raised in nearby Washington, D.C., which was then racially segregated. Jones had a difficult, impoverished childhood; early on, his father left the family, and his mother, who could neither read nor write, supported her children by cleaning houses and working at various menial jobs in an upscale hotel restaurant. "I don't even pretend to begin to say what my mother went through when she went out to work each morning," Jones told Mary Ann French. "She could have gotten up one morning and gotten on the bus and never come back. But she didn't. She always came back in the evening." Jones's younger brother was mentally retarded and was eventually institutionalized. When Jones was about 14, his younger, more extroverted sister, with whom he was very close, was sent to live with relatives in Brooklyn, New York, to give her a chance at a better life. By Jones's count, the family moved within Washington on some 18 occasions, "for one reason or another—the roof would leak or there would be some other defect," as he recalled to an interviewer for the *Washington Post Book World* (August 24, 2003). The frequent relocations made it very difficult for him to maintain friendships. He described his childhood summers in an article for the *Washington Post Magazine* (August 7, 1994), "Moving Pictures: In Search of Summers Past." Of the summer of 1964, he wrote, "I am unable to make friends with the children on Sixth Street because my heart is unable to take it anymore, unable to extend itself, knowing that in a few months or a year we will move again and the friends will be lost and I will have to start all over." Reflecting on what his life was like when he was an older teenager, he noted, "Though I am close to friendless, in a way it is not a great hurt. It may well be what saves my life, saves me from being devoured by the streets, saves me from the shaky love of a girl who would have given me a baby and sent me bumbling off into a raw kind of manhood." A saving grace of the poor neighborhoods where Jones lived, he has recalled, was the sense of community conveyed by the adult residents. While his mother washed dishes in a restaurant all night when he was about three, in "a house of neighbors who treat us like their own children, my sister and I sleep without fear alone in our room until our mother returns in the early morning."

As a boy Jones found solace in reading. With money he earned by running errands or collecting empty soda bottles, he bought comic books, with *Archie, Richie Rich,* and *Casper the Friendly Ghost*

among his favorites. (The rise in the price of comic books from 10 to 12 cents "broke his heart," as Linton Weeks wrote in the August 16, 2003 issue of the *Washington Post.*) At 13 Jones began to read more sophisticated works—including Richard Wright's novel *Native Son* and the autobiography of the singer and actress Ethel Waters—books that impressed him with the richness of experience and the sense of human possibility they reflected. Jones attended Cardozo High School, in Washington, where he became an honors student in English. He told Rachel L. Swarns for the *New York Times* (October 16, 2003) that he had to sign his mother's name to his report cards, because she could not do so.

During high school Jones chanced to meet a Jesuit teacher at the College of the Holy Cross, in Worcester, Massachusetts. At that teacher's suggestion, Jones applied to Holy Cross, where he was admitted and received a scholarship. Jones originally majored in mathematics, but switched to English when he did not do well in a calculus course. (The reason, he later found out, was that he had needed glasses and was not seeing the numbers on the blackboard properly.) "It surprised me that I was competitive" at Holy Cross, Jones said to Linton Weeks. "The public schools in Washington had given me a pretty substantial education." He graduated in 1972; in his sophomore year he had begun to write fiction.

After college Jones returned to Washington and took care of his mother, who was then ill, while working sporadically. After her death, in January 1975, Jones continued to have trouble finding work and stayed for a time in a shelter for homeless people. The year 1976, however, saw two positive developments: *Essence* magazine accepted one of his short stories and paid him $400 (the magazine's staff had trouble locating him to send him the check); and he found steady work, answering telephones at the American Association for the Advancement of Science, where he spent three years. At a writers' conference at George Mason University, in Virginia, Jones met the novelist John Casey, who encouraged him to pursue creative writing in graduate school. Jones chose the program at the University of Virginia, because it was close to Washington and because James Alan McPherson, whose short stories Jones had enjoyed in college, taught there. Jones studied there from 1979 to 1981, earning an M.F.A. degree. He told Lawrence P. Jackson for the *African American Review* (Spring 2000) that he learned more from the literature courses he took than from the writing courses. Since then, teaching creative writing from time to time at various colleges, he has tried to do as "thorough a job as I can, point by point, almost line by line if there's time, because I didn't think that I got that when I was in graduate school." In 1983 Jones landed a job at Tax Analysts, a nonprofit company based in Arlington, Virginia, that assists tax professionals in understanding changes in regulations; he remained there for nearly two decades as a writer and proofreader for the organization's publication *Tax Notes*.

Meanwhile, Jones continued to publish short stories in various magazines, including *Essence* and *Callaloo*. His book *Lost in the City*, a collection of 14 short stories, appeared in 1992. The city of the title is Washington, D.C., where many African-Americans from the Deep South have come to improve their lot. There they make modest gains in security and prosperity but still struggle to hold their families together. Most of the stories are told from a female point of view. "Jones has near-perfect pitch for people," Michael Harris noted in the *Los Angeles Times Book Review* (July 12, 1992). "A motherless girl who raises pigeons, old women stirred by a lightning storm to remember the dark rural past, a boy whose demanding lady boss at a grocery store becomes his best friend, a man who finds a new lifestyle knocking on strangers' doors in search of his runaway daughter, a woman whose father, imprisoned 25 years for killing her mother, wants to get back into her life—whoever they are, he reveals them to us from the inside out." As Jonathan Yardley wrote for the *Washington Post Book World* (June 21, 1992), when a woman in one of the stories tells her daughter, "God don't put no more on us than we can bear," Jones "puts that proposition to the test. Though there are many themes in his work, none is more important than the daily struggle of ordinary people against terrible odds. Some of these are imposed from without: Discrimination and segregation, though only occasionally brought to the forefront, are stunting, inescapable realities. But so too are those imposed from within, by people who have ignored or forgotten a grandfather's advice: 'Don't get lost in the city.'" Jones's collection was nominated for a 1992 National Book Award and won the PEN/Hemingway Award for first fiction. In 1994 Jones received a Lannan Literary Award, with a stipend of $50,000; he was also awarded a $20,000 grant from the National Endowment for the Arts.

In early 2002 Jones's job at Tax Analysts was phased out. That development, as Jerome Weeks wrote in the *Dallas Morning News* (October 6, 2003), gave Jones "the jolt" he needed to finish the novel he had begun years earlier; the money from his awards—and his frugal lifestyle—allowed him to concentrate on his writing full-time. Since college, when he had learned that some African-Americans had owned slaves, Jones had nurtured the idea of writing a novel on the subject. Over the years he had collected and read many books on the slave era but had made a conscious decision not to become overly influenced by historical facts; he told Linton Weeks that he "didn't want the research to get in the way of the people and the world I had already imagined."

The Known World was published in 2003. The novel suggests that slavery corrupts absolutely, exempting no one, whether slave or master. The novel focuses on Henry Townsend, who was born a slave but whose parents have purchased the family's freedom; he acquires his own plantation and slaves and is mentored by Robbins, his former master. By the time of his early death, Henry has acquired more than 30 slaves, who are left to his wife. Henry watches from beyond the grave as the overseer Moses, who has begun an affair with Henry's widow, plots to betray his family and the other slaves. Meanwhile, news of slave revolts and escapes leads the whites in the novel to doubt even their seemingly devoted slaves, with the result that "cozy certainties become unmoored," as Gene Seymour phrased it in New York *Newsday* (August 24, 2003). "Justice, love and the sanctity of life are worn away and ultimately disfigured by the habit of treating people of color as property."

Jones's unusual subject attracted reviewers' attention, but it was the quality of his writing that drew praise. Ron Franscell noted for the *Denver Post* (August 31, 2003) that the "biblical rhythms" of Jones's prose "lend depth to a story about profound moral confusion." In the *New York Times* (August 14, 2003), Janet Maslin pronounced the novel to be "stunning" and added, "In no way is Mr. Jones's work morally black and white. Racial lines here are intriguingly tangled and not easily drawn. . . . With its eloquent restraint and simplicity, *The Known World* penetrates a realm of contradictions and takes the measure of slavery's punishments." In March and April 2004 Jones won the National Book Critics Circle Award and the Pulitzer Prize for fiction, respectively, and in September of that year he was awarded a $500,000 MacArthur Fellowship (widely referred to as a "genius grant"). The large increase in his bank account notwithstanding, Jones told Deborah Solomon for the *New York Times Magazine* (October 10, 2004) that he did not intend to change his lifestyle much. "I don't want to own anything that I can't fold up and bring into my apartment," he declared.

In 2006 Jones published *All Aunt Hagar's Children*, a collection of short stories, some of which had previously appeared in the *New Yorker*. Like the tales in *Lost in the City*, those in the newer volume are set mostly in Washington, D.C., and certain characters appear in both books. *All Aunt Hagar's Children* includes "A Rich Man," in which an ex-Pentagon employee settles into a retirement community in downtown Washington and begins to cheat on his wife with a series of increasingly younger mistresses; "Resurrecting Methuselah," in which a woman ponders the best ways to save her failing marriage and properly educate her daughter; and "Root Worker," in which a doctor confronts the limits of modern medicine when her own ailing mother consults a voodoo practitioner. Dave Eggers, echoing sentiments expressed by many critics, wrote for the *New York Times Book Review* (August 27, 2006, on-line) that "the collection manages to stun on every page; there are too many breathtaking lines to count."

Jones currently lives in Washington, D.C., in a sparsely furnished apartment. He is unmarried and spends many solitary hours reading. Rachel L. Swarns reported that when reviews of *The Known World* began to appear, Jones "had no car, no cellphone and no fax machine to cope with the flurry of interview requests. Now he has a driver to ferry him to literary events and a fax machine, all courtesy of his publisher. He has decided against buying a cellphone, fearing it could seem too pretentious." Jones told William L. Hamilton for the *New York Times* (August 31, 2006, on-line), that he had, however, made certain minor changes: "Because of all the stuff we went through when I was a kid, I don't ever want to eat another cabbage sandwich."

Of the recurring themes in his work, Jones told Robert Fleming for *Publishers Weekly* (August 11, 2003), "I refuse to write about ignorance, despair and weakness, [or] about people going to clubs and doing dumb things. . . . I want to write about the things which helped us to survive: the love, grace, intelligence and strength of us as a people."

—S.Y.

Suggested Reading: *African American Review* p95+ Spring 2000; *Denver Post* (on-line) Aug. 31, 2003; *Los Angeles Times Book Review* p6 July 12, 1992; (New York) *Newsday* D p32 Aug. 24, 2003; *New York Times* C p18 June 11, 1992, (on-line) Aug. 14, 2003, (on-line) Aug. 31, 2006; *New York Times Book Review* (on-line) Aug. 27, 2006; *New York Times Magazine* p17 Oct. 10, 2004; *Publishers Weekly* p254 Aug. 11, 2003; *Washington Post* G p1 July 22, 1992; *Washington Post Book World* p3 June 21, 1992; *Washington Post Magazine* p8+ Aug. 7, 1994

Selected Books: *Lost in the City*, 1992; *The Known World*, 2003; *All Aunt Hagar's Children*, 2006

Courtesy of Solidaridad Publishing

José, Francisco Sionil

(see-O-neel)

Dec. 4, 1924– Novelist; journalist

The Filipino author Francisco Sionil José, who signs his work F. Sionil José, was introduced to American readers in 1992 when Random House published *Three Filipino Women,* a collection of three novellas that expanded upon *Two Filipino Women,* an earlier version of the book that had been published in the Philippines in 1981. It is a testimony to the American publishing industry's tendency to ignore the literature of the non-Western world that his introduction came so late. He had been writing for about 40 years, and his books, which are all written in English, had been translated into more than 20 languages before they were made available in the U.S. Indeed, José was known almost everywhere else. His international reputation is such that some critics have conjectured that he will soon be awarded the Nobel Prize in literature. He has already received the Asian equivalent: in 1980 he won the Ramon Magsaysay Award for journalism, literature, and creative communication arts. Random House has since attempted to familiarize American audiences with his work, publishing a number of his other novels throughout the 1990s, including: *Sins* in 1996; *Dusk,* known as *Po-on* (1984) in the Philippines and other countries, in 1998; *Don Vicente*, which includes two novels—*Tree* (1978) and *My Brother, My Executioner* (1979)—in 1999; and *The Samsons*, which contains *The Pretenders* (1962) and *Mass* (1979), in 2000.

While José's introduction to American readers came in the 1990s, his introduction to American publishers took place four decades earlier. In 1955 he traveled to New York City with a manuscript of *Tree* and met the literary critic Malcolm Cowley, who was an editor at Viking Press at the time. After reading the manuscript, Cowley introduced José to an agent, asked him to edit the work—presumably to make it more appealing to American readers— and promised to publish it. José returned to the Philippines and began working on the manuscript, but after a week, he asked himself, as he told David Streitfeld for the *Washington Post* (July 12, 1998), "For whom am I writing this? I realized I was writing not for the Americans, but for my own people." Maintaining his identity as a Filipino writer, he decided, was more important than gaining access to the lucrative American literary market, and he thus abandoned the task Cowley had given him. His commitment to his Filipino identity has remained an important element of his authorial persona. "I belong to the English tradition because I write in English," he has said, Lito B. Zulueta reported for the *Philippine Daily Inquirer* (May 27, 2001), "but my tradition, too, is my village, the Ilocanos, and this unhappy country we call Filipinas." Thus, when his books began being published internationally, he told his editors, according to Streitfeld, "Make all the changes and corrections you want, but there's one thing—Don't make me less Filipino." Having insisted that he is first and foremost a Filipino, José is a national treasure in the Philippines and has attained this distinction despite his criticism of Filipino society.

A member of the native ethnic group known as the Ilocanos, Francisco Sionil José was born on December 4, 1924 and grew up on a farm in Rosales, a village in the northern part of the Philippines. Unlike previous generations of children in his socioeconomic class, he received an education, because the U.S. colonial administration introduced a public-school system to his region, and he has said, according to Lito B. Zulueta, "If not for the Americans, I would have been a dirt poor farmer in Ilocos, toiling and tilling the land." He developed a love of reading at an early age, which his mother did everything she could to encourage. "When she found out I was reading everything I could lay my hands on, even the old newspapers that were used to wrap fish," José told David Streitfeld, "she'd go around scrounging books from people in town." He read late into the night under a streetlight, because he often could not afford the kerosene for the homemade lamp that he had fashioned out of a pomade jar. After finishing high school, José studied medicine at the University of Santo Tomas, in Manila, but gave it up to pursue writing. He became the editor of the student newspaper, the *Varsitarian*, and received encouragement from such mentors as the Spanish Dominican writer Juan Labrador and Paz Latorena, one of the first generation of Filipino writers in English.

During this time he also sold short stories to weekly magazines in order to support his mother and to pay for the education of his brother and sister. Starting in 1947, José wrote for the national Catholic weekly *Commonweal*. He left the university in March 1949, after he landed a job as an assistant editor for the United States Information Service (USIS) in the Philippines, a position he kept for a year, after which he worked as an associate editor at the *Manila Times*. By the end of the 1950s, José had not simply established himself as a professional journalist and fiction writer but was also an important figure among the

Filipino intelligentsia; he also founded his country's chapter of PEN, the international organization of poets, playwrights, and novelists. He published his first novel, *The Pretenders*, in 1962. The fourth volume in the chronology of his five-volume Rosales Saga, *The Pretenders* tells the story of the impoverished Antonio Samson, who wins a scholarship to Harvard University shortly after World War II, earns his degree, and returns to the Philippines idealistically hoping to become a professor and use his talents to improve his country. Instead he marries Carmen Villa, the daughter of a wealthy businessman, Don Manuel, and is obliged to use his talents to promote his father-in-law's business and maintain the status quo. The conflict between his ideals and his existence eventually leads Samson to commit suicide. The novel received high praise and has become standard reading in the Philippines. Nonetheless, when the novel—packaged with the final book in the series, *Mass* (1979)—finally appeared in the U.S. in 2000, reviews were less than stellar. Carina A. del Rosario, writing for the *International Examiner* (August 14, 2001), complained, "Carmen Villa is the tempting city girl, luring Tony away from his roots, embodied by his cousin, Emy. Don Manuel Villa represents the manipulative elite. All the characters, though, are just too one dimensional, too predictable. While José tackles an important aspect of Filipino history and identity, *The Pretenders* comes off as a cliche." The book, however, has always been regarded as a classic in literary markets outside of the U.S.

Following the success of *The Pretenders*, José opened up a bookstore in Ermita, the tourist district of Manila. He initially called it Erehwon (*nowhere* spelled backwards) but changed its name to Solidaridad Bookshop, in homage to the underground, revolutionary newspaper of that name published during Spanish rule. He also opened his own publishing house, called Solidaridad as well, and began publishing his own books and those of other Filipino writers. In 1966 he became the editor and publisher of *Solidarity*, a journal of current affairs, ideas, and arts, with financial help from the Congress for Cultural Freedom, an organization sponsored by the U.S.'s Central Intelligence Agency (CIA). The connection between his journal and the CIA led a newspaper to publish an article in 1967 that accused him of being a covert agent. He vehemently denied the charge and successfully sued for libel.

In 1968 he published his first book of short stories, *The God Stealer, and Other Stories*. He has since published four other collections: *Waywaya, and Other Short Stories From the Philippines* (1980), *Platinum: Ten Filipino Stories* (1983), *Olvidon, and Other Stories* (1988) and *Puppy Love and Thirteen Short Stories* (1998). None of these collections are available in the U.S., though José's short stories are an important element of his oeuvre. The themes of these stories are the same as those of his novels, according to Markus Ruckstuhl for *BusinessWorld* (December 3, 1999): "The continuous search for the truth, for social justice and a moral order is the foundation on which all José's novels and short stories are built and erected." The stories are also a major part of modern Filipino literature. Thus Greg Sherridan, writing for the *Australian* (January 9, 1998), advised, "if you want an easier introduction to Filipino literature, his short stories are exquisite."

In 1978, 23 years after he showed his manuscript to Cowley, José published *Tree*, the second volume of the Rosales Saga, and the following year, he published the third, *My Brother, My Executioner*. When the two novels appeared under the title *Don Vicente: Two Novels* in the U.S. in 1999, Ricco Villanueva Siasoco of the *Boston Globe* (July 25, 1999) criticized *Tree* for having "a skittish, episodic structure." He went on to note that the story revolves around a number of "archetypal characters who populate the unnamed narrator's childhood" and concluded that it reads more "like the interconnected story collections so popular today . . . [and so] fails to deliver an overarching punch." Siasoco found *My Brother, My Executioner* more satisfying: "The second book," he wrote, "gives us a more linear narrative. Luis Asperri Vicente learns of his father's complicity in the devastation of a small village where Luis's impoverished mother and grandfather lived. It is Luis's struggle to reconcile the trappings of his birth and his conflicting social values that imbues the tale with a dimension absent from *Tree*." A critic for *Kirkus Reviews* (June 15, 1999), by contrast, found the second novel "much weaker" than *Trees*, which, the reviewer said, "is distinguished both by its narrator's eloquently conflicted feelings and by the facility with which José creates a rich parade of characters." David Walton, writing for the *New York Times* (February 6, 2000), found both novels equally compelling, observing that "José's storytelling is direct and accessible, his characters and story lines drawn together by the symbol of the great balete tree that stands in the center of Rosales, 'a guardian over the land and our lives, immemorial like our griefs.'"

José followed *Tree* with *Mass,* the last book in the Rosales Saga and the one he had the most trouble publishing. Under the dictatorship of Ferdinand Marcos, whom José publicly criticized, the government-run schools' subscriptions to *Solidarity* were cancelled and the profitability of his publishing company suffered. José, therefore, could not afford to print any books and, as Michael J. Ybarra explained for the *Los Angeles Times* (May 17, 1998), "other local houses refused to touch the novel, which included a portrait of a ruthless ruler named Marcos." José eventually sold the book to a publisher in Holland, where it was published in 1982, and used his advance to print it in Manila in 1979. *Mass* tells the story of Antonio Samson's illegitimate son, José Samson, who first gets involved in the criminal underworld of Manila in

the early 1970s but then rejects that life to become an anti-Marcos leftist. Regarding it as more interesting than *The Pretenders,* the novel with which it was published in the U.S., Christopher Atamian of the *New York Times* (October 29, 2000) noted, "The author's message is clear: colonialism may have come and gone, but the Filipino people must now bear the burden of fighting their own governing classes. At times the novel reads too much like a Marxist treatise on class exploitation, but over all, this book is a fascinating and worthwhile introduction to a culture and history too often ignored in the West."

In 1981 José published *Two Filipino Women,* and the book became *Three Filipino Women* when it was published in the U.S in 1992. "All three stories," Joseph Coates wrote for the *Chicago Tribune* (June 18, 1992), "are about successful intellectual men in love with women superior to them in strength, integrity and commitment; all, probably intentionally, follow a pattern: first, strong involvement with the enchantress, then separation, eventual reconciliation, and then the fatal results of it due to the man's inadequacy." Robert DiAntonio, writing for the *St. Louis Post-Dispatch* (July 12, 1992), suggested that the stories were allegorical as well as realistic when he called attention to the parallel between the women in the stories and the Philippines; the writing, DiAntonio wrote, is "harshly realistic as it chronicles the lives of three beautiful women who, like the Philippines itself, have long been victimized." Lynne Bundesen for the *Los Angeles Times* (August 13, 1992) took another perspective, arguing that the stories present a microcosm of Filipino culture. "Open this book and you will be taken deep into the mentality and geography of the Philippines," she wrote. "The characters created in these novellas speak a language they are trying to make their own, and it is through the often idiosyncratic use of that language that these stories are told." Bundesen concluded, "The reader of this slim volume of well-crafted stories will learn more about the Philippines, its people and its concerns than from any journalistic account or from a holiday trip there."

Po-on, the first book in the Rosales Saga and the last to be printed, was published in the Philippines in 1984 and later in the U.S. under the title *Dusk* (1998). Beginning in 1872 in Po-on, a village in the Ilocos region, and spanning 20 years, the novel tells the story of the Samson family's migration to Rosales and dramatizes, through the events surrounding this migration, the beginning of the Philippines' quest for independence. Discussing the importance of his saga in the introduction to the U.S. edition, José suggested that it helps to fill a void left by historians. "*Dusk,*" he wrote, according to Frank Gibney for the *New York Times* (August 2, 1998), "is simply the story of a family, or rather of a peace-loving man who led his clan in its flight from the narrow coastal plain of the Ilocos in northern Luzon to the central plains. It is also a story of Spanish tyranny, and the Philippine response to it and to the American intrusion into our islands after the Spaniards left. All too often, our history is adorned with heroes of high station; there is nothing written about the common people, the foot soldiers who die in the hundreds so that their generals may live." Bruce Allen, writing for the *Boston Globe* (June 7, 1998), was disinterested for the most part in José's historical intentions and called the novel "a melodramatic and generally absorbing tale of a native family's displacement, victimization, and transformation." Allen went on to observe, "Although *Dusk* is dominated by its author's political agenda, it's a strongly atmospheric story distinguished by its sensuous physical descriptions and several vivid foreground figures." Other reviewers agreed. A writer for *Kirkus Reviews* also found that the quality of José's writing saved the novel from being mere political propaganda. "The obvious political agenda," the reviewer wrote, as quoted by David Streitfeld, "overwhelms the narrative, but José's luminous evocations of the land and the life are fair compensations.'"

After finishing the Rosales Saga, José published four other novels: *Ermita* (1988), *Gagamba: The Spider Man* (1991), *Viajero* (1993), and *Sin* (1994), which was published as *Sins* (1996) in the U.S. These novels also examine Filipino society. *Sins*, for instance, recounts the life of Don Carlos Corbello in the form of a deathbed confession, though not exactly a pious one, for Corbello, as Julie Shiroishi noted for *AsianWeek* (October 3, 1996), "alternately takes great pride in his skill as an international businessman and seducer of women." Like almost everything José writes, the story is not simply about its character, who becomes, as a writer for *Kirkus Reviews* (March 1, 1996) observed, "a metaphor for the behavior of the Filipino elite, who suppress the population and squander national resources while amassing great personal fortunes." Thus Pico Iyer wrote for the *New York Times* (May 26, 1996), "In the end, *Sins* reveals itself as a somewhat old-fashioned and even earnest argument for land reform and a moral reminder that the sins of the father will be visited on the son. Yet it leaves one with the lingering suspicion that Mr. José, like his antihero, may be concealing more than a touch of romanticism beneath his affected cynicism."

For more than 40 years, José's bookstore, which he runs with his wife, Maria Teresita (Tessie), has served as his home and also as a place for him to meet with other Filipino intellectuals—including judges, writers, and businessmen—for roundtable discussions on issues affecting his country. On the second floor, he can be found socializing with friends over a meal, that is, when his schedule allows him to stay at home. He has often been away, lecturing in other Asian countries and more recently in the U.S. In 1986 Corazon Aquino ousted Marcos to become the first woman president of the Philippines. Aquino promised

changes in the government and improvements for the country—but two years into her term, when those changes had failed to materialize, a disappointed José told Seth Mydans for the *New York Times* (February 28, 1988), "If you are a Filipino like I am, it's so wonderful to get away—to get away from this dirt, from this tension, from this anarchy, from the uncollected garbage in the street." Still, he refuses to emigrate. His seven children, all of whom live in the U.S., would like him to move there, but "Manila is like a very ugly son that only a mother can love, but I love it," he explained to Michael J. Ybarra. "Whatever is negative about it—and there is a lot that is negative about my country—it is what sustains me." Indeed, whatever problems have beset the country he loves, José has retained a sense of optimism and said, according to Rustica C. Carpio for the *Philippine Daily Inquirer* (May 15, 2000), "I do not think that life is absurd or that we are headed toward mass perdition; the very act of living is a creative act. Always, as we go from day to day, we make our existence known, we assert ourselves above and beyond all the prison that nature and the tyrannies of our time have imposed on us. This is not an act of the artist but of man as well."

—A.R.

Suggested Reading: *Los Angeles Times* E p1 May 17, 1998; *Philippine Daily Inquirer* p10 May 27, 2001; *Washington Post* X p15 July 12, 1998

Selected Books: *Three Filipino Women*, 1992; *Sins*, 1996; *Dusk*, 1998; *Don Vicente*, 1999; *The Samsons*, 2000

Judt, Tony

Jan. 2, 1948– Historian

Tony Judt has earned an impressive reputation for his exacting scholarship, his unusually clear and vigorous prose, and his willingness to propose and defend controversial positions. In such books as *Past Imperfect: French Intellectuals, 1944–1956* (1992), *The Burden of Responsibility: Blum, Camus, Aron, and the French Twentieth Century* (1998), and *Postwar: A History of Europe since 1945* (2005), among others, Judt has voiced skepticism about the viability of the European Union (EU) and offered stinging critiques of such important thinkers as Simone de Beauvoir and Jean-Paul Sartre, whom he considers—along with the political left in western Europe during much of the 20th century—apologists for the brutalities of the Soviet dictator Joseph Stalin. Most recently, Judt has put himself at the center of debates about Israel and the failure of American left-wing intellectuals to oppose, with sufficient vigor, the ongoing war against Iraq—ideas that have made him the subject of sometimes vituperative criticism and even, arguably, something akin to censorship. Such controversies seem to follow naturally from Judt's opinion that historians—particularly historians of recent events—must at times make people uneasy. He told Donald A. Yerxa, for *Historically Speaking: The Bulletin of the Historical Society* (January/February 2006, online): "The historian's task is not to disrupt for the sake of it, but it is to tell what is almost always an uncomfortable story and explain why the discomfort is part of the truth we need to live well and live properly. A well organized society is one in which we know the truth about ourselves collectively, not one in which we tell pleasant lies about ourselves. Historians have a special role in this. . . . So, yes, we have a disruptive duty. This is one of the reasons why I get so annoyed with those of my colleagues who only write for each other. We have a duty to the larger community. We can only perform that duty by writing good professional history."

Tony Robert Judt was born on January 2, 1948 in London, England, and raised in the city's East End. His mother was a child of Jewish immigrants from Russia, and his father had come to England from Belgium. Often said to have come from a long line of rabbis, Judt became actively involved in Israeli politics and the Zionist movement at 15, when he joined Dror, a left-wing Zionist youth organization (now known as Habonim Dror); he was later named the group's national secretary. Judt and his associates in Dror encouraged British Jews to resettle in Israel and coordinated relief shipments to what was then a relatively poor and still-young nation. Throughout the 1960s Judt frequently traveled to Israel and for a time he worked on a kibbutz, or cooperative farm. After finishing his secondary education, he matriculated to King's College at the University of Cambridge, in England, but dropped out, in 1967, to return to Israel following the nation's dramatic victory in the Six-Day War. After serving as a translator for international volunteers who were assisting the Israeli army, Judt went back to King's College, where he earned his bachelor of arts degree in history, in 1969, and four years later his doctorate, with a dissertation entitled "The French Socialist Party, 1920–1924." Judt also studied at the Ecole Normale Supérieure in Paris, France.

Judt's teaching career began in 1972, when he joined the faculty of King's College as a fellow, a post he held until 1978. That year he left England for the U.S., where he took up a post as an assistant professor at the University of California, at Berkeley. Two years later he returned to England to serve as a fellow at St. Anne's College at the University of Oxford. Since 1987, the year he left St. Anne's, he has been a professor of history at the Institute of French Studies at New York University (NYU), in New York City. In 1995 he founded the Remarque Institute at NYU, and ever since that time he has served as the institute's director.

According to its Web site, the institute was founded "to support and promote the study and discussion of Europe, and to encourage and facilitate communications between Americans and Europeans."

Judt's first book, *Reconstruction du parti socialiste: 1921–1926* (1976), was based on his dissertation. It chronicles the renaissance of the French Socialist Party following World War I. Examining the internal dynamics of the party, Judt found that radical rather than moderate elements tended to exert the most influence. The work received a mixed critical reception among its largely academic audience.

Judt returned to French politics in his second book, *Socialism in Provence: A Study in the Origins of the Modern French Left, 1871–1914* (1979). Trying to understand the appeal of socialism in the south of France in the late 19th and early 20th centuries, Judt argued, somewhat controversially, that the socialists won the votes of Provençal peasants by promising to materially improve their lives, instead of appealing to already existing radical tendencies. Praising Judt's "richly nuanced presentation," Leslie Derfier offered a largely positive but still critical assessment of the book for the *American Historical Review* (June 1980): "The peasant-socialists themselves seldom come alive [in the book]; individuals are named only to illustrate abstractions; and there seems little appreciation of what they were fighting for. I also found the book overstructured, inevitable perhaps, given its division into descriptive and analytical halves. But when the writing rises above its analytical monotone . . . it is very good indeed." A reviewer for *Choice* (January 1980) gave the book a somewhat warmer reception: "It is a well-written book with extensive notes for each chapter and an excellent bibliography. Judt's approach is most interesting, but the appeal of this work will be confined almost entirely to specialists in the field."

Judt's third book, *Marxism and the French Left: Essays on Labour and Politics in France, 1930–1981* (1986), brought together five essays on the broad topic of the reception in France of the ideas of Karl Marx and his ideological descendents. Judt considered Marxism less as a grand theory and more as a loosely organized set of ideas that affected people's everyday lives. While noting that "even for the generalist in French culture, this book is difficult to read," Marthe Lavallee-Williams, writing for *America* (August 29–September 5, 1987), commended Judt's careful analysis and his ability to make "the intricacies of French daily life more understandable, if not palatable, to American readers. [Judt's] command of interacting forces—demographic, economic and financial—clarifies the apparent contradictions cloaked under the appeal of Marx and Lenin for sophisticates and railway workers alike." Jack Hayward wrote for the *Times Literary Supplement* (July 18, 1986): "Like other scholars, [Judt] regards the French Right as counter-revolutionary, reacting against the Left. This may be too simple a way of dismissing the religious, elitist and more recently capitalist values which have affirmed positive and not simply negative political norms. He is on firmer ground when he argues that the French Left has been badly split in its attitude to the state and legitimate authority, notably over whether to accept the broader-based, 'bourgeois' republican tradition. . . . While Judt has not yet quite attained the mastery of French left-wing history of a George Lichtheim (to whose memory his book is dedicated), he has written a well-informed and persuasive reinterpretation of an old French Left that is now receding beyond recall, except for historians."

In 1989 Judt served as editor of *Resistance and Revolution in Mediterranean Europe, 1939–1948*, an essay collection devoted to the rise of communism in such Mediterranean countries as Yugoslavia, Greece, France, and Italy during the middle of the last century. H. R. Kedward, a reviewer for *History* (October 1990), praised the volume in general but faulted the essay on France for only distantly engaging with the Mediterranean part of that country. Kedward concluded: "All students of communism and resistance (and the two are not seen as coextensive) will be stimulated by these perceptive chapters."

Judt's next book, *Past Imperfect: French Intellectuals, 1944–1956* (originally published in French, in 1992, as *Passé imparfait: Les intellectuels en France, 1944–1956*), took French writers and philosophers of the postwar period to task for acting as apologists for the Soviet Union. Though many of the figures Judt examined— whether existentialists, as with Sartre and Beauvoir, or left-wing Catholics, as with Jean-Marie Domenach and Emmanuel Mounier—were not communists themselves, they nonetheless argued for the virtues of the Soviet system, particularly when set against Western democracies, which, to their lights, often committed similarly appalling acts. A final section of the book pricks at the continuing enthusiasm for French intellectuals among left-wing American academics.

Reviews of the book were generally positive, though often divided along political lines. Some critics, typically those writing for more liberal publications, felt that Judt took a simplistic approach to a complex subject, while reviewers from politically conservative publications praised the book almost uniformly. In a review for the *American Spectator* (February 1993), M. D. Carnegie wrote: "Judt has written a spectacularly damning work of scholarship that will curdle the blood of those who have wandered happily through the pages of twentieth-century French literature. Though originally intended for a French audience, and a scholarly one at that, the book is fine reading. There is an excellent section on the continuing legacy of French intellectual life, as

well as a keen overview of the language of rights in France, and how it has come to differ so greatly from its Anglo-American counterpart." Frederic Raphael offered more measured praise for the London *Sunday Times* (February 7, 1993), describing the book as "closely documented and often entertaining" and arguing that Judt "succeeds in both understanding almost everything and pardoning almost nothing. Merciless but rarely smug . . . this is two-thirds of an excellent book. It tails off in the last section, which seems to have been appended at the instance of an American publisher. Instead of pursuing his post-war theme, Judt turns away to deride fellow-American academics who whore after the ideas of [Jacques] Derrida and [Jacques] Lacan and Roland Barthes long after they have passed their quote-by date." Carlin Romano, however, in an extended and highly critical review for the *Nation* (April 26, 1993), portrayed Judt as a careerist and a reactionary and responded with particular indignation to the book's portrait of Sartre. Noting that "Judt utterly trashes [Sartre] as a man and thinker," Romano added: "Judt's sleight of hand in *Past Imperfect* consists of focusing on the four years from 1952 to 1956, during which Sartre decided to commit himself to the project of Soviet Communism by tactically declining to criticize it publicly, and then writing as though that attitude governed Sartre in the whole twelve years under study. . . . The agenda, plainly, is to destroy Sartre's credibility, and counter-evidence gets brushed aside in the process." Romano concluded: "In the end, it is Judt, rather than Sartre and his circle, who comes across as intellectually narrow. He often writes as though he's infuriated by their failure to share his simple moral logarithms, or his forty-years-later conclusion that the corruption and failure of communist ideology in Russia and Eastern Europe during the era under study should have eternally· invalidated their interest in Marxism. One can easily imagine Judt active in the great French purge . . . of collaborators after 1945; he's that kind of guy."

A Grand Illusion?: An Essay on Europe (1996) brought together a series of three lectures that Judt gave in Bologna, Italy, in 1995, on the question of the European Union's efforts to forge a singular European identity. In the book Judt argues that a truly united Europe is not only unlikely, it is also a facile attempt to sweep the continent's regional and local problems under the rug. Brad Hooper wrote for *Booklist* (September 15, 1996): "Judt . . . takes a middle-road approach, finding no historical inevitability behind the idea of Europe as a tightly cohesive entity. The concept, he shows, is of recent origin; and defending his thinking with fact and reason, he concludes that the likelihood of an 'ever-closer union' than exists today is 'slim indeed.'" Stanley Hoffmann gave the book a mixed review for *Foreign Affairs* (January–February 1997), praising Judt's "analytical clarity" but faulting his "descriptive complexity." Hoffmann wrote: "[Judt] concludes that a 'truly united Europe' is so unlikely that it would be 'unwise and self-defeating to insist upon it.' In his view, '"Europe" is more than a geographical notion but less than an answer,' and has become 'little more than the politically correct way to paper over local difficulties, as though the mere invocation of the promise of Europe could substitute for solving problems and crises that really affect the place.' While any skeptical student of the EU would agree with the main lines and conclusions of his provocative argument, its bracing analysis suffers from exaggerations, contradictions, and omissions." William Safran, on the other hand, writing for the *Review of Politics* (Spring 1997), found the book "a welcome antidote to the Euro-romanticism of many U.S. political observers and of their tendency to exaggerate the importance of institutional factors." Safran added: "The book reminds us, refreshingly, of what Europeans—and Americans writing about postwar Europe—often leave out of their discussion: the revival of traditional nationalism and the recycling of Communist apparatchiks into nationalist demagogues; and the persistence of heterophobia, and in particular of antisemitism, in Germany, France, and the 'democratizing' countries of Eastern Europe, and the almost studied forgetfulness about the cultural role once played by Jews." Describing the book as "an original and well-founded analysis," Max Beloff, in a critique for the *Washington Times* (October 20, 1996), felt that its "only fault . . . and it is a rare one" is being "far too short. A longer book would have enabled Mr. Judt to answer some of the doubts that his rapid survey of some two millenniums is bound to produce in the reader's mind."

With *The Burden of Responsibility*, Judt returned to the theme of the moral responsibility of French intellectuals of the postwar period. The book, based on lectures originally given at the University of Chicago, offers a kind of mirror image of *Past Imperfect*. Instead of dissecting a group of writers who failed to live up to their intellectual ideals, the book praises Leon Blum, Albert Camus, and Raymond Aron for their regard for humanity, their learning, and their unwillingness to sacrifice their ideals for politically expedient ends. S. D. Armus, for *Choice* (May 1999), remarked: "In selecting Leon Blum, Albert Camus, and Raymond Aron, [Judt] has deliberately chosen modern French thinkers whose honesty and bravery are in stark contrast to some of their contemporaries. . . . Still, the choice of these three particular men is somewhat puzzling. Camus and Aron, surely, are worthy of praise, but both have been nearly deified in the past decade, and Judt has nothing new to say about them. Blum, however, was in need of a reassessment, and the author does him a service by reviving him here. Judt's style is, as always, his strongest point, and the clear presentation of these minibiographies makes up for some of the weaknesses in this rather

minor book." Tzvetan Todorov, writing for the *New Republic* (December 28, 1998), felt that *The Burden of Responsibility* "displays the same qualities of deep learning, lively writing, and subtle, considered judgments" as *Past Imperfect*, adding: "One might argue with this or that detail of Judt's presentation; but certainly he has seized upon the proper heroes. From these exemplary figures, one may learn something valuable and urgent about the role of intellectuals in public life."

In *The Politics of Retribution in Europe: World War II and Its Aftermath* (2000), a volume of essays Judt co-edited with István Deák and Jan T. Gross, a group of noted European scholars studied the problem of guilt among Europe's post–World War II generation, as leaders on both sides of the conflict sought to place the war within the context of their national identities. Donald Bloxham, writing for *History* (July 2001), described the book as "a fine example of comparative history," while Derek W. Urwin remarked for the *English Historical Review* (June 2001): "In various general chapters the editors successfully impose upon the whole a comparative framework that draws attention both to a general European pattern and to marked East-West differences. . . . The outcome is a book of consistently high analytical quality, which possesses a degree of cohesion that is normally difficult to achieve in an edited collection."

Judt's most recent book, *Postwar: A History of Europe Since 1945*, a massive 900-page tome, examines the evolution of modern Europe over the past 50 years, placing particular emphasis on the historical importance of the Holocaust. As Joe Schlesinger noted for the Toronto *Globe and Mail* (December 31, 2005): "Judt . . . argues that 'Auschwitz is the most important thing to know about World War Two.' Not because of the sheer number of the dead, but rather because of the indifference to the Holocaust—and even complicity in it—of just about every nation in Europe. That indifference—all too often motivated by outright anti-Semitism—lasted well beyond the war." Judt also makes the case that the years between the end of World War II and the collapse of the Soviet block, beginning in 1989, will be seen historically as a sort of "interim age"—in essence, a very long epilogue to the bloodiest conflict in human history.

The book was widely praised, for the most part, though some critics were put off by its considerable length. Alan Ryan, for the *New York Review of Books* (November 3, 2005), declared that Judt "brings to *Postwar* an astonishing range of knowledge and an intense political, intellectual, and emotional engagement; these are nicely offset by the intellectual distance that the Channel and the Atlantic have helped to provide and by a wry sense of the innumerable ways in which events play tricks on all of us. The result is a book that has the pace of a thriller and the scope of an encyclopedia; it is a very considerable achievement." On the other hand, a reviewer for the *Economist* (November 19, 2005), while acknowledging that Judt was "particularly good on the centrality of the Holocaust to the new Europe," felt that the "grand and important themes" that Judt brings up are mostly set aside in favor of familiar information: "His discussion is chronological not thematic, and the main ideas get lost in what is now a familiar story, although the story is told with some skill. Nevertheless, few books of nearly 1,000 pages justify their length, and *Postwar* is no exception. When Lord Beaverbrook was sent a 700-page biography of his fellow press magnate, Lord Northcliffe, he dispatched it unread to the University of New Brunswick, saying, 'It weighs too much.' Sadly, *Postwar* is likely to suffer the same fate." *Postwar* was a finalist for the 2006 Pulitzer Prize for general nonfiction.

In addition to the works listed above, Judt co-edited *Language, Nation, and State: Identity Politics in a Multilingual Age* (2004) and *With Us or Against Us: Studies in Global Anti-Americanism* (2005), both with Denis Lacorne. The recipient of a fellowship from the John Simon Guggenheim Foundation, Judt is a fellow of England's Royal Historical Society and a member of the American Academy of Arts and Sciences. Since 1991 he has held the title of Erich Maria Remarque Professor of European Studies at NYU, and in 2006 he earned the additional honor of being named a University Professor. ("University Professorships," according to the Web site of the Office of Public Affairs at NYU, "are conferred upon outstanding scholars in recognition of the interdisciplinary dimension and breadth of their work.") Judt has also held academic posts at the Institut d'Etudes Politiques and the Ecole des Hautes Etudes en Sciences Sociales, both in Paris, France, and at the Institut für die Wissenschaften vom Menschen in Vienna, Austria, where he has been a permanent fellow since 1996.

In the October 23, 2003 issue of the *New York Review of Books*, Judt published an article entitled "Israel: The Alternative," in which he argued that Israel should abandon its status as a Jewish state. "In a world where nations and peoples increasingly intermingle and intermarry at will; where cultural and national impediments to communication have all but collapsed; where more and more of us have multiple elective identities and would feel falsely constrained if we had to answer to just one of them; in such a world Israel is truly an anachronism," Judt wrote. "And not just an anachronism but a dysfunctional one. In today's 'clash of cultures' between open, pluralist democracies and belligerently intolerant, faith-driven ethno-states, Israel actually risks falling into the wrong camp." The idea immediately drew an outpouring of responses, most of them strongly critical of Judt's idea. Commentaries soon appeared in other publications, and the *New York Review of Books* received more than 1,000 letters in the week after

the piece was published. Perhaps the most frequently cited counterargument to Judt came from Leon Wieseltier, an editor at the *New Republic*, for which Judt had served as a contributing editor since 1999. "Judt calls his article 'Israel: The Alternative,'" Wieseltier wrote for the *New Republic* (October 23, 2003). "But let us read strenuously. A bi-national state is not the alternative *for* Israel. It is the alternative *to* Israel. Judt and his editors have crossed the line from the criticism of Israel's policy to the criticism of Israel's existence. The right in Israel and America are therefore greatly in their debt: They have given credence to the suspicion that the criticism of Israel's policy is always nothing other than the criticism of Israel's existence." In a statement laden with irony, Wieseltier added: "They have taken the heroic step of calling for the dissolution of the Jewish state." Judt's name was soon removed from the masthead of the *New Republic*. In the three years since that article appeared, Judt has from time to time made other comments on Israel that have brought him criticism, though none as strong as that generated by this first piece.

Tony Judt lives in New York City with his wife, Jennifer Homans, a dance critic who writes primarily for the *New Republic*, and their two children, aged 9 and 12.

—C.M./D.R.

Suggested Reading: *America* p114 Aug. 29–Sep. 5, 1987; *American Historical Review* p642 June 1980; *American Spectator* Feb. 1993; *Booklist* p214 Sep. 15, 1996; *Choice* p1,494 Jan. 1980, p1,683 May 1999; *Economist* p88 Nov. 19, 2005; *English Historical Review* p763+ June 2001; *Forward* p1 Dec. 26, 2003; *Historically Speaking: The Bulletin of the Historical Society* (on-line) Jan./Feb. 2006; *History* p545 Oct. 1980, p434+ July 2001; (London) *Sunday Times* Features Feb. 7, 1993; *Mother Jones* (on-line) Dec. 20, 2005; *Nation* p562+ Apr. 26, 1993; *New Republic* p42+ Dec. 28, 1998; *New York Review of Books* p16+ Nov. 3, 2005; Remarque Institute Web site; *Times Literary Supplement* p782 July 18, 1986; (Toronto) *Globe and Mail* D p16 Dec. 31, 2005; *Washington Times* B p8 Oct. 20, 1996

Selected Books: *La Reconstruction du parti socialiste: 1921–1926*, 1976; *Socialism in Provence, 1871–1914: A Study in the Origins of the Modern French Left*, 1979; *Marxism and the French Left: Essays on Labour and Politics in France, 1830–1981*, 1986; *Past Imperfect: French Intellectuals, 1944–1956*, 1992; *A Grand Illusion?: An Essay on Europe*, 1996; *The Burden of Responsibility: Blum, Camus, Aron, and the French Twentieth Century*, 1998; *Postwar: A History of Europe Since 1945*, 2005; as editor— *Resistance and Revolution in Mediterranean Europe, 1939–1948*, 1989; *The Politics of Retribution in Europe: World War II and Its Aftermath* (with István Deák and Jan T. Gross),

2000; with Denis Lacorne—*Language, Nation, and State: Identity Politics in a Multilingual Age,* 2004; *With Us or Against Us: Studies in Global Anti-Americanism,* 2005

Courtesy of the Miami Book Fair

Julavits, Heidi

1968(?)– Novelist; editor

The novelist and editor Heidi Julavits is among a coterie of young writers, including Dave Eggers and Vendela Vida, who have been praised for bringing a much-needed dose of vitality to the world of American letters. She has published three novels: *The Mineral Palace* (2000), *The Effect of Living Backwards* (2003), and *The Uses of Enchantment* (2006). Additionally, she has published numerous short pieces in *Esquire, Story, McSweeney's, Harper's Bazaar, Glamour, Time* and the *New York Times Book Review,* among other periodicals. She is the founding co-editor of the *Believer,* an advertising-free monthly literary magazine with an extensive presence on the Web.

Born in about 1968, Heidi Julavits grew up in Maine, graduated from Deering High School, and completed the writing program at Columbia University, in New York City. Following her graduation from Columbia, Julavits worked as a waitress in New York City, before catching her first major break with the short story "Marry the One Who Gets There First," which appeared in *Esquire* in 1998. (She garnered a book deal shortly thereafter.)

Julavits had begun writing *The Mineral Palace* in 1996. Set during the Great Depression, the novel focuses on Bena Jonssen, the wife of a doctor, who has just moved with her family to Pueblo, Colorado, encountering Bonnie Parker (of "Bonnie and Clyde" fame) along the way. Once settled, Bena begins writing for the local newspaper and helps to restore the town's crumbling landmark, the Mineral Palace. In the midst of her endeavors, however, she falls in love with another man. The novel was well received. A critic for *Publishers Weekly* (July 31, 2000) opined, "Julavits can be a magician with language, spinning brilliant metaphors and investing descriptive scenes with almost palpable dimensionality. Her enthusiasm with words sometimes spills over into hyperactive verbiage, however, resulting in such forced images as 'bacon thinner than a wedding veil.' Several key scenes are shriekingly melodramatic, and prosthetic limbs turn up all too frequently among the eccentric characters (and animals). While Julavits can justly be criticized for overwriting, however, her narrative has the drive to keep readers hooked." Jeff Giles, writing for *Newsweek* (September 18, 2000), remarked, "*The Mineral Palace* is a marvelous debut novel: harrowing, poetic and tragic enough to satisfy both [William] Faulkner and Oprah [Winfrey]. . . . Julavits's prose can be astonishingly dark, and there are times when her plot is too hectic and her many symbols so overripe and heavy that they just about fall off the tree. Still, she's such a gifted, visceral writer . . . that even her most painful visions can be beautiful to behold."

In Julavits's next novel, *The Effect of Living Backwards,* Alice and Edith, two sisters on their way to Morocco, become embroiled in a skyjacking engineered by a group of unlikely terrorists. "Surprising role reversals and hairpin turns of perspective permeate this novel," Art Winslow observed for the *Chicago Tribune* (July 20, 2003). He added, "In [this] entertaining, picaresque tale of what may or may not be a true hijacking, by characters who may or may not be what they seem or indeed who may or may not exist outside Alice's own head, Julavits also conducts an epistemological inquiry into how we know what we know. In too many ways to ignore, this fabulist concoction is also a clever homage to *Alice's Adventures in Wonderland,* but with terrorism, both interpersonal and institutional, as its satiric backdrop." Though some reviewers again chided Julavits for what they deemed a predilection for overwriting, the critical response was quite favorable. In a typical notice, Taylor Antrim, writing for the *New York Times Book Review* (June 22, 2003), described the work as "savage and funny. The book is improbable, sure, but so wildly inventive that you hardly care."

In 2006 Julavits published *The Uses of Enchantment.* (The title is a reference to a 1976 work of the same name by the now-discredited child psychologist Bruno Bettelheim, in which he discusses the importance of fairy tales and their dark themes to a child's development.) The protagonist of Julavits's book is a 16-year-old girl named Mary, who disappears one day from her New England prep school, only to reappear a few weeks later, unharmed and claiming to be unaware of what happened to her during those weeks. She is sent to a psychologist, who becomes convinced that the Mary has faked the entire incident, based on similarities between her account and a centuries-old local legend involving an abducted girl and witchcraft. "Readers angered by ambiguity should avoid this book," Julie Wittes Schlack wrote for the *Boston Globe* (October 19, 2006). "But those who have the courage and optimism to take novels seriously (as Julavits, editor of the *Believer* magazine, clearly does) will find themselves haunted by it in the best sense of the word." A reviewer for the *New Yorker* (November 6, 2006, on-line) concurred, writing, "Julavits expertly keeps the reader baffled until the end, but beneath the mystery is a sophisticated meditation on truth and bias."

Julavits married her second husband, the writer Ben Marcus, in the summer of 2002. The couple divide their time between Brooklin, Maine, and New York City, where Marcus teaches creative writing at Columbia University.

—P.B.M.

Suggested Reading: *Chicago Tribune* C p1 July 20, 2003; Fail Better Web site; *New York Observer* p1 May 12, 2003; *New York Times Book Review* p16 June 22, 2003; *Pittsburgh Post-Gazette* (on-line) Sep. 7, 2003; *Publishers Weekly* p66 July 31, 2000

Selected Books: *The Mineral Palace*, 2000; *The Effect of Living Backwards*, 2003; *The Uses of Enchantment*, 2006

Julian Wasser/Courtesy of Random House

Kaiser, Robert Blair

Dec. 3, 1930– Journalist; nonfiction writer

The journalist and author Robert Blair Kaiser has spent much of his career writing about the Catholic Church, portraying some of its famous and infamous figures, as well as those from the world of popular culture. He covered the Second Vatican Council for *Time* during the early 1960s, and his first book, *Pope, Council, and World: The Story of Vatican II* (1963), a detailed chronicle of the council's first session, was an international best-seller. In 1970 Kaiser published an extensive account of the 1968 murder of the presidential candidate Senator Robert F. Kennedy in *"R.F.K. Must Die!": A History of the Robert Kennedy Assassination and Its Aftermath*, for which he benefited from access to Kennedy's killer, Sirhan Sirhan. After enjoying a career as a freelance writer during the 1970s and early 1980s, Kaiser returned to the Vatican as a subject, publishing *The Politics of Sex and Religion: A Case History in the Development of Doctrine, 1962–1984* (1985), an account of the Catholic Church's controversial ban on artificial contraception. In 2002 Kaiser published a memoir, *Clerical Error: A True Story.* Kaiser's most recent work, *A Church in Search of Itself: Benedict XVI and the Battle for the Future* (2006), is an assessment of the struggle between traditionalists and progressives within the Catholic Church.

Robert Blair Kaiser was born on December 3, 1930 in Detroit, Michigan. After his parents divorced, Kaiser went to live with his mother in Phoenix, Arizona. Kaiser's mother, although not religious herself, enrolled him in a Catholic grammar school. "Both my mother and my father (whom I visited in the summers) were making other, romantic friends and I hated that," Kaiser wrote in *Clerical Error: A True Story.* "My mother was in her early thirties, and she had every right to try to make a new life for herself, and so did my father. I couldn't see it then. I made it clear to both of them that I wouldn't tolerate any fooling around, which meant that I'd find a way to leave them both. Now, I started looking to the Church as both mother and father. I thought the Church could give me a refuge from all this, this messy marriage-and-divorce business." Kaiser found that his Catholic education gave him a moral anchor during his confused childhood, and he eventually converted

KAISER

to Roman Catholicism. At 14 Kaiser earned a scholarship to Loyola High School, a Jesuit boarding school in Los Angeles, California.

During his high-school years, Kaiser decided that he wanted to become a Jesuit priest. "The Jesuits had helped me run away from home [when I was 14]," Kaiser recalled in *Clerical Error.* "By my senior year, it seemed like a natural thing to pass right on into the Order itself." Kaiser joined the Sacred Heart Novitiate, a Jesuit seminary, in Los Gatos, California, and he pursued his undergraduate education at the Jesuit-run Santa Clara University, in Santa Clara, California. "As I look back now on that life in the Novitiate, I see it as kind of boot camp, the kind you find in the U.S. Marine Corps," Kaiser wrote in his memoir. "The discipline was supposed to make us into the kind of men who could take orders, so that, later on, we'd be the kind of shock troops our superiors (or even, in special cases, the pope himself) could send anywhere in the world, on any mission. It was also a life that seemed designed to keep us psychologically immature. But of course, this is one reason I joined the Jesuits in the first place: to keep from growing up, like some latter day Peter Pan."

In 1950 Kaiser completed the first phase of his Jesuit training and took his first vows. That same year he began his juniorate, the next phase of his training, at Mount St. Michael's in Spokane, Washington. Since he never graduated from Santa Clara University, Kaiser enrolled at Gonzaga University, in Spokane, receiving his B.A. in 1952. Kaiser remained at Gonzaga, earning his M.A. in philosophy in 1955.

After completing his juniorate, Kaiser began his regency, a three-year teaching phase and the final part of his training before he was ordained as a Jesuit priest. For two years Kaiser taught at St. Ignatius High School, in San Francisco. Although he enjoyed teaching and supervising the production of the school's newspaper, Kaiser soon found himself at odds with many of his Jesuit superiors for what he believed was their rigid formalism and strict enforcement of rules. In 1957 Kaiser abandoned his plans to become a Jesuit priest and returned to his mother's house in Phoenix.

Kaiser then had to decide what he would do with his life. "I had all the training necessary to become a teacher, but that would put me into another ivory tower," Kaiser wrote in his book. "I wanted to enter the real world, come down off my arid mountaintop and plunge into a cool blue pool. I wanted a world to float in, one that would caress me all over and lap around my ears. My goal as a Jesuit, to make a better world, was terribly abstract. First, I thought, I'd like to know more about the world-as-it-was. My best entree to that real world, I decided, was not teaching but reporting for the local newspaper." After applying unsuccessfully for a job with the *Arizona Republic* in Phoenix, he managed to get a job as a call taker and chart maker

for the *Daily Racing Form.* A short time later, the *Arizona Republic* hired Kaiser as a police reporter, and he eventually covered other beats. Kaiser married in 1959 and then went to work as a correspondent for *Time.*

In 1962 *Time* sent Kaiser to Rome to cover the Second Vatican Council, a gathering of the world's Catholic bishops that was called by Pope John XXIII to discuss reforming the Catholic Church. Since the council's sessions were closed to the public, Kaiser obtained information by drawing on the many contacts he had made in Rome and at the Vatican. One of Kaiser's scoops for *Time* was a story about how the pope had set up a commission to study the use of artificial contraceptives, which were prohibited by Catholic doctrine. In December 1962 Kaiser wrote his second cover story on the pope for *Time* when it named the pontiff "Man of the Year."

Every Sunday during this time, Kaiser and his wife, Mary, held dinner parties at their apartment in Rome. Their guests included bishops, theologians, Jesuit priests, and many others. "Our spacious apartment, with its huge picture windows and sparkling marble floors, became something of a gathering place for conciliar progressives," Kaiser recalled in his book. "Mary was often the only woman in the house, and she became an unflappable hostess." One time, a friend of Kaiser's brought a guest to the party—an Irish Jesuit named Malachy Martin, a progressive theologian and professor at the Vatican's Pontifical Biblical Institute. Martin impressed Kaiser by telling him he was a personal friend of the Reverend Loris Capovilla, the pope's private secretary. Martin became a regular guest at the Kaisers' home, and Kaiser often used him as a source.

Kaiser's first book, *Pope, Council, and World,* appeared in 1963. (The book was published as *Inside the Council: The Story of Vatican II* in Britain.) In this work Kaiser detailed the struggle between traditionalists and progressives to shape the direction of the council and the future of the Church. Kaiser's "account of the issues involved, of the great events and of the personalities engaged, is first-class writing and always fair, but there emerges from it a strange picture of press frustration and an equally frustrated lack of understanding by the Vatican officials," a reviewer observed for the *Times Literary Supplement* (September 27, 1963). "To them the press representatives were intruders, laymen who lacked the theological knowledge to appreciate the issues, and therefore needed instruction. . . . Mr. Kaiser writes as the representative of an anxious and would-be friendly world, and his book, always searching and sometimes caustic, might do something to bring home to the members and officials of Vatican II that the world would like to see a dove bringing an olive branch from the ark." In his review for *America* (August 31, 1963), W. H. Fanning had mixed feelings about the book. "The result of Kaiser's diligence and background is a remarkable record," Fanning wrote. "*Pope, Council, and World* also gives a sweeping vision of the *aggioriornamento* or updating movement in the Church." Fanning, however, faulted Kaiser for writing from a partisan viewpoint and over-simplifying the struggle between the council's traditionalists and progressives. "Kaiser has put together a valuable, broad picture of the Church updating itself under Pope John's skillful hand," he added. "It is only unfortunate that the author's presentation is so one-sided that it will alienate many who might otherwise be won."

Shortly after the publication of this book, Kaiser discovered that Malachy Martin had seduced his wife. One day, after returning to Rome from a trip, Kaiser noticed that his wife had become emotionally distant and began to suspect that Martin was having an affair with her. Kaiser's suspicions were confirmed when private detectives he hired found that Mary went to several hotels to meet the priest. "I lost 20 [pounds] the week I found out," Kaiser recalled to Rory Carroll, a reporter for the London *Observer* (March 17, 2002). "I was drinking a lot." Kaiser's marriage, which had produced two young children, eventually ended in divorce. The Jesuits defrocked Martin after Kaiser shared with them copies of love letters the priest had sent to Mary.

In 1964 Kaiser left Rome and returned to the U.S. After covering the presidential race for *Time*, Kaiser left the magazine in 1966 to work as a freelance writer. In 1970 Kaiser published his second book, *"R.F.K. Must Die!"*. The book recounted the assassination of the New York senator, who was also the brother of the slain President John F. Kennedy and a candidate for the Democratic Party's nomination for president in 1968. On June 5 of that year, Robert Kennedy was shot after winning the California Democratic primary and died the next day. The assassin, a 24-year-old Palestinian immigrant named Sirhan Sirhan, was immediately arrested. It was believed that Sirhan shot Kennedy, on the one-year anniversary of the start of the Six-Day War, because he hated the senator for his strong pro-Israel views. In 1969 Sirhan was convicted of murder and sentenced to death. In 1972, however, his sentence was commuted to life in prison after the Supreme Court of California declared the state's death penalty unconstitutional. In 1968 Kaiser signed a contract with Sirhan that gave him the exclusive rights to the assassin's story. Kaiser then agreed to contribute a part of his royalties from the book to Sirhan's defense. In order to determine what motivated Sirhan, Kaiser interviewed Bernard L. Diamond, the chief psychiatrist retained by the defense, and Diamond allowed Kaiser to observe sessions in which Sirhan was put under hypnosis. During the writing process, Sirhan threatened Kaiser's life, and Sirhan's family filed suit to prevent publication of the book, but they were unsuccessful.

The title of *"R.F.K. Must Die!"* is taken from a note Sirhan scribbled in his diary several weeks before the assassination. When discussing the book in the *Saturday Review* (October 17, 1970), F. J. Cook pointed out that, while readers may be suspicious of the work because Kaiser signed a contract with Sirhan, Kaiser produced a relatively unbiased examination of what occurred. "One anticipates that this will be another one-sided, 'authorized' version of events, but it is not," Cook wrote. "It is an honest book, one that so enraged Sirhan he tried to stop its publication: and, simply because Kaiser did have a unique inside vantage point, he is able to develop step by step the portrait of a character so weird he baffled psychiatrists, his own attorneys, and perhaps, in the end, even himself." The reviewer added that Kaiser "is no all-out conspiracy buff. He tries simply to present the facts as he found them. Not until almost the end of his story does he attempt any deep interpretation of those facts." In the *New York Times Book Review* (November 15, 1970), Thomas S. Szasz, a professor of psychiatry, wrote that the book "is a valuable storehouse of information, even though many of the events described in it have been reported before." Szasz, however, faulted Kaiser for uncritically accepting Diamond's theory that Sirhan, through his automatic writing, had programmed himself to carry out the assassination in the same way magnetic tape programmed computers of the time. "In science, theories are constructed to fit facts," Szasz observed; "in courtroom psychiatry, 'facts' are constructed to fit theories. It is absurd, therefore, to judge Sirhan's act without carefully considering [other, relevant] nonpsychiatric facts. Sirhan is a man, not a computer."

Kaiser next turned to less controversial subjects, assisting the celebrated attorney Melvin Belli and the football player Pat Haden with their autobiographies. *Melvin Belli: My Life on Trial: An Autobiography* was published in 1976, and *Pat Haden: My Rookie Season with the Los Angeles Rams* appeared on shelves a year later. Kaiser then took a position writing for the *New York Times* from 1979 to 1981. In 1981 he began teaching journalism at the University of Nevada, in Reno, and was eventually named chairman of the university's journalism department. In 1984 Kaiser was hired as a columnist by the *San Diego Tribune*.

Kaiser's next book about Catholicism was *The Politics of Sex and Religion*. In it Kaiser examined the Catholic Church's teachings on sex and artificial contraception. According to Kaiser, Pope Paul VI decided to reaffirm the Church's ban against artificial contraception in his encyclical *Humanae Vitae* (1968), despite the fact that a commission set up by John XXIII had recommended some changes in the Church's stance. "[While] reading the introduction, I thought for a while I would not be able to recommend the book. It has the tone of bland, *Time*-style advocacy journalism, which achieves its effects through the use of flavorful but low-fiber adjectives instead of chewier nouns and verbs," Robert G. Hoyt observed in his review for *Commonweal* (January 17, 1986). "In the rest of the book, fortunately, Kaiser's analysis emerges mostly out of the events he records; so do his characterizations of the principal players and of what was at stake for them. On those parts of the story of which I have independent knowledge, I found his reporting essentially accurate. . . . And the book is interesting: a considerable feat." By contrast, the Rev. John R. Connery dismissed the book in his review for *Theological Studies* (December 1985). "[Kaiser] was a reporter for *Time* in Rome during an important part of this period, and had access at least to much secondhand information about what went on in the commission meetings," Connery wrote. "Since he is not a theologian, one cannot expect a sophisticated theological account of this controversy. More problematic, however, is the fact that he was not an unbiased observer. This reader will sense the bias in favor of contraception right from the first pages. The present reviewer also followed this controversy very closely, and on the basis of his own reading of it as well as the slant of the book toward contraception and the lack of firsthand information and/or any kind of documentation, he would have to question the reliability of the author's account."

In 1994 Kaiser assisted the actor Jamie Farr with the writing of his book, *Just Farr Fun.* Kaiser's 1997 play, *Jubilee 2000: A Musical Celebration,* financed by the archdiocese of Phoenix, Arizona, combined his interests in pop culture and the Catholic Church. The play, staged at local venues, was described by Tom Roberts for the *National Catholic Reporter* (January 9, 1998) as a "zany walk through Christian history." In 1999 Kaiser began covering the Vatican for *Newsweek.*

In 2002 Kaiser published *Clerical Error: A True Story,* in which he recalled the 10 years that he spent studying to become a Jesuit priest, how he became involved in journalism, and his experience covering Vatican II for *Time,* including the events that led to the dissolution of his marriage. In his review of *Clerical Error* for the *National Catholic Reporter* (March 8, 2002), Arthur Jones noted that the book's "narrative picks up speed, with a tension rooted in mounting sadness. What's going to happen? This is tragedy without much comedy, a tragedy the description of which the finicky reader may regard as a tad voyeuristic. Not so in my judgment. Candor, not prurience, is the key to understanding what Kaiser is about." Jones observed that the book "would be unbelievable were Kaiser not telling it with such frankness. It rings accurate because it oozes such pain. Did we need to know all this? For its insights into a wicked Martin, yes." By contrast, a reviewer for *First Things* (November 1, 2002) panned the book: "This memoir makes for painful reading, much like watching a drunk stagger across a busy freeway and wondering whether he'll make it to the other side. There are moments of humor, usually unintended, in the author's depiction of prominent liberals who played a part in the Council and gathered regularly at Kaiser's Sunday evening salon. The praise bestowed on his achievements, and the envy of others, are amply treated. The book ends with Mr. Kaiser, wobbling but upright in the middle of life's freeway, still raging and shaking his fist at the oncoming cars, although it is now late at night and the traffic has slowed."

In 2005 Kaiser, working for *Newsweek*, covered the election of Pope John Paul II's successor, Cardinal Joseph Ratzinger, who took the name Benedict XVI upon assuming the papacy. To the more progressive elements within the Church, the appointment of Ratzinger, who was decidedly conservative, was a disappointment. Kaiser profiled the new pope, as well as five contemporary cardinals, for *A Church in Search of Itself.* "The highlights of the longtime Vatican-watcher Robert Blair Kaiser's account of the state of the Roman Catholic Church are his vividly drawn profiles of Catholics who perform quietly dramatic acts of compassion, creativity and resistance," R. Scott Appleby wrote for the *Washington Post Book World* (May 7, 2006). "These agents of enculturation—that is, adapting Christian belief and practice to local cultures—resist not only fundamentalists and secular despots, Kaiser observes, but also Vatican enforcers who attempt to stifle 'homegrown' forms of Christianity." But, Appleby continued, "dividing the Catholic world into the 'party of change' and the 'party of no change' drains nuance and complexity from the profiles of six cardinals that form the spine of Kaiser's narrative."

Kaiser married a second time, in 1966, and has a child from his second marriage, in addition to the two from his first. He divides his time between Rome and Phoenix, Arizona.

—D.C.

Suggested Reading: *America* p216 Aug. 31, 1963; *Commonweal* p20+ Jan. 17, 1986; *First Things* p63 Nov. 1, 2002; *National Catholic Reporter* p3 Jan. 9, 1998, p18 Mar. 8, 2002 *New York Times Book Review* p5 Nov. 15, 1970; *Saturday Review* p29+ Oct. 17, 1970; *Theological Studies* p734+ Dec. 1985; *Times Literary Supplement* p767 Sep. 27, 1963; *Washington Post Book World* p9 May 7, 2006

Selected Books: *Pope, Council, and World: The Story of Vatican II,* 1963; *"R.F.K. Must Die!": A History of the Robert Kennedy Assassination and Its Aftermath,* 1970; *The Politics of Sex and Religion: A Case History in the Development of Doctrine, 1962–1984,* 1985; *Clerical Error: A True Story,* 2002; *A Church in Search of Itself: Benedict XVI and the Battle for the Future,* 2006

Jerry Bauer

Kay, Jackie

Nov. 9, 1961– Poet; short-story writer; novelist; playwright

Pigeonholed early in her career as a black, lesbian, Scottish writer, Jackie Kay has since achieved artistic success in a broad range of literary forms—including plays, unclassifiable biographical essays, literary short stories, and poetry for both children and adults—bringing her a wider audience than such narrow descriptors would suggest. Her major collections of verse for adults—*The Adoption Papers* (1991), *Other Lovers* (1993), *Off Colour* (1998), and *Life Mask* (2005)—have won her some of the highest literary prizes awarded in England and Scotland, and her novel *Trumpet* (1998) earned her strong praise from reviewers in Anglophone countries around the world. Kay's use of autobiographical elements in her writing, particularly in *The Adoption Papers*, have sometimes prompted journalists and critics to see too literal a connection between her life and work, a tendency Kay finds tiresome but natural. "We can't be scornful or scoff at this compulsion, this desire to know what's true and what's not," she told Teddy Jamieson for the Glasgow *Herald* (May 27, 2006). "But in a way it's all true and it's all not true and I quite like to write close to the edge of things, exploring the border country that exists between true and false, fact and fiction, real life and imagined life. But I hope it won't just be read as 'this happened to me.'"

Jacqueline Margaret Kay was born on November 9, 1961 in Edinburgh, to a white mother (a Scottish nurse) and a black father (a Nigerian studying in the forestry-and-agriculture department at the University of Aberdeen). At the age of five months (many sources say at birth), she was adopted by a white couple, John and Helen Kay, who raised her in Bishopbriggs, a suburb of Glasgow, alongside an older brother, Maxie, who was also adopted and also black. Helen Kay was a primary-school teacher and John "didn't have a proper job," as Kay told Jamieson. Instead, he worked in a variety of capacities for the British Communist Party, which his wife also strongly supported. Immersed in political life, Kay attended rallies, took her place in antiapartheid marches, and wrote letters of political protest or solidarity from an early age. "We got meat from the party butcher every Saturday morning," she told David Robinson for the *Scotsman* (January 12, 2002). "If we needed a carpet put down, there'd be a party carpet fitter, there'd be a party plumber, party everything." Another aspect of her childhood that helped shape her political sensibilities was the frequent racist bullying she and her brother endured as the only black children in their otherwise white community.

Kay has told interviewers that she feels grateful for having the adopted parents she had. "It was a very happy combination that I happened to end up with people who were so different, so ahead of their times," she told Jackie McGlone for the Glasgow *Herald* (October 16, 1993). "I'm sure I wouldn't write now if I hadn't been brought up by them," she added, noting that her home had been filled with books and that she had often been taken to poetry readings and other cultural events. After years of telling interviewers that she had never tried to contact her birth parents, Kay has in recent years contacted both. According to Jamieson, Kay has prepared a manuscript about her 2003 reunion, in Nigeria, with her birth father; she is uncertain about publishing it, in part because of her desire to respect his privacy. She told Jamieson that the contrast between her image of him—"a cross between Paul Robeson and Nelson Mandela or something"—and the reality was "quite shocking."

Between the ages of 10 and 16, Kay studied acting two times a week at the Royal Scottish Academy of Music and Drama, in Glasgow, but she eventually despaired of a stage career because she was excluded from the vast majority of roles due to her skin color. Instead she embraced literary pursuits. Growing up she had particularly enjoyed *Anne of Green Gables* and other novels by Lucy Maud Montgomery. "I loved that book because [Anne] was adopted too," Kay told Robinson. "She had red hair and got picked on." (The deep influence of this early reading on Kay's life was evidenced when she later named her son after a character in the book. In the book Matthew "was the kindest man," she told Robinson. "So I called my son that because I wanted him to be kind too. And yes, he is.") At age 11 Kay composed a short novel, set in the U.S., called "One Person, Two Names," which told the story of a black girl who passed as white. In her teens Kay showed a selection of her poems to the Scottish novelist and poet Alasdair Gray, and he assured her that she was "a writer, no doubt about it at all, a writer," as she told Catherine Lockerbie for the *Scotsman* (January 16, 1993).

Kay first publicly acknowledged her homosexuality while studying English at the University of Stirling, in central Scotland, where she also became a staunch feminist. "I was really, really angry, an angry feminist, shockingly angry and annoyed at the inequalities of the world and seeing them all afresh and actually feeling like it was all some sort of plot in that way you do. I'm glad I got out of it," she told Jamieson.

After graduating from the university, in 1983, she started her literary career in London, where she supported herself with a variety of jobs. The first selection of her poetry published in book form came in 1984, with the appearance of *A Dangerous Knowing: Four Black Women Poets*. Described by Terri Jewell for the Australian journal *Hecate* (November 30, 1986) as "a gift," the book brought together work by Barbara Burford, Grace Nichols, Gabriela Pearse, and Kay. Jewell characterized Kay's voice in the poems as "assertive and irreverent" and concluded, "I could read a whole lot more of her work." Kay also contributed fiction to two books—sometimes mistakenly referred to as novels—*Everyday Matters 2: More Short Stories by Women* (1984) and *Stepping Out: Short Stories on Friendships between Women* (1986), and returned to the theater, this time as a playwright. The drama company Gay Sweatshop produced two of her early plays, *Chiaroscuro* (published in 1986 but first performed in 1985 under the title *The Meeting Place*) and *Twice Over*. Published in 1989 as part of *Gay Sweatshop: Four Plays and a Company*, *Twice Over* is the story of an elderly gay woman whose acquaintances recognize her sexuality only after her death. Reviewing its U.S. premier, Gerald Nachman described the play in the *San Francisco Chronicle* (March 10, 1992) as "a mildly amusing if less than revelatory look at the closeted lives of lesbians a generation ago (or indeed, today)."

Kay cemented her reputation as a poet in 1991, after becoming one of the winners of the annual Eric Gregory Award from Britain's Society of Authors and publishing her first major collection, *The Adoption Papers*. At the heart of the collection is a series of poems about adoption written in the voices of a black daughter and both of her white mothers, the one who gave birth to her and the one who adopted her. In the London *Independent* (December 29, 1991), William Scammell described the book as "moving" and pointed to "Kay's talent for getting under the skin and into the voices of the streetwise and fancy-free." In 1992 *The Adoption Papers* earned Kay two major Scottish literary awards: the Scottish Arts Council Book Award and the Saltire Society Scottish First Book of the Year Award. (Kay shared the Saltire prize with the poet Christopher Whyte.) Additionally, one poem in *The Adoption Papers*, "Black Bottom," won the

best single poem commendation from the Forward Arts Foundation.

Also in 1992, after roughly four years of motherhood, Kay published a collection of poetry for young people, *Two's Company*, that drew on her own childhood experiences. Joanna Carey, in a review for the London *Guardian* (September 5, 1992), called the poems "funny, sad, and thoughtful" and "resolutely individual." In 1993 the book won the annual poetry award from the journal *Signal: Approaches to Children's Books*. In June 1992 Kay's *Twice through the Heart*, a retelling of the real-life murder of an abusive husband by his wife, was broadcast on the television channel BBC2 as part of an unusual series of documentaries in verse. An adaptation of the piece as a song cycle, set to music by the British composer Mark-Anthony Turnage, debuted in June 1997 at the Aldeburgh Festival, in England.

Early in 1993 Kay's play *Every Bit of It*, about two women who meet on a train and are brought together by their love of the 20th-century blues singer Bessie Smith, opened in Glasgow's Tron Theatre. Arguing that the drama felt "more like an idea for a painting than a play," Joyce McMillan wrote for the London *Guardian* (January 21, 1993): "Once the basic situation is established, Kay seems at a loss to know how to develop her script or bring it to a close. The strength of the scenario, the conviction of the performances, and the power of the poetic writing keeps the piece going for about 50 of its 90 minutes. . . . But the dialogue becomes dangerously weak and repetitive; the ending . . . is a serious mistake; and [the production] leaves the structural weaknesses of the piece highly exposed." Similarly faint praise followed the premier of Kay's play *Twilight Shift*, about two working-class men in a Scottish mining community who become romantically involved. In the play, McMillan wrote, again for the London *Guardian* (November 3, 1993), Kay "takes a strong situation . . . and writes it up with a kind of self-conscious, image-making lyricism that emphasizes the power of language to conjure pictures out of darkness, and fill simple physical facts, like the dirt and danger of the mines, with metaphorical meaning. But somehow, the link between the drama and the poetry remains unforged: the most gripping sequences are the ones in which Kay abandons the metaphorical mode and goes straight to the heart of the confrontation that drives the drama."

Kay's next major poetry collection, *Other Lovers*, received strong reviews when it appeared later in 1993. In the London *Observer* (December 26, 1993), Adam Thorpe wrote, "Kay's diction is as far as you can get from back-beating melancholy: anxious, and angry, the odd moments of reverie are all the more effective, proof that she's always in full control of her ambitious art." In a review for *World Literature Today* (June 22, 1994), Bruce King compared *Other Lovers* to *Adoption Papers* and found it "a more consistent volume, showing an increased range of form, voices, emotions, imagery, and situations." To King, "Kay is at her best when the subject is someone else or there are several characters, so her own feelings of alienation, of not belonging, and her desire to identify, to love, have other people through or against which to define themselves." The book was one of three recipients of the 1994 Society of Authors Somerset Maugham Award, given annually to the best books written by authors younger than 35.

In 1994 Kay's next book of children's verse, *Three Has Gone*, was published. Praised by reviewers for its playfulness and lightly handled technical control, the book dealt with difficult themes. As a reviewer for the London *Independent* (November 20, 1994) wrote, "Although always entertaining, [Kay's] work puts across the realpolitik of family life, and of a child's experience, with such poems as 'Divorce' and 'Attention Seeking.'" Published in 1997, Kay's next work, *Bessie Smith*, told the story of the singer's life, sometimes through imagined reconstructions, alongside incidents from Kay's own experience. Calling the book an "engrossing olio of biography, autobiography, poetry, and fiction," Mike Tribby, in a review for *Booklist* (February 1, 1998), noted that, in keeping with the book series in which the work appeared, Kay emphasizes Smith's romantic attachments to women. But, he added, Smith's "music and career are amply and lovingly detailed as well; indeed, this is primarily a warm, personable, evocative, and pleasing portrait of 'the Empress of the Blues' that is also interesting as a study of two strong artistic female characters (Kay herself is the second) and the connections between their seemingly disparate lives."

Kay's book on Bessie Smith grew out of another project she had already begun, a novel inspired by the story of the jazz pianist, saxophonist, and bandleader Billy Tipton. Born Dorothy Tipton, Billy spent most of his adult life—through a long, high-profile career and five marriages—as a man. When Tipton died, in 1989, of a perforated ulcer that he refused to have treated (apparently for fear that the doctor would detect the secret that he had kept from his wives, band-mates, and adopted children), Kay was stirred to tell a story similar to Tipton's own. "What touched me particularly," Kay told Andrea Stuart for the London *Independent* (August 8, 1998), "was a quote from his adopted son who said, 'He will always be Daddy to me.' It was a story that was both ordinary and extraordinary. Ordinary in that he was still 'daddy', and extraordinary in that the son accepted his father's construction of his identity, and that is both radical and challenging." The result, *Trumpet*, gave its main character, Joss Moody, only a single marriage and a single child and used a range of narrators to tell his tale.

The book was widely praised in the U.K. and the U.S. for its warm, respectful portrayal of a life that other writers might have rendered as merely sensational. In the London *Guardian* (August 29, 1998), Katy Emck noted that Kay "cleanly sidesteps both prurience and pretentiousness. Although the pull of the book cannot help deriving from the reader's curiosity about the minutiae of how Joss Moody pulled it off [and] what sex was like with her 'wife' . . . , Kay makes a point of marginalizing these concerns." Emck concluded: "*Trumpet* is written in clear, spare prose which is full of poetic touches such as the description of death, when 'the whole face opens out as if it has been finally understood'. The qualities of sympathy and tenderness in this novel make it special, and make Kay a writer to respect." The *Guardian* awarded the novel its prestigious fiction prize, in December 1998; Dan Glaister wrote for the paper (December 4, 1998) that the prize had been bestowed on the book for "the way it marries ambition with understatement; for the strength of the writing; for its fascinating subject material; and for the way it engages with the great emotions without ever becoming sentimental." Some reviewers, however, found fault with Kay's characterization and pacing, as well as her knowledge of jazz, though almost all of them seemed to consider the novel, on balance, worth reading. For the on-line magazine *Salon* (March 10, 1999), Mary Elizabeth Williams wrote, "Kay writes with quiet assurance, skipping back and forth both in time and among characters with the deftness of a knowing guide. Her only weakness may be ambition: To the already complicated story of gender crossing she adds race mixing, a thread she keeps picking up and putting down erratically. And she might have been able to convey her point about love conquering all without making both Millie and Joss so darn nice and noble. Their marriage may indeed have been a meeting of soul mates, but if Joss Moody was so all-fired-up perfect, he'd have been the first jazz musician of his kind in history." In addition to the *Guardian* award, *Trumpet* was given the Authors' Club First Novel Award, in 2000, and that same year was short-listed for Ireland's most prestigious literary award, the International IMPAC Dublin Literary Award. A play version of *Trumpet*, adapted and directed by Grace Barnes (with input from Kay), was first mounted in Scotland, in 2005, and was produced again, in 2006, as part of the Queerupnorth Festival, in Manchester, England.

Two other books by Kay were published in 1998. One was another major collection of verse, *Off Colour*. Short-listed for the 1998 T. S. Eliot Prize for Poetry, the book was widely praised by reviewers. In the Glasgow *Herald* (December 17, 1998), Hayden Murphy considered the collection "an articulate fight against apathy" and "a clinical yet emotional deconstruction of false pity and pieties." Implicitly contrasting this book with Kay's previous collections, Murphy wrote: "Racism and prejudice are still the natural enemies but now she sees them in the context of an inherently healthy society. That she is prepared to jettison automatic reactions and regenerate her own fulfilled responses gives this book an authoritative feel." Later that year Kay published another collection of children's verse, *The Frog Who Dreamed She Was an Opera Singer*. The book was described by Lindsey Fraser for the London *Guardian* (November 17, 1998) as "a most welcome new collection from a poet whose love of words, sounds and rhythms is matched by an apparently boundless imagination and curiosity." Fraser added, "This collection, taken as a whole, recalls the varied pace of childhood, the sunny moments when anything—even an opera singing frog—seems possible, and those darker times when nothing seems right."

Over the next four years, Kay worked on a second novel about the actress and singer Hattie McDaniel, who, as a supporting actress in the film *Gone with the Wind* (1939), became the first African-American ever to win an Academy Award. With that project never published and seemingly never completed, Kay's first work of fiction after *Trumpet* became a book of short stories. Entitled *Why Don't You Stop Talking* (2002), the collection brought together 13 stories about odd, occasionally fantastical characters, almost all of them women and many of them tied to Scotland. The book received almost uniform and unqualified praise in Great Britain and Ireland. In the *Irish Times* (January 26, 2002), Arminta Wallace wrote that every one of the pieces in the collection "is individually memorable, glowing with its own eerie light like a gemstone set in a bracelet. Taken together, though, they form an unusually coherent examination of Kay's chosen themes . . . of alienation, transformation and the nature of self in a world where to be 'Scottish' means you have incorporated bits of Jamaica or Trinidad or Ireland or even, sometimes, England." Kay's other 2002 work of fiction was the children's novel *Strawgirl*, about a Scottish girl called Maybe (her real name is Molly) who fights to defend her family farm after the death of her Nigerian father, with the help of the seemingly imaginary title character. The book was described by Alice Ferrebe for *Scotland on Sunday* (November 10, 2002) as "a deeply democratic novel that gives equal weight to the feelings of children, adults and animals alike. A simple story, it is crammed with complex ideas and gorgeous poetry—to cows, to trees, to family and to friends, imaginary or otherwise."

Published in 2005 to generally positive reviews, Kay's next collection of poetry, *Life Mask*, contained poems about recovering after the breakup of a long romantic relationship and a woman's reunion with her strange birth father. Anna Millar, in a review for *Scotland on Sunday* (April 24, 2005), termed the book "a lucid rite of passage," adding, "Kay's unerring fascination with how fragile and fluid identity can be, how people can reinvent themselves, and how gender and race are resolutely unfixed, are all addressed here, simply and without pretension." In the London

Sunday Times (October 23, 2005), Alan Brownjohn offered more mixed praise. "Kay is a direct, punch writer, using quirky terms and ideas to express vulnerable truths in this hit-and-miss fourth collection." Kay's most recent book is another collection of short stories, *Wish I Was Here*. Published in June 2006, the book's reviews have been mixed, if generally positive.

Along with her other awards, Kay became one of four poets honored in 2003 with the Cholmondeley Award, given annually by the Society of Authors in recognition of "the achievement and distinction of individual poets." In January 2005 she received an honorary doctorate from the University of Warwick, in England. Later that same year, she became one of four 20th-century Scottish poets—and the only living one—to have a bronze sculpture of her head placed in the Edinburgh Business Park, which is described on its Web site as "Scotland's Most Prestigious Business Park."

Between roughly 1991 and 2004, Kay's partner was her fellow Scottish poet Carol Ann Duffy. Kay now lives in Manchester with her son, Matthew, who was born in about 1988; Matthew's father is the London-born Guyanese poet Fred D'Aguiar, a close friend who offered to co-parent with Kay and who remains devoted to their son. "I always wanted to be a mother. So being gay didn't stop me," she told Teddy Jamieson.

—D.R.

Suggested Reading: British Council Web site; (Glasgow) *Herald* p8 Oct. 16, 1993; (London) *Guardian* p10 Dec. 5, 1998; (London) *Sunday Times* June 12, 1994, Dec. 20, 1998, Oct. 23, 2005; *Scotsman* p4 Jan. 12, 2002

Selected Books: *Adoption Papers*, 1991; *Two's Company*, 1992; *Other Lovers*, 1993; *Three Has Gone*, 1994; *Bessie Smith*, 1997; *Off Colour*, 1998; *Trumpet*, 1998; *The Frog Who Dreamed She Was an Opera Singer*, 1999; *Strawgirl*, 2002; *Why Don't You Stop Talking*, 2002; *Life Mask*, 2005

Kearney, Meg

(KAR-nee)

June 3, 1964– Poet

Meg Kearney composed the following autobiographical statement for *World Authors 2000–2005*:

"Mother Goose's nursery rhymes, children's Bible stories, Brothers Grimm fairy tales, even a Giant Golden Book of *The Iliad and the Odyssey* with marvelous illustrations were just some of the books that filled the house where I grew up. Born on June 3, 1964, I was the youngest of three

Courtesy of Meg Kearney

Meg Kearney

adopted children. My older sister and brother and I were all born in New York City, adopted at very young ages by Joe and Trudy Kearney, and brought to live in LaGrange, a little town east of Poughkeepsie, New York. My father was a school principal—my principal from kindergarten through sixth grade—and my mother was a nurse and bibliophile. Both of my parents read to me when I was young, which might be why I grew up loving books, and started to write stories of my own in second grade. I can remember sitting on the hearth in the living room, scribbling away with my paper and pencil, while Dad sat in his chair beside me reading the paper or watching a ball game on TV, and Mom sat across the room with a book in her lap.

"My parents were very encouraging of my early literary attempts. Dad went so far as to bring my hand-written stories to school so his secretary could type them. I wrote my first 'full-length book,' a tale about Pocahontas (this was long before the Disney version), in fifth grade. Dad's secretary typed all eighty pages, leaving room for my own illustrations. Then when I turned twelve, my uncle and aunt gave me a little blank book. It was the most beautiful object I'd ever seen, measuring maybe five by four inches, filled with rice paper gilded at the edges. The cloth cover was embroidered with a Chinese design, all reds and golds.

"I knew that whatever I wrote in that book had to be very special and very short. That's when I started writing poems. I'd draft each piece until I thought I had it right, then copy it carefully into the little book. Unfortunately, that book is lost now. I'm sure the poems were dreadful, but because of

that book I discovered that poetry was my passion and never wrote fiction again.

"It wasn't long after I started writing poems—I know I was still in sixth grade, and it was nearing my birthday in June—that I decided to read one to Mom. I sat her down on the bed in my room, and proceeded to read her a short lyric in which I wondered if my birthmother was thinking about me, wondered if she remembered my birthday. When I finished the poem, I looked up to see that Mom's face had turned pale—she bore a look I didn't recognize. She must have mumbled something like 'That's very nice, dear,' but I don't honestly recall; I do know she fled the room.

"That moment was very powerful, and taught me two essential things. While my parents and brother and sister talked openly at home about the facts of our adoption, we never discussed our feelings. This was something I'd not thought about before, though it made a kind of sense, as we never spoke about us kids being adopted at all outside the walls of our house. In reading that poem to Mom, I discovered that wondering about my birthmother, expressing a bit of melancholy over the fact that I didn't know what she looked like or why she gave me away—was taboo territory. I wasn't supposed to 'go there.' At the same time, I realized that this poetry stuff had a lot of power. After all, it made my mother run from my room. So I continued writing poems—I never really felt any choice in the matter—but I didn't show them to anyone for years.

"It was in college that I took my first poetry workshop. Instead of asking his students to bring in poems they'd already written, our professor assigned us poets to read, and then asked us to respond to them with our own poems. This meant that I was going to have to share my writing with someone, but I trusted this professor because I thought he had good taste: we read Wallace Stevens and William Carlos Williams, Emily Dickinson and Gertrude Stein, Yeats and Rilke, Hopkins and Rimbaud. How could I not be inspired? At some point during the semester, I had a one-on-one conference with the professor, who started the session by reading me one of my own poems. Just the idea of it was mind-boggling, and I sat there stiffly, as if waiting for a blow. But while he read the poem, a miracle occurred: he began to weep. I was stunned. Again, the power of poetry had been confirmed. There was no doubt I was going to stick with this poetry thing.

"It was this same professor who made me enter one of my poems in a contest sponsored by the Hudson Valley Writers Association (HVWA), which sponsored a literary magazine and had a poetry group that met weekly. I entered the contest and won, much to my astonishment. The people at HVWA were friendly and soon welcomed me into the group. I attended some of their peer workshops, but never had the guts to read my work.

"While I knew I wanted to be a poet, I also knew that there was no way to make a living at it. Teaching poetry never actually entered my mind. At first I thought I would be a journalist, but by the time I was a sophomore in college I'd switched my major from journalism to English. After graduation, I ended up working in the corporate communications department of a gas and electric utility in upstate New York. For my first few years I wrote and edited the company's weekly newsletter; then, after a short, baffling stint as a purchasing agent, I coordinated educational programs: giving power plant tours, teaching children about electrical safety, and running the speakers bureau. It was an odd life for a poet, and though I had a few colleagues I could talk with about books, there was no one I could talk with about poetry. Luckily, I was asked by the people from HVWA to serve as one of the poetry editors for the organization's literary magazine, *Echoes*, which introduced me to a couple of women I could finally talk with about poetry. We started running some poetry workshops in local high schools, which was terrifying and fun, but also made me feel like an imposter. Who was I to teach poetry to kids? I'd only published a couple of poems here and there. I felt that I knew nothing. Teaching underlined that feeling.

"It was in the summer of 1989 that I discovered The Frost Place, a center for poetry and the arts in Franconia, New Hampshire. I was still working the utility job, and applied to participate in the Frost Place's annual Poetry Festival without believing I'd actually get in. There was no way I could have anticipated how that acceptance would change my life. Here was a group of people who loved poetry as much as I did, who didn't think it strange that I didn't own a television and would rather read a book than go to the mall. Here was a place—free from the hierarchies and envies of the corporate world (I had no idea that such things could be found in the poetry world, and remained blissfully ignorant of that for another year or two)—where poetry was spoken of with passion and intelligence. The faculty was astounding, and included Heather McHugh, John Engels, Molly Peacock, and William Matthews, with whom I would later study as a graduate student. I'd found a place like no other; I'd found my tribe. I was a baby poet, but I'd found a place where I could grow up."

Kearney has been involved with the world of American letters in one capacity or another since the mid-1980s, when she joined the Hudson Valley Writers Association (HVWA) of upstate New York. This local writers' group provided her with the opportunity to teach at various middle and high schools as a visiting poet and to serve as one of three editors of *Echoes*, a quarterly poetry

magazine. In 1994 she moved to New York City and joined the National Book Foundation, sponsor of the National Book Awards and numerous literary educational programs. There, Kearney's myriad responsibilities included directing its Summer Writing Camp, a nine-day inter-generational program for aspiring writers with demonstrated talent and financial need. The camp, which Kearney was responsible for launching when she was hired by the foundation, began with 12 students (all teens) and one writer in residence its first year; after its first decade, it was accepting an average of 48 students, ranging in age from 14 to 70 and representing more than 25 states. Those accepted received full fellowships, allowing them to participate in workshops and to benefit from individual tutoring from published writers (who have included such award-winning authors as Jessica Hagedorn, Norma Fox Mazer, Jacqueline Woodson, Cornelius Eady, and Kimiko Hahn). So successful was the program under Kearney's direction that the foundation was able to publish, with the help of Black Classic Press and Henry Holt and Company, four collections of the work produced by the camp's participants. Kearney was also responsible for the foundation's American Voices program, which is designed to inspire Native American writers of all ages. Kearney sees American Voices as something that can help revive the voices of a people who have been silenced or ignored for centuries. "We want them to tell their story rather than have others tell it for them," Kearney explained to Scott Winter for the North Dakota *Bismarck Tribune* (April 27, 2000).

Besides writing grants and setting up programs to help others improve their writing, Kearney worked on honing her own craft throughout the 1990s and began to gain some recognition for her efforts. Her poems appeared in prestigious literary magazines, including the *Black Warrior Review*, *Ploughshares*, the *Gettysburg Review*, *Tar River Poetry*, and *Washington Square*. In the late 1990s, while she was working on her master's degree in creative writing at the City College of New York (CCNY), she also started to win awards, including the Geraldine Griffen Moore Award in Creative Writing in 1997, fellowships to the Virginia Center for the Creative Arts (1998, 1999, 2000, 2004), and both a *New York Times* fellowship and the Alice M. Sellers Academy of American Poets Prize in 1998. In 2001 she was the recipient of an Artist's Fellowship from the New York Foundation for the Arts. The awards were valuable to her development, Kearney told *World Authors*, in that "they gave encouragement," but each time she won, she went on to say, with refreshing humility, that she sometimes wondered if an award committee "had made some kind of mistake."

Outside the small circle of poetry-journal readers and editors and the world of award committees, Kearney remained largely unknown. This changed in 2001. Donald Hall, the well-known American poet, introduced Kearney to a wider audience of readers in his foreword to *An Unkindness of Ravens*, Kearney's first book of poems, which was published by BOA Editions. Kearney, Hall observed, has produced "a book of reticence and revelation, secrecy and surprise." Hall continued: "Few poems are narrative, but something like a story emerges from these lyrics alive with hurt and splendor. Although the poems radiate personal feelings, we have no sense of confessional poetry as deliberate self-revelation; Kearney's confessional is Catholic." Hall later noted that poems' value derived not simply from the importance of their themes: "Whatever place her poems come from," he wrote, "their beauty lies in their language." Picking up on the themes in Hall's introduction, Zoe Randall, writing for the *American Book Review* (Jan./Feb. 2003), discussed both the power of Kearney's Catholic sensibility and her use of language. "Kearney's world is full of Catholic shame and sin; it is as dark as the confessional itself," Randall wrote. "In 'The Prodigal Mother,' her Molly 'cannot enter the house'; there is no one 'to say she is forgiven, to say / there will be roast lamb, dancing—.' Molly lies

. . . face-
down in the dirt, legs sprawled,

lace petticoat revealing a torn
thigh. Have you no modesty, Molly?
. . .
. . . The woman sits down
in the dirt, thinking of Jesus. Molly,
slumped on her lap, stares into her

own empty chest."

Randall concluded: "Kearney's wonderful use of enjambment punctuates and extends meaning and pain." The Catholicism that haunts Kearney's poems has continued to receive attention; Debra Galant in the *New York Times* (October 10, 2004), for example, recently noted that hers is "the poetry of a lapsed Catholic girl who spends a lot of time in bars," and warned, "One poem, with a title that can't be printed in a family newspaper, employs a particularly hilarious metaphor for a certain sex act."

The Catholic themes were not the only element of the poems that caught the attention of critics: the craft with which Kearney created the poems and arranged them as a collection has also earned critical respect. Commenting upon the power of the poems as individual entities, a reviewer for the *Bloomsbury Review* observed, as quoted on Kearney's Web site, "Meg Kearney is a true find, and her poems are a reminder that the strongest poetry always arrives when the first-person speaker is dominant. The confident tone, the surprise of each moment, and the stories woven around deep imagery give Kearney's work an unforgettable twist." Anne-Marie Oomen, in a review for *ForeWord Magazine* (2002, on-line),

called attention to the narrative power of the collection, noting, "Though any one of these poems will stand alone, when they are read as a whole, a deeply emotional narrative of a lost family surfaces. The poems of the third section, 'Adoptive Measures,' explore both the personae of a mother who gives up her child and the 'surrendered' daughter, growing into the invented memory of both the mother and daughter who longs to fill in the blanks of life and make whole all the empty parts. 'I search faces / on the street, at the supermarket, laundromat: I try / not to be rude; I stroke my chin—Do I have your nose? / Would you turn your head?'"

While her poems had appeared in two anthologies—*Where Icarus Falls: A Poetry Anthology* (1998) and *Urban Nature: Poems About Wildlife in the City* (2000)—before the publication of *An Unkindness of Ravens*, since her first book was published Kearney's poems have been included in such anthologies as *Poets' Grimm: 20th Century Poems from Grimm Fairy Tales* (2003), *Never Before: Poems about First Experiences* (2005), *Shade 2006: An Anthology of Poetry and Fiction* (2006), *The Book of Irish American Poetry from the 18th Century to the Present* (2006), and *Conversation Pieces: Poems that Talk to Other Poems* (2007). Kearney also co-edited *Blues for Bill: A Tribute to William Matthews* (2005), an anthology of poems written by such poets as Sharon Olds, Stanley Plumly, and David Wojahn and gathered to honor the memory of the well-respected poet and teacher William Matthews, with whom Kearney had studied. Her work has also appeared in *Poetry* magazine, the most prestigious poetry journal in the U.S.

Her second book, *The Secret of Me*, was published in the fall of 2005 by Persea Books, an independent publisher located in New York City that is dedicated to publishing, according to its Web site, "works that endure by meeting high standards of literary merit and relevance." *The Secret of Me*, Kearney told *World Authors*, is "a collection of poems written in the voice of 14-year-old girl named Lizzie McLane," an aspiring poet who happens to be an adopted child, although "a strong narrative line runs throughout the book and holds the poems together." Indeed, the narrative element to the collection is so strong that a critic for *Kirkus Reviews* (November 1, 2005) referred to it as a "novel-in-verse." The critic continued: "A real balance of personal exploration as an adoptee and new teenage emotions creates a powerful blend in a warm character ready to connect and sustain that bond to readers. No only will adolescents feel expertly sensitized to issues of adoption, they will get a good dose of real poetry with unique and inspiring language so often sacrificed for story in this genre." The book concludes with an afterword, a guide to poetics, a collection of the main character's favorite poems, and recommended books and Web sites.

In 2005 Kearney resigned from the National Book Foundation. She had, by that time, become the associate director, but she left to take the position of director of the creative-writing program at Pine Manor College, in Chestnut Hill, Massachusetts. Her first responsibility was to set up the Solstice Summer Writers' Conference, a gathering of writers and students who participate in panel discussions, readings, and workshops in fiction, nonfiction, and poetry. At the same time, she developed the master of fine arts in creative writing program at Pine Manor College. Her third book is tentatively called "Redemption Arcade."

—A.R.

Suggested Reading: *American Book Review* p26+ Jan./Feb, 2003; *Bloomsbury Review* Mar./Apr. 2002; *ForeWord Magazine* (on-line) 2002;

Selected Books: *An Unkindness of Ravens*, 2001; *The Secret of Me*, 2005

Jonathan Exley

Kellerman, Jonathan

Aug. 9, 1949– Novelist

When Jonathan Kellerman's first crime novel, *When the Bough Breaks*, came out, in 1985, he wasn't sure it would be a success. The book concerned the unsavory theme of child abuse and featured two protagonists unusual for the mystery genre: a child psychologist named Alex Delaware and Milo Sturgis, an overweight, gay Los Angeles Police Department operative. That year, however, the nation's attention was captured by frequent news stories about alleged sexual abuse at a preschool in California, and *When the Bough Breaks* seemed timely and relevant. It won several industry awards and became a surprise best-seller. Kellerman, himself a practicing psychologist for more than a decade before becoming a full-time writer, has now written numerous best-selling books featuring Alex Delaware. He told Jennifer Levitsky for Bookreporter.com (January 22, 1997), "[Alex Delaware] is my Walter Mitty fantasy. I decided, finally, to write what I knew but I'm a rather boring fellow, married with kids, dogs, etc., and could never get into the trouble he does. I'd like to think I share his compassion and curiosity about people and, certainly, some of the more technical aspects of psychology that find their way into the novels emerge from my own experience. Oh yeah, he's also in much better physical shape." Occasionally, Kellerman also writes a book focusing on a female homicide detective named Petra Connor, a nonfiction volume about child psychology, or a stand-alone mystery. (A stand-alone mystery refers to one not featuring a recurring main character.)

Jonathan Kellerman was born on August 9, 1949 in New York City to Sylvia Fiacre and David Kellerman. The family lived on the Lower East Side of Manhattan, then a decaying neighborhood, but they soon moved to a more middle-class area in the borough of Queens. When Kellerman was nine, his family relocated to California, where he eventually attended the University of California, at Los Angeles (UCLA), earning his bachelor's degree in 1971. While there he worked on the *Daily Bruin*, the school's newspaper, producing editorial cartoons, as well as articles. As a senior, Kellerman, who was also an accomplished guitarist and earned money as a freelance musician, won a Samuel Goldwyn Writing Award for fiction.

While he loved writing and thought that he might publish fiction as a sideline one day, Kellerman did not think of it as a possible way to earn a living. He was most interested in biology and human behavior, and in 1974 he earned a doctoral degree in psychology from the University of Southern California (USC). Kellerman then served internships in clinical psychology and pediatric psychology at the Childrens Hospital of Los Angeles (CHLA) and was a postdoctoral fellow at the facility.

In 1975 Kellerman began conducting research into the psychological effects of the plastic bubble units used to isolate children with cancer and other diseases from outside contagions, and in 1977 he helped establish CHLA's innovative Psychosocial Program at the Division of Oncology, an accomplishment of which he remains exceedingly proud. Besides publishing many articles in professional journals, he detailed his approach in the book *Psychological Aspects of Childhood Cancer*, which he published in 1980. He also authored *Helping the Fearful Child: A*

Parents' Guide to Everyday and Problem Anxieties in 1981. (In 1998, prompted by a spate of highly publicized school shootings, he returned to the topic of child psychology with *Savage Spawn: Reflections on Violent Children.*)

Kellerman worked long days at the hospital and maintained a private practice, but for a few hours each night he wrote fiction in his unheated garage. He has described himself during that period to several interviewers as "a failed writer with a really good day job." Determined to make it in the world of fiction, Kellerman eventually began writing full-time. He wrote on his official Web site, "Having written novels for 13 years without any success, [*When the Bough Breaks*] was my (alleged) final attempt to publish full-length fiction before having to face up to monumental inadequacy. I say alleged because it's unwise to underestimate the power of the obsessive-compulsive personality, so who knows what it would've taken to get me to finally knock it off? I quit my job as a medical school professor to write *Bough,* and struggled to remedy what I felt were my two main deficiencies as a writer: cowardice about exploring my own life experiences, and inadequate plot. I finished the book in 1981, whereupon it was promptly rejected by several agents, one of whom opined, 'You'd be a good non-fiction writer.' Another said, 'I kind of like it, but my secretary doesn't.'" He continued, "The book sat in a drawer for two years until I connected with the gentleman and scholar who's remained my agent and close friend for twenty years, Barney Karpfinger. He sold it quickly. Finally, I was a writer, not a delusion-wracked loser. My advance payment was so small that I could've flipped burgers at McDonalds and done better. The publisher held the book until 1985, not really sure how to classify it and fully intending to relegate it to instant obscurity."

Despite such expectations, the novel became a best-seller and won several industry awards, including the prestigious Anthony Boucher and Edgar Allan Poe prizes. In *When the Bough Breaks,* Kellerman introduced Alex Delaware, a character partially modeled on himself. Delaware works with his friend, a Los Angeles homicide detective named Milo Sturgis, who happens to be gay. The two struggle to solve a mystery that hinges on the testimony of a reluctant child, who has been traumatized by the events she has witnessed. In a review of *When the Bough Breaks* in the *Chicago Tribune* (June 1, 1986), Clarence Petersen asserted that with the novel, "Kellerman steps directly into the front rank of American suspense story writers." He praised Kellerman's plotting and noted that every "walk-on character is a small masterpiece of memorable characterization, and the dialogue is unerringly realistic." The book was made into a 1986 made-for-television movie starring Ted Danson. (This is the only Kellerman book adapted for the screen; although others have been optioned, the pictures have ultimately not been made. Kellerman has been told by several film-industry

figures that his novels are too cerebral or complex for commercial adaptation; in one notable instance, Kellerman himself backed out of a movie deal when the director wanted to give Delaware a limp.)

Kellerman's second Alex Delaware novel, *Blood Test* (1986), involves the oncology ward of a hospital, a milieu with which the writer was intimately familiar. A child has disappeared, and if he does not get chemotherapy soon, he will die. "Among the guilty are a deranged horticulturist who specializes in flowers of evil and a holistic cult whose practices may give pause to even the most jaded vice and narcotics squads," David Lehman wrote in *Newsweek* (June 9, 1986). "As one character exclaims, 'California has become a sanctuary for the psychic refuse of the world!' *Blood Test* renders this atmosphere of nouveau depravity and trendy nuttiness vividly but not ostentatiously. It's a relentlessly intelligent thriller."

"To some extent Alex Delaware is me, taken to the extreme,'" Kellerman told Leslie Cohen for the *Jerusalem Post* (November 14, 1997). He explained that as a psychologist at CHLA he "encountered incredible things, like children whose parents had been murdered." Background knowledge, such as Kellerman's experience of the court system, in which he frequently had to testify as an expert witness, gave a further aura of authenticity to his books, although Kellerman admitted to Cohen that he had never "encountered anything as gross and disgusting as some of the things Alex" encounters.

Kellerman continued to write mysteries featuring Delaware, generally publishing one a year and landing regularly on best-seller lists. These included *Over the Edge* (1987), *Silent Partner* (1989), *Time Bomb* (1990), *Private Eyes* (1992), *Devil's Waltz* (1993), *Bad Love* (1994), *Self-Defense* (1995), *The Web* (1996), *The Clinic,* (1997), and *Survival of the Fittest* (1997). In his books he explored such topics as Munchausen by Proxy Syndrome, a rare form of child abuse in which parents simulate illness in their kids to earn attention for themselves; assisted suicide; and mood-altering drugs. Throughout the series Delaware and Milo Sturgis continued to develop as characters, and their personal lives were explored in some detail. (Milo's sexuality, in particular, has drawn comment from readers, with some applauding Kellerman's decision to play against stereotyping by making his tough LAPD detective gay and others questioning how a straight, married writer has the temerity to try to portray a gay figure.)

Kellerman has written a number of books outside the series, allowing him to introduce other protagonists and themes. *The Butcher's Theater* (1988) follows a team of Israeli detectives as they try to capture a serial killer in Jerusalem. Kellerman, a devout Orthodox Jew, studied in Israel in 1968 and has occasionally returned to visit the country since then. His main character is

Superintendent Daniel Sharavi, an ex-soldier maimed in the Six-Day War. "At its heart, the book is a police procedural, with Israeli police and Israeli bureaucracy and Israeli politicians, each with their own agenda," Mort Kamins wrote for the *Los Angeles Times Book Review* (March 13, 1988). "A Mephistophelian murderer is on the loose, and a specially formed team of cops fights to solve the puzzle before he kills again, and before the killings of Arab women threaten to tear apart the delicate web of Jerusalem's Arab-Jewish relations." Kellerman brought Sharavi back as a consultant to the LAPD in *Survival of the Fittest*.

Kellerman and his wife, fellow mystery writer Faye Kellerman, have continued to practice Judaism devotedly, finding no conflict between their religious life and the violence that they write about. They have pointed out that the Bible is not lacking in stories of crime and violence. "In the Torah and the Gemara [Jewish texts], you get an unflinching view of everything," Kellerman told Cohen. "The first family act was homicide," he said, referring to the murder of Abel by Cain.

In *Billy Straight*, his 1998 novel, Kellerman featured a female detective, Petra Connor of the LAPD. (She had appeared previously as a minor character in an Alex Delaware book.) Connor is on a mission to find Billy, a 12-year-old homeless boy who has witnessed a murder. David Lehman, writing for *People* (January 18, 1999), called Billy "a kind of urban Huckleberry Finn, a heroically resourceful boy." Marilyn Stasio of the *New York Times Book Review* (January 24, 1999) found Connor "bland" but agreed, "the kid is irresistible." Connor was featured again in *A Cold Heart* (2003), in which she teams with Delaware and Sturgis, and *Twisted* (2004), in which she is partnered with Isaac Gomez, a brilliant young man from a disadvantaged background who adds his epidemiological and sociological knowledge to her forensic skills. Reviewers have hinted that Gomez deserves to reappear in a series of his own.

In *The Conspiracy Club*, published in 2003, Kellerman introduced another detective, a young psychotherapist named Jeremy Carrier who works in a large urban hospital. Kellerman explained on his Web site, "I wanted to write from the perspective of a psychologist who wasn't Delaware—someone younger, tormented, with a troubled past. This novel probably tapped into my need to explore a decade and a half working as a hospital psychologist." In the book Carrier's girlfriend has been murdered. Although he is emotionally devastated himself—and becomes a suspect—Carrier is drawn into the investigation. A reviewer for *Library Journal* (December 15, 2003) called *The Conspiracy Club* a "classic mystery with little gore."

Reviewing *Therapy*, Kellerman's 2004 Alex Delaware novel, a *Publishers Weekly* (April 5, 2004) critic summed up Kellerman's career, noting that over the years he has satisfied "the reading public's hunger for mysteries featuring compassionate, intelligent protagonists, interesting secondary characters (including complex villains), strong plot lines and clear, unpretentious writing."

In 2004 Kellerman and his wife published their first collaborative effort, *Double Homicide*. The book consists of two novellas: *In the Land of Giants*, set in Boston, and *Still Life*, set in New Mexico. The authors did not include any of the main characters for which they are known (in the case of Faye Kellerman, a policeman named Peter Decker and his Orthodox Jewish wife, Rina Lazarus) and have given no indication of who wrote which novella. They plan to release several more such collaborative volumes, each set in a new geographic locale.

The Kellermans and their four children live in Los Angeles. One son, Jesse, is a playwright and novelist. Kellerman has pointed out in interviews that family connections did not help the young writer; his parents' contacts declined to look at the manuscript for his first novel, *Sunstroke* (2006), and he was forced to find an agent and publisher on his own.

Interviewers—while commenting on how affectionate and respectful of each other the couple seem—frequently ask them if sharing a profession causes tension in their household. Kellerman told Alden Mudge for the BookPage Web site, "Faye and I were married 12 or 13 years before either of us got published. It wasn't as if the two of us met at a writer's conference and brought these egos in. Faye was 18 when I met her; I was 21. To the extent that we've grown up at all, we've grown up together. The fact that our relationship was solid before we got published really helped." (Faye was a dentist before leaving her practice to write full-time.) Kellerman admitted to Mudge, however, "I'm always wary of interviews like this. What happens is that we come across as disgustingly smug and goody two-shoes. Honestly, we don't have any big skeletons in our closets."

Kellerman's latest Alex Delaware books are *Rage* (2005), in which the psychologist becomes embroiled in the murder of a newly released convict, and *Gone* (2006), in which he investigates the demise of a young actress.

—S.Y.

Suggested Reading: *Booklist* p5 Sep. 1, 2004; *Chicago Tribune* C p42 June 1, 1986; *Federal Probation* p94+ Dec. 1999; *Jerusalem Post* p22 Nov. 14, 1997; *Los Angeles Times Book Review* p13 Mar. 13, 1988, p11 Jan. 24, 1999; *New York Times Book Review* p24 Jan. 24, 1999; *People* Jan. 18, 1999; *Publishers Weekly* p54 Oct. 13, 2003, p42 Apr. 5, 2004; *Washington Post Book World* p5 Nov. 23, 1997

Selected Books: nonfiction—*Psychological Aspects of Childhood Cancer*, 1980; *Helping the Fearful Child: A Parents' Guide to Everyday and Problem Anxieties*, 1981; *Savage Spawn:*

Reflections on Violent Children, 1999; Alex Delaware series—*When the Bough Breaks*, 1985; *Blood Test*, 1986; *Over the Edge*, 1987; *Silent Partner*, 1989; *Time Bomb*, 1990; *Private Eyes*, 1992; *Devil's Waltz*, 1993; *Bad Love*, 1994; *Self-Defense*, 1995; *The Web*, 1996; *The Clinic*, 1997; *Survival of the Fittest*, 1997; *Monster*, 1999; *Dr. Death*, 2000; *Flesh and Blood*, 2001; *The Murder Book*, 2001, *Therapy*, 2004; *Rage*, 2005; *Gone*, 2006; Petra Connor series—*Billy Straight*, 1998; *A Cold Heart*, 2003; *Twisted*, 2004; other fiction—*The Butcher's Theater*, 1996; *The Conspiracy Club*, 2003; children's books—*Daddy, Daddy, Can You Touch the Sky?*, 1994; *Jonathan Kellerman's ABC of Weird Creatures*, 1995

Khadra, Yasmina

Jan. 10, 1955– Novelist

Yasmina Khadra is the pseudonym of Mohammed Moulessehoul, formerly a high-ranking officer in the Algerian army, who wrote under his wife's name to evade the censorship and opprobrium of the Algerian government. Though his most recent novels—which include *The Swallows of Kabul* (2004), *The Attack* (2006), and *The Sirens of Baghdad* (2007)—were written in the safety of his new home in Aix-en-Provence, France, far away from the political turmoil of his homeland, he has continued to use his feminine nom de plume. He has said in interviews that he continues to do so to honor the courage of Algerian women.

Khadra submitted the following autobiographical statement, which has been translated from the original French, to *World Authors 2000–2005*:

"My name is Mohammed Moulessehoul and I was born January 10, 1955 in Kenadsa, in the Algerian Sahara to a plumber father and a nomad mother.

"In 1956, my father joins the ranks of the National Liberation Army that arose to declare war on France for Algerian independence.

"July 1962, the time of independence; my father has become an officer and opts for a military career.

"In September 1964 my father places me in the Revolutionary Cadets' School in order to make me an officer. That military school has been created for orphans of the war of liberation. I am nine years old and I have neither the strength nor the courage to oppose my father's decision. I therefore become a little soldier at the age of nine.

"Rejecting my painful situation and unable to stand the high walls of the fortress, which sicken me, I find in books the sole means of escape. At the age of 13, I begin to write in order to re-create the world that has been wrenched from me.

"At 17, I write my first collection of stories, *Houria*.

"After 11 years in the Cadets' School and obtaining my 'Bac' [degree], I am sent, in 1975 to the Military Academy to take up the career of an officer in the mechanized infantry. In 1978, freshly promoted to second lieutenant, I join a combat unit deployed at the front.

"1984, the publication of my first works in Algeria and France, respectively *Houria* and *Amen!*.

"1985, I marry Amal Yasmina Khadra Benaboura.

"1988, after six books published under my own name and the slight 'notoriety' that follows, the military hierarchy decide to have me closely watched and my books placed under censorship. Refusing to account to the censors for my writing, I give up literature. I become depressed. My wife suggests that I write under a pseudonym, clandestinely. What to take for a pen name? My wife tells me, 'You have given me your name for life, I give you mine for posterity.' Yasmina Khadra is thus born.

"February 1990, the birth of my son, Mohammed.

"1991, civil war erupts in Algeria. I join the special forces and am engaged in the antiterrorist struggle until the end of my military service in September 2000.

"April 1993, the birth of my daughter Ghizlene.

"1997, *Morituri* comes out in France under the pseudonym Yasmina Khadra. Then it appears in other European countries.

"September 2000, entering the profession of novelist, I quit the army to dedicate myself to literature. I leave Algeria and go, with my wife and children, to Mexico for several months.

"I return to France in January 2001. I am still here."

In 2001, when Khadra revealed his true identity to the press, he disappointed the French literary establishment, which had believed that it had finally found the authentic voice of an Arab woman. According to Stuart Jeffries, writing for the London *Guardian* (June 22, 2005), Khadra's fans were particularly disturbed to discover that he was "an Algerian army officer with three decades of military experience behind him. And not just an army officer, but one who had led a struggle against armed Islamist radicals and who, as a result, faced opprobrium in the French media for being tainted with the blood of civilians killed in brutal oppression by the north African state." Algeria, which had gained its independence from France in 1962, had already suffered through tumultuous decades, when, in the early 1990s, Islamic guerrillas began waging war against the government. It is estimated that from the onset of violence until 2000, when President Abdelaziz Bouteflika pardoned all members of the Islamic

Yasmina Khadra

Salvation Army, nearly 150,000 people were killed in the violence.

First lionized, then despised, Khadra had a hard time in Europe. The International Parliament of Writers (IPW), which had promised to support and protect the writer's family for two years while he worked to resettle outside of Algeria, withdrew its funding. (Representatives from the IPW told the press that it was Khadra who broke off his relationship with the organization.) "There were many misunderstandings because people found it hard to understand a writer who was a soldier," Khadra told Jeffries. "I had to really fight against those who did not appreciate my work because they pigeonholed me as some sort of brute who was responsible for military massacres. In the eight years I led the fight against terrorism, there were no massacres." In response to those among the leftist literati who accused him of having civilian blood on his hands, Khadra published a short memoir *L'Imposture des mots* (which translates as "the deceitful word"), in 2002. "It is about the shock of a man who dreamed of literature from behind the walls of a barracks for nearly 36 years," he told Giles Tremlett for the London *Guardian* (January 3, 2002). "I thought only soldiers liked fighting. I have discovered that intellectuals hit harder and hurt more."

Khadra's work was first translated into English in 2000, when Toby Press released *Les agneaux du Seigneur* (1998) as *In the Name of God*. The novel unfolds in Ghachimat, a small Algerian village that is isolated from the political turmoil of the capital city, Algiers. When a young man proposes marriage to the mayor's daughter and is rejected, he volunteers to join a band of Islamic guerrilla fighters, the *mujahideen*, in Afghanistan in order to escape the village and his embarrassment. He later returns to the village heavily armed and filled with newfound religious fervor, sparking a wave of violence as the residents divide themselves along religious lines. "*In the Name of God* becomes a classic revolutionary tale of perverted ideals and lust for power, property and revenge," Christine Wald-Hopkins wrote for the *Tucson Weekly* (August 17, 2000, on-line). "The traditional is overthrown. Historical artifact is razed in the name of principle. Education is curtailed and civil rights rescinded. The spurned lover turns his personal rejection into political statement; religion sanctions hate crime. The novel is violent and wrenching. But it's also compelling and thought-provoking."

Though *A Quoi revent les loups?* (2000) literally translates as "what do wolves dream about?," its English translation was published simply as *Wolf Dreams* (2003). Nafa Walid, the novel's protagonist, wants to escape his wretched, impoverished life in Algiers. After briefly serving as a chauffeur for a rich, decadent family, Walid becomes enraged over the gap between the elite and the poor and eventually joins the Islamic fundamentalists who are attempting to overthrow the government. "Khadra's portrait of Walid's transformation jumps awkwardly between the spare story-telling style reminiscent of Albert Camus' *The Outsider* to political expose," Rosalie Rayburn wrote for the *Albuquerque Journal* (July 13, 2003), "but his portrait of the religious fervor and thuggish violence that has characterised Algeria over the past decade rings chillingly true."

Morituri, the first in a series of police procedurals that sold well in Europe, was originally published in France in 1997 and finally translated into English in 2003. The Latin title, which translates as "we who are about to die," is a reference to the salute that Roman gladiators were forced to give Caesar before entering the ring. Though ostensibly a detective novel about a police inspector—Brahim Llob, who is tasked with finding the kidnapped daughter of one of the country's most influential power brokers—the book offers a particularly gruesome description of the ravaged Algerian streets that Llob must traverse in his quest. "This writing was a therapy," Khadra told Elaine Ganley for the Dubuque, Iowa, *Telegraph Herald* (March 30, 2003). "It allowed me to stay lucid. It allowed me to shield myself from a torment that wouldn't stop." The author went on to explain to Ganley that *Morituri* had been written in a haze, following an incident on November 1, 1994, in which he saw a group of young boys torn apart by a bomb planted at a cemetery.

"Khadra writes with a vehemence that comes from his memory of a different, more benign and beautiful Algiers that once was and might again be," Paul Skenazy wrote, reviewing *Morituri* for the *Washington Post Book World* (November 23, 2003). "The book rushes forward propelled by that rage. There are beautifully engineered vignettes and stunning, sharp bits of dialogue. Khadra is often able to finesse the prosaic bits of information-gathering and interviews with suspects that hobble less intelligent mystery writers. The harsh brilliance of the prose is quirky, though: Wonderful lines alternate with overly abstract and convoluted baroque phrasings, and the passive voice often disrupts the forward tumble of action. But on the whole this is a remarkable entrance to a world that remains unknown to too many of us." In the *New York Times Book Review* (November 23, 2003), Marilyn Stasio took umbrage with the "overly respectful translation" by David Herman, writing that his inability to temper the "feverish idiom" of the French text has caused the author's "apocalyptic vision of a society" to lose its "righteous political rage, along with its profound sorrow."

Originally published as *Les hirondelles de Kaboul* (2002), *The Swallows of Kabul* is set in Afghanistan and follows two married couples as they suffer under the rule of the Taliban, an Islamic fundamentalist group that held power from 1996 to 2001, dispensing harsh punishments to anyone who violated *sharia*, a strict form of Islamic law. According to Ben Ehrenreich, writing for the *Village Voice* (February 3, 2004), Khadra was not entirely successful at describing this new setting: "To a secularly minded Algerian, perhaps even more than to an American, Afghanistan represents a sort of black hole of religious fanaticism. It was the place where Algerian jihadis went to learn to fight and kill, so it's no surprise that *The Swallows of Kabul* is not about Afghanistan at all. The city Khadra describes, with its palm trees and humidity, more closely resembles North Africa than Central Asia. But it's more a mythic hell than any locatable human geography. Kabul is not a living city but 'a dark antechamber, where the points of reference are obscure; a puritanical ordeal; something latent and unbearable.'" Nonetheless, many critics chose *The Swallows of Kabul* as one of the best novels of 2004, including the editors of the *San Francisco Chronicle* (December 12, 2004). A reviewer for that paper wrote: "Life under the Taliban is a complex nightmare of rigid codes and violence, and its laws take their brutal toll on everyone, especially the story's couples. Disturbing and mesmerizing, the beautifully written *Swallows* puts a human face on the suffering inflicted by the Taliban."

Double Blank (2005) is a translation of another book in the Inspector Llob series, *Double blanc* (1997). In this novel the inspector is assigned to find the murderer of a senior-ranking diplomat, and while pursuing his investigation, he provides the reader with a cross section of Algerian life. "For the many not conversant with current Algerian politics, this will serve as an easy-to-digest guide to life under a military regime constantly threatened by religious extremists," a staff writer noted for *Publishers Weekly* (January 31, 2005).

"Llob, whose Mike Hammer–like comfort level with violence is highly disturbing, is too unattractive a character to engage readers emotionally. The oppressive atmosphere and the unfamiliar location will make it a challenge for this deserving series to find a wide U.S. readership." Paul Skenazy, writing for the *Washington Post* (June 5, 2005), also took note of the novel's deviation from the detective genre: Khadra "wastes little time on the personal pleasantries or detailed descriptive passages that give local color (and expanded page counts) to most detective novels these days. Llob's family, present in *Morituri* in brief asides that offered a semblance of human warmth, are now in hiding, dismissed in a sentence along the way. Jump-cuts move us from scene to scene, eliminating the locating shots that provide backdrop in most books. Instead there are the cunning observations: a prostitute who dresses in a chador and wears nothing underneath, for example. . . . There is nothing user-friendly about Khadra's writing. But if you want to peek into the dark side of a country in dissolution, there's no finer guide."

In *Autumn of the Phantoms* (2006), a translation of *L'Automne des Chimeres* (1998), Inspector Llob once again casts his critical gaze on the corruption and violence of Algeria. The inspector, paralleling the real-life struggles of his creator, has run afoul of the Algerian government for writing a book—also titled *Morituri*—under the pen name Yasmina Khadra. "This narrative doubling, which might seem overly postmodern in another story, deepens the menace hanging over Llob," a staff writer noted for *Publishers Weekly* (December 12, 2005). "Following the funeral of one of Llob's oldest friends, killed by the radical Islamists who are waging war on the Algerian government, Llob lives through bombings, terrorist attacks and waves of threats from superiors who could have him killed without the slightest repercussion. Like an existential novel, Llob's book aims to speak hard truths in simple language, and there's more than a touch of Camus in its bleak view of a society in which power and cruelty are synonymous." Susanna Yager, writing for the London *Sunday Telegraph* (April 30, 2006), acknowledged that the plot of "this brief, brilliantly atmospheric novel," was rather thin—but, she continued, "its picture of a country living under a repressive and corrupt government and the daily threat of terrorist attack is memorable and deeply moving." The most recent installments in the Inspector Llob series, *Le dingue au bistouri* (1999) and *La part du mort* (2004), have yet to be translated into English.

Khadra's *The Attack* is set amid the Israeli-Palestinian conflict. The main character, Amin Jaafari, is a Tel Aviv–based surgeon of Arab descent who has remained relatively apolitical—that is, until his wife dies in a terrorist attack. He is shocked to discover that she is suspected to have been the suicide bomber. Setting out to find the truth, Jaafari tours the Middle East, receiving a first-hand education on the politics of the region. "*The Attack* seems at first to be a conventional page-turner—until you realize the quest is going nowhere but toward the next dead end and Jaafari's next brutal beating," David Gates wrote for *Newsweek* (June 5, 2006). "Finally, the terrorist who recruited his wife explains it to him: she was too contented. . . . Dr. Jaafari concludes that he hasn't 'learned anything redemptive'—and it's the moment when he finally seems human. Khadra isn't in the redemption business: his true subject isn't terrorism, but blindness and ambiguity, which have been around before there were headlines to rip them out of." Kamila Shasmie, writing for the *New Statesman* (July 10, 2006), concurred that while the novel is steeped in current affairs, it is more nuanced than the reader might initially expect: "The characters are not mere mouthpieces—above all else, this is a novel about a man who feels himself betrayed. Amin Jaafari's very human drama is the heart of this thoughtful and affecting work."

The Sirens of Baghdad, the English translation of Khadra's *Les sirènes de Bagdad* (2006), is scheduled for publication in May 2007. It is the tale of a young man from a small Iraqi village who joins the insurgency fighting the 2003 U.S.–led invasion of his country.

—S.Y.

Suggested Reading: (London) *Guardian* (on-line) Jan. 3, 2002, (on-line) June 22, 2005; (New York) *Newsday* D p31 Feb. 15, 2004; *New York Times* E p7 Feb. 17, 2004; *New York Times Book Review* p7 Feb. 29, 2004; *Tucson Weekly* (on-line) Aug. 21, 2000; *Village Voice* p52 Feb. 3, 2004; *Washington Post Book World* p13 Nov. 23, 2003, p13 June 5, 2005

Selected Books in English Translation: *In the Name of God*, 2000; *Morituri*, 2003; *Wolf Dreams*, 2003; *The Swallows of Kabul*, 2004; *Double Blank*, 2005; *The Attack*, 2006; *Autumn of the Phantoms*, 2006; *The Sirens of Baghdad*, 2007

King, Laurie R.

Sep. 19, 1952– Novelist

Laurie R. King has distinguished herself as one of the most popular—and acclaimed—contemporary authors of mystery fiction. Whether she is writing her Sherlock Holmes–inspired Mary Russell series (which finds the retired Holmes sleuthing with a new partner, his gifted young wife, Russell); the police procedurals known as the Kate Martinelli mysteries (about a tough female cop in San Francisco); or one of her evocative stand-alone novels, King is known for suspenseful tales filled with vivid characters and colorful details. To date, King's novels have sold nearly two million copies worldwide and have been published in 18 languages.

Laurie R. King was born in Oakland, California, on September 19, 1952, the second of three children. Her father, Roger, worked a variety of jobs, including stints as a nurseryman, real-estate agent, gas-station attendant, and furniture repairman; he had a penchant for change that often uprooted his family. As King recalled in an autobiographical statement published on her official Web site, "We moved so often when I was young, it wasn't until high school that I entered the same school in September that I'd been in the previous June. By then, I'd more or less given up on the tedious process of making friends, since libraries were always nearby, and books were much better companions anyway. So for most of my childhood, in Santa Cruz and San Jose, California, then the suburbs of Tacoma, Washington, I lived in a community of fictional

individuals—those of Walter Farley and Marguerite Henry and Albert Payson Terhune; Ray Bradbury and Robert Heinlein and Isaac Asimov; Rosemary Sutcliff and Madeleine L'Engle." She concluded, "So as we migrated up and down the West Coast, I was at home, because there were always libraries." King has estimated that she had moved more than 20 times by the time she finished high school.

Despite her interest in reading, King was generally a mediocre student. "High school found me more interested in science fiction than science, reading novels than writing papers," she wrote in her autobiographical statement, "and my lackluster grades hardly encouraged counselors to seek me out with the stimulation of college dreams." She continued her education only because an aunt with whom she was living after high school insisted that she enroll at the local community college. Inspired by a philosophy teacher named Norman Miller, whom she writes, "was the first to suggest that religion was a passion that could permeate all life, a drive like any other, not some ethereal wimpiness," she transferred to the University of California, at Santa Cruz, to major in religious studies. There, she completed a senior thesis on "The Role of the Fool in Western Culture" and earned her degree in 1977. King married Noel Q. King, a faculty member of the religious-studies program, that same year.

The couple spent several years traveling around the globe to such places as England, Australia, New Zealand, South America, and India, whenever Noel King had breaks from teaching at the university. Meanwhile, King returned to her religious studies, concentrating on Old Testament

Courtesy of Random House

Laurie R. King

theology at the Graduate Theology Union, part of the University of California, at Berkeley. After completing a graduate thesis titled "Feminine Aspects of Yahweh," in 1984, she earned her master's degree.

For the next several years of her marriage, King dedicated herself to being a wife, mother, and homemaker. In 1980 she gave birth to a daughter and in 1983, a son. In the early 1980s the couple purchased a crumbling 80-year-old farmhouse on two acres of land, which required King to dedicate much of her time to renovating the home and tending the garden. In 1987, when her son entered preschool, providing her with three free mornings each week, she began to write fiction. "The thing is, in California, everyone's writing a novel," she noted in an interview posted on her Web site, "Or a screenplay, if you're south of Big Sur, which I'm not. . . . Half my husband's students had dense, two-ream novels, generally of an experimental nature, to share with the world. Granted, mine was only a third that long and possessed a rudimentary plot, but still, nobody assumed that a manuscript in the hand was worth a hardback on the shelf." Despite her academic background in religion—or, in a sense, because of it—King found herself well equipped to undertake the process of writing an novel. She explained, "Had I not been so caught up in a subject as basically, well, useless as theology, I might have been employable with my Master's [degree], but at the end of those years, I had two kids, a house that was no longer about to fall down around our ears, a lot of odd skills, and, suddenly, the desire to write fiction."

King's first novel featured a new twist on Sir Arthur Conan Doyle's classic Sherlock Holmes mysteries. She envisioned a young female heroine who would become Holmes's apprentice and, ultimately, his equal in intellect, boldness, and detection skills. As she described in her autobiographical statement, "I sat down with the Waterman fountain pen I had bought on the Oxford high street [in London] the summer before and wrote on a canary pad the words: 'I was fifteen when I met Sherlock Holmes, fifteen years old with my nose in a book as I walked the Sussex Downs, and nearly stepped on him.' And like that, I was a writer." Mary Russell became the protagonist of King's first Holmesian mystery; the author completed the first draft in only 28 days. As she began sending the manuscript regularly to publishers, she also started writing the next book in the series, in which Russell develops from a young girl into a mature woman. (This novel eventually became the third book in the series, *A Letter of Mary*, published in 1997.) When that book was completed, she promptly embarked on another mystery story altogether, this one about Kate Martinelli, a tough female cop in San Francisco who is investigating the murder of three girls.

In about 1989 King decided she could no longer continue the time-consuming process of mailing her manuscripts to publishers. "I realized that I had sufficient energy either to write, or to shop the stuff around, but not both," she noted on her Web site. "That's when I went looking for an agent. . . . I wrote to five agencies in the San Francisco area (New York? Where's that?) and had various responses from each, but Linda Allen was the only agent who liked both Mary Russell and Kate Martinelli without hesitation. I threw myself at her feet." Ultimately, it took nearly two more years for Allen to sell one of King's books to a publisher, St. Martin's Press. When she did, it was not a book in the Mary Russell series, but rather the Kate Martinelli novel, *A Grave Talent* (1993).

In *A Grave Talent* Martinelli and her embittered partner are on the heels of a murderer, after the bodies of three children are found near a reclusive community just outside of San Francisco. Martinelli begins to suspect an eccentric artist with a criminal past who lives in the area. However, the story takes a number of haunting twists before the case is solved. One of the unique aspects of the novel was King's choice to depict Martinelli as a lesbian. "Kate is the perfect example of the writer's cliche that your characters both choose you and write the story," King told Dana Stabenow for *Mystery Writers International* (2002, on-line). "If I'd stopped to think about the effrontery of a straight writing a gay character, I probably would have backed away from it. But I was writing a story about a cop, an outsider in a lot of ways, and Kate just, er, 'came out' that way." *A Grave Talent* was received warmly by both fans and critics of the mystery genre, and King received the prestigious

Edgar Award for best first novel from the Mystery Writers of America, as well as Britain's John Creasey Award.

Although King did not initially conceive the Kate Martinelli mystery to be one in a series, she was prompted by her editor to bring Martinelli back for another book. As she recalled in her autobiographical statement, "A topic I had been pushing around in the back of my mind for some time came into play: What would a holy fool look like in twentieth century America?" (King had some experience with this topic since her undergraduate thesis had explored the role of such characters.) In *To Play the Fool* (1995), Martinelli investigates the murder of a homeless man and his dog in Golden Gate Park. As she studies the case, she focuses on a homeless man everyone calls Brother Erasmus, who communicates only in biblical and literary quotes. Martinelli begins to suspect that Erasmus knows more than he is saying. To uncover the truth of his identity and his past, she elicits the help of the dean of the University of California's Graduate Theological Union and her own lover, Lee, a psychotherapist who had been severely injured at the close of the earlier novel. *To Play the Fool* received widespread critical praise. As Rex E. Klett noted for *Library Journal* (February 1, 1995), "The author presents her homeless characters with honesty and compassion, much in the way she describes the relationship between Kate and her lover or her police partner, Al. A fitting and well-done sequel to the award-winning *A Grave Talent*."

In the next Kate Martinelli novel, *With Child* (1996), the title character's lover, who has been rendered a paraplegic by her injuries, has left her to spend time on an island off the coast of Washington state. Meanwhile, her partner, Al, is getting married, and Martinelli agrees to watch his precocious 12-year-old stepdaughter, Jules, while he and his wife set off on their honeymoon. Martinelli is also busy tracking a serial killer on the loose in the Pacific Northwest. When Jules disappears from a motel near Portland, Martinelli embarks on a desperate search to find the girl, who resembles the killer's other victims. Critics again responded to King's vivid and natural portrayal of the gutsy female detective, as well as her emphasis on broadening the character through several complex new relationships. Dick Adler wrote for the *Chicago Tribune* (January 7, 1996), "Martinelli is the kind of person you'd like to know and talk with over many lunches, a smart and tough woman confident in her lesbian sexuality but feeling the pangs of childlessness, especially since her relationship with her crippled lover is in a state of limbo." A *Publishers Weekly* (December 4, 1995) reviewer opined, "Although readers may connect pieces of the puzzle sooner than Kate, the pleasure of her company and the accelerating suspense preceding the climax make for a compelling read." *With Child* received nominations for the Edgar Award and Britain's Orange Award.

In the next book in the series, *Night Work* (2000), Martinelli and her partner begin investigating a string of unusual murders, in which all of the victims are men who have been formerly accused of physically abusing women or children. In the course of the inquiry, they encounter a group of feminists known as the Ladies of Perpetual Disgruntlement, members of which have been seeking minor acts of revenge against known abusers. Although Martinelli initially sympathizes with the cause, she becomes increasingly alarmed as the murders continue. In the course of the investigation Martinelli explores the topic of goddess worship; the figure of Kali, the Hindu goddess of creation and destruction, figures prominently in the plot. As a reviewer wrote for *Publishers Weekly* (January 17, 2000), "King's ability to turn esoteric religious concepts into key narrative points makes this a highly unusual—and memorable—novel." Nancy McNicol, writing for *Library Journal* (January 2000), affirmed, "King once again gives the reader a superbly structured plot played off a set of intellectually stimulating characters whose bold philosophical stances and varied professional backgrounds result in confident and often unexpected behavior. Fans of the three previous Martinelli books will be gratified to witness the continuing evolution of relationships among the recurring characters while newcomers will easily find their way into this suspenseful tale."

In 2006 King, borrowing a theme from her other series, published *The Art of Detection*, in which Martinelli investigates the murder of a Sherlock Holmes fanatic. A reviewer for *Publishers Weekly* (April 24, 2006, on-line) called the book an "intelligent, satisfying novel of suspense" and concluded, "Fans of both series will be well rewarded." King has attributed her success with the Martinelli books, in large part, to the development of the characters and their relationships with each other. "Any good novel, mystery or otherwise, is a story told on a number of levels," she explained in an interview on her Web site. "The Martinelli books (which aim at being both good and novels) are first of all mysteries—good, entertaining stories. They also follow the development of Kate herself from a strongly defensive person (in *A Grave Talent*) who hides behind a nickname and gives out nothing of herself to others, into a woman able to commit herself to friendship. Around her are woven together the lives of the other series characters, her partner, her lover, her community, and their stories."

The modern-day police procedurals offered King a significant change from the characters and style of her Mary Russell novels, which, in contrast, she composed in first-person, formal British English. As she noted on her Web site, the variety "keeps me from becoming tired of the characters and myself." With the success of *A Grave Talent*, King was able to publish the first book in the Mary Russell series, *The Beekeeper's Apprentice*, in 1994. The book is set in 1915, after the legendary detective Sherlock Holmes, at age 54, has retired to a cottage in the Sussex Downs to keep bees. Although King's assertion of Holmes's age in 1915 met with some scrutiny, she maintained that references in Arthur Conan Doyle's original stories verify the detective's approximate age. As she explained in the essay "A Holmes Chronology," posted on her Web site, the perception that Holmes was an aging detective, well into his middle years, is in fact the result of Sidney Paget's popular drawings of the character for the *Strand Magazine*; secondary literature—written by various literary critics and not by Conan Doyle—about the life of Holmes; and stage and film productions of the stories, in which Holmes is often portrayed by older actors. King noted, "In conclusion, readers familiar with the Holmes canon who encounter the Russell books assume that the author has violently manipulated the chronology for her own purposes, to make a younger Holmes who is hence both more active and more believable as the partner of a young woman. In fact, I have merely restored Holmes to his proper years, and freed him up for a long and healthy middle age."

In addition to her reinterpretation of Holmes's age, King's overall approach to the genre proved unique. In *The Beekeeper's Apprentice* and the following Mary Russell novels, King focuses more on Russell than on Holmes. This, she explained, allowed her to tackle the stories in an original manner, without being bound by the traditional Holmesian canon. "I thought [Holmes] needed a change," she told Stabenow, "of the sort that opened up the aspects of his personality not previously explored during his Baker Street days. Mary Russell is his opposite—young, female, Twentieth Century, feminist, theologian, half American—and yet she is precisely the same in how she sees the world and how she approaches problems. He needed a challenge, and he got one." In addition, by narrating the tales through the lens of Russell's experience, King was able to appeal to the sensibilities of young female readers, who may have found themselves largely absent from the original stories. In her *Washington Post* (February 20, 1994) review of *The Beekeeper's Apprentice*, Pat Dowell opined, "By an act of creative will, King has relieved Holmes of the worst effects of his misogyny and, by so doing, salved the old hurt that comes to every female reader of literature, usually at a very young age, when she realizes with great disappointment that she is excluded by most great authors of adventure from the circle of presumed readers and fellow adventurers: that sinking feeling that 'They didn't mean me.'"

At the start of *The Beekeeper's Apprentice*, the 15-year-old Russell encounters Holmes, who initially mistakes her for a boy, while walking in the countryside near the Sussex Downs. The two strike up a friendship, and the young woman becomes the detective's apprentice, ultimately assisting him in solving the mystery of an American senator's kidnaped daughter. Along the way, King introduces several characters from the original series, including Dr. Watson, whom Russell comes to call "Uncle John," and Holmes's brother Mycroft. The novel was applauded by both fans and critics, who praised King's style and humor, as well as her depiction of Holmes pitted against an intellectual equal. Reviews also acknowledged King's ability to evoke the novel's setting—the British countryside before World War I—with vivid authenticity. *The Beekeeper's Apprentice* was named a notable young-adult book by the American Library Association and was nominated for the Agatha Award for best novel.

At the start of the next Mary Russell mystery, *A Monstrous Regiment of Women* (1995), Russell is one week shy of her 21st birthday, having just completed her studies in theology at the University of Oxford. When she is introduced to Margery Childe, the leader of a women's group known as the New Temple of God (which combines feminism, theology, and social activism) she becomes drawn into the temple's inner circle. After one of the members is murdered, Russell convinces Holmes to assist in locating the dead woman's brother, who had developed a heroin addiction during World War I. King juxtaposes the murder mystery with another suspenseful subplot—that of the deepening affection developing between Russell and Holmes. *A Monstrous Regiment of Women* was hailed as a significant achievement, what Dick Adler, writing for the *Chicago Tribune* (September 3, 1995), called "a book that is as audacious as it is entertaining and moving." He continued, "What gives King's books such a rich and original texture is the character of Mary—totally believable in her own right, a tall and gangling orphan with a restless intellect and a great store of moral and physical courage. And because Mary is the center of the story, Holmes himself becomes more interesting—a dark, roving, refreshingly fallible figure." Many critics also praised King's attention to historical detail, as well as her accurate depiction of several social issues, including the condition of women in 1920s London and the experience of life following World War I. The book earned King the Nero Wolfe Award for best novel.

Set three years later, in 1923, *A Letter of Mary* (1997) finds Russell and Holmes happily settled into married life. Russell is working on an academic paper in theology when an archaeologist friend who has recently returned from Palestine arrives at the couple's Sussex home. With her, she brings a papyrus scroll that was possibly written by Mary Magdalene. (The author of the mysterious letter refers to herself as an apostle of Jesus Christ.) When the archaeologist is suddenly murdered, Russell and Holmes set out to uncover the truth behind the historical scroll. Besides the novel's intriguing investigation, a reviewer for *Publishers*

Weekly (November 18, 1996) found King's real achievement to be "her depiction of the complex relationship between two individualists. Almost 40 years apart, they're fondly indulgent of one another's idiosyncrasies and share intellectual camaraderie, companionable humor and sexual attraction. . . . If you can't imagine the misogynist Sherlock Holmes sharing domestic bliss, this novel will make you a believer."

In *The Moor* (1998), King brings Russell and Holmes to Dartmoor, the scene of Arthur Conan Doyle's most famous Sherlock Holmes mystery, *The Hound of the Baskervilles* (1902). The only full-length Holmes novel that he ever wrote, it follows Holmes and his partner, Watson, as they trace a legendary demon dog said to be roaming the moors near Devon. In King's updated tale, Holmes finds himself on the moors once again, tracking the Hound of the Baskervilles 20 years later with his wife, after a man is found dead beside the footprints of a large dog. As the couple work their way through the moors, they interview a number of colorful characters, including a mysterious American who has taken ownership of Baskervilles Hall. *The Moor* was widely celebrated as an inventive and suspenseful tale, despite being what one *Publishers Weekly* (November 17, 1997) reviewer called "hobbled by the slow coalescence of its subplots." Nevertheless, the reviewer added, "King, always a fluent writer, is a wonder at combining the original 'Hound' tale with a real person (Baring-Gould) and modern themes (land fraud) into a new, captivating story." The reviewer was referring to Sabine Baring-Gould (1834–1924), a writer and scholar who actually lived in the area and who figures in the plot of the novel. In her laudatory review for *Booklist* (January 1–15, 1998), Emily Melton wrote, "The dark, foreboding Devonshire moors form a perfect backdrop for this mesmerizing tale. Add King's devilishly clever plot and eccentric characters, her ability to achieve a perfect balance between serious mystery and lighthearted humor, and the charm with which she develops the captivating relationship between Holmes and Russell, and the result is a superbly rich read that would please Doyle himself."

The fifth book in the Mary Russell series, *O Jerusalem* (1999), is set in 1919 and therefore takes place chronologically just after the first. Here, Russell is a 19-year-old Oxford student who remains Holmes's apprentice, partner, and platonic soul mate, though she has not yet become his wife. When Holmes is stalked and nearly killed by a dangerous female adversary, he and Russell take refuge in Palestine, which has recently come under British rule. (Throughout the novel, Russell remains disguised as a young man.) Once in Palestine, the duo are met by two Arab guides, Ali and Mahmoud, who lead them on a journey through the desert. By chance, they encounter two seemingly unrelated murders, which ultimately set them on the trail of a dangerous foe intent on destroying Jerusalem. Despite what several critics

found to be a weak plot, most reviews praised King's decision to resurrect the romantic tensions of the first Mary Russell novels. Writing for the *Washington Post* (July 18, 1999), Maureen Corrigan observed that the book "returns to the fascinating, shadowy, psychological terrain of [Russell and Holmes's] courtship. King enjoys playing around with boundaries and encouraging her characters to transgress them." Dick Adler wrote for the *Chicago Tribune* (June 6, 1999), "It's an inspired move on King's part, because it also gives her the chance to do what she does better than virtually anyone else in the field: connect us, by thousands of details of language, custom, history and sensual impressions, to an alien environment. . . . King puts us into each scene so quickly and completely that her narrative flow never falters."

In the novel *Justice Hall* (2002), the characters of Ali and Mahmoud reemerge in a surprising twist. At the novel's start, Russell and Holmes have just returned to Sussex following their adventures in Dartmoor, only to learn that the two Bedouin spies with whom they traveled in Palestine are actually English aristocrats: Ali is Alistair Hughenfort, and Mahmoud is his cousin Marsh, the seventh Duke of Beauville. However, Marsh has little interest in being a duke and hopes to return to Palestine after handing his estate over to the next rightful heir. Russell and Holmes are called in to investigate the shadowy Hughenfort line. King used the opportunity to explore the conceits of the British aristocracy. Despite the premise that the two clever sleuths had not previously recognized Ali and Mahmoud as British—a precept that some critics found implausible—most reviews praised the story as another captivating mystery.

In *The Game* (2004), Russell and Holmes are sent by Mycroft to India, to search for a missing British spy, who turns out to be Kimball O'Hara, the protagonist of the famous Rudyard Kipling novel *Kim*. A reviewer for *Publishers Weekly* (January 26, 2004, on-line) wrote, "If for some Mary Russell is too perfect a character to be as enduringly compelling as Holmes, all readers will appreciate the grace and intelligence of King's writing in this exotic masala of a book." Russell and Holmes made their next appearance in *Locked Rooms* (2005). The book finds the pair returning to San Francisco to settle Russell's family estate. "King's re-creation of San Francisco, especially the backstory during the devastating 1906 earthquake, is superb, and it's a pleasure to see the unusually competent Russell struggling with her own psyche," a reviewer wrote for *Publishers Weekly* (April 25, 2005). "The plot may be a bit thin, but the narrative has real momentum, the characters are engaging and the prose, as always, is intelligent, evocative and graceful." "King not only marvelously evokes the bygone days of 1920s San Francisco but she also adds layer after complex layer to this believably rendered relationship," Sarah Weinman wrote for the Passaic County, New

Jersey, *Herald News* (July 31, 2005). "A light touch, well-handled flashbacks and excellent pacing make *Locked Rooms* a thoroughly entertaining read."

In addition to the books in her two distinct series, King has written three stand-alone mysteries that have allowed her to bring new protagonists to the page. In the first, *A Darker Place* (1999), Anne Waverly, a professor of religious studies at a small university, agrees to infiltrate a religious cult to gather information for the FBI. Since the death of her husband and young child in a commune's mass suicide 18 years earlier, Waverly has frequently worked as an undercover infiltrator of potentially dangerous cults. In the process of her investigation, Waverly finds herself confronting her own painful past, as well as the group's distorted beliefs. The novel received generally high praise from critics, who applauded King's genuine characters and well-researched exploration of life inside a cult. As Mary Stasio observed in the *New York Times* (March 7, 1999), "King's solid research into alternative religious sects makes the desert commune feel like a real place, while her taut pacing insures that an air of menace hangs over the strange rituals that go on there. But the strongest appeal of the story lies in its superb characters, especially the children who become Anne's charges." Adding to the praise of King's characters, Nancy McNicol for *Library Journal* (January 1999) opined, "King's theological background serves her well in this stand-alone thriller. Anne Waverly is competent and believable in each of her dual roles, and her vulnerability makes her an accessible narrator. King's facility for creating one-of-a-kind characters continues to expand."

In her next thriller, *Folly* (2001), King presents another troubled protagonist, the 52-year-old Rae Newborn, an artist who suffers from severe clinical depression. Newborn has endured the loss of her second husband and young child in a car accident, as well as a brutal attack by muggers in the driveway of her California home. To escape her dire circumstances, she decides to move to the San Juan Islands off of Washington state, where she has recently inherited a 150-acre island. There, she sets about rebuilding "Folly," a home—now burned to its foundation—that her great-uncle Desmond built in the 1920s. Desmond had suffered his own demons after witnessing numerous horrors during World War I. Shortly after completing the structure, he vanished and was never heard from again. In the course of constructing her own sanctuary—a process that King recounts in great detail—Newborn uncovers and solves a murder that puts her own life at risk. *Folly* received generally mixed reviews. Although critics again praised King's skill at crafting an intriguing mystery, they lamented aspects of the plot. As one reviewer noted for *Publishers Weekly* (January 15, 2001), "While King skillfully portrays psychological illness, the book's sheer complexity

of detail is overwhelming. There's more than the average mind can keep straight, and the passages about rebuilding Folly, especially, have a tendency to bog down." A critic for the *Toronto Star* (March 11, 2001) found that "The story seems more a work of engineering than of imagination, and the characters come only in blacks and whites with little shading." Despite such reviews King received the Macavity Award from Mystery Readers International for the book.

In her next nonseries mystery, *Keeping Watch* (2003), King centers the story around Allen Carmichael, who appeared as a minor character in *Folly*. A middle-aged man haunted by his experiences in Vietnam, Carmichael works outside the law, abducting abused children and placing them in good homes; he is actually part of an extensive underground network dedicated to the cause. In what is to be his last rescue, Carmichael "kidnaps" Jamie O'Connell, a 12-year-old computer fanatic who has suffered physical and psychological abuse at the hands of his father, a well-known entrepreneur. As Carmichael uncovers the details of Jamie's childhood, he finds the case may not be what it seemed on the surface. *Keeping Watch* received near unanimous praise from critics, who found the story powerful and well written. One reviewer for *Kirkus Reviews* (December 1, 2002) called the book "a gripping, intricately plotted psychological thriller, full of subtle twists." Writing for *Booklist* (January 1–15, 2003), GraceAnne A. DeCandido opined, "Some stories scour the soul. This one is full of things that hurt: scary, horrible, humiliating things. It is also an exquisitely wrought exploration of the many different kinds of love. . . . Along the way, King, in her excoriating, gorgeous prose, ignites the jungles of Vietnam, the sly worlds of computer gaming, life in the Pacific Northwest, and the kind of offhand devotion brothers can give each other. King works layers within layers like carved ivory spheres and makes a tale that holds one taut on every page."

In 2004 King ventured away from the mystery genre to publish *Califia's Daughters*, set in the near future. Using the pen name Leigh Richards, King describes a postapocalyptic period in which women outnumber men—who are prized mainly for their reproductive abilities—by a dozen to one. A. M. Dellamonica wrote in a review for the SciFi Channel Web site, "Complex and satisfying, *Califia's Daughters* delivers both as an action-adventure novel and a triumph of world-building." On her Web site King explained why she had experimented with a new genre: "I have a confession to make: My first love was science fiction. Before Dorothy L. Sayers and Josephine Tey entered my life, my heart belonged to Isaac (Asimov), Robert (Heinlein), and Theodore (Sturgeon). Other worlds, a grand vision of the universe, the furthest possibilities of humanity—what's not to adore?"

In 1997 King was given an honorary doctorate from the Church Divinity School of the Pacific. She received the Gail Rich Award (an arts prize) the following year. In addition, her short story "Paleta Man," collected in *Irreconcilable Differences* (2003), edited by Lia Matera, was nominated for an Edgar Award. King's short stories have appeared in *Thrilling Tales* (2003), *Crime Through Time* (2003), and the literary magazine *McSweeney's*. She has also written the introduction to a recent edition of Arthur Conan Doyle's *Hound of the Baskervilles*, published by Random House in their Modern Library Classics series, and a chapter on writing historical mysteries in *Writing Mysteries* (2002), a guide by the Mystery Writers of America, edited by Sue Grafton and Jan Burke.

Laurie R. King resides in northern California, with her husband, Noel, and her two children, Zoe and Nathanael.

Despite her prolific output, King once noted in an interview, as posted on her Web site, that the hardest part of writing a novel often is mustering the confidence. "Not that confidence is ever truly attained," she explained, "I am always both exhilarated and terrified when I set off on a hundred-thousand-word novel, not knowing how I'm going to get to the end. More often than not, I reach the 120 page mark and think, I'm not going to be able to do it this time. It is a work of trust to push forward, to have faith that the back of the mind will carry on through the darkness and into the light. . . . Perhaps by the fiftieth book, it might get easier."

—K.D.

Suggested Reading: *Chicago Tribune* Books p4 Sep. 3, 1995, Books p6 Jan. 7, 1996, Books p8 Feb. 7, 1999, Books p3 June 6, 1999; *Kirkus Reviews* p1,721 Dec. 1, 2002; Laurie R. King's Web site; *Mystery Readers International* (online), 2002; *Publishers Weekly* p55 Dec. 4, 1995, p64 Nov. 18, 1996, p56 Nov. 17, 1997, p46 Jan. 17, 2000, p55 Jan. 15, 2001; *Washington Post* X p5 July 18, 1999

Selected Works: Mary Russell novels—*The Beekeeper's Apprentice*, 1994; *A Monstrous Regiment of Women*, 1995; *A Letter of Mary*, 1997; *The Moor*, 1998; *O Jerusalem*, 1999; *Justice Hall*, 2002; *The Game*, 2004; *Locked Rooms*, 2005; Kate Martinelli novels—*A Grave Talent*, 1993; *To Play the Fool*, 1995; *With Child*, 1996; *Night Work*, 2000; *The Art of Detection*, 2006; other fiction—*A Darker Place*, 1999; *Folly*, 2001; *Keeping Watch*, 2003; *Califia's Daughters*, 2004

Kinsella, Sophie

Dec. 12, 1969(?)– Novelist

The British author widely known as Sophie Kinsella has written a series of books typifying the genre that has come to be called "chick lit"—novels about single women navigating their 20s and 30s in a frenzy of romantic, professional, and financial misadventures. Inspired by the hugely successful *Bridget Jones's Diary*, published by Helen Fielding in 1996, the ubiquitous, pastel-colored books are witty, lighthearted romps that often take place in London or New York. Kinsella's popular Shopaholic series chronicles the travails of Becky Bloomwood, a financial journalist with a devastating weakness for designer accessories. Kinsella herself was once employed, in her 20s, as a financial journalist, a fact that is noted in her promotional biographies, which also cheekily note her impeccable credit. These biographical sketches do not normally reveal that Sophie Kinsella is actually a pen name for the author otherwise known as Madeleine Wickham, who has written seven novels in a style vastly different from the pithy, girlish irreverence of the Shopaholic series. "When I had the idea for Shopaholic, I wanted it to be my secret project," Wickham—or Kinsella, as she is generally referred to in the press—told Karyn Miller for the London *Mail on Sunday* (May 4, 2003). "Writing under a different name meant that it didn't matter if the book was a disaster—I could always go back to my other books. And this book was to be different from my Madeleine Wickham books—lighter, funnier and younger. . . ."

Wickham's foray into chick lit proved immensely successful; her first title, *The Secret Dreamworld of a Shopaholic* (2000; published in 2001 in the U.S. as *Confessions of a Shopaholic*), tapped into the psyches of her target audience. "I get hundreds of letters from female fans, asking me if I could have possibly read their diaries or peeked in their closets," she told Waheeda Harris for the *Vancouver Sun* (April 17, 2004). The positive response to the flighty fashionista was so strong that Kinsella continued the series with *Shopaholic Abroad* (2001; published in the U.S. in 2002 as *Shopaholic Takes Manhattan*); *Shopaholic Ties the Knot* (2003); *Shopaholic and Sister* (2004); and *Shopaholic and Baby* (2007).

Though the genre is often criticized for its relatively predictable plots and heroines—young women fretting over lovers and examining handbags with the same breathless zeal—Kinsella does not mind that the Shopaholic series is not considered serious literature. "I am proud to be a 'chick lit' author," she told Miller. "I like the silly, chatty humour. I'm not trying to win the Booker Prize—I want to entertain people."

Sophie Kinsella was born Madeleine Wickham in London, England, to academic parents. (Some sources list the date of her birth as December 12,

Robin Matthews/Courtesy Transworld Publishers

Sophie Kinsella

1969.) She and her two younger sisters grew up on Putney Hill, near Wimbledon, and as a child, she studied music and dance. She was also an avid reader. "When I was 10, I was addicted to Noel Streatfeild [a British writer]," she told a reporter for the London *Daily Telegraph* (July 19, 2003). "*Ballet Shoes*, *White Boots* [both part of a series known as the Shoe Books], and other tales of middle-class families, in which one child tends to be a promising ballerina and generally has a sibling who is a prodigy at acting or music. Talents are taken very seriously and the greatest prize is a professional engagement, which often helps the family finances. As a stage-struck dance pupil, these stories were my idea of heaven."

Kinsella was a student at the Sherborne School for Girls, a well-regarded private school in Dorset. Later, she attended the University of Oxford, studying philosophy, politics, and economics. Upon graduating, Kinsella went to work for a financial publication called *Pensions World*, writing "the most boring articles in the world," as she recalled to a reporter for Bookreporter.com (November 14, 2003). After that, she wrote for the magazine *Resident Abroad*. Her heart was not in her financial writing, however—"I was never very good at facts!" she told a reporter for the Canadian *National Post* (April 3, 2004)—and she felt dissatisfied with her journalistic career. Eventually, she decided to try her hand at fiction. "I used to commute to work on the train and read endless paperbacks, and I'd find myself thinking, 'I could do that,'" she recalled to the *National Post* reporter. She found fiction "very natural, much more so than financial reports," although she kept her new endeavor hidden from her co-workers. Her

first book, *The Tennis Party*, was written mainly during her lunch breaks, after work, and on the weekends. It was published in 1995, and, in her mid-20s, she became a first-time, best-selling author.

The Tennis Party "was well-marketed," Kinsella told Rita Zekas for the *Toronto Star* (March 22, 2003), explaining her debut novel's unpredicted success. "It was released in Wimbledon and it was all about playing tennis, drinking Pimms, and sleeping with other people's husbands." Wickham went on to write other novels under her own name: *A Desirable Residence* (1996), *Swimming Pool Sunday* (1997), *The Gatecrasher* (1998), *The Wedding Girl* (1999), *Cocktails for Three* (2000), and *Sleeping Arrangements* (2001). Writing for the London *Guardian* (March 29, 2003), Nicholas Clee called the novels "astute social comedies, with something of the flavour of the plays of Alan Ayckbourn." Though she enjoyed the success of her books, Wickham decided she wanted to try her hand at a different, lighter kind of writing. As she often recounts in interviews, inspiration hit on a day that she opened a crippling credit-card statement that caught her off guard. That moment was the seed for her first Shopaholic book. After completing *The Secret Dreamworld of a Shopaholic*, Wickham sent it to her unwitting publisher under the pseudonym Sophie Kinsella. (Sophie is her middle name, and Kinsella is her mother's maiden name.)

The Secret Dreamworld of a Shopaholic is the story of Becky Bloomwood, a 20-something financial journalist and out-of-control spendthrift. Hounded by her credit-card company and her bank—both of which are owed unspeakable sums of money by the flighty heroine—Becky conjures up increasingly off-the-wall excuses to explain her inability to pay back her debt. As she invents crisis after creative crisis, she continues to spend money she doesn't have on clothes, shoes, and a flurry of accessories. Kinsella meant the book to be funny, blithe, and breezy—nothing like the novels she penned under her real name. It was, at first, a project she took on for fun. "I had no idea it would even be published let alone become a success," she told a reporter for the *Ottawa Citizen* (March 23, 2003). "I used to sit in my room, typing away, laughing at my own jokes and saying to myself, 'Yeah, I find this funny, but is anyone else going to find this funny? Does anyone else see the world like this?'" According to the sales figures, many people identified with Becky Bloomwood. The book was a best-seller in both Britain and the U.S., where it was published the next year under the title *Confessions of a Shopaholic*.

The book's success prompted Kinsella to write a sequel, *Shopaholic Abroad*, which transplanted Becky's misadventures to the shopping mecca of New York City. Highlights from the book include a scene in which Becky exercises a nearly ulcer-inducing act of willpower when she manages to leave a shoe store with a pair of (admittedly pricey) lilac sandals—without bowing to the temptation of purchasing the same pair of shoes in a color described as clementine. Like the first book written under the Kinsella name, *Shopaholic Abroad* became a best-seller in England and in the U.S., where it was published the following year with the title *Shopaholic Takes Manhattan*.

Kinsella's third book in the series, *Shopaholic Ties the Knot*, takes place once again in New York, where Becky is working, appropriately, as a personal shopper. Its plot centers around Becky's wedding to the millionaire she had met and fallen in love with in the previous book—a charmer by the name of Luke, whose mother is an icy socialite intent on making her son's wedding a lavish extravaganza at the legendary Plaza Hotel. When Becky realizes that her parents back in London are planning a comparatively modest hometown affair, she tries to manage attending both, with chaotic results. "Sure it's silly. Sure, it's pretty unbelievable," Shelley Boettcher wrote for the *Calgary Herald* (March 22, 2003). "But it's the perfect novel for a couch potato on a lazy Sunday afternoon." Kinsella had fun "researching" the book; her methodology, she told interviewers, included visits to the couture shop of the wedding-gown designer Vera Wang to try on dresses.

Shopaholic Ties the Knot was intended to be the final book in the Shopaholic series. Kinsella's next novel was a stand-alone comedy called *Can You Keep a Secret?* (2003). The book begins as the heroine, Emma Corrigan, a jittery marketing assistant, becomes so nervous on a turbulent flight to London that she spills her most personal secrets (including her dress size) to a total stranger—a handsome man who, she discovers the following day, is actually the shadowy owner of her company. Hannah Stephenson, writing for the U.K. Newsquest Regional Press (June 11, 2003), called *Can You Keep a Secret?* a "witty, clever read." In 2004 Kinsella sold the movie rights to *Can You Keep a Secret?* (The film version, which will reportedly star Kate Hudson, has not yet been released.)

Despite her original intention, Kinsella did not shelve her Shopaholic series for long. She released a fourth Shopaholic novel in 2004. In it Becky discovers, to her grave dismay, that she has a long-lost sister who hates to shop. The book, titled *Shopaholic and Sister*, was already ranked number six on the *New York Times* best-seller list when it was published, based solely on preorders from eager fans. She then took another break from the series to write *The Undomestic Goddess* (2005), a comic look at a female attorney who, after a disastrous day at the office, decides to take a job as a housekeeper—despite not knowing how to cook or iron.

Kinsella's latest book, *Shopaholic and Baby* (2007), finds Becky Bloomwood pregnant and anxious to acquire the best strollers and most fashionable infant clothing. When asked why she thinks so many people can relate to her bumbling heroine, Kinsella responds, as she told a reporter for Teenreads.com (November 2003), "I think there is a bit of Becky in all of us. People love to laugh at their own flaws—and who hasn't bought some totally useless item because it was half-price?" While she recognizes that Becky is "in some ways shallow and silly," Kinsella maintains that deep down, Becky Bloomwood is a good person, "incredibly warm, loving, and feisty—and always resourceful." By contrast, the critic Lynn Crosbie, who bashes the genre as "Jane Austen by way of multiple lobotomies," called Becky an "empty husk" and one of chick lit's many "pathological narcissists, whose lives are putridly executed as extensions of their unwarranted self-love," in an article for the *Toronto Star* (April 28, 2002).

Kinsella has not published a Madeleine Wickham book since she began her Shopaholic venture. As Karyn Miller wrote, "These days, Madeleine Wickham has been virtually killed off, so that the author can devote herself to her chick-lit books." Nevertheless, in 2004 her publisher reprinted several of Wickham's books, hoping to capitalize upon some of the success of her later chick-lit efforts. In publishing circles, consequently, Kinsella straddles both identities; newspaper articles often refer to her using both her real and adopted name. Kinsella has no problem reconciling this duality. "What other job would allow you to reinvent yourself, take a new name, do things totally differently and not burn any bridges?" she asked Miller.

Kinsella contributed to the short-story collection *Girls Night In* (2004), the proceeds of which went to War Child, an international humanitarian-aid charity. She currently lives in London with her husband, Henry, a high-school teacher she met at Oxford. They have two sons, Freddy and Hugo.

—L.S.

Suggested Reading: *London (Ontario) Free Press* D p10 Apr. 14, 2004; *Ottawa Citizen* C p10 Mar. 23, 2003; Sophie Kinsella's Official Web site; *Toronto Star* D p15, Apr. 28, 2002

Selected Books: as Madeleine Wickham—*The Tennis Party*, 1995; *A Desirable Residence*, 1996; *Swimming Pool Sunday*, 1997; *The Gatecrasher*, 1998; *The Wedding Girl*, 1999; *Cocktails for Three*, 2000; *Sleeping Arrangements*, 2001; as Sophie Kinsella—*The Secret Dreamworld of a Shopaholic*, 2000; *Shopaholic Abroad*, 2001; *Shopaholic Ties the Knot*, 2002; *Can You Keep a Secret?*, 2003; *Shopaholic and Sister*, 2004; *The Undomestic Goddess*, 2005; *Shopaholic and Baby*, 2007

Kirby, David

Nov. 29, 1944– Poet; critic

The poet David Kirby is the author of *The Opera Lover* (1977), *Sarah Bernhardt's Leg* (1983), *Saving the Young Men of Vienna* (1987), *Big-Leg Music* (1995), *My Twentieth Century* (1999), *The House of Blue Light* (2000), *The Travelling Library* (2001), and *The Ha-Ha* (2003), collections of poetry praised for their humor and vivid narrations in an era when narrative poetry is unfashionable. Kirby the poet coexists with—and complements—Kirby the critic, whose works include *American Fiction to 1900: A Guide to Information Sources* (1975), *America's Hive of Honey: Or, Foreign Influences on American Fiction through Henry James: Essays and Bibliographies* (1980), *The Sun Rises in the Evening: Monism and Quietism in Western Culture* (1982), *A Dictionary of Contemporary Thought* (1984), *Plural World: An Interdisciplinary Glossary of Contemporary Thought* (1984), *Mark Strand and the Poet's Place in Contemporary Culture* (1990), *Boyishness in American Culture: The Charms and Dangers of Social Immaturity* (1991), *Portrait of a Lady and The Turn of the Screw: Henry James and Melodrama* (1991), *What Is a Book?* (2002), and *Ultra Talk* (2007). His "method has a singular kind of candor and appeal," Graham Christian wrote for *Library Journal* (May 15, 1999).

David Kirby was born on November 29, 1944 in Baton Rouge, Louisiana, to Josie and Thomas Austin Kirby. His father chaired the English department at Louisiana State University. According to his poem "At the Grave of Harold Goldstein," Kirby was "yanked summarily / from the cookies-and-milk milieu of Baton Rouge High / and set down without preamble" at Catholic High School, as punishment for adolescent misdeeds. He attended Louisiana State University, receiving his bachelor's degree, in 1966, and then earned his doctorate from Johns Hopkins University, in Baltimore, Maryland, in 1969. That same year Kirby got a job teaching at Florida State University, in Tallahassee. He remained there throughout his academic career, advancing to become the W. Guy McKenzie professor of English. Kirby is married to the poet Barbara Hamby, who often appears as a character in his poetry.

In 2004 Kirby contributed the following statement to *World Authors 2000–2005*:

"I began to write poetry when I began to write: my first poem (lost to the ages, regrettably) was a five-year-old's attempt to placate his angry mother. At the same time, we were always big readers in my family, so that all through my school days, I found it as natural to go from reading to writing as I did from sleeping to waking, say. Indeed, both acts seemed like natural functions to me, as necessary as any other.

"All that changed when I went away to Johns Hopkins University to pursue the doctorate. At Hopkins, there were two separate programs, the Ph.D. in English curriculum (in which I was enrolled) and the Writing Seminars, which granted an M.F.A. Ne'er the twain did meet: the English students thought of the Writing students as a garretful of absinthe-swilling bohemians, and the Writing students thought of the English students as an ant heap of over-analytical drones. They were right, too: in those days, forecasters were predicting a shortfall of humanities Ph.D.s, so my doctoral program was a three-year accelerated version, meaning that I and my classmates read English nonstop for 36 months. With all that critical analysis going on, there was barely time for food and sleep, much less poetry.

"The year that I got my doctorate, the forecasters discovered that they had been wrong and that there were plenty of humanities Ph.D.s after all. So the three-year program was abandoned, but not before I had written and defended a dissertation on Henry James, been hooded by my major professor at graduation, and accepted a position at Florida State University, on whose campus I appeared in 1969, brimming with the worldly wisdom that only a 24-year-old possesses. I rather quickly mined my dissertation for five articles and developed other scholarly projects, but then, to my surprise and joy, the poetry began to return. My heroes have always been those who are both writers and critics, including John Dryden, Matthew Arnold, Henry James, and Virginia Woolf, to name just a few. I am aware that I am better known as a poet than a critic, partly because of the ease of thinking 'he's a poet' rather than 'he's a critic of 19th-century U.S. literature with a particular interest in the post-Civil War novel.' But I really do divide my time almost equally between analyzing literature and trying to create it. By trying to make myself the best American writer I can be as well as the best analyst of American writing, I devise for me, my readers, and my students a mental and emotional life that strives to be like American culture itself, i.e., action-packed.

"A few years ago, I got tired of reading (and writing) the 2"x4" I-looked-out-my-window-and-here's-what-I-saw poem and decided to let the poems be as long as they wanted to and say whatever they needed to say. In doing so, I was influenced by the poet David Antin but also by monologuist Spalding Gray and cartoonist Stan Mack, he whose *Village Voice* cartoons about New York street life were always accompanied by the tag line, 'Guaranteed: All Dialogue Reported Verbatim.' Mainly, of course, I was trying to do what Whitman does and offer a first-person speaker as a proxy for all humanity. I called these new poems my 'memory poems,' though I recently learned that Byron had used the same term for some of his autobiographical works. Also, I decided to counter the looseness of the poems' contents with a sawtoothed stanza I was pretty proud of until I opened the *Norton Anthology* one day to teach Marianne Moore to a roomful of sophomores and blushed when I realized she had beat me to it. Ah, well, no new thing under the sun, as Ecclesiastes says.

"The first memory poems (there were four in my 1995 book *Big-Leg Music*) were more or less journalistic, reporting events chronologically. Then the texture of the poems became more complex, almost Talmudic in character as 'unrelated' events began to crowd in and commentary piled upon commentary. My next collection, *My Twentieth Century*, consists of 20 memory poems, the first 18 of which are of the older, journalistic type and the last two of which are these newer, busier memory poems. The title poem itself is of this newer type; accepting it and another for *Northwest Review*, poetry editor John Witte wrote: 'What a pleasure to accept two of your sly, energetic, ribald, wonderful poems. . . . Many, many thanks. We were swept away.' And reviewing an anthology I was in, Judith Kitchens referred to 'David Kirby's hilarious roundabout forays into his own mind,' a humbling reminder that someone else can usually describe what you're trying to do better than you can.

"What's next? Who knows. . . . Something different, surely: 10 years ago I had no idea that what I'd be doing now would be as radically dissimilar to what I was doing then as it is. One reads and one writes and one listens to other people and one's work evolves, half-consciously and half through persistence and luck. I really feel everyone should be off writing his or her own poetry, but anyone interested in this project should know I have a web site, which I'll update as changes occur."

When Kirby's collection of poems, *Saving the Young Men of Vienna* won the 1987 Brittingham Prize for poetry, Mona Van Duyn, who announced the winner, called Kirby a "generous poet," Peter Klappert reported for the *Southern Review* (Winter 2000). Van Duyn continued: "In 'The Peaceable Kingdom' of a David Kirby poem the framing of an identifiable voice and a strong, encompassing closure brings and binds together the paradoxical, the funny, the sad, the messy, the precious in aesthetic concord. His palette is brighter and braver for its inclusion of the often-scanted hues of statements, idea, vivacity of language and an interest in beings beyond the self." Like Walt Whitman, the famed 19th-century American poet, Kirby writes poems—in both the first and third person—that are grounded in the notion of inclusiveness, something perhaps most pointedly illustrated by his diction, which encompasses everything from the academic to the colloquial.

Klappert illustrated that quality of Kirby's work through a brief discussion of "The Death of Fred Snodgrass," a poem from *Sarah Bernhardt's Leg* that reads, as Klappert quotes it, "San Francisco, / April 6, 1974. / It says here / in the *Chronicle*: /

'Fred Snodgrass, / who muffed / an easy fly ball / that helped / to cost / The New York Giants / the 1912 / World Series, / died yesterday / at age 86.' / F**k you, / Fred Snodgrass. / Some things / we never forget." Klappert goes on to write: "A colloquial, conversational voice ('It says here,' 'Some things / we never forget') reads a well-made newspaper sentence full of baseball language and responds with apt slang—in this case, an obscenity. Is the speaker reading aloud? The last four lines certainly sound like it, but the first two mimic the dateline of a short news item: 'San Francisco, / April 6, 1974.' So it's a kind of report. But a report on what?" Observing that Kirby's real interest lies not in Snodgrass but in people's inability to forget having failed at things that are usually easy to accomplish, Klappert concluded, "the poem is a report on Homo sapiens, and it's the product of notable intelligence, even wisdom, though it masquerades as a Bronx cheer."

The qualities of Kirby's work on which both Klappert and Van Duyn comment have reemerged throughout Kirby's career, despite the difference that can be found among his books. Meg Harlan, writing an assessment of *The House of Blue Light* for the *New York Times Book Review* (November 12 2000), thus observed, "The loquacious style of Kirby's poetry can sometimes resemble the riffs of a brainy stand-up comedian. In the 18 long poems in [this volume], which span anywhere from three to six pages, tragicomical trains of thought run at a frenetic pace. . . . Kirby's structure—stanzas of long, alternatively indented lines that easily accommodate the cadences of conversation—contributes to the sense of a casual artistry at work. Yet in relating seemingly autobiographical, spryly digressives sagas about work, marriage, travel and even the joys of mediocre movies, Kirby makes the narrative poem . . . amusing, lively and relevant enough for contemporary tastes. While his language is at times gratingly prosaic . . . , Kirby's strings of lyric vignettes are often inspired." Commenting on the same book, Jamey Hecht wrote for *American Book Review* (July/August 2001), "I can't help but enjoy [Kirby] with a light heart, disarmed, refreshed, and reminded of how wide the field of poetry has become now that modernism is over." Ann K. Van Buren noted for *Library Journal* (September 1, 2000), "Kirby lifts the heavy veil of seriousness that poetry often wears."

Similarly, in *The Ha-Ha*, a book of poems about traveling with his wife to such places as Florence, Paris, and Hawaii, "Kirby reveals his fondness for irony, presenting us with numerous situations in which opposites blend, where the beautiful and the horrible and the comic and the serious exist simultaneously. This strategy increases the poetry's emotional impact considerably, reminding us that nothing ever is simple or clean; that the good, the bad and the ugly usually are entwined around each other like the noodles in a bowl of spaghetti," Stephen B. Armstrong wrote for *Battle Creek (Michigan) Enquirer* (December 7,

2006). Andy Brumer, more pointedly remarking upon Kirby's mixture of high and low culture, remarked for the *New York Times* (December 14, 2003): "The stream-of-consciousness and jazz-based rhythms of Kerouac and Ginsberg meet the surreal, philosophical musings of Wallace Stevens, with an occasional dose of cathartic confessionalism à la Robert Lowell. In 'Americans in Italy,' Kirby paints an empathetic portrait of his fellow tourists and muses upon the postmodern conjunction of high and popular culture: 'I am passed by dozens of my countrymen and women, / most of whom are dressed as though they're here / not to look at the Botticellis and the Ghirlandaios / but to play city-league softball or mow the lawn.' Artless lines like these ring clear as a bell. A few others, however, succumb to a self-satisfied sense of their own cleverness."

Kirby's criticism shares with his poetry the same mixture of elite and popular discourse, something perceived by Floyd Skloot, who wrote for the *Harvard Review* (Spring 2003) that in *What Is a Book?*, Kirby "has a flair for combining scholarship, earthy wisdom and humor in his work." Skloot concluded: "His essays intend to get at the heart of Why and How we write or read. But . . . some things just don't lend themselves to analysis and definition. As a result, Kirby often finds himself stymied at exactly the point when he is attempting to be clearest. . . . Looking at criticism and at writing itself, he keeps coming up against 'the thing you can't explain.' *What Is a Book?* ends up being unable to answer most of the questions it asks. But it remains a provocative and entertaining pastiche in which Kirby offers many keen, resonant observations." While in *Ultra Talk*, which contains essays on topics as diverse as Johnny Cash, Shakespeare, St. Teresa of Avila, and Emily Dickinson, a reviewer wrote for *Publishers Weekly* (January 22, 2007), "Kirby's general thesis is that the best art is art that's appreciated by both the elite and the general public over a long period of time, and in his academic essays about Shakespeare and Whitman, he demonstrates this bridging with an effortless combination of anecdote and quotation."

Kirby, whose most recent book is *The House on Boulevard St.* (2007), has also written biographies—*Grace King* (1980) and *Herman Melville* (1993); writing manuals—*Diving for Poems* (1985) and *Writing Poetry: Where Poems Come from and How to Write Them* (1989); and two children's books with A. Woodman—*The Cows Are Going to Paris* (1991) and *The Bear Who Came to Stay* (1994).

—S.Y./A.R.

Suggested Reading: *American Book Review* p29 Jul./Aug. 2001; *Battle Creek (Michigan) Enquirer* D p7 Dec. 7, 2006; *Choice* p1,136 Apr. 1984; *Library Journal* p377 Feb. 15, 1984, p200 Sep. 1, 1985, p99 May 15, 1999; *New York Times Book Review* p26 Nov. 12, 2000; *Parnassus: Poetry in Review* p124+ 1998; *Southern Review* p196+ Winter 2000, p34+ Winter 2001

Selected Books: poetry—*The Opera Lover*, 1977; *Sarah Bernhardt's Leg*, 1983; *Saving the Young Men of Vienna*, 1987; *Big-Leg Music*, 1995; *My Twentieth Century*, 1999; *The House of Blue Light*, 2000; *The Travelling Library*, 2001; *The Ha-Ha*, 2003; *The House on Boulevard St.: New and Selected Poems*, 2007; critical studies— *American Fiction to 1900: A Guide to Information Sources*, 1975; *America's Hive of Honey: Or, Foreign Influences on American Fiction through Henry James: Essays and Bibliographies*, 1980; *The Sun Rises in the Evening: Monism and Quietism in Western Culture*, 1982; *A Dictionary of Contemporary Thought*, 1984; *Plural World: An Interdisciplinary Glossary of Contemporary Thought*, 1984; *Mark Strand and the Poet's Place in Contemporary Culture*, 1990; *Boyishness in American Culture: The Charms and Dangers of Social Immaturity*, 1991; *Portrait of a Lady and The Turn of the Screw: Henry James and Melodrama*, 1991; *What Is a Book?*, 2002; *Ultra Talk*, 2007; biographies—*Grace King*, 1980; *Herman Melville*, 1993; writing manuals—*Diving for Poems*, 1985; *Writing Poetry: Where Poems Come from and How to Write Them*, 1989; juvenile literature—*The Cows Are Going to Paris* (with A. Woodman, illustrated by C. L. Demarest), 1991; *The Bear Who Came to Stay* (with A. Woodman, illustrated by H. Stevenson), 1994

Kirshenbaum, Binnie

1964(?)– Novelist; short-story writer

Binnie Kirshenbaum's short stories and novels evoke the modern-day world of Jewish New York, with its distinctive dialect, culture, and sensibilities. She has become particularly noted for creating quirky, complex, and supremely memorable female characters. Discussing the arc of Kirshenbaum's career, Frances Taliaferro wrote for the *Washington Post* (February 8, 2004), "Her gift for neurotic comedy has deepened into a more humane generosity; she hasn't become just another fast, funny urban smartmouth." Kirshenbaum's last novel, *An Almost Perfect Moment* (2004), elicited numerous critical accolades and cemented Kirshenbaum's preeminent status among an emerging generation of Jewish writers.

Born in about 1964, Binnie Kirshenbaum was raised in Bronxville, New York. Having chosen to live in a neighborhood that was not primarily Jewish, her family rarely practiced their religion. "As much as my parents tried to be good parents, I came to really resent how much they insisted upon assimilation," she told Judith Solomon for the *Jerusalem Report* (August 23, 2004). At 20 Kirshenbaum moved to New York City to attend Columbia University, renting an apartment a few doors down from Darech Amuno, a landmarked synagogue. "My Jewish consciousness developed when I came to New York," she told Solomon. "I began to see the richness of the heritage, to see that there were just these incredibly wonderful people who were Jewish, who were brilliant and exciting and smart and talented. Instead of feeling embarrassed that I was this princess, I began to feel, hey, you know, this is really terrific. We come from a remarkable people. Little by little it just grew and grew and grew." After earning her bachelor's degree in 1980, she attended Brooklyn College, from which she earned an M.F.A. She is currently a professor at Columbia.

The protagonist of Kirshenbaum's first book, a young-adult novel titled *Short Subject* (1989), is Audrey, a girl estranged from her peers and floundering at school. To escape reality she immerses herself in 1940s gangster films. Soon Audrey is talking and acting like the characters she sees in the movies, and eventually she runs afoul of the authorities when her imitations begin to involve actual stealing. "The story's resolution is too easy. . . and the joke of the tough-talking little loser who escapes into celluloid dreams wears a litle thin," Hazel Rochman wrote for *Booklist* (November 15, 1989). "Still, it's a good joke, and first-novelist Kirshenbaum creates a believable world, even if it sometimes seems more like the New York of early Woody Allen and Philip Roth than that of today." Rochman concluded, "The first-person narrative is comic and vulnerable, so that while we laugh and sympathize with Audrey, we also realize that she's not seeing it all, and that her dream roles increase in flamboyance as her problems become more desperate." Judie Porter offered a similarly mixed review for *School Library Journal* (September 1989), remarking, "The book is well written and contains some unique qualities; however, in the final analysis, poor Audrey suffers too much from being the victim of a movie buff's nostalgia trip."

Kirshenbaum's first short-story collection, *Married Life and Other True Adventures* (1990), included several previously published works and was described by Penny Kaganoff for *Publishers Weekly* (April 6, 1990) as "astute, mildly zany, and often wickedly funny." An eclectic array of characters people the collection, including a woman who marries in order to get health insurance and a husband and wife who trek to Eastern Europe in order to preserve their faltering marriage.

Kirshenbaum's first adult novel, *On Mermaid Avenue* (1992), details the exploits of its narrator, Monarose, and her best friend, Edie, "two determinedly kooky New York women," as Charles Solomon described them for the *Los Angeles Times* (April 10, 1994). Edie and Mona, who frequent New York's Coney Island amusement park, choose poverty over jobs, concluding, "We can't hold down a career and pursue happiness at the same time," as quoted by Laurie Muchnick for *New York Newsday* (July 25, 1993). Solomon found *On Mermaid Avenue* wanting, opining that, "as is often the case with regional novels, it doesn't travel well," and that Edie "emerges as less a free spirit than an irresponsible clod whose high jinks include vandalism and breaking and entering." Muchnick offered a decidedly different take on the work, commenting, "Kirshenbaum's writing is swift and witty, and she has created an enchantingly concrete, if slightly surreal, fictional world." Muchnick concluded, "Like cotton candy, *On Mermaid Avenue* is sticky and sweet with lots of pizzazz and very little nutritional value to weight it down."

The protagonist of *A Disturbance in One Place* (1994), Kirshenbaum's next novel, carries on two extramarital affairs simultaneously—while also pursuing a third. Already involved with an artist and a university professor, the nameless narrator believes that her unconquered new flame might be her soul mate. In typical Kirshenbaum fashion, *A Disturbance in One Place* is highly comic, yet it is also "a dark and powerful look at a troubled spirit," as a *Publishers Weekly* (February 27, 1995) reviewer observed. Evelin Sullivan, writing for the *Review of Contemporary Fiction* (Fall 1995), concurred with this assessment, stating that the book's "look at the wounds of a solitary pilgrim is close and unflinching, sad, disturbing, and often very funny. The result is a compelling, highly intelligent and profoundly moving work."

Kirshenbaum's second collection of short fiction, entitled *History on a Personal Note* (1995), contains 16 stories in which "belonging—in a family, a community or a culture—is an underlying theme," as Michele Leber noted for *Library Journal* (April 15, 1995). The compilation's title piece and several others center on the relationship between two friends—a New York Jew and a southerner—and examine such varied topics as the reunification of Germany, the Kennedy family, and sitcoms. Jacqueline Carey, writing for the *New York Times Book Review* (July 2, 1995), opined, "Most of the stories emphasize ethnicity and current events with mixed results. . . . Ms. Kirshenbaum seems to want to write in the Grace Paley mode, but when a Paley Italian or a Paley Jew talks about the 'coloreds,' there is no mistaking the author's attitude toward those remarks—or, despite it, her compassion for the character who is speaking. Politics in its broadest sense is an integral part of many of her characters' lives; in Ms. Kirshenbaum's stories, by contrast, we mostly get headlines. And although her prose is fluid and inviting, [Kirshenbaum] never comes close to the poetic heights of her master. Then again, who does?"

Pure Poetry (2000), Kirshenbaum's next novel, is a poetry manual of sorts, with each chapter bearing the name of a poetic device that is then illuminated in the narrative that follows. The novel's main character is a marginally famous poet named Lila Moscowitz who is renowned for her profane (yet structurally traditional) verse. Moscowitz is suffering from a profound case of writer's block. Her personal life is in shambles: she quarrels with her family, fears leaving her apartment, and is still struggling to get over her recently remarried ex-husband, Max, a German blood relative of the Nazi war criminal Albert Speer. Sarah Ferguson, writing for the *New York Times Book Review* (March 26, 2000), disliked Kirshenbaum's use of poetic terms to structure each chapter, complaining that "the device quickly deteriorates into a 'Where's Waldo?' game that will appeal only to the most determined readers." Ferguson continued, "Kirshenbaum's prose style is fluid, and promising flashes of her dry humor occasionally light up the story. For the most part, though, *Pure Poetry* is anything but." Barbara Fisher, writing for the *Boston Globe* (March 26, 2000), contradicted Ferguson's assessment in her review, stating "This novel is a deeply satisfying marriage of form and content. And also a very funny, smart, and moving story."

Hester Rosenfeld, the protagonist of Kirshenbaum's next book, *Hester Among the Ruins* (2002), is the daughter of German Jews who fled to the U.S. following the rise of the Nazis. In order to better understand the Holocaust, Hester, a historian by profession, travels to Munich, where she begins a torrid affair with Heinrich Falk, a German history professor. Of the relationship, Hester muses, "Only destiny could think up an attraction this intense and this perverse," as quoted by Katharine Weber for the *New York Times Book Review* (May 12, 2002). Weber characterized the work as "a sly and very black comedy. . . . The truth has been present on every page of this complex and painfully funny novel: there is no forgiveness, no forgetting." Writing for the *New York Times* (February 8, 2002), Richard Eder described *Hester Among the Ruins* as an "enticing, brainy and dark novel about one of the entangling enigmas of modern history," adding that "Ms. Kirshenbaum's comedy has fizz and bite. She handles interrogation, passionate love, her two characters and what they seem to represent with disconcerting sleight of hand."

Kirshenbaum "mixes biblical lore with Brooklyn culture in her latest novel [*An Almost Perfect Moment*], a tragicomic tale of mah-jongg, thwarted love and the mysteries of faith in 1970s Canarsie," a reviewer for *Publishers Weekly* (January 26, 2004) wrote. The focal point of the story is Valentine Kessler, an attractive Jewish teenager who, after noting a resemblance between herself and a depiction of the Virgin Mary, strives to emulate the New Testament figure. Other singular characters abound in *An Almost Perfect*

Moment, including Valentine's obese mother and her mah-jongg partners; John Wosileski, a sallow teacher who develops a romantic attachment to Valentine; and Ms. Clarke, a fellow teacher who possesses a comely figure offset by an acne-ravaged face and a secret longing for Mr. Wosileski. After an unsatisfactory tryst with Wosileski, Valentine, although technically a virgin, becomes pregnant. "What makes the novel fun is Kirshenbaum's breezy writing style and her shrewd observations about human nature," Thrity Umrigar observed for the *Boston Globe* (April 18, 2004). "She can sting you with a line that captures completely John's plodding sense of failure. And she can leave you chuckling at her description of the daily games of mah-jongg that Valentine's mother, the 273-pound Miriam Kessler, plays with her three Jewish girl friends." Nevertheless, Umrigar continued, "the novel's greatest strength is the knowing, affectionate look back that Kirshenbaum casts at Jewish life in the Brooklyn of the 1970s." In a similarly positive review, Frances Taliaferro stated, "The real wonder of *An Almost Perfect Moment* is that, halfway into it, you've begun to care about Kirshenbaum's characters. They're deeply, even ludicrously flawed, but they're not figures of fun because they all carry the existential burden of loneliness and the fear that 'in time it would mutate into something worse than loneliness: the surrender to it.'"

In 1996 *Granta* magazine named Kirshenbaum one of America's best young novelists. Among her other accolades are awards from *Today's First*, a public-television program, and the *San Francisco Review of Books*. She is the recipient of a Goodman Writing Award and a New York Foundation for the Arts fellowship. She currently lives in New York City with her husband and is working on her next novel, which is to be called "Greater Than Love."

—P.B.M.

Suggested Reading: *Booklist* p652 Nov. 15, 1989; *Boston Globe* C p4 Mar. 26, 2000, C p3 Feb. 10, 2002, E p7 Apr. 18, 2004; Columbia University Web site; *Library Journal* p118 Apr. 15, 1995; *Los Angeles Times* R p7 Mar. 21, 2004; New York State Writers Institute Web site; *New York Times* E p41 Feb. 8, 2002; *New York Times Book Review* p12 July 2, 1995, p23 Mar. 26, 2000, p20 May 12, 2002, p14 Feb. 15, 2004; *Publishers Weekly* p229 Jan. 26, 2004; *School Library Journal* p250 Sep. 1989; *Washington Post* T p6 Feb. 8, 2004

Selected Books: *Short Subject*, 1989; *Married Life and Other True Adventures*, 1990; *On Mermaid Avenue*, 1992; *A Disturbance in One Place*, 1994; *History on a Personal Note*, 1995; *Pure Poetry*, 2000; *Hester Among the Ruins*, 2002; *An Almost Perfect Moment*, 2004

Knight, Stephen

1960– Poet; novelist; critic

Stephen Knight has published a novel, *Mr. Schnitzel* (2000), and three collections of verse: *Flowering Limbs* (1993), *The Sandfields Baudelaire* (1996), and *Dream City Cinema* (1996); he has also written a book of children's verse, *Sardines, and Other Poems* (2004). In 1987 he won a major prize dedicated to young British poets, the Eric Gregory Award from the British Society of Authors, and five years later he took the top spot in the National Poetry Competition, sponsored by Britain's Poetry Society, after having twice come in as a runner-up. Similarly short-listed two times for the T. S. Eliot Prize for Poetry, Knight won the Book of the Year Award from the Arts Council of Wales, in 2001, for *Mr. Schnitzel*. He has also gained a following among readers of the *Times Literary Supplement* and other large-circulation publications in which his poems, as well as his reviews of fiction and verse, often appear. Knight views the remembered trials of adolescence and the troubles of urban living through a unique lens, crafting poems that are "effective in terms of comic invention and the languid atmosphere of dread they conjure," as Tim Dooley wrote for the *Times Literary Supplement* (January 7, 1994). Robert Potts, writing for the London *Guardian* (August 5, 2000), called him "one of Britain's best, if undervalued, poets."

Stephen Knight wrote the following statement for *World Authors 2000–2005* before the publication of *Mr. Schnitzel* and *Sardines*:

"I was born in Swansea, south Wales in 1960 and began writing at sixteen, soon after my family moved closer to the sea. My earliest attempts at poetry sprouted from a long-haired adolescence of morose, clifftop walks and awkward silences at home. Pretty standard fare, I should say. The gawkiness has gone, but water seeps into my writing to this day.

"I read English at Jesus College, Oxford, and, after a few years adrift, attended the Bristol Old Vic Theatre School. Since 1987, I have worked sporadically as a theatre director, first at the Thorndike Theatre in Leatherhead, Surrey, and latterly as a freelance. My poems began appearing in magazines and anthologies in 1983, though my first book—*Flowering Limbs*—did not appear for another 10 years. I review poetry and fiction for the *Times Literary Supplement*, tutor for the University of Glamorgan's MPhil in Writing, and do whatever else it takes to make ends meet.

"I no longer live in Wales though I still regard the country as my imaginative home. To many Welsh speakers, a monoglot like me is as good as English, though as far as my English neighbours are concerned I am unmistakably Welsh. A writer could do worse than live in this kind of no man's land. The poems I have written in a phonetic Swansea accent—gathered in *The Sandfields Baudelaire*—are glancing references to this condition.

"My taste for quotidian surrealism owes as much to a boyhood love of Marvel and DC comics as it does to my later enjoyment of writers (Swift, Kafka, etc) whose perspectives are, in all senses, funny. I have found the germs of poems in images of the dugong—a creature once said to have been mistaken for a mermaid—the memory of monstrous faces in the curtains that hung in my bedroom when I was small, or a 1980s news report about the trade in human organs. Lately, the more bizarre elements of my writing have faded, a change which has coincided with a move towards prose and a forthcoming novel, 'Mr. Schnitzel.'

"Displacement, surfaces and a weak purchase on solid ground figure in my poems, which may have something to do with being the Welsh son of an Austrian mother, the source of a not unpleasant sense of separateness throughout my childhood. The rented rooms I lived in during my twenties were also mines of poetic material. I have no idea why.

"While I can suggest origins, the outcomes of poems are (for me) necessarily vague. I wouldn't bother to travel if I knew the destination beforehand, and the day I fully understand my reasons for writing is the day I stop altogether."

Being from Wales has meant that Knight's work is often overshadowed by the most famous Welsh poet of the 20th century, Dylan Thomas, who also hailed from Knight's hometown. "Growing up in Swansea, I did everything I could not to be influenced by Dylan Thomas's writing," Knight told Rebecca Hansell for the *South Wales Evening Post* (October 20, 2001). "My poems are very different from his. I wanted to be recognised as a poet in my own right, rather than just covering old ground." That recognition began to come fairly early in his career, particularly when his poem "The Mermaid Tank" won him the National Poetry Competition. His first book, *Flowering Limbs*, soon followed and was warmly received by the British poetry establishment; Robert Potts called it "an impressive, appropriately surreal account of adolescence." In an earlier article for the London *Guardian* (January 16, 1997), Potts praised the versatility Knight demonstrated in *Dream City Cinema*: "Whether in villanelle, sonnet, or freer (yet faultlessly cadenced) forms, Knight makes his bleak, fantastical situations utterly compelling." Describing the book as "a thematically unified paean to decay and marginality" and "song-like, brilliantly musical," Potts concluded that it was "impossible to recommend this book too strongly." Neither the chapbook *The Sandfields Baudelaire* nor *Sardines, and Other Poems* were widely reviewed.

For *Mr. Schnitzel* Knight drew on another aspect of his background, his mother's Austrian upbringing and his own visits to that country when he was young. The book is divided into seven sections, each one relating a fairy tale told to the main character, Stephen, by his father, known as Mr. Schnitzel. Each of those stories is then extensively annotated by Stephen, who puts them in the context of his family's dynamics. "Some of the material [in *Mr. Schnitzel*] is autobiographical, but there's also some fiction blended in," Knight told Hansell. "A lot of my readers just assume it's all true because it reads like a memoir, which it isn't. Even my mother was confused. When she read it, she kept apologising because she couldn't remember events that hadn't happened!"

Knight's innovative storytelling method and careful writing won him strong praise from critics. Fellow novelist Patricia Duncker named *Mr. Schnitzel* among the best books of 2001 in a canvass of prominent writers conducted for *New Statesman* (December 3, 2001); the novel, Duncker wrote, was "magnificent" and "made me roar and weep in equal measure." In a critique for the London *Times* (July 29, 2000), Michael Arditti observed: "While whimsy may be the keynote of the stories, the foot-notes present a far bleaker picture of Stephen's parents' unhappy marriage. Their incompatibility, manifested most dramatically when the family is away on these holidays, becomes increasingly apparent when they return to their everyday lives at home. The contrast between the highly coloured fiction and the sombre commentary also creates a potent image for the disparity between childhood fantasy and the harsh reality of the adult world." Maggie O'Farrell, writing for the London *Observer* (July 23, 2000), also emphasized the footnotes, which she called "often surreal and tangential, reflecting the complex and impenetrable currents of connections that any family group can build up. . . . Reading a book in this way is more of a challenge than it seems. You can't decide whether to interrupt the fairytale to follow the footnote or read it through and then go back. I experimented with both, and the result is much the same—a layered, slightly blurred but curiously satisfying narrative. In revealing the real-life parallels and explanations for the father's tales, it manages to expose that alchemical process of how fact turns into fantasy and then into fiction."

Knight lives in London. A veteran teacher, he has held positions at such institutions as the University of Glamorgan, in South Wales, and Goldsmiths College, part of the University of London. Suzi Feay surveyed poets about their income for the London *Independent on Sunday* (March 7, 2004) and wrote that "Knight puts his poetry income at a rather precise 42 per cent of his total; of that, 9 per cent comes from book sales." Knight also told Feay that at that time he was unable to write poetry because of his teaching commitments: "I am currently overseeing the work of 33 postgraduate students at three universities. This entails reading a quantity of their writing (mostly novels-in-progress and short stories) every day. The last thing I want to do when that's done is go and write a poem. At the moment, it would feel like an indulgence. The money is negligible and who wants to read it anyway?"

—S.Y.

Suggested Reading: British Council Web site; (London) *Guardian* p5 Jan. 13, 1993, T p16 Jan. 16, 1997, Saturday Pages p9 Aug. 5, 2000; (London) *Independent on Sunday* Features p16+ Mar. 7, 2004; (London) *Observer* p12 July 23, 2000; (London) *Times* July 29, 2000; *South Wales Evening Post* p21 Oct. 20, 2001; *Times Literary Supplement* p18 Jan. 7, 1994

Selected Books: poetry—*Flowering Limbs*, 1993; *The Sandfields Baudelaire*, 1996; *Dream City Cinema*, 1996; fiction—*Mr. Schnitzel*, 2000; children's verse—*Sardines, and Other Poems*, 2004

Krüger, Michael

(KROO-ger)

Dec. 9, 1943– Poet; novelist; editor

The German poet, novelist, and editor Michael Krüger has been compared to such authors as Milan Kundera, Franz Kafka, and Samuel Beckett, but his admirers have always mentioned his unique ludic gifts, as well as his thematic interest in the power of art. Rather than being a benign source of pleasure, art in Krüger's work is almost a force of nature, sometimes invigorating and sometimes crippling the protagonists of many of his novels, including *Das Ende des Romans* (1990), translated by Ewald Osers as *The End of the Novel* (1992); *Der Mann in Turm* (1991), translated by A. Leslie Willson as *The Man in the Tower* (1993); and *Die Cellospielerin* (2000), translated by Andrew Shields as *The Cello Player* (2004). In *Himmelfarb* (1993)—published in English in 1994, under the same title and again translated by Willson—the protagonist is a social scientist rather than an artist, but he is his own creation, perhaps a work of art. Art also figures largely in Krüger's poetry, the form in which Germans first came to know his work. His books of verse include *Diderots Katze* (1978), translated into English by Richard Dove as *Diderot's Cat* (1994); *Brief nach Hause* (which can be translated as "letter home," 1993); and *Nachts, unter Bäumen* (1996), which Dove translated as *At Night, Beneath Trees* (1998), a volume that also contained *Brief nach Hause*. David Scrase, reviewing *Nachts, unter Bäumen* for *World Literature Today* (Winter 1997), called the book "deeply satisfying" and remarked: "Krüger's poetic writing has progressed over a period of a quarter of a century from deeply philosophical dialogues to more lyrical musings on the problematic relationship of nature and civilization. . . . City and country, the indoors and outdoors, art and life—all is appropriate in Krüger's poems." Eileen Battersby, reviewing Krüger's collection of short prose pieces *Aus dem Leben eines Erfolgsschriftstellers* (1998), translated by Karen Leeder as *Scenes from the Life of a Best-Selling Author* (2002), wrote for the *Irish Times* (November 9, 2002): "If there is a message among the insights [in this book] it could be that art may not hold the answers to life, it does however offer a more attractive alternative."

Michael Krüger was born on December 9, 1943 in Wittgendorf, a tiny village in the German state of Saxony Anhalt, which became part of East Germany in 1949. Krüger, however, grew up in West Berlin. He attained the German degree *abitur*, which lies somewhere between an American high-school diploma and an associate's degree, and later attended the Free University of Berlin, studying, by most accounts, philosophy and literature. Between 1962 and 1965 he worked as a bookseller in London, England, and in 1968, having returned to Germany, he co-founded, with the publisher, biographer, and outspoken cultural critic Klaus Wagenbach, an annual literary review called *Tintenfisch*. That same year he began to work in Munich as an editor for the publishing house Carl Hanser Verlag, one of Germany's most prestigious literary publishers; he became a director for the company in 1986 and is currently a managing partner.

In 1976 Krüger started the literary magazine *Akzente* (which translates as "accents") and released his first book, a poetry collection entitled *Reginapoly*. Krüger's next book of verse was *Diderot's Cat*, which William Scammell, writing for the London *Independent* (February 20, 1994) judged "enjoyable"; rather than being a self-involved poet, Krüger is instead, Scammell argued, "a cool, puzzled archaeologist of our (and Germany's) strange times."

Michael T. O'Pecko, reviewing *At Night, Beneath Trees* for *Library Journal* (March 1, 1998), called the volume "beautifully translated" and "highly interesting." O'Pecko added: "Krüger has an unusual gift for expressing evanescent feelings and subtle ideas in deceptively simple, richly detailed, and realistic language." Krüger's other books of poetry include *Lidas Taschenmuseum* (1981), *Aus der Ebene* (1982), *Wiederholungen* (1983), *Die Dronte* (1985), *Idyllen und Illusionen* (1989), *Wettervorhersage* (1998), and *Kurz vor dem Gewitter* (2003). Krüger's poetry has brought him, among other commendations, the 1986 Peter Huchel Prize and the 1994 Ernst Meister Prize.

The End of the Novel, Krüger's first book to appear in English, is the story of a writer who revises his novel, a bildungsroman that he originally dreamed would be the great European novel, until almost nothing of it is left. The writer's decision to have his principal character commit suicide forces him "to abandon," as Roger Moss noted for the London *Independent* (January 25, 1992), "whole chunks of discussion on ethics, philosophy, the place of sin, of knowledge and of pessimism in modern life; until finally yielding up the dismembered manuscript to a stranger whom he never sees again, and stepping free into the sunlit world 'as if I were the only being on earth.'" Moss added: "Krüger seems much less committed to the silencing of literary noise than his title might suggest. The way he holds on to sex and satire—those familiar devices for keeping desire and value-judgement alive in language—suggests the same. . . . Krüger's writing doesn't have the courage of its lack of convictions. Rather than being refreshed by the loss of the imagination in the modern world, he seems to regret it, and with it a good deal of the challenge of modernity." By contrast, Sven Birkerts, writing for *New York Newsday* (March 22, 1992), argued that an important motif in contemporary thought is "that of ending, of finishing up" and that writers "from [Samuel] Beckett on have been exploring the dimensions of the frayed hole that was left when God and the promises of coherent—if not transcendent—meaning vanished." Krüger's "artful touch," Birkerts felt, allowed him to give life to those weighty concerns without having the book collapse into ponderousness: Krüger "is able to view his hyperserious hero through a comic lens. He is repeatedly the foil of inscrutable characters who step forth from nowhere to hurl their peculiar selves at him. When the waitress at the inn [where Krüger goes every evening] lays claim to him, moving in to occupy his cottage and his bed, he responds with a Buster Keatonish unflappability. Like some character in Beckett, he neither helps nor hinders the woman."

The eponymous man in *The Man in the Tower* is a German artist who lives both in a real tower in France and in the metaphoric ivory tower of the refined artist—a person who, faced with a creative impasse in his painting, passes the time by translating Dante. While his life is uneventful in many ways, the painter, who is never named, does become involved in a murder investigation and an affair, raging all the while against contemporary society. "You spend the whole novel waiting for something to happen," Leslie Wilson wrote for the London *Independent* (June 6, 1993). Diana Hinds, also writing for the London *Independent* (May 29, 1993), made a similar point, calling the novel "a curious story in which things fail to happen." For Hinds, however, the seeming pointlessness of the narrative is offset by "the pleasures of Michael Krüger's crisp, clean prose, well translated here by Leslie Willson, and his tone of detached amusement." Wilson, however, disagreed about the quality of Willson's translation, writing: "The messy structure is the writer's own, but the occasional burst of confused language appears to be over-literalism on the part of the translator (no relation of mine)." Patrick McGrath, in his critique of the novel for the *New York Times Book Review* (April 4, 1993), quoted the narrator's argument that each work of art "should be a systemization of vanished beauty, an obituary . . . and afterward, a powerful, abiding silence should prevail." That silence, McGrath contended, is "not the silence of death and aridity. It is, rather, the emptiness out of which new artistic life can spring. Sure enough, in a jolting, ill-lighted train compartment moving through a bare landscape shortly before Christmas, the painter returns creatively to life. And so this brilliant dark squib of a novel comes to its close, on a note, albeit ironic, of affirmation."

The narrator of *Himmelfarb* is an aging German ethnologist and travel writer named Richard, who has constructed an enviable career for himself— but only by plagiarizing the unpublished work of a man he had left for dead some 50 years earlier, Leo Himmelfarb. A German Jew on the run from the Nazis, Himmelfarb had guided Richard through the Brazilian rain forests early in World War II, and his writings gave evidence of an intellectual adventurousness far beyond Richard's capacity. Decades later, when Himmelfarb writes to Richard, drawing his attention to the injustice he has committed, Richard is suddenly forced to examine his past life. "In conception," a reviewer for *Publishers Weekly* (July 11, 1994) noted, "Krüger's mendacious bookworm has clear echoes of Beckett and [Saul] Bellow, but the wry philosophical tone that colors his reflections on his odd life lived in history's margins is quite distinctive. A tale rooted in the reveries of so stunted and unlikable a personality won't be to all tastes; but those who prefer the whimper to the bang will find much to admire in Krüger's deft shadings." A reviewer for the London *Sunday Times* (October 9, 1994) called it a "precise, elegant story, as resonant and challenging as many novels twice its length," one that "touches on a great deal, not least the obsessive, irritable nature of old age, and beautifully re-creates the feverish atmosphere of the jungle." In 1996 *Himmelfarb* was awarded the Prix Médicis Etranger, a French literary prize given annually to an outstanding foreign work.

Krüger's comedic skills were in high relief in his send-up of the literary world, *Scenes from the Life of a Best-Selling Author*. Nicholas Lezard noted for the London *Guardian* (September 27, 2003) that *Scenes* "is a catalogue of deadpan oddities: the father who dies of idleness; the grandfather, with a library dedicated to books about nothing, who sits by a door which itself opens on nothing; or the uncle who hopes to prove that the history of the world is due to misprints. Meanwhile, everyone is terrorised by a gang of monstrous aunts, who live in perpetual outrage and anti-intellectual despair." The pieces in this collection, Lezard concluded, "have the unmistakable tang of real inspiration, of weird, audacious comic genius. Krüger's style is a high-risk enterprise, not so much following in

Kafka's footsteps as matching his pace on the other, more comic side of the street. That he is able to work in the area of the fable, treating reality as a canvas that can be scribbled all over rather than something to be dutifully reported, shows his nerve." While emphasizing Krüger's comic skills, Eileen Battersby also noted that *Scenes* contains "several moments of deep feeling" and argued, "No matter how odd the stories appear, they always manage to stay just this side of the surreal."

The eponymous cellist of *The Cello Player* is a young Hungarian named Judit who comes from Budapest to Munich in order to live and study at the conservatory. In Munich she lives with the narrator, a German composer whom she calls Gyorgy. Formerly her mother's lover and possibly Judit's father, the composer made a small fortune writing music for television shows but now is struggling to produce an opera about Osip Mandelstam, the great Russian poet who died in a Stalinist purge. Judit frustrates Gyorgy's attempts to complete the opera and, bringing in an assortment of strange guests, all but takes over his home. A reviewer for *Publishers Weekly* (December 1, 2003) observed that this "ironic, subtly crafted story shows how domestic give-and-take can make the simple negotiations of living add up to an 'incomprehensible life.'" Robert Schwarz, for *World Literature Today* (Winter 2001), maintained that Krüger needed to be the "lucid stylist" he is "in order to portray an artist torn between a deeply felt inner mandate . . . and the siren call of material success." *The Cello Player*, he concluded, "is a nuanced novel with overtones of a wry humor. What lingers in the mind is the botched passion of a human being bullied by the reality of his ego." Noah Isenberg, writing for the *New York Times Book Review* (May 16, 2004), praised the translation for retaining "much of the original idiom, cadence and narrative flow of Krüger's lively German prose" and argued that the book's settings and Krüger's storytelling techniques meant that "*The Cello Player* has perhaps less in common with other postwar German fiction than with the writing of Milan Kundera or Vladimir Nabokov, both of whose romantic exposition and fine ironic touches resonate here." For Carol Herman, writing for the *Washington Times* (January 4, 2004), *The Cello Player* is not just "a story of domestic intrigue and disappointment," it is also "an allegory of the ravages of Eastern Europe after WWII. The poems of Osip Mandelstam . . . reveal postwar suffering even as they reveal the narrator's inner turmoil."

In 2002 Krüger published *Das falsche Haus* (which can be translated as "the wrong house"). Gregory H. Wolf, writing for *World Literature Today* (July–September 2003), described the book as "an intriguing novella" told by a reporter who "exhibits humor, biting sarcasm, social criticism and a general exasperation with bourgeois society and the poseurs he encounters every day." Wolf added: "Krüger continually piques the reader's interest by compounding confusing situations with even more confusing and mysterious episodes, none of which are ever resolved. In this way, Krüger delivers a postmodern text in which closure and constant dissonance are the norm." An English-language edition of Krüger's most recent novel, *Die Turiner Komödie* (which can be translated as "the Turin comedy," 2005), is reported to be forthcoming.

In 2003 Krüger provided the introductory text for a monograph on the German photographer Candida Höfer. The following year a partial portrait of Krüger—more precisely, a lithographic rendering of his eyes—and a somewhat opaque text related to him were published as part of the book *Unrecounted*, a collaborative undertaking by the German émigrés Jan Peter Tripp, an artist, and W. G. Sebald, a writer. (Sebald died in a car crash three years before the book was published, putting Tripp in the position of making some of the pairings between his partial portraits and Sebald's texts.) Reviewing *Unrecounted* for the *New Republic* (July 25, 2005), Michael Andre Bernstein quoted the text set under Krüger's eyes: "They say / that Napoleon / was colour-blind / & blood for him / as green as / grass."

Among the many awards Krüger has received is the Großer Literaturpreis from the Bavarian Academy of Fine Arts. He is also the author of the essay collection *Vorworte, Zwischenbemerkungen, Nachrufe* (2003).

Krüger lives in Munich, Germany, and despite holding an executive position at Carl Hanser Verlag, still finds time to write two hours a day, thanks in part to his being "a very bad sleeper," he explained to Dennis Lythgoe for the Salt Lake City *Deseret Morning News* (February 8, 2004). "Sometimes I write poetry and sometimes I write novels, but the pen is producing. Everyone in my office has a computer, but I'm too stupid for that, I have to confess. I have a pencil and notebook in my pocket and that is how I write." Nonetheless, Krüger finds writing "a very, very difficult thing. Everyone can write, but writers can't write. My mother, who was not a writer, could write. She could write a 20-page letter, and it was beautiful— but she never wrote a book. Now I sit over a white piece of paper and I constantly quarrel with the words, and the words are nasty to me. Writing is torture. But I have to do it."

—S.Y.

Suggested Reading: *Library Journal* p92 Mar. 1, 1998; (London) *Independent* p29 Jan. 25, 1992; (London) *Sunday Times* Oct. 9, 1994; (London) *Times* June 3, 1993; *New York Newsday* p34 Mar. 22, 1992; *New York Times Book Review* p12 Apr. 4, 1993, p26 May 16, 2004; *Washington Times* B p6 Jan. 4, 2004; *World Literature Today* p144 Winter 1997, p146+ Winter 2001

Selected Books in English Translation: fiction— *The End of the Novel*, 1992; *The Man in the Tower*, 1993; *Himmelfarb*, 1994; *Scenes from the Life of a Best-Selling Author*, 2002; *The Cello Player*, 2004; poetry—*Diderot's Cat*, 1994; *At Night, Beneath Trees*, 1998

Kunzru, Hari

Dec. 1969– Novelist

The hype preceding Hari Kunzru's debut novel, *The Impressionist* (2002)—due to the notoriously large advance that the author received—seemed to some critics to overshadow the work itself, although reviewers generally praised Kunzru's efforts. David Kipen, writing for the *San Francisco Chronicle* (April 7, 2002), termed it "a picaresque stitch, a deadly serious book about race and empire that can still put a reader on the floor with the exquisitely timed comic understatement of its language."

Hari Kunzru was born in December 1969 in London, England, to an Indian father and English mother. He was raised in Essex, then studied English literature at Wadham College at the University of Oxford. Upon his graduation, in 1991, Kunzru moved to London but could not find steady employment. Consequently, he returned to academia, studying at the University of Warwick, in Coventry, where he met the editor of *Wired* and began writing technology pieces for the magazine. He soon branched out into other areas, writing for the *Economist*, the London *Daily Telegraph*, and the London *Guardian*, among others. However, Kunzru became increasingly devoted to his own material, working often on *The Impressionist*, which he conceptualized in 1989. After securing an agent in 1999, Kunzru sent off drafts of *The Impressionist* to various publishers. Dutton offered Kunzru an astounding sum, the equivalent of $1.8 million, for the U.S. and U.K. publishing rights.

The Impressionist follows the chameleon-like existence of Pran Nath, a half-Indian, half-English boy who becomes a master at manipulating his identity. He begins life as a pampered child in India, unaware of his British blood and believing himself to be the son of a wealthy Kashmiri merchant. When a housekeeper reveals his half-breed identity, he is thrown out on the street, where he learns to survive as a sex slave. He subsequently reinvents himself as a servant to a depraved missionary in Bombay before moving on to England, where he conceals his Indian ancestry

Chris Jackson/Getty Images

Hari Kunzru

to pass as an aristocratic Oxford student named Jonathan Bridgeman. "In certain ways Kunzru is almost too ambitious," Nick Rennison wrote in a review for Amazon.com. "There is so much crammed onto the pages of *The Impressionist* that some of it, almost inevitably, doesn't work as well as it might. However, as the shapeshifting Pran Nath moves from one identity to another, knockabout farce mixes with satire, social comedy with parody. And beneath the comic exuberance and linguistic invention, there is an intelligent and occasionally moving examination of notions of self, identity, and what it means to belong to a class or society." Daniel Mendelsohn wrote for *New York* (April 8, 2002), "You're likely to buzz through Kunzru's 400 pages in a rush of pleasure, and only afterward might you wonder, as I did, why it doesn't affect you more—why what you remember is your pleasure in the author's craftsmanship rather than the tragedy of the wrenching tale he tells. . . . If you were able to care about Pran more, to feel with him (as opposed to merely for him), this remarkable debut would be great instead of very good. Still, if *The Impressionist* is better at surfaces than at depths, it's a remarkable book that should leave a lasting impression."

Kunzru's second novel, *Transmission* (2004), is the story of Arjun Mehta, a reclusive man who leaves his home in India for—and is ultimately disappointed by—a high-tech job in the U.S. "We've retailed this whole vision of a global future," the author told Steven Zeitchik for *Publishers Weekly* (June 21, 2004). "There's a highly mobile [set] who works and expands our wealth. But we've forgotten a whole other part: the

class who pays for it, who are trapped in the logic of one place." Kunzru continued: "I wouldn't call it an anti-technology book. I love the ability of technology to produce a world where I can burrow into some wonderful stuff. But one of the most pernicious ideas is that we live in an Information Age. Yes, it's true, people in the U.K. are not hewing coal. They're in call centers. You can say objectively that it's a better life. But there's a price."

Janet Maslin described *Transmissions* as a "deft comedy of global manners and cyberpranks" in her review for the *New York Times* (May 17, 2004). "If *Transmission* starts out with an eye for literate social satire that suggests Martin Amis or Zadie Smith," she continued, "it winds up in a Chuck Palahniuk paranoid daydream of systematic unraveling. . . . While the book presents such kaleidoscopic absurdities as an Indian film crew's bewilderment at the stags' heads and violent tartans it encounters in Scotland . . . it also evokes the essential sweetness and bewilderment of everyone in this story. Good-humored even when it overheats into a conspiracy-theory finale, *Transmission* potently reaffirms this author's initial promise."

Kunzru lives in London. He is also a freelance journalist and editor. He has received the Betty Trask Award and the Somerset Maugham Award and was short-listed for the Guardian First Book Award and the Whitbread Award. He was also chosen as the winner of the John Llewellyn Rhys Award, but refused to accept the prize, accusing its sponsor, the London *Mail on Sunday*, of following racist editorial policies.

—P.B.M.

Suggested Reading: *BBC News* (on-line); Hari Kunzru Web site; *New York* (on-line) Apr. 8, 2002; *San Francisco Chronicle* (on-line) Apr. 7, 2002

Selected Books: *The Impressionist*, 2002; *Transmission*, 2004

Kurth, Peter

July 27, 1953– Nonfiction writer

Peter Kurth is a journalist and biographer who has made his career, in large part, by writing about extraordinary women living through extraordinary times. He has published books about Anna Anderson, the woman who claimed to be the youngest daughter of the last czar of Russia; the American journalist Dorothy Thompson, who warned against the rise of fascism in Europe throughout the 1930s; and the revolutionary modern dancer Isadora Duncan, among other figures. He has also written for a number of major magazines and newspapers on a wide range of topics, including politics, royalty, and AIDS.

Peter Kurth was born on July 27, 1953 in Tulsa, Oklahoma, the son of W. Frederick Kurth and the former Constance Schindler. In 1975 he received a bachelor's degree from the University of Vermont. He soon began writing for a variety of publications, including *Cosmopolitan, Harper's Bazaar*, the *New York Times Book Review*, the *New York Observer*, and *Vanity Fair*.

In 1983 Kurth published his first book-length biography, *Anastasia: The Riddle of Anna Anderson*. On the evening of July 16, 1918, Nicholas II, the deposed Russian czar, was murdered, along with his family, by a band of Bolsheviks. Rumors persisted that at least one of his children had managed to escape. In 1920 a young woman was pulled, nearly drowned, from a Berlin canal. She refused to reveal her identity to the police and was sent to an asylum. Nurses there remarked on her uncanny resemblance to Princess Anastasia, the youngest of the czar's daughters. When confronted, the young woman, who adopted the name Anna Anderson, admitted to being the princess. She was never accepted by the remaining members of the extended royal family, then living in Germany. Kurth, however, contends that Anna Anderson was indeed Anastasia and in his book offers the tantalizing bits of evidence that led him to this conclusion.

The reviews of *Anastasia: The Riddle of Anna Anderson* focused on whether or not critics felt Kurth had convincingly proved that Anna was Anastasia. Carol Verderese wrote for the *New York Times Book Review* (January 8, 1984): "Kurth thoroughly retells this much told story and convincingly argues that Anastasia was not killed by a Bolshevik firing squad. . . . [Her grandmother and others] rejected Anastasia, the author argues, because of her emotional instability and the possibility that she may have borne an illegitimate child between her alleged escape from Russia and her arrival in Berlin." On the other hand, a critic for the *Economist* (January 14, 1984) argued, Anastasia's story "was disastrous on all counts. No single part of it was ever proved. . . . For all the massive research behind the book, Mr. Kurth's partisanship blinds him to the accepted criteria, whether historical or judicial, of truth." In the early 1990s the British Home Office's Forensic Sciences Service performed mitochondrial DNA testing on the remains of the assassinated royals and ruled that Anna Anderson, who had died in 1984, was not a relative. Despite this ruling, Kurth has stood by his findings. In an essay posted on his official Web site he writes, "I knew Anna Anderson for more than 10 years and have been acquainted with virtually everyone involved in her quest for recognition over the last quarter-century: friends, lawyers, companions, neighbors, journalists, historians, Russian and European royalty and aristocratic families—a wide array of competent witnesses who didn't hesitate to acknowledge her

as the daughter of the tsar. My experience of her character, my thorough knowledge of her case, and, it seems to me, probability and common sense all convince me that she was indeed Anastasia of Russia."

Kurth published his next book, *American Cassandra: The Life of Dorothy Thompson*, in 1990. The famed 20th-century journalist was given the nickname Cassandra by one of President Franklin Roosevelt's lieutenants because, like the mythical Cassandra whose dire prophecies were ignored, Thompson's early warnings against Nazism and fascism went unheeded throughout the 1930s. As the head of the foreign bureau of the *Philadelphia Public Ledger*, Thompson interviewed Adolf Hitler in 1931. The resulting article so angered the German leader that Thompson became the first American reporter expelled from that country. In 1936 Thompson became a columnist for the *New York Herald Tribune*. Her outspoken stance on women's issues, war, and the New Deal, among other topics, soon made her one of the most popular reporters of the era.

In addition to covering Thompson's work, Kurth examined her sometimes rocky private life, including her three marriages (one to the novelist Sinclair Lewis) and her lesbian affairs. The biography received generally favorable reviews. In the *Chicago Tribune* (June 24, 1990), John Maxwell Hamilton opined, "Kurth writes very well, and his characterization is excellent. Though admiring Thompson, he is balanced in reporting her weaknesses. As the story moves along, picking up steam when she begins to achieve wide popularity, the reader is drawn into her passions and private tribulations. In the end, her death [in 1961] becomes a personal loss." Thomas Griffith, in the *New York Times Book Review* (July 29, 1990), held a similar opinion: "Peter Kurth . . . skillfully uses this new book to explore the riddles within the personality of Dorothy Thompson, quoting lavishly from her voluminous personal papers, which can be both candid and mawkish, and also very touching."

In 1995 Kurth returned to the topic of Russia with *Tsar: The Lost World of Nicholas and Alexandra*, a coffee-table book with photographs by Peter Christopher. It received very positive reviews. Francine du Plessix Gray wrote for the *New York Times Book Review* (October 29, 1995), "It has been common wisdom that most books as physically dazzling, as gorgeously illustrated, as Peter Kurth's *Tsar* are accompanied by vapid nontexts. Mr. Kurth's narrative is a striking exception to the rule . . . [and] is amply documented and compellingly written." Brad Hooper offered a similar opinion in his review for *Booklist* (October 1, 1995), calling it "a remarkably comprehensive overview of the reign of the last czar and his consort. . . . Kurth sensitively documents the imperial family's suffering as prisoners of the Bolsheviks and their eventual execution." The book was written a few weeks after the DNA results of the royal remains were made public, and Kurth, who had been denied the chance to update *Anastasia* by his publishers, was able to address the issue briefly in this volume.

Kurth next published *Isadora: A Sensational Life* (2001), a comprehensive work on the life of the famed dancer Isadora Duncan. In the book, which took 10 years to write, he examined her revolutionary dance style, which sometimes shocked and puzzled audiences, and delved into her tumultuous life. (Duncan had three children by three different men; two of the children died tragically in an automobile accident. Duncan herself died in a notoriously freakish accident, when her billowing scarf caught in the rear wheel of her car, breaking her neck.) Tom Beer, writing for *Biography Magazine* (December 2001), proclaimed: "Peter Kurth . . . treats Duncan's life with great flair. Though it is difficult today to fully appraise her innovations—her dances were never filmed—Kurth recognizes Duncan as a performer in the largest possible sense: charismatic, commanding, and provocative." In a review for the London *Guardian* (January 27, 2002, on-line), Jann Parry wrote: "Kurth does not assess her legacy or analyse her dancing. His concern is to rescue her from earnest scholars and looney wannabes by recording her life as completely as possible, letting readers make their own judgements."

Isadora was written during a tumultuous time in Kurth's own life. He wrote in an article for the on-line magazine *Salon* (November 12, 2001): "When I began the research for *Isadora*, [my lover] had just died of 'AIDS-related complications.' I had nothing to do but ward off panic. An editor . . . mentioned Isadora Duncan over lunch. I had a lot of different lives at that time. I was driven, dashing, never stopping, always leaving. I had a separate life in London from the one in New York, a third life in Paris, a generic life for traveling, a gay life, a writing life, a life for tea with duchesses and a life in Vermont—'home,' where I grew up, went to college, got married and divorced, wrote my first book, met [my lover] and lost him." (Kurth had also been diagnosed as HIV-positive in the late 1980s.)

During this period Kurth was also thrust into the spotlight as his family's spokesperson. Twenty years before, his two young nieces had been abducted by their father, Stephen Fagan, who charged that Kurth's sister Barbara was an unfit mother. Finally discovered hiding in Florida, Fagan was arrested on kidnapping charges. The girls, remaining loyal to their father despite evidence that he had acted inappropriately, refused to speak to their mother, and the entire family was thrust into a maelstrom of attention from the tabloids and television talk shows. Kurth won widespread praise for his reasoned and polished presence in the midst of the media circus.

In addition to his frequent contributions to *Salon* and other publications, Kurth is a regular columnist for *Seven Days*, a magazine based in Vermont; for this work he recently earned an award for outstanding commentary from the Association of Alternative Newsweeklies. He is often called upon by the hosts of National Public Radio programs and various television news magazines to provide commentary on his many areas of interest.

—K.D.

Suggested Reading: *Biography Magazine* p36 Dec. 2001; *Booklist* p250 Oct. 1, 1995; *Chicago Tribune* XIV p3 June 24, 1990; *Christian Science Monitor* p11 Sep. 21, 1983; *Economist* p81 Jan. 14, 1984; *Library Journal* p102 Apr. 15, 1990; *New York Times* C p4 Aug. 8, 1990; *New York Times Book Review* p18 Jan. 8, 1984, p12 July 29, 1990, p15 Oct. 29, 1995; *New Yorker* p105 Sep. 17, 1990; Peter Kurth's Web site

Selected Books: *Anastasia: The Riddle of Anna Anderson*, 1983; *American Cassandra: The Life of Dorothy Thompson*, 1990; *Tsar: The Lost World of Nicholas and Alexandra*, 1995; *Isadora: A Sensational Life*, 2001

Laird, Nick

1975– Poet; novelist

Originally known as the husband of the successful novelist Zadie Smith, Nick Laird achieved literary prominence of his own in 2005—the year in which he published his first book of poems, *To a Fault*, and his first novel, *Utterly Monkey*. Praising his ability to lead his "reader out into a sort of no-man's land of the mind," Rachel Campbell-Johnston wrote for the London *Times* (January 22, 2005) that Laird's poetry "explores those spaces—so inscrutable and yet so instinctively sensed—that stretch between what is present and what is possible, what is earthbound and what can soar." It is for his poetry that Laird has garnered the most admiration; when his novel came out, critics found that its strengths often rested on the elements that seemed most influenced by his poetic training. Jane Shilling observed for the London *Times* (April 23, 2005), for example, that Laird's prose is characterized by a "generous, rolling style that . . . is underpinned by an observing eye and an endearing weakness for a colourful adjective." In November 2005 Laird was named the most-promising poet of the year by the Ireland Chair of Poetry Trust; the prize entitled Laird to a period of residence in an artists' retreat. Paul Durcan, the noted Irish poet who named the winner, observed in his announcement, as quoted on the Web site for Radio Televis Eireann (RTE): "It does not happen often, but it does happen: A first book of poems is published and a star is born. Such a book is *To a Fault* and such a new-born star is Nick Laird."

Courtesy of W. W. Norton

Nick Laird

Nick Laird was born in 1975 in Cookstown, County Tyrone, Northern Ireland. His father, Alastair Laird, was an insurance broker; his mother, Carol, worked in her husband's office. The young Laird wrote his first poem at the age of four, about his teddy bear: "Bouncy bouncy on the bed— happy couple, me and Ted!" he recalled to Lucy Alexander for the London *Times* (April 30, 2005). In school he earned straight As and wrote prize-winning essays, although in interviews he is self-deprecating about his accomplishments: "I don't think I was an overachiever," he told Louise East for the *Irish Times* (April 16, 2005). "I just always found everything intensely interesting." Laird came of age during a period of turmoil in Northern Ireland—known as the Troubles—in which tensions between the largely Protestant unionists, or loyalists (those favoring a continued union with the United Kingdom), and the largely Catholic nationalists, or republicans (those seeking a unified Ireland), frequently resulted in outbreaks of violence. In interviews Laird has recalled the difficulties of living in such an environment: "It's not normal to be stopped every day by soldiers with guns who look in your schoolbag," he told Gold. "It's not normal to not be able to get to school because masked men have closed the roads and kicked the windows in at your dad's office."

After high school Laird went to the University of Cambridge, in England. He studied English literature, something his parents allowed him to do only on the condition that he enter law school after he had completed his undergraduate degree. During his second year at Cambridge he started a writers' group and became the editor of a journal, the *May Anthologies*. Through that journal he met

Zadie Smith, who had submitted a short story. "It was just head-and-shoulders above anything else," he told Louise Carpenter for the London *Sunday Telegraph* (July 24, 2005). The two were close friends for a while before they started dating. A year after they met, both Laird and Smith entered a creative-writing competition, the prize for which was £60 worth of book tokens (gift certificates). Laird won—but three weeks later, Smith, having written about 100 pages of a novel, signed a £250,000 book deal for what would become *White Teeth* (2000), her acclaimed debut. "You just can't compete with that, there's no point," Laird told Carpenter.

After graduating from Cambridge, Laird fulfilled his promise to his parents and entered law school. He did not expect to actually work as a lawyer, planning to quit once he had qualified, but after finishing law school, he landed a position at a prominent law firm, Allen & Overy, where he remained for six years, working in international litigation. He also served briefly in the inquiry into Bloody Sunday—January 30, 1972, the notorious day in which British troops opened fire on unarmed Irish Catholics who were protesting British rule in Northern Ireland.

While working as a lawyer, Laird held on to his desire to be a poet, writing during his lunch hour and at night. Soon his poems and book reviews began to appear in the pages of the *Times Literary Supplement* (*TLS*) and a number of literary journals in Britain and Ireland. By 2002 his reputation was beginning to grow; he won the TLS/Blackwell's Poetry Competition, and his poems were included in *New Writing 11*, an anthology of young British writers published by Picador. Reviewers of the publication praised his work for being among the best in the volume. Murrough O'Brien, in his review for the London *Independent on Sunday* (April 28, 2002), for example, called him one of "the real jewels in this compilation," a writer who reveals "a sensibility at once humorous and compassionate." Allan Massie, writing for the *Scotsman* (April 6, 2002), called him "a poet with a cool, assured voice."

Such attention did not afford Laird the leisure to make writing his full-time job, and he continued working as a lawyer. By 2003, however, he was feeling overworked and demoralized. "There was one seven-month period where I had one day off," he told Alexander. He took a sabbatical and traveled to Harvard University, in Cambridge, Massachusetts, where Smith was then teaching as a Radcliff Institute Fellow; he took up a writing fellowship, allowing him time to complete his first book of poems, *To a Fault*. "Then, the day I got back to the office, I was back in the same chambers with the same client and the same technical expert on the same case," he told Alexander. A few months later, in November 2003, he resigned in order to write. "It didn't seem brave," he told Alexander. "I was so hacked off with the job, I had to do something. I had a couple of months where

I was a bit shaky financially, but it's worked out well." (Several sources erroneously state that he gave up his job in early 2004, after his real break as a writer came.) Having completed a draft of his first novel, *Utterly Monkey*, he showed it around to several publishers; a bidding war ensued, leading to a lucrative two-book deal for £100,000 from Fourth Estate, a prestigious literary publisher in England.

To a Fault was published at the beginning of 2005. The book's poems deal with, among other things, relationships, both familial and romantic, and the Troubles in Northern Ireland. Such themes have led readers to see them in an autobiographical light, something Laird has attempted to dissuade readers from doing, explaining to Carpenter, "Poems are only true about the emotion at the time and then you move on. . . . I don't want to use the word therapy because I don't think writing is therapy, although it is a way of clarifying things. Writing is so strange, especially writing poetry, because you're supposed to be sensitive and attuned, and yet also tough-skinned and able to accept all this criticism of your work and your life." The book garnered almost entirely positive reviews. Belinda McKeon praised the collection for the *Irish Times* (January 8, 2005): "Memorable enough, upon first reading, to stitch themselves into the mind and to be found there days later, still smarting, still holding strong, are the poems in which Laird braves exploration of a father-son relationship which is not so much damaged by dread and guilt as sustained by them." She added, "Born when the Troubles were still young, and having grown to adolescence in their most savage years, Laird approaches violence without fanfare, even without gravitas. . . . His perspective on sectarian bloodshed seems so close, so accustomed as to be almost neutral, venturing no judgments and offering no polished laments. Pervading the collection, however, is an anger which is interesting, though unsettling, in its lack of focus." Sam Leith, writing for the London *Daily Telegraph* (January 15, 2005), noted, "*To a Fault* is an impressive, attentive, worked-over collection, the production of someone who has been reading poetry carefully and critically for years and is fully in control of his effects. That's not to say its learning is arid, either: there are tender love poems here, and dark jokes. The whimsically complex title of the collection is characteristic. Laird had partly in mind [William Butler] Yeats's poem 'To a Shade'—attracted by the idea of addressing something inanimate. But it also has the effect of a cliche quietly, Muldoonishly unpicked [an allusion to Paul Muldoon, a poet from Northern Ireland] to yield something more: the idea of rift; and a hint, in the background, of blame."

Utterly Monkey, which was published about four months after *To a Fault*, tells the story of five days in the life of Danny Williams—a young Protestant lawyer from the fictional Northern Ireland town of Ballyglass (reportedly based on Laird's hometown) who works in a top London law firm. Danny hates his job: as Michiko Kakutani summarized for the *New York Times* (January 6, 2006), "He hates the monotonous hamster-wheel routine. He hates his pompous, patronizing boss. He hates the poisonous office politics. Most of all, he hates being a lawyer who has to work on closing deals he hates—like the one that would result in the acquisition and downsizing of a company and put thousands of people in Northern Ireland out of work." At the same time, he appreciates the money and is enamored of a colleague, a young black woman named Ellen. (Some critics have noted that the character of Danny has a lot in common with Laird and that Ellen bears a strong resemblance to Zadie Smith, although Laird denies that the book is autobiographical). Danny's life gets turned upside down when Geordie, a childhood friend, shows up at Danny's London apartment, rekindling old, not always happy, memories and starting new problems—Geordie has fled Northern Ireland with £50,000 that his girlfriend stole from a loyalist paramilitary group. Some loyalist thugs are close on Geordie's tale, and soon he and Danny find themselves caught up in a plot to bomb the Bank of England.

The book received a generally positive, if qualified, response. Jane Shilling called it "a novel rich in both achievement and promise, by a writer who can actually write." Stephen Knight, writing for the London *Independent on Sunday* (May 22, 2005), observed, "The prose of *Utterly Monkey* is brisk and frictionless, hurrying readers past the story's coincidences and unlikely twists. Consequently, it lacks texture; colourless dialogue furthers the plot more than it develops characters, and Laird's milieu is only sparsely detailed. This is a matter of choice rather than inability. When the writing does attend to minutiae, the results are vivid, and Laird has a nice line in witty observations." Similarly, Brandon Robshaw, writing for the London *Independent* (May 31, 2005), complained, "The story never really does come to a boil, as various plot strands peter out. A flashback to the murder of a schoolteacher has curious little consequence, for example. And between events are long stretches of descriptive writing, enjoyable in themselves but hardly accelerating the narrative drive." In 2006 *Utterly Monkey* earned Laird the Betty Trask Award, which is given annually to a work of traditional fiction by the Society of Authors and which Laird shared with two other authors, Peter Hobbs and Nicola Monaghan.

Laird and Smith were married in September 2004. They live in Kilburn, a northern section of London. Laird has told reporters that they try to keep a firm schedule of writing in the mornings—Laird on their house's first floor and Smith on the second. He is currently working on a book of poems, tentatively titled "The War Artists" and a musical about Kafka, a collaboration with his wife and the composer Adam Andrusier. His next novel, "Glover's Mistake," will be released in the U.K. later in 2007. He does some legal consulting, but his days are mostly consumed with writing—his goal is to write 1,000 words each day. His efforts have so far won him the Eric Gregory Award, in 2004, and the Rooney Prize for Irish Literature, in 2005. He was short-listed for the Forward Poetry Prize for best first collection, in 2005, and both the Commonwealth Writers Prize and the Dylan Thomas Prize (for writers under 30), in 2006.

—A.R.

Suggested Reading: *Irish Times* p12 Jan. 8, 2005, p19 Apr. 16, 2005; (London) *Daily Telegraph* p12 Jan. 15, 2005; (London) *Evening Standard* C p10 Mar. 4, 2004; (London) *Guardian* p6 May 3, 2005; (London) *Independent* May 31, 2005; (London) *Independent on Sunday* p23 May 22, 2005; (London) *Sunday Telegraph* p1 July 24, 2005; (London) *Times* p15 Jan. 22, 2005, p42 Apr. 30, 2005

Selected Books: *To a Fault*, 2005; *Utterly Monkey*, 2005

Darlene Devita/Courtesy of Random House

Landay, William

July 25, 1963– Novelist

Since the publication of his first novel, *Mission Flats* (2003), William Landay has often been compared to such writers as Scott Turow, who, like Landay, went from being a prosecutor to a novelist; and Dennis Lehane, another mystery writer whose work often deals with the seedy side of Boston, Massachusetts. All three authors share the distinction of having won praise for their impressive combination of suspenseful plotting, careful writing, and full character development. Reviewing *Mission Flats* for the on-line magazine *January* (September 2003), Sarah Weinman noted the comparisons Landay's background and subject matter had elicited and added: "It's my belief that it won't be long before future debut novelists will be compared to a list of authors topped by Landay

himself. *Mission Flats* is much more than a remarkable debut; it's one of the best efforts in crime fiction so far this year. Whether that places undue expectations on the author's future career will, of course, remain to be seen, but with *Mission Flats*, he's off to a flying start."

Born in Boston on July 25, 1963, Landay earned his undergraduate degree from Yale University, in New Haven, Connecticut, and his law degree, in 1990, from Boston College Law School. After working for several years as an assistant district attorney (ADA) in Middlesex County, Massachusetts, Landay gave up his post in order to work on a novel. "I liked being a lawyer," he remarked to an interviewer for Bookreporter.com (February 2, 2007). "I'm a little conflict-averse—probably I would not have lasted forever as a trial lawyer. But I enjoyed my time as an A.D.A., especially the great people I worked with." Landay added that he considered the change of profession "more a matter of turning toward something than turning away. I'd always dreamed of being a writer and I figured, as I was turning 30, that I'd better get to it before time ran out." At the beginning, Landay told a reporter for his law school's alumni magazine, *BC Law* (Fall–Winter 2004, on-line), "I was very intimidated. Writing a novel is so outside the realm of most people's experience. It's like climbing a very high mountain and not knowing whether you'll reach the top." After two years Landay had one manuscript to show for his trouble, but it and the novel that followed never made it into print. To support himself during those years, he drew on his retirement money and worked here and there, tending bar, moonlighting as a Web developer; he even returned, for a year, to being a prosecutor. "If you want to have a family and kids and mortgages and all that," Landay told the Bookreporter.com interviewer, "it's wise to get through the whole unpublished writer phase of your life first."

An unusual murder mystery, *Mission Flats* is told from the perspective of the small-town police chief Ben Truman and relates the investigation into the death of a man whose body was found in a lakeside cabin near Truman's hometown of Versailles, Maine. The corpse is revealed to be a district attorney from Mission Flats, an imaginary neighborhood described as the roughest in Boston. In order to clear his own name of suspicion and to get out of Versailles—where he has been trapped since giving up trying to earn his doctoral degree in order to take care of his ailing mother—Truman heads to Boston to uncover the truth about the murder. He soon begins to doubt that the suspect being pursued by the Boston police, Harold Braxton, is actually guilty, especially after uncovering clues tying this case to the murder of a police officer more than 20 years earlier.

Mission Flats earned generally positive reviews. In a critique for the *Boston Globe* (September 28, 2003), Jim Fusilli wrote: "[Landay] captures the ragtag detachment of the criminal justice system, portraying the police as public servants compelled to dispense justice when there's no other recourse. Though his narrative lurches and meanders on occasion, Landay lets his knotty story untie methodically, resulting in an ending that's genuinely shocking. Though Truman seems at times an ill-suited guide to this world of men and their machinations, in the end only he could have ushered us through Landay's shrewd tale." Writing for the *New York Times Book Review* (October 5, 2003), Marilyn Stasio observed: "[Landay] writes with eloquent intensity, even a sense of despair, about the no-win ethical choices that can corrupt or otherwise crush a good cop." *Mission Flats* won the British Crime Writers' Association John Creasey Memorial Dagger for best debut novel in 2003.

In early 2007 Landay published his second novel, *The Strangler*. Set in Boston in 1963, the book revisits a real-life series of murders and sexual assaults attributed to a figure known as the Boston Strangler. A man named Albert DeSalvo confessed to the 11 murders police had attributed to the killer and to two more as well. Even with that confession, however, the evidence against him was too weak to bring charges against him, leaving the case unsolved to this day and feeding suspicions that more than one person had been involved in the crimes. More central to the book, however, is the story of three brothers—Joe, Michael, and Ricky Daley—who work on either side of the law and their father, a Boston policeman who dies while on duty.

Laura Wilson, in a critique for the London *Guardian* (February 24, 2007, on-line), called the tale of the Daleys "the stronger of the two storylines" but judged the book as a whole "meaty" and "ambitious" and "made all the more powerful by an author unafraid to tackle the complexities of moral ambiguity." To Patrick Anderson, writing for the *Washington Post* (February 5, 2007), the story of the Boston Strangler functions in the novel partially as a symbol for "a bigger story of crime and corruption" in Boston's West End: "If I read him correctly, [Landay is] saying that, yes, someone was strangling these women, but at the same time crooked cops, vicious mobsters, greedy businessmen and compliant politicians were strangling a great American city." Anderson noted that there was "some ugly violence in the story" but added: "There are also interesting digressions on everything from lock-picking to migraine headaches, from the mysteries of religion to the difficulties of love." Calling the book "an impressive and satisfying performance" and "genre fiction, but of a high order," Anderson concluded by judging Landay "a writer to watch."

Landay is married and lives in Boston. At the moment in 2001 when he heard he had sold *Mission Flats*—reportedly for a sum approaching $1 million—he and his wife were in their obstetrician's office, only minutes away from taking their first glimpse, via ultrasound, of the baby that is now their oldest son, Ted.

In a detailed essay available on his Web site, Landay explained why he has allowed only the barest amount of biographical material about him to become available. Distinguishing between attitudes he attributed to the great French novelist Gustave Flaubert (1821–1880), who maintained a low profile during his life, and the much more forthcoming American writer Ernest Hemingway (1899–1961), Landay wrote: "I prefer the Flaubert approach. I am a private person. That is one reason novel-writing appeals to me: Novelists—all storytellers—approach the world through misdirection, from oblique angles, through stories. We come on like crabs, scuttling up to the truth sideways. A more direct, forthright sort of person would be writing essays or memoirs or some other form that addresses the world head-on. More important, I believe each novel has to stand on its own. Either it has the stuff or it doesn't. The reader should not have to look outside the book cover for proof that it is convincing, moving, and authentic. My books are the only credential that matters."

—C.M.

Suggested Reading: *BC Law* (on-line) Fall–Winter 2004; *Boston Globe* H p6 Sep. 28, 2003; *Buffalo News* F p4 Oct. 5, 2003; *January* (on-line) Sep. 2003; (London) *Guardian* (on-line) Feb. 24, 2007; *New York Times Book Review* p20 Oct. 5, 2003; *Washington Post* C p3 Feb. 5, 2007; William Landay's Web site

Selected Works: *Mission Flats*, 2003; *The Strangler*, 2007

Stephane de Sakutin/AFP/Getty Images

Laporte, Geneviève

(lah-PORT, zhawn-vee-
EHV)

1926(?)– Poet; memoirist

One of the 20th century's most iconic figures and arguably the era's greatest artist, Pablo Picasso earned a reputation as a womanizer who drove two of his former lovers to suicide and another into a mental institution. But the French poet, memoirist, children's author, and documentary filmmaker Geneviève Laporte, who had a surreptitious affair with the Spanish artist during the 1950s and was the subject of a number of his later works, remembers a very different man: "He has been cast as a macho, a monster, a cad, who extinguished cigarettes on the cheek of his wife. But look at these drawings—there is nothing but tenderness, no?" she told a reporter for Agence France-Presse (June 24, 2005), as she gestured to the drawings from her personal collection, 20 of which she auctioned off, to the delight of the art world, during the summer of 2005.

Many have noted that Picasso's drawings of Laporte lack the harshness typically found in his portraiture. In 1997, when the State Hermitage Museum, in St. Petersburg, Russia, held an exhibition of Picasso's pieces featuring Laporte, the curators described them as emerging from his "Tender Period" or "Geneviève Period." "I think we had a special relationship because we both were poets," she told a reporter for the *China Daily* (June 25, 2005). The key to the relative health of their friendship and love affair may have been that Laporte did not let her role as Picasso's muse come

to define her. Consequently, when the relationship with Picasso soured, she had already established herself as a notable young poet. Indeed, she went on to publish several volumes of verse and win the 1999 Prix Maïse Ploquin-Caunan from the Académie Française for her collection *La sublime porte des songes* (which translates as "the sublime door of dreams"). In addition to her poetry, Laporte has authored two children's books and two memoirs; she has also produced a number of documentary films.

Geneviève Laporte was born in about 1926 and raised in France. Her father worked in the chemical industry and her mother was an art enthusiast. Laporte was a promising young student, who began writing poetry at an early age. During the Nazi occupation of France in World War II, she joined the Resistance, serving as the president of the Front National Étudiant (FNE), a student organization, at her Paris high school, Lycée Fénelon. She and other FNE members founded the broadsheet newspaper *La Voix de Fénelon* (which translates as "the voice of Fénelon").

The *La Voix* staff became enraged when a band of fascists raided the 1944 Paris Salon d'Automne—an annual exhibition that showcased innovations in painting and sculpture—and threw several of Picasso's paintings out the windows. The students wanted to interview Picasso for their newspaper but were afraid to approach him. "Naturally, Picasso was known to us by name only, and had the reputation of being unfriendly to journalists and even of refusing to see them," Laporte wrote in *Sunshine at Midnight: Memories of Picasso and Cocteau* (1975). They decided to draw lots for the unpleasant task. Laporte drew the short stick and found herself timidly knocking on the door of Picasso's famous Parisian studio on the Rue des Grandes-Augustins. To her surprise, Picasso received her graciously—until she ventured to inform him that young people did not understand his paintings. According to John Lichfield for the London *Independent* (June 20, 2005), Picasso retorted, "Since when do you have to explain the language of painting? Do you understand the language of potato chips?"

Picasso, then 63 years old, was amused with this innocent schoolgirl, who reminded him of a model that he had painted nearly 40 years earlier, and he asked her to return after the article was published. Over that winter Laporte developed a friendship with the artist, frequently visiting his studio, where they discussed art and literature while innocently sipping hot chocolate. "I was certainly perfectly naive," Laporte stated, as quoted by Angela Doland for the Associated Press (June 17, 2005). "He told me [later], 'You can't imagine how much I wanted to touch your hair, but I didn't dare.' . . . He could have been my grandfather! Ooh la la, if he had touched my hair, I would have taken off running."

LAPORTE

After graduating from Fénelon, Laporte traveled to Britain and later the U.S. For the next seven years Picasso maintained a platonic relationship with her, waiting until she was in her mid-20s before attempting to seduce her. A spring thunderstorm precipitated the beginning of their romance in 1951: "I said I was going home. And at that moment, I swear, it was like in a fairy tale," Laporte recalled, according to Doland. "The room grew dark, and through the skylight I saw a sky like I've never seen before, except in Congo during tropical storms. He told me, 'Wait a little while, there's going to be a storm.' And bada boom: lightning, thunder, hail." That afternoon they began an intense love affair that would last two years.

For the duration of his romance with Laporte, Picasso was living with the painter Françoise Gilot, with whom he had two children. Gilot and Picasso had a tumultuous relationship and during a particularly difficult period in the summer of 1951, Picasso left her, taking Laporte with him to Saint Tropez on France's Mediterranean coast. The French poet Paul Éluard and his wife Dominique also joined them. "I was at the point of killing myself," Picasso confessed to Éluard, according to Karl Green for *International Auctioneers* (January 2005). "[Laporte] made me laugh. Laugh do you understand? Laugh." To which Éluard replied, "Even if she had made you cry, she would have saved you."

Laporte says that Picasso was not only a tender paramour but also an excellent teacher. "We spoke about painting, about magic, about esotericism—about everything," Laporte recalled to Green, "He was extremely cultivated, Picasso, in so many fields. He had me read St. John of the Cross, Balzac and the Marquis de Sade." Genevieve served as Picasso's muse; he drew her constantly while they were in St. Tropez, depicting her as a harem courtesan, a sphinx, and, most famously, in a sailor's shirt in *Geneviève au tricourt marin*. Picasso in turn encouraged Laporte to write poetry and promised to illustrate her first book. After the sojourn in St. Tropez, Picasso returned to Gilot but continued his romance with Laporte.

In the fall of 1953, Gilot left Picasso permanently; the following day he asked Laporte to move into his home in Vallauris, a small town in southern France. In response Laporte snapped that he needed to change the sheets first. "After all [Gilot] had left their house in Vallauris only the night before," she explained to Green. "With hindsight, my reaction was probably due to all that Vallauris represented for me. . . . It represented the side of Picasso's life that took him away from me—in a way, he cheated on me with Vallauris. But that's with hindsight. At the time, I only knew that I didn't want to go there." Her refusal marked the beginning of the relationship's demise. Later, Jean Cocteau—the versatile French artist who distinguished himself in painting, poetry, fiction, ballet, opera, and film—told Laporte that she had saved her own skin by ending the affair.

Though their affair was deteriorating, Picasso and Laporte continued to correspond about her upcoming book of poetry. Her verse reminded him of the innovative French poet Guillaume Apollinaire, Picasso said, though Laporte thought he was simply flattering her. She was also unconvinced by Éluard's praise, so a mutual friend showed her work to Jacques Audiberti, a French poet, novelist, and playwright famous for his extravagant use of language and rhythm. Audiberti was so enthusiastic about Laporte's collection that he sent her an essay on the art of poetry to serve as the introduction. Picasso supplied the illustrations as promised and also helped her select which poems to include. With an initial print run of 200 copies, *Les cavaliers d'ombre* (variously translated as "knights of darkness" or "dark knights") was published in 1954 and quickly sold out due largely to Picasso's cachet. "I was not altogether surprised that 'the book', as Picasso called it, was a success with bibliophiles," Laporte wrote in *Sunshine at Midnight*, "though I never for a moment believed that it was due to my poems."

Laporte first met Jean Cocteau in the summer of 1954; they were introduced by a publisher who wanted both of them to contribute to a collection of poetry. After reading *Les cavaliers d'ombre*, Cocteau pronounced, according to Laporte's recollection in *Sunshine at Midnight*, "You are a true poet. Most of what I am asked to read nowadays is mere sing-song. But not *your* poems, *you* exist." Cocteau offered to illustrate Laporte's second volume of poetry, *Sous le manteau de feu* (which translates as "under the coat of fire"). He gave Laporte 12 sketches for the book, which was published in 1955. Laporte later authored *Le Soleil éblouie* (which translates as "the blinding sun"), another poetry collection that also featured illustrations by Picasso.

Eventually Laporte stopped seeing Picasso altogether and in 1959 married a fellow member of the Resistance. The marriage, which did not last long, produced one son. Laporte continued to write poetry but supported herself mainly by working in public relations and as a journalist. She later became interested in documentary film and produced 18 films on Africa. In 1999 she was awarded the Prix Maïse Ploquin-Caunan—an annual poetry prize from the prestigious Académie Française—for *La sublime porte des songes*, a collection of poetry that included illustrations by Picasso and the French painter Yves Brayer.

Laporte did not write or speak publicly about her relationship with Picasso for nearly 20 years after they parted ways. Then, one day at a luncheon with the head of Agence France-Presse, someone suggested that she write about her experiences with the artist. After considerable reflection Laporte decided to go forward with the project in order "to rehabilitate the memory of Pablo," as she explained to Green. "There have been many negative things written about Picasso. That he was cruel and heartless, that he was stingy. . . . I never experienced any of that. To me, he was always tender, kind, and generous to a fault." That Picasso, who famously described the women in his life as either "goddesses or doormats," had a destructive influence on his lovers is hard to deny: both his mistress Marie-Thérèse Walter and his second wife Jacqueline Roque committed suicide, while another lover, the artist Dora Maar, had to be institutionalized after a nervous breakdown. Consequently, Laporte's tender recollection stood in marked contrast to the sordid tragedy with which Picasso's romantic life is often associated. "When a man has several lovers, each one has a tendency to say, 'I was the one he loved the most,'" Laporte explained to Green. "I don't claim that. But there was something about our relationship that was different from all his others—I am a poet; Picasso was a poet himself, and greatly admired poetry. It may be because of this that I had a different experience with Picasso."

In 1973, the year of Picasso's death, Laporte published the memoir *Si tard le soir, le soleil brille.* An English translation, *Sunshine at Midnight: Memories of Picasso and Cocteau,* followed in 1975. Ann Pryor, reviewing the work for *Best Sell* (December 1975), wrote that while Laporte's "unnecessarily flowery language and obvious grammatical errors" might be the fault of the translation, the book's "shallow content" was its greatest flaw; "Laporte has either chosen to tell us very little or has very little to tell." Robin Kaplan for *Library Journal* (February 1, 1976) agreed that Laporte's book left many questions unanswered, but noted that "her memoir conveys something of Picasso's warmth and charm." Louise Bernikow, writing for the *New York Times Book Review* (November 9, 1975), saw the work as less a biography of Laporte or Picasso, than a "book about how Great Men in intimacy are much like everyone else." Laporte later published *Un Amour secret de Picasso* (1989; which translates as "a secret love of Picasso") and three children's books—*Du petit Pablo au grand Picasso* (2003; "from little Pablo to the great Picasso"), *Le grand Picasso* (2004; "the great Picasso"), and *Du petit Wolfgang au grand Mozart* (2006; "from little Wolfgang to the great Mozart").

In the course of their relationship, Picasso had given Laporte a number of his drawings. For many years they hung, unnoticed by visitors, on Laporte's apartment walls. After the publication of *Si tard le soir, le soleil brille,* however, her insurer convinced her that it was no longer safe to keep the artwork in her apartment, so she deposited them in a bank vault. They remained there for decades, until a friend persuaded her to sell them; at least they would be on view, her acquaintance reasoned. "On several occasions, Pablo told me that he was very hurt when friends sold drawings that had been gifts from him. He once said to me, 'If anyone ever tells you that these drawings have any value, tear them up,'" Laporte explained to Green. "For me, there was never any question of selling them,

anyway, in spite of the fact that I could have lived very well all this time by selling only one or two a year. I once told a friend that I wanted to be buried with them. My friend replied that if I did that, I wouldn't rest in peace very long." Laporte couldn't bear the idea of throwing out what she saw as love letters from Picasso, but she also wasn't interested in leaving them to her family. "For my relatives it can't be the same," she stated, as quoted in *China Daily* (June 25, 2005). "They can't have the same relationship I have with these drawings."

On June 27, 2005 at the Hôtel Dassault, in Paris, the Artcurial Briest Poulain Le Fur auction house offered 20 sketches (some sources stated 18), a few engravings, and a pendant that Picasso had given to Laporte. Most of the various ink, charcoal, and pencil sketches were of her, and many were inscribed with the phrase "Pour Geneviève" (For Geneviève). The auction raised almost $1.9 million, which Laporte earmarked for the creation of an animal welfare foundation. The Picasso Museum in Paris purchased "Odalisque," a sketch of Laporte reclining nude on a bed, for $575,357—about three times the estimated price and the most that one of his drawings from 1951 had ever sold for. "His work of the postwar period don't typically earn as much as earlier ones," Francis Briest, the auctioneer, stated, according to Rachid Aouli for the Associated Press Worldstream (June 27, 2005).

The day of the auction, a thunderstorm hit Paris. "It is very strange. It was in a storm that I fell into the arms of Pablo and this week the storm came back," Laporte remarked, as quoted by Charles Bremner for the London *Times* (June 28, 2005). "He was either furious because I was selling or saying 'Thank you, mission accomplished.'"

—J.C.

Suggested Reading: Associated Press June 17, 2005; *China Daily* June 25, 2005; *International Auctioneers* p16+ Jan. 2005; (London) *Independent* p6+ June 20, 2005

Selected Books: *Sunshine at Midnight: Memories of Picasso and Cocteau,* 1975

Larson, Erik

Jan. 1, 1954– Journalist; nonfiction writer

"I'm not a historian; I'm a writer who tries to find stories and bring them to life," Erik Larson explained in an interview with Ronald Kovach for the *Writer* (September 2003). "I love trying to capture atmosphere, landscape, events, in prose. I love sinking into the past. What I'm trying to do for my readers is allow them to just fall into another time, and ideally not emerge until the book is done, with a changed sense of the past."

Courtesy of the Miami Book Fair

Erik Larson

Erik Larson was born on January 1, 1954 in Brooklyn, New York, and grew up in Freeport, Long Island, New York. He studied Russian culture and history at the University of Pennsylvania, where he received a bachelor's degree, in 1976. Two years later, in 1978, he received a master's degree from the School of Journalism at Columbia University, in New York City.

While working as a journalist, Larson published articles in *Harper's*, the *New Yorker*, and the *Atlantic Monthly*; spent two years at *Time*; and then served two stints at the *Wall Street Journal*, for which he wrote stories that often involved a historical element. "I've always been interested in history," Larson explained in an interview archived on the University of Oregon's Literary Nonfiction Web site. "I majored in history in college, although I never intended to be a historian. I also found, afterwards when I was writing feature stories for the *Wall Street Journal*—and maybe it's the stories I picked or just the way I think—there was always a historical component to my stories. In many cases, the historical component was one of the richest parts of the piece—the most interesting, the most compelling. And they were often funny. Any good piece of journalism, any good piece of writing, has a strong historical component. I'm convinced of that."

In 1992 Larson published his first book, *The Naked Consumer: How Our Private Lives Become Public Commodities*, a study of how information is gathered about consumer spending habits and how that information is used in direct-marketing campaigns. He describes how companies take information from a variety of sources—the U.S. Census Bureau, banks, medical records, credit cards—to create profiles of an individual's spending habits, based on their income, credit history, and even ethnicity. The book received generally favorable reviews. In the *New York Times Book Review* (January 24, 1993), Scott Huler proclaimed: "[Larson] manages to make the stories behind those mass mailings into a narrative that is both a highly informative research presentation and something of a detective story. . . . Mr. Larson delves into the world of mailing lists and census data, passive television meters and Universal Product Codes, introducing such concepts as 'smart mail' and 'recombinant information.'. . . [He] chattily describes emerging methods by which data gatherers learn increasingly intimate details of our lives. And though he is sometimes strident—finding Orwellian portent, for example, in just about every event that happened to occur in 1984—his tone of alarm is borne out by his research."

Larson's second book, *Lethal Passage: How the Travels of a Single Handgun Expose the Roots of America's Gun Crisis* (1994), grew out of a series of articles he wrote for the *Wall Street Journal* about the gun culture in the U.S. After learning of a series of drive-by shootings in his neighborhood that took place in about 1980, he began to investigate how teenagers were able to acquire guns with such apparent ease. To illustrate this point, he traced the history of one particular gun, a Cobray M-11/9, that was used by a 16-year-old boy named Nicholas Elliot to kill his teacher and terrorize other teachers and students at his school in Virginia Beach in 1988. A reviewer for the *Economist* (April 30, 1994) noted: "The chapters alternate, effectively, between [a] broad gun culture and the chilling details of Nicholas's day of revenge. . . . Mr. Larson's purpose is to expose, in plain unvarnished prose, the awful laxity of America's gun industry. He does it as well as it could and should be done." Clifford Krauss, writing for the *New York Times Book Review* (March 20, 1994), remarked: "*Lethal Passage* . . . sometimes suffers for its hyperbolic rhetoric—as when it suggests that 'Nicholas in effect carried with him the good wishes of an industry and a culture.' But its argument that too many unqualified people are carrying guns in America today is persuasive."

Though Larson's first two books dealt with contemporary social issues in a historical context, his next book, *Isaac's Storm: A Man, a Time, and the Deadliest Hurricane in History* (1999), focused directly on a historical event, albeit an obscure one. Throughout his career he had been interested in writing suspenseful stories; he even made attempts to write novels, though none were published. With *Isaac's Storm*, however, he discovered how to take elements of fiction—suspense, plot, detailed place descriptions—and inject them into a nonfiction work. On September 8, 1900 a devastating hurricane hit Galveston, Texas. In a narrative structure similar to *Lethal Passage*, the author focused both on the event, in this case the hurricane, and on a single individual, Isaac Cline, chief of the U.S. Weather Bureau in Galveston. Although many meteorologists declared that the hurricane would hit central Texas, Cline and his supervisor, Willis L. Moore, dismissed their warnings, an error in judgment that cost the lives of between 6,000 and 8,000 people.

Isaac's Storm received enthusiastic reviews. A. E. Staver, writing for *Choice* (April 2000), called it a "riveting book." In the *New York Times Book Review* (September 12, 1999), W. Jeffrey Bolster wrote: "[Larson's book,] richly imagined and prodigiously researched, pulls readers into the eye of the hurricane, and into everyday lives and state-of-the-art science. It is a gripping account, horridly fascinating to its core, and all the more compelling for being true. . . . Few historical reconstructions sustain such drama." Writing for the *New Statesman* (October 11, 1999), Rebecca Adams declared: "This book is gripping, informative and imaginative from start to finish. Larson combines abundant 'human interest' with a good dollop of history and just enough science. He is clear and succinct on the mechanics of these meteorological demons, and his lyrical descriptions of harmless water droplets swelling into gigantic, lethal, airborne armouries stir the spirit. . . . As this book reminds us, weather experts are still only making educated guesses much of the time and when they get it wrong, hurricanes can be as unpredictable and deadly as ever they were."

In *The Devil in the White City: Murder, Magic, and Madness at the Fair That Changed America* (2003), Larson evokes the scene of the famous Chicago World's Fair of 1893, which was also known as the World's Columbian Exposition, because it celebrated the 400th anniversary of Christopher Columbus's landing in the New World. (The fair showcased a number of significant inventions—most notably the Ferris wheel, the first zipper, and Aunt Jemima pancake mix—and displayed a wide variety of exhibits from different cultures, including mummies, belly dancers, and cannibals.) Larson tells the story of the fair's architect, Daniel H. Burnham, who overcame numerous obstacles to build the "White City" (so named because of the fair's many white-painted buildings); Larson juxtaposes this tale with a darker story that was unfolding at the same time, a spree of murders that occurred in the vicinity of the fair. H. H. Holmes, reputedly America's first urban serial killer, was a doctor believed to have killed dozens of people, mostly young women, in some cases supplying his medical classes with their skeletons. Larson's factual account suggests that the events in Chicago in 1893 marked the birth of the 20th century, with all its wondrous progress and gruesome horrors.

Nominated for the National Book Award for nonfiction, *The Devil in the White City* received generally positive reviews. Janet Maslin, writing for the *New York Times* (February 10, 2003), noted

that Larson "relentlessly fuses history and entertainment to give this nonfiction book the dramatic effect of a novel, complete with abundant cross-cutting and foreshadowing. Ordinarily these might be alarming tactics, but in the case of this material they do the trick. Mr. Larson has written a dynamic, enveloping book filled with haunting, closely annotated information. And it doesn't hurt that this truth really is stranger than fiction." A reviewer for *Publishers Weekly*, as quoted on Amazon.com, wrote, "Larson is most interested in industriousness and the new opportunities for mayhem afforded by the advent of widespread public anonymity. This book is everything popular history should be, meticulously recreating a rich, pre-automobile America on the cusp of modernity, in which the sale of 'articulated' corpses was a semi-respectable trade and serial killers could go well-nigh unnoticed."

In Larson's most recent book, *Thunderstruck* (2006), he explained how the success of one inventor relied on the actions of a murderer. When Guglielmo Marconi first introduced his system of radio telegraphy—the first form of wireless communication—to English audiences in 1896, the scientific community remained skeptical. Marconi earned respect for his invention, however, when it helped to apprehend H. H. Crippen, an Englishman who had fled to Canada after murdering his overbearing wife. "In addition to writing stylish portraits of all of his main characters, Larson populates his narrative with an irresistible supporting cast," James L. Swanson wrote for *Publishers Weekly* (August 14, 2006). "He remains a master of the fact-filled vignette and humorous aside that propel the story forward. *Thunderstruck* triumphantly resurrects the spirit of another age, when one man's public genius linked the world, while another's private turmoil made him a symbol of the end of 'the great hush' and the first victim of a new era when instant communication, now inescapable, conquered the world."

Larson and his wife, the physician Christine Gleason, live in Seattle, Washington, with their three daughters. The author counts among his influences John Steinbeck, Ernest Hemingway, Raymond Chandler, Ross MacDonald, and Leo Tolstoy. He writes either on a computer or on a yellow legal pad in his home office, generally from 4 a.m. to about 7 a.m., then breaks to spend time with his family before they leave for work and school. At about 8:30 he returns to writing and continues until about noon. "Ideally I will stop the writing process in mid-sentence or mid-paragraph, knowing exactly where I will have to go the next day," he remarked in his interview with Kovach. "I think that is the single most critical rule for a writer: Stop at a point where you know you can pick up the next day."

—C.M.

Suggested Reading: *Booklist* p1,739 Jan. 1–15, 1999; *Economist* p100 Apr. 30, 1994; *Library Journal* p100 Oct. 1, 1992; *New Statesman* p55 Oct. 11, 1999; *New York Times* E p1 Feb. 10, 2003; *New York Times Book Review* p16 Jan. 24, 1993, p46 Sep. 12, 1999; *Washington Post Book World* Cp4 Feb. 13, 2003; *Writer* p20+ Sep. 2003

Selected Books: *The Naked Consumer: How Our Private Lives Become Public Commodities*, 1992; *Lethal Passage: How the Travels of a Single Handgun Expose the Roots of America's Gun Crisis*, 1994; *Isaac's Storm: A Man, a Time,and the Deadliest Hurricane in History*, 1999; *The Devil in the White City: Murder, Magic, and Madness at the Fair That Changed America*, 2003; *Thunderstruck*, 2006

Lau, Evelyn

July 2, 1971– Poet; memoirist; novelist; short-story writer

Discussing the prostitutes she occasionally passes on the street more than a decade after she herself was one of them, Evelyn Lau wrote in her second memoir, *Inside Out: Reflections on a Life So Far* (2001), "Their eyes are masked in makeup, their legs elongated by short skirts and stiletto heels. I remember, and I don't want to remember. I expect them to see it in my face, this memory, this mutual knowledge. I feel that the ordinary clothes in which I am dressed are a sham, an adopted disguise, along with all the other trappings of my ordinary life. That somewhere a pin could be pulled and it would all fall away, all come tumbling down. And I would land back on the street corner where, for a long time, I felt I belonged, as I had never belonged anywhere before." The passage captures the psychic double existence Lau was forced to assume both before and after she ran away from home at the age of 14 and ended up selling herself on the streets. An honor student whose parents expected her to pursue a career in medicine or law, she hid from them her desire to be an author—holing up in her bedroom and stashing her writings between the pages of her textbooks. Now established as one of the most important young writers working in Canada today, Lau has produced two memoirs, four books of poetry, two collections of short stories, and a novel.

Born on July 2, 1971 in Vancouver, British Columbia, Canada, Evelyn Lau grew up in a conservative Chinese-Canadian household. She began to think about becoming a writer, despite her parents' wishes, when she was just six. "I'm six years old and in grade one, and already an incorrigible bookworm. I was sitting in my classroom, looking at my book, and I felt as if—this

is so embarrassing—I got so much pleasure out of reading that I should give other people pleasure with something I'd written. That was where I started," she told Brian Fawcett for *Books in Canada* (May 1993). Lau demonstrated that she had talent early on. By 1984 she was publishing poetry in both Canada and the U.S. and was one of 12 writers to win an essay-writing contest, the prize for which was a meeting with Pope John Paul II. Her parents, nonetheless, forbade her to write, and while she wasn't argumentative and seemed to be complying with their wishes, achieving high grades and practicing piano every day as they demanded, she continued to write in secret. At the age of 14, she could no longer tolerate the repressive atmosphere of her home and ran away.

Lau was taken in by an aging hippie who forced himself on her, taking her virginity. Out of her parents' home for less than a week, Lau responded by attempting suicide and was placed in a psychiatric ward. Upon her release, she was returned to her parents, from whom she again ran away. For the following 22 months, she submersed herself in street life, turning to drugs and prostitution. All the while, she kept writing, keeping diaries of her day-to-day experiences. At the age of 16, she realized that drugs had become a bigger part of her life than even writing. "That totally destroyed me," a reporter for the Associated Press (July 23, 1988) quoted her as saying. She again attempted suicide and again found herself in a hospital. When she was released, she was made a ward of the state, rather than returned to her parents, and by the time she was 17, she had found a publisher for her diaries. She had also won a Canadian Council grant for $13,000 Canadian (about $10,700 in U.S. currency). In 1989 *Runaway: Diary of a Street Kid* was released by HarperCollins. The book achieved best-seller status and was turned into a made-for-TV-movie, *The Diary of Evelyn Lau* (1993), starring Sandra Oh. The book garnered positive, if qualified, reviews, proving it had been published for more than its sensational subject matter. Bruce Serafin wrote for the *Toronto Star* (October 7, 1989), "Lau—who is now 18—is that very rare thing in the literary world, a child prodigy." Serafin, however, went on to point out that her talent had not yet fully developed. "As a piece of writing," he noted, "*Runaway* has flaws. It is repetitious, excruciatingly self-involved. You read it at great speed, skipping and bouncing from page to page. But there are many remarkable moments in it, and taken all in all, it seems to be a valuable book." Other reviewers responded similarly. Darlene James, in a review for *Maclean's* (November 13, 1989), for example, observed, "the writing—and the writer—are often infuriating. The sections written when Lau was taking prodigious amounts of methadone and LSD are redundant to the point of tedium. She is sometimes self-pitying and self-aggrandizing at the same moment—'I could become one of the top writers in Canada, or I could

Courtesy of Doubleday

Evelyn Lau

be a drug addict, or I could die. Those are the choices. . . .' Still, the book also yields passages of great power in which Lau's anger sizzles on the page. At those times, it is a shock for the reader to recall that the words were penned by an adolescent."

The year after *Runaway* was released, Lau became the youngest person ever to receive the Canadian Authors' Association award for most promising writer under 30 and published her first book of poems, *You Are Not Who You Claim* (1990). Gerry Shikatani, writing for the *Toronto Star* (November 24, 1990), acknowledged that Lau was "frequently original and subtle" and that her poetry could be "evocative and provocative." However, he pointed out that "those who seek other levels of writing might better shop elsewhere. A lack of restraint often leads Lau into melodramatic excess ('Her hands stretched out / to fill the void') or dreary statement ('reputations are dependent upon other people / their needs and their inadequacies . . .')." Despite such mixed reviews, Lau won the Milton Acorn Memorial People's Poetry Award for the book in 1991.

Lau's second book of poems, *Oedipal Dreams*, was published in 1992 and was nominated for the Governor-General's Award for poetry. The poems pressed, according to Malcolm Parry for the Canadian newspaper the *Vancouver Sun* (September 24, 1992), "the same buttons [that *Runaway* had pressed] . . . , as in this to a psychoanalyst with whom, two poems later, she will make love: 'sometimes you speak as if there were a child in the room / when there is only me. / I spoke for years as if there were a crowd in the room / when there was only you.'" Others greeted

the book more enthusiastically. A writer for the *Vancouver Sun* (October 31, 1992) reported that the Canadian poet Irving Layton had called Lau "the poet I've been waiting for" and said, "her future success is inevitable." The *Sun* article also noted that the writer Marilyn Bowering had said the poems show us "a brutal sexual psychic underworld made bearable only by poetry's peculiar power to open and staunch wounds at one and the same time."

After writing *Oedipal Dreams*, Lau returned to prose and wrote her first book of short stories, *Fresh Girls, and Other Stories* (1993). The book led the poet Susan Musgrave to proclaim, as Ken McGoogan reported in the *Calgary Herald* (September 25, 1993), "What [the novelist] Anne Rice does for vampires, Evelyn Lau does for sex: fills us with a kind of longing for perverse pleasure and pain." For Lau, the book marked a turning point; writing it forced her to become more self-conscious about her work. She told Joel Yanofsky for the Montreal *Gazette* (October 9, 1993), "The truth is I'm less sure of my writing now than I was when I was 16 because now I know what good writing is. . . . I'm trying to get better." Yanofsky believed she had. "*Fresh Girls*," he wrote, "is a dazzling fictional debut—a beautifully crafted collection of short stories about the ugliest side of our nature, about the obliteration of desire by shame, love by cruelty." Anna Asimakopulos, also writing for the Montreal *Gazette* (October 2, 1993), similarly observed that Lau's "writing, though disturbing, is compelling" and noted that "the stories . . . are all fast-paced. They can be read in one sitting. But like an addiction, they beg to be reread. And, like the raised red welts on the body of one of Lau's characters, the stories linger long after they're finished." Other reviewers were less enthusiastic. Sharon Drache, in a critique for *Books in Canada* (October 1993), called the stories "disappointing" and wrote, "Lau writes a lot about sex but without humour or insight. There is a tiresome sameness to these stories that renders them indistinguishable and ultimately forgettable."

Lau next published a book of poems, *In the House of Slaves* (1994). Like *Fresh Girls* it had, as Philip Marchand wrote for the *Toronto Star* (April 9, 1994), "a heavy sado-masochistic accent," a quality that prompted Marchand to call Lau the "author most in danger of exhausting her theme." Other reviewers were less discouraging. Heather Mallick, in a review for the *Toronto Sun* (May 1, 1994), wrote that Lau "has done a rather good job of demystifying sado-masochism in her latest collection of poems. She captures sordidness very well—how odd it is to do disgusting things at Christmas, for instance. 'There was blood on the sheets, so red, so festive.'"

In 1995 Lau published a novel, *Other Women*, which seemed to respond to Marchand's jibe in its total lack of prostitutes or sleazy back streets. "I was hoping people would see this book in terms of subject matter as a leap from what I was writing about in the past," she was quoted as saying by the Canadian Press Newswire (September 13, 1995). The novel tells the story of Fiona, an artist who is in the midst of an unconsummated but long-term affair with Raymond, a married middle-aged man. Focusing on Fiona's thoughts, the novel, according to Margaret Gunning for the *Vancouver Sun* (September 2, 1995), becomes "convoluted and internal, an endless inner monologue of pain: 'The days passed and I could not stop thinking about, waiting for, you. It was like some faulty wiring in my brain was causing a single tape of experience to loop around and around,' Fiona observes, summing up one of the main problems with the book." Gunning later qualified her criticism and declared, "In spite of its narrow emotional track, *Other Women* can't be dismissed as a poor effort. Evelyn Lau couldn't write badly if her life depended on it, and her prose is full of breathtaking phrases and images." Other critics were more comfortable with the form of the novel as a whole. "It is written in chapters of alternating voice, going from the third person to the first, as though miming Fiona's effort to gain perspective," Andre Alexis wrote for the *Toronto Star* (September 23, 1995). "It also lurches unpredictably in time, going forward and backward, returning obsessively to incidents, places, moments and things. For all that, it is not particularly confusing or off-putting: the logic of the transitions is emotional, rather than linear, and it effectively pulls you into Fiona's emotional state."

Four years passed before Lau's next book, a collection of short stories called *Choose Me* (1999), appeared. During these years, Lau sought to expand her horizons and become more in tune with people living ordinary lives. Five of her first six books had been either directly or indirectly influenced by her experience on the streets as a teenager. As Andreas Curtis, in an article for *Toronto Life* (March 1999), observed, "she followed up *Runaway*'s success with three acclaimed books of poetry and a collection of short stories that all mined the landscape of young hookers, empty sex and profound loneliness." To break out of that mold, Lau spent, as Daniel Gerard reported for the *Toronto Star* (March 20, 1999), "the past few years 'trying to enter a new life, encounter other lives and be able to write about those.'" *Choose Me* is populated by a teacher, a photographer, a journalist, and a woman working in a clothing store, among other ordinary people. One character is a prostitute but "only as an afterthought," Gerard notes. Lau told Gerard, "I don't think it's so much a development of my writing as it's a development in my knowledge." Many critics complained, however, that the stories were simply obsessive, if disguised, retellings of her two-year affair with W. P. Kinsella, a writer in his 60s who sued Lau after she published an essay about their life together. Each story is about a

couple in which the man is at least 20 years the woman's senior. Lau found the comparison between the stories and her life tiresome, complaining to Joel Yanofsky for the Montreal *Gazette* (May 15, 1999), "I think what I have found most difficult . . . is the efforts on behalf of some reviewers to see these fictional stories as explicitly about the relationship between me and Bill [Kinsella]. The *National Post*, for example, said all the male characters in the book are Bill. The stories have been discounted as having any kind of merit as a result of the perception that they are autobiographical." Other critics found different flaws. Nikki Abraham, for example, observed in *Books in Canada* (April 1999) that the plot lines of all the stories were practically the same. A young woman falls for an unavailable older man in a position of authority, pursues him till he succumbs to her advances, and then becomes disenchanted with him, particularly because of his aged body. Abraham qualified her criticism by observing, "Actually, there are some differences among the various female narrators, their men, and their relationships to them. However, these differences are not deep enough to dispel the sensation of trudging through the same psychological territory. . . ; essentially the same relationship is being described in each of the seven stories." Writing for the *Toronto Sun* (April 18, 1999), Heather Mallick, by contrast, called *Choose Me* "the best work the alarmingly talented Lau has ever produced" and ventured that if it were "presented properly by her publisher, it could well become a literary landmark. For it's the writers who demolish cherished myths [in this case, the myth that older men are wise, generous, and attractive] . . . who win fame."

Lau followed *Choose Me* with a collection of personal essays, *Inside Out: Reflections on a Life So Far*, which describes, as Jennifer Van Evra wrote for the *Vancouver Sun* (March 24, 2001), "the skewed rationale behind her experience with bulimia; dissects the flat, dreary landscape of depression with a surgeon's precision; explores her compulsion toward relationships with older, fatherly, unavailable men, and reflects on how her days on the street to this day pervade her life." For a writer who had complained to Joel Yanofsky that "it's not her work that's being scrutinized, it's her personal life," publishing a second memoir might have seemed an odd move, but as Lau explained to Van Evra, this book was all about the writing process, "about going through numerous drafts and polishing and trying to make sure every word was in the right place. For me, the craft in the book is far more important than the subject matter." The care Lau had put into the book was noted by critics. "Lau writes with astonishing frankness, handling with clarity and occasional shocking beauty subject matter most of us would probably avoid or deny, even to ourselves," Robert Wiersema wrote for *Quill & Quire* (March 2001). Charles Mandel, in a review for the *Calgary Herald* (March 31, 2001), agreed, writing, "This is powerful writing, the naked fear and uneasy feelings coming off the page like sour sweat. Lau's essays are confessions of inadequacy, of doubt, of need." Similarly, Philip Marchand proclaimed in the *Toronto Star* (March 11, 2001), "Perhaps through sheer persistence, Lau has mastered the plain style—there is no hint of guile or artifice in her prose. Such simplicity is deceptive. You don't write this way without hard work and talent."

Lau's fourth book of poetry, *Treble,* was published in 2005 by Raincoast Books. It was, Susanne Hiller explained for the Canada *National Post* (April 23, 2005), "vintage Lau. One section, titled 'Fatal Attraction' deals mostly with adultery involving married men who will never leave their wives. But there is material—the struggle for love, the desire to establish deeper relationships—that reflects her life today." Other critics found the collection disappointing. Ian LeTourneau wrote for *Books in Canada* (December 2005), "For the most part, *Treble* was filled with unsurprising, pedestrian narrative poems. . . . Narrative poetry, I'll admit, is not my cup of tea, but I can appreciate it when it's done well. And by 'well' I mean that it contains a vocabulary that is not anemic, has purpose, and still contains some powerful (or at least useful) metaphors and images. . . . Many of Lau's poems are too melodramatic for my taste. Poems like 'The Corn Maze' come with language that scores high on the histrionic scale: 'other couples / stumbled in defeat. They crushed past us / in the heat.' Still, Lau . . . can write a decent line, such as in 'Domesticity #2,' where she writes about a face 'folded in on itself, / an origami of anger.' That's a brilliant image. But it's too bad she chokes the rest of her poems with unnecessary verbiage."

—A.R.

Suggested Reading: *Books in Canada* p13+ May 1993, p16 Apr. 1999; (Canada) *Vancouver Sun* D p7 Oct. 31, 1992, C p4 Nov. 17, 1992; *Maclean's* p81 Nov. 13, 1989, p72+ Oct. 11, 1993; *Toronto Star* M p13 Oct. 7, 1989, G p1 Oct. 21, 1989, G p13 Nov. 24, 1990

Selected Books: *Runaway: Diary of a Street Kid,* 1989; *You Are Not Who You Claim,* 1990; *Oedipal Dreams,* 1992; *Fresh Girls, and Other Stories,* 1993; *In the House of Slaves,* 1994; *Other Women,* 1995; *Choose Me,* 1999; *Inside Out: Reflections on Life So Far,* 2001; *Treble,* 2005

Le Guin, Ursula K.

Oct. 21, 1929– Novelist; short-story writer; poet; translator; children's book author; critic

Ursula K. Le Guin is widely hailed as one of the most important authors of science-fiction and fantasy stories, a distinction enhanced by the fact that she is a woman who has succeeded in genres that, prior to her appearance, were largely the domain of men. The author of almost 20 novels and more than 100 short stories, Le Guin enjoys a considerable base of devoted fans; moreover, although she writes in genres that are traditionally disparaged by the literary establishment, she has been festooned with critical praise. The notoriously fastidious critic Harold Bloom has called her "a superbly imaginative creator and major stylist," as quoted by Ellen Emry Heltzel in the *Portland Trailblazer* (September/October 2000), and the author John Updike has similarly commended her in the *New Yorker.* Among her honors are a National Book Award, five Hugo Awards, five Nebula Awards, the Kafka Award, a Pushcart Prize, and the Howard Vursell Award of the American Academy of Arts and Letters. Le Guin established her reputation with *The Left Hand of Darkness* (1969), a highly acclaimed science-fiction novel about a human who visits a distant planet where the inhabitants are genderless. That novel, which has been applauded for its feminist themes and intellectual

Michael Buckner/Getty Images

observations, belongs to a series of novels known as the Hainish cycle—named after the universe wherein they are set—which also includes the novels *The Dispossessed: An Ambiguous Utopia* (1974) and *The Telling* (2000), among others. Le Guin's well-known fantasy series, the books of

Earthsea, takes place in an imaginary world populated with wizards and witches; it begins with *The Wizard of Earthsea* (1968) and includes *The Farthest Shore* (1972). She has also published realistic novels, such as *Very Far Away from Anywhere Else* (1976), in addition to children's books, essays, poetry, and works of translation. Although the majority of Le Guin's stories deal with the fantastical and the alien, they emphasize human nature and human relationships, providing her with an opportunity to explore such themes as feminism, sexuality, race, nationalism, the environment, politics, and the dangers of unchecked technological progress.

Ursula K. Le Guin was born Ursula Kroeber in Berkeley, California, on October 21, 1929, the daughter of Alfred Louis Kroeber, a respected anthropologist, and Theodora (Kracaw) Brown Kroeber, a writer, chiefly of children's books. Alfred L. Kroeber's work with Ishi, a Native American reported to be the last member of his cultural group, was memorialized by Theodora Kroeber in the classic work *Ishi in Two Worlds* (1961). Ursula had two older brothers, Theodore Charles and Karl, and an older half-brother, Clifton, from her mother's previous marriage to Clifton Spencer Brown. After the death of Alfred L. Kroeber, Theodora Kroeber married John Quinn, in 1968.

The academic environment in which young Le Guin grew up filled her with a great respect for cultural diversity. She was introduced to the tradition of fantasy through her father's retelling of Native American legends, her reading of the fairy tales of the Norwegian folklorist Peter Christian Asbjørnsen, and the children's stories of the Irish-born Celtic revivalist Padraic Colum, among other myths and legends. At about the age of 12, as Le Guin later recalled in her autobiographical essay "A Citizen of Mondath" (included in her nonfiction collection *The Language of the Night* [1979]), she picked Lord Dunsany's *A Dreamer's Tales* off a living-room bookshelf and began to read, "Toldees, Mondath, Arizim, these are the Inner Lands. . . ." It was, she wrote, a defining moment: "What I hadn't realized, I guess, is that people were still making up myths. One made up stories oneself, of course; but here was a grownup doing it, for grownups, without a single apology to common sense, without an explanation, just dropping us straight into the Inner Lands. . . . I had discovered my native country." Another influence on her development was her discovery of the *Tao-te Ching*, a philosophical work attributed to the historical Chinese philosopher Lao-tzu. Other influences over the years have ranged from the English Romantic poets to the Italian fantasy novelist Italo Calvino and the Polish science-fiction writer Stanislaw Lem.

Le Guin began writing stories when she was nine. At 11 she submitted one to the science-fiction magazine *Amazing Stories* but was rejected; discouraged, she refrained from trying to publish her work for nearly a decade. By the time she graduated from high school, she had lost interest in science-fiction stories altogether, having moved on to classic literature, including the works of Leo Tolstoy. At Radcliffe College, in Cambridge, Massachusetts, she studied French and Italian, specializing in Renaissance literature, and received her B.A., in 1951. The next year she earned her master's degree at Columbia University (with a thesis on "Ideas of Death in Ronsard's Poetry") and began work on a Ph.D. In 1953 she received a Fulbright grant to spend a year in France researching her doctoral dissertation on the poet Jean Lemaire de Belges. En route to France, she met Charles Le Guin, a history professor, whom she married in Paris on December 25, 1953. Following her marriage, she cut short her doctoral program to keep in step with her husband's academic itinerary; she taught French at Mercer University, in Macon, Georgia, in 1954 and at the University of Idaho, in 1956. In 1958 the Le Guins settled in Portland, Oregon, where Charles Le Guin began teaching history at Portland State University.

Despite giving up her doctoral studies, Le Guin did not stop writing. Much of her early work was poetry, some of which was published in small magazines. She wrote five unpublished novels between 1951 and 1961, one set in contemporary San Francisco and four in Orsinia, a fictional (though nonfantastic) Central European country, which was also the setting for some short stories she wrote at the time. One of the short stories, "An die Musik," was published in *Western Humanities Review* (Summer 1961). Several publishers rejected the novels on the ground that the material seemed "remote." "It *was* remote," Le Guin observed in "A Citizen of Mondath." "It was meant to be. Searching for a technique of distancing, I had come on this one. Unfortunately, it was not a technique used by anybody else at the moment, it was not fashionable, it did not fit into any of the categories."

One category Le Guin eventually found her way into was science fiction, which she resumed reading in 1960. She was inspired by the stories of Cordwainer Smith (the pseudonym of Paul Linebarger), which persuaded her that sophisticated writing could be done in the genre. When first trying her hand at science fiction, she knew as yet too little science to use it as a framework and so wrote what she describes as "fairy tales decked out in space suits." The tales were first published by Cele Goldsmith Lalli, the editor of *Fantastic Stories of Imagination*. The first to appear, in September 1962, was "April in Paris," an agreeable time-travel story, more fantasy than science fiction, in which black magic romantically unites four lonely people from different eras. The second was "The Masters" (February 1963), her first genuine science-fiction story, set in a post-catastrophic world where science is proscribed because of the havoc it has wrought; the story's heroes are two defiant adventurers brought to inquisitorial justice for secretly studying mathematics. The third was "Darkness Box" (November 1963), about a king who vainly tries to halt time, change, and mortality by shutting darkness into a box and throwing it in the sea. "The Word of Unbinding" (January 1964), was, along with a later story, "The Rule of Names," the prelude to the Earthsea novels. Another story, published in *Amazing Fact and Science Fiction Stories* (also edited by Cele Goldsmith Lalli) in September 1964, was "The Dowry of Angyar," later retitled "Semley's Necklace"; that work was the first of her Hainish stories.

Based partly on the Norse Odin myths, the Hainish cycle, also known as the Novels of the Ekumen, covers approximately 2,500 years of future history beginning about 350 years from now. An original race from the planet Hain colonizes a League of All Worlds, seeding other habitable planets in our galaxy, including Earth, with human life. In the dark age following a galactic war, the several far-flung humanoid settlements, varying enormously in culture and, in some instances, in biology, forget their common origin and have to struggle to recognize one another as human. All of the Hainish stories take place long after the war, when contact is gradually being reestablished. In *Rocannon's World* (1966; published together with *The Kar-Chee Reign* by Avram Davidson) the hero is Gaveral Rocannon, an interstellar ethnologist marooned on the primitive planet Fomalhaut II whose fearlessness in adapting to the ways of its five sentient races is rewarded with the gift of telepathy or "mindspeech." Telepathy is also in common use in *Planet of Exile* (1966; published together with *Mankind Under the Lease* by Thomas M. Disch), set some 1,000 years later on Gamma Draconis III, where a colony of "civilized" humans look upon the native Tevarians as savages but ultimately unite with them in common defense against a race of marauding nomads; the military alliance culminates in a mutual cultural and genetic adaptation. The setting of the third Hainish novel, *City of Illusions* (1967), is an Earth subjugated by the Shing—invaders who have turned mindspeech into "mindlying." The hero is Falk, an amnesiac messenger from Gamma Draconis III who, after remembering his true identity, joins it to his new Earthly persona and, thus balancing the two sides of his personality, able to detect mindlying and destroy the Shing. (*Rocannon's World*, *Planet of Exile*, and *City of Illusions* were also joined and published as *Three Hainish Novels* in 1967.)

Le Guin's short story "Winter's King" provided the seed for her novel *The Left Hand of Darkness*, which many critics and fans consider to be the crowning achievement of the series and which remains one of her most popular books. She has described the novel as, in part, a feminist "thought experiment," exploring what would happen in a society free of sexual role-playing, although her main concern was not with sexuality but with fidelity and betrayal. Its protagonist is Genly Ai, an envoy of the Ekumen of Known Worlds (the sophisticated commercial-cultural-mystical successor to the imperialistic League of All Worlds). He is on a recruiting mission on the glacial planet Gethen (also called Winter), the inhabitants of which are androgynous except during their monthly "oestrus cycle," when they can mate either as men or women. Genly Ai's political quest turns into a personal odyssey, in which he is transformed by the Gethenian freedom from gender stereotypes, by the social and psychological ramifications of that liberation, and by his relationship with Estaven, an exile from both of the opposing societies on Gethen. *The Left Hand of Darkness* won the Nebula Award of the Science Fiction Writers of America and the Hugo Award of the World Science Fiction Convention.

Also belonging to the Hainish series were the novellas *Vaster than Empires and More Slow* (1971), which was collected in *The Wind's Twelve Quarters* (1975), and the Hugo Award–winning *The Word for World is Forest* (1972), which was republished as a separate book in 1976. In the former, Osden, a misanthropic interplanetary explorer with "wide-range bioempathic receptivity" finally finds the love of his life in the sentient vegetation of an Edenic planet. *The Word for World is Forest* was inspired in part by the author's readings about sleep and dream research and in part by her revulsion at the Vietnam War. In the novella, an expedition from Earth (which has been reduced to a concrete desert) goes to the planet Athshe, where it finds an "inferior," tiny, green-skinned people (dubbed "creechies" by the invaders) who live symbiotically with their ecology and whose men are responsible for "thinking"—a combination of waking consciousness and dreaming—while the women take care of tribal activities. Enslaved and forced to take part in the destruction of their planet, the peaceful Athsheans are driven to violence and the brink of insanity.

The Hainish cycle began an extended hiatus after the publication of *The Dispossessed: An Ambiguous Utopia* (1974), which won both the Hugo Award and the Nebula Award for the best science-fiction novel of 1974, and with the related short story "The Day before the Revolution," which won the Nebula Award for best short story of 1974. The novel is set on Anarres, a barren planet where anarchist settlers have established a less-than-perfect egalitarian community, and on Urras, the rich, spoiled sister planet—similar to our own—from which the settlers emigrated 170 years earlier. The protagonist is Shevek, a brilliant physicist who grew up on Anarres but whose freewheeling genius is stymied there. Ambivalent, he moves to Urras and then, finally, back to Anarres. "The contrasting worlds on Anarres and Urras have been realized with painstaking intelligence," Helen Rogan observed for *Time* (August 5, 1974). "Le Guin's characters, especially

Shevek and his family, are complex and haunting, and her writing is remarkable for its sinewy grace."

In 2000 Le Guin returned to the novels of the Ekumen with the publication of *The Telling*. In this novel a character named Sutty is one of four observers on the planet Aka, a world less technologically advanced than the rest of the Ekumen. Aka's government has begun to pursue a program that eliminates any ideas that make people recall the past; through this process the Aka government hopes to become as technologically developed as other worlds. Through investigation Sutty discovers an underground group of storytellers who preserve ideas through a process called "telling." Like its predecessors, *The Telling* received exceptional reviews. "Le Guin presents a masterpiece that is heartwarming, life-affirming and touching," Kurt Lancaster wrote for the *Christian Science Monitor* (September 7, 2000). "Her vision is truthful not only to [the] characters, but like good science fiction, to our contemporary age." Jackie Cassada agreed, writing for *Library Journal* (July 2000): "This parable of the modern world's headlong rush towards monocultural sterility exemplifies the author's elegant simplicity and keen insight."

Perhaps equally well known, Le Guin's Earthsea books have also received strong critical and popular acclaim. Whereas the Ekumen novels are science fiction, the Earthsea books belong to the genre of fantasy. Fundamental to the series are the rules of magic prevailing in the fictional Earthsea Archipelago, especially the rule of names, which is drawn from Sir James George Frazier's *The Golden Bough*: true names identify inner realities, and knowledge of them gives power over the realities. The first volume, *The Wizard of Earthsea*, relates the coming of age of the young wizard Ged, an apprenticeship in which he learns to control his "shadow," with its pride, temper, fear, jealousy, hatred, and other flaws of character, so that he may use his magical powers for good without endangering himself or others.

The second volume is *The Tombs of Atuan* (1970), a Newbery Honor Book. That novel, highly sexual in its symbolism, chronicles the descent of Ged into the underworld to rescue Arha, a young priestess consecrated to the service of ancient dark powers called the "Nameless Ones." The third volume, which won the National Book Award for children's literature, is *The Farthest Shore*. In it, Ged, now older and a master wizard, embarks on his greatest adventure of all, a confrontation with death. He makes a young apprentice his heir in magic as he goes on a quest to prevent magic from disappearing from Earthsea. Along the way Ged must confront his past and the shadow of death, undergoing a form of psychological evolution that, critics have noted, closely follows the broad outlines of the theories of the psychologist Carl Jung.

Tehanu: The Last Book of Earthsea (1990) picks up the story after Ged's return from his adventures in *The Farthest Shore*. Though now stripped of his powers, Ged uses his human skills to save Therru, an abused child, who later emerges as a powerful witch. The reviews were generally favorable. Writing for *Horn Book* (May/June 1990), Ann A. Flowers remarked: "Eighteen years after the publication of *The Farthest Shore*, Ursula K. Le Guin has flawlessly and seamlessly taken up her story where she left off. . . . [This is a] beautiful expression of mature love; a thoughtful, brilliant achievement." Robin McKinley was equally appreciative in the *New York Times Book Review* (May 20, 1990): "*Tehanu* is a major novel by a major novelist. It is deceptively short, and written in a deceptively simple style. . . . The very best thing about this novel is its sense of growth, of distance traveled as well as time passed."

Le Guin had intended to conclude the Earthsea series with *Tehanu*, but a decade later, finding she had more to write about the fictional world, she published *Tales from Earthsea* (2001), a collection of stories that occur either before or after the events of the original novels. Intended primarily for readers already familiar with the series, it also contains an essay on the history of Earthsea, as well as information about its people, languages, and magic. In a review for the *Christian Science Monitor* (May 3, 2001), Kurt Lancaster raved, "Le Guin's writing pulses with purity. These stories sail the reader to a foreign land full of genuine wonder. . . . The best works of fantasy reveal the power of spirit to overcome the entropy of morality, as Le Guin proves with her latest set of tales from Earthsea."

Le Guin has also published another novel in the Earthsea series, *The Other Wind* (2001), which, to some critics, turned the world of Earthsea on its head. The story focuses on Alder the Sorcerer, a man deeply troubled by the death of his wife, as he begins having dreams about a wall that separates the land of the living from the land of the dead; the wall is on the verge of being breached, leaving the dead to invade the land, and the master wizard Ged sends Alder on a quest to stop the looming disaster. In an article for the *New York Times Book Review* (October 7, 2001), Gerald Jonas proclaimed: "At the age of 72, Le Guin has brought to bear on her youthful creation the hardheaded, cleareyed, ultimately optimistic view of human nature that she has forged during an extraordinarily productive and thoughtful career. Reading her latest, I was grateful to have before me a work of art that embodies this lesson: When the good band together, they can accomplish miracles."

In addition to the Ekumen and Earthsea books, Le Guin has written several notable freestanding novels. In *The Lathe of Heaven* (1971), Dr. William Haber, a psychiatrist in Portland, Oregon, is assigned the case of George Orr, a man whose dreams come true. Although George is deeply disturbed by his ability to alter reality with his dreams, Dr. Haber seeks to use the power of his patient for the purpose of "improving" the world—with disastrous results. Theodore Sturgeon, writing for *National Review* (February 4, 1972), called the novel "beautifully wrought," and added that the author's "perceptions of such matters as geopolitics, race, socialized medicine and the patient/shrink relationship are razor-sharp and more than a little cutting." Two television films of *The Lathe of Heaven* have been produced, the first by the Public Broadcasting Service (PBS) in 1980; the second by the A&E network in 2002.

Le Guin's other major novels vary greatly in subject matter and styles. The only fantasy to be found in *Very Far Away from Anywhere Else*, a novella about a teenage friendship, is in the minds of the protagonists, Paul and Natalie, sensitive young people who give each other the strength to resist pressures to conform. By contrast, the American small-town world of *The Beginning Place* (1980) evolves into a dreamlike reality in which two young people make the difficult passage from adolescent to adult sexuality together. In *Malafrena* (1979), a historical romance set in the fictional Central European country of Orsinia in the 1820s, when young European visionaries dreamed of revolution against reactionary governments, a Byronic hero struggles with the dilemma of freedom versus commitment. The science-fiction novella *The Eye of the Heron* (1983) is concerned with the odds against pacifism and nonviolent resistance in a violent society, and it carries forward the exploration of feminism that Le Guin began in *The Left Hand of Darkness* and *The Dispossessed*. In *Always Coming Home* (1985), an experimental work set in California's Napa Valley in a distant, postapocalyptic future, Le Guin depicts the conflict between the Kesh, a spiritual and harmonious people, and the war-making Condors. The book was packaged with an audiocassette of "Kesh music" (contributed by composer Todd Barton). Samuel R. Delany, writing for the *New York Times Book Review* (September 29, 1985), remarked: "With high invention and deep intelligence, *Always Coming Home* presents, in alternating narratives, poems and expositions, Ursula K. Le Guin's most consistently lyric and luminous book in a career adorned with some of the most precise and passionate prose in the service of a major imaginative vision."

Le Guin has also published numerous short-story collections. Her earlier collections include *Orsinian Tales* (1976) and *The Compass Rose* (1982). *Buffalo Gals, and Other Animal Presences* (1987), a compilation of more than two dozen short tales and poems, borrows from the tradition of talking-animal myths. *Searoad: Chronicles of Klatsand* (1992) is a collection of short fiction featuring four generations of mother-daughter relationships in the fictional town of Klatsand, Oregon. A reviewer for *Ms.* (March/April 1992) wrote: "No science fiction here, but a book of exquisite, linked stories about a small Pacific Coast town and its people. As always, Le Guin is a heartbreakingly beautiful writer." Le Guin's other collections include *A Fisherman of the Inland Sea* (1994); *Four Ways to Forgiveness* (1995), which contains four interconnected science-fiction novellas, set in the Hainish universe, about slavery and liberation; and *Unlocking the Air, and Other Stories* (1996), a selection of 18 fictional pieces. Several of the stories in *The Birthday of the World, and Other Stories* (2002) are also set in the Hainish universe. A reviewer for *Publishers Weekly* (January 14, 2002) called that collection "evocative, richly textured and lyrically written" and noted: "Deeply concerned with gender, these eight stories, although ostensibly about aliens, are all about ourselves: love, sex, life and alienation are all handled with illuminating grace. Le Guin's overarching theme, the journey, informs her characters as they struggle to come to terms with themselves or their worlds."

In *Changing Planes* (2003), a collection of 15 linked short stories, the narrator explains that a friend of hers, a woman named Sita Dulip from Cincinatti, discovered that she had the ability, while enduring the boredom and general unpleasantness of airport waiting rooms, to transport herself, with a twist of her mind, into another plane of existence. Each story offers an "interplanary" travelogue, describing the journeys of Sita and other travelers to mysterious alien worlds, which despite their oddity are similar in ways to our own. "We see ourselves, our habits and behaviors, reflected in these alien landscapes," Nick Owchar wrote for the *Los Angeles Times* (September 5, 2003). "Rather than providing escape from the humdrum, which science fiction and fantasy mostly do, Le Guin offers insight. . . . Such moments of alien deja vu make Le Guin's books a pleasure to read, and one finishes *Changing Planes* in awe of her imagination."

Le Guin has written a number of books for children and young adults, most notably the popular Catwing books, illustrated by J. Schlinder, which feature the adventures of four flying cats who escape a dangerous and dirty city and find a loving home with two children in the country. The series includes *Catwings* (1988), *Catwings Return* (1989), *Wonderful Alexander and the Catwings* (1994), and *Jane on Her Own* (1999). Crescent Dragonwagon, reviewing *Catwings* for the *New York Times Book Review* (November 13, 1988), remarked: "[Le Guin's] dialogue, humor, skill as a storyteller and emotional veracity combine near-flawlessly in a story that is both contemporary and timeless." Le Guin's other children's books include *Leese Webster* (1979), *Cobbler's Rune* (1983), *Solomon Leviathan* (1988), *A Visit from Dr. Katz* (1988), *Fire and Stone* (1989), *Fish Soup* (1992), *Buffalo Gals, Won't You Come Out Tonight* (1994), *A Ride on the Red Mare's Back* (1992), *Tom Mouse* (2002), *Gifts* (2004), and *Voices* (2006).

Le Guin has published a number of poetry collections and chapbooks, including *Wild Angels* (1974), *Hard Words* (1981), *Wild Oats and Fireweed* (1988), *Blue Moon over Thurman Street* (with Roger Dorband, 1993), *Going Out with Peacocks* (1994), *Sixty Odd: New Poems* (1999), and *Incredible Good Fortune: New Poems* (2006). She is also the author of three books of criticism and several essay collections. She has translated works into English, including the *Tao Te Ching*, and edited several anthologies of science fiction.

Ursula K. Le Guin and her husband, Charles, have three grown children—Elizabeth, Caroline, and Theodore—and three grandchildren. They live a very private life in Portland, Oregon.

—K.D.

Suggested Reading: *Christian Science Monitor* p21 Sep. 7, 2000, p21 May 3, 2001; *Horn Book* p338 May/June 1990; *Library Journal* p3641 Nov. 1, 1971 p146 July 2000; *Ms.* P62 Mar./Apr. 1992; *National Review* p107 Feb. 4, 1972; *New York Times Book Review* p31 Sep. 29, 1985, p40 Nov. 13, 1988, p38 May 20, 1990, p19 Oct. 7, 2001; Ursula K. Le Guin's Official Web site; *Science Fiction Studies* p1+ Mar. 1976; Bucknall, Barbara J. *Ursula K. Le Guin*, 1981; De Bolt, Joe. *Ursula K. Le Guin*, 1979; Olander, Joseph D. and Martin Harry Greenberg. *Ursula K. Le Guin*, 1979; Slusser, George Edgar. *The Farthest Shores of Ursula K. Le Guin*, 1976

Selected Books: novels—*Rocannon's World*, 1966; *Planet of Exile*, 1966; *City of Illusions*, 1967; *A Wizard of Earthsea*, 1968; *The Left Hand of Darkness*, 1969; *The Tombs of Atuan*, 1970; *The Lathe of Heaven*, 1971; *The Farthest Shore*, 1972; *The Dispossessed: An Ambiguous Utopia*, 1974; *The Word for World is Forest*, 1976; *Very Far From Anywhere Else*, 1976; *Malafrena*, 1979; *The Beginning Place*, 1980; *The Eye of the Heron*, 1983; *Always Coming Home*, 1985; *Tehanu: The Last Book of Earthsea*, 1990; *The Telling*, 2000; *The Other Wind*, 2001; short fiction—*The Wind's Twelve Quarters*, 1975; *Orsinian Tales*, 1976; *The Compass Rose*, 1982; *Buffalo Gals, and Other Animal Presences*, 1987; *Searoad: Chronicles of Klatsand*, 1991; *A Fisherman of the Inland Sea*, 1994; *Four Ways to Forgiveness*, 1995; *Unlocking the Air, and Other Stories*, 1996; *Tales from Earthsea*, 2001; *The Birthday of the World, and Other Stories*, 2002; children's books—*Catwings*, 1988; *Catwings Return*, 1989; *Fish Soup*, 1992; *A Ride on the Red Mare's Back*, 1992; *Buffalo Gals, Won't you Come Out Tonight*, 1994; *Wonderful Alexander and the Catwings*, 1994; *Jane on Her Own*, 1999; *Tom Mouse*, 2002; *Gifts*, 2004; *Voices*, 2006; poetry collections—*Wild Angels*, 1974; *Blue Moon over Thurman Street* (with Roger Dorband), 1993; *Going Out with Peacocks*, 1994; *Sixty Odd: New Poems*, 1999; *Incredible Good Fortune: New Poems*, 2006; translations—*Lao*

Tzu: Tao Te Ching, 1997; *Selected Poems of Gabriela Mistral*, 2003; *Kalpa Imperial: The Greatest Empire that Never Was*, 2003; criticism—*Dancing at the Edge of the World: Thoughts on Words, Women, Places*, 1989; *The Language of the Night: Essays on Fantasy and Science Fiction*, 1979; *Steering the Craft: Exercises and Discussions on Story Writing for the Lone Navigator of the Mutinous Crew*, 1998; *The Wave in the Mind: Talks and Essays on the Writer, the Reader, and the Imagination*, 2006

Courtesy of Random House

lê thi diem thúy

(LAY TEE YIM TWEE)

1972– Novelist; performance artist

The Vietnamese author lê thi diem thúy (like the poet e.e. cummings, lê spells her name with all lowercase letters) based her first novel, *The Gangster We Are All Looking For* (2003), on her childhood experiences as one of the Vietnamese "boat people" of the late 1970s; many residents left the country after the end of the Vietnam War, in 1975, fleeing aboard whatever boats—even the most crudely made ones—were available. Though her own struggles inspired her novel, she emphasizes that it is a work of fiction—not a memoir. "It mirrors places I've [been], both geographical and emotional, but I didn't enter into it as a recollection of my own experiences and memories," she told Sarah Anne Johnson for the *Writer* (February 2004). "I entered into it with these characters and followed them. I'm much more excited about the things that happen that I never anticipate. . . . Also, I didn't want to write a memoir because I wanted people to engage with these characters and *this* narrator, not because she was me or because it had happened to me, but because *this* happens in the world. The experience of displacement is a profound one and is one that so many people have gone through."

Born in the village of Phan Thiet, on the coast of South Vietnam, in 1972, lê left the country with her father in a small fishing boat when she was six years old. They were picked up by a U.S. Navy vessel and taken to a refugee camp in Singapore. Although lê's birth name was Trang, her father mistakenly reported it as Thuy, the name of lê's older sister. After Thuy drowned two years later, lê kept her sister's name. This was the second child that the family had lost; the eldest son drowned in the ocean off of Vietnam when he was six. "I feel the presence of these older siblings," lê told David Mehegan for the *Boston Globe* (June 2, 2003). "I still don't think I am the oldest." Lê and her father eventually made their way to San Diego, California, where, after two years, her mother and a sister were able to join them.

Lê later attended Hampshire College, in Massachusetts, where she received a degree in cultural studies and postcolonial literature. During a semester abroad, in 1993, she traveled to France, where for the first time she truly felt like an American. "Being in France and not hearing English every day," she told Mehegan, "helped clarify how I hear English and carry it inside me." After graduating, in 1994, lê became a performance artist, recounting her childhood tales. One of these performances, "Red Fiery Summer," featured material that later became part of her first novel. She has performed at venues throughout the U.S. and Europe, including the Whitney Museum of American Art and the Vineyard Theater, both in New York City.

In 1996 lê published the prose piece "The Gangster We Are All Looking For" in the *Massachusetts Review*. A portion of that story was republished in the Readings section of the April 1996 issue of *Harper's*. The New York City–based literary agent Nicole Aragi saw the excerpted piece and drove up to Bard College, in Annandale-on-Hudson, New York, where lê was performing "Red Fiery Summer." "It was incredible," Aragi told Mehegan. "There was something very quiet about it, but it had the most astonishing impact. It's true of her writing as well. She doesn't expose everything." Aragi encouraged the young artist to develop the piece as a book.

The Gangster We Are All Looking For contains five episodic chapters about the life of a Vietnamese refugee family, as told through the eyes of the family's daughter. The girl and her father, whom she calls Ba, are the first to arrive in Southern California, where they are temporarily supported by a sympathetic but condescending American family. The girl's mother, Ma, arrives

later, and the reunited family struggles to endure the bitter forces of loss, alienation, and memory. In a review for the *Los Angeles Times* (June 8, 2003), Peter Zinoman wrote, "In this richly rendered Vietnamese family portrait, the narrator, whose intricate and persuasive self-representation emerges indirectly from her precise descriptions of her parents and of the world around her, is the most memorable character. The evolution of her ambiguous sexuality and her efforts to cope with a mysterious family tragedy drive the narrative." In New York *Newsday* (July 6, 2003), Laurie Stone called *The Gangster We Are All Looking For* a "luminous, quirky first book," and noted that its "originality issues from [lê's] use of language. It's as if words are controlled substances—her joy, addiction and means of escape." Stone added that, like a performance piece, "the narrative skips back and forth in time and flies over space—such as the water separating California and Vietnam—with transitions triggered by visual images, emotional echoes and sounds."

Lê's work has been anthologized in *The Best American Essays 1997, Half and Half: Writers on Growing Up Biracial and Bicultural* (1998), and *The Very Inside: An Anthology of Writings by Asian & Pacific Islander Lesbians* (1998). She currently lives in Northampton, Massachusetts.

—C.M.

Suggested Reading: *Boston Globe* B p7 June 2, 2003; (New York) *Newsday* D p31 July 6, 2003; *Los Angeles Times* p10 June 8, 2003; *Writer* p4 Feb. 2004

Selected Books: *The Gangster We Are All Looking For*, 2003

Lee, Andrea

1953– Novelist; short-story writer; journalist

Andrea Lee has made a specialty of crafting stories about women who, usually when they are out of their own milieu, come to realizations concerning their lives or their relationships. In writing about those experiences, Lee shines a hard, bright light on her characters, one that has often dazzled critics. Her first book was a work of nonfiction: *Russian Journal* (1981), an objective glimpse into the lives of people in the Soviet Union at a time when—its serious economic and other troubles notwithstanding—no one realized it would last only a decade longer; her linguistic abilities allowed her to form friendships with Russians of many descriptions. Her novel *Sarah Phillips* (1984) is a thinly veiled autobiography that traces the coming-of-age of a black American woman, at home and abroad, during the heyday of the civil rights movement and afterward. Lee's well-

Filippo Gallino/Courtesy of Random House

Andrea Lee

received collection of short stories, *Interesting Women* (2002), tells of women in exotic locales undergoing moments of crisis or change in their lives, and her latest novel, *Lost Hearts in Italy* (2006), tells of the collapse of a couple's marriage.

Andrea Lee was born in 1953 in Philadelphia, Pennsylvania, and grew up in a middle-class family. "I've been composing fiction since I was four years old and annoyed my family with recitations of long, loud epic tales of which I was, of course, the heroine," Lee said during an interview for the Random House Web site (September 2002). In her early teens, she continued, she "began seriously writing short stories," which "seemed quite natural, a way not only of entertaining myself but also of getting at the hidden themes and patterns I was beginning to discern in life around me." Lee's father, the Reverend Charles Lee, the pastor of the historic First African Baptist Church, was generally considered to be a dynamic preacher and was active in the civil rights movement. Lee was educated at a private elementary and secondary school, the Baldwin School, in Bryn Mawr, Pennsylvania, and graduated from Harvard University, in Cambridge, Massachusetts, where she obtained her B.A. and M.A. degrees in English literature.

In 1978 Lee's then-husband, who was working toward a doctorate in Russian history at Harvard, won a 10-month fellowship to study in the Soviet Union. Lee accompanied him; her first book, *Russian Journal*, which appeared initially as a series of pieces in the *New Yorker* during the Cold War between the Soviet Union and the U.S., is the account of what it was like to be a young American

woman among the Russian people. Lee, who spoke Russian, wrote in the book that it was "easy to make a number of Russian friends from outside the restricted circle normally accessible to foreigners. Since we lived on rubles, stood in queues and rode the metro with ordinary Russians we got a view of life in Moscow and Leningrad [now St. Petersburg] that was very different from that of the diplomats and journalists we knew." In 35 vignettes Lee described how she taught English to Jews trying to emigrate; went to a women's bathhouse, where she encountered "hooligans," as the high-spirited women cavorting there called themselves; and attended such ceremonial events as the May Day parade, which celebrated the triumph of communism in Russia. She provided such an entrancing snapshot of life for an American in Russia that many reviewers observed that her book, unlike other travel books, inspired in them a desire to visit that country. Walter Clemons noted in *Newsweek* (October 19, 1981) that the "oddest illumination of the book" was that Lee found Russians to be fascinated by American culture and, at the same time, nostalgic for the days of the czar.

While critics had strikingly different takes on *Russian Journal*, most agreed on its excellence. A *Library Journal* (October 1, 1981) reviewer found Lee's style "eager and delighted and outgoing" and the book modest and engaging. Walter Clemons remarked that Lee "records what she saw and heard with unassuming delicacy and exactness" and took note of her extraordinary ability to make friends—which extended even to the man she took to be a KGB operative assigned to spy on Lee and her husband. In the *New Republic* (February 24, 1982), Christopher Booker lauded Lee's objectivity: "One of her strengths is that she does not attempt any sweeping analysis of Soviet life or 'the Russian character.' She keeps strictly within the compass of describing only the people she meets and what she sees. But how well she observes and records it all! . . . The dark, oppressive underside of Soviet life is constantly present in the background, but all the more forcefully for being so understated." He added that Lee "sees with . . . a novelist's eye." On the other hand, in *Freedomways* (No. 2, 1982), M. L. Patterson saw *Russian Journal* as a form of red baiting: "The Soviet Union in all of its political and cultural complexity, contradictions, historical richness and profound importance in today's world was not encompassed by Ms. Lee's vision. . . . She doesn't even relate her Afro-American identity to the story. . . . Lee's highly subjective views paint a picture of the Soviet Union that has the net effect of reinforcing the fanatical anti-communism, warmongering and bellicosity so much in vogue currently." *Russian Journal* was nominated for a National Book Award.

Lee became a contract writer for the *New Yorker* and published many short stories in that magazine and other prominent journals. Her next book, *Sarah Phillips* (1984), was classified as a novel, but many saw it as so autobiographical as to be considered a memoir. The title character, like the author, is a light-skinned black woman who grows up in an upper-middle-class family during the civil rights era; she is sent to private schools, where she is sometimes the only nonwhite student, and to exclusive summer camps. Her parents give vocal support to civil rights activities while separating themselves from the participants. Sarah and her brother are restricted to watching protests on television, because their mother fears their contact with the black masses, and although their father thunders in favor of civil rights from the pulpit of the church of which he is the pastor, he criticizes poor black people. The novel opens after Sarah has graduated from Harvard and is living in Paris with friends, gratifying the "lively appetite for white boys" she has declared herself to have. She has fully broken away from her family's values and traditions, even having refused baptism in her father's church at the age of nine. Eventually, however, she finds the life she has chosen for herself unacceptable as well. She then undertakes an exploration of her heritage, in order to find a new, more self-realizing identity.

Many reviewers, although they found *Sarah Phillips* a dazzling literary production in many ways, took issue with its lack of a resolution in the area of Sarah's attempt at finding her cultural identity. Laura Obolensky, a *New Republic* (November 19, 1984) reviewer, praised the passage in the novel in which Sarah refuses baptism, noting that in "artfully lean prose, Lee draws compelling portraits of each of the Phillipses, vividly captures the mood of the black congregation as it sits packed 'in a near-visible miasma of emotion and cologne,' and etches a multiplicity of minor but unfailingly haunting characters. . . . Through Sarah's truculent and often droll refusal to submit to baptism by immersion . . . , Lee comes closest to explaining Sarah's later rebellion. . . . Ultimately, however, *Sarah Phillips* makes for a disconcerting read. . . . What remain deeply troublesome sociological issues are treated tangentially, or with a tone of detachment often bordering on the sardonic. The moral and emotional conflict that should rend [Lee's] narrator as she struggles between two worlds, neither of which really claims her allegiance, is never demonstrated."

Donald B. Gibson, writing for the *African American Review* (Spring 1995), however, concluded that the "book is far more complicated than it at first appears. If *Sarah Phillips* were simply a celebration of the lightness of Sarah's color and the privilege of her class, then the book might be as politically contemptible as some readers have seen it as being. But . . . the author is firmly aware of the tensions produced by the intersections of race, class, and color. The novel is something of a confessional enterprise, in which the author acknowledges the stress and guilt resulting not only from her failure to embrace her African past but also—and just as painfully—from her simultaneous denial of her father and mother, her personal, direct connections to the African American community and its past."

In *MELUS* (Spring 1999) Don M. Enomoto took the position that the novel *Sarah Phillips* was a characteristic product of the "postmodern world. Because Lee occupies a unique position as both a writer and participant in this world . . . her vision departs from 'traditional' black literature. *Sarah Phillips* attempts to define the literary and psychological 'boundaries' of this new social order. In creating a new aesthetic that more accurately reflects the condition of black Americans at the end of the twentieth century, Lee explores the ambiguous terrain where issues of race, class, and gender intersect." Enomoto concluded that the lack of a definitive resolution in *Sarah Phillips* "is an inherent aspect of Lee's complex, innovative, and sophisticated vision."

Lee told an interviewer for the Random House Web site, "Journalism has always seemed restrictive to me, with its stodgy rules of time and place, and its dogmatic insistence on having characters who are actually alive! I'm always aware of how much better magazine and newspaper pieces would be if one combined, exaggerated, or rounded off actual events—just the sort of thing that makes for dishonest journalism, and good fiction. Besides, I am timid and lazy by nature and detest doing the legwork, the probing and questioning that makes a great journalist. I prefer to spy on people from a distance and then retire to my computer to invent backgrounds and adventures for them." Nonetheless, for profiles in the *New Yorker*, she has spent time dining with and interviewing such celebrities as the fashion designers Gianni Versace (she conducted the last interview he gave before he was murdered) and Luciano Benetton.

Meanwhile, Lee has continued her career as a notable short-story writer. In 2002 she published *Interesting Women*, a fiction collection. The stories deal mainly with women in exotic surroundings. In a story called "Brothers and Sisters Around the World," which originally appeared in the *New Yorker* (February 7, 2000), an American black woman and her French husband vacation in Madagascar, one of the many exotic tropical locales that he insists they visit. There, the wife's animosity toward two women who befriend her husband leads her to commit an act that, paradoxically, causes them to feel a kinship with her. Many of the stories in *Interesting Women* are concerned with female bonding, moments when women share their secrets.

In the *New York Times Book Review* (May 12, 2002), Jennifer Schuessler wrote that while "race gives Lee's book a subtle charge, her real subject is a sort of international sisterhood." At the same time, she contended, Lee "writes fiction that is concerned with the many ways of being a foreigner—in your own home, your own country, even your own marriage." Schuessler concluded by noting that the encounters between women in the book, to quote one of Lee's narrators, "turn out to be schoolgirl crushes in disguise, instant friendships that last as long as it takes to swap tales of love and desperation. In short, an ephemeral traffic of souls that is about as revolutionary as flowers pressed in rice paper." Kate Bolick noted for New York *Newsday* (April 7, 2002, on-line) that "as willful and mysterious as these women often are, what really makes them interesting are their relationships with each other. Whether married with children, unattached and on the prowl or independent divorcees, they rarely consider their men to be more than well-heeled interlopers. The vagaries of female friendship—in all its complicated, platonic potency—are primary to these stories." Bolick further observed that it was rare "to find the abstruse dynamics of adult female friendships explored in fiction in the first place. That the author brings such droll intelligence to the effort is even better. . . . Yet refreshing and amusing as these observations are, the stories themselves are often static. In most cases, they feel less like stories and more like rambling, descriptive anecdotes." By contrast, in *Publishers Weekly* (February 18, 2002), a reviewer commented that in reading *Interesting Women*, "you know you're in the presence of an author fully able to, as [one] narrator says, 'picture an endless mazurka of former wives, husbands, lovers, children, and assorted hangers-on, not excepting au pairs, cleaning women and pets.' The stories are full of tension—sexual, material, racial. . . . They . . . provide instant and sophisticated gratification."

Lee's latest novel, *Lost Hearts in Italy*, appeared in 2006. The novel focuses on the dissolution of Mira Ward and Nick Reiver's marriage. The young couple moved to Italy, in the 1980s, after the bank Nick works for transferred him. On her way to join him, Mira meets Zenin, an Italian billionaire, with whom she soon begins a long-lasting affair. Critics, as they did when Lee had published her first novel, called attention to the autobiographical elements in the story, noting that Mira shares much with Lee, and Lee told Liane Hansen for an interview on NPR (August 27, 2006), "I think that Mira could be seen as, say, *Sarah Phillips* grown up." Reviews were more harsh than those of Lee's earlier books. Lucy Ellmann, writing for the London *Guardian* (September 23, 2006), complained: "This novel is a painstaking inquiry into an adulterous love affair and its aftermath. It adheres to a rigid formula: in strict rotation, chapter after chapter, each of the three people involved gets an equal say, starting with some scene from the present, followed by one from the past—the 1980s—when the triangular liaison took place. This is then rounded off quite unnecessarily with the thoughts of some innocent bystander. The book is full of muffled guilt and anger, but it's hard to see from where these emotions emanate. The characters are puppets, whom we care little about. They eventually split up and marry other people. So what?" Similarly disappointed, Erica Wagner wrote for the *New York Times* (July 2, 2006), "Lee has a talent for descriptive writing, and the passages in this novel that describe, say, Nick and Mira's romantic afternoon at Cerveteri, the Etruscan city of the dead just outside Rome, are pleasing and evocative. And the novel, overall, is not onerous to read. But I kept wondering why I was bothering with these people, and why the author kept feeling the need to drive her points, such as they are, home so firmly. The device of placing little codas, in which minor characters are given a perspective on the main events, is one of the book's more annoying tricks. It's not a shock to discover that the deckhand on Zenin's yacht is a little jealous of the old guy. It's possible for a novel—and unfortunately, this is just such a novel—to be both too particular, and not particular enough. It's a shame, but there are no surprises here, however much even the author herself might have wished for them." Not everyone was so harsh. Carlin Romano, writing for the *Philadelphia Inquirer* (August 27, 2006), praised "the lustrous, textured canniness of Lee's sentences" and went on to observe: "At least one reviewer has suggested that *Lost Hearts* is overwritten the way Mira is so often overdressed. *Mi dispiace, ma* ('I'm sorry, but') Lee's prose shimmers so effectively that this critic concludes, *al contrario*, that too much contemporary American is underwritten."

In the early 1990s Lee married her second husband, Ruggero Aprile di Cimia, who is a baron, and the couple now live in a 600-year-old villa in Turin, Italy, with Lee's daughter and son. Discussing her feelings about Italy with the Random House interviewer, Lee said, "I don't feel like an expatriate. Nor do I feel in any way Italian. In Italy, though I feel completely at home in my family and my household, I feel like a mindful sojourner—someone with deep knowledge of and few illusions about the country around me. Affectionate, but always slightly detached, always foreign. The more I live in Italy, the more passionately American I feel, though in a very profound, not visible sense. Outwardly, I've taken on a protective coloration of the society around me—wearing the clothes, eating the food, adopting superficial customs—but inwardly I'm engaged in a continuous meditation on the curious mixture of libertarianism and Puritanism that makes up America, and how that contrasts with the burden of tradition in Europe. When I come back to the States—which I do at least four times a year—I feel the combination of blessed relief and critical detachment one feels when coming back from college to your childhood home. America seems gloriously big, rich, sprawling, extravagant, bursting with energy, creativity and convenience. At the same time, it seems oddly provincial— unaware of the world outside—naively moralistic, materialistic and race-obsessed, in a way that seems oddly frozen in time. I revel in America when I come home for my two months each summer, but I walk around feeling slightly foreign. All in all, I live between two worlds, which is not at all a bad thing for a writer."

—S.Y.

Suggested Reading: *African American Review* p164+ Spring 1995; *Library Journal* p1,920 Oct. 1, 1981; *MELUS* p209+ Spring 1999; *New Republic* p36 Feb. 24, 1982, p41 Nov. 19, 1984; *New York* (on-line) April 15, 2002; (New York) *Newsday* (on-line) Apr. 7, 2002; *New York Times Book Review* p13 May 12, 2002; *New Yorker* p42+ July 28, 1997, p74+ Feb. 7, 2000; *Newsweek* p102 Oct. 19, 1981; *Washington Post* p10 Oct. 25, 1981

Selected Books: nonfiction—*Russian Journal*, 1981; fiction—*Sarah Phillips*, 1984; *Interesting Women: Stories*, 2002; *Lost Hearts in Italy*, 2006

Scott Wintrow/Getty Images

Lehane, Dennis

Aug. 4, 1965– Novelist; short-story writer; playwright

Dennis Lehane has become known for creating multifaceted characters and gripping plots. In addition to writing the best-selling series of books featuring the detectives Patrick Kenzie and Angela Gennaro, Lehane is the author of the critically acclaimed stand-alone novels *Mystic River* (2001), which was made into an Academy Award–winning movie in 2003, and *Shutter Island* (2003),

as well as a volume of short pieces, *Coronado* (2006). Several of his books are set in or around the Dorchester section of Boston, Massachusetts, the gritty, working-class neighborhood in which he was raised; all of them—in the opinions of many reviewers—display a keen understanding of both human psychology and the elements that make up compelling fiction. His writing, like that of the celebrated authors Elmore Leonard and Raymond Chandler, blurs the distinction between pulp fiction and the "literary novel." Discussing the popularity of the mystery genre, Lehane noted during a *Newsweek* (February 19, 2001) interview, "We've become disillusioned with so-called literary fiction. People don't want to be told that life sucks and let's read about it for the next 250 pages. They kinda know that, that life is mundane, that life is very boring. But they're not just reading for escapism. They're reading to work stuff out, and for that they're looking for stories a little larger than life—characters going through extreme situations, grandly passionate and tragic things. And mysteries do that better than anything."

The youngest of five children, Dennis Lehane was born on August 4, 1965 and grew up in Dorchester. His parents were Catholic immigrants from County Cork, in Ireland; his mother was a school cafeteria worker, his father a warehouse foreman for the Sears retail company. In interviews Lehane has spoken with pride about his parents' struggles. "I love what I do," Lehane remarked in an interview with Louise Jones for *Publishers Weekly* (June 21, 1999), "but I'm no hero. My father worked the same job for 37 years and I don't think he loved it. That's heroism, doing the job and working toward retirement to support your family. That's awe-inspiring."

When Lehane was six years old, a new world opened up for him when his mother took him to the local public library. In a sense, reading gave him experiences he could not otherwise have had in his everyday life, and it served as a refuge from the sometimes violent conflicts in his neighborhood, which were fueled in part by racial tensions. Those conditions, which reached their peak in the 1970s, have informed Lehane's writing since the beginning of his career.

Lehane began his college education at the University of Massachusetts, in Boston, and transferred soon afterward to Eckerd College, a small school in St. Petersburg, Florida. He received his bachelor's degree in creative writing in 1988 and immediately entered a master of fine arts program in creative writing at Florida International University, in Miami. There, he honed his craft under the tutelage of such noted writers as John Dufresne, James Hall, Les Standiford, and Lynne Barrett. (Lehane had begun writing short fiction as an undergraduate but was unwilling to send anything out for publication until his writing improved.)

During his apprenticeship Lehane often imitated the minimalist style of the famed short-story writer Raymond Carver. Later, on a lark, he wrote a mystery novel and showed it to his creative-writing teacher at Eckerd, Sterling Watson. Watson was so impressed with Lehane's novel that he showed it to his former student Ann Rittenberg, who had by that time become a literary agent. Rittenberg, in turn, agreed to represent Lehane and sent the novel to Claire Wachtel at the publishing house Harcourt Brace; it was accepted for publication there on June 17, 1993. Lehane remarked in his interview with Jones: "My publishing career is such a fluke. I got to it a lot faster than I expected. I have no publishing horror stories."

The novel, *A Drink before the War* (1994), which became a critically acclaimed best-seller, features the private detective duo Patrick Kenzie and Angela Gennaro. Patrick, who narrates the novel, and Angela bring to their work both the street smarts they honed in Dorchester, where they were childhood friends, and their personal troubles: Patrick is haunted by the abuse he suffered at the hands of his father, while Angela has to contend with a husband who occasionally beats her. In the novel they are hired by two state senators to track down an African-American cleaning woman who has stolen some sensitive documents. After finding the woman, the detectives realize that the materials she has taken point to political corruption and child prostitution. In a review of *A Drink before the War* for *Booklist* (November 15, 1994), Emily Melton noted: "Lehane offers slick, hip, sparkling dialogue that's as good as it gets, a plot that rockets along at warp speed, and [a] wonderfully original, in-your-face crime-solving duo. . . . A terrific first novel and, one hopes, the beginning of a superb series." Writing for *Library Journal* (November 1, 1994), Rex E. Klett remarked: "Lehane's minimal use of literary references helps establish character, as do his frequent allusions to child abuse and wife battering. Rough and tumble action for a high energy, likable pair." *A Drink before the War* won a Shamus Award from the Private Eye Writers of America.

In Lehane's second entry in the Kenzie-Gennaro mysteries, *Darkness, Take My Hand* (1996), the detectives are on the trail of a serial killer, whose crimes have left the neighborhood in shock and the police baffled. As Angela's marriage falls apart and Patrick finds love, the partners discover that the killer may have a connection to their own pasts. In *Booklist* (July 1996), Emily Melton wrote: "Lehane's latest is an explosive story that is at once gut-wrenchingly violent and achingly melancholy. . . . In a series of heart-stopping climaxes that grow ever more terrifying and bloody, Patrick and Angie lose nearly everything. Lehane's perfectly crafted plot leers, teases, taunts, and lulls, scattering bits of humor and heartbreak among the soul-chilling episodes of death and destruction. A tour de force from a truly gifted writer."

Sacred, the third Kenzie-Gennaro mystery, was published in 1997. In this outing the detectives are kidnapped by a dying billionaire named Trevor Stone, who promises them a handsome monetary reward if they help track down his missing daughter. Their investigations lead them to the cult-like Church of Truth and Revelation and to a series of murders. Ahmad Wright, in *Library Journal* (June 15, 1997), declared: "With its fast-paced plot, Lehane's . . . newest will be a winner with adventure buffs." David Pitt agreed, writing for *Booklist* (June 1–15, 1997), "This is Lehane's third novel . . . and it's devilishly twisted, a kind of Elmore-Leonard-meets-*The-Sting* in which everyone is trying to con everyone else. The characters are well drawn (especially the billionaire and his daughter, who keep revealing new things about themselves, right up until the last scene), the mystery perplexing, . . . and the conclusion deeply satisfying. *Sacred* is a first-class novel that will delight anyone who loves an intricate mystery."

The Kenzie-Gennaro series continued with *Gone, Baby, Gone* (1998), which finds the detectives on the trail of a missing four-year-old girl whose mother, a junkie and prostitute, has stolen $200,000 from a drug dealer. Patrick and Angela, meanwhile, become romantically interested in each other. When the money is recovered by the police, they offer to exchange it for the safe return of the young girl—an offer fraught with problems for everyone involved, including Kenzie and Gennaro. Pam Lambert wrote for *People* (August 10, 1998), "Lehane's evocative prose lures us into the labyrinth of this chilling, masterfully plotted tale into that dark place where men try to play God and everyone gets hurt." Reviewing the book for New York *Newsday* (August 4, 1998), Adam Mazmanian noted, "[Lehane's] crisp dialogue, the oddball supporting cast and the Kenzie-Gennaro romance provide much-needed lightness to what is, ultimately, a dark and harrowing tale." (Plans have been announced to adapt the book for film.)

In *Prayers for Rain* (1999), the most recent Kenzie-Gennaro crime novel, Patrick Kenzie and his friend Bubba Rogowski try to dissuade a man from continuing to stalk a woman; soon afterward the stalker's victim leaps naked to her death from a Boston landmark. The apparent suicide leads Patrick to turn for help to Angela, with whom he has ended his partnership and romance. In a review for *Booklist* (April 15, 1999), Wes Lukowsky wrote, "This fifth Kenzie-Gennaro novel again features well-armed heroes who exact their own brand of vigilante justice in a Boston where the police are inept and/or helpless. As in all the best hard-boiled series, each entry reveals more about the principal characters and their relationships in a violent, uncaring world. . . . Lehane has worked his way into the top echelon of crime writers." Wilda Williams, writing for *Library Journal* (June 15, 1999), was more critical, noting,

"Lehane's love of Boston, its neighborhoods, and its people shines through his hard-edged prose. However, the overly convoluted plot is at times unbelievable, and the gruesome violence . . . is extreme and not for the squeamish."

Taking a break from the Kenzie-Gennaro series, Lehane penned *Mystic River* (2001). That novel, written in third person, focuses on three friends: Sean Devine, Jimmy Marcus, and Dave Boyle. One day in 1975, while the more street-smart Sean and Jimmy look on helplessly, a pair of strange men, pretending to be law-enforcement officers, order 11-year-old Dave to get into their car; Dave is then held prisoner for several days. Twenty-five years later the three friends are reunited in their old neighborhood, following the murder of Jimmy's 19-year-old daughter. That reunion—as well as the investigation into Jimmy's daughter's death—forces them to confront what happened to Dave on that day in their childhood. In the *New York Times Book Review* (February 18, 2001), Marilyn Stasio praised *Mystic River*, calling it a "powerhouse of a crime novel. . . . Lehane spares nothing in his wrenching descriptions of how a crime in the neighborhood kills the neighborhood, taking it down house by house, family by family. Although his deeply scored characterizations of the three former friends carry the soul of his story, Lehane's penetrating studies of their neighbors—including some of the strongest and saddest women you'll ever meet in this genre—are no less vital." Writing for *Newsweek* (February 19, 2001), Malcolm Jones concluded that *Mystic River* "is Lehane's best book by far. Like all his writing, it shimmers with great dialogue and a complex view of the world—what Lehane likes to call 'comic fatality'—where every hero is a little soiled and more than slightly compromised." The novel was adapted for the screen in 2003 by the actor and director Clint Eastwood; the film brought Academy Awards to Sean Penn, who was named best actor for his performance as Jimmy, and Tim Robbins, who won in the best-supporting-actor category for his portrayal of Dave.

Lehane's next novel, *Shutter Island* (2003), was another departure from the Kenzie-Gennaro series. The book, a historical psychological thriller, is set in 1954 on the fictional island of the title, which houses a mental hospital for criminals. As the story opens U.S. Marshall Teddy Daniels and his partner, Chuck Aule, are on their way to the island to investigate the disappearance of Rachel Solando, a woman who drowned her three children two years ago. No one knows how she got out of the hospital, a place where nothing is what it appears to be. Following on the heels of the critically acclaimed and immensely popular *Mystic River*, *Shutter Island* received mixed reviews. "Lehane's strength is dialogue and a relentless penetration into the minds of his characters. In *Shutter Island*, it is Teddy Daniels that Lehane inhabits, luring the reader to suspend belief and join him," Rob Mitchell wrote in a review for the *Boston Herald* (May 13, 2003). "Reminiscent of John Fowles' *The Magus*, *Shutter Island* envelops, encircles and floats inside-out. The ambiguous ending may disappoint some, but it is effective and cries out for a second reading to discover how and where Lehane manages his crafty manipulation." In *People* (April 21, 2003), Edward Nawotka declared, "Although Lehane's latest doesn't have the multifaceted power of his 2001 bestseller *Mystic River* . . . he has crafted a thriller as exciting as an elaborate video game (now Teddy makes his way down a craggy cliff to recover an important clue; now he's sneaking into a fort). If you like books that will make great movies, then this one is for you."

In 2006 Lehane published *Coronado*, which contains five short stories—most previously published elsewhere—and the titular play, which had been mounted, to little fanfare, off-Broadway at the end of 2005. Many reviewers expressed a preference for Lehane's longer fiction. Calling the collection "merely a stopgap for fans," Clea Simon wrote for the *Boston Globe* (September 11, 2006, on-line), "At his best, [Lehane] gives us deft portraits of . . . stunted lives, implying the forces behind them without pity or exaggeration. But in the five short stories and one play that make up *Coronado*, he rarely has the chance to fulfill that promise. Instead, we get the misery without the understanding, the strangled voices without any real insight into what is making such poor creatures writhe." Simon conceded, however, that the first line of Lehane's story "Until Gwen," which originally appeared in the June 2004 issue of *Atlantic Monthly*, is "perhaps the best in contemporary noir": "Your father picks you up from prison in a stolen Dodge Neon with an eight ball in the glove compartment and a hooker named Mandy in the backseat."

Lehane's experiences as a writing student have inspired him to teach writing classes himself, first at Tufts University and then at the Harvard Extension School. For several years, until 2004, he was a member of the faculty of the University of Southern Maine Stonecoast M.F.A. program. In interviews he has been highly critical of the "high/low" debate within the literary world, which finds some arguing that character is all-important and others maintaining that plot is the key to a good novel. In an interview with Jillian Abbott for the *Writer* (May 2004), Lehane offered his own take on the subject: "Starting in the 1960s and continuing through the 1980s, plot became a dirty word in literary circles. Fiction lost its way. A great novel comes when there is beauty of language, illumination of character and a great plot. All three elements are necessary." He elaborated on that point in an interview with Edward Nawotka for *Publishers Weekly* (April 14, 2003): "You can't separate character—which is what the higher set champions—and plot—which is what the other side defends. They are both in service to each other. If you go to any great work of art, you talk about plot all day and then you talk about character all day. Just give me a well-written book." Lehane, who has written episodes of the acclaimed HBO television series *The Wire*, lives in Jamaica Plain, a suburb of Boston, with his wife, Sheila, and their dogs.

—C.M.

Suggested Reading: *Boston Herald* p46 May 13, 2003; *Chicago Tribune* V p6 Dec. 28, 1994; *Entertainment Weekly* p105+ Apr. 4, 2003; *Newsweek* p58+ Feb. 19, 2001; *People* p43 Aug. 10, 1998; *Publishers Weekly* p40+ June 21, 1999, p43+ Oct. 23, 2000, p39+ Apr. 14, 2003; *Writer* p66 Aug. 2002, p16+ May 2004

Selected Books: *A Drink before the War*, 1994; *Darkness, Take My Hand*, 1996; *Sacred*, 1997; *Gone, Baby, Gone*, 1998; *Prayers for Rain*, 1999; *Mystic River*, 2001; *Shutter Island*, 2003; *Coronado*, 2006

Leighten, Patricia

Nov. 11, 1946– Art historian

Patricia Leighten is a professor of art history at Duke University, in Durham, North Carolina, and the author of *Re-Ordering the Universe: Picasso and Anarchism, 1897–1914* (1989) and *Cubism and Culture* (2001), which she co-wrote with Mark Antliff. In 2007 Antliff and Leighten will publish their second collaboration, "A Cubism Reader: Documents and Criticism, 1906–1914." Her next solo project, the book "A Politics of Form: Art, Anarchism and Audience in Avant-Guerre Paris," is due out the same year. She has studied and teaches the history of photography, as well as late 19th and early 20th century art, and she is particularly captivated by the connection between visual culture and both the politics of interpretation and the politics of representation.

The daughter of George David Leighten and the former Barbara Edith Greeno, Patricia Leighten was born on November 11, 1946 in Providence, Rhode Island. She studied for her bachelor of arts degree at the University of Massachusetts, in Boston, graduating summa cum laude in 1973. She then earned her master's degree from Rutgers University, in New Brunswick, New Jersey, in 1975, and her doctorate in art history from the same institution in 1983. While there she co-founded the *Rutgers Art Review* and served as the publication's editor in chief from 1979 to 1980. Leighten began her academic career as a lecturer at the University of Delaware, in Newark, for the 1982–83 school year. The subsequent year she was promoted to assistant professor of art history, and she became an associate professor in 1988. She remained at the University of Delaware until

approximately 2002; since that time she has taught art history at Duke University. As of early 2006 she also chaired the department.

With the publication of several articles in the mid- and late 1980s, Leighten became one of the forerunners in her field to apply a revisionist interpretation to the history of cubism, arguing that the movement—which shunned such traditional techniques as perspective, foreshortening, modeling, and chiaroscuro, instead emphasizing the flat, two-dimensional, fragmented surface of the picture plane—should be placed in the context of the intellectual and cultural atmosphere of the period. Leighten's first book, *Re-Ordering the Universe*, examined the impact that politics, particularly the anarchist movements in Barcelona and Paris, had on the early work of the Spanish painter Pablo Picasso. She argued that the anarchist influence was evident "not only in style but in content as well, in the collages of autumn, 1912, which came to fruition during the First Balkan War, when Picasso and his bohemian milieu were deeply agitated by world events and preoccupied with issues of pacifism, militarism and war," as quoted by David Cottington in *Cubism and Its Histories* (2005). While many art historians had written about the wordplay that Picasso created by including newspaper clippings in his paintings, Leighten made the radical suggestion that the viewer should actually read the articles, not just the headlines, in the clips, which detail such noteworthy events as the signing of an armistice treaty and a description of cholera victims piled high. "[This book] is deliberately revisionist, setting out to explode the myth created by Picasso, and accepted by several generations of art critics and historians, that his Cubist-period paintings were revolutionary only in form. . . ," George Woodcock, wrote for the *New Leader* (June 12–26, 1989). "This is one of a number of valuable recent books examining the turn-of-the-century era when Modernism in art and literature was born. It is stimulating, informative and well-argued. Anyone studying the history of Cubism and related movements should read *Re-Ordering the Universe* to rectify the myth that Pablo Picasso and his coterie really believed that significance lies only in form." John Russell, in the *New York Times Book Review* (June 11, 1989), wrote: "Picasso in Barcelona, Picasso in Montmartre, Picasso in Horta de Ebro, Spain, Picasso and Braque—'roped together like mountaineers'—all are standard fare. But Patricia Leighten's book proves that in all these contexts it is still possible to resee, to reread and to rewrite. . . . This is a most remarkable book, and one to which all future students of Picasso will be indebted, even if they do not agree with some of its more absolute assertions." *Re-Ordering the Universe* was nominated for a CINOA prize for art history by La Confédération Internationale des Négociants en Oeuvres d'Art, a international confederation of 32 art and antique dealers' associations.

The following year, in 1990, Leighten was the recipient of the Arthur Kingsley Porter Prize for her article "The White Peril and l'art negre: Picasso, Primitivism, and Anticolonialism," which originally appeared in *Art Bulletin* and was later included in *Race-ing Art History: Critical Readings in Race and Art History* (2002), edited by Kymberly N. Pinder. In 2001 Leighten co-authored *Cubism and Culture* with Mark Antliff, a fellow professor of art history at Duke University. This book, which covered the advent of cubism from its origins in primitivism to its political observations on race and colonialism, was a part of the publisher Thames & Hudson's World of Art series. Writing for the London *Independent on Sunday* (December 2, 2001), Tim Hilton described the book as a "welcome addition" to the series, one "which places the [cubism] movement within a political background" and explores the relation of particular paintings to "the themes of French colonialism, anarchism, and the wavering nationalism of the First World War."

Leighten has received numerous awards throughout her career, including a postdoctoral fellowship from the J. Paul Getty Trust (1985–86), a Samuel H. Kress Senior Fellowship from the Center for Advanced Study in the Visual Arts at the National Gallery of Art (1989–90), and a fellowship from the John Simon Guggenheim Memorial Foundation (1990–91). She has served on the editorial board of *Art Bulletin* and the board of directors for the College Art Association.

—C.M.

Suggested Reading: Duke University Web site; (London) *Independent on Sunday* p16 Dec. 2, 2001; *New Leader* p21 June 12, 1989; *New York Times Book Review* p13 June 11, 1989

Selected Works: *Re-Ordering the Universe: Picasso and Anarchism, 1897–1914,* 1989; *Cubism and Culture* (with Mark Antliff), 2001

Leimbach, Marti

July 16, 1963– Novelist

Marti Leimbach first came to the attention of the literary world with *Dying Young* (1990), a novel that not only garnered an impressive $500,000 advance for its unknown young author, who had written it when she was only 25, but also managed to appeal to fans of both the literary novel and the popular page-turner. Inspired partially by the declining medical conditions of Leimbach's mother and maternal grandparents, all of whom died between the completion of the novel's first draft and its publication, the novel told the story of a young woman emotionally caught between two men, one of them dying from leukemia. Since writing *Dying Young* Leimbach has produced four additional novels, perhaps the most notable of which, *Daniel Isn't Talking* (2006), was culled from her experiences as the mother of a child with autism. On her official Web site, Leimbach commented that when speaking about *Daniel Isn't Talking*, "I find people leaning toward me. *My nephew is autistic, my son, my grandchild, my brother. . . .* It seems there are more and more of us whose lives have been changed by autism or another developmental disability. Perhaps it is not so surprising, therefore, that a book like this has emerged from the ashes of my life; the story is all around us."

Marti Leimbach was born Martha Grace Leimbach on July 16, 1963 in Washington, D.C.; she has at least two siblings, a sister and a brother. Her father, Leonard LaSalle Leimbach, was an attorney; he committed suicide when she was four. Her mother, the former Mary Finkenstaedt, was a

Mark Lawrence Photography/Courtesy of Random House

journalist, and her career made an early and lasting impression on Leimbach. "I began writing because I could not imagine any other profession," Leimbach wrote on her Web site. "My mother, a journalist, was forever at the typewriter or on the phone, and I thought in the natural progression of things I would do the same."

Leimbach attended public schools in Potomac, Maryland, before going on to Harvard University, in Cambridge, Massachusetts. Set on following her mother into journalism, Leimbach initially took expository writing classes at Harvard but later branched out, taking her first fiction-writing class with the novelist and short-story writer Mary Robison. Calling that first class "a great introduction to the world of fiction writing," Leimbach added on her Web site: "You had to somehow survive among peers who were so dead smart, so well read, so tremendously confident (it seemed) in their own abilities as writers. You had to pick your way carefully through the array of different voices and opinions, not be crushed by criticism or overly flattered by generous comments. In short, you had to be your own person, your own writer, and do what you did best—if you could figure out what that was."

After graduating magna cum laude from Harvard, in 1987, Leimbach won a Regents Fellowship to study at the University of California, at Irvine, for the 1987–88 school year, under the literary scholar Donald Heiney, who wrote fiction under the pen name MacDonald Harris. While studying with Heiney, Leimbach began her first novel, which did not have a firm title until much later. Unable to buy a computer of her own, in part because she had to save money to visit her mother and grandparents, all of whom were then dying of cancer, Leimbach worked on the book at odd hours at the university's computer lab, which never closed. She recalled in an interview with Jean Crichton for *Publishers Weekly* (June 16, 1989): "At five in the morning, as I was writing the last chapter, I thought, 'Well, I can't make this any better right now. They're going to have to get another writer in here, because this is the best I can do.'" The manuscript nonetheless went through several subsequent revisions, two of them guided by Heiney and Robison, as well as Robison's husband, James, who is also an author. Another revision was guided by one of the most powerful editors in the field, Nan A. Talese. In early 1989 Talese had bought the book's American hardcover publishing rights for Doubleday, providing Leimbach with a substantial part of the $500,000 she received for the book before publication. "When I read the manuscript, I was very impressed with Marti's talent," Talese told Jean Crichton. "I felt the combination of her talent, the story and the significance of the subject matter would earn the advance back." Leimbach, who was 25 at the time of the sale, clearly felt that the money was needed. "I was ready to do whatever it took," she told Becky Aikman for *New York Newsday* (August 7, 1989). "I was terribly out of money, so I figured out that the 'Total' brand of oatmeal actually provides all your necessary vitamins. I had it every day, the same thing. It precluded the necessity for vitamin pills, which are very expensive, and for vegetables and all sorts of products that you just can't keep forever in one of those mini-refrigerators."

Dying Young tells the story of Victor Geddes, a 33-year-old man stricken with leukemia who refuses further chemotherapy and instead advertises for a caretaker to help him ease his way out of life. Hilary Atkinson, a shoplifter six years

his junior and several rungs beneath him on the social ladder, soon takes the position. A romance develops between the two, and after moving to Hull, a small town on the coast of Massachusetts, they enjoy a relatively peaceful life together. Then they meet Gordon, who not only befriends the couple but soon becomes romantically involved with Hilary. Describing the novel as "a simply told tragic love story," Michelle Heinemann, in the *Times Literary Supplement* (July 20 1990), argued that "Leimbach writes smoothly about a prickly subject—death." What "gives *Dying Young* its sharp focus," Heinemann added, is "Hilary's clear and wry perspective," but despite this "clarity," the book "leaves the reader hungry for something a bit more substantial." Barbara Hoffert, in *Library Journal* (December 1989), called Leimbach's debut a "touching, well-wrought story. . . . Leimbach offers some remarkably astute perceptions on death's power to confound our expectations and love's power to confound death as she moves toward an ending that is both satisfying and unexpected." A film adaptation of *Dying Young*, starring Julia Roberts and directed by Joel Schumacher, appeared in theaters in 1991; the paperback edition of the book was published at the same time and spent more a month on the *New York Times* best-seller list.

Leimbach used a first-person narrator in both *Dying Young* and her follow-up novel, *Sun Dial Street* (1992), but in the second book she wrote from the perspective of a man—"something," Leimbach commented on her Web site, "I will never do again as I found it an unnecessary impediment to the whole process. I was only 26 when I started the book and felt about 105 when I finally wrote the last page." In the book the narrator, Sam Haskell, a 25-year-old manager for a number of small-time rock bands, leaves Massachusetts for Los Angeles, traveling partially on business and partially to see his sister, Ginny, and his mother, Lois, who has bipolar disorder and, Sam finds out when they meet again for the first time in four or five years, has begun calling herself Jewel. While sparring verbally with his difficult family, Sam begins a romance with a married woman, Lucy. Though the book seems to turn into a mystery novel, when Eli—Lucy's ex-boyfriend as well as Ginny's—is murdered, his killer is never revealed. Writing for the *Financial Times* (February 20, 1993), Stephen Amidon argued: "By making her narrator a man, Leimbach has robbed the slim story of the emotional power that might have saved it. Sam's voice only rarely rings true, and his musings about the inner lives of the other characters are downright annoying. The result is a book that reads like a hasty and ill-conceived novelisation of a melodramatic film." Dan Cryer, writing for *New York Newsday* (April 13, 1992), also commented somewhat disparagingly on the book's cinematic qualities but did find some merits to the book. "None of these people are particularly likeable," Cryer wrote about the characters, "though Hollywood might find them attractive. They have the depth of the storyboard. Still, Leimbach has an ear for witty dialogue . . . [and some scenes] are tense with edgy dark comedy."

Love and Houses (1997), Leimbach's third novel, met with considerably greater praise. The book was written after Leimbach had married; moved to London, England; and had her first child, with her second on the way. "I was unbelievably happy," Leimbach commented on her Web site, adding: "All writers, at some time in their lives, experience a book that 'writes itself' without any effort at all. Such was the case with *Love and Houses*." The novel takes a lighthearted look at abandonment, telling the story of Megan Howe, a fiction writer who is seven months pregnant when her husband, Andy, a bookseller, leaves her. In addition to expecting a baby, Meg also has an apartment on the market and plans to turn a former schoolhouse into the family's new home. The return of one of Megan's ex-boyfriends, Theo Clarkson, eventually forces her to choose between him and her husband. Like many critics Barbara Quick, writing for the *New York Times Book Review* (April 13, 1997), highlighted Meg's willingness to comment on everything around her. "The structure of *Love and Houses*," Quick wrote, "owes more to stand-up comedy than the novelist's tradition: it's a breathless riff filled with irreverent dialogue and painful anecdotes that make you laugh out loud." Calling the book "entertaining" and "witty," Catherine Park, writing for the Cleveland *Plain Dealer* (July 20, 1997), found that the commentary sometimes drags the rest of the novel down. "At moments, *Love and Houses* descends into sappy, overblown contemplation of its title theme. In fact, Meg's tepid insights into the rather thin love-house parallel are the only cracks in the foundation of an otherwise warm and captivating novel."

Falling Backwards, Leimbach's fourth novel, was published in the United Kingdom in 2002. Considered a love story, the novel describes the shadow cast over the lives of a married couple, Rebecca and James, by their shared memory of James's first wife, Lea. On her Web site, Leimbach explained her motivations for writing the book: "I became interested in the idea of the past being a kind of constant draw, like a weight you carry that can pull you back into itself unless you continue to exert effort against it. I tried to imagine what would happen to a couple that could not let go of a past event, or a past love. From this emerged the idea of a person inadvertently being just that weight which pulls others back to her." Though not widely reviewed the novel was praised in the Gloucester, England, *Citizen* (March 17, 2001): "*Falling Backwards* is a haunting and lyrical account of emotional dependencies that can be deeply destructive, driving apart those who feel the need to be together to survive. Above all, Marti Leimbach has crafted a moving tale that explores the demands imposed by impossible and idealised love."

The idea and some of the specific incidents in Leimbach's next novel—about a mother struggling with her son's autism and its effects on her marriage—came to her as a result of her experiences in dealing with her son's own case of autism. Though the cause of autism and a number of related disorders is not known, autism in particular is diagnosed when certain symptoms—including delays in linguistic and social development and in certain kinds of play—are detected in children younger than three. Children with autism tend to have marked patterns of interest or behavior, being drawn, for example, to certain types of objects or feeling a compelling need to order and arrange objects. In the case of Leimbach's son, the disorder did not clearly manifest itself until after he received a vaccination for measles, mumps, and rubella, when he was 19 months old, and, in an article in the London *Sunday Telegraph* (February 4, 2001), Leimbach expressed her fear that the vaccine had brought on the disorder and acknowledged that she felt guilty for having allowed her doctor to administer it to her son. Leimbach's suspicions about what caused her son's disorder and her fear that she was somehow to blame are widely shared by parents of autistic children, as is the marital trouble that Leimbach and husband experienced after their son's symptoms began to appear.

In *Daniel Isn't Talking* Melanie Marsh, an American living in London with her husband, Stephen, fights to provide her second child, Daniel, the treatment necessary for him to deal with his autism. Where most people want to put Daniel in a special school, Melanie works with an Irish behavioral therapist and successfully helps steer her son toward managing his disorder; all the while her marriage is taking a clear turn for the worse. Eve Conant, in the *New York Times Book Review* (April 9, 2006), followed many critics of Leimbach's earlier novel *Sun Dial Street* by remarking that the characters in *Daniel Isn't Talking* "seem to be itching to get off the page and onto the set; layers of personality are sacrificed for plot expediency and straight-to-the-screen dialogue. But Leimbach's semiautobiographical novel . . . is timely and uplifting, even if her characters narrowly escape central casting." In the *Washington Post* (May 21, 2006), Suki Casanave wrote that the novel "manages to be about autism without being just about autism. Instead, it's about tangled relationships, compassionate moments, fear and joy." Leimbach, Casanave concludes, "puts us face-to-face with the early stages of coming to grips with raising an autistic child, exposing the inner life of a feisty mother and her frantic rescue attempts. Melanie's breakdown and eventual recovery, powered in part by some important self-discoveries in the book's final pages, give us reason to hope that, in the face of things to come, she and others like her can manage to find their way."

Marti Leimbach teaches in the creative-writing program at the continuing education division of the University of Oxford. She lives in England with her husband, Alastair David Rolfe, whom she married in 1991, and their two children, Imogen Violet and Nicholas Sebastian. Nicholas, who was nine as of April 2006, plays the guitar, enjoys school, and can interact with friends and family. While he still displays symptoms of autism—for example, refusing to let anyone touch his toes or clip his toenails and needing to sit in what he takes to be the middle seat in the middle car in a train— he "manages his autism so that it is not as great a disability as it could have been," Leimbach wrote in another article for the London *Telegraph* (February 26, 2006), as cited on her Web site. Leimbach added: "I can see that within this child lies an intelligence different to my own but no less valid. I can see also that his path in life will be challenging. Am I afraid of what may happen in the future? Yes, but I am comforted by how gentle people are with him, how they forgive his averted gaze, his nervous rocking, his long speeches. It ignites in me a flame of hope, not that he will be 'normal' but that he will be accepted and loved for who he is, however different."

—C.M.

Suggested Reading: *Chicago Tribune* VI p2 Feb. 4, 1990; *Financial Times* II p22 Feb. 20, 1993; (Gloucester) *Citizen* p27 Mar. 17, 2001; *Library Journal* p171 Dec. 1989, p162 Feb. 15, 1997; (London) *Sunday Telegraph* p4 Feb. 4, 2001; (London) *Sunday Times* p10 Mar. 5, 2006, p50 Apr. 2, 2006; Marti Leimbach's Web site; *New York Newsday* p1+ Aug. 7, 1989, p20+ Jan. 7, 1990, II p63 Apr. 13, 1992; *New York Times Book Review* p22 Jan. 14, 1990, p20 Apr. 13, 1997, p23 Apr. 9, 2006; *People* p 45 Apr. 10, 2006; *Publishers Weekly* p46+ June 16, 1989; *Times Literary Supplement* p782 July 20, 1990

Selected Books: *Dying Young*, 1990; *Sun Dial Street*, 1992; *Love and Houses*, 1997; *Falling Backwards*, 2002; *Daniel Isn't Talking*, 2006

Levine, Judith

(luh-VEEN)

Sep. 20, 1952– Journalist; essayist; critic

The essayist and critic Judith Levine's feminist-inspired works, which explore the impact of history, culture, politics, and the marketplace on the personal life, particularly in terms of sex and gender, have earned her a reputation in literary circles as a firebrand and made her the object of political attack. Her most recent book, *Not Buying It: My Year without Shopping* (2006) offers a critical take on American consumer culture.

Judith Levine contributed the following autobiographical statement to *World Authors 2000–2005*:

"For better and for worse, I am the child of outsiders. Their outsiderness was partly chosen. They were Jews, but atheists; communists during McCarthyism, civil rights activists when segregation was rampant, early and fierce opponents of the war in Vietnam and of the many subsequent wars waged by the U.S. My mother once said she's never worked for a cause that won (that's not quite true. The Vietnam War did end; feminism, of which she was a premature proponent, won too, in spite of backlash). And yet they were utopians: they believed in a better world. Pessimism of the intellect, optimism of the will: that's what animated my parents, and me. Or, as immigrants imbued with American can-doism but shadowed by Russian Jewish gloom might put it, 'We'll make a perfect world—god willing, we should live so long!'

"Outsiderness is a condition, maybe even a requisite, of criticism: what W. E. B. Dubois called the 'double consciouness' of the marginalized, who also live inside the majority (often hostile) culture. But my family's criticalness is also temperamental. We analyze, and yes, we find fault. We attack and we defend. Emotionally, that can be tough on a child. It can be tough on an adult—and on those around her, too. I hope that years of therapy, Buddhism, and relationships both loving and not, have helped turn some of my combativeness to reasoned strategy for change, and some of my defensiveness to resiliency and the strength to stand up for my beliefs. What is left of the tendency to analyze what's wrong with people, I hope, is emotional acuity and honest self-interrogation. Writing a memoir tries these skills. I tried to put them into *Do You Remember Me?: A Father, a Daughter, and a Search for the Self*, a memoir of my family's dealing with my father's Alzheimer's and a critique of the medicalization of aging and dementia.

"I've often been asked why I choose topics that get me into hot water. My first book, about 'man-hating' and the antagonisms between the sexes, drew charges that I myself was a man-hater (for the record, I'm in a longterm relationship with a man, and some of my best friends . . .). *Harmful to Minors: The Perils of Protecting Children from Sex*, a defense of young people's sexual pleasure, was attacked by the Right as 'advocacy for pedophilia.' My mother hated *Do You Remember Me?* And *Not Buying It: My Year without Shopping*, which is a critique, but by no means an unequivocal condemnation, of consumer culture, has drawn accusations that I'm trying to bring down the U.S. economy.

"Am I a masochist, or what? Actually, I'm prepared to attack those in need of attacking, but unlike many journalists, it's hardly my favorite thing to do. I don't enjoy being attacked, either. I'm not a contrarian; I don't get a kick out of being against things just because other people are for them. In fact, I sometimes long to agree with the majority (I'd probably make more money if I did). And while I have principles, I'm not ideological. My utopian vision isn't a blueprint; polemic—that is, one-sided argument with all the complications edited out—generally bores me.

"The one statement that might describe my work, and my attitude in general, is: 'It's not that simple.' I'm drawn to the gray areas, not the blacks and whites.

"One reason it, whatever it is, is never simple is that, as the old feminist slogan put it, the personal is political, and increasingly, the political is personal (I also write a column called 'Poli Psy,' on 'the public uses and abuses of emotion.'). That's the connection that intrigues and moves me as an activist, a writer, and a person. It's why none of my personal writing is just about me or my friends or family; I don't think my own life is that interesting on its own, and anyway, just telling it leaves out half the story. Talking with a woman who swears by astrology and other 'spiritual systems,' as she put it, I said I didn't believe that the stars, or some transcendent beings or spirits, shape our lives. Didn't I believe in forces bigger than me, she asked, bigger than individuals? Of course, I said. And what would that be? she asked.

"That force is history. I think of myself not just as the sum of my personal biography—my family, personality, or body—but as a creature of history.

"History—that is, culture, political movements and events, the economy, the environment in the particular time and place I live—is written on my intimate life, on my feelings and relationships, my hopes and desires, even on my body, its pains and pleasures, the meanings of its survival and its mortality. Politically, I don't accept the idea that 'private' or 'personal' issues such as abortion, interpersonal violence, or even shopping are distractions from the 'real' world-changing stuff like wars and the doings of Great Men. Nor are the arts and popular culture 'escapes' from real life. They are real life. I'm a nonfiction writer because I like going out into the world to work, and also because I'm not good at making up stories. But I don't see my journalistic 'stories,' or my 'subject,' as different from that of many novelists, filmmakers, or playwrights. That story is the daily life of regular people, including myself, against a backdrop of history."

Judith Levine was born on September 20, 1952, in the New York City borough of Queens, to Theodore and Charlotte (Peterson) Levine. Her father was a psychologist, and her mother was an administrator at, among other places, the Margaret Sanger Research Bureau, a birth-control clinic. Levine pursued her undergraduate degree at the City College of New York (now the City University of New York), from which she graduated magna cum laude, in 1974. She was then admitted to the master's program at the prestigious school of journalism at Columbia University, in New York City, earning her degree in 1979. Throughout the 1970s, while attending both City College and Columbia, she worked a variety of jobs, as a waitress, daycare teacher and bicycle messenger.

In the 1980s Levine embarked on a full-time career in writing, contributing freelance feature articles and reviews—from a feminist perspective—on a range of provocative subjects, from sexual etiquette to drug use; her work appeared in a variety of publications, including the left-leaning alternative journal *Utne Reader* and the women's lifestyle magazines *Glamour* and *Mademoiselle*. Levine served as a contributing editor to *New York Woman* from 1991 to 1992.

In the latter year she published her first book, *My Enemy, My Love: Man-Hating and Ambivalence in Women's Lives* (1992), in which she analyzed the traditional gender roles and addressed the relationship between misandry (hatred of men) and feminism in contemporary society. Levine argued that much antimale feeling in women has its origin in father-daughter relations, particularly those involving discrimination or abandonment. Such misandry express female anger while paradoxically trapping both genders in familiar roles, thereby perpetuating the causes of anger. Critics praised Levine for her bravery in tackling such a sensitive subject. Eunice Lipton, writing for the *Women's Review of Books* (May 1992), observed, "Levine uses humor brilliantly to force confrontation with . . . stereotypes. She also takes all forms of culture seriously." To Lipton the book represented "a significant breakthrough in terms of dealing with theoretically difficult material in a perfectly accessible way." At the same time Lipton thought that Levine "hasn't really dissected the relationship between man-hating and ambivalence, or rather . . . she senses there is no instrumental relationship there." Lipton added: "I do believe that Levine wrote *My Enemy, My Love* with immense passion and hope. She wrote it for men as well as for women. While the book legitimizes the continuing rage of women . . . it also attempts to convince men of the hopelessness—and ultimate loneliness—of their emotional lives."

In the mid-1990s Levine started work on her controversial second book, *Harmful to Minors: The Perils of Protecting Children*, in which she expressed the view that sexual activity among children and teenagers is a healthy and natural part of growing up. She also took issue with the lack of sex education available to American children in public schools and with laws designed to prevent sex among children and teenagers, asserting that both contribute to a culture of fear surrounding sex and prevent meaningful discussion of the topic. Her findings, based on research conducted from 1996 to 2000, included indications that children were not harmed by exposure to sexually explicit material, which in turn suggested, according to Levine, that sexual relationships between adults and teenagers are not uniformly devastating.

After completing her manuscript, Levine approached editors at several major publishing houses, initially meeting with rejection. In 2001 the University of Minnesota Press officials agreed to publish the manuscript, only after five academic experts had verified that the book's arguments were based on comprehensive research. Douglas Armato, director of the press, told an interviewer for Fox News Web site (April 2, 2002) that he believed that the book's arguments would spark public debate among its readers. The controversy surrounding Levine began in March 2002—a month prior to her book's publication—following an article filed by the Newhouse News Service, in the wake of a major scandal in the Roman Catholic Church involving the decades-long cover-up of the issue of priests charged with sexually abusing children. The article contained a quote from Levine, who said in effect that a sexual relationship between a priest and a young person "conceivably" could be positive. (At 14, Levine had been involved in a summer-long, nearly consummated romance with a camp counselor almost twice her age.)

Although Levine said in subsequent interviews that she opposed any sexual relationship between an adolescent and an authority figure, the publication of Harmful to Minors nonetheless created another controversy, in part because she endorsed a change in America's various age-of-consent laws that would bring them in line with those in other countries. Levine's assertion that teenagers are sexual beings who pursue sexual relationships with older people out of sheer curiosity, as well as her suggestion that statutory-rape laws are based on unrealistic expectations drew criticism from many conservative media commentators and activists, who accused her of condoning child abuse. Vocal opposition to Levine's book came from, among others, Robert H. Knight, the director of the Culture and Family Institute (an affiliate of the conservative Christian group Concerned Women for America), who asked Minnesota Governor Jesse Ventura to stop publication of the book, which was being published under the auspices of the University of Minnesota. On her nationally syndicated radio talk show, Laura Schlessinger also condemned Levine, calling her an advocate of pedophilia. (It was later discovered that neither Schlessinger nor the colleague who had brought Harmful to Minors to her attention had read much of the book.)

Levine answered Schlessinger's charge in an interview with Amy Benfer for Salon (April 19, 2002, on-line): "The first thing I have to say is that no sane person would advocate pedophilia. . . . What I say is that it is possible for teens to tell the difference between coercion and consent, and that most statutory rape prosecutions have to do with conflict within the family over the sexual lives of their children, most often their teen girls or gay boys. Trying to adjudicate or deal with those conflicts in the context of criminal law . . . is really a primitive instrument for trying to figure out how young people can have relationships of true consent." Levine also had her share of defenders, among them spokespersons for the American Booksellers Foundation for Free Expression, the Association of American Publishers, the PEN American Center, and the National Coalition Against Censorship.

Benfer reported that Harmful to Minors: The Perils of Protecting Children from Sex sold out of its initial print run of 3,500 copies less than a month after its publication, triggering a second printing of 10,000. Critical assessments of the book were mixed. Louise Armstrong wrote for the Women's Review of Books (June 2002), "It becomes hard to share Levine's jubilant optimism that teaching girls to understand and proclaim and act on their own sexual desire is key to putting them in charge of their sexual destiny. In the world that we live in, it is far more likely that such advocacy will simply further the child-as-seducer myth that has plagued young girls for centuries." Levine received qualified praise from Deborah Roffman, writing for Psychology Today (July/August 2002): "Levine articulately addresses the moral issues intrinsic in sexual decision-making. Yet nowhere does she offer strategies for helping children and adolescents develop skills for moral thinking. . . . In a popular culture that glorifies sex at every turn, promotes the sexualization of children at earlier and earlier ages and continues to model unhealthy gender-role stereotyping and relationships, Levine's call for a new approach to sex education is important—but inadequate. Our children's best hope is not, as Levine suggests, that we simply give them permission and enjoy sex and then step out of their way. Rather, we must stay close enough to help them learn how to deal with sex in the most positive and healthy ways." The Sex Information and Educational Council of the United States (SIECUS) recognized Harmful to Minors as one of the 40 most influential works ever published about sexuality. The book received the 2002 Los Angeles Times Book Award for current interest. The judges considered the book "a cogent and passionate critique of the war against young people's sexuality," as quoted by J. Michael Kennedy for the Los Angeles Times (April 27, 2003). "An uncompromising humanist and feminist, Judith Levine exposes the moral panic behind such policies as 'abstinence-only' sex education and insists on adults' responsibility to give affirmative support to children's and teenagers' sexual development."

In her next book, *Do You Remember Me?: A Father, a Daughter, and a Search for Self* (2004), Levine chronicled her father's lengthy struggle with Alzheimer's disease and its effects on the relationships within her family. The book examines society's inability or unwillingness to accept those no longer capable of rational thought. "One of the main points of the book is that self is not something that exists autonomously," Levine explained to Rachel Sarah for the northern California Jewish newsweekly *J.* (June 11, 2004, on-line). "This sense that you're not just yourself— that you live in a community and have a social responsibility to others—is a strong Jewish precept. You don't just have to save yourself. You have to heal the world. That was a very strong part of my upbringing." A reviewer for *Publishers Weekly* (April 19, 2004) called the book "a daughter's poignant homage to a father she came to best after he lost his mind" as well as "a searing indictment of how America treats its disabled and a cautionary tale for aging baby boomers."

The idea for Levine's most recent book, *Not Buying It: My Year without Shopping* (2006), her critique of American consumer culture, came to her when she made a New Year's resolution in 2004—after going on a spending spree that "maxed out" her credit card. "I was interested in investigating what role consuming has in my life. That was really my motivation, and I thought it'd be easy to go for a week or a month, even three months, so I thought, 'Let's try to do a really extreme experiment and go for a whole year,'" she told Jessica Bennett in an interview for *Newsweek* (March 31, 2006, on-line). For that year Levine and her partner, Paul Cillo, limited their spending to items they regarded as bare necessities—such as hygiene products, food, a *New York Times* subscription, and Internet access—while foregoing luxuries, including credit cards, new clothes, digital and premium cable-television service, meals in restaurants, movies in theaters, Starbucks coffee, and fresh-cut flowers. They relied heavily on library books, free concerts, and public transportation. The experiment revealed a great deal to Levine about her own attitude toward shopping. "I tended to think of myself as a pretty uninterested shopper," she told Bennett. "[But] as soon as I stopped buying things, I realized how important buying things is—not just for the things, but for the experiences. I missed movies a lot, but I also learned that by taking recreational shopping or impulse shopping . . . out of your life, for me it eliminated a lot of the worrying that I do about money. It freed up a lot of emotional space for me, not to mention time. I learned that just a little bit of consciousness goes a long way, and it has unexpected rewards."

Critics considered the book both interesting and insightful. Sandra Tsing Loh, writing for the *Atlantic Monthly* (July–August 2006), observed,

"Levine's yearlong Visa-free journey reveals a hitherto-invisible realm. Without the whirl of buying, vast quantities of time open up—and not just from a lack of purchased entertainment; consuming itself takes time. . . . But perhaps Levine's most pointed observations are political. She is no fan of [President George W.] Bush—he who advised patriotic citizens, post-9/11, to go shopping. But she's troubled too with her fellow Democrats' click-and-buy approach to political organizing." Marjorie Kehe wrote for the *Christian Science Monitor* (March 7, 2006): "[Levine is] a sharp and witty writer. . . . My one complaint about *Not Buying It* would be that—in a true spirit of minimalism—it could have been shorter. Although Levine argues that 'politics is a form of consumption,' the section about the 2004 election seemed to me a bit like padding, as if Levine were worried that, alone, the account of her experiment might not be interesting enough. (It is.) But otherwise, this honest and humorous tale of a nonspending year is well worth putting aside a few hours to read. (Perhaps instead of a movie or two.) By thinking harder about how it would feel to consume less we might just make ourselves—and our planet—a lot better." *Not Buying It* has been translated into five languages.

Levine's weekly column Poli Psy appears in the Vermont-based publication *Seven Days*. In 2005 the Association of Alternative Newsweeklies awarded her the prize for best political column; she was also named the recipient of the Richard J. Margolis Award, in 1993. She has co-founded three organizations: the National Writers Union, a trade union of contract and freelance writers; No More Nice Girls, a street theater group that promotes abortion rights; and Take Back the Future. She also serves on the board of directors of the National Center on Reason and the Vermont chapter of the American Civil Liberties Union (ACLU). Levine and Paul Cillo divide their time between Brooklyn, New York, and Hardwick, Vermont. Among other activities, she enjoys cooking; she is a lover of cats.

—B.M.

Suggested Reading: *J.* June 11, 2004 (on-line); Judith Levine's Web site; *Newsweek* (on-line) Mar. 31, 2006; *Psychology Today* p70 July–Aug. 2002; *Publishers Weekly* p53 Apr. 19, 2004; *Salon* (on-line) Apr. 19, 2002; *Village Voice* July 3–9, 2002; *Women's Review of Books* p1+ June 2002

Selected Books: *My Enemy, My Love: Man-Hating and Ambivalence in Women's Lives*, 1992; *Harmful to Minors: The Perils of Protecting Children*, 2002; *Do You Remember Me?: A Father, a Daughter, and a Search for Self*, 2004; *Not Buying It: My Year without Shopping*, 2006

Levine, Philip

Jan. 10, 1928– Poet

Philip Levine has distinguished himself as one of the most important poets of his generation, known for his conversational style and sparse use of language. Detroit, his hometown, serves as the backdrop for much of his material; Levine's poems emphasize the city's despairing conditions, the decay resulting from race riots and poverty, and the heavy influence of blue-collar industry; yet, he also depicts the inner lives of Detroit's inhabitants, giving life to rugged, working-class characters often ignored in poetry. A reviewer for *Magill Book Reviews* (February 15, 1990) noted, "No other poet—except for James Wright in his Ohio Valley poems and a relatively unknown poet, Peter Oresick—has written of the American working class with [such] clarity, dignity, and empathy. Far from being romanticized or idealized, Levine's workers are drawn in all their anger, frustration, and hopelessness of their dreams. . . . The value of workers and their lives and the accompanying urban melancholy constitute major themes in Levine's poetry, themes too often neglected in art, and about which no one writes with more conviction." Levine has not limited himself to poems about Detroit, however. Throughout his extensive body of work, he has explored the themes of history, anarchy, the experience of Jewish immigrants, death, and remembrance. In two of his recent books, *What Work Is* (1991) and *The Simple Truth* (1994)—which won the National Book Award and the Pulitzer Prize for poetry, respectively—Levine tackles the nature of work and the manner in which the senses can capture one's personal history.

In June 2003 Philip Levine contributed the following statement to *World Authors 2000–2005*:

"Looking back at my life in poetry—I'm now 75—very little strikes me as planned and yet almost nothing seems accidental. What important decisions did I make that have kept me so long at this enterprise? Perhaps there were none. One thing for certain: there was never that cinematic moment that arrives just in time after an all-night pursuit of the absolute and brings the dawn with its message: You will be a poet. I do remember important moments in the pursuit of the poem but none involve decisions. At age six my older brother asked why I had thrown a particular stick away as unsuitable for my purposes. I answered: 'It lacks flexibility.' He was utterly charmed by my vocabulary. At thirteen I climbed a copper beech in a small grove near my house one night and composed a talk to the night sky; I was speaking in a voice I barely recognized as my own but one I liked. At seventeen a teacher loaned me a collection of the poems of Wilfred Owen, and I was astonished that a man who died in WW I could so perfectly enunciate the whole spectrum of feelings I had regarding WW II, which I expected would soon destroy me. Most of the other school day memories involving poetry blur into the miasma of boredom that came with 'scanning' poems like 'Snowbound' and memorizing sonnets by Shakespeare I didn't understand.

"At age eighteen I read some of the little gnomic poems of Stephen Crane and immediately sat down to write a handful of my own, which were no good but not much worse than Crane's. A month or two later I read T. S. Eliot for the first time, and I fell in love with this thing called modern poetry. About this time my teacher at Wayne University, a Mr. Sinclair, informed me that I had a great gift for writing, and though he disagreed with most of what I wrote—I had turned in a personal essay calling for the end of all legal restraints & the creation of a society in which wealth was shared & all class differences eliminated—I'd almost convinced him by the force of my writing. 'You should become a writer,' he said. Of such little things a life is born. At the time I was reading John Dos Passos, Theodore Dreiser, and Sherwood Anderson, and I felt powerfully influenced by their portrait of the strengths of the American character and the ills of our society; I thought I would do something similar in poetry, and my writing would in turn influence my generation & those to come.

"At about age twenty-five, while working in an auto factory in Detroit to support my writing life, it struck me that though my poems influenced no one—since almost no on read them—I loved writing them more than anything else I had ever done. I also realized there was much more to the art than I had mastered working largely on my own. The next year, I went off to study with a poet whose work I admired, Robert Lowell; he revealed very little enthusiasm for my work. That was at the University of Iowa; the second semester I ran out of money and lied my way into John Berryman's class, and in him I found the mentor I needed, and having worked with him for sixteen weeks, I knew it would be pointless to look for another teacher. Berryman had, fortunately, given me a road map for further study on which one book led to another and still another.

"Since then I've largely made my living as a teacher of writing and literature, and through teaching I met people who enriched my life and my writing, both colleagues (Peter Everwine and Charles Hanzlicek come to mind) and students (Larry Levis, Ernesto Trejo, Sherely Ann Williams and many more). From the beginning my family has been very supportive of my effort to be a poet: when I was young my mother and my twin brother, Eddie, wildly exaggerated my talent, which is what I needed. From the age of twenty-six it's been my wife, Franny, who has been both my best critic and my most constant support. One thing has never changed: when I'm at my best as a writer I truly don't know what I'm doing and yet the results are me; no matter how strange the work is it feels familiar and right. I don't have an explanation for this and don't need one."

Philip Levine was born on January 10, 1928 in Detroit, Michigan. His parents, Harry A. Levine and the former Ester Pristol, were both Russian-Jewish immigrants who had met in the U.S. and settled in Detroit, where Levine's father and grandfather jointly owned an auto-parts business. When Levine was just five years old, his father died suddenly, reducing the family to near poverty. For the rest of Levine's youth, his mother worked tirelessly to support her three sons, thus exposing Levine to the challenges of the lower-middle class. A bright child, he loved reading from an early age and began composing poetry at the age of 13. Levine attended Detroit's Wayne University (now Wayne State University), where he furthered his affection for poetry. After receiving his bachelor's degree, in 1950, he worked for several years as a machinist in various local factories, becoming close friends with many of his blue-collar co-workers. As he recalled to Gary Pacernick in an interview for the *Kenyon Review* (Spring 1999), "The men became my friends; the women became my friends, not always romantic, just friendships. Yeah, I got close to them and realized that their lives weren't that different from my own. When they found out, for example, [that] I'd finished college . . . They said, 'What do you want to be, Phil?' 'Well, I'd like to be a poet.' 'Ain't that some [expletive]. You want to be like Edgar Allen Poe?' They knew Edgar Allen Poe but that was about it. They had a very good-natured attitude toward me. 'You graduated from Wayne?' 'Yeah, I graduated from Wayne.' 'And you're working here on the night shift with me. Well, I never went to college. I guess I wasn't so dumb after all.'" During this period, Levine "married badly," as he recalled in a statement for *World Authors 1970–1975*, and quickly divorced. He also refused military service in the Korean War, a difficult and controversial decision that he later declared one of the best of his life.

After a short stint at the University of Iowa, in Iowa City, in 1953, Levine earned an M.A. from Wayne University, in 1954, and moved south for a year, to explore the mountains of North Carolina and the wetlands of Florida. While living in North Carolina, he married Frances Artley, an actress and costumer, on July 4, 1954. As Levine later recalled in a discussion group at Davidson College, as printed in *TriQuarterly* (Winter 1995), this period was one of the few in which he doubted his future as a poet. "I thought I'd made a drastic step that might mean I would never become the amazing poet I had seemed destined to become. I had just gotten married. I had fallen in love with a woman who had a young child, and so we married. I thought, 'Look what a foolish thing love has driven me to do. I must now be a responsible human being. I'm only twenty-six years old and I've thrown my young life away.'" Nevertheless, Levine persisted with his writing, often spending full days walking through the mountain towns of North Carolina. "As I got further and further into it I realized I was carrying out research," he said. "I was researching myself as well as these people and their place. . . . I found [George] Saintsbury's *History of English Prosody* in the local library, never had been read, pages uncut, and I poured over that. I'd been trying to write poetry for ten years, and I still didn't know how to do it and knew I didn't know. But I was getting clues and I was also learning how to research poems: you keep your eyes open, your ears open, all your senses open. The world responds to you, and you respond to the world. It goes on that way, it never ends."

In 1955 Levine returned to school, attending the University of Iowa's prestigious creative-writing program, where he studied under the influential poet John Berryman. Levine paid tribute to Berryman in his 1994 collection of personal essays, *The Bread of Time: Toward an Autobiography*, in which he dedicated one chapter to his poetic mentor. Here he described Berryman as a gifted and inspirational teacher, who often made high demands of his students but gave a great deal in return. While he was engaged in graduate study, Levine also worked as a faculty member in the university's English department. In 1957 he earned his M.F.A. and was awarded a poetry fellowship to study at Stanford University, in Palo Alto, California, under the poet Yvor Winters. Winters—then an elderly and stylistically rigid poet—was in many ways Levine's opposite, but the young writer, who was then still experimenting with a range of styles, found the experience worthwhile. "I think Yvor Winters was good for me in spite of how bad a teacher he was," Levine told Pacernick. "He was good for me because I wasn't a kid anymore. I turned thirty during the year I worked with him. I was not particularly upset when he didn't like what I wrote. I didn't like a good deal of what he praised and liked himself, so it didn't really matter." Levine explored his unique relationship with Winters in *The Bread of Time*, and critics often praised the portraits of his two mentors as particularly insightful.

In 1958 Levine joined the faculty at Fresno State College (now the Fresno campus of California State University), where he became a professor of English, in 1969. (Levine retained this position until he retired, in 1992; he also served as a professor of English at Tufts University, in Massachusetts, from 1981 to 1988.) After settling in California, he began publishing poems in a number of eminent literary journals. Although these early formal poems were highly accomplished, Levine's technical skills were often overshadowed by his powerful content. After winning the Joseph Henry Jackson Award from the San Francisco Foundation, in 1961, for his manuscript "Berenda Slough and Other Poems," Levine was able to publish his first poetry book, *On the Edge*, in 1963. The book's unsettling poems, many of which had been included in the earlier manuscript, were generally praised for their economy and directness, as well as Levine's mastery of traditional forms of verse. These poems were often infused with a tragic conviction that to live is to fail, human dignity decays, and courage often flounders; Levine presented an angry voice and dark vision, particularly in a group of four monologues attributed to deserters from the French Colonial Army during Algeria's war for independence. Despite what some critics found to be an overly pessimistic stance, most reviewers agreed the book was a remarkable debut.

His second volume, *Not This Pig* (1968), featured poems about the experiences of outcasts, underdogs, and criminals, as well as more personal poems. "A New Day" offered the realization that "what we get is what we bring," as quoted by Denis Donoghue for the *New York Review of Books* (April 25, 1968), while in the longer poem "Silent in America: Vivas for Those Who Have Failed," Levine presented his observations of contemporary American life. Levine explained to Wen Stephenson for the *Atlantic Monthly* (April 8, 1999, on-line), the latter poem came out of an experience in which his jaw had been wired shut after being broken in a mugging. "I spent two months listening," he said. "I just listened to everybody: my children, my friends, my wife, my brother. They were boring the hell out of me! I became aware of how language was being used— usually not to communicate but to disguise, to obfuscate. It was only two months of my life, but it was a powerful experience." Of this poem, Bill Katz, writing for *Library Journal* (January 1, 1968), noted, "[Levine has] much to tell us about ourselves and our surroundings." Overall, Levine's second collection was well received by critics, although some reviewers found the poems to be occasionally uneven. "[This book shows Levine] to be a poet of growing power and strangeness," Judson Jerome observed for the *Saturday Review* (June 1, 1968), adding, "Often his mysteriousness seems mere vagueness, lack of focus, but in moments of precision his poems perform beautifully."

Levine followed up this successful collection with the books *5 Detroits* (1970), *Thistles: A Poem Sequence* (1970), *Pili's Wall* (1971), *Red Dust* (1971), and *They Feed They Lion* (1972). Many of the poems in these works dealt with themes of travel—reflecting Levine's experiences of living in Spain for two years—and of his exposure to the Spanish-speaking poets Miguel Hernandez, Rafael Alberti, Pablo Neruda, Antonio Machado, and Cesar Vallejo, as well as postwar Polish poetry. However, Levine's poetry returns frequently to Detroit, focusing largely on the city's bewildered inhabitants. One of his most famous pieces, the title poem "They Feed They Lion," which Levine composed in the aftermath of Detroit's devastating 1967 race riots, evokes the communal strength and rage of industrial workers. The last stanza reads:

From my five arms and all my hands,
From all my white sins forgiven, they feed,
From my car passing under the stars,
They Lion, from my children inherit,

From the oak turned to a wall, they Lion,
From they sack and they belly opened
And all that was hidden burning on the oil-stained earth
They feed they Lion and he comes.

Writing for the *Yale Review* in 1972, as quoted on the Modern American Poetry Web site, Marie Boroff described this poem as "a litany celebrating, in rhythms and images of unflagging, pistonlike force, the majestic strength of the oppressed, rising equally out of the substances of the poisoned industrial landscape and the intangibles of humiliation. Its language is an extraordinary meld of high rhetoric and illiterate linguistic forms, galvanized by intensity and feeling."

Levine's next three works—*1933* (1974), which again dealt with subjects of Detroit's industrial and Jewish-immigrant communities; *New Season* (1975), a short pamphlet; and *On the Edge and Over: Poems Old, Lost, and New* (1976)—were also well received. Robert Mazzocco wrote for the *New York Review of Books* (April 3, 1975), "Levine's is a daunting, brooding art, often without solace. . . . He can create the sense of milieu, the sound, feel, geography of a place, a time, a people, the flavor of what's been happening among us and what continues to happen, which seem to me almost totally lacking in most other serious poetry today."

In his next work, *The Names of the Lost* (1976), Levine undertakes a more personal exploration of his own life, recollecting events from his Detroit childhood; his family; and his years in Spain, Italy, and California with philosophical depth and left-wing political zeal. Despite some critics' reservations about the authenticity of emotion behind some of the poems, the collection won significant acclaim, with Jay Parini writing for *Poetry* (August 1977), "This collection confirms Levine as one of our essential poets. His dark vision is central to our experience in this century, and *The Names of the Lost* will be read for a long time to come." For this work Levine was awarded the Lenore Marshall Award for best American book of poems, in 1976. He continued to explore these themes in *7 Years from Somewhere* (1979) and *Ashes: Poems New and Old* (1979), which earned the National Book Critics Circle Award in 1980. For *Ashes*, Levine also garnered the 1980 National Book Award for poetry, while *7 Years from Somewhere* was named a notable book by the American Library Association.

Most reviews of Levine's next book, *One for the Rose* (1981), discussed the accessibility of the poet's language, with critics both praising and lamenting his characteristic style. "Levine's poems have the rare and laudable virtue of readability;" Richard Tillinghast wrote for the *New York Times* (September 12, 1982), "they carry the charm and vitality of the poet's distinctive speaking voice, which is by turns assertive and tough or humorously self-deprecating. . . . The other side of this poet's accessibility is a frequent flatness of diction and an overreliance on the line break for emphasis." Writing for the *Times Literary Supplement* (July 2, 1982), Jay Parini observed, "Levine is America's pre-eminent poet of the working class, and his personae dwell among factories, cheap rented housing, polluted landscapes, and the ordinary objects of daily life. . . . [His] short, flat lines and swiftly running enjambment give the unwary reader the illusion that he is reading prose chopped up arbitrarily into verse. This accusation holds true of his less good poems; the successes are dazzling and frequent." Despite condemnations of what Herbert Leibowitz, writing for the *New York Times* (October 7, 1979), described as "threadbare language"—Levine once told an interviewer he was not interested in language itself but rather in the meaning behind it—literary critics continued to applaud the poet's attention to powerful everyday themes. In reviewing *Selected Poems* (1984), Edward Hirsch wrote for the *New York Times* (August 5, 1984), "[Levine] is not always the most elegant or felicitous writer, but his work is ultimately carried forward and transmuted by passion, by a stubborn will to remember and testify." *Selected Poems* was nominated for the 1984 Los Angeles Times Book Prize.

After publishing *Sweet Will*, a slim collection of 16 poems, in 1985, Levine wrote *A Walk with Tom Jefferson* (1988), in which he again highlighted Detroit's urban landscape. Narrating the title poem is Tom Jefferson, an old black man who migrated to Detroit in the late 1920s to get work in a Ford plant. Through the years, he has married, seen the race riots of 1943, served in World War II, and lost his son to the Korean War; he now lives in a dilapidated part of the city, where most of the homes had been looted, destroyed, and abandoned years before. Nevertheless, Jefferson endures, tending to his winter garden and surviving with a strong sense of both honor and humor. In another poem, "Buying and Selling," Levine presented an autobiographical sketch of himself at age 30. Overall, *A Walk with Tom Jefferson* was deemed a critical success. Writing for the *Kenyon Review* (Fall 1989), Paul Mariani called the work "an exceptional book by an exceptional poet." "Moreover," he added, "it signals Philip Levine's determination to continue in the direction taken in his previous book, *Sweet Will*, towards a more meditative, all-inclusive voice in a line which goes back to Wordsworth and Keats."

In 1991 Levine published the collected work *New Selected Poems*, as well as a new volume of poems, *What Work Is*, in which he explored the essence of work and its place in the lives of the lower-middle class. Daniel L. Guillory wrote for *Library Journal* (May 1, 1991), "This collection amounts to a hymn of praise for all the workers of America. These proletarian heroes, with names like Lonnie, Loo, Sweet Pea, and Packy, work the furnaces, forges, slag heaps, assembly lines, and loading docks at places with unglamorous names like Brass Craft or Feinberg and Breslin's First-Rate

Plumbing and Plating." Beyond his authentic depictions of manual labor, Levine crafts rich characters, each with their own dreams, as they succumb to the repetitive and monotonous tasks of life. In the book's title poem, he wrote, as quoted by the *Los Angeles Times* (September 15, 1991): "We stand in the rain in a long line / waiting at Ford Highland Park. For work. / you know what work is—if you're / old enough to read this you know what / work is, although you may not do it." *What Work Is* was hailed as "one of the most important books of poetry of our time," by David Baker, writing for the *Kenyon Review* (Summer 1992). He added, "Levine's insistence on attending to the particularities of personality and character, on seeing distinction in the face of blurring abuse, and on demanding the restorative authority of song wrenched out of the pain and grime of such detail—these are the primary materials of his art." For this collection, Levine was awarded the Los Angeles Times Book Prize and the National Book Award for poetry, both in 1991.

In Levine's next book, *The Simple Truth* (1994), he offered more reflective poems, exploring his personal history and lessons gleaned from the past. One of the more well-known pieces, "On the Meeting of García Lorca and Hart Crane," described a meeting between the two men, whom Levine describes in the poem as "the two / greatest poetic geniuses alive." In other poems, Levine evoked recollections of his parents and other family members. In the book's title poem, he writes:

> Some things
> you know all your life. They are so simple and true
> they must be said without elegance, meter and rhyme,
> they must be laid on the table beside the salt shaker,
> the glass of water, the absence of light gathering
> in the shadows of picture frames, they must be
> naked and alone, they must stand for themselves.
> My friend Henri and I arrived at this together in 1965
> before I went away, before he began to kill himself,
> and the two of us to betray our love. Can you taste
> what I'm saying?

The Simple Truth was a critical success, with Fred Muratori for *Library Journal* (November 1, 1994) noting, "Levine's third book of new verse in six years offers further proof that since turning 60 his drive to explain his relationship to the world has never been stronger. . . . Though the usual touchstones of his work . . . are ever present, this collection is more consistently narrative and elegiac than previous ones, elevating the minutiae of personal remembrance to an almost mythic significance." The volume earned Levine the 1995 Pulitzer Prize in poetry.

After publishing a collection titled *Unselected Poems* (1997), containing verses that had been left out of his three previous books, Levine wrote *The Mercy* (1999). The title poem described Levine's mother's emigration to the U.S., in 1913, on a ship called the *Mercy*. Overall, the collection deals with themes of journey, "from innocence to experience, and youth to age, and clarity to confusion and back again, and life to death," as the poet told Joel Brouwer for the *Progressive* (August 1999). Many of the poems took the forms of elegies, including "The Return," in which Levine sought to better understand his father's early death, and "The Secret," in which he discussed his mother's death at age 94. Several poems continue Levine's exploration of the harsh working-class life while others, such as "He Would Never Use One Word Where None Would Do," examine questions about the effectiveness of language. Critics praised *The Mercy* as an important literary contribution. Writing for *World Literature Today* (Winter 2002), David Rogers declared, "Craft in *The Mercy* is a control of voice so complete it amounts to a spiritual discipline. It is discipline in observation and choice of detail governed by creative love. What Levine sees is taken into himself. It emerges transformed in these remarkable poems." Adam Kirsch wrote for the *New York Times* (April 18, 1999), "*The Mercy* is one of Levine's finest books, and it has many virtues."

In a review for the *New York Times* (November 21, 2004), Terrence Rafferty suggested that Levine had titled his most recent collection of poetry, *Breath* (2004), "perhaps in honor of what this writer won't waste trying to convince us he has all the answers." Rafferty continued, "Levine just wants to tell us why he writes poems, why anyone would bother to write poems: for the feeling, on those rare days, that you can take the world in and then push it out transformed, and that the process will seem 'automatic, this entering and exiting, / my body's essential occupation without which / I am a thing.'" Selecting *Breath* as one of his favorite books from 2004, the reviewer Tom Chandler wrote for the *Providence Journal* (December 26, 2004), "These tough, muscular poems continue his [Levine's] trademark themes of righteous anger at injustice and the celebration of working-class lives."

Throughout his career Levine has received numerous honors and awards, including several grants from the National Endowment for the Arts (1969, 1976, 1981, and 1987—he refused one in 1970); the Frank O'Hara Prize from *Poetry* (1973 and 1974); a grant from the National Institute of Arts and Letters (1973); an award of merit from the American Academy of Arts and Letters (1974); the Levinson Prize from *Poetry* (1974), two Guggenheim fellowships (1974 and 1981); the Harriet Monroe Memorial Prize for poetry from the University of Chicago (1976); the Golden Rose Award from the New England Poetry Society (1985); the Ruth Lilly Award from the Modern Poetry Association and American Council for the Arts (1987); and the Elmer Holmes Bobst Award from New York University (1990). He was elected a chancellor of the Academy of American Poets in 2000. In addition to his memoir, *The Bread of Time: Toward an Autobiography*, Levine published the prose book *So Ask: Essays, Conversations, Interviews* in 2002.

Levine—who has also translated books of poetry, most recently a 2007 edition of *Tarumba*, by the Mexican poet Jaime Sabines—lives in New York City and in Fresno, California, with his wife of nearly 50 years. The couple share four sons. Levine told Pacernick the most incredible thing about his life has been not his poetry, but his marriage. "I will have been married forty-three years come this summer," he said in the 1999 interview. "And people say, Boy was that smart. But let me tell you I was not thinking with my head. My wife and I were driven to each other for irrational purposes. We've been able to live together a long, long time and still enjoy each other's company a great deal. I'd rather be with her than anybody else in the world, and so it's been a great blessing for me, that and fatherhood too, which has its difficulties, but it's been terrific too. . . . I was a guy who grew up believing that marriage was a trap and having children was a greater trap. What I've discovered is that's not true at all. It makes a human being out of you, and the rewards go on and on and on."

—K.D.

Suggested Reading: *Atlantic Monthly* (on-line) Apr. 8. 1999; *Kenyon Review* p170+ Fall 1989, p166+ Summer 1992, p9+ Spring 1999; *TriQuarterly* p67+ Winter 1995; *World Literature Today* p154 Winter 2002

Selected Books: *On the Edge*, 1961; *Not This Pig*, 1968; *5 Detroits*, 1970; *Red Dust*, 1971; *They Feed They Lion*, 1972; *1933*, 1974; *On the Edge and Over: Poems Old, Lost, and New*, 1976; *The Names of the Lost*, 1976; *7 Years from Somewhere*, 1979; *Ashes: Poems New and Old*, 1979; *One for the Rose*, 1981; *Selected Poems*, 1984; *Sweet Will*, 1985; *A Walk with Tom Jefferson*, 1988; *New Selected Poems*, 1991; *What Work Is*, 1991; *The Simple Truth*, 1994; *Unselected Poems*, 1997; *The Mercy*, 1999; *Breath*, 2004

Lindqvist, Sven

(lind-KVIST, SVEN)

1932– Memoirist; nonfiction writer

Sven Lindqvist submitted the following autobiographical statement to *World Authors 2000–2005*:

"How did I become a writer? How did I become the sort of writer that I am—not a journalist, not a novelist, not a poet, not a playwright, not a critic, not an explorer but using some of the skills of these trades to create a genre all my own. How did I become Sven Lindqvist?

Ulla Montan

Sven Lindqvist

"A decisive experience was a little book that I read when I was 9 years old. In spite of its innocent title—*In the Shade of the Palms*—it was the most gruesome book I had ever read. It was the diary of a Swedish missionary, Edward Wilhelm. He came to Congo in 1892 and witnessed some of the atrocities committed by the colonial regime of King Leopold.

"Travelling up the Congo, Sjoblom saw a small boy beaten until his body was 'a piece of bloody flesh that quivered for every lash.' Sjoblom counted 60 lashes. Then the boy lay there in his torment, wriggling like a worm, and every time the captain passed, he gave him a couple of kicks.

"At dinner the whites bragged about their exploits. 'Only the whip can civilize the black,' they said. 'The best of them is not too good to die like a pig.'

"I read this with tremendous empathy. I had myself been flogged. Not in the same way, for sure, but enough to identify with the black boy.

"But even more I identified with Sjoblom. I wanted to become like him. Not a missionary, maybe, but one who travelled the world and experienced it. I wanted to be an eyewitness to the injustices and cruelties and report on them. Like Sjoblom I wanted to sound the alarm and appeal to world opinion.

"Sjoblom reported what he saw to the Congo Balolo Mission in London. In May 1897, he appeared in London at a meeting arranged by the Aborigines Protection Society. His intense gravity and dry, detailed, rather pedantic way of speaking, had a great impact. Sjoblom's testimony on the mass murders in Congo made the front page of the *Times* and received widespread publicity.

"I was at an age when one devours adventure books of every kind. But after having read Sjoblom's diary, I realized that all the other books I had read had one thing in common—they were made up. They were just stories. The things that were told had not happened. The people they were about never existed.

"Sjoblom's diary, with all its imperfections, was so much more powerful reading than anything I had read before just because it was about real events happening to real people. This experience came to determine my own writing.

"A few years later my mother and her sisters had a religious awakening through the Oxford Movement for Moral Rearmament. Meetings were held in our living room in a Stockholm suburb. We all sat in a circle, each with a pen and a notebook, to write down what God said to us. All I had to do was to go completely quiet inside and rub out all my own thoughts and I would hear God's voice.

"But I couldn't do it. God never said anything to me. All the others wrote down God's words, but I couldn't hear His voice. Not the first time, not the second time, not the third time either.

"The situation got embarrassing. There we sat and I felt everybody's eyes on me. This time I had to write something. So I gave in to group pressure and started to cheat. I made up something that I thought God might say to me and wrote it down just as if He had really said it.

"That was the first time I wrote something that wasn't an exercise in handwriting or spelling. This is where my writing career began. It began with my putting myself in God's place and pretending that my words were God's words, even though they were just something that I had made up.

"When we showed each other our notebooks, I got a lot of praise. Uncle Richard read a few lines aloud. Aunt Mani had tears in her eyes. My mother glowed with pride. I was the only one who knew that it was all made up.

"Once the deception had begun, there was no going back. Every week I had to sit there and make up something on God's behalf which He unfortunately had not said to me. These meetings went on all through the winter. I got deeper and deeper into the deception. It was a great relief when at last it was over.

"And when, as a young man, I began writing short stories and chapters of novels I felt a powerful inner resistance. I didn't want to make things up. I didn't want to pretend to be God.

"It was a great relief when I found a way of writing that liberated me from fiction. I learned to write in my own name, with my own voice, about things that I had seen and experienced myself—without having to make it up. The deception was over at last. It wasn't God talking. It was me.

"This was such a great discovery for me, that I wrote a whole book about it, my first book: *Ettförslag,* (A Proposal, 1955). What I proposed was a new literary form, *eine Wahrheitskunst,* an 'art of truth.'

"I called this new literary form 'essay' but I was careful to distinguish it from the chatty British gentleman's essay and from the mere organising and analyzing of facts.

"The essay *'has to be a drama of dialogue between facts, a poem about the smell, sound and shimmer of facts, a novel about the relations between facts and their birth, life and death.'*

"That was what I wanted to do. That is what I have done, in more than thirty books over more than fifty years. I am still doing it."

———

The author of more than 30 books in Swedish, Lindqvist is best known to English-language readers for his travel essays and memoirs, which often display a distinctly leftist political bent. In particular, his works have frequently examined the impact of Europeans on Third World nations and how racism, colonialism, and conflict have shaped these countries. Lindqvist's interest in such subjects stems from his childhood fascination with foreign places, an interest that he concedes his career has well satisfied. "I really had two great childhood ambitions, to write and to travel," he remarked, according to Richard Gott for *High Life* (May 2000), the magazine of British Airways, as reprinted on Lindqvist's Web site. "To see the world was extremely important, that was the sublime thing, to go there and to have been there. But I also wanted to write, though not necessarily about travelling, because I got such an immense pleasure out of reading; it occurred to me that the pleasure of creating such text would be even more satisfying. I have been able to fulfil both these ambitions, and in this way my life has been immensely successful, because I've hardly done anything else, other than the two things that I really really wanted to do when I was a small boy."

Sven Lindqvist was born on March 28, 1932 in Stockholm, Sweden. His parents, Oscar Lindqvist and the former Signhild Bergenfalk, were both teachers. Growing up in a neutral country largely unaffected by World War II, Lindqvist enjoyed a relatively sheltered upbringing given the time period. "The world outside Sweden in my childhood," he recalled to Gott, "was the missionary who came to Sunday School and told us about his experiences in Africa or China, or wherever. Often he would have some fascinating objects to show us, of native artistry. There were also books in which you could find woodcuts or other black-and-white pictures that seemed quite out of this world. Very simple by today's standards, they gave you an enormous lust to go there." At the age of 15, Lindqvist left Sweden for the first time, becoming the first person in his family ever to go overseas. As he recollected to Sophie Harrison in an interview for *Granta* (online), "*Nobody I knew had every been out of Sweden!* I was Columbus, going out into the great

unknown. And what did I see? I went to Germany and I saw cities, cities as big as London, just razed to the ground, not a single house left standing. That was in 1947, and it was a very formative experience." Lindqvist also spent the summer of 1948 living in England, in the town of St. Albans, outside London, where he stayed with a British family.

After reading *The Glass Bead Game* (1943), a novel by Herman Hesse, Lindqvist decided to study the Chinese language. (Set in the 23d century, the novel follows Joseph Knecht as he struggles to master the glass bead game, a deeply esoteric hobby pursued by his society's intellectual elite.) "It struck me," Lindqvist recalled to Gott, "that in order to understand the game of glass beads you would have to learn some Chinese." He subsequently studied literature and Chinese at the University of Stockholm, the latter subject under the renowned sinologist Bernard Karlgren. During the Korean War, which was fought from 1950 to 1953, Swedish troops participated in the conflict under the auspices of the U.N.; Lindqvist, however, declared himself a conscientious objector and performed national service instead. In 1961 Lindqvist traveled to Beijing, China, to study at Peking University, becoming one of the first Westerners admitted to the institution. Upon completing his coursework, he remained in Beijing, serving as a cultural attaché for the Swedish embassy. Lindqvist's stay in China provided the inspiration for his first major written work, *Kina inifrån*, which was published in Swedish in 1963 and translated into English two years later, under the title *China in Crisis*. The book chronicles Lindqvist and his wife's experiences while attending Peking University during the 1961–62 school year. The work also recounts their visit to the island of Formosa, today known as Taiwan, where Chiang Kai-shek's Nationalist government retreated, following its defeat by communist forces in 1949. The book received mixed reviews in the U.S., which at the time did not recognize the Chinese communist government. For *Harper's Magazine* (October 1965), J. A. Cohen wrote, "[This] book includes a devastatingly accurate analysis of Chiang Kai-shek's demoralized military dictatorship on Formosa. Although little is new in Lindqvist's interpretation, it is a readable, balanced, and useful contribution to the popular literature. In some respects his comments are dated. . . . Also, the economic situation on the mainland has shown significant improvement since his departure. Unfortunately, the last few chapters are little more than digests of well-known academic studies." Writing for the *Saturday Review* (October 9, 1965), M. H. Fried noted, "[This book] can be read very quickly, and with fascination. . . . Unfortunately, the presentation of problems and solutions is vague; what we get are impressions, mostly the author's, and not any real grasp of what went on. . . . Lindqvist's Main-landers are shadows, and his information no better than—perhaps not as good as—what our experts dredge from an intense scrutiny of the Chinese press. . . . The clearest impression that remains with me is that of an impassable gulf between Lindqvist and the Chinese who surrounded him. . . . [His] remarks about current political opinion in Taiwan are superficial."

Upon returning to Sweden from overseas, Lindqvist took up doctoral studies in the history of literature at the University of Stockholm, completing his Ph.D. in 1966. Since then, he has, on average, written approximately one book every two years. However, few of these have been translated into English. Two notable exceptions from his early career are *Slagskuggan. Latin amerika inför 70-talet* (1969), which was published in English as *The Shadow: Latin America Faces the Seventies* (1972); and *Jord och makt i Sydaamerika* (1974), which was translated as *Land and Power in South America* (1979). Both volumes were written following extended travels in Latin America, where Lindqvist catalogued the many inequities and injustices that afflicted the region. Among his more popular works yet to appear in English are *En gift mans dagbok* (1978) and *En älskares dagbok* (1981), which roughly translate as "The Diary of a Married Man" and "The Diary of a Lover," respectively. With *Gräv där du står* (1978), or "Dig Where You Stand," Lindqvist spurred a social movement of sorts. The book encourages workers to research the companies that employed them. In examining the documented history of the Swedish cement industry, for which his grandfather worked, "Lindqvist found nothing except crudely argued assumptions that management was always right and the shareholders always vastly more important than the workers, whose main contribution was to obstruct growth and progress," Patrick Wright observed for the *London Review of Books* (August 23, 2001). Consequently, Lindqvist proposed that workers rather than management compose the history, thereby developing a different narrative, one that would take their contributions into account. In the years after the book's publication, more than 10,000 workers followed Lindqvist's example and began researching their jobs.

In 1988 Lindqvist completed *Bänkpress*, a memoir recalling how in middle age he developed a passion for bodybuilding. Later translated into English by Sarah Death, under the title *Bench Press* (2003), the book describes how a conversation with a skinhead bodybuilder in a gym sauna led Lindqvist to take up the sport. More a philosophical treatise on the meaning of bodybuilding than an instruction manual, *Bench Press* also details how the author used bodybuilding as a means to reconcile his youth as a pudgy, awkward child. Writing for the London *Independent on Sunday* (January 19, 2003), Mark Simpson remarked, "*Bench Press* muses philosophically and poetically on bodybuilding,

childhood, dreams and politics . . . Often thought-provoking in a whimsical way, and rich with a poetic charm, it never manages to fascinate in quite the way it seems to want to." Michael Glover, for the *Spectator* (January 13, 2003), a British magazine, observed, "After the marvellous and truly thought-provoking interlude of philosophical debate in its opening pages between the author and the skinhead—is the body changeable or should it be regarded as fixed, like nature? Does wanting to be strong mean that you despise weakness?—the book begins to suffer from what can only be described as alarming sidereal drift: body-building as auto-sculpture; a brief, spasmodic world history of body-building and gymnastics; shifts in the changing male ideal; sun worship; Arnold Schwarzenegger, biggest of the big; and, perhaps most intriguing of all, the fact that [the author of the Sherlock Holmes mysteries] Sir Arthur Conan Doyle was one of the judges of the first international body-building contest in 1901."

Lindqvist's next work to appear in English translation was *Exterminate All the Brutes* (1996), which was initially published in Swedish as *Ultrota varenda jävel* in 1992. The impetus for the book originated in Lindqvist's childhood reading habits; as he relates in the work, the history tomes he found on his parents' bookshelves described 19th-century European colonialists in Africa as heroes attempting to "civilize" the continent. However, one volume, by a Swedish missionary named Edward Wilhelm Sjoblom, stood in sharp contrast, instead suggesting that Western ventures in Africa were not civilizing exercises but merely efforts to expand European economic interests. The work goes on to recount Lindqvist's own personal journey through the Sahara. "The book begins as as a chronicle of travel," Paul L. Wachtel remarked for the *Washington Post* (April 14, 1996), "but Lindqvist's travel is far from an idle pleasure jaunt. As he puts it pithily and chillingly, he is telling the story 'of a man traveling by bus through the Saharan desert and, at the same time, traveling by computer through the history of the concept of extermination.'" R. James Tobin, a reviewer for *Library Journal* (March 1, 1996), remarked, "With a provocative title taken from [Joseph] Conrad's *Heart of Darkness*, Lindqvist offers a disjointed but powerful essay on racist genocide perpetrated in the name of European civilization against 'primitive' dark peoples destined by nature, in the view of some of the most respectable scientists of the 19th century, to die out. . . . Lindqvist's work, translated from the Swedish, is persuasive, readable, and highly recommended for general readers."

Published in Sweden in 1994, *Ökendykarna* was translated into English six years later by Joan Tate, under the title *Desert Divers* (2000). *Desert Divers* grew out of Lindqvist's experiences in the Sahara Desert while writing *Exterminate All the Brutes*. Throughout the memoir Lindqvist returns to the books about Africa he read as a child as he discusses why so many Western authors (himself included) have been drawn to the Sahara. Writing for the *New Statesman* (August 7, 2000), Richard Canning proclaimed, "Mixing confessional narrative, literary analysis and history, *Desert Divers* is a neat, accessible work that, for westerners drawn to the vast reaches of this desert, asks all the right questions. Equally shrewd, it refuses easy answers." Nicholas Howe, for *Research in African Literatures* (Summer 2003), observed, "Lindqvist is something more than the desert romantic he characterizes in *Desert Divers*; he is, truly, a desert mystic. Or, he wishes to be. But something holds him back from making that final walk alone into the desert from which there is no return. Lindqvist has a sharp eye for detail, for the facts of the lived life, whether they be the practices of his fellow human beings or the literal terrain he moves through. He does not have the obliviousness to the here and now that makes for a successful mystic."

Lindqvist returned to the idea of Western racism in *Antirasister: Människor och argument i kampen mot rasismen 1750–1900* (1995), which was translated into English by Joan Tate as *The Skull Measurer's Mistake: And Other Portraits of Men and Women Who Spoke Out Against Racism* (1997). Throughout the text Lindqvist sketches vivid portraits of men and women who defied the racism that dominated their particular time periods. The title is taken from the life of Freidrich Tiedemann, a surgeon from the Napoleonic era, who, by measuring the skulls of assorted people, concluded that Europeans did not possess the largest brains—a finding that outraged many but struck a blow against the racist ideology that dominated Western thought. He also recalls more famous events, including Benjamin Franklin's confrontation with a mob intent on killing Native Americans. A critic for *Kirkus Review* (April 15, 1997) proclaimed, "[Lindqvist] honors courageous visionaries from the 18th century to the mid-20th centuries who stood up to the prevailing racism of their time—a well-intentioned notion only partially carried off. . . . This is a useful, unpretentious volume that may give context and hope to the fight against racism, while admittedly charting no new territory."

Lindqvist's most recent book in English translation is *A History of Bombing* (2001), which was originally published in Sweden as *Nu dog du: bombernas århundrade* (1999). As the title suggests, the work presents a historical overview of bombs, from their earliest usage up through their impact on the wars of the late 20th century. Robert Winder, writing for the *New Statesman* (May 14, 2001), remarked, "[Lindqvist's] book is a disquieting ramble through the long and inglorious love of blitzkrieg that is one of the truest hallmarks of western civilisation. It is learned, yet concise; doom-laden, yet light. He begins with the earliest Chinese attempts to fire pellets out of bamboo canes, and ends with the snazzy American missiles

that went screaming into Iraq. In between, he ticks off (in both senses of the term) the technical advances that have fuelled our colossal urge to kill." For the *English Historical Review* (June 2002), Simon Ball was more critical of Lindqvist's thesis: "The author is particularly hard on Britons and Americans who try to draw a distinction between their actions and those of the Nazis. Lindqvist's reading of history is wholly ideological; it is a closed system that will brook no contradiction. As one might expect in a book whose form was modelled on a series of adventures for boys, this is puerile work. Indeed, the most interesting paragraphs are about the seven-year-old Lindqvist's fear of being bombed—given Sweden's neutrality, a fate that he, happily, avoided. The most revealing paragraph reveals the sixteen-year-old Lindqvist lecturing the English family who had offered him hospitality on the evil that their countrymen had perpetrated on the Germans [during World War II]."

Lindqvist's first marriage, to the former Cecilia Norman, produced two children, Aron and Clara, before ending in divorce in the 1980s. Lindqvist is now married to Agneta Stark, an economist. Since 1951 he has been a contributor to the Swedish daily periodical *Dagens Nyheter*. Between 1967 and 1974 he was a member of Sweden's Royal Commission. Lindqvist has received numerous awards for his work over the years, including the Dobloug Prize from the Swedish Academy, in 1969; he is the recipient of an honorary doctorate from the University of Uppsala and an honorary professorship from the government of Sweden. He is a member of the Swedish Union of Authors.

—C.M.

Suggested Reading: *Granta* (on-line) June 2001; *High Life* May 2000; (London) *Independent* p9 May 12, 2001; *Saturday Review* p60 Oct. 9, 1965; Sven Lindqvist's Web site

Selected Works in English Translation: *China in Crisis*, 1965; *The Shadow: Latin America Faces the Seventies*, 1972; *Land and Power in South America*, 1979; *Exterminate All the Brutes*, 1996; *The Skull Measurer's Mistake*, 1997; *Desert Divers*, 2000; *A History of Bombing*, 2001; *Bench Press*, 2003

Courtesy of Kelly Link

Link, Kelly

1969– Short-story writer; editor

When her debut short-story collection, *Stranger Things Happen* (2001), was published, Kelly Link was immediately heralded as one of the best new voices in the fantasy genre. She received numerous prizes for her work, including a World Fantasy Award for "The Specialist's Hat" and a Nebula Award for "Louise's Ghost," both of which appeared in the collection. Her second collection, *Magic for Beginners* (2005), only cemented her reputation. With her husband, she runs Small Beer Press, an independent publisher of innovative fiction.

Kelly Link was born in 1969. In an interview with Gabriel J. Mesa for the Milk Of Medusa Web site, she recalled her transient childhood: "My dad was a minister in Tennessee where he taught in a seminary and then we moved to Florida, also for his work. When I was in high school my parents divorced and I moved with my mother to live in North Carolina. So I've lived pretty much all over the East Coast." She was an avid reader as a child, particularly of science fiction and fantasy. "My dad read me all the [J. R. R.] Tolkien books, and my mom read me C. S. Lewis, and then my dad started passing me books by writers like Frank Herbert and Robert Heinlein," she explained to Ron Hogan for an interview posted on the Beatrice Web site (2001). "And I'd go to the library and get everything I could. I read a lot of Ursula K. Le Guin."

Link attended Columbia University, in New York City. "When I was picking colleges I picked New York because I wanted to see as many musicals as possible," she joked to Mesa. "I'm a little ashamed of that now. I saw *Phantom of the Opera* way too many times." Link earned an M.F.A. at the University of North Carolina, at Greensboro, before moving to Boston, where she was a member of the Cambridge Science Fiction Writers Workshop. She also worked in a popular bookstore called Avenue Victor Hugo, where she met her future husband, Gavin Grant. Grant had been managing the store, but left to earn more money temping at a large company. He had access to a photocopier and began printing a zine (a small magazine) called *Lady Churchill's Rosebud Wristlet.* The name was chosen simply because Grant and Link liked the sound of it and because they found Lady Randolph Churchill (the mother of Winston Churchill, a British prime minister) to be an interesting historical figure.

Link's work—often ghost or detective stories with a twist—began appearing in small literary magazines in the mid-1990s. She was approached by Steve Pasechnick, the head of Edgewood Press, in Boston, who wanted to publish a collection of her writing. She set about writing a few new stories to add to the collection, but Pasechnick disliked this new work, and the two made a joint decision to abandon the project.

When Link and Grant moved from Boston to the New York City borough of Brooklyn, they founded Small Beer Press. "We'd seen how magazines and books get put together," Link told Hogan. "When we moved to New York, we talked to a couple friends about helping us with copyediting, we got advice on printers." She continued, "We read a lot of books on fonts and layouts. We looked at a lot of small-press books that weren't well designed, and figured out why they didn't work. And I'd worked in bookstores for seven years, so had [my husband]; we knew what good books were supposed to look like." The couple continued to publish *Lady Churchill's Rosebud Wristlet,* as well as occasional chapbooks. *Stranger Things Happen* was the company's first book-length effort.

Stranger Things Happen garnered several glowing reviews. The fact that the self-published book was even noticed by newspaper and magazine critics surprised many observers, but Link explained to Mesa, "Even though it's a small press label, in every other way we're sort of counterfeiting all the stuff real books have, such as blurbs that are going to catch somebody's eye. With a lot of small presses, people are doing them for love, so they don't necessarily have time to get them out to review places like *Kirkus* or *Publishers Weekly* or maybe they don't even know about them. But these places have deadlines that you have to meet, and then once the books have been reviewed by *Publishers Weekly* or *Kirkus* there's a better chance that libraries or bookstores will seek the books out."

The pieces in *Stranger Things Happen* range from a genuine ghost story ("The Specialist's Hat") to a postmodern fairy tale ("Travels With the Snow

Queen") to a detective story that lampoons Nancy Drew ("The Girl Detective"). Deeming the book "the best collection of fantasy (defined broadly) stories to appear in a good long while," Gregory Feeley found much to praise in his review for the *Washington Post Book World* (August 26, 2001): "*Stranger Things Happen* is a tremendously appealing book, and lovers of short fiction should fall all over themselves getting out the door to find a copy." In the *New York Times Book Review* (November 11, 2001), Andrew O'Hehir wrote, "Link can handle slapstick comedy and Gothic horror; her stripped-down prose is light on description but rich in evocation and subterranean meaning. She embraces fantasy to its fullest sense and in doing so transcends all considerations of genre. . . . At their best, her stories have the vibrancy, the buzzing resonance and the oddly insistent quality of dreams. They aren't linked to one another, at least not in the sense that they share settings or characters, but they all draw water from the same clear, cold, deep well."

In 2003 Small Beer Press published *Trampoline*, a collection of stories edited by Link. It includes work by Karen Joy Fowler, Carol Emshwiller, and Christopher Rowe, among other writers. (Link has since co-edited, for St. Martin's Press, several editions of *The Year's Best Fantasy & Horror.*) That same year Link contributed a fairy-tale-inspired story titled "Catskin" to *McSweeney's Mammoth Treasury of Thrilling Tales.* Her short story "Stone Animals," originally published in the journal *Conjunctions*, was reprinted in *The Best American Short Stories 2005.*

Link next published *Magic for Beginners*, a collection that included the title story, which features a group of schoolgirls whose lives begin to resemble those of characters in a TV series, and "The Hortlak," in which zombies frequent a 24-hour convenience store. Michael Knight, in an assessment for the *New York Times Book Review* (August 7, 2005), called *Magic for Beginners* "a potent blend of horror and magic realism and postmodern absurdism, but it's also not any of those things exactly—she's a hard writer to put your finger on. . . . [but] it's not hard to see why fiction like hers might turn some readers on." Rebecca Meacham agreed, writing for the *Women's Review of Books* (July/August 2006), "Link's second collection is enchanting and highly potent. While some stories flow and puddle without resolution, each piece is complex and piquant. . . . This is the substance of ordinary life steeped in the delights and terrors of imagination—it is a medicinal brew." In a review for the *Boston Globe* (September 25, 2005), Peter Berbergal opined, "Link's stories are delightfully playful, almost precocious, as she creates palimpsests of secret passages, hidden doors, quiet pulses of deeper meaning. Don't look for unexpected twists or tight resolutions. Nevertheless, many images linger, and the characters are memorable, real people placed in

impossibly strange circumstances, sometimes of their own making."

Kelly Link has been the recipient of both the prestigious Hugo Award and the Nebula Award, given for outstanding writing in the genres of science fiction and fantasy.

—K.D.

Suggested Reading: Beatrice Web site; Milk of Medusa Web site; *New York Times Book Review* p15 Nov. 11, 2001, p13 Aug. 7, 2005; *Salon* (on-line) Nov. 8, 2001; Small Beer Press Web site; *Washington Post Book World* p10 Aug. 26, 2001; *Women's Review of Books* p12+ July/Aug. 2006

Selected Books: *Stranger Things Happen*, 2001; *Magic for Beginners*, 2005

Liss, David

1966– Novelist

"I feel like one of my goals as a historical novelist is to de-romanticize the past," David Liss told Robert Birnbaum in an interview for *Identity Theory* (on-line). "With the best history we have and the best theory we have, [I want to] give readers a sense of what it might have been like to have experienced a certain kind of existence in the past. It's a risky decision. I know." For Liss, the author of such highly regarded novels as *A Conspiracy of Paper* (2000) and *The Coffee Trader* (2003), who abandoned doctoral studies in English literature to pursue his calling as a writer, the risky decision has paid enormous dividends and helped to establish a unique niche for him in the historical-fiction market.

David Liss was born in 1966 and grew up in southern Florida. After high school he attended Syracuse University, in New York, from which he received a B.S. "I always wanted to write fiction," Liss recalled to Birnbaum. "After I graduated from college, I tried to write a book and it was very, very bad. It hadn't yet occurred to me that it was very bad because I was twenty-two years old and hadn't yet figured this out. I was a victim of the American cultural myth that genius requires no work. That if you have to work at something then you are not really gifted at it. So I said, 'I can't do this, I'll do something else.'" Liss opted for graduate school and, he assumed, an eventual doctorate in English literature; he subsequently received master's degrees from both Georgia State University, in Atlanta, and Columbia University, in New York City. His principle area of study was how the concept of modern personal finance was influenced by the mid-18th-century novel.

However, while writing his doctoral dissertation at Columbia, Liss recalled to Birnbaum, "I just decided I wanted to take another crack at fiction." The decision to forego his studies was a complicated one: Liss was aware of the constraints that a potential university professorship would have on his time; if he wanted to receive tenure, "it would be at least another seven years before I would have a chance to tinker around with fiction." Consequently, after receiving a grant to complete his doctoral thesis, Liss instead used the money to finance the writing of his first novel, *A Conspiracy of Paper*. The historical setting of the book was one with which Liss was familiar: "I chose to write about 18th century British culture and economics because it was something I knew about," he explained to Birnbaum. "I had been researching *A Conspiracy of Paper* for years before I even knew I was going to write it. Because I had such limited time, I wanted to write something I knew about and not take on an entirely new project."

A Conspiracy of Paper takes place in London in 1719, amid the expansion of the so-called South Sea Bubble, a period of wild financial speculation that soon led to a market crash. The protagonist is Benjamin Weaver; dubbed the "Lion of Judah" during his boxing days, Weaver has since retired from professional pugilism due to injury and become the 18th-century London equivalent of a private eye, a "protector, guardian, bailiff, constable-for-hire and thief-taker," as Liss described him. Weaver is hired to investigate an apparent suicide that his client believes was murder; this same client also suggests that Weaver's father's demise was the result of similar foul play.

James Polk wrote for the *New York Times Book Review* (February 20, 2000), "What makes *A Conspiracy of Paper* so readable is that Liss manages to create a number of arresting side plots featuring everything from the London underworld to boxing to social mores to English anti-Semitism. And all these sketches are populated with a thoroughly mixed bag of characters, varying from the Dickensian to the Orwellian." In a critique for the *New York Times* (February 21, 2000), Christopher Lehmann-Haupt agreed, writing, "The author has the leisure to explore every aspect of early 18th-century London life from the precarious relations of Jews with English society to the way the underworld was organized to the behavior of people high and low." He concluded, "*A Conspiracy of Paper* is an evocation of English history that you can happily get lost in for days." The book captured the prestigious Edgar Award, a prize awarded to mystery authors, in the category of best first novel. Liss had some reservations concerning his designation as a mystery or thriller author, telling Birnbaum, "I don't want to be limited to writing genre mysteries. I might someday write something that is strictly a genre mystery without any literary pretensions. I might never write another mystery again for as long as I live. I like keeping my options open." The rights to the movie version of the book were sold to

Miramax, and a film was tentatively slated for production, but the project has since been shelved.

With *The Coffee Trader* Liss shifts focus from 18th-century London to 17th-century Amsterdam as he details the plight of Miguel Lienzo, a Portuguese Jew who has fled his homeland in the face of religious persecution and hopes to make his fortune in the Netherlands. During his graduate-school studies, Liss had been intrigued by the Dutch of the 17th century but had never had the opportunity to delve into the subject. However, as he explained to Sybil Steinberg for *Publishers Weekly* (January 27, 2003), "Being a full-time novelist gave me a chance to dive into that world. And since a great deal of what made the 17th-century Dutch so interesting was their new modes of doing business, another book about business made sense to me." For Miguel, however, "doing business" in Amsterdam is exceedingly difficult, due in large part to the collapse of the sugar market and rampant anti-Semitism. In debt and forced to live in his brother's basement, he discovers the beneficial effects of coffee and believes that, through his manipulation of the market for the commodity, he can make the fortune thus far denied him. Erica Noonan, reviewing the work for the *Boston Globe* (April 29, 2003), wrote, "[Liss] has written a largely enjoyable, occasionally transporting tale of financial intrigue. . . . His writing is smooth and elegant—like a good cup of coffee."

Liss's third novel, a sequel to *A Conspiracy of Paper* entitled *A Spectacle of Corruption* (2004), chronicles Benjamin Weaver's unraveling of a nefarious election plot. "No one comes out smelling too well in this one," Liss told Birnbaum. A critic for *Publishers Weekly* (January 5, 2004) wrote, "Mystery and mainstream readers with a taste for gritty historical fiction will relish Liss's glorious dialogue, lively rogues, fascinating setting and indomitable hero." The Scottish writer James Buchan, however, criticized Liss's reliance on expository dialogue to clarify the novel's complicated plot and his occasional lapse into anachronism. "The effect" of these lapses, Buchan wrote for the *Washington Post Book World* (March 28, 2004), "is to break the spell of the book, like a stage actor dropping out of character. The question is whether Liss has settled into a sort of Weaver franchise, in which plots become more complex, action more brutal, language and morals less authentic and characters more simple, or whether he sets off again in search of the only thing a novel cannot do without, which is novelty."

Set in Florida, in 1985, *The Ethical Assassin* (2006) is Liss's first novel to take place in contemporary America. The protagonist, Lem Altick, begins selling encyclopedias door-to-door to pay for his education at Columbia University, in New York City, and discovers an almost preternatural ability to sell people things they do not need or cannot afford. He is about to complete one such sale in a dingy, beat-up trailer, when

Melford Kean, a strident vegan and the eponymous ethical assassin, bursts in and shoots his potential clients. Kean, not expecting witnesses but not willing to take Altick's life, forces him to grab the gun and fire the last two bullets, killing the couple and inextricably tying Altick to Kean over the course of the book's many twists and turns. Knowing Liss's own veganism and interest in animal rights, Debby Waldman, writing for the *Edmonton Journal* (May 7, 2006), argued that Kean's "anti-meat rants" make the book seem "less like fiction than like propaganda. It's the one glaring weakness in an otherwise rollicking read that manages to strike an impressive balance of suspense and humour." Oline H. Cogdill of the Fort Lauderdale *Sun-Sentinel* (March 5, 2006) was less troubled by Kean's speeches, writing: "*The Ethical Assassin's* premise has the potential to fall flat at any moment and there are, briefly, long-winded passages that bog down the story. But these moments are quite a few, and Liss' inventiveness at delivering a totally bizarre and completely believable plot continues to win over the reader."

Liss, an avid baseball fan, lives with his wife, a university professor, in San Antonio, Texas. They have one daughter. On his Web site Liss noted that his follow-up to *The Ethical Assassin* takes place in New York City and Philadelphia, Pennsylvania, in the 1790s and is expected to be published in 2008.

—P.B.M.

Suggested Reading: *Boston Globe* E p2 Apr. 29, 2003; David Liss's Web site; *Edmonton Journal* D p11 May 7, 2006; (Fort Lauderdale) *Sun-Sentinel* p20 Mar. 5, 2006; *New York Times* E p11 Feb. 21, 2000; *New York Times Book Review* p34 Feb. 20, 2000; *New Yorker* p91 Mar. 6, 2000; *Publishers Weekly* p234 Jan. 27, 2003; Random House Web site; *Washington Post Book World* p6 Mar. 28, 2004

Selected Books: *A Conspiracy of Paper*, 2000; *The Coffee Trader*, 2003; *A Spectacle of Corruption*, 2004; *The Ethical Assassin*, 2006

Lochhead, Liz

Dec. 26, 1947– Poet; playwright; performance artist

Though relatively unknown outside Britain, Liz Lochhead is one of the most celebrated authors to emerge from her native Scotland in the last half century; she is widely regarded as "a national treasure" and Scotland's "greatest living playwright," according to Brian Logan for the London *Guardian* (August 7, 2003). Though Lochhead is sometimes dismissed by English critics as a regional writer, several of her plays, including *Mary Queen of Scots Got Her Head Chopped Off* and *Perfect Days*, which captured a Fringe First Award at the 1998 Edinburgh Festival, have achieved a degree of recognition that far outstrips Lochhead's supposed parochial status. In addition to her dramatic works, Lochhead has published several poetry collections, and her work has been widely anthologized. She is credited with injecting a powerful feminine—and feminist—perspective into the overwhelmingly male-dominated fraternity of Scottish letters. "For 25 years," Gillian Glover observed for the *Scotsman* (June 6, 2003), "Lochhead has been the distinctive female voice of Scotland. Gallus [Scottish slang meaning daring or cheeky], inquisitive, accusing and playful. Angry and tender by turn. She has hectored, cajoled and entertained through every possible medium and register."

Liz Lochhead was born on December 26 (Boxing Day), 1947 in Motherwell, County Lanarkshire, Scotland, the eldest of two daughters of John Lochhead, a local official, and the former Margaret

Forrest, a homemaker; she was raised as a Presbyterian. In 1952 the family moved from Motherwell to the mining village of Newarthill, also in Lanarkshire, where Lochhead attended Newarthill Primary School and later Dalziel High. Growing up, Lochhead noticed a disjunction between the language used in and out of the classroom; the language of everyday life was a distinctive Scots English with its own accents, inflections, and vocabulary. In school, however, students were instructed—and expected to speak—in proper Oxbridge English, a mode of language alien to them. Experiencing those two linguistic styles proved beneficial for Lochhead; as the author explained to Glover, "I feel sorry for the monoglot Oxbridge standard English speakers, because they don't have the experience of shifting register. Being Scottish is an advantage because we all learn the post grown-up English voice at school, then to have other registers gives you a wonderful opportunity for irony."

After completing secondary school, Lochhead attended the Glasgow School of Art, and she dates her first attempts at writing to those years. "Going to art school's a good thing to do for a writer," she explained to Glover. "It encourages you to make things, and you don't think it's any big deal. A poem, a pot, you know [what] you need at the beginning is courage, not inhibition." After graduating, in 1970, Lochhead started a career as an art teacher at various schools in Glasgow and Bristol. However, she soon felt herself drawn more strongly toward literary endeavors. In 1971 Lochhead began attending a creative-writing class taught by Philip Hobsbawm at Glasgow University's Department of Adult Education. "She made a huge impression," Hobsbawm recollected to a reporter for the *Scotsman* (December 1, 2001). "Her poems showed a striking talent: very original, rhythmically quite extraordinary. I can still remember them."

Lochhead's first collection of poetry, *Memo for Spring*, was published in 1972 and captured a Scottish Arts Council Book Award. It reflected a traditional Scottish sensibility, albeit one with a strong feminine tilt. *Memo for Spring*, Edwin Morgan wrote for *Contemporary Poets* (1996), "made an immediate impact with its freshness and truth of experience," adding that the work's "appeal was direct, and yet the writing used more verbal devices than might appear at a glance or on a first hearing."

During the next few years, Lochhead's poems appeared in print sporadically, and in the late 1970s, she gave up teaching to concentrate on her writing and theatrical endeavors. In 1978 she began performing her poetry onstage with Marcella Evaristi in a theatrical revue entitled *Sugar and Spice*. In the ensuing years, Lochhead returned frequently to the stage to perform poetry and monologues.

Lochhead's first play, *Blood and Ice*, debuted in 1980 and was published in 1982. Set in 1816, in the area around Lake Geneva, on the French and Swiss border, the play explores the relationships among the writers Percy Bysshe Shelley, Lord Byron, and Mary Wollstonecraft Shelley. The initial reviews were scathing, as Ruth Wishart recollected for the London *Guardian* (July 24, 1985): "The drama critic from the *Guardian* clearly felt that honesty was the only defensible policy: 'Liz Lochhead, for all her evident intelligence which she will try to wear on her sleeve, has no idea of dialogue, less of plot, and less still of what constitutes drama.' [T]he man from the *Birmingham Post* said he'd rather, on balance, have been at the dentist." Nevertheless, the work went through numerous revisions and returned to the stage several times after its initial run. Kate Clanchy, writing for the *Scotsman* (January 13, 1997), observed, "Lochhead's trademark strengths are clearly emergent in [*Blood and Ice*]: there is a strong central female character who grows in stature as she is battered and wronged, a lively cynic—Byron—lovingly presented, a symbolic social conscience in the form of a maid, and several moments of [pretension]-busting wry humour."

Still devoted to poetry, Lochhead published her second collection, *The Grimm Sisters*, in 1981; David Droz, describing the volume for the British Council Web site, observed, "The Lochhead themes and style are most evident—the collection is made up of ironic retellings of fairytales and myths. The texts are provocative and full of humour, and tend towards dramatic monologues. Their style is not meditatively lyrical, but rather, poetry which should be read aloud."

Lochhead followed that, in 1984, with *Dreaming Frankenstein and Collected Poems, 1967–1984.* Lochhead's next volume, *True Confessions and New Clichés,* was published in 1985. Lochhead explained to Wishart that the impetus to write the work arose from a desire to overcome the thorough trashing she had received from critics reviewing *Blood and Ice.* "Within three months [of *Blood and Ice*]," Lochhead told Wishart, "I'd written *True Confessions* and in performing that I got rid of some of the ghosts." The work was replete with singular and amusing female characters from Lochhead's Glasgow. Wishart praised the work, remarking, "*True Confessions and New Cliches* underscores [Lochhead's] talent as a humorist, sending up the female condition in a way that demonstrates her belief that not only are we all sisters under the skin but that we screw up in remarkably similar fashion."

Also in 1985, Lochhead's innovative Scots translation of *Tartuffe,* by Jean-Baptiste Poquelin, known as Molière (1622–1675), opened on the stage. (Lochhead would later adapt another work of Molière's, *Le Misanthrope,* into Scots.) *Tartuffe* marked a turning point for Lochhead's work; it was the first of her plays to possess what a reviewer for the *Scotsman* (December 1, 2001) called her "fizzing linguistic flamboyance." The play was published as *Tartuffe: A Translation into Scots from the Original by Molière* (1985).

In 1986 another collection of poetry, *For Bram Stoker: A Sequence of Poems,* was published. During those years Lochhead also wrote numerous plays, most of which failed to bring her notice outside of Scotland. However, in 1987, with the production of *Mary Queen of Scots Got Her Head Chopped Off,* Lochhead finally began to receive widespread critical respect for her talents as a dramatist. The gothic *Mary Queen of Scots Got Her Head Chopped Off*—"one of the finest Scottish plays of recent years," as a writer for the *Scotsman* (March 4, 1994) observed—debuted at the Edinburgh Festival Fringe. The play is Lochhead's fractured take on the title character. (Mary, raised a Catholic, nominally ruled Scotland, officially a Protestant country, from almost the moment she was born, in 1542, but in practice only between 1561 and 1567. Forced to abdicate the throne, she was imprisoned for nearly a year before fleeing, in 1568, to England, where she was once again put in prison, this time by her sister, Elizabeth I, who kept Mary there for almost two decades before she was executed, ostensibly against Elizabeth's wishes.) Lochhead's play "pits independent feminine sensibilities against male orthodoxy, allows for humour and irreverence and for parallels to be drawn between the past and the present," Edwin Morgan remarked. "Prose and verse, song and action, come together in [this] extremely effective play." Opining that Lochhead "takes a fresh and moving look at Scottish history and the myths that run through it," Hamish Lennox nevertheless described the script for the London *Times* (September 9, 1989) as "a scruffy mongrel of Old Scots and inert modern Ameringlish." Despite the occasional mixed review, *Mary Queen of Scots Got Her Head Chopped Off* secured Lochhead's place as one of Scotland's most gifted and promising playwrights. It was published, in 1989, along with another play of Lochhead's, in a volume entitled *Mary Queen of Scots Got Her Head Chopped Off; and Dracula.*

In 1991 Lochhead published another volume of poetry, *Bagpipe Muzak*; three years later she scripted *Latin for a Dark Room*, a short film that was selected for production by the Tartan Shorts initiative, which sought to encourage the nascent Scottish film industry. A reviewer for the *Scotsman* (March 28, 1994) described the short as "a bittersweet tale of romance and defeat set in Victorian Edinburgh." The film starred Siobhan Redmond, a longtime friend of Lochhead.

The comedy *Perfect Days*, widely considered Lochhead's defining work, opened at Edinburgh's Traverse Theatre during the 1998 Edinburgh Festival and captured a Scotsman Fringe First Award. (First published in 1998, the play appeared in a revised edition the following year.) The central character, played at the festival by Redmond, is Barbs Marshall, a Glasgow hairdresser in her late 30s with a unique array of friends and family. Barbs desperately wants to have a child but can't seem to find a suitable partner and so opts for artificial insemination. Dan Glaister, writing for the London *Guardian* (August 26, 1998), described the play's robust reception: "The critics have raved, calling it 'lethally observant' and 'pebble-dashed with . . . a brilliant, transforming shower of unforgettable one liners.'" Glaister also sought to place the work within the context of Lochhead's career: "Although [Lochhead] has had her successes, and has climbed up the writerly career ladder—a stint as a writer in residence at the [Royal Shakespeare Company], respectable sales of plays and poems, courted by television—there is a sense that *Perfect Days* is something she wanted to get off her chest, an admission that yes, this is froth, but it is profound, it touches audiences and it is real." Reflecting on the play's success in an interview for the London *Guardian* (January 6, 1999), Lochhead remarked, "Of course, *Perfect Days* is not what I had hoped for—no play ever is—but I've never written anything that satisfies other people in quite this way. In some ways, it's been a bit like a fairy tale."

Lochhead followed up the success of *Perfect Days* with *Britannia Rules*, the first half of which was based on a one-act play she had written in 1983 entitled *Shanghaied*. The beginning of *Britannia Rules* details the lives of three poor children who are evacuated to the country during World War II, taking up residence on a pastoral estate with an upper-class girl. In the latter half of the play, which takes place on Coronation Day, 1953 (when Queen Elizabeth II was crowned), the children have aged and returned to their respective socioeconomic milieus. "It is much gentler in the second act, less dramatic," Lochhead told Jackie McGlone for the *Scotsman* (September 8, 1998), "but all the characters have some kind of dilemma to face. In the first part, it's about four wee people trying to stay sane in a world gone mad." "It is not a very subtle play," Eddie Gibb observed for the London *Guardian* (September 17, 1998), "but given the central theme—British identity—it's an interesting idea for this doyenne of Scottish theatre to be addressing." Gibb concluded, "Lochhead couldn't have been any plainer about this play's theme of identity, and in the second half she hammers home the message at the expense of character development. . . . *Britannia Rules* works well enough as a populist comedy, but by relentlessly playing for laughs Lochhead undersells the kernel of a fascinating idea—that Scots are not all left-leaning republicans." Joyce McMillan, writing for the *Scotsman* (September 14, 1998), offered considerably higher praise for *Britannia Rules*, stating, "there's simply no resisting the sheer intelligence and breadth of vision in Lochhead's writing, its infectious humanity, its sense of history, its hugely creative—and still quite unusual—capacity to laugh with the ordinary people of [Scotland] rather than at them." The play was published in 2003.

In 2000 Lochhead translated the ancient Greek tragedy *Medea*, by Euripides, into Scots. The work was named Scottish Book of the Year by the Saltire Society, becoming the first play to receive Scotland's highest literary award. Lochhead's translation updated the Greek myth of Medea and Jason. In Euripides' version of the story, the two meet during Jason's quest for the Golden Fleece and then marry and have children. Jason, however, soon finds a more politically advantageous marriage and sets about divorcing Medea—who promptly kills their children and Jason's fiancée. Reviews were exceptional. "In *Medea*," a critic for the *Scotsman* (December 1, 2001) observed, "Ms. Lochhead makes the Greeks of Corinth speak Scots and Medea herself speak a fractured, refugee's English."

Misery Guts, Lochhead's Scots adaptation of *Le Misanthrope*, debuted in Scotland in 2002. The play's main character is Alex Frew, a Scots art critic who finds himself eternally disappointed with the modern world and often in trouble for his sharp observations about Scottish politics and culture. As the play progresses, Alex falls for a devious television starlet and quarrels with the media baron Dougald Scougall. Ultimately, he decides to retire to the country to write nature poems. "Liz Lochhead and the Royal Lyceum Theatre Company have triumphed with this scorcher of a show that is surely now the hottest ticket in town," Kenneth Speirs wrote for the London *Daily Mail* (March 29, 2002), adding, "But watch out it burns, it burns."

Returning to the ancient Greek tragedies for inspiration, Lochhead crafted a trilogy entitled *The Thebans,* in which she reworked for modern Scots consumption Sophocles' *Oedipus* and *Antigone,* separating the two with a brief play, drawn mostly from Euripides, about Jocasta, the mother and wife of Oedipus. Explaining her fascination with those ancient tales, Lochhead told Mark Brown for the *Scotsman* (August 3, 2003), "They are incredible stories. There's no subtext, they are subtext. People speak out their internal dilemmas, and that's incredibly powerful. As a dramatist it gives you a sense of how bloodless plays are now." In a review for the *Scotsman* (August 7, 2003), Joyce McMillan characterized the trilogy, which debuted on stage and was published in 2003, as "an impressive and sometimes thrilling achievement," noting: "Here, [Lochhead] writes not in Scots but in a sinewy Scot-inflected English, as if she had now brought all the riches gathered in her long journey through the language of Scotland to bear on the creation of a new and edgier post-modern English. . . . In the age of the visual image, Liz Lochhead remains [a] dramatic poet whose works can make the stage vibrate with energy and dynamism."

Lochhead's most recent collection of poems, *The Colour of Black and White* (2003), was "garlanded with good reviews," as Robert Dawson Scott wrote for the London *Times* (August 4, 2003). "The many fans of [Lochhead's] poetry can relax," Lesley Duncan wrote for the Glasgow *Herald* (June 7, 2003). She "is in top form." One of the most noted poems in the collection contrasts the language Lochhead learned in school with that used outside: "It wis January / and a gey dreich day / the first day Ah went to the school / so my mum happed me up in ma / good navy-blue napp coat wi the red tartan hood," Lochhead begins, but when the child enters the school and the poem comes to an end, the poem's opening is revised: "It was January / and a really dismal day / the first day I went to school." Clair Wills wrote for the *Times Literary Supplement* (December 12, 2003), "Lochhead's ear for the rhythms of popular language is put to particularly good use in her portrayal of women-to-women relations, such as in 'Clothes' or 'Little Women', a beautifully judged poem about schoolgirls making and breaking friendships." Lochhead, Wills added, "is one of the greatest champions of female community."

In 2004 Lochhead's play *Good Things* had its premier at the Perth Theatre, in a production mounted by Scotland's Borderline Theatre Company. The action of the play, which was published in 2006, takes place in a thrift store and concerns Susan, a volunteer at the store, who, nearing 50 and single, is struggling with her love life and with a home life made difficult by an aging father and a raging daughter.

Lochhead married Tom Logan, an architect, in 1986. They make their home in Glasgow. In addition to writing plays and poems, Lochhead travels around Scotland and England—as well as overseas on occasion—to perform and teach. Lochhead is renowned for the aid she offers other aspiring authors and is credited with helping to create, as Wills stated, "a woman-friendly Scottish literary milieu very different from the opening decades of the last century."

In 2005 Lochhead was made Glasgow's poet laureate. Early that same year she was named to an advisory group for the National Theatre of Scotland. Lochhead has received honorary degrees from the University of Edinburgh and the Glasgow Caledonian University and has been the recipient of numerous writing fellowships. Summing up Lochhead's place in Scottish letters, Joyce McMillan wrote for the *Scotsman* (September 14, 1998), "Liz Lochhead is not only [Scotland's] finest craftswoman-playwright, but also a political and cultural observer of terrifically sharp insights."

—P.B.M.

Suggested Reading: British Council Web site; (Glasgow) *Herald* p12 Apr. 25, 1995; (London) *Guardian* p15 Aug. 26, 1998, p14 Jan. 6, 1999, p14 Aug. 7, 2003; *Scotsman* p12 Sep. 8, 1998, p11 Sep. 14, 1998, p10 Mar. 8, 1999, p16 Dec. 1, 2001, p13 June 6, 2003, p10 Aug. 3, 2003, p6 Aug. 7, 2003; *Times Literary Supplement* p6 Dec. 12, 2003

Selected Books: plays—*Blood and Ice,* 1982; *Tartuffe: A Translation into Scots from the Original by Molière,* 1985; *Mary Queen of Scots Got Her Head Chopped Off; and Dracula,* 1989; *Perfect Days,* 1998; *Medea,* 2000; *Misery Guts,* 2002; *The Thebans,* 2003; *Britannia Rules,* 2003; *Good Things,* 2006; poetry collections—*Memo for Spring,* 1972; *The Grimm Sisters,* 1981; *Dreaming Frankenstein and Collected Poems: 1967–1984,* 1984; *True Confessions and New Clichés,* 1985; *For Bram Stoker: A Sequence of Poems,* 1986; *Bagpipe Muzak,* 1991; *The Colour of Black and White,* 2003

Long, David

Mar. 6, 1948– Novelist; short-story writer

David Long has achieved critical success as a short-story writer and novelist, but without the fame that might have accompanied it. Frank D. Miele described Long in *Poets & Writers* (May/June 1997) as "the most lamentable of all creations—a writer's writer—one who is widely recognized as a master by his peers yet has never quite caught on with the general public." Long's fiction has appeared in numerous periodicals, including the *New Yorker,* *Story,* and *GQ,* and he has published three volumes of short stories, *Home Fires* (1982), *The Flood of '64* (1987), and *Blue Spruce* (1995), and three novels, *The Falling Boy* (1997), *The Daughters of*

Courtesy of David Long

David Long

up contemporary poetry, especially the lapidary work of John Haines, Robert Bly, Gary Snyder, and many others. When I began to write, as an adult, I wrote poems in this tradition, but in grad school I was seduced away by the short story, and for the next 20-odd years, with the exception of the occasional personal essay, I wrote almost nothing but stories.

"The turning point in my publishing life came in 1990, when I landed a story in the *New Yorker,* which also landed me my agent, Sally Wofford-Girand, and later, a book contract with Scribner that included a novel. I was not at all sure I was up to it. I'd come of age in the time of the Big Novelists—the Mailers and Styrons and Bellows, et al; I somehow felt I'd be struck down for the sin of pride if I attempted a novel. It turned out to be more a matter, as John Gregory Dunne observed, of laying a lot of pipe. I finished the first novel, *The Falling Boy*; it was published, and from then on I wanted to write nothing but novels.

"There are writers who blurt out great quantities of narrative, often endless permutations of their own lives, then boil this material down into art. I'm not like that. I work slowly, revising continually. I'm more of a mosaic maker: *this stone, this stone, this stone.* I'm constantly aware of constructing an artifact. Bits of my personal experience go into the story, but I don't set out to write about myself. I agree with Milan Kundera, who says that the subject of fiction isn't 'reality' but 'existence'—that is, its fundamental strangeness—and that a character is 'an experimental self.' While telling significant human stories remains essential, what drives me, day by day, is the attempt to make good sentences—intelligent, surprising, economical, attitude-rich. The hardest part of novel writing has proven to be not the delayed gratification, or the problem of managing the bigger scale; it's the business of going to work so many days in a state of ignorance. Without ignorance, there's no discovery, of course, but it's a bit nerve-wracking. Someone once said: You see as far as your headlights shine. Very true. The hard part is having faith that your lights will keep turning up new stretches of road.

"Finally, I continue to be nourished by what I read. In recent years, I've gotten more driven and disciplined about my reading, keeping an elaborate set of lists, and reading many more works from earlier times, and from the rest of the world. A few of my literary heroes: Alice Munro, Cormac McCarthy, William Maxwell, José Saramago, William Faulkner, John Updike, Joyce Carol Oates, Philip Roth . . ."

Simon Lamoreaux (2000), and *The Inhabited World* (2006). Terrence Rafferty, describing Long's oeuvre for the *New York Times Book Review* (September 24, 2006), explained that there is "a kind of sad story that Long has been telling for more than 20 years now . . . : a tale of everyday, getting-by existence in America, where joys can be sudden and painfully intense, and sorrows can be, too, and the trick is not to let the blues get the better of you. This is, of course, more easily said than done: it takes the sort of sustained energy that can, like electricity on a sweltering midsummer day, simply fail and leave you stranded (there's no way of knowing for how long) in a smothering darkness."

David Long sent the following autobiographical statement to *World Authors 2000–2005*:

"I was born in Boston in March 1948 and brought up in rural Massachusetts, the only child of two Midwesterners—my father was a labor relations lawyer for a steel company, my mother an amateur cellist. After Pomfret School in Connecticut and Albion College in Michigan, where I met my wife, Susan Schweinsberg, I took a two-year detour through Hartford Seminary (this was the height of the Vietnam War), then came West to study creative writing with Madeline DeFrees, Richard Hugo, and William Kittredge at the University of Montana. In 1975, my wife's job as a medical librarian took us to Kalispell, Montana, where we stayed until the late 1990s. Our older boy, Montana, was born in 1976, our younger, Jackson, in 1981.

"I'm a prime example of Saul Bellow's dictum: 'A writer is a reader moved to emulation.' Toward the end of my undergraduate years, I began soaking

David Long was born on March 6, 1948 to Jean Dimond and John H. Long. He grew up in the small town of Lunenberg, Massachusetts. Long earned a master's degree in religious studies from the

Hartford Seminary, in Connecticut, in 1972. In 1974 he received an M.F.A. degree from the University of Montana, at Missoula.

Long started his writing career as a poet, publishing a collection of verse, *Early Returns*, in 1981. He had been encouraged, however, by William Kittredge, one of his creative-writing teachers, to concentrate on short stories. His first collection, *Home Fires*, was published to great acclaim in literary circles. Most of the eight stories take place in Montana or other places in the northern Rockies, but, James W. Grinell wrote for *Studies in Short Fiction* (Summer 1983), "All eight transcend their particular locale and enter the realm of universality, most often by examining the theme of lost love—lost through misunderstanding or missed communication, inexorability or desertion."

The Flood of '64 is also set largely in "Big Sky Country," as Montana is nicknamed for its spectacular vistas. Rena S. Kleiman, in a wholly positive critique for the *Los Angeles Times Book Review* (April 19, 1997), singled out for particular praise the story "Great Blue," in which a boy spends the summer with his dying grandfather: "When the grandfather says, 'Hardly seems fair, does it?' we can hear Long saying the same thing about the victims everywhere: of cancer, of jail, of mob justice, of floods—of whatever is big, inescapable, and out to get you. . . . Long is at home in this big country, where events are larger than life, and we feel that comfort in his writing voice. There are no light bulbs going off, no epiphanies—but he has such a strong sense of these people and this place that you want to sit back and say 'OK. Put another log on—it's a long night.' And let him weave his storyteller's yarns about you."

The best stories in *Blue Spruce*, a collection that took him seven years to write, were described by Michael Upchurch for the *Chicago Tribune* (March 26, 1995) as "unostentatious on the surface" but with an "interior richness." Upchurch wrote, "There is a sense in each tale, of a whole life—or even several lives—being examined and distilled . . . . [along with] an abiding respect for the mysteries of behavior." A reviewer for *Publishers Weekly* (January 16, 1995) noted that the stories in *Blue Spruce* "come alive at unexpected moments with a sudden forcefulness." Calling the writer a "true craftsman," the reviewer continued, "Long's voice has an unerring pitch, and his insight is equally impressive."

Mark, the protagonist of Long's first novel, *The Falling Boy*, has married his childhood sweetheart, Olivia, longing not only for her, but for the stable family he believes she represents. That stability is elusive, and he winds up having an affair with her sister. "Long's achievement in this novel is that he makes us care for everyone who has a stake in Mark's life, from his grandmother to his wife and children, to his in-laws and even his co-workers," Floyd Skloot wrote for the *Sunday Oregonian* (July

20, 1997). "Also he makes the fixing of a marriage as interesting as its breakage." David L. Ulin, in a similarly laudatory review for New York *Newsday* (July 6, 1997), commented that Long eschews sentimentality "in the service of something more profound. The world in which Mark and Olivia find themselves is at once organic, unforgiving and deeply, relentlessly real. And by allowing that world to stand for itself, Long has created an exquisite novel, a sublime piece of literary artistry that never backs away from the messy tangle of life."

Miles, the main character of Long's next novel, *The Daughters of Simon Lamoreaux*, is also entangled with two sisters, causing Andrew O'Hehir to quip, in a review for the *New York Times* (August 6, 2000, on-line), "It's safe to say that David Long has a thing for sisters." In the book a girl named Carly Lamoreaux disappears before a date with Miles, then a prep student, never to be seen again. Miles subsequently marries, unhappily, and in the midst of a trial separation, some quarter-century after Carly's disappearance, he is contacted by her sister, Julia, who is desperate to solve the mystery. "As gripping as Long's explorations of sisterhood are, his real subject is not sisters per se but the men who love them," O'Hehir wrote. "If fiction about the strangled emotional life of the American male has become its own genre, packed with its own clichés, few of the writers who have worked this territory can match Long's vivid characterization, his blend of cleareyed sympathy and critical distance and his old-fashioned gift for storytelling. *The Daughters of Simon Lamoreaux* has the propulsive power and mystery of a Gothic romance, but the world it creates is a complicated and contemporary one, in which men and women are shaped by random events and rarely know themselves as well as they think they do." The book received near-universal praise; Bonnie Johnston, in a representative review for *Booklist* (April 15, 2000), opined that "in addition to being an intriguing mystery, Long's novel is a captivating story about the healing potential of love in the face of tragedy."

The Inhabited World, Long's latest novel, is a ghost story of sorts. Evan, who committed suicide a decade before, now haunts the house in which he once lived. Maureen, the current occupant, is contemplating doing the same after a failed love affair with a married man. Although Evan is not visible or audible to Maureen, he longs to draw on his own experiences to help her. In an interview posted on Long's official Web site, he explained, "I wanted to avoid the conventions of ghost fiction. I didn't want the novel to be about spooking the living, and I didn't want it to be a fairytale—like the movie *Ghost*, for example, where there's a hugely sentimental moment of contact between the dead guy and his widow." Long continued, "The word 'ghost' never appears in the book. All during the time I was writing it, the working title was *Purgatorio*. I wanted my character to be in an intermediate place. He knows he's not alive, yet he's not in a state of total nothingness. he's somewhere between life and death. His task is to try to understand *why*. Is it permanent? Is there a purpose behind it? *Why* him?" Terrence Rafferty noted, "*The Inhabited World* is, on some level a cautionary tale. . . . But it doesn't read like one, because Long fills it with unpredictable, vigorously imagined minor characters, good jokes, stray beauties of landscape (the Pacific Northwest) and even some precisely observed and deeply appreciative evocations of what used to be called the pleasures of the flesh. The novel wouldn't work if Long weren't able to convey the keenness of the joys his hero has left behind, and he is able, emphatically."

Over the course of his career, Long has been the recipient of an O. Henry Award, a Pushcart Prize, and a Rosenthal Prize from the American Academy of Arts and Letters, among other honors. He began, almost three decades ago, keeping a log of all the books he reads, and he posts on his Web site various lists—including his favorite plays, memoirs, and short-story collections (along with quirkier lists made up of Estonian novels and books from the year he was born). "These are not lists of Best Books. There's a multitude of great novels and story collections I've never read (or read and don't much like)," he told Ron Hogan for the on-line publication *Beatrice* (August 20, 2006).

"No, this is my list; it's biased, personal. These are works that still get under my skin. These are the ones that have marked me, that have sprung me from the here and now, or taught me what art is capable of—that have, in fact, become indispensable to my life as an artist." While Long is inarguably serious about literature, he does not believe in taking himself too seriously; in an effort to relax his students, he once brought a sack of novelty glasses—with comic noses and mustaches attached—to a class he was teaching, passing them out and donning a pair himself.

—S.Y.

Suggested Reading: *Beatrice* (on-line) Aug. 20, 2006; *Booklist* p1,524 Apr. 15, 2000; *Chicago Tribune* C p5 Mar. 26, 1995; *Los Angeles Times Book Review* p3 Apr. 19, 1987; *New York Times Book Review* Sep. 24, 2006; *Ploughshares* p236 Fall 1995; *Publishers Weekly* p49 Mar. 27, 2000, p34 Mar. 13, 2006; (Spokane, Washington) *Spokesman Review* D p3 Sep. 4, 2005; *Studies in Short Fiction* p140 Summer 1983; *Sunday Oregonian* G p3 July 20, 1997

Selected Books: *Early Returns*, 1981; *Home Fires*, 1982; *The Flood of '64*, 1987; *Blue Spruce*, 1995; *The Falling Boy*, 1997; *The Daughters of Simon Lamoreaux*, 2000; *The Inhabited World*, 2006

MacSweeney, Barry

July 17, 1948–May 9, 2000 Poet

Barry MacSweeney burst onto the poetry scene in England at the age of 19, with the publication of his first collection, *The Boy from the Green Cabinet Tells of His Mother* (1968). Over the course of his career, he wrote more than 20 volumes of poetry but waged a fierce battle with alcoholism the entire time. MacSweeney never got to see his final collection or enjoy the critical attention it brought him; *Wolf Tongue* (2003) was published three years after his death from alcohol-related complications.

The son of Patrick MacSweeney and the former Lilian Calvert, Barry MacSweeney was born on July 17, 1948 in Newcastle upon Tyne, Northumberland, England. He studied at the Broadwood Primary School and the Rutherford Grammar School. He was raised in poverty in Newcastle, but he often escaped his dismal surroundings by traveling to the moorland surrounding the city. He left school at age 16 to become a cub reporter for the Newcastle *Evening Chronicle*, but returned for the 1966–67 academic year to study journalism at Harlow Technical College, in Essex.

Moira Conway/Courtesy of Bloodaxe Books

MacSweeney had subsequent stints on a variety of newspapers, eventually rising to the position of deputy editor of the *Shields Gazette*. Journalism, however, was not his main interest. He had been writing poetry since the age of seven; his first effort, as he often recalled, was about daffodils and crocuses. He continued to write poems as a young adult, in the evenings after work. He also began drinking during those hours. "I'd very rarely go to the pub after work because I wrote all the time at home," he explained to David Whetstone for the Newcastle *Journal* (November 25, 1997). "I'm an accomplished cook so I would have some food and that would be an excuse to open a bottle. Then I would get to work on the poems. I drank at home where you don't have the encouragement of closing time. If you get drunk [at home] you are not going to fall down in the street."

In Newcastle during the 1960s, poetry was experiencing a resurgence. Poets, young and old, flocked to the area; Basil Bunting was receiving long-overdue recognition as the country's major modernist poet, Tom Pickard was organizing a series of influential readings at the Morden Tower (a medieval venue on the city walls), and John Silkin had reestablished his quarterly poetry journal, the *Stand*, after moving from Leeds. MacSweeney was influenced by the native poets surrounding him and gained an appreciation for the American poets who visited to give readings.

In the spring of 1967 MacSweeney organized the Sparty Lea Poetry Festival, a 10-day event during which poets from all over England convened in the small village of Sparty Lea to read, write, talk, and (reportedly) drink copiously. Attendees included the poet J. H. Prynne, who became a lifelong friend to MacSweeney, and Andrew Crozier, the co-founder of the *English Intelligencer*, which was instrumental in introducing many new poets to the reading public. The festival has been widely credited as a seminal event in the revival of British poetry.

MacSweeney began publishing poems in small literary magazines, and he soon came to the attention of Michael Dempsey, then the editor of Hutchinson's New Authors imprint, which published *The Boy from the Green Cabaret Tells of His Mother*. The book proved to be widely popular, and MacSweeney found himself a pivotal fixture in the counterculture arts world. He was mentioned in *Vogue*, and as an ill-conceived publicity stunt his publisher nominated him—not yet 20 years old—for the poetry professor's chair at the University of Oxford. He received just three votes and managed to nearly ruin his reputation as a serious poet. "He felt ridiculed," Jackie Litherland, a fellow poet who later became MacSweeney's confidante and companion, told Gordon Burn for the London *Guardian* (June 1, 2000). "They trashed him. He was just a kid. He found it very difficult to get published after that. He was seen as a 60s fashion victim. The talent didn't diminish, but his manuscripts were rejected."

Burn described MacSweeney's career trajectory: "[He] disappeared into the alternative universe of the little magazines; of fugitive publications and small editions." He continued, "As a last resort, he would Roneo [copy] his poems and send them out to the hardcore [group] of 20 people." MacSweeney and his first wife, the poet Elaine Randell, founded Blacksuede Boot Press, named after the type of boots worn by the singer Bob Dylan. Along with publishing some of MacSweeney's poetry, Blacksuede also published the work of Randell, Crozier, and Prynne.

MacSweeney's published volumes include *The Last Bud* (1969), *Six Sonnets for Nathaniel Swift* (1969), *Flames on the Beach at Viareggio* (1970), *Brother Wolf* (1972), *Fools Gold* (1972), *Black Torch* (1978), and *Odes* (1978). Much of his work chronicled his unease with the social and political situation in Britain, as well as such personal topics as his childhood. By the early 1980s, however, he was publishing less and drinking more. He often agonized over sending his work to larger publishing companies. When he sent his collection, *Ranter*, to the editors at Bloodaxe Books, a prestigious poetry press, it was initially rejected, and although it was published by another company in 1985, he found the rejection demoralizing. MacSweeney's personal life was not going well either; after divorcing Randell, he married for a second time, in 1983, to Lesley Bourne, and this marriage lasted just three months. His drinking worsened, and he repeatedly checked himself into detox clinics, never with any lasting success.

In 1993, however, MacSweeney was excited about one bright spot in his life—the upcoming publication of his collection *The Tempers of Hazard*, which also featured the work of Chris Torrance and Thomas A. Clark, by Paladin Books. That same year the media mogul Rupert Murdoch acquired the imprint and, at the advice of his accountants, ordered the company to pulp all books that had not made a profit, including *The Tempers of Hazard*. MacSweeney was devastated; his drinking worsened and he lost his job at the *Shields Gazette*, where he had been employed for eight years. His life improved somewhat after he began a relationship with Jackie Litherland, whom he courted with trips to the countryside and elaborate meals during his sober periods. Yet even she was unable to prevent MacSweeney's drinking binges. In June 1995 he suffered alcohol-induced convulsions and had to be placed on a life-support machine in a hospital.

After receiving an award of £10,000 from the Royal Literary Fund, MacSweeney used the money to book himself into a well-regarded detox clinic. For a time it seemed as if he had recovered. He began to chronicle his drinking life in a collection of poems, which was ultimately published as *The Book of Demons* in 1997. The collection included a reprint of the 1995 poem sequence *Pearl*, about his relationship with a mute classmate, and was widely regarded as one of his best works. Michael Bradshaw, in the *Richmond Review* (on-line), wrote, "The *Book of Demons* has an amplitude of line and diction, a plentitude of horror. This is not a sinister minimalist horror of cuts and thrusts but an extravagant and wide howling with lots to say . . . and therefore endlessly vociferous, so that a yearning is felt back into the pre-linguistic silence from which Pearl fought so hard to emerge. The pain of both language strangled and language unleashed are felt in abundance." In 1997 MacSweeney won the Paul Hamlyn Foundation Award, which carried a monetary prize of £15,000.

Despite such successes, MacSweeney continued to drink; during the last years of his life he was drunk almost continually and suffered horrible hallucinations. He broke several limbs in various falls and often collapsed in public. He died on May 9, 2000. Gordon Burn quoted a poem by MacSweeney that seemed to predict the manner of his death: "One day choke on it, tongue / jammed backwards down / throat's clogged highway."

Shortly after MacSweeney's death Litherland edited a collection of his selected poems, *Wolf Tongue*, which was published by Bloodaxe in 2003. In a review for the *Times Literary Supplement* (December 19–26, 2003), Patrick McGuinness called the selected poems a "work of

rare intensity and power: as harrowing a journey into the interior, and as true a witness to its times and places, as can be found in recent poetry." John Sears wrote for *Pop Matters* (August 13, 2003, on-line) that MacSweeney was a poet "doomed to flashes of political optimism made only more futile by the deepening historical gloom they illuminate, a situation expressed most powerfully in the final lines of the final poem of this remarkable collection: 'We are not stone, but we are in the grinder. / Everything is lost, and we are dust and done for.'"

—C.M.

Suggested Reading: (London) *Guardian* p24 May 18, 2000, p2 June 1, 2000; (London) *Independent* p7 May 13, 2000; (Newcastle) *Journal* p11 Nov. 25, 1997; *Richmond Review* (on-line); *Times Literary Supplement* p16 Dec. 19–26, 2003

Selected Books: *The Boy from the Green Cabaret Tells of His Mother*, 1968; *The Last Bud*, 1969; *Six Sonnets for Nathaniel Swift*, 1969; *Flames on the Beach at Viareggio*, 1970; *Brother Wolf*, 1972; *Fools Gold*, 1972; *Black Torch*, 1978; *Odes*, 1978; *Blackbird*, 1980; *Ranter*, 1985; *The Book of Demons*, 1997; *Wolf Tongue*, 2003

Magris, Claudio

(MAH-greece, CLOW-dee-oh)

Apr. 10, 1939– Novelist; essayist; translator; playwright

The work of the Italian scholar, translator, and writer Claudio Magris, who has often been named as a possible future recipient of the Nobel Prize in literature, is, like its author, steeped in the culture of Trieste, Italy, Magris's birthplace. Between 1867 and 1918 Trieste was a prosperous seaport of Central Europe as a part of the Austro-Hungarian Empire and became a cultural center, with notable artists such as Italo Svevo (1861–1928), James Joyce (1882–1941), and Umberto Saba (1883–1957) living there at various times. As it is both a seaport and artistic mecca, the city became a place where various ethnic groups mixed freely. At the same time, however, the city, at least in the period in which Magris grew up, drew attention to the ability of borders to seem impermeable, and he observed, as Eric Solsten explained for the Library of Congress Information Bulletin (December 1999, on-line) that "a constant theme in his writing . . . was borders of every kind: national, political, social, psychological and linguistic. He stated that his fascination with borders no doubt stems from the fact that he grew up in Trieste, which is on the

Courtesy of PEN American Center

border between Italy and Yugoslavia. As a very young child, he could travel eastward from Trieste, but with the creation of the Iron Curtain after World War II, these well-known areas suddenly were closed to him." Magris's books have received numerous awards and have been translated into many languages; his works in English translation include *Danube* (1989), *Inferences from a Sabre* (1990), *A Different Sea* (1993), and *Microcosm* (2000).

The only child of Duilio and Pia (de Gisogono) Magris, Claudio Magris was born on April 10, 1939 in Trieste, Italy, where he grew up. As a port on Italy's northeastern border with Slovenia, formerly part of Yugoslavia, Trieste has always been a cosmopolitan city where Italians, Germans, and Slavs have lived among one another for centuries, and Magris is something of a reflection of the city of his birth; although he is predominantly of Italian ancestry, with some Slavic blood, one of his grandfathers was in the Austrian navy at the time when Trieste was the central port of the Hapsburg Empire. Living so close to Austria and Germany prompted his early interest in German literature, which he studied while attending the Universita degli Studi di Torino, in Turin, Italy, receiving his degree in 1962. After completing his dissertation on the Hapsburgs, he published it under the title *Il mito absburgico nella letteratura austriaca moderna* (which can be translated as "the Hapsburg myth in modern Austrian literature"), in 1963. He then began translating works by such authors as Henrick Ibsen, Heinrich von Kleist, Arthur Schnitzler, and Georg Büchner into Italian and also writing criticism, publishing his second scholarly study, which was about the German writer Johann Jacob Wilhelm Heinse and called *Wilhelm Heinse*, in 1968, the year he took a position as a lecturer in German studies at the Universita degli Studi di Trieste. Magris would remain in Trieste until 1970, when he was appointed a professor of German language and literature at the Universita degli Studi di Torino. The following year he published *Lontano da dove: Joseph Roth e la tradizione ebraico-orientale* (which can be translated as "far from where: Joseph Roth and the Eastern-Jewish tradition") and in 1974 he published *L'anarchico al bivio: Intellettuale e politica nel teatro di Dorst* (which translates as "the anarchist at the crossroad: intellectualism and politics in the theatre of Dorst"), a book he had written with Cesare Cases.

During these years Magris also wrote for various European newspapers and periodicals and was a reviewer and essayist for *Corriere della Sera*, arguably Italy's leading national daily. Some of his journalistic writings were collected as *Dietro le parole* (which can be translated as "behind the words") in 1978—the year he returned to the Universita degli Studi di Trieste to become a professor of German studies—and as *Itaca e oltre* (which can be translated as "Ithaca and beyond"), in 1982. Among his essays are pieces on the German writer and composer E. T. A. Hoffmann, the Norwegian dramatist Henrik Ibsen, the Italian novelist and short-story writer Italo Svevo, the Austrian author Robert Musil, the German painter and writer Herman Hesse, and the Argentinean

writer Jorge Luis Borges. He has also published, with Angela Ara, *Trieste: Un'identità di frontiera* (which can be translated as "Trieste: a frontier identity," 1982) and with Italo Zannier *Giuseppe Wulz* (1984), as well as written a number of other scholarly works, including *L'altra ragione: Tre saggi su Hoffmann* (which can be translated as "the other reason: three essays on Hoffman," 1978), *L'anello di Clarisse* (1984), *Quale totalità* (1985), and a collection of essays called *Utopia e disincanto: Saggi, 1974-1998* (which can be translated as "utopia and disenchantment: essays, 1974-1998," 1999).

Magris's reputation outside Europe, however, rests primarily on his fiction and literary travel writing, all of which he published after he was 40. His first novel, *Illazioni su una sciabola*, appeared in 1984. Translated by Mark Thompson as *Inferences of a Sabre*, the novel finds the author returning to his childhood in Trieste and recalling the Cossacks—Russians opposed to communist rule in the Soviet Union who fought on the German side during World War II. "I was a little boy of five or six in Udine," Magris told Richard Gott for the London *Guardian* (August 3, 1990), "when it was occupied by the Cossacks. I saw these strange soldiers with their families and their horses, sometimes camels, and I understood that these men were completely different from us." An epistolary work, the novel tells the story of Father Guido, who attempts to make sense of what happened to the commander of the Cossacks, Pjotr Nikolaievich Krasnov, whom he cannot be certain that he ever met. Although placed in a fictional setting, Krasnov was in fact the real leader of the Cossack regiment. Part of the losing side during the Russian Revolution of 1918, Krasnov moved to Berlin in the 1920s and, in his old age, was forced by the Nazis to lead the Cossacks against the Soviet Union during World War II. Krasnov, according to some accounts, was killed on May 2, 1945 by Italian partisans, but Magris and others claim that he was handed over to the Soviet authorities and, in 1946, hanged in Moscow. In this slight book, which ran to 77 pages in the English edition, Magris used Krasnov's story to relate the various betrayals that the Cossacks faced during the war. In a review for the London *Independent* (August 4, 1990), Hugo Barnacle called the novel "a fine piece of watchmaker's prose, beautifully printed and bound" and complimented the author on his "good, pure style."

Two years later Magris published the literary travel book *Danubio* (1986)—which was translated into English by Patrick Creagh under the title *Danube*—and earned international renown as a keen observer of Central European culture and as an Italian author of considerable significance. In *Danube*, Magris uses a trip down the Danube River—the chief waterway of the Austro-Hungarian Empire and the ancient northern border of the Roman Empire—to explore Central European history and culture, particularly its evolution. As he moves down Europe's second-longest river to the Black Sea, he passes through Germany, where the river originates, as well as Austria, Hungary Yugoslavia, Romania, and Bulgaria. As the book was written at the height of the Cold War, these countries were then in the grip of the Soviet Union, so many of his reflections discuss the people living behind what Winston Churchill once described as the Iron Curtain, but he also recounts historical and cultural events that occurred near the Danube and helped to shape Central Europe's remarkable and often violent history.

English-language critics were generally united in their praise of *Danube*. In the London *Times* (July 13, 1989), William Hobson wrote, "Magris is an acute and inspiring critic, making one long to read or go back to the vast number of writers from Marcus Aurelius to Canetti on whom he draws. But he himself also writes with great beauty and artistry. An undercurrent of nostalgia runs through this book. He mourns, for instance the classical concept of life . . . before the advent of post-modernism and the imprisonment of living at one remove from reality. But nostalgia and melancholy have always been characteristic of Central Europe, just as it has always taught that destinies are not irreparable. Magris attempts not so much to answer the questions as to show how to approach them. At one point he says: 'The river of life flows in our veins . . . and at every heartbeat, it deposits in us a little of the silt of time, which one day will rise as high as the heart; but now that torrent does not overwhelm, but cradles us.' This is the universal theme of *Danube*." In the London *Independent* (July 1, 1989), Ian Thomson wrote, "*Danube* is not simply a masterpiece of travel; it is an odyssey. . . . Magris is always lyrical about the magical allure of water—'a bright clear surface like that of a calm sea barely ruffled to froth and wind, more unfathomable than the depths. That display their cavernous obscurities, and evoking a gentle, a reticent infinity.' Worn out at his journey's end, he reaches the Black Sea, where a strange breed of Russians with long patriarchal beards fish in the delta from canoes. The book ends on a melancholy note with this haunting line from the Triestino poet Biagio Marin: 'Lord let my death be like the flowing of a river into the great sea.' Perhaps, after all, *Danube* is really an elegy."

Magris's second novel, *Un altro mare* (1991), which was published in English as *A Different Sea*, tells the story of a young man named Enrico living a rootless life in the early part of the 20th century. As an intellectual he longs for existential truth and, in order to find it, travels from Gorizia, a city in Austria-Hungary, to South America. Returning to Europe after many years, he discovers that his schoolyard friend Enrico, who had been something of a philosophical inspiration for him during his journeys, has committed suicide, leaving him alone to face the coming onslaught of political -*isms* that will tear Europe apart: communism,

nationalism, and fascism. Unlike its predecessors, *A Different Sea* found critics divided over its merits. "It is a novel of great intellectual ambition," Michael Glover wrote in his review for the *Financial Times* (July 24, 1993), "exercised within a small compass, but fails because Magris has not succeeded, for all his scholarly credentials, in breathing life into the central character." On the other hand, Richard Gott, the literary editor of the London *Guardian* (July 27, 1993), observed, "This is a very short book, yet Magris packs in as many ideas, events, and characters as can be found in a novel ten times as long. Not a word is wasted, nor is there ever a moment when the reader does not thirst to turn the page. . . . [Magris] belongs among that small band of writers for whose forthcoming works one awaits with impatience."

Magris returned to travel writing in the 1990s, publishing *Microcosmi*, in 1997. Translated by Iain Halliday as *Microcosms*, the book details Magris's visits to cafes, homes, inns, and other gathering places of northern Italy, interweaving discussions of local history and folklore with descriptions of the lives of the people he meets. In the process the author manages to show his readers Italy through both his eyes but also the eyes of its inhabitants, while he reflects on the region's rich and often tangled history. In the London *Independent* (July 29, 1999), Mark Thompson wrote, "Despite [a] redemptive upward curl that closes many episodes of the book, *Microcosms* is overcast with a pathos that is more affecting because [it is] not really confessed or explored. . . . Magris's writing has never been more intimate than in the beautiful last chapter. Suffering lurks in the margins of *Microcosms*, whose places are theatres of memory, chosen for their power to provoke personal recollection. This power sustains the narrative. . . . Below the carapace of allusions lies an oblique memoir of family life, celebrating its cycles of repetition, renewal and loss. English readers unfamiliar with the terrain may need stamina, which will be rewarded." Nicholas Howe, writing for the *New Republic* (September 2, 2002), observed, "Even if it makes one want to travel to Trieste and its environs, *Microcosms* is not a travel book. Instead, it testifies to the saving vision that can come only from an insider learned in the ways and the histories of a place and yet free of all provinciality. To love the incongruities of one's native place, to have read everything that has been written about one's city, to write of home with a cosmopolite's style: these are the qualities that make *Microcosms* one of the most remarkable portraits of place written in our time."

In addition to the works discussed above, Magris has written a number of plays, including *Stadelmann* (1988), *Le voci* (1991), and *La mostra* ("the show," 2001). Three of his plays are due to be published in English, in 2007, in a collection called "Three Plays," which will include *Le voci* (which is to be entitled "Voices"), *Essere già stati* ("To Have Been"), and *Stadelmann*. A fierce critic of postmodern thought, many of Magris's works overtly or obliquely criticize the demise of a more traditional attitude toward life. In his interview with Richard Gott for the London *Guardian*, Magris described postmodernism in Italy: "In Italy it is now an entire culture. There are some groups of intellectuals who are not just studying and interpreting and analysing the process, but are often actually celebrating the postmodern, seeing it as the twilight, not just of certainty, not just of truth, but of values themselves. They celebrate this farewell to values as a liberation. . . . I think sometimes that intellectuals have no sense of responsibility. I remember some colleagues at the end of the 70s telling their students that Bach and pornography were the same thing. They knew very well the distinction between them, and it was a lack of responsibility to teach that—like rich people telling poor people that money is not important." Despite his dissatisfaction with the contemporary cultural milieu, Magris denies that his work is sentimental or nostalgic—two adjectives often used to describe his writing. "Absolutely not," he told Mark Thompson for the *Guardian* (October 16, 1992). "Or only for what should be, not what was. Tenderness, yes, but if I'm interested in your grandmother's love affairs, it's not because of the good old days when she was young. Anybody's love is important, eternal, whether it happened a century ago or yesterday. You don't signify more than your grandmother, not because of nostalgia—because of respect for human feeling. Otherwise the feelings of those killed in Auschwitz matter less than ours as we sit comfortably in the Café San Marco. Which isn't true."

Magris, whose last novel, *Alla cieca* (which can be translated as "blindly") appeared in 2005, has received numerous prizes and awards for his work, including the Austrian Medal of Honor in the Arts and Sciences from the Austrian Ministry of Education, Arts, and Sports and the Goethe Medaille from the Goethe Institutes for the promotion of German language study abroad and international cultural cooperation (both in 1980), the Premio Aquileia and Premiolino (both in 1983), the Premio Bagutta (1987), the Premio Antico Fattore (1988), the Premio Juan Carlos I (1989), the Premio Grinzane Piemonte (1999), the Erasmus Prize (2001), and the Austrian State Prize for European literature (2006). He also holds honorary doctorates from a number of universities and was named, in 2001, to a chair at the College de France.

Married to Marisa Madieri since August 20, 1964, Claudio Magris has two sons, Francesco and Paolo. From 1994 to 1996 he served as a member of the upper house of the Italian parliament.

—C.M.

Suggested Reading: (Canada) *Vancouver Sun* A p19 July 8, 2000; *Chicago Tribune* p3 Oct. 11, 1989; *Financial Times* p25 July 24, 1993; (Glasgow) *Herald* p12 July 17, 1993; (London) *Guardian* p28 Aug. 3, 1990, p25 Oct. 11, 1991, p16+ Oct. 16, 1992, p8 July 27, 1993; (London) *Independent* p32 July 1, 1989, p28 Aug. 4, 1990, p5 July 29, 1999; (London) *Times* July 13, 1989, Sep. 27, 1993; *New Republic* p31 Sep. 2, 2002; *New York Newsday* B p8 Feb. 9, 1995; *Scotland on Sunday* July 25, 1993; *Washington Times* E p9 Oct. 16, 1989

Selected Books in English Translation: *Inferences from a Sabre,* 1984; *Danube,* 1986; *A Different Sea,* 1991; *Microcosms,* 1997

Courtesy of Canongate Books

Maine, David

Nov. 28, 1963– Novelist

David Maine has received widespread critical praise for his three novels: *The Preservationist* (the British edition of which bears the title *The Flood,* 2004), *Fallen* (2005), and *The Book of Samson* (2006). Retelling familiar Old Testament stories, Maine's work, Alan Rauch wrote for the *Charlotte Observer* (December 18, 2005), intelligently examines "the Biblical text and extrapolates from the scraps of information provided in the Old Testament to generate a fictional history." In the process, Maine more than simply brings to life well-worn tales, he reinterprets them, providing them with, as Janet Maslin wrote for the *New York Times* (November 2, 2006), "a startlingly contemporary tone." She went on to observe: "Though the tone of his books is wonderfully mischievous, their essential seriousness is beyond question. Here is a beguiling, original writer who is determined to reinterpret the Bible's humanity in ways that make sense in the modern world."

One of three children, David Maine was born on November 28, 1963 and raised in Farmington, Connecticut. After completing high school, he attended Oberlin College, in Ohio, where, besides studying, he performed in a rock-and-roll band called Jackhammer and the Power Tools, using the stage name Buzz Saw. In the late 1980s he entered the M.F.A. program at the University of Arizona, earning his degree, in 1991. While in Arizona he met Uzma Aslam Khan, who also attended the M.F.A. program and who has since achieved recognition as a novelist. After working for a few years in the mental-health systems of Massachusetts and Arizona, Maine married Kahn, and in 1995 the couple moved to Morocco, where Maine taught English until 1998, when he moved, with his wife, to Lahore, Pakistan. Maine continued to teach English in Pakistan, and after a few years in his new country, he began writing his biblical novels, starting his first in the wake of the September 11, 2001 terrorist attacks on the World Trade Center in New York City and the Pentagon in Washington, D.C. "Religious devotion is more of a public commodity in Pakistan than in the U.S., and this has allowed me to loosen up and write about people who express that devotion publicly," he explained to Edward Nawotka for *Publishers Weekly* (January 26, 2004). "Sure, there are publicly devout figures in the States," he continued, "but in general it's considered good etiquette to keep your religious ideas to yourself— at least in New England, where I'm from. In Pakistan there is no such compulsion."

Perhaps unconsciously affected by the September 11 terrorist attacks, he acknowledges, Maine turned to a tale of universal disaster, the biblical story of the flood, when his writing took a religious turn. "It seems possible," he told Nawotka, "that the general gloomy world view [of the period] affected my thinking and writing," though he also noted, "I like animals. I do remember that, even as a little kid, Noah made a real impression on me. I used to wonder how they got all those animals on one boat." The novel, the *Preservationist,* retells the flood story from the point of view of Noah and the handful of family members who join him on his ark and was greeted with enthusiastic reviews. Elena Seymenliyska, writing for the London *Guardian* (March 4, 2006), for instance, proclaimed that the book "marked Maine out as a natural storyteller and a man of unbridled imagination." Melvin Jules Bukiet observed for the *Washington Post* (June 27, 2004), "This story is familiar to anyone with a smidgen of biblical knowledge. Yet as the story has come down to us in Hebrew or Sunday school versions, it's usually viewed through a shortsighted lens that perceives its protagonist as a person rather like one of us who's confronted with a dilemma. The surprise in Maine's version comes from his

transformation of that perception through the gritty integrity of his vision of the prediluvial world." Taking a more tempered view, Christine Wald pointed out for the *Denver Post* (July 11, 2004) that the story was "a bit thin as it sets out," but went on to say that "Maine's book grows into a fascinating, layered tale. Just realizing the logistics of Noe's enterprise is an exercise in creativity." (*Noe* is the Greek/Latin form of the Hebrew *Nôah* and is the spelling favored by Maine.)

Maine returned the following year with *Fallen,* a novel that opens on the deathbed of Cain, who, by killing his brother Abel, became humankind's first murderer. Tracing Cain's story backwards, the narrative ends with the expulsion of his parents, Adam and Eve, from Paradise. Janet Maslin wrote for the *New York Times* (September 8, 2005) that Maine's first novel "turns out to have been a dry run for this quirky, delectable, much more daring book." *Fallen,* she went on to write, "is a risky, original undertaking. It is not one of those parasitical fables that siphon all their inspiration from borrowed material. Mr. Maine uses 40 chapters (a number with much biblical resonance, starting with Noah and the flood) to reconstruct the early book of *Genesis* in reverse, as a way of amplifying hindsight and regret." Other reviewers were equally impressed. "The portrayal of Adam, Eve and their children is astonishing," Hugo Barnacle wrote for the London *Sunday Times* (April 23, 2006). "They retain their mythical, archetypal quality, yet are utterly, quirkily credible. The reader may find it impossible to see *Genesis* any other way afterwards." Not everyone, however, was as enthusiastic. Complaining about Maine's decision to start his story from the end and move backwards, Ron Charles wrote for the *Washington Post* (October 2, 2005), "On the whole, I found this structure more clever than engaging. . . . Going the wrong way, we don't have much to look forward to after the fratricide. And the unique conditions of the world at this time further compound the story's dramatic problem: As Maine moves back toward the beginning of humanity, his cast of characters must shrink, the brothers grow less and less interesting until they finally disappear in utero, and we're left with a long section about Adam and his wife wandering around outside Paradise."

Maine's third novel, *The Book of Samson,* portrayed the biblical story of Samson, a soldier from ancient Israel with superhuman strength. Samson is able to help the Israelites conquer their enemies, the Philistines, until his lover, Delilah, or Dalila (the form of the name that Maine uses), discovers and reveals that the source of his power is his hair. The Philistines cut Samson's hair, robbing him of his strength and imprisoning him before one last burst of energy allows him to destroy the Philistine temple and everyone inside, including himself. General knowledge of story's outline did not detract from the novel's power.

"The reader," Janet Maslin observed for the *New York Times* (November 2, 2006), "knows the book's blueprint and can make certain assumptions about where its narrative is heading. Once again Mr. Maine finds a way to defy those expectations. Despite the overeager way he touts the tale of Samson and his notorious barber-paramour, Dalila . . . this book ultimately reaches for a very different theme from that of sexual betrayal. It is more searingly focused on violence committed in the name of God." Amy Wilson, reviewing the book for the Kentucky *Lexington Herald Leader* (December 10, 2006), called attention to Maine's ability to use the original tale to his own advantage, observing: "What Maine does is flesh out Samson as surely Samson was flesh. He has let Samson, heavily enchained and suddenly blind and waiting for his slow torturous death inside a temple devoted to a god not his own, reel out his version

of events. That he comes off as truly and completely blind and yet . . . innocent at the same time is testament to Maine's appreciation of the complexities of religion and the men who try to practice it."

David Maine continues to live in Lahore, Pakistan, with his wife.

—R.E.

Suggested Reading: *Denver Post* F p9 July 11, 2004; (London) *Guardian* p28 Oct. 9, 2004, p16 Mar. 4, 2006; (London) *Sunday Times* p50 Apr. 23, 2006; *New York Times* E p6 June 28, 2004, E p9 Sep. 8, 2005, E p1 Nov. 2, 2006; *Publishers Weekly* p111 Jan. 26, 2004; *Washington Post* T p6 June 27, 2004, T p4 Oct. 2, 2005

Selected Books: *The Preservationist*, 2004; *Fallen*, 2005; *Book of Samson*, 2006

Ulla Montan/Courtesy of Henning Mankell

Mankell, Henning

Feb. 3, 1948– Novelist

The Swedish novelist, playwright, and theater director Henning Mankell is best known to English-speaking readers for his popular series of detective novels featuring Kurt Wallander, a dour and dyspeptic police inspector in Ystad, a city in the southern Swedish province of Skåne. The first book in the series, *Faceless Killers*, was also the first to appear in English translation, in 1997. Most of the Wallander novels have been translated into English, including *The Dogs of Riga*, *The White*

Lioness, *Sidetracked*, *The Fifth Woman*, and *One Step Behind*. (The English translations, however, have not been published in their original order.) The series has been a huge international success, selling more than 20 million copies worldwide and spawning numerous films. In Germany, for example, Mankell's brooding detective sells more books than J. K. Rowling's Harry Potter series. "Apart from his uncommon skill at devising dense, multilayered plots, Mankell's forte is matching mood to setting and subject," Marilyn Stasio wrote for the *New York Times* (May 4, 2003). "Whether it's a magisterial storm at sea or the 'gray mud, gray trees, gray sky' of a barren town in the dead of winter, the bleak imagery in these books is both a reflection of Wallander's state of mind and a comment on the greater darkness that he senses creeping over his country and his world." Mark Lawson observed for the London *Guardian* (September 21, 2002), "Wallander has an unusual physical and psychological complexity. . . . The detective's private desperation is set against a growing public sense that quiet, liberal, boring Sweden is heading towards anarchy. . . . It's this social pessimism that makes Mankell a global rather than a local author." Mankell retired Wallander after nine novels but has continued to publish other books, including *Chronicler of the Winds* and *Before the Frost*, a novel featuring Wallander's daughter, Linda, who also joins the Ystad police force.

Henning Mankell was born on February 3, 1948 in Stockholm, Sweden. His father, Ivar, was a judge; his mother was a librarian. Mankell's mother left the family before he was two years old; Mankell and his older sister, Helena, remained with Ivar, who moved the family north to Harjedalen, a deeply forested province with long, dark winters. They lived in an apartment above the courthouse with his father's mother, who taught

Mankell to write when he was about six. The experience inspired him, as he told Ian Thomson for a profile in the London *Guardian* (November 1, 2003): "[I] can still remember the miracle that I could make a sentence, then more sentences, telling a story." He added, "The first thing I wrote was a one-page summary of Robinson Crusoe, and I'm so sad I don't have it any more: it was the moment I became an author." He also read incessantly and developed a fascination with Africa. He told Thomson, "Africa was the most exotic place I could conceive of—the end of the world—and I knew I would go there one day."

In 1961 Mankell's father moved the family to the more southern town of Boras, where Mankell attended secondary school. He dropped out at the age of 16 and became a seaman; from 1964 to 1966 Mankell was a stevedore on a ship carrying coal and iron to European and American ports. He found much of the work boring, but at the same time, Mankell told Thomson, it was his "real university" and "a romantic, Conradian dream of escape" (a reference to the author Joseph Conrad).

After his stint at sea ended, Mankell spent time in Paris. In 1968 he went back to Sweden to work in theater, becoming a stagehand in Stockholm. By that time, he had written his first play, "about Swedish colonial interests in 19th-century South America," he told Thomson. It received positive reviews, although Mankell told Thomson it was "not very good." In 1972 he published his first novel, *The Stone-Blaster.*

In his early 20s Mankell's dream of visiting Africa was fulfilled: "I don't know why, but when I got off the aeroplane in Africa I had a curious feeling of coming home," he told Thomson. Over the following years he spent time in various parts of the continent, settling, in 1987, in Maputo, Mozambique, where he accepted a position running the Teatro Avenida, the national theater—the region's first professional theater. He has spent the rest of his life shuttling between Sweden and Africa, all the while writing novels, which are generally set in Sweden, though often written in Africa. "[I have] one foot in the sand and the other in the snow," he told Nicci Gerrard in an interview for the London *Observer* (March 2, 2003, on-line). "I am like an artist who must stand close to the canvas to paint, but then stand back to see what he has painted. My life has that movement. Some things you can only see at a distance." He also writes and directs plays in Mozambique.

Kurt Wallander made his debut, in 1991, in Mankell's novel *Faceless Killers.* Mankell wrote the book shortly after returning to Sweden, in 1989, as a response to the heightened tension and racially motivated violence that had followed a recent influx of immigrants to the country. As he recalled to Thomson, "Racism is a crime, and I thought: okay, I'll use the crime story. Then I realised I needed a police officer." He selected the name Wallander from a telephone directory. "It was May 20 1989 (I looked it up in an old diary)

when Kurt was born." "Beginning with *Faceless Killers,* readers could sense a new voice had come onto the scene," Robert Rosenberg wrote for the *New York Sun* (July 16, 2003). "The tone was darker, more somber than that of Mankell's forerunners Maj Sjowall and Per Wahloo, creators of the Martin Beck books in the 1970s." Rosenberg continued, "*Faceless Killers* introduces Wallander at a turning point in his life and career: He is 40 years old; his wife is divorcing him; his troubled teenage daughter is going off to Stockholm, her life and future uncertain; his father, who has rejected him for becoming a policeman, is in the early stages of Alzheimer's; and his mentor on the police force, the thoughtful and thorough Rydberg, is slowly fading out of his life." Meanwhile, Sweden has been recently inundated with immigrants, provoking neo-Nazi agitation as well as a general sense of unease.

In *Dogs of Riga* (1992; published in English in 2002) two Latvian corpses, apparently tied to the Russian Mafia, are found floating on a life raft off the coast of Sweden. "Certain now that he lacks the stomach for the escalating levels of violence in modern society, the despondent inspector has an anxiety attack that lands him in the hospital," Marilyn Stasio recounted in her review of the book. Nevertheless, Wallander, now 43, must travel to Riga to investigate; there he encounters widespread government corruption, "which opens his eyes to the chilling reality of life in the totalitarian Eastern Bloc: grim, harrowing and volatile," a reviewer noted for *Publishers Weekly* (March 31, 2003). "There's a pervasive sense of Scandinavian gloom," the reviewer continued, "in Wallander and in the novel, that might be difficult for some American readers, but this is a very worthy book—a unique combination of police procedural and spy thriller that also happens to be a devastating critique of Soviet-style Communism."

Wallander investigates the mysterious disappearance of a Swedish woman in *The White Lioness* (1993; published in English in 2003). After her corpse turns up, other corpses follow, and the investigation unexpectedly leads to a group in South Africa that is planning to assassinate Nelson Mandela. (The story takes place in the early 1990s, after Mandela was released from prison but before he became president.) "Wallander becomes involved more deeply than his police responsibilities require," Marcel Berlins noted in the London *Times* (May 10, 2003). "A member of his family is drawn into the circle of violence and his mental stability is put in question. Wallander remains one of the most impressive and credible creations of crime fiction today, and the Swedish policing scenes are, as usual, excellent. But the South African angles, setting up and developing the Mandela conspiracy, are limp and the characters unbelievable." Morag Fraser, writing for the Melbourne *Age* (May 24, 2003), concurred: "Mankell is thorough in his research [regarding

South Africa], but somehow it all seems schematic when compared with the flesh and blood of his Everyman cop who is working himself towards diabetes and worrying, in his specifically Swedish way, about the state of the world."

Sidetracked (1995; published in English in 1999) involves a serial killer who has been scalping his victims. Wallander takes over the case, while also investigating the apparent suicide of a young girl who set herself on fire. "[Wallander] juggles the two stressful inquiries while trying to cope with a delicately poised love affair, a difficult daughter and a father declining in dementia," Berlins wrote for the London *Times* (November 11, 2000). "Even though some of the answers are revealed well before the end, the tension continues almost until the last page. [Wallander] is a dedicated cop with a messy personal life, hard-working to the point of exhaustion, often irascible, and uncomfortable swallowing the orders of his masters. He is tough yet compassionate, cynical about his work while passionately believing that evil-doers must be caught." The investigation, however, has the Ystad police going in circles. "While they tread water, Mankell fills us in about a country that pulled itself out of material poverty only to plunge into the spiritual poverty of the welfare state and its eroded present," Eugen Weber wrote for the *Los Angeles Times* (August 24, 2003). "When we got rid of the old society where families stuck together," Mankell writes, as quoted by Weber, "we forgot to replace it with something else." "For all the excitements of the [novel's] plot, at its heart lies a passionate concern with the nature of political life in modern Sweden, and in particular the compromising of its traditional social democratic values," Tom Holland wrote for the London *Daily Telegraph* (November 18, 2000). "Perhaps this doesn't sound like the most thrilling of recommendations, and yet it is Mankell's understated anger at the state of his country which helps give his gripping and often extremely lurid story its strong moral force." Mankell won the 2001 Crime Writers' Association Macallan Gold Dagger Award for *Sidetracked*.

One Step Behind (1997; published in English in 2003) is considered by many to be the masterpiece of the Wallander series. The story begins with the disappearance of three young people who had gone out celebrating Midsummer's Eve; shortly thereafter Wallander's colleague Svedberg, who has been investigating the disappearance, is shot to death. When the bodies of the youngsters turn up, the cases begin to merge. Wallander, who discovers he has diabetes, pursues the murderer but is increasingly debilitated by his disease. "Wallander assiduously strips away layer after layer, dredging up fragments of conversations and crime-scene clues that lead him closer and closer to the killer, who plays him cleverly and remains one step ahead until the brutal end," Francine Fialkoff wrote for *Library Journal* (February 15, 2002). "The book is not only an intriguing puzzle,

but a moving description of a man trying to keep faith with a dead friend," Jane Jakeman wrote for the London *Independent* (October 12, 2002). "In the last resort, Wallander must tackle his enemy without the easy answer of the gun. This is the best aspect of crime fiction: a gripping plot plus the exploration of character and relationships that reverberate around murder." A *Publishers Weekly* (January 21, 2002) reviewer observed: "Wallander, whose frazzled personal life is further impaired by the diabetes he ignores, works himself to exhaustion, sidestepping official procedure and making intuitive leaps to find the cold-blooded killer." The reviewer added, "The glum tone of the book . . . reflects a crumbling Swedish society: government corruption is widespread; honest cops are disillusioned by abuses in high officialdom; rifts among social classes and between Swedes and recent immigrants abound. Mankell's writing is deadpan and stark, the plotting meticulous and exacting."

After penning two more books for the Wallander series, Mankell decided to retire the beloved character. "I did this out of respect for myself and my readers," he explained to Thomson. He then wrote the stand-alone mystery *The Return of the Dancing Master* (2000; published in English in 2003). In this book detective Stefan Lindman is diagnosed with cancer; learning that a former colleague has been brutally murdered, he tries to distract himself from his own condition by diving into the investigation. "What he uncovers is an unexpected neo-Nazi presence at the heart of contemporary Swedish society," Ian Thomson wrote for the London *Sunday Telegraph* (October 26, 2003). "Mankell's anger at the state of his country lends *The Return of the Dancing Master* a refreshingly old-fashioned moral force and sense of disquiet." "The unrelenting Lindman turns out to be an innovative investigator, though those seeking fast-paced action rather than meticulous introspection will be disappointed," a *Publishers Weekly* (March 1, 2004) reviewer observed. "Secrets are slowly and methodically teased from the evidence, and by the satisfying end readers with a taste for the unusual will find Lindman, and the mystery he solves, not in the least bit ordinary."

He returned to the Wallander family, in 2002, publishing *Before the Frost* (2002; published in English in 2004), in which Wallander's daughter, Linda, upon completing her police training, finds herself drawn into a strange mystery involving animals set on fire and the murder of a local cultural historian. "A complex (but wholly credible) narrative connects these events with a terrorist plot led by a survivor of the 1978 mass suicide in Jonestown, Guyana," a reviewer noted for *Publishers Weekly* (January 31, 2005). "As always with Mankell, the mystery is connected to larger issues—the decline of Swedish civility, of course, but also the danger of religious fundamentalism (the events are set in the weeks before [the terrorist attacks against the U.S. on September 11, 2001])—but polemics never trumps suspense in this extraordinarily compelling drama."

Chronicler of the Winds (2002; published in English in 2006) tells the story of Nelio, a 10-year-old boy from a small African village. After revolutionaries seeking to overthrow the country's dictator raze the village, Nelio escapes to a nearby port city, where he joins scores of other abandoned children and becomes their reluctant leader. "[Mankell] vividly depicts in this heartbreaking fable the ongoing tragedy of Africa's disenfranchised," a reviewer wrote for *Publishers Weekly* (April 17, 2006). "At times the narrative strays too far from Nelio's story and the tone slips into a kind of magical realism, but it's impossible not to be moved by the tale of Nelio's short and painful life." Rebecca Stuhr for *Library Journal* (May1, 2006) called it "timely and well worth reading," adding, "Mankell's novel is about the broken legacy of colonialism and the greed and the violence that follow in its wake."

In *Depths* (2004; published in English in 2006) the main character is Lars Tobiasson-Svartman, a naval engineer who, during World War I, is sent by the neutral Swedish government on a secret mission to find navigable channels for the Swedish navy, in case they are forced to participate in the war. Lars feels unloved by his wife and discovers, on a supposedly deserted island, a woman named Sara; they have an affair, and Sara becomes pregnant. As the war continues, so does Lars's unfaithfulness to his wife, and his skill with taking soundings becomes a contrary metaphor for his inability to explore his own depths. John Preston for the London *Sunday Telegraph* (October 15, 2006) worried that Mankell might be forgoing his gifts as a writer of thrillers in hopes of achieving literary success. "The symbolism," Preston wrote, "could hardly be more clunky—there's an awful lot about internal and external depths—and even the descriptive passages have an overcooked feel about them." On the other hand, Paul Binding, for the London *Independent* (October 6, 2006), called the book "mesmerically fascinating" and argued that despite its careful rendering of its historical setting, the book has "much of the folk-ballad about it: relentless progress to a terrible conclusion; intimate relationship to place. Readers of the Kurt Wallander novels can now appreciate that, for Mankell, his existentially isolated characters are as important as his sociological interests."

Mankell continues to divide his time between Sweden and Mozambique. "What Africa has taught me is that the worst thing in the world is the fact that there is so much suffering that is absolutely unnecessary," he told Gerrard. He has contributed to the creation of the Memory Books project in Africa, in which people dying of AIDS are asked to write down their memories for their children. "Books are messengers," Mankell told Gerrard.

"Like the diary of Anne Frank, they speak for the dead."

In 1998 Mankell married Eva Bergman, a daughter of the filmmaker Ingmar Bergman. He has four sons from previous relationships.

—S.Y.

Suggested Reading: (London) *Guardian* p28 Sep. 21, 2002, p20 Nov. 1, 2003; (London) *Observer* (on-line) Mar. 2, 2003; (London) *Times* (on-line) May 10, 2003; *New York Sun* July 16, 2003; *New York Times* VII p27 Apr. 14, 2002

Selected Books in English Translation: *Faceless Killers*, 1991; *The Dogs of Riga*, 1992; *The White Lioness*, 1993; *Sidetracked*, 1995, *Chronicler of the Winds*, 1995; *The Fifth Woman*, 1996; *One Step Behind*, 1997; *The Return of the Dancing Master*, 2000; *Before the Frost*, 2002; *Depths*, 2006

Manning, Kate

Novelist

The plot of Kate Manning's debut novel, *Whitegirl* (2002)—in which a beautiful blonde is attacked, and authorities believe that her estranged husband, an African-American athlete-turned-actor, is the culprit—will undoubtedly remind readers of the famous trial of O. J. Simpson (in which the football player was accused of murdering his wife, Nicole). Manning, however, had no intention of rehashing the details of that legendary court case: "I wanted to write about the racial awakening of a naive white woman in the context of a relationship, and to look at the gap between the way white people experience race and the way black people do. I hope that the book sparks some interesting conversations," Manning told Bella Stander, in an interview posted on Stander's literary Web site.

When Manning was a young girl, her family relocated frequently: during a 12-year period, Manning attended 10 different schools. This disjointed childhood, however, did not dampen her innate eagerness to learn nor her natural intelligence. In 1979 she graduated from Yale University, in New Haven, Connecticut, and subsequently taught English in Japan and worked in refugee relief in Thailand. Following her return to the U.S., Manning found employment as a freelance writer for the *Nation*, which is based in New York City, and helped organize the magazine's 1981 American Writers Congress. She then began a career in television journalism, becoming a producer of a PBS documentary series for which she won two Emmy Awards. Manning eventually left her job to raise her three children, using her scarce spare time to focus on her writing. (She had been "writing fiction and putting it in drawers for years," as she told Stander.)

The idea for *Whitegirl* came to Manning in her sleep, she told Stander: "[I] sat up in bed in the middle of the night and said, 'This is a good story.'" The novel, which took more than five years to write, opens with Charlotte, a former model, recovering from a knife attack. The authorities have arrested her African-American husband, Milo, a former ski champion who is now an actor, but Charlotte isn't sure if Milo is responsible or not. While recuperating, she examines her 20-year relationship with him, in an effort to figure out why their life together fell apart. As the book opens, Charlotte is reflecting: "I was not always a white girl. I used to be just Charlotte. A person named Charlotte Halsey. But when I met Milo, when I fell in love with him, I became White, like a lit lightbulb is white. In the mirror there is my skin the color of sand, hair the color of butter, eyes blue as seawater. just so bleachy white I am practically clear. In a heavy snowfall you'd have trouble picking me out." She describes her husband: "Milo is black, what they call 'Black,' only not to me. Brown skin, a shade the newer catalogues would call *cinnamon stick* or *cocoa*. . . . You in your sunny kitchen, or your office cubicle, or your shopping mall might not mind that the word *black* means 'soiled and dirty,' means 'characterized by the absence of light' or 'evil or wicked or gloomy.' God knows, I could have cared less myself, before."

The book received mixed notices. A reviewer for *Publishers Weekly* (January 28, 2002, on-line) described *Whitegirl* as "admirably nonexploitative in affect [with] real depth on many issues black and white." The reviewer cautioned, however, "Readers who need the mystery solved and it is one of the compelling reasons to read on may be disappointed by the ambiguous ending." Martha Southgate, writing for the *New York Times Book Review* (March 3, 2002), noted, "Manning can be a clever writer," but concluded that she could "exhibit a tin ear in racial matters. . . . [There is] an unconvincing tone about interracial relationships that pervades the book."

Manning lives in New York City with her husband and children. Stander noted the author's slim figure and flaxen hair, but pointed out that despite their physical similarities, Manning and the fictional Charlotte have little else in common. "Like any fiction writer, the whole story comes from my life and none of it does," Manning told Stander. "What matters to me is that the characters feel true to life; that a reader follows them and feels their feelings and understands their motives and mistakes."

—P.B.M.

Suggested Reading: Bella Stander's Web site; Mostly Fiction Web site; *New York Times Book Review* p16 Mar. 3, 2002; *Publishers Weekly* (on-line) Jan. 28, 2002

Selected Books: *Whitegirl*, 2002

Star Black/Courtesy of HarperCollins

Manrique, Jaime

(man-REEK)

June 16, 1949– Novelist; poet

Jaime Manrique is part of many worlds. He is a poet, novelist, and author of nonfiction treatises as well as a teacher. Hailing from Colombia, he was schooled in the ways of Latin *machismo*, but he has openly professed his homosexuality. Now living in New York City, he is a naturalized American citizen whose experiences as a new immigrant remain fresh to him. These dichotomies pervade his writing, which often challenges the reader's preconceived notions of a subject.

Jaime Manrique was born on June 16, 1949 in Barranquilla, a regional capital on the northern coast of Colombia. His parents were Gustavo Manrique, a married plantation owner and a member of the country's white ruling class, and Solidad Ardila, a poor woman from the countryside, whom he took as a mistress. Gustavo, who eventually left Ardila for a younger mistress, did not publicly acknowledge Manrique and his younger sister, but did provide them with some financial support. When Manrique was about seven years old, he moved with his mother and sister to Bogota. At 12 he began writing poetry. Asthmatic and frequently unable to attend school, he entertained himself by reading prodigiously. By his teens he had read most of the great 19th-century European novels.

Manrique also loved movies and would often skip school in order to see whatever was playing at his local theater. At 14 he watched *The Man with the Green Carnation* (also known as *The Trials of*

Oscar Wilde, 1960), a film about the life of the homosexual British writer Oscar Wilde. That movie allowed Manrique to put a name on his own often-confused sexual identity. The pervasive homophobia and machismo in Colombia left him, however, with feelings of guilt and isolation, and it was not until the mid-1960s, when he moved to Florida with his family, that he finally felt free to openly acknowledge his homosexuality. (It took him longer to discuss the issue with his mother, who was supporting the family as a domestic worker.)

In 1972 Manrique earned a bachelor's degree from the University of South Florida, in Tampa. In 1975 he received a Colombian national poetry award for his first collection, *Los adoradores de la luna* (which translates as "those who adore the moon"). In 1977 he studied writing at New York City's Columbia University, with the homosexual Argentinean writer Manuel Puig, who is best known for the 1976 novel *The Kiss of the Spider Woman*. The city fascinated the young poet, and with the exception of a single trip back to Colombia in 1979, he has never returned to his native country.

In 1978, after completing Puig's seminar, Manrique published *El cadáver de papa*, which became a best-seller in Colombia, but caused some controversy there because it featured a gay protagonist who kills his wealthy father and then, dressed in drag, tries to seduce his father-in-law. He next published *Notas de cine: confesiones de un critico amateur* (1979), a collection of essays about his love of film. In 1983 Manrique published his first English-language novel, *Colombian Gold: A Novel of Power and Corruption*, a political thriller set in his native country, which received positive reviews.

Between 1988 and 1993 Manrique served as a part-time faculty member at Eugene Lange College, a small liberal-arts facility that is part of the New School University, in New York City; during roughly the same period (1989–91), he was a writer in residence at the New School for Social Research, part of the same university. After beginning work in 1992 as an associate professor at Goddard College in rural Vermont, he published a semiautobiographical novel, *Latin Moon in Manhattan*, the story of Sammy (Santiago) Martinez, a homosexual Colombian American poet who is hoping to finish an epic poem about Christopher Columbus—while trying to make his way in a New York City filled with homeless people, drug addicts, undercover policeman posing as prostitutes, and gun-toting store owners. The novel received mixed reviews. In the *Los Angeles Times* (March 15, 1992), Virgil Suarez wrote: "*Latin Moon in Manhattan* is an original debut by an obviously talented writer, but many parts of his novel lack unity and direction. The reader can't help but feel overwhelmed by all the incongruous, haphazard incidents that take place over a few days. Something is lost in Sammy's

guilt-driven, passive detachment as he merely witnesses the events of his life without much interaction. . . . But it is a fast-paced, good book because, after all the comic-tragedy, many parts of it are picaresque and rambunctiously funny." Cristina Garcia wrote for the *Washington Post Book World* (February 2, 1992), "A lot goes on in *Latin Moon in Manhattan* but in essence, very little happens. Substantial themes, such as being gay in a virulently macho society or the tragicomic ingestion of pop icons by new immigrants, are touched upon but not wrestled with in any meaningful way. The potentially fascinating terrain of what it means to be cross-cultural in America is only superficially explored, or else sacrificed to the dizzying momentum of roisterous lunacies."

In Manrique's next book, *Twilight at the Equator* (1997), Sammy Martinez remains a central character. The book, a collection of connected stories, also focuses on the life of Sammy's maternal grandmother. In his writing, Manrique drew largely on the life of his own grandmother, who had been born in a town settled by runaway slaves. "The town is what is known as a palenque, a settlement made in the early 19th century by runaway Black slaves who chose the site for its remoteness," he told Eleanor Levine for the New York *Amsterdam News* (April 5, 1997). "My mother's family had originated in this village, and my grandfather and his children had lived there until they moved to El Banco almost half a century ago. In writing that part of the book, I think I came very much in touch with my African side. Until I visited my grandmother, I hadn't realized how African her community was." The book also contains tales of Martinez pretending to be a Chicano from Texas to satisfy an irrational employer and commencing an affair with a young film student. Levine wrote, "Jaime Manrique's subject matter is racism, politics, immigration, homophobia and domestic conflicts. This is a gay, Hispanic man of color who writes about the politics of his homeland and his adopted country. He is a master of description—description of tropical foliage, Colombian food and incidents of daily life that make it real. You feel like you are there. . . . *Twilight at the Equator* shares with *Latin Moon in Manhattan* a humor, sadness and feelings of alienation which are lyrically transcribed." Ilan Stavans, in his review of the novel for the *Washington Post Book World* (May 11, 1997), wrote, "Manrique is adept at ridiculing the style known in the United States as magical realism. Indeed, his fiction often reads like a response to the Latin-American masters of the '60s; his characters, for one thing, are globetrotters and sinners, but they are neither mystical nor magical; they thrive in urban centers and seem allergic to Western values. But what truly characterizes his style is his obsession with homosexuality—an obsession that is becoming more and more evident as Manrique matures."

Eminent Maricones: Arenas, Lorca, Puig, and Me (1999), Manrique's next book, was described by Daniel Reitz for the on-line magazine *Salon* (June 25, 1999) as "part memoir, part biography, part gay literary criticism, part journalism." Reitz continued, "*Eminent Maricones* is Jaime Manrique's celebration of himself and his place in the pantheon of homosexual Hispanic letters. For the author to include his own experiences alongside those of two celebrated Latin American writers (Manuel Puig and Reinaldo Arenas) and one Spanish icon (Federico García Lorca) may sound like hubris, but it makes perfect sense within the structure of this slim but significant volume." The book, which includes six essays that had previously appeared separately in various publications, received mixed reviews. Daniel Mendelsohn, in the *New York Times Book Review* (October 10, 1999), called it a "flawed but intermittently fascinating memoir." George De Stefano, writing for the *Nation* (September 6–13, 1999), noted: "The book's title alludes to Lytton Strachey's *Eminent Victorians*; by coupling 'maricon' (faggot) with 'eminent,' Manrique destigmatizes the pejorative and makes the point that the outcast sexuality of his beloved writers is inextricable from their greatness as men and artists. . . . Though Manrique's subjects come to bad ends, he never depicts them as exemplars of gay victimhood. They are brilliant, groundbreaking artists. . . . Manrique brings to their stories a novelist's eye for the telling detail and a poet's gift for metaphor and condensation. He also offers the unique perspective of a bilingual, bicultural writer shaped by Bogota and Greenwich Village. . . . His double vision yields insights into Puig, Arenas and Lorca unavailable to a writer less attuned to the complex interplay of culture and sexuality, as well as that of race and class in Latino and Anglo societies."

Manrique's latest book is the historical novel *Our Lives Are the Rivers* (2006), which concerns the life of Manuela Sáenz, the mistress of General Simón Bolívar, who secured independence from Spain for a large portion of South America. "On the surface, this new novel may look like a complete departure from the rest of my work. But if you scratch that surface, you'll discover *Our Lives* contains themes that I've explored in my other novels: politics, the corruptive nature of power, gender-bending, exile, illegitimacy, the oppression of women, society's rejection of those who dare to be different," Manrique told an interviewer for the HarperCollins Web site. "Like all my heroes, Manuela is an outcast. To paraphrase Flaubert: 'Manuela Sáenz *c'est moi.*'"

Between 1998 and 1999 Manrique, who lives in the New York City borough of Manhattan, served as an adjunct assistant professor at Columbia University. Since 2002 he has been an associate professor there. In addition to his other works, Manrique has written the poetry collections *Scarecrow* (1990), *My Night with Federico García*

Lorca (1997), and *Tarzan, My Body, Christopher Columbus* (2001), which contains poems written over the course of a quarter century. With Joan Larkin, Manrique served as the translator for *Sor Juana's Love Poems: In Spanish and English* (2001). He edited, with Jesse Dorris, the collection *Bésame Mucho: New Gay Latino Fiction* (1999). He often visits the neighborhood of Jackson Heights, in the New York City borough of Queens, an area sometimes called Little Colombia. "I think it is quite possible for Colombians to spend a great deal of their lives in these 20 or 30 blocks," Manrique told James Dao for the *New York Times* (October 9, 1992). "They can eat Colombian meals and watch Colombian television, listen to Colombian radio and talk to other Colombians. Maybe it will snow once in a while and that will make it different from Colombia, but that's about it. There's something a little artificial about creating a Little Colombia in the middle of Queens, but there are psychological reasons. Like my mother, who lives in Florida. She still gardens as if she were in Colombia. She has guava trees and pineapples. It's probably the only way she can stay here. Otherwise, it would be unbearable."

—C.M.

Suggested Reading: *Los Angeles Times Book Review* p11 Mar. 15, 1992; *Nation* p28 Sep. 6–13, 1999; (New York) *Amsterdam News* p24 Apr. 5, 1997; *New York Times* B p1 Oct. 9, 1992; *New York Times Book Review* p38 Oct. 10, 1999; *Washington Post Book World* p9 Feb. 2, 1992, p11 May 11, 1997

Selected Books in English Translation: fiction—*Colombian Gold*, 1983; *Latin Moon in Manhattan*, 1992; *Twilight at the Equator*, 1997; *Our Lives Are the Rivers*, 2006; nonfiction—*Eminent Maricones: Arenas, Lorca, Puig, and Me*, 1999; poetry—*Scarecrow*, 1990; *My Night with Federico García Lorca*, 1997; *Tarzan, My Body, Christopher Columbus*, 2001; as editor—*Bésame Mucho: New Gay Latino Fiction*, 1999; as translator—*Sor Juana's Love Poems: In Spanish and English*, 2001

Marquis, Christopher

Nov. 13, 1961–Feb. 11, 2005 Journalist; novelist

"Often you find journalists who are talented reporters but not good writers, or good writers who are not very good reporters. Chris was both, as well as a very decent human being," the former *Miami Herald* Latin American editor Don Bohning recalled to Juan O. Tamayo for the *Miami Herald* (February 13, 2005) on the occasion of Christopher Marquis's death. Known primarily as a journalist, Marquis also used his talent with words to write fiction, and he published, in 2003, *A Hole in the Heart,* the novel that must remain his only contribution to literature but had been expected, when it was released, to launch his career in fiction, earning Marquis a place on *Book Magazine*'s "Ten Writers to Watch" list.

The son of Harold and Nancy Marquis, Christopher Marquis was born on November 13, 1961 and raised in Kentfield, California. (He had two brothers, Matthew and Jeff, and a sister, Julie.) He graduated from Redwood High School, in 1979, and then entered the University of California, at Berkeley, earning a bachelor's degree in literature in 1984. He got his first experience as a journalist working as an intern for the *Baltimore Sun,* while still a student, in 1982, and after Berkeley he went to the Graduate School of Journalism at Columbia University, in New York City, where he received a master's degree. He became a freelance journalist, working for *La Nacion* in Argentina, the beginning of his work on Latin America, a place he had fallen in love with, as Tamayo reported, "on a 1981 college class trip to Guatemala, when gunmen killed a town mayor who wanted electricity and water for his people. 'In one chilling day, I had been initiated into an unpredictable world of remarkable leaders and monumental injustice,' he wrote." In 1987 he found a staff position with the *Miami Herald,* starting out as suburban reporter but quickly earning a place on the city staff and then the foreign staff. "You could tell he was a great storyteller. And as time went on, we wanted him more and more covering Latin America," Mark Seibel, who was the foreign editor at the *Miami Herald* during Marquis's early years with the paper. In 1989 the paper sent Marquis to its Washington bureau, where he served as its Latin America policy writer. In 2000 he became a reporter for the Washington bureau of the *New York Times.*

Marquis was not content with being only a reporter. He had always dreamed of being a novelist, and despite the demands of his newspaper career, he worked on his fiction and found a publisher for his novel, *A Hole in the Heart.* The book's protagonist, Celestine "Bean" Jessup, is a young woman adrift; unsure of what she wants to do with her life after graduating from San Francisco State University, she takes a job as a substitute teacher at an elementary school in Eyak, Alaska—population 2,500. (The evocative locale was a natural choice for the author. While studying at the University of California, at Berkeley, Marquis worked in fish canneries in Alaska during summer breaks.) In Eyak Bean meets a fisherman and carpenter named Mick, whom she soon marries. When Mick is killed in a climbing accident on Mount McKinley, his estranged mother, Hanna, arrives at Bean's home and moves in with her. Bean and Hanna, a prickly chain-smoker suffering from arthritis, develop a lasting relationship, and the unusual domestic arrangement continues even as Bean returns to San

Francisco and finds a new love. Explaining his decision to create a female protagonist, Marquis said, Anneli Rufus reported for the *East Bay Express* (September 24, 2003), "This may sound odd for such an intimate portrait, but I wanted to establish some distance between myself and my character. I had chosen to deal with subjects that in some hands could come off as melodramatic or even maudlin. I wanted a more dispassionate view, a lighter touch infused with humor, to explore the weighty questions of what happens after your life blows apart. . . . I have been blessed with a lot of strong-willed women in my life, and I've spent a lot of time listening to them. That said, I did have some rather embarrassing conversations with my female confidantes to get the sex scenes right."

A reviewer for *Publishers Weekly* (August 11, 2003) called *A Hole in the Heart* a "witty, offbeat first novel" and wrote that the "twists and turns in the plot are deftly executed, and Marquis's ironic, compassionate humor tempers the pathos of Bean's hangdog existence. Like Anne Tyler, Marquis has a knack for creating hapless characters who radiate humanity." Writing for the *Denver Post* (August 24, 2003), Robin Vidimos tempered her praise, opining: "Christopher Marquis, in his debut novel, tells a quirky tale that is as much an emotional journey as a physical one. . . . *A Hole in the Heart* is a book both heartfelt and wise, despite the occasional bumps." Other reviewers focused on those bumps. Dolores Derrickson, writing for the Denver *Rocky Mountain News* (September 18, 2003), observed, "Marquis does a good job of drawing us into Bean's story." Derrickson, however, went on to complained that the "characterizations remain weak" and concluded: "In the end, *A Hole in the Heart* leaves nothing but the void the title might predict."

Marquis, while staying with his brother Matthew in San Francisco, died of complications caused by AIDS on February 11, 2005. At the time, he had been working on his second novel, which was to be set in Argentina. Among the honors he received during his life was being made a Nieman fellow at Harvard in 1998 and 1999.

—C.M./A.R.

Suggested Reading: *Denver Post* EE p3 Aug. 24, 2003; *Miami Herald* B p5 Feb. 13, 2005; *Publishers Weekly* p257 Aug. 11, 2003; *Rocky Mountain News* D p15 Sep. 18, 2003

Selected Books: *A Hole in the Heart,* 2003

Martel, Yann

June 25, 1963– Novelist

"I write simple books and I view my readers as my equals," the Canadian author Yann Martel told Aida Edemariam for the London *Guardian* (October 23, 2002). "In a novel, you must amuse as you elevate. You mustn't be too much of a storyteller, because the reader feels kidnapped, taken in but left with nothing. You have to be a bit challenging. You really have to do a bit of everything. And at the end of the day people do come back to art." This philosophy may help explain the success of Martel's award-winning novel, *Life of Pi* (2001). The book—an unlikely tale of a young Indian boy who survives a shipwreck only to find himself aboard a lifeboat accompanied by a 450-pound Bengal tiger—received both popular and critical acclaim, spending months on the best-seller lists and winning its author the prestigious Booker Prize, which carries with it a $75,000 award. A reviewer for *Publishers Weekly* (April 8, 2002) called *Life of Pi* "a fabulous romp through an imagination by turns ecstatic, cunning, despairing and resilient. . . . [It is] an impressive achievement." Suzy Hansen, writing for the on-line journal *Salon* (August 1, 2002), labeled it "a preposterous but utterly enchanting story." And, despite Martel's opposition to gratuitous narratives, a writer for the Toronto *Globe and Mail* observed, as quoted on the Random House Web site, "A storyteller, in order to enchant, must lie, and then convince us that he is not lying. This novel is all about storytelling."

Yann Martel was born in Salamanca, Spain, on June 25, 1963 to Canadian parents who worked as diplomats. His father, Emile, was pursuing his doctorate at the time; upon its completion, the family moved from Salamanca to Portugal, and then to Alaska, where his father took a teaching job at the University of Alaska. (In addition to working as a diplomat, Martel's father is an award-winning poet. His mother, Nicole, is a translator.) The family moved often, settling temporarily in such places as Costa Rica, France, Mexico, and Canada. "We were pretty nomadic," Martel told Graeme Smith for the Toronto *Globe and Mail* (June 14, 2004). Despite his many travels, Martel had many pets while growing up, which may have contributed to his interest in featuring animals in his work. "As kids, we all go through a phase where we're obsessed with pets," he told Adam Langer in an interview for *Book* magazine (November/December 2002). In Costa Rica, Martel's pets included rabbits, birds, a dog, and a monkey, whose short life Martel attributed to "existential anxiety." Martel's interest in the animal kingdom also comes from his sense of nature as something of a utopia. As he told Langer, "I've never owned a car, which means I'm pretty much a prisoner of the city. And because of that, my mind seeks to escape it and I slightly idealize nature . . . so I guess that leads to a certain interest in animals." Conversely, religion, another guiding theme in *Life of Pi*, is notable for its absence from Martel's upbringing—his parents were totally secular. "My parents are the children of the Quiet Revolution, which was a time in Quebec in the '60s when the city just basically threw the whole Catholic Church in the garbage can and people left the church in droves," he told Langer. "Quebec went from being the most backward Catholic province in Canada to being the most secular, forward-looking, progressive socially. And my parents are children of that time, so I grew up in a household where nothing good or bad was said about religion. It just didn't exist."

In his youth Martel thought about going into politics and also considered such academic pursuits as anthropology and philosophy. He eventually attended Trent University, in Ontario, and obtained a degree in the latter. After graduating, he took a number of odd jobs to earn money, including working as a dishwasher, a tree planter, and a security guard. He also traveled extensively, not settling in any one place for long. "I've lived nine years in Paris in all," he explained to Langer, "two times for four years and then another year with a girlfriend. . . . I spent a year in India. I've bummed around Europe a fair bit; I went to South America once, Morocco, Turkey." Montreal became Martel's home base when he was 28; at about that time he decided to seriously try his hand at writing. In 1991 the Canada Council for the Arts bestowed on Martel a writing grant. He subsequently penned "a couple of bad plays, some bad short stories, and a bad novel," as he told Aida

Edemariam. The "bad short stories" were in fact a collection that comprised his first published work, *The Facts Behind the Helsinki Roccamatios* (1993). The collection garnered critical praise. Eric Henderson, in his review for the Canadian newspaper the *Vancouver Sun* (September 4, 1993), wrote, "Martel's exuberant writing makes reading an intense experience. . . . [He] has the ability to make us feel deeply for his characters even though we may interact with them in an unconventional way." For the collection Martel was awarded Canada's $10,000 Journey Prize. The "bad novel" in question was his 1996 book, *Self*, a fictitious exploration of a man's transformation into a woman, along the lines of Virginia Woolf's *Orlando* (1928). Though it was well received—Charles Foran, writing for the *Ottawa Citizen* (July 7, 1996), called the book "an intelligent and entertaining meditation on sexuality, language, and identity"—Martel has told interviewers that he is not happy with the book. "It's a terrible novel," he told Langer. "I think it should disappear." Nevertheless, *Self* was short-listed for the Chapters First Novel Award in 1996.

In 1997 Martel embarked on another writing project, thanks to another grant from the Canada Council for the Arts. He traveled to India—for the second time—in search of inspiration. However, as he recounted in an essay for the Powell's Books Web site titled "How I Wrote *Life of Pi*," he fell into a terrible rut. "One night I sat on my bed and wept, muffling the sounds so that my neighbors would not hear me through the thin walls. Where was my life going? Nothing about it seemed to have started or added up to much. I had written two paltry books that had sold about a thousand copies each. I had neither family nor career to show for my 33 years on Earth. I felt dry and indifferent. Emotions were a bother. My mind was turning into a wall. And if that weren't enough, the novel I had planned to write in India had died." Then one day, while climbing a hill in Bombay, he recalled a review he had read many years earlier of a book by the Brazilian writer Moacyr Scliar. The book was *Max and the Cats*—but all Martel could remember was that it was about a boy who survives a shipwreck when emigrating with his family to Brazil. The boy ends up on a lifeboat with a jaguar. "Suddenly, my mind was exploding with ideas. I could hardly keep up with them," he recalled. "In jubilant minutes whole portions of the novel emerged fully formed: the lifeboat, the animals, the intermingling of the religious and the zoological, the parallel stories." Furthermore, Martel said, "I now had a reason to be in India."

Martel spent two years doing research for *Life of Pi*. The first six months were spent in India, where he visited zoos in order to accurately portray a zookeeper, who is the main character's father in the book, as well as the peculiarities and natural characteristics of orangutans, meerkats, tigers, and other animals that make an appearance. It took him a while to decide which animal would be the main protagonist. "At first, I had an elephant in mind . . . ," he explained in his essay for the Powell's Books Web site. "But the image of an elephant in a lifeboat struck me as more comical than I wanted. I changed to a rhinoceros. But rhinos are herbivores and I could not see how I could keep a herbivore alive in the high seas. And a constant diet of algae struck me as monotonous for both reader and writer, if not for the rhino." Martel eventually decided on the animal that, he explained, "in retrospect seems the obvious one: a tiger." Also, in order to capture the essentials of the religions that Pi explores with such innocent gusto in the beginning of the story, Martel visited churches, mosques, and Hindu temples. After six months visiting zoos and houses of worship, he returned to Canada to read. "I read the foundational texts of Christianity, Islam, and Hinduism. I read books on zoo biology and animal psychology. I read castaway and other disaster stories." The result, published in 2001 in Canada by Random House, was the story of Piscine Molitor Patel, nicknamed Pi, whose father owns a zoo in the Indian village of Pondicherry. When Pi is 16, the family sets sail for Canada to start a new life; along the way, the Japanese freight ship they are on sinks. Pi escapes to find himself adrift on the open sea in a 26-foot lifeboat—accompanied by a wounded zebra, an orangutan, a hyena, and a Bengal tiger named Richard Parker. The animals don't all get along, and after some in-fighting only Pi and the tiger are left.

In addition to being a tale of survival (Pi is out at sea on the lifeboat for more than 200 days), *Life of Pi* is a meditation on religion. Pi, who grew up practicing his native Hinduism as well as Christianity and Islam, is skeptical of agnostics (as is Mantel, who found himself becoming more religious as he researched the book). "Doubt is useful for awhile," Pi says early in the novel, as quoted by Charles Matthews for the *San Jose Mercury News* (June 2, 2002). ". . . But we must move on. To choose doubt as a philosophy of life is akin to choosing immobility as a means of transportation." Pi's diverse religious background (although it had been the cause of some consternation for his parents as well as the local priest, pandit, and imam he sought out for guidance) leads him to reason in "his typically idiosyncratic way," Suzy Hansen noted in her review of the book. "Hindus, in their capacity for love," Pi observes, as quoted by Hansen, "are indeed hairless Christians, just as Muslims, in the way they see God in everything, are bearded Hindus, and Christians, in their devotion to God, are hat-wearing Muslims." When observing Muslims pray, he comments, "Why, Islam is nothing but an easy sort of exercise. . . . Hot-weather yoga for Beduins." "His naiveté can be silly," Hansen remarks, "but ultimately it's an open-mindedness, a way of turning things upside down to see them differently, that serves him well."

The celebrated Canadian novelist Margaret Atwood, in a review for the London *Sunday Times* (May 5, 2002), called *Life of Pi* "a terrific book. It's fresh, original, smart, devious, and crammed with absorbing lore. . . . [It's] a boys' adventure for grownups." Charles Matthews praised Martel's deftness in treading the line between narrative authority and self-conscious fantasy. "[*Life of Pi* is] a most implausible tale made plausible by Martel's skill—the skill of any good writer of adventure fiction—at working with details (about animals, about the sea, about survival skills) that at least have the appearance of being authoritative and factual. We believe in Pi Patel and Richard Parker and that a 16-year old boy and a Bengal tiger could co-exist for 227 days on a boat 'three and a half feet deep, eight feet wide and twenty-six feet long, exactly.'" *Life of Pi* was short-listed for the Canadian Governor General's Literary Award for Fiction as well as the Commonwealth Writers Prize. It won the Hugh MacLennan Prize for Fiction (2001), the South African Boeke Prize (2003), and the Booker Prize (2002), the top literary award in Britain.

The publicity around the award, however, soon gave way to a controversy that threatened to undermine Martel's success; the Brazilian media accused Martel of "copying" or "borrowing" from *Max and the Cats*, which Moacyr Scliar had published in 1981. Scliar, one of Latin America's most critically acclaimed authors, told Larry Rohter for the *New York Times* (November 6, 2002), "My reaction is one of mixed feelings. . . . In a certain way I feel flattered that another writer considered my ideas to be so good, but on the other hand, he used that idea without consulting me or even informing me. An idea is intellectual property." A small but fiery controversy ensued, much to Martel's dismay, and the recently heralded author found himself on the defensive in interviews. He maintained that he had read only a review of the book, not the book itself, and insisted that he had been forthcoming about his debt to the novel. "In the essay [for the Powell's Books Web site] and in every interview I've done, print radio and television, I've mentioned where I got my premise," Martel told a participant in a "question & answer" session sponsored by the London *Guardian* (November 26, 2002, on-line). "It was public knowledge for months before the Brazilian press decided to turn it into a scandal." The controversy eventually died down, and Martel himself was absent from most of it. He was living in Germany at the time, teaching at the Free University in Berlin.

Recent interviews have found Martel still basking in the acclaim of *Life of Pi*, while struggling to write a novel that lives up to its success—a difficult mission, given that the book tour took him to 21 counties and that the sales have made him considerably wealthy. "I could be a one-hit wonder and that's it," he told Graeme Smith. "I'll be known as, 'Remember that guy who wrote *Life of Pi*, about that boy in the lifeboat with his tiger?'" After a year and a half without writing, Martel is at work on a new book, also featuring animals. The story is a Holocaust parable starring a monkey and a donkey in a dystopian universe. Some sources claim he published a collection of short stories, in 2004, entitle "We Ate the Children Last," and while a short story with that title did appear in the July 17, 2004 edition of the London *Guardian*, no collection is available.

Yann Martel, whose partner is the novelist Alice Kuipers, lives primarily in Canada, a country he described for the London *Guardian* Q&A as "a wonderful political act of faith that exists atop a breathtakingly beautiful land." In addition to writing, he travels extensively, does yoga, and is a regular volunteer at a palliative-care unit in Montreal. When it comes to his work, he describes himself as a slow but "hardworking" writer, pausing only to use the phone and make tea. "When I'm in front of my computer I can spend hours on end getting sentences down from the dream world on to my screen," he told a participant in the London *Guardian* Q&A. "It's a joy."

—L.S.

Suggested Reading: *Book* (on-line) Nov./Dec. 2002; (London) *Guardian* (on-line) Nov. 26, 2002, Oct. 23, 2002; Powell's Books Web site; *Salon* (on-line) Aug. 1, 2002; (Toronto) *Globe and Mail* (on-line), June 14, 2004

Selected Books: *The Facts Behind the Helsinki Roccamatios*, 1993; *Self*, 1996; *Life of Pi*, 2001

Martin, George R. R.

Sep. 20, 1948– Novelist; short-story writer; screenwriter

While George R. R. Martin has been known to readers of fantasy and science fiction since he began publishing books, in the 1970s, he did not reach a wider audience until he began the Song of Ice and Fire series, a yet-to-be-completed sequence of novels whose first four books have reached the *New York Times* and *USA Today* best-seller lists, among others. Martin, who has won many fantasy-genre awards, including six Locus Awards, is noted for injecting gritty realism into a genre often labeled as escapist and characterized by fairy-tale simplicity. Most critics have agreed that the characters in the Song of Ice and Fire series are complex, fully realized human beings who drive the plot as much as they are driven by it. The series has elicited comparisons to J. R. R. Tolkien's *Lord of the Rings* trilogy for its intricate and extensive underlying mythology, which Martin has drawn with uncommon vividness and detail. Already, the

Szymon Sokół

George R. R. Martin

first four books in the series—*A Game of Thrones* (1996), *A Clash of Kings* (1999), *A Storm of Swords* (2000), and *A Feast for Crows* (2005)—fill over 4,000 pages. Martin has attributed their unusual length to his desire to ensure that the details of the stories are "put clearly into the mind's eye" of each reader—"and that takes wordage," as he explained to Roz Kaveney for Amazon.com (Great Britain). The Song of Ice and Fire books have been translated into German, French, Italian, Spanish, Swedish, Dutch, Japanese, Portuguese, Croatian, Russian, Polish, Hungarian, Finnish, and Esperanto.

One of the three children of Raymond Collins Martin, a longshoreman, and Margaret Brady Martin, George Raymond Richard Martin was born on September 20, 1948 in Bayonne, New Jersey. His sisters are Darleen (Martin) Lapinski and Janet (Martin) Patten. Raised in a household in which the only pets allowed were fish and turtles, Martin made the most of the situation: he named his turtles and created adventures for them, set in a toy castle. His first short story, written during his childhood, was titled "Turtle Castle." Martin also honed his craft early on by writing and telling scary stories to his neighborhood playmates. "I would write in block printing in those old black-and-white marbled notebooks," he recalled to Tasha Robinson for SciFi.com. "I would write out these monster stories by hand and sell them to the other kids for a nickel. A nickel was a lot of money in those days; you could get a Milky Way, with two nickels you could get a comic book. So I'd sell the stories and give a dramatic reading of the stories as well, because my audience didn't actually read that well."

Martin attended the Mary Jane Donohue School, a public elementary school, and Marist High, a Catholic college-preparatory institution. While there he became an avid comic-book collector and began submitting his fiction to amateur comic "fanzines." He earned a B.S. degree in journalism and graduated summa cum laude from Northwestern University, in Evanston, Illinois, in 1970, then earned an M.S. in journalism from the same school in 1971. As a conscientious objector, Martin did not fight in the Vietnam War; rather, he completed alternative service through the Volunteers in Service to America (VISTA) program, from 1972 to 1974. From 1973 to 1976 he also directed chess tournaments for the Continental Chess Association, after which he became a journalism instructor at Clarke College, in Dubuque, Iowa, until 1976. He was a writer in residence at the college from 1978 to 1979.

Martin married Gale Burnick in 1975. When the marriage ended, in 1979, he became a full-time writer. In 1974 Martin had won a Hugo Award for his novella *A Song for Lya*. His novel *Dying of the Light*, a romance set on the dying planet of Warlorn, was nominated for the same award in 1977. That year he also published the short-story collection *Songs of Stars and Shadows* and edited *New Voices in Science Fiction: Stories by Campbell Award Nominees*. In 1979 his short story "Sandkings" won the Hugo and Nebula Awards, and his short story "The Way of Cross & Dragon" won the Hugo. In 1981 he published the short-story collection *Sandkings* and collaborated with Lisa Tuttle on the novel *Windhaven*, set in a world of small islands where all communication is conducted through the Flyers, a society of elite hang-glider pilots.

Dubuque had once been a major manufacturer of steamboats, and while Martin was at Clarke College, he became fascinated with them. His novel *Fevre Dream* (1982) is about a steamboat captain who goes into business with a vampire who seeks to teach his fellows to live peacefully among humans. In 1983 Martin published *The Armageddon Rag*, which follows the journalist Sandy Blair as he investigates the ritual murder of an ex-promoter of the defunct rock band Nazgul. Blair, still steeped in the 1960s culture of his youth, discovers an odd plot to resurrect Nazgul, which had dissolved after its lead singer was murdered onstage in the late 1960s. Clarence Peterson, reviewing the book for the *Chicago Tribune* (January 20, 1985), declared, "Martin . . . has mastered the suspense writer's craft." *The Armageddon Rag* won a Balrog Award for best fantasy novel in 1984. Also in 1983 Martin published the short-story collection *Songs the Dead Men Sing* and co-edited, with the science-fiction writer Isaac Asimov, *The Science Fiction Weight-Loss Book*, a collection of science-fiction short stories that, according to Lois A. Strell in *School Library Journal* (October 1983), "deal with people's obsessions with fat in the present and future." Martin's next book was the short-story collection *Nightflyers* (1985).

In 1986 Martin published *Tuf Voyaging*, a group of tales about the adventures of Haviland Tuf, a humble space traveler who acquires a "seedship" equipped with gene-cloning capabilities that he uses to tackle problems on a host of exotic planets. A reviewer for *Publishers Weekly*, as quoted on Amazon.com, wrote, "These colorful tales mostly skirt the more interesting and prickly issue of Tuf's playing god to fundamentally change the cultures he encounters. Still, the seed-ship is a wonderful idea and Tuf . . . is a droll hero."

Also in 1986 Martin took his first job in television, as story editor for *The Twilight Zone* (1985–87), a new version of the classic series. In 1988 he became a producer for the TV series *Beauty and the Beast*; the following year he was promoted to co-supervising producer. The show, which ran from 1987 to 1990, was a modern-day version of the classic fairy tale. Catherine (Linda Hamilton) is an assistant district attorney in New York City who meets and is transformed by Vincent (Ron Perlman), a creature whose head and face resemble those of a lion and who lives in a secret society of outcasts underneath the city. Martin also worked on various other film and TV projects, including *Doorways*, a pilot he wrote for Columbia Pictures Television, which he also executive produced. His story "Nightflyers" was made into a feature film in 1987, and "Sandkings" was made into a two-hour movie for the TV series *The Outer Limits* in 1995. Most of his efforts, however, were never scheduled for broadcasting.

Martin has said that working in television improved his ear for dialogue and sense of narrative structure but frustrated him, too, because he often felt that his creative vision had been compromised. He began working on the Song of Ice and Fire series partly in reaction to what he saw as the limitations of writing for film and TV. "Television and film were an interesting few years, I learned a lot from it, but it would never replace books as far as I'm concerned," he told Alex von Thorn for the Canadian Web site voyageur.idic.ca. "Certainly, for a writer, books are the ultimate art form. You're everything when you write a book; you're the writer, you're also the director, you're all the actors, the set director, the costume designer, the special effects guy." The idea for the series had come to Martin in 1991, when, for no apparent reason, there came into his mind an image of a litter of wolf pups lying in the snow beside their dead mother. The vividness and power of the image spurred him to write what became chapter one of *A Game of Thrones* (1996), in which young Bran Stark, along with his brother and half-brother, rescue six dire-wolf pups—one for each of them, their two sisters, and their little brother. (In actuality, the dire wolf has long been extinct.) Their father, the nobleman Ned Stark, is subsequently called away from the family home, Winterfell Castle, to assist his old friend King

Robert Baratheon, prompting a reshuffling of power on the continent of Westeros that leads to both open and secret warfare. Martin's fictional world is defined by unpredictable seasons—long summers of plentitude end abruptly in bitter winters that rage for years on end. Much of *A Game of Thrones* follows Ned Stark as he uncovers a plot by the king's wife, Cersei Lannister, and her clan to seize control of the seven kingdoms of Westeros. The book also chronicles the adventures of Daenerys Targaryen, the exiled daughter of a deposed king, who is cast among a wandering tribe of horsemen and may have a link to the world's last remaining dragons. A further subplot involves Ned Stark's illegitimate son, John Snow, who is sent to the north of Westeros, where a 700-foot-tall wall of solid ice borders a forbidding wilderness full of giants and the dreaded, undead "Others."

Martin, who relates his story through alternating chapters told from the points of view of various characters, set out to create an epic tale on a scale similar to that of the *Lord of the Rings* series. Though Martin's series features a huge cast of characters, a wealth of intricate subplots, and a complex history and mythology, much of his creation remains an undercurrent in the fast-moving plot. Martin told Linda Richards for *January Magazine* (January 2001), "I think you have to do the back story in a book like this like an iceberg: most of which would be below the surface. Just enough to show that something huge is there."

A Game of Thrones won nearly universal praise. "Like the best epic fantasy and the best historical fiction, *A Game of Thrones* is about individuals and the effects of vast and small events on their lives," Phyllis Eisenstein wrote for the *Chicago Sun-Times* (August 11, 1996). "Reminiscent of T. H. White's *The Once and Future King*, this novel is an absorbing combination of the mythic, the sweepingly historical, and the intensely personal." A reviewer for *Publishers Weekly*, as quoted on Amazon.com, wrote, "It is fascinating to watch Martin's characters mature and grow, particularly Stark's children, who stand at the center of the book. Martin's trophy case is already stuffed with major prizes, including Hugos, Nebulas, Locus Awards and a Bram Stoker. He's probably going to have to add another shelf, at least."

The second installment in Martin's trilogy is *A Clash of Kings* (1999), wherein the continuing battle between the Starks and Lannisters is told. Also joining the fray are King Robert Baratheon's two brothers, Renly and Stannis, who have as much antipathy toward each other as they do toward the Lannisters. The book also follows Daenerys Targaryen, as she struggles for survival in the exotic reaches of the land, and John Snow, who experiences the coming plague from the north firsthand. A critic for *Kirkus Reviews* (December 1, 1998) wrote that among the many rewards of reading *A Clash of Kings* are "a backdrop of convincing depth and texture; intricate, flawless plotting; fully realized characters; and restrained, inventive magical/occult elements." In the *Santa Fe New Mexican* (May 9, 1999), Terry England argued that, far from being escapist (a label often applied to fantasy), the novel offers valuable commentary on contemporary life, including "our attitudes about women and men, about our love of war, about how [easily] we lie for the simplest of reasons and how easy it is for us to deceive those we profess to love and honor."

In 2000 Martin published *A Storm of Swords*, the third novel in the Song of Ice and Fire series. The war among the Starks, Lannisters, and Baratheons continues to rage, while in the north John Snow finds himself among the barbaric Wildlings as they try to invade the seven kingdoms. His half-brother Bran is in peril as Winterfell Castle is besieged, and Daenerys Targaryen continues her difficult rise to power as the keeper of the last three surviving dragons. Terry England, writing for the *Santa Fe New Mexican* (December 17, 2000), noted that Martin's series had "vaulted him into the top ranks of science fiction and fantasy publishing" and that the "books do something that happens rarely: Break away from the commonplace." In the Cleveland, Ohio, *Plain Dealer* (December 3, 2000), Julie E. Washington wrote, "Martin creates a gorgeously and intricately textured world, peopled with absolutely believable and fascinating characters."

Many reviewers have agreed that the characters are the strength of Martin's Song of Ice and Fire series, particularly within the genre of fantasy, in which characters often fall into clear categories of good or evil. "I look for ways to make my characters real and to make them human, characters who have good and bad, noble and selfish, well-mixed in their natures . . . ," Martin told Tasha Robinson. "I read too much fiction myself in which you encounter characters who are very stereotyped. They're heroic-hero and dastardly-villain, and they're completely black or completely white. And that's boring, so far as I'm concerned. It's also unreal." Martin's heroes also break the conventions of the fantasy genre in that they are far less glamorous than the norm: Tyrion Lannister is a gnarled, sometimes ruthless dwarf who is also witty and kind; Samwell Tarly is obese and afraid of physical confrontation but displays courage and loyalty in critical situations; and Lady Brienne, a giant coarse-featured woman uncomfortable with her femininity, is one of the realm's fiercest warriors. As Julie E. Washington noted, Martin further highlights the disparity between the romantic and harsh reality by using a plot line that involves Ned Stark's captive daughter, Sansa, "a dangerously naive girl who believed the songs about fair maidens and brave knights. She learns, in the most brutal ways possible, that life is not a song." Martin told Tasha Robinson, "I think there's a requirement, even in fantasy—it comes from a realm of the imagination and is based on fanciful worlds, but there's still a necessity to tell the truth,

to try to reflect some true things about the world we live in. There's an inherent dishonesty to the sort of fantasy that too many people have done, where there's a giant war that rips the world apart, but no one that we know is ever really seriously inconvenienced by this."

In 2001 Martin published *Quartet: Four Tales from the Crossroads*, which includes "Black and White and Red All Over," about a group of journalists who track Jack the Ripper through Victorian Manhattan; "Starport," an unproduced screenplay; *Skin Trade*, a werewolf novella that won the World Fantasy Award; and *Blood of the Dragon*, a precursor to *A Game of Thrones*, which won a Hugo Award. A reviewer for *Kirkus* (May 1, 2001) described *Blood of the Dragon* as being "for fans only."

The fourth book in the Song of Ice and Fire series, *A Feast for Crows,* was published, in 2005; it focuses on the story of Cersei, and her attempt to seize power in the seven kingdoms. Polly Shulman called the novel, in a review for New York *Newsday* (November 27, 2005) "a fast-paced, emotionally complex, masterfully written adventure," but she noted that it only "takes some of the characters forward through the next stage of their intrigues, journeys and wars. . . . The rest are left hanging from their cliffs until the next book." Terry Dowling, writing for the *Australian* (December 10, 2005), observed, "Nothing is one-dimensional in Martin's work, and there are new characters and subplots aplenty, but with nine dynasties and a series cast of more than 30 characters playing out their dramas across centuries, it is the Seven Kingdoms setting itself that is the central character here." Nicole Child, writing for the *Daily Californian*, as cited on the University Wire (December 5, 2005), thought this addition to the series failed to live up to its predecessors, noting "favorite characters such as Jon Snow, Tyrion and Bran don't appear in the volume." She went on to write: "Unfortunately, while Martin tries to make up for the missing characters . . . by adding new ones, it isn't the same as in previous books. The characters just don't tick the same way when they aren't influenced by other important characters. It's difficult hearing Cersei Lannister curse her dwarf brother Tyrion, when the reader has no idea where Tyrion is at the moment." The forthcoming titles in the Song of Ice and Fire series are "A Dance with Dragons," a book that grew out of *A Feast for Crows*, which had grown too big; "The Winds of Winter"; and "A Dream of Spring."

In 2006 Martin published *The Ice Dragon*, a book adapted from a story that appeared in 1980, in *Dragons of Light*. The story concerns Adara, a seven-year-old girl who was born on the coldest day of the coldest year and who becomes a cold, remote child. More interested in ice lizards than people, she forms a bond with the ice dragon, which helps her defeat invaders that threaten her family. "As in most children's stories, the lessons of courage, sacrifice and love for family are intertwined throughout," Terry England wrote for the *Santa Fe New Mexican* (November 12, 2006)

Martin—who is the editor of the long-running Wild Card series of books, featuring collaborations by various authors—is a member of the Writers' Guild of America and the Science Fiction & Fantasy Writers of America (of which he was south-central regional director from 1977 to 1979 and vice president from 1996 to 1998). He lives in Santa Fe, with his partner, Parris; his dog, Mischa; and his two cats, Augustus and Caligula.

—P.G.H.

Suggested Reading: *Daily Oklahoman* D p18 Aug. 15, 2003; *January Magazine* (on-line) Jan. 2001; (Monroe, Louisiana) *News-Star* D p6 Apr. 27, 2003; *Santa Fe New Mexican* D p4 Aug. 25, 1996; SciFi.com; SF Site Web site

Selected Books: *A Song for Lya and Other Stories*, 1976; *Dying of the Light*, 1977; *Songs of Stars and Shadows*, 1977; *Sandkings*, 1981; *Windhaven* (with Lisa Tuttle), 1981; *Fevre Dream*, 1982; *The Armageddon Rag*, 1983; *Songs the Dead Men Sing*, 1983; *Nightflyers*, 1985; *Tuf Voyaging*, 1986; *Portraits of His Children*, 1987; *A Game of Thrones*, 1996; *A Clash of Kings*, 1999; *A Storm of Swords*, 2000; *Quartet: Four Tales from the Crossroads*, 2001; *Blood of the Dragon*, 2001; *Skin Trade*, 2001; *A Feast for Crows*, 2005; *The Ice Dragon*, 2006: as editor— *New Voices in Science Fiction: Stories by Campbell Award Nominees*, 1977; as co-editor (with Isaac Asimov)—*The Science Fiction Weight-Loss Book*, 1983

Selected Television Shows: as story editor—*The Twilight Zone*, 1985–87; as producer—*Beauty and the Beast*, 1988–89; as co-supervising producer—*Beauty and the Beast*, 1987–90

Debra Martin/Courtesy of Random House

Martin, Lee

Oct. 2, 1955– Novelist; memoirist; short-story writer

After troubles in his youth ranging from repeated abuse by his father to a period of delinquency as an adolescent, Lee Martin began to write stories— some fictional, some true, some occupying an unusual space in between, but all of them offering readers a clear-eyed understanding of the world rather than expressions of victimization or idealized portraits of small-town life. His books, which include *The Least You Need to Know* (1996), *From Our House* (2000), *Quakertown* (2001), *Turning Bones* (2003), and *The Bright Forever* (2005), are marked by a lyrical prose style, grounded in natural speech, that conveys struggle and succeeding triumph. Martin remarked in the *Writer* (December 2005): "I often think that writing is a very spiritual pursuit, not so much in terms of traditional religion but in the terms of communing with the world and its people."

Lee Martin wrote the following autobiographical statement for *World Authors 2000–2005*:

"I grew up in Illinois, the only child of Roy Martin and Beulah Read Martin. My father was a farmer, and my mother was a grade school teacher, and they found each other later in life rather than sooner; my father was 38 when they married, and my mother was 41. I wasn't in their plans, but on October 2, 1955, four years past their wedding, there I was.

"A little over a year later, my father lost both of his hands in a farming accident, the episode that begins my first memoir, *From Our House*. He continued to farm with his prosthetic hands and with my mother's help, and my own as I grew older. Many times, when I was frustrated with some task—trying to loosen a rusted bolt, for example—I'd say to him, 'I can't.' Without fail, he'd respond, 'Can't never did anything.' And we'd keep at it until we got the job done. So he taught me—this man who wasn't highly educated himself—that the challenge, no matter how daunting, was always a test I could pass if I only kept trying.

"I believe that my father's accident, combined with my mother's devotion and goodness, made me aware at an early age that the world could be a frightening and yet beautiful place. My father could be a brutal man; my mother was timid and without guile. Imagine the three of us transplanted from that farm in southern Illinois—Lukin Township in Lawrence County to be exact, about ten miles southwest of the itty-bitty town of Sumner—to Oak Forest, a southern suburb of Chicago, which is exactly what happened in the autumn of 1963. My mother took a teaching position in the Arbor Park School District, and we started a string of six years where we spent the school year in our apartment in Oak Forest and the summers on our farm downstate. I felt myself caught between the culture of the city and that of the country, never fully belonging to either and always carefully negotiating my way with whatever people I happened to be among at a particular time. I was becoming a writer even then, though I didn't know it. I was developing the sensibility of someone, to borrow from Henry James's advice to the novice writer in 'The Art of Fiction,' 'upon whom nothing is lost.'

"I've taken great pleasure over the years in seeing what sense I can make of the world and the people in it by writing stories and essays and novels, and, yes, even the occasional poem, though I pretty much left poetry behind me with the angst of my teenage years. My father was an expert storyteller, and such talent was a powerful currency in the rural culture we finally returned to when I began high school in Sumner. A storyteller always had something to say and many hours were passed in pool halls, barbershops, diners, and on front porches, with men vying for center stage. I was a shy kid who listened to those stories, read a good deal, and eventually started spinning tales of my own on the page. Along the way—from Sumner High School, to Olney Central College, to Eastern Illinois University—I was fortunate enough to have excellent teachers who encouraged my creativity and love of language. In 1975 I married Debra Goss, and she's been my first reader—or should I say 'first listener' since I read everything aloud to her—ever since, from my days in the MFA program at the University of Arkansas, to my doctoral program at the University of Nebraska, Lincoln, and to teaching positions in Memphis, Tennessee; Harrisonburg, Virginia; Denton, Texas; and, finally, here in Columbus at Ohio State University, where I currently direct the creative writing program.

"The music language makes when it's artfully arranged is something that's always extremely important to me. Often it's a voice I hear that first brings me to the page. In my first novel, *Quakertown*, it was a voice of pride and joy jouncing up from a thriving African-American community in 1920s Texas. In my second novel, *The Bright Forever*, it was a chorus of voices, all desperate to tell the story of a young girl's disappearance in a fictional small Indiana town in 1972. In my first book, a collection of stories called *The Least You Need to Know*, I was just starting to hear the plain-spoken and yet lyrical voices of sons telling the stories of their imperfect fathers, a voice I would claim as my own in the story of my relationship with my own father in *From Our House*. I've been working at the craft of fiction and literary nonfiction for a good while now, and still it's the voice that urgently needs to tell a story that compels me. I've had some good fortune along the way, most recently my novel, *The Bright Forever*, being named a 2006 Pulitzer Prize finalist in fiction. Not bad, I can't help noting, for a boy who wasn't meant to ever see the light of day. Maybe that's why I've always been interested in the stories of who we are in this world I was never meant to see. I have to document it, remake it with each story or essay or novel, for fear at any moment it might be gone."

In 1995 Martin won the Mary McCarthy Prize for short fiction, a contest sponsored by Sarabande Books, for the manuscript that became his short-story collection, *The Least You Need to Know*, which Sarabande published as part of his prize. The stories in the book widen out from Martin's childhood experience of father-son relationships and often feature, Karen Angel noted in the *New York Times Book Review* (July 14, 1996), "endings in which the young protagonist's world is shattered by a selfish paternal act." Martin's principal theme, Angel added, is "the irrevocable nature of the destructive actions, which leads his characters to long for an ability to rewind the clock. What they learn, however, is just how easily a life can come apart." A reviewer for *Publishers Weekly* (May 6, 1996) gave a slightly less enthusiastic assessment: "Throughout the book, Martin's writing is sensitive and lucid, only occasionally veering into the florid. The characters he writes about are utterly real, if somewhat uniform (the fathers are tough and mysterious, the mothers have quirky hobbies like eggshell painting). But their concerns and joys are perfectly identifiable and voiced with passion."

Martin forged his next book, the memoir *From Our House*, out of the materials of his actual childhood, when he was buffeted by a father given to fits of anger and violence and comforted by a tender-hearted mother. "For most of my life, I balanced on the thin line between my father's brutality and my mother's compassion," Martin remarked in an essay reprinted in *Harper's* (January 2000) that drew on material from his memoir. "While Martin never calls his mother an enabler or his father an abuser," a reviewer for *Publishers Weekly* (May 8, 2000) noted, "by age 16, years of family dysfunction had turned him into a shoplifter, burglar and arsonist, putting him close to 'becoming ruined beyond return.'" The reviewer concluded that "this moving family album, suffused with forgiveness and reconciliation, binds up the wounds." Gina Kaiser offered a similar assessment in *Library Journal* (May 1, 2000): "Martin shows how he and his father learn to overcome their shame and control their rage. The honest and straightforward description of their relationship and their obvious affection for each other completely involve the reader."

Having exorcized the ghosts of his parents in his previous books, Martin used his next book, *Quakertown*, to bring to light a bitter episode in the history of Denton, Texas, where he taught at the University of North Texas (UNT). The eponymous Quakertown was a Denton neighborhood which was settled after the Civil War by African-Americans. The novel takes place in 1921, when the town's white leaders decide they want to put a park in the spot where Quakertown then stands. Two families share center stage: one led by a white banker, Andrew Bell, who is organizing the plan to do away with Quakertown; the other headed by his black gardener, "Little" Washington Jones, whom Bell recruits to act as his ambassador of sorts to the people of Quakertown. Among the problems they face, however, is the long-simmering passion between Bell's son, Kizer, and Jones's daughter, Camellia, who is already engaged to a black man, a bootlegger named Ike Mattoon. Jabari Asim, writing for the *Washington Post Book World* (July 1, 2001), noted that "though *Quakertown* is by no means a thriller, its . . . pages pass by in a blur as Kizer blunders through his affair with Camellia and their parents stumble toward freefall. Amid swirling racial tension, there are couplings, confrontations, torchings, gunfire and death, each misstep leading to another and enveloping the town like a Texas twister." Martin, Asim added, "skillfully builds suspense by introducing characters that seem easy to classify as bigots, bullies or warriors—then complicates matters by showing that courage and cowardice sometimes inhabit the same skin. . . . In his richly dramatic re-imagining of the events behind Quakerstown's demise, Lee Martin has written one of the finest novels of the year." Sandra Scofield, writing for the *Chicago Tribune* (August 5, 2001), offered a more mixed assessment, praising the development of the plot in the novel's first half, as it builds toward Camellia and Ike's marriage, but describing the remainder of the novel as "an epic soap opera," in which "Martin's empathic impulse overcomes his craftsman's instinct for restraint. He tosses in new characters in new settings. The plot shatters into fragments and then is wrapped up with a couple of jumps and an epilogue." Scofield concluded: "When Martin draws back from his inventory of emotions and focuses on moments of sharp sensory observation, he can take your breath away. But he doesn't trust the reader to see below the surface without a written guide; he doesn't leave anything to the pleasure of discovery and the apprehension of a second meaning. Everything is there, on the page, exhausted."

Martin fictionalized the lives of some of his real ancestors in *Turning Bones*, which derives its title from a Madagascan custom of dancing with the bones of dead relatives in order to propitiate those ancestors. "Martin appropriates this tradition for his own uses," Sarah Huffines observed in the *Midwest Quarterly* (Autumn 2004). "He imagines the stories of past generations, and dances with these individuals, appeasing them for his own perceived shortcomings as successor to the Martin line." An only child who has made the decision not to have children, Martin is the last member of a family that left behind no detailed written records of their history, forcing Martin to imagine, for example, what it was like for one 19th-century Martin to buy a slave or to take as his second wife a woman 36 years his junior. "All of these stories, which center on turning points in their protagonists' lives, are set in fully realized versions of the past," Margaret Quamme wrote for the *Columbus Dispatch* (November 30, 2003). "They work as historical fiction. But what makes *Turning Bones* remarkable is the way Martin moves fluidly between these fictions and his attempts to be honest about his own life. . . . Martin generously shares the origins of these stories and in the fictions that result. In writing them, he seems to have felt his way into the points of view of people who used to drive him crazy and to have found a way, at least in part, to forgive himself of his own shortcomings. This is fiction as a means of grace."

In *The Bright Forever* Katie Mackey, a nine-year-old girl from a prominent small-town family, disappears one evening in 1972; four days later she is found murdered. Three decades pass, and the townspeople involved in the events around Katie's death begin to tell her story. The chief suspect in the murder is the girl's lonely, strange math tutor, but another possibility is an alcoholic drifter who has come to town, married a middle-aged woman, and blackmailed the teacher for his involvement with Katie, whose death soon prompts another murder. "While the killer's identity is fairly clear, Martin sustains a nagging doubt, serving his theme of the shattering of small-town innocence, the guilt behind the Norman Rockwell façade," a critic for *Kirkus Reviews* (March 1, 2005) observed. Conan Putnam, writing for the *Chicago Tribune* (May 29, 2005), found that by having the chapters narrated from multiple points of view, Martin makes "a larger point . . . about guilt, the ways stories are constructed and the truth of the human heart." Putnam felt, however, that "perhaps because [the narrators of the novel] are older, their voices are too soft, elegiac and tinged with self-consciousness to be as unobtrusive as they need to be to make the full impact of their stories deeply felt." In a review for the *Washington Post* (May 27, 2005), Carolyn See wrote: "*The Bright Forever* is a deeply traditional novel, 'literary' in the old-fashioned sense. That's both the good news and the bad news.

Those who crave the kind of obscurely comforting narrative that used to be found in public libraries in the 1940s and '50s will take to this book because, despite its occasional gore, its overall tone is as soft and giving as one of mom's old blankets. Those who prefer an edgier take on matters of life and death might be well advised to give the book a pass. This is not a novel that lends itself to draconian judgments. It's true to itself, and for many, that will be enough."

Martin is the co-editor, with Jeffrey Skinner, of *Passing the Word: Writers on Their Mentors* (2001). A compendium of writers' commentaries on their teachers and works that show those same teachers' influences, the book was described by Amy Strong for *Library Journal* (June 1, 2001) as "a fine collection that honors writing teachers and showcases the talents of the next generation."

Among the many honors Martin has received is a $20,000 National Endowment for the Arts grant, made in 2000, that enabled him to finish researching and writing *Quakertown*.

—S.Y.

Suggested Reading: *Chicago Tribune* C p4 Aug. 5, 2001, C p3 May 29, 2005; *Columbus Dispatch* C p9 Nov. 30, 2003; *Kirkus Reviews* p252 Mar. 1, 2005; *Library Journal* p126 May 1, 2000; *Midwest Quarterly* p96+ Autumn 2004; *New York Times Book Review* p16 July 14, 1996; *Publishers Weekly* p74 May 6, 1996, p213 May 8, 2000; *Washington Post* C p3 May 27, 2005; *Washington Post Book World* p3 July 1, 2001; *Writer* p66 Dec. 2005

Selected Books: *The Least You Need to Know*, 1996; *From Our House*, 2000; *Quakertown*, 2001; *Turning Bones*, 2003; *The Bright Forever*, 2005; as editor—*Passing the Word: Writers on Their Mentors* (with Jeffrey Skinner), 2001

Chris Watt/Courtesy of Random House

McCall Smith, Alexander

Aug. 24, 1948– Novelist; nonfiction writer

Before the late 1990s Alexander McCall Smith was noted chiefly as a law professor, writer of texts on legal and ethical issues, and author of more than 20 well-reviewed children's books. That changed in 1998, with the publication of *The No. 1 Ladies' Detective Agency*, the first in a series of books focusing on Mma Precious Ramotswe, the matronly, wise proprietor of a detective firm that is named after her. Clea Simon observed for the *Boston Globe* (October 16, 2002) that McCall Smith—who grew up in Rhodesia, now Zimbabwe, the son of white, Scottish-born parents—had run an enormous risk in making his detective a black African woman: "Despite his years spent on that continent, his essentially European background, not to mention his gender and cultural biases, could have made these books patronizing, his Precious Ramotswe an embarrassing stereotype. That she is not. That she is, in fact, a strong independent, and endearing model for contemporary women anywhere, is a testimony to his skill." McCall Smith has also written other light-hearted series, including one featuring Professor Dr. Moritz-Maria von Igelfeld, a pompous German philologist; one whose protagonist is Isabel Dalhousie, an editor and amateur sleuth; and one, originally serialized in the *Scotsman*, that follows the exploits of an eclectic group of apartment dwellers.

Alexander McCall Smith was born on August 24, 1948 in Chipinga, in the African nation then called Rhodesia. His parents, Daphne Woodall and Sandy McCall Smith, were Scottish; his father was the public prosecutor in the Rhodesian town of Bulawayo. McCall Smith pursued a university education in Edinburgh, Scotland, earning his LL.B. in 1971 and his Ph.D. in law in 1979 from Edinburgh University. He returned in the 1970s to Africa, where he had grown up, soon after receiving his law degree. In addition to helping establish the first law school in Botswana, McCall Smith wrote, with Kwame Frimpong, *The Criminal Law of Botswana*, which was published in 1992. He also wrote the code for criminal law for the newly emerging government of Lesotho. Other titles on legal jurisprudence by McCall Smith include the 1994 volume *Law and Medical Ethics*, written with J. K. Mason; *Justice and the Prosecution of Old Crimes: Balancing Legal, Psychological, and Moral Concerns*, published in 2000 in collaboration with Daniel W. Shuman; and *Errors, Medicine, and the Law*, written with Alan Merry, which appeared in 2001. Smith has also edited numerous legal compilations, such as *The Forensic Aspects of Sleep*, on which he collaborated with Colin Shapiro. McCall Smith's distinguished legal career included a stint as a visiting professor of law at Southern Methodist University, in Dallas, Texas, in 1988, and the post of professor of medical law at the University of Edinburgh.

McCall Smith's career in popular literature began with children's books, among them *The White Hippo* (1980) and *Children of Wax: African Folk Tales* (1989), written under the name R. A. McCall Smith. Despite the gruesome nature of many events portrayed in the latter book, such as humans being attacked and mutilated by animals, the tales "have a quiet poetry that makes them memorable," according to a reviewer for the Glasgow *Herald* (May 14, 1994). "They are also very strange—people turn into animals and vice versa, and acceptance of the supernatural is total—but underlying all the stories are two strong social messages: help your neighbours, and don't damage the land." In an assessment of McCall Smith's book *Jeffrey's Joke Machine* (1990), illustrated by Robert Bartelt, Eleanor Ironside wrote for the London *Sunday Times* (October 21, 1990), "It is difficult, even as a cynical adult, not to be tickled at the notion of a machine being funny." Also in 1990, with *Akimbo and the Elephants*, illustrated by Mei Yim Low, McCall Smith began a series, focusing on a boy who goes on safaris; the books came to include *Akimbo and the Lions* (1992) and *Akimbo and the Snakes* (2006), among others. He has also written a children's series featuring an enterprising nine-year-old girl named Harriet Bean and one whose protagonists are a pair of sleuthing siblings, Max and Maddy Twist. McCall Smith's 1992 stand-alone book, *Springy Jane*, illustrated by Elke Counsell, is a story about a girl with springs in her knees. After she performs a heroic deed, the springs rust. "An elegy for lost youth?" a reviewer for the London *Independent* (July 19, 1992) asked.

Heavenly Date, and Other Stories, a 1995 work, is a volume for adults. Ali Smith described it in the *Scotsman* (July 8, 1995) as a "light, traditional collection with moments of suspense and richness" and an overall theme: "the courtship ritual, the excitements and dangers of 'dating.'" Smith concluded, "McCall Smith's real interest lies . . . not in the 'itchings of the flesh,' but in the distances between people. Much of the time he leaves his characters in the dark when it comes to love and its physical reality, or shows their desperation to keep the worldly spaces they inhabit pure."

When McCall Smith published *The No. 1 Ladies' Detective Agency*, he shot to international literary fame. The heroine of the series is Mma Precious Ramotswe, a "traditionally built" (that is, rather large) black woman from Botswana who uses her inheritance from her father to establish the country's only female-run detective agency. Ramotswe (always referred to as "Mma," the local polite form of address) has been through much in her 30-odd years, including marriage to an abusive husband, and has acquired a measure of wisdom. "We help people with the problems in their lives," she says. "We are not here to solve crimes." Some of her cases involve crimes nonetheless, but thanks to Mma Ramotswe's "profound commonsense, missing husbands are found, imposters exposed, stolen property returned," David Robinson wrote for the *Scotsman* (May 7, 2002), in a profile of McCall Smith. "Violence is rare, corruption negligible, cynicism unknown" in Mma Ramotswe's practice. She is joined in her enterprise by Mma Makutsi, a stellar graduate of a secretarial college, and Mr. J. L. B. Matekoni, whom she will later marry. These characters, joined by several others, such as Howard Moffat (named for a real-life doctor and clergyman who is an old friend of McCall Smith's), live and work mostly in Gaborone, in Botswana. McCall Smith told Robinson that the books in the series are not "fairy stories," since "there are people like [Mma Ramotswe]. In Africa there is a spiritual dimension to life that is increasingly rare here [in Scotland]."

The Precious Ramotswe series now comprises several novels: *Tears of the Giraffe* appeared in 2000, followed by *Morality for Beautiful Girls* (2001), *The Kalahari Typing School for Men* (2002), *The Full Cupboard of Life* (2003)—for which McCall Smith won the remunerative SAGA Award for Wit, a prize given only to writers over the age of 50—*In the Company of Cheerful Ladies* (2004), and *Blue Shoes and Happiness* (2006); another, "The Good Husband of Zebra Drive," is scheduled for publication late in 2007. The cases depicted in the books seldom involve violent criminality but deal, rather, with domestic dilemmas that are universal and involve questions of ethics, morality, and the conduct of everyday affairs. As McCall Smith told Martin Arnold in an interview for the *New York Times* (December 12, 2002), he made Ramotswe a detective because a person in that line of work "sees lots of interesting and entertaining things in people. . . . There's no crime in the books, but there are her insights, and little stories about little ordinary difficulties like adultery, badly behaved husbands."

Alida Becker, reviewing *The No. 1 Ladies' Detective Agency*, *Tears of the Giraffe*, and *Morality for Beautiful Girls* for the *New York Times Book Review* (January 27, 2002), noted that all the "bustle" in the novels "is much less about whodunit than why. It's also very much about the variety and resilience of a nation to which [McCall] Smith . . . seems utterly devoted. As, of course, is

Mma Ramotswe, who recognizes the difficulties her country faces—poverty, disease and drought, to name just a few—but would never choose to live anywhere else. Not even America." Becker found Mma Ramotswe to be a kind of homespun philosopher: "Sitting in her ocher-walled office with its tin roof and itinerant chickens, Mma Ramotswe sips redbush tea and ponders the ethics of her cases: the wife who wants the detective to steal back the car her husband has stolen; the grief-stricken mother who, with Mma Ramotswe's deft application of a little blackmail, might be reunited with a young grandson. How to act? Or whether to act at all? 'I think,' she concludes toward the end of *Morality for Beautiful Girls*, 'that there are some matters that are best left undisturbed. We don't want to know the answer to everything.'"

A chorus of critical praise greeted each book in the *No. 1 Ladies' Detective Agency* series. Rosemary Goring, reviewing *The Kalahari Typing School for Men* for the Glasgow *Herald* (June 8, 2002), spoke for many of her colleagues when she lauded McCall Smith's "subtle wit and understated compassion. . . . Seemingly simple and old-fashioned, yet acute and at times profound, [McCall Smith's fiction] is a salutary corrective to the traditional Western way of seeing the world. Though set in contemporary Botswana, it is redolent of a previous age, a reflection, perhaps, of a people with little material security who are consequently more closely concerned with their neighbours. Yet though it sounds a comforting place, it is also a landscape stalked by fear: poverty, diseases such as Aids, and the anxiety that even in this once near idyllic environment, life is not as safe as it had been. McCall Smith's talent is to depict the contradictions of this community, and of his delightful heroine, with the minimum of fuss. A narrative pared to the quick, so plainly recounted that each sentence has the weight of truth, this is fiction for the connoisseur." The series was optioned for the screen by the director Anthony Minghella.

McCall Smith surprised his fans by next introducing a series focusing on Professor Dr. Moritz-Maria von Igelfeld. The first book, *Portuguese Irregular Verbs*, named after the professor's opus, was written in 1997 but not published until 2003; that novel was followed shortly thereafter by *The Finer Points of Sausage Dogs* and *At the Villa of Reduced Circumstances*. Von Igelfeld is a German Romance philologist, "ineffably pompous," as David Robinson described him in the *Scotsman* (August 23, 2003), and "an intellectual pratfall waiting to happen." He is frequently invited to speak at conferences and is so flattered by the invitations that he fails to investigate the conferences' topics; as a result he often finds himself in situations with high potential for embarrassment. He quarrels with his nemesis, Professor Dr. Detlev Amadeus Unterholzer, at the Institute of Romance Philology

in Regensberg, where "he pursues his studies with blithe disregard to the world around him," according to Robinson. In *The Finer Points of Sausage Dogs*, for example, von Igelfeld is mistaken for an expert on canine health and invited to Arkansas to talk about dachshunds. Unwilling to disabuse his audience of their illusions, he pretends to be that expert.

Another of McCall Smith's series features an amateur detective named Isabel Dalhousie. In *The Sunday Philosophy Club* (2005); *Friends, Lovers, Chocolate* (2006); and *The Right Attitude to Rain* (2006), Dalhousie, a Scottish woman of independent means who edits a journal of applied ethics, investigates murders on the side—all the while pondering weighty questions of moral responsibility. While some reviewers found Dalhousie's intellectual moralizing less interesting than Precious Ramotswe's homespun wisdom, McCall Smith's many fans made the new franchise a commercial success.

McCall Smith, said to have been inspired by Armistead Maupin's popular *Tales of the City* series, about a San Francisco apartment building, wrote a series of vignettes that originally appeared in the *Scotsman* in 2004 and were compiled into book form in 2005. The stories follow a cast of characters—an eccentric widow, a precocious young child along with his overbearing mother, and a vain rugby fan, among them—who live in a Georgian apartment building in Scotland. The books, *44 Scotland Street* and *Espresso Tales*, like McCall Smith's other fictional offerings, were eagerly snapped up by *Scotsman* readers and fans of his previous series.

In his legal practice, which often consists of offering ethical advice to the public on matters of current concern, such as the determination of fault in medical errors, McCall Smith honed his ability to portray contradictions, a skill evident in his fiction as well. "The law must be very careful about blaming people for negligence. Negligence is not necessarily culpable," he wrote in an essay published in the London *Times* (June 13, 2000). "What is criminal is recklessness, which is the deliberate taking of an unjustified risk with somebody else's life. There may be some doctors who do that and they may well merit criminal prosecution, but we should be very careful to identify them as a very small minority. . . . After all, one thing the law should be able to do is to distinguish between that which is an inevitable part of being human—being unable to perform tasks perfectly 100 per cent of the time—and that which is truly blameworthy." Upon the publication of *Errors, Medicine and the Law* (2001), which McCall Smith wrote in collaboration with Alan Merry, Anthony Daniels noted for the London *Sunday Telegraph* (August 12, 2001) that the authors discuss the making of errors in medical practice "in a calm, subtle and lucid fashion, all the more timely because of the hysteria created by lurid newspaper stories. . . . They . . . believe that it is more important to improve standards than to exact retribution, often unjustly."

McCall Smith lives in Edinburgh with his wife, a doctor; they have two daughters. He is a founding member of, and bassoonist in, the Really Terrible Orchestra, which performs in Edinburgh and has endeared itself to audiences with humorous versions of classical music. He is also vice chairman of the Human Genetics Commission of Great Britain and Britain's representative to the UNESCO bioethics commission. McCall Smith makes frequent trips to Botswana, where he regularly visits an orphanage that journalists surmise he supports financially.

—S.Y.

Suggested Reading: *Boston Globe* D p2 Oct. 16, 2002; (Glasgow) *Herald* p4 May 14, 1994, p12 June 8, 2002; (London) *Independent* p36 July 19, 1992; (London) *Sunday Telegraph* p13 Aug. 12, 2001; (London) *Sunday Times* (on-line) Oct. 21, 1990; (London) *Times* (on-line) June 13, 2000; *New York Times* E p3 Dec. 12, 2002; *New York Times Book Review* p12 Jan. 27, 2002; *Publishers Weekly* p75+ July 22, 2002, p58 Mar. 24, 2003; *Scotland on Sunday* p27 Nov. 8, 1998; *Scotsman* p17 July 8, 1995, p8 May 7, 2002

Selected Books: fiction—*Heavenly Date, and Other Stories*, 1995; *The No. 1 Ladies' Detective Agency*, 1998; *Tears of the Giraffe*, 2000; *Morality for Beautiful Girls*, 2001; *The Kalahari Typing School for Men*, 2002; *The Full Cupboard of Life*, 2003; *Portuguese Irregular Verbs*, 2003; *The Finer Points of Sausage Dogs*, 2003; *At the Villa of Reduced Circumstances*, 2003; *In the Company of Cheerful Ladies*, 2004; *44 Scotland Street*, 2005; *Espresso Tales*, 2005; *The Sunday Philosophy Club*, 2005; *Friends, Lovers, Chocolate*, 2006; *The Right Attitude to Rain*, 2006; *Blue Shoes and Happiness*, 2006; children's books—*The White Hippo*, 1980; *Children of Wax: African Folk Tales*, 1989; *Jeffrey's Joke Machine*, 1990; *Akimbo and the Elephants*, 1990; *The Five Lost Aunts of Harriet Bean*, 1990; *Harriet Bean and the League of Cheats*, 1991; *The Bursting Balloons Mystery*, 1997; *The Chocolate Money Mystery*, 1997; *Akimbo and the Lions*, 2005; *Akimbo and the Snakes*, 2006; *The Cowgirl Aunt of Harriet Bean*, 2006

McCourt, James

July 4, 1941– Novelist

James McCourt has received high praise from critics; in 1994, the renowned if controversial literary critic Harold Bloom listed McCourt's work in *The Western Canon*, Bloom's chronology of the essential works of Western literature. McCourt's debut novel, *Mawrdew Czgowchwz* (pronounced "Mardu Gorgeous"), was published in 1975; a comedic tale about a fictional Czech opera singer of that name who enchants the New York City opera scene, it attracted considerable attention and is today considered a cult classic. With the publication of his subsequent books—*Kaye Wayfaring in "Avenged": Four Stories* (1985), *Time Remaining* (1993), *Delancey's Way* (2000), and *Wayfaring at Waverly in Silver Lake* (2002)—McCourt became known for his packed, scintillating prose, riddled with ideas, witticisms, and countless cultural references, from celebrated gay icons to political figures to New York City bathhouses. As Leo Carey wrote for the *New York Times* (September 8, 2002), "His narratives proceed through eddying internal monologues interspersed with dense conversational passages. . . . Whatever may have happened is usually less important than all the witty things that can be said about what happened. For McCourt's characters, conversation is an art, or possibly a sport. He makes no attempt to imitate ordinary speech, and everyone—whether movie producer

or child—speaks with hyperreal articulacy." His most recent book, *Queer Street: The Rise and Fall of an American Culture, 1947–1985: Excursions in the Mind of the Life* (2004), provides a lengthy survey of urban gay culture in the post–World War II era. McCourt is a longtime contributor to the *New Yorker* and *Film Comment*, and his articles have appeared in a number of other publications. Discussing his work as a whole, McCourt informed William Moses Hoffman for the *Los Angeles Times* (October 31, 1993). "I don't write novels. The novel is an English middle-class product. It is undeniably wonderful—[I] love Dickens—with plots and all that. Myself, I write tales. They go on and on, then just stop. I belong to the Irish tradition of storytelling. Or as they used to say at the Danceteria [a notorious Manhattan disco]: 'F—— art, let's dance.'"

James McCourt was born on July 4, 1941, the second of three sons, in Flushing, a neighborhood in the New York City borough of Queens, and raised in nearby Jackson Heights. McCourt's parents were Irish Americans and devout Roman Catholics. His father worked as a timekeeper on the New York waterfront, while his mother taught in Catholic elementary schools. Introduced at a young age to opera and the theater by his parents, the extroverted McCourt developed a keen interest in drama and created his own stage shows to perform at friends' houses. As a teenager McCourt dated girls; his romantic relationships, however, were physically chaste, something he at first attributed to his Catholic upbringing. "But," he told Hoffman, "I might have been more suspicious. . . . All in all, I was having a pretty rough time, and sometimes I was beat up for being queer." After finishing high school, McCourt entered Manhattan College, a Catholic college located in the Bronx, in 1958, but later matriculated at New York University. In the late 1950s McCourt began frequenting the standing-room section at the Old Metropolitan Opera House, a notorious meeting place for the city's gay men who, at the time, as McCourt recalled, were fierce opera lovers with preferences for certain divas. After college, intent on pursuing a career as an actor and playwright, McCourt left Manhattan and his friends from the Metropolitan Opera House for New Haven, Connecticut, where he enrolled in the Yale School of Drama. There he met his future partner, Vincent Virga. McCourt dropped out of the drama school in 1965 and moved with Virga to London, where the two worked various dead-end jobs, though McCourt authored plays from time to time. Over the next several years, McCourt traveled back and forth between New York and London, teaching for a time at Seton Hall University, in New Jersey, before settling in New York, in the late 1960s.

Back in New York, McCourt immersed himself in the city's vibrant cultural scene, associating with famous drag queens and such celebrities as the artist Andy Warhol and the musician Lou Reed. In 1972, with Virga working as a typesetter for the Susan Sontag–edited *New American Review*, McCourt had a chapter of what would eventually become *Mawrdew Czgowchwz* published in the journal. Sontag took McCourt on as a protégé and introduced him to editors at Farrar, Strauss, and Giroux, who agreed to publish his first novel, though it was another three years before McCourt completed the work.

The title character of *Mawrdew Czgowchwz* is an opera diva with impeccable vocal talent. The work chronicles her explosion onto the opera scene and the resentment her skill engenders in her rivals. Christopher Lehmann-Haupt, writing for the *New York Times* (June 15, 1984), called it "a hilarious high-camp, low-comedy romp through New York City's high-culture mélange." "McCourt is unfailingly exact about every detail of operaphilia and about such '40s esoterica as the murder of composer-conductor Alexander Hollenius by Christine Radcliffe," Walter Clemons wrote for *Newsweek* (January 27, 1975). "McCourt," Clemons opined, "is an ecstatic fabulist, robustly funny and inventive, and touchingly in love with his subject." Patrick Giles, in an article for the *Los Angeles Times* (July 7, 2002), proclaimed, "Once Mawrdew Czgowchwz sings, the town, its new diva—and American fiction itself—are never again the same. . . . McCourt, in his first work, waved his pen to produce a place for himself among the major American writers of our day. Enchantment is the modus operandi of *Mawrdew Czgowchwz*: action, characters, diction and tone whisk the

reader into a state of blissful, jaw-dropping belief." Giles continued, "This isn't really so much a novel about opera as it is a grand masque celebrating the harmony possible between art and life and the redemptive potential for greatness in both."

Kaye Wayfaring in "Avenged" (1984) consists of four stories about Kaye Wayfaring, a two-time Oscar nominee who hopes to finally capture the award with her performance in the upcoming film *Avenged*. In the first story Kaye sits on a rock in New York City's Central Park, thinking about the role while reminiscing about her tragic childhood. In the second story, Kaye considers the four possible endings for *Avenged*—death by fire, earth, water and air—while at the same time recalling a memory about a Yale Drama School production of Shakespeare's *Twelfth Night* in which she played the role of Viola. In the third section, Kaye attends the premiere party for *Avenged* and travels via train to rendezvous with her lover, a son of Mawrdew Czgowchwz. In the book's final episode, Kaye attends a Hollywood soiree, visits the place of her mother's suicide, and then falls asleep. "Apparently realizing that high camp has its limits, [McCourt] tries to branch out into sentiment and drama," Christopher Lehmann-Haupt observed for the *New York Times* (June 15, 1984), concluding that the book was less successful than its predecessor: "There are occasional pleasures to be found in this scramble. . . . [But] it is difficult for Mr. McCourt to resist the wisecrack. After a while not only does this tendency interrupt the emotional flow of the novel, but it also begins to irritate."

In 1993 McCourt published *Time Remaining*. The book is composed of two novellas, the first of which, "I Go Back to the Mais Oui," serves as a prelude to the second and longer piece, "A Chance to Talk." In the former, Danny Delancey, a gay performance artist in his 40s, recollects the wild and campy culture of gay life in New York City in the days before AIDS. Danny recalls the bars and the baths and alludes to such memorable figures as Judy Garland, Frank O'Hara, and Jackson Pollock, as well as McCourt's own Kate Wayfaring and Mawdrew Czgowchwz. In "A Chance to Talk," Odette O'Doyle—a drag-queen ballerina from Ireland—and Danny travel together aboard a train bound from New York City to the South Fork of Long Island as Odette recounts how she traveled to Europe and scattered the ashes of eight of her friends, all of whom had succumbed to AIDS. "Odette's recitations are brilliant, touching, funny, self-deprecating: flamboyance warmed with wisdom. McCourt is no easy writer, but his way with disorder and sorrow—early and late—is not to be missed," a writer for *Kirkus Reviews* observed, as archived on Amazon.com. "Age and AIDS give these frothy, entertaining evocations of New York's gay subculture all the melancholy resonance of a last call at the piano bar," a critic opined for *Publishers Weekly*, also quoted on Amazon.com. "To those who comprehend its nuances, this book will surely give pleasure; the rest of the reading public may be somewhat bewildered. A tour de force of high camp, Manhattan-style, this collection proves McCourt is a dazzling practitioner of the lost language of queens."

Danny Delancey and Odette O'Doyle resurface in McCourt's next work, *Delancey's Way*. Danny, a gay reporter for the *East Hampton Star*, relocates to Washington, D.C., with Odette in tow, in order to cover the incoming session of Congress and the subsequent Republican dismantling of the nation's environmental statutes. Reviews of the novel were mixed. "There are vague intimations of a plot circulating through the pages of [the novel]," Bill Goldstein wrote for the *New York Times Book Review* (February 27, 2000), "but what stands out more memorably is the astonishing pantheon of cultural icons erected with name-dropping specificity: [Barbara] Stanwyck, Judy [Garland], Truman Capote, Bea Lillie, Leo Lerman, [Samuel] Beckett, Dorothy Malone in *Written on the Wind* and more." Goldstein continued, "What one character calls the 'anecdotal resonance of yesteryear' is, finally, the animating force of *Delancey's Way*—for it is easier to grasp hold of song titles and references to the Kennedy brothers' sexual peccadilloes than it is to navigate through pages of stilted conversation that pass in a blur. . . . *Delancey's Way* is a novel deeply inside its own beltway." Vince Passaro, writing for New York *Newsday* (February 24, 2000), averred, "[McCourt's] take on manners and society is so elaborate, fanciful and light it quickly drifts into a state of Byzantine complication and self-referentiality, and becomes almost impossible to read." However, Robert E. Brown, in a review for *Library Journal*, as quoted on Amazon.com, offered considerable praise for the work: "Sometimes this book is funny, and sometimes it's very funny. What it is, is an acidic romp through the political high and low roads of Washington."

In *Wayfaring at Waverly in Silver Lake*, McCourt returns to the character of Kaye Wayfaring, now an aging movie actress living in Los Angeles's Silver Lake neighborhood. The book is arranged into seven interlocking stories, each of which is tied to one of the seven deadly sins (as set forth in the Christian tradition). In the first story, which deals with pride, Kaye visits the resting place of her childhood friend Marilyn Monroe; in ensuing chapters, Kaye appears as an Irish pirate queen in a motion picture and upbraids a party crasher at a Halloween costume bash for dressing up like a dead Monroe. Kaye's son Tristan also surfaces in the work, narrowly escaping a heroin overdose delivered by a crazed biker. Reviews of the book were mostly positive. "McCourt," David Rollow observed for the *Boston Globe* (October 6, 2002), "is insidious, like reality. His stories refer forward and backward, crisscross, and they sneak up on you in more surprising ways: they are so light and airy, so full of laughter, wordplay, and tomfoolery

that it's a mystery how they turn suddenly moving. . . . *Wayfaring at Wavery in Silver Lake* is damned funny, a constant delight, and a work of art through and through." A critic for *Publishers Weekly*, as quoted on Amazon.com, offered tempered praise: "Though funny and smart enough for two books, [*Wayfaring at Waverly in Silver Lake*] falls short of gratification."

Queer Street: Rise and Fall of an American Culture, 1947–1985: Excursions in the Mind of the Life, is a nostalgic paean to the New York City of McCourt's youth. As narrated by the loquacious Queer Temperment (Q. T. for short), it offers a complex look at the effects that assimilation has had on gay community. "[The book] is as much a vision of gay culture right after [World War II] as an adventure in the mind of the 62-year-old Mr. McCourt," Felicia R. Lee observed for the *New York Times* (December 29, 2003). "In 577 pages, *Queer Street* combines memoir, essays, bits of dialogue, lines from movies and walk-ons in an attempt to describe the social and cultural evolution of gay life in the 20th century." McCourt's account serves as a defense of the gay lifestyle and sensibility that existed prior to the activism of Stonewall (the first public protest by homosexuals against police harrassment, in 1969) and the increasing mainstream acceptance of homosexuality. As Edmund White observed for the *Los Angeles Times* (November 30, 2003): "McCourt's book is not a study of gay rights and certainly not of gay sexuality; instead it is a sly and resolutely disorganized homage to a vanished sense of humor." Today's gay liberationists, McCourt writes, as quoted by George Chauncey for the *New York Times* (December 31, 2003), "would wipe camp, along with lipstick, mascara, eye shadow and hair coloring, off the face of homosexual experience." The book has received considerable praise. Chauncey likened the book to "a long conversation with a gay uncle who insists on occupying center stage. He can be frustrating at times. . . . But then he takes your breath away by raising the curtain on a world you barely knew existed, and you can only gaze in wonder." "A fierce critical intelligence animates every page of *Queer Street*," Maureen N. McLane wrote for the *New York Times Book Review* (December 14, 2003). "[The book offers] a sustained argument against the contempt of the newly, self-satisfiedly, liberated, those who dismissed their elders as a pathetic, self-hating, closeted crew. At times McCourt sounds like nothing so much as an exasperated parent, vexed by the children's flagrant disregard for their elders' wisdom." According to Sara Nelson for the *New York Observer* (November 24, 2003), "[*Queer Street*] may be one of the bravest, most enlightening literary and cultural histories to appear in a long time."

McCourt has lived with Vincent Virga, a photo editor, since 1965. The couple divide their time between New York City; East Hampton, on Long

Island; Washington, D.C.; and the Republic of Ireland. McCourt cites Herman Melville, Virginia Woolf, and James Joyce as his major influences as a writer. He also lists Bette Davis as his favorite subject: "A diva is a woman whose voice and manner drives you nuts," McCourt told Hoffman, "Bette had both. . . . Her voice and manner had that ability to transform your inner life. It is a religious feeling that some feel for the Blessed Virgin."

—P.B.M.

Suggested Reading: *Boston Globe* H p7 Oct. 6, 2002; *Los Angeles Times* p30 Oct. 31, 1993, R p5 July 7, 2002; *New York Observer* p8 Nov. 24, 2003; *New York Times* E p1 Dec. 29, 2003, E p18 Dec. 31, 2003; *New York Times Book Review* p16 Sep. 8, 2002, p7 Dec. 14, 2003

Selected Books: *Mawrdew Czgowchwz*, 1975; *Kaye Wayfaring in "Avenged": Four Stories*, 1984; *Time Remaining*, 1993; *Delancey's Way*, 2000; *Wayfaring at Waverly in Silver Lake*, 2002; *Queer Street: The Rise and Fall of an American Culture, 1947–1985: Excursions in the Mind of the Life*, 2004

McFarland, Dennis

1950– Novelist; short-story writer

Dennis McFarland "is a novelist of quiet eloquence," a reviewer for *Publishers Weekly* (February 23, 2004) commented. Since the publication of his debut book, *The Music Room*, in 1990, McFarland has become one of the most respected talents in contemporary American fiction. His primary strengths as a writer are his hypnotic prose, his piercing dialogue, and his complex, three-dimensional characters. Thematically McFarland's novels "have all been concerned with the nervous relationship between the present and the past and the protean role that memory plays in shaping individuals' sense of themselves," as Michiko Kakutani observed for the *New York Times* (February 27, 2001).

Dennis McFarland was born in 1950 in Alabama, and grew up in Mobile. "Without invading the privacy of my family too much," McFarland told Dan Cryer for New York *Newsday* (April 22, 2001), "I can say that I had a very difficult childhood. . . . I had a kind of childhood that I've had to spend a lot of time sorting out." McFarland took piano lessons as a youngster and had eventually planned on pursuing a career in music. After completing high school he went on to college but attended to his studies only sporadically, often changing schools and taking extended time off. He lived for a while in California, where he drank heavily and experimented extensively with drugs. Nevertheless, McFarland emerged from this period of youthful excess, and in 1974 he received a music degree from Brooklyn College, part of the City University of New York. However, "by the time I got my degree in music I had lost interest in it," McFarland explained to Wendy Smith for *New York Newsday* (June 26, 1994). Plagued by stage fright, McFarland found it difficult to perform in public.

Having renounced his musical aspirations, McFarland opted to try his hand at writing. "Deciding to write was a desperate act," he told Smith. "I didn't know what I was doing, so I started trying to remember what people had suggested to me. English teachers in high school and college had told me I wrote very well, and I thought, 'Okay, I'll try it.'" The aspiring author spent the next several years "working in total isolation, teaching myself to write," as he recalled to Smith. Eventually he entered the writing program at Goddard College, in Vermont, where he came under the tutelage of the noted author Frank Conroy. "I was very ripe for instruction," McFarland told Smith, "and I just blossomed in that six-month period; [Conroy] taught me things that still inform my work."

After completing his course of study at Goddard, McFarland moved on to Stanford University, in California, where, in 1981, he began a Wallace Stegner teaching fellowship in creative writing. He spent the next five years there, but his tenure at Stanford was far from a happy one. "I wasn't being published and was very frustrated; I felt that nobody cared whether I kept writing or not. I was getting lovely letters from competitions saying, 'Congratulations, you're one of the ten finalists,' and my response was to crumble up the letter and throw it across the room because I hadn't won. I had this script in my head for my life, and it was entitled 'Almost'; that was my doom. I was abusing alcohol and being self-destructive in all kinds of ways," McFarland explained to Smith. Therapy helped McFarland come to terms with some of these issues and provided the impetus for him to commence work on *The Music Room*. While writing *The Music Room*, McFarland continued to teach creative writing at Goddard and at Emerson College, in Massachusetts.

Published in 1990, *The Music Room* was a smashing success both critically and commercially. The money made from the book allowed McFarland to curtail his teaching; at the time, as he explained to Matthew Gilbert for the *Boston Globe* (July 17, 1990), he welcomed the respite: "That way, if and when I go back [to teaching], I'll return with some freshness. I felt like I was saying the same thing over and over. I would enjoy occasionally doing a workshop, or maybe working with an individual, but I would be very happy never to have to teach again. I never saw teaching as a career."

The protagonist of *The Music Room* is Martin Lambert, a man in his late 20s, separated from his unfaithful wife and living in San Francisco. While vacuuming his home Martin receives a call from the New York City police informing him that his brother, Perry, has committed suicide. Martin heads home for the funeral, holing up in his late brother's apartment, where he recalls their troubled early years—a childhood corrupted by their parents' alcoholism and by the family's wealth, which served to isolate Martin and Perry from their peers. Martin soon begins an affair with his deceased brother's pregnant girlfriend, comes to terms with his own drinking, and struggles to understand the implications of his brother's act. Reviewing *The Music Room* for *Newsweek* (May 28, 1990), David Gates commented, "McFarland is a Divine Watchmaker of a novelist. He balances character against character: competent cellist Martin and gifted composer Perry, Martin's cheating wife and Perry's faithful girlfriend." Gates added, "McFarland more than compensates for first-novelistic excesses with dialogue you can hear—especially the drunk scenes—and details you can see. A desk in a precinct house is 'one of those sad grey metal obstructions with a rubber-coated top scored by countless fingernail gashes.'" In a review for the *Boston Globe* (April 9, 1990), Matthew Gilbert singled out McFarland's prose for particular praise, noting that it "has a musical, musing quality. Syntactical flourishes wind through chapters, providing a hypnotic rhythm in much of *The Music Room*," marking a "trend away from the spare minimalism so popular through the 1980s, toward a narrative unafraid of rich sensory detail. Even as he charts a tale of emotional emptiness, his landscape is rocky and rough, without the stark barrenness that minimalist writers have exploited." Christopher Lehmann-Haupt, reviewing the novel for the *New York Times* (April 23, 1990), commented, "The details of Mr. McFarland's prose are brilliantly vivid, whether they invoke Lambert's almost romantically intemperate past, or Perry's doomed search for redemption, or Marty's sometimes comically tortured dreams." Not all of the novel's reviews were wholly positive, however: Matthew Gilbert commented on "the author's awkwardness with plot," and Jonathan Yardley, in an assessment for the *Washington Post* (May 9, 1990), faulted several aspects of the work, remarking that "its narrator is earnest but disagreeably self-absorbed, its depth of feeling in time becomes merely overwrought, its sentimental denouement is both predictable and disappointing, and its use of certain dramatic devices is maladroit." Despite these perceived shortcomings, *The Music Room* briefly appeared on the *New York Times* best-seller list, a rarity for such literary novels, and marked McFarland as one of the bright new lights of American fiction. McFarland's talents were obvious even to Yardley, who stated, "Purely as a writer, [McFarland] is the real thing, which is to say something of a rarity these days and cause enough to celebrate his arrival."

In McFarland's second novel, *School for the Blind* (1994), Francis Brimm, an aging photographer hoping to finish out his days in quiet solitude, retires to his childhood home in Florida, where Muriel, his unmarried older sister, has lived throughout her life. The chapters of the book alternate between Francis's and Muriel's point of view. One morning Francis has a vision of a photograph he had taken in France at the end of World War II of a young French woman whose hair was cut off by her fellow citizens as punishment for having a child by a German soldier. For Francis, the episode begins an extended examination of his earlier life; similarly, Francis's return leads Muriel to explore her own turbulent past and to confront unpleasant memories she has long suppressed, including that of her father's suicide. "If the novel has flaws," Christopher Lehmann-Haupt observed for the *New York Times* (May 12, 1994), "they are sometimes a heavy-handed symbolism and gratuitous literary references to the likes of [Anton] Chekhov, [Joseph] Conrad, [William Butler] Yeats, [James] Joyce and [George] Eliot." Nevertheless, Lehmann-Haupt described *School for the Blind* as an "accomplished" novel, possessed of a prose that "soars . . . with equal suppleness [to that of *The Music Room*] but takes a welcome turn for the droll." Sven Birkerts, in a critique for the *New York Times Book Review* (May 22, 1994), described the work as "an affectingly oblique meditation on age and time and the long-term wages of denial." In a glowing review for the *Boston Globe* (May 22, 1994), Richard Dyer praised what he termed "the interwoven textures and images of McFarland's writing—the supple rhythms of its sentences, the articulations of its strong simple and intricate structure." *School for the Blind*, he continued, "is a book meant to be read aloud, shared with someone you care about. It is a book in tune with itself that chimes in the resonant spaces of our common experience; every heart will return its echo."

McFarland's third work, the ghost story *A Face at the Window*, reminded many reviewers of the work of Henry James, particularly his novel *The Turn of the Screw*. McFarland's protagonist here is Cookson Selway, "a 43-year-old guy whose main life theme has been Self-Aware bumping into Self-Destruct," as Gail Caldwell remarked for the *Boston Globe* (March 16, 1997). Born and raised in the American South, Selway had led a life of excess in the 1970s, selling drugs and using the proceeds to finance a second career as a restaurateur. Eventually Selway managed to clean up his act, giving up the substance abuse and successfully emerging from his malaise to lead a quiet domestic life outside Boston. Soon after sending their daughter away to boarding school, Selway and his wife travel to London for a vacation. At the hotel Selway begins to hear piano music playing that no one else can discern. He speaks with a teenager at breakfast who has apparently been dead for over half a century, and soon more ghosts emerge. Michiko Kakutani, writing for the *New York Times* (March 14, 1997), was highly critical of *A Face at the Window*, opining, "By the end of the book, the reader is so tired of Cookson's self-pitying self-inventories, so weary of his efforts to determine whether the ghosts are projections of his unconscious or real emanations from the spirit world, that one doesn't really care what effect they have on his search for self-knowledge and redemption." Kakutani concluded, "one hopes . . . [*A Face at the Window*] represents a curious detour in an otherwise estimable career." Carolyn See offered a more balanced critique for the *Washington Post* (May 16, 1997), stating, "If all books were perfect, critics wouldn't have much to do. But *A Face at the Window* could almost put a critic out of business. So much of it is terrific, and just part of it comes up wanting. Unfortunately, it's a crucial part. This is a ghost story, and the ghosts are boring beyond words." Gail Caldwell had fewer reservations about the novel, describing it as "a pleasant immersion: clever without being contrived, thoughtful without being maudlin," adding, "Because Dennis McFarland is a writer of considerable depth, it is also something more: a novel about lost sons and daughters, lost selves, wandering about in those fogbound outer territories, trying to get themselves home."

The senseless murder of Malcolm Vaughn, a married father gunned down in full view of his family, is the event that drives *Singing Boy* (2001), McFarland's next novel. In it McFarland explores the emotional impact Malcolm's death has on those closest to him: his wife, Sarah; his eight-year-old son, Harry; and his best friend, Deckard, a troubled Vietnam veteran. According to Judith Warner, writing for the *Washington Post* (April 2, 2001), the grief McFarland describes is one in which "there are only layers and layers of pain—backward-looking pain for the adults, forward-leaning pain for Harry whose intelligence, imagination and budding artistic talent will always bear the inscription of a random act of violence." Allegra Goodman, in a critique for the *New York Times Book Review* (March 4, 2001), opined, "McFarland writes with such integrity about Sarah, Deckard and Harry that the reader can't help sharing their proud, exclusionary grief." Judith Warner effused, "Grief appears, in this beautiful gasp of a book, to have a life of its own. It is caused by inexplicable untoward events; it is eased by the same. It is so deep and so palpable that it envelops the reader. . . . And that, indeed, is the novel's only weakness, if weakness it be: The evocation of sadness and loss is so good and so real that it can make reading *Singing Boy* literally painful."

In his next novel, *Prince Edward*, published in May 2004, McFarland examines events in Prince Edward County, Virginia, during the summer of 1959. Unwilling to desegregate their schools, the county's leaders opt instead to close them. The novel is told from the perspective of Benjamin Rome, the 10-year-old son of an ardent white segregationist. "The foreground of this fine and affecting novel is alive with the sights and sounds of a sweltering Virginia summer," a reviewer wrote for *Publishers Weekly* (February 23, 2004), "but it is the author's real achievement to make it simultaneously clear that in the barely perceived background a world is turning upside down."

McFarland's next novel, "Letter from Point Clear," which is scheduled to be published in summer of 2007, is about the Owen family of Point Clear, Alabama. The Owen children have lived away from their hometown for several years as the novel opens. However, the youngest, Bonnie, feels obliged to return home and take care of her sick father. After he dies she falls in love with and marries an evangelical preacher who helps her give up her self-destructive lifestyle. Unaware of the changes their sister has made to her life, Bonnie's siblings, Ellen and Morris, come home when they hear about her marriage, hoping to help her out of her most recent mistake. Meanwhile, the preacher finds out that Morris is gay and sets out to save him.

McFarland is married to the author Michelle Blake Simons. Together they have two children. McFarland's short stories have appeared in the *New Yorker*, and his work has been featured in *The Best American Short Stories 1990* and *Prize Stories 1991: The O'Henry Awards*, among other compilations. He currently lives with his family in Massachusetts.

—P.B.M.

Suggested Reading: *Boston Globe* p33 Apr. 9, 1990, p61 July 17, 1990, B p15 May 22, 1994, N p15 Mar. 16, 1997, D p1 Mar. 18, 2001; Henry Holt and Company Web site; *New York Times* C p14 Apr. 23, 1990, C p17 July 12, 1990, C p20 May 12, 1994, C p34 Mar. 14, 1997, E p8 Feb. 27, 2001; *New York Times Book Review* p12 May 22, 1994; p8 Mar. 4, 2001; *Newsweek* p74 May 28, 1990; *Publishers Weekly* p46 Feb. 23, 2004; *Washington Post* B p2 May 9, 1990, X p5 June 19, 1994, B p2 May 16, 1997, C p8 Apr. 2, 2001

Selected Books: *The Music Room*, 1990; *School for the Blind*, 1994; *Face at the Window*, 1997; *Singing Boy*, 2001; *Prince Edward*, 2004

Elena Seibert/Courtesy of Random House

McGrath, Patrick

(mick-GRAW)

Feb. 7, 1950– Novelist; short-story writer

Shortly after Patrick McGrath published *Spider* (1990), his second novel, a critic for the *Economist* (December 8, 1990) wrote, "McGrath's dark imagination is offset by a polished prose style and urbane wit, as if mocking the self-complacency of a society that ignores the symptoms of its own sickness." By this point in his career—after a collection of short stories, *Blood and Water and Other Tales* (1988), and a novel, *The Grotesque* (1989)—McGrath had established a reputation as one of the strongest Gothic writers of his generation, counting among his literary predecessors such figures as Edgar Allan Poe, H. P. Lovecraft, Roald Dahl, Oscar Wilde, Evelyn Waugh, and Nathaniel Hawthorne. He followed these first books with four novels—*Dr. Haggard's Disease* (1993), *Asylum* (1997), *Martha Peake* (2000), and *Port Mungo* (2004)—and a collection of three novellas, *Ghost Town: Tales of Manhattan Then and Now* (2005). Through the years, McGrath has, Allan Brown noted in the London *Sunday Times* (August 5, 2001), "finessed a world in which the most prosaic of situations coagulate into nightmare as wrong paths are taken, bad decisions are made and the grip on reality gradually loosens." As a contemporary practitioner of the Gothic literary tradition that started in the 18th century, McGrath often straddles the line between popular and literary writing. "The architecture of [my] books is obviously Gothic," he told Brown, "but hopefully there's something more literary

going on too. The focus is a close interest in familial and sexual relationships, and how obsession kicks in when disorder occurs in the psyche."

The oldest of four children, Patrick McGrath was born in London, England, on February 7, 1950 to Patrick and Helen (O'Brien) McGrath and grew up, from the age of five, in Crowthorne, a town west of London, on the grounds of a high-security institution for the criminally insane, Broadmoor Hospital, where his father served as the medical superintendent. Some commentators have traced the origin of McGrath's novelistic worlds to this childhood environment, but McGrath denies the connection. "In that orderly mental hospital, the truly disturbed men and women were secluded in parts of this great massive institution where the children of staff would never encounter them," he told Donald Clarke for the *Irish Times* (July 3, 2004). "What we encountered were well gardened terraces, sports fields, patients on the way to recovery who worked on the estate. It was an England of a past time. It was a benign and actually rather serene place." McGrath has, however, acknowledged to Andre Chautard, for the *Los Angeles Times* (January 8, 2003), that "many of the stories that were told at the dinner table involved . . . spectacular crimes [committed by those interned in the hospital], and as a small boy I was drinking this stuff up. And not coincidentally, I think, I began reading Edgar Allan Poe when I was about 10 years old." After finishing secondary school, McGrath went to the University of London, where he studied literature and earned his degree, with honors, in 1971. McGrath then left for Canada and, with the help of his father's professional contacts, found work as an orderly in a mental hospital. He later moved to Vancouver, British Columbia, Canada, taking classes at Simon Fraser University before moving on to the Queen Charlotte Islands, in northwestern Canada, near Alaska. He held a teaching position at a kindergarten there but, he told Chautard, "I was no good at it. I couldn't control them. I had discipline problems with my kindergarten class, and I knew that education was not for me. And a long-ago dream of writing fiction returned to me." McGrath then quit teaching, built a log cabin, and began to write.

McGrath's first stories failed to interest publishers, but the experience of writing them inspired him. "I found that being a writer beats everything," he told Kate Kellaway for the London *Observer* (May 2, 1993). "I loved not having to be socially useful. I loved the fact that you could write and get away with it. I found it intoxicating and I haven't outgrown that feeling." Intent on establishing a writing career, McGrath moved, in 1981, to New York City with Orshi Drozdik, his girlfriend at the time. (Drozdik is now an internationally acclaimed artist, known for works with feminist themes.) In New York McGrath edited a computer magazine and served as a contributing editor for the literary magazines *Bomb* and *Between C & D*. (McGrath was among the writers anthologized in *Between C & D: New Writing from the Lower East Side Fiction Magazine*, published in 1988.) McGrath's work for these small magazines helped establish his reputation as the "first postmodern gothic storyteller," a phrase used on the jacket of his first book, *Blood and Water and Other Tales*, according to John Blades for the *Chicago Tribune* (February 28, 1988). In a review of the book, Blades commented that if the phrase "means a writer who is out to mock and satirize, to draw and quarter his predecessors, with a prose style that has more wicked edges than [a] medieval mace, then his publisher's description is right on the money." By contrast, Sue Martin, writing for the *Los Angeles Times* (February 28, 1988), felt that "some of these tales are silly, some are gross and some are actually pretty good. In this slim volume of 13 stories, we've got a little of everything: a haunted Southern mansion, complete with bayou and Spanish moss; a crawling hand, vampires of a sort and various and sundry other creepies, fringe dwellers and eccentrics. They're all off-kilter and tend toward the macabre and horrific. Patrick McGrath has a facility for setting his scenes (anywhere from India, to English moors, to New York City) and for flavorful description, but a lot of the stories tend to the banal, structurally, punctuated with a bizarre ending." The book was a finalist for the Horror Writers Association's 1988 Bram Stoker Award for superior achievement in a collection of short fiction.

McGrath's first novel, *The Grotesque*, takes the form of an internal monologue by Sir Hugo Coal, a mute and misanthropic country gentleman confined to a wheelchair. Coal's unreliable narrative details his version of the events that led to the murder of Sidney Giblet, the prospective husband of Coal's daughter, Cleo, and the accident that turned Coal into a quadriplegic. "Contemplating Mr. McGrath's ingenuity, skill and daring in creating this rare species of book," Susan Kenny wrote for the *New York Times* (May 28, 1989), "one can do no better than echo Sir Hugo contemplating his life: 'As a connoisseur of ironies, I cannot, now, help recognizing just how rich this one is.'" Less awed—but impressed nonetheless—Michiko Kakutani wrote for the *New York Times* (April 21, 1989): "There are times when his Grand Guignol tastes lead him to embroider his story with gratuitously gruesome details—squashed and mutilated insects, a carnivorous toad that nearly devours someone's severed finger, pigs fattened on human flesh and then turned into Christmas sausages. Such descriptions seem both needlessly gross and unnecessary—Mr. McGrath is such an ingenious manipulator of discomfort and suspense that he needn't rely on such cheap and obvious devices. His storytelling can stand triumphantly on its own."

McGrath's second novel, *Spider*, is told through the journals of Dennis "Spider" Cleg, a man institutionalized for his mother's murder, which Spider believes was actually committed by his father. The novel is divided into two chronological sequences: one takes place before World War II, when Spider was a child, and the other in London in the late 1950s, after Spider's release from a mental hospital. Spider's continuing psychological problems mean, as Cary Kimble noted for the *Washington Times* (January 21, 1991), that "the only thing that is evident in this murky story is that Spider is not stable enough to have been discharged into the world." The narrator's unreliability led Michael Harris, writing for the *Los Angeles Times* (October 14, 1990), to suggest that *Spider* "may be a novel about mental illness that masquerades as a thriller. Or it may be a thriller whose impact is blurred by the derangement of its narrator. Either way, it's a suspenseful and evocative [work]." Others, while acknowledging the quality of McGrath's prose, found fault with the novel as a whole. In the London *Independent* (June 8, 1991), Andrew St. George observed, "McGrath has created a serious situation for a trivial character; and since he gives no points of purchase on reality, it becomes difficult to engage with or care about his creation."

In 1991 McGrath helped to give definition to the genre in which he worked by editing a fiction collection with Bradford Morrow called, in the U.S., *The New Gothic: A Collection of Contemporary Gothic Fiction*, which was published the following year in Britain as *The Picador Book of the New Gothic*. It includes a range of works by such literary stars as Martin Amis, Jeanette Winterson, Joyce Carol Oates, and Angela Carter, as well as such established horror writers as Peter Straub and Anne Rice. The introduction to the anthology notes the line of continuity between the older Gothic style, with its ghosts and clanking chains, and the new Gothic, which might include those elements but focuses largely on depraved psychological states. "Were Poe to come upon this collection," McGrath writes in the book's introduction, as quoted by Tom Shone for the London *Sunday Times* (January 24, 1993), "he might perhaps be bewildered by the various accents and settings of the work, but he would certainly recognise and applaud the spirit animating them. This is the New Gothic."

McGrath's third novel, *Dr. Haggard's Disease*, tells the story of Dr. Edward Haggard's brief love affair and lifelong obsession with Fanny Vaughan, the wife of the senior pathologist at the mental hospital where he worked in the years before World War II. Many critics responded to *Dr. Haggard's Disease* in much the same way they did to McGrath's previous works, simultaneously praising the quality of the writing and finding the work, as a whole, disappointing. In the *New York Times* (May 21, 1993), Michiko Kakutani wrote, "Initially the reader is mesmerized by Dr.

Haggard's tale. We keep turning pages, hypnotized by Mr. McGrath's nimble prose and eager to find out what really happened. Unfortunately, the payoff is a letdown." Sven Birkerts, in a review for *New York Newsday* (May 2, 1993), called attention to elements that may have left readers disappointed but concluded that the novel rose above these elements: "The last sentence is calculated to bring a shudder, a gasp. Is this art or sensational melodrama? We nearly have a photo finish, but McGrath's grace and daring, his vision of the transfiguring power of love, give the nod to art."

McGrath set his next novel, *Asylum*, in an institution much like Broadmoor. Told, characteristically, by an unreliable narrator, Peter Cleave, an older physician at the hospital, the book relates the story of another affair and subsequent obsession, this time between the wife of a forensic psychiatrist, Stella Raphael, and a murderous sculptor and psychiatric patient, Edgar Stark. In a review for the London *Independent* (August 24, 1996), D. J. Taylor wrote, "While all this is written up with huge attack and intensity, full of shrewdly observed dilemmas and incidental drama, McGrath can't avoid—in fact, rather seems to welcome—a kind of staginess which in consequence seems mildly tongue-in-cheek." Taylor also contended that, as a psychiatrist, the narrator "has the professional habit of explaining motivation . . . rather than demonstrating it. The result is a novel so tightly controlled by its voice that characters end up stifled." To Adam Mars-Jones, writing for the London *Guardian* (August 25, 1996), *Asylum* suggested "an attempt to break out of the confinements of the Gothic genre McGrath has made his own, to crack open the chrysalis and extend wings throbbing with new blood. But his readership may prefer the horrors of his larval stage." Others praised this effort as among McGrath's best. "By pushing familiar passions to extremes and by glossing familiar psychological concepts with religious notions of sin and guilt and redemption," Michiko Kakutani wrote for the *New York Times* (February 14, 1997), "Mr. McGrath has managed to construct a chilling story that works as both a Freudian parable and an old-fashioned gothic shocker. In showing how a seemingly ordinary housewife ended up in love with a violent psychopath, he connects the dots in her story in such a way that they form a narrative that feels as inevitable as it is scary." In 1996 the book was short-listed for Britain's prestigious Whitbread Novel Award (now one of the Costa Book Awards) and earned a nomination for one of that year's British Fantasy Society Awards.

With *Martha Peake*, McGrath changed direction slightly, placing his Gothic story within the 18th century, when Horace Walpole's *The Castle of Otranto* (1764) established the Gothic mode, rather than in the mid-20th century. A central symbol in the novel is the Englishman Harry Peake's rape of his daughter, Martha. Pregnant with her father's child, Martha flees England for America, landing in Boston in 1774 and becoming involved with the American Revolution through her American cousins. The plot serves in part as an opportunity for McGrath to meditate on storytelling and how countries come to understand their own past. "I wanted to get at the mythical element within every nation's own history," McGrath said in an interview with the London *Observer* (August 20, 2000). "The simplifications that occur; the distortions that occur in history, or within the transmission of historical fact into national narratives." McGrath's willingness to wrestle with these questions using a genre associated with popular entertainment found favor with many critics. "One of the most pleasing things about *Martha Peake* is that it doesn't see the haunted house terrors which the late eighteenth century liked so much as an irrelevant diversion from its more serious inquiries," Philip Hensher wrote in a review also appearing in the London *Observer* (August 20, 2000). "Rather, those serious inquiries . . . exist alongside and within a Gothic world view. It feels like a real understanding of the period, and a big step forward in our understanding of ourselves." Anthony Quinn, writing for the London *Sunday Times* (August 27, 2000), also noted the unusually thoughtful intentions behind the novel but questioned their effectiveness: "In its historical scope and imaginative reach this is certainly [McGrath's] most ambitious novel yet, while the beautifully precise and elegant prose maintains the satisfying purr of a luxury-car's engine. The sly indirection and evasiveness are also present and correct—all that is missing is the pleasurable sensation of horror that the last page traditionally delivers."

McGrath's next novel, *Port Mungo*, is split between scenes of the New York City art world and life on the Gulf of Honduras, in a coastal town that gives the novel its name. McGrath explores the effects of these surroundings on two artists, Jack Rathbone and Vera Savage, and their daughters, Peg and Anna. Some critics found the book reminiscent of McGrath's earlier novels, but Richard Lacayo argued in *Time* (May 31, 2004) that it was "not about anything so simple as abnormal psychology. It's about the brutal impulses available to anyone, especially artists, who would let slip the loose restraints of civilization." Others, while pleased with the novel, were unsure how to respond to it. "At the end of this immensely clever and tautly composed novel," Christopher Benfey wrote for the *New York Times* (May 30, 2004), "the admiring reader may be left with a corresponding shadow of a doubt. Is *Port Mungo* a seriously meant meditation on the shadowy wellsprings of art and love, its carefully contrasted characters embodying the fraught polarities of this radioactive field? Or is it, rather, a cunningly contrived device of smoke and mirrors, with secrets passing for mysteries, and gothic conventions . . . smuggled in for added frissons?"

McGrath's next book, *Ghost Town: Tales of Manhattan Then and Now*, comprises three novellas, all set in New York City. The first takes place during the War of Independence, the second during the Civil War, and the last in the weeks after the September 11, 2001 terrorist attacks. Despite this range of historical settings, most reviewers treated the book as a response to the events of September 11. In the *Washington Post* (September 16, 2005), Carolyn See wrote, "McGrath's first purpose—if I read correctly—is to issue a strong corrective to self-absorbed New Yorkers, who live exclusively in the here and now. Sept. 11 may or may not have changed the world as we know it— that remains to be seen. But that morning's destruction was certainly not the first in the city, and perhaps not even its bloodiest." Eileen Battersby, writing for the *Irish Times* (September 17, 2005), found that the book "convincingly evoked a sense of the horrors endured by New York through its history." Others found the book uneven. Max Byrd, in a review for the *New York Times* (September 4, 2005), lamented McGrath's departure from "his vivid psychological studies of characters on the brink of madness." McGrath, Byrd wrote, "has lost his way" with the stories set in the 18th and 19th centuries, "perhaps because historical fiction requires at least some mundane fidelity to facts and perhaps because New York is simply too epic and sprawling a subject."

McGrath, who has had three of his novels—*The Grotesque*, *Spider*, and *Asylum*—turned into films, divides his time between New York and London. In 1991 he met and, a few months later, married the actress and director Maria Aitken. Though Aitken has children from previous marriages, she and McGrath have had none of their own, for while "McGrath occasionally ponders what it would have been like" to be a father, as Tim Teeman reported for the London *Times* (December 28, 2002), "he has long held that artistic and family life are mutually exclusive."

—A.R.

Suggested Reading: *Chicago Tribune* C p3 Feb. 28, 1988; *Economist* p103 Dec. 8, 1990; *Irish Times* p76 July 3, 2004, p13 Sep. 17, 2005; (London) *Guardian* p16 Aug. 25, 1996; (London) *Independent* p29 June 8, 1991, p6 Aug. 24, 1996; (London) *Observer* p13 Aug. 20, 2000; (London) *Sunday Times* (on-line) Jan. 24, 1993, Aug. 27, 2000, Aug. 5, 2001; *Los Angeles Times* p3 Jan. 8, 2003; *New York Times* C p29 Apr. 21, 1989, VII p7 May 28, 1989, C p25 May 21, 1993, C p38 Feb. 14, 1997; *Washington Post* C p3 Sep. 16, 2005; *Washington Times* F p2 Jan. 21, 1991

Selected Books: novels—*The Grotesque*, 1989; *Spider*, 1990; *Dr. Haggard's Disease*, 1993; *Asylum*, 1997; *Martha Peake*, 2000; *Port Mungo*, 2004; short fiction—*Blood and Water and Other Tales*, 1988; *Ghost Town: Tales of Manhattan Then and Now*, 2005

McIntosh, Matthew

1977(?)– Novelist

Well (2003), the debut work of fiction by Matthew McIntosh, is not a novel in the traditional sense. It has no central narrative and no main character— except perhaps that of Federal Way, Washington, a blighted, blue-collar suburb on the outskirts of Seattle. Here desolate junkies, punk rockers, barflies, and dropouts subsist on menial jobs, if they work at all; while some are hopeful, most are resigned to their lot, disillusioned, suffering, unsure of the future and unsure of themselves. These characters, whom McIntosh introduces in first-person testimonials or third-person sketches, struggle to build lives for themselves in a place where few dreams come true. "Just as Raymond Carver put obscure Northwest backwaters like Prosser and Toppenish on the literary map, Matthew McIntosh's debut novel, *Well*, stakes a claim for lowly Federal Way as the rich new locus of unexamined lives," Mark D. Fefer wrote for *Seattle Weekly* (September 3, 2003, on-line). "But don't look for his book to show up on any Chamber of Commerce recommended-reading list. As portrayed by 26-year-old native son McIntosh, the good citizens of Federal Way are relentlessly un-well."

Other than his age—he was born in about 1977—and the fact that he is from Federal Way, McIntosh has revealed little about his personal life to the press. "My thing is, I don't particularly want people to know anything about me," he explained in an interview with Spencer Brown that is posted on McIntosh's Web site. "I don't want to be famous. I'd like my book to be famous, but the rest, I'd prefer to stay out of, as much is possible. I don't have the mindset that I'll sell myself if that's what it takes to make my book sell. I think if you give in to that kind of pressure, it'll affect the way you write, and what you write about. You've got to be able to keep your distance, because it's distance that allows you a clearer perspective on the world."

When asked by Peter Wild, in an interview posted on the Bookmunch Web site (June 8, 2003), how he would introduce his book to readers, McIntosh replied: "I'd tell them it's a novel with a large, broad cast of characters, composed of short pieces all dependent on one another in forming the shape and movement of a larger narrative, some sections a paragraph long, some fifty pages, taking place in a suburb of Seattle, USA, having to do with (among other things) modern hope and hopelessness, alienation and abandonment, disconnection, faith, love, pills, violence, old vs. young, the loss of community, the state of waiting, what it's like being alive in time today, the sense that the world once must have offered such promise but somehow, sometime before anyone can remember, it reneged. It's an attempt to take the reader on a trip through the psychic makeup and experience of a people around the turn of the millennium." Referring to that same interview, in which McIntosh said that writers working in more conventional forms "should be retiring soon," Fefer opined that "the young author fell short in his quest to expand our definition of a novel, to create something grand and [Robert] Altman-esque, something more than a patchwork. There is something, too, just slightly patronizing in McIntosh's depiction of uneducated, blue-collar stiffs uniformly consumed with rage and despair. Is it really fair to presume that a guy who sweeps up at KeyArena resents his lot and hates his life?"

Although Fefer was disappointed with the novel, *Well* received mostly positive notices. In a review for the *Washington Post* (August 12, 2003), Chris Lehmann wrote, "Readers who've been burned one too many times in the giddy self-referenced hall of mirrors that is postmodern fiction could be forgiven for asking themselves some variation of 'How long, Lord, how long?' But they would be unwise. For Matthew McIntosh, young and despondent though he may be, is the real thing—a tremendously gifted and supple prose hand, recounting all manner of human distress and extremity in an assured and generous voice, balancing, as all honest practitioners of the fictional art must, the delicately pitched forces of fate, remorse and grace." Martha Southgate, in her review for the *Chicago Tribune* (August 20, 2003), was more reserved in her praise, noting, "*Well* is a promising first novel, if a flawed one. . . . McIntosh shows a remarkable facility for capturing different voices, the way people speak and think in their most private moments. And some of the vignettes reverberate in the way of fine short stories. But because McIntosh has chosen to give no narrative structure to the book, I put it down not entirely satisfied." Still, she concluded, "McIntosh is a writer to keep an eye on. It remains to be seen if his promise can be put in the service of a fully imagined novel."

—C.M.

Suggested Reading: *Chicago Tribune* C p6 Aug. 20, 2003; *Los Angeles Times* R p14 Sep. 21, 2003; Matthew McIntosh's Web site; *Washington Post* C p3 Aug. 12, 2003

Selected Books: *Well*, 2003

McPhee, Martha

June 25, 1964– Novelist; nonfiction writer

Martha McPhee is the daughter of John McPhee, the acclaimed *New Yorker* staff writer and the author of more than 20 books. Michiko Kakutani, in an assessment for the *New York Times* (June 17, 1997), affirmed that McPhee "shares her [father's] gift for fine, lapidary prose. . . . Blessed with a poet's ear for language and a reporter's eye for detail, she proves . . . also a gifted novelist, a writer with the ability to surprise and move us." McPhee used not her celebrated father, however, but her stepfather, Dan Sullivan, as the inspiration for her character Anton Furey, a charismatic figure who appears in the novels *Bright Angel Time* (1997) and *Gorgeous Lies* (2002). In between those novels McPhee collaborated with her sisters—Jenny (also a novelist) and Laura (a photographer)—to write *Girls: Ordinary Girls and Their Extraordinary Pursuits* (2000), an account of young women who are successful at various activities. Spurred by accounts of American girls' dwindling self-esteem and lack of ambition—problems not readily apparent in John McPhee's accomplished daughters—the trio sought out girls who were making art, advancing feminism, and becoming sports and chess champions. McPhee's latest novel is *L'America* (2006).

Martha McPhee was born on June 25, 1964 and attended Bowdoin College, in Brunswick, Maine, majoring in art history and Italian literature. She graduated in 1987. (McPhee first made her professional mark as a translator; in 1994 she and her sister Jenny translated Pope John Paul II's *Crossing the Threshold of Hope*, a theological and philosophical tract originally written in Italian.) Also in 1994, she earned an M.F.A. from Columbia University, in New York City.

Martha McPhee wrote the following essay, describing her unique family situation and early years, for *World Authors 2000–2005*:

"My elementary school teachers used to sit with me after school in the principal's office as I waited for my mother or stepfather to pick me up. Inevitably they were late. Between them they had ten children—all different ages, all in various schools. At one point or another a large portion of the ten had attended Johnson Park, my elementary school. In the principal's office, painted lime green, the teachers would engage me in conversation as we passed the time—up to two hours it could be that I'd wait. The question they always wanted to understand was how I was related to so many kids who had passed through the school. At one point or another each of my teachers had had one (sometimes two) other member of my family in their classrooms and each child had had at least one parent (sometimes two) who differed from mine. This was the beginning of the divorce boom, the early 1970s, and blended families were not yet a known quantity. Sitting in the office, wearing one of my sisters' dresses (too big for me) and tights too small (the crotch hanging somewhere mid-thigh), I'd draw diagrams to explain my connection to all these children. They'd ask more questions, curiosity apparent in

Courtesy of Harcourt

Martha McPhee

the curl of their lips, and I'd answer—often lying if it made the story better. As it turned out, later when I was grown and writing novels, stories about my family would be the fodder for my imagination—the real intersecting with the invented to become story. My first novel, *Bright Angel Time*, and my second, *Gorgeous Lies*, both rose from the beautiful wreckage of my childhood. (My family is happy to know, however, that my third novel, in progress as I write this essay, is not inspired by them.) With the early stories of my family (divorce intrigue, Jesuit priests and Gestalt therapists, an illegitimate child or two, dreams of utopia) designed to entertain my teachers I learned the allure and the power of narrative. And I'd spin these tales tirelessly until my stepfather's turquoise Cadillac pulled up to the curb, the horn beckoning me. Kids would be spilling from the doors, chaos dancing around the car—my own little cloud. With a kiss on the cheek the teachers would send me off.

"I loved telling stories, but as a child I never dreamed of being a writer. I was terrible in school. I couldn't spell. Critical essays were simply impossible for me. I thought you had to be smart to be a writer. 'But you are smart,' my mother would say. She knew everything that I was good at and she knew the size of my imagination. For her my lack of interest in school had nothing to do with my intelligence. And as we grew up, to all her daughters she would say, 'You can do anything you want.' She had wanted to be a writer herself, but life got in the way. She wasn't going to let 'life' get in the way of her daughters' lives. As an eight-year-old she was already encouraging me to write a novel. As a 20-year-old, on the basis of a letter

written home from Europe, she was encouraging me to submit work to *The New Yorker*. When I started writing with serious intentions she became my tireless editor, reading my novels so many times she knows them by heart.

"But back to when I was small and bad in school and believing myself not smart enough to be a writer. My father was a writer and he was very smart. From a young age he discouraged his daughters from writing absolutely. He knew well the sacrifice required to succeed. He warned all of us never to be writers. 'It's a miserable profession,' he'd say, as he struggled through some piece of nonfiction that he was working on and that was going badly. He knew the price of long hours of solitude. He'd add realism to his warning, 'The average annual income of a writer is $800 a year.' But when he saw that my interest was serious and when he saw that I was worried because I couldn't spell well, he let me know that spelling wasn't necessary for good writing. 'A copy editor can fix that,' he said. Indeed, he let me know that good writers often couldn't spell. He named Flannery O'Connor as an example—showed to me her letters with all their errors. He said a writer writes. It's a need, a compulsion that trumps everything else. It's like breathing. It is not a choice.

"Thirteen years into writing professionally, into carving out pockets of time, into finding odd corners and empty spaces in which to plant myself and my computer, into finagling finances, into surviving the disappointments and rewards of publishing, into balancing motherhood and artistic drive, I can see quite clearly the weave of belief and compulsion. I love to tell stories. I always have. It's a need, I agree. The imagination with its big ideas for novels and characters floats parallel to my ordinary daily life, somehow both ephemeral and deeply solid, suspended there by my side as a permanent fixture begging me to grab hold of it and make it real."

The narrator of *Bright Angel Time* is Kate Cooper, whose life in New Jersey with her mother, Eve, and geologist father is orderly and unexceptional. When Kate is eight, however, her father abandons the family to live with another woman, and Eve embarks on a relationship with Anton, a larger-than-life gestalt therapist with four children of his own. Kate, her two sisters, and her mother join Anton and his children on a cross-country tour in a turquoise camper. "And we're off: poker, drugs and whiskey; sensitivity training and Esalen; freedom and love and jealousy; religion and the geological history of the American Southwest; crimes and hatreds and deception and lust; the abandonment of family life in favor of family lifestyle — all experienced through the eyes of a funny, intelligent and spiritual child," Sam Sifton wrote for the on-line magazine *Salon* (June

11, 1997). Despite some initial reservations, Sifton was impressed by the novel: "The author's surname is McPhee. Flip the book over and check out the dust jacket photograph of her: classic intelligent-babe pose, lips pursed and glossy, hair long and silken. John McPhee's daughter? Oh, Christ, one thinks at first. . . . Because for every nepotistic bit of recognition afforded to Martha McPhee on the occasion of her debut novel (which is actually quite good), there will be an equal number of unkind shots from the petit literoisie. McPhee's a legacy child on the ivy-trimmed campus of New York publishing (Dad's an institution at the *New Yorker*, with myriad books published by Farrar, Straus & Giroux); it's impossible, standing in the metaphorical quad, to look at her novel and not think she has a lot to prove. But in spite of any initial impulse to sneer, I found *Bright Angel Time* a carefully wrought and intelligent novel—and a pre-adolescent, feminine road novel at that. McPhee somehow manages to align familial dysfunctionality and love against a background of ridiculous early-'70s utopianism. That's difficult work for anyone, and to her credit McPhee pulls it off." Walter Kirn, in an assessment for the *New York Times Book Review* (May 25, 1997), was equally impressed, writing, "At a time when psychological memoirs are the favored literary means of recapturing childhood confusion, Ms. McPhee's novel is a welcome reminder of the power of metaphor—of fiction—to shape and interpret the chaos of early experience. . . . In [the] best scenes—a desert acid trip, a family argument in a roadside diner—events are allowed to speak for themselves, without the benefit of piped-in commentary." He concluded, "Like the current spate of childhood memoirs, [this] is a story of abuse—or at least spectacular neglect. What places it a notch above those other books is its expansive sense of history, of circumstances beyond the purely domestic. . . . [Kate's] intimations of eternity make her something more than an innocent victim, a tabula rasa scarred by cruel adults. She's a shipwrecked child of the universe whose imaginative reach exceeds her mortal grasp."

Gorgeous Lies, which was nominated for a National book Award, revisits Kate and the rest of the blended Cooper-Furey clan years later, as Anton is dying. The book opens, "They loved Anton. Every single one of them. Alice most of all. She was his youngest. Eve loved him. She was his wife. Agnes loved him. She was his ex-wife. Lily loved him. She was his lover. They all loved him. The little beady-eyed preacher woman, the woman who sold ducks, Eve's divorce lawyer who always had a different girl on his arm, the Strange couple from down the road. (That was their name, Strange, and they were strange, with dramatic drawn-out English accents, though they were not English—he a poet and a banker, she an aging actress.) The Furey kids loved him, of course. He was their father. The Cooper girls tried to hate him, but what they really wanted was for him to love them. Love them big and wide and infinitely, like a father. The Cooper girls were not his children. Once, they had all lived at Chardin—all the children, that is. Long ago in the 1970s." A reviewer for *Publishers Weekly* (July 22, 2002) called the book "invigorating if convoluted" and praised McPhee's "offbeat writing style and poetic metaphors." The year that *Gorgeous Lies* was published saw an astonishing display of productivity for the McPhee family. As Martha McPhee told the Barnes & Noble interviewer: "Of all of them I am in awe. The list includes my husband, Mark Svenvold's *Elmer McCurdy: The Life and Strange Afterlife of an American Outlaw* (Basic Books), my sister Jenny McPhee's paperback of her first novel *The Center of Things* (Ballantine Books); my half-sister Joan Sullivan's memoir *An American Voter: My Love Affair with Presidential Politics* (Bloomsbury); my father John McPhee's 25th book of nonfiction, *The Founding Fish* (FSG); [and] my sister Sarah McPhee's work of art historical research, *Bernini and the Belltowers: Architecture and Politics of the Vatican* (Yale University Press)."

McPhee's latest novel, *L'America*, is the story of Beth, an American raised on a commune, and Cesare, a prosperous young Italian: the two meet on an Aegean island and begin a long romance. Calling the book "a sensuous and finely modulated tale," Donna Seaman wrote for *Booklist* (March 1, 2006), "With adroit sleight of narrative hand, McPhee dramatizes cultural contrasts, the unending repercussions of first love, the gradual metamorphosis of the self, the erotics of heartbreak, and the consolation of beauty." Michiko Kakutani, in a review for the *New York Times* (May 30, 2006), found the book less deserving of praise, opining, "Martha McPhee's ungainly new novel, *L'America*, reads like a shotgun wedding between Henry James and Nora Roberts, between James's international theme (probing the tension between American innocence and European sophistication) and the sappy conventions and even sappier language of a romance novel."

McPhee's foray into nonfiction, *Girls: Ordinary Girls and Their Extraordinary Pursuits*, was appreciated by many critics. A young reviewer for the pop-culture magazine *Bust* (on-line) wrote, "Reading *their* [stories] makes me realize that I *have* a story, which I sometimes forget. And in an age when it seems like you're nobody if you aren't on MTV, it's nice to be reminded that just doing your thing, no matter what it is, will make you a star." Similarly, a reviewer for the library journal *VOYA* (on-line) lauded the inclusion of such subjects as "seven-year-old composer-pianist Evelyn Saylor and chess player Khadeejah Gray, to twelve-year-old online investor Stephanie Formas to twenty-year-old environmental activist Kory Arvizu Johnson," and opined, "The photographs are, quite simply, gorgeous. The black-and-white studies of these remarkable young women are the haunting work of Laura McPhee, an award-winning photographer who captures the intensity of each girl's pursuit. Novelists Jenny and Martha McPhee are clearly their father's daughters. They begin each chapter with moving essays that summarize the progress women have made over the years and the doors that have opened for this new generation of motivated girls."

Martha McPhee's work has appeared in *Zoetrope*, the *New Yorker*, *Vogue*, and *Redbook*, among other publications. She teaches creative writing at Hofstra University, in Hempstead, New York.

—S.Y.

Suggested Reading: *Christian Science Monitor* p13 May 6, 1997, p17 Jan. 24, 2001; *Los Angeles Times Book Review* p12 Oct. 6, 2002; *New York Times* (on-line) Apr. 14, 2003; *New York Times Book Review* p9 May 25, 1997; *Publishers Weekly* p107 Sep. 25, 2000; *Times Literary Supplement* p24 June 20, 1997; *Washington Post* C p2 Sep. 2, 2002

Selected Books: fiction—*Bright Angel Time*, 1997; *Gorgeous Lies*, 2002; *L'America*, 2006; nonfiction—*Girls: Ordinary Girls and Their Extraordinary Pursuits* (with J. McPhee and L. McPhee), 2000

Courtesy of Ohio University

Mda, Zakes

(EM-da)

Oct. 6, 1948– Playwright; novelist; poet

Zakes Mda has been acknowledged as one of South Africa's leading voices, writing plays and novels that examine apartheid—the government-sanctioned policy of racial, economic, and social segregation in place there until the 1990s—and its aftermath, as well as broader issues of a more universal scope. Though called a magic realist by many critics, Mda has said that he has not been influenced by such celebrated masters of the genre as the Colombian writer Gabriel García Márquez. His work instead stems from the great oral traditions of South Africa, in which tribal histories are often peppered with magical elements. Though

he is sometimes denounced for being a critic of the new South African government, which, in his opinion, has not carried out needed political reform, Mda believes that the only loyalty he owes as an artist is to deliver compelling, thought-provoking stories to his readers.

The eldest child of five (four boys and a girl), Zakes Mda was born Zanemvula Kizito Gatyeni Mda (an IsiXhosa name that translates to "bringer of rain" or "one who comes with the rain") on October 6, 1948 in the Herschel District of the Eastern Cape Province in South Africa. (The Eastern Cape is a particularly poor, barren area; despite this, it has been home to many of South Africa's leading political figures, including Nelson Mandela, Thabo Mbeki, and Walter Sisulu.) His parents, Ashby Peter Solomzi, a lawyer, and Rose Nompumelelo Mda, a nurse, moved the family to Johannesburg shortly after Mda's birth, and later to Soweto. Mda, who has said he developed his sense of narrative, in part, from the comic books he devoured as a youngster and still loves, returned to the Herschel District to visit his grandparents during school holidays. Eventually his parents, unhappy with the potential for a teenager to get into trouble in Soweto, sent him to school there. His father joined him in Herschel, to set up a law practice.

In addition to being a lawyer, Mda's father, a vocal opponent of apartheid, was a founding member of the African National Council's (ANC) Youth League, which had been formed in 1943, and a founding member of the Pan-African Congress, formed in 1959 as a political-action movement. In the early 1960s he was arrested for his anti-apartheid activities, and when he was released, in 1963, he went into exile in neighboring Lesotho; the rest of the family followed him soon after.

While attending Lesotho's Peska High School between 1965 and 1969, Mda began writing plays. His work, which he wrote in English, took on a polemic tone after he began reading about activist Steve Biko's Black Consciousness Movement, which sought a nonviolent end to white rule. (Mda, at that time, felt most comfortable with English, because he had lost touch with IsiXhosa, his native language, and was not yet proficient in Sesotho, the language used in Lesotho.) Mda was also greatly influenced by such politically aware playwrights as Athol Fugard, Joe Orton, Harold Pinter, Dukuza ka Macu, and Wole Soyinka. He studied at the International Academy of Arts and Letters in Switzerland and in 1976 earned a bachelor of fine arts degree.

Mda's first major play, *We Shall Sing for the Fatherland*, written in 1973 and performed in 1978, won an Amstel Merit Award. Its two main characters are ex-soldiers who find themselves without homes or jobs a decade after their country has achieved independence. His next major play, *The Hill*, whose main characters are veteran workers in a South African gold mine, was written in 1978 and won him Amstel playwright of the year honors in 1980 (although some sources state 1979 or 1983). Those works, along with another play, *Dark Voices Ring*, brought Mda considerable fame in his home country and were collected into the book *We Shall Sing for the Fatherland and Other Plays* (1980). On the strength of the book he was admitted to Ohio University, from which he earned both a master's degree in theater and a master's degree in mass communications. While living in the United States, his play *The Road* (written in 1982), won the 1984 Christina Crawford Award from the American Theater Association.

Mda returned to Africa in 1984 and spent the next year as a program director at Radio Lesotho, in Maseru. He then became a professor at the National University of Lesotho, in Roma, a position he held until 1992. Concurrently, in 1989 Mda earned a doctorate from the University of Cape Town; his dissertation was published in 1993 as *When People Play People: Development Communication through Theater*, which detailed ways in which theater can transmit important information to the illiterate and disenfranchised.

Meanwhile, Mda continued to write plays, primarily about the brutality of apartheid, and earned a measure of international respect and renown. These plays were later collected into two volumes: *The Plays of Zakes Mda* (1990)—which includes *Dead End*, *We Shall Sing for the Fatherland*, *Dark Voices Ring*, *The Hill*, and *The Road*—and *And the Girls in Their Sunday Dresses* (1993)—which includes the titular play (about an anti-apartheid activist and a prostitute who become friends while waiting for food aid to be distributed), *The Final Dance* (a long poem), *Banned* (a radio play), and *Joys of War* (an anti-war piece that has been compared to the work of the German writer Bertolt Brecht). In addition to these works, Mda wrote two additional plays, *The Nun's Romantic Story* (1991) and *The Dying Screams of the Moon* (1992), while serving as a writer in residence at the University of Durham, in England.

In 1995 alone, five of Mda's plays were produced by major South African theater companies over the course of six months—an unprecedented achievement for any South African playwright and especially noteworthy for a black one. In the *Dictionary of Literary Biography* (2000), Bhekizizwe Peterson observed: "What sets his dramatic work apart from other theatrical accounts is Mda's rare acumen to distill from the absurdities and grotesque experiences of apartheid South Africa credible characters whose profound humanity, pathos, and resilience shines whatever the odds stacked against them."

After the end of apartheid, Mda's writing changed in some respects. Whereas previously, his artistic endeavors and the politics of his homeland were indivisible, now he was free to write about more universal aspects of the human condition and to experiment stylistically. "My main mission now is to tell a story, rather than to propagate a political message," Mda told Benjamin Austen for *Harper's* (February 2005). "During apartheid it was the other way around." It was not until after 1994, when the country's first free, multiracial elections were held, signaling a new era in South African history, that Mda produced a novel. He explained to Rebecca L. Weber for africana.com, "During apartheid we didn't really have the luxury to sit down and focus on one piece of work that would take months and months on end to complete. . . . During apartheid, generally, with black writers, we focused on short stories. We focused on plays, and on poems. You see, those are much more immediate. You write a poem because you are going to perform it that afternoon at a funeral or at a street rally. . . . You write a play because there are issues that must be put on the table. Our work was highly political and it was used as a weapon against apartheid." He continued, "So during this period of transition things were more relaxed. There were no longer any demands on us— demands that were imposed by ourselves, as oppressed citizens of South Africa. . . . We could afford now to sit back and write our novels. Today, for the first time in the history of literature in South Africa, you will find more novels than ever before."

Mda's first novel, *Ways of Dying* was published by Oxford University Press in 1995, when Mda was a visiting fellow at Yale University. It has since been translated into many languages. It tells the story of Toloki, a young man who becomes a professional mourner—someone paid to wail and moan over the deceased at funerals. In a review for *Choice* (March 1996), J. Lavieri called the book "a fine debut for Mda as a fiction writer" and opined, "What [the acclaimed novelist and social commentator] Chinua Achebe has done for Nigeria, Mda appears capable of doing for South Africa." In *World Literature Today* (Winter 1996), Brenda Cooper wrote, "Ultimately . . . the novel is about ways of living: the pleasure of cake and onions, of romance, of the commitment to comforting the bereaved and seeking a serious purpose to life in a society battling to undergo change."

Mda's next novel, *She Plays with Darkness*, originally published in 1995, takes place over the course of almost three decades in Lesotho and focuses on the lives of a pair of fraternal twins, Radisene and Dikosha. While Radisene makes his way through life as something of a scam artist (an insurance hustler, his specialty is securing burial contracts before his competitors), his sister, Dikosha, renounces much of the physical world, including marriage, to commune with ancestral spirits through dance. John C. Hawley, in a review for *America* (July 5–12, 2004), wrote, "Like a Greek drama, Mda's conclusion suggests that if a contemporary South Africa is not going to surrender to its recurring tragedies, it will need both aspects of its personality—its world of spirits and stories and dances, and its world of canniness and energetic construction. . . . Mda's novels invite the reader into a strangely atmospheric and surreal world in which actual historical events and, in some cases, actual historical figures, enter the frame of our view and play their part, and time moves along."

In 2002 Mda published his third novel, *The Heart of Redness*. (The title is derived from the fact that the Xhosa of the Eastern Cape traditionally wore clothing dyed with red ocher, which also stained their skin. When missionaries arrived on the Cape, those Xhosa who converted to Christianity began to wear European-style garb and began to refer to the non-converted, whom they considered backwards and unsophisticated, as the Red People.) The novel takes place in Qolorha, a seaside community in South Africa, where the villagers have been feuding for generations over issues of tradition and modernization. Tony Eprile wrote for the *New York Times Book Review* (August 11, 2002), "[This] is a brilliant critique of [the] cult of newness. . . . Mda has responded to South Africa's rapid changes and unpredictable transitions with a work that is itself a new kind of novel: one that combines Gabriel García Márquez's magic realism, social realism, and a critical re-examination of the South African past." In the *New York Review of Books* (January 16, 2003), Norman Rush was more critical, writing, "I sense in Mda an extreme, almost religious impulse to identify with forebears who have, irrationally or not, given up everything in the struggle against an ultimately unstoppable adversary. . . . This brings us . . . to the great omission in Mda's work. . . . The AIDS pandemic is absent, totally absent, here. That's an impossibility. The single greatest threat facing South Africa is not glanced at." He concluded, "With AIDS omitted, Mda has created a novel that is, finally, an escapist dream, a fable more than a parable." Benjamin Austen was dismissive of such assessments of Mda's work and pointed to Rush's review in particular. "It is hard to imagine any present-day American novel being dismissed as inconsequential on the grounds that it did not address the War on Terror, job loss, or the current blight of reality television," Austen wrote. "Novels are generally esteemed for their artistry and their reckoning of the human condition, not for direct assaults on time-bound societal issues."

Mda's next novel was *The Madonna of Excelsior* (2004). In it he weaves a tale based on a notorious South African trial of the early 1970s in which six Afrikaner (white South African) men and 14 black women from the town of Excelsior, in the rural northeastern part of the country, were convicted—under the Immorality Act of 1949—of miscegenation (sexual contact between people of different races). Some of the men involved committed suicide in the wake of the media attention paid to the trial, and Mda had often wondered how the children produced by those unions had fared. He traveled to the village to do research and found most residents reluctant to discuss the incident. "Fortunately I went to a bar," Mda told Weber. "There were some black guys drinking bottles there on the floor. One of them stood up and said, 'Hey, I can help you. In fact, my mother was one of those women. I have a sister as a result of those events.' He took me around [and is] my very close friend now. I stole many things from his life." Mda added, "Of course, he goes around Excelsior now calling himself Viliki [the novel's protagonist]—boasting that it was him in the book!"

The Madonna of Excelsior focuses on one of the accused women, Niki, who has slept with an eminent white farmer, and follows her children— the mixed-race Popi, who becomes a town councillor, and her black half-brother, Viliki, a political activist—into adulthood. A reviewer for the *Economist* (February 28, 2004) called Mda a "marvellous storyteller" and wrote, "His . . . villains are [those] who count not on their ability but on their skin colour to win promotion, and the former leaders of the struggle, now town councillors, who allocate subsidised houses to themselves, their girlfriends, mothers and grandmothers. These are sub-themes in a novel exercised mainly by the interaction between people of different colours as they come to terms with their pasts, presents and futures. Corrupt members of South Africa's new black elite will nonetheless find *The Madonna of Excelsior* makes uneasy bedside reading. So will their white apologists." In a review for *America* (July 5–12, 2004), John C. Hawley wrote, "The real allegory in this novel is represented by the two races that need each other to produce the child that is the new South Africa."

Mda followed *The Madonna of Excelsior* with *The Whale Caller* (2005), a novel set in Hermanus, a coastal South African village, that tells the story of a man who is simply referred to as the Whale Caller. He attracts the attention of Sharisha, a whale who thrashes her tail and joyfully leaps through the air in response to his blowing his kelp horn. The Whale Caller's life becomes complicated and an odd love triangle emerges, when he falls in love with Saluni, the town drunk. "It's worth swallowing this bizarre scenario for the compelling love story that follows between the whale-caller and an equally eccentric drunk, and for the unusual perspective this novel gives on the 'new' South Africa. Mda manages to combine dry humour and social commentary with passionate romance and pagan ritual," Kate Owen noted for the London *Sunday Telegraph* (August 13, 2006). A *Publishers Weekly* (October 24, 2005) reviewer, by contrast, observed, "Mda's unconvincing fifth novel [is] a hodgepodge of allegory, pop psychology, faux naïve diction and occasional references to the new South Africa." The reviewer concluded, "The symbolism at the heart of this novel (the unattainable whale) is pushed so ludicrously far and left so carelessly unmoored to believable characters or real-world specifics that the novel drifts away from the reader."

Zakes Mda, whose next novel, "Cion," is set to be released n the summer of 2007, is married and has five children. In recent years he has taught at the University of Vermont, in Burlington, and the University of Witwatersrand, in Johannesburg.

Though he divides his time between the United States and South Africa and continues to be a prolific writer, he has found time for several additional pursuits. He is an avid beekeeper, the director of the Southern African Multimedia AIDS Trust, a dramaturge at the Johannesburg's Market Theatre, and a serious artist who has mounted several exhibits of his paintings.

—C.M.

Suggested Reading: *America* p25+ July 5–12, 2004; *Choice* p1126+ Mar. 1996; *Economist* p81+ Feb. 28, 2004; *Harper's* p85+ Feb. 2005; *New York Review of Books* p29+ Jan. 16, 2003; *New York Times* p9+ Aug. 11, 2002; *Newsweek* p2 Sep. 9, 2002; (South Africa) *Sunday Times* p17 Oct. 13, 2002

Selected Books: play collections—*We Shall Sing for the Fatherland and Other Plays*, 1980; *The Plays of Zakes Mda*,1990; *And the Girls in Their Sunday Dresses*, 1993; novels—*Ways of Dying*, 1995; *She Plays with Darkness*, 1995; *Heart of Redness*, 2002; *The Madonna of Excelsior*, 2004; *The Whale Caller*, 2005; poetry—*Bits of Debris*, 1986

Menashe, Samuel

Sep. 16, 1925– Poet

Samuel Menashe is sometimes referred to as one of the last bohemian poets, someone who has spurned the traditional road of literary networking and self-promotion and followed his own idiosyncratic tastes. Menashe lives on the fifth floor of a walk-up tenement house in New York City's Greenwich Village, where he crafts his poems the old-fashioned way: not with a computer or typewriter, but with a pen. Although his poems—which are usually very short—have been published over the years in many respectable journals, including the *New Yorker* and the *Times Literary Supplement*, he has had difficulty publishing books of his work. In recent years he has achieved greater recognition, primarily due to the praise and promotion of such fellow writers as Dana Gioia and Billy Collins. In 2005 the Poetry Foundation selected Menashe for the inaugural Neglected Masters Award; the prize included $50,000 and a commitment from the Library of America to publish a volume of his work. As Gioia observed in the introduction to Menashe's *The Niche Narrows: New and Selected Poems* (2000), according to the Poetry Foundation's Web site, "The public career of Samuel Menashe demonstrates how a serious poet of singular talent, power, and originality can be largely overlooked in our literary culture."

Samuel Menashe was born on September 16, 1925 in New York City. His parents, Russian-Jewish immigrants, raised him in the New York City borough of Queens, where his father owned a dry-cleaning and laundry business. Menashe's parents were intelligent people, he explained in an interview with Julie Salamon for the *New York Times* (October 10, 2003, on-line). "It is assumed that immigrant parents means ignorant parents. . . . Part of the American image of your achievement is that you are a self-made man, that you are totally other than your parents rather than you are a continuation."

Menashe studied at Townsend Harris High School, an elite public school. He then attended Queens College, part of the City University of New York, with the idea of eventually becoming a doctor. However, after the U.S. entered World War II, in 1941, he felt compelled to join the army. He enlisted when he turned 18, in 1943. After receiving training at the Infantry School in Fort Benning, Georgia, he was dispatched to Europe. His company, the 87th division, landed in France in 1944 and fought through to Belgium and Germany. They also participated in the Battle of the Bulge, in which his company began fighting one morning with 190 men and ended the day with only 29 men left standing.

Menashe was about 20 years old when the war ended in 1945. He was discharged the next year, unsure of what he was going to do with his life. "When I came back, I heard people talking about what they were going to do next summer," he

Richard M. Gummere/Courtesy of the American Poets
Project

Samuel Menashe

explained to Salamon. "I was amazed that they could talk of that future, of next summer. As a result, I lived in the day. For the first few years after the war, each day was the last day. And then it changed. Each day was the only day."

Between 1946 and 1947 Menashe continued his studies at Queens College under the G.I. Bill; feeling restless, however, he returned to France to study at the Sorbonne, of the University of Paris, from which he received a degree in literature, in 1950. Though he had acquired an interest in becoming a writer, he assumed he would write short stories, not poems. "In my twenty-fourth year—without [foreseeing] it the day before—with no thought of being a poet, I woke up one winter night under the bare windows of my room in Paris," Menashe explained in an interview conducted in January 1984 with Fred Bornhauser, published in *Contemporary Authors*, Volume 115 (1985). "Thrust among the stars by this sudden awakening, I began my first poem, which tells this experience. In my day, one did not decide to be a poet or take courses to become one. One never expected to meet a poet."

Since being a professional poet is not often a lucrative profession, Menashe tried teaching in order to support himself. But he was not suited to life as an academic, so he began working at a number of odd jobs, including stints as a tour-guide director, a French tutor, a waiter, and a poetry lecturer aboard cruise ships. He soon settled in Greenwich Village, where he started to perfect his terse, controlled style of poetry. He specialized in very short poems, many of which were no more than 10 lines long. He was soon being published in a number of respected literary magazines,

including *Harper's*, *Commonweal*, the *Antioch Review*, and the *Yale Review*.

Unfortunately for the struggling young poet, the literary establishment in New York took little interest in his type of short poetry and he was unable to find a publisher willing to put out a book of his work. He decided to visit England in search of prospects, although he had been cautioned that the literary scene there was no better. After spending some months in London, however, he sent his poems to Kathleen Raine, a poet at the University of Cambridge. She passed the manuscript along to a friend, Victor Gollancz, who published it in 1961 under the title *The Many Named Beloved*. Barry Ahearn, in an article for *Twentieth-Century Literature* (Summer 1996), quotes an untitled poem from the collection: "A flock of little boats / Tethered to the shore / Drifts in still water . . . / Prows dip, nibbling." Ahearn praised Menashe's ability to find vitality in this serene image: "To put it simply, we are in the presence of a poem that sees all things as living. We need no longer hunt for invisible energies; to Menashe they are limpidly present."

Despite the favorable response that *The Many Named Beloved* received in England, Menashe had no easier time breaking into the literary establishment in the United States. This was due, in part, to his own unwillingness to do those things that, in the eyes of some critics, are the requirements for achieving success as a poet in America. As Dana Gioia has observed in an essay published on his Web site: "There are, of course, several reasons for Menashe's continuing obscurity. He has lived a bohemian life in an age of academic institutionalism. He has not worked as a teacher, editor, or critic—the common paths to literary visibility. But the major cause of his obscurity, I suspect, is strictly literary. Menashe has devoted his entire poetic career to perfecting the short poem—not the conventional short poem of 20–40 lines beloved of magazine editors, but the very short poem."

Menashe's first book of poetry to be published in America was *No Jerusalem But This* (1971). A collection of short poems meditating on Jewish themes, it received rave reviews. In the *New York Review of Books* (July 22, 1971), Stephen Spender wrote, "Nothing seems more remarkable about . . . [Menashe] than that his poetry goes so little remarked. Here is a poet who compresses thoughts and sensations into language intense and clear as diamonds." Grace Schulman wrote in a review for the *Nation* (March 6, 1972). "Sparse, almost gnomic in their simplicity, the poems are structured in sentences but unpunctuated for the sake of a free conversational flow and images that are not contained. That enables the poet to avoid the monotony such simplicity might otherwise threaten, for the images, unenclosed, seem to explode from the narrow lines."

Menashe had better luck with publishing his books in the early 1970s. *No Jerusalem But This* was followed by another collection, *Fringe of Fire*, in 1973, and a third, *To Open*, in 1974. In the latter collection, the poet wrote of love and friendships, recollections of dreams and his parents, and of his own mortality. Like its predecessors, *To Open* received generally favorable reviews. Writing for the *Christian Science Monitor* (August 28, 1974), Victor Howes proclaimed: "The art of Samuel Menashe is a jeweler's art; his poems are small, precision-cut, gem-like, and give off little sparks and splinters of flame. . . . What impresses in the individual poems is their laser-beam intensity. What impresses in the aggregate is Menashe's scope. He ranges from Japanese haiku to Taoist saying, from Persian proverb to elemental prayer." He concluded, "[Menashe's] inner rhymes, his assonances, his occasional plays upon words make even the simplest-seeming statement a construct to read again with heightened attention." "[Menashe's poems] are spare, strong, and clear. They are also deceptively simple," a reviewer observed for *Choice* (December 1974). "Menashe makes use of rhymes in various combinations, all of which feel natural to eye and ear because the poet communicates with the reader as if he knew him personally. . . . He is a fine artist, to be read for enjoyment and to be admired for craftsmanship."

Menashe's work was subsequently included in various anthologies and textbooks, but he did not publish another book until 1986, when *Collected Poems* was printed by the National Poetry Foundation. The volume assembled some of Menashe's unpublished poetry along with the contents of his three previous collections; it was generally well received by critics. In the *New York Times Book Review* (March 8, 1987), Michael Heller wrote: "Donald Davie, in his short but useful introduction to Mr. Menashe's volume, suggests that the poet's accomplishment is most apparent when his poems approach 'the shape of a conversational utterance, of something one might say.' I would argue that Mr. Menashe's poems are most powerful when they just barely meet our conversational norms. I can't imagine anyone saying the poem entitled 'Dreams,' but I can hear in it a power of poetic form that I hear in no one else."

In 2000 Talisman House Publishers printed *The Niche Narrows: New and Selected Poems*. Several of the collection's poems deal with the themes of death and dying. In one such poem, entitled "At Millay's Grave," Menashe writes, as quoted on the Poem Tree Web site: "Your ashes / In an urn / Buried here / Make me burn / For dear life / My candle / At one end— / Night outlasts / Wick and wax / Foe and friend."

In 2001 the U.S. poet laureate Billy Collins invited Menashe to give a reading at the Library of Congress. Michael Schaffner, in a review of the event for the Big City Lit Web site (December 2001), remarked, "Menashe establishes an immediate and intimate rapport with his audience. This results from no performer's trick, but from the simple presence of his wry, avuncular figure and the puckish glint in his eye. When he speaks, the sound is full, yet gentle, and underscores the deliberate way he summons one of his short pieces from memory, then lays it on the audience like a taste from his drink, or a rare coin he would rather share than keep."

Two years after receiving a $200 million gift from the heiress Ruth Lilly, the Poetry Foundation established the Neglected Masters Award to "bring renewed critical attention to the work of an under-recognized, significant" American poet, according to the foundation's Web site, and Menashe was selected as the first recipient. As part of the prize the Library of America published a collection of his work, *Samuel Menashe: New and Selected Poems* (2005). "The fact that they decided to do this, to recognize what they call neglected masters, is unbelievable," Menashe told Stephen Kinzer for the *New York Times* (October 7, 2004). "After so many years of unsuccessful hunting on the streets of Manhattan, it's pretty great to have a New York publisher."

Samuel Menashe continues to live in the same Greenwich Village apartment in which he has resided for the past several decades. Though the apartment is cluttered with books and papers, it has been described as light and airy, its walls decorated by paintings done by personal friends. When not composing poetry in his apartment, Menashe travels by subway to write in New York City's Central Park. He also gives regular readings at his local public-library branch.

—C.M.

Suggested Reading: *Choice* p370 May 1972, p1,478 Dec. 1974, p1,694 July/Aug. 1987; *Christian Science Monitor* p10 Aug. 28, 1974; *Nation* p314 Mar. 6, 1972; *New York Review of Books* p3 July 22, 1971; *New York Times* (online) Oct. 10, 2003; *New York Times Book Review* p22 Mar. 8, 1987; *Twentieth-Century Literature* p294+ Summer 1996

Selected Books: *The Many Named Beloved*, 1961; *No Jerusalem But This*, 1971; *Fringe of Fire*, 1973; *To Open*, 1974; *Collected Poems*, 1986; *The Niche Narrows: New and Selected Poems*, 2000; *Samuel Menashe: New and Selected Poems*, 2005

Nicolas Asfouri/AFP/Getty Images

Mistry, Rohinton

(MIS-tree, roh-HEEN-
tuhn)

July 3, 1952– Novelist; short-story writer

Several critics, including Brooke Allen, writing for the *Atlantic Monthly* (September 2002) and Eileen Battersby, for the *Irish Times* (June 1, 2002), have placed the Indian-born Canadian writer Rohinton Mistry among the world's greatest living novelists. Mistry's first book—a short-story collection originally titled *Tales from Firozsha Baag* (1987) but published in the U.S. as *Swimming Lessons, and Other Stories from Firozsha Baag* (1989)—established him as a significant new voice in contemporary English fiction. His first novel, *Such a Long Journey* (1991), brought him three major awards and was short-listed for one of the Anglophone world's most important literary honors, the Booker Prize. (Both of his subsequent novels were also near-winners for the Booker.) Commenting on *Such a Long Journey* for the *New York Review of Books* (June 20, 1996), Hilary Mantel wrote that in that book Mistry appeared to "carry a mirror for us down the dusty highways of India, through the jostling Bombay streets, behind compound walls and into the huts and houses where the millions sit, reinventing themselves, constantly reciting the stories of their own lives and times. . . . Human decency came shining through."

Mistry's wealth of finely detailed characters and his ability to meld major historical moments with small-scale dramas have prompted critics to compare the sprawl and scope of his books to those

of such 19th-century novelists as Charles Dickens, Honoré de Balzac, and Leo Tolstoy. Reviewing Mistry's third novel, *Family Matters* (2002), for the *New Yorker* (September 30, 2002), John Updike, one of the writers Mistry admired most when he was growing up in Bombay, attributed to Mistry's fiction "liveliness, precision, weight . . . and the broad sympathy that calls [these qualities] into being." Updike added, "In a world of hurry and quick artistic killing, Mistry has kept the patience to tease narrative and moral interest out of domestic life." While Mistry's fiction has an undeniably tragic tenor—violence, disease, and civic deterioration pervade his books, and his characters often suffer horrible fates—his novels and short stories also frequently take ludic turns.

Now translated into more than 25 languages, Mistry's work might be said to have sprung from his brow whole, much as Athena, the Greek goddess of war, emerged from the brow of Zeus, already armed for battle. Mistry had experienced life—coming of age during a tumultuous period in Indian history, studying mathematics and economics to please his practically minded family, marrying, immigrating to Canada, and working there in a bank—and almost as soon as he sat down to write about it, he began winning awards. "Mistry's talent was waiting for him, educated, confident, and fully formed, when he first conjured it up," Jamie James wrote in the *Atlantic Monthly* (April 2000). James compared Mistry to a person sitting down to play the piano for the first time after merely listening to records and immediately playing as well as the greatest pianist.

Mistry's novels and most of his stories are set in India, which he left in 1975. Asked by Battersby whether he was afraid of losing touch with India by staying away too long, Mistry replied: "No, it is my culture. It is the place where I was born, where I grew up and lived for 23 years of my life. It is the place that shaped my imagination." Not an autobiographical writer in the narrowest sense, Mistry is instead, as Battersby wrote, "more like a medium through which his vibrant, complex stories filter." Battersby continued: "Family is [Mistry's] theme, or perhaps it is not. His preoccupation is life in general rather than in particular—change, the passing of time and the things people not so much do to themselves as permit to happen to them. . . . Mistry succeeds in creating the illusion that he does not manipulate his characters, but is merely reporting on the circumstances they find themselves in. This is a clever, subtle device; his authorial presence is far more intrusive than his gentle art might suggest."

Rohinton Mistry was born on July 3, 1952 in Bombay (now Mumbai), India; he has three brothers and one sister. Mistry's father, Behram, worked in advertising, and his mother, Freny, ran their middle-class home. (Coincidentally, Mistry's wife is also named Freny.) Mistry's family are Parsis. A tiny minority group constituting well under .01 percent of India's population, Parsis practice the monotheistic religion of Zoroastrianism, and in India they have achieved a prominence in society disproportionate to their numbers.

Mistry was educated at Bombay University, where he studied mathematics and economics; in 1975 he received his degree. Alongside these practical pursuits, however, Mistry also wrote and performed music, casting himself, he told Ron Graham for *Toronto Life* (February 1997), as the Bob Dylan of Bombay. "I wasn't much of a rebel," Mistry added. "It was cool to have bell-bottoms and a beard and big hair, and there were some student protests about the running of the university, but I couldn't help seeing it as a watered-down imitation of a rebellion." While still a student Mistry became engaged to Freny Elavia, also a Parsi, and soon after his graduation he left India for Toronto, Canada. (Some sources say Freny preceded him to Toronto and married him there; others say they were married in India). "It was always accepted that there was no future in India," he told Battersby. "In the past we always went to England, it was a tradition. Later this became the US, but the US lost its shine. So for my generation, it was Canada."

In Toronto Mistry took a job as an accounting clerk for the Canadian Imperial Bank of Commerce (better known as CIBC) and later began taking night courses in English and philosophy at the University of Toronto, earning a second bachelor's degree, in 1984. His wife, a teacher, was interested in literature and, growing tired of hearing Mistry say he would like to write, told him he should enter a story in the newly established Hart House Literary Contest, an annual competition held by the *Hart House Review*, a literary magazine associated with the university. He won the contest, in 1983, with what has always been described as the first story he had ever written. The following year he repeated his success, and at the end of 1985, with the financial help of his wife and a grant from the Canada Council for the Arts, he put his career at the bank behind him and began writing full-time.

Mistry's first book, published in Canada as *Tales from Firozsha Baag* and in the U.S. as *Swimming Lessons, and Other Stories from Firozsha Baag*, won him immediate recognition. The 11 stories in the book are set primarily in an imaginary slice of Parsi-dominated Bombay called Firozsha Baag, among the residents of which is Kersi, a recurring character in the collection who seems to serve as a stand-in for the author. In the last story in the collection, "Swimming Lessons"—considered by many critics to be book's finest tale—Kersi, now an immigrant living in Toronto, sends a copy of his collection of short stories back to Bombay for his parents, whose responses differ. His mother believes that Kersi must miss Bombay terribly, because he writes about it instead of his present reality, while his father feels pleased that his son has achieved "artistic distance."

Reviews for the collection were almost uniformly positive, with many of them suggesting that the book announced the arrival of a major writer. Perhaps the only negative comments about the collection came from Janette Turner Hospital, in a nonetheless largely positive critique for the *Los Angeles Times Book Review* (March 5, 1989). While arguing that "there are cultural nuances in Bombay that Mistry conveys with the skill of a master" and that "he conveys sparsely and powerfully the tug of war between compassion and the survival instinct," Hospital also contended that Mistry occasionally employed "heavy-handed symbolism" and that the final story contained a number of what she characterized as "extremely sexist observations about women." Nancy Wigston, writing for the Toronto *Globe and Mail* (May 2, 1987), offered a more typical assessment: "Behind the crumbling walls of Firozsha Baag, Mistry shows much of what is admirable and pitiable in human nature. His writing is moving and comic, and he leaves behind a tangible closeness to this 'foreign' milieu. We can only be grateful that this extraordinarily talented young writer has been moved to share the flavor of his memories with his new neighbors." Michiko Kakutani, in an assessment for the *New York Times* (February 3, 1989), quoted a passage in the book in which one character, Jehangir, comments on another, Nariman, a storyteller: "Jehangir said that Nariman sometimes told a funny incident in a very serious way, or expressed a significant matter in a light and playful manner. And these were only two rough divisions, in between were lots of subtle gradations of tone and texture. Which, then, was the funny story and which the serious? Their opinions were divided, but ultimately, said Jehangir, it was up to the listener to decide." Kakutani added: "The same description might well be applied to these tales." The collection was short-listed for the 1987 Canada Council for the Arts Governor General's Award for best fiction.

The setting for Mistry's first novel, *Such a Long Journey*, is another Bombay apartment complex inhabited largely by Parsis. The chief character, Gustad Noble, is an ill-paid bank clerk who remembers a more prosperous time and struggles to maintain dignity and some joy for himself and his family. Gustad achieves perhaps his only triumph when he gets a street artist to paint a galaxy of saints, gods, and prophets of every religion on a wall outside the apartment building. Formerly treated as a public urinal, the wall is then treated as a shrine—until it is destroyed for a road-widening project. The last event, the result of government corruption rather than necessity, is only one of the many ways in which the political troubles facing India in the early 1970s find their way into the novel. Among the others is India's intervention into a war within Pakistan, a conflict that led, in 1971, to the former province of East Pakistan declaring independence and becoming Bangladesh.

"Against this tragic backdrop," Robert DiAntonio opined for the *Jerusalem Post* (May 8, 1991), "Rohinton Mistry writes one of the most powerful and intriguing novels of recent memory." For Richard Eder, writing for the *Los Angeles Times Book Review* (April 21, 1991), "*Such a Long Journey* . . . is authentically Dickensian." The novel, Eder added, "can be garish and contrived, and indulgent and self-indulgent in the marshaling of its story, but its major characters and some of its minor ones are unforgettable and deeply and broadly moving. That is, as they individually move us, their world moves and cracks around them." James Wood, writing for the London *Guardian* (February 28, 1991), called *Such a Long Journey* "a first novel of brilliance and galloping comedy." Wood declared that what was most impressive about the novel is "that in it the world . . . appears as a wonder. Bombay surges and clamours, it presses in on the novel's hero, Gustad Noble. Gustad finds this world oppressive, exhausting, but wondrous. Mistry fills his pages with description. First, because such describing is a joy (and a joy to the reader). Second, because his novel strives to explain the labour-pains of a country born into premature modernity. Mistry's Bombay is in a state of comic decay. . . . It is a rare pleasure to read a contemporary novel with such faith in the patient accumulation of narrative evidence. Gustad, for instance, is offered to us in all his foolish, but also strangely heroic complexity. By the end of the novel, we understand his stubbornness and insouciant trust in others." In addition to being short-listed for the Booker, *Such a Long Journey* won the Governor General's Award (1991), the Commonwealth Writers Prize for best book (1992), and the Smithbooks/Books in Canada First Novel Award (1991; now called the Amazon.ca/Books in Canada First Novel Award). A film version of the story, directed by Sturla Gunnarsson, was released in Canada in 1998.

The main characters of Mistry's next novel, *A Fine Balance* (1995), are Dina Dalal, a youngish Parsi widow who has set up a tailoring shop in her living room in order to remain independent and avoid remarriage; Maneck, Dina's tenant, a Parsi college student from a remote village; and Ishvar and his nephew Omprakash, two Dalit tailors who work as her assistants and live in the apartment as well. (Dalits, more often referred to in the West as untouchables, are a group of well over 100 million Indians who are considered by Hindu tradition to be less than human because they are employed in various proscribed professions. In the past and to varying degrees at present, a Dalit who so much as cast a shadow on someone of higher caste—or more precisely, someone who had a caste, since untouchables are considered to be without caste—was thought to have polluted that person.) Dina's private troubles are mirrored by a host of public ones, most brought on by the corrupt administration of Prime Minister Indira Gandhi, who in 1975, having been convicted of electoral

fraud by the High Court of Allahbad, declared a state of emergency and, together with her son Sanjay, began brutally suppressing all opposition, while at the same time waging what amounted to a war against the country's poor—a plan that included the forced sterilization of thousands.

In *A Fine Balance* the confluence of these private and public woes means that many of the characters in Mistry's book meet terrible ends. Elaine Kalman Naves asked Mistry during an interview for the Montreal *Gazette* (November 11, 1995) whether he knew from the outset "the overwhelmingly tragic way the book would end." Mistry answered: "I half knew it. I knew I wanted to write about 1975 when the Emergency was declared. It lasted about 18 months but it was a horrific time which could have been 18 years for the people who were affected by it. When you're dealing with such a grim situation, you know you can have humor. . . . it's essential of course, it's what gets us through it all, but the basic nature of the book would be about the tragedies that took place during those 18 months—there was no way around it."

Tom Adair, writing for *Scotland on Sunday* (March 3, 1996), described the book's final sections, when the surviving characters are reunited nearly a decade after the main events of the story, as "three successive, brilliantly written, unforgettably poignant scenes, portraying irretrievable loss, a trampled dream, and defiant love across the barricades of caste. Then, an unexpected stroke of Tolstoyan dimensions strikes through the action. Surprising but apt, it knells to a close a novel of equally Tolstoyan force. The book's final sound is not one of anguish, but of laughter . . . the final echo in a book which will live and linger in the mind of anyone wise enough to read it and keep it at hand. A major achievement." A reviewer for the *Financial Times* (March 30, 1996) argued that the fine balance the characters seek is that "between hope and despair," adding: "The problem facing the main characters—and by inference all Indians—is how do they survive in this madhouse? Mistry contends that the principal bulwarks against the violence and insanity of Indian life were patterns of kith and kinship—close, warm, loving relations between family and friends. And the worse the situation, according to Mistry, the greater the loyalty and friendship." Brooke Allen noted Mistry's "keenly developed feeling for the absurd: there is hardly a page in all of his fiction that isn't funny on one level or another. What makes the final pages of *A Fine Balance* heartbreaking is not that we see the protagonists' lives so hideously diminished but that in spite of it all they are still laughing." *A Fine Balance* won the 1995 Giller Prize, one of Canada's most prestigious literary awards; the 1996 Commonwealth Writers Prize for best book; the Royal Society of Literature's 1996 Winifred Holtby Award for regional literature; and the 1997 Los Angeles Times Book Prize for fiction. It was short-listed for the Booker Prize, the International IMPAC Dublin Literary Award, and the Irish Times International Fiction Award, as well. The novel experienced a dramatic increase in sales—some press reports described a tenfold rise in the number of copies in print—after it was selected, in November 2001, by Oprah Winfrey for her television book club.

Mistry wrote his next novel, *Family Matters,* from the perspective of Nariman Vakeel, a retired professor of English. Nariman has given over his apartment in a building named Chateau Felicity to his stepchildren, Jal and Coomy Contractor, the son and daughter, respectively, of the widow he married because his Parsi family would not approve his union with a Christian woman. Charged with taking care of Nariman in his old age, the children turn out to be ungracious in the extreme. When Nariman, already weakened by Parkinson's disease, becomes disabled by a fall, Jal and Coomy find a pretext to dump the old man on his only daughter, Roxana, and her husband, Yezad, and their three children, all of whom live in a two-room flat in an area dubbed Pleasant Villa. "All this unfolds against a mid-1990's Bombay that is . . . stewing in corruption," John Sutherland observed for the *New York Times Book Review* (October 13, 2002). "Is the city being destroyed by sectarianism . . . or by the general push and pull of a bustling, heterogeneous society?" The book "gives no easy answer" to such a question, Sutherland wrote, adding: "Occasionally Mistry celebrates Bombay's cultural diversity. . . . But the more pervasive image of the city is of gangsterism, cronyism, impervious bureaucracy, destitution and decay—a landscape of 'crumbling plaster, perforated water tanks and broken drain pipes.' This is an India to escape from, not an India to reform." Shashi Tharoor, writing for the *Washington Post Book World* (October 27, 2002), called the book "wonderful" and noted that its title "can be read both ways: It concerns family matters, and it is founded on the essential premise that families matter." In an otherwise overwhelmingly positive review, Tharoor did detect "a few flaws: some minor characters whose two-dimensionality seems unworthy of Mistry's skills; a dramatic event or two that he does not do enough to rescue from contrivance; the occasional lapse into over-explication. . . . And there is a gratuitous side-swipe about Indian authors writing 'magic-realist midnight muddles' [a reference to Salman Rushdie and his revered novel *Midnight's Children* (1980)] that a wiser editor might have persuaded Mistry to excise." Tharoor concluded: "But these are minor failings in a superb work that confirms Rohinton Mistry's reputation as a novelist of the highest quality." Short-listed for the 2002 Booker Prize, Mistry was passed over in the end—fellow Canadian Yann Martel won with *Life of Pi* (2001)— but *Family Matters* did take the Kiriyama Prize for Asian and Pacific Rim fiction in 2002 and the Canadian Authors Association Award for fiction in 2003.

In late 2002, while touring the U.S. to give readings and speak to journalists as part of a tour to support *Family Matters,* Mistry cut his trip in half and abruptly returned to Canada after being repeatedly subjected to additional security checks of a sort that are supposed to be random. "'Random' in quotation marks," Mistry told Judy Lightfoot for the *Seattle Post-Intelligencer* (November 6, 2002). "My wife and I were cheerfully told, on our first flight, that we had been selected for a random check. We thought, 'Oh, what luck.' But then it happened every single flight, 100 percent."

In December 2003 Mistry's agent announced that the author had signed a contract for a new book, though no information about its subject matter or date of publication was given. In 2004 Mistry was awarded $225,000 by the Pierre Elliott Trudeau Foundation for his contributions to public policy, making him the first person from outside academia ever to be named a Trudeau Fellow.

For 18 years Rohinton Mistry lived with his wife, Freny, in Brampton, a suburb of Toronto, but they have since moved elsewhere in Ontario. He refused to divulge to Judy Stoffman, writing for the *Toronto Star* (March 31, 2002), exactly where, because in the past he has been overwhelmed by fans visiting his home. "You'd be surprised the ways people have of finding where you live," he told Stoffman. Though clearly critical in some ways of his adopted home, Mistry described Canada to Eileen Battersby as "a good place to live, a good place to write."

In an article for *Time* (April 22, 1996), the noted writer Pico Iyer opined, "The field of candidates for the title of Great Indian Novelist is as crowded these days as for its American equivalent, but few have caught the real sorrow and inexplicable strength of India, the unaccountable crookedness and sweetness, as well as Mistry."

—S.Y.

Suggested Reading: *Atlantic Monthly* p126+ Apr. 2000, p165+ Sep. 2002; *Economist* R p14 Apr. 20, 1996; *Financial Times* Books p11 Mar. 30, 1996; *Irish Times* p53 June 1, 2002; *Jerusalem Post* May 8, 1991; (London) *Guardian* Feb. 28, 1991; *Los Angeles Times Book Review* p2 Mar. 5, 1989, p3 Apr. 21, 1991; *Maclean's* p54 Apr. 22, 2002; *Meanjin* p210+ Vol. 54, No. 2, 1995; (Montreal) *Gazette* H p1 Nov. 11, 1995; *New York Review of Books* (on-line) June 20, 1996; *New York Times* C p32 Feb. 3, 1989; *New York Times Book Review* p7 Oct. 13, 2002; *New Yorker* p140+ Sep. 30, 2002; *Scotland on Sunday* p13 Mar. 3, 1996; *Time* p90 Apr. 22, 1996; (Toronto) *Globe and Mail* May 2, 1987; *Toronto Life* p64+ Feb. 1997; *Toronto Star* D p3 Mar. 31, 2002; *Washington Post Book World* T p5 Oct. 27, 2002; *World Literature Today* p239+ Spring 1999

Selected Books: short fiction—*Tales from Firozsha Baag*, 1987 (published in the U.S. as *Swimming Lessons, and Other Stories from Firozsha Baag*, 1989); novels—*Such a Long Journey*, 1991; *A Fine Balance*, 1995; *Family Matters*, 2002

Moriarty, Laura

Dec. 24, 1970– Novelist

Laura Moriarty's debut novel, *The Center of Everything* (2003), marked a fresh departure from the standard coming-of-age story, which is considered by some critics to be an over-used convention. It earned Moriarty considerable admiration among publishing professionals, who lauded her ability "to get into the heads of young people, retaining their innocence, while at the same time understanding that their optimism may not evolve into happiness," in the words of Leigh Haber, an editor at Hyperion, as quoted by Natalie Danford for *Publishers Weekly* (January 27, 2003). (The novelist Laura Moriarty is not to be confused with the poet nor the legal-issues writer who both share her name.)

Laura Eugenia Moriarty was born on December 24, 1970, in Honolulu, Hawaii, one of four daughters. (She does not use her middle name professionally, adding somewhat to the confusion surrounding the trio of writers named Laura Moriarty.) She grew up in a military family and spent much of her childhood in the western and southeastern U.S., particularly in Montana, and eventually settled with her family in the small town of Bozeman. At age 17 Moriarty left Montana to attend the University of Kansas, in Lawrence. After initially planning a career in medicine, Moriarty became interested in writing while enrolled in a study-abroad program at the University of Malta. "I thought I wanted to go to medical school, so I signed up to take all these organic chemistry and physiology classes. . . . I couldn't keep up. I dropped out in February, and I needed money. . . . The only job I could get was an illegal one, working at a bar. I don't know anything about mixed drinks, and I don't speak Maltese. I think I was supposed to stand behind the bar [and] be American and female and smile, but I ended up squinting at people a lot, so eventually, I was in the back doing dishes. That was the year I started writing," she told an interviewer for the Barnes and Noble Web site.

After abandoning her medical studies, Moriarty specialized in social work and received, in 1993, a bachelor's degree from the University of Kansas. Two years later she became a graduate student in English at the same institution. Her reading of the English classics, along with her position as a teaching assistant in undergraduate writing classes, helped to hone her creative-writing skills. Moriarty earned her Master of Arts degree, in 1999, and entered the university's Ph.D. program. A few months after she had begun, finding that the rigors of pursuing a doctorate were not conducive to her writing, she applied for the George Bennett Fellowship for creative writing at Phillips Exeter Academy, a renowned boarding school in New Hampshire. She was awarded the fellowship, and during the 2000–01 academic year, she completed the novel in New Hampshire by maintaining a well-organized schedule that consisted of four hours of writing and four hours of reading each day. At the end of her fellowship, Moriarty moved to Portland, Maine, and worked as a social worker, until Hyperion Books gave her a $400,000 advance for her novel.

The Center of Everything is set during the 1980s in the fictional Kerrvill, a small town in rural Kansas. It takes its title from the locale; Moriarty wrote in the novel, "If you look at a map of the world, the United States is usually right in the middle, and Kansas is in the middle of that. So right here where we are, maybe this very stretch of highway we are driving on, is the exact center of the whole world, what everything else spirals out from." The narrator is Evelyn Bucknow, who is 10 years old as the book opens. Evelyn is caught between her religious-minded grandmother, Eileen, and her single, unemployed mother, Tina, who becomes pregnant following an affair with her married boss and gives birth to a severely disabled boy. Mameve Medwed, writing for the *Boston Globe* (August 24, 2003), described *The Center of Everything* as "beautifully evocative" and compared the story's narrator to such classic literary characters as Scout Finch of Harper Lee's *To Kill a Mockingbird* and Holden Caulfield of J. D. Salinger's *The Catcher in the Rye*. "Evelyn's voice," she concluded, "illuminates the most mundane observations, turning the ordinary extraordinary. As the child nears adulthood, her intelligence so widens and transcends her horizon that the reader, like Evelyn Bucknow herself, is not in Kansas anymore." Janet Maslin wrote for the *New York Times* (June 30, 2003), "[This] debut novel has the makings of something wearily familiar: the Midwestern mother-daughter coming-of-age story. . . . Happily, Ms. Moriarty's artful, enveloping book is a lot more interesting than its genre initially suggests. It traces not only stormy adolescence, but also the essential stages of Evelyn's moral and intellectual evolution. The author makes fine use of simple, small-town events, refracting and re-examining them through Evelyn's changing perceptions."

Not all of the reviews were congratulatory however. Barbara Quick, writing for the *San Francisco Chronicle* (July 13, 2003, on-line), called the novel "a work of only modest accomplishment that frequently teeters over the chasm of banality. . . . The problem with this book [is] it's sanitized and it's all on the surface. We never get inside the characters enough to feel convinced of their uniqueness and humanity. Tina is a sugar-coated version of the bad mom, not bad enough to be a downer. Evelyn's best friend and romantic rival never comes across as anything more than a dumb bunny. The boy they both want to marry is a cipher with dreamy eyes and curly hair. Evelyn somehow manages to go through puberty in the book without ever mentioning it at all."

Since it was first published, *The Center of Everything*, which had an initial printing of 100,000 copies, has been translated into French and Croatian. Moriarty's book was also chosen as a main selection of the Book-Of-The Month Club and the Literary Guild. The novel was featured as

a *USA Today* Summer Reading Pick, a Book Sense Top 10 Pick and a Barnes and Noble Book Club feature title. Moriarty, whose next novel, "The Rest of Her Life," is scheduled to be published in August 2007, lives in Lawrence, Kansas, with her husband and daughter.

—P.B.M./B.M.

Suggested Reading: *Boston Globe* D p7 Aug. 24, 2003; *New York Times* p18 July 12, 2003; *Orlando Sentinel* F p10 Aug. 3, 2003; *Publishers Weekly* p130 Jan. 27, 2003; *San Francisco Chronicle* (on-line) July 13, 2003

Selected Books: *The Center of Everything*, 2003

Judy Natal/Courtesy of Graywolf Press

Mullen, Harryette Romell

July 1, 1953– Poet

"I think that I have always felt that what I wrote was somewhere between what I heard and what I read," the poet Harryette Romell Mullen told Elisabeth A. Frost in an interview for *Contemporary Literature* (Fall 2000). As an African-American growing up in still-segregated areas of the country, much of what Mullen heard was gospel music and hymns along with the language of the people around her—a mix of everyday speech from the children she played and went to school with and her family's own studiously precise brand of English. Mullen has also long been devoted to the written word, an attachment she relates to her family's deep love of

books. "All my immediate relatives had jobs that required literacy—teaching and preaching, doing office work, or doing social work. There was the street or the playground on one hand and home, school, church, and books on the other. There are always different camps." Dense with allusions and wordplay and strongly informed by her background in literary theory, Mullen's poetry speaks to an unusually broad audience for a contemporary poet, especially one drawn to the techniques and ideology of experimental poetry. "Some of this experimental poetry seems to be only for the inner inner circle—the poet's poets," Mullen told Alyson Ward for the *Fort-Worth Star-Telegram* (November 17, 2002). Mullen added: "I'm trying to go away from the little tiny circle in the middle and go out into those outer concentric circles. With each book, I learn a little bit more how to do that." Mullen has published several collections of poetry, winning particular praise for *Trimmings* (1991), *S*PeRM**K*T* (1992), *Muse & Drudge* (1995) and *Sleeping with the Dictionary* (2002). This last won her a spot as a finalist for three of the country's top prizes for poetry, the Los Angeles Times Book Prize, the National Book Critics Circle Award, and the National Book Award.

Harryette Romell Mullen was born on July 1, 1953 in Florence, Alabama, one of two children, both girls, of James Otis Mullen and Avis Ann Mullen, who met and married while students at Talladega College, a historically African-American institution located about 80 miles north of Montgomery. Mullen's grandfathers and great-grandfathers were Baptist ministers; another grandfather was a printer; and both her grandmothers taught school, as did Mullen's mother. After Mullen's parents divorced, Mullen's mother bore primary responsibility for raising the children, a burden that meant Mullen and her sister "always knew we had to be quiet and entertain ourselves," she told Hogue. Deeply committed to education, Mullen's mother—who went on to earn a doctoral degree at the University of Texas, at Austin, the year after Mullen received her bachelor's—carefully policed her daughters' way of speaking, pushing them closer to the style of English popularly identified at that time with educated whites. Her mother and grandmother's deep religious devotion also meant that, though her mother had one time played in a school band with the great jazz saxophonist Ornette Coleman, she restricted her children's exposure to music that did not stray too far from religious hymns and gospel, leaving her daughter to develop an appreciation for the blues and other secular musical forms only later in life.

At some point in her early childhood Mullen's father moved to Chicago, Illinois, and when she was about three or four, Mullen, her sister, and her mother took up residence in Fort Worth, Texas. At first the family lived in an almost entirely African-American neighborhood, where their way of speaking made them seem "seditty or dicty or proper," as Mullen told Calvin Bedient for a special issue of the journal *Callaloo* (Vol.19, No. 3, 1996) devoted to her and her work. Speaking of the same situation in an interview with Cynthia Hogue for *Postmodern Culture* (January 1999, on-line), Mullen said, "We were segregated in a black community!" The Spanish used by her neighborhood's one Mexican American family added a further touch of linguistic complexity that, augmented by studying Spanish later in life, often finds its way into Mullen's work. When Mullen was about 11 years old, the family moved within Fort Worth and became the first African-Americans in their new neighborhood. "The next door neighbors packed overnight bags and went to a motel so that they would not have to spend a single night next to us," Mullen told Bedient. "Another neighbor used to let his German Shepherd dog out to chase my sister and me while we rode our bicycles to the Book Mobile" Mullen has also recalled neighbors vandalizing her family's lawn and breaking a window with a rock. The dislocation Mullen felt in her new home was deepened by a certain rootlessness that she felt because her home, her school, and her church were, though within Fort Worth, in different neighborhoods.

Mullen began reading before she entered school and was writing from an early age—"since I could hold a pencil," she told Hogue. Part of the impulse was practical, since the distance separating her from her father meant that writing was her primary way of keeping in touch with him, but she and her sister also wrote and illustrated stories and poems simply to pass the time. Mullen also experimented with crafting her own alphabet and even attempted to make up an entire language, having been impressed by the so-called Elvish languages J.R.R. Tolkien elaborately created for his fantasy novels *The Lord of the Rings*. She published her first poem while she was still in high school. Dutifully written to fulfill a school assignment, this early poem of Mullen's was entered into a competition by the teacher who assigned it and, after winning, appeared in a local newspaper. Still, Mullen imagined she would become a teacher like her mother and grandmothers and treated writing more like a hobby. At the University of Texas, at Austin, Mullen studied English and worked on the main student newspaper, the *Daily Texan*, writing editorials "on race subjects usually," as she told Hogue, and at a sister publication that focused on issues affecting African-American called *Black Print*.

In the absence of a coherent African-American studies curriculum, Mullen took classes in African and Afro-Caribbean literature, as well as African-American folklore. Taught by a white professor and with Mullen as the only African-American in the room, the folklore class made Mullen feel "alienated," she told Frost, "because the folklore that I knew was the folklore that you know if you go to church, if you are on the school playground, if you are leading a very sheltered, lower-middle-class life in a black community. And the folklore that was being taught was collected in prisons, pool halls, or on the street corners. It was the lore of the men on the streets. No wonder I didn't understand it." At the same time, the university's active African-languages department allowed Mullen to hear a number of important African and African diaspora writers read their work, while friends who were writers kept her in touch with local poetry readings. After trying her hand at reading her own work one night, Mullen started to take her writing more seriously and began publishing her poems as early as 1976, the year after she earned her degree. Between 1975 and 1978 Mullen worked as an instructor at Austin Community College, and from 1978 to 1981 she served as a visiting writer and workshop leader in the Texas Commission on the Arts' Artists in Schools Program.

Mullen's first collection of poetry, *Tree Tall Woman*, was published in 1981. In her interview with Hogue, Mullen said that she thought this book was "really about relations among black people, whether it's family or intimate relationships or just being in the world as a person who has a particular perspective, but it was not having continually to point out that I was writing from a black perspective. That was just part of the work." The aesthetic Mullen describes here was a reflection of and a response to one of Mullen's primary influences, the Black Arts Movement, itself an outgrowth of the civil rights and Black Power movements. Describing to Hogue some of the aspects of the Black Arts Movement that influenced her, Mullen singled out "the idea that there was a black culture and that you could write from the position of being within a black culture." Similarly, in a 1997 interview with Farah Griffin, Michael Magee, and Kristen Gallagher, available on the University of Buffalo Web site, Mullen argued that "all of that sixties activism had to do with black people saying, well, you know, we have been here a long time and we're still not really here, so we need to build something of our own. . . . This was a time when large numbers of black people said, 'We've been beating on this wall for so long, but it's still there. We need to just turn elsewhere and create something for ourselves, and create an alternate identity that has to do with being black and does not necessarily have to do with joining the rest of America.' And I think that was very important, I think it was useful, I think it was a moment of clarity." (The movement also influenced a writer of an earlier generation, Gwendolyn Brooks, pushing Brooks to write verse that was more obviously engaged with the political world; Mullen has often cited Brooks as a fundamental influence for her work.)

In the last 10 years, though, Mullen has cast doubt on some of her early ways of thinking about black culture and language—ways of thinking shared to some degree by other writers involved in the Black Arts Movement. In her early work, she told Hogue, "I felt I knew what it was to write in a black voice and it meant a sort of vernacularized English. I think that it's much more complicated than that." In her interview with Griffin, Magee, and Gallagher, Mullen applied her altered perspective more specifically to Tree Tall Woman, telling them that her work in that book was "very much in the tradition of the 'authentic voice.' Most of those poems have a persona who speaks from the black family, from the black community, with a certain idea of who was a black person. Without even consciously thinking about it, I suppose I more or less assumed a black person was someone with Southern roots and someone who ate collard greens and someone who was probably a Protestant. Once I left the South, I had to rethink all of that." In a 1999 interview with Christopher Myers for the magazine Index (on-line), she identified the voice she used in Tree Tall Woman as the one her mother put on to mock Mullen and her sister's occasional use of so-called African-American dialect, as distinct from so-called Standard English.

By fall 1983 Mullen had moved to California, where she joined the University of California, at Santa Cruz, as a graduate student in literature. In 1987 she earned her M.A.; three years later she earned her Ph.D., with a dissertation entitled "Gender and the Subjugated Body: Readings of Race, Subjectivity, and Difference in the Construction of Slave Narratives." (A revision of the dissertation was scheduled to be published by Cambridge University Press in 1999 as Freeing the Soul: Race, Subjectivity, and Difference in Slave Narratives, and the book is listed on several bibliographies; however, no record of it appears in the Library of Congress and, according to the on-line database WorldCat, only three libraries in the world list it in their catalogs, two of which give the year of publication as 1997.)

Mullen continued writing poetry in graduate school and gradually came under the influence of a group of writers in nearby San Francisco who were associated with an avant-garde school of writing called language poetry (sometimes rendered as L=A=N=G=U=A=G=E P=O=E=T=R=Y). Generally eschewing narrative, meditation, and clear subject matter in favor of re-imagining language by means of unorthodox, even willfully nonsensical syntax that sometimes grew out of word games or collage, language poetry also dovetailed to some degree with the type of literary theory—especially feminist theory—that Mullen studied while working on her Ph.D. At the same time, Mullen began developing an interest in the work of the early-20th-century writer Gertrude Stein, principally the collection of prose pieces Tender Buttons: Objects, Food, Rooms (1914) and less directly the novella "Melanctha: Each One As She May," which first appeared in Stein's Three Lives (1909). Often written in sentences that might be syntactically simple but are nonetheless difficult to comprehend, Stein's work had at first thwarted even as devoted a reader as Mullen. "I remember . . . thinking," she told Hogue, "'I can't read this! I can't understand it!' I felt frustrated but it was intriguing. I thought, 'She acts like she thinks she knows what she's doing.'" Eventually, with more time and a stronger graduate education under her belt, Mullen learned to appreciate Stein's "elegance," as she told Hogue. "By using words and the syntactical structures over and over again—often there's a series, a list, and the only punctuation is periods and commas—she is boiling down language to the absolute, essential elements. I began to understand that that was a different way to use language, a way of using language that forces the reader either to throw it down, or else if you stick with it, to enter another subjectivity." In 1988 Mullen moved to Ithaca, New York, where she worked as an instructor at Cornell University, and two years later—the same year that she earned her doctorate—she became an assistant professor.

In 1991 Mullen published her second book, a collection of short prose poems called Trimmings. A striking departure from Tree Tall Woman, Trimmings was inspired in both method and subject by Stein's Tender Buttons. Both books share an affection for simple words and lists and are suffused by a lightly handled but intense eroticism. Mullen told Barbara Henning in an exchange of letters published on the Web site for the Poetry Project of St. Mark's Church in-the-Bowery (in the East Village neighborhood of New York City)—that the poems in Trimmings were generated in part by making lists—initially of "words referring to anything worn by women" and then a series of lists inspired by those words. In some instances Mullen rewrites Stein's earlier text, expanding it to include a more direct discussion of race, as well as male-female sexual encounters. Taking up one of Stein's most famous "objects" in

Tender Buttons, "A Petticoat"—which reads, in its entirety, as Frost transcribes it for the interview with Mullen that she published, "A light white, a disgrace, an inkspot, a rosy charm"—Mullen recast it as: "A light white disgraceful sugar looks pink, wears an air, pale compared to shadows standing by. To plump recliner, naked truth lies. Behind her shadow wears her color arms full of flowers. A rosy charm is pink. And she is ink. The mistress wears no petticoat or leaves. The other in shadow, a large, pink dress."

In an afterward titled "Off the Top," Mullen wrote, "*Trimmings* was for me a way to think about women and language." The book's first reviewers seemed to pick up on both these ideas and Mullen's indebtedness to Stein. In the *Antioch Review* (Winter 1993), Molly Bendall noted Stein's influence but wrote that Mullen "brings her own contemporary African American female voice to these poems." Bendall concluded, "These wonderfully sparkling variations turn our language over and inside out in a postmodern mode (very vogue) and, as fancy as songs and jazz riffs, they stay seamless. We become infatuated and caught up in the music while still coming away asking ourselves, What are these trimmings we're trimmed with? What are these trappings we're trapped in?" In the *Women's Review of Books* (February 1993), Elisabeth Frost offered similarly emphatic praise: "Mullen puts on language like clothing, implying that women 'put on' identity like items of dress. These relationships among femininity, clothes and language are beautifully orchestrated in word-play that dramatizes complex issues about gender and culture without offering easy or predictable answers." Eileen Myles offered more qualified praise in a November 1991 review in the *Voice Literary Supplement*. Acknowledging that she increasingly appreciated Mullen's book the more she read it, Myles wrote that Mullen's use of prose rather than verse implied "a universe of real objects, each one serving a different need. If longer, perhaps, their resemblances would grow. As they stand, these trimmings are an imaginary wardrobe. As readers we look for the hook that makes them work, supplying the narrative, which is our part of the game."

S*PeRM**K*T was published in 1992. Like *Trimmings*, *S*PeRM**K*T* grows in part out of Mullen's love of Stein, moving, as Mullen and many critics have noted, from the "objects" of her second book to "food." This interest is hinted at in the book's title, which reads like a neon sign for a supermarket with the *u*, *a*, *r*, and *e* burnt out. "In a way, you can think of that as 'you are what you eat,'" Mullen told Emily Ann Williams in an interview for the *African American Review* (Winter 2000). The book, she explained to Williams, is a way of "looking at the supermarket as a kind of synecdoche of consumer culture. It is also a world of language, because everything in the supermarket is labeled." At the same time, the letters in Mullen's title that remain suggest the book's interest in sexual politics and give it its most common pronunciation, *sperm kit.*

Reviewers were almost uniformly positive about the book. In the *MultiCultural Review* (March 1994), Aldon L. Nielsen wrote, "Mullen's prose poems carry on Gertrude Stein's explorations of the curious connections between food, form, and sexuality, but Mullen also interrogates those questions of race which Stein so often evades or papers over." The critic Stephen Yenser, in the *Yale Review* (April 1994), pointed readers to the last part of *S*PeRM**K*T*, which reads, in Yenser's transcription, "Flies in buttermilk. What a fellowship. That's why white milk makes yellow butter. Homo means the same. A woman is different. Cream always rises over spilt milk. Muscle men drink it all in. Awesome teeth and wholesale bones. Our cows are well adjusted. The lost family album keeps saying cheese. Speed readers skim the white space of this galaxy." Yenser then comments: "The ground covered in this small space—from the churn through the dairy section of the market to the Milky Way—is breathtaking. Not even Mullen's white space should be speed-read."

Mullen has said that the publisher of *S*PeRM**K*T*, the small poetry press Singing Horse, did not lose money on the book—a resounding success in the often grant- or bequest-funded world of poetry publishing—and that she was asked to submit another manuscript for publication. The result appeared in 1995 as *Muse & Drudge*. The title refers to what Mullen has often identified as the two roles of women in the male-centered literary tradition, where women ostensibly serve to inspire art as muses while, behind the scenes, doing the drudge work of washing, cooking, cleaning, and taking care of children that makes the male artists' other work possible. Formally, the book's playful, highly referential language and the fact that it reads as a single poem tie it to *Trimmings* and *S*PeRM**K*T*. At another formal level, however, the work is also a departure, since Mullen uses quatrains, rather than prose or more varied verse forms. Thematically, Mullen focuses on African-American women in a way that reaches back most clearly to *Tree Tall Woman*, though in this case Mullen's ideas are more obviously informed by literary theory. Mullen asked Frost in her Fall 2000 interview, "When you think about a black woman in this culture, which one is she going to be? She could be either one, the black woman as a beast of burden or as a postmodern diva."

As with *S*PeRM**K*T*, reviews of *Muse & Drudge* were generally positive. In a long scholarly discussion of the book in the journal *Women's Studies* (1998), Frost argues that in *Muse & Drudge* "Mullen has composed a long poem as blues: fragmented and improvisational, disjunctive in its continuities. Mullen mixes the influences of avant-garde groups too often considered in isolation: like poets of the Black Arts Movement, Mullen experiments with speech-based idiom, but, like Language-influenced writers, she launches her cultural critique by rejecting the rules of syntax and fashioning a distinctively visual, punning, and allusive play with language." In the *Georgia Review* (Fall 1996), Fred Chappell argued that Mullen "is trying to make a viable modern poetry out of African American speech rhythms and folk forms, attacking traditional materials in a radical but conservative style," according to a citation of Chappell's review in a 1997 bibliography in the *Mississippi Quarterly*. Mullen's work, Chappell also noted, shows "a sophisticated mind using unsophisticated tools." The publication of *Muse & Drudge* in 1995 coincided with Mullen's move from New York to Los Angeles, where she began teaching at the University of California. (She became a full professor at UCLA in 2003.)

In 2002 Mullen published *Sleeping with the Dictionary*. The title was inspired by a night of troubled sleep. "One night I'm tossing and turning in bed," Mullen told Ward, "and something is poking me in the back. What is it? It's the corner of my American Heritage dictionary." Less literally, the title also hints at the book's unapologetic, even giddy embrace of language, encompassing everything from jazz-inspired scatting to a parody of the formal language used in airplane announcements to two revisions of William Shakespeare's sonnet 130. (In Shakespeare, the sonnet begins "My mistress' eyes are nothing like the sun." In Mullen the first line reads, in one version, "My Mickey Mouse ears are nothing like sonar"; in another, "My honeybunch's peepers are nothing like neon.")

Mullen's growing reputation and the book's early acclaim led to a greater number of reviews and slightly more qualified praise than had generally greeted her earlier work, with multiple reviewers pointing to the poem "Jinglejangle" as an instance of the occasional lapse of Mullen's powers. The writer of a review in *Publishers Weekly* (December 17, 2001) called *Sleeping with the Dictionary* "no less conventional, and more diverse" than her previous books and concluded: "All of the work here is full of such energy, invention and pleasure that the dictionary surely awoke refreshed." In the *Village Voice* (March 19, 2002) David Mills wrote, "Mullen's infectious linguistic torques can entrance readers, lulling them into believing that she is merely engaged in a cozy dialectic with Messrs. Webster and Roget. But she sculpts sardonic and insightful poems. . . . Ultimately, *Sleeping* excavates the semi-permeable relationship between jabberwocky and logic. Mullen writes about being 'licked all over by the English tongue.' Reading her innovative intellectual congresses and titular poem's bawdy allusions, I realized I'd become a literary Peeping Tom." Describing the book as "contrived but not overly predictable," Hoke S. Glover III wrote in the *Black Issues Book Review*

(July–August 2002): "At the heart of Mullen's literary technique is sampling—or what the academy calls intertextuality. This idea of laying down rhythm over rhythm, blending the familiar with the old is nothing new. Restructuring and reworking, not just the melody or the notes, but the structure of the music itself, the style, the phrasing of the whole thing is part and parcel of Mullen's oeuvre."

In addition to being selected as a finalist for the Los Angeles Times Book Prize, the National Book Critics Circle Award, and the National Book Award, Mullen won the 1994–95 Gertrude Stein Award in Innovative American Poetry and the 1994–95 Rockefeller Fellowship at the University of Rochester's Susan B. Anthony Center for Women's Studies. In April 2005 she was named a recipient of a John Simon Guggenheim Memorial Fellowship.

Widely anthologized, Mullen is also the subject of a growing body of academic criticism. Among the books with significant discussions of her work are: *Extraordinary Measures: Afrocentric Modernism and Twentieth-Century American Poetry* (2000) by Lorenzo Thomas, *Everybody's Autonomy: Connective Reading and Collective Identity* (2001) by Juliana Spahr, *A Boundless Field: American Poetry at Large* (2002) by Stephen Yenser, and *The Feminist Avant-Garde in American Poetry* (2003) by Elisabeth Frost.

Mullen, who is divorced, lives in West Los Angeles. In June 1999, Mullen's poem "Wipe that Smile Off Your Aphasia" appeared on the city's buses, one of which she takes to work—"a very un-L.A. thing to do," she told Emily Ann Williams. Mullen's sister Kirsten, the inspiration for the poem "Kirstenography" in *Sleeping with the Dictionary*, is also a writer.

—D.R.

Suggested Reading: *Callaloo* p651+ Vol. 19, No. 3, 1996; (Fort Worth) *Star-Telegram* p1 Nov. 17, 2002; *Los Angeles Times* V p1 Nov. 18, 2002; *Postmodern Culture* (on-line) Jan. 1999

Selected Books: *Tree Tall Woman*, 1981; *Trimmings*, 1991; *S*PeRM**K*T*, 1992; *Muse & Drudge*, 1995; *Sleeping with the Dictionary*, 2002; *Blues Baby: Early Poems*, 2002; *Recyclopedia: Trimmings, S*PeRM**K*T, and Muse & Drudge*, 2006

Jack Pierson/Courtesy of Eileen Myles

Myles, Eileen

*Dec. 9, 1949– Poet; prose writer; playwright;
performance artist*

Eileen Myles found a place early in her life in New York City's downtown poetry scene, where for a time she directed—and shared her work at—the St. Mark's Poetry Project. Her poetry has been collected in such volumes as *The Irony of the Leash* (1978), *A Fresh Young Voice from the Plains* (1981), *Sappho's Boat* (1982), *1969* (1989), *Not Me* (1991), *Maxfield Parrish* (1995), *Skies* (2001), and *Sorry, Tree* (2007). Myles makes light of the distinction between poetry and her other writings, which she considers to be part of her poetic practice, leading her to publish such multi-genre works as *School of Fish* (1997) and *On My Way* (2001). Her ostensibly fictional, heavily autobiographical prose works *Bread and Water* (1987), *Chelsea Girls* (1994), and *Cool for You* (2000) have also been lauded. "I think a kind of fragmented writing and thinking can be the way the mind operates," she told Daniel Kane in an interview for the Web site of the Teachers & Writers Collaborative (January 1999). "I also think that when we look down at a page, we might want something more suggestive—more full, more narrative—with more handles. One doesn't have to decide one way or the other. I know that in paintings, I like ones that are abstract and ones that are representational. I like poetry that's abstract and poetry that tells a story and has real things. I kind of like to do it both ways." Long politically active and widely admired for her complex and challenging depictions of gender, Myles also earned some measure of fame for having run, in

1992, as a write-in candidate for president. "I realized that if I ran for president," Myles told Anthony DellaFlora for the *Albuquerque Journal* (February 15, 1998), "I could do that performance as a campaign—be a poor candidate, be a lesbian candidate, be a working-class candidate, be a poet candidate."

Eileen Myles wrote the following statement for *World Authors 2000–2005*:

"I went into a bookstore in Harvard Square in maybe 1966 (I was 16) and picked up a book in the poetry section called *Back in Boston* by Ted Berrigan and Ron Padgett and Aram Saroyan. I think those three guys. It was very idiomatic and minimal and sort of documented just their trip to Boston. I was taken by their audacity, and how easy they made it look. I had always admired the part of the comic book written in the balloon and their little book had the strength and the rhythm of that miraculous writing. I liked personal video too when I first saw it in the Museum of Fine Arts in Boston—some guy just standing there talking about himself. That was possible too!

"So much of what was in the air in the early sixties to late seventies both before and since I've entered the art world was an intimate sort of art making within life that appeared to validate its own attempt as it went along. An art without boundaries, undecorous, a stepping up and continuing. Which excited me. I discovered Frank O'Hara's poetry just before I moved to New York in 1974 and right after that was introduced to the poetry of James Schuyler who later became a friend and informal teacher. O'Hara impressed me by his direct use of speech rhythms in poetry, and Schuyler was like that also, yet there was a deep visual magic simplicity in his way of making a statement that thundered like no one else's. I also found Gertrude Stein's work around this time (*Lectures in America*) and was smitten by the prospect of a woman boldly explaining literature to the world and by extension declaring her own genius. I picked up Henry Miller, first in *Tropic of Capricorn*, describing the laughing misery of life on earth, the American Earth. You could complain, he taught me. It was doable. I read Jill Johnston's columns in the *Village Voice* which later became *Lesbian Nation* and her candor about her sexuality and her daily art life in New York were a model for raucous female possibility now.

"All of these landmarks of personal statement and accounting in art—and I include the films of Andy Warhol too, that tedium, all of these proposed to me in a variety of stylistic montage the idea that experience was intrinsically valuable. Punk rock said it too. Art can meet life head-on.

"Yet my work's grown more abstract and narrative over time. Abstract in that what's become personal in my work is where my body goes—so I started to find a language for how the world opens and closes around us and began to see making poetry as a way to score that process. I ran for President in 1992 because at 40 I could, and because by entering the body politic as a candidate I could make implicitly political poetry just by being ordinary. My candidacy exalted the ordinary which is what I've always 'meant.' I've been writing fiction since 1980 and now I'm entirely intrigued by the form of the novel. It seems completely unstatic, but requires a lot more footwork, a more separate building time which I feel burdened and relieved by because it keeps me out of the world some, which I like. But fiction allows my poetry to collapse and reorganize more readily; I'm finding the rhythm of all that to be the real subject of it—not even time, but signature. Which might be as autobiographical as you get."

Eileen Myles was born on December 9, 1949, in Cambridge, Massachusetts, the daughter of Terrence Myles, a mail carrier, and Genevieve Preston Hannibal, a secretary. Myles has written extensively about growing up in a working-class environment in Boston and about her father's alcoholism and grandmother's mental illness; her father's early accidental death—a blow that struck Myles when she was 11—and her years of Catholic schooling are also frequent subjects in her work. After high school she attended the University of Massachusetts, in Boston, and told Holland Cotter, for the New York Times (May 30, 2001), that at college she "was a total townie and very aware of it." In 1971 she earned her degree and three years later relocated to New York City, where for a short time she took part in a graduate program at Queens College. The same year that she moved to New York she gave a reading of her work at the legendary punk-music club CBGB. The experience helped inspire her to begin studying, in 1975, at the Poetry Project at St. Mark's Church-in-the-Bowery (in the East Village neighborhood of New York City), under the direction of such poets as Ted Berrigan, Alice Notley, and Paul Violi. Her informal apprenticeship under these and other teachers lasted until 1977, but she maintained a day-to-day involvement with the organization for at least a decade. The Poetry Project, she told Cotter, "was dedicated to the idea of the working artist. You could just walk in, sit down and take a class. It was all free."

Also in 1977 Myles began publishing a literary magazine called Dodgems (generally given as dodgems), which lasted through 1979. Her first book of poems, The Irony of the Leash, was followed, in 1979, by Polar Ode, a book she co-authored with a fellow poet, Anne Waldman, and another collection, A Fresh Young Voice from the Plains. Around this same time she became acquainted with the poet James Schuyler, who employed her as a secretary.

The seven years separating her poetry collections Sappho's Boat and 1969 were in part spent in Mexico, writing the prose stories brought together in Bread and Water. During this time, though, Myles also began to move beyond the alcoholism that had marked her early years, and her new-found sobriety gave her an altered sense of the world around her. "I stopped drinking in the '80s, and that's when I started really spotting the homeless," she told Anthony DellaFlora. "I saw them and I saw their pain when I first stopped drinking, in a very intense way, and I started feeling sort of politicized."

Having already worked, in 1980, as an instructor at the St. Mark's Poetry Project, she became, in 1984, the organization's artistic director, a position she held until 1986. Five years later she published Not Me, which received strong praise from critics. C. Carr, writing for the Voice Literary Supplement (June 1991), characterized the poems in Not Me as "observations of quotidian life" and argued that "Myles is an observer-poet more than a philosopher-poet. . . . Very seldom do her words call attention to their wordness." In a critique for the Kenyon Review (Spring 1992), Robyn Selman called the book "at least in part the autobiography of an American outlaw. At its core is the story of a woman who long ago parted company with social expectations" Comparing Myles to Schuyler but also acknowledging that she might not reach his lyrical heights, Selman still felt that "when Myles's poems bump and lumber, they do so the way real city sidewalks do."

Appearing two years after her quixotic presidential bid—which nonetheless succeeded in getting her name on the vote tallies in 28 states—Myles's story collection Chelsea Girls brings together 28 short prose pieces that, over their loosely chronological course, chart her upbringing in Massachusetts and her early experiences of New York life. Erika Taylor, writing for the Los Angeles Times Book Review (November 6, 1994), argued that Myles's egocentrism both elevated and undermined the collection. The book, Taylor wrote, "is so unabashedly solipsistic, so confidant in its own self-absorption, that [Myles] takes chances and has pay-offs few other writers would be willing to risk. . . . It would be easy to dismiss Chelsea Girls as poetic hot air if Myles weren't so smart and funny. Somehow, she manages to hold our attention in spite of the closed-in quality of her work. This is writing with big courage, big talent and a big self image." Other critics responded less warmly. Writing for the Review of Contemporary Fiction (Spring 1995), Michelle Latiolais noted that such cultural icons as Allen Ginsberg and Robert Mapplethorpe make appearances in the book and added: "Reading Chelsea Girls I found myself thinking that material this populated with the famous and the infamous, this studded with the iconography of a decade, should be a bit more interesting and fun to read, but too many of Chelsea Girls's pages are rather artlessly done diary entries. There are sections, however, where Myles really writes her subject and the result is stunning."

Maxfield Parrish brought new poems by Myles together with all of the poems from *Sappho's Boat* and a small selection of work from *The Irony of the Leash*. Myles's next book of newly collected work was *School of Fish*, which in addition to verse also features Myles's provocative essay "The Lesbian Poet," which she first presented as a lecture at the St. Mark's Poetry Project. In a critique for the *Harvard Gay & Lesbian Review* (Fall 1997), Gabrielle Glancy called the book "upliftingly dark" and added: "This book comforts as it disarms, knits up as it unravels. In past works, Myles has relied more heavily on the blunt edge of a tough and tender 'sex-ability' to reel you in with hard-headed verse. *School of Fish* is the work of a seasoned 'troubadour,' unafraid of night waters."

Myles next book, *Cool for You*, is an autobiographical novel that retraces some of the ground covered in *Chelsea Girls*, particularly regarding Myles's Boston-area upbringing. In the novel, however, Myles also goes into detail about her grandmother's mental illness and institutionalization—and her own involvement with similarly impersonal places. The reviews of the book were largely positive, with many critics commenting on Myles's use of autobiography and her handling of first-person narration. In an analysis of the book for the *Nation* (January 1, 2001), Chris Kraus argued that, unlike such writers as Sylvia Plath and Susanna Kaysen, both authors of autobiographical accounts of institutionalization, "Myles has no particular belief in the possibility of a fully integrated female self. She doesn't think her experience will be redeemed. The circumstances of Myles's life . . . are no more dire than those of millions who daily feel the disparity between their own lives and the surfaces of upper-middle-class life that are projected blandly on TV and intricately probed in most contemporary literary fiction. What's harrowing is the detail in which this disparity is experienced and recorded." Kate Clinton, writing for the *Progressive* (January 2001), called the book "a straight-ahead story about a working class Irish American girl in horrible schools and creepy jobs." Clinton added, "The first-person point of view . . . is so vivid, dissociated, self-aware, and flat-out poetic in its description of day-to-day survival and transcendence that it verges on claustrophobic in its realization of setting, character, and plot. In some places, I had to force myself to look up and away from the words and gasp for air." To Charles Shipman, writing for the *St. Louis Post-Dispatch* (November 5, 2000), *Cool for You* appeared "to be more a collection of scenes from the author's life than a fictional narrative. . . . The book jumps from scene to scene, event to event with little explanation as Myles surveys her life, particularly her childhood in Boston. This is disconcerting at first, but gradually you settle in and simply let Myles tell her story." While maintaining that "the writing is sometimes too fragmented to follow and occasionally becomes a tad melodramatic," Shipman also felt that "Myles has an undeniable gift for capturing the small details and mundane events that shape our lives. She's also capable of writing with tremendous sensitivity, and because she never slips into sentimentality, her tender passages are all the more affecting."

In 2001 Myles published both *Skies* and *On My Way* (sometimes given as *on my way*). A critic for *Publishers Weekly* (January 21, 2002) wrote that the books "give ample evidence of the strengths and idiosyncrasies" of Myles's work and added that *Skies* "beautifully portrays the sweet metaphysical tragedy of having to bear lonely witness to one's own experiences." In a critique for the *Village Voice* (April 2, 2002), Cathy Hong called attention to Myles's "moxie for politics," " lyric zeal," and "anarchic post-feminist energy" and described her poetic style in *Skies* and elsewhere as "plainspoken and personalized." Hong added, "The sky is a perfect muse for Myles: Its panoramic oscillations are swifter than the speed in which she could jot them down. She freezes the flashes of cloud formations the way she freezes incidental moments of her life. But as much as these poems are visually impressionistic, they are also visionary. The sky is not only a manifestation of our evanescent identities, it is a hovering witness to the city's turbulence, the melancholic absence of lost love, and its outlaw, borderless condition is Myles's own utopian space. . . . Meditative, brave, and insouciant, Myles has a limitless thirst for marrying poetry with her social agenda."

In addition to poems and stories, Myles has also written a number of plays, including *Joan of Arc: A Spiritual Entertainment* (co-authored with Barbara McKay and Elinor Naven, 1979), *Patriarchy* (co-authored with Naven and Ann Rower, 1980), *Our Town* (co-authored with Tom Carey, 1982), *Feeling Blue* (1988), *Modern Art* (1990), and *Our Sor Juana* (1994). Most of these works enjoyed only limited runs, but she presented her solo performance work *Leaving New York* on tour in 1990. She also wrote the libretto for the opera *Hell* (2004), with music written by Michael Webster. She has been a frequent contributor to such publications as *Art in America*, the *Nation*, and the *Village Voice*.

After years of teaching on a part-time basis for such New York City institutions as the Parsons School of Design, New York University, and the New School for Social Research, Myles took on a full-time position as a professor in the literature department at the University of California, at San Diego, in 2002. On her Web site EileenMyles.net (she also maintains EileenMyles.com and the two have slightly different content), Myles described her position in San Diego as: "Professor of Fiction Writing, Poetry Writing, Short Fiction, Poet's Novel, Writing between Genres, The Libretto, and Pathetic Literature."

Myles began publicly identifying herself as a lesbian in the mid-1970s and has long put her sexuality at the center of her poetic and political identities. Her ideas about gender, however, remain fluid. She has sometimes suggested that she feels more like a man than a woman and just as often insisted on her femaleness. Reviewing *School of Fish* for the *Nation* (July 21, 1997), Jonathan Taylor argued that Myles's presentation of her sexuality was "something [she] has always practiced with playful mordancy" and illustrated his point with a quotation from that book. "If I am / not a / man," Myles wrote, "how could / I be so / incredibly / important."

—S.Y.

Suggested Reading: *Albuquerque Journal* D p2 Feb. 15, 1998; EileenMyles.com; EileenMyles.net; *Kenyon Review* p167 Spring 1992; *Los Angeles Times Book Review* p6 Nov. 6, 1994; *Nation* p39 July 21, 1997, p32+ Jan. 1, 2001; *New York Times Book Review* p13 July 29, 2001; *Progressive* p35 Jan. 2001; *Publishers Weekly* p71 June 27, 1994, p85+ Jan. 21, 2002; *Review of Contemporary Fiction* p173+ Spring 1995; *St. Louis Post-Dispatch* C p10 Nov. 5, 2000; Teachers & Writers Collaborative Web site Jan. 1999; *Village Voice* p68+ June 27, 2000, p53 Apr.2, 2002; *Voice Literary Supplement* p29 June 1991

Selected Books: *The Irony of the Leash*, 1978; *A Fresh Young Voice from the Plains*, 1981; *Sappho's Boat*, 1982; *Bread and Water*, 1987; *1969*, 1989; *Not Me*, 1991; *Chelsea Girls*, 1994; *Maxfield Parrish*, 1995; *School of Fish*, 1997; *Cool for You*, 2000; *On My Way*, 2001; *Skies*, 2001; *Sorry, Tree*, 2007

Thos Robinson/Getty Images

Nafisi, Azar

1950(?)– Memoirist; literary scholar

A lover of Western literature and a teacher of English literature in her native Iran, Azar Nafisi went from being an excited supporter of the 1979 Iranian Revolution to an out-of-work dissident, having been pushed out of her position as a professor after a series of political and religious conflicts with administrators and outside authorities. Official censure, however, did not stop her from teaching, and she surreptitiously began a literary discussion group in 1995 with some of her female students, which, for a period of two years, met regularly to discuss Western novels and criticize the Iranian government. *Reading Lolita in Tehran* (2003) is Nafisi's critically lauded memoir of her experiences leading that discussion group. (The title refers to Vladimir Nabokov's 1955 novel *Lolita*.) "Much of the artistry of this book is in Nafisi's ability to interweave the political, the imaginative, and the personal," John R. Rachal noted in a review for the *Journal of Higher Education* (July/August 2006). The students in Nafisi's class set aside the regular pressures of the outside world in order to explore new modes of being, and, as Rachal pointed out: "In so doing, their pursuit of education becomes an act of defiance, of insubordination. Escape, argument, solidarity, freedom, curiosity . . . all commingle in this refuge for free thought in an apartment in revolutionary Tehran. In their Thursday morning literary conversations, Nafisi and her fellow subversives explore the actions and psyches of fictional people who inhabit worlds created by the imagination. In the process, they plumb, amid the reality of war and theocratic oppression, the liberating and redemptive power of art."

Azar Nafisi was born in Tehran in about 1950 to a highly prominent family. (Some sources, seemingly deriving their information from a version of the on-line resource Wikipedia, state that her birth year is 1955—a somewhat improbable date, given that this would have made her about 17 when she received her undergraduate degree.) Her father, Ahmad Nafisi, was a mayor of Tehran, and later, during Nafisi's youth, spent about four years in jail on charges seemingly manufactured by the shah, Mohammed Reza Pahlavi. Nafisi's mother, Nezhat Nafisi, became one of the first women elected to the *Majlis*, Iran's main parliamentary body, in 1963, the same year that Iranian women were first given the right to vote.

At the age of 13 Nafisi left her native Iran, living first in Lancaster, England, where she finished her secondary education. Married impulsively before she was 18, she joined her husband in attending the University of Oklahoma, in Norma. According to information posted on the Web site of the University of Oklahoma's College of Arts and Sciences, Nafisi earned a B.A. in English and philosophy, in 1972, an M.A. in English, in 1974, and a Ph.D. in English and American literature, in 1979; her doctoral dissertation, about the mid–20th century memoirist and critic Mike Gold, was entitled "The Literary Wars of Mike Gold: A Study in the Background and Development of Mike Gold's Literary Ideas, 1920–1941." (Her dissertation was written under a slightly different transliteration of her last name: Naficy.) During this time she divorced her first husband—after much wrangling. She married her second, Bijan Naderi, in 1977. Both Nafisi and her new husband were active participants in the international Iranian student movement, which opposed the rule of the shah and American involvement in Iranian affairs.

In 1979 the student movement and other external and internal pressures, particularly the influence of the exiled Ayatollah Khomeini, combined to force the then-ailing shah from power, and Nafisi returned to her home country that same year to take up a teaching position in the English department at the University of Tehran. "I think that if Harvard or Oxford or Cambridge had offered me a job, I would not have felt so nervous and so honored as when I went into the hallowed halls of the University of Tehran," Nafisi told Zlatica Hoke for the *Voice of America News* (June 23, 2003). "The amount of time I spent just preparing myself for this first day is something that I'll never forget." After making a similar point in *Reading Lolita*, Nafisi went on to describe the university as "the navel, the immovable center to which all political and social activities were tied. When in the United States we read or heard about the turmoil in Iran, the University of Tehran seemed to be the scene of the most important battles."

Nafisi's work as a teacher was made difficult by the upheaval all around her and by members of the radicalized student body who viewed Western literature as a tool of imperialism. Moreover, the Islamic conservatives who took the reins of the revolution required that women conform to strict specifications of behavior and dress. Refusing to don a veil, Nafisi was fired from the University of Tehran in 1981 or 1982. In the late 1980s she returned to academia, teaching at the Free Islamic University and at the Allameh Tabatabai University; at some point in her career she held a fellowship at the University of Oxford, in England. Recalling the difficulties of the period in an interview with Wen Stephenson for the PBS show *Frontline* (on-line), Nafisi stated, "Life in academia was like guerilla warfare, from not wearing my veil

properly to the books I taught and the meetings I organized, to the liberal way I treated students." After another political disagreement, she resigned from teaching in 1995.

Exiled from academic life, Nafisi organized an informal book group with seven of her former female students. Since several of the books were banned, the women had to meet in secret; they read works by such authors as Nabokov, F. Scott Fitzgerald, Henry James, and Jane Austen. The books often served as springboards for critical discussions of the culture and politics of Iran. After meeting for two years, the group disbanded in 1997, following Nafisi's departure to the United States. Those clandestine meetings formed the basis for Nafisi's *Reading Lolita in Tehran.*

Reading Lolita in Tehran, Paul Allen wrote for the London *Guardian* (September 13, 2003), "is a highly personal memoir combined with literary criticism. . . . [It is] a story that is vivid, often heroic and sometimes funny in a ghastly way." Michiko Kakutani, reviewing the book for the *New York Times* (April 15, 2003), hailed it as "a visceral and often harrowing portrait of the Islamic revolution in that country and its fallout on the day-to-day lives of Ms. Nafisi and her students. It is a thoughtful account of the novels they studied together and the unexpected parallels they drew between those books and their own experiences as women living under the unforgiving rule of the mullahs. And it is, finally, an eloquent brief on the transformative powers of fiction—on the refuge from ideology that art can offer to those living under tyranny, and art's affirmative and subversive faith in the voice of the individual."

Perhaps the only critical note sounded against the book came three years after its publication, when another Iranian-born academic living in the U.S., Hamid Dabashi, blasted *Reading Lolita in Tehran* in the English-language Egyptian newspaper *Al-Ahram* (June 1–7 2006). Dabashi argued that "one can now clearly see and suggest that this book is partially responsible for cultivating the US (and by extension the global) public opinion against Iran, having already done a great deal by being a key propaganda tool at the disposal of the Bush administration during its prolonged wars in such Muslim countries as Afghanistan (since 2001) and Iraq (since 2003)." Dabashi called the book "reminiscent of the most pestiferous colonial projects of the British in India"—namely, the creation of a group of "native informers" who would make it easier to subjugate the masses. He characterized Nafisi as "the personification of that native informer and colonial agent, polishing her services for an American version of the very same project." Asked about those comments for an article by Richard Byrne that appeared in the *Chronicle of Higher Education* (October 13, 2006), Nafisi refused to address them specifically, simply saying, "I don't consider [Dabashi's] recent writings worth responding to."

Certainly, though, Dabashi was correct to consider the book influential. Adopted almost instantly by literature teachers and reading groups, the book spent a total of over two years on the *New York Times* best-seller list. It has now been translated into 32 languages and sold hundreds of thousands of copies, transforming Nafisi from a relatively unknown academic into a significant media figure. She is reported to be working on two books: "The Republic of the Imagination," which her official biography on the Web site of the Steven Barclay Agency describes as "about the power of literature to liberate minds and peoples"; and "Things I Have Been Silent About," slated for publication in late 2008 and characterized as "a memoir about her mother."

Nafisi is currently a fellow at the Johns Hopkins University School of Advanced International Studies, in Washington, D.C., and the director of an organization within the school called the Dialogue Project. On its Web site the organization is described as "a multi-year initiative designed to promote—in a primarily cultural context—the development of democracy and human rights in the Muslim world." The Dialogue Project, according to the site, "also hopes to educate those in non-Muslim communities . . . in the complexities and contradictions that govern both Western relationships with and life in many predominantly Muslim societies around the world." Nafisi has written for the *Washington Post*, the *Wall Street Journal*, the *New York Times*, the *New Republic*, *Social Research*, and other publications. She is the author of a 1994 scholarly book, written in Farsi, the title of which has been translated as "anti-terra: a critical study of Vladimir Nabokov's novels." Nafisi has spoken occasionally of translating and revising that text, enriching it with some of the ideas she did not include when writing the earlier version, knowing that they would keep the book from being printed.

Nafisi lives with her husband, Bijan Naderi, in Washington, D.C. The couple have two children, Negar and Dara. "How do you define your own status in this country," Robert Birnbaum asked Nafisi in an interview for the on-line magazine *Identity Theory* (February 5, 2004). "Exile, émigré, a citizen of the world?" Nafisi responded: "I would like to think of my own status as what you called 'citizen of the world' or a 'citizen of a portable world,' if not of the world. Lots of times you can feel as an exile in a country that you were born in. And you discover that there are people all around the world with whom you share the same values."
—P.B.M./D.R.

Suggested Reading: *Frontline* (on-line); *Identity Theory* (on-line) Feb. 5, 2004; *Journal of Higher Education* p743+ July/Aug. 2006; (London) *Guardian* Sep. 13, 2003; *Voice of America News* June 23, 2003

Selected Books: *Reading Lolita in Tehran*, 2003

Courtesy of Gary B. Nash

Nash, Gary B.

July 27, 1933– Historian

The author of more than 20 books, most recently *The Unknown American Revolution* (2004) and *The Forgotten Fifth* (2006), the historian Gary B. Nash is best known for his revisionist interpretations of early American history, specifically his reassessments of the influence of minorities and the causes of the Revolutionary War. His authoritative research has been widely praised by academics and general readers alike, and he has earned considerable plaudits for his ability to synthesize a wide variety of source material into a compelling narrative.

A history professor at the University of California, at Los Angeles (UCLA), since 1966, Nash came to national prominence during the 1990s, when as associate director of the National Center for History in the Schools at UCLA, he contributed to the development of the National History Standards Project, which sought to enhance the history education curriculum in primary and secondary public schools. The project was mandated by Congress and overseen by Lynne Cheney (the wife of current Vice President Dick Cheney), who was then head of the National Endowment for the Humanities (NEH). During his involvement with the project, Nash found himself embroiled in the American culture wars, as conservative critics, Lynne Cheney among them, faulted the standards initially proposed for being too politically correct and overly critical of the United States. Since that time Nash has stressed the importance of a balanced history curriculum, one that honors significant figures and events without glossing over less savory aspects of the American past.

Gary Baring Nash was born on July 27, 1933 in Philadelphia, Pennsylvania, to Ralph C. Nash and the former Edith Baring. He received his education at Princeton University, in New Jersey, where in 1955 he earned a bachelor of arts degree in history. After graduation Nash joined the U.S. Navy; he served for the next three years. Following his discharge he returned to Princeton, taking up doctoral studies in history at the university's graduate school, where he also served as assistant to the dean, from 1959 to 1963. In 1964 Nash completed his Ph.D. and spent the next two years teaching at Princeton, first as an instructor and then as an assistant professor of history.

Nash moved to Southern California in 1966, after accepting an assistant professorship at UCLA. He was made a full professor in 1974. From 1984 to 1991, he served as the dean of undergraduate curriculum development. He was associate director of the National Center for History in the Schools from 1988 to 1994 and director of the center since 1994. Between 1992 and 1996, he co-chaired the National History Standards Project, an experience he detailed in his book *History on Trial* (1997), which was co-authored by Charlotte Crabtree and Ross Dunn.

Nash made his name as a revisionist historian—one who reevaluates conventional beliefs by examining sometimes neglected historical documents. His writings have typically focused on the early American colonies up through the establishment of the republic. His first book, *Quakers and Politics: Pennsylvania 1681–1726* (1968), analyzed the role played by Quakers in shaping Pennsylvania society and politics. A reviewer for *Choice* (March 1969) characterized *Quakers and Politics* as "an important book for any colonial American collection," declaring it a "comprehensive, authoritative, and well written account . . . [which shows how] the strong Quaker tradition of antiauthoritarianism engendered a negative attitude toward political control, whether exercised by the proprietor, upper-class Quakers, or imperial agents." A critic for the *Virginia Quarterly Review* (Spring 1969) proclaimed the work a "brilliant investigation,'" as well as "the best single volume on the early history of Pennsylvania and one that has meaning for the early history of other American colonies." The Pacific Coast Branch of the American Historical Association named *Quakers and Politics* the top book of the year in the American history category.

Nash followed up *Quakers and Politics* with a collection of essays entitled *Class and Society in Early America* (1970). By examining birth and death certificates, tax lists, and marriage licenses, rather than the accounts of colonial elites, Nash sought to more clearly define the socio-economic structure of colonial society, an area of scholarship over which modern historians have considerable disagreement. In her critique for the *American*

Sociological Review (December 1971), Suzanne Keller observed, "The problem of evidence and inference in history, in this case of American colonial history, is at the heart of this compact collection of essays and commentaries. The introductory essay by Nash is a model of clarity and substance which sets the tone for the entire volume." A reviewer for *Choice* (May 1971) remarked, "The author is convinced that the 'literary' interpretations have not exposed an accurate picture of American society, but he seems to believe that modern scholarship will prevail. A provocative volume which bears close scrutiny."

In 1970, with Richard Weiss, Nash co-edited *The Great Fear: Race in the Mind of America*, an anthology of essays discussing the issue of race throughout American history, from the earliest interactions between European settlers and Native Americans, to the 19th-century immigrant waves and the modern plight of Mexicans living in the U.S. A writer for *Choice* (July 1971) commented, "The time span covered by the contributors ranges from colonial times to the present, but naturally each essay is an intensive discussion of a specific facet of the problem, such as Larry Kincaid's essay on racial attitudes during the Civil War and Reconstruction, Stanley Coben's 'The failure of the melting pot' and Peter Loewenberg's 'The psychology of racism' which is the best concise treatment that exists." F. A. Burdick wrote for *Library Journal* (December 1, 1970), "This collection of essays by a group of young historians provides a new view of such central issues in black history and the history of racism as the origins of racism in Colonial America, racial attitudes during the Civil War and Reconstruction, and racism in industrialization." "The pieces," Burdick continued, "reflect no single interpretive theme, but rather the desire to summarize existing scholarship and delineate new ideas and perspectives. They are of uniformly high quality and scholarship, and should interest the informed reader."

With *Red, White, and Black: The Peoples of Early America* (1974), Nash returned to the issue of race in America as he compared the three groups present during the colonial period: white settlers, African slaves, and Native Americans. In a review for the *American Anthropologist* (June 1975), Ernest Schusky wrote, "For anthropologists [*Red, White, and Black*] is a useful introduction to some revisionist thought in history, and the work is a warning that historians are undertaking problems once thought the province of anthropology." Schusky took particular note of "Nash's review of Black culture," which "ably points up the positive adjustments of Africans in the New World." Schusky concluded, "His critique of the earlier hypotheses that neglected an active African role are a valuable summary for the non-historian." A reviewer for *Choice* (October 1974) observed, "[The author] cites the contribution of each culture and carefully avoids any suggestion that one was superior to another. He avoids, also, the traditional emphasis on politics and the role of the elite." "His treatment of the adaptation of blacks to slavery," the critic continued, "stresses African culture and cultural survivals, with a sound synthesis of recent literature on slavery in the British and Latin American colonies. Finally Nash dispels the legend of unlimited opportunity and success among the white colonists, summarizing the recent work of demographers and social historians that shows that economic growth brought increasing social stratification and a large property-less class."

Following the publication of *The Private Side of American History: Readings in Everyday Life* (1975), Nash's next major work was *The Urban Crucible: Social Change, Political Consciousness, and the Origins of the American Revolution* (1979), in which he used primary sources from three major colonial cities—New York, Philadelphia, and Boston—to demonstrate how social change and a growing political consciousness in the colonies helped spark the Revolutionary War. J. R. Pole wrote for the *Times Literary Supplement* (April 11, 1980), "Professor Nash's book is one of the finest works on colonial America since the revival of interest that began some twenty-five years ago; and his enormously thorough research, discriminating judgment and lucid exposition will place the problems [he examines] in the forefront of historical attention for the next generation of colonial historians. Historians of the economic and social history of other parts of the Western world will also have to reckon with [his] findings." Pole found the wide spectrum of source material one of the books key strengths: "In addition to the usual newspapers, business records and diaries and letters [Nash] has forced speech from tax lists, poor relief records, wills, inventories, deed books, mortgages and wage records. When these are put together with the accounts we already have, familiar episodes sometimes take new forms." Ultimately, Pole concluded, "The side of the story [Nash] tells has never been so comprehensively told, nor with such humanity." In a similarly positive vein, C. W. Akers wrote for the *New England Quarterly* (June 1980), "No book makes clearer that the French wars, in which some merchants acquired a fortune from profiteering, exacted a devastating price from ordinary urbanities. Likewise, when viewed from the bottom up, all the major political and economic developments from 1690 to 1776 take on a broad new dimension that demands inclusion in future colonial histories. The side-by-side comparisons of the three towns in each period reveal hitherto unnoticed or unemphasized differences, as well as similarities, in the conditions faced by the lower classes. Nash documents his contention of increasing urban poverty and a concentration of wealth with an impressive body of quantitative evidence." A finalist for the Pulitzer Prize in history, *The Urban Crucible* was nominated for a

host of other awards and won the Commonwealth Club of California's Silver Prize in Literature.

Nash authored or collaborated on a number of notable works during the 1980s, among them *Struggle and Survival in Colonial America* (1981), for which he served as co-editor, with David G. Sweet, and *Race, Class and Politics: Essays on American Colonial and Revolutionary Society* (1986). He was one of six authors of *The American People: Creating a Nation and a Society* (1986), and a co-editor, with Ronald B. Schultz, of *Retracing the Past: Readings in the History of the American People* (1986). In *Forging Freedom: The Formation of Philadelphia's Black Community, 1720–1840* (1988) Nash explored the evolution of Philadelphia's African-American community from 1720, as it dealt with shifting white racial attitudes, from early cooperation to segregation. Thomas J. Davis, writing for *Library Journal* (May 1, 1988), stated, "Nash's masterful work of historical detection and recreation details the black struggle that made Philadelphia *the* urban black center of post-Revolutionary America. Nash weaves the tale of black successes and tragedies using information from public records and private papers." For *Choice* (November 1988) D. W. Hoover described the volume as "a welcome addition to the literature on Philadelphia blacks," concluding that "Nash's sophisticated work will be the standard in the future."

Nash expanded on racial themes in his subsequent work, *Race and Revolution* (1990), a collection of three essays adapted from several lectures he had delivered at the University of Wisconsin. These lectures, and the resulting book, examined why the first emancipation movement in the United States had failed. Previous scholarship held that slavery survived the Revolutionary War due to the implacability of Southern political leaders, who felt the morally repugnant institution was an economic necessity, but in *Race and Revolution* Nash proposed that racism in the northern portions of the country was just as responsible for slavery's continued existence. David Szatmary wrote for *Library Journal* (October 1, 1990), "Relying upon recent scholarship, the author provides an insightful, well-written investigation which will appeal to scholars and the general public." Reviewing the work for *Choice* (June 1991), R. Detweiler observed, "Generations of historians have blamed the failure of abolitionism at the end of the 18th century on the intransigence of the South, but this revisionist account determines that northern racism and hypocrisy played just as important a role. Nash finds that . . . northern leaders failed to take advantage of the great opportunity to end slavery at the onset of the new nation."

Following *Race and Revolution*, Nash co-authored *Freedom by Degrees: Emancipation and Its Aftermath in Pennsylvania, 1690–1840* (1991) with Jean R. Soderlund. Nash's other books of the period include *American Odyssey: The United*

States in the Twentieth Century (1991) and *Lessons From History: Essential Understandings and Historical Perspectives Students Should Acquire* (1992), which he co-edited.

In 1992 Nash agreed to co-chair the National Historical Standards Project after Lynne Cheney (who heading the NEH from 1986 to 1993) requested the assistance of the National Center for History in the Schools. The goal of the project was to establish educational standards for history instruction. These standards were developed after consultation with academic historians, school administrators, and politicians in Washington, D.C. In an article posted on the History News Network Web site (November 8, 2004), Nash recalled, "Though approved by a national council, half of whose members were her appointees and endorsed by thirty major professional and public interest organizations, the standards were dismissed by Ms. Cheney as having no redeeming value." In particular, Cheney felt too much attention had been paid to such embarrassing historical events as the rise of the Ku Klux Klan and the Red Scare of the 1950s and too little paid to such historical figures as Robert E. Lee or the Wright brothers. In *History on Trial: Culture Wars and the Teaching of the Past* (1997), Nash, along with co-authors Charlotte Crabtree and Ross Dunn, recounted the political firestorm created by the standards project and its impact on the teaching of American history in the United States. For the *Christian Science Monitor* (October 6, 1997), Gregory M. Lamb observed that *History on Trial* "offers an important resource to parents, teachers, administrators, government officials, or anyone trying to understand how history can be most effectively taught in the 1990s. Brightly written and solidly researched, it is itself a model of good scholarship, bringing light to a troubled chapter in recent American history." A more critical analysis came from Sean Wilentz for the *New York Times Book Review* (November 30, 1997), who wrote, "A predictable collection of conservative publicists and polemicists, led by Rush Limbaugh, amplified Cheney's charges and tried to turn the history standards debate into a cause celebre. . . . Roughly half of *History on Trial* is devoted to a description of these events and of the authors' ultimately successful efforts to vindicate a revised version of their proposed guidelines. It is, unmistakably, a partisan account." "In retrospect, at least," Wilentz continued, "the authors seem to have been mighty naive in thinking that their efforts to bring the new social history into America's classrooms would provoke little political response. More important, they offer few second thoughts about the genuine deficiencies in their original proposals."

Nash returned to one of the central themes of his writing—race in America—with his next work, *Forbidden Love: The Secret History of Mixed-Race America* (1999). Intended for adolescent readers, *Forbidden Love* highlighted the contributions of biracial people to the United States. Brent Staples, in a critique for the *New York Times Book Review* (September 12, 1999), declared, "Nash shows clearly that mixed-race people have been with us always, using cross-cultural skills to great advantage in art, diplomacy and civic leadership." "But," Staples noted, "the title *Forbidden Love* is misleading, especially for adolescent readers, for a book that dwells more on broad social themes than on the intimate details of individual lives. . . . *Forbidden Love* would have benefitted greatly from a little more research into the lives of Nash's more famous subjects, especially Walter White, who was executive secretary of the N.A.A.C.P. in the late 1940's." Writing for *Booklist* (May 15, 1999), Hazel Rochman commented, "The alluring title and cover don't quite fit the scholarly, detailed, sometimes heavy, style but many readers will want to know more about the longstanding taboos and the fight for tolerance, past and present. In many ways, this is also a history of American racism. . . . Nash draws on science, literature, politics, art, and music, and especially on popular culture, with words and period prints that show the vicious stereotypes." "What will hold teens," Rochman concluded, "are the many personal stories that are woven into the political struggles: stirring accounts of 'interracial renegades' who defied convention and stood up for love."

In his subsequent work, *First City: Philadelphia and the Forging of Historical Memory* (2001), Nash examined "how Philadelphians remembered, celebrated, and forgot their past from the eighteenth century until the present," Richard Stott wrote for the *Journal of American History* (March 2003). Central to Nash's analysis was how Philadelphia's public institutions—its museums and libraries, for example—dealt with particular moments in the city's past. Stott praised the work, dubbing it "well-crafted." A writer for the *American Historical Review* declared, as quoted on the Web site of the University of Pennsylvania Press, "[*First City*] represents well the tensions and opportunities that await writers seeking to push the craft of history to a new level of self-awareness and creativity."

With *The Unknown American Revolution: The Unruly Birth of Democracy and the Struggle to Create America* (2004), Nash sought to redefine the Revolutionary War as less a noble and heroic struggle against a foreign colonial power than a bloody civil conflict fraught with bitter divisions and political rivalries. In addition, the work drew attention to the previously unrecognized importance of American Indians to the colonists' cause. For the *New York Review of Books* (September 22, 2005), Edward S. Morgan wrote, "In the closing pages of his book Nash denies that his unknown Revolution was a failed revolution. Rather, he says, it was an incomplete one. His defeated slaves, Indians, women, and farmers passed the torch to later generations to carry on what they had begun. Perhaps he is right. Perhaps the success of egalitarian, democratic movements after the launching of the new national government can be seen as a continuation of the disparate movements he describes. But they were disparate." "Despite Nash's scrupulous and comprehensive scholarship," Morgan stated, "he has not succeeded in making them a coherent whole, a revolution in themselves. The known Revolution was national, a successful joining of thirteen colonies into a 'perpetual union,' capable of effecting egalitarian reforms on a continental scale." For the *New Leader* (May/June 2005), Henry F. Graff proclaimed, "In his incisive *The Unknown American Revolution*, revisionist historian Gary B. Nash . . . offers no salute to George Washington as the signal figure in the achievement of independence. Instead, he singles out what he perceives to be a rich spirit of democracy simmering throughout colonial American society and coalescing as the ideology of the new nation. Recognizing that the new nation needed a hero—an 'infallible divinity'—and found one in the Virginian, the author proceeds to paint Washington as less than admirable in the eyes of many who were closest to him." Graff noted, "The texture of American history is not smooth, Nash contends, and his fruitful research will fascinate anyone with traditional impressions of the colonial world."

Nash's most recent book, *The Forgotten Fifth: African Americans in the Age of Revolution* (2006), is a study of black Americans during the Revolutionary War. (The title refers to the fact that during the revolutionary period, a full fifth of the nation's population was black.) According to the Harvard University Press Web site, "[In the book] Nash tells of revolutionary fervor arousing a struggle for freedom that spiraled into the largest slave rebellion in American history, as blacks fled servitude to fight for the British, who promised freedom in exchange for military service. The Revolutionary Army never matched the British offer, and most histories of the period have ignored this remarkable story. The conventional wisdom says that abolition was impossible in the fragile new republic. Nash, however, argues that an unusual convergence of factors immediately after the war created a unique opportunity to dismantle slavery. The founding fathers' failure to commit to freedom led to the waning of abolitionism just as it had reached its peak. In the opening decades of the nineteenth century, as Nash demonstrates, their decision enabled the ideology of white supremacy to take root, and with it the beginnings of an irreparable national fissure. The moral failure of the Revolution was paid for in the 1860s with the lives of the 600,000 Americans killed in the Civil War."

Now professor emeritus at UCLA, Nash has received numerous awards for his work over the years. He is an elected member of the American Philosophical Society, the American Antiquarian Society, the Society of American Historians, and the American Academy of Arts and Sciences. From 1994 to 1995 he served as president of the Organization of American Historians. He is also the recipient of the University of California Distinguished Emeriti Award and the Defense of Academic Freedom Award from the National Council of Social Studies. He has served on numerous editorial advisory boards, prize and nominating committees, and faculty advisory committees.

Nash has been married twice: to Mary Workum on December 20, 1955 and to Cynthia Shelton on October 24, 1981. His first marriage, which ended in divorce, produced four children: Brooke, Robin, Jennifer, and David. Nash and his current wife live in Pacific Palisades, California.

—C.M.

Suggested Reading: History News Network Web site; UCLA Web site

Selected Books: *Quakers and Politics: Pennsylvania, 1681–1726*, 1968; *Class and Society in Early America*, 1970; *Red, White, and Black: The Peoples of Early America*, 1974; *The Urban Crucible: Social Change, Political Consciousness and the Origins of the American Revolution*, 1979; *Race, Class and Politics: Essays on American Colonial and Revolutionary Society*, 1986; *Forging Freedom: The Formation of Philadelphia's Black Community, 1720–1840*, 1988; *Race and Revolution*, 1990; *History on Trial: Culture Wars and the Teaching of the Past* (with Charlotte Crabtree and Ross Dunn), 1997; *Forbidden Love: The Secret History of Mixed-Race America*, 1999; *First City: Philadelphia and the Forging of Historical Memory*, 2001; *The Unknown American Revolution: The Unruly Birth of Democracy and the Struggle to Create America*, 2004; *The Forgotten Fifth: African Americans in the Age of Revolution*, 2006

Nasrin, Taslima

1962– Novelist; poet; journalist; memoirist

Taslima Nasrin was forced to flee her native country, Bangladesh, in 1994, because of a *fatwa*, or Islamic religious ruling, against her in response to her 1993 book *Lajja*. Nasrin had become a target of fundamentalist ire several years before for her newspaper and magazine columns, which openly criticized Islam for its oppression of women. Living in exile, she continues to be an outspoken critic of the repression she encountered in Bangladesh, which she says is inextricably linked to the influence of Islam (and religion in general) in daily life. "Every single religion tends to suppress women," she said at a meeting organized by the Norwegian Humanist and Ethical

Jon Levy/AFP/Getty Images

Taslima Nasrin

Association in Oslo, Norway, as reported by Barbro Sveen for *Humanist* (March/April 1995). "That is why religion and women do not get on very well together. Therefore—if we are of the opinion that women have a right to be human beings—we have to separate religion from the state. It is only in a secular society that women can rely on being free." A staunch atheist, Nasrin believes that Islam is inherently misogynistic, regardless of the form in which it is practiced: "I don't find any difference between Islam and Islamic fundamentalists," she told Matt Cherry and Warren Allen Smith for *Free Inquiry* (Winter 1998–99), as posted on the Council for Secular Humanism Web site. "I believe religion is the root, and from the root fundamentalism grows as a poisonous stem. If we remove fundamentalism and keep religion, then one day or another fundamentalism will grow again. I need to say that because some liberals always defend Islam and blame fundamentalists for creating problems. But Islam itself oppresses women. Islam itself doesn't permit democracy and it violates human rights. And because Islam itself is causing injustices, so it is our duty to make people alert. It is our responsibility to wake people up, to make them understand that religious scriptures come from a particular period in time and a particular place." Noted for her blunt style, Nasrin has recently published two volumes of her autobiography, which recount her childhood and early career as a doctor. Both books, along with several of her other works, have been banned in Bangladesh.

Taslima Nasrin was born in 1962 in Mymensingh, a small town in what was then East Pakistan, the daughter of a physician father, Rajab Ali. She was the third child in the family, following two brothers and preceding a sister. Her childhood was turbulent; she was sexually abused by an uncle and a male cousin beginning at age five, and in 1971 her family (except for her father) temporarily fled to the countryside to escape the violent war in which East Pakistan won its independence from West Pakistan and became Bangladesh. Her father beat his children, but he also encouraged his eldest daughter to become a doctor. Her mother, distraught by her husband's philandering, became devoutly religious and tried to pass along her beliefs to her children. Taslima was not enthusiastic about such forced worship, which included reading the Koran in Arabic without knowing its meaning. "When I was 14 or 15 years old, I found the Bengali translation of the Koran, and I learned what God says in the verses," she recounted to Cherry and Smith. "I was surprised to read wrong information about the solar system in the Koran—for example, that the sun is moving around the earth and the earth is not moving but standing still because of the support of the mountains. The inequalities and injustices against women and the people of different faiths in the Koran made me angry. If any religion allows the persecution of the people of different faiths, if any religion keeps women in slavery and keeps people in ignorance, then I cannot accept that religion. As an individual, I wanted to serve people irrespective of religion, race, and gender. And instead of having irrational blind faith, I preferred to have a rational logical mind."

Although Nasrin did well in science at school, she loved literature from an early age. She began writing when she was 15, composing poetry for literary journals and, from 1978 to 1983, editing the literary magazine *Senjuti*. She also served as president of a literary organization while studying at Mymensingh Medical College, from which she graduated in 1984 with an M.B.B.S. (a bachelors degree in medicine and surgery). She later moved to the Bangladeshi capital, Dhaka, to complete her residency training as an anesthesiologist. For the next eight years she worked in public hospitals and in a government gynecology clinic, where she witnessed physical injuries to women that would later lead her to speak out. "When I was at the hospital in Dhaka, I treated so many seven- or eight-year-old girls who were raped by their male relatives, some 50 or 60 years old," she said at an appearance at the Asia Society in New York City, as reported by Thulani Davis for the *Village Voice* (November 19, 2002). "I treated them, and I remembered when I was raped."

Nasrin's first volume of poetry, *Shikore Bipul Khudha* (which can be translated as "hunger in the roots") was published in 1986, and was followed by *Nirbashito Bahire Ontore* (which can be translated as "banished without and within") in 1988. The success of the latter volume provided Nasrin with the opportunity to begin writing for several progressive Bangladeshi newspapers and magazines in 1989. Her columns frequently dealt with the oppression of women; she attacked political and religious tenets that discriminate against women, eliciting both ardent support and angry opposition. "All the editors wanted me to write because letters showed there was popular interest from women. Also from men. They found it shocking," she told Irshad Manji for *Herizons* (Winter 2003). "Before me, women would write love stories or advice on childcare and cooking. I wrote something different. Even the fundamentalists—male chauvinists who hated me—they used to read me." In 1990 Islamic fundamentalist groups began organizing demonstrations denouncing the atheism and sexual content in Nasrin's work. A number of demonstrators broke into the newspaper offices where she worked; others sued her editors and publishers. Nasrin was attacked in public several times and was largely confined to her house. She continued to publish, however. Her poetry collections from this period include *Amar kichu jay ase na* (which can be translated as "I couldn't care less," 1990), *Atale antarin* ("captive in the abyss," 1991), *Balikar Gollachut* ("game of the girls," 1992), and *Behula eka bhasiyechila bhela* ("Behula floated the raft alone," 1993). In addition, the essay collection *Nirbachito Kolam* appeared in 1991 (it was published in English in 2004 as *Selected Columns*), followed by *Jabo Na Keno? Jabo* ("why shouldn't I go? I will go") and *Nosto Meyer Nosto Godyo* ("fallen prose of a fallen woman") in 1992 and *Choto Choto Dukkho Kotha* ("stories of pain") in 1994. She also published three novels, *Oporpokkho* ("opposition," 1992), *Sodh* (1992, published in English as *Getting Even* in 2002), and *Nimontron* ("invitation," 1993).

It was the publication of the novella *Lajja,* in February 1993, that incensed Islamic fundamentalists in Bangladesh to the point that they issued a fatwa against Nasrin. *Lajja*—published in English as *Shame* in 1997—addressed the violence between Hindus and Muslims resulting from the destruction of the Babri Masjid mosque in India, in December 1992; it recounted the suffering of a fictional Hindu family in Bangladesh at the hands of Muslim fundamentalists after the mosque's destruction. (Many members of the Hindu minority in Bangladesh were threatened with violence by Bangladeshi Muslims, who account for 90 percent of that nation's population. India's ruling party, the Bharatiya Janata Party, widely promoted *Shame* in India—an act which inflamed anti-Muslim sentiment there, thus further angering many Bangladeshis.) The controversial book quickly sold 60,000 copies before being banned by the government. Janet Ingraham, in a review for *Library Journal* (November 1, 1997), called it "a seething indictment of oppression and religious fundamentalism couched precariously as a novel." Ingraham added, "This important work is impassioned but difficult to read. [It is] more

reportage and protest than story." In *World & I* (May 1997) Charles R. Larson characterized the book as "a docudrama of [Nasrin's] time," adding, "Lengthy passages of factual material are woven through her narrative, often appearing as the lists of atrocities that were happening in Bangladesh during the troubled time of her story. And yet, when she wants to jump beyond the level of outrage, there are moments of powerful insight in her story, vignettes of the humanity for which her characters have searched."

Soon after the book's publication, Muslim fundamentalists accused Nasrin of conspiring against Islam, and the group Soldiers of Islam issued a fatwa against her and placed a bounty of 50,000 taka (equivalent to approximately $1,250) on her head after she remarked in the *New Statesman*, a British political journal, that the Koran ought to be thoroughly revised. Because devout Muslims believe the Koran is the word of God, many viewed Nasrin's statement as blasphemous. Nasrin has claimed that it was misquoted and that she was criticizing the Islamic legal code rather than the holy text itself. In a letter of correction to the *New Statesman*, she argued that religious scripture was irrelevant to the modern world and called instead for a civil code granting women equality with men. "My view on this issue is clear and categorical," she wrote, as reported by Meredith Tax for the *Nation* (November 18, 2002). "I hold the Koran, the Vedas, the Bible, and all such religious texts determining the lives of their followers as 'out of place and out of time.' We have crossed the sociohistorical contexts in which these were written and therefore we should not be guided by their precepts. . . . We have to move beyond these ancient texts if we want to progress."

As the controversy surrounding *Shame* grew, a coalition of 14 political and civic organizations united to demand Nasrin's execution by hanging; in addition, the coalition organized demonstrations, many of which turned violent, and led a general strike that lasted a week and brought Bangladesh to a standstill. Nasrin's passport was confiscated, and she was forced to quit her job. In June 1994 the government, invoking a seldom-used law, filed a case against her for injuring the religious sentiments of the people. Because she feared she would be killed by fellow inmates or guards in prison, Nasrin went into hiding just before officers came to arrest her. (While the government of Bangladesh is secular, Islamic fundamentalist groups wield considerable power. Many speculated that the charges against Nasrin were a means of appeasing such groups.) Processions calling for her death shook the streets of the capital; one demonstration attracted 100,000 participants, some of whom threatened to release thousands of poisonous snakes if their demands were not met. Among those voicing support for Nasrin were the international writers' organization PEN, Amnesty International, the International

Humanist and Ethical Union, and the National Organization for Women. After several months in hiding, Nasrin escaped to Sweden with the assistance of the Women Writers' Committee of International PEN. A Bangladeshi court sentenced her in absentia to a one-year prison term in 2002.

Nasrin has continued to write prolifically in exile, publishing the poetry volumes *Ay kasta jhepe, jiban debo mepe* (which can be translated as "pain come pouring down, I'll measure out my life for you," 1994), *Nirbashito Narir Kobita* ("poems from exile," 1996), *Jolopodyo* ("water lilies," 2000), *Khali Khali Lage* ("feeling empty," 2001), and *Kicchukhan Thako* ("stay for a while," 2005) . Her other novels include *Phera* (1993; which was translated into English as *Homecoming*, 2005), *Bhromor Koio Gia* ("tell him the secret," 1994), and *Forashi Premik* (which was translated into English as *French Lover*, 2002). In 1995 a collection of English poems, *The Game in Reverse*, appeared in the U.S. "The poems' strength lies in the strong feminist voice that details the imperatives of male dominance," Uma Parameswaran wrote in *World Literature Today* (Spring 1996). "The power exerted by men over women is expressed in poem after poem." These two volumes were followed by *100 Poems* (1997); *Love Poems* (2004), a selection of the love poems from Nasrin's previous books; and *All about Women* (2005).

In 1998 Nasrin returned to Bangladesh to visit her dying mother. Because the government has repeatedly denied her applications to return to the country, she entered Bangladesh illegally; when it became known that she had returned, fundamentalist groups once again called for her death. Nasrin continues to hope that she will one day be able to return to her homeland. "I have never mentally settled into exile," she told Manji. "I live with the dream that one day I will return permanently. I have even asked my family to leave everything in my house exactly the way it was— my books, my clothes, my papers, my pictures, the pen on my desk. Exile is a bus stop for me."

The first volume of Nasrin's autobiography, *Amar Meyebela*, was published in 1999 and banned by the Bangladeshi government on the grounds that it might damage the existing social system and offend the religious sentiments of the people. (Nasrin created the word *Meyebela* when writing her columns in Bangladesh, because there was no word for a girl's childhood years in the Bengali language.) The book was translated as *My Girlhood* for an edition published in India, in 2001, and as *Meyebela: My Bengali Girlhood* for the 2002 U.S. edition. A reviewer for *USA Today* (September 24, 2002) characterized the book as "a richly detailed story of a traditional upbringing amid difficult change. Set when East Pakistan was gaining independence under the new name of Bangladesh, the memoir juxtaposes the cruelty of war and famine with the sweet friendships and games of childhood. As Nasrin grows older, the games give way to other, often darker, matters: the

arranged marriages of her friends, a cousin's death after a botched abortion and her own encounters with sex abuse." In *Kirkus Reviews* (July 1, 2002), a critic noted, "The writing is personal and understandably angry, although this is its weakness, since Nasrin seems to imply—without giving any wider context for readers to judge by— that the horrors she details are universal. . . . By 14, Nasrin had become critical of her family, her country, and her faith. A raw and impassioned account of the making of a young feminist." Jeff Zeleski, writing for *Publishers Weekly* (June 3, 2002), called the book a "moving but uneven memoir. . . . Nasrin writes hauntingly of a childhood of confusion and pain. . . . The memoir shows the young Nasrin trying to make sense of taboos (why isn't her mother allowed to go to the movies?) and the mysteries of adulthood (why doesn't any grownup seem happy?). . . . But Nasrin's tale—consistently heartbreaking and sometimes gorgeously written—grows disorganized as it progresses: the chronology becomes confusing, anecdotes get repeated, and the abrupt ending leaves many questions unanswered." In 2002 Nasrin published the second volume of her autobiography, *Utal Hawa* ("wild wind"). *Utal Hawa* chronicles her life from ages 16 to 26, including her marriage to the Bangladeshi poet Rudra Mohammad Shahidullah, and was also banned by the government of Bangladesh. Nasrin has continued to write autobiographical books, publishing *Dwikhondito* ("split into two," 2003), *Ko* ("speak up," 2003) *Sei Sob Ondhokar* ("those dark days," 2004), and *Ami Bhalo nei, tumi bhalo theko prio desh* ("I am not fine, but you stay well my beloved country," 2006). These later books have yet to be translated into English.

Nasrin has contended that it is impossible to be both a feminist and a practicing Muslim. "If you are a Muslim, it means you are obeying Allah's words, which are totally against women," she explained to Manji. "If you are a feminist, it means you support women's rights and you cannot be religious. Actually, I don't understand how women can be religious because religion is made for men, for their own pleasure. Most of Hinduism's gods are female, but look at how women in Hindu society are treated. Reform efforts by Muslims should focus on removing religious laws." In addition, she is dismissive of the argument that promoting equal rights in essentially patriarchal societies is tantamount to cultural imperialism. "Some people try to portray female genital mutilation as culture," she told Manji. "Does that mean it should be followed? I love my culture—my food, my music, my clothing—but I never, ever accept torture as being culture." Nasrin has also voiced strong support for the separation of church and state. "People who live according to their religious belief should be respected," she said, as reported by Sveen. "But I have also seen the other side of religion—the one that results in violence, rapes, persecution, and death. I have seen groups of people professing the same religion fight each other bitterly. I have also witnessed how millions of Hindus have been obliged to leave their country just because they are Hindus and not Muslims. I asked myself: is this religion?"

Nasrin has often been compared to Salman Rushdie, the Indian author who went into hiding after his 1988 book *The Satanic Verses* so outraged Islamic fundamentalists that the Ayatollah Khomenei issued a fatwa against him. Although Rushdie defended Nasrin in an open letter written in 1994, she publicly criticized Rushdie after he apologized for *The Satanic Verses.* "I believe he showed cowardice in declaring his Islamic faith and calling on the publisher of *The Satanic Verses* neither to issue the book in paperback nor to allow it to be translated," she told the *Middle East Quarterly*, as quoted by Lianne George for the *National Post* (November 13, 2002).

Some literary critics have called Nasrin a talentless self-promoter whose success depends on her blunt and sometimes shocking language rather than on the merits of her prose and poetry. "Had they been written by a Westerner, many of Nasrin's poems would be dismissed as literarily thin political tracts," Nomi Morris wrote for *Maclean's* (October 9, 1995). However, Nasrin and her defenders contend that, as far as the fatwa is concerned, critical reaction is beside the point. "I don't think I'm a great philosopher, political leader or writer," she told Morris. "I was a medical doctor writing to express myself. I don't think I should be killed for it."

Nasrin's work has been the inspiration for both an opera and a film. The American composer and musician Steve Lacy based his opera *The Cry* on a September 1994 poem, "Happy Marriage," about a Muslim woman trapped in an abusive marriage, which Nasrin wrote for the *New Yorker*. *The Price of Freedom*, a short film about Nasrin's life directed by the Australian filmmaker Mathew Kelley, premiered at the 2003 Singapore International Film Festival.

Nasrin received India's Ananda Prize in 1992 for *Nirbachito Kolam*, and in 1994 she was awarded the Kurt Tucholsky Prize from Swedish PEN, the Human Rights Award from the government of France, Le Prix de l'Edit from the French town of Nantes, and the Sakharov Prize for Freedom of Thought from the European Parliament; also in 1994 she was named feminist of the year by the Feminist Majority Foundation. Her other honors include the Monismanien Prize from Uppsala University, in Sweden (1995), an honorary doctorate from Ghent University, in Belgium (1995), the International Humanist Award from the International Humanist and Ethical Union (1996), the Binodon Bichitra Award (1999), the Ananda Award for *Amar Meyebela* (2000), the Erwin Fischer Award from the Internationaler Bund der Konfessionslosen und Atheisten (2002), and the Freethought Heroine Award from the Freedom

from Religion Foundation (2002). In 2002 *Meyebela: My Bengali Girlhood* won the *Los Angeles Times*'s prize for best nonfiction book of the year.

Nasrin writes in her native tongue, Bengali, but her works have been translated into some 20 other languages, including Hindi, Urdu, Malayalam, Assamese, Kannada, Oriya, Nepali, English, French, German, Swedish, Norwegian, Italian, Icelandic, Serbo-Croatian, Arabic, and Persian. She has been divorced three times (and says she was beaten by her husbands). Since her exile she has lived in Sweden and France. She has been a research scholar at Harvard University's John F. Kennedy School of Government, studying the secularization of Islamic countries, and is currently a senior editor for *Free Inquiry* magazine, published by the Council for Secular Humanism. She writes occasional pieces for other publications, primarily in Europe.

—K.E.D.

Suggested Reading: *Free Inquiry* (on-line) Winter 1998–99; *Herizons* p18+ Winter 2003; *Nation* p34+ Nov. 18, 2002; *Village Voice* p55 Nov. 19, 2002; *World & I* p283+ May 1997

Selected Books in English Translation: poetry— *Light Up at Midnight, Selected Poems*, 1992; *The Game in Reverse*, 1995, *100 Poems*, 1997; *Love Poems*, 2004; *Homecoming*, 2005; *All about Women*, 2005: fiction—*Shame* 1997; *French Lover*, 2002, *Meyebela: My Bengali Girlhood*, 2002; *Getting Even*, 2002: nonfiction—*Selected Columns*, 2004

Newman, Sandra

1965– Novelist

Sandra Newman made her literary debut in 2002, with the publication of the novel *The Only Good Thing Anyone Has Ever Done*, and was welcomed into the literary community by the novelist Jonathan Safran Foer, who provided a blurb for her novel's cover. Commenting on that fact, Sharyn Wizda Vane wrote for the *Austin American-Statesman* (May 23, 2003), "At risk of sounding like a Blockbuster placard, if you liked Foer's form-bending *Everything Is Illuminated*, you'll love *Good Thing*, which mixes prose, poetry, lists and outlines in an engagingly eccentric story about identity and seeking the truth about one's past." Newman thus established herself as an important experimental novelist, one whom even the reviewers, usually skeptical about the value of experimental prose, found successful. "You could be forgiven for thinking that its title could just as easily have been *Everything Microsoft Word Has Ever Done*. It's all here: bullet-pointed lists, numbered lists, underlining, big type, small type and so on. Yes, it's an experimental novel," Scarlett Thomas wrote for the London *Independent on Sunday* (March 24, 2002), but concluded: "But don't go away—it's actually rather good. . . . You realise that experimental formats actually have a use (and become, in the hands of this author, poetry). It is hard not to be charmed by this. It feels like Elmore Leonard with more depth, and a twist of post-structuralism. The dialogue is pitch-perfect, with laugh-out-loud lines. The story is nuts, of course. By the end at least two of the characters have seen God, one has left in a spaceship and one has been transformed by a miracle. In places—hell, in the whole thing—this is overdone. But there is some breathtaking writing here, and this is an exhilarating read."

Sandra Newman was born in 1965 and adopted when she was about two weeks old by Sheldon and Louise Newman, a middle-class couple who failed to provide a happy home in Chelmsford, Massachusetts, where Newman grew up. Her adopted mother suffered from depression, spending five years of Newman's childhood in hospitals before committing suicide, when Newman was 13. At this point Sheldon Newman, and Jeff, Sandra's older brother, who had also been adopted, led separate lives. "The house had three storeys. Jeff lived on the top, dad had the middle and I lived in the basement and we didn't really meet or speak," Newman told Anna Pukas for the London *Daily Express* (April 6, 2002). "My brother and I had been close as children but after mother got ill, we were both trying to pretend that our family didn't exist. There was a sort of sibling rivalry that went wrong." When she was 18, Newman went to London and enrolled in Polytechnic of Central London to study for a degree in English and Russian; there she became a radical socialist. Upon completing her degree she began to write unpublishable short stories and novels, while doing temp work to support herself, including a stint as a blackjack player. She got the job by answering a classified ad placed by a gambler who was putting together a team of players. Newman competed in tournaments around the globe, including in Malaysia and Katmandu. "We were paid a salary and travelling expenses and we could keep a percentage of our winnings," Newman explained to Pukas. "It was quite a good living and I was an excellent player." In a twist arguably stranger than fiction, when she was 25, Newman's biological father, Richard Grossman, got in touch with her. He was a wealthy writer who lived in the gangster Bugsy Siegel's castle in Hollywood, and he put her in touch with her biological mother, Sally Greenawalt, who worked for NASA but had studied Russian in college. (The castle was eventually sold to the pop singer Madonna.)

Originally published in the U. K., *The Only Good Thing Anyone Has Ever Done* follows Chrysalis Moffat—a troubled young woman who had been born in Peru and adopted by an American family. She now lives in California—on a "madcap, deranged and heartbreaking spiritual quest for self-determination and identity," as Adrienne Miller wrote for *Esquire* (on-line). Following the death of her adopted mother, Chrysalis learns that much of what she had believed about herself is false. Consequently, she hides beneath her bed for an extended period, agonizes over her unfinished doctoral thesis, and assists her brother in setting up a scam to fleece the unwitting public. (The two enlist a fake guru and turn their inherited mansion into the Tibetan School of Miracles to prey on gullible spiritual seekers.) Eschewing traditional narrative structure, Newman tells the story through a unique series of lists interspersed with poetry and seemingly random interludes in the style of business reports. Miller called the book "a witty, imaginative debut from a young novelist with dazzling intellectual resources." In a review for *Pop Matters* (on-line), Phoebe Kate Foster wrote, "[The book might seem] confusing, peculiar, improbable and hard to follow. And, to some extent, that's correct. However, it is also charming, eclectic, entertaining, un-put-downable even if you don't quite understand what's going on, and it may well become a cult classic." "In a debut novel full of deft twists and unexpected intersections," Chris McCreary wrote for the *Review of Contemporary Fiction* (September 22, 2003), "Sandra Newman's narrative spans a world's worth of exotic locations and manages to weave together plotlines as diverse as germ warfare, professional blackjack, and New Age quackery."

In 2002 Newman was nominated for the London Guardian First Book Award. She signed a two-book deal when she found a publisher and is reportedly working an autobiographical novel about her journeys among various members of her biological family, with whom she eventually forged relationships.

—P.B.M./A.R.

Suggested Reading: *Austin American-Statesman* E p1+ May 23, 2003; *Esquire* (on-line); (London) *Daily Express* p45 Apr. 6, 2002; (London) *Independent on Sunday* p16 Mar. 24, 2002; *Pop Matters* (on-line); *Review of Contemporary Fiction* p125 Sep. 22, 2003

Selected Books: *The Only Good Thing Anyone Has Ever Done*, 2002

Niffenegger, Audrey

1963– Novelist

Since the 2003 publication of her first novel, *The Time Traveler's Wife*, Audrey Niffenegger has seen the book achieve widespread critical and commercial success; it was chosen for the *Today Show*'s book club, and the actor Brad Pitt purchased the movie rights. Not so long ago, however, Niffenegger was best known for other work. "I'm a printmaker, and I make artist books," she explained during a September 17, 2003 interview with Matt Lauer for the *Today Show*. "I started learning how to set type by hand and do letter press and how to bind a book by hand. . . . I've always just loved books as objects." She continued, "I've also made paintings that don't have any words in them, and so now I've finally made a book [*The Time Traveler's Wife*] that doesn't have any pictures." Capitalizing on the success of her novel, Niffenegger was finally able to publish two graphic novels that she had created earlier, *The Three Incestuous Sisters* (2005) and *The Adventuress* (2006).

Audrey Niffenegger was born in South Haven, Michigan, in 1963. As a young child, attending St. Joan of Arc School, in Skokie, Illinois, she was interested in art and book making. "I was the kid everybody thought was snotty because I was so internal," she told Pam DeFiglio for the *Chicago Daily Herald* (February 6, 2007). "I'd take a sheet of paper and fold it up small and write a book." After graduating from Evanston Township High School, she attended the School of the Art Institute of Chicago, earning her B.F.A., in 1985. She then moved to New York City, but a garbage strike sent her running back to the Chicago area. "There were piles of garbage 20 feet high everywhere. I had friends living in these unbelievable ratholes," she told DeFiglio. "And I decided I could be an artist just as well in Chicago." She earned her M.F.A. from Northwestern University, in the Chicago suburb of Evanston, in 1991. Two years later she began teaching at Columbia College Chicago, an arts-focused institution where she continues to work. Her classes include writing, letterpress printing, and fine-book production.

Although it includes elements of science fiction, *The Time Traveler's Wife* is primarily a love story. The protagonists are Clare, an art student, and Henry, a librarian who happens to have a genetic defect that allows him to travel to different points in time. Clare initially met Henry when she was six years old and he was 36; they married when she was 23 and he was 31. The two characters struggle to maintain a relationship as Henry bounces around in time and Clare remains in the present. The novel was widely praised. Dorman I. Shindler, in a review for the *Denver Post* (September 21, 2003), wrote, "Her characters [are] so true and the denouement so bittersweet yet perfect that readers won't begrudge her the extra room to tell a tale of two lovers who overcome all obstacles—including time itself—to live and love together." Calling the book "both compelling and unsettling," Kathy Balog opined for *USA Today* (September 24, 2003, on-line), "[Niffenegger] writes with the unflinching yet detached clarity of a war correspondent standing at the sidelines of an unfolding battle. She possesses a historian's eye for contextual detail."

In 2005 Niffenegger published an oversized graphic novel, *The Three Incestuous Sisters*, a strange tale of three sisters—the pretty Bettine, talented Clothilde, and clever Ophile—who share a house by the sea. A reviewer for *Publishers Weekly* (August 1, 2005) praised the full-page aquatint illustrations—etchings that affect the tones of watercolor washes—describing them as "evocative and [Edward] Gorey-esque" and noting that "they tell the story more than the minimalist prose does." In a review for the *Chicago Tribune* (September 11, 2005), Brad Thomas wrote, "Niffenegger's virtuosic printmaking skills allow her to create open and dramatic images that convey a story in a way words cannot. Ultimately her works are in service of the story, but each image embodies an autonomy that can make the story seem secondary. Each plate is imbued with a somber beauty and intensity that will draw the reader/viewer back for more thorough and rewarding scrutiny."

As with *The Three Incestuous Sisters*, the original version of Niffenegger's other graphic novel, *The Adventuress*, had been produced by hand, with Niffenegger preparing the plates for the illustrations and printing and binding the volumes. Consequently the initial copies of the books sold for $10,000 each. "The original must be exquisite," Margaret Reynolds wrote, reviewing *The Adventuress* for the London *Times* (September 16, 2006), "but even in reproduction the result is as haunting as Niffenegger's fiction." Niffenegger, who wrote and illustrated *The Adventuress* while in college, devised the storyline by selecting 10 images from her sketch books and attempting to connect them through a narrative. The heroine is a thin woman who wears nothing but elbow-length gloves. Created by an alchemist, she falls in love with Napoleon and later gives birth to a cat. The book is "whimsical but never silly and the images, carefully detailed in shades of green, are lovely," Nina Caplan wrote for the London *Evening Standard* (September 26, 2006).

Niffenegger is currently working on a novel, "Her Fearful Symmetry," and a graphic novel, "The Library." In a November 16, 2006 interview with Allen Pierleoni for the *Sacramento Bee*, Niffenegger described herself as a "spinster without any current appendages." She collects taxidermied specimens.

—C.M.

Suggested Reading: *Chicago Sun-Times* Features p59 Sep. 17, 2003; *Denver Post* E p2 Sep. 21, 2003; *San Francisco Chronicle* M p2 Sep. 28, 2003; *USA Today* (on-line) Sep. 24, 2003

Selected Books: novels—*The Time Traveler's Wife*, 2003; graphic novels—*The Three Incestuous Sisters*, 2005; *The Adventuress*, 2006

Terry Pollack/Courtesy of Wesleyan University Press

Notley, Alice

Nov. 8, 1945– Poet

A second generation member of the so-called New York School of poets and "one of the most distinctive voices in contemporary American poetry," according to R.D. Pohl in an article for the *Buffalo News* (May 2, 1993), Alice Notley has written numerous collections of verse. Among her more notable works are the feminist epic *The Descent of Alette* (1996); *Mysteries of Small Houses* (1998), which earned her the 1998 Los Angeles Times Book Prize for poetry and a 1999 Pulitzer Prize nomination; and *Disobedience* (2001), which was awarded the 2002 Griffin Poetry Prize. Notley is the widow of the poets Ted Berrigan and Douglas Oliver, and she recently edited collections of both of their work.

Born on November 8, 1945, in Bisbee, Arizona, Alice Notley was raised in Southern California, in the town of Needles, where her father owned and operated an automotive store. Located in the desert, Needles "was frighteningly lonely and empty, and I was dying to get away from it," Notley told Jennifer Dick in an October 2001 interview for

Double Change (on-line). After graduating from high school, Notley entered Barnard College, in New York City, completing her bachelor's degree in English, in 1967. She then went to the University of Iowa's Writers' Workshop, in Iowa City, with the intention of writing fiction. Once there, however, Notley "almost instantly started writing poems," as she told Maureen Holm in an interview for the *Poetry Calendar* (February 2000), which was republished on the Lyric Recovery Web site. "I got interested in the fact that there was this control on one page," she told Holm. "I think most fiction writers write by the sentence and paragraph, but my stories were written painstakingly, almost syllable by syllable." However, Notley did not particularly enjoy her initial experience at the University of Iowa and took a year off at one point to travel, spending time in San Francisco, Spain, and Morocco. After returning to Iowa, Notley found the situation there had improved somewhat: "When I came back, some new poets had arrived, including my future husband, Ted Berrigan," Notley explained to Holm. "I began reading people like Frank O'Hara, Gregory Corso and Allen Ginsberg instead of Robert Lowell and Sylvia Plath, and it made a great difference. I needed both a more casual voice, a freer line and a sense of happiness in poetry."

After completing her master of fine arts degree in 1969, Notley moved with Berrigan to an apartment on St. Mark's Place, in New York City, where they became associated with the Poetry Project at St. Mark's Church on the city's Lower East Side. Berrigan was a charter member of the second generation of the New York School of poetry, which Peter Schjeldahl described for the *New York Times Book Review* (January 17, 1982) as a "continuing academy-without-walls of the gritty and urbane." For the *Chicago Review* (January 1, 1999), Notley herself defined the New York School, whose first generation included John Ashbery, Kenneth Koch, and Frank O'Hara, as "successive groups of poets responsive in their writing to New York as a community and as an international city." (Elsewhere, the New York School poets have been characterized by the influence of modernism and surrealism on their work.) With the publication of her first poetry collection, *165 Meeting House Lane*, in 1971, Notley became associated with the New York School herself. After marrying Berrigan, in 1972, Notley gave birth to two sons, Anselm and Edmund.

Over the next decade, Notley authored a number of poetry collections, among them *Phoebe Light* (1973), *Incidentals in the Day World* (1973), *Alice Ordered Me to Be Made* (1976), *Songs for the Unborn Second Baby* (1979), *When I Was Alive* (1980), *Waltzing Matilda* (1981), and *How Spring Comes* (1981), which earned her the 1981 Poetry Center Book Award. In the latter two works, Peter Schjeldahl commented, "[Notley] proves herself a virtuoso of the word games and mingled voices, rhapsodic and goofy by turns, that characterize poetry decisively influenced by, among others, Frank O'Hara. . . . Small twists with big effects, writerly tricks that tickle and stab, are Miss Notley's forte, correlatives of a sensibility that shuttles riskily between fantasy and reality, literary dandyism and a daily life of family, friends and money worries." Overall, Schjeldahl wrote, "The growing strength of Alice Notley's writing seems to me one of the more heartening developments in current poetry. Miss Notley is easily the most authentic and effective poet in many years to emerge from the Lower East Side division of what is loosely called 'the New York School.'" Following the publication of *How Spring Comes*, Notley wrote an autobiographical work entitled *Tell Me Again* (1982).

On July 4, 1983 Ted Berrigan died from liver disease. The grieving process was difficult for Notley, and she sank into a profound depression. The poems written by Notley during this period— many of which are contained in her 1988 collection *At Night the States*—are noteworthy for their gloom and clipped brevity. Prior to *At Night the States* and subsequent to *Tell Me Again*, Notley authored three other collections—*Sorrento* (1984), *Margaret & Dusty* (1985), and *Parts of a Wedding* (1986). While mourning Berrigan, Notley reconnected with one of his old friends, the English poet and novelist Douglas Oliver, whom she married in 1988.

The next decade was a busy one for Notley. After *At Night the States*, she wrote *Homer's Art* (1990), and from 1990 to 1992 she taught at the Maryland Institute College of Art, in Baltimore, while publishing a poetry magazine with Oliver entitled *Scarlet*. Notley and Oliver moved to France in the summer of 1992 and wrote a collaborative work, *The Scarlet Cabinet: A Compendium of Books* (1992). Over the next four years Notley had several more poetry collections published, among them, *Selected Poems of Alice Notley* (1993) and *To Say You* (1994).

Inspired by "Inanna's Descent into the Underworld," an epic poem from ancient Sumeria, *The Descent of Alette* (1996) was Notley's attempt at a new, feminist epic poetry. "Inanna's Descent into the Underworld," details the continually frustrated plight of the goddess Inanna as she tries to enter hell, where her sister is the reigning deity. "I used that as a pattern for near inaction," Notley told Maureen Holm. "There are no fights, no battles. What happens is really an internal thing, the way a myth or a dream is internal and moves in place much of the time. I had to define for myself what an epic poem was. I invented a measure for it, a line that has a very particular sound, and it's vivid, rhythmic, very musical." Richard Gehr, writing for New York *Newsday* (December 29, 1996), described *The Descent of Alette* as a "fractured feminist epic" and a "hallucinatory description of a necropolitan subway descent." *The Descent of Alette* employs quotation marks

extensively: in a sample quoted by Susan McCabe for the *Antioch Review* (Summer 1998), the poem reads, "'One day, I awoke' '& found myself on' 'a subway, endlessly' 'I didn't know' 'how I'd arrived there / or' 'who I was' 'exactly' 'But I knew the train' 'knew riding it' 'knew the look of' 'those about me'." Though some reviewers expressed confusion over the use of the quotes and the work as a whole, McCabe declared, "Notley's poetic project fuels itself by a kind of ecstatic search for new ways of being, reimagined ways of inhabiting a gendered world."

Notley's *Mysteries of Small Houses* (1998), a nominee for the 1999 Pulitzer Prize and the winner of the 1998 Los Angeles Times Book Prize for poetry, was described as "an extraordinary accomplishment," "powerful [and] deeply compelling," "both intimate and historical," and "fearless and innovative" by the judges on the Pulitzer Prize committee, according to David Shaw in a report for the *Los Angeles Times* (April 24, 1999). "Notley offers in this volume a moving, funny, absorbing autobiography of a sensibility as well as a lived life," Mary Oliver wrote for the *Chicago Tribune* (December 20, 1998). In describing the work, Notley told Maureen Holm that she had not intended to write an autobiography: "My intention was and still is to re-center the 'I' in poetry. People have become very unsure how to use it, when to use it, and whether it represents anything real besides a physical reference." The work does, however, recount Notley's life—her childhood in the Southwest, her time at Barnard, her disappointing experience in Iowa—while calling into question our notions about individual identity. "On first reading," Oliver wrote, "these poems seem stream-of-consciousness ruminations; on second reading, one recognizes the stringently self-inquiring mind at work amidst the flow." In one poem quoted by Oliver, entitled "Experience," Notley wrote, "So glad I don't have to write / in the styles of the poetries I was taught / they were beautiful and unlike me / positing a formal, stylized woman. / But I am the poet, without doubt. / Experience is a hoax."

Notley's mission in writing *Disobedience* (2001) was to find a form that joined all the components of her previous work; more specifically, she sought to fuse "autobiography as daily commentary and daily involvement in politics (I mean politics by virtue of one's being oneself, and part of the world), along with fictional narrative, with characters, and fantasy and dream," Notley explained to Brian Kim Stefans for *Publishers Weekly* (August 27, 2001). "*Disobedience*," she continued, "reacts against everything, and is concerned with breaking down barriers, for example, the barriers that separate waking consciousness and dream consciousness, the barriers that separate narratives of real life, fictional narratives and dream accounts as genres." In one poem quoted on the Griffin Poetry Prize Web site, Notley writes:

Have forgotten the other you . . .
that sense that some other entity knows one intimately
from the inside.

It's probably part of oneself
why shouldn't it be
why shouldn't part of one, be "god?"

Could "god" "know" a "person?"
if god is ground
god could be in a person, could be like a person
having to mimic our every idiocy.

In their citation for *Disobedience*, the Griffin Prize judges remarked, "In an unsentimental interrogation of the will, the soul and the common being the long poem 'disses' the orthodoxies of political power, sex, and philosophy. *Disobedience* does what only the best poetry can do in times like these, surprise, denounce, dissent."

Shortly after Douglas Oliver died in Paris, on April 21, 2000, Notley edited *Arrondissements* (2003), a collection of his poetry. Earlier she had edited a posthumous anthology of Ted Berrigan's work entitled *The Sonnets* (2000), and in 2005 the University of California Press published *The Collected Poems of Ted Berrigan*, which she also edited. Anselm and Edmund Berrigan, her sons, are both poets themselves.

In addition to the honors listed above, Notley is also the recipient of a 1983 GE Foundation award, a 2001 award from the American Academy of Arts and Letters, the Poetry Society of America's 2001 Shelly Memorial Award, and numerous fellowships and grants. Notley currently lives in Paris, France, where she edits the magazine *Gare du Nord*. In addition to poetry, Notley enjoys the visual arts, particularly painting in watercolor and creating collages; some of her visual works are pictured in her poetry collections.

In 2006 Notley drew on previous books and chapbooks, as well as uncollected work, for *Grave of Light: New and Selected Poems, 1970-2005*. The book afforded critics the opportunity to assess Notley's career as a whole. Writing for *Booklist* (September 15, 2006), Janet St. John wrote: "Notley's poems tell the story of her artistic development and bear witness to the multitude of styles and influences that Notley has explored. From second generation New York School to 'language' and prose poetry to mythical epics, Notley as artist is like a hero on a fantastical journey. She descends into subterranean worlds of dream and ascends to heights of philosophical thought, but also remains rooted in the dirt of politics and the tedium of the everyday life." The book, St. John concluded, "should have something for everyone."

—P.B.M.

Suggested Reading: Academy of American Poets Web site; *Buffalo News* p10 May 2, 1993, F p8 Dec. 3, 2000; *Double Change* (on-line); Griffin Poetry Prize Web site; *Jacket* (on-line); Lyric Recovery Web site; *New York Times Book Review* p13 Jan. 17, 1982

Selected Books: *165 Meeting House Lane*, 1971; *Phoebe Light*, 1973; *Incidentals in the Day World*, 1973; *Alice Ordered Me to Be Made*, 1976; *A Diamond Necklace*, 1977; *Songs for the Unborn Second Baby*, 1979; *When I Was Alive*, 1980; *Waltzing Matilda*, 1981; *How Spring Comes*, 1981; *Tell Me Again*, 1982; *Sorrento*, 1984; *Margaret & Dusty*, 1985; *Parts of a Wedding*, 1986; *At Night the States*, 1988; *Homer's Art*, 1990; *The Scarlet Cabinet: A Compedium of Books* (with Douglas Oliver), 1992; *Selected Poems of Alice Notley*, 1993; *To Say You*, 1994; *Close to Me & Closer. . . (The Language of Heaven) and Désamère*, 1995; *The Descent of Alette*, 1996; *Mysteries of Small Houses*, 1998; *Disobedience*, 2001; *Coming After: Essays on Poetry*, 2005; as editor—*The Sonnets*, 2000; *Arrondissements*, 2003; *The Collected Poems of Ted Berrigan*, 2005

Marc Atkins/Courtesy of Bloodaxe Books

Oliver, Douglas

Sep. 14, 1937–Apr. 21, 2000 Poet; novelist

Though some critics called his writing outmoded and overly formal, Douglas Oliver's poetry was indisputably vibrant and politically aware. He had been publishing poetry since the late 1960s, but Oliver's reputation was finally cemented with the publication of two long poems: "The Infant and the Pearl," (1985), which examines England under the leadership of Prime Minister Margaret Thatcher, and *Penniless Politics* (1991), a book-length poem that describes a communal society rising from the ashes of a decaying New York City. In these poems, and indeed in the majority of his work, Oliver exhibited a remarkable ability to produce highly structured material that still possessed spirit, passion, and vulnerability.

The youngest of three children, Douglas Oliver was born to Scottish parents on September 14, 1937 in Southampton, England. He was raised in Branksome, near Bournemouth, in a run-down estate built in the 19th century for Sir Percy Florence Shelley, the son of the legendary poet. Other literary influences echoed through the area; Robert Louis Stevenson wrote the classic horror novel *The Strange Case of Dr. Jekyll and Mr. Hyde* (1886) in Bournemouth, and Stevenson's work remained a lifelong fascination for Oliver.

Oliver attended the Bournemouth School but was terribly unhappy there. He left at age 16 and joined the Royal Air Force shortly thereafter. Upon his discharge he became a journalist, writing first for local newspapers in Cambridge and Coventry, and later, during the 1960s, after he had moved to France, for Agence France-Presse.

Oliver married Janet Hughes, a schoolteacher, in 1962. They had three children: Kate, Tom, and Bonamy. Tom, who had been born with Down's Syndrome, died before his second birthday, right around the time Oliver's first collection of poems, *Oppo Hectic* (1969), was published by Ferry Press. Tom would become a central figure in his father's later work, most notably in a volume titled *In the Cave of Suicession* (1974). To write that work, Oliver traveled to an abandoned lead mine called Suicide Cave, in Derbyshire's Peak District, and stayed there many nights over a period of months, sometimes typing as he sat in the dark.

In 1972 Oliver left France to return to England. He entered the University of Essex to study literature. On his graduation day, the university offered him a teaching position, and when not teaching, Oliver wrote. In 1973 he published his first novel, *Harmless Building*, which described a dysfunctional family in a small town on the south coast of England. He also wrote *The Diagram Poems* (1979), which were based on the activities of guerrillas in Uruguay. Oliver sympathized with the guerrillas, in part because of their steal-from-the-rich and give-to-the-poor sensibilities. Though his left-leaning politics were always apparent in his poetry, critics particularly noted their presence in this collection.

With the rise of the British prime minister Margaret Thatcher's right-wing government during the early 1980s, Oliver's uneasiness with the state of the world increased. He suffered from nervous anxiety, which manifested itself in psoriasis, among other symptoms. During this period of his life, he left England frequently, first as a boxing correspondent in Italy for the London *Spectator*—boxing was another lifelong passion—and then, in 1982, as a lecturer at the British Institute in Paris.

Journalism assignments also took him to such places as Granada and Haiti. Due in part to his lengthy absences, his marriage to Hughes disintegrated.

Oliver's distrust of Thatcher was the impetus behind "The Infant and the Pearl," which has been called one of his greatest works. The piece was inspired by "Pearl," an anonymous allegorical poem written in the 14th century. In "The Infant and the Pearl" Oliver uses the allegory and rigid stanza structure of the earlier piece to skewer Thatcher and members of her government, who—in his opinion—allowed partisanship to polarize the nation. He wrote, as quoted by Nicholas Johnson in the London *Independent* (April 26, 2000), "She was wearing / a pearly suit, not silver-rose / pink, since sadly we seem to be sharing / a black and white world. . . ."

Kind, a book of collected poems, was published in 1987, furthering Oliver's reputation and winning him a wider readership. That same year some of his early work was featured in *A Various Art*, a well-regarded anthology edited by Andrew Crozier. The year was noteworthy for Oliver for other reasons, as well. While at the University of Essex Oliver had met a married couple, two poets named Ted Berrigan and Alice Notley. Berrigan had died in 1983, and in 1987 Oliver renewed his friendship with Notley and soon married her.

The new couple moved to New York City—Notley is an American—and Oliver found work as a computer programmer in a cancer hospital and as a contact tracer for patients with HIV, the virus that causes AIDS. Oliver lived with Notley on the Lower East Side, an area of the city then decaying and ridden with crime. He became a fixture of the poetry scene in lower Manhattan, frequently participating in readings and slams, at which the audience weighed in with criticism. He began work on *Penniless Politics*, an epic poem published in England, in 1991. In this piece Oliver envisions a section of the Bronx and Brooklyn breaking away from the rest of the city (and the rest of the United States) to form a utopia, in which multiculturalism and socialism are the norm. (The poem even includes the text of the new nation's Constitution.) In a review for the London *Guardian* (April 7, 1992), Howard Brenton remarked: "What was the shock like reading T. S. Eliot's *The Waste Land* when it was published in 1922? I think I know. I've just read Douglas Oliver's epoch-making long poem, *Penniless Politics*. I never thought I would ever read anything like it in the 1990s. *Penniless Politics* sets the literary agenda for the next 20 years." The poem might not have received such attention had it consisted merely of political polemic. Critics also praised the beauty of Oliver's writing, as in this description of an urban market quoted by Brenton: "As cabbage leaves drift on / the sidewalk, and cherries, / squashed, bleep / their stones, ice sparkles / under broccoli, the washed / beans seep / water through slats of wood / out at Hunt's Point, and it's only 6:30 / the wholesale market already / almost done, the rest of the / city / barely waking as the dawn / gleams on unsold boxes of / onions . . ."

In 1992 Oliver and Notley moved to Paris, and Oliver returned to his teaching post at the British Institute. Between 1996 and 1998 several small publishers anthologized a number of his previous published works. (Oliver was committed to supporting independent imprints, particularly those run by fellow poets.) In 2000 Bloodaxe (founded by the poet Neil Astley) published *A Salvo for Africa*, an optimistic collection in which Oliver argued that the continent could rise above its problems, despite those who believe corruption, warfare, and disease pull all hope (and aid money) into a never-ending abyss.

Douglas Oliver died on April 21, 2000 following a long battle with cancer. In 2003 his widow completed the editing of *Arrondissements*, a collection of three long poems about Paris, "The Shattered Crystal," "China Blue," and "The Video

House of Fame." "Video games and Parisian wanderings serve as brilliantly unpolished microcosms in this posthumous collection," a reviewer wrote for *Publishers Weekly* (February 23, 2004).

Oliver is frequently remembered not only for his poetry, but for his gentle nature and generosity.

—C.M.

Suggested Reading: *Chicago Review* p79 Jan. 1, 1999; *Financial Times* p13 Dec. 17, 1994; (London) *Guardian* p38 Apr. 7, 1992, T p7 Jan. 17, 1995, T p10 Jan. 23, 1997, p28 May 6, 2000; (London) *Independent* p6 Apr. 26, 2000

Selected Books: *Oppo Hectic*, 1969; *Harmless Building*, 1973; *In the Cave of Suicession*, 1974; *The Diagram Poems*, 1979; *Kind*, 1987; *Penniless Politics*, 1991; *Selected Poems*, 1996; *A Salvo for Africa*, 2000; *Arrondissements*, 2003

Tom Cogill/Courtesy of University of Virginia Public Affairs

Orr, Gregory

Feb. 3, 1947– Poet; nonfiction writer

With the publication of his first poetry collection, *Burning the Empty Nests* (1973), Gregory Orr achieved a place in the first rank of American poets. "Last night's dreams disappear. / They are like the sink draining: / a transparent rose swallowed by its / stem," he wrote in "Washing My Face," from that volume. Critics responded

favorably to his plainspoken expressions of isolation. "Everything is seen as if from a distance: silhouettes of experience, contours of feeling," Herbert Leibowitz wrote for the *New York Times Book Review* (August 12, 1973). "The Poet, alone, gazes at empty beds, rooms, streets and fields. . . . Only an occasional figure steps forward, as from a hallucination, to menace him with death or loss of identity." Orr has been deeply involved with reading, writing, and teaching poetry since he was young, and he has written at length about how these activities have helped him recover from the paralyzing grief of having, at the age of 12, accidentally killed one of his brothers—an event that figures prominently in his poetry and in his widely praised memoir *The Blessing* (2002). Orr explores the redemptive qualities of verse in the nonfiction book *Poetry as Survival* (2002). In the preface to that book, "Everywhere and Always," Orr wrote: "I lived for about four years after my brother's death without any hope at all. Nothing that I found in my culture sustained me. . . . . Then, thanks to Mrs. Irving, the librarian in my small public school, I discovered poetry. . . . In the small 'honors English' class that Mrs. Irving taught in my senior year, she had us write all kinds of things: stories, sketches, plays, haiku. I wrote a poem one day, and it changed my life. I had a sudden sense that the language in poetry was 'magical,' unlike language in fiction: that it could create or transform reality rather than simply describe it. That first poem I wrote was a simple, escapist fantasy, but it liberated the enormous energy of my despair and oppression as nothing before had ever done. I felt simultaneously revealed to myself and freed of my self by the images and actions of the poem. I knew from that moment on that all I wanted to do was write poems." Steven Cramer, looking back at Orr's career in a review of *The Caged Owl: New and Selected Poems* (2002) for *Poetry* (July 2003), wrote: "We all know examples of poets who garner early acclaim, then either lose their gifts or reuse them until they're so much gift-wrapping. Blessed with the curse of fame at twenty-six, Orr became neither a one-hit wonder nor a recycler of self-derivative tunes. Instead, he has quietly attended, and attended to, his own thirty-year singing school. Burdened with the curse of 'a long story / of torment' to tell, this mature lyricist has found, for himself and for us, the form that affirms."

Gregory Orr contributed the following autobiographical statement to *World Authors 2000–2005*:

"Many of the events of my early years are covered in a recent memoir (*The Blessing*, Council Oak Books, 2002). I was born on February 3, 1947 in Albany, New York. My father was in medical school at the time and we lived in a farmhouse without hot water 40 minutes southwest of the city in the Heldeberg Hills, though my parents had both been born and raised in cities. We eventually settled in the rural Hudson Valley about 50 miles south of Albany in the hamlet of Germantown, where my father was a country doctor. Probably the pivotal event in my life happened when I was 12 and was responsible for the death of a younger brother, Peter, in a hunting accident. This was not the first sudden death of a sibling—when I was three, a brother who was four climbed out of his crib one night, swallowed some sugar-coated pills, climbed back to bed, and died. More uncannily, I learned on the day of Peter's death that my father, when he was a boy about my age, had killed his best friend in a similar hunting accident. Neither of my parents could or would discuss my brother's death with me, and I became seriously withdrawn out of grief and horror at what I had done. When I was 14, our remaining family (two brothers and an infant sister and my parents) moved to Haiti, where my father intended to work for a year as a doctor at a backwoods, American-run hospital, the Hopital Albert Schweitzer in Deschapelles. I loved Haiti and I was grateful to be far from my guilt about my brother's death, but about eight months into our stay there, my mother died overnight from complications following a surgical procedure at the hospital. We returned to the States and my father subsequently remarried.

"While still in high school, I joined a civil rights organization, the CORE (Congress of Racial Equality) chapter in the nearby city of Kingston, New York. Ultimately, my interest in these political projects would take me to Mississippi as a volunteer in the summer of 1965. My experiences there and in rural Alabama involved numerous beatings and jailings and one very terrifying kidnapping at gunpoint and could perhaps be summarized as 'violent misadventures.'

"I first attended Hamilton College (1964–66), but the fit was bad and I transferred to Antioch College (1966–69) in hopes that I could learn more about poetry writing, which was, by then, my single passion. After I graduated from Antioch, I attended the MFA program at Columbia University, studying with Mark Strand and Stanley Kunitz. When I realized that Kunitz had made wonderful poems by, among other things, assimilating and transforming childhood trauma, I knew I had found a guide and mentor for my own project. While working at a bookstore near Columbia, I met my future wife, Trisha. After completing my MFA degree (1969–1971), I accepted a three-year fellowship in the University of Michigan's Society of Fellows. I saw a copy of my first collection of poems (*Burning the Empty Nests*, Harper and Row, 1973) at our wedding. Following my three years in Ann Abor, I accepted a job at the University of Virginia, where I have been since 1975. I have two daughters, Eliza (born 1982) and Sophia (born 1986). My wife is a still life painter.

"My own life since coming to Virginia has been rather uneventful, in a good sense, as compared to my childhood and adolescence. I founded and designed Virginia's Master of Fine Arts Writing Program in 1983 and served as its first director. For the most part, however, my adventures concern the lyric poets whose work I love: Keats, Blake, Yeats, Wordsworth, Dickinson, Whitman, Roethke. My whole life I've enjoyed speculating on the urgent purposes and functions of the lyric poem and that preoccupation finally took the form of a book, *Poetry as Survival* (University of Georgia Press, 2002). My own poetry collections are as follows: *Burning the Empty Nests* (1973), *Gathering the Bones Together* (1975), *The Red House* (1980), *Salt Wings* (a chapbook, 1980), *We Must Make a Kingdom of It* (1986), *New and Selected Poems* (1988), *City of Salt* (1995), *Orpheus and Eurydice* (2001), *The Caged Owl: New and Selected Poems* (2002), and *Concerning the Book that Is the Body of the Beloved* (2005)."

Orr's first book of poetry grew out of his M.F.A. thesis, which was also titled "Burning the Empty Nests." Reviewing the book for *Poetry* (December 1973), David Lehman joined other critics in noting the surrealistic cast and restrained expressiveness that characterized many of its verses: "The absence of explicit political references in . . . Orr's very impressive first book of poems functions as part of a strategy of reticence, a pointing outward to a larger silence against which (as [Samuel] Beckett would say) we have sinned. . . . Precise phrasing begets precise imagery; the succinctness of Orr's writing goes hand in hand with a visual sense of bareness, of stark landscapes in which humanity and nature confront and converge, with [René]

Magritte-like transformations." To some reviewers these surrealistic touches at times seemed mannered. Though Herbert Leibowitz praised Orr for having "an immaculate style of latent violence and inhibited tenderness," he also described the poems as "monodies, as if Orr were an opera singer with the range of one octave, suspicious that more versatile rhythms would corrupt the purity of his voice. Uninflected, the poems are frozen in their surrealistic reflexes and two dimensional surface. Orr's syntax permits no spontaneity, no play with language out of which wild surmises might come." In 1997 *Burning the Empty Nests* was reissued by the Carnegie-Mellon University Press, as part of its Contemporary Classics series.

The sequence of seven poems that gives *Gathering the Bones Together* its title takes up the subject of Orr's tragic hunting accident, and other poems in the volume are concerned with similar questions of mortality and memory. Noting that "the presence of death is strong in the book," Seamus Cooney, in a review for *Library Journal* (June 1, 1975), considered Orr to be staying in "the vein of dream imagery seen in his *Burning the Empty Nests*" but felt that *Gathering the Bones Together* "includes more poems anchored in a referentially real world. . . . Though they are technically un-adventurous and lack rhythmic or syntactic vigor, at their best these poems are quietly convincing." J. F. Cotter, writing for *America* (August 16, 1975), argued that in Orr's verse "suffering and the courage to speak the truth develop an awareness of others' losses" and the speaker in his poems is not consoled by "false hopes or facile answers." Orr's, Cotter added, "is a life that has died to itself to be reborn in a woman's love and in a simple reverence for leftover things: a spider's web, a buried egg or a shell. People and objects are not mere subjects of verse or symbols; they are the hands that reach out for his salvation."

The Red House, Orr's next book of verse, took on a wide range of subject matter and received similarly disparate reviews. In an extensive essay for the *New York Times Book Review* (October 12, 1980), Charles Molesworth assessed Orr and other poets of roughly that same generation—including such important figures as Charles Simic, Louise Glück, Ted Kooser, and David St. John—and found them largely wanting, with the exceptions of Marilyn Hacker and Alfred Corn, two poets associated with the movement known as neo-formalism. Comparing *The Red House* with Orr's earlier collections, Molesworth wrote that the third book "has much plainer writing, with a concentration of subjects drawn from rural Virginia. But the typical poem still exhibits a drifting dreaminess; there are no exclamations or sharp rhetorical edges." Molesworth concluded: "Mr. Orr's poetry looks easy to write, and with good reason, for it shows no sense of traditional lyric possibilities before, say, the last decade, and little musicality or invention." D. L. Guillory, on the other hand, writing for *Library Journal*

(November 1, 1980), judged Orr's work "vividly phrased and undeniably human. Light filters through the cracks of a barn 'the way sword-blades/pierce a magician's box.' The ground is 'toothed with dew,' and smells of every kind abound, the pungent scent of 'wine and kerosene,' the familiar odor of 'sweat, dirt and flesh.'. . . Orr is still haunted by 'the invisible and unforgiving dead,' the ghosts of his brother and father. This mixture of pleasure and pain makes *The Red House* readable and true."

After publishing *Salt Wings*, *We Must Make a Kingdom of It*, *New and Selected Poems*, *City of Salt*, and *Orpheus and Eurydice*, Orr published *The Caged Owl: New and Selected Poems*. Warmly received, the book afforded critics the opportunity to assess the whole of Orr's career. In a critique for the *Harvard Review* (Fall 2002), Floyd Skloot wrote that Orr "has long been among our most austere and urgent poets" and argued that over the years "Orr's subject matter has remained consistent, and his Imagist sense of poetry as radically compressed human speech has held firm." Skloot added: "Orr's work deepens and opens steadily, with reality outside his guiltswamped mind finding its way more and more fully into the poems. Pain is not all he knows, but his intimacy with trauma serves as a filter for everything else, so that when love or joy or wonder burst through, the effect for a reader is as explosive as for the poet himself." While offering a mixed appraisal of Orr's early work, Steven Cramer praised the more recent verse included in *The Caged Owl*, remarking, "Complexity conveyed by a limpid style is Orr's late excellence." To Hank Lazer, writing for the *American Poetry Review* (November–December 2003), "Orr's greatest accomplishment is the sequence of poems" first printed in *Orpheus and Eurydice*, most of which are reproduced in *The Caged Owl*. In those poems, Lazer added, "Orr incorporates the resonance of myth and story he has learned so well, and this sequence displays Orr's most sustained musicality. Most remarkable, though, the framing myth of Orpheus and Eurydice allows Orr to make a complete departure from the recurring autobiographical stories that have been central to his writing."

Orr took a further leap with *Concerning the Book that Is the Body of the Beloved*. Sloughing off his restrained lyricism and much of the specific subject matter that had preoccupied him since his earliest work, Orr plunged into "a confident, mystical, expansive project, whose very clear short poems (almost 200 of them) constitute a meditation and ritual for grieving a lost beloved," as a *Publishers Weekly* (September 12, 2005) reviewer noted. Though that reviewer felt some of the "poems can be overbroad in focus," Gail Wronsky, writing for the on-line poetry journal *Slope* (Winter 2007, on-line), praised the "direct lucidity" of the collection and called the book "as marvelously refreshing and bold, even in its gentleness—as challenging, sly, and wise—as any work recently published in the U.S." Joining other critics in comparing Orr's work in this instance to that of William Blake and Walt Whitman, Wronsky went on to acknowledge that it might sit uncomfortably with some readers: "This book will, I'm afraid, be dismissed by people who do find it 'simple,' dismissed because it refers to things we find 'Too embarrassing to be spoken.' Don't be embarrassed or cynical concerning the book *Concerning the Book That is the Body of the Beloved.* It anticipates and annihilates both of those approaches. It offers itself unpretentiously and with profound spiritual dignity."

In addition to his work as a poet, Orr is an accomplished essayist and critic. His first book of nonfiction prose, *Stanley Kunitz: An Introduction to the Poetry* (1985), was praised by reviewers as a comprehensive and insightful exploration of the work of one of the most important American poets of the late 20th century. B. Wallenstein, writing for *Choice* (November 1985), found the book "excellent not only in revealing the work of an important and much neglected American poet, but also in examining the ways lyric poetry achieves its eminence." Similarly, Leland Krauth, in a critique for *Library Journal* (August 1985), praised Orr's "unfailingly deft and illuminating" interpretations and added: "Later critics may do more with Kunitz's sources, his techniques, or his place in the ranks of 20th-century poets, but no one is likely to cast more light than Orr on what Kunitz himself described as his 'beating back/ To find what forces made him man.' Orr's incisive study will become a standard reading of this important poet." After publishing the collection *Richer Entanglements: Essays and Notes on Poetry and Poems* (1993), Orr co-edited, with Ellen Bryant Voigt, *Poets Teaching Poets: Self and the World* (1996), a selection of essays by writers and students associated with the M.F.A. creative-writing program at Warren Wilson College, in Asheville, North Carolina.

Orr's memoir, *The Blessing*, recounts his tumultuous youth and his later attempts to come to terms with the many tragic events he endured. Separated into four sections, the book first details the hunting accident that killed Orr's brother Peter, then delves further into Orr's family, drawing attention, for example, to his father's addiction to amphetamines—a drug Orr himself would later use, at his father's invitation. The time immediately after Peter's death, during which Orr's family remained resolutely silent, is the subject of the third part of the book, while the fourth concerns Orr's struggles during the civil rights movement and his subsequent way of understanding what he had done (and what had happened to him) as a child. The event had remained shrouded in silence among members of Orr's family, and crafting the book was, Orr has said, almost the only way he had left to reconcile himself to his experiences. "Six years ago, my father was beginning to die of prostate cancer, and I thought finally we might be able to talk," Orr told Joseph Barbato for *Publishers Weekly* (September 16, 2002). "But he said, 'No, you don't talk about things like that.' That opened the wound up all over again. Here is this person, who is dying, the last person I can talk to about this, and he won't talk." Orr then decided: "I am just going to have to write my way out of this in a memoir." Orr received offers from publishers for the project, but, he told Barbato, "They wanted me to sensationalize the story of my family. Curse my soul, I listened and wrote that book. But I realized it wasn't the way I wanted to represent my life." Council Oak Books, a smaller press, as Orr explained to Barbato, "let me write the book I wanted to write."

Reviews of *The Blessing* were markedly positive. "Orr has distilled the anguish of his youth right clown to its holy bones in a breathtaking chronicle of long-term shock and the arduous road to expiation," Donna Seaman wrote for *Booklist* (October 15, 2002). "In each poemlike chapter, tension, sorrow, and darkness give way to the mystical beauty of metaphor as Orr struggles to make sense of yet another horror." Andrea Hollander Budy, in a review for the Little Rock *Arkansas Democrat-Gazette* (August 15, 2004), wrote: "Throughout the narrative, Orr the adult writer is able to render, without self-indulgence or self-pity, Orr the anguished child. The circumstances that surround the accident, for example, involve Orr's submissive mother and reckless father, but the writer neither holds them directly responsible, nor attempts to implicate them." Budy concluded by calling the book "engaging and satisfying" and noted that readers are "left thankful that a once-doomed child found his way through enumerable suffering and was able to deliver his riveting and difficult tale in graceful prose that is clear, direct and memorable."

Published the same year as *The Blessing*, *Poetry as Survival* considered the therapeutic and transformative value of lyric poetry—for Orr and for other writers, past and present, and also for readers. The book received generally positive reviews, though some critics argued against his emphasis on lyric poetry and with his wider description of poetry's value. Charlotte Stewart, writing for *Tulsa World* (October 19, 2003), observed: "Of course the power of Orr's argument is grounded in his own remarkable suffering and survival. And it is rendered even more compelling by its presentation within the context of historical evidence that shows the personal lyric's range and durability in human life—as well as by Orr's subtle and astute descriptions of the mysterious selves in which we struggle to center our lives."

Orr has won major awards at virtually every stage of his career. Among the honors conferred on him are: the Discovery Award from the Poetry Center of the Young Men's–Young Women's Hebrew Association (1970), the University and College Poetry Prize from the Academy of

American Poets (1970), the Virginia Prize for Poetry (1984), and the American Academy of Arts and Letters Award in literature (2003). He has been a Guggenheim Foundation fellow (1977–78) and a National Endowment for the Arts fellow (1978–79 and 1989–90), and in 2000 he received a fellowship from the Rockefeller Foundation.

Orr lives in Charlottesville, Virginia, with his wife, Trisha. Though Orr has often emphasized that he was able to overcome his childhood troubles through making and reading poetry, Joseph Barbato wrote, "Orr agrees that marriage and family have [also] helped heal him. 'I'm a happy person,' he blurts out."

—S.Y.

Suggested Reading: *America* p77 Aug. 16, 1975; *American Poetry Review* p43+ Nov.–Dec. 2003; *Choice* p450 Nov. 1985; *Library Journal* p1,135 June 1, 1975, p2,331 Nov. 1, 1980, p97 Aug. 1985, p93 Mar. 18, 2002; *Milwaukee Journal Sentinel* E p7 Apr. 14, 2002; *New York Times Book Review* p5 Aug. 12, 1973, p14 Oct. 12, 1980; *Poetry* p173 Dec. 1973, p211+ July 2003; *Publishers Weekly* p93 Mar. 18, 2002, p47 Sep. 16, 2002, p43 Sep. 12, 2005; *Slope* (on-line) Winter 2007; *Writer* p13+ July 1998

Selected Books: poetry—*Burning the Empty Nests*, 1973; *Gathering the Bones Together*, 1975; *The Red House*, 1980; *Salt Wings*, 1980; *We Must Make a Kingdom of It*, 1986; *New and Selected Poems*, 1988; *City of Salt*, 1995; *Orpheus and Eurydice: A Lyric Sequence*, 2001; *The Caged Owl: New and Selected Poems*, 2002; *Concerning the Book that Is the Body of the Beloved*, 2005; nonfiction—*Stanley Kunitz: An Introduction to the Poetry*, 1985; *Richer Entanglements: Essays and Notes on Poetry and Poems*, 1993; *The Blessing*, 2002; *Poetry as Survival*, 2002; as editor—*Poets Teaching Poets: Self and the World* (with Ellen Bryant Voigt), 1996

Stephanie Rausser/Courtesy of Random House

Orringer, Julie

June 12, 1973– Short-story writer

There is a blurb on the cover of Julie Orringer's collection of short stories, *How to Breathe Underwater* (2003), in which her fellow writer Charles Baxter states: "There is a headlong energy in Julie Orringer's stories that I find quite remarkable." An interviewer for the Powell's Books Web site concurred, writing, "Energy is right. At times, Orringer's sentences practically cartwheel down the page."

Born in Miami, Florida, on June 12, 1973, Orringer was raised in New Orleans, Louisiana, and Ann Arbor, Michigan, among other towns. She explained to Robert Birnbaum for the *Morning News* (October 22, 2003, on-line), "My family moved a lot because my parents were physicians and they were early on in their training when I was born. In fact, they were in their third year of medical school [at the University of Miami] when I was born. And that made it hard for me in certain ways—as an elementary school kid because I was the new kid and it took me a long time to dig in. That was hard enough to begin with and I was this awkward, gangly, bookish kid who would rather sit in the library and read chapters in books than trade stickers on the playground." (Orringer is of Jewish descent, a fact that she has said cemented her feelings of being an outsider, particularly in New Orleans, where the biggest event of the year, Mardi Gras, is a Christian-based festival.) She told Birnbaum, "I think things were made a lot more difficult by the fact that my mother was diagnosed with breast cancer when I was 10. And so from very early on I had to begin contemplating the idea that I would lose her and experiencing the uncertainty that that threw into our lives. . . . she was sick for 10 years before she died." Despite such hardships, Orringer, who has one brother and one sister, retains fond memories of her childhood. "My first exposure to writing came when I was three years old, when my father sat down with me and made me a little book out of tiny pieces of paper he'd stapled together," she told an interviewer for the Barnes & Noble Web site. "He was the one who taught me that a book was not just something you could read, but something you could create. Soon

I began composing the stories with him. Some of our early titles were *The Bowling Party, The Very Tiny Owl, The New Baby,* and *The Time We Went to Hollywood.*"

Orringer briefly considered pursuing a career in medicine but changed her focus to creative writing after attending an inspiring lecture by the author Denis Johnson while in college. Her parents, themselves creative—her father had studied journalism for a time, and her mother was an accomplished musician, dancer, and gymnast—were supportive of the decision. Orringer graduated from Cornell University, in Ithaca, New York, in 1994; two years later she earned an M.F.A. from the Writers' Workshop at the University of Iowa, where she studied under such luminaries as Frank Conroy, Marilynne Robinson, and James Alan McPherson. She then moved to San Francisco, where she roomed with two fellow Iowa alumni and wrote. She earned money as a fertility-clinic receptionist, warehouse worker, concierge, and calligrapher, among other positions. In 1997 the *Yale Review* accepted her short story "What We Save." "I was totally ecstatic," she told Colleen Dougher for the Florida-based arts magazine *City Link* (November 5, 2003, on-line). "I couldn't believe that that was going to happen. And then, it was very scary, because that meant that the story was going to be out there and other people were going to read it." The story won the *Yale Review*'s Smart Family Foundation Award for best story that year. In 1998 her story "When She Is Old and I Am Famous" was published in the *Paris Review* and won that journal's Discovery Prize. The following year Orringer was awarded a Stegner Fellowship at Stanford University, in California, which provided her with tuition for a workshop and a cash stipend. "Suddenly," she told Dougher, "it wasn't just a matter of trying to put together a couple of hours after a full day's work. Writing *became* the day's work, and that was an incredible liberation."

The title of Orringer's first book, *How to Breathe Underwater,* proved puzzling to some readers; typically, short-story collections take their names from one of the included stories, but *How to Breathe Underwater* contains no tale by that title. "The title came to me rather late in the process," Orringer explained to Birnbaum. "I didn't know when I was putting the stories together that this was going to be the thematic umbrella. And I was working on [the story 'Isabel Fish'] and I came to that moment when the narrator is trying to imagine what's ahead as she begins scuba lessons. She is coming off a rather awful incident with a car accident and a drowning and it seemed to me this phrase, this idea of trying to breathe under water was something that maybe had some larger resonance for the other stories as well. They tend to be about young women who are in between childhood and adulthood. They are about people who are at a moment of an incredibly difficult transition in their lives." She continued, "I feel like the title has something to do with how hard it is to

redefine yourself after a loss or trauma or as you are entering this new period of your life. And yet we somehow do it anyway."

In addition to "Isabel Fish," *How to Breathe Underwater* contains eight other stories, including, "Pilgrims," about two siblings' strange Thanksgiving celebration the year their mother is dying of cancer; "Stations of the Cross," about a young Jewish girl attending her friend's Holy Communion; and "Care," about a drug-addicted aunt who is put in charge of her six-year-old niece for the day. Reviewers were impressed: Lisa Dierbeck wrote for the *New York Times Book Review* (October 19, 2003), "Orringer has a gift for the dramatic. Because of her assured voice, restraint and eye for detail, she never sacrifices believability in favor of the theatrical. . . . The harsh landscape in which Orringer's characters dwell corresponds to the fierce beauty of her writing. Even the grimmest of these stories conveys, along with anguish, a child's spark of mystery and wonder." Donna Seamen wrote for *Booklist* (September 1, 2003), "Radiant in their explicit sensory descriptions, penetrating in their eviscerating discernment of both the cruelty and resiliency of children, and exquisitely attuned to the overwhelming tide of emerging sexuality, Orringer's unnerving and fiercely beautiful stories delve to the very core of life's mysteries."

Orringer lives in San Francisco with her husband, the writer Ryan Harty, whom she married in 2000. (The pair met at the Iowa Writers' Workshop.) Her upcoming novel—about a young Hungarian Jew who receives a scholarship to study architecture in Paris in the late 1930s, when strict quotas prohibit him from studying at a Hungarian university—was inspired in part by her grandfather.

—P.B.M.

Suggested Reading: Barnes & Noble Web site; *Booklist* p61 Sep.1, 2003; *City Link* (on-line) Nov. 5, 2003; *Morning News* (on-line) Oct. 22, 2003; *New York Times Book Review* p18 Oct. 19, 2003

Selected Books: *How to Breathe Underwater,* 2003

Oyeyemi, Helen

1984– Novelist; playwright

The literary world has always celebrated writers who have displayed considerable talents at an early age. Notable historic examples include Mary Shelley, who had written the classic novel *Frankenstein* (1818) by age 19, and John Keats, who published his first collection of poetry in 1817, at age 22. More recently, S. E. Hinton wrote

© Sarah Wood/Courtesy of Bloomsbury

Helen Oyeyemi

her most acclaimed novel, *The Outsiders* (1967), at 16, and Joyce Maynard published *Looking Back: A Chronicle of Growing Up Old in the Sixties* (1973) at 19. Recently admitted to those select ranks is Helen Oyeyemi, the author of the critically acclaimed novel *The Icarus Girl* (2005). The novel, completed just before Oyeyemi's 19th birthday, started a bidding war among prospective publishers in England, and the young author, who recently completed her undergraduate studies at the University of Cambridge, is currently working on her second.

Helen Oyeyemi, the oldest of three children, was born in Nigeria in 1984 and moved to Lewisham, England, when she was four, so her father could study at Middlesex University. (He is now a special-education teacher.) In an article published in the London *Guardian* (February 2, 2005, on-line), she wrote, "I have the muddled perspective of someone who is in a Nigerian cultural framework, but not of it, being carried along by a culture at a distance from its source and its pervading influence. I'm a mix of first- and second-generation Nigerian—I was born 'back home,' where I feel more comfortable in my skin, but I am still often baffled by certain Nigerian ways."

As a child she often felt alienated from the real world, but she had a deep connection to an imaginary friend named Chimmy and the characters in the books she read. Literature of all types was a central focus of her life from early on. "You can read a lot of books and the main characters are white people—especially in the classics—and after a while you forget that you're not white, almost, because it's this big pervasive

culture," she told Anita Sethi for the London *Guardian* (January 10, 2005, on-line). "And then you find books like *Yoruba Girl Dancing* [by Simi Bedford] and you think: it's just as interesting to be Nigerian in England as it is to be white in England."

Oyeyemi suffered from depression during her early teenage years, but when she tried discussing it with her parents, she discovered they did not really understand the problem, "because people don't get depressed in Nigeria," as she explained to Helen Brown for the London *Daily Telegraph* (January 8, 2005). "They were like, 'Cheer up, get on with it.'" She elaborated to Sethi: "In Nigeria, the problems are so much more immediate and more real, like you're not getting any electricity or any water, you actually have to struggle and stuff. [So my parents thought], it's fine [in England], what's your problem?"

At age 15 Oyeyemi took an overdose of painkillers and sleeping pills and was hospitalized. After checking out of the hospital, she began seeing a psychiatrist. "He asked me what I read and I started telling him about Edwin Muir and Sylvia Plath [writers who both famously suffered from severe depression]," she told Brown. "He was, like, 'Yeah, I like them too.' I don't know if that was his idea of therapy, but I walked out of there thinking, 'This is not going to help me go back to school and feel like a normal person.'" Oyeyemi continued to read voraciously and also began to write. Her stories were sometimes spooky or existential in nature, but the writing helped relieve her depression. A vacation to Nigeria with her family also proved therapeutic, and she found herself well on the way to recovery.

While studying for her university admission exams (called the A-levels in England), Oyeyemi began to write *The Icarus Girl*. She spent seven solitary months on the project, and no one knew what she was writing. (Her parents believed that it was a long exam-related essay.) Oyeyemi told Heather V. Eng for the *Boston Herald* (June 22, 2005), "I had an offer from Cambridge depending on the (A-level) results. I didn't tell my parents I was writing [the book]. They would go crazy because they'd be like, 'You know you have to get these grades so you can go to Cambridge!' But I kept thinking I had to keep on with the story because it might just go away." Oyeyemi had been writing short stories for years, and she told Felicia R. Lee for the *New York Times* (June 21, 2005) that writing *The Icarus Girl* "came really, really easily. But I think it came easy because I didn't think it was a novel. It was just kind of a story that kept getting longer, so I didn't get scared or anything."

Oyeyemi sent her first 20 pages to Robin Wade, a literary agent, who called her the next day wanting to see more. Oyeyemi sent Wade the roughly 150 pages that she had completed. On the basis of those pages a bidding war broke out for the publishing rights. The novel was ultimately sold to Bloomsbury as part of a two-book deal for a reported advance of £400,000. Although both the publisher and the author claim that figure to be inflated, they have not publicly confirmed a different amount. Oyeyemi learned of the sale on the same day she was informed that she had gained admission to Corpus Christi College at the University of Cambridge, in England. (After studying social and political sciences, in 2006 Oyeyemi earned her undergraduate degree.)

The plot of *The Icarus Girl* centers on eight-year-old Jessamy Harrison, the biracial daughter of a Nigerian mother and a British father. Jessamy, a troubled child who prefers to stay in seclusion writing haikus, has periodic tantrums when forced into social situations. Jessamy's parents send her to Nigeria for the summer, hoping that some time spent with her extended family will help her. In Nigeria she finds little in common with her cousins and begins to feel just as isolated there as she had in London. One day she meets a barefooted girl named Titiola, or TillyTilly, who seems to know all about her. No one else ever sees TillyTilly, a character Oyeyemi had used initially in a short story she had written at age 13. At first TillyTilly's companionship is a comfort to Jessamy, but when the family returns to London, TillyTilly's influence on Jessamy grows increasingly malevolent.

Oyeyemi made great use of both native Nigerian folklore and Christian imagery in the book; she told Eng, "I think I've always been quite interested in folklore and [folk] tales. I think they're the best way to access a culture, more so than food or music or anything like that." Her parents were Christians, Oyeyemi has told interviewers, but they also ascribed to many superstitions; her mother warned, for example, that writing someone's name in red ink would cause that person's death or that whistling in the house invites evil spirits.

The reviews for *The Icarus Girl*, although tinged with some reservations, were largely positive. Peter Parker wrote for the London *Times* (January 23, 2005, on-line), "Oyeyemi's ambitious first novel . . . succeeds best when it deals with Jess's dual inheritance and the tensions experienced by a 'half-and-half child.' The author plays numerous sophisticated games with notions of twinship and identity and, perhaps because at 20 she is not far removed from it, convincingly re-creates the not altogether attractive world of small girls. A more practised writer might have resisted the temptation to slip briefly into the consciousnesses of other characters, which feels rather like a narrative cheat, but the principal flaw in this otherwise impressive novel is the amount of time devoted to Jess's other world. Listening to other people's dreams can become tedious, and reading about them runs the same risk. Used more sparingly, this device would be fine, but Jess's excursions into fantasy (if that's what it is) are both lengthy and repetitive. For these reasons, *The Icarus Girl* is not quite the literary marvel that advance publicity has suggested. It is nevertheless a highly auspicious

fictional debut." A reviewer for the London *Telegraph* (January 30, 2005, on-line) had a similar assessment of Oyeyemi's strengths and weaknesses as a first-time novelist: "The mystical elements in the narrative are not totally convincing and Oyeyemi rather loses control of her material in the second half. But for a first novel from someone who was still at school when she wrote it, *The Icarus Girl* is an astonishing achievement. There is not a trace of the preciousness that so often characterises teenage fiction: just simple, well-drawn characters, crisp dialogue and an enviable grasp of the rudiments of storytelling." In the *New York Times* (July 17, 2005), Lesley Downer examined the hype surrounding Oyeyemi's youth and the size of her advance, and asked, "But does the book stand on its own? Would we think it was good if we knew nothing about the author?" She concluded, "Deserving of all its praise, this is a masterly first novel—and a nightmarish story that will haunt Oyeyemi's readers for months to come." *The Icarus Girl* was nominated for the British Book Awards *Decibel* Writer of the Year Award and the Commonwealth Writers' Prize for best first book.

Helen Oyeyemi has written two plays, *Juniper's Whitening* and *Victimese*, which were published in one volume in September 2005. Her second novel, *The Opposite House*, is due out in June 2007.

—C.M.

Suggested Reading: Bloomsbury Web site; *Boston Globe* B p10 June 20, 2005; (London) *Daily Telegraph* p12 Jan. 8, 2005; (London) *Guardian* (on-line) Feb. 2, 2005; (London) *Times* (on-line) Jan. 23, 2005; *New York Times* E p1 June 21, 2005

Selected Books: *The Icarus Girl*, 2005; *The Opposite House*, 2007

Packer, George

1960– Journalist; novelist

George Packer submitted the following autobiographical statement to *World Authors 2000–2005*:

"I grew up on the campus of Stanford University, in a house full of books. At our dinner table my father, who taught law, held forth on politics (it was the 1960s—there was a lot to talk about), and my mother, who wrote fiction, told stories of her raucous Alabama childhood. I was raised between the rigor of analysis and the pleasure of imagination, and perhaps because I was closer to my mother—especially after my father suffered a massive stroke in 1969, when I was eight—the ambition to be a writer, which flickered on and off throughout my youth, always

Alex Wong/Getty Images for Meet the Press
George Packer

meant becoming a fiction writer. But I wasn't one of those children who from a very early age knew he wanted to be a writer and lived continuously in his imagination and made up stories to get revenge for the petty humiliations of living. I also wanted to be a politician, a soldier, a basketball player, and an actor.

"My earliest literary effort, aside from a few nonsense poems, was an autobiographical sketch, written when I was seven, that shows an inclination toward historical fact more than invention: 'I was born to early. Luckely I lived. About two months later my mom named me. She named me GEORGE. I didn't cry much. My sister was born earlier than me. All this happened when Dwight D. Eisenhower was President. The year, 1960. When I was three on November twenty second 1963 John F. KENNEDY WAS MURDERED! A man named Oswald did it. A week afterward the police were taking Oswald to a nother jail, when man named Jack Ruby shot Oswald because Oswald shot Kennedy. When I was five, Johnson was running for President against Goldwater. Johnson won. When I was six, Johnson was Anaugurated. When I was seven, I voted for McCarthy.'

"I was thrilled and terrified by the Kennedy assassination, and by the upheavals that followed. I was also thrilled and terrified by *Where the Wild Things Are*, in which Max sets sail from his room and rules over the beasts of foreign shores. These two passions, as far as I knew then, had nothing to do with each other. I spent a lot of time projecting myself into various characters, and my first love in grown-up literature was Shakespeare's *Julius Caesar*, which my father assigned me to read the

summer I turned 12 and which I immediately staged with a group of friends, casting myself as Brutus.

"That summer's reading list turned out to be my father's last bequest to me; he took his own life that December. For a number of years after his death, I lost the ability to lose myself in literature; I cut myself off from its dangerous allure; something in my imaginative life switched off. But at the same time, under the solitary influence of my mother, I now wanted to be a fiction writer more than anything else, and in these inauspicious circumstances I began a series of adolescent forays that turned out badly. I took my models all too literally: I wanted to be Dickens, Conrad, Fitzgerald, Faulkner, Joyce, and the evidence lies in stories so derivative that a good many of them were set in the 19th century. It was all very self-conscious, intellectualized, and second-hand. Writing meant writing like the writers I liked; it certainly didn't mean writing from my own life, which I didn't care to examine too closely, and which hardly seemed a subject worthy of literature.

"I was a much better student than writer, but all through high school and college—I attended Yale from 1978 to 1982—whatever success I enjoyed seemed like a consolation prize. In a writing class I was told that my fiction sounded like Henry James, only not as good. By the time I went off to West Africa with the Peace Corps, three weeks after graduation, I had pretty much abandoned the thought of a literary career. Eighteen months by myself in a little village in Togo undermined the considerable intellectual defenses I had raised 10 years earlier in the aftermath of my father's suicide. I went home with no idea what to do next; my plan of becoming an English professor lay in ruins. As it happened, the way back took me through Barcelona, and in a bookshop on the Ramblas I picked up a copy of George Orwell*'s Homage to Catalonia*.

"On the airplane I read the first sentence: 'In the Lenin Barracks in Barcelona, the day before I joined the militia, I saw an Italian militiaman standing in front of the officers' table.' Something in the simple rhythm and clarity of the words resonated deeply. And the 'I' that appeared so forthrightly, asserting the kind of authority that comes from having gone through an experience, yet without calling attention to itself—this 'I' was probably the most important word I'd ever read. It gave me the courage I needed.

"Back in the U.S., living in Boston and working on construction jobs, I started to write about my time in Africa. I wrote an essay about the boy who lived with the family next door and over a period of weeks kept stealing things from my house. The effect of that sentence of Orwell's didn't show right away. In my first draft the essay began, ponderously, 'Corruption has been in the news lately.' But by the time I had finished, the falseness and evasions of many years had been squeezed out by the sheer pressure of the experience itself, and the first sentence read: 'A trail of muddy footprints appeared on my kitchen wall one day, six months after I had come to Togo, West Africa as a Peace Corps volunteer.' It's hard to say just what about this sentence, and this essay, was so liberating. I, literally, had at last made it into my own prose. But I didn't want my appearance to lead the reader down an endless hole of narcissism. The 'I' allowed me to take in the physical world, the human beings around me, and the larger significance of our actions. At the time I barely knew what an essay was, but I somehow grasped that its purpose wasn't mere self-examination, but reflection on the world.

"The essay eventually became a part of my first book, *The Village of Waiting*, which was published, to my innocent surprise, in 1988. By luck and effort, the writing of that book showed me what I wanted to do as a writer and how to do it. I wanted to use the pleasure of narrative, of drawing characters and scenes in a story that happened to be true, to think through ideas. The ideas in this book, and in my other book of nonfiction, *Blood of the Liberals*, have largely to do with society and history. In this sense, I'd stumbled across a way to reconcile the influences of my father and my mother, but in a literary form that I could make my own. What I hope to achieve in any book is a fusion of literary art and moral, even political, purpose. But my writing years have coincided with a time of political quiescence in America, the sovereignty of private life, and it isn't clear whether the kind of books I want to keep on writing will have a wide readership.

"As it turned out, I continued to write fiction, published two novels—*The Half Man* and *Central Square*—and hope to write another some day. For certain states of being, and certain subjects—for example, marriage—only fiction will do. I've also worked as a journalist for *The New York Times Magazine*, the *New Yorker*, and *Dissent*. But neither of these forms allows me the freedom that came with the first piece I ever published, that essay about the stealing: the freedom to speak directly to the reader, from my own experience, about things that I hope matter to us both."

George Huddleston Packer was born in 1960 in California. His mother is a writer and using the name Nancy Huddleston Packer she has published several writing guides and short-story collections, including *The Women Who Walk* (1989) and *Jealous-Hearted Me, and Other Stories* (1997). Packer's father, Herbert, was a law professor at Stanford University, in Palo Alto, California, and the author of two important studies of the American legal system—*Ex-Communist Witnesses: Four Studies in Fact Finding* (1962) and *The Limits of the Criminal Sanction* (1968)—

among other works; he committed suicide in 1972. George's sister, Ann Packer, is also a writer; she has published a well-received collection of short fiction, *Mendocino, and Other Stories* (1994), and a best-selling novel, *The Dive from Clausen's Pier* (2002).

George Packer's first book, *The Village of Waiting* (1988), which was published while he was still in his 20s, describes his experiences as a Peace Corp worker in Togo, in West Africa, in a village whose name means "wait." He portrayed with sympathy people destined to wait perhaps forever for the benefits of development. According to Gail Pool, writing for the *Christian Science Monitor* (November 8, 1988), Packer's "story is skillfully written, neither melodramatic nor despondent. Other visions of what he saw—and other responses—are possible, but he conveys his own with honesty. Many who have done fieldwork in the third world may recognize elements of his experience, from the shock of cultural difference and doubting of one's purpose to rituals such as the BBC news at 6. Those who have not may come to understand why a young 'white foreigner who'd come on an enlightened mission, and once there managed to keep his eyes open, quickly lost his bearings in the face of it.'"

Packer next turned to fiction; *The Half Man* (1991), set in a country resembling Indonesia, concerns an American journalist, Daniel Levin, whose personal problems interfere with his reports on a rebel leader. "Unsurprisingly for this type of novel, every encounter with natives becomes freighted with metaphysical (or metaphorical) significance, with Levin weighed down by his whiteness, his Americannes and his naivete," a reviewer wrote for *Publishers Weekly*, (August 9, 1991). "Packer writes evocatively, but the predictability of the relationships and of the story itself grinds him down as his protagonist's helplessness grows. As it stands, *Half Man* strains after the halfway mark."

Packer's second novel, *Central Square* (1998), is set in Cambridge, Massachusetts, during the cold winter months. Joe Amouzou, an African-American who has just returned from a yearlong stay in Africa, successfully passes himself off as an African musician and in the process interacts with a wide cross section of local residents. "Packer has a good feel for the sunlight-deficient lives of a typical New England winter," a reviewer wrote for *Publishers Weekly* (August 17, 1998), "but the novel is more than a few deft portraits of selected urban existences. It is a graceful meditation on the moral longing and often doomed effort that go into reinventing oneself." Reviewing the novel for *Ploughshares* (Winter 1998), Don Lee wrote, "*Central Square* is a searing, trenchant elegy of the passion that once fueled the ideals of socialism, love, spirituality, racial harmony, class, and art—all attempts to commune with a larger purpose. The novel's plot doesn't quite meet its potential, but Packer writes with intelligence and honesty, and *Central Square* stands not only as an evocation of a neighborhood, but also as an important survey of our culture."

For *Blood of the Liberals* (2000), Packer returned to nonfiction, examining the evolution of American liberalism through the history of one family—his own. First Packer recounted the story of his maternal grandfather, George Huddleston, an agrarian populist who represented Alabama in the U.S. Congress from 1915 to 1937. As a member of the urban, intellectual middle class, Herbert Packer was an "Adlai Stevenson Democrat" and "New Deal liberal." Finally, in an autobiographical section, George Packer explains how his own views of liberalism, rooted in volunteerism and political activism, developed during his studies at Yale University and while he was in the Peace Corp. Charles K. Piehl wrote for *Library Journal* (August 2000), "Packer's combination of personal and historical perspectives, as well as his considerable skill at conveying them, make this work both challenging and enjoyable. Written for the lay reader, it nonetheless avoids oversimplification." *Blood of the Liberals* received a Robert F. Kennedy Book Award.

In the summer of 2003 Packer traveled to Iraq to report on the aftermath of the U.S.–led invasion. He was awarded the Ed Cunningham Memorial award from the Overseas Press Club and was nominated for the Michael Kelly Award for his article "War After the War," which was published in the November 24, 2003 issue of the *New Yorker*. In its citation, which is posted on the organization's Web site, the jury for the Michael Kelly Award praised Packer for helping Americans to make sense of the conflict in Iraq: "Twenty years from now, students looking for a definitive account of the troubled aftermath of the U.S. invasion of Iraq will no doubt turn to George Packer's deeply reported 20,000-word piece in *The New Yorker*. Packer weaves the stories of individual Iraqis and Americans into a compelling narrative that provides readers with a wide-angle view of the situation in Iraq. His ability to get Iraqi civilians and American soldiers to open up to him and reveal their doubts and fears about the U.S. occupation makes his piece all the more riveting."

Unlike most prominent liberals, Packer supported military action in Iraq during the run-up to the invasion—but he never wrote about his support for the war at that time because he remained ambivalent about his position. "The reporting I did before the war was more of: What are the questions here and what are the difficulties it poses whether you are a liberal or a conservative, [or] whatever? I basically found it impossible to say no to a war that would get rid of Saddam Hussein," Packer explained to Robert Birnbaum in an interview for the on-line magazine the *Morning News* (January 2, 2006). "It was not a Council on Foreign Relations strategic calculation. It was a really individual and non-rational feeling."

In *The Assassin's Gate: America in Iraq* (2005), readers can trace the development of Packer's disillusionment with the war. Beginning with its lackluster effort at postwar planning before the invasion, George W. Bush's administration is depicted as overrun with ideologues who issued dictates from Washington that were of no help—and often a great hindrance—to the well-intentioned soldiers and diplomats on the ground in Iraq. "George Packer's brutal analyses and trenchant on-the-spot reportage for the *New Yorker* magazine over the past two years provide the core of this devastating critique," a reviewer wrote for the *Economist* (October 15, 2005). "It re-confirms the now familiar but appalling facts: that once the Americans' high-tech military superiority had rapidly overwhelmed Mr Hussein's force in the conventional phase of war, there was, amazingly, no plan whatsoever for the future, beyond a sublime belief in the assurances of a coterie of Iraqi exiles that harmony ('sweets and flowers') would magically replace the dictatorship. . . . Much of this is old hat, previously described by Mr. Packer in the *New Yorker* and by others elsewhere. Where he scores most is in portraying the psychology of Iraqis, their ambivalence to the liberation/occupation ('I wanted both sides to lose,' says one quite typical Iraqi doctor), their fractiousness and fatal vulnerability to absurd conspiracy theories, as they try to creep out from under the debilitating shadow of Mr. Hussein."

Most of the nation's top newspapers—including the *Los Angeles Times*, the *New York Times*, and the *Washington Post*—placed the *Assassins' Gate* on their lists of the best books of 2005. It won the Helen Bernstein Book Award for Excellence in Journalism from the New York Public Library and the Cornelius Ryan Award from the Overseas Press Club of America. It was also short-listed for the Council on Foreign Relation's Arthur Ross Book Award, receiving an honorable mention.

—S.Y.

Suggested Reading: *American Prospect* p40+ Dec. 4, 2000; *American Scholar* p143+ Autumn 2000; *Atlantic* p98 Sep. 1988; *Columbia Journalism Review* p56+ Sep.–Oct. 2005; *Economist* p89 Oct. 15, 2005; *New York Times* (on-line) Aug. 23, 2000; *New York Times Book Review* p9 Aug. 27, 2000; *Ploughshares* p226+ Winter 1999; *Washington Monthly* p59 Apr. 1989; *Washington Post Book World* p4 Feb. 9, 1992

Selected Books: nonfiction—*The Village of Waiting*, 1988; *Blood of the Liberals*, 2000; *The Assassin's Gate: America in Iraq*, 2005; fiction—*The Half Man*, 1991; *Central Square*, 1998

Courtesy of Canongate Books

Packer, ZZ

Jan. 12, 1973– Short-story writer

The graduate of a string of prestigious universities and the winner of a major award from the Mrs. Giles Whiting Foundation years before she had even published her first book, ZZ Packer became the "darling of the book world," as Julia Chaplin noted for *Interview* (January 2001), with the appearance of her story "Drinking Coffee Elsewhere" in an issue of the *New Yorker* (June 19 and 26, 2000) featuring fiction writers who had never published there before. Describing a young African-American woman coming to terms with her outsider status at Yale University, the story suggested a writer with an unusually rich gift for drawing humor and painful insights out of the events of everyday life. Three years after the story appeared, Packer published her first collection, also titled *Drinking Coffee Elsewhere*, and critics almost universally agreed that the stir created by that story had been justified. Andrew Guy Jr., writing for the *Houston Chronicle* (May 9, 2003), described Packer's stories as "the beginning arc in the career of a writer with the kind of voice that hasn't been heard since Terry [McMillan, the author of *Waiting to Exhale*] convinced book publishers that, yes, black people do read." Mick Cochrane, reviewing Packer's collection for the *Buffalo News* (March 9, 2003), called her "a tremendously talented young writer who doesn't feel the need to announce her genius or prove on every page that she's edgy. The world, she obviously knows, is full of sharp edges, thank you very much. She does what the best artists do: Takes pains to show us—with clarity and compassion—

the ragged, sometimes sinister, almost always heartbreaking mess we make of things, and in the face of that, the possibility of decency, generosity and courage." Explaining her aesthetic sensibility to Michelle Griffin, for the Australian newspaper the *Age* (June 5, 2004, on-line), Packer said: "You know that sound the garbage truck makes in the morning when it's backing up? And it's so familiar you don't even hear it—it's just part of the texture of everything around you, it's so familiar. That's the kind of experience I'm trying to get at."

ZZ Packer was born Zuwena Packer on January 12, 1973 in Chicago, Illinois. *Zuwena* is said to mean "good" in Swahili, while *ZZ*, she told Robert Birnbaum for the on-line magazine *Identity Theory* (April 29, 2003), "is just this nickname that I've had ever since I can remember." At five Packer moved with her family to Atlanta, Georgia. About six years later her parents divorced, and Packer and her mother left Georgia for Louisville, Kentucky, where she stayed until leaving for college. Packer's mother and grandmother were members of a historically black Pentecostal denomination of Christianity. Though reared in this tradition, Packer stopped attending church after leaving her mother's home. "I was pretty sceptical even as a child," Packer told Griffin. "I didn't buy into the institutionalised nature of organised religion. What I reacted to was the rigidity and authoritarian nature of really strict religion."

Packer was a devoted reader from a very young age. "I always read way ahead of me," she told Jean Nash Johnson for the *Dallas Morning News* (February 19, 2004). "I remember reading [Emily Brontë's 1847 novel] *Wuthering Heights* when I was 10, and I would fall asleep, but I'd stick with it until I finished." Still, Packer's skill at math and science and her interest in robots had led her to imagine a career as an engineer rather than a writer, and she spent some of her summers during high school in programs designed to cultivate young scientists. In turn, these programs exposed her to a set of elite universities that otherwise might have seemed extremely remote. "There is no way in Louisville, Kentucky that I would have been able to see these colleges," Packer told Birnbaum. "People wouldn't even have been pointing me to these colleges."

At 17 Packer left Louisville for Yale University, in New Haven, Connecticut. After initially pursuing a science-related degree, Packer switched to the humanities. "I knew I'd be good at medical school," Packer told Kim Curtis for the Associated Press (May 27, 2003). "But I'm so flaky I didn't know that I'd be a good doctor. I became an English major, but I had no idea what I was going to do with it. I just knew that I loved it." In February 1994, while she was still at Yale, she published what appears to be her first short story, "Sometimes You Get Lucky," in *Seventeen*. (Though many sources describe Packer as having published her first piece in *Seventeen* at the age of 19, no earlier citation under Packer's name could be found, whether for fiction or, as at least one source maintains, nonfiction. It is possible that the story was written and sold to *Seventeen* several years before it saw print.)

After earning her degree from Yale, in 1994, Packer began attending the Writing Seminars at Johns Hopkins University, in Baltimore, Maryland, where she worked with such famed writers as Stephen Dixon, John Barth, and Francine Prose. Packer earned her M.A. from Johns Hopkins, in 1995, and followed that with two years of teaching in Baltimore-area public high schools. In 1999 she completed the M.F.A. program at the Iowa Writers' Workshop, at the University of Iowa, where she had continued her writing education under such teachers as Frank Conroy and James Alan McPherson. (Packer paid tribute to McPherson's work in an essay for the January/February 2002 issue of *Poets & Writers*.) After Iowa Packer went to Stanford University, in Palo Alto, California, where she received a coveted Stegner Fellowship and subsequently stayed on as an adjunct lecturer.

Prior to the publication of "Drinking Coffee Elsewhere" in the *New Yorker*, Packer published the story "Geese" in the book *25 and Under: Fiction* (1997), edited by Susan Ketchin and Neil Giordano; "Speaking in Tongues" in *The Workshop: Seven Decades of the Iowa Writers' Workshop* (1999), edited by Tom Grimes; and "Brownies" in *Harper's* (November 1999). "Brownies" also appeared in *The Best American Short Stories 2000*, edited by E. L. Doctorow and Katrina Kenison. Packer's story "Every Tongue Shall Confess," after first appearing in *Ploughshares* (Fall 2002), appeared in the 2003 edition of *The Best American Short Stories*, edited by Walter Mosley and Katrina Kenison, and that same year's edition of *New Stories from the South: The Year's Best*, edited by Shannon Ravenel.

The eight stories that comprise *Drinking Coffee Elsewhere* deal for the most part with African-American women and girls who struggle with their feelings of being outsiders. Evadne Anderson, reviewing the book for the Montreal *Gazette* (June 14, 2003), judged the book a "tour de force" and wrote: "All [of Packer's characters] are questioning, in a world that offers no acceptable answers but, rather, invites, coerces or bullies them to resign and accept the status quo, as defined by pastor or parent, Ivy League dean, peer or pimp. They are obstinate but never wrong-headed; some are charming but never precious. They strongly believe that they have an inalienable right to be independent." To Joy Press, writing for the *Village Voice* (March 4, 2003), the characters are mostly "goody-goodies," which Press defined as "young, wholesome African American women caught at a formative moment, ducking bitterness as it settles in around them. Packer forces them up against the rough surface of the world and watches them lose their way: The quiet honor-roll student unraveled by alienation and sadness at Yale, where she's

deemed a dangerous rebel; the teenaged debate-team whiz who ends up on his own at the Million Man March, ditched by his misguided slacker dad; the well-meaning woman who wants to teach high school in inner-city Baltimore but can't connect with her troubled charges." To Press, the pieces in Packer's collection felt "refreshingly subtle and unresolved. They don't call attention to themselves; in fact, they shun irony and linguistic bravado. Sometimes her fondness for pathos weighs the stories down, makes them feel a little too much like virtuous parables. But in the book's more organic pieces, Packer's characters feel inseparable from the messy sociopolitical landscape, feet firmly planted in our world." Named one of the best books of 2003 by the *San Francisco Chronicle* and a notable book of the year by the *New York Times* and the American Library Association, *Drinking Coffee Elsewhere* also received a 2004 Alex Award from the Young Adult Library Services Association and was a finalist for the 2004 PEN/Faulkner Award for fiction.

Packer currently makes her home in Pacifica, California with her husband Michael Boros, a software marketing executive whom she married in 2001. She playfully dubbed Boros "Mr. Packer" in her essay on their relationship "Being Mr. Packer," printed in *Why I'm Still Married: Women Write Their Hearts Out on Love, Loss, Sex, and Who Does the Dishes* (2006), edited by Karen Propp and Jean Trounstine. In addition to winning the Mrs. Giles Whiting Foundation Writers' Award, in 1999, Packer has also received a Rona Jaffe Writers Foundation Grant (1997), a Bellingham Review Award (1999), and a Guggenheim Fellowship (2005). She is currently working on a novel about the Buffalo Soldiers, a name given to the African-American regiments of U.S. troops who in the years directly after the Civil War fought against Native Americans on the western frontier. Packer told Heidi Benson, for the *San Francisco Chronicle* (September 16, 2003): "I've done my own personal research [for the book], asking my grandmother about life as a child of sharecroppers in Mississippi and researching sharecropping and labor, which led me to the great migration, when blacks moved north for more opportunities. But you don't hear about those who moved west. The more I learned about blacks in the west and the Buffalo Soldiers, I became fascinated [by] the idea of recently emancipated people in the regular army being used to put Indians on reservations. It's an interesting moral conundrum and a neglected part of history."

—P.B.M./D.R.

Suggested Reading: *Buffalo (New York) News* E p5 Mar. 9, 2003; *Dallas Morning News* E p1 Feb. 19, 2004; *Houston Chronicle* Zest p18 May 9, 2003; *Identity Theory* (on-line) Apr. 29, 2003; (Montreal) *Gazette* J p4 June 14, 2003; *San Francisco Chronicle* D p1 Sep. 16, 2003; *Village Voice* p58 Mar. 4, 2003

Selected Books: *Drinking Coffee Elsewhere,* 2003

Courtesy of Carolyn Parkhurst

Parkhurst, Carolyn

Jan. 18, 1971– Novelist

Carolyn Parkhurst's innovative first novel, *The Dogs of Babel* (2003), received many positive reviews, but most critics attribute the book's commercial success to the plaudits offered by the best-selling author Anna Quindlen on the *Today Show*. After Quindlen's appearance *The Dogs of Babel* rocketed up the best-seller list, holding on for months. She followed this auspicious debut with *Lost and Found* (2006), a satire of reality television.

Born on January 18, 1971 in Manchester, New Hampshire, Parkhurst was raised in Waltham, Massachusetts. She dreamed of writing novels in her youth. "When I was about ten, I tried to write a novel called *Dress of Many Generations*. It was about a young girl who finds a dress in her grandmother's attic; every time she puts it on, she's transformed into one of the women who wore it before her," she wrote in an essay posted on the Powell's Books Web site. "It never got beyond the outline stage, although I enjoyed drawing pictures of the dress. When I was in high school, sick of cramming for the SATs, I decided that my first book would be a futuristic novel about a world where everyone has to take a standardized test to enter society." She matriculated at Wesleyan University, in Middletown, Connecticut, where she received her B.A. in English. She obtained an M.F.A. in creative writing from American University, in Washington, D.C. Prior to the publication of *The Dogs of Babel*, Parkhurst's work appeared in a number of literary journals, including the *Crescent Review*, the *North American Review*, and the Hawaii *Review*.

The Dogs of Babel (released as *Lorelei's Secret* outside the U.S. and Canada) centers on Paul Iverson, a linguist whose wife has died under mysterious circumstances. Using his linguistic expertise, Iverson tries to teach his dog to communicate, thinking that the canine may have witnessed his wife's last moments. "There's a real issue of getting readers to suspend their belief when your premise is a man who is trying to teach his dog to talk. That might be a hard thing for readers to buy," Parkhurst told Jay MacDonald for *BookPage* (on-line). "My hope is that, as you learn more about Paul and what he's like, it's believable that he might follow this unlikely course. . . . I think every dog owner has wondered, what is my dog thinking? What do they make of what they observe about my life? I wish it were true that we could talk and find out what they're thinking, but I don't think it's ever going to happen."

Describing *The Dogs of Babel* as "an unforgettable debut," Kristine Huntley wrote for *Booklist* (June 2003), "The brilliance of Parkhurst's novel lies in the subtle buildup of emotion as Paul digs deeper and deeper to discover the truth about the woman he loved, who may have worn a mask even when with him." Though most critics were positive, some reviews were tempered with criticism; Lev Grossman, writing for *Time* (June 16, 2003), observed, "*The Dogs of Babel* is a neatly, almost perfectly constructed novel, but its flawlessness is also its biggest flaw. It's too pretty: it lacks the messiness of reality, and as a result it feels smaller than life."

Parkhurst drew inspiration for her second novel, *Lost and Found*, from a pop phenomenon. "Like a lot of people, I like the drama of reality shows—even though a lot of them aren't very good, and there are questions about how 'real' they really are, part of the fun lies in the idea that you're watching events that might actually have an effect on someone's life," she told Scott Butki for Blogcritics.org (Aug. 30, 2006). "I thought that the drama and structure of a reality show, along with the fact that I'd be placing my characters in an intense, pressure-cooker-type environment, would provide a good backbone for a novel."

The reality show at the heart of Parkhurst's novel is loosely based on CBS's *Amazing Race*, a program in which teams of two or four race around the world. The individuals comprising the two-person teams competing in the fictional competition are a hodgepodge of personalities. "Parkhurst's characters include a mother-daughter team dealing with a tragic secret, a husband and wife who believe religion will keep them faithful to heterosexuality, brothers divorced within a year of each other, and former child stars hoping to jump-start their careers," Carol Memmott wrote for *USA Today* (May 25, 2006). "You think the bickering is bad on TV? Just wait until you hear what Parkhurst imagines they're really thinking and saying off-camera."

Parkhurst has been married since 1998 and resides in Washington, D.C. She has one son, who was born the day after she completed *The Dogs of Babel.* "I love to travel and to cook," she wrote on the Barnes & Noble Web site, "although I haven't had much of a chance to do either one since my son was born." She also collects masks and enjoys crossword puzzles.

—P.B.M.

Suggested Reading: Carolyn Parkhurst's Web site; Mostly Fiction Web site; *People* p53 June 16, 2003; *Time* p68 June 16, 2003

Selected Books: *The Dogs of Babel*, 2003; *Lost and Found*, 2006

Courtesy of HarperCollins

Patchett, Ann

Dec. 2, 1963– Novelist; memoirist

Ann Patchett's novels, *The Patron Saint of Liars* (1992), *Taft* (1994), *The Magician's Assistant* (1997), and *Bel Canto* (2001), have featured settings ranging from the American South to South America, as well as principal characters of varying race, nationality, and sexual persuasion. Many reviewers have commented on the extraordinary sense of place found in her works. Rather than exploring the more negative aspects of life under trying circumstances, Patchett has created transformative havens in such locales as a home for unwed mothers, a Memphis blues bar, a small town in Nebraska, and a sequestered South American mansion, scenes from which her characters often emerge, despite all their hardship, with an attitude of renewal. Writing in the *New York Times Book Review* (November 16, 1997), Suzanne Berne referred to Patchett's use of "flashy paradoxes" and noted that they served to encourage "a struggle with credulity," which she saw as being one of the novelist's aims: "Improbable relationships can flourish; strange havens do exist," something Patchett further proved when she released, in 2004, her memoir, *Truth & Beauty*, which told of the conservative Patchett's close friendship with the flamboyant Lucy Grealy, a writer who died in 2002.

Ann Patchett was born on December 2, 1963 in Los Angeles, California. Her father, Frank Patchett, was a detective in the Los Angeles Police Department. Her mother, who was born Jeanne Wilkinson, was a nurse and went on to publish her first, highly successful novel, *Julie and Romeo*, in her 60s, under the name Jeanne Ray. When Patchett was six years old, her parents divorced. She then moved with her mother and sister to Nashville, Tennessee, her mother's hometown. There, Patchett earned low grades at the Catholic school she attended sporadically. Her family "had very peculiar circumstances," Patchett told Elizabeth Bernstein in an interview for *Publishers Weekly* (October 13, 1997). "[My mother] was a very loving mother, but we were scrambling; we had bigger things going on in our lives than whether or not I could read." She learned to read nonetheless, and what praise she won from her teachers came as the result of her writing and storytelling abilities. She submitted her poems to the *New Yorker* and *Seventeen* magazines when she was in high school. "I believe that my gift in this world," Patchett told Bernstein, "is not that I'm smarter or more talented than anyone else: it's that I had a singular goal. I don't want other stuff: friends, kids, travel. What makes me happy is writing." When she enrolled in Sarah Lawrence College, in Bronxville, New York, in 1980, she was determined to become a poet.

Patchett changed her focus after signing up for a fiction-writing class taught by the novelist Allan Gurganus, "to escape a poetry writer's block," as Elizabeth Bernstein reported. In that course, "I just completely found myself," Patchett recalled. "I took to fiction like a duck to water." Just before she graduated, her story "All Little Colored Children Should Learn to Play Harmonica," about a large black family in the 1940s, was published in a 1984 issue of the *Paris Review.* (The story has since been anthologized numerous times and adapted for the stage.) She continued her apprenticeship at the Iowa Writers' Workshop, earning an M.F.A. degree in 1987. After receiving her degree, Patchett went through an emotional rough patch, which included the ending of a brief marriage. She left a teaching post at Allegheny College, in Meadville, Pennsylvania, to return to her mother's home in Nashville; while working there as a waitress, she came up with an idea for a book. She then landed a fellowship at the Fine Arts Work Center in Provincetown, Massachusetts, where she completed her manuscript, which was published as *The Patron Saint of Liars* (1992).

The novel concerns Rose, a young woman who runs away from her husband and, two months pregnant, lands in St. Elizabeth's, a Catholic home for unwed mothers, in Kentucky. Rose, who is then trained as a cook, remains at the home after giving birth to her daughter, Cecilia. She marries (bigamously) Son, the handyman for the home, who raises Cecilia as his own child. *The Patron Saint of Liars* was described by several reviewers as creating a "magical" and "healing" atmosphere. Alice McDermott wrote in the *New York Times Book Review* (July 26, 1992), "Ann Patchett has written such a good first novel that among the many pleasures it offers is the anticipation of how wonderful her second, third and fourth will surely be. . . . The world of St. Elizabeth's and of the novel itself . . . retains some sense of the miraculous, of a genuine, if unanticipated, power to heal."

In *Taft*, her 1994 novel, Patchett turned, as she had in "All Little Colored Children Should Learn to Play Harmonica," to portrayals of African-Americans. John Nickel, the narrator, is the manager of a bar in Memphis, Tennessee. He is also a frustrated jazz drummer, having given up his career in music to earn a steady living for his girlfriend and their son, Franklin. After he has put his girlfriend through nursing school, she leaves him, taking Franklin with her. Fay Taft, a white, working-class 17 year old, then arrives in Memphis with her younger, drug-involved brother, Carl, after the death of their father. Fay becomes a waitress in Nickel's bar, and Nickel, tormented by longing for his own son, becomes a surrogate parent to Fay and Carl.

In an interview with Elizabeth McCracken, her friend and fellow writer, for Ballantine Books Reader's Circle (on-line), Patchett explained both how she had come to choose a black man as the narrator and why there is a constant, lurking sense of danger and violence in the novel: "When I had all my characters and my story, I set about to find a narrator. It's a little like a casting call. I tried out different characters, started the book from different points of view. I never intended John to be the narrator, but in the final analysis he was the most reliable person I had to work with. I did not set out to have a black male narrator. He was simply the character who was my best bet. . . . When John says he can think of half a dozen things worth dying for, I think he's not talking about specific things but a general sense of honor. He is a heroic character. . . . He would die trying to do the right thing. . . . As for the violence in the book and John's awareness of that violence, that comes from my perception of what it must be like to be a black man in the south (or anywhere in this country, for that matter)." Patchett went on to recall that "growing up in Nashville in the late sixties, I remember the Klan stood out on Music Row every weekend with their white hoods and German shepherds. . . . John understands that the world is a dangerous place in a way that Franklin and Fay and Carl absolutely do not understand. The intersection of one character's understanding and another character's naivete is a fearsome and tender place. It is a perfect place to set a novel."

"Like his creator, Nickel speaks with a voice that is both someone else's and his own," Diana Postlethwaite wrote in the *New York Times Book Review* (October 16, 1994). "Ms. Patchett brings three rich narratives together, exploring Nickel's relationship with his son, Franklin; Nickel's relationship with Fay and Carl, and Nickel's imagining of Taft's relationship with his son and daughter. What could be merely a literary parlor trick—keeping three stories in the air at once—becomes, in Ms. Patchett's telling, as resonant as a blues song, each story harmonizing with and answering the others." Richard Eder, writing in *New York Newsday* (October 6, 1994), was equally enthusiastic about *Taft*, declaring it to be "light-voiced, almost lilting, about sorrowful things." He concluded that Patchett had managed "the lightness and the sorrow with an equilibrium that does both justice," creating "a moving emblem of fatherhood's rarely explored passion." Patchett was awarded the Janet Heidinger Kafka Prize for *Taft* in 1995.

The Magician's Assistant, Patchett's 1997 novel, explores a different kind of passion—that of a woman for a gay man. Sabine has been the assistant to Parsifal, a magician, for two decades; she lives in Los Angeles with Parsifal and his Vietnamese lover, Phan, until Phan dies of AIDS. Parsifal, believing he will soon follow Phan in death, marries Sabine to make her his widow, so she can benefit financially. After he dies, much sooner than expected, the inconsolable Sabine—left alone in a large house—must deal with the fact that Parsifal lied about his past: instead of the dead, upper-class relatives he invented, his family members are living, working-class residents of Nebraska, whom she visits. "When Parsifal died she lost the rest of his life, but now she had stumbled on 18 years," Patchett wrote, as quoted by Suzanne Berne in the *New York Times Book Review* (November 16, 1997). "Eighteen untouched years that she could have; early, forgotten volumes of her favorite work. A childhood that could be mined month by month. Parsifal would not get older, but what about younger?"

"The muted tone of this narrative matches Sabine's tentative moves in the void of her loss; yet Patchett's sweet and plangent voice often reminds one of Laurie Colwin in its evocation of love that transcends sexual boundaries and in the portrayal of reassuring patterns of domesticity," the *Publishers Weekly* (July 14, 1997) reviewer wrote. "Patchett's ability to evoke sense of place . . . is near magical in itself. If the narrative moves at a deliberately slow pace, it's rich with the rewarding contrast between the precise mechanics of magic tricks and the real possibility of magic in daily life." Other reviewers, such as Veronica Chambers, writing for *Newsweek* (October 13, 1997), also found wizardry in *The Magician's Assistant*. "We read Patchett's novel with the same pleasure and awe of an audience watching a chained Houdini escape from an underwater chamber," she wrote. "As Patchett portrays families, few things are as true as the magician's tease: the closer you get, the less you can see."

Patchett has allowed her sense of fun free rein in the essays she has written for such magazines as *Gourmet* and *Vogue*. In a back-page piece published in the *New York Times Magazine* (July 23, 2000), Patchett wrote ironically of her surprise that her mother, Jeanne Ray, had become a best-selling novelist; Patchett slyly revealed her own feelings of jealousy and rivalry while pretending the opposite sentiments: "My mother's success is hardly her own fault. Wasn't I the one who did the pushing? Didn't I snatch up her manuscript like a foundling left on the doorstep and rush it to my agent . . . ? If I had wanted my mother to stay a nurse, I would have given her a kiss upon her forehead after reading her book and said, 'Oh, Mom, I think it's so sweet that you tried to write a novel.' And she would have thrown it in the fireplace." Reporting the comment of a producer for the TV show *48 Hours*—which ran a story on Ray—to the effect that Ray's success could boost the sales of Patchett's own books, Patchett wrote, "Let's be honest here. My mother has written an extremely funny book about 60-year-olds finding true love and great sex in a florist's cooler. I just finished a novel about opera and Peru. If *48 Hours* calls me again, chances are pretty good it's going to be because they've misplaced Mom's phone number."

Patchett's reference to Peru notwithstanding, *Bel Canto*, her 2001 novel, is set in an unnamed South American country. (She did reveal in her *Publishers Weekly* interview that the book's action was inspired by events in Lima, Peru, in 1996, in which the Tupac Amaru rebel guerrillas seized the Japanese ambassador's residence and took a large number of hostages.) Patchett explained to Elizabeth Bernstein that she wanted the characters in her novel to speak different languages, noting that she was "very interested in the idea of foreignness, of people coming from different countries finding a way to communicate." In *Bel Canto*, about 200 foreign diplomats have gathered in a vice-presidential palace to celebrate the birthday of a visiting Japanese electronics executive who loves opera. A great opera star has been invited to perform, the hope being that the Japanese mogul will be moved to invest in the host country's industry. Absent from the party is the country's president, who is at home watching his favorite soap opera; the terrorists who burst into the party hoping to capture the president are thus forced to hold everyone else as hostages. Many are

soon released, leaving Roxane Coss, the opera star, to endure a long period in the company of opera lovers and hardened guerrillas—a group in which she at first believes herself to be the only woman. "As the days drag on," a writer for *Publishers Weekly* (April 16, 2001) noted, the hostages' "initial anguish and fear give way to a kind of complex domesticity, as intricately involved as the melodies Roxane sings during their captivity." Patchett observed in an interview published in the *New York Times* (April 2, 2002) that *Bel Canto* was "more ambitious in terms of its narrative structure" than her other novels. "The characters were more heroic; they were people who tried so hard to be their best selves," she added.

"Roxane's uncanny effect on people is meant to symbolize the transformative power of art, the way in which art and culture are as inevitable as the beauty and desire that inspire them," Daniel Mendelsohn wrote for *New York* (June 18, 2001). "Literature, music, horticulture, drama, language, religion, cuisine, pedagogy: These are the elements of civilization itself, and Patchett's optimistic point is that they will spring up in the most inhospitable of places. 'Who knew that being kidnapped was so much like attending university?' one of the characters jokes at what proves to be the end not of a nightmare but of a culture-filled idyll, a time-out-of-time in which politicians and corporate tycoons and terrorists get a prolonged taste of literature, art, music—'all the brilliant things we might have done with our lives if only we suspected we knew how.'" "While at first Patchett's tone seems oddly flippant and detached," the *Publishers Weekly* reviewer observed, "it soon becomes apparent that this light note is an introduction to her main theme, which is each character's cathartic experience. . . . Patchett proves equal to her themes; the characters' relationships mirror the passion and pain of grand opera, and readers are swept up in a crescendo of emotional fervor." James Polk, writing in the *New York Times Book Review* (June 10, 2001), complained that many of the "humanizing details" Patchett brought to her descriptions of the guerrillas' activities "diminish the story's taut ambivalence, making some scenes near the end sound almost like accounts of a Boy Scout jamboree." Still, he concluded, "*Bel Canto* often shows Patchett doing what she does best—offering fine insights into the various ways in which human connections can be forged, whatever pressures the world may place upon them." Patchett received the PEN/Faulkner Award for *Bel Canto* in 2002. The novel also brought her the Orange Prize, awarded only to women writing in English.

In 2002 Patchett lost her close friend and fellow writer Lucy Grealy to a heroine overdose, and a few weeks later wrote an article about her for *New York*. Feeling the article left too much unsaid, Patchett spent the following years writing *Truth & Beauty* (2004), a memoir about her relationship with Grealy, which had begun when the two women entered the Iowa Writers' Workshop and became roommates. (Grealy is best remembered for *An Autobiography of a Face* (1994), a memoir about her childhood struggle with cancer and the reconstructive surgeries that she had to endure afterwards, because her treatment caused part of her jaw to disintegrate.) "Patchett portrays her friend as a rare being, an embodiment of truth and beauty, a brilliant and courageous woman who attracted many ardent and giving admirers to her bright blaze. The reader is left in awe of Grealy's intelligence, resiliency, vitality and audacity, and deeply affected by the boon and burden of Patchett's devotion to her. And Patchett makes palpable the shock of the abrupt termination of their grand alliance," Donna Seaman wrote for the *Atlanta Journal-Constitution* (May 9, 2004). She concluded: "A generous and virtuoso performance, Patchett's testament to friendship is at once elegiac and celebratory, gracefully balanced between emotion and reason, alight with understanding and beautifully, and truthfully, shadowed by the vagaries of fate, the obdurateness of personality, the mystery of being." Others, however, were not as impressed, comparing Patchett's memoir to Grealy's own and finding Patchett's lacking. "While *Truth & Beauty* is highly readable," Jocelyn McClurg wrote for *USA Today* (May 11, 2004), "the language rarely rises to the poetic heights of Grealy's autobiography. But if

this honest book sends new readers out in search of Grealy's memoir, Patchett will have served her friend's memory well." Patchett was awarded the 2004 Heartland Prize for non-fiction for her effort.

Patchett lives in Nashville, where her partner, Karl, a surgeon, also lives. "Karl and I have been together for 10 years but we've never lived together. We see each other every day and we'll separate only when one of us dies, but I really, really like living alone. And writing is all about being alone. I like other people, I'm very close to my family but so much of what I do involves sitting on the sofa and staring like an idiot. If I'm engaged by other people all the time, I just don't need to engage with writing," she told Murray Waldren for the *Weekend Australian* (October 23, 2004).

—S.Y.

Suggested Reading: Ann Patchett's Official Web site; *Gentlemen's Quarterly* p207+ Nov. 1997; *New York Times* E p1+ Aug. 26, 2002; *New York Times Magazine* p66 July 23, 2000; *Publishers Weekly* p52+ Oct. 13, 1997; *Vogue* p78+ Apr. 1995, p120+ Mar. 1997

Selected Books: *The Patron Saint of Liars*, 1992; *Taft*, 1994; *The Magician's Assistant*, 1997; *Bel Canto*, 2001; *Truth & Beauty*, 2004

Peace, David

Apr. 9, 1967– Novelist

Andy Beckett, writing for the *London Review of Books* (September 23, 2004), commented that David Peace's novels all "carry a distaste that suggests a moralist at work." Similarly, Guy Somerset, writing for the Wellington, New Zealand, *Dominion Post* (June 19, 2004), characterized Peace's novels as "rank with corruption and violence and . . . written in a style so spare and fractured as to make James Ellroy [a writer of hard-boiled crime fiction] read like Maeve Binchy [a writer of best-sellers particularly popular with female readers]." Peace's first four novels, each named after the year in which the story takes place, earned him a reputation as a serious and highly ambitious crime writer. With his two most recently published books, he has moved outside the traditional subjects of crime fiction but has retained his deep interest in corruption and in the recent history of his native England. Peace's novels are distinguished by the rigorous research he conducts in preparation for writing about a period that other writers might have been content to describe from memory. (He long ago left the U.K. for Japan.) Discussing his novel *The Damned Utd* (2006) with Tim Adams for

the London *Observer* (December 31, 2006), Peace said that he tried to strike a balance between research and imagination: "I really have to hold on to the idea that it is a novel. You feel responsibility and obligation to the truth, though, obviously, and I researched it as closely as I could. Everything that can be fact is fact. People say to me it is always raining in your books. But if it is raining on the day I say it was then it certainly was raining on that day, I guarantee."

In early 2006 David Peace wrote the following autobiographical account for *World Authors 2000–2005*:

"I was born in Ossett, West Yorkshire, in 1967. I attended Batley Grammar School, Wakefield District College, and the former Manchester Polytechnic, from which I graduated in 1991. Unemployed and unpublished, I went to Istanbul in 1993 to teach English. I moved to Tokyo in 1994, also to teach English. I married in 1996 and now have two children. My first novel, *Nineteen Seventy-Four* was published by Serpent's Tail in the U.K. in 1999. Then followed *Nineteen Seventy-Seven* (2000) and *Nineteen Eighty* (2001). Also in 2001 I gave up teaching English in order to write 'full-time.' *Nineteen Eighty-Three* was published in 2002. Together, these first four books form the Red Riding Quartet. Following the completion of this quartet, I changed to Faber and Faber, who published *GB84* in 2004. I have been very fortunate that some of these books have been translated into French, Italian, Japanese, German, and Russian and also won some prizes, etc. This year, 2006, will see the publication of *The Damned Utd.* Forthcoming, over the next five years, are: 'Tokyo Year Zero,' 'Tokyo Occupied City,' and 'Tokyo Regained.' Also, 'UK-DK' and 'The Yorkshire Rippers.'"

Peace was born on April 9, 1967 to Basil Dunford Peace and Felicity Wilkinson, both teachers; he has at least one sister and one brother. During Peace's youth Yorkshire was the setting for a series of 13 brutal murders of women that were carried out by a former truck driver named Peter Sutcliffe, better known as the Yorkshire Ripper. Though Sutcliffe had begun assaulting women as early as 1969—and committed his first murder in 1975—his habit of choosing prostitutes for victims meant that it was not until June 1977, when he killed a 16-year-old girl named Jane McDonald, who had no connection with the sex trade, that he became a source of national anxiety. Peace lived about five miles away from where McDonald was murdered, and the search for her killer became a defining fascination. "Me and my brother," Peace told Somerset, "we were big fans of Sherlock Holmes and Marvel comics, and we thought we would try to solve the case, and set up a little office. We used to keep the cuttings in a file and everything." Peace became convinced that his father was the killer, only changing his mind when an audiotape, purporting to come from the Ripper himself, suggested the killer had an accent markedly different from his father's. Even once Sutcliffe had been captured and convicted of 13 killings, in 1981, the story of the Ripper continued to fascinate. Peace and other people interested in those killings have cast doubt on whether Sutcliffe committed all the crimes for which he was found guilty, and the police, who interviewed Sutcliffe at least a dozen times in connection with the killings before almost accidentally capturing him, have been strongly criticized for their incompetence, not least in accepting the audiotaped hoax and a related group of letters. "There has always been this air of not everything being known," Peace told Tim Teeman for the London *Times* (August 12, 2000). "I believe Sutcliffe was responsible for some of his crimes and more that he hasn't admitted, but I also believe that he was not responsible for all the murders that he was convicted of." Peace wrote in an essay for the British magazine *Crime Time* (on-line) that coming of age in Yorkshire during that period was possibly "the single biggest influence" on his writing.

When he was about 26, Peace followed his parents into teaching, though he has told interviewers that he chose to begin teaching English as a second language primarily to escape his life as an unsuccessful writer in England, where he was unable to publish any of his prose fiction or have any of his screenplays produced. (Among the scripts he wrote during this time was a feature-length film about the cartoon character Scooby-Doo. Based on the legend of the Flying Dutchman, the film would have been, as Peace described it to Somerset, "very, very scary and very, very dark.") In *Crime Time* Peace wrote that it was "difficult to feel any affection towards either the work or that period of my life because both involved so much sacrifice, disappointment and hurt for many people, not only myself. That said, the obsessions were the same: the Yorkshire Ripper—that time and that place. So the initial research and early texts continue to inform and inspire my current writing on a daily basis."

Living among people so closely affected by crime has perhaps also given Peace an unusually strong sense of the ethics of writing about the subject. "Crime," Peace observed in his *Crime Time* essay, "is brutal, harrowing and devastating for everyone involved, and crime fiction should be every bit as brutal, harrowing and devastating as the violence of the reality it seeks to document. Anything less at best sanitises crime and its effects, at worst trivialises it." "Crime fiction," he continued, "has both the opportunity and the obligation to be the most political of any writing or any media, crime itself being the most manifest example of the politics of the time. . . . I believe the crime writer, by their choice of genre, is obligated to document these times and their crimes, and the writer who chooses to ignore this responsibility is then simply exploiting, for his or her own financial or personal gratification, a genre that is itself nothing more than an entertainment industry constructed upon the sudden, violent deaths of other, innocent people and the unending suffering of their families."

Peace's first published novel, *Nineteen Seventy-Four*, was also the first entry in the Red Riding Quartet, a series inspired by the American writer James Ellroy's L.A. Quartet: *The Black Dahlia* (1987), *The Big Nowhere* (1988), *L.A. Confidential* (1990), and *White Jazz* (1992). (The titles of Peace's quartet are sometimes spelled out and sometimes given as numerals. An additional variation comes when the numerals are spelled out but the compound numbers they represent are not hyphenated—hence the occasional rendering of their titles as *Nineteen Seventy Four*, etc.) Peace's book follows a young reporter, Eddie Dunford, trying to understand the disappearances of a number of young girls in West Yorkshire at the end of 1974. In time Dunford's investigation leads him to feel that the disappearances are somehow related to the people and institutions controlling the city, including the police, who exist in an environment in which, George Needham wrote for *Booklist* (November 1, 1999), "corruption [is] as pervasive as oxygen." Needham compared Peace's book to George Orwell's classic *Nineteen Eighty-Four* (1949) and wrote that both books are about "the ultimate destruction of the soul at the hands of a dystopian society." Peace's book, Needham added, "presents not a warning about the future but a rueful tale of the shabby and unethical recent past upon which our current reality is built." Andy Beckett noted that Peace casts the world around Dunford "in apocalyptic terms. . . . As the narrator speeds round Leeds's grey ring of motorways, in ceaseless midwinter rain and darkness, he comes across burning gypsy caravans, corrupt property developers, [pedophiles], and a police force that beats and kidnaps and burgles with the impunity of a private army." Writing for the *New York Times Book Review* (February 20, 2000, on-line), Marilyn Stasio called the volume "a bundle of spastic nerves and jumpy tempos, hard to hold in your hand but harder to put down." Stasio particularly commended Peace's writing, arguing that "Peace's riveting style of one-word sentences, one-sentence paragraphs and monosyllabic obscenities pounds the page in the same staccato rhythms of the jackhammers in Eddie's skull. Although the ugliness of it is unrelenting, there's no getting away from the music of such pain." D. J. Taylor, on the other hand, writing for the London *Guardian* (September 4, 1999), judged the novel "completely gratuitous." He took Peace to task for his frequent use of profanity and added: "Peace's trademark trail of pared-down sentence-long paragraphs, often used when he [wants] to recapitulate the plot . . . can sometimes render the proceedings irritatingly staccato. No question of David Peace's ability, but even in the shadowy world of modern-day noir, there is such a thing as over-egging the pudding."

Two men—the police detective Bob Fraser and the cynical crime reporter Jack Whitehead, both antiheroes at best—take turns narrating the second book in the Red Riding Quartet, *Nineteen Seventy-Seven*. Though the novel details the opening of the investigation into the Ripper case, Peace concerns himself less with the killings themselves than with, as Michael Arditti noted for the London *Daily Mail* (July 28, 2000), "the culture of misogynistic violence in which Peter Sutcliffe thrived and which permeates Peace's police force." Nicola Upson, writing for *New Statesman* (September 4, 2000), observed: "The darkness of *Nineteen Seventy Seven* emerges seamlessly out of the first book into a fictionalised account of the early stages of the Ripper inquiry: vice flourishes in the Chapeltown district of Leeds; women lie in parks and on waste ground with their skulls smashed in by a blunt instrument; and the public, slow to respond to the killing of prostitutes, is eventually driven to outrage by the murder of a 16-year-old student. . . . With a human landscape that is violent and unrelentingly bleak, Peace's fiction is two or three shades the other side of noir."

The investigator at the center of *Nineteen Eighty*, the third book in the quartet, is Peter Hunter, perhaps the most upright member of the heavily compromised West Yorkshire police force. Alongside Hunter's story come the "spirit voices" of each of the 13 victims, who recapitulate their "last desperate seconds, mingled with the confession of their killer and their autopsy details," Nick Hasted noted for the London *Guardian* (August 2, 2001). "I thought about the presence the victims had in my life at the time [of the killings]," Peace told Hasted. "They were reduced to photographs. Every time [the Ripper] killed, these same photos would come out in the papers, and it was like they were trapped in that one image. I wanted to portray the unremitting bleakness of that, that these were brutal, harrowing crimes, the consequences of which we're still living with." Commenting on Peace's idea "that since crime in reality affects people's lives in terrible ways, it shouldn't be treated lightly in crime fiction," Peter Guttridge wrote for the *Observer* (September 2, 2001), "*Nineteen Eighty* provides a bleak portrait of those times, written in a stylised prose that takes a few pages to attune to but which admirably suits the subject matter. It's black and moving but, pace Peace, it's also highly entertaining. But then it is crime fiction, which, at root, notwithstanding all the many claims for significance, is entertainment."

Told by three men, each of whom had made some appearance in Peace's earlier books, *Nineteen Eighty-Three*, the last of the Red Riding Quartet, has the "most complex structure," David Marley wrote for the London *Independent* (December 14, 2002). "Peace's prose is relentlessly bleak in its narrative content, but also in its depiction of the decaying, grey urban landscape. These factors come together to create a strong and affecting atmosphere. . . .This is fiction that comes with a sense of moral gravity, clearly opposed to diluting the horrific effects of crime for the sake of bland entertainment. . . . Peace's series offers a fierce indictment of the era."

In 2003 Peace was named one of Britain's best young novelists by the literary magazine *Granta*, and the following year he enjoyed wide success with the publication of *GB84*, a fictionalized account of the miners' strike that pitted Britain's highly conservative prime minister Margaret Thatcher against Arthur Scargill, the Marxist leader of the National Union of Mineworkers. Beginning in March 1984 and lasting roughly a year, the sometimes-violent strike ended in defeat for the workers and triumph for the government, dividing a country worn down by pervasive unemployment and dominating the media to the point of stultification. "A lot of the time you were just really sick of it," Peace told Jasper Rees for the London *Daily Telegraph* (March 6, 2004). "You just wished it would go away. I was in a band and we got to play loads of benefit concerts. You've got to be careful you don't romanticise it, but there was an upsurge in local activism and artistic expression." Peace's account of the strike was viewed by many critics as being hardly romanticized at all. Calling *GB84* "a horrible novel," Sukhdev Sandhu wrote for the London *Daily Telegraph* (March 13, 2004) that it was "dark to the point of being dystopic. Joyless and unremittingly nasty. A bloated profanosaurus that seems even longer than its 460 pages, it is obscene, almost entirely lacking in humour, and repetitive to the point that most readers' eyes will glaze over. And yet, although it stretches the very limits of readability, it's also a startling and magnificently monologic work, all the more compelling for having almost nothing in common with most literary fiction in Britain these days." Sandhu placed Peace's novel in the category of "avant-pulp" and, while noting that the book "will not be to everybody's taste," concluded: "But, like a freeway pile-up, it has a vile and lingering fascination that is not easy to forget." Euan Ferguson noted for the London *Observer* (February 29, 2004) that Peace "has said he felt an 'almost incredible amount of anger and guilt' as he learnt more details of the ways in which the sacrifice and solidarity of striking miners were undermined by government, police and media: anyone with a brain and a conscience will empathise as these same details, these true details, emerge." Ferguson criticized Peace for overloading the book with too many subplots and commented: "Sadly, despite the undoubted skill and passion Peace brings to his subject, the subplots tend to infuriate. *GB84* is a valuable read, but you have to immerse yourself in it, give up a weekend: and my fear is that too many readers, like the miners themselves, will simply give up and go back to work." Terry Eagleton, calling the strike "a bare-knuckled confrontation between the capitalist state and the working-class movement, a self-consciously epochal affair on both sides," argued for the London *Guardian* (March 6, 2004) that Peace's work went counter to the common assumption that "leftwing politics and literary realism . . . go together. In fact, a lot of traditional popular culture is magical, romantic and fantastic to its core. And much of the finest leftwing art has seen the need to revolutionise form and technique, rather than simply pumping new political materials through old literary channels." Peace's narrative, Eagleton judged, was "a bold mixture of thriller, monologue, theatre script, chants, slogans, crime story, sexual subplot and documentary fiction" and "a crowded, ambitious, quick-moving novel, and as such is the literary equal of the epic events it commemorates."

With his novel *The Damned Utd* Peace returned once again to the year 1974 and fictionalized another piece of British history, this time the smaller-scale drama of soccer coach Brian Clough's 44-day reign as the head of Leeds United. As a seven-year-old, Peace saw the first game in which Clough coached Leeds, and the experience stayed with him for decades. Clough, who died in 2004, while Peace was still working on the book, had been a fierce critic of Leeds's often vicious and unsportsmanlike behavior, making his appointment to the position of head coach a surprise to many sports fans. His career at Leeds was cut short in part by an extraordinarily poor record, with the team winning only a single game under his charge, but his brief tenure is more often remembered for his willful alienation of many of his players. On his first day he announced to the team, according to Tim Adams, writing for the London *Observer* (December 31, 2006): "Gentlemen, I might as well tell you now. You lot may have won all the domestic honours there are and some of the European ones but, as far as I am concerned, the first thing you can do for me is to chuck all your medals and all your caps and all your pots and all your pans into the biggest f**king dustbin you can find, because you've never won any of them fairly. You've done it all by bloody cheating."

The Damned Utd proved a critical and popular success. Adams called it "the only football book worth having—or giving—this Christmas" and wrote that it depicted "the life of Brian in all of its blunt glory." As with Peace's other books, critics often focused on his signature style, and in this case most felt that the style suited the subject. Tim Souster, in a critique for the *Times Literary Supplement* (August 11, 2006), wrote: "Peace's treatment of this material is original. His writing is sharp-edged and condensed, governed by repetition. . . . Action is described in short, blunt sentences, and descriptions come in the form of verbless fragments, with harsh rhythms and a biblical flavour. . . . The effect is obsessive, manic, a perfect fit for Clough." Leo McKinstry, reviewing the book for the London *Sunday Telegraph* (September 24, 2006), joined other critics in praising Peace's decision to narrate the book from two points of view: one giving Clough's first-person account of his time at Leeds, and the other a second-person rendering of his more successful period at the helm of the soccer team for Derby County. McKinstry concluded: "Though the outline of Clough's career is well-known, it is difficult to put down this book because it has its own dark momentum as Clough heads for the sack from the Leeds board: 'They hate me. In the shadow of the stands. On the steps of Elland Road. In the light of the cameras and the spits of the rain.' The quality of the writing is sustained right to the end of this saga, as Clough is turned into an almost Lear-like tragic figure, noble in the depths of his raging absurdity." A film adaptation of *The Damned Utd* is reported to be in the works, with Stephen Frears directing from a script written by Peter Morgan.

Peace's next series of novels will be a trilogy that examines Tokyo from 1946, when the city began rebuilding after World War II, through 1964, when it hosted the Summer Olympic Games.

David Peace lives in Tokyo, Japan, with his wife, Izumi, and their children, George, born in 1997, and Emi, born in 2000. Peace has often told interviewers that being so far from England has in some ways made it easier for him to write about the world he knew growing up. At times, however, the distance has made it difficult for him to participate in the type of events many young authors use to further their careers. When *Granta* honored Peace by placing him alongside such fiction-world luminaries as Zadie Smith for their selection of the best young British novelists, for example, Peace could not fly back to the U.K. in time to be photographed with the rest of the group.

—S.Y.

Suggested Reading: *Booklist* p509 Nov. 1, 1999; *Crime Time* (on-line); (London) *Daily Mail* p56 July 28, 2000; (London) *Daily Telegraph* p12 Mar. 6, 2004, p8 Mar. 13, 2004; (London) *Guardian* p8 Sep. 4, 1999, p12 Aug. 2, 2001, p26 Mar. 6, 2004; (London) *Independent* p31 Dec. 14, 2002, p20+ Mar. 5, 2004; (London) *Observer* p16 Sep. 2, 2001, p17 Feb. 29, 2004, p10+ Dec. 31, 2006; *London Review of Books* p25+ Sep. 23, 2004; (London) *Times* Aug. 12, 2000; *New Statesman* p43 Sep. 4, 2000; *New York Times Book Review* p28 Feb. 20, 2000; *Times Literary Supplement* p23 Aug. 11, 2006; (Wellington, New Zealand) *Dominion Post* p10 June 19, 2004

Selected Books: *Nineteen Seventy-Four*, 1999; *Nineteen Seventy-Seven*, 2000; *Nineteen Eighty*, 2001, *Nineteen Eighty-Three*, 2002; *GB84*, 2004; *The Damned Utd*, 2006

Perkins, Emily

1970– Novelist; short-story writer; newspaper columnist

"I think failure is more inherently interesting than success. It's like the old cliché about everybody being happy in the same way, but misery being fascinatingly individual. The gap between expectation and achievement is something I've explored in all my work," Emily Perkins, the author of a book of short stories, *Not Her Real Name* (1996), and two novels, *Leave Before You Go* (1998) and *The New Girl* (2001), told Serena Allott for the London *Daily Telegraph* (June 30, 2001). To investigate that gap Perkins has employed the talents that she developed as a child actor, using "the skills of performance on the page," as Bill Manhire, a poet and an important figure in New Zealand literary circles, told Simon Robinson for *Time Australia* (August 12, 1996). In the process she has created fictional worlds filled with characters who are, as Christina Patterson wrote for the London *Observer* (May 31, 1998), "overwhelmed and immobilised by the limitations implicit in any choice. . . . They are intensely aware of their 'self -packaging' and barely capable of communication devoid of irony."

Emily Perkins was born in 1970 in Christchurch, New Zealand, and grew up in Auckland and Wellington, large New Zealand cities. She began her professional life as an actress, first doing commercials and then, when she was 15, landing the role of a drug-using teenager in a television soap opera. That show was canceled after a year, and for the rest of the 1980s and in the early 1990s, Perkins struggled through auditions, landed some terrible parts, studied at the New Zealand Drama School in Wellington, and tried to work as a waitress. "I hated serving people. I had no sense of

balance, a low boredom threshold and an inability to say 'Would you like some of today's delicious apple cake with that?' with any sincerity at all," she told Nigel Jones for the London *Guardian* (September 24, 1998).

When Perkins was 22, feeling, as she told Jones, "that acting wasn't the real me," she abandoned her thespian aspirations and turned to writing, enrolling in a course taught by Manhire at Victoria University, in Wellington. Within a year Perkins had published her first story, and shortly thereafter, she moved to London. "I'd just had my first story published here in *Sport* [a New Zealand literary magazine] and thought 'if I really wanted to keep doing this, then I'd really better get out there and see some new things," she told Megan Lane for the Wellington *Evening Post* (March 17, 1999). In London Perkins found a job in the sales department of the Bloomsbury publishing company, where she remained until 1996, the year her first book, *Not Her Real Name* (1996), was published.

Not Her Real Name, a collection of 12 short stories about 20-somethings, established Perkins as an adept observer of her generation. Ursula Owen wrote for the London *Observer* (August 4, 1996), "Emily Perkins's first collection *Not Her Real Name* (Picador) is the best evocation I've read of what it's like to be an urban young woman in these postmodern times: she makes you laugh, weep and squirm." Stephen Oxenham, writing for *World Literature Today* (Spring 1997), found Perkins's stories broader in scope, calling attention to their "grasp of the human predicament, its comedy and ironic potential." He continued, "[Perkins]is adept at creating a tension in which catastrophe is encountered, experienced, and survived, and the constant, fluent readjustment to reality is a signal characteristic of her characters. . . . Perkins is urban, urbane,

599

reflecting a quality of some good current New Zealand writing which says, 'This is good writing from New Zealand, not just good New Zealand writing.'" Others, however, found Perkins predictable. Elizabeth Young and Paula Tumulty complained for the London *Guardian* (August 16, 1996) that the stories were "brat-packy and 'postmodern' in character. They display, to begin with, the Jay McInerney Machinations: the erratic, charmless use of the present tense and the second person singular. There is, too, that meaningfully meaningless tendency to randomly terminate a story. Then there's the Douglas Coupland Consciousness—'He worries that he worries too much'—and the Bret Easton Ellis Ennui: 'Nothing much happens' and, for a change, 'Nothing's happening, nothing's happening, nothing's happening. Nothing's happening.' Plus the inevitable transposable people with ordinary names and nose-rings. And the background drone of quoted pop songs."

Perkins followed her short stories with *Leave Before You Go,* a novel that is set largely in New Zealand, where Daniel, a London art-school dropout, ends up after smuggling heroin out of Thailand. For many, the novel solidified the reputation that Perkins had begun to acquire when her stories first appeared. "Amid the noisy chorus of twentysomething novels, Emily Perkins's distinctive voice . . . stands out for its lightness and authenticity," Lisa Allardice wrote for the London *Observer* (August 15, 1999). "The ambiguous titles suggest the emotional emptiness at the centre of her work, in which characters are always leaving, going, lying or just plain drifting, as a way of escaping from themselves. . . . An appropriately aimless storyline tingles with snappy dialogue and smart observations. The claustrophobia and boredom of Perkins's Auckland is palpable. As well as capturing the mood of a disaffected generation, her depiction of loss and betrayal is painfully convincing." Similarly, Caroline Gascoigne observed for the London *Sunday Times* (June 14, 1998), "Events [in the novel] start to pile up—an affair, a break-up, a walk-out from a job, a fling, a pregnancy . . . but the various crises, like the characters, fail to develop. Life just keeps on happening. Which, in the end, is precisely Perkins's point." Others were less impressed. Iain Sharp, while acknowledging for the Auckland *Sunday Star-Times* "that Perkins remains a dab hand at transcribing the non-consequential conversations of twentysomething slackers, drifters and wannabes," he went on to complain, "Overall, the book reads like a slight little tale that has been stretched to seven or eight times its natural length. As entertainment, I'd put it on a par with . . . a weaker episode of *Seinfeld.* Readable but not riveting. Not a disgrace exactly, but definitely a disappointment."

Three years later Perkins published her second novel, *The New Girl,* about a university teacher, Miranda, who arrives in a small town to recover from a failed love affair and escape the dark secrets of her past life. The inspiration for the story, Perkins told Caroline Baum for the Sydney *Sun-Herald* (August 4, 2002), was "a scandal at a university in New Zealand in which a young woman had exerted undue influence on some first-year students, and I wondered about that situation and imagined a situation where the mentor's agenda is not entirely benign, where she has some kind of sinister history." In the novel Miranda sets up a self-improvement class for a group of teenage girls just after their final year of school. The actual activities of the group, however, consist of smoking marijuana, exchanging fashions, and gossiping. Miranda has a brief affair with one girl's alcoholic father, and another girl, Julia, develops a crush on her. "Miranda is an agent of destruction. She asks hard questions and brings the disasters she is running away from with her; she is a kind of Eve, or Pandora, opening a box of knowledge and leaving in the middle of the fall-out," Gaby Wood explained for the London *Observer* (July 22, 2001) and went on to observe, "Perkins has a wonderfully light touch; she is a master of dialogue and plain speech, a casual [Raymond] Carver for our times." Sophie Ratcliffe, reviewing the novel for the London *Times* (July 14, 2001), perceived some flaws, noting that "the ending ties up some plot points a touch hastily, perhaps," but concluded that "on the whole [the story] is beautifully paced, with set-piece descriptions countered by wit as dry as her New Zealand summer . . . [and] though set in an Antipodean backwater, the novel is emotionally located in a nowheresville so evocative that I felt that Perkins must have read my old diaries. For as each character reveals a desire for affection, 'like me, like me, like me' becomes the leitmotif in more ways than one. Touching on the difference between liking and being alike, *The New Girl*'s greatest strength is the way it questions our presumptions of identity."

Perkins is also the editor of *The Picnic Virgin* (1999), a compilation of short works by contemporary New Zealand writers, published by Victoria University Press.

Perkins is married to Karl Maughan, a New Zealand artist noted for his lushly realistic paintings of gardens. She writes a humorous column, Her Outdoors, for the London *Independent on Sunday*, in which she discusses the details of her daily life. In one column (June 29, 2003, on-line), for example, she bemoaned her husband's absence on their wedding anniversary: "This is Somebody Else's Outdoors, namely my husband's, who for purposes of anonymity I shall call Karl Maughan (am not interested in protecting his privacy right now). On our wedding anniversary he leaps out of bed, shoves a cup of tea at me and buggers off to Venice for the Biennale. I get the kids dressed, take the eldest to nursery, realise the youngest has mouth ulcers and that's why he's on a starvation diet, book him into the doctor although I know there's nothing we can do but wait out the misery until the ulcers disappear of their own accord, trundle off to the pharmacy for Bonjela [ointment], meditate on four years of marriage and the daily thrill and romance of it. . . ."

In 2006 Perkins was awarded a Buddle Findlay Sargeson Fellowship, which includes living quarters in New Zealand and a cash stipend. She reportedly used it to work on her next novel, tentatively titled "Novel About My Wife."

—S. Y.

Suggested Reading: (London) *Daily Telegraph* p8 June 30, 2001; (London) *Independent* p32 Sep. 22, 1996; (London) *Independent on Sunday* p26 Feb. 16, 2003, p18 June 29, 2003; (London) *Observer* p16 May 31, 1998, p14 Aug. 15, 1999, p16 July 22, 2001; (Sydney) *Sun-Herald* p32 Aug. 4, 2002; *Time Australia* p84 Aug. 12, 1996; *World Literature Today* p465 Spring 1997

Selected Works: novels—*Not Her Real Name, and Other Stories*, 1996; *Leave Before You Go*, 1998; *The New Girl*, 2001; as editor—*The Picnic Virgin*, 1999

Petterson, Per

July 18, 1952– Novelist

Per Petterson—who is known as "Norwegian literature's knight of masculine sensitivity," according to Boyd Tonkin, the literary editor of the London *Independent* (May 3, 2006)—is one of his country's best-selling authors. He has also has earned a great deal of notice in the English-speaking world with the recent translations of three of his novels, most notably *Out Stealing Horses*, which won Britain's 2006 Independent Foreign Fiction Prize, an award shared by author and translator (in this case, Anne Born). Petterson's other novels available in English (also translated by Born) include *To Siberia*, which was inspired by his mother's adolescence in Nazi-occupied Denmark, and *In the Wake*, which explores the aftermath of a boating accident based on a real-life tragedy suffered by the author's family.

Per Petterson was born in Oslo, Norway, on July 18, 1952. Little has been written in English about his private life, though it is known that he was trained as a librarian and has worked as a laborer, bookseller, and translator. In interviews he has admitted to being influenced by such writers as Knut Hamsun, the Norwegian Nobel laureate, and Raymond Carver, whose work he discovered in the 1980s, while working in a bookstore that imported foreign literature. "It was like coming home," Petterson said of the experience with Carver, as quoted by Boyd Tonkin. His initial literary success came in 1987, with the publication of his first short-story collection, *Aske i munnen, sand i skoa* (which translates as "ash in his mouth, sand in his shoe"). Two novels quickly followed: *Ekkoland* (1989) and *Det er greit for meg* (1992), which translate as "Echoland" and "it's fine by me," respectively. These early works recount the lives of young, working-class men living on the outskirts of Oslo in the mid-20th century.

Petterson's first novel to be translated into English translation was *Til Sibir* (1996), which was published as *To Siberia* in the U.K., in 1999. Set before and during World War II, the story is narrated by a young Danish woman living in a small town in Jutland. She longs to escape her life—particularly her drunken grandfather and religious mother—by moving to Siberia. Meanwhile, her brother and closest confidant, Jesper, joins the resistance against the Nazi occupation of Denmark and later flees to Morocco. The novel, which depicts the lives of working-class people as they struggle to survive under extraordinary circumstances, was nominated for the Nordic Council's Literature Prize.

In the Glasgow *Herald* (December 10, 1998), John Cairney wrote that *To Siberia* "seems set to establish [Petterson's] international reputation," and described it as "an exceptionally well-told novel, with strong characterisation and a beautifully paced and balanced plot." Sharon Norris wrote for the *Scotsman* (November 14, 1998), "Although this is not the first novel to deal with the brother-sister relationship, Petterson is clearly a writer of great talent and originality. His female narrator is utterly convincing, and although the structure of the novel is such that we know early on that one of the central characters dies, the author manages to retain the reader's interest to the end. We care enough to want to know why. If there are any criticisms to be levelled here, it is possibly that *To Siberia* falls into the now cliched category of Brooding Scandinavian Novel. Perhaps it is just the publishers in this country which have effectively created such a genre. Either way, do not be put off, for this is a beautifully written if wistfully sad novel and, just as important, skillfully translated."

Petterson's next novel, *I kjølvannet* (2000), was translated as *In the Wake* and published in 2003 in the U.K. and in 2006 in the U.S. Though not technically a memoir, much of the author's own experiences went into the novel, which depicts the lives of a writer named Arvid Jansen and his brother after a tragic accident aboard a ferry boat claims the lives of several family members. (The book recalls the fire aboard the *Scandinavian Star* on April 7, 1990, in which many people were killed, including the author's parents, younger brother, and niece.) In the novel, Arvid only fully feels the impact of the loss some six years afterwards, when he realizes that none of them will ever return. He has difficulty writing and drinks too much; every attempt to distract himself from his grief only brings back painful memories, not only of the tragedy but also of his youth. Arvid's surviving brother is equally despondent; his grief leads to the end of his marriage and a suicide attempt.

Reviewing *In the Wake* for the London *Independent on Sunday* (February 9, 2003), Paul Binding wrote, "For all its fidelity to the author's experiences, this is emphatically a novel, not a memoir, and not merely because Petterson has occasionally departed from actual facts (his anguished brother didn't attempt suicide). *In the Wake* accords all its characters, narrator included, an objective validity belonging wholly to fiction. The movements from the inner life of recollection and resentment to bemused, groping encounters with others have a wonderful artistic intricacy, each a skein in a flawless whole." A *Publishers Weekly* (May 1, 2006) reviewer opined, "Despite the gloomy subject matter, Arvid is a witty, self-deprecating narrator who fought with his family while they were alive and misses them terribly now that they're gone. This novel won several literary prizes in Europe. . . . The events may not feel as immediate to American readers, but many will find Arvid's path of loss and redemption affecting nonetheless."

The same year that *In The Wake* was published in Britain, Petterson's novel *Ut og stæle hester* (2003) became a best-seller in his home country and garnered both the Norwegian Critics Prize for Literature and the Booksellers' Prize from the Norwegian Booksellers Association. In the novel, which was published in English translation as *Out Stealing Horses* (2005), an elderly widower named Trond takes up residence in a run-down cottage on the outskirts of a small village in Norway just as winter is about to set in. There he reflects on the summer he spent at age 15 in a cabin in the woods with his father. One day that season he went with his friend Jon to ride a neighbor's horses without permission (the activity that gives the book its title), thereby setting in motion a chain of events that deeply affect his life.

"There is touching humour in parts to *Out Stealing Horses*, a gentle, personal kind," Gloria Trapezaris wrote for the London *Daily Express* (November 4, 2005). "Trond's life is an orderly set of rules—something he readily admits is an attempt to emulate his long-lost father's efficiency. He needs to wash and put on a fresh shirt for dinner, to always keep his home neat and tidy. It is not a sad story but one of a man in control. The narrative is a beautiful balance between an anchored sentience and a naturally-flowing stream of consciousness. Petterson writes with robust unpretentiousness, and his prose may be unadorned yet it is porous with atmospheric sentiment. His story gathers pace like growing up, and stimulates heart and mind like a brisk country walk." Boyd Tonkin, writing for the London *Independent* (December 14, 2005), noted: "On the face of it, *Out Stealing Horses* offers little new. Per Petterson creates a reflective narrator who, widowed and alone on the brink of the millennium, looks back to the summer of 1948 that changed forever his sense of his parents, his world and himself. It's almost a Hollywood set-up, as the 15-year-old Trond has to negotiate a fatal accident that plunges his best friend into trauma, his father's extra-marital affair and imminent desertion, and even the wartime Nazi-defying heroics that lie behind this family crisis. Yet Petterson does it all with immense subtlety and assurance, so this familiar coming-of-age plot sparkles like the northern sunlight on the river that winds and surges through the forest, and through the action of the novel."

Per Petterson lives in a rural village in Norway.
—C.M.

Suggested Reading: (London) *Daily Express* p48 Nov. 4, 2005; (London) *Guardian* (on-line) May 3, 2006; (London) *Independent* p48 Dec. 14, 2005, p20 May 3, 2006, p22 May 5, 2006; (London) *Independent on Sunday* p16 Feb. 9, 2003; *Scotsman* p18 Nov. 14, 1998

Selected Books in English Translation: *To Siberia*, 1999; *In the Wake*, 2003; *Out Stealing Horses*, 2005

Picoult, Jodi

May 19, 1966– Novelist

Jodi Picoult has taken on such controversial issues as spousal abuse, pedophilia, infanticide, mercy killing, and televangelism in her books: *Songs of the Humpback Whale: A Novel in Five Voices* (1992), *Harvesting the Heart* (1993), *Picture Perfect* (1995), *Mercy* (1996), *The Pact: A Love Story* (1998), *Keeping Faith* (1999), *Plain Truth* (1999), *Salem Falls* (2001), *Perfect Match* (2002), *Second Glance* (2003), *My Sister's Keeper* (2003), *Vanishing Acts* (2005), *The Tenth Circle* (2006), and *Nineteen Minutes* (2007). Joy Dickinson observed in the *Dallas Morning News* (June 25, 2000), "No matter how secure a reader's convictions about a particular issue, Ms. Picoult will surely shake them up." Dickinson wrote in a later review for the *Dallas Morning News* (April 29, 2001) that Picoult "has carved her own niche with her novels—one part romance, one part courtroom thriller, two parts social commentary." For Ann Hood, writing for the *Washington Post Book World* (May 5, 2002), "Picoult has become a master—almost a clairvoyant—at targeting hot issues. . . .

Jodi Picoult

Diving into murky moral territories where characters struggle with feelings that range from vengeance to guilt to sorrow and everyplace in between is a trademark of Picoult's fiction."

Picoult composed the following autobiographical piece for *World Authors 2000–2005*:

"I grew up in a very suburban part of Long Island, that in the 1970s was full of potato and sod farms and is now dominated by strip malls. Where I live, now, in New Hampshire, the nearest Starbucks is an hour away and the closest thing we have to a mall is a Walmart. I have a younger brother, Jon, who is now married and living in suburban Connecticut. My parents do not quite understand how a child from a row-house development grew into a woman who now lives on 13 acres with a cow, but I feel much more comfortable in my adopted state than I do when I go back to visit my parents.

"I went to a public school in Smithtown, NY— one that was not distinctive in any way but for a few teachers who really encouraged me to write. Maybe because of this, I got to Princeton thinking I knew it all already. My first creative writing workshop there was with Mary Morris. She sat me down on the floor, handed me a glue stick, scissors, and construction paper, and told me to cut and paste based on what the class directed. I left there in tears and went to her office hours three days later, to ask why she'd done that to me. 'Because you needed it,' she said, 'and because you could take it.' Well, I wanted to show HER. I edited that piece to within an inch of its life, and when she told me to send it off to a magazine, I did. A few months later *Seventeen* called and said they

wanted to pay me $2000 for my piece. I immediately called my mom to tell her I was going to be a writer. 'That's nice,' she said. 'Who's going to support you?'

"I fully believe that if not for Mary Morris's guiding hand and my mother's reality check, I wouldn't be where I am now. I still keep in touch with Mary, and my mother is one of my first readers—and biggest fans. My father and I work annually on a parody of 'The Night Before Christmas,' set in the property/casualty industry and printed in *Business Insurance*, a trade magazine where my dad has a regular column. It's a little like writing in Greek, because I know nothing about his industry (except that it always seems to be in dire straits, according to him), and that absolutely nothing rhymes with 'reinsurance recoverable.' He gives me a list of topics to cover, and I try to put them into iambic pentameter, and after several hours of cursing, I hand him a draft.

"I have three children—all of whom have been affected, I think, by having a mom with a very unlikely career. My oldest used to pull books off the shelves at libraries and open them up to the author photo in the back and crow, 'Mommy!'— even if it happened to be Stephen King—because that was the place where his mother's picture tended to be. I think, now that he's older he a) knows I'm better looking than Stephen King and b) believes that you truly can be anything you want if you set your heart on it, which in his case may be a singing paleontologist. My middle son has always been a poet—in fact I used many of his incredible observations to create the character of Nathaniel in *Perfect Match*. And my youngest, my daughter—well, this year she hit second grade and her teacher called me in September to ask if I'd mind typing up her short story. Apparently, it was 33 pages long. 'Ah!' I told her teacher. 'So that's where the gene went!' I have high hopes of one day being like Mary and Carol Higgins Clark.

"I think that having kids, and the world's greatest husband, and a bucolic country life are what allow me to write the things I tend to write. No one will ever accuse me, I think, of writing a fluff book—or indeed of addressing anything short of a weighty and sometimes devastating topic . . . and many people who meet me are surprised to find out that I'm a pretty happy person, given that choice of subject matter. But I think I can crawl through the dark side of life and love because I know, at five o'clock, I can go back downstairs to a place that's safe. If I had any less of a support network in my family, I don't know that I'd be able to write the things I do. And those topics—I *need* to write them. There are plenty of other authors out there who think the purpose of a novel is to wrap things up neat and tidy at the end . . . but I disagree. I'd rather spill out the can of worms and watch a thousand different readers stuff them back in a thousand different ways. If a book doesn't leave you thinking, in my opinion, it hasn't done its job."

PICOULT

Jodi Lynn Picoult was born on May 19,1966. She grew up in Nesconset, Long Island, the daughter of nominally Jewish but not highly religious parents—Jane Picoult, a nursery-school administrator, and Myron Picoult, an insurance, securities, and financial analyst. Picoult obtained her B.A. degree from Princeton University, in New Jersey, in 1987, and a master's degree in education from Harvard University, in Cambridge, Massachusetts, in 1990. (She married Timothy Warren van Leer, also a graduate of Princeton, in 1989.)

In addition to working for a time on Wall Street, Picoult has been a textbook editor and a junior-high-school teacher; in 1991, however, she gave up outside jobs for full-time writing. *Songs of the Humpback Whale* was published the following year. The debut novel is told by five distinct narrators: Jane, a speech pathologist who was abused as a child; her husband, Oliver, an oceanographer whom she has abandoned after a fight; her daughter, Rebecca, who travels with her on a cross-country journey; her brother, Joley; and her lover, Sam. Ellen R. Cohen, a reviewer for *Library Journal* (June 1, 1992), wrote, "This uniquely constructed first novel, the literary equivalent of counterpoint in music, is told in five voices whose polyphonic development delineates a multifaceted love story on different levels for different individuals. . . . The characters' contrapuntal recollections offer psychological insights into their lives. These insights lead to growth, second chances, and love. Charming and poignant, Picoult's novel is even better after a second reading." While praising the book's "structural tour de force," Judith Grossman complained in a critique for the *Women's Review of Books* (July 1992), "Despite its pleasures, *Songs of the Humpback Whale* left me finally troubled and disheartened. . . . The women characters inhabit an airless emotional hothouse from which no escape is seen; the initially strong sympathy Jane in particular arouses becomes exhausted before the end, so entirely contingent on one man after another is her existence."

Picoult next published *Harvesting the Heart*, about Paige, an ambivalent and frightened young mother who must come to terms with the fact that her own mother had abandoned her years before. Karen Ray wrote for the *New York Times* (January 16, 1994), "Although the caramel-smooth prose of Ms. Picoult's novel, with its alternating points of view, aims for equity, Nicholas [Paige's husband] is the less-realized character. But this imbalance is hardly a flaw. After all, neither life nor novels deal out such material fairly. This story belongs to Paige O'Toole Prescott—and to the lucky reader."

Picture Perfect, Picoult's next book, follows Cassie Barrett, an anthropologist who falls in love with Alex Rivers, a Hollywood star, while acting as a consultant on a movie set. A reviewer for *Publishers Weekly* (January 16, 1995, on-line) found little to like in the book, writing, "After a whirlwind romance, Cassie becomes the new Mrs. Rivers, toast of filmdom's beautiful people. But all is not bliss for the newlyweds: Alex's tortured past just won't let go, and Cassie must bear the brunt of his emotional scars. Perhaps attempting to salvage the predictable plot, Picoult administers to Cassie's bland character a dose of adrenalin-pumping amnesia. She also throws in a dollop of Native American culture and a noble savage who skirts the periphery of Cassie's tumultuous existence, always ready with sage advice, spiritual healing techniques and warm embraces. Some rather prettily told Indian legends are added to the mix, but the total effect is wide of the mark."

Reviewers were kinder to Picoult's next effort, *Mercy*, about an elderly husband who gives in to his cancer-stricken wife's pleas to help her end her life. Calling the novel "a sensitive exploration of the balance of love," a *Publishers Weekly* reviewer (June 24, 1996, on-line) wrote, "What could have been a competent, topical novel about a mercy killing becomes, in Picoult's hands, an inspired meditation on love." Polly Paddock concurred in a review for the *Boston Globe* (August 17, 1996), opining, "Picoult writes with a fine touch, a sharp eye for detail and a firm grasp of the delicacy and complexity of human relationships," and calling *Mercy* "a quietly powerful book that examines the boundaries of love and loyalty, courage and forgiveness."

The Pact concerns a suicide pact—between two teenagers whose families have been close friends for 18 years—gone wrong. In an article posted on her official Web site, Picoult explained that her inspiration for the novel was a student she had once taught: "I had a hundred kids . . . and one little girl was suicidal. We all knew—her parents, her guidance counselor, and her four subject teachers. It was decided that all of us would work hard to keep her focused, and present. My job, as the English teacher, was to get her to write in a journal and to meet with her daily after school to talk about what she'd written. I got pregnant that year, and left teaching to have my first son, Kyle. My husband and I moved out of state; and my first novel was published. I embarked on a new career . . . but I never forgot about that student. I never forgot what it felt like to be someone else's lifeline. . . . And I knew, when I started to write my fifth book, that my subject matter was going to involve teen suicide." Picoult went on to explain that the book marked a turning point in her career: "Not only was it the book that put me on the literary map as a writer—it also was the first one that made me fall in love with research. Since writing it, every novel I've tackled has started with hands-on research, experiences that have taken me from courtrooms to prisons, from Amish homes to Eskimo villages to haunted homes."

In *Keeping Faith* Picoult examines issues of organized religion, the modern media, and the medical profession. The book follows Mariah White, struggling through the aftermath of a painful divorce, and her daughter, fittingly named Faith, who copes by talking to an entity she calls her "guard." When Faith begins quoting from the Bible, which she has never read, and showing signs of stigmata, the pair get caught up in a maelstrom of attention from the media, religious groups, and social-service workers. In a critique for *Publishers Weekly* (February 22, 1999, on-line), widely echoed by others, a reviewer wrote, "Fans of Picoult's fluent and absorbing storytelling will welcome her new novel, which, like *Harvesting the Heart*, explores family dynamics and the intricacies of motherhood, and concludes, as did *The Pact*, with tense courtroom drama. . . . Picoult's pacing stabilizes the increasingly complicated plot, and the final chapters, in which Mariah fights for Faith's custody in court, are riveting. The mother-daughter relationship is all the more powerful for being buffeted by the exploitative and ethically questionable domains of medicine, media, law and religion; these characters' many triumphant transformations are Picoult's triumphs as well."

The protagonist of *Plain Truth* is an Amish teenager who hides her pregnancy and gives birth in secret. Kristina Lanier wrote for the *Christian Science Monitor* (June 22, 2000), "[Picoult] sets a big task for herself in *Plain Truth*, but she pulls it off—avoiding sentimentality and even maintaining the cultural tension and thriller-like guessing game into the book's final scenes. Picoult's strength, though, lies in sculpting solid characters and a thoughtful, well-researched, and well-paced yarn." In a review for the *Library Journal* (April 1, 2000), Penny Stevens found the book's surprise ending unconvincing but went on to praise the pace of the story, concluding, "[Picoult] offers an interesting look into Amish culture and beliefs."

Salem Falls took on the hot-button issue of inappropriate relationships between teachers and students. Wrongfully convicted of statutory rape, the book's main character, Jack St. Bride, loses his teaching job and is sent to prison; upon his release he moves to a small New Hampshire town to make a fresh start but finds that suspicion has followed him. The book was a indisputable commercial success, but a reviewer for *Publishers Weekly* (February 19, 2001, on-line) warned, "Picoult tastefully tackled touchy subject matter in *Plain Truth*, but she tips toward sensationalism here. That may gain her readers in the short run, but could undermine her reputation over time."

The reviewer's fears seemed unjustified: Picoult continued to produce a string of highly popular novels, including *Perfect Match*, which deals with the issue of pedophilia; *Second Glance*, which touches on eugenics and the paranormal; *My Sister's Keeper*, which examines the question of whether a healthy sibling should be forced to donate bone marrow to a sick one; *Vanishing Acts*, about child abduction; and *The Tenth Circle*, which contains themes of date rape and the wisdom of revenge.

Picoult's latest novel is *Nineteen Minutes*, which a reviewer for *Publishers Weekly* (January 1, 2007) called a "brilliantly told new thriller." The book looks at how bullying can contribute to high-school violence; the title is a reference to a school shooting—which takes 19 minutes and leaves 10 people dead—at the center of the plot. The *Publishers Weekly* reviewer concluded, "The author's insights into her characters' deep-seated emotions brings this ripped-from-the-headlines read chillingly alive."

Picoult and her family currently live in Hanover, New Hampshire, with a bevy of pets.

—S.Y.

Suggested Reading: *Chicago Tribune* T p3 Mar. 11, 1994; *Christian Science Monitor* p17 June 22, 2000; *Dallas Morning News* SR p9 June 25, 2000, AS p12 Apr. 29, 2001; *Entertainment Weekly* p60 Mar. 24, 1995, p60 June 11, 1999; *Kirkus Reviews* p20 Jan. 2003; *Library Journal* p124 Nov. 15, 1998; *Orlando Sentinel* (on-line) June 5, 2002; *People* (on-line) May 8, 2000; *Publishers Weekly* (on-line) Jan.16, 1995, June 24, 1996, Feb. 22, 1999, Feb. 19, 2001, Jan. 1, 2007; *Washington Post* C p4 May 26, 2000; *Washington Post Book World* p6 Apr. 8, 2001, p6 May 5, 2002; *Women's Review of Books* p29 July 1992

Selected Books: *Songs of the Humpback Whale: A Novel in Five Voices*, 1992; *Harvesting the Heart*, 1993; *Picture Perfect*, 1995, *Mercy*, 1996; *The Pact: A Love Story*, 1998; *Keeping Faith*, 1999; *Plain Truth*, 1999; *Salem Falls*, 2001; *Perfect Match*, 2002; *Second Glance*, 2003; *My Sister's Keeper*, 2003; *Vanishing Acts*, 2005; *The Tenth Circle*, 2006; *Nineteen Minutes*, 2007

Pierre, DBC

1961– Novelist

DBC Pierre, winner of the 2003 Booker Prize for his first novel, *Vernon God Little: A 21st-Century Comedy in the Presence of Death*, may be one of the most controversial winners in the history of the prestigious award. Pierre's novel has been lauded by British critics, who have compared it to such classics as Mark Twain's *The Adventures of Huckleberry Finn* and J. D. Salinger's *Catcher in the Rye*, but it has received a much chillier reception on the other side of the Atlantic. Though John Carey, chairman of the Booker committee, insisted that the novel—a dark comedy set in the fictional town of Martirio, Texas—was selected purely for its literary value, many American critics believed that Europeans, angry with the U.S. for its decision, earlier that year, to wage war in Iraq without the approval of the U.N., were drawn to a book that reaffirmed their negative stereotypes

Eamonn McCabe 2003/Courtesy of W. W. Norton

DBC Pierre

about Americans. Describing *Vernon God Little* as "a vigorous but unimaginative compendium of every cliche you've ever heard about America in general and Texas in particular," the *New York Times* (November 5, 2003) reviewer Michiko Kakutani wrote that the Booker committee's "assessment probably says more about British attitudes toward the United States than about literary taste."

Pierre grabbed more headlines that year by claiming to have led a dissolute life as a drug addict, con man, and roisterer. "I've always been an artist," he said after receiving his award, according to Emily Bearn, in an article for the London *Sunday Telegraph* (October 19, 2003). "When you hear things about my past, you have to realise I was struggling with the art beast. I knew I was living a life that others might one day vicariously live. It was either write or take a length of rope and hang myself."

The novelist calling himself DBC Pierre was born Peter Warren Finlay in Reynella, near Adelaide, Australia, in 1961. His parents were English, but his father's career, as a scientist specializing in crop genetics, kept the family moving around the globe. The Finlays lived briefly in the U.S. before settling in Mexico, where Pierre attended a private school alongside the sons and daughters of wealthy American expatriates. Although he was not a good student, his artistic abilities were recognized by his teachers and family, and while still in high school, he began working as a freelance graphic designer and cartoonist. When Pierre was still a teen, his father was stricken with a brain tumor and traveled to New York City, accompanied by Pierre's mother, to

receive medical care. The couple left Pierre responsible for the family home. He took that responsibility lightly, inviting his drug-using friends to spend time there and driving around recklessly. His father died when he was 19. Shortly afterward the family lost its fortune when the Mexican government nationalized the country's banks. Pierre has told interviewers that he felt that he had to make up for the losses somehow and began to gamble heavily. He also became addicted to cocaine, heroin, and other drugs.

Pierre returned to Australia as an adult, but did not feel at home there nor in any of the European countries in which he lived. During this peripatetic time in his life, he settled briefly in Spain, where he befriended the American artist Robert Lenton. When Lenton left to return to the U.S., in about 1987, Pierre told him that he would assist the artist in selling his apartment; Pierre sold the apartment as promised but pocketed the money to feed his drug addiction. (Shortly before receiving the Booker Prize, which includes a £50,000 cash award, Pierre contacted Lenton and offered to repay the money from the apartment plus interest.) Commenting on his wilder years, he told Emily Bearn: "Strange to say, there wasn't ever any real wickedness behind my behaviour. My mind was always informed by an unrealistic confidence that I'd pull a rabbit out of the hat the next morning. I had a confidence I'd be immediately successful and it led me to ignore the rights of these folks. I thought, 'OK, I'll keep this 10 grand back because I can double it.' Whenever something's gone sour, it's always been based on my belief that I'd pull off some kind of creative work."

In 1991, however, Pierre hit bottom. "I arrived at my thirtieth birthday a couple hundred grand in debt," he told Dave Weich, in an interview for the Powell's Books Web site. "Some of it I'd achieved deceitfully; [the rest] was just good people who'd had faith and either invested or loaned me at some point, and their faith had been completely dashed. I was a kid that everyone said would do things one day. I never knew what these would be or how that would happen. So I hit thirty with a bang and every type of substance, then it all stopped and I went into treatment for a couple years. Counseling and that. They brought me back down to the real world where you're clearly not going to make a couple hundred grand to pay everyone back, and if all you can do is fry chicken that's what you're going to have to do. I came down to ground level, then spent from thirty to thirty-seven reconstituting myself and discovering what, if anything, I could do." Earlier in his life Pierre had been given the nickname "Dirty Pierre" (a reference to an incorrigible cartoon character) by one of his friends; after his reform he changed it to DBC (Dirty But Clean) Pierre.

Pierre was inspired to write his first novel, *Vernon God Little*, in 1999, after watching a television news piece about a 13-year-old

American boy who had murdered some of his classmates in school. "The kid had just destroyed his whole life and other people's lives and I looked at him and it just seemed he couldn't possibly have been, in the true sense, responsible for that," Pierre wrote for a BBC News Internet forum (October 29, 2003). "It seemed such a motif of the times we were in—the frustrations. These are like the bubbles around the edges of the pot—the culture we live in now is being heated up from the bottom commercially and there's pressure to be this and do that, buy this etc. and I just took this as one of the more sinister bubbles rising from that pot." The author insists that he began working on the novel before the 1999 Columbine High School massacre, in which two alienated teenagers—Dylan Klebold and Eric Harris—went on a shooting rampage, killing several fellow students before taking their own lives. Nonetheless, *Vernon God Little* focuses on the fallout from a similar killing spree, carried out in a Texas high school by a bullied loser named Jesus Navarro. Vernon Little, who happens to be a friend of Jesus, is falsely accused of being an accessory to the crime. Made to play the "skate-goat," as he puts it, Vernon flees to Mexico.

In 2003 *Vernon God Little* won the Whitbread First Novel Award and was the upset winner of the Booker Prize for Fiction, the most lucrative literary award in Great Britain. Having retained the British nationality of his parents, Pierre was eligible for the Booker, which is awarded only to Britons or Commonwealth citizens. According to a press release posted on the Booker Prize Foundation Web site, John Carey described *Vernon God Little* as "a coruscating black comedy reflecting our alarm but also our fascination with modern America." Though Pierre has said that his book was more about the evils of the modern world in general than a critique of American culture in particular, American critics were harsher on the work than their British counterparts. Chris Lehmann, a reviewer for the *Washington Post Book World* (December 2, 2003), took the "cheap and undemanding social" satire personally, if not jingoistically. "There's nothing in particular to be made of this teeth-grindingly feeble stab at satire and virtual random-search engine of potty humor—except, of course, that it was the 2003 recipient of the prestigious Booker Prize, for the best novel produced in the far-flung former British Empire," Lehmann wrote. "The plot is so leaden, its jokes so drearily predictable and its main characters so contemptuously rendered that it's hard not to see the selection itself as a Vernon Little–style obscene gesture directed at an America presently enjoying precious little esteem in European opinion—and whose commander in chief, it scarcely needs reminding, is the former execution-happy governor of the blighted, bloated and bigoted Lone Star State that so heartlessly persecutes the young Vernon Little." Michiko Kakutani found that Pierre "evinces a certain raw energy and an instinctive ability to orchestrate suspense," but complained that "his characters are all crude caricatures" and "his efforts to satirize the sort of media feeding frenzies that almost routinely ensue after tragedies today are neither revealing nor acute" She concluded: "In trying to score a lot of obvious points off a lot of obvious targets, Mr. Pierre may have won the Booker Prize and ratified some ugly stereotypes of Americans, but he hasn't written a terribly convincing or compelling novel."

Commenting on how the British view American culture, Sarah Lyall wrote for the *New York Times* (November 16, 2003), "British complaints about the United States are like those of a lover in a dysfunctionally passionate relationship. Its anger, frustration and disgust are corollaries of its love." Citing *Vernon God Little* as an example, she notes that the book "may be a devastating dissection of the American media and celebrity culture, with extended riffs on gluttony, hypocrisy and the death penalty, among other things, but at the same time it has been celebrated by some as a vibrant example of the playfully creative possibilities of American English." John Carey told Lyall: "Reading his [Pierre's] book made me think of how the English language was in Shakespeare's day, enormously free and inventive and very idiomatic and full of poetry as well. America is where the language is going forward."

Reviews were mixed for Pierre's second novel, *Ludmila's Broken English*, in which he attempted to address the issue of globalization through parallel storylines that follow a pair of British conjoined twins shortly after they are separated and an impoverished woman from the Caucasus who gets drawn into a mail-order bride scam. While a reviewer for *Publisher's Weekly* (March 20, 2006) described the book as a "maddeningly entertaining encore," another critic, writing for *Kirkus Reviews* (April 1, 2006), complained that nothing seems to mean much in "this stick-figured, incongruously plotted, gratuitously indulgent novel." A reviewer for the *New Statesman* (March 13, 2006) took a more moderate stance, praising "the novel's great comic innovation—the salty vernacular spoken by its collection of grotesque degenerates in their Caucasus mountain hideaway," but also noting that "Pierre's prose splinters into a clamour of competing idioms."

Pierre lives in Leitrim, Ireland, with his girlfriend.

—S.Y.

Suggested Reading: (London) *Sunday Telegraph* p3 Oct. 19, 2003; (New York) *Newsday* B p2 Oct. 29, 2003; *New York Times* E p1 Nov. 5, 2003, IV p1 Nov. 16, 2003; Powell's Books Web site; (Queensland, Australia) *Courier Mail* p9 Oct. 17, 2003; *Village Voice* (on-line) Oct. 29–Nov. 4, 2003; *Washington Post Book World* p3 Dec. 2, 2003

Selected Books: *Vernon God Little: A 21st-Century Comedy in the Presence of Death*, 2003; *Ludmila's Broken English*, 2006

David Westing/Getty Images

Pinter, Harold

Oct. 10, 1930– Playwright; screenwriter; novelist; poet

In the late 1950s and early 1960s, Harold Pinter emerged as one of the most original playwrights in the Anglophone tradition. In the intervening years his stature has only grown, culminating, in 2005, with the Swedish Academy conferring on Pinter that year's Nobel Prize for Literature. Frequently compared to his artistic master and later friend, Samuel Beckett, Pinter has typically presented theatergoers with a wider and more frankly comic world than Beckett usually did. The characters in their plays do, however, share a clipped, sometimes opaque, way of speaking and a willingness to meet the absurdities of their situation with grim, if not necessarily disciplined, determination. Describing the accomplishments that earned him the Nobel Prize, the Swedish Academy, according to its Web site, noted that Pinter—an accomplished screenwriter, actor, and director as well playwright—"restored theatre to its basic elements: an enclosed space and unpredictable dialogue, where people are at the mercy of each other and pretence crumbles. With a minimum of plot, drama emerges from the power struggle and hide-and-seek of interlocution."

Harold Pinter was born in Hackney, an impoverished neighborhood in London, England, on October 10, 1930. He was the only child of Hyman (Jack) Pinter, a tailor, and Frances Moskowitz, whose father conducted business under the last name Mann. According to Michael Billington's book *The Life and Work of Harold Pinter* (1997), there is no evidence that the Pinter family was from Portugal or Spain or that the name had once been da Pinta, though such claims frequently appear in treatments of Pinter's life antedating Billington's biography. Pinter's parents were Jewish, as were many people in Hackney. At the same time their neighborhood was also home to a substantial group of organized and virulent anti-Semites, both before and after World War II, giving the young Pinter a day-to-day sense of violence waiting around each corner. When the war began, in 1939, Pinter was evacuated to the country, as were many other children in urban areas in Britain. Pinter ended up in a castle in Cornwall, where he stayed for only a year before returning to London. He finished his secondary education at the Hackney Downs School, an all-boys institution, where he excelled at both acting and sports, matching or breaking school records in track and earning awards for his skills at soccer and cricket, a sport that remains one of his chief enthusiasms. His leading performances in such plays as *Macbeth* and *Romeo and Juliet* were greeted with acclaim from his peers and an enthusiastic drama teacher. After graduating, in 1948, he was given a grant to attend the Royal Academy of Dramatic Art (also in London), but feeling out of place he left after only a matter of months. He turned 18 that same year, making him eligible for the military's draft; Pinter, however, refused to go. "I was simply not, absolutely not, going to join the army," Pinter told Anne-Marie Cusac for the *Progressive* (March 2001). "Because I had seen the Cold War beginning before the hot war was over." After two trials Pinter managed to escape with only fines, rather than a prison sentence. (Great Britain's national service requirement was abolished in 1960.)

Over the next decade he lived the peripatetic life of an actor in the waning age of traveling repertory companies. He took roles in classical and contemporary plays, sometimes under a stage name, David Baron, and performed on the radio. Between engagements he worked as a doorman, salesman, waiter, and dishwasher and wrote poems and short stories, some of which appeared in English literary magazines during that time. He also drafted an autobiographical novel, *The Dwarfs*, which he revised decades later and published in 1990, partially in celebration of his 60th birthday. In 1951 he began a two-year tour in the company of the venerable Shakespearian actor Anew McMaster (whom he later celebrated in the pamphlet-length book *Mac: A Memoir* [1968]). In 1953, while working with another repertory company, he met the actress Vivien Merchant, and the two married in September 1956; their son Daniel was born two years later. During that time, Pinter also encountered the work of the famed Irish playwright and novelist Samuel Beckett. The affinity between the two men's work has been a refrain in commentary on Pinter from early on, yet many critics point out that while Pinter's plays may be absurd in ways that align him with Beckett, the fundamental situations in Pinter's early plays are usually realistic—grounded in a particular place, with characters speaking in carefully observed regional accents. The two men had enough in common, however, to become friends for many years.

Pinter decided to try his hand at playwriting after coming across a strange scene at a party in 1957, when he happened to spy two people in a small room: a big man wearing a cap, seated, and a small man with bare feet, standing. The big man was silent, but the little man was chattering on brightly, feeding the other as if he were a child. Pinter described the scene to a friend who taught drama at the University of Bristol, in southwest England, and was asked to work it up into a play for student production. The result, which took only days to write and debuted in Bristol that same year, was a short play called *The Room*. Like most of Pinter's early work, *The Room* is set in a single, confined space. The characters are Rose, a talkative woman; her husband, Bert, whom she mothers; and a succession of visitors who threaten their sanctuary in various ways. The most mysterious of the visitors is a blind black man who insists that he has claims on Rose. She, in turn, insists that she does not know him. Though arguably journeyman work, the play contains many of the elements that critics identify with Pinter's early "comedies of menace"—his careful reproduction of the irrelevancies and evasions of ordinary speech and the anxiety-inducing sense that nothing is certain, that unfamiliar rules are operating, often in the service of disaster. At the end of the play, for example, Bert turns on the blind man and beats him cruelly, but instead of Bert suffering punishment for what he has done, it is Rose who, just before the curtain falls, goes blind. Decades after he wrote *The Room*, Pinter recalled in an interview with Stephen Schiff for *Vanity Fair* (September 1990) that watching its first performance was pivotal to his career. The experience was "so extraordinary," he told Schiff. "I got really wildly drunk on that occasion—but what I'm really talking about is the dizziness of the event to a young man. I never quite recovered from that. I realized I was a marked man."

Not long after *The Room*, Pinter wrote his next play, *The Dumb Waiter* (1957; sometimes spelled *The Dumbwaiter*). Here two professional killers await their orders in a squalid basement room in an otherwise empty house. They know they will be told to kill someone, but the victim's identity has yet to be revealed. They talk, read the newspaper, argue about soccer and grammar, and eat cookies. Suddenly a dumbwaiter in the wall clatters down, bearing a demand for "Two braised steak and chips. Two sago puddings. Two teas without sugar." This order, so unlike the one they had expected, is followed by others. Anxious, afraid of discovery, and bewildered by the calls for increasingly unfamiliar food, the two men send up their pathetic and inadequate provisions until

nothing is left. The play ends when another order comes down and one of the killers draws his gun on the other.

Pinter's first full-length play, *The Birthday Party*, was also written in 1957 and premiered at the Cambridge Arts Theatre in 1958. Set in a shabby seaside boarding house modeled on the type Pinter had stayed in as an actor, the play focuses on Stanley, an indolent, self-indulgent man who claims without conviction that he was once a concert pianist of promise and that his career had been ruined by jealous enemies. All he has done, by the time the play begins, is exploit the generosity of his motherly landlady, Meg. Then two mysterious strangers arrive and begin to cross-examine Stanley in a bizarre way. Between them they accuse him of every kind of evil—of betraying the "organization" and practicing religious heresy, of embezzlement and murder, of unspecified crimes against Ireland, cricket, big business, and the Catholic martyr Oliver Plunkett. This is followed by a kind of ritual humiliation of Stanley at what is supposed to be Stanley's birthday party. After insisting that it is not actually his birthday anyway, Stanley collapses into a benumbed silence. The next morning—clean and bowler-hatted—he is led away to a waiting car and an unknown fate.

The Birthday Party was the first of Pinter's plays to be performed professionally. A month after its premiere, however, when it moved to the Lyric Theatre in London, it was derided by critics on its opening night and closed after only a week. Though *The Birthday Party* later became a film (which was released in 1967), with a screenplay by Pinter himself, and has now come to be thought of as one Pinter's indisputable masterpieces, the failure of the play sent the playwright, then out of work and with a wife and small baby to support, into despair. Help came from two sources: the American producer Roger L. Stevens, who bought the options on Pinter's next three plays, and Donald McWhinnie of the BBC's drama department, who commissioned a radio play. Called *A Slight Ache* and first broadcast in 1959, the play has since been staged repeatedly. The main characters are a middle-aged couple, Edward and Flora, who become obsessed with an old match seller outside their house and invite him in. Once indoors, he cannot be persuaded to say or do anything whatsoever. The weak and talkative Edward, increasingly worried and suspicious, batters himself into a breakdown against the other man's monumental silence. Flora, however, finds herself taken with a man who so obviously needs her attention. In the end, under Flora's guidance, tramp and husband exchange roles.

Though Pinter had already won some recognition for his work by 1959, it was during that year that he achieved his first popular successes with the sketches he wrote for the theater revues *One to Another* (in which *The Black and White* and *Trouble in the Works* first appeared) and *Pieces of*

Eight (to which Pinter contributed *Special Offer, Getting Acquainted, Last to Go,* and *Request Stop*). But his real arrival as a major figure in the British theater came in 1960, when his second full-length play, *The Caretaker*, opened in London at the Arts Theatre Club, subsequently moving to the Duchess Theatre in the West End, where it ran for more than 400 performances. Crossing the Atlantic the play opened at the Shubert Theatre in New Haven, Connecticut, in September 1961, and moved to the Lyceum in New York City a month later. Acclaimed by both British and American critics, it firmly established Pinter's reputation in the theater world.

The setting of *The Caretaker* is a junk-filled attic in a derelict London house. Two strange brothers live in the attic and interact with a degraded old vagrant who tries to bluster and wheedle a place in this unattractive company. As in Pinter's earlier plays, there is a sense of menace in *The Caretaker*, but it does not come from outside the play's one room, as it does in the previous works. It resides in the isolation of the three characters and their inability to communicate. Each is tragically and comically lost in his own fantasies: the old derelict Davies, with his bigotry and transparent lies; the older brother, Aston, numbed by electric shock treatment; and the younger brother, Mick, who alternately torments and flatters Davies, offers him a job as caretaker of the house, encourages him to insult Aston, and finally uses the insult as an excuse to throw him out (presumably his intention all along). *The Caretaker* won the London *Evening Standard*'s award for best play in 1960; it was equally successful the following year in New York City and has since been staged all over the world; a film version, directed from a screenplay written by Pinter himself, appeared in 1963. It remains one of most analyzed of all of Pinter's plays, according to a scholarly study conducted by Kimball King and Marti Greene, which appears in the collection *Pinter at 70: A Casebook* (2001).

The most conventional and approachable of Pinter's plays, *A Night Out*, was written the same year as *The Caretaker* and produced on radio and television in 1960 before reaching the stage in 1961. It is a more or less comic account of a young man's attempt to throw off the domination of his possessive mother by visiting a prostitute. Acting out his need for rebellion, the young man bullies the woman, accusing her of his mother's faults, before returning meekly to the status quo. *The Dwarfs*, another of Pinter's radio plays broadcast in 1960, was adapted from his then-unpublished novel; it too was subsequently adapted for the stage, albeit in an expanded form. *The Dwarfs* marks the first time Pinter used interior monologue in a play, offering the audience unusually direct insights into the thought processes of the character Len, whose relationships with two friends and ideas about himself provide the theme of this difficult play. Some of the ideas of *The Dwarfs* are also pursued in two subsequent television plays:

The Collection (1961) and *The Lover* (1962). The first is a complicated social comedy turning on the question of whether Bill, a clothes designer, slept with Stella, a married colleague, at a fashion show in Leeds; each concedes and then denies that this has happened. Whether the accusation is true or false remains unclear, as do the natures of the characters. At first the wife at the center of *The Lover* appears to have taken a paramour, but it eventually emerges that the lover is her husband, who visits her in the afternoons, taking on a different name and persona in order to fulfill their mutual need for fantasy and excitement.

By 1963 Pinter's plays had brought him financial success and widespread professional acclaim. A burgeoning industry of scholarly commentators developed as well, with the critic John Russell Taylor offering detailed analyses of Pinter's work in his book *The Angry Theatre: New British Drama* (1962), and Martin Esslin providing a similar treatment in *The Theatre of the Absurd* (1961). Taylor gave particularly glowing praise, describing Pinter's plays as "the true poetic drama of our time, for [Pinter] alone has fully understood that poetry in the theatre is not achieved merely by couching ordinary sentiments in an elaborately artificial poetic diction." Taylor continued: "Instead he has looked at life so closely that, seeing it through his eyes, we discover the strange sublunary poetry which lies in the most ordinary object at the other end of a microscope." Though he would later encourage political interpretations of his early work, Pinter was initially resistant to critics' detecting symbolic meanings behind the stories he scripted. As he told Joseph Morgenstern for the *New York Herald Tribune* (September 10, 1961), "I feel very strongly about the particular, not about symbolism." Pinter was similarly resistant to being labeled an absurdist. "Sometimes I feel absurd," he told an interviewer for New York *Newsday* (November 26, 1962), "sometimes I don't."

During this same time, Pinter was also active as a director and screenwriter. A long association with the Royal Shakespeare Company began in 1962, when Pinter and Peter Hall co-directed an adaptation of his earlier teleplay *The Collection* at London's Aldwych Theatre. Though Pinter would go on to direct or co-direct dozens of more plays, films, and television adaptations of plays over the course of the next 40 years—more often taking up other people's plays, particularly his friend Simon Gray's, than his own—his early directorial efforts were aimed at staging his own works. He directed *The Lover* and *The Dwarfs* at the Arts Theatre Club in 1963 and *The Birthday Party* in 1964. Pinter also wrote screenplays for four films based on the work of other writers: *The Pumpkin Eater* (1963; adapted from the novel by Penelope Mortimer), *The Quiller Memorandum* (1965; adapted from the novel by Adam Hall), and two films directed by Joseph Losey, *The Servant* (1963; adapted from the novella by Robin Maugham) and *Accident* (1966;

adapted from a novel by Nicholas Mosley). *The Servant* (in which Pinter played a small role) was particularly successful with critics, winning awards from the New York Film Critics Circle for best screenplay and the British Screenwriters Guild.

Pinter wrote his third full-length stage play, *The Homecoming*, in 1964. It opened in a Royal Shakespeare Company production at the New Theatre in the Welsh city of Cardiff, before appearing at the Aldwych Theatre in London, beginning on June 3, 1965. Teddy, the long-absent son of an East End Jewish family, returns to London from America, where he has made good as a scholar and critic. Dominated all his life by his father and brothers, Teddy can now be considered a success—not least because he has married a beautiful woman—and he expects his family to offer the respect and admiration he thinks he deserves. But once in London, Teddy is treated by his family as ever, while his enigmatic wife, Ruth, makes such a strong impression that Teddy's family suggests that she abandon her husband and children and stay with them as their communal mistress. She accepts their proposition, and Teddy returns to America alone. The play enjoyed a great success in London and later in New York City, where the same production opened at the Music Box Theater in 1967 and where it received the New York Drama Critics Circle Award. For many critics *The Homecoming* represents Pinter's highest achievement as a dramatist.

In 1965 the television play version of *Tea Party* was broadcast first in England by the BBC and, the following week, rebroadcast across Europe. It is a study in paranoia based on a short story Pinter had written in 1964 about a rich man who marries a society woman but falls in love with his secretary as well. Another television play from this time, *The Basement*, derives from a very early sketch called "Kullus," dating back to 1949 and later published in Pinter's *Poems and Prose, 1949–1977* (1978). It is an unusually abstract study, with some of the quality of a writer's exercise, centering on the struggle between two men for the ownership of a girl and a room. The two works later appeared on the stage in a September 1970 double bill at the Duchess Theatre in London. A similar double bill ran at the Aldwych Theatre the year before, when two short plays by Pinter, *Silence* (written in 1968) and *Landscape* (written in 1967), appeared on the stage for the first time. The first of a series of plays deeply concerned with memory, *Landscape* is about an aging couple, a housekeeper and her husband, also a servant, who sit at a table in the house in which they work and exchange what seem to be reminiscences but are actually distinct monologues. In *Silence*, two men and a woman muse, mostly privately but sometimes in conversation, about their relationship with each other and the almost-forgotten past.

Pinter's next full-length play, *Old Times*, written in 1970, also explores the uncertainty of memory. In the play a married couple, Deeley and Kate, live in the country in a converted farmhouse. They await the arrival of Kate's friend Anna, whom Kate has not seen since they shared a flat in London as young secretaries. Anna arrives (or rather her presence on stage is revealed), and at that point the high-comedy banter of the opening scene gives way to a subtle but increasingly ferocious contest of memory between Deeley and Anna—about the words from popular songs of the 1940s, about how Deeley picked up Kate in a movie theater showing the film *Odd Man Out* (1947), about the man (was it Deeley?) Anna remembers crying on Kate's bed. The prize they fight for is Kate. Is she the Kate of Anna's youth or the Kate essential to Deeley's image of himself? It gradually becomes clear that she is neither. Appearing first in a Royal Shakespeare Company production at the Aldwych Theatre in June 1971, *Old Times* was greeted with rapturous critical praise, and it remains among Pinter's most frequently revived and discussed plays.

By the early 1970s, Pinter had cemented his reputation as a dramatist with a combination of artistic triumphs and an increasingly steady array of honors. At the same time his actual output as a playwright was slowing. An extremely fertile stretch of playwriting between about 1957 and 1967 gave way to a period more focused on screenwriting and directing. In 1970 he directed James Joyce's sole play, *Exiles* (1915), and followed that in 1971 by directing the first of many plays by his friend Simon Gray, *Butley*, which he would direct as a film in 1973. Also in 1970 he adapted the Irish writer Aidan Higgins's first novel, *Langrishe, Go Down* (1966), for film; the screenplay was eventually reworked and filmed as a television movie that premiered in 1978, with Pinter playing one of the roles. Pinter gave over virtually the whole of 1972 to another adaptation: distilling for the screen the early-20th-century French masterpiece *A la recherche du temps perdu*, a more than 3,000-page novel, written by Marcel Proust between roughly 1909 and his death in 1922. (The most famous translation of its title into English is *Remembrance of Things Past*, but a more literal and now somewhat more common translation is *In Search of Lost Time*.) Proust's novel is enormously complex and meditative and famously short on what serves in most films as action. The screenplay had originally been commissioned by Losey, with whom Pinter had collaborated on a 1970 adaptation of L. P. Hartley's novel *The Go-Between* (1953). Though eventually published on its own in 1977 and performed on radio in 1995 as *The Proust Screenplay* and on the stage in 2000 as *Remembrance of Things Past*, Pinter's screenplay has never been filmed, despite being almost universally praised, even by scholars of Proust; it is thus arguably the most famous unmade film of all time.

After finishing work on the Proust script, Pinter returned first to short forms, writing the roughly 20-minute-long play *Monologue* in 1972, which was broadcast by the BBC, in April 1973. Like other plays by Pinter, *Monologue* takes place in a single room and details the power struggles between two men for the affection of a woman. In this case the woman (like the blind man in *The Room*) is black, and her presence and the presence of the main character's rival are both evoked only indirectly, in the pause-punctuated monologue that gives the play its name. In 1974 Pinter took a turn at adapting another posthumously published literary work, F. Scott Fitzgerald's *The Last Tycoon* (1941), which was released in 1976 as a slow-moving, poorly received film by the director Elia Kazan. Also in 1974 he directed John Hopkins's play *Next of Kin* for London's National Theatre, where he had been made an associate director the year before by his longtime collaborator Peter Hall. In April 1975 the National Theatre mounted, in the Old Vic Theatre, Pinter's first full-length play since *Old Times*, just as Pinter's home life was collapsing around him. Written in 1974 and called *No Man's Land*, the play is about a rich English writer named Hirst, who, after meeting the comparatively obscure and certainly poorer poet Spooner at a pub, invites Spooner back to his fancy home, where he regales him with drinks. The play received mixed reviews when it opened but was an unquestionable success with the public, in part because of the performance of the legendary actor John Gielgud as Spooner. (Gielgud reprised his role the next year for the play's first run in New York City.)

By the time *No Man's Land* opened there, Pinter's life had become the subject of almost daily headlines in the British press; in July 1975 his first wife, Vivien, had filed divorce papers and gone public with the name of Pinter's mistress, Lady Antonia Fraser, a biographer and politically committed public figure. The scandal not only forced Pinter and Fraser into seclusion while divorce proceedings ground on for years, it also prompted Pinter's son to change his last name to Brand. Pinter's marital problems had, for a time, disastrous artistic consequences as well, with Pinter unable to work on a new play for over two years after Vivien took her case public. Instead, Pinter threw himself into directing and performing, bringing versions of *Blithe Spirit* by Noel Coward, *The Innocents* by William Archibald, and *Otherwise Engaged* by Simon Gray to the stage, some in London but many in New York City. Pinter's long-contained political convictions began to emerge around this same time, first in 1973, with his public censure of the U.S. for its role in a coup that overthrew the democratically elected leftist leader Salvador Allende in Chile and installed the dictator Augusto Pinochet.

The play that brought Pinter back to the stage was *Betrayal*. Written in roughly three months and opening in London in a National Theatre performance in November 1978, it features another of Pinter's triangles among two men (Jerry and Robert) and a woman (Emma). Recounting in detail (but also reimagining) an affair Pinter had during his first marriage but before he became involved with Fraser, the play was initially considered an examination of his breakup with his first wife and received forcefully negative reviews in London. New York reviewers were more receptive when the play opened there in 1980, and it won Pinter a second New York Drama Critics Circle Award. Pinter wrote a screenplay for *Betrayal* in 1981, and the film was released, to sometimes ecstatic reviews, in 1983.

The same year that *Betrayal* debuted in London, Pinter directed Simon Gray's play *The Rear Column*, and the following year he staged Gray's *Close of Play*. In 1980 he revived a long-buried, expressly political play he had written in 1958 called *The Hothouse* and gave it its first performance, in April 1980. Set in a governmental research institution, the play features a one-time colonel named Roote, who leads the crazed psychological experiments that are at the thematic heart of the play. In 1981 he staged another work by Gray, *Quartermaine's Terms*, as well as the play *Incident at Tulsa Hill* by Robert East. That same year the movie version of John Fowles's 1969 novel *The French Lieutenant's Woman* was released to widespread acclaim, particularly for Pinter's screenplay, which showed the same ingeniousness in its approach to Fowles's difficult, self-referential text that had been in evidence in the Proust screenplay. Pinter went on to earn an Academy Award nomination for best adapted screenplay. Also in 1981 the first of three short plays that would for a time be collected under the title *Other Places* was broadcast on BBC radio. Called *Family Voices*, the play was written in 1980 and includes three speakers (a young man, his mother, and his ghostly father), who come together to tell the story of the time the young man decided between his natural family and the strange approximation of a family he had found at a boarding house far away. When *Family Voices* reached the stage in 1982, it was joined to two other shorts, *A Kind of Alaska* and *Victoria Station*, both written that year. *Victoria Station* is an especially short sketch about a dispatcher for a taxi company who fluctuates from boredom to outrage to despair. Unique among Pinter's stage writing, *A Kind of Alaska* adapts the work of another writer, the neurologist Oliver Sacks, whose popular book *Awakenings* (1973) recounts how a pharmaceutical had been used to "reawaken" patients who had been suffering under the sleep-like symptoms of the disease encephalitic lethargica. Pinter had read *Awakenings* around the time of its release, and nearly a decade later he woke up suddenly inspired to write a story about an English high-society woman from earlier in the century who returns to normal consciousness thanks to a drug and, after carrying on anachronistically, slowly descends once again into a kind of coma. Of all the parts of *Other Places*, *A Kind of Alaska* arguably earned the most enthusiastic response at the time—not least from Sacks himself—and it remains the most often revived.

Though for Pinter the late 1970s and early 1980s were a time of sustained artistic recognition and increased political activity—particularly on behalf of writers suffering at the hands of authoritarian states—his personal life during this time was more troubled. His divorce from Vivien was finally granted in 1980, not long before he and Fraser married, but by then Vivien, unable to contain her despair over the breakup, had already fallen into an alcoholic spiral that killed her in 1982. She was only 53 and still one of the most famous and highly regarded actresses in England, especially for her many performances in her husband's plays.

During much of the 1980s, Pinter's output as a playwright was slight in comparison to his work for film. His plays showed a directly political cast that his screenplays generally did not; however, his film adaptations of Margaret Atwood's allegorical novel *The Handmaid's Tale* (1985), Ian McEwan's *Comfort of Strangers* (1981), and Franz Kafka's *The Trial* (1925) belie any neat distinction between the two types of work. In 1983 Pinter helped out the antinuclear revue *The Big One* by submitting a sketch called *Precisely*, which presents an after-work conversation, implicitly about nuclear war, that two men have over drinks. Longer but still contained in only a few brief scenes, *One for the Road* takes place in an unspecified country in which a government official is responsible for the brutal treatment of three members of a single family. First staged in 1984 on a double bill with *Victoria Station*, *One for the Road* took the place of *Family Voices* when *Other Places* was presented in Brighton and London in 1985. That year Pinter also traveled to Turkey with the American playwright Arthur Miller as part of a five-day-long visit meant to draw attention to the country's record of suppressing writers critical of the country's government. Soon after he returned, Pinter began sketching a new play, *Mountain Language*, but set the work aside for three years. His ever-growing political rage at his own country drove him to finish it in 1988, the same year it appeared on television and on the stage at the National Theatre. Though somewhat more grounded in place than *One for the Road*, the play covers similarly bleak territory during its approximately 20 minutes. In four quick scenes set in a camp, the play shows the lives of a group of prisoners who are said to be "mountain people" and whose natural language, different from the language of the guards, is banned. By turns violent and almost eerily quiet, full of the sort of pauses that have made Pinter's plays famous, the work has

been restaged many times since its initial performance, which got a mixed reception. The most famous revival took place in London, in 1996; a group of Kurds (the minority ethnicity living in Iraq, Iran, and parts of Turkey that first inspired Pinter's play) put on a performance that went awry when a passerby spotted them in their military costumes and called the police. Arrested, the Kurdish actors, like the prisoners in Pinter's play, were forbidden to speak their native language.

Pinter's plays during the 1990s were for the most part just as densely constructed and deeply committed to political expression, but the better part of his time was given over to political protests, writing poetry, directing, and performing more actively than he had for many years. The first play of the decade takes its title from a speech by American president George H. W. Bush, who described what he called a "new world order" that had come into place after the fall of the Soviet Union and its allied powers in Eastern Europe. Pinter's *New World Order* lasts only 10 minutes and is an allegory about power and a statement against torture: two men discuss the fate of a third, who is blindfolded and bound.

After years of suggesting to interviewers that he would perhaps never write another full-length play ("Something's happened, I think, to my creative juices," he told Stephen Schiff in 1990), he surprised the London theater world in 1993 with his first full-length play since *Betrayal*. Called *Moonlight*, the play opened at the relatively small Almeida Theater in September 1993. The story examines the aging and difficult Andy and his relationship with children, particularly his two estranged sons and his more forgiving daughter. The play's direct, heartfelt themes struck a deep chord with audiences and critics, who offered it a warmer welcome than any Pinter had received since *The Caretaker*.

Pinter's next play, *Ashes to Ashes*, was completed three years later. While preparing a revival at the Bristol Old Vic, in March 1996, of Reginald Rose's famous drama *Twelve Angry Men*, Pinter suddenly was taken with the desire to write. After 10 days he had completed *Ashes to Ashes*, which debuted at the Royal Court Theatre in September of that year. A compact chamber drama, the play never specifies the nature of the relationship between its two characters, a woman named Rebecca and a man named Devlin, both of them in early middle age. They discuss the woman's experiences, near violent but erotic, with an old lover. The play's ambiguities led some critics in London to complain that all of its elusiveness made for an unsatisfying experience. As Pinter approached his 70th birthday, he wrote his most recent original play, *Celebration*, which premiered on a double bill with *The Room* at the Almeida Theatre in March 2000. Considered by many critics to be funnier and more accessible than *Ashes to Ashes*, *Celebration* takes place in an expensive restaurant where three sets of couples—

two mafia men and their wives at one table and one more sophisticated couple at another—discuss their marriages and, in the case of the isolated couple, their infidelities as well.

Though *Pinter's People*, a collection of 14 sketches assembled by other hands from the past five decades of Pinter's work, enjoyed a successful run at London's Theatre Royal Haymarket in early 2007, Pinter has yet to write another play since *Celebration*. In March 2005 he openly declared his intention never to take another turn at drama.

A major retrospective of Pinter's work was launched at New York City's Lincoln Center for the Performing Arts in 2001, with nine of his plays performed in a single month, alongside a retrospective of 10 of the films he scripted over the years. A similar but smaller festival of Pinter's work took place in Dublin to coincide with his 75th birthday. Only a few days later, he received a call from the chairman of the Nobel Prize committee. According to a transcript of a conversation with Michael Billington that appeared in the London *Guardian* (October 14, 2005, on-line), Pinter's first response to hearing that he had won was an arguably Pinteresque pause. "I was very moved by this even though I hadn't really taken it in," he told Billington. "Why they've given me this prize I don't know."

In his Nobel lecture, reproduced on the Swedish Academy's Web site, Pinter distinguished between the type of truth he seeks in art, which can be contradictory even when it is political in intent, and the truth he demands as a citizen. Pinter argued that "the majority of politicians, on the evidence available to us, are interested not in truth but in power and in the maintenance of that power. To maintain that power it is essential that people remain in ignorance, that they live in ignorance of the truth, even the truth of their own lives. What surrounds us therefore is a vast tapestry of lies, upon which we feed." Pinter excoriated the U.S. government for what he considered its willful abuses of power and indifference to the truth. Pinter concluded: "I believe that despite the enormous odds which exist, unflinching, unswerving, fierce intellectual determination, as citizens, to define the real truth of our lives and our societies is a crucial obligation which devolves upon us all. It is in fact mandatory. If such a determination is not embodied in our political vision we have no hope of restoring what is so nearly lost to us—the dignity of man."

Among Pinter's other awards are the Alfred Toepfer Stiftung Shakespeare Prize for contributions to European culture (1970); the Austrian State Prize for European literature (1973); the Laurence Olivier Award for best new play for *Betrayal* (1979); the Pirandello Prize (1980); the David di Donatello Prize (1982); the Elmer Holmes Bobst Award for arts and letters (1984); the David Cohen Prize for Literature (1995); the Hermann Kesten Medal from the German branch of the international human rights and literature organization PEN for his commitment on behalf of persecuted and imprisoned writers (2001); PEN's S. T. Dupont Golden Pen Award for a lifetime of distinguished service to literature (2001); and the Premio Europa per il Teatro (2006). He has received more than a dozen honorary degrees, including ones from universities in England, Scotland, Ireland, Italy, Greece, Bulgaria, and the U.S.

Diagnosed with cancer in 2002, Pinter remains in frail health. Nonetheless, in October 2006, he gave 10 performances of Beckett's *Krapp's Last Tape* (1958) at the Royal Court Jerwood Theatre Upstairs in London, England, where he lives with his wife.

—D.R.

Suggested Reading: HaroldPinter.org; *Vanity Fair* p219+ Sep. 1990; Billington, M. *The Life and Work of Harold Pinter*, 1996; Gordon, L. (ed.) *Pinter at 70: A Casebook*, 2001

Selected Plays: *The Room*, 1957; *The Birthday Party*, 1957; *The Dumb Waiter*, 1957; *A Slight Ache*, 1958; *The Hothouse*, 1958; *The Caretaker*, 1959; *A Night Out*, 1959; *Night School*, 1960; *The Dwarfs*, 1960; *The Collection*, 1961; *The Lover*, 1962; *Tea Party*, 1964; *The Homecoming*, 1964; *The Basement*, 1966; *Landscape*, 1967; *Silence*, 1968; *Old Times*, 1970; *Monologue*, 1972; *No Man's Land*, 1974; *Betrayal*, 1978; *Family Voices*, 1980; *Victoria Station*, 1982; *A Kind of Alaska*, 1982; *One for the Road*, 1984; *Mountain Language*, 1988; *The New World Order*, 1991; *Party Time*, 1991; *Moonlight*, 1993; *Ashes to Ashes*, 1996; *Celebration*, 1999

Selected Films: as screenwriter—*The Caretaker*, 1963; *The Servant*, 1963; *The Pumpkin Eater*, 1964; *The Quiller Memorandum*, 1966; *Accident*, 1967; *The Birthday Party*, 1968; *The Go-Between*, 1970; *The Homecoming*, 1973; *The Last Tycoon*, 1976; *The French Lieutenant's Woman*, 1981; *Betrayal*, 1983; *Turtle Diary*, 1985; *Reunion*, 1989; *The Handmaid's Tale*, 1990; *The Comfort of Strangers*, 1990; *The Trial*, 1993; as director—*Butley*, 1974; as actor—*Mansfield Park*, 1999; *Catastrophe*, 2000; *The Tailor of Panama*, 2001

Selected Television Programs: as screenwriter—*Langrishe Go Down*, 1978; as director—*The Rear Column*, 1980; *The Hothouse*, 1982; *Mountain Language*, 1988; *Party Time*, 1992; *Landscape*, 1995; *Ashes to Ashes*, 1998

Selected Books: *The Proust Screenplay* (with Joseph Losey and Barbara Bray), 1977; *Poems and Prose, 1949–1977*, 1978; *The Dwarfs*, 1990; *Harold Pinter: Plays 1*, 1996; *Harold Pinter: Plays 2*, 1996; *Harold Pinter: Plays 3*, 1997; *Harold Pinter: Plays 4*, 1998; *Various Voices: Poetry, Prose, Politics: 1948–1998*, 1998; *The Disappeared and Other Poems*, 2002; *Press Conference*, 2002; *War*, 2003

Porter, Roy

Dec. 31, 1946–Mar. 3, 2002 Historian

When Roy Porter died unexpectedly at the age of 55, he was widely mourned in academia and among popular audiences, who appreciated his erudite yet witty and accessible books. "He is the model of a popular historian—appearing on talk shows, writing book reviews, being consulted by governments—but is still admired by academics for the rigor of his research and the sweep of his knowledge," Sarah Lyall wrote for the *New York Times* (April 24, 1999). Many concurred with Andrew Miller, writing for the *New York Times Book Review* (March 21, 2004), that Porter's was "a career that ended far too soon." Such lamentations seemed a touch ironic, however, given that Porter was one of the most prolific writers of his—or any—generation. By the time he retired, in 2001, he had published, depending on various estimates, anywhere from 80 to 100 books. "Because of his intellectual curiosity, Porter's work ranged widely and included a notable social history of London," Jeremy Black wrote for the *Times Higher Education Supplement* (October 24, 2003). "Yet most of it is best comprehended through the interrelated themes of the histories of medicine and science, the 18th century and the English Enlightenment. Scarcely a narrow span—and in Porter's fertile hands these themes were probed far, and profitably, leading to a careful typology of the nature of Enlightenment ideas in Britain with an emphasis on its practicality."

The son of a jeweler, Roy S. Porter was born on December 31, 1946 and raised in London in "a stable if shabby working-class community completely undiscovered by sociologists," as he once famously described it. In 1959 the family moved to the more genteel suburb of Norwood. Porter showed early promise in his studies, and after attending Wilson's School, in the Camberwell district of London, he was accepted into Christ's College at the University of Cambridge. There he was a student of John Plumb, a famous scholar, who "had a vision of history as being accessible to everybody," Porter told Lyall; that approach was influential on the young scholar. He graduated with high honors in history, in 1958, and received a Ph.D. in the history of science, in 1974.

In 1970 Porter became a research fellow at Christ's College. Two years later he was named the director of history studies at Churchill College at the University of Cambridge and later promoted to dean. In 1979 he became a senior lecturer at the Wellcome Trust Centre for the History of Medicine at University College London (UCL). He was happy to return to London, having disliked the hierarchical displays and intellectual posturing at Oxford. He was promoted to the position of full professor at UCL in 1993 and retired in September 2001. While pursuing his scholarly career, Porter also served as a public intellectual, appearing frequently on such popular British radio and television programs as *Night Waves*, *Making Waves*, *That's History*, and *Kaleidoscope*.

Porter's first book, *The Making of Geology: Earth Science in Britain, 1660–1815* (1977), was based on his doctoral thesis, which traced the emergence of one of the most controversial scientific disciplines. "As the title indicates, Porter's study confines itself to the British," K. L. Taylor wrote for *Science* (January 13, 1978), "but this limitation helps make possible what is perhaps the most interesting and valuable feature of the book, its consistent focus on the social as well as the intellectual currents out of which geology materialized." Porter's "ability to see and describe the larger issues embodied in the early theories of the earth, which he rightly calls scientific myths, is quite exceptional," according to a reviewer for *Choice* (March 1978). "Geologists may feel that he overemphasizes the social, as opposed to the theoretical, aspects of the science. Yet they will learn much from his account and will find his bibliography invaluable."

In his next book, *English Society in the Eighteenth Century* (1982), Porter examined in more general terms the time period that most interested him and dealt "admirably with the manifold ways of interpreting the century as a whole," according to Asa Briggs for the London *Guardian* (May 23, 1982). Five years later Porter began building his extensive bibliography on the history of medicine with the publication of three books: *Disease, Medicine, and Society in England, 1550–1860*, an extended essay on the impact of disease on the English before the advent of publicly funded medical care; *A Social History of Madness: The World through the Eyes of the Insane*; and *Mind-Forg'd Manacles: A History of Madness in England from the Restoration to the Regency*.

Mind-Forg'd Manacles draws its title from a line in the poem "London" by the English poet and painter William Blake. Relying on literature, diaries, letters, medical writings, court cases, and historical works, Porter compiled an assortment of ideas about insanity from the 18th century and traced pivotal changes in the development of psychiatry. "While the book will mostly interest scholars, others will enjoy his descriptions of, for example, the treatment of George III's madness, the practices at the Bethlem ('Bedlam') insane asylum and the 'moral therapy' of the York Retreat, as well as the other vignettes that are woven into this social history of madness. Mr. Porter . . . knows the period very well and he writes in an engaging style, but the book is mainly descriptive; he attempts little integration of the information he presents." Noting that the author takes particular interest in the treatment of deranged women, Austin MacCurtain wrote for the London *Sunday Times* (July 1, 1990), "Porter is not only sophisticated about theory and a formidable researcher and scholar but also so readable as to be actually funny at times; he has written a book

Franzisca Augstein/Courtesy of W. W. Norton

Roy Porter

which says as much about society as about those excluded from it."

Porter's second book on the topic, *A Social History of Madness,* received more attention than the first and remains one of his better-known works. The book examines the plight of the mentally ill in a variety of historical and social contexts. Porter drew on many and varied sources—from Margery Kempe (1373–1438), an English religious writer, to Sigmund Freud (1856–1939), the Austrian founder of psychoanalysis. Marina Warner, writing for the *New York Times Book Review* (September 4, 1988), noted that Porter sees the history of madness as a history of power, one in which the voices of the deranged have often been suppressed: "It takes a historian like Mr. Porter . . . to pay attention to the prolix confessions, self-vindications and jeremiads of the insane, to unearth a pamphlet like 'A Receipt to Make a Lunatic . . . and a Sketch of a True Smiling Hyena' and communicate the sense it makes with sympathy and humor." Warner praised the "pugnacious yet soft-spoken" book, which "gives us new ears to listen to the so-called ravings and gibberish of the mad," but expressed disappointment that it was so Eurocentric. "His one chapter on America seems little more than a gesture," she wrote. "Following upon *Mind-Forg'd Manacles,* published last year, this book necessarily goes over some of the same ground. More damaging, however, the most searching passages of *A Social History of Madness* are drawn from the 18th-century material covered there, as if some excellent bottles had been left undrunk at that feast and the author could not face setting them aside."

For the publisher Palgrave Macmillan's series *Historians on Historians,* Porter contributed *Gibbon: Making History* (1988), an assessment of the work of the 18th-century historian Edward Gibbon. The book "is an excellent piece of work; muscular, lucid, suitably dogmatic and on the basics well equipped," John Kenyon wrote for the *Times Literary Supplement* (December 15, 1989). "It also displays a sense of humour. . . . It will prove perfectly acceptable to the non-academic reader whose commitment to Gibbon, or to any other historian, does not extend to the dense mechanics of textual analysis or the week-by-week detail of a major biography." Though Anthony Lentin, writing for *History Today* (July 1989), felt that "Porter reminds us why all students of history should read, enjoy, respect and learn from Gibbon," he noted two faults in the book: "First, though full of excellent quotations from Gibbon, it lacks any references to enable the reader to look them up. Second, while his main thesis is that 'Gibbon was extraordinarily self-aware as to how history was necessarily the creation of the shaping intellect, indeed of the imagination,' Porter omits for lack of space the kind of detailed *explication de texte* that would best bring this out. On the other hand he provides probably the best possible bibliographical essay."

In *Health for Sale: Quackery in England, 1660–1850* (1989), Porter explored the social and political context that allowed medical charlatans to flourish as they crossed the English countryside peddling spurious potions that they claimed would cure all sorts of ailment. Pat Rogers, writing for the *Times Literary Supplement* (October 20, 1989), declared, "Porter's handling of the subject is lively, sensitive to a broad range of sociopolitical issues, and replete with telling detail. . . . His citation of the many newspaper advertisements preserved in the Wellcome [Institute] collection and the British Library adds a rich texture to his argument on the development of medical marketing." After examining the book in its 2001 reprint, which was published as *Quacks: Fakers & Charlatans in English Medicine,* Mark S. R. Jenner wrote for the *English Historical Review* (June 2002), "It is clear that the author's energetic prose has stood the test of time and that it is one of the best of Porter's books and probably the most compelling outline of the workings of the English medical marketplace in the long eighteenth century."

In 1990 Porter published *The Enlightenment,* an entry in Palgrave Macmillan's Studies in European History series, and two year later he published another biography, *Doctor of Society: Thomas Beddoes and the Sick Trade in Late-Enlightenment England.* Beddoes, who lived from 1760 to 1808, embodied the romantic ideal in that his pursuits were far-ranging; in addition to his interest in science, he also concerned himself with literature and politics. Beddoes "called the Medicine of his day 'lucrative homicide' and thought long and hard about the place of the doctor in society and the social, economic and political roots of ill-health and how to eradicate them," according to Ann Dally for *History Today* (November 1992). "As one would expect, Porter's book is about much more than Beddoes. Through Beddoes he gives us insight into such things as medicine in the eighteenth century against a background of the Enlightenment, the advancement of scientific medicine, the idea and possibilities of reform, attitudes to quacks and the development of popular instruction in the art of health." In the *Times Literary Supplement* (February 21, 1992), James C. Riley noted, "For Roy Porter, Beddoes is interesting because he wrote so vigorously on many issues relating to the culture of sickness and medicine, not because his opinions were valuable. Yet Beddoes does not allow Dr Porter to go very far in exploring several of the issues raised in his introduction. Beddoes listened carefully to things his patients said and tried to interpret them, Porter observes, but only briefly in the main text do his insights into language surface. . . . What we do learn from Porter's close reading of Beddoes's writings is that he recognized cultural forms and causes of sickness and was deeply pessimistic about them."

Porter's attachment to the city of London, dating from the time he spent there as a youth, was evident in *London: A Social History* (1995). David Cannadine noted in his review for the London *Independent* (October 23, 1994), "This is a very clever, very important and very angry book. It is clever because it is by Roy Porter, and if that alone is not sufficient recommendation, it should be added that this is much the best and bravest thing he has yet written. It is important because it makes the whole sweep of London's unique history comprehensible and accessible in a way that no previous writer has ever managed to accomplish. And it is angry because it begins and concludes with a slashing, unanswerable indictment of Thatcherite misrule and mismanagement, which have reduced what was once the greatest city in the world to its present parlous and pitiable plight." Though Michael Elliott, writing for the *Washington Post* (May 7, 1995), found Porter's dire predictions about the financial future of London too negative, the critic declared that "his book deserves to be an instant classic."

For another 1995 publication, *The Facts of Life: The Creation of Sexual Knowledge in Britain, 1650–1950,* Porter and his co-author, Lesley Hall, mined sex manuals published over a 300-year period to trace the development of attitudes about sexual disorders, morality, pleasure, and propriety. Peter Bradshaw wrote for the London *Evening Standard* (March 13, 1995), "With erudition and energy, Porter and Hall show how sexual knowledge—or at any rate a literature of sexual knowledge—grew, but was increasingly splintered and made problematical." In the London *Sunday Times* (January 29, 1995),

Philippa Gregory wrote, "This large and scholarly study is invaluable for historians of ideas: provocative, inspiring and thoughtful. But the title is misleading. This book is not about the facts of life it is about versions of the facts: how they were imagined, mythologised, discovered, disseminated and exploited. It is about the conveying of information: not the tale itself, but the telling and the tellers."

Gout: The Patrician Malady (1998), which was written with G. S. Rousseau, illustrates how cultural concepts about the body and its ailments influence medical treatment. In their introduction, Rousseau and Porter note that in modern times gout is viewed as a "disease of the *ancien régime* and the Old World," an ailment that the "idle and licentious" brought upon "their own heads, or rather feet, by outrageous overindulgence," but "in truth gout is very much still with us; it continues to threaten males in the developed world, and globally it is spreading." Furthermore, they point out, "the glaring neglect of gout draws attention to biases" among medical historians, who prefer to study such lethal epidemic diseases as the bubonic plague or AIDS. "By exploring the ways gout was represented, both medically and culturally, the authors uncover its essentially ambiguous qualities," Ludovic Hunter-Tilney wrote for the *Financial Times* (February 26, 2000). "Was it an hereditary disorder or one brought on by lifestyle? Was it Nature's way of righting the body or an ailment which itself had to be cured? Should it be purged from within or soothed by applying an ointment (a medieval authority recommended puppy boiled with cucumber, rue and juniper)? These questions tied in with debates about politics, class and gender, and they are expertly unravelled in the book. Gout's history resounds far beyond the chink of empty port bottles."

Considered one of Porter's finest books, *The Greatest Benefit to Mankind: A Medical History of Humanity* (1998) is a sweeping survey of the contributions that medicine has made to civilization from ancient Greece to modern times. The title for the book is taken from a quotation by Samuel Johnson, whose opinion of the field was far more optimistic than Porter's. "I kind of wanted the publishers to put a question mark at the end" of the title, he told Sarah Lyall. "I'm a great fan of Samuel Johnson, but I didn't want people to take the title as an assertion. I wanted them to take it as a possibility."

"One of the abiding impressions left by this astonishingly erudite historical survey of medicine is the enormous intellectual effort across all cultures to try and understand the origins of illness," Jon Turney wrote, reviewing *The Greatest Benefit to Mankind* for the *Financial Times* (January 3, 1998). "Another is what perilous lives we have led, especially since we created cities to live in. Porter's meticulous account of medical thinking and practice is punctuated by regular bulletins about which plague was ravaging urban populations in which parts of the globe at the time. There is prodigious labour here, as well as generous helpings of wit. And if no-one can reasonably be expected to be truly stylish over 800 pages, Porter manages it most of the time. . . . This fine book is much more than a chronicle of the rise of modern medical science. It is also a splendidly salutary reminder of the precariousness and pain of the human lot through most of our history." In the *Los Angeles Times Book Review* (April 12, 1998), Andrew Scull wrote, "*Benefit to Mankind* is in some respects even more ambitious than anything else [Porter] has written to date, aspiring to provide nothing less than 'a medical history of mankind' from hunter-gatherer societies to high-tech Western medicine at the dawn of the new millennium, and everything in between. In almost all relevant respects, it must be accounted a triumph: simultaneously entertaining and instructive, witty and thought-provoking, a coherent overview comprising within its 832 pages an elegant and moving set of reflections on our collective efforts to grapple with disease and debility and to come to terms with the frailties of our flesh." *The Greatest Benefit to Mankind* won the Los Angeles Times Book Prize for history, in 1998.

In *The Creation of the Modern World: The Untold Story of the British Enlightenment* (2000)—which was published in Britain that same year as *Enlightenment: Britain and the Creation of the Modern World*—Porter argued that such British figures as John Locke, David Hume, and Isaac Newton had contributed more to the Age of Reason than had been indicated in previous assessments by historians, who tended to focus more on the intelligentsia of France and Germany. "The reader who consults the book's 88-page bibliography may feel that England has not had quite such a raw deal as Porter suggests," James A. Galloway wrote for the *Lancet* (December 23, 2000). "We must, however, be grateful for whatever motivated the author, for he has produced a valuable and fascinating account of an extraordinarily dynamic culture, and of the emergence of an intelligentsia whose influence upon the development of the modern world has been incalculable." *The Creation of the Modern World* was awarded the Wolfson History Prize and short-listed for the British Academy Book Prize.

Bodies Politic: Disease, Death, and Doctors in Britain, 1650–1900 (2001), examines that period's artistic representations of the body and various medical themes and contains more than 100 illustrations. According to Mark S. R. Jenner, writing for the *English Historical Review* (April 2002), "Porter's text is as lively as the many satirical prints which he reproduces. . . . *Bodies Politic* deserves a wide readership and will certainly stimulate further research in the field." Roy Herbert, writing for *New Scientist* (June 2, 2001), described *Bodies Politic* as "a feast for mind and eye," in which the evolution of perceptions of the medical industry is "told with lots of humour and copious extracts from contemporary writing."

Though Porter retired from his teaching post in 2001, he continued to write, telling his friend Habie Schwarz, in a personal letter that was later published in the London *Guardian* (March 13, 2002), that, in addition to learning to play musical instruments and gardening, "Scribbling goes on too. . . ." Porter suffered a heart attack and died on March 3, 2002, while riding his bike a short distance from his home in the parish of St. Leonards-on-Sea, in East Sussex. He was survived by his companion, Natsu Hattori (press accounts vary as to whether the two were married), and his mother.

Just two days before his death, Oxford University Press published another of Porter's books on mental illness, *Madness: A Brief History*. The relatively slender volume—258 pages long in its first American edition—provides an overview of cultural concepts about mental illness from antiquity to modern times. Noting that "this readable yet rigorous little book" was written with a "global slant," Antoinette Brinkman wrote for *Library Journal* (March 1, 2002) that a "wealth of facts and literary references illuminate how people went from believing that supernatural forces cause mental illness to their reliance on more rational and naturalistic explanations, culminating in today's combination of the medical and psychosocial models." In the *New Statesman* (February 11, 2002), Julian Keeling explained that "Porter doesn't really attempt to answer what madness is. Instead, he concentrates on a few core questions: Who has been identified as mad? What has been thought to cause their condition? And what action has been taken to cure or secure them? He has given himself a big subject, but manages to reduce it to a little more than 200 pages with skill and restraint. What makes this book so satisfying, however, is Porter's ability to combine broad brush strokes with telling little details of the lives of the mad and their minders, and their uneasy symbiosis."

Blood and Guts: A Short History of Medicine (2003) was published posthumously. Based on Porter's university lectures on the social history of medicine, the volume is divided into subtopics: disease, doctors, the body, the laboratory, therapies, surgery, the hospital, and medicine and modern society. "Even on the printed page he maintains a conversational tone that makes the topic wholly accessible," a reviewer wrote for *Publishers Weekly* (February 24, 2003). In a review of *Blood and Guts* for the London *Independent* (December 7, 2002), Chandak Sengoopta wrote, "Historians of medicine will come and go; many will contribute profusely to the discipline in their own ways. Roy Porter's personal blend of learning, generosity and near-universal accessibility, however, is unlikely ever to be matched. They just don't make them like that any more, as I realised again while leafing through this book."

Though Porter had also completed *Flesh in the Age of Reason: The Modern Foundations of Body and Soul* (2003) before his death, he did not have time to complete the notes and index. Most reviews lamented the fact that the book, which examines changing notions about the body and soul during the Enlightenment, would be Porter's last. "For those of us who knew, admired and loved Porter, reading this book is necessarily an acutely painful pleasure," Simon Schama wrote for the London *Guardian* (September 27, 2003, on-line). "For it is mercilessly clear that when Porter died last year at the age of 55, he was at the height of his powers. The book is great Porter, which is to say the best history anyone could ever want to read. Never was the presence of the author so strong: deeply serious in the depth of his philosophical inquiry yet wearing his massive erudition lightly. As always in his work, exacting arguments of intellectual history are made accessible as narrative; the ideas themselves not suspended in some realm of disembodied play, but fleshed out as the title of the work implies and embedded in the lived historical experience of thinkers both mighty and paltry. . . . The exhilaration of reading this shockingly vital and exuberant book is punctuated by the mournfulness of realising there will not be another like it."

Porter was a fellow in the British Academy and an honorary fellow in the Royal College of Physicians and Royal College of Psychiatrists. Over the course of his career, Porter edited and co-edited numerous scholarly and reference books, frequently collaborating with a number of different colleagues, most often W. F. Bynum and Mikuláš Teich. He co-edited at least three anthologies with his ex-wife, Dorothy (Watkins) Porter. According to various press accounts, Porter was married and divorced either three or four times. His obituary in the London *Daily Telegraph* (March 6, 2002) noted: "Porter struck an incongruous figure: part unshaven urban guerrilla; part leather-clad biker; part Costa playboy with a fist of rings, unbuttoned shirt, medallion and hairy chest; and part unworldly academic in Cornish pasty shoes. Yet he had the ability to make his subject come alive, and his seminars attracted the brightest and best."

—S.Y.

Suggested Reading: *Chicago Tribune* C p3 June 1, 1988; *Financial Times* p5 Jan. 3, 1998, p4 Feb. 26, 2000; *Harper's* p87+ Mar. 2004; (London) *Evening Standard* p29 Mar. 13, 1995, p57 Oct. 30, 2000; (London) *Guardian* (on-line) Sep. 11, 1987, Books p4 Feb. 26, 2000, (on-line) Sep. 29, 2003; (London) *Independent* p4 Oct. 21, 1994, p28 Oct. 23, 1994; p11 June 16, 2001, p6 Mar. 6, 2002, p23 Dec. 7, 2002; (London) *Independent on Sunday* p19 Oct. 5, 2003; *Los Angeles Times Book Review* p3 Apr. 12, 1998; *New Statesman* p42+ Jan. 9, 1998, p50+ Feb. 11, 2002; *New York Times* B p9 Apr. 24, 1999; *New York Times Book Review* p30 Apr. 10, 1988, p7 Sep. 4, 1988, p6

Dec. 24, 2000, p11 Mar. 21, 2004; *Washington Post Book World* p1 May 7, 1995, p15 Feb. 22, 2004

Selected Books: *The Making of Geology: Earth Science in Britain, 1660–1815,* 1977; *English Society in the Eighteenth Century,* 1982; *Mind-Forg'd Manacles: A History of Madness in England from the Restoration to the Regency,* 1987; *A Social History of Madness: The World through the Eyes of the Insane,* 1987; *Disease, Medicine, and Society in England, 1550–1860,* 1987; *Gibbon: Making History,* 1988; *Health for Sale: Quackery in England, 1660–1850,* 1989; *The Enlightenment,* 1990; *Doctor of Society: Thomas Beddoes and the Sick Trade in Late-Enlightenment England,* 1992; *London: A Social History,* 1995; *The Facts of Life: The Creation of Sexual Knowledge in Britain, 1650–1950* (with Lesley Hall), 1995; *Gout: The Patrician Malady* (with G. S. Rousseau), 1998; *The Greatest Benefit to Mankind: A Medical History of Humanity,* 1998; *The Creation of the Modern World: The Untold Story of the British Enlightenment,* 2000; *Bodies Politic: Disease, Death, and Doctors in Britain, 1650–1900,* 2001; *Madness: A Brief History,* 2002; *Blood and Guts: A Short History of Medicine,* 2003; *Flesh in the Age of Reason: The Modern Foundations of Body and Soul,* 2003

Powell, Sophie

1980– Novelist

Sophie Powell impressed critics and readers alike with her debut novel, *The Mushroom Man* (2003), which combines Celtic lore with modern family drama. In the Malaysia *New Straits Times* (May 7, 2003), U-En Ng described the novel as "an astonishing debut that unmasks the unforgiving light of adult reason as a poor, mottled sham. The central idea underpinning Powell's remarkable story is deadly serious. It concerns the way a child's imagination can be stifled by an over-enthusiastic parent."

Born in 1980, Powell was raised mostly in London, England, but spent many weekends on her family's sheep farm in the Brecon Beacons, in Wales, where she often picked mushrooms with her grandmother, sister, and brother. "Our farm is appropriately entitled Rhandir-y-beirddion, which translates as 'Land of the Poets' in Welsh, and it really is the most magical place on earth: It overlooks a Roman castle (Carregg Cennen Castle) and even has a tumulus (a Roman burial mound) by the stream," Powell wrote for an autobiographical statement posted on the Penguin Group Web site. Long fascinated with fairy tales and myths, she received her undergraduate degree in Classics from Trinity College at the University

Courtesy of Sophie Powell

Sophie Powell

of Cambridge, in England. While a student, her short story "At the End of the Line" was selected by the best-selling novelist Zadie Smith for the 2001 issue of *The May Anthologies*, composed of new writings by students from the University of Oxford and the University of Cambridge.

Though *The Mushroom Man* is inspired by her experiences on the family farm, Powell did not begin writing the novel until after she moved to New York City, where she was pursuing her M.F.A. in creative writing at New York University. "Amidst the urban, chaotic jam-packedness of New York, I hankered after the rural stillness of our sheep farm in Wales," she wrote on the Penguin Group Web site. She arrived in New York shortly before the terrorist attacks of September 11, 2001 and completed her novel within the first three months in the city.

The Mushroom Man begins as the protagonist, six-year-old Lily Newman, accompanies her mother on a trip to visit her aunt's Welsh farm. During her visit, Lily becomes fixated on a fairy tale about a hermit, the Mushroom Man, who lives in the nearby forest. After fashioning umbrellas from the wild mushrooms to protect the fairies from the rain, he is rewarded with immortality and the power to turn people invisible. Lily sets out to find the hermit and goes missing. The adults believe that she has been abducted by a child predator.

"The irony and humor which characterizes the novel is always oscillating between addressing serious issues and making fun of everyone and everything," Powell explained on the Penguin Group Web site. "The children's world versus the adults' world—whose vision is the most correct?"

Though describing *The Mushroom Man* as "as ephemeral and light as the forest fairies it depicts so well," Karen Karbo, writing for the *New York Times* (March 30, 2003), felt that Powell "has managed to create a world where the sad adult business of estrangement, mourning and betrayal coexists with the unseen childhood world of light and happiness, and that's no small feat. The Welsh countryside has never seemed so alluring, or the existence of simple magic, despite the nasty disappointments of adult life, so probable."

A reviewer for *Publishers Weekly* (December 9, 2002) described *The Mushroom Man* as a "charming debut" and "touching comedy that explores childhood fantasies as well as messy adult truths about family relationships." The reviewer continued, "Powell neatly juggles many elements here: sibling rivalry, a marriage gone sour, widowhood. Her wry, playful prose, assured voice and unerring eye for detail make her one to watch." On the other hand, Jeff Guinn, writing for the *Fort-Worth Star-Telegram* (March 23, 2003), offered the young author more qualified praise: "Powell is the literary equivalent of a major-league baseball hotshot rookie who demonstrates great promise as a hitter but still strikes out far too often. *The Mushroom Man*, Powell's first novel, has its moments, but it's obviously the product of a still-inexperienced writer who hasn't yet learned how to move efficiently from one story high point to the next." The novel has been translated into Italian, Korean, and Japanese.

After completing her M.F.A., in 2003, Powell taught for a time at New York University. She is now living in Boston, teaching at Boston College and Lesley University, and serving as assistant director of the Abroad Writers' Conference. She visits the family farm whenever possible and enjoys helping with such chores as lambing and sheep sheering.

—C.M.

Suggested Reading: *New York Times* VII p4 Mar. 30, 2003; Penguin Group Web site; *Publishers Weekly* p59 Dec. 9, 2002

Selected Books: *The Mushroom Man*, 2003

Pynchon, Thomas

May 8, 1937– Novelist; short-story writer; essayist

Once requested to supply information about his life to the reference publication *Who's Who*, Thomas Pynchon, the famously private novelist, short-story writer, and essayist, thought of "inventing a life, indicating that he was born in Mexico, that his parents were Irving Pynchon and Guadalupe Ibarguengotia and that he was 'named Exotic Dancers Man of the Year in 1957' and 'regional coordinator for the March of Edsel Owners on Washington (MEOW) in 1961,'" Mel Gussow reported for the *New York Times* (March 4, 1998), citing letters that Pynchon had written between 1963 and 1984 to his then-agent, Candida Donadio. Pynchon's refusal to make himself available to the media has meant that he is almost universally described as a recluse—a label he dismisses out of hand. In one of the few comments that he has ever made to the media—comments he was drawn into making after a CNN camera crew filmed him surreptitiously—Pynchon told a writer for CNN.com (June 5, 1997), "My belief is that 'recluse' is a code word generated by journalists . . . meaning, 'doesn't like to talk to reporters.'"

Pynchon's determination to protect his privacy, besides minimizing the amount of available biographical information on him, has allowed mythologies to be built up around his life and work. Over the years people have asserted that he was actually the alter-ego of someone else, with possibilities including William Gaddis and J. D. Salinger; such anonymous figures as the antitechnology eco-terrorist the Unabomber; or the writer of a series of letters signed, pseudonymously, Wanda Tinasky. The idea has even been mooted that Pynchon is not an individual at all but a committee of writers publishing under a pseudonym. His notoriety can thus seem as tied to his elusiveness as to his work. His importance as a writer, however, rests on the rich imagination, inventive storytelling techniques, and extraordinarily dexterous writing style, as well as the striking knowledge of history, science, world literature, and popular culture, that he exhibits in his fiction—to some degree in the handful of short stories he has published, the majority of which are collected in *Slow Learner* (1984), but above all in his novels: *V.* (1963), *The Crying of Lot 49* (1966), *Gravity's Rainbow* (1973), *Vineland* (1990), *Mason & Dixon* (1997), and *Against the Day* (2006). "Pynchon thinks on a different scale from most novelists," Luc Sante wrote for the *New York Review of Books* (January 11, 2007), "to the point where you'd almost want to find another word for the sort of thing he does, since his books differ from most other novels the way a novel differs from a short story, in exponential rather than simply linear fashion. Pynchon's work has absorbed modernism and what has come after, but in its alternating cycles of jokes and doom, learning and carnality, slapstick and arcana, direct speech and poetic allusiveness, high language and low, it taps into something that goes back to the Elizabethans, who potentially addressed the entire world, made up of individuals with differing interests and capacities."

The Pynchon family—whose earliest recorded member arrived in England from Normandy in the 11th century with William the Conqueror—had already distinguished itself in America's historical landscape prior to the appearance of Thomas Pynchon's novels. The first American to bear the family name was William Pynchon (1590–1662), who emigrated from England, in 1630, as one of the patentees of the Massachusetts Bay Colony, and founded, in the same year, Roxbury, Massachusetts, now a part of Boston but at that time a distinct town. In 1636 William founded Agawam, which, in 1640, was renamed Springfield. When Springfield was incorporated the following year, William was, according to most sources, made the town magistrate by the General Court of Boston and allowed to preside over Springfield's legal matters—exclusive, that is, of capital crimes. (William may have nonetheless, as an associate of the General Court, had a hand in trying some capital cases, including that of Margaret Jones, whose execution, in 1648, is taken to be the first successful prosecution of a New Englander for the crime of being a witch.) In 1650 William published the theological tract *The Meritorious Price of Our Redemption*, which argued primarily that Christ did not atone for the sins of humanity by spending the three days between death and resurrection burning in Hell— the predominant view at the time. Condemned as heretical by the same General Court with which William had long been associated, the book was burned, in 1651, in Boston's marketplace. In 1652 William, unable to mollify the authorities and keep his convictions intact, escaped to England, leaving his properties in the care of his son, John Pynchon (1621–1703), who ran the family's fur-trading and meatpacking businesses—through which he amassed considerable wealth—and served, like his father, in various official capacities in Springfield. (This history is parodied in *Gravity's Rainbow* in the guise of the history of Tyrone Slothrop's ancestors.)

The Pynchons maintained a significant place in New England for generations after William's departure, and in 1851 they found themselves written into literary history, when Nathaniel Hawthorne—whose own ancestor, William Hathorne, had arrived in America, in 1630, as a part of the expedition that established the Massachusetts Bay Colony—used the name "Pyncheon" in *The House of the Seven Gables*. The book fictionalizes the consequences for Hawthorne's ancestors of their part in the infamous Salem witchcraft trials, which began some 30 years after William Pynchon died. Hawthorne felt obliged to write a letter of apology, after two members of the Pynchon family objected to his use of their name. The Pynchons continued to flourish into the early 20th century, when they ran Pynchon & Company, a prominent stockbrokerage firm, which went bankrupt as a result of the 1929 stock-market crash.

Thomas Ruggles Pynchon Jr. was born on May 8, 1937 in Glen Cove, Long Island, New York, the oldest of the three children of Thomas Ruggles Pynchon Sr. and Catherine Frances (Bennett) Pynchon. (Clifford Mead, in the 1989 book *Thomas Pynchon: A Bibliography of Primary and*

Secondary Materials, gives her first name as Katherine, and biographers have generally followed Mead, but the spelling of her name with a *K* is used neither in her husband's obituary nor her own.) He has a sister, Judith, and a brother, John. His father, an engineer (some sources say a surveyor), presided over the local Republican club and served briefly as a town supervisor for Oyster Bay, where the family had begun to live, in the early 1940s, in the part designated East Norwich. Beginning in the mid-1960s, Pynchon's father became a partner with Kahler and Pynchon, an engineering and surveying firm, and then an associate partner and eventually partner with the engineering firm Sidney B. Browne & Son. After giving up the latter position, in 1994, he served as a consultant, never retiring, his daughter observed on the occasion of his death, in 1995. "Speaking for my brother," Judith Pynchon told Justin Martin for New York *Newsday* (July 23, 1995), "I hope that [his success] will not overshadow my father's accomplishments in his long and productive life." Thomas Pynchon's mother—an active member of her community, having been, for example, a founding volunteer of the East Norwich Public Library—was a registered nurse at the Glen Cove Community Hospital (now the Glen Cove Hospital) until she retired, in 1955; she died in 1996.

Growing up, Pynchon was a fan "of spy fiction, novels of intrigue, notably those of John Buchan . . . [as well as those of] E. Phillips Oppenheim, Helen MacInnes, Geoffrey Household, and many others," he revealed in the introduction to *Slow Learner.* In high school Pynchon wrote a column for his school newspaper, the *Oyster Bay Purple and Gold,* called "The Voice of the Hamster," under the pseudonyms Roscoe Stein, Boscoe Stein, and Bose, as well as some articles—including "The Boys" and "Ye Legend of Sir Stupid and the Purple Knight"—under his own name. In these brief pieces Pynchon was already using the kind of bizarre names favored in his fiction and employing a wry sense of humor, as well as displaying his abiding interest in misfits and collective behavior. In 1953 he graduated, at age 16, from Oyster Bay High School, where he was class salutatorian and the recipient of the Julia L. Thurston award as the senior with the highest average in English. In the fall of the same year, he entered Cornell University, in Ithaca, New York, on a scholarship. He adamantly refused to submit his photograph to the freshman register and has continually refused to allow himself to be photographed for publication. Aspiring to become a physicist, he majored in engineering physics and earned a reputation for being both studious and responsible, as Jules Siegel, a fellow student at Cornell during the 1953–54 academic year, recalled in an article that he wrote for *Playboy* (March 1977): "Tom Pynchon was quiet and neat and did his homework faithfully. . . . He got $25 a week spending money and managed it perfectly, did not cut class and always got grades in the high 90s. He was

disappointed not to have been pledged to a fraternity, but he lacked the crude sociability required for that. . . . He was, if anything, a very private person." Gifted at math, Pynchon impressed his physics professors to such a degree that, according to Frank D. McConnell's article in *Contemporary Novelists* (1986), "one of his former teachers still wonderingly remembers his apparently voracious appetite for the complexities of elementary particle theory." While Pynchon later formally changed his major to English, physics remained a cardinal interest, as illustrated by his fascination with the concept of entropy early in his career and, as David Goldblatt wrote for *Arts & Book Review* (December 15, 2006), his more recent "engagement with the dilemmas of mathematics and physics" in *Against the Day.*

At the end of his sophomore year, Pynchon left Cornell for the U.S. Navy. He spent part of his two years in the service at the naval base in Norfolk, Virginia, and during that period he kept company with Anne Cotton, a young woman who worked for an intelligence agency in Washington, D.C. He introduced her to jazz at Washington nightclubs, while she stimulated his interest in opera, an interest that would later manifest itself in his fiction. Pynchon's attitude toward literature also changed during his two years away from Cornell. In his introduction to *Slow Learner,* Pynchon described coming across, in 1956, an issue of the *Evergreen Review,* which showcased the work of Beat writers, whose aesthetic seemed starkly opposed to the modernist tradition that he was absorbing at Cornell. Pynchon wrote in his introduction that for him and others of the period, "It was not a case of either/or, but an expansion of possibilities. I don't think we were consciously groping after any synthesis, although perhaps we should have been." Louis Menand, writing for the *New York Review of Books* (June 12, 1997), thus calls Pynchon "the unlikely offspring of Jack Kerouac and the Cornell English department."

Pynchon returned to Cornell in the fall of 1957. The Russian-émigré novelist Vladimir Nabokov was then teaching at the school, and it has become a piece of the Pynchon lore that the young writer studied under him. Though no firm evidence exists to prove that was the case, many people interested in Pynchon's life have considered it likely that he at the very least sat in on some of Nabokov's lectures. Charles Hollander, in the article "Pynchon's Politics: The Presence of an Absence," written for *Pynchon Notes* (Spring–Fall 1990) and reproduced on the Web site Vheissu.info, quoted an acquaintance of Pynchon's during his Cornell years, Robert H. Eisenman, as saying: "Everybody who was anybody audited the legendary Nabokov lectures, to hear the showman on Emma, Anna, and Gregor Samsa. It was a very large lecture hall with no attendance monitors, so auditors caught individual lectures as they pleased. Pynchon would have known that." Siegel suggested at least that level of acquaintance between the two authors when he wrote that Pynchon had found Nabokov's Russian accent difficult to understand.

Pynchon became more involved with the campus literary scene during his second period at Cornell. He served on the editorial staff of the undergraduate literary magazine, the *Cornell Writer*, which published several poems and stories by his close friend, the late writer, folk singer, and self-styled revolutionary Richard Fariña, to whom *Gravity's Rainbow* is dedicated. Pynchon also wrote in this period a never-performed musical, in collaboration with Kirkpatrick Sale, called *Minstral Island*, which is set in 1998, in an IBM-controlled dystopia. Five of Pynchon's six published stories also appeared during these years: "The Small Rain" (which was originally published in the *Cornell Writer*, March 1959), about a peacetime military operation to clean up a hurricane-torn region of Louisiana; "Mortality and Mercy in Vienna" (*Epoch*, Spring 1959), an involved tale set at a party that erupts into violence; "Low-lands" (*New World Writing*, March 1960), a story that is about a middle-class man retreating into adolescent fantasies to avoid adult responsibilities and that features the first appearance of the character Pig Bodine—"a recurring avatar" in many of Pynchon's later books, as Menand noted for the *New Yorker* (November 27, 2006); "Entropy" (*Kenyon Review*, Spring 1960), which is set in the midst of a lease-breaking party and explores both social and physical chaos; and "Under the Rose" (*Noble Savage*, May 1961), a spy story that evolved into the third chapter of *V.*

On obtaining his B.A., with distinction in all subjects, in 1959, Pynchon was offered the Woodrow Wilson Fellowship and a job teaching creative writing at Cornell but turned both down, making, instead, an unsuccessful application for a fellowship from the Ford Foundation to write an opera libretto. Around that time, while staying with friends in the Greenwich Village section of New York City, he also began to work on *V.*

In 1960 Pynchon moved to Seattle, Washington, where, between February 1960 and September 1962, he worked for the Boeing Company as an engineering aide and technical writer, while completing *V.* A member of the team supporting the Minuteman missiles, Pynchon is said to have had a high-level security clearance and to have written for an internal newsletter called the *Bomarc Service News*, not the *Minuteman Field Service News* as was once believed. In December 1960 he published the article "Togetherness" in *Aerospace Safety*. Walter Bailey, another employee at Boeing during that time, described Pynchon to David Cowart, according to Cowart's paraphrase in his book *Thomas Pynchon: The Art of Allusion* (1980), as "a taciturn and withdrawn young man whose apparent misanthropy did not make him particularly well-liked."

In late 1962 Pynchon went from Washington State to California and from there to Mexico. In 1963, shortly after *V.* was published, *Time* sent a photographer to Mexico City to photograph Pynchon for an article on the book. According to an often-repeated account, the photographer arrived at the door of Pynchon's apartment only to have Pynchon flee through a window and catch a bus to a remote Mexican village. In Mexico, another well-worn story goes, the locals, amused by Pynchon's florid mustache, called him Pancho Villa, after the famed general in the Mexican Revolution.

An encyclopedic work, *V.* combines two plots: one, set in the U.S. in the mid-1950s, involves an Italian-Jewish drifter named Benny Profane, who seems determined to perfect his "schlemielhood"—the state of being a victim—and who meets up with and befriends a crowd in New York City called the "Whole Sick Crew"; the other plot—skeletal, nonlinear, and more fragmentary—concerns the quest of an adventurer named Herbert Stencil to track down V., a mysterious and corrupt woman, described by David Cowart as a "kind of Nazi Venus, a nightmare vision of the eternal feminine," whose initial recurs in the journals of his father, an agent with the British foreign office, and who reappears under various names and guises in such diverse places as New York, Paris, Alexandria, Florence, Malta, and South Africa. Filled with bizarre incidents and a cast of bohemian characters, *V.* became a cult book of the 1960s. Its style reminded critics, variously, of Nathanael West, William Faulkner, Lawrence Durrell, and Vladimir Nabokov. Others found that its experimental approach and bizarre humor recalled the work of such authors as Joseph Heller, William S. Burroughs, John Barth, and Kurt Vonnegut.

In a fit of enthusiasm, Richard Poirier called *V.*, as Kenneth Kupsch noted in an article on the novel for *Twentieth Century Fiction* (Winter 1998), "the most masterful first novel in the history of literature." Charles G. Gros, writing for *Best Sellers* (April 1, 1963), felt that "reading *V.* is like listening to a scholarly but erratic documentation of Hell by a disinterested onlooker while verbal sewage and vignettes of all that is most disgusting in mankind alternate with sociological asides, sardonic and blasphemous attacks on Christianity, [and] Freudian tidbits." George Plimpton, for the *New York Times Book Review* (April 21, 1963), found *V.* "as complicated and varied as a Hieronymus Bosch triptych" and credited Pynchon with "a vigorous and imaginative style, a robust humor, a tremendous reservoir of information . . . and, above all, a sense of how to use and balance these talents." The critic for *Newsweek* (April 1, 1963) asserted: "This splendid first novel is simply a picture of life, as first-rate novels always are, reflecting a creative force of great originality, complexity, and breadth." *V.* earned Pynchon the 1963 William Faulkner Award for best first novel.

Pynchon reportedly began work on *Gravity's Rainbow* upon the publication of *V.,* but along the way he wrote his sixth—and, to date, last—short story, "The Secret Integration" (*Saturday Evening Post,* December 1964); his first essay in a popular publication, "A Journey into the Mind of Watts" (*New York Times Magazine,* June 12, 1966); and his second novel, *The Crying of Lot 49.* "The Secret Integration" explores the issue of racial integration through the eyes of children who create a fantasy world in which racial distinctions are inconsequential, at the same time that their parents are intimidating a black couple who recently moved into their neighborhood. "A Journey into the Mind of Watts" considers the 1965 racial riots in a black section of Los Angeles, and concludes: "Far from a sickness, violence may be an attempt to communicate, or to be who you really are." In *Pynchon: A Collection of Critical Essays* (1978), Joseph W. Slade described the article as "a skillful piece of journalism" that "traces the ironies of black life in a prosperous white city."

Pynchon's second novel, *The Crying of Lot 49*—segments of which appeared in *Esquire* and *Cavalier*—was more accessible to the general reader than its predecessor, perhaps because of its strong and unified plot and its length of fewer than 200 pages. It focuses on Oedipa Maas, a California housewife who, as "executor, or she supposed executrix, of the estate," as she is described in the novel, of her former lover, the real estate mogul Pierce Inverarity, stumbles upon what appears to be a conspiracy directed by a mysterious, ubiquitous, and centuries-old postal service, the Tristero. In the novel Pynchon uses the Second Law of Thermodynamics (which describes entropy, or energy loss) as a metaphor for a deteriorating civilization. In *The Grim Phoenix: Reconstructing Thomas Pynchon* (1978), William M. Plater noted that *The Crying of Lot 49* had "a tightly controlled plot based on the highly successful movie formula, an economy of dialogue, plausible fantasy, and characters that are at least imaginable." Those characters included rock 'n' roll singers, right-wing extremists, and other denizens of the subculture of southern California. But to Arthur Gold, writing for *Book Week* (April 24, 1966), *The Crying of Lot 49* seemed "a curiously dead novel." Pynchon himself appeared to accept the latter view, calling it in a letter to his agent around the time that he completed it, Gussow reported, "a short story, but with gland trouble," and hoping she could "unload it on some poor sucker." He later wrote for his introduction to *Slow Learner* that in it, especially when contrasted with "The Secret Integration," "I seem to have forgotten most of what I thought I'd learned up till then." Nevertheless, the book earned Pynchon the 1967 Richard and Hinda Rosenthal Foundation Award of the National Institute of Arts and Letters.

Very difficult to summarize because of its complexity, *Gravity's Rainbow,* Pynchon's third novel, interweaves at least five major stories and numerous minor ones. The ostensible protagonist, or antihero, is Tyrone Slothrop, an American lieutenant stationed in London, England, during the blitz, who has erections on precisely those spots on which German V-2 rockets will land. He deserts to avoid becoming a toy of the Allied authorities, who want to exploit his special characteristic. The novel follows Slothrop's adventures from London to the Casino Hermann Goering in the south of France, and on a journey across Germany. In the end, taking on a number of personæ, including the war-correspondent Ian Scuffling, the cartoonlike character Rocketman, the actor Max Schlepzig, and the mythical pig hero Plechazunga, Slothrop comes close to losing his personhood. Michael Wood, assessing the novel for the *New York Review of Books* (March 22, 1973), saw *Gravity's Rainbow* as "a tortured cadenza of lurid imaginings and total recall that goes on longer than you can quite believe. Its characters, like those in *V.,* are marginal people, layabouts, dropouts, gangsters, failed scientists, despairing spiritualists, spies, SS men, dancing girls, faded movie stars. . . . The mythical population of the book runs from King Kong to [John] Dillinger to Fu Manchu to Tannhauser, with lyrics by [Rainer Maria] Rilke and T. S. Eliot, and there are plenty of songs . . . and limericks and gags." Wood went on to note that Pynchon could "intuit huge canvases from small details, whole cultures from a fragment of stone." Richard Locke, in an assessment for the *New York Times Book Review* (March 11, 1973), called *Gravity's Rainbow* the "longest, most difficult and most ambitious novel" to appear in the U.S. since Nabokov's *Ada,* and Walter Clemons, who noted for *Newsweek* (March 19, 1973) that "it isn't plausible to call a novel great the week it's published," classified it as "at the very least, tremendous." Lawrence Wolfley, in an essay for the Modern Language Association journal *PMLA* (October 1977), saw *Gravity's Rainbow* as "shot through with the particular Freudian thinking" represented by the classical scholar and philosopher Norman O. Brown, who equated repression of sexuality with death and destruction. For Wolfley, who considered Pynchon's novel "one of the greatest of our time," *Gravity's Rainbow* "dramatizes the perpetual struggle of life against death" by "joyfully embracing and celebrating all the death instincts of Western man in a style of unmediated euphoria." Praise for the novel was not unanimous, however. John Gardner, in his book *On Moral Fiction* (1978), referred to Pynchon's "winking, mugging despair" and argued: "[Pynchon], in *Gravity's Rainbow,* carelessly praises the schlock of the past (King Kong, etc.) and howls against the schlock of the present which, he thinks, is numbing and will eventually kill us. We may defend *Gravity's Rainbow* as a satire, but whether it is meant to be satire or sober analysis is not clear." Robert Alter, writing for the *New York Times Book Review* (August 10, 1980), called its brand of apocalypticism juvenile and disapproved of its excessive use of sex and scatology.

A debate over the quality of the novel also arose among those responsible for awarding the Pulitzer Prize in 1974. The three judges on the prize committee unanimously selected *Gravity's Rainbow* as the best novel of 1973, but the 14-member Pulitzer advisory board overruled them, dismissing the huge novel as "obscene" and "unreadable." Consequently, no Pulitzer Prize for fiction was awarded that year. *Gravity's Rainbow* did receive the 1974 National Book Award for fiction, sharing it with Isaac Bashevis Singer's *A Crown of Feathers*. Pynchon did not attend the awards ceremony. Rather he sent the stand-up comedian and self-styled "world's greatest expert on everything," Professor Irwin Corey, to accept the $1,000 prize for him. Pynchon was also designated the winner of the Howells Medal of the American Academy and Institute of Arts and Letters for *Gravity's Rainbow*, which was judged the best novel of the previous five years, but he turned it down. "The Howells Medal is a great honor, and being gold, probably a good hedge against inflation too," Pynchon wrote in a letter to the Academy, as Bill Roeder reported for *Newsweek* (June 2, 1975). "But I don't want it. Please don't impose on me something I don't want. It makes the academy look arbitrary and me look rude." He concluded: "I know I should behave with more class, but there appears to be only one way to say no, and that's no." The Academy announced the award anyway and kept the medal in the institute's headquarters in New York, "gathering luster there not simply because it is gold but by the honor that Thomas Pynchon, however unwillingly, has given it," William Styron, a previous winner, explained, according to Roeder.

For about a decade Pynchon published nothing. Then, in 1983, when the novel *Been Down So Long It Looks like Up to Me* (1966) by his college friend Fariña was reissued, Pynchon wrote an introduction to the book that included a brief autobiographical sketch, recalling how he had met Fariña and some of their college high jinks, as well as a description of how Pynchon reacted to the news of Fariña's death. The following year he published a brief but notable essay, "Is It O. K. to Be a Luddite?," in the *New York Times Book Review* (October 28, 1984). Pynchon's essay uses C. P. Snow's celebrated lecture "The Two Cultures"—which drew a sharp distinction between scientific and literary culture—as a jumping-off point for understanding the Luddite tradition (that is, the tradition of rejecting technological advancement) in art and history, casting it as a revolt against authority and arguing that Ludditism will be altered by the computer revolution. "Will mainframes attract the same hostile attention as knitting frames once did? I really doubt it," Pynchon wrote, adding: "Machines have already become so user-friendly that even the most unreconstructed of Luddites can be charmed into

laying down the old sledgehammer and stroking a few keys instead."

Apparently because his short stories had been circulating for years in pirated pamphlet editions, Pynchon decided to publish five of the six stories—including "The Secret Integration" but excluding "Mortality and Mercy in Vienna"—in the volume *Slow Learner,* along with an introduction, in which he offered more autobiographical anecdotes and criticized what he considered the inadequacies of his own early attempts at fiction. Peter S. Prescott, in a review for *Newsweek* (April 9, 1984), pronounced the book a "minor disaster," but Christopher Lehmann-Haupt, writing for the *New York Times* (March 29, 1984), praised the stories for their "unusual narrative vigor and inventiveness." Helen Dudar took a middle ground in her *Chicago Tribune* (April 8, 1984) review, calling the stories "flabby and only marginally interesting" but claiming that *Slow Learner* was "a fascinating display of the feeling for style and imagined event this greatly talented and intelligent man had by the time he was twenty-one." In 1988 Pynchon was awarded a fellowship—commonly called the "genius grant"—from the John D. and Catherine T. MacArthur Foundation.

The title of Pynchon's fourth novel, *Vineland,* is taken from Vinland, the name that Leif Ericson gave to America when he landed on its shores sometime around 1,000 AD, and in the novel it serves as the name of a fictional northern California county in which the story is largely set. (Vineland, New Jersey, was also the home of Pynchon's aunt, Angeline Roth, at the time of his father's death.) Called "a recovery of the lost history of a progressive left coast" by John Leonard for the *Nation* (October 5, 1998), *Vineland* unfolds in 1984—a year that calls to mind George Orwell's novel of that name and, pointedly, the height of Ronald Reagan's presidency—and tells the story of Zoyd Wheeler, an aging hippie who has been living off mental-disability checks, and his daughter Prairie, who is searching for her absent mother, Frenesi Gates, a radical filmmaker who betrayed her ideals when she fell in love with and began working for Brock Vond, a federal agent. For the previous 14 years Frenesi, who is also Zoyd's ex-wife, has been working for the government. Her job has now been lost to budget cuts, and Vond reappears, trying to kidnap Prairie in an attempt to reestablish his dominance over Frenesi.

The book received mixed reviews. Salman Rushdie, writing for the *New York Times* (January 14, 1990), greeted it enthusiastically, arguing, "There is enough in *Vineland* to obsess the true, mainlining Pynchomane for a goodly time." Rushdie added: "What is perhaps most interesting, finally, about Mr. Pynchon's new novel is what is different about it. What is interesting is the willingness with which he addresses, directly, the political development of the United States, and the slow (but not total) steamrollering of a radical tradition many generations and decades older than flower power." Daniel Vilmure, by contrast, called the novel, for the *St. Petersburg (Florida) Times* (January 28, 1990), "unworthy of [Pynchon's] talent, and of 17 years of silence better left unbroken." Wendy Steiner, writing for the London *Independent* (February 3, 1990), concluded: "The pleasure we usually take in Pynchon's inventions is blunted by the book's general crudeness. Instead of an intricate structure of worlds-within-worlds and a richness that no amount of reading can exhaust, we have gags laid over heavy-handed irony."

Following *Vineland*'s publication, a group of letters signed by Wanda Tinasky and published in the Boonville, California, *Anderson Valley Advertiser*, between 1983 and 1988, began to be attributed to Pynchon. Bruce Anderson, the paper's editor, thought he saw parallels between Tinasky's and Pynchon's styles and decided *Vineland* was the novel set in Northern California that Tinasky had claimed she was writing. (Pynchon denied he had anything to do with the letters, and in the late 1990s, the scholar Don Foster proved Thomas Hawkins, a minor Beat poet, had written them. Coincidentally, Hawkins often put forward the idea that Gaddis's and Pynchon's novels were written by Jack Green, the pseudonym of John Carlisle, a minor 20th-century literary critic and the publisher of an underground Manhattan newspaper in the late 1950s and early 1960s called simply *Newspaper*.)

In the early 1990s Pynchon published a number of short pieces, including an introduction to the posthumous collection of Donald Barthelme's writings called *The Teachings of Don B.: Satires, Parodies, Fables, Illustrated Stories, and Plays* (1992); an essay on sloth called "Nearer, My Couch, to Thee" for the *New York Times Book Review* (June 6, 1993), which was reprinted in *Deadly Sins* (1993), a collection of eight essays by eight writers, each one addressing one of the so-called cardinal sins (or, in the case of the eighth essay, despair); and an introduction to Jim Dodge's novel *Stone Junction*, in 1997, the same year that Pynchon's fifth novel, *Mason & Dixon*, was published. During this period Pynchon also became, largely against his will, a somewhat more public figure. In 1994, when *The John Larroquette Show* was preparing to air an episode on which Pynchon was mentioned, the show's eponymous star—a devoted Pynchon fan and a collector of first editions of Pynchon's work—sent Pynchon the script; he surprised many people involved in the show by sending back, through his agent, comments about it and requests for changes. "In a weird way, we got him to rewrite the script," Larroquette told Scott Williams for the Associated Press (March 7, 1994). In 1996 and 1997, working largely from Internet databases, journalists from such publications as *New York* magazine and the London *Times*, as well as camera crews from CNN, tracked Pynchon down at his home in New York

City, captured images of him on film, and sometimes exchanged words with him, not all of them printable. "Let me be unambiguous," Pynchon told the CNN.com reporter. "I prefer not to be photographed."

When *Mason & Dixon*, a novel Pynchon had been working on since the 1970s, appeared, the novelist T. Coraghessan Boyle wrote for the *New York Times* (May 18, 1997), "This is the old Pynchon, the true Pynchon, the best Pynchon of all. *Mason & Dixon* is a groundbreaking book, a book of heart and fire and genius, and there is nothing quite like it in our literature, except maybe *V.* and *Gravity's Rainbow*." The book is narrated by the Reverend Wicks Cherrycoke, who amuses his sister's family with the story of the surveyor Jeremiah Dixon and the astronomer Charles Mason, who are primarily remembered for drawing, in the mid-1760s, the Mason-Dixon line, the traditional boundary between America's North and South. The novel begins in around 1760, when Mason and Dixon first met, after having been hired by the British Royal Society to observe, from South Africa, the Transit of Venus—that is, a time when that planet crosses in front of the sun. Some 250 pages later, Mason and Dixon arrive in America, where they meet a host of characters both historical and fantastic, including George Washington; Thomas Jefferson; Benjamin Franklin; Armand Allègre, a French chef who is stalked by the French scientist Jacques de Vaucanson's mechanical duck; and Captain Zhang, a Chinese feng shui expert. The resulting novel is not simply an entertaining tale but also, as Melvin Jules Bukiet pointed out for the *Chicago Tribune* (May 11, 1997), a serious exploration of "a moment that [Pynchon] considers the boundary in time limning the divide between the modern world and its antecedents. Soon to come are the American and Industrial Revolutions, but meanwhile an agrarian society—ready to collapse under the collateral onslaughts of technology and commerce—awaits the two rather minor men who set off to define space in the New World."

The response to *Mason & Dixon* was generally positive. Deborah L. Madsen, writing for the London *Times Higher Education Supplement* (May 23, 1997), described the novel as "the successor to *Gravity's Rainbow* . . . that *Vineland* . . . was not" and "a gigantic, sprawling, epic narrative," adding: "It has stature, grandeur, importance, weight. Above all else, it is an historical novel. The wealth of period detail is astounding, from the characters' 18th-century diction and the narrator's prose style to the mannerisms, incidental details and minutiae of everyday life that give texture to Pynchon's historical recreation." Corey Mesler, writing in a similar vein for the Memphis, Tennessee, *Commercial Appeal* (June 1, 1997), called *Mason & Dixon* a novel "as rich, as devious, as preposterous," and "as big as America. It just might be The Great American Novel. It is certainly

Pynchon at his best, which is saying something. And, if this is not his finest novel (the delirium of having just enjoyed it must be tempered with historical perspective) it is undoubtedly his most entertaining." To Rick Moody, writing for the *Atlantic Monthly* (July 1997), the novel "is obviously meant to quash the idea that *Gravity's Rainbow* was some sort of fantastic lucky break. It is self-consciously intent on dealing with American literature on the most ambitious scale imaginable. And it succeeds magnificently." Dissenting from those views, J. Bottum wrote for the *Weekly Standard* (May 19, 1997), "There's Thomas Pynchon the literary event and then there's Thomas Pynchon the writer of novels. The literary event seems stronger than ever. . . . But as far as Thomas Pynchon the novelist goes, we seem to have come at last to the end of him. The unreadable hodgepodge that is *Mason & Dixon*—nearly 800 pages of the absurdist adventures of the surveyors of the boundary between Pennsylvania and Maryland, written in a deliberately annoying mockery of 18th-century prose and narrated by a clergyman with the typically Pynchonesque name of Cherrycoke—confirms what his oddly casual *Vineland* had suggested: With his self-indulgence and lack of literary discipline, Thomas Pynchon has wrecked himself. Now 60, with only two novels in the last 24 years, he will never deliver on his promise."

In 2003 Pynchon wrote a forward to an edition of Orwell's *Nineteen Eighty-Four* (1949), which was published to celebrate the 100th anniversary of Orwell's birth. Reinterpreting the significance of the novel, Pynchon argued that it was not so much an allegory of the Stalinist Soviet Union as a warning about totalitarianism, to which the U.S., Britain, and other democracies around the world are not immune. Around that time Pynchon also changed his attitude about being publicly heard, agreeing to lend his voice to an episode of the animated television series *The Simpsons*. (Earlier in his career, a woman who claims to have been a former lover of Pynchon's, as Andrew Gordon wrote for an essay in *The Vineland Papers* [1994], "once offered to arrange for Pynchon to speak in a university auditorium. She told him she could assure his anonymity by having him speak through a microphone from behind a screen. He refused: 'They would still be able to recognize my voice.'") Pynchon was heard on two episodes: "Diatribe of a Mad Housewife," broadcast on January 15, 2004, and "All's Fair in Oven War," broadcast on November 14, 2004. In both Pynchon, pictured with a bag over his head, simultaneously mocked and maintained his much-discussed reclusiveness. In the first episode he stands on the sidewalk next to a sign reading "Thomas Pynchon's House" and responds to a request for a blurb about Marge Simpson's novel *The Harpooned Heart* by saying, in a distinct New York accent, "Here's your quote: 'Thomas Pynchon loved this book—almost as much as he loves cameras.'" He then calls out to passing cars: "Hey, over here, have your picture taken with a reclusive author! Today only, we'll throw in a free autograph. But, wait! There's more!"

In June 2006, under an entry marked "Untitled Thomas Pynchon (Hardcover)," Amazon.com posted an announcement—and briefly removed it, fueling speculation that readers were being hoaxed—that described the contents of a new Pynchon novel. Signed by Pynchon, the description ended with the mock warning: "The author is up to his usual business. Characters stop what they're doing to sing what are for the most part stupid songs. Strange sexual practices take place. Obscure languages are spoken, not always idiomatically. Contrary-to-the-fact occurrences occur. If it is not the world, it is what the world might be with a minor adjustment or two. According to some, this is one of the main purposes of fiction. Let the reader decide, let the reader beware. Good luck." That novel, readers soon learned, was *Against the Day*.

Set in the era between the 1893 Chicago World's Fair and the late 1910s and covering territory as far-flung as Colorado and Siberia, the novel—arguably as resistant to summary as *Gravity's Rainbow*—is loosely built around the conflict between Scarsdale Vibe, an industrialist, and Frank, Reef, and Kit Traverse, the sons of Webb Traverse, an anarchist whom Vibe has had killed. While Webb's sons set out to avenge their father's death, other plots swirl around in the novel, bringing with them dozens of additional charters—all of them, J. Peder Zane wrote for the Raleigh, North Carolina, *News & Observer* (December 24, 2006), "stamped by their epoch's promise and march toward death." Zane saw two general categories of characters. One is composed of such people as Vibe, "the forces of the day—pitiless champions of status quo." The other is made up of a group of "inconvenient dreamers standing 'against the day'—who seek to fly above or transcend [their opponents'] rapacious world and the even crueler force of time, which eventually claims us all."

Critics were divided over the novel's value. Ira Nadel wrote for Canada's *Vancouver (British Columbia) Sun* (December 2, 2006), "*Against the Day* is history blended with culture, time and space, all wrapped up in a single work that challenges our ideas and tests our perseverance. . . . Picking up the text, rather than peering at it, will reveal an optimism and self-confidence that is bracing. . . . And while it may be impossible to answer clearly the question of what's happening, you should let the experience overtake you." Menand, in his *New Yorker* review, offered a more tempered assessment, writing: "All of Pynchon's novels . . . are long, rambling, multilayered, underplotted, quasi-unfinished monsters. But with this one there is the feeling that the magician has fallen in love with his own stunts, as though Pynchon were composing a pastiche of a Pynchon novel. Still, none of this is simple self-indulgence." Arguing that Pynchon was using the book's overwhelming number of characters, events, and settings as "a simulation of the disorienting overload of modern culture," Menand concluded: "As always, it's an amazing feat. Pynchon must have set out to make his readers dizzy and, in the process, become a little dizzy himself." Steven Moore, writing for the *Washington Post Book World* (November 19, 2006), observed, "Pynchon fans will accept this gift from the author with gratitude, but I'm not so sure about mainstream readers. While *Against the Day* isn't as difficult as some of Pynchon's other novels, its multiple story lines test the memory, and some folks may be scared off by the heady discussions of vectors, Brownian movements, zeta functions and so forth, not to mention words and phrases from a dozen languages scattered throughout. . . . Not for everybody, perhaps, but those who climb aboard Pynchon's airship will have the ride of their lives. History lesson, mystical quest, utopian dream, experimental metafiction, Marxist melodrama, Marxian comedy—*Against the Day* is all of these things and more."

Besides the works discussed above, Pynchon has published two reviews: one (first published in *Holiday*, December 1965) of Oakley Hall's novel *Warlock* (1958) and another (*New York Times Book Review*, April 10, 1988) of Gabriel García Márquez's *Love in the Time of Cholera*. He has written liner notes for *Spiked! The Music of Spike Jones* (1994), a CD compilation of music by the mid-20th–century performer Spike Jones, and *Nobody's Cool* (1996), an album by the American rock band Lotion and "perhaps the only album in rock history that is better known for its liner notes than for its music," a writer for the All Music Guide Web site remarked. Pynchon has also published open letters in support of fellow writers, specifically Salman Rushdie and Ian McEwan. In a note for the *New York Times Book Review* (March 12, 1989), reproduced on the Spermatikos Logos Web site, Pynchon thanked Rushdie—whose novel *The Satanic Verses* (1988) had brought him death threats—"for recalling those of us who write to our duty as heretics." More recently, when McEwan was accused of plagiarizing a source for his novel *Atonement* (2001), Pynchon joined other writers in defending him. In a letter to the London *Daily Telegraph* (December 6, 2006), Pynchon remarked that "for McEwan to have put details from" the source in question—which McEwan had also cited—"to further creative use, acknowledging this openly and often, and then explaining it clearly and honorably, surely merits not our scolding, but our gratitude."

Pynchon's work is the subject of numerous essays, a number of monographs, and, since 1979, an academic journal called *Pynchon Notes*; in 2001 the Swiss-born filmmakers Donatello and Fosco Dubini released the documentary *Thomas Pynchon: A Journey into the Mind of <P.>*. At the end of 2006, the artist Zak Smith published his *Pictures Showing What Happens on Each Page of Thomas Pynchon's Novel* Gravity's Rainbow. Discussing Pynchon in the decades before *Slow Learner* was published, Helen Dudar, who interviewed some of his acquaintances for her 1984 *Chicago Tribune* article, portrayed Pynchon as "a restless, rootless man who lives, as unencumbered as possible, from place to place and coast to coast in borrowed or sublet quarters. He seems to walk in and out of people's lives as if they were rest stops on a transcontinental highway. . . . He is good company and a fairly accomplished cook, tending toward vegetarianism. . . . His friends are expected to honor his lust for anonymity, introducing him to their friends by whatever fake name he is using."

Now married, Pynchon has apparently abandoned his itinerant existence and lives in New York City with his wife and agent, Melanie Jackson, and their son, Jackson. The television correspondent Charles Feldman, in a report for the CNN program *The World Today* (June 5, 1997), observed: "Fans may be disappointed to learn Pynchon leads a somewhat conventional life in New York City." On the same broadcast Nancy Jo Sales, the author of a famously invasive article on Pynchon's private life for *New York* (November 11, 1996), added: "He shops at neighborhood stores. He has lunch with other writers. He spends weekends in the countryside with his family."

In 1999 Pynchon wrote an article called "Hallowe'en? Over Already?" for *The Cathedral School Newsletter,* a publication put out by his son's school. Accompanying the piece was a one-line biography: "Tom is a writer."

—A.R.

Suggested Reading: *Atlantic Monthly* p106+ July 1997; *Book World* p3 Apr. 22, 1984; (Canada) *Vancouver (British Columbia) Sun* C p8 Dec. 2, 2006; *Chicago Tribune* XIV p36+ Apr. 8, 1984; CNN.com July 5, 1997; *Confrontation* p44+ Nov. 1985; (London) *Independent* p30 Feb. 3, 1990; *New York Review of Books* p22+ Mar. 22, 1973; *New York Times* p 59+ Oct. 16, 1978, E p1 Mar. 4, 1998; *New York Times Book Review* p1+ Mar. 11, 1973; *New Yorker* p170+ Nov. 27, 2006; *Newsweek* 100+ Apr. 9, 1984; *Playboy* 97+ Mar. 1977; Spermatikos Logos Web site; *St. Petersburg (Florida) Times* D p6+ Jan. 28, 1990; *Washington Post Book World* p10 Nov. 19, 2006; *Weekly Standard* p36+ May 19, 1997; Clerc, Charles, ed. *Approaches to Gravity's Rainbow*, 1983; Foster, Don. *Author Unknown: On the Trail of Anonymous*, 2000; Levine, George, and David Leverenz, eds. *Mindful Pleasures: Essays on Thomas Pynchon*, 1976; Pearce, Richard, ed. *Critical Essays on Thomas Pynchon*, 1981

Selected Books: *V.*, 1963; *The Crying of Lot 49*, 1966; *Gravity's Rainbow*, 1973; *Slow Learner*, 1984; *Vineland*, 1990; *Mason & Dixon*, 1997; *Against the Day*, 2006

© Eric England/Courtesy of Houghton Mifflin

Randall, Alice

May 4, 1959– Novelist; songwriter; biographer

When the country-music songwriter Alice Randall turned her attention to penning fiction in the late 1990s, neither she nor anyone else expected that her first novel would spark a national debate about intellectual property rights. Shortly before her novel *The Wind Done Gone* was published, in 2001, Randall and her management team were sued by the estate of Margaret Mitchell, which claimed that Randall had written an unauthorized sequel to Mitchell's novel, *Gone with the Wind* (1936). Randall, however, argued that her book was not a sequel, but merely a parody of Mitchell's romantic view of the pre–Civil War South. The court eventually decided in favor of allowing the publication of Randall's novel—but not before the literary world was polarized by the issue.

Writing *The Wind Done Gone* was a direct response to Mitchell's novel, which Randall felt depicted black people in the antebellum South in an unrealistic and unflattering manner. "I was offended that this book had taken slavery and turned it into an entertainment," she told Julie Salamon for the *New York Times* (March 16, 2004, on-line). "I did not want that book to sit on the shelf unrebuked and unscorned. I wanted to make an assault on the text for my daughter."

Mari-Alice Randall was born on May 4, 1959 in Detroit, Michigan, the daughter of George Randall, the owner of a dry-cleaning business, and Bettie Randall, a government analyst. After spending her formative years in Washington, D.C., Randall studied at Harvard University, in Cambridge, Massachusetts. In 1981 she earned a bachelor's degree in English and American literature. One night, while studying in her dorm room, she was inspired to become a country-music songwriter. "It was in sophomore year, I think," she recalled to Troy Patterson in an interview for *Entertainment Weekly* (July 27, 2001). "I took a screenwriting class, and I was spending a couple of days typing a 110-page script, and I got so bored with whatever pop-rock radio station I was listening to that I decided to turn on the country station. It was a joke, something to distract me. And I was immediately struck that there was this Metaphysical quality [relating to a school of 17th-century poets] to some of the strategy in country lyrics."

Soon after her graduation Randall settled in Nashville, Tennessee, considered the country-music capital of the world, to try to make it as a songwriter. She befriended the singer-songwriter Steve Earle after one of his shows and discussed her dreams with him. Earle was encouraging, and over the next few years she worked diligently, vowing not to quit the business until she had a number-one song. Her lyrics—which fused feminist, literary, and cultural references into country rhythms—soon earned her a number of fans. She became known for songs that transcended the usual topics of the genre; she has written about such sensitive topics as lynching ("The Ballad of Sally Ann") and slave casualties ("I'll Cry for Yours, Will You Cry for Mine?"). Moe Bandy, a popular singer, recorded "Many Mansions," a song Randall co-wrote with Carol Ann Etheridge, and Tricia Yearwood, a country superstar, recorded "XXX's and OOO's: An American Girl," a song co-written by Matraca Berg. That latter song became a number-one record, the first country song ever co-written by an African-American woman to top the charts. In 1994 it was used as the theme song for a television movie, *XXX's and OOO's*, for which Randall also wrote the screenplay. (The plot concerned the ex-wives of a group of country-music stars, who bond over their shared experiences.) Randall wrote other screenplays and drafted adaptations for such notable works as *Their Eyes Were Watching God*, *Brer Rabbit*, and *Parting the Waters*. While such work was lucrative, she was enjoying even greater success with her songwriting; more than 30 of her compositions have thus far been recorded by various country artists.

As a child Randall had read *Gone with the Wind*, Margaret Mitchell's novel of the old South, and had been, like many readers, enchanted by the character of Scarlett O'Hara, a Southern belle who schemes her way back to prosperity during and after the Civil War. But as a person of mixed-race ancestry, Randall was bothered by the fact that Mitchell included no mixed-race characters in her book, especially since such people were very much evident in the South of that era. After rereading the book as an adult, Randall decided to revisit its characters by parodying its events in a novel of her own. Her main character, Cynara, is Scarlett's half-black sister, fathered by Gerald O'Hara. As Cynara relates, from her point of view, the events that took place in *Gone with the Wind*, her perspective undermines the myths of the old South, particularly the notion that there was complete separation between the races. Other characters from Mitchell's novel appear under different names, including Ashley and Melanie Wilkes as, respectively, "Dreamy Gentleman" and "Mealy Mouth," and also Scarlett's husband, Rhett Butler, as "R," who becomes Cynara's lover. Randall also added more dimension to the characters of the slaves in Mitchell's book, who were often portrayed as comical or simpleminded. "I think those portrayals are poisonous," Randall explained in an interview posted on CNN.com (June 22, 2001), "and I've tried to create an antidote to that poison. Cynara is the main character, and she's highly intelligent, refined, yet a passionate woman. Mammy and other house servants have complex minds and complex motivations in my novel. As I've said, this is an antidote to the poisonous portrayals of blacks in the first novel, as one-dimensional childlike or animal-like stereotypes."

Shortly before *The Wind Done Gone* was to be released, the trustees of Margaret Mitchell's estate filed a lawsuit, claiming that the new novel was an infringement of Mitchell's copyright. In addition, they argued that the use of Mitchell's characters in settings after the era in which *Gone with the Wind* takes places resulted in an unauthorized sequel being created. (The Mitchell estate has authorized only one sequel to the book thus far. Written by Alexandra Ripley and titled *Scarlett*, it was published in 1991.) On April 20, 2001 a U.S. district court judge prohibited the publication of *The Wind Done Gone* on the grounds that it was "unabated piracy."

The American literary establishment, including the novelists Pat Conroy, Harper Lee, and Toni Morrison, as well as the noted historians Shelby Foote and Arthur M. Schlesinger Jr., rallied to Randall's cause, and some even testified on behalf of the defense. An appeal was filed by Houghton Mifflin and was heard in an Atlanta court on May 25, 2001, at about the time advance copies had already been sent to book reviewers. The reviews found their way into print in newspapers and magazines across the country, some of them on the op-ed pages rather than in the book sections. (Advance copies of the book were selling for several hundred dollars each on e-Bay, the on-line auction site.) The Atlanta court eventually concluded that the book was a parody and therefore not an infringement on Mitchell's copyright, and *The Wind Done Gone* was published that June, according to schedule.

Despite the publicity surrounding the publication of the novel, *The Wind Done Gone* received mostly scathing reviews. Few critics agreed with Karen Traynor, who, for *Library Journal* (May 1, 2001), called the parody a "sometimes cryptic but always fascinating story. . . . Through the eyes of Cynara and the other now freed slaves, we get unique perspectives of life on a Southern plantation and of the Reconstruction era. Randall, an established country songwriter, uses language and idiom to haunting and poetic effect. Fans of Toni Morrison's *Beloved* will enjoy this well-written historical fiction." More critics tended to agree with Megan Harlan, who for the *New York Times Book Review* (July 1, 2001) observed: "When a United States Court of Appeals overturned an injunction, won by the Margaret Mitchell estate, that would have prevented the publication of Alice Randall's parodic sequel to *Gone With the Wind*, it was a victory for the author and for First Amendment rights. Alas, the legal battle surrounding this first novel is more interesting than the book itself, which never rises to the promise of its clever, controversial premise." Terry Teachout, in another representative critique, wrote for the *National Review* (August 20, 2001), "This first novel by author Alice Randall has been . . . written up in *O: The Oprah Magazine*, and staunchly defended on the editorial page of the *New York Times*, proving for the umpteenth time that the most efficient way to publicize bad art is to hire a lawyer and try to suppress it."

Alice Randall's second novel, *Pushkin and the Queen of Spades*, was published in May 2004. The protagonist of the book is Windsor Armstrong, a Harvard-educated black matriarch whose son, Pushkin X, becomes engaged to a white lap dancer. Reviews were decidedly mixed. "*Pushkin and the Queen of Spades* shares with *The Wind Done Gone* . . . an ambitious engagement with history," Gayle Pemberton wrote for the *Women's Review of Books* (July 2004). She went on to observe that if the novel "can be said to resemble any novel, it is Ralph Ellison's *Invisible Man*, even though Windsor tells us that Pushkin X is 'invincible' and anything but 'invisible.' Randall, like Ellison, builds a narrative of enormous scope on allusion and pun. However, she locates her narrative in the center of one of the major shortcomings of *Invisible Man*: Randall's is an exploration and affirmation of the love in the black family and, yes, of the possibility of love across the racial line. In this, she goes where very few African-American men or women in fiction have dared to go. That daring is not met with performance, however, and a story as hyperbolic as this one requires a lighter touch. Randall's prose can be maddeningly melodramatic, making a soap opera out of the fundamentally humorless Windsor's efforts to come to terms with Pushkin X's choice." Rebecca L. Ford, writing for the *Chicago Tribune* (June 13, 2004), found the novel to be "brainy, funny and filled with literate insider references, traversing an arc that spans from Afro-Russian poet Alexander Pushkin (whose great-grandfather was an African slave given to Czar Peter the Great as an exotic gift) to martyred rapper

Tupac Shakur. Randall pulls back the curtain on the urban, marginally middle-class, post-Great Migration village that raised her eccentric, black, bourgeois, intellectual heroine, Windsor Armstrong."

Randall has since published *My Country Roots: The Ultimate MP3 Guide to America's Original Outsider Music* (2006), a collection of 100 playlists for downloading, which was compiled with Carter and Courtney Little, and *A Biography on Booker T. Washington* (2007), which she wrote with David Ewing, for the Amistad Black Life Series. (Amistad is an imprint of HarperCollins.)

Alice Randall's first marriage produced a daughter, Caroline. She is now married to her co-author, David Ewing, an attorney who is a ninth-generation resident of Nashville and the great-great-grandson of the first African-American lawyer in Tennessee. Randall serves on a number of museum and historical-society boards, including the African-American Historical and Genealogical Association, the Andrew Jackson

Slave Descendant Project, and the Family Cemetery Project, among others. She is particularly interested in the topics of enslaved women and children in the American South and former slaves who went on to notable academic achievement. She herself now teaches, as a writer in residence, at Vanderbilt University, in Nashville, Tennessee.

—C.M.

Suggested Reading: *American Libraries* p30 June-July 2001; CNN.com June 22, 2001; *Entertainment Weekly* p22+ July 27, 2001; Houghton Mifflin Web site; *Library Journal* p128 May 1, 2001; *National Review* p44+ Aug. 20, 2001; *New York Times* (on-line) Mar. 16, 2004; *New York Times Book Review* p16 July 1, 2001; *Publishers Weekly* p13 June 4, 2001

Selected Books: *The Wind Done Gone*, 2001; *Pushkin and the Queen of Spades*, 2004; *A Biography on Booker T. Washington* (with David Ewing), 2007

Ravel, Edeet

1955– Novelist; short-story writer

Edeet Ravel holds multiple degrees in Jewish Studies and in English, disciplines she has put to good use in her published works, which include the innovative prose poem *Lovers: A Midrash* (1994) and the novels *Ten Thousand Lovers* (2003), *Look for Me* (2004), and *Wall of Light* (2005), which together form a trilogy about love and war in Israel. As Andrew Armitage noted for the Ontario *Owen Sound Sun Times* (November 17, 2005): "Each of Ravel's novels in the trio can be read alone. Still, while they are only vaguely linked, one builds upon the other until the whole is a rich tapestry of what life [in Israel] is like." In addition to her literary output and her 20-year teaching career at various Canadian universities, Ravel regularly travels to Israel to do volunteer work. The Israeli-Palestinian conflict and its moral implications form the thematic framework for much of her writing; however, while many examinations of the ongoing bloodshed tend towards the polemical, Ravel successfully avoids such criticism. In a review of *Ten Thousand Lovers* for the Toronto *Globe and Mail* (March 1, 2003), Nancy Richler commented, "Ravel . . . is unflinching in her exploration of the moral and emotional conflicts of her characters and of the country in which they live, but the light she shines is as compassionate as it is clear-eyed, illuminating each character's full humanity and revealing the beating heart of the state of Israel as well as its wounded spirit."

Edeet Ravel wrote the following autobiographical statement for *World Authors 2000–2005*:

Yudit Avi-Dor/Courtesy of Random House

"When I look at my writing, I see recurring themes of exile, identity and a quest for integration emerging again and again. I suppose this has to do with my own history. I was born in a community that was essentially a utopian experiment, and in this experimental society children were separated from their parents at birth and lived in communal children's houses. Furthermore, the kibbutz itself was newly founded when I was born, and its members were acutely aware that the land had belonged to Palestinians, now displaced, only seven years earlier. In addition, we were told that we were surrounded by a nameless, faceless 'enemy' against which we had to be on guard. When I was four, and again when I was seven, the family moved to Montreal—first on an extended visit, and then for good. I had to adjust to a very different culture, and I found the transition difficult. I lost my language, Hebrew, to a large extent, and that loss of fluency remains painful to this day. Like many Israelis who became citizens of other countries, I felt that I didn't entirely belong to any place.

"As a child growing up in a highly idealistic environment, I was taught to care about the weak and the oppressed. Today many former kibbutz children are involved in human rights and do the sort of work I do. I find it unbearable to stand by when I see suffering, and in Israel I feel it is my duty to do something to help, because I am part of that reality. When I work on behalf of Palestinians at checkpoints I am deeply saddened, and this is true not only of the other Israeli women I work with but of many of the soldiers, an increasing number of whom refuse to serve in the Occupied Territories. I see a reality many Jews and Israelis don't get to see, and if they did, they would be more determined to work towards ending the Occupation of the West Bank and the Gaza Strip. I have to remain hopeful that peace is possible, and indeed I think there is enormous potential for the two nations, Palestinian and Israeli, to get along. I dream of the day when we will be having soccer matches with one another.

"Apart from my political work, what has given me a sense of direction and purpose in my life are my daughter and of course my writing. Raising my daughter has been a deep and glorious experience and has taught me so much about myself and about the strange thing we call life. As for writing, I have seen myself as a story-teller since I was a very young child. I always knew that I would spend my life trying to capture in words what goes on beneath the surface. This has made me insatiably curious. There is almost nothing on this planet that does not interest me in one way or another. I believe that ultimately the only things that can save us as a race are compassion and a sense of humour. Compassion will keep us from destroying ourselves and our planet. A sense of humour will keep us from despairing as we struggle against all the obstacles in our way."

———————————

In the late 1940s Ravel's parents, who were originally from Montreal, helped found a Marxist collective, Kibbutz Sasa, after having moved to the Middle East as members of the Zionist youth movement Hashomer Hatza'ir. In 1955 Ravel was born on the kibbutz. "Edeet is an archaic word, no longer in use, and never in common use, even in ancient times. It is an adjective used to describe

arable land," she explained in an interview posted on the HarperCollins Web site. "But Israeli parents just choose that name because they like the sound of it. My theory is that it is a version of Edith, adopted by Europeans who came to Israel, but I can't prove it!"

Ravel, who has a brother and a sister, showed early promise as a writer: at 16, back in Montreal, she won a Canadian short-story competition; the piece was subsequently anthologized. In 1973, after completing high school, Ravel returned to Israel to attend Hebrew University, in Jerusalem, where she remained for the next five years, completing her bachelor's and master's degrees in English literature. Returning to Canada, Ravel acquired an additional master's degree in creative writing; she later obtained an M.A. and Ph.D. in Jewish studies from McGill University, in Montreal. Recalling her academic work, Ravel told Bill Gladstone for the *Forward* (October 31, 2003), "I went to Israel to study English literature and I went to McGill University to study Jewish Studies. I did it all upside down." In 1981 Ravel began teaching. She gave courses on the Holocaust, biblical exegesis, and Hebrew literature at McGill; she taught creative writing at Concordia University; and she was an English instructor at John Abbott College. (Both Concordia and John Abbott are located in Montreal, as well.)

Ravel's debut work, *Lovers: A Midrash,* was published in 1994 by a Montreal press and won the Norma Epstein National Writing Award; it was subsequently translated into Hebrew. "Part of the Jewish heritage," Iris Winston explained in an article for the *Ottawa Citizen* (March 19, 1995), "the Midrash is a way of exploring biblical texts by using one story to explain another. Beginning as oral literature—learned conversations or parables told by men in synagogues and study houses—the Midrash was eventually transcribed." Ravel made extensive use of this form in the feminist-tinged prose poem *Lovers: A Midrash*, which offers a modern interpretation of Solomon's Song of Songs. "What attracted me [to the form] is that the midrash looks at life as a puzzle," Ravel told Charlie Fidelman for the Montreal *Gazette* (February 9, 1995). "I didn't want readers to have everything spelled out for them." Using the midrash, Ravel examines "spiritual, parental, passionate and obsessive love, as well as the absence of love and love for one's vocation," according to Fidelman. Among the characters introduced are a Jewish woman who becomes enamored with an Arab student, British men who respond to a personal ad promising amorous attention in return for a night on the town, and a rabbinical student with homoerotic inclinations. *Lovers: A Midrash* won considerable praise for its ambitious format: "Bringing [the midrash] to bear on the theme of love is a master stroke (apart from death, what subject is more ultimately hard to pin down?)," Carol A. Davison wrote for the Montreal *Gazette* (April 15, 1995). "Doing so by way of the

Song of Solomon, a biblical text that has been alternately interpreted as an allegorical celebration of God's relationship with the church and a woman's sexual-spiritual love of a man, is craftier still." While some reviewers felt Ravel's use of the midrash, with its fragmented and episodic structure, was not always successful, the book's overall critical reception was highly positive: in a letter posted on Amazon.com, the esteemed Israeli novelist A. B. Yehoshua wrote that Ravel had "succeeded in assimilating the midrashim [plural form of midrash] of the past and in transforming them into a unique spiritual apprehension of the modern world. This is a remarkable accomplishment. Even more remarkable is that your [Ravel's] midrash is written with humour and compassion." The novelist Elizabeth Spencer, whose comments appear on the book's cover, wrote, "*Lovers: A Midrash* is an intriguing experiment, part myth, part aphorism, laced through with recurrent cries and episodes of private emotion. In drawing on her own passions, Edeet Ravel evokes passionate echoes from the reader."

Ravel next prepared the screenplay for the 1998 Joyce Borenstein documentary *One Divided by Two: Kids and Divorce.* Borenstein filmed interviews with youngsters whose parents had divorced, and *One Divided by Two* is composed of clips from the interviews, as well as a series of animated segments written by Ravel, "including one that looks at the complicated world of stepfamilies by creating an entangled family tree," as Tanya Davies noted for *Maclean's* (August 17, 1998). The film became available to schools in September 1998 and was aired on Canada's Vision-TV in December 1998.

Ravel had been writing for nearly three decades and had completed eight novels before she sent *Ten Thousand Lovers,* the one she considered her best, to publishers. Headline, a British company, discovered the work among a heap of unsolicited manuscripts and published it in 2003. It became a best-seller in Canada and was nominated for the Koret Jewish Book Award and the 2003 Governor General's Award, Canada's highest literary honor. The Toronto *Globe and Mail* named it one of the top-ten books of the year; *Quill & Quire* ranked it among the year's five top novels; and Hadassah, the Women's Zionist Organization of America, placed it in the top four. Ravel's much-acclaimed and widely translated novel details the doomed romance between an inexperienced young linguistics student named Lily and Ami, a conflicted interrogator for the Israeli military; the title refers to the 10,000 lives lost to date in the violence that has plagued Israel since its founding, in 1948. The couple meet when Ami offers Lily a ride as she hitchhikes from Jerusalem to Tel Aviv; their romance quickly blossoms and, after Lily becomes pregnant, they marry. The characters, Ravel said in an interview with Kinneret Globerman posted on the JBooks Web site, are

drawn in part from her own life: "Most of Lily's Jerusalem adventures are based on actual experiences I had. Ami resembles my first husband, Yaron, in some ways." Disturbed by his job yet afraid to quit for fear of being replaced with a less humane interrogator, Ami believes the occupation of the West Bank and Gaza Strip is corrupting Israel's soul. He ultimately decides to resign his post. Fatefully, he agrees to conduct one last interrogation, with tragic results.

Lily's numerous digressions on Hebrew etymology are included in the narrative; Hebrew came into conversational use only in the late 19th century, and consequently new words had to be invented to reflect the realities of the evolving world. "[Ravel's] etymological forays provide fascinating, insightful glimpses into the development of the Israeli psyche in the brief history of the state's existence," Nancy Richler wrote. While some critics felt that Ravel's supposed political agenda was, at times, intrusive, the work received significant praise. Remarking on the political gulf separating many Israelis, particularly on the subject of the Palestinian territories, Bill Gladstone remarked for the *Forward* (October 31, 2003, on-line): "Like a self-enclosed world, [Ravel's] book is a thing of integrity, true to itself and so deeply felt that it somehow manages to bridge the gap." A reporter for *Ha'aretz* (March 15, 2003) similarly stated, "Ravel's strength lies not only in fantasizing about the beauties of Israel, but in allowing the menacing and the terrible to become part of her portrait of Israeli life. This is a wonderful book, compelling not only for its literary merit but because it expands our grasp of what 'Israeli' means."

Look for Me (2004), the second book of the Tel Aviv trilogy, chronicles the exploits of Dana Hillman, an Israeli photographer and peace activist. For the past 11 years, Hillman has been searching for her husband, who mysteriously disappeared from the hospital after being badly burned in an accident. When Hillman finally receives a clue to his whereabouts, she sets out to find him. In the shadow of the success of *Ten Thousand Lovers*, Ravel's second installment proved disappointing to some reviewers. "There's something about *Look for Me*, and the portrait of Dana Hillman in particular, that doesn't quite work," Robin McGrath wrote for the Newfoundland, Canada, *St. John's Telegram* (August 22, 2004). "It's trying too hard, or something. Dana is simply too naive, too gifted, too loveable, too stupid. It fails to ring true."

The final installment in the trilogy, *A Wall of Light*, begins: "I am Sonya Vronsky, professor of mathematics at Tel Aviv University, and this is the story of a day in late August. On this remarkable day, I kissed a student, pursued a lover, found my father, and left my brother." Deaf since the age of 12, Sonya, now 32, spends part of her remarkable day trying to pass through barriers separating part of Israel from a Palestinian area in order to find the lover she mentions at the novel's beginning, an Arab taxi driver. Ravel also weaves into the novel excerpts from a diary written by Sonya's nephew during the 1980s and early 1990s and letters, dating from 1957, sent by her mother to what was then the Soviet Union. Though *A Wall of Light* was nominated for the Giller Prize (a top Canadian book award), many critics offered the book only tempered praise. Describing the novel as "a seriously flawed work," Michael Greenstein remarked for the Toronto *National Post* (December 17, 2005): "For all the novel's pleasures, there is scant thickness of thought, and its similes run thin in the absence of more sophisticated metaphor." Both Greenstein and Nancy Wigston, in a review for the *Toronto Star* (October 2, 2005), singled out Sonya's attachment to the Arab driver for particular criticism, but Wigston lauded Ravel's work overall, writing: "Skillfully juggling the weight of the multi-layered past with the bright intensity of the present, Ravel has written a book that shimmers with suspense, mystery, and wit."

In 2007 Ravel published a series of books for young adults about a girl named Pauline, who retells the story of her life to give it the drama of her favorite books. Each of the books is titled *Pauline, Btw* and is subtitled, in the order in which it appears: *The Thrilling Life of Pauline de Lammermoor*, *The Mysterious Adventures of Pauline Bovary*, *The Secret Journey of Pauline Siddhartha*, and *The Trials and Tribulations of Pauline Luxemburg*. Ravel also has a novel forthcoming, "Tell Tony We Miss Him." Set in Montreal in the 1960s and 1970s, the novel tells the story of four teenagers whose parents survived the Holocaust. Ravel has also, in preparation for the French translation of *Look for Me*, returned to the novel and made a number of substantial revisions, including altering the ending. (The revisions will appear in English in future editions of the novel, and the revised ending is currently available on Ravel's Web site.)

Ravel is active in the peace movement in Israel. "We are Jews and we feel that all the Jewish values that we believe in are being destroyed by the occupation," Monique Beaudin quoted Ravel as saying, in the Montreal *Gazette* (April 17, 2002). Ravel describes her peace work, which sometimes involves negotiating between Israeli soldiers and Palestinians at checkpoints, as "very traumatic," according to Pat Donnelly for the Montreal *Gazette* (October 21, 2003). "You spend most of your time trying not to cry."

Twice divorced, Ravel has a daughter, Larissa, by her second husband. She and her daughter live in Guelph, Ontario. Despite her dual citizenship, Ravel told Globerman, "I see myself as an Israeli who ended up living in Canada by accident. Audrey Thomas [a Canadian writer] once said, 'My branches are in Canada, but not my roots.'"

—P.B.M.

Suggested Reading: *Canadian Press* Oct. 20, 2003; Edeet Ravel's Web site; JBooks Web site; *Maclean's* p49 Aug. 17, 1998; (Montreal) *Gazette* F p4 Feb. 9, 1995, H p3 Apr. 15, 1995, A p1 Apr. 17, 2002, I p5 Mar. 8, 2003, D p1 Oct. 21, 2003; *New York Times Book Review* (on-line) Feb. 15, 2004; *Ottawa Citizen* B p4 Mar. 19, 1995; (Toronto) *Globe and Mail* D p15 Mar. 1, 2003; *Toronto Star* D p6 Oct. 2, 2005

Selected Books: *Lovers: A Midrash*, 1994; *Ten Thousand Lovers*, 2003; *Look for Me*, 2004; *A Wall of Light*, 2005

Ray, Jeanne

Aug. 1937– Novelist

A registered nurse for more than 40 years, Jeanne Ray did not consider becoming a novelist until shortly after her 60th birthday. One day while standing in line at her grocery store, she encountered a magazine rack displaying the blaring headlines "Great Sex at 20, 30, 40!" and "How to Be Fabulous at Fifty." Yet, Ray observed, none of the covers seemed to speak to her age group. "I thought, why isn't there a Great Sex at 60?" she explained to Barbara McMahon for the London *Evening Standard* (August 25, 2000). "Aren't we entitled to a love life or are we supposed to be too thrilled about taking our grandchildren to swim practice even to think about sex? I have never found birthdays depressing before, but I really felt I was being ignored. I was angry that somehow society had forgotten I was still an intelligent, attractive, sexual human being." To overcome her dismay, Ray set about writing a love story centered around two 60-something characters. The result, *Julie and Romeo* (2000), which is a loose comic re-invention of William Shakespeare's *Romeo and Juliet*, became a surprise hit that year, topping the *New York Times* best-seller list and selling more than 500,000 copies; it has since been translated into six languages and optioned for film by Barbra Streisand's production company. Ray, whose daughter is Ann Patchett, the award-winning author of such novels as *The Magician's Assistant* (1997) and *Bel Canto* (2001), followed up her debut novel with *Step-Ball-Change* (2002), *Eat Cake* (2003), and the sequel *Julie and Romeo Get Lucky* (2005).

Jeanne Ray was born Jeanne Wilkinson in August 1937, the daughter of a cabinetmaker and a homemaker with only an eighth-grade education. Ray spent her childhood in California, where she dreamed of becoming a writer and venturing off to Paris. However, as she recalled to Rosemary Herbert for the *Boston Herald* (June 9, 2000), "My parents said that was a ridiculous thing for a young woman to embark upon." "The practical thing to do was to become a nurse," she continued, "which I deluded myself into thinking was a romantic career. It was a question of wearing black and going to Paris to write or wearing white and taking care of broken bodies." At the age of 21, Ray had a whirlwind romance with Frank Ray, a police officer. The couple married after dating for only two months and eventually had two children. However, after 10 years of marriage, as Ray told Herbert, "Finally we just outgrew each other. I moved to Nashville [Tennessee] for a change, and my second husband was the doctor I worked for." Ray's second marriage lasted for 20 years but again resulted in divorce. "I was 49 [at the time of the divorce] and my 50th birthday was grim. I'd been taught love is for the young and I thought I'd die alone," Ray told Peter Sheridan for the Tennessee Express (September 22, 2000). "Then I met Darrell, my third husband—and the passion was still there." Ray married Darrell, a retired Presbyterian minister, in the early 1990s. Of her challenge in finding long-lasting love, she told McMahon, "I hate the fact that I have been married three times because it makes me sound flighty." Nevertheless, she asserted that her present husband is "the one, absolutely, that I want to spend the rest of my life with. But had I met him when he was 20, I wouldn't have appreciated him."

Ray had always enjoyed her career as a nurse, yet throughout her life she continued writing, most often in journals and stories that she kept private. When at age 60 she began feeling alienated by today's youth-oriented culture, Ray began pouring her feelings out on her computer each night. "There was fire in my belly," she told McMahon, "and at first I just wanted to get it all off my chest, but then it evolved into Julie and Romeo. I thought people in their sixties needed a love story. The world is such a youth and beauty-oriented society that anyone born before the Second World War is considered aged and decrepit. Our problems and our joys are not the concerns of folks at large. But we can be in love, we are still sexual creatures, we are not just dried-up old beans." Before long, Ray had composed 150 pages of what she thought would make an inspirational story for older people. With much trepidation, she showed her first draft to her novelist daughter. "That was so scary," Ray recounted to Deborah Norville in an interview broadcast on the CBS Early Show (July 9, 2002). "I just can't begin to tell you. It's scarier than being on television . . . because I knew she would be very honest with me . . . and I was afraid she would say, 'Mom, keep your day job.'" But, as Patchett recalled in that same interview, "I knew it was going to be fine. I mean, we had talked about it. We'd talked about the plot in the story. I was anxious to see it, and it immediately was clear to me that this was something that was not only good but really saleable." Patchett helped Ray edit the manuscript before she passed it on to her own agent, who was equally pleased with the material.

The agent put the book up for auction and promptly sold it to the Harmony Books division of Random House for a six-figure sum. "My new editor called to say she's so happy to have the book," Ray reminisced to Leslie Garcia for the Chicago Tribune (November 10, 2000). "Then, 15 minutes later, she called and said Barbra Streisand had optioned it [for film]. That was quite a day."

Julie and Romeo (2000), set in Somerville, Massachusetts, tells the story of two 60-something florists who own rival shops in their town—the Jewish Julie Roseman, who is recently divorced after 35 years of marriage, and the Catholic Romeo Cacciamani, a widowed, Italian father of six. When Julie and Romeo both attend a small-business trade show in Boston, they find themselves falling passionately in love—despite a long-standing feud between their two families. (Years earlier the two protagonists had actually thwarted an attempted elopement between Romeo's son and Julie's daughter.) The tale takes a number of comic twists as the couple's respective offspring and Romeo's 90-year-old mother go to extreme lengths to sabotage the blossoming relationship. Ray includes a number of references to Shakespeare's Romeo and Juliet, drawing, for example, a parallel between the tomb where Romeo and Juliet often met and the refrigerated room where the modern-day Romeo and Julie keep their flowers. The novel was a surprise hit. Kim Hubbard wrote for People (December 18, 2000), "It's a pretty cornball idea, recasting Shakespeare's tragedy as a tale of two 60ish florists. But in the hands of first-time novelist Ray, . . . it works amazingly well." Hubbard concluded, "Wise, winsome and refreshingly optimistic about late-in-life love, Julie and Romeo does the Bard proud." In a laudatory review for Victoria (February 2001), Michele Slung opined, "Jeanne Ray, whether she's tangling or untangling the threads of her main characters' moonstruck, star-crossed lives, has produced a novel that manages to be comic, sexy and heartwarming, all at the same time. While she clearly adores her modern-day Montagues and Capulets, she's also wonderfully tough-minded about them, recognizing how people would sooner lose sight of the most important thing—love—than willingly give up control."

Despite the overwhelming success of Julie and Romeo, Ray felt apprehensive about tackling her second novel, Step-Ball-Change. For help and encouragement she often turned to Patchett. "It's funny," Patchett told Sherryl Connelly for the New York Daily News (June 5, 2002), "but I feel like I have a 16-year-old daughter. I am always giving her advice, which she pointedly does not take. Then she comes back and says, 'Oh, you were right.'" From the outset, however, Ray knew the message she wanted to convey in her second novel. "I wanted to write about how, if a marriage is solid, two people can work through things," she explained. "Of course, the book is also about adjusting and adapting to change."

Step-Ball-Change, which takes its title from a tap-dance step that moves the dancer forward and then backward, presents the story of Caroline McSwain, a 60ish wife and mother of four adult children, who is also a dance instructor in her hometown of Raleigh, North Carolina. When Caroline's only daughter, Kay, a 30-year-old public defender, announces that she is engaged to Trey Bennett, of the town's most influential bloodline, the family begins preparations for an extravagant, 1,000-guest wedding. Complicating matters, Kay might still be in love with Jack, a charming district attorney. Meanwhile, Caroline's temperamental sister Taffy, recently separated from her husband, moves into the house (which is undergoing extensive renovations) for an extended visit with her ankle-biting dog. Caroline's life spins out of control as she works to juggle the demands of her dance studio and her family; yet as Jeff Zaleski wrote for *Publishers Weekly* (May 6, 2002), "Her love for her family helps her to keep things on track."

Ray herself had always entertained dreams of becoming a dancer, so her lead character allowed her to connect with one of her own passions. "I think [Caroline] came from me," she told Stephanie Swilley for *BookPage* (May 2002, online). "I'm sure she hasn't made as many mistakes as I have made, and probably did a better job in many ways, but the basis [is] pretty much me."

Step-Ball-Change received mixed reviews, yet most critics praised the light, comical, and heartwarming elements of the story. Cheryl Ossala wrote for *Dance Magazine* (November 2002), "Grand themes—acceptance, self-knowledge, love—and Ray's amusing turns of phrase allowed me to forgive her less-than-grand plot and two-dimensional characters." Jeff Zaleski added, "Although Ray allows the sap level to rise a little too high as the inevitable picture-perfect ending rolls around, she has a gift for lively dialogue that makes the characters (Caroline and Tom especially) snap into place."

Ray's novel *Eat Cake* presents another story of domestic commotion; it centers around Ruth Nash, an aging housewife who loves to bake. In the book's opening lines, Ruth declares, "This is a story of how my life was saved by cake," as quoted by Tamara Butler for *Library Journal* (April 15, 2003). Ruth, whose teenaged daughter is perpetually moody and whose son has just left for college, finds herself in the midst of a family crisis when her husband, Sam, loses his job as a hospital administrator and has difficulty obtaining another. In addition, Ruth learns that her estranged father, Guy, a nomadic lounge singer, has broken both of his wrists and needs a place to recover. Despite the fact that Ruth's mother, Hollis, already lives in the home, Ruth takes in Guy and is soon dealing with her parents' acrimonious relationship. As Sam struggles with his joblessness, Ruth gets an idea— to make money by selling her cakes—that becomes a family effort. The novel, which comes complete

with the fictional Ruth's own cake recipes, was generally well received. "While it might be said that this is a predictable and undemanding book," Danise Hoover wrote for *Booklist*, as quoted on Amazon.com, "it is also a comforting one, and perhaps signals a new genre that might be called 'domestic fantasy.'"

In 2005 Ray published *Julie and Romeo Get Lucky*, a sequel to her first novel. Early on in the story, Romeo throws his back out while making love to Julie and consequently spends the rest of the novel in bed. Most of the action revolves around Julie's 8-year-old granddaughter, Sarah, who is obsessed with playing the lottery and watching a DVD of the 1970s version of *Willy Wonka & the Chocolate Factory*.

Although Ray briefly retired from nursing before the publication of her second novel, she told Connelly that she missed the sense of community she had gained from working with patients. "I got really depressed not being part of a family of patients," she said. "So I went back to work one day a week and that solved all my problems." Ray currently lives in Nashville, Tennessee, with her third husband, Darryl, with whom she shares 10 grandchildren. Speaking of her newfound career as a novelist, she told McMahon that she hopes it can serve as an inspiration for other aging men and women. "Don't waste time," she offered. "I never thought at this age I'd be an author, so this is the time to pursue artistic things, travel or take up a hobby you always dreamed about."

—K.D.

Suggested Reading: *Boston Herald* A p42 June 9, 2000, A p22 June 16, 2002; *Chicago Tribune* News p7 Nov. 10, 2000; *Raleigh News and Observer* C p1 June 24, 2002

Selected Books: *Julie and Romeo*, 2000; *Step-Ball-Change*, 2002; *Eat Cake*, 2003; *Julie and Romeo Get Lucky*, 2005

Rayfiel, Thomas

1958– Novelist; short-story writer

In praising *Colony Girl* (1999), the second and perhaps most well-received of Thomas Rayfiel's novels, Susie Linfield commented for the *Los Angeles Times* (October 7, 1999) that the work's "protagonist and narrator, Eve, is utterly original, indeed sui generis. Yet at every moment, Eve is absolutely credible; she has all the qualities of an authentic person, albeit one you have never met before. Eve shows us just what a writer with a truthful imagination can achieve; she is the triumph at the heart of this marvelous new novel." Rayfiel's other novels include his debut work, *Split-Levels* (1994), as well as his two sequels to

Thomas Rayfiel

Colony Girl, *Eve in the City* (2003) and *Parallel Play* (2007). Rayfiel has also authored a serial novel, *Lutwidge Finch*, for *Zingmagazine*, and his short fiction has appeared in such journals as the *Antioch Review* and *Grand Street*.

Born in 1958, Rayfiel graduated from Grinnell College, in Iowa, in 1980. He worked as a screenwriter before embarking on a career as a novelist. *Split-Levels*, published in 1994 by Simon & Schuster, chronicles the return of Allen Stanley to his suburban childhood home, where his father has recently been discovered dead in the bathtub, his wrists slashed. Allen, who is in his 30s, steadfastly avoided going home for years; as he now takes charge of his deceased father's affairs, his homecoming forces him to confront his own troubled childhood—including the unexplained disappearance, when he was just a boy, of his older sister. Unfortunately, Allen's efforts to come to terms with the past become increasingly complicated as the police begin to suspect him of having a hand in his father's death, while his childhood friends bring up earlier rumors that his father was a pedophile. Describing the work as an "intriguing first novel," Marilyn Stasio wrote for the *New York Times Book Review* (May 29, 1994): "Mr. Rayfiel has a little trouble keeping the hero from turning into a zombie. But his bizarre tormentors are palpable enough, and there is something seductively malignant about the surreal suburban landscape through which they wander." Reena Jana, for the *San Francisco Review of Books* (June/July 1994), similarly described *Split-Levels* as a "wonderfully edgy first novel," in which "Rayfiel articulates the American suburb with an eye so exact, so clinical, and so critical that he

transforms Everyman's life, fantasies, and nightmares from the so real into the surreal." Rayfiel, Jana continued, "has a gift for catering to the short attention span of a TV viewer and succeeds brilliantly in building suspense, creating surprise, and recreating the rhythms of real-world speech."

Eve, the teen-aged protagonist of Rayfiel's second novel, the coming-of-age story *Colony Girl*, lives with her mother in the Colony, the rural-Iowa commune of a religious cult. Gordon, the sect's charismatic leader, is an amoral charlatan who may also be Eve's father. Gordon forces those in the Colony to lead a monastic existence without electricity or other comforts, while he grows wealthy and indulges himself with television and prescription opiates. Richard Eder, for the *New York Times* (September 29, 1999), observed, "Eve is explorer and adventurer in transit between two countries: the Colony, once familiar and now, to her maturing eyes, turned foreign; and the world just outside, which she seizes on with the wacky lucidity of a bright visitor from very far away." After sneaking out of the Colony and drinking too much at a local party, Eve is assisted by Joey Biswanger, with whom she becomes enamored—although she later falls for Joey's father, Herb. As the story continues, Gordon decides to marry Eve's best friend, while permitting Eve herself to work in town as a highway flagman. Eve soon uncovers Gordon's corrupt relationship with town officials and threatens to blow the whistle. According to Eder, *Colony Girl* "is truly about . . . adolescent discovery and the corkscrew byways that lead to it." "The writing in *Colony Girl* is bright and knowing, without being arch," Lynna Williams commented for the *Chicago Tribune* (October 3, 1999). "It is especially strong in its descriptions of the physical, including the Iowa landscape and Eve's sexual explorations." Overall, Williams concluded, "Rayfiel has written a charming and disturbing novel; the fullness of the imaginative portrait of the Colony can only add to our understanding of group belief and adolescent girls." According to Eder, "[It] is the titupping flow of Eve's speculative and wonderfully discordant narration" that binds the book together. "It is a stream that makes her mishaps and odd victories into a journey and not just sights along the way. No Mississippi runs through Arhat, Iowa, but here as in *Huckleberry Finn* the real river is the narrator's voice. What a voice it is."

An older, wiser Eve resurfaces in Rayfiel's third novel, *Eve in the City*. Now 17, Eve has left the Colony and Iowa behind her and taken up residence in New York City. She meets Viktor, an immigrant from Mingrelia (a region of the former Soviet Republic of Georgia), at a coffee shop and obtains a job at his rather unsavory bar. After work early one morning Eve witnesses an apparent stabbing and reports the incident to the police. The detective charged with investigating the crime develops a paternal attachment to Eve; she, meanwhile, falls for a painter she meets at an art gallery. Eve begins searching on her own for the stabbing victim and soon uncovers more than she bargained for. "[Eve] is quite as splendid as in the first book, and this gives *Eve in the City* moments of acute, astonished delight," Richard Eder observed for the *New York Times Book Review* (September 21, 2003). "And certainly Rayfiel has a grittily haunting feel for New York." However, Eder faulted Rayfiel's development of the work's secondary characters, remarking, "The elaborate complications that whirl these figures about manage only to turn them into fantastical doodles, Wonderland figures serving to befuddle Eve's Alice. So do a couple of splashy hyperplots." Moreover, Eder added, "the author can be as lost in New York as his character is. The adventures that test her and the people she comes up against have an artificially constructed quality; they are willed wonders." A reviewer for *Publishers Weekly* (September 22, 2003) offered a similarly mixed critique, remarking, "Improbable encounters are necessary to advance the plot toward a conclusion that strains credibility; at times the narration is choppy and the chronology cloudy." However, the reviewer continued, "What shines through is Rayfiel's knowledge of, and affection for, the public and peripheral worlds of New York City."

Rayfiel's fourth novel, *Parallel Play*, returns to the story of Eve. Now 27 and living in Brooklyn, she finds herself married to an older doctor, Harvey Gabriel, and thrust into motherhood. Taking care of her seven-month-old daughter, Ann, proves more onerous than joyful to Eve, and her troubles are compounded when she runs into her ex-boyfriend Mark. She also begins to suspect that her pediatrician is trying to steal away her husband. A reviewer for *People* (January 22, 2007) called the novel "a fast and feisty read" and praised Rayfiel's writing as "full of energy."

Carolyn See, in a review for the *Washington Post* (January 12, 2007), complained about the narrow lives led by Eve and *Parallel Play*'s other characters. "No young woman can exist in a plot with just a husband and a baby," See wrote, "so wouldn't you know it, right on Page 4, along comes the invidious ex-boyfriend, popping up serendipitously at the playground." See agreed, however, with Rayfiel's argument, presented in a reader's guide appended to the book, that American women are given a highly idealized, possibly even false, idea of motherhood. "The act of giving birth doesn't automatically endow every woman with a full-blown maternal instinct—far from it," See wrote. "You can be the sweetest person in the world and be felled by postpartum depression and a disinclination to have much to do with your demanding baby."

Rayfiel and his wife, Claire, a potter, reside in the New York City borough of Brooklyn. They have two children.

—P.B.M.

Suggested Reading: *Chicago Tribune* C p5 Oct. 3, 1999; *Los Angeles Times* E p3 Oct. 7, 1999; *New York Times* E p8 Sep. 29, 1999; *New York Times Book Review* p15 May 29, 1994, p15 Sep. 21, 2003; *Publishers Weekly* p85 Sep. 22, 2003; *San Francisco Review of Books* p45 June/July 1994

Selected Books: *Split-Levels*, 1994; *Colony Girl*, 1999; *Eve in the City*, 2003; *Parallel Play*, 2007

Anna Wilcox/Courtesy of Random House

Redhill, Michael

June 12, 1966– Poet; novelist; short-story writer; playwright

Unlike writers who work in a single genre throughout their careers, Michael Redhill has found success alternately as a poet, playwright, novelist, and short-story writer. In 2001, when he was already a recognized figure in Canadian poetry and drama, his first novel, *Martin Sloane*, was published to great acclaim and was presented with both the Amazon.ca/Books in Canada First Novel Award and the Commonwealth Writers' Prize for a first novel from Canada or the Caribbean; his first collection of short stories, *Fidelity* (2003), was also widely praised. Redhill has suggested that the recognition he received is evidence of Canada's blossoming sense of literary identity. "It's a very good time to be a first-time novelist in Canada, it's a very good time to be a writer in Canada, it's a very good time to be a reader in Canada," Redhill said at the Amazon.ca/Books in Canada awards ceremony, as quoted by James Cowan for the Toronto *National Post* (October 2, 2002). "This is

an early stage in our cultural-literary history where we're reading ourselves first. We're not waiting for confirmation from outside our borders that what we're doing is worthwhile, and I think that's a very important stage in our development."

Michael Redhill was born in Baltimore, Maryland, on June 12, 1966 to Marshall and Linda (Strasberg) Redhill. His family later moved to Canada, and he attended high school in Toronto. He returned to the U.S. for the academic year 1984–85 to study at Indiana University, in Bloomington, but was unhappy there. He then transferred to York University, in Toronto, where he studied film production and screenwriting, before transferring, in 1989, to the University of Toronto, from which he received his bachelor's degree in English, in 1992.

Redhill first began publishing poetry in 1985, when one of his pieces was accepted by *Poetry Toronto*. Other acceptances quickly followed, in such periodicals as *Excalibur*, *Quarry*, *Toronto Life*, and *Capilano Review*, among others. Redhill's first major poetry collection, *Impromptu Feats of Balance*, appeared in 1990, a year after his chapbook *Temporary Captives*. In the early 1990s Redhill, while continuing to write and publish poetry, also saw several of his plays produced, including *Be Frank* (1991), *The Hanging Gardens of Willowdale* (1992), *Heretics* (1992), *Information for Visitors to Warsaw* (1993), and *The Monkey Cage* (1993).

Central to Redhill's second collection of poetry, *Lake Nora Arms* (1993), is a feeling of nostalgia for places and people long gone. (Interestingly, while there is a Nora Lake, known for its abundant trout, in northwest Ontario, Lake Nora Arms is also the name of a reportedly disreputable apartment complex near Indiana University.) In a critique of the collection for *Quill & Quire* (December 1993), a reviewer noted: "*Lake Nora Arms* . . . shows Redhill already building and expanding upon an impressive early talent. . . . Redhill is at his best . . . when the straightforward 'I' of [a] poem surges forward in undeniable authenticity and seems to soar from the page. Such moments certainly make you want to read more by this fine young poet."

Following the success of *Lake Nora Arms*, Redhill's poetry was included in two anthologies published in 1995: *Breathing Fire* and *The Last Word*. In 1996 he served as the editor for *Blues and True Concussions*, a poetry anthology, and also wrote two theatrical pieces: *Lake Nora Arms*, a dramatization of his poetry collection, and *Building Jerusalem*. Redhill's third collection of poetry, *Asphodel*, was published in 1997.

Building Jerusalem is one of Redhill's most frequently mounted plays and became, in 2001, the first of them to be published in book form. The play—about a group of wealthy Victorians welcoming the 20th century on New Year's Eve 1899—struck a chord with many viewers, who saw parallels as their own century gave way to a new one. In the *Toronto Star* (January 10, 2000), Vit

Wagner remarked: "The emerging portrait is of a society ruled by formality, even at play. The insistence on propriety is deftly captured in writer Michael Redhill's mimicry of Victorian banter, which is sometimes cutting but seldom uncouth. It all seems very quaint at times, but a deeper purpose emerges. [Director Ross] Manson and company peel back the veneer of decorum to show how the violence and dislocation of the 20th century is contained in the attitudes espoused by some of the characters. Imaginatively conceived and smartly performed, *Building Jerusalem* is a timely cautionary reminder that the future is not always what we expect."

In 2000 Redhill's play *Doubt* debuted in a production directed by Leah Cherniak. The protagonist, an author of a series of mysteries, has writer's block. While he is working in his apartment one day, a mysterious woman comes out of his bedroom; at the same time characters from his current novel appear and attempt to perform what he's written thus far. In a review for the *Toronto Star* (May 12, 2000), Robert Crew had a mixed reaction to the play: "There's no doubt about it. *Doubt* is an engaging piece of theatrical whimsy. . . . It's fun, in a virtuoso kind of way, but without any of the depth associated with a similar riff by someone such as Tom Stoppard. . . . Despite some inventive staging and some genuinely funny moments, one doubts that *Doubt* has very much to say."

The publication of Redhill's first novel, *Martin Sloane*, was met with a considerable amount of fanfare in his native country. Redhill had proven himself an adept editor, poet, and playwright, and many critics eagerly awaited his first novel, to see if the writer was similarly skilled in long fiction. The novel, which took Redhill a decade to write and was revised more than 12 times, told the story of Jolene Iolas, a college student in upstate New York, who falls in love with an older Irish artist, the Martin Sloane of the title. One night Martin vanishes, never to be heard from again, and Jolene come to terms with his desertion.

Martin Sloane received solidly favorable reviews. Writing for the *Vancouver Sun* (May 5, 2001), Annabel Lyon proclaimed: "Redhill is neither a vague nor an obscure writer. His turns of phrase often combine solid, well-hewn familiarity with leavening flashes of wit or beauty." Brian Bethune noted for *Maclean's* (May 14, 2001): "For a first novel, even one polished through a dozen drafts over 10 years, *Martin Sloane* is remarkably assured. . . . Redhill's years of effort are apparent in more than his seamless prose. That craftsmanship, together with his understanding of basic human nature, allowed him to pull off the memorable character of Jolene, whose life is shattered when Martin gets up one night and simply disappears, forever." Todd Pruzman, in the *Washington Post* (August 25, 2002), agreed, writing: "Like Martin's enigmatic sculpture, *Martin Sloane* unveils itself with an offhand disquiet that is easily overlooked but, once revealed, very difficult to dislodge."

The novel's success ensured that Redhill's next collection of poetry, *Light-Crossing* (2001), received a great deal of press. In a review for the *Vancouver Sun* (April 21, 2001), Mark Cochrane offered this assessment: "Smart but not cerebral, rarely sentimental, and attentive to pleasure and loss in equal measure, *Light-crossing* is a gorgeous, big-hearted book that transcribes the carnal minutiae of being alert and alive, lustful and loving, muscular and sad. It is everything contemporary lyric poetry can be, but almost never is." A critic writing for *Quill & Quire* (June 2001) agreed, noting: "Despite the span of time it took to write the poems—Redhill admits some were composed as early as 1988—the book is a remarkably unified collection, held together by a strong sense of place and a gradually evolving consciousness that begins with meditations on one-night stands and ends up basking in the exhausting pleasures of fatherhood."

Redhill's short-story collection *Fidelity* features a divorced couple trying to maintain a semblance of love in their relationship, a married man obsessed with a young co-worker, a father unable to deal with his teenage daughter's sexuality, and a thrice-married man whose current wife wants him to get a vasectomy, among other characters. The collection was widely praised. Kevin Canfield, in an assessment for the *Atlanta Journal-Constitution* (May 2, 2004), called it "evocative and uncommonly wise," and noted: "Like the finest practitioners of his art, Redhill understands that most of us are more alike than we'd care to admit. His slim book of stories examines these commonalities with uncommon wisdom." In the *Atlantic Monthly* (April 2004), Benjamin Schwarz opined: "Ambiguous, undramatic, attentive to detail (the bantering sarcasm that settles on a divorced couple's conversation; an office manager's meddlesome tone), these stories will inevitably be described as 'quiet.' But make no mistake: every one will leave the reader shaken."

Redhill's play *Goodness* was first mounted in Canada in 2005 and was published that same year. The narrative concerns a Jewish playwright, named Michael Redhill, who investigates a World War II–era massacre that killed many members of his family. In August 2006 the play was performed in Scotland as part of the Edinburgh Fringe Festival and won the Best of Edinburgh Prize, presented by the Carol Tambor Theatrical Foundation. *Goodness* received a number of strongly positive reviews, with Neil Cooper, a critic for the Glasgow *Herald* (August 18, on-line), calling it a "searingly intense study." Others, however, found its self-referential qualities off-putting. Lyn Gardner, writing for the London *Guardian* (August 18, 2006, on-line), called the play "compelling" but argued that "Redhill dresses it up with all sorts of distracting and tricksy framing devices. Redhill himself even appears in a subplot that only detracts from the main thrust of the play with its emphasis on the author and the audience's responsibility."

Redhill's second novel, *Consolation*, was released in Canada in 2006 and in the U.S. in 2007. The novel is in part an exploration of the city of Toronto during two eras, the mid–19th century and the late 1990s, which are linked in the novel by a set of photographs, taken in the 1850s by an immigrant Englishman, Jeremy Hallam. Though some reviewers found Redhill's prose overwrought—and attributed that to his background as a poet—many critics praised Redhill's novel for its textured evocation of the city. Nancy Schiefer, in a review for the *London (Ontario) Free Press* (October 28, 2006, on-line), remarked: "Although Redhill's novel is at its descriptive best with 19th-century Toronto, it is cognizant, too, of the sights and sounds of today's city. Taken together, Redhill's leisurely 'tale of two cities' is a well nuanced book, its narrative threads combined convincingly."

Between 1986 and 1990 Redhill served as publisher and co-editor of *Yak*, a Toronto-based literary magazine he founded as a student. He has been an editor for a number of other magazines and small publishers, including Coach House Press. He is currently the publisher and a contributing editor of *Brick*, one of Canada's leading literary journals.

Michael Redhill lives in Toronto with his partner, Anne Simard; they have two sons. Redhill told Richard Helm for the *Edmonton Journal* (December 3, 2006) that the family would be living in France for a year beginning in July 2007, partially to distance himself from what he called the "hothouse flower quality" in Canadian culture.

—C.M.

Suggested Reading: *Atlanta Journal-Constitution* L p5 May 2, 2004; *Atlantic Monthly* p111 Apr. 2004; (Canada) *Vancouver Sun* H p21 May 5, 2001, D p21 Apr. 21, 2001; *Edmonton Journal* B p1 Dec. 3, 2006; (London) *Guardian* (on-line) Aug. 18, 2006; *London (Ontario) Free Press* (on-line) Oct. 28, 2006; *Maclean's* p67 May 14, 2001; *Quill & Quire* p24 Dec. 1993, p47 June 2001; *Toronto Star* J p5 Apr. 10, 1997; *Washington Post Book World* p7 Aug. 25, 2002

Selected Books: poetry—*Impromptu Feats of Balance*, 1990; *Lake Nora Arms*, 1993; *Asphodel*, 1997; *Light-Crossing*, 2001; fiction—*Martin Sloane*, 2001; *Fidelity*, 2003; *Consolation*, 2006; plays—*Building Jerusalem*, 2001; *Goodness*, 2005

Reed, Kit

1932(?)– Novelist; short-story writer

Few modern American writers can claim to be as prolific and as versatile as Kit Reed. In a career spanning five decades, she has written more than 20 novels and various collections of short stories, as well as primers for aspiring authors. She has written for adults and juveniles, for fans of thrillers and readers of literature, in experimental styles and within the realm of science fiction. Whatever the style or subject matter, however, critics have applauded Reed's deft writing and characterizations. Her short fiction has been published in the *Yale Review, Transatlantic Review, Missouri Review, Magazine of Fantasy and Science Fiction, Tampa Review, Texas Review*, and *Voice Literary Supplement*, as well as *Cosmopolitan, Redbook*, and *Omni*, among other periodicals. Reed has also been a reporter and book reviewer for a variety of newspapers and magazines and teaches a fiction workshop at Wesleyan University, in Middletown, Connecticut.

Kit Reed wrote the following autobiographical statement for *World Authors 2000–2005*:

"Probably the most important thing about me as a writer is that I grew up a military kid.

"Until I moved to Connecticut as an adult, I'd never lived in one place for more than two years at a time. We went where the Navy took us; my father was in submarines. I was in four different fourth grades—New London; Panama, where I went from the base to school in Cristobal; New London again; then after Christmas break, St. Petersburg, Florida. By the time I finished college, we'd moved a dozen times.

"As a result, I grew up with the idea that the inconvenience is always temporary, and if you don't like what's going on right now, cheer up. You can always move. All those moves made me observant. Walking into a new school in a new place, which I did so many times, sharpens your faculties. You need to pick up local customs fast or you will be ostracized. To make it in any school you need to wear what they wear, and you need to know it down to the details, like sock cuffs turned up or socks turned down. You learn how to walk the walk and, more important, how to talk the talk.

"It sharpened my ear for dialog and for nuances like the difference between 'Hi' (St. Paul's School in St. Petersburg) and (Beaufort High School on the Inland Waterway) 'Hey.' Even today I echo the cadences of people I'm with—the clipped speech or the drawl, the apposite slang. It's a way of blending in. In school, it was a survival tactic. Kids don't have adults' mitigating social graces. If you're at all different, they may not tar and feather you, but they *will* peck you to death.

"But there's more. There's always more. Military kids don't always get to keep their fathers. Mine was lost in the Coral Sea. His sub went missing with all hands aboard when I was in fifth grade. Now, military kids know, but don't always want to admit it: Missing in Action usually turns out to mean, *dead*.

"In an odd way all this makes me resilient. When you're caught short in childhood by the death of a parent, it teaches you the essential importance of a Plan B. This is particularly useful to people who grow up to be novelists. So much of fiction is written on spec, so many hopes ride on each story or novel that wise writers learn never to count on any one submission. In art as in life, everybody needs a fallback plan.

"I wrote my first novel in Honolulu, Hawaii when I was going on five. I was already telling myself a running bedtime story about Dick and Daisy, Brenda and Rusty, who all lived together on a ranch, but the novel I dictated to my mother was about my stuffed rabbit, Harbor Wilson. It was called *Harbor Plots her Plans*.

"When she read it back, I made her erase some side remark I'd made that she had dutifully copied in. Not part of the story! I added an illustration to fill the empty space. It was the first of a series of Harbor books; I sent the last one off to the publishers of the 36 Oz books I read a dozen times. My jacket copy shimmered in my head: 'Kitten Craig is twelve years old and has her own horse.' They were, I'm happy to report, extremely kind when they sent it back.

"Most embarrassing sentence committed when young? From the second page of a radio play called 'The Banditti,' which never did get to page three: 'Good heavens, Deanna ejaculated.'

"I didn't write much in high school because by then we were in South Carolina, where cute boys were. My mother managed the Officers' Club at Parris Island for a spell. Seven kids from Parris

Island rode to Beaufort every morning, rattling around inside an olive drab city bus marked U.S.M.C. From there I went to Georgetown Visitation Convent in Washington, D.C. for a year of lockdown. Matched doberman pinschers posted at the front and back stairs, to keep THEM out or US in. In spite of stupendously bad math scores, the College of Notre Dame of Maryland was gracious enough to let me in. I did OK. I started to write again. I did a series of short stories as a senior thesis, one banned from the college magazine because it concerned an affair. Still, the nuns were cool. They taught us that we could do anything we wanted in life.

"Then I went to work at the *St. Petersburg Times*, one of the country's best independent newspapers, and the real training began. As one of four women on cityside, I did everything from obits to TV coverage. I learned to bash out drafts on the manual typewriter, sentence by sentence, word by word, and if it wasn't good enough, go back to the top and do it until it was right. It's the way I compose. Brick by brick by brick. Computers make it easier because I don't have to throw the typewriter carriage after every line. I can do more drafts, because I don't get as tired.

"In my career I've had at least six agents, but only one husband. I met Joseph Reed when we were nineteen and we've been hanging out together ever since. We married the year after we finished college and moved to Great Lakes Naval Training Center in Illinois. Voila, I lost my job. For six months I edited a government house organ and in my spare time—there was plenty of it—wrote a gang of stories.

"In New Haven, where Joe went to graduate school, I worked for the *New Haven Register*. It's hard to be temperamental about your prose when praise comes from a guy talking around a cigar. I interviewed a woman published for the first time after fifteen years. Inspired, I sent out one of the Great Lakes stories. It sold. It was like my first shot of heroin. I never quit. I had a baby, my first of three. Voila, I was out of work. I started a novel. It became *Mother Isn't Dead She's Only Sleeping*, my first.

"I got a Guggenheim on the strength of my second, and a grant from the Abraham Woursell Foundation after the third. I've had things optioned for the movies. The psychological thrillers I wrote as Kit Craig earned more money than I'm used to. If you prorated my earnings over a lifetime you'd find I probably make less than a preschool aide. I'm working with fiction writers at Wesleyan University—but only, as I've been telling myself for far too long, until I make enough money to quit.

"People who don't know me ask the classic question, 'Why do you write?' I do it because I do it. It's who I am."

Kit Reed was born in San Diego, California, to John R. Craig and the former Lillian Hyde. (Some sources list the year of her birth as 1932.) Her father was in the U.S. Navy, so the family moved frequently throughout her childhood, living in Honolulu, Hawaii; New London, Connecticut; Washington, D.C.; St. Petersburg, Florida; Beaufort, South Carolina; and Panama—among other locales.

Reed, a Roman Catholic, received a bachelor's degree from the College of Notre Dame, in Baltimore, Maryland, in 1954. On December 10, 1955 she married Joseph Wayne Reed Jr., a writer, painter, printmaker, and professor, with whom she now has three children: Joseph McKean Reed, John Craig Reed, and Katherine Reed Maruyama. During her early career Reed worked primarily as a reporter. After graduating from Notre Dame she worked for 18 months for the *St. Petersburg Times*, and when the Reed family moved to Connecticut, in 1956, she joined the staff of the *Hamden Chronicle*. From there she moved to the *New Haven Register*, for which she also reviewed books. She was named New England Newspaperwoman of the Year by the New England Women's Press Association in both 1958 and 1959.

In 1959 Reed left the newspaper business to become a novelist. Her first book, *Mother Isn't Dead, She's Only Sleeping*, was published in 1961. While it was not a great commercial success, her second novel, *At War as Children* (1964), received more critical notice. In this autobiographical novel, three friends, who come of age during World War II, travel around the country as "Navy brats." They watch their mothers silently worry, dreading an official visit from the Navy indicating that their husbands have been killed during military duty. The friends drift apart over the years but come together again during college, at a time when one of them is facing a difficult religious crisis. H. C. Gardiner, in a review for *America* (February 29, 1964), wrote: "Mark this novel as one of the best conceived and most convincingly executed Catholic novels of many a year. I don't know that the author will be thankful for my putting this label on it; so I hasten to say that it is by no stretch of the imagination Catholic in the sense of being a preachment or of handling an obviously theological or moral situation. . . . The book is anything but stuffy. The dialogue between the young people strikes the ear as absolutely authentic. . . . Finally, the climax—which fairly bursts upon the reader in the last two pages or so— is a great surprise, and yet on reflection it seems obvious that such a climax had been building ever since Denny's spiritual crisis. The quiet inevitability of this climax is the crowning evidence of the sure touch with which Mrs. Reed faced the challenge of writing such a novel. It is Catholic—unobtrusively, but unmistakably."

In *The Better Part* (1967), Reed explores life through the eyes of Martha Ewald, the teenage daughter of a state correctional official at an institution for delinquent girls; her best friend is the son of the institution's psychiatrist. During the course of the novel, Martha helps one girl escape from the facility. Margaret Parton, in the *Saturday Review* (May 20, 1967), opined, "Simultaneously an allegory and a straightforward story, *The Better Part* shimmers with the fascinating puzzlement of a superbly crafted optical illusion. A bitter book, perhaps, but honest and inevitable." Pamela Marsh, in a review for the *Christian Science Monitor* (July 29, 1967), asked, however, "Would an intelligent man really encourage his young and sensitive daughter to spend all her time gossiping with the inmates?"

Reed then published the short-story collection *Mr. Da V., and Other Stories* (1967), before moving into the world of science fiction for her next novel. (Her ventures into the genre are often called "speculative fiction" by her readers, as a way to differentiate them from conventional science fiction; Reed told *World Authors* that she "prefers character-based cultural criticism to stories based in science or rocketry.") In the novel *Armed Camps* (1969), set in the year 2001, a frightened girl escapes from a pacifist commune, while a young man with a military family background revolts against his upbringing. B.D. Allen complained in *Library Journal* (June 15, 1970), "[In this] allegory on the ironies in our responses to violence . . . the two plots, finally, effectively collide, but it's hard to be really convinced because much of the novel's 'message' lies flatly at the level of the obvious and predictable." F.L. Ryan suggested in *Best Sellers* (July 1, 1970) that the author's "purpose in this novel is to bring into focus that time element over which witches brood and middle-aged people worry, the future. . . . Mrs. Reed uses the 'I' narrator in both stories and the responses of these narrators have the immediacy and sharpness that an 'I' narration can present. On the other hand, I felt that Mrs. Reed was rushing to her point and in the process sketching the characters rather than letting them expand and become significant through this expansion."

Reed's next book, *Cry of the Daughter*, was published in 1971. In *Tiger Rag* (1973) Reed continued to experiment, this time using multiple monologues, as well as letters, to create an intriguing character study. The plot follows a woman named Dorothea, who is forced to confront her past when the death of a childhood friend causes painful memories to surface. In a review for the *Washington Post* (October 16, 1973), Carole Horn noted, "Kit Reed excels as a wordsmith, expanding her meanings with sure, delicate, but precise phrases. . . . From the first sentence, metaphors run into one another, producing the threads mingled consciously or unconsciously to form the story's unusual tapestry. Yet the book is not entirely satisfying. It seems to lack symmetry; shifts from one person's interior monologue to the next do not seem inevitable, as they do, for instance, in Virginia Wolf's *The Waves*. And it

seems more a challenging, abstracted, well-executed intellectual puzzle than a real story. The author puts us in the minds of her characters, but not, somehow, into the heart of the matter."

In her next novel, *Captain Grownup* (1976), Reed introduced her readers to Willard Michaels, a once-promising journalist and aspiring writer who, after his marriage collapses, gives up on his dreams and moves to Connecticut to teach English at a local high school. Completely lost and without direction in his life, Michaels latches onto one of his students, Susan Velma Hinners, and hopes through her to find some purpose. Margo Jefferson remarked in *Newsweek* (April 19, 1976), "Kit Reed offers a gallery of sharply drawn minor portraits along the way: from Michael's college buddies, once brash and hearty, now baffled and a bit sour, to Susan's eccentric family, thriving on guilt, unhappiness and threats of violence. She writes a rapid-fire, wise-cracking prose that can tumble—witness the book's title—into cuteness. But most of the time her blend of sentiment and sting is just right."

Reed began to teach English and writing at Wesleyan University, in 1974, and continued to steadily produce a stream of literary and science-fiction novels and short stories—including *The Killer Mice* (1976), *The Ballad of T. Rantula* (1979), *Magic Time* (1981), *Other Stories and the Attack of the Giant Baby* (1981), *Blood Fever* (1982, as Shelley Hyde), *Fort Privilege* (1985), *Catholic Girls* (1987); she also published two nonfiction manuals, *Story First: The Writer as Insider* (1982) and *Revision* (1989).

Reed found the popularity and wide readership that had previously eluded her with *Gone* (1992), a psychological thriller she wrote under the pen name Kit Craig, in which the widow of a submarine commander is kidnaped by her former neighbor. Following her abduction, it is up to her teenage children and their four-year-old brother to save her. In a review for *Newsweek* (June 22, 1992), Tom Post cheered, "[This is] a tightly wound psycho-thriller written with terrifying understatement by Kit Craig, a.k.a. Kit Reed, who teaches writing at Wesleyan University. . . . *Gone* is the first thriller by Craig, who, under her real name, is the author of a half dozen literary novels. It is a fine pop debut, a riveting and menacing adventure to the last page." Writing for *Library Journal* (May 1, 1992), Rebecca House Stankowski proclaimed, "In this fast-paced thriller, novelist Kit Reed (*Catholic Girls*) has taken on a new pseudonym as well as a new genre. . . . Of course, the idea of two teenagers and a child embarking on a cross-country rescue mission is silly, but the author's portrait of Cleve, the seductive psychopath, is so stunning that it's easy to forget the ridiculous premise—and hard to put down the book."

Reed followed this novel with a collection of short stories, *Thief of Lives* (1992), which received mixed reviews. Carol Anshaw, writing for the *Washington Post* (November 20, 1992), complained: "The economics of publishing seems to demand that a collection be so long and hold so many stories before it can be bound and sold at a profit—in this case, a fiscal policy that had not served the author well. *Thief of Lives* would have been much stronger if a quarter of these stories had been left quietly behind in the author's drawer." In his assessment for the *New York Times Book Review* (January 17, 1993), Greg Johnson wrote, "Ms. Reed is clearly a resourceful and often witty writer. Although this uneven, perhaps too eclectic gathering contains some stories that seem dated or derivative, it is also distinguished by several masterly examples of the form." Reed's other books of this period include *Little Sisters of the Apocalyse* (1994), *Straight* (1995), *Closer* (1997), and *Some Safe Place* (1998).

In *J. Eden*, Reed's 1996 novel, a trio of middle-aged New York City couples rent a farmhouse in Massachusetts for the summer, hoping that a break from the hustle and bustle of the city will help them sort out their lives. The novel received mostly favorable reviews. In *Small Press* (July/August 1996), Geraldine Levy wrote: "The story is told from 11 points of view, a device that, in less skilled hands, might do little more than solicit sympathy for the narrators. But Reed manages to create all the suspense and momentum of a mystery, thanks to incisively drawn characters, vivid details and penetrating insights." Michael Sledge noted for the *New York Times Book Review* (April 21, 1996), "Why this group, inclining toward envy rather than affection, self-pity rather than self-awareness, might choose to spend any time together at all, much less an entire season, is the biggest mystery here. At summer's end, a tragedy blows in to spur the inevitable epiphanies, but they come too late and with too little preparation. Yet despite the flatness of its adult characters, *J. Eden* sometimes strikes home—particularly when it inhabits the world of the children, whose frenetic play only masks a deep craving for parental affection. To win that love, they offer up the one thing they feel they have to give: a terrible willingness to bear the responsibility for their parents' unhappiness."

Weird Women, Wired Women (1998), a collection of 19 short stories, was met with almost universal praise. Ted Leventhal wrote for *Booklist* (March 15, 1998), "Kit Reed notes in the introduction that her fiction is hard to categorize, rejecting the generic label 'science fiction.' Her humorous, ironic prose could best be described as *The Feminine Mystique* meets *The Twilight Zone*. . . . She is versatile as well as prolific, with her prose evolving over the years from brief comic sketches ('The Wait') to layered, nuanced novellas (*War Songs*). She seems transfixed on the conflicting roles of modern women: mother and wife, breadwinner and homemaker. The complex relationship between mothers and daughters is also a frequent theme of her fiction, entertained in such clever stories as 'The Were-mother' and 'The Mothers of Shark Island.' Reed revisits these themes again and again, and the work suffers from repetition. However, her unique blend of humor makes the book definitely a worthwhile read." In the *New York Times Book Review* (July 19, 1998), Enid Shomer wrote, "Beauty pageants, hi-tech motherhood, fat farms, game shows—nothing involved in shaping women's expectations is immune from [Reed's] satiric scrutiny. . . . Most of these stories shine with the incisive edginess of brilliant cartoons, though 'The Mothers of Shark Island' and a few others are so dampened by bitterness that they fail to ignite. The best take the form of darkly comic rants by women who have too zealously pursued what they thought was happiness. While Reed calls these stories 'speculative fiction,' they are less fantastic than visionary, uncovering humor and horror where others have seen only clothes, make-up and recipes snipped from the newspaper."

Some of Reed's more recent works include *Seven for the Apocalypse* (1999), *@expectations* (2000), and *Thinner Than Thou* (2004). In the latter, a satire of the American obsession with body image, an anorexic girl is abducted and taken to an unusual convent-like institution, and an obese girl is forced into a concentration camp of sorts for the overweight. A reviewer for the *School Library Journal* (May 10, 2004, on-line) wrote, " Reed . . . rips into the dangerous pursuit of body perfection at the expense of the soul in this stinging and mordantly witty satire. . . . With this sharp-eyed look at America's obsession with image, Reed provides much food for thought and reaffirms her position as one of our brightest cultural commentators." Writing for *People* (July 15, 2004), Lynn Andriani remarked, "With an ear for dialogue and a truly wild imagination, Reed . . . populates her scary book with believable characters, including Annie Abercrombie, an anorexic teenager taken hostage by the nuns, and Kelly, the obese friend also targeted by the better-bod squad. A clever what-if, Reed's tale is provocative as well as amusing."

Like many of its predecessors, Reed's most recent story collection, *The Dogs of Truth* (2005), met with considerable praise. A reviewer for *Publishers Weekly* (July 25, 2005) wrote, "Reed . . . transforms the ordinary into the extraordinary in this impressive story collection. . . . No matter how absurd, these horror stories still sting with truth and ring with humor, often ending with an odd happiness."

Reed's most recent novel, *The Baby Merchant* (2006), is set in a future in which children have become the rarest commodity. A reviewer for *Publishers Weekly* (March 13, 2006) wrote, "Set in an all-too-plausible future world with a falling birth rate, closed borders and lengthy adoption waiting lists, Reed's provocative SF novel explores the lengths desperate people will go to become parents."

Kit Reed, who currently lives in Connecticut with her husband, has been the recipient of the Abraham Woursell Foundation Literary Grant, a Guggenheim fellow, and a Mellon fellow of the Aspen Institute for Humanistic Studies. In 1974 she was a visiting writer in India. In 1990 she served as the American coordinator for the Indo-U.S. Writers Exchange. Reed is also a member of a number of literary organizations, including the Writer's Guild of America, the National Book Critics Circle, and the Authors League Fund, among others.

When asked by Gwyneth Jones for *Infinity Plus* (June 19, 2004, on-line) why she began teaching creative writing, Reed replied, "I prefer to think of it as working with writers who want to write fiction. Creative Writing is a phrase that makes me want to throw up. As if writing is like playschool finger painting or sandbox stuff. Creative is, I think, a loose and loathsome word for what is, essentially, a demanding obsession. Or an exacting discipline."

—C.M.

Suggested Reading: *America* p289 Feb. 29, 1964; *Best Sellers* p130 July 1, 1970; *Booklist* p1,203 Mar. 15, 1998; *Infinity Plus* (on-line) June 19, 2004; *New York Times Book Review* p36 Mar. 8, 1964, p21 Jan. 17, 1993, p26 Apr. 21, 1996, p18 July 19, 1998; *Newsweek* p91 Apr. 19, 1976, p55 June 22, 1992; *People* p47 July 5, 2004; *Publishers Weekly* p42 May 10, 2004, p53 July 25, 2005, p46 Mar. 13, 2006; *Saturday Review* p42 May 20, 1967; *Small Press* p65 July/Aug. 1996; *Washington Post* B p6 Oct. 26, 1973, C p2 Nov. 20, 1992

Selected Books: *Mother Isn't Dead, She's Only Sleeping*, 1961; *At War as Children*, 1964; *The Better Part*, 1967; *Mr. Da V., and Other Stories*, 1967; *Armed Camps*, 1969; *Cry of the Daughter*, 1971; *Tiger Rag*, 1973; *Captain Grownup*, 1976; *The Killer Mice*, 1976; *Other Stories and The Attack of the Giant Baby*, 1981; *Fort Privilege*, 1985; *Catholic Girls*, 1987; *Gone*, 1992; *Thief of Lives*, 1992; *J. Eden*, 1996; *Closer*, 1997; *Weird Women, Wired Women*, 1998; *@expectations*, 2000; *Thinner Than Thou*, 2004; *Dogs of Truth*, 2005; *The Baby Merchant*, 2006

Reuss, Frederick

(ROYCE)

Oct. 2, 1960– Novelist

Frederick Reuss, despite a childhood and youth spent largely in such places as Ethiopia, Nigeria, India, and Germany, has chosen to set most of his novels in such iconic American locales as the Midwest, Atlantic City, and New York. Reviewers have praised the extraordinary voices Reuss gives the protagonists of his books, which include *Horace Afoot* (1997), *Henry in Atlantic City* (1999), *The Wasties* (2002), and *Mohr* (2006). Reuss "cares deeply about how we fashion our thoughts and consciousness" and examines "the dark philosophical and psychological labyrinths in which we search for glimmers of ourselves," as Veronica Scrol wrote for *Booklist* (July 1999).

Reuss composed the following autobiographical statement for *World Authors 2000–2005*:

"I was born in Addis Ababa, Ethiopia in 1960, where my father, (Berlin-born Jewish refugee) was serving his first posting as a U.S. Foreign Service Officer. From Ethiopia we moved to Nigeria, to India, and then, in 1969, to Washington, D.C., where my brothers, my sister and I made our first entry into suburban American life and Dad made his entry into the Vietnam war, where he was sent on 'temporary duty' to the U.S. Embassy in Saigon. Mom (New York Irish/Scottish Catholic) saw to it that we all continued the Catholic education that was begun at Presentation Convent in Madras.

Sophie Reuss/Courtesy of Unbridled Books

America seemed a perfect paradise. Television! No beggars or poor people (within view, anyway). Changing seasons. Drinkable water—directly from the faucet! Smooth roads. Big cars. Climate controlled grocery stores with names like Safeway and Giant where huge shopping carts were loaded to over-capacity with colorfully packaged foods (frozen TV dinners were a much hankered after novelty). The Vietnam war (and Dad) seemed very far away; but both were brought nearer by the reel to reel tapes he would send home containing his 'letters' (hope-rich baritone, noisy traffic and what we imagined to be bombs exploding in the distance) interspersed with selections from The Beatles.

"In 1970, Dad returned from Vietnam (peptic ulcers). I became a fully-acculturated suburban American boy. In 1974 we moved to Dusseldorf, West Germany, where I worked to become a fully-acculturated German teenager, and 'discovered' (probably in very nearly this order) Kurt Vonnegut, Ezra Pound, Frank Zappa, James Joyce, Allen Ginsberg, Franz Kafka, Fyodor Dostoyevsky, Thomas Mann, Henry Miller, Gary Snyder, The Mahavishnu Orchestra, Jack Kerouac, Tangerine Dream, William Burroughs, the films of [Rainer Werner] Fassbinder and [Pier Paolo] Pasolini, Miles Davis, Paul Klee and Joseph Beuys. I wrote poems and long strange letters and was encouraged in my literary pursuits by two very understanding teachers.

"In 1978 I entered Antioch College where I majored in philosophy. I also began to (try to) write fiction. In 1981 I returned to Germany where I spent one year at the University of Tübingen reading philosophy. Never fully tempted to pursue an academic (or any) career, I moved to New York City after finishing college and tried to support myself in a variety of odd and useless jobs while trying to write fiction. In 1985, I moved upstate to the Catskill mountains. Over the next three years I acquired a curious new discipline—the ability to sit down every day, listen to my imagination, and write for long stretches at a time. In 1988, I threw all the results of this curious new discipline into the trash, returned to Madras and, by a miracle, found my old nanny, Gertie. I hadn't seen her since leaving Madras at nine years old. She was old, sick, and living in the worst poverty. It was one of the saddest and most frightening things I have ever seen, but it also brought the world into focus and filled me with a peculiar sense of hope. I stayed in India for four months, then returned to Washington, got married, and eventually completed my first novel. I have two daughters and continue to write fiction.

"The novel is the form that I am most impelled to. While I can't say that I am consciously possessed by any one specific, or urgent theme, my novels do tend to portray characters in various states of dislocation, whose identities have in some way become obscured or effaced entirely. I wouldn't know how to go about trying to explain the emergence of this theme in my work without falling into some paradigmatic, theoretical trap. One of the great challenges in writing fiction is avoiding traps (I am tempted to say one of the great traps a person can fall into is the writing of fiction). Reading and writing are imaginative acts, and the imagination is a mysterious gift that needs only fresh air and exercise."

Frederick Reuss was born on October 2, 1960 in Ethiopia as an American citizen. He completed his B.A. degree at Antioch College, in Yellow Springs, Ohio, in 1983. The protagonist of his first novel, *Horace Afoot*, is Quintus Horatius Flaccus (called Horace), whom Jeff Druchniak, in a review for the *Michigan Daily* (March 17, 1999, on-line), describes as an "armchair philosopher and designated local eccentric of Oblivion, U.S.A., a place he chose to live in merely for its name." Horace, who holds down no regular job, choosing instead to live frugally on an inheritance, shuns human contact and the conveniences of modern technology. "I hate internal combustion engines and the civilization that has been built on them," he says, as quoted by David Sacks for the *New York Times* (December 28, 1997, on-line). "I read in 'Selected Philosophical Essays' that hatred of civilization is not necessarily an irrational projection onto the world of personal psychological difficulties. So I know it's not just me." Sacks called *Horace Afoot* a "charming, unexpectedly poignant first novel" that "combines two strands of plot: a sly satire of Midwestern life and a restrained account of how a closed heart comes to be unlocked. Much of the novel involves Horace simply walking around the town, viewing his fellow citizens with the same shallow pity or mistrust that they reserve for him. . . . Horace's perambulations create a vivid mosaic of the town, its gap between rich and poor, its downsized defense plant, squalid roadways, glorious cornfields. Frederick Reuss's deft prose and eye for detail give the setting both realism and universal overtones." In a review for *Library Journal* (October 1, 1997), Patrick Sullivan called the book "interesting and thoughtful," while Druchniak characterized it as "one of the most charming first novels a reader may run across."

Like Horace, the six-year-old protagonist of Reuss's next book, *Henry of Atlantic City*, is decidedly eccentric. Henry lives in the hotel attached to the Atlantic City casino for which his father, an embezzler, works as head of security. He is befriended by a blackjack dealer and amateur philosopher named Sy, who introduces him to the Gnostic gospels. Henry possesses am astounding memory and proceeds to learn the gospels by heart; he comes to believe that he has an angel whispering in his ear and that he himself might be a saint. When his father goes on the lam, Henry is consigned to a series of foster homes and orphanages—generally perplexing everyone he meets. "Throughout these lonely adventures, Henry views everything through a whimsical Gnostic lens: the casino's garish classical decor, for example, with its Bacchus Room and Gladiator Lounge, neatly coincides with Henry's fascination with early Christianity (he compares a casino bigwig to the sixth-century Emperor Justinian)," Megan Harlan wrote for the *New York Times* (November 28, 1999, on-line). "While Reuss's eccentric wordplay can occasionally feel stilted, he achieves a brilliant tonal balance between Henry's idealistic spiritual visions and the tawdry, disappointing world he inhabits. The result is an inventive and moving parable about a boy who finally learns to have faith in himself." A reviewer for *Publishers Weekly* (June 28, 1999, on-line), opined, "Reuss's manner—a spare third-person narrative, sticking largely to terms and phrases Henry knows—becomes a courageously concentrated show of authorial control and tonal fidelity (though it does slip up a bit near the end). Henry's thoughts, and his speeches to other characters, mix quotes from Gnostic scriptures and Byzantine history with his questions about the mechanics of a befuddling adult world. Everything Henry sees gets a Byzantine gloss: cars can be chariots, and a tycoon Henry meets becomes the emperor Justinian. The play of past and present, heretical theology and life-experience, through Henry's consciousness yields some neat, sophisticated jokes. More often Reuss achieves a brilliant pathos, reminding us that at any age 'loneliness is the most meaningless treasure in existence.'"

The Wasties is narrated by Michael "Caruso" Taylor, a university English professor suffering from the condition that is causing him to grow progressively more infantile and dependent on others. (He calls the malady "the wasties.") "Although we're never told the exact nature of Caruso's condition—physical, psychological, or some combination—the novel traces his regression from adulthood to adolescence to infancy," Laura Stickney explained in a review for the *Washingtonian* (on-line). "First he revels in the shock value of obscene words and his new smoking habit; later he yearns for walkie-talkies and bath toys. His passionate love for his wife transforms into a child's adoration for his mother; his nurse becomes his babysitter. A former English professor, Caruso populates his fantasies with characters from his studies—allusions that are always humorous and sometimes quite clever. Beat poet Allen Ginsberg is in his yoga class; naturalist John Muir bums cigarettes from him in the park." Stickney continued, "Caruso's observations are by turns hilarious and devastating, and even as he gradually loses his sanity, they often ring true. . . . Reuss manages to keep a book with little actual dialogue engrossing through both humor and humanity. Although at times I just wanted to shake Caruso and tell him to grow up, his increasingly desperate plight and quirky perspective kept me interested. He may be mute, but his words speak volumes." A reviewer for *Publishers Weekly* (July 29, 2002, on-line) praised the book's "loopy charm" and predicted, "The cultish appeal of *Henry of Atlantic City* and *Horace Afoot* won Reuss a small following of devoted readers. *The Wasties* won't broaden his reach, but should satisfy most fans."

The protagonist of Reuss's latest novel, *Mohr*, is a real-life figure: a German physician and minor novelist named Max Mohr, who also happens to be the author's great-uncle. As the Nazis came to power, Mohr escaped from Germany, leaving behind a wife and young daughter. He traveled to Shanghai to practice medicine and died there a few years later, never reunited with his family. Reuss explained his decision to use his relative's experiences as the basis for a novel in an interview posted on the Unbridled Books Web site: "The decision to write the story of Max Mohr as a novel was not difficult. The further I delved into Mohr's life and times, the more I came to understand that history is narrative, an imaginative act in which the past is inscribed onto the present and given meaning. In writing the book, I had privileged access to rich and diverse materials—newspapers, books, films, private correspondence, oral histories and, finally, photographs. It was these last objects that focused my attention and concentrated my imagination most fully. More than anything else, they seemed at once to narrow and to increase the distance between me and those real people who once lived." Some of those photos are interspersed throughout the text of the novel, impressing many reviewers. Elizabeth Kiem, for example, wrote for *Flak Magazine* (on-line): "Without the photographs, *Mohr* would be a different book altogether. Reuss may be in large company as an author whose work is inspired by an old family portrait, but he enters a smaller confederacy when he ponders the essence of photography and its transcendent reality: 'What moves you in looking at these old snapshots of people who were long gone before you entered the world isn't nostalgia, but a thrilling sense of connection,' he writes. He asks, 'Can feelings be preserved in photography, the way love letters can be written on a typewriter?' His answer is ambiguous, for while *Mohr* is a testament to the endurance of emotion on photo-paper, it is also an exercise in invention. The feelings telegraphed by these pictures are strong indeed, but they are enforced by an imagined urgency and an embellished plot." A reviewer for *Publishers Weekly* (May 15, 2006, on-line) wrote, "Reuss succeeds in giving vivid shape to Mohr's life—the major events (including possible WWII spy intrigue in China) and the mundane (taking foxglove to keep his pulse regular). If not a man in full, the book contains a man kaleidoscopic."

Frederick Reuss lives in Washington, D.C., not far from American University, with his two daughters and his wife, a manufacturer's representative. Bob Thompson, in a profile of Reuss for the *Washington Post* (July 10, 2006, on-line), referred to her position as the "family's real-world job." Of writing literary fiction, Reuss told Thompson, "Needless to say, it's not a good way to make a living."

—S.Y.

Suggested Reading: *Booklist* p1924 July 1999; *New York Times* (on-line) Nov. 28, 1999; *New York Times Book Review* p5 Dec. 28, 1997, p20 Nov. 28, 1999; *Publishers Weekly* (on-line) June 28, 1999, July 29, 2002; Unbridled Books Web site; *Washington Post* (on-line) July 10, 2006; *Washington Post Book World* p5 Oct. 12, 1997

Selected Books: *Horace Afoot*, 1997; *Henry of Atlantic City*, 1999; *The Wasties*, 2002; *Mohr*, 2006

Rhodes, Dan

1972– Novelist; short-story writer

When Dan Rhodes was anointed by the prestigious literary magazine *Granta* as one of the best young British writers in 2003, he responded with characteristic modesty: "The other people on [the list] seem to be pretty clever compared to me," the novelist told Peter Wild for the Bookmunch Web site (June 3, 2003), "so I can't help thinking that I'm only on it because of some kind of clerical error." After the publication of his first novel, *Timoleon Vieta Come Home: A Sentimental Journey* (2003), and two short-story collections—*Anthropology, and a Hundred Other Stories* (2000) and *Don't Tell Me the Truth About Love* (2001)—Rhodes began telling the press that he was ready to retire from writing. "Right now I have no imagination or motivation, and it's a fantastic feeling," he told Wild. "I wasn't able to switch off for six and a half years, and now I've managed it. I'm very reluctant to go back to writing. I wrote obsessively, to the detriment of every other aspect of my life. . . . Maybe I'll write something else one day, but if I do I'm hoping I would be obliged to approach the work from a completely different angle." The following year, however, he published his second novel, *The Little White Car* (2004)—albeit under the pen name Danuta de Rhodes, and another book, *Gold*, is scheduled for publication in 2007. In an interview for the London *Independent* (February 16, 2005), Rhodes described a writer's life as "a fantastic job, when you're a few months ahead of the bailiffs and your publisher isn't trying to kill you. I almost never have to set my alarm clock, so I'm in no position to grumble. I don't see it as a sustainable way of life, so I'm determined to enjoy it while it lasts."

Dan Rhodes was born in 1972 in England. He has two older sisters. According to various press reports, his parents own a pub in the town of Tunbridge Wells, in southeast England. (Though more than one source reported that his father was a bricklayer, the author has refuted this on his Web site.) He was not the most promising student at the Tunbridge Wells Grammar School for Boys and failed his English A-level (a college-placement test), but he did attend the University of Glamorgan, in Wales, as a student of the humanities. Rhodes later returned to the university to pursue a master's degree in creative writing, which he completed in 1997—but before that, he held a series of menial jobs that would not interfere with his writing, working on a fruit and vegetable farm, in the stockroom of a bookstore, and behind the counter of his parents' pub. He also taught for a while in Ho Chi Minh City, South Vietnam.

His first collection of short stories, *Anthropology, and a Hundred Other Stories*, consists of 101 darkly humorous tales of love, each told in 101 words and organized alphabetically by their one-word titles. "Effortless to read, amusing, and yet coloured by a deep sadness about the passing of things, these prose haikus display a psychological and verbal precision that ranges across anecdote, character and, sometimes, a whole compressed life," Gareth Evans wrote for the London *Independent* (March 11, 2000). "You might be able to finish this attractive volume over a long coffee, but you will want to hold on to the truths it so skillfully offers." In the *Washington Post* (September 19, 2000), Jabari Asim observed that Rhodes's stories combined the "surreal irony" of the comedian Steven Wright and "macabre playfulness" of the comics artist Gary Larson: "Although Rhodes's gimmick may sound like those mathematical experiments favored by Georges Perec and other writers associated with France's Oulipo group [which promoted the use of constrained writing techniques], his fiction more closely resembles the sardonic monologues of stand-up comedians. . . . Rhodes's abrasive style isn't for everyone, but I found his book a refreshing change of pace." (A later edition of the book used the subtitle *101 True Love Stories*.)

Rhodes's second short-story collection, *Don't Tell Me the Truth About Love*, was more traditional than his previous effort, containing seven fully fleshed tales. Once again, however, the author skewered modern romance. "These are fairy tales written in the detached, ethereal tones of the brothers Grimm, with an elegant simplicity that lets you find the humour if you want to," Toby Clements wrote for the London *Daily Telegraph* (February 10, 2001). "But as in all good fairy tales, desolation and madness lurk just around the corner. . . . Needless to say, none of these cautionary tales ends happily ever after, but Rhodes's narrative skill, his clear diagrams and his wrong-footing humour sweeten the pill immeasurably." The reviewer for *Publishers Weekly* (January 9, 2006) was less impressed with Rhodes's sophomore effort: "Rhodes's characters possess the uncomplicated, pared-down dimensions of archetype, such as the old professor of 'The Carolingian Period,' who's been intoning the same lecture at the School of Architecture for 30 years and is undone in a moment by a pretty auditor's attention. . . . Rhodes aims for parable and, despite inventiveness, comes closer to pat."

Rhodes's first novel, *Timoleon Vieta Come Home: A Sentimental Journey*, was published in 2003. The title character is a mongrel belonging to Carthusians Cockroft, a somewhat dissolute and embittered English composer who lives in a crumbling farmhouse in the Umbria region of Italy and spends his time chasing after men. Although devoted to his pet, Cockroft agrees to set him loose in Rome, a city unfamiliar to the dog, when his latest romantic conquest demands that he do so. The dog tries to find his way home, and as he crosses the Italian countryside, the novel sketches the histories of the humans he encounters. "These stories are lively and moving in themselves, but structurally they are gratuitous, like quite a few of the vignettes that pop up throughout the book, while their characters have the one-dimensionality of folktale—the plots drive them, rather than the other way around," Justine Jordan wrote for the London *Guardian* (April 12, 2003). "They lack the depth that is vital to a narrative of loose connections (think of David Mitchell's multilayered *Ghostwritten*). With its tone of sing-song certainty and its surface clarity, *Timoleon Vieta Come Home* will be the same every time you read it, like a fairy tale. Indeed, sometimes it reads like a story for exceedingly cynical, unshockable children (which is perhaps a compliment). Yet it is charming, original, funny, biting and wise." Michiko Kakutani, the *New York Times* (August 12, 2003) reviewer, described the novel as "part shaggy dog tale, part fairy tale, part Lassie takeoff, and a quite thoroughly original debut." She noted that in the hands of another writer the events of the novel "might sound overly contrived, but Rhodes manages to serve them up with an anomalous blend of humor, heartfelt emotion and old-fashioned storytelling verve. He has written a beguiling and resonant little novel." *Timoleon Vieta Come Home* won the Authors' Club Best First Novel Award and the Quality Paperback Book Club's New Voices Fiction Award in 2003 and was short-listed for the John Llewellyn Rhys Prize and Le Prince Maurice Prize in 2004.

In 2004 Rhodes published his second novel, *The Little White Car*, under the pen name Danuta de Rhodes, for whom the author created a humorous biography: "Danuta de Rhodes was born in 1980 and spent much of her childhood in Paris, Milan and Rio de Janeiro. She started writing features for fashion magazines at the age of 12 and her first screenplay, the romantic comedy *Le Cochon d'Inde*, was produced when she was just 14," according to the back flap of the book's first edition. Ostensibly an addition to the popular chick-lit genre, *The Little White Car* is about a Parisian woman who wakes up one morning with a hangover, no memory of the night before, and an unexplained dent in her car. After turning on the morning news, she realizes that she is the person responsible for the crash that killed Diana, Princess of Wales. "*The Little White Car* is in almost every sense a piece of fluff, which scarcely

distinguishes it from everything else in the chick-lit genre, but it reads smoothly and in spots is a fair amount of fun," Jonathan Yardley wrote for the *Washington Post* (September 16, 2004, on-line). "One senses that Danuta has her tongue firmly in cheek from first page to last, but then maintaining that pose for so long a stretch is, in and of itself, something of an accomplishment. . . . It's a clever (and more than slightly irreverent) conceit upon which to construct a novel, but Dan/Danuta brings it off, in the process sending up chick lit and just about anything else that crosses the screen." Caryn James, writing for the *New York Times Book Review* (October 24, 2004, on-line), maintained that the "pleasures of this book are enhanced by knowing the true identity of the fabulous Danuta, the Dame Edna of hot young novelists." Dan Rhodes, she added, "certainly belongs on a list of the most gifted new fiction writers, although this latest book is simply a witty diversion."

Rhodes is married and lives in Scotland.

—S.Y.

Suggested Reading: Dan Rhodes's Web site; *Irish Times* p60 Mar. 29, 2003; (London) *Daily Telegraph* p5 Feb. 10, 2001, p12 Mar. 22, 2003; (London) *Guardian* Features p8 Apr. 9, 2003, Saturday Pages p27 Apr. 12, 2003; (London) *Independent* Features p10 Mar. 11, 2000; *New York Times Book Review* (on-line) Oct. 24, 2004; *Washington Post* (on-line) Sep. 16, 2004

Selected Books: *Anthropology, and a Hundred Other Stories*, 2000; *Don't Tell Me the Truth About Love,* 2001; *Timoleon Vieta Come Home: A Sentimental Journey*, 2003; *The Little White Car,* 2004

Robinson, Marilynne

Nov. 26, 1943– Novelist; essayist

Like such writers as Henry Roth and Ralph Ellison before her, Marilynne Robinson made a celebrated fiction debut, whetting her readers' appetites for a second novel that would not appear for decades. Her first book, *Housekeeping* (1980), the story of two girls left in the care of their unconventional aunt, "is a nearly perfect work, still as singular . . . as when it was published," in the words of Mona Simpson, writing for the *Atlantic Monthly* (December 2004). "The book . . . found its place in that category of cherished marvels that happen only once in a lifetime, like certain comets." Robinson followed up *Housekeeping* with two works of nonfiction: *Mother Country* (1989), a diatribe against the British cover-up of contamination of the Irish Sea with nuclear waste from a plutonium reprocessing plant, and *The Death of Adam: Essays on Modern Thought* (1998),

Kirk Murray/Courtesy of the University of Iowa
Marilynne Robinson

an examination of where received ideas, such as Darwinism, Freudianism, and mistaken beliefs about the theology of John Calvin, have led society. Twenty-four years after her first book appeared, Robinson caused a stir in the literary community with the publication of her second novel, *Gilead*, which takes the form of a letter from an aged father to his very young son. Paul Bailey, observing in the London *Guardian* (May 3, 2003) that the narrator of *Housekeeping* "walks . . . among the lost," added in a comment that might apply equally to *Gilead*, "It is Robinson's gift to convey what it is like to be in that peculiar, yet familiar, condition of loneliness." In the *Los Angeles Times* (December 12, 2004), Merle Rubin described Robinson as "a consummate artist, a scrupulous scholar, a believing Christian and a genuinely radical thinker" and wrote that she "approaches whatever she undertakes with the kind of gravitas one seldom encounters today. In place of the buzzwords and half-baked ideas that pass for conventional wisdom, she offers something truly unconventional and certainly much closer to wisdom." *Gilead* won both the 2004 Pulitzer Prize and the 2005 National Book Critics Circle Award for fiction.

The writer was born Marilynne Summers on November 26, 1943 in Sandpoint, Idaho, to John J. Summers, who worked for lumber companies, and Ellen (Harris) Summers, a homemaker. Robinson and her brother, David, now an art professor at the University of Virginia, represented her family's fourth generation of Idahoans. In her essay "My Western Roots," included in the 1993 volume *Old West–New West: Centennial Essays* and available on the University of Washington Web site,

Robinson wrote about the "lonesome" quality—a word she used in a positive way—of the areas where she grew up: "I remember when I was a child . . . walking into the woods by myself and feeling the solitude around me build like electricity and pass through my body with a jolt that made my hair prickle. I remember . . . thinking, there is only one thing wrong here, which is my own presence, and that is the slightest imaginable intrusion—feeling that my solitude, my loneliness made me almost acceptable in so sacred a place."

Robinson read a great deal as a child. "I find that the hardest work in the world—it may in fact be impossible—is to persuade easterners that growing up in the West is not intellectually crippling," she wrote in "My Western Roots." She added that some people, on learning that she is from Idaho, have asked questions to the effect of, "Then how were you able to write a book?" In fact, Robinson and her fellow students at Coeur d'Alene High School were made familiar with classical literature. Her Latin teacher, Mrs. Bloomburg, "trudged us through Cicero's vast sentences, clause depending from clause, the whole cantilevered with subjunctives and weighted with a culminating irony. . . . And at the end of it all, I think anyone can see that my style is considerably more in debt to Cicero than to Hemingway." (She added, "I admire Hemingway.") Robinson has often declared, as she did in the *New York Times Book Review* (May 13, 1984), that as a writer she was "influenced most deeply by the 19th century Americans—Dickinson, Melville, Thoreau, Whitman, Emerson and Poe. Nothing in literature appeals to me more than the rigor with which they fasten on problems of language, of consciousness—bending form to their purposes, ransacking ordinary speech and common experience, rummaging through the exotic and recondite, setting Promethean doubts to hymn tunes . . . always, to borrow a phrase from Wallace Stevens, in the act of finding what will suffice."

Robinson attended Brown University, in Providence, Rhode Island, where her brother was a senior when she was a freshman; she studied American literature, particularly that of the 19th century, and took creative writing courses taught by the novelist John Hawkes. After graduating, in 1966, Robinson returned west to enroll at the University of Washington, in Seattle, where she earned a Ph.D., in 1977, with a dissertation entitled "A New Look at Shakespeare's *Henry VI, Part II*: Sources, Structure, and Meaning." She went next to France, where she taught at the Université de Haute Bretagne, in Rennes, until 1979. Robinson has also taught in such institutions as Amherst College, the University of Massachusetts, Skidmore College, and the University of Kent in England (as a visiting professor in 1983–84). In 1991 she moved to Iowa City to join the faculty of the University of Iowa Writers' Workshop.

Meanwhile, Robinson continued to work on the novel she had begun as a graduate student. That book, *Housekeeping*, soon came to be considered a 20th-century American classic. The novel is narrated by Ruth, who describes how she and her sister, Lucille, left orphans by the suicide of their mother, come under the guidance of their deeply eccentric Aunt Sylvie. Sylvie's behavior leads Lucille to seek refuge in the home of one of her teachers, after which she lives a conventional life in the town and has no contact with her sister or aunt. Ruth, meanwhile, is drawn to Sylvie and accompanies her on an odyssey into the wilderness. "Set in the Pacific Northwest, the novel is steeped in images of mountains, lakes and forests," Lisa Durose wrote for *ANQ* (Winter 1997), adding: "Much of the haunting lyricism of Robinson's prose stems directly from the powerful and mysterious landscape she vividly describes."

Reviewers unanimously praised *Housekeeping*. Anatole Broyard noted for the *New York Times* (January 7, 1981), "It's as if in writing it, [Robinson] broke through the ordinary human condition with all its dissatisfactions, and achieved a kind of transfiguration. You can feel in the book a gathering voluptuous release of confidence, a delighted surprise at the unexpected capacities of language, a close, careful fondness for people that we thought only saints felt." Broyard concluded that Robinson "works with light, dark, water, heat, cold, textures, sounds and smells. She is like the Impressionists, taking apart the landscape to remind us that we are surrounded by elements, that we are separated from one another, and from our past and future, by such influences. . . . She knocks off the false elevation, the pretentiousness, of our current fiction. Though her ambition is tall, she remains down to earth, where the best novels happen." The *Time* (February 2, 1981) critic, Paul Gray, observed that *Housekeeping* "brilliantly portrays the impermanence of all things, especially beauty and happiness, and the struggle to keep what can never be owned." In the years after its publication, *Housekeeping* became the subject of many academic studies and dissertations; some viewed it as a feminist text, because it focuses on women living in and making their way through the wilderness without male companionship. The novel was nominated for the Pulitzer Prize for fiction and the PEN/Faulkner fiction award. It won the Richard and Hinda Rosenthal Award, given by the American Academy and Institute for Arts and Letters, and the PEN/Hemingway award (for best fiction by a previously unpublished author). *Housekeeping* was made into a 1987 film by the director Bill Forsyth.

The impact of Robinson's debut was such that readers and critics eagerly awaited a follow-up novel. The writer turned, however, to nonfiction. She explained in an interview with Margo Hammond for the *St. Petersburg (Florida) Times* (November 7, 2004), "Fiction writing is just my mental life, or my spiritual life, but I have to put together an adequate mind, in a sense, to be able to write fiction. And the way that I do that is by writing other things." She was inspired to write her second book, *Mother Country: Britain, the Welfare State, and Nuclear Pollution*, after reading an article in England, where she was then teaching, about the risks of exposure to nuclear waste. Robinson then investigated the contamination of the Irish Sea and its surroundings by Britain's nuclear-industrial complex at Sellafield. There, nuclear waste was received from other countries, plutonium was extracted from it, and the detritus was dumped into the environment, causing widespread ecological damage. "To understand Sellafield," Jason Sherman wrote for the *Toronto Star* (February 24, 1990), Robinson "realized that she'd have to place Britain's social and economic history under the microscope." That involved an attempt to "re-educate" herself, as she told Jason Sherman, by reexamining the works of British thinkers she had always believed to be critics of the social and economic status quo, such as George Orwell and George Bernard Shaw—whom she now found to be "defenders of the very structures they apparently want to dismantle," as Sherman phrased it. In *Mother Country*, an indictment of the British government, Robinson wrote, "I am angry to the depths of my soul that the Earth has been so injured while we were all bemused by supposed monuments of value and intellect, vaults of bogus cultural riches. . . . The grief borne home to others while I and my kind have been thus occupied lies on my conscience like a crime."

After delving into 600 years of British history, Robinson concluded—according to Susan Slocum Hinerfield, writing for the *Los Angeles Times Book Review* (July 23, 1989)—that "beneath the famous civility the British have always wasted lives and credited the idea of human surplus" and that in Great Britain, "there is a lack 'of positive substantive personal and political rights.'" Merle Rubin, writing for the *Los Angeles Times Book Review* (December 12, 2004), agreed that the "heartfelt and disturbing" book was about "how a country like Britain, long regarded as a bastion of liberty, fair play, decency and democracy, could allow the welfare of its citizens to be gravely endangered by the plutonium at Sellafield (formerly called Windscale)." Peter Gorner wrote for the *Chicago Tribune* (July 12, 1989), "Frightened and furious, [Robinson] has written a venomous essay in the tradition of 19th century novelists, and it is a chilling and poignant scream of outrage." Some scientists, however, including Max Perutz, a Nobel Prize–winning chemist, writing for the *New York Review of Books* (November 23, 1989), condemned *Mother Country* as presenting "monstrous exaggerations of the dangers presented by Sellafield." Robinson's book was banned in Great Britain but named a finalist for the National Book Award in the U.S.

In *The Death of Adam: Essays on Modern Thought*, Robinson explored the works and ideas of past thinkers, including the 19th-century German political philosopher Karl Marx and the 19th-century British naturalist Charles Darwin, as a way of examining contemporary social attitudes—in which she found an overreliance on received viewpoints and what might be called knee-jerk cynicism. In particular, she sought to defend the ideas—often misrepresented, in her view—of the 16th-century theologian John Calvin. Merle Rubin wrote for the *Christian Science Monitor* (January 14, 1999) that *The Death of Adam* "is both original and somber, brimming with fresh insights and perspectives that could well help to elevate the level of our public discourse." In a critique for *Magill Book Reviews* (1999), Lois A. Marchino found Robinson "particularly adept at making connections between attitudes and events and between the myths society clings to and the realities of survival that are at stake if these myths are not re-examined. . . . The humanitarian vision which shapes each of the essays makes this a profound work at both the levels of individual self-understanding and of understanding contemporary culture."

Robinson's long-awaited second novel, *Gilead*, appeared in 2004, after a relatively brief period of composition that began in 2001 and lasted roughly two years. The book's protagonist, John Ames, is a 76-year-old pastor in the small town of Gilead, Iowa; the novel takes the form of a letter he writes to his seven-year-old son, to be read after Ames's death. In recounting his own life, Ames describes his grandfather, also a preacher, who held services during the Civil War era while wearing a pistol, and his father, who rebelled against the grandfather by becoming a pacifist. *Gilead* addresses the theme of fathers and sons, in both the familial and Christian senses; its plot hinges on the return to town of a fellow minister's prodigal son, who is named after Ames. James Wood, writing for the *New York Times Book Review* (November 28, 2004), called the novel "religious, somewhat essayistic and fiercely calm," as well as "a beautiful work—demanding, grave and lucid." Wood added: "There is . . . something remarkable about the writing in *Gilead*. . . . Robinson's words have a spiritual force that's very rare in contemporary fiction." Philip Connors, writing for New York *Newsday* (November 21, 2004), observed, "[Ames's] yearning to understand the mysteries of the human heart, and his awareness that those mysteries would hardly be more clear were he allowed another hundred years to ponder them, give his letter, in the end, an almost unbearable poignancy. Imagining his son reading the letter in adulthood grants us the pleasure of extending the life of this austere, beautiful novel long beyond the last page."

Robinson has two adult sons from her marriage, which ended in divorce. She has described herself as a Congregationalist Christian.

—S.Y.

Suggested Reading: *ANQ* p31+ Winter 1997; *Atlantic Monthly* p135+ Dec. 2004; *Chicago Tribune* C p5 July 12, 1989; *Christian Science Monitor* p20 Jan. 14, 1999; *Critique* p95+ Winter 1989; (London) *Guardian* p37 May 3, 2003, p31 Sep. 25, 2004; *New York Times* C p18 Jan. 7, 1981, C p11 Nov. 25, 1987; *New York Times Book Review* p14 Feb. 8, 1981, p7+ May 13, 1984, p14 Feb. 7, 1999, p1 Nov. 28, 2004; *New York Times Magazine* p63+ Oct. 24, 2004; *Toronto Star* M p17 Feb. 24, 1990

Selected Books: fiction—*Housekeeping*, 1980; *Gilead*, 2004; nonfiction—*Mother Country: Britain, the Welfare State, and Nuclear Pollution*, 1989; *The Death of Adam: Essays on Modern Thought*, 1998

Mitch Butler/Courtesy of Hazel Rowley

Rowley, Hazel

Nov. 16, 1951– Biographer

Hazel Rowley is the author of several well-received biographies of major 20th-century writers. *Christina Stead: A Biography* (1993), her first book, was warmly praised for its thorough examination of its subject, a critically appreciated but oft-neglected novelist. *Richard Wright: The Life and Times* (2001) focused on Wright's journey from humble beginnings in Mississippi to the heights of literary fame. In her most recent book, *Tête-à-Tête: Simone de Beauvoir and Jean-Paul Sartre* (2005), Rowley explores the relationship between Beauvoir, a feminist icon and author *The Second Sex* (1949), and Sartre, who popularized the philosophy known as existentialism in such works as *Being and Nothingness* (1943) and *No Exit* (1944). The French couple's unconventional relationship has been a source of much gossip and intrigue, as they pursued romantic liaisons with countless others—often swapping or sharing sexual partners—all the while maintaining a firm commitment to each other that lasted until Sartre's death, in 1980.

Rowley contributed the following third-person statement to *World Authors 2001–2005*:

"Hazel Rowley was born in London, England, on November 16, 1951. In 1960, her father, Derrick Rowley, was appointed Professor of Immunology at the University of Adelaide, South Australia. Hazel Rowley well remembers the month-long boat voyage across the world the family made when she was eight. (She has an older brother and younger sister.) Her father took his sabbatical years in Switzerland and Germany, and the family accompanied him. Hazel Rowley studied French and German at the University of Adelaide, gained First Class Honours, and in 1973 she won a German Exchange Fellowship (DAAD) for two years in Freiburg, Germany, which she followed by a year in Strasbourg, France. During the 1970s, Rowley, who had been active against the Vietnam War and apartheid in South Africa, was also steeped in the women's movement. The subject of her Ph.D. was Simone de Beauvoir and Existentialist autobiography.

"Travel and cultural difference are central to Rowley's writing. She wrote her first book, about that famous wandering writer, the expatriate Australian novelist Christina Stead, while teaching literary studies at Deakin University, Melbourne. *Christina Stead: A Biography* (Heinemann, 1993) garnered considerable international acclaim. It was a *New York Times* Notable Book, and in Australia it won the National Book Award for Nonfiction. In December 1996, after 13 years as a university professor (in an article in *The Australian*, she commented that she had enjoyed the tail end of an era when academic life in the humanities was profoundly fulfilling), Rowley found herself dismayed by the anti-intellectualism and 'rationalizations' of the new regime.

"She left her senior academic post in Literary Studies at Deakin University and moved to the United States, where she wrote *Richard Wright: The Life and Times* (Holt, 2001) while affiliated with the W.E.B. Du Bois Institute for Afro American Studies at Harvard. The book had cover reviews in the *New York Times*, *Washington Post*, *Chicago Tribune* and the *Philadelphia Inquirer*, and was listed among the *Washington Post* Best Books of the Year.

"Rowley moved to Paris to write *Tête-à-Tête: Simone de Beauvoir and Jean-Paul Sartre* (HarperCollins, 2005). In this book, Rowley returned to a relationship that had marked her earlier life. She had interviewed Simone de Beauvoir in Paris in 1976. Now, with the distance of passing years, she wanted to know the truth about that famous relationship that Beauvoir had somewhat idealized in her memoirs. Rowley was open to what she would find. *Tête-à-Tête*, which has been translated into over a dozen languages, has once again reaped international acclaim.

"Hazel Rowley currently divides her time between New York City and Paris. 'I don't write books about subjects I already know a lot about,' she says. 'I write books to learn. The writing is an adventure, a voyage of discovery. I always take a huge risk with my books. They keep me awake at 3 in the morning. They frighten me, and excite me. I invest a great deal of personal passion in them. They change my life.'

"Rowley has written numerous articles and reviews, and her essays have twice appeared in *The Best Australian Essays*. An outspoken writer and passionate speaker herself, she finds herself drawn to subjects who challenge conventions. As a biographer, she has focused on writers who have had the courage to challenge the state of the world, in their lives and in their writing."

Although Christina Stead, the subject of Rowley's first book, is not widely known today, she is considered by many to be a leading figure in 20th-century literature. Stead was born in 1902 in Australia. Her mother died when she was two; her father was a complex man, a self-educated naturalist who was confident in his own goodness and wisdom but whose self-absorbed insensitivity to others terrified his children. Stead later immortalized him as the character Sam Pollit in her best-known novel, *The Man Who Loved Children* (1940). Stead left Australia in her mid-20s, settling in England and working as a secretary. She struck up a relationship with her boss, the Marxist writer William J. Blake; although married, Blake fell in love with Stead, and the two adopted a peripatetic life. Stead was a devout Stalinist, even after such events as the 1956 Hungarian Revolution began to cause other idealistic leftists to abandon their fealty to the Soviet Union. During World War II the couple lived well in the U.S., but after McCarthyism and Cold War hostility to communism forced them to Europe, she and Blake fell on hard times, eking out what money they could from free-lance writing assignments. She kept writing novels, but had little luck getting them published. Then, in 1966, *The Man Who Loved Children* was reprinted with an introduction by the literary critic Randall Jarrell, who called it "one of those books [whose] own age neither reads nor praises, but that the next age thinks is a masterpiece," as quoted by Elizabeth Ward for the *Washington Post* (October 2, 1994). Stead's reputation enjoyed a major boost, but her productive literary years had passed. Shortly thereafter Blake died; Stead returned to Australia, where she led a lonely existence until she died, in 1983.

"Hazel Rowley's is not the first biography of Christina Stead, but it is the most complete and detailed account of her life to date," Merle Rubin wrote for the *Los Angeles Times* (November 20, 1994). "Rowley . . . very ably demonstrates the close connection between Stead's life and her fiction, without falling into the dangerous habit of mistaking the one for the other. Stead drew many of her characters and situations from real-life family, friends and acquaintances. Her portraits, fueled by obsessive love or strong hatred, may well have distorted the facts, but uncovered deeper truths about human nature, laid bare by the intensity of her re-imagining." "Rowley's account of Stead's life provides as intensely detailed, absorbing and complex a portrait as any of her subject's fictional characters," Diane Cole wrote for *New York Newsday* (October 2, 1994). "Her reconstruction of Stead's early years allows us rare insight into the way the artistic imagination can spin parallel worlds in fiction out of the most hurtful realities. And her portrait of Stead's hellish Grub Street life confirms that, whatever new horrors of the publishing world we read today, being a serious artist has never been easy. Perhaps the final miracle is not simply that Christina Stead had the gift to create, but that she found the will to persevere." Rowley won Australia's CUB Banjo Award in 1994 and was named a finalist for the Festival Award for Literature for *Christina Stead*.

In 1996 Rowley resigned her post at Deakin University, complaining, in an article for the *Australian* (December 18, 1996) that higher education was severely devaluing the humanities, primarily through ill-conceived funding requirements and unrealistic publishing demands. "Research, writing and teaching is what I do best; it's my passion," she wrote. "And I've just taken what they call an 'early retirement package.' Why? The new regime is so opposed to the spirit of free inquiry and reflection, imagination or challenge, that it is no longer possible to think creatively, let alone stretch oneself to the limit of one's intellectual capacity. The word from our leaders is loud and clear: 'I don't care what you publish. Just publish.' God knows who's going to do the reading."

Rowley moved to the U.S. and became associated with the W. E. B. Du Bois Institute for Afro-American Studies at Harvard University, in Cambridge, Massachusetts. She began research for a biography of Richard Wright, one of the most important African-American writers of the 20th century, best known for his novel *Native Son* (1940) and his autobiography *Black Boy* (1945). She had some trepidations about the project, as she told Frank Campbell in an interview for the *Weekend Australian* (December 1, 2001). "'Did I dare? . . . Would I, as a white woman from Australia, ever be able to understand, let alone convey, the experience of a black man in America?'"

Richard Wright was the first best-selling black author in the U.S., and he had a profound influence on such celebrated black writers as Ralph Ellison and James Baldwin. The latter once said, as quoted by John Freeman for the *American Scholar* (Autumn 2001), "In *Uncle Tom's Children*, in *Native Son*, and above all, in *Black Boy*, I found expressed, for the first time in my life, the sorrow, the rage, and the murderous bitterness which was eating up my life and the lives of those around me." Wright was born in Mississippi in 1908, when racial segregation was a way of life in much of the South. Beset by poverty, he had little education, but he became a voracious reader on his own initiative. He later moved to Chicago, worked menial jobs, and eventually joined the Communist Party. He published his first book, *Uncle Tom's Children*, in 1938. *Native Son*, which he published two years later, told the story of Bigger Thomas, a frustrated, uneducated black man who accidentally murders a white woman. Wright's protagonist was "the angriest, most violent antihero ever to have appeared in black American literature," Rowley wrote in her biography, as quoted by Hardy Green for *BusinessWeek* (September 24, 2001). Following the unprecedented success of *Native Son* and *Black Boy*, Wright achieved considerable wealth as well as the respect of American intellectuals; he married and settled in New York City, but too restless to stay put, he moved the family to France, where he fell in with such literary luminaries as Sartre, Beauvoir, and Gertrude Stein.

Reviews of *Richard Wright* were mixed. "Rowley's writing is clear, concise, and thankfully shorn of the kind of academic mumbo-jumbo that often sinks works by scholars attempting to write about real people's lives," Amy Alexander wrote for the *Boston Globe* (October 21, 2001). "Overall, Rowley wisely lets Wright's correspondence, and the recollections of his surviving friends, family members, and other living associates, paint a vivid picture of a man who was as complicated as he was talented." Michael Anderson, in a review for the *New York Times* (August 26, 2001), agreed that Rowley "has a daunting dedication to primary sources and her documentation is meticulous," but concluded, "For all its additions to the record, Rowley's biography seems irritatingly opaque; neither the man nor his achievement comes into focus. . . . With but token gestures toward interpretation and analysis—her discussions of the individual books are at best cursory—Rowley has, in effect, assembled only the makings of a biography." Eric Arnesen, writing for the *Chicago Tribune*, praised Rowley for providing a "richly textured sense" of Wright's daily life in the 1940s and '50s and commended the chapters on his years in Paris and his 1953 voyage to Africa, but complained that Wright's "lengthy and tortured relationship to communism and the American

Communist Party is . . . given short analytical shrift. . . . Rowley appears interested neither in exploring the evolution of Wright's political and philosophical ideas nor in placing them in their broader context." Daniel Garrett opined for *World Literature Today* (April–June 2003), "Rowley's biography of Wright may not be elegant or eloquent (it is rather plain and slow-moving) but it is the most factual and fair—and the most intelligent— biography of Wright that I am aware of, and it allows future generations to inherit a Wright who is whole, at once man, thinker, and writer."

In *Tête-à-Tête* Rowley delved into the lives and relationships of Beauvoir and Sartre. The two met in Paris in 1929, when they were students preparing for university exams. Sartre, although a notoriously unattractive individual, was intelligent, charming, and had a way with women, and the two promptly fell in love; both sought to flout traditional bourgeois conventions, and their relationship, which lasted for the next five decades, was far from ordinary. "Sartre proposed a pact," Louis Menand wrote for the *New Yorker* (September 26, 2005). "They could have affairs, but they were required to tell each other everything. As he put it to Beauvoir: 'What *we* have is an *essential* love; but it is a good idea for us also to experience *contingent* love affairs.'" Numerous affairs did indeed follow, which Rowley carefully delineated in her biography. Sartre was a prolific seducer of young women, although by admission he preferred cuddling to sex. Beauvoir, who in interviews denied having sex with women, in fact had affairs with many of her infatuated female students, as well as long-term affairs with such noted figures as the writer Nelson Algren and the filmmaker Claude Lanzmann. All the while, Sartre and Beauvoir, in the name of "transparency," would report back to each other about their various dalliances.

For research, Rowley conducted interviews with several former lovers, and she received cooperation from Beauvoir's daughter Sylvie Le Bon de Beauvoir, who furnished her with access to previously unpublished letters. However, Arlette Elkaïm-Sartre, another daughter, refused to allow publication of many of Sartre's letters, and Rowley was forced to cut some material for the European edition and paraphrase some for the American release.

Reviews of the book were laudatory. "Without undue prurience, Rowley romps through the major entanglements, loves, triangles, friendships and affairs engaged in by the authors," a reviewer wrote for *Publishers Weekly* (August 1, 2005). "Though Beauvoir is the heroine of the book, Rowley offers revealing insights into Sartre: including the extent to which he juggled, depended upon and supported his many mistresses and the compulsive need he had to seduce women far more beautiful than he, despite his tepid sensuality. Intrigues aside, however, Rowley concludes that, for both Sartre and Beauvoir, the most enduring commitment was not to each other or their many lovers but to their writing, politics and philosophical legacy." "As Rowley states at the outset, her book is neither a full-scale biography . . . nor a study of [the couple's] work. It is rather 'the story of a relationship,'" Heller McAlpin wrote for the *Los Angeles Times* (December 11, 2005). "Is *Tête-à-Tête* just high-brow gossip? With her use of well-chosen quotations from letters, memoirs, novels, essays and interviews, Rowley captures not just her subjects' sexual shenanigans but also their voices, their unflagging work ethic and their drive to unfetter mankind from self-imposed limitations. An admiring but balanced portrait emerges of activist intellectuals determined to practice the freedom they preached. Rowley summarizes their ideas with impressive clarity and brevity. She also points out unsavory or misguided aspects of their behavior, such as Sartre's heartless descriptions of taking a lover's virginity or his long support of Stalinist communism." "Rowley is an engrossing narrator," Christina Nehring wrote for the *New York Times* (December 4, 2005). "Her book tells Beauvoir and Sartre's repellent, inspiring and unlikely tale more completely and concisely than it has ever been told before." *Entertainment Weekly* (December 30, 2005) named *Tête-à-Tête* one of the best books of the year.

—S.Y.

Suggested Reading: *Australian* p13 Dec. 18, 1996; *Boston Globe* E p5 Oct. 31, 2001; *Chicago Tribune* C p1 Sep. 2, 2001; *New York Times* VII p26 Dec. 4, 2005; *New Yorker* p141+ Sep. 26, 2005; *Weekend Australian* R p8 Dec. 1, 2001

Selected Books: *Christina Stead: A Biography*, 1993; *Richard Wright: The Life and Times*, 2001; *Tête-à-Tête: Simone de Beauvoir and Jean-Paul Sartre*, 2005

Royte, Elizabeth

May 6, 1960– Journalist; nonfiction writer

As a freelance writer for some of the most popular American magazines, Elizabeth Royte has written on a wide variety of topics; she has produced articles that detail the heartbreaking realities of war and others that gently satirize the stranger customs of the contemporary scene. She has been particularly interested, however, in environmental issues, as is reflected in her two critically acclaimed books, *The Tapir's Morning Bath: Mysteries of the Tropical Rain Forest and the Scientists Who Are Trying to Solve Them* (2001) and *Garbage Land: On the Secret Trail of Trash* (2005).

Elizabeth Royte wrote the following autobiographical statement for *World Authors 2000–2005*:

Courtesy of Elizabeth Royte

Elizabeth Royte

"I was born on May 6, 1960, in Boston, and spent my childhood in Chelmsford, then a fairly rural suburb northwest of the city. My father, Paul Royte, is from Maine: he's a psychologist who spent most of his career working in public schools. My mother, Eleanor Kalfin Royte, is from New York. She taught kindergarten at the beginning of her career and then, as an early-childhood teacher educator, became the director of the Child Study Center at Simmons College. I graduated a year early from my local high school, then attended Bard College, graduating with a degree in English in 1981. I have one child, Lucy, who was born in 1999.

"I don't remember having literary aspirations as a child, but my mother remembers me announcing that I wanted to write and illustrate children's books when I grew up. I started out taking classes in creative writing at Bard but gravitated toward nonfiction. After graduation, I moved to New York City and worked as an editorial assistant at Conde Nast publications. I found the atmosphere less than stimulating, quit after one year, and took an internship at *The Nation Magazine*, where I learned the useful skills of fact checking, proofreading, and getting along with editors. When my internship ended, I stuck around for another year, working for The Nation Institute, the magazine's social action arm, then went out on my own. I worked for a year at *Geo*, a hybrid travel-and-nature magazine; when it folded I started writing freelance. I did book reviews for small downtown weeklies, and got proofreading and copy editing work at *Rolling Stone, Manhattan, Inc.* (now defunct) and other publications. My clip file grew.

"One winter day, an editor at an uptown weekly contacted me to write a piece about professional dog walkers, and then another piece about restaurant inspectors. I liked this editor, but soon he left the weekly for a job at the *New York Times Magazine*. It was a turning point in my career as well, for this editor assigned me a feature story on the great Harvard biologist Edward O. Wilson. I traveled with Wilson to a research station in Panama, where he was collecting *Pheidole*, the world's largest genus of ants. The story appeared on the cover of the *New York Times Magazine*, and soon after, editors at other publications began phoning me to offer work. It was at about this time, the mid-1990s, that I began writing almost exclusively about the environment and the outdoors. I traveled widely and wrote pieces on public-lands grazing, forensic entomology, eco-saboteurs, Mexican free-tailed bats, microbiologists, wild dogs in Africa, extinctions in Hawaii, and conservationists in Brazil. For *Outside* magazine, where I'm listed on the masthead as a correspondent, I wrote adventure travel stories and, for a couple of years, the Wild File column, which answers readers' questions about the natural world. The magazines to which I contributed include: *National Geographic, The New Yorker, Harper's, Smithsonian, Outside, New England Monthly, Esquire, The New York Times Magazine, Vogue, Life, Conde Nast Traveler,* and others.

"I didn't have a strong science background, but I seemed to have a fascination with the natural world, or at least with those who study it. (As a child, I had spent a lot of time outdoors—swimming, canoeing, hiking, and skiing—but I had never made a serious study of nature. Now, in my early thirties, I realized that what I most enjoyed was writing about those who can share their knowledge of—and their enthusiasm for—the natural world, people who can explain its inner workings. I was drawn to scientists' precision and confidence, their strange language, and customs.

"My visit to the rainforest with E. O. Wilson spurred me to write my first book, *The Tapir's Morning Bath: Mysteries of the Tropical Rain Forest and the Scientists Who Are Trying to Solve Them* (Houghton Mifflin, 2001), about a community of researchers at the Panamanian field station I'd visited so long ago. The rainforest was everything it's generally cracked up to be, but the field biologists I met there—narrowly focused, hypercompetitive, and sometimes a little bit undersocialized—were the real draw for me. They knew the forest inside out, but they also embodied, unlike scientists who study partial organisms on a lab bench, a sort of gee-whiz infatuation that's currently unfashionable but does, I think, speak to something in all of us. The book explores the value of basic research and evolutionary studies, and it examines the schism between studying biodiversity and working to preserve it.

"I spent the better part of 1998 living in Panama at the field station, got married that same year, had a baby the following winter, and then moved from Manhattan to Brooklyn. The book was published in September of 2001.

"Looking for a new book subject, I considered writing about the Bronx Zoo but realized the daily commute from Brooklyn would kill me. I was still interested in scientists but got drawn into a strange quest: to follow the many different streams of garbage that left my home and write about their widespread social and environmental impact. The result of these efforts was *Garbage Land: On the Secret Trail of Trash* (Little, Brown 2005). I continue to write for magazines today."

Royte's first book, *The Tapir's Morning Bath*, is an account of the year she spent on Barro Colorado Island, in the Panama Canal, shadowing researchers from the Smithsonian Tropical Research Institute and taking careful notes on how they studied the unusual biodiversity of the rainforest. Describing the book as a "mischievous report," a reviewer for the *New Yorker* (October 8, 2001) noted that though Royte is not a scientist, "she gamely tags along with researchers as they pursue spider-monkey dung and doctoral degrees, while stealthily collecting her own data on *Homo academicus* and its mating habits in the wild." The reviewer concluded that the book, which is "by turns comic and poetic," provides "the pleasure of a long, meandering excursion, in which the act of observing is its own reward." In the *New York Times* (October 7, 2001), Ann Finkbeiner, who praised Royte's decision to present the material as a "profile of a community," wrote: "Profiles of communities often fail in least four ways: the number of participants in the conversation is usually more than a reader can keep straight; the reader misses a central voice, a point of identification; the science gets cut-and-pasted into the text in a single compulsory lump, as does the history; and the story line is hard to track. But Royte is a remarkable writer, and nails all four. . . . The central voice is the author's, and she's a perfect guide: intensely curious, smart, occasionally unimpressed, a little relentless and so personal she lets us watch her taking a pregnancy test." *The Tapir's Morning Bath* was selected as a notable book by the *New York Times* in 2001.

In the introduction to Royte's second book, *Garbage Land*, she explained the impetus for her distasteful quest to find out what happens to her refuse: on Earth Day 2002, while paddling a canoe through the "diarrheal brown" waters of the Gowanus Canal in Brooklyn, watching as Sierra Club members plucked trash from the water, she began to wonder about her own complicity in the environmental devastation around her. "Before this day I'd wondered only idly how my detritus disappeared," she wrote. "You can't live in New York or any big city and not be aware that vast tonnages of waste are generated daily. If you're unlucky enough to be around during a garbage strike or an extended snow emergency, those tonnages assume a visceral reality. But most of the time that reality is virtual, because somehow our unwanted stuff keeps disappearing. It moves away from us in pieces—truck by truck, barge by barge— in a process that is as constant as it is invisible." For the next year, Royte followed the trail of her own and then other people's refuse, from its origin to its final resting places in landfills, wastewater treatment plants, and in the ecosystem.

Garbage Land paints a bleak picture, one in which the insatiable appetites of American consumers have caused the nation's municipal waste stream to nearly triple since 1960. "It's a fascinating, sometimes tiring, often depressing tour," William Grimes wrote for the *New York Times* (July 15, 2005). "Ms. Royte . . . is a dogged reporter and a vivid writer, which means that her catalog of crimes against nature hits the senses hard. . . . Unpleasant odors are the least of it. As she makes her rounds, Ms. Royte cites a blizzard of studies, statistics and experts to prove that the garbage problem threatens to bury us all. The numbers, flying from every direction, are alarming, and they are meant to be. Americans now throw out 4.3 pounds of garbage each day, 1.6 pounds more than they threw away 30 years ago." While Glenn C. Altschuler, writing for the *Boston Globe* (July 3, 2005), criticized Royte for not offering a program for reform—describing her as a "modern-day, modernist muckraker, exhibiting more irony, realism, and resignation than righteous indignation"—many reviewers agreed with the sentiments of Donna Seaman, who, in her review for *Booklist* (June 15, 2005), described *Garbage Land* as "fascinating, appalling, and—thanks to [Royte's] keen first-person journalism, commonsense skepticism, and amusing personal asides—downright entertaining."

Royte's writing can also be found in such anthologies as *Why Moths Hate Thomas Edison: And Other Urgent Inquiries into the Odd Nature of Nature* (2001), *Naked: Writers Uncover the Way We Live on Earth* (2004), and *The Best American Science Writing* (2004). Royte lives with her husband, Peter Kreutzer, and daughter, Lucy, in the Park Slope neighborhood of Brooklyn.

—S.Y.

Suggested Reading: *Boston Globe* K p6 July 3, 2005; *Detroit Free Press* (on-line) Aug. 7, 2005; *New York Times Book Review* p15 Oct. 7, 2001; *New Yorker* p87 Oct. 8, 2001

Selected Books: *The Tapir's Morning Bath: Mysteries of the Tropical Rain Forest and the Scientists Who Are Trying to Solve Them*, 2001; *Garbage Land: On the Secret Trail of Trash*, 2005

Ruff, Matt

Sep. 8, 1965(?)– Novelist

Matt Ruff has distinguished himself as a writer capable of crossing wide boundaries between genres. His first two books, *Fool on the Hill* (1988) and *Sewer, Gas and Electric: The Public Works Trilogy* (1997), were classified as fantasy and science fiction, while his most recent novel, *Set This House in Order: A Romance of Souls* (2003), about two individuals afflicted with multiple personality disorder, has been called "equal parts literary fiction and psychological thriller," according to Nestor Ramos, writing for the *Sunday Oregonian* (March 2, 2003). Ruff told readers in a 1998 on-line chat, as archived on the *Event Horizon: Science Fiction, Fantasy, Horror* Web site, "I think of myself as a generic storyteller who is happy to write in any genre that strikes my fancy."

Matt Ruff contributed the following autobiographical statement to *World Authors 2000–2005*:

"I like to joke that I am the child of a mixed marriage: North American and South American. My father was born in 1922 to a family of Midwestern dairy farmers. He entered the Lutheran ministry, and after the failure of his first marriage came east to work as a hospital chaplain in New York City. My mother, ten years younger, was a missionary's daughter who grew up battling snakes and scorpions in the jungles of Brazil.

"They made an odd couple. My father was a quiet, non-confrontational person. Mom was a born warrior: boisterous and tough, always game for a fight and sometimes spoiling for one. Our house in Queens served as Ellis Island for other immigrating South American relatives, and this, along with a religious schism within the family—my mother's mother and one of her brothers were converts to Mormonism—provided plenty of opportunities for argument, even when Dad and I weren't in the mood.

"It's probably no coincidence, then, that my novels feature characters of different backgrounds, temperaments, and beliefs being thrown together, often with volatile results, although my protagonists' fictional debates tend to be very controlled and Socratic affairs compared to the theological free-for-alls that used to break out at the Ruff house.

"I decided I wanted to be a writer when I was five years old. While I did occasionally write short stories to entertain my friends or to try to impress girls, my emphasis from the beginning was always on longer works. I must have started at least half a dozen novels while I was still in grade school, always abandoning them before the end but each time getting a little farther along.

"The first novel I actually completed was a semi-autobiographical religious drama called *The Gospel According to St. Thomas*, about a minister's son who comes to question his faith. *St. Thomas* was intended, among other things, to break the news to my parents that I wasn't growing up to be the devout Lutheran they'd hoped for. The whole time I was writing it I was imagining their reaction; Dad, I figured, would take it well (and he did), but I anticipated a royal set-to with Mom. Naturally, she chose that exact moment in history to turn pacifist. While cleaning my room one day she found the manuscript and read it without bothering to ask permission. Not only did she not blow her top, she thought the book was really good. So I was the one who ended up getting mad, partly because of the violation of privacy, but mainly because I felt cheated. I was rebelling, God damn it! How dare she not be outraged?

"At least I'd proven I could finish a novel, if I was passionate enough about its subject. As I was in college now, fast approaching the day when I would have to start paying for my own food, I started thinking about another book, one that would be good enough not just to tame my mother, but to actually be published, and save me from having to get a real job.

"I started writing *Fool on the Hill* near the end of my sophomore year at Cornell University. Rather than choose a single plot, I took four different story ideas—one about a lovelorn writer who gets drawn into a storytelling contest with the Greek god Apollo, one about a dog and a cat in search of heaven, one about a group of modern day knights and ladies, and one about a clan of magically inclined Little People—and wove them together, using Ithaca and the Cornell campus as a backdrop. Even allowing for my multicultural upbringing, this kitchen-sink approach really shouldn't have worked, but I turned out to have a knack for complex narratives.

"I finished the first draft of *Fool* just in time to submit it as my senior thesis for Honors English. The members of the thesis committee were both impressed and appalled: after allowing me to graduate summa cum laude, they changed the rules, limiting future fiction submissions to a maximum of 80 pages.

"Meanwhile one of my professors, the novelist Alison Lurie, gave me the address of her literary agent Melanie Jackson, and told me to send her a copy of my manuscript once I'd revised it. Melanie liked the book, and by October of that year had sold it to Atlantic Monthly Press. Published in 1988, *Fool on the Hill* gained an early cult following that continues to this day. I've been writing full time ever since.

"Where *Fool on the Hill* was a comic fantasy, my second novel, *Sewer, Gas and Electric: The Public Works Trilogy*, was a science-fiction satire, and my most recent book, *Set This House in Order: A Romance of Souls*, is a mainstream drama about two people with multiple personalities. I didn't consciously plan to write in a new genre each time, but I like the challenge of not repeating myself, and I've never been short of ideas. The hard part is deciding what not to write; since I've only got a finite amount of time left, and since I take, on average, four or five years to finish a book, I want to make each one count."

Matt Ruff was born in the mid-1960s—an occasional source lists September 8, 1965 as his date of birth—and began writing early in life. He explained on his official Web site, "Traditionally you're supposed to start with short stories and work your way up to longer fiction, but I guess I never liked the thought of using up a good idea in only ten pages, so from the beginning, I worked almost exclusively on novels. My early attempts weren't very good, but since my parents were still paying for my room and board at that point, it didn't matter. I kept trying, and got a lot of practice."

Ruff attended Cornell University in Ithaca, New York, where he majored in English. As he recalled in an interview for Amazon.com, as posted on his Web site, "My most embarrassing moment came in a college creative writing seminar when the teacher asked everyone to describe what they were working on. Most of the students were busy with short stories; the woman to the left joked that she was 'taking notes for a novel.' Then came my turn: 'Well, I've written two books already, and I'm working on a third . . .' It came out like I was bragging, but by that point, I'd been writing for over a decade and a half, so it would have been strange if I *hadn't* finished a novel."

Ruff completed a draft of his first novel, *Fool on the Hill*, between his sophomore and senior years at Cornell and became a published novelist while still in his early 20s. *Fool on the Hill*, set in and around the campus of Cornell University, features the fictional graduate student and aspiring novelist Stephen Titus George, who encounters a number of fantasy characters in his effort to battle evil and find true love. When George learns to write without paper, he begins composing a volume about the history of Cornell, a mythical book that had been started more than a century earlier by a Greek god known as Mr. Sunshine. Along the way, S. T. George (or St. George), as he comes to be called, battles a number of evil creatures, including Rasferret the Grub and his army of magical rats. The story features several fantastical subplots, including one in which a telepathic dog and a jovial cat search for Heaven.

Reviewers appreciated the book's complex, multilayered plot. Albert E. Wilhelm, writing for *Library Journal* (October 15, 1988), called Ruff's treatment "remarkably inventive." He added, "Ruff's exuberant tale will appeal strongly to readers with a taste for the fabulous." Sharon Miller opined for United Press International (January 6, 1989), "This outrageous book has almost anything you could ask for, heroes and villains, romance and adventure, humor and tears. The humans, the talking cats and dogs and the sprites all get their fair share of drama as Ruff moves expertly from one group to another. All this makes for a book that is satisfying and fun to read." Despite a persistent rumor among fans that Ruff later "disowned" this novel, the author refuted the claim on his Web site, explaining, "Because it was my first published novel, I can't help being critical of *Fool on the Hill*—when I wrote it I thought it was perfect, and now I know it was just the best my 20-year-old self could do, and this bugs me—but *Fool* is still my baby and it always will be."

Ruff's next work, *Sewer, Gas and Electric: The Public Works Trilogy*, is structured with three individual sections, each exploring society in the futuristic setting of 2023. The book's main character, Harry Gant, is an egocentric billionaire, working to build a new Tower of Babel. Gant's ex-wife, Joan Fine, is investigating the murder of a Wall Street millionaire who tried to thwart Gant Industries. (The victim was apparently beaten to death with a copy of Ayn Rand's *Atlas Shrugged*.)

Sewer, Gas and Electric, part science-fiction novel and part political farce, explores the ways in which technology can go wrong. The first section looks at the general state of the world in 2023, when the entire black race has been eradicated by a mysterious plague and replaced with androids called Electric Negroes. In the book's second section, a computer-resurrected image of Ayn Rand assists Fine in her murder investigation. Here Ruff picks apart Rand's theory of Objectivism, as outlined in *Atlas Shrugged*. (Objectivism emphasizes objective reality, reason, self-interest, and capitalism.) The third section includes an android rebellion and a fast-paced climax.

Reviews of *Sewer, Gas and Electric* were generally mixed, although many critics praised the scope of Ruff's work and his comic tone. The novel was often compared to the works of Thomas Pynchon, Joseph Heller, and Kurt Vonnegut. Ellen Gilchrist wrote for the *Washington Post* (February 16, 1997), "Matt Ruff is a protean talent but he has a disquieting tendency to soar one moment and fall into sophomoric doggerel the next. . . . One minute his writing is among the best that American literature has yet produced, and one is willing to forgive him any indulgence, any sly homage to Vonnegut, or whomever. The next instant, he will toss in some juvenilism that makes one want to toss the book back on the stacks in disgust." A critic for *Publishers Weekly* (October 28, 1996) wrote, "Told with breezy good humor, this exuberantly silly tale will find an audience among admirers of the day-glow surrealism of Steve Erickson and the tangled conspiracy theories of David Foster Wallace. What is absent here are the carefully honed language and the attention to nuance and character necessary to prevent Ruff's own Tower of Babel from sagging under the weight of his pell-mell special effects." Despite such mixed reviews, Gilchrist concluded, "Don't count

Ruff out. He just might be the fellow whom American literature's been seeking for a long time. When he's good, he's very, very, very good."

In *Set This House in Order: A Romance of Souls* (2003), Ruff presents two characters afflicted with multiple personality disorder (MPD). Andy Gage is a 29-year-old man whose psyche was destroyed when he was three years old by his abusive stepfather. In response, he developed a series of distinct personalities, each vying for control of his body. Unlike many other MPD sufferers, Andy has not taken steps to reintegrate these fragments into a single persona—the treatment most psychiatrists consider desirable. Instead, he has devised a system that allows his roughly 100 alternate personalities to exist harmoniously, by imagining that the individual "souls" are co-existing in one "house." Andy takes a janitorial job at a software company in Seattle, Washington, and is introduced to Penny, an MPD sufferer who is at first unaware of her disorder. In the course of the novel, each character must confront the torture and abuse that triggered their respective disorders, and Andy attempts to solve the mystery of his stepfather's murder to determine if one of his own identities was responsible.

Set This House in Order received widespread acclaim, with many critics praising Ruff's realistic portrayal of a complicated mental disorder, as well as his humorous and ironic tone. Writing for the *San Francisco Chronicle* (February 9, 2003), Barbara Quick declared the novel "a stunning feat of literary craftsmanship," adding, "What is amazing is that Ruff has managed to make of this

material a novel that is not only gripping for all its 479 pages, but also at times laugh-out-loud funny. . . . Conceptually the thing is terribly clever." Gail Caldwell, writing for the *Boston Globe* (February 16, 2003), found the work "funny, wildly inventive, and emotionally astute," as well as "a shockingly likable suspense story." She noted, "What seems more extraordinary [than the shifting narration] is how thoroughly [Ruff] has imagined the turmoil, symptomatology, and constant internal negotiations of a fragmented personality. Not to mention how much he has made us care for every one of the demi-characters presented here."

Matt Ruff lives in Seattle, Washington, with his wife, Lisa. According to his Web site, he is currently working on two projects: a science fiction–style novel of paranoia titled *Bad Monkeys*, which is slated for publication in August 2007, and a fantasy novel, about a fugitive who makes a deal with the devil, tentatively called "Suit of Lights."
—K.D.

Suggested Reading: *Boston Globe* E p6 Feb. 16, 2003; *San Francisco Chronicle* p3 Feb. 9, 2003; *Sunday Oregonian* D p9 Mar. 2, 2003; *Washington Post* C p14 Nov. 21, 1988, X p4 Feb. 16, 1997

Selected Books: *Fool on the Hill*, 1988; *Sewer, Gas and Electric: The Public Works Trilogy*, 1997; *Set This House in Order: A Romance of Souls*, 2003

Rushdie, Salman

June 19, 1947– Novelist; nonfiction writer

Salman Rushdie has established himself as a distinguished voice of contemporary literature through his elaborate and often phantasmagoric forays through a post-colonial, multi-ethnic landscape. His novels—marked by imaginative storylines, inventive wordplay, and a brimming exuberance—explore themes of religion, pop culture, history, and politics in a style that, although undoubtedly unique, has raised comparisons to the magical realism of Gabriel García Márquez. His widely acclaimed second novel, *Midnight's Children* (1981), which chronicled the fate of India in the decades before and after that nation gained its independence from Britain, was awarded the Booker Prize in 1981. Twelve years later the novel was named the "Booker of the Bookers"—the best novel to have won the Booker fiction prize in the award's 25-year history. The novel for which Rushdie became a household name, *The Satanic Verses* (1988)—the title refers to verses deleted from the Koran—was

judged blasphemous by the Islamic Iranian leader Ayatollah Ruhollah Khomeini, who subsequently proclaimed a death sentence on the author. Forced to live as a fugitive for nearly a decade, Rushdie continued writing, producing such notable works as *Haroun and the Sea of Stories* (1990) and *The Moor's Last Sigh* (1995) before the Iranian government officially removed its support for the death sentence. Rushdie has remained highly productive, writing the novels *The Ground beneath Her Feet* (1999), *Fury* (2001), and *Shalimar the Clown* (2005), in addition to generating a wealth of nonfiction material and maintaining his tireless advocacy for freedom of speech. In an interview with Carlin Romano for the *Philadelphia Inquirer* (September 25, 2005), Rushdie discussed the influence he commands in certain circles as someone who has famously suffered under extreme intolerance. "If this unusual access or fame came my way for unusual reasons," he said, "the thing to do is to put it to work. Send it back out to work."

Ahmed Salman Rushdie was born into a Muslim family in Bombay (now known as Mumbai), India, on June 19, 1947, two months before India gained

Rossano B. Maniscalchi/Courtesy of Random House
Salman Rushdie

its independence from Britain and the Indian subcontinent was partitioned into the nations of India (predominantly Hindu) and Pakistan (predominantly Muslim). Rushdie has said in interviews that his childhood was happy, if uneventful, and that he acquired an appreciation for books at an early age. Rushdie's paternal grandfather was an accomplished poet in Urdu, the national language of Pakistan. Rushdie's father, Anis Ahmed Rushdie, a businessman educated at the University of Cambridge, in England, was a student of both Arabic and Persian literature, as well as European literature; at bedtime he read to Rushdie and his three sisters, mostly from fairy tales at least partly inspired by *The Thousand and One Nights*. His mother, the former Negin Butt, was, as Rushdie once recalled in an interview, "the keeper of the family stories. She has a genius for family trees; forests of family trees grow in her head, and nobody else can possibly understand their complexity." By the time Rushdie was five he wanted to be a writer, although the desire remained a rather vague one until he was in his early 20s.

Rushdie sees himself as the son of three spiritual "mothers"—India, Pakistan, and England. In 1961, at age 14, he was sent to Rugby, an elite English public school (which is the equivalent of a private school in the U.S.). Having grown up enamored of the culture represented by his English and Scottish teachers at Bombay's Cathedral School, he arrived full of expectations that England would be a "magical" place. While he was impressed with his teachers at Rugby, his high spirits were dashed because of abuse from his classmates, who subjected him to "minor persecutions and racist

attacks," as he recounted to John Haffenden for *Novelists in Interview* (1985). He later realized that he received such treatment not only because he was Indian but also because he lacked the interest and ability for sports. (He did excel at chess and table tennis.) "If I had been able to bat elegantly at cricket and play field hockey," he once speculated, "I would have been accepted by my peers, been captain of the eleven, and grown up as a kind of ultra-rightist Indian businessman."

During holidays at home in Bombay, Rushdie never mentioned to his parents his difficulties at Rugby. When his parents joined the Muslim exodus from predominantly Hindu India and moved to Karachi, Pakistan, in 1964, Rushdie, who loved Bombay, felt doubly displaced. In time he became accustomed to Karachi, but he found it lifeless in comparison with his bustling hometown. He was also repelled by the cultural repressions he discerned in Pakistan, such as laws regarding the segregation of men and women, one of the facets of Islamic culture that he would later describe in his novels *Shame* (1983) and *The Satanic Verses*.

After his experience at Rugby School, Rushdie was reluctant to follow his parents' plan for him to go on to the University of Cambridge. On a visit home in 1965, he told his parents that (although a place had already been reserved for him at Cambridge) he would not return to England. The domestic argument that ensued was probably exacerbated by the emotional impact of the war then raging between India and Pakistan. In interviews Rushdie has recalled his confusion over the war. Both sides had what he saw as a "technical claim" on him, and he had difficulty regarding India, his birthplace, as the enemy. "And yet if somebody's dropping bombs on you," he pointed out to Michael T. Kaufman for the *New York Times* (November 13, 1983), "there is really only one reaction you can have toward them, which is not friendly. So I was very deranged by it, and in the end my parents more or less forcibly threw me on a plane to England."

Once enrolled at Cambridge, Rushdie was pleasantly surprised to find that persecution by his peers was a thing of the past. Among his fellow students he found many kindred spirits, and "intelligence ceased to be a factor in one's encounters," he recalled in his interview with Haffenden. He majored in history, partly because it "included everything else, anyway," and he pursued an interest in acting by joining Footlights, the esteemed Cambridge theatrical club.

After receiving his master's degree with honors from Cambridge, in 1968, Rushdie acted for a year at the Oval House (a fringe theater in a working-class London neighborhood)—although he came to doubt his abilities as an actor. Leaving the theater, he spent a year working as an advertising copywriter before turning his hand to fiction. His first novel—the story of a Pakistani holy man who acquires a large following of businessmen, politicians, and generals who then use him as a pawn in a political takeover—has never been published; in interviews he has described it as a failure.

Grimus (1975), Rushdie's first published novel, was written after he had returned to the writing of advertising copy on a part-time basis. Based on a Persian narrative poem, *Grimus* is a fable of magical realism, the story of an American Indian who receives the gift of immortality and embarks on a search for life's meaning. Though a commercial failure, the book drew favorable critical attention, especially among science-fiction buffs. Mel Tilden, in the *Times Literary Supplement* (February 21, 1975), described it as "engrossing and often wonderful. . . . [It is] science fiction in the best sense of the word." He added, "It is one of those novels some people will say is too good to be science fiction, even though it contains other universes, dimensional doorways, alien creatures, and more than one madman."

Rushdie's second novel, *Midnight's Children* (1981), established the author's reputation as a major new literary talent. During the five years it took him to write the book, Rushdie continued to live on his income from the ad agency for which he wrote copy two days a week. By the time he completed the final draft, however, his ability to write advertisements was blocked by his thorough distaste for the people and practices in the industry. He quit his job with trepidation, unsure that anybody would even publish *Midnight's Children*. "After all," he explained to Amanda Smith in an interview for *Publishers Weekly* (November 11, 1983), "the first novel had not done anything commercially, certainly, and this one was a quarter of a million words long and a bit weird, and it wasn't what the English normally like to hear about India. It wasn't about the Empire, and it wasn't about maharajahs and young English girls and it wasn't about rape."

Midnight's Children reflects Rushdie's belief that the individual cannot be separated from his or her environment and that national histories make sense only in the form of individual lives, and vice-versa. The book allegorically chronicles the history of India through the lives of 1,001 children whom Rushdie imagines having been born during the midnight hour that ushered in the day of India's independence from Great Britain—August 15, 1947. Two of these children, both boys, were born in the same Bombay nursing home on the very stroke of midnight, one the child of wealthy Muslim aristocrats, the other a boy born to a penurious Hindu street singer and a departing British colonist. A nurse switches the two infants, radically altering and entwining their fates. The child of the streets, Saleem Sinai, is raised with all the benefits and privileges of India's upper class; the other boy, Shiva, is raised by the street singer. Saleem, the novel's narrator-protagonist, is in his 30s when the novel begins. After relating the three

decades of family history that preceded his birth, Saleem recounts his own personal history, including his discovery, at a young age, that he has the power of telepathy; through his gift, he learns that all of "midnight's children" are possessed of magical abilities, such as the power to see into the future, travel through time, or change one's gender; the closer to midnight their time of birth, the greater their gifts. Shiva, to whom the hour gave the gifts of war, becomes India's most decorated war hero, as well as Saleem's mortal enemy.

Saleem's life story parallels that of independent India—from a euphoric natal celebration through a gifted childhood to an adulthood that is common, blemished, and tired. The book's allusive and fanciful design was intended by Rushdie to create dual reverberations, anchoring Saleem's stories at once in the Western picaresque tradition of *Tristram Shandy* and the *Decameron* on the one hand and the Indian cultural and mythic tradition on the other. Saleem's huge nose, for instance, recalls not only that of Cyrano de Bergerac, but also the trunk of India's elephant-headed god of literature, Ganesh.

The central theme of *Midnight's Children*, the decline and destruction of the hopes born with India's independence, came to Rushdie during the repressive and sometimes brutal state of emergency that was imposed by Prime Minister Indira Gandhi in 1975 as the climax of what Rushdie has described as "the peculiarly monarchic style of government" in which she recast Indian democracy. In his view, two of the effects of the state of emergency were the final shattering of the dream of India's founding fathers and the open emergence of previously covert corruption and strong-arm politics. In chronicling that emergence, Rushdie hoped to stimulate "certain kinds of conversation which were not taking place in India and Pakistan," he told an interviewer.

In a review of *Midnight's Children* for the *New Republic* (May 23, 1981), C. R. Larson cheered, "Salman Rushdie has written a dark and complex allegory of his nation's first 31 years. The narrative conveys vindictiveness and pathos, humor and pain, and Rushdie's language and imagery are brilliant." Charles Michener, writing for *Newsweek* (April 20, 1981), concurred, "Salman Rushdie . . . is a brilliant new aspirant to the ranks of V. S. Naipaul and Milan Kundera—private storytellers with public visions who cast contemporary nobodies into the whirlpool of current events and watch them come up, gasping for air. . . . Rushdie's prose is splendidly pickled." "*Midnight's Children* sounds like a continent finding its voice," Clark Blaise wrote in the *New York Times Book Review* (April 19, 1981). "Of course there a few false notes. There is a shorter, purer novel locked inside this shaggy monster. A different author might have teased it out, a different editor might have insisted upon it. I'm glad they didn't. . . . The flow of the book rushes to its conclusion in counterpointed harmony: myths intact, history accounted for, and a remarkable character fully alive." In addition to winning won the Booker Prize for fiction, *Midnight's Children* also claimed the James Tait Black Memorial Prize for fiction and the English-Speaking Union Award.

The setting of Rushdie's next novel, *Shame* (1983), is a country that is "not Pakistan, or not quite"; the narrator seems often to be, quite overtly, Rushdie himself. Using a nonlinear narrative style, with many asides on history, politics, and literature, he tells a contemporary fairy tale concerning several remarkable people whose lives exemplify honor, shame, and shamelessness. The most central of these are two archrivals for supreme power in their country—General Raza Hyder, an Islamic fundamentalist, and Iskander Harappa, a rich Westernized demagogue who becomes prime minister. Their extensive stories, replete with suggestive incidents and bizarre details, closely parallel the real-life tragedy of recent Pakistani history and the successive regimes of Zulfikar Ali Bhutto and General Mohammed Zia ul-Haq. Yet it is the women in their families who come to dominate the novel. "I had thought before I began," the narrator explains, "that what I had on my hands was an almost excessively masculine tale, a saga of sexual rivalry, ambition, power, patronage, betrayal, death, revenge. But the women seem to have taken over; they marched in from the peripheries of the story to demand the inclusion of their own tragedies, histories, and comedies, obliging me to couch my narrative in all manner of sinuous complexities, to see my 'male' plot refracted, so to speak, through the prisms of its reverse and 'female' side."

Reviews of *Shame* were mostly favorable. "Rushdie's second novel is a comic fusion of reality and fantasy, a captivating blend of narrative skill, imagination, and wit," Paul E. Hutchison wrote for *Library Journal* (November 1, 1983). "Some of Mr. Rushdie's devices misfire; others are so exaggerated that the reader simply backs away, untouched and unamused," Robert Towers wrote for the *New York Times Book Review* (November 13, 1983). "And yet the book in its own peculiar fashion works. *Shame* can, I think, be best enjoyed if we see it not as a novel but as one of those unclassifiable works in which certain writers of the 18th century excelled—[Jonathan] Swift in *Gulliver's Travels*, Voltaire in *Candide*, [Laurence] Sterne in *Tristram Shandy*." "*Shame* should consolidate [Rushdie's] position as one of the finest young writers around," Paul Stuewe averred in a review for *Quill & Quire* (December 1983). "This novel . . . teems with interesting characters, dramatic events, and marvelous verbal inventions. Like its predecessor, it recreates an exotic but thoroughly believable world that is a delight to experience."

After completing his first nonfiction work, *The Jaguar Smile: A Nicaraguan Journey* (1987), about a visit he had taken to the Latin American country the previous year, Rushdie published his well-known and highly controversial novel *The Satanic Verses* (1988), which incensed many Muslims around the world who believed the work to be derogatory. The book, published in September, was banned in October by the Indian government, and several other countries subsequently banned it as well. In the ensuing months it provoked book burnings and violent demonstrations by Islamic fundamentalist groups in India and Pakistan, some of which resulted in injuries and deaths. On February 14, 1989 the orthodox Iranian leader Ayatollah Ruhollah Khomeini charged Rushdie with blasphemy and issued a *fatwa*, or religious edict, calling for his execution. A multimillion-dollar reward was established by an Iranian "charity" to be paid to whomever carried out the fatwa. Rushdie was forced to go into hiding, and the British government provided him with 24-hour police protection.

The source of offense in Rushdie's novel was its apparent association of the Islamic prophet Muhammed with diabolism. The novel features a religion that resembles Islam and whose prophet is named Mahound (which also happens to be the name of a satanic figure in medieval Christian mystery plays). Furthermore, it features a scribe altering the prophet's dictation, thereby impugning the authority of the Koran, the holy book of Islam. The title of the novel is derived from an incident in the life of Muhammed, who, in order to please the polytheistic citizens of Mecca, once added two verses to the Koran to elevate three of their favorite goddesses to the status of angels. Sometime later, Muhammed removed the verses, explaining that they had been inspired by Satan.

In Rushdie's novel, a terrorist's bomb blows up a jetliner flying over the English Channel. Two passengers, an Indian movie actor named Gibreel Farishta and a British television star named Saladin Chamcha, survive—but the experience transforms them into archetypes of good and evil, an angel and a devil. The novel proceeds in a complex narrative involving metamorphoses, dreams, and revelations. In critical circles the book (for which Rushdie's publisher, Viking Penguin, had paid a staggeringly high advance of $850,000) received mixed reviews. Edward B. St. John, for *Library Journal* (December 1988), praised it, writing: "Rushdie spins a huge collection of loosely related subplots that combine mythology, folklore, and TV trivia in a tour de force of magic realism that investigates the postmodern immigrant experience." A. H. Mojtabai, writing for the *New York Times Book Review* (January 29, 1989), offered a more critical assessment: "As a display of narrative energy and wealth of invention, *The Satanic Verses* is impressive. As a sustained exploration of the human condition, it flies apart into delirium. . . . Does it require so much fantasia and fanfare to remind us that good and evil are deeply, subtly intermixed in humankind?" Bharati Mukherjee, in a review for the *Voice Literary Supplement* (March 1989), remarked: "Excellent books must be perfect; great books can stumble. *The Satanic Verses* has too many tangential subplots, too much undramatized narration, and too many pages where the major characters simply are not present ever to be confused with workshop excellence. Inevitably, the book will be characterized as bloated; I prefer to think of it as swollen with irritated life. This book completes a trilogy [with *Midnight's Children* and *Shame*] that must be swallowed whole, python-style, hair, horns, and hooves intact." *The Satanic Verses* won the Whitbread Novel Award in 1988.

Rushdie remained in hiding for the next several years; he continued to appear occasionally at social gatherings and literary events, but only after taking elaborate safety precautions, always accompanied by personal bodyguards. He lived in a series of safe houses and made certain never to disclose the address of where he was staying; only a few trusted friends were given a phone number where he could be reached. Such precautions were necessary, as the furor over the book showed no signs of abating. In 1991 an assailant attacked an Italian translator of *The Satanic Verses*, demanded Rushdie's address, then wounded the man with a knife. Several days later a Japanese translator of the novel was killed in Tokyo. In 1993 a mob of Islamic extremists in Turkey set fire to a hotel where Azin Nesin, a noted Turkish author who had translated the novel, was staying; the conflagration left 40 dead and 145 injured. Only a few months earlier, the Iranian government had publicly reaffirmed the proclamation calling for Rushdie's death.

The period of living as a fugitive was very difficult for Rushdie. In addition to the lack of freedom, the social isolation, and the accompanying paranoia, his second wife, the author Marianne Wiggins, with whom he spent the first year of the fatwa, left him and subsequently criticized him in the press. (The couple divorced in 1993.) He survived, as he told Nina Darnton for the *New York Times* (January 17, 1996), because of his belief that he was fighting not only for his life and the right to be heard but also for "the art of the novel, the voice that nobody owns." Rushdie continued to write throughout these trying years. He produced a children's book, *Haroun and the Sea of Stories* (1990), which, through its fanciful plot, conveyed a message about the power of storytelling and the error of artistic repression. The book, which Philip Weiss, in a review for *Esquire* (January 1993), described as "magically inventive," won the Writer's Guild Award for best children's book. (Many critics have pointed out that the book, because of its sophistication and depth, can also be enjoyed by adults.) A collection of Rushdie's journalistic writing, *Imaginary Homelands: Essays and Criticism 1981–1991*

(1991), was followed in 1992 by a book-length essay on the classic film *The Wizard of Oz*, and by *East, West* (1994), a book of short stories. In 1993—after Rushdie received a measure of public support from British prime minister John Major and U.S. president Bill Clinton, both of whom met with the author—Rushdie began making more public appearances, although he was still in hiding and living under constant police protection. In May 1995 the Iranian government conceded that it would not enforce the fatwa against Rushdie—but also stated that withdrawing it was not a viable option. "Nobody can touch the theoretical aspects of the fatwa unless he wants to commit suicide," a senior Iranian official told the London *Sunday Telegraph* (May 22, 1995). "The Iranian government is not going to send anyone to assassinate Salman Rushdie—that's for sure."

The Moor's Last Sigh, Rushdie's first novel since *The Satanic Verses*, was published in England in 1995. In an interview with Maya Jaggi for *New Statesman and Society* (September 8, 1995), the author described the book as the "completion of what I began in *Midnight's Children, Shame*, and *The Satanic Verses*—the story of myself, where I came from, a story of origins and memory. But it's also a public project that forms an arc, my response to an age in history that began in 1947 [with India's independence]. That cycle of novels is now complete."

Set in India, *The Moor's Last Sigh* centers around a family that is in the business of importing and exporting spices. Moraes "Moor" Zogoiby, the book's main character and narrator, is of mixed ancestry. His father is Jewish; his mother, Aurora, is Catholic and reputedly a descendant of the Portuguese explorer Vasco da Gama. Aurora is also a well-known artist whose masterpiece, called "The Moor's Last Sigh," has been stolen. Moor tries desperately to help recover the painting but is hampered by an affliction that causes him to age twice as fast as normal humans. The novel satirizes Indian politics as rife with corruption, and also contains a parody of the Hindu fundamentalist leader Bal Thackeray; as a result, Rushdie once again found himself in hot water, this time with the Indian government, which banned imports of the novel. Additionally, Shiv Sena, a Hindu fundamentalist movement in India, sought to ban the sale and printing of the book in New Delhi, India's capital, as well as in other major Indian cities.

The critical response to *The Moor's Last Sigh* was enthusiastic. Brad Hooper, writing for *Booklist* (November 1, 1995), remarked, "The plot does not unfold—it floods like a river gone over its banks, exploding with incredible events and larger-than-life characters, and to be carried along is to ride beautiful prose through the colliding and conjoining of races and religions that have gone into the making of the fabric of Indian history and culture. [It is] a marvelously wrought novel, guaranteed to entrance." In *Library Journal*

(December 1995), Edward B. St. John proclaimed, "This rich and very readable novel is filled with playful allusions to postwar Indian history, world literature, pop culture, and Rushdie's own recent travails. On a par with the marvelous *Midnight's Children*, this is Rushdie's best work in years." A reviewer for the *Economist* (September 9, 1995), while finding the novel to be less impressive than *Midnight's Children*, noted that "it is still a mavellously inventive display of verbal dexterity; an exuberant, entertaining, zestful novel which proves, if proof were needed, that Mr. Rushdie's spirit remains undiminished."

In an interview with Nisid Hajari for *Entertainment Weekly* (February 9, 1996), Rushdie confirmed that the death sentence had done little to diminish his artistic drive and creative sensibility. "The *fatwa* could have damaged me as an artist by making me more cautious or more strident. [With this novel] I wanted to say, 'I'm not going to become either . . . because those are both the *fatwa*'s creatures. And I'm not going to be the *fatwa*'s creature. I'm going to go on being the writer I was." *The Moor's Last Sigh* won the Whitbread Novel Award in 1995.

In 1999 Rushdie published *The Ground beneath Her Feet.* A modern-day retelling of the mythical story of Orpheus and Eurydice, the book concerns the lives of a singer-songwriter duo, Vina Apsara and Ormus Cama, as recounted by their friend Umeed "Rai" Merchant, a photographer. Ormus has the remarkable ability to hear popular songs 1,001 days before they become hits, but is unable to hear the lyrics to these songs, and Vina aids him in discovering them. The world they inhabit is one parallel to our own, one in which a fictional person named Jesse Garon Parker, not Elvis Presley, records "Heartbreak Hotel" for Sun Records and where Lee Harvey Oswald's gun jams when he tries to kill President John F. Kennedy. The book received mixed reviews. Michael Wood, writing for the *New York Times Book Review* (April 18, 1999), called it an "exuberant and elegiac new novel—and to my mind [Rushdie's] best since *Midnight's Children*." However, several reviewers echoed Paul Gray's assessment in *Time* (April 26, 1999): "No novelist currently writing in English does so much with more energy, intelligence and allusiveness than Rushdie. . . . But for all Rushdie's brilliance, the parts of this novel seem greater than the sum of its whole." In the *National Review* (May 17, 1999), James Gardner came to a similar conclusion but noted that "it would be unfair to suggest that [this] is an entirely bad book. Rushdie differs from the [Thomas] Pynchons of the world in that, from page to page, he is almost invariably funny and interesting. Even if the grand strategy of [this novel] is, to be frank, dull and uninspired, Rushdie is one of the very best writers we have, as is clear even in a novel as flawed as this one." (The rock band U2 subsequently recorded a song, "The Ground beneath Her Feet," which was inspired by the novel; Rushdie, who is a friend of the band, appeared on stage during their 1999 tour.)

In Rushdie's novel *Fury* (2001), a University of Cambridge professor named Malik Solanka, originally from Bombay, quits his academic career to produce a television show wherein an animated doll, called Little Brain, meets important thinkers from the past. The show becomes wildly popular, and Solanka winds up moving to New York City to start a new life for himself. Solanka is an unhappy man, however, who leaves behind his wife and his three-year-old son, in part because he has uncontrollable violent impulses and is afraid he may hurt his family. Transplanted to New York City in the year 2000, a time of decadence, turmoil, and millennial paranoia, he tries to get a grip on his unraveling life and the equally unraveling world around him.

Reviews of *Fury* were often withering, with James Wood calling it, in an extensive critique for the *New Republic* (September 24, 2001), "a novel that exhausts negative superlatives." In the *Atlantic Monthly* (September 2001), Brooke Allen wrote: "Rushdie lives, as the saying goes, in interesting times, and he has all the mental equipment necessary for skewering contemporary values and fears. But the book's promising beginning is soon drowned out by more typically Rushdian overkill: the cacophony of voices, plots, opinions, allegory, puns, magical realism, multicultural mythology, historical clues, and pop-culture references he has never attempted to edit. He cannot trust the story he is telling to hold its own." A reviewer for the *Economist* (August 25, 2001) wrote, "Although *Fury* starts well, combining acuity of description with thumping readability, it soon loses its way. Mr. Rushdie is usually too effervescent a writer to be pompous, but here he is drawn into making overwrought and grandiose pronouncements on the state of America. . . . Less furious than spurious, this will not be counted one of his best books." Some critics were more sympathetic. Merle Rubin, writing for the *Christian Science Monitor* (September 6, 2001), found *Fury* to be "an acrid, sharp, self-critical portrait of an angry man in an anger-inducing world."

In 2002 Rushdie published *Step across This Line: Collected Nonfiction 1992–2002*, an assortment of essays on such topics as rock music, football, literature, politics, and international conflicts. The action in Rushdie's most recent novel, *Shalimar the Clown* (2005), begins in the 1990s in Los Angeles, California, where the main character, Max Ophuls, a former diplomat, and his adult daughter, India, reside. While Laura Miller, writing for the *New York Times* (October 23, 2005), acknowledged that Los Angeles is "admittedly a difficult city to grasp," she argued that Rushdie rendered it with "cheap facility." "Cascading clauses are a Rushdie trademark; they can be taken as a manifestation of abundant imagination or as a symptom of poor writerly discipline, depending on the reader's tastes. It's hard, though, to see them as anything but laziness when they're misapplied. 'The decentered promiscuous sprawl of this giant invertebrate blob, this jellyfish of concrete and light, made it the true democratic city of the future,' is a fancy about Los Angeles that's grievously out of touch with the vacuum-sealed lives of the city's affluent," Miller wrote. After Max is murdered by the title character, Shalimar, the novel returns to the story of their first encounter, 30 years earlier, in the long-disputed region of Kashmir, which crosses the borders of Pakistan, India, and China. Here too, according to Miller, Rushdie's descriptions are lacking. "Rushdie has no gift for pastoralism and he evokes the fabled natural beauties of Kahmir as if he were a man who knew them primarily through the medium of embroidery motifs," she wrote. "But if Rushdie cannot make you see and smell and feel the loveliness of life in Kasmir, he does, finally, make a commanding story of its loss. It is a place where the frontiers between the words 'Hindu' and 'Muslim' had 'grown smudged and blurred,' but it will be dragged into the sectarian brutality of the 20th century all the same." Arguing that "Rushdie's importance as a novelist is partly attributable to his willingness to engage with big subjects," John Sutherland wrote for the London *Evening Standard* (September 5, 2005), "*Shalimar the Clown* depicts a world in which 'nationality' is an obsolete concept. The novel explores, with more sensitivity than any political scientist ever could, the forces which are clashing in a world which no longer has clearly defensible or invadable frontiers. . . . 'Everywhere,' writes Rushdie, 'is now a part of everywhere else.'" The book, Sutherland added, "finds [Rushdie], in my judgment, writing at his best."

The Iranian government lifted the fatwa against Rushdie in September 1998, though some fundamentalist groups continue to agitate for his death. In 2000 Rushdie left London to settle in New York City—a move that was harshly criticized in the British press as a betrayal of the country that had supported and protected him during his years underground—and began a relationship with Padma Lakshmi, a 29-year-old model originally from southern India whom he married in 2004. Rushdie has two sons who live in England: Zafar, from his marriage to his first wife, Clarissa Luard; and Milan, by his third wife, Elizabeth West. Zafar, now in his late 20s, is reported to be writing a book about his childhood, much of which was spent under the fatwa, and Rushdie told Carlin Romano that Milan, who is approaching 10, might also have literary ambitions. "I'm very happy for him to take over the family business," Rushdie said.

—K.D.

Suggested Reading: *American Film* p16+ Dec. 1984; *Atlantic Monthly* p138+ Sep. 2001; *Booklist* p435 Nov. 1, 1995; *Christian Science Monitor* p14+ Sep. 6, 2001; *Economist* p88 Sep. 9, 1995, p66 Aug. 25, 2001; *Esquire* p71+ Jan. 1993; *Library Journal* p134 Dec. 1988, p159 Dec. 1995; (London) *Independent Extra* p16 Oct. 13, 2006; *New Republic* p40 May 23, 1981, p32+ Sep. 24, 2001; *New York Review of Books* p12 May 6, 1999; *New York Times Book Review* p3+ Nov. 13, 1983, p3 Jan. 29, 1989, p7 Apr. 18, 1999; *Newsweek* p89 Apr. 20, 1981; *Philadelphia Inquirer* H p1 Sep. 25, 2005; *Time* p99 Apr. 26, 1999; *Washington Post* B p1+ Nov. 25, 1993; Haffenden, John. *Novelists in Interview*, 1985

Selected Books: fiction—*Grimus*, 1975; *Midnight's Children*, 1981; *Shame*, 1983; *The Satanic Verses*, 1988; *Haroun and the Sea of Stories*, 1990; *East, West*, 1994; *The Moor's Last Sigh*, 1995; *The Ground beneath Her Feet*, 1999; *Fury*, 2001; *Shalimar the Clown*, 2005; nonfiction—*The Jaguar Smile: A Nicaraguan Journey*, 1987; *Imaginary Homelands: Essays and Criticism 1981–1991*, 1991; *The Wizard of Oz (BFI Film Classics)*, 1992; *Step across This Line: Collected Nonfiction 1992–2002*, 2002

Catherine Cabrol/Courtesy of Random House

Sa, Shan

Oct. 1972– Novelist; poet

Shan Sa is the pseudonym of a Chinese-born author who, in 1990, moved to France, where she now enjoys a high-profile literary career. A poetry prodigy, Sa has now also written a number of novels in the language of her adopted country, including *Porte de la paix celeste* (1997), *Les Quatre vies du saule* (1999), *La Joueuse de go*

(2001), *Impératrice* (2003), *Les Conspirateurs* (2005), and *Alexandre et Alestria* (2006); she has also published a volume of poetry in French, *Le Vent vif et le glaive rapide* (2000), and a book combining text, painting, and calligraphy, *Le Miroir du calligraphe* (2002). In 2003 *La Joueuse du go* was published in English as *The Girl Who Played Go* and proved a critical and commercial success. Sa's *Impératrice* then appeared, in 2006, as *Empress*. Anthea Lawson, in an assessment for the London *Times* (May 14, 2003), called Sa's prose "graceful and trance-like: her fights are a whirling choreography of flying limbs and snow, her emotions richly yet precisely expressed. So spellbinding is the atmosphere created that this reviewer reached the horrifying denouement without having noticed that she didn't even know the characters' names."

Shan Sa was born Yan Ni in 1972 in Beijing, China; her pseudonym has been translated as meaning "wind rustle" (or "rustle of wind") or "wind scatter." (Some international sources give her birth name as Yan Ni-Ni and list her date of birth as October 26 or 28.) She often spent the summers of her youth in Manchuria, a region that appears frequently in her novels. The child of literature professors, Sa received great support from her family for her artistic endeavors: her relatives taught her calligraphy, and her grandmother strongly urged Sa to become a painter. She began writing at the age of seven, published her first book of poetry at eight, and a few years later won a Chinese national poetry contest for children. She also studied music extensively.

In 1989, having already published at least two additional volumes of poetry, Sa, struck by the horror of the Chinese government's repression and massacre of protesting students in Tiananmen Square, decided to leave her native land, and in 1990, after completing her Chinese secondary education, she relocated to France, where her father was teaching at the time. Though she had studied English before leaving China, Sa, had little or no command of French when she first arrived; she thus struggled during her initial studies in France, which were done at the Ecole Alsacienne, a private secondary school. She nonetheless succeeded in obtaining her baccalauréat—the French equivalent of a high-school diploma—in 1992, and in 1994, after two years of studying philosophy at the Catholic Institute of Paris, a private university, she began working as as an assistant to the acclaimed artist Balthus (1908–2001) before penning her first novel.

Porte de la paix celeste (which translates as "door of celestial peace") recounts the Tiananmen massacre and its aftermath through the eyes of the book's two main characters; it captured France's prestigious Goncourt Prize in the debut-novel category. Building on the success of *Porte de la paix celeste*, Sa wrote the novel *Les Quartre vies du saule* (which translates as "the four lives of the willow"), which was awarded a Prix Cazes. The work tells the stories of four characters whose lives span four centuries of Chinese history. Departing from the medium of the novel, Sa published the poetry collection *Vent vif et le glaive rapide* (which translates as "the sharp wind and the fast sword").

Sa's third novel, *La Joueuse du go*, was inspired by the life of her grandmother and earned its author another Goncourt Prize, this time in the category of high-school literature. Translated into English by Adriana Hunter, *The Girl Who Played Go* is set in a small town in Manchuria during the Japanese occupation, which began in 1931 and ended with Japan's surrender at the end of World War II. The story concerns two very different characters whose lives intersect over the board game go, in which players place small stones on a grid in an attempt to surround their opponents' stones. In the novel an anonymous Japanese soldier is ordered to infiltrate the Chinese resistance and hopes to do so by circulating among the city's go players. While doing so he meets a Chinese schoolgirl, and the two strike up an unlikely friendship over the game board. The story is told from both perspectives in alternating chapters. "As their [go] match stretches out," Sarah A. Smith observed for the London *Guardian* (May 24, 2003), "both find their certainties wrecked. When the Japanese army moves towards Beijing, the game breaks up. Neither player is a victor." Sha, Smith continues, "does not hold back in describing the cruelty of the Japanese, nor the courage of the resistance. But this is an extremely even-handed book, which gives a picture too, in the details of the soldier's letters home, of the Japanese mindset. It is a story worth telling, and intriguingly told." Jennifer Reese praised the work for *Entertainment Weekly* (October 17, 2003), remarking, "Despite some lyrical excesses and a slow start, this unlikely love story . . . is beautiful, shocking, and sad."

Sa followed *The Girl Who Played Go* with *Le Miroir du calligraphe* (which translates as "the mirror of the calligrapher"), a work that combined a variety of artistic modes and highlighted the intermingling of Asian and Western influences in the author's work. As described on the Web site of the Bureau International de l'Edition Francaise, Sa's "ink drawings and paintings, made up of a subtle play of black and grey, with the vigor of incendiary colors, vacillate between the traditional Chinese style and Western contemporary art."

The appearance of Sa's fourth novel, *L'Imperatrice,* was accompanied by a squabble between two publishers over the right to publish the book. The battle was widely reported in the French press, and Sa was accused of a lack of loyalty to her original publisher. Researching the book for over a year before beginning to write it had already taken its toll on Sa. "I suffered so much for this book," she told Annabel Walker for the *South China Morning Post* (April 10, 2005). "I did so much research that all the documentation nearly killed my inspiration." Based on the life of China's only female emperor, Wu Zetian, who ruled at the turn of the eighth century AD, the book tells the story of a well-born but not well-to-do young woman, called Heavenlight, who goes from being a courtesan to marrying the emperor and later leads the state herself, becoming Empress Wu. Linda Gampert for the *Oregon Daily Emerald* (June 1, 2006) called *Empress* "lushly written" and wrote that it "masterfully retells a time and place unlike our own in so many ways but the undertones of jealousy and despair will still resonate with readers today." Ann Mah of the *South China Morning Post* (August 20, 2006) described the book "as ornate and intricate as an embroidered Imperial gown" and concluded: "Heavenlight is a commanding character, but her story is hampered by overly florid prose and careening plot twists. Meticulously researched, rich in language and detail, filled with majestic pageantry, *Empress* is nevertheless a worthy tribute."

Sa's fifth novel, *Les Conspirateurs* (which translates as "the conspirators") follows a young Chinese woman whom the CIA is trying to recruit in order to investigate a French politician. Eventually she becomes enmeshed in the lives of two other spies, one American, the other French. With *Alexandre et Alestria* Sa returned to a historical setting, during the conquests of the famed Macedonian king Alexander the Great (the Alexandre mentioned in the title).

Besides the battle over publishing rights, Sa has been at the center of another controversy. Some critics have expressed disbelief that a young immigrant who learned French as a second language could have produced such beautifully written novels. They accuse her editors of heavily revising much of her work and question which portions Sa can rightfully claim as her own. Sa's defenders have been quick to charge such critics with xenophobia and excessive national pride.

"My home is Beijing, I live in Paris and I'm looking for somewhere to settle down in New York or LA," Sa told Walker, adding: "My dream is to live nowhere. . . . When I stay somewhere for a long time I feel suffocated because you're exposed to that country's particular point of view. When I go away I discover what's happening in other places and it's like oxygen to me. It gives me more lucidity."

—P.B.M.

Suggested Reading: *Library Journal* p100 Oct. 15, 2003; (London) *Guardian* (on-line) May 24, 2003; (London) *Times* p20 May 14, 2003; *New York Times Book Review* p24 Oct. 26, 2003; *Oregon Daily Emerald* (on-line) June 1, 2006; *Publishers Weekly* p43 Sep. 29, 2003; *South China Morning Post* p7 Apr. 10, 2005, p6 Aug. 20, 2006

Selected Works in English Translation: *The Girl Who Played Go*, 2003; *Empress*, 2006

Saffron, Inga

1957– Journalist; nonfiction writer

Before she began her tenure as the Moscow correspondent for the *Philadelphia Inquirer*, which lasted from 1994 to 1998, Inga Saffron had tasted caviar (salted sturgeon eggs) only twice, as far as she could remember. During her stay in Russia, however, she developed a taste for the delicacy; in those days caviar was so common and cheap—peddlers hawked it on streets of Moscow—that Saffron often ate it for breakfast. Although she now writes mostly about architecture, her taste for sturgeon eggs grew into an obsession, culminating in her first book, *Caviar: The Strange History and Uncertain Future of the World's Most Coveted Delicacy* (2002).

Saffron was born in 1957. She studied French and intellectual history at both the University of Pennsylvania, in Philadelphia, and New York University, in New York City, but did not earn a degree from either institution. While working as a reporter for the *Courier News*, in Plainfield, New Jersey, she first became interested in urban planning when city officials razed a section of a downtown neighborhood. "They told me it was urban renewal," she explained Sasha Issenberg for *Philadelphia Magazine* (April 2003). "I knew at that moment I wanted to write about what happens to cities as a result of those urban-renewal policies."

Later, when she returned from her stint in Moscow, Saffron told her editors at the *Philadelphia Inquirer* that she was not interested in the high-profile positions that are usually afforded returning foreign correspondents and instead opted to be the paper's architecture critic, writing the weekly column Changing Skyline. According to Issenberg, it is a role that Saffron has defined "widely, writing about policy and planning, and celebrating preservation and public spaces. Many weeks, she sounds like a crusading city columnist who happens to have a passing interest in architecture." As Saffron explained on Skyline Online, her Weblog (more commonly known as a blog), she strives to "look at architecture and planning with a civilian's eye. If an artist exhibits a bad painting in a museum, no one forces you to go see it. But when designers and developers put up a building in a prominent spot in your city, all of us have to live with it." Admitting that her column rarely addresses the design of new structures, Saffron explained to Issenberg: "I wish I had an opportunity to write about beautiful, interesting buildings, but they hardly ever happen in Philadelphia. . . . I think American cities are at a really critical point. Philadelphia could go either way: It could thrive, or it could cease to exist. Some days, it looks like things are going to be okay. Some days, it can't go on." Her muckraking and insightful criticism earned her a nomination for the Pulitzer Prize in 2004.

In her first book, *Caviar*, Saffron examined the history of one of the world's most sought-after delicacies. In Russia, caviar had progressed in stature from pig feed to peasant food to aristocratic delicacy. The collapse of the Soviet Union, where the government had strictly controlled the market, has meant disaster for the sturgeon, and the once-abundant fish now faces an increased threat from poachers and pollution. "Written with an elegance befitting the subject, *Caviar* is a fascinating work of culinary and environmental history," Karen Dukess wrote for *USA Today* (October 21, 2002). "It is peopled with colorful characters who have tied their fortunes to caviar, from the Greek sea captain who figured out how to transport the perishable delicacy to Europe, to the smugglers brazen enough to fly into JFK [airport] with suitcases of fresh caviar, to the scientists who devised a way to use DNA testing to detect inferior or illegal caviar. Perhaps most indicative of caviar's legendary mystique are the fish farmers raising sturgeon, which take 10 years to mature before eggs can be harvested. For the roe of any other fish, this probably would be a foolhardy pursuit. But this is caviar, which, as Saffron writes, is not just about taste, but 'is a culinary Rorschach that unleashes our deeply held notions about wealth, luxury and life.'" A reviewer for *Publishers Weekly* (October 15, 2002) wrote, "Saffron has taken an off-beat but intriguing topic, and, through her elegant and detailed prose, created a book worthy of gourmands and amateur historians alike."

Saffron lives in Philadelphia, Pennsylvania, and is married to the novelist and short-story writer Ken Kalfus, who was nominated for a National Book Award for his novel *A Disorder Peculiar to the Country* (2006). They have one daughter, Sky Kalfus. "Saffron is a graceful woman whose voice trembles slightly as she chooses her words," according to Issenberg, "and there's no reason to believe that picking fights is in her nature. Instead, her eloquent outrage comes from a feeling that bad architecture is a crime against civilization."

—P.B.M.

Suggested Reading: *Philadelphia Inquirer* (on-line); *Philadelphia Magazine* April 2003; *USA Today* (on-line) Oct. 21, 2002

Selected Books: *Caviar: The Strange History and Uncertain Future of the World's Most Coveted Delicacy*, 2002

Salih, Al-Tayyib

(SAH-lih, al-tie-YIHB)

1929– Novelist: short-story writer

The novel *Season of Migration to the North* by the Sudanese author Al-Tayyib Salih, who writes in Arabic, was described by the late critic Edward Said "as one of the finest works of modern Arabic literature," according to the Canadian Broadcasting Company's Web site. Salih, who is generally referred to in the media as simply Tayyib Salih, has won a preeminent place in the canon of world literature; *Season of Migration to the North* "richly deserves its classic status and a wider readership, as it is one of the best novels to have been written in Arabic, perhaps the best," according to Robert Irwin, in a critique for the London *Times Literary Supplement* (December 19–26, 2003).

Al-Tayyib Salih was born in 1929, in the Northern Province of Sudan. The Arabic speakers of the area are divided into numerous ethnic or supratribal groupings; Salih's particular group consists predominantly of small farmers but was also renowned for producing Islamic scholars. Consequently, the study of Islam formed the basis of his early education. A gifted student, Salih attended secondary school in Khartoum, and then—though he had initially planned to pursue a career in agriculture in his home country—traveled to London, where he obtained an advanced degree. After completing his studies Salih began a career in broadcasting, eventually rising to become the head of drama for the British Broadcasting Company's Arabic Service division. He also served as the director general of information in the Persian Gulf state of Qatar and worked for the United Nations Educational, Scientific, and Cultural Organization (UNESCO) in both Paris and Qatar.

For Salih writing was always a hobby rather than a career. This was due in part to the poor financial remuneration Arabic writers have historically received—a result of rampant piracy. As Irwin noted, "In the Arab world it has always been all but impossible to earn a living by writing novels." Irwin quoted Salih's introduction to the 2003 edition of *Season of Migration to the North*, "It is true that I have become well-known all over the place but of course renown without recompense is no consolation for a writer."

Season of Migration to the North first appeared in a Lebanese literary magazine, in 1966, and was translated into English by Denys Johnson-Davies three years later for the Heinemann African Writers Series; it was republished in 2003 by Penguin Classics. It is currently banned in Salih's native Sudan. The book's narrator is a Sudanese native who has returned to his homeland following seven years of schooling in England. In his village he becomes friends with a newcomer named Mustafa Sa'eed whose singular story is revealed as the novel progresses. Like the narrator, Sa'eed spent time studying in England and eventually became a well-regarded academic. He also embarked on a series of frenetic love affairs with white women. Vowing "to liberate Africa with my penis," as quoted by Irwin, Sa'eed ensnared young women with his exotic charm, eventually driving three of them to suicide. After murdering one of his lovers, Ša'eed was sentenced to seven years in prison. Upon his release, he married and raised a family. Once his story is told to the narrator, Sa'eed disappears, leaving his family in his new friend's care, and it is believed that he has committed suicide by drowning himself in the Nile. With Sa'eed's apparent demise, a locked room in his house is opened to the narrator, who finds it filled with works of Western literature.

Season of Migration to the North betrays undeniable echoes of Joseph Conrad's *Heart of Darkness*: Salih "has studied it carefully and become, in a sense, the master of Conrad's narrative, so that he is able to play strange games with it and reshape and invert it," Irwin noted. "*Season of Migration to the North* is a melodrama of passion and violence, but it is also a political novel with sharp things to say about imperialism (which is compared to a contagion, to sexual desire and to the curse of Tutankhamun's tomb), as well as about post-colonialism." David Pryce-Jones offered high praise for the novel in the *New York Times Book Review* (July 23, 1989), calling it "a brilliant miniature of the plight of Arabs and Africans who find themselves no longer sustained by their past and not yet incorporated into a viable future. Swift and astonishing in its prose, this novel is more instructive than any number of academic books."

The Wedding of Zein, and Other Stories was initially published in English in 1969. Like much of Salih's work, the stories take place in the town of Wad Hamid. In this work, as Irwin observed, "Salih has abandoned his study of Conrad and Freud [in *Season of Migration to the North*] and has turned instead to the folkloric repertoire of Sudanese Sufism. We hear no more of educated men with minds like knives." "These three stories . . . show what happens when a considerable sophistication and resourcefulness of technique is applied to traditional storytelling material," a critic for the London *Guardian* opined, as quoted on the Heinemann Web site.

The short novel *Bandarshah*, published in English in 1996, tells the tale of a man who is unable to remember his name and who speaks a language that no one understands. Villagers care for him and teach him the Koran. Rehabilitated, the amnesiac marries, has children, and becomes, after his death, a town legend. According to the UNESCO Publishing Web site, "As readers, we become the amazed spectators of village politics, initiation ceremonies, weddings, floggings and burials—scenes peopled with a cast of genies, devils, and houris—and encounter the mysticism

of the Arab world described in a prose so absorbing and fascinating that we want to return to read it again and again."

Salih has written a number of highly regarded short stories, with occasional English translations found in compilations of Arabic literature.

—P.B.M.

Suggested Reading: Canadian Broadcasting Company Web site; Heinemann Web site; *Los Angeles Times* V p12 Apr. 27, 1989; *New York Times Book Review* p15 July 23, 1989; *Times Literary Supplement* p25 Dec. 19–26, 2003; Unesco Publishing Web site

Selected Books in English Translation: *Season of Migration to the North*, 1969; *The Wedding of Zein, and Other Stories*, 1969; *Bandarshah*, 1996

Schine, Cathleen

1953– Novelist

Over the past 20 years, the novelist Cathleen Schine has "perfected the underappreciated art of the domestic comedy," Claire Dederer wrote for the *New York Times Book Review* (October 19, 2003). Since her debut novel, *Alice in Bed*, was published, in 1983, Schine has earned comparisons to the august likes of Jane Austen, George Eliot, and Gustave Flaubert. Schine, Dederer continued, "loves the chat of families, their intimate gossip. Her elegant writing has a down-home appeal: you dig in happily and eat it all up."

Cathleen Schine was born in Bridgeport, Connecticut, in 1953 and raised in nearby Westport. During her days in high school and later at Sarah Lawrence College, in Bronxville, New York, she frequently penned "what she calls pretentious poetry," as Dan Cryer reported for *New York Newsday* (April 11, 1993). Medieval history began to supplant her interest in writing at Sarah Lawrence, and she transferred to Barnard College, in New York City, to focus on the topic. After earning her bachelor's degree from Barnard, in 1976, Schine entered the University of Chicago, where she took up graduate studies in medieval history. "I tried to be a medieval historian," Schine explained in an interview posted on the Barnes & Noble Web site, "but I have no memory for facts, dates, or abstract ideas, so that was a bust." While on a fellowship in Florence, Italy, prior to dropping out of graduate school, "Schine found herself more drawn to buying shoes than to perusing manuscripts," as Cryer reported. Upon returning to New York, Schine applied to become a buyer at Bloomingdale's department store. "I had an interview," Schine told the Barnes & Noble interviewer, "but they never called me back. I really had no choice. I had to be a writer."

Schine began her writing career doing occasional pieces for the *Village Voice* and eventually became a regular columnist. She then landed a position as a copy editor at *Newsweek*. Regarding her stint at that newsmagazine, Schine informed the Barnes & Noble interviewer, "My grammar was good, but I can't spell, so it was a challenge. My boss was very nice and indulgent, though, and I wrote *Alice in Bed* on scraps of paper during slow hours."

"The idea of a story about a young woman who spends a year in bed suffering from a mysterious and painful joint disease does not immediately inspire confidence," Caroline Seebohm wrote, critiquing *Alice in Bed* for the *New York Times Book Review* (June 5, 1983). "But Cathleen Schine is no ordinary writer, and in this striking first novel she has created an extremely funny heroine whose hospital year is suffused with wit, pathos and frequently sex." A host of memorable characters orbit around Alice Brody, the upper-middle-class Jewish protagonist, as she lies in her bed in Connecticut, variously dreaming, pondering her past, chatting on the phone, or scribbling letters to her friends. (Schine was inspired by her painful recuperation from hip surgery at age 20.) John Updike offered a mixed review for the *New Yorker* (August 1, 1983), opining, "Miss Schine's glancing, skipping style, while it makes Alice's yearlong ordeal bearable to read about, does not do well at creating the weave, the thickening circumstances, of a novel. . . . Things just happen in this book." Still, *Alice in Bed* earned much praise from literary commentators. Michiko Kakutani wrote for the *New York Times* (July 4, 2003), "Out of these bare bones of a plot, Miss Schine has fashioned a fluently written story and found an engaging voice." Ray Anello, writing for *Newsweek* (June 13, 1983), termed the work a "buoyant first novel," and added, "Schine has a knack for seeing the reality behind eccentric behavior and for laughing when she might just as easily be in tears."

Schine married the film critic David Denby in 1981. They had two children, Max and Thomas, and Schine took a hiatus from writing novels in order to raise them. After a seven-year interlude between novels, Schine revisited Alice Brody, now an avid birdwatcher, in *To The Birdhouse* (1990), a work M. G. Lord described for the *Washington Post* (May 20, 1990) as "part adventure story, part comedy of manners and part wartime drama."

In the book, Alice's mother, Brenda, is dating Louie Scifo, a thoroughly undesirable lout. When Alice convinces her mother to break things off with him, a feud erupts; Scifo slashes the family's tires and breaks into their home to hide a poisonous spider under Brenda's pillow, and the Brodys retaliate by adding Scifo's name to junk-mail lists and sending him off on time-consuming, pointless errands. While some reviewers questioned the meaning of the reference to Virginia Woolf's 1927 novel *To the Lighthouse* in the work's title and found Schine's prolonged digressions on birdwatching tiresome, the author nevertheless continued to earn critical plaudits. "One of the primary joys in this funny, light, entertaining novel is Cathleen Schine's graceful prose style," Lee Smith wrote for the *New York Times Book Review* (May 20, 1990). Elizabeth Guiney Sandvick, writing for *Library Journal* (May 15, 1990), observed, "Schine's flair for darkly humorous scenes reveals her characters at their worst and funniest. The bizarre and zany ending seems contrived, but the author's keen eye for satiric detail wins over the reader." Michiko Kakutani concluded for the *New York Times* (May 1, 1990) that Schine "has given us, in Alice and Louie, two delightfully quirky characters who deserve a permanent place in the pantheon of comic creations."

The title of Schine's 1993 book, *Rameau's Niece*—"a novel of ideas dressed up as Manhattan marital comedy," as Chris Goodrich declared for the *Los Angeles Times* (March 23, 1993)—echoes that of *Rameau's Nephew* by the 18th-century French philosopher Denis Diderot. Margaret Nathan, Schine's heroine, achieves renown after writing a biography of Charlotte de Montigny, an obscure figure from the 1700s. Soon Margaret tires of her egotistical academic husband, Edward, and heads off to Europe to work on her second book, which focuses on a subversive philosophical tract she had discovered during the research for the biography. "In the end," Angeline Goreau observed for the *New York Times Book Review* (March 21, 1993), "Margaret arrives at the moral of her story: real truth lies in cultivating one's own garden. But happiness must be won before it can be enjoyed." Goreau qualified her praise by noting the work's abrupt ending and wrote that she found it "difficult to entirely reconcile the tone of Margaret's redemption with the ribald absurdity of what comes before." Nevertheless, Goreau concluded, "We are encouraged to forgive these failings, however, by the sheer delight of listening to Cathleen's Schine wonderfully inventive comic voice summoning up a woman driven to the brink of madness by theory. Ms. Schine sweeps through the life and manners of the intelligentsia with an eye for detail so sure and an ear for pretension so finely tuned that we believe her entirely—well, almost—when she tells us that the emperor has no clothes."

The protagonist of Schine's 1995 novel, *The Love Letter*, is Helen McFarquhar, a divorcée who owns a bookstore in a small coastal town near New York City. While in the process of writing the novel, Schine worked in a bookstore to better understand the dynamics of running such an enterprise, and, as she told the Barnes & Noble interviewer, she "discovered that selling books is an interdisciplinary activity, the disciplines being: literary critic, psychologist, and stevedore."

The eponymous love letter is sent to Helen by Johnny Howell, a college student on summer vacation. Despite the vast age difference, Helen begins a tempestuous affair with the youth and refuses to end it even in the face of enormous logistical complications. *The Love Letter* "is a book of wit and charm," Jonathan Yardley wrote for the *Washington Post* (May 3, 1995), "but its central premise is riskier than Schine is able to bring off; she asks the reader to suspend disbelief, but she fails to earn what she asks for." The chief criticism of the work "isn't that the affair is improbable or unbelievable," Yardley continued, "but that Johnny is so unlikely a partner to it." Michiko Kakutani wrote for the *New York Times Book Review* (May 16, 1995), "*The Love Letter* may lack the satiric edge and scholarly resonance of *Rameau's Niece*, it may evaporate instantly from the reader's mind, but it remains a delightful exercise in literary wit, a perfect summer screwball comedy." A film adaptation of *The Love Letter*, starring Kate Capshaw and Blythe Danner, premiered in 1999.

The Evolution of Jane, Schine's 1998 novel, follows Jane Barlow Schwartz, a young woman who travels to the Galapagos Islands in the course of examining a friendship gone wrong. Schine explained to Emily Gordon for New York *Newsday* (October 25, 1998), "I was trying to write a book about friendship and was having a lot of trouble, and then I started thinking about Darwin, putting those two things together—the idea of friendship and the idea of evolution, the mystery of change." What Schine concludes about friendship from her research—as illustrated in *The Evolution of Jane*— she informed Gordon, is that "it's a mistake. I think it's just a mutant, what Darwin called a sport—a freak of nature. Family ties make sense, and romantic ties make sense in evolutionary terms, but friendship—I don't know." Christopher Lehmann-Haupt wrote for the *New York Times* (October 12, 1998) that Schine's novel was "consistently amusing and provocative, [and] remains a great pleasure to read. But it works better intellectually than in the gut, where the best fiction has to make its presence felt." Grace Fill, writing for *Booklist* (July 1998), was more effusive in her praise: "Told with witty sophistication, this is an entertaining story that does not lack substance."

In *She Is Me* (2003), the main character, Elizabeth, is tapped to write a screenplay adaptation of Flaubert's *Madame Bovary*. Elizabeth relocates to Los Angeles with her daughter and boyfriend to work on the movie and to care for her widowed grandmother and mother, both of whom have contracted cancer. "As with past Schine novels," Lisa Kreidner wrote for the *Washington Post* (September 14, 2003), "the message of *She is Me* is that sooner or later, even the most sensible soul must let down her guard and let passion blow through her. . . . The neat ending may be a tad pat, but Schine's bemused confection convinces us that true love is indeed possible, at least for those willing to take some risk." Claire Dederer wrote, "Schine's women are mothers and daughters, but they're also Emma Bovary—quality

adulterers. Schine allows them to be many things at once, and when we're done reading about them, most other women in most other novels seem a little emotionally impoverished."

Schine left David Denby at the beginning of 2000. (In 2004 he wrote a book, *American Sucker*, about his experiences after the separation, which was amicable. The book focuses on his attempt to make enough money in the stock market to buy Schine's share of their Manhattan apartment.) Schine currently divides her time between New York City and Venice, California. Besides her novels, she writes frequently for *Vogue*, the *New Yorker*, the *Village Voice*, and the *New York Times*, among other publications. Schine's next novel, *The New Yorkers*, which is about the romantic entanglements of city dwellers who meet while walking their dogs, is due out in May 2007.

—P.B.M.

Suggested Reading: Barnes & Noble Web site; iVillage Web site; *New York Newsday* p32 Apr. 11, 1993; *New York Times* C p17 May 1, 1990, C p16 May 16, 1995, E p7 Oct. 12, 1998; *New York Times Book Review* p14 June 5, 1983, p15 May 20, 1990, p13 Mar. 21, 1993, p17 Apr. 20, 1993, p9 Oct. 19, 2003; *Washington Post* C p2 May 3, 1995, T p10 Sep. 14, 2003

Selected Books: *Alice in Bed*, 1983; *To the Birdhouse*, 1990; *Rameau's Niece*, 1993; *The Love Letter*, 1995; *The Evolution of Jane*, 1998; *She Is Me*, 2003

Segev, Tom

Mar. 1, 1945– Journalist; historian

Tom Segev is one of Israel's best-known journalists and authors. A member of an unofficial group of Israeli scholars known as the "New Historians," he challenges what he considers myths about Israel's turbulent history. Segev draws on a wide range of primary sources, including Israeli government archives and important private diaries, to reconstruct the past, regardless of whether the truth reflects positively or negatively on Israel's image and leaders. Among Segev's most controversial books are *1949: The First Israelis*, which sheds light on Israel's mistreatment of Arabs living in Palestine during the 1948 war of independence and the miserable conditions that some Jewish immigrants experienced after their arrival in the country; *The Seventh Million: The Israelis and the Holocaust*, which shocked many readers by alleging that Zionist leaders did little to rescue their fellow Jews from the Nazis during World War II; and *One Palestine, Complete: Jews and Arabs under the British Mandate*, which asserts that the British maintained a pro-Zionist policy during its administration of Palestine.

Courtesy of Henry Holt

Tom Segev

Segev's iconoclasm has sparked criticism from other scholars, who accuse him of selectively interpreting the historical record to suit his revisionist agenda and left-wing views. "When I go to research a story, sometimes the official version is true, sometimes the myth is true, and sometimes, well, let's see what the evidence is that I find," he explained to Susie Linfield for New York *Newsday* (May 12, 2002). "My real commitment is to the story itself. But there are people in Israel who say, 'Who gives you the right to kill my myth?' I don't go for that. I think it's much more exciting to grow up, become self-critical, [and] explore your past."

Tom Segev was born on March 1, 1945 in Jerusalem, in what was then the British mandate of Palestine. His parents were Jewish refugees who had fled Nazi Germany in 1935. On November 29, 1947 the U.N. passed a resolution calling for the division of Palestine into separate Jewish and Arab states. The news was greeted with excitement by most Jews, anxious for a state of their own, but with less enthusiasm by Arabs; a short time later, fighting broke out between the groups. The state of Israel declared its independence, on May 14, 1948, the day the British mandate expired. Before a full day had passed, the Arab nations of Egypt, Lebanon, Syria, Iraq, and Transjordan (later Jordan) invaded Israel with the aim of destroying the new state. Israel successfully repelled the invasion, but the war dragged on for more than a year (during which time Segev's father was killed in action) until armistice agreements were reached with Egypt, Lebanon, Syria, and Transjordan.

Segev attended Israel's National Defense College and then enrolled at Hebrew University, in Jerusalem. He graduated with a bachelor's degree

in political science and history. Segev next pursued a doctorate in history at Boston University, in Massachusetts. His dissertation profiled many of the commanders who ran the Nazi death camps during World War II, and in 1971 he earned his doctorate.

After returning to Israel, Segev began a career as a journalist. He wrote for such Hebrew-language newspapers as *Ma'ariv*, *Al Hamishmar*, and *Kol Yisrael*. In 1977 he began writing a weekly column for *Ha'aretz*, one of Israel's most prominent papers. For several years during the 1980s, Segev served as the co-editor of *Koteret Rasheet*, a left-wing, Hebrew-language magazine.

In 1984 Segev published his first book in Hebrew; the English translation appeared two years later as *1949: The First Israelis*. Drawing on declassified government archives and other primary sources, Segev chronicled the new Jewish state during its first several years. The book became a best-seller in Israel, sparking heated controversy for its challenge to the popular version of history that most Israelis are taught in school. The Israeli government has maintained that hundreds of thousands of Arabs living in Israel were encouraged to flee by their leaders and were told that they would return to their homes right after Israel was defeated by invading Arab armies. Segev showed that Israeli forces themselves, in fact, expelled thousands of Arabs. He argued that the looting of Arab property by Israelis was widespread and that the Israeli's government's efforts to stop this abuse were unsuccessful. Segev also documented tensions between secular and religious Jews in the new state and instances in which Israelis of European origin mistreated and discriminated against Jewish immigrants from Arab countries, who were often comparatively less educated and had different customs.

To bolster its population Israeli officials encouraged immigration and welcomed hundreds of thousands of Jews from Europe and the Middle East. Segev wrote that at the time Israel was not prepared to absorb large numbers of immigrants and that thousands of Jews who came to the country hoping for a better life were forced to live in miserable conditions in detention camps. "This book should be required reading for all who want to understand the Arab-Israel conflict," Elmore Jackson wrote for the *New York Times Book Review* (February 2, 1986). "The story is all here—the upheaval and violence that followed the United Nations partition resolution in November 1947 and the proclamation of the State of Israel in May 1948; the insecurity of Jewish settlers as they attempted to make their way in what were or had been predominantly Arab areas; and the parallel insecurity of Arab residents who had difficulty deciding whether to seek shelter behind Arab armies or to stay and face uncertain treatment in a largely Jewish state. It is deplorable but not surprising that atrocities took place. What is new in Mr. Segev's book is the wealth of graphic and substantiated detail, which sheds light on Israel's leaders in this early period." In his review for the *Los Angeles Times Book Review* (March 16, 1986), Marvin Seid also praised the book, writing that Segev "recounts some of the less prideful events that occurred in Israel during and immediately after its war of independence." The reviewer observed that Segev "lets the record speak for itself. Many will not like what it says. . . . But what happened [back then] left a deep imprint on Israeli society and national attitudes. Understanding the present demands an honest confrontation with the past. *1949* is an important contribution to understanding."

In 1989 Segev adapted his doctoral dissertation for the book *Soldiers of Evil: The Commandants of the Nazi Concentration Camps.* In it he profiled 55 of the men who ran the camps in which millions of Jews and others were murdered during World War II. Segev interviewed some of the commandants who were still alive and their families. He found that the men were not fanatics or even devout followers of the Nazi ideology but still willingly followed orders to murder innocent people without question. *Soldiers of Evil* received mixed reviews. "While [Segev's] account handily details the biographies of many of these nonentities who achieved an immortality of sorts, it doesn't really tell us anything new; and anyway the life and times of the more infamous ones have been written up before," Meir Ronnen observed for the *Jerusalem Post* (August 11, 1989). "Originally research for Segev's doctorate in history, this book does not suggest why the doctorate was awarded, for the conclusion it comes to is that there really isn't any earth-shaking conclusion to be drawn, save the pretty obvious one that it was simply circumstances that put these veteran and willing careerists in charge of the camps and dictated their response to the challenge of performing an unpleasant task on behalf of the German people." By contrast, in his critique for the *Los Angeles Times Book Review* (February 19, 1989), Peter Sichrovsky argued that the book was "an important step toward the demythologization of the perpetrators." He wrote, "Neither psychological nor sociological explanation is offered. Instead, the 55 men themselves, or their wives and children, take the floor. The system of duty and obedience described is one that an official in that era would no more have thought to question than he would have thought to question the daily movement of his bowels. Came the order to kill the Jews, one did it. Came the order to shoot women and children, one did it. Had the order come to stone redheads only, one would have done it, and this not because of any underlying conviction but only because the order had come. The title of the book, *Soldiers of Evil*, is therefore well chosen."

Segev's third book, which was first published in Hebrew in 1991, appeared in English translation two years later as *The Seventh Million: The Israelis and the Holocaust.* Using primary sources, Segev examined the response of Zionist leaders to the Holocaust during World War II and how subsequently Israeli attitudes toward the Holocaust gradually changed. Segev dissented from the commonly accepted portrait of Zionist leaders heroically attempting to save as many Jews as possible from the death camps. He argued that some Zionists leaders did very little to help the Jews because they remained focused on their primary goal of establishing a Jewish homeland in Palestine. In the new Jewish state, some Zionists looked down on Holocaust survivors, faulting them for failing to offer any resistance to the Nazis.

Segev explained that several high-profile events, including Israel's negotiation with what was then West Germany over war reparations and the 1961 trial of the Nazi war criminal Adolf Eichmann forced many Israelis to confront the terrible reality of the Holocaust after years of silence and indifference. In his review for the *New York Times* (May 5, 1993), Herbert Mitgang wrote that Segev "makes an original contribution to the literature of the Holocaust from still another perspective." Calling the book "richly detailed and well researched," Mitgang opined, "Artifacts in Holocaust museums and memorials in Israel, Europe and the United States continue to be reminders of genocide and inhumanity in this dying century. So are such written testaments as *The Seventh Million.*" In the *Wall Street Journal* (July 15, 1993), Amy Dockser Marcus wrote that the book was "a compelling and disturbing work that begins with the Nazi rise to power and ends with the Persian Gulf 60 years later." Marcus also faulted it in several areas: "The book's major flaw is that Mr. Segev's sharp voice frequently gets lost in the overwhelming wealth of detail he has uncovered. The early chapters on the prestate leaders' reactions to the Holocaust, particularly that of Israel's first prime minister, David Ben-Gurion, are fast-paced and riveting. But in subsequent sections of the book, particularly on subjects that have been already well-documented elsewhere, such as the 1961 trial in Jerusalem of the Nazi war criminal Adolf Otto Eichmann, Mr. Segev shies away from providing the kind of interpretation that is critical in a work of this magnitude and gets bogged down recounting minute developments in the innumerable ideological disputes between the various political factions."

Segev next chronicled the history of Britain's administration of Palestine in his book *One Palestine, Complete: Jews and Arabs under the British Mandate* (2000), which was originally published in Hebrew in 1999. Segev asserted that the British, contrary to what is often written by historians, favored the creation of a Jewish state in Palestine. "I was surprised when I first started to sit in the archives, to find that the documents told a completely different story than what we were all taught at school," Segev explained to Moshe Temkin for the *Jerusalem Report* (September 13,

1999). "We learned that we ran the British out of Palestine, that they were horrible and oppressive rulers, and that we built our country despite their efforts to ruin the Zionist prospect. In fact, Israel was created with their full assistance and sponsorship. It was the Arabs who ran them out. The British became sick of Palestine after putting down the Arab Revolt in 1939." *One Palestine, Complete* sharply divided reviewers. "Segev is a skillful writer and the book is an engaging read," Amos Perlmutter wrote in the *National Review* (March 19, 2001). "Yet despite the fact that he has consulted nearly every book on his subject written in Hebrew or English, including unpublished diaries, none of this material adds an iota of new information. Instead, *One Palestine, Complete* reshuffles the facts under the guise of a new interpretation." Perlmutter criticized Segev for downplaying the importance of the British White Paper, which was adopted on March 13, 1939, terminating Jewish immigration to Palestine and denying refuge to many Jews who were later killed by the Nazis. By contrast, in *Middle East Policy* (June 1, 2001), Philip Wilcox hailed the book. "Segev weaves a fascinating tale that brings to life the struggle between Jews and Arabs in Palestine under British rule from the perspective of all three parties," Wilcox wrote. "Drawing on newly mined archives and personal diaries of major and minor participants, he adds color and human drama to this tragic conflict and makes some controversial but well-supported judgments. Segev's approach is sometimes acerbic, but it is also compassionate and nonpartisan, true to his reputation as one of Israel's leading 'post-Zionist' writers." Wilcox concluded that by "illuminating a formative chapter of the [Arab-Israeli] conflict, this book should help Israelis and Palestinians understand themselves and their history more clearly and honestly, as they struggle to come to terms with each other." In 2001 the book was honored with the National Jewish Book Award.

In his next book, *Elvis in Jerusalem: Post-Zionism and the Americanization of Israel* (published in the U.S. in 2002), Segev argued that American culture is transforming Israel, gradually displacing the predominant Zionist ideology. While many critics see such Americanization exclusively in the form of new McDonald's fast-food restaurants and Dunkin' Donuts shops springing up throughout Israel, Segev sees instead a beneficial trend, which is introducing the virtues of tolerance, pragmatism, and individualism to the country. In the *Los Angeles Times Book Review* (May 19, 2002), Walter Laquer was impressed by Segev's arguments. "In *Elvis in Jerusalem*, [Segev] deals with certain cultural trends in Israel over the last decade, and [the book] appears at a time when these issues are not exactly on the top of our agenda," Laquer wrote. "But the comments of a shrewd observer are still of interest, not only to professionals in the field of cultural studies but to anyone interested in understanding the continuing debates in Israel over its ideological foundations." By contrast, David Margolis dismissed the book in his review for the *Jerusalem Report* (June 30, 2003). "Ironically, [Segev's] unsatisfactory book is, in some ways, itself an artifact of the imported American style—irreverent, breezy, charming, full of interesting facts and factoids, [but] not deep," Margolis observed. "His approach is selectively anecdotal and fragmentary, with stories strung together disproportionately to suit a political intent."

Tom Segev currently lives in Jerusalem. He has been a guest professor at Hebrew University and a senior fellow at the Bildner Center for the Study of Jewish Life at Rutgers University, in New Jersey. The first American edition of *1967: Israel, the War, and the Year that Transformed the Middle East* is slated for publication in May 2007.

—D.C.

Suggested Reading: *Jerusalem Post* (on-line) Aug. 11, 1989, Apr. 16, 1993; *Jerusalem Report* p56+ Sep. 13, 1999, p41 June 30, 2003; *Los Angeles Times Book Review* p1 Mar. 16, 1986, p6 Feb. 19, 1989, p11 May 19, 2002; *Middle East Policy* (on-line) June 1, 2001; *National Review* (on-line) Mar. 19, 2001; *New York Times* C p21 May 5, 1993; *New York Times Book Review* p13 Feb. 2, 1986; *Wall Street Journal* A p10 July 15, 1993

Selected Books in English Translation: *1949: The First Israelis*, 1986; *Soldiers of Evil: The Commandants of the Nazi Concentration Camps*, 1989; *The Seventh Million: The Israelis and the Holocaust*, 1993; *One Palestine, Complete: Jews and Arabs under the British Mandate*, 2000; *Elvis in Jerusalem: Post-Zionism and the Americanization of Israel*, 2002

Seiffert, Rachel

1971– Novelist; short-story writer

Rachel Seiffert's debut, *The Dark Room* (2001), which consists of three interlocking novellas, was warmly welcomed in literary circles and short-listed for the prestigious Booker Prize. As with that first book, all of her subsequent work has explored the fallout of war and one generation's guilt over another's transgressions. "Despite the big themes," Lorna Bradbury wrote for the London *Telegraph* (January 28, 2007, on-line), "Seiffert's fiction isn't as earnest as this sounds. The substance of her work is personal lives: the intricacies of human behaviour and the peculiar dances we weave around each other. She is interested in the moments we find ourselves cut off from the world, adrift from our lovers and families. She is an excellent dramatist of human failure."

Rachel Seiffert was born in Oxford, England, in 1971. Her German mother had moved to England in the 1960s, when she married Seiffert's Australian father, an academic then working in Oxford. As a child Seiffert spent a significant amount of time in Germany, visiting her grandmother there during summer recesses. In school she was often bullied and called a Nazi. As a child she believed that being German was a bad thing, even though she then had little knowledge of the Nazi regime or the Holocaust. "I've been aware my whole life of German guilt," she told Bradbury.

The Dark Room, Seiffert's first novel, traced the effects of the Third Reich's reign over three generations of Germans. In the book's first section, which covers the period from 1921 to 1945, a photographer chronicles Adolf Hitler's rise to power; in the second section a 12-year-old girl searches for her grandmother at the end of the war, after her parents, members of the Nazi Party, are arrested by the invading allied forces; in the final section a young teacher struggles to understand his grandfather's membership in the Waffen-SS, a notoriously brutal combat unit. "None of the three main characters commit atrocities; the focus is on their emotional lives and their varying awareness of national guilt. They are preoccupied with personal goals that shed light on the Germany they inhabit," David Sacks wrote for the *New York Times Book Review* (May 13, 2001). "Seiffert writes lean, clean prose. Deftly, she hangs large ideas on the vivid private experiences of her principle characters." A reviewer for the *Economist* (May 12, 2001) was equally laudatory, calling the book "a very readable, imaginative attempt to hold essential truths in living memory." *The Dark Room* won a Los Angeles Times Book Prize for first fiction and a Betty Trask Award.

For a full year after the publication of her book, while she was traveling to promote it, Seiffert suffered from a serious depression. "It took me a while to work out why I was sad all the time, and then it occurred to me that if you begin each day getting up and talking about the Holocaust over breakfast with someone you've never met before, it's no surprise you feel low," she told Helen Pidd for the London *Guardian* (January 29, 2007). "My whole life, since I developed some sort of political conscience, I've been used to thinking about the Holocaust. But it was the day-in-day-out-ness of promoting *The Dark Room* that got to me. It sounds very dramatic to say this, but it felt very invasive. Writing it was hard, but it wasn't as hard as talking about it afterwards."

In 2004 Seiffert published *Field Study,* a widely praised collection of short stories. "Though her settings are sharply rendered," a reviewer wrote for *Publishers Weekly* (June 14, 2004), "Seiffert often omits crucial bits of information, turning her stories into puzzles, sad games, as in 'The Crossing,' in which a mother and children are helped across a river by a man whose accent betrays him as an enemy in an unspecified conflict. In 'Second Best,' the last, longest and best story of the collection, Seiffert allows herself more specificity in time and place (Poland and Berlin, 1996), as well as a more complete exploration of her characters' thoughts and feelings. Disciplined, spare and unsentimental, these are accomplished, often moving tales."

In Seiffert's most recent novel, *Afterwards*, the protagonist, Alice, is frustrated that the men in her life are keeping her at arm's length. As is later revealed, both her boyfriend, Joseph, and recently widowed grandfather are concealing the fact that they each killed someone while serving in the military. "While Joseph suffers post-traumatic stress disorder, it is very difficult to feel sympathy for his rages and lows when he remains closed not only to his girlfriend, but also to the reader. Alice speaks of love and longing, but the lack of detail and depth makes her feelings forgettable," Amy Crowther wrote for the *Irish Independent* (February 11, 2007). "The germ of a decent read is here, but the lack of flesh and emotion could leave readers with a heavy sense of frustration." On the other hand, Bradbury wrote that "*Afterwards* is a daring work, sure to gain [Seiffert] greater recognition. It is her first sustained novel, more substantial than anything she has written before, and more integrated, with a greater degree of momentum and urgency."

Before becoming a successful writer, Seiffert worked in the film industry as an editor and director. She told Pidd that her spare prose style is likely the result of her experience editing films: "In cutting rooms, there's a big emphasis on pace. In the film world it's all about moving on the story, so I want to put in the minimum to convey what is there. . . . I really don't like describing the tone of voice people speak in: 'He said, gruffly', 'He said, wryly.' That really annoys me. And I don't like too much description, full stop, or adjectives. Why do I need to know that someone has a piggy nose, or freckles? Each reader will imagine the piggy nose or the freckles in their own way anyway."

Seiffert's short story "Blue" was short-listed for the Macallan Short Story Award in 1999; in 2001 her short story "The Crossing" won the PEN David T. K. Wong Award. Though Seiffert has lived most of her life in Oxford and Glasgow, she recently moved to Berlin, Germany. She has two children, Edie and Finlay.

—C.M.

Suggested Reading: *Economist* p90 May 12, 2001; *Library Journal* p128+ May 1, 2001; (London) *Guardian* Features p12 Jan. 29, 2007; (London) *Telegraph* (on-line) Jan. 28, 2007; *New York Times Book Review* p30 May 13, 2001

Selected Books: *The Dark Room*, 2001; *Field Study*, 2004; *Afterwards*, 2007

Karen Fernandez/Courtesy of Random House

Selvadurai, Shyam

1965– Novelist

Shyam Selvadurai left civil war and political turmoil in his native Sri Lanka (formerly Ceylon) to find success as a novelist in Canada. A gay man of mixed Sinhalese and Tamil heritage, Selvadurai writes about characters in his turbulent homeland who struggle to maintain their sexual identity and individuality against the enormous pressures of family and society. Selvadurai made his literary debut with the highly acclaimed *Funny Boy: A Novel in Six Stories* (1994), which follows the homosexual awakening of a Tamil boy and his family's repeated efforts to get him to conform to traditional heterosexual male roles. Discussing the writing process with Claus Anthonisen for the *Windsor Review* (March 2001, on-line), Selvadurai observed: "When the characters start to take care of themselves, when they start to do things you didn't expect them to, that is the most exciting part of the novel; it's the moment when you know the novel is working, that it's found its voice, and its DNA so to speak. . . . It's a moment of joy, but also of fear."

One of four children, Shyam Selvadurai was born in 1965 in Ceylon. (In 1972 the country's name was changed to Sri Lanka.) He and his siblings grew up in a privileged environment. His father, who is Tamil, coached the Davis Cup tennis team. His mother, who is Sinhalese, was a doctor. As a child Selvadurai enjoyed reading and writing. He often staged plays, which he wrote himself, in his parents' living room.

In contrast to the family's domestic harmony, ethnic tensions between the Sinhalese majority and the Tamil minority divided the island nation, which had earned its independence from Great Britain in 1948. In 1983 the tensions between the Sinhalese and Tamils exploded into civil war; the Tamil Tigers, a militant separatist group, clashed with the police and government troops. Colombo, Sri Lanka's capital, experienced massive riots, which devastated large parts of the city. Fearing for their children's safety, Selvadurai's parents took the family to Canada, in 1985. "If not for us, [my parents] would have stuck it out," Selvadurai told Joel Yanofsky for the Montreal *Gazette* (October 8, 1994). The adjustment was difficult. "The problem with coming to Canada wasn't culture shock, it was class shock," Selvadurai recalled to Yanofsky. "What was hard was going from thinking to yourself, in Sri Lanka, as being a cut above everybody else, which was preposterous, to everyone here thinking you are a cut below because of the color of your skin." Because she was not allowed to practice medicine in Canada, Selvadurai's mother had to take a job as a file clerk.

When he was 21 years old, Selvadurai revealed to his parents that he was gay. "I think it made it easier for them to accept it because they knew that there were greater possibilities for happiness here [in Canada], than there would have been in Sri Lanka [where homosexuality is illegal]," Selvadurai told Ray Deonandan for *India Currents* (April 30, 1996). "In Sri Lanka, I think they would have said, 'We realize that you are gay, and we know that it's not a sickness.' But it would have made them very unhappy because I couldn't have been accepted and happy there."

Selvadurai enrolled at York University, in Toronto. "I actually thought I was going to be a director, but then I took a playwright's course, and it really turned me on to writing," he told Claus Anthonisen. "I had a very good teacher, Matthew Corrigan, at York, who gave me the basics, who understood that writing was actually a craft—like dance, or visual art. As a teacher, he knew he had to teach us the craft of writing, and that inspiration, and all that other experimental stuff would come much later, and that we'd have to do it on our own. What we needed to do was get a good grounding." Selvadurai graduated with a Bachelor of Fine Arts degree. He then wrote a few pieces for Canadian television and worked in a bookstore.

In 1990 Selvadurai began writing fiction, producing a novel that was, as he told Yanofsky, "a piece of crap." Selvadurai's professional break came when he published a story, "Pigs Can't Fly," about a young boy's homosexual awakening, in a small literary magazine. The critic and editor Alberto Manguel was impressed with the story and contacted Selvadurai. "Alberto wanted to publish it in his anthology of gay literature," Selvadurai recalled to Yanofsky. "He also said he'd passed the story on to his agent, Lucinda Vardley, and she'd be calling me. Within an hour, she was on the phone telling me how much she loved the story and was I writing anything else? I told her it was the first part of a novel. She said that when I was done I should show it to her." In 1994 Selvadurai published his first book, *Funny Boy: A Novel in Six Stories*, in Canada and England. (The book was published in the United States in 1996 as *Funny Boy: A Novel*.) Set in Sri Lanka during the 1970s and early 1980s, the novel is narrated by Arjie, a Tamil boy who gradually discovers that he is gay and resists the pressures of his family to abandon his sexual identity. The similarities between Arjie and Selvadurai led many readers and reviewers to conclude that *Funny Boy* was an autobiographical novel. "People think I'm Arjie," Selvadurai told Michael J. Glitz for the *Advocate* (June 22, 1999, on-line), "but they're wrong. With *Funny Boy* I knew the autobiographical question would come up, so I was actually careful to keep myself out of it."

Funny Boy received extensive acclaim. "Throughout, the book evokes an alert and sensitive child's growing awareness of adult hypocrisies and duplicities and, in doing so, presents the child narrator's views and speculations innocently but translucently, so that the underlying adult realities, especially where racial overtones are involved, shine through and we come to dread what the narrator does not yet foresee," Christopher Levenson wrote for the *Ottawa Citizen* (September 19, 1994). "Although all the stories interconnect, they can be read separately since they are self-contained. When read in sequence, they . . . [create] characters and situations that live in their own right, not simply for the impact on the protagonist." In the *New York Times Book Review* (April 14, 1996), Edward Hower recommended the novel. "Throughout *Funny Boy*, Shyam Selvadurai writes as sensitively about the emotional intensity of adolescence as he does about the wonder of childhood," Hower wrote. "He also paints an affectionate picture of an imperfect family in a lost paradise, struggling to stay together in troubled times. Arjie's parents and relatives may not be able to understand his inability to fit into a conventional sexual identity—but he learns that despite this, he can always count on their love." In 1994 *Funny Boy* was nominated for the prestigious Giller Prize, which annually honors the best Canadian novel or short-story collection published in English. *Funny Boy* won the SmithBooks/Books in Canada First Novel Award, now called the Amazon.ca/Books in Canada First Novel Award, in 1995, and the Lambda Literary Award for gay-men's fiction, in 1997.

In the mid-1990s Selvadurai's parents began spending six months in Sri Lanka each year to escape Canada's harsh winters, and in 1997 Selvadurai returned to his native land for the first time since emigrating. He and his partner, Andrew, spent a year living in a spacious house in Colombo that his parents had rented for them. Selvadurai spent much of his time doing research in governmental archives for his second novel. "I needed to be back in Sri Lanka to understand

emotionally how difficult it is [as a gay man] to do even a small action like riding a bicycle or writing a letter," Selvadurai explained to Glitz. "How much courage it takes to do that—and the consequences of it."

Selvadurai was unnerved when the police came one day to search his rented house for Tamil rebels. (Because of his Tamil surname, he was automatically suspicious in the eyes of the authorities.) Because homosexuality was still a criminal offense in Sri Lanka, Andrew quickly moved his belongings into a separate room in a frantic effort to conceal the nature of their relationship. When a policeman asked Selvadurai if he was indeed Tamil, Selvadurai confirmed that he was, but noted that his mother was Sinhalese. "With a curt wave of his hand, he dismissed this last fact," Selvadurai wrote in an article for *Time* (August 18, 2003). The incident angered him. "If the importance of my Sinhalese identity was irrelevant, how unthinkable this must be, my gay identity," he wrote. "In this country that I still considered my home, I could never be at home. Andrew and I were never again completely at ease in our own house."

In 1999 Selvadurai published his second novel, *Cinnamon Gardens*. Set in the 1920s, the book follows Annalushmi, a young woman, and Belandran, her uncle, a closeted homosexual, as they defy their families' wishes and society's conventions to seek personal happiness. The characters both live in Cinnamon Gardens, an affluent area of Colombo. Inspired by England's suffragette movement, Annalushmi refuses to marry the man picked by her parents and instead pursues a career as a teacher. Belandran, who is married and the father of a daughter, resumes a homosexual relationship with a man he had met in London two decades earlier. (Belandran's father had forced him to give up the relationship and marry.)

Most reviewers praised *Cinnamon Gardens*. "Selvadurai has written an almost Victorian novel, with the lives of his characters intertwined and interrelated, rich with the heat and scent of British colonial overlay on an ancient society," GraceAnne DeCandido wrote for *Booklist* (May 15, 1999). "Wry references to love, always in terms of fever or illness, grace notes of description for a lock of hair or the fold of a sari, and elegant chapter headings taken from the *Tirukkural*, the famed work of Tamil philosophy, add to the ambience generated by this beguiling novel." Bill Richardson lauded *Cinnamon Gardens* for *Quill & Quire* (December 1998): "[The novel] draws its strength from those old-fashioned, momentum gathering narrative imperatives of plot, character, and setting. These take on a particular buoyancy in a novel that unfolds, as this one does, in a traditional society at a pivotal historical moment when its underpinnings are being rattled loose." The reviewer added, "Now and again, the seams come apart so that we can see all the careful research with which *Cinnamon Gardens* has been stuffed, but this is a minor quibble. [Selvadurai] is a gifted storyteller, and this is a graceful, absorbing, and intelligent novel." *Cinnamon Gardens* was nominated for the Trillium Book Award.

In late 2005 Selvadurai published *Swimming in the Monsoon Sea*, his first work of young-adult fiction. Set in Sri Lanka in 1980, the novel tells the story of Amrith, a 14-year-old boy living with an adoptive family after the mysterious death of his mother and the earlier disappearance of his abusive, alcoholic father. The arrival of Amrith's cousin, Niresh, a freewheeling Canadian two years his senior, disrupts Amrith's insular, privileged world. Heather Birrell for *Books in Canada* (December 2005) praised Selvadurai's control over character development and his exploitation of setting: "Selvadurai gives Amrith just the right amount of fumbling insight into his new self-awareness, sensibly forgoing a focus on the 'issue' for a more nuanced treatment of the whole person in language both workaday and lyrical. Also successful is the author's use of the moody monsoon sea of the title as a reflection of (and counterpoint to) Amrith's shifting disposition." Writing for the *Washington Post Book World* (October 2, 2005), Elizabeth Ward described the novel as "that rare thing, a coming-of-age story that transcends labels and deserves to be called literature, plain and simple." Ward concluded: "As much a paean to a time, a place and a class as a coming-of-age story, *Monsoon Sea* puts the standard American 'teen issue' novel to shame."

In 2005 Selvadurai also edited the short-story anthology *Story-Wallah!: A Celebration of South Asian Fiction.*

Shyam Selvadurai lives in Toronto.

—D.C.

Suggested Reading: *Advocate* (on-line) June 22, 1999; *Booklist* p1,643 May 15, 1999; *Books in Canada* p39 Dec. 2005; *India Currents* p7 Apr. 30. 1996; (Montreal) *Gazette* Books p12 Oct. 8. 1994, J p3 Oct. 24, 1998; *New York Times Book Review* p22 Apr. 14, 1996; *Ottawa Citizen* B p3 Sep. 18, 1994; *Quill & Quire* p31 Dec. 1998; Shyam Selvadurai's Web site; *Washington Post Book World* p11 Oct. 2, 2005; *Windsor Review* (on-line) Mar. 2001

Selected Books: *Funny Boy: A Novel in Six Stories*, 1994; *Cinnamon Gardens*, 1999; *Swimming in the Monsoon Sea*, 2005; as editor—*Story-Wallah!: A Celebration of South Asian Fiction*, 2005

Senna, Danzy

1970– Novelist

In both of Danzy Senna's critically praised novels, *Caucasia* (1998) and *Symptomatic* (2004), the author has drawn from her own experiences growing up in a mixed-race family to scrutinize the racial tensions that doggedly persist in American society. "One of the things I'm sort of wary of in the multiracial movement is a denial of the persistence of racism," she told Rebecca L. Weber for *Africana* (July 6, 2004). "In this Tiger Woods model, we're all just happy to be mixed, and we're so cute and we're so Benetton. There are still issues that you confront being mixed. There are really difficult experiences that you have if you appear white and you're not white."

Danzy Senna was born in 1970 in Boston, Massachusetts, to a black father and a white mother who were both active in the civil rights movement. Her mother, Fanny Howe, is a novelist and poet; her father, Carl Senna, is a journalist and the author of *The Black Press and the Struggle For Civil Rights*. In an article titled "The Mulatto Millennium," which was published in the anthology *Half and Half: Writers on Growing Up Biracial and Bicultural* (1998), Senna explained the complexities of her feelings about her mixed heritage: "I was born in 1970, when 'black' described a people bonded not by shared

Courtesy of Blue Flower Arts

complexion or hair texture but by shared history. Not only was I black (and here I go out on a limb), but I was an enemy of the people. The mulatto people, that is. I sneered at those byproducts of miscegenation who chose to identify as mixed, not black. I thought it wishy-washy, an act of flagrant assimilation, treason, passing even. It was my parents who made me this way. In Boston circa 1975, mixed wasn't really an option. . . . Let it be clear—my parents' decision to raise us as black wasn't based on any one-drop rule from the days of slavery, and it certainly wasn't based on our appearance, that crude reasoning many black-identified mixed people use: if the world sees me as black, I must be black. If it had been based on appearance, my sister would have been black, my brother Mexican, and me Jewish. Instead, my parents' decision arose out of the rising black power movement, which made identifying as black not a pseudoscientific rule but a conscious choice."

After graduating from high school, Senna moved to California to pursue her B.A. at Stanford University. "I was pre-med in college as an attempt not to become a writer like [my parents]," she told Weber. "I failed all my science and math classes, so I decided to go with the family trade." She graduated with honors, in 1992, and then returned east to work as a researcher and reporter for *Newsweek*. In 1996 Senna obtained her M.F.A. from the University of California, at Irvine. From 1996 to 1997 she served as a contributing editor to *American Benefactor*.

Caucasia takes place in Boston in the 1970s, a time of profound racial unrest for the city. Birdie, who is biracial and appears to be white, watches as her parents' marriage falls apart. Her radical intellectual father, Deck, gets a new black girlfriend who doesn't acknowledge Birdie; meanwhile, her mother, Sandra, devotes all her energy to the movement. Soon Sandra's political activities put the family in danger. Deck and his girlfriend disappear with Birdie's darker-skinned sister, Cole, and Sandra and Birdie go underground, settling in New Hampshire and passing as the widow and daughter of a Jewish professor. Amidst the uncertainty, Birdie struggles to reconcile her biracial heritage, occupying as she does a nebulous region in which she is a member of both races but accepted by neither. Alisa Valdes, writing for the *Boston Globe* (March 7, 1998), called the work "a well-crafted coming-of-age story that escapes the confines of race, all the while digging to its complex core. . . . Despite a few small flaws, . . . [it is] a stunning debut from one of the most promising writers Boston has produced this decade."

Senna's second book, *Symptomatic* (2004), is the story of two biracial women who are passing for white. "*Symptomatic* carries off plot twists and turns with a focused, vivid language that brings out every telling detail about being a newcomer both to New York City and to the inner landscape of an authentic self," Elizabeth Aoki wrote for the *Seattle Times* (July 4, 2004). "[Senna] plays with stereotypes and duality masterfully, delivering telling snapshots of a white hairdresser whose dialogue comes straight out of a rap video, or a

dreadlocked African-American artist mixing with Manhattan's martini culture." While most other critics were not as impressed with Senna's sophomore effort, Alan Cheuse, a reviewer for National Public Radio's *All Things Considered* (May 17, 2004), reminded readers that "*Symptomatic* is still a book by a truly interesting young writer whose work you'll want to follow from now on."

—P.B.M.

Suggested Reading: *Boston Globe* C p7 Mar. 7, 1998; *New York Times* E p2 May 4, 1998; *Seattle Times* (on-line) July 4, 2004

Selected Books: *Caucasia*, 1998; *Symptomatic*, 2004

Courtesy of Harvard University Press

Shelby, Tommie

Dec. 29, 1967– Philosopher

Until 2005 Tommie Shelby was, in many respects, a typical scholar, teaching at a university, attending conferences, and publishing articles for the benefit of those who share his academic interests. With the publication of *We Who Are Dark: The Philosophical Foundations of Black Solidarity* (2005), a profound reassessment of the influence of identity politics on African-American social movements over the last century, Shelby made that rare transition from obscure scholar to public figure. His study has garnered notices in such popular publications as the *New York Times Book Review* (January 15, 2006), in which it was described as "a new theory of black identity built atop the ruins of the old." *We Who Are Dark* has also led major figures in the field of African-American studies to laud Shelby's work as capable of reinvigorating the continuing struggle of African-Americans to fashion an American culture free of racism. The eminent sociologist and historian Orlando Patterson, in an E-mail cited by the editors of the *New York Times Book Review* (January 8, 2006), wrote, "My attraction to Shelby's book is that he has done, much better and at a more appropriate time, what I had tried to do, at about his age, 30 years ago. I think that identity politics, while once instrumental in the early stages of cultural and political emancipation, has long outlived its purpose. . . . I am pessimistic about black progress as long as African-American leaders have a vested interest in promoting, indeed celebrating, the very identity politics that drags down the majority of black people, especially the young."

Tommie Shelby submitted the following autobiographical statement for *World Authors 2000–2005*:

"I was born December 29, 1967 in Vienna, Georgia, near where my great-grandmother owned a small farmhouse. I grew up largely in Jacksonville, Florida, with a brief stint during my teenage years in Los Angeles. I am the oldest of six, with three brothers (one, Christopher, now deceased) and two sisters, and my mother, Vernell, raised us mostly on her own, though she did have considerable help, especially with me and my brother Chris, from my grandmother, Mattie Brock. I never knew my biological father, who refused to take any responsibility for me. I sort of knew my stepfather, but he and my mother divorced in 1982 and I haven't seen or spoken to him in almost twenty-five years. I can't say I ever missed him. My mother, who died in 1999, gave birth to me at the age of seventeen. She was among the many black single mothers who struggle to escape ghetto poverty and to give their children a chance to create decent lives for themselves in an unjust society. Her life was hard and short, but she had [a] gentle and kind spirit. I loved her loud and infectious laugh, which was most robust when she was running a 'Boston' on you in Bid Whist!

"As a boy, I had absolutely no interest in school or books. Only sports, popular music, and girls occupied my mind at the time. Yet it was not lost on me that without an education my life could easily be as difficult as the one my mother faced. The first in my family to attend college, I enrolled at Florida A & M University in 1986. I had a lot of catching up to do and so spent much of my first two years in college, including summers, developing my writing and reading skills. At first I tried my hand at majoring in business administration but luckily discovered the life of the mind as my calling and ultimately chose philosophy as my principal disciplinary focus. Philosophy suits my temperament—introspective,

brooding, questioning. At age twenty, I faced a difficult and life-altering choice: should I be a Christian or a philosopher? Many thinkers whom I admire (for example, Martin Luther King, Jr. and Cornel West) have regarded this as a false choice and have maintained their commitment to Christianity and philosophy. I found this an impossible reconciliation. I chose philosophy and have no regrets. My family has never been able to understand this decision, but to their credit they continue to embrace me as they always have, with warmth and unconditional love.

"I was fortunate to have many mentors who nurtured and encouraged my desire to become a scholar. David Felder, a philosophy professor at Florida A & M, almost single-handedly prepared me for graduate school. At the University of Pittsburgh, where I earned my doctorate, Tamara Horowitz (now deceased) was devoted to making sure I succeeded in completing my studies. Kwame Anthony Appiah and Bernard Boxill, two distinguished philosophers, have supported me from my undergraduate days to the present. I have never been inclined to take all the credit for my achievements (you know, that familiar petite-bourgeois conceit that all is due to 'self-reliance'), for I know that without the goodwill of others, too many to mention, I'd probably be working some dead-end job, feeling deeply unfulfilled—or worse.

"After earning my Ph.D. in 1998, I accepted the position of assistant professor of philosophy at Ohio State University. This was a wonderful job with great colleagues, but my interests were shifting away from Marxism's contribution to meta-ethics (the subject of my dissertation) toward questions of race. Thus I sought out an institutional environment where I thought I might better pursue this new interest. Much to my surprise and delight that place turned out to be Harvard's highly esteemed Department of African and African American Studies. There I learned a tremendous amount about the black experience from my eminent colleagues in related fields, and this set me on the path to doing interdisciplinary work rather than limiting myself to the insular world of academic philosophy.

"Yet I do think of myself first and foremost as a political philosopher. My work is strongly influenced by three political traditions—black nationalism, Marxism, and liberalism—and I seek to draw the best from each as I take up contemporary issues of race and class. I've written essays on each of these traditions, highlighting their relevance to the continuing problems of racism and economic inequality. I'm also passionate about making the African American philosophical tradition more widely known and appreciated among scholars and laypersons. My book, *We Who Are Dark: The Philosophical Foundations of Black Solidarity*, was an attempt to merge these two interests.

"My best friend, Derrick Darby, and I co-edited a collection of essays entitled *Hip Hop and Philosophy: Rhyme 2 Reason.* He and I grew up under similar circumstances and share a deep love for both philosophy and hip hop music. We thought it would be fun and educational to try to, as it were, 'mix' the two, with the hope of drawing young people from the 'hip hop generation' into the lovely if sometimes rarefied world of philosophy.

"In 2002 I met Jessie Scanlon, a journalist and an editor, and we were married on July 23, 2005. We split our time between Cambridge, Massachusetts and Brooklyn Heights. I hope someday that we will write a book together on journalism and democracy, but for now I'm satisfied with being as content as I've ever been."

Tommie Shelby graduated magna cum laude from Florida A&M University, in Tallahassee, with a bachelor of arts degree in philosophy in 1990. After earning his doctorate from the University of Pittsburgh, in 1998, he took a position as an assistant professor at Ohio State University, in Columbus. Only two years later Shelby left Ohio to become an assistant professor in the Department of African and African American Studies at Harvard University, in Cambridge, Massachusetts. He soon began publishing articles about the African-American experience in a variety of academic journals—including the *Fordham Law Review*, *Philosophy and Public Affairs*, *Political Theory*, the *Philosophical Forum*, *Social Theory and Practice*, the *Journal of Social Philosophy*, and *Ethics*—and was later promoted to become the John L. Loeb Associate Professor of the Social Sciences and of African and African American Studies. As a Harvard professor, Shelby began to draw the attention of critics, even before the majority of his work was published. The linguist John H. McWhorter, who has argued that the discourse on African-Americans should not emphasize their victimization, wrote for *City Journal* (Spring 2002) that Shelby and other professors in his department at Harvard were teaching "victimology in its Sunday best," noting that Shelby's course on Marxist theories of racism, "unpacks 'the role of capitalist development and expansion in perpetuating racial inequality' and boasts a reading list that can serve as a primer on how to rage (articulately) against the machine."

Ignoring such criticism, Shelby continued his work, seeking to demonstrate the ideological systems that allowed those in the West to justify slavery and discriminatory practices and to show that African-American thought, even that which derives from popular culture, has addressed important philosophical questions. With the latter purpose in mind, he edited, with Derrick Darby, *Hip Hop and Philosophy: Rhyme 2 Reason* (2005),

a collection of essays that reveal how "rap classics by Lauryn Hill, OutKast, and the Notorious B.I.G. can help us uncover the meanings of love articulated in Plato's Symposium," how "Run-D.M.C., Snoop Dogg, and Jay-Z can teach us about self-consciousness and the dialectic in Hegel's *The Phenomenology of the Spirit*," and how "Rakim, 2Pac, and Nas can shed light on the conception of God's essence expressed in Aquinas's *Summa Theologica*," according to the Open Court Publishing Company's Web site. "These philosophers," the publisher concluded, "delight in showing how a love for rhymes over beats and for pure reason, far from being incompatible, can be mastered and mixed to contemplate life's most profound mysteries."

At the end of 2005, *We Who Are Dark*, a study that belied the criticism of such commentators as McWhorter, was published. In it Shelby not only critiqued Western culture from the perspective of the African-Americans who have suffered systematic oppression but also examined African-American thought, dissecting, as *Publishers Weekly* (August 22, 2005) reported, "the history of black political thought from W. E. B. Du Bois to Malcolm X in order to arrive at a new political philosophy that takes black solidarity as its foundation. [Shelby] does an excellent job of summarizing the central tenets in black political thought, from Booker T. Washington's beliefs about self-reliance to Marcus Garvey's more radical strain of black independence. His approach to history is rigorous and genuinely critical. Shelby finds merits and flaws in almost every political theory he discusses, leading to an evenhanded, meticulously thought-out argument that builds upon the best elements of black political thought." The solidarity for which Shelby called, however, is not grounded in racial identity, a notion he regarded "as dangerous as biological conceptions of race," but, Patterson observed in his review for the *New York Times* (January 8, 2006), the author "goes much further, rejecting all forms of positive black identities." For Shelby, African-American solidarity is a condition determined by a shared history: "What holds blacks together as a unified people with shared political interests," he writes, as quoted by Dan Coleman for the Durham, North Carolina, *Chapel Hill Herald* (January 14, 2006), "is their racial subordination and their collective resolve to triumph over it." Shelby calls attention to the diversity among blacks and "urges readers to question the significance of this [black] solidarity in the complex world of post–civil rights era America," Laura A. Moore observed in her review for the *Harvard Crimson* (December 2, 2005, on-line); he asks them, in effect, to refashion the concept of black solidarity so that it can become more inclusive, capable of embracing "homosexuals, feminists, mixed-race individuals, and members of various socioeconomic groups," according to Moore.

Shelby has won myriad academic awards, including the Harvard University Certificate of Distinction in Teaching and the Ford Foundation Postdoctoral Fellowship for Minorities. He remains a professor at Harvard and has recently been lecturing throughout the U.S., promoting his book and the notion that African-American solidarity movements must be reimagined to remain effective.

—A.R.

Suggested Reading: (Durham, North Carolina) *Chapel Hill Herald* p2 Jan. 14, 2006; *Harvard Crimson* (on-line) Dec. 2, 2005; *New York Times Book Review* p10 Jan. 8, 2006; *Publishers Weekly* p51 Aug. 22, 2005

Selected Works: *We Who Are Dark: The Philosophical Foundations of Black Solidarity*, 2005; as editor—*Hip Hop and Philosophy: Rhyme 2 Reason* (with Derrick Darby), 2005

JD Sloan/Courtesy of Random House

Shepard, Jim

Dec. 29, 1956– Novelist; short-story writer

The fictional writings of Jim Shepard "operate in a shadowy middle ground between history and invention, taking stories we think we know and recasting them, until they reveal new facets of themselves," David L. Ulin wrote for the *Los Angeles Times* (April 28, 2004). Shepard often incorporates characters and events from history and popular culture, using them as a springboard for further rumination about troubling questions of

morality and fate. In his recent novel *Project X* (2004), for example, he writes about two middle-school boys who, alienated and unfairly persecuted by their peers, resort to violence reminiscent of the notorious school shooting at Columbine High School, in Colorado, in 1999. *Love and Hydrogen* (2004), a collection of short stories, includes pieces about Attorney General John Ashcroft; John Entwistle, the deceased bassist for the rock band the Who; and the *Hindenburg*, the famous German airship that crashed in 1937.

For an author whose work attracts strong praise, Shepard is surprisingly little known, and the majority of his books are out of print. His work has been marginalized in some respect because of the lingering biases of a literary establishment that tends to frown upon the use of popular culture in serious art. His fictional interests also move toward the outlandish, setting him apart from the current trend of depicting such familiar fare as marital woes and modern-day anomie. These very traits, however, have earned him the respect of other authors who see him as carving out new territory—bringing him the double-edged distinction of being known as a writer's writer. In a promotional blurb on the book jacket for *Love and Hydrogen*, the author Dave Eggars effused: "[Shepard] gives us red-blooded characters who leave the living room and fly, kayak, dive, search, and emerge from swamps to devour unwitting campers. Stories about dissolving marriages are fine, but how about two gay engineers on the Hindenberg? Or a 19th-century man searching for a giant half-shark/half-whale? These are uniformly bold and exhilarating stories. Let's hope Shepard becomes as influential as he should be. He's the best we've got." Another prominent admirer, Michael Chabon, who featured Shepard in his anthology *McSweeney's Mammoth Treasury of Thrilling Tales*, has attributed his lack of popularity to his fictional diversity. "He's extremely difficult to pigeonhole," Chabon told Ulin. "That works against an artist in any form. But there's so much to him as a writer, so much more than just his use of pop tropes. He's got incredible range. In fact, it's almost as if he's creating his own mini-genre. He can do everything. He can be serious, comic, dark, nostalgic; he never seems to repeat himself."

Jim Shepard was born on December 29, 1956 in Bridgeport, Connecticut, to Albert R. Shepard and the former Ida Picarazzi. His extended family was primarily composed of working-class Italians; his mother had come from Italy when she was a child and his father was half-Italian, with some Welsh and Irish ancestry. On his mother's side he had more than two dozen first cousins—many of whom helped to infuse his childhood with Italian culture as well as a flair for storytelling.

In 1978 Shepard received his bachelor's degree from Trinity College, in Hartford, Connecticut, making him the first member of his family to receive a college education. Shepard had written stories as a child—mostly about monsters—but never seriously considered writing as a career until college. At Trinity he enrolled in a writing workshop, but he was initially discouraged by an instructor who belittled his fledgling attempts. Then something changed: "I wrote in a completely different way," he explained to Amanda Smith in an interview for *Publishers Weekly* (January 31, 1994). "It was voice-driven—something that came to me in the middle of the night—and I squatted on my little bedroom floor and wrote . . . and was very excited about it." The same professor who before had dismissed Shepard now urged him to send the story to the *Atlantic Monthly*. Though the *Atlantic* rejected that piece, its editors asked to see more of Shepard's work, and within a month the magazine had accepted one of his stories.

Shepard earned his M.F.A. from Brown University, in Providence, Rhode Island, in 1980, after which he joined the staff of the University of Michigan, in Ann Arbor, as a lecturer in creative writing; he held that position until 1983. "The idea of myself as a professor was burlesque," he told Smith. "I thought it quite silly for a long time. [The author] Charlie Baxter has a great phrase for it: he calls it 'the fraud police.' It took me quite a while to realize that the fraud police weren't going to come into my classroom and carry me out." In 1983 he took a position as an assistant professor of English at Williams College, in Williamstown, Massachusetts. In 1990 he became an associate professor and five years later was made a full professor. Still at Williams, he currently holds the title J. Leland Miller Professor of English.

Flights (1983), Shepard's first novel, tells the story of Biddy Siebert, an adolescent boy living in Connecticut with his parents and a seven-year-old sister, Kristi. His life is hardly ideal; his parents have moved throughout his childhood, leaving him bereft of friends. The action unfolds over a nine-month period, in which Biddy gives up all of his other interests in favor of an overwhelming desire to learn everything about airplanes. When his father, Walt, tries to encourage his interest in aviation by taking him aboard a friend's plane, Biddy decides to steal the plane and pilot it himself. In a review for *Library Journal* (August 1983), T. F. Smith wrote, "The young boy's inner and outer self and his environment are depicted with sensitive, lyrical realism. The secondary characters have vitality, and the tensions of the story are masterfully controlled. [This] is a fine first novel." Tom Alessandri, writing for *America* (December 3, 1983), observed: "*Flights* is a rousing success for what it does *not* do. It avoids pandering to our current taste for flash, chase and perversion. Rather, in its sensitive realism, it examines a comfortably ordinary family in Connecticut, as they survive events through four holidays one year. *Flights* is a dramatic exercise in the sheer panic of growing up, and a palatable treatise on happiness. . . . In its soaring conclusion, [this novel] wonderfully documents Biddy's decision to put his life together."

Shepard's second novel, *Paper Doll* (1986), focuses on the young and inexperienced members of a U.S. Air Force squadron stationed in England during World War II. The crew of one bomber—the *Paper Doll* of the title—are American men in their late teens and early 20s; they joke, drink, argue, run around with English girls, and bond with one another as they make practice runs in their B-17F Flying Fortress, waiting for the day when they get the "go-call" to begin a real bombing run over Germany. Some of the novel's major characters include Bobby Bryant, a gentle boy whose mission in high school was to never stand out; Gordon Strawberry, a small, blond, underage soldier who likes to sing; and Lewis Peeters, a jokester with unbelievable luck in battle. The novel received mostly favorable reviews. Robert Towers, in the *New York Review of Books* (December 18, 1986), wrote: "One could complain that the beginning is so slow that it may lose readers too impatient to get their bearings. While plausibly characterized, Bryant is insufficiently developed to serve as a real center of consciousness or a primary focus for the reader's sympathies (though it may be argued that the author, whose major concern is the group's experience, has purposely declined to lend much weight to a single character). A few anachronisms creep into an almost perfect evocation of the speech and the attitudes of the early 1940s. But the faults are minor compared to what has been achieved. . . . *Paper Doll* is simultaneously the most moving and the least sentimental novel of the Second World War that I have yet read." In the *Washington Post* (October 22, 1986), Jonathan Yardley proclaimed: "Though [Shepard] is far too young to have any personal experience or memory of World War II, *Paper Doll* aches with verisimilitude. The boyish banter of the crew, the relations between American aviators and British civilians, the looming awareness of life's fragility—Shepard has got it all exactly right. *Paper Doll* is a lovely book, as funny as it is sad, filled with life even as it confronts death; Jim Shepard has written much more than a mere love story."

Shepard's novel *Lights Out in the Reptile House* (1990) takes place in an unnamed fascist state in which spying on citizens and arrests by the secret police are the norm. The central character, a teenager named Karel Roeder, has few cares in the world beyond his friend Leda Schiele and his after-school job at the Reptile House at the local zoo. Leda is more politically aware than Karel, who has little interest in overthrowing the current dictatorship. However, Leda soon influences Karel, and he finds himself developing a conscience about conditions in his country. The book received several positive notices. Dan Cryer, writing for *New York Newsday* (February 18, 1990), noted that the novel "is written with such graceful lucidity and such restless storytelling power that it becomes a political fable for the ages. Without books like this, literature would be poorer and history indeed would be wholly tragic."

However, Lynn Freed, in the *New York Times Book Review* (February 25, 1990), penned a scathing review: "Although the publishers of *Lights Out in the Reptile House* compare it to J. M. Coetzee's masterpiece, *Waiting for the Barbarians*, these books have little in common except the construct of an anonymous fascist state. Except for a few flashes of eloquence, Mr. Shepard's writing is clumsy and inelegant, his book heavy with reported speech and action, with emotions told rather than shown. It is filled with cumbersome sentences."

Freed's trouncing of *Lights Out* dealt a painful blow to Shepard's career. Initial reviews had been positive, but after Freed's critique, no other reviews of the book followed. "I was devastated," Shepard recalled in an interview with Dan Cryer for *New York Newsday* (February 20, 1994). "There was this period of five or seven months of not writing, of waiting for someone else to review the book and say, 'Well, it's a failure,' but there was just silence." Eventually Shepard began writing again after being coaxed by his friend Edward Hirsch, a poet who had been similarly attacked by a noted critic. Hirsch urged him to channel his anger into determination and not self-pity. Shepard returned to publication with *Kiss of the Wolf* (1994).

The protagonist of *Kiss of the Wolf*, Joanie Mucherino, has been married for 12 years when she is deserted by her husband and forced to raise her son, Todd, with the aid of her extended family. She has little love in her life, but she finds herself strangely attracted to Bruno, a local tough guy who has been interested in her for years. Bruno, however, turns out to be a misogynist who brings more menace than romance into her life. At her son's confirmation party, she spurns Bruno's aggressive advances and flees in her car. In her hurry to get away, she accidentally hits and kills a man crossing the street. She speeds off, only to discover later that the man she killed was a friend of Bruno's—and that her admirer has sworn to track down the killer.

"This is a spare, modern tale with realistic characters and a suspenseful plot that turns on a single fateful incident," Anne Gendler wrote for *Booklist* (January 15, 1994). "Eleven-year-old Todd, Joanie, Joanie's mother, and Joanie's long-time admirer Bruno alternate with a third-person narrator to tell the story, which is at once morbid and gripping." "Shepard expertly captures the insularity of Italian American life," Ralph Sassone opined for the *Voice Literary Supplement* (June 1994). "As a choral work, his novel is brilliant, funny, pitch-perfect; the characters' voices convey not only distinct personalities but a distinctively ethnic (i.e., working-class Italian) way of being. . . . Shepard is especially acute whenever Bruno Minea barrels through; every word and gesture is right." Sassone did offer some negative remarks: "Shepard seems to be caught between his desire to give a vibrant character center stage and

his need to keep the reader in suspense. The result is a compromise that makes his otherwise graceful novel seem creaky, even a touch confused. *Kiss of the Wolf* compels anyway. . . . And the novel builds to a genuinely terrifying final showdown." Richard Brausch praised the work in the *New York Times Book Review* (February 20, 1994): "Christopher Isherwood once wrote that it is far more difficult to write stories of terror—those that excite dread and awe—than stories of horror, which merely cause alarm, loathing and disgust. *Kiss of the Wolf* is from the former mold, and even as it makes us laugh, it succeeds in conveying the terror of a slowly closing net of suspicion and circumstance."

Shepard's first collection of short stories, *Battling against Castro* (1996), also received generally positive reviews. Robert E. Brown, in a review for *Library Journal* (July 1996), described the work as "intelligent and imaginative," adding: "These pieces excel as short fiction, although they could also be germs for novels. The real winner here is the grimly bizarre 'Ida,' where a boy finds himself quarterbacking a nightmare version of the 1975 NFL championship game, with his father coaching on the sidelines and sending his mother on 70 brutal carries in his backfield." Tom De Haven, in a piece for the *New York Times Book Review* (July 21, 1996), was more reserved in his praise: "The 14 stories in Jim Shepard's first collection are almost bewilderingly various in style and subject, but each is delivered with consummate skill. And several are so imaginative and mysterious and have such distinctive voices that they seem certain to take up permanent residence in a reader's memory. On the downside, Mr. Shepard, for all his virtuosity, can be miserly with characterization . . . and he has a frustrating habit of merely stopping—of stomping on the brake—rather than ending a story." De Haven concluded, "[Shepard's] finest work in this collection appears in two stories that read like mini-novels. 'Mars Attacks' is that rarest of rarities—a tour de force that actually manages to be more than just a structural novelty [and] 'Nosferatu,' which purports to be a journal kept by the German film director F. W. Murnau during the creation of his famous 1922 vampire movie, feels like a masterpiece to me."

Shepard subsequently turned his short story about Murnau into a full-length novel, also titled *Nosferatu* (1998). Through a series of fictional journal entries, Shepard relates how the German director became fascinated with "Nosferatu: A Tale of Horror," a short story by Heinrik Galeen, and became determined to make it into the film that would ultimately launch his career. In a review for the *Times Literary Supplement* (June 5, 1998), Keith Miller cheered: "First of all, a congratulatory swirl of the cloak to Jim Shepard for devising a fictional form which, if not wholly new, gives at least a fresh twist to the often cumbersome genre of fictionalized biography. The core of [*Nosferatu*] takes the shape of an unedited production diary kept by the filmmaker F. W. Murnau on the set of his 1922 masterpiece *Nosferatu*. . . . The conceit allows Shepard smoothly to present us with a good deal of technical information about this most heroic period in the history of cinema, while offering, as it were, a long close-up on the director's troubled spirit. . . . There is an enjoyable dryness in Shepard's handling of detail which stops us from taking things too seriously." "This is [a] dark and brooding saga," Susan Gene Clifford wrote for *Library Journal* (April 15, 1998). "Indeed, Shepard seems a bit obsessed with Murnau himself. His style is driving and fraught with passion. Not a novel for everyone, it is nonetheless noteworthy for its unique fusion of story and style. The reader is propelled through the plot by Shepard's intensity of language and cadence."

Shepard's novel *Project X* derives its subject matter from the horrific shooting that took place at Columbine High School on April 20, 1999, when two teenage boys gunned down several of their classmates in a premeditated assault. Shepard's story is narrated by Edwin Hanratty, an unhappy and antisocial youth who resides at the bottom of the school's pecking order. "I'm the kid you think about . . . when you want to make yourself feel better," Edwin informs the reader, as quoted by Stephen Metcalf for the *New York Times Book Review* (January 25, 2004). Edwin receives little emotional support at home, where his father's spiteful behavior creates an atmosphere of aggression. Edwin falls in with another reject, a boy known as Flake, who coaxes Edwin into devising a scheme for getting revenge against their peers.

The book was widely praised. "[*Project X*] is the latest contribution to the mini-canon of works devoted to understanding the [Columbine] massacre, and it may be the most probing and sensitive," Metcalf wrote. "[Shepard] lays down innocuous sentence after innocuous sentence until you find, to your surprise, your heart lurching." "Shepard makes these miserable characters sympathetic and even funny, . . . but avoids easy sociological explanations for their predicament," a reviewer for *Publishers Weekly* (November 24, 2003) wrote. "The two boys, who have only their alienation to cling to, are often snotty and off-putting, and bat away all helping hands; there are also hints of deeper pathologies. With a pitch-perfect feel for the flat, sardonic, 'I-go-then-he-goes' language of disaffected teens, Shepard explores how, in two disturbed minds, the normal adolescent obsessions with competence, mastery and status take on disastrous proportions, and the search for social belonging becomes a life-or-death matter."

"What I wanted to do [with *Project X*]," Shepard explained to Ulin, "was to give a glimpse of the kind of mind that finds everything apocalyptic. With kids this age, it's like they're at a crossroads every 20 minutes. They have no perspective, which is what makes everything so dire." "Edwin is ethically passive," Shepard told Ulin. "I write about characters like that because it's an easy way to implicate the reader but also because I'm interested in how people get involved in things without making conscious decisions of any kind."

For his next book Shepard returned to the short-story form; *Love and Hydrogen* contains 22 tales about a variety of subjects. In the title story two gay airship mechanics fall in love while flying in the doomed *Hindenburg*. In "John Ashcroft: More Important Things than Me," Shepard brings together an assemblage of actual statements made by the former U.S. attorney general that reveal his human side. "The Creature from the Black Lagoon" offers a retelling of the classic 1954 film from the perspective of the monster. The collection drew high praise from critics. "Shepard burrows into his protagonists with the ego-erasing intensity of a character actor, building his effects not with flashy gestures but through small but telling observations," Amanda Heller wrote for the *Boston Globe* (February 29, 2004). "Shepard obviously has a lock on the new American paranoia, and his voice should be essential reading," John Freeman wrote for the *Chicago Tribune* (February 22, 2004). "Shepard loves to take risks, and his success rate is admirable. In this collection of 22 stories, only three are duds. . . . Shepard has a knack, though, for writing about nearly any kind of experience and making it immediate."

Shepard has served as the editor for several collections, including *You've Got to Read This: Contemporary American Writers Introduce Stories that Held Them in Awe* (1994), with Ron Hansen; *Unleashed: Poems by Writers' Dogs* (1995), with Amy Hempel; and *Writers at the Movies: Twenty-Six Contemporary Authors Celebrate Twenty-Six Memorable Movies* (2000). He has contributed to such publications as the *New Yorker*, *Esquire*, *Harper's*, and *Redbook*. He lives in Williamstown, Massachusetts, with his wife, Karen, and their two children, Aidan and Emmett.

—C.M.

Suggested Reading: *America* p360 Dec. 3, 1983; *Booklist* p901 Jan. 15, 1994, p1,096 Mar. 1, 1998; *Library Journal* p1,505 Aug. 1983, p167 July 1996; *Los Angeles Times* E p4 Apr. 28, 2004; *New York Newsday* p23 Feb. 18, 1990, p32 Feb. 20, 1994; *New York Review of Books* p29 Dec. 18, 1986; *New York Times Book Review* p9 Nov. 9, 1986, p27 Feb. 25, 1990, p8 July 21, 1996, p9 Jan. 25, 2004; *Publishers Weekly* p64+ Jan. 31, 1994; *Times Literary Supplement* p22 June 5, 1998; *Voice Literary Supplement* p5 June 1994

Selected Books: novels—*Flights*, 1983; *Paper Doll*, 1986; *Lights Out in the Reptile House*, 1990; *Kiss of the Wolf*, 1994; *Nosferatu*, 1998; *Project X*, 2004; short fiction—*Battling against Castro*, 1997; *Love and Hydrogen*, 2004

Claudio Vazquez/Courtesy of Random House

Shipler, David K.

Dec. 3, 1942– Journalist; nonfiction writer

David K. Shipler has written about some of the most complex matters of our times, including life inside the former Soviet Union, relations between Arabs and Jews, racial issues in America, and the struggles of the working poor. Both historian and policy wonk, Shipler not only details the various problems of each of these subjects but also offers viable solutions. As quoted by the editors of *Who's Who in America* (2001), he has said, "I have been governed professionally by the conviction that an open society needs open examination of itself to survive. Defining problems, inspecting blemishes, probing wounds, and exposing injustice are the required pastimes of a free people. Nothing intelligent can come from ignorance. If information does not guarantee wisdom, it is at least a prerequisite, for the only wise course is through knowledge. To write about current affairs, then, is to play a small role in a great endeavor."

David Karr Shipler was born on December 3, 1942 in Orange, New Jersey. His father, Guy Emery Shipler Jr., was a journalist; his mother, the former Eleanor Karr, was a teacher. He studied at Dartmouth College, in Hanover, New Hampshire, and in 1964 received a bachelor's degree. After graduating, he served in the U.S. Naval Reserve and was discharged, in 1966, with the rank of lieutenant.

Shipler's first big break in journalism also came in 1966, when he was hired as a news clerk at the *New York Times*. Two years later he was promoted to full reporter, a position he held until 1973. He then became the paper's foreign correspondent in

Saigon, where he covered the end of America's involvement in Vietnam. After the fall of South Vietnam, in 1975, Shipler transferred to the paper's foreign office in what was then the Soviet Union. As the newspaper's Moscow correspondent between 1975 and 1979 (the last two years of which he spent as bureau chief), he became intimately acquainted with life in the former Soviet Union and with a wide variety of people who lived there. Though many people during the time in which Shipler was based in Moscow believed that the Soviet people yearned for American-style democracy and free-market capitalism, he found that many Soviet citizens preferred their ordered society and saw individual freedom as a blueprint for societal chaos. Though there were, according to Shipler, few true Marxist believers in the Soviet Union then, many had come to accept the inequality of the system because they were dependent upon it for their survival. Most became adept at taking advantage of the existence of special privileges, black-market purchases, and educational and employment opportunities for party loyalists. Ultimately, Shipler's impressions of the land formed the basis of his first book, *Russia: Broken Idols, Solemn Dreams* (1983).

In the *New York Times Book Review* (November 20, 1983), Marshall D. Shulman wrote: "Mr. Shipler's volume is a biopsy taken from Soviet society . . . to measure change during a period of mounting tension abroad and tightening controls at home. . . . With a sensitive and compassionate eye, Mr. Shipler set himself the task of feeling and recording the state of mind of the people with whom he was able to come in contact. . . . He has succeeded admirably. He captures the contradictory feelings that beset all travelers to the Soviet Union, the paradoxes that abound in Soviet life and the subjective ambiguities that torment all feeling observers in Moscow." Writing for the *Christian Science Monitor* (March 28, 1984), Robert Marquand opined: "It is true that cultural observations such as Shipler's can be extremely subjective—due, in part, to the kinds of Russians attracted to a Western journalist and to the inherent limitations the Western press endures in a closed society. Still, in terms of background, documentation, and general sweep, this book is on target. From the sheer volume of interactions with all varieties of Russians, the inclusions of many jokes and anecdotes, and the wide range of subjects covered, it is clear that the author has fought his way clear to an understanding of the underlying dynamics of contemporary Russia."

After leaving the Soviet Union, in 1979, Shipler became the *New York Times* bureau chief in Jerusalem, Israel. During the five years he spent there, he became versed in the deeply ingrained attitudes Jews and Arabs hold towards one another and how those attitudes are rooted in religious and cultural teachings. *Arab and Jew: Wounded Spirits in a Promised Land* (1986), Shipler's book on the subject, won a Pulitzer Prize, in 1987, and was made into a television documentary in 1989.

In a review for *Commentary* (January 1987), Edward Alexander declared: "[This] book purports to eschew the political dimensions of the Arab-Israeli conflict in order to concentrate on 'the human dimension.'. . . [Yet], from Shipler's style of examining 'attitudes' and 'impressions,' political implications inevitably arise. . . . To be evenhanded or morally impartial between two sides in a conflict when one side happens to be contending for the destruction of the other is to become a moral nonentity. To avoid the appearance of being such a nonentity, you must either redefine the conflict in the Middle East . . . to one between Jewish nationalism and the nationalism of Palestinian Arabs exclusively; or you must dodge this unpleasant business of destructive intention altogether by stressing the cultural identity of Palestinian nationalism. Shipler does both." Ronald Sanders wrote for the *New York Times Book Review* (September 28, 1986), "This is a definitive report of enormous size that, while exhaustively covering the whole often familiar ground, manages to do so with remarkable freshness and originality. . . . [It] seems to leave no aspect of the complex Arab-Jewish relationship untouched, ranging through such contrasting topics as war and friendship, terrorism and intermarriage, reciprocal myths and understandings, social and sexual attraction and repulsion, conflicting nationalisms, . . . all presented in an abundance of narratives, anecdotes and conversations that never seem hackneyed."

In his next book Shipler examined a relationship as complex as that of Arabs and Jews—that of black and white Americans. A sweeping study of race covering all strata of American society, *A Country of Strangers: Blacks and Whites in America* (1997) not only focuses on the racial attitudes of both groups but suggests ways in which race relations could be improved. Not all critics, however, were willing to agree with Shipler's diagnosis—or his cure. Alan Wolfe, writing for the *New Republic* (September 29, 1997), opined: "Any good conversation presupposes equality among the speakers; each has something to say and is expected to say it. But the 'dialogue' that Shipler urges goes only one way. . . . His examples paint a picture of black America represented not by those who have struggled against persistent discrimination to make it, but by those who, in insisting that black success is impossible in racist America, send out a message of numbing resignation. And his white America is symbolized not by those who have taken dramatic strides to move beyond the racism of their parents' generation, but by those so ashamed of themselves that they take pleasure in confessing to sins they never committed." (The November 10, 1997 issue of the *New Republic* carried a spirited response from Shipler, who denied holding the views attributed to him by Wolfe and wrote that Wolfe "pretends to embrace 'facts' and eschew 'feelings' but he falsifies facts and lets his feelings run wild."

Wolfe returned the vitriol, calling Shipler's ideas for helping to improve race relations in America "well-meaning, but hopelessly patronizing.") By contrast, Kwame Anthony Appiah, writing for the *New York Times Book Review* (November 16, 1997) called *A Country of Strangers* an "engaged and engaging new book," adding that it "provides something that statistics alone will not: the rich fabric of the everyday workings of race in this nation as reported by a thoughtful journalist who has searched widely through the country to map the geography of its racial feeling."

To research *The Working Poor: Invisible in America* (2004), Shipler crisscrossed the country, visiting sweatshops in Los Angeles, mill towns in New Hampshire, and housing projects in Washington, D.C. He met people of diverse ethnic backgrounds and circumstances to create a composite picture of the millions of poor people in America. Shipler's book stresses the vicious cycle of poverty, as exemplified by Caroline Payne, a single mother of four who tried to move up the ladder of employment at the local Wal-Mart, only to be prevented from doing so because of her appearance; she had lost her teeth because she lacked health insurance, and Wal-Mart supervisors felt she didn't meet the image they wanted to project. "If she had not been poor," Shipler remarked in his book, "she would not have lost her teeth, and if she had not lost her teeth, perhaps she would not have remained poor."

A reviewer for *San Francisco Chronicle* (March 14, 2004) noted that Shipler "claims that neither liberal nor conservative analysis adequately addresses the complexities of poverty today. His sprawling, compassionate take on the situation of the country's 35 million working poor describes with clear-eyed sympathy the individuals and families who sustain the seemingly limitless appetite for low-wage work and should provide ammunition to policymakers—if there are any—who wish to seriously engage the project of eliminating poverty in America."

Reviewing the book for the *Washington Post Book World* (March 7, 2004), Eric Schlosser praised it—with some reservations: "*The Working Poor* is not an easy read, and the darkness of the subject is only partly to blame. Shipler's hard work deserves a better editor. The structure of the book is sometimes confusing, and it would have benefitted from a tighter focus, with fewer individual portraits and digressions. But this is an essential book. Even those who lack pity and compassion should be concerned about what is now happening to the poor." He continued, "*The Working Poor . . .* should be required reading not just for every member of Congress, but for every eligible voter. Now that this invisible world has been so powerfully brought to light, its consequences can no longer be ignored or denied."

Since leaving the Jerusalem bureau of the *New York Times*, David K. Shipler has worked as the paper's Washington bureau chief (1985–87) and chief diplomatic correspondent (1987–88). Between 1988 and 1990 he was the senior associate at the Carnegie Endowment for International Peace, in Washington, D.C. After spending a year (1984–85) as a guest scholar at the Brookings Institution, a non-partisan think tank, Shipler taught at a number of schools, including the American University School of International Service, in Washington, D.C., and Princeton University, in New Jersey, where he has been a Woodrow Wilson visiting fellow since 1990. In 1998 he was a writer in residence at the University of Southern California, Los Angeles. He holds honorary degrees from several institutions, including Middlebury College, in Vermont.

Shipler has been married to Deborah S. Isaacs since 1966. They have three children: Jonathan Robert, Laura Karr, and Michael Edmund.

—C.M.

Suggested Reading: *Christian Science Monitor* p20 Mar. 28, 1984; *Commentary* p66 Jan. 1987; *New Republic* p27 Sep. 29, 1997; *New York Times* C p7 Nov. 11, 1983, A p17 May 26, 1992, E p8 Feb. 18, 2004; *New York Times Book Review* p1 Nov. 20, 1983, p1 Sep. 28, 1986, p11 Nov. 16, 1987; *San Francisco Chronicle* M p2 Mar. 14, 2004; *Washington Post Book World* p3 Mar. 7, 2004; *Wavelength* p8+ May 1989

Selected Books: *Russia: Broken Idols, Solemn Dreams*, 1983; *Arab and Jew: Wounded Spirits in a Promised Land*, 1986; *A Country of Strangers: Blacks and Whites in America*, 1997; *The Working Poor: Invisible in America*, 2004

Bruno Vincent/Getty Images

Shriver, Lionel

May 18, 1957– Novelist

Until recently, the work of the novelist Lionel Shriver was critically acclaimed but unknown to the vast majority of the book-buying public. Her prominence rose significantly in 2004, when she received the prestigious Orange Prize for her 2003 work *We Need to Talk About Kevin*. The narrator of that novel is a woman, Eva, whose teenage son has murdered several of his classmates and a teacher; the novel raised some eyebrows in the literary establishment, due less to the violence described in the story than to Eva's openly negative attitude toward motherhood. *We Need to Talk About Kevin* is not the first of Shriver's works to explore controversial views on the part of her protagonists; *Game Control* (1994), for example, features a character whose beliefs about human population control warrant the label "extremist." "If you don't allow yourself to write characters who do disagreeable things—if you only allow yourself to write about what you would be glad for your readers to imitate in real life—then you're pretty much constrained to characters who help little old ladies across the street and rescue cats from trees," Shriver told Andrew Lawless for the Three Monkeys Online Web site.

The writer was born Margaret Ann Shriver on May 18, 1957 in Gastonia, North Carolina, the second of the three children—and the only daughter—of Donald W. Shriver, a Presbyterian theologian who later became associated with Union Theological Seminary, in New York, and Peggy (Leu) Shriver, who became an administrator for the National Council of Churches. Shriver was raised mainly in Raleigh, North Carolina, and in New York City. She has described her parents as "Adlai Stevenson Democrats"; in an interview with Rachel Cusk for the London *Guardian* (October 4, 2003), she gave her mother and father credit for "the fact that I'm very engaged with moral matters, though that always sounds, if nothing else, unentertaining. So I come at these issues with a certain perversity, always looking at the hard case." Shriver decided at age seven that she would be a writer. At eight she rejected her feminine name because, as many sources have reported, she felt that men had an easier time in the world; she called herself Tony before adopting, at 15, the name Lionel. "I felt alienated from femininity—I've always had a sense of myself as fundamentally androgynous," she said, as quoted by Luke Leitch in the London *Evening Standard* (June 8, 2005). Also at eight, already reflecting on one of the themes that would inform *We Need to Talk About Kevin*, Shriver "foreswore motherhood," as she wrote in an essay that appears on the Reading Group Guides Web site. She and her brothers, she added, "were annoying. We were loud and sneaky and broke things. At eight, maybe I was simply horrified by the prospect of being saddled with myself."

In an interview posted on the Barnes & Noble Web site, Shriver identified Joseph Heller's novel *Catch-22*, about characters in World War II, as the work that has most influenced her as a writer. The "first 'grown-up' novel I ever read," *Catch-22* "convinced me that fiction for adults needn't be humorless, or laborious to read," she said. She recalled reading the book at 12 and having read it "eight times by the time I hit the tenth grade," explaining that there is "an amoral, anarchic quality to Heller's satire that struck a chord." Shriver attended Columbia University, in New York, receiving her B.A. degree in creative writing in 1978 and her M.F.A., in the same specialty, in 1982. During her lengthy talk with Robert Birnbaum for the Web-based magazine *Identity Theory* (July 24, 2003), Shriver said that she chose Columbia because, thanks to her father's association with Union Theological Seminary, "I didn't have to pay for it." As for the decision to pursue a degree in writing, she admitted, "It's not a very difficult degree to earn. There is no science to creative writing and it feels very self-indulgent. I have always been aware that most of the great writers of the past didn't go to workshops. It's always seemed a little embarrassing to me. On the other hand, I did want to get published. I badly needed some connections, which is why most people go to these programs. It's not to learn to write finer sentences."

After graduating from Columbia Shriver taught English in several colleges in New York. Then, in 1985, she began to lead the life of an expatriate and world traveler. She spent six months touring Western Europe and another half-year living on a kibbutz in Israel before going to Belfast, Northern Ireland, where she intended to stay for nine months to research a book. (It was eventually published as the novel *The Bleeding Heart*.) As it turned out, she lived there for 12 years, during which she made visits of as long as a year to Nairobi, Kenya; New York; Bangkok, Thailand; and Vietnam. She reported from all of those places for the *Wall Street Journal*, the *Economist*, the *Philadelphia Inquirer*, the *Jerusalem Post*, and the London *Guardian*, as well as other media outlets. Living abroad, she told Robert Birnbaum, "gives you a different perspective."

Shriver's first novel, *The Female of the Species* (1987), is set in Kenya. The main character, Gray Kaiser, is an anthropologist who encountered an isolated tribe in 1948 and has returned on the eve of her 60th birthday to make a film about her discoveries. The story is narrated mainly by Errol, Gray's assistant, who watches as Gray becomes obsessed in Kenya by Raphael, a 24-year-old whose manipulative, dominating behavior evokes Gray's memories of another man she once knew. In the *New York Times Book Review* (July 19, 1987), Katherine Bouton wrote that *The Female of the Species* was unusual for a first novel in that it was not apparently autobiographical but "totally imagined. . . . That fictive quality is both the novel's weakness and its promise. . . . It is . . . hard not to admire the breadth and consistency of Lionel Shriver's inventiveness and the exuberance of her imagination."

The New York City borough of Queens is the setting of Shriver's 1988 novel, *Checker and the Derailleurs*. Checker, a 19-year-old, charismatic drummer in a rock band, is in love with the 29-year-old Syria, a glassblower, but has arranged her marriage to the band's saxophonist, an illegal immigrant. The critic for the *Magill Book Reviews* (on-line) noted that the novel's "premise of loss and renewed life is well developed," and Ethan Bumas remarked for *Library Journal* (May 15, 1988) that the novel "is at its best funny, clever, and touching."

Shriver's next novel was *The Bleeding Heart* (1990, published in Great Britain in 1992 as *Ordinary Decent Criminals*). Its 30ish protagonist, Estrin, like Shriver herself, has gone to live in Belfast amid violent conflict between Unionists, who want Northern Ireland to remain part of Great Britain, and Republicans, who want the region to join the rest of the Irish Republic. Estrin meets Farrell, a former bomb dismantler for both sides who becomes a conciliator at political conferences between the two factions. A *Publishers Weekly* (July 20, 1990) reviewer found the novel to be "ultimately tragic, . . . woven through with threads of Irish politics and the anguish of people whose lives can take meaning only from external cues. Shriver's writing is outstandingly lucid and bright, with an original blend of American and Irish whimsical irony." Margaret Walters noted for the London *Independent* (June 21, 1992) that the novel is "a love story, and a surprisingly moving one. But Shriver's edgy, accurate wit, her ear for rhetorical inflation and self-deception, and her refusal to be conned by personal or political platitudes expand her novel: its real subject is the seductiveness and the sadness of Belfast itself."

Shriver wrote for the *New Statesman* (June 10, 2002) that in "demographic terms, for more than a century westerners have seemed unable to decide what they fear most. The precipitous drop in European fertility rates has produced anxiety about numerical dwindling. . . . Yet the sixfold increase in worldwide population during the same period has prompted a contrary fear of crushing biological overload. Given the emotive nature of these opposing horrors—'we are about to disappear!' v 'we are being overrun!'—it is less surprising that population issues have filtered into the western literary canon than that their direct treatment in mainstream literature is rare." Shriver published *Game Control* (1994) to address the issue in a fictional format. Noting that most literature about the population problem is futuristic and that, in it, the feared swarms of humanity have not yet arrived, she wrote, "By contrast, my own more mainstream *Game Control* is set in modern-day Nairobi," and its "irascible protagonist is . . . convinced that we are reproducing ourselves into extinction, and is therefore researching a pathogen that would neatly decimate a third of the world's population overnight." The character Calvin, a demographer, was once concerned with conserving elephants on a game preserve; now, his "game" is the human animal. He and two other characters exemplify approaches to the population problem: Eleanor, a liberal social worker distributing birth-control materials to people who do not use them properly, falls in love with Calvin, whose solution to both elephant and human overpopulation involves culling. Wallace, a retired population worker, has come to feel that humans can provide the solution to their own problems and that, therefore, the more people the better.

"The three are not so much people as opportunities for argument, certainly in the first half of the book, as the impressive arrays of theories and statistics are laid out," Sylvia Brownrigg wrote for the London *Guardian* (May 3, 1994). "In the second, the rather overwrought plot takes over and they each take on the looming presence of characters in a science fiction drama." Marek Kohn, who reviewed *Game Control* for the London *Independent* (April 10, 1994), felt that the satire in Shriver's novel had fallen short. "To believe that [Eleanor] would fall in with [Calvin's] schemes, even conditionally," he wrote, "demands that we both accept the terms of the problem and grasp the horror contained within it. If those requirements were met, we'd be seduced, like [Eleanor], into thinking the unthinkable, and the potential for a monstrous comedy could be unleashed. . . . The trouble with *Game Control* is that it's funny, but not appallingly so."

The central character in *A Perfectly Good Family* (1996) is Corlis McCrea, who, like Shriver herself, is the middle child between two brothers. Upon the death of their mother, the McCrea children return to North Carolina to settle her estate. The assets are to be divided four ways, not three, with the fourth share going to the American Civil Liberties Union, which the liberal parents supported. For the siblings to get possession of the family mansion, their old home, two of them must form an alliance; Corlis is torn between her brothers, the elder a wild and promiscuous drinker, the younger a repressed conservative. "Shriver cleverly contrives to precipitate her characters into a traumatic free-for-all, an obstacle course of horribly loaded preferences," Alex Clark noted in the London *Guardian* (March 29, 1996). "For children brought up in a world of moral imperatives, this gift of self-determination,

immediately qualified by the need for co-operative action, is a distinctly double-edged sword. . . . Choice, Shriver underlines, is enslavement as well as liberation, and *A Perfectly Good Family* is a fine illustration of that point." Fanny Blake, reviewing the novel for the London *Independent* (May 5, 1996), was equally positive: "Often funny and always intelligent, this is a sharply observed history of the redoubtable McCrea family, shot through with sardonic wit and black comedy."

Double Fault (1997) is a story of the marriage of two professional tennis players. After Willy, once an up-and-coming star in the sport, is eclipsed by her husband, Eric, and sidelined by injury, she can scarcely bear the thought of his victories. The book received mixed notices. The *Publishers Weekly* (June 30, 1997) reviewer complained of Shriver's seeming didacticism, commenting that the novelist "stacks the deck against Willy, whose defeatist family and embittered coach have filled her with mean-spirited insecurities, so that her final sacrifice for Eric (equally cocky but more individualized and just plain nicer) is also, unfortunately, her only really instinctive, unprogrammed gesture in the book." Louise Redd, by contrast, wrote for the *Dallas Morning News* (September 21, 1997), "Though *Double Fault* is crammed with Willy's failures, her final tragedy has the effect of turning up the volume just a notch on all her previous angst. Ms. Shriver throws out no false note of hope, no hoopla about the resiliency of the good ol' human spirit. . . . She has written a gorgeous, compelling tragedy in which she stays with her game every step of the way."

Although most reviewers of her work placed Shriver in the top rank of contemporary literary novelists, that assessment was not reflected in the sales figures of her books. That changed in 2004, when she won the Orange Prize for her novel *We Need to Talk About Kevin*, published the previous year. (Ironically, given Shriver's stated attitude about femininity, the Orange Prize is presented only to women.) Shriver explained in her essay on the Reading Group Guides Web site that two factors had moved her to write the novel: her new ambivalence about her longstanding refusal to have children, now that she was in her early 40s and facing "the imminent closure of the reproductive window"; and news stories about shootings of teens by their classmates, in particular the highly publicized 1999 murders in Columbine, Colorado. Those incidents added to her fear about parenthood the possibility that her child "might turn out to be a killer." The narrator of *We Need to Talk About Kevin* is Eva, who reveals in letters to her husband, from whom she is separated, her negative feelings about parenthood. Her son, Kevin, at the age of 15, has massacred several of his schoolmates and a teacher. Has Eva's dislike of her son contributed to Kevin's amorality, or has his innate criminality caused her to turn away from him? "I think *Kevin* has attracted an audience,"

Shriver wrote in a piece for the London *Guardian* (February 18, 2005, on-line), "because my narrator, Eva, allows herself to say all those things that mothers are not supposed to say."

A *Publishers Weekly* (March 24, 2003) reviewer called Shriver's "the most triumphantly accomplished" of a number of fictional works inspired by real-life shootings. The reviewer added that *We Need to Talk About Kevin* is "a harrowing, psychologically astute, sometimes even darkly humorous novel, with a clear-eyed, hard-won ending and a tough-minded sense of the difficult, often painful human enterprise." For Zoe Green, writing for the London *Observer* (February 27, 2005), the "novel is an elegant psychological and philosophical investigation of culpability with a brilliant denouement. . . . Eva's voice carries this novel, which is as much a psychological study of her as it is of Kevin and, although her reliability as a narrator becomes increasingly questionable as she oscillates between anger, self-pity and regret, her search for answers becomes just as compulsive for the reader."

Shriver's next novel, *The Post-Birthday World* (2007), is about Irina McGovern, an American children's book illustrator living in London; she is enmeshed in an apparently happy relationship with Lawrence Trainer, another American expatriate, who makes his living as a terrorism expert. Her life becomes complicated when she goes out with her longtime acquaintance Ramsey Acton, a professional snooker player, and suddenly has the urge to kiss him. The rest of the story follows the dual strands of Irina's life after the near breach of fidelity and the fantasy she constructs about what might have happened if she had given in to her urge. Christine Smallwood wrote for *Book Forum* (on-line), "Shriver tells both versions of the story, in alternating chapters, to draw out the consequence of her protagonist's choice (and/or lack thereof.) Canoodling awaits ye who enter here!" A reviewer for *Publishers Weekly* (November 20, 2006, on-line) wrote, "With Jamesian patience, Shriver explores snooker tournaments and terrorism conferences, passionate lovemaking and passionless sex, and teases out her themes of ambition, self-recrimination and longing. The result is an impressive if exhausting novel."

Lionel Shriver is married to a jazz drummer and divides her time between London, England, and New York City.

—S.Y.

Suggested Reading: *Dallas Morning News* p91 Sep. 21, 1997; (Glasgow) *Herald* p6 July 24, 1993; *Identity Theory* (on-line) July 24, 2003; *Jerusalem Post* B p9 May 10, 2002; *Library Journal* p94 May 15, 1988; (London) *Guardian* p13 May 3, 1994, T p17 Mar. 29, 1996; (London) *Independent* p36 June 21, 1992, p28 Apr. 30, 1994, p36 May 6, 1996; (London) *Observer* p16 Feb. 27, 2005; *Magill Book Reviews* (on-line);

New Statesman p38+ June 10, 2002; *New York Times Book Review* p13 July 19, 1987; *Publishers Weekly* p52 July 20, 1990, p65 June 30, 1997, p55 Mar. 24, 2003; *Washington Post* D p3 June 30, 1987, E p3 Nov. 20, 1990

Selected Books: *The Female of the Species*, 1987; *Checker and the Derailleurs*, 1988; *The Bleeding Heart*, 1990; *Game Control*, 1994; *A Perfectly Good Family*, 1996; *Double Fault*, 1997; *We Need to Talk About Kevin*, 2003; *The Post-Birthday World*, 2007

Shteyngart, Gary

1972– Novelist

Gary Shteyngart's debut novel, *The Russian Debutante's Handbook* (2002), won extensive praise from critics. Taylor Antrim, writing for the *New York Observer* (June 10, 2002), echoed the sentiments of many when describing Shteyngart as "one of the most talented and entertaining writers of his generation." His second book, *Absurdistan* (2006), secured that reputation; Liza Nelson and Kyle Smith, writing for *People* (June 19, 2006), described the comic novel as "a *Catch-22* for the age of short attention spans."

Born Igor Shteyngart in Leningrad, in the former Soviet Union, in 1972, the writer came with his family to the U.S. at the age of seven and grew up in the New York City borough of Queens. During the 1990s he lived for a time in Prague, in the Czech Republic, and later graduated from Oberlin College, in Ohio, with a degree in politics. He then returned to New York City, where he worked as a writer at several nonprofit organizations and attended the graduate writing program at Hunter College. His work impressed one of his instructors, the novelist Chang-Rae Lee, who passed the manuscript for *The Russian Debutante's Handbook* along to his publisher, Riverhead Press.

The Russian Debutante's Handbook recounts the adventures of Vladimir Girshkin, a Russian-Jewish emigre to the U.S. who seeks, as Shteyngart writes, "the final destination of every immigrant's journey: a better home in which to be unhappy," as quoted by Fritz Lanham for the *Houston Chronicle* (June 21, 2002, on-line). Girshkin is a troubled man in his mid-20s; having attended a progressive Midwestern liberal-arts college, he ekes out a drab existence as an immigration clerk in New York City, befriending eccentric characters and searching for love. Deemed a failure by both his mother, an avid capitalist and entrepreneur, and his father, a suicidal and criminally minded doctor, Girshkin relocates to Prava, a fictional city in Eastern Europe, where he cultivates ties to the Russian mob and attempts to make a living by bilking Western expatriates.

Gary Shteyngart with his family's pet bear.

Courtesy of Bloomsbury

Laura Miller, reviewing *The Russian Debutante's Handbook* for the on-line magazine *Salon* (June 20, 2002), wrote that although it is a novel about the immigrant experience, it is not "one of those solemn tales of wistful dislocation." She characterized it instead as "a blisteringly funny, almost frighteningly energetic novel of adventure, perfidy and even a car chase or two." Lanham likewise declared, "What Shteyngart does so well is convey the immigrant's divided sensibility in language that's fresh, wry and witty." "This is a picaresque, sprawling story, so precisely imagined that you can't help giving in to the pleasure of it and losing yourself in the improbabilities of its 450-page span," Antrim opined. "Girshkin's narrative mixes acerbic observations of mid-90's post-collegiate culture, obsessive insecurity and irrepressible libido with an affecting longing to be a fully realized American. It's a strong, tasty cocktail." For *The Russian Debutante's Handbook* Shteyngart was awarded the Stephen Crane First Fiction Award. The novel was named a *New York Times* notable book for 2002 and was also named one of the best books of the year by a variety of publications, including the *Washington Post Book World* and *Entertainment Weekly*.

Shteyngart began writing his second novel, *Absurdistan*, five or six days before the terrorist attacks on the U.S. of September 11, 2001. "Strangely enough, I set [the novel] close to the Middle East, in the former Soviet republics bordering with Iran and Caucuses region," he told Grinberg. "I'd just got back from that part of world and decided to write a book about oil and oil politics when suddenly the book had acquired uncanny timeliness. Still, I had to put it away after 9/11. . . . I took a month and went back to writing. But I worried at the time that in the novel I have a lot of violence and buildings being set on fire. And in the parts I'd already written, there were references to the World Trade Center."

Misha Vainberg, the antihero at the center of *Absurdistan*, is the spoiled, obese son of a Russian gangster. Having spent more than a decade living in the U.S., he considers himself an American. But when he tries to return home, after attending his father's funeral in St. Petersburg, the U.S. government denies him reentry, leaving him stranded in the fictional post-Soviet nation Absurdistan, attempting to obtain a fake Belgian passport. "Everything in Shteyngart's frustrated world—characters, countries, landscapes—strives for U.S.–style culture and prosperity, a quest that gives shape to the melancholy and hysteria of Shteyngart's Russia," a reviewer wrote for *Publishers Weekly* (March 13, 2006). "Extending allegorical tentacles back to the Cold War and forward to the War on Terror, Shteyngart piles on plots, characters and flashbacks without losing any of the novel's madcap momentum, and the novel builds to a frantic pitch before coming to a breathless halt on the day before 9/11. The result is a sendup of American values abroad and a complex, sympathetic protagonist worthy of comparison to America's enduring literary heroes."

Shteyngart currently lives in New York City and teaches fiction writing at Hunter College. His writing has appeared in numerous publications, including the *New Yorker* and *Granta*.

—P.B.M.

693

Suggested Reading: Gary Shteyngart's Web site; *Houston Chronicle* (on-line) June 21, 2002; *New York Observer* p18 June 10, 2002; *Salon* (on-line) June 20, 2002

Selected Books: *The Russian Debutante's Handbook*, 2002; *Absurdistan*, 2006

Siddons, Anne Rivers

Jan. 9, 1936– Novelist; nonfiction writer

"Sometimes, I can feel in my bones a woman who's been dead 100 years wagging her finger at me, telling me that a lady doesn't make waves, a lady doesn't confront," Anne Rivers Siddons told Cynthia Ganz and Gail Cameron Wescott for *People* (September 16, 1991). "Sometimes I find myself deferring to some old gentleman with no sense at all. It's not easy to escape." Siddons is the author of *Heartbreak Hotel*, *Peachtree Road*, *Colony*, *Downtown*, *Low Country*, and several other novels whose heroines, like her, are natives of the U.S. South. While her commitment to the South is absolute, as she has told interviewers, she has strived to escape the mindset associated with the stereotypical Southern belle and with the romanticized notions about the South that have long manifested themselves in popular culture. Because she believes that she depicts the South "as it really is," as she told Ganz and Wescott, Siddons has rejected comparisons of any of her novels to Margaret Mitchell's Pulitzer Prize–winning Civil War epic *Gone with the Wind* (1936), but like that immensely popular book, many of hers have become best-sellers. "What's intriguing about Siddons is how much she transcends the usual parameters of fluff fiction, both in terms of literary finesse and penetrating intelligence," the literary critic and essayist Donna Seaman wrote for *Booklist* (May 15, 1994). Siddons began her professional life as a designer and layout artist for advertising firms; she later prepared copy for ads as well. In the early 1960s she was an editor at *Atlanta* magazine; her nonfiction pieces have appeared in that magazine and others, among them *Gentlemen's Quarterly*, *Redbook*, *Georgia*, *House Beautiful*, *Lear's*, *Goodlife*, and *Southern Living*. She has also published a collection of essays and the travel guide *Go Straight on Peachtree: A McDonald City Guide to Atlanta* (1978).

The only child of Marvin Rivers, a prosperous lawyer, and the former Katherine Kitchens, a high-school secretary, the writer was born Sybil Anne Rivers on January 9, 1936 in Atlanta, Georgia. Like the members of six previous generations of her family, she was raised in the nearby town of Fairburn. By her own account, her parents expected her to become something of a Southern belle; her goals, therefore, were supposed to be marriage and homemaking rather than a career outside the home. In high school she earned top grades, served on the cheerleading squad, and was selected homecoming queen. In her senior year she was named Centennial Queen of Fairburn. She also wrote occasional pieces for the local Fairburn newspaper.

After her high-school graduation, in 1954, Siddons enrolled at Auburn University, in Alabama. She studied architecture before changing her major to illustration. As an undergraduate she joined a sorority and "did the things I thought I should," as she told a HarperCollins interviewer a few years ago, as quoted on the Fantastic Fiction Web site. "I dated the right guys. I did the right activities." Her extracurricular pursuits included writing for the campus newspaper, the *Auburn Plainsman*. One year, when she held the post of *Plainsman* editor, she wrote what she described to the HarperCollins interviewer as "an innocuous, almost sophomoric column" for the paper in support of racial integration. Auburn University administrators asked her not to print the editorial, but she did so anyway; when it was published, a statement appeared alongside it in which the administrators declared that the college did not support integration. After a similar editorial by her appeared in a later issue of the *Plainsman*, Auburn administrators stripped her of her editorship.

After Siddons received a B.A.A. (bachelor of applied arts) degree, in 1958, she attended a few classes at the Atlanta School of Art. According to *Contemporary Authors* (1999), in about 1959 she began working in the advertising department of the Retail Credit Corp., where she prepared ad designs and layouts. From 1961 to 1963 she held a similar position with Citizens & Southern National Bank; there, her responsibilities grew to include copywriting, and she gained a newfound appreciation of her talents as a writer. Before that time, she told the HarperCollins interviewer, "writing came so naturally that I didn't value it. I never even thought that it might be a livelihood, or a source of great satisfaction. Southern girls, remember, were taught to look for security."

In 1963 Siddons quit her job at the bank to join the staff of *Atlanta*, then edited by Jim Townsend, whom *Time* once dubbed "the father of city magazines." Founded two years earlier by the Atlanta Chamber of Commerce, *Atlanta* is among the oldest of American city magazines. While there, Siddons covered many events connected with the civil rights movement. Decades later, writing for *Atlanta* (May 2001), she recalled that she and her colleagues "knew, with pride, . . . that Atlanta was the epicenter of the civil rights movement, and that its great hero and master spirit, Dr. Martin Luther King, Jr., was one of our own. Many of us at the magazine knew personally some of Dr. King's lieutenants, ridiculously young men who had stared impassively down gun barrels and been clubbed and hosed and dogged in a half dozen cities across the wounded South. They were our heroes. They still are mine."

In 1966 Siddons married Heyward L. Siddons, a business executive, and became stepmother to his four young sons (Lee, Kemble, Rick, and David) from his previous marriage. The next year she left *Atlanta* to work at Burke-Dowling Adams, an advertising agency. In 1969 she was hired by Burton Campbell Advertising, where she remained until 1974. During that time she received a letter from Larry Ashmead, an editor at Doubleday, who had admired some of her *Atlanta* articles and wondered whether she might be interested in writing a book. Assuming it to be a prank by someone who had swiped some Doubleday stationery, Siddons tossed the letter away. Several weeks later Ashmead tracked her down, and soon afterward she signed a contract with Doubleday for a collection of essays and a novel. The former, *John Chancellor Makes Me Cry*, was published in 1975; the latter, *Heartbreak Hotel*, in 1976.

The essays in *John Chancellor Makes Me Cry* (most of which appeared earlier in *Atlanta*, *Georgia*, or *House Beautiful*) are devoted to such subjects as Siddons's memories of one of her grandfathers; her reactions to the evening news on TV; her husband's and her work in advertising; her stint as her husband's nurse during his bout with the flu; a trip she took to New York City; a stray cat that she adopted; and her experiences while on jury duty. In a review for *Library Journal* (June 15, 1975), Patricia Goodfellow cheered: "These random essays . . . show great variety, wit, and a lively, polished style. Some of the domestic vignettes rival [those of the humorist] Erma Bombeck. . . . A few of these selections are a shade too trendy and . . . may date rapidly; but on the whole, [it is] a stylish, enjoyable collection." Bombeck herself wrote for the *New York Times Book Review* (April 13, 1975) that Siddons's essays "combine humor, intimacy and insight into a marriage." The one "that gives readers the most insight" into Siddons, in Bombeck's view, describes a month in which Siddons experienced several painful emotional blows in succession.

The heroine of Siddons's semiautobiographical novel *Heartbreak Hotel*, Maggie Deloach, is a beautiful, popular 1950s college student whose life takes an unexpected turn after she writes a pro-integration article for her campus newspaper. In the *New York Times Book Review* (September 12, 1976), Katha Pollitt wrote, "This is a marvelously detailed record of a South as gone with the wind as Scarlett O'Hara's."

The House Next Door (1978), Siddons's next book, is a horror novel that Stephen King, known worldwide for his own horror novels, praised in his nonfiction book *Danse Macabre* (1981), a critique of such tales; indeed, he ranked it with Shirley Jackson's classic 1959 novel *The Haunting of Hill House*. Writing *The House Next Door*, Siddons told Bob Summer for *Publishers Weekly* (November 18, 1988), was "something of a lark. It's different from anything I've ever written, or probably ever will. But I like to read occult,

supernatural stories. Some of the world's great writers have written them, and I guess I wanted to see what I could do with the genre."

The plot of the novel *Homeplace* (1987) centers on Micah Winship, a successful journalist, who returns to her childhood home in a small Georgia town after an absence of more than 20 years. A previously scheduled break from her job and her daughter's visit with Micah's ex-husband have made it possible for Micah to help care for her dying father, to whom she feels no sense of duty. Against her will, she finds herself becoming involved with the happenings of her town. In a *Washington Post* (August 3, 1987) review, Alice Digilio wrote, "Siddons is a fine teller of tales. . . . And by the time we've turned the last page and the hammock has ceased to rock, some of the old wisdom about human nature and love has been reaffirmed. In Siddons' world the genuine triumphs over the sham; the trivial falls down before the significant. And needless to say, love conquers all. Of course, that's why we escaped to read in the hammock in the first place."

Siddons's first resounding commercial success came with *Peachtree Road* (1988). That novel is set in Atlanta and spans four decades, beginning during the early days of World War II, when James Bondurant deserts his wife and three children. Mother and children find a home with Bondurant's brother and sister-in-law, who have a seven-year-old son named Shep. The boy soon bonds with his younger cousin Lucy, who later creates havoc in the lives of people close to her. In the *Washington Post* (October 14, 1998), the novelist Ellen Feldman noted that while Siddons was sometimes guilty of overwriting, *Peachtree Road* "is also a carefully wrought [novel] that somehow manages to retain the grace and delicacy of the world it mourns. More important, it is a compulsively readable book. Siddons is a born teller of tales. Just when we think we know the story of Lucy and Shep Bondurant, the author pulls us up with a double-twisted ending that recasts everything that has gone before. Like the gracious old houses that line it, *Peachtree Road* is a world we live in and carry with us long after we leave it."

Siddons followed *Peachtree Road* with *King's Oak* (1990), *Outer Banks* (1991), *Colony* (1992), and *Hill Towns* (1993). (In 1992 she had signed a three-book contract with HarperCollins worth about $3.25 million, and in 1994 she inked a deal with them totaling $13 million.) *Colony*, still arguably one of Siddons's most popular books, is about a southern native named Maude, who beginning in 1922 spends every summer with her disapproving mother-in-law and other members of her husband's clan in a wealthy coastal enclave in Maine. The *Virginia Quarterly Review* (Autumn 1992, on-line) described *Colony* as a "beautifully crafted novel" with a "roomy narrative."

Downtown (1994) is about the coming-of-age of Maureen "Smoky" O'Donnell in mid-1960s Atlanta. After a sheltered childhood, Smoky becomes a journalist for the city's newest magazine, *Downtown*, and comes in contact with a rich aristocrat, a free-spirited photographer, and participants in the civil rights movement, among others. In a *Library Journal* (June 15, 1994) review, Joyce Smothers wrote, referring to a best-selling contemporary American novelist and one of the greatest American playwrights of the 20th century, respectively, "Echoes of Pat Conroy and Tennessee Williams can be heard in half a dozen apocalyptic scenes, keeping us flipping through the last 200 pages of this hefty chronicle of Atlanta in the Sixties. . . . Siddons . . . has drawn on memory to create a satisfying historical romance spiced with wry humor." Donna Seaman, in an assessment for *Booklist* (May 15, 1994), wrote of the story, "It's 1966, and change is in the air, especially in the newly glamorous mecca of Atlanta. . . . Siddons devotes a lot of ink to describing the conflicting dynamics of this time and place and often seems overwhelmed by material we sense is close to her heart. In fact, for the first 100 pages or so, she seems to be driving with the brakes on. When she does let loose, she treats us to some irresistible romance as well as an unusual, if cursory, dramatization of the struggle between the Black Panthers and followers of Martin Luther King, Jr."

Merrit Fowler, the main character in Siddons's *Fault Lines* (1995), is "a self-sacrificing housewife who is tempted to walk away from her old life," as Joanne Wilkinson described her for *Booklist* (September 1, 1995). Married to a workaholic and emotionally depleted by the burdens of caring for her sickly mother-in-law, Merrit follows her daughter to her sister's home in California. In the aftermath of a devastating earthquake, the three women reevaluate their lives and ambitions. *Fault Lines* reminded Wilkinson of both Robert Waller's *Bridges of Madison County* (1992) and Anne Tyler's *Ladder of Years*. "It's apparent from the get go, though," she noted, "that Siddons is working more along the lines of Waller's melodrama than Tyler's wry sendup. . . . There's enough Sturm und Drang in this one to register 8.0 on the Richter scale, and Siddons pumps up every scene with overly lush prose and strangled dialogue. . . . Hollywood glam, a natural disaster, anorexia—everything, in fact, but the kitchen sink. . . . Read it and weep." Shannon Dekle, in a review for *Library Journal* (September 15, 1995), agreed: "Siddons has produced another heart-wrenching drama of Southern women. . . . As in *Downtown*, Siddons deliciously portrays the story of three women who have failed to find internal happiness . . . [and] keeps readers absorbed until the climactic ending."

As Siddons's novel *Up Island* (1997) opens, the protagonist, Molly Redwine, is grappling with the death of her mother, her father's resulting depression, her husband's desertion, and her son's imminent departure from home. In hopes of making a fresh start, Redwine uproots herself from her native Atlanta and settles in Martha's Vineyard, in Massachusetts, where, among other activities, she ministers to both a cancer patient and a pair of swans. In a review for *People* (June 9, 1997), Kim Hubbard wrote, "Siddons manages to make Molly's island interlude, which might easily feel contrived, come across as just the step this particular sort of strong-willed woman would take. The action drags in places; obviously smitten with the Vineyard's rolling landscape, the author seems determined to catalog its every delight. Yet Molly's journey to healing, and her discovery that families come in more forms than she could ever have imagined, make *Up Island* an affecting read." *Up Island* and its successors *Low Country* (1998) and *Nora, Nora* (2000) appeared on many best-seller lists.

Siddons's novel *Islands* (2004) also examines the idea that families are what we make of them. In *Islands*, four friends meet once a year on one or another of the three barrier islands near Charleston, South Carolina, to share, with the intimacy of blood relations, their losses, joys, and challenges. "As always, Siddons writes with a graceful lushness, evoking the wild salt marshes of the coast and Charleston's candlelit drawing rooms with equal ease," Nancy Pate wrote for the *Chicago Tribune* (May 13, 2004). "*Islands* doesn't have the depth of *Colony*—perhaps her best book—but it will have readers longing for sandy beaches and carefree days spent with good friends who feel like family."

Sweetwater Creek (2005), spent 15 weeks on the *New York Times* best-seller list. In it the author described the coming-of-age of a 12-year-old girl named Emily Parmenter. In the opinion of Claudia Smith Brinson, writing for the *Chicago Tribune* (September 28, 2005), it is Siddons's "best work."

In the early 1980s, according to Cynthia Sanz and Gail Cameron Wescott, Siddons's growing renown led to strains in her marriage. "But we got some counseling," her husband, Heyward Siddons, who is 11 years her senior, told the *People* reporters, "and it made me grow up, and the jealousy turned to admiration and greater love." At the time of that conversation, every evening the couple would read aloud whatever Anne Siddons had written that day, as part of the editing process. In 1998 Siddons and her husband moved their primary residence from Atlanta to Charleston, South Carolina. She writes in a separate building in the yard of their house, which was built in the 18th century. She also maintains a condo in an Atlanta high-rise and spends summers with her husband in their house in Brooklin, Maine, where many of his ancestors lived.

—C.M.

Suggested Reading: *Atlanta Magazine* p100+ May 2001; *Booklist* p1645 May 15, 1994, p7 Sep. 1, 1995; *Chicago Tribune* p4 May 13, 2004; *People* p33 June 9, 1997, p41 July 31, 2000; *Publishers Weekly* p55+ Nov. 18, 1988; *Southern*

Living p100+ Sep. 1994; *Washington Post* B p3 Oct. 14, 1988; Walsh, William J. *Speak, So I Shall Know Thee: Interviews with Southern Writers*, 1993

Selected Books: nonfiction—*John Chancellor Makes Me Cry*, 1975; *Go Straight on Peachtree: A McDonald City Guide to Atlanta*, 1978; fiction—*Heartbreak Hotel*, 1976; *The House Next Door*, 1978; *Fox's Earth*, 1981; *Homeplace*, 1987; *Peachtree Road*, 1988; *King's Oak*, 1990; *Outer Banks*, 1991; *Colony*, 1992; *Hill Towns*, 1993; *Downtown*, 1994; *Fault Lines*, 1995; *Up Island*, 1997; *Low Country*, 1998; *Nora, Nora*, 2000; *Islands*, 2004; *Sweetwater Creek*, 2005

Sisman, Adam

Mar. 17, 1954– Biographer

Adam Sisman has won acclaim as the biographer of such notables as the historian A. J. P. Taylor, the 18th-century figures James Boswell and Samuel Johnson, and the writers Samuel Taylor Coleridge and William Wordsworth. He told an interviewer for the Penguin Publishers Web site, "I feel that it's not for me as a biographer to judge my subjects—I leave that to the reader. When I wrote about A.J.P. Taylor, I was amazed how many people said I had showed him to be deceitful, or a scoundrel, or whatever—and an equal number of people who said I was too fair to him! What I try to do is to present as vivid and truthful a portrait as possible, though I can't imagine writing a biography of someone I didn't have some sympathetic feeling for. As for Boswell, well, of course I identified with him completely: struggling to write a book, staving off his creditors, under pressure from publishers and rival biographers, constantly breaking off work on the book to try and earn enough money to live on—that was me, just as it was Boswell."

Adam Sisman wrote the following autobiographical statement for *World Authors 2000–2005*:

"I was born in London on 17 March 1954. My parents were living in Italy at the time, and my mother came back to England for the birth. When I was about four, my parents brought my younger sister Lucy and me back to England, and the family settled in west London. I was educated at St Paul's in Hammersmith, a public school dating back nearly 500 years with a fine academic reputation. My teachers encouraged an interest in history and literature, and I was torn between the two when it came to deciding what to study at university. I was also interested in science and mathematics, particularly pure mathematics.

"My parents came from impoverished middle-class backgrounds, so that when they married they were virtually penniless. Both had their education interrupted by the war and neither went to university, though my father subsequently attended art school, afterwards becoming a graphic designer. He first worked in advertising and then in book and magazine publishing, doing sufficiently well to make us a modestly affluent family by the mid-1960s. At some stage my mother went back to work, and after a succession of secretarial jobs, she re-trained as a social worker.

"My parents read widely and the house was always full of books. Though neither was particularly political, both took it as axiomatic that one should support the Labour Party and that only dullards voted Conservative. One of my early memories was of my mother joining the annual march organised by the Campaign for Nuclear Disarmament; the route passed close to our house in Chiswick, and I watched it pass.

"When I was in my early teens my parents divorced, and my mother subsequently remarried a doctor, a Polish Jew by origin, more purely intellectual than either my father or my mother, and over the years both a friend and a stimulus to me. Neither of my parents was Jewish, though our unusual surname often meant that we were mistaken for such by Jews and non-Jews alike. I like to think that this has helped to free me from ever harbouring anti-Semitic thoughts. It helped too that St Paul's was a very cosmopolitan school, with a large intake of Jewish boys. I relished the prevalent atmosphere of free intellectual inquiry and debate.

"My teens were a time of student revolt, and I suppose I was influenced by the mood of the times like a great many other people. I attended the Grosvenor Square demonstrations against the Vietnam War and various rallies against the South African regime. I joined the Anti-Apartheid Movement, the only political party I have ever been a member of. None of this was very considered; I also attended the Rolling Stones' free concert in Hyde Park and various other pop concerts in the same spirit of vague liberation. I railed against the advantages that my parents had worked hard to provide. One aspect of this was that I resisted the sensible decision to sit the Oxford and Cambridge examinations; deciding that these were bastions of unfair privilege, I opted instead for Sussex University. In retrospect, I think I was influenced as much by Sussex's radical reputation as anything else. The result was disappointing: I found few barriers to overturn and I felt less intellectually engaged than I had been at school. Many of my fellow-students were influenced by the then fashionable structuralist philosophers, who left me cold; maybe I was too stupid to understand them. I may not have tried hard enough.

"I left Sussex with a mediocre degree in history and was lucky to obtain a job as a very junior editor at Oxford University Press. Quite quickly I was promoted to become a commissioning editor. Over the next dozen years I worked for a number of

London publishers. It was a time of enormous change in book publishing, as small companies were swallowed up by larger and larger conglomerates. By the end of the 1980s I was out.

"At OUP I had met another junior editor, who became my wife. She too made a successful career in publishing (more successful than me) before falling foul of a management reshuffle. By the early 1990s we had two small children and no jobs.

"I always wanted to be a writer, without having any idea what I wanted to write about. I began to write a biography of the historian A.J.P. Taylor, inspired by a posthumously published correspondence in the London Review of Books, in which Taylor asserted the benefits to a scholar of writing for a popular readership. He claimed that the discipline of writing reviews and newspaper articles helped him to write his own books, improving his prose and leading him to develop his ideas on paper. I was intrigued by this argument, and by the counter-argument that writing worthless ephemera debased the scholar's calling. As an editor I had spent much of my career encouraging scholars to reach out to an audience beyond that of their colleagues. Taylor was interesting to me too in that he saw himself as an outsider, a gadfly, an irritant to The Establishment (a term he coined). I enjoyed his irreverence and his puckish sense of humour. And he wrote about many of the historical issues that interested me most: the origins of the two world wars, for example.

"Taylor had died in 1990, and my biography was the first to appear, meaning that in tracing the course of his life and work I was exploring country that had been visited by no one else—except, of course, Taylor himself. I found it exhilarating to form conclusions and put forward hypotheses without reference to previous authorities.

"My Taylor biography sold well, and was enthusiastically received by reviewers. Hugh Trevor-Roper (Lord Dacre), who did not always come off winner in his clashes with Taylor, generously described my book as 'a first-class biography.' Norman Stone, a former pupil of Taylor's, found it 'so good as almost to constitute unfair competition. . . . As a description of post-war social-intellectual history, I do not know that this book has ever been bettered. . . . If there is anything wrong with this book, it is the English vice of fair-mindedness.' The book also received favourable reviews from other historians, including David Cannadine, Raymond Carr, Peter Clarke, Richard Overy, John Keegan, and Martin Gilbert and journalists such as Alan Watkins, Anthony Howard, Geoffrey Wheatcroft, and Robert Harris. Many of the reviewers drew attention to the clarity of the writing, which, according to Lord Beloff, 'would have pleased Taylor himself.' The book was shortlisted for the James Tait Black Memorial Prize and longlisted for the old NCR Award.

"I now began to write articles and reviews, most often for The Observer, though I have also written for The Sunday Times, the Evening Standard, The Spectator, and The Independent on Sunday, the Irish Times, the Washington Post, and various other publications. Over the years I have done numerous broadcasts for BBC and foreign radio stations, and appeared in several television programmes. In 1990 I co-founded a small copywriting business, Words. I have also worked as a consultant to various publishers, and have ghost-written several books.

"My wife had made a successful literary debut with a witty romantic comedy (followed since by two more), which was bought by publishers around the world. She remarked that we now controlled the means of production. We decided to move to the country, to a house near Bath.

"I spent a long time trying to decide what to write next. The sensible choice would have been to build on the success of my Taylor book. But I decided, against all advice, that my next book should be quite different. Writing a biography had focussed my attention on the process, and led me to the greatest of all biographies, Boswell's life of his friend Samuel Johnson. Like millions before me, I was captivated by the interplay between biographer and subject, and amused by the multiple ironies that occur when the writer becomes a character in his own book. I knew instinctively that I wanted to explore these issues, but it took me a long time before I found the form that suited me best—a biography not of a man, but of a book. Boswell's Presumptuous Task was published in the UK in November 2000, and subsequently in the USA. Like my Taylor book, it has been very widely reviewed, and has been praised by critics on both sides of the Atlantic, being described as 'a treat' (Hilary Spurling), 'brilliant' (Michael Holroyd), 'extraordinarily gripping' (Richard Holmes), 'fabulously entertaining, deft and witty' (Philip Hensher), and 'unputdownable' (Francis Wheen). The book has been shortlisted for the Whitbread Biography Prize, the Duff Cooper Biography Prize and the James Stern Silver Pen Award for Non-fiction, and longlisted for the Samuel Johnson Prize.

"I see myself as a writer, rather than simply as a biographer. I am interested in ideas as well as personalities, and by the interaction between the two. My aim is to write intellectually daring and exciting books to a high scholarly standard. Most of all I write to give pleasure to the reader: to stimulate, to entertain, to amuse, and perhaps even to delight."

When Sisman sat down to write *A.J.P. Taylor*, he set himself the task of bringing narrative consistency to the controversial and, in some ways, contradictory life of one of Britain's most famous 20th-century historians. Considering himself a radical liberal, Taylor made much of his working-class roots in northern England, where he was born and raised, but, as an adult, he avoided taking up the life his parents had led. Similarly, he was an anti-establishment figure who desired to be made a lord—that is, a member of the British Parliament's House of Lords—and an adamant socialist who fostered a devotion to the extreme right-wing media mogul Lord Beaverbrook. As a historian, however, Taylor seemed to have positioned himself firmly on the left, regarding his work as a tool in the fight against conservative forces. He famously asserted, as a reviewer for the *Economist* (February 19, 1994) reported, "History is the great propagator of doubt . . . It is sceptical of authorities; of historians; of our own views, and those of others." At the same time, Taylor observed, the *Economist* article continued, "The task of the historian is to explain the past; neither to justify nor to condemn it. Study of history enables us to understand the past; no more and no less."

Sisman's biography was published to general acclaim, in 1994. The *Economist* declared that it was "comprehensive and impeccably researched [as well as] beautifully crafted. With such a complex subject as Taylor, that is no mean achievement." The reviewer also suggested that Taylor would have approved of it, observing, "Sisman examines Taylor's views and ways but holds back from judging him either as a man or as an historian" and that he "weaves [Taylor's memorable epigrammatic wit] into his narrative to telling effect." Sisman would later reveal, in an article for the London *Guardian* (November 18, 2000), that writing biographies, as Taylor said of writing histories, propagated doubt. "Writing biographies teaches scepticism," he wrote. "When writing . . . a biography of . . . A. J. P. Taylor, I was startled to find how many people I interviewed told me stories I knew not to be true, or testified to events from the point of view of a witness on occasions when I knew they could not have been present. Even professional historians were guilty—not of lying but simply as victims of that strange human tendency to believe they had been present at a scene only imagined from a description. The mind rearranges events into what seems a rational progression, making order out of chaos." Peter Clarke wrote for the *London Review of Books* (January 27 1994), "Sisman has done enough research to prune the dense foliage of legend which Taylor himself lovingly propagated through his peculiar mixture of vanity, perversity and desire to entertain." Martin Gilbert, writing for the London *Guardian* (January 25, 1994), found that "portraying Taylor sympathetically, but in all his moods and stances, Adam Sisman has done both the historian and his readers a great service."

Continuing to explore the art of biography, Sisman turned to James Boswell, the author of the most renowned biography ever written in English,

The Life of Samuel Johnson. Boswell's Presumptuous Task: The Making of the Life of Dr. Johnson, Sisman's 2000 book, is the history of how a biography of a great man came to be written by a man regarded as considerably less than great. James Boswell, the son of a Scottish nobleman, had studied philosophy in Scotland, but moved, when he was 22, to London, where he met and befriended the literary celebrity Samuel Johnson. During the 21-year friendship that followed, Boswell indefatigably took notes and researched Johnson's life, and seven years after Johnson's death, Boswell published one of the few English biographies to attain the status of an important piece of literature.

Ross Leckie, writing for the London *Times* (September 22, 2001), opined that "[if] Boswell's biography of Johnson was innovative because it revealed the whole man, here Sisman does the same for Boswell." Leckie went on to praise Sisman's "meticulous and sympathetic reconstruction" of Boswell's life, finding that the book was "better than just biography at its best" because "Sisman also gives a gripping account of the survival and transmission of Johnson and Boswell's letters and manuscripts." Richard Eder was similarly impressed, writing for the *New York Times* (August 2, 2001), "[Sisman] points up the artistry with which the vain and self-doubting Boswell—foundering in distraction, compulsive drinking and sex, and the dreadful mess he made of his life—wrote his biography." Critics, however, were not unanimous in their approval. Miranda Seymour, in a review for the *Atlantic Monthly* (September 2001), complained, for example, that "Sisman's sparkling, companionable, and intelligent account" leaves out the "darker, demon-ridden side to James Boswell's nature."

Sisman next book concerned what is perhaps the most famous friendship in English literary history: that of the poets William Wordsworth and Samuel Taylor Coleridge, the two main figures in the early years of the literary Romantic Period. The book, *The Friendship: Wordsworth and Coleridge*, was released in England in 2006 and in the U.S. in 2007. Jonathan Bate, writing for the London *Guardian* (December 16, 2006), complained that Sisman had spent too much time discussing the years before Wordsworth and Coleridge met. "The decision to devote so much space to the two men's separate lives before their poetic convergence is a tactical disaster. It means that when Sisman does finally turn to their lives together, he has no space to create a sense of place, to bring alive the wider circle of family and friends, or for more general reflection on literary friendship, inspiration and collaboration, the crucial idea of poetry as 'conversation' or the significance of anonymous publication (neither poet's name was on the original title-page of *Lyrical Ballads* in 1798)." Others, however, were more impressed. A reviewer for *Publishers Weekly*, (November 20, 2006) for example, noted, "Sisman . . . provides an extensive background to their relationship, delineating in particular the political landscape that so influenced both men's thinking . . . elegantly weav[ing] the two men's stories together. Knowing how people tend to justify their own actions, Sisman is appropriately skeptical of their own accounts of their lives, using them to propose the most likely scenarios rather than as hard fact. Though lengthy, this book engages the reader's attention, freely mixing larger questions of politics with gossip, which helps bring to life figures long reified in the public imagination. At times there is too much detail, which doesn't enhance an already overloaded story explored extensively elsewhere. But Sisman does open up to the general reader the personal interactions that led to the birth of Romanticism."

Sisman lives in Holcombe, Somerset, just south of Bath, in southwest England. He is married to the popular novelist Robyn Sisman.

—S.Y.

Suggested Reading: *Atlantic Monthly* p141+ Sep. 2001; *Economist* p103 Feb. 19, 1994; *History Today* p56+ May 1994; (London) *Guardian* (on-line) Jan. 25, 1994, p18 Mar. 5, 1995, S p3 Nov. 18, 2000; (London) *Times* P p21 Sep. 22, 2001; *New Criterion* p61 Mar. 2001; *New York Times* (on-line) Aug. 2, 2001

Selected Works: *A.J.P. Taylor*, 1994; *Boswell's Presumpuous Task: The Making of the Life of Dr. Johnson*, 2000; *The Friendship: Wordsworth and Coleridge*, 2006

Chris Jackson/Getty Images

Smith, Ali

Aug. 24, 1962– Novelist; short-story writer; playwright

Ali Smith's work has been influenced by modernists of the early 20th century, particularly the Irish novelist and short-story writer James Joyce and the American poets Wallace Stevens and William Carlos Williams. In her fiction Smith has continued the experimental tradition of those literary giants, defying readers' expectations through her use of form and through the kinetic nature of her narratives and viewpoints. In her books, the story collections *Free Love*, *Other Stories and Other Stories*, and *The Whole Story*,

and *Other Stories* and the novels *Like*, *Hotel World*, and *The Accidental*, Smith has often written about lesbian love, but she resists the label "lesbian writer"—as she resists categories in general. Smith told Anna Burnside in an interview for the Glasgow *Sunday Herald* (October 7, 2001), "We all live in boxes and if there's one thing I want to do it's push the edges of boxes and make them open."

Ali Smith was born on August 24, 1962 in Inverness, Scotland, to Donald Smith, an electrician who worked on hydroelectric projects, and Ann Smith, a bus conductor and switchboard operator. Her family was Catholic. The youngest of five children, Smith has told interviewers that her childhood was a happy one. "It's very safe to be the fifth child in a family," she told Gillian Bowditch for the London *Sunday Times* (October 14, 2001). "The next brother was seven years older than me so I had the benefits of an only child as well as belonging to a big family." As a child Smith was an enthusiastic reader; by the time she was eight years old, she had read *Dubliners*, by James Joyce, *Animal Farm*, by George Orwell, and *Gulliver's Travels*, by Jonathan Swift. Despite the sense of security she enjoyed, Smith was "conscious that she was different long before she understood what that difference was," as Bowditch phrased it. Smith and another girl were "deeply in love" with each other, as the writer told Bowditch. "Growing up knowing most things are not about you, that you are excluded from most things, makes you feel different. There is nothing like feeling different to make you a writer. Any foreignness, any exile, any sense of the outside position is incredibly important."

Smith's parents, who had been forced by circumstance to leave school at age 14, were determined that their children pursue university degrees. As an undergraduate Smith attended Aberdeen University, in Scotland, earning an M.A. degree, in 1984, and an M.Litt. degree the following year. During her college years Smith felt ambivalent about her sexual orientation. She dated men, which "was terrible and . . . fine," she said to Bowditch. "It was terrible because it was a mistake and it was fine because it was real. I don't think I'll ever live such a double life again." Upon leaving Aberdeen Smith went on to study for a doctorate in literature at Newnham College, a women's institution at the University of Cambridge, in England; her advisers, however, considered her proposed thesis topic, "Modernism and Joy in Irish and American Literature," to be too broad, and she left the program. By that time she had begun writing plays. Smith next taught English at Strathclyde University, in Scotland, an experience she reportedly found loathsome.

During that time Smith suffered what was diagnosed in 1992 as chronic fatigue syndrome. She went on sick leave and "had two months of not doing anything at all, lying on my back and being unable to move," as she told Bowditch. "It was absolutely terrifying. You just lie there waiting for things to change. Then you stop waiting for anything. You just close down." She added that her illness was "a phenomenally life changing, life stopping thing. . . . It was a visionary experience. You're faced with a different world and, if you are going to live, you have to renegotiate this world. The illness was the catalyst for my next stage. It allowed me to write." After six months of sick leave, Smith left her teaching post and returned to Cambridge, where she lived with her partner, Sarah Wood. Smith received disability payments and consulted an expert on chronic fatigue syndrome. Meanwhile, she and Wood wrote a number of plays that had well-received stagings at the Edinburgh Fringe Festival. In 1994 Smith won the Macallan Scotland on Sunday short-story competition with "Text for the Day."

Smith's first book was a collection of short stories, *Free Love*, published in 1995. Many of the stories deal with lesbian love, and perhaps for that reason Smith struggled to get it published before Virago, a press that specializes in feminist books, took it on. Critical reception of *Free Love* was excellent. Kristina Woolnough wrote for *Scotland on Sunday* (June 18, 1995) that with "deceptively uncluttered language," Smith "homes in on the pinpoints of pain involved in the awakening of selfhood, first love . . . first sexual experiences . . . the flint of unshakeable memories in the whirl of the present, the transience of love. . . . The tension and interplay between what Smith is saying and how she says it is the most striking feature of her writing." For a London *Sunday Times* (July 9, 1995) reviewer, most of the stories are about "the ways in which people come together, and are separated again." The stories, the reviewer found, are "brief, rather fragmented . . . , yet they are often memorable as well." *Free Love* won the Saltire First Book Award.

Smith's next book, the novel *Like* (1997), was also greeted enthusiastically. Its principal characters are Amy Shone, a scholar whose nervous breakdown has left her unable to read; her seven-year-old daughter, Kate, with whom Amy lives an itinerant life; and Amy's old friend, called Ash, who wants to be Amy's lover. The cause of Amy's breakdown is not fully revealed, but as Claire Messud wrote for New York *Newsday* (August 13, 1998), "Smith's novel is wise even in its obliqueness, in its masking of what cannot be known. . . . In often incandescent prose, with a quicksilver capacity to inhabit the psyches of her characters, Ali Smith has composed a lingering threnody of love." In the London *Guardian* (July 20, 1997), Christina Patterson gave *Like* qualified praise, writing that the stories of Amy and Ash "are beautifully written in precise, poetic prose that successfully evokes the love of like for like. But they do remain separate stories, echoing against each other with great subtlety, but not, finally, working as a novel."

With *Other Stories and Other Stories*, which appeared in 1999, Smith established a pattern she has followed since: alternating story collections with novels. The book contains stories about the Other, the narrator's lover, who is addressed as "you," and stories about other people; the latter include "Kasia's Mother's Mother's Story," in which a woman seems to be caught in a war zone, and "Blank Card," which depicts the effect of anonymously sent flowers on a pair of lovers. "On the surface, the tales appear disparate, but on deeper consideration, there are myriad connections," Denyse Lyon Presley wrote for the London *Independent* (April 4, 1999), noting also that "through pared down prose [Smith's] tales uncover some essence of truth without recourse to overt didacticism."

Smith's *Hotel World* (2001), a novel, follows five characters who inhabit a hotel and its periphery. One is the ghost of Sara, a 19-year-old chambermaid who as a result of a bet has died from a fall down a hotel dumbwaiter. Another is Sara's sister, who mourns her obsessively and takes to a life in the streets outside the hotel; there, the narrative also focuses on Else, a tubercular beggar. Inside the hotel are Lise, the desk clerk, who is having a nervous breakdown, and Penny, an ad copywriter who turns out blurbs for the hotel chain. "The one uniting factor that brings together these individual threads is not so much the hotel or [Sara's] death, as the haunting, dream-like note Smith has imbued into every line," Adam Vaughan wrote for the *Richmond Review* (on-line). The critical response to *Hotel World* was mainly positive. In the minority was Chauncey Mabe, who wrote for the Fort Lauderdale, Florida, *Sun-Sentinel* (January 30, 2002), "As if another example were needed to prove that literary modernism is utterly played out, along comes . . . Ali Smith with a novel chock full of the sort of dreary, self-conscious narrative trickery that was already threadbare by the middle of the last century." Most, however, agreed with Vicky Hutchings, who wrote for the *New Statesman* (May 21, 2001), "Smith's writing is haunting and acute." In Great Britain *Hotel World* was placed on the short lists for the Booker Prize and the Orange Prize.

In keeping with her pattern, Smith's next book was a collection, *The Whole Story, and Other Stories*, which was published in 2003. The stories include one that begins, "I was on my way across King's Cross station concourse dodging the crowds and talking to you on my mobile when Death nearly walked into me," and another in which the narrator falls in love with a tree. The title of the collection is ironic, since, as Laura Baggaley noted for the London *Observer* (May 25, 2003), "Throughout, Smith shifts the narrative perspective so that 'I' becomes 'you,' making us question whether it is possible to grasp the complete story." Baggaley also observed, "Smith's prose captures moments in time like those sharp, seemingly insignificant memories which stick in the mind. Her protagonists share memories and we follow the workings of their minds, absorbing past and present, reflection and reminiscence. Reading this collection is like reading a brain in the process of thinking, flitting between subjects, every detail vivid." Writing for the *Miami Herald* (March 21, 2004), Connie Ogle called *The Whole Story, and Other Stories* "wonderfully strange and exhilarating."

In Smith's most recent volume, the novel *The Accidental* (2006), a mysterious woman named Amber enters and changes the lives of the Smart family, whose members are Eve, an author with writer's block; her philandering husband, Michael, a college literature professor; the suicidal Magnus, Eve's teenage son from a previous marriage; and Astrid, her 12-year-old daughter. In an assessment of *The Accidental* for the *Threepenny Review* (Spring 2006, on-line), Sigrid Nunez declared, "Smith's writing is so fine, it is naturally the first thing one wants to praise. Her cleverness and exuberance, her unflagging verbal virtuosity, delight the reader page after page. But stylistic tour de force is hardly Smith's only concern, and though *The Accidental* is not a realistic novel, its characters are not only believable but brimming with life." *The Accidental* won the Whitbread Novel Award and was short-listed for both the Booker Prize and the Orange Prize.

A production of Smith's first full-length play, *The Seer*, was mounted in 2006 after a five-year delay. Susan Irvine, writing for the London *Sunday Telegraph* (June 4, 2006), described it as "a kind of metaphysical farce exploring the relation of truth to fiction. . . . In *The Seer* the invisible wall between art and life is permeable, allowing us to question what a real existence might be, with a humour at times so plain silly that the audience forgets itself and gets carried away across the fourth wall, too, in a moment that is both cheesy and strangely moving."

Melissa Denes wrote for the London *Guardian* (April 19, 2002, on-line) that Smith "strikes you as a generous person—in the space of an hour she will have recommended at least five writers," and she added that Smith, who reviews fiction for the *Guardian*, "doesn't like to take on anything she instinctively knows she won't like." The writer is a political liberal, as suggested by her desire, which she revealed to the *Scotsman* (June 7, 2001), to "lock [former British prime minister Margaret Thatcher] in a room and punch her—and I've got quite a good right hook." With her partner, Sarah Wood, and Kasia Boddy, Smith edited *Brilliant Careers: The Virago Book of Twentieth-Century Fiction* (2000). She also selected the stories for *Shorts3: The Macallan/Scotland on Sunday Short Story Collection* (2000).

—S.Y.

Suggested Reading: *Atlantic Monthly* p139+ Jan. 2002; *Boston Globe* G p3 Jan. 20, 2002; (London) *Guardian* p17 July 20, 1997, (on-line) Apr. 19, 2003; (London) *Observer* p16 May 25, 2003; (London) *Sunday Times* (on-line) July 9, 1999; *Miami Herald* M p6 Mar. 21, 2004; (New York) *Newsday* B p2 Aug. 13, 1998; *Publishers Weekly* p51 Mar. 1, 2004; *Review of Contemporary Fiction* p256 Summer 1998; *Scotland on Sunday* S p11 June 18, 1995; *Washington Post* C p4 Jan. 22, 2002

Selected Books: *Free Love*, 1995; *Like*, 1997; *Other Stories and Other Stories*, 1999; *Hotel World*, 2001; *The Whole Story, and Other Stories*, 2003; *The Accidental*, 2006; as editor— *Brilliant Careers: The Virago Book of Twentieth-Century Fiction* (with K. Boddy and S. Wood), 2000; *Shorts3: The Macallan/Scotland on Sunday Short Story Collection*, 2000

Sorokin, Vladimir

Aug. 7, 1955– Novelist; playwright; screenwriter

The controversial Russian writer Vladimir Sorokin has become notorious for his sexually explicit and violent prose. He often mimics the conventions of socialist realism—the style of writing mandated in 1932 by the Union of Soviet Writers, notable for its strict adherence to and glorification of Communist Party doctrine—only to shock his readers with depictions of rape, cannibalism, and murder. Sorokin's prose has been heavily influenced by the pop art of Erik Bulatov, who subtly altered socialist realist work with personal and political slogans. "Thanks to Bulatov's pictures I suddenly saw this formula: everything is culture [and] lends itself to pop art," he told Sergei Shapoval for the *Moscow News* (October 18, 1992). "Every utterance set on paper is a dead thing which can be manipulated at will. For me it was like the discovery of nuclear energy."

Vladimir Georgievich Sorokin was born on August 7, 1955 in Moscow, Russia, to a moderately prosperous family. His father was a professor of metallurgy, and his mother was a homemaker. He told Olga and Alexander Nikolayev for the *Moscow News* (September 6, 2000), "I loved playing with anything [as a child], sand, 12 sticks, chess pieces. My parents and teachers were not amused and kept telling me that it was time I grew up at last." Sorokin, who stuttered badly as a child, is a fan of all genres of music from the classical work of Richard Wagner to modern rock; he told the Nikolayevs, "The most powerful influence of my youth came from music." He was interested in art as well. From the ages of eight to 13, he studied at an art workshop held at Moscow's Pushkin Museum.

In 1972 a Russian newspaper published some of Sorokin's poetry. In the mid-1970s he joined a loose group of artists and writers who became known as the Moscow conceptualists. The conceptualists, who included Bulatov, contended that it was impossible to depict reality accurately and thus the conventions of traditional art should be rejected or subverted. In 1977 he married a music teacher named Irina, and that same year he graduated from the Moscow Institute of Oil and Gas, where he had studied engineering. Rather than pursuing an engineering job, he turned to book illustration to support his family. (Irina gave birth to twin daughters, Anna and Maria, in 1980.) He has since illustrated more than 50 books. He continued to write for his small circle. "I had a glimmer of hope that some emigre journal might one day publish a story," he told Shapoval. "But I did not think of books, let alone of translations into foreign languages."

Sorokin's stories were published abroad but were available in Russia only in *samizdat* editions, underground printings used to distribute suppressed literature. "All my life I have been writing for myself and myself only," he told David Hoffman for the *Washington Post* (July 12, 2002). "I have a simple approach: Literature is a narcotic. Without it, we can't survive, as without art in general. If it's a drug and I am a person producing a narcotic, then my main task is to make it strong enough and clean. How they take it, how they distribute it, how they sell it and how it works— this is not my business." In 1992 Sorokin's work was finally published in Russia. Of that first volume, *Vladimir Sorokin: Sbornik Rasskazov*, Anatoly Korolyov wrote for the *Moscow Times* (May 25, 2005), "It's clear that the book spelled the end of Soviet literature. Sorokin turned a monstrous magnifying glass on the molecules of Soviet existence, the building blocks of the country's ideological carcass, and mixed the innocent pathos of party literature with existential nightmares."

Sorokin's first novel, *Ochered'*, was initially published in 1985 by the Paris-based journal *Syntaksis* and has since been translated into nine languages. (The English-language edition, *The Queue*, was published in 1988.) It consists almost entirely of the conversations of Russian shoppers as they wait in line for days to purchase an unspecified item of clothing. During the queuing, a common occurrence in 1980s Russia, the shoppers engage in conversations about sex, politics, and other queues; romances occur; and at one point some shoppers manage to steer the line into a bar so that everyone can enjoy a drink. Sorokin used various graphic devices to indicate the behavior of his characters, including printing dialogue upside down when some characters become drunk and leaving pages blank when a character falls asleep.

In 1992 (various sources list other dates) Sorokin published *Serdtsa Chetyrekh* (generally translated as "four stout hearts"), which was a finalist for Russia's first Booker Literary Prize (now the Booker–Open Russia Literary Prize). A parody of a detective thriller, the novel tells the story of four adventurers who have their hearts ripped out and turned into dice. The novel contained such a high level of violence and gore that workers at the publishing house where it was printed reportedly walked off their jobs in protest. Later that same year Sorokin published *Mesiats v Dakhau*, a novella. (*A Month in Dachau*, the English-language translation, was published in 1994.) The protagonist of the piece is a Soviet writer who takes a business trip to the Dachau concentration camp, created by the Nazis in World War II. When he arrives, he discovers that the camp is still functioning and falls in love with a double-headed female prison guard. Viktor Yerofeyev, writing for the *Moscow News* (January 1, 1993), called the book "a beautiful baroque piece symbolizing literature's triumph over life. It is also an accurate record of German-Russian tedium."

In 1994 Sorokin published *Norma* (which translates as "the norm"), an experimental work that consists of eight unconnected pieces written in a variety of styles. Each section ends in a breakdown of grammar and syntax. The prevailing metaphor in the book involves human feces, which the characters are forced to eat. According to David Gillespie and Elena Smirnova, writing for the Literary Encyclopedia Web Site, "Sorokin not only deconstructs the falsity and corruption of Soviet reality; he travesties that reality as absurd, grotesque and irredeemable."

Also in 1994 Sorokin published the 400-page *Roman* (which translates as "a novel"). It begins like a classic Russian novel in an idyllic setting— but turns horrific when the lead character, bitten by a wolf during a hunt, slaughters his neighbors and family. Gillespie and Smirnova wrote, "Sorokin sets out to subvert and destroy the much-vaunted heritage of Russian literature, rejecting the notion of 'high' art and the moral lessons it is meant to instill." Korolyov commented that such work "not only parodied the classics but undermined all of their postulates, from humanism and belief in Jesus Christ to faith in the people and hope for the little guy." In Sorokin's 1995 novel, *Tridtsataia Liubov' Mariny* (which translates as "Marina's 30th love"), the title character, a music teacher who was raped repeatedly as an adolescent, seeks to find liberation through sexual encounters. She can achieve sexual fulfillment only with other women, until she meets a man committed to communism. Marina then pledges to become a model Soviet citizen and subverts her own desires for the greater good. While *Tridtsataia Liubov' Mariny* received little attention in Russia, it was reviewed at least 40 times in Germany. Sorokin expressed some shock that his writing had found such an audience. "I did suppose that people of my psychosomatic type exist, but there proved to be more of them than I thought. Honestly, it was a surprise for me," he told Shapoval. He theorized, though, that his popularity in Germany could be explained "by the fact that the Germans have also passed through totalitarianism."

In 1999 a screenplay Sorokin wrote with the director Alexander Zeldovich was filmed as *Moskva* (*Moscow*). A parody of the Russian playwright Anton Chekhov's *Three Sisters*, the film tells the story of a mother and two daughters who move to Moscow, where they buy a nightclub. The movie is set in a post-Soviet milieu of underworld dealings, sex, and drugs and showed Moscow in such a state of moral decay that one Russian newspaper sued the film's producers for defaming the city. Writing for *Variety* (September 25, 2000), Deborah Young commented that *Moskva* was an "overly long but ultimately chilling study of life in the Russian capital today" and compared it to "a Chekhov play gone criminally insane." *Moskva* became Russia's first entry into the Venice Film Festival in a decade.

Sorokin has also branched out into theater. He has written several plays, among them *Shchi*, the name of a traditional Russian soup, which opened at Moscow's South-West Theater in 1999. The play takes place in a totalitarian world in which forbidden recipes are guarded by dissidents—as manuscripts were in the Soviet Union. Sorokin's play *Dostoevsky-Trip* also premiered in 1999, at the Theater Na Yugo-Zapade, in Moscow. The play focuses on a group of homeless people who try an experimental drug that is named for the Russian novelist Fyodor Dostoevsky. After becoming intoxicated, each junkie assumes the role of a character from Dostoevsky's 1869 novel *The Idiot*. "Sorokin, by first finding common ground among people of different eras and then blowing away the modest comfort that provides, left us in naked confrontation with the cruelties, the paradoxes and the impossibly hard choices that modern life foists upon those living it," John Freedman wrote for the *Moscow Times* (November 19, 1999). Among

Sorokin's more experimental plays is *Dismorphomania*, a *Hamlet* parody set in a psychiatric ward that was staged at the Alexei Levinsky Studio.

In 1999 Sorokin published the novel *Goluboye Salo*. (The title is usually translated as "blue lard" or "blue fat." "Blue" is also Russian slang for "homosexual.") A surrealist science-fiction story, it takes place in the middle of the 21st century, when a group of scientists in Siberia are cloning famous Russian writers. These writers, including Dostoevsky and Chekhov, produce blue lard when they write, and this substance is used to fuel a space station on the moon. The novel then switches time periods to 1954, when Stalin; his successor, Nikita Khrushchev; Adolf Hitler; and one of Hitler's chief lieutenants, Heinrich Himmler, plan to inject the blue fat to make themselves immortal. The book did not receive much attention until 2002, when a conservative Russian youth group, Moving Together, began protesting the novel as pornographic. The group found a long homosexual encounter between clones of Stalin and Khrushchev particularly offensive. During their protests, members of Moving Together destroyed copies of the novel. "I can't remember the last time books were destroyed in Moscow," Sorokin told Gary Shteyngart for the *New Yorker* (March 10, 2003). "Even in the Stalin era and during the revolution they didn't do this. They killed people, but treated books well." A member of Moving Together filed a lawsuit against Sorokin for publishing pornography, and the Moscow police began an investigation. Sorokin denied that his book was pornographic. "It's a novel, a work of literature," Sorokin told Hoffman. "So it uses explicit language and doesn't leave a lot to the imagination, but that doesn't make it pornography. Literature, like culture, has to have teeth if it wants to keep pace with the crazy times we live in. Culture shouldn't be like a neutered tomcat: comfortable, fat and predictable." The police probe raised the specter of Soviet-era censorship. Mikhail Shvydkoi, Russia's minister of culture, remarked that while he was not a fan of Sorokin's work, "that doesn't mean that [such writers] must be ostracized and expulsed from literature," as he was quoted as saying by a reporter for United Press International (June 29, 2002). The writer and critic Alexander Kabakov also came to Sorokin's defense. "Some experts might consider a few of his scenes to be pornographic, but that alone can't make him a pornographic author," Kabakov told Maura Reynolds for the *Los Angeles Times* (July 12, 2002). "I believe he is too cold-headed for that. He writes from his head rather than from his emotions." Thanks to the controversy, sales of *Goluboye Salo* jumped dramatically, and the book entered into several printings, a rarity for contemporary Russian fiction. Prosecutors also investigated Sorokin's novel *Lyod* (2002), about a mystical race of supermen, but dropped the case in July 2002. Of the police probes, Sorokin told a reporter for the Associated Press (July 29, 2002), "I consider this matter absurd, vicious and humiliating to me as a writer and humiliating to Russian literature as a whole." Sorokin and his publisher later filed suit against Moving Together, arguing that the group had published excerpts of his books without permission. Prosecutors dropped the criminal case against Sorokin in April 2003.

Sorokin's has also written works that are more optimistic and less explicit than the novels that caused such controversy. In 2001 he published *Pir* (which translates as "the feast"), a collection of 13 stylistically varied stories that revolve around food. Each story takes place in a different country. "I have long been fascinated by the mystery of cooking and eating, one of the most powerful and archaic processes in the world," Sorokin told the Nikolayevs. "But it was in Japan, after I encountered a totally different food culture, that the idea of my book assumed its final shape. . . . Overall, there emerges a symbol of food as a language with lots of dialects but which is a universal communication tool."

In 2002 the film *Kopeyka* (*The Kopeck*), based on a script by Sorokin and the film's director, Ivan Dykhovichnyj, was released. The film follows the various owners of a Kopeck—a Soviet automobile—over the course of 30 years. The owners include a KGB agent, a prostitute, and an avant-garde artist. The film was later nominated by the Russian Film Academy for a Nika Award for best screenplay. Sorokin's next script to be filmed was *4* (2004), directed by Ilya Khrjanovsky. Four years in the making, the film is a surrealistic tale of three Russians. It was nominated for best picture at the Gijón International Film Festival. Writing for *Variety* (October 4, 2004), Leslie Felperin noted that the movie "will unsettle even the most blasé heavy metal or horror movie fan." Calling it "seriously weird," she remarked that some audiences would enjoy the picture's "bawdy comedy, bravura sound design and uncanny atmosphere," while it would "baffle others." Sorokin also wrote the screenplay to *Veshch'* (2002), directed by Dykhovichnyj, and *Cashfire* (2002), directed by Alexander Zeldovich.

Sorokin's 2004 novel, *Put Bro* (which translates as "Bro's way"), is a prequel to *Lyod*. In the *Moscow Times* (September 24, 2004), Victor Sonkin wrote, "Sorokin makes the sophomoric wish to be superhuman sound absurd and funny—exactly the way it should."

In 2005 the Bolshoi Opera premiered *The Children of Rosenthal*, a new opera with a libretto by Sorokin and a score by the avant-garde composer Leonid Desyatnikov; it was the first new opera the state-funded theater had commissioned in 30 years. Sorokin and Desyatnikov had met during the production of *Moskva,* for which Desyatnikov wrote the music. The two formed a friendship and professional relationship. "Desyatnikov's complex compositional method is similar to my sensibility," Sorokin told Vadim Prokhorov for the London *Guardian* (March 16, 2005). "Also, he is a natural and original melodist." The opera tells the story of the clones of famous classical musicians who are created by a Soviet scientist. After the breakup of the Soviet Union, the composers fall on hard times. Almost all of the opera's characters die, after an evil pimp gives them poisoned vodka. Although he admitted he had never read any of Sorokin's work, Sergey Neverov, a deputy in the Duma, a Russian governmental body, attacked the opera based on a television report, and the Duma's Culture Committee mounted an investigation of the work. "It is not decent for the stage of the Bolshoi Theatre," Neverov told Kester Kenn Klomegah for the Inter-Press Service (April 19, 2005). Several dozen protesters from Moving Together also picketed the opera, and bomb threats were called in to the theater on opening night. The evening proceeded without incident, however. The seats of the Bolshoi were completely filled, and the cast made several curtain calls to sustained applause.

In 2006 New York Review Books published *Ice*, a translation of *Lyod*, as part of its NYRB Classics series. The novel begins as a chunk of extraterrestrial ice falls to Earth in Siberia, awakening a strange sensation in a select few—all of whom are blond-haired and blue-eyed. Describing *Ice* as a novel that comments "adroitly on Europe's 20th century nightmares," Jon Fasman wrote for the *Los Angeles Times* (January 7, 2007): "The notion of a small, elite group that wreaks unimaginable havoc and death for higher reasons echoes the terrors of Stalinism. The novel's awakened are inspired to kill innocent people by space beings who transmit their messages through ice; Stalin's elite were inspired by the pseudoscientific scribblings of a German thinker interpreted by a bald, goateed Russian and then implemented by a Georgian peasant. Which is more comprehensible? All commit unspeakable atrocities without a shred of guilt because they believe their mission frees them from moral restraints. . . . If all of this sounds as if it makes for heavy reading, don't worry. *Ice* is a thriller in the truest sense: In addition to a swift and sure plot, reading it affords the thrill of discovering something new."

Sorokin lives in southwest Moscow with his wife and daughters. In order to earn a living he has taken various jobs, including teaching Russian literature and language in Japan. He described himself to the Nikolayevs as "an accomplished introvert who peeps out now and then."

—G.O.

Suggested Reading: *Los Angeles Times* p3 July 12, 2002; *Moscow News* Oct. 18, 1992, Sep. 6, 2000; *Moscow Times* May 25, 2005; *New Yorker* p42 Mar. 10, 2003

Selected Books in English Translation: *The Queue*, 1988; *A Month in Dachua*, 1994; *Ice*, 2006

Soueif, Ahdaf

(soy-EF, ah-DEF)

1950– Novelist; short-story writer; essayist; translator

Born in Egypt but educated in England, Ahdaf Soueif writes works that articulate the difficulties of belonging to two cultures, participating in both but never fully at home in either. Like other notable Egyptian writers, such as the Nobel Laureate Naguib Mahfouz, Soueif explores such themes as post-colonialism, Arab culture, and Muslim identity, but she does so from a distinctly female perspective, focusing on the lives of women and their public and private struggles to define themselves. Whether in her insightful essays; short stories, which are described by critics as delicate, lyrical, and sparse; or her lengthy novels, in which she ambitiously tackles questions of history and geography in an attempt to hone in on the vacillating identity of her female protagonists, Soueif is known for creating a richly textured world of sights, sounds, and smells; indeed, her attention to detail and sweeping scope has earned her a reputation as Egypt's George Eliot (the 19th-century author of *Middlemarch*). "Every picture is made up of detail," Soueif told Lynn Cline in an interview for the *Santa Fe New Mexican* (April 4, 2003). "Detail is what makes it real, what makes the reader 'live in' the scene. And it's in the detail that—I think—the most subtle effects are achieved."

Ahdaf Soueif was born in 1950 in Cairo, Egypt, into a family of Muslim intellectuals. Her father, Mustafa Soueif, was a psychology professor at Cairo University. Her mother, Fatmah Musa, was a professor of English at the same institution. Between the ages of four and eight, Soueif lived in London, where her mother was studying for a doctorate at the University of London. During this time Soueif learned to read English and acquired a passion for English literature, reading widely of the classics; among her favorites were George Eliot and the 20th-century French author Colette. "Reading became my passion—probably my favorite activity," Soueif recalled to Cline. "I think the idea must have formed itself in my head very early on that one day I would write stories. . . . It seems to have always been there. My sister and brother tell me that I was full of stories every day when we came back from school."

Soueif returned to Cairo when she was eight and began attending private school. She studied English literature at Cairo University, receiving her B.A., in 1971. She earned a master's degree in English and American literature, in 1973, from the American University in Cairo, then moved to England, where she earned a doctorate in linguistics from Lancaster University, in 1978. In 1981 she married an Englishman, Ian Hamilton, a respected poet, biographer, critic, and editor. She and Hamilton moved back and forth between London and Cairo for several years before eventually settling in an old Victorian house in Wimbledon. With Hamilton she had two sons, Omar Robert and Ismail Richard, born in 1984 and 1989 respectively. At this time Soueif worked briefly in academia, teaching for short periods in Cairo and at King Saud University, in Riyadh, Saudi Arabia.

Soueif began writing fiction in English as soon as she completed her doctorate. While she assumed she would eventually write in Arabic, in which she is also fluent, this turned out not to be the case. "The sentences kept coming in English," she explained in a February 28, 2000 lecture at Brunel University, Uxbridge, Middlesex, as posted on the university's Web site. "What was happening was that dialogue came to me in Arabic but narrative came in English. After a while of this I just gave up, and decided that the stories were coming in English and there we were." Soueif attributes this development to the difference "between the spoken Arabic and the written Arabic," adding that "the classical standard Arabic is a written language which you only ever hear in formal lectures or on the news, and so on, but the language that you use every day is the colloquial, and it's quite a bit different. So the fact that you can use colloquial Arabic well doesn't necessarily mean that you can write well in classical Arabic. . . . I operate in Arabic perfectly well. I write essays and criticism and letters and reports and so on, but I simply cannot write fiction in Arabic. . . . It becomes a blunt instrument in my hand."

Soueif's first book of fiction, *Aisha*, was published in 1983. The work is a collection of short stories, each focusing on a woman named Aisha, who, like Soueif herself, is an Egyptian with a British education. The primary theme of the stories is the conflict Aisha experiences as she negotiates her identity between these two different worlds. The book was well received by critics and was short-listed for the Guardian Fiction Award.

In the Eye of the Sun (1992) started out as two short stories, but eventually grew into a sprawling 800-page novel. The protagonist is a Muslim Egyptian girl named Asya al-Ulama, a daughter of respected academics whose experience of the world is very much shaped by her knowledge of English literature. The story takes place between 1969 and 1980, and begins with Asya during her days as a university student in Cairo. She falls in love with handsome Saif Madi, a slightly older, Westernized Muslim, and after a prolonged courtship the two marry. Although she loves her husband, the relationship leaves her sexually unfulfilled, and at length she departs to pursue a Ph.D. in northern England. There she finds sexual awakening in the arms of a progressive Englishman named Gerald Stone. The love affair, which is ultimately unrewarding—Asya derides the self-centered Stone as a "sexual imperialist" for his history of having girlfriends from developing countries—brings about the dissolution of Asya's marriage to Saif, who is outraged when he discovers his wife's infidelity. Asya's coming-of-age story takes place against a background of 1970s sexual politics, the Six-Day War (the 1967 conflict between Israel and the Arab nations of Egypt, Jordan, and Syria), and the social and psychological aftereffects of British colonialism. (The book's title derives from the poem "Song of the Wise Children" by Rudyard Kipling, who is often remembered as a champion of European imperialism.)

In the Eye of the Sun, which took Soueif four years to write, was largely autobiographical, as she explained to Hind Wassef for the *Cairo Times* (April 30, 1998, on-line): "These characters and incidents that have been swirling around in my mind for years have been fictionalized, put into a structure, and now I can stop thinking about them. It is like housekeeping. You clear this accumulation by working it out into fiction." Soueif has said that, in working on the novel, the character of Asya came to her first; as she developed her protagonist, however, Soueif found it necessary to elaborate the story's historical and political context. "We Egyptians are indivisible from our history," she explained to Wassef. "I don't know if this is particular to us as a people who have had so many wrenchings in their history, so many waves of occupations followed by national resurgence then another occupation and so on. It is this that gives us this compulsion to go back to find out who we are."

In the Eye of the Sun was well received by critics in the West. Leila Ahmed, writing in the *Washington Post Book World* (June 13, 1993), hailed it as "something of a landmark. It is the first novel I know of that successfully renders an Arab, Egyptian Muslim reality in English. Without losing the authentic tones, images, voices and complicated politics of Arabic life, Soueif manages to assimilate that world seamlessly into the familiar universe of the English language and the imaginative and moral world of English literature." "Creating ambience—and, importantly, ambience from a rare female perspective—is what this author does best," Silvie Drake opined for the *Los Angeles Times* (September 26, 1993). "She shows us the special intimacy of women working together in kitchens, young girls sharing secrets, children playing, elders nattering and generations finding strength in the bustle and emotional cacophony they share. Through it all there is Asya the child, the teen-ager, bride, daughter, woman, searching for her voice in a world defined by men." In the Arab and Muslim countries of Africa and the

Middle East, however, *In the Eye of the Sun* received mixed reviews. Some critics there praised the work, calling it an Arabic novel written in English. The explicit depictions of sexuality, however, drew hostile remarks from many Muslim reviewers, who judged the scenes of adultery to be particularly offensive. The novel was banned in some Arab countries for its portrayal of sexuality in the harem.

Soueif's next book, *Sandpiper* (1996), was, like *Aisha*, a collection of related short stories. The female protagonists—some of whom had appeared in *In the Eye of the Sun*—hail from diverse cultural backgrounds: Arab, English, American, and Greek. Four of the volume's seven stories had been previously published in such periodicals as *Granta* and the *London Review of Books*. Uju Asika, writing in the *Weekly Journal* (June 3, 1997), described the stories as "linked by a subtext of crumbling identities, emotional fragility and the claustrophobia of personal relationships. . . . Soueif once more refuses to tiptoe around taboo subjects and proves that she is unafraid of the dark side of life." Edward Said, a noted Arab scholar and Soueif's close friend, praised her as "one of the most extraordinary chroniclers of sexual politics now writing," as quoted by Tunku Varadarajan for the London *Times* (February 24, 1996). *Sandpiper* received the Cairo International Bookfair Award for best collection of short stories in 1996.

In the novel *The Map of Love* (1999), Soueif relates a panoramic family saga through two interweaving stories, both of which take place in Egypt; one is set at the beginning of the 20th century, the other in the present day. In 1997 in New York, an American journalist named Isabel Parkman discovers an old trunk filled with documents, journals, and letters, some of which are in English and some in Arabic. Isabel, recently divorced, is enamored with an Egyptian man named Omar, who suggests that she take the trunk with her to Cairo, where his sister Amal—a divorcee who lived in the West for some time before returning to Egypt—can help her translate the Arabic. Isabel meets Amal in Egypt, and together the two begin to unearth a century-old love story. The letters belonged to Lady Anna Winterbourne, Isabel's great-grandmother, a widowed Englishwoman who left London and traveled to Egypt, which at the time was under British colonial rule. The adventuresome and politically conscious Anna comes to understand a great deal about Egyptian politics, the racism of British imperialists, Islamic culture, and the difficulties of being a woman in a man's world. Eventually, she meets a brooding Egyptian nationalist, Sharif al-Baroudi; the two fall in love, and in 1901 the unlikely couple get married. Meanwhile, in present day Cairo, Isabel and Amal become friends and discover that, since Sharif is Amal's grandmother's brother, they are in fact distant cousins.

Soueif spent two years doing background research for *The Map of Love*; she began, however, with no more than the idea for a simple love story: "I was interested in a romantic novel set in the desert, in the romantic tradition where the man and woman start off with antipathy and then it turns to affection and then you have this combustion," she explained to Tom Collins for the *Albuquerque Journal* (April 4, 2003). "And then it turned serious on me, when I started positioning the characters. It became clear to me that I didn't want to just write a story in the tradition of 19th century English women's travel literature. I wanted to write something else. And so the politics came in really in a secondary way, almost organically." Once she had broadened her focus, she took great care in her depiction of the politics and history of Egypt. She was particularly concerned with addressing some of the stereotypes that exist about the country. "Everyone is aware of Ancient Egypt," she explained to Libby Brooks for the London *Guardian* (August 2, 1999). "The perception is that there was this great Pharonic period and that now Egypt is a developing country. That hurts me enormously because we may be developing in terms of microchips and making our own aeroplanes, but in the ways that matter, the ways of civilisation, we're there, and have been for a long time."

The Map of Love was enthusiastically received by readers and critics alike. "It is a magnificent work," Brooks wrote, "reminiscent of [Gabriel García] Márquez and [Isabel] Allende in its breadth and confidence." "The bland title belies the rich plots that play out and become one in a complicated story gracefully told," Jules Verdone commented for the *Boston Globe* (December 18, 2000). "[Soueif] gives each major character a discrete voice and makes an exchange in 1899 impossible to mistake for a recent conversation. Somehow she manages to do so without a lot of affectation. . . . The women she creates are resilient, bold, affectionate, and resourceful. They bend and defy and endure." Annette Kobak, writing for the *New York Times* (October 1, 2000), called *The Map of Love* "a wonderfully accomplished and mature work of fiction." Kobak added, "The novel's use of . . . historical strands is never tendentious, and its title suggests a more subtle purpose: to show how love can grow in the interstices between different countries, even between different times. And love here encompasses a far broader map than just romance: love of country, of nature, of language, of sensual pleasures; love between siblings, family members, friends, generations; love even between the living and the dead." *The Map of Love* was translated into Arabic by Soueif's mother.

In March 2003, coinciding with the American invasion of Iraq, Soueif wrote an editorial for the London *Guardian* (March 13, 2003), criticizing the Western media for its superficial depiction of Arab women as hapless victims, instead of recounting the daily struggles of women for autonomy and the preservation of their families and culture. "Arab women are generally portrayed [by the Western media] as victimised, subservient. They sit next to silent, wide-eyed children in Iraqi hospitals, they stumble among the ruins of their homes in Jenin. Many in the west seem to think they need to be dragged out from under their veils and scolded into standing up for themselves. But as we all try to block, to temper, to survive the coming horror, it is crucial for sympathisers in the west to understand the truth. . . . I'm asked what Arab women are doing in these critical times. They are doing what they have to do: toughing it out, spreading themselves thin, doing their work, making ends meet, trying to protect their children and support their men, turning to their friends, their sisters and their mothers for solidarity and laughs. There was a quieter, more equable time when women's political action was born of choice, of a desire to change the world. Now, simply trying to hold on to our world is a political action."

In 2004 Soueif published *Mezzaterra: Fragments from the Common Ground*, a collection of cultural commentaries and political essays, many of them reprinted from the London *Guardian*. Reviews of the book were somewhat divided along ideological lines, with those who agreed with the anti-Zionist theme of many of the pieces applauding the volume. A *Publishers Weekly* (September 5, 2005) reviewer noted, "The 38 pieces collected here . . . establish Soueif as the intellectual heir to Edward Said." Soueif's most recent book, *I Think of You* (2007), is a collection of select stories that appeared originally in *Aisha* and *Sandpiper*.

In 2004 Soueif translated into English Mourid Barghouti's memoir *I Saw Ramallah*. She has worked at the Al Furqan Center for Islamic Studies, preserving and publishing ancient Islamic manuscripts. She has published essays and reviews in numerous international periodicals, including *Akhbar al-Adab*, *al-Arabi*, *Cosmopolitan*, *Granta*, the London *Observer*, the *London Review of Books*, the London *Sunday Telegraph*, *New Society*, *Nisf al-Dunya*, *Sabah al-Kheir*, and the *Washington Post*. Soueif was the chair of the judging panel for the 2003 Orange Prize for fiction, a prestigious award open only to women.

Soueif's husband, Ian Hamilton, died in December 2001. She currently divides her time between England and Egypt.

—A.I.C.

Suggested Reading: *Albuquerque Journal* p1 Apr. 4, 2003; *Boston Globe* C p6 Dec. 18, 2000; Brunel University Web site; *Cairo Times* (on-line) Apr. 30, 1998; *Kirkus Reviews* Aug. 1, 2000; (London) *Guardian* p4 Aug. 2, 1999; (London) *Times* Feb. 24, 1996; *Los Angeles Times Book Review* p15 Sep. 26, 1993; *New York Times* VII p30 Oct. 1, 2000; *Santa Fe New Mexican* P p14 Apr. 4, 2003;

Washington Post Book World p6 June 13, 1993; *Washington Times* B p8 June 13, 1993; *Weekly Journal* p20 June 3, 1997

Selected Books: *Aisha*, 1983; *In the Eye of the Sun*, 1992; *Sandpiper*, 1996; *The Map of Love*, 1999; *Mezzaterra: Fragments from the Common Ground*, 2004; *I Think of You: Stories*, 2007

John D. McHugh/AFP/Getty Images

St. Aubyn, Edward

1960– Novelist

Edward St. Aubyn was born in 1960, in the English district of Cornwall, which, according to Suzi Feay for the London *Independent* (April 18, 2006), the "St. Aubyns seem to own." The author has often described his aristocratic father as brutal and sadistic, and after the publication of his Patrick Melrose trilogy, in which the five-year-old hero is raped by his father, speculation arose as to whether St. Aubyn had been similarly victimized as a child. He initially refused to confirm or deny such speculation but later admitted that he had been sexually abused by his father from the age of five to eight. His parents divorced shortly after the abuse ended—though his mother did not learn about it until years later—and soon after they split he was sent off to the Westminster School, in London. While attending the prestigious boarding school, St. Aubyn began using drugs, and by age 16 he was addicted to heroin. His bad habits continued while he studied at the University of Oxford, and he claims to have been under the influence of drugs during the final examination for

his degree, which, according to his own account, he passed with the lowest grade in his class.

Independently wealthy from an early age, St. Aubyn spent most of his youth drinking and loafing about in a drug-induced haze, and he experienced occasional overdoses. "I don't know if they were suicide attempts or not," he told Julia Llewellyn Smith for the London *Times* (June 14, 1994). "I didn't see any point in living." Eventually, he sought counseling, and in 1988, two years after his father's death, he began writing his first novel. "Once I started writing, I decided to stop the analysis. I didn't need it any more," he told Rachel Cooke for the London *Observer* (January 8, 2006, on-line). "If it [writing] does have any therapeutic value, the only way to get access to it is to write without any therapeutic intent. You transform experience into, for want of a better word, art." Nevertheless, St. Aubyn found working on his first novel—a semiautobiographical story of a materially endowed but emotionally deprived child—a harrowing experience. "I'd been told by my father that if I ever told anyone about what had happened, he would kill me," he told Cooke. "So to write a novel about it was an enormous transgression."

That fictionalized account of his childhood, *Never Mind*, was published in 1992, with the five-year-old protagonist, Patrick Melrose, standing in as the author's alter ego. The novel is set in southern France, where the family is vacationing in luxury. During the trip Patrick is neglected by his alcoholic mother, tortured by his sadistic father, and thrown into the company of their rather unappetizing friends. "This novel slices open the gilded apple that is the minor British aristocracy," a reviewer wrote for the Glasgow *Herald* (November 21, 1992). "While they are excessively civilised on the surface, discussing philosophy over gourmet meals, underneath, these people's lives are rotten. St Aubyn anatomises with cruel brilliance a goodly apple rotten at the heart; one hopes his friends don't recognise themselves." (It is a convention among some writers in the U.K. to leave off the period when abbreviating such words as Saint.) Many critics, noting the author's delight in raking his upper-class peers over the coals, compared him to the early-20th-century satirist Evelyn Waugh, who likewise skewered high society with his sardonic wit. "Moving in and out of the heads of his seven characters," Amanda Craig wrote for the London *Independent* (February 22, 1992), "St Aubyn can be sarcastic, viciously funny ('he had the sullen air of a man who looked forward to strangling poultry'), and blunt about English manners ('a high proportion of outright rudeness and gladiatorial combat')." Most reviewers agreed with Craig that "St Aubyn's characters are hateful, but all too real."

When the reader next encounters Patrick, in the second volume of the trilogy, *Bad News* (1993), the disturbed young protagonist—now a 22-year-old with a drug habit that costs thousands of dollars a week—must travel to New York City to claim the ashes of his recently deceased father. Again, St. Aubyn drew praise from critics for his dark humor: "Funeral parlours, drug dealers, airhead girls, and crass fellow-passengers on aircraft are all grist to St Aubyn's savagely funny mill," Phil Baker wrote for the London *Sunday Times* (December 12, 1993). "His distinctively English misanthropy finds plenty of targets in America, and a wackier strain of humour breaks through with Patrick's multiple personalities: internal characters like The Fat Man, Humpo Languid, and Mr President all use his head 'like a cheap hotel'." Nick Foulkes, writing for the London *Evening Standard* (November 12, 1992), described *Bad News* as a "vivid, acutely written book; a cross between [Hunter S. Thompson's] *Fear and Loathing in Las Vegas*, [Jay Mcinerney's] *Bright Lights Big City* and [Charles Jackson's] *The Lost Weekend*, seasoned with a pinch of [Evelyn Waugh's] *The Ordeal of Gilbert Penfold*." As in most of the aforementioned classics, the central character in St. Aubyn's novel tears recklessly through town, binging on drugs and alcohol: "St Aubyn attempts to and often succeeds in capturing the mentality of the addict," Foulkes wrote. "He is good when describing the interaction of various drugs and their effects. He offers stomach-churning accounts of injections, while conveying effectively the simultaneous feelings of self-loathing and self-destructive romance as well as the serious drug user's contempt for those who flirt with narcotics and view them merely as faintly licentious weekend entertainment."

By the time St. Aubyn concluded the series with *Some Hope* (1994), Patrick had reached the age of 30. The author's "bleak view of mankind . . . is milder here, and there is even, as the title suggests, a glimmer of hope ahead, some sort of lightening of the skies," according to Lindsay Duguid in a review for the London *Independent* (July 10, 1994). Once again, the author takes aim at the upper crust, going so far as to include Princess Margaret, the younger sister of Queen Elizabeth II, not only as a character but also as a symbol of the "dehumanising caste system of polite society," according to Catherine Milton for the London *Times* (June 16, 1994). While Milton argued that the Patrick Melrose trilogy stood only "a slim chance of standing out from the literary flotsam and jetsam of fin de siecle Britain," Gabriele Annan, writing for the *New York Review of Books* (March 25, 2004), praised the novels—which were released later in the U.S. as one volume, *Some Hope: A Trilogy* (2003)—as "hilarious and harrowing by turns, sophisticated, reflective, and brooding." Noting the tendency of British reviewers to compare St. Aubyn to Waugh, Annan boldly proclaimed to find the former's books both funnier and sadder: "Like Waugh's novels, they are set among the English upper classes, but whereas Waugh loved toffs (even if he sometimes made fun of them) St. Aubyn loathes them, and mocks them relentlessly and with venomous wit. His sociological and psychological insight is penetrating, especially where the two categories overlap. The dialogue is brilliant too, with every character speaking and thinking in his or her own idiom. Metaphors explode like rockets to illuminate meaning, and only very rarely detonate just a little over the top."

In St. Aubyn's first stand-alone novel, *On the Edge* (1998), Peter Thorpe, a middling, thirtysomething English banker, throws away everything to chase after a free-spirited German girl, Sabine, with whom he has had a brief affair. He looks for her at such New Age institutions as a commune in Scotland and the Esalen Foundation, in California, where he meets an unusual set of American spiritual seekers. While Christina Koning, writing for the London *Times* (May 9, 1998), acknowledged that "some of his [St. Aubyn's] jibes at the expense of 'alternative' religions are quite amusing," she complained that "it has been done before—notably by John Updike and Evelyn Waugh," and felt that, by this point, "the jokes have worn thin." Most critics, however, agreed with Lindsay Duguid, who wrote for the London *Sunday Times* (May 31, 1998) that though St. Aubyn may have taken aim at easy targets, his execution was praiseworthy: "This is not difficult material to send up. St Aubyn records it all from a poised satirical stance; not quite sneering, not quite complicit, his attitude is a mixture of incredulity and amusement. When he slows down, however, and loses himself in description . . . his writing is impressive and unexpectedly moving."

St. Aubyn received mixed reviews for his next novel, *A Clue to the Exit* (2000), in which screenwriter Charlie Fairburn sells his home in St. Tropez and moves to a luxurious French hotel, after being told that he has only six months to live. "St Aubyn manifestly prides himself on a spare and rigorously clear prose style, and understandably so—it can be playful and lingeringly witty, this improbable mix of grace and baldness," Zoe Williams wrote for the London *Evening Standard* (September 11, 2000). "It can also be imperious to the extent that the book appears to be curling away from your crude gaze as you read the bleeding thing. Some of the details are wilfully, comically arcane in Charlie's book, or extracts thereof, the protagonists have a long and delightful riff about the component structures of the synapses, and the potential for coherent quantum events therein. Other episodes are icy and distant—reading this book is like nothing so much as going on a series of very polite, highly sophisticated dates with a man who says something engaging once every other course, and spends the rest of the time playing so hard to get that no woman with any sense would let him go to the loo on his own. . . . The dialogue throughout is arch, beautifully turned stuff. But overall, the effect is curiously unsatisfying, never drawing you in for long enough to get away with the intermittent disdain of its tone, or the outright enigma of its characters."

Continuing his reign as the premier chronicler of the decadent English aristocracy, St. Aubyn brought back Patrick Melrose for *Mother's Milk* (2006). Patrick, who is now married with two children and works as a lawyer, struggles to adjust to his new role as a responsible family man. Though John Williams, writing for the London *Mail on Sunday* (February 12, 2006), praised the opening sequence (in which Patrick's five-year-old son, Robert, recalls his own birth) as a "brilliantly done" passage that will cause "the reader to think afresh about the beginning of life," the reviewer complained that the novel is oddly unsatisfying. "Patrick aside, it's peopled by characters too contrived to engage the reader," Williams wrote, "and even Robert is more a prescient authorial conceit than a real child." Angel Gurria-Quintana disagreed, however, arguing in the *Financial Times* (January 28, 2006) that while the author's scathing depictions of the pitiful parenting skills of the elite "would verge on caricature were St Aubyn a less precise observer" of the environment which he knows so well, "his ability to convey emotional nuances underpinning the posh grotesques . . . makes this beautifully written novel funny, disturbing and heart-rending."

St. Aubyn, known as Teddy to his friends, was married in 1987 to Nicola Shulman, but the union ended after three years. Though he reportedly spends most of his time in rural France, with his second wife and young son, St. Aubyn became an American citizen in about 2003. "Teddy is an elegant man of great warmth, great wit, great presence of mind and impeccable manners," Patrick McGrath wrote. "His mode of speech is the languid drawl, often sinking to a near-inaudible murmur, but punctuated often by gusts of raucous laughter."

—S.Y.

Suggested Reading: *Bomb* p76+ Fall 2003; (Glasgow) *Herald* p7 Nov. 21, 1992; (London) *Independent* p28 Feb. 22, 1992, p36 July 10, 1994, p12 May 23, 1998; (London) *Times* June 14, 1994; *New York Review of Books* p32+ Mar. 25, 2004

Selected Books: *On the Edge*, 1998; *A Clue to the Exit*, 2000; *Some Hope: A Trilogy*, 2003; *Mother's Milk: A Novel*, 2006

Stern, Amanda

1971(?)– Novelist; comedy writer; nonfiction writer

In her first novel, *The Long Haul* (2003), Amanda Stern depicts the relationship between a nameless female narrator and her boyfriend. A critic for *Publishers Weekly* (October 20, 2003) described the book: "Stern's slim debut, centered on the tumultuous six-year affair between a needy, self-absorbed young musician referred to only as 'the Alcoholic,' and the unnamed, enabling narrator, paints a rich picture of mid-1990s undergraduate and postcollege anomie. Details of the Gen-X experience—drinking at dive bars; going to rock shows attended by a 'United Nations' of 'fraternity brothers, sorority sisters, punks, skater kids, techno freaks'—are cleanly rendered, and Stern's tone is a spot-on mix of nostalgia, sympathy and ennui. . . . Stern shows the dysfunctional relationship in its moments of light (the first blush of affection; an ill-conceived nighttime quest for a corkscrew) and darkness (fighting; a miscarriage; an attempted rape). Though the narrator is sometimes frustratingly passive, she is also articulate and skillful at telling her own sharp, dark coming-of-age story."

Amanda Stern was born and raised in the Greenwich Village section of New York City. In a piece for the *New York Times Magazine* (December 30, 2001), she reminisced about Etan Patz, a small boy abducted from her neighborhood in 1979: "In the third grade, I lived on Macdougal Street. My

Steve Wiley

world was green Pumas and striped Lacoste sweatshirts. At 3 feet 5 inches and 40-odd pounds, I, too, could have been snatched by anyone, but I wasn't the one taken. One Friday morning in 1979, Etan Patz walked to the corner of West Broadway and Prince and disappeared into never." She wrote, "My generation was shrinking. I couldn't take the not knowing. If you're missing, do you still exist? Was it the same as death or worse? These thoughts plagued me. I was awake the day my childhood ended, watched it slip from me right there on the evening news."

As a young adult Stern spent a number of years working as an assistant to such film directors as Terry Gilliam, Hal Hartley, Ted Hope, James Schamus, and Ang Lee. She was the creator of the radio comedy *The Cindy Something Show*, which she hosted and produced for the Pseudo Online Network, a Web-based media company, for three years. She also served as co-host of the on-line comedy program "This is Not a Test," which was available on MSN.

Stern is well-known in New York City's arts community for curating and hosting a reading-and-music series at Happy Ending, a massage parlor-turned-bar on the Lower East Side of Manhattan. "The last thing I wanted was to create a traditional reading series. I have to sit through it every week and God knows I could bore myself to death via C-SPAN, and at home nonetheless. So when I started mentally constructing the events, I tried to think about what it was I wanted to see, but more importantly, what it was I was trying to say," she explained to Janine Armin for Bookslut.com. "I arrived at this: Not all writers are as boring as carcasses. Sure, some are. But I'm not interested in spending time with them. I am interested not only in how writers think and view the world, but almost more so in the other things they can do. I'm always taken by the hidden talents of my peers, and so it was this aspect that I set the guidelines for Happy Ending. And the guidelines are that the authors must do something they've never done before onstage. They must take a risk, outside of reading in public. It's not that the terms are so interesting, it's what the authors do with these terms that make the events so entertaining." She continued, "The other aspect of the show involves musicians with stories of their own to tell. The musicians are usually local—emerging or accomplished—singer-songwriters, and they play five original tunes and one cover song of their choice (the first year, the musicians had to cover '80s songs only, and it was amazingly fun, but after a year, enough.) Underneath that, there are some other things that add to what's already a semi-lighthearted event. For one thing, the venue is outstanding. It's this unique blend of swank and kitsch that I love."

The Long Haul took Stern nine months to write. "*The Long Haul* was based on a relationship I had with an alcoholic, but the book, in a very real sense, is less about that specific relationship than it is about a certain prototype," she explained to Kevin Sampsell for *Word Riot* (on-line). "What I tend to do in my work is rely on actual lived moments of my past and explode them. So, in each chapter in *The Long Haul* I can point to at least one or two things that actually happened to me, or to us, but more often than not, the thing that occurred was a premise and the story I end up writing is a

false realization of that premise or a fictional interpretation of what might have happened if say, we DID find a young girl when driving in an ice storm, or if I did stalk a patient of the free therapist I was seeing. So, I suppose the skin of the novel is real but what holds the skin in place is fiction."

Reviews of the book varied widely. "Reading Amanda Stern's debut novel, *The Long Haul*, is like showing up at some underground concert venue, anticipating the breakout performance by a local indie-rock celebrity, and then having him show up drunk, only to poetry-slam you about his abusive mother, his perverted uncle, and his penchant for self-scarification and suicide before smashing his guitar, giving you the finger, and stumbling dramatically out the door," John Barnard wrote for the Baltimore *City Paper* (December 3, 2003, on-line). "The chapter-vignettes, while perhaps revealing as 'slices of life,' do very little in terms of story or character development. What we're left with is a disjointed series of snapshots of a world in which nobody has a name or a profession, and everyone is tortured, codependent, and prone to sexual assault or self-mutilation. It's a world so devoid of reality that there's no possible Archimedean point from which the suggested 'extremity' of our protagonists' lives can gain any purchase. The characters simply drift through these episodes, chugging beers, lying on the couch, weeping, smoking, criticizing others, and more or less begging the reader to jump in, slap them, and point out that this sort of self-indulgence, never mind its life-defeating qualities, won't even make for good fiction." In a review for *Library Journal* (December 2003, on-line), Andrea Kempf strongly disagreed, writing, "Stern's poetic depiction of codependency enhances this heartbreaking story of a young college student who becomes the girlfriend of an alcoholic rock musician. . . . Each haunting vignette demonstrates her identification with the lost, the damaged, the brutalized. Stern is a writer and a poet with the ability to select just the right phrase to create the sense of despair and hopelessness that her protagonist experiences. Her first novel has a ring of truth that comes from close observation and/or personal experience. With its self-destructive main characters, this moody novella will strongly resonate with those who came of age in the 1990s."

Stern—who currently lives in the New York City borough of Brooklyn and teaches in a public middle school—is working on a novel tentatively titled "The Guthrie Test," which she expects to complete by the time "my nine year old niece has [her own] children," as she quipped on her Amazon.com Weblog. The novel, like *The Long Haul*, will explore themes of addiction and relationships.

Stern has been the recipient of writing fellowships at Yaddo and the MacDowell Colony. "Lately, I've been doing some of my best writing in Cape Cod," she told Armin. "When I arrived home from MacDowell in December I realized that I loved nature. Having been born and raised in Greenwich Village I was an avowed concrete elitist, but that's been slipping with age, and I get a lot of perspective when I leave here."

—C. M.

Suggested Reading: Amanda Stern's Web site; (Baltimore) *City Paper* (on-line) Dec. 3, 2003; Bookslut.com; *Ottawa Citizen* C p10 Oct. 19, 2003; *Publishers Weekly* p37 Oct. 20, 2003; *Word Riot* (on-line)

Selected Books: *The Long Haul*, 2003

Stern, Steve

Dec. 21, 1947– Novelist; children's book writer

Much like one of the South's most acclaimed writers, William Faulkner, the native Tennessean Steve Stern has centered most of his novels and short stories in one Southern locale—but unlike Faulkner, whose Yoknapatawpha County existed only in his fiction, Stern writes about a historical place, the Pinch, a Depression-era, Jewish-immigrant enclave in Memphis. "I have a love-hate relationship with the South," Stern told Morris Dickstein for the *New York Times Book Review* (March 1, 1987). "I don't understand why I continue to return there. So 'Southern writer' is a label I'm uncomfortable with. As for being a 'Jewish writer,' well, that feels strange, too. There was very little Jewish content in my growing up. I'm just drawn to Jewish sources and Jewish folklore the same way I seem to be drawn to the damn South. If there's anything that made my being Southern and Jewish necessary and important to my fiction, it's that the combination of the two serves to provide a sense of community."

Steve Stern supplied the following autobiographical statement to *World Authors 2000–2005*:

"Growing up, I had a tenuous relation to my own heritage. Tenuous to non-existent. Raised in a Reform synagogue in Memphis, Tennessee, which had expunged most vestiges of Old World tradition from its liturgy, I had little knowledge of or interest in the Jewish past. Classically assimilated and unbelieving, I was pleased that nothing beyond the map of Jerusalem on my face identified my otherwise invisible religious provenance. But that was before I had begun to write fiction. Once I did, I was assaulted by echoes from an undigested past, and in my case the echoes tolled louder than the original noise. Helpless to do other than listen, I was shocked and surprised (I still am) by how seductive I found the music. So seductive, in fact, that I could have wished myself lashed more

securely to the mast of the 20th century. Enticed despite myself, however, I began to imagine the mysterious transit of the blood in my own body's arteries: how it might have issued initially from the heart of some bearded Talmudist conning his Hebrew text in a tumbledown studyhouse in Pshitsk, how the blood had thinned over time to an eventual trickle as it branched like a river delta toward a desert suburb in Tennessee. It was a comfortable, nostalgic conceit. But there must also have been something of the Huck Finn impulse left over from my Southern heritage at work, an adventuring impulse that made me want to untether myself from my own moment in time, to build a raft and paddle upstream to visit that noisome old Talmudist.

"It was a longer and more arduous journey than I'd counted on. En route I wrote a story called 'Lazar Malkin Enters Heaven' about an old man too obstinate to die, who is dragged off to paradise by a frustrated malech hamovess, the Angel of Death, while still alive. I thought myself very clever. But not long after, having begun the process of following the echoes back to their source, I discovered the legend of Enoch to whom only a couple of lines are devoted in the Book of Genesis. 'He walked with God, and was not,' says the verse, and that was apparently all it took to trigger among the rabbis, for whom Scripture was a kind of trampoline, a whole mystical literature about Enoch the cobbler, who for his righteousness was translated to heaven alive. There he became the recording archangel Metatron who sits at God's right hand. I read about Serah bat Asher, the original prototype of the Wandering Jew, who endured on earth for many centuries before she too was taken to heaven alive. Then there were the tales of the prophet Elijah, who regularly commutes between heaven and earth in his tatterdemalion disguise, dispensing mischief and mitzvot [a meritorious or charitable act] in equal portions; and the cautionary legend of 'The Four Who Entered Paradise'—'. . . and only Rabbi Akiba descended in peace'; for it's a dangerous business to trespass in heaven. Suddenly I didn't feel so clever anymore. Having tugged at the branches of my meager sapling of a story, I'd pulled up a root system as large as a giant sequoia's."

Steve Stern was born on December 21, 1947 in Memphis, Tennessee, to Rose (Lipman) Stern, a homemaker, and Sol Stern, a grocer. After earning his bachelor's degree in English from Rhodes College (also in Memphis), in 1970, Stern led something of a bohemian life, living in various places, including New Orleans, London, and a commune in Arkansas. He was often unemployed during that time, which he described to Elizabeth H. Brandon, writing for *Rhodes* (Winter 2006), as a decade "full of false starts." He settled down long enough to earn his M.F.A. in creative writing from the University of Arkansas, in Fayetteville, in 1977.

Stern's big break came in 1981, when he won the O. Henry Award for the short story "Isaac and the Undertaker's Daughter," which originally appeared in the literary magazine *Epoch* (Spring–Summer 1979). That piece became the titular story of his first book, which was published in 1983 and received the Pushcart Writer's Choice Award. "These seven stories [in *Isaac and the Undertaker's Daughter*], written with great brio, portray zany Jewish family life ever so slightly haunted by demons," Susan Sontag wrote, according to the Lost Roads Publishers Web site. "Steve Stern may be a late practitioner of the genre, but he is an expert one. Whiplash sentences, lots of energy and charm."

That same year, 1983, Stern took a job with the Center for Southern Folklore's Ethnic Heritage Program, for which he recorded the memories of surviving residents of the Memphis neighborhood known as the Pinch; in the city's early days, it was called "Pinchgut," in reference to the malnourished look of the Irish railroad workers who shared the neighborhood with Jewish merchants. Stern told Roy Hoffman for the *New York Times* (November 12, 1986) that the recollections of these elderly Jewish residents "lent a vitality to my stories I could never conjure on my own." In 1984 Stern published his first novel, *The Moon and Ruben Shein* (1984), the tale of a writer who inherits a wife and a mistress, after his literary mentor commits suicide. While the book garnered some critical praise, it received little publicity.

From 1985 to 1986 Stern worked as a visiting lecturer at the Memphis College of Art, and in 1987, while teaching at the University of Wisconsin, Madison, he published his second collection of stories, *Lazar Malkin Enters Heaven.* Morris Dickstein praised the book, calling Stern "a prodigiously talented writer from Memphis, who arrives unheralded like one of the apparitions in his own stories." All of the stories in the collection are set in the Pinch, with the exception of the concluding story, "The Ghost of Saul Bozoff," which is set in a New England writers' colony much like the MacDowell Colony in New Hampshire, which Stern had visited as a fellow in 1985. In this metafictional story, Saul Bozoff, a writer who serves as Stern's alter ego and reappears in his later work, is haunted by the spirit of a young Jewish woman who died in the early 20th century. She convinces Bozoff to collaborate with her in the writing of the stories that she was unable to complete due to her untimely death. "'The Ghost and Saul Bozoff,' [is] more like a self-reflective essay than a fully realized piece of fiction," Dickstein wrote. "It deals with a brooding writer—the archetypal figure of Jewish anxiety and self-doubt—who, finding himself surrounded by natural beauty in an idyllic New England writers'

colony, is quite incapable of doing any work." Dickstein concluded: "Reaching back to a neglected corner of the Jewish psyche, [Stern] has taken well-worn materials and turned them alchemically into something rich and strange."

Though *Lazar Malkin Goes to Heaven* was critically acclaimed and won the Edward Lewis Wallant Award for Jewish American literature, the book did not enjoy great commercial success, due in part to a lawsuit that delayed the release of the paperback edition. One of Stern's characters shared the name of a deceased resident of the Pinch, and one of that man's descendants sued both the author and his publisher, Viking. Though the descendant did not win his suit, Stern was careful to select a fairly common Jewish surname for the hero of his next novel, *Harry Kaplan's Adventures Underground* (1991). Also set in the Pinch, it is the story of a 15-year-old boy, Harry, whose father moves the family from Brighton Beach, Brooklyn, to Memphis, so that he can open a pawn shop with the help of his slightly crooked brother, Morris. Harry escapes from his dreary world by reading adventure stories and is brought back to reality only by the Great Flood of 1939—at which point his life begins to mimic the stories he so admires. "Steve Stern has written a novel that evokes many of the virtues (inventiveness, playfulness, great narrative energy) of Harry's romantic literary models; unfortunately, it also shares some of their flaws," Francine Prose wrote for the *Washington Post Book World* (March 31, 1991). "What boys' adventure stories lack—and why few adults read them—are certain felicities and freshness of language, depth of perception and characterization, and that sense of form and control that makes us feel that experience is being reshaped and transformed into art. . . . Reading Steve Stern's novel seems, at moments, like spending time with a boy Harry's age—the kid keeps reaching too far, trying too hard, miscalculating and failing. Even so, he's much more endearing than many cooler, knowing adults who have learned precisely how much (and how little) to offer, and to give." Jay Rogoff, however, writing for the *Sewanee Review* (Winter 1993), argued that Stern "has done as much as anyone to further the art of Jewish southern writing," noting that "through two books of short stories and this, his second novel, *Harry Kaplan's Adventures Underground*, he has concocted a southern-fried chicken plate of picaresque, fable, and fantasy garnished by shimmering prose, shrewd characterizations, and hilarious invention."

In *A Plague of Dreamers* (1994), which includes three novellas, Stern related the tales of a trio of eccentric loners living in the Pinch, a place that Mark Shechner, writing for the *Chicago Tribune* (January 30, 1994), described as "a magic kingdom along Memphis, Tennessee's North Main Street": "Here the supernatural exchanges marriage vows with the domestic; the dream life jostles the commercial; teen-age boys climb trees into the collective unconscious; death is provisional; golems, devils and fallen angels in shabby rooms watch reruns of *The Millionaire* on television." According to Stuart Schoffman, in a review for the *Jerusalem Report* (June 2, 1994), "*A Plague of Dreamers* is a post-modern celebration of Jewish vitality, a joyous melting-down and recasting of traditional lore, a grab-bag of ideas liberated from the intellectuals who invented them. For Stern and his heroes, the past is an albatross transformed into a phoenix, a gilgul, or reincarnation, that honors the ancient masters whose language is lost to Americans, but whose stories are too strong and stubborn to die."

With *The Wedding Jester* (1999), which won the National Jewish Book Award, Stern continued to "stake out his own unique territory where history and myth intersect, where Jewish legends, mysticism and ancient traditions implode into the everyday with dazzling and unforeseen consequences," according to a reviewer for *Publishers Weekly* (May 10, 1999). For example, in the title story, a bride who is holding her wedding at an old resort in the Catskills becomes possessed by the dybbuk (a restless spirit or demon) of an old Borscht Belt comedian. Once in front of the alter, she begins to spew forth a stream of jokes in the man's voice—that is, until Saul Bozoff exorcises the dybbuk with a kabbalistic kissing technique. "This irreverent, classic story plumbs Jewish humor as a source of strength, a survival tool, a vehicle to resist cant and conformity," the *Publishers Weekly* reviewer wrote. "Stern's tales utterly transport readers into a fully realized world, whether the setting is the neurotic, Seinfeld-like milieu of a Manhattan writer ('Bruno's Metamorphosis'), or czarist Russia's Jewish ghetto and New York's Lower East Side ('Romance'), or Stern's favorite haunt, a Memphis, [Tennessee] Jewish community in uneasy coexistence with its gentile neighbors ('Tale of a Kite'). With empathy and bracing wit, Stern's enjoyable stories seismically chart the collision of the Old World and the New, of undying religious traditions and modern secularism, of lust and love, faith and doubt."

Saul Bozoff appears again in *The Angel of Forgetfulness* (2005), sharing the narrative with Nathan Hart, a journalist for a Yiddish newspaper in the early part of the 20th century. Together they relate a multitude of interwoven stories: in 1969, when Bozoff is a student at Columbia University, in New York City, an elderly woman gives him a copy of one of Hart's manuscripts, "The Angel of Forgetfulness," which relates the tale of Mocky, an angel who, in 17th-century Russia, becomes mortal for the love of a woman. Back in his own time, Hart attempts to seduce a lovely young girl with his manuscript, and within that narrative the reader is introduced to the adventures of Mocky's son, Nachman Opgekumener. In the *Washington Post Book World* (April 3, 2005), Michael Dirda described the novel as "touching, funny and dizzying as well as delicate in its virtuosity," and praised Stern's adeptness at interweaving a "clutch of narratives that, we gradually come to realize, are fugal variations on the same story." Dirda argued, "Steve Stern isn't as well known as he should be, but he belongs in the same company as Stanley Elkin and Cynthia Ozick, Michael Chabon and Mark Helprin, Melvin Jules Bukiet and Philip Roth. All of these might be thought of, very loosely, as innovative and restless practitioners of contemporary American-Jewish fantasy." A critic for *Kirkus Reviews* (December 15, 2004) also compared Stern's work to that of other great Jewish writers, albeit in a less flattering manner, noting that Bozoff, a "neurotic, virginal, self-pitying character," who may as well have stepped "straight from the pages of Woody Allen, Philip Roth and Bernard Malamud." The reviewer further complained that while the "time periods of the three narratives offer Stern rich potential," the author "seems never to have met a detail, character or subplot he didn't like, unleashing a torrent of verbiage that obscures and overwhelms his considerations of art and reality, heaven and earth."

Stern has also published two children's books *Mickey and the Golem* (1986) and *Hershel and the Beast* (1987). He told David Margolis, in an interview for the *Jerusalem Report* (April 8, 2005), that he is working on a novel about a Southern suburban boy who finds a frozen rabbi from Eastern Europe in his family's freezer.

Stern was briefly married in the 1980s and has no children. He first began teaching at Skidmore College, in Saratoga Springs, New York, as a visiting lecturer in 1988; he now teaches English there as a full professor.

—S.Y.

Suggested Reading: *Chicago Tribune* C p6 Jan. 30, 1994; *Jerusalem Post* July 17, 1991; *Jerusalem Report* p46 June 2, 1994, p40 Apr. 18, 2005; *Los Angeles Times* E p23 Mar. 11, 2005; *Los Angeles Times Book Review* p6 May 24, 1987; *New York Times* C p1 Nov. 12, 1986, E p3 Apr. 25, 2005; *New York Times Book Review* p11 Mar. 1, 1987; *Sewanee Review* Winter 1993; *Washington Post Book World* p8 Mar. 31, 1991, p15 Apr. 3, 2005

Selected Books: fiction—*Isaac and the Undertaker's Daughter*, 1983; *The Moon and Ruben Shein*, 1984; *Lazar Malkin Enters Heaven*, 1986; *Harry Kaplan's Adventures Underground*, 1991; *A Plague of Dreamers*, 1994; *The Wedding Jester*, 1999; *The Angel of Forgetfulness*, 2005; children's fiction—*Mickey and the Golem*, 1986; *Hershel and the Beast*, 1987

Szpilman, Wladyslaw

(SHPIL-man, vwah-DEE-
swahf)

Dec. 5, 1911–July 6, 2000 Memoirist

While Wladyslaw Szpilman was first and foremost a musician, he is equally known as the author of an affecting memoir, *The Pianist*, which he wrote shortly after World War II. The story of his survival during the Nazi occupation of his native Poland, the book was made, in 2002, into an acclaimed film, which won three Academy Awards.

Szpilman was born in Sosnowiec, Poland, on December 5, 1911, into a family of accomplished musicians. He studied the piano at the Chopin School of Music, in Warsaw, and in 1931 he traveled to Berlin, Germany, to continue his studies. There he began composing some of his most memorable pieces. In 1935 he returned to Poland to work as a pianist for Polish State Radio, in Warsaw. In September 1939, while Szpilman was performing Frédéric Chopin's "Nocturne in C Sharp Minor," the studio was bombed, as the Nazis invaded the city.

Like all the other Jews in the city, Szpilman was forced to live in the infamous Warsaw Ghetto, and one day, along with his entire family, he was taken to a railyard to be transported to Treblinka, a notorious Nazi death camp. Szpilman was pulled from the line by a policeman who recognized him from the local cafés, where the musician sometimes played the piano. His parents and siblings were sent to Treblinka, where they ultimately perished. Szpilman hid in a succession of apartments owned by non-Jewish friends, and even after the city was practically deserted, he remained—finding shelter in bombed-out houses and scavenging for food. "Afterwards, when the story emerged, he was called the Robinson Crusoe of Warsaw," Jay Rayner wrote for the London *Observer* (March 28, 1999, on-line). "It gives the tale a romantic edge, but there is no romance here, no poetry, just a bleak animalistic survival."

One day, as Szpilman was trying to use a fireplace poker to open a can of food he had scavenged, he was discovered by a German officer, Wilm Hosenfeld, whom he describes in his memoir as "the one human being wearing a German uniform that I met." Hosenfeld, a music lover, was moved to help Szpilman after hearing that he was a pianist. (Fortuitously, there was a piano in the home in which Szpilman had been scavenging, and he played Chopin's "Nocturne in C Sharp Minor" as proof of his talent.) Hosenfeld found Szpilman a safe hiding place and occasionally visited, bringing news and food. In this way Szpilman survived the war, and in 1945 he wrote *The Pianist*.

The book was first published in Poland, in 1946, but it was soon suppressed by Communist authorities, who were unhappy that the book featured a German hero and contained laudatory descriptions of the anti-Communist Polish underground. Szpilman, unconcerned that the memoir was out of print—he did not really consider himself an author—went on to become the director of music at the state-run radio station (from 1945 to 1963), composed an estimated 500 more pieces of music, and established a career as an international concert pianist. In 1998, thanks in large part to the efforts of Szpilman's son Andrzej, who lived in Germany, the book was translated and published in that country. (Because Szpilman never talked about the war, Andrzej had been unaware, throughout most of his childhood, of his father's experiences; at the age of 12, however, he came across the memoir hidden on a high shelf.) The book was translated into English and published in the U.S. in 1999. Marie Marmo, writing for *Library Journal* (August 1999), called the memoir "an important addition to Holocaust literature," and in a review for the *Times Literary Supplement* (April 23, 1999), David Pryce-Jones observed: "The simplicity of what [Szpilman] had to say is terrifying."

Szpilman died on July 6, 2000 in Warsaw, a city he had refused to abandon despite the hardships he had suffered there. "It is the only city in the world where I can live," he had told Karen Glaser, in an interview for the *Jewish Chronicle* (March 19, 1999, on-line).

A film version of *The Pianist* was released in 2002; it won Academy Awards in the categories of best director (Roman Polanski), best actor (Adrien Brody), and best adapted screenplay. Andrzej Szpilman, now a doctor, attended the awards ceremony. "Szpilman is played in the film by Adrien Brody," Roger Ebert wrote for the *Chicago Sun-Times* (Jan. 3, 2003, on-line). "We sense that his Szpilman is a man who came early and seriously to music, knows he is good, and has a certain aloofness to life around him. More than once we hear him reassuring others that everything will turn out all right; this faith is based not on information or even optimism, but essentially on his belief that, for anyone who plays the piano as well as he does, it must." Ebert continued, "Polanski himself is a Holocaust survivor, saved at one point when his father pushed him through the barbed wire of a camp. He wandered Krakow and Warsaw, a frightened child, cared for by the kindness of strangers. His own survival (and that of his father) are in a sense as random as Szpilman's, which is perhaps why he was attracted to this story. . . . By showing Szpilman as a survivor but not a fighter or a hero—as a man who does all he can to save himself, but would have died without enormous good luck and the kindness of a few non-Jews—Polanski is reflecting, I believe, his own deepest feelings: that he survived, but need not have, and that his mother died and left a wound that had never healed." The film, Ebert concluded, "refuses to turn Szpilman's survival into a triumph and records it primarily as the story of a witness who was there, saw, and remembers."

—C.M.

Suggested Reading: *Chicago Sun-Times* (on-line) Jan. 3, 2003; *Choice* p1,351 Mar. 2000; *Jewish Chronicle* (on-line) Mar. 19, 1999; *Library Journal* p116 Aug. 1999; (London) *Observer* (on-line) Mar. 28, 1999; *Times Literary Supplement* p30 Apr. 23, 1999

Selected Books in English Translation: *The Pianist,* 1999

Alberto Pizzoli/AFP/Getty Images

Tabucchi, Antonio

(tah-BOO-key)

Sep. 23, 1943– Novelist; short-story writer; translator

Over the past 30 years, Antonio Tabucchi's oeuvre has put him at the forefront of postmodern Italian literature. "If a politician's job is to soothe people, to show that all's well because of his or her presence, mine is to disturb people, to sow the seeds of doubt," Tabucchi remarked in an interview with Asbel Lopez for the *UNESCO Courier* (November 1999, on-line). "The capacity to doubt is very important for human beings. For heaven's sake, if we don't have any doubts, we're finished!" Because of their often plotless structure and oneiric atmosphere, Tabucchi's books have sometimes elicited doubts from reviewers but few, however, have questioned his talent.

While traveling through Europe by rail as a young man, Tabucchi had read a verse by the Portuguese poet Fernando Pessoa. Always an ardent lover of books, Tabucchi then embarked upon a lifelong fascination with the Portuguese language and its literature, and with the help of his wife, Maria José de Lancastre, a native of Lisbon, he has since translated most of Pessoa's works into Italian. Portugal also became the setting for many of his own pieces, and eventually, he wrote a novel, *Requiem: A Hallucination*, in his adopted language.

Antonio Tabucchi was born on September 23, 1943 in Pisa, Italy. At that time the Nazis had invaded the country, and the Allies had responded by bombarding Pisa. Many of the windows in the local hospital had been blown out, and doctors had sent home all of their patients—except Signora Tabucchi, who was already in labor. Tabucchi told Graham Fawcett for the London *Independent* (July 7, 1991), "My father came to fetch us the next day. On his bicycle. It was his only means of transport. My mother sat on the crossbar, holding me in her arms. The road was a mass of bomb craters. Every so often my father had to get off his bike, wheel us down into a crater and up the other side, and then remount and cycle on." Fawcett commented that Tabucchi related the story as though he himself—at just one day old—truly remembered the events and was not simply reciting an oft-repeated family tale. "This touches a more consistent feeling I get from reading a work [by Tabucchi] such as *The Woman of Porto Pim* [1983]: one minute I think I am being told the truth, the next, the narrator seems to be taking me for a ride. Was this my problem, I asked him, or his trick?" Tabucchi responded, "*The Woman of Porto Pim* is a small book about shipwrecks. Real shipwrecks, existential, psychological, all sorts of shipwrecks. And to shipwreck the reader is something which appeals to me."

Little has been published in English-language sources about Tabucchi's childhood, but the writer told Fawcett that he had grown up in his maternal grandparents' home in the village of Vecchiano, where he found his first literary influences. "[My grandparents] were old people who would have their friends round in the evenings and tell each other stories of Tuscany and the First World War, which they had all fought in," Tabucchi told Fawcett. "My grandfather told me about the firing squad he'd watched. It was at their house that I learned to listen." He also came to love many of the authors he found in the library of an intellectual uncle, an unpublished playwright.

Tabucchi attended the University of Pisa, and during his breaks he traveled throughout Europe, following the paths of the authors he admired. It was during one of his journeys through Paris that he stumbled upon a book by Pessoa. His fascination with one particular poem, "Tabacaria" (which means tobacco shop), and Pessoa's use of heteronyms inspired him to learn Portuguese. (The term heteronym, which also refers to sets of words that are spelled the same but have different pronunciations and meanings, means, in a literary sense, imaginary characters who write in various styles. A heteronym differs from a simple pen name in that its creator develops an entire fictitious persona to go along with it.) Pessoa predominately employed three heteronyms (in addition to using his own name and style)— Alberto Caeiro, Ricardo Reis, and Alvaro de Campos—but according to some sources, he occasionally used some 70 others. (The book that Tabucchi had discovered in the Parisian bookstall near the Gare de Lyon was attributed to Alvaro de Campos.)

Tabucchi began translating Pessoa's works into Italian and was inspired to visit Portugal, especially Lisbon. In 1969 he graduated from the University of Pisa, after completing his thesis, "Surrealism in Portugal." He furthered his education at the Scuola Normale Superiore di Pisa, a university center for teaching and research, and after graduation, in 1973, he accepted a post teaching Portuguese language and literature at a school in Bologna, Italy. Two years later his first novel, *Piazza d'Italia*, was published. Tabucchi told Asbel Lopez, "My first novel . . . was an attempt to write history that hasn't been written, history as written by the losing side, in this case the Tuscan anarchists. My books are about losers, about people who've lost their way and are engaged in a search."

In 1978 Tabucchi began teaching Portuguese literature at the University of Genoa, a post he held until 1987. In 1984 his short novel *Notturno indiano* (released five years later in English translation as *Indian Nocturne*) was published; in 1987 it was awarded France's Prix Médicis for best foreign novel. *Indian Nocturne* is the story of a nameless European man who travels throughout India—equipped with a *Lonely Planet* guidebook—in the dream-like state of an insomniac. The narrative unfolds via his conversations with various characters. Amy Edith Johnson, in a representatively mixed notice, wrote for the *New York Times Book Review* (July 16, 1989), "Tabucchi manages to convey a great deal in these few pages. It is a rich portrait of slivers of the country, an impressive construction though one with little solidity or meat to it." Similarly, Geoffrey Moorhouse, in a review for the London *Guardian* (December 25, 1988), generally enjoyed the book but complained, "The ending . . . is opaque; and we are left pondering some bits and pieces of illusion."

In 1991 Tabucchi was awarded a chair at the University of Siena, where he still teaches for half of the year. (He spends the other half in Portugal.) In 1994 he published *Requiem: A Hallucination*— his first and only book written in Portuguese. The short novel takes place on a hot Sunday in July, when the narrator, via oneiric visions, explores Lisbon. He meets friends, family, and an assortment of locals, but his main goal is to reach an appointment with a poet reminiscent of Pessoa. Detailed attention is given to eating and drinking throughout the text, and Tabucchi has included recipes for various dishes eaten by his main character.

The blurriness of *Requiem*'s narrative emphasizes the mental state of the narrator, who is trapped between dream and reality. Tabucchi explained the importance of this particular state on his writing process: "I converse with my characters in the moments between waking and sleeping— when the super-ego relaxes its control and the cautious surveillance of the intellect is dulled," he told Harriet Paterson for the London *Independent* (May 14, 1994). "Only then does one become open, without received ideas."

As the title suggests, death is a prominent theme in the book, but there is a redemptive quality in the text. "Although *Requiem* deals with death," Tabucchi told Paterson. "It is light-hearted: the dead return to life and start feasting. They have the chance to revisit past misunderstandings, seek explanations. It is a luxury, a Freudian analysis of oneself." Ronald De Feo wrote for the *Nation* (June 6, 1999), "In the hands of a less accomplished and more solemn writer all of this material might have become exceedingly heavy, depressing and mawkish, but Tabucchi balances the somberness with such good spirits that the novel, which is as much meditation as hallucination, is actually great fun to read."

For Tabucchi's next novel, *Sostiene Pereira* (*Pereira Declares*), he returned to writing in Italian. The book, published in 1996, remained on the Italian best-seller charts for months and became his most well-known novel to date. Set in the 1930s, during the first years of Antonio Salazar's dictatorship in Portugal, the novel tells of an intellectual who directs the cultural page of a Lisbon daily newspaper, *Lisboa*. The protagonist's life is significantly altered when he hires a young man to write obituaries for public figures who have not yet died. The book provided Tabucchi with a vehicle in which to express his fervent anti-fascist sentiments. Anthony Constantini wrote for *World Literature Today* (Summer 1995), "*Sostiene Pereira* has been received extremely well by the critics, especially the progressive ones. They see it as a well-developed example of sociopolitical engagement wherein the private life and public life of an individual merge to create a character representing the intellectual's situation during the period of Fascism." He continued, "However, this unanimous praise is, to say the least, suspicious, and could very well be dictated by Italy's political situation in the early part of 1994 . . . [when Silvio Berlusconi, the prime minister elected in April of that year, established an ultra–right wing government, the first in more than three decades]. It could be that the progressive intellectuals saw this book as an interpretation of their current convictions." Other critics separated the novel from the concurrent political climate in Italy. Paterson, writing again for the London *Independent* (January 6, 1996), examined the novel in light of Tabucchi's previous works: "Tabucchi's writing has taken on a new departure. It is less abstract and cerebral, more directly concerned with character than in the past. Surrealism and dreamlike ambiguity have given way to firmer ground—to a thoroughly unified examination of the transformation of one's heart." She concluded, "Tabucchi has created that rare thing, a literary character so real that he possesses a life independent of the book that temporarily framed him."

In 1997 Tabucchi published *La testa perduta di Damasceno Monteiro* (translated into English as *The Missing Head of Damasceno Monteiro* in 2000), again choosing a political theme. The novel was based on an actual unsolved incident, in which a man had been murdered and decapitated in an office of the Republican National Guard (RNG), a paramilitary security organization. Tabucchi's protagonist, Firmino, a young journalist, chronicles the events and interviews witnesses: a crew of intellectuals, transvestites, Gypsies, and lower-class workers. The novel attracted increased interest soon after its publication, when an RPG officer confessed to the real-life murder and was subsequently sentenced to 17 years. "*The Missing Head of Damasceno Monteiro* is a gripping read," Marion Lignana Rosenberg wrote for the on-line magazine *Salon* (January 5, 2000). "Lithe, elegantly plotted and, with its unblinking scrutiny of the measures deployed against 'people aiming to subvert our culture,' disconcertingly timely for readers on both sides of the Atlantic." Michael Pye, in a review for the *New York Times* (February 20, 2000), was critical of Tabucchi's didactic bent and believed that "much of [the novel] works very well, but you should be warned about Tabucchi's tendency to slam the door on the captive reader and start a seminar. Indeed, explicit thought sometimes upsets Tabucchi's book the way explicit sex upsets lesser writers—because although it's great fun, it makes you suspicious of everything else." Still, he concluded, "You may sometimes want to snort with exasperation and send Tabucchi's book [skidding] across the room. But, then again, when did you last find a novel this interesting?"

Tabucchi's most recent book in English translation, *It's Getting Later All the Time,* was published in 2006. An epistolary novel divided into 18 chapters, *It's Getting Later All the Time* features 17 letters written by men to an unnamed woman or women; the final letter is from a woman who universally addresses all of the men, offering advice and answering their questions. "Taken linearly, these letters . . . don't make any more sense than scenes in a Fellini movie. But . . . to look for logic is to miss the point," Andrew Ervin wrote for the *New York Times* (September 24, 2006). "The subtle relationships between the

letters turn out to be more thematic than literal, though they eventually come together in a brilliantly unexpected way."

For his contributions to literature, Antonio Tabucchi was named to the order of Infante Dom Henrique by the president of Portugal, and the French government named him Chevalier des Arts et des Lettres. Tabucchi is a regular contributor to the Italian newspapers *Corriere della Sera* and *El Pais*, and he continues to publish work about Pessoa, including *The Last Three Days of Pessoa* (1994)—a metaphysical recounting of the end of the poet's life. (In 2000 *The Last Three Days of Pessoa* was published in a volume that also includes *Dream of Dreams*, in which Tabucchi imagines the dreams of such figures as the painter Caravaggio, the poet Arthur Rimbaud, and the psychoanalyst Sigmund Freud.)

Tabucchi, who has written many works not yet available in English translation, is a founding member of the International Parliament of Writers (IPW), an organization that helps writers who are in exile for political reasons. He and his wife, a fellow academic to whom he has been married since 1970, have a daughter who, he has said, "is more Portuguese than Italian and a son who is more Italian than Portuguese," as Robert Gray quoted for *Eclectica* (October/November 2005, on-line).

—F.C.

Suggested Reading: *Eclectica* (on-line) Oct./Nov. 2005; *Hindu* (on-line) Nov. 2, 2000; (London) *Independent* p26 July 7, 1991, p31, May 14, 1994, p11, Jan. 6, 1996; *Nation* p802 June 6, 1994; *New York Times* VII p17 Feb. 20, 2000, VII p22 Sep. 24, 2006; *UNESCO Courier* (on-line) 1999; *World Literature Today* p565 Summer 1995

Selected Books in English Translation: *The Woman of Porto Pim*, 1983; *Indian Nocturne*, 1989; *Requiem: A Hallucination*, 1994; *Pereira Declares*, 1996; *The Missing Head of Damasceno Monteiro*, 2000; *It's Getting Later All the Time*, 2006

Tartt, Donna

Dec. 23, 1963– Novelist

To read Donna Tartt's first novel, *The Secret History* (1992), "is to undergo an esoteric initiation rite—to join a secretive cult made up of more than 5 million readers in 24 countries," A. O. Scott wrote for the *New York Times Book Review* (November 3, 2002). The novel, begun while Tartt was a student at Bennington College, in Vermont, and published when she was 28, focused on a group of highly intellectual young men and

Bruno Vincent/Getty Images

Donna Tartt

women engaged in debauchery and, ultimately, murder—and turned its author into an instant celebrity. "This moody thriller," Vanessa Thorpe wrote for the London *Observer* (July 28, 2002), "has entered the cult literary canon, alongside J. D. Salinger's *The Catcher in the Rye* and Joseph Heller's *Catch-22*." A decade passed before the appearance of Tartt's second novel, *The Little Friend*, the story of a pre-adolescent girl's obsession with avenging the death of her brother. The general consensus among critics was that the new novel was worth the wait.

Donna Tartt was born on December 23, 1963 in Greenwood, Mississippi, to Don Tartt, who was active in local politics, and his wife, Taylor. Her parents took her when she was very young to Grenada, Mississippi, where her grandmothers and what she has termed a "bevy" of great-aunts helped to raise her. A precocious child, she wrote her first poem at the age of five and published a sonnet in a literary journal at 13. (She managed such accomplishments despite, or perhaps because of, the fact that when she was a child and had a cough, her great-grandfather would give her a mixture of whiskey and codeine-laced cough syrup; she wrote in *Harper's* [July 1992] that she consequently spent much of her childhood in a hallucinatory state.)

In the private high school she attended, Tartt became a cheerleader. During that period she also read the works of George Orwell; his novel *Animal Farm* "upset me a little, especially the end," but its "statement ALL ANIMALS ARE EQUAL, BUT SOME ANIMALS ARE MORE EQUAL THAN OTHERS echoed sentiments that I recognized as prevalent in the upper echelons of the

cheerleading squad," Tartt wrote in the essay "Team Spirit," published in *Harper's* (April 1994). She added that the cheerleaders fell into two categories: the "snobs," the girls who were from wealthier families, had "flat chests, and were skittish and shrill," and the "sluts," who were "from poorer families, and much better liked in general. . . . Physically and economically, I fell into the category of snob, but I did poorly in school and was not gung ho or clubbish enough to fit in very well with the rest of them." Also, as she wrote in her essay, "I was fourteen years old then and failing algebra and the fact that I was failing it worried me as I would worry now if the Mafia were after me, or if I had shot somebody and the police were coming to get me."

Her math grades notwithstanding, Tartt enrolled at the University of Mississippi, at Oxford, in 1981. Her literary efforts during her freshman year drew the attention of the novelist Willie Morris, who was a writer in residence at the university. For the London *Guardian* (July 20, 2002), Tartt contributed a tribute to Morris, who died in 1999. "Never," she wrote, "will I forget my naive astonishment at discovering that there existed another person who loved words in much the same sputtering and agonised way that I did, who fought them and cursed them and cried over them and stood back, dazzled and agog in admiration of them. After all those years isolated in my hometown, shut up in my bedroom reading books, I had thought I was the only person in the world so afflicted." Morris recommended Tartt to Barry Hannah, also a writer in residence, who admitted her to his graduate course in short-story writing. Morris and other teachers at the school persuaded Tartt to transfer to Bennington College because of its well-known writing program and because she craved the sort of less-restrictive environment it offered. At Bennington she began to work on *The Secret History*. Also while there she became friends with the writers Jill Eisenstadt and Bret Easton Ellis; she would dedicate *The Secret History* to Ellis, who read the novel in manuscript form during the eight years she spent writing it. Ellis also introduced her to the literary agent Amanda Urban, who was as smitten with Tartt's writing as Morris and Hannah had been. As a result *The Secret History* was sold to the highest bidder—Knopf—for $450,000, became a best-seller, and established Tartt as a noteworthy young author.

The Secret History's title comes from that of a work by the sixth-century Byzantine historian Procopius, which details the goings-on of that region and era. Tartt's novel is set at the fictional Hampden College, in Vermont, in modern times, but harkens back to an earlier period. "I think we have much more in common now with the ancient Greeks than with, say, a medieval Christian," Tartt explained to Susannah Hunnewell in an interview for the *New York Times Book Review* (September 13, 1992). "We really do live in an age of new paganism. By the time Plato was writing, the Greek gods were as abstract as God is to us now. . . . No culture since the Greeks has had such a cult of youth as we have," she added. In the novel a small group of students fall under the spell of Julian, a charismatic teacher of classics with Dionysian pretensions, who proclaims, "The more cultivated a person is, the more intelligent, the more repressed, then the more he needs some method of channeling the primitive impulses he's worked so hard to kill." The students decide to "enter the unseen world" of "emotion, darkness, barbarism" by staging a bacchanal—a Dionysian orgy in the woods—involving a return to what Julian calls a "nonrational, pre-intellectual state," in which "dancing, frenzies, slaughter, visions" occur. All of these take place, and a farmer becomes the sacrificial victim. When one of the group, Bunny, who did not participate in the "rites," finds out about the murder, he blackmails the others. The members of group, who have now been joined by the narrator, Richard, a working-class outsider, decide to silence Bunny by killing him.

Critical response to *The Secret History* amounted to an almost universal recognition of Tartt's talent and originality as a writer—with some cavils about the excesses to which she had gone. A *Publishers Weekly* (June 29, 1992) reviewer found the best parts of the book to be those in which "Tartt describes the effect of the death on a small community, the behavior of the victim's family and the conspirators' emotional disintegration. Here her gifts for social satire and character analysis are shown to good advantage and her writing is powerful and evocative." Nancy Wood, writing for *Maclean's* (October 12, 1992), felt that Tartt's writing was "strongest when she finds poetry in everyday events: the sights and smells of a campus, the familiarity of certain television shows." She found the "obscure discussions about Greek philosophers and poets," into which the characters enter, to be somewhat pretentious on the part of the author. For the *New York Times* (September 4, 1992) reviewer Michiko Kakutani, the group of elitist students in the novel "are all such chilly customers" that "they do not so much lose their innocence as make a series of pragmatic, amoral decisions. As a result, real guilt and suffering do not occur in this novel; neither does redemption. The reader is simply left with a group portrait of the banality of evil." Nevertheless, Kakutani found the novel "a ferociously well-paced entertainment," which "succeeds magnificently. Forceful, cerebral and impeccably controlled, *The Secret History* achieves just what Ms. Tartt seems to have set out to do: it marches with cool, classical inevitability toward its terrible conclusion."

The fact that there was a 10-year interval between the publication of *The Secret History* and that of Tartt's second novel, *The Little Friend*, which appeared in 2002, meant that the latter book was greeted both with éclat and with a degree of scrutiny that it might not otherwise have received.

Tartt told Vanessa Thorpe that the story of a 12-year-old girl trying to avenge the hanging death of her brother is "a scary book about children coming into contact with the world of adults in a very frightening way." *The Little Friend*, set in a small Mississippi town like that of Tartt's own childhood, starts with a prologue in which nine-year-old Robin is found hanging from a tupelo tree near his family's home. The family proceeds to fall apart; the mother takes drugs and the father leaves for a job in another town. After 12 years have passed, Harriet, an infant at the time of the death, obsessively plots vengeance on Danny Ratliff, now a young man and an amphetamine addict, who Harriet believes murdered her brother. Danny and his brothers manufacture drugs in a shed on the edge of the town and are, in A. O. Scott's words, "like an infernal mirror image of Harriet's own family."

Some reviewers found that while Tartt's narrative skills had taken a downward turn with *The Little Friend*, her power to describe emotional states, particularly "the peculiar geography of childhood in all its dreamlike intensity and ennui," as Michiko Kakutani phrased it for the *New York Times* (October 17, 2002), had grown. Kakutani found that the "strongest portions of *The Little Friend* deal not with Harriet's vigilante actions but with her mundane, day-to-day life." Kakutani continued, "Tartt's portrait of the . . . family possesses all the detail and luminosity of an old platinum photograph." Daniel Mendelsohn, who reviewed *The Little Friend* for the *New Yorker* (October 28, 2002), observed that the novel "takes the shape of a murder mystery, but it's not really about a death at all. It's about a way of life. . . . The apparently haphazard accumulation of detail . . . leads to the true heart of Tartt's book: the recognition, crucial to adulthood, that we are all guilty, to some extent, and that we inevitably hurt those we love. Each of the seven sections of *The Little Friend* explores a guilty act. . . . However obliquely, this novel demonstrates the way in which guilt resides in the very fabric of a certain kind of small-town culture. . . . The terrible price that Harriet and those around her pay for her self-knowledge justifies her closing insight—a tragic but also decidedly Southern one—that 'victory and collapse were somehow the same thing.' . . . *The Little Friend* doesn't get where it was headed . . . , but there's no question that it takes you somewhere worth going."

Between the publication of *The Secret History* and that of *The Little Friend*, Tartt spent most of her time in New York City, with intervals in upstate New York and Grenada, Mississippi, her hometown. The success of *The Secret History* enabled her to buy a house near Charlottesville, Virginia. She has published stories in *Gentleman's Quarterly*, *Harper's*, and the *New Yorker*. The narrator of *The Secret History* remarks, "I suppose at one time in my life I might have had any number of stories, but now there is no other. This is the only story I will ever be able to tell"; it was feared for a time that the statement might apply to Tartt herself. On the topic of why her books take so long to write, Tartt told Caroline Frost for BBC Four (August 22, 2003, on-line) that she can remain "moving a comma round very happily for hours." Tartt said, "If I could write a book a year and maintain the same quality, I'd be happy [to]. But I don't think I'd have any fans."

—S.Y.

Suggested Reading: *Harper's* p60+ July 1992, p37+ Apr. 1994; (London) *Guardian* p28 July 20, 2002; (London) *Observer* p3 July 28, 2002; (London) *Sunday Times* (on-line) June 2, 2002; *New Republic* p47+ Oct. 19, 1992; *New York Times Book Review* p3 Sep. 13, 1992, p11 Nov. 3, 2002; *New Yorker* p109+ Oct. 28, 2002; *Time* p69 Aug. 31, 1992, p74 Oct. 21, 2002; *USA Today* D p8 Oct. 15, 2002

Selected Books: *The Secret History*, 1992; *The Little Friend*, 2002

Teachout, Terry

Feb. 6, 1956– Journalist; critic; editor

The journalist, critic, and editor Terry Teachout is the author of *The Skeptic: A Life of H. L. Mencken* (2002), about the notoriously opinionated and controversial journalist whose writings for the *Baltimore Sun* in the early 20th century helped define the age. In 1995 Teachout, who has had a longstanding interest in Mencken, edited a collection of the critic's previously unpublished writings, titled *A Second Mencken Chrestomathy*, intended as a sequel to Mencken's own best-selling 1949 anthology *A Mencken Chrestomathy*. Teachout is also the editor of *Ghosts on the Roof* (1989), a collection of writings by Whittaker Chambers, and *Beyond the Boom: New Voices on American Life, Culture, and Politics* (1990), an assortment of essays by Teachout and other members of the Vile Body, a circle of young conservatives that Teachout founded in New York City. Teachout's autobiography, *City Limits: Memories of a Small-Town Boy*, was published in 1991. He is the music critic for *Commentary*, a former editor of *Harper's*, and a frequent contributor of articles on music, dance, and literature to such publications as the *New York Times*, *New Criterion*, *Time*, the *National Review*, the *Washington Post*, and the *Wall Street Journal*.

Terry Teachout was born on February 6, 1956 in Cape Girardeau, Missouri, and grew up in nearby Sikeston. His parents were H. H. Teachout, a hardware salesman, and the former Evelyn Crosno, a typist. Between 1972 and 1974, before deciding to go to college, he played bass in a country and bluegrass band in southeast Missouri. For a time in 1974 he attended St. John's College, in Annapolis, Maryland, a school devoted to the study of "great books," but he later transferred to William Jewell College, in Liberty, Missouri, from which he received his bachelor's degree, in 1979. From 1983 to 1985 he attended the University of Illinois, in Urbana-Champaign. Teachout worked his way through school as a music critic for the *Star and Times* in Kansas City, Missouri, a position he held from 1977 until 1983. In 1985 he received an offer from *Harper's* to serve as an assistant editor; the following year he was promoted to senior editor. In 1987 he became an editorial writer for the *New York Daily News* and served in that capacity until 1993.

In 1989 Teachout edited *Ghosts on the Roof*, a collection of writings by Whittaker Chambers, the American writer and editor who is best known for accusing, in the late 1940s, the U.S. State Department official Alger Hiss of being a Communist and a spy. Teachout's book assembles many of Chambers's essays, reviews, articles, and short stories that were published between 1931 and 1950 in such periodicals as *New Masses*, the *American Mercury*, the *National Review*, *Time*, and *Life*. In a critique of the book for the *National Review* (June 2, 1989), Joseph Sobran wrote: "[Here] we finally meet Chambers alone, without the shadow of the Hiss case, though its foreshadowing is here and there inescapable. . . . [Included] are thoughtful essays on [James] Joyce, [George] Santayana, [Franz] Kafka, and Charles Beard, light pieces on travel books and movies. . . . These articles disclose a mind that was ready for anything, eager for challenges, never so committed in advance that it could be put on the defensive, not even by a scholarly apologia for the Soviet Union."

The next year Teachout edited *Beyond the Boom: New Voices on American Life, Culture, and Politics* (1990). The 15 essays included in this collection reflect the thoughts of a group of conservative writers, editors, and economists known as the Vile Body, a literary salon founded by Teachout that has since disbanded. Contributors to the collection included Teachout, Richard Brookhiser, Walter Olson, George Sim Johnston, Susan Vigilante, Maggie Gallagher, Richard Vigilante, Roger Kimball, Donna Rifkind, Andrew Ferguson, Bruce Bawer, John Podhoretz, Dana Mack, Lisa Schiffren, and David Brooks. Depending on the political leanings of the reviewer, the collection was either praised or derided. In the *National Review* (October 15, 1990), Priscilla L. Buckley remarked: "Like most compilations, *Beyond the Boom* has flaws . . . but its sins are for the most part the venial sins of exuberance. This is the nearest thing yet to that serious book that cries out to be written on a generation—the Woodstock generation—whose unexpunged sins have poisoned America's cultural and spiritual landscape for the successor generation, and the rest of us." By contrast, John Elson, in *Time* (December 3, 1990), wrote: "The anthology's contributors, for the most part, are stronger on aphorism and assertion than on analysis. They also indulge in an awful lot of navel gazing, often in a tone of self-satisfied righteousness."

In 1991 Teachout published *City Limits*, his memoir about growing up in small-town Missouri, struggling to find his direction, and ultimately deciding to move to New York City to pursue a writing career. He wrote the book, as he told Wendy Smith in an interview for *Publishers Weekly* (November 25, 2002), "because the experience of being born in a small town and moving to a big city is one of the most important themes in American literature, and I thought it had not been written about with sufficient sympathy. Most of these books were written by people who hated where they came from." Reviews of Teachout's autobiography were mixed. In the *National Review* (October 21, 1991), Brad Miner proclaimed: "Mr. Teachout's remembrances are presented with charm and wit, and they provide a passage into one's own past. . . . How Terry Teachout, a shy, musically gifted boy, comes from Missouri to Gotham . . . and becomes a writer of growing reputation, is a story of some fascination." Jane Smiley, writing in the *New York Times Book Review* (November 10, 1991), opined: "Mr. Teachout's prose has a lively rhythm and good pacing. Even so, . . . it's hard to share the author's amazement at the trip from Sikeston to Manhattan. In fact, readers who still live in the Midwest might share my feelings of annoyance at the eerie sentimentality of [some of] Mr. Teachout's recollections." Smiley continued, "On the whole, it's probably better for even a good writer, like Mr. Teachout, to write his or her memoirs later rather than sooner. Mr. Teachout seems to know what interests him about his life, but has less of a grasp on what's interesting about it to others."

H. L. Mencken, in the months before he suffered a disabling stroke in late 1948, had assembled an anthology of his writings that he titled *A Mencken Chrestomathy*. (A chrestomathy is a volume of collected passages or stories of an author. Mencken's publisher, Alfred Knopf, objected to the title on the grounds that customers, not knowing what it meant, would refrain from buying it; Mencken insisted and proved otherwise.) The book became a best-seller and has been reprinted numerous times. Mencken had also started to prepare a second volume, but after the stroke deprived him of the ability to read and write, he abandoned the project. Teachout, who began researching Mencken in the early 1990s in order to write his biography, discovered the manuscript for the intended sequel in a neglected library closet. Mencken had selected the material, noted its sources, and added a few explanatory comments. Teachout edited and organized the collection and published it as *A Second Mencken Chrestomathy*

(1995). In a review for the *Baltimore Sun* (January 29, 1995), Charles A. Fecher wrote: "The first question that has to be asked is, of course, this one: is the second *Chrestomathy* as good as the first? Well, no, not really. Mencken, with a remarkable critical objectivity in approaching his own writings, selected for the first one the very best of his work over the years. It was good, and he knew that it was. . . . At the same time—and perhaps because the material in it is less familiar—this second *Chrestomathy* is capable of bringing as much enjoyment as the first. As Mr. Teachout notes, of the 238 pieces brought together here, 147 have never before appeared in book form and 62 come from books that are no longer in print. Thus it reads almost like a fresh new work."

After years of research, Teachout published *The Skeptic: A Life of H. L. Mencken* (2002), which explored all aspects of his subject's life. Teachout had access to a wealth of information, including Mencken's three-volume autobiography, two early biographies, and diaries and manuscripts that Mencken wrote late in life but that his will specified were to be published only decades after his death. Mencken's journalism, marked by his contrarian spirit and witty invective, was frequently offensive to many: he was anti-Semitic, thought blacks were inferior to whites, disparaged democracy, voiced pro-German sentiments during World War I and II, and derided Franklin D. Roosevelt as the worst kind of politician. Yet he was also seen as the scourge of ignorance and hypocrisy, and he is remembered as one of America's greatest journalists. "Teachout makes no apologies for Mencken's deep blemishes and controversial views, but examines them in the context of the writer's German roots, his personal and social isolation, his lack of formal education, and his coming of age in an era that was far less modern than his writing conveys," Mary Leonard noted in the *Boston Globe* (March 6, 2003). "Indeed, Mencken was a man of great contradictions, and Teachout is at his most insightful in capturing them. Mencken was a sedentary cigar-chomping hypochondriac who embraced social Darwinism with a vengeance and felt his stock was superior to most. He was cruel and brawling in his columns but tender in his love letters to his ailing wife, Sara." In the *Christian Century* (April 5, 2003), David Stewart proclaimed: "Terry Teachout's book makes clear the energy of Mencken's writing and editing, his breathtaking industry in writing so much and so variously over so many years, and the steadfastness with which he held to his beliefs."

In 2004 Teachout published *A Terry Teachout Reader*, a collection of his essays and reviews from the previous 15 years, and *All in the Dances: A Brief Life of George Balanchine*, in which Teachout argues that the famed choreographer is as important to the development of the arts in the 20th century as the painter Henri Matisse and the composer Igor Stravinsky. Reviews for *All in the*

Dances were mixed; while a critic for *Publishers Weekly* (October 11, 2004) found the book "pithy, conversational and vivid," Laura Jacobs, writing for the *Washington Post* (November 28, 2004), described it as "a lumpily chronological, strangely argumentative hike through Balanchine's life, with quotes and stories recycled from older books of first-hand reporting."

Terry Teachout has been married to Elizabeth Cullers, an opera coach, since 1980; they live in New York City. He continues to serve as a contributing writer for *Commentary* and *Time* and has been an arts columnist for the *Washington Post* since 1999. A collection of Teachout's journalism was published by Yale University Press as *A Terry Teachout Reader* (2004). Regarding future projects, he told Wendy Smith, "I don't contemplate writing another biography, though I'm really glad I did [Mencken]. I'm a scholar manqué, like a lot of journalists, and to do a fully annotated book based on primary source material was my chance to be a full professor without having to put up with all the nonsense. I'm not sure I need to do it again.

Mencken was a very personal project: about the man I have my doubts, about the writer I have none."

—K.D.

Suggested Reading: *Baltimore Sun* F p5 Jan. 29, 1995; *Boston Globe* D p7 Mar. 6, 2003; *Chicago Tribune* C p1 Dec. 22, 2002; *Christian Century* p41 Apr. 5, 2003; *Commonweal* p234 Apr. 5, 1991; *National Review* p48 June 2, 1989, Oct. 15, 1990, p40 Oct. 21, 1991; *New York Times Book Review* p14 Nov. 10, 1991; *Publishers Weekly* p249 Nov. 25, 2002; *Time* p114 Dec. 3, 1990

Selected Books: nonfiction—*City Limits: Memories of a Small-Town Boy*, 1991; *The Skeptic: A Life of H. L. Mencken*, 2002; *All in the Dances: A Brief Life of George Balanchine*, 2004; *A Terry Teachout Reader*, 2004; as editor— *Ghosts on the Roof*, 1989; *Beyond the Boom: New Voices on American Life, Culture, and Politics*, 1990; *A Second Mencken Chrestomathy*, 1995

Tin Moe, U

(tin moe, oo)

Nov. 19, 1933–Jan. 23, 2007 Poet; children's book writer

Despite being one of Burma's most famous and celebrated poets, U Tin Moe fled his home country, which is also known as Myanmar, in 1999, choosing exile in Europe over the harsh treatment to which government authorities had subjected him during the previous decade. U Tin Moe's poetry had become widely popular in the late 1950s, during Burma's brief spell as a republican democracy. A 1962 military coup overthrew the democratic government, however, and an increasingly repressive regime was instituted. In 1988 he joined the newly formed National League for Democracy (NLD), an opposition group. In 1991 he was jailed for his pro-democracy activities and his poetry banned. Released in 1995, he was recognized as a victim of the military regime and hailed as a hero for his actions against it.

U Tin Moe was born Ba Gyan on November 19, 1933 in Kanmye (sometimes written Kan Mye), a village in the Taungtha township, which is part of the Myingyan district of Burma's centrally located Mandalay Division. (The country is divided into 14 administrative divisions.) His parents were U Ba Oh, a tailor and trader, and Daw San Hte. (U is a Burmese honorific, generally translated as uncle, used when referring to respected adult males; Daw, or aunt, is an honorific for adult women.)

Strongly influenced by the Burmese poet U Wun (often called Minthuwun), U Tin Moe first started writing poems when he was a teenager. In 1951 he founded a library in Kanmye. In 1954 he left for Yezagyo High School in the neighboring Magwe division, where he founded another library. Around this time U Tin Moe began submitting his poetry to literary magazines. While several publications rejected his poetry, the popular literary journal *Ludu* (which can be translated as "the people") accepted some of his works.

As U Tin Moe was finishing up his high-school education, the newly independent Burmese government was attempting to create an intellectual class. Formerly a British colony, Burma had been conquered by Japan during World War II. In 1945 Burmese armed forces (which Japan had earlier helped organize) collaborated with the British to expel the Japanese occupiers. In 1948 Britain granted Burma its independence, and the country became a republic. To help usher in a new age for independent Burma, the government sought out such potential scholars as U Tin Moe: after completing high school, with high distinction, in 1957, he was personally invited to study at Rangoon University by the professor of Burmese there and by the Burmese minister of education. However, he did not have the economic means to travel to Rangoon and so stayed near Yezagyo to teach English and math at an elementary school. When the professor who had recruited U Tin Moe found that he had not matriculated, he arranged instead for the fledgling writer to attend the nearby Mandalay University. Before U Tin Moe began college, he studied as a novice at the well-known Shweyesaung Buddhist Monastery in Mandalay.

U Tin Moe continued writing at Mandalay University. He was the vice-president of the Writers' Association there from 1958 to 1959 and was made president the following academic year. In 1959 he published his first collection of poems, *Hpan-mi-ein* (which can be translated as "poems of the glass lantern"), through the *Ludu* publishing house. "When I published this collection I was quite tentative; I had quite a bit of trepidation," he told Dr. Kyi May Kaung for an interview broadcast on Radio Free Asia (September 2000), as translated by Kaung and posted on the pro-democracy Burma Project Web site. "In those days you didn't publish a poetry collection just like that." For the collection, he was awarded the National Literary Prize for Poetry from Myanmar's Literary Institute (Sarpay Beikman). "I had more confidence and courage [after I won the prize] and I was able to keep writing poetry consistently," U Tin Moe told Kaung. One of the poems included in this collection was "The Great Guest," one of his shortest poems but probably his most quoted: "The cheroot's burnt down / The sun is brown / Please take me back." (A cheroot is a kind of cigar.) In 1963 he published another collection, *Songster in a Boat*, which contained 70 poems and included English translations.

U Tin Moe graduated from Mandalay University in 1965, with a bachelor's degree in Burmese language and literature, Far Eastern history, and Pali (the liturgical language of Theravada Buddhism). During and after his studies at Mandalay—from 1957 until 1967—he also worked as a teacher at private schools in Mandalay, Myingyan, and Rangoon. Until the mid-1980s he worked as a compiler and assistant editor at Rangoon University's translation and publishing department.

In 1962 General Ne Win led a military coup that forced the civilian government under Premier U Nu out of power. Ne Win's regime, proclaiming itself the Revolutionary Council, discarded the country's constitution and ruled by martial law, nationalized the industrial and commercial sectors, and outlawed opposing political parties. Shortly after the coup Ne Win established the Press Scrutiny Board, which limited freedom of speech by requiring writers to register all literature intended for publication and censoring books, songs, advertisements, and magazines.

Despite the newly imposed censorship, U Tin Moe continued writing poetry. During 1966 and 1967 he was the poetry editor for the popular *Ludu Daily News*, but the publication was shut down when the government imposed a ban on all newspapers in 1967. The next several decades in Burma were marked by increasing repression, a foundering economy, and clashes among rebel political factions and separatist ethnic groups.

During the 1970s U Tin Moe became more involved in efforts to educate and care for children. For one of his children's books, whose title is generally translated as either "Ma Ni and her little umbrella" or "Ma Nee with umbrella," published in 1970, he received the National Literary Prize for Children's Literature. He told Kyi May Kaung that the primary influences for his children's work were Maung Thein Han (better known as Zawgyi) and Minthuwun: "For me, these two fine gentlemen are the two great poets whom I hold in the deepest respect. I grew up with their poems and I like their work so much." In 1971 he founded the Mothers' School Nursery Center. From 1975 until 1985 he was a member of the children's-literature committee in the government's Social Welfare Department. During those same years he was a member of the prize board of Burma's *Dokyaungtha Journal*.

In 1988 U Tin Moe joined the resistance to Burma's government, becoming a member of the newly formed NLD, led by the democracy advocate Daw Aung San Suu Kyi, the daughter of the military general who had helped win Burma's independence in 1947. In 1989 he joined the NLD's Central Intellectuals' Working Group (also called the Intellectual Consultatory Committee). His official entry into the movement coincided with increased protests against the government and more violent repression of peaceful political protesters: in 1988 the military government killed several thousand student demonstrators.

During the next several years, U Tin Moe focused his poetry on supporting the pro-democracy movement, and his works were widely circulated in underground rebel circles. "When I was younger I wrote about my village, my neighborhood, about the place I came from," he told Kyi May Kaung. "About upper Burma—the customs, the pagoda festivals. About harvesting peanuts. I was born and grew up in Taungtha Township—so I wrote about it with a sense of great affection. But as I grew older and more educated, [my] world expanded. I started to write not only about village and rural life in Upper Burma, but about the life of the majority, about the life experiences of all the people of Burma. I wrote about politics too. All this started to become very interesting to me. Before 1988, I did not write much that could be said to be political, but after the mass pro-democracy movement that started in 1988, politics became a part of the lives of the people of Burma. And so I, as one man, one person, amongst the people of Burma—I also wanted to be free. I was dissatisfied with the oppression. I do not like being bound up. I also wanted to breathe the zephyrs of freedom, the little fresh breezes."

When the military government allowed elections to be held, in 1990, the NLD overwhelmingly won them, but the governing State Law and Order Restoration Council (SLORC) refused to call parliament into session—an action that would have ceded authority of Burma to the NLD—and instead sentenced dozens of prominent NLD members to long prison terms.

U Tin Moe, who had, for the time being, escaped imprisonment, was named chief editor of the literary magazine *Pe-phu-hlwa* (which can be translated as "palm leaf manuscript") in 1991. After the publication of the December 1991 issue, the first he had edited, the government arrested him and closed down the magazine. His arrest coincided with those of about 900 students (according to Amnesty International) demonstrating for the release of Daw Aung San Suu Kyi, who had been under house arrest since July 1989 and had won the 1991 Nobel Peace Prize.

After being imprisoned for six months without being charged, in June 1992 U Tin Moe was sentenced to four years for violating the 1962 Printer and Publishers Registration Law, which required all written material designed for publication to be registered with the Press Scrutiny Board. He was imprisoned at Insein jail, infamous for reports of prisoner abuse. Within a year Amnesty International and other human rights groups were lobbying for his release.

At Insein U Tin Moe was denied all reading and writing materials. One of his only comforts during his imprisonment was the discovery of his poem "The Great Guest" scrawled on a jail wall by a previous prisoner. Facing increasing international scrutiny into their human rights practices, in April 1992 the Myanmar government announced that it would gradually release political prisoners they no longer considered a threat to national security. During the next three years the government released more than 2,000 political detainees. U Tin Moe was released on February 4, 1995, nine months before his sentence was over. (Daw Aung San Suu Kyi was also released in 1995, rearrested in 2000, released in 2002, and rearrested again in May 2003.)

While U Tin Moe was allowed to write for magazines and newspapers, authorities warned him not to resume his political activities. One of his collections of poems, whose title has been translated as "desert years," which he submitted to the Press Security Board in the late 1970s, was finally published in 1998. Shortly after the publication of this volume, U Tin Moe once again earned the ire of the Burmese government: one of his poems, the title of which means "the light of Suu," written in 1999 about Daw Aung San Suu Kyi's British husband, who had died that year (after being denied a visa to visit his wife one last time), was circulated underground and broadcast on the Norway-based Democratic Voice of Burma radio station. After the broadcast U Tin Moe's name and works were once more banned. Concluding that he would be imprisoned again if he stayed in Burma, he fled to join his daughter in Belgium (where she had married), in April 1999. According to advocacy groups, the government had issued a ban against U Tin Moe's travel, but he tricked immigration officials by acquiring a passport bearing his birth name, Ba Gyan, allowing his exit to be overlooked by military officials until they heard him being interviewed on foreign radio stations. According to an article written by Pauk Sa for the government-run *New Light of Myanmar* newspaper (July 21, 2001, on-line), the government had readily granted U Tin Moe a temporary visa so that he could visit his daughter in Belgium. He was granted political asylum in the United States, in August 2000.

Thereafter U Tin Moe divided his time between California and Belgium and continued to write poems decrying Burma's military regime. "Now, poetry is my main pursuit and obsession," he told Kyi May Kaung. "I write poetry all the time, even when I am traveling."

U Tin Moe has published more than 15 poetry books, educational books, and essay collections. While living in the U.S., he wrote regularly for the South Korean *Millennium Window Journal,* Thailand's *New Era Journal,* and Japan's *Ahara Journal* and also hosted a show devoted to Burmese literature on U.S.–sponsored Radio Free Asia. All of his works, as well as any image bearing his likeness, remain banned in Burma, but are often smuggled in and distributed illegally.

In 2002 U Tin Moe was awarded a Hellman-Hammett Grant, distributed by Human Rights Watch to writers who have, according to the organization's Web site, "been victims of political persecution and are in financial need." In 2004 he was one of the top three honorees of the Prince Claus Awards, distributed annually by the Prince Claus Fund for Culture and Development in conjunction with the Dutch government. U Tin Moe's award carried a purse of about $46,000.

U Tin Moe's wife, Daw Myint Myint San, who ran a preschool in Rangoon, died in 1990. They had four daughters and a son; their youngest daughter, Mo Cho Thinn, has written several popular short stories.

On January 23, 2007, U Tin Moe was at a Los Angeles teashop with a friend when he suddenly collapsed and died.

—S.H.

Suggested Reading: *Irrawaddy* (on-line) Jan. 2001; *Observer Worldview* (on-line) May 12, 2002

Selected Books in English Translation: *Songster in a Boat*, 1963

Tirone Smith, Mary-Ann

Feb. 6, 1944– Novelist; memoirist

Mary-Ann Tirone Smith first won critics' attention with such literary novels as *The Book of Phoebe* (1985), *Lament for a Silver-Eyed Woman* (1987), *The Port of Missing Men* (1989), and *Master of Illusion* (1994), before establishing her reputation as an author of well-honed thrillers, with such works as *An American Killing* (1998), *Love Her Madly* (2002), *She's Not There* (2003), and *She Smiled Sweetly* (2004). More recently, she has written a memoir, *Girls of Tender Age* (2005). She has attempted to maintain a sense of continuity through it all, explaining during an interview, coinciding with the release of *Love Her Madly* and available on the Mostly Fiction Web site, "In all of my books, I have explored the theme of injustice, whether it be Arab nations using Palestinians as pawns or innocent men being wrongly accused. I find writing suspense to be especially stimulating in some ways in that some kind of injustice is at the heart of every mystery." Writing her first thriller, *An American Killing*, was, she added, "extremely rewarding. I found I did not have to compromise my literary integrity to write a novel of substance that was also a real page-turner. My intent as a writer has always been to write a good book about real issues. It's very possible to do this in any genre."

The second child of Maurice and Florence (Deslauriers) Tirone, Mary-Ann Tirone was born on February 6, 1944 in Hartford, Connecticut, and grew up in a working-class family in Hartford's Charter Oak Terrace, a 1,000-unit housing project built at the beginning of World War II. Her father, known as Yutch or Yutchie, spent all of his working life at the Abbott Ball Company, a ball-bearing factory, first as a heat treater in the hardening room and later as a foreman. Her mother was a data processor at the Aetna Life Insurance Company until she married; she was a homemaker during the early years of Tirone Smith's life. When Florence later returned to data processing, this time working at Connecticut General during what was known as the "housewife shift"—that is, during afternoon and evening hours—she began spending her free time away from home, golfing, bowling, and playing cards, and Maurice took over some of the household responsibilities. Tirone Smith believes these changes had a positive effect on her home life, which was, while not unhappy, made difficult by a mother who always seemed to be approaching a nervous breakdown and by the family's need to accommodate itself to Tirone Smith's autistic older brother, Tyler, who could not, for example, bear to hear loud noises and made increasing demands on the family as he grew older. "For all intents and purposes," she told Carole Goldberg for the *Hartford Courant* (January 8, 2006), "my mother left home when I was 7, and I am not sure what would have happened [otherwise]. I knew even as a kid that it was better for her to have a separate life."

In the midst of her dysfunctional family life, Tirone Smith fell in love with fiction while listening to her father tell stories as he was tucking her into bed at night. After she learned to read, she began dreaming of becoming a writer. "I remember handing in my first theme paper, not knowing how the teacher would respond," she told Jack Cavanaugh for the *New York Times* (September 15, 1991). "And then the teacher . . . told me, 'Your writing flows like a river.' Well, I was so thrilled, and it gave me so much inspiration and encouragement." She further honed her skills while attending Central Connecticut State University (CCSU), where she studied psychology and English, earning her degree in 1965. Particularly useful to her future as a writer, she has said, were a psychology course in which she had to write a 100-page autobiography and a history course in which the professor, William O. Williams, gave fascinating lectures that presented history as a series of stories. Tirone Smith has drawn upon the love of history that Williams inspired in a number of her novels.

Tirone Smith did not, however, immediately pursue her dreams of becoming a writer. She joined the Peace Corp 10 days after her graduation from CCSU and spent the next two years in Cameroon, where she was responsible for setting up a public library. When she returned to Connecticut, she married Jere Patrick Smith in 1968 and later had two children, Jene Maria and Jere Paul, again putting her dreams on hold. Still, she used what free time she had between parenting duties to write, eventually producing her first novel.

The Book of Phoebe is a coming-of-age story about Phoebe Desmond, whose mother named her after the younger sister of Holden Caulfield, the main character of J. D. Salinger's quintessential coming-of-age-tale, *The Catcher in the Rye*. Phoebe—whose voice resembles Caulfield's in its precociousness and distrust of phoniness—is a Yale student who becomes pregnant and travels to Paris, where her friend Marlys lives, to have the child and give it up for adoption. In Paris, Marlys arranges for Phoebe to stay with Ben Reuben, an artist. Phoebe and Ben fall in love, and when Ben becomes curious about Phoebe's decision not to have an abortion, she answers his questions by giving him a journal she had written at the age of 13. The journal contains a fictionalized account of an episode involving her brother Tyrus, whom most of the family considers mentally ill and who has been locked in the attic, where he, like Tirone Smith's own brother, reads books about World War II. The remainder of the novel develops both plot strands, and the "technical difficulties involved in weaving together the two tales are for the most part worked out quite neatly," Rebecca Goldstein observed in the *New York Times* (July 14, 1985). Goldstein went on on to argue, though, that Tirone Smith does not fully distinguish Phoebe's voice at 13 from her voice at 19. "The younger Phoebe's powers of expression are so extraordinary for a child of her age that, despite self-avowals of giftedness, they approach the borders of unbelievability. The elder Phoebe does not seem to have made any substantial progress beyond her former precocious self. Where, we might ask, are the signs of the three and a half years she has studied at Yale? What was she studying? A smart kid like Phoebe should have got a lot more out of a first-class education."

The Book of Phoebe was followed two years later by *Lament for a Silver-Eyed Woman*. This second novel drew upon Tirone Smith's experience in the Peace Corp; it tells the story of Mattie Price, a woman who aspires to become a writer, and Jo Parsons, a passionately idealistic political activist. Having become friends as children in the 1950s, Mattie and Jo grow closer as they become adults, attending the same exclusive women's college, traveling together in Europe and Hawaii, and finally joining the Peace Corp. Both are stationed in Cameroon, but their lives follow different directions thereafter. Mattie returns home and marries a man whose estranged father was a Nazi, while Jo, newly married to a leader in the Palestine Liberation Organization, moves to a refugee camp outside Beirut, Lebanon. Called Shatila, the camp was the site, in 1982, of a massacre of hundreds of people, the majority of them Palestinian refugees—an event that Tirone Smith partially depicts at the end of the novel. "Throughout, Smith keeps the reader riveted, her voice first jaunty and irreverent, then increasingly portentous as events turn tragic," a reviewer for *Publishers Weekly* commented, as cited on Amazon.com. "This is a novel about friendship, love and loyalty, about betrayal, and about justice. While there are some lapses in credibility, on the whole the book makes a vivid impact."

Tirone Smith's third novel, *The Port of Missing Men,* tells the story of Lily Neelan, who has just won two gold medals at the 1936 Olympics in Germany and is now returning to the U.S. on a luxury liner with her mother, Gertie. Having prostituted herself to raise her daughter, Gertie is now looking for a wealthy husband and eventually finds Albert Rexhault, a German businessman. Lily and Gertie subsequently embark on a yearlong social tour, during which a number of characters—including Lily, Gertie, and Albert—confront, among other things, the lack of fathers in their lives. In the *New York Times* (May 7, 1989), Fannie Flagg wrote: "Reading this delightfully unexpected, offbeat little book is like taking a ride on the Crazy Mouse at the carnival: you never know what twists or turns it will take next." Grace Lichtenstein, however, concluded in the *Washington Post* (June 27, 1989), that "there is something missing in this *Port* besides men. The book lacks a core. Lily is a swell kid, yet she is almost too sane, given her background and the circumstances in which she finds herself, for us to take her seriously. She is intelligent and perky and spontaneous, attributes that put her light years ahead of most real-life, narrowly focused teenage girl athletes. But when she dives, we are told, she is so perfect that she makes almost no splash. That's the problem with the book."

In her fourth novel, *Masters of Illusion: A Novel of the Connecticut Circus Fire*, Tirone Smith engaged with the history of her hometown, using the Hartford circus fire of July 6, 1944, which killed almost 170 people, as the starting point for her story. "The fire was such a legend in Hartford," Tirone Smith told Jocelyn McClurg for the *Hartford Courant* (May 22, 1994). "People talked about it all the time. Then the anniversary would come around and people would say, 'What were you doing when you heard about the fire?'" In *Masters of Illusion*, Tirone Smith tells the story of the fire and its decades-long aftermath through the character Margie Potter. Six months old at the time, Margie escapes the fire with only injuries while her mother dies in it. When she is about 17, Margie falls in love with a man 10 years her senior, Charlie O'Neill, who has been fixated on that night's events for most of his life. The two marry and, over the next 25 years, investigate the fire's cause, which Charlie believes was arson. Margie at first serves as a spur to Charlie's quest but later becomes dissatisfied with her role. She then acts as Charlie's "psychiatrist" to help him resolve his obsession. This psychological approach, Jim Shepard wrote for the *Los Angeles Times* (October 30, 1994), "leaves the reader unsurprised when, in keeping with the therapeutic model, the principals are finally released by the novel's truth when the cause of the fire emerges. Their release is our disappointment. We feel the opportunity lost: a gifted writer, a compelling subject and a dauntingly complicated tangle of conflicts, all resolved into a too-neat bundle." Others found the novel disappointing as well. Tirone Smith, Josh Rubins observed for the *New York Times* (June 26, 1994), "has got hold of a powerful hook: the long-ago circus fire, with its lingering mystery and enduring damage, as a metaphor for all half-remembered childhood devastations. Unfortunately, *Masters of Illusion* never quite lives up to its resonant premise. The complex relationship between Margie and Charlie deconstructs, disappointingly, into a lecture on co-dependency straight off the self-help shelf. The narrative remains oddly static, interrupted by a series of increasingly melodramatic revelations. And Ms. Smith's blunt, earthbound prose, at times an effective reflection of Margie's immersion in pop culture, more often seems a mismatch for the story's ambitious reach."

Following *Masters of Illusion,* which had elements of a mystery, Tirone Smith wrote *An American Killing,* a book in which she fully embraced the thriller genre, consciously seeking a way to make enough money to live off her fiction. Tirone Smith told Karen Carlin for the *Pittsburgh Post-Gazette* (September 6, 1998) that before beginning *An American Killing,* "I had immersed myself in very commercial books that I loved—*The Name of the Rose, Gorky Park, Smilla's Sense of Snow, Presumed Innocent.* These were books that made the best-seller list, but were serious, well-written books, written by people who had a knowledge of things. Then I thought about the thread that made them commercial, and it was murder." While acknowledging that *An American Killing* was "truly a departure in that it is a suspense novel," Tirone Smith insisted to Carlin that the change was superficial, saying, "But it's the same [as my other books] in that I set out with an image. The image begins to grow, and I start writing about what I'm seeing. In this case . . . somebody was murdered, a whole family." Set in Washington D.C., the novel tells the story of Denise Burke, a true-crime writer whose husband, a domestic adviser to President Clinton, is in a position to give her access to Washington insiders, most importantly Congressman Owen Allen Hall. Burke and Hall have an affair, and she begins investigating for him a group of murders in his district. Writing *An American Killing* was lucrative, and Tirone Smith was relieved of the need to pen contract books and press releases—work she had done for years for extra cash. Some critics were so impressed by the book that they expressed a desire for Tirone Smith to turn Burke into a character for a series. Gail Cooke wrote for the *Milwaukee Journal Sentinel* (November 3, 1998), for example, "With Denise Burke, Smith has created a witty, plucky and thoroughly likeable heroine whom we want to meet again. When she returns, it is hoped she'll bring her best friend, FBI Agent Poppy Rice."

Tirone Smith has yet to revive the character Burke, but she has placed Rice into her own series, the first installment of which was *Love Her Madly.* As with *Masters of Illusion,* Tirone Smith drew on an actual event to generate the story for this novel, modeling the life of her main character, Rona Leigh Glueck, on Karla Faye Tucker, the first woman executed in Texas since the Civil War. The execution was more controversial than such events usually are not simply because Tucker was a woman but also because she had become, during her time in prison, a born-again Christian and had earned such defenders as the televangelist Pat Robertson. In the novel, Rice, convinced of Glueck's innocence, investigates the murders that brought Glueck her death sentence only to have the case take an unexpected turn on the day of Glueck's execution. "This fiction is loaded with brand names and big names that give the story a delightful sense of reality," Paul Lomartire wrote for the Cox News Service (February 1, 2002). Calling Rice "sexy and bawdy and brazen enough to be unique among the too-many serialized fiction cops out there," Lomartire suggested that if Tirone Smith "keeps her heroine as fresh as this book, she's got a hit on her hands." Others were less impressed. In the *Los Angeles Times* (January 30, 2002), Dick Lochte argued that neither Glueck nor Rice "is all that lovable. Rona Leigh is either a formerly homicidal druggie-turned-Christian-bliss ninny or a still-homicidal, druggie-turned-sly sociopath. Poppy, the book's narrator, is an arrogant I'm-right-and-you're-an-idiot kind of fun gal whose vaunted irreverence and hardball feminism lead to such charming asides as her speculation that, since Jesus stopped 'a gang of fellows from stoning an adulteress to death,' the adulteress must have been 'pretty.' . . . Love her madly? Mmmmm, maybe not."

Despite the reservations of some critics, the first Poppy Rice novel was a success, and Tirone Smith followed it with two more, *She's Not There* and *She Smiled Sweetly.* In the first, Rice attempts to take some time off on Block Island, Connecticut, only to stumble upon a body on the beach. Marilyn Stasio, writing for the *New York Times* (February 9, 2003), called *She's Not There* "an accomplished whodunit with a solid premise, well-observed characters and a great setting." In the *Houston Chronicle* (June 01, 2003), Amy Rabinovitz offered more tempered praise, writing: "There's an air of made-for-TV movie about the whole thing that may put off some readers. Others will be thoroughly entertained. With its cast of eccentric islanders and dozens of possible ways the story can play out, the book has a sense of expectancy balanced with charm and warmth. Count on this as a book that works for long airport waits or a mindless day at the pool." The second novel, *She Smiled Sweetly,* brought Rice to Boston to investigate a young woman's murder-by-drowning. In the *Hartford Courant* (June 6, 2004), Carole Goldberg noted that by the novel's end "justice has been served and the mysteries have been solved" and "fans of the series will be looking forward to another go-round with Poppy and her gang."

In 2003, however, Tirone Smith suspended work on the series in order to write a memoir. Inspired by an essay on her childhood published in August 2002 in the *Hartford Courant,* the memoir, *Girls of Tender Age,* recounts her growing up in Hartford and the events leading up to the 1953 murder of an 11-year-old friend, Irene Fiederowicz, by Robert Nelson Malm, a man who had a history of sexual violence. The two stories are presented in alternating chapters, one chapter dealing with Tirone Smith's youth, the next recounting Malm's journey toward Hartford, until they collide—Irene dead and the community left to struggle with the consequences. The memoir, Julia Scheeres wrote for the *New York Times* (January 22, 2006), "peers into the dark spaces between the street lights in a quiet residential neighborhood. Something sinister lurks just off the page, and it creeps closer and closer until the memoir's two story lines twist together. Yet despite its grim topics, Smith's book is infused with acerbic wit. The reader pictures her as the wisecracking patron on the next bar stool, nursing a tumbler of bourbon and talking out of the side of her mouth. Smith's deadpan delivery and comedic timing . . . give the narrative spark." Nancy Connors, in the Cleveland *Plain Dealer* (January 29, 2006), wrote that *Girls of Tender Age* "is a very good story" but "not perfect by any means." Tirone Smith, Connors ventured, "could have used a good editor at times."

With the exception of her two years in Cameroon, Tirone Smith has resided her entire life in Connecticut. She currently lives with her husband in East Haven.

—A.R.

Suggested Reading: *Hartford Courant* G p1 May 22, 1994, G p1 Jan. 8, 2006; *Los Angeles Times* p11 Oct. 30, 1994; Mostly Fiction Web site; *New York Times* VII p11 July 14, 1985, VII p24 May 7, 1989, 12 Connecticut Weekly Section p8 Sep. 15, 1991, 14 Connecticut Weekly Section p6 Jan. 22, 2006; *Pittsburgh Post-Gazette* F p8 Sep. 6, 1998; *Washington Post* B p4 June 27, 1989

Selected Books: fiction—*The Book of Phoebe*, 1985; *Lament for a Silver-Eyed Woman*, 1987; *The Port of Missing Men*, 1989; *Master of Illusion*, 1994; *An American Killing*, 1998; *Love Her Madly*, 2002; *She's Not There*, 2003; *She Smiled Sweetly*, 2004; nonfiction—*Girls of Tender Age*, 2005

Touré

1971– Journalist; music critic; fiction writer

Since he began writing for *Rolling Stone* magazine more than a decade ago, Touré has established himself as one of America's best writers on music; his work has also appeared in the *New Yorker*, the *New York Times*, and *Playboy*, among other publications. In 2002 he published his first work of fiction, *The Portable Promised Land*, a collection of 24 short stories celebrating both the humor and the beauty of black popular culture. He later expanded upon these themes in the novel *Soul City* (2004), and a collection of his previously published magazine articles, *Never Drank the Kool-Aid* (2006).

Touré was born in 1971 in Boston, Massachusetts. Touré, a West African surname, is the first name given to him by his mother; the writer dropped his last name more than a decade ago and refuses to reveal it, describing it on his Web site as "something that came automatically, like fries with a burger." After attending prep school in Connecticut, where he became an avid tennis player, he spent three years at Emory University, in Atlanta, Georgia, then dropped out and headed to New York City to pursue a writing career. In 1992 he was hired by *Rolling Stone* to work as an unpaid intern. "I was the worst intern they ever had," he told Philip Connors in an interview for New York *Newsday* (July 21, 2002). "I never did what they told me to do. I delegated work to the other interns so I could chat up the writers and editors." Though he was fired from the job, he had become friends with a record-review editor, who assigned him to write a 100-word

Evan Agostini/Getty Images

album review on a freelance basis. Soon he was working as a freelance reviewer for *Elle*, the *Source*, and the *Village Voice*, in addition to *Rolling Stone*.

Over the next 10 years, Touré moved up the ladder at *Rolling Stone*, eventually becoming a senior correspondent and contributing editor. He has interviewed some of music's most important young artists, including Jay-Z, Notorious B.I.G., Tupac Shakur, and Mary J. Blige, and has written cover stories on Lauryn Hill, DMX, and Alicia

Keys. Touré has the distinction of being *Rolling Stone*'s first African-American staff writer.

Meanwhile, Touré took several classes in nonfiction writing at Columbia University, in New York City, hoping to eventually complete an M.F.A. degree. The first story that he wrote for his first fiction-writing class, "The Sad, Sweet Story of Sugar Lips Shinehot, the Man with the Portable Promised Land," tells of a black saxophone player who makes a deal with the devil so that white people are invisible to him. That story received positive responses from Touré's fellow students, and when the semester ended, he enrolled in another fiction course. When he read another story, "A Hot Time at the Church of Kentucky Fried Souls," to that class, however, it was panned by his classmates. Touré was so discouraged by the experience that he stopped taking classes at Columbia altogether. A year and a half later, however, "A Hot Time" won an award from the short-fiction magazine *Zoetrope: All-Story*. The magazine's editor in chief, Adrienne Brodeur, encouraged Touré to keep writing fiction. He followed Brodeur's advice and soon found a publisher for his work.

The resulting book, *The Portable Promised Land*, is a collection of 24 short stories that are based on urban folk tales and that both poke fun at and celebrate African-American popular culture. Most of the stories are set in a fictional metropolis, Soul City. One story, "The Steviewondermobile," describes Huggy Bear Jackson and his much-loved 1983 Cadillac, which is equipped with a $25,000 stereo system specially designed to play only Stevie Wonder songs. Even though the Steviewondermobile cannot go above 25 miles per hour and sometimes comes to a dead stop because the stereo system overtaxes the electric system, Huggy's life revolves around his car. "Everyone in Soul City was devout, but not everyone was a Stevie-ite," Touré wrote in the story. Other musical "religions" and sects represented in the city include "Milesism, Marlyties, Coltranity, the Sly Stonish, the Ellingtonians, Michael Jacksonism."

Other pieces in Touré's collection are more meditative in tone, particularly "My History," which imagines what the world would be like if the civil rights leader Martin Luther King Jr. had not been assassinated and the basketball icon Earvin "Magic" Johnson had never contracted HIV. Renee Graham, reviewing the collection for the *Boston Globe* (July 1, 2002), wrote that Touré "establishes himself as a vital new voice in fiction. Popping with energy and edginess, *The Portable Promised Land* is an inspired ode to the methods and madness of those who know being black isn't just a matter of race—it's a state of mind, and a state of grace."

In his first novel, *Soul City*, Touré continued to build on the themes he had developed in *The Portable Promised Land*, according to Aissatou Sidime for the *Chicago Tribune* (January 26, 2005): "Touré revives some of the same concepts, such as

vehicles with radios that only play the music of a single musician or band, i.e. the (Marvin) Gayemobile. But he expands them into full-fledged utopia in which all things, from street names to the leading industries, reflect black culture." The novel follows Cadillac Johnson, a writer for *Chocolate City Magazine* who is sent to Soul City to cover a mayoral election—a contest that essentially determines who will serve as the city's deejay. While Sidime praised the novel as a "hilariously honest social commentary," the author Patrick Neate, writing for the *Washington Post* (October 20, 2004), described it as "a kind of African American utopia imagined by someone raised on the pop-culture staples and stereotypes of black identity—someone who found his politics in Public Enemy, his history watching *Roots* and his hero in John Shaft."

In a review for *Library Journal* (March 1, 2006), Robert Morast wrote that *Never Drank the Kool-Aid*, a collection of Touré's previously published magazine articles, "doesn't differ much from other anthologies by contemporary pop culture writers. Not only does Touré dish on intimate moments shared with secluded superstars (witness him and Prince engage in a pick-up basketball game), but he also ponders the importance of and/or disappointment in icons (why Michael Jordan is a failure despite being an undisputed champion). But there is a saving grace to this seemingly mundane offering: Touré himself. . . . With prose that bridges two worlds, he stands out from the glut of scribes trying to make a name writing about African American culture." According to a reviewer for *Publishers Weekly* (January 2, 2006), "Touré has a knack for putting his subjects at ease, and he blends their intriguing candor with apt observations on the nature of their careers. He describes his own place in events without overshadowing the story itself. He's just interested in bringing us along for the ride, even if that means sitting shotgun while DMX pulls a full-speed 180 in a Cadillac Escalade on Sunset Boulevard."

Since 2005 Touré has served as a writer, host, and consulting producer for Black Entertainment Television (BET). He currently lives in the Fort Greene neighborhood of Brooklyn, in New York City. In March 2005 he married Rita Nakouzi, a consultant on fashion and lifestyle trends.

—H.T.

Suggested Reading: *Black Issues Book Review* p12+ July/Aug. 2002; (New York) *Newsday* D p31+ July 21, 2002

Suggested Books: fiction—*The Portable Promised Land*, 2002; *Soul City*, 2004; nonfiction—*Never Drank the Kool-Aid*, 2006

Trope, Zoe

1986– Memoirist

Zoe Trope's memoir, *Please Don't Kill the Freshman* (2003), would have been a remarkable achievement for any author, but for a writer who had yet to finish high school, the accomplishment was all the more notable. In an interview posted on Powell's Books Web Site, Trope told Dave Weich that she hopes her book will lead people to "see that teenagers can write and that we can think about things; it's a fledgling hope for respect for youth. I know that there are so many kids who've written to me or who've talked to me at readings who are insightful and have something to say. And it really frustrates me when people shut off teenagers."

Zoe Trope is the punning pseudonym of a young woman who was born in 1986 and grew up outside of Portland, Oregon. Though she does not reveal many details about her parents in order to maintain her anonymity, she has stated in interviews that they have been very supportive. "My dad's a lot like me," she told Weich. "Our birthdays are two days apart, and we're both outgoing, obnoxious, funny, rambunctious people. We work really well with my mother, who's just this solid, poker-faced woman." In the eighth grade Trope took an after-school writing course taught by Kevin Sampsell, a published author and owner of a small, local publishing house called Future Tense Publishing. "I'd picked up Kevin's book during the class," Trope told Weich. "They said he was a published Portland author, so of course I went to my library, and they had a copy of *How to Lose Your Mind with the Lights On*. I remember I started reading it in the car as my mom was driving me home. . . . It's just insane, surreal stuff, but I absolutely loved it because it wasn't like anything else I'd read. There wasn't a specific beginning, middle, and end to each story, and there was something really evocative and interesting and powerful about everything in the book."

Sampsell described his young student as "very rambunctious and sort of disruptive, but in a fun way," according to Whitney Joiner for the on-line magazine *Salon* (October 27, 2003). He was impressed by her talent, and the two continued to communicate after the class ended. Later, when Trope was in high school, he took some of the poetic, funny journal entries that she had shown him and compiled them into a short book, about 13,000 words long, which he published and sold in local book stores. After the author Joe Weisberg called Sampsell to arrange a reading in Portland for his novel, *10th Grade*, which is also about a high-school sophomore, Sampsell sent him a copy of Trope's chapbook. Weisberg in turn forwarded it to his agent, who eventually signed Trope to a contract. The agent encouraged Trope to expand on the work in order to begin showing the manuscript to big-name publishers. She extended the time period covered in the memoir to the end of her sophomore year, and HarperCollins agreed to publish the book under its young-adult imprint.

In *Please Don't Kill the Freshman* Trope recalls her first two years of high school: "We follow along as [Trope is] publishing her chapbook. Falling in love, giving her first readings, taping pictures to her locker, crafting her international debut, bursting with hormones, staring self-doubt in the face, and trying to finish her homework in the meantime," according to Weich. Trope writes about complex issues—including sexual orientation—that are not typical of the young-adult genre. Her biting critiques have also drawn the ire of officials at her high school who objected to some of the characterizations, although Trope had changed all the names. Trope was lauded by Jeffrey Hastings in *School Library Journal* (October 1, 2003) for her "precociously perceptive and preternaturally poisonous pen." Michaela Bancud, writing for the *Portland Tribune* (August 26, 2003, on-line), opined, "At times overwrought, at times brilliant, [Trope] captures the intensity of teenage life—the betrayal, frustration and heartbreak—as perhaps only a teenager truly can."

Since the publication of her memoir, her work has appeared in *Curve Magazine* and *The Oregonian*, among other publications. Trope, who refuses to be photographed in order to maintain her privacy, graduated a year early from high school, in 2003. She is currently studying art history at Oberlin College, in Ohio. She told Weich that many people have expressed jealousy over her early success: "Just accept the simple fact that I was extremely lucky. I was in this class, and a guy called Powell's [Books], and he sent my chapbook to an agent, and the agent sent it to the publishers, and the publishers picked it up? It is a weird chain of events that I really didn't have a lot of control over. I'm getting better at handling people being bitter or jealous or just not liking the book."

—P.B.M.

Suggested Reading: *Portland Tribune* (on-line) Aug. 26, 2003; *School Library Journal* Oct. 1, 2003; Zoe Trope's Web site

Selected Books: *Please Don't Kill the Freshman*, 2003

Tucker, Lisa

Novelist; short-story writer

Before writing the novels *The Song Reader* (2003), *Shout Down the Moon* (2004), and *Once Upon a Day* (2006), Lisa Tucker waited on tables, cleaned offices, taught math, and toured the Midwest with a jazz band, among other pursuits. "I started writing fiction in 1995 for no other reason than that

I loved reading it," she told an interviewer for the Barnes & Noble Web site. "I'd never had a creative writing course or attended a workshop; I didn't know any writers. I still feel there's something so magical about just plunging in and learning the craft as you go." She signed with an agent in 1997 but did not catch the attention of a publisher until 2001, when she switched agents. "The four years in between were hard, though I never stopped writing," she told the interviewer. "Hanging next to my desk, I have a cheap little purple ribbon that I bought at a school supply store, the kind given out to the kids who don't win the prize: 'I try my best.' I wanted to succeed, of course, but mainly I wanted to live up to that."

Tucker grew up in a small town in Missouri. While her home had few books, it did have a record player, and she grew up loving music. Listening to the songs' lyrics, she discovered she loved words as well. Tucker won a scholarship to the University of Pennsylvania, from which she graduated in 1984. Despite receiving financial aid, she worked long hours at odd jobs to support herself while studying literature. "[College] made me realize that even as a poor kid from Missouri, I was capable of living in the world of thought," she told Caroline Tiger for the University of Pennsylvania *Gazette* (July/August 2003, on-line). Tucker then went on to earn a graduate degree in mathematics from Villanova University, also in Pennsylvania.

The Song Reader is set in a Missouri town similar to the one in which Tucker grew up. The novel tells the story of two sisters, Mary Beth and Leanne, whose father has left them and whose mother has just died. Forced to make ends meet, Mary Beth, the elder of the two, performs what she calls song readings—by analyzing the songs stuck in the heads of her patrons, she provides insight into their problems and recommends strategies to help overcome them. "I think everybody senses that music has something to do with memory," Tucker told Kevin Howell for *Publishers Weekly* (March 17, 2003, on-line). "When you're driving down the street and hear a song from a high school dance on the radio, you find yourself thinking about that dance. The song triggers the memory, in the same way that the smell of chalk can make you think of your first-grade class. I came up with the idea of song reading when I realized these triggers wouldn't have to come from outside ourselves. We don't normally find ourselves smelling chalk for no reason, but we can find ourselves humming a song we haven't heard in years for no obvious reason. I couldn't help wondering: why that particular song? Why now? Could the song have entered your mind at this point in your life because it was telling you something you needed to know?"

A reviewer for *Publishers Weekly* (March 17, 2003, on-line) wrote, "Tucker's assured debut novel is an achingly tender narrative about grief, love, madness and crippling family secrets. . . . This intoxicating debut may remind [readers] of Shirley Jackson's *We Have Always Lived in the Castle* and Pat Conroy's *[The] Prince of Tides*, but it's not lost in their shadows." Jen Talley Exum agreed in a review for *Romantic Times Book Reviews* (on-line): "This is a beautiful and bittersweet debut that explores the meaning of family and memory. . . . It brings colorful, small-town Missouri to vivid life through quirky characters and silly love songs. It's easy to accept the idea that the soundtracks of our lives hold meaning; it's more difficult to acknowledge what that meaning is. That's what Mary Beth and Leeann are forced to do, in a story at once funny and touching, heartbreaking and wise."

Tucker's next novel, *Shout Down The Moon*, follows the adventures of Patty Taylor, a single mother supporting her young son by singing in a band. Roberta O'Hara wrote for Bookreporter.com, "Lisa Tucker's debut novel, *The Song Reader*, was an original and engrossing premise coupled with compelling writing. With that one book Tucker cemented herself as a strong new voice, a talented writer to watch for in the future. Now in her sophomore effort, *Shout Down the Moon*, Tucker proves that *The Song Reader* was no fluke; she has more stories to tell." A reviewer for *Publishers Weekly* (December 22, 2003, on-line) opined, "Tucker's compulsively readable tale deftly moves over the literary landscape, avoiding genre classification; it succeeds as a subtle romance, an incisive character study and compelling woman-in-peril noir fiction."

Tucker's latest novel, *Once Upon a Day*, follows the developing relationship between a widowed doctor and a young woman whose life has been unusually sheltered. (Tucker did not entirely abandon her usual musical themes; the young woman sings to herself to halt her panic attacks, and another character becomes a jazz singer.) A reviewer for *Publishers Weekly* (November 28, 2005, on-line) wrote, "An exceptionally empathetic storyteller, Tucker has created a haunting, gripping novel that brims with graceful writing and fragile characters. This should be catnip for book clubs, whether they devour it as a page-turner about parenting and family or discuss its subtle meditations on fate and coincidence, wealth and poverty, freedom and safety, fairy tales and American dreams."

Tucker is married and has a son; the family lives in northern New Mexico. (Her husband is a software developer and jazz composer.) Her short work has been published in *Seventeen* and *Pages*, among other periodicals, and is included in the anthologies *Lit Riffs* (2004), which features stories based on popular songs, and *Cold Feet*, which contains stories with marital themes.

—P.B.M.

Suggested Reading: Lisa Tucker's Web site; *Publishers Weekly* (on-line) Mar. 17, 2003, Dec. 22, 2003, Nov. 28, 2005; University of Pennsylvania *Gazette* (on-line) July/Aug. 2003

Selected Books: *The Song Reader*, 2003; *Shout Down the Moon*, 2004; *Once Upon a Day*, 2006

Courtesy of Nancy E. Turner

Turner, Nancy E.

1953– Novelist

Nancy E. Turner is the author of *These Is My Words: The Diary of Sarah Agnes Prine, 1881–1901* (1998), *The Water and the Blood* (2001), and *Sarah's Quilt: A Novel of Sarah Agnes Prine and the Arizona Territories, 1906* (2005). All are about women who triumph over hardship and prove the essential durability of the human spirit; the difficulties depicted in *These Is My Words* and *Sarah's Quilt* are faced by pioneer women on the American frontier in the 19th century, while those in *The Water and the Blood* are confronted by a young woman in bigoted, small-town America at the beginning of World War II.

In 2003 Nancy E. Turner provided the following autobiographical statement for *World Authors 2000–2005*:

"Born in Dallas, Texas in 1953, I spent my youngest years in Santa Ana, California, and Scottsdale, Arizona. Living in the shadow of Disneyland's Matterhorn may have enhanced my imagination, for, each night, if my sisters and I were good, we were allowed stay up, sit in the front yard, and watch the 9:00 p.m. Disneyland fireworks show, and I believed if some of the 'fairy dust' from the fireworks fell on me while I was thinking happy thoughts, I might be able to fly.

"On the way to becoming 'a writer,' I have been a mother, a wife, a dog trainer. I've taught piano lessons and directed vocal and handbell choirs, played piano and organ in churches, sewn Halloween costumes, decorated cakes, and been a teacher's aide in a one-room schoolhouse in the Petrified Forest National Park. I've earned money from such sundry professions as: seam snipper in a pants factory, real estate agent (at which I bombed), church music director, executive secretary, and restoration aide to a paleontologist specializing in Pleistocene fossils. I've always loved science, but I'm dreadful at math, which means I only get to admire from a distance. However, I cut my reading eye teeth on Isaac Asimov and Ray Bradbury, sneaking them from my dad's stash of 'grownups only' books off the top shelves. Combine Nancy Drew mysteries and *Little House on the Prairie* by Laura Ingalls Wilder, toss in *Gone With the Wind*, which I read for the first time when I was 10, and—well—you get the idea. There was nothing I wouldn't read.

"In 1969 I fell in love in high school with a blond-haired boy with a broken leg he'd gotten in football practice. By the time he graduated, we were engaged, and within a month, Uncle Sam sent him Greetings from the U.S. Army, and he was drafted. I'd been trying to get the funds and paperwork completed to be a foreign exchange student in Germany for my senior year of high school, and when he was told he was going to Germany, my parents gave permission for us to marry. The plan was that he'd go there and I'd go as his wife, live on base housing, and finish high school in Germany. The Army is not aware that people make plans however, and they decided he was needed in Vietnam, so I was stuck at home to finish school in 1971. Our daughter was born in 1973, and our son in 1976. We've been married now 31 years. Can it really be that much time has passed? There must be a book there, somewhere. . . .

"In 1992, when my son was in high school and my daughter was a sophomore in college, my husband took a promotion that meant a raise and a move to Tucson. The opportunity to get a degree was staring me in the face, but I was intimidated by the atmosphere at the University of Arizona, so I enrolled at Pima Community College. I studied much harder than I ever had before. In the middle of everything, though, I dropped out for a semester to finish the manuscript for *These Is My Words*, not thinking it could actually become a novel. With an Associate's degree in hand, I enrolled at the U. It took seven years—start to finish—but I completed a Bachelor's degree in Fine Arts Studies with a triple major in creative writing, music, and studio art at the University of Arizona in December 1999. I graduated with a G.P.A. of 3.85 and two published novels under my belt.

"*These Is My Words* is not a story about my family, but it is inspired by the strength found between a few lines of memoir, a battered newspaper clipping, and the lines deeply worn into the face of my great-grandmother, Sarah Agnes Prine, on a fading daguerreotype. *These Is My Words* has received critical acclaim around the world by notable writers like Mary Stewart and Rosamunde Pilcher. It has been released in three foreign languages, and in audio and large print format. It was on the London *Times* best seller list from May 10, 1999 to June 1, 1999. Literary awards include: Arizona Library Association Adult Author of the Year, 1999, *The Arizona Daily Star* book list of "Best Picks" for 1998, *Good Housekeeping* Magazine Book of the Month, plus serialization, March, 1998. It was a finalist for the 1999 WILLA (Cather) Award, the 2000 Audie Award for Audio, nominated for the 1998 Pulitzer Prize, 1998 Western Heritage Award, 1998 Christopher Award for moral standard of excellence in literature. It was National Public Radio 'Book Week' Novel of the Week, Johannesburg, South Africa, a book club selection for Doubleday Book Club and The Literary Guild Book Club.

"*The Water and the Blood* came out in October, 2001. Based in a fictional town in East Texas, the story opens on Halloween night in 1941 when a group of high school seniors commit a terrible crime. The main character, a young woman with the moniker of 'Frosty,' has been drawn into the deed by misplaced rage. They all assume that they've gotten away with the act, and go on with their lives. Just a few short weeks later, Pearl Harbor is bombed by the Japanese Navy. For these young people, their world instantly becomes global instead of centered in a small pocket of a small town. The declaration of war sends each of the characters on a different path, and throughout the story, we see the evolvement of Frosty's character until she realizes that she has to make a fateful choice."

These Is My Words, as the title implies, takes the form of diary entries. A reviewer for *Publishers Weekly* (January 5, 1998, on-line) found it an effective device: "When she begins recording her life, Sarah Prine is an intelligent, headstrong 18-year-old capable of holding her own on her family's settlement near Tucson. Her skill with a rifle fends off a constant barrage of Indian attacks and outlaw assaults. It also attracts a handsome Army captain named Jack Elliot. By the time she's 21, Sarah has recorded her loveless marriage to a family friend, the establishment of a profitable ranch, the birth of her first child—and the death of her husband. The love between Jack and Sarah, which dominates the rest of the tale, has begun to blossom. Fragmented and disjointed in its early chapters, with poor spelling and grammar, Sarah's journal gradually gains in clarity and eloquence as she matures. While this device may frustrate some

readers at first, Taylor's deft progression produces the intended reward: she not only tells of her heroine's growth, but she shows it through Sarah's writing and insights. The result is a compelling portrait of an enduring love, the rough old West and a memorable pioneer."

Sarah's Quilt, a sequel, met similar praise. For *Publishers Weekly* (April 18, 2005, on-line), a reviewer wrote, "Older, tougher, wiser, Sarah enchants with her plainspoken energy and honesty. The title may suggest a gentle tale of domestic comfort, but the book is as straightforward, gritty and persistent as the woman who inspires it and as memorable as the landscape where she carves out her life."

Between the novels featuring Sarah Prine, Turner published *The Water and the Blood*, which a *Publishers Weekly* (October 8, 2001, on-line) reviewer called a "beautifully written portrait of Southern religious repression and racism." Turner soon returned, however, to the heroine based on her great-grandmother. The next installment of Sarah Prine's adventures, set at about the time of the Mexican Revolution of 1910 and tentatively titled "The Star Garden," is due to be released in late 2007. Turner, who has three grandchildren, sewed the quilt that is set to be featured on the book's cover.

—S.Y.

Suggested Reading: *Booklist* p986 Feb. 15, 1998, p54 Sep. 1, 2001; *Library Journal* p173 Feb. 15, 1998; *Publishers Weekly* p43+ Oct. 8, 2001; *Washington Post Book World* p7 Feb. 22, 1998

Selected Books: *These Is My Words: The Diary of Sarah Agnes Prine, 1881–1901*, 1998; *The Water and the Blood*, 2001; *Sarah's Quilt: A Novel of Sarah Agnes Prine and the Arizona Territories, 1906*, 2005

Udall, Brady

1957(?)– Short-story writer; novelist

"I believe a book can't just be all darkness, all dark notes," the novelist and short-story writer Brady Udall remarked in an interview with Robert Birnbaum for the on-line journal *Identity Theory* (July 21, 2002). "That's too easy—to be that nihilistic. I owe my characters some opportunity at hope or redemption. It's not going to be the redemption that the reader expects. They are not going to be happily married and live happily ever after and become President of the United States, or something. There has to be at least the opportunity for that. I respect my characters. That might sound corny, but I can't just hurt them and kill them just for my purposes. It would be too much for me to do that."

Born in a rural part of northeastern Arizona, reportedly in 1957, Brady Udall hails from a famous political family, of which former Secretary of the Interior Stewart L. Udall and former Congressman Morris K. Udall were members. As a child and young adult, he had little idea about what he wanted to do when he grew up—though he was certain he wanted to avoid manual labor. "I grew up working on a farm and I knew I sure as heck didn't want to do that for the rest of my life," Udall noted in an interview with Jeanette Kwok (March 13, 2001), as posted on the Web site for Udall's novel, *The Miracle Life of Edgar Mint.* "I remember being out in the alfalfa fields in the hot sun hauling hay, sweaty, dirty, exhausted, and thinking: once I leave for college I will never do a job like this again. I will find something where I can sit in an air-conditioned office, sip lemonade, listen to music if I want to, and type on a computer. So I became a writer."

Udall kept his ambitions to himself for many years. In high school he would occasionally write a story and show it to his English teacher to gain some encouragement, but that was the extent of his self-promotion. While studying for his undergraduate degree at Brigham Young University, in Provo, Utah, he majored in sociology because he never wanted to "let on that I would try my hand at writing," as he noted in an interview with Ron Hogan for the Beatrice Web site.

After graduating from college, in 1992, Udall, a member of the Church of Jesus Christ of Latter-Day Saints (also known as Mormons), served as a missionary in Brazil and Korea, where he taught English. Returning to the U.S., he attended the prestigious Iowa Writers' Workshop, receiving his M.F.A. in 1995. "I didn't go [to Iowa] to learn how to write," he noted in his interview with Birnbaum. "I thought I already knew how. I pretty much did. They offered me money and a fellowship. Two years, not having to work, just going to school. That's where I wrote my first collection of stories."

Udall's work initially received notice while he was in his first year at Iowa. Carol Houck Smith, a book editor at W. W. Norton, was sufficiently impressed by a handful of his short stories to offer him a two-book deal. His first book, *Letting Loose the Hounds* (1997), was a collection of short stories. Set mostly in locales in which Udall has lived, such as rural Utah and Arizona, the stories depict the lives of ordinary men and women who have suffered or continue to suffer under the weight of common modern American problems, including divorce, dead-end jobs, and broken dreams. Still, despite the characters' disillusionment, they are able to find the humor in often tragic situations.

Letting Loose the Hounds received generally favorable notices. In her review for *Library Journal* (January 1997), Charlotte L. Glover wrote: "Udall breathes fresh life into tales of the modern West, where cowboys drive pickup trucks, Native Americans live in mobile homes, and the desert is just past the next subdivision. . . . These bittersweet stories of men and women are tinged with comedy." She added, "The characters speak in the first person and their words flow with the raw emotions and natural [dialogue] of a Sam [Shepard] play. The writing is full of colorful language, slang, and the rhythm of everyday speech. Characters rage, curse, and contemplate without pausing for breath while the reader is propelled forward because, as the old woman in [the story] 'Snake' says, 'somebody hand over their whole life to you and you got to be a little curious.' Udall . . . has a bright future in fiction."

Jim Shepard, writing for the *New York Times Book Review* (March 2, 1997), had reservations about the collection but was mostly positive: "Mr. Udall's indebtedness to his contemporary predecessors is sometimes clear. A host of his narrators share Rick Bass's characters' fierce devotion to passion, to intensity itself. Other characters have Denis Johnson's ear for a dialogue so understated in the face of crisis that it approaches the realm of the non sequitur. . . . Finally, though, Mr. Udall is his own man. There are the occasional tics (everyone seems to have a name like Bach Abercorn or Hyman Dimbatt), and occasionally the characters' inability to communicate is too closely paralleled by the story's surrender in the face of the unnamable. (What is it that's causing all this self-destructiveness? Well, sometimes it's a mystery.) But the best stories provide the tools with which to solve such mysteries and are suffused, besides, with the 'ache of sadness at the measures we have to take, the desperations and last resorts.'"

In 2001 Udall published his first novel, *The Miracle Life of Edgar Mint.* Two experiences inspired him to write the story: growing up near a Native American reservation and meeting his wife's ex-boyfriend, who had been run over by a mail truck in his youth. Combining these two stories he created the character of Edgar Mint, a half-Apache boy who gets his head run over by a mail truck while playing on the reservation one day. He miraculously survives the accident—brought back to life by a shady doctor—and is sent to a hospital to recover. He regains all his abilities except for the ability to write, but when a hospital friend supplies him a typewriter, he begins using it avidly. Meanwhile, since his alcoholic mother had left him even before finding out whether he had survived, he is sent to a boarding school for Native American delinquents where he is routinely tortured—and at one point almost killed—by his fellow students. Afterwards, he becomes the foster child of a dysfunctional Mormon family in a Utah suburb, where he tries to lead a normal life but finds himself continuously menaced by the doctor who, having saved him, has now taken an obsessive interest in the boy. Edgar, meanwhile, undaunted despite his difficulties, decides to track down the mailman who ran him over and offer him forgiveness.

The novel received largely positive reviews. In *Newsweek* (June 15, 2001), Malcolm Jones declared: "If they gave prizes for the best first line of a first novel, Brady Udall would have no competition: 'If I could tell you only one thing about my life it would be this: when I was seven years old the mailman ran over my head.' Fine, we're all paying attention now. But the truly noteworthy thing about Udall is that once he's got our attention, he knows what to do with it. Even though [the novel] could be described as the Apache version of *David Copperfield*, the truth is, it's like nothing else you've read. . . . By the end of the story the only unbelievable thing is that Edgar Mint is nothing but a figment of Udall's imagination. That's the real miracle here." Jennifer Reese, in the *New York Times Book Review* (July 1, 2001), called *The Miracle Life of Edgar Mint* a "rambling and generous first novel. . . . Contemporary fiction is full of cynical, world-weary protagonists. One of the strengths of this big, uneven novel—it reads at times like a John Irving novel touched up by Roy Blount Jr.—is the lovely and complex character of Edgar, an innocent whose struggle to survive is at odds with his fundamentally gentle nature. . . . Other characters are less rich, the denouement seems

rushed, and the book is too long. But it is also sweet, sad and refreshing."

Brady Udall is a past recipient of a Bread Loaf Fellowship, a James Michener Fellowship, an Iowa Arts Fellowship, and an Arizona Commission on the Arts Fellowship. He has been the winner of the *Playboy* College Fiction Contest and the *Sunstone* Fiction Contest. His short stories and essays have been published in a number of journals and periodicals, most notably *Esquire, Gentlemen's Quarterly, Story*, and the *Paris Review*. He has taught at such institutions as the University of Idaho, in Moscow, and at Southern Illinois University, in Carbondale. Udall and his wife, Kate, have two sons.

—C.M.

Suggested Reading: Beatrice Web site; BookBrowse Web site; *GQ* p192 May 2003; *Identity Theory* (on-line); *Library Journal* p152 Jan. 1997; *New York Times Book Review* Mar. 12, 1997, p16 July 1, 2001; *Newsweek* p91 June 25, 2001

Selected Books: *Letting Loose the Hounds*, 1997; *The Miracle Life of Edgar Mint*, 2001

Ullmann, Linn

Aug. 9, 1966– Literary critic; novelist

Over the past 10 years, the novelist Linn Ullmann has earned worldwide acclaim for her anti-heroic and thematically nuanced narratives about ordinary and often unsympathetic characters. Her four novels—three of which have been translated into English under the titles *Before You Sleep* (1999), *Stella Descending* (2003), and *Grace* (2005)—are notable not only for their thematic power but also for their stylistic beauty, a quality Ullmann constantly struggles to achieve. As she recently revealed in an article for *Time Out* (March 15, 2006), "There are days when writing is easy, fun even. Other days, I'll simply settle for getting the thing done, to finish before deadline. I will be a genius some other time. Writing to finish is a bit like getting through a sleepless night without panicking. There's a lot to be said for finishing. This, by the way, is why editors invented deadlines. If there were no deadlines, writers wouldn't write, least of all finish. So if I'm lucky, if I don't get the flu, or the children don't get the flu, or something else happens (of major or minor consequence), I will finish and feel really good for about five minutes—before I begin thinking that I was mad to have written this, the words are all scrambled. I will have to do it all over again."

Ulla Montan/Courtesy of Random House

The daughter of the Norwegian actress Liv Ullmann and the renowned Swedish film director Ingmar Bergman, Linn Ullmann was born in Oslo, Norway, on August 9, 1966 and spent much of her youth accompanying her mother around the world. With such famous parents, Ullmann found herself in the public eye from the moment she was born. As a child she appeared in a number of films, including *Utvandrarna* (*The Emigrants,* 1971), *Nybyggarna* (1972), *Viskningar och rop* (*Cries and Whispers*, 1972), and *Höstsonaten* (*Autumn Sonata,* 1978). In the early 1980s, Ullmann settled with her mother in New York City. While attending the Professional Children's School in Manhattan, she modeled for a time but found the work uninteresting. "Modeling for me is like playing dress-up," she remarked, according to George Hackett and Mary Murphy for *Newsweek* (September 26, 1983). "Acting is what I really want to do." However, before long Ullmann lost interest in acting as well. In the mid-1980s she shifted her focus toward humanitarian endeavors. Working with the United Nations Children's Fund (UNICEF), Ullmann served as a youth ambassador from late 1986 through late 1987, and hosted a video called *A Toy Is What You Make It* (1987), which depicts how children from Kenya, Peru, Sri Lanka, and Turkey fashion toys from inexpensive material. Reflecting on her youthful idealism, Ullmann remarked, as quoted by Douglas Keay for the London *Times* (July 13, 1987), "I wasn't a part of the Sixties, but I was born into them. And it seems to me they had lovely ideals which kind of floated away. And now we're so competitive about life. If only there could be some kind of embrace." During this same period, she was also "toying with writing" according to Keay. Upon completing her bachelor's degree in English at New York University (NYU), in 1988, Ullmann took up graduate studies; however, within a year she left school and returned to Norway. A few months after arriving in Oslo, in 1989, she married Espen Toendel, a 34-year-old lawyer.

In Norway Ullmann worked in journalism, as a radio reporter, but maintained an interest in the literary arts, co-editing the journal *Vagant*. In the early 1990s she became a literary critic for *Dagbladet*, a prominent Norwegian newspaper. Later that decade Ullmann edited the 1997 volume *Men jeg bor her ennå* (which can be translated as "but I live here, still"), an anthology of work by contemporary Norwegian authors; co-wrote two elementary-school social-studies texts; and penned *Yrke: regissør* (1998, the title means "profession: director"), an examination of the life and films of the Norwegian director Arne Skouen. During this period Ullmann also tried her hand at fiction writing, which she found very trying at first. "I had to put that part of me, the critic, in a deep, dark cellar before I could start writing," she remarked, as quoted by Gillian Glover for the *Scotsman* (March 2, 2000). "I tried several times to start the book before I finally pierced whatever I needed to pierce to get into it. I kept hearing that critical voice in my head, and it was making me write very boring prose." Once this critical voice was suppressed, Ullmann produced *For du søvner* (1998), which almost instantly turned her into an international literary star. In the year after its debut, the work was widely translated—the English version, by Tiina Nunnally, was entitled *Before You Sleep*—and published in 14 countries, garnering accolades from critics throughout the globe.

Set in New York, and Oslo, *Before You Sleep* details the story of three generations of woman from a Norwegian family as told by Karin Blom, a notorious liar from the family's third generation, to her seven-year-old nephew as he struggles to stay awake for a call from his mother, Karin's sister, Julie. Karin's voice, that of a woman described by Catherine Lockerbie for the *Scotsman* (July 6, 1999) as "a fine fin-de-millennium woman, unstoppably feisty, all appetite and assertion," was for some the strongest element of the book. As Eileen Pollack, writing for the *Boston Globe* (October 24, 1999), noted, "*Before You Sleep* succeeds in every way a novel should succeed, but its most captivating feature is the voice of its young protagonist. Karin Blom is that most engaging of narrators, a young cynic who can't avoid loving what she scorns." Ullmann was quite proud of her narrator, stating, as quoted by Lockerbie in a later article for the *Scotsman* (August 7, 1999), "I wrote [*Before You Sleep*] in opposition to sad female victims in novels. My heroine drinks like crazy, seduces any man she wants. I wanted to make it wild and funny and aggressive. In Scandinavia now you see the development of more dangerous, omnipotent female characters, and in a way, mine is a product of Norwegian folk tales. She is fantastic, triumphant!" Others, however, found Karin to be the book's primary shortcoming. Dominic Black, in a review for *Scotland on Sunday* (March 12, 2000), described the novel as "a self-conscious, showy and untidy attempt to explore family relations and their disintegration," and continued, "*Before You Sleep* doesn't know what kind of novel it wants to be, and succeeds spectacularly in being none of them." Black went on to complain that Karin's voice "plagues the reader throughout this rambling narrative. She introduces us to her extended family, her mother, sister, father and lovers, in a knowing, 'isn't that profound in its oddity' tone that, within the first 10 pages, makes one want to reach into the print and throttle her."

Despite the occasional negative review, *Before You Sleep* proved to be the beginning of a fruitful literary career. In 2001 Ullmann completed her second novel, *Når jeg er hos deg*, which was translated into English as *Stella Descending*. Told from the perspective of multiple narrators, the novel opens with Stella falling off the roof of an apartment building; she may have slipped or jumped, or her husband may have pushed her. What follows is an examination of Stella's past and those with whom she has spent it in an attempt to unravel the mystery not only of her death but also of her entire life. The work received largely positive reviews. Writing for the London *Independent* (January 23, 2004), Paul Binding applauded the power of Ullmann's prose even while calling attention to what he perceived as the book's flaws: "Ullmann's grasp of the ambiguous natures of her people, and her understanding of their backgrounds, is admirably strong. The governing metaphor of the fall, and of the density of those two seconds, is at once poetic and intellectually satisfying." Nevertheless, Binding continued, "What for me at times vitiates the novel's success, however, is Ullmann's inclusion of material extraneous to this central image." "*Stella Descending* is surrealistic—not just in the vague modern sense of the word, as a synonym for 'odd' or 'weird' or 'unsettling,'" Michael Harris wrote for the *Los Angeles Times* (August 24, 2003), "but also in the original 1920s sense: as a work of art that blurs the borders between mundane reality and the reality of fantasies and dreams. This is a characteristic of Ingmar Bergman's films that Ullmann . . . seems to have inherited, along with an interest in secrets festering beneath the placid surface of Scandinavian life."

Originally published in Norway as *Nåde* (2002), Ullmann's third novel, *Grace*, has been her most critically successful to date. As the work, begins, the protagonist, Johan Sletten, learns that he is dying of cancer and has six months to live. Ullmann proceeds to explore this cowardly man's attempt "to face his end with something resembling dignity and courage," as Sam Thompson noted for the London *Guardian* (February 25, 2006), and, in the process, builds a portrait of a sad, mediocre figure, whose one saving grace is his relationship with his second wife, Mai, a pediatrician 17 years his junior. Moving between the past and the present, Ullmann patches Sletten's story together in a collage-like manner. Among the revelations that emerge are the circumstances surrounding Johan's father's death—after Johan made a deal with Death to take his father instead of his gravely ill mother. Ullmann likewise evokes the events leading up to the demise of Johan's first wife, Alice—whom, Ullmann writes, as quoted by Thompson, "he would have run . . . over himself" if a black station wagon had not done it first. Other strands of the narrative include the trivial incidents leading to Johan's estrangement from his son, and the state of his relationship with Mai—whom he loves beyond measure and whose love he is amazed to receive. Critics were dazzled. "Ullmann stunningly and consistently illuminates the nuances of people who love each other taking leave and the confluence of emotions: fear, loss, pain, relief and release are all intimated in her exquisitely subtle prose," Victoria A. Brownworth observed for the *Miami Herald* (February 20, 2005), going on to note, "This dense and immensely compelling novel lingers in the memory, beautiful, haunting and just a little frightening." Similarly, Bruce Bawer remarked for the *New York Times Book Review* (January 30, 2005), "An elegant stylist with an original voice (and a top-notch translator,

Barbara Haveland), [Ullmann] is especially good at capturing moments of poignancy, often with a trace of gallows humor. Thus, feeling unwell one day, Johan catches himself 'searching Mai's face with something like suspicion, much as a passenger on a plane will search the flight attendant's face when the plane begins to shudder and the cabin lights go out. Is this it? Are we crashing now?'"

Ullmann's fourth novel, *Et Velsignet Barn* (which translates as "a child blessed"), was published in Norway in 2005; it has yet to be translated into English. Ullmann, who divorced her first husband, is now married to Niels Fredrik Dahl, one of Norway's most respected living writers. The couple reside in Oslo with their four children and their dog, Brando. Aside from her fiction, Ullmann writes a political and cultural column for the daily newspaper *Aftenposten*.

—A.R.

Suggested Reading: *Boston Globe* C p3 Oct. 24, 1999; (London) *Independent* p23 Jan. 23, 2004; (London) *Times* July 13, 1987; *New York Times Book Review* p21 Jan. 30, 2005; *Scotland on Sunday* p13 Mar. 12, 2000; *Scotsman* p9 Aug. 7, 1999; *Time Out* p41 Mar. 15, 2006

Selected Works in English Translation: *Before You Sleep,* 1999; *Stella Descending,* 2003; *Grace,* 2005

Upchurch, Michael

Feb. 5, 1954– Novelist; critic

Michael Upchurch, while working steadily as a book and theater critic for such publications as the *Chicago Tribune*, the *New York Times Book Review*, the *Oregonian*, the *San Francisco Chronicle*, the *Seattle Times*, and the *Washington Post Book World*, has also published four novels. Set in locales from Seattle, Washington, to Washington, D.C., *Jamboree* (1981), *Air* (1986), *The Flame Forest* (1989), and *Passive Intruder* (1995) are peopled with diverse and nuanced characters that have earned Upchurch critical notice.

Michael Upchurch was born in Rahway, New Jersey, on February 5, 1954, the son of Edward Upchurch, an engineering consultant, and the former Patricia O'Neill. During a childhood he described for the *American Scholar* (Winter 1999) as "peripatetic," Upchurch lived in Holland and England, as well as the United States. He was educated at the University of Exeter, in Devon, England, where in 1975 he received a bachelor's degree in English literature.

Upchurch soon moved to North Carolina, where he worked as a bookstore clerk while writing his first novel. In 1979 he moved to New York City and had sold the book to a publisher within a year. *Jamboree* follows several families from New Jersey enjoying an outing with the Boy Scouts. One of the scouts, Chris Castle, has a father who was killed in the Vietnam War and an English stepfather, and in the course of the book he comes to terms with his family history, as well as his feelings about duty and ceremony. In a review for the *Washington Post Book World* (June 7, 1981), Charles Trueheart noted that the novel is primarily about war: "It is not hard to spot, in Upchurch's spare and remarkably acute sketches of the [Boy Scout] Jamboree, a central concern with war, and the way its memory and specter washes over generations and spills into civilian life."

Upchurch continued working in bookstores and as an administrative assistant while trying to sell his next novel. *Air* is set during the late 1970s in Washington, D.C.; it features Arleen, an unpopular young woman who comes to the nation's capital from North Carolina to work at a scientific publisher. Spending her evenings at various nightclubs, Arleen meets and falls in love with a New Wave musician named Andrew. The duo marry and become part of the 1980s conservative movement spearheaded by Ronald Reagan's election to president. *Air* received varying reviews. A critic for *Kirkus Reviews* (May 15, 1986) wrote that Upchurch "has captured—brilliantly and almost photographically—a period of recent history, the pause before Reagan." A critic for *Publishers Weekly* (May 9, 1986), however, was confounded by the novel, wondering if the author had "crafted a self-conscious satire or a serious novel? Are Arleen and Andrew supposed to inspire or frighten?" In answer to that, Upchurch told an interviewer for *Contemporary Authors* (1997), "I intended satire to a degree, but of characters who were too troubled to serve simply as targets. Arleen and Andrew were certainly never intended to 'inspire.' (I hate preaching in fiction.) Instead, they're conundrums, as most of my characters are."

Upchurch's third novel, *The Flame Forest*, is set in England, and details an unlikely love triangle between three teenagers: Jim Ward, a steadfast and quiet youth, and Roberta and Peter Lindquist, twins who have recently moved to his village. Peter, a homosexual, is attracted to Jim, who is in turn attracted to Roberta (who conceals a mental illness throughout the narrative). Calling *The Flame Forest* "a novel to be read and admired" in the *San Francisco Chronicle* (July 9, 1989), Mark Childress praised Upchurch's writing, adding that "most of his scenes and sentences are beautifully wrought, and his delicate tracing of an adolescent's brush with madness takes on the quality of a fable or fairy tale." Douglas Greenwood, in the *Washington Post Book World* (September 3, 1989), also had many positive things to say in his review:

"There are several unforgettable scenes in *The Flame Forest*, some reminiscent of Kingsley Amis's comic inventiveness in *Lucky Jim*, others in the vein of the wild imaginings of Franz Kafka or Nathaniel West." He concluded, "If there is any 'message' in this provocative novel, it is not that innocence is always lost, but that in spite of the slings and arrows of outrageous fortune, we are scarred for life in ways that we may not understand when we are young."

With his next novel, *Passive Intruder*, Upchurch gave the traditional ghost story a modern twist. In it, a 24-year-old receptionist named Susan Pond marries an older photographer named Walker Popman. A year after their marriage they take a three-week trip crossing the continental United States to celebrate their anniversary. In every city they visit, the pair sees a ghostly image of a woman in their snapshots; they finally spot her in person at a museum in Chicago. Moments after the sighting, Walker dies of a heart attack. In the *New York Times Book Review* (November 5 1995), David Willis McCullough found much to praise in *Passive Intruder*: "Michael Upchurch . . . is a stylist who works best with the smoke and mirrors of the human psyche. In his latest work, relationships are often oblique; logic is unimportant. Mr. Upchurch is that rarest of ghost-story writers, one who doesn't seem the least bit interested in making physical settings themselves seem ghostly. To him, everything is in the mind or the memory—or on a badly developed roll of film. But then, of course, *Passive Intruder* is not really a ghost story at all, but a surprisingly seductive meditation on mourning."

Michael Upchurch lives in Seattle, Washington, with his partner, the film critic John Hartl. He lists among his major influences the novelists Christina Stead and Henry Green.

—C.M.

Suggested Reading: *American Scholar* p130+ Winter 1999; *Chicago Tribune* V p3 Jan. 10, 1996; *Library Journal* p89 Oct. 15, 1995; *New York Times Book Review* p12 Nov. 5, 1995; *Washington Post Book World* p4 Sep. 3, 1989

Selected Books: *Jamboree*, 1981; *Air*, 1986; *Flame Forest*, 1989; *Passive Intruder*, 1995

Urrea, Luis Alberto

(oo-RAY-ah, loo-EES
ahl-BARE-toh)

*Aug. 20, 1955– Nonfiction writer; short-story
writer; poet*

In novels and short stories, books of nonfiction, and volumes of poetry, Luis Alberto Urrea has illuminated the experiences of impoverished Mexicans and those Mexican-born people who, like him, have crossed the border to live in the U.S. He is perhaps best known for his "border" trilogy, comprising the nonfiction works *Across the Wire: Life and Hard Times on the Mexican Border* (1993), *By the Lake of Sleeping Children: The Secret Life of the Mexican Border* (1996), and *Nobody's Son: Notes from an American Life* (1998), which describe the plight of the poor in Tijuana, Mexico, and Urrea's own difficult growing-up years. The writer continued his chronicle of the destitute of his native country with *The Devil's Highway* (2004), an account of the ill-fated journey of 26 Mexican men through the desert toward the Arizona border. Urrea's poems have been collected in volumes including *The Fever of Being* (1994) and *Ghost Sickness* (1997), and he is the author of the fiction works *In Search of Snow* (1994), *Six Kinds of Sky* (2002), and *The Hummingbird's Daughter* (2005). In an observation that might be applied to Urrea's body of work as a whole, Jennifer Modenessi wrote in her review of *The Hummingbird's Daughter* for the *Contra Costa Times* (July 3, 2005), "There's . . . an earthy dose of the everyday spiking Urrea's prose—mud, stink and death counterbalance some of Urrea's more otherworldly themes and keep the book firmly grounded in the loam."

One of six children, Luis Alberto Urrea was born on August 20, 1955 in Tijuana, Mexico. His father, Alberto, came from Sinaloa, Mexico, and traced his heritage to the Basque region of northern Spain; his mother, Phyllis, was a white woman from New York. "My mother was a New Yorker with a bohemian flair, but deeply conservative views," Urrea told Daniel Olivas during an interview for the Elegant Variation Weblog (June 2005). "My father was a Mexican military man and cop with a poet's soul." His father had had an important security post on the staff of the president of Mexico until about 1954, when he fell out of favor with his superiors. "One of the stories he always used to tell us," Urrea said to Ernie Grimm for the *San Diego Reader* (June 24, 2004, on-line), "was that he had been asked to perform a task he could not get himself to perform, and he had been paid $2000 in a check from the president of Mexico that he had never cashed. And after he had died, when I went through his papers, I found the check. . . . You can assume what it was; they must have wanted him to kill someone." After Urrea's father lost his position on the president's staff, the family fell on

hard times; his parents commuted across the border to San Diego, California, where his father worked for a tuna cannery and his mother for a department store. Because Urrea was then left in the care of Mexican women, his first language was Spanish, and he has recalled thinking as a small boy that his mother was insane because she spoke English, which he did not understand. Urrea has described his parents' marriage as volatile and recalled that he himself was mistreated by members of his extended family. Such experiences, he has said, have informed the tragicomic nature of much of his writing. (He had health problems as well, contracting tuberculosis in Tijuana.) One source of solace during his boyhood was his relationship with his godparents, Abelino and Rosario García, who appear in fictional form in *In Search of Snow* and *The Fever of Being*.

When Urrea was three years old, his family moved to San Diego. They lived in the largely African-American neighborhood of Logan Heights before moving to the mostly white San Diego suburb of Clairemont when Urrea was in the fifth grade. In Clairemont, "far from being the athlete and army captain my father wanted, and even farther from being the crew-cut Ivy League lawyer my mother wanted, I was this post-beatnik art kid," Urrea told Daniel Olivas. He attended Clairemont High School, which later became known as the model for the 1982 film *Fast Times at Ridgemont High*. At the suggestion of a teacher, Urrea read a book of poems by Stephen Crane, which so impressed the teenager that he began trying to imitate Crane in writing his own poetry. He was also influenced by the lyrics of the songwriter Leonard Cohen. In about 1970 he bought a copy of the poetry volume *The Lords and the New Creatures*, by the rock-music icon Jim Morrison, "and that was it," as Urrea told Ernie Grimm. "I was hooked on poetry." Urrea was the first member of his family to attend college, majoring first in drama, then in writing, and earning a bachelor's degree from the University of California, at San Diego, in 1977. One of his teachers there was the writer Ursula Le Guin. Urrea wrote and illustrated *Frozen Moments*, a book of short stories and poetry, as his senior thesis; the university paid for a few copies of the work to be published in 1977.

"Once college was over, I hung out, dude," Urrea wrote for his Web site. "Me and my gang spent every night driving around with tankfuls of 35 cent gas." During that time he also wrote lyrics for a rock band, worked as a movie extra ("Don't ask—it's too humiliating," he wrote for his Web site), and wound up clerking in an all-night grocery store. He began to emerge from that seemingly aimless lifestyle when Ursula Le Guin included one of his stories in her anthology *Edges* in 1980. Then Cesar Gonzalez, whom Urrea has identified as an important figure in his life, got him a position as a teaching assistant in the Chicano Studies program at Mesa College, in San Diego. Urrea also began doing work with Spectrum Ministries, under E. G. Von Treutzchler III, who ministered to a group of people living in desperately poor conditions in a district called the Borderlands, in Tijuana, and who became an additional mentor for the young writer. In 1982 Urrea was tapped by Harvard University, in Cambridge, Massachusetts, to teach writing workshops. Meanwhile, he did graduate work at the University of Colorado, at Boulder, earning his M.F.A. degree in 1987, the year he became an associate professor at Massachusetts Bay Community College. He taught writing on a freelance basis from 1990 to 1996 and at the University of Southwestern Louisiana from 1996 to 1999. In the latter year he began teaching at the University of Illinois, at Chicago, where he now has tenure.

Urrea's first book to be issued by a major publisher, *Across the Wire*, is an account of the people living in almost subhuman squalor 20 minutes from downtown San Diego. Urrea wrote "with unflinching candor and raw clinical detail about the very worst manifestations of the disease, brutality and sexual degradation that afflict the men, women and children who live in the Borderlands," Jonathan Kirsch observed in the *Los Angeles Times* (February 10, 1993). "And if the reader is rendered sick at heart or sick to the stomach by the particulars of human misery, so be it. 'Poverty *is* personal: it smells and it shocks and it invades your space,' Urrea writes. 'You come home dirty when you get too close to the poor'. . . . But Urrea refuses to abandon the hope of redemption, no matter how remote it may seem, and so, curiously enough, *Across the Wire* is *not* a tale of unrelieved despair." Kirsch called the book "a work of investigative reporting that is also a bittersweet song of human anguish." David Unger, writing for the *New York Times Book Review* (February 21, 1993), hailed *Across the Wire* as "testimonial literature at its best." The book was selected for a Christopher Award in 1994.

In 1994 Urrea published his first collection of poetry, *The Fever of Being*, as well as his debut novel, *In Search of Snow*. The latter book is set in Arizona in the 1950s and follows Mike McGurk, a man in his late 20s, as he drifts through life in the company of his father, a mechanic and sometime bare-knuckle brawler. "Urrea wrests strange, beautiful poetry out of a mean, lean desert terrain . . . in this impressive first novel, a blend of deadpan humor, picaresque adventure and search for self," a *Publishers Weekly* (February 7, 1994) reviewer observed. Ray Gonzalez pointed out in the *Nation* (July 18, 1994) that *In Search of Snow*—along with other books then being published by Chicanos—represented a sign that Chicano literature was being fully integrated into the mainstream, since the book was not relegated to small-press publication or dependent on word-of-mouth sales efforts, as works by Mexican American writers had been in the past. *In Search of Snow* "is a joy to read because Urrea is not

sticking to the somber tone so common among other young Chicanos now writing," Gonzalez opined, noting that Urrea "has a flair for creating strong characters and bringing them alive in a blend of drama, slapstick comedy and cinematic technique."

Urrea returned to nonfiction, and to the poor sections of Tijuana, for *By the Lake of Sleeping Children*. On the California side of the Tijuana/U.S. border, as Urrea observed, are luxurious houses and swimming pools; those are visible from the other side, where an enormous garbage dump provides the only livelihood for the wretchedly deprived population. "The politically constructed divide maps the geography of Urrea's bifurcated identity," Ronald Takaki remarked in the *Washington Post Book World* (December 15, 1996), "his Mexican father and American mother, his birth in Tijuana, and his growing up in San Diego." Takaki quoted Urrea as writing, "My father raised me to be 100 percent Mexican, often refusing to speak English to me, tirelessly patrolling the borders of my language. . . . And my mother raised me to be 100 percent American: she never spoke Spanish . . . If, as some have suggested lately, I am some sort of 'voice of the border,' it is because the border runs down the middle of me. I have a barbed-wire fence neatly bisecting my heart." Carolyn Alessio, who reviewed the book for the *Chicago Tribune* (December 15, 1996), found that Urrea had "portray[ed] the poverty and desperation of his native Tijuana in a language both truthful and improbably poetic."

In *Ghost Sickness*, Urrea's second collection of poetry, the narrator of the poems travels by car through the desert of the American Southwest, driven by the ghost of his father in one section and taking the wheel himself in the later sections. "By the last stanza in this collection," Sharon Preiss noted in the *Tucson Weekly* (February 16, 1998), "the words and sounds—the feelings—are those of relief. At last we hear harmonious music, a voice that, having traveled through the discord of the abyss, is now clear and still. The ghost has been laid to rest, and peace envelops this difficult landscape of memory, image, word, and sound."

Nobody's Son is the concluding volume of Urrea's border trilogy. It is both a memoir and a meditation on "la raza," the joys and sorrows of being a Mexican American. Part of the sorrow, for Urrea, stemmed from the wealth of anti-Mexican sentiment he encountered—from people including his own mother, who asked him why, when he was teaching at Harvard, he could not call himself Louis instead of Luis. "You are not a Mexican!" she declared. "This is not, however, just a book about race," a *Publishers Weekly* (August 10, 1998) reviewer wrote. "In fact, it's just as much about writing, and at its best Urrea's staccato phrases build up to a vivid, often brutal image." Rebecca Martin, writing for *Library Journal* (October 1, 1998), noted the "energetic and darkly humorous" nature of Urrea's book, and added, "The essential tone, however, is of self-deprecating humor about the challenge of explaining a dual identity, a task he accomplishes with passion and understanding." *Nobody's Son* won an American Book Award in 1999.

Vatos (2000) is a collaboration between Urrea and the photographer Jose Galvez, in which *vatos*, "street slang for dude, guy, pal, brother," are celebrated in photographs and Urrea's poem "Hymn to Vatos Who Will Never Be in a Poem." Tom Mayo, writing for the *Dallas Morning News* (October 1, 2000), called the book a "deeply rhythmic litany . . . that is by turns haunting and inspiring." *Wandering Time: Western Notebooks* (2000), written in sections corresponding to the seasons of the year, is an account of Urrea's travels through the western United States and of the people he encountered along the way. The book includes references to many writers who influenced his own takes on travel and nature—references that "are refreshing details in an otherwise bland piece," in the opinion of Cynde Bloom Lahey, writing for *Library Journal* (February 15, 1999). In *World Literature Today* (Summer 2000), however, Catharine E. Wall praised the book, writing, "Urrea has illustrated well one of his own adages, that 'a good writer must excel at two things: poking around and paying attention.'"

Urrea's next work of fiction, *Six Kinds of Sky*, is a collection of short stories dealing with the grief-stricken, broken-down, and wretchedly poor—largely Mexican Americans—in the West. "Class struggle, official corruption, the remote distance of the U.S.A. and its concerns, perhaps stereotypical Mexican themes, are brought to life by the characters that populate this fiction and the gentle humor with which most of them are etched," Richard J. Murphy remarked in the *Review of Contemporary Fiction* (Fall 2002). Urrea, a *Publishers Weekly* (January 21, 2002) reviewer noted, "is a poetic writer who draws strong characters and wears his literary compassion on his sleeve, and he uses all of his gifts to full advantage here." *Six Kinds of Sky* received a Book of the Year Award from the editor's of *ForeWord*.

The Devil's Highway is the true story of 26 men who in May 2001 walked through the desert from Veracruz, Mexico, to the Arizona border, to try to get into the U.S. Fourteen of the men died on the way. Urrea told the story in novelistic fashion, concentrating on the men's emotions and on the horrifying details of what happens to those who almost literally burn to death in the desert. Emiliana Sandoval, writing for the *Detroit Free Press* (March 28, 2004), called *The Devil's Highway* "a beautiful book about a horrible trip." Chris Lehmann, writing for the *Washington Post Book World* (March 28, 2004), noted, "Urrea spares the reader none of the grisly details. He describes the six stages of hyperthermia—stress, fatigue, syncope, cramps, exhaustion and stroke—with a poet's practiced eye." Urrea was awarded the

Lannan Foundation's literary prize for nonfiction in 2004, and *The Devil's Highway* was nominated for a Pulitzer Prize.

The Hummingbird's Daughter, the novel Urrea published in 2005, took 20 years to write. It tells in a romantic and magical-realist fashion the story of his distant relative Teresita Urrea, who was born in 1873—in the time of the vicious dictator Porfirio Diaz—and who, because of her healing powers, was known as the Saint of Cabora. The illegitimate daughter of a wealthy rancher, Teresita was born to a teenage girl her father had seduced. Eventually her father made Teresita part of his household and had her educated. She was further trained by Huila, a medicine woman, and belief in her powers grew after she was raped and murdered (or so everyone thought) by a ranch hand, only to rise before the mourners at her own wake. Because of her revolutionary fervor, she was declared an enemy of Diaz. David Hiltbrand observed for the *Philadelphia Inquirer* (May 31, 2005, on-line) that *The Hummingbird's Daughter* is "an extraordinary example of what can transpire when a remarkable story is granted to a truly gifted writer," and called the novel "an epic as steeped in lore and magic, in beauty and suffering, in religion and passion, as old Mexico itself." "Poor, illegitimate, illiterate and despised, Teresita is the embodiment of the dictum that the last shall be first, and her ascension over the course of 500 pages is a myth that is also a charmingly written manifesto," Stacey D'Erasmo remarked in the *New York Times Book Review* (July 3, 2005). Urrea's "brilliant prose is saturated with the cadences and insights of Latin-American magical realism," a *Publishers Weekly* (April 18, 2005) reviewer wrote, noting that the book is "sweeping in its effect, employing the techniques of Catholic hagiography, Western fairy tale, Indian legend and everyday family folklore against the gritty historical realities of war, poverty, prejudice, lawlessness, torture and genocide. Urrea effortlessly links Teresita's supernatural calling to the turmoil of the times, concealing substantial intellectual content behind effervescent storytelling and considerable humor."

Urrea lives in Naperville, Illinois, with his second wife, Cindy, a journalist whom he calls Cinderella. The couple have three children: Eric, Megan, and Rosario. Urrea has at least one child from his previous marriage. He is a professor of writing and English at the University of Illinois. "My favorite place is Colorado. My favorite food is salad, though I'm a sucker for a good buffalo burger," Urrea announced on his Web site. "I don't drink and I don't smoke and I, like everybody else in America today, have diabetes. I hate diabetes, but I love being alive."

—S.Y.

Suggested Reading: *Boston Globe* D p8 Apr. 25, 2004; *Chicago Tribune* C p1 Dec. 15, 1996; *Contra Costa Times* (on-line) July 3, 2005; *Dallas Morning News* C p11 Oct. 1, 2000; *Library*

Journal p88 Oct. 1, 1998; *Los Angeles Times* E p6 Feb. 10, 1993, E p5 Sep. 5, 1994; *Los Angeles Times Book Review* p12 May 15, 2005; *Nation* p98+ July 18, 1994; *New York Times* E p2 Nov. 10, 2004; *New York Times Book Review* p9 Feb. 21, 1993, p8 July 3, 2005; *Philadelphia Inquirer* (on-line) May 31, 2005; *Publishers Weekly* p71 Feb. 7, 1994, p18 Aug. 10, 1998, p65 Jan. 21, 2002, p44 Apr. 18, 2005; *Washington Post Book World* p1 Dec. 15, 1996, p3 Mar. 28, 2004

Selected Books: nonfiction—*Across the Wire: Life and Hard Times on the Mexican Border*, 1993; *By the Lake of Sleeping Children: The Secret Life of the Mexican Border*, 1996; *Nobody's Son: Notes from an American Life*, 1998; *The Devil's Highway*, 2004; fiction—*In Search of Snow*, 1994; *Six Kinds of Sky*, 2002; *The Hummingbird's Daughter*, 2005; poetry—*The Fever of Being*, 1994; *Ghost Sickness*, 1997; *Vatos* (with Jose Galvez), 2000

Courtesy of Random House

Vanderbes, Jennifer

1974– Novelist; short-story writer; playwright

"*Easter Island* was, in many ways, my own personal protest against the autobiographical first novel," Jennifer Vanderbes wrote for the *Washington Post Book World* (December 7, 2003), attempting to explain why her literary debut had been a historical novel instead of a memoir, typically a more popular and profitable genre for new writers. Though her happy, uneventful childhood was partly to blame for her decision, she

also makes it clear that she had originally desired to separate the art from the artist. "After publishing my novel, I know that even if it were feasible to separate art and artist for the reader, for the writer, such separation is impossible," she wrote in the *Washington Post Book World*. "The funny thing is that, even if you avoid autobiographical fiction, life still tangles you up with your work. The novel set in the faraway place I'd never been eventually brought me to the island, twice, where I met people who reminded me of characters I thought I'd invented. And in the end, I've come to realize that there is a lot of me and my life in the novel, and that whatever I know about the world did seep in there, through the layers of history and science; it's simply that this all happened in ways too complicated to articulate to others, and perhaps too scary to articulate to myself."

Jennifer Chase Vanderbes was born in New York City, in 1974, and raised in the borough of Manhattan. Her father made travel documentaries, and her mother wrote copy for ads. She began keeping a journal at age 12, after she first read *The Diary of Anne Frank*. After she graduated from the prestigious Dalton School, in Manhattan's Upper East Side neighborhood, she attended Yale University, in New Haven, Connecticut, earning a bachelor's degree in English literature. She then accepted a position at the *Pittsburgh Post Gazette*, but quickly discovered that the life of a reporter left her too exhausted to work on her creative writing, so she quit and moved to Beaufort, South Carolina, a small shrimping town. Taking a job as a waitress, she dedicated her free time to writing. "There were no distractions. None at all," she told Marie Arana for the *Washington Post Book World* (December 7, 2003). After a year of waitressing, she returned to school, later earning her M.F.A. from the Iowa Writers' Workshop, at the University of Iowa, in Iowa City. She received writing fellowships from the University of Wisconsin, as well as Colgate University, in Hamilton, New York. Prior to the publication of *Easter Island*, Vanderbes's short story "The Hat Box" appeared in the anthology *Best New American Voices 2000* and her play *The Applicant* was staged at New York's Soho Repertory Theatre's Summercamp 2000 Festival.

In an interview posted on the Book Passage Web site, Vanderbes explained why she had chosen Easter Island, located more than 2,000 miles off the coast of Chile, as the setting for her first novel: "For years, I'd heard about Easter Island. I knew that it was the most remote inhabited island in the world, and I knew it was famous for its enormous stone statues. But it wasn't a place I thought of writing about until . . . I was reading an excerpt from the journal of a British archaeological expedition that was there in 1914, who, in the midst of describing their excavations and their anthropological research, mentioned that the German fleet had anchored there for a week, claimed not to have any newspapers, and then left without so much as a mention that the whole world had gone to war. It was then that the isolation of this place really became palpable for me. I began to see this remote island as a place where various interesting story elements—archaeology, Polynesian culture, intrepid Edwardian travelers, Germany's WWI fleet—could literally, converge."

Published in 2003, *Easter Island* weaves together three stories taking place over the course of six decades. The first is set in 1913, when Elsa Pendleton journeys to Easter Island with her new husband, an aging anthropologist; they are accompanied by her disabled sister, Alice. Ron Charles wrote for the *Christian Science Monitor* (May 29, 2003), "The intensely private, beautifully intimate moments captured here between these sisters are, in fact, like nothing I've read anywhere else." In the midst of the narrative, Vanderbes chronicles the real-life German admiral Graf Von Spree's retreat to Easter Island with his fleet at the outset of World War I. The third portion of the novel leaps ahead to the 1970s to follow Greer Faraday, a young graduate student who travels to the island to study pollen dispersal while recovering from the loss of her husband.

"Vanderbes takes shortcuts with this modern story that sometimes make it less satisfying than the older one, but again she's brilliant at portraying emotional ambiguities," Charles commented. Overall, the work was well received. Critics marveled at Vanderbes's success in seamlessly connecting these complex and disparate stories: Harlan, for example, commented, "As this island lays bare each woman's character, Vanderbes ultimately connects their stories with assured and hair-raising subtlety."

Easter Island has been translated into 16 languages, according to the author's Web site. Vanderbes was awarded a Guggenheim Fellowship in 2006. She lives in New York City.

—P.B.M.

Suggested Reading: *Christian Science Monitor* (on-line) May 29, 2003; Jennifer Vanderbes's Web site; *San Francisco Chronicle* (on-line) June 29, 2003; *Washington Post Book World* p5 Dec. 7, 2003

Selected Books: *Easter Island*, 2003

Vanderhaeghe, Guy

(VAN-der-hayg)

Apr. 5, 1951– Novelist; short-story writer

Guy Vanderhaeghe grew up in a small town on the plains of the Canadian province of Saskatchewan, and the worlds he has created in his fiction have often drawn much of their inspiration from his intimate knowledge of that landscape and the people who inhabit it. Praised for his short stories early in his career, Vanderhaeghe has come to be seen as an exceptional historical novelist, and his two most recent novels—the first parts of a projected trilogy—are regarded as superb examples of literary Westerns in a league with the writings of Cormac McCarthy. Reviewing Vanderhaeghe's second novel for the *Boston Globe* (June 13, 1990), Robert Taylor noted: "Vanderhaeghe is not a household name here [in the U.S.]; now and then referred to as 'a Canadian prairie writer,' he is, to put it differently, one of the best novelists on either side of the border."

Guy Vanderhaeghe wrote the following autobiographical statement for *World Authors 2000–2005*:

"I was born, raised, and received my elementary and high school education in Esterhazy, Saskatchewan, a small agricultural and mining community. My father, Clarence Vanderhaeghe, worked as a labourer, mill worker, and part-time farmer, my mother, Alma, as a secretary. I am an only child, which may have increased my solitary tendencies and encouraged my love of reading. For

Margaret Vanderhaeghe

many years there was no library in my hometown, my parents were not 'bookish' or university educated, but my mother was determined that I receive an education, so I was allowed to read anything that happened to fall into my hands: comic books, 40-year-old copies of *The Boy's Own Annual* lent me by an elderly English lady, Zane Grey's westerns, the plays of Eugene O'Neill, *Reader's Digest Condensed Books*, and the novels of John O'Hara and Erskine Caldwell, which my teachers considered highly inappropriate for a child my age.

"In 1968, I enrolled at the University of Saskatchewan where I completed a B.A. with a double major in English and history. I married my wife Margaret and entered graduate school to do an M.A. in British imperial history in 1972. These years were a time of rising Canadian cultural nationalism, and for the first time in my life I was exposed to Canadian literature, books that had had no part in my high school curriculum, were still largely ignored or dismissed by academics, and mostly absent from the shelves of bookstores. The work of Robertson Davies, Mordecai Richler, Margaret Atwood, Alice Munro, Mavis Gallant, Margaret Laurence, Robert Kroetsch, and Rudy Wiebe came as a revelation to me, engendering a sense of excitement. Spurred on by this work, I published my first short story in a newly created Saskatchewan literary journal, *Grain*, while still a student. Throughout that decade, I produced short stories influenced by the work of Alice Munro and American writers such as Flannery O'Connor and Eudora Welty whose stories, like mine, had their roots in their experience of small town life. These stories were later collected in two books, *Man Descending* (1982), which won the Governor-General's Award for Fiction and the Geoffrey Faber Memorial Prize in Great Britain, and *The Trouble with Heroes* (1983). My first novel, *My Present Age* (1984), a black urban comedy, was something of a departure from this early work. It was followed in 1989 by the novel *Homesick*, which was a co-winner of the City of Toronto Book Award, and a return to the material and themes of my two previous collections of short stories. A third collection of short stories, *Things As They Are?*, was published in 1992.

"With the encouragement of the stage director Bill Glassco, I grew interested in theatre in the '90s. *I Had A Job I Liked. Once.* was first performed at Persephone Theatre in Saskatoon, Saskatchewan and won the 1992 Canadian Authors' Association Award for Drama. By then, my former interest in history had reasserted itself and research in a provincial archive led to *Dancock's Dance*, a play loosely based on an incident in the North Battleford Insane Asylum whose patients assumed many of the duties of the staff and helped run the institution during the crisis of the Spanish influenza pandemic of 1919.

"Until this point, I had been wary of attempting historical fiction, feeling that my training as an historian would be difficult to reconcile with the artistic demands of the novel. However, in 1996 I published *The Englishman's Boy*, a double narrative dealing with the Cypress Hills Massacre of 1873 (a little known event with important ramifications for the history of Canada) and a movie producer's plan, 50 years after that bloody episode, to make a film based on the recollections of a participant in the slaughter. *The Englishman's Boy* won the Governor-General's Award for Fiction, two Saskatchewan Book Awards, and was short-listed for the Giller Prize, and the International IMPAC Dublin Literary Award. The second novel of a projected historical trilogy set in Montana, Alberta and Saskatchewan in the 1870s, *The Last Crossing*, appeared in 2002. It won three Saskatchewan Book Awards, The Canadian Booksellers' Ex Libris Prize, and was chosen as the winner of the Canadian Broadcasting Corporation's Canada Reads program in 2004.

"All of my writing, whether set in the past or the present, has been a response to the landscape, people, and culture of the Canadian prairies. It is also a product of the Canadian literary nationalism that was such a force in the Seventies, and helped mould the attitudes of a generation of writers. That sense of literary mission is perhaps best exemplified in a letter from Robert Kroetsch sent to Ken Stange during those years of ferment. 'The notion that you can be universal without a rock-hard sense of the particular is a notion that has destroyed much Canadian writing from Callaghan's novels to some of the Frye-inspired "myth poetry."' I have always been an unapologetic literary regionalist, although I hope not an insular one. While remaining committed to Kroetsch's position, I have been stimulated by a wide variety of national literatures, by the writers of the American South, the British comic novelists, and, in particular, the 19th-century Russian writers. I have drawn freely from their example as a way of learning how to write my place, my time."

Vanderhaeghe was born on April 5, 1951. He has sometimes said that the main source of excitement for him in Esterhazy was the Maple Leaf Theatre, which showed two movies a week. "My mother really liked movies," he told Beverley Slopen for the *Toronto Star* (August 10, 1996). "She would take me to anything, whatever it was, talking her way past the age restrictions." He also traveled with his father on the rodeo circuit, "sleeping in the backs of trucks, in barns and in granaries," as he told Candis McLean for an article in a now-defunct Canadian publication, the *Alberta Report* (September 6, 1999). On those trips he encountered an assortment of characters whose colorful language left a lingering impression.

Vanderhaeghe earned a B.Ed. from the University of Regina, in Saskatchewan, in 1978. He continued to live in Saskatchewan, working as an archivist for the university from 1973 to 1975, before going on to act as an editor and researcher for medical-related businesses from 1976 to 1981, first in Regina and then in Saskatoon; this period was interrupted by a spell teaching high-school English and history in Herbert from 1978 to 1979. He became a full-time writer in 1981.

Vanderhaeghe had written stories from the time he first learned to read and write but stopped when he was a teenager. "I didn't want to be known as a brain," he told John Bemrose for *Maclean's* (September 23, 1996). Much later, while studying for his master's degree, he was diagnosed with diabetes, and fearing for his long-term health, he pushed aside plans for an academic career and devoted himself to what he had always wanted to do: write. There was little opportunity for a writer to support himself in Saskatchewan, however, and he began teaching creative writing at the University of Ottawa, in Ontario. That period was the only time he lived outside his native province, and life there did not agree with him. "I had a vague fear of what would happen to me," he told Nick Miliokas for the Toronto *National Post* (December 27, 2002), adding: "I was afraid that I would become a nostalgic writer, that I would top off at [the age of] 30. If I'd stayed there forever, I might not have written the books I've written."

Vanderhaeghe's first collection of short stories, *Man Descending*, was greeted with wide acclaim. In *Western American Literature* (November 1983) Aritha van Herk called the pieces brought together for the collection "good stories, extraordinary stories" and added: "They have the smell, the look, the accent of fiction that introduces an archetypal but strange world, a world that predates fiction. It is a world born out of Saskatchewan, a Saskatchewan idiosyncratically and flavorfully itself rather than a romantic rendition of prairie and sky." W. P. Kinsella, in a review for *Books in Canada* (August–September 1982), called the stories "delightful" and singled out "Drummer" for particular praise, calling it "a teaching model for the short story—voice, tone, mood, character development, are all used to perfection." Cary Fagan, in a critique for the *Canadian Forum* (September 1982), found the collection more uneven. "Vanderhaeghe," Fagan added, "is one of the few Canadian writers who sounds occasionally too slick, as if he had his eye on the *New Yorker*, but I admire him even for that ability."

Written before *Man Descending*, Vanderhaeghe's next collection of stories, *The Trouble with Heroes*, appeared the year after his first book and was not as well received. Anthony Bukoski wrote for *Books in Canada* (March 1984) that "Vanderhaeghe possesses great talent and promise, but in this early work he has fallen a bit short." Although also generally critical of the collection, Matthew Clark noted in *Quill & Quire* (June 1994) that "every story [in the book] has its virtues" and argued that "Vanderhaeghe's greatest gift is his ability to make his stories matter to the characters and to the reader."

Ed, the antihero of Vanderhaeghe's first novel, *My Present Age*, appeared as one of the many downward-spiraling characters in *Man Descending*. The trajectory of Ed's life continues its fall in *My Present Age*, in which Ed, separated from his wife, Victoria, gives up his job, cashes in his life insurance, and sits around his apartment, reading. Ed attempts to get Victoria back and to find her when she runs away from him. Hugh M. Crane, writing for *Library Journal* (September 1, 1985), found "too many digressions and flashbacks, padding the plot and muddying the theme of the powers and dangers of the imagination. More seriously, Victoria, a stereotypical yuppie, seems unworthy of the effort to regain her." Norman Shrapnel, in a review for the London *Guardian* (June 5, 1986), expressed the opinion that *My Present Age* seemed like a throwback to the so-called angry young man novels of the 1950s, "with an anti-hero living near the end of his tether, devising complex rituals to keep hysteria at bay, landing himself in predicaments which, however entertaining to the reader, are no laughing matter to the victim." Shrapnel concluded: "Funny he [Ed] may be, and sometimes fatuous. . . . Yet we feel he is genuinely at the receiving end, truly suffering from life." Martin Seymour-Smith, in a review for the *Financial Times* (June 7, 1986), called the novel "realism at its best" and "compulsively readable." The book, Seymour-Smith added, "gives a memorable picture of teeming city [that] Ed . . . haunts in his pathetic quest—and, above all, it presents us with wholly credible people."

Vera, the main character in *Homesick*, Vanderhaeghe's next novel, is a woman whose "nearly relentless self-pity discourages readers from the generous impulses they might otherwise feel toward her, for in fact she has legitimate grievances," Douglas Bauer wrote for the *New York Times Book Review* (June 17, 1990). Vera has been embittered by her mother's early death, which led her father to pull her out of high school and make her his housekeeper and the caretaker for her younger brother. After her own early widowhood, Vera leaves Toronto to return to small-town Saskatchewan, where she is once again forced to act as a housekeeper for her father, Alec, and her own 12-year-old son, Daniel. Elaine Kendall, writing for the *Los Angeles Times* (June 15, 1990), agreed that Vera is "one of the least lovable heroines in recent fiction." But, she observed, "the real heroine of this novel is the Canadian landscape, portrayed with a lyrical sensitivity that enlarges our comprehension of characters shaped by its extremes." She added that although "the emphasis in *Homesick* is upon place rather than character, old Alec Monkman is a memorable portrait of a plain man forged by poverty, annealed by personal tragedy and hidebound by the rigid limits of the small provincial town in which he has spent his life."

Vanderhaeghe returned to the short-story form with the collection *Things as They Are?*, and for some reviewers the collection confirmed his place among such skilled Canadian practitioners of short fiction as Alice Munro, Mavis Gallant, and Margaret Atwood. Bryan Demchinsky, writing for the Montreal *Gazette* (September 19, 1992), maintained that Vanderhaeghe had opened "the clearest window" on Saskatchewan and that most of his stories "are contained within the experiences of boys and men" with a background similar to that of the author. The characters' "inchoate emotions and habits of mind," Demchinsky added, "are distilled into scenes that will be startlingly familiar for those from the region and recognizable to everyone else. At least two of the stories, 'Man on Horseback' and 'Loneliness Has Its Claims,' are classics. The other eight are merely very, very good." Barbara Black wrote, in another review for the Montreal *Gazette* (June 12, 1993), that in the same way that "Munro writes from a feminine point of view in the best sense of the word, Vanderhaeghe writes about being a man." Black added, "Vanderhaeghe writes wonderfully about the demons of childhood, too: the bullying teacher, the embarrassing father, the shabby mother, the high school bravado that can go horribly wrong. He can be funny and tender and tough, everything you want in a man, or a short story." To Helen Lillie, writing for the Glasgow *Herald* (June 11, 1994), Vanderhaeghe "is an expert in dramatising the subtle unhappiness which builds up between people when communication is incomplete. . . . This is strong stuff and exceptionally well done but it isn't always pleasant reading."

Vanderhaeghe next novel, *The Englishman's Boy*, brought him especially emphatic praise. A complex interweaving of stories from 1873 and 1923, its theme is the distortion of memory and the broader distortion, by commercialization or other means, of history. The 1873 narrative concerns a band of American wolf hunters and whiskey traders who pursue a group of Assiniboine (also called Nakoda, in recognition of their descent from one branch of the Sioux) over the Canadian border in hope of getting back at the Assiniboine for having stolen some of the wolf hunters' horses. The wolfers, as they are called, end up slaughtering some of the Assiniboine—men, women, and children alike. In Vanderhaeghe's rendering the action of this strand in the narrative centers around Shorty McAdoo, the eponymous Englishman's boy, who rides with the wolf hunters and later becomes a Hollywood stuntman. In the strand of the narrative set in 1923, a young filmmaker, Damon Ira Chance, commissions a budding screenwriter—the Saskatchewan native Harry Vincent, who narrates this part of the novel from a distance of 30 years—to track down McAdoo and draw from him the story of what happened in the Cypress Hills. By that time Shorty is an old man pursued by memories of the wrongs he has committed. Vincent Banville wrote for the *Irish Times* (September 30, 1997), "There is a tragic grandeur in the rise and fall of Chance's presumptuous design, and in his efforts to use wealth and power to overcome the dignified reticence and single-minded honour code of the old cowboy. . . ." Banville found a "mighty swirl

of colour and happenstance, as the hunters draw closer to their quarry and Harry Vincent manages to extract the secret from McAdoo. Both climaxes end in violence, as befits lives lived on the razor edge. *The Englishman's Boy* is a big novel of action and ideas, and if melodrama does intrude from time to time, well, what's the harm." Katharine Weber, writing for the *Los Angeles Times Book Review* (September 28, 1997), called *The Englishman's Boy* "essentially such a good idea that each segue from past to present to past again is a graceful little leap between subtly matched gestures and images. Vanderhaeghe has brought together two familiar and essentially American settings and linked them in an imaginative and surprising way with his outsider's sensibility. His novel tells us the American frontier story in our own vernacular; it is hard to refrain from invoking [Nathanael West's] *The Day of the Locust* when considering how the novel ends, just as it is inevitable that both [Larry McMurtry's] *Lonesome Dove* and [Cormac McCarthy's] *All the Pretty Horses* come to mind when one savors the chapters set in the Montana territory."

Told with a mix of first- and third-person narration, *The Last Crossing*, the second in Vanderhaeghe's proposed historical trilogy about the northern prairies, concerns two English brothers, Addington and Charles Gaunt, who travel to the U.S. at the behest of their father to find Charles's twin, Simon. Often described by critics as Christ-like, Simon is "a tender person," Art Winslow wrote for the *Chicago Tribune* (February 15, 2004), and "a catalyst for much good in the family." Winslow praised the manner in which Vanderhaeghe created "an ensemble of voices in which a few characters speak for themselves, at times outside the direct scene-by-scene action of the novel. There is enough differentiation in the voices that it works well, not always the case when novelists attempt it, and the technique allows for some wonderful asides." The reviewer for the London *Observer* (February 15, 2004), Salley Vickers, enjoyed the "many . . . entertaining or disturbing characters," and the adroit use made by Vanderhaeghe of "many dichotomies—between race, class, gender, religion and family—which reverberate as the story unfolds." She judged the novel "beautifully written—neither gratuitously stark nor tortuously embellished." John Vernon, in an assessment for the *New York Times Book Review* (February 22, 2004), compared *The Englishman's Boy* and *The Last Crossing* and found the latter "by far the richer novel, though its richness is nothing if not studied and deliberate." (Vernon called the story "as carefully constructed and laboriously pieced together as a Lego Taj Mahal.")

Both *The Englishman's Boy* and *The Last Crossing* were significant best-sellers in Canada. A Canadian television miniseries based on *The Englishman's Boy*, with a script by Vanderhaeghe himself, finished shooting in late fall 2006 and is planned to be broadcast sometime in 2007. The miniseries will also serve as Vanderhaeghe's dramatic debut: he plays a bartender in a Western saloon. His wife, Margaret Nagel, a painter, was cast as a prostitute.

Guy Vanderhaeghe remains attached to his origins in the great western prairies of Canada. In contrast to the popular vision of a windswept and largely empty wilderness, most people in the prairies live in cities. Vanderhaeghe and his wife, also a Saskatchewan native, live in Saskatoon, where, since 1993, he has taught as a visiting professor at St. Thomas More College.

—S.Y.

Suggested Reading: *Alberta (Canada) Report* p38+ Sep. 6, 1999; *Boston Globe* p53 June 13, 1990; *Chicago Tribune* C p4 Feb. 15, 2004; *Financial Times* Weekend p16 June 7, 1986; (Glasgow) *Herald* p17 June 11, 1994; *Library Journal* p214 Sep. 1, 1985; *Los Angeles Times* E p18 June 15, 1990; *Los Angeles Times Book Review* p11 Sep. 28, 1997; *Maclean's* A p64 Nov. 30, 1992; p46 Sep. 23, 1996; *New York Times Book Review* p15 June 17, 1990; *Quill & Quire* p32 June 1984; (Toronto) *National Post* PM p11 Dec. 27, 2002; *Toronto Star* H p11 Aug. 10, 1996; *Western American Literature* p267+ Nov. 1983

Selected Books: short fiction—*Man Descending*, 1982; *The Trouble with Heroes*, 1983; *Things as They Are?*, 1992; novels—*My Present Age*, 1984; *Homesick*, 1989; *The Englishman's Boy*, 1996; *The Last Crossing*, 2002

E.D.L.M./Courtesy of Random House

Vida, Vendela

1972(?)– Novelist; nonfiction writer; editor

"I like to write about something I'm not," Vendela Vida, co-editor of the literary magazine the *Believer*, told Joshunda Sanders for the *San Francisco Chronicle* (August 27, 2003). "In my 20s, I wrote about girls; in my 30s, I wrote a book about New York while living in San Francisco." While working on her first book, *Girls on the Verge: Debutante Dips, Drive-bys, and Other Initiations* (1999), she traveled the country to interview young women from a wide variety of cultural and economic backgrounds, amassing so much research that it crowded her tiny New York City apartment. Wanting a respite from research, she next published her first novel, *And Now You Can Go* (2003), which was followed by *Let the Northern Lights Erase Your Name* (2007).

Vida was born in about 1972 and raised in Pacifica and San Francisco, California. Her father was a native San Franciscan, and her mother emigrated to the U.S. from Sweden. One night, when she was 10, her family was watching the film version of Ernest Hemingway's novel *A Farewell to Arms*, and she began to cry. "I kept thinking the woman's arms would get cut off," she told Sanders. "Then I thought, 'Writers are really sneaky.' It was the first time I really understood the power of metaphor." A graduate of Middlebury College, in Vermont, Vida interned at the *Paris Review* prior to obtaining her M.F.A. from Columbia University, in New York City.

Vida's first book, *Girls on the Verge*, was published when she was 27 years old. Compiled from interviews with an eclectic array of teenage girls, *Girls on the Verge* is a nonfiction account of Vida's encounters with and analysis of young women partaking in various coming-of-age rituals, including sorority rushes, debutante balls, gang initiations, and marriages. Vida also participated in several of these events in her attempt to understand the role they play in forming an identity. The crux of Vida's argument, as quoted by Alissa Quart for the on-line magazine *Salon* (September 16, 1999), is that since "time and feminism have liberalized sexual mores," our contemporary maturity rituals are no longer primarily sexual; rather, they are rites of "personal choice." Following *Girls on the Verge*, Vida worked various odd jobs, including waiting tables, consulting on a marketing campaign for Tampax, and writing subtitles for a Thai film.

Vida wrote her first novel, *And Now You Can Go,* while she was visiting Costa Rica. The narrator, Ellis, is a 21-year-old art-history student at Columbia University whose journey of self-discovery begins with an unsettling encounter with a gun-wielding man in New York City. The man demands neither her money nor sex; he intends to commit suicide but doesn't want to die alone, so he plans to shoot Ellis and then himself. In an attempt to console him, she finds herself reciting poetry, and soon the man apologizes and runs off. The rest of the book deals with the emotional aftermath as Ellis goes about her life but continues to reflect on the incident. Stephanie Zacharek, writing for the *New York Times Book Review* (August 24, 2003), termed the work "a swift, fleet novel, a spare but polished miniature that isn't ashamed to strive for small truths instead of great lumbering ones. . . . Vida writes with a sense of urgency, and with leapfrogging good humor. She has no use for her character's self-pity, and doesn't expect us to be interested in it either." A critic for *Publishers Weekly* (July 7, 2003) observed, "Despite the high drama of the start, this is an unsentimental tale, in which the classic brush with death elicits a sense of awe as well as anger, and conventional notions of therapy and reconciliation are overturned. The end, unfortunately, arrives just as the book began—abruptly—and the reader longs for something more. Nevertheless, this remains an intriguing and auspicious debut."

Vida's second novel, *Let the Northern Lights Erase Your Name,* opens shortly after the death of the man that Clarissa Iverton has always believed was her father. After sorting through some old papers, however, she discovers her birth certificate, which lists a different man. Clarissa leaves her New York City home and sets out to find this mysterious man and her mother, who had abandoned the family 14 years earlier. Her sojourn leads her to the Northern reaches of Europe. "Novels about unhappy young people who seek to escape their dysfunctional families and find a new identity are almost a genre to themselves," Leslie Patterson wrote for *Library Journal* (November 1, 2006), "but the vivid scenes of Lapland, with its reindeer, northern lights, and Ice Hotel, give this novel a unique twist." In *Booklist* (December 1, 2006), Donna Seaman wrote, "With skilled distillation, Vida evokes a culture on the brink of extinction and a legacy of loss as her anxious yet adventurous protagonist throws herself on the mercy of strangers in an otherworldly realm of deep cold, hard drinking, a hotel constructed of snow and ice, the northern lights, and long memories. Brilliantly distilled, blade-sharp, and as dangerously exhilarating as skating in the dark."

In April 2003 Vida married Dave Eggers, the author of the best-selling book *A Heartbreaking Work of Staggering Genius.* She is one of the founding editors of the *Believer,* which launched in March 2003, and she edited *The Believer Book*

of *Writers Talking to Writers* (2005), a collection of interviews with such noted writers as Zadie Smith, Ian McEwan, and Z. Z. Packer.

—P.B.M.

Suggested Reading: (London) *Guardian* (on-line) Sep. 23, 2003; *New York Times* B p11 May 17, 2003; *New York Times Book Review* p6 Aug. 24, 2003; *Salon* (on-line) Sep. 16, 1999; *San Francisco Chronicle* D p1 Aug. 27, 2003

Selected Books: nonfiction—*Girls on the Verge,* 1999; novels—*And Now You Can Go,* 2003; *Let the Northern Lights Erase Your Name,* 2007; as editor—*The Believer Book of Writers Talking to Writers,* 2005

Frederick M. Brown/Getty Images

Vowell, Sarah

Dec. 27, 1969– Essayist; critic; radio commentator

Since making her debut on the National Public Radio program *This American Life,* in 1996, Sarah Vowell has developed an audience of loyal listeners with her witty and self-deprecating personal essays. When asked to explain Vowell's appeal, Ira Glass, the show's host and producer, told David Daley for the *Chicago Sun-Times* (April 23, 2000), "Both in her style of writing and the way she sounds when she reads on the radio, there's no else like her. There's no other writer who feels so passionately about Van Halen's 'Jump' and the Andrew Jackson presidency—hating them both. Her vision of what the country is, and what she should be writing about, is totally her own. She's utterly in step with the current moment and out of step with the current moment. She's in touch with contemporary culture and the things people in their 20s are interested in, but it's all informed with a level of attention and idealism about America as a place you would expect from somebody much older and tweedier." Vowell credits her success to the personal, intimate style of storytelling she uses to convey her observations on American history and pop culture, which are delivered in a voice that is far less sonorous than those typically associated with broadcast fame. "I do sound like a cartoon character," Vowell told Edward Guthmann for the *San Francisco Chronicle* (October 23, 2003, on-line). "My voice was always a liability because it's so peculiar. [But] for the radio listeners who like me, that's part of the reason they like me." In 2004 she lent her distinctive voice to the animated film *The Incredibles*. With the success of such best-selling essay collections as *Take the Cannoli: Stories from the New World* (2000) and *Assassination Vacation* (2005), Vowell has scaled back her involvement in *This American Life*, though she remains a contributing editor.

Sarah Vowell was born—eight minutes after her twin sister, Amy—on December 27, 1969 in Muskogee, Oklahoma. Her father was a gunsmith, and her mother was a beautician. When she was 11 (some sources state 12), Vowell moved to the city of Bozeman, Montana, which she described to Dan Webster for the Spokane, Washington, *Spokesman-Review* (April 13, 2004, on-line) as a life-changing event: "It was the most important thing that ever happened to me . . . moving to a town that had a library. In Oklahoma, our school had one shelf with some books on it." She attended public school and became heavily involved in the music department. "I was this sad, lonely kid but there was this whole infrastructure to throw myself into. I joined the chorus, the band, and the head of the music department gave me trumpet lessons," she said during a 2005 lecture at New York University, in New York City, according to the College Board Web site. After graduating from high school, she enrolled at Montana State University, in Bozeman, where she initially devoted herself to music but quickly abandoned that to study modern languages with the goal of becoming an art-history professor. Vowell worked part-time as a disc jockey and news reporter at KGLT, the college's student-run radio station, and was a staff writer for the student newspaper, for which she reviewed art, books, and music. When the music critic and writer Greil Marcus visited the campus for a lecture, she was assigned to interview him, and after reading the resulting article, he asked her to submit additional writing samples. Marcus showed her work to the editors of the New York City–based magazine *Artforum*, who were so impressed that they asked her to write a book review. She wrote another article for the magazine

the following year, in 1994, and later began contributing to *Art Papers* and the *New Art Examiner*.

After receiving her bachelor's degree in modern languages, in 1993, Vowell moved to Washington, D.C., interning at the Smithsonian Institution. She then lived in San Francisco, California, where she worked for an antiquarian-map dealer. She applied—unsuccessfully—to pursue her graduate studies in art history at the University of California, at Berkeley. "I didn't get in for various reasons. One of them, they said, was that I was interested in too many things and they couldn't see me sticking with art history. I was devastated, but they were so right," Vowell told Robert K. Elder for the *Chicago Tribune* (November 6, 2002). In 1995 she enrolled in the art-history program at the School of the Art Institute of Chicago, which was the only graduate program to which she had been accepted. While attending school, she taught classes and served as a music reviewer for *City Pages*, a weekly newspaper that is distributed in Minneapolis and St. Paul, Minnesota.

Inspired by her experiences while working at KGLT, Vowell spent 1995 listening to music and current events on American radio and recording her impressions in a journal, which was published in 1997 as *Radio On: A Listener's Diary*. In addition to surveying popular music, she provided personal observations on currents events, ranging from the suicide of Kurt Cobain, the lead vocalist of the rock band Nirvana, to the bombing of the Alfred P. Murrah Federal Building, in Oklahoma City. Howard Hampton, who reviewed the book for the *Village Voice* (March 11, 1997), enjoyed Vowell's "conversational, let-it-blurt directness," noting that "she doesn't mince words or fall back on stillborn jargon in place of saying what she really means." Nonetheless, some critics complained about the format of Vowell's debut. "The journal form of *Radio On* has limitations, and it allows for self-indulgence," Bud Kliment wrote for the *Chicago Tribune* (June 29, 1997). "Vowell has admirable powers of description, but many of the entries merely recount the programming she has heard. Without her commentary or reaction, they seem like listening exercises. And while Vowell's snarly outlook is one of the book's strengths, sometimes she just comes across as bratty and sophomoric, talking back to the talking box, with neither speaker saying much." Marc Allan, writing for the *Indianapolis Star* (June 16, 1997), complained that "Vowell's observations, while immediate, aren't tied together cohesively. Plus, she spends too much time trashing Rush Limbaugh (a too-easy target) and not nearly enough time discussing Howard Stern, whose influence is far more interesting and complex." In recognition of Vowell's freshman effort, *Newsweek* named her the best new nonfiction writer of 1997.

After earning her master's degree, in 1996, Vowell accepted a position as a music critic at the *San Francisco Weekly*, which lasted only six months; though Vowell had won an award for her music journalism, she quickly realized that she was not as passionate about music as writing. "One reason I couldn't sustain myself as a music critic was just that I was never one of those record collector people who cared about every little thing about a band, who can't wait to see what record comes out every week," she told Todd Inoue for *Metroactive* (October 19, 2005, on-line). "For me, it was always more obsessive. I could listen to the same Jonathan Richman song over and over again. I came at it as a fan, but not a 'follow the beat' kind of fan. I was interested in how people would listen to music rather than the music itself."

While living in Chicago Vowell had befriended Ira Glass, who had co-hosted, with Gary Covino, *The Wild Room*, a weekly program that aired on the Chicago public radio station WBEZ. At the time Glass was also in the process of developing a new program, *This American Life*, which would consist of a series of stories centered around a new theme each week. Glass and Vowell were having dinner one night, in 1996, when Vowell told him about a letter that she had received from Scott Lee, a fan of the Seattle punk group the Fastbacks, which she had praised in one of her articles. Lee had also enclosed a book containing statistical information about the group, including a page with a pie chart of the material that each drummer for the group had contributed over the years. "I was just making conversation and [Glass] said, 'Can I get a tape recorder?'," Vowell told Adrian McCoy for the *Pittsburgh Post-Gazette* (March 21, 2002). Glass convinced her to produce a radio piece on Lee for *This American Life* and later offered her a position as a contributing editor. "I just had a hunch about that show," she told Inoue. "I thought, 'If I was in Chicago, I'd be able to work on that show more,' which turned out to be true. I became an editor the second I got back to Chicago. I started doing a lot of radio stories and that changed the writing I was capable of."

On the eclectic weekly radio series—which, according to Inoue, "is now considered the pinnacle of recorded storytelling" and, as of 2005, had a nationwide audience of 1.7 million—Vowell read her personal essays, which contained her witty, self-deprecating observations on subjects ranging from her youth, daily life, politics, history, and pop culture—all delivered in a distinctly high-pitched voice. "Sounding like a kid sometimes works to my advantage. It makes what I say seem more surprising," she told Gary Mullinax for the Wilmington, Delaware, *News Journal* (January 31, 2004). "If I talk about the Spanish-American War, people pay attention: Why is that seven-year-old talking about Cuba in 1898? Or like my story going to the Bush inauguration. I said some pretty mean things about the president, but because I sound like a nice kid I can get away with it more."

In 1998 Vowell produced a one-hour radio documentary for *This American Life* in which she and her twin sister, who are one-eighth Cherokee, retraced the path that their ancestors took during the Trail of Tears—an event lasting from 1838 to 1839, in which 14,000 tribe members were forcibly relocated from their lands in the southeastern U.S. to eastern Oklahoma. Poorly equipped and subjected to the cruelty of federal troops, a reported 4,000 perished on the trip. "I loved reading all the books and doing all the research and going to the sites and interviewing people and thinking about it," Vowell told Edward Guthmann. "But the way the radio listeners responded to that story really kind of inspired me because they seemed so thirsty for it. I mean, they liked my story, but they seemed just as thirsty for the actual knowledge—for the facts."

Vowell's fascination with American history was first sparked by her grandfather and father, both of whom loved the topic; she and her sister often traveled with their father to visit Civil War battlefields and other historical sites. As she recalled during an interview with Terry Gross, the host of the NPR program *Fresh Air* (September 16, 2002), "My father and my grandfather . . .would always talk about history just as 'history starring our family,' you know, so the reason we were all born in Oklahoma was because of Jacksonian Indian removal policy, because of the removal of our Cherokee ancestors on the Trail of Tears to eastern Oklahoma. So that's why we were there. Or the Civil War wasn't just some abstract thing; our great-great-grandfather was in it, as a Confederate. Or, you know, the Depression was something that happened to my grandparents, and one day a guy shows up for supper and my grandmother feeds him and he leaves $20 under the dinner plate, and that was Pretty Boy Floyd." Following the airing of her Trail of Tears documentary, Vowell began receiving letters from listeners whose own knowledge of American history was not as expansive. "People do not know as much about American history as they would like," she told Robert Birnbaum in an interview for *Identity Theory* (October 7, 2002, on-line). "When they are drawn to it the thing they come up against is a lot of really dull writing. One thing that I do that expert scholar types do not, is joke around or talk about what it's like to go there now. [I] think about some idea relating to it and I write it in a nice easy essay form where I pick the really interesting bits and talk about that instead of some entire dreary messy chronology. I have a mission when I do historical stories, since I'm not an expert. I would like to be entertaining about it."

In the summer of 1999, Vowell moved from Chicago to New York City, and the following year she published her second book, *Take the Cannoli: Stories From the New World*, a collection of her most memorable essays from the monologues on her radio program, recounting such diverse subjects as the homemade cannon that her father built and her obsession with Francis Ford Coppola's masterpiece *The Godfather* (from which she drew the title of her book). Writing for *Booklist* (March 1, 2000), GraceAnne A. DeCandido described the collection as "sharp and engaging" and praised the author for her wit: "From its opening salvo, where [Vowell] describes her relationship with her father the gunmaker, to her hilarious set piece on touring Disneyworld with an extremely urban gay friend, we are in for a lot of good conversation." On the other hand, Rick Marin wrote for the *New York Times Book Review* (April 9, 2000) that Vowell's essays "contain everything I find irritating and boring about PRI [Public Radio International] and National Public Radio. Self-indulgent monologues. Received wisdom passing for irreverence. Cozy smugness. . . . [Vowell] is no stranger to the 'I' word. Let me put it another way: Spalding Gray talks less about himself. . . . Reading 219 pages of Vowell made me want to buy a consonant."

In Vowell's third book, *The Partly Cloudy Patriot* (2002), which she titled after a quote from the Thomas Paine pamphlet *American Crisis* (1776), she adopted a more serious tone. The majority of the 19 personal essays included in the book explore American patriotism through the analysis of such events as the 2000 presidential election and the September 11, 2001 attacks on New York City and Washington. (She did, however, include some more irreverent pieces, including a chapter titled "Tom Cruise Makes Me Nervous.") Reviewing the collection for the Curled Up With a Good Book Web site, Amanda Cuda wrote, "It's possible to glean something from Vowell's writing, even if you don't share her politics. In her essay 'Democracy and Other Things,' Vowell speaks about the fateful speech then–Vice President Al Gore made to a bunch of high school students during his presidential campaign, in which he was quoted in the *New York Times* as taking credit for discovering Love Canal. But the students claim that paper changed a word of his speech, which changed the entire meaning of the talk. Even if those who detest Gore and find him an insufferable braggart will find the testimony of the high school kids compelling. However, Vowell's piece also shows sympathy for the reporter who allegedly misquoted him. Her clear-eyed approach to the situation is both compelling and refreshing. Fans of Vowell's meditations on popular culture and her family will also find much to love in the book as well, including a hilarious story about her Montana-based family celebrating Thanksgiving dinner at her New York apartment. . . . *The Partly Cloudy Patriot* does contain the occasional misstep, such as a bizarre short essay that reads like one of those Larry King columns Norm MacDonald used to spoof on *Saturday Night Live*. Yet Vowell is still a priceless voice in American culture—even when you can't actually hear her voice."

In 2004, after hearing Vowell's voice on the radio, the writer and director Brad Bird offered her a role in *The Incredibles* (2004), his animated film about a family of superheroes who must conceal their powers to live among everyday people. Although Vowell had rejected previous offers to provide the voices for animated characters, she accepted the role of Violet, the teenage daughter who possesses the power of invisibility and ability to create force fields. "In my real life I'm more of a walking Woody Allen movie," she told Anthony Breznican for the Associated Press (November 17, 2004). "I'm afraid to drive and I can't swim and all that stuff so it is incredibly thrilling and fun to listen to my voice do things that, when it's in my regular body, it would never get to do."

The following year, in March 2005, Vowell published *Assassination Vacation*, in which she humorously detailed her visits to the sites connected with the assassinations of Presidents Abraham Lincoln, James A. Garfield, and William McKinley. In his review for *America* (April 4–11, 2005), Peter Duffy wrote that Vowell "has done her homework, providing lucid descriptions of the murders and agile summations of the scholarly assessments of each era. She has a great eye for odd bits of lore, and she relishes discovering the forgotten and ignored." Though Vowell reportedly tested the material for *Assassination Vacation* at New York City comedy clubs, Duffy felt that her "jokes occasionally fall flat, and sometimes her anecdotes veer toward the cutesy." He suggested that "some of the passages would probably have worked better on radio, where, as with Garrison Keillor, Vowell's inimitable delivery adds an additional layer of meaning and expression to the text." But, Duffy concluded, "overall this is a delightful read, full of wonderful surprises about our nation's history."

In July 2005 Vowell joined the staff of the *New York Times* for three weeks as a temporary replacement for the op-ed columnist Maureen Dowd. Vowell has also contributed articles to *Esquire*, *Gentleman's Quarterly*, the *Los Angeles Times*, *Time*, and the *Village Voice*, among other publications. She is a regular guest on *Late Night with Conan O'Brien* and has made appearances on *The Daily Show with Jon Stewart*, *Late Show with David Letterman*, and *Nightline*, as well as performing at numerous comedy festivals. She serves on the board of directors for 826NYC, a nonprofit organization that encourages school-age children to develop their writing skills.

When not touring to promote her books, Vowell enjoys quiet evenings at home in her New York City apartment.

—B.M.

Suggested Reading: *Chicago Tribune* C p1 Nov. 6, 2002; *Metroactive* (on-line) Oct. 19, 2005; (Spokane, Washington) *Spokesman-Review* (on-line) Apr. 13, 2004; *This American Life* Web site; *Washington Post* T p27 Apr. 17, 2003

"Like Gentileschi's important works . . . provides an imaginative and respectful point of view to a compelling woman's story." Kristine Huntley offered similar praise in her review for *Booklist* (December 1, 2001): "a moving celebration of the power of art. . . . *The Passion of Artemisia* offers a vivid portrait of a complex female artist who doggedly pursues her passion despite seemingly overwhelming obstacles."

Born in 1871, Emily Carr, the protagonist of Vreeland's novel *The Forest Lover*, dedicated her life to painting the landscape and inhabitants of Canada's Pacific coast in a bold, expressionist style. (She is especially remembered for her captivating depictions of tribal totem poles.) As Vreeland shows, however, Carr's predilections clashed with the sensibilities of the era, earning her the disapproval of her family and the public; only late in life would Carr receive the recognition she deserved. Vreeland describes Carr's treks through the wilderness and her encounters with the area's indigenous population; she "creates an Impressionist canvas of Emily Carr's life, based on fact and imagined into what Carr might call 'something bigger than fact: the underlying spirit, all it stands for,'" as Judith Long wrote for New York *Newsday* (January 25, 2004). However, as with *The Passion of Artemisia*, some reviewers found Vreeland's portrait of Carr idealized: "Vreeland so loves Emily Carr that she fashions her into a feminist New Age icon, a woman who runs with the trees," Michael Agger commented for the *New York Times Book Review* (February 8, 2004). Nevertheless, "One of the pleasures of this beguiling novel," a reviewer for *Publishers Weekly* (November 24, 2003) observed, "is the way Vreeland . . . has acquired a painter's eye; her descriptions of Carr's works are faithful evocations of the artist's dazzling colors and craft." The reviewer continued: "There are few dramatic climaxes; instead Vreeland emphasizes Carr's relationships with her rigidly conventional siblings and with her mentors and colleagues. She vividly describes the obstacles Carr faced when she ventured into the wilderness and in her periods of near poverty and self doubt."

The stories in Vreeland's collection *Life Studies* explore some of the ways in which art has touched the lives of those involved only peripherally, if at all, in its creation. The book is divided into two sections of eight stories each. The settings in the first section, "Then," are historical, while in the other, "Now," they are essentially contemporary; a single story bridges the gap, in a section titled "Interlude." "Anyone who has been caught under the spell of great art will already understand the wisdom of Vreeland's fiction," Mary Houlihan remarked for the *Chicago Sun-Times* (January 2, 2005). "With this collection of stories, the art enthusiast continues her mission to preach a vibrant, intelligent sermon about the life-changing power of art." Kelly Jane Torrance, in a review for the *Washington Times* (January 30, 2005), called the collection "the work of a great talent" but found the stories themselves frequently flawed. "Ms. Vreeland has an enviable talent for prose, sometimes even great prose. But that stimulating style often seems wasted on stories that simply do not go anywhere." The book, Torrance noted, "is, in the end, something of propaganda."

Luncheon of the Boating Party, Vreeland's latest novel, "tracks Auguste Renoir as he conceives, plans and paints the 1880 masterpiece that gives her vivid fourth novel its title," according to a reviewer for *Publishers Weekly* (February 19, 2007). The reviewer further explained: "Renoir, then 39, pays the rent on his Montmartre garret by painting 'overbred society women in their fussy parlors,' but, goaded by negative criticism from [his friend the novelist] Émile Zola, he dreams of doing a breakout work." To that end Renoir gathers a party of 13 men and women who spend several Sundays drinking and socializing, as the artist attempts to capture them on canvas. The reviewer concluded, "Vreeland achieves a detailed and surprising group portrait, individualized and immediate."

Vreeland's books have won her numerous literary prizes over the years. *Girl in Hyacinth Blue* captured *ForeWord Magazine*'s award as best novel of the year for 1999, the journal *Inkwell*'s 1999 Grand Prize for Fiction, and the 1999 San Diego Book Awards' Theodore Geisel Prize, among others; it was also a finalist for the 1999 Book Sense Book of the Year prize and a nominee for the 2001 International Dublin Literary Award. Vreeland herself was named storyteller of the year by *Independent Publisher* for 1999 and woman of the year (1999–2000) by *San Diego Writers' Monthly*. *The Passion of Artemisia* won Vreeland a second Theodore Geisel Award, in 2002, and *Life Studies* brought her a third, in 2005.

Vreeland married Joseph "Kip" Gray, a software engineer, in November 1988. They have no children and currently live in San Diego. In addition to her novels, Vreeland has written more than 250 articles for a variety of periodicals on topics ranging from art to education to skiing. "What English Teachers Want," her instructional pamphlet for high-school and community-college writers, published in 1995, is used by educational institutions across the country. Her short fiction has appeared in the numerous journals, including *Ploughshares*, *New England Review*, the *Missouri Review*, *Alaska Quarterly Review*, *Calyx*, and *So to Speak*.

—P.B.M.

Suggested Reading: *Book* p69 Mar./Apr. 2002; *Booklist* p69 Sep. 1, 1999, p607 Dec. 1, 2001; *Boston Globe* TV WK p4 Feb. 2, 2003; *Chicago Sun-Times* p13 Jan. 2, 2005; *Chicago Tribune* CN p1 Mar. 11, 2002, C p2 Feb. 11, 2004; *New York Times* E p3 Mar. 9, 2000; *New York Times Book Review* p29 Dec. 19, 1999, p24 Feb. 8, 2004; *Publishers Weekly* p35 Jan. 14, 2002, p39 Nov.

24, 2003; Susan Vreeland Web site; *Washington Post* T p6 Feb. 17, 2002, T p10 Feb. 22, 2004; *Washington Times* B p8 Jan. 30, 2005

Selected Books: novels—*What Love Sees*, 1988; *Girl in Hyacinth Blue*, 1999; *The Passion of Artemisia*, 2002; *The Forest Lover*, 2004; *Luncheon of the Boating Party*, 2007; short fiction—*Life Studies*, 2005

Frazer Harrison/Getty Images

Wagner, Bruce

1954– Novelist; screenwriter

"I grew up a few doors from [the Oscar-winning actor] Broderick Crawford," in Beverly Hills, California, Bruce Wagner told Erik Himmelsbach for the *Los Angeles Times* (August 28, 1996). "When I was 10, his girlfriend overdosed and died. One day she simply wasn't there anymore." This tragedy, occurring as it did just a year after Wagner's family moved to the area, "was the beginning of the Hollywood Babylon for me," the author told Bernard Weinraub for the *New York Times* (August 28, 1996), referring to the popular 1975 exposé of that name by Kenneth Anger. As in Anger's book, the dark underbelly of Hollywood is the dominant motif in Wagner's work: his novels and screenplays evoke a nightmarish vision of Hollywood in which, beneath the sunshine and the glamour, lies a sordid world of excess and insanity. However, his work is not all darkness and gloom: "I do write about degradation, but in the context of many other things," the author contended to Irene Lacher for the *Los Angeles Times* (January 29,

2002). In fact, Wagner told Weinraub, "[My] fantasy is to create a world like [Charles] Dickens's," with its formal structure and verdant language. "Dickens is like a beacon for me. He should be for all writers."

Bruce Wagner, the son of Morton and Bunny Wagner, was born in Madison, Wisconsin, in 1954. When his son was eight years old, Morton moved the family to Beverly Hills, buying a house on Rodeo Drive. Though Morton (currently a stockbroker in New York City) was in the entertainment business, working in radio and briefly as a producer for *The Les Crane Show*, the family stood on one of the lower rungs of the Beverly Hills social ladder. Nevertheless, at Buena Vista Elementary School and Beverly High, Wagner came into contact with some of Hollywood's most illustrious youngsters— including the offspring of Elizabeth Taylor—and socialized at some of the area's most exclusive homes, gaining insights into the lives of the elite while remaining on the outside himself. Wagner ran into Groucho Marx on occasion and, "lived right down the street from the Beverly Wilshire Hotel," the author informed Himmelsbach. "I would see Warren Beatty and Julie Christie there all the time. I could see Barbara Hutton wheeled down when she died. That was my youth, so that's why I write so much about this town."

At the age of 16, Wagner dropped out of high school, left his parents' home, and began to work variously at a Century City bookstore and as a limousine and ambulance driver. At one point he traveled to San Francisco, "where he wound up," Wagner recounted to Weinraub, "in a halfway house for people who could not cope." Returning to Los Angeles after his San Francisco sojourn, Wagner obtained a position as a limousine driver at the Beverly Hills Hotel, for which he chauffeured a variety of clients, including Orson Welles, Olivia de Havilland, Audrey Hepburn, and members of the Saudi royal family.

He enjoyed the job but at age 25 decided to try his hand at screenwriting. Collaborating with another author, Wagner produced the script for a comedy entitled *Young Lust*. The script was quickly purchased and made into a film, but it was never released. The next several years were difficult for Wagner. Although he disliked acting he accepted occasional roles to earn money; his most notable part was in the 1987 comedy *One Crazy Summer*, with John Cusack and Demi Moore, in which he played a mentally unbalanced character.

The horror director Wes Craven provided Wagner with his next major screenwriting opportunity. The two had met through a mutual acquaintance, and later, as Wagner recalled to Dan Epstein for *Spiked* magazine (on-line), when Craven was asked to do another *Nightmare on Elm Street* movie, "he called me out of the blue to work with him on it. It was a very generous offer and I had a huge amount of fun working on that movie."

The film that resulted, *Nightmare on Elm Street III: Dream Warriors*, was released in 1987 and was positively received for an installment of a horror-film series. Wagner next wrote the script for the 1989 film *Scenes from the Class Struggle in Beverly Hills*, a caustic look at the wealthy inhabitants of the town and the people who serve them.

In his early 30s and inspired by the stories of F. Scott Fitzgerald, Wagner penned a series of short fiction pieces about a frustrated writer named Bud Wiggins. Wagner self-published about 1,000 copies of the collection in 1988 and sold them at a West Hollywood bookstore. The work sold well and was excerpted in *Esquire*; on that basis Random House offered Wagner a book contract. Released in 1991, his first novel, *Force Majeure* "paints a picture of Tinseltown so bleak it makes Jackie Collins [known for writing sexually explicit best-sellers] look like Barbara Cartland [a writer of genteel romances]," Kevin Allman wrote for the *Los Angeles Times* (September 16, 1991). The central character is Bud Wiggins who, like Wagner in his earlier days, drives a limo and searches endlessly for his big break while careening towards a mental breakdown. The cast of characters includes Bud's oddball mother, his neglectful agent, and a host of other bizarre people. "Wagner," Tony Cohan wrote for the *Washington Post* (October 4, 1991), "is a gifted writer with a morbid, quirky wit, a canny sensibility loosed among the palms. . . . Wagner details the nightmarish triple-think and paranoid symbology of every Hollywood transaction." David Finkle, writing for the *New York Time Book Review* (September 29, 1991), remarked, "The novel will delight movie buffs; it's the revenge of a cynical Hollywood scribe, tickling and testing the system from within."

Following up on the success of *Force Majeure*, Wagner teamed with the movie director Oliver Stone to create an offbeat miniseries for ABC entitled *Wild Palms*. Shown in May 1993, *Wild Palms* was set in an Orwellian, futurist Los Angeles. It starred James Belushi as Harry Wycoff, an honest attorney who, while working for a television station, stumbles onto a mind-control plot involving drugs and holograms and masterminded by a monomaniacal senator played by Robert Loggia. Described by Wagner as "a techno-shamanistic melodrama," and by one of its cast members as "*Dynasty* on peyote," according to Steve Weinstein, writing for the *Los Angeles Times* (May 9, 1993), *Wild Palms* received a mixed critical response. In a review for the *Los Angeles Times* (May 14, 1993) Howard Rosenberg stated, "Some credit is due *Wild Palms* for at least daring to dream. In essence, though, it creates its own hologram, an eyeful of image with nothing to touch, feel or hold on to." Mary Harron, writing for the London *Independent* (November 7, 1993), offered a different perspective: "*Wild Palms* should be watched like opera; for its gorgeous images, its emotional set-pieces and its high style.

And don't worry if you can't follow the plot. That just makes it more like the modern world." Wagner's next television project, the two-hour science-fiction movie *White Dwarf*, premiered on May 23, 1995. (Wagner co-wrote the script with Francis Ford Coppola.) *White Dwarf* takes place in the year 3040 on the planet Rusta, which is being torn apart by a civil war.

Wagner's second novel, *I'm Losing You* (1996), was the first in his cell phone trilogy (so-named because the books derive their titles from the parlance of cell phone users). Dubbed "a heartless novel about a town [Los Angeles] without pity," by John Clark in a nevertheless positive review for the *Los Angeles Times* (August 4, 1996), *I'm Losing You* earned Wagner significant literary accolades. As in *Force Majeure*, Wagner introduced an intricate web of fascinating characters whose lives intersect in unexpected ways. There's Gina, "the delusional masseuse," as Anita Gates wrote for the *New York Times Book Review* (August 18, 1996), "who refers to herself as 'the thief of energy.' ('Took as much energy from her as I could,' she writes of the recipient of a two-hour massage, 'and it just drained and drained, like venom from a snake.')"; there's also Severin, Gates added, "who hasn't left his hillside house near the Hollywood sign since 1981, because he's waiting for a telephone call about his script. To pass the time, he sits by the pool and monitors car phone conversations." Overall Gates lauded the work, stating, "Mr. Wagner has a satirist's eye and ear for various levels of hope and awareness. . . . *I'm Losing You* may stop short of brilliance, but it's pretty fabulous and its message is trenchant." Janet Maslin, in a review for the *New York Times* (July 30, 1996), called the book a "poisoned dart of a novel," and added that it "sees the film world's ironies with pitiless clarity and creates a savage, shocking tableau. . . . The book's cacophony of glib, abrasive and evilly funny voices creates a vision of soullessness colliding with mortality." The work "put Wagner on the map as the most lucid and pitiless of Hollywood's novelistic observers," Dwight Garner declared for the *New York Times Book Review* (November 16, 2003).

In 1999 the film version of *I'm Losing You*, directed by Wagner himself, came to the silver screen. The finished product "[bore] surprisingly slender resemblance to [the] book," as Janet Maslin noted for the *New York Times* (July 16, 1999). Wagner explained the discrepancy to Jan Breslauer for the *Los Angeles Times* (July 16, 1999), "I wanted to preserve the soul of my book without the almost pornographic savagery that the first part of it includes." Maslin concluded that while Wagner's film "successfully echoes his book's bleak resonance . . . his straightforward ability with a camera is no match for what he can do on the page."

In Wagner's next installment of the cell phone trilogy, *I'll Let You Go* (2001), he offered "a Dickensian epic about the disparities between the richest and poorest in present-day Los Angeles," as John Freeman remarked for the *Boston Globe* (February 3, 2002). The book chronicles the Trotter family, a Los Angeles clan of eccentric billionaires, and Amaryllis, an 11-year-old orphan living on the streets. "Here," Freeman opined, "Wagner devotes the same poetic exactitude to portraying life in the gutter as he does the peccadilloes of Hollywood's rich and famous." Though, on the whole, *I'll Let You Go* enjoyed a respectable critical reception—with Michiko Kakutani for the *New York Times* (January 2, 2002) terming it "virtuosic"—some reviewers were disappointed. David Abrams wrote for *January* (May 2002), "The book is too long by even the most generous of Dickensian standards." Abrams concluded, however, "Draggy finish aside, *I'll Let You Go* is well worth the reader's time and patience." Similarly, Sudip Bose, writing for the *Washington Post* (February 3, 2002), noted that that while the book "might be self conscious at times, even a bit contrived . . . [it] ultimately succeeds, for it champions elements of fiction too often neglected in contemporary literature—plot, character, suspense."

In 2001 another film adaptation of *I'm Losing You* was released. Also directed by Wagner, *Women in Film*, as the picture was titled, concentrated on one chapter of the novel. The film was composed of documentary-style interviews with three actresses, who detail their struggles to break into the motion-picture industry. The film received a very limited release.

Still Holding (2003), the final chapter of Wagner's cell phone trilogy, is "the hippest, funniest and most angrily humane novel written about Hollywood in the last 20 years, and it bumps Wagner up to another level as a novelist," Dwight Garner raved for the *New York Times Book Review* (November 16, 2003). *Still Holding* details the plight of the Buddhist superstar Kit Lightfoot; while studying to play a brain-damaged character in a film, Lightfoot is attacked by an autograph seeker. In a cruel twist, the beating causes Lightfoot to lapse into an advanced vegetative state. "As always," Melvin Jules Bukiet wrote for the *Los Angeles Times* (November 2, 2003), "Wagner evinces a fine ghoulish relish for those aspects of human nature that are Hollywood's stock in trade: avarice, covetousness, vainglorious self-promotion, self-delusion and the infinite gradations of degradation and despair."

Bertie Krohn, the narrator of *The Chrysanthemum Palace* (2005), is an actor in his 30s and the son of the creator of TV's longest-running space opera, *Starwatch: The Navigators*. The novel also details the lives of two other children of successful celebrities: Clea Fremantle, a childhood friend of Bertie Krohn and the daughter of an actress who earned three consecutive Academy Awards but committed suicide when Clea was young; and Clea's lover, Thad Michelet, a moderately successful actor and novelist who struggles with his hateful father, a

Pulitzer Prize–winner several times over and a perennial candidate for the Nobel Prize. Karen Campbell, in a review for the *Boston Globe* (March 21, 2005), called the book's prose "intricate and inventive" and added, "*The Chrysanthemum Palace* reads a little like a potboiler: more surface than substance, with lots of name dropping, melodrama, and tales of colorful excess. It's diverting, even involving, but not particularly emotionally engaging; the characters seem more flash than real blood and guts." A critic for the *New Yorker* (February 14, 2005) argued: "This slender novel lacks the kaleidoscopic frenzy of Wagner's 'cell-phone' trilogy, and its more limited range gives his relentlessly up-to-the-minute pop-trivia references a somewhat airless feel. Still, [Wagner's] ability to eviscerate the absurdities of Hollywood, while occasionally hinting at its basic humanity, remains undiminished."

Wagner's most recent novel, *Memorial* (2006), follows the lives of four members of a dysfunctional Los Angeles family, each of them willing to do virtually anything they can for money or fame. While some previous critics questioned the value of Wagner's method of describing Hollywood, particularly his constant name-dropping, many found *Memorial* to offer a complex and rewarding portrait of Los Angeles. Danna Schaeffer, in a critique for the *Sunday Oregonian* (November 5, 2006), called the book "extraordinary: large of vision, deep and engrossing" and Pankaj Mishra, assessing the novel for the *New York Times* (October 8, 2006), remarked: "Wagner may again seem trapped in the persona of a haughtily amoral author, briskly rubbing his readers' faces in the grotesqueries available through the local Yellow Pages. But *Memorial* also records a softening of mood and a growing curiosity about other possibilities of being. Behind the clamorous, disheveled prose, the tirades and philippics, one senses a moral intelligence missing from much contemporary fiction that aspires self-consciously to a Nabokovian poise and beauty."

Wagner was married to the actress Rebecca De Mornay for a brief period in the early 1990s. Some observers suggest that Wagner's somber mien, shaved head, and black outfits mask his true character. His friend, the actress and screenwriter Carrie Fisher, told Irene Lacher, "He's a really kind, tender guy, and that's the surprise of him because he certainly doesn't look like that. . . . He's a nice Jewish boy who loves his mother."

—P.B.M.

Suggested Reading: *Boston Globe* B p11 Mar. 21, 2005; *Los Angeles Times* F p1 Aug. 16, 1991, E p1 Aug. 28, 1996, V p1 Jan. 29, 2002, *New York Times* II p34 May 16, 1993, C p9 Aug. 12, 1996; *New York Times Book Review* (on-line) Dec. 8, 2003; *Spiked* (on-line); *Sunday Oregonian* O p16 Nov. 5, 2006

Selected Books: *Force Majeure*, 1991; *I'm Losing You*, 1996; *I'll Let You Go*, 2001; *Still Holding*, 2003; *The Chrysanthemum Palace*, 2005; *Memorial*, 2006

Selected Screenplays: *Nightmare on Elm Street III: Dream Warriors*, 1987; *Wild Palms*, 1993; *White Dwarf*, 1995; *I'm Losing You*, 1999; *Women in Film*, 2001

Courtesy of Ronald Wallace

Wallace, Ronald

Feb. 18, 1945– Poet; literary critic; short-story writer

Ronald Wallace has—somewhat deceptively—focused his poems and criticism on the lighter aspects of human experience. For someone who has written a poem called "The Bad Snorkeler" ("He's a wetsuit full of damage, a trip mine / of enthusiasm") and a book entitled *God Be with the Clown*, Wallace frequently—and surprisingly—bases his writing on a sense of mortality and the deep sadness at the heart of life. He has won critical approbation for his poetry collections: *Plums, Stones, Kisses & Hooks* (1981), *Tunes for Bears to Dance To* (1983), *People and Dog in the Sun* (1987), *The Makings of Happiness* (1991) *Time's Fancy* (1994), *The Uses of Adversity* (1998), and *Long for This World: New and Selected Poems* (2003). Wallace's volumes of criticism, *Henry James and the Comic Form* (1975), *The Last Laugh: Form and Affirmation in the Contemporary American Comic Novel* (1979), and *God Be with the Clown: Humor in American Poetry* (1984), have

been deemed to occupy a valuable niche in the literature on American writing. His book of fiction, *Quick Bright Things* (2000), comprising interrelated short stories, has also been praised.

For *World Authors 2000–2005*, Ronald Wallace wrote:

"I was born on February 18, 1945, in Cedar Rapids, Iowa, and grew up in St. Louis, Missouri. My first stories, written in block letters at the age of four, were modeled on the Dick and Jane primer I read in pre-school: 'I HAVE A FATHER HIS NAME IS BILL-WALLACE. I LIKE HIM HE IS A NICE FATHER. SOME TIMES I PLAY WITH HIM. HE GAVE ME SOME PAPPR. I DREW ON IT. I HAVE A MOTHER HER NAME IS LO-WALLACE. ONE TIME SHE PLAYED BALL WITH ME. SHE GAVE ME TWO HATS ONE HAT IS BLUE ONE HAT IS DARK BROWN AND LIGHT BRAWN. I HAVE A HOME. IT HAS A KICTH AND A LIVING-ROOM. IT HAS A BASEMENT AND A ATICK. MY MOTHER WROKS IN THE KICTH.' My mother, always my biggest fan, kept these efforts, along with all my subsequent writings, on a special display shelf devoted to my published work. The domestic themes—the importance of family, home, play, writing, and parent-child relations—have remained a central strand in my fiction and poetry.

"In grade school I read all the books in the classroom libraries—*Clara Barton: Girl Nurse; Thomas Alva Edison: Boy Inventor; Bartholomew and the Oobleck*—and won a spelling bee and an award for penmanship. At the age of 10 I moved to Rock Hill, a suburb of St. Louis, and although I was not particularly happy there, it is a time and place I keep coming back to in my writing. It was 1955. The cold war was in full swing; the Russians were about to launch Sputnik; I was in love with a fat red-headed girl with thick glasses; and my father had contracted multiple sclerosis, a progressive degenerative disease which would slowly paralyze him and foster a conflict in our relationship which would find its way into every book I would write.

"I kept a diary—a little gold affair with a lock—something only girls did and which, therefore, had to be kept secret. Writing for me was necessary, useful, and dangerous—if my friends found out, I would be laughed at. I read voraciously—*Uncle Scrooge* comics, *Mad Magazine, Humbug*, The Hardy Boys, Nancy Drew, and later (a result of sneaking downtown to used bookstores on the streetcar to used bookstores) pulp horror and science fiction by H. P. Lovecraft, August Derleth, Ray Bradbury, Theodore Sturgeon, and Robert Heinlein. It was there that I also discovered Mary Shelley's *Frankenstein*, Shirley Jackson's 'The Lottery,' and William Faulkner's 'A Rose for Emily.'

"In ninth grade I had my first revelation about the power and mystery and exhilaration of poetry. It was in Mrs. Alexander's English class, the last class of the day. The class clown had brought some plastic vomit, and toward the end of the period he placed it on the floor beside him, gagged loudly and raised his hand. Mrs. Alexander sent him off to the nurse and called for the janitor, who, seeing the prank for what it was, played along by sprinkling some sawdust on the vomit and sweeping it up into his dustbin. The class by now in hysterics, Mrs. Alexander gave up trying to restore order and instead just passed out some mimeos for us to read silently. They were Emily Dickinson poems, and, as I read them, the class and its laughter faded, Mrs. Alexander, asleep on her desk, faded, and I was left in the presence of the rare and strange feeling (as I would later learn Emily Dickinson herself had put it) as if the top of my head were taken off. I didn't understand the poems, but I felt their power—their joy and exhilaration and surprise and whimsy—and when the bell rang, I didn't hear it. I knew at that point that I wanted to be able to do what Emily Dickinson had done for me. I wrote poetry in secret, I read poetry in secret, and I dreamed of one day being a real poet and writer.

"I attended The College of Wooster where I edited the school newspaper and co-founded a literary magazine, the *Shaft*, and met my wife, Peg, who, with my daughters Molly and Emily, and my sister Teri-Ann, would provide central themes for my work. After college, I attended graduate school at the University of Michigan, specializing in English and American literature from 1780–1970 and writing a PhD dissertation on Henry James which would later become *Henry James and the Comic Form*, the first of three books I would write on humor in American literature (*The Last Laugh: Form and Affirmation in the Contemporary American Comic Novel; God Be With the Clown: Humor in American Poetry*). My own poetry and fiction has always reflected the accessible comic voice I discovered in Donne and Marvel, Whitman and Dickinson, and Frost and Stevens, along with the intense lyricism I found in Gerard Manley Hopkins, Dylan Thomas, and Sylvia Plath.

"In 1971, my wife and I sold everything we owned and traveled in Europe where, in a farmhouse in Grindelwald, Switzerland, I committed myself to seriously writing poetry. These, my first published poems, were instrumental in securing me a teaching position at the University of Wisconsin-Madison where, since 1972, I have developed a creative writing program, established a poetry series (Brittingham and Pollak prizes) through the University Press, founded a literary magazine (*The Madison Review*) and implemented a post-MFA Institute for Creative Writing, while teaching poetry and fiction workshops and introductory literature. My six books of poetry—*Plums, Stones, Kisses & Hooks* (which was rejected ninety-nine times before finding a publisher), *Tunes for Bears to Dance To, People and Dog in the Sun, The Makings of Happiness, Time's Fancy, The Uses of Adversity*—and my one collection of interconnected short stories—*Quick Bright Things*—have all explored

themes of childhood, family, illness, father-son conflicts, domestic love, parenthood, mortality, art, travel, the natural world (my wife and I own an old farm on 40 acres in the hills of Richland County, Wisconsin, where we've raised goats and chickens and several large gardens, and where I've done considerable writing—the farm provides the setting for many of my stories and poems), and the importance of tolerance, good temper, sympathy, and humor in human affairs.

"I'm an avid volleyball player, and my co-ed team, The Grapes of Wrath, continues to whup the youngsters—at least occasionally."

Wallace, currently the Felix Pollak Professor of Poetry and Halls-Bascom Professor of English at the University of Wisconsin, in Madison, earned his B.A. in 1967 and his doctoral degree in 1971. He described his workspace at the university to Daina Savage for the Lancaster, Pennsylvania, *Intelligencer Journal* (October 12, 2001) as "probably the most beautiful office in the world. Even though I'm in the middle of town, it doesn't feel like it when you look out the window." He gives a somewhat bleaker (yet humorous) view of his working conditions in the poem "Literature in the 21st Century," which is included in the volume *Long for This World: New and Selected Poems*:

> Sometimes I wish I drank coffee
> or smoked Marlboros, or maybe cigars—
> yes, a hand-rolled Havana cigar
> in its thick, manly wrapping,
> . . .
> and I'd be writing about war and old losses—
> man things—and not where I am, in this
> pristine and sensitive vessel, all
> fizzy water, reticence, and care, all reduced
> fat and purified air, behind my deprived
> computer, where I can't manage even
> a decaf cap, a mild Tiparillo, a glass of
> great-taste-less-filling light beer.

Wallace's first book, *Henry James and the Comic Form*, derived from his thesis, has been cited by Harold Bloom (in his volume *Modern Critical Interpretations: Henry James's* The Ambassadors) and other literary scholars as an important work of James criticism. His other books of literary scholarship examine the humour in the works of such writers as John Barth, John Hawkes, Ken Kesey, and Vladimir Nabokov (in *The Last Laugh*) and John Berryman, Emily Dickinson, Robert Frost, and Wallace Stevens (in *God Be With the Clown*); they are also considered thoughtful and worthy volumes.

Wallace is known to the general reading public, however, primarily as a poet. He told Savage, "Poetry needs to be entertaining. My comic poems go over well with an audience, but I want people who come to my reading[s] to say that they didn't realize serious poetry that makes them think would also be funny." He continued, "[Robert] Frost said poetry is play. If not, it's a fraud."

Wallace's poetry often includes autobiographical detail in his poetry. In "Off the Record," from *The Makings of Happiness*, he writes of his father:

In the attic I find the notes
he kept in college
over forty years ago: Hooray
for Thanksgiving vacation! he wrote
in the margin of Psych 102.
And for a moment I can see him there,
feel the exuberance surge through
that odd cell of his body
where I am still
a secret code uncompleted, a piece
of DNA, some ancient star-stuff.
And then I find a recording of me
from 1948, when he was twenty-two
and I was three, and I can see,
from my perch up on his shoulders
from stopping at the gaudy arcade,
plugging his lucky quarter into the future where we'd
  always be.
Maybe imagination is just
a form of memory after all, locked
deep in the double helix of eternity.
Or maybe the past is but one more
phantasmagoric invention we use
to fool ourselves into someone else's shoes.
It's not my voice I want to hear
on memory's fading page, on imagination's disk.
It is my father's in the background
prompting me, doing his best
to stay off the record, his hushed
instructions vanishing in static.

Yet, as a reviewer noted for *Publishers Weekly* (September 26, 1994, on-line), "Part of what sets [him] apart from other poets who write about personal and family life is his virtuosity with complex forms." Wallace frequently uses such traditional poetic forms as the sonnet, the villanelle, and the sestina, among others. *The Uses of Adversity*, Wallace's 1998 collection, is composed of 100 sonnets. In preparation for the book, he spent an entire year writing at least one sonnet a day. "By May 29, 1995, the 365th day of my project, the act of writing a sonnet a day had become so familiar it was something of an addiction," he wrote for a 1997 issue of the Associated Writing Programs (AWP) *Writer's Chronicle*, as reprinted on his official Web site. "I even considered continuing for another year, but decided that that way lay madness. I didn't want to become Merrill Moore, who . . . for all his world-record 50,000 sonnets, is an-all-but-forgotten figure in American poetry."

Long for This World contains selections from *The Uses of Adversity*, as well as from Wallace's other poetry collections: *Plums, Stones, Kisses & Hooks, Tunes for Bears to Dance To, People and Dog in the Sun, The Makings of Happiness*, and *Time's Fancy*. A reviewer for the *St. Louis Post-Dispatch* (December 7, 2003) called the poems "by turns fresh, compassionate [and] whimsical" and praised Wallace's "remarkable ease and eloquence." *Long for This World*—which contains such poems as "The Assistant Professor's Nightmare," "The Belly Dancer in the Nursing Home," and "Why I am Not a Nudist"—was included in the newspaper's list of best books of 2003. That year Wallace's work was also represented in the volume *Best American Poetry 2003*, edited by Yusef Komunyakaa.

Besides writing his own poetry, which has been widely anthologized, Wallace edits two University of Wisconsin Press Poetry Series; he is also the editor of *Vital Signs: Contemporary American Poetry from the University Presses* (1989), which Charles Guenther described for the *St. Louis Post-Dispatch* (December 24, 1989) as a "highly successful showcase" for Pittsburgh, Princeton, Wesleyan, and Yale, among other university presses. (Guenther particularly applauded Wallace's inclusion of a large number of female poets.)

Wallace has not confined himself to poetry and literary criticism: he is also the author of a volume of interconnected short stories, *Quick Bright Things*, which a reviewer for *Publishers Weekly* (January 10, 2000, on-line) described as "a broad and often moving [work that] recounts the travails and triumphs of a Midwestern man from boyhood to middle age." The reviewer singled out the title story as "deft and thematically satisfying." In a 2001 issue of the AWP *Writer's Chronicle*, as reprinted on his official Web site, Wallace recounts that he had originally begun writing short stories in an effort to win "Florida State University's 'World's Best Short Short Story Contest,' the prize for which is a hundred dollars and a crate of Florida oranges and publication in *Sundog* magazine." He continued, "I tried to win that contest for a decade. This year [2001] I did finally win . . . which must qualify me (for fifteen minutes at least) as something of an authority on the form."

Ronald Wallace has been the recipient of many honors over the course of his career, including: a Vilas Associateship, several Council for Wisconsin Writers Book Awards, several Wisconsin Arts Board Grants, a Helen Bullis Prize, a Porter Butts Award for the creative arts, a Robert E. Gard Foundation Award, and a Lynde and Harry Bradley Major Achievement Award. In 1994 he was named a Wisconsin Library Association Notable Author.

—S.Y.

Suggested Reading: *American Literature* p146+ Mar. 1985; *Apalachee Quarterly* p119+ Vol. 39 1993; *Choice* p273 Oct. 1984; *Georgia Review* p176+ Spring 1999; (Lancaster, Pennsylvania) *Intelligencer Journal* p3 Oct. 12, 2001; *New York Times Book Review* Feb. 27, 2000; *Paris Review* p117 Winter 1999; *Publishers Weekly* p47 Jan. 10, 2000, (on-line) Sep. 26, 1994; *St. Louis Post-Dispatch* C p5 Dec. 24, 1989, C p11 Dec. 7, 2003; *Transactions* p137+ Vol. 81 1993; *Wisconsin Academy Review* p45+ Mar. 1998

Selected Books: poetry—*Plums, Stones, Kisses & Hooks*, 1981; *Tunes for Bears to Dance To*, 1983; *People and Dog in the Sun*, 1987; *The Makings of Happiness*, 1991; *Time's Fancy*, 1994; *The Uses of Adversity*, 1998; *Long for This World: New and Selected Poems*, 2003; criticism—*Henry James and the Comic Form*, 1975; *The Last Laugh: Form and Affirmation in the Contemporary American Comic Novel*, 1979; *God Be with the Clown: Humor in American Poetry*, 1984; fiction—*Quick Bright Things*, 2000; as editor—*Vital Signs: Contemporary American Poetry from the University Presses*, 1989

Ross Land/Getty Images

Walters, Minette

Sep. 26, 1949– Novelist

"One of the most often repeated criticisms of the crime genre is that it is formulaic writing: you use the same place, the same characters, but with a different death each time," Minette Walters observed in an interview with Eve Tan Gee for *Crime Time* (on-line). "In other words, you don't have to think too hard about the next book. In one way I can see that this is a criticism that can be levelled, and I felt that I really wanted to change direction with each book."

Unlike such celebrated crime-fiction writers as Arthur Conan Doyle and Agatha Christie, Minette Walters has no single recurring character, such as Sherlock Holmes or Miss Marple, to unify her works. Yet this absence hasn't stopped her from becoming one of the most popular British crime novelists of her era; her books have won many

awards and have been translated into more than 20 languages. Several have been adapted into popular television films. Despite the unavoidable comparisons to Agatha Christie novels, Walters's mysteries aren't polite discussions about murder but vividly realistic portraits of death, told in unsparing detail. "In a typical Christie, death tends to become incidental as everyone moves on into the drawing room for tea," Walters noted in an interview with Barry Came for *Maclean's* (March 8, 1999). "In my books, I really do not want the reader to have any doubt that I regard death—violent death—as something absolutely vile and shocking."

Minette Caroline Mary Walters was born on September 26, 1949 in Bishop's Stortford, England. She is the daughter of Samuel Henry Desmond Jebb, an army captain, and the former Minette Colleen Helen Paul, an artist. She studied at the Godolphin School and Durham University, from which she received a bachelor's degree in French and German literature. She started writing fiction, although she confessed to Came, "It was all terribly surrealist, a lot of crap basically, totally unpublishable." In 1972 she began working in magazine journalism and eventually joined the London offices of *Woman's Weekly Library*, where she served as the editor of the hospital-romances section. "I had to find eight novelettes a month," she explained in her interview with Came. "Each had to be 30,000 words long, about doctors and nurses. It was wretchedly difficult." On a colleague's dare, she began writing the romances herself and was soon making more money from that than from editing. In about 1977 she quit her editing position.

Walters, however, did not spend long as a freelance romance writer. In 1978 she married Alec Hamilton Walters, a business consultant. The first of her two sons was born in 1979 and the second in 1982. Until the boys went off to boarding school, near the end of the 1980s, she stopped writing in order to focus on raising them. However, with the house empty and her creative juices flowing, she decided to write a crime novel—something that had been a lifelong dream. Her first novel, *The Ice House*, was published in 1992. Set in an old English mansion, the novel centers around the discovery of a decaying, unidentifiable corpse in the mansion's abandoned ice house. Phoebe Maybury, a recluse who lives in the mansion with two female housemates, had been suspected of murder following the disappearance of her husband a decade before, but the police had never been able to substantiate the speculation. Now, with the discovery of this body, Phoebe again finds herself the subject of uncomfortable scrutiny, as well as rumors of lesbianism and witchcraft. Felicia Lamb, writing for the London *Mail on Sunday* (August 15, 1993), declared: "Don't miss this startling, witty, original story of three independent women shut away in a large country house. . . . [This is a] super-accomplished first novel, full of surprises, violence and love." *The Ice House* became a best-seller and won the prestigious Crime Writers' Association (CWA) John Creasey Award for best first crime novel.

In *The Sculptress* (1993), Olive Martin, an unpleasant, overweight, menacing woman, is serving a life sentence for the brutal murder (and dismemberment) of her mother and sister. In prison she spends her days sculpting figures—and subsequently dismembering them. Rosalind Leigh, a journalist and author suffering from writer's block, is coerced by her publisher into writing about Martin and the murders. Although Rosalind is at first repelled by the idea, she interviews Martin and quickly becomes intrigued by the woman; Martin insists she is guilty, but Rosalind begins to suspect that she may in fact be innocent after all. *The Sculptress* became a best-seller and was the winner of the 1994 Edgar Allen Poe Award for best mystery novel. In a review for the London *Guardian* (August 10, 1993), Matthew Coady noted: "Behind scenes of provincial life, Walters manipulates a plot bursting with surprises, in which deception, inheritance and hidden sexual passion all have their part. It amply confirms the promise of her first novel, finding time for a glimpse at a variety of English prejudice and ending on an ambiguous note." Marcel Berlins, writing for the London *Times* (May 7, 1994), observed, "Walters's use of such a thoroughly unsympathetic person as Olive to carry the story is dangerous. But then she is a risk-taker, not frightened of overstatement. In all her books, there are characters burdened with an excess of eccentricity and feyness; and she is not always in control of her dialogue. But these are small penalties to pay for the pleasure of reading a rare talent possessed of such unnerving imagination."

The focus of *The Scold's Bridle* (1994) is a severely dysfunctional family. When Mathilda Gillespie is found dead in her bathtub with her wrists slit, her blood full of alcohol and barbiturates, and her face covered by a medieval torture device—the scold's bridle of the title— police have to slog through a slew of possible murder suspects. Despised by everyone in her village, Mathilda has made her share of enemies over the years, including her own daughter and granddaughter. Yet, when it is discovered that the dead woman has left her fortune to Sarah Blakeney, her physician, the doctor must use all of her investigative powers to uncover the true murderer. Patrick McGrath, writing for the *New York Times Book Review* (October 2, 1994), expressed mixed feelings about the novel: "Narrative momentum is quickly established and briskly sustained as we learn more about the constellation of characters involved with Mathilda Gillespie. Of particular fascination is her granddaughter, Ruth, a nasty piece of work in the early chapters but a girl who is later shown to be the victim of a vicious young man called Dave. . . . Dave is a horrifying piece of

contemporary social reality and his presence is utterly disruptive. . . . Here on the one hand is a mythic England where right is clearly distinguished from wrong and the law is upheld by established institutions. At the same time we have Dave's England, much more violent and sordid and troubling, so much so that it requires a heavy psychological gloss to be made sense of at all. The two uneasily coexist in these pages . . . [and] produce a sort of muddle." Most reviews, however, were positive. "Articulate and sophisticated prose, complicated plot, imaginative characters, and psychological intensity give this British title high marks," Rex E. Klett opined for *Library Journal* (October 1, 1994). Lynn McAuley wrote for the *Ottawa Citizen* (June 26, 1994), "Walters is a sensitive, intelligent writer. In a lesser writer's hands, the scold's bridle . . . would become an awkward and obtuse symbol. Instead, Walters cleverly uses it to tell tales of incest, child abuse and sexual humiliation. While the plot is fast and tricky, it is Walters' characters that give the novel legs. They are all interesting, surprising and painfully human." The book won the CWA Gold Dagger Award for fiction, considered the most prestigious award in the crime-fiction genre.

In *The Dark Room* (1996), Jinx Kingsley, the daughter of the multimillionaire Adam Kingsley, wakes up in a hospital with no memory of why she is there. She is covered in bandages, apparently as a result of a failed suicide attempt. She soon learns the reason she supposedly attempted suicide: her fiancé, Leo, has run off with her best friend, Meg. When the murdered bodies of Meg and Leo turn up, Jinx finds herself the number-one suspect. Mary Scott, writing for the *New Statesman and Society* (October 13, 1995), noted: "Motivation is at the heart of *The Dark Room*. Like all the best detective fiction it challenges readers to work out how a particular character would act faced with specific circumstances. In this case there's a sharp, subtle twist; the narrator must figure out what *she* might have done. . . . It's a richly original premise and one that Minette Walters exploits to full dramatic effect." Scott added, "The quest for truth is punctuated by touches of humanity that lift this novel way above others of its genre." Emily Melton offered tempered praise in a review for *Booklist* (January 1–15, 1996), observing: "Walters's previous novels have garnered prestigious awards and rave reviews, and her fourth book may do the same. . . . [She] is masterful at tantalizing the reader with odd clues, subtle nuances, obscure hints, and titillating glimpses into the characters' checkered pasts, and she uses rapier-sharp, psyche-probing character analyses and a tightly constructed plot to further lure her readers. Too bad that halfway through the 350-plus pages of 'did she or didn't she,' the story loses momentum. Even though Walters pulls things back together with a slam-bang ending, the book isn't her best effort."

In *The Echo* (1997) Amanda Streeter's husband, suspected of having been involved in a multimillion-pound fraud, has disappeared. At the same time, a dead vagrant has been found in Amanda's garage. When Michael Deacon, a journalist, discovers that Amanda has paid for the vagrant's funeral, he begins to suspect a connection between the two—a connection that may lead to the discovery of Amanda's husband. Though popular with the reading public, the novel received mixed reviews. Writing for *Booklist* (February 1, 1997), Emily Melton opined: "Walters is a gifted storyteller whose rich, dark tales of psychological suspense have led critics and fans to compare her favorably with Ruth Rendell. Her latest book, though, is as baffling and unsettling as wandering through an elaborate maze, with the attendant frustrations, wrong turns, and dead ends. But for readers who persevere, there's also the ultimate reward of arriving in the center of the maze and finally comprehending the ultimate logic of its layout. . . . There's plenty to like about Walters' latest—rich emotion, psychological intrigue, and deliciously tantalizing mystery—but the plot is looser, stranger, and slightly less compelling than her usual efforts. Still, it's a strong showing." Natasha Cooper, writing for the *Times Literary Supplement* (March 7, 1997), noted that the novel "almost collapses under the burden of all the themes it has to carry. These include: the failures of the community-care system, homelessness, the damage done to children by their parents, sin and atonement, actual and emotional patricide, [and] the genetic roots of mental illness. . . . Much of *The Echo* is powerful, and, after a slowish start, it becomes quite gripping. It is also much bigger and more ambitiously constructed than most crime novels, with lengthy quotations from imaginary books, reviews, articles, police memos and a psychiatric session to puzzle and inform the reader. But it does not quite work. . . . Minette Walters has considerable talent and is concerned with important issues, but it is hard to escape the feeling that if she could have taken this novel more lightly, . . . it would paradoxically have carried more weight."

In *The Breaker* (1998), the naked body of a young woman is discovered on a beach. Police determine that she was drugged, raped, then strangled; eerily, her fingers appear to have been deliberately broken. At the same time, a three-year-old girl is found wandering alone through the streets of a nearby town; it soon becomes clear she is the daughter of the victim. Three major suspects emerge in the grisly case: the woman's sexually frustrated husband; the handsome, deceptive actor who found the body; and a lecherous high-school teacher with a bad drug habit. Each time the police build an effective case, new evidence turns up that unsettles their efforts. In *Booklist* (March 1, 1999), David Pitt wrote: "[Walters] just keeps getting better. Her latest is a wonderfully convoluted whodunit that will perplex even expert villain spotters. Her characters are carefully constructed: they're real people, not crime-novel stock figures. . . . This fine novel is sure to be a best-seller, and it deserves to be. Not only Walters' fans but anyone who likes a smart, well-constructed mystery will be spellbound until the final scenes have been played out." Writing for the *New York Times Book Review* (June 27, 1999), Marilyn Stasio remarked: "Ambiguity is an art, and Minette Walters has perfected it in *The Breaker*. . . . The suspense is killing—but only because the psychology is sound."

With *The Shape of Snakes* (2001), Walters delved further into the psychological motivations of her characters. Mrs. Ranelagh, a school teacher, has spent the past 20 years obsessed with the death of her neighbor, "Mad Annie," a black woman who suffered from Tourette's syndrome. Ranelagh had found the woman dying in the gutter one night, her skull shattered. The police report called the death an accident, but Ranelagh, aware of the vicious torment Mad Annie received from her racist neighbors, remains convinced that she had been murdered. Ranelagh makes inquiries of her own and assembles a mass of photos, testimony, E-mails, and correspondence, with which she hopes to reopen the case and pinpoint the murderer. As her quest for justice reaches a zealous pitch, with even her husband falling prey to her suspicions, people begin to wonder why she cares so much, and whether or not she herself has something to hide. "Walters succeeds where many a literary novelist has failed by grounding her complex rumination on the nature of contemporary society within the structure of a gripping crime novel," Joanne Wilkinson observed for *Booklist* (May 1, 2001). "This is a bold psychological thriller that practically revels in unpleasant, unsettling themes, and yet it is almost impossible to put down." Marilyn Stasio, in the *New York Times Book Review* (July 22, 2001), noted: "I have learned never to trust the narrator in Minette Walters's subtle psychological mysteries. These complex characters can be cunning, deceitful, even mad—which is exactly what makes them such absorbing company. . . . Although the narrator obviously has a hidden agenda, the master manipulator here is Walters, whose commanding control over her inflammatory material—and her readers—distracts the eye from potential murder suspects and directs the mind to the everyday acts of casual inhumanity that are the real issue."

In 2002 Walters published *Acid Row*. In the novel Nicholas Franek, a music teacher and a known pedophile, lives in Acid Row, one of Britain's blighted urban housing estates. The other residents, already in a furor over the presence of a pedophile, erupt into violence after an unsettling combination of events: Sophie Morrison, a young doctor, is kidnapped by Franek and his father (himself a convicted murderer and rapist), and a 10-year-old girl named Amy, last seen on the estate, is abducted. In the *New Statesman* (October 29, 2001), Amanda Craig suggested: "The isolation of the elderly [on the estate], the frustration of teenagers with nothing to do and nowhere to go, the struggle for decency and kindliness in adversity, all are well drawn. By weaving a suspenseful tale of courage and error around this grim territory, Walters addresses the ills of modern Britain as few literary novelists have dared to do." However, Craig added, "The effort to be kind glosses over the real mess and horror of life on a sink estate [a British term for a dilapidated housing project]. Increasingly the novel, as it progresses, comes to resemble a screenplay, with the locations and viewpoints stated, rather than described. Walters is an intelligent and compassionate writer, but she is now producing much too fast." Marilyn Stasio, in the *New York Times Book Review* (July 21, 2002), remarked: "Walters focuses on a few key households—including one in which [Franek and his father] are holding a female physician hostage—and methodically tracks the trajectory of violence as it spreads from house to house on a wave of escalating anger. The tension is fierce, but not as piercing as her group portrait of social outcasts for whom 'the pedophile was just an excuse for the boiling resentment of Acid Row's underclass.'"

Walters's next novel, *Fox Evil* (2003), opens with a murder in the small Dorset village of Shenstead. Colonel James Lockyer-Fox's wife, Ailsa, had been found dead on the terrace of Shenstead Manor, wearing only her nightgown. Though the coroner's inquest has cleared her husband of suspicion, James begins receiving a number of threatening phone calls accusing him of her murder as well as a number of other crimes. James, increasingly depressed and isolated, asks his good friend Mark Ankerton, a lawyer based in London, to help clear his name. What Ankerton discovers, however, is a group of nomadic squatters, the Travelers, who are led by a malevolent man calling himself Fox Evil. A reviewer for *Publishers Weekly* (April 14, 2003) observed: "This psychological thriller . . . should satisfy both aficionados of the traditional English cozy and readers who prefer mysteries with a grimmer edge." The reviewer added, "The writer's many fans will thoroughly enjoy this hefty, stand-alone mystery, but psychological thriller readers who are more interested in thrills than psychology may find the going a bit too slow and the eventual denouement too complicated by half." Dorman T. Shindler, writing for the *Denver Post* (June 29, 2003), noted, "As readers delve into this novel, the subplots will seem wildly disparate and unrelated, as if a net had been cast too widely. Then Walters . . . tightens her auctorial fist, pulling the strings together, catching up her readers and the various subplots in an intricate meshwork of plot, character and prose. Not many writers can touch upon the subjects of homelessness, the gypsy lifestyles of a society's disaffected and even genetic

disposition while sustaining forward momentum in a suspenseful, crime novel." *Fox Evil* brought Walters another CWA Gold Dagger Award for fiction.

Wrongful convictions and problems of evidence take center stage in *Disordered Minds* (2004). In the 1970s Howard Stamp, a 20-year-old mentally retarded man, was sent to prison for murdering his grandmother—although the case was flawed and he recanted his confession. Three years into his sentence, he committed suicide. Now, some years later, an anthropologist named Jonathan Hughes takes up Stamp's case. As his investigation unfolds Hughes comes into contact with George Gardener, who has long been convinced of Stamp's innocence. However, as both Hughes and Gardener soon realize, the real killer is determined to make sure that the case remains closed. In a review for the *Times Literary Supplement* (December 5, 2003), Natasha Cooper observed: "Crime fiction provides an excellent outlet for rage, which may be why it appeals so much to women, both as writers and readers. Minette Walters has always been one of the angriest crime writers, which may partly explain why she has also been one of the most popular." Cooper added, "The narrative is interspersed with newspaper clippings, witness statements, emails and letters, giving readers the clues they need to solve the murder. These are the most effective parts of the novel. The narrative itself is not as compelling as usual, and some of the dialogue is so unlikely that it makes the characters themselves less credible than they should be. But the rage [Walters displays] is splendid." "As before, Walters demonstrates a knack for these damaged characters and great skill in the mechanics of suspense," Mark Lawson wrote for the London *Guardian* (December 13, 2003, on-line). "A good crime novel combines factual authority with the benefits of invention; and the orderly mind of Minette Walters has brought off another."

The Tinder Box (2004) was originally commissioned by an organization representing Dutch publishers and booksellers, and when it first appeared, in 1999, the book was given away for free (after the purchase of another book) in stores across the Netherlands, as part of an annual event called Book Week. The novella centers around the murders of two women in the village of Sowerbridge. The prime suspect is a young Irishman, Patrick, and when he is charged with the crime, his parents and their neighbor attempt to prove his innocence and uncover the anti-Irish sentiment that they feel is responsible for Patrick's arrest. "BritCrime writer Minette Walters is in a slump, a deep, deep trough," Gary Curtis wrote for the Ontario *Hamilton Spectator* (October 23, 2004), adding: "Her characters are, as always, well-etched, but her story saunters and wanders." Others found Walters's command of the form impressive. Layla Dabby wrote for the Montreal *Gazette* (December 18, 2004), "Walters is perfectly comfortable with the tight, concise writing required by the novella's brevity, and tremendously effective in capturing the suspicions and hatred permeating Sowerbridge."

Walters returned to the novel form with *The Devil's Feather* (2005). Inspired by a visit Walters took to Sierra Leone, the book tells the story of Connie Burns, a journalist who has become intrigued by a series of rapes and murders in Sierra Leone and by the neglect and eventual death of an elderly woman with Alzheimer's who once lived in the country cottage, in England, where Burns is now hiding from the man she believes did the killings that she investigated in Africa. "This time the lady famous for an imagination that's as savage as it is fertile has excelled herself," Richard Dismore wrote in a critique for the London *Sunday Express* (September 11, 2005). Larry Gandle, in a review for the *Tampa Tribune* (September 24, 2006), recognized Walters's skill as a writer but argued that since *The Sculptress* her work has been "uneven. Unfortunately, *The Devil's Feather* will not go down as one of her high points." While praising the book's "vivid and fully realized characterizations," Gandle concluded that "the banal plot sinks the novel as a whole."

Minette Walters lives in an 18th-century manor house in a rural part of Dorset, England, with her husband; they have two adult sons, Roland and Philip.

—C.M.

Suggested Reading: *Booklist* p244 Oct. 1, 1994, p749 Jan. 1–15, 1996, p907 Feb. 1, 1997, p1,105 Mar. 1, 1999, p1,643 May 1, 2001; *Crime Time* (on-line); (London) *Guardian* p9 Aug. 10, 1993; (London) *Mail on Sunday* p43 Aug. 15, 1993; (London) *Sunday Express* p39 Sep. 11, 2005; (London) *Times* May 4, 1994; *Maclean's* p62+ Mar. 8, 1999; (Montreal) *Gazette* H p4 Dec. 18, 2004; *New Statesman* p32 Oct. 13, 1995, p55 Oct. 29, 2001; *New York Times Book Review* p30 Oct. 2, 1994, p26 June 27, 1999, p22 July 22, 2001, p16 July 21, 2002; *Ottawa Citizen* B p3 June 26, 1994; *Publishers Weekly* p46 Apr. 14, 2003; *Tampa Tribune* p7 Sep. 24, 2006; *Times Literary Supplement* p21, Mar. 7, 1997, p22 Dec. 5, 2003

Selected Books: *The Ice House*, 1992; *The Sculptress*, 1993; *The Scold's Bridle*, 1994; *The Dark Room*, 1996; *The Echo*, 1997; *The Breaker*, 1998; *The Shape of Snakes*, 2001; *Acid Row*, 2002; *Fox Evil*, 2003; *Disordered Minds*, 2004; *The Tinder Box*, 2004; *The Devil's Feather,* 2005

Webb, Charles

1939– Novelist

The author of more than half a dozen novels, most of them praised by reviewers for their deft dialogue and fast-moving plots, Charles Webb is best known for his first, *The Graduate*, published in 1963 and four years later made into the iconic film starring Dustin Hoffman and Anne Bancroft. In the decades since its release, the film has grossed more than $100 million and spawned a highly successful stage adaptation, but it has brought Webb a total of only $30,000, all of which he gave away many years ago. In 2006 Webb, facing intense financial pressure brought on by his wife's illness and their zealous, longstanding revolt against materialism, called attention to their plight and soon found a publisher for the sequel to *The Graduate*. Called "Home School," the novel is currently slated for publication in the U.K., sometime in 2007. Both parts of the story grew out of the life of the author, who, like his most famous characters, dropped out of society early in life. "It's hard," Webb's wife explained in an interview with Alan Franks for the London *Times* (March 10, 2001). "If you saw the way we lived, and have to live, to keep this point of view. We deny ourselves practically every comfort there is. We have no furniture. It's a choice. Either you subscribe to the comforts that money can buy, or you stand for something else. We stand for something else. We have always stood for something else."

Charles Richard Webb was born in 1939 (some sources state June 9) in San Francisco, California, the son of a wealthy heart surgeon. Raised in Pasadena, California, Webb graduated from the Midland School, in Los Olivos, California, in 1957, and went on to study American history and literature at Williams College, in Williamstown, Massachusetts. In 1960 Webb met his future wife, Eve Rudd, while they were still students. The daughter of New England prep-school teachers and the descendant of a Connecticut governor, Eve was studying at Bennington College, in Vermont, and shared Webb's contempt for money and privilege. Not long after they met, she dropped out of college, pregnant with Webb's child. Eve's mother, Josephine Rudd, quickly arranged a shotgun wedding, but it was called off after Eve had an abortion. (Josephine Rudd has often been considered the inspiration for Mrs. Robinson, perhaps *The Graduate*'s most famous character, but Webb, who had a contentious relationship with his mother-in-law, has insisted that the character is an embroidered version of one of his parents' friends, whom he admired from afar.) Eve's parents threw other barriers in their way, but the pair married nonetheless, in 1962, the year after Webb earned his B.A. from Williams. By that time he had already begun writing *The Graduate*.

In the novel a well-to-do young man named Benjamin finishes college and returns to his parents home in California, dissatisfied with his life and full of the conviction that his education was worthless. Over the ensuing months he puts off any decisions about his future while embarking on an illicit relationship with one of his parents' wealthy friends, Mrs. Robinson. In the midst of the affair, he falls in love with her daughter, Elaine, but loses her after his affair becomes known. Immediately after Elaine exchanges vows with another man, with everyone still gathered at the church, Benjamin cries out to her, convincing her of his love. The two run from the church and hop onto a bus, the driver and the other passengers stunned to see a woman in a wedding dress and a man in a torn shirt boarding in a such a state of panic. The novel's final sentence ("The bus began to move.") does not even hint at what their future might be, only that they are heading ineluctably toward it.

Like all but one of Webb's future novels, the story is told primarily through dialogue, a method that has divided critics over the years but did allow much of *The Graduate* to be reproduced word-for-word on the screen. One of Webb's strongest artistic influences in this regard was the playwright Harold Pinter, whose early play *The Caretaker* (1960) Webb had seen on a trip to London. "In *The Graduate*," Ambrose Clancy wrote for the *Los Angeles Times* (May 14, 2002), "you can see Pinter's influence, especially the deadpan sense of menace beating at the heart of ear-perfect exchanges. Question marks are eliminated where they would normally be employed, which adds a note of alienation between characters who aren't terribly interested in answers anyway but are conversing by rote, barely hearing one another."

The book was a modest commercial success upon its initial publication and earned mixed critical reviews. For *Harper's* (February 1964), K. G. Jackson pointed to the novel's "driving immediacy" and called Webb's ear for dialogue "excellent." The book, Jackson added, "is not without humor, one is entirely involved, and though the story starts moving slowly one feels a latent tension and it seems entirely inevitable when it ends with the speed and mindless drive of a runaway locomotive." Charles Shapiro in the *Saturday Review* (October 19, 1963) also noted that the book features "some fairly humorous sexual and social adventures" but added: "Webb's parody of Ben's parents and Ben himself is too forced and far too heavyhanded. They are a bit too foolish to be real and not foolish enough to be truly funny. And when Ben gets around to going to bed with the wife of his father's partner and then gets involved with the lady's daughter the novel becomes inept and ridiculous." Adapted for the screen by Calder Willingham and Buck Henry and directed by Mike Nichols, *The Graduate* became the highest grossing film of 1968, earning some $50 million in

the U.S. alone. In 1998 the American Film Institute ranked *The Graduate* the seventh-best American movie of all time.

The film dramatically increased the sales of Webb's novel but brought him no income directly, since he had opted to settle years earlier for the lump sum of $20,000. In the wake of the film's success, its producer, Lawrence Turman, gave Webb another $10,000, which also gave Turman the rights to the characters and thus control over the sequel. (The sequel rights ultimately wound up in the hands of the French production company Canal Plus; as of the end of 2006, Webb is attempting to regain his rights through the French courts.) Webb has insisted repeatedly in interviews that he is glad not to have profited from the film and often distances himself from both his novel and the film by refusing to discuss them, going so far at one point as to pay a lawyer to keep the phrase "By the author of *The Graduate*" off the cover of one of his later novels. In 1991 he ceded control of the book's copyright to the Anti-Defamation League of B'nai B'rith (ADL), a nearly century-old organization founded to combat anti-Semitism. "Though neither [my wife] nor I are Jewish," Webb told Clancy, "we gave the rights to the ADL because we felt they had influenced us in a profound way, to understand prejudice in all of its forms and victims."

Around the time the film was being made, Webb and his wife moved to Hollywood, but they quickly grew disenchanted with that life. "I'd had this dream of becoming a real Hollywood type—with the car, the house on the beach, everything," Webb recalled in an interview with Jane Fryer for the London *Daily Mirror* (April 19, 2006). "But we couldn't handle it. In retrospect, I think we were deeply shocked by the success of it all. We were very startled by the attention and just sort of withdrew from it. We wanted to remove ourselves from all the hoopla, the materialism of it, and I suppose we've been trying to do that ever since." Having decided to leave Hollywood and divest themselves of material goods, the Webbs returned their beachfront stucco bungalow to the real-estate agent who sold it to them—who, in turn, reportedly gave the house to his daughter—and moved back to Williamstown, Massachusetts, where they bought another house. It too was soon given away, this time to the Massachusetts Audubon Society. Their third house, bought in Hastings-on-Hudson, New York, in 1976, was also donated; according to some reports, a fourth home was also purchased and given away. "None of this seems very rational in retrospect," Webb told Richard Leiby for the *Washington Post* (December 20, 1992).

Webb continued to write fiction steadily for about 15 years after publishing *The Graduate*. His second novel, *Love, Roger* (1969), told the story of Roger Hart, who wants nothing more than to be left alone. His goal in life is complete stability, with nothing happening to upset his routine of doing very little as a travel agent, but over the course of the novel he undergoes a series of misadventures that play havoc with his carefully ordered life. Howard Junker, writing for *Newsweek* (May 5, 1969), called the book "tightly written" and "funny" and "a document of the times." Commenting on Webb's particular brand of absurdity, Junker wrote: "Absurdity used to mean . . . how bizarre and terrifying everyday events could become. It is Webb's vision to see the absurd in nonthreatening, perfectly normal normalcy, the American Dream without ambition, the American Tragedy without tears." L. R. Huish, writing for *Library Journal* (June 1, 1969), commented: "This second novel by the author of *The Graduate* will delight his fans but may distress those readers who dislike outspoken sex. . . . The book is well written, often funny, and holds the reader's interest. However, one cannot say that there is any plot line, character development, or even verisimilitude."

The Marriage of a Young Stockbroker (1970), Webb's next novel, explored the life of William Alren, a middle-class man whose existence seems on the surface as ordinary as any other suburbanite's. Alren's marriage, however, cannot satisfy his relentless carnal interests, and he often fantasizes about sex and even leaves work once to watch pornography. John Thompson, in a review for *Harper's* (March 1970), called the novel "a clever suspense story with an extremely meretricious happy ending tacked on." The main character, Thompson continued, "is presented from the beginning as a dangerous psychopath, a compulsive voyeur and sexual misfit, and, in one scene after another, his wife seems in mortal danger. . . . It is strange that the author could make us so aware of the menace of this stupid and aimlessly driven young man, and then in the end ask us to believe that all this is really innocence, and that he is rescuing his wife from the hideous country-club set for a lifetime of wedded bliss." A. H. Norman, in an assessment for *Newsweek* (March 16, 1970), judged that Webb had "essentially written a screen-play, and a good one, but with distracting narrative passages stuck in as filler. One must visualize the book in order to read it. William's interior monologues dominate the inaction, and although his mind is paranoiac enough for several marriages, it can't support the characters Webb is less concerned about." *The Marriage of a Young Stockbroker* was adapted for the screen in 1971; it was a box-office failure.

In 1974 Webb published *Orphans and Other Children*, a collection of two novellas ("The Last Usher" and "Gwen") and a short story ("Mediterranean Estates"). Like the novels that preceded it, the collection was praised by some for its well-rendered dialogue and precise observations but criticized by others for its spare style and seeming pointlessness. A critic for the *New Yorker* (September 2, 1974) observed: "With a curious fascination, Webb writes of uptight people who yearn to break out and sometimes do—but only through desperate, grotesque lunges. . . . In each case, the observer [who narrates the story] is pounced upon, aroused, tempted, and very nearly ruined by characters . . . who feel that they have found the answers to life's riddles, or who at least want to force answers on others. Mr. Webb's narrative is marked by smooth, understated dialogue that unwraps each person's pretenses layer by layer, and this is admirable. What is not so admirable is the sniggering amusement that the author often exhibits toward his lost souls. Mr. Webb has too much talent to be wasting time on titillating the unhappy and repressed." For the *Times Literary Supplement* (April 4, 1975), David Lodge wrote: "[Webb] is a writer who scarcely seems to be trying: but his seeming artlessness is deceptive. His basic device, simple but effective, is to use first-person narrators but to eliminate all the report of the narrator's inner feelings, responses, motives, etc. . . . [This method] produces a delicate, wry, laconic comedy of embarrassment. . . . [The technique is] highly cinematic, since the omission of introspection puts all the weight of meaning on to speech and gesture, between which Mr Webb maintains a subtle and amusing counterpoint. There is a soft—indeed a sentimental—core to these stories, too; but the technique of understatement prevents them from cloying and the writer does not seem to be claiming more for them than they are worth. Their achievement is slight, but not negligible."

Webb's next book, the novel *The Abolitionist of Clark Gable Place* (1975), addressed the issue of racism in modern-day California. The main character is Kenneth Ward, a recently divorced man who is minding a home on Clark Gable Place, outside Los Angeles, during its owner's absence. One day an African-American man named Eugene Cowles comes to the door selling subscriptions for a youth rehabilitation center at his church. Ward sees an opportunity to conduct a social experiment by inviting Cowles and his adult children to live with him in the house; the results are disastrous. "Long before the savage end [of the book] the story would have trailed away into a kind of ritual helplessness were it not for Mr. Webb's splendid nonchalant dialogue," William Feaver wrote for the *Times Literary Supplement* (April 16, 1976). The dialogue's tone, Feaver adds, "is quiet, jargonic, bemused. When desperation comes the tone shrills a little but then resumes its former level. Events overtake the dialogue and Mr Webb's ending transforms the neat fable into a crafty tragedy." For the *New York Time Book Review* (May 18, 1975), John Yohalem also praised the novel's dialogue, calling it "pointed and careful, almost free of any false note," but found that the novel's lack of descriptive material muddled the narrative, creating seemingly haphazard contradictions in the characters and making the comprehensible parts of them seem shallow. Yohalem concluded: "Webb, who is an expert technician, a fine dramatic craftsman and recorder of speech patterns, has attempted to support too much on too little. He has played for the high stakes of defining his times, and he has lost, but not ignobly."

By the mid-1970s Webb's books had begun to reach an ever smaller audience, despite their generally favorable reviews. He published two more novels in that decade, *Elsinor* (1976) and *Booze* (1978). The latter was sold to a group of investors who, working from the assumption that the book was not going to sell many copies, took it on as a tax write-off. (As Richard Leiby pointed out: "If the scenario sounds familiar, it is. It was not unlike the improbable plot of Mel Brooks's 1968 movie, *The Producers*.") Written quickly and only haphazardly edited, *Booze* takes the form of an internal monologue by an alcoholic artist who paints only oranges. Praised by a critic, the artist shrugs off calls to show his work because he considers what he actually produces to be far less important than the process of creating them. Webb has distanced himself from the novel ("I don't think it's a good book," he told Leiby), but Leiby called *Booze*, the only one of Webb's novels that contains no dialogue, "a seductive work, full of eccentric insights and engaging characters."

In about 1982 Webb and Rudd divorced for political reasons, partially in protest over the fact that nowhere in the U.S. at that time was it possible for same-sex couples to marry or join in a civil union and partially because the pair had come to the conclusion that marriage somehow violated their constitutional rights. (According to Clancy, they remarried around 1998, "in order to smooth the emigration process to Britain," where they now live.) About the same time as the divorce, Rudd dropped both her first and last names and began calling herself Fred, which became her sole legal name in about 1985. The choice of name was an act of protest—as was Fred's daily routine of shaving her head—and of solidarity. "Fred sounded like such a friendly name," she told Charles E. Claffey for the *Boston Globe* (April 21, 1992). "When I met other Freds, I learned that they tended to be a downtrodden lot. Freds have an inferiority complex. I hoped to change that." (The Freds that she met have sometimes been cast as a California self-help group dedicated solely to the troubles attendant to bearing that name. Webb told Clancy that this story was true "but the original impetus was for other reasons. 'My father always wanted a boy' would be closer to the mark.")

By the late 1990s Webb and Fred had given away not only a succession of houses but also the income from Webb's writing and Webb's share in his father's estate, which they reportedly gave to their younger son. For much of the time they lived in California, but they also spent a year in France and lived for periods in Massachusetts and New Jersey. They supported themselves at menial jobs— cleaning houses, working as clerks in stores, acting as custodians for a nudist colony—and

periodically appealed to the public for help. Webb also occasionally promised a new book, announcing plans for a sequel to *The Graduate* as early as 1992, but within months of that announcement began dismissing the idea.

In 2001, having emigrated to the U.K., Webb completed work on *New Cardiff*, his first novel in 23 years, which was published in the U.S. in 2002. In the novel an English artist named Colin flees to the U.S. after being dumped by his longtime girlfriend, Vera. For no particular reason he settles in New Cardiff, Vermont, where he paints people who strike his fancy, including Mr. Fisher, who runs the motel at which Colin is staying. He soon begins a romance with Mandy Martin, a nursing-home worker, but their budding relationship runs into trouble when Vera tracks Colin down in New Cardiff. The novel was illustrated by Fred, whose drawings are presented as Colin's own. Calling the book "a good-natured, consistently amusing romp through the vicissitudes of no-longer-so-young love," Merle Rubin wrote for the *Los Angeles Times* (January 14, 2002), "Webb once again tells his story largely through dialogue, displaying his considerable flair for comedy, not to mention his sharp ear for the voices of his characters and the cadences of contemporary conversation. . . . Webb, who like Colin has lived on both sides of the Atlantic, has a great deal of fun gently and affectionately satirizing both sets of national characteristics." Xan Brooks, in a review for the London *Guardian* (April 14, 2001), however, argued that the book "wavers constantly between warm, homely simplicity and trite sentimentality. It gives us contours for characters and stage directions in place of prose. But in reducing his art to such self-sufficient hippy basics, the author runs the risk of leaving little but a featherweight romance that lacks dramatic punch. In its no-frills style, *New Cardiff* reads less like a novel and more like a screenplay." The rights to adapt the novel for the screen were sold even before the book appeared, and in 2003 the adaptation was released under the title *Hope Springs*.

Webb's name began to surface in the media in 2006, when it was reported that he and Fred were facing eviction from their apartment in Hove, East Sussex, England because they owed roughly £2,000 in back rent and were in debt for an additional £30,000. Webb told reporters at the time that Fred had suffered a nervous breakdown in 2001 and that he had spent most of his time taking care of her, leaving him little opportunity to sell his next novel, "Home School." An autobiographical sequel to *The Graduate,* the novel is said to draw on Webb and his wife's experience of pulling their sons out of school and "un-schooling" them—illegally—at home. Benjamin, Elaine, and Mrs. Robinson all make a return appearance. "Not a lot of people picked up on it, but the title of *The Graduate* was supposed to convey it was about education," Webb told Jill Lawless for the Canadian Press (May 31, 2006).

"Benjamin is disenchanted with education, and once his kids enter the system he finds it intolerable."

Webb and Fred currently live in England. Their son John, born in about 1965, earned his Ph.D. in comparative government from Georgetown University, in Washington, D.C., in 1993, and is an internationally recognized expert on the Russian petroleum industry. Their other son, David, born in about 1968, has been described as a performance artist, but in 2001 Alan Franks characterized David's work as "living on his grandfather's inheritance." Webb explained to Franks: "There is no need to film or write anything down. [David] visits friends, goes to Starbucks, reads magazines. As long as he is using the money, his performance will go on."

—C.M.

Suggested Reading: (Glasgow) *Herald* p20 Mar. 9, 2001; *Harper's*, p118 Feb. 1964, p110 Mar. 1970; *Library Journal* p2,252 June 1, 1969; (London) *Daily Mail* p22 Apr. 19, 2006; (London) *Guardian* p10 Apr. 14, 2001; (London) *Times* Mar. 10, 2001, p3 Apr. 18, 2006, p28 May 30, 2006; *Los Angeles Times* Features p3 Jan. 14, 2002; *New Yorker* p82+ Sep. 2, 1974; *Newsweek* p113 May 5, 1969, p104 Mar. 16, 1970; *Saturday Review* p37 Oct. 19, 1963; *Sunday Tasmanian* Jan. 22, 1989; *Times Literary Supplement* p353 Apr. 4, 1975, p455 Apr. 16, 1976; *Washington Post* F p1 Dec. 20, 1992

Selected Books: *The Graduate*, 1963; *Love, Roger*, 1969; *Marriage of a Young Stockbroker*, 1970; *Orphans and Other Children*, 1974; *The Abolitionist of Clark Gable Place*, 1975; *Elsinor*, 1976; *Booze*, 1978; *New Cardiff*, 2002

Courtesy of Scott Weidensaul

Weidensaul, Scott

1959– Nonfiction writer

The natural historian Scott Weidensaul has written more than two dozen books—some of them about the birds of prey that are his particular area of specialty and some covering various other aspects of the natural world. Weidensaul is the author of, among other volumes, *The Birder's Miscellany: A Fascinating Collection of Facts, Figures, and Folklore from the World of Birds* (1991), *Discover Birds* (1991), *Seasonal Guide to the Natural Year: A Month by Month Guide to Natural Events, Mid-*

Atlantic (1992); *Seasonal Guide to the Natural Year: A Month by Month Guide to Natural Events, New England and New York* (1993), *Mountains of the Heart: A Natural History of the Appalachians* (1994), *Raptors: The Birds of Prey* (1996), *Living on the Wind: Across the Hemisphere with Migratory Birds* (1999), *The Ghost with Trembling Wings: Science, Wishful Thinking, and the Search for Lost Species* (2002), and *Return to Wild America: A Yearlong Search for the Continent's Natural Soul* (2005). His most recent effort, *Of a Feather: A Brief History of American Birding*, is scheduled to be released late in 2007. Janice P. Nimura wrote for the *Los Angeles Times* (August 25, 2002), "Scott Weidensaul ranks among an elite group of writer-naturalists—Bruce Chatwin, John McPhee and David Quammen come to mind—whose straightforward eloquence elevates ecology to the level of philosophy."

Scott Weidensaul contributed the following autobiographical statement to *World Authors 2000–2005*:

"I am, in a sense, a transplanted native of the region about which I so often write. Just before I was born, in 1959, my parents moved to Levittown, the soulless, newly constructed mega-suburb just outside Philadelphia, but—and for this I am endlessly grateful—by the time I was in elementary school they returned to the Appalachians of eastern Pennsylvania, where their roots are deep. The fact that I was born elsewhere still comes as a shock to me when I think about it, for I am so much a product of these gentle mountains where I still live, that it is only with an effort that I remind myself I am not, strictly speaking, a local.

"For a boy like me, hooked on nature and with an urge to run wild, the ridges of Pennsylvania were a wonderful place to grow up; Ashland Mountain rose out of our backyard, and before I was 12, I was hiking, camping and fishing all over it and the neighboring hills. But this was also the edge of the anthracite mining belt, and the next valley to the north was a moonscape of unreclaimed strip mines, black culm banks and lifeless streams running orange with acid mine drainage—enough to turn me into an ardent conservationist from an early age. My preoccupation with nature excluded most other activities except reading, at which I was gluttonous, and a minor talent for art. I was the kind of kid who dragged home every animal he could find, and whose room his mother dreaded cleaning, never sure what might be living under the bed. An early passion was snakes, and when it came time for college, I had my sights set on a biology degree and a career as a herpetologist. Ability, or the lack thereof, intervened; I couldn't do higher math to save my life, including the kinds of statistical analyses that are the stock in trade of a biologist, and so switched majors, figuring I'd take a stab at being a wildlife artist. It was not until some years later, when I was out of college and trying to make a living as an animal illustrator, that I faced a second unpleasant truth: I wasn't terribly good at it. Not bad, necessarily, but my talent was middle-of-the-road at best, and my prospects were not bright.

"Writing had never been a consideration. I enjoyed it, and was reasonably adept at it, but the notion of being a writer never really occurred to me until 1978, when I began to write and illustrate a weekly natural history column for a local newspaper. That led, a year or two later, to a full-time reporting job—and in this I was remarkably lucky, for the paper, the Pottsville *Republican*, had just won a Pulitzer Prize for investigative reporting, and despite its size enjoyed a national reputation. Staffed with fine editors and writers, it was a marvelous place to learn the craft, and I spent eight years there in a variety of niches, the final three doing investigative work.

"All the while I continued to write about nature, which remained my prime interest. Since the late 1980s I've made my living as a freelance writer of natural history in newspapers, magazines like *Smithsonian* and *Audubon*, and in books. It's been a fine excuse to pick subjects that I enjoy, and about which I would like to learn more, and to immerse myself in them for extended periods. Such was the case in the early 1990s when I wrote *Mountains of the Heart*, a personal exploration of the natural and cultural history of the Appalachians—not just the famous (and infamous) hills of southern Appalachia, but the entire sweep of the range from Alabama to the northern tip of Newfoundland.

"One particular interest of mine has always been birds, and especially the phenomenon of migration; since the mid-1980s, I have banded hawks, owls and other birds to study their movements. (In this, I enjoy a hint of the wildlife biology career I once sought.) Researching my 1999 book *Living on the Wind* allowed me to spend the better part of three years traveling from Alaska to South America, following the waves of migratory birds that unite the hemisphere with their movements—working for a month on a ranch in the Argentine pampas with scientists studying hawks, or assisting a Jamaican ornithologist with his studies in the thorn-scrub forests of that island.

"Another interest—one that deepens as I get older—is humanity's relationship with the natural world, and how each molds the other. Even those for whom nature is not a daily obsession have, it seems, what E.O. Wilson calls 'biophilia,' an innate attraction to wild places and wild animals, and it has been my great good fortune to make a living by sharing it with them. The British naturalist David Attenborough once described humans as 'the compulsive communicators,' and I have often thought of myself as a compulsive explainer—a sharer of the larger joys and delights of the natural world with those who, for whatever reason, haven't noticed."

Weidensaul does not write from an ivory tower: an active field researcher, he has, for more than two decades, banded hawks each fall and has recently started an ambitious project to study the northern saw-whet owl (*Aegolius acadicus*), a small raptor. He is one of the very few bird experts in the U.S. licensed to band hummingbirds and is currently conducting research into the increasing number of western hummingbirds now appearing in the eastern part of the country for the winter. (Bird banding is a practical research tool that allows for the study of migration patterns, social structure, life span, and population growth, among other variables. Because putting the identification bands on individual wild birds requires capturing and handling them, bird banding requires a federal permit.)

Weidensaul has distinguished himself as a writer by choosing topics about which he is especially passionate. *Mountains of the Heart: A Natural History of the Appalachians*, for example, is his paean to the region in which he grew up. Scott Shalaway described the book for the *Charleston (West Virginia) Gazette* (June 4, 1999) as a "first-hand account of [Weidensaul's] travels from one end of this ancient mountain chain to the other, from Alabama to Newfoundland. He writes of the plants, wildlife and people that shaped the Appalachians, and more importantly, of the geological forces that built and then tore down the eastern spine of North America." Shalaway continued, "Weidensaul's books are more than good reads, they're journeys through time and space. Journeys that most of us will never be able to duplicate. Oh, we might travel a portion of Virginia's Skyline Drive, or hike a few miles of the Appalachian Trail, but we can't devote two years to seeing it all. Instead, we can tag along with

Weidensaul and make him our personal tour guide." Merrill Slavin, in a review for the *Roanoke Times* (February 26, 1995), was equally impressed, writing, "Weidensaul's thoughtful and loving look at the mountains of his heart is an intimate, one-of-a-kind revelation of the diversity and beauty which is the Appalachians."

Weidensaul has always been particularly interested in birds of prey. His exhaustive guide *Raptors: The Birds of Prey* was originally published, in 1996, and proved so popular that it was re-published, in 2001, as *The Raptor Almanac: A Comprehensive Guide to Eagles, Hawks, Falcons and Vultures*. Weidensaul, by all accounts a scrupulous, thoughtful person, posted a disclaimer on his Web site, stating, "Readers should be aware that this reissue of my 1996 book was done by the publisher without my knowledge, and was marketed as an entirely new title even though it was not revised or updated in any way. While I am pleased the book is again in print, I am embarrassed to see that Lyons Press (an imprint of Globe Pequot) has promoted it as though it was a new book." Despite his mixed sentiments, the newly titled book was a critical success and was given an honorable mention at the 2001 National Outdoor Book Awards.

Although Weidensaul's work had always been well reviewed, he reached new heights of acclaim when *Living on the Wind: Across the Hemisphere with Migratory Birds* became a finalist for a Pulitzer Prize for general nonfiction in 2000. Reviews were almost universally positive. David Tomlinson wrote for *New Scientist* (March 27, 1999), "*Living on the Wind* stands out among bird books. . . . It is a book to be read, not looked at; there isn't a single picture of a bird to enliven its 400 pages. And it matters not a jot because Weidensaul writes so well. . . .Thought-provoking, provocative, informative, [this is] not only an outstanding book on bird migration, it's also one of the best books I have read for a long time." Nancy Bent, in an assessment for *Booklist* (March 15, 1999), praised the volume's "factual and yet lyrical" style, while Paddy Woodworth described it for the *Irish Times* (October 11, 2003) as "authoritative and beautifully written."

Weidensaul's next volume, *The Ghost with Trembling Wings: Science, Wishful Thinking, and the Search for Lost Species*, explored extinction and the occasional reappearance of supposedly vanished species. A reviewer for *Publishers Weekly* (May 20, 2002, on-line) described the book: "Approximately 30,000 species of animals and plants go extinct every year. Weidensaul's narrative concerns those rare occurrences when a supposedly extinct animal makes a surprise reappearance, and the much more frequent occasions when scientists or civilians only think they've sighted a vanished creature. His suspenseful naturalist detective stories take readers all over the globe to Madagascar, Indonesia, Peru, Costa Rica in search of these lost species. In the swamplands of Louisiana, the author and his guide brave swarming mosquitoes and deadly vipers to check out reports of an ivory-billed woodpecker. Weidensaul recounts famous success stories, like the recovery of the coelacanth, a fish believed to be extinct for about 80 million years until fishermen landed one off the coast of South Africa in 1938, as well as various wild goose chases and his own obsessive search for the South American cone-billed tanager. Along the way, he shows how humans and nature have unwittingly conspired to condemn animals to oblivion, such as the dozens of Great Lakes fish species lost to overfishing and the inadvertent introduction of parasitic lampreys from canals built in the 19th century. For the most part, though, Weidensaul's gracefully written book strikes a hopeful note, reveling in the exhilaration of the searches themselves: the greatest gift these lost creatures give this too-fast, too-small, too-modern world [is] an opportunity for hope." *The Ghost with Trembling Wings* garnered many such positive notices. "By turns harrowing and elegiac, thrilling and informative, [the book] takes the reader to exotic places like the hinterlands of Mato Grosso in western Brazil, where swarms of sweat bees plague those in search of the elusive cone-billed tanager," Michiko Kakutani, the notoriously hard-to-impress reviewer, wrote for the *New York Times* (June 5, 2002, on-line). "Mr. Weidensaul . . . demonstrates his ability both to communicate the startling marvels of nature he has observed firsthand and to regale us with tales of scientific derring-do, plucked from the annals of natural history." Robert Winkler wrote for the *Christian Science Monitor* (August 8, 2002), "[*The Ghost with Trembling Wings*] is a virtuoso presentation that can be dizzying, even exhausting, yet in this it reflects the wild world as Weidensaul found it."

In 1953 the bird expert Roger Tory Peterson and the British naturalist James Fisher set out on a 100-day, 30,000-mile trek—from Newfoundland to Florida, into Mexico, through the Southwest, the Pacific Northwest, and into Alaska. In 1955 they published an account of their trip, *Wild America*. As the book's 50th anniversary approached, Weidensaul decided to recreate the trip, hoping to discover how North America's natural landscape had changed over the past half century. He published his own findings in *Return to Wild America: A Yearlong Search for the Continent's Natural Soul*. A reviewer for *Publishers Weekly* (August 22, 2005, on-line) wrote, "In the midst of environmental-policy gloom and global-warming doom, Weidensaul's poetic account of his travels to several scattered wilderness oases of North America is an unexpected tonic. . . . This engrossing state-of-nature memoir, making a vibrant case for preserving America's wild past for future Americans, promises to become a classic in its own right." Irene Wanner, in a review for the *Seattle Times* (November 25, 2005, on-line), wrote, "Weidensaul writes with passion and skill, allowing his curiosity to roam thoroughly around each region he visits," and concluded, "He does a masterful job of balancing history and science with personal experience, making the book interesting and informative not only to birders, but also to anyone who venerates North America's vast, fragile beauty."

Besides writing for an adult audience, Weidensaul has published books introducing children to the joys of natural history; these include *A Kid's First Book of Birdwatching* (1990), which was packaged with a tape of bird songs, and *Max Bonker And The Howling Thieves* (1996), a picture book in which a bumbling dog detective investigates the mysteries of the Amazon Rainforest.

Weidensaul has retained his original love of art and is a founding board member of the Ned Smith Center for Nature and Art, near Millersburg, Pennsylvania. The center is named for the late naturalist and artist Ned Smith (1919–85) and houses hundreds of original paintings, field sketches, and manuscripts donated by Smith's widow. Weidensaul has published *The Wildlife Art of Ned Smith* (2003) and *Ned Smith's Game News Covers: The Complete Collection* (2006).

Scott Weidensaul regularly teaches at the Hog Island Audubon Camp, off the coast of Maine. His other annual activities include banding migrant songbirds crossing the Gulf of Mexico each April, as part of the Hummer/Bird Study Group at Fort Morgan, Alabama; from the beginning of October to Thanksgiving each year he also coordinates a major research project under the auspices of the Ned Smith Center, to learn more about the northern saw-whet owl, which is described on his Web site as "the smallest owl in the East and one of the most enigmatic birds in North America."

—S.Y.

Suggested Reading: *Charleston (West Virginia) Gazette* D p1 June 4, 1999; *Choice* p776 Jan. 1997; *Irish Times* Oct. 11, 2003; *Library Journal* p62 Mar. 15, 1996; *Los Angeles Times* L p8 Feb. 12, 1995, R p10 Aug. 20, 2002; *New Scientist* p45 July 20, 1996, p50 Mar. 27, 1999; *New York Times* (on-line) June 5, 2002; *Publishers Weekly* (on-line) May 20, 2002, Aug. 22, 2005; *Roanoke Times* Feb. 26, 1995; *School Library Journal* p169 Oct. 1998; *Washington Post Book World* p11 Dec. 17, 2000

Selected Books: *The Birder's Miscellany: A Fascinating Collection of Facts, Figures, and Folklore from the World of Birds*, 1991; *Discover Birds*, 1991; *Seasonal Guide to the Natural Year: A Month by Month Guide to Natural Events, Mid-Atlantic*, 1992; *Seasonal Guide to the Natural Year: A Month by Month Guide to Natural Events, New England and New York*, 1993; *Mountains of the Heart: A Natural History of the Appalachians*, 1994; *Raptors: The Birds of Prey*, 1996; *Living on the Wind: Across the Hemisphere with Migratory Birds*, 1999; *The Ghost with Trembling Wings: Science, Wishful Thinking, and the Search for Lost Species*, 2002; *The Wildlife Art of Ned Smith*, 2003; *Return to Wild America: A Yearlong Search for the Continent's Natural Soul*, 2005; *Ned Smith's Game News Covers: The Complete Collection*, 2006

Courtesy of Lauren Weisberger

Weisberger, Lauren

1977– Novelist

The Devil Wears Prada (2003), the tale of a young woman's ill-fated stint as a personal assistant to a domineering fashion editor, is Lauren Weisberger's commercially successful debut novel. Weisberger was born in 1977 and grew up in Allentown, Pennsylvania. In 1999 she graduated from Cornell University, in Ithaca, New York, and landed a job as a personal assistant to Anna Wintour, the editor of the renowned fashion magazine *Vogue*. Weisberger told Sherryl Connelly for the New York *Daily News* (April 14, 2003) that she accepted the job despite the fact that "high fashion was not anything I knew anything about." After a year Weisberger left *Vogue* for a position at *Departures*, a travel magazine, and began penning her novel while enrolled in a writing seminar.

The Devil Wears Prada, published by Doubleday, tells the story of Andrea Sachs, a recent college graduate who obtains a coveted position as a personal assistant to Miranda Priestly, the tyrannical editor of a top-tier fashion magazine. Given Weisberger's resume, most critics assumed that Priestly was a direct send-up of Wintour. Kate Betts, a magazine editor, reviewed the book for the *New York Times* (April 13, 2003), calling it a "thinly veiled roman à clef." Betts continued, "Having worked at *Vogue* myself for eight years and having been mentored by Anna Wintour, I have to say Weisberger could have learned a few things in [the year she worked at *Vogue*.] She had a ringside seat at one of the great editorial franchises in a business that exerts an enormous influence over women, but she seems to have understood almost nothing about the isolation and pressure of the job her boss was doing." Weisberger spent much of her time in interviews refuting the charge that Wintour was the sole inspiration for Priestly, claiming instead that the character was a composite of the bad bosses that every worker occasionally suffers.

Besides accusations that she was being vindictive and ungrateful to her former employer, Weisberger was plagued by denunciations of her writing skill. Claire Dederer, reviewing the book for Amazon.com, called Weisberger's prose "inept [and] ungrammatical," and in a *Booklist* review, as archived on the same Web site, Kathleen Hughes found the characters "shallow and two-dimensional." Despite such criticisms, the hardcover edition of *The Devil Wears Prada* was listed for more than 20 weeks on the *New York Times* best-seller list. Its success "ushered in the modern 'underling-tell-all' genre, abetted by other revenge-of-the-employee tales like *The Nanny Diaries*, by Emma McLaughlin and Nicola Kraus," according to Anna Bahney for the *New York Times* (May 25, 2006).

Weisberger reportedly received a six-figure sum for the film rights to her novel. The cinematic version of *The Devil Wears Prada* received largely positive reviews, and critics were particularly pleased with Meryl Streep's performance as Miranda. Reviewing the film for the *New York Times* (June 30, 2006), A.O. Scott wrote that while the moral of the novel is rather simple—"nobody, however glamorous, successful or celebrated, has the right to treat another person the way Miranda treats her assistants"—the lesson in the film is "not quite so unambiguous." He continued: "The literary Miranda is a monster. Ms. Weisberger, restricting herself to Andy's point of view and no doubt giving voice to her own loathing of the real-life editor on whom Miranda is modeled, resisted the temptation to make her villain a complex (or even a terribly interesting) character. But the screen Miranda is played by Meryl Streep, an actress who carries nuance in her every pore, and who endows even her lighthearted comic roles with a rich implication of inner life. With her silver hair and pale skin, her whispery diction as perfect as her posture, Ms. Streep's Miranda inspires both terror and a measure of awe. No longer simply the incarnation of evil, she is now a vision of aristocratic, purposeful and surprisingly human grace. And the movie, while noting that she can be sadistic, inconsiderate and manipulative, is unmistakably on Miranda's side."

Weisberger's second novel, *Everyone Worth Knowing* (2005), follows Bette, a young professional who quits her career in finance to work for a publicity firm that eventually asks her to serve as the beard (phony girlfriend) to a gay British aristocrat. In a review for the *New York Times* (October 2, 2005), Liesl Schillinger wrote that this "fatuous, clunky" novel was unlikely to silence the author's critics. "She has in no way strengthened her writerly muscle," Schillinger continued, "but she has wised up: she no longer believes in the purple unicorn of job satisfaction." Addressing such criticism for the on-line magazine *Salon* (November 1, 2005, on-line), Rebecca Traister wrote, "Of course, chick-lit beat-downs are nothing new. In the decade or so that the genre has been popular, we have heard a repeated chorus of despair: that chick-lit novels like *Everyone Worth Knowing* are reducing literary heroines to shallow, one-dimensional cliches of urban femininity—[the cocktail] cosmos and clotheshorses and gays. Yet, Weisberger did not invent chick lit, nor is she particularly emblematic of it. . . . At this point, we shouldn't be surprised by the treatment of Weisberger and her peers. Beating on 'women's' fiction—and dismissing certain literary trends as feminine rubbish—has a history as long as the popular fiction itself."

Weisberger currently lives in New York City. She also writes freelance magazine articles, and her short story, "The Bamboo Confessions," was published in the chick-lit anthology *American Girls about Town* (2004). In her free time Weisberger enjoys overseas travel.

—P.B.M.

Suggested Reading: (New York) *Daily News* (on-line) Apr. 14, 2003; *New York Times Book Review* p30 Apr. 13, 2003; *Salon* (on-line) Apr. 24, 2003

Selected Books: *The Devil Wears Prada*, 2003; *Everyone Worth Knowing*, 2005

Welsh, Louise

1967– Novelist

Louise Welsh, a novelist who uses her love of antiques and history to create riveting mysteries, is seen by many critics as one of the leading lights of modern Scottish writing. Her debut novel, *The Cutting Room* (2002), which is about an auctioneer who uncovers evidence of a sexually charged murder among the belongings of a wealthy, deceased man, was inspired by her years as a secondhand-book dealer and received extremely positive reviews on both sides of the Atlantic. Her

Timm Schamberger/AFP/Getty Images

Louise Welsh

follow-up, *Tamburlaine Must Die* (2004), was
concerned with the still-mysterious death of the
legendary Elizabethan playwright Christopher
Marlowe and came about as a result of her avid
historical studies.

Louise Welsh was born in Edinburgh, Scotland,
in 1967. Because her father, John Welsh, was in the
Royal Air Force (RAF), her family moved around
a great deal during her childhood—first to
Singapore, then to Kilmarnock, in Scotland, then
England, and, finally, back to Edinburgh. When
her father retired from the RAF, he worked as a
sales representative, and her mother, Ena, worked
as a cleaning woman. Because they moved so
frequently, Welsh's parents did not accumulate
many books, though both were enthusiastic
readers; one of her earliest memories is of her
father reading Robert Louis Stevenson's *Treasure
Island* to her. Reading was a habit they passed on
to their two daughters, who haunted the local
library at least once a week. "I have always read
anything, anything at all," Welsh told Anna
Burnside for the London *Sunday Times* (July 21,
2002). "One time when I was in the library I
remember panicking and thinking, what will
happen when I've read all of these books? It was a
terrible thought when I was a child. Then when
you get older, you realise that you're not going to
be able to read all the books you want to read." She
also developed a love of antiques at an early age
and spent many Saturdays as a teenager
rummaging through antiques fairs.

After graduating from Craigmount High School,
in Edinburgh, Welsh studied history at the
University of Glasgow, in the early 1980s. "Oddly,
these years were the only time I didn't write," she

told Mike Wilson for the London *Sunday Times*
(August 14, 2005). "I wrote a lot when I was a
teenager and I felt the urge to return after I
graduated, but when I was a student my own
writings were no doubt awful essays." After
completing her undergraduate degree, Welsh
worked in an office but didn't find it to her liking.
With few job offers in sight, she decided on a bold
plan—to open her own secondhand bookstore.
"Through people I knew I discovered some space
was becoming available just off Byres Road [in
Glasgow]," she recalled to Colin Waters for the
Glasgow *Sunday Herald* (July 28, 2002). "I began
by buying books at jumble sales, and through a
gradual process, was able to fill the shop." Among
her regular customers during the seven years she
ran the bookstore were the novelists Alasdair Gray
and Bernard MacLaverty.

Welsh enjoyed putting her shop together, but
after a point she began to look for something new.
"I'd run the shop for seven years and I felt I'd got
as far as I could with it," she told Waters. "I began
to ask myself if this was really something I wanted
to do until I was 60. By that point, I had begun to
write more seriously and the shop was taking up
too much time. In the early years, it was exciting
as I was finding out so much, but once I'd learned
how to do it, some of the appeal went, especially
as I was working 12-hour days." A friend suggested
that she enroll in a master's program in creative
writing that was jointly offered by the University
of Glasgow and the University of Strathclyde.
Though she was initially hesitant about going, she
found the writing workshops to be extremely
beneficial to her, enabling her to write with
confidence from a variety of perspectives. At some
point one of her teachers, the novelist Zoë
Wicomb, suggested that she write a novel. Before
long she was crafting a mystery involving a lanky,
gay auctioneer named Rilke, who, after purchasing
some items from a recently deceased man named
Roddy McKindless, comes across a massive stash
of pornography, including "snuff" pictures—
images depicting the murder of a woman for sexual
purposes. The pornography collection intrigues
Rilke, who begins to research a girl in one of the
images to discover if she has in fact been
murdered.

Shortly after *The Cutting Room* was published,
in 2002, it was named one of the five best debut
novels of the year by Katharine Viner and Melissa
Denes, writing for the London *Guardian* (March
23, 2002). In the *New York Times Book Review*
(March 30, 2003), Sophie Harrison wrote, "*The
Cutting Room* is a remarkable first novel. Like all
the best exponents of the genre, Louise Welsh sets
up her template and then manipulates it, using the
glamour of crime to examine more humdrum kinds
of suffering and loss. She piles on the atmosphere
to produce a Glasgow that is predictably dark and
yet still plausible. She is playfully referential; one
reason this novel is such fun to read is that it feels
as though the author's enjoying herself. When

Rilke goes looking for sex in a city park, for example, it's as though he's stepped straight into a piece of British noir. . . . A less confident writer might have toned down the foreboding, for fear of committing a Glasgow cliche; Welsh heightens it instead, to fantastically gothic effect." A reviewer for *Publishers Weekly* (February 23, 2003) wrote: "Yet another talented Scottish author makes a debut with this dark and twisty thriller, boasting a highly unusual hero and a compelling background that shows extensive inside knowledge. . . . Welsh obviously knows her auction business, and also how to keep an intriguing story moving. She is not good at action, however, and the actual climax, in which the mystery of McKindless's death is solved, is oddly muted and unconvincing. This is one of those books, however, in which the journey is infinitely more beguiling than the destination." *The Cutting Room* won the John Creasey Memorial Dagger Award from the Crime Writers' Association and was nominated for the Orange Prize for Fiction. A film version, staring the actor Robert Carlyle, is currently in production.

Tamburlaine Must Die (2004), Welsh's second novel, was set in Elizabethan England and looked into the still-unsolved murder of Christopher Marlowe, William Shakespeare's literary rival. Though Marlowe disappeared in 1593, and rumors of his demise began circulating shortly thereafter, no explanation of his death was offered until 1925, when the scholar Leslie Hotson happened upon some paperwork in a public records office that detailed an inquest held by the Queen's coroner. According to the records from the inquest, Marlowe died at a house in Deptford, South London, on May 30, 1593. He was stabbed through the eye by Ingram Frizer, with whom he had been fighting over the payment of a bill. While Frizer was sent to prison, he received a pardon from the Queen only 28 days later, leading many to speculate, and with good reason, that the playwright had not been killed by accident; Marlowe had served as a secret service agent, and at the time of his murder, faced charges that he was an atheist who was promoting his antireligious views through his plays. Welsh's slim novel, which is presented as if Marlowe wrote it himself, uses the latter conspiracy theory as the basis for the story, in which the playwright is accused of heresy and blasphemy by the Queen's Privy Council, which had discovered heretical verses signed by Marlowe's most famous character, Tamburlaine, popping up all over London.

Welsh's sophomore effort received somewhat mixed reviews. "Welsh captures the underbelly of 1690s London with touches of frightening realism," Joseph M. Eagan wrote for *Library Journal* (December 2004). "In the company of unsavory characters, Marlowe is portrayed as a violent and drunken protagonist whose degeneracy overwhelms his genius. Unfortunately, the narrative fails to convey adequately the sense of trepidation and urgency that one would expect

from such a desperate man, while the language seldom reflects the literary talent of its alleged author. The preponderance of description over action, a thin plot, and a predictable denouement also detract from the novella's suspense." In the *Nation* (March 21, 2005), Daniel Swift remarked that *Tamburlaine Must Die* "fictionalizes Marlowe's last days with novelistic wit and interpretive imagination. Welsh is no academic. . . . But every line of *Tamburlaine Must Die* is informed by a thorough grasp of not only the day-to-day of Marlowe's life but also a sympathetic willingness to imagine the in-between."

Welsh, who has won a Robert Louis Stevenson Memorial Award from the National Library of Scotland, is currently at work on a new novel. "It's set in Glasgow and a little bit in Germany and it has a male narrator," she told Adrian Turpin for the London *Sunday Times* (July 25, 2004). "That's all I'm saying, except that it has no sex in it yet. It hasn't been needed, though it would be a shame if it continued like that. I've been responsible for choosing the books for a women's reading group recently and they always complain when there's no sex."

Welsh's success as a popular author came while she was in her mid-30s, an experience that she believes was ultimately beneficial to her. "I'm lucky because I wasn't 21 when this happened to me," she told Turpin. "I'm lucky I've got good grounding." For a time she taught writing courses at the University of Glasgow but has since given up teaching to concentrate on her writing. She lives in Glasgow with the novelist Zoë Strachan.

—C.M.

Suggested Reading: Canongate Books Web site; (London) *Sunday Times* Features p5 July 21, 2002, Features p3 July 25, 2004, Features p3 Aug. 13, 2005; *Nation* p27+ Mar. 21, 2005; *New York Times Book Review* p5 Mar. 30, 2003;

Selected Works: *The Cutting Room*, 2002; *Tamburlaine Must Die*, 2004

White, Emily

1966– Nonfiction writer

While serving as the editor of the Seattle-area alternative weekly paper the *Stranger* in the late 1990s, Emily White planned to write an article about girls who had been labeled "sluts"—but she needed to find subjects. Dan Savage, her co-worker and a nationally syndicated sex columnist, let her place an ad in his column; it read, "Are you or were you the slut of your high school?" When her phone began ringing off the hook and her inbox filled with E-mails, White realized that she had touched upon a phenomenon that merited further study. In 2002 she published her examination of the topic, *Fast Girls: Teenage Tribes and the Myth of the Slut* (2002). "I think high school is a mirror of society and the rest of life," White told John Marshall for the *Seattle Post-Intelligencer* (March 16, 2002). "I think that, by looking at what happens to some girls in high school, we can better understand the state of women and how much work needs to be done before equality is attained."

Emily White was born in 1966 and raised in Portland, Oregon. Despite her interest in the effects of being known as a slut, she had no such reputation in her youth. White told Marshall that in high school she had been "a well-behaved, unobtrusive goody-goody." After graduating from Catlin Gabel, a private secondary school in Portland, she studied at Sarah Lawrence College, in Bronxville, New York; Stanford University, in Palo Alto, California; and the University of Oxford, in England. While at Oxford she grew interested in the writings of French feminists and was later enamored with the Riot Grrrl movement, a feminist punk scene that began in Olympia, Washington, in the 1990s. She spent a period as a writer in residence at the Richard Hugo House, a literary center in Seattle. From 1995 to 1999 she served as the editor in chief of the *Stranger*, which she left after receiving the advance to write her first book.

While researching *Fast Girls* White interviewed 150 women. The book documents not only their adolescent experiences but also how their lives have unfolded since. White examined the reasons the stereotype has proliferated over the years, particularly in suburban high schools, where, she discovered, usually at least one girl in every class was branded as such. "The one real surprise in a book that includes 'the Myth of the Slut' in its subtitle is that White had absolutely no interest in investigating whether the girls who were saddled with that name were indeed 'fast girls,' whether what they were alleged to have done was myth or truth," John Marshall wrote. "[Her] focus is instead on 'myth' as a pervasive archetype that can be found at high schools in small towns and suburbia throughout America." White told Marshall: "It's the public ritual that I'm most interested in. I'm not interested in these girls' private lives. I do not care about that, and I am not about to make moral judgments."

White's book, which touches on Jungian archetypes and mob mentality, received varying reviews. In a review for *Library Journal* (March 1, 2002), Linda Beck called it "an excellent sociological study about girls, women, and sexuality." However, in the *New York Times Book Review* (April 21, 2002), Suzy Hanser disagreed, writing: "Despite White's earnestly braving the cruel and confusing world of high school, her findings about the mysterious 'slut,' and the drab white suburbs she lives in, are mostly predictable. . . . White's observation—that girls called sluts tend to come from the lower classes or

those who dress or act differently from the norm—holds true for any type of adolescent ridicule. Part of the problem is that White seems to have become caught up in the lives of a few wounded young women." On the other hand, a reviewer for *Publishers Weekly* (February 25, 2002) felt that White should have dedicated less space to cultural analysis: "Though her tone is accessible to general readers, White's book is a bit more academic than recent titles on similar subjects. . . . The stories of White's interviewees paint a textured, harrowing picture of high school life, and readers will wish she had devoted more space to these powerful testimonies."

White works as a freelance writer, and her work has appeared in such publications as the *New York Times Book Review* and New York *Newsday*. Her next book, scheduled for publication in mid-2007, is tentatively titled "You Will Make Money In Your Sleep: From Boom to Bust with Dana Giacchetto in the 1990s." The upcoming book was twice afforded mention in the notorious *New York Post* gossip column Page Six. On October 26, 2006 the *Post*'s columnist Richard Johnson wrote: "Emily White has written a book about Dana Giacchetto, the money manager to the stars who turned out to be a flimflam artist—but she certainly is *not* his ghostwriter, as we called her [in a column from October 20, 2006]. 'He cooperated, but he has no editorial control,' said White. . . . White has known Giacchetto since 1990 in Seattle, where her husband, Rich Jensen, worked for Giacchetto's Sub Pop Records, the label of grunge god Kurt Cobain of Nirvana. Giacchetto was flying high with such investors as Leonardo DiCaprio, Cameron Diaz, Gywneth Paltrow, Matt Damon, Ben Affleck, Tobey Maguire and Mike Ovitz when he was arrested in 2000 and charged with defrauding them of nearly $10 million. He was sentenced to 57 months in federal prison. . . . He's paying monthly restitution to his victims, some of whom are suing now for the 'access fees' Scribner paid to Giacchetto through his lawyer Ron Fischetti."

—C.M.

Suggested Reading: *Library Journal* p126 Mar. 1, 2002; *New York Times Book Review* p29 Apr. 21, 2002; *Seattle Post-Intelligencer* E p1 Mar. 16, 2002

Selected Books: *Fast Girls: Teenage Tribes and the Myth of the Slut*, 2002

Willis, Sarah

1954(?)– Novelist

In the fiction writing of Sarah Willis, many of the characters and places bear a striking resemblance to those she has known in her own life; as she wrote for the Book Sense Web site: "There is always a brother who gets beaten up by his sister, and often a beautiful blond mother. Also, I like to write about a place I have spent many of my summers, a place I love, Chautauqua, New York." But, she adds, "I can't write about myself. My stories are about someone else, which means I have to see these places, these people, these events in my life, through someone else's eyes, the eyes of my narrator. . . . I want to write characters who are not me, but who are, really, partly me. I want diversity, and I want a feeling that we are all the same in some basic way." Her first novel, *Some Things That Stay* (2000), about a teenage girl trying to find her place in the world, was named a notable book of the year by the *New York Times* and won the Cleveland Arts Prize for Literature and the Stephen Crane Award for First Fiction from the Book-of-the-Month Club. Her other novels are *The Rehearsal* (2001), *A Good Distance* (2004), and *The Sound of Us* (2005). She also writes short stories, which have appeared in many publications, including *Book Magazine, Confrontation, Crescent Review*, and the *Missouri Review*.

Sarah Willis was born in about 1954 in Cleveland, Ohio. Her father, Kirk Willis, was an actor and director at the Cleveland Play House; he died when she was 12. Although traumatized by the loss, she began to write poetry shortly thereafter. When she was 16 she dropped out of her high school and instead attended a small Quaker school. In 1971 she started working at the Free Clinic of Greater Cleveland, a health center for the uninsured. She worked there over the next 10 years, while also attending the Cuyahoga Community College, in Cleveland, and Otterbein College, in Westerville, Ohio. In 1978 she received a B.F.A. in theater from Case Western Reserve University, in Cleveland. She married, had two children, and divorced. When she was 34 she started studying creative writing through non-degree courses at Cleveland State University; soon her short stories began to be published, and she started teaching public writing workshops at the university. She founded the East Side Writers' Group, also in Cleveland. One of her short stories was nominated for the Pushcart Prize.

Willis's first novel, *Some Things That Stay*, was published in 2000. Tamara, the narrator, is near her 15th birthday at the start of the novel. She and her two younger siblings are forced to move every year because their father, a landscape painter, requires varied scenery for inspiration. After the family moves to a farmhouse in upstate New York, Tamara becomes acquainted with a poor family across the road whose son initiates Tamara into sex and whose daughter helps her get in touch with religion—something her atheistic parents have spurned. Things become difficult for Tamara when her mother is stricken with tuberculosis and sent to a sanatorium. "It is Tamara's attempt to understand her mother's absence—as a punishment, as a test, as divine justice, as a curse, as a liberation and a condemnation—that is the real subject of this novel," Susie Linfield noted in the *Los Angeles Times* (February 24, 2000). Carol Anshaw, writing for the *Women's Review of Books* (July 2000), praised Willis's realistic description of Tamara's gradual sexual initiation as something not often seen in fiction. "And there's a lot about this book," she added, "that's notable in this same small way, the striking of small, clear notes of truth. . . . Aside from minor faults . . . Willis has set out a meticulously detailed coming of age narrative that could belong to no one but her protagonist. She has created a novel that nicely fills the narrow space on the bookshelf reserved for small, well-made stories."

In *The Rehearsal* (2001), Willis's second novel, she again presents a family headed by an artistic father who is unaware of the real needs and feelings of his wife or his children. Will Bartlett, the resident director of a theater company in Pittsburgh, is planning to stage a performance of John Steinbeck's novel *Of Mice and Men*. In order to engender a sense of reality and authenticity, he has invited all the actors to stay in the barn at his summer house in Chautauqua, New York, where they will live together for a month, developing their characters. While Will is absorbed in his production, the living arrangement puts strain on the rest of his family—his wife, Myra, who has to do all the cooking and cleaning; his 16-year-old daughter, Beth, a lover of theater who idolizes her father and resents her mother; and his eight-year-old son, Mac, who is shy and completely uninterested in acting. "The novel's third-person point of view moves from character to character, including all the Bartletts . . . and most of the actors," Miranda Schwartz observed for the *Chicago Tribune* (February 24, 2002). "This surfeit of views grows frustrating: Just when we are involved in the thoughts of one character, Willis pulls us away to the next and the next. . . . We want to hear more from some tellers, like Myra and Beth, and less from others—Mac and the actors." Although Schwartz called Willis's first novel "first-rate" and "nearly seamless," she found that *The Rehearsal* fell short of the author's aims. "In both novels, Willis is interested in taking characters to their breaking point and seeing what happens to them. She puts them through crises natural and domestic to see what they are made of. Both books scrutinize the making of art and the concomitant effect on those around the artist. Writing about visual mediums such as painting and theater is challenging, as they must be seen to be fully experienced. *The Rehearsal* doesn't come alive with the breath of theater." Caroline See, writing for the *Washington Post* (October 19, 2001), described the novel's narrative technique as "a brave undertaking, but it leads to what seems to be an oversimplification of the characters." See continued, "Myra is the sole character here who is allowed any depth and complexity. Still, the idea of an old-time theater group as a parable for change is charming; there are theatrical allusions aplenty, including a genuine *Tempest*. And Sarah Willis is a writer of great skill."

In *A Good Distance* Willis explores the nuances of memory through a story about Alzheimer's disease. The protagonist, Jennifer Morgan, is in her 40s and living in Cleveland. She had grown up in the city but had left when she was a teenager, after her father died and her relationship with her mother, Rose, deteriorated. After many years she returned and is now raising a family of her own, but she is haunted by the past and hopes to achieve some reconciliation with her mother. Before she can, Rose falls ill with Alzheimer's. Instead of placing her mother in a nursing home, Jennifer takes her in, but the strain may prove too much for her own family, as dealing with Rose leaves her little time or energy for her husband of three years, Todd, and her rebellious teenage daughter. "The book makes an uncommonly good yarn out of a desperately common situation," John Freeman wrote for the *Atlanta Journal-Constitution* (April 8, 2004). "Setting up this family dynamic is impressive, but what makes *A Good Distance* remarkable is the way Willis brings each character to life, bestowing quirks and sheltered secrets in the most natural of fashions." Freeman added, "*A Good Distance* shows how sad Rose's decline is and helps us appreciate what it does to Jennifer, too. . . . This is a deeply sad book, one whose sadness comes not from melancholia but a clear-eyed recognition of life's inescapable facts." "Willis artfully builds on the blunt impasse of Rose's condition to create a narrative driven by corrosive secrets and gritty revelations on both sides," Deborah Mason wrote for the *New York Times Book Review* (June 13, 2004). "The plot also sets up a sly dichotomy—a daughter seemingly in control of her memory versus a mother who is not. That tosses in another curveball when it comes to rival versions of the truth. . . . Eventually, we learn how Jenny's true story differs from the one she has always told. 'What we see, and what we remember is as malleable as clay,' Willis writes. 'It carries our fingerprints.' She tracks these fingerprints on the two women's memories. . . . As Willis uncovers these memories, she shows how even the most independent self is never a solitary creation; there will always be someone to remind us that, despite our most devious denials, our histories are entwined." Mason added that the tone in which those memories are conveyed "give[s] the novel its jolting credibility." She concluded: "An artfully defiant work of fiction, *A Good Distance* stubbornly hews to the unruliness of life as it is negotiated daily, and as that negotiation shapes our stories, whether we like it or not."

The Sound of Us tells the story of Alice Marlow, a 48-year-old woman living in Cleveland. An interpreter for the deaf, Alice is single with no children and leads a lonely life. One night she receives a telephone call from a frightened six-year-old girl who cries that her mother has disappeared. Alice goes to her apartment, finds the girl alone, and has no choice but to call the authorities; as a social worker takes the dark-skinned Larissa Benton into custody, Alice realizes she has developed a strange attachment to the little girl—and she becomes determined to help Larissa find her way through Cleveland's child-welfare system. "Willis allows for ambiguity in her moving story," a reviewer wrote for *Publishers Weekly* (May 16, 2005). "When Michelle, Larissa's white, wayward mother, returns, she's neither a villain nor a victim; Alice, who converses with her dead twin brother, is not a saint. When Michelle moves into Alice's home to be closer to her daughter the narrative reaches its height of tension; Willis shows both the safety and generosity of Alice's world and the unpredictable but loving home that Michelle would provide. A careful, tender story of the complex bonds of motherhood, this novel doesn't shy away from its problems, but still comes to rest on the side of its wonders."

Sarah Willis lives in Cleveland Heights and is working on a new novel. She contributes essays to the *Plain Dealer Sunday Magazine* and has taught creative-writing classes at several writers' workshops and colleges.

—S.Y.

Suggested Reading: *Chicago Tribune* C p2 Feb. 24, 2002; *Los Angeles Times* E p3 Feb. 24, 2000; *New York Times Book Review* p18 June 13, 2004; *Washington Post* C p2 Oct. 19, 2001; *Women's Review of Books* p40 July 2000

Selected Books: *Some Things That Stay*, 2000; *The Rehearsal*, 2001; *A Good Distance*, 2004; *The Sound of Us*, 2005

Winchester, Simon

Sep. 28, 1944– Nonfiction writer; journalist

When Simon Winchester graduated from the University of Oxford, in 1966, he intended to pursue a career in geology. He worked briefly on oil rigs in the North Sea and as a prospector in Africa before discovering that he was "an extremely bad, incompetent geologist," as he told Michael J. Ybarra for the *Los Angeles Times* (April 24, 2004). While still in Africa, Winchester retreated to his tent one night to read James Morris's *Coronation Everest*, a book that

Simon Winchester

chronicled Edmund Hillary and Tenzing Norgay's historic climb up the highest peak in the world. "I read this book, and instantly I knew this is what I wanted to do," Winchester told Yvonne Nolan for *Publishers Weekly* (August 27, 2001). "It was about going on adventures and then telling people back home about those adventures. I wrote to . . . Morris and said I've just read *Coronation Everest* and basically my question is, 'Can I be you?'" Morris replied, and following his advice, Winchester returned to England to work as a reporter, later establishing a name for himself by covering the conflicts between Protestant and Catholic militants in Northern Ireland. Over the next three decades, he reported on such historic events as the formation of Bangladesh, the Jonestown massacre, and the assassination of the Egyptian president Anwar Sadat. He also published such highly praised travelogues as *The Sun Never Sets: Travels to the Remaining Outposts of the British Empire, Korea: A Walk through the Land of Miracles*, and *The River at the Center of the World: A Journey Up the Yangtze and Back in Chinese Time*. Pico Iyer, writing for the *New York Times Book Review* (April 28, 1991), described Winchester as an "exceptionally engaging guide, an intrepid English traveler of the old school, at home everywhere, ready for anything, full of gusto and a seemingly omnivorous curiosity."

Midway through his career Winchester began to worry that publishers would soon stop financing his far-flung travels, particularly since the sales for his books were generally disappointing. He thus began writing historical nonfiction. He pored over locked-away files and letters at Broadmoor, an English asylum for the criminally insane, and

learned the intricacies of lexicography for *The Professor and the Madman: A Tale of Murder, Insanity, and the Making of the Oxford English Dictionary*, which, in 1998, catapulted Winchester to best-seller lists for the first time. He applied the same approach, the illumination of scientific history through biography, in *The Map That Changed the World: William Smith and the Birth of Modern Geology* and later revisited the topic that made him famous with *The Meaning of Everything: The Story of the Oxford English Dictionary*. In a review of the latter book for the *Wilson Quarterly* (Autumn 2003), Clive Davis declared that in the overcrowded field of historical nonfiction, "Winchester's unobtrusive erudition and droll turn of phrase set him apart from the rest of the journalistic pack." Winchester's most recent books—*Krakatoa: The Day the World Exploded, August 27, 1883* and *A Crack in the Edge of the World: America and the Great California Earthquake of 1906*—examine important geological events.

When Simon Winchester was born, on September 28, 1944 in London, England, to Bernard Winchester and the former Andree de Wael, his father, a British soldier who had been captured on D-day, was languishing in a German prison camp. "I've often thought it must have been quite a strain for my father," Winchester told Nolan. "He'd had a miserable time in Braunschweig POW Camp. He presumably wanted to come back to a woman who would look after him and be nice and tender. Instead, there was this seven-month-old strapping baby. I was sent off to boarding school in Dorset at the age of five, and I often think that was just my father saying, 'Look, I want to just be with your mother, thank you. And you've already intruded too much into my life. So go away!'" When Winchester was 14, his father disappointed him by accepting a job in the U.S. and then backing out. Young Winchester was so determined to see America, however, that shortly after graduating from boarding school, he hitchhiked his way across North America, traveling as far north as Montreal, Canada, and as far south as Mexico City—spending only $18 in the process. "People were so kind," he told Ybarra. "I just adore this country. I love the geology of America." Later, in 1976, Winchester published the travelogue *American Heartbeat: Some Notes from a Midwestern Journey*.

When Winchester returned to England, he tried to join the British Royal Navy but was rejected due to his color blindness. He then enrolled at St. Catherine's College, at the University of Oxford. After earning an M.A. degree in geology, in 1966, he accepted a job prospecting for copper in the Ruwenzori Mountains in western Uganda. Following the advice of James Morris (who published books under the name Jan Morris after undergoing a sex-change operation, in 1972), Winchester returned to England and in 1967 took a job as a correspondent for the Journal, a small newspaper in Newcastle upon Tyne. In 1970 he was hired by the Manchester Guardian and sent to Northern Ireland to cover the increasingly frequent clashes between Protestant and Catholic militants. "Before Northern Ireland, I was no-one," Winchester told a reporter for *Sunday Life* (September 19, 2004). "And then I came and covered the beginnings of the story, and managed to survive it. For me it was a formative time as a journalist. It was an amazing story to cut my teeth on." His experiences there also served as the basis for his first book, In Holy Terror: Reporting the Ulster Troubles, which came out in England in 1974 and was published in the U.S. the following year as *Northern Ireland in Crisis: Reporting the Ulster Troubles.*

From 1972 to 1976 Winchester served as the Guardian's correspondent in Washington, D.C., covering, among other things, the Watergate affair and the resignation of President Richard Nixon. After a stint reporting from New Delhi, India, from 1977 to 1979, he returned to Washington as the chief U.S. correspondent for the London *Daily Mail.* In 1980 the firm Faber and Faber was set to publish Winchester's second book, *Their Noble Lordships: The Hereditary Peerage Today,* an unflattering portrait of the upper ranks of British society, when writs filed by five noblemen—who claimed that the book contained factual errors—forced the publisher to recall and pulp the first edition. The revised edition, published in 1981, was largely praised by critics, especially for the humorous anecdotes Winchester had collected through his extensive interviews.

By the time the U.S. edition—which was published as *Their Noble Lordships: Class and Power in Modern Britain*—reached bookstores, in 1982, Winchester was serving time in an Argentinian prison. While covering the Falkland Islands War for the London *Sunday Times* (for which he had begun working as a feature writer the year before), he had been mistaken for a British spy. He was released after three months and detailed that experience in the book *Prison Diary, Argentina* (1983), which failed to impress most reviewers; Malcolm Deas, writing for the *Times Literary Supplement* (February 10, 1984), called it "an ephemeral, sentimental and frustrated book." In 1983 Winchester also published *Stones of Empire: The Buildings of the Raj,* a survey of British architecture in India and Pakistan, for which he supplied the photographs and captions and his mentor, Morris, wrote the text.

In the mid-1980s Winchester moved to Hong Kong, where he reported on the Pacific region for the London *Guardian,* among other publications, and conducted some of the research for his next book, *The Sun Never Sets* (1985; published as Outposts in Britain), a travelogue of his journeys to the remaining British colonies, including Bermuda, Gibraltar, and St. Helena. It took Winchester three years to visit nearly all of the populated lands still under British rule, and

reviewers were delighted with his observations. Andrew Harvey, writing for the *New York Times Book Review* (June 1, 1986), termed *The Sun Never Sets* a "warm, superbly written book," which serves not only as "a vivid account of far-flung islands" but also as "a meditation, by turns funny, melancholic and mocking, on the decline of modern Britain."

In 1987 Winchester began writing books and freelance articles full-time, and the following year he published Korea. To research that account of the people and history of the Republic of Korea, he traversed the country from the southern tip of the peninsula to the North Korean border. In a review for the London *Guardian* (July 15, 1988), Ruth Grayson described the book as "immensely readable" and praised Winchester for his thorough research.

In *Pacific Rising: The Emergence of a New World Culture* (1991), Winchester argued that the primacy of the nations with coastlines along the Atlantic Ocean would soon fall to the increasing influence of those of the Pacific Rim. The peoples of the Pacific were beginning to experience "an inchoate, undefined sense of oneness, of coterminous identity," he wrote, according to a reviewer for the *Economist* (February 23, 1991). Noting that the author "goes to elegant, erudite and amusing lengths" to convey that sense of identity as well, the *Economist* reviewer nonetheless remained unconvinced: "The quarter or more of the world's population who live around the rim of the Pacific are too diverse to be cutely grouped as the 'Pacific man' in the 'Pacific century,' so readily defined by fund managers and futurologists." Pico Iyer, on the other hand, found that "the singular charm of the book" is that Winchester "has no time for dull geopolitical surveys or dutiful claims of cultural unity; instead, he simply assembles a colorful encyclopedia of facts, adventures and perspectives based on his travels," presented with "a storyteller's fluency and panache."

In 1992 Winchester published *Pacific Nightmare: How Japan Starts World War III, A Future History,* a speculative work in which a catastrophic war is sparked by the British handover of Hong Kong to the Chinese in 1997. Malcolm Bosse wrote for the *New York Times Book Review* (October 18 1992) that *Pacific Nightmare* "illustrates both the strengths and the weaknesses" of the future-history genre: "The author's reach for authenticity often leads to so much detail that the reader must wade through it. . . . And the book has no emotional focus, since no single character, either fictional or historical, takes center stage, not even for a few pages. But each event is closely reasoned, precisely delineated. The writing and thinking are never shoddy. Wonderfully odd bits of information dot the pages."

In 1994 Winchester—traveling by boat, car, train, plane, bus, and on foot—followed the course of the Yangtze River (also called the Changjiang), which originates in the highlands of Tibet and snakes across China, emptying into the Pacific Ocean. He chronicled his experiences in *The River at the Center of the World* (1996), examining what he described as the "delicious strangeness of China," as quoted by a reviewer for *Publishers Weekly* (September 16, 1996). "Wryly humorous, gently skeptical, immensely knowledgeable as he wends his way along the 3900 miles of the great river, Winchester provides an irresistible feast of detail about the character of the river itself, the landscape, the cities, villages and people along its banks . . . ," the reviewer wrote. "Winchester is comfortable with the country's long, complex history and politics, and he writes about them with an easy grace that defies the usual picture of China as an enigma wrapped in a conundrum."

Not long after Winchester had struck out on his own as a freelance writer, he began to fear that he might "slide into a middle age of extreme penury," as he told Ybarra. Though many of his books received positive reviews, their sales were dismal; one of his books reportedly sold only 11 copies. Then, as he told Dave Weich for the Powell's Books Web site, while reading Jonathon Green's *Chasing the Sun: Dictionary-Makers and the Dictionaries They Made* (1996), Winchester noticed an intriguing footnote: "Readers will of course be familiar with the story of W. C. Minor, the convicted, deranged, American lunatic murderer, contributor to the OED." No one before Winchester had thought to write a book about the relationship between James Murray, editor of the *Oxford English Dictionary*, and William C. Minor, an American expatriate and Civil War veteran who had contributed thousands of entries to the first edition of the dictionary while confined to an English asylum for the criminally insane.

Though Winchester's publisher at the time passed on the project and advised him to drop it, HarperCollins agreed to publish *The Professor and the Madman* (1998)—which proved to be his breakthrough. The book was a best-seller in both Britain and the U.S. and thus far has sold more than a million copies worldwide. *The Professor and the Madman* (which was published as *The Surgeon of Crowthorne* in Britain) also received many critical accolades. "This book is representative of a type seen frequently of late . . . ," Benjamin Griffith wrote for the *Sewanee Review* (Summer 1999). "Winchester's superb account of Murray's first visit to Broadmoor and the growing friendship between the two scholars is a high point." David Walton, writing for the *New York Times Book Review* (August 30, 1998), called it an "imaginative retelling of these two 'inextricably and most curiously entwined' lives." Winchester wrote about a greater number of people involved in the creation of the *Oxford English Dictionary* in *The Meaning of Everything* (2003), which was short-listed for a British Book Award for history book of the year. In reviewing it for the *Los Angeles Times* (October 19, 2003), Robert McCrum wrote that its subject was "perfectly suited to Winchester's magpie mind. Winchester's account is an affectionate and frankly partisan study of the making of a great dictionary. It is also an offbeat portrait of an extraordinary society."

Interviewing Winchester shortly after Mel Gibson's production company bought the film rights to *The Professor and the Madman*, Mel Gussow reported for the *New York Times* (September 7, 1998) that the author sounded like a "newly retired explorer." Winchester told Gussow, "I think the idea of settling down and writing books about strange episodes in history, which somehow illuminate something rather greater, would be a nice way to spend a life, if I can wean myself from travel." He seemed unable, however, to completely abandon his peripatetic ways, visiting the Kosovar refugee camps in Macedonia for his next book, *The Fracture Zone: A Return to the Balkans* (1999). Having traveled through the region decades earlier on a road trip from Vienna, Austria, to Istanbul, Turkey, he was shocked by the "Bruegel-scene of mass misery" he discovered in a once-peaceful country that was being torn apart by conflicts between the ethnic Macedonians and the Albanian minority, as quoted by a reviewer for *Publishers Weekly* (September 27, 1999). "Taking a fatalistic attitude," the reviewer continued, Winchester "views the region's problems as little more than the fruit of 'classic Balkan hatreds, ancient and modern.' Still, Winchester's extensive interviews make his book notable. Almost every page contains the reflections of ordinary citizens, who reveal to Winchester their hatreds, their troubles and their hopes, lending richness and authenticity to his account. His unsentimental descriptions of the area's destroyed mosques, burned houses and virulent graffiti serve as a poignant reminder that the effects of war last long after the planes are gone."

Winchester's next book, *The Map That Changed the World* (2001), tells the story of William Smith, a British canal digger who labored for 22 years to create the first geological map, which was published in 1815. Though Smith is now known as the father of modern geology, he lived in poverty and obscurity, receiving little recognition for his work, until 1831, when he received the Geological Society of London's highest award and a lifetime pension from the king. "Winchester's such a fine historian, journalist and stylist that he manages to make this whole genre (popular science history refracted through partial biography) seem absolutely new," Kathryn Hughes wrote for the *New Statesman* (July 2, 2001). Hughes also praised the author for pointing out that Smith's discoveries—which contradicted the biblical tale of creation—paved the way for the crisis of faith in the Victorian age.

In *Krakatoa* (2003), Winchester described the 1883 eruption of the eponymous volcano—which was so powerful that the force of the explosion altered the configuration of the Sunda Strait, and the flow of lava and shower of rock and ash resulted in the formation of new islands in the Indian Ocean. "*Krakatoa* is a trove of wonderfully arcane information," Janet Maslin wrote for the *New York Times* (April 25, 2003). "The author has been able to attach so many tentacles to a single event . . . that there seems to be nowhere he can't go. . . . This manner of amplifying science or history with odd, figurative footnotes has become extremely popular; just read a full-length book about salt, for example. But since *The Professor and the Madman* . . . Winchester has emerged as the leading practitioner of the method. He incorporates research that ranges far and wide, serving up both real and cocktail-party science. And all the while, in scattering these trails of bread crumbs, he keeps track of his story's central path."

While packing the research materials for *Krakatoa*, Winchester noticed that the event was often lumped together with such other great natural disasters as the 1906 earthquake that devastated San Francisco, California. Realizing that the centennial of that event was fast approaching, he set to work on *A Crack in the Edge of the World* (2005). As Bryan Burrough noted for the *New York Times Book Review* (October 9, 2005), Winchester's book "is not a straightforward account of the earthquake and subsequent fire but a first-person melange of geology textbook and travelogue grafted onto a recounting of the events that destroyed San Francisco 100 years ago," and though the text is accompanied by charts, maps, and a glossary, "they adorn sections mined with passages as impenetrable as bedrock."

Winchester continues to contribute articles to U.S. and British publications, among them *Harper's Magazine*, *Smithsonian*, *National Geographic*, the *Spectator*, *Granta*, the *New York Times*, and the *Atlantic Monthly*. He has also written for and hosted television documentaries and has frequently contributed to the BBC radio show *From Our Own Correspondent*. In 2006 Winchester was made an Officer of the Order of the British Empire (OBE) by the queen of England in a ceremony at Buckingham Palace.

Winchester, who has been married twice, has three children (four, according to some sources) from his first marriage. He owns an apartment in New York City, a cottage on the Scottish island of Luing, and a small farm in the Berkshires, in Massachusetts.

—S.Y.

Suggested Reading: *Boston Globe* D p8 Apr. 20, 2003; *Economist* p93 Feb. 23, 1991, p119 May 16, 1992; *New Statesman* p47 July 3, 1998; (New York) *Newsday* B p9 Aug. 12, 2001; *New York Times* E p1 Sep. 7, 1998, E p9 Sep. 16, 1998, E p43 Apr. 25, 2003; *New York Times Book Review* p10 Apr. 28, 1991, p12 Aug. 30, 1998, p24 Dec. 5, 1999, p18 Oct. 9, 2005; *Publishers Weekly* p44 Aug. 27, 2001; *Smithsonian* p156+ Apr. 1987; *Washington Post Book World* p6 Jan. 16, 2000

Selected Books: fiction—*Pacific Nightmare: How Japan Starts World War III, A Future History*, 1992; nonfiction—*Northern Ireland in Crisis: Reporting the Ulster Troubles*, 1975; *American Heartbeat: Some Notes from a Midwestern Journey*, 1976; *Their Noble Lordships: Class and Power in Modern Britain*, 1982; *Stones of Empire: The Buildings of the Raj* (with Jan Morris), 1983; *Prison Diary, Argentina*, 1983; *The Sun Never Sets: Travels to the Remaining Outposts of the British Empire*, 1985; *Korea: A Walk through the Land of Miracles*, 1988; *Pacific Rising: The Emergence of a New World Culture*, 1991; *Small World* (with Martin Parr), 1995; *The River at the Center of the World: A Journey Up the Yangtze and Back in Chinese Time*, 1996; *The Professor and the Madman: A Tale of Murder, Insanity, and the Making of the Oxford English Dictionary*, 1998; *The Fracture Zone: A Return to the Balkans*, 1999; *The Map That Changed the World: William Smith and the Birth of Modern Geology*, 2001; *Krakatoa: The Day the World Exploded, August 27, 1883*, 2003; *The Meaning of Everything: The Story of the Oxford English Dictionary*, 2003; *A Crack in the Edge of the World: America and the Great California Earthquake of 1906*, 2005

Wolfe, Alan

June 10, 1942– Political scientist; sociologist

"Alan Wolfe is one of our best social critics," Richard Madsen wrote for the *American Journal of Sociology* (January 1998). "Few contemporary sociologists have been as prolific, as wide ranging, and as capable of reaching a large, general, educated public, and few have offered commentary that is so consistently well informed and well balanced." Wolfe, who has taught sociology and political science at some of America's most prestigious institutions, established his reputation as an incisive social observer through the publication of such books as *Marginalized in the Middle* (1996), *Moral Freedom: The Search for Virtue in a World of Choice* (2001), *The Transformation of American Religion: How We Actually Live Our Faith* (2003), and *Return to Greatness: How America Lost Its Sense of Purpose and What It Needs to Do to Recover It* (2005). Americans, he has posited, continually reinvent themselves to find pragmatic bridges over the troubled waters of public policy. In *One Nation, After All: What Middle-Class Americans Really Think About: God, Country, Family, Racism, Welfare, Immigration, Homosexuality, Work, the Right, the Left, and Each Other* (1998), Wolfe observed that middle-class Americans "understand that what makes us one nation morally is an insistence on a set of values

Courtesy of Boston College

Alan Wolfe

capacious enough to be inclusive but demanding enough to up-hold standards of personal responsibility."

Alan Wolfe wrote the following autobiographical statement for *World Authors 2000–2005*:

"Philadelphia is my home town. I've always felt a certain significance to that fact, even though I left home 40 years ago and rarely go back. Being urban but not a New Yorker was just the right combination for someone like me, the first in my family to attend college. There was enough of a city around to fall in love with music, art, and books. But nothing in Philadelphia was quite so overwhelming as everything in Manhattan. Baseball players get seasoning in the minor leagues; the same—forgive me, Philadelphians—is true of writers.

"I was trained to become an academic but I became a writer instead. It never occurred to me when I began my training that the two were at odds, perhaps because the doctoral program I attended—in Philadelphia, of course—was, despite its Ivy League status, not one of the most distinguished in the country at the time. Penn was glad to have me, and I still feel indebted to those who taught me. But when one of the professors there tried to get me to adopt him as my mentor, going so far as to outline the career I would follow if I just attached myself to his research plans, I instinctively rebelled. I did not get then, as I still do not get now, the point of working with others when it comes to ideas. Academics may do that, but writers do not. Writers have things to say and can only say them in their own voice. Publishing in academic journals with a long list of co-authors

can be valuable, but it is not writing. Had not my distaste for narrow-gauge research disrupted the usual path to academic success, the timing of my entrance into adulthood would have. Through no fault of my own I was born in a year, 1942, that would make the tumultuous events of 1968 occur just as I was trying to decide what to do with my life. When people turn 26, they typically begin to think about careers and families. When I turned 26, I thought about assassinations, riots, and wars. The public took over the private. I would, like so many others of my generation, protest. But I would also write, assuming, of course, that someone would publish me.

"The person who initially did so was Carey McWilliams, editor of the left-leaning the *Nation*, the first important writer I ever knew—his books on California are classics—and a man who seemed to reach out across the generations to encourage me. 1968, as it happens, was the year I moved to Manhattan to accept a job teaching at a newly opened "experimental college" on Long Island. When Carey asked me to visit him in his Greenwich Village office, I began to think of myself as a New York intellectual, even as my politics in those days came equipped with obligatory disdain for the anti-communist stance so many of the previous generations of New York intellectuals (bravely, I now realize) took.

"One thing led to another, which is a way of saying that the *Nation* led to the *New Republic*. The book pages of *TNR*, edited ever since I have written in them under the watchful eyes of Leon Wieseltier, became my major outlet, and it is to Leon that I feel my strongest sense of obligation both as a writer and as a thinker. I have learned my liberalism through Leon, a man for whom reason and passion are exquisitely combined in defense of hard-won common sense. And it was Leon who encouraged me to write honestly, a fundamental ingredient of writing well. The chips fell as chips do, and I found myself, as I put it, somewhat ironically, *Marginalized in the Middle*, the title of the book of essays that grew out of my writing for *TNR*. Politically, the middle was not the best place to be as the country's political class became divided into ideological camps. But intellectually the middle was the only place from which one could draw on the strengths of both liberalism and conservatism, and while my sympathies remained closer to the former than the latter, even as some of my 1960s comrades shifted sharply to the right, I felt that both were important in grasping the complexities of American politics.

"Writing for a general interest magazine such as the *New Republic* should have led me to disdain academic scholarship even more, but actually the reverse took place. Secure that I had a platform and something to say when standing upon it, I rededicated myself to the academic world, even developing a specialty in religion and politics. (Typically, perhaps, I chose a somewhat marginalized specialty; religion declined as a subject of academic interest the more it grew as a reality in American public life). And if being a non-believer fascinated by religion was not enough, I also found myself, a thoroughly secular Jew, teaching at a Catholic University.

"Boston College works for my academic side in much the same way that my affiliation with the *New Republic* works for my non-fiction writer side. Because Catholic colleges and universities have more of a sense of mission than secular ones, and because their tradition is so intertwined with the history and philosophy of Western Europe, BC is an institution that respects and rewards those who take on big subjects. It is the perfect academic home for me, and it does not surprise me that I have become more productive than ever since arriving here.

"In the past couple of years a number of aspiring academics have contacted me because, of all things, they want to be writers. Despite Fox News, short attention spans, and iPods, the supply of individuals who want to write reflectively on serious political topics does not seem to be drying up. That's good news all around, for those who write, those who read, and those whose lives are changed by what people write even if they never read them."

Alan Wolfe was born on June 10, 1942 to Jean Birnbaum and Leon L. Wolfe, in Philadelphia, Pennsylvania. In 1963 he received his bachelor's degree in political science from Temple University, in Philadelphia. He conducted graduate studies in political science at Vanderbilt University, in Nashville, Tennessee, from 1964 to 1965, before pursuing his doctorate, which he earned in 1967, in the same field at the University of Pennsylvania, in Philadelphia. He has taught sociology and political science at Rutgers University, in New Jersey (1966–68); the State University of New York's College at Old Westbury (1968–70); the City University of New York's Richmond College (1970–78); the University of California, at Santa Cruz (1977–79); the University of California, at Berkeley (1978–80); the University of Aarhus, in Denmark (1987–88); Columbia University, in New York City (1989); and the City University of New York's Queens College and Graduate Center (1979–89). In 1991 he was appointed the dean of the graduate faculty of political and social science at the New School, in New York City. He then taught political science and sociology at Boston University, in Massachusetts, and since 1999 he has served as the director of the Boisi Center for Religion and American Public Life at Boston College.

Wolfe's first book, *The Seamy Side of Democracy: Repression in America* (1973)—in which he argued that repression is an integral part of the theory of liberalism—was seen by most reviewers as polemical rather than an example of serious scholarship. "The book suffers from overgeneralizations and evidence which is clearly selected to fit the political bias of the author," R. L. Satow wrote for *Library Journal* (September 1, 1973). "The Marxist propositions which the author attempts to prove are worded in a tautological way, making it impossible to disprove them. . . . Basing this generalization on the fact that most 20th-century repression in America has occurred during Democratic Administrations, [Wolfe] disregards the fact that this might be related to the Democrats being in power during both world wars." In contrast his second book, *The Limits of Legitimacy: Political Contradictions of Contemporary Capitalism* (1977), a discussion of the contradictions inherent in a liberal democracy, drew praise from those who agreed with Wolfe's position and castigation from those who disagreed with him—though the latter were fewer than the former. "Unflinching in its perception and encyclopedic in its documentation, this book is an important work on contemporary politics," John Bokina wrote for *Library Journal* (December 1, 1977). "It ought to transcend its immediate interest to political scientists and theorists and attain a wider readership among everyone concerned with the prospects for democracy." However, M. N. Rothbard, the critic for *American Historical Review* (June 1978), observed that Wolfe's "aim was to present a history of the modern 'capitalist' state, but there is no history here."

Wolfe wrote *America's Impasse: The Rise and Fall of the Politics of Growth* (1981) in part to refute President Ronald Reagan's insistence that economic growth for the nation necessarily resulted in prosperity for all of its citizens. In Wolfe's view, public social ideals are more important to the nation than the satisfaction of individuals' desires for more consumer goods. "Again and again [Wolfe] makes the point that even in the quarter-century of prosperity after 1945 any strategy which began by simultaneously attempting to provide a secure environment for investment and a decent environment for the poor would end by emphasizing the former objective over the latter," W. B. Hixon wrote for *Commonweal* (March 12, 1982). "Wolfe has no doubts that Reagan's particular version of 'growth politics,' with its emphasis on 'business freedom and military strength,' will lead to the same end; for in his view our society has already been 'victimized by the program now being advanced to save it.'" Hixon felt that Wolfe had made that point well but was "less persuasive in explaining the crucial historical context." On the other hand, a reviewer for *Choice* (April 1982) argued that *America's Impasse* "should be regarded as one of the more important books recently published."

With *Whose Keeper?: Social Science and Moral Obligation* (1989), Wolfe began taking a different approach to his work. "His previous works were framed, roughly, by a horizon of Marxist political economic assumptions," Jean Bethke Elshtain wrote for *Commonweal* (January 12, 1990). "But, having become the father of two small children, and having continued to think rather than allow his reflections to ossify into the dogmas of either the left or the right, Wolfe has accomplished a minor miracle. He has written a book that offers genuinely fresh insights into the ever more intractable dilemmas of modernity." In the book he suggests the creation of a new civil morality that would stem from a reinvigorated sense of community, in which individuals, with the guidance of the social sciences, would be better able to balance the needs of both distant and intimate others. "Wolfe's provocative survey of the breakdown of civil society spares neither right-wing champions of 'economic freedom' nor left-liberal advocates of an expanded welfare state, " Michael Kazin wrote for the *Washington Post Book World* (October 15, 1989). "The single-minded pursuit of self-interest, argues Wolfe in terms that parallel a charge often made by conservative evangelicals, is a siren call that makes for lonely people and a culture lacking the common moral narratives which would nourish its spirit and inspire debate about its principles." At the same time, Wolfe was also troubled by the Scandinavian welfare state, which he described, according to Kazin, as "a system whose citizens view the state as a purveyor of services that demand the steady payment of revenues but little in the way of commitment or participation."

In *The Human Difference: Animals, Computers, and the Necessity of Social Science* (1993), Wolfe called for a return to a more moral and humanistic approach to academic studies, taking particular issue with postmodernism and the philosophies that underlie the animal rights and deep ecology movements. "It is time for them [social scientists] to find a way of studying human beings that takes full account of the distinctiveness of the human beings they study," Wolfe wrote in the introduction. "*The Human Difference* is a defense of humanism. . . . We are a puzzling species, capable of doing great things while also capable of wreaking great harm. . . . The more we learn about how we act and think, the less likely we will feel the need to model our understanding of ourselves on the study of other animal species or computers." Arthur Frank, writing for *Contemporary Sociology* (March 1994), found the book "biting, generous, witty, introspective, provocative, and ecumenical; . . . nothing short of a new philosophical anthropology for contemporary sociology." Randall Collins, the reviewer for the *American Journal of Sociology* (March 1994), found Wolfe's "cool and even-handed style" a contrast to "the polemical tactics so often associated with these topics." However, he noted that environmentalists "are hardly an intellectual challenge to the existence of sociology, and Wolfe's argument here is a bit like fighting off a mouse with a bludgeon."

Though Wolfe's 1996 book, *Marginalized in the Middle,* is a collection of previously published articles (most of which were written for the *New Republic*), Richard Madsen argued that the book "is more than the sum of its parts; Wolfe has revised and reframed his previously published essays so as to construct a general argument about the role of the social critic in modern American society." After briefly discussing what he deems the "golden age" of American criticism, the 1950s and 1960s, Wolfe outlined how he believes social criticism should and should not be conducted by critiquing the work of contemporary critics. "He aims his criticisms at a wide range of targets spanning the contemporary political and theoretical spectrums: for example, feminists like Judith Lorber and Catharine MacKinnon, theorists of race like Andrew Hacker, rational choice theorists like Richard Posner, scholar/policy advocates like Theda Skocpol, and communication theorists like Deborah Tannen," Madsen wrote. "These thinkers have gone at least partially wrong, in Wolfe's view, because they are not sufficiently grounded in empirical data, not based in sufficiently broad theories, and/or have not properly reconciled the tension between describing what is and advocating what ought to be." Sanford Pinsker, writing in *Society* (September/October 1997), agreed with most of Wolfe's arguments, particularly "the general spirit with which he seeks to defend the importance of an ongoing, vigorous criticism." Pinsker took issue with Wolfe, however, on the idea that social criticism can be accomplished in an atmosphere "free of polemical argument, much less of a political identification."

For *One Nation, After All,* Wolfe spoke with 200 middle-class Americans from the suburbs of Tulsa, Boston, Atlanta, and San Diego, skewing his sample to include more Southerners and Christians than others, and discovered that, despite the impression left by public opinion polls, there is no great political divide in America. "The evidence in this book reveals that the news media—which habitually portray the country as bitterly divided over moral, racial and social issues—are profoundly out of touch, and perhaps even incapable of grasping the full complexity of what and how Americans think," Brent Staples wrote for the *New York Times Book Review* (March 8, 1998). "For the most part, Wolfe suggests, Americans practice a kind of 'capacious individualism,' trying to be faithful to their own values while, to the largest possible extent, respectful and nonjudgmental of others' values. But he is so overwhelmed by the goodness of common folk that he sometimes fails to question what they tell him. This is clearly the case in discussions of race, where people rarely express their most honest negative feelings—and often don't know what those feelings are, given that the most crucial ones are subconscious. Excessive optimism aside, *One Nation, After All* is a fascinating and often stirring tour through an America that the news media and would-be culture warriors seem not to know. " Seymour Martin Lipset, writing for the *Wilson Quarterly* (Summer 1998), found that all "is not entirely right with *One Nation*'s approach." He pointed to the problem of identifying who exactly is in the middle class: "To identify oneself with the upper class is boastful; to identify oneself with the lower class is invidious. So when presented with this three-class question, nearly everyone reports middle-class status. Back in 1948, however, the social psychologist Richard Centers asked respondents if they were upper class, middle class, working class, or lower class. Given the fourth choice, a plurality of respondents—between 35 and 45 percent in the United States and elsewhere—placed themselves in the working class." But, Lipset continues, "Despite this flaw, *One Nation* is a thoughtful, provocative, and data-rich book."

Drawing from another survey of American thinking, Wolfe next wrote *Moral Freedom*, a summation of Americans' ideas about morality. According to George Scialabba, writing for the *American Prospect* (April 23, 2001), Wolfe came to the conclusion that "Americans have come to accept the relevance of individual freedom, not only in their economic life, but in their moral life as well," and in fact, the idea of moral freedom has become the "defining characteristic of the moral philosophy of Americans." Wolfe's survey produced evidence of what he saw as a consensus among Americans that morality is no longer to be imposed by rules and censorship but emerges from individual desires and needs. "Wolfe sees moral freedom as freedom's third great age—its final and most radical stage," Stanley Kurtz wrote for *Policy Review* (June/July 2001). "For Wolfe, the age of moral freedom succeeds the nineteenth century triumph of economic freedom and the twentieth century victory of political freedom." According to Kurtz, however, "Wolfe's survey questions—and his manner of interpreting them—effectively caricature and marginalize traditional moral views," and, the reviewer argued, "what Wolfe actually demonstrates is the existence of a wide variety of clashing views." Reviewing the book for *America* (August 13-20, 2001), James F. Keenan protested that there is "something terribly domesticated about Wolfe's data and analysis." He concluded, "What does Wolfe's 'search for virtue in a world of choice' have to say about the international choices America makes when its citizens' moral concerns do not, generally speaking, go beyond their borders? I could find no answer to that question."

In *The Transformation of American Religion: How We Actually Live Our Faith*, Wolfe drew the same conclusions as he had in his previous books: religious institutions are changing in accordance with the dominant American culture of "self-esteem." According to Michael Massing, writing

for the *Nation* (October 6, 2003), Wolfe is so "intent on showing how American culture has transformed religion, he ignores the many ways in which religion has transformed American culture," and consequently fails to acknowledge the intolerance of such evangelical groups as the Promise Keepers, which exclude women and express a deep antipathy toward homosexuals. "The evangelicals in his book all seem to be tolerant, moderate and nonjudgmental. He is able to arrive at such a conclusion, however, only by glossing over—and sanitizing—some of the more disturbing trends in American religion. . . . Wolfe goes so far as to maintain that conservative Protestantism is promoting 'the emergence of biblical feminists, women who try to combine their commitment to evangelical faith with an equally strong commitment to women's-equality.' Thus does a movement that denies women the right to teach Sunday school become, for Wolfe, an incubator of feminism. . . . Given the huge impact evangelical Christians are having on America, there's an urgent need for more insight into their world. That world needs to be explored without condescension and cynicism—but also without the kind of whitewashing offered in *The Transformation of American Religion*."

Although Wolfe has expressed faith in and admiration for the American people as a whole, he used his discontent with the presidency of George W. Bush as the motivation for *Return to Greatness: How America Lost Its Sense of Purpose and What It Needs to Do to Recover It* (2005). "Wielding history as a political cudgel has become a favorite tactic of the right's intellectual enemies in recent years," Gary Rosen wrote for the *New York Times Book Review* (April 3, 2005). "*Return to Greatness* joins a growing literature—by Garry Wills, Michael Lind, Kevin Phillips and others—determined to show the parallels between the Republican ascendancy and one or another ugly chapter of the American past. Variations abound. Is Bush (or before him, Newt Gingrich) more a Gilded Age plutocrat or a Klansman, a McCarthyite, a swaggering Davy Crockett or a reactionary sectionalist a la John C. Calhoun? Whatever the invidious comparison—and here, it must be said, Wolfe is relatively restrained—the history-telling is obviously of the potted variety, either over-schematic or simply tendentious. Footnotes and elaborate typologies cannot hide what amounts to sophisticated name-calling." Charles Kupchan, writing in the *Washington Post Book World* (April 3, 2005), tended to agree: "Wolfe's approach is promising; after all, the electoral appeal of Bush's foreign policy stems at least partially from the president's ability to equate his ambitious agenda with American ideals. But Wolfe's follow-through is lacking. His analysis ultimately falters because the differences he draws between goodness and greatness—as well as the respective policy agendas of these traditions—are confused and confusing, limiting the book's ability to illuminate America's current predicament."

Wolfe has served as the editor for numerous texts, including *Political Analysis: An Unorthodox Approach* (1972), with Charles A. McCoy; *America at Century's End* (1991); and *School Choice: The Moral Debate* (2003). He is a contributing editor for the *New Republic* and the *Wilson Quarterly*, and he frequently contributes articles to *Commonweal*, the *New York Times*, *Harper's*, the *Atlantic Monthly*, and the *Washington Post*, among other publications.

Alan Wolfe is married to a Dane and told Michael Cromartie in an interview for *Christianity Today* (March/April 2004, on-line) that there was a "Kierkegaardian culture" in his family, referring to the 19th-century Danish philosopher Søren Kierkegaard. "Kierkegaard is largely missing in American religion," he complained. "I don't think there's enough brooding going on."

—S.Y.

Suggested Reading: *America* Aug. 13, 2001; *American Journal of Sociology* p1399 Mar. 1994, p1073+ Jan. 1998; *Christianity Today* (on-line) Mar./Apr. 2004; *Commonweal* p150 Mar. 12, 1982, p36+ Nov. 7, 2003; *Nation* p32+ Oct. 6, 2003; *New York Times Book Review* p6 Mar. 8, 1998, p18 Apr. 3, 2005; *Society* Sep./Oct. 1997; *Washington Post Book World* p9 Oct. 15, 1989, p1 Feb. 15, 1998, p5 Apr. 3, 2005; *Wilson Quarterly* p112+ Summer 2001

Selected Books: *The Seamy Side of Democracy: Repression in America*, 1973; *The Limits of Legitimacy: Political Contradictions of Contemporary Capitalism*, 1977; *The Rise and Fall of the 'Soviet Threat': Domestic Sources of the Cold War Consensus*, 1979; *America's Impasse: The Rise and Fall of the Politics of Growth*, 1981; *Whose Keeper?: Social Science and Moral Obligation*, 1989; *The Human Difference: Animals, Computers, and the Necessity of Social Science*, 1993; *Marginalized in the Middle*, 1996; *One Nation, After All: What Middle-Class Americans Really Think About: God, Country, Family, Racism, Welfare, Immigration, Homosexuality, Work, the Right, the Left, and Each Other*, 1998; *Moral Freedom: The Search for Virtue in a World of Choice*, 2001; *The Transformation of American Religion: How We Actually Live Our Faith*, 2003; *Return to Greatness: How America Lost Its Sense of Purpose and What It Needs to Do to Recover It*, 2005; as editor—*An End to Political Science: The Caucus Papers* (with Marvin Surkin), 1970; *Political Analysis: An Unorthodox Approach* (with Charles A. McCoy), 1972; *America at Century's End*, 1991; *School Choice: The Moral Debate*, 2003

Wood, Michael

July 23, 1948– Nonfiction writer

Through his popular documentary films and books of history, Michael Wood has established a reputation for crafting interesting and informative histories of monumental subjects in a style that is accessible to a general audience. In the early 1980s, after training as an academic and a journalist, Wood began making documentaries for television and since that time he has made almost 100 history and travel documentaries for British and American television, and for many of these projects he has written companion books that have been praised by critics. He has explored such diverse subjects as Medieval Europe, the Trojan War, the Spanish Conquistadors, and William Shakespeare—always with an eye for uncovering those parts of the past that might better our understanding of the relevance and importance of historical events and people. A self-described "popularizer," he looks at his output, according to an interview with Arthur Unger for the *Christian Science Monitor* (June 3, 1986), as "a cross between historical journalism and detective work."

Michael David Wood was born on July 23, 1948 in Manchester, England, the son of George Wood and the former Elsie Bell. He received his early education at Manchester Grammar School and

Courtesy of Maya Vision International

earned an undergraduate degree from Oriel College at the University of Oxford. He did postgraduate research on Anglo-Saxon history, but was unable to complete his thesis because of financial difficulties.

For many years Wood was a television journalist, first with ITV from 1973 to 1976 and then with the BBC from 1976 to 1979, when he began making such television documentaries as *In Search of Offa* (1979), *In Search of Arthur* (1980), *In Search of Eric Bloodaxe* (1981), and *In Search of Alfred the Great* (1981). Wood's first companion book, *In Search of the Dark Ages*, was published in 1981, the same year in which the documentary of the same name was first broadcast and Wood's book *Great Railway Journeys of the World* also appeared. Wood made documentaries for the BBC until 1986, then switched over to Central TV, for which he worked until 1991. Wood subsequently joined Maya Vision International, an independent film and television production company based in London.

In Search of the Trojan War (1985) was Wood's companion volume to a six-part television documentary of the same name. Both the series and the book examine the historical evidence of the Trojan War, paying particular attention to the archeological clues that suggest the existence of the ancient city of Troy, which was allegedly destroyed by the Mycenae and other Greek kingdoms some 3,000 years ago. Wood outlines the development of the legend of Troy as it progressed from Homer's epic poem *The Iliad* through medieval and Renaissance-era embellishments. The BBC series was a major success, leading Unger to comment that "In London, Michael Wood is known as the man who caused a sellout of Homer's classics in the main bookshops." A women's magazine, furthermore, nominated Wood as "hunk of the month." The series was subsequently broadcast in the U.S. on PBS. Wood's companion volume was equally well received by critics. Phoebe-Lou Adams, in a review for the *Atlantic Monthly* (May 1986), wrote: "For anyone interested in the connection, if any, between Homeric epic and Bronze Age reality, Mr. Wood is a stimulating guide and detective. He writes well too." Jackson P. Hershbell wrote for *Library Journal* (April 15, 1986), "Though not a professional archaeologist, Wood shows a fine grasp of the various problems presented by the Homeric epics, and writes well about sometimes complicated archaeological, linguistic, and historical matters."

Wood's next book, *Domesday: A Search for the Roots of England* (1986), attempted to explain how the Domesday book was not only the official census of England in 1086 but also included the status of every citizen of the realm, including his or her land and property holdings. Covering the period from 1066—the year William the Conqueror invaded England—to 1154, Wood's book chronicles life in England during the Saxon and Celtic era and through the early post-Domesday period. Writing for *Library Journal* (June 1, 1988), Richard C. Hoffmann observed: "Wood's book stems from his BBC television series of the same

name . . . and partakes of that medium's analytical fuzziness and gripping immediacy. The content and production of the original Domesday book provide the basis for a wide-ranging exploration of the culture's origins." Rita G. Keeler, in *School Library Journal* (December 1988), proclaimed: "Like Wood's other book in the same format (*In Search of the Dark Ages*), [this work] reflects a felicitous ability to bring the past to life without compromising solid scholarship."

The period of the late 1980s and early 1990s saw Wood covering a variety of topics for television. He hosted *Art of the Western World* (1989), wrote the script for *Travels: The Sacred Way* (1991), and hosted *Legacy: The Origins of Civilization* (1991), for which he also wrote a companion volume. (Published in the U.K., in 1992, under the same title as the television show, Wood's companion book did not appear in the U.S. until 1994, when it was titled *Legacy: The Search for Ancient Cultures*.) Wood then published *The Smile of Murugan: A South Indian Journey* (1995), a book detailing his journey through the state of Tamil Nadu, in southern India, which he made several years earlier with his girlfriend, Rebecca Ysabel Dobbs, whom he later married. (Murugan, a Hindu deity and the son of Lord Shiva, is worshiped by the Tamil people.) Fascinated with the belief systems and the values of the Tamil people, Wood presents in his book a discussion of the region's culture and history, from prehistoric times through to the present day. In a review for the London *Sunday Times* (December 3, 1995), Philip French noted: "Wood makes a journey to Madras to see some middle-class Indian friends and listen to their opinions. Although this is interesting enough, it does not hold the book together. I had a sense that the author's attention was wandering, leaving an indiscernible subtext hovering beneath the words. The opening and closing sections of *The Smile of Murugan* are odd confections of jottings and irrelevancies. The high point is the middle of the book, when Wood is on his video-bus pilgrimage to south India's sacred temples. Here there is enough momentum to carry the narrative forward and keep you turning the pages."

Wood returned to the topic of the ancient world with *In the Footsteps of Alexander the Great* (1997), a companion book to the BBC series of the same title. In about 334 BCE, Alexander, the king of Macedonia and conqueror of the Persian Empire, led his army of approximately 40,000 from Greece into Persia, beginning a march of conquest that would cover 22,000 miles in 11 years. He built an empire stretching across parts of what is today the Middle East, Russia, and India—more than two million square miles in all. Wood's book explores the life of Alexander and relays Wood's own adventure retracing Alexander's route with a film crew to create the documentary. In the *New York Times Book Review* (November 23, 1997), D. J. R. Bruckner wrote: "Relying on Greek and Roman sources, Wood tells a glorious story with some very dark shadows. On the whole he gets it right, and his writing is clear and crisp. The harrowing tale of his own trek over the same ground makes clear how heroic Alexander's army was. And in a dozen countries, in cities and villages, in desert camps and on mountains of the Hindu Kush, he found that Alexander is fiercely alive in poetry, songs and folk tales, in the imaginations of millions." Mary Carroll, in a critique for *Booklist* (November 15, 1997), remarked: "If some BBC/PBS travel documentaries are the video equivalent of a lush coffee-table book, others are more challenging. . . . Wood's exploration of the lands through which Alexander the Great and his armies marched falls into the latter category; in traveling from Macedonia east to the Himalayas, Wood examines shifting notions of Alexander himself over the centuries, demonstrating how each era's assumptions and attitudes color its interpretation of the quasi-legendary leader. This tie-in volume is well (though not lavishly) illustrated with a mixture of Alexandrine art from a variety of cultures, landscapes that capture the wide range of geographies through which Alexander and his imperial armies passed, and portraits of cultures (in Turkey and the Persian Gulf, Afghanistan and Pakistan to the Hindu Kush) in which the influence of that long-ago juggernaut is still visible. A thoughtful, often fascinating narrative."

Wood explored the medieval roots of his native country with the widely praised book *In Search of England: Journeys into the English Past* (1999). Sherie Posesorski, in the *New York Times Book Review* (May 28, 2000), proclaimed this volume to be "a collection of illuminating essays on the pastiche of myths and facts that has shaped England's national identity. With scholarly zeal, journalistic skepticism and narrative flair, Wood, a veritable archaeologist of myth, examines key iconic figures, places and texts that have come to represent the idea and ideals of the English." Ronald Hutton, in the *Times Literary Supplement* (December 10, 1999), opined: "Where the book triumphs—and where it was designed to excel—is in two very different respects. One is to bring home to general readers the range and complexity of source material for a study of medieval England; and here the film-maker's eye comes into its own. Better than any historian for decades, Wood brings home not just the ways in which buildings, landscapes and written texts may be read, but the sensual beauty of encounters with them. . . . Its other purpose is to delineate an English identity at a time when a British one is threatened by devolution; and Wood manages to invest Englishness with a romanticism more commonly associated with the other nationalities of these islands."

In *Conquistadors* (2000) Wood portrays the Spanish conquest of the Americas in the 16th century through the exploits of such notorious explorers as Hernan Cortés. As Wood describes his own travels (which were filmed for the BBC series of the same name) through the Aztec and Inca lands that were ravaged many centuries ago by the conquistadors, he discusses the destruction of those empires as well as the cultural and religious influences of the Europeans on contemporary Latin America. Critiquing the book for the *MultiCultural Review* (December 2001), James C. Harrison noted that Wood "retraces the routes of Hernan Cortés's campaign against the Aztecs, Francisco Pizarro's war against the Incas, Gonzalo Pizarro and Francisco Orellana's incredible journey into the interior of South America, and Cabeza de Vaca's arduous march through North America. The story he writes is part history and part travelogue but all informative. He demonstrates sympathy for both the Spaniards and the indigenous people. . . . Supplementing his story is a wealth of fabulous photographs that bring the reader closer to the tale Wood is spinning."

Wood's *Shakespeare* (2003) was the companion volume to the four-part BBC documentary *In Search of Shakespeare* (2003), which was also the title used for the book's British publication. Relying on contemporary historical research and some of his own investigative work, Wood provides a portrait of William Shakespeare as a product of the turbulent times in which he lived. One of the more notable propositions Wood makes is that Shakespeare and his family were secretly Catholic, although that religion was forcibly suppressed in Elizabethan England after a series of violent oscillations in the official state religion. Critics were divided on the question of Shakespeare's Catholicism, though most were united in praise of Wood's work. In *America* (November 10, 2003), Tom O'Brien commended Wood for writing a "sterling biography . . . enlivened by excellent illustrations of the Elizabethan era." O'Brien added: "Wood assiduously shows how Shakespeare's life was framed by earthshaking philosophical and religious transitions. . . . A Catholic connection feels stretched, as if Wood or the BBC felt they needed to publicize the series as groundbreaking. Fortunately, Wood makes a subtler case." Trygve Thoreson, writing in *Booklist* (October 1, 2003), concurred with O'Brien's assessment, noting: "Wood has crafted a book of substance and originality. . . . [He] presents a portrait of Shakespeare as very much a child of Stratford, a poet for whom the people of the village and countryside of his youth were always a part of his conscious, creative life. We are also given a convincing portrait of the artist's struggles in the unpredictable world of the Elizabethan theater. . . . A highly readable, informative, and artfully illustrated volume for bardolaters and common readers alike."

To prepare for *In Search of Myths and Heroes* (2005), the companion piece to the BBC documentary series of the same name, Wood and his team traveled to 19 countries seeking to understand the historical origins and contemporary significance of such legends as the Queen of Sheba, King Arthur, Shangri-La, and Jason and the Golden Fleece. On his journeys Wood discovered, as he told Judith S. Gillies for the *Washington Post* (November 13, 2005), that "the power of the story in the culture was more important than historical fact," adding: "It's important to show how stories like these can take on a life of their own and become so important in the culture." The text left some critics wanting. "It's all quite fascinating," Brian J. Buchanan observed for the Nashville *Tennessean* (October 30, 2005), "though the presentation is hobbled in places by inadequate maps that refuse to indicate various places insisted upon in the text. . . . Still, in its audacious plunge into old time, this book will drag your imagination into worlds both dreamt of and possibly real."

Other television documentaries that Wood has hosted include *Hitler's Search for the Holy Grail* (1999) and *Top 10 Egypt* (2003). He is the winner of the University of Oxford Matthew Arnold Memorial Prize in English and is a fellow of the Royal Historical Society. He lectures widely in both the U.S. and Britain. His reviews and articles have appeared in the London *Telegraph*, the London *Evening Standard*, *Literary Review*, the London *Times*, *Dialogue*, the London *Guardian*, and New York *Newsday*, among others.

Wood married Rebecca Dobbs in 1988. They live with their two daughters in North London, England.

—C.M.

Suggested Reading: *America* p31+ Nov. 10, 2003; *Atlantic Monthly* p100 May 1986; *Booklist* p540 Nov. 15, 1997, p294 Oct. 1, 2003; *Christian Science Monitor* p31 June 5, 1986; *Library Journal* p80 Apr. 15, 1986; (London) *Sunday Times* Dec. 3, 1995; Maya Vision International Web site; *MultiCultural Review* p84+ Dec. 2001; (Nashville) *Tennessean* D p51 Oct. 30, 2005; *New York Times Book Review* p29 Nov. 23, 1997, p18 May 28, 2000; *Times Literary Supplement* p9 Dec. 10, 1999; *Washington Post* Y p3 Nov. 13, 2006

Selected Books: *In Search of the Dark Ages*, 1981; *In Search of the Trojan War*, 1985; *Domesday: A Search for the Roots of England*, 1986; *Legacy: A Search for the Origins of Civilization*, 1992; *The Smile of Murugan: A South Indian Journey*, 1995; *In the Footsteps of Alexander the Great*, 1997; *In Search of England: Journeys into the English Past*, 1999; *Conquistadors*, 2000; *Shakespeare*, 2003; *In Search of Myths and Heroes: Exploring Four Epic Legends of the World*, 2005

Yarbrough, Steve

Aug. 29, 1956– Novelist; short-story writer

Steve Yarbrough comes from the rich storytelling culture of Mississippi, where such noted writers as William Faulkner, Eudora Welty, and Tennessee Williams got their start. "You have big shoes to fill if you're a writer from Mississippi," Yarbrough told Kathey Clarey for the *Fresno Bee* (September 20, 1998). "I think Mississippi is the best place in the world for a writer to grow up," he has said, as quoted in an article posted on the Mississippi Writers and Musicians Project Web site. "It's not a bland place, and people there tend to be very passionate about life."

Steve Yarbrough was born in Indianola, Mississippi, on August 29, 1956 to John and Earlene Yarbrough. He graduated from Indianola Academy, in 1975, and then went on to study at the University of Mississippi, in Oxford. He earned a bachelor's degree in philosophy and English literature there, in 1979, and a master's degree in English literature, in 1981. In 1985 he received an M.F.A. in creative writing from the University of Arkansas, in Fayetteville, where he studied under fellow Mississippi writer James Whitehead. After completing his education Yarbrough taught for four years at the Virginia Polytechnic Institute, in Blacksburg. In the late 1980s he moved to Fresno,

Courtesy of Random House

California, to teach creative writing at California State University, in Fresno. In 1992 he lived in Poland for a brief time; while there he met his wife,

Eva, who now translates Polish books into English. They have two daughters, Magda and Tosha.

Yarbrough's first collection of short stories, *Family Men*, was published in 1990. The tales in the collection revolve around such ordinary people as Sara, a housewife and government clerk, who has become alienated from her friends and family by her bigoted husband; Moody, a wheelchair-bound man who is crippled shortly after his wedding; and Uncle Cecil, an alcoholic estranged from most of his family members. A critic reviewing the collection for the *Arkansas Democrat-Gazette* (February 3, 1991) noted: "In the story-telling tradition of the South, Steve Yarbrough writes short fiction that captures the essence of a region he knows firsthand. But the characters and situations they struggle with transcend labels and have universal appeal."

Mississippi History (1994), Yarbrough's second collection of short stories, features similarly sympathetic characters. They struggle with mortgage payments, the rising cost of healthcare, lost jobs, and racial intolerance. Yarbrough looks at his protagonists' lives through the long lens of history and shows that the problems facing these ordinary people have roots in the troubled history of the American South. In the title story a rift develops between two young friends—one Christian, the other Jewish—when the Christian boy finds an anti-Semitic joke amusing. In "Hungarian Stew," Malina, a Polish exchange student, falls in love with Jack, a Mississippi native; the relationship is complicated by the fact that Malina has a husband back in Poland with whom she shares a long history. In the *New York Times Book Review* (November 6, 1994), Suzanne Berne wrote: "Mr. Yarbrough's characters are ungainly, unpoetic, earnest people who work at understanding how the past has snagged their lives; they are grateful to be even partly successful. For them, a revelation comes slowly, and when it arrives, it's nothing fancy. As a lonely history teacher who falls in love with his aunt concludes about himself: 'Something's wrong, and you're the one it's wrong with.'"

Yarbrough's third collection of stories, *Veneer* (1998), features such memorable characters as a Persian Gulf War veteran struggling to adjust to life at home, a young woman worried that her husband will leave her for someone skinnier, and a man remembering a disastrous Fourth of July celebration. In her profile of Yarbrough, Kathey Clarey wrote that the book "takes the reader on a variety of journeys, some of them poignant, some of them downright funny. At the core of each is an understanding of human beings and how they can be shaped by their environments and/or families. . . . Yarbrough's talent for description drops you right into the humid Mississippi Delta country or the streets of a Polish city." A reviewer for *Publishers Weekly* (July 27, 1998), observed: "In his measured, observant prose, Yarbrough . . . evokes not the sentimentalized or Gothicized

South but one that is warm, engaging and recognizably human."

During the summer of 1996 Yarbrough sold a then-unpublished manuscript titled *The Oxygen Man* to Hollywood producers, who in turn asked him to write the screenplay. Unfortunately, two of the producers who backed the project quit, his option expired, and another screenplay he wrote became the focus of a legal battle. "Hollywood isn't a good business for novelists and short-story writers to spend a lot of time in," he explained to Clarey. "The track record of adapting work isn't good. . . . One time I got a call telling me I had to write a scene where a car blew up. It hadn't been in the novel or the screenplay, but they needed a visual depiction of violence." Still, Yarbrough saw benefits from his short stint in the movie industry. "The amount of money they pay you [for the screenplay] is amazing," he told Clarey. "You can buy a house from what you get, even if the movie isn't made." Yarbrough's time in Hollywood also helped him land representation with the exclusive ICM Agency, which sold *The Oxygen Man* to a publisher within three weeks. The novel, Yarbrough's first, appeared in 1999.

The oxygen man of the title is Ned Rose, a restless middle-aged man who lives with his sister. He works at night, checking the oxygen levels in the catfish ponds on a farm in Mississippi; the farm is owned by Mack Bell, with whom Ned shares a troubled history. Frank Caso wrote for *Booklist* (April 15, 1999), "This novel mixes well the classic elements of the family cycle of cause and effect, hidden and imminent violence, and the long gestation before restitution." In *Library Journal* (May 1, 1999), Judith Ann Akalaitis wrote: "Yarbrough cleverly and clearly illustrates life unfolding in a small Mississippi town through subtle references to race relations and town politics as well as detailed description of the natural surroundings. His intimate descriptions of his characters' lives make them real." W. E. Reinka, reviewing *The Oxygen Man* for *Independent Publisher* (May/June 1999), called it "a brilliant debut novel [that] portends a major literary career."

Yarbrough's next novel, *Visible Spirits* (2001), is set in the American South at the turn of the 20th century, when the progressive politics of Reconstruction were giving way to the segregationist Jim Crow laws. The central characters of the novel are two brothers, Tandy and Leighton Payne. Leighton is the mayor and the editor of the local newspaper; Tandy has just come back into town hoping to reclaim his family's plantation. He is disgusted that his brother has abandoned their agrarian traditions to write and edit a progressive newspaper that demands equality between the races. Tandy focuses much of his bigotry on Loda Jackson, the town's black postmistress. When he writes a hate-filled letter to Leighton's paper about Loda, Leighton refuses to publish it, forcing both the brothers and the town's other citizens to a reckoning. Writing for *USA Today* (June 7, 2001), J. Ford Huffman opined: "*Visible Spirits* is a compelling look at moral courage, full of passion about a time when the gilded age and the guilty of all ages collided." In the *Rocky Mountain News* (June 15, 2001), Jennie A. Camp noted: "Yarbrough handles admirably the turn-of-the-century racial tensions of a society . . . presenting us with an engaging story, believable (and frequently infuriating) characters and a glimpse of ourselves that is both disturbing and surprisingly insightful."

Yarbrough's next novel, *Prisoners of War* (2004), recalls the German prisoners who were sent to dozens of camps throughout the South to work as day laborers and farm hands during World War II. During the summer of 1943, Loring, Mississippi, hosts many of these men. At the same time, some of the town's black residents realize they are unwilling to fight for a country that has done them so much wrong. In the *Biloxi Sun Herald* (March 21, 2004), Scott Naugle wrote: "One finishes Steve Yarbrough's *Prisoners of War* with a strong feeling that the author respects his readers. This is not common today. . . . The plot moves along briskly, tension builds, the characters are true to form, and the ending is the unexpected ending that a reader gets with a good story. On the surface, and going no deeper, this is a fine novel meticulously written. Going deeper into the well, though, brings rewards." Prisoners of War was short-listed for the 2005 PEN/Faulkner Award for fiction.

The End of California (2006), also takes place in Loring, Mississippi. Pete Barrington, a 42-year-old doctor, returns to Loring under the cloud of an adulterous affair with a patient. Having lived for more than two decades in California, Barrington and his wife and daughter struggle with adjusting to life in what feels like a foreign environment, and Barrington is forced to confront a place and a past that he was only able to escape because of his looks and football talent. In an interview for the *Fresno State News* (June 12, 2006, on-line), Yarbrough said that part of what he wanted to deal with in the novel "was the question of what California has always meant to people in the rest of the country. Like my main character, I grew up in Mississippi, then moved to the Golden State, so I feel as if I've got one foot in each world. And they are indeed separate worlds, if not separate universes." *The End of California* received generally positive reviews, and many critics paid particular attention to Yarbrough's character development. "Yarbrough's story blends elements we have seen in other novels—the small town South, the football hero grown up, passions that reach back to high school, a little incest and a lot of extramarital sex, racial tensions, hypocrisy among the pious," Patrick Anderson wrote for the *Washington Post* (June 12, 2006). "But it all works because Yarbrough knows his characters so well, cares for them so deeply and writes of them in prose that is graceful, precise and packed with surprises."

Steve Yarbrough has received numerous awards for his work, including a National Endowment of the Arts fellowship for fiction writing and a Pushcart Prize for his short story "Preacher." Though he and his family now live in California, he maintains close ties to his Southern roots and frequently visits Mississippi to lecture.

—C.M.

Suggested Reading: *Arkansas Democrat-Gazette* Feb. 3, 1991; *Biloxi Sun-Herald* H p2 Mar. 21, 2004; *Dallas Morning News* Mar. 25, 2004; *Booklist* p1514 Apr. 15, 1999; Fresno State News (on-line) June 12, 2006; *Library Journal* p113 May 1, 1999; *Los Angeles Times* p3 June 19, 2001; *New York Times* (on-line) Feb. 8, 2004; *New York Times Book Review* p19 Nov. 6, 1994; *Rocky Mountain News* D p22 June 15, 2001; *Time* p82 June 7, 1999; *USA Today* D p4 June 7, 2001; *Washington Post* C p10 June 12, 2006

Selected Books: short fiction—*Family Men*, 1990; *Mississippi History*, 1994; *Veneer*, 1998; novels— *Oxygen Man*, 1999; *Visible Spirits*, 2001; *Prisons of War*, 2004; *The End of California*, 2006

Young, Kevin

1970– Poet

"Kevin Young is, simply put, one of the hottest commodities in poetry today," David Ingle observed for *Flagpole* magazine (April 7, 1999, on-line). Young's nomination for the National Book Award for poetry, for his collection *Jelly Roll: A Blues* (2003), further cemented his place as one of the preeminent voices in American poetry. Integrating the rhythms and styles of the blues and hip-hop with African-American vernacular, Young has developed an innovative style that is, in its use of musical structures as a framework, reminiscent of such acclaimed poets as Langston Hughes. In *Jelly Roll* Young built upon the success and promise of his two earlier award-winning collections, *Most Way Home*—his 1995 debut— and *To Repel Ghosts: Five Sides in B Minor,* a 2001 poetic homage to the late artist Jean-Michel Basquiat. Young's articles and poems have appeared in such publications as the *New Yorker*, the *New York Times Book Review*, the *Kenyon Review*, the *Paris Review*, *Callaloo*, and *Paideuma*. He has also edited such poetry anthologies as *Giant Steps: The New Generation of African American Writers* (2000), *Blues Poems* (2003), and *Jazz Poems* (2006), as well as a 2004 selection of verse by the famed American John Berryman.

An only child, born in 1970 in Lincoln, Nebraska, to what he has described as a family of musicians, storytellers, and ministers, Young moved around frequently as a youngster,

Kay Hinton/Emory Creative Group

Kevin Young

relocating six times before the age of 10. Early on he showed an interest in writing; he first penned adventure stories but took up poetry at the age of 13.

Young was especially influenced by his grandfather Mack, who was involved in zydeco music and played the fiddle; he told Abe Aamidor for the *Indianapolis Star* (October 21, 2003), "I like to think I can hear my grandfather's music in my head." After finishing high school Young entered Harvard University, in Cambridge, Massachusetts, and studied poetry under Seamus Heaney and Lucie Brock-Broido. In 1992 he earned a bachelor's degree. While at Harvard Young was awarded an Academy of American Poets Prize and participated in the Dark Room Collective, an organization dedicated to helping young black artists. Following his graduation from Harvard, Young entered Stanford University, in California, where he remained for two years on a Stegner fellowship and studied with the poet Denise Levertov.

While at Stanford, in 1993, Young completed his debut collection, *Most Way Home*, which was later selected for the National Poetry Series. *Most Way Home* earned Young the John C. Zacharis First Book Award from the journal *Ploughshares* and Emerson University. Don Lee wrote for *Ploughshares* (Winter 1996–1997), "The book reflects a personalized, largely imagined view of African American history in this century, loosely based on stories from Young's Louisiana family. It considers the dialectic of home and displacement, and the myths and fierce nostalgia that join the two." The work, Lee added, is divided into four sections which together "create a narrative arc." The first section examines a family evicted from

their land; in the next portion a visit to a carnival sideshow is recounted; a woman describes her childhood in the third section; and in the last Young addresses "more contemporary and urban landscapes." *Most Way Home* earned Young extensive critical praise: Lucille Clifton, the poet and editor who chose the book for the National Poetry Series, wrote, as quoted on Amazon.com, "This young poet's gift of storytelling and understanding of the music inherent in the oral tradition of language recreates for us an inner history which is compelling and authentic and American." A reviewer for the *Voice Literary Supplement*, as quoted by Don Lee, observed, "In Young's alchemy, succulent scraps are gathered from daily life, distilled, and emerge, finally, as portable nuggets of home, carried wherever the poet may travel."

When his tenure as a Stegner fellow came to an end, Young entered Brown University, in Providence, Rhode Island, in pursuit of an M.F.A., which he was awarded in 1996. Young then joined the faculty of the University of Georgia as an assistant professor of English and African-American Studies. While there, Young edited the anthology *Giant Steps:The New Generation of African American Writers* (2000). The volume, which Young intended to counter expectations of what black writing should be, includes work by relatively unknown authors all born prior to 1960, including John Keene, Daniel Jerome Wideman, Natasha Tretheway, and Allison Joseph. "The range of ideas, aesthetic styles and political perspectives [contained in the book] is startling," Walton Muyumba wrote for the *Chicago Tribune* (February 20, 2000).

To Repel Ghosts: Five Sides in B Minor is Young's 117-poem tribute to the controversial 1980s-era artist Jean-Michel Basquiat, who died in 1988 at the age of 28 after a frenzied period of impressive artistic creation and personal excess. Of the work, Young told Lee, "This is not biography . . . nor is it hagiography. Rather, I think it's closer to discography, riffing off his work while recording parts of his life. It's a long poem, a jam session in his honor, bringing in many figures from his time and from history, whether they are musicians, graffiti artists, comedians, or, as Basquiat put it, 'Famous Negro Athletes.'" *To Repel Ghosts* was a finalist for the Academy of American Poets' James McLaughlin Prize. Donna Seaman, writing for *Booklist* , as quoted on Amazon.com, offered profuse praise in a representative review, stating, "Young's magnum opus scats, talks, shouts, and sings a story that encompasses not only one man's tragedy but that of a nation: the persistence and virulence of racism." A revised version of the book appeared in 2005 as *To Repel Ghosts: Remixed from the Original Masters.*

The title of Young's next collection, *Jelly Roll: A Blues* (2003), plays on the same sexual references that the early jazz pianist and composer Ferdinand

Joseph Lamothe did when he called himself Jelly Roll Morton. Though the book takes similarly playful turns, it also explores the gloomier elements of human feeling. John Hawn wrote for the *Indianapolis Star* (April 20, 2003), that the book's "more than 100 short poems—some only two lines long—combine the lexicon of blues and jazz with the conciseness and imagery of haiku. . . . Young maintains the essence of the blues—which is inherently rife with cliches—while reshaping them into a vibrant form. He entwines the familiar blues form and poetry into something that involves not just the ear and eye, but the tongue, as well." Brian Phillips, writing for *Poetry* (February 2004), called the book "plump and play-acting" and its poems "rarely more than a fan's eager notes, a sophisticate's predilections." Phillips added: "On the page Young's poems look minimal, thin couplets in a field of white space, but this long book is a surfeit of its own technique; Young seems to have left nothing out. Even in its many poems on heartbreak, this work flashes the easy grin of a writer being generous with himself." Like other critics Phillips took Young to task for using what he described as "affected dialect." Labeling the use of such phrases as "mom'n thems" and "Dear, I needs" "mere strategic typography" and "not Young's voice," Phillips argued: "Any book subtitled *A Blues* is likely to include blues slang; but when the Harvard-educated Young calls a sexual partner 'Rider,' the effect is decidedly uncomfortable. The word sounds more natural coming from the Rolling Stones." Published the same year as *Jelly Roll*, Young's anthology *Blues Poems* showcases writing inspired by blues music and features work by a wide range of authors, including Langston Hughes, Allen Ginsberg, Charles Wright, Yusef Komunyakaa, and Gwendolyn Brooks.

Young's collection *Black Maria* (2005) derives its name from the slang term used to describe either a police van or a hearse. (The second word in the title is pronounced mah-RYE-ah.) An attempt to recreate a film noir in verse, this book-length sequence of short, linked poems—winkingly described on the cover as having been "produced and directed" by Young—as tells the story of poetic detective A.K.A. Jones as he pursues the mysterious Deliah Redbones through the streets of Shadowtown. Joel Brouwer, in his review for the *New York Times* (May 1, 2005), writes that though the "initial promise of narrative coherence helps to draw you into the world of Shadowtown," the book is more atmospheric than plot-driven, which leaves the text without any of the plot twists that are typical in the film noir genre. "And that leads to a more general question: Why bother reading *Black Maria* at all, when you could go to the movies instead?" Brouwer writes. "Young's answer, I imagine, would be that there are some things that only poetry can do, and one of these is to reduce things to their essences. *Black Maria* is a sort of periodic table of film noir. It's less a

detective story than a compilation of the elements that make up all detective stories."

Young's next book, *For the Confederate Dead* (2007), plays on the title of the poet Robert Lowell's highly regarded 1964 collection *For the Union Dead*. A selection of elegies for public figures and personal acquaintances, Young's book was greeted with generally positive reviews, though as with many of Young's books, critics often commented that it seemed overlong. Laurel Maury, writing for the *Los Angeles Times Book Review* (January 21, 2007), called the collection "lively and excellent" and Young's work "a good antidote" to the idea that "poetry is difficult, obtuse or only for strange eggheads." Maury argued that Young's book and Lowell's "are very different. Lowell sought to yank a definition of his nation from a mix of aging Puritanism and middle-aged desperation. Young is also on a nation-defining mission, but it's as though he believes that the South and blackness were left out of Lowell's equation. Lowell is the greater poet, but Young is fun, full of unself-conscious music and isn't a sucker for middle-aged sorrow. His poems are often sad, but they never dote on their sadness. . . . Young's poems always give a sense of an outer world of people, beauty, family, a place where mourners gather after a funeral and sing Bob Marley songs. (As a poet, he owes more to Marley than to Lowell.) *For the Confederate Dead* gives an open-eyed vision of a complete world."

After holding an endowed chair in poetry at Indiana University, in Bloomington, Young became the Atticus Haygood Professor of English and Creative Writing and the curator of the Raymond Danowski Poetry Library, both at Emory University, in Atlanta, Georgia. In May 2005 Young married Kate Tuttle, the senior executive editor of the *African American National Biography*, a joint project of the W. E. B. Du Bois Institute for African and African American Research at Harvard University and Oxford University Press. He commutes between Atlanta and his home outside Boston.

—P.B.M.

Suggested Reading: *Boston Review* Summer 1998; *Chicago Tribune* Books p5 Feb. 20, 2000; *Flagpole* (on-line) Apr. 7, 1999; *Indianapolis Star* E p8 Apr. 20, 2003, E p5 Oct. 21, 2003; *Los Angeles Times Book Review* p10 Jan. 27, 2007; *Nation* p28+ May 9, 2005; *Ploughshares* Winter 1996–97, p186+ Spring 2006; *Poetry* p299+ Feb. 2004; *Publishers Weekly* p58 Nov. 25, 2002; *Washington Post* T p13 Aug. 31, 2003

Selected Books: *Most Way Home*, 1995; *To Repel Ghosts: Five Sides in B Minor*, 2001; *Jelly Roll: A Blues*, 2003; *To Repel Ghosts: Remixed from the Original Masters*, 2005; *Black Maria*, 2005; *For the Confederate Dead*, 2007; as editor—*Giant Steps: The New Generation of African American Writers*, 2000; *Blues Poems*, 2003; *John*

Berryman: Selected Poems, 2004; *Jazz Poems*, 2006

Margaret Randall/Courtesy of City Lights Books

Zamora, Daisy

June 20, 1950– Poet

"I propose to women that we throw out the walls, dive off of cliffs without wings, and have faith in our own hearts, in our own thoughts," the poet Daisy Zamora told Leslie Ruiz Baldelomar for the Nicaraguan newspaper *La Prensa* (January 22, 2004, on-line), as translated by *Current Biography International*. One of Nicaragua's most acclaimed and respected authors, Zamora became famous for poems and essays that captured the revolutionary zeal of the Sandinista rebellion in the 1970s. In a country in which poetry represents the soul of a people—where the poet Rubén Darío (1867–1916) is still revered as a veritable patron saint of Nicaraguan culture—Zamora occupies a unique position, speaking for both the fighters of the revolution and the women whose voices were too often drowned out by their male compatriots, even as they fought side by side. Her 1988 collection, *En Limpio se Escribe la Vida* (which translates as "life on a clean slate"), was called "the first poetic and feminist manifesto that undermines patriarchal definitions of the family, reproduction, housework, and the 'double day'" by the scholar Greg Dawes, as quoted by George Evans in his introduction to Zamora's collection *The Violent Foam*. She is a prolific writer; her work has appeared in more than 40 anthologies and been translated into several languages, including Dutch,

French, English, Italian, German, and Russian. "Her poetry, more than feminist, is humanist," Baldelomar wrote, "because through it she comes out against war and in favor of harmony between human beings and the environment. It goes from the personal to the political, from the private to the public." Zamora's status as a female revolutionary was hardly unique; many women had active roles in the Sandinista movement, which in theory condemned sexism as a continuation of social and economic oppression. In practice, however, sexism often persisted even within the movement, and Zamora's experience provided a dual perspective on rebellion and repression. As Maria Dolores Bolivar wrote for *Imagen* (August 6, 2000, on-line), as translated by *Current Biography International*, "Daisy Zamora exposed her private life to everyone, and spoke out powerfully against the repression that she has experienced as a woman, knowing that she is not alone. Her cause is reflected in the lives of many Nicaraguan women who still have not reached true equality in society." Richard Siken, reviewing *Clean Slate: New and Selected Poems*, a translated compilation published in 1993, for *Tucson Weekly* (February 27, 1997, on-line), wrote, "Yes, Daisy Zamora is a political poet, but perhaps not for the reasons you might think. Ultimately, [she] is trying to do one simple thing: She is trying to be herself. But for a woman in Latin America, speaking out for yourself is a political act. . . . [Zamora] has no hidden political agenda, but she does challenge the cultural inheritance that would encourage her silence."

Daisy Zamora was born in Managua, Nicaragua, on June 20, 1950 to a wealthy family with liberal political leanings. Her father was killed when she was a young girl, assassinated by political enemies. While Zamora had a traditional Catholic education, the political tumult that surrounded her as she came of age, coupled with her family's liberalism, radicalized her in early adulthood. From the time she was young, Zamora enjoyed writing. She experimented with poetry during her adolescence and published her first poem, "Un niño muerto en la carretera" (which translates as "a dead child on the road"), when she was still a teenager. (The poem appeared in *La Prensa Literaria* on September 3, 1967.) In the early 1970s Zamora attended the Universidad Centroamericana, in Managua, where she studied psychology. After receiving her degree, she enrolled in the Instituto Centroamericano de Administracion de Empresas (Central American Institute of Business Administration) and earned a postdoctoral degree. Later she studied painting at the Escuela Nacional de Bellas Artes, in León, Nicaragua.

Zamora's personal history is intertwined with that of modern Nicaragua itself; she joined the Sandinista movement while still in college, when it was beginning to make headway across the country. The Sandinista movement, a clandestine

Marxist group formally known as the Frente Sandinista de Liberación Nacional (FSNL), was founded on July 23, 1961, by university students seeking to overthrow the repressive regime of the Somoza family, which had ruled Nicaragua since 1936. The Frente Sandinista took its name from the nationalist Augusto César Sandino, who had used guerrilla tactics to protest repeated American interventions in his country's affairs during the early 20th century. Murdered in 1934 by General Anastasio Somoza's troops, Sandino came to be regarded as a martyr for Nicaraguan freedom. Two years later, General Somoza launched a coup against President Juan Bautista Sacasa, gaining control of the country in a rigged election in 1936. He then ruled Nicaragua for 20 years, maintaining friendly relations with the U.S. and American business interests and enriching himself in the process. After he was assassinated, in 1956, his two sons took control of the presidency and the army and set about quashing dissent, using increasingly harsh methods.

When the Sandinistas organized their resistance, in the 1960s, their support came mainly from poor rural Nicaraguans and students; they also had the backing of the Cuban revolutionary leader Fidel Castro, whom the U.S. was actively trying to overthrow. In the decade that followed, however, economic crises, the growing disparity between the rich and the poor, and increasingly blatant instances of political corruption in the Somoza government brought the rebels more and more support from Nicaragua's mainstream and its wealthier, educated classes. In December 1972 a massive earthquake struck the city of Managua, killing 20,000 people and leaving 250,000 homeless. When international aid poured in, the Somoza-led National Guard pocketed most of it, leaving much of the city in ruins and the population without much-needed assistance. This stoked the already simmering outrage against the corrupt regime, and the FSNL gained support and momentum. On January 10, 1978 the editor of the left-leaning newspaper La Prensa, Pedro Joaquín Chomorro, who was a vocal critic of the Somoza regime, was murdered, and the Sandinistas responded with a surge of attacks in the cities and countryside, overwhelming the National Guard. This marked the beginning of the end for the Somozas; the family fled on July 17, 1979. Two days later, the Sandinistas took control of the capital.

Zamora had joined the Sandinistas during the 1970s, after graduating from college and marrying Oscar-René Vargas, a sociologist who was also in the movement. She and her husband lived and worked at a sugar mill in Chinandenga. Together they organized a support network for their fellow combatants; Zamora's duties included raising funds for the purchase of weapons and transporting weapons and fighters. Later on she and Vargas moved to Managua, where she worked as a translator for a magazine; their home doubled as a safe house for rebels and a storehouse for weapons. Using a smuggled scanner, Zamora also tapped into the radio communications of Somoza's National Guard. In the late 1970s, she went to work at Radio Sandino, the clandestine radio station of the Sandinista movement. There she produced a show titled The Sandinista Woman, which dealt specifically with the experiences of women revolutionaries in the struggle for Nicaragua, zeroing in on the considerable sacrifices and hardships they had endured. During the final months leading up to the Sandinistas' victory in 1979, Zamora came to be known as the voice of the movement. With the victory of the Sandinistas, she was given a prominent position in the new government, being named vice minister of culture under the priest and poet Ernesto Cardenal.

Although Zamora contributed much to the Sandinista movement, she is better known for her role as a poet and a writer whose work interweaves political themes with the universal imagery of war as well as deeply personal remembrances. Her early work was introspective and autobiographical; much of it was about love. The poetry she produced as the Sandinistas made gains in their fight, however, reflected the heightened tension of a revolution in the works, if not necessarily through battleground imagery, then in her descriptions of the everyday strength of women and ordinary people. As a critic wrote for Publishers Weekly (July 12, 1993, on-line), "Emerging from torment, her poems assume a wry irony; in one poem she writes in the voice of an 'unemployed' housewife, in another she instructs would-be beauty queens. On a more tender note, she makes peace with her mother and seeks to learn about her matrilineal heritage." Other poems dealt more directly with revolution and its harsh realities, such as "Commander Two," about a female combatant, and "Emilia, the Nurse," about a nurse who is angry at American intervention in Nicaragua. Her poem "It Was a Ragged Squadron," written in September 1978, described the fear and apprehension of watching a fellow comrade walk into potentially dangerous territory: "Your boots sank into the pliant earth / and you raised a whitish mist at every step / (Time must have slowed down for us.) / Dionisio, all the comrades watched you / our hearts beating uselessly / beneath the full moon."

The Sandinistas ruled Nicaragua from 1979 until 1990. For much of that time the country was torn by warfare between the victorious revolutionaries and their enemies, the contras, who had powerful American support. In 1990 the revolutionaries were defeated in a democratic election—an event that shocked and demoralized many, Zamora included. In an essay published in the compilation Sandino's Daughters Revisited (1996), edited by Margaret Randall, Zamora excoriated the party for failing to live up to its own ideals or carry out all the reforms envisioned by its supporters. During this troubled period, she continued to write as well as teach and serve as vice minister of culture. Besides poems, she wrote a short story called "Las Fotos de la Pulga" (1988), which translates at "the photos of the flea."

In 1992 Zamora published *Riverbed of Memory*, translated by Barbara Paschke and featuring poems about war and remembrance whose overarching metaphor was often the poet's own body. This is one of Zamora's most frequently employed methods. "It is important for a woman to be aware of and to recover her own body because we have been told too many times that we were born to make sure that humankind doesn't disappear; we need to have a consciousness of our own selves and our own bodies. . . . Having this consciousness that each human being is an individual and has this uniqueness has enabled me to write these poems. Maybe this perspective is nothing new for men, but for a woman, having this consciousness is important." The following year Zamora published *Clean Slate: New and Selected Poems*. This collection was translated by a mother/daughter team, Margaret and Elinor Randall (the former of whom was also a Sandinista combatant) and featured works written since 1968, including the epic "Radio Sandino," which sets a radio report alongside the speaker's most personal childhood recollections. In 1994 Zamora published *Life for Each*. Containing new, often sensual poems, and printed in a bilingual format, with Spanish poems facing English translations by Dinah Livingstone, the collection was well received. A critic for *Poetry London* called each poem "alive and performable," and a reviewer wrote in *Ore* magazine, "This is poetry born out of personal and political struggle, painful to read yet all the more inspiring for that," as quoted on the publishing company Katabasis's Web site.

Zamora's *The Violent Foam* was published by Curbstone Press in a bilingual format in 2002. The English translations were the work of George Evans, an American poet to whom Zamora is now married. Longer than her previous books, *The Violent Foam* focuses on the same social-justice issues that have defined Zamora from her days as a revolutionary, while placing them in a present-day context. Jen Hofer, in an article for the *American Book Review* (November–December 2002) titled "Under Permanent Crossfire: Poetry and Revolution," noted the poems' accessibility as well as their serious subject matter: "Many poems in *The Violent Foam* speak specifically to [social-justice] issues on an individual, deeply human level, to, for example, the hypocrisy of national leaders who 'speak out in defense of the poor, / of children, women, / of justice,' yet dump all their 'fury . . . / and . . . impotence because [they] don't have a custom-made world, / . . . on the weak / who appear in the statistics.'"

Zamora's most recent collection of poetry, which has yet to be translated into English, is *Fiel al corazón: Poemas de amor* (which translates as "faithful to the heart: love poems"). She has received numerous awards for her work, and in 2006 she was honored as Woman Writer of the Year by the National Congress and the National Association of Artists in Nicaragua.

Daisy Zamora lives in San Francisco, California. She served as a visiting professor at the University of California, at Santa Cruz, from the spring of 2002 through the fall of 2003. She enjoys teaching Americans, she told Leslie Ruiz Baldelomar: "Something very curious happens with my students. They [start to realize] that the history of the United States is very linked to that of Central America."

—L.S.

Suggested Reading: *American Book Review* Nov.–Dec. 2002; Curbstone Press Web site; *La Prensa* (on-line) Jan. 22, 2004; *La Prensa Literaria* (on-line) Sep. 27, 2002

Selected Books in English Translation: *Riverbed of Memory*, 1992; *Clean Slate: New and Selected Poems*, 1993; *Life for Each*, 1994; *The Violent Foam*, 2002

Zuber, Isabel

July 28,1932– Novelist; poet

In her debut novel, *Salt* (2002), Isabel Zuber tells a rich tale of rural life in North Carolina at the turn of the 20th century. When Gary Carden, interviewing the author for *Smoky Mountain News* (March 13, 2002, on-line), commented that the novel's main character seemed "poised between two worlds"—namely the past and future—Zuber replied: "As a child, I romanticized the past and begged my father to tell me 'something old-timey,' but I would not want to go back to that time—to poverty, prejudice, inferior medical care. Even so, I know full well that much has been lost in terms of invaluable connections with the land and the community. There is a quote from my introduction to the poems about my father [*Winter Exile*] that sums this up: I hope [these poems] will also honor a lost way of life that, while it was rock hard and often painful, was also beautiful, moving and satisfying in a way that we may not be able to recover."

The daughter of Herman Roland Eggers, a university administrator, and Elizabeth Mae (Pennington) Eggers, a homemaker, Isabel Zuber was born on July 28, 1932 in Boone, North Carolina. Her family would gather to hear her father read aloud after their evening meal, and as a child she dreamed of writing novels. "I started one when I was seven years old," Zuber told Patty Smith for *Blackbird* (December 15, 2003, on-line). "I wrote two whole pages about something I knew absolutely nothing about, the war between Texas and Mexico." She graduated from Appalachian State University, also in Boone, with bachelor's degrees in English and library science, in 1954. Later, in 1988, she earned a master's degree in library science from the University of North Carolina, at Greensboro. In 1969 she accepted a position at the Z. Smith Reynolds Library at Wake Forest University; she remained there until her retirement, in 2001.

While pursuing her career in library science and raising her two children—Jonathan and Elizabeth—she continued to write poetry and short stories, scribbling bits and pieces in various notebooks whenever she found a spare moment. According to Kim Underwood for the *Winston-Salem Journal* (March 17, 2002), Zuber's "personal mantra has been 'Penelope Fitzgerald, Penelope Fitzgerald. . . .'" (Fitzgerald, who twice won the prestigious Booker Prize, did not begin writing until she was in her 60s.)

When Zuber finally found a stretch of uninterrupted time to work on her novel, she found the bits of text that had accumulated over more than 20 years came together easily. *Salt*, which won the First Novelist Award from Virginia Commonwealth University, tells the story of the spirited Anna Maude Stockton, a young girl who spends her days helping her mother tend to the family farm and playing with her sister, Nell. Though her father is a wastrel, Anna enjoys his war stories and folk tales. When Anna is sent to work for a wealthy family, whose home boasts an extensive library, she develops a passion for books. Her love of learning is subsumed, however, by her marriage to the twice-widowed John Bayley, a coarse farmer with whom she eventually has five children.

The novel was widely praised. In the *New York Times Book Review* (June 30, 2002), Betsy Groban declared it to be "a sweeping first novel, a panorama of rural life in early 20th-century America. . . . Zuber gets the historical details right, and her characters' emotions (especially Anna's—romantic, tender and full of quiet desperation) are handled just as deftly." Calling it "a beautiful first novel," Yates Forbis wrote for the *Tallahassee Democrat* (September 29, 2002): "Zuber draws on her own family history and legends to tell this story. Recently at a family reunion, her aging great-aunt, who had had *Salt* read aloud to her, called her niece to her side and said, 'Honey, you wrote it righter than you know.' Honest praise for an honest and powerful book."

R.C. Scott, writing for the *Washington Times* (June 2, 2002), praised *Salt*, noting that Zuber "brings her poet's precision to this first novel, to give an exacting and moving account of courage, persistence, and the power of family." In fact, before turning novelist, Zuber had published two collections of poetry: *Oriflamb* (1987), which won the chapbook contest held by the North Carolina Writers Network, and *Winter's Exile*, which was published in 1997. She has been the recipient of the Lee Smith Award for fiction from the Appalachian Writers Association and a University of Tennessee Press short-story prize. Her poetry and short stories have appeared in several publications, including the *American Voice*, *Poetry*, *Now & Then*, *Pembroke Magazine*, and *Shenandoah*.

Zuber lives in Winston-Salem, North Carolina. She is currently working on her second novel, which is about four sisters raising their nephew in a small Southern textile town.

—C.M.

Suggested Reading: *New York Times Book Review* p21 June 30, 2002; *Tallahassee Democrat* E p4 Sep. 29, 2002; *Washington Post* C p4 Mar. 22, 2002; *Winston-Salem Journal* D p1 Mar. 17, 2002

Selected Books: poetry—*Oriflamb*, 1987; *Winter's Exile*, 1997; novel—*Salt*, 2002